Nov. 28–Dec. 1, 2011
Scottsdale, AZ, USA

Association for
Computing Machinery

Advancing Computing as a Science & Profession

MM'11

Proceedings of the 2011 ACM
Multimedia Conference

Sponsored by:

ACM SIGMultimedia

Volume 2

Association for
Computing Machinery

Advancing Computing as a Science & Profession

The Association for Computing Machinery
2 Penn Plaza, Suite 701
New York, New York 10121-0701

ISBN: 978-1-4503-0616-4 (Digital)

ISBN: 978-1-4503-1358-2 (Print)

Additional copies may be ordered prepaid from:

ACM Order Department
PO Box 30777
New York, NY 10087-0777, USA

Phone: 1-800-342-6626 (USA and Canada)
+1-212-626-0500 (Global)
Fax: +1-212-944-1318
E-mail: acmhelp@acm.org
Hours of Operation: 8:30 am – 4:30 pm ET

ACM Order Number: 433117

Printed in the USA

Message from the General Chairs

We are delighted to welcome you, on behalf of the entire organizing committee, to the 19th ACM International Conference on Multimedia ACM Multimedia 2011 (MM'11), held between November 28th and December 1st, 2011, in Scottsdale, Arizona, USA.

ACM Multimedia (MM) is the flagship conference of the Special Interest Group on Multimedia (SIGMM), which profiles cutting-edge scientific developments and showcases innovative industrial multimedia technologies and applications. The conference aims to promote intellectual exchanges and interactions among scientists, engineers, students, multimedia users, and artists through various events, including keynote talks from leaders in the area, oral and poster sessions focused on research challenges and solutions, workshops in up-and-coming key areas of research, technical and industrial demonstrations of prototypes and commercial products, tutorials, research and industrial panels, doctoral symposium, mentoring events, scientific competitions (including an open source software and a multimedia grand challenge competition), and interactive art exhibits.

Our key motivation while organizing the MM'11 conference was to find innovative ways to design an "inclusive" conference program: lowering the barriers between various MM sub-communities, boosting the cross-fertilization of ideas among the contributors and attendees across the various MM events, and maximizing the return-on-investment for the MM'11 participants. Examples of this new approach include the following:

- New plenary poster sessions, where *all* contributors (i.e., authors of long and short research papers, of workshop papers, and contributors to all other MM'11 events) are invited to share poster versions of their contributions with the rest of the MM'11 community. These plenary poster sessions allow conference participants to get a quick idea of interesting things happening in the multiple parallel sessions they cannot clone themselves to attend!
- Workshops were aligned with the other MM'11 events, instead of being held on a separate "workshops day" where many workshop participants never got to know the main conference and vice-versa. Our aim was to integrate workshops (which were chosen, in the first place, to represent emerging topics that complement the areas covered by the main technical program) organically with the other conference events and encourage broader participation by registrants in all conference and workshop programs.
- These innovations aimed to eliminate barriers in the program had to be supported by corresponding innovations in the MM'11 registration policies. Thus, we have instituted an "all-in-one" registration fee structure, which covers attendance to all MM'11 events, including presentation and poster sessions, panels, demonstrations, tutorials, and workshops.
- By keeping the overall registration fee lower than recent years and by shaving one day off from the conference program, we also reduced the overall participation cost for most of the MM'11 attendees.

A travel grants program, generously supported by the National Science Foundation (NSF) and SIGMM, also helped us lower the barrier for participation for many students and, as of this writing, a full 30% of the registrants to MM'11 are students. We also have a number of mentorship activities, including women mentoring event, organized and sponsored by SIGMM, a Doctoral Symposium program, which (in addition to having regular panels and presentations as before) this year opened up its doors to all student authors who want to present posters at the event, a panel on "*Job Opportunities and Career Perspective for Fresh Graduates of the Multimedia Community*", and a new "*vis-a-vis meeting with researchers*" social event where graduate students will meet and exchange ideas and receive guidance with internationally recognized researchers in their research area.

Of course, apart from the above, MM'11 also continued with programs that proved to be extremely successful in the past. We have continued with the well-established and highly successful Open Source Software Competition, with special emphasis this year on instructional open source software designed for educational use in teaching multimedia-related courses at undergraduate or graduate level. Like the previous years, the Multimedia Grand Challenges competition attracted challenges from many leaders of the multimedia industry, including HP, Technicolor, Nokia, Yahoo, Huwei, and 3D Life, and proposals from all over the world. Similarly, this year's industrial exhibits program, which complements the MM technical demonstrations program, will focus on cutting-edge research prototypes, including system and product demonstrations from many industrial leaders, such as IBM, FX Palo Alto Labs, Microsoft Research, Exalead, and Yacast. The panels program emphasizes opportunities and challenges faced by researchers, industry, and open-source communities in multimedia and thus covers timely topics, such as "*Smart Games*", "*Towards Synergy Between the Open Source and the Research Multimedia Communities*", and "*Innovating the Multimedia Experience*".

We are enthused to report that MM'11 includes three exciting keynote talks by three industry and academic leaders in multimedia research: Alex Pentland, Head of the MIT Human Dynamics Lab, Genevieve Bell, Director of the Interaction and Experience Research at the Intel Labs, and Arnaud Robert, Senior Vice President of Technology at The Walt Disney Studios. Last, but certainly not the least, we are proud that MM'11 hosts the prestigious SIGMM Technical Achievement Award presentation to Prof Shih-Fu Chang (Columbia University) and his award acceptance speech.

We would like to acknowledge those who have contributed to the success of MM'11. First of all, we would like to thank all authors who submitted papers to the technical program, various workshops, and other events of MM'11. We also thank the authors of the accepted papers who will present their work in MM'11 and the panelists and keynote speakers who have accepted to participate in the conference to discuss current and future challenges in the field of multimedia and to propose innovative solutions. We are grateful to the members of the various program committees and external reviewers who have helped put together a high-quality program and would like acknowledge members of the various MM'11 organizing committees and many student volunteers for their invaluable help at every step of the process. We would like to thank the staff of ACM and Sheridan for their continuous support and the Conference Management Toolkit Team (CMT) at Microsoft for letting us use CMT for handling the submission and review workflows of MM'11. Finally, we would like to thank our sponsors (as of this writing), Google, IBM, Microsoft, FxPal, Technicolor, Qualcomm, Springer, Yahoo!, Arizona State University, and the University of Texas at Dallas, who have extended their generous support to MM'11. We would also like to thank the National Science Foundation (NSF) and SIGMM for their generous support for the MM'11 student travel award program

We hope that you will enjoy the ACM MM'11 conference.

K. Selçuk Candan
Sethuraman (Panch) Panchanthan
Balakrishnan (Prabha) Prabhakaran
ACM MM'11 General Chairs

Message from the Technical Program Chairs

We have an exciting technical program at ACM Multimedia 2011. The process to select the technical program included several innovations. These innovations — guided by the recent report by a select SIG Multimedia committee — include the following: move to technical areas instead of tracks, each submitted paper had a primary area and an optional secondary area set by the authors at the time of submission, and an author rebuttal phase.

The ten areas were as follows:

- Multi-modal Integration and Understanding in the Imperfect World
- Media Analysis and Search
- Scalability in Media Processing, Analysis, and Applications
- Multimedia Systems and Middleware
- Media Transport and Sharing
- Multimedia Security
- Media Authoring and Production
- Location-based and Mobile Multimedia
- Human, Social, and Educational Aspects of Multimedia
- Arts and Contemporary Digital Culture

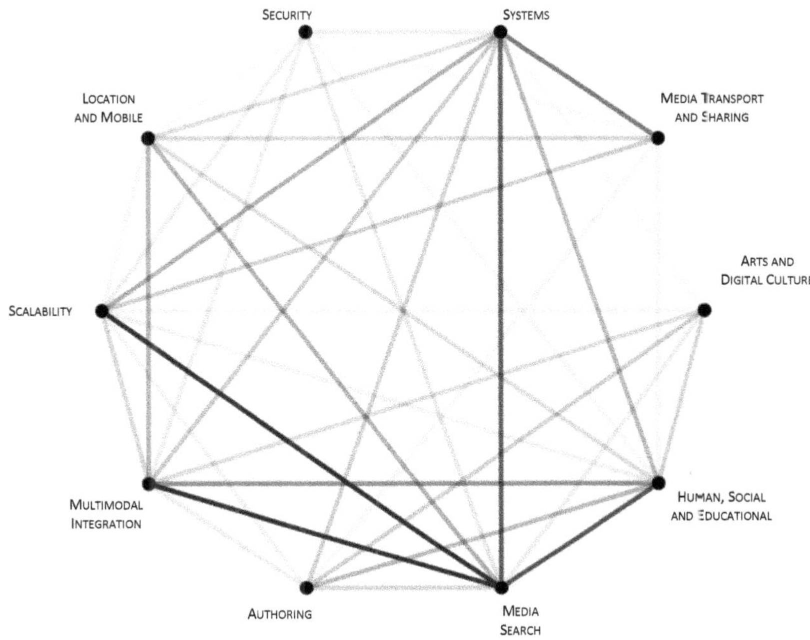

CROSS-LINKAGES BETWEEN PRIMARY AND SECONDARY AREAS

The areas — chosen in consultation with the broad SIG Multimedia community — reflect core research areas (e.g. multimedia systems and middleware), as well as different multimedia research contexts (e.g. location-based mobile multimedia). Typically, each area had two area chairs managing the review process; media analysis and search was an exception: due to the large number of submissions (39%), we assigned six area chairs to manage this area. The figure above shows the relationship between areas in the papers submitted for review— there is an edge between two areas when a paper has both areas specified in the paper. In the figure, edges with higher strength are more opaque.

Many authors specified both primary and secondary areas, resulting in the assignment of two reviewers from the primary area and one reviewer from the secondary area. In the minority of cases when there was no secondary area, we assigned all three reviewers from the primary area. The selection of reviewers from two different areas, allowed for a cross-disciplinary evaluation of the submitted paper. In past conferences a paper submitted to one of the four tracks was exclusively evaluated by reviewers from that track. Additionally, to increase the responsibility of the chairs as well as to give more credit to their work on their accepted paper, we have indicated the name of the AC that was supervising the reviewing process and which recommended the paper for acceptance.

The conference was highly competitive with low acceptance rates. We received a total of 666 submissions which included 335 long papers and 331 short papers. Subsequent to the initial notification, authors had one week to rebut the criticisms of the papers. After the rebuttal phase, the area chairs led a discussion with the reviewers on the merits of each paper, which included the author rebuttals. In the end, we accepted 58 long papers, with an acceptance rate of 17.3%, and 120 short papers with an acceptance rate of 36.3%. We additionally recommended 52 long papers to appear as short papers. The figure below shows the distribution of primary areas for all papers. We selected three papers were selected for the best paper and best student paper session. We solicited nominations from each area, for best student paper and best paper competition. The technical program chairs selected three from the nominations.

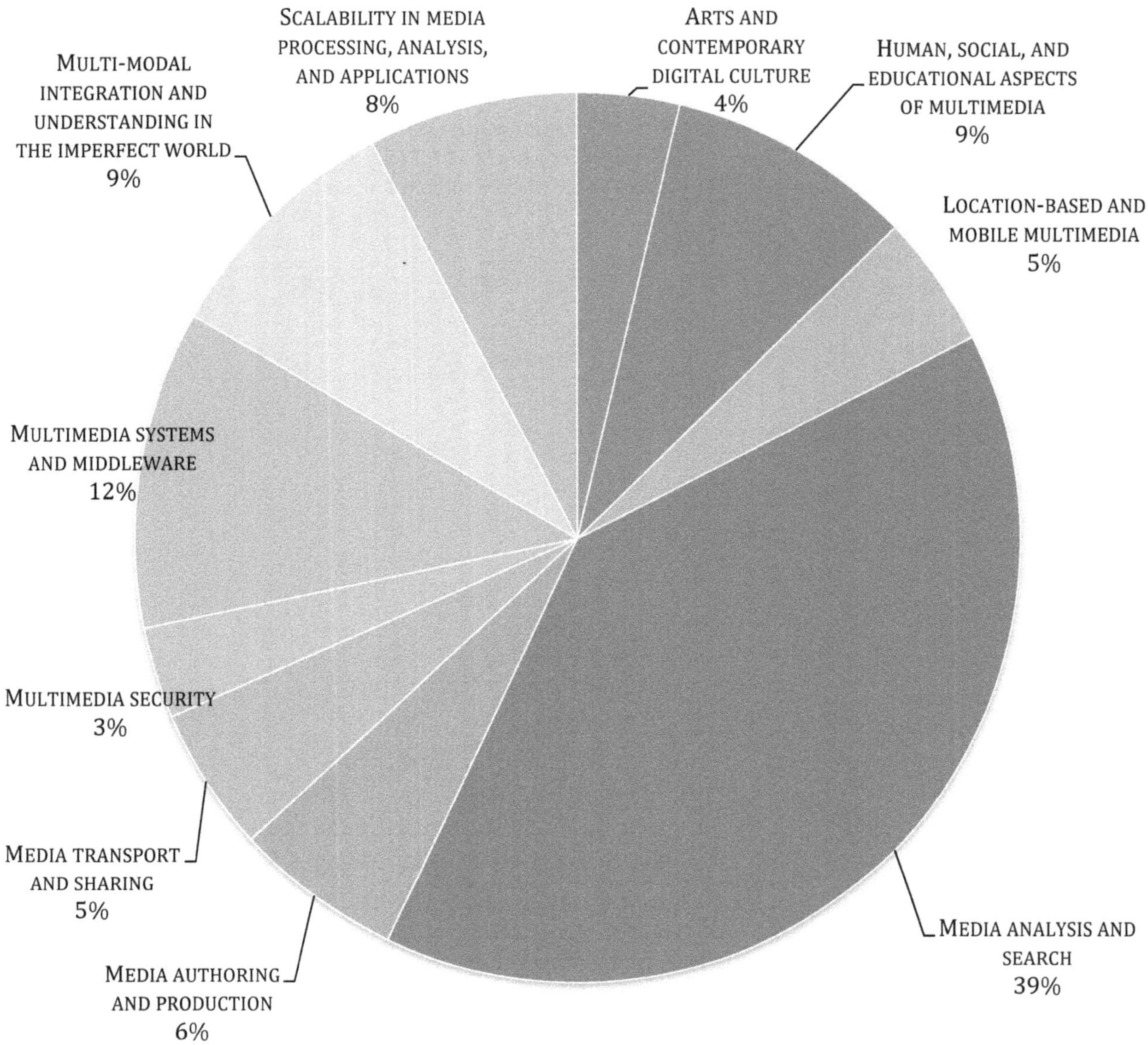

We would like to thank all of our area chairs and reviewers who volunteered a significant amount of their time to ensure a high quality program.

Hari Sundaram,
ACM MM'11,
Technical Program Chair
Arizona State University, USA

Wu-Chi Feng,
ACM MM'11,
Technical Program Chair
Portland State University, USA

Nicu Sebe,
ACM MM'11,
Technical Program Chair
University of Trento, Italy

Table of Contents

Short Papers: Session 2

Short Papers: Session 3

ACM Multimedia 2011 Conference

General Chairs: K. Selçuk Candan *(Arizona State University, USA)*
Sethuraman Panchanathan *(Arizona State University, USA)*
Balakrishnan Prabhakaran *(University of Texas at Dallas, USA)*

Local Arrangement Chairs: Vineeth Nallure Balasubramanian *(Arizona State University, USA)*
Baoxin Li *(Arizona State University, USA)*

Technical Program Committee Chairs: Wu-Chi Feng *(Portland State University, USA)*
Nicu Sebe *(University of Trento, Italy)*
Hari Sundaram *(Arizona State University, USA)*

High-Risk High-Return Papers Chairs: Ramesh Jain *(Portland State University, USA)*
Ralf Steinmetz *(TU Darmstadt, Germany)*
Svetha Venkatesh *(Curtin University, Australia)*
Michelle Zhou *(IBM Research, USA)*

Multimedia Grand Challenge Chairs: Gerald Friedland *(ICSI, University of California at Berkeley, USA)*
Yohan Jin *(MySpace, Inc., USA)*

Tutorials Chairs: Jiebo Luo *(University of Rochester, USA)*
Thomas Plagemann *(University of Oslo, Norway)*
Zhongfei Zhang *(Binghamton University, USA)*

Panels Chairs: Shahram Ghandeharizadeh *(University of Southern California, USA)*
Forouzan Golshani *(California State University Long Beach, USA)*
Stefan Gobel *(TU Darmstadt, Germany)*

Technical Demo Chairs: Vincent Charvillat *(University of Toulouse, France)*
Shervin Shirmohammadi *(University of Ottawa, Canada)*
Roger Zimmerman *(National University of Singapore, Singapore)*

Industrial Exhibit Chairs: Deepak Turaga *(IBM T. J. Watson Research Center, USA)*
Dulce Ponceleon *(IBM Almaden, USA)*
Ajay Divakaran *(Sarnoff Corporation, USA)*

Workshop Chairs: Jin Li *(Microsoft Research, USA)*
Maria Luisa Sapino *(University of Turin, Italy)*
Borko Furht *(Florida Atlantic University, USA)*

History Preservation Chairs: Alberto Del Bimbo *(University of Florence, Italy)*
Chabane Djeraba *(University of Lille, France)*
Carsten Griwodz *(University of Oslo, Norway)*

Web Chairs: Xiaohu Guo *(University of Texas at Dallas, USA)*
Daragh Byrne *(Dublin City University, Ireland)*

Sponsorship Chairs:	Abdulmotaleb El Saddik *(University of Ottawa, Canada)* John R. Smith *(IBM T. J. Watson Research Center, USA)* Wolfgang Klas *(University of Vienna, Austria)* Yong Rui *(Microsoft Research Asia, China)*
Publicity and Social Media Chairs:	Romulus Grigoras *(University of Toulouse, France)* Marcel Worring *(University of Amsterdam, The Netherlands)* Laurent Amsaleg *(CNRS-IRISA, France)*
Doctoral Symposium Chairs:	Yu-Ru Lin *(Arizona State University, USA)* Vincent Oria *(NJIT, USA)*
Travel Grant Chairs:	Jong Wook Kim *(Teradata, USA)* Tao Mei *(Microsoft Research Asia, China)* Antonio Picariello *(University of Naples, Italy)*
Proceedings Chairs:	Marco Patella *(University of Bologna, Italy)* Xavier Anguera *(Telefonica R&D, Spain)*
Interactive Art Exhibit Chairs:	Todd Ingalls *(Arizona State University, USA)* David Tinapple *(Arizona State University, USA)*
Open Source Software Competition Chairs:	Wei-Tsang Ooi *(National University of Singapore, Singapore)* Pablo Cesar *(CWI, The Netherlands)*
Finance and Registration Chairs:	Ming Li *(California State University Fresno, USA)* Shu-Ching Chen *(Florida International University, USA)*
Industrial Panels Chairs:	Khaled El-Maleh *(Qualcomm, USA)* Haohong Wang *(TCL Research America, USA)*

ACM Multimedia 2011 Program Committees

Location-Based and Mobile Multimedia Chairs:
Gang Hua *(IBM Research, USA)*
Daniel Gatica-Perez *(Idiap Research Institute, Switzerland)*

Location-Based and Mobile Multimedia:
Jianfei Cai *(Nanyang Technical University, Singapore)*
Roberto Cesar *(University of San Paulo, Brazil)*
Tim Cheng *(University of California Santa Barbara, USA)*
Radek Grzeszczuk *(Nokia Research Center Palo Alto, USA)*
Ton Kalker *(Huawei Technologies, USA)*
Stephan Kopf *(University of Mannheim, Germany)*
Thommen Korah *(Nokia Research Center Hollywood, USA)*
Paisarn Muneesawang *(Naresuan University, Thailand)*
Timo Ojala *(University of Oulu, Finland)*
Nuria Oliver *(Telefonica, Spain)*
Michael Rohs *(University of Munich, Germany)*
Enrico Rukzio *(University of Duisburg-Essen, Germany)*
Eckehard Steinbach *(Munich University of Technology, Germany)*
Ye-Kui Wang *(Huawei Technologies, USA)*
Hongkai Xiong *(Shanghai Jiao Tong University, China)*
Yu Zheng *(Microsoft Research Asia, China)*

Scalability in Media Processing, Analysis, and Applications Chairs:
Xian-Sheng Hua *(Microsoft Research Asia, China)*
Lei Chen *(Hong Kong University of Science & Technology, China)*

Scalability in Media Processing, Analysis, and Applications:
Edward Chang *(Google Inc., USA)*
Michel Crucianu *(CNAM, France)*
Bin Cui *(Peking University, China)*
Alan Hanjalic *(TU Delft, The Netherlands)*
Ichiro Ide *(Nagoya University, Japan)*
Vincent Oria *(NJIT, USA)*
Malcolm Slaney *(Yahoo, USA)*
Jingdong Wang *(Microsoft Research Asia, China)*
Shuicheng Yan *(National University of Singapore, Singapore)*
Jun Yang *(Carnegie Mellon University, USA)*
Xiangmin Zhou *(CSIRO, Australia)*
Xiaofang Zhou *(University of Queensland, Australia)*

Multi-Modal Integration and Understanding in the Imperfect World Chairs:

Cees Snoek *(University of Amsterdam, The Netherlands)*
Marco Bertini *(University of Florence, Italy)*
Alexander Hauptmann *(Carnegie Mellon University, USA)*

Multi-Modal Integration and Understanding in the Imperfect World:

Andrea Cavallaro *(Queen Mary University of London, UK)*
Yinpeng Chen *(Arizona State University, USA)*
Stefanie Nowak *(Fraunhofer IDMT, Germany)*
Tamara Berg *(Stony Brook University, USA)*
Daragh Byrne *(Dublin City University, Ireland)*
Josep Casas *(Technical University of Catalonia, Spain)*
Rita Cucchiara *(University of Modena, Italy)*
Fernando de la Torre *(Carnegie Mellon University, USA)*
Abdulmotaleb El Saddik *(University of Ottawa, Canada)*
Benoit Huet *(Eurecom, France)*
Yu-Gang Jiang *(Columbia University, USA)*
Michael Lew *(Leiden University, The Netherlands)*
Rainer Lienhart *(Augsburg University, Germany)*
Wei-Hao Lin *(Google Inc., USA)*
Suzanne Little *(Open University, UK)*
Joao Magalhaes *(NOVA University of Lisbon, Portugal)*
Vasileios Mezaris *(ITI-CERTH, Greece)*
Adrian Ulges *(DFKI, Germany)*
Remco Veltkamp *(Utrecht University, The Netherlands)*
Rong Yan *(Facebook, USA)*
Ichiro Ide *(Nagoya University, Japan)*

Media Analysis and Search Chairs:

Tat-Seng Chua *(National University of Singapore, Singapore)*
Lexing Xie *(Australian National University, Australia)*
Bernard Merialdo *(Eurecom, France)*
Marcel Worring *(University of Amsterdam, The Netherlands)*
Qi Tian *(University of Texas at San Antonio, USA)*
Kiyoharu Aizawa *(University of Tokyo, Japan)*

Media Analysis and Search:

Laurent Amsaleg *(CNRS-IRISA, France)*
Xavier Anguera *(Telefonica R&D, Spain)*
Yiannis Avrithis *(NTUA, Greece)*
Noboru Babaguchi *(Osaka University, Japan)*
Juan Cao *(Chinese Academy of Sciences, China)*
Liangliang Cao *(University of Illinois at Urbana-Champaign, USA)*
Shih-Fu Chang *(Columbia University, USA)*
Xinyi Cui *(Rutgers University, USA)*
Mohamed Daoudi *(LIFL, France)*
Tri Do *(Idiap Research Institute, Switzerland)*
Dan Ellis *(Columbia University, USA)*
Ed Fox *(Virginia Tech, USA)*
Yuli Gao *(Google, Inc., USA)*
Zan Gao *(Beijing Univ. of Posts and Telecommunications, China)*
Mei Han *(Google, Inc., USA)*
Allan Hanbury *(Vienna University of Technology, Austria)*
Richard Hong *(Hefei University of Technology, China)*
Winston Hsu *(National Taiwan University, Taiwan)*
Hayley Hung *(University of Amsterdam, The Netherlands)*
Rongrong Ji *(Columbia University, USA)*
Qifa Ke *(Microsoft Research, USA)*
Lyndon Kennedy *(Yahoo! Research, USA)*
Yannis Kompatsiaris *(CERT-IT, Greece)*
Jiebo Luo *(University of Rochester, USA)*
R Manmatha *(University of Massachusetts Amherst, USA)*
Stéphane Marchand-Maillet *(University of Geneva, Switzerland)*
Tao Mei *(Microsoft Research, USA)*
Frank Nack *(University of Amsterdam, The Netherlands)*
Paul Natsev *(IBM Research, USA)*
Chong Wah Ngo *(City University of Hong Kong, China)*
Noel O'Connor *(CLARITY, Ireland)*
Bo Qiu *(Institute for Infocomm Research, Singapore)*
Shinichi Satoh *(NII, Japan)*
Behzad Shahraray *(AT&T Labs Research, USA)*
Heng Tao Shen *(University of Queensland, Australia)*

Media Analysis and Search (continued):

Jialie Shen *(Singapore Management University, Singapore)*
Alan Smeaton *(Dublin City University, Ireland)*
Julian Stottinger *(Vienna University of Technology, Austria)*
Hao Tang *(HP Labs, USA)*
Jinhui Tang *(Nanjing University of Science and Technology, China)*
Jasper Uijlings *(University of Trento, Italy)*
Koen Van de Sande *(University of Amsterdam, The Netherlands)*
Roelof van Zwol *(Yahoo! Research, USA)*
Jun Wang *(IBM Research, USA)*
Meng Wang *(National University of Singapore, Singapore)*
Ye Wang *(National University of Singapore, Singapore)*
Lynn Wilcox *(FX PAL, USA)*
Xiao Wu *(Southwest Jiaotong University, China)*
Zhipeng Wu *(University of Tokyo, Japan)*
Dong Xu *(Nanyang Technical University, Singapore)*
Eric Zavesky *(AT&T Labs Research, USA)*
Zheng-Jun Zha *(National University of Singapore, Singapore)*
Cha Zhang *(Microsoft Research, USA)*
Lei Zhang *(Microsoft Research Asia, China)*

Media Authoring and Production Chairs:

Susanne Boll *(University of Oldenburg, Germany)*
Dick Bulterman *(CWI, The Netherlands)*

Media Authoring and Production:

Cyril Concolato *(Telecom ParisTech , France)*
Ritendra Datta *(Google Inc., USA)*
Andreas Girgensohn *(FX PAL, USA)*
Luiz Fernando Gomes Soares *(PUC-RIO, Brasil)*
Fons Kuijk *(CWI, The Netherlands)*
Rodrigo Laiola Guimaraes *(CWI, The Netherlands)*
Qian Lin *(HP Labs, USA)*
Wei-Hao Lin *(Google Inc., USA)*
Feng Liu *(Portland State University, USA)*
Frank Nack *(University of Amsterdam, The Netherlands)*
Maria Pimentel *(ICMC-USP, Brasil)*
Cecile Roisin *(Grenoble University – INRIA, France)*
Lloyd Rutledge *(Open University, The Netherlands)*
Ansgar Scherp *(University of Koblenz-Landau, Germany)*
Jacco van Ossenbruggen *(VU University, The Netherlands)*

Multimedia Systems and Middleware

Chairs: Pål Halvorsen *(University of Oslo, Norway)*
Wei-Tsang Ooi *(National University of Singapore, Singapore)*

Multimedia Systems and Middleware: Dewan Tanvir Ahmed *(University of Ottawa, Canada)*
Laszlo Boszormenyi *(Klagenfurt University, Austria)*
Vincent Charvillat *(IRIT - University of Toulouse, France)*
Sheng-Wei Chen *(Academia Sinica, Taiwan)*
Yen-Kuang Chen *(Intel, USA)*
Touradj Ebrahimi *(EPFL, Switzerland)*
Alexander Eichhorn *(Simula Research Lab, Norway)*
Romulus Grigoras *(University of Toulouse, France)*
Ravindra Guntur *(National University of Singapore, Singapore)*
Hermann Hellwagner *(Klagenfurt University, Austria)*
Andreas Mauthe *(Lancaster University, UK)*
Ketan Mayer-Patel *(UNC-Chapel Hill, USA)*
Sebastien Mondet *(University of Oslo, Norway)*
Klara Nahrstedt *(University of Illinois at Urbana-Champaign, USA)*
Nabil Sarhan *(Wayne State University, USA)*
Karsten Schwan *(Georgia Institute of Technology, USA)*
Timothy Shih *(National Central University, Taiwan)*
Ralph Steinmetz *(TU Darmstadt, Germany)*
Jingtao Wen *(Tsinghua University, China)*
Chuan Wu *(University of Hong Kong, China)*
Ja-Ling Wu *(National Taiwan University, Taiwan)*
Michael Zink *(University of Massachusetts Amherst, USA)*

Media Transport and Sharing Chairs: Reza Rejaie *(University of Oregon, USA)*
Surendar Chandra *(FX PAL, USA)*

Media Transport and Sharing: Kevin Almeroth *(University of California Santa Barbara, USA)*
Grenville Armitage *(Swinburne Univ. of Technology, Australia)*
Nina Bhatti *(HP Labs, USA)*
David Choffnes *(University of Washington, USA)*
Mark Claypool *(Worcester Polytechnic Institute, USA)*
Walid Dabbous *(INRIA, France)*
Wu-Chi Feng *(Portland State University, USA)*
Tristan Henderson *(University of St. Andrews, UK)*
Cheng-Hsin Hsu *(Deutsche Telekom, Germany)*
Sugih Jamin *(University of Michigan, USA)*
Sebastian Kaune *(TU Darmstadt, Germany)*
Dejan Kostic *(EPFL, Switzerland)*
Charles (Buck) Krasic *(Google Inc., USA)*
Baochun Li *(University of Toronto, Canada)*
Nazanin Magharei *(University of Oregon, USA)*
Sue Moon *(KAIST, South Korea)*
Misha Rabinovich *(Case Western Reserve University, USA)*
Sanjay Rao *(Purdue University, USA)*
Kave Salamatian *(University of Savoy, France)*
Subhabrata Sen *(AT&T Labs, USA)*
Anees Shaikh *(IBM T. J. Watson Research Center, USA)*
Nalini Venkatasubramanian *(University of California Irvine, USA)*
Joerg Widmer *(IMDEA, Spain)*
Roger Zimmermann *(National University of Singapore, Singapore)*

Multimedia Security Chairs: Qibin Sun *(Institute for Infocomm Research, Singapore)*
Tian-Tsong Ng *(Institute for Infocomm Research, Singapore)*

Multimedia Security: Feng Bao *(Institute for Infocomm Research, Singapore)*
Li Bin *(Shenzen University, China)*
Rainer Böhme *(University of Munster, Germany)*
Ee-Chien Chang *(National University of Singapore, Singapore)*
Robert Deng *(Singapore Management University, Singapore)*
Gwenael Doerr *(Technicolor, France)*
Sabu Emmanuel *(Nanyang Technological University, Singapore)*
Xinting Gao*(Institute for Infocomm Research, Singapore)*
Alex Kot *(Nanyang Technological University, Singapore)*
Ching-Yung Lin *(IBM Research, USA)*
Siwei Lyu *(SUNY Albany, USA)*
Ee Sin Ng *(Cambridge University, UK)*
Yun-Qing Shi *(NJIT, USA)*
Tieniu Tan *(Chinese Academy of Sciences, China)*
Min Wu *(University of Maryland, USA)*

Human, Social, and Educational Aspects of Multimedia Chairs:

Massimo Zancanaro *(Fondazione Bruno Kessler, Italy)*
Mor Naaman *(Rutgers University, USA)*

Human, Social, and Educational Aspects of Multimedia:

Elisabeth Andre *(University of Augsburg, Germany)*
Tico Ballagas *(Nokia Research Palo Alto, USA)*
Frank Bentley *(Motorola Mobility Applied Research Center, USA)*
K. Selçuk Candan *(Arizona State University, USA)*
Marc Cavazza *(University of Teesside, UK)*
Pablo Cesar *(CWI, The Netherlands)*
Keith Cheverst *(Lancaster University, UK)*
Gregorio Convertino *(Palo Alto Research Center, USA)*
Matthew Cooper *(FX PAL, USA)*
Aiden Doherty *(University of Oxford, UK)*
Berna Erol *(Ricoh California Research Center, USA)*
Leonardo Giusti *(MIT, USA)*
Erik Grönvall *(Aarhus University, Denmark)*
Alex Jaimes *(Yahoo! Research, USA)*
Ramesh Jain *(University of California Irvine, USA)*
Antonio Krueger *(DFKI, Germany)*
Oswald Lanz *(Fondazione Bruno Kessler, Italy)*
Bruno Lepri *(Fondazione Bruno Kessler, Italy)*
Venet Osmani *(CREATE-NET, Italy)*
Matthias Rehm *(University of Aalborg, Denmark)*
Nicu Sebe *(University of Trento, Italy)*
Börkur Sigurbjörnsson *(Yahoo! Research, USA)*
Ramanathan Subramanian *(University of Trento, Italy)*
Hari Sundaram *(Arizona State University, USA)*
Raphael Troncy *(Eurecom, France)*
Svetha Venkatesh *(Curtin University, Australia)*
Justin Weisz *(IBM T.J. Watson Research, USA)*
Michelle Zhou *(IBM Research, USA)*

Arts and Contemporary Digital Culture Chairs: Aisling Kelliher *(Arizona State University, USA)*
David A. Shamma *(Yahoo! Research, USA)*

Arts and Contemporary Digital Culture: Barbara Barry *(One Laptop Per Child, USA)*
Joanna Berzowska *(Concordia University, Canada)*
Elizabeth Churchill *(Yahoo! Research, USA)*
Luca Farulli *(Academy of Fine Arts of Venice, Italy)*
Karrie Karahalios *(Univ. of Illinois at Urbana-Champaign, USA)*
Jofish Kaye*(Nokia Research Palo Alto, USA)*
Andruid Kerne *(Texas A&M, USA)*
Ann Morrison *(HIIT, Finland)*
Edgar Roman-Rangel *(Idiap Research Institute, Switzerland)*
Jurgen Scheible *(Aalto University, Finland)*
Sha Xin Wei *(Concordia University, Canada)*

Open Source Software Competition Chairs: Wei-Tsang Ooi *(National University of Singapore, Singapore)*
Pablo Cesar *(CWI, The Netherlands)*

Open Source Software Competition Evaluation Members: John Adcock *(FX PAL, USA)*
Xavier Amatriain Rubio *(Netflix, USA)*
Marco Bertini *(University of Florence, Italy)*
Andrea Vedaldi *(Oxford University, UK)*
Mathias Lux *(Klagenfurt University, Austria)*
Ye Wang *(National University of Singapore, Singapore)*
Ketan Mayer-Patel *(UNC-Chapel Hill, USA)*
Sebastien Mondet *(University of Oslo, Norway)*
Hendrik Knoche *(EPFL, Switzerland)*
Pavel Korshunov *(EPFL, Switzerland)*
Cyril Concolato *(Telecom ParisTech , France)*

Multimedia Grand Challenge Chairs: Gerald Friedland *(ICSI, University of California at Berkeley, USA)*
Yohan Jin *(MySPace, Inc., USA)*

Multimedia Grand Challenge: Patrick Perez *(Technicolor, France)*
Qian Lin *(HP Labs, USA)*
Kaushal Kurapati *(Yahoo! Research, USA)*
Timo Pekka Pylvanainen *(Nokia Research Center Tampere, Finland)*

Doctoral Symposium Chairs: Yu-Ru Lin *(Arizona State University, USA)*
Vincent Oria *(NJIT, USA)*

Doctoral Symposium: Cristian Borcea, *(NJIT, USA)*
K. Selçuk Candan *(Arizona State University, USA)*
Cees Snoek *(University of Amsterdam, The Netherlands)*
Michelle Zhou *(IBM Research, USA)*
Michel Crucianu *(CNAM, France)*
Surendar Chandra *(FX PAL, USA)*
Valerie Gouet-Brunet *(CNAM, France)*
Maria Luisa Sapino *(University of Turin, Italy)*
Ichiro Ide *(Nagoya University, Japan)*
Shinichi Satoh *(NII, Japan)*

ACM Multimedia 2011 Additional Reviewers

Parag Agarwal *(Microsoft, USA)*
Nikolaus Bee *(Augsburg University, Germany)*
Joan-Isaac Biel *(Idiap Research Institute, Switzerland)*
Damian Borth *(DFKI, Germany)*
Liangliang Cao *(IBM Research, USA)*
Axel Carlier *(National University of Singapore, Singapore)*
Robert Ming-Yu Chen *(Carnegie Mellon University, USA)*
Shu-Ching Chen *(Florida International University, USA)*
Yan-Ying Chen *(National Taiwan University, Taiwan)*
Wen-Huang Cheng *(Academia Sinica, Taiwan)*
Zhiyong Cheng *(Singapore Management University, Singapore)*
Tzu-Hsuan Chiu *(National Taiwan University, Taiwan)*
Wei-Ta Chu *(Nanyang Technical University, Singapore)*
Sashikanth Damaraju *(Texas A&M University, USA)*
Chi Tai Dang *(Augsburg University, Germany)*
Daisuke Deguchi *(Nagoya University, Japan)*
Lei Ding *(Ohio State University, USA)*
Cem Direkoglu *(Dublin City University, Ireland)*
Lixin Duan *(Nanyang Technical University, Singapore)*
Abdallah El Ali *(University of Amsterdam, The Netherlands)*
Gwenn Englebienne *(University of Amsterdam, The Netherlands)*
Marin Ferecatu *(CNAM, France)*
Rogerio Feris *(IBM Research, USA)*
Mingchen Gao *(Rutgers University, USA)*
Thomas Gloe *(Dresden University of Technology, Germany)*
Luke Gottlieb *(International Computer Science Institute, USA)*
Benjamin Guthier *(University of Mannheim, Germany)*
William Hamilton *(Texas A&M University, USA)*
Matthew Hill *(IBM Research, USA)*
Steven Hoi *(Nanyang Technical University, Singapore)*
Liang-Chi Hsieh *(National Taiwan University, Taiwan)*
Min-Chun Hu *(Nanyang Technical University, Singapore)*
Minqing Hu *(Teradata, USA)*
Chun-Hsiang Huang *(Nanyang Technical University, Singapore)*
Adam Janin *(International Computer Science Institute, USA)*
Matthias Kirchner *(Dresden University of Technology, Germany)*
Felix Kistler *(Augsburg University, Germany)*
Yin-Hsi Kuo *(National Taiwan University, Taiwan)*
Namhee Kwon *(Incentica Lab, USA)*
Wen-Yu Lee *(National Taiwan University, Taiwan)*
Tayeb Lemlouma *(IRISA, France)*
Chuanjun Li *(PROS Pricing, USA)*
Xirong Li *(University of Amsterdam, The Netherlands)*
Yen-Liang Lin *(National Taiwan University, Taiwan)*
Dong Liu *(Columbia University, USA)*
Tinglin Liu *(Rutgers University, USA)*
Wei Liu *(Columbia University, USA)*
Zhiyuan Liu *(Google Inc., USA)*
Zhu Liu *(AT&T Labs, USA)*
Wenjun Lu *(University of Maryland, USA)*
Mathias Lux *(Klagenfurt University, Austria)*
Zhigang Ma *(University of Trento, Italy)*
Kevin McGuinness *(Dublin City University, Ireland)*
Michele Merler *(Columbia University, USA)*
Robert Mertens *(International Computer Science Institute, USA)*
David Monaghan *(Dublin City University, Ireland)*
Joe Munoz *(Hatch Labs, USA)*
Spiros Nikolopoulos *(CERTH, Greece)*
Naoko Nitta *(Osaka University, Japan)*
Yin Qu *(Texas A&M University, USA)*
Giuseppe Rizzo *(Eurecom, France)*
Daniel Rule *(MySpace, USA)*
Philipp Schaber *(University of Mannheim, Germany)*
Klaus Schöffmann *(Klagenfurt University, Austria)*
Christian Schulze *(DFKI, Germany)*
Sancho Sebastine *(Datran Media,USA)*
Xiance Si *(Google Inc., USA)*
Jacopo Staiano *(University of Trento, Italy)*
Junwoon Suh *(Sarnoff Corporation, USA)*

Myunghoon Suk *(University of Texas at Dallas, USA)*
Jichao Sun *(NJIT, USA)*
Tomokazu Takahashi *(Gifu Shotoku Gakuen University, Japan)*
Yan Tang *(AMD, USA)*
Giorgos Tolias *(NTUA, Greece)*
Avinash Varna *(Intel, USA)*
Johannes Wagner *(Augsburg University, Germany)*
Yichu Wang *(University of California, Santa Barbara, USA)*
Zhiyu Wang *(Google Inc., USA)*
Hazem Wannous *(Telecom Lille, France)*
Andrew Webb *(Texas A&M University, USA)*
Kenji Yamada *(AT&T Interactive, USA)*
Keiji Yanai *(University of Electro-Communications, Japan)*
Xin Yang *(University of California Santa Barbara, USA)*
Victoria Yanulevskaya *(University of Trento, Italy)*
Xiangqian Yu *(NJIT, USA)*
Gloria Zen *(University of Trento, Italy)*
Shaoting Zhang *(Rutgers University, USA)*
Lin Zhong *(Rutgers University, USA)*

ACM Multimedia 2011 Sponsors & Supporters

Financial Support Provided by the Following Sponsors:

Gold: Google

Silver: ASU, Qualcomm, UTD

Bronze: FXPAL, IBM, Microsoft, Springer science+business media, technicolor, Yahoo!

Contributor: Cambridge University Press

Student Travel Award Provided by the Following Federal Agency:

NSF

Analysis of Cypriot Icon Faces using ICA-Enhanced Active Shape Model Representation*

Guifang Duan*
The Institute of Science and Engineering, Ritsumeikan University
Kusatsu, Japan
gfduan@fc.ritsumei.ac.jp

Neela Sawant*
†College of Information Sciences and Technology, The Pennsylvania State University
University Park, PA
nks125@ist.psu.edu

James Z. Wang†,‡
‡Office of International Science and Engineering, National Science Foundation
Arlington, VA
jwang@ist.psu.edu

Dean Snow
Department of Anthropology, The Pennsylvania State University
University Park, PA
drs17@psu.edu

Danni Ai
Graduate School of Science and Engineering, Ritsumeikan University
Kusatsu, Japan
gr041083@ed.ritsumei.ac.jp

Yen-Wei Chen
College of Information Science and Engineering, Ritsumeikan University
Kusatsu, Japan
chen@is.ritsumei.ac.jp

ABSTRACT

Religious iconography is an integral component of the cultural heritage of Cyprus, which was once a part of the great Byzantine empire. On one hand, icons exhibit strict adherence to conventional symbols, poses and apparel. On the other hand, there is a great variety in the style of depiction that can be attributed to different schools and periods. This paper proposes an active shape model (ASM) based technique for icon face representation that can be used for style comparison and attribution. For centuries-old icons suffering from loss of paint, cracks and added noise from digitization artifacts, we apply an independent component analysis (ICA) technique to enhance the paintings' original work. The experimental results show that our method can effectively characterize Cypriot icons.

Categories and Subject Descriptors

I.4 [**Image Processing and Computer Vision**]: Enhancement, Feature Measurement (Feature Representation)

General Terms

Algorithms, Theory, Experimentation

Keywords

Cyprus, Byzantine, Iconography, Active shape model, Independent component analysis

*Duan and Sawant have equal contributions.

*Area chair: Aisling Kelliher and David A. Shamma

MM'11, November 28–December 1, 2011, Scottsdale, Arizona, USA.

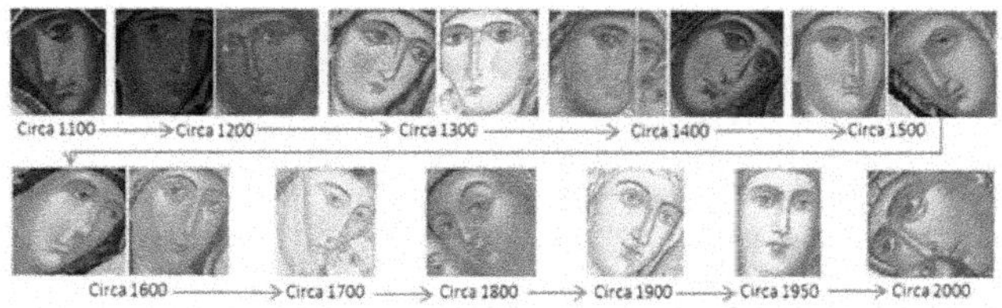

Figure 1: Style variations in the depiction of Mary

1. INTRODUCTION

Iconography is one of the most defining characteristics of the Byzantine empire seated at Constantinople from 330 AD to 1453 AD. Icons are religious artworks that depict important characters and events in the orthodox Christian belief, offering a spiritual comfort through familiarity and at the same time confirming the unchanging truths of Christianity. The constancy is a direct result of a church canon that dictated repetition and copying of subject matter, facial features and poses [3]. For example, Mary, Jesus, saints and angels are depicted with halos. Angels and some saints such as John the Baptist, are conferred wings to emphasize their role as messengers. Even specific colors are used to distinguish the different themes in icons. White color, symbolizing the unrealized essence of God, is used only to depict the resurrection and transfiguration of Jesus. Gold represents heaven while red and blue colors are used to represent divine and human life respectively. These features are ubiquitous in the surviving icons found in many European and Mediterranean countries that were once a part of the Byzantine empire.

Icons from Cyprus present one of the more challenging case-studies in Byzantine iconography. While the content of icons strictly adheres to the church canon, there are distinctive stylistic trends that can be traced to socio-political changes in the last millennium. Fig. 1 shows the faces of sixteen icons of Mary selected from different periods in Cypriot iconography. The strict Byzantine style circa 1100 is identified by ascetic or non-humanized faces. Icons are depicted in complete spiritualization emphasizing smooth lines and flat

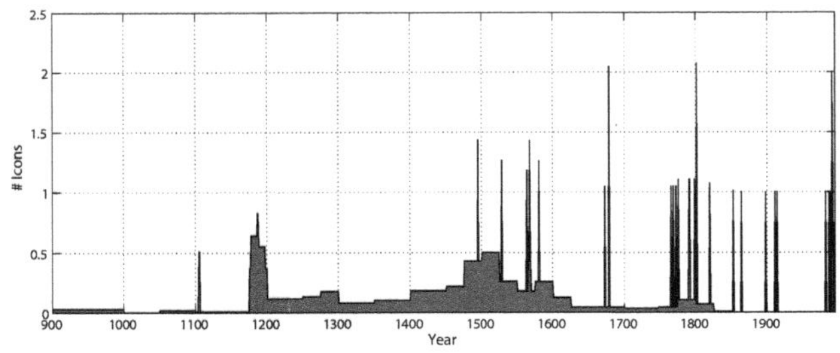

Figure 2: Temporal distribution of icon dataset

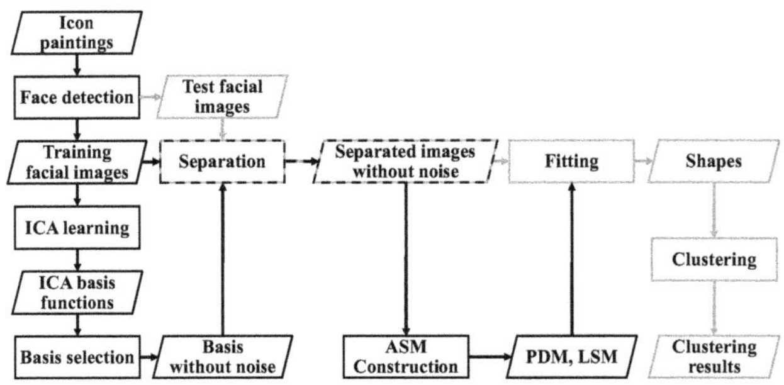

Figure 3: System flowchart

contours with careful shunning of naturalistic effects. Facial contours are accented with red, brown and black lines. The next two icons in the Comnenian style are characterized by strong accent on contours, flat clear colors and semitic features in faces. The third group of icons circa 1300 coincides with the reign of the Frankish kings. The attempt to render intense red cheeks is a noticeable characteristic from the late Comnenian period. For the next two centuries, the Venetian rulers brought a simultaneity of Latin and Christian Orthodox culture under which icon art flourished and two main factions came into existence: Italo-Byzantine (renaissance influence) and Palaeologan (conservative Byzantine). The icons circa 1400 and 1500 indicate western borrowings in the slight humanization of faces in the Italo-Byzantine style. Some 16th century icons depict seriousness in expression, large features and intense tonal gradations. After Cyprus fell to Ottoman Turks in 1571, many artists abandoned the country. A few artists developed individual styles that deviated from established schools and strict Byzantine form. The example icon circa 1800 is attributed to the school of Ioannis Kornaros, specifically to Hiermonk Charalambos. This style is characterized by round fat faces with narrow foreheads and arched eyebrows. By late 19th and early 20th century, western style of icon painting such as the Russian icon art became a major influence on Cypriot art. Icons from this period are known for their strong naturalism. Finally icons in post-independence Cyprus show a return to the strict Byzantine style similar to circa 1100.

Our collection encompasses 400 icon faces. The exact year of production is known for recent icons. Remaining icons have been analyzed by art historians and assigned to specific centuries. The plot of temporal density distribution in Fig. 2 shows the diversity of icon images. The area bounded between two years on the temporal axis (X-axis) indicates the average number of icon faces available in that time period. The spikes in the distribution (magnitude 1) correspond to paintings associated with specific production years. On the other hand, if a painting is associated with a century (such as the 12th), its density is distributed uniformly across the entire century (from 1101 to 1200). The location and style metadata is available for most icons.

1.1 Problem Definition

The problem of icon style identification and attribution is of great interest to art historians. The knowledge required to solve such inference problems is not coded in any church canon but is scholastically acquired by studying icons in detail. In this paper we propose a technique to represent and compare icons based on an automated characterization of facial features. Such tool may aid analysis of painting styles and provide an independent judgment to supplement expert opinions. The timely nature of this study may germinate many directions to preserve Cypriot cultural heritage and demonstrate the use of technology for societal good.

1.2 Related Work

The most relevant work in the analysis of Byzantine art involved automatic icon classification into categories such as Jesus, Mary, different angels and saints using explicit encoding of icon depiction rules obtained from a 16th century manual by Monk Dyonsios [8]. The rules cater to the proportions and general appearance of postures, hair and beard styles, apparel and symbols for different icons. The authors encoded these rules using Fuzzy logic, detected face components such as eyes, nose, beard, moustache and computed between-component distances and proportions. One similarity between their approach and the proposed work is the focus on facial features of icons. However, our focus is on using unsupervised techniques to identify stylistic trends not explained by color codes and written rules.

In other notable work, the research on cultural heritage spans globally. Pham conducted a style classification on Vietnamese folk paintings using color and deformable shape descriptors [7]. Classification of traditional Chinese paintings has been addressed in [6] using Brush-stroke analysis and in [5] using color, shape and texture analysis.

2. SYSTEM OVERVIEW

Centuries-old icons suffer from loss of paint and cracks. If images are obtained by scanning icon plates, artifacts such as punch holes are introduced. To handle this issue, we propose an image enhancement strategy using independent component analysis (ICA) [4]. We then apply Active Shape Model (ASM) [2] to extract facial features from ICA-enhanced icon images. As our goal is style comparison, we use a clustering approach whereby icons of different deities are grouped together if drawn in similar styles.

Fig. 3 presents the flowchart of the proposed scheme for icon face representation. The first step after acquisition of icon images is to detect faces and divide the data into train and test partitions. The training faces are processed using ICA to identify basis with maximum signal noise separation. Faces enhanced using the learned basis are input to the ASM-based feature extraction module. For the present work, we only focus on the shape information and accordingly convert color images to gray-scale. Finally, images are clustered using the extracted shape features. We now discuss the four main aspects of the system: face detection,

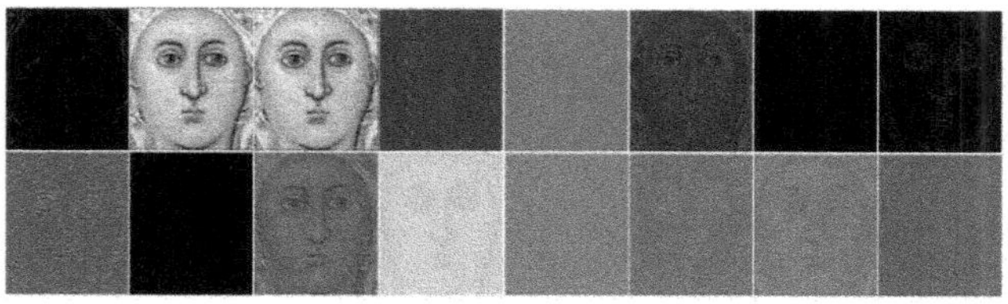

Figure 4: The separated images by 16 basis functions of ICA (contrast enhanced for illustration)

ICA decomposition and noise separation, ASM fitting, and facial feature extraction.

2.1 Face Detection

Designing icon-specific face detectors similar to Viola-Jones human face detection [9] is difficult as training requires thousands of positive samples. We have only a limited collection of faces from Cyprus, many of which are severely deteriorated. The existing detectors trained on human faces were able to detect icon faces with 65.4% precision and 29.8%. recall. Therefore, we employed manual supervision to precisely extract faces from all icon images.

2.2 ICA Decomposition and Noise Separation

The presence of noise influences local structure around facial landmarks, leading to a failure in precise feature extraction. Such noise cannot be mitigated using a conventional low-pass filter. In stead we propose an ICA-based method to get a better result. ICA is a statistical technique for decomposing a complex dataset into independent components by a linear transform. It is widely used for blind signal separation [1]. Since the basic rules of icon depiction are the same, we assume they are drawn from a blind signal source. The deterioration is treated as a noise, which we need to separate using ICA. The goal is to identify noise-free basis functions and construct ASM over enhancement of images separated by these basis functions.

To train ICA, we sampled 10,000 patches from random positions in icon face images as the training set. Each patch sample is 4×4 pixels in size, thus, we obtained 16 basis functions. An image can be decomposed into 16 components by projecting on to the subspace formed by the basis. Suppose a Cypriot icon face image is mixed by several unknown signals, it can be separated into 16 independent images as shown in Fig. 4. Using the separated images, we empirically identified projections with and without noise. For ASM construction, we choose images corresponding to the second and the third basis (the second and the third figure in the top row of Fig. 4).

2.3 ASM Construction

Originally introduced by Cootes et al.[2], ASM has been successfully applied for automatic shape extraction of deformable objects such as face, hand, and vertebra. Compared to the active contour models or snakes, ASM adds considerable variability to structure representation.

For point distribution models of ASM (PDM), we manually selected 44 landmark points (as shown in Fig. 5) to represent the shape of each Cypriot icon face. To reduce the influence of noise, each image of the training set is projected onto the 2nd and the 3rd basis of the ICA basis functions. The projected images are combined into a single image by overlapping and intensity normalization. Further, the combination is smoothed using a low pass filter. Resulting relatively noise-free images are used to train local structure models (LSM). One limitation of our approach is that the shape model does not handle large pose variations (tilted faces of some icons). We propose to remedy this issue by training additional shape models for different poses.

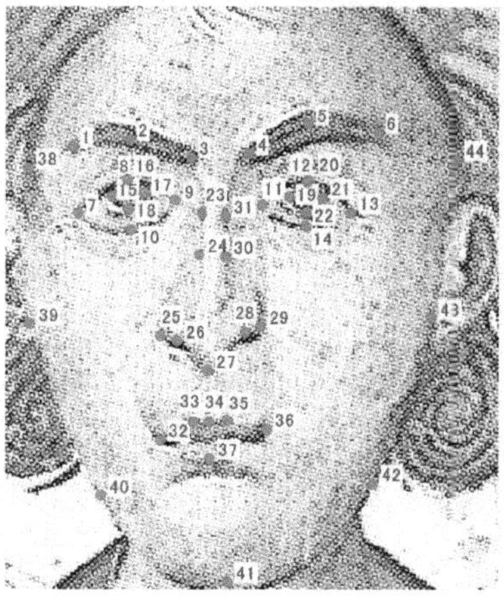

Figure 5: The 44 facial landmarks

2.4 Facial Feature Representation

Two types of representations can be extracted from active shape models. The x, y locations of landmarks are concatenated into a Type-1 representation. Since each face is represented by 44 landmarks, the dimension of a shape vector is 88. In order to reduce the influence of pose variations, shape features are normalized by Generalized Procrustes Analysis (GPA) [2]. This approach helps align shapes by minimizing the sum of distances of each of the N shapes from the mean.

An alternate Type-2 feature representation can be computed by modeling the inner distances of all landmarks from a fixed landmark. As shown in Fig. 5, the point of the nose needle (the point of No. 27) is selected as a reference point and its distance from each of the remaining 43 points is concatenated into a feature vector. These distances represent local shape composition. The local shape feature of the ith face can be denoted as a 43 dimensional vector: $\mathbf{d}_i = [d_1^i, d_2^i, \cdots, d_{43}^i]$, and normalized to account for size variations as: $\hat{\mathbf{d}}_i = \mathbf{d}_i/\sqrt{\mathbf{d}_i{}^T\mathbf{d}_i}$.

3. EXPERIMENTAL RESULTS

To limit the complexity introduced by large pose or viewpoint variation, we performed pilot experiments on frontal icon faces. A number of images suffering from heavy noise, low resolution and missing facial features were not included. Image sizes were normalized to 640×640 pixels.

3.1 Automatic Shape Extraction by ASM

We used a leave-one-out strategy to learn active shape models. In each setting, one image is used to test the model learned over the remaining images. The manually marked landmarks of a test image were not included in training but used as the ground truth for performance assessment. To determine the number of modes in point distribution models, the fraction of total variation is kept at 95%. The aver-

Figure 6: Fitting results by (a) conventional ASM and (b) proposed ASM with ICA

Figure 7: Clustering icons with Type-1 features (left) and with Type-2 features (right)

age mean square error (MSE) from our implementation is only 11.85% of that obtained from the conventional ASM (average MSE 440.84). Fig. 6 compares the sample results of automatic shape extraction obtained using conventional ASM and the proposed approach with ICA. It is seen that our method is significantly more accurate in locating and correctly annotating the required facial landmarks.

3.2 Clustering Icons with Style Similarity

We clustered the facial features of icons using the K-means algorithm. Fig. 7 shows the resultant groupings computed on Type-1 (GPA-normalized location features) and Type-2 features (inner distances from nose point) respectively.

Qualitative observations indicate that the Type-1 features yield more reasonable groupings as compared to the Type-2 features. The groupings also show a promising ability to draw parallels across different periods of the Cypriot art and by extension of the Byzantine art. Consider cluster 5 in both types of clustering results in Fig. 7. The last two icons from circa 1982 and 1192 respectively, are both drawn in the style of strict Byzantine. This is a purely computational support to art historians' belief that post-independence, the icon art in Cyprus returned to the traditional Byzantine art. Also, the first two images in the third clusters show icons of Saint Timon ($\sim$1575) and Jesus Christ ($\sim$1400) drawn in the Palaeologan style. These examples demonstrate how techniques for image analysis can be used to match an unknown icon to other icons with known metadata and automatically infer the attributes of the unknown icon.

4. CONCLUSION

Cypriot icons present an intriguing case study of cultural heritage. We presented a scheme for icon face representation using active shape model. Shape models for frontal poses were learned using icon images enhanced with independent component analysis. The experimental results showed that the adapted ASM method exceeds the conventional ASM approach in representing noisy Cypriot icons. Two types of facial features were constructed and used to group icons of similar styles. Overall, we find that the present research direction holds great promise in analyzing icons. This system can be extended to Byzantine art from other regions. One major task for future work is to systematically evaluate icon groupings with the help of art historians.

5. ACKNOWLEDGMENTS

This material is based upon the work supported by the National Science Foundation under Grant Nos. 0347148 and 0949891. The computational infrastructure was provided by the Foundation through Grant No. 0821527. Part of the work of J. Z. Wang is done while working at the Foundation. Any opinion, findings, and conclusions or recommendations expressed in this material are those of the authors and do not necessarily reflect the views of the National Science Foundation. The authors thank Sorin Hermon of the Cyprus Institute for his guidance in the initial phases of the project.

6. REFERENCES

[1] Y.-W. Chen and G. Duan. Independent component analysis based ring artifact reduction in cone-beam ct image. In *IEEE Image Processing*, pages 4189–4192, November 2009.

[2] T. F. Cootes, C. J. Taylor, D. H. Cooper, and J. Graham. Active shape models - their training and application. *Computer Vision and Image Understanding*, 61(1):38–59, January 1995.

[3] R. Cormack. *Byzantine Art.* Oxford university press, New York, 2000.

[4] A. Hyvärinen and E. Oja. Independent component analysis: Algorithms and applications. *Neural Networks*, 13(4-5):411–430, May/Jun 2000.

[5] S. Jiang, Q. Huang, Q. Ye, and W. Gao. An effective method to detect and categorized digitized traditional chinese paintings. *Pattern Recognition Letters*, 27(7):734–746, May 2006.

[6] J. Li and J. Z. Wang. Studying digital imagery of ancient paintings by mixtures of stochastic models. *IEEE Transactions on Image Processing*, 13(3):340–353, March 2004.

[7] B. Pham. Image indexing and retrieval for a vietnamese folk paintings gallery. In *DICTA'05*, pages 73–80, 2005.

[8] P. K. Tzouveli, N. Simou, G. B. Stamou, and S. D. Kollias. Semantic classification of byzantine icons. *IEEE Intelligent systems*, 24(2):35–43, March/April 2009.

[9] P. Viola and M. Jones. Robust real-time face detection. *International Journal of Computer Vision*, 57(2):137–154, May 2004.

A Creation-Tool for Contemporary Dance using Multimodal Video Annotation

Diogo Cabral[1], João Valente[1], João Silva[1], Urândia Aragão[1], Carla Fernandes[2], Nuno Correia[1]
[1]CITI, Departamento de Informática, Faculdade de Ciências e Tecnologia, FCT, 2829-516 Caparica
[2]CLUNL, Faculdade de Ciências Sociais e Humanas, FCSH, 1069-061 Lisboa
Universidade Nova de Lisboa, Portugal
diogocabral@di.fct.unl.pt, {p110356, jms19199}@fct.unl.pt,
urandia.aragao@gmail.com, carla.fernandes@fcsh.unl.pt, nmc@di.fct.unl.pt

ABSTRACT
This paper presents a video annotator that supports multimodal annotation and is applied to contemporary dance as a creation tool. The Creation-Tool was conceived and designed to assist the creative processes of choreographers, working as a digital notebook for personal annotations. The prototype, developed for Tablet PCs, is a real-time multimodal video annotator based on keyboard, pen and voice inputs. In addition, a remote control for mobile devices was added to the system. Two types of annotations were defined: annotation marks and regular annotations. The annotations marks are defined by a keyword and an icon, in contrast to regular annotations that do not have a pre-defined structure. Motion tracking defines the dynamic behavior of the annotations and voice input complements the other modalities.

Categories and Subject Descriptors
H.5. Information interfaces and presentation: H.5.1 Multimedia Information Systems-*Video*; H.5.2 User Interfaces- *Input devices and strategies*, *Interaction styles*

General Terms
Experimentation, Human Factors.

Keywords
Annotations, Video Annotations, Pen-based Video Annotations, Tablet PCs, Contemporary Dance

1. INTRODUCTION
Creative processes of choreographers, or other authors in the performative arts, involve several rehearsal iterations where video based annotation can significantly enhance the process. The TKB (A Transmedia Knowledge-Base for contemporary dance) is a transdisciplinary project that aims at designing and constructing an open-ended multimodal knowledge-base to document, annotate and support the creation of contemporary dance pieces.

In the context of the TKB project we developed a "Creation-Tool", which constitutes the object of this paper. The Creation-Tool enables to record and augment video materials with personal annotations during the rehearsal periods of a particular work.

Pen and touch as input methods offer the opportunity to craft new user experiences that are uniquely well suited to how people naturally work with pen and paper. Additionally, pen-based technology combined with digital video allows the association between handwritten annotations, or sketches, with video segments, called pen-based video annotations [4].

The Creation-Tool supports the capture and multimodal annotation of video content, in real-time. The annotations associated to video content can be text, ink strokes or audio. The prototype was developed for Tablet PCs exploring bimanual pen and touch interaction. Motion is an essential element in dance and graphical video annotations can require motion tracking methods. Graphical notes should follow the associated video elements [4], in order to maintain their context. Therefore, this work also explores pen-based or text graphical video annotations, combined with motion tracking.

2. A Creation-Tool for Contemporary Dance
This section presents the video annotator used as a creation tool for contemporary dance. Choreographers can use the system to analyze and improve their work, by recording and annotating a rehearsal, or a live performance, for a later review or for sharing notes with the performers. Remote audio capture and control were implemented, thus allowing more freedom of movements and gestures, essential on dance performance environments. Motion tracking methods are being applied to video annotations, in order to maintain their context. The video content associated with the annotations is tracked and the annotations follow it along the video. The application is also able to capture up to two video input streams.

The prototype is being developed for Tablet PCs, and currently a HP Touchsmart tm2-2150 Tablet is being used. It is implemented in C++, using OpenCV[1], openFrameworks[2] and Qt GUI[3] frameworks.

The Creation-Tool interface was designed to explore a bimanual input, using human touch and a stylus. Presently, the touch input is used for mode and tool switching, exploring the non-preferred hand mode switching [12]. In addition, a remote control interface was developed, using the TouchOSC[4] application. This remote interface allows the user to control application features, via the Open Sound Control (OSC)[5] Protocol, which works on a Wi-Fi network. Figure 1 shows the Creation-Tool and the different input modalities. It runs on a Tablet PC, allowing pen and touch

Area Chair: Aisling Kelliher

MM'11, November 28–December 1, 2011, Scottsdale, Arizona, USA.

[1] http://opencv.willowgarage.com/wiki/

[2] http://www.openframeworks.cc/

[3] http://qt.nokia.com/

[4] http://hexler.net/software/touchosc

[5] http://opensoundcontrol.org/

inputs, and uses a mobile device (iPod Touch) combined with a Bluetooth microphone for audio annotations.

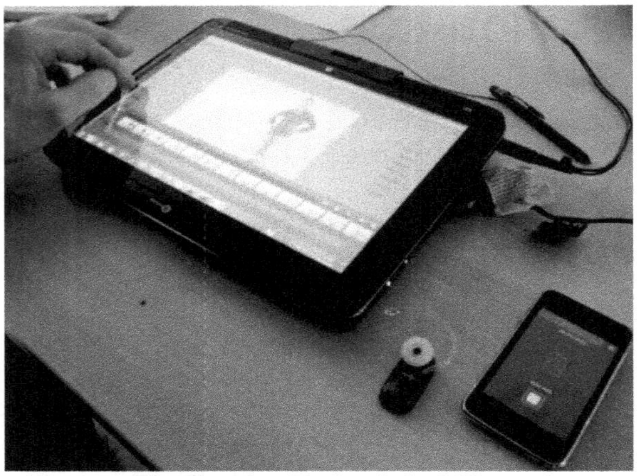

Figure 1. The Creation-Tool and the Different Input Modalities.

3. Interface Design

The interface design started from the analysis of the user needs, technical specifications and required content and features. Two choreographers with different creation processes and needs were involved from the beginning of the tool development.

Figure 2. Creation-Tool Main Interface.

The video annotator interface is composed of a video display area, presenting a live or pre-recorded stream, in which it is possible to augment the content with annotations (Figure 2). It is also possible to annotate in the area around the video window, avoiding the occlusion of video elements by the user notes. All annotations are shown in a timeline, as well as the corresponding video frames.

The menus and tool bars are organized in five sections: on the upper left side, there is the *system menu* and, on the left side, the *tools bar*. On the upper right side, the *project menu* manages all the content and files and, on the right side, *the toolsets* (related with tools bar, e.g., line color, line width, eraser) are included. At the bottom, the *timeline* is used for video and notes navigation. The timeline can be dragged down and partially hidden, avoiding the occlusion of tool buttons, video content and annotations. Sizes and spacing between buttons are related with the touch screen specifications in order to have a better performance.

In order to allow more freedom of movements and gestures, essential on dance performance environments, some application features can be controlled remotely with a mobile device via OSC. The device (e.g., iOS or Android based device) uses the TouchOSC application to send messages to the system through a graphical interface, such as starting and finishing a voice annotation or starting and stopping a video capture.

4. Video Annotations

Aiming at responding the needs of the choreographers, two types of annotations were defined: annotation marks and regular annotations. The annotation marks are concepts, defined by the choreographer. These marks are represented by a keyword, such as "lights" or "bravo", and have a correspondent icon, in contrast to regular annotations that do not have a pre-defined structure. In order to add a mark, the user presses the corresponding button in the annotation marks bar and for its removal, presses on the added mark (Figure 4).

Figure 3. Annotation Marks.

Regular annotations can be made using three different inputs: keyboard (virtual or physical), pen and voice. The pen-based and voice inputs allow two distinct types of interactions not supported by the keyboard. The voice annotations, combined with a wireless microphone and a remote control, provide an instantaneous and location-independent method of annotation. Pen-based video annotations afford the user, in this case the choreographer, the ability to sketch over a video stream, allowing more freedom in the creative process.

4.1 Voice-based Annotations

The Creation-Tool enables the recording of voice annotations. This feature is achieved by using the libsndfile[6] and RtAudio4[7] frameworks. The system produces a sound file for each annotation made and a main sound file for the background sound of the video. Currently, the user explicitly defines the annotation time interval, using the audio annotation button. A Bluetooth microphone and the TouchOSC interface can be used for the recording of remote annotations. A voice recognition method will be applied in the future to transcribe voice annotations to text, as well as the recording from two different input audio devices, one recording audio annotations and the other capturing the background sound.

4.2 Graphical Annotations

The Creation-Tool has two types of graphical annotations: (1) text-based annotations and (2) pen-based annotations. Even though text has a semantic representation, it also has a graphical form. Text annotations are written using a keyboard or a stylus. Pen-based annotations can be used for sketching or handwritten writing. In order to maintain their context, i.e., to maintain the association between a note and the corresponding video feature, graphical video annotations can use motion tracking.

---

[6] http://www.mega-nerd.com/libsndfile/

[7] http://www.music.mcgill.ca/~gary/rtaudio/

4.2.1 *Text-based Annotations*

The text-based annotations can be written using a physical or virtual keyboard. This input method allows one to write regular text annotations using a text box (Figure 4).

Figure 4. Text Based Annotation.

The system uses the virtual keyboard available in the Windows Tablet PC Input Panel. Text annotations have their search mechanism facilitated, since no recognizer is needed, as in pen and voice annotations.

4.2.2 *Pen-based Video Annotations*

The system implements the concept of pen-based video annotations, i.e., a set of time ink strokes, with spatial and temporal dimensions. As previously mentioned, pen-based annotations allow more freedom in the creative process (Figure 5). The user can also use the handwriting recognizer available in the Windows Tablet PC Input Panel to transform pen-based annotation into text.

Figure 5. Pen-based Annotations

4.2.3 *Motion Tracking*

With the goal of tracking dancers in the scene, an object tracking library is under development. An initial version of the framework is already in place, with a couple of trackers already implemented. OpenCV version of the CAMSHIFT tracker [1] allowed for a quick way to test the object tracking framework. This tracker has proven rather limited for use in actual dance videos, especially whenever the dancers are being tracked and parts of the background have similar color histograms. In order to improve the system, an attempt of background subtraction was tried but it was too sensitive to illumination changes to be useful for this application.

A second tracker (Figure 6) works by point matching between successive frames. It detects the interest points using the FAST [14] corner detector, builds BRIEF [3] descriptors out of those interest points, and then computes the Hamming distance between them to match between frames. The tracker needs to be trained with the object of interest starting position and proceeds to detect interest points in that area's neighborhood. The mean and standard deviation of the points' movement are calculated and the outliers are pruned, preventing that interest points in the background affect the performer's tracked position. Problems still occur, however, when the background's and the performer's movement are similar.

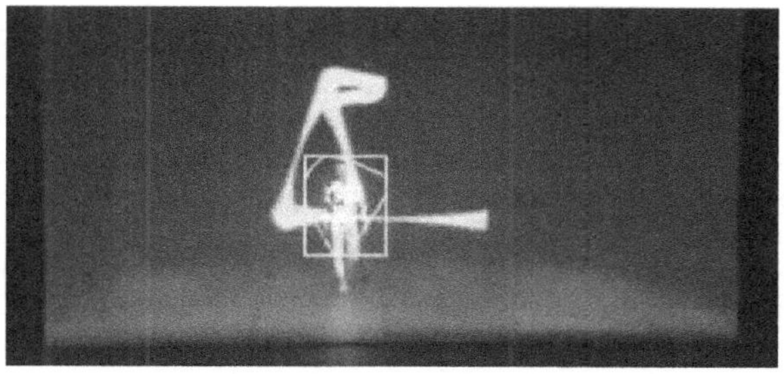

Figure 6. FAST+BRIEF Tracking: Dancer and background have different types of motion. (*.txt* choreography: S. Jürgens)

4.3 Annotations Storage

The annotations are stored in a XML file. Each annotation type is stored in a different node. Each node contains the reference to the first frame and the last frame, which defines the annotation time interval. Stored information includes the format attributes for ink and text notes, the reference to the sound file for audio notes and the points (x,y) that defined ink annotations.

5. Related Work

Video is crucial to capture dance movements, gestures or choreographies. In order to add and share information, personal or other, to this type of content, video annotators are becoming important in dance environments. Nonetheless, different types of video annotators, with different modalities, were developed in the last decades.

5.1 Video Annotator for Dance Performance

Danvideo [11] is a system for semi-automatic authoring and access to dance archives. The system allows the dance expert to annotate manually the video content using macro and micro features of the video content (semantic annotations). VideoTraces [6] allows users to capture video and to annotate it by talking and gesturing. The system enables one to capture, save and organize video clips. Audio and gestures are overlaid on the video and preserved in a resulting "video trace".

Our Creation-Tool has the aim to work as a digital notebook, for choreographers. Therefore, it requires more natural and fluid methods of video annotation, like pen-based annotations and voice annotations.

5.2 Video Annotators

Over the last 30 years, different types of video annotators were developed in order to add information to this medium. Aiming to capture more real and natural annotations, different modalities, like text (keyboard based), voice and sketching (pen-based), were tried.

5.2.1 *Text-based Video Annotators*

The VideoAnnEx [15] allows video text-based annotation. The system associates a video region to an annotation, but they are shown separately. The AntV [8] system allows multimedia annotations, in the form of text, images or videos, over the main video window. Nonetheless, the AntV annotation spatial positions are not changed in time. In our work, we consider that text annotations have a graphical dimension and, therefore, should also be overlaid on top of the video content and follow video features.

5.2.2 *Voice-based Video Annotators*

The Video Traces, the Ambulant Player [2] and, more recently, the WaC [5] tool, allow voice recording as video annotations. Our Creation-Tool allows video annotations based on recorded voice, but adds the possibility of remote annotation, by using a wireless microphone and a remote control.

5.2.3 Pen-Based Video Annotators

Systems like the NoteLook [7] or the WaC, explored the idea of sketching video annotations on the top of a single video frame. Nonetheless, this association loses the temporal dimension of video content. Marquee [16] allowed the association of ink strokes to a video segment but in separated interfaces. In the LEAN [13] system, it is possible to annotate a video segment, or a particular frame, and browse the video based on these annotations. In Videotater [9], the annotations are associated to a video segment, on the global timeline. In these two projects, annotations have a temporal association but do not track the video motion features. In the Ambulant Player project, pen annotations are dynamic and have their spatial path explicitly defined by the user. A recent work [10] explores graphical video annotations combined with motion tracking, but does not consider the particular case of pen-based annotations and the tracking feature needs a long time of video pre-processing. In our system, we implement and explore the concept of pen-based video annotations [4], allowing a fluid method of video annotation and in which the annotations do not lose their context.

6. Preliminary Tests and Discussion

A preliminary usability test with a choreographer was done, simulating a dance rehearsal. For this test, a regular and HD webcams, connected to a Windows Tablet PC were used to capture the scene to be annotated. In addition, a Bluetooth headset was used for audio annotations and an iPod Touch as a remote control.

The main interface was well perceived. Nonetheless, some interaction problems were observed. The major interaction difficulties were related with the ability to use touch and pen simultaneously in the Tablet PC. The pen usage blocks touch mode, which makes a true pen+touch interaction difficult to achieve. It is also important to improve the recording buttons, as well as the timeline's hiding mechanism, so they can be performed with more fluid gestures. The annotation marks interaction has to be improved, since pressing the used mark to define its endpoint distracted the choreographer. The input for text and audio annotations did not present major difficulties.

7. Conclusions and Future Work

A real-time multimodal video annotator, used as a Creation-Tool for contemporary dance, was described in this paper. The prototype, developed for Tablet PCs, explores pen and touch interaction. The system allows text, ink and voice annotations. Two types of annotations were also defined: annotation marks and regular annotations. The annotations marks are defined by a keyword and an icon, in contrast to regular annotations that do not have a pre-defined structure. In addition, a remote control interface, running on mobile devices, was implemented. The tool was conceived to assist the creative processes of choreographers, working as a digital notebook for personal annotations.

The main interface of the Creation-Tool was well perceived, but particular interaction features should be improved. The system is still under development and some important steps have yet to be performed, such as the integration of the main interface with the motion tracking framework and more complete usability tests. Annotations will also include hypermedia notes, allowing the user to annotate video content with different media, such as images, web pages or other videos.

8. ACKNOWLEDGMENTS

This work is partially funded by the project "TKB - A Transmedia Knowledge Base for contemporary dance" (PTDC/EAT/AVP/098220/2008 funded by FCT/MCTES), the UTAustin-Portugal, Digital Media, Program (SFRH/BD/42662/2007 FCT/MCTES) and by CITI/DI/FCT/UNL (PEst-OE/EEI/UI0527/2011). We would like to thank the choreographers Rui Horta and Stephan Jürgens for their suggestions and help.

9. REFERENCES

[1] Bradski, G. R. 1998. Computer Vision Face Tracking For Use in a Perceptual User Interface. *Intel Technology Journal, 2*, 2, 12–21.

[2] Bulterman, D. 2004.Animating peer-level annotations within web-based multimedia. In *EuroGraphics Multimedia Workshop* 2004, Euro-graphics Association, 49–57.

[3] Calonder, M., Lepetit, V., Strecha, C. and Fua, P. 2010. BRIEF: binary robust independent elementary features. In *Proc. ECCV'10* . Springer-Verlag, 778-792.

[4] Cabral, D. and Correia, N. 2009. Pen-Based Video Annotations: A Proposal and a Prototype for Tablet PCs. In *Proc. INTERACT '09*. Springer-Verlag, 17-20.

[5] Cattelan, R. G., Teixeira, C., Goularte, R., and Pimentel, M. C. 2008. Watch-and-comment as a paradigm toward ubiquitous interactive video editing. *ACM Trans. Multimedia Comput. Commun. Appl.* 4, 4, 28 -52.

[6] Cherry, G., Fournier, J., and Stevens, R. 2003. Using a digital video annotation tool to teach dance composition. *Interactive Multimedia Electronic Journal of Computer-Enhanced Learning.*

[7] Chiu, P., Kapuskar, A., Reitmeier, S., and Wilcox, L. 1999. NoteLook: taking notes in meetings with digital video and ink. In *Proc. ACM MM '99*. ACM, 149-158.

[8] Correia, N. and Chambel, T. 1999. Active video watching using annotation. In *Proc. ACM MM '99*. ACM, 151-154.

[9] Diakopoulos, N. and Essa, I. 2006. Videotater: an approach for pen-based digital video segmentation and tagging. In *Proc. UIST '06*. ACM, 221-224.

[10] Goldman, D. B., Gonterman, C., Curless, B., Salesin, D., and Seitz, S. M. 2008. Video object annotation, navigation, and composition. In *Proc. UIST '08*. ACM, 3-12.

[11] Kannan, R., Andres, F., and Guetl, C. 2010. DanVideo: an MPEG-7 authoring and retrieval system for dance videos. *Multimedia Tools Appl.* 46, 2-3, 545-572.

[12] Li, Y., Hinckley, K., Guan, Z., and Landay, J. A. 2005. Experimental analysis of mode switching techniques in pen-based user interfaces. In *Proc. CHI '05*. ACM, 461-470.

[13] Ramos, G. and Balakrishnan, R. 2003. Fluid interaction techniques for the control and annotation of digital video. In *Proc. UIST '03*. ACM, 105-114.

[14] Rosten, E. and Drummond, T. 2006. Machine learning for high-speed corner detection. In *Proc. of ECCV (1)*. 430-443.

[15] VideoAnnEx, http://www.research.ibm.com/VideoAnnEx/

[16] Weher, K. and Poon, A. 1994. Marquee: a tool for real-time video logging. In *Proc. CHI '94*. ACM, 58-64.

Flower Power*

Gianluca Monaci
Philips Research
Eindhoven, The Netherlands
gianluca.monaci@philips.com

Tommaso Gritti
Philips Research
Eindhoven, The Netherlands
tommaso.gritti@philips.com

Fabio Vignoli
Philips Retail Solutions
Eindhoven, The Netherlands
fabio.vignoli@philips.com

Wouter Walmink
studio:ludens
Eindhoven, The Netherlands
wouter@studioludens.com

Maarten Hendriks
Little Mountain
Eindhoven, The Netherlands
maarten@littlemountain.nl

ABSTRACT

Flower Power is an interactive installation that creates immersive light atmospheres by capturing the colors of flowers and re-projecting them in the environment. A camera is suspended over a flower bed and its position depends on the positions of the visitors around the installation, which are detected using presence sensors. The image captured by the camera is rendered into the surrounding environment as a suggestive, saturated light scene. The participants can thus give the power to their favorite flower to set the overall light experience. In this paper we describe the motivation and the realization of the installation, and we discuss insights and reactions collected during the 2010 STRP Festival.

Categories and Subject Descriptors

J.5 [**Computer Applications**]: Arts and humanities; H.5.3 [**Group and Organization Interfaces**]: Collaborative computing, Synchronous interaction

General Terms

Algorithms, Design, Human Factors

Keywords

Interactive installation, ambient interaction, real-time video rendering, light feedback

Figure 1: Main intents of the installation: attract the attention of the visitors, invite the participants to discover the beauty of flowers, stimulate interaction with the installation, the environment and other visitors.

1. INTRODUCTION

Flower Power is a collaborative, interactive installation that creates immersive experiences by capturing the colors of flowers and re-projecting them in the environment in the form of saturated, changing lights. *Flower Power* was installed at the STRP Festival [1], one of the largest art and technology festivals in Europe. As a counterweight and extension to the technical environment present all around at STRP Festival, *Flower Power* was designed as an oasis of nature where the beauty of flowers is extracted to create interactive light effects. A camera suspended over a bed of colorful flowers moves towards the visitors present around the installation. The colors of the flowers, captured by the camera, are then transmitted to the surrounding environment using colored lights placed all around the installation.

The principal intents of the installation are represented in Figure 1. First, we want to attract the attention of the visitors with a colorful environment mixing nature and light. We aim at stimulating the discovery of the beauty of flowers, that are enhanced, enlarged, blown-up through the camera and the lights. We want to encourage the interaction of the visitors with the installation, that responds to people presence. We want to mediate visitors' interaction with the environment, by setting the whole light atmosphere moving the camera over the flower bed. We also want to favor joint collaboration and exploration with other participants, by discovering how the installation responds to the presence of multiple visitors.

2. RELATED WORK

In recent years, artists have presented a growing num-

*Area chair: David Shamma

MM'11, November 28–December 1, 2011, Scottsdale, Arizona, USA.

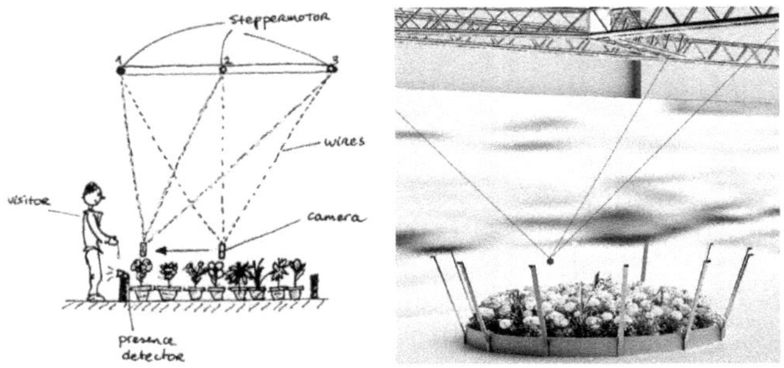

Figure 2: Conceptual phase of *Flower Power*: first sketch [left] and 3D rendering [right].

ber of interactive and immersive installations, following the progress and accessibility of technologies and computer software [2, 3]. Some of these installations also involve light, such as the works of Golan Levin [4], Camille Utterback [5] and Matthias Oostrik [6]. Golan Levin's *Motion Traces* translates in real-time the position of people and their motion, detected in a lobby space, into adaptive video projections and color room illumination. Along a similar line, in Camille Utterback's *Abundance*, human presence and motion in a square are mapped into colored patterns projected onto a 3-story building. Matthias Oostrik's *MotionWall* and *Bijlmer Moodwall* are large LED walls placed in public spaces that react to people presence creating colorful light shapes that follow the passersby.

In this work, we aim at stimulating a more explicit interaction of visitors with light, empowering them to create the whole lighting atmosphere through the individual or collaborative discovery of the colors of flowers.

3. INSTALLATION DESCRIPTION

The core of *Flower Power* a bed of flowers over which is suspended a camera. The position of the camera is determined by the people's presence around the installation. The camera continuously captures close-up images of the flowers, which are translated in real-time into a light scene in the surrounding environment. A schematic sketch and a 3D rendering of the installation, drawn during the conception phase, are shown in Figure 2.

Flower Power is controlled by a processing engine, the *Experience Player* (see Figure 3). The Experience Player is a programmable processing unit that can handle multiple sensor inputs and multiple output signals through scripts in LUA [7], an open source scripting language. The Experience Player receives as input visitors' presence determined by infrared (IR) presence detection sensors. A *Camera Positioning Script* determines the position of the camera, which is controlled by three stepper motors that extend or reduce the length of the wires that hang the camera over the flowers. The image grabbed by the camera is sent back to the Experience Player, where a *Light Rendering Script* converts it into a light atmosphere. Figure 3 shows a schematic representation of the *Flower Power* installation's processing flow.

3.1 Camera installation and activation

About 100 plants with flowers of different colors were placed into a circular space of 2m of diameter. A Philips SPC2050 webcam was suspended at close distance over the flower bed, attached to three fabric wires of variable length.

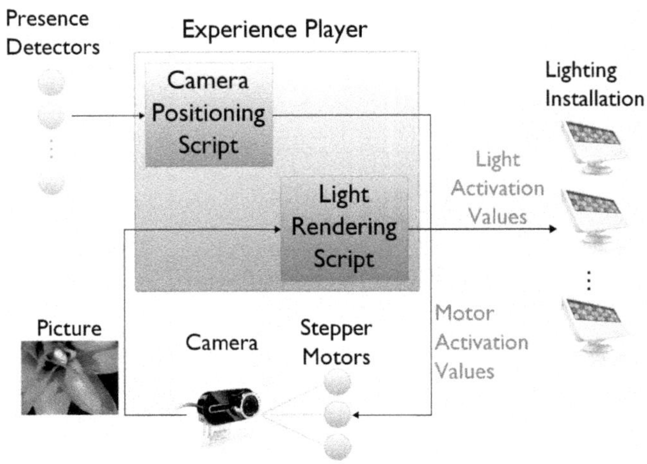

Figure 3: *Flower Power*'s processing flow is controlled by the Experience Player. Presence information is fed to the Camera Positioning Script, which determines the camera location and sends the activation values to the stepper motors. The camera grabs a picture of the flower bed that is fed to the Light Rendering Script. This script transforms the image into light activation values, and thus a light atmosphere.

By changing simultaneously the length of the wires using stepper motors, the camera is displaced over the flowers while maintaining it at a constant distance from them. The Camera Positioning Script in the Experience Player assigns the position of the camera based on the input of twelve active IR presence detectors placed around the flowers. The detection range of the detectors is about 1m. If a visitor approaches the installation and is detected, the camera moves towards him/her. If several persons are present, the Positioning Script moves the camera towards the barycenter of the positions of the detected participants. If nobody is present, the Positioning Script displaces the camera according to a pseudo-random pattern. Figure 4 shows the flower bed installed at the STRP festival. The camera, hanging from three wires, and one of the twelve presence detectors are highlighted in the picture.

3.2 Light installation and rendering

The light scene was set using 110 LED colored light sources of different type and size. The luminaires were placed along the walls and on the ceiling of a large space of about 14m × 6m and of 3m height surrounding the flower bed (see Figure 4). All light channels could be addressed using a DMX controller. The value of each channel (R, G, B) of each light was set in real-time such that the overall light scene would match the image captured by the camera.

3.2.1 Light Rendering Script

The image capture by the *Flower Power* camera is translated in real-time into a light scene using a custom-made light rendering algorithm. The Light Rendering Script has to fulfill two major requirements: 1) fidelity, it has to be able to produce evocative, immersive light atmospheres that match the captured images; 2) speed, it has to work fluidly in real-time to provide immediate, intuitive feedback to the visitors. To obtain this we adopt a calibration-based system,

Figure 4: The *Flower Power* installation at the STRP festival 2010. The camera, one of the presence detectors and one of the screens showing the camera live view are highlighted with white boxes.

ImagiLight, that is presented in [8]. The calibration, done to characterize the lighting system, is performed only once at installation phase.

For calibration, a second camera (not the one placed over the flower bed) captures images of the lighting effect of each luminaire on the environment. We acquire one image per channel, activated to its maximum driving value. A standard RGB camera is used as capturing device. At the end of the process, a *light palette* composed of images showing the effect of each primary of each light source on the environment is available. These images are stored as basic elements that the system uses to map the effect of each light on the environment. At each given time instant, the Rendering Script receives an input image from the camera suspended over the flower bed and uses these palette images to compute in real-time the light activation values that create a light scene as close as possible to the input image. This computation is done using a sparse image approximation algorithm, described in [8]. The activation values for each channel are sent via DMX to the lights. An image captured by the installation's camera [left] and rendered light atmosphere [right] are shown in Figure 5. It can be observed that the overall light scene is faithful to the input image, while being a suggestive abstraction of it with its saturated colors and its smooth, abstract shades.

4. INTERACTIONS AND IMPRESSIONS

Flower Power was installed at the 2010 STRP Festival, one of the largest art and technology festivals in Europe, with about 30.000 visitors in 2010. This 10-days event features a multidisciplinary program including interactive art, light art, concerts, theatrical and dance performances, experimental music, discussions, films, lectures, video art, animation and workshops. During the day the festival was typically attended by a diversified crowd of students, members of the technology and art community and general public. In the evenings, the attendees were mainly young people coming to assist to the numerous concerts. Figures 4, 5 and 6 show the *Flower Power* installation at the event. For a video impression, please visit [9].

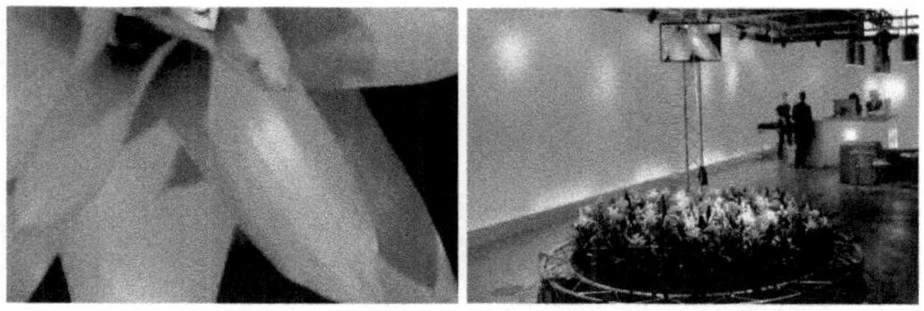

Figure 5: Image captured by the installation's camera [left] and rendered light atmosphere [right].

During the whole festival we observed the visitors interacting with the installation and we informally collected impressions about Flower Power. In particular, in the first day of the event we actively sought remarks and criticisms to grasp the impressions and expectations of the audience and tune the behavior of the installation.

We noticed that part of the visitors were oblivious to the relation between the flowers/camera and the light scenery. This emphasized how important it is to provide real or imaginative linkage between cause and effect. In this installation, the link was strengthened by two displays (one is highlighted in Figure 4) that showed the image from the camera that was the input for the light installation, providing a "stepping stone" between the two.

Tuning the speed of the camera was a challenge. A fast pace was favorable to keep the installation responsive, so people could decipher how they were affecting it. On the other hand, a slow pace was favorable for smooth and relaxed overall light changes. This seems to be a recurrent challenge in installations that need to be both responsive and noticeable by casual passersby while overall not being too dominating. Here we decided to have fast-paced stepper motors controlling the camera position to obtain a more reactive feedback.

Other remarks concerned the presence detection mechanism. The twelve presence sensors, placed around the flower bed at uniform distance, had a narrow sensing field, leaving regions in between them where attendees were not detected. To solve this issue, we placed on the ground in front of each sensor a red marker indicating the optimal sensing area of the detectors. The red round markers are visible in Figure 4.

Because of the diversity of the crowd in different week days and at different time of the day, we could observe a number of different interaction styles with the installation. At daytime the density of visitors was lower, favoring the interaction by individuals and small groups which could carefully observe the installation (Figures 1 and 6(a)-(b)). Visitors at a distance were attracted by the large walls illuminated by the changing, saturated light, and typically started to look at the installation without interacting. Once they were close enough to realize they could influence the light effects by attracting the camera, they started to move around the central circle and look closer to the flowers and the camera itself. Small groups of people typically engaged in collaborative interaction to coordinately drive the camera towards interesting parts of the installation. We observed a group of school kids talking and instructing each other in order to control the camera. Teamwork and leadership arose.

At nighttime, during concerts and live performances, a large crowd was typically surrounding *Flower Power* (Figure 6(c)), creating chaotic camera motion and dynamic light-

Figure 6: Visitors interacting with the *Flower Power* installation: individuals or couples (a),(b), large crowd (c), one participant finds a shortcut to set his favorite light atmosphere (d).

ing effects. In these situations, while there was no explicit control of the camera by the visitors, the installation was appreciated for the generation of suggestive atmospheres.

The mechanism by which the light atmosphere was set was understood by most visitors once the screens were mounted next to the flower bed. This encouraged the interaction and stimulated the participants to discover the plants that were magnified by the camera and the lighting system, as can be seen in Figures 1 and 6. Interestingly, several participants experimented ways to interact with the installation that were not foreseen. Because most attendees did not know how the sensors worked, some people were dancing, jumping or wiggling in front of the sensors to make the camera move closer or faster. Once people understood the relation between camera and light atmosphere, they started to place objects in front of the camera to modify the light settings, going beyond the possible flowers' color palette. In Figure 6(d) for example, one visitor places the blue screen of his phone in front of the camera, creating in this case a surprising blue effect.

The 2010 STRP Festival introduced the first field trial of the *eSphere* system [10], which allowed visitors to connect to the art work exposed. A small subset of the festival's participants received an RFID chip with which they could give feedback about works and performances in terms of tags. At the end of the festival, a tag cloud for each art work was also generated. The tag cloud of *Flower Power* is shown in Figure 7. The installation was tagged 216 times, witnessing a considerable interest. The most recurring terms associated with *Flower Power* are definitively positive, and are consistent with the installation's objective: *colorful, beautiful, cool, social, interactivity, flower, cute, light.* Few more original and evocative terms were also mentioned, such as *Turkish delight* or *potpourri.*

Figure 7: Tag cloud of *Flower Power.*

5. DISCUSSION

In this paper we described *Flower Power*, an interactive installation that allows participants to discover the beauty of flowers and to collaboratively influence the overall light atmosphere. The installation was well perceived by the audience, as witnessed by our observations and by the feedback to the eSphere system. In particular, participants appreciated the interesting and surprising interaction between visitors, nature and surrounding environment through motion and light.

Flower Power provides useful, innovative insights and tools for the development of future applications. From a technological point of view, we introduced here the *Experience Player*, a flexible platform to handle and process multiple input and output signals, making it ideally suited to support all kind of multimedia interactive installation. A second novelty is the *Light Rendering Script*, which provides a fast and efficient way to translate visual information into light settings for arbitrarily complex lighting infrastructures. The tool can be employed in a range of light-based installations as well as in light designing and architecture.

Concerning the user interaction aspects, visitors were impressed by the beauty of the light effects they could generate through the flowers, although some of the attendees preferred to short-circuit the logic of the installation by using their own colored objects to set the light atmosphere. This observation was particularly inspiring and in the future we plan to investigate a more direct, physical interaction of individuals and crowds with light and space.

6. REFERENCES

[1] STRP Festival. `www.strp.nl`.
[2] Oliver Grau. *Virtual Art: From Illusion to Immersion.* The MIT Press, 2003.
[3] Robert Kronenburg. *Flexible: Architecture that responds to change.* Laurence King Publishers, 2007.
[4] Golan Levin and Collaborators. Motion traces. `http://www.flong.com/projects/a1`.
[5] Camille Utterback. Projects. `camilleutterback.com/projects`.
[6] Matthias Oostrik. `http://www.magdatt.nl`.
[7] The programming language LUA. `www.lua.org`.
[8] Tommaso Gritti and Gianluca Monaci. Imagilight: a vision approach to lighting scene setting. In *Proceedings of ACM Multimedia*, 2011.
[9] Flower power videos, 2011. [Online] Available: `https://sites.google.com/site/tommasogritti/publications/flowerpower_videos`.
[10] eSphere. `www.e-sphere.nl`.

Crowdsourcing Visual Detectors for Video Search

Bauke Freiburg
Video Dock
Panamalaan 1b, 1019 AS
Amsterdam, The Netherlands
bauke@videodock.nl

Jaap Kamps
ISLA, University of Amsterdam
Science Park 904, 1098 XH
Amsterdam, The Netherlands
kamps@uva.nl

Cees G.M. Snoek
ISLA, University of Amsterdam
Science Park 904, 1098 XH
Amsterdam, The Netherlands
cgmsnoek@uva.nl

ABSTRACT

In this paper, we study social tagging at the video fragment-level using a combination of automated content understanding and the wisdom of the crowds. We are interested in the question whether crowdsourcing can be beneficial to a video search engine that automatically recognizes video fragments on a semantic level. To answer this question, we perform a 3-month online field study with a concert video search engine targeted at a dedicated user-community of pop concert enthusiasts. We harvest the feedback of more than 500 active users and perform two experiments. In experiment 1 we measure user incentive to provide feedback, in experiment 2 we determine the tradeoff between feedback quality and quantity when aggregated over multiple users. Results show that users provide sufficient feedback, which becomes highly reliable when a crowd agreement of 67% is enforced.

Categories and Subject Descriptors: H.3.3 Information Storage and Retrieval: Information Search and Retrieval
General Terms: Algorithms, Experimentation, Performance
Keywords: Semantic indexing, video retrieval, information visualization

1. INTRODUCTION

Social tagging platforms like YouTube and Vimeo are effective for sharing complete videos, but users requiring access to video fragments have no other choice than to inefficiently browse through an entire video of interest [8]. For a long time, automated video-fragment classifiers promise to alleviate the manual burden of localizing specific video fragments. Despite good progress in video concept classification, the performance of automated methods still varies [9], which can be attributed to the amount of training data used. In this paper we study social tagging at the video-fragment level using a combination of automated content understanding and the wisdom of the crowds.

Area Chair: David Shamma.

MM'11, November 28–December 1, 2011, Scottsdale, Arizona, USA.
Copyright 2011 ACM 978-1-4503-0616-4/11/11 ...$10.00.

We start from the state-of-the-art in concept detection [11], and we investigate how visual tagging by an online crowd might support video access at the fragment level. Crucial in such a crowdsourcing study is user tagging motivation. In-depth studies on motivations for visual tagging are many, emphasizing in particular organizational, social, and gaming aspects [5, 2, 1], or Fame, Fortune, Fun, and Fulfillment [6]. An additional motivation for (visual) tagging is the creation of new information. For example when incorrect individual tags are aggregated in the right way their collective judgement might be highly reliable [13]. In fact, a crowdsourcing evaluation can be as reliable as an expert evaluation [12]. However, it is well known that in online communities 90% of users never contributes [7]. To assure participation of the remaining 10% of users, micro payments are often offered [4], or the social impact is emphasized, especially within a dedicated user community. Surprisingly, exploiting the crowd for video labeling at the fragment level is scarce [8, 14, 3], to the best of our knowledge in combination with automated visual analysis non-existing even.

The main research question in this paper is: *can user tags from crowdsourcing be beneficial to a system that automatically predicts labels for video fragments?*. We divide this question into the following sub-questions: *i)* Does a concept-based video search engine provide enough incentives for users to provide labels, without receiving payment or other compensation? *ii)* Are the resulting labels of sufficient quality compared to expert labels, when aggregated over multiple users? In order to answer these question, we develop a video search engine for a dedicated user-community that allows for easy fragment-level crowdsourcing. We highlight the case study in which we evaluate our research next.

2. CROWDSOURCING CASE STUDY

We study the merit of crowdsourcing visual detectors for video search within a cultural heritage context. To maximize user participation, we motivate online users by providing them with access to a selection of exclusive, full-length concert videos. While our case study is limited to the cultural heritage domain by design, the principle of combining visual detectors with crowdsourcing is general and applicable to *any* multimedia retrieval, authoring, or visualization application open for cultural engagement.

2.1 Concert Video Search Engine

We developed an online video search engine for rock concerts [10]. Our search engine uses archived video footage of the Pinkpop festival. This annual rock festival is held

Figure 1: Eleven common concert concepts we detect automatically, and for which we collect user-feedback.

Figure 2: Timeline-based video player where colored dots correspond to automated visual detection results. Users can navigate directly to fragments of interest by interaction with the colored dots, which pop-up a feedback overlay as displayed in Figure 3.

since 1970 at Landgraaf, the Netherlands. All music videos have been recorded during the 40 years life cycle of the festival. We cleared copyright for several Dutch and Belgian artists playing at Pinkpop, including gigs from *K's Choice*, *Junkie XL*, and *Moke*. The amount of footage for each festival year varies from only a summary to almost unabridged concert recordings, even including raw, unpublished footage. The complete video archive contains 94 concerts covering 32 hours in total.

We create detectors for 11 concert concepts following a state-of-the-art implementation [10]. We select the concepts based on frequency, visual detection feasibility, previous mentioning in literature and expected utility for concert video users (summarized in Figure 1). We consider a video fragment a more user-friendly retrieval unit compared to more technically defined shots or keyframes. We create fragment-level detection scores from frame-level scores by aggregating the concept scores of all the frames in the processed videos. The fragment algorithm was designed to find the longest fragments with the highest average scores for a specific concert concept [10]. Users may provide feedback on these automatically detected fragments using our feedback mechanism.

2.2 Feedback Mechanism

The main mode of user interaction with our video search engine is by means of the In-Video Browser, see Figure 2. The timeline-based browser enables users to watch and navigate through a single video concert. Little colored dots on the timeline mark the location of an interesting fragment corresponding to an automatically derived label. To inspect the label, users simply move their mouse cursor over the colored dot. By clicking on the dot, the player instantly starts the specific fragment in the video. If needed, the user can manually select more concept labels in the panel on the left of the video player. Too maintain overview, the In-Video

Figure 3: Harvesting user feedback for video fragments (top to bottom). The thumbs-up button indicates agreement with the automatically detected label, thumbs-down disagreement. Three key frames represent the visual summary of the fragment. Users may correct wrong labels, adapt fragment boundaries, or suggest additional labels (in Dutch).

browser automatically launches with a maximum of twelve fragments on the timeline interface every time a user starts a concert. These twelve correspond to the most reliable fragment labels. Once the timeline becomes too crowded as a result of multiple selected labels, the user may decide to zoom in on the timeline to retrieve fragments for a specific, smaller part of the video.

An important aspect of the In-Video browser is that the user viewing experience is interrupted as little as possible, the video continues to play while the user interacts with the browser. In the graphical overlay that appears while the fragment is playing, the label is shown together with the

Table 1: Results for Experiment 1: User Incentive.

	Fragments		Feedback			Positive		Negative	
Visual Concept	$\sum$	%	$\sum$	%	*Avg*	$\sum$	%	$\sum$	%
Singer	117	23%	851	24%	7.3	782	26%	69	14%
Audience	87	17%	800	22%	9.2	697	23%	103	20%
Stage	82	16%	499	14%	6.1	462	15%	37	7%
Drummer	70	14%	560	16%	8.0	429	14%	131	26%
Guitar player	61	12%	335	9%	5.5	274	9%	61	12%
Close-up	35	7%	182	5%	5.2	174	6%	8	2%
Over the shoulder	20	4%	110	3%	5.5	102	3%	8	2%
Pinkpop logo	11	2%	93	3%	8.5	49	2%	44	9%
Pinkpop hat	10	2%	73	2%	7.3	48	2%	25	5%
Hands	9	2%	31	1%	3.4	23	1%	8	2%
Keyboard	8	2%	33	1%	4.1	17	1%	16	3%
Total	510	100%	3,567	100%	6.4	3,057	100%	510	100%

duration and thumbnails of the first, middle and last frame. With the thumbs-up and thumbs-down buttons the user indicates whether she agrees with the automatically suggested label or not. We refer to this feedback as a positive or negative user tag. If the user indicates that the label is incorrect, she may indicate to the system what the correct label for the video fragment should be, chosen from the predefined labels or a new suggestion from the user. The overlay disappears within a few seconds, but instantly after user-feedback, see Figure 3 for a typical feedback sequence.

3. EXPERIMENTAL SETUP

3.1 Field Study

The video search engine was available online from December 2009 to February 2010. In these three months almost ten thousand users, mainly from the Netherlands and Belgium, visited the site and used the system to watch concert videos with the in-video browser. Due to press releases by the different organizations involved, online media was the main source for traffic. A total number of 958 users provided feedback on the video fragment labels, which is a common participation rate for online communities [7]. From this user base, we classify 578 members as active users because they provided multiple tags. The average active user provided feedback on six different fragments, but two labels on different fragments is the most common. In this study we restrict ourselves to the positives and negative user tags. Additional feedback like suggestions for other labels or new start/end times are not taken into account for the current study. All user feedback was stored in a database together with the users IP addresses and user sessions.

3.2 Experiments

In contrast to standard retrieval evaluation tasks, where the user information need is captured in a standard model, our field study is done in a non-controlled environment, with real users and real-world user behavior. The effect is that little is known about the participating users, except for their IP-address and session-id. We conduct two experiments. In the first experiment: **User Incentive** we gather user tags and we evaluate whether the In-Video browser and the automatically labeled video fragments indeed encourage the users to provide feedback for free on a diverse set of concerts and fragments. The more challenging research question is whether users put enough effort in the tags so that they become reliable at an aggregated level. Therefore, the goal of the second experiment: **Quality vs Quantity**, is to verify the reliability of the user tags. This is performed by comparing the (aggregated) user tags with an expert-labeled ground truth.

4. RESULTS

4.1 Experiment 1: User Incentive

The question that we tried to answer with this experiment is whether a concept-based video search engine provides enough incentives for users to provide labels, without receiving payment or other compensation. We summarize the feedback statistics over the 11 visual concepts in Table 1. We received feedback on a total of 726 different fragments, but we focus our study on the 510 fragments that received at least two judgements. In total these fragments received 3,567 different tags distributed over 62 concerts. The feedback distribution shows that the four most common labels have received 75% of the user feedback. The feedback per fragment varies depending on the visual label from an average of 3.4 (Hands) to 9.2 (Audience).

There are multiple reasons why a fragment could have received more or less feedback: 1) presence of the visual concept varies per video, 2) detectors perform better for specific labels, 3) users could evaluate some labels better than others, and so on. In this non-controlled field study we could not collect all the data that is needed to analyze the dependencies of all those variables. It could be expected that users would be more easily motivated to provide negative feedback on incorrect suggested labels. We also investigated the relation between positive and negative judgements for each of the fragments (data not shown), from which we conclude that the user tags are independent of the quality of the automatically detected fragment label. Coming back to the question we started with, we conclude that within the context of our case study users had sufficient incentive to provide labels.

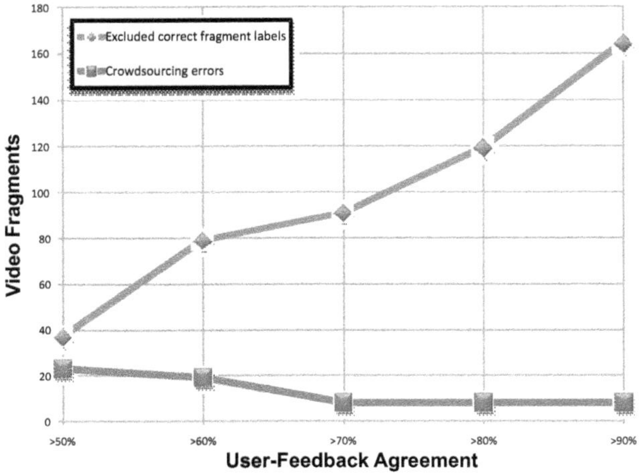

Figure 4: Results for Experiment 2: Quality vs Quantity. Simply relying on a majority vote of the crowd results in most correct fragments, albeit with 23 errors. We observe a best tradeoff between quality and quantity of crowdsourcing visual detectors for a user agreement of 67%.

4.2 Experiment 2: Quality vs Quantity

The question that we tried to answer with this experiment is whether the resulting labels are of sufficient quality compared to expert labels, when aggregated over multiple users. We have in total 510 fragments, where we now assume the expert label to be correct, and investigate for how many of them we would have obtained the same label when imposing a minimum agreement threshold on the crowdsourced labels. We plot the percentage of agreement among user-provided labels versus the number of video fragments in Figure 4. The ground truth shows that the quality of the suggested labels is high. As much as 85% of the automatically suggested labels correspond with the ground truth. If the simple evaluation principle of the majority is used, only 23 fragments have received tags that do not match with the ground truth, which in our case corresponds to a loss of 37 training samples. When we further increase the threshold for a positive or negative agreement the number of fragments receiving the wrong label is gradually reduced to 8 fragments only, but the number of excluded training samples increases rapidly. For a conservative user agreement of 80%, for example, 119 fragments are ignored. We observe that a threshold of 67% provides a well-chosen balance between the 8 errors and the 422 fragments that can be used as a correction mechanism, or as reliable training examples for a new round of detector learning.

5. CONCLUSION

The main research question of this paper was: can user tags from crowdsourcing be beneficial to a system that automatically predicts labels for video fragments. We developed a video search engine for a dedicated user community in the domain of concert video allowing for easy fragment-level crowdsourcing. The user-feedback mechanism of the In-Video browser made it possible to harvest positive and negative user judgements on automatically predicted video fragment labels.

For this case study two experiments are conducted. The first experiment showed that users provided enough feedback. Analysis of the collected data proved that users provided the feedback to the video-fragment labels without a preference for incorrect labels. The second experiment showed that 85% of the automatically suggested labels corresponds with the ground truth. We observe that an aggregation threshold of 67% provides a well-chosen balance between errors in the user judgements and the amount of reliable training examples remaining. If the threshold is enforced, the error rate in the training examples is less than 2%. Within the context of our case study, we conclude that crowdsourcing can be beneficial to enhance and improve automated video content analysis. How the new information can be exploited for incremental learning of visual detectors is an interesting question for future research.

6. ACKNOWLEDGMENTS

We thank our users for providing feedback. We are grateful to the Netherlands Institute for Sound and Vision. This research is supported by the projects: BSIK MultimediaN, FES COMMIT, Images for the Future, and STW SEARCHER.

7. REFERENCES

[1] L. Ahn. Games with a purpose. *IEEE Computer*, 39(6):92–94, 2006.

[2] M. Ames and M. Naaman. Why we tag: Motivations for annotation in mobile and online media. In *Proc. CHI*, 2007.

[3] R. Gligorov, L. B. Baltussen, J. van Ossenbruggen, L. Aroyo, M. Brinkerink, J. Oomen, and A. van Ees. Towards integration of end-user tags with professional annotations. In *Proc. Web Science*, 2010.

[4] A. Kittur, E. H. Chi, and B. Suh. Crowdsourcing user studies with mechanical turk. In *Proc. CHI*, 2008.

[5] C. Marlow, M. Naaman, D. Boyd, and M. Davis. HT06, tagging paper, taxonomy, Flickr, academic article, to read. In *Proc. Hypertext*, 2006.

[6] P. Marsden. Crowdsourcing. *Contagious Magazine*, 18:24–28, 2009.

[7] J. Nielsen. Participation inequality: Encouraging more users to contribute, 2006. `http://www.useit.com/alertbox/participation_inequality.html`.

[8] D. A. Shamma, R. Shaw, P. L. Shafton, and Y. Liu. Watch what I watch: using community activity to understand content. In *Proc. MIR*, 2007.

[9] A. F. Smeaton, P. Over, and W. Kraaij. Evaluation campaigns and TRECVid. In *Proc. MIR*, 2006.

[10] C. G. M. Snoek, B. Freiburg, J. Oomen, and R. Ordelman. Crowdsourcing rock n' roll multimedia retrieval. In *Proc. ACM Multimedia*, 2010.

[11] C. G. M. Snoek and A. W. M. Smeulders. Visual-concept search solved? *IEEE Computer*, 43(6):76–78, 2010.

[12] R. Snow, B. O'Connor, D. Jurafsky, and A. Y. Ng. Cheap and fast—but is it good?: evaluating non-expert annotations for natural language tasks. In *Proc. EMNLP*, 2008.

[13] J. Surowiecki. *The wisdom of crowds: why the many are smarter than the few.* Random House, 2005.

[14] R. van Zwol, L. Garcia, G. Ramirez, B. Sigurbjornsson, and M. Labad. Video tag game. In *Proc. WWW*, 2008.

A Mobile Interactive Robot for Gathering Structured Social Video

Alexander Reben
MIT Media Lab
75 Amherst St
Cambridge, MA 02139
areben@media.mit.edu

Joseph Paradiso
MIT Media Lab
75 Amherst St
Cambridge, MA 02139
joep@media.mit.edu

ABSTRACT

Documentaries are typically captured in a very structured way, using teams to film and interview people. We developed an autonomous method for capturing structured cinéma vérité style documentaries through an interactive robotic camera, which was used as a mobile physical agent to facilitate interaction and story gathering within a ubiquitous media framework. We sent this robot out to autonomously gather human narrative about its environment. The robot had a specific story capture goal and leveraged humans to attain that goal. The robot collected a 1st person view of stories unfolding in real life, and as it engaged with its subjects via a preset dialog, these media clips were intrinsically structured. We evaluated this agent by way of determining "complete" vs. "incomplete" interactions. "Complete" interactions were those that generated viable and interesting videos, which could be edited together into a larger narrative. It was found that 30% of the interactions captured were "complete" interactions. Our results suggested that changes in the system would only produce incrementally more "complete" interactions, as external factors like natural bias or busyness of the user come into play. The types of users who encountered the robot were fairly polar; either they wanted to interact or did not - very few partial interactions went on for more than 1 minute. Users who partially interacted with the robot were found to treat it rougher than those who completed the full interaction. It was also determined that this type of limited-interaction system is best suited for short-term encounters. At the end of the study, a short cinéma vérité documentary showcasing the people and activity in our building was easily produced from the structured videos that were captured, indicating the utility of this approach.

Categories and Subject Descriptors

H.5.2 User Interfaces (D.2.2, H.1.2, I.3.6)

General Terms

Design, Experimentation, Human Factors.

Keywords

HRI, Social Robotics, Interaction, Automatic Documentary

Aera Chair: Aisling Kellihera

1. INTRODUCTION

A robotic camera called Boxie was built that had a goal of actively capturing a story about its environment and the people within it. That is, that the robot had a specific story capture goal and leveraged its mobility and interactivity together with the capabilities of the ubiquitous sensor network to achieve that goal. This device also allowed for an active first person view that many passive distributed media capture systems don't enable [1]. It can also reach areas that 3rd person systems do not cover by its inherent mobility. In these blind areas the robot either recorded data there or prompted others to move it to an area where sensors are active.

The novel approach to this system is that it enables activities of interest to be effectively and actively captured by leveraging human empathy and interaction as a social robot. Sociable robots can be defined as robots which leverage social interactions and cues in order to attain the internal goals of the robot [2]. Through this empathy and interaction, this engagement encouraged the person interacting with the robot to share their story, in a meaningful way. Similar robots have been developed that leverage humans to achieve simple goals using empathy [3]. We evaluated the effectiveness of different forms of interaction which were developed on the robot platform. This interaction design and testing in real world scenarios was the focus of the investigation. The robot acts as a facilitator to coax those who may not initially be inclined to interact with the system to share their stories. The documentary that was created started small scale, at the immediate level of the person interacting with the robot, and expanded through that interaction to encompass stories from others who subsequently encountered the robot. As the style of the documentary is cinéma vérité, it provokes the subjects.

A narrative "thread" followed the robot through its interactions and path of story goal achievement. Through this, we can see how the robot's users are connected within the story line, through the robot's interactions. This provides a way to incorporate social interaction within the framework of ubiquitous media systems. This system is the first we know of that has the specific goal of actively capturing a documentary within a ubiquitous media environment by leveraging human intelligence, interaction and emotion. This novel approach created a rich story capture system within and outside of ubiquitous media frameworks.

2. INTERACTION DESIGN

As with all social robots, interaction design plays a pivotal role in their success. The first step in the design of a sociable robot that leverages humans is to consider the interaction with the user. There are several factors that determine the success of such a system. The factors for our particular system were overall "cuteness", interaction simplicity, appearance and behavior.

2.1 Appearance

Appearance is an important factor in addressing interactivity and usability of a robot. Since the robot would be relying on its cuteness in order to leverage humans, special care was taken in the design of its appearance. The overall aesthetic of the robot was box-shaped with a bottom mounted track drive. We chose this shape because of its simple lines and familiar appearance. The physical characteristics of most importance included eye size, eye spacing and position, head size, and body proportions. The eyes of the robot were chosen to be large and circular. Geldart et al. determined that figures with larger eye sizes were found to be more attractive by both adults and children [4]. This eye geometry yielded the "cutest" looking results in the prototypes. The eyes were set far apart and low on the head, making the robot appear naive and young. The head was made large in relation to the torso, a 3:2 ratio was found to be most aesthetically pleasing. A short squat body was the most childlike configuration (see Figure 1). We also considered how the user would hold the robot. The only way to test how a user might approach holding the robot was to develop physical prototypes and ask users to grasp the robot in the most natural way.

Figure 1. Boxie the robot.

2.2 Subject Acquisition

The overall interaction paradigm for the robot was that of "active" story gathering. Bergström et al. determined that an active robot in a crowded public area (that of a shopping mall) was most successful in eliciting interactions with passers-by if it took an active role in the human acquisition process [5]. It was also found that humans will adjust their positions in order to be "noticed" by the face of the robot. The idea of a human being "noticed" was a central consideration in the interaction design of the robot. To be noticed, the robot needed a face and a gaze. It also needed to recognize the user and acknowledge their presence. This also placed the camera embedded in the robot's eye in a position to have a face-to-face interview with the subject.

2.3 Engagement

The main mechanism the robot uses to leverage humans is cuteness. Our emotional reactions and empathy for cute things is hardwired into our brains through evolution. The subject of cuteness has been long studied by evolutionary psychologists. The reaction we have to cute things originates with the need to care for babies [6]. The cuteness of babies motivates parents to care for and protect them. We used the cuteness of the Boxie robot to draw users in and keep them engaged. The cuteness paradigm we chose to use is that of the lost and helpless child. It was felt that if the robot was perceived as a helpless and lost "child-bot" that user's instincts would engage and they would interact with the robot until they were able to help it. A major consideration was how to engage the user and keep them engaged without making the user feel suspicious of the robot.

"...the rapidity and promiscuity of the cute response makes the impulse suspect, readily overridden by the angry sense that one is being exploited or deceived." [7]

We avoided this pitfall by carefully molding the interaction with the robot to gradually ask the user to work more for the system. The robot also interacted in a two-way fashion, giving the user something in-kind to their input. For example, when the user told the robot something about themselves, the robot would tell it something about itself. With this approach, we avoided the perception by the user that they were being used by the system, making the interaction enjoyable and effective.

2.4 Behavior

Creating behavior that was "cute" was not as immediately apparent as designing the physical appearance. The behavior of the robot needed to be scripted, just as an actor would be. The particular behavior of the robot depended on its motive and its current situation. Depending on the goal of the system, the robot modified its behavior to best achieve the objective. The voice and movement of the robot were the main avenues through which to represent behaviors.

Through movement, we could play with the personality of the robot dynamically. Non-verbal behavior can express as much as and augment the content of verbal communication [8]. Movement is an important factor for displaying expression in robots with constrained appearances such as Boxie [9]. The nominal movement behavior of the robot was to seek out people while getting stuck or lost. The robot was made to act naive by appearing to not know where it was going. By appearing lost, people around the robot would be compelled to help it, just as they would with a lost child or helpless animal. When the robot got itself suck, its behavior was reminiscent of a wounded animal or a child in need. For example, if the robot wedged itself in a corner or under an obstacle, it squirmed around back and forth as if it was trapped. The robot would detect if it was stuck by using its distance sensor and accelerometer. When the robot got itself stuck, it would raise slightly off the ground, which could be detected by an increase in acceleration due to gravity and an increase in the robot to floor distance. It would wait to detect reflected body heat of a nearby human or time-out in software and move again. When the robot came to a complicated intersection, it moved back and forth as if it was searching or confused about what it should do. This confusion led people to believe the robot was lost or helpless to find its way. The robot slowed down before this behavior to mimic hesitance or fear of the path ahead. When the robot sensed a human it stopped in the direction of the human and motioned toward them, indicating that it would like to initiate a conversation. This indication of conversational intent was an important factor in the capture of a human for interaction [10].

Past research has found that behavior plays a crucial role in attempting to get a user to perform an action for a system. One robot that did produce a tangible output from its users was shaped like a trash can, and would rove around trying to elicit children to deposit trash. The robot could not complete its goal on its own without the interaction of the children. The robot utilized vocalizations and behaviors to try to elicit trash from the children. It was found that the robot could achieve its goal if the robot was moved toward an area with trash by the children [11].

2.5 Story Capture

The type of story we chose to capture was the documentary. We crafted a script for the robot to speak in order to capture a story about the current place the robot was in. The childlike voice of the robot was scripted in such a way as to complete the robot's goals. Two scripts were produced and implemented. One involved giving the user simple commands while the other added personality and provided a two way conversation. The intent was to study the difference in user responses in comparing the types of scripts implemented. In "Relational agents: a model and implementation of building user trust" it was found that adding "small talk" to the interaction paradigm of an embodied agent increased the user trust for that agent [12]. At the beginning and end of each script, the robot would make an edit point in the internal camera. This separated the individual interactions inside the robot, effectively pre-editing and sorting the footage. The scripts interviewed those that the robot found so that the video shot would be able to be assembled into a coherent documentary. The place in the robot's script was advanced by the subject acknowledging they were done speaking by pressing a button on the side of the robot's head. The interviewees would speak directly to the robot looking at the robots "face" (hence camera) during the capture process (Figure 2). (see reference [13] for detailed scripts).

Figure 2. Example of face-to-face interaction from the view of the robot.

When the robot was finished roving for the day, it was retrieved and the video was downloaded along with the data to indicate how to edit to documentary together. This data was used to form a video showing the robot's journey and its interaction with people.

3. RESULTS

3.1 Interaction Time

The minimal amount of time to complete the full useable interaction sequence was a little over 3 minutes. A full useableinteraction sequence was defined as interaction with the robot to the point of being a useable narrative (over 90% question completion rate). In a sample group of 15 subjects, a clear separation between full interaction and partial interaction was seen at the 2.5 to 3 minute mark [13]. We used this mark to identify the videos which were full useable interaction vs. partial interaction. There exists a large spike of interactions which lasted for less than 1 minute. The majority of these interactions were found to be, through analysis of the video and question progression, either users pushing the button and walking away or not choosing to continue interacting with the robot after quickly investigating it. It was found the 70% of the interactions fell into this "partial interaction" category while 30% fell into the "full useable interaction category" [13]. Note that it was to be expected that the number of complete interactions would be low. This was due to the fact the complete interactions took a disproportionally large amount of time vs. incomplete interactions. Since the time the robot was roaming was finite, more incomplete interactions could be recorded vs. the number of complete ones. Furthermore, complete interactions implied a full commitment to the robot, which required more time of the participant.

3.2 Robot Abuse

An interesting trend emerged; users who did not complete the full interaction also tended to mistreat the robot – i.e. handle it roughly. We measured how mistreated the robot was by using simple accelerometer data to infer how it was handled, hit or shaken. While users who reached the full interaction stage attained an average maximum G force of 2.4 (Figure 3), those who did not complete the interaction fully reached an average maximum of 4.9 Gs, over twice as much (Figure 4)[13]. While 2.4 Gs is within the limit of normal acceleration of the robot (associated with handling and tilting), a force of 4.9 Gs indicates rough handling and a few interactions where the robot was placed back on the ground roughly. There is a clear split between the interaction types. This data could be used to sense a bad interaction for either automatic editing or for the robot to take action and try to evade this type of person.

3.3 Documentary Production

The video gathered from the robot was able to be used to generate a coherent documentary about the spaces it had visited. After a week of roaming a space, we were easily able to extract enough footage to generate an edited documentary lasting 5 minutes 25 seconds [13]. We captured a total of 50 clips which equated to roughly an hour of raw footage, about a third of which were useable. We were able to use the footage from both partial and full interactions, with each type lending their own character to the story. Because of the way in which the raw video was automatically sorted by the button pushes of the users after each segment of interaction, this video [14] was straightforward to assemble and has been well received by all who have viewed it.

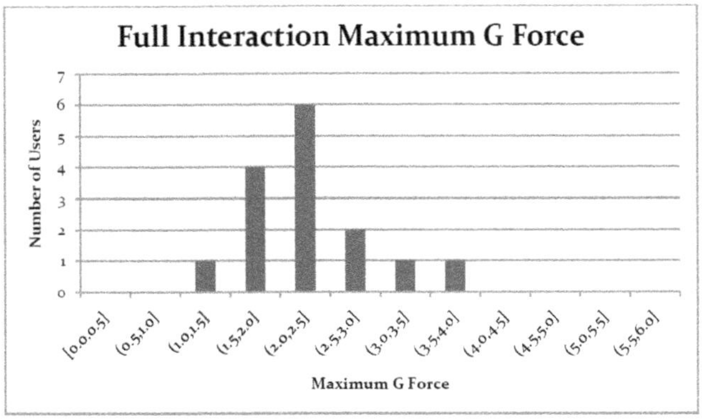

Figure 3. Distribution of maximum G forces encountered during full interactions.

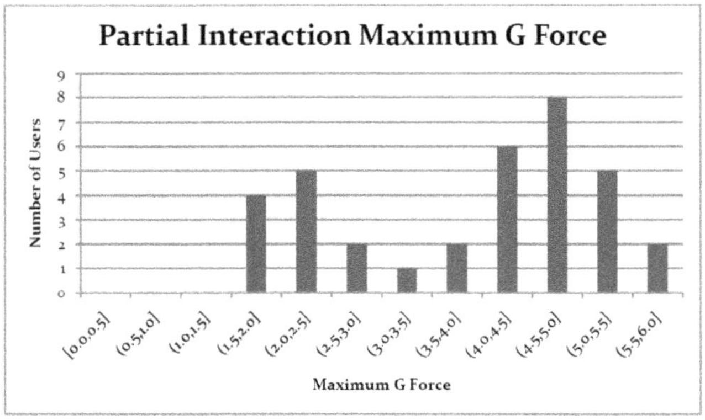

Figure 4. Distribution of maximum G forces encountered during partial interactions.

4. CONCLUSIONS

The creation of a physical agent to facilitate interaction resulted in a successful story-capturing robot, which effectively engaged people to extract structured interviews about its environment. Success was measured as the ability to create a coherent cinéma vérité style documentary with the robot's footage. It was found that 30% of the interactions captured were "complete" interactions. Results suggested that changes to the system would only produce incrementally more "complete" interactions, as external factors like natural bias or busyness of the user come into play (as it was set loose in an active workplace). The types of users who encountered the robot were fairly polar; either they wanted to interact or did not - very few partial interactions went on for more than 1 minute. It was also determined that this type of limited-interaction system is best suited for short-term encounters. At the end of the study, a coherent movie was easily produced from the video clips captured, proving that their content and organization were viable for story-making.

Some suggestions can be made for the development of future agent-based physical story capture systems. Keep the interaction as interesting as possible as users are more likely to share stories if the agent also shares back with the user. Anthropomorphize the system to create a connection with the person you are trying to leverage. Have the agent offer them something in exchange for their interaction. Make the agent seem like it needs the user. Be transparent with the purpose of the agent, as users are prone to be skeptical about a system that needs them but does not tell them why. Try not to be annoying since there is a fine line between attempting to capture a user and annoying them; the system is most effective just before that line. Look "good" because the agent should look the part. This is as important a consideration as the technology inside.

5. ACKNOWLEDGMENTS

We acknowledge the MIT Media Lab and its research sponsors for supporting this work, together with our colleagues, particularly Mat Laibowitz, Nan-Wei Gong and the rest of Responsive Environments and Sheng-Ying Pao for their help and support.

6. REFERENCES

[1] M. Laibowitz, 2010. *Distributed narrative extraction using wearable and imaging sensor networks*, PhD. Thesis, MIT Media Lab.

[2] C. Breazeal, 2004. *Social interactions in HRI: the robot view*, Systems, Man, and Cybernetics, Part C: Applications and Reviews, IEEE Transactions on, vol. 34, pp. 181-186.

[3] K. Kinzer, Tweenbots, Accessed 2011, http://www.tweenbots.com/

[4] S. Geldart, et al., 1999. "Effects of eye size on adults' aesthetic ratings of faces and 5-month-olds' looking times," *PERCEPTION-LONDON-*, vol. 28, pp. 361-374.

[5] N. Bergström, et al., 2007. Modeling of natural human-robot encounters," School of Computer Science and Engineering, Royal Institute of Technology, Stockholm, Sweden, 2008. Tavel, P. *Modeling and Simulation Design*. AK Peters Ltd., Natick, MA.

[6] D. Dutton, 2003. "Aesthetics and evolutionary psychology," *The Oxford Handbook of Aesthetics*, pp. 693–705.

[7] N. Angier, "The Cute Factor," in *The New York Times*, ed. New York, 2006.

[8] B. DePaulo, 1992. "Nonverbal behavior and self-presentation," *Psychological Bulletin*, vol. 111, pp. 203-243.

[9] C. L. Bethel and R. R. Murphy, 2006. "Affective expression in appearance constrained robots," presented at the *Proceedings of the 1st ACM SIGCHI/SIGART conference on Human-robot interaction,* Salt Lake City, Utah, USA.

[10] S. Satake, et al., 2009. "How to approach humans?: strategies for social robots to initiate interaction," presented at the *Proceedings of the 4th ACM/IEEE international conference on Human robot interaction*, La Jolla, California, USA.

[11] Y. Yamaji, et al., 2010. *STB: human-dependent sociable trash box*, presented at the Proceeding of the 5th ACM/IEEE international conference on Human-robot interaction, Osaka, Japan.

[12] T. Bickmore and J. Cassell, 2001. "Relational agents: a model and implementation of building user trust," presented at the Proceedings of the SIGCHI conference on *Human factors in computing systems*, Seattle, Washington, USA

[13] A. Reben, 2010, *Interactive Physical Agents for Story Gathering*. Master's thesis. MIT Media Lab, Cambridge, MA, USA.

[14] A. Reben, Boxie, Accessed 2011, http://boxie.media.mit.edu

Abstract Rendering of Human Activity in a Dynamic Distributed Learning Environment

Andreea Danielescu
Arizona State University
School of Arts Media + Engineering
Tempe, AZ 85281
1.480.965.9438
lavinia.danielescu@asu.edu

Ryan P. Spicer
Arizona State University
School of Arts Media + Engineering
Tempe, AZ 85281
1.480.965.9438
ryan.spicer@asu.edu

David Tinapple
Arizona State University
School of Arts Media + Engineering
Tempe, AZ 85281
1.480.965.9438
david.tinapple@asu.edu

Aisling Kelliher
Arizona State University
School of Arts Media + Engineering
Tempe, AZ 85281
1.480.965.9438
aisling.kelliher@asu.edu

Shawn Nikkila
Arizona State University
School of Arts Media + Engineering
Tempe, AZ 85281
1.480.965.9438
shawn.nikkila@asu.edu

Sean Burdick
sean.burdick.ee@gmail.com

ABSTRACT
Contemporary distributed enterprises present challenges in terms of demonstrating community activity awareness and coherence across individuals and teams in collaborating networks. *Building with a Memory* is an experiential media system that captures and represents human activity in a distributed workplace over time. The system senses and analyzes movement in two workspaces in a mixed-use building with the results rendered in an informative ambient display in the building entryway. We describe the design and development of the system, together with insights from two studies of the installation and promising future directions.

Categories and Subject Descriptors: J.5 [Computer Applications]: Arts and Humanities – *fine arts*.

General Terms: Algorithms, Design, Human Factors.

Keywords: Memory, motion tracking, ambient presence.

1. INTRODUCTION
Within distributed organizations, building and maintaining mutual awareness across individuals is vital to ensure the development of a strong sense of communal achievement. For enterprises employing adaptable spaces, the activity dynamics of employees must be generally understood by the entire community to inform efficient collaboration. Such challenges provide opportunities for the development of technical, social and environmental responses aimed at increasing community awareness and understanding.

Prior responses to these challenges have addressed the awareness shortfall, ranging from artistic interventions (Jeremijenko's *"Live Wire"*) [12], to more utilitarian solutions [13]. Informed by insights from these works and others, our research examines the mediated cultivation of community activity awareness in a dynamic, distributed learning environment.

Figure 1: The dynamic light panels and video display of the *Building with a Memory* system

We present *Building with a Memory*, an experiential media system [11] that uses a network of sensors and output devices to capture and represent the history of human activity across related spaces. The system analyzes and renders both the current level of physical activity in the sensed spaces, and that same activity contextualized over time, through colored lighting and a video display.

The system is distributed across three spaces (two sensed and one for display) in a multi-use university building that is evolving into a hub for the host academic unit and surrounding campus communities. This well-trafficked location provides an ideal setting for observing, analyzing and rendering emergent human activity. Our system aims to present meaningful value for regular, occasional and one-off building visitors, without compromising individual privacy. To do so, the system understands human activity as an aggregation characterizing the large-scale dynamics in the two sensed spaces, where no one individual is directly identifiable. Analysis of this activity is visually represented on a panel display and two variable-color, lighting fixtures The visual representation plays automatically, providing a straightforward entry point for new visitors while also encouraging repeated *unfocused* or low-effort engagement by familiar workers [6].

The work described in this paper builds extensively on an earlier prototype detailed in [3] with significant technical, conceptual and

*Area Chair: Nicu Sebe

MM'11, November 28–December 1, 2011, Scottsdale, Arizona, USA.

aesthetic improvements. New technical contributions include a networked architecture with an extensible API, sensing in multiple spaces and refined mappings of activity to feedback.

2. RELATED WORK

In crafting *Building with a Memory*, we draw on several areas of inquiry. Within the workplace context, research into the ambient representation of presence and activity has produced novel installations from both academic and commercial entities. Within the visual realm, the role of light and color in conveying meaning about human activity reveals a historical record of traditional, digital and interactive artistic explorations that serve to situate and direct our work. The works of Mark Rothko, Hans Hofmann, Moris Louis and Barnett Newman inspire the aesthetic of our system's light panel display while James Turrell and Olafur Ericsson inspired our use of light field schemas.

2.1 Artistic Exploration of Human Movement

There is a rich history of interactive art exploring the sensing and representation of human activity in space, either explicitly or implicitly (Utterback's *Aurora Organ* or *Abundance*; Snibbe's *You are Here*; Rokeby's *San Marco Flow*; Viegas' *Artifacts of the Presence Era*). These pieces explore a variety of dynamics in terms of the relationship between sensed activity, archiving, and reflection. In works like *Impossible Geographies* [5], *Motion Traces*, and *Abundance*, users' actions map directly to feedback. In *San Marco Flow* and *You are Here*, the sensed space is separate from, or larger than, the feedback space. As a result, those sensed may be unaware of their participation. These works also vary in their representation of the history of human activity. *You are Here, San Marco Flow* and *Abundance* represent individual activity directly; *Aurora Organ* and *Impossible Geographies* represent activity abstractly.

Other research involves semi-public workspace displays that present visualizations meaningful primarily to 'insiders' [10]. These projects range from pragmatically functional to deliberately abstract. We seek to balance between these two poles and to render activity for familiar insiders and visitors.

2.2 Activity through Optical Flow

Computer vision offers a multitude of techniques for analyzing and understanding human activity, including blob tracking, face recognition, and gesture recognition [1,7]. These methods are often used to identify people rather than protect their privacy. We aim instead to understand activity at a much coarser granularity – to record general levels of activity rather than individual actions.

Optical flow is regularly used as input to more complex algorithms, such as Support Vector Machines [2,9]. We use raw optical flow data because it provides coarse measures of activity, but cannot be used to identify individuals. This maintains privacy, while still extracting information. This low-complexity method also makes it easier to move toward low cost sensor nodes.

3. SYSTEM OVERVIEW

Building with a Memory captures information about human activity, through fixed video sensors. A central server receives and archives this data and provides an API for feedback devices to access both current and historical activity. The activity is analyzed and rendered through a situated flat panel display and variable-color, indirect lighting fixtures (see Figure 2).

3.1 Sensing

Each sensor node includes a computer connected to a wide-angle USB video camera. Our application captures video at a resolution

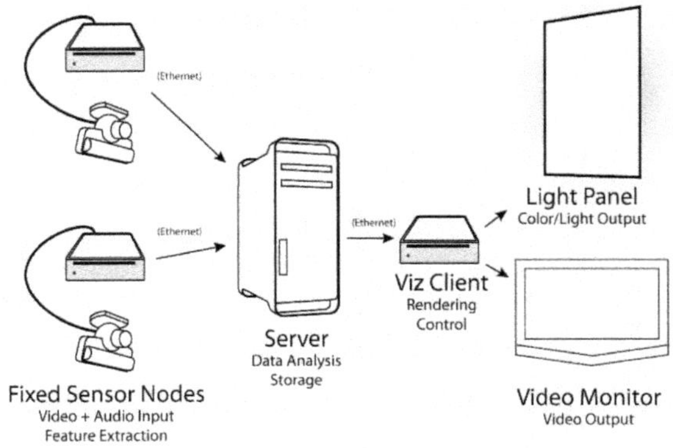

Figure 2: The architecture of the installation.

of 320x240 at three frames per second. The application performs Lucas-Kanade optical flow analysis to extract motion vectors and streams them to the archival server via TCP/IP. The choice of frame-rate provides a balance between capturing movement and minimizing server and network load. Raw video is not saved or transmitted, thus protecting the anonymity of individuals in the space and further reducing bandwidth and storage requirements.

3.2 Archival

The archival server receives the data from the sensor nodes and saves it to disk, with the prior ten minutes of activity kept in memory. The server can provide the current or historical data for any room, either in terms of raw or normalized magnitudes. The system averages the total optical flow magnitude from the last 90 frames, implementing a low-pass filter to emphasize macro-scale patterns rather than local spikes. We select the sum of the magnitude of optical flow vectors for each frame as the primary feature for our visualization since it provides a direction-invariant metric. The server archives all optical flow vectors for each frame allowing for additional features to be calculated in the future.

3.3 Feedback

Building with a Memory provides feedback through a video display and LED lighting. All feedback shares a common color mapping based on the conventions used in heat-maps [4], weather maps (as in www.weather.com) and television shows displaying thermal cameras, making it familiar to observers in a Western cultural context (Figure 4).

The video display renders the previous week's activity both as a line-graph and on a floor plan contextualizing the sensed spaces in the building (Figure 3). A playback head automatically scrubs across the historical data, highlighting an hour-wide window. The average activity level for the window is represented in the color of the room on the floor plan. The video display also shows the current activity level of each sensed space to the right of the line graphs, updating every ten seconds. This update rate minimizes network traffic and discourages people from manipulating the visualization by intentionally moving around in the space.

The LED light panels (Figure 5) located to each side of the display, present the average of current activity levels. The light panels use 12 clusters of red, green and blue Philips LEDs to wash the walls surrounding the installation with color. This provides an ambient indication of the building's current activity level.

Each light panel contains an XBee 802.15 radio, an Arduino Pro microcontroller, and three LED driver boards (see Figure 5). Each LED is individually addressable, allowing for the development of complex patterns of color. Passive cooling is used to avoid adding cooling fans that would detract from the ambiance of the piece.

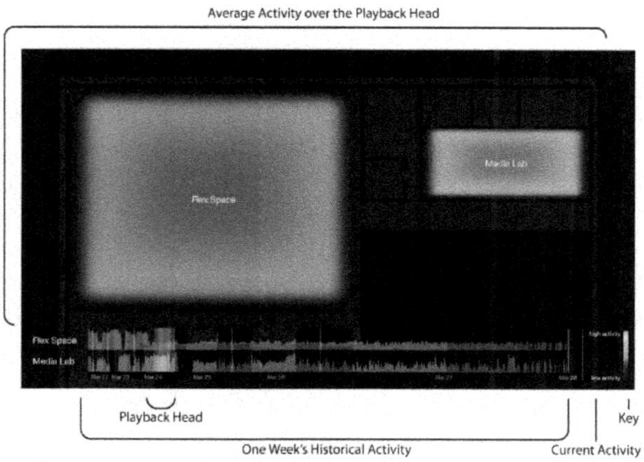

Figure 3: The on-screen visualization.

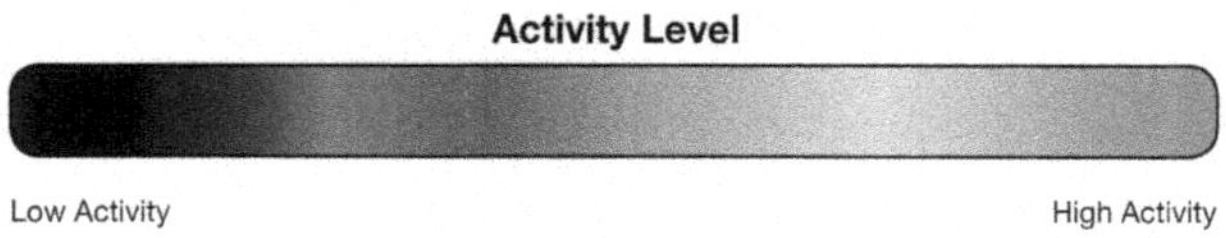

Figure 4: The color mapping is defined as a linear gradient in HSL color space.

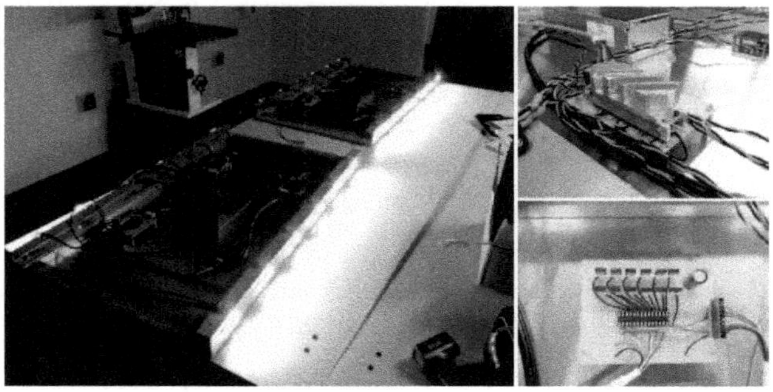

Figure 5: Light panel construction

4. EVALUATION METHODOLOGY

Evaluating this type of system formally presents many challenges. The system includes both novel and standard approaches in terms of design, engineering, aesthetics and implementation. Due to this overlap, we consider the taxonomy of technical/quantitative analysis and aesthetic/qualitative evaluations proposed in [8]. We are interested in whether the data reveals meaningful patterns of activity, and community understanding of, the installation.

Building with a Memory was installed in February 2011. Sensors were installed in a computer lab (*Media Lab*) and a lecture / performance space (*Flex Space*). The feedback was located in the entry hallway (see Figure 6).

4.1 Activity Pattern Analysis

We focus on two time periods: an open house that took place in February 2011 and a normal week of activity during March 2011. For both of these periods we can detect identifiable events such as lectures, dance performances and class changes.

Accurately capturing events in large environments can be challenging due to restricted space for camera placement. In both spaces, cameras were placed in ceiling corners. The cameras could not be mounted overhead due to low ceilings and obstructions. This caused activity in those corners to register a greater optical flow magnitude than activity in the opposite corner. The magnitudes were normalized with respect to each individual room to compensate for differences in room size.

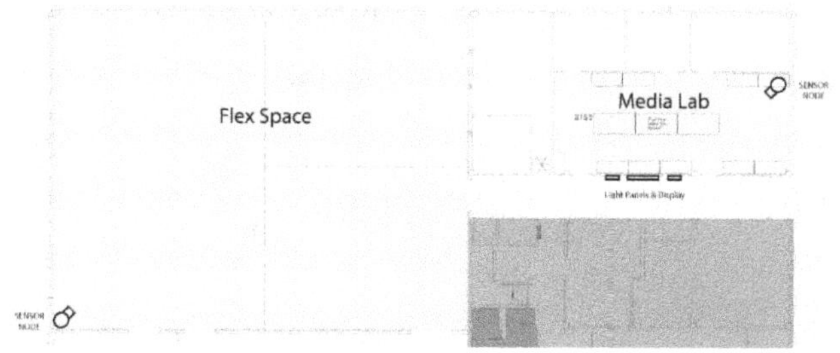

Figure 6: Floor plan of the building in which the sensing nodes and visualization are installed. Light shading indicates camera sensor fields of view.

The data was first down-sampled using a windowing technique. Anything under the noise floor was removed. To smooth the data, a 10-frame window was moved across the data, with a 5-frame overlap between successive windows. For each window, the minimum value was used to remove the influence of the large spikes due to switching the lights in the space on or off. If the minimum value was below the noise floor, implying missing data, the mean of the magnitude was used instead. This technique provides us with less noisy data that is more easily analyzed.

4.2 User study

Through surveys, we evaluated the installation's impact on stakeholders' knowledge of activity in the building. Participants recruited from the community were asked to describe their use of the building's facilities and to estimate the level of activity in the building for the week prior to interacting with the installation. They were also asked about their interest in a direct measure of building activity. A week later, after interacting with the installation, participants were asked to complete the survey again. This allowed changes in awareness promoted by the installation to be subjectively measured. Participants were asked whether they found the installation distracting or informational and whether they would like to be provided with the information on a website or through a mobile application.

5. RESULTS

Informal feedback was received throughout the month the project was displayed. The general response was positive. Administrative leaders in several university departments expressed a desire to integrate the system into workspaces they managed. Viewers were attracted to the form of the installation and to the ideas expressed. Several spectators commented that the installation's feedback could be used to understand activity such as water/power use.

5.1 Activity Pattern Analysis Results

We first consider the building opening celebration. The event included periods in which guests explored numerous interactive installations, listened to speeches, and observed dance and laptop music performances. The Media Lab contained one exhibit. Half of the Flex Space was configured as an auditorium, while the other half contained interactive exhibits. We focus on the Flex Space, where most of the evening's events occurred (Figure 7). We can determine from the graph that the dance performance and the laptop orchestra's entrance into the space generated substantial activity levels. At other points, people moved between the spaces engaging with exhibits, generating constant levels of activity.

Our second example looks at the activity of a typical week in the building. Figure 8 depicts activity in the Flex Space throughout one week in March 2011. This data demonstrates very different patterns of activity from the Open House event. The Flex space is currently used as a lecture hall on Tuesdays and Thursdays. The

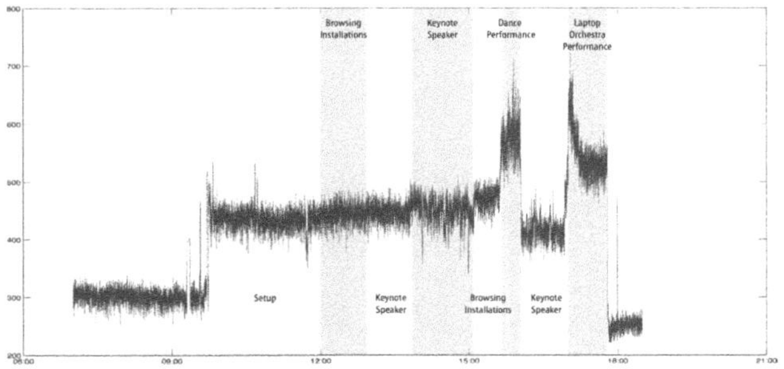

Figure 7: Flex space activity during the open house.

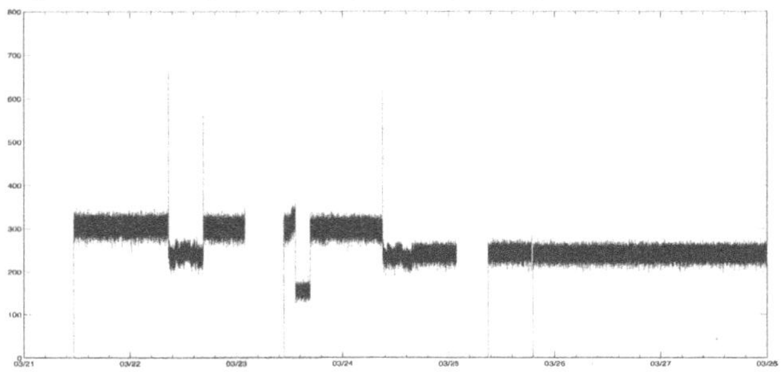

Figure 8: Flex space over one week in March 2011.

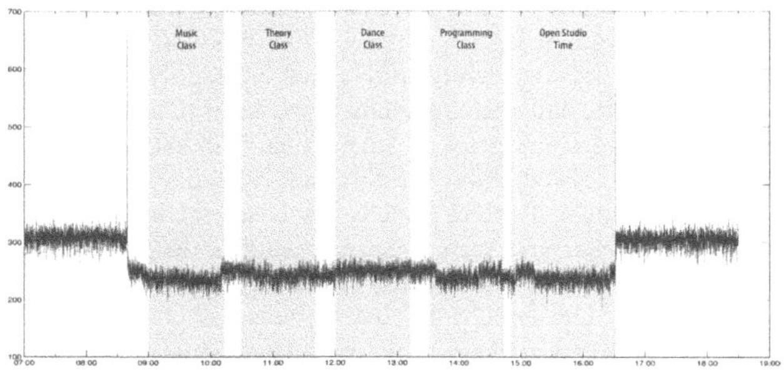

Figure 9: Flex space on Tuesday of the week in March (7 am to 6:30 pm).

periodicity of these activities is visible, including heightened levels of activity during the dance related classes (see Figure 9). This space is relatively unused the rest of the week. The Media Lab is not displayed as the activity in that space is unremarkable.

5.2 User Study Results

Our pre-survey revealed surprising attitudes towards the workspaces. Twelve community members responded to the survey, including faculty, staff, and students. Although the number of survey respondents was limited, several observations can still be made. Of those surveyed, most were interested in activities in the Media Lab and wanted to know when they could enter to use the computers or socialize, pointing to the Media Lab as the primary locus for community activity. Interest was divided between spaces for staff and faculty who monitor both locations.

Based on the survey, community members assumed that the Media Lab space was active at night, even though it is closed and locked after 8pm. In general, the Media Lab was perceived to be more active than it actually is, and more active than the Flex Space. This reveals a bias in how the spaces are programmed.

In the post-survey, participants reported interest in seeing the system expanded to other spaces in the building, including a fabrication and electronics lab. Respondents spent about a minute looking at the display, indicating minimal attention was required to make sense of the design. They felt the installation was not distracting, and were not concerned with the presence of cameras.

6. FUTURE WORK

The *Building with a Memory* system presents many opportunities for continued research. These include the development of additional sensing techniques and the roll out of new interfaces tailored for smart-phone access. Along the aesthetic dimension, the mappings of human activity to color may need to be rethought based on the addition of new sensors (both static and mobile) and new sensing modalities. These changes must be considered in terms of their contribution to the local community.

In the near future, we intend to deploy a mobile application that allows stakeholders to browse activity levels of the sensed spaces at various levels of granularity. Given our survey results, we would also like to add sensors to additional workspaces.

Future sensing advances include integrating our optical-flow system into more complex human-motion tracking algorithms, such as blob tracking or dynamic background subtraction, which could more precisely localize individuals. We are investigating the integration of acoustic feature detection into the sensor nodes to classify types of activity in the space.

7. ACKNOWLEDGMENTS

Building with a Memory is supported by the Office of the Vice-President for Research and Economic Affairs, the Graduate Research Support Program, and the Graduate College at Arizona State University. The authors also wish to thank Andrew McCord for his contribution to the project.

8. REFERENCES

[1] Aggarwal, J. K. and Cai, Q. (1997). Human motion analysis: a review. Proceedings IEEE Nonrigid and Articulated Motion Workshop. an Juan , Puerto Rico, IEEE Comput. Soc: 90-102.

[2] Ali, S. and Shah, M. (2010). *Human action recognition in videos using kinematic features and multiple instance learning.* IEEE transactions on pattern analysis and machine intelligence **32**(2): 288-303.

[3] Danielescu, A., Spicer, R., Tinapple, D., Kelliher, A. and Campana, E. (2010). Building with a memory: responsive color interventions. Proceedings of the international conference on Multimedia. Firenze, Italy, ACM: 1409-1412.

[4] Friendly, M. (2009). *The History of the Cluster Heat Map.* American Statistician **63**(2): 179--184.

[5] Gemeinboeck, P. (2005). Impossible geographies of belonging. Proceedings of the 13th annual ACM international conference on Multimedia. Hilton, Singapore, ACM: 567-570.

[6] Hallnäs, L. and Redström, J. (2001). *Slow Technology -- Designing for Reflection.* Personal Ubiquitous Comput. **5**: 201-212.

[7] Moeslund, T. B. and Granum, E. (2001). *A Survey of Computer Vision-Based Human Motion Capture.* Computer Vision and Image Understanding **81**(3): 231-268.

[8] Sengers, P. (2006). Autobiographical design. CHI 2006 Workshop on Theory and Method for Experience-Centred Design. New York, NY, USA, ACM Press.

[9] Sidenbladh, H. (2004). Detecting Human Motion with Support Vector Machines. 17th IAPR International Conference on Pattern Recognition. Cambridge, UK. **2**: 188-191.

[10] Streitz, N., Röcker, C., Prante, T., Stenzel, R. and Van Alphen, D. (2003). *Situated interaction with ambient information: Facilitating awareness and communication in ubiquitous work environments.* Human-Computer Interaction (HCI International 2003).

[11] Sundaram, H. and Rikakis, T. (2008). *Encyclopedia of Multimedia*, Encyclopedia of Multimedia,

[12] Weiser, M. and Brown, J. S. (1995) *Designing Calm Technology* http://www.ubiq.com/hypertext/weiser/calmtech/calmtech.htm.

[13] Wren, C. R., Ivanov, Y. A., Kaur, I. and Leigh, D. (2007). *SocialMotion: Measuring the Hidden Social Life of a Building.* Location- and Context-Awareness. J. HIGHTOWER, B. SCHIELE and T. STRANG. **4718:** 85-102.

"WaterTouch": An Aquatic Interactive Multimedia Sensory Table based on Total Internal Reflection in Water

Steve Mann, Ryan Janzen, Jason Huang
University of Toronto
http://wearcam.org/watertouch/

ABSTRACT

We propose a water-based multitouch multimedia user-interface based on total-internal reflection as viewed by an underwater camera. The underwater camera is arranged so that nothing above the water surface is visible until a user touches the water, at which time anything that penetrates the water's surface becomes clearly visible.

Our contribution is twofold: (1) computer vision using underwater cameras aided by total internal reflection; (2) hyperacoustic signal processing (frequency shifting) to capture the natural, acoustically-originating sounds of water rather than using synthetic sounds.

Using water itself as a touch screen creates a fun and playful user interface medium that captures the fluidity of the water's ebb and flow. In one application, a musical instrument is created in which acoustic disturbances in the water (received by underwater microphones or hydrophones) are frequency-shifted to musical notes corresponding to the location in which the water is touched, as determined by the underwater computer vision system.

Categories and Subject Descriptors

H.5.2 [**Info. systems**]: Interfaces & pres.—*User Interfaces*; I.4.9 [**Computing Methodologies**]: Image Processing and Computer Vision; J.2 [**c.apps.**]: Physical sciences & engineering; J.5 [**c.apps.**]: Arts & humanities—*Music*

General Terms

Theory, Design, Human Factors

Keywords

Hydraulophone, Total internal reflection, Tangible User Interface, ORGANic User Interface, Human Computer Interaction, Musical Instrument, Touch Screen, Waterplay

We wish to thank Jonti-Craft, Inc. for providing their "Sensory Table" into which we installed the WaterTouch.
* Area Chair: David Shamma

MM'11 November 28–December 1, 2011, Scottsdale, Arizona, USA.

1. INTRODUCTION

1.1 Background and related work

Water has a history of use in human computer interaction [11], public sculpture [9], and water therapy [2].

Water has also been used in hydraulophones [8], which use pressurized jets of water as a tactile user-interface. In general, tangible user interfaces have proven themselves in many applications of human-computer interaction. For example Ishii's bottles [3], and the Music Cube [1] form notable examples of tangible interfaces.

Benjamin Franklin invented a musical instrument which he called the armonica, making sound from fingers rubbing on tuned pieces of glass while wet. Sometimes also referred to as glass harmonica, this instrument consisted of a row of spinning glass disks or goblets all mounted to a single metal shaft spun by a foot treadle.

While playing glass armonica underwater, we found, in our previous work [7], that the water imparted interesting attributes to the sound, but we wanted some additional versatility, and the option to have a high Q-factor (less damping) at certain times during our performances. In order to achieve this, we used a spinning glass cylinder, which produced sound continuously along its entire length.

We picked up the sound by way of a geophone (contact microphone) in the cylinder, and transmitted it wirelessly to a computer. A computer vision system, connected to a camera, detected the 1-dimensional position where the rod was touched.

This information was used to control the attributes of one or more (depending on the number of fingers touching) bandpass filters affecting the original physical sound. The instrument was used in a variety of public performances (street performances, underwater performances, etc.). See Fig 1(c),(d).

Glass was chosen so as to make an approximate refractive index match with the liquid (water) in which it was immersed. With this matching of refractive indices, the glass cylinder appeared almost invisible in the water. Using underwater cameras looking upwards, at an angle greater than the critical angle of total-internal-reflection, the image of the fingers was strongly enhanced, such that the camera could much more easily pick up the fingers while ignoring everything else in the scene (Fig 1(c),(d)). Additionally, tiny water waves produced by the sound vibrations (acoustic sound production in the glass) were visible, so that the camera could actually pick up some of the ripples from the sound waves in the scene.

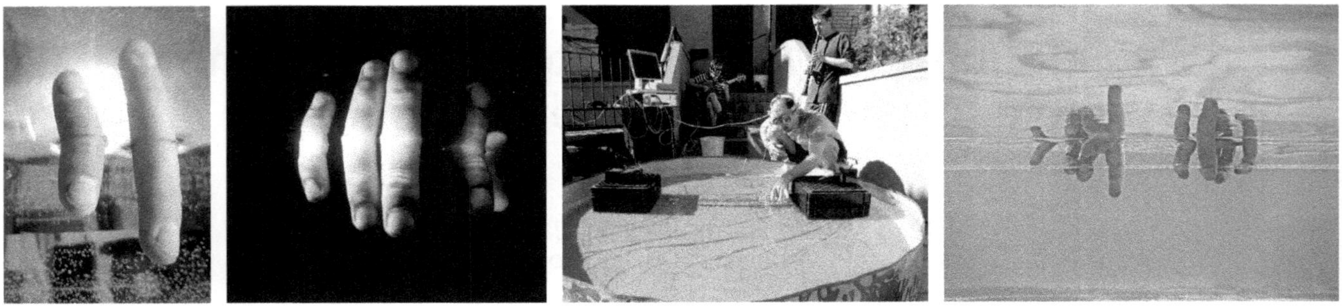

(a) (b) (c) (d)

Figure 1: **WaterTouch uses true total internal reflection.** (a) Placing the camera underwater, and having it look up at an angle, makes it possible to see the fingers as they disturb the light gathered by total internal reflection. This gives rise to a hyper-sensitivity in the image plane, making visible subtle motion- and sound-induced ripples in the water. With carefully constructed computer vision, a high-speed camera can function as an optical pickup of acoustic phenomena, much like an electric guitar having an optical pickup. Together with an array of geophones, hydrophones, and microphones, this provides a multiply acoustic instrument having a richly acoustic physicality. Fingers that penetrate the surface can appear as if floating in a disembodied state (b), making computer vision, tracking along the flat air-water boundary layer, and accurate 3D localization trivial. (c) and (d) show our earlier experiments with an underwater friction-idiophone, where underwater (plus wearable overhead) cameras "look" at a glass cylinder and detect 1-dimensional motion.

1.2 Relation to other touch screens

Many touch screens work on the principle of frustrated total internal reflection [12][10] (*i.e.* affecting an evanescent wave by touching the surface outside it). WaterTouch works on *true* total internal reflection, *i.e.* the user actually penetrates the surface material.

Water gives depth and dimensionality to the surface. Its randomness, unpredictability, and unique properties, create a fun, plaful, and fascinating form of interaction that even a 2 year old child can immediately relate to!

2. WATERTOUCH

We now describe the watertouch interface. Unlike our early 1-dimensional experimentation which required glass, this work purely uses the surface-tension layer of water as the sole surface of visual and acoustic interaction.

It is based on a product called a "Sensory Table" manufactured by Jonti-Craft, a company based in Wabasso, MN, USA. The product consists of a transparent acrylic tub on wheels that can be filled with sand or water to give children a variety of sensory experiences.

The name 'Sensory Table' arises because the sand or water are used to stimulate the senses, not because the table has any sensors in it. But we can easily add sensing apparatus to turn the Sensory Table into a human-computer interface.

Typically we use one or more underwater cameras, along with underwater listening devices (hydrophones) and a data projector. Projectors serve two roles: (1) structured lighting for active computer vision; (2) display of information to the user. This can be achieved by an infrared projector or other infrared light source for the structured vision, and a visible light projector for the display of information to the user.

Unlike a solid touch screen, where only the tips of the fingers touch a two-dimensional (2D) surface, the WaterTouch uses computer vision to capture finger motion in three dimensions (3D), while also capturing some of the random or idiosyncratic behaviour of water that generally gives the user-experience an aquatic feel. See Fig 2.

Fingers that penetrate the surface appear as if floating in a disembodied state, as shown in Fig 1(b). Inserting a black background at the far end of the pool causes the underside of the water surface to also become black, and when lit from above, the fingers become very clearly distinguishable.

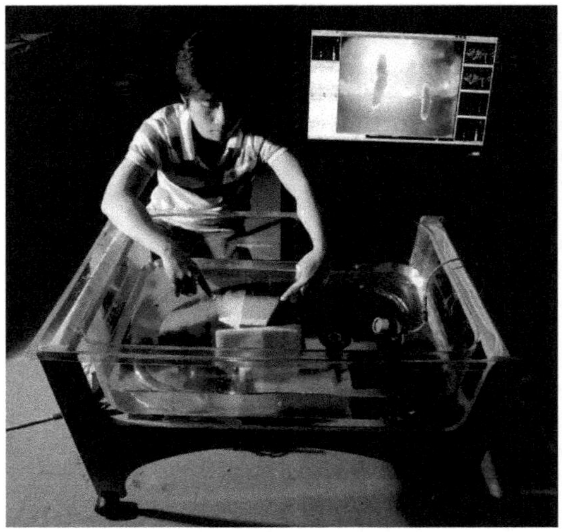

Figure 2: WaterTouch, with projector and active computer vision (infrared illumination, infrared and visible light sensing), underwater using total internal reflection. The use of water also gives a volumetric effect visible throughout the water. Unique properties of water create an interesting and sensory-rich space for play and exploration.

3. TOTAL INTERNAL REFLECTION UNDER A RIPPLED WATER SURFACE

To achieve total internal reflection, the camera's angle of viewing (akin to angle of incidence for light emission) must be beyond the critical angle at the water surface. We use Snell's law:

$$\frac{\sin\theta_1}{\sin\theta_2} = \frac{n_2}{n_1} \tag{1}$$

where n_1 and n_2 are the indices of refraction of water and air, respectively, and θ_1 and θ_2 are the angles of incidence and transmission. The critical angle when looking from underwater up at a flat air-water interface is $\theta_c \doteq 48.6°$ (found by setting θ_2 to 90° for the onset of total internal reflection).

The camera angle θ_{CAM} must be sufficiently shallow to ensure total internal reflection over the entire viewing area under the water surface. This requirement becomes even more harsh when surface waves are present.

Ripples or waves are created in our water trough by the movement of fingers. Capillary waves are the most common type of water waves for this size of setup, as opposed to deep water gravity waves. Small capillary waves can be

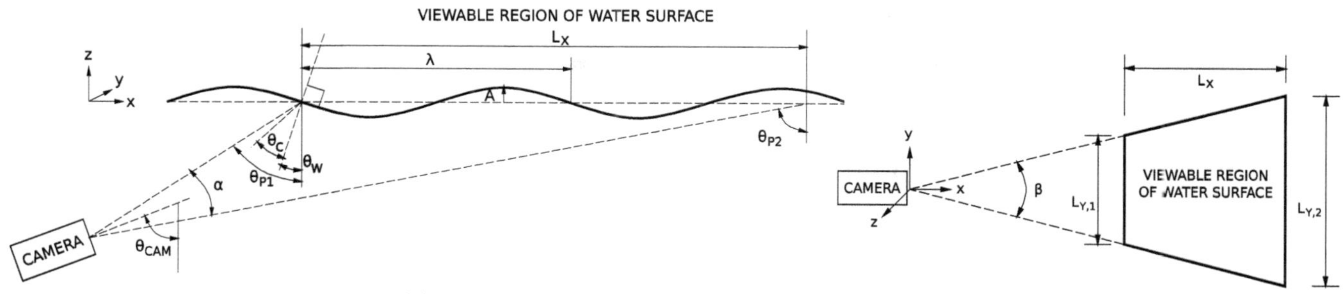

(a) (b)

Figure 3: (a) Camera viewing the water surface from underneath, with total internal reflection (side view). The worst-case scenario has surface waves propagating in the x-direction either towards or away from the camera, which gives the most strict requirement on the camera angle to achieve total internal reflection. (b) Overhead illustration of the underwater total-internal-reflection haptic area.

approximated as sinusoidal waves, as in:

$$z_w(\vec{r},t) = A\sin(k(\vec{r}\cdot\hat{r_t}) - \omega t) \tag{2}$$

with $\vec{r}$ as position in (x, y), t as time, $\hat{r_t}$ as the direction of wave travel, k as the wave number, and ω as the angular frequency of the water wave.

For total internal reflection, we need the top peripheral viewing angle (see Fig 3(a)) to be sufficiently large:

$$\theta_{P1} > \theta_c + \theta_w(\vec{r},t) \tag{3}$$

at all times, where $\theta_w(\vec{r},t)$ is the angle of the water surface. To be true at all times, we consider a wave travelling in the x direction, moving towards or away from the camera.

$$\begin{aligned}
\max\{\theta_w(\vec{r},t)\} &= \sup\left\{\tan^{-1}\frac{\partial z_w}{\partial \vec{r}} : \vec{r}, t\right\} && (4)\\
&= \sup\left\{\tan^{-1}\left.\frac{\partial z_w}{\partial x}\right|_{y=0} : x, t\right\} && (5)\\
&= \sup\left\{\tan^{-1}\left(Ak\cos(kx-\omega t)\right)\right\} && (6)\\
&= \tan^{-1}(Ak)_{max} && (7)\\
&= \tan^{-1}\left(2\pi\frac{A}{\lambda}\right)_{max} && (8)
\end{aligned}$$

where λ is the wavelength.

For a camera with viewing angle α, we have $\theta_{P1} = \theta_{\mathrm{CAM}} - \frac{\alpha}{2}$, and so we place the camera at an angle such that:

$$\theta_{\mathrm{CAM}} > \frac{\alpha}{2} + \sin^{-1}\left(\frac{n_2}{n_1}\right) + \tan^{-1}\left(2\pi\frac{A_{max}}{\lambda_{min}}\right) \tag{9}$$

to maintain total internal reflection over the viewing area.

4. TRANSFORMING FROM IMAGE COORDINATES TO PHYSICAL, RECTANGULAR COORDINATES

Since the camera is placed on an angle, the water surface area viewed by it is trapezoidal. The trapezoidal region subtends a solid rectangular cone of α degrees high and β degrees wide, for a camera aspect ratio of $\beta : \alpha$.

We make a transformation to relate what is viewed on the camera to the real, physical space along the water surface.

A point (X, Y) in a X_{MAX} by Y_{MAX} image, transforms to the physical coordinates:

$$\begin{aligned}
x &= d_{\mathrm{CAM}}\tan\left(\theta_{\mathrm{CAM}} - \alpha\left(\tfrac{X}{X_{\mathrm{MAX}}} - \tfrac{1}{2}\right)\right) && (10)\\
y &= x\tan\left(\beta\left(\tfrac{Y}{Y_{\mathrm{MAX}}} - \tfrac{1}{2}\right)\right) && (11)
\end{aligned}$$

with an origin as shown in Fig 3, and camera depth d_{CAM}.

The total size of the haptic area is: (for $\theta_{\mathrm{CAM}} + \frac{\alpha}{2} < 90°$)

$$L_x = d_{\mathrm{CAM}}\cdot\left(\tan\left(\theta_{\mathrm{CAM}} + \tfrac{\alpha}{2}\right) - \tan\left(\theta_{\mathrm{CAM}} - \tfrac{\alpha}{2}\right)\right) \tag{12}$$

$$L_{y,1} = d_{\mathrm{CAM}}\cdot 2\tan\left(\tfrac{\beta}{2}\right)\tan\left(\theta_{\mathrm{CAM}} - \tfrac{\alpha}{2}\right) \tag{13}$$

$$L_{y,2} = d_{\mathrm{CAM}}\cdot 2\tan\left(\tfrac{\beta}{2}\right)\tan\left(\theta_{\mathrm{CAM}} + \tfrac{\alpha}{2}\right) \tag{14}$$

Although many modern television displays and cameras are HDTV (16:9 aspect ratio), much of the underwater video cameras commonly in use still use the NTSC standard (4:3 aspect ratio). This aspect ratio is also standard for VGA, SVGA, DVGA. So, as an example, for cameras with a 4:3 aspect ratio, it can be helpful to orient the camera in a sideways orientation, so $\beta : \alpha = 3 : 4$. This is a way to make the haptic surface more square than rectangular, so L_x is nearly equal to $(L_{y,1} + L_{y,2})/2$.

5. MULTITOUCH IMAGE PROCESSING OF UNDERWATER FINGERS

Detecting fingers and interpreting their motions involved several steps. The first was to use skin tone masking, based on ratios of red:green, red:blue and green:blue for each pixel.

After masking according to a set of possible skin tones, the masked image was converted to greyscale, and two iterations of erosion were applied to reduce noise in the finger boundaries: first, vertical erosion, then horizontal erosion.

We then applied canny edge detection to extract contours from a binary version of the eroded image. The contour boundary was numerically expanded by 20% in order to fill in gaps between finger sections that the masking may have opened up. The set of all enclosed regions of the given frame were unioned with those from the previous frame, creating a set-union type of moving average filter.

Canny edge detection was applied a second time to the modified finger regions, and then their centroids were calculated. The (X, Y) coordinates were transformed to physical (x, y) coordinates. Finger area created a third dimension, z.

The result was a tactile user-interface that was responsive to finger motion. We designed a system that created musical tones, where the vertical placement of fingers controlled frequency and horizontal placement controlled amplitude.

Furthermore, the surface was multitouch, which meant that multiple fingers inserted in the water created a musical chord. For example, three fingers could be inserted to play a D-minor chord, and so on.

6. FINGERS VS. BUBBLES

We chose to embrace the idiosyncracies of the water surface, using a separate detection system that detects bubbles and splashes independently from the fingers, thus creating a new user input space.

Fluid flow creates a large set of phenomena in response to finger motion. Surface tension, alone, leads to various kinds of waves, bubbles, splashes, atomizations and droplet mergers. All of these complex phenomena are controllable, and the human being at a young age gets a very keen sense of how they function, intuitively.

We created a separate detection scheme for bubbles and splashes using colour matching based on the hues associated with the reflections of waves and bubbles at various angles.

As a demonstration, we had the bubble interface control a polyphonic tone generator, and the result was a gamut of controllable sounds in sync with the visual turbulent splashes.

7. LIQUID PROJECTION SCREEN

Water in the vessel was able to make the projection display visible, given a small concentration of impurities in ordinary drinking water. With water alone, the projection is cast in a similar way as sunlight making visible rays of light permeating a deep lake.

It is also possible to use other materials as a projection screen. Oil, such as vegetable oil, floats on the water surface and adds a different scattering characteristic for viewing the projection.

8. WATERTOUCH AS A HYPERACOUSTIC MUSICAL INSTRUMENT

Inherent in the WaterTouch system is a high degree of idiosyncratic behavior that is specifically aquatic. Every time the surface is touched, ripples and waves are generated.

These disturbances, some turbulent and some laminar, create underwater sound, over a wide spectral range. A great deal of the frequency spectrum extends below the range of human hearing. Since many of these disturbances are controllable by fingers, we chose to embrace these sounds by capturing them and shifting them up to desired notes on a musical scale, where the degree of shift depended on the location of touch on the surface. In this way, our WaterTouch system, when used as a musical instrument, is a hyperacoustic instrument.

Unlike a hyperinstrument[5] in which position sensors, etc., *add* synthetic sounds to an acoustic instrument, hyperacoustic instruments *use* the acoustically-originated sound as their primary computer input/output and process that sound based on additional sensors or inputs [6].

To make this new hyperacoustic instrument as expressive as possible, we wished to bring the subsonic and ultrasonic sounds into the audible range. In a way similar to (but not the same as), superheterodyne radio reception, signals can be downshifted and upshifted by means of using an oscillator in the process of frequency-shifting and various forms of selective sound filtration. However, unlike what happens in a superheterodyne receiver, we prefer to scale frequencies logarithmically rather than linearly, in order to better match the frequency distribution of human perception. [7]

This digital signal processing is, in a general sense, a filtering operation, which may be highly nonlinear in certain situations. The frequency-shifter was implemented on a computer system having a broadband analog to digital converter, *i.e.* an A to D converter that responds all the way down to 0Hz (DC), and up to approx. 40kHz. Computer vision was performed on the same computer system, with the resulting multitouch (x, y) coordinates controlling multiple amplitudes and pitches, depending on the number of fingers inserted. One mode had a continuum of available pitches, while another mode constrained the pitches to a diatonic scale.

What we have done is brought the ultra-low frequencies (easily controllable by a user when touching the water [4]) into the audible range, in response to a real-time visual multitouch analysis of finger motion across the water surface.

9. CONCLUSIONS

We successfully implemented and demonstrated "WaterTouch", a user-interface based on a Sensory Table (Water Table). The apparatus was equipped with sensors that resulted in a water-based touch screen that captured the randomness and idiosyncratic behavior of water waves, ripples, bubbles, and similar phenomena, in response to user input.

The use of total internal reflection, in a pool with an underwater camera, created a situation in which tracking became very simple. For example, fingers inserted into the water were immediately visible, completely disembodied, against a pure black background. This made the computer vision tracking extremely easy. Moreover, the simple algebraic projective geometry of the air-water boundary made it very easy to locate, in multiple dimensions, anything that penetrated the water's surface.

10. FUTURE WORK

The use of a lake as a touch surface is being explored as part of a grander vision of turning an entire lake into the world's largest musical instrument. Our hope is that this work helps with the creation of an Ontario Water Centre to help teach the world about the importance of clean lakes, rivers, and about water conservation (ongoing collaboration with the Ladies of the Lake, Georgina, Ontario, Canada).

11. REFERENCES

[1] M. B. Alonso and D. V. Keyson. *MusicCube: making digital music tangible.* ACM CHI, 2005.

[2] K. Devereux et al. Effects of a water-based program on women 65 years and over: a randomised controlled trial. *Australian Journal of Physiotherapy*, 52(2):102–8, 2005.

[3] H. Ishii. Bottles: A transparent interface as a tribute to mark weiser. *IEICE Trans. on Info. and Systems*, pages Vol. E87–D, No. 6, pp. 1299–1311, June 2004.

[4] R. Janzen and S. Mann. Arrays of water jets as user interfaces: Detection and estimation of flow by listening to turbulence signatures using hydrophones. In *Proc. ACM MM '07, September 24-29, Augsburg, Germany*, pages 505–8, 2007.

[5] T. Machover. Hyperinstruments: A composer's approach to the evolution of intelligent musical instruments. In W. Freeman, editor, *Cyberarts*. Spartan Books, San Francisco, 1991.

[6] S. Mann, R. Janzen, and R. Lo. Hyperacoustic instruments: Computer-controlled instruments that are not electrophones. In *Proc. ICME2008*, pages 89–92, 2008.

[7] S. Mann, R. Janzen, R. Lo, and C. Aimone. Inventing...to make a badly tuned...instrument play in perfect harmony. In *Proc. ICMC '07, Aug. 27-31*, volume 1, pages 105–112, 2007.

[8] S. Mann, R. Janzen, and M. Post. Hydraulophone design considerations: Absement, displacement, and velocity-sensitive music keyboard in which each key is a water jet. In *Proc. ACM MM '06, October 23-27, Santa Barbara*, pages 519–528, 2006.

[9] P. Richards. *The Wave Organ.* Exploratorium (acc. 2005-8), http://www.exploratorium.edu/visit/wave_organ.html.

[10] H. Seichter et al. Multitouch interaction for tangible user interfaces. *IEEE International Symposium on Mixed and Augmented Reality*, pages 213–214, 2009.

[11] K. van Mensvoort. *Datafountain: Money translated to water.* Online documentation by the inventor, http://www.koert.com/work/datafountain/, 2005.

[12] D. Yeliussizov et al. Multi-touch sensing using frustrated total internal reflection. *Proc. App. Inf. and Comm. Tech. (AICT)*, pages 1–4, 2009.

Quality of Experience Evaluation of Voice Communication Systems using Affect-based Approach*

Abhishek Bhattacharya
Florida International University
School of Computing and Information Sciences
Miami, FL 33199
abhat002@cs.fiu.edu

Wanmin Wu
University of Illinois at Urbana-Champaign
Department of Computer Science
Urbana, IL 61801
wwu23@cs.uiuc.edu

Zhenyu Yang
Florida International University
School of Computing and Information Sciences
Miami, FL 33199
yangz@cs.fiu.edu

ABSTRACT

The voice communication industry is undergoing a rapid phase change with continuously evolving technologies such as cellular, mobile and Internet telephony. Effective evaluation of system performance is becoming critical, which will serve as an important instrument for service providers to monitor and manage quality. Recently, *Quality of Experience* (QoE) metrics are found to be more valuable quality assessment mechanism since they are more closely related to human perception as compared to traditional QoS-based techniques. In this paper, we investigate a new affect-based approach for QoE evaluation. Our hypothesis states that QoE in voice communication is correlated to user's *affective behavior*, which will vary across networking conditions. We conduct extensive user study based on natural human-human voice communication. The experimental results indicate very promising prospect of this approach.

Categories and Subject Descriptors

H.1.2 [**Information Systems**]: Models and Principles – *human factors*; H.5.1 [**Information Interfaces and Presentation**]: Multimedia Information Systems

General Terms

Experimentation, Human Factors, Measurement

Keywords

Quality of Experience, affect computing, voice communication

1. INTRODUCTION

The voice communication industry is undergoing a rapid phase change with technologies such as cellular, mobile and Internet telephony replacing the conventional telephone systems. Traditional performance evaluation methods are very much system-oriented where *Quality of Service* (QoS) metrics have been the de facto standard for voice communication. Recently, there is a paradigm shift towards user-oriented methodology with the introduction of human-centric computing in the systems area [12], and the concept of Quality of Experience (QoE) is gradually gaining popularity [13, 8]. In practice, system developers have applied QoE assessment techniques, ranging from user feedback [7], QoS-based user experience estimation [16] to media quality analysis [4].

User feedback methods obtain explicit input from the user for quality measurement, like in the popular format of *Mean Opinion Score* (MOS) where users are asked to complete a questionnaire based on a 1-to-5 scale. The main disadvantage is its *intrusiveness* and the issue of scaling quality with numbers. A good amount of research has been done in QoS-based estimation methodologies [16], where QoE is estimated by modeling from the underlying QoS parameters (e.g., delay, loss rate). These methods are essentially objective approximation of QoE due to lack of user engagement. Thus, they cannot cover all QoE dimensions that may affect human perception and experience [7]. Media quality analysis methods assess the quality by measuring the distortion of the signal based on certain analysis models like signal-to-noise ratio (SNR), e.g., the state-of-the-art standard of *Perceptual Evaluation of Speech Quality* (PESQ) as specified in ITU-T P.862. However, these methods fail to consider factors such as various listening levels, sidetone/talk echo, and conversational delay/interaction [7].

In this paper, we investigate the usability of *affective computing* in evaluating QoE of voice communication. Affective computing deals with the analysis of human emotional variables naturally revealed during the user-system interaction. In the process, emotions have been shown to have strong association with user experience regarding interest, satisfaction, motivation and performance [15]. Using signal processing, linguistic analysis, and psycho-physiological techniques, automated emotion recognition is feasible by aggregating affective cues from multi-modal user input such as facial expression, speech, body gesture, and neuroimaging [17]. Guided by the above evidences, we hypothesize that QoE or the user perception of quality in voice communication is correlated to his/her *affective behavior* (e.g., pitch, voice, timing and articulation), which will vary across networking conditions. To the best of our knowledge, the analysis of af-

*Area chair: Dr. Mor Naaman.

MM'11, November 28–December 1, 2011, Scottsdale, Arizona, USA.

fective behavior and its role in the QoE evaluation of voice communication is an unexplored area.

The front end of our proposed affect-based QoE evaluation framework performs feature extraction to derive samples. The set of information sources are drawn from three major categories of affective signals involving *acoustic*, *lexical* and *discourse* features as suggested by previous research in emotion detection [17, 5, 14]. Each information source is processed separately and then a decision-level classifier fusion mechanism is adopted for deriving the final predicted quality. A block diagram of the entire framework is shown in Figure 1 with the details described in Section 2. A subset of data samples are used to train classification modules using machine learning tools. Then, the rest of the data samples are used for performance testing of quality prediction. Finally, the accuracy analysis is provided by comparing the output of the affect analysis framework (i.e., QoE estimation) with the user feedback.

Our contributions in this paper are the followings. *We provide a new affect-based methodology of QoE evaluation in voice communication.* Different from previous approaches, we propose to assess quality directly from the user affective responses. Therefore, *our method has the advantage of deriving subjective QoE measures in an implicit and non-intrusive manner.* The experimental results indicate very promising prospect of this approach. Regarding boarder impacts, as the communication systems become more media-rich and interactive (e.g., spatial audio, 3D/immersive space), measuring QoE via indirect methods will become more challenging [8]. Therefore, our work represents an important pioneering step towards the understanding of QoE for the future generation of communication systems.

In the remainder of the paper, Section 2 presents the details of the framework. Section 3 describes the methodologies and settings of the experiment. Section 4 highlights the results and the paper concludes with Section 5.

2. AFFECT ANALYSIS FRAMEWORK

Our affect-based QoE analysis framework consist of three primary stages: *Feature Extraction*, *Classification*, and *Fusion*. In feature extraction module, three major categories of affective signals are extracted including *acoustic*, *lexical*, and *discourse* features. After feature extraction, the affective responses are analyzed individually by the classification module of each category. In the last stage, the results are then combined to generate the final output of the framework (i.e., QoE estimation). We follow the general methodologies and technical justifications as presented in [14] for the design of the framework. We briefly introduce each module of the framework in the following sections. An overview of the framework is shown in Figure 1.

2.1 Feature Extraction

Acoustic (A). We consider 22 different acoustic attributes related to segmental and suprasegmental information of speech signals. These attributes are derived from turn-level statistics and transformations in the domains of *fundamental frequency*, *energy*, *duration*, and *formants*. The module of acoustic feature extraction was implemented using `openSMILE` tool [9] which is an open-source software that can extract many low-level acoustic features and statistic functionals. The 22 acoustic attributes form the base feature set (denoted as *Base*). Generally, not all features are equally significant for affective analysis and irrelevant ones can be eliminated from the base feature set. For performance enhancement, we perform a feature selection procedure by employing *leave-one-out* method and the *nearest neighborhood* rule for enhancing accuracy. For the purpose of comparing different approaches, we generate two subsets from the base feature set, one has 10 best features (denoted as $f10$) and the other has 15 best features (denoted as $f15$) since they are practical choices from a total of 22 considering both efficiency and performance. Lastly, we obtain another feature set by performing *Principal Component Analysis* (PCA) on the base feature set (denoted as *PCA*). We select PCA since it is a popular technique that can reduce the number of dimensions considerably without affecting performance.

Lexical (L). Lexical features are used to model salient or distinctive words for various expressions by the notion of *mutual information* [10] to establish the correlation between words and different QoE levels. Denote the vocabulary $V = \{v_1, v_2, ..., v_n\}$ and the set of quality levels $Q = \{q_1, q_2, ..., q_m\}$. In our case, we choose $m = 3$ (i.e., levels of "*Good*", "*Average*", and "*Bad*"). The mutual information can effectively quantify the amount of information between a specific word and a quality level as in (1):

$$I(v, q) = \log \frac{\Pr\{q|v\}}{\Pr\{q\}} \quad (1)$$

for $v \in V$ and $q \in Q$. Intuitively, if a word v is correlated with a quality level q, then $\Pr\{q|v\} > \Pr\{q\}$ and $I(v,q)$ is positive. If there is no correlation, then $\Pr\{q|v\} = \Pr\{q\}$ and $I(v,q)$ is zero. If v makes q less likely, $I(v,q)$ is negative. Given an utterance, the *action* for quality level q_k is an effective indicator for matching each word with its saliency w.r.t quality levels, which can be calculated as in (2):

$$a_k = \sum_{i=1}^{n} O_i I(q_k, v_i) + \log(q_k) \quad (2)$$

where O_i is the likelihood that word v_i is recognized in the utterance by the speech recognition module. Finally, we use $\{a_0, a_1, a_2, a_0 - a_1, a_1 - a_2, a_2 - a_0\}$ as the feature set for the lexical information since the action values and their differences can help to distinguish between the different quality categories. We leverage on the Automatic Speech Recognition (ASR) system from the `HTK Toolkit` of Cambridge University for translating text output from voice signals.

Discourse (D). We take a simplified approach in discourse features by modeling only *repetition*, which is found to be the most important indicator of trouble in communication [5]. We choose from 1-word to 5-word repetitions and formulate the discourse feature set as: number of 1-word repetition, number of 2-word repetitions, and likewise.

2.2 Classification and Fusion

The original data set contains samples tagged with user quality feedback, which is divided into training set ($\approx$ 75%) and testing set ($\approx$ 25%). For the initial training phase, samples of the training set are utilized to build a classifier. During the testing phase, samples of the testing set are fed into the classifier (with user feedback removed) which will output QoE predictions. Then, the output is used to compare with the user feedback. We choose two basic types of classifiers: *Support Vector Machines* (SVM) and *k-Nearest Neighbors* (*k*NN) mainly due to their effectiveness and performance benefit. Four variants of SVM are employed as

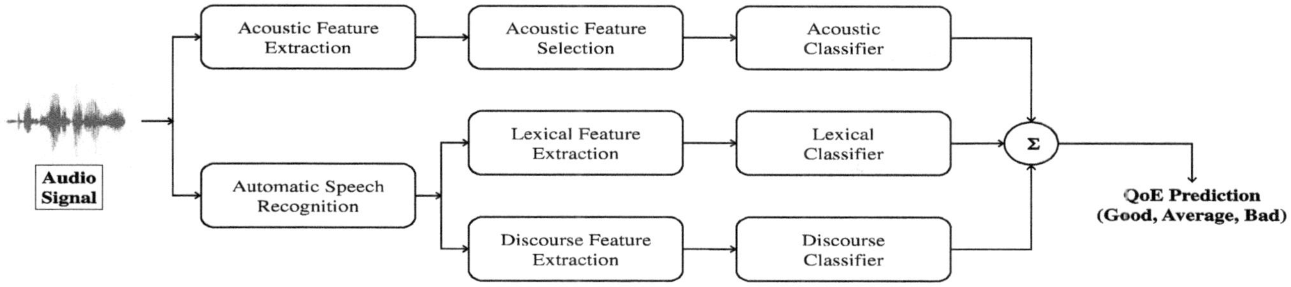

Figure 1: Block diagram of the affect analysis framework.

follows: (1) *SVM*: uses fixed training and testing sets (for testing the baseline performance of the classifier), (2) *SVM-5CV*: divides the data into five randomly chosen sets of equal size and applies 5-fold cross-validation (for compensating the small size of the training/testing set) , (3) *SVM-5WC*/*SVM-10WC*: employs 2-layer hierarchical SVM model that trains 5 and 10 bottom-layer weak classifiers (*5WC* and *10WC* respectively) and a top-layer meta-classifier (for improving the classification accuracy). For kNN classifier, we train two derivatives as follows: (1) *kNN*: similar to that of *SVM* with $k = 10$ (baseline classifier and $k = 10$ provides best result with tractable complexity), (2) *kNN-5CV*: similar to that of *SVM-5CV* with an iterative number of nearest neighbors from $k = 1$ to 15 (improved classifier accomodating for small size of the dataset).

The fusion process involves with the aggregation of predicted output from each information sources (i.e., acoustic, lexical, discourse) to generate a single output value. We employ *decision-level* fusion (simple and found to be effective) that takes results from multiple classifiers to compute a single value by averaging the results from each classifier. For the software, we use the tools of `libSVM` [6] for SVM classifiers and `Weka` [11] for kNN classifiers.

3. EXPERIMENTAL DESIGN

We designed the user study experiment for the examination of the following research hypothesis.

H: *The user perception of voice communication quality is correlated to his/her affective response, which will vary across networking conditions.*

The main purpose of the experiment was to collect two types of data: audio signal of user conversation and the user quality feedback. For that purpose, we engaged a pair of participants at the two ends in natural conversation through a *Voice over Internet Protocol* (*VoIP*) connection. During the test, we tuned the QoS parameters of delay, loss rate and bandwidth to simulate various networking conditions. We expect that the affect state of user as reflected from his/her voice will change accordingly, as well as his/her subjective perception of the communication quality. Thus, we recorded the voice conversation and asked the user to rate the quality. The collected data were used for training and testing by the affect analysis framework in the previous stage (Section 2).

3.1 Network and System Setup

We installed two desktop computers with Intel i686 Core 2 Quad CPU 32-bit (2.39GHz) and 2GB RAM running Linux kernel (Ver.2.6.31.5) at each end of a VoIP connection. We configured a third computer to be used as a layer-2 bridge for connecting the two VoIP end computers using the Linux `brctl` utility. To simulate various networking conditions (delay, loss rate and bandwidth), we tuned the traffic flow between the two VoIP end computers by applying `dummynet` on the bridge computer. The QoS class was modeled as the tuple of $\langle$delay(d), bandwidth(b), loss-rate(l)$\rangle$. We found five different QoS classes (C_1,C_2,C_3,C_4,C_5) ranging from best to worst by a pilot study of differential quality levels.

We organized each test session based on a maximum 15-minute run. Each session is divided into multiple intervals and the size of each interval was fixed to 20 seconds (considering previous research and the possible interference to the user, we chose 20 seconds as the fixed timescale for each test interval).[1] The final VoIP experiments were made by randomly alternating among the QoS classes ($C_1 \backsim C_5$) at each interval and then applying the setting to the VoIP network environment through the `dummynet` pipes. In this study, we employed a trichotomous or 3-point scale decision of perceptual quality levels: "*Good*", "*Average*", and "*Bad*". Each interval was saved as one sample after it was tagged with QoS class labels and user quality level feedback. We used the library of `PortAudio` [2] to record audio signals from the microphone into `wav` files, and deployed `PJSIP` [1] as the VoIP software with G.711 codec.

3.2 Participant and Conversation Model

We recruited 15 participants from two mid-level undergraduate CS classes of Java Programming and Computer Networks.[1] All students were proficient with English language (6 native, 7 advanced and 2 intermediate speakers). Among them, 11 were male and 4 were female, between 18-38 years of age ($M = 25.54$, $SD = 3.38$). They had a mean of 3.67 years of using VoIP service and all claimed to have been using at least one VoIP service in the past (with the most popular being Skype followed by GTalk). Each participant was asked to complete an Entry Questionnaire at the beginning of the study for collecting background/demographic information, and their previous experience with VoIP if any. We wanted to invoke neutral and natural conversation from the participants. The ITU recommendation also suggests that the content should be "neither so interesting nor so disagreeable or boring" [3]. It is observed that in some cases the conversation itself might have invoked emotional responses

[1]The ITU-T recommendation for the subjective assessment of sound quality also suggests the clip duration from 15 to 20 seconds, and the minimum number of participants in an experiment to be between 10 and 20 [3].

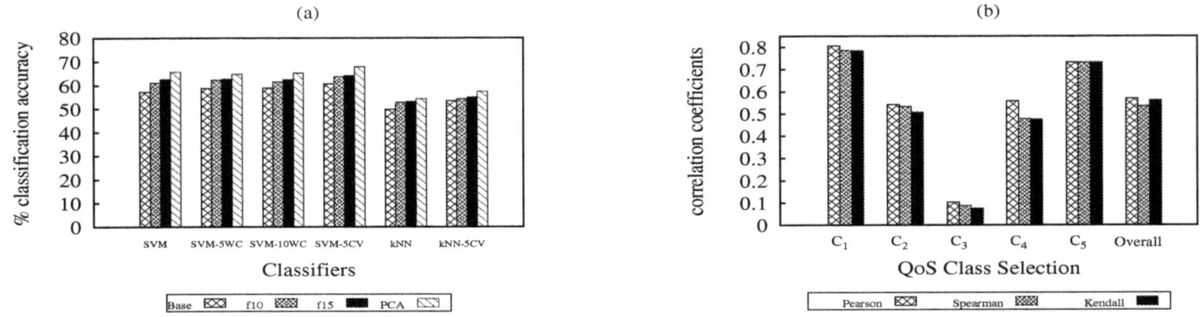

Figure 2: (a) Classification accuracy with different feature sets versus varying classifiers from the combination of all affective sources (A+L+D), (b) Correlation tests of the quality prediction from the testing samples.

that are not related to communication quality perception. In our preliminary experiment, we tried to filter out "emotional noise" from the perspective of conversational content by considering features such as salient words and repetitions. Note that, such drawback is inherent in any type of subjective assessment including MOS.

4. RESULTS

In this section we present the experimental results of our study. Figure 2(a) shows the cross-view of results based on all affective sources (A+L+D) with different feature selection schemes and classifiers. In all cases, the PCA feature selection scheme provides the highest performance. The $f10$ and $f15$ selection schemes provide comparable accuracy which is consistently higher than the base set. Comparing different classifiers, it is observed that *SVM-5CV* gives the highest accuracy. As a short summary, the best performance is achieved with SVM 5-fold cross-validation and PCA-based feature selection, which gives an accuracy of 67.9%.

The results of correlation between the user quality feedback and the quality prediction are given for each QoS class in Figure 2(b) using different calculation methods (Pearson, Kendall and Spearman). It is observed that different network QoS classes have varied correlation impact: QoS classes of C_1 and C_5 demonstrate the highest correlation, C_2 and C_4 stay as the intermediate cases, while C_3 has the lowest correlation. The implication we can draw here is that QoE prediction tends to be more accurate if the underlying networking condition is either very good (i.e., C_1) or very bad (i.e., C_5), and becomes less accurate for mid-range (i.e., C_3) networking conditions. The finding also suggests that we should be more careful to apply QoS-based estimation.

5. CONCLUSION

We have conducted a user study to investigate an affect-based approach of QoE evaluation in voice communication, which represents a new and unexplored area. We evaluated the effectiveness of this approach by using various affect features and classification techniques to discriminate different quality perceptions and compare with user feedback. The accumulated evidence supports our initial hypothesis of exploiting affective responses as the predictor of subjective experience of quality due to its correlation with human cognitive perception. Although we refrain from claiming that our methodology can cover the entire spectrum of QoE evaluation factors, our study does provide contributory illustrations for affective information to be considered as a relevant and valuable indicator.

6. ACKNOWLEDGMENT

This study is supported by the National Science Foundation (NSF) under CSR-1116023. The presented views are those of authors and do not represent the position of NSF.

7. REFERENCES

[1] PJSIP:. http://www.pjsip.org/.
[2] PortAudio:. http://www.portaudio.com/.
[3] ITU-T rec. bs.1284-1: General methods for the subjective assessment of sound quality, 2003.
[4] ITU-T Rec. G.107. The E-model, a computational model for use in transmission planning, 2005.
[5] A. Batliner, K. Fischer, R. Huber, J. Spilker, and E. Nöth. How to find trouble in communication. *Speech Commun.*, 40, 2003.
[6] C.-C. Chang and C.-J. Lin. libSVM: a library for support vector machines. http://www.csie.ntu.edu.tw/ cjlin/libsvm, 2001.
[7] K.-T. Chen, C.-C. Tu, and W.-C. Xiao. OneClick: A framework for measuring network quality of experience. In *INFOCOM 2009, IEEE*, 2009.
[8] T. Ebrahimi. Quality of multimedia experience: past, present and future. In *ACM*, MM '09, NY, USA, 2009.
[9] F. Eyben, M. Wöllmer, and B. Schuller. OpenSMILE: the munich versatile and fast open-source audio feature extractor. In *ACM*, MM '10, NY, USA, 2010.
[10] A. Gorin, S. Levinson, L. Miller, A. Gertner, A. Ljolje, and E. Goldman. On adaptive acquisition of language. In *ICASSP, 1990*, volume 1, Apr. 1990.
[11] M. Hall, E. Frank, G. Holmes, B. Pfahringer, P. Reutemann, and I. H. Witten. The weka data mining software: an update. *SIGKDD Explor. Newsl.*, 11, November 2009.
[12] A. Jaimes, N. Sebe, and D. Gatica-Perez. Human-centered computing: a multimedia perspective. In *ACM*, MM'06.
[13] R. Jain. Quality of experience. *Multimedia, IEEE*, 11(1), jan.-march 2004.
[14] C. M. Lee and S. Narayanan. Toward detecting emotions in spoken dialogs. *IEEE TSAP*, 13(2), march 2005.
[15] D. Nahl. Learning the internet and the structure of information behavior. *J. Am. Soc. Inf. Sci.*, 49, 1998.
[16] B. Sat and B. W. Wah. Playout scheduling and loss-concealments in voip for optimizing conversational voice communication quality. In *ACM*, MM'07.
[17] Z. Zeng, M. Pantic, G. Roisman, and T. Huang. A survey of affect recognition methods: Audio, visual, and spontaneous expressions. *Pattern Analysis and Machine Intelligence, IEEE Transactions on*, 31(1), 2009.

A Multi-layer Hybrid Framework for Dimensional Emotion Classification

Mihalis A. Nicolaou
Department of Computing
Imperial College London, U.K.
mihalis@imperial.ac.uk

Hatice Gunes
EECS, Queen Mary
University of London, U.K.
haticeg@ieee.org

Maja Pantic
Imperial College London, U.K.
U. of Twente, The Netherlands
m.pantic@imperial.ac.uk

ABSTRACT

This paper investigates dimensional emotion prediction and classification from naturalistic facial expressions. Similarly to many pattern recognition problems, dimensional emotion classification requires generating multi-dimensional outputs. To date, classification for valence and arousal dimensions has been done separately, assuming that they are independent. However, various psychological findings suggest that these dimensions are correlated. We therefore propose a novel, *multi-layer hybrid framework* for emotion classification that is able to *model inter-dimensional correlations*. Firstly, we derive a *novel geometric feature set* based on the (a)symmetric spatio-temporal characteristics of facial expressions. Subsequently, we use the proposed feature set to train a multi-layer hybrid framework composed of a *temporal regression layer* for predicting emotion dimensions, a *graphical model layer* for modeling valence-arousal correlations, and a final *classification and fusion layer* exploiting informative statistics extracted from the lower layers. This framework (i) introduces the *Auto-Regressive Coupled HMM* (ACHMM), a graphical model specifically tailored to accommodate not only inter-dimensional correlations but also to exploit the internal dynamics of the actual observations, and (ii) replaces the commonly used Maximum Likelihood principle with a more robust final classification and fusion layer. Subject-independent experimental validation, performed on a naturalistic set of facial expressions, demonstrates the effectiveness of the derived feature set, and the robustness and flexibility of the proposed framework.

Categories and Subject Descriptors

H.1.2 [**User / Machine systems**]: [Human information processing]; I.2.10 [**Vision and scene understanding**]: [Video analysis]; I.5.2 [**Design Methodology**]: [Feature evaluation and selection, Classifier design and evaluation]

* Area Chair: Massimo Zancanaro

General Terms

Human Factors, Feature evaluation and selection, Classifier design and evaluation, Experimentation

1. INTRODUCTION

Traditionally, research in the field of automatic emotion recognition has focused on recognizing discrete, basic emotional states (e.g. happiness, sadness) from posed data acquired in laboratory settings [4]. However, these models are deemed unrealistic as they are unable to capture the non-basic and subtle affective states exhibited by humans in everyday interactions. In order to accommodate such subtle expressions, researchers have started adopting a dimensional description of human emotion where an emotional state is characterized in terms of a number of latent dimensions [10]. Two dimensions are deemed sufficient for capturing most of the affective variability: valence and arousal (V-A), signifying respectively, how negative/positive and active / inactive an emotional state is.

Due to the aforementioned reasons, automatic, dimensional and continuous emotion recognition has increasingly attracted the interest of the affective computing researchers in recent years. Wollmer et al. [13], quantize the V-A dimensions into 4 or 7 levels and use Conditional Random Fields (CRFs) for classification from audio cues. Other works discriminate the emotions into more coarse classes such as positive vs. negative [9], by combining audio-visual cues via Coupled Hidden Markov Models (CHMMs) and likelihood space fusion, while the work of [14] utilizes a dynamic Bayesian network combined with Long-Short Term Memory (LSTM) Neural Nets, performing regression and quantizing the results into four quadrants.

Various findings in psychology (i) postulate the existence of inter-dimensional correlations between the valence and arousal dimensions [8, 7], and (ii) suggest that there exist asymmetrical variations on the human face (left vs. right, lower vs. upper hemiface) depending on whether the subject is expressing a positive or a negative emotion [2, 11]. Although such features have been used for other human behavior understanding problems they have not been explored for dimensional emotion prediction. The work presented in this paper takes into account these findings, and differs from the previous works on automatic dimensional emotion prediction by proposing the following contributions.

(A)symmetric features. We derive a set of geometric spatio-temporal meta-features from facial feature point trackings. We show how the derived feature set enables better prediction accuracy compared to the initial set of raw fea-

tures (i.e., facial feature point locations).
Auto-Regressive Coupled Hidden Markov Models (ACHMM). We introduce the ACHMM, a novel HMM variant specifically tailored for capturing inter-dimensional patterns and observation dynamics. To the best of our knowledge, this paper pioneers the use of ACHMM.
A multi-layer hybrid framework. We propose a novel multi-layer hybrid classification framework composed of three distinct layers: (1) A *regression layer* generating the continuous A-V prediction (using LSTM), (2) a *graphical model layer* trained on the predicted emotion dimensions to capture the correlations between the continuous emotion descriptions (using ACHMM), and (3) a final *discriminative classification and fusion layer* (using SVM) for incorporating informative statistics extracted from both the regression and the graphical model layer, replacing the commonly applied (but less effective) Maximum Likelihood principle.

More specifically, the proposed framework aims to capture specific, intra-dimensional statistics via the regression layer, and subtle, emerging inter-dimensional patterns via the graphical model layer. Outputs from both layers are combined via a final discriminative classification layer that estimates a set of statistics over the previous two layers and uses this information for *classifier fusion*. To date, no such work has been attempted for dimensional emotion classification. Subject-independent experimental validation, performed on a naturalistic set of facial expressions, demonstrates the effectiveness of the derived feature set, and the robustness and flexibility of the proposed multi-layer hybrid framework.

2. DATA SET

We used the Sensitive Artificial Listener (SAL) Database [3] for this work. It contains naturalistic audio-visual conversational data taking place between a participant and a human operated avatar. Each avatar has a different personality (happy, gloomy, angry or pragmatic). The recordings were made in controlled laboratory settings with one camera, microphones, uniform background, and constant lightning conditions. Only data from 4 subjects have been continuously annotated by 3-4 coders along the V-A dimensional (emotion) space. Representative frames together with their facial point trackings are shown in Fig. 1. In total, we used 61 positive and 73 negative episodes ($\approx$ 30,000 frames) capturing transitions to an emotional state and back (e.g., going from nonpositive to positive and back to non-positive).

3. FEATURE EXTRACTION & SELECTION

In this section, we explain how we process and select the facial features used for training the first-layer regressors.

Similarly to [12], we track 20 facial feature points which represent the facial expression of the subject in any given frame (see Fig. 1). This is referred to as the *original feature set*. We register each set of points in a given frame to the corresponding coordinate system centered at the fixed point of the face (the average of the inner eye points and the tip of the nose). We thus end up with a simple translation applied to every point in every frame (also using the fixed point itself as a feature).

Motivated by psychological findings [1, 2, 11], we extract various symmetrical features, in an attempt to capture facial asymmetry manifestations. These features include distances between points on the left vs. right hemiface, and the upper vs. lower hemiface (e.g., the distance between left & right eyebrow, between upper & lower eyelid, etc.). For each of these symmetric pairs of points (p_l, p_r), we extract the angle, the coordinate distance $\langle p_l - p_r \rangle$, and the Euclidean distance $(||p_l - p_r||)$. Subsequently, we derive a new set of features to capture the temporal aspect of a given expression. For every point $p =< x_p, y_p >$ we extract the velocity in x and y directions: $< \frac{dx_p}{dt}, \frac{dy_p}{dt} >$. We also fit a set of overlapping windows of length w to an n-degree polynomial $y^w(x^w) = a_n x^n + \cdots + a_0$ (t represents the current frame, and the window is defined as $[t-w, t+w]$). By doing so, we derive the $n+1$ coefficients $([a_n \ldots a_0])$. In summary, the *full feature set* (fs) consists of facial feature point coordinates registered to the fixed point $(< x, y >_{rfp})$, a vector defined by subtracting the two symmetric points $< x, y >_s$, symmetric angles (π), symmetric distances $(||.||)$, velocities $(\frac{dp}{dt})$, and polynomial fitting coefficients $(a_n t^n)$.

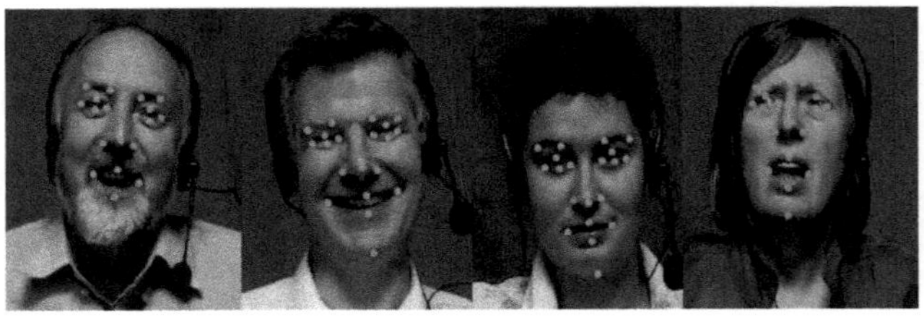

Figure 1: Examples from the SAL data set along with the extracted 20 points, used as (original) features for facial expression recognition.

In order to select the appropriate features for the problem at hand, we apply Correlation Based Feature Selection (CFS) [5] on the full feature set. The CFS ranking results show that the top ranked features correspond to velocity, point (a)symmetry and polynomial coefficients, signifying the importance of the temporal and (a)symmetric characteristics of facial expressions. We conducted further experiments with LSTM Neural Nets (LSTM-NN) to verify this finding. The obtained results showed that using *the derived feature set* reduced the Mean Squared Error (MSE) both for valence and arousal. Our experiments also showed that including the polynomial coefficients caused the accuracy to decrease.

4. PREDICTION & CLASSIFICATION

The final feature set (omitting polynomial features) obtained is used to train a multi-layer hybrid prediction and classification framework. This 3-layer hybrid framework incorporates a prediction layer for each emotion dimension, a graphical model layer for capturing inter-dimensional emotion correlations, and a final discriminative classification layer incorporating statistics extracted from both layers. In the following sections we firstly describe the employed models, and subsequently explain the structure of the proposed hybrid framework.

4.1 Long-Short Term Memory Neural Nets

LSTM Neural Nets (LSTM-NN) [6] are a form of Recurrent Neural Networks (RNN), which in contrast to traditional RNNs enable the learning of temporal information longer than a few time steps. In LSTM-NNs a typical node is replaced with a memory cell. The cell maintains the given state of the network, which is considered to be representative of the *previous* (and the *future*, in the bidirectional case) sequence inputs. A set of gates provide 'read, write, reset' operations on the cell state.

4.2 Auto-Regressive Coupled HMM

By merging two common HMM variants, the Coupled HMM and the Auto-Regressive HMM, we propose the Auto-Regressive Coupled HMMs (ACHMM) for the problem of capturing inter-dimensional emotion correlations and structure. The ACHMM is a Dynamic Bayesian Network modeling observation dependencies (not only on the abstract state level, but also conditioned on the actual observations) and capturing the inter-stream structure. CHMMs are structured specifically to model interactions between multiple processes. Assuming that we have two streams of observations, at each time t, we have two hidden nodes and two nodes modeling each observation stream. The state of each hidden node at time t depends on the hidden states of both hidden nodes at $t-1$. By augmenting CHMM with auto-regression, we relax the assumption that the observation depends only on the current state of the model. The distribution of the observation at each time t is now conditioned both on the current hidden state as well as the previous observation. An ACHMM with two streams of observations is illustrated in Fig. 2(a) (see the HMM nodes).

4.3 The Multi-layer Hybrid Framework

The multi-layer hybrid framework we propose is illustrated in Fig. 2. The framework has three distinct layers: (1) a *regression layer* (LSTM-NN) which generates the continuous prediction for each emotion dimension, (2) a *graphical model layer* (ACHMM) that models the inter-dimensional structure, and (3) finally, a *discriminative classification layer* (SVM) incorporating statistics from the lower layers. More specifically, the regression layer is expected to capture specific, intra-dimensional statistics which would serve as intermediate features for more accurate classification of an emotion dimension. The graphical model layer on the other hand, is able to capture subtle, emerging inter-dimensional patterns which seamlessly contribute to the classification of a given sequence.

Let us consider the **LSTM-ACHMM$_{\mathbf{ML}}$** model. Firstly, the LSTM-NNs are trained using the optimal feature set obtained in Section 3. Two separate LSTM-NNs are trained as regressors, one for each emotion dimension. Let $\mathcal{D}$={Valence, Arousal} be the set of emotion dimensions. The continuous prediction generated by each LSTM-NNs at time t represents the observation modeled by each component of the ACHMM at time t. Due to the structure of the ACHMM, for $t = [2, N]$, the observation O_{dt} generated for each emotion dimension $d \in \mathcal{D}$ depends directly on the previous observation for this dimension O_{dt-1}, and the state of the hidden node H_{dt}. Furthermore, the hidden state H_{dt} depends on the previous hidden states of both dimensions (H_{At-1} and H_{Vt-1}) due to the coupled nature of the model. Classification is obtained using Maximum Likelihood (ML) principle.

In order to combine the distinct qualities of the aforementioned models, we add a final *classification and fusion layer* to the framework. This layer exploits a set of statistics from the two lower layers, and uses these features to the aim of classifier fusion using SVMs. Thus, it not only *replaces* the ML-based classification with the discriminative classification of SVMs, but also provides a more robust learning of inter-dimensional patterns and structure via classifier fusion.

Let us now consider the 3-layer hybrid model of **LSTM-ACHMM$_{\mathbf{SVM}}$**. Firstly, from the LSTM-NN prediction, for each dimension $d \in \mathcal{D}$ and sequence s, we extract the following feature vector $f_{\text{LSTM},d}(s)$:

$$\langle \bar{posf}_d(s), \bar{negf}_d(s), \bar{sum}_d(s) \rangle$$

where $\bar{posf}_d(s)$ and $\bar{negf}_d(s)$ correspond to the percentage of frames with positive/negative output for dimension d, and $\bar{sum}_d(s)$ is the average value of the (sequence) output for this dimension. From the ACHMMs, we extract a subset of the statistics that characterize the model. Again, for each sequence s and dimension d, we obtain the feature vector $f_{\text{ACHMM},d}(s)$:

$$\langle \hat{ll^+}_d(s), \hat{ll^-}_d(s), \mathbf{M\bar{P}E_d(s)} \rangle$$

Where $\hat{ll^+}_d(s)$ and $\hat{ll^-}_d(s)$ are the normalized (using the sequence length, $\hat{ll}_d(s) = \frac{ll}{|s|}$) class likelihoods generated by the model. $\mathbf{M\bar{P}E_d(s)}$, also known as the most probable explanation, refers to the most probable state that each hidden node is at time t. Out of a total of St_n states, let $|St(h_i, St_j)|$ be the number of time steps that the hidden node h_i is at state St_j. Then for each $\bar{St}_j$, a new feature (representing the percentage of time that the hidden node is at every state) is generated as $\bar{St}_j = \frac{|St(h_i, St_j)|}{|s|}$. The feature vector fed into the SVM classifier is described as:

$$\langle f_{\text{LSTM,Val}}(s), f_{\text{LSTM,Ar}}(s), f_{\text{ACHMM,Val}}(s), f_{\text{ACHMM,Ar}}(s) \rangle$$

Notice that statistics extracted for both emotion dimensions are fed into the classifier, thus enabling more robust learning of inter-dimensional patterns and structure.

5. EXPERIMENTAL SETUP & RESULTS

For our experiments, we use the bidirectional LSTM-NNs with one hidden layer. The ACHMMs have 3 hidden states for each hidden node, with each observation modeled by a mixture of 2 Gaussians. We use SVMs with an RBF kernel and optimize the parameters via cross-validation on the training set. The proposed multi-layer hybrid framework is evaluated for two classification tasks: (i) V-A hemispheric classification (positive vs. negative for the valence dimension, and active vs. inactive for the arousal dimension), and (ii) V-A quadrant classification (positive/active, negative/active, positive/inactive, and negative/inactive). All experimental evaluation is obtained by performing *leave-one-subject-out cross-validation.* The results obtained are shown in Table 1. The LSTM results refer to the regression results mapped from the LSTM-NNs onto the valence / arousal classes (via majority voting). When we compare these results to the results obtained from the hybrid LSTM-ACHMM$_{ML}$ model (by applying ML over the ACHMM), the LSTM-NN results provide better $F1$ scores for the valence and arousal classes. The quadrant classification results, however, show that the hybrid model improves the classification results (an 8% increase in the F1 score). This finding supports our assumption that modeling inter dimensional correlations helps in capturing (more) subtle class variances. Finally, the proposed multi-layer hybrid framework (LSTM-ACHMM$_{SVM}$) outperforms both its ML coun-

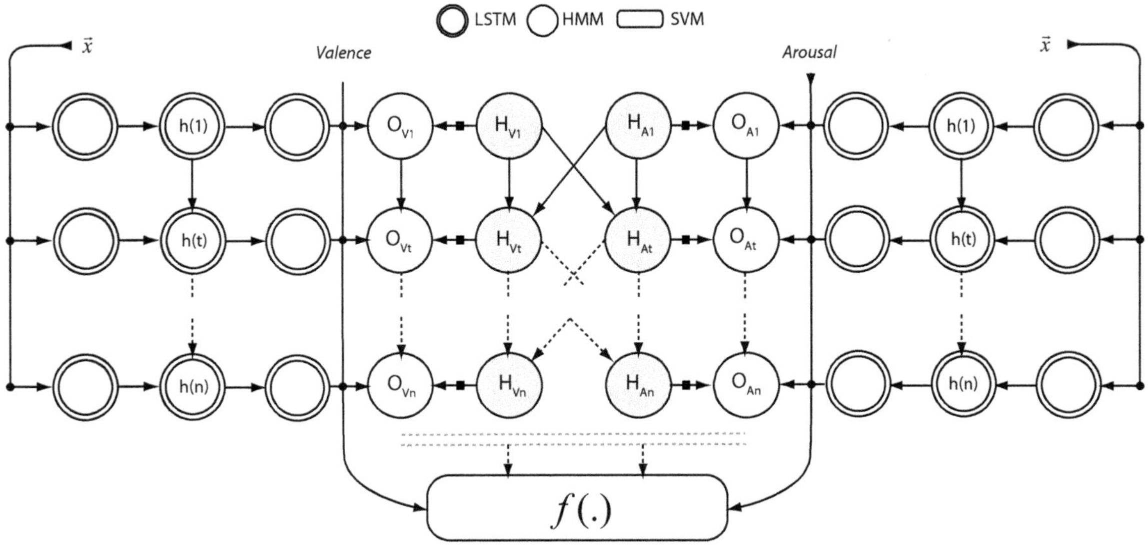

Figure 2: Illustration of the 3-layer hybrid framework employed. The graphical model employed is an ACHMM, where shaded nodes represent hidden nodes and filled squares represent a mixture of Gaussians.

Table 1: Experimental results (ACC: accuracy, PREC: precision, REC: recall) for valence (positive/negative), arousal (active/inactive), and quadrant classification.

Layer(s)	Model	Valence				Arousal				Quadrant			
		ACC	PREC	REC	F1	ACC	PREC	REC	F1	ACC	PREC	REC	F1
layer 1	LSTM	80	83	81	80	80	80	75	75	71	60	60	58
layers 1, 2	LSTM-ACHMM$_{ML}$	72	76	70	69	75	67	60	58	67	66	66	66
layers 1, 2, 3	LSTM-ACHMM$_{SVM}$	86	87	86	**86**	84	83	79	**79**	84	90	75	**77**

terpart and the simpler LSTM-based classification in all classification tasks. LSTM-ACHMM $_{SVM}$ achieves an accuracy of 86% and 84% for valence and arousal (hemispheric) classification, respectively, compared to an accuracy of 80% and 71% using LSTM-NNs (for the same classification task). The most significant increase in accuracy is obtained for quadrant classification where the LSTM-ACHMM$_{SVM}$ framework improves both the classification accuracy (from 71% to 84%) and the F1 score (from 58% to 77%).

6. CONCLUSIONS

This paper presented a novel multi-layer hybrid framework that derives (i) symmetric spatio-temporal features, (ii) introduces (and pioneers the use of) ACHMM, and (iii) combines a dynamic regressor (LSTM-NNs), a structured graphical model (ACHMM), and a discriminative classification and fusion scheme (SVM) for subject-independent dimensional emotion prediction and classification. Comparative evaluation, performed on a naturalistic data set of facial expressions, showed that the proposed framework provides an increase in accuracy and robustness in all classification tasks. Specifically, our results indicate that by modeling inter-dimensional covariances we can learn complex and subtle class variances more robustly. Overall, the proposed framework is highly flexible due to its layered nature. It can be easily extended and applied to other multi-dimensional (and/or multi-modal) classification problems.

7. ACKNOWLEDGMENTS

This work has been funded by the European Research Council under the ERC Starting Grant agreement no. ERC-2007-StG-203143 (MAHNOB).

8. REFERENCES

[1] J. Borod et al. Facial asymmetry while posing positive and negative emotions. *Neuropsychologia*, 26(5):759 – 764, 1988.
[2] J. Borod et al. Neuropsychological aspects of facial asymmetry during emotional expr. *Neuropsychology Rev.*, 7:41–60, 1997.
[3] E. Douglas-Cowie et al. The HUMAINE database. In *ACII*, pages 488–500, 2007.
[4] H. Gunes and M. Pantic. Automatic, dimensional and continuous emotion recognition. *IJSE*, 1(1):68–99, 2010.
[5] M. A. Hall. Correlation-based feature selection for discrete and numeric class machine learning. In *ICML*, pages 359–366, CA, USA, 2000.
[6] S. Hochreiter and J. Schmidhuber. Long short-term memory. *Neural Comput.*, 9:1735–1780, November 1997.
[7] R. Lane et al. *Cognitive Neuroscience of Emotion.* Oxford University Press, 2000.
[8] P. A. Lewis et al. Neural correlates of processing valence and arousal in affective words. *Cerebral Cortex*, 17:742–748, 2007.
[9] M. Nicolaou et al. Audio-visual classification and fusion of spontaneous affective data in likelihood space. In *ICPR*, pages 3695–3699, 2010.
[10] J. A. Russell. A circumplex model of affect. *Journal of Personality and Social Psychology*, 39:1161–1178, 1980.
[11] B. B. Schiff and B. MacDonald. Facial asymmetries in the spontaneous response to positive and negative emotional arousal. *Neuropsychologia*, 28(8):777 – 785, 1990.
[12] M. Valstar et al. How to distinguish posed from spontaneous smiles using geometric features. In *ICME*, pages 38–45, 2007.
[13] M. Wollmer et al. Abandoning emotion classes - towards continuous emotion recognition with modelling of long-range dependencies. In *Interspeech*, pages 597–600, 2008.
[14] M. Wollmer et al. Combining long short-term memory and dynamic bayesian networks for incremental emotion-sensitive artificial listening. *IEEE J-STSP*, 4(5):867 –881, 2010.

Transforming Clinical Rehabilitation into Interactive Multimedia

Catherine H. Vuong[1,2,3], Todd M. Ingalls[1], James J. Abbas[2,3]
[1]School or Arts, Media and Engineering, Arizona State University, Tempe, AZ, USA
[2]Center for Adaptive Neural Systems, Arizona State University, Tempe, AZ, USA
[3]School of Biological and Health Systems Engineering, Arizona State University, Tempe, AZ, USA
{catherine.vuong, todd.ingalls, jimmy.abbas}@asu.edu

ABSTRACT

There has been an increased interest in using interactive multimedia as a mechanism for physical rehabilitation, including the direct usage of off-the-shelf games and gaming systems. Although, these games have been shown to have physical and psychosocial benefits in the elderly; they were limited when participants had significant physical and/or cognitive disabilities. The limited success in the use of gaming systems to promote rehabilitation may largely be due to the fact that the games being played on them were not designed with rehabilitation in mind and thus they do not necessarily target specific the symptoms or conditions of the disorder.

However, if designed correctly and for rehabilitation, interactive multimedia and gaming systems have significant rehabilitation potential. We believe for a system to effective in promoting rehabilitation, its approach must be based in the clinical techniques used to treat the symptoms and the principles of neural science behind the disorder. In this paper, we describe and approach to Parkinson's rehabilitation using this methodology.

Categories and Subject Descriptors

J.3 [**Life and Medical Sciences**]: Health; H.5.2 [**Information Interfaces and Presentation**]: User Interfaces – *auditory (non-speech) feedback, screen design, interaction styles*; I.6.4 [**Simulation and Modeling**]: Model Validation and Analysis

General Terms

Design, Experimentation, Human Factors

Keywords

Interactive Multimedia, Parkinson's Rehabilitation, Visual Cueing, Visual Feedback, Optical Flow

1. INTRODUCTION

Since the introduction of the Nintendo Wii in 2006, there has been a growing interest in the possibility of using interactive multimedia as a mechanism for physical rehabilitation, including the direct usage of off-the-shelf games and gaming system [9,13,15]. In some cases, the use of these games has been shown to improve movement parameters, however, the improvements have been limited [9]. The limited success in the use of gaming systems to promote rehabilitation may largely be due to the fact that the games being played on them were not designed with rehabilitation in mind and thus they do not necessarily target specific symptoms or conditions. In particular, current games suffer several severe limitations for use in rehabilitation as they: 1) do not always require the full extension of movement, 2) can induce frustration as games may be too difficult for a population needing rehabilitation, 3) lack the capability to track progress or adjust to individual's current ability based upon clinically relevant parameters.

*Area Chair: Massimo Zancanaro

MM'11, November 28–December 1, 2011, Scottsdale, Arizona, USA.

Regardless of the shortcomings in using pre-existing games to target rehabilitation, we argue that movement-control gaming system technology can be utilized in physical rehabilitation if the games are designed in such a way as to maximize therapeutic effects. Interactive multimedia has been used in physical rehabilitation of Parkinson's disease [3] and stroke [5,14].

To maximize therapeutic effects of an interactive multimedia system, three things should be taken into consideration: 1) the clinical techniques being emulated, 2) the neural science behind the disease and, 3) the multimedia paradigms being used. Therefore, it will not be a one system fits all. Each approach (and system) will be different depending on the disease, symptoms and multimedia techniques used; however, one approach may be able to treat multiple disorders.

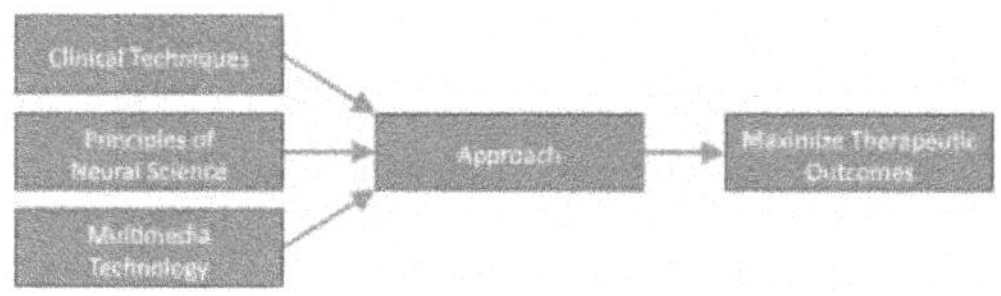

Figure 1. Method to designing interactive multimedia to maximize therapeutic effect.

For a multimedia system to be effective in targeting neural rehabilitation, there must be a clear understanding of the symptoms and techniques used to treat the symptoms.

Understanding the neural science can give us clues on how to target (or not target) the flow of visual and auditory information. We may not always have a full picture of the disease or condition, as much of these questions are a part of ongoing research in neural science. There are, however, theories to suggest that neurorehabilitation may provide a mechanism to bypass (or supplement) the diseased or damaged areas of the brain.

In this paper, we will describe an approach to Parkinson's rehabilitation and initial system manifestation. As this is the first system developed from this approach it has been designed for in-clinic use. In this system, participants with PD will be asked to reach and/or step toward virtual targets. The target location(s) will be controlled by a physical therapist. An example of the final system can be seen in Figure 2.

2. SPECIFIC EXAMPLE – LARGE EXERCISES IN PARKINSON'S DISEASE

Parkinson's disease (PD) is neurodegenerative movement disorder characterized by decrease amplitude and speed of movement, difficulty initiating movement, tremor, rigidity and postural instability [12]. It is a progressive disease that starts unilaterally and spread bilaterally, progressing from mild unilateral reduction in arm swing and resting tremors to confinement to bed or wheelchair [8,10]. There is no cure, however, different measures, most notably physical therapy, can be taken in the early stages to stave off the symptoms.

Figure 2. Clinic-based system. System was designed by integrating clinical techniques, principles of neural science, and multimedia techniques.

2.1 Clinical Symptoms and Techniques

PD is characterized by hypokinetic (slowness) movement. People with PD show an increase in gait disturbances, including: reduced speed, reduced stride length, reduced stride length regulation, and reduced cadence; during the later stages shuffling gait, festination, freezing and falls are common [12]. Also common during the early stages of PD are micrographia and monotone voice. Micrographia is characterized by reduced handwriting size, clarity, speed, and increased hesitation during writing. During the later stages, non-movement symptoms, such as dementia, depression, respiratory problems, sleep disturbance, sexual dysfunction, personality changes may appear [12]. Dyskinesia (involuntary movement) are also frequent during the later stages of the disease due to pharmacological treatment. Physical therapy, particularly Training BIG and visual cueing, has been used to delay the onset of the symptoms and postpone the need for pharmacological intervention.

2.1.1 Large Exercises

Intense amplitude exercises, such as Training BIG, a widely adopted physical rehabilitation protocol for PD [6,7], have been shown to increase the speed and amplitude in non-training tasks in people with PD. These exercises are done in the presence of a physical therapist and participants are asked to focus on the sensory awareness of the movement 'bigness.' The 'bigness' of the movement is relative to the typical movement patterns of PD. Examples of BIG movements might include, swinging the right arm across the body while fully extended the right leg then switching sides. Another is reaching the right arm up while stretching the right leg back, then swinging the right arm back and the left arm up while stepping back onto the right leg and fully extending the left leg forward; then alternating sides [7]. These tasks have been shown to be effective as they target reduced amplitude of movement with increase amplitude of movement. However, this technique has it limitation; without the constant observation of a physical therapist the size of the movement may decrease; a participant may not be moving as big as he/she feels.

2.1.2 Visual Cueing

Visual cueing, such as lines or markers on the floor, has been shown to increase the stride length, stride length regulation, and velocity in people with PD. The most effective cues were perpendicular to the walking path and spaced one step length apart [11]. Though the exact cause of the marked change is not known; it has been suggested that visual cues may trigger a step, draw attention to the stepping process, or provide dynamic visual feedback. Thus the key mechanism can be attributed to two key features: landmarks and optical flow.

Landmarks. The perpendicular line and markers on the floor are landmarks; much like mile-markers on a freeway, they help the participant to identify how far he/she has gone or stepped. These landmarks are most effective when they are placed one-step length apart. Each landmark can help to trigger a movement and draw attention to the stepping process.

Optical Flow. The absence of improvement in the presence of stroboscopic illumination suggest that the lines or makers on the floor provide dynamic visual feedback about the participants movement [1,2,11]. As the participant walks the line/markers flow down the participant's field of view. This feedback combined with feedback about their limb placement on the floor may contribute to the increase stride length and stride length regulation.

Approach. Using large amplitude movement to increase amplitude and speed of movement. Visual cues provide landmarks to increase amplitude of movement. Optical flow provides dynamic information about movement.

2.2 Principles of Neural Science

PD is a neurodegenerative disease caused by the degeneration of the dopaminergic pathways in the basal ganglia. The basal ganglia is composed of two pathways, the direct and indirect pathway, that are believed to be responsible for the generation of movement. The direct pathway is responsible for facilitating movement; while the indirect pathways is responsible for inhibiting movement. The misregulation of dopamine results in a reduced excitation of the direct pathway and reduced inhibition of the indirect pathway [4].

2.2.1 Hypokinetic and Progressive

PD is a hypokinetic movement disorder affecting the whole body [12]. It is a progressive disease that starts unilaterally and spread bilaterally, progressing from mild unilateral reduction in arm swing and resting tremors to confinement to bed or wheelchair; which varies from person to person [8,10]

The design of the system should therefore take into account the stage of the disease. If the system was design for the early stages of the disease, subjects should be encouraged to stand and explore their full range of motion. If the system was designed for the later stages of the disease, subjects may not be able to stand for long periods of time or at all; therefore, the system should be designed to allow a subject to be sitting.

2.2.2 Sensory Perception

People with PD, during the early stages, retain their ability to move in the presence of visual cues and to produce large amplitude movements. This helps to reaffirm that the problem with PD is either in muscle activation or sensory feedback. In either case, visual feedback allows for compensation in reaching target goals.

During visual cueing and large exercises the visual feedback allows users to realize their reduced amplitude of movement and compensate [6,7,11]. The carry-over effect from the visual cueing suggests that the visual feedback alters perception of movement in the somatosensory processing and/or the sensory-motor integration; thus, allowing people with PD to compensate for the reduce somatosensory feedback or muscle activation.

The integration of visual cues, training BIG, and visual feedback to provide participants with their position information can be used to increase a participant's sensory awareness.

2.2.3 Age of onset

Since the average age of onset is 60 years old, people with PD may suffer from other ailments (i.e. dementia, hip replacement, memory-loss, etc.); even if these symptoms are not normally associated with PD [5,12]. These items should be taken into consideration. It is important to mention, most of these adults did not grow up playing video games or computers. Therefore, in designing our system, demographics must be taken into consideration. The system should be simple enough for the participant to use, while still providing meaningful feedback. The system should not be high impact as this may be detrimental to those with hip/knee replacement or the elderly participant.

Approach. Because of the progressive nature of PD, the system: 1) should allow for participants to perform tasks either standing or sitting, 2) should be designed to track movement patterns over time, and 3) should be designed to facilitate long-term rehabilitation. Because of the age-of-onset, the system should be simple to learn, easy to follow, and low-impact.

2.3 Multimedia Technology

2.3.1 Choice of development system

Although it is extremely enticing to develop for the current gaming mediums, it is also important to realize there are other mediums available for development and the use of an alternate medium for development does not mean that the approach will not be transferrable to current or future gaming platforms.

One of the important advantages of using an alternate medium is cost; this includes monetary and time cost. Developer kits for commercial gaming system are expensive and unnecessary during the design phase of the approach. In addition, most of these developer kits have system specific libraries that will take time to learn and may not be transferrable to a different platform.

It is also possible to emulate technology available in motion gaming systems. The Playstation 3 Move and the Xbox Kinect use camera(s) to track position in 3-dimensions; if 3-dimensions are not necessary, motion can be tracked in 2-dimensions by using an infrared web-camera. In addition, development on a personal computer has many advantages: 1) information from the individual sessions can easily be saved, accessed and, analyzed. 2) libraries are not new and there is a strong support system, and 3) it does not require technology specific to the development platform that may or may not be transferable to other platforms. It is important to note that the Playstation 3 Move and Xbox Kinect attachments can be purchased separately and access through USB.

Approach. Motion technology can be implemented using low-cost alternatives, such as infrared web-cameras

3. REALIZATION

We were able to draw the following concepts from the clinical techniques, principles of neural science, and multimedia technology.

Clinical Techniques. Using large amplitude movement to increase amplitude and speed of movement. Visual cues provide landmarks to increase amplitude of movement. Optical flow provides dynamic information about movement.

Principle of Neural Science. Because of the progressive nature of PD, the system: 1) should allow for participants to perform tasks either standing or sitting, 2) should be designed to track movement patterns over time, and 3) should be designed to facilitate long-term rehabilitation. Because of the age-of-onset, the system should be simple to learn, easy to follow, and low-impact.

Multimedia Technology. Motion technology can be implemented using low-cost alternatives, such as infrared web-cameras.

Using these concepts we were able to design an approach appropriate for PD rehabilitation. In our approach, large amplitude exercises in the upper and lower extremities will be visually cued;

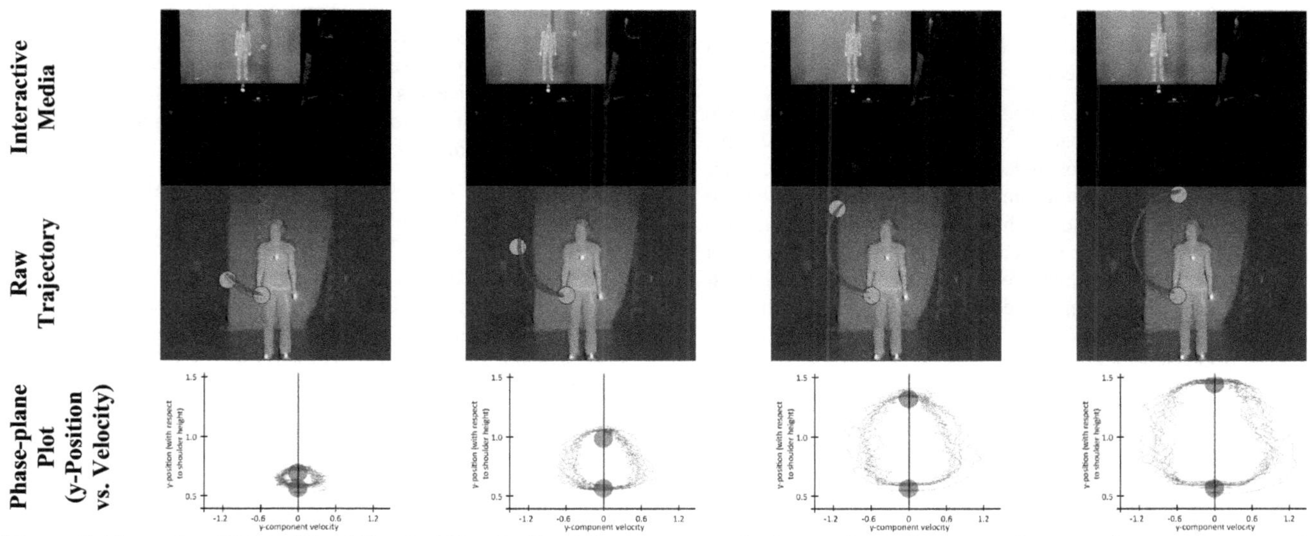

Figure 3. Example of Right Hand Vertical Reach. Participants were asked to perform four sets of ten reaches, each set was done from resting to 1) 45, 2) 90, 3) 135, and 4) 180°. From these reaches, we can see that velocity increases with amplitude of movement.

participants will be given visual feedback based on their physical position. The visual cues will be flexible to allow for long-term rehabilitation. Any system designed from this approach will allow for the participant to be standing or sitting, simple to learn, easy to follow, and low impact. The system will also be able to track their movement patterns over time. The initial system manifestation was design for use inside a rehabilitation clinic to determine the effectiveness of the approach and to gather quantitative data.

In this system, participants are asked to step and/or reach toward virtual targets (visual cues) on the screen. Targets are designed to be flexible using a drag-and-drop paradigm. As a result, targets can be moved to increase amplitude of movement or facilitate sitting or standing position. Targets can also be turned on or off to encourage unilateral, bilateral (opposing or reciprocal) movement.

Participants wear retroreflective markers on both their feet and in the center of the torso; in each hand they hold an incandescent flashlight that emits in both visible and infrared (IR) light. The marker/flashlight locations and the participants silhouette are tracked in 2-dimensions using an IR camera. This design can easily be translated to the Playstation 3 Move or the Xbox Kinect. The videostream from the IR camera is saved for post-processing and to track movement pattern progression over time.

Although the initial system was designed for use inside a physical therapy clinic, with some slight modifications, this approach could be applied to an in-home system. Some reconsideration would have to be given to the multimedia paradigm targeting long-term engagement.

4. DISCUSSION

The initial system manifestation was tested using non-impaired able-bodied subjects to test the effectiveness of the system (and approach). Participants were asked to perform a variety of reaching and stepping tasks. Shown in Figure 3, is a sample set of data from right hand vertical reach. In this exercise participants were asked to perform four sets of ten reaches, each set was done from resting to 1) 45, 2) 90, 3) 135, and 4) 180°.

This simple test showed an increase in velocity with higher amplitude of movement; consistent with clinical techniques (visual cueing and Training BIG) that says increasing amplitude of movement increases velocity of movement; and although it was only tested in non-impaired able-bodied participants the results may be translated to PD participants. In understanding the clinical techniques we were more accurately able to target the symptoms using the interactive multimedia.

In addition, visual feedback helped participants to better perceive their relative location in space. During the initial reaches/steps, participants often overshot or undershot the target location. After visually seeing their silhouette and marker location, they were able to correct their movement. This will be of particular interest in people with PD, as their movement is not always as large as they perceive. In the next stage, we will be performing a pilot test using PD subjects to determine effectiveness of the approach.

5. REFERENCES

[1] Azulay, J. P., Mesure, S., and Blin, O. Influence of visual cues on gait in Parkinson's disease: contribution to attention or sensory dependence? J Neurol Sci. 248(1-2). 192-195

[2] A012 Azulay, J. P. , Mesure, S. , Amblard, B. , Blin, O. , Sangla, I. , and Pouget, J. Visual control of locomotion in Parkinson's disease. Brain. 122 (Pt 1). 111-20

[3] Camurri, A., Mazzarino, B., Volpe, G., Morasso, P., Priano, F., and Re, C. Application of multimedia techniques in the physical rehabilitation of Parkinson's patients. Journal of Visualization and Computer Animation. 14(5). 269-278

[4] Dauer, W. and Przedborski, S. Parkinson's disease: mechanisms and models. Neuron. 39(6). 889-909

[5] Duff, M., Chen, Y., Attygalle, S., Herman, J., Sundaram, H., Qian, G., He, J., and Rikakis, T. An adaptive mixed reality training system for stroke rehabilitation. IEEE Trans Neural Syst Rehabil Eng. 18(5). 531-41

[6] Farley, B. G., Fox, C. M., Ramig, L. O., and McFarland, D. H. Intensive Amplitude-specific Therapeutic Approaches for Parkinson's Disease: Toward a Neuroplasticity-principled Rehabilitation Model. Topics in Geriatric Rehabilitation. 24(2). 99-114

[7] Farley, B. G. and Koshland, G. F. Training BIG to move faster: the application of the speed-amplitude relation as a rehabilitation strategy for people with Parkinson's disease. Exp Brain Res. 167(3). 462-467

[8] Goetz, C. G., Poewe, W., Rascol, O., Sampaio, C., Stebbins, G. T., Counsell, C., Giladi, N., Holloway, R. G., Moore, C. G., Wenning, G. K., Yahr, M. D., and Seidl, L. Movement Disorder Society Task Force report on the Hoehn and Yahr staging scale: status and recommendations. Mov Disord. 19(9). 1020-8

[9] Higgins, H. C., Horton, J. K., Hodgkinson, B. C., and Muggleton, S. B. Lessons learned: Staff perceptions of the Nintendo Wii as a health promotion tool within an aged-care and disability service. Health Promot J Austr. 21(3). 189-95

[10] Hoehn, M. M. and Yahr, M. D. Parkinsonism: onset, progression and mortality. Neurology. 17(5). 427-42

[11] Lewis, G. N., Byblow, W. D., and Walt, S. E. Stride length regulation in Parkinson's disease: the use of extrinsic, visual cues. Brain. 123 (Pt 10). 2077-90

[12] Morris, M. E. Movement disorders in people with Parkinson disease: a model for physical therapy. Phys Ther. 80(6). 578-597

[13] Saposnik, G., Teasell, R., Mamdani, M., Hall, J., McIlroy, W., Cheung, D., Thorpe, K. E., Cohen, L. G., Bayley, M., and {Stroke Outcome Research Canada (SORCan) Working Group}. Effectiveness of virtual reality using Wii gaming technology in stroke rehabilitation: a pilot randomized clinical trial and proof of principle. Stroke. 41(7). 1477-84

[14] Subramanian, S., Knaut, L. A., Beaudoin, C., McFadyen, B. J., Feldman, A. G., and Levin, M. F. Virtual reality environments for post-stroke arm rehabilitation. J Neuroeng Rehabil. 4. 20

[15] Yong Joo, L., Soon Yin, T., Xu, D., Thia, E., Pei Fen, C., Kuah, C. W. K., and Kong, K.-H. A feasibility study using interactive commercial off-the-shelf computer gaming in upper limb rehabilitation in patients after stroke. J Rehabil Med. 42(5). 437-41

Socially Relevant Simulation Games: A Design Study*

Ramin Tadayon
Arizona State University
College of Technology and Innovation
7001 East Williams Field Road
Mesa, Arizona 85212
rtadayon@asu.edu

Ashish Amresh
Arizona State University
College of Technology and Innovation
7001 East Williams Field Road
Mesa, Arizona 85212
amresh@asu.edu

Winslow Burleson
Arizona State University
School of Computing, Informatics, and Decision Systems Engineering
699 South Mill Avenue
Tempe, Arizona 85281
winslow.burleson@asu.edu

ABSTRACT

Socially Relevant Simulation Games (SRSG), a new medium for social interaction, based on real-world skills and skill development, creates a single gaming framework that connects both serious and casual players. Through a detailed case study this paper presents a design process and framework for SRSG, in the context of mixed-reality golf swing simulations. The SRSG, entitled "World of Golf", utilizes a real-time expert system to capture, analyze, and evaluate golf swing metrics. The game combines swing data with players' backgrounds, e.g., handicaps, to form individual profiles. These profiles are then used to implement a golf simulation game using artificially controlled agents who inherit the skill levels of their corresponding human users. The simulation and assessment modules provide the serious player with tools to build golf skills while allowing casual players to engage within a simulated social world. A framework that incorporates simulated golf competitions among these social agents is presented and validated by comparing the usage statistics of 10 PGA Golf Management (PGM) students with 10 non-professional students.

Categories and Subject Descriptors

I.6.8 [**Simulation and Modeling**]: Types of Simulation/Gaming

General Terms

Design

Keywords

Simulation, social gaming, golf swing analysis, real-time motion capture, background assessment

*Area chair: Massimo Zancanaro

MM'11, November 28–December 1, 2011, Scottsdale, Arizona, USA.

1. INTRODUCTION

Game developers distinguish between realistic simulations, referred to as "serious games", and games intended to incorporate social networks and interaction, referred to as "social games". Most game designs fall into one category or the other. Consequently, each of these types of games tends to be adopted by a specific target audience. Despite the separate game development processes this distinction has created, the possibility exists to make a game socially relevant without losing the requirements of a simulation or serious game. This paper presents a design process; example title, the World of Golf; and in-depth case study, that effectively blends the two forms to create Socially Relevant Simulation Games (SRSG).

2. BACKGROUND

2.1 Serious Games

Serious games serve to educate, rather than entertain. Their primary purpose is to provide an interactive means by which a knowledge domain can be transferred to the player [9]. The audience for these games depends upon the subject matter present in the game. It consists of players who wish to train or learn a specific skill set, including experts and players who are already somewhat knowledgeable in the subject matter presented in the game, and often a serious game provides direct, visual means by which these players can assess themselves [12]. Many simulation games can thus be considered serious games[6].

Based on Moizer's work, we define a "serious game" as a game that:

1) Is intended to educate or train the player.

2) Contains a direct (usually visual) means of assessing skill or learning.

3) Employs a game interface which provides the above two features.

2.2 Social Games

The goal of "social gaming" is to incorporate, as seamlessly as possible, the social interactions and networks which occur in the real world in a virtual environment [11]. As such, the audience for social games includes players who wish to socialize and interact within this virtual environment[1][3]. Social games may provide little benefit for single-player gameplay, and some may not include single-player functionality at all. Also, since the focus of a social game is on the social interaction, the game itself becomes a platform to facilitate this interaction [5], and thus the details of the game's subject matter are considered less significant. Facebook games are a modern example of this gaming category [4].

We define a "social game", or a game which is "socially relevant", as a game that:

1) Requires little or no knowledge about the game's subject domain in order for a player to enjoy the game.

2) Employs an interface, central to enjoyment of the game, that is designed to connect its player base through multiplayer gameplay.

3. A DESIGN FRAMEWORK FOR SOCIALLY RELEVANT SIMULATION GAMES

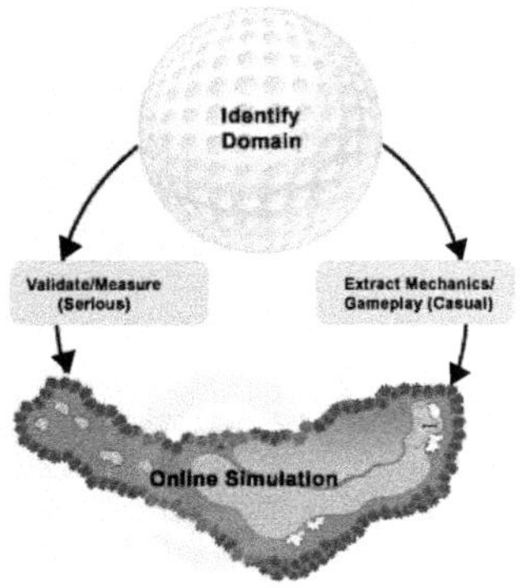

Figure 1: SRSG Design Flow Diagram

We have developed a framework for SRSG that includes a three-step design and development process, focusing on the design of the simulation, consistent interfaces for all users, and social hooks.

Step 1. *Simulation*: In this step the development team designs the simulation, or core serious game aspects, of the SRSG in a manner that ensures that it realistically and convincingly models the level of skill and domain knowledge of users.

Step 2. *Consistent Interfaces*: After completing Step 1, the development team must translate elements of the interface that has been developed to provide a consistent interface which is both informative and simple to understand for both casual and expert players.

Step 3. *Social Hooks*: Expand the completed simulation with social hooks and features to attract and entertain the casual audience.

Using the same process, games which are currently simulations can be modified and expanded into social simulations using steps 2 and 3. The design process is illustrated in Figure 1.

4. WORLD OF GOLF

To demonstrate the efficacy of the SRSG design process we employed it to create the World of Golf as a generalizable SRSG. It is a golf swing simulation that includes a simple, yet powerful method for facilitating online social gaming. We chose this subject domain because it includes easily measurable metrics of skill and performance and is an activity which facilitates social interaction among players.

4.1 Step 1: Design of a Simulation

In order to create an accurate simulation and to complete the first step of our design process, we begin by establishing metrics which can serve as criteria for assessment and training. This process is critical for any simulation to be considered "serious", and the amount and types of metrics depend on the subject matter taught by the simulation.

4.1.1 Golf Swing Metrics

In general, metrics for the first step of the SRSG design process should be chosen based on two requirements:

1) The metrics should be accurately measurable using the chosen method of input.

2) The metrics combined should form an accurate assessment of a player's skill level in the subject domain.

With these goals in mind, World of Golf's game engine uses five golf swing metrics to determine what to look for in a player's golf swing. They are as follows:

1. Club Speed - The vector representing the force acting upon the ball at time of collision, vimpact, is directly affected by the speed of forward motion with which the player swings [7].

2. Club Face - The angle of the club head's face - open, closed or square - affects the direction of travel and curvature of the shot [10].

3. Club Path - The path traveled by the club head during the swing influences direction of flight. This influence increases as club speed increases [8].

4. Centeredness at Contact - The distance travelled and direction of a ball are both influenced by how close the ball was to the club head's "sweet spot".

5. Angle of Approach - The steepness of the angle at which the club head approaches the ball during the swing affects how far the ball travels and how curved its path becomes [2].

These five metrics interact to form a near-precise measure [8] of the flight path of the ball after contact, and help World of Golf satisfy the first step of the social simulation design process.

4.1.2 Swing Assessment

The next step is to design an interface which brings the learning elements in the simulation to the player. In the general case, this includes both player input and feedback from the simulation. By establishing this interface, we complete step 1 of the design process. For this purpose, World of Golf utilizes real-time capture of 3-axis data from the Wiimote's accelerometer. The user holds the accelerometer with the y-axis pointing downward toward the ball and the z-axis facing in the direction opposite the shot. The x-axis represents the displacement of the club handle toward or away from the golfer.

The club then forms a "swing plane" which intersects a "ground plane" to represent a club path, as indicated in Figure 2. Deviations from this plane by the club head result in changes to the centeredness of contact, and a different club path results in a new swing plane altogether.

4.2 Step 2: Design of an Interface

Having completed the first step, we now arrive at the second part of the SRSG design process, the development of a uniform interface which includes features targeting both expert and casual audiences. In general, the interface for

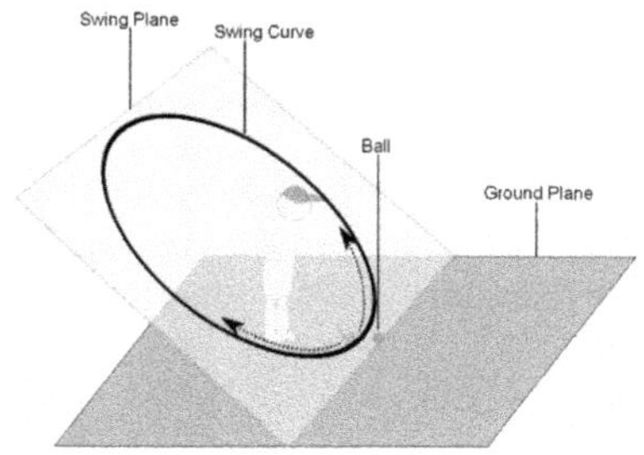

Figure 2: Planar Swing Model

a SRSG should be designed so that, while some elements target expert audiences and some focus on casual audiences, all elements are accessible, to a reasonable extent, by both audiences.

The interface displays a set of bars which represent the magnitude of movement of the golf club on the x, y, and z axis, along with the numeric values themselves. The bars are used as a form of visual feedback which is simplistic enough for casual players to determine how powerful and how steady their swing was, while at the same time providing the raw numeric values for use by experts to determine where improvement should be made in their swing. The goal of this design strategy is to satisfy the requirements in step 2 of the design process (to develop a uniform interface that engages both targeted audiences).

4.3 Step 3: Social Hooks and Attractive Features

The remaining task is to fulfill the requirement of a socially relevant game. Since at this point, we have already developed a complete game, the goal is to expand the game with social hooks and features which facilitate player interaction. In order to fulfill this third and final step of the SRSG design process, World of Golf includes a "golf world" module. This module was incorporated into the design to allow players to get visual feedback on their performance and skill level. Values for each metric are used to compose a virtual golf player, an artificial agent whose play style and swing depend directly upon these retrieved values.

This module serves as the social hook which connects players, both casual and expert, to other players through their avatars in the game world, creating interactions typical in a social network game [4]. When a casual player is matched against an expert player, the system automatically adjusts the performance requirements to keep the gameplay balanced, allowing for a fair match despite the difference in skill between the two players. This connection between the two audience groups completes the final step of the design process, making the game enjoyable for both groups.

5. EVALUATION

To demonstrate that World of Golf satisfies the requirements of the SRSG design process, we evaluate it as a simulation. While this evaluation is not a core part of the design process, it is useful in ensuring that one has met the requirements of both gaming categories. Since the "Golf World" interface is yet to be complete, we leave the evaluation of World of Golf as a social game for future work, and instead focus on the serious game elements of the prototype. In order to determine the validity of the real-time assessment performed by the software, the system was evaluated by comparing profile assessments of golf students against those of non-golf students. The goal of the evaluation was to ensure that the assessment rating scored by a golf player is consistently higher than the rating scored by a player who is a beginner or who does not play golf.

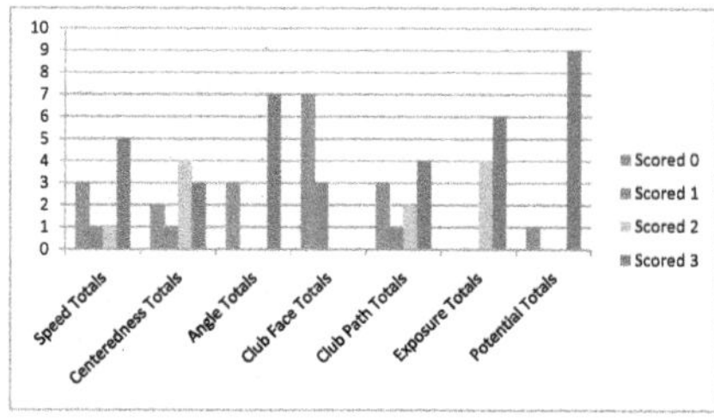

Figure 3: Swing Assessment Scores for PGM Students

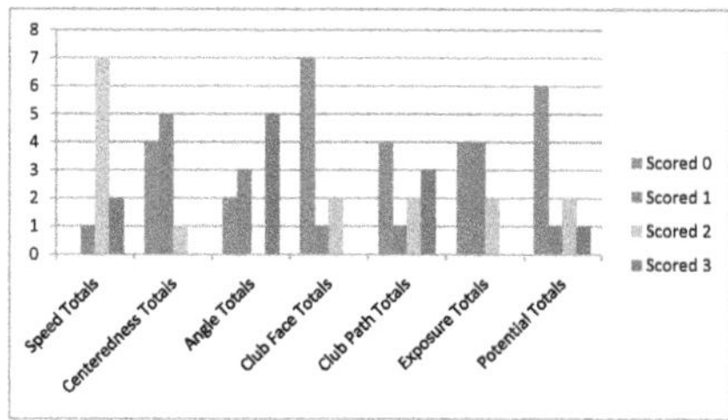

Figure 4: Swing Assessment Scores for Non PGM Students

5.1 Procedure

The study was performed at a driving range of a PGA Golf Management (PGM) program housed in a university. 10 PGM students and a control group of 10 non-PGM students anonymously participated in the evaluation. Each student was instructed to swing the Wii remote until he or she was satisfied with the last swing. Each student also completed the questionnaire along with his or her swing and an anonymous profile was created for that student.

Students were scored on each of the five metrics (club speed, club face, club path, centeredness at contact, angle of approach) as well as on level of exposure to the sport and level of potential. All students were given the same set of instructions and tested under the same condition. Number of attempts varied, and only the last swing attempt was given a score. The score represented the overall swing performance for each student.

5.2 Results

For the questionnaire module, the responses of PGM students indicated both high levels of exposure and high potential. Worth noting is that none of the PGM students tested scored below a "2" in exposure, as indicated in Figure 3. This indicates that the scaling on exposure should be increased to account for professional players, as the soft-

Averages	Speed	Centeredness	Angle	Club Face	Club Path	Exposure	Potential
PGM	1.8	1.8	2.1	0.3	1.7	2.6	2.7
Non-PGM	2.1	0.7	1.8	0.5	1.4	0.8	0.8

Figure 5: Swing Assessment Averages

ware in its current state did not differentiate well between the students themselves. The range of exposure levels for non-PGM students was slightly more evenly distributed, as shown in Figure 4, though no non-PGM student scored a "3" in exposure among those tested.

For the swing metrics, scores of PGM students tended toward extremes, whereas those of non-PGM students varied less. 5 indicates the averages of students tested in each of these metrics for both PGM and non-PGM students. Non-PGM averaged higher in speed, and their club faces were more likely to be open club faces. They scored an average of 2.1 in speed, beating the PGM students by 0.3, and 0.5 in club face, beating the PGM students by 0.2.

For centeredness, club angle, and club path, PGM students scored consistently better on average than non-PGM students. In centeredness, PGM students scored 1.8 on average, 0.7 higher than that of the control group. In angle, they averaged 2.1, beating the non-PGM testers by 0.3. In club path they held an 0.3 point advantage as well, scoring 1.7 in comparison to 1.4 for non-PGM.

5.3 Analysis

The advantage in speed and openness of club face in non-PGM students can be accounted for by the observation that these students, most likely as a result of inexperience, focused on swinging the club with as much force as possible, giving much less consideration to the accuracy of their swing or the steadiness at the point of impact. The reasoning might be that these students interpreted a "good" golf swing as one with the greatest speed at impact with the ball. Their grips on the Wii remote were less steady, causing the wrists to rotate significantly at impact and the club face to switch often to an open position.

While PGM students scored lower in speed and club face metrics, their swings were far more steady and precise on average. Based on similar reasoning, the PGM students would focus less on putting force in their shot and tended to focus more on maintaining proper shoulder, wrist and body positioning during the swing. This scored them almost an entire point higher on average in centeredness and gave them approach angles and club path scores which indicated a more experienced golf swing. Based on the scores output by the software, PGM students performed better overall and indicated far higher levels of experience and potential, a result which supports the validity of World of Gold as a simulation.

6. CONCLUSION

World of Golf demonstrates that through a framework for SRSG that applies a three- step design process, it is possible to create a game which satisfies the interests of both experts and casual players, and do so without isolating the gameplay experience of the two groups. This design study applies the SRSG design process to a physical simulation involving motion detection and synthesis; however the design process could theoretically be applied to any simulation whose subject matter involves some form of social interaction, using the criteria and requirements described. In addition to providing a strategy for the development of new, socially-aware simulations, the proposed design model encourages the expansion of pre-existing simulation games without modification of the core elements, allowing them to engage a larger audience.

7. ACKNOWLEDGMENTS

The authors would like to thank Geoffrey Huston, Assistant Coordinator of the PGA Golf Management Program at Arizona State University, for dedicating his time and providing continued support in this project, and the PGM program for their cooperation during the evaluation process.

8. REFERENCES

[1] N. Ducheneaut and R. J. Moore. The social side of gaming: a study of interaction patterns in a massively multiplayer online game. In *Proceedings of the 2004 ACM conference on Computer supported cooperative work*, CSCW '04, pages 360–369, New York, NY, USA, 2004. ACM.

[2] Y. Ishii, M. Awaji, and K. Watanabe. Stability of golf club motion and emg when swinging. In *SICE-ICASE, 2006. International Joint Conference*, pages 2344 –2347, 2006.

[3] M. C. Juan, M. Alcañiz, L. Gamberini, I. Zaragoza, and F. Martino. Shared virtual environment (sve): a framework for developing social games. In *Proceedings of the international conference on Advances in computer entertainment technology*, ACE '07, pages 258–259, New York, NY, USA, 2007. ACM.

[4] B. Kirman, S. Lawson, and C. Linehan. Gaming on and off the social graph: The social structure of facebook games. In *Computational Science and Engineering, 2009. CSE '09. International Conference on*, volume 4, pages 627 –632, 2009.

[5] T. Manninen. Interaction in networked virtual environments as communicative action: social theory and multi-player games. In *Groupware, 2000. CRIWG 2000. Proceedings. Sixth International Workshop on*, pages 154 –157, 2000.

[6] J. Moizer and J. Lean. Toward Endemic Deployment of Educational Simulation Games: A Review of Progress and Future Recommendations. *Simulation and Gaming*, 41(1):116–131, 2010.

[7] S. M. Nesbit. A three dimensional kinematic and kinetic study of the golf swing. *Journal of Sports Science and Medicine*, 4(4):499–519, 2005.

[8] S. M. Nesbit and R. McGinnis. Kinematic analyses of the golf swing hub path and its role in golfer/club kinetic transfers. *Journal of Sports Science and Medicine*, 8(2):235–246, 2009.

[9] L. P. Rieber, L. Smith, and D. Noah. The value of serious play. *EDUCATIONAL TECHNOLOGY*, 38(6):29–36, 1998.

[10] K. Watanabe and M. Hokari. Measurement of 3-d loci and attitudes of the golf driver head while swinging. *Systems, Man and Cybernetics, Part A: Systems and Humans, IEEE Transactions on*, 36(6):1161 –1169, 2006.

[11] N. Yee, J. Bailenson, M. Urbanek, F. Chang, and D. Merget. The unbearable likeness of being digital: The persistence of nonverbal social norms in online virtual environments. *CyberPsychology & Behavior*, 10(1):115–121, 2007.

[12] M. Zyda. From Visual Simulation to Virtual Reality to Games. *Computer*, 38(9):25–32, 2005.

Context-based Friend Suggestion in Online Photo-Sharing Community *

Ting Yao [1], Chong-Wah Ngo [1], Tao Mei [2]
[1] City University of Hong Kong, Kowloon, Hong Kong
[2] Microsoft Research Asia, Beijing 100080, P. R. China
tingyao.ustc@gmail.com; cwngo@cs.cityu.edu.hk; tmei@microsoft.com

ABSTRACT

With the popularity of social media, web users tend to spend more time than before for sharing their experience and interest in online photo-sharing sites. The wide variety of sharing behaviors generate different metadata which pose new opportunities for the discovery of communities. We propose a new approach, named context-based friend suggestion, to leverage the diverse form of contextual cues for more effective friend suggestion in the social media community. Different from existing approaches, we consider both visual and geographical cues, and develop two user-based similarity measurements, i.e., *visual similarity* and *geo similarity* for characterizing user relationship. The problem of friend suggestion is casted as a contextual graph modeling problem, where users are nodes and the edges between them are weighted by *geo similarity*. Meanwhile, the graph is initialized in a way that users with higher *visual similarity* to a given query have better chance to be recommended. Experimental results on a dataset of 13,876 users and ~1.5 million of their shared photos demonstrated that the proposed approach is consistent with human perception and outperforms other works.

Categories and Subject Descriptors

H.4.m [**Information Systems Applications**]: Miscellaneous

General Terms

Algorithms, Performance, Experimentation.

Keywords

Friend suggestion, social media, user similarity.

1. INTRODUCTION

With the rapid development of Web 2.0 technologies, online photo-sharing communities become increasingly popular. This offers users a distribution outlet for sharing their experience and interest with others [3]. Finding potential friends with similar interest in the social community will facilitate photo-sharing and browsing experience, as well as improve the effectiveness of user-target advertising.

In practice, most of the online communities allow users to self-create a set of interest groups, and then users can find friends and join their interest groups based on the group titles and tags. Since these interest groups are self-organized, plenty of groups usually fall into a similar topic [11], which leads to the difficulties for users to search for their interest groups, friends and photos. For example, 19,929 groups are returned by searching with the keyword *sport* in Flickr [6].

To address this problem, some online communities have provided the auto-suggestion function. For example, questionnaire based schemes ask users to do a set of psychological tests and then suggest friends according to the user-provided answers [15]. Usually, these tests require users to passively answer hundreds of questions. This is tedious and not succinct. A more common approach, for instance in [5], is by recommending common friends between users. This auto-suggestion approach is not fully automatic and requires human intervention.

Some works have also been done to explore the online rich media to automatically discover user relationship. Bhattacharyya *et al.* quantify user similarity based on user profiles such as location, hometown, activities, interest, favorites, and professional association [2]. Roth *et al.* suggest friends based on an implicit social graph, which is formed by user interaction with contacts and groups of contacts [12]. Li *et al.* propose to use location history to mine the user similarity and then recommend the potential friends, in which the location is only limited within tens of cities [9]. In brief, these applications focus on only one single cue. The rich media in the social communities are not fully exploited.

In real life, the chance that two persons will travel together to the same places and take similar photos would be higher when they share similar interest. Motivated by this observation, we propose a method to suggest friends for users, named *context-based friend suggestion*, by mining the user-shared photos and the geo-locations of their photos in the online photo-sharing community. Mathematically, we model the community as a graph in which the nodes represent users and the edges evaluate their relation strength. Specifically, given a *query user* (i.e., user who will be suggested friends), the graph is biased with the preference towards the users who take similar photos (higher similarity in visual appearance of the shared photos) as the query user, and further-

*Area chair: Mor Naaman

MM'11, November 28–December 1, 2011, Scottsdale, Arizona, USA.

more, the relation is weighted by the geo-location similarity. Therefore, we develop two user-based similarities, i.e., *visual similarity* and *geo similarity*, between a pair of users. The *visual similarity* indicates the similarity of users' shared photos in visual appearance, and it is filtered by photo tags and refined based on the representative photos which are selected based on photo comments and views. The *geo similarity* expresses the similarity of user experience and is defined based on the geographic distance of the shared photos.

The main contributions of this paper are two-fold. First, we propose a friend suggestion method in online photo-sharing community by leveraging multiple contexts, including user-contributed photos, their associated tags and geo-locations, as well as user behaviors like viewing and commenting. To the best of our knowledge, the proposed friend suggestion method represents one of the first attempts towards leveraging a variety of contexts for friend suggestion. Second, we develop two user-based similarity measurements, i.e., *visual similarity* and *geo similarity*, based on the multiple contexts of users' photos in online photo-sharing site.

The remainder of this paper is organized as follows. Section 2 provides a brief review of related work. Section 3 presents the proposed friend suggestion. Section 4 shows experiments and Section 5 concludes the paper.

2. RELATED WORK

Mining user relationship in the social network attracts more and more attentions in recent years [1][4][8][10]. Agrawal *et al.* analyze the social behavior of people on the newsgroups [1]. Li *et al.* develop a scalable community discovery solution for large-scale text document corpus [8]. To leverage more data types and their hidden relations, Cai *et al.* propose to learn an optimal linear combination of different relations, which can best meet the user expectation, to discover the hidden community [4]. Lin *et al.* propose a community discovery method through analysis of time-varying and multi-relational data in the rich media social network [10]. The ability to mine user relations also drive various applications. Bhattacharyya *et al.* quantify the user similarity based on user profiles [2]. Roth *et al.* suggest friends based on the implicit social graph formed by users' interactions with contacts and groups of contact [12]. Wu *et al.* present a friend recommendation system which focuses on people's visual appearances on portraits photos [15]. Li *et al.* propose to use location history to mine the user similarity and then recommend the potential friends [9].

3. CONTEXT-BASED FRIEND SUGGESTION

The basic idea of the proposed *context-based friend suggestion* is to recommend a list of friends that have similar interest with a given query user based on multiple contexts in online photo-sharing site. The framework is shown in Fig.1. In an online photo-sharing community, each user shares several photos with geo-locations, provides a set of textual tags to describe photo contents, and attracts some views and comments from the other users. For a given query user, the photo tags are first used to roughly select the potential users and filter out most of users, and then the selected users are ranked to obtain an initial friend list based on the user similarity in terms of visual appearance of their shared representative photos (*visual similarity*). The representative photos are obtained by considering the photo comments and

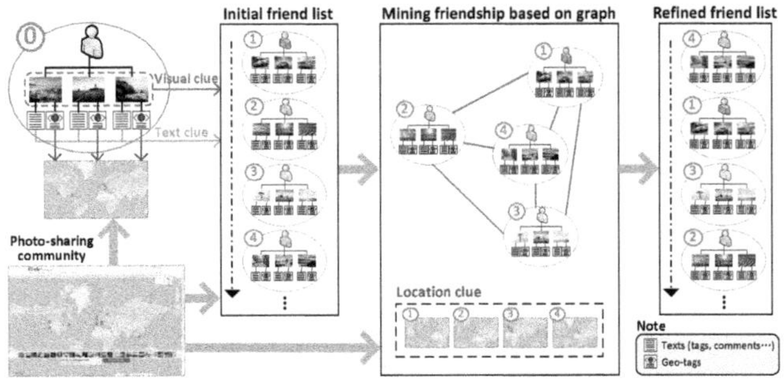

Figure 1: The flowchart of context friend suggestion.

views. Meanwhile, based on a large number of photos with geo-locations, we build a *geographic vocabulary* and represent each user by a set of *geographic words* obtained by vector quantizing the geo-locations into geographic vocabulary. Based on the *geographic words*, the *geo similarity* between each two users is obtained. Assuming that two users are likely to travel to the same places and take similar photos when they share similar interest, we build a graph to model the user friendship, in which, users are nodes biased with *visual similarity* to the query user, and edges between the nodes are weighted by their *geo similarity*. Through a propagation process, we can explicitly detect the user friendship strength and suggest a friend list to the query user.

3.1 Visual Similarity

The *visual similarity* is calculated based on the visual cues of users' representative photos. The representative photos are obtained according to the comments and view numbers of photos, assuming that the more the comments and views, the higher the quality of a photo. Specifically, if the number of views and comments in a photo exceeds the average view/comment number of the photo in an album, this photo will be selected as a representative one.

Denote R_u as the feature vector of representative photos of user u, then we can define the *visual similarity* between user u_i and u_j as follows:

$$s_v(u_i, u_j) = \min_{\mathbf{v}_i \in R_{u_i}, \mathbf{v}_j \in R_{u_j}} \cos(\mathbf{v}_i, \mathbf{v}_j), \quad (1)$$

where $\cos(\mathbf{v}_i, \mathbf{v}_j)$ is the cosine similarity by measuring the angle between the feature vectors of photos $\mathbf{v}_i$ and $\mathbf{v}_j$. We adopt the scale-invariant feature transform (SIFT) descriptor with a Difference of Gaussian (DoG) interest point detector [13]. The interest point is referred to as a local salient patch, each associated with a 128-dimensional feature vector. We further use K-means to cluster the similar patches into "visual words," and use the Bag-of-Word (BoW) model to represent each photo, as it has proven to be effective for object recognition [13].

3.2 Geo Similarity

The *geo similarity* is obtained based on the geographic distance of users' shared photos. First, we randomly collect a large number of photos with geo-locations (GPS coordinates). Then, we build a *geographic vocabulary* by using K-Means clustering and quantize each photo's geo-location into clusters like a "word" in a text document. In this way, all photos of a user will be represented as a set of *geographic words*.

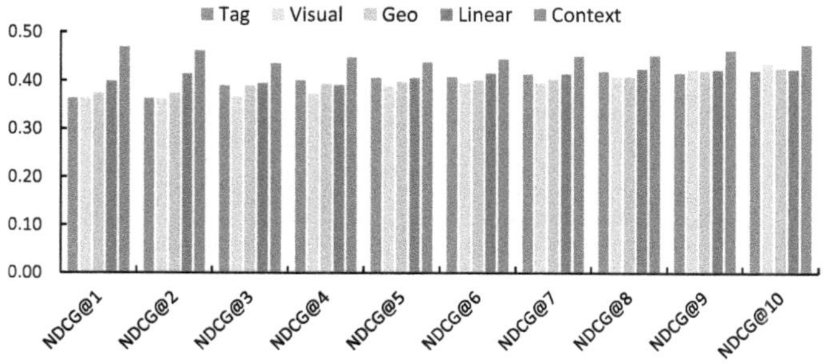

Figure 2: Subjective evaluation on friend suggestion.

Let K denote the size of the *geographic vocabulary*. Then each user can be represented by a vector of K dimensions, $\mathbf{g} = [g_1, g_2, \dots, g_K]$, where each element g_i indicates the number of ith words in a user's photo album. In other words, there are g_i photos fall into the ith geographic words. Let $\mathbf{g}_i$ and $\mathbf{g}_j$ denote the geo representations of the user u_i and u_j respectively, then the *geo similarity* is calculated by the cosine similarity:

$$s_g(u_i, u_j) = \cos(\mathbf{g}_i, \mathbf{g}_j). \quad (2)$$

3.3 Context-based User Similarity

For a given query user q, let $\mathcal{U} = \{u_1, u_2, \dots, u_N\}$ denote a set of N users. The objective is to rank these users according to the friendship with the query user q. The higher a user is ranked, the more similar interest they have. Let $G(\mathcal{V}, \mathcal{E})$ denote a connected graph, where nodes $\mathcal{V}$ correspond to the N users, initialized with the *visual similarity* between the users and query user, and edges $\mathcal{E}$ indicate the *geo similarity* between these nodes. We form the affinity matrix $\mathbf{S}_g = [s_g(u_i, u_j)]$ defined by an $N \times N$ symmetric similarity matrix on the edges of the graph, in which the element $s_g(u_i, u_j)$ is the *geo similarity* between user u_i and u_j, and $s_g(u_i, u_i) \equiv 0$. We construct the matrix $\mathbf{F} = \mathbf{D}^{-1/2}\mathbf{S}_g\mathbf{D}^{-1/2}$ in which $\mathbf{D}$ is a diagonal matrix with its (i,i)-element equal to the sum of the ith row in $\mathbf{S}_g$. Following the method introduced in [16], we use the regularization framework and the cost function as follows

$$Q(\mathbf{s}) = \tfrac{1}{2}\Big(\sum_{i,j=1}^{N} s_g(u_i, u_j)\Big\| \tfrac{s(u_i,q)}{\sqrt{D_{ii}}} - \tfrac{s(u_j,q)}{\sqrt{D_{jj}}} \Big\|^2 + \mu \sum_{i=1}^{N} \|s(u_i, q) - s_v(u_i, q)\|^2\Big), \quad (3)$$

where $s(u_i, q)$ is the *context-based user similarity* of the user u_i and the query user q. The μ ($\mu > 0$) is the regularization parameter. The first term of Eq.(3) is the smoothness constraint, which defines the global consistency of the *geo similarity* over the graph. The second term is the fitting constraint that discourages large deviation from the initial scores of *visual similarity.*

Then the final *context-based user similarity* is given by

$$\mathbf{s}^* = \mathrm{argmin}_{\mathbf{s}} Q(\mathbf{s}). \quad (4)$$

By differentiating $Q(\mathbf{s})$, we can obtain

$$\frac{\partial Q}{\partial \mathbf{s}}\Big|_{\mathbf{s}=\mathbf{s}^*} = \mathbf{s}^* - \mathbf{F}\mathbf{s}^* + \mu(\mathbf{s}^* - \mathbf{s}^0) = 0, \quad (5)$$

where $\mathbf{s}^0$ represents the vector of *visual similarity.* We define $\alpha = \frac{1}{1+\mu}$ and matrix $\mathbf{I}$ as an identity matrix with diagonal element being 1 and the others 0. We can derive that

$$\mathbf{s}^* = (1-\alpha)(\mathbf{I} - \alpha\mathbf{F})^{-1}\mathbf{s}^0. \quad (6)$$

After obtaining the final *context-based user similarity* to the query user, the users are ranked accordingly to obtain the refined friend list.

Figure 3: The representative photos of top five suggested friends for the query user with *Flickr* ID "14489732@N00."

4. EXPERIMENTS

4.1 Dataset

We conducted experiments on a dataset collected from *Flickr*, which includes 13,876 users and ~1.5 million user-shared photos. Each photo has textual tags, geo-location, comments and view number from others. In this dataset, each user has at least five photos and each photo has geo-location information. In our experiments, the numbers of visual words and clusters based on GPS information are both set to 2,000 empirically [13]. The tradeoff parameter α is set to 0.9. The sensitivity of α will be analyzed in details in section 4.2.3.

4.2 Evaluations

We compared our context-based friend suggestion (Context) with the following four methods in both subjective and objective experiments:

- Tag: A *tag similarity* measured by the number of common tags on the users' photos. The higher the number of common tags, the more similar the two users.
- Visual: A *visual similarity* determined by estimating the visual similarity of user representative photos as described in Section 3.1.
- Geo: A *geo similarity* measured by exploring the similarity based on the geographic distance of users' photos as mentioned in Section 3.2.
- Linear: A linear fusion of Tag, Visual and Geo.

4.2.1 Subjective User Study

We randomly selected 1,000 users as the query users. The similarity of each user pair was manually labeled by three subjects on a scale of 1-3: (1) dissimilar (totally different interest), (2) similar (somewhat relevant interest), and (3) strongly similar (almost same interest). We adopted the Normalized Discounted Cumulative Gain (*NDCG*) as the performance metric [7].

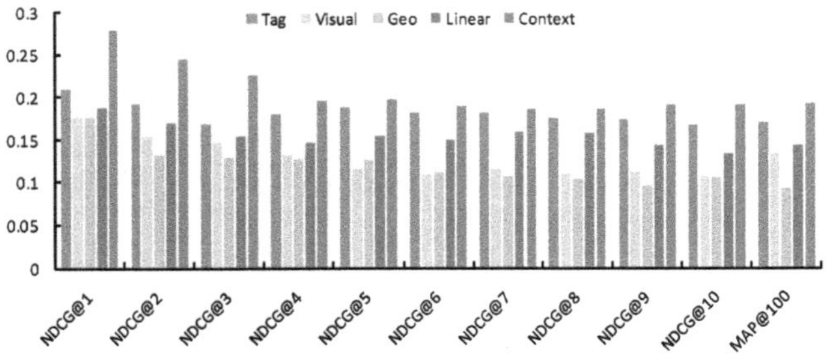

Figure 4: Objective evaluation on friend suggestion.

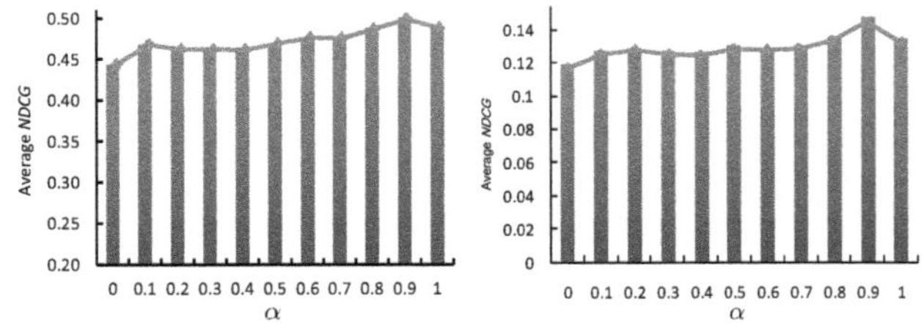

(a) Subjective user study (b) Objective evaluation

Figure 5: The performance curve with respect to the parameter α.

Fig.2 shows the experimental results. We can see that Context outperforms the others and achieves the best performance at different depth of *NDCG*. From the results, user similarity obtained by combining multiple contexts can express the user relationship more objectively and accurately, compared with the results using single cue. In contrast to the linear fusion, the superiority of Context indicates the effectiveness of jointly exploring user-based *visual similarity* and *geo similarity* over a graph model.

Fig.3 shows the top five users' representative photos to a query user according to the final user similarity. From the representative photos of each user, we can see that these photos are similar with each other. These users are likely to have similar interest and thus are potential candidates for friend suggestion.

4.2.2 *Objective Evaluation of Friend Suggestion*

The objective evaluation was conducted according to the *contacts* function in Flickr site, which is organized by users themselves. If a user exists in the other user's contact list, we view the two users as friends. We first filtered out the users who have no contacts in Flickr site or in our user set. After filtering, we obtained 2,975 users and took them as the query users. Since there are only two scales (in or not in contact list), we can also adopt the non-interpolated Mean Average Precision (*MAP*) [14] as another measurement. Fig.4 shows that the proposed Context also achieves the best performance at different depth of *NDCG* as well as *MAP*.

4.2.3 *Parameter Sensitivity*

In this section, we analyzed the sensitivity of the parameter α in Eq.(6). Fig.5 shows the *NDCG* performance with respect to different values of α. The *NDCG* score is obtained by averaging the top 20 results of all the query users. From the figure, we can see that the performance curve is smooth when α varies in a range from 0 to 1. The performance is not sensitive to the change of the parameter, which indicates the robustness of our method. The best performance is achieved when $\alpha = 0.9$.

5. CONCLUSIONS

We have presented our friend suggestion approach in online photo sharing community by leveraging multiple contexts, including user shared photos, associated geo-location, text cues (photo tags) and social behaviors (comments and views). Based on multiple contexts, we develop two types of user-based similarity, called *visual similarity* and *geo similarity*. Accordingly, we use a graph model to combine the two similarities. Future work includes the dynamic weighting of context cues according to their importance. We are also interested in exploring other applications of friend suggestion, such as interest group suggestion and auto-generation.

6. ACKNOWLEDGEMENTS

The work described in this paper was partly supported by a grant from the Research Grants Council of the Hong Kong Special Administrative Region, China (CityU 119709).

7. REFERENCES

[1] R. Agrawal, S. Rajagopalan, R. Srikant, and Y. Xu. Mining newsgroups using networks arising from social behavior. In *Proceedings of WWW*, Budapest, May 2003.

[2] P. Bhattacharyya, A. Garg, and S. F. Wu. Analysis of user keyword similarity in online social networks. *Social Network Analysis and Mining*, Oct 2010.

[3] D. Boyd and N. Ellison. Social network sites: Definition, history, and scholarship. *Journal of Computer-Mediated Communication*, 13(1):210–230, 2008.

[4] D. Cai, Z. Shao, X. He, X. Yan, and J. Han. Mining hidden community in heterogeneous social networks. In *Workshop on Link Discovery: Issues, Approaches and Applications*, Chicago, 2005.

[5] Facebook. http://www.facebook.com/.

[6] Flickr. http://www.flickr.com/.

[7] K. Jarvelin and J. Kekalainen. Cumulated gain-based evaluation of ir techniques. *ACM Transactions on Information Systems*, 20(4):422–446, 2002.

[8] H. Li, Z. Nie, W.-C. Lee, C. Giles, and J.-R. Wen. Scalable community discovery on textual data with relations. In *Proceedings of CIKM*, Napa Valley, Oct 2008.

[9] Q. Li, Y. Zheng, X. Xie, Y. Chen, W. Liu, and W.-Y. Ma. Mining user similarity based on location history. In *Proceedings of GIS*, Irvine, 2008.

[10] Y.-R. Lin, J. Sun, P. Castro, R. Konuru, H. Sundaram, and A. Kelliher. Metafac: Community discovery via relational hypergraph factorization. In *Proceedings of KDD*, Paris, June 2009.

[11] R.-A. Negoescu, B. Adams, D. Phung, S. Venkatesh, and D. Gatica-Perez. Flickr hypergroups. In *Proceedings of ACM Multimedia*, Beijing, Oct 2009.

[12] M. Roth, A. David, D. Deutscher, and et al. Suggesting friends using the implicit social graph. In *Proceedings of KDD*, Washington DC, 2010.

[13] J. Sivic and A. Zisserman. Video google: A text retrieval approach to object matching in videos. In *Proceedings of ICCV*, 2003.

[14] TRECVID. http://www-nlpir.nist.gov/projects/trecvid/.

[15] Z. Wu, S. Jiang, and Q. Huang. Friend recommendation according to appearances on photos. In *Proceedings of ACM Multimedia*, Beijing, 2009.

[16] D. Zhou, O. Bousquet, T. Lal, J. Weston, and B. Schölkopf. Learning with local and global consistency. *Advances in Neural Information Processing Systems*, 2003.

Music Visualization: Predicting the Perceived Speed of a Composition – Misual Project –*

Anastasia Gumulia
University of British Columbia,
NTT Communication Science
Labs., 3-1, Morinosato
Wakamiya, Atsugi
Kanagawa, 243-0198, Japan
anastasia.gumulia@gmail.com

Bartłomiej Puzoń
AGH University of Science
and Technology,
NTT Communication Science
Labs., 3-1, Morinosato
Wakamiya, Atsugi, Kanagawa
243-0198, Japan
bpuzon@o2.pl

Naoko Kosugi
NTT Communication Science
Labs., 3-1, Morinosato
Wakamiya, Atsugi
Kanagawa, 243-0198, Japan
kosugi.naoko@lab.ntt.co.jp

ABSTRACT

This paper discusses how people feel the speed of tunes and proposes a way to express it with images. In Misual Project, the research is done to provide people with a way to learn/know music other than by listening to it. This paper focuses on the speed feeling of music, since it is an important musical characteristic for listeners. Although tempo itself is an important indicator of the speed of music, we found that the number of notes per time unit and rhythms (combination of regular and dotted notes) are also important. How and how much these factors contribute to the speed feeling is investigated in listening tests with simple tunes. The factors are visualized so that people can intuitively imagine how fast a tune is. A selection of famous tunes is visualized and the advantage of music visualization is discussed. The visualization allows us to look at a tune as a whole and to compare tunes.

Categories and Subject Descriptors

H.5.1 [**Information Interfaces and Presentation**]: Multimedia Information System; H.5.5 [**Information Interfaces and Presentation**]: Sound and Music Computing—*Signal analysis, synthesis, and processing*; J.4 [**Social and Behavioral Sciences**]: Psychology

General Terms

Design, Experimentation, Human Factors

Keywords

music visualization, music speed, music psychology

*Area chair: Massimo Zancanaro

MM'11, November 28–December 1, 2011, Scottsdale, Arizona, USA.

1. INTRODUCTION

Music has been a part of our everyday lives. Nowadays, there's a tremendous amount of music available and so little time. Because of this, the authors are researching ways for listeners to roughly imagine how the music sounds without having to listen to all of it. In our music visualization [6], multiple musical elements are extracted and put together in an image, which will help people to grasp the music as a whole and compare tunes from various aspects.

This paper focuses on the speed feeling of music, where speed refers to how fast/slow people feel a piece of music is. It is one of the most important pieces of information for listeners and composers because it can convey a message to affects listeners' emotions [8, 10]. Many studies are focusing on the effect of music tempo (beats per minute) on people's behaviour, including talking, shopping, and eating [9, 5, 3]. But obviously tempo is not the only element that affect people's speed feeling, since some people perceive tempo as being halved or doubled [7]. This means real tempo will not always give listeners the correct perception of the speed feeling of music. However, few studies have investigated what gives people the speed feeling besides tempo. In this paper, other musical elements that contribute to the speed feeling and how these elements contribute to the speed feeling are examined in listening test with simple tunes.

2. RELATED WORK

In *This is Your Brain on Music,* Levitin describes that music is both *ubiquitous* and *antique.* In fact, there is no single culture that has not been exposed to it. Collier & Hubbard showed that the interaction between tempo and frequency influences how people rate the speed of music [2]. They found that frequency exaggerates people's judgement of speed, i.e., high frequency pushes people to rate a fast tempo to be faster than it is and vice versa. However, research on how people rate the speed of music is still rare.

Nowadays, many kinds of music visualization are available. The forerunner might be the Windows Media Player. The colorful screen varying according to the music volume seems to be useless, however we sometimes enjoy spending time listening to music and following the changing shapes on the monitor. Musicream [4] and Musicovery [1] provide us a way to select music by connecting colors and shapes to it.

3. MUSICAL ELEMENTS THAT GIVE US SPEED FEELING

To find which musical elements give people the speed feeling, the authors decided to investigate a selection of well-known classical tunes. Among the selected pieces, there were some with a clearly distinguishable tempo and beat (Bach's *Preludes* in C major and C minor) and ones where the tempo is hard to follow (tap) for an untrained ear (Bach's *Toccata* in D minor, Chopin's *Nocturne op. 32 No. 1*, Schumann's *Träumerei*). Additionally, orchestral (*Hungarian Dance No. 5* by Brahms) and choral (*Verdi's Dies Irae* from *Messa Da Requiem*) were analysed. After discussions, the authors determined two musical elements that seemed to have the strongest effect on the speed feeling: existence of dotted notes and number of notes per time frame.

3.1 The effect of dotted notes

Artificial tunes were used at this stage so that the participants could focus on only one element as they listened to the tunes. Some elements that might contribute to the effect of dotted notes to the speed feeling were observed. They included the flow feeling from the continuous melody, the pattern of the notes, tempo, and the ratio of dotted notes. Hereafter, dotted1 refers to dotted notes with 3:1 ratio and dotted2 refers to dotted notes with 7:1 ratio.

From this experiment, it can be concluded that the effect of dotted1 is different from dotted2. In general, dotted1 has a tendency to give a slower feeling in comparison to regular notes. However, dotted2 gives both slower and faster feeling compared to regular notes.

3.2 Discussion about speed feeling

From these sets of experiments, we know that the number of notes per time frame and the existence of dotted notes affect how people feel the speed of music. The bigger the number of notes per time frame, the faster people feel the tune to be. Meanwhile, the effect of dotted notes is different across individuals. From the first experiment, we can see that dotted notes contribute to the speed feeling. However, the effect of dotted1 is different from dotted2. Dotted1 tend to give people a slower feeling. However, dotted2 gives both slower and faster feeling. This might be due to the closeness between notes in dotted2. In dotted2, the dotted notes were followed by sixteenth notes. The interval between a dotted note and a sixteenth note was very long and the one between a sixteenth notes and the next dotted notes was very short. In dotted2, people do not have enough time to process the sixteenth notes. Besides, the location of the sixteenth notes did not fall on strong beats. Therefore, it is hard for people to memorize this pattern which leads them to interpret it differently every time they hear this kind of rhythm. In dotted1, the dotted notes were followed by eight notes, which had a longer duration than the sixteenth notes in dotted2. People have more time to process the eight notes and this gives them the impression of slower feeling than for the regular notes. The eighth notes fell on less strong beats, but were still more obvious than the sixteenth notes in dotted2. It is easier for people to divide a quarter note into two eight notes than into four sixteenth notes.

Another observation that we made is that tempo does contribute to the effect of dotted notes on the speed feeling. Dotted1 always gives a slower feeling no matter what the tempo is. However, dotted2 gives different feeling as the tempo changes. At 80 BPM, dotted2 add to the slower feeling of the tempo. However, dotted2 gives both slower and faster feelings at 120 BPM. At 160 BPM, dotted2 adds to the faster feeling that the tempo already has. This might be because the duration of sixteenth notes is very short at fast tempo, which gives people a faster feeling than the eight notes in dotted1.

Table 1: Shapes to express existence of dotted notes

◯	successive notes in the ratio of $\simeq$ 1:1
▷	successive notes in the ratio of $\simeq$ 1:3 or 3:1
◁	successive notes in the ratio of $\simeq$ 1:7 or 7:1
□	successive notes in other ratio

We conducted several experiments about speed feeling of music. From the experiments that we have done, the most surprising thing was that when we changed two regular notes in real tunes to the combination of one dotted note and one regular note which duration was half of the original regular notes, we actually felt the tempo was changed. We suspect the flow feeling is caused by a continuous increase/decrease of intervals in a real tune. When a real tune has this kind of trend, it feels as if the tune was flowing nicely and causes the speed to be felt different. Therefore, the interval variation was done in this experiment. At medium intervals, no matter what kind of notes were used, the tendency was towards a slower feeling. However, at high intervals, no obvious tendency was observed. This might be because the flow feeling given by a real tune is not only caused by the increase/decrease of intervals but also by another combination of several elements.

4. VISUALIZATION

4.1 Design of music image

Based on the results and discussion in Sections 3, we focused our visualization on the two musical elements for speed feeling: the number of notes per a certain time unit, called here **onset density**, and the existence of dotted notes, or in other words, the ratio of dotted notes and regular notes. The existence of dotted notes is depicted with shapes based on the duration ratio between successive notes (Table 1). The number of notes is expressed by the size of the shapes. As the foundation of images, we used the temporal transition of volume. This also gives us the length information of music pieces.

4.2 Data acquisition

We extract volume data and note onset times from MIDI data to depict volume transitions and the existence of dotted notes using Matlab with Christine Smit's Midi Tools. The onset data are divided into time windows. The note ratio R_i in each window is $R_i = \max(d_i, d_{i+1}) / \min(d_i, d_{i+1})$, where d_i is the onset-to-onset duration of the i-th note. The ratio category R'_i is defined as follows:

$$R'_i = \begin{cases} \text{1:1} & \text{if } R_i < 1.1 \\ \text{3:1} & \text{if } 2.5 < R_i < 3.5 \\ \text{7:1} & \text{if } 6.5 < R_i < 7.5 \\ \text{other} & \text{otherwise} \end{cases} \quad (1)$$

The number of occurrences of each category is then counted. The **dominant note ratio** of a time window is a note ratio category that occurs most frequently. If two categories have the same number of representants, the highest category is selected (assumed order of categories: irregular > 7:1 > 3:1 > regular).

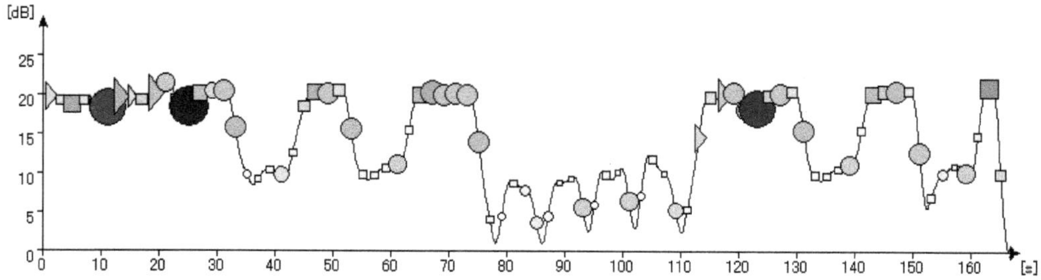

Figure 1: Visualisation of *Hungarian Dances No.5.*

To obtain loudness information, we convert MIDI files into a 44.1 kHz/16bit/mono WAV files using Timidi95 v2.0. The power of the signal is computed using the root mean square method with a 0.5-s window.

4.3 Data visualization

The viewer is implemented in Python, using standard library module Tkinter.

The existence of dotted notes is depicted using shapes from Table 1 according to dominant note ratio. They are placed on the loudness curve. Their sizes are determined by the onset density, and are correlated with the lightness of the shape's interior to facilitate reading.

The loudness is represented on a standard two-dimensional time versus loudness plot with time on the x-axis and loudness on the y-axis. As the viewer is independent from the data acquisition method, the loudness model can be changed without any need to alter the viewer. The data is smoothed with a moving average filter with 1-s window to remove high-frequency changes. Then, the outcome is shifted so that the lowest value above 30 dB is treated as 0. In order to compare the duration of tunes, the x-axis resolution is fixed.

4.4 Visualization results

We have configured the viewer so that every 270 pixels on the x-axis correspond to one minute of music. The shapes represent the onset density within a time window of 2 s. Radii of circles and radii of the circumcircles of squares can vary between 3 and 16 pixels. The vertical edge of triangles can vary between 6 and 32 pixels. The biggest figure represents ten onsets per second. The color of the shape's interior grows darker as the number of onsets increases. In the following sections, $\{a\text{-}b\}$ denotes a section of the plot between seconds a and b and $\{c\}$ denotes a characteristic spot at the second c of the plot.

4.4.1 J. Brahms - Hungarian Dance No. 5

Hungarian Dance No.5 is visualized in the Fig. 1. When confronting the imagination with the music itself, this vivid composition is indeed likely to raise a vigorous, positive mood. The initial loud fragment depicted in {0-30} became one of the recognizable musical phrases among classical music. Its energetic character can be deduced from high loudness level, varying dominant note ratio and varying onset density. The characteristic fast passages are depicted clearly in {12} {25} and {127}. The sudden, substantial changes of the loudness level of the composition are easily visible on the visualization. The noticeable rests in the music are indicated by spots with low onset, for example at {51}.

The repetitive structure of the quietest fragment of the composition is reflected in {78-110}. One can observe similar pattern of shapes (small circle, two squares, big circle) on each of the four lobes – the only spot that breaks this relation is the circle at {83}. The short, fast passage heard just before the music falls silent at the end of every lobe is indicated by large circles on the falling slopes of the curve.

4.4.2 J. Pachelbel - Cannon

The majority of listeners would rate the Pachelbel's composition as a slow, relaxing tune due to its regularity and calm nature. This character can be judged properly from the visualization. The Fig. 2 is a visualization of Pachelbel's *Cannon in D.* The tune starts with a longer then assumed series of notes of the same length – indicated on the graph by the 1:1 ratio dominance. This series continues past {44} and ends at {65}. Inside the series, the tremolo embellishing the melody is clearly distinguishable at {43}. {118} depicts another tremolo found in the tune. {0-65} and the energetic climax {88-109} give a feeling of regularity and order. This is represented on the graph by the lack of rapid loudness, onset density changes and the unchanging dominant note ratio. The variation of those three parameters in sections {65-88} and {110-149} matches the irregular character of the music in these sections. The loudness curve properly shows the silence at {68} and {80}.

4.4.3 A. Dvorak - Humoresque

Humoresque is visualized on Fig. 3. Two tracks of a MIDI file are shown on a common time axis. The top plot represents the right hand part of the score while the bottom plot represent the left hand part.

The composition is built from three patterns repeated many times: the first pattern is present in {0-34}, {52-70} and {106-124}, the second in {34-70} and {124-142} and the third in {70-88} and {88-106}. The similarity of {0-34}, {52-70} and {106-124} is indicated on the visualization by the consistent dominance of the 3:1 note ratio. Additionally, {52-70} and {106-124} share visibly similar accompaniment pattern. {34-70} and {124-142} are linked by the characteristic accompaniment where irregular note ratio is dominant.

The strong accent of the composition on {88-106} is visible on the image because of the increased loudness level and onset density. Both parameters increase also on the bottom plot. In turn, the softening accent (the final arpeggio) is indicated by locally increased onset density ({140}).

4.5 Comparison of all tunes

It is obvious that the longest and calmest tune is *Cannon* (Fig. 2). It also might be the most stable, since there is less changes in the dominant note ratio throughout the tune. The onset density varies most frequently in *Hungarian Dance No. 5* (Fig. 1). Thus, it might be the tune that will give us the most dynamic changes in speed feeling. On the other hand, the dominant note ratio varies most frequently

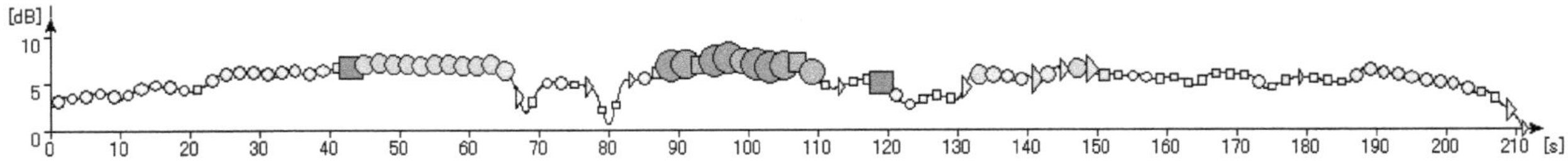

Figure 2: Visualisation of Pachelbell's *Cannon in D major.*

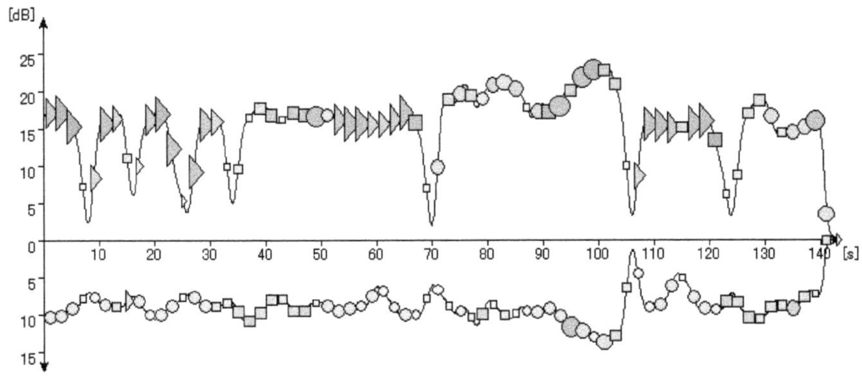

Figure 3: Visualisation of Dvorak's *Humoresque*. The top graph shows the melody, the bottom shows the accompaniment.

in *Humoresque* (Fig. 3). Thus, it might be the tune that will give us the comfortable changes in speed feeling based on rhythm changes. Although the loudness level of *Hungarian Dance No. 5* and *Humoresque* is almost the same, each of the main changes are different: many onset density changes can be seen in *Hungarian Dance No. 5* and many dominant note ratio changes in *Humoresque*. This may cause different impression for each tune. We can see climax parts in each tune in their own style, such as increase in the onset density or changes in dominant note ratio.

5. CONCLUSION

This paper discussed elements that affect people's speed feeling of music and proposed a way to visualize it. The number of notes per time unit and dotted notes were the two elements besides tempo that affected people's judgement about how fast the tune is. These elements were extracted in every constant time interval and depicted with shapes, such as circles, triangles, and squares. They were put on a contour figure generated from volume transition. The number of notes was visualized with the size of the shapes. We made a viewer that visualized the existence of dotted notes, the number of notes, volume transition, and the length in an image. Three famous tunes were visualized with the viewer. We confirmed that some of the characteristics could be appropriately expressed in the images. Although certain degree of training is needed while interpreting the visualization, the examples show that visualization of onset density, dominant note ratio, loudness and the length of a tune may help people to imagine how fast a piece of music is, how it sounds and what kind of emotion it causes. Thus, this visualization will allow people to imagine how (fast) the music sounds before listening to it. This means it can provide people a new way to learn/know music other than listening to it.

Acknowledgments

This research is granted by the Japan Society for the Promotion of Science (JSPS) through the "Funding Program for Next Generation World-Leading Researchers (NEXT Program)", initiated by the Council for Science and Technology Policy (CSTP).

6. REFERENCES

[1] http://musicovery.com/.

[2] W. Collier and T. Hubbard. Judgments of happiness, brightness, speed, and tempo change of auditory stimuli varying in pitch and tempo. *Psychomusicology*, 17(1/2):36–55, 1998.

[3] S. Eroglu, K. Machleit, and J. Chebat. The interaction of retail density and music tempo: effects on shopper responses. *Psychology and Marketing*, 22(7):577–589, 2005.

[4] M. Goto and T. Goto. Musicream: New Music Playback Interface for Streaming, Sticking, Sorting, and Recalling Musical Pieces. In *Proc. of ISMIR*, pages 404–411, 2005.

[5] M. Jungers, C. Palmer, and S. Speer. Time after time: The coordinating influence of tempo in music and speech. *Cognitive Processing*, 1(2):21–35, 2002.

[6] N. Kosugi. Misual – Music Visualization based on Acoustic Data. In *Proc. of the 12th International Conference on Information Integration and Web-based Applications & Services (iiWAS2010)*, pages 607–614, 2010.

[7] N. Kosugi, Y. Nishihara, T. Sakata, M. Yamamuro, and K. Kushima. A Practical Query-By-Humming System for a Large Music Database. In *Proc. of the 8th ACM International Conference on Multimedia*, pages 333–342, 2000.

[8] D. Levitin. *This Is Your Brain on Music: The Science of a Human Obsession.* Paw Prints, 2008.

[9] S. Oakes. Musical tempo and waiting perceptions. *Psychology and Marketing*, 20(8):685–705, 2003.

[10] B. Vickhoff. *A Perspective Theory of Music Perception and Emotion.* Text, University of Gothenburg, Mar. 2008.

Kinship Verification from Facial Images Under Uncontrolled Conditions *

Xiuzhuang Zhou[§,‡], Junlin Hu[*], Jiwen Lu[†], Yuanyuan Shang[§,‡], Yong Guan[§,‡]
[§]College of Information Engineering, Capital Normal University, Beijing, China
[‡]Beijing Engineering Research Center of High Reliable Embedded System, Capital Normal University, China
[*]College of Information Science and Technology, Beijing Normal University, Beijing, China
[†]School of Electrical and Electronics Engineering, Nanyang Technological University, Singapore
E-mail: zxz@xeehoo.com; hujunlin@msn.com; lujiwen@pmail.ntu.edu.sg; syy@bao.ac.cn; guanyong@mail.cnu.edu.cn

ABSTRACT

In this paper, we present an automatic kinship verification system based on facial image analysis under uncontrolled conditions. While a large number of studies on human face analysis have been performed in the literature, there are a few attempts on automatic face analysis for kinship verification, possibly due to lacking of such publicly available databases and great challenges of this problem. To this end, we collect a kinship face database by searching 400+ pairs of public figures and celebrities from the internet, and automatically detect them with the Viola-Jones face detector. Then, we propose a new spatial pyramid learning-based (SPLE) feature descriptor for face representation and apply support vector machine (SVM) for kinship verification. The proposed system has the following three characteristics: 1) no manual human annotation of face landmarks is required and the kinship information is automatically obtained from the original pair of images; 2) both local appearance information and global spatial information have been effectively utilized in the proposed SPLE feature descriptor, and better performance can be obtained than state-of-the-art feature descriptors in our application; 3) the performance of our proposed system is comparable to that of human observers.

Categories and Subject Descriptors

I.4.9 [**Computing Methodologies**]: Image Processing and Computer Vision–Applications

General Terms

Algorithm, Performance, Experimentation.

Keywords

Face Analysis, Kinship Verification, Image Descriptors.

*Area chair: Mor Naaman.

Figure 1: Samples of our kinship database. From top to bottom are the Father-Son (FS), Father-Daughter (FD), Mother-Son (MS) and Mother-Daughter (MD) kinship relations, respectively.

1. INTRODUCTION

Facial image analysis have been widely investigated in the computer vision and multimedia computing community, and a large number of such methods have been proposed for various practical applications, such as face recognition [12], facial expression recognition [6], gender classification [9], ethnic classification [8] and human age estimation [7]. While great successes have been made in these areas, there are a few attempts on automatic face analysis for kinship verification, possibly due to lacking of such publicly available databases and great challenges of this problem.

Recently, Fang *et al.* [5] attacked the challenge of kinship verification by using facial feature extraction and selection methods and their empirical results has verified this possibility. While encouraging results were obtained, there are still two shortcomings of their method:

- Their method was evaluated on a comparatively small dataset (150 pairs), such a small dataset may be insufficient to demonstrate the effectiveness of face image analysis-based kinship verification.
- Facial images in [5] were collected under a controlled environment such that only upright frontal images with normal illumination and natural facial expression were accepted for verification. In many real world applications, there may be some variations on pose, expression, occlusion and illumination of the acquired face images, and it is of great significant to investigate kinship verification under uncontrolled conditions.

Different from previous work in [5], the main purpose of this research is to drive the kinship verification from facial images research more towards real scenarios. Instead of being limited to well-cropped faces with costly manual annotations, we focus on fully-automatic kinship verification from face images under uncontrolled conditions that imposes no restrictions in terms of pose, lighting, background, expression and ethnicity on the face images (Figure 1 shows several example images), such that a fully automatic and real-time system which takes general face images as inputs can be achieved. Moreover, we further propose a new spatial pyramid learning-based (SPLE) feature descriptor for face representation. Since SPLE can utilize both local appearance and global spatial face information for feature representation, better performance can be obtained than state-of-the-art feature descriptors in our system. Experimental results are presented to demonstrate the efficacy of our proposed approach.

2. PROPOSED APPROACH

To automatically classify kinship relation from facial images, we are facing two questions. First, what characteristics are crucial for kinship verification? Second, how to make decisions based on these characteristics? To answer these questions, we will discuss several feature representation methods and present a new one in Section 2.1 together the SVM classifier in Section 2.2.

2.1 Representation

Raw pixel is the most straightforward representation for face images. However, it may be not a good choice for face analysis task because it usually suffers from the illumination and expression variations. To overcome these effects, many local descriptors have been proposed in the literature. For example, Ahonen *et al.* [1] proposed a local binary pattern (LBP) method to describe the micro-structure of the face. Since LBP is encoded by a handcrafted design, many LBP variants [1, 11] have been proposed to improve the performance of the original LBP method. However, these methods still apply the handcrafted strategy, and it is very difficult to obtain an optimal encoding method manually. To address this problem, Cao *et al.* [3] recently proposed a learning-based method by using a unsupervised learning approach to encode the local micro-structures of the face into a set of discrete codes. While better performance can be obtained, this feature descriptor still suffer from one shortcoming: the spatial information were totally discarded in the LE method because a conventional clustering technique, e.g. k-means, was used to obtain the histogram and the spatial information cannot be effectively reflected in such feature histograms.

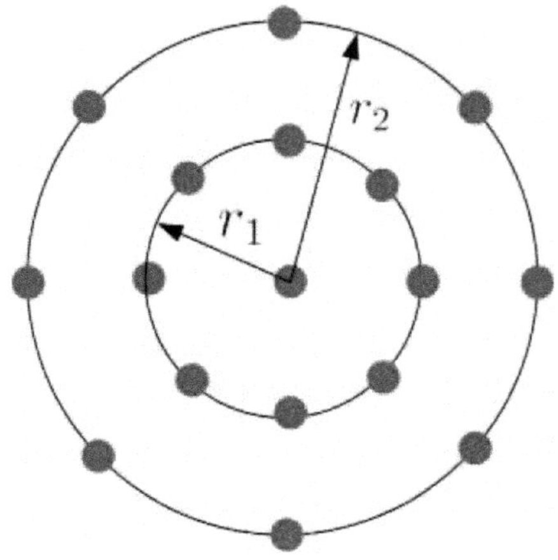

Figure 2: The sampling method used in our SPLE method.

To make better use of the spatial information, we propose a spatial pyramid learning-based (SPLE) feature descriptor for face representation, works as below

Step 1: For each pixel, we sample its neighboring pixels in a ring-based pattern to form a low-level feature vector. Similar to LE, we sample $r * 8$ pixels at even intervals on the ring of radius r. In our experiments, we empirically set $r_0 = 0$, $r_1 = 1$ and $r_2 = 2$, such that 25 (1+8+16) pixels are sampled to construct a feature vector for each pixel, as shown in Figure 2.

Step 2: Normalize the sampled feature vector into unit length such that it can be more robust to illumination variant.

Step 3: Randomly select $2N_1$ pairs of face images to construct a training set, in which N_1 pairs are with kinship relations and the other N_1 pairs are not with kinship relations, respectively.

Step 4: Perform K-means on the the training set to quantize all feature vectors into M discrete types, and make the simplifying assumption that only features of the same type can be matched to one another. Now, for each face image with size of $p \times q$, it will be encoded as a $1 \times M$ histogram-type feature vector.

Step 5: Construct a sequence of grids at resolution $0, \cdots, L$, such that the grid at level l has 2^l cells along each dimension. We extract the LE feature in each cell and concatenate them into a long feature vector. In our experiments, M and L are empirically set to be 200 and 2, respectively, such that the final feature vector is 4200-dimensional (200 + 200*4+200*16).

2.2 Classifier

After obtaining feature representation of each face image, different classifiers can be applied. Since our kinship verification is a binary classification problem and support vector machine (SVM) has demonstrated excellent performance for such tasks, we here apply SVM for classification. Different from the previous SVM-based face verification approaches which use the difference of any two positive or negative face samples as features, we use an normalized absolute histogram difference (NAHD) of a pair of samples as features for SVM learning.

Let $F_1 = [F_{11}, F_{12}, \cdots, F_{1D}]$ and $F_2 = [F_{21}, F_{22}, \cdots, F_{2D}]$

be two SPLE feature representations of two face images I_1 and I_2, we define NAHD as follows:

$$V(I_1, I_2) = \frac{|F_1 - F_2|}{\sum_{t=1}^{D} |F_{1t} - F_{2t}|} \quad (1)$$

We can observe that the elements in $V(I_1, I_2)$ are non-negative and hence the histogram intersection kernel can be used for calculate the similarity of two feature vectors V and U, described below as:

$$sim(V, U) = \sum_{t=1}^{D} \min(V_t, U_t) \quad (2)$$

Having obtained the kernel matrix, we can apply the conventional SVM for kinship verification. In our experiments, the RBF kernel was used for similarity measure of each pair of samples.

3. EXPERIMENTAL RESULTS

3.1 Dataset

Currently, there is no publicly available face image database with kinship relations. In this study, we collected 1000 images from the internet through an online search for images of public figures or celebrities and their parents or children. We pose no restrictions in terms of pose, lighting, background, expression, age, ethnicity and partial occlusion on the images used for training and testing. We adopt the Viola-Jones face detector to detect the face region in each image, and correctly detect 800+ face images, each is size of 64×64. We selected 100 pairs of face images for each of the four kinship relations (Father-Son (FS), Father-Daughter (FD), Mother-Son (MS) and Mother-Daughter (MD)) to construct the dataset, such that 800 images are totally used.

For each of the four subset, we construct 100 pairs of positive (true) samples and 100 pairs of negative (false) samples. The positive samples are the true pairs and the false samples are each parent with a randomly selected child from the children images who is not his/her true child. Figure 3 shows some positive and negative samples we used in our experiments.

3.2 Experimental Settings

For each of the four kinship subsets, we perform 5-fold cross validation for the 100 pairs positive and 100 pairs negative samples. We compared the performance of SPLE with the following four face feature descriptors:

- **PCA** [10]: This method has been widely used for a large number of face analysis tasks, and it can also work for the scenario when the face images are collected under uncontrolled conditions. The feature dimension for PCA was empirically set to be 100 in our experiments.

- **LBP** [1]: We followed the parameter setting of LBP in [1] and used 59 bins to describe each face image.

- **HOG** [4]: HOG (histogram of gradient) was originally proposed for human detection and was recently applied to face recognition [2]. Here, we followed the parameter setting of HOG in [3] and used a b-bin HOG descriptor for face representation.

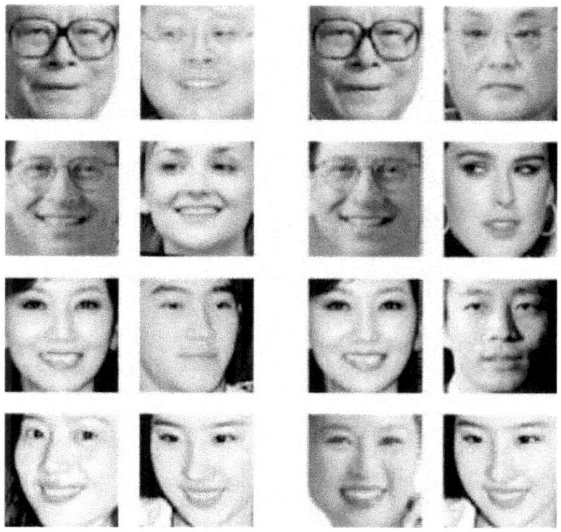

Figure 3: Positive (left) and negative (right) samples used in our experiments.

Table 1: The classification accuracy (%) of different feature descriptors on different subsets.

Method	F-S	F-D	M-S	M-D	Mean
PCA	59.00	51.50	61.50	61.50	58.38
LBP	62.50	59.75	63.25	60.75	61.56
HOG	57.50	50.50	59.50	58.00	56.38
LE	61.75	58.50	68.75	69.50	64.62
SPLE	63.50	61.50	72.50	73.50	67.75

- **LE** [3]: This method is a newly proposed face feature descriptor and shows better performance than other popular face feature descriptors such as LBP and HOG [3]. We used 200 bins for LE to encode a histogram feature for each image.

3.3 Results and Analysis

Table 1 shows the classification accuracy of different feature descriptors on different kinship subsets. As can be seen from this table, the proposed SPLE method outperforms PCA, LBP, HOG and LE with gains in accuracy of 4.50%, 1.00%, 2.00%, and 1.25% on the F-S subset, 10.00%, 1.75%, 11.00%, and 3.00% on the F-D subset, 11.00%, 9.25%, 13.00%, and 3.75% on the M-S subset, and 12.00%, 12.75%, 15.50%, and 4.00% on the M-D subset, respectively. Moreover, we can also observe from this table that all feature descriptors obtain worse performance on the Father-Daughter subset than those on the Mother-Son and Mother-Daughter subsets, which indicates that it is more challenging to recognize the Father-Daughter relation than others from facial images.

Now, we investigate the parameter sensitivity of the proposed SPLE feature descriptor. There are two important parameters: the discrete types M and the spatial pyramid L. Figures 4 & 5 show the classification accuracy of SPLE versus different number of discrete types and different spatial pyramid levels, respectively. We can easily see from the two figures that SPLE is stable to varying parameters. This shows the relative insensitivity of M and L and hence it is easy to select appropriate values of SPLE to obtain good performance.

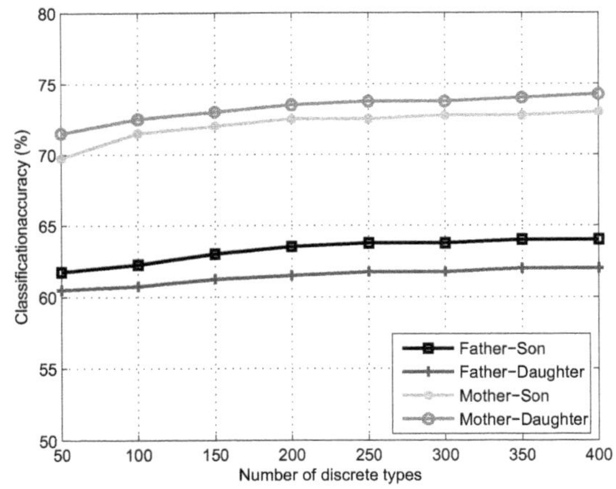

Figure 4: Classification accuracy (%) of SPLE versus different number of discrete types.

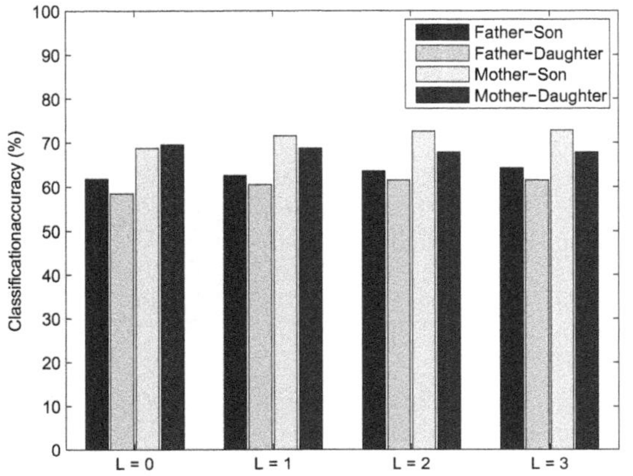

Figure 5: Classification accuracy (%) of SPLE versus different number of spatial pyramid levels.

As an important baseline, the human ability in kinship verification from facial images is also tested. From each of the above four subsets, we randomly selected 100 pairs of face samples, 50 are positive and the other 50 are negative, and presented them to 20 human observers (10 males and 10 females) with age of 20 to 30 years old. None of them received training on the task before the experiment. There are two stages in the experiment. The difference is that, in the first stage (HumanA), only the cropped face regions are shown, while, in the second stage (HumanB), the whole original color images are shown. HumanA intends to test kinship verification purely based on face, while HumanB intends to test kinship verification based on multiple cues including face, hair, skin color, and background. Note that the information provided in HumanA is the same as that provided to the algorithms. Table 2 shows the classification accuracy of human ability on kinship verification on different kinship subsets. We can observe from Tables 1 & 2 that our proposed automatic kinship verification approach can obtain better performance than HumanA, and performs slightly worse than HumanB, which further indicates that some other cues such as hair, skin color, and background also contribute to kinship verification.

Table 2: The classification accuracy (%) of human ability on kinship verification on different kinship subsets.

Method	F-S	F-D	M-S	M-D	Mean
HumanA	63.00	60.00	68.00	72.00	65.75
HumanB	68.00	66.00	76.00	78.00	72.00

4. CONCLUSION

To the best of our knowledge, this paper is the first attempt to investigate kinship verification from facial images under uncontrolled conditions. Our method does not require manual human annotation of face landmarks and the kinship information is automatically obtained from the original pair of images. Moreover, we further proposed a new spatial pyramid learning-based (SPLE) feature descriptor for face representation, and experimental results have shown that the performance of SPLE is not only significantly better than that of the state-of-the-art feature descriptors, but also comparable to that of the human observers.

5. ACKNOWLEDGE

This work was partially supported by the grant from the National Natural Science Foundation of China (No. 11178017) and Beijing Nova Program (No. 2008B57).

6. REFERENCES

[1] T. Ahonen, A. Hadid, et al. Face Description with Local Binary Patterns: Application to Face Recognition. *PAMI*, 28(12):2037–2041, 2006.

[2] A. Albiol, D. Monzo, A. Martin, J. Sastre, and A. Albiol. Face Recognition Using HOG-EBGM. *Pattern Recognition Letters*, 29(10):1537–1543, 2008.

[3] Z. Cao, Q. Yin, X. Tang, and J. Sun. Face Recognition with Learning-based Descriptor. In *CVPR*, pages 2707–2714, 2010.

[4] N. Dalal and B. Triggs. Histograms of Oriented Gradients for Human Detection. In *CVPR*, pages 886–893, 2005.

[5] R. Fang, K. Tang, N. Snavely, and T. Chen. Towards Computational Models of Kinship Verification. In *ICIP*, pages 1577–1580, 2010.

[6] B. Fasel and J. Luettin. Automatic Facial Expression Analysis: A Survey. *Pattern Recognition*, 36(1):259–275, 2003.

[7] G. Guo, Y. Fu, C. Dyer, and T. Huang. Image-Based Human Age Estimation by Manifold Learning and Locally Adjusted Robust Regression. *IEEE Trans. on Image Processing*, 17(7):1178–1188, 2008.

[8] S. Gutta, J. Huang, P. Jonathon, and H. Wechsler. Mixture of Experts for Classification of Gender, Ethnic Origin, and Pose of Human Faces. *IEEE Trans. on Neural Networks*, 11(4):948–960, 2002.

[9] B. Moghaddam and M. Yang. Learning Gender with Support Faces. *PAMI*, 24(5):707–711, 2002.

[10] M. Turk and A. Pentland. Eigenfaces for Recognition. *Journal of Cognitive Neuroscience*, 3(1):71–86, 1991.

[11] L. Wolf, T. Hassner, and Y. Taigman. Descriptor Based Methods in the Wild. In *ECCVW*, 2008.

[12] W. Zhao, R. Chellappa, P. Phillips, and A. Rosenfeld. Face Recognition: A Literature Survey. *ACM Computing Surveys*, 35(4):399–458, 2003.

VastMM-Tag: A Semantic Tagging Browser for Unstructured Videos

Mitchell J. Morris
Columbia University
530 West 120th Street
New York. NY 10027
+01 (646) 775-6092
mjm311@columbia.edu

John R. Kender
Columbia University
530 West 120th Street
New York. NY 10027
+01 (212) 939-7115
jrk@cs.columbia.edu

ABSTRACT

Quickly accessing the contents of a video is challenging for users, particularly for unstructured video, which contains no intentional shot boundaries, no chapters, and no apparent edited format. We approach this problem in the domain of lecture videos using machine learning and semantic display techniques. We extend an existing video browser, through a display of these machine-learned semantic labelings to provide the user with a multi-timeline semantic view. Each timeline corresponds to one semantic label and indicates the label's probable presence or absence in the associated frames. We also provide a full Boolean algebra over these labels, in order to accommodate more complex queries, such as 'text or code, but no instructor'. Finally, we quantify the effectiveness of our features and our browser through user studies on various tasks. We find that users follow a nearly fixed pattern of access, alternating between the use of these tags and keyframes, and also between the use of 'word bubbles' and the player. We show that the tag algebra is integral to the time efficient use of tag timelines, saving up to 27% of the time for various retrieval tasks.

Categories and Subject Descriptors

H.5.1 [**Information Interfaces and Presentation**]: Multimedia Presentation Systems – *Video*, H.5.2 [**Information Interfaces and Presentation**]: User Interfaces – *Interaction Styles*, I.2.10 [**Artificial Intelligence**]: Vision And Scene Identification – *Video Analysis*, I.4.9 [**Image Processing and Computer Vision**]: Applications

General Terms

Performance, Design, Experimentation, Human Factors.

Keywords

Unstructured Video, Semantic Tagging, Tagging User Interface, Machine Learning of Tags, Tag Algebra

*Area Chair: Massimo Zancanaro

1. INTRODUCTION

Universities regularly record their lectures for their students and make them available as supplements to attending classes or as studying aids. However, standard media players only allow a user to play, fast-forward, rewind, or skip about the video.

Previous browsers have added various tools to assist the user in scanning through the material [5]. We have extended an existing video browser that includes thumbnails, speaker and visual segmentation cues, keywords/phrases, and a visual speaker list [2] with a new method to provide users with semantic information about the video's contents, displayed in a multi-timeline view. The semantic labeling is done using automatic video frame classifiers built from Support Vector Machines, using the Sort-Merge feature selection method [7]. Each timeline indicates the sections of the video that contain the corresponding semantic concept.

Although much work has been done on semantic browsers for edited videos, there is comparatively little work on unstructured videos, such as home videos or the casual capture of lectures, and even less on the automatic tagging of sections of unstructured videos [5]. There are websites and services which automatically generate keyword-style tags by analyzing the audio portion of a video; however, visual concepts are not recognized and no tag timelines are displayed [4].

VASTMM [3] is a video browser designed to work with unstructured video. Virtual shots determined by foreground motion and by the similarity of spoken words are displayed along a timeline to assist in video browsing. The shot boundaries identifying keyframes, and the recognized spoken words are displayed in 'bubbles' along separate timelines of the video; see the lower left quadrant of Figure 1. A user can use either the keyframes or the words to jump to sections of interest.

2. VASTMM-TAG

In standard video retrieval engines, video classification techniques are used for answering queries against a database of videos. Users formulate a query and then the system displays to the user a series of video segments of potential interest [5]. In this video browser context, classification of individual keyframes or shots is not often used, particularly for unstructured video. We apply automatic semantic tagging to enhance the video browsing experience through tagged frame highlighting, multimodal timelines, and tagged-segment-only playback.

2.1 Machine Learning Techniques

To label key frames with semantic tags we use an SVM implementation, LibSVM [1], to learn high-level concepts based on a very large library of extracted image features. We use the Sort-Merge feature selection algorithm with Keeper Heuristic to reduce the dimensionality of the features [7]. This heuristic method of selecting good feature sets preforms at least as well as a baseline consisting of the entire set of features; since the entire set is usually redundant, its absolute performance is actually suboptimal. As suggested in [7] we used Haar Wavelet features for finding the concept of `text` and FFT features for finding `code`. When Sort-Merge is applied to `text`, it reduces the number of features from 576 to 32, yet with an increase in accuracy. Similar results occurred with `text` and `presenter`.

2.2 Segment Labeling

VastMM-Tag is a novel system to demonstrate the augmentation of video browsers with semantic tag information; see Figure 1. The original VASTMM browser demonstrated the utility of visual segmentation and verbal topic bubbles [2]. However, it made no attempt to address image features or semantic concepts above the signal level; VastMM-Tag adds tag timelines.

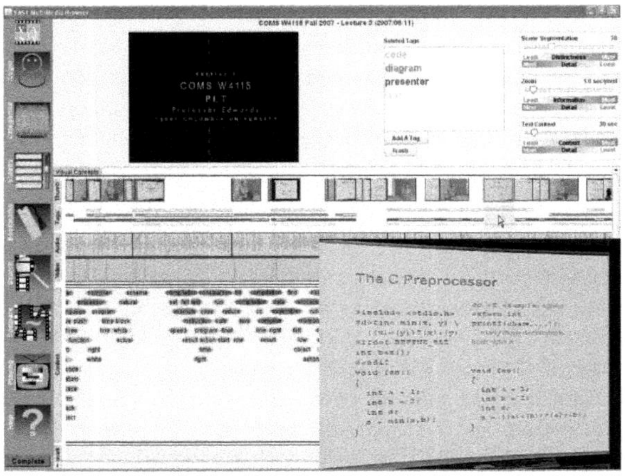

Figure 1: Screenshot of VastMM-Tag browser in action. The tag timelines are the colored bars below the keyframe array. The cursor is hovering over the tag timelines, selecting the tags `code` and `text` (shown in green and yellow respectively). The gray highlight is showing the boundaries of the currently selected 'shot'. The keyframe representing that shot is displayed in the lower right hand corner.

2.2.1 Video Segmentation

The first step in generating the tag time lines is to segment the otherwise unstructured video, into intuitive 'scene' or 'shot' boundaries based on gross motion properties and change in the audio track. Each boundary is assigned a confidence value [3]. The boundaries are used to decompose the video into simulated shots. The first frame from each shot is used as a representative keyframe. When users view a video in the browser, they are allowed to select what level of confidence is appropriate for their task by using a slider; a high confidence value results in fewer but longer segments being displayed. The browser then uses these confidences to partition the video into segments. Each segment starts with a cut, ends with another cut, and has a thumbnail to represent the segment. The segment is labeled with the confidence of the beginning cut [2].

2.2.2 Tag Definition

We have generated semantic labels for visual concepts of `text`, `code`, `presenter` and `diagram`. `Text` means there are words for viewer to read on the screen, `code` means that 'text' is also some sort of computer code, `presenter` indicates that the frame includes the person delivering the lecture, and `diagram` represents the presence of diagrams, whether hand-drawn and computer-generated. The groundtruth for each of the tags in each of the video frames was collected with a web-based tagging tool we developed to allow a fast tagging method.

2.3 MULTI-TAG TIMELINES

The multi-tag timeline is the defining characteristic of VastMM-Tag. It shows the user a number of timelines, each corresponding to a semantic tag. This display gives the user an overview of where in the video semantic concepts occur or co-occur with each other. The interface defaults to display 5 tag timelines at once to the user. This is in the middle of the range of what is considered useful working memory.

2.3.1 Selecting Tags

When the user first opens a video, the timeline section of the display is blank, as is the Selected Tags box. As each tag is selected, a new time line is added to the timeline view. The tags are colored by the order in which they are added: the colors, in order, are green, red, blue, orange, and magenta. The order and coloring of the timelines match the ordering and coloring in the Selected Tags box as can be seen in Figure 1.

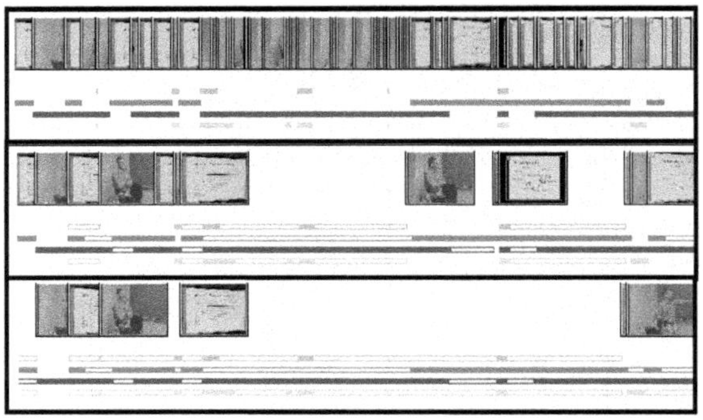

Figure 2: A close up of the timeline section of the browser at varying scene segmentation levels. From top to bottom, the shots show cut confidence 0 (most permissive), 30, and 100 (least permissive). Rigid boundaries cause localization losses.

2.3.2 Interpreting Timelines

For each selected tag, a correspondingly colored timeline is displayed as in Figure 2. These timelines are drawn based on the video segments automatically generated by the browser. The hollow bars seen in Figure 2 are drawn to indicate uncertain tag presence resulting from a heuristic merger of video segments when the cut confidence threshold is not at its most permissive.

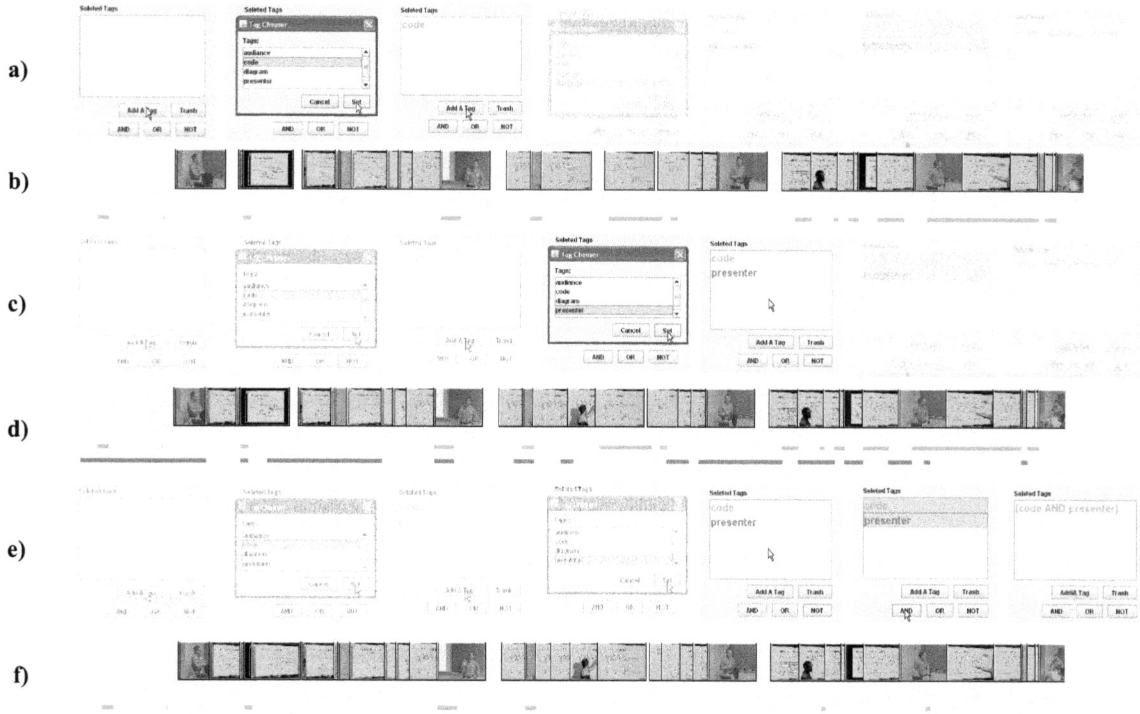

Figure 3: Walkthrough of the tag algebra process. a) The selection of tag `code`. b) The display of the `code` timeline, in green. c) The additional selection of the tag `presenter`. d) The immediate additional display of the additional `presenter` timeline, in red. e) The creation of a composite `code and presenter` timeline by selecting the components and selecting AND. f) The removal of the component timelines, and the display of the new `code and presenter` timeline, in green.

2.3.3 Using the Tag Algebra

A tag algebra is available to enable users to create timelines that are derived from the basic tags, using the Boolean operations of AND, OR, and NOT. To create such a composite timeline, the user first selects the component tags they are interested in by adding them to the displayed list of timelines. Next the user highlights the tags they want to operate on and the operation they want to perform. The two operand timelines are then removed and replaced with the resultant which receives the color and position of the first operand. A walkthrough of the process is shown in Figure 3. This mode of interaction is based on the UI methods used for performing Boolean operations on 3D models, such as in the 3D graphics editing tool Maya.

Table 1: User study browser configurations and average time to completion in seconds.

'Word Bubbles'	X	X	X	X
Play	X	X	X	X
Keyframes	X	X	X	
Tags		X	X	X
Tag Algebra			X	X
Total Users	4	4	4	3
Avg. Completion (sec)	39.9	33.1	24.3	102.4

Regardless of the segmentation confidence, the boolean operation is carried out on the individual base segments, namely those that are displayed when the cut confidence is set to most permissive. Then as the cut confidence threshold is adjusted, the drawing of the timelines is carried out using the same method as for non-Boolean timelines. Thus, first the algebra is preformed, and then the same heuristic-based adjustments are made, and finally the uncertainty of locality is displayed using hollow bars. This form of multi-timeline display is one step beyond the state of the art. For example, the one-off MSNBC debate viewer [8] only allowed the displaying of a single (hand-generated) tag timeline, not the union or intersection of them.

3. USER STUDIES

To evaluate how users take advantage of the system, a preliminary user study has been conducted with 15 university students. The users were assigned to different browser configurations, but each user was asked to complete the same 5 search tasks. These consisted of: "Find a shot of a diagram", "Find sections of the video where the presenter stands alone", "Find the slide where just-in-time compliers is being talked about", "Find a diagram incorporating computer code", and "Find a keyframe matching Example D".

Users were allowed enough time to take each task to a successful completion, so completion rates were identically 100% throughout. Table 1 shows the configurations used, the number of users who used each configuration, and the average search time for each configuration. We noticed that when users became familiar with the video after repeated search tasks, they would exploit a working memory of the video. The transition between the start of a task and the first usage of one of the indicated interface objects is best attributed to such direct recall. We call this state 'Memory'. We observed that in some of the tasks the user behavior went directly from 'Memory' to 'End'. This transition represents those completions where the user happened to be already looking at the target segment, or remembered exactly where the segment was.

4. CONCLUSIONS

4.1 Paired Behaviors

From the data from the user study, we noticed a number of user patterns. In the transition diagrams supported by this evidence there is a strong association between three interface element pairs: the 'Word Bubbles'-Play pair; the Tags-Keyframes pair, and to a lesser extent the Play-Keyframes pair; see Figure 4.

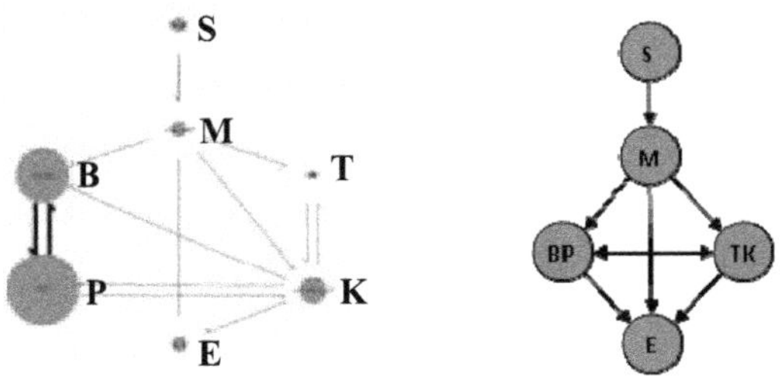

Figure 4: On Left, user interface transition diagrams for browser configuration with tag algebra. On right a composite graph of user interface transitions aggregated over all interface configurations and users, where S = Start, M = Memory, B = 'Word Bubbles', P = Player, T = Tags, K= Keyframes, E = End.

4.2 Course-Fine Strategy

These alternating behaviors suggest that there is a three-tiered approach to completing the search task, in which a user will first use a coarser level of search before proceeding to a finer level. The coarsest level used is the user's own memory, if it exists. Mid-level search is either the use of the 'word bubbles' or the tag timelines. The finest level of search consists of confirming the target location by either watching/hearing the video, or by referencing the keyframes. From these observations (Figure 4) we can conclude that there is a grammar that describes the most frequent search strategies of the users:

$$S\ M\ (\ BP \mid TK\ )^*\ E$$

where S = Start, M = Memory, BP = the alternation between 'Word Bubbles' and Player, TK = the alternation between Tags and Keyframes, and E = End.

4.3 Tags Are Useful

An observation draw from Table 1 is that tag timelines assist the users in finding sections of the video to carry out their search. Tag algebra further reduces the needed time to complete a search as shown in Table 1. The usage pattern diagrams suggest that when users do not have the algebra, they will modify their timelines during the search. However, when the algebra is available, they only need to create the timelines once. We also note that keyframes are a critical partner with tags; even with the algebra, not having keyframes to summarize the video makes the times explode. Tags are most useful when they appear with a mid-frequency; tags that appear too often provide no useful information; those that appear sparsely can be overlooked.

5. FUTURE WORK

The pairing of the 'Word Bubbles'-Play usage and the Tags-Keyframes usage was surprising. We hypothesize that these two separate search strategies represent two different mind sets, with 'Word Bubbles'-Play search corresponding to users searching for audible cues, and Tags-Keyframes search corresponding to users searching for visual cues. Based on suggestions by the users, we will explore the utility of bridging this aural-visual difference by allowing users to create additional Tags that correspond to Words. That is, in addition to the machine-derived visual tags, users can ask for a semantic timeline that visualizes the location of an ASR-detected word. We are also executing an extended IRB-approved observational study using students taking a university course, who will use the VastMM-Tag interfaces to view lectures. Their usage habits will be monitored to assess how these interface components are used in an undirected situation.

6. ACKNOWLEDGEMENTS

This research was supported in part by NSF grant IIS-0713064

7. REFERENCES

[1] Chang, C.-C. and Lin C.-J. 2001. LIBSVM : A Library for Support Vector Machines. www.csie.ntu.edu.tw/~cjlin/libsvm.

[2] Haubold, A. and Kender, J. R. 2007. Analysis, User Interface, and their Evaluation for Student Presentation Videos. In Multimedia and Expo, 2007 IEEE International Conference on.

[3] Haubold, A. and Kender, J. R. 2007 VAST MM: Multimedia Browser for Presentation Video. In Image and Video Retrieval, 2007 International Conference on.

[4] Law-To, J., Grefenstette, G. and Gauvain, J.-L. 2009, VoxaleadNews: robust automatic segmentation of video into browsable content. Proceedings of the 17th ACM international conference on Multimedia, 2009

[5] Lee, H., Smeaton A. F. and Furner J. 1999. User Interface Issues for Browsing Digital Video. 21st BCS IRSG Colloquium on IR (Glasgow, UK, 1999)

[6] Li, F.C., Gupta, A., Sanocki, E., He, L. and Rui, Y. 2000. Browsing digital video. In Proceedings of the Conference on Human Factors in Computing Systems (The Hague, Netherlands, 2000). CHI '00. 169-176.

[7] Morris, M. J. and Kender, J. R. 2009. Sort-Merge Feature Selection and Fusion Methods for Classification of Unstructured Video. International Conference on Multimedia and Expo, 2009.

[8] MSNBC Debate Viewer. 2008 http://www.globenewswire.com/newsroom/news.html?d=151266

Expanding the Point — Automatic Enlargement of Presentation Video Elements *

Qiyam Tung Ranjini Swaminathan Alon Efrat Kobus Barnard
University of Arizona
1040 E. 4th St.
Tucson, AZ 85721
{qtung, ranjini, alon, kobus}@cs.arizona.edu

ABSTRACT

We present a system that assists users in viewing videos of lectures on small screen devices, such as cell phones. It automatically identifies semantic units on the slides, such as bullets, groups of bullets, and images. As the participant views the lecture, the system magnifies the appropriate semantic unit while it is the focus of the discussion. The system makes this decision based on cues from laser pointer gestures and spoken words that are read off the slide. It then magnifies the semantic element using the slide image and the homography between the slide image and the video frame. Experiments suggest that the semantic units of laser-based events identified by our algorithm closely match those identified by humans. In the case of identifying bullets through spoken words, results are more limited but are a good starting point for more complex methods. Finally, we show that this kind of magnification has potential for improving learning of technical content from video lectures when the resolution of the video is limited, such as when being viewed on hand held devices.

Categories and Subject Descriptors

K.3 [**Computing Millieux**]: Computers and Education – *Computer Uses in Education*; H.5 [**Information Systems**]: Information Interfaces and Presentation – *Multimedia Information Systems*

General Terms

Algorithms

Keywords

lecture, video, magnification, laser, speech, mobile, learning

*Area chair: Massimo Zancanaro

1. INTRODUCTION

Many universities offer video lectures as a way to bring classes to students who cannot physically attend courses. Examples include MIT OpenCourseWare [1], Stanford on iTunes [2], and UC Berkeley Extension Online [3]. Such online materials also benefit students who can attend classes as lecture videos are helpful for reviewing concepts. There is potential educational value in using mobile devices, such as cell phones, to watch these videos. However, as lecturers increasingly rely on electronic slides (e.g., PowerPoint) to present their topics, it also becomes important that the user should be able to read the slides in the video. This problem is particularly important when the lecturer attempts to draw students' attention to a specific semantic unit (word, bullet, or image) using laser pointers or by speaking about it. We therefore propose to automatically magnify those elements as the video is presented to the user so that the text is easily readable and therefore understandable. Our contributions are as follows:

- Identifying **semantic units** in each slide, such as bullet points, groups of bullets, and images.
- A method for robustly identifying the position of each semantic unit on a presentation slide.
- Identifying events, which are a lecturer's attempt to draw attention to a semantic unit, based on analysis of speech transcript and aligning them to times in the video corresponding to each semantic unit. We consider a spoken word *aligned* to a bullet if we know what bullet it belongs to.
- Identifying events based on laser pointer gestures.
- Augmenting the video by backprojecting an enlarged sharp image of this semantic unit, taken from the full-resolution slide.

We have demonstrated the usefulness of our technique towards increasing readability of lecture videos by exposing two randomly selected groups of students to two videos, one with magnification and one without. The assumption is that when the lecturer knows that the laser pointer would be used to enhance the video, he would use it in a manner similar to the way it is used in the aforementioned videos. We found that the average scores of those who watched the magnified video were higher and statistically significant. We have also tested our algorithm that detects when semantic units are highlighted by laser points and found that the identified semantics units were very similar to those identified by humans. These experiments are detailed in Section 5.

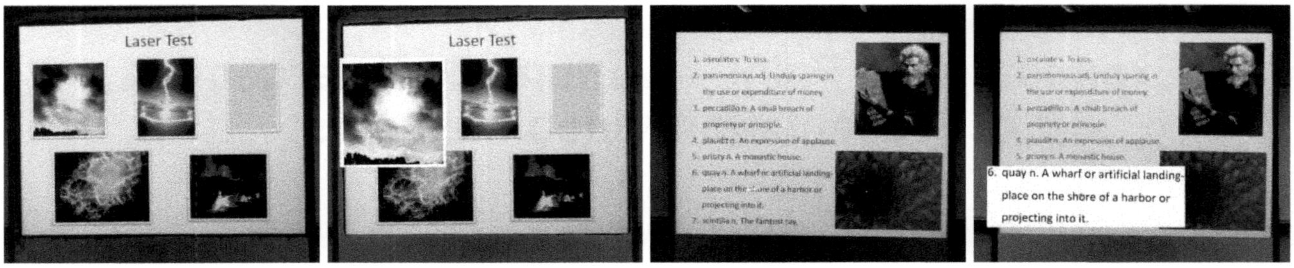

Figure 1: Two snapshots from videos played with (first and third from the left) and without magnification. A semantic unit (image, bullet, or word) is magnified when triggered by a laser gesture. A semantic unit is also magnified for a length of time when a word from the bullet is read.

2. RELATED WORK

Several methods have been proposed for improving the quality of understanding for lecture videos. An hour-long video can be hard to navigate. One of the ways to make lecture videos more useful is by indexing it by its presentation slides, as shown by Fan *et al.* [4]. Their system, the Semantically Linked Instructional Content (SLIC) project, identifies slides in a video by finding the mapping, a homography, between a presentation slide and a video frame. Using this information, the SLIC system allows the users to browse the lecture by slides. Furthermore, they [5], as well as others ([6] [7]) are often able to find accurate homographies that enable them to project the slide back into the video, making the slide look clean and sharp. For our purposes, having accurate homographies allows us to determine where the semantic units are within each frame of the video. With this, we can identify when this semantic unit is being highlighted by a laser pointer as they now share the same coordinate system.

Even with backprojection, lecture material can be difficult to read on the small screen of a mobile device. This is a significant concern as mobile devices have long been considered as an important educational tool and much effort and development have been put into mobile learning [8]. Thornton and Houser [9] show that students benefit from using mobile devices as a learning tool. They sent e-mail lessons to students' phones to promote learning in regular intervals. They have found that 93% of the students found it a useful teaching method. There has also been success in integrating mobile devices into the classroom, as Dyson *et al.* show in [10]. Students participated in a lecture by texting responses to activities using their cell phones, giving quick feedback on the understanding of the class. These studies suggest a trend towards using smartphones for educational purposes. Our system will help enhance the understandability a lecture video.

3. IDENTIFYING SEMANTIC UNITS

In order to magnify a semantic unit, we need to know where it is located within the slide. This is obtained using methods such as [5]. Our first step is to identify an accurate *bounding box* of a single word, bullet, or image in the slide. We do this by analyzing the original presentation files, such as Microsoft PowerPoint files. Microsoft has adopted the Office Open XML (OOXML) format since 2007 [11], which is published as an open standard. However, this format does not specify the coordinates of words or images, so we have developed a method for finding the locations based on modifying text color described in detail below, effectively identifying their positions. We have also developed a general technique that finds the boxes by parsing the presentation file, which requires minimal knowledge and assumptions about the format. If the presentation file's semantic units, such as text and images, can be found and colored, this technique can be expanded to suit many other forms. We have demonstrated it for PowerPoint files, but it is applicable to similar formats such as KeyNote and OpenOffice presentations.

Finding bullet bounding boxes. We define words to be strings of characters separated by blank spaces. A *bullet point* is similar to a word as it is an item in a list whose items start after the typographical symbol of a bullet or any other numbering scheme. Due to space constraints, we will describe just the algorithm for finding bullet bounding boxes. The process for finding bounding boxes for each word is similar.

First, we create uniquely colored bullet points in the PowerPoint file. Note that the bullets in the original presentation are not necessarily uniquely colored, so we change each bullet point's color again to create a second version with a different set of unique RGB values. The results are two PowerPoint files whose bullets are uniquely colored. The two sets of slides are exported to images. We emphasize that the coloring of the slides is only a means of identifying the bounding boxes and does not affect the slides presented to the user.

We now identify the coordinates of the corners of the bullet point's text by comparing the two corresponding images. For each image, we retain a bullet-color correspondence. Note that it is possible that some images or background colors match the bullet's RGB values. Hence, we created two sets of uniquely colored bullets. We then compare each corresponding pixel of the two augmented images. When we find a color difference, we reference the table of bullet-color correspondences and identify which bullet it belongs to. This guarantees that we will find the pixels of a bullet point because only bullet points will be colored differently. Then, for each bullet, we find the minimum and maximum x and y coordinates to derive its bounding box.

Finding image bounding boxes. To find the bounding boxes for images, we adopt a similar technique. We replace the original image with a monochromatic image. The size of the replaced image does not matter as PowerPoint rescales it to the desired size. Once this is done, we can follow the same algorithm for images as we did for bullets.

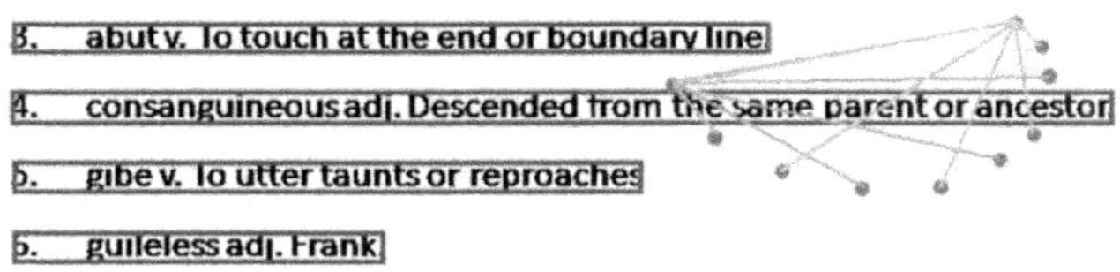

Figure 2: This figure illustrates how our algorithm works. The rectangles around the word indicate the bounding boxes (not part of the original slide). The points represent a laser dot sequence moving from left to right. For the sake of clarity, only a subset of all possible lines are drawn.

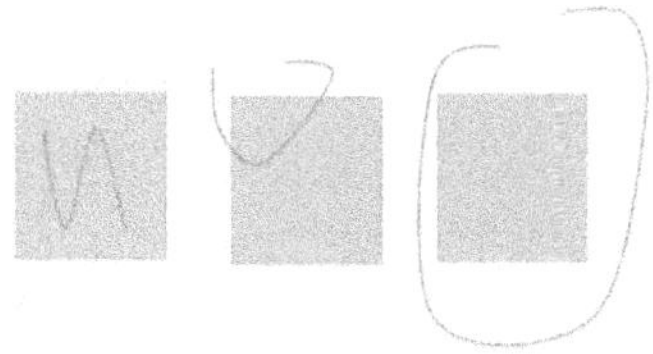

Figure 3: The curves represent examples of the paths of a laser gesture. The laser gestures can be arbitrary and do not necessarily fall inside the box. For all three cases, our algorithm can still identify which bounding box the laser is highlighting.

4. IDENTIFYING AND MAGNIFYING EVENTS

Next, we describe how to identify at which frames a semantic unit is being discussed in the lecture video. We achieve this based on speech and laser pointer use. Once identified, we magnify the element in the video frame coordinate system. We use the algorithm described by Fan *et al.* [5] to find the homographies for slides to frames and thus the time at which the slide is shown in the video. A homography is a transformation that maps points between two planes as seen by a projective camera. In other words, this operation describes the relationship between a slide and its projection in the video. The bounding boxes in the slide combined with the homography specify where the semantic units are located within the video frame coordinate system. In the following sections, we will describe how we determine at what time to magnify a semantic unit.

Speech events. In a lecture, the speaker may utter words that appear in a bullet of the slide. When the words in a bullet are read from a slide and are correctly mapped to their corresponding spoken words, we obtain times (i.e. video frame number) for when a bullet should be magnified.

Swaminathan *et al.* [12] show how to align speech transcript to the words on slides in the context of improving the transcript. This was done by creating an HMM for expected phoneme sequences for each slide, allowing for words to be skipped or additional words to be inserted, which often occurs as speakers embellish their main points. This benefits us because once we know which bullet a spoken word belongs to, it also informs us the time at which a bullet is being discussed.

From our experiments, we use the timing information accompanying the speech transcript and follow the algorithm outlined by Swaminathan *et al.* to create time boundaries for each bullet. The boundary for each bullet is created by using the minimum and maximum timestamps of all words in a bullet.

Laser pointer events. In addition to identifying speech-based events, we also identify events where the laser pointer is used to highlight bullets or images. We use the technique used by Winslow *et al.* [13] to find the laser points. Then we use the homography transformation to map the laser point to find where it appears in the slide's coordinate system.

Our algorithm uses a voting scheme based on line intersections to determine the semantic unit being discussed. Given a laser *gesture*, a small time interval of continuous laser points, we compute a set of line segments from all the pairs of laser points (see Figure 2). This provides a notion of the movement of the laser points in the video. For example, the first two points (leftmost points in the figure) fall outside of the box. However, the segment between the two points intersects the box, so the algorithm counts that as a vote. Furthermore, this method approximates the area of a convex polygon that contains all the laser points. Thus, this method can be thought of as a method of calculating the area intersections of two polygons. In the rightmost example in Figure 3, the laser points determine a path that curves around a semantic unit's bounding box. Even though the points never fall within the box, it will still get votes from the resulting line segment intersections.

5. EXPERIMENTS

We ran three sets of experiments measuring how well the spoken words are aligned to text bullets, how accurately our algorithm identifies semantic unit through laser gestures, and how effective magnification is in learning.

Speech alignment. In this experiment, we tested how well our method can identify the time boundaries of a bullet (or part of a bullet) when it is read off the slide. Since our algorithm can only identify bullets whose slide words appear in the transcript, we ran our algorithm on 3 videos in which the lecturer often read off the words of a slide.

We compared the estimated bullet time boundaries to the boundaries created manually, which was done by identifying which bullet words were read from the slide. We use precision and recall to estimate how good the results are. Specifically, precision is $\frac{t_p}{t_p+f_p}$ and recall is $\frac{t_p}{t_p+f_n}$, where t_p, f_p, and f_n are true positives, false positives, and false negatives, respectively. The number of true positives is obtained by intersecting ground truth and estimated time boundaries and the remaining milliseconds of the estimated bullet time boundary are considered false positives. Similarly, false negatives are the number of milliseconds of a non-bullet time interval incorrectly predicted by our algorithm.

Table 1 shows that the average precision and recall are 32% and 37.6%, respectively. While the results may not be good enough to make magnifying semantic units based on speech practical by itself, it provides useful information for more complex methods, such as identifying bullets through topic similarity.

Laser pointer event test. In this experiment, we tested our algorithm's accuracy of identifying semantic units with laser pointers.

	Precision	Recall
Talk 1	0.290	0.375
Talk 2	0.369	0.409
Talk 3	0.317	0.343
Average	0.320	0.376

Table 1: The precision and recall of bullet time alignment.

	No Magnification	Magnification
Total Correct	74	86
Total Incorrect	87	33
Score	0.460	0.723

Table 2: The table lists the data from the user study. It is partitioned into the group that watched the video with magnification and the group that did not.

We have used 9 short 30-second videos. In the video, the lecturer used a laser pointer to highlight semantic units with simple gestures like circling and underlining. Three graduate students watched and created a ground truth sequence of semantic units highlighted for each video. The ground truth from each student was in perfect agreement.

To test the accuracy of our algorithm, we checked to see whether it correctly identified the order of semantic units highlighted by lecturer. To do this, we computed the edit distance (using the Unix *diff* program) between the ground truth and the machine generated sequence. The error rate is defined as $error = \frac{e}{l}$, where e is the number of edits and l is the length of sequence of semantic units. There were a total of 8 edits out of a sequence of length 59, which gives us a error rate of 13.6%. However, the errors were due to the fact that our laser tracking algorithm lost track of the laser point for a few frames, changing a single gesture into two gestures. Otherwise, our algorithm yields the same semantic unit sequence as the ground truth data.

Effectiveness of Magnification. One problem with viewing lecture videos on a handheld device is that the small screen size makes the contents of the slide difficult to see. By enlarging the bullet based on laser-based events, we simultaneously help the viewer find the relevant bullet and also make it easier to read. Our hypothesis is that users who see magnified bullet points will be more likely to remember the content of the bullet point as opposed to those who do not. To test this, we randomly show our participants one of two videos, one with magnification and one without.

To measure the effectiveness of the enlargement, we created a questionnaire by sampling GRE-level nouns. We showed each participant a 50-second video with two slides containing around 10 definitions of these uncommon nouns (e.g., "gynecocracy"). To focus the participant's attention to particular nouns, a lecturer would use a laser pointer to highlight them. The screen size were chosen so as to simulate a typical smartphone. Students randomly viewed either the original video or a video in which enlargement was performed on the highlighted bullets. Once the video ended, they were automatically redirected to a questionnaire on the definitions of the highlighted nouns.

To measure the correctness of each group, we counted the percentage of total correct answers, In our experiments, there were a total of 40 responses. 23 of those saw the original video and 17 saw the magnified video.

From table 2, we see that participants who viewed the magnified video answered more questions correctly and made fewer mistakes. This is reflected by the scores of the users who did and did not watch the magnified video, which are 72.3% and 46.0%, respectively. Assuming that the answers from each group are normally distributed, we use Welch's t-test to show that the scores are statistically significant. The p-value of 0.0092 confirms that participants generally perform much better at remembering the definitions of bullets when they were magnified.

6. CONCLUSION

We demonstrated a method for magnifying relevant semantic units. Our experiments suggest that our method of identifying semantic units by laser pointer is accurate insofar as human judgment is concerned and when the laser points themselves have not been missed. Though our speech-based events are less accurate, it is a good first step to relating spoken words to bullets. Finally, our user study shows that our method of enlarging semantic units can potentially help users remember the lecture contents.

7. REFERENCES

[1] "MIT OpenCourseWare," 2010, `http://ocw.mit.edu/OcwWeb/web/home/home/index.htm`.

[2] "Stanford on iTunes," 2010, `itunes.stanford.edu/`.

[3] "UC Berkeley Extension Online," 2009, `http://learn.berkeley.edu/`.

[4] Q. Fan, K. Barnard, A. Amir, A. Efrat, and M. Lin, "Matching slides to presentation videos using sift and scene background matching," .

[5] K. Fan, Q.and Barnard, A. Amir, and A. Efrat, "Accurate alignment of presentation slides with educational video," .

[6] X. Wang and M. Kankanhalli, "Robust alignment of presentation videos with slides," .

[7] G. Gigonzac, F. Pitie, and A. Kokaram, "Electronic slide matching and enhancement of a lecture video," in *Visual Media Production, 2007. IETCVMP. 4th European Conference on.* IET, 2008, pp. 1–7.

[8] J. Attewell and C. Savill-Smith, "Learning with mobile devices: research and development," *mLearn 2003 book of papers*, 2003.

[9] Patricia Thornton and Chris Houser, "Using mobile phones in education," in *WMTE '04: Proceedings of the 2nd IEEE International Workshop on Wireless and Mobile Technologies in Education (WMTE'04).*

[10] L.E. Dyson, A. Litchfield, E. Lawrence, R. Raban, and P. Leijdekkers, "Advancing the m-learning research agenda for active, experiential learning: Four case studies," *Australasian Journal of Educational Technology*, vol. 25, no. 2, pp. 250–267, 2009.

[11] "ECMA," 2008, `http://www.ecma-international.org`.

[12] R. Swaminathan, M. E. Thompson, S. Fong, A. Efrat, A. Amir, and K. Barnard, "Improving and aligning speech with presentation slides," *Int. Conf. Pattern Recognition (ICPR) 2010.*

[13] A. Winslow, Q. Tung, Q. Fan, J. Torkkola, R. Swaminathan, K. Barnard, A. Amir, A. Efrat, and C. Gniady, "Studying on the move: enriched presentation video for mobile devices," in *2nd IEEE Workshop on Mobile Video Delivery (MoViD), in conjunction with INFOCOM*, 2009.

Sharing Rectangular Objects in a Video Conference*

Senthil Kumar
Bell Laboratories
Alcatel Lucent
Murray Hill, NJ 07974
senthil.sk.kumar@alcatel-lucent.com

Sreedal Menon
Bell Laboratories
Alcatel Lucent
Bangalore, India
sreedal.menon@alcatel-lucent.com

Francis Zane
Bell Laboratories
Alcatel Lucent
Murray Hill, NJ 07974
francis.zane@alcatel-lucent.com

ABSTRACT

This paper presents a novel method for sharing rectangular objects in a video conference. During these sessions, users often want to share a printed document or other planar rectangular objects (a photograph, the whiteboard on the wall, etc.) with the other participants. If the object is simply held in front of the camera (or if the camera is turned towards the object), the object will undergo perspective distortion and a rectangular object will appear in the video as a quadrilateral. In addition, a handheld document will not be steady and it will be difficult for other users to read its contents. In this paper, we present an algorithm that uses real-time predictive keystone correction to automatically lock on to object and present it with the proper orientation and shape.

Categories and Subject Descriptors

H.4.3 [**Information Systems Applications**]: Communications Applications: Computer conferencing, teleconferencing, and videoconferencing; H.5.1 [**Information Interfaces and Presentation**]: Multimedia Information Systems; H.5.3 [**Group and Organization Interfaces**]: Web-based interaction; I.2.10 [**Vision and Scene Understanding**]: Video Analysis

General Terms

Algorithms

Keywords

Keystone correction, Remote collaboration

1. INTRODUCTION

Sharing content is a key part of remote collaboration, and sharing purely virtual content (files, desktops) is part of many collaboration systems. However, when people are physically co-located, they also do this naturally by using whiteboards, drawing on a piece of paper, turning around their mobile phone to show others, and many other gestures. However, when the are collaborating through a video conference, these natural methods become much more difficult to use effectively.

When presenting such an object to the camera, it is likely to be too small to be seen effectively by the camera without careful positioning. Even when it is big enough, it is likely not place entirely square to the camera plane. A camera pointed at a whiteboard on the wall or at a piece of paper on the table likely sees the object from an angle that transforms the simple rectangle into some quadrilateral shape. Finally, unless the object is mounted in some fashion, the

(a) (b)

Figure 1: An example of sharing a note. The picture on the left shows the scene seen by the camera and the picture on the right shows the image that is shared with the other participants in the conference.

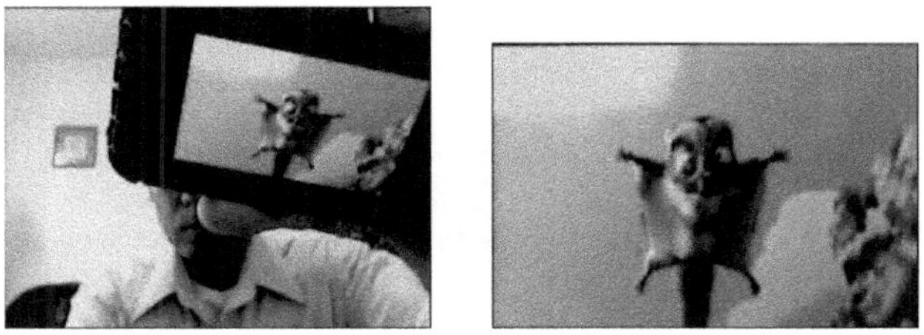

(a) (b)

Figure 2: An example of sharing a video. Normally, unless the user keeps the handheld device steady (Figure a), it would be difficult for others to view the content. Our system locks onto the video and presents it with the proper orientation and shape (Figure b).

*Area chair: Massimo Zancanaro

MM'11, November 28–December 1, 2011, Scottsdale, Arizona, USA.

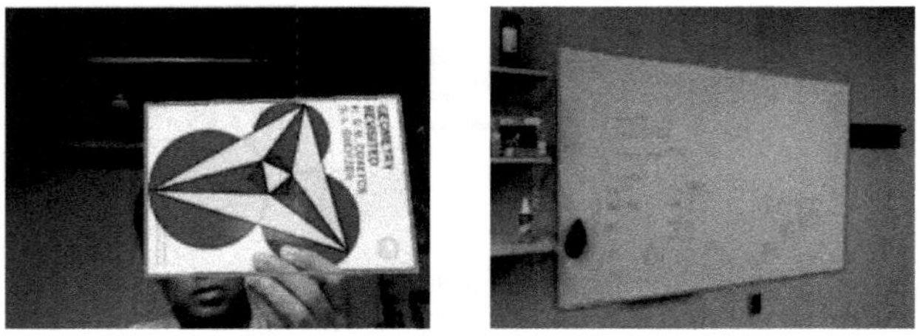

(a) (b)

Figure 3: The object may be held by the user or it may be fixed in the scene

object will drift back and forth even as the user attempts to hold it steady making it difficult to look at the content. A physically present viewer has the ability to move his head to improve his viewing angle, but a remote user (seeing only the projection captured by the camera) does not have that option.

The common thread is that in a large range of these situations, we have prior knowledge that the object is actually a rectangle - a whiteboard, a poster, a sheet of paper, a smartphone screen - that has been deformed because of its projection onto the camera. This deformation (referred to as keystoning) can then be reversed by tracking the object and estimating the transformation it has undergone, then inverting it to restore it to its original configuration. Through this, the remote user is then able to see the object in a natural way (Figures 1 and 2).

In this paper, we present an algorithm for real-time predictive keystone correction that automatically locks onto object and presents it with the proper orientation and shape. Even if the user moves the object around, the other participants will see a steady keystone corrected image sequence. We describe the problem in more detail in Section 2 and propose a solution. That solution is refined in Section 3. Section 4 provides some conclusions.

2. KEYSTONE CORRECTION

Our problem is to identify a rectangular object of interest in the scene and perform keystone correction of its image. The object of interest need not be of a uniform color or texture (see Fig 2(a) and Fig 3(a)). The object may be held by the user or it may be stationary on a table or a wall (Fig 3(b)). Before attempting to identify the object of interest, we first need to define what we mean by the object of interest because there can be multiple rectangular objects in the scene. For this, we look at two different cases. The first case corresponds to the situation where the object is held by the user and the second case corresponds to the case where the object is stationary (a paper on the table or a whiteboard on the wall, etc). In the first case, we assume that the user initially picks the object from somewhere and then moves it into the camera's field of view. Once the object is in the camera's field of view, the user may or may not hold the object steady. In this case, the object that we are looking for is a quadrilateral that moves into the field of view and may or may not move after that. In fact, we are actually looking for the largest quadrilateral that satisfies the above constraint because the object held by the user may contain multiple rectangles.

For the second case, where the object is stationary, we assume that the object of interest is the largest quadrilateral in the scene. This assumes that the user has zoomed the camera in on the object so that it is the largest in the scene.

We employ slightly different algorithms for the two cases and the user selects the appropriate algorithm at runtime by using a simple GUI.

Identifying objects of interest is a fundamental problem in computer vision. In our case, if the object of interest is of a uniform color or texture, we could use one of the many well known segmentation algorithms. However, as shown in Figures 2(a) and 3(a), the only constraint on the object is that it is a rectangle. Image matting techniques such as grab-cut [5, 3] can separate such objects from the background but they require user intervention where the user has to manually mark some pixels as foreground pixels and some other pixels as background pixels (grab-cut can be used in an automated manner but it does not run in real-time).

In our approach, we identify the object of interest by identifying all quadrilaterals in the image and then determining the quadrilateral that corresponds to the object of interest. We explain the steps below.

Given an input image, our algorithm first identifies the lines in the scene by performing edge detection followed by the Hough transform. For edge detection, we use the canny edge detector with a low threshold which results in a large number of edge pixels. These edge pixels are grouped into contours and small contours are eliminated. Hough transform is applied to the pruned edge image which results in a set of lines. We next consider the set of all possible quadrilaterals that can be formed by these lines. Any four lines can form a valid quadrilateral as long as no three of them are parallel. Groups of lines that form quadrilaterals that are too small to be the object of interest are not considered. We identify all valid quadrilaterals in the scene and represent them with their 4 vertices. Having done this, the next step is to pick the quadrilateral that corresponds to the object of interest. Here the algorithm employs different approaches depending on whether the object is held by the user or not.

For the case where the object is stationary (a whiteboard on the wall or a paper on the table), we choose the largest quadrilateral in the image as the object of interest. For the case where the object is held by the user, we wait until a new quadrilateral shows up in the image and then employ a tracking algorithm to track the quadrilateral from one frame to the next. For tracking, we use as features the corners of the quadrilaterals. The feature vector at each corner consists of the normalized RGB values at the corner and the output of the Harris corner detector [1]. This allows us to successfully determine the quadrilateral of interest.

Once we determine the corners of the quadrilateral of interest, that quadrilateral can be easily warped into a rectangle (see, for example, cvGetPerspectiveTransform and cvWarpPerspective in [1]). To do this, we need to specify the corners of the rectangle to which we want to map the quadrilateral. We can choose a rectangle of arbitrary size as long as its aspect ratio matches that of the object being tracked. Our software uses a default aspect ratio of 1.5 but this ratio can be adjusted by the user using a slider. Note that the user does not have to know the actual aspect ratio - he simply adjusts the slider until the corrected image "looks" correct.

Some examples are shown in Figure 4. The tracking algorithm works well in most cases. However, when the object is moved in front of another rectangle in the background,

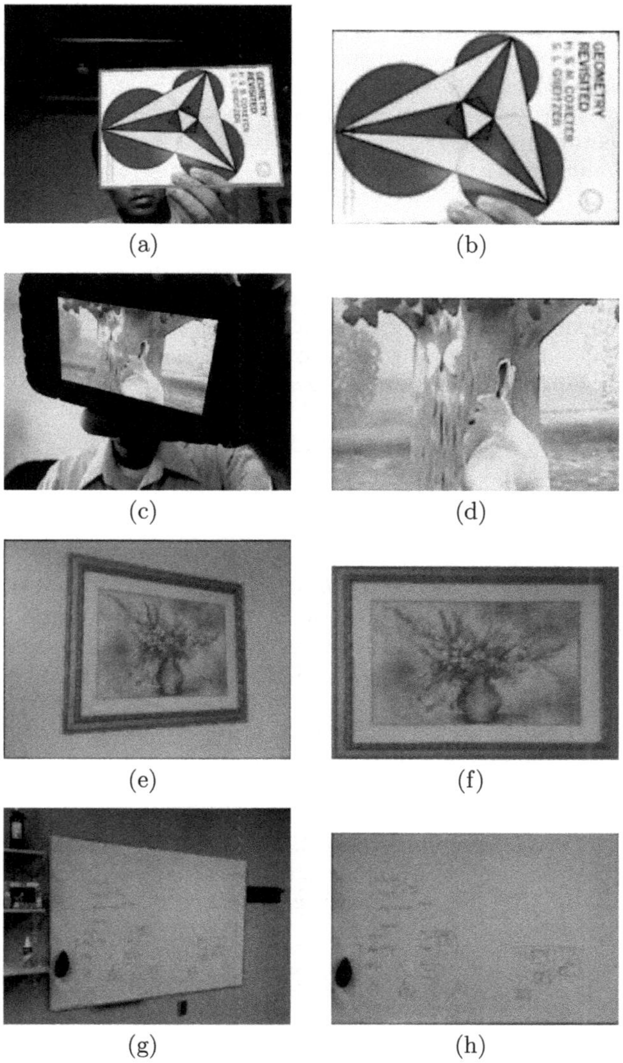

(a) (b) (c) (d) (e) (f) (g) (h)

Figure 4: Some examples of sharing. The pictures on the left show what is seen by the camera and those on the right show what is shared with the other participants in the conference.

tracking may fail sometimes when one or more edges from one rectangle are close to edges of the second rectangle. To alleviate this problem, we use a predictive approach to tracking as explained next.

3. PREDICTIVE TRACKING

The most important feature that will help us identify the right quadrilateral is that the transformations that happen to it in the 2D projected plane should correspond to valid transformations in the reverse projection (3D world). This can be ensured through two ways. One is to actually do the reverse projection and test after estimating the camera and projection matrices. There are a lot of algorithms that try to address the problem of estimating the camera and projection matrices from a set of points tracked across frames [4]. But these are computationally intensive and lead to huge delays in the processing pipeline. The easier and more efficient alternative is to look at the transformations in the 2D plane and, based on statistical reasoning, predict if the transformation can be a valid transformation in the 3D world from which the projection was done. We have experimented with the second option and found that it works very well.

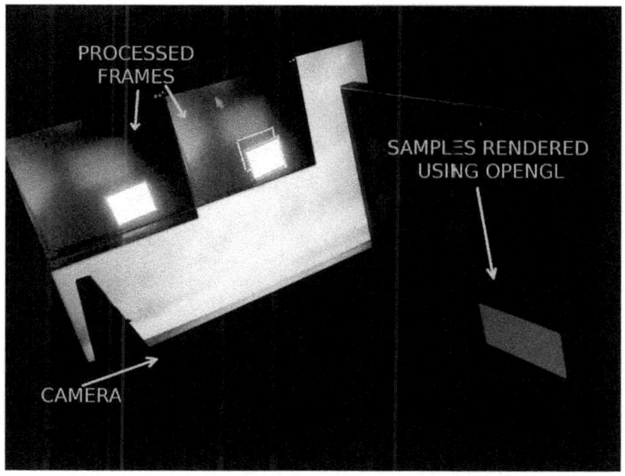

Figure 5: Experimental Setup

Experimental Setup.

We generated a big dataset automatically using openGL to generate valid projections of 3D transformations (translation and rotation) of rigid right quadrilaterals. The transformations were generated randomly to account for all variations that are possible in the real 3D space. These projections were captured through a camera and processed as described in Section 2. From the outputs of this process, feature values were extracted and the detected quadrilateral transformations were labeled as valid transformations. To generate the negative class samples, valid transformations were done but the objects were made to go beyond the boundary of the screen, leading to invalid, shear transformations.

For predicting the validity of a transformation as seen on the 2D plane in the 3D world, we used as features, values associated with the location of the corner points before the transformation and those after it. We normalize these values to ensure better predictability, train and run a support vector classifier [7, 2, 6] to predict the binary variable represented by validity of a transformation. The features we used for this purpose are the normalized corner positions, the angles at each corner, the lengths of the four sides and the support for each edge from the hough transform.

On top of this, to account for the human aspects, a part of the dataset, ~2000 data points were generated on actual human labeling of detected quadrilaterals of rectangular objects held by them in front of the camera.

Observations.

As can be seen from the results of the experiments (Figures 6 and 7) the SVMs are generalizing well. The cross validation accuracy peaks within 100-200 support vectors. The fall in accuracy beyond that shows overfitting while the lower accuracies before that shows lack of data points. The fact that ~100 support vectors is able to predict the labels for more than 12000 sample points with close to 100% accuracy shows that this process is indeed very powerful.

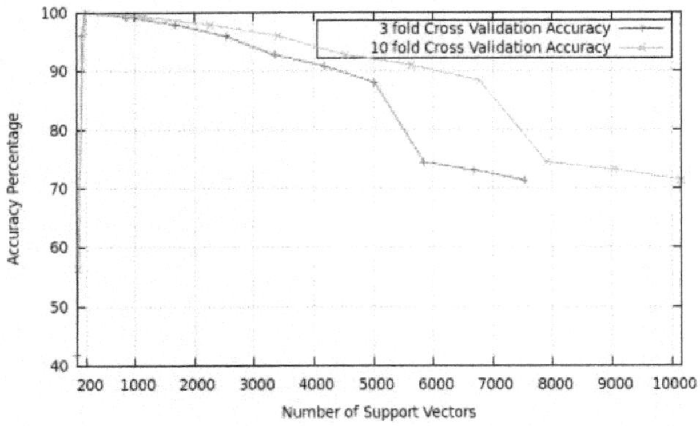

Figure 6: ν-SVM Accuracies with increasing no of SVs

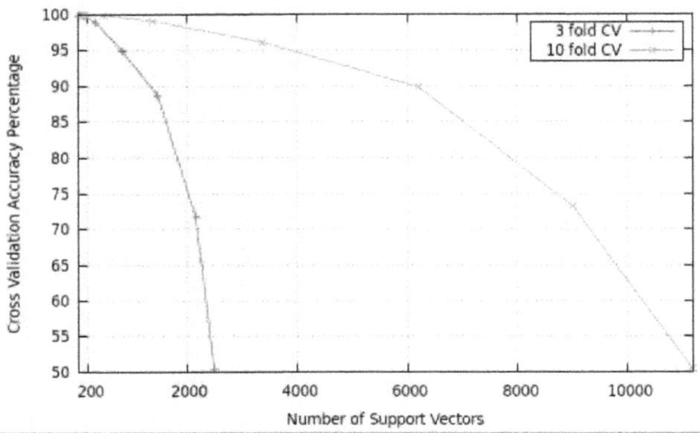

Figure 7: c-SVM Accuracies with increasing no of SVs

This SVM based approach in conjunction with the algorithm described in Section 2 provides a reliable mechanism that allows us to track the object of interest.

4. CONCLUSIONS

This paper presented an algorithm for sharing rectangular objects in a video conference. The object of interest is shared without any perspective distortion and without any jitter or motion artifacts. This work is part of a larger immersive communications project in our lab.

5. REFERENCES

[1] G. Bradski and A. Kaehler. *Learning OpenCV: Computer Vision with the OpenCV Library.* O'Reilly Media, 2008.

[2] C. J. C. Burges. A tutorial on support vector machines for pattern recognition. *Data Min. Knowl. Discov.*, 2(2):121–167, 1998.

[3] Y.-Y. Chuang, B. Curless, D. H. Salesin, and R. Szeliski. A bayesian approach to digital matting. *Proceedings of IEEE CVPR*, pages 264–271, 2001.

[4] S. J. Maybank and O. D. Faugeras. A theory of self-calibration of a moving camera. *International Journal of Computer Vision*, 8(2):123–151, 1992.

[5] C. Rother, V. Kolmogorov, and A. Blake. Grabcut - interactive foreground extraction using iterated graph cut. *Proceedings of ACM SIGGRAPH*, pages 309–314, 2004.

[6] B. Schölkopf, A. Smola, R. Williamson, and P. L. Bartlett. New support vector algorithms. NeuroCOLT Technical Report NC-TR-98-031, Royal Holloway College, University of London, UK, 1998. Published in Neural Computation 12(5):1207–1245, 2000.

[7] V. Vapnik. An overview of statistical learning theory. *IEEE Transactions on Neural Networks*, 10(5):988–999, 1999.

Biased Metric Learning for Person-Independent Head Pose Estimation*

Hao Ji[1], Fei Su[1,2]
[1] School of Information and Communication Engineering
[2] Beijing Key Laboratory of Network System and Network Culture
Beijing University of Posts and Telecommunications, Beijing, China
jihaogood@gmail.com, sufei@bupt.edu.cn

ABSTRACT

In this paper, a new biased metric learning (BML) method is proposed for human head pose estimation problem. Traditional approaches focus on modeling a smooth low-dimensional manifold embedded in the high-dimensional feature space. Such manifold-embedding methods, linear or nonlinear, suffer from one common drawback, that all neighbors are identified based on the Euclidean distance in the original feature space. However, the nature local structure of data is always corrupted by various factors in this original feature space. The proposed BML method aims at obtaining a global optimal linear transformation from the input feature space into a new semantic space which is characterized by pose angles. The metric is trained with the goal that local semantic structure of data with same label is preserved while the biased distance of differently labeled data is maximized. The learning process also reduces to a convex optimization by formulating it as a semidefinite problem (SDP). Numerous experiments demonstrate the superiority of our BML method over several current states of art approaches on publicly available dataset.

Categories and Subject Descriptors

I.4.9 [**Image Processing and Computer Vision**]: Applications; I.2.6 [**Artificial Intelligence**]: Learning; I.5.4 [**Pattern Recognition**]: Applications

General Terms

Algorithms, Experimentation

Keywords

Metric Learning, Semidefinite Programming, Human Head Pose Estimation

*Area chair: John Doe-add appropriate name

MM'11, November 28–December 1, 2011, Scottsdale, Arizona, USA.

1. INTRODUCTION

Human head pose estimation is a hot research topic in computer vision due to its significant role in many real applications. For examples, the estimation of head pose angle is always a first key in multi-view face recognition system [1]. Head pose estimation also plays an essential role in driver attention monitoring [2] and many human computer interaction (HCI) applications.

The existing methods for head pose estimation can be broadly divided into three categories [3]: (1) Template based method such as Active Appearance Model (AAM) is used to learn the primary modes of variation in shape to predict the head pose [4], which always suffers from poor facial features location with low resolution face images. (2) Classification based method divides head images into discrete pose classes [5], while the underlying order property of pose angle is lost in the classification process. (3) Manifold based method, currently state of the art method for head pose estimation , consider that each high-dimensional face image lies on a low-dimensional continuous manifold constrained by the pose variations [6].

Traditional manifold based methods, supervised or unsupervised, determine the target neighbors and the local structure by Euclidean distance in the feature space, which is always corrupted by various factors, such as illumination change, expression variation, different sampling strategy and image noise. The manifold constructed based on Euclidean distance in the original feature space can not reveal the nature structure of data .

Our work is inspired in part by the prowess of biased manifold framework [6] and the metric learning models [7]. The novelties and contributions of the proposed method are: (1) The process of pose estimation is transferred to the semantic space through a simple linear transformation, which yields much better results than in the original feature space. (2) The underling order property of pose angle is utilized to guide our learning process. For example, the relationship between samples labeled 1° and 2° is viewed different to the relationship between samples labeled 1° and 5°, this kind of order information is always lost in classification based methods. (3) The process of biased metric learning is formulated as a semidefinite problem (SDP) [8]. Since SDP is convex, global optimum is warranted.

The rest of this paper is organized as follows. Section 2 details our biased metric learning process. Extensive experiments on public database FacePix [9] are presented to show the robustness and superiority of our method over other

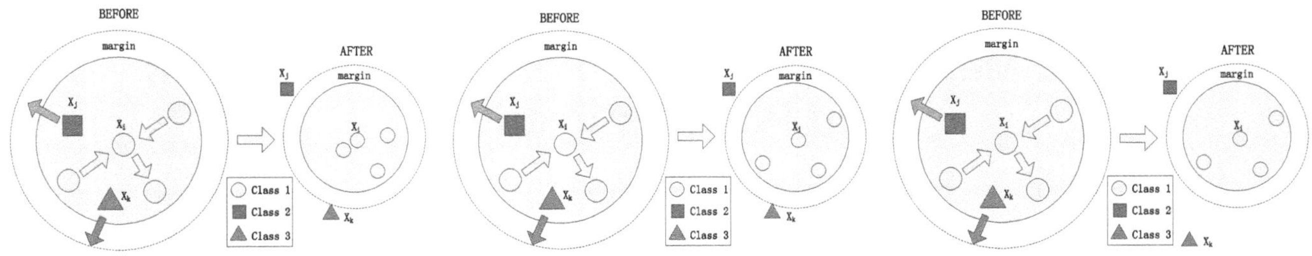

(a) Weinberger' s approach [9] (b) Xiao' s approach [13] (b) Our approach

Figure 1: Schematic illustration of the three different metric learning method. Each figure shows the situation of data from 3 classes before and after transformation. Here we only take one data $\mathbf{x}_i$'s neighborhood as example, the label difference $abs(y_i - y_k) > abs(y_i - y_j)$. Local structure of same labeled data is corrupted in figure (a), the order property is lost in figure (b), our BML method utilizes the order property while preserve the local structure shown in figure (c).

state-of-the-art methods in Section 3. Finally, Section 4 gives a conclusion.

2. BIASED METRIC LEARNING

2.1 Definition of Distance Metric Learning

Let $\{(\mathbf{x}_i, y_i)\}_{i=1}^n$ donate a training set of n labeled head images with $\mathbf{x}_i \in \mathbf{R}^d$ and discrete pose angle y_i. The goal of metric learning is to learn a linear transformation $\{\mathbf{L} : \mathbf{R}^d \rightarrow \mathbf{R}^d\}$, which we will use to compute distance between samples as:

$$D(\mathbf{x}_i, \mathbf{x}_j) = \|\mathbf{L}(\mathbf{x}_i - \mathbf{x}_j)\|_2. \tag{1}$$

We can also rewrite eq. (1) parameterized by Mahalanobis matrix $\mathbf{M}$ as:

$$D(\mathbf{x}_i, \mathbf{x}_j) = \|(\mathbf{x}_i - \mathbf{x}_j)\|_{\mathbf{M}} = \sqrt{(\mathbf{x}_i - \mathbf{x}_j)^T \mathbf{M} (\mathbf{x}_i - \mathbf{x}_j)}. \tag{2}$$

where $\mathbf{M} = \mathbf{L}^T\mathbf{L}$ and M is required to be positive semidefinite. In particular, Euclidean distances are recovered by setting $\mathbf{M}$ to be equal to identity matrix. In order to reduce the impact of various factors such as illumination change, expression variation and sampling strategy, we aim at learning a transformation from corrupted feature space to the semantic space which is characterized by labels of the data.

2.2 Biased Metric Learning

Balasubramanian et al. [6] proposed a biased manifold framework to estimate head poses. Distances are biased according to the difference between their labels, which have been demonstrated as an effective approach to construct the local structure of samples. The biased distance is defined as

$$\hat{d}(i,j) = f(i,j)d(i,j) = \left(\frac{P(i,j)+\beta}{max_{i,j}P(i,j)+\epsilon-P(i,j)}\right)^{\alpha} d(i,j) \tag{3}$$

where $f(i,j)$ is the biased coefficient, $P(i,j)$ is the absolute difference between the angle y_i and y_j, ϵ ensures the denominator not to be zero, α is a control parameter, β is the label noise, $d(i,j)$ is the Euclidean distance between $\mathbf{x}_i$ and $\mathbf{x}_j$. The biased coefficient $f(i,j)$ ensures small distance between similarly labeled samples, otherwise large distance. We aim at using this biased coefficient to guide our metric learning process to get improved estimation results.

Weinberger et al. [7] train the metric that pull target neighbors with same labels closer together while push differently labeled samples further apart. However, the interior nature structure of samples in the semantic space may be corrupted, which is illustrated in Fig.1(a). The structure of the same labeled samples (yellow circles) is damaged which is not a good choice for head pose estimation. Xiao et al. [10] find a way to keep the interior structure, but the order property of pose angle is lost. All samples with different labels are considered no difference to the target sample, the estimation process is reduced to a classification based program. Fig.1(b) shows this drawback that although samples from class2 (blue square) and class 3 (red triangle) have different pose angle, they are considered no difference to $\mathbf{x}_i$. In other words, misjudging the pose of $\mathbf{x}_i$ to class 2 or class 3 makes no difference, which will lead to deteriorated estimation results.

BML utilizes the order property of pose angle by incorporating biased coefficient in the metric learning process. Our goal is to maximize the local biased Mahalanobis distances between target object and its neighbors with different labels, while preserve the interior local structure of samples with same label in the semantic space. Fig.1(c) shows the transformation using BML. While the absolute difference $P(i,k) > P(i,j)$, which means $abs(y_i - y_k) > abs(y_i - y_j)$, the transformation will push $(\mathbf{x}_k)$ further than $(\mathbf{x}_j)$. This transformation will definitely improve the ultimate estimation results. So the biased metric learning task could be formulated as:

$$\boxed{\begin{gathered} \max \sum_{i,j} \varphi_{i,j} \|\mathbf{L}(\mathbf{x}_i - \mathbf{x}_j)\|^2 f(i,j) + \alpha \sum_{i,j} \phi_{i,j}\xi_{i,j} \\ s.t. \ \|\mathbf{L}(\mathbf{x}_i - \mathbf{x}_j)\|^2 + \xi_{i,j} = \hat{d}_{i,j}^2 \quad \phi_{i,j} = 1 \\ \xi_{i,j} >= 0 \end{gathered}} \tag{4}$$

where $f(i,j)$ is the biased coefficient, $\xi_{i,j}$ is a slack variable to enure the feasible set is not empty, $\hat{d}_{i,j}$ is the biased distance, $\{\phi_{i,j}, \varphi_{i,j}\} \in \{0,1\}$. $\phi_{i,j} = 1$ donate $\mathbf{x}_j$ locates in the neighborhoods of $\mathbf{x}_i$ with same label using the biased distance, otherwise $\phi_{i,j} = 0$. $\varphi_{i,j} = 1$ donate $\mathbf{x}_j$ locates in the neighborhoods of $\mathbf{x}_i$ with different label using the biased distance, otherwise $\varphi_{i,j} = 0$.

Recall that the distance metric learning can be stated in two ways: to learn a linear transformation $\mathbf{x}_i \rightarrow \mathbf{L}\mathbf{x}_i$ or, equivalently, to learn a Mahalanobis metric $\mathbf{M} = \mathbf{L}^T\mathbf{L}$. We may reformulate eq. 5 as convex optimization over the cone

Algorithm 1 Biased Metric Learning for Head Pose Estimation

Train Stage:

(1): Crop and scale-normalize each head image to certain size for train.

(2): Extract HOG features [11] from each normalized image to obtain $(\mathbf{x}_1, y_1), ..., (\mathbf{x}_N, y_n)$, where $\mathbf{x}_i$ is the feature vector and y_i is the corresponding pose angle.

(3): Identify neighborhoods of each sample using eq. 3 to get the local structure.

(4): Learn the biased metric $\mathbf{M} = \mathbf{L}^T\mathbf{L}$ by solving the SDP problem in eq. 5.

Test Stage:

(1): Crop and scale-normalize each head image to certain size for test.

(2): Extract HOG feature from each test image to obtain feature vectors $\mathbf{x}_{N+1}, ..., \mathbf{x}_{NN}$.

(3): Project test data from original feature space to the semantic space $\tilde{\mathbf{x}}_i = \mathbf{L}\mathbf{x}_i$.

(4): Estimate the pose angles of test data using KNN in the transformed space.

of positive semidefinite metric $\mathbf{M}$. So we obtain the loss function:

$$\begin{gathered} \max \sum_{i,j} \varphi_{i,j}(\mathbf{x}_i - \mathbf{x}_j)^T\mathbf{M}(\mathbf{x}_i - \mathbf{x}_j)f(i,j) + \alpha \sum_{i,j} \phi_{i,j}\xi_{i,j} \\ s.t.\ (\mathbf{x}_i - \mathbf{x}_j)^T\mathbf{M}(\mathbf{x}_i - \mathbf{x}_j) + \xi_{i,j} = \hat{d}^2_{i,j} \quad \phi_{i,j} = 1 \\ \xi_{i,j} >= 0 \\ \mathbf{M} \succeq 0 \end{gathered} \tag{5}$$

The function is convex and it is a standard semidefinite program (SDP). Several SDP packages can solve this kind of problem efficiently [12][13]. Algorithm 1 summarizes the whole procedure of BML for head pose estimation.

3. EXPERIMENTAL RESULTS

In this section, to demonstrate the efficiency of our proposed biased metric learning method, comprehensive experiments are conducted on FacePix database [9], a famous publicly available database for head pose estimation.All face images are scale-normalized to 60×60. HOG [11] is then used to extract the image features. Part of samples of the FacePix databases are shown in Fig.2. Mean Absolute Error (MAE) is used to evaluate the performance of the system by averaging the absolute difference between the estimated pose angle and the ground truth. Experimental results show that our algorithm indeed works stably and efficiently compared to other state of the arts methods.

3.1 Manifold Visualization

In order to check whether the biased metric can find the nature local structure of the data, we evaluate the performance of two famous manifold-embedding methods, Locally Linear Embedding (LLE) [14] and Laplacian Eigenmaps (LE) [15]. The local neighborhoods is constructed using the biased metric instead of Euclidean distances. 10 subjects's face images with pose variation between [-90°,+90°] at 4° increments are used to obtained the low-dimensional

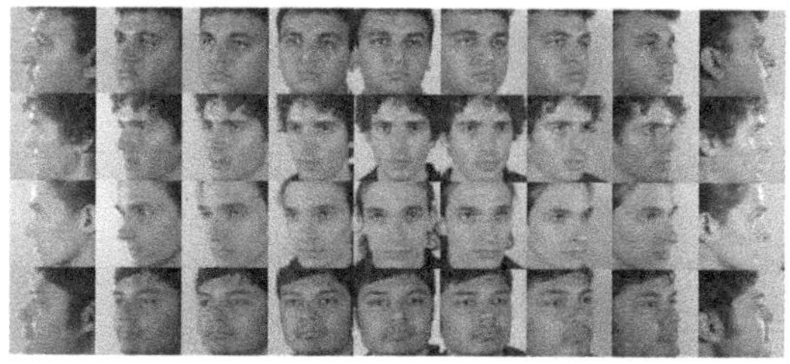

Figure 2: Sample images from the FacePix database.

manifold embedding. Fig.3 shows the 2-D and 3-D view of the manifold embedding using our biased metric. Apparently, both LLE and LE can discover an apparent trend of head pose angles.

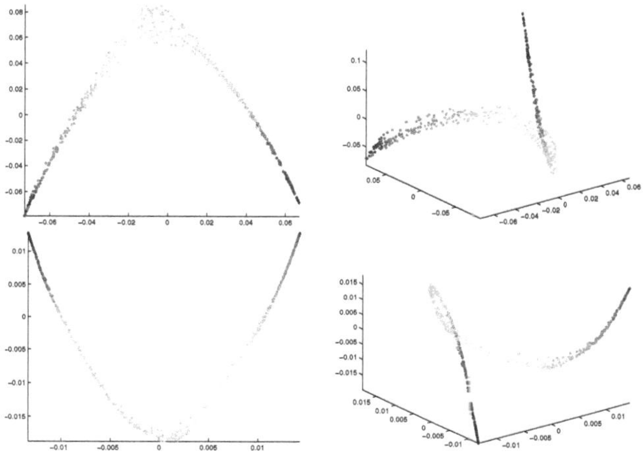

Figure 3: The manifold embedding of 10 subjects with pose variation between [-90°,+90°] at 4° increments. Biased metric is used to construct local neighborhoods. The first row shows the 2D and 3D manifold embedding of LLE. The bottom row shows the 2D and 3D manifold embedding of LE. The number of neighbors k is set to 20.

3.2 Quantitative evaluation

In this work, we considered a set of 2184 face images, consisting of 24 individuals (91 images per subject) with poses angles varying from -90° to +90° with increments of 2°. 21 subjects are used as training data, the rest are used as test data. The number of neighbors selected is uniformly fixed at 50. Fig. 4 shows the head pose estimation accuracy across the whole pose angles from -90° to +90° with increments of 2°.

We also compare our method with other five state-of-the-art methods for head pose estimation, such as Ridge Regression, Support Vector Regression [16], Graph Embedded Analysis [5], Biased Manifold Estimation [6] and Weighted KNN. RR is a linear regressor, SVR is nonlinear using RBF kernel. To test the robustness of methods to different sampling strategy, we sample data varying from -90° to +90° with different angle increments (2°, 4°, 6°, 8°, 10°). The quantitative results with different sampling strategy are presented in Table 1. With increasing sampling interval, most

Table 1: **Head pose estimation performances under different sampling strategy varying from 2° to 10° angle intervals.**

Pose Sampling Variation	2-degree	4-degree	6-degree	8-degree	10-degree
Ridge Regression	7.402	7.604	7.908	8.014	8.165
Support Vector Regression	5.682	6.120	6.420	6.614	7.088
Graph Embedded Analysis	3.483	7.851	8.151	8.751	9.991
Biased Manifold Estimation	3.088	4.171	5.271	5.679	6.462
Weighted KNN	4.363	3.951	3.858	3.418	2.923
Biased Metric Learning	**2.481**	**2.405**	**2.301**	**2.173**	**1.971**

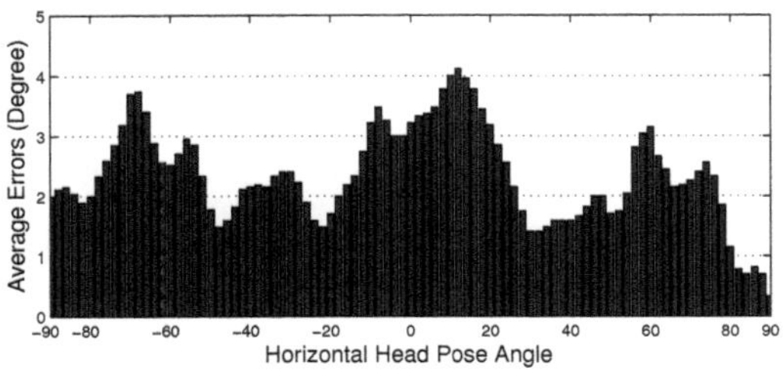

Figure 4: Average error of head pose estimation across -90° to +90°.

methods are influenced more or less and have an apparent performance decrease. KNN-based methods (WKNN and BML) seem robust to different sampling strategys. As sampling interval grows, the disparities of samples with different labels become large , which is good for KNN-based methods but always results in overfitting for regression-based methods. Our Biased Metric Learning method outperforms other methods apparently with lowest MAE.

4. CONCLUSIONS

In this paper, we propose a biased metric learning method for head pose estimation. By a linear transformation from feature space to the semantic space which characterized by head pose, even simple method such as KNN become quite competitive compared to other estimation methods. Local structure of same labeled data is preserved while biased distances between differently labeled data are maximized. We also formulate the problem as a semidefinite problem (SDP). Since SDP is convex, no local minima need to worry about. The experimental results on FacePix database demonstrate the robustness and superiority of our method over other state-of-the-art methods.

5. ACKNOWLEDGMENTS

This work is supported by the National Natural Science Foundation of China (90920001 and 61062012), the Scientific Research Foundation for the Returned Overseas Chinese Scholars, State Education Ministry, and the Fundamental Research Funds for the Central Universities.

6. REFERENCES

[1] J. Tu, T. Huang, and Y. Xiong, "Calibrating head pose estimation in videos for meeting room event analysis," *ICIP*, pp. 3193 – 3196, 2006.

[2] E. Murphy-Chutorian and M. Trivedi, "Head pose estimation for driver assistance systems: A robust algorithm and experimental evaluation," *Intelligent Transportation Systems*, pp. 709 – 714, 2007.

[3] E. Murphy-Chutorian and M. Trivedi, "Head pose estimation in computer vision: A survey," *TPAMI*, vol. 31, pp. 607 – 626, 2009.

[4] J. Xiao, S. Baker, I. Matthews, and T. Kanade, "Real-time combined 2d + 3d active appearance models," *CVPR*, pp. 709–714, 2004.

[5] Y. Fu and T. Huang, "Graph embedded analysis for head pose estimation," *AFGR*, pp. 3–8, 2006.

[6] V. Balasubramanian, J. Ye, and S. Panchanathan, "Biased manifold embedding: A framework for person-independent head pose estimation," *CVPR*, pp. 1–7, 2007.

[7] Q. Weinberger, J. Blitzer, and K. Saul, "Distance metric learning for large margin nearest neighbor classification," *NIPS*, 2006.

[8] L. Vandenberghe and S. Boyd, "Semidefinite programming," *SIAM Review*, pp. 49–95, 1996.

[9] D. Little, S. Krishna, J. Black, and S. Panchanathan, "A methodology for evaluating robustness of face recognition algorithms with respect to variations in pose angle and illumination angle," *ICASSP*, vol. 2, pp. 89–92, 2005.

[10] B. Xiao, X. Yang, Y. Xu, and H. Zha, "Learning distance metric for regression by semidefinite programming with application to human age estimation," *MM*, 2009.

[11] N. Dalal and B. Triggs, "Histograms of oriented gradients for human detection," *CVPR*, vol. 1, pp. 886–893, 2005.

[12] D. B. Borchers, "a c library for semidefinite programming," *Optimization Methods and Software*, vol. 11, pp. 613–623, 1999.

[13] J. F. Sturm, "Using sedumi 1.02, a matlab toolbox for optimization over symmetric cones," *Optimization Methods and Software*, vol. 11, pp. 625–653, 1999.

[14] S. Roweis and L. Saul, "Nonlinear dimensionality reduction by locally linear embedding," *Science*, pp. 2323–2326, 2000.

[15] M. Belkin and P. Niyogi, "Laplacian eigenmaps for dimensionality reduction and data representation," *Journal of Neural Computation*, vol. 15, pp. 1373–1396, 2003.

[16] E. Murphy-Chutorian and M. Trivedi, "Head pose estimation for driver assistance systems: A robust algorithm and experimental evaluation," *Intelligent Transportation Systems*, pp. 709–714, 2007.

Next Photo Please: Towards Visually Consistent Sequential Photo Browsing*

Dong Liu
School of Computer Sci.& Tec.
Harbin Institute of Technology
Harbin 150001, P. R. China
dongliu.hit@gmail.com

Shuicheng Yan
Department of ECE
National Univ. of Singapore
Singapore 117576, Singapore
eleyans@nus.edu.sg

Hong-Jiang Zhang
Microsoft Adv. Tech. Center
49 Zhichun Road
Beijing 100080, P. R. China
hjzhang@microsoft.com

ABSTRACT

Sequential photo browsing has become the most important function in the desktop and online image repository management systems, where existing systems typically display the photos in default orders such as the lexicographic order of the photo filename or the chronological order of the photo taken time. However, these browsing orders, especially when the browsing speed is fast, ignore the vision persistency characteristic of human visual systems, which results in inconsistent visual experience for photo viewers. To address this issue, we construct a photo relationship graph based on various kinds of visual features that complementarily reflect human visual perception. Then the seeking of visually consistent photo browsing sequence is cast into a traveling salesman problem which seeks an optimal path with minimum visual distance within the graph structure. Experiment results on sequential browsing of Flickr photo groups indicate that the proposed method clearly beats the other sequential photo browsing methods in terms of visual consistency.

Categories and Subject Descriptors

H.5.2 [**Information Interfaces and Presentation**]: User Interfaces

General Terms

Performance, Experimentation, Human Factors

Keywords

Vision Persistency, Sequential Photo Browsing, TSP

1. INTRODUCTION

Increasing popularity of digital cameras and mobile photo cameras has resulted in gigabytes of digital photos sitting on our storage devices or on the web. People take photos to record their lives easily with one-click shot and the cost of taking and storing a photo has been reduced to be zero. As a result, digital photos are becoming part of our daily lives.

Typically, digital photos are testimonials of the events, scenes or objects in our lives, which are used to refresh our memories about the life experiences. It is therefore becoming increasingly important to provide good support for the photo owners to browse the photo collections. Currently, the popular commercial desktop photo management softwares such as ACDSee [1] and Microsoft Digital Image Suite [2] all provide user-friendly interface for photo browsing. Besides, photo browsing has also become a key ingredient of the online photo sharing systems such as Flickr [3] and Picasa [4]. There are mainly two paradigms for browsing photo collections in current systems. In the first paradigm, the users are presented with a set of photos in a two-dimensional grid of thumbnails on the screen. However, it can only display photos using thumbnail (miniature) versions and thus prevents the users from the content details of the individual photos. The second paradigm further overcomes the above drawback by displaying photos with their original resolutions in a sequential manner, which has become the most important photo browsing approach in current systems.

The key issue in the sequential photo browsing is the browsing order of the photo sequence, where the existing systems typically display the photos in a collection in one of the following manners: (1) the lexicographic order of the photo filename; (2) the chronological order of the photo taken time. However, these browsing orders totally ignore the *persistence of vision* characteristic [5] of human visual perception systems, which is closely related with visual experience of human beings. Persistence of vision is the phenomenon of the eye by which an afterimage is thought to persist on the retina. That is to say, if an user views an image at one time point, the appearance of the image will continue to have a visual stimuli on the user's biological vision system. The ignorance of this property in sequential photo browsing may cause inconsistent visual experience for the photo viewers, especially when the photos are browsed in a fast speed. As an example, Figure 1(a) illustrates a photo browsing sequence from Flickr[1]. From the figure we can observe that the photos in the browsing sequence are not consistent in the visual contents, and bring abrupt visual variations to the photo viewers.

The issues associated with the existing sequential image browsing methods motivate us to develop visually consistent method to enhance user's visual experience in sequential photo browsing. The photos in Figure 1(a) show a com-

*Area chair: Mor Naaman

[1] http://www.flickr.com/groups/640498@N21/pool/show

MM'11, November 28–December 1, 2011, Scottsdale, Arizona, USA.

Figure 1: (a) A photo browsing sequence from Flickr. As can be seen, the displaying order is not smooth in terms of visual consistency. (b) A visually consistent photo browsing sequence that orders the displayed photos based on visual contents.

pelling example of where we can improve the visual consistency of the photo browsing sequence. Although the sequence is not optimal in terms of visual consistency, each photo has its visual neighbors in the sequence. If we align the photos in the sequence based on their visual similarities, the subsequent photos will become more smooth in terms of visual consistency, which can be illustrated in Figure 1(b). Finding the visual consistency between the photos and align them accordingly is the basis of the photo browsing method proposed in this paper.

There are two main difficulties in finding visually consistent photo browsing sequence. The first is the image processing required. Note that the images in a collection may have an entirely separate set of visual features that are common among the whole collection, which have a great impact on the visual similarity/distance estimation. For example, some images are similar in terms of color features while others are similar with respect to texture features. Therefore, we look for different kinds of visual features to complementarily reflect the properties of human visual perception.

The second difficulty is that even after we estimate the image similarities/distances based on complementary visual features, we still need a mechanism to seek a photo browsing sequence that reflects visual consistency. Towards this goal, we infer a photo relationship graph, where the photos are linked to each other based on their visual distance. Then the visually consistent photo sequence seeking task can be intuitively cast into a Traveling Salesman Problem (TSP) [6] since we are looking for an optimal path in a connected graph where each vertex (image) has to be visited (ordered) exactly once. We will show that this method can effectively construct visually consistent photo browsing sequence that enhances user's visual experience in photo browsing.

The main contributions of this paper are as follows:

- We propose a visually consistent sequential photo browsing method to visualize the photos in an collection. As our best knowledge, this is the first effort towards improving visual consistency issues in sequential photo browsing.
- We propose to use complementary visual features to construct a graph between the images. We also employ the TSP solver to seek an optimal path in the graph as the desired photo browsing sequence that reflects visual consistency.

2. RELATED WORK

Our work is first related to the visualization methods in image browsing applications. Several research efforts have been dedicated to improve the user's experience in image browsing. Combs et al. [7] have proposed a zoomable user interface to make better use of screen space than the generally applied scrolling. Rodden et al. [8] have further investigate whether it benefits the users to have the sets of thumbnail images arranged according to their mutual visual similarities. The arrangements are created using the multidimensional scaling (MDS) algorithm which treats the inter-object dissimilarities in some high dimensional space, and then attempts to approximate them in a low dimensional output space. Despite these efforts have shown encouraging results, we can see that they only focus on organizing a collection of thumbnail images in a two-dimensional grid plane, whereas there is still a severe lack regrading improving user's experience in sequential photo browsing.

From the aspect of seeking an order from a given image collection, our method is slightly related to the image ranking works in the image retrieval discipline. For example, Jing et al. [9] have proposed the VisualRank algorithm, relying on analyzing the visual link structures among the images, to rank the returned image set of text queries. Liu et al. [10] have constructed the relevance between the tags and the image contents, and utilized the tag relevance information to rank image search result of the tag queries. The focus of these works is to differentiate the images that are relevant to the query keywords from those that are irrelevant, which, however, is essentially different from the sequential photo browsing method introduced in this work, where the images are ranked in term of visual consistency.

3. OUR APPROACH

In this section, we cast the seeking of visually consistent photo browsing sequence into a TSP problem on a graph structure. We first discuss the low-level representations for the images, and then present how TSP can be utilized to seek an optimal path in the graph structure.

3.1 Feature Representations

As aforementioned, the individual low-level features for representing the images in a collection, when used alone, are often too restrictive for the breadth of image contents that need to be handled. Therefore, we turn to the complementary features instead. More specifically, we represent each image with a 418-dimensional feature vector composed of three kinds of low-level global visual features. The first is color moments over 5×5 fixed grid partitions [11], where the first 3 moments of 3 channels of CIE Luv color space are extracted, which results in a 255-dimensional feature vector per image. The second is Gabor texture [12] where we take 8 scales and 8 orientations of Gabor transformation and further use their means and standard deviations to represent the whole image which results in 128-dimensional feature vector. The third is a 75-dimensional edge direction histogram [13], which is taken as the line direction distribution of an image and represents the global information of shape in an image.

3.2 Browsing Sequence Seeking as TSP

We now formulate the seeking of visually consistent photo browsing sequence as a TSP. Assume we are given an image collection $\mathcal{X} = \{x_1, x_2, \ldots, x_N\}$ where N denotes the total number of images. We first construct a salesman graph G. To do this, we set up a city i for each image $x_i \in \mathcal{X}$. For graph adjacency construction, we aim to build up the edge linkages between the city vertices. Given two city vertices i and j, and their corresponding low-level feature representations x_i and x_j, we are to put one edge if and only if the two cities are nearby enough. In this work, we employ the mutual k-nearest neighbor strategy to create the nearby relationship between the cities. Specifically, two cities i and j are linked with an edge if image x_i is among the k nearest neighbors of image x_j and vice versa. Here the k nearest neighbors are measured by Euclidean distance and the parameter k is fixed as 50. Note that the adjacent relations defined above are symmetric and consequently the constructed adjacent salesman graph is undirected.

The next task is to establish the real-valued (symmetric) distances between any pair of cities, which represent the pairwise visual dissimilarities between the images. In this work, we associate the edge between vertices i and j with a dissimilarity measure d_{ij}, which is calculated as follows,

$$d_{ij} = \begin{cases} \|x_i - x_j\|^2, & \text{if i and j are connected,} \\ +\infty, & \text{otherwise,} \end{cases} \tag{1}$$

where x_i and x_j denote the low-level features of the two images and $\|\cdot\|$ denotes the ℓ_2 norm.

The goal of TSP is to find a *Hamiltonian cycle*, i.e., a sequence which visits each vertex (city) in the graph exactly once and then returns to the starting vertex, with the least weight in the graph [6]. Formally, we define a tour of cities (images) as a cyclic sequence π of cities $\{1, 2, \ldots, N\}$ where $\pi(i)$ represents the city that follows the city i on the tour. The TSP problem is then formulated as the optimization problem to find a permutation π that minimizes the length of the tour defined by

$$\min \sum_{i=1}^{N} d_{i\pi(i)}. \tag{2}$$

For this minimization task, the tour length of $(N-1)!$ permutation vectors have to be compared. This results in a problem which is very hard to solve and in fact known to be NP-complete problem [14]. To find the optimal tour, Held et al. [15] present a dynamic approach to solve the TSP, an optimization problem that is defined as follows: Given a subset of city vertices (excluding the first city) $S \subset \{2, 3, \ldots, N\}$ and $l \in S$, let $d^*(S, l)$ denote the length of the shortest path from city 1 to city l, visiting all cities in S in-between. For $S = \{l\}$, $d^*(S, l)$ is defined as d_{1l}. Then the shortest path for larger sets with $|S| > 1$ is

$$d^*(S, l) = \min_{m \in S \backslash \{l\}} \left(d^*(S \backslash \{l\}, m) + d_{ml}\right). \tag{3}$$

Finally, the minimal tour length for a complete tour which includes returning to city 1 is

$$d^{**} = \min_{l \in \{2,3,\ldots,N\}} \left(d^*(\{2, 3, \ldots, N\}, l) + d_{l1}\right). \tag{4}$$

Using the last two equations, the quantities $d^*(S, l)$ can be computed recursively and the minimal tour length d^{**} can be found. In a second step, the optimal permutation $\pi = \{1, i_2, i_3, \ldots, i_N\}$ of city vertices 1 through N can be computed in reverse order, starting with i_N and working successively back to i_2. The procedure exploits the fact that a permutation π can only be optimal, if

$$d^{**} = d^*(\{2, 3, \ldots, N\}, i_N) + d_{i_N,1} \tag{5}$$

and, for $2 \le p \le N-1$

$$d^*(\{i_2, i_3, \ldots, i_p, i_{p+1}\}, i_{p+1}) = d^*(\{i_2, i_3, \ldots, i_p\}, i_p) + d_{i_p, i_{p+1}}. \tag{6}$$

Because the images are linked together in a graph via complementary visual features that reflect human visual perception, the shortest tour found by TSP solver will correspond to a smooth image sequence in which the subsequent images are visually consistent, which essentially improves the visual experience in sequential image browsing.

Table 1: The details of the photo groups.

Name	Photo #	Name	Photo #
Germany	163	Widelife	1,221
Korea	493	Sunrise	286
Nature	183	London	204
New York	157	Thailand	500
Paris	265	Manasquan	333
Exposure	185	Shanghai	365
Bombay	719	China	500
HongKong	136	NewBook	157

4. EXPERIMENTS

In this section, we conduct extensive experiments to evaluate the performance of the proposed sequential photo browsing method by comparing it with the other sequential photo browsing methods.

4.1 Datasets and Methodologies

We perform the experiments on 16 public photo sharing groups[2] that are collected from Flickr. These photo sharing groups are captured by different people at different locations around the world and contain diverse visual contents, including cityscape, landscape, wide life, etc. Table 1 illustrates the detailed information of these albums. To evaluate the performance of the visually consistent sequential photo browsing method, we employ the following two sequential photo browsing methods as comparison baselines.

- Browsing the photos in each photo group based on the lexicographic order of photo filename, which will be referred to as *browsing by filename.*
- Browsing the photos based on Affinity Propagation (AP) clustering algorithm [16]. For each photo group, we first employ the AP clustering algorithm to divide the photos into a number of clusters. Then the photo browsing sequence can be obtained in a two-step manner: (1) For each cluster, we calculate the average value of all pairwise distances between the images in the cluster and then order the clusters according to the obtained values. (2) The images within each cluster can be ordered according to their distances to the cluster center. We name this method as *browsing by AP* in the experiment.

[2]http://www.flickr.com/groups/

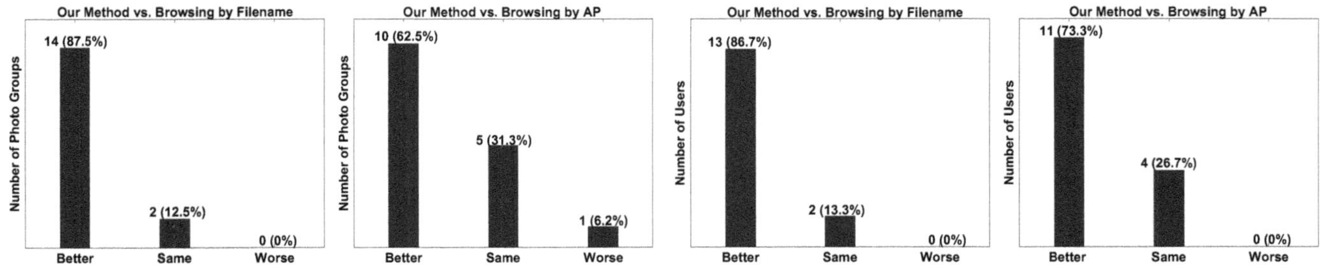

(a) Per-Group Evaluation (b) Overall Evaluation

Figure 2: (a) Per-group comparisons between our proposed and browsing by filename and browsing by AP methods on the 16 photo sharing groups. (b) Overall comparison between our proposed method and the other two browsing methods from the 15 users.

For each photo group in Table 1, we use both the two baseline methods and our proposed method to generate photo browsing sequences. Therefore, there are totally 48 (3×16) photo browsing sequences for evaluation. To validate the performance of each photo browsing method, we resort to a human judgement procedure. We invite 15 graduate students to view each photo browsing sequence and accordingly manually label the visual consistency. To simulate the fast browsing in real scenarios, we arrange the browsing as a dynamic sequence where the time interval between two subsequent images is 0.1 seconds. Since it is impractical to ask the evaluators to views hundreds or even thousands photos in a photo group at a time, we only provide a fragment of the photo sequence, which consists of the top 20, median 20 and last 20 photos in the given photo sequence, for displaying. To avoid the bias on the evaluation, the participants do not have any prior knowledge about the method adopted by this work.

We provide two evaluation approaches to justify the performance of three sequential photo browsing methods. (1) Per-group evaluation. In this approach, based on the comparisons of the photo browsing sequences generated by our proposed method and the browsing by filename (or browsing by AP) method, the human evaluators are asked to assign score "2", "1" or "0" to indicate that our proposed method performs better, same and worse than the browsing by filename (browsing by AP), respectively. (2) Overall evaluation. After viewing the photo browsing sequences on all photo groups, the evaluators are asked to make overall comparisons between the proposed method and other two browsing methods. They are asked to judge whether the proposed method works "better" (score 2), "same" (score 1) or "worse" (score 0) than the other sequential photo browsing method.

4.2 Experimental Results and Analysis

The evaluation results for the 15 users are illustrated in Figure 2. In Figure 2(a), we present the average number of the photo groups which have score "2", "1" or "0" assigned by the human evaluators. Form the figure, we can have the following observations. (1) The visually consistent sequential photo browsing method performs better than the browsing by filename method over 14 groups, closely over 2 groups and worse on 0 group. This clearly demonstrates the effectiveness of exploiting visual content information in the task of sequential photo browsing. (2) Comparing to the browsing by AP method, the proposed method performs better over 10 groups, closely over 5 groups and worse only over 1 group, which owes to the fact that the TSP algorithm is able to obtain optimized photo sequence for browsing. Figure 2(b) shows the overall evaluation results. All 15 users consider the proposed method performs no worse than the other two sequential photo browsing methods. Specifically, 86.7% and 73.3% users report that the proposed method is better than the other counterpart.

5. CONCLUSIONS

We have introduced a visually consistent sequential photo browsing method that displays the photos in a sequence in terms of visual consistency. Based on an image relationship graph constructed with complementary visual features, the seeking of visually consistent photo browsing sequence is cast in a traveling salesman problem over the graph structure. Experiment results on real Flickr photo groups have confirmed the effectiveness of the proposed method. For future work, we will apply the proposed photo browsing method into the application of photo-to-video transformation, which will be a promising method to enhance the visual consistency in the video contents.

6. REFERENCES

[1] ACDSee. http://www.acdsee.com/.
[2] Microsoft Digital Image Suite. http://www.microsoft.com/products/imaging.
[3] Flickr. http://www.flickr.com.
[4] Picasa. http://picasa.google.com.
[5] A. Joseph and B. Fisher. The Myth of Persistence of Vision. *Journal of the University Film Association*, 30(4), 1978.
[6] E. Lawler, J. Lenstra, A. Kan and D. Shmoy. The Traveling Salesman Problem. *Wiley*, 1985.
[7] T. Combs and B. Bederson. Does Zooming Improve Image Browsing? In *ICDL*, 1999.
[8] K. Rodden, W. Basalaj, D. Sinclair and K. Wood. Does Organisation by Similarity Assist Image Browsing? In *CHI*, 2001.
[9] Y. Jing and S. Baluja. VisualRank: Applying PageRank to Large-Scale Image Search. *TPAMI*, 30(11), 2008.
[10] D. Liu, X.-S. Hua, L. Yang, M. Wang and H.-J. Zhang. Tag Ranking. In *WWW*, 2009.
[11] M. Stricker and M. Orengo. Similarity of Color Images. In *SPIE*, 1995.
[12] B. Manjunath and W.-Y. Ma. Texture Features for Browsing and Retrieval of Image Data. *TPAMI*, 18(8), 1996.
[13] A. Vailaya, A. Jain and H.-J. Zhang. On Image Classification: City Images vs. Landscapes. *PR*, 31(12), 1998.
[14] D. Johnson and C. Papadimitriou. Computational Complexity, 2009.
[15] M. Held and R. Karp. A Dynamic Programming Approach to Sequencing Problems. *Journal of SIAM*, 1962.
[16] B. Frey and D. Dueck. Clustering by Passing Messages between Data Points. *Science*, 315(5418), 2007.

Towards Understanding User Tolerance to Network Latency in Zoomable Video Streaming*

Ngo Quang Minh Khiem Guntur Ravindra Wei Tsang Ooi
Department of Computer Science
National University of Singapore
Singapore 117417
{nqmkhiem,ravindra,ooiwt}@comp.nus.edu.sg

ABSTRACT

We conducted a user study with 35 participants viewing 5 video clips to understand user tolerance to network latency when zooming and panning in zoomable video streams. With zooming or panning, unseen spatial regions in a frame are revealed and momentarily in an unknown state until data arrive from the server. To handle such unknown state, two common concealment schemes are used, namely Black scheme and Low-Res scheme. Black scheme renders the newly revealed region as black pixels, while Low-Res covers the unknown part with data from a low resolution video stream, which is additionally streamed by the server. In the context of these schemes, our study based on the simulation of delays shows that users are more tolerable to delay in Low-Res scheme. Up to 94% of participants can tolerate 1 second delay and 80% can tolerate up to a delay of 2 seconds in Low-Res scheme, while only 77% of participants can tolerate 1 second delay in Black scheme. The tolerable delay in zoomable video streaming is higher than thresholds found in some high interactive multimedia applications.

Categories and Subject Descriptors: H.5.1 [Multimedia Information Systems]: Evaluation H.4.3[Communications Applications]: Video

General Terms: Experimentation, Human Factors

Keywords: Zoomable Video, Delay Tolerance, Network Latency, Region-of-Interest Streaming, Concealment Scheme

1. INTRODUCTION

For the past few years, the proliferation of digital video cameras has widely enabled the capturing and publishing of High-Definition (HD) videos (1920x1080 pixels). Consumers, however, are increasingly watching videos on mobile devices that have limited screen size and display resolution. Due to the mismatch between captured and displayed resolutions, many of captured details are lost or cannot be clearly seen. This fact has led to the introduction of new interactions namely *zoom and pan* in video playback.

Zoomable video allows users to zoom and pan around a video to watch a Region-of-Interest (RoI) at a higher resolution. Support for zooming and panning during video playback is easily achieved if videos are stored locally. We, however, are interested in supporting zooming and panning in the *streaming* context. When the client zooms in/out or moves a RoI, data corresponding to the new RoI co-ordinates needs to be fetched. Due to network latency, when users request for a RoI, they may experience a delay, between the instant the RoI changes and instant the data for the new RoI arrives.

In the server-client architecture, network latency is dominated by round-trip time while in peer-to-peer architecture, delay is due to various components which are influenced by protocol design. An attempt to characterize users' interactions with zoomable video was presented in [3]. One of the findings in that paper was that users actively and frequently interact (zoom/pan) with zoomable video. It was shown that 70% of the time the user interactions were spaced less than 1.6 seconds apart. In such cases, users may frequently experience a long waiting time before the new requested RoI arrives for viewing. Being kept waiting for every interaction may cause users to feel annoyed and lose interest in trying to use zooming or panning. Hence, the ultimate goal of zoomable video streaming system would be defeated.

Motivation. Past research on zoomable video has focused on encoding of zoomable video to support dynamic cropping of RoIs and understanding the influence of encoding parameters on zoomable video [7]. There is, however, no comprehensive study of users' tolerance to network latency in streaming of zoomable video. Such understanding is important since it can help in designing a system that is more responsive to frequent user interaction. Knowing tolerance levels to network delay helps us decide whether prefetching and caching are necessary for a streaming system of zoomable videos. For instance, if users can only tolerate a very low network delay (e.g., less than 1 second), prefetching or caching may be necessary to improve response time. In the context of peer-to-peer streaming of zoomable video, knowing maximum user tolerance to delay, we can build a better peer-to-peer streaming protocol for requesting or disseminating data of RoIs among the peers.

Approach. Being aware of the importance of understanding users' tolerance to network latency, we conducted a user study with 35 participants. The goal was to measure users' tolerable delay in two commonly used concealment schemes. The two concealment schemes attempt to minimize the wait time in response to a change in RoI. In the absence of the concealment scheme, the user interface waits for data belonging to the new RoI to arrive. During that interval, the video frame is frozen there by resulting in an unpleasant user experience. The concealment schemes attempt to quickly respond to a change in RoI. The first scheme moves the RoI to the new position as soon as user requests for a change. Newly revealed regions are rendered in 'black' as the data for these regions has not

*Area chair: Hari Sundaram

MM'11, November 28–December 1, 2011, Scottsdale, Arizona, USA.

yet arrived. Once the data arrives, these regions are rendered with the correct pixel values. We refer to this scheme as *Black*. The second concealment scheme relies on the existence of a low resolution video stream which is always streamed by the server. In response to a change in RoI, the newly revealed regions are rendered with data from the low resolution stream. Once the requested data arrives , these new regions are displayed at the correct resolution. We refer to this scheme as *Low-Res*. Using these two schemes, we study user tolerance to delay in the context of zoomable video streaming.

The rest of our paper is organized as follows. Related work is discussed in Section 2. We describe our zoomable video interface, two concealment schemes in Section 3 and details of experiments in Section 4. Results of the user study are presented and discussed in Section 5. We conclude our paper in Section 6.

2. RELATED WORK

User tolerance to network latency and its effects has been well studied for many networked multimedia applications. ITU-T G.114 standards suggest that an end-to-end delay of at most 400 ms is recommended for general network planning [1].

In the context of streaming of progressive meshes, most users can tolerate up to 1 second of delay when the data rate is sufficiently high (100 KBps) [4]. The reason for such high tolerable delay is due to the progressive nature of this application.

User tolerance to network latency and its effects in multi-player networked games has also been studied. Game genre differ in game nature and user interaction models, so does the user tolerance to delay. For Real Time Strategy (RTS) games which emphasize more on strategy, a study with the popular game Warcraft III found that users feel the smoothness for latencies between 0 ms and 500 ms. They start perceiving a degrade in game experience at some point between 500 ms and 800 ms [8]. For MMORPGs, a study with EverQuest 2 found that the game still runs smoothly with very high latency of 1250 ms [6]. For first person shooting, a study with the Unreal Tournament 2003 game has shown that a delay of 100 ms is noticeable while network latency of 200 ms is annoying [2].

3. ZOOMABLE VIDEO PLAYER

In this section we describe the zoomable video interface and two concealment schemes we used for the user study.

3.1 Zoomable Video Interface

We have previously implemented a web-based video player that allows users to zoom and pan around a High Definition (HD) video viewed in a small display. Figure 1 shows a screenshot of the zoomable video interface. On top is the main video display of small size 320x180, which simulates the scenario of watching a video under resource constraints (e.g., mobile devices with small screen size). A thumbnail window of size 160x90 is displayed in the bottom-left corner of the interface. The thumbnail view always shows a scaled-down version of the source video to provide users with the context of a RoI. The small rectangle on the thumbnail depicts a RoI. The region outside this small rectangle is made transparent so that the selected RoI more visible. The bottom-right corner of the interface shows control buttons for users to zoom in/out or move the RoI. Panning can also be done by dragging on the main display window, or clicking on the thumbnail display, while zooming is also possible with scroll wheel of a mouse.

Our zoomable interface can support six different zoom levels (0 to 5). The smallest zoom level 0 (by default) is equivalent to viewing the whole original video (1920x1080) at the display size 320x180 and hence, at the lowest level of detail. Watching a RoI

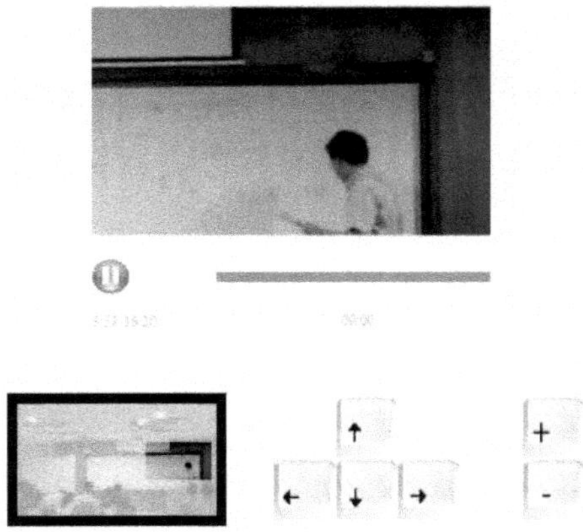

Figure 1: Snapshot of Zoomable Video Interface

at higher zoom level is equivalent to cropping a RoI at higher resolution and scaling it down to fit the display size of 320x180. For instance, at zoom level 5, a region of size 320x180 is cropped from original video and displayed. At level 4, a cropped region of size 640x360 from original video is scaled down to fit the main display.

3.2 Concealment Schemes

In this section, we explain in more detail the concealment schemes for which we measure the users' delay tolerance. When zooming or panning to change a RoI, a client sends the request and waits for the data of the new RoI to arrive. New RoI and the previous RoI may be overlapping. If so, part of the new RoI can be obtained from the previous RoI. Both *Black* and *Low-Res* concealment schemes maintain the continuity in viewing experience of users by displaying parts of RoI with data already available. In case the overlapping region comes from a RoI at different zoom level, upscaling or downscaling is necessary before rendering. Specifically, when users pan, the new RoI remains at the same resolution as the previous RoI. The overlapping part only needs to be re-located at its relative position within the new RoI on main display. In the case of zooming in, i.e., viewing a sub-region of current RoI at higher details, that sub-region of current RoI (at lower zoom level) is scaled up. With zooming out, i.e., viewing a larger RoI that contains the current RoI, the current RoI is scaled down and re-located at its correct position in the new RoI on the display.

The difference between Black and Low-Res concealment schemes lies in how they *conceal unavailable* parts of new RoI. Black scheme maintains the simplicity by rendering newly revealed part as region of black pixels while waiting for new data to come. Low-Res scheme, however, requires the additional transmission of thumbnail video, which is a very low resolution version of the original video (shown at the bottom left of our interface). Thumbnail video requires much less bandwidth and hence, should be readily available at client sides. Low-Res scheme covers any unfilled part of new RoI with pixels upscaled from the corresponding region of thumbnail video. Figure 2 illustrates how two schemes fill up the newly revealed region for each interaction (pan to move RoI to the right, zoom in and zoom out). Note that in the case of zooming in, there is no any newly revealed region. Regions seen as black in Black scheme appear blur in Low-Res scheme. It is due to the scaling up of pixels from thumbnail video.

In both schemes, users can still experience the smoothness when zooming or panning although they may see some blurring or blacking effects. By providing the responsiveness, we believe users' experience of delay is becoming less painful. We conducted a user study described in the following sections to understand how users tolerate delays in Black and Low-Res concealment schemes.

4. USER STUDY

Video Clips. In this user study, we are using five different video clips captured by a HD camera. There are three videos of magic tricks (*Clock, Transfer, Dice*), one video of gymnastics performance (*Gym*) and one video of lecture (*Lecture*). In magic clips, the magician performs various tricks with the dices and the cards. For gymnastics video, a team of gymnasts perform on the floor of an indoor stadium. The lecture video captures a lesson in a university classroom where the lecturer uses the whiteboard to write notes. Participants can use our zoomable video interface to zoom or pan around in these videos to watch some region at higher resolutions. For example, the number on a dice or a card, the face or the movement of a gymnast, hand-writing of the lecturer on the whiteboard, etc. The camera is fixed and static in all clips. Videos are encoded with high quality to ensure the good viewing experience of RoIs at different zoom levels. Length of videos is about 3 to 5 minutes except lecture video of 16 minutes.

Experimental Setup. We conducted the user study on a PC with an Intel Core 2 Quad CPU 9550 at 2.83 GHz, 3 GB of RAM and running Windows XP. Firefox 3.6 browser was used to open the web-based player. All experiments were done in our research lab. The machine was connected to our central server. Test clips were pre-downloaded and stored on the local machine. This was to make sure the simulated delay was totally under our control and not affected by the actual network delay.

The simulation of effects of network latency in our system when users zoom or pan was implemented in the video player itself. Specifically, the video player delays the rendering of entire frames of newly requested RoI and shows only available parts of RoI instead. The entire frames are displayed after the delay expires.

Pilot Study. Before the actual user study, we conducted a pilot study with 8 users to find out the proper range of delay. We observed that most of these users rejected all test cases with delays over 4 seconds and none of them could distinguish among the delays below 1 second.

Experiment Parameters. Based on the pilot study, we used the delay range from 1 second to 5 seconds with the step size of 1 second. Each of these five delay values was *randomly* assigned with a video in the set of five clips. Different delay values were assigned with different videos. A delay and a video together formed a *configuration* and hence, we had 5 different configurations. We tested these configurations for the two concealment schemes. As such, a total of ten test cases were presented. Note that for different participants, the same delay value might not be associated with the same video. The fixed coupling between a delay and a video might result in the fairness issue among delay values due to the differences among the content of videos.

The same video content should not be watched multiple times in an experiment session. Being familiar with video content, participants may lose interest in watching or interacting with a video and hence, their evaluation of corresponding test cases are affected. As such, we used different videos for different delay values to alleviate this issue. Note that with current experiment setup, each video is viewed exactly twice in any experiment session.

Test cases were presented in a random order. There was no preference to any delay value or concealment scheme. We did not use the *method of limits* (i.e., start from some delay value (very low or very high) and keep increasing or decreasing the delay until the user's maximum tolerance level has been reached) [5]. For our study, this method is prone to the error of habituation since a participant's tolerance level may have been adapted to the gradual change of delay and hence, is possibly improved beyond the actual level.

Experiments. A total of 22 male and 13 female participants, mostly from the university participated in this paid experiment, None of them had visual impairment or used this zoomable video interface before. Three participants, however, had previous experiences with zoomable video.

The participants were briefed about the user study and what to do in order to complete this experiment. They were first asked to read the instructions and watch a demo video on how to use this zoomable video interface. This was followed by a practice session to make sure they were familiar with different ways to zoom and pan before starting the actual experiment. In this practice session, there was no latency introduced in the interface, i.e. a participant would see the new RoI without any delay after performing zooming or panning actions. This was to *normalize* the differences among user expectations. Since not every participant had viewed zoomable video before, it was crucial that they should share the same expectation of a good streaming of zoomable video. The clip in this practice session was not used for the test cases.

Each participant was registered as a new session on the server. Users' interactions and answer choices were logged into our server database. For each session, five configurations (delay and video) were randomly generated to form 10 test cases. Ten test cases were presented to the participant in a random order. The delay value of each test case was not revealed. Participants were not even told about the presence of delay in these test cases. We, however, let the participants know that some blurring or blacking effects seen during zooming or panning were due to different implementations. For each test case, a participant is asked to watch and interact (zoom/pan) with a video. Each test case was followed by a question *"Do you find the responsiveness when zooming and panning acceptable?"* asking participants to evaluate the responsiveness of zooming or panning. The answer was given in the form of Yes/No Optional Buttons. The next test case is displayed if a participant selects and confirms his answers. Participants were not allowed to go back to previous test cases to change their answers.

5. RESULTS AND DISCUSSION

To understand how well users tolerate network latency when zooming and panning in two concealment schemes, we plot Figure 3. For every delay value in each scheme, we measure the percentage of participants who rated that delay value as *acceptable*. Note that it is allowed if a participant rejects some delay value while accepting longer delay values since user tolerance to delay may vary in different video content.

Results. The Figure 3 shows that for Black concealment scheme, only 77% of users can tolerate 1 second delay. There is a significant drop in acceptance percentage when the delay is 2 seconds (31%) and only less than 20% of participants can tolerate a delay up to 5 seconds for Black scheme. The delay tolerance levels of participants are significantly higher in Low-Res scheme. Up to 94% of participants can tolerate delay of 1 second and 80% can tolerate 2 seconds. Surprisingly, more than half of participants (51%) can tolerate up to a delay of 5 seconds.

Discussion. More users were tolerable to delays in the Low-Res scheme than Black scheme. This finding is as expected. In Low-Res scheme, when users change the RoI, they can see the newly revealed part of the RoI immediately, though at a low resolution. Even with 1 second or 2 seconds of latency, most users still found such delays acceptable. In Black scheme, the new part of RoI appears as black and hence, many users felt unpleasant when seeing nothing for new part of interest during waiting time. Low-Res

Figure 2: Concealment Schemes (Top row: Black scheme. Bottom row: Low-Res scheme).

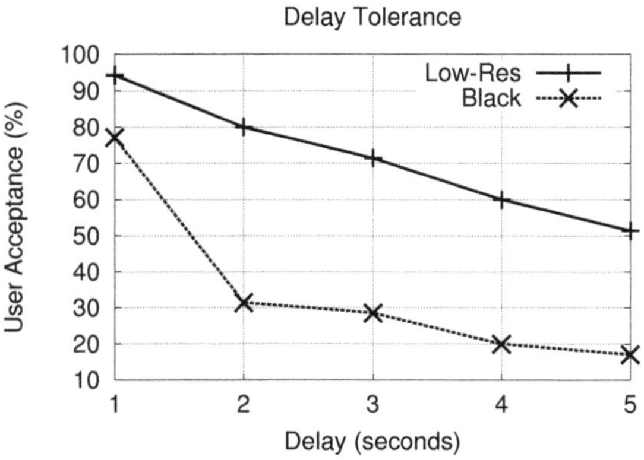

Figure 3: Delay Tolerance

scheme, while requiring the additional transmission of thumbnail video to viewers, has more users tolerable to delays.

The tolerable delay value in viewing zoomable video streams is higher than thresholds found in some high interactive multimedia applications, such as networked games. The reason for such a high latency is possibly because they can see the display of new RoI, in part or at low resolution, immediately. Both schemes attempt to "conceal" the presence of network latency by quickly responding to user interactions with zoomable videos. The users' tolerable network latency of 1 second is a good news for any peer-to-peer streaming systems of zoomable videos, since a requesting peer has more time to find other peers that have data for the entire or part of new RoI, or data are allowed to be forwarded through multiple hops to reach a requesting peer. Prefetching and caching in zoomable videos are necessary to quickly provide data of new RoIs in the presence of high network latency, since user tolerance starts degrading beyond 1 second.

6. CONCLUSION

This paper presented the findings of our user study on how much network latency users can tolerate in interactions with zoomable videos and how their tolerance levels degrade in the presence of network latency. We also show how the choice of concealment scheme helps improve delay tolerance levels of users. These findings, we believe, can be incorporated into designing a system for streaming of zoomable video that provide both good Quality of Experience (QoE) and Quality of Service (QoS).

Acknowledgments

This research work is supported by National University of Singapore Academic Research Fund under the research grant WBS:R-252-000-368-112, and NExT Search Center, funded by the Singapore National Research Foundation & Interactive Digital Media R&D Program Office, MDA, under the research grant WBS:R-252-300-001-490.

7. REFERENCES

[1] ITU-T Recommendation G.114 - one-way transmission time.

[2] T. Beigbeder, R. Coughlan, C. Lusher, J. Plunkett, E. Agu, and M. Claypool. The effects of loss and latency on user performance in Unreal Tournament 2003. In *Proceedings of NetGames '04*, pages 144–151, Portland, OR, Aug. 2004.

[3] A. Carlier, G. Ravindra, and W. T. Ooi. Towards characterizing users' interaction with zoomable video. In *Proc. of International Workshop on SAPMIA'10*, Florence, Italy, October 2010.

[4] R. N. De Silva, W. Cheng, W. T. Ooi, and S. Zhao. Towards understanding user tolerance to network latency and data rate in remote viewing of progressive meshes. In *Proceedings of NOSSDAV '10*, pages 123–128, Amsterdam, The Netherlands, 2010.

[5] G. Fechner. *Elements of Psychophysics: Volume 1*. Holt, Rinehart and Winston New York, 1966.

[6] T. Fritsch, H. Ritter, and J. Schiller. The effect of latency and network limitations on MMORPGs: a field study of EverQuest2. In *Proceedings of NetGames '05*, pages 1–9, Hawthorne, NY, Oct. 2005.

[7] N. Quang Minh Khiem, G. Ravindra, A. Carlier, and W. T. Ooi. Supporting zoomable video streams with dynamic region-of-interest cropping. In *Proc. of MMSYS '10*, Phoenix, Arizona, USA, 2010.

[8] N. Sheldon, E. Girard, S. Borg, M. Claypool, and E. Agu. The effect of latency on user performance in Warcraft III. In *Proceedings of NetGames '03*, pages 3–14, Redwood City, CA, May 2003.

Socialising through Orchestrated Video Communication *

Marian Ursu Pedro Torres
Vilmos Zsombori Michael Frantzis
Department of Computing
Goldsmiths, University of London
{m.ursu,p.torres,v.zsombori,
m.frantzis}@gold.ac.uk

Rene Kaiser
Institute of Information and Communication
Technologies
JOANNEUM RESEARCH
rene.kaiser@joanneum.at

ABSTRACT

We report on the development of a video communication medium through which groups of people situated in different physical locations can naturally talk to each other, see and hear each other, and engage in social entertaining activities. Participants are free to move within their space and behave in a manner closer to collocated experiences. Essentially, this is implemented as a multi-location, multi-camera, hands-free video conferencing system between groups, with integrated support for entertaining activities. In this paper we focus on automatic orchestration, the reasoning process that applies screen grammar to best support the communication. We present a formal model for representing orchestration rules and discuss initial evaluation results.

Categories and Subject Descriptors

I.2.4 [**Artificial Intelligence**]: Knowledge Representation Formalisms and Methods—*representations (procedural and rule-based), representation languages*; H.4.3 [**Information Systems Applications**]: Communications Applications—*video conferencing*

General Terms

Design, Experimentation, Human Factors, Languages

Keywords

Multi-location Videoconferencing, Orchestration, Social Entertainment

Acknowledgements

The research leading to these results has received funding from the European Community's Seventh Framework Programme (FP7/2007-2013) under grant agreement no. ICT-2007-214793.

*Area Chair: Mor Naaman

MM'11, November 28–December 1, 2011, Scottsdale, Arizona, USA.

1. INTRODUCTION

We are working towards the development of a video-based virtual communication and interaction space in which dispersed groups of people are able to naturally talk to each other, and to create and share moments of fun, by engaging in entertaining social activities. In simple terms, this interaction mode can be described as a *multi-location, multi-camera, hands-free* video conference, with integrated support for engagement in social entertaining activities between groups of people who already know each other, such as family and friends. This work has been motivated in [8].

The aim is for the communication technology to create as natural and immersive a communication medium as possible between groups. Participants are free to move within their spaces and behave in ways close to a collocated unmediated interaction. Multiple cameras offer the benefit of different perspectives on each location and the system is responsible for providing the best support for the communication channels at each time during the interaction, seamlessly integrating the entertaining activities that are taking place. This process is called *automatic orchestration*. Orchestration is about developing new *screen grammars* for *video-mediated communication and play* and expressing it in a computational form amenable to automatic application during the interaction. The main requirements we chose include: (i) *pragmatics* — all that is important to be seen in each location is indeed shown; (ii) *autonomy* — absence of *direct* instructions to orchestration; (iii) *transparency* — end users' perception of the communication medium should be minimal; (iv) *aesthetics* — screen storytelling grammar employed to better convey what is *pragmatically* required.

Work related to the overall paradigm has been the main topic of a EuroITV workshop[1]. Related research in interactive TV narratives investigates automatic creation of TV productions which adapt to viewers requirements at the time of delivery both with pre-recorded content [7] and live content [4]. A major distinction to our approach regards the roles played by the end users — actors vs spectators.

Intelligent virtual camera planning [2] deals with the automatic planning of camera placement and movement, sometimes including also shot composition, in order to achieve the best narrative effect. Most of this work, although closely related, is carried out in virtual worlds, where there are fewer constraints regarding the cameras and far more information regarding the world itself. Extensions to the real physical

[1]Enhancing Social Communication and Belonging by Integrating TV Narrativity and Game-Play, EuroITV 2009.

world exist [6], but they are quite limited in scope. Automatic orchestration of camera panning and zooming has been explored for video conferencing among children [9].

Research in social TV attempts to enhance the social experiences surrounding the watching of TV programmes, for example, by providing communication support for those separated in space and possibly time alongside the watching of the same TV content. Representative samples of recent research, including various approaches to this concept and surveys of the state of the art can be found in [1, 3]. The aim of establishing communication channels between people situated in different locations, with a view to sharing and enhancing the entertainment experiences is perfectly aligned with ours.

2. FORMALISATION

2.1 Architecture

The architecture of the Orchestration Engine (OE) is presented in Figure 1. The design approach is *centralised* — one engine for the whole system — and *declarative* — the knowledge bases are separate from the reasoning procedures. The OE receives primitive events from the ANALYSIS modules from all the locations, which analyse the local audio visual streams and extract low-level contextual information (e. g. voice activity from a particular person). The OE also receives input regarding the game state from the GAME ENGINE (e. g. whose turn it is or if there has been a winning move).

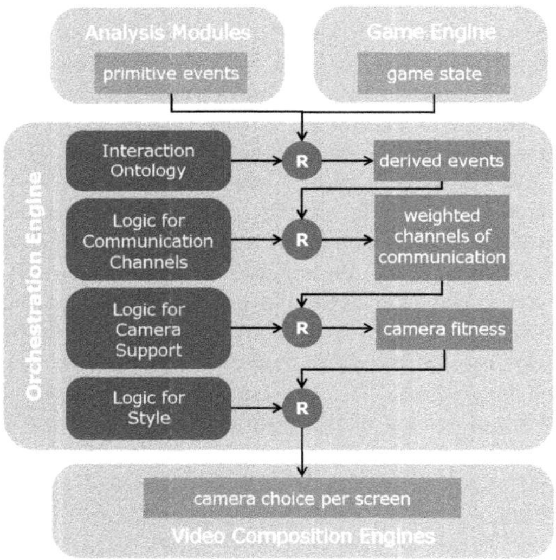

Figure 1: Architecture of the OE

Via an INTERACTION ONTOLOGY module (IO), the OE lifts the primitive events into *high-level events*, a process that identifies certain sequences of primitive events (e. g. start and stop voice activity) and assigns them a more significant meaning (e. g. dialogue). These events are further transformed into *channels of communication*, on the basis of a static knowledge base — the logic for the inference of communication channels. The next step in the inference is to determine *camera fitness* with respect to each location — i. e. which camera from each location is best suited to cover the local events from the point of view of another location. The knowledge base on which this process is determined by the geometric configuration of the system and has to be recalculated if the position of the people in the room or the positions of the cameras change. If provided with updated information of people and camera positions, the (static) *logic for camera support* can be used to determine the fitness of each camera with respect to every location. Finally, there are *stylistic constraints*. They may impose or forbid certain camera transitions for aesthetic purposes, for example, to prevent too frequent cuts. The result of the orchestration reasoning process is, for each location, a choice of a local camera for each of the other locations, which is communicated to and effected by the local VIDEO COMPOSITION ENGINES.

2.2 Interaction Ontology

The ANALYSIS modules identify communication features, in real-time, from the audio and visual streams of all locations. They are sent to the OE as timestamped events, e. g. `voice(start,personID,timestamp)`. The GAME ENGINE also sends events that happen in the game space, e. g. `winning_move(personID)`. We referred to both of these types of events as *primitive*.

The OE maintains a *state* of the overall social interaction and communication context, represented as a set of *higher-level* events, e. g. `dialogue(personID,personID)`. The primitive cues are extracted from each location *independently* of the others, but the OE integrates them in the overall *state*. The OE recomputes the *state* each time it receives a new primitive event, on the basis of the definitions stated in an "interaction ontology", a knowledge base currently expressed in OWL2. So far we have concentrated on classifying sequences of lower-level *voice activity* events into more meaningful conversational events, namely monologue, dialogue, group discussion and silence. To define them, we took only the start time of each speech into account, and neglect the duration, overlaps and gaps of each event. Whilst still quite simplified, this approach provided overall good results. Nevertheless, we encountered problems with regards to the efficiency of reasoning and a newer implentation of this cue lifting module which dropped the ontology approach in favour of Complex Event Processing is reported in [5].

2.3 Communication Channels and Rules

Channel inference rules map the high-level cues into channels of communication. These channels are captured by a dynamic three-dimensional matrix **C** with entries, C_{ijk}, between 0 and 1; **C** is recomputed after each change in the *state* of the system. The value of C_{ijk} is the weight of the channel from person i to person j as perceived by person k: 0 means no channel, whereas 1 means maximum importance. The need to introduce the third index, k, derives from the fact that a conversation between two people may be of different relevance to different observers. For example, if the channel inference module receives a dialogue event between person i and person j a rule may raise the weight of all channels C_{ijk} for every k. The rise in weight could be greater if $k = i$ or $k = j$ and lower otherwise to express the fact that, when person i is talking to person j, the conversation is more important to person i and person j than to some other person. This dialogue rule could be stated as:

$$\begin{cases} i = j \;\Rightarrow\; C_{ijk} = 0 \\ i \neq j \;\Rightarrow\; \begin{cases} k = i \vee k = j \;\Rightarrow\; C_{ijk} = 1, C_{jik} = 1 \\ k \neq i \wedge k \neq j \;\Rightarrow\; C_{ijk} = 0.2, C_{jik} = 0.2 \end{cases} \end{cases}$$

Similar rules are used for silence, monologues, group discussion and unknown states. More generally, the inference rules may control the weights of channels of communication based on any kind of event raised via the IO that may be introduced in the future. The contributions coming from all different audiovisual states are all added into a single **C** matrix and subsequently normalised for each observer.

The support given by each camera to each channel of communication is captured by a four-dimensional matrix **S** with entries, S_{ijkc}, between 0 and 1. The value of S_{ijkc} is the support given by camera c to the channel from i to j as perceived by k. The fitness of camera c with respect to the location L is defined as

$$\phi_L(c) = \sum_{ij} \sum_{k \in L} C_{ijk} \cdot S_{ijkc}. \quad (1)$$

The way camera fitness is defined implies that the choice of a camera over another is made considering superposition of partial fitnesses concerning different triples of people (i, j, k). Essentially, the fittest camera for a location is the one that provides the most support over all channels involving the observers in that location.

The matrix **S** is determined using *support rules*. A support rule may state, for example, that, if person i and person k are in the same location — which implies they can see each other without the support of the system — and there is a channel of communication from i to j, the support for observer k of a camera showing a close up of person j is 1. In other words, support will be 1 if k can see both people involved in the dialogue. Support rules, in general, may consider the proportion a person occupies on the screen — seeing a wide shot with three people when we just want to see one is worse than seeing a close up of that person — and the angle at which they look at the camera — to cover a dialogue, a camera that shows a front shot is more useful than one that shows the person at an acute angle. For brevity, details of these rules are left out. According to our formulation, the support matrix $\mathbb{S}$ may vary with time (e. g. if people move, different cameras will give different support) and the OE will make its decisions accordingly. This feature will be useful when there are cues providing information on real-time position of people and cameras.

Style rules aim both (i) to avoid too frequent or infrequent camera changes and (ii) to constrain transitions between types of shots. A style rule may state that a camera change is not allowed more frequently than every 2 seconds or that, after 60 seconds of showing the same feed, a different camera should be picked even if it is not the best choice. As for transitions, a style rule may state that a close-up of a person cannot be followed by a close-up of another person in the same room without going through a wide-shot of both people, to avoid disorientation. In summary, the OE computes the fitness of each camera with respect to every location according to (1) and then chooses the most fit camera at each location that satisfies all the style constraints.

3. EVALUATION

The concept of orchestration was evaluated through three sets of experiments — Figure 2. In the first set of experiments, we worked with 8 participants who were organised in different combinations of groups of 2 and 3 and swapped between the two rooms. We fixed the following characteristics:

Games	Set-up	Video Mediation
Charades Pictionary	2/3 persons per location persons not always in wide-shot limited change of position orchestration: **needed**	**1 fixed** camera **4 mobile** cameras **live manual** editing
Scrabble Poker	2 persons per location both persons always in wide shot no change of position orchestration: **optional**	**5 fixed** cameras **live manual** editing
Electronic board game Guessing games	2 persons per location both persons always in wide shot no change of position orchestration: **optional**	5 **fixed** cameras **live manual** editing

Figure 2: Experimental Set-ups

(i) two locations; 2/3 people per location; (2) non-mediated audio link — the two locations were set adjacent to each other, but with no direct visual connection; (3) one TV set in each location; one room received a manually orchestrated video stream edited from 5 cameras from the other location; the other location received a static stream.

Figure 3 illustrates three shots available to the orchestration process to cover a group of friends playing *Pictionary* with other friends in another location. Cam_A is a wide shot, used to cover both the sofa and the armchair, Cam_B is used for showing the game board, but also for allowing the person at the board to communicate with the other location, and Cam_C is used to show the person in front of the armchair when he becomes active. Besides having different roles in supporting communication, these shots also serve different aesthetic functions.

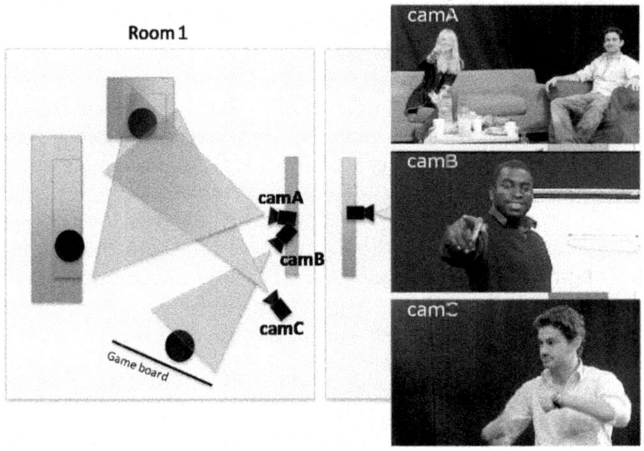

Figure 3: Example of functional shots

Within this first set, we carried out three trials of experiments in a total of 15 hours or interaction including social game play and informal communication. We informally interviewed the participants after each trial. The most significant overall aspect, mentioned by all those who received the orchestrated stream, was that they became immersed in the communication and stopped noticing the editing from multiple cameras. They were able to *naturally* communicate with the people in the other room, without perceiving the way in which the medium facilitated this. We regard this as an important result. The principles of *transparency* and indirectly that of *pragmatics* seem to have been satisfied. There were also interaction sessions in which the editing was noticed by the participants. However, overall, the results strengthen our conviction that screen grammar has the potential to improve video-mediated communication between groups.

In a second set of evaluation experiments for automatically orchestrated communication we kept the dependency on ANALYSIS, but removed the requirement for real-time computation for all the software components, and also the reliance on the VCE. Instead, we used a non-linear editing suite which we called *off-line automatic orchestration.* For this, we carried out a one day trial involving 5 participants, work colleagues and friends, organised in different groups of 2. The set-up consisted of two separate rooms, communicating via mediated audio and video. The games played were *Ludo* and *Tabu.* For both rooms, the audio and video streams were *static* during the interaction, but one of the locations had three fixed cameras continuously recording, with the front wide camera being of sufficiently high quality to be used for virtual cameras. The real-time experience was not orchestrated, but automatically orchestrated streams were subsequently constructed and evaluated. ANALYSIS was carried out off-line on the recorded footage as a stand alone process. It produced a description of features synchronised with the audio-visual content. Orchestration was then ran, taking these primitive cues as input. It produced a description of all the editing decisions and exported them as FinalCut-Pro XML files. The edited streams were then watched and evaluated by those participating in the experience as well as by others. The overall impression was again encouraging: the orchestrated stream was considered as more interesting and versatile than the static wide when the orchestration logic was complete — i. e. when it included interpretation of primitive cues into more meaningful information, the refinement of channels of communication, the use of camera support rules and, finally, stylistic rules.

The third and final set of experiments was carried out for *real-time automatic orchestrated interaction.* The set up consisted of two separate rooms, each having 1 central and 2 lateral cameras, the central one also supporting virtual cameras. The game played was an electronic version of the board game *Space Alert.* Apart from informal evaluation sessions carried out by the members of the team that developed the system, there have been two 90 minutes evaluation sessions, carried out by a group of 5 people. The initial ambition was to have all the processes running automatically. Unfortunately, the extraction of primitive cues in real time was insufficiently reliable. This led to more or less random editing decisions and its effect was clearly disturbing. For example, at times, instead of showing the person talking, the system showed a close-up of the other person in the room. Therefore, to decouple the orchestration process from the unreliability of the cues, primitive cues were injected manually by a human operator observing the activity in the room. Orchestration using such primitive cues was deemed as interesting and with clear exploitation potential in video mediated communication.

4. CONCLUSIONS AND FUTURE WORK

We have described a framework for orchestrating video communication for social interaction between groups of people via a multi-location, multi-camera, hands-free system. To the best of our knowledge, this is the first attempt to develop a screen grammar for social interaction and the necessary formal models and associated tools to express and reason with it.

From manual orchestration experiments we have elicited a set of orchestration rules and devised a formal model for their implementation in an automated system. We have implemented such a system and evaluated it both off-line and in real time. The preliminary results were promising. Our immediate research agenda includes a number of trials specifically designed for the evaluation of orchestrated communication, that are to be carried out with a more significant number of participants and quantitative evaluation methods, as we take these initial positive evaluations as sufficient to motivate further developments.

We have concluded that an expressive set of orchestration rules can be defined using a formalism based on the concept of channels of communication. We aim to extend this model further by using first-order logic to describe those rules. Moreover, we plan to enrich the current model with the ability to reason more generally with time. For that purpose, we will bring temporal constructs into first-order logic, allowing the system to reason about sequences of high-level events.

5. REFERENCES

[1] Special issue on social interactive television. *Internationl Journal of Human-Computer Interaction*, 24(2):113–238, 2008.

[2] M. Christie, R. Machap, J.-M. Normand, P. Olivier, and J. Pickering. Virtual camera planning: A survey. In *Smart Graphics*, number 3638 in LNCS, pages 40–52. Springer, 2005.

[3] D. Geerts, G. Harboe, and N. Massey. Workshop on social interactive television. In *Interactive TV: A Shared Experience, TICSP Adjunct Proceedings of EuroITV 2007*, pages 119–142. TICSP, 2007.

[4] M. Gude, S. M. Grünvogel, and A. Pütz. Predicting future user behaviour in interactive live tv. In *EuroITV 2008: Changing Television Environments*, number 5066 in LNCS, pages 117–121. Springer, 2008.

[5] R. Kaiser, P. Torres, and M. Höffernig. The interaction ontology: Low-level cue processing in real-time group conversations. In *Proc. of 2nd Intl. Workshop on Events in Multimedia*, pages 29–34, NY, USA, 2010. ACM.

[6] A. Ranjan, J. Birnholtz, and R. Balakrishnan. Improving meeting capture by applying television production principles with audio and motion detection. In *Proc. of CHI '08*, pages 227–236, NY, 2008. ACM.

[7] M. F. Ursu, M. Thomas, I. Kegel, D. Williams, M. Tuomola, I. Lindstedt, T. Wright, A. Leurdijk, V. Zsombori, J. Sussner, U. Myrestam, and N. Hall. Interactive tv narratives: Opportunities, progress, and challenges. *ACM Trans. Multimedia Comput. Commun. Appl.*, 4(4):1–39, 2008.

[8] D. Williams, M. F. Ursu, P. Cesar, K. Bergström, I. Kegel, and J. Meenowa. An emergent role for tv in social communication. In *EuroITV '09: Proc. of the 7th European Conference on Interactive Television*, pages 19–28. ACM, 2009.

[9] S. Yarosh, K. Inkpen, and A. Brush. Video playdate: toward free play across distance. In *Proc. of the 28th Intl. Conf. on Human Factors in Computing Systems*, pages 1251–1260. ACM, 2010.

Perceptual Coding of Recorded Telemanipulation Sessions*

Fernanda Brandi, Eckehard Steinbach
Institute for Media Technology
Technische Universität München
Munich, Germany
{fernanda.brandi,eckehard.steinbach}@tum.de

ABSTRACT

Efficient recording and replay of telemanipulation sessions require the compression of the occurring visual-haptic signals. To this end, we propose two distinct approaches which take into consideration known limitations of human visual and haptic perception. We compare both schemes to the state-of-the-art approaches and show that a substantial additional data reduction can be achieved while maintaining good overall haptic and visual performances.

Categories and Subject Descriptors

E.4 [**Coding and Information Theory**]: Data compaction and compression

General Terms

Algorithms, Experimentation, Human Factors, Performance

Keywords

data reduction, haptics, perceptual coding, playback, signal compression, signal recording, telemanipulation

1. INTRODUCTION

Real-time haptic interaction sessions can be recorded and later replayed to one or more users [4]. During an offline haptic application the user is not required to actively control the teleoperator. Instead, the operator passively receives all the forms of feedback available (e.g. forces, visual and auditory content) produced in a previous real-time interaction and thus can relate to the recorded actions being replayed [5]. In this way, the subject can assess all the routines previously performed by the original operator of the real-time haptic session.

Previous works [5, 1] have proposed different manners to compress haptic signals for playback. Both approaches have utilized the well-known Weber's Law to selectively reduce the amount of haptic data. This relation has been broadly employed for haptic data compression and the reader is invited to read [3] for a more comprehensive take on this topic.

2. PROPOSED OFFLINE HAPTIC DATA COMPRESSION SCHEME

Two different approaches are proposed in this work. We propose to record all the haptic data acquired during the real-time haptic session, therefore, not only the force feedback signal is recorded (as in [5]) but also the position signal. This scheme is presented in Figure 1.

Since the communication loop is opened during replay of the recorded session, both force-feedback and position modalities can be independently post-processed without affecting each other. Thus, different perceptual signal compression schemes are designed in this work taking into account the specific properties of each recorded haptic modality. The force-feedback signal is compressed by exploiting

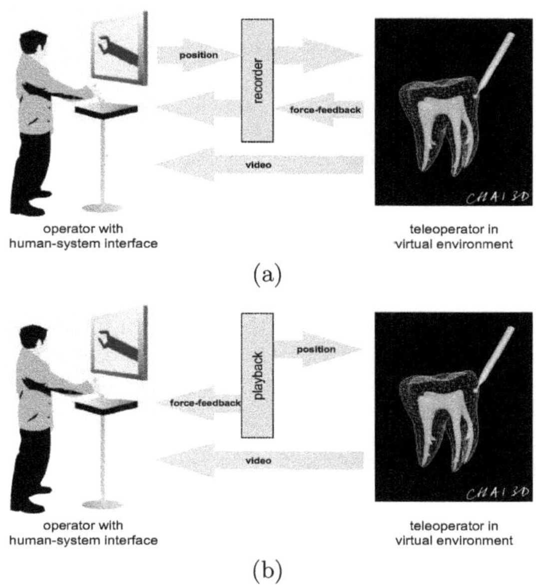

Figure 1: In (a) both position and force-feedback signals are recorded from a real-time haptic session. In (b) the recorded force signal is directly played back to the operator and the position signal is sent to the teleoperator where the visual information is regenerated and transmitted to the user.

*Area chair: Mor Naaman

MM'11, November 28–December 1, 2011, Scottsdale, Arizona, USA.

limits of human *haptic* perception using Weber's Law, and the position signal is compressed by exploiting limits of human *visual* perception [2] since its only feedback is delivered through the visual display.

2.1 Force-Feedback Signal

Inspired by [1], a novel force-feedback signal compression scheme is proposed. After the recording of a telemanipulation session, the goal is to reconstruct the force-feedback signal using only a few key samples referred to in the following as *support points*. The reconstructed signal should be entirely contained in between the perception thresholds (i.e. *deadbands* calculated using the original data and Weber's Law) since any data fluctuation within these boundaries is said to be indistinguishable [3].

The following four steps describe the algorithm for the compression of force data.

2.1.1 Initialization Stage

The first step is to quantize the three-dimensional force-feedback signal to enable the use of entropy coders. The quantization uses a reversed logarithmic function which leads to smaller steps around zero and larger steps towards greater absolute force intensity values. This spacing is designed to accommodate Weber's Law which asserts that weaker stimuli generate tighter deadband intervals and stronger stimuli generate larger deadband intervals.

The quantization points contained within the deadband thresholds of a recorded sample, $\mathbf{x}_n$, are considered the *candidates*, $\mathbf{c}_{n,m}$, to be a support point, $\mathbf{s}_i$. In this case, the recorded signal has N samples, each time instant (i.e. sample) n has a variable maximum number, $m_{max}(n)$, of candidate points and i is indexing the still unknown total number of support points, I_{init}, determined in this stage. The algorithm then starts selecting one of the $m \leq m_{max}(n)$ candidate points for the first time instant, $n = 1$, and tries to connect it to a candidate point of the next time instant, $\mathbf{c}_{n+1,m}$. The two points define a line segment $\mathbf{l}_i$ (with a time interval $d_i = n_{end} - n_{start}$) which is tested regarding the deadband thresholds. If there is no deadband violation along this segment, then the candidate point, $\mathbf{c}_{n+1,m}$, is saved and the algorithm proceeds testing the next ending point, $\mathbf{c}_{n+2,m}$ (using the same starting point $\mathbf{c}_{n,m}$). This procedure continues until a deadband violation occurs. In this case, the remaining m candidate points in that same ending time instant, $n + d_i$, are tested for a non-violating segment. In case it succeeds, the algorithm further continues its search incrementing the time instant. Otherwise, the ending point (and also the starting point in case it is the first line segment) is saved as a support point, $\mathbf{s}_i$. When $n = N$, the initialization algorithm stops and stores the set of support points $SP_{init} = [\mathbf{s}_1, ..., \mathbf{s}_{I_{init}}]$.

2.1.2 Relaxation Stage

After determining the initial number of support points, I_{init}, the reconstructed signal can assume a zigzag form as shown in Figure 2(b). These sudden signal variations can potentially disturb the user during playback. To address this issue, we propose a relaxation stage in which the support points in SP_{init} can be rearranged in order to minimize the reconstructed signal distortion. These points can be moved not only spatially (changing their intensity values) but also temporally (changing their time instants).

This phase of the algorithm tests each support point, $\mathbf{s}_i$, analyzing the overall signal distortion for both line segments, $\mathbf{l}_i$ and $\mathbf{l}_{i+1}$, connected to it. In case the current support point location provides the smallest distortion, then $\mathbf{s}_i$ is not changed. Otherwise, the candidate point coordinates that provide the minimum local distortion overwrite the coordinates in $\mathbf{s}_i$. This process is repeated until points are no longer altering their locations. It is important to note that the tested points in this stage are again taken from the quantization points defined in the previous stage. Also, for each new triple of points $\mathbf{s}_{i-1}$, $\mathbf{s}_i$ and $\mathbf{s}_{i+1}$ there is a deadband violation check to guarantee that the reconstructed segments $\mathbf{l}_i$ and $\mathbf{l}_{i+1}$ are contained within the perception thresholds.

For the task of minimizing the segments' deviation, we introduce a novel distortion metric which is an adaptation of the known formula of the *mean squared error* (MSE). This formula was modified so it also takes into consideration the psychophysical aspects of human perception. This metric is referred to as the *weighted mean squared error* (WMSE) and can be described as

$$WMSE = \frac{1}{N} \sum_{n} ||\mathbf{x}_n - \hat{\mathbf{x}}_n||^2 \frac{1}{k||\mathbf{x}_n||} \quad (1)$$

where N is the total number of acquired samples, $||\ .\ ||$ denotes the length of a vector, $\mathbf{x}_n$ is the nth original sample, $\hat{\mathbf{x}}_n$ is the nth reconstructed sample and k is the deadband parameter. It can be observed that for a constant deviation $||\mathbf{x}_n - \hat{\mathbf{x}}_n||$, the larger $||\mathbf{x}_n||$ is, the weaker is the influence of this deviation in the overall summation.

The relaxation stage produces a set of support points $SP_{relax} = [\mathbf{s}_1, ..., \mathbf{s}_{I_{relax}}]$ that decreases the reconstructed signal's distortion if compared to the previous stage and thus can improve the subjective quality of the displayed signal. The effectiveness of the relaxation stage is illustrated in Figure 2(c). Note that the reconstructed signal is now closer to the original one and the zigzag effect is eliminated.

2.1.3 Optimization Stage

Whenever the support points cease to be rearranged in the relaxation stage, the optimization stage checks if there are any support points that can be removed from the set SP_{relax}. After the relaxation some support points may be aligned and hence can be suppressed while segments are merged together. Comparing Figure 2(b) and 2(c) it can be observed that not only the points were rearranged in the relaxation stage but also that a support point (around 50 ms in this example) was removed. If points are dropped in this stage generating a new set $SP_{optim} = [\mathbf{s}_1, ..., \mathbf{s}_{I_{optim}}]$, the algorithm returns to the relaxation stage to adjust the remaining support points. Otherwise, it skips to the coding stage. This stage increases the compression ratio while maintaining the low distortion of the reconstructed signal.

2.1.4 Coding Stage

The last stage employs an entropy coder on the resulting set of support points SP_{optim}. The quantization points determined in the initialization stage and utilized throughout all the previous stages help to decrease the support points' entropy and therefore can enable a stronger signal compression. In this work, a Huffman coder was utilized to encode the final support points. A description of the decoding and reconstruction processes is ommited in this work since they

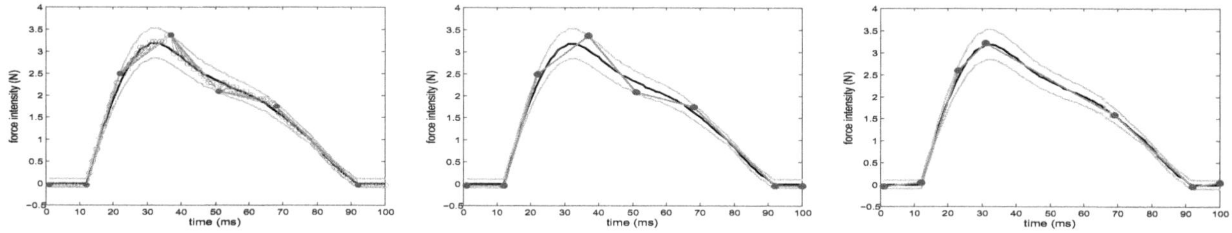

(a) (b) (c)

Figure 2: The central black curve shows the original recorded signal with its deadband thresholds depicted as the upper and lower green curves. The initialization process (a) is illustrated by the red line segments which connect the support points in blue and the candidate points in red. (b) shows the set SP_{init} of support points (blue) and the connecting line segments (red) that will be relaxed in the second stage. Finally, (c) shows the resulting support points after the relaxation and optimization stages.

can be straightforwardly performed using a Huffman decoder and linear interpolation of the decoded support points.

2.2 Position Signal

As shown in Figure 1, the only information that the user receives concerning the position signal is provided visually, hence, a novel data reduction approach is proposed in this work taking into account the human visual perception limitations.

The human sight is characterized by a relatively low temporal resolution, especially if compared to the haptic sense which demands display rates of up to 1 kHz. Although a fair motion illusion can be provided with refresh rates of approximately 20 Hz, there might exist visual artifacts such as flickering and judder that can be avoided when higher display rates are employed [6]. The adequate refresh rate for the position signal is investigated in the experimental evaluation.

The proposed position signal compression scheme involves three basic stages which will be presently described.

2.2.1 *Subsampling Stage*

The position signal can be uniformly subsampled to rates usually utilized for video signals. Therefore, the original 1 kHz haptic rate can be decreased to rates that can vary from 15 Hz up to 100 Hz depending on the actions performed by the operator during the recording session.

2.2.2 *Differential Coding Stage*

Instead of directly saving the subsampled position signal composed by the support samples $\mathbf{s}_i$, we propose to encode only the differences (in each axis a) between subsequent support samples referred to as $\Delta s_{i,a}$. Moreover, we pre-define uniform quantization steps based on a given $\Delta s_{max} = \max_i(\Delta s_{i,a})$. This adaptive quantization process better accommodates the quantization intervals to the $\Delta s_{i,a}$ values generated with a certain subsampling rate. This stage is included in this work to decrease the entropy of the encoded samples and ultimately improve the overall data compression performance.

2.2.3 *Reconstruction Stage*

To minimize the visual artifacts, the support samples can be used to regenerate the missing samples and thus, provide a higher refreshing rate. Two upsampling methods are tested in this work: the *hold last sample* approach wherein the last displayed support point is continuously replicated, and the support sample *linear interpolation* approach. The latter is expected to have a considerably better performance especially if the teleoperator takes part in a real (i.e. not virtual) scenario wherein automated equipments are highly sensitive to abrupt signal changes.

3. EXPERIMENTS AND RESULTS

We recorded a 12-second haptic interactive virtual session using the CHAI3D library and the Force Dimension omega.6 haptic device. The data was processed offline and the two proposed schemes were evaluated independently.

Each experiment had fifteen participants. The haptic and visual artifacts were individually explained to the subjects at the beginning of each experiment and reference sessions with uncompressed signals and with strong artifacts were made available to the subjects. The sessions were randomly displayed to the participants and after each session they should give their ratings according to the following marks: *excelent=100, good=75, fair=50, poor=25, very bad=0.*

3.1 Force-Feedback Signal

In this experiment the proposed scheme is tested against the state-of-the-art approach [5]. The tested deadband parameter k could assume values from 10% up to 90%. The pre-quantization of the samples to yield the candidate support points was performed using 2^B levels where $B = 6, ..., 9$ bits. The signals reconstructed after the *initialization* stage (using the support points set SP_{init}) and after the *optimization* stage (using the support points set SP_{optim}) were also compared to evaluate the effectiveness of the relaxation and optimization stages.

For the subjective tests, three different schemes were evaluated: the approach presented in [5] (referred to as "traditional deadband" in the experimental results graphs), the proposed approach utilizing $B = 6$ bits *not including* the relaxation and optimization stages and *including* the relaxation and optimization stages The deadband parameter k could assume five different values: 10%, 30%, 50%, 70% and 90%.

It can be observed in Figure 3(a) that for identical deadband parameter values k, the proposed approach substantially outperforms the reference scheme [5]. Our work's improvement can also be clearly observed in Figure 3(b) which shows considerably reduced bitstream sizes attaining better

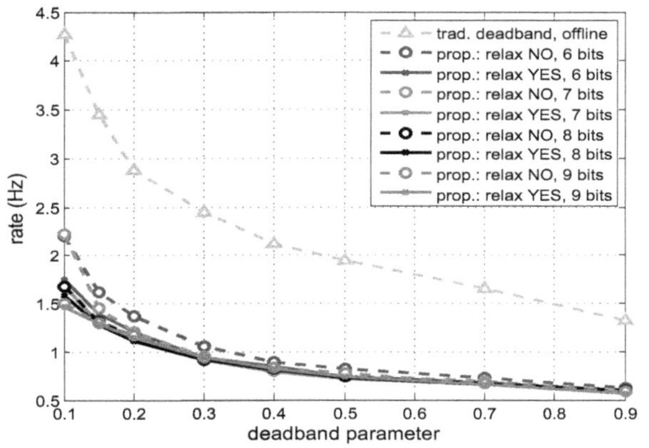

(a)

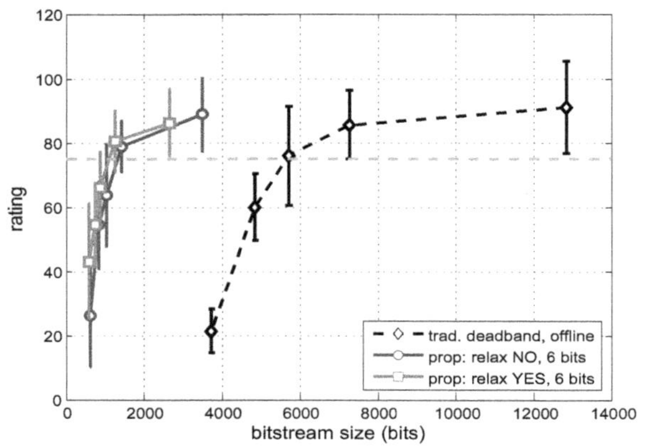

(b)

Figure 3: Objective and subjective results evaluating different force-feedback signal compression schemes. The green dashed line in (b) indicates the lower threshold that reflects non-disturbing sessions.

subjective ratings. This means that even if one decides to apply more conservative values for the deadband parameter k (thus, decreasing the compression ratio of the bitstream to around 96% of its original size), the total data reduction performance and the subjective ratings are still strongly encouraging for the approach presented in this work.

3.2 Position Signal

In this experiment the proposed approach is tested using two reconstruction methods: the hold last sample and the linear interpolation. The pre-quantization of the maximum difference Δs_{max} was performed using 2^B intervals in which $B = 4$ or $B = 8$ bits. The decreased sampling rate could assume 6 different values: 10, 20, 30, 40, 60 and 80 Hz.

Observing Figure 4, it can be seen that the hold last sample approach leads to the worst performance. Participants often noticed a flickering artifact during these sessions. Furthermore, the displaying of linearly interpolated signals is more agreeable to the users even at lower refreshing rates.

Concerning the data compression ratio, the proposed approach achieved values around 98% (display rate at 20 Hz) which by far outperforms [5] since in the latter all visual information (i.e. video) needs to be stored. Aiming at a more advantageous trade-off between subjective results and data

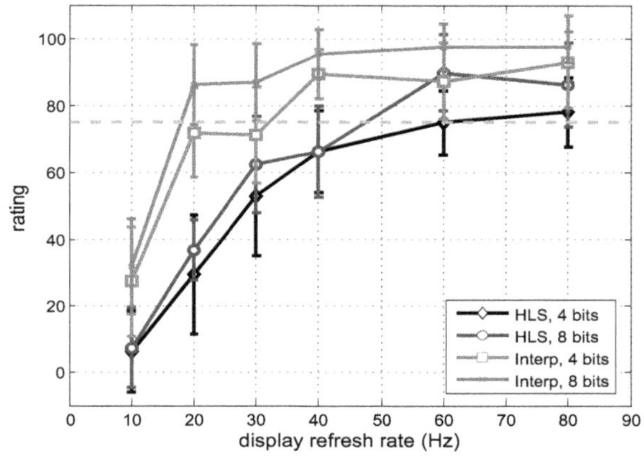

Figure 4: Subjective results (mean and standard deviation) evaluating different position signal compression schemes. The green dashed line indicates the lower threshold that reflects non-disturbing sessions.

reduction, the use of more quantization bits combined with the linear interpolation as the signal reconstruction method seems to be the best choice.

4. CONCLUSION

In this work we introduce two novel schemes to compress recorded haptic data. In both approaches, well-known psychophysical limitations of human perception are exploited. The presented schemes are specifically designed for the different haptic modalities (e.g. position, force-feedback). The proposed force-feedback signal compression approach is based on Weber's Law. The presented position data signal compression scheme accounts for human visual perception limitations, in particular the ability of perceiving motion.

We compare the proposed schemes to the state-of-the-art approach in [5] and show that a substantial additional data reduction can be achieved while maintaining good performance for the haptic and visual experiences.

5. REFERENCES

[1] F. Brandi and E. Steinbach. Minimizing the number of support points in perceptual offline haptic compression. In *IEEE Int. Symposium on Haptic Audio-Visual Environments and Games*, Phoenix, USA, Oct. 2010.

[2] E. B. Goldstein. *Sensation and Perception.* Wadsworth, 6th edition, 2002.

[3] P. Hinterseer, S. Hirche, S. Chaudhuri, E. Steinbach, and M. Buss. Perception-based data reduction and transmission of haptic data in telepresence and teleaction systems. *IEEE Trans. on Signal Processing*, 56(2):588–597, Feb. 2008.

[4] K. L. Holland, R. L. Williams II, R. R. Conatser Jr., J. N. Howell, and D. L. Cade. Implementation and evaluation of a virtual haptic back. *Virtual Reality Society Journal*, 7(2):94–102, 2004.

[5] J. Kammerl and E. Steinbach. Deadband-based offline-coding of haptic media. In *ACM Multimedia*, Vancouver, Canada, Oct. 2008.

[6] A. Punchihewa and D. G. Bailey. Artefacts in image and video. In *Image and Vision Computing*, New Zealand, 2002.

Automatic Modeling of *Personality States* in Small Group Interactions

Jacopo Staiano
DISI-University of Trento
via Sommarive 14
Povo, Italy
staiano@disi.unitn.it

Bruno Lepri
MIT Media Lab and FBK
20 Ames Street,
Cambridge, MA, USA
lepri@fbk.eu

Ramanathan Subramanian
DISI-University of Trento
via Sommarive 14,
Povo, Italy
subramanian@disi.unitn.it

Nicu Sebe
DISI-University of Trento
via Sommarive 14
Povo, Italy
sebe@disi.unitn.it

Fabio Pianesi
FBK
via Sommarive 18
Povo, Italy
pianesi@fbk.eu

ABSTRACT
In this paper, we target the automatic recognition of *personality states* in a meeting scenario employing visual and acoustic features. The social psychology literature has coined the name *personality state* to refer to a specific behavioral episode wherein a person behaves as more or less introvert/extrovert, neurotic or open to experience, *etc*. Personality traits can then be reconstructed as density distributions over personality states. Different machine learning approaches were used to test the effectiveness of the selected features in modeling the dynamics of personality states.

Categories and Subject Descriptors
H.1.2 [**User/Machine Systems**] [Human information processing]

General Terms: Algorithms, Measurement, Human Factors

Keywords: personality states, modeling, Big Five Traits, modeling dynamics

1. INTRODUCTION
It is customary for us to describe people as being more or less *talkative*, *bold* or *sociable*. We employ these descriptors in our daily life to explain and/or predict others' behavior, attaching them to well-known and new acquaintances. *Extraversion*, the trait dimension they refer to, is so familiar that we continuously exploit it inconspicuously. Similarly, we talk about other people being more/less prone to anger and frustration (*Neuroticism*), responsible or attentive (*Conscientiousness*), and so on. These descriptors relate to traits comprising the well-known Big Five model of personality [1].

* Area Chair: Mor Naaman

MM'11, November 28–December 1, 2011, Scottsdale, Arizona, USA.

The importance of personality for technology and human-computer interaction has also been acknowledged. Studies have shown that personality traits determine people's attitudes towards machines [14] and conversational agents [13]. It has been argued that social networking websites could increase the chances of a successful relationship by analyzing text messages and matching personalities [2], and that tutoring systems would be more effective if they adapt to the learner's personality [7]. Moreover, given its relevance in social settings, information on people's personality can be useful for providing personalized support to group dynamics.

Several works have explored automated personality analysis [9, 11], often targeting the Big Five model of personality [1] of which Extraversion is a major dimension. The general approach is to isolate promising behavioral correlates of the targeted traits for classification or regression, adopting a thin-slice perspective. In particular, some works have focused on the well-known correlation between Extraversion and prosodic features [11] - higher pitch and higher variation of the fundamental frequency, higher voice quality and intensity - while others such as [9], have also considered verbal cues, including many relating to syntax, content, utterance type, *etc*. More recently, Lepri *et al.* [8], exploited medium-grained behaviors enacted in group meetings and related to social attention (social gaze) for automatically predicting *Extraversion*.

All these approaches to the automatic recognition of personality have more or less implicitly adopted the so-called 'person perspective' on personality [3]: for a given behavioral sample, classify whether the sample belongs to an extrovert or introvert (or equivalently, to a neurotic or an emotionally stable, and so on). The problem with this approach is that it assumes a direct and stable relationship between, *e.g.*, being extravert and acting extravertedly (*e.g.*, speaking loudly, being talkative, *etc*.). On the contrary, extraverts can sometimes be silent and reflexive, while introverts can at times exhibit extraverted behaviors. Similarly, people prone to neuroticism need not always exhibit anxious behavior, while agreeable people can sometimes be aggressive. While the person perspective has often dismissed these fluctuations of actual behavior as statistical noise, it has been recently suggested by Fleeson [3] that they are meaningful. The social psychology literature has coined the term *personality states* to refer to concrete behaviors (including ways of acting, feeling and thinking) that can be described as having a similar content to the corresponding personality traits. In other words, a personality state describes a specific behavioral episode wherein a person behaves more or less, introvertly/extravertly, more or less neurotically, *etc.* Personality can then be reconstructed through density distributions over personality states, with parameters such as means, standard deviations, *etc.*, summarizing what is specific to the given individual.

In this paper we address the automatic classification of personality states corresponding to the Big Five traits [1], in multi-party meetings. Hence we will be concerned with classifying whether people behaved extravertedly/introvertedly; neurotically or in an emotionally stable manner; in a conscientiousness or careless way; agreeably/disagreeably or creatively/uncreatively. To the best of our knowledge, this is the first work targeting such a qualitative characterization of human behavior in a computational setting, opening new perspectives for the automatic recognition of personality and its relationships to actual behaviors.

2. THE MISSION SURVIVAL CORPUS

We performed our experiments on meeting videos from the Mission Survival corpus. The Mission Survival II corpus [11] is a multimodal annotated collection of video and audio recordings of meetings in a lab setting. In each meeting, four participants are seated around a table and engaged in the Mission Survival Task (MST), which is used in experimental and social psychology to elicit decision-making in small groups [5]. The objective of the "Mission Survival" task is to reach a consensus on how to survive a disaster scenario, *e.g.*, a plane crash in an uninhabited island. The group has to select a limited number of (up to 15) items critical for survival. Each group member needs to convince the others regarding the utility of a particular item.

The recording equipment consisted of five Fire-wire cameras, four placed in the corners of the room and one directly above the table, and four web-cameras installed on the meeting table. Speech activity was recorded using four close-talk and six table-top microphones along with seven T-shaped microphone arrays, in order to obtain optimal coverage of the environment for speaker localization and tracking.

2.1 Personality states

Our experiments were conducted on 4 meeting videos extracted from the Mission Survival corpus (with a total number of 16 subjects and with a total run-time of 120 minutes). The video stream corresponding to each meeting participant was split into 5-minute long slices, making for a total of 108 clips.

Personality state annotation was performed by 30 volunteers (researchers and graduate students) using the Ten Item Personality Inventory [4], a 10-item questionnaire developed to obtain a brief measure of the Big Five dimensions. Annotators were required to assess a participant's personality based on the 5-minute slices containing a close-up view of the subject with the synchronized audio. Contextual information (the behavior of the other meeting participants) was available only through the audio channel. Each video was annotated by three different annotators, and each annotator saw a given subject no more than once. The wordings of the 10 items were modified in order to reflect the different goal of our exercise; hence, rather than asking to assess how much the item "Extraverted, enthusiastic" applied to the subject, it asked about how much it applied to the behavior he/she exhibited in the given audio-video slice.

In Table 1, we report the global means and standard deviations computed from the annotated personality states. For 16 participants, the average score (5.07 in a range from 1 to 7) for Neuroticism is quite high, while the mean score for Openness (creativity, complexity) is relatively low (3.95).

In order to perform the classification experiments, scores were quantized (Low/High) for each personality state by taking the median score as a threshold. Table 2 reports the transition probabilities for each personality state. As can be seen, our subjects showed a good degree of consistency in their behaviors: if a person was behaving extravertedly/introvertedly at time *t* he/she was more likely to continue behave the same way at *t*+1. The only exceptions in this regard are (a) the transition from a disagreeable to an agreeable behavior; it appears that participants tend to persist in disagreeable behaviors. (b) Also, a transition from an emotionally stable behavior to a neurotic behavior is as likely as continuing with an emotionally stable behavior.

Table 1. Means and standard deviations for personality states

Trait	Mean	Standard deviation
Extraversion	4.18	1.66
Agreeableness	4.55	1.05
Consciousness	4.99	1.12
Neuroticism	**5.07**	1.04
Openness	**3.96**	1.25

Table 2. Transition probabilities for each personality state

Extraversion	L	H
L	0.688	0.312
H	0.296	0.704
Agreeableness		
L	0.471	0.529
H	0.259	0.741
Conscientiousness		
L	0.604	0.396
H	0.386	0.614
Neuroticism		
L	0.500	0.500
H	0.386	0.614
Openness		
L	0.681	0.319
H	0.311	0.689

3. FEATURE EXTRACTION

A total of 37 features, including both low-level features and high-level features, were automatically extracted from the meeting corpus.

3.1 Low-level features

We focused on two classes of features: 'Activity' and 'Emphasis' [10], measuring vocal signals in social interactions. Activity, implying conversational activity level, usually indicates interest and excitement. It is measured by the *z*-scored percentage of speaking time (mean and standard deviation of energy per frame, average length in seconds of voiced segments and of speaking segments, fraction of spoken time and voicing rate). For this purpose, the speech stream of each participant is first segmented into voiced and non-voiced segments, and then split into speaking and non-speaking segments. Emphasis is often considered a signal indicating the strength of the speaker's motivation. Moreover, the consistency of emphasis (lower the variations, higher the consistency) could be a signal of mental focus, while variability may signal an openness to influence from other people. Emphasis is measured by the variation in prosody, *i.e.* pitch and amplitude. For each voiced segment, the mean energy, frequency of the fundamental formant and the spectral entropy are extracted (mean of formant frequency, confidence in formant frequency, spectral entropy, value of the largest autocorrelation peak, location of the largest correlation peak, number of the largest autocorrelation peak, time derivative of energy in frame). The mean-scaled standard deviation of these extracted values is then estimated by averaging over longer time-periods (standard deviation of formant frequency, confidence in formant frequency, spectral entropy, value of the largest autocorrelation peaks, location of the largest autocorrelation peaks, number of the largest autocorrelation peaks, and time derivative of energy in frame).

3.2 High-level features

Social attention features were extracted by jointly processing the audio-video channels using the hierarchical approach developed in [8]: the output of a Cylindrical Head Model [15] head-pose tracker was used as a proxy for the subject's gaze and fine-tuned with the output of a sub-pixel accurate visual-gaze estimation system [16]. Social attention features were defined as the outcome of joint processing of head-pose and visual-gaze: for each subject, in every frame, *Attention Given* (to at least one of the other participants) and *Attention Received* (from at least one of the other participants) were thus available.

The audio channel was processed through use of a Voice Activity Detection system based on the long-term spectral divergence algorithm detailed in [12]. Speaking time was calculated as the percentage of frames in which voice activity was detected over the duration of the processed slice.

For every participant p, the audio-visual features were then fused in order to obtain *Attention Given While Speaking* (the percentage of p's speaking time during which he/she devotes visual attention to at least one of the other members of the group), *Attention Given While Not Speaking* (the percentage of p's non-speaking time during which he/she devotes visual attention to at least one of the other members of the group), *Attention Received While Speaking* (the percentage of p's speaking time during which he/she receives visual attention from at least one of the other group members), and *Attention Received While Not Speaking* (the percentage of p's non-speaking time during which he/she receives visual attention from at least one of the other group members).

4. FEATURE SELECTION

Correlation-based feature selection is a subset selection technique whose objective is to determine the optimal subset of features [6]. This method evaluates the merit of a subset of features computing the individual predictive ability of each feature along with the degree of redundancy between them. The preferred and selected features using this approach are the features highly correlated with the target value and with low inter-correlation values. This method is used in conjunction with a search strategy, typically the `Best First' search that makes a search in the space of features subsets, using a greedy hill-climbing with a backtracking facility. The search may start with an empty set of features and search forward (forward search) or with the full set of features and search backward (backward search), or at any point search in both directions, forward and backward. We employed the forward search feature selection technique.

The selection has been based on 10-fold cross validation; features selected in at least 8 folds were chosen to train and test the models. The features selected for each personality trait are as follows:

1) *Extroversion* – mean of {attention given, attention received, attention received while not speaking, formant frequency, spectral entropy, energy in frame};
2) *Neuroticism* – mean of time derivative of energy in frame;
3) *Agreeableness* – mean of {formant frequency, confidence in formant frequency}, standard deviation of {spectral entropy, number of autocorrelation peaks};
4) *Openness* – mean of {attention received, formant frequency, spectral entropy};
5) *Consciousness* – mean of {attention received, attention received while speaking, attention received while not speaking, formant frequency, value of largest autocorrelation peak}.

5. AUTOMATIC RECOGNITION OF PERSONALITY STATES

A set of machine learning algorithms, both generative (Naïve Bayes, Hidden Markov Models) and discriminative (Support Vector Machines) were used to evaluate the effectiveness of the selected features in modeling the dynamics of personality states. Each algorithm was evaluated in 5 binary classification tasks, one per personality trait. The leave-one-meeting-out strategy was employed, thus 4 models for each personality state were trained on a 3-meetings subset, evaluating them against the remaining one, and finally averaging the results.

The first classifier we applied is Naïve Bayes, a simple probabilistic classifier that applies the Bayes theorem and assumes that the presence/absence of a particular feature of a given class (*e.g.*, a personality state) is unrelated to the presence/absence of other features. The main advantage of using Naïve Bayes is that it only requires a small amount of training data to estimate the parameters (means and variances) necessary for classification. As discussed in connection with Table 2, there are certain regularities in personality state change that a sequential model might be able to capture. Hidden Markov Models were exploited to this end; they consider the temporal correlation between the samples and define the prior probability of the classes in the current sample as depending upon the posterior probabilities of the classes in the previous sample. More precisely, a left-to-right HMM model for each personality state (one for extrovert/introvert; one for neurotic/emotionally stable; and so on) was represented as follows: t, time: $y(t)$, the feature vector; $x(t)$, the personality state; $p(x)$, the priors for the personality states; $p(x(t)|x(t-1)$, the personality states transitions probabilities; $p(y(t)|x(t))$, the conditional distribution of the observed feature vector given the current personality state at time t. We assumed speaker independence and the feature sequences (one per subject) from all the four meetings were used to train a single HMM. The training was done using the standard Expectation Maximization (EM) algorithm. For prediction, each person is represented by an independent instantiation of the same Markov process. Thus, four independent HMMs represent the four people in a meeting.

For classification, we used the standard Viterbi algorithm to compute the most likely sequence of personality states. Finally, we also tested the performance of a powerful discriminative approach. In particular, we used Support Vector Machines (SVMs) as classifiers. The bound-constrained SVM classification algorithms with a linear and with a RBF kernel were used. The cost parameter C and the RBF kernel parameter γ were estimated through the grid technique by means of 10-fold cross validation.

Furthermore, the cost parameter C was weighted for each class with a factor inversely proportional to the class size.

6. RESULTS AND DISCUSSION

Table 3 reports accuracy results. Bold figures identify values that are significantly better ($p<.05$) than the relevant criteria, represented by the classifiers that use the priors (binomial tests with Bonferroni correction).

Table 3. Summary of classification results

	NB	HMM	SVM (lin)	SVM (rbf)
Extra	**0.694**	**0.731**	**0.648**	**0.676**
Neurot	**0.639**	0.574	**0.63**	**0.62**
Agreable	0.583	0.481	0.574	0.583
Opennes	0.5	0.5	0.546	0.547
Conscien	**0.583**	0.547	0.575	0.555

Extraversion is the best-recognized behavioral quality: extravert/introvert behaviors are easier (using the considered features) to distinguish than, *e.g.*, Openness. Neuroticism is the second best recognized quality, an interesting result considering that it is obtained by using just one feature, the (mean of the) speech energy derivative. The results for the other states are either non-significant or barely significant (as for Conscientiousness with Naïve Bayes).

HMMs yield interesting results only with Extraversion and in this case, they perform statistically better than linear or rbf SVMs. Since in the ground truth, personality states such as Openness and Conscientiousness show temporal properties similar to those of Extraversion, the ineffectiveness of HMM to isolate them is probably due to the limited predictive power of the selected features. Finally, SVM classifiers with linear and RBF kernels have similar performance scores.

In general, it seems that the considered non-verbal features have a good power in discriminating between introvert and extrovert behaviors, a result that emphasizes the important role of vocal (*e.g.*, pitch) and social attention features not only for recognizing the Extroversion trait (as widely documented by studies in social psychology and in the automatic analysis of behavior), but also for the recognition of behaviors expected from the trait. The encouraging results obtained for the Neurotic dimension, employing a single feature are also notable. Putting them together with the results concerning Extraversion, and noting that the two corresponding traits are also referred to as Positive and Negative Affect respectively, it can be concluded that the quality of affect, as it surfaces in actual behaviors, is a most readily detectable characteristic among those constituting the Big Five taxonomy.

We have just begun work concerning a highly complex phenomenon: automatic characterization of the quality of behaviors in terms of personality states. Still, preliminary results appear to have proven its feasibility, opening the way to a new and exciting research area.

7. AKNOWLEDGEMENT

Bruno Lepri's research is funded by PERSI project inside the Marie Curie COFUND – 7th Framework. The work of Jacopo Staiano, Ramanathan Subramanian, and Nicu Sebe was partially supported by the FIRB S-PATTERNS project.

REFERENCES

[1] Costa, P.T., and McCrae, R.R. Four ways why five factors are basic. *Personality and Individual Differences*, 13(6): 653-665, 1992.

[2] Donnellan, M.B., Conger, R.D., and Bryant, C.M. The Big Five and enduring marriages. *Journal of Research in Personality*, 38: 481–504, 2004.

[3] Fleeson, W. Towards a structure- and process-integrated view of personality: Traits as density distributions of states. *Journal of Personality and Social Psychology,* 80: 1011-1027, 2001.

[4] Gosling, S. D., Rentfrow, P. J., & Swann, W. B., Jr. A Very Brief Measure of the Big Five Personality Domains. *Journal of Research in Personality*, 37: 504-528, 2003.

[5] Hall J., and Watson W. The effects of a normative intervention on group decision-making performance. *Human Relations*, 23(4): 299–317, 1970.

[6] Hall, M. A. Correlation-Based Feature Selection for Discrete and Numeric Class Machine Learning. *Proc. 17th Int'l Conf. Machine Learning*, 359-366, 2000.

[7] Komarraju, M., and Karau, S. J. The relationship between the Big Five personality traits and academic motivation. *Personality and Individual Differences*, 39: 557–567, 2005.

[8] Lepri, B. Subramanian, R., Kalimeri, K., Staiano, J., Pianesi, F., and Sebe, N. Employing Social Gaze and Speaking Activity for Automatic Determination of the Extraversion Trait. In *Int'l Conf. on Multimodal Interfaces*, 2010.

[9] Mairesse F., Walker M.A., Mehl M.R., and Moore R.K. Using Linguistic Cues for the Automatic Recognition of Personality in Conversation and Text. In *Journal of Artificial Intelligence Research* 30: 457-500, 2007.

[10] Pentland, A. *Honest Signals.* MIT Press, 2008.

[11] Pianesi, F., Mana, N., Cappelletti, A., Lepri, B., and Zancanaro. M. Multimodal Recognition of Personality Traits in Social Interactions. In *Int'l Conf. on Multimodal Interfaces*, 2008.

[12] Ramirez, J., Segura, C., Benitez, C., de la Torre, A., and Rubio, A. Efficient voice activity detection algorithms using long-term speech information. *Speech Communication*. 42(3-4): 271-287, 2004.

[13] Reeves, B., and Nass, C. *The Media Equation*. University of Chicago Press, 1996.

[14] Sigurdsson, J.F. Computer experience, attitudes toward computers and personality characteristics in psychology undergraduates. *Personality and Individual Differences*, 12(6): 617–624, 1991.

[15] Valenti, R., Sebe, N., and Gevers, T. Combining Head Pose and Eye Location Information for Gaze Estimation. In *IEEE Trans. Image Processing*, 2011.

[16] Valenti, R., Staiano, J., Sebe, N., and Gevers, T. Webcam-based Visual Gaze Estimation. In *Int'l Conference on Image Analysis and Processing*, 662–671, 2009.

Snap & Play: Auto-Generate Personalized Find-the-Difference Mobile Game *

Si Liu†
Institute of Automation,
Chinese Academy of Sciences
China-Singapore Institute of
Digital Media, Singapore
sliu@ia.ac.cn

Qiang Chen†
Department of ECE,
National University of
Singapore, Singapore
chenqiang@nus.edu.sg

Jian Dong
Department of ECE,
National University of
Singapore, Singapore
a0068947@nus.edu.sg

Shuicheng Yan
Department of ECE,
National University of
Singapore, Singapore
eleyans@nus.edu.sg

Changsheng Xu
Institute of Automation,
Chinese Academy of Sciences
China-Singapore Institute of
Digital Media, Singapore
csxu@ia.ac.cn

Hanqing Lu
Institute of Automation,
Chinese Academy of Sciences
China-Singapore Institute of
Digital Media, Singapore
luhq@ia.ac.cn

ABSTRACT

According to the year 2010 report of the Entertainment Software Association [5], 42% of USA heads of households reported playing games on mobile devices, rising quickly from the 20% in 2002 and bringing huge market for mobile games. In this paper, by taking the popular game, Find-the-Difference (FiDi), as a concrete example, we explore new mobile game design principles and techniques for enhancing player's gaming experience in personalized, automatic, and dynamic aspects. Unlike traditional FiDi game, where image pairs (source image vs. target image) with M different patches are manually produced by game developer and players may feel boring or cheat after practicing all image pairs, our proposed Personalized FiDi (P-FiDi) mobile game may be played under a new Snap & Play mode. The player may first take photos with one's mobile device (or select from one's own albums). Then, these photos serve as source images, and the P-FiDi system automatically generates the counterpart target images by sequential operations of aesthetic image quality enhancement, image patch and differentiating style joint selection, music adaptation, dynamic difficulty level determination, and ultimate automatic image editing with a rich set of popular differentiating styles used in traditional FiDi game. Finally, the player enjoys the unique gaming with one's own (instant) photos and music, and the freedom to have new gaming image pairs any time. The user studies show that the P-FiDi mobile game is satisfying in terms of player experience.

†indicates equal contribution. This work was done when the first author was a Research Assistant in Electrical and Computer Engineering Department, National University of Singapore.
*Area chair: Gang Hua and Daniel Gatica-Perez

MM'11, November 28–December 1, 2011, Scottsdale, Arizona, USA.

Figure 1: (a) Snap & Play gaming mode for Personalized FiDi (P-FiDi) mobile game, where the instantly captured photo is used as source image, and the system auto-generates the counterpart target image with M different patches. (b) The interface for the basic version of P-FiDi. For better viewing, please see the original color pdf file.

Categories and Subject Descriptors

I.2.1 [**Artificial Intelligence**]: Applications and Expert Systems; H.5.1 [**Information Interfaces And Presentation**]: Multimedia Information Systems

Keywords

Personalized, Snap & Play, Games With a Purpose, Automatic, Dynamic, Advertisement, Edutainment

1. INTRODUCTION

In this paper[1], by taking the popular game, Find-the-Difference (FiDi), as a concrete example, we explore new mobile game design principles and techniques for enhancing player's gaming experience in personalized, automatic, and dynamic aspects. FiDi game is very popular and welcomed.

[1]This is a simplified version, please check our website for the long version.

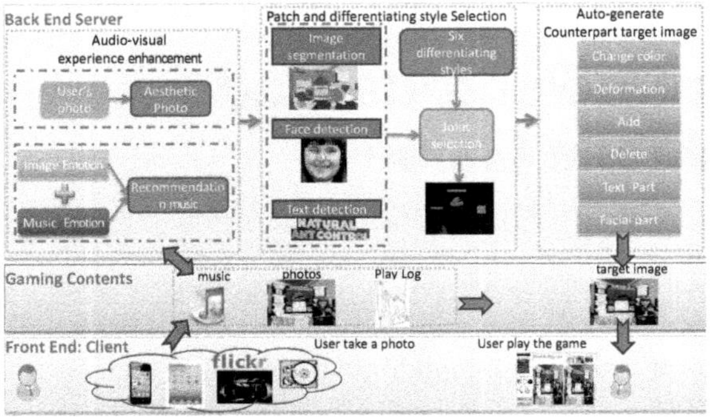

Figure 2: The proposed framework for the automatic and dynamic P-FiDi mobile game. For better viewing, please see the original color pdf file for all images.

There are averagely about 180,000 players simultaneously online at 8 : 00 pm in the QQ game[2], the biggest online game society in China. A typical interface is shown in Figure 1(b). There are two images displayed in pair. The left image is called source image, while the right one is called target image. The source image and the target image are almost the same except for M (generally 5) small different patches between them. The differences can be produced using many different change/differentiating styles, such as color change, deformation, adding new items, deleting existing items and so on. The player can gain the corresponding score by identifying each difference within pre-set time. Despite the success of traditional FiDi game, it is imperfect as many other general games. First, the target images are generated manually by software experts, which is generally very time-consuming. Second, the provided images are specifically provided by game developer, which may not well fit player' taste, and thus the player will be easy to feel boring. Finally, the available number of image pairs is limited and the involved differences for each image pair are fixed, and thus an experienced player can remember all the different patches and their corresponding differentiating styles, which may easily lead to cheat in gaming process. On the other hand, through playing FiDi, the player can develop the capability of observation, relax mood and simultaneously browse many high-quality photos. Owing to its popularity and the close relation with multimedia techniques, we select FiDi as the example in this paper to investigate how to enhance user gaming experience with multimedia techniques.

2. SYSTEM OVERVIEW

To provide player individually unique experience, we design and implement the P-FiDi system by considering the following key elements. (1) The most important quality we emphasize is **naturalness**. All the generated patches with changes should visually look seamless with the source image. (2) We target a **personalized** system which serves each individual player with tailored visual & audio experience and difficulty level setting. (3) The overall system is **automatic** and **dynamic**, the latter of which guarantees the freshness of the game and avoids the possible boring sense. These key elements severe as guidelines for us to design the entire mobile game.

The flowchart of the P-FiDi system is shown in Figure 2. First, user uploads a source image to the system either by taking a photo or choosing an existing photo. Meanwhile, the meta data of user personal music are sent to the back-end along the the source image. The whole back-end processing contains three components sequentially. The first component aims to provide unique audio-visual experience to player. Visually, the source image may be aesthetically enhanced. For audio part, the emotion of the source image is extracted/estimated and the music with consistent emotion is recommenced as gaming background music. In the subsequent patch and differentiating style selection phase, the photo is segmented into smaller patches. Face, facial component alignment and text detection are also used to generate some semantic patches if available. They all serve as the processing units in the following steps. According to the gaming rules, up to M (5 in this work) patches are selected to perform changes and their corresponding differentiating styles are determinated simultaneously. In figure 2, the patch-style selection matrix is represented by a map, where each segments are colored according to their corresponding to their differentiating style. Finally, the patches undergo the selected changes and the counterpart target image is generated. Finally the target image along with the recommended music is sent back to the front-end, and the user plays with the generated image pair with the selected background music. The system records the player's performance information, which is used to adjust difficulty level dynamically.

[2]http://qqgame.qq.com

3. TECHNIQUE DETAILS

3.1 Visual-Audio Experience Enhancement

3.1.1 Photo-Quality Aesthetic Enhancement

An implicit purpose of the P-FiDi game is to browse many esthetic images. Moreover, a key factor to foster player's adhesion is the pleasant gaming experience. However, most players are not professional photographer, so it is necessary and important to first perform photo-quality aesthetic enhancement when necessary.

To enhance the aesthetic effect of photos and better attract the mobile game players, some user-provided photos may need pre-processing. We mainly focus on two categories of photos for such a pre-processing, a) images containing single foreground objects, and b) scene images containing no definite foreground, such as landscapes or seascapes [2].

3.1.2 Background Music Recommendation

For P-FiDi game, proper background music may promote the game experience. In our implementation, the music is from the music album in one's mobile device. We mainly consider two factors in the background music recommendation process: user's own preference and the cross-modality image-music emotion consistency

By combing the user preference score p and the emotion similarity m, the final recommendation level r for each music track can be computed as:

$$r = \alpha p + (1 - \alpha) m, \quad (1)$$

where α is a tunable parameter, which is set as 0.7 in our implementation. Finally, the music with the maximal r is selected as background music.

3.2 Patch and Differentiating Style Selection

The first step of fully automatical creation of the counterpart target image is to select some basic processing units as the candidate change receivers. Basically, we need determine where to change and how to change, which is a patch-style joint selection process. Based on this process, further image editing operations can be conducted to change each selected patch with the determined differentiating style accordingly.

3.2.1 Changeable Unit Generation

To reduce the computational cost, we use mean-shift algorithm [4] to decompose the source image into several small size patches, which serve as the basic processing units in the P-FiDi system. Besides the segmented patches, two other kinds of semantic patches are dealt with separately, i.e the face area [12]and text area.

3.2.2 Patch-Style Joint Selection

Patch-Style Joint Selection Matrix: The selected patches and potential adopted differentiating styles combination are represented as an $N \times K$ indicator matrix S, where K is the number of candidate differentiating styles,

The non-zero elements S_{ij} indicates that the i-th patch is selected to undergo the change with the j-th differentiating style. Each row represents a patch and each column corresponds to a differentiating type.

Objective for Overall Fitness: The patch-style fitness matrix C is of the same size as S, with element C_{ij} corresponding to the preference of patch i to undergo the j-th differentiating style. The definition of C shall be given in Section 3.3.

Objective for Spatially Dispersed Distribution: To synchronize with gaze movement on the image, it is intuitively reasonable to distribute the changed patches dispersedly in the image. To describe the patches' spatial distances, we define an $N \times N$ matrix D, with each element describing the pairwise spatial distance between two image patches. We also define a matrix $R \in \mathbb{R}^{N \times (N \times K)}$ to sum over s for each patch. In the i-th row, the $(i-1) \times K + 1$ to the $(i \times K)$-th elements are of value 1 and others are zeros. Then $(Rs)_i$ indicates how many differentiating styles have been selected for the i-th patch.

There also exist some extra constraints over s to guarantee the validity of the patch-style joint selection.

Binary Property Constraint: First, s should be binary, namely, $s \in \{0,1\}^{(N \times K) \times 1}$.

Total Change Number Constraint: To ensure the total number of changes is M, we have $\sum_{i=1}^{N \times K} s_i = M$.

Each Patch with at Most One Change: It is natural to restrict that each patch can only undergo one differentiating style, namely, $(Rs)_i \leq 1, \forall\, i \in \{1, 2, \cdots, N\}$.

Change Style Diversity: The diversity is important to enhance the interestingness of the game, and the system should generate as many kinds of changes as possible for each image. Specifically, we restrict that each image cannot contain one certain differentiating style for more than twice. So we define a $K \times (N \times K)$ indicator matrix T.

Overall Formulation: In summary, the patch-style joint selection problem is formulated as follows:

$$\begin{aligned} \max_{s} \quad & c^T s + \frac{1}{2M} s^T R^T D R s \\ s.t. \quad & (Rs)_i \leq 1, \forall\, i \in \{1, 2, \cdots, N\}; \\ & (Ts)_j \leq 2, \forall\, j \in \{1, 2, \cdots, K\}; \\ & \sum_{i=1}^{N \times K} s_i = M; \quad s \in \{0,1\}^{(N \times K) \times 1}. \end{aligned} \qquad (2)$$

This optimization problem can be transferred to a specific Binary Quadratic Programming problem [9]. However, the optimal solution cannot be obtained in polynomial time. There exist many solutions, e.g MOSEK [1], to relax this problem either using Semidefinite Programming or spectral relaxation [9]. But optimal solution need huge amount of computation.

3.2.3 Criterion for Patch-Style Fitness

In P-FiDi system, the number of changes is fixed to be M, and theoretically, each patch can undergo any kind of change. However, each differentiating style has its preference in patch properties. For example, adding small items onto flat region is more natural and easier to implement than onto complicated regions. We enumerate the definition for style-specific fitness, and present four features for judging whether one patch is suitable for one specific differentiating style, i.e. patch size, shape of patch, local contrast and color variance. The fitness value of a patch for differentiating style j is finally trained with a weighted sum of these features.

3.3 Auto-Generate Counterpart Target Image

In this subsection, we elaborate on auto-generating the counterpart target image with various image editing operations over the selected patches with their corresponding determined differentiating styles from the six candidate styles: changing color, deformation, adding items, erasing items, text change and facial change.

Changing Color: In P-FiDi system, two methods, color transfer [11] and color harmony[3], are adopted to change the color of the selected patch. The specific change method is determined randomly. The randomness of color change strategies further strengthens the system to be more dynamic.

Deformation: To deform a selected patch, we first generate a mesh (grid) G over this region. Then we map this mesh onto a predefined template or randomized mesh $\hat{G}$. Every grid in the mesh has one-one correspondence with the original mesh G. For each grid, we use color interpolation to generate the new texture. Finally, the obtained new texture for the given region is embedded into the original image using Possion Editing [10].

Adding Items: We adopt two methods to add items into the image. The first is to insert a small item into the selected patch. We collect 120 categories of small items, including animals, daily tools, vegetables, and so on. The category of the item to insert is determined by the scene property of the source image. For example, it is more natural to add a clock rather than an ambulance into an indoor image. The second method is to copy the selected patch to its neighborhood. We scan every patch around the selected patch, and choose the flattest one as the destination patch. Then we use alpha matting [13] to implement the patch copy.

Erasing Items: The fourth differentiating style is to remove and then refill the selected patch.Two inpainting methods are implemented for such a purpose. One is based on examples [7], and the other is based on solving Partial Differential Equations (PDE) [8].

Text Change: The fifth differentiating style is related with texts. We apply a text detector [6] to obtain the text region in the source image. Then based on the detected text parts, we project the pixels towards the bottom border of the text bounding box. Based on the projected histogram, we can segment the text into several letters. After obtaining the letters, three types of changes can be done, i.e., changing letter's color, copying certain letter to its surrounding position and switching the letters' order.

Facial Change: For the last differentiating style, we first use the state-of-the-art level face detector [12] to localize the face region. Then a template matching method is applied to align the face so that we can localize the eyebrow, eye, nose mouth, and facial contour. Then we can proceed several changes such as enlarging (shrinking) the eyes or mouth, lengthening (shortening) the eyebrow. Even more, we can add some items to the face such as mole or ink spot. These changes are subtle and hard to be recognized even if it is on the face.

4. EXPERIMENTS

In this section, we systematically evaluate the P-FiDi mobile game. 400 images from two contributors (also participants of user studies) and 30 advertisement posters from Flickr.com are used as the personalized photo album. These daily photos record many ordinary life moments, such as children's birthdays, friends' graduation ceremonies, friends gathering, spring outing and so on. In total, 30 friends of the two contributors are invited to participate the user-studies. There are 20 females and 10 males. Their ages vary from 10 to 50.

4.1 User Experience: P-FiDi vs. FiDi

As the game interface design is not the focus of this work, we focus on the quality of the generated source-target image pairs for player experience study and the image pairs from P-FiDi and traditional FiDi games are all played with the same gaming interface in Figure 1. For comparison, we randomly download 15 source-target image pairs from Tecent QQ website, referred to as QQ-FiDi, and another popular FiDi website [3], referred to as Web-FiDi, respectively. The source-target image pairs from these two popular FiDi game providers are used as baselines and sent to the 30 players. Another 15 images pairs are randomly selected from the personalized photo album and also sent to each player. The order of QQ-FiDi, Web-FiDi and P-FiDi is shuffled randomly for each player. After players have played all the 45 image pairs, they are asked to evaluate these three systems from five aspects: 1) image naturalness, 2) interestingness, namely whether playing the game is of fun, 3) style variation richness, 4) content affinity, namely whether the game gives the player an intimacy feeling, and 5) games with a purpose (GWAP), namely whether the players may acquire some extra information by playing the game.

All the evaluations are categorized into five levels, i.e. $\{1, 2, 3, 4, 5\}$, indicating 'very bad', 'bad', 'average', 'good' and 'very good', respectively. The average statistics from the 30 participants are shown in Figure 3. From the results, it is observed that, overall, P-FiDi outperforms the other two baselines, and the superiority is very obvious in terms of GWAP and content affinity aspects. Possible explanations include: 1) players are the friends of the photo contributors, and thus they may feel these source-target image pairs very familiar and attractive, and 2) players can obtain much useful information by playing with commercial posters, e.g., the players shall know when the movie 'king's speech' is going to release by playing with its movie poster. The image naturalness of the P-FiDi system is comparable with, though slightly worse than, QQ-FiDi. It is reasonable since the target images from QQ-FiDi are all manually designed by experts and the images are all carefully selected.

[3]http://spotthedifference.com/explorer.asp

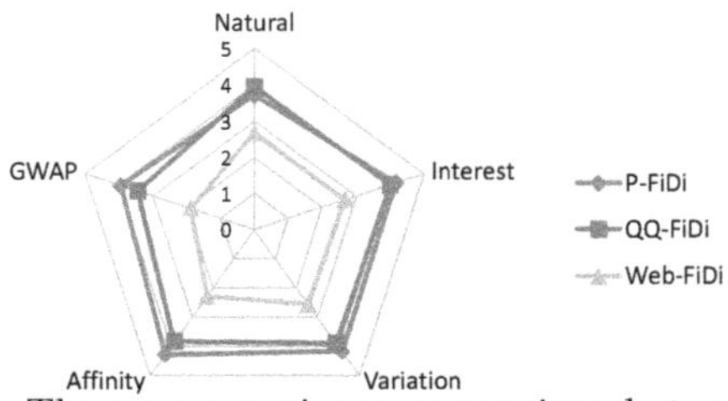

Figure 3: The user experience comparison between P-FiDi and two baselines from five aspects.

Figure 4: Some results of P-FiDi. The changed parts are annotated with yellow ellipse or arrow.

4.2 Discussions

To show P-FiDi is technically feasible in generating natural target images with desirable differentiating styles, the combinational results are shown in Figure 4. More results along with the front-end of the P-FiDi[4]are available online. These results well validate the technical feasibility of the P-FiDi system.

5. ACKNOWLEDGMENTS

This work is supported by the CSIDM Project No.CSIDM-200803 partially funded by a grant from the National Research Foundation (NRF) administered by the Media Development Authority (MDA) of Singapore. This work was also supported by the National Natural Science Foundation of China (Grant No. 60903146, 60833006), and 973 Program (Project No. 2010CB327905).

6. REFERENCES

[1] The MOSEK optimization software.

[2] S. Bhattacahrya, R. Sukthankar, and M. Shah. A framework for photo-quality assessment and enhancement based on visual aesthetics. *MM*, 2010.

[3] D. Cohen-Or, O. Sorkine, R. Gal, T. Leyvand, and Y. Xu. Color harmonization. *TOG*, 2006.

[4] D. Comaniciu and P. Meer. Mean shift: A robust approach toward feature space analysis. *TPAMI*, 2002.

[5] entertainment software association. Essential facts about the computer and video game. 2010.

[6] B. Epshtein, E. Ofek, and Y. Wexler. Detecting text in natural scenes with stroke width transform. In *CVPR*, 2010.

[7] A. Criminisi, P. Prez, K. Toyama. Object Removal by Exemplar-Based Inpaintin. In *CVPR*, 2003.

[8] Tony F. Chan and Jianhong Shen. Non-Texture Inpainting by Curvature-Driven Diffusions. *JVCIR*, 2000.

[9] C. Olsson. Solving large scale binary quadratic problems: Spectral methods vs. semidefinite programming. In *CVPR*, 2007.

[10] P. Pérez, M. Gangnet, and A. Blake. Poisson image editing. In *SIGGRAPH*, 2003.

[11] E. Reinhard, M. Ashikhmin, B. Gooch, and P. Shirley. Color transfer between images. *IEEE Comput. Graph. Appl.*, 2001.

[12] P. Viola and M. Jones. Robust real-time face detection. *IJCV*, 2004.

[13] A. Levin, D. Lischinski and Y. Weiss. A Closed Form Solution to Natural Image Matting. In *CVPR*, 2007.

[4]A simplified version for ease of distribution `http://sites.google.com/site/pfidifidi/personlized-fidi`

Fast Detection of Noisy GPS and Magnetometer Tags in Wide-Baseline Multi-Views *

Aveek Shankar Brahmachari
Computer Science and Engineering
University of South Florida
Tampa, FL 33620, USA.
abrahmac@mail.usf.edu

Sudeep Sarkar
Computer Science and Engineering
University of South Florida
Tampa, FL 33620, USA.
sarkar@usf.edu

ABSTRACT

We propose an algorithm for detection of noisy GPS and magnetometer tags in wide-baseline camera views. Our algorithm neither needs densely sampled views nor does it need a single visually connected path through all the views in the dataset. We use vision-based estimates of mutual rotation and translation between cameras to compute a measure of confidence on the correctness of the associated GPS and magnetometer tags. The vision algorithm can find the epipolar geometry between two wide-baseline images without needing pre-specified correspondences. We have two versions of our approach; one that requires geometric pose estimation between all pairs of images and a faster version that uses a pre-filter based on photometric comparison of images to quickly reject non-overlapping views from further geometric consideration. We show qualitative and quantitative results on the Nokia Grand Challenge 2010 Dataset. We find that magnetometer readings are more accurate than GPS readings.

Categories and Subject Descriptors

I.4.1 [**Image Processing and Computer Vision**]: Digitization and Image Capture—*Camera calibration*

General Terms

Algorithms, Experiments

Keywords

Epipolar Geometry, Wide-baseline Images, Image Collection

1. INTRODUCTION

Images tagged with GPS and magnetometer information are becoming common. However, their reliability is questionable partly due to unavoidable environmental constraints such as presence of tall buildings, cloudy days, etc., and partly due to low quality sensors. We propose a vision-based method for the detection of noisy GPS and magnetometer tags in an unordered collection of wide-baseline views. The problem of refining GPS and magnetometer tags figured in the Nokia Grand Challenge [8]. So far, no research work has directly addressed this challenge problem. The Nokia Grand Challenge dataset is a hard dataset containing images captured using a mobile phone that has a camera and is equipped with GPS and magnetometer sensors. The visual connectivity in this dataset is very sparse as we have shown in [4]. This is unlike most other landmark scene datasets used in current research [1, 2] in scene reconstruction and other applications [10, 7, 13, 5, 12, 9]. We use the Nokia Grand Challenge dataset in our research and consider the problem of detection of noisy GPS and magnetometer tags.

Detection of noisy GPS and magnetometer tags has not been addressed in vision research to the best of our knowledge. However, GPS and vision sensor fusion have been researched for applications such as localization of a query image in a dataset of GPS tagged images [7, 13] and bridging of GPS outages in Mobile Mapping Vehicles [9]. In all such applications, the visual connectivity among images is dense in terms of the 3D scene they capture. Snavely [10] proposed the use of GPS pose as initialization to bundle adjustment of images that are very well-connected in terms of the 3D scene they capture. However, as we find in the current study, the GPS and magnetometer tags are not reliable to be accepted as initializations to bundle adjustment especially for wide-baseline images.

For each image, we compute the pairwise epipolar geometries with respect to the other neighboring images. In the exhaustive version, the neighbors are all the other images, but in the faster version, the neighboring images are decided based on photometric comparison of the image features. Epipolar geometry estimation is the most expensive part of the process, especially when we have wide baselines. The photometric pre-filter results in significant savings. To quantify the correctness of the GPS tags, we use the maximum of cosine similarity between the vision based estimate of unit translation vectors over all the neighboring epipolar geometry estimates and the respective GPS based unit translation vectors. We compute a similar quantity for the magnetometer based rotation estimates to quantify magnetometer errors. We also visually display the epipolar lines based on GPS and magnetometer estimates and those based on vision estimates to qualitatively characterize the extent of the errors.

*Area chair: Daniel Gatica-Perez

MM'11, November 28–December 1, 2011, Scottsdale, Arizona, USA.

2. ALGORITHM COMPONENTS

Given N images $I_1, \cdots, I_N$ with the ith camera GPS position in Earth Centered Earth Fixed (ECEF) coordinates $\mathbf{X_i} = (x_i, y_i, z_i)$ and magnetometer based orientations $\mathbf{O_i} = (\psi_i, \theta_i, \phi_i)$, we need an estimate of confidence of the GPS positions and magnetometer orientations. This estimate of confidence can then be incorporated into 3D view estimation algorithm [10] or by an algorithm that constructs a photo tour through the views [4].

For a pair of images (I_i, I_j), let $\mathbf{T^v_{ij}}$ and $\mathbf{R^v_{ij}}$ be the vision-based estimate and $\mathbf{T^g_{ij}}$ and $\mathbf{R^m_{ij}}$ be the GPS based estimate of translation unit vector and rotation in terms of Euler's angles, respectively.

2.1 Vision-based Rotation and Translation

For wide-baseline views, epipolar geometry estimation is a hard problem since the rate of outliers in initial photometrically established feature correspondences is high and the number of inliers is low. We use the Balanced LOcal and Global Search (BLOGS) algorithm [3] to estimate the rotation and translation between two camera views. BLOGS estimates the epipolar geometry between two views by employing complementing local and global searches based on the Joint Feature Distributions [11] and a distribution based on the feature appearances. This search finds the best minimal set of correspondences, i.e. 8 pairs of correspondences in our case as we use the 8-eight point algorithm to estimate the epipolar geometry. To constrain the search, we restrict it to a set of putative correspondences. Given all match scores between feature pairs from two images in the form of a similarity matrix, ρ, the match pairs that exhibit highest similarity along both their respective rows and columns, are selected to be the putative correspondences $\mathbf{X_{ij}}$ between images I_i and I_j. BLOGS avoids degenerate correspondence configurations by checking for the mutual scatter in each pair of correspondences in the minimal set of correspondences. An example of a degenerate sample would be all points lying on a plane.

Based on the best minimal set of correspondences, we estimate the fundamental matrices $\mathbf{F_{ij}}$. From this, using the intrinsic calibration matrices $\mathbf{K_i}$ and $\mathbf{K_j}$ for the two views, we estimate the essential matrix as $\mathbf{E_{ij}} = \mathbf{K_j}^T \mathbf{F_{ij}} \mathbf{K_i}$. This essential matrix, $\mathbf{E_{ij}}$, is then decomposed into a translation vector, $\mathbf{T^v_{ij}}$, and a rotation matrix, $\mathbf{R^v_{ij}}$ [6].

2.2 Which Vision Estimate to Use?

We use how well the fundamental matrix $\mathbf{F_{ij}}$ fits the putative correspondence set $\mathbf{X_{ij}}$ as an estimate of the confidence in the vision estimates of the rotation and translation. We compute this fit measure using a robust combination of the Sampson's distance, which is an excellent approximation of the geometric re-projection error. We refer the reader to [6] for details regarding the mathematical form of the Sampson distance. We denote the Sampson's distance of the k-th putative correspondence between images I_i and I_j by $\delta_{ij}(k)$. These individual errors of the putative correspondences (both inliers and outliers) need to be combined into one overall error measure. However, instead of simply summing them, we consider a robust combination form that allows us to weigh down outliers. We choose Welsh's weight function as our robust combination kernel to arrive at the error combination given by

$$\gamma(\mathbf{F_{ij}}|\mathbf{X_{ij}}) = \frac{1}{|\mathbf{X_{ij}}|} \sum_{k=1}^{|\mathbf{X_{ij}}|} \exp\left(-\frac{\delta_{ij}(k)}{\sigma}\right), \tag{1}$$

where $|\mathbf{X_{ij}}|$ is the cardinality of the putative correspondence set. The negative exponential in the Welsh's weight function suppresses the effect of outliers. Correspondences with very large Sampson's errors will not contribute to the overall cost. The sum of such exponentials gives an M-estimate of the fundamental matrix fitting quality. In our experiments, we have fixed $\sigma = 10^{-4}$.

This fit error can also be looked upon as a geometric inlier rate estimate, i.e. estimate of the fraction of putative correspondences that are "explained" by the fundamental matrix estimate. This inlier rate estimate should be high, but not too high. High inlier rates could also arise from degenerate configurations, e.g. planar scenes. We want to ignore epipolar geometry estimates based on such degenerate configurations as they will not result in reliable estimates of rotation and translation. We employ the following geometric test flag to decide whether to use the corresponding vision estimates:

$$G_{ij} = \left(\tau_3 \geq \gamma(\mathbf{F_{ij}}|\mathbf{X_{ij}}) \geq \max\left(\frac{\tau_1}{|\mathbf{X_{ij}}|}, \tau_2\right)\right). \tag{2}$$

Thus, the estimated inlier rate should be between an upper and lower value, with the lower value constrained to result in at least τ_1 number of inlier correspondences. In our experiments, we used $\tau_1 = 20$, $\tau_2 = 0.1$, and $\tau_3 = 0.75$. Note that this means that the epipolar estimate should have at least 20 correspondences as its support. Similar thresholds have been used in [10].

2.3 Tag Confidence Estimation

The dot product of the unit translation vectors from GPS, $\mathbf{T^g_{ij}}$, and that from vision, $\mathbf{T^v_{ij}}$, is indicative of the correctness of the GPS associated with the two images. We denote this dot product by g_{ij}. Similarly, the product of cosine of the difference between Euler angles from magnetometer, $\mathbf{R^m_{ij}}$, and the vision rotation estimate, $\mathbf{R^v_{ij}}$, is a measure of confidence in the magnetometer tags of the image pair. We denote this cosine product by m_{ij}. For each image, I_i, we consider the vision estimates of mutual rotation and translation with other images, I_j, for which the test flag G_{ij} (Eq. 2) is true. We compute the confidences in the GPS and magnetometer tags for image I_i, denoted by g_i and m_i, respectively, using:

$$g_i = \max_{j \in \{G_{ij}=T\}} g_{ij} \quad \text{and} \quad m_i = \max_{j \in \{G_{ij}=T\}} m_{ij}. \tag{3}$$

The confidence in an image tag is based on the quality of conformance with vision-based estimates that we get when paired with other images.

2.4 Speed-up using Photometric Estimates

The estimation of epipolar geometry between two images is the most computationally expensive part. Moreover, as captured by Eq. 3, we ignore estimates that do not satisfy the test involving geometric inlier rates (Eq. 2). For a dataset with wide baseline views, as is our case, a large number of vision estimates would be ignored. We designed a test based on just photometric properties that can do equally well. This can replace the geometric test in Eq. 3 and thus restrict the epipolar estimation process only to limited cases.

The photometric similarities between all possible correspondence pairs can be represented as a matrix, ρ. The maximum along both rows and columns of this matrix form our putative set of correspondence, $\mathbf{X_{ij}}$. Let ρ_{kr} and ρ_{kc} be the second highest values in the row and column, respectively, for the k-th putative match. The confidence in a putative correspondences could be related to how different these second maximums are from the similarity of the putative correspondences, which is the maximum along the corresponding row and the column. The more is the difference, more is the confidence in the match being correct. We use the following combination to result in a normalized confidence for the k-th putative match.

$$w_{ij}(k) = (1 - \exp^{-\rho_k})^2(1 - \frac{\rho_{kr}}{\rho_k})(1 - \frac{\rho_{kc}}{\rho_k}) \qquad (4)$$

The combination results in high confidence values for putative matches with high similarities *and* those for which the next best matches have low similarities. Using these confidence weights over the putative matches, $\mathbf{X_{ij}}$, we define the photometric similarity between the two images as

$$P_{ij} = 1 - \exp\left(-\kappa \log |\mathbf{X_{ij}}| \frac{\sum_{k=i}^{|\mathbf{X_{ij}}|} w_{ij}(k)}{|\mathbf{X_{ij}}|}\right). \qquad (5)$$

It is exponentially related to the average confidence over the putative matches, $\frac{\sum_i w_{ij}(k)}{|\mathbf{X_{ij}}|}$, and the number of putative matches, i.e. the $\log |\mathbf{X_{ij}}|$ term. This increases with the number of putative correspondences and their average confidence. The constant term κ is fixed based on training data. In our experiments, we used $\kappa = 3$. Although our approach is not feature specific, we have used SIFT features in this research. For other features the value of κ might vary.

We can replace the $G_{ij} = TRUE$ test in Eq. 3 with $P_{ij} = TRUE$ test. In other words, instead of using actual geometric inlier rate and number of inliers, we use a photometric measure that can be computed easily. Also, to bound computational cost, we restrict to epipolar estimation only to top-n best photometric matches to any given image.

3. RESULTS

The Nokia Grand Challenge dataset consists of widely spaced images and also has GPS and magnetometer tags which makes it a suitable test bed. It has two sub-datasets - one is a 'Demoset' containing 105 images and another is a 'Lausanne' set containing 243 images. κ in the Eq. 5 is estimated over the 'Demoset' in Nokia Dataset. We show results on the 'Lausanne' set. All 243 images from the Lausanne dataset were sub-sampled to size of 192×256 for evaluation of photometric similarity matrix. Pose-estimates were evaluated at size of 384×512 for these images.

3.1 GPS and Magnetometer Errors

In Fig. 1(a) we show a histogram of our estimated GPS tag confidence measure given in Eq. 3. Ideally all the values should have been close to 1, capturing the fact that there is at least one other image in the dataset with which the GPS and vision-based translation estimates are in agreement. This shows that there are many noisy GPS tags. On the other hand, the histogram of our estimated magnetometer tag confidence (Fig. 1(b)) shows that most of the values are close to 1. In general the magnetometer tags are more reliable than the GPS tags, at least on the Nokia dataset.

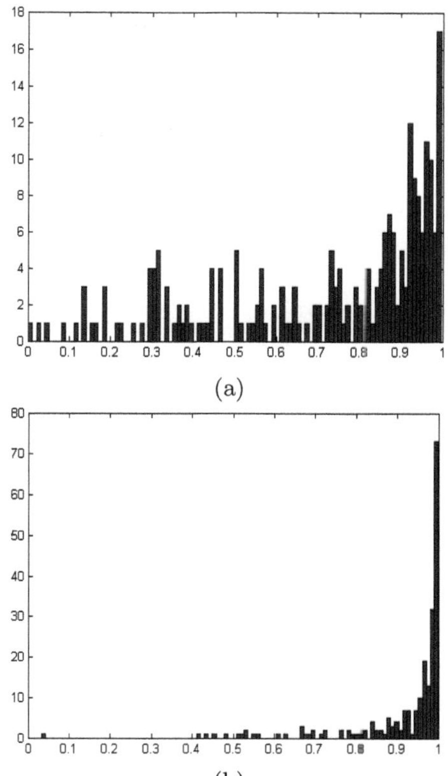

Figure 1: Histogram of confidence in (a) GPS and (b) magnetometer tags as validated by vision-based estimates for 243 images in the Nokia Grand Challenge Dataset. The confidence values range from 0 to 1, with 0 denoting no-confidence and 1 being highly certain.

3.2 Comparison of Epipolar Lines

In the absence of actual ground truth, epipolar lines serves as qualitative check of the correctness of our result. In Fig. 2, we show two examples of the quality of the fundamental matrix from vision and from magnetometer and GPS tags. The epipolar lines should pass exactly through the points corresponding to marked points on the left most images. While the vision based estimates were found to be accurate, the GPS and magnetometer based fundamental matrices were found to be far from accurate for most image pairs. The first image pair is the one that has highest support for its GPS and magnetometer based fundamental matrix in the entire dataset.

3.3 Geometric vs. Photometric

The photometric estimate is a good predictor of the geometric match between two images. On the 'Lausanne' test data, we found that there was 95.6% match, i.e. pairs of images that were found to have high photometric similarities also had high geometric inlier rates. On a single machine with Intel Dual Core processor @1.80 GHz, using Matlab, the run time for exhaustive geometric processing, i.e. computing epipolar geometry for every pair of images in the set of 243 images was 21 hrs 38 mins 24 secs. As comparison, using a photometric filter, the time required was reduced drastically to 27 mins 18 secs.

Figure 2: Examples of quality of epipolar estimates based on GPS/magnetometer data and vision data for some image pairs from the Nokia dataset. The left column shows few reference points on one of the images pairs. The middle column shows the corresponding epipolar lines on the other image pair based on the GPS/magnetometer estimates. In the right column we see the epipolar lines based on the vision estimates.

4. CONCLUSION

We saw that it is possible to solve the problem of detection of erroneous GPS and magnetometer tags in images without solving the greater problem of 3D estimation. We do need an algorithm to estimate the epipolar geometry between wide baseline images, which can be computationally expensive. However, photometric comparison of images can be used to significantly reduce the cost by restricting the need for epipolar estimation to only a limited set of image pairs. The parameters of our algorithm were trained using the smaller 'Demoset' in the Nokia Challenge and we demonstrated the performance on the larger 'Lausanne' dataset. These datasets are more difficult in terms of 3D spacing between views and view-overlap than the those used in current works. Greater number of GPS tags were found to be unreliable than magnetometer tags. The next obvious question is whether vision can be used to rectify these GPS tags. This is our future interest.

5. REFERENCES

[1] S. Agarwal, N. Snavely, I. Simon, S. Seitz, and R. Szeliski. Building rome in a day. In *Proceedings of ICCV*, pages 72–79, Kyoto, Japan, 2009.

[2] Y. Avrithis, Y. Kalantidis, G. Tolias, and E. Spyrou. Retrieving landmark and non-landmark images from community photo collections. In *Proceedings of ACM Multimedia*, pages 153–162, Firenze, Italy, October 2010.

[3] A. Brahmachari and S. Sarkar. BLOGS: Balanced Local and Global Search for non-degenerate two view epipolar geometry. In *Proceedings of ICCV*, pages 1685–1692, Kyoto, Japan, 2009.

[4] A. Brahmachari and S. Sarkar. View Clustering of Wide-Baseline N-Views for Photo Tourism. In *Proceedings of SIBGRAPI*, Maceió, 2011.

[5] A. Hakeem, R. Vezzani, M. Shah, and R. Cucchiara. Estimating geospatial trajectory of a moving camera. In *Proceedings of ICPR*, volume 2, pages 82 –87, Hong Kong, 2006.

[6] R. Hartley and A. Zisserman. *Multiple View Geometry in Computer Vision*. Cambridge University Press, NY, USA, 2000.

[7] S. Khan, F. Rafi, and M. Shah. Where was the picture taken: Image localization in route panoramas using epipolar geometry. In *Proceedings of ICME*, pages 249–252, Toronto, Canada, 2006.

[8] T. Pylvanainen. Nokia Challenge 2010: Where was this Photo Taken, and How? `http://comminfo.rutgers.edu/conferences/mmchallenge/2010/02/10/nokia-challenge/`.

[9] R. Roncella, F. Remondino, and G. Forlani. Photogrammetric bridging of GPS outages in mobile mapping. In *VIII Videometrics*, pages 308–319, 2005.

[10] N. Snavely, S. Seitz, and R. Szeliski. Photo tourism: Exploring image collections in 3d. In *SIGGRAPH06*, pages 835–846, Boston, Massachusetts, USA, 2006.

[11] B. Triggs. Joint feature distributions for image correspondence. In *Proceedings of ICCV*, pages 201–208, Vancouver, British Columbia, Canada, 2001.

[12] A. Wu, E. Johnson, and A. Proctor. Vision-aided inertial navigation for flight control. *Journal of Aerospace Computing, Information and Communication*, pages 348–360, 2005.

[13] W. Zhang and J. Kosecka. Image based localization in urban environments. In *Proceedings of 3DPVT*, pages 33–40, Washington DC, USA, 2006.

Video-based Image Retrieval*

Linjun Yang
Microsoft Research Asia
linjuny@microsoft.com

Yang Cai †
Zhejiang University
yangcai1988@gmail.com

Alan Hanjalic
Delft University of Technology
a.hanjalic@tudelft.nl

Xian-Sheng Hua
Microsoft Bing
xshua@microsoft.com

Shipeng Li
Microsoft Research Asia
spli@microsoft.com

ABSTRACT

Likely variations in the capture conditions (e.g. light, blur, scale, occlusion) and in the viewpoint between the query image and the images in the collection are the factors due to which image retrieval based on the Query-by-Example (QBE) principle is still not reliable enough. In this paper, we propose a novel QBE-based image retrieval system where users are allowed to submit a short video clip as a query to improve the retrieval reliability. Improvement is achieved by integrating the information about different viewpoints and conditions under which object and scene appearances can be captured across different video frames. Rich information extracted from a video can be exploited to generate a more complete query representation than in the case of a single-image query and to improve the relevance of the retrieved results. Our experimental results show that video-based image retrieval (VBIR) is significantly more reliable than the retrieval using a single image as a query.

Categories and Subject Descriptors

H.3.3 [**Information Storage and Retrieval**]: Information Search and Retrieval

General Terms

Algorithm, Experimentation, Performance

Keywords

Content-based image retrieval, video-based image retrieval

1. INTRODUCTION

Content-based image retrieval following the Query-by-Example (QBE) principle generally requires an example image as a query to search for similar images or near-duplicates. Although extensive research efforts have been invested in improving QBE-based image retrieval, the level of retrieval reliability is still insufficient. This is mainly due to the likely variations in the capture conditions (e.g. light, blur, scale, occlusion) and viewpoint between the query image and the images in the collection. This query-collection mismatch has been difficult to resolve due to insufficient invariance of the visual features used to represent the query and the collection images in view of the factors mentioned above.

While, for instance, the SIFT features [4] are effective in general, they are still insufficiently capable of handling the variations such as occlusion. Furthermore, in a typical SIFT-based image representation using visual words [7], the visual word quantization degrades the retrieval reliability to trade off for the scalability of the retrieval system. However, even if the problems related to the varying capture conditions can be avoided, the likely mismatch between the query and collection images in terms of the viewpoint from which an object or a scene are captured still remains the main obstacle for the successful practical adoption of QBE-based image retrieval.

Figure 1 illustrates the problems discussed above on the use case in which different images showing an Oxford building are used as queries to retrieve relevant images from the Oxford Building dataset [1]. Although these different queries are largely visually similar and show the same target object, the retrieval performance varies greatly for different query images, as indicated by the curve.

While the example in Fig. 1 is used to illustrate the query-collection mismatch problem as the main reason for unreli-

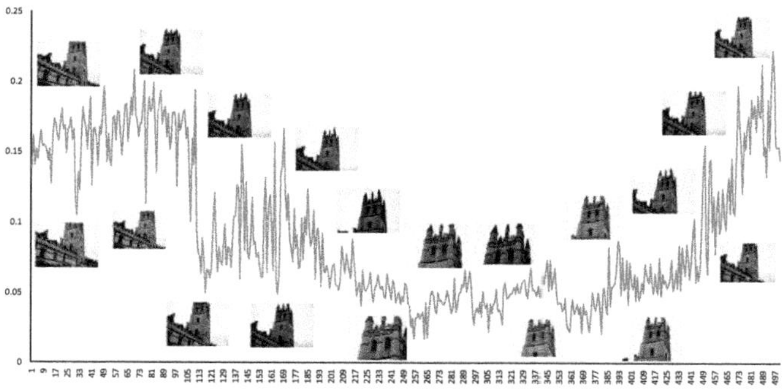

Figure 1: Illustration of the variance in the retrieval performance using different captures of the same visual object as query.

†This work was performed while Yang Cai was a research intern at Microsoft Research Asia.
*Area chair: Daniel Gatica-Perez

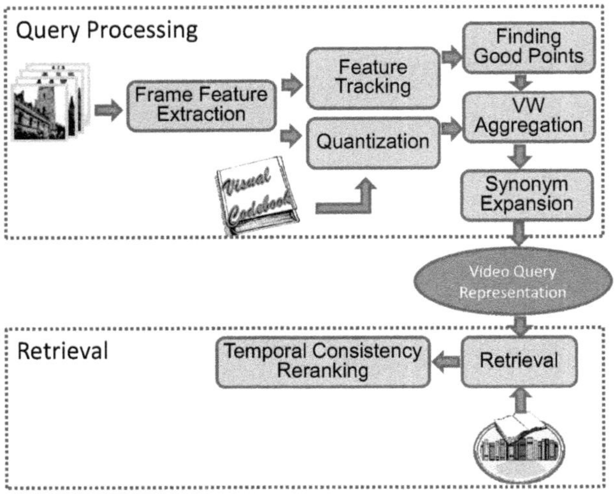

Figure 2: The flowchart of the proposed VBIR approach zooming in on the query processing and retrieval steps.

able QBE-based image retrieval, this example also reveals a potential effective solution to this problem. Multiple images of the same object that are characterized by different capture conditions and viewpoints could, namely, be aggregated together in order to extract the information for creating a more robust representation of the query object, a representation that is more complete than if any of the individual images are used as query alone. Although multiple images of the same object can be collected in various ways, a video capturing the object provides the most intuitive way to generate such a complex query, as it removes the need for the user to decide about the type and number of images to take for the same object. We therefore refer to this promising solution to the query-collection mismatch problem further as *video-based image retrieval* (VBIR) and introduce in this paper an approach for efficiently and effectively implementing this solution for a real-life use scenario.

The paper is organized as follows. We describe the proposed VBIR approach and its key components in Section 2. Then, the experimental evaluation of the proposed approach is presented in Section 3, followed by conclusions in Section 4.

2. THE PROPOSED APPROACH

Figure 2 illustrates the flowchart of the proposed VBIR approach. In the query processing step, we first process the query video into frames, from which SIFT features are extracted. Then, we perform feature tracking among the detected SIFT feature points over adjacent video frames and then find "good" points, which are stable and therefore able to represent the query well. After that, the good points are aggregated into a histogram to obtain a first improved query representation. This representation is then further expanded based on the mined synonyms. In the retrieval step, temporal consistency reranking is introduced to further refine the search result obtained by a general image retrieval model based on the expanded query. In the following, we will describe the elements of the flowchart in Figure 2 in more detail.

2.1 Corresponding SIFT points among frames

First, we track the SIFT points over all video frames to construct the corresponded point sequences. For each pair of temporally adjacent frames in the query video, we firstly track the SIFT points detected in the previous frame using Lucas and Kanade optical flow algorithm [5] implemented in OpenCV and modified using image pyramids [2]. Then, the tracked positions in the subsequent frame are further aligned to the detected SIFT points. The process is repeated for each pair of adjacent frames in the query video to produce many corresponded point sequences, each of which comprises a sequence of tracked SIFT points across video frames.

All the corresponded point sequences obtained using the procedure described above comprise the set $\mathcal{S}$, where $\mathbf{S}_k = \{p_i^j\}$ is the kth element of $\mathcal{S}$ and represents the kth point sequence and p_i^j represents the jth SIFT point in the ith frame.

2.2 Finding good points

We assume that a good point that is reliable for retrieval should have the following properties. First, it can be tracked and corresponded in multiple adjacent frames, which states that it is stable and clearly identifiable. Second, it should gravitate towards the center of the frame, which is due to our observation that people usually tend to put the object of interest in the center of the frames when capturing a video, so the central points are more likely to be related to a users' search intent.

Based on the above assumptions, we design a set of criteria to evaluate the goodness of points. For each point p_i^j, its corresponded point sequence is denoted as $\mathbf{S}(p_i^j)$. Then, the goodness of p_i^j is defined by Eqn. (1) as a combination of two terms, the *stableness* term and the *center-awareness* term,

$$G(p_i^j) = \alpha \times \frac{Len(\mathbf{S}(p_i^j))}{FrameCount} + (1-\alpha) \times Cent(p_i^j). \quad (1)$$

Here, α is a parameter to control the respective contributions from the two terms, and $FrameCount$ is the number of frames in the query video, which is used for normalization. $Len(\mathbf{S}(p_i^j))$ denotes the number of frames being tracked in the point sequence $\mathbf{S}(p_i^j)$ to represent the stableness of the point. The center-awareness term $Cent(\mathbf{S})$ is defined to reflect the assumption that the object near the center of the image is of more importance. Considering the occasional departures of intended objects from the central image area, we use the average distance of all the points in the tracked sequence to represent the center-awareness of each point in the sequence. The center-awareness of point p_i^j is defined as,

$$Cent(p_i^j) = -\frac{\sum_{p \in \mathbf{S}(p_i^j)} d(p,c)}{Len(\mathbf{S}(p_i^j)) \times d(0,c)}. \quad (2)$$

Here, d denotes the distance from point p to the frame center c, and $d(0,c)$ represents the distance from the origin of the frame to the center.

2.3 Aggregating visual words

The query video is represented as a histogram, denoted as $\mathbf{q}$, where each bin q_i corresponds to a visual word w_i in the vocabulary. Then, for each visual word, we aggregate its occurrence in all frames, divided by the number of frames in the query video, as the value in the corresponding bin of the query histogram. Representing the query as an aggregated histogram is a convenient way to take into account all the appearances of the query object in different frames with variations including scales, viewpoints, and lighting. It utilizes the redundancy in the video to achieve a comprehensive representation of the object of interest captured by the query video. In addition, compared with that of fusing the retrieval results using different video frames as query, which requires multiple scan of the database [6], the aggregation of visual words into a single query representation makes the retrieval process more efficient.

2.4 Synonym expansion

One of the advantages of a video compared to a single image is that it may contain a wide range of different appearances of the same object. This redundancy provides useful information for deriving the relations between the features extracted in different frames. Stavens et al. [8] used such information to learn the parameters for feature description. In this paper, this information is utilized to construct the synonym relations among visual words to partially address the imperfections due to visual word quantization.

For each visual word w_i, its term count in all frames of the query video is denoted as tc_i and the number of points in a corresponded point sequence $\mathbf{S}_k$ being quantized as w_i is denoted as $tc_i(\mathbf{S}_k)$. Then we can construct an affinity matrix M with the element m_{ij} defined as follows,

$$m_{ij} = \frac{\sum_k \min(tc_i(\mathbf{S}_k), tc_j(\mathbf{S}_k))}{tc_i}, \qquad (3)$$

with the diagonal elements set to zero.

The affinity matrix is then used to generate a contextual histogram from the aggregated query histogram so that the term counts of synonymous visual words can boost each other to alleviate the problem of quantizing similar feature descriptors into different visual words.

The contextual histogram is generated as,

$$cq = M \cdot q. \qquad (4)$$

This histogram is then combined with the aggregated query histogram into the new query representation,

$$q_{new} = \beta q + (1 - \beta) M \cdot q. \qquad (5)$$

Using the new query representation, we can construct the vector space model based on the standard *tf-idf* scoring function known from text information retrieval to compute the similarity between the query video and images in the collection:

$$q_v = q_{new} .* idf. \qquad (6)$$

Here the operator $.*$ stands for element-wise vector multiplication, while *idf* is a vector where idf_i represents the *idf* (inverted document frequency) of the visual word w_i.

2.5 Temporal consistency reranking

While many frames in the query video have been utilized to achieve a robust query representation, the noisy information spread in the frames may also get aggregated to produce an amplified negative effect on the query quality. Hence, to suppress this negative effect while keeping the advantages of visual word aggregation, we propose a reranking approach to adjust the search result achieved in the above steps by taking the temporal consistency of the visual content into consideration.

The reranking approach is based on our assumption that the false matches between the query video frames and the database images should not be consistent among temporally adjacent video frames. In other words, since temporally adjacent frames usually do not exhibit great changes in their appearance and all contain the object of interest, the similarity scores computed between a relevant image in the collection and adjacent frames in a video should not change greatly. However, for a mismatch, a high similarity score obtained on one video frame, e.g. due to noise in feature representation and capture conditions, will most likely be followed by a low score on the next video frame. In view of this, we choose to rerank the images in the top of the results list based on the temporal consistency information.

For each image I_i in the top of the results list, we compute the similarity scores between that image and all frames in the query video based on the vector space model with *tf-idf* weighting, denoted as $v(I_i, F_k)$, where F_k represents the kth frame in the query video. Then, by regarding $v(I_i, F_k)$ as a function of k, we can compute the gradient of the function as

$$g_i^k = v(I_i, F_{k+1}) - v(I_i, F_k). \qquad (7)$$

The absolute values of the gradients are then averaged to reflect the temporal consistency of the matching scores for temporally adjacent frames:

$$\tilde{g_i} = \frac{\sum |g_i^k|}{FrameCount}. \qquad (8)$$

The average gradient is then combined with the similarity score computed in Section 2.4 to obtain a new reranking score for the top-ranked results,

$$r_i = -\tilde{g_i} + \gamma \bar{r}_i, \qquad (9)$$

where $\bar{r}$ is the initial ranking score.

We noticed that some of the query videos are highly dynamic due to camera shake. For such a query video, all the images in the database may have a high average gradient, which implicitly increases the impact of temporal consistency on reranking. We use the mean of average gradients of the top-ranked images as the measure of the dynamics degree of the query video, which is then used to weight the average gradient term to achieve a new reranking function. In this way, the expression in Eqn. (9) can be modified as

$$r_i = -\frac{\tilde{g_i}}{\frac{1}{N}\sum_{i=1}^{N} \tilde{g_i}} + \gamma \bar{r}_i, \qquad (10)$$

where N is the number of top-ranked images to be considered in reranking.

3. EXPERIMENTS

3.1 Experimental setup

To set a benchmark for video-based image retrieval and allow for comparison of other methods with the approach proposed in this paper, we chose the publicly available Oxford building dataset [1] as the image collection. The Oxford building dataset comprises 5062 images crawled from Flickr[1] using 11 landmarks of Oxford University as queries.

[1]http://www.flickr.com

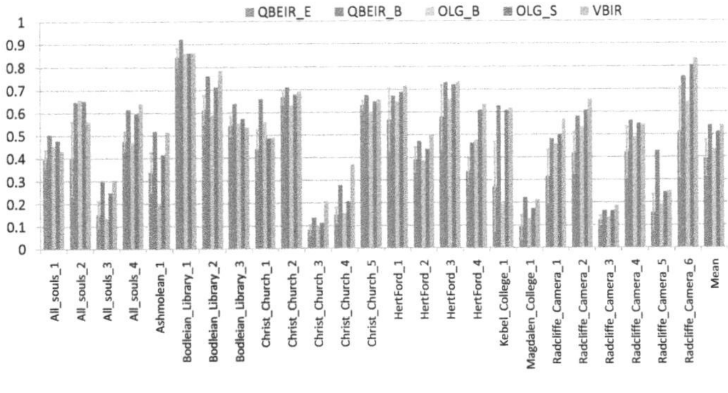

Figure 3: The performance comparison of QBE based image retrieval and VBIR. QBEIR_E shows the mean and the standard deviation of the MAP of image retrieval using single frames in the query video, QBEIR_B is the best possible performance of retrieval using a single frame.

To collect the query videos for our experiments, we used the 11 landmark names as query to search for suitable videos in YouTube. Finally we obtained 15 videos for 8 landmarks, while for the other 3 landmarks we were not able to find any relevant videos. Since not all the parts in these videos are about the corresponding landmarks, we selected those segments exactly describing the landmarks as query video clips in our experiments. Consequently, 25 video clips were selected as queries. The ground-truth corresponding to each landmark in the Oxford building dataset is still used as the ground-truth for the video-based image retrieval experiments. The key frames in the query videos and the images in the database were down-sampled to 300*300 by preserving the aspect ratio and then SIFT features were extracted. A 100K visual vocabulary was constructed using Robust Approximate Kmeans [3].

The Average Precision (AP) is used to evaluate and compare the various methods, which is defined as the average of the precisions computed at all recall levels. The Mean Average Precision (MAP) is the average of the APs across all queries.

3.2 Performance comparison

We implemented QBE-based image retrieval as a baseline to be compared with the proposed VBIR concept. Specifically, we used each frame in the query videos individually to query the image database to simulate QBE-based image retrieval. The average performance with standard deviation and the best possible performance for each query video using different frames as query are illustrated in Figure 3. The methods in [6], which fuse the retrieval scores by using each frame individually as query were also implemented and used for comparisons, including fusion by summing all scores (OLG_S) and fusion by taking the maximum (OLG_B).

We can see from Figure 3 that QBE-based image retrieval suffers from a dramatic performance variation, which demonstrates its insufficient reliability. Intensive camera motion such as zoom in/out in HertFord_v1, and large changes of light conditions due to different shooting angles in videos Christ_Church_v1 and Radcliffe_Camera_v1 cause that the object of interest is described at a broad range of capture conditions, which can only in part match the conditions at which collection images have been captured. This causes large variation in the retrieval performance if video frames are used individually as query. However, such information can be put into a good use to improve the retrieval performance by using the whole video clip as query, as proposed in this paper.

Figure 3 also allows for a comparison between the performances of VBIR and QBE-based image retrieval. We can see that the performance of VBIR is significantly better than the expected performance of QBE-based image retrieval. The improvement was computed as 36.37% in terms of MAP. Furthermore, for 24 among 25 query videos VBIR can achieve a performance boost compared to the average performance of QBE-based image retrieval. In particular, the MAP of VBIR is even larger than the expected performance of QBEIR by a margin of the standard deviation for 19 queries. This demonstrates that the incorporation of the information contained in all video frames has a clear potential for improving the reliability of the retrieval performance. Finally, we can see that VBIR achieves a comparable result with the best possible performance of QBEIR. This means that, by using a video as query, we can achieve a result similar to the best one achievable by using an arbitrary single image as query.

The proposed VBIR approach further outperforms OLG_B and OLG_S by 23.95% and 5.81% and in 84% and 80% queries, respectively. While VBIR achieves a better performance compared to its competitors, it also exhibits a better efficiency in terms of the retrieval part. While OLG_B and OLG_S cost 5.2s to complete the retrieval part for one query, VBIR only needs 1.2s for the same task.

4. CONCLUSION

We proposed in this paper a new image search framework that we refer to as the *video-based image retrieval* (VBIR) framework. VBIR makes it possible to search for images and related information using a short video clip taken on the object of interest as query. The approach underlying the proposed framework includes mining of the useful information from all frames of the query video and using this information to refine the query representation and in this way improve the retrieval performance. The experimental results show that video-based image retrieval significantly improves the retrieval reliability over that of using a single image as query.

5. REFERENCES

[1] http://www.robots.ox.ac.uk/~vgg/data/oxbuildings.

[2] G. Bradski and A. Kaehler. *Learning OpenCV: Computer Vision with the OpenCV Library.* O'Reilly, Cambridge, MA, 2008.

[3] D. Li, L. Yang, X.-S. Hua, and H.-J. Zhang. Large-scale robust visual codebook construction. In *ACM Multimedia*, 2010.

[4] D. G. Lowe. Distinctive image features from scale-invariant keypoints. *Int. J. Comput. Vision*, 60(2):91–110, 2004.

[5] B. D. Lucas and T. Kanade. An Iterative Image Registration Technique with an Application to Stereo Vision. In *Proc. of the 1981 DARPA Imaging Understanding Workshop*, 1981.

[6] J. Sivic, F. Schaffalitzky, and A. Zisserman. Object level grouping for video shots. 2004.

[7] J. Sivic and A. Zisserman. Video google: A text retrieval approach to object matching in videos. In *ICCV*, 2003.

[8] D. Stavens and S. Thrun. Unsupervised learning of invariant features using video. In *CVPR*, 2010.

Location-Aware System Based on a Dynamic 3D Model to Help in Live Broadcasting of Sport Events *

Roberto Yus
University of Zaragoza
Maria de Luna 1
Zaragoza, Spain
ryus@unizar.es

Eduardo Mena
University of Zaragoza
Maria de Luna 1
Zaragoza, Spain
emena@unizar.es

Jorge Bernad
University of Zaragoza
Maria de Luna 1
Zaragoza, Spain
jbernad@unizar.es

Sergio Ilarri
University of Zaragoza
Maria de Luna 1
Zaragoza, Spain
silarri@unizar.es

Arantza Illarramendi
Basque Country University
Manuel de Lardizabal s/n
San Sebastián, Spain
a.illarramendi@ehu.es

ABSTRACT

Broadcasting sport events in live is a challenging task because obtaining the best views requires taking into account many dynamic factors, such as: the location and movement of interesting objects, all the views provided by cameras in the scenario (some of them wireless, mobile, or attached to moving objects), possible occlusions, etc. Therefore, a technical director needs to manage a great amount of continuously changing information to quickly select the camera whose view should be broadcasted.

In this paper, we present a location-aware system that helps technical directors in the broadcasting task, using a 3D model updated continuously with real-time location data retrieved from the scenario. They can indicate in run-time their interest in certain moving objects and the system is in charge of selecting the cameras that provide the kind of views required.

Categories and Subject Descriptors

H.2.4 [**Database Management**]: Systems – Query processing; H.3.4 [**Information Storage and Retrieval**]: Systems and Software; H.5.1 [**Information Interfaces and Presentation**]: Multimedia Information Systems

General Terms

Algorithms, Management

Keywords

Content selection in run-time, 3D model, multiple camera management

*Area chair: Gang Hua

MM'11, November 28–December 1, 2011, Scottsdale, Arizona, USA.

1. INTRODUCTION

Broadcasting organizations are considering the combined use of professional cameras with low-cost cameras controlled remotely to reduce the production cost. However, that solution has a serious impact in one of the most complex and critical tasks in a live content production environment: the more cameras are employed, the more images are available, and therefore the more complicated the work of the technical directors is. Technical directors have to make quick decisions in live broadcasting scenarios to select, among the available video sources, the best video stream to broadcast.

In this paper, we present a system that, using 3D models as basis, assists technical directors in the difficult task of selecting in live the best candidate video signals coming from static or moving cameras. Here we improve the ideas proposed in [4] by considering 3D scenarios, and so we tackle problems like occlusions and computing the percentage of an object being viewed by a camera. Thus, the system supports an expressive specification of the kind of view that must be obtained (e.g., a side view showing at least a 60% of the object, etc.). So, we could highlight the following benefits provided by the proposed system:

- It manages information about the features of video cameras to select those that could satisfy the requirements of the technical director (the kind of views needed on certain target objects).
- It considers the 3D representation and orientation of the objects, in addition to the features of the cameras (focus, pan, tilt, etc.), to recreate the camera views (taking occlusions into account).
- It ranks the cameras presented to the technical director. For example, the percentage of the required object that each camera can provide can be selected as a ranking criterion.

The rest of the paper is structured as follows. In Section 2, we explain how objects in a scenario are modeled. In Section 3, we describe the approach proposed to obtain the cameras that can provide the specified views, based on different 3D computations. In Section 4, we present an experiment that shows the efficiency of the system in terms of processing time. In Section 5, we review some related works. Finally, conclusions and future work are included in Section 6.

2. MODELING THE OBJECTS

To model objects in the scenario, a generic class *Object* is defined, which represents the set of entities in the scenario. An *Object* is represented by the tuple:

<id, name, loc, extent, centroid, frontV, topV, cams>

where *id* is a unique identifier of the object, *name* is the name of the object, *loc* is the location of the object (its 3D coordinates), *extent* is the volume occupied by the object, *centroid* is the centroid of the object extent, *frontV* and *topV* are normal vectors pointing towards the front and the top of the object, respectively[1], and *cams* is the list of cameras attached to the object (if any).

In order to define the extent of the object, a 3D mesh created by using an external modeling package (e.g., Autodesk 3ds Max, Blender, etc.) should be made available to the system. Besides, the normal front and top vectors must be defined for this 3D model in order to allow the system to distinguish between the different kinds of views of the object (top/bottom, front/rear, left/right, or any combination of two or three elements chosen from the three previous pairs). In this way, the system will be able to answer queries retrieving, for example, cameras focusing a certain object, cameras recording a top view of an object, etc. Figure 1 shows the 3D model that has been created to represent the rowing boats of the use case explained in Section 4, their normal vectors, and some example views that we could obtain.

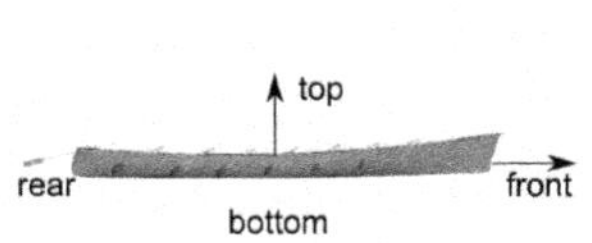

(a) Side view

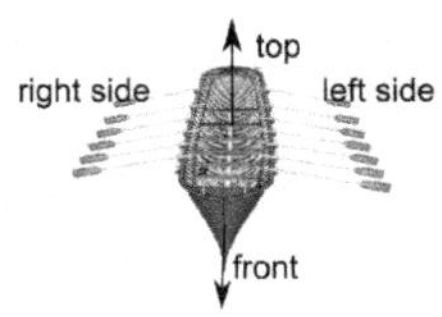

(b) Front/top view

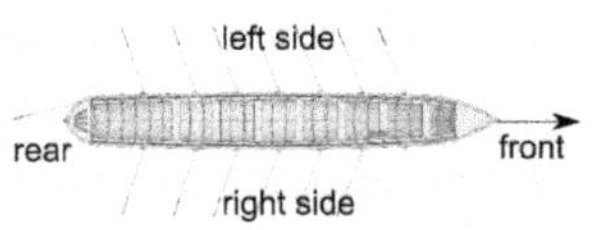

(c) Top view

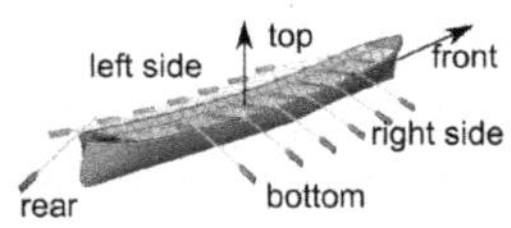

(d) Rear/right/top view

Figure 1: Different views of an object

3. 3D SELECTION OF CAMERA VIEWS

In this section, we explain how the system, based on the use of a 3D model, computes the answers to the queries requesting camera views on certain target objects. First, we explain how the percentage of the target object viewed by a camera is computed. Then, we explain how the system computes the kind of view (front/rear, top/bottom, right/left) of an object that a camera is providing.

[1]The current orientation of the object is provided by a compass and a 3D accelerometer.

3.1 Percentage Viewed of the Target Object

In [4], the keywords *full* or *incomplete* can be specified as a parameter for a query in order to indicate that a complete or any view of the target object must be obtained. However, this simple approach has some limitations. On the one hand, a *full* view means that the camera is focusing the whole object. Therefore, even if only a small percentage of the object is not in the view, the corresponding camera will be excluded from the answer. On the other hand, if the technical director asks for an *incomplete* view, cameras focusing a very small percentage of the object will be also part of the answer.

Our new proposal solves these limitations by supporting queries that ask for a certain minimum percentage[2] of an object or a certain minimum percentage of a specific view of the target object (defined by the corresponding vectors, as explained in Section 2).

In order to compute what a camera is viewing, we recreate the scene in a 3D engine by taking into account the camera features (current focus, pan, tilt, etc.) and the 3D models of the objects. Then, we use 2D projections (obtained by rendering the 3D scene) to calculate the percentage of an object that is viewed by that camera. For this purpose, we have used *JMonkeyEngine* (JME)[3], a Java game engine with advanced graphics capabilities supported through *OpenGL 2.0* via *Lightweight Java Game Library* (LWJGL). We update the location and direction of the objects and cameras in the 3D scenario continuously every second, to obtain accurate results. Since the system has less than one second to perform all the calculations, an efficient approach has been developed to obtain the answers as soon as possible, which is evaluated in Section 4.

There exist two situations where a camera could have an incomplete view of an object: 1) when the target is partially or fully occluded by another object, and 2) when the target does not fit the field-of-view (FOV) of the camera. In the following, we summarize the computation of the percentage that a given camera is viewing of a certain target object (illustrated by using the scene of Figure 2(a)):

1. The scene is recreated in the 3D engine using the location, direction, and 3D models of objects viewed by the camera that we are considering.

2. The target object is painted completely in red, including the parts outside the FOV of the camera, and the other objects in the scenario are painted in transparent green, in order not to hide the target object (see Figure 2(b)).

3. The current FOV is painted in transparent blue to select what the camera is currently viewing (see Figure 2(c)).

4. If the target does not fit completely the FOV, the virtual camera in the 3D model is moved backwards until it views the target object completely. This movement allows the system to obtain a render covering the full object while it does not affect the perspective of the scene (see Figure 2(d)).

[2]We believe that specifying a maximum percentage is not very useful, but it could be added easily to the system, if needed.

[3]`http://www.jmonkeyengine.org/`

5. A 2D projection of the 3D scene is rendered, and then the system obtains the percentage of the target object viewed by the camera[4]:

$$\frac{\#pixels\ not\ occluded}{\#pixels\ of\ target\ object}$$

   Using the image of Figure 2(d), the system obtains that the camera views 41% of the target object (the second boat). Notice that the visible part of the target object is shown in magenta because of its red and blue channels and the occluded part inside and outside the FOV are shown in white and yellow, respectively.

Due to the use of different color channels, the system is able to manage occlusions in different situations, and the above computations are performed with a single render and iteration.

(a) Scene in *Google Earth*

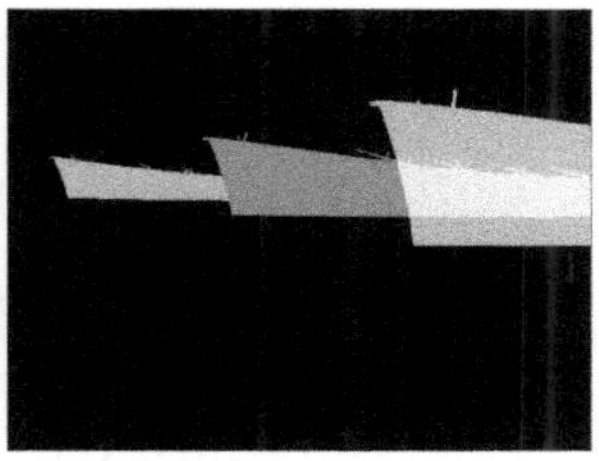

(b) Selecting the target

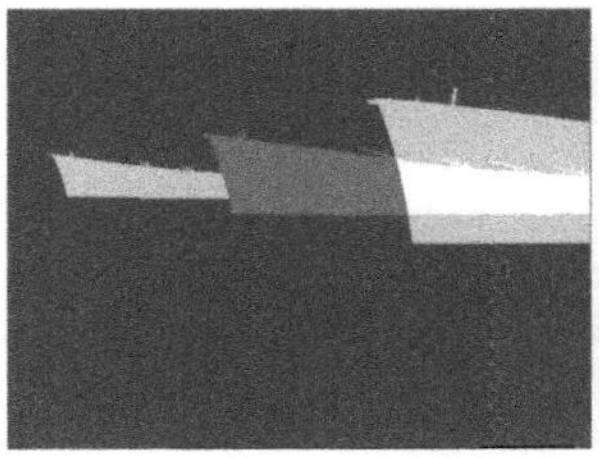

(c) Painting the FOV

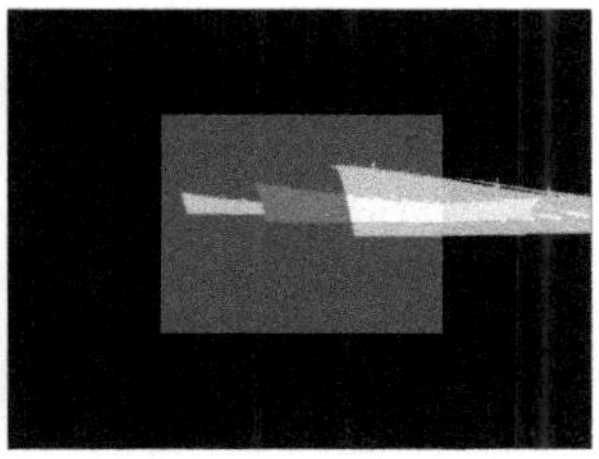

(d) Full view of target object

Figure 2: Sample computation of the percentage of a target object in a view

The percentage of the target object viewed by each camera can be used to rank the answer presented to the technical director (cameras viewing a higher percentage of the target object are presented first).

3.2 Queries About Specific Views of an Object

A technical director could be interested in obtaining cameras focusing a target object but retrieving a certain kind of view. For example, he/she could be interested in obtaining the cameras that are providing a rear/top/right view of a rowing boat (as seen in Figure 1(d)). To do that, the system needs to obtain the parts of the object belonging to the views requested. As the 3D model of the objects can be complex, selecting the parts of the target that belong to a view can be a difficult and time-consuming task. So, we have used an approach based on *light sources* and *illumination*. The idea is to illuminate only the wanted view by using a directional light source, and thus making it only visible. Besides, by using different colors for each light source, the system can simultaneously check several views in a single pass.

Figure 3 shows an example of this technique, when a technical director queries the system to obtain cameras retrieving a right/top view of a target object. A light source (red) has been set to "select" the parts of the object that belong to the top view and another light source (green) "selects" the parts that belong to the right side view. With this single image, and analyzing the color channels of the pixels, the view of the target object provided by this camera is classified as a predominantly top/right side view (the camera is viewing a 78% of the top and a 92% of the right of the object), and so is returned to the technical director as part of the answer set.

Figure 3: Sample computation of the kind of view of a camera shot

4. EXPERIMENTAL EVALUATION

For the experimental evaluation we have considered a specific sports scenario: the traditional rowing races in San Sebastian, Spain. The scenario has four rowing boats equipped with a *Pan-Tilt* camera and moving according to real GPS location data captured during the race in 2010. Besides, there are other three fixed cameras placed in usual positions for TV cameras. Let us suppose that we want to retrieve the cameras that can view at least 70% of a certain boat. This query will be evaluated continuously, and so the answer will be always kept up-to-date. The proposal is based on the location-dependent query processing system LOQOMOTION [3], which enables the continuous query processing needed to automatically update (as necessary) the set of ideal camera selections.

In our experiment, we want to evaluate the processing time needed by the system to compute the views of the seven cameras in the scenario. As the location, direction, and other parameters of the objects and cameras in the scenario are updated every second, the system has to be able to perform the processing in less than one second to provide the technical director with updated information.

In Figure 4 we represent the time needed by the system to compute the views of all the cameras (vertical axis) for every time instant during the race (horizontal axis). The tests were run on an Intel Core i5-480M with graphics card NVIDIA GeForce GT 540M. As our approach is based on the use of a 3D engine, the processing time depends on the graphics card (the graphics card used is in the mid-range). Notice in Figure 4 that the maximum time needed by the system was 0.17 seconds. The highest delays are reached when most of the cameras do not focus the target boat and their rotation has to be computed to obtain what the cam-

[4] *pixels of target object*: red channel $\neq 0$
non-occluded: red & blue channels $\neq 0$, green channel $= 0$

eras will see. The minimum processing time needed was 0.078 seconds, very close to the average time (0.085 seconds). Therefore, this test shows that the system achieves the processing time requirements needed for a dynamic environment as the one explained before.

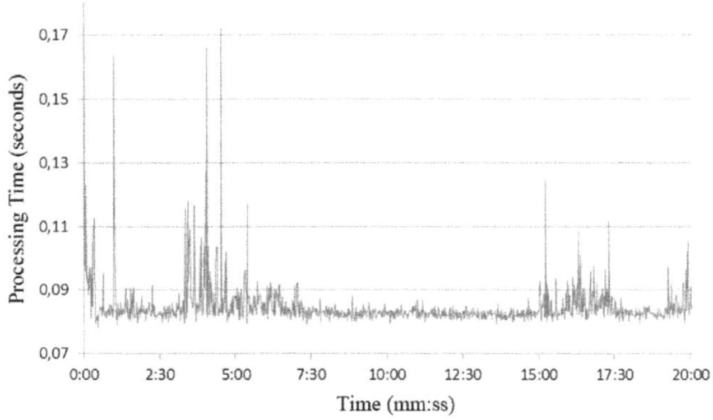

Figure 4: Processing time

5. RELATED WORK

A number of works have focused on the specific problem of helping producers of sport videos. For example, as part of the *APIDIS* (*Autonomous Production of Images based on Distributed and Intelligent Sensing*) project, in [1] the authors present a system that helps the video production and video summarization in the context of basketball games. The work presented in [2] tackles the problem of summarizing videos of soccer games by applying different image processing algorithms to analyze the input videos. In [6] the problem of video summarization, based on metadata describing the semantic content of MPEG-7 videos, is considered in the context of baseball games. Cricket and soccer videos are used to validate the work in [5], which exploits audio features (such as an increase in the audio level of the voice of the commentators or the cheers of the audience) to extract excitement clips from sport videos.

All these works perform an automatic video processing in an offline way, while our approach is based on real-time processing; although some works explicitly mention the possibility of live broadcasting [7], they do no consider moving cameras. Besides, they use image processing techniques (which could fail, for example, for the detection of specific objects located far or partially hidden by others), while our approach is based on a 3D model updated continuously with the current locations and directions of objects and cameras in the scenario. So, our proposal can complement the above approaches.

6. CONCLUSIONS AND FUTURE WORK

In this paper, we have presented a system that helps technical directors in the difficult task of broadcasting sport events in live. The system makes use of a 3D model of the objects in the scenario. This model is continuously refreshed (every second) by taking into account the locations, and other parameters, of the moving objects and cameras. The technical director can query the system in order to obtain the cameras that fulfill his/her demands. The main features of this proposal are:

- 3D models of the objects and camera features (focus, pan, tilt, etc.) are considered to recreate the scenario. In this way, we do not need to analyze real camera sequences. Indeed, our approach can be a good complement for image processing techniques.
- The approach supports an expressive way to indicate the kind of view that must be obtained. More specifically, it supports the definition of the viewpoint required (front/rear, top/bottom, side) and the minimum percentage of coverage of the target object that must be provided.
- The cameras presented to the technical director can be ranked, for example, according to the percentage of the required target object that can be provided.

Moreover, the proposal is quite flexible, and so new functionalities could be added to the system without relevant changes to the main architecture. Thus, we plan to adapt the system to other sports scenarios such as classic cycling. Besides, we will also consider situations where exploiting multimedia information provided by mobile devices carried by spectators or tourists would be interesting.

7. ACKNOWLEDGMENTS

This research work has been supported by the CICYT project TIN2010-21387-C02. We also thank Francisco J. Serón for his technical support.

8. REFERENCES

[1] F. Chen and C. D. Vleeschouwer. Personalized production of basketball videos from multi-sensored data under limited display resolution. *Computer Vision and Image Understanding*, 114(6):667–680, June 2010.

[2] A. Ekin, A. M. Tekalp, and R. Mehrotra. Automatic soccer video analysis and summarization. *IEEE Transactions on Image Processing*, 12(7):796–807, July 2003.

[3] S. Ilarri, E. Mena, and A. Illarramendi. Location-dependent queries in mobile contexts: Distributed processing using mobile agents. *IEEE Transactions on Mobile Computing*, 5(8):1029–1043, August 2006.

[4] S. Ilarri, E. Mena, A. Illarramendi, and G. Marcos. A location-aware system for monitoring sport events. In *Eight International Conference on Advances in Mobile Computing & Multimedia (MoMM 2010)*, pages 305–312. ACM Press, Austrian Computer Society (OCG), November 2010.

[5] M. H. Kolekar. Bayesian belief network based broadcast sports video indexing. *Multimedia Tools and Applications*, 2011. Online First, published online: 9 July 2010, doi:10.1007/s11042-010-0544-9.

[6] N. Nitta, Y. Takahashi, and N. Babaguchi. Automatic personalized video abstraction for sports videos using metadata. *Multimedia Tools and Applications*, 41(1):1–25, January 2009.

[7] J. Wang, C. Xu, E. Chng, H. Lu, and Q. Tian. Automatic composition of broadcast sports video. *Multimedia Systems*, 14(4):179–193, September 2008.

Real-Time 3D Interaction with Deformable Model on Mobile Devices

Ziying Tang
Department of Computer and Information Sciences
Towson University, USA
ztang@towson.edu

Orkun Ozbek
Department of Computer Science
Tufts University
USA
Orkun.Ozbek@tufts.edu

Xiaohu Guo
Department of Computer Science
University of Texas at Dallas
USA
xguo@utdallas.edu

ABSTRACT
Mobile-based augmented reality is an emerging technology that provides immersive experiences over wireless networks. Its applications, such as 3D streaming, have become more and more popular on mobile devices. However, most of these applications do not support real-time 3D interactions. Consequently, mobile users can only watch or browse 3D contents passively instead of actively interacting with 3D objects. In this paper, we propose a novel method that allows mobile users to change a model's shape and motions through interactions via mobile touch screen and obtain feedbacks in real-time. To accelerate computational speed and reduce communication load, we compute 3D deformations using a spectral representation. Moreover, a progressive deformation streaming technique is proposed to reduce the effect of interaction delay between the server and mobile clients. Our experimental results indicate that our method provides real-time interaction feedback, offering satisfactory user experiences.

Categories and Subject Descriptors
H.5.1[[**Information Interfaces and Presentation**]: Multimedia Information Systems- animations.

General Terms
Algorithms, Human Factors, Performance

Keywords
Progressive Streaming, 3D Model, Mobile Application.

1. INTRODUCTION
With the development of tele-communication and tele-immersion applications, 3D streaming has attracted increasing attentions. Researchers have also extended its application to mobile devices, thanks to their portability and fast-growing wireless networks. Some mobile devices are equipped with 3D displays and 3D cameras [2], making 3D streaming on mobile devices an interesting and promising research area.

In order to share 3D dynamics remotely, image-based techniques such as 3D video have been proposed. Compared to 2D video, 3D video consists of a sequence of depth images which can be used to reconstruct 3D virtual scenes. Nevertheless, 3D video needs to be captured offline and pre-processed, as such, remote users cannot receive real-time feedback. Another disadvantage of 3D video is that it does not support user interactions: watching and browsing virtual data are the only options available for remote users. When streaming 3D video on mobile devices over wireless networks, new challenges, such as limited bandwidth and slow rendering speed, arise. In general, 3D video requires a Gbps bandwidth to ensure good qualities, which is far beyond the capacity of most wireless networks (Mbps).

Another way of sharing 3D contents is streaming virtual models directly, known as model-based streaming technique. To share 3D dynamics based on it, 3D animations are created and transferred. Depending on the requirements of applications, the server can send the original data, a simplified data with low resolutions, or partial of models to remote clients. Mobile clients render the 3D object locally according to their own view directions. Compared to image-based techniques, model-based streaming techniques are more flexible, since the model is stored on the mobile device. However, 3D animation has to be pre-generated offline and user interactions with 3D models are still very limited.

In this paper, we propose a novel method to enable real-time 3D interactions with virtual objects through mobile devices. Our method allows users to change model's shape and motions actively in addition to watching and browsing. Specifically, adopting a spectral technique, a powerful server is used to perform deformation computations according to users' manipulations. We are able to not only reduce transmission loads significantly but also improve computing speed remarkably. Moreover, a new progressive deformation streaming approach is developed to minimize the effects of interaction delay between the server and mobile clients. Remote mobile users can view a coarse version of the shape and motion changes under interaction immediately, while waiting for the detailed deformation being transferred from the server. A special case when the wireless service is not available is also discussed.

There are several novelties in our work. First, we extend the mobile-based 3D interactions to support active user manipulations in real-time. Second, applying spectral techniques, we are able to improve computational efficiency and reduce streaming loads. Third, we solve the network related interaction delay problem by proposing a new progressive deformation streaming algorithm.

2. RELATED WORK
Generally, two areas of previous researches related to our work, namely streaming on mobile devices and 3D deformations.

3D model streaming has long been an active research topic and been used in many applications. To support mobile devices with

*Area Chair: Daniel Gatica-Perez

small screens and limited computing resources, Duguet and Drettakis [4] propose to use simplified point-based models to replace mesh-based models. Doran et al. [3] suggest a progressive streaming way for mobile clients to view a 3D tree Model. From a different point of view, some approaches [7, 9] follow the image-based technique i.e. 3D video, instead of directly streaming 3D models. They use a server to render the 3D model at the viewpoints specified by the clients to solve the rendering speed problem on mobiles. However, they also bring other problems such as delays between the server and mobile clients.

In computer graphics area, researches on 3D deformation have explored how to quickly simulate more realistic and nature movements of 3D soft objects. Some of them follow the spectral method which is very related to ours. For instance, Karni and Gotsman suggest to use spectral representations of 3D models to achieve better compression results in 2000 [6]. Later, similar idea has been utilized to compute mesh deformations [1, 8], and to compress and stream 3D mesh [5]. Tang et al. [10] further extend it in a collaborative virtual environment, where 3D surface deformations are shared in real-time.

3. REAL-TIME 3D INTERACTION

We would like to provide mobile users a flexible and interactive way to manipulate 3D virtual data and receive feedbacks instantly. In our method, 3D interactions have two kinds:

- Simply browsing: rotation and zoom in/out;
- Deformation operation: change the shape or motion of the 3D model.

In general, computing 3D deformation is very time-consuming and describing deformation requires a large amount of data. The limited computing capability of mobile devices and the relatively slow connectivity of wireless networks pose challenges to complete deformation on mobile. Hence, instead of mobile devices, a powerful server is used to complete deformation computation. Additionally, we adopt a spectral technique and describe deformations using a small number of frequencies to ensure fast speed and low streaming loads. However, the using the computation server brings the network latency which leads to a new interaction delay problem. To reduce the effect of interaction delay, we propose a progressive deformation streaming algorithm, which can also be used to support local computing when the server is not accessible due to the lack of wireless service.

3.1 Spectral Deformation

Using *manifold harmonics* (MH) [6], we can transfer the geometric representation of a 3D model into frequency domain, and vice versa. When solving the Laplacian-based deformation over the spectrum of low frequencies, it only requires a little computational cost so that achieve real-time 3D interactions. In this section, we briefly review the linear Laplacian-based variational method for mesh deformation, and a detailed introduction could be found in [1, 8].

Denote the manifold surface before and after the deformation as S and S'. We define the displacement before and after deformation as $\mathbf{d} = \mathbf{p}' - \mathbf{p}$, where $\mathbf{p}$ and $\mathbf{p}'$ represent the same point on S and S' respectively. During deformation, the user can specify some constraints over some vertices as interaction points to manipulate the surface. Suppose there are c constraints in total. Then the deformation is described as:

$$\begin{pmatrix} \mathbf{A} & \mathbf{B} \\ \mathbf{B}^T & \mathbf{0} \end{pmatrix} \begin{pmatrix} \mathbf{d} \\ \boldsymbol{\gamma} \end{pmatrix} = \begin{pmatrix} \mathbf{0} \\ \mathbf{d}' \end{pmatrix} \tag{1}$$

where $\mathbf{A}$ is an $n\times n$ coefficient matrix, and n is the number of vertices of the model. $\mathbf{B}$ is an $n\times c$ matrix with $B_{ij}=1$ if the j-th constrain is for vertex v_i, and $B_{ij}=0$ otherwise, and $\boldsymbol{\gamma}$ is a vector containing the Lagrange parameters.

The size of linear system (1) is $(n+c)\times(n+c)$, which is normally very large, because a 3D model can have thousands vertices. For example, for a simple Lion model with 2500 vertices (n=2500) and 3 selected constraints (c=3), we get a 2503×2503 matrix.

By employing the MH and selecting only the first m low frequencies, we can largely reduce the size of the linear system from $(n+c)\times(n+c)$ into $(m+c)\times(m+c)$ as

$$\begin{pmatrix} \mathbf{H}^T\mathbf{A}\mathbf{H} & \widetilde{\mathbf{B}} \\ \widetilde{\mathbf{B}}^T & \mathbf{0} \end{pmatrix} \begin{pmatrix} \tilde{\mathbf{d}} \\ \boldsymbol{\gamma} \end{pmatrix} = \begin{pmatrix} \mathbf{0} \\ \mathbf{d}' \end{pmatrix} \tag{2}$$

where $\widetilde{\mathbf{B}}$ is an $m\times c$ matrix with $\widetilde{\mathbf{B}}_{kj} = \mathbf{h}_i^k$ if the j-th constrain is for vertex v_i, and $B_{ij}=0$ otherwise, $\tilde{\mathbf{d}}$ is the displacement vector in frequency domain and $\mathbf{H}$ is manifold harmonic bases. Compared with $(n+c) \times (n+c)$, the linear system (2) with size $(m+c) \times (m+c)$ is much smaller, because m is only the first few low frequencies. Follow the previous example: for the Lion model, if we use first 50 frequencies (m=50) to compute deformation, the size of the linear system is 53×53. Therefore, we have m instead of n unknown variables, where $m \ll n$, so the computational cost of solving the linear system can be reduced remarkably.

3.2 Progressive Streaming

In our scenario, the mobile-based 3D interaction allows the viewer to change the motions or shapes of the 3D model. Even though deformation cost has been largely reduced by the use of the spectral method, it is still too heavy for mobile devices, especially for very large model and complex movements. Therefore, a powerful server is utilized to perform the task and send results to mobile clients. When we follow the traditional Server-Client (S-C) approach, users need to forward interactions to the server and wait the returned update. Therefore, at least one round trip network delay (RTD) is required before the mobile user is able to visualize results of his/her interactions. We call this delay an *interaction delay*, as illustrated in Figure 1. The interaction delay can greatly impact the user experience of interactive applications, and this delay, amplified by the limited bandwidth and unstable wireless networks of mobile devices can be relatively long. For example, based on our experiments, the RTD from an iPhone user at USA to a server at India can reach 2.527 second in the afternoon using 3G wireless. Therefore, traditional S-C method is no longer able to fulfill our requirements, leading to the necessity of better solutions.

As explained previously, deformation can be computed using a $O(m)$ method in the spectral domain. A special feature of the spectral representation is that for a 3D model low frequencies represent the model structure while high ones encode the details. This fact allows us to select only first m frequencies to calculate deformation. In addition, different frequencies can express the model in different level of details (LODs). Note that the LODs here are in the spectral domain. Inspired by these unique characteristics, we analyze the interaction delay problem from a new perspective. It is ideal to get an instant feedback to ensure satisfying user experience, even though the delay introduced by the unstable wireless condition is not in the scope of our study. Instead of just passively waiting for the feedback from the server, we calculate a rough deformation result on the mobile using a very small number of frequencies, and provide users an instant interaction response. Meanwhile, the detailed deformation

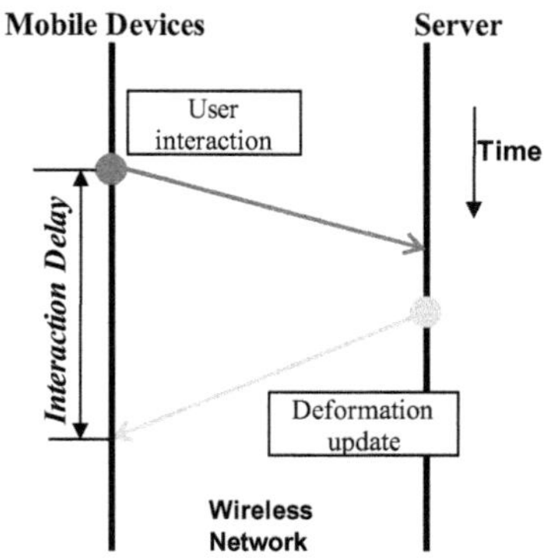

Figure 1. Interaction Delay between mobile devices and the server.

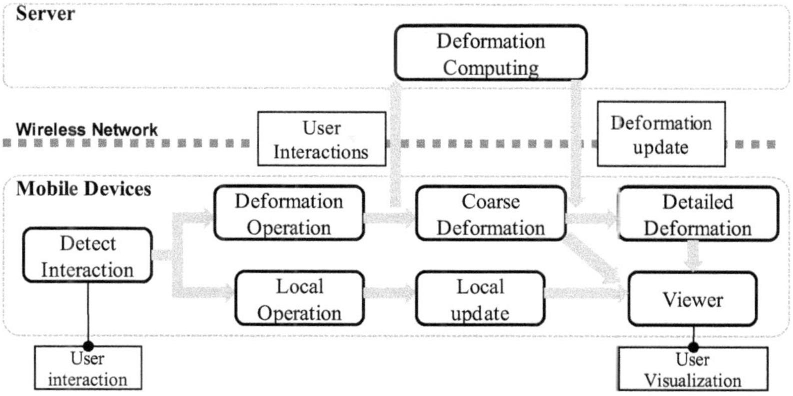

Figure 2. Pipeline of the proposed progressive deformation streaming method.

described by a larger number of frequencies is computed by and streamed from the server to increase the LODs progressively, adapting to the capability of the mobile device and wireless network conditions.

Based on the analysis above, we propose the new progressive deformation streaming (PDS) algorithm, whose pipeline is illustrated in Figure 2. First, based on wireless conditions, we decide to use traditional S-C architecture or PDS method. Next, if the PDS method is chosen, we detect user interactions on mobile devices, and separate them into two categories: local browsing e.g. rotation, and deformation operations. Then, the interactions of the latter case are passed to both the server and local computing module. After that, mobile clients compute a coarse result using a very small number of frequencies and provide an instant feedback to users; meanwhile the server calculates the same deformation in high LOD. Finally, the motion updates are streamed back to clients, providing detailed results progressively.

3.3 A Special Case

Our progressive deformation streaming technique is mainly designed for the case when the wireless condition is not satisfying and the communication latency between the server and mobiles clients is long. However, it is not limited to this case only. It is known that mobile devices connect to the web via wireless networks when they are within the range of a hotspot. Even though nowadays wireless networks have covered most of the cities, there are still some places out of the range. Thus, when wireless service is not available, mobile devices cannot communicate with the server, no matter in which architectures. In this situation, the local deformation computing, which is the core part in our PDS algorithm, is the only solution to get feedbacks.

Table 1. Model statistics and computing time.

	Model	Bunny	Dinosaur	Lion
	#Vertex	502	1252	2502
	Pre-computing Time (mobile)	2.139	5.572	10.76
Running Time	Coarse result (mobile)	0.124	0.324	0.633
	Increase LOD (mobile)	0.071	0.153	0.327
	Server Computing	0.0058	0.0105	0.0193

Similarly, we can compute a coarse result quickly on mobile, and slowly improve LODs using the update calculated locally.

4. EXPERIMENTAL RESULTS

We implement the real-time 3D interactions and the proposed progressive streaming algorithm on a Windows XP PC with Intel Core2 Duo 2.93GHz CPU and 2GB DDR2 RAM, a MacBook-Pro and some iPhones. Clients are tested on some iPhones. iPhone clients communicate with the PC server through 3G wireless with bandwidth less than 1Mbps.

Table 1 lists the testing models' statistics and time costs of our experiments. The server's running time using 100 frequencies and mobiles' speed using 10 frequencies at different stages are included. The time mentioned in the table refers to one single deformation, and is measured based on seconds. As we can see from the table, mobiles are able to finish coarse computing in a fraction of second, even for large model such as Lion. Thus, it is true that we are able to provide users an instant interaction feedback. Increasing LOD on the mobile is the speed of improving deformation results after receiving the detail information from the server, and this time cost is very small. Additionally, the server computing speed is quite fast, so the RTD is the dominating delay for the whole procedure. The pre-computing time, which consists of loading the model and initializing the deformation, is relatively longer compared with running time, but it only needs to carry on once offline, and does not affect the real-time performance.

The number of frequencies (m) used to compute deformation is the key factor which determines the speed of our algorithm. For most of the models, we can get very good and detailed results using 200 frequencies (m=200). The left side of Figure 3 shows the relationship between the computing time and m used for the

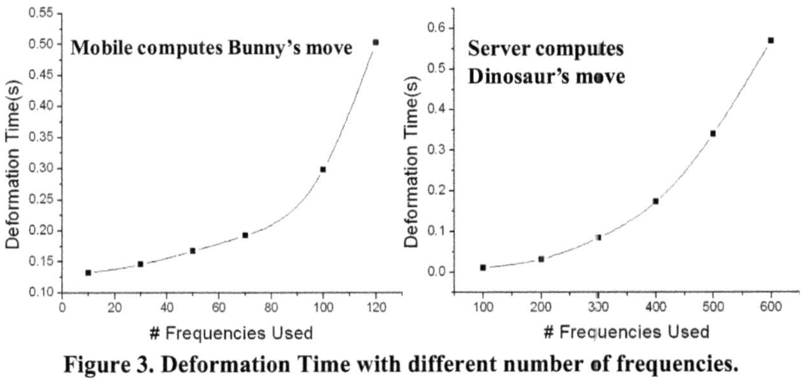

Figure 3. Deformation Time with different number of frequencies.

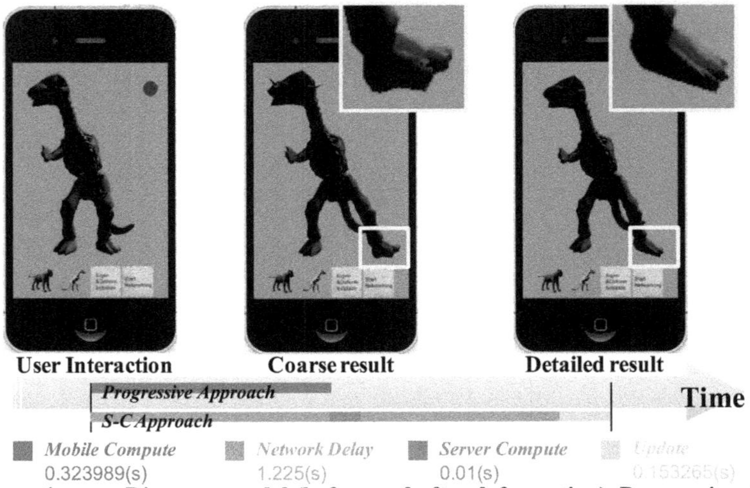

Figure 4. Deformation interactions on Dinosaur model (before and after deformation). Progressive Approach provides user a coarse result in 0.3 second. Traditional Server-Client Approach needs about 1.388 second to provide user a feedback.

Bunny model on the mobile devices. Similarly, the right side of Figure 3 shows the speed of the server for the Dinosaur model. It is clear that even for a larger model like Dinosaur with more frequencies used, the server's speed is much faster, indicating that mobile cannot quickly get very good results alone. Moreover, we notice that even though the increase of m leads to the increase of the computing time, the performance of the overall system is very effective. Generally, the steaming load, which is related to m, is only several KB in all our experiments. The value of m is not fixed and we can adjust it depending on the size of the model, network conditions and application requirements.

Figure 4 demonstrates the deformation streaming results of the Dinosaur model in a setting where the server is at Turkey and the mobile user is at USA. During testing, the RTD delay is about 1.2 second. As shown in the figure, while the mobile user can get a coarse feedback in about 0.3 second following the PDS method, he has to wait for about 1.4 second to view the deformation if the traditional S-C approach is used. Note that this waiting time can be much longer if it is in a highly congested network and rash hour such as the weekday afternoon. Therefore, the network delivery delay is the bottleneck. Note that the communication delay for uploading the constraints to the server and retrieving the updates from the server are almost the same, because the streaming load in our system is very small for both cases.

5. CONCLUSION AND FUTURE WORK

We have developed a novel method for mobile users to interact with 3D objects and receive interaction feedbacks instantly. Our method enables mobile clients to modify 3D models' shape and motions in real-time in addition to watching and browsing them. Following the Server-Client architecture, a spectral method is adopted to compute deformations using frequencies to ensure low cost and high speed. Moreover, we propose a new progressive deformation streaming approach to reduce the interaction delay effect between the server and mobile clients. This allows mobile users to view interaction results quickly in a coarse version while waiting for details from the server. Our experiments of several 3D models on the iPhone confirm the effectiveness of the proposed method. Our works can be extended to include multiple mobile users in a collaborative system. We also plan to compare with other applications and perform user studies in the future.

6. REFERENCES

[1] Botsch, M. and Sorkine, O. 2008. On linear variational surface deformation methods. *IEEE Transactions on Visualization and Computer Graphics*, 14(1), 213–230.

[2] Chhaya, M. Samsung W960 First Mobile Phone with a 3D Display. http://phonerpt.com/samsung-w960-first-mobile-phone-with-a-3d-display/

[3] Doran, A., Mondet, S., Grigoras, R., Morin, G., Ooi, W. and Boudon, F. 2009. A demonstration of MobiTree: progressive 3D tree models streaming on mobile clients. In *Proceeding of ACM international conference on Multimedia.* 955-956.

[4] Duguet, F. and Drettakis, G. 2004. Flexible Point-Based Rendering on Mobile Devices. IEEE Computer Graphics and Applications, 24(4), 57-63.

[5] He, Y., Chew, B., Wang, D., Hoi, C. and Chau, L. 2009. Streaming 3D meshes using spectral geometry images. In *Proceeding of ACM international conference on Multimedia.* 431-440.

[6] Karni, Z. and Gotsman, C. 2000. Spectral compression of mesh geometry. In *Proceedings of ACM SIGGRAPH 2000.* 279–286.

[7] Lamberti, F. and Sanna, A. 2007. A Streaming-Based Solution for Remote Visualization of 3D Graphics on Mobile Devices. *IEEE Transactions on Visualization and Computer Graphics*, 13(2), 247-260.

[8] Rong, G., Cao, Y. and Guo, X. 2008. Spectral mesh deformation. *The Visual Computer*, 24(7-9). 787– 796.

[9] Shi, S., Kamali, M., Nahrstedt, K., Hart, J., and Campbell, R. 2010. A high-quality low-delay remote rendering system for 3D video. In *Proceeding of ACM international conference on Multimedia.* 601-610.

[10] Tang, Z., Rong, G., Guo, X. and Prabhakaran, B. 2010. Streaming 3D Shape Deformations in Collaborative Virtual Environment. In *Proceeding of IEEE Virtual Reality*. 183-186.

Keyframe Presentation for Browsing of User-generated Videos on Map Interfaces

Jia Hao, Guanfeng Wang, Beomjoo Seo, Roger Zimmermann
School of Computing, National University of Singapore, Singapore 117417
[haojia,wanggf,seobj,rogerz]@comp.nus.edu.sg

ABSTRACT

To present user-generated videos that relate to geographic areas for easy access and browsing it is often natural to use maps as interfaces. A common approach is to place thumbnail images of video keyframes in appropriate locations. Here we consider the challenge of determining which keyframes to select and where to place them on the map. Our proposed technique leverages sensor-collected meta-data which are automatically acquired as a continuous stream together with the video. Our approach is able to detect interesting regions and objects (hotspots) and their distances from the camera in a fully automated way. Meaningful keyframes are adaptively selected based on the popularity of the hotspots. Our experiments show very promising results and demonstrate excellent utility for the users.

Categories and Subject Descriptors

H.3.5 [**Information Storage and Retrieval**]: On–line Information Services—*Web-based services*; I.4.8 [**Image Processing and Computer Vision**]: Scene Analysis—*Sensor Fusion*

General Terms

Algorithms, Measurement, Performance

Keywords

Hotspot detection, visible distance, keyframe extraction

1. INTRODUCTION

We consider the problem of presenting user-generated outdoor videos on a map interface for easy browsing and viewing. Creating such videos is now popular and easy due to the technological advances in camera systems. Specifically, smartphones can now record good-quality video and they are carried by millions.

For videos that relate to geographic locations, regions or objects, map-based interfaces are a natural way to present them and make them available for browsing and viewing. Example interfaces are Bing Maps and Google Earth. Two aspects are crucially important for a good thumbnail presentation solution: (1) relevant keyframes must be extracted to show the most salient features of a video and (2) the keyframe thumbnails need to be placed in accurate locations on the map-based interface.

Existing solutions are limited in that they allow users to post videos based on a single GPS location, usually the initial camera position, and a single keyframe is placed there. However, this approach is unsatisfactory under two common conditions: (a) user mobility results in videos taken along some trajectory, so a single thumbnail location is insufficient to describe the video, and (b) the location of the most salient object in the video is often not at the position of the camera, but may in fact be quite a distance away. Consider the example of a user videotaping the pyramids of Giza – he or she would probably need to stand at a considerable distance. However, any user looking for videos of the pyramids would most likely zoom into their actual location.

Here we present our novel and unconventional solution to address the above two challenges. We do not restrict the movement of the camera operator and hence assume that mobile videos may be shot along some trajectory. In the first phase, to obtain the viewable scenes, we continuously collect GPS location and viewing direction information (via a compass sensor) together with the videos. This is easily achievable today as smartphones contain all the necessary sensors for recording videos that are annotated with meta-data. In the second phase we process the sensor meta-data of multiple videos to identify hotspot regions containing important objects or places. The third phase computes a set of visible distances between the camera locations and the hotspots. Finally, in the last step we leverage all the resulting information to extract relevant keyframe thumbnails and place them in their correct location on a map-based interface. Based on our results we believe that our approach provides high utility to the users in a fully automatic process that requires no manual intervention.

Existing work on visible distance estimation relates to the field of adaptively adjusting vehicle speeds [4, 3], which does not have the same goal as our work. The visible distance we aspire to estimate is the distance between the camera location and the key objects in the video frames. To the best of our knowledge, our method is the first to investigate this kind of *effective visible distance* for video. Most existing keyframe extraction techniques are based on the signal content of video streams [7, 6]. Due to the time-consuming pro-

*Area Chairs: Gang Hua

cedure of video decoding and the complex computations involved, these methods lack scalability. Different from them, our keyframe extraction method can be more efficient and light-weight because it utilizes only the video meta-data.

2. FRAMEWORK DESIGN

Our framework consists of four phases: data collection, hotspot estimation from profiling, visible distance R estimation, and keyframe extraction. In Section 2.1, we present how to collect videos and their sensor measurements. Section 2.2 describes how we generate a popularity map that captures how often an area is pointed at by camera views and how we infer most popular locations. In the rest of this paper we term such a location (or its grid cell representation on a 2D map) as "hotspot". Such hotspots can be a part of an attraction or consist of a more diffuse area that contains no specific physical objects but may be of interest to users (e.g., a beautiful valley). To estimate R accurately, we then associate a camera view with the closest hotspot in Section 2.3. Finally Section 2.4 presents our keyframe extraction algorithm which utilizes all the results of the previous steps.

2.1 Data Collection

A camera positioned at a given point P in geo-space captures a scene whose covered area is referred to as the camera field-of-view (FOV, also called the *viewable scene*). We adapt the FOV model introduced in our prior work [1], which describes a camera's viewable scene with four parameters: camera location P, camera orientation α, viewable angle θ and maximum visible distance R^{max} (see Eqn. 1).

$$FOV \equiv \langle P, \alpha, \theta, R^{max} \rangle \tag{1}$$

The camera position P consists of the latitude and longitude coordinates read from a positioning device (e.g., GPS) and the camera direction α is obtained based on the orientation angle provided by a digital compass. R^{max} is the maximum visible distance from P at which a large object within the camera's field-of-view can be recognized. The angle θ is calculated based on the camera and lens properties for the current zoom level [2]. To acquire sensor-annotated videos we have written two custom recording apps for Android and iOS smartphones. When a mobile device begins to capture video, the GPS and compass sensors are turned on to record the location and orientation of the camera. Our data-acquisition software fetches such sensor values as soon as new values are available. Video data are processed in real-time to extract frame timecodes (t_f). All collected meta-data (i.e., location, direction, frame timecode and video ID) are combined as a tuple and uploaded to a server.

Figure 1(a) illustrates the concept of visible distance R estimation based on hotspots. Along the camera trajectory (black line segments), the camera views (blue arrows) tend to point to some areas (red circles) more frequently, and R can be determined as the distance between such popular areas, i.e., hotspots, and the camera locations.

2.2 Hotspot Detection

First, a target space is assumed on a 2D geographical map which is partitioned into equally-spaced square grid cells. For estimating the hotspots in the space, we use a grid counting-based popularity method. Our algorithm maintains a data structure for every map grid cell containing a

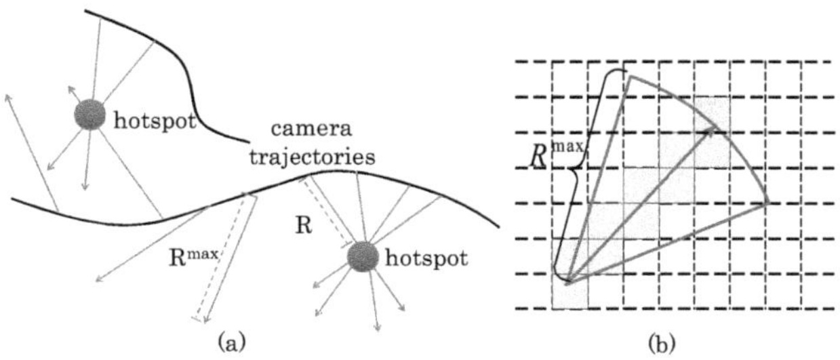

Figure 1: (a) Conceptual illustration of visible distance estimation. (b) Coverage model.

monotonically increasing counter of interest. Without prior knowledge on the underlying landmarks or attractions, it is incremented whenever its grid cell is visually covered by an FOV. We investigate a line-based coverage model who uses a line vector with length R^{max}. Its center is at the GPS location, and its heading is the camera direction – see Figure 1(b). With this model we increase the counters of all the grid cells only along the center line. The rationale is that users tend to focus on objects located at the median plane of the FOV.

Among all the grid cells, we then compute the local maxima of the map and determine them as hotspot if their probability is higher than those of all their neighboring cells and their differences exceed a certain threshold.

2.3 Effective Visible Distance Estimation

Let H be a set of estimated hotspots computed from the previous stage. When new sensor values related to a camera view arrive in the system, they are transformed into a measurement vector $\mathbf{X} = \{\mathbf{x}_1, ..., \mathbf{x}_{|H|}\}$, where $\mathbf{x}_i$ consists of the subtended angle a of a compass value to the hotspot $i \in H$ and the Euclidean distance d to the hotspot. We estimate the effective visible distance R by the closeness – in terms of lower angular disparity – to a hotspot and select the closest one. Eqn. 2 expresses R as the distance to the hotspot which is most likely pointed to by a camera view, by choosing the minimum subtended angle.

$$R = \{\underset{x_i}{\text{argmin}}\ (x_i.a)\}.d \tag{2}$$

2.4 Keyframe Extraction

We analyze the visual similarity between frames and select the keyframes with sufficient content change.

2.4.1 Visual Similarity Measurement

We derive an overlap ratio of a projected line between two FOVs to approximate the visual similarity between two frames. To illustrate the analysis, let us consider the diagrams in Figure 2, with a reference FOV located at $A(0,0)$, directing its angle to North along the y-axis, and a target FOV whose location is at $B(x,y)(x \geq 0)$, offset by angle difference γ. The angle of view is $2 \times \beta$ and R is the viewable distance. Our goal is to determine by how much FOV B overlaps with FOV A.

In the first step we limit the problem to the case of $0 \leq \gamma \leq \beta$ as depicted in Figure 2. We denote the vertical ordinate of the intersection point of FOV B's left ray and y-axis as l. For the case of $l \leq R$ (see Figure 2(a)), from A's perspective the overlap ratio (simplified as a line) by B is:

$$sim(f_A, f_B) = \frac{R \tan\beta + (R - l)\tan(\beta - \gamma)}{2R\tan\beta} \tag{3}$$

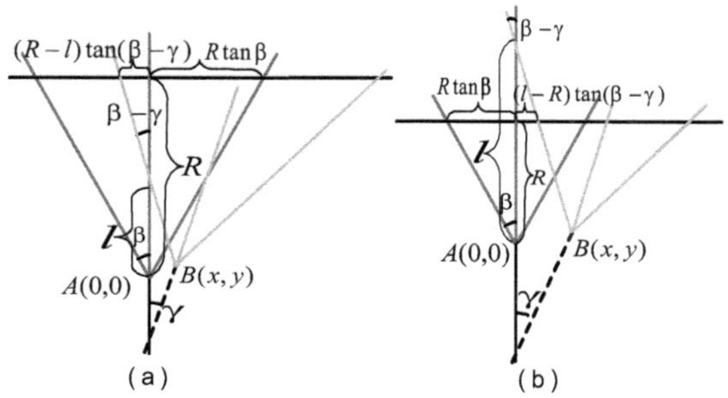

Figure 2: Overlap ratio of the projected line between two FOVs.

If l is greater than R (see Figure 2(b)), the overlap ratio is:

$$sim(f_A, f_B) = \frac{R\tan\beta - (l - R)\tan(\beta - \gamma)}{2R\tan\beta} \quad (4)$$

If $\beta \le \gamma \le 2 \times \beta$, the ratio is reduced to the same result as shown in Equation 3 ($l \le R$) and Equation 4 ($l > R$).

Similar equations can be easily derived for the situation when $\beta \le -\gamma \le 2 \times \beta$ and $-\beta \le \gamma \le 0$. If there does not exist an intersection point of FOV B's ray and the y-axis, that is, $\gamma \ge 2 \times \beta$ or $\gamma \le -2 \times \beta$, there exists no overlap, and hence we set the ratio to zero. Furthermore, if y is no less than R, there is no overlap either.

2.4.2 Keyframe Selection

Given a video sequence $S_i (i = 0, 1, ...N - 1)$ of N frames as input, every frame is represented as an FOV. Let f_i be the FOV representing the ith frame, where i denotes the index of the currently processed frame. At every arriving new frame, an FOV is obtained to represent its visual content. The first frame is always chosen as a keyframe. The similarity score $sim(f_{last}, f_i)$ between the FOV of the current frame f_i and the FOV of last extracted keyframe f_{last} needs to be calculated. If this similarity score is lower than a given threshold T, the current frame is selected as a new keyframe and stored for later use when new frames will arrive.

3. EXPERIMENTS

To evaluate the performance of our framework, we recorded 71 video sequences of sensor-annotated, mobile videos. These videos were collected in the Marina Bay area in Singapore with Samsung Galaxy S and Motorola Droid smart–phones running Android 2.2. The real trajectories of these test videos are shown in Figure 3. The average length of test videos is 130s, the resolution is 720×480 pixels, and the frame rate is 24 frames per second. The sampling rate for the location and orientation sensor information is 1 sample per second. All FOVs of the test videos are within a rectangular area which is separated into 100×100 cells. The size of each cell is about 20×18 m^2. Due to limited space, we only present the detailed results for one video, namely v8636(00:05:07).

3.1 Hotspot Detection Results

Figure 3 is a snapshot from Google Maps which shows the hotspots detected from a popularity map obtained from our coverage model. The green lines are the trajectories for the 71 videos, and the red points are the hotspots that were detected. The labeled hotspots "A, B, C, D, E, H, G" all represent the locations of landmarks or are locations near landmarks (A: Clifford Pier; B: The Fullerton Hotel Singapore; C: Merlion; D, E: Esplanade; G: The Float; H: Marina Bay Sands). However, "F" is located in the water, in the center between those landmarks. "F" can be eliminated through some filtering method.

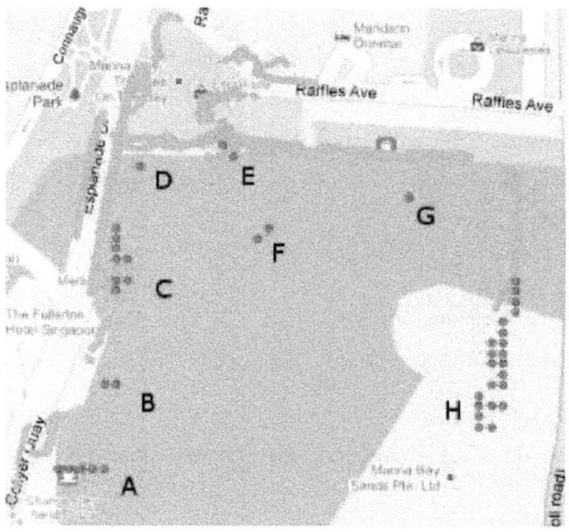

Figure 3: Hotspot detection results.

3.2 Effective Visible Distance Statistics

To evaluate our estimation of the effective visible distance, we manually collected ground truth data. For each video frame represented by the corresponding FOV, we found the most important object in the frame based on human perception, located the object in Google Earth, and then obtained its latitude and longitude. Afterwards, the distance between the camera location and the object was calculated as the ground truth effective visible distance. The frames in transition or containing ambiguous content (even users could not identify the most important object) were discarded. Figure 4 shows the comparison between the ground truth and the estimated effective visible distance for video v8636. Except for some miss estimations due to the incorrect understanding of the hotspots, the estimated distances match very well with the ground truth data. For instance, for the frame at time 40, the estimated distance R is 712 m. Correspondingly, we can observe from the actual picture that the focus of the picture is Marina Bay Sands, which is very far away. For the frame at time 120, the focus is the Merlion, which is nearby. Accordingly, the estimated distance R is 20 m.

3.3 Keyframe Extraction and Placement Results

The results for the proposed keyframe extraction algorithm are dependent on the threshold T, which determines the final number of keyframes that will be generated. The dependency of the number of keyframes on the threshold T is illustrated in Figure 6. If we set a relatively high threshold value, we might obtain a large number of keyframes with most of them being similar to each other. On the other hand, if we set a relatively small threshold value, the number of keyframes will be less and it is possible that some content between keyframes will be missed. Based on these observations and taking into consideration that mobile phone applications have battery constraints where similar keyframes should be avoided, we selected a threshold of 0.55 as a good compromise for the algorithm.

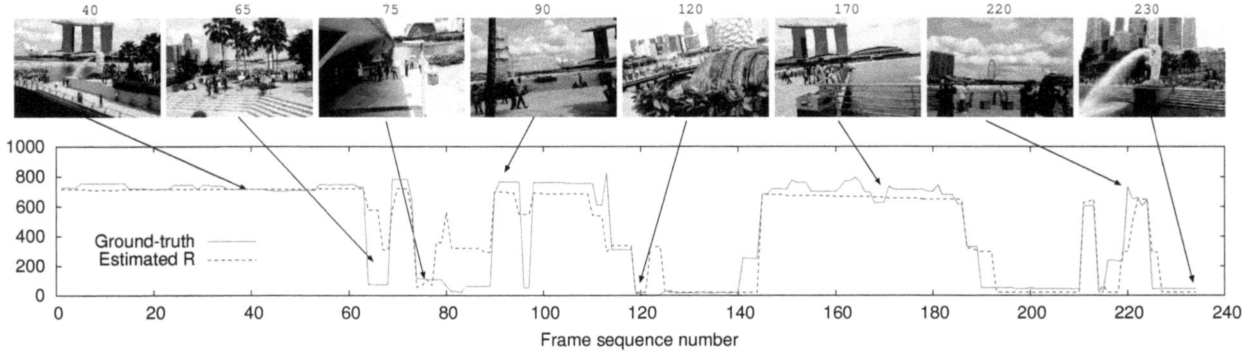

Figure 4: Comparison between the ground-truth and the estimated visible distance R for video v8636.

Figure 5: Selected keyframes of video v8636 for the proposed keyframe selection algorithm.

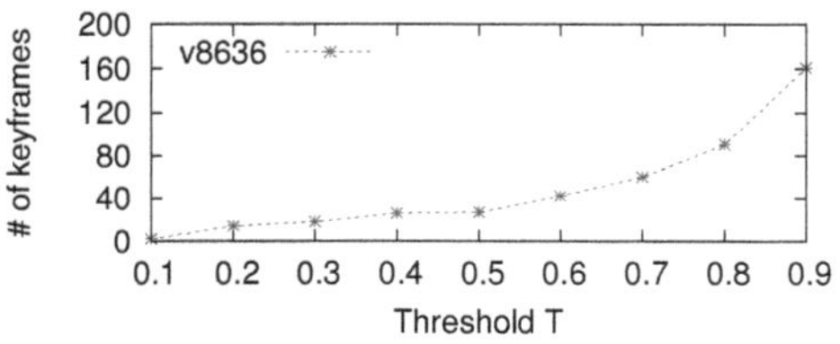

Figure 6: The number of keyframes as a function of the threshold T using video v8636.

Figure 5 shows the the keyframe extraction result of our algorithm which successfully generates a compact keyframe set with adequate coverage for the original video and is computationally fast and efficient.

By applying hotspot detection, visible distance estimation and keyframe extraction, we can utilize a map-based user interface to present user-collected videos. The keyframe placement algorithm has been implemented in a demonstration system [5] which illustrates that when a user navigates along the video trajectory on the map, the corresponding thumbnails for the video keyframes are displayed at the estimated (far or near) locations.

4. CONCLUSIONS

In our study we presented an approach to detect hotspots and their distances from the camera in a fully automated way. We then leveraged that information to obtain an effective keyframe extraction method. The experimental results show that our technique is very effective for presenting user-generated outdoor videos on a map interface for easy browsing and viewing.

Acknowledgments

We would like to acknowledge that this research was carried out at the Centre of Social Media Innovations for Communities (COSMIC), sponsored and supported by the Singapore National Research Foundation and Interactive & Digital Media Program Office, MDA.

5. REFERENCES

[1] S. Arslan Ay, R. Zimmermann, and S. H. Kim. Viewable Scene Modeling for Geospatial Video Search. In 16th *ACM Intl. Conference on Multimedia*, pages 309–318, 2008.

[2] C. H. Graham, N. R. Bartlett, J. L. Brown, Y. Hsia, C. C. Mueller, and L. A. Riggs. *Vision and Visual Perception.* John Wiley & Sons, Inc., 1965.

[3] N. Hautière, R. Labayrade, and D. Aubert. Real-time Disparity Contrast Combination for Onboard Estimation of the Visibility Distance. *IEEE Transactions on Intelligent Transportation Systems*, 7(2):201–212, 2006.

[4] D. Pomerleau. Visibility Estimation from a Moving Vehicle using the RALPH Vision System. In *IEEE Transactions on Intelligent Transportation Systems*, pages 906–911, 1997.

[5] B. Seo, J. Hao, and G. Wang. Sensor-rich Video Exploration on a Map Interface. In 19th *ACM Intl. Conference on Multimedia*, 2011.

[6] W. Wolf. Key Frame Selection by Motion Analysis. In *ICASSP*, pages 1228–1231, 1996.

[7] H. Zhang, J. Wu, D. Zhong, and S. Smoliar. An Integrated System for Content-based Video Retrieval and Browsing. *Pattern Recognition*, 30(4):643–658, 1997.

Detecting and Identifying People in Mobile Videos

Xunyi Yu
University of Massachusetts, Amherst
Amherst, Massachusetts, 01002
yuxunyi@gmail.com

Aura Ganz
University of Massachusetts, Amherst
Amherst, Massachusetts, 01002
ganz@ecs.umass.edu

ABSTRACT

In this paper, we propose a system capable of detecting and identifying people in videos captured by smart phones. We discuss the challenges to extend existing location aware multimedia applications from annotating static landmarks in distance to annotating dynamic people in close range with significant pose variations. We propose to use a hybrid video and RF tracking system to enable accurate observer and target localization, and extract part models comprised of Maximally Stable Color Regions for each target. The model can efficiently detect possible positions of targets in the video, which are then used as dynamic landmarks to calibrate the camera orientation. Finally, positions of all targets in the video are jointly estimated using both visual features and spatial constraints. Experiments show that our approach can locate identified targets in video with significantly higher accuracy than back-projection using camera orientation estimations from accelerometers and magnetometers.

Categories and Subject Descriptors

I.5.4 **[Pattern Recognition]** Applications – *Computer Vision;* H.5.1 **Information Interfaces and Presentation (e.g., HCI)]:** Multimedia Information Systems – *Video*

General Terms

Algorithms, Measurement, Experimentation

Keywords

People detection, camera calibration, feature fusion.

1. INTRODUCTION

The proliferation of smart phones with embedded camera, GPS, and orientation sensors has spurred a whole set of location and context aware applications. One capability of particular importance to these applications is accurately recognizing and locating targets on screen or on recorded videos. A lot of progress has been made by fusing location and orientation sensor information with visual features, leading to improved user experience of augmented reality applications, and better annotation of mobile videos, etc. Still, most applications today can only deal with large scale static landmarks such as architectures in distance.

In this paper, we explore the possibility of annotating the living components of an environment, i.e., people in close surrounding of the user. We propose a system that can detect and identify people with arbitrary poses, e.g. standing, sitting or lying on the ground, in videos captured from the smart phone held by a moving observer. This new capability can potentially lead to location aware mobile applications with more social networking elements that enable users to know who's who on the screen, or even better, read people's "mind", e.g. their Facebook pages superimposed on their image.

We propose a general framework that enables detecting and identifying people on mobile videos, composing of the following components. 1) Introduce the hybrid video and RF tracking system as the infrastructure to improve localization accuracy of the observer and the targets. 2) Propose individualized person detection based on part models with Maximally Stable Color Regions features. 3) Use people as dynamic landmarks to calibrate mobile camera orientation. 4) Jointly estimate people positions in mobile video using visual features and spatial constraints.

2. CHALLENGES AND RELATED WORK

There are challenges in several aspects to extend existing approaches from annotating static landmarks in distance to annotating moving people in close range with pose variations.

Observer and target localization: When the targets and the observer are close by, even small localization errors will cause large deviations in back-projection target positions. Existing applications typically use GPS or indoor WiFi localization system to determine the location of the observer, which could be off several meters [6]. Thus they can only handle large scale landmark targets with known locations that are at least tens of meters away, in which distance the relative localization error of the observer is small. For people annotation application, both the observer and the targets need to be localized, and they are often only meters apart. In this case, it is even difficult to determine whether the targets are within the field of view of the camera using GPS or RF localization. Specialized ultrasound or UWB ranging devices can be used to achieve higher localization accuracy [4]. But these devices are not widely on market yet, and are also subject to many issues that affect localization accuracy in practice, e.g. body attenuation and multi-path

Camera orientation: Many applications use the direction of gravity and magnetic north given by accelerometers and magnetometers embedded in smart phones to derive the orientation of the cameras. To get accurate orientation estimations, the user typically needs to stand still, and can only pan the camera slowly. When the user is walking, the acceleration stem from body movements and hand shake makes it difficult to estimate the direction of gravity from accelerometers. Although gyroscopes can be used to improve the responsiveness of the relative orientation estimation, it cannot remove the bias of

*Area Chair: Gang Hua

MM'11, November 28–December 1, 2011, Scottsdale, Arizona, USA.

absolute orientation estimation introduced by inaccurate gravity direction estimated under acceleration.

Visual features: Visual features applicable to rigid static landmarks, e.g. architectures, are not appropriate for non-rigid human bodies under pose and view variation [5]. Despite relative success in detecting upright pedestrians [9], it is still a non-trivial task to detect people with arbitrary poses, e.g. people lying or sitting on the ground in our experiments. Given the detection, it is still challenging to establish correspondence even between upright standing people observed in different cameras, i.e. the people re-identification problem in surveillance video [3].

Fusion of location, orientation and visual features: Visual features are often used to calibrate camera parameters. For existing landmark annotation applications, dense features on architectures are typically used and 3D point clouds of these features are generated from an excessive number of photos taken at different locations and orientations [7]. For places of tourist interest, these features and photos are abundant to find. However, for people annotation application we considered, the environment may lack distinguishing features, e.g. cameras pointing down on people on a park lawn. Also, it may be costly to acquire 3D point clouds for the environment.

3. SYSTEM OVERVIEW

We propose a general framework to address the above challenges. First we use a hybrid video and RF tracking system as the infrastructure to accurately locate the observer and the targets [8]. Fixed mounted cameras can detect human targets and achieve localization accuracy within a meter, but they cannot find out the identities of the targets. GPS or WiFi can only locate targets with less accuracy, but targets' identities are explicit. We propose to use a hybrid video and RF tracking system that can locate people accurately using video, while using complimentary RF signals to find out their identity.

Given more accurate ground locations of the observer and the targets, the back-projection position of targets on screen can still be way off due to inaccuracy of camera orientation sensors under acceleration. So we use people as dynamic landmarks to calibrate the camera orientation in the system, which has the advantage of not requiring pre-established 3D cloud map of dense features of an environment.

To detect possible positions of a target in the mobile video, we build individualized part models using the background separated blobs of the target in the video captured by the fixed camera tracking system. The body parts are composed of Maximally Stable Color Regions of different colors and scales. Regions of similar colors and scales to body centers collect votes from nearby body part regions, and those with votes passing a threshold will be used as candidates. This approach is very efficient as oppose to using a moving window to detect body parts, as there are typically only tens of regions meeting color and scale constraints of an individual, as oppose to tens of thousands of searching windows of different positions, rotations and scales in a generic part model human detector [1]. The approach is specifically developed to deal with people with significant pose and view variations, e.g. those sitting or lying on the ground. When the targets to be detected are standing, we can use pedestrian detectors to further reduce the false positive rate.

There are typical multiple candidate detections for a target, especially when he dresses in similar colors to others or is close in appearance to the background. We only use the initial detections to calibrate the camera orientation. We perform searching on camera orientation space on each frame by matching initial detections to the back-projection target positions. There are typically multiple local optimums of similar values in the camera orientation space for a single frame due to large numbers of false detections and ambiguities in matching. So we apply temporal camera movement constraints, and find the most consistent camera parameters over a time window.

After the best camera orientation is found, the back-projection target position may still not coincide with the actual location of a target, due to localization errors of the observer and the targets on the ground plane. If we use detections closest to the back project position of the target as the final detection, multiple targets may be matched to the same region, or regions that should be other targets' body parts. We use shortest spanning tree to approximate the constraints between all targets, and use the max-product algorithm to find the final annotation of targets in the field of view using both visual features and spatial constraints.

4. PEOPLE DETECTINO IN MOBILE VIDEO

In this section, we assume that ground location of the observer and the targets are given by the hybrid video and RF tracking system, and focus on the detection of human targets under inaccurate camera orientation sensor inputs and residual localization errors of the observer and the targets.

4.1 Part models with Maximally Stable Color Regions

We observe that human clothing and body color is quite distinct from background colors, and will form Maximally Stable Color Regions [2] corresponding to upper and lower body clothing, and exposed skin regions. The feature is also invariant over a range of scales, different poses and viewing angles. Thus color regions extracted from body blobs detected by fixed cameras mounted way above the head level in distance can be reliably detected in videos taken by hand-held cameras in close range at head level from a very different view angle. So we build part model detector for an individual target using his blob in the fixed camera to detect him in the mobile video.

We use the following model to evaluate the visual score of stable color regions r_l as the center of the body of the ith person based on the color and scale of itself and nearby regions according to the part model,

$$Vscore_i(r_l) = A(r_l)C(r_l, p_{i0})\left(\sum_{m,k} A(r_m)C(r_m, p_{ik})\right), \quad (1)$$

where r_m is the mth region within the body dimension after rescaling according to the distance between the target and the observer, and p_{ik} is the kth body part of the model for the ith target we extracted. Function $C(\ )$ evaluates the similarity of a region to a body part, based on color and scale. Note that when a target is close to the observer, body parts extracted are often breaking into smaller regions. Thus we only use scale of the reference body part to limit the maximum size of region. Function $A(\ )$ measures the area of the region, so that evidence from many smaller regions can be accumulated. Note that in our model, body parts other than the body center contributed additively to the overall score instead of multiplicatively as typically found in part model for articulation estimation, to account for part fragmentations and occlusions [1]. Figure 1 shows the detection result for three targets in a video frame with part models built from their blobs in the fix camera.

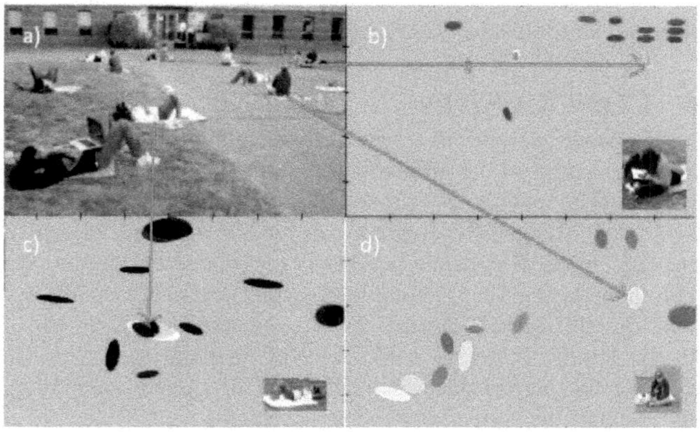

Figure 1: Target detection with individualized MSCR part models, a) mobile video, b) c) d) candidate detections of three targets respectively, brighter color indicates higher score, red arrows indicate the correct correspondences. Target's image patches from the fixed camera is on lower right.

4.2 Camera Orientation Estimation

The Maximally Stable Color Region based detection is not very discriminative when a target's clothing is not very distinct from others or from the background. To ensure a low false negative rate, we often end up with a very high false positive rate, i.e. multiple detections for a target. So the number of incorrect correspondence, i.e. the outliers, may dominate the data. Also, the number of targets is limited, and there are localization errors of the observer and targets. So there are typical multiple local optimums in the camera parameter space and the correct camera orientation may not be the global optimum. So we do not use RANSAC algorithm typically used in camera calibration to get a point estimate of the camera parameters, but first find all local optimums for a frame, and then apply the temporal constraint of smooth camera movement to filter the camera orientation.

We observe that camera roll is usually near zero, as the observer will try to keep the camera level to the ground. The pitch of the camera only varies in a relatively small range, as the observer usually pitches the camera slightly downward to center on the people on the ground plane. The yaw of the camera changes more abruptly, when the observer pans the camera, or changes his heading. Due to the lack of a gyroscope in our phone, the yaw from orientation sensors is very inaccurate, subjecting to orientation sensor lag along with inaccuracies caused by acceleration. For each frame, we calculate the matching score for camera pitch and yaw within a search window centered on orientation sensor outputs, of width 40° and 120° respectively. During observer movement, camera roll can deviate slightly from zero. This effect is compensated during joint people detection.

We assume that the position of a person follows a normal distribution centered on the back-projection position, with variance being larger when the target is closer to the observer. For each target in the field of view given an orientation, visual scores of different detections are attenuated by spatial mismatches, the best detection will be used to calculate the average visual and spatial score for a rotation as

$$Rscore(\mathbf{R}) = \frac{1}{N}\sum_{i=1}^{N}\max_{j \in D_i}\left(Vscore_i(r_{ij})p\left(p_{ij} \mid p_i^b(\mathbf{R}), \sigma_i^2\right)\right)P(N), \quad (2)$$

where r_{ij} and p_{ij} are the region and position of the *j*th detection of the *ith* person, and $p_i^b(\mathbf{R})$ is the back-projection position of the *ith* person given camera orientation $\mathbf{R}$. $P(N)$ is the probability that there are *N* targets in the field of view. For efficiency concern, we do not apply one-to-one correspondence constraint at this stage, so one region may be used by multiple targets.

The number of states for camera pitch and yaw is very large. So instead of trying to find the best camera orientation in the entire orientation space, we use non-maximal suppression to find local optimums of the score function for a frame, to form new states for that frame. Then we evaluate the transition probability between states in adjacent frames by evaluating the distance between two rotations. If gyroscope is available, we can use the angular speed estimate to calculate the transition probability. Otherwise, we consider the camera movements to be equally likely on any direction within an angular speed limit. We do not use optical flow to estimate angular speed, as using people as landmarks has exactly the same effect. Given the states and their transition probability, we use Viterbi algorithm to find the most likely sequence of camera orientation.

4.3 Joint Target to Region Correspondence

In the previous stage, we find the best mode of the camera orientation, but the back-projection target position can still be off tens of pixels as we are confined to the local optimums of the distribution on each frame, and there are residual localization errors of the targets and the observer. Now we use both visual features and spatial constraints between the targets to find jointly the screen position of all targets. At this stage, we only use absolute target position to threshold candidate detections, while rely on more relative target position to find the best correspondence, as it is more robust to residual back-projection errors.

We use a graphical model to model the correspondence between all targets and their initial detections. Nodes in the graph are the people in the field of view of the camera. The initial detections within a threshold of the back-projection position of a person are the states of his corresponding node. Assuming that the target is equally likely to be anywhere within the threshold of the back-projection position, the prior distribution of a node is proportional to its detections' visual scores. We assume that the position of one person follows a normal distribution centered at the position of another person plus the offset between their back-projection positions. This relative spatial relationship is used to calculate the conditional probability between two states of two nodes.

The *maximum a posteriori* estimation of the resulting fully connected graphical model cannot be calculated efficiently. So we use the shortest spanning tree between all targets in the field of view as an approximation. The distance between two nodes is determined by both their spatial distance of back projections, and similarity of their appearance. So people near each other with similar appearances are more likely to be adjacent neighbors, with their spatial constraints directly enforced, and thus less likely to collide into each other. With the tree approximation, we find the *maximum a posteriori* detections for all targets using the Max-Product algorithm. Figure 2 shows an example of using the method to further improve annotation accuracy over direct back-projection. Note how the residual back-projection errors for targets on the upper-right portion of the screen are removed.

Figure 2: a) Back-projection positions of targets, b) Positions of best body centers, red lines indicting edges in the tree.

5. EXPERIMENT

We focus on the evaluation of the accuracy of camera orientation calibration using people detected with Maximally Stable Color Regions part models, and the accuracy of estimated positions of people with tree approximation using both visual features and spatial constraints. In the experiment, we only use fixed camera tracking to locate people, without actually applying the hybrid RF system to find out targets' unique identities that are required for an application to query target information from a database, to rule out the influence of identification errors evaluated in [8].

The experiment is conducted on a 30 by 30 meters area, mostly covered by a Cannon HG21 video camera mounted on the third floor of a nearby building. There are 40 people sitting or lying on the ground, and one observer walking through them with a Motorola Droid smart phone with accelerometers and magnetometers taking videos of the scene and the people at 800x480 resolution. The ground locations of the observer and the targets are given by the fixed camera tracking system using homography. We process 120 seconds video at 10 frames per second in a batch mode.

Of the 120 seconds video, our algorithm finds camera orientation successfully for 78 seconds of the video. For the remaining video, the algorithm finds the incorrect local optimum, resulting in target back-projection errors over two times the body height for most targets. Incorrect camera orientation is primarily due to sharp turns of the observer or lack of people in the field of view when the observer moves to the peripheral of the experiment area. As a comparison, if we use global optimum of individual frames without applying temporal constraint, camera orientation estimate is successful for only 56 seconds of video. If the phone is equipped with gyroscope, the transition probability across different frames can be modeled more accurately and could lead to better camera calibration.

Of the 78 seconds video with acceptable camera orientation estimation, we pick 30 frames and manually annotate the body center for each target. The back projection error of target position is 45 pixels in average, and 0.29 body height of the corresponding target on average. As a comparison, the back projection error with camera orientation given by the embedded accelerometer and magnetometer is 211 pixels, and 1.43 body height. By fusing visual features and spatial constraints, and using Max-product algorithm to find corresponding regions as body centers for all targets jointly, about half of the back-projection target positions that do not overlap with the targets are now centered on the targets. The reduction of position estimate error on average is not obvious, due to a few incorrect correspondences, and the mismatch between manually annotated body centers and regions found by the algorithm. Note that in applications with standing targets, the annotation accuracy can be significantly improved after using shape and gradient information, and part models with stronger constraints between parts, to reduce false detections.

6. CONCLUSION

In this paper, we present a system that use hybrid video and RF tracking system as the infrastructure, to calibrate mobile camera, and annotate people in mobile videos. We show how to use Maximally Stable Color Regions part models for target detection, and use targets as dynamic landmarks for camera calibration. We also show that by fusing visual features and spatial constraints, we can find the correspondence from candidate detections to all targets jointly. In future work, we will integrate gyroscopes to improve the performance and efficiency of camera calibration, and evaluate the system on moving pedestrians.

7. REFERENCES

[1] M. Andriluka, S. Roth and B. Schiele, "Pictorial structures revisited: People detection and articulated pose estimation," in *Computer Vision and Pattern Recognition, 2009. CVPR 2009. IEEE Conference on,* 2009, pp. 1014-1021.

[2] P. -. Forssen, "Maximally stable colour regions for recognition and matching," in *Computer Vision and Pattern Recognition, 2007. CVPR '07. IEEE Conference on,* 2007, pp. 1-8.

[3] N. Gheissari, T. B. Sebastian and R. Hartley, "Person reidentification using spatiotemporal appearance," in *Computer Vision and Pattern Recognition, 2006 IEEE Computer Society Conference on,* 2006, pp. 1528-1535.

[4] X. Liu, M. Corner and P. Shenoy, "SEVA: Sensor-enhanced video annotation," *ACM Trans.Multimedia Comput.Commun.Appl.,* vol. 5, pp. 24:1-24:26, August, 2009.

[5] K. Mikolajczyk and C. Schmid, "A performance evaluation of local descriptors," *Pattern Analysis and Machine Intelligence, IEEE Transactions on,* vol. 27, pp. 1615-1630, 2005.

[6] M. Park, J. Luo, R. T. Collins and Y. Liu, "Beyond GPS: Determining the camera viewing direction of a geotagged image," in *Proceedings of the International Conference on Multimedia,* Firenze, Italy, 2010, pp. 631-634.

[7] X. Xiao, C. Xu and J. Wang, "Landmark image classification using 3D point clouds," in *Proceedings of the International Conference on Multimedia,* Firenze, Italy, 2010, pp. 719-722.

[8] Xunyi Yu and A. Ganz, "Global identification of tracklets in video using long range identity sensors," in *Advanced Video and Signal Based Surveillance (AVSS), 2010 Seventh IEEE International Conference on,* 2010, pp. 361-368.

[9] Zhenjiang Li, Kunfeng Wang, Li Li and Fei-Yue Wang, "A review on vision-based pedestrian detection for intelligent vehicles," in *Vehicular Electronics and Safety, 2006. ICVES 2006. IEEE International Conference on,* 2006, pp. 57-62

Multiple Object Localization by Context-Aware Adaptive Window Search and Search-Based Object Recognition

Fang-Erh Lin, Yin-Hsi Kuo, Winston H. Hsu
National Taiwan University, Taipei, Taiwan
{espblue, kuonini}@gmail.com, winston@csie.ntu.edu.tw

ABSTRACT
Multiple object localization and recognition has been an important problem in recent years not only because of its difficulty to be time efficient but also due to many different schemes of widespread applications. In many previous works, only a limited amount of object models contribute to less computational time. However, they tend to not work efficiently together with large-scale database. In this paper, we propose a context-aware adaptive window search algorithm and search-based object recognition system to recognize and localize multiple objects in an image with a large-scale database. Since we tackle this problem with the idea that users can get brief information of an item immediately after taking only a snapshot, a low response time is also taken into account. We implement the algorithm within a large-scale book recognition system and present experimental results that demonstrate the efficiency of our algorithm in terms of detection recall, precision, and speed compared to the baseline and efficient subwindow search (ESS) approaches.

Categories and Subject Descriptors
H.3.3 [**Information Storage and Retrieval**]: Information Search and Retrieval – *retrieval models, search process.*

General Terms
Algorithms, Performance, Design, Experimentation

Keywords
Multiple object localization, image retrieval, window estimation.

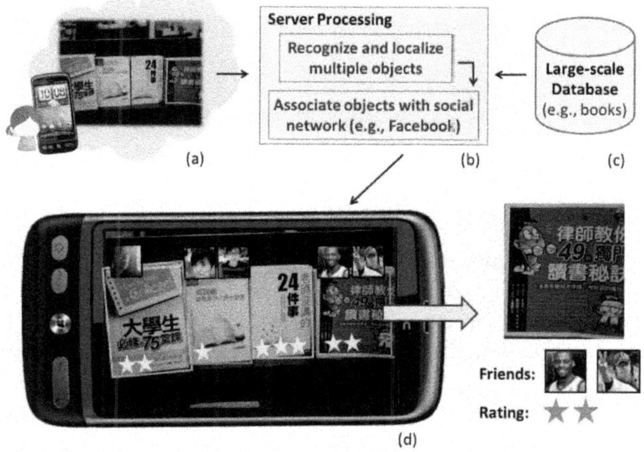

Figure 1. An application scenario of the multiple object localization and recognition problem. (a) Whenever users want to know the comments or other information of products in stores, they can take a photo by mobile phones and upload it to the remote server. (b) After recognizing and localizing multiple items, objects in the image can be detected and related information can be retrieved from social networks. (c) The recognition system is constructed by a large-scale database (e.g., million-scale object images). (d) Take books as example, users can see ratings of books and those friends who have read the books, by mobile phones. (Best seen in color.)

1. INTRODUCTION
With the increasing popularity and more and more types of sensors being equipped on smart phones, the number of applications implemented on smart phones has been growing fast recently. Also, thanks to the prevalence of high-bandwidth mobile networks, it has been promising to acquire related information from a large-scale database by taking a snapshot using mobile phones and then sending the image to remote server for object recognition. As Figure 1 shows, consider a customer in a bookstore who wants to know comments and evaluations for each book on the bookshelf. Additionally, with social networks such as Facebook and aNobii [1], the customer may even be able to know which friends have read those books before. Using the systems demonstrated in [5][11], the customer takes a snapshot of one book each time with the camera-phone. The camera-phone sends the query image over the mobile network to a remote server and waits for related data of the book returned from the server after the item is recognized. However, to view the comments of all the books on the bookshelf, the customer has to take many snapshots and spend time on communication between the camera-phone and the server. Under this situation, proposing an algorithm to localize and recognize multiple objects efficiently is necessary.

In recent years, *multiple object localization and recognition* has been an important problem. To localize objects efficiently, a branch-and-bound approach named Efficient Subwindow Search (ESS) [6] was proposed to decrease the computational cost and outperform the original sliding window method. The branch-and-bound scheme repeatedly decreases the possible regions from the input image to bound the desired object using visual word histograms. Recently, Tom Yeh et al. proposed a data-dependent multi-class branch-and-bound formalism that bounds the region of interest based on features' positions [12]. The authors in [10] proposed a Steiner tree model to solve multiple object detection and localization problem. This method selects windows most likely to contain the objects of interest by segmenting the entire image and post-processing such as merge and trim. By Steiner tree model, it selects regions and detects objects efficiently. These methods above all improve the speed to localize objects; however, for problems that contain larger-scale (i.e., millions of) object models in the database, such methods all fail to achieve real-time processing due to scalability issues.

Through these previous works [10][12], it is obvious that multiple object recognition and localization problem is important but not

*Area Chair: Gang Hua

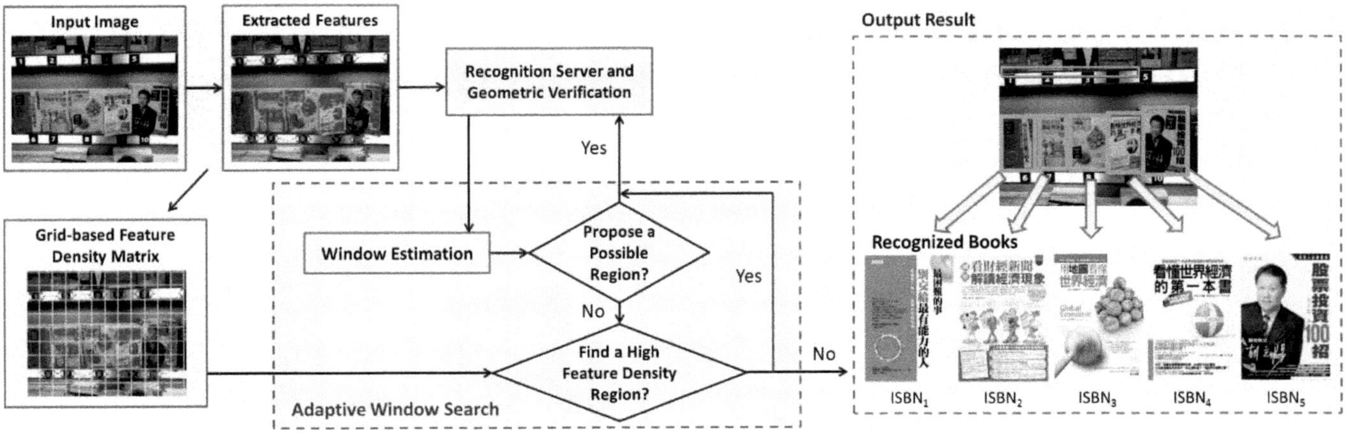

Figure 2. System diagram. Once the image is sent to the server, its features will be extracted and used to calculate a grid-based feature density matrix. At first we retrieve similar images for the input image and verify the spatial consistency between the features of input image and images in database, in order to find an initial region containing the book. Then we find other regions of interest by adaptive window search, integrating the information of the initial region and the feature density matrix. The result is output if there is no other high feature density region to retrieve. ISBNs for each recognized book enable us to retrieve other information (e.g., brief introduction, price, rating, comments) through social networks (e.g., Facebook, aNobii).

addressed properly. Therefore, we design an algorithm to efficiently localize multiple objects with a large number of object models and recognize objects by a search-based recognition system.

To summarize, the main contributions of this work are:

- Proposing a method to solve the multiple object localization problem by a search-based object recognition system.
- A database of the search-based object recognition system constructed of 251,000 images. To the best of our knowledge, it is the largest-scale database in the multiple object recognition and localization problems.
- A scheme with a considerably low response time and applicable in mobile augmented reality.

2. SYSTEM OVERVIEW

Figure 2 provides an overview of our system, which is mainly divided into two parts, the adaptive window search process and the object recognition process. For the object recognition part, we have downloaded a large amount of object images from a product selling website (Section 3.1) and constructed an online query system (Section 3.2). In order to locate the informative regions in the query image, the grid-based feature density matrix is calculated and provided to find the candidate regions which may contain objects. First we query the input image by the recognition system, and get the initial region using geometric verification to check feature matching consistency. The adaptive window algorithm proposes a region of interest relying on information provided by the initial region or the feature density matrix. Then, images similar to the proposed region will be retrieved and checked for spatial consistency to find matched objects. By repeating these steps, objects in the input image will be localized and recognized gradually. Details for the adaptive window search process will be explained in Section 4.

3. OBJECT RECOGNITION SYSTEM

3.1 Collecting Data

In the multiple object localization problem, we start from multiple book localization due to the application scheme and the easier data collection.

In order to collect a sufficient amount of book images, data from a large book selling website [2] is crawled. The metadata of each book (title, ISBN, price and comments) is fetched as well. There are no websites collecting book spines. Therefore, book images in our database only consist of book covers.

3.2 Recognition and Geometric Verification

After the image data is collected, a bag-of-feature-points is extracted from each book image. We have tried different local image detectors such as Harris-affine, Hessian-affine and Maximally Stable Extremal Region [8], and different descriptors such as SIFT [7] and SURF [3] for better recognition accuracy. Finally we adopted Hessian-affine detector and SIFT descriptor. For fast searching through a large-scale database, each book image is quantized to a set of visual words through a vocabulary tree. Because of the superiority in efficiency of inverted indexing, we retrieve books with similar visual word histograms efficiently.

Because different books usually have dissimilar covers and users only care about the images exactly shown in the query image, in the book recognition process we only focus on N candidate images (e.g., the five best-matching images) and perform a geometric consistency check to find the correct matching book. The spatial verification is done by RANSAC to find spatial consistency between the features of the query image and candidate images. The candidate image with the largest and above-a-threshold number of matching inliers is chosen as the correct matching book, and will be returned to the adaptive window process. Moreover, an affine model from the correct matching book in the database to the query image is generated by matching inliers. It enables us to bound the region of the book in query image.

4. MULTIPLE OBJECT LOCALIZATION

There are some common characteristics of book display on bookshelves in bookstores. Books in the same bookshelf are often put densely together. However, due to the complexity and variety of covers, the approach to segment covers of different books does not work as in [4]. It is hard to find main edges between books by edge detection and get the dominant direction using Hough transform. Therefore, we design a context-aware adaptive window search method which proposes regions by already matched books in a row-based manner (Section 4.2.1), and a grid-based feature density matrix for supporting information (Section 4.2.2).

Figure 3. Flow chart of adaptive window search. The number on each mask denotes the sequence number. No. 1 is the initial region after querying the input image and that spatial consistency is verified. Regions No. 2~6 are proposed by window estimation and verified through the recognition system. After scanning all the adjacent areas, No. 7 is recommended via feature density matrix, and then previous steps are repeated. Cyan marks are extracted features of the image.

4.1 Baseline Algorithm

To the best of our knowledge, there has been no similar work that uses search-based recognition system in large-scale database to detect multiple objects. Therefore, we propose a simple algorithm as the baseline method. The recognition result of the input image may be influenced by noisy visual words such as features of bookshelves. However, it is still possible to get book images which show up in the input image if more similar images are selected and checked by geometric verification. First we send a request to the recognition server that recognizes the whole input image, and perform a spatial verification for the top 10 ranked similar images. After selecting the best-matching image, we remove the features in the matched region from original input image and send a new request. By repeating these steps, features sent to the recognition server become less and the recognition of other books will not be easily affected by visual words of already-recognized books, which pose as noise for recognizing remaining books. Therefore, we can retrieve all the matching books after repeating requests many times.

4.2 Adaptive Window Search (AWS)

4.2.1 Window Estimation

Empirically, although visual features of all the other books in the input image represent background clutter when we focus on a specific book, it is still possible to get the best-matching image, which is one of the books in the input image, returned from the recognition system, if the query image is the whole input image. Therefore, we assume that the best-matching image after geometric verification, as returned from the recognition system, is one of the books in the input image (e.g., No. 1 in Figure 3). We retrieve not only the affine model of the best-matching book but also the approximate size of the book. Due to the fact that all books are about the same size and that books near each other are always packed together, we can estimate the size and position of the books near the currently recognized one (e.g., No. 2 or 6 in Figure 3). The estimated region is sent to the recognition system for retrieving the answer that whether there is any book in this region. Only at most five best-matching books will be checked by spatial consistency to find the best-matching result. The affine model will also be adjusted to the correct region that contains books, and then the revised region and size of the newly recognized book are used to propose the next assumption. The process stops when the remaining region is too small to recognize a book.

Table 1. Results for recall, precision and speed by applying baseline and AWS algorithms. Oracle result is performed by recognizing ground truth books.

Algorithm	Oracle	Baseline	AWS
Recall	78.06%	47.10%	**65.16%**
Precision		90.12%	**90.99%**
Processing Time per Book		19.95 s	**4.42 s**

4.2.2 Grid-based Feature Density Matrix

The method described in Section 4.2.1 can only localize objects in the same row if one of those books is recognized first as shown in Figure 3 (No.2~6). For other books not recognized and localized yet, we adopt another observed characteristic in bookstores to decrease the time spent in selecting query regions and reduce the amount of features to process. The vacancy between different rows of bookshelves usually contains few features while the covers of books can have a large amount of features extracted, as shown in Figure 3. A grid-based feature density matrix can be computed to measure where the vacant space may be and where books show up. If the window search stops because of getting close to a border, we check the density matrix to find another high density region to start up the sliding window process again until the density of the remaining region is smaller than a threshold.

5. EXPERIMENTS AND DISCUSSIONS

5.1 Implementation Details

The recognition system and feature extraction for input images are implemented in C code in order to fulfill real-time retrieval. We chose MATLAB to develop geometric verification process and adaptive window search algorithm for easier matrix operation and convenient image processing.

5.2 Dataset and Ground Truth

To construct a large scale database, we use a set of over 251,000 book images crawled from [2]. The average dimension for each image is 200 x 280 pixels. Hessian-affine and SIFT features are extracted from each book image. A set of features of randomly selected 20 thousand images are used to train a hierarchical vocabulary tree with 6 levels and 10^6 leaf nodes. Note that we adopt this approach on Oxford buildings dataset and find it comparable with the baseline reported in [9]. For testing dataset, we take 27 photos containing 155 books in the bookstore. The localization is considered positive if its intersection with a ground truth bounding box divided by their union is greater than 80% and the recognition result is correct.

5.3 Baseline and Adaptive Window Search

As shown in Table 1, only 47.1% books are detected by the baseline algorithm but 90.12% books are recognized correctly, while 65.16% books are detected and 90.99% recognized correctly by adaptive window search. Some localization results are shown in Figure 4. The processing time shown in last row of Table 1 is the average of overall time spent on recognition and geometric verification for all testing images divided by the sum of recognized books. Average processing time for each book is 19.95 seconds by baseline and 4.42 seconds by AWS.

5.3.1 Recognition Results and Precision

As shown in Table 1, adaptive window search performs better than the baseline method by ignoring the cluttered background features and focusing on the feature matching in the proposed region. However, the book images we took in the bookstore are

Figure 4. Examples of multiple object localization and recognition using baseline and AWS algorithms. The upper images are results of the baseline algorithm, and the bottom ones are results of AWS. Yellow bounding boxes are the localization results.

affected by lighting; also, sometimes the books are wrapped in an extra cover, which makes them look differently from images in the database. It may cause true negative. There is another situation that the cover of a book is mild with few features, resulting in that matching inliers will be too less to pass the threshold. Moreover, the layout of books on bookshelves in the bookstore may not be orderly, for example, one of the books is placed vertically while the book next to it is laid down, or books with covers revealed are put together with others with spines laid outside. For above situations, achieving high recall in book localization is very challenging. Oracle testing results shown in Table 1 prove the difficulty recognizing books in bookstore with situations mentioned above. Only 78.06% of ground truth books can be recognized by the recognition system. Compared to oracle testing results, AWS achieves 83.47% recognition recall. With the help of geometric verification, the books are almost recognized correctly in the detected region and get a high precision rate.

5.3.2 Speed

Localization and recognition in adaptive window search algorithm is four times faster than the baseline. The main reason why the baseline method takes such a long time to localize and recognize each is that there are more book images that have to be checked by geometric verification for each round than AWS. Besides, there are also more features in each recognition step because all the features in input image have to be seen except for those in matched regions. Nevertheless, with AWS, the number of features sent to the recognition server is smaller than baseline because only those in the proposed region are sent. The proposed region contains fewer noisy features, and the feature matching step has less chance to be affected by the cluttered background. Therefore, we only have to care about the first image matching result, on whether the number of its inlier features is large enough. Also, empirically, the number of images needed to be checked by spatial verification can also be reduced to at most five. For these reasons, AWS does decrease the time to recognize and localize objects.

5.4 Comparisons with Similar Works

We adopt ESS [6] as a geometric verification method in baseline algorithm. The recall rate is 21.94% and the precision is 79.07%, and it takes 90.04 seconds for each book. The localization results by ESS are worse than by RANSAC. Therefore, it is difficult to propose a probable region contains book and it takes longer time to recognize and localize books.

Considering the worst case that there are no books in the input image, branch-and-bound method in [6][12] may take a large amount of iterations to converge to the optimal solution. By AWS, if the best-matching image retrieved from the recognition server for the input image does not pass the threshold after geometric verification, the process automatically stops proposing any region of interest. Therefore, the way of AWS handling the worst case is more efficient than previous works.

6. CONCLUSIONS AND FUTURE WORKS

We have proposed an efficient adaptive window search algorithm to select possible regions that contain books and send them to the recognition server for image matching and geometric verification. AWS can be applied to other recognition system with large-scale database (e.g., logos of daily objects). The results show that with AWS, we obtain an improvement around 4 times in speed and 20% in recall. After recognizing and localizing multiple books, applications can be designed to use the information of books such as ISBN as bridge to retrieve more related data through social network. As future works, we will speed up the geometric verification and perform this application combined with aNobii [1] and Facebook using mobile phone.

7. REFERENCES

[1] http://www.anobii.com/.

[2] http://www.books.com.tw/.

[3] Herbert Bay et al. SURF: Speeded up robust features. *CVIU*, 2008.

[4] David Chen et al. Building book inventories using smartphones. *ACM Multimedia*, 2010.

[5] Stephan Gammeter et al. Server-side object recognition and client-side object tracking for mobile augmented reality. *CVPR Workshop*, 2010.

[6] Christoph H. Lampert et al. Beyond sliding window: object localization by efficient subwindow search. *CVPR*, 2008.

[7] David G. Lowe. Distinctive image features from scale-invariant keypoints. *IJCV*, 2004.

[8] Jiri Matas et al. Robust wide baseline stereo from maximally stable extremal regions. *BMVC*, 2002.

[9] James Philbin et al. Object retrieval with large vocabularies and fast spatial matching. *CVPR*, 2007.

[10] Olga Russakovsky et al. A Steiner tree approach to efficient object detection. *CVPR*, 2010.

[11] Sam S. Tsai et al. Mobile product recognition. *ACM Multimedia*, 2010.

[12] Tom Yeh et al. Fast concurrent object localization and recognition. *CVPR*, 2009.

Clustering Geo-tagged Photo Collections Using Dynamic Programming *

Matthew Cooper
FX Palo Alto Laboratory
Palo Alto, CA USA
cooper@fxpal.com

ABSTRACT

This paper describes methods for clustering photos that possess both time stamps and geographical coordinates as metadata. We present a two part method that first analyzes photos' time and location information to independently partition the photos into multiple clusterings. A subset of the detected clusters is then selected for the final photo clustering using an efficient dynamic programming procedure that optimizes a clustering fitness score. We propose fitness measures to produce clusterings that are coherent in space, time, or both. One group of scores directly measures within-cluster inter-photo distances. A second set of scores measures clusters' consistency with the reference clusterings. We present experiments that validate our method using multiple data sets.

Categories and Subject Descriptors

H.3.1 [**Information Systems**]: INFORMATION STORAGE AND RETRIEVAL—*Content Analysis and Indexing Indexing Methods*

General Terms

Algorithms, Management

Keywords

Digital photo organization, event clustering, digital libraries

1. INTRODUCTION

As digital photography continues its explosive growth, personal photo collections require more powerful management tools. A common organizational step for consumers prior to either sharing photos with others or creating personal albums is the grouping of photos, often around events. Automatic processing plays an increasingly important role here as personal photo collections grow in scale. The growing availability of geographic information recorded at photo capture represents an opportunity to enhance automatic management tools. Newer digital cameras and more commonly smart phones record latitude and longitude coordinates with photos.

In this paper, we process location and time metadata for event-based photo clustering within a dynamic programming (DP) framework. We order the photos by time and segment the photo collection into contiguous partitions by analyzing inter-photo similarity in both time and space independently. This generates a set of reference clusterings that each characterize the collection's structure in either time or space at a specific scale. The clusters comprising the reference clusterings are candidates for inclusion in the final photo clustering. We examine multiple clustering fitness scores for optimization by DP. The first scores measure within-cluster dissimilarity in either time or space. We next take an ensemble clustering perspective to assimilate the structural information within the reference spatial and temporal clusterings. We propose a score to quantify the shared information between a candidate cluster and the reference clusterings. Using this score, the DP procedure selects clusters to maximize this shared information. We describe our method in detail below and present experiments on several datasets demonstrating a high level of performance.

2. RELATED WORK

Events provide a natural framework for organizing both digital photos and more general multimedia collections [15]. A number of time-based approaches to event-based photo clustering have been presented [7, 11]. [5] presented a dynamic programming method for temporal photo clustering that we extend here to incorporate location information. Naaman, *et al.* [9] performed early work on clustering combining time and location information. Initially, time alone is used to over-segment the photos. Recorded locations are independently hierarchically grouped in clusters. In a third pass, temporal segments that belong to the same location cluster are merged. Pigeau, *et al.* [3, 10], also present a multi-pass system. The first pass performs clustering using mixture models learned jointly on the time and location data with a variational approach to determine model order. In a second pass, clusters are grouped using information measures and the mixture parameters. Cao *et al.* [4] studied hierarchical image annotation using event clustering of photos. Their method first processed time and then location using mean shift clustering. In contrast, we compute tempo-

*Area chair: Daniel Gatica-Perez

MM'11, November 28–December 1, 2011, Scottsdale, Arizona, USA.

ral and spatial reference clusterings of the photo collection separately, but select a subset from the union of detected clusters. Our approach is non-parametric and cluster selection is performed via DP to directly optimize cluster fitness measures.

Ensemble clustering refers to the class of problems in which a final clustering must be determined given a set of available clusterings. In this context, various information theoretic criteria for clustering assessment have been studied [13]. We require that a clustering S labels each of the N photos as a member of exactly one cluster $s \in S$, and that each cluster s is contiguous in time order.[1] The mutual information between two clusterings R and S is:

$$I(R;S) = \sum_{r \in R, s \in S} P(r,s) \log \left(\frac{P(r,s)}{P(r)P(s)} \right) \quad (1)$$

$$\text{where } P(r) = \frac{|r|}{N} \text{ and } P(r,s) = \frac{|r \cap s|}{N}$$

Direct application of mutual information favors over segmentation. To counter this, normalized forms have been proposed [12, 13]. We use the normalized mutual information (NMI):

$$NMI(R;S) = \frac{I(R;S)}{\sqrt{H(R)H(S)}} \quad (2)$$

where $H(R) = -\sum_{r \in R} P(r) \log(P(r))$ is the entropy of R.

Becker *et al.* [2] used NMI for event-based grouping of shared multi-user photo collections in a setting analogous to the TREC event detection and tracking task [14]. Given a number of information streams, the goal is to identify events and then group photos belonging to each event. Becker *et al.* compiled photos from Flickr with user annotated event tags from upcoming.org for testing. Their approach combined supervised classification with NMI measures for clustering. We use dynamic programming to construct a photo clustering with maximum average NMI with a set of reference clusterings. In contrast to [2], we perform unsupervised clustering of *single user* photo collections. We assume non-overlapping event clusters that partition the user's photo stream in time order.

3. PHOTO CLUSTERING

We cluster photos in two steps. The first step assembles a set of *reference clusterings* to characterize the structure of the photo collection. The second step builds a final clustering as a subset of candidate clusters from the reference clusterings. A DP procedure constructs the final clustering to share maximal information with the reference clusterings by optimizing a mutual information score.

3.1 Building reference clusterings

We assemble reference clusterings by segmenting the time-ordered photos into clusters with high pairwise similarity. This process is performed independently using both temporal and spatial similarity at multiple scales. Denote the time and location of the nth indexed photo by t_n and l_n, respectively. For temporal clustering, we follow [5] which builds a hierarchical temporal partitioning using an exponential set of inter-photo similarity measures:

$$s_\tau(i,j) = \exp\left(-\frac{|t_i - t_j|}{\tau}\right) \quad , \quad (3)$$

where τ is varied to produce a set of temporal reference clusterings across a range of scales. For spatial reference clusterings, we use the distance between photo locations to construct a similar hierarchical spatial partitioning:

$$s_\sigma(i,j) = \exp\left(-\frac{d_g(l_i, l_j)}{\sigma}\right) \quad . \quad (4)$$

d_g is the approximate geodesic distance.[2] Each value of σ generates a spatial reference clustering. We add each clustering calculated using either (3) or (4) for a specific value of σ or τ into the set of reference clusterings $\mathcal{R}$. The set of all constituent clusters in $\mathcal{R}$ are candidates for potential selection by the DP procedure described below.

3.2 Cluster selection

We efficiently select the subset of candidate clusters that comprise the final photo clustering using a standard DP procedure for grouping an ordered set of objects [6, 8]. We represent each candidate cluster by the indices of its boundaries, and denote the set of all boundaries by $\mathcal{B}$. Generally, $\beta = |\mathcal{B}| \ll N$, the number of photos. We present two sets of scores for optimization via DP.

3.2.1 Content-based selection

The content-based cost of the cluster with boundary indices b_i and b_j is the total pairwise distance between the cluster's photos:

$$C_F(b_i, b_j) = \sum_{m,n=b_i}^{b_j - 1} d(m,n) \quad . \quad (5)$$

We consider two distance measures:

$$d(m,n) = \begin{cases} |t_m - t_n| & \text{for temporal selection} \\ d_g(l_m, l_n) & \text{for spatial selection} \end{cases} \quad . \quad (6)$$

DP successively builds minimum cost partitionings with k clusters based on the minimum cost partitioning with $k-1$ clusters. $E_F(b_j, k)$ is the optimal partitioning of the photos indexed $1, \cdots, b_j$ with cardinality k and is computed iteratively:

$$E_F(b_j, k) = \min_{b_i \in \mathcal{B}, k \le b_i \le b_j} E_F(b_i, k-1) + C_F(b_i, b_j) \quad , \quad (7)$$

The result is a set of minimum cost partitionings with cardinality[3] $3 \le K \le \beta$. A traceback step identifies the clusters in each optimal clustering. The total clustering cost $E(N, K)$ decreases monotonically with K. We heuristically select the optimal cardinality, K^*, based on the ratio of change in the total clustering cost:

$$K^* = \underset{2 \le k \le \beta - 1}{\operatorname{argmax}} \frac{E_F(N,k)}{E_F(N,k+1)} \quad . \quad (8)$$

3.2.2 Using normalized mutual information

An advantage of the DP framework is that it can select from the combined set of candidate clusters detected using

[1] Throughout, we refer to a labeling S of all N photos as a clustering, and to any of its constituent elements $s \in S$ as a cluster that labels some subset of the photos.

[2] See http://en.wikipedia.org/wiki/Great-circle_distance

[3] We define $b_1 = 1$, and $b_\beta = N$.

either spatial or temporal similarity. However, it is not clear how to effectively fuse the spatial and temporal distances of (6) into a combined distance in (5). Instead, we use NMI to integrate the spatial and temporal information in the reference clusterings $\mathcal{R}$. Using DP, we construct the clustering S to maximize the average shared information with each clustering $R \in \mathcal{R}$:

$$\frac{1}{|\mathcal{R}|} \sum_{R \in \mathcal{R}} NMI(R;S) \ . \tag{9}$$

This score prefers candidate clusters that are consistent in both time and space or across multiple scales. To apply DP, we decompose this total score into terms associated with a single candidate cluster $s \in S$. Define:

$$I(s;R) = \sum_{r \in R} P(r|s) \log \left(\frac{P(r|s)}{P(r)} \right) \ , \tag{10}$$

and notice that

$$NMI(R;S) = \frac{1}{\sqrt{H(S)}} \sum_{s \in S} P(s) \frac{I(s;R)}{\sqrt{H(R)}} \ . \tag{11}$$

Let s_{ij} be the cluster of photos between indices b_i and b_j. We then define a score for maximization by DP as in (5):

$$C_{NMI}(b_i, b_j) = \frac{1}{|\mathcal{R}|} \sum_{R \in \mathcal{R}} P(s_{ij}) \frac{I(s_{ij};R)}{\sqrt{H(R)}} \ , \tag{12}$$

This score is inserted into (7), replacing minimization (of within-cluster dissimilarity) with maximization (of average NMI with $\mathcal{R}$). Note we have neglected the $H(S)$ term from (11) in the score of (12). The DP procedure thus maximizes a scaled form of the average NMI:

$$E_{NMI}(S) = \frac{1}{|\mathcal{R}|} \sum_{R \in \mathcal{R}} \frac{I(R;S)}{\sqrt{H(R)}} \ . \tag{13}$$

The $H(R)$ terms implicitly weight each reference clustering R, generally emphasizing clusterings with fewer clusters. This is consistent with the intuition that clusters detected at coarser scales are more important.

As before, the DP procedure produces a set of clusterings of different cardinalities, and we select the final cardinality K^* to maximize the average NMI of (9) directly. We consider the range of possible values, $3 \leq k \leq \beta$ and perform the traceback to select the clusters that maximize the score of (13). We denote the resulting clustering with cardinality k by S_k, and compute its entropy. We then scale the clustering score $E_{NMI}(S_k)$ to determine the average NMI. We select the final clustering with cardinality:

$$K^* = \underset{3 \leq k \leq \beta}{\operatorname{argmax}} \left(\frac{1}{\sqrt{H(S_k)}} E_{NMI}(S_k) \right) \ . \tag{14}$$

4. EXPERIMENTS

We test our clustering methods using multiple data sets. We assess performance with the B^3 score [1, 2] which is the geometric mean of the per-photo precision and recall averaged over the collection. The first data set consists of two users' personal photographs accumulated over 15 months. The two sets contain 1036 and 413 photos respectively and include timestamps *without* location information. In this case, our method integrates structural information across temporal scale for photo clustering. We compute reference clusterings from the photos' timestamps by varying τ in (3) using the similarity-based method of [5]. We then apply the DP methods of Section 3.2.1 and 3.2.2 and compare performance with the confidence measure method described in [5] as a baseline. Table 1 shows that the DP method using the NMI score described in Section 3.2.2 achieves superior performance.

Table 1: Summary statistics for temporal photo clustering. Per-photo precision and recall are computed across the two single user data sets.

Clustering Method	Average Precision	Average Recall	B^3
[5]	0.714	0.855	0.778
Sec. 3.2.1	0.887	0.628	0.735
Sec. 3.2.2	0.951	0.915	0.932

The next data set is described in [2] and publicly available[4]. Photos are collected from Flickr with user annotated event tags from the upcoming.org website. We filtered the dataset, first removing photos without geotags and then grouping photos by user. We retained per-user photo sets with at least 350 photos and 10 events, producing 32 single-user data sets with a total of 37,434 photos. We compute temporal reference clusterings as above, and compute spatial reference clusterings similarly by varying σ in (4).

We examine several variants of each DP method for testing. We compare using temporal reference clusterings (TIME), spatial reference clusterings (SPACE), and both (COMBO). Each DP method uses the constituent clusters of $\mathcal{R}$ as candidates for selection. The content-based DP method of Section 3.2.1 selects clusters to minimize the cost of (5) using either temporal (TIME) or spatial (SPACE) distance as in (6). The NMI-based DP method of Section 3.2.2 selects clusters according to the NMI score of (12) using temporal reference clusterings (TIME), spatial reference clusterings (SPACE), or both (JOINT).

Experimental results appear in Table 2 The strictly temporal baseline of [5] achieves $B^3 = 0.680$ ($P = 0.943, R = 0.531$), underperforming the proposed DP methods. Content-based DP, described in Section 3.2.1, shows substantial variation in performance with different usage of spatial and temporal information for both building reference clusterings and cluster selection. While this approach improves on the performance of the temporal baseline, matching the configuration to a given data set is a critical practical consideration which may require a training stage or prior knowledge of the data or photographers.

In the absence of training data, it's often desirable to use all available information. An advantage of the NMI-based DP procedure of Section 3.2.2 is that it integrates available information in a principled framework both for building reference clusterings and also for cluster selection. Although combining the temporal and spatial information in both steps does not provide optimal performance (COMBO/JOINT $B^3 = 0.852$), it does essentially match the best performing system for content-based DP (SPACE/TIME, $B^3 = 0.879$). Also, the variation in performance with configuration is relatively limited using the NMI score. More gener-

[4]http://www.cs.columbia.edu/~hila/wsdm-data.html

Table 2: **Summary statistics for photo clustering using a subset of the upcoming data from [2].**

Content-based DP: Section 3.2.1				
Reference Clusterings	Cluster Score	Average Precision	Average Recall	B^3
TIME	TIME	0.727	0.865	0.790
TIME	SPACE	0.560	0.651	0.602
SPACE	SPACE	0.487	0.918	0.636
SPACE	TIME	0.859	0.900	0.879
COMBO	TIME	0.742	0.811	0.775
COMBO	SPACE	0.497	0.690	0.578
NMI-based DP: Section 3.2.2				
Reference Clusterings	Cluster Score	Average Precision	Average Recall	B^3
TIME	TIME	0.944	0.733	0.825
TIME	SPACE	0.902	0.905	0.904
TIME	JOINT	0.946	0.761	0.844
SPACE	SPACE	0.905	0.881	0.893
SPACE	TIME	0.903	0.932	0.917
SPACE	JOINT	0.906	0.926	0.917
COMBO	TIME	0.943	0.736	0.826
COMBO	SPACE	0.904	0.880	0.892
COMBO	JOINT	0.940	0.780	0.852

ally, the NMI-based DP methods perform at a higher level than the content-based DP methods. The best performing NMI variations achieve the highest level of performance of all tested methods.

5. SUMMARY

In this paper, we present methods for clustering photos with timestamps and geographic information using dynamic programming. Motivated by ensemble clustering, we propose an NMI score for selecting clusters that share maximal average information with a set of reference clusterings. The reference clusterings characterize the photo collection's structure in space and time across multiple scales. The NMI-based method shows the best experimental performance in large scale tests.

Our present approach applies to any ordered data with heterogeneous attributes that can characterize the data's structure. In future work, we hope to incorporate other modalities including content-based similarity of photos and text tag-based similarity which is increasingly available. We expect these extensions of this method to further enhance our automatic clustering results. Additionally, we aim to extend the method to unordered collections by looking beyond clustering via dynamic programming.

6. REFERENCES

[1] E. Amigó, J. Gonzalo, J. Artiles, and F. Verdejo. A comparison of extrinsic clustering evaluation metrics based on formal constraints. *Inf. Retr.*, 12:461–486, August 2009.

[2] H. Becker, M. Naaman, and L. Gravano. Learning similarity metrics for event identification in social media. In *Proc. of the ACM Intl. Conf. on Web Search & Data Mining*, WSDM '10, pages 291–300, New York, NY, USA, 2010. ACM.

[3] P. Bruneau, A. Pigeau, M. Gelgon, and F. Picarougne. Geo-temporal structuring of a personal image database with two-level variational-bayes mixture estimation. In *Adaptive Multimedia Retrieval Workshop (AMR'08)*, 2008.

[4] L. Cao, J. Luo, H. Kautz, and T. S. Huang. Image annotation within the context of personal photo collections using hierarchical event and scene models. *IEEE Trans. on Multimedia*, 11:208–219, February 2009.

[5] M. Cooper, J. Foote, A. Girgensohn, and L. Wilcox. Temporal event clustering for digital photo collections. *ACM Trans. Multimedia Comput. Commun. Appl.*, 1(3):269–288, 2005.

[6] W. D. Fisher. On grouping for maximum homogeneity. *J. of the American Statistical Association*, pages 789–798, December 1958.

[7] A. Graham, H. Garcia-Molina, A. Paepcke, and T. Winograd. Time as essence for photo browsing through personal digital libraries. In *Proc. of the ACM/IEEE-CS Joint Conf. on Digital libraries*, JCDL '02, pages 326–335, New York, NY, USA, 2002. ACM.

[8] J. Hartigan. *Clustering Algorithms.* John Wiley and Sons, 1975.

[9] M. Naaman, Y. J. Song, A. Paepcke, and H. Garcia-Molina. Automatic organization for digital photographs with geographic coordinates. In *JCDL '04: Proc. of the ACM/IEEE-CS Joint Conf. on Digital libraries*, pages 53–62, New York, NY, USA, 2004. ACM.

[10] A. Pigeau and M. Gelgon. Building and tracking hierarchical geographical & temporal partitions for image collection management on mobile devices. In *MULTIMEDIA '05: Proc. of the ACM Intl. Conf. on Multimedia*, pages 141–150, New York, NY, USA, 2005. ACM.

[11] J. Platt, M. Czerwinski, and B. A. Field. Phototoc: automatic clustering for browsing personal photographs. In *Information, Communications and Signal Processing, 2003 and the Pacific Rim Conf. on Multimedia*, volume 1, pages 6–10, 2003.

[12] A. Strehl and J. Ghosh. Cluster ensembles — a knowledge reuse framework for combining multiple partitions. *J. Machine Learning Research*, 3:583–617, March 2003.

[13] N. X. Vinh, J. Epps, and J. Bailey. Information theoretic measures for clusterings comparison: Variants, properties, normalization and correction for chance. *J. Machine Learning Research*, 11:2837–2854, October 2010.

[14] C. L. Wayne. Multilingual topic detection and tracking: Successful research enabled by corpora and evaluation. In *Intl. Conf. on Language Resources and Evaluation*, 2000.

[15] U. Westermann and R. Jain. Toward a common event model for multimedia applications. *IEEE MultiMedia*, 14:19–29, January 2007.

Combining Image and Text Features: A Hybrid Approach to Mobile Book Spine Recognition

Sam S. Tsai[1], David Chen[1], Huizhong Chen[1], Cheng-Hsin Hsu[2], Kyu-Han Kim[3]
Jatinder P. Singh[4], Bernd Girod[1]
[1]Department of Electrical Engineering, Stanford University, Stanford, CA 94305, USA
[2]Department of Computer Science, National Tsing Hua University, Hsinchu, Taiwan
[3]HP Laboratories, Palo Alto, CA 94304, USA
[4]Deutsche Telekom R&D Laboratories USA, Los Altos, CA 94022, USA
[1]{sstsai, dmchen, hchen2, bgirod}@stanford.edu, [2]chsu@cs.nthu.edu.tw
[3]kyu-han.kim@hp.com, [4]j.singh@telekom.com

ABSTRACT

Despite the successful use of local image features for large-scale object recognition, they are not effective in recognizing book spines on bookshelves. This is because some book spines contain only text components that do not yield distinguishing image features. To overcome this issue, we develop a new approach that combines a text-based spine recognition pipeline with an image feature-based spine recognition pipeline. The text within the book spine image is recognized and used as keywords to search a book spine text database. The image features of the book spine image are searched through a book spine image database. The search results of the two approaches are then carefully combined to form the final result. We implement the proposed hybrid book recognition pipeline used in a book inventory management system, and conduct extensive experiments to evaluate its performance. The experimental results show that while text-based or image feature-based systems only achieve a recall of ∼72%, the proposed hybrid system achieves a recall of ∼91%.

Categories and Subject Descriptors: H.3.3 Information Storage and Retrieval:Information Search and Retrieval - Search Process
General Terms: Algorithm, Design

1. INTRODUCTION

Manually managing items on a bookshelf is a tedious and time consuming task. To solve this issue, research groups have developed automated management systems to identify books on the shelves. One way to recognize the books is to tag each book with an identifier such as an RFID or barcode and read the tag using a specialized reader. Another way is to use images from a digital camera for identifying books [2,3,5,7–9,12]. Deploying camera-based book recognition solutions is more cost-effective because there is no need to attach physical tags to individual books.

Among the camera-based systems, Chen et al. [2,3] and Matsushita et al. [9] use image features for robust recognition. In [2,3], Chen et al. describe a system that builds book inventories using smartphones. They take a picture of a bookshelf and identify the book spines in the image. Furthermore, they use location sensors to attach location information to each book. In [9], Matsushita et al. propose an interactive bookshelf based on a camera-projector system. They use the imagery from cameras to recognize items removed from the bookshelf and project light signals to guide the user. These systems leverage local image features for recognition and gain invariance to scale, rotation, illumination changes, and occlusion. However, experimentally, we found that their recognition performance was fairly low: a recall of merely ∼72%. Their poor performance on some book spines can be attributed to the fact that image features were developed primarily for natural scenes and thus do not work well with images that have plain texts.

To overcome this issue, we develop a new hybrid recognition system that combines a text-based recognition pipeline and an image feature-based recognition pipeline for more accurate book spine recognition. We use camera-phones to take pictures of a bookshelf. The query image is sent over a network to a server where the bookshelf image is processed. The individual book spines are extracted and passed to the text-based and image feature-based recognition pipelines for recognition. Independently, the two pipelines propose recognition results, and we combined them to form the final recognition result. Our experimental results show that this hybrid system achieves a performance substantially better than those of the text-based and image feature-based systems.

The main contributions of our work are as follows:

- Design and implementation of a novel hybrid book spine recognition system which achieves superior recognition accuracy compared to a text or image feature-based approach.
- Development of a method to robustly recognize spine texts from bookshelf images for spine recognition: We extract book spines from the bookshelf image and remove the perspective distortion. Text is localized using a detection method based on Maximally Stable Extremal Regions (MSER) and Stroke Width Transform (SWT) [4] and recognized using Optical Character Recognition (OCR). Recognized texts are used as keywords to search a spine text database with a dictionary built from the spine text in the database.

The rest of this paper is organized as follows. We discuss the related work in Sec. 2. We describe the proposed system in Sec. 3. We report experimental evaluation results in Sec. 4.

2. RELATED WORK

Recognizing books on shelves has been considered [2,3,5,8,9,12]. Crasto et al. [5] present an interactive bookshelf based on a camera-projector system where they use the color histogram of the book spines to identify books. Matsushita et al. [9] also introduce

The authors would like to thank Area Chair Marcel Worring for all the help during the review process. This work was done while C. Hsu, K. Kim were with Deutsche Telekom R&D Laboratories, USA.

MM'11, November 28–December 1, 2011, Scottsdale, Arizona, USA.
Copyright 2011 ACM 978-1-4503-0616-4/11/11 ...$10.00.

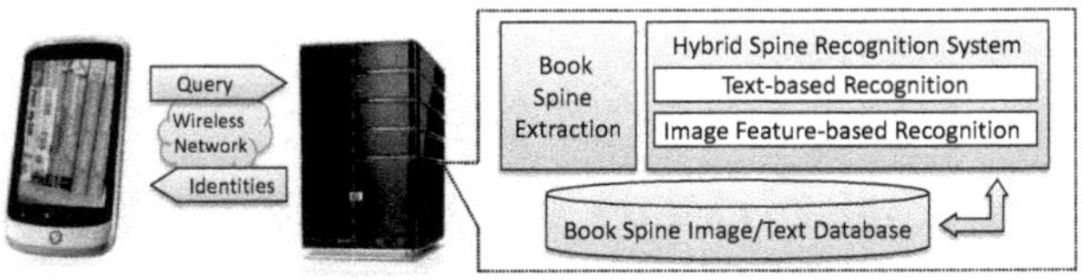

Figure 1: Mobile book spine recognition system.

an interactive bookshelf while using a different approach for book recognition. Instead of recognizing the book spines directly, they recognize book covers using local image features when books are being removed from the shelf. Loechtefeld et al. [8] suggest using optical tracking methods to identify books from shelves using camera phones while using a pico projector to display guidance information. Chen et al. [2, 3] leverage SURF features [1] for recognizing books using their spine images. They use smartphones to take images of bookshelves and extract the book spines from the images. Each book spine is then queried against a book spine image database. Location information from the mobile device is used to build a location-aware book inventory. In [12], Quoc and Choi develop a framework for recognizing books on bookshelves using robots with cameras. They find individual book spines by detecting the straight lines within the image. From the segmented book spines, they detect the text positions using edges and use character recognition to read the text.

3. MOBILE BOOK SPINE RECOGNITION

The architecture of our system is illustrated in Fig. 1. On the camera-phone, a lightweight application guides the user to take a picture of the bookshelf. The query image of the bookshelf and location data is sent to a server. On the server, book spines are first extracted from the image of the bookshelf. Then, each book spine image is identified using a recognition system which consists of a text-based recognition pipeline and an image feature-based recognition pipeline. The recognized results are sent back to the user and also passed to a book management system that creates a location aware inventory [3] which keeps track of each book's location.

3.1 Book Spine Extraction

We illustrate the steps to extract the individual book spines in Fig. 2. To extract the individual book spines from the image of the bookshelf we first detect lines that resemble book boundaries as shown in Fig. 3(b). Then, we form a quadrilateral that encloses the book spine using the two ends of the boundary lines as vertices. The region within the quadrilateral is extracted from the image and reprojected to form a rectangular region as shown in Fig. 3(c). In the case where a book spine is not fully found due to cropping, we extend the boundary lines to have the same length as the boundary lines of spines that were correctly detected.

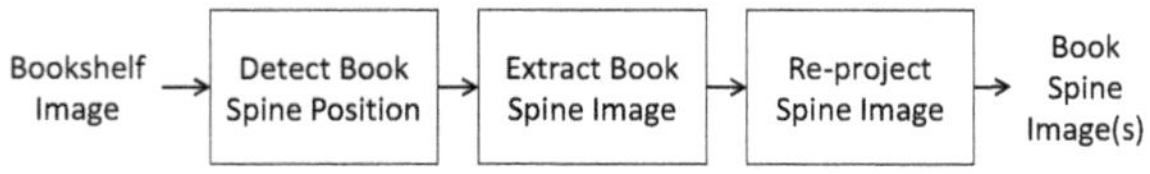

Figure 2: The building blocks to extract book spine images.

3.2 Book Spine Recognition

To recognize the book spines, we match each extracted spine to an online database of book spines. As shown in Fig. 1, we use hybrid recognition system that consists of a text-based recognition pipeline and an image feature-based recognition pipeline. From each book spine image, we detect and recognize the text on the spines and use it as keywords to search a book spine text database. Similarly, image features are extracted from the book spine images and matched to a book spine image database. We combined the results of the two pipelines to form the final output.

(c)

Figure 3: (a) Original image of a bookshelf. (b) A line detection algorithm is used to find the spine boundaries from the original image. (c) The extracted book spines are reprojected into rectangle regions.

3.2.1 *Recognizing Spines with Text*

The text on the book spines typically contains the title and the author names, which can provide effective keywords to search for the book. To use the text on the book spines, the text within the extracted book spine image has to be automatically recognized. The process of recognizing the text on the book spines and using the text to identify the book is shown in Fig. 4.

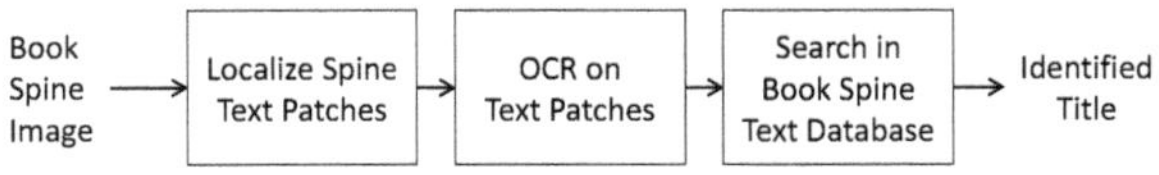

Figure 4: The building blocks for spine recognition based on text.

First, we detect text in the extracted book spine image using a text detection algorithm based on MSER and SWT [4]. MSERs are detected from the image and pruned using Canny edges, forming the character candidates. Stroke widths of the character candidates are found based on distance transforms. Then, they are pairwise linked together based on their geometric property to form text lines. The algorithm localizes the text within the book spine image and also filters out graphical components on the book spine. The localized text is then extracted from the book spine image and denoised using an edge-preserving filter. Fig. 5(a) shows the text patches extracted from the book spine image. Finally, the individual text patches are passed to an OCR engine for recognition. Words that are recognized from each local text patch, as shown in Fig. 5(b), are used as keywords to search a book spine text database.

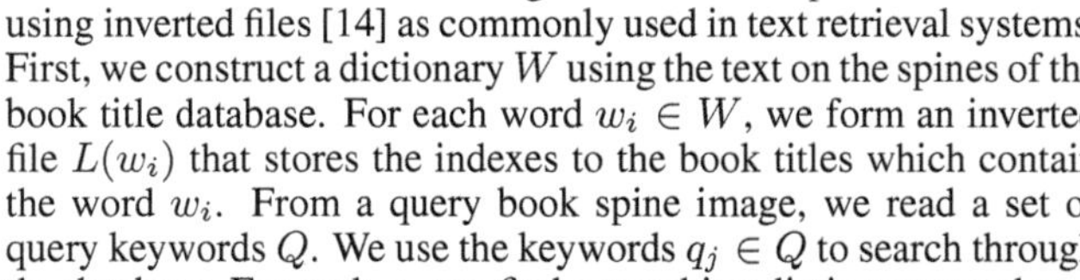

(b)

Figure 5: (a) Localized text patches extracted from the book spines. (b) The words recognized using an OCR engine.

To facilitate the search, we organize the book spine text database using inverted files [14] as commonly used in text retrieval systems. First, we construct a dictionary W using the text on the spines of the book title database. For each word $w_i \in W$, we form an inverted file $L(w_i)$ that stores the indexes to the book titles which contain the word w_i. From a query book spine image, we read a set of query keywords Q. We use the keywords $q_j \in Q$ to search through the database. For each q_j, we find a matching dictionary word m_j. We investigate two approaches to find matching words: (1) *Exact word matching*, where we find m_j as the exact same word as q_j. If no exact matching word is found for q_j, then q_j is ignored from Q. (2) *Nearest neighbor word matching*, where we find m_j as the closest distance word to q_j according to the editing distance $d(q_j, m_j)$.

It satisfies the criteria that $d(q_j, m_j) \leq d(q_j, w_i), \forall w_i \in W$. Finally, we calculate the score for the kth book spine as follows:

$$s_t(k) = \sum_j I(k \in L(m_j)), \quad (1)$$

where $I(\cdot)$ is the indicator function which is assigned one if k is in $L(m_j)$ or zero otherwise. We also consider the score when it is further weighted using *tf-idf* (term frequency-inverse document frequency) [13]. *tf* weights the word according to the number of occurrences within the spine text, and *idf* weights the score based on the how many different titles the word has occurred in.

3.2.2 *Recognizing Spines with Image Features*

In the image feature-based recognition pipeline, we use image features to match the query book spine to a database of book spine images. From the query spine, we extract SURF features [1] and use them to match the spines to a database of book spine images using a vocabulary tree with soft binning [10, 11]. A small set of top scoring candidates from the vocabulary tree are geometrically verified by estimating an affine model between the two spine images using RANSAC [6]. We use the number of consistent feature matches after geometric verification as the score $s_i(k)$. The score of the book spines where no consistent geometrical model is found are set to zero.

3.2.3 *A Hybrid Approach*

We combine the results of the text-based recognition pipeline with the image feature-based recognition pipeline to form the final result. A linear combination is used, as suggested by [15]. For the text-based recognition pipeline, the score $s_t(k)$ for database spine k is calculated as using Eq. (1). For the image feature-based recognition pipeline, the score $s_i(k)$ for database spine k is the number of feature matches after geometric verification. The hybrid score $s_h(k)$ for book spine k, is calculated by linearly combining scores from the two pipelines as follows:

$$s_h(k) = s_t(k) + \lambda \cdot s_i(k). \quad (2)$$

λ is experimentally determined to be 10. The value roughly corresponds to the ratio of the number of image features to the number of words of typical book spines. Finally, a threshold ϕ is used to determine whether a book spine image is confidently matched. When $s_h(k) > \phi$, the system declares that the book spine is an identified match. Otherwise, the system responds to the user that no match has been found.

4. EXPERIMENTAL RESULTS

To evaluate the recognition performance of our system, we construct a database of 2300 book spine images, which are collected from a library and a book store in Stanford University. We have implemented three book spine recognition algorithms: image feature-based, text-based, and hybrid. We segment book spine images and label the title and authors for each book spine. For the text-based recognition pipeline, we construct a book spine text database from all the labeled text. The resulting dictionary consists of a total of 5398 words. For the image feature-based recognition pipeline, we construct a vocabulary tree using SURF features extracted from the database book spine images. For query images, we took 50 photos of bookshelves using camera-phones, including Nokia N95, N97, and Motorola Droid, with 5MP cameras. We take pictures of bookshelves in different orientations, illuminations, and perspectives.[1]

We use SVGA (1024x768) images, resized from the full-sized images, to evaluate the recognition performance of our hybrid recognition system. Text is detected from each book spine image and the text within the localized patch is recognized using the Tesseract OCR engine.[2] We limit the allowed recognized characters to only alphanumerical letters and a reduced set of punctuations and notations. If not specified, the recognized query keywords are matched to the dictionary using Nearest Neighbor (NN) word matching, and the scores are weighted using *tf-idf*. Image features are extracted from the book spine images and quantized through the vocabulary tree. The top 50 scoring titles are geometrically verified using RANSAC to find the total number of feature matches.

We evaluate the recognition performance using precision and recall on the extracted 454 book spines. The precision is the percentage of correctly identified titles out of the declared correct titles. The recall is the percentage of correctly identified titles out of all query spines. Precision and recall can be varied by adjusting the threshold ϕ, which we use to decide whether the top scoring match is a declared match (Sec. 3.2.3). A lower ϕ means the top scoring match is easily accepted as the correct one, which would lead to lower precision but high recall. A higher ϕ would require a high score for a correct match and leads to higher precision but lower recall.

4.1 Recognition Performance

In Fig. 6, we show the precision-recall curves of the text-based, image feature-based, and hybrid system. Compared to the image feature-based system, text-based system achieves higher recall when the precision is lower than 87%. The image feature-based system achieves higher recall when the precision is higher. At a precision of 95%, the text-based system achieves a recall of less than 40% while the image feature-based system achieves a recall of 72%. Both systems are substantially outperformed by the proposed hybrid system. At a precision of 95%, the proposed system has a recall of 91%, which is 51% and 19% higher that the text-based and image feature-based systems, respectively.

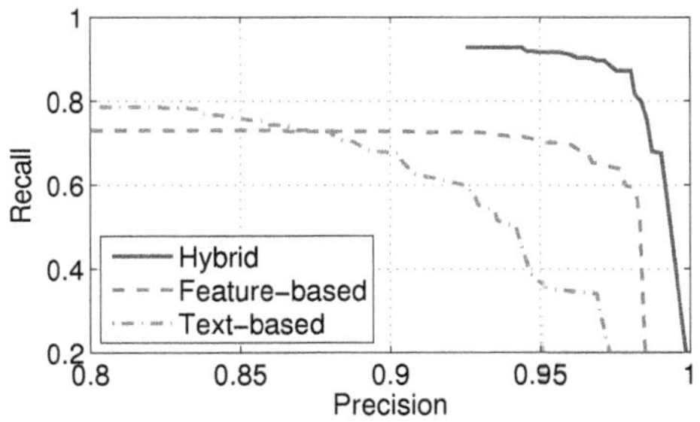

Figure 6: The recognition performance of the three systems.

To gain insights on why the proposed hybrid system substantially outperforms the other two systems, we closely examine the book spines that are correctly recognized by text-based and image feature-based systems. The number of spines for which both identify correctly is ~58% of total number of spines. This indicates that the two systems are suitable to different types of spines. As shown in Fig. 7(a), spines with text that have generic fonts tend to be harder for the image feature-based system to recognize due to the similarity between visual features. However, character recognition on generic fonts has higher accuracy because the OCR engine is trained to recognize these fonts. On the other hand, spines with graphical components and cursive text, such as the spine shown in Fig. 7(b), are rather challenging to OCR engines. In contrast, image features of these spines are fairly distinctive. Hence, by combining the text-based and image feature-based systems, we mitigate the misses and improve the overall recognition performance.

We investigate how the system performs when combined using a different λ. In Fig. 8, we show how λ affects the recall at different precisions. The best recall is obtained at a λ value of ~10. We observe that the best λ is roughly the same at various precisions.

We evaluate the recognition latency on a 3.2 GHz i7 server with 8 cores and 6 GB memory. Spine extraction is performed in 0.10

[1] http://msw3.stanford.edu/~sstsai/BookSpineSearch

[2] http://code.google.com/p/tesseract-ocr/

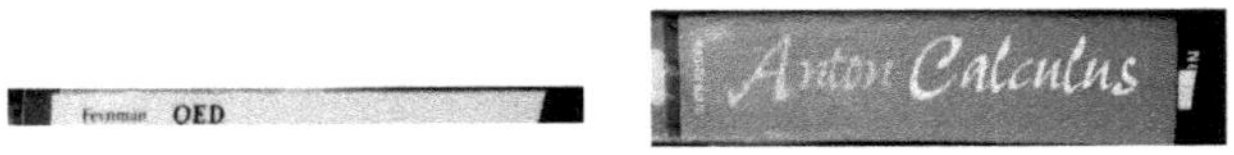

(a) (b)

Figure 7: (a) Spines with generic text can be recognized by the text-based system but not the image feature-based system. (b) Spines that vary more in style can be recognized by the image feature-based system but not the text-based system.

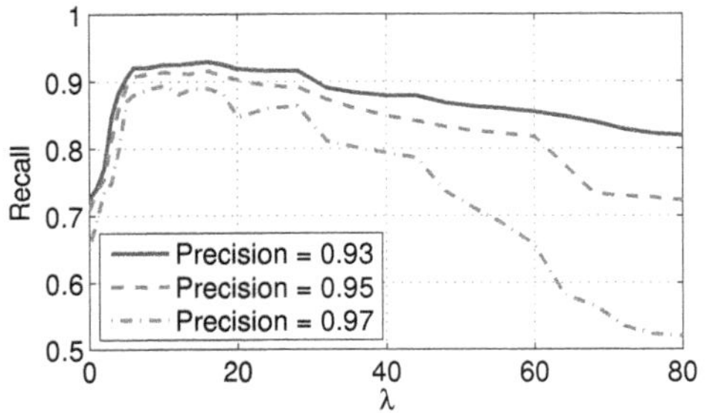

Figure 8: The recall at different precisions for the hybrid scheme using varying values of λ.

seconds which is required for all systems. The recognition latency for the text-based recognition pipeline is 0.22 seconds per spine image. The recognition latency for the image feature-based recognition system is 0.57 seconds per spine image. We evaluate the latency using our query images, which contains an average of ~10 books per query. While processing the spines in parallel, the average recognition latency is 1.24 seconds.

4.2 Text-based Spine Recognition Evaluation

We further evaluate the performance of the text-based recognition pipeline which was not considered in previous works. We show in Fig. 9 the recall performance of the top scoring title for different resolutions using different scoring schemes. We observe for all different image sizes, using simple exact word matching scheme performs worst. Using the NN word matching to match the keyword to the dictionary helps improve the recognition performance by ~8% for all different resolutions. With the additional *tf-idf* weighting, another ~8% improvement can be observed. That is, a total of ~16% improvement on recall can be gained by choosing a better scoring scheme.

The word recognition performance of the correctly identified titles is shown in Fig. 10 for exact word matching and NN word matching. We only consider words that have three or more characters. Using NN word matching, we in effect do spell checking and achieve a recognition performance improvement of ~9% over exact word matching.

The word recognition performance drops when the resolution is lowered. However, we observe that the recall performance of the top scoring title improves no more than 5% when the spine height is above 768 pels. This suggests that SVGA sized images are sufficient when network bandwidth is scarce.

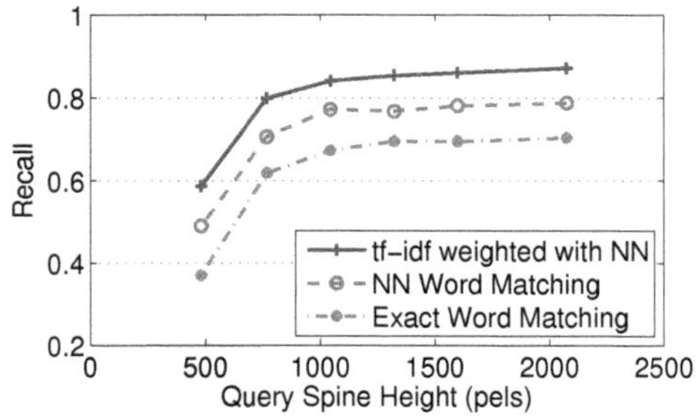

Figure 9: The recall performance of the top scoring book spine for three spine text database search schemes.

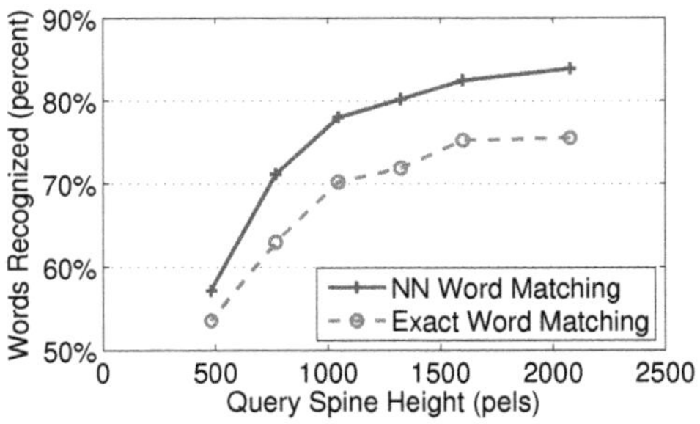

Figure 10: Word recognition performance of the correctly identified titles for different spine resolutions.

5. CONCLUSIONS

We have presented a new hybrid recognition system for identifying books on a bookshelf for use in book management systems. From a query image of a bookshelf, we extract the individual book spine images. Text is detected from the book spine images and used as keywords to search through a book spine text database. The text-based recognition system achieves high recall but low precision. We extract image features from the book spine images and use them to match the spines to a book spine image database. The image feature-based recognition system achieves a moderate recall at high precision. We combine the text-based recognition system with the image feature-based recognition system to form a hybrid recognition system. Through extensive experiments, we demonstrated that the hybrid scheme achieves a significantly higher recall of 91%, when the image feature-based and text-based systems have recall of 72% and 40% respectively.

6. REFERENCES

[1] H. Bay, A. Ess, T. Tuytelaars, and L. V. Gool. Speeded-up robust features (SURF). *Computer Vision and Image Understanding*, 110(3), 2008.

[2] D. Chen, S. Tsai, K.-H. Kim, C.-H. Hsu, J. P. Singh, and B. Girod. Low-cost asset tracking using location-aware camera phones. Number 1, San Diego, California, USA, 2010.

[3] D. M. Chen, S. S. Tsai, B. Girod, C.-H. Hsu, K.-H. Kim, and J. P. Singh. Building book inventories using smartphones. In *Proc. ACM Multimedia (MM'10')*, MM '10, Firenze, Italy, 2010. ACM.

[4] H. Chen, S. S. Tsai, G. Schroth, D. M. Chen., V. Chandrasekhar, G. Takacs, R. Vedantham, R. Grzeszczuk, and B. Girod. Robust text detection in natural images with edge-enhanced maximally stable extremal regions. In *International Conference on Image Processing*, 2011.

[5] D. Crasto, A. Kale, and C. Jaynes. The smart bookshelf: A study of camera projector scene augmentation of an everyday environment. In *Proc. IEEE Workshop on Applications of Computer Vision (WACV'05)*, Breckenridge, CO, January 2005.

[6] M. Fischler and R. Bolles. Random sample consensus: a paradigm for model fitting with applications to image analysis and automated cartography. *Communications of the ACM*, 24(6), 1981.

[7] D. Lee, Y. Chang, J. Archibald, and C. Pitzak. Matching book-spine images for library shelf-reading process automation. In *Proc. IEEE International Conference on Automation Science and Engineering (CASE'08)*, Arlington, VA, September 2008.

[8] M. Loechtefeld, S. Gehring, J. Schoening, and A. Krueger. Shelftorchlight: Augmenting a shelf using a camera projector unit. *UBIProjection 2010 - Workshop on Personal Projection*, 2010.

[9] K. Matsushita, D. Iwai, and K. Sato. Interactive bookshelf surface for in situ book searching and storing support. In *Proceedings of the 2nd Augmented Human International Conference*, New York, NY, USA, 2011.

[10] D. Nister and H. Stewenius. Scalable recognition with a vocabulary tree. In *Proc. IEEE Conference on Computer Vision and Pattern Recognition (CVPR'06)*, New York, NY, June 2006.

[11] J. Philbin, M. Isard, J. Sivic, and A. Zisserman. Lost in quantization: Improving particular object retrieval in large scale image databases. In *Proc. IEEE Conference on Computer Vision and Pattern Recognition (CVPR'08)*, Anchorage, AL, June 2008.

[12] N. Quoc and W. Choi. A framework for recognition books on bookshelves. In *Proc. International Conference on Intelligent Computing (ICIC'09)*, Ulsan, Korea, September 2009.

[13] G. Salton and C. Buckley. Term-weighting approaches in automatic text retrieval. *Information Processing and Management*, 24(5), 1988.

[14] I. H. Witten, A. Moffat, and T. C. Bell. Managing gigabytes: Compressing and indexing documents and images. 1999.

[15] T. Yeh and B. Katz. Searching documentation using text, ocr, and image. In *Proceedings of the 32nd international ACM SIGIR conference on Research and development in information retrieval*, New York, NY, USA, 2009.

Knowledge Propagation in Large Image Databases Using Neighborhood Information*

Michael E. Houle
National Institute of Informatics, Tokyo, Japan
meh@nii.ac.jp

Vincent Oria
New Jersey Institute of Technology, NJ, USA
oria@njit.edu

Shin'ichi Satoh
National Institute of Informatics, Tokyo, Japan
satoh@nii.ac.jp

Jichao Sun
New Jersey Institute of Technology, NJ, USA
js87@njit.edu

ABSTRACT

The aim of this paper is to reduce to a minimum the level of human intervention in the semantic annotation process of images. Ideally, only one copy of each object of interest would be labeled manually, and the labels would then be propagated automatically to all other occurrences of the objects in the database. To that end, we propose a neighbor-based influence propagation approach *KProp* which builds a voting model and propagates the knowledge associated to some objects to similar objects. We show that *KProp* can perform efficiently through matrix computations and achieve better performance with fewer labeled examples per object.

Categories and Subject Descriptors

H.2.4 [**Systems**]: Multimedia Databases

General Terms

Algorithms

Keywords

Neighborhood, Image Annotation, Classification

1. INTRODUCTION

Practical methods for the indexing and querying of large-scale image databases often require that the images be annotated with semantic information beforehand. Unfortunately, due to the high costs associated with human annotation, or the unavailability of cameras with GPS functionality or other special devices, the number of labeled objects is often severely limited.

*Area chair: Lei Chen

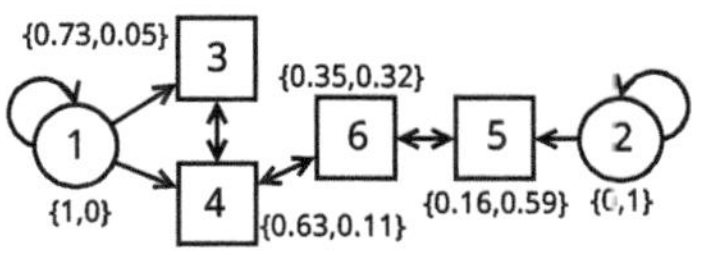

Figure 1: Applying *KProp* in classification of 6 faces.

Analysis of textural information or correlation of visual features and keywords can be applied to the problem of automated image annotation [6, 11, 12]. Such methods, however, usually assume the associated information to be content-descriptive terms that can be searched within a word dictionary or an ontology tree. Other solutions have been based on queries, or on supervised (or semi-supervised) machine learning techniques [3, 8].

In this paper, we propose a new method, *KProp*, that seeks to propagate labels from initially annotated data objects to new data objects that resemble them, according to a user-supplied measure of similarity. *KProp* builds an influence graph derived from neighborhoods of the objects with respect to the similarity measure, and then propagates knowledge scores through the graph from those nodes corresponding to objects with apriori semantic annotations. Intuitively, our method builds a voting model based on the hypothesis that similar objects should share the same semantic interpretations with high probability.

Figure 1 illustrates this idea by applying *KProp* to classify 6 face images. Face 1 and 2 are labeled as A and B, respectively. Scores measuring the degree of association between labels and faces are propagated from labeled faces 1 and 2 to unlabeled faces 3 to 6. The stabilized scores are given in braces beside each face with the first value corresponding to A and the second to B. The details of the score computation and interpretation will be described later.

The propagation of information within the neighborhood graph bears a superficial resemblance to variants of the well-known PageRank algorithm for web page search [10]. PageRank generates visit probability scores through the web link graph for a browsing session modeled as a random walk; these probabilities are calculated through an iterative process that propagates probability values through the link graph. RankCompete generalizes PageRank for simultaneous image ranking and clustering [2]. SimRank derives a graph whose nodes and edges represent data objects and the relationships between them, and uses it to compute the structural-context similarity of two objects [7].

The remainder of this paper is organized as follows. The description of *KProp* appears in Section 2, divided into two phases: graph construction and knowledge propagation. In Section 3, we present and discuss experimental results for a simple object dataset and a face dataset. We conclude this paper in Section 4.

2. INFLUENCE PROPAGATION MODEL

Let D be a set of n data objects, with each object associated with a subset of label set $L = \{\lambda_1, \lambda_2, \cdots, \lambda_t\}$, representing the current state of knowledge about the object. If the label set $L(o_i)$ associated with object $o_i \in D$ is empty, then o_i will be said to be *unlabeled*; otherwise, o_i will be referred to as *labeled*. Given an initial labeling of m objects of D, with the remaining objects initially unlabeled, the goal is to determine an $n \times t$ score matrix S whose elements $s_{i,j}$ $(1 \leq i \leq n, 1 \leq j \leq t)$ measure the degree of association of object o_i with label λ_j.

KProp operates in two phases, by first modeling object similarity information as an object neighborhood graph (Section 2.1), and then propagating knowledge scores through the graph according to certain weighting and combination rules (Section 2.2).

2.1 The Influence Graph

The modeling of object relationships as graph edges often arises naturally according to the specific data domain. In some domains, such as web pages with embedded hyperlinks, scientific papers with citations, and user-item pairs in a recommender system, the similarity relationships are explicitly indicated by link structure, references, or pairings as the case may be. Here, we consider the case where no explicit object pairings are defined, but where a pairwise similarity measure (or distance measure) exists. We will make the natural assumption that knowledge should be shared and propagated between objects whose similarity is sufficiently high.

Let us denote the symmetric pairwise distance between two objects $o, o' \in D$ by $d(o, o')$. Given an object o, the distance function d determines a ranking of the objects of D relative to o. More precisely, the rank of o' relative to o is given by $\rho(o, o') = |\{z \in D|\, d(o, z) < d(o, o')\}|$. Uniqueness of ranks is guaranteed only if all pairwise distance values between objects of D are unique; if desired, this can be achieved by breaking ties arbitrarily yet consistently.

The set of objects to which o is allowed to propagate its knowledge will be called the *region of influence* of object o. Regions of influence can be defined in terms of neighborhoods of o with respect to the distance d. This can be done in many ways, most straightforwardly in terms of thresholds on either the distance of its members to o, the rank of its members in distance order from o, or both. The values of these thresholds can be constant, or can depend on the specific object o at which the region of influence is based.

Let $\tau_\rho(o)$ and $\tau_d(o)$ be positive threshold values for object distances and ranks, respectively. In this paper, we will consider regions of influence of the following general form:

$$\mathit{Infl}(o) = \{z \in D|\, d(o, z) \leq \tau_d(o) \wedge \rho(o, z) \leq \tau_\rho(o)\}.$$

We will say that an object o *influences* object o' if o' lies within a *region of influence* associated o.

We model object relationships as a directed *influence graph* $G(V, E)$, with the node set partitioned into $V = V_l \cup V_u$, where V_l and V_u represent the initially-labeled (*source*) object set and initially-unlabeled (*non-source*) object sets, respectively. E is composed of three types of edges:

1. $\forall v \in V_l$, $\langle v, v \rangle \in E$;
2. $\langle v, u \rangle \in E$ whenever $v \in V_l$, $u \in V_u$ and v influences u;
3. $\langle u, u' \rangle, \langle u', u \rangle \in E$ whenever $u, u' \in V_u$, and either $u \in \mathit{Infl}(u')$, or $u' \in \mathit{Infl}(u)$ (or both).

It can be observed that each $v \in V_l$ has a self-edge, and all other edges lead to nodes of V_u. This construction prevents objects whose labels are known in advance from being influenced by other objects. For a pair of non-source nodes $u, u' \in V_u$, the influence is applied in both directions, even if the influence relationship is unidirectional.

In general, there are several difficulties associated with the selection of a distance threshold for the region of influence. Choosing a distance threshold value for each specific object typically requires more domain knowledge than is commonly available. Even when uniform thresholds are employed, effective threshold values may vary from instance to instance. Due to the effects of high dimensionality or other factors, distance values may not be able to discriminate effectively between objects of the same class as that of o, and objects of classes different from that of o.

Rank thresholds have an important advantage over distance thresholds in that they do not require an explicit interpretation of distance values. Choosing a fixed rank threshold k — that is, considering k-nearest neighbor (k-*NN*) sets of the objects — compensates for local variations in data density in a way that distance thresholds cannot.

Although distance thresholds can be used together with rank thresholds for some applications, in this paper we will consider only rank thresholds. To promote the connectivity of the influence graph, we adopt the convention that both edges $\langle u, u' \rangle$ and $\langle u', u \rangle$ are introduced whenever $u \in k\text{-}NN(u')$ or $u' \in k\text{-}NN(u)$ (as reflected in the definition of the influence graph stated earlier). The bidirectional edges also prevent non-source nodes that are otherwise unreachable from source nodes from constantly propagating 0 scores to the other nodes.

In this paper, the problem of choosing a practical value of the rank threshold k will be addressed empirically.

2.2 Label Propagation

We first give a simplified version of the scoring model behind our label propagation approach, in Section 2.2.1. We then present a more rigorous treatment of our method for computing *KProp* label scores in Section 2.2.2.

2.2.1 A Simplified Scoring Model

For the data objects of $D = \{o_i | 1 \leq i \leq n\}$, we assume that pairwise distances $d(o_i, o_j)$ are available in advance for all $1 \leq i, j \leq n$. Scores associated with the propagation of each label λ are computed separately (and can be performed in parallel). When propagating scores for label λ, source nodes of objects pre-associated with λ are assigned initial scores of 1, while all other nodes are given initial scores of 0. Let $N(a) \subseteq V$ denote the set of all nodes from which an edge is directed to $a \in V$. Let $R^q_\lambda(a)$ denote the score of a with respect to λ in the q-th iteration. The final score of node a with respect to λ can then be iteratively computed according to the following formula, until convergence:

$$R_\lambda^{q+1}(a) = \begin{cases} R_\lambda^q(a) & \text{if } a \in V_l \\ df \cdot \frac{\sum_{b \in N(a)} R_\lambda^q(b)}{|N(a)|} & \text{if } a \in V_u \end{cases} \quad (1)$$

Here, df is a damping factor ($0<df<1$) used to penalize nodes that are far away from the knowledge sources, and to accelerate the convergence rate.

Figure 1 illustrates the converged state of the propagation procedure for a simple face set, where face 1 and 2 are labeled as person A and B, respectively. The damping factor df was set at 0.9.

Basically, Equation 1 indicates that the score of a node a for a specific label λ is decided by a weighted average of all its incoming neighbors' scores for λ. The scores of source objects — either 0 or 1 — remain unchanged.

This simple propagation model can be intuitively regarded as a form of voting mechanism with feedback. For simplicity, assume that the labels refer to class membership. Labeled objects know their classification status, and provide suggestions to nearby unlabeled objects. Depending on which label scores are being propagated, source objects iteratively transmit information about themselves as recommendations for their neighboring objects. Non-source objects iteratively ask their neighbors (both source and non-source objects) for their recommendation, and weight and combine the results. Although exact distance or similarity information can be utilized for weighting scores, we adopt a simple averaging scheme: once the neighbors of an object have been decided, they will be treated uniformly.

2.2.2 *Computing Influence Scores*

We now formulate the *KProp* procedure in terms of iterative matrix multiplications of a propagation matrix with the score matrix. Let object o_i correspond to row i and column i of the $n \times n$ adjacency matrix A of the influence graph $G(V, E)$:

$$a_{i,j} = \begin{cases} 1 & \text{if } \langle j, i \rangle \in E, \\ 0 & \text{otherwise.} \end{cases}$$

Note that the rows for source objects have the value 1 on the major diagonal and 0 in all other locations, and that for non-source objects the matrix is symmetric with 0 for all entries on the major diagonal.

Entries of the $n \times n$ propagation matrix P can be computed by:

$$p_{i,j} = \begin{cases} a_{i,j} & \text{if node } i \in V_l, \\ df \cdot \frac{a_{i,j}}{\sum_{q=1}^{n} a_{i,q}} & \text{otherwise.} \end{cases}$$

Let object $o_i \in D$ correspond to row i of the score matrix S, and let label $\lambda_j \in L$ correspond to column j of S. Entries of the $n \times t$ initial score matrix S^0 can be computed as:

$$s_{i,j} = \begin{cases} 1 & \text{if object } i \text{ is associated with knowledge } \lambda_j, \\ 0 & \text{otherwise.} \end{cases}$$

Let S^q be the state of the score matrix in the qth iteration. S^q is computed from the previous state according to the formula

$$S^q = PS^{q-1}. \quad (2)$$

The iteration continues until each element $\delta_{i,j}^q$ in $\Delta^q = S^q - S^{q-1}$ falls within the bound $\delta_{i,j}^q \leq \varepsilon$, where ε is a user-specified tolerance value.

Let f be the iteration at which convergence is achieved. As will be seen later, given a propagation matrix P, each column $C_j^f (1 \leq j \leq t)$ of S^f is entirely decided by its corresponding column C_j^0 of the initial score matrix S^0. C_j^f will turn out to be an eigenvector of the propagation matrix P for the eigenvalue 1.

THEOREM 1. *Given a propagation matrix P corresponding to an influence graph $G(V, E)$, the sequence of score matrices (S^q) in Equation 2 converges to a unique matrix S^f.*

3. EXPERIMENTAL RESULTS

KProp was compared with query- and learning-based methods on two datasets: *ALOI-100* and *Google-23*. Details of the experimental framework and evaluation method are explained in Section 3.1. Section 3.2 describes the datasets used in the experiments, and Section 3.3 gives a brief discussion of the results.

3.1 Experimental Framework

The parameters $k = 10$ and $df = 0.9$ were chosen experimentally for *KProp*. The tolerance value ε was set at 10^{-6}.

As a baseline method for the evaluation, we implemented a simplified version of the query-based method presented in [8], which for each unlabeled object u first finds its nearest labeled object v, and then assign t to u if t is a label of v. We refer to this method as *Bestmatch*, and to our implementations of supervised and semi-supervised learning methods as *SVM* and Laplacian *SVM*(*LapSVM*) [9], respectively. Multi-class classifiers were trained using the linear kernel, and the number of nearest neighbors chosen for the construction of the Laplacian graph was 10.

For simplicity, we require that each object be associated with at most one label. Throughout all experiments, L_2 was used as the distance measure. To ensure that no object remained unlabeled by *Bestmatch*, *SVM* or *LapSVM*, no score- or distance-based acceptance threshold was applied when assigning a label to an object. No such guarantee exists for *KProp*, however. Although k is chosen so as to allow most unlabeled objects to be reachable from labeled objects, some objects may be very distant or unreachable. Such objects would remain unlabeled at the termination of *KProp*, thereby counting as incorrect label assignments.

We modify the usual definition of *recall* to be the proportion of correct label assignments to the total number of unlabeled objects:

$$recall = \frac{\sharp(unlabeled\ objects\ correctly\ assigned\ a\ label)}{\sharp(unlabeled\ objects)}$$

3.2 Datasets

ALOI-100 We collected the images of the first 100 objects from the ALOI image dataset [5], each object being associated with 108 images captured from different orientations under different conditions. Each image is represented by a 641-D vector based on color and texture histograms [1] and has the corresponding object ID as its ground truth class label.

Google-23 We queried the names of 23 celebrities in Google Image Search[1] and crawled 11811 images, from which 6686 faces were extracted and manually labeled with one of

[1]http://images.google.com

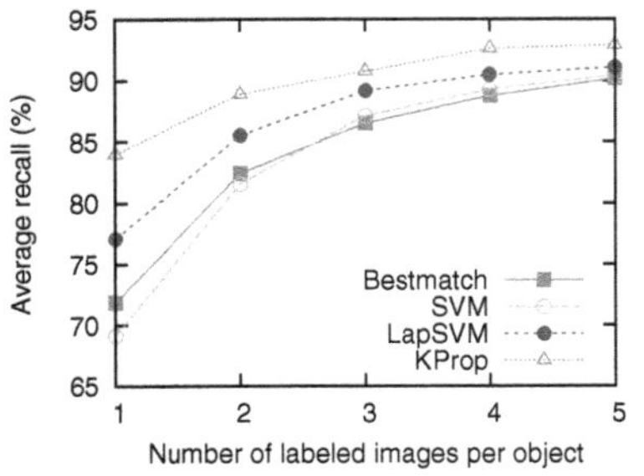

Figure 2: Average recall of 5 runs on ALOI-100.

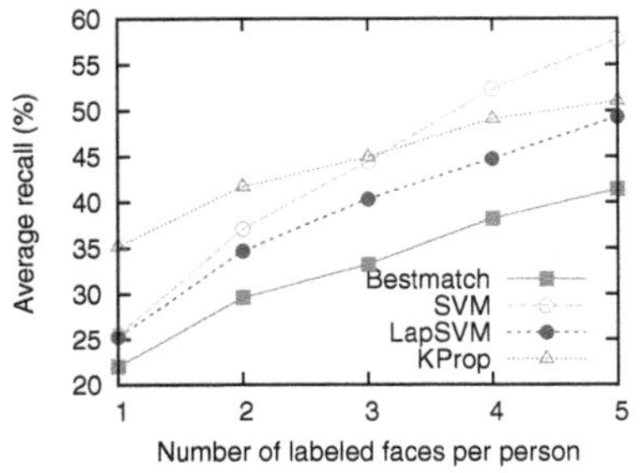

Figure 3: Average recall of 15 runs on Google-23.

the 23 names. Each face was described as a 1937-D vector [4].

In both datasets, each experimental run was initialized by randomly selecting 1 to 5 images from each class for initial labeling. Performance curves expressing average recall values are plotted in Figures 2 and 3.

3.3 Discussion

It can be observed from Figure 2 that *KProp* has consistently better results on *ALOI-100* than its competitors, particularly in the case where when only one image is labeled per object. There, it achieves an average recall of 84%, 9% better than its nearest competitor, *LapSVM*. As the number of prelabeled images increases, the performance gap narrows.

From Figure 3, we can see that when the number of prelabeled images per class is 3 or fewer, *KProp* outperforms the other methods tested. When one face per person is prelabeled, *KProp* outperforms the runner-up *SVM* by 38% on average recall. *SVM* outperforms our method when label size reaches 4.

The relative performance of *KProp* can be explained in terms of the transitivity of object relationships. *ALOI-100* is a simple dataset of which images are taken in gradually changing conditions, and thus a path from a labeled image to an unlabeled image of a common object could be well established. Conversely, such transitivity is not found in the face dataset: when face a is similar to face b, and b is similar to face c, it is often the case that a does not resemble c. *SVM*, by not relying on the transitivity of similarity information, can avoid such errors when the number of positive training examples is sufficiently large. Any ambiguous objects are classified once, and incorrect decisions will not be propagated. This is also a possible explanation as to why *SVM* outperforms *LapSVM* in *Google-23*, since the latter method involves unlabeled objects in the training process.

4. CONCLUSION

We have proposed *KProp* as a neighborhood-based approach for the propagation of knowledge associated to a few objects of interest to an entire image database. By modeling objects in an influence graph, degrees of association between objects can be computed efficiently through matrix operations. Experiments results on simple object and noisy face datasets show the effectiveness of our approach when the number of prelabeled objects per class is very small. Although our approach is not a substitute for learning-based classifiers, it illustrates how semantic information can be effectively propagated locally when the similarity relationship exhibits a high degree of transitivity.

5. REFERENCES

[1] N. Boujemaa, J. Fauqueur, M. Ferecatu, F. Fleuret, V. Gouet, B. L. Saux, and H. Sahbi. IKONA: Interactive Generic and Specific Image Retrieval. In *International workshop on Multimedia Content-Based Indexing and Retrieval (MMCBIR'2001)*, September 2001.

[2] L. Cao, A. Del Pozo, X. Jin, J. Luo, J. Han, and T. S. Huang. Rankcompete: simultaneous ranking and clustering of web photos. In *Proceedings of the 19th international conference on World Wide Web*, pages 1071–1072, 2010.

[3] C. Cusano, G. Ciocca, and R. Schettini. Image annotation using SVM. In *Society of Photo-Optical Instrumentation Engineers (SPIE) Conference Series*, volume 5304, pages 330–338, December 2003.

[4] M. Everingham, J. Sivic, and A. Zisserman. "Hello! My name is... Buffy" – automatic naming of characters in TV video. In *Proceedings of the British Machine Vision Conference*, 2006.

[5] J.-M. Geusebroek, G. J. Burghouts, and A. W. M. Smeulders. The amsterdam library of object images. *International Journal of Computer Vision*, 61(1):103–112, January 2005.

[6] D. R. Hardoon, C. Saunders, S. Szedmák, and J. Shawe-Taylor. A correlation approach for automatic image annotation. In *Advanced Data Mining and Applications*, pages 681–692, 2006.

[7] G. Jeh and J. Widom. Simrank: a measure of structural-context similarity. In *Proceedings of the eighth ACM SIGKDD international conference on Knowledge discovery and data mining*, pages 538–543, 2002.

[8] A. Makadia, V. Pavlovic, and S. Kumar. A new baseline for image annotation. In *Proceedings of the 10th European Conference on Computer Vision: Part III*, pages 316–329, 2008.

[9] S. Melacci and M. Belkin. Laplacian Support Vector Machines Trained in the Primal. *Journal of Machine Learning Research*, 12:1149–1184, March 2011.

[10] L. Page, S. Brin, R. Motwani, and T. Winograd. The pagerank citation ranking: Bringing order to the web. Technical Report 1999-66, Stanford InfoLab, November 1999.

[11] R. Shi, C.-H. Lee, and T.-S. Chua. Enhancing image annotation by integrating concept ontology and text-based bayesian learning model. In *Proceedings of the 15th international conference on Multimedia*, pages 341–344, 2007.

[12] B. Sigurbjörnsson and R. van Zwol. Flickr tag recommendation based on collective knowledge. In *Proceeding of the 17th international conference on World Wide Web*, pages 327–336, 2008.

Edge-Preserving Single Image Super-Resolution*

Qiang Zhou[1], Shifeng Chen[1], Jianzhuang Liu[1,2] and Xiaoou Tang[1,2]
[1]Shenzhen Key Laboratory for Computer Vision and Pattern Recognition
Shenzhen Institutes of Advanced Technology,Chinese Academy of Sciences, China
[2]Department of Information Engineering, The Chinese University of Hong Kong, China
{qiang.zhou,shifeng.chen}@siat.ac.cn, {jzliu,xtang}@ie.cuhk.edu.hk

ABSTRACT

This paper proposes a novel approach to single image super-resolution. First, an image up-sampling scheme is proposed which takes the advantages of both bilateral filtering and mean shift image segmentation. Then we use a shock filter to enhance strong edges in the initial up-sampling result and obtain an intermediate high-resolution image. Finally, we enforce a reconstruction constraint on the high-resolution image so that fine details can be inferred by back projection. Since strong edges in the intermediate result are enhanced, ringing artifacts can be suppressed in the back projection step. We compare our algorithm with several state-of-the-art image super-resolution algorithms. Qualitative and quantitative experimental results demonstrate that our approach performs the best.

Categories and Subject Descriptors

I.4.3 [**Image Processing and Computer Vision**]: Enhancement

General Terms

Algorithms, Experimentation

Keywords

Image Super-Resolution, Edge-Preserving

1. INTRODUCTION

The goal of single image super-resolution is to recover a high-resolution image from a low-resolution image. Image super-resolution is important in many applications of multimedia such as playing a video on a higher-resolution screen. Although much work has been available, super-resolution has not be solved very well yet. As pointed out in [2], the generation process of a low-resolution image can be modeled as smoothing and down-sampling a high-resolution image. Single image super-resolution is a challenging problem because there is inevitable information loss in down-sampling and the number of unknowns in the recovery exceeds the number of observed data.

Previous approaches to super-resolution can be categorized into three groups: interpolation based, reconstruction based, and learning based. The comparison of different approaches is summaried in Table 1. Interpolation based methods [1, 9] do not introduce high-frequency information. Therefore, their results often appear over-smooth and have jagged artifacts along the edges.

The reconstruction based approaches [4, 5, 14] are formulated under the framework of enforcing a reconstruction constraint and imposing prior knowledge on high-resolution images. The reconstruction constraint requires that the high-resolution image via smoothing and down-sampling should be as close as possible to the low-resolution image. In [13], Shan et al. utilize the heavy-tailed distribution prior of natural image gradient for image/video super-resolution. Different from above mehtods, statistical edge features between the low-resolution and high-resolution image are used in [5, 14]. In these methods, the imposed prior is not true for arbitrary images and many artifacts (e.g., ringing) may appear in the high-resolution image.

The category of learning based approaches [6, 15, 19, 18, 11, 21, 10],also known as image hallucination techniques, is originally proposed in [6] for learning high frequency details that do not appear in the low-resolution image from a number of training examples. The framework can be formulated by a Markov Random Field (MRF) and solved by belief propagation. The learning based methods are often time-consuming. To speed up their algorithm, Sun et al. [15] propose to learn only the primal sketch priors (e.g., edges, ridges, and corners) for image hallucination. In [21], sparse representation is incorporated into the learning step. Recently, Sun et al. [16] propose a context-constrained hallucination method which pays much attention to textural regions. Because of insufficient training examples, high frequency artifacts often appear in the results of a learning based approach.

Almost all image super-resolution methods [6, 15, 4, 13, 14, 21] need an initial high-resolution image for latter steps via up-sampling the input low-resolution image. Previous approaches often use interpolation methods (e.g., bicubic interpolation) to obtain the initial high resolution result. Such a simple method severely degrades the final result. In this paper, we propose a novel up-sampling method to ob-

*Area chair: Lei Chen

MM'11, November 28–December 1, 2011, Scotsdale, Arizona, USA.

Table 1: Comparison of different super-resolution approaches.

Categorization	Description	Disadvantages
Interpolation based	using different interpolation techniques	over-smooth, jagged artifacts
Reconstruction based	using reconstruction constraint and image prior	ringing artifacts, imposing additional prior
Learning based	learning high frequency details from training set	high frequency artifacts, relying training set

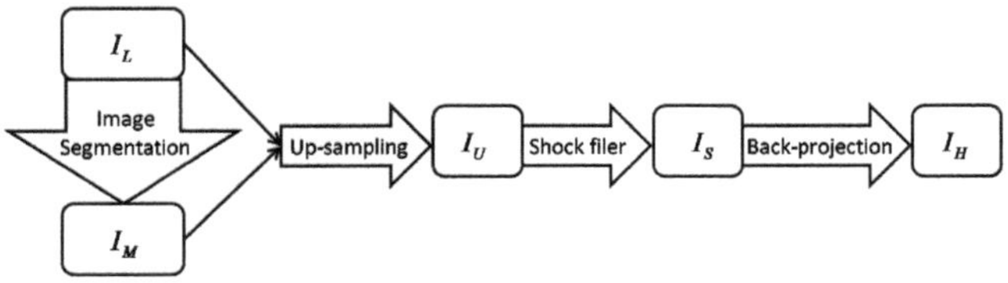

Figure 1: Framework of our approach.

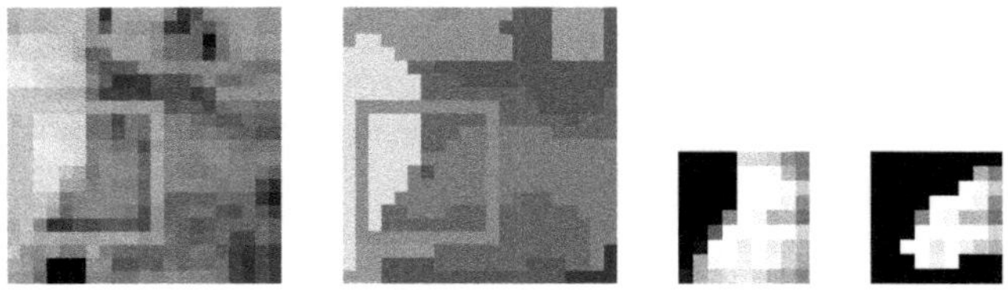

(a) (b) (c) (d)

Figure 2: Illustration of the soft-edge and hard-edge constraints in our up-sampling scheme. (a) One patch of a low-resolution image (Fig. 4 (a)). The blue pixel is the current center and the red rectangle denotes its filtering neighborhood region. (b) The result of mean shift segmentation. (c) The bilateral filtering weight $BF(p_l, q)$ for the blue pixel. (d) The final up-sampling weight $BF(p_l, q)M(p_l, q)$ for the blue pixel. A larger intensity in (c) and (d) denotes a larger weight value. These values are scaled for visualization.

tain the initial high-resolution result. Our scheme incorporates a soft-edge and a hard-edge constraints in up-sampling. The soft-edge constraint is enforced via bilateral filtering [17] which smoothes the image while preserving edges. The hard-edge constraint is enforced after applying the mean shift image segmentation algorithm [3].

After obtaining the initial result via up-sampling, we use the complex shock filter [7] to enhance strong edges in the high-resolution image, instead of imposing prior knowledge on the high-resolution image which is used in most previous methods [4, 13, 5, 14]. These methods with a prior have two main disadvantages. First, the prior is not suitable for all images. With it imposed, many artifacts may be introduced to the high-resolution image or the result appears over-smooth. Second, solving for a high-resolution image with a prior is computationally expensive.

Finally, we enforce a reconstruction constraint on the high-resolution image and the final result is solved by back projection [8]. The results obtained by the original back projection [8] often suffer from ringing artifacts. Due to the combination of up-sampling scheme and the complex shock filter, our algorithm obtains results without noticeable ringing artifacts.

Compared with previous work, our algorithm has two advantages. The first is that it works without any prior and thus can handle arbitrary images. The second is that it preserves edges excellently.

2. FORMULATION OF OUR APPROACH

Let I_L be the input low-resolution image, I_U be the initial high-resolution result obtained by our up-sampling method, I_S be the intermediate result after the shock filter, and I_H be the final high-resolution image. The framework of our algorithm is shown in Fig. 1.

2.1 Up-Sampling

In previous image up-sampling algorithms, the filter is constructed considering only spatial information with useful intensity information discarded. Motivated by bilateral filtering in [17], we propose a novel up-sampling scheme considering both spatial and intensity information. Bilateral filtering can be defined as

$$B(p) = \frac{1}{W(p)} \sum_{q \in \Omega} I(q) G_{\sigma_s}(\|p - q\|) G_{\sigma_r}(\|I(p) - I(q)\|), \quad (1)$$

where I is the input image, and Ω is the set of all pixels of the image, p and q denote pixel locations over the image, and $W(p)$ is the normalization constant at p, and G_{σ_s} and G_{σ_r} are two Gaussian functions with standard deviations σ_s and σ_r, respectively.

The intuition of bilateral filtering is to smooth the image using pixels which are close both in the spatial domain and the intensity domain. We call this as soft-edge constraint. In our algorithm, to interpolate a target pixel, we choose its nearby pixel with similar colors. In order to preserve edges better, we also propose a hard-edge constraint. We first perform segmentation on the input low-resolution image by the mean shift algorithm [3]. Then for each pixel, we use only pixels in the same segment for up-sampling.

Let I_M be the result of mean shift image segmentation. By combining both the soft-edge constraint and the hard-edge constraint, our up-sampling is formulated as

$$I_U(p_h) = \frac{1}{W(p_h) + \beta} (\sum_{q \in \Omega} BF(p_l, q) M(p_l, q) I_L(q) + \beta I_L(p_l)), \quad (2)$$

$$BF(p_l, q) = G_{\sigma_s}(\|p_l - q\|) G_{\sigma_r}(\|I_L(p_l) - I_L(q)\|), \quad (3)$$

$$M(p_l, q) = \begin{cases} 1 & \text{if } I_M(p_l) = I_M(q) \\ 0 & \text{if } I_M(p_l) \neq I_M(q) \end{cases}, \quad (4)$$

where β is a balance parameter, p_h is pixel position in the high-resolution image, and p_l is the position in the low-resolution image corresponding to p_h. If the coordinates of p_l are not integers, $I_L(p_l)$ and $I_M(p_l)$ are obtained by nearest interpolation on the low-resolution image. The term $\beta I_L(p_l)$ in (2) is used to emphasize the importance of the filter center p_l.

Fig. 2 gives an example to illustrate the soft-edge constraint and hard-edge constraint. From this example, we can see that the color of each pixel in the high-resolution

(a) (b) (c) (d)

Figure 3: Comparison of different algorithms at 3× magnification on the "mickey" and "Lena" images. (a) Bicubic interpolation. (b) Sharpen bicubic (bicubic interpolation + unsharp mask in Adobe Photoshop). (c) Back projection. (d) Our approach. (Better viewed on the screen with more than 400% zooming-in.)

image is determined by both the soft-edge and hard-edge constraints.

2.2 Shock Filter

Based on the up-sampling result I_U, a shock filter is employed to enhance strong edges in the high-resolution image. The shock filter is a blind deconvolution technique and originally developed in [12] for image enhancement. The classical 2D shock filter formulation is:

$$I_t = -\text{sign}(I_{\eta\eta})\|\nabla I\|, \tag{5}$$

where $\nabla I = (I_x, I_y)_T$ and $I_{\eta\eta} = I_{xx}I_x^2 + 2I_{xy}I_xI_y + I_{yy}I_y^2$ denote the gradient and the second derivative, respectively.

The drawback of the original shock filter is that it is very sensitive to noise. Consequently, it enhances both true edges and noise. Later improved shock filter algorithms have been proposed. In this paper, we choose the complex shock filter in [7] to obtain the enhanced image. General 2D complex shock filter is defined as

$$I_t = -\frac{2}{\pi}\arctan(a\text{Im}(\frac{I}{\theta}))\|\nabla I\| + \lambda I_{\eta\eta} + \tilde{\lambda} I_{\xi\xi}, \tag{6}$$

where $I_{\xi\xi} = I_{xx}I_y^2 - 2I_{xy}I_xI_y + I_{yy}I_x^2$, $\lambda = re^{i\theta}$ is a complex scalar, $\tilde{\lambda}$ is a real scalar, the parameter a controls the sharpness of the slope near zero, θ is the phase angle of the complex part, and $\text{Im}(\frac{I}{\theta})$ denotes the complex part of $\frac{I}{\theta}$. More details can be found from [7].

Then we update I_S by the following operation:

$$I_S^{t+1} = I_S^t + I_t * d_t \tag{7}$$

where d_t is a iteration step. In our experiments $d_t = 0.1$ and the initial input in the iteration procedure is I_U.

2.3 Reconstruction Constraint Refinement

The obtained intermediate result I_S often does not satisfy the reconstruction constraint. Reconstruction error is defined as

$$E(I_L, I_H) = I_L - (I_H \otimes g)\downarrow_s, \tag{8}$$

where $\otimes$ is the convolution operator, g is a spatial filter, and $\downarrow_s$ denotes the down-sampling operator with factor s. The

(a) (b) (c) (d)

Figure 4: Comparison with a reconstruction based method at 3× magnification on the "Hat" image. (a) Original image zoomed-in by nearest interpolation. (b) Bicubic interpolation. (c) Result by [13]. (d) Our approach. (Better viewed on the screen with zooming-in.)

(a) (b) (c) (d) (e)

Figure 5: Comparison with another reconstruction based method at 3× magnification on the "Zebra" image. (a) Original image zoomed-in by nearest interpolation. (b) Bicubic Interpolation. (c) Back Projection. (d) Result by [4]. (e) Our approach. (Better viewed on the screen with zooming-in.)

reconstruction constraint requires that the high-resolution image after smoothing and down-sampling should be as close as possible to the input low-resolution image.

As in many image super-resolution methods [15, 14, 4, 13], the reconstruction error can be minimized by the back projection algorithm [8] which is an iterative gradient-based minimization method:

$$I_H^{t+1} = I_H^t + (((I_H^t \otimes g)\downarrow_s - I_L)\uparrow_s) \otimes f \tag{9}$$

where I_H^t is the high-resolution image at iteration t, and g and f are a spatial filter and a Gaussian "back projection" filter, respectively. The intermediate result I_S is used as the initial I_H at the first iteration. In our experiment, the standard variances of g and f are set to $s/2$.

3. EXPERIMENTAL RESULTS

We compare our approach with bicubic interpolation and sharpen bicubic interpolation (using the "unsharp mask" in Adobe Photoshop with the default parameters on the result of bicubic interpolation), and back projection [8] on the "mickey" and "Lena" images in Fig. 3. As shown in the zooming-in region, bicubic interpolation over smoothes the whole image, especially at strong edges. The Sharpen bicubic and back projection methods introduce ringing artifacts on salient edges. The edges of our result are sharp without noticeable artifacts.

Fig. 4 shows the comparison of our approach with a reconstruction based method using the gradient heavy-tailed distribution prior [13] (the code is downloaded from `http://www.cse.cuhk.edu.hk/~leojia/projects/upsampling`) on the "Hat" image, where the results by bicubic interpolation is also given. In Fig. 5, we compare our approach with another reconstruction based method using the soft edge smoothness prior [4] (the results are downloaded from `http://vision.`

(a) (b) (c) (d) (e)

Figure 6: Comparison with the learning based method at 3× magnification using the "Man" image. (a) Original image zoomed-in by nearest interpolation. (b) Back projection. (c) Result by [4]. (d) Result by [21]. (e) Our approach. (Better viewed on the screen with zooming-in.)

Table 2: RMS values obtained by sveral methods. The best results are in bold.

Images	Bibubic	BP[8]	[13]	[21]	Ours
Man	3.4621	3.3399	4.9643	3.5426	**3.0115**
Zebra	3.9180	3.7476	5.3520	3.9090	**3.6105**
Fire	3.0549	**2.2970**	2.6483	2.6483	2.4373
KNhair	3.6888	3.2124	4.9028	3.6311	**3.1747**

`eecs.northwestern.edu/research/IP/SR`) on the "Zebra" image. The method in [13] suppresses the details in the texture region, such as the region in the rectangle. The result obtained by [4] suffers from ringing artifacts because the imposed prior may not be compatible with the input low-resolution image. On the other hand, our approach preserves the details and sharp edges in the high-resolution results.

In Fig. 6, we compare with a learning based method [21] (the matlab code can be obtained from `http://www.ifp.illinois.edu/~jyang29/`) on the "Man" image. We observe that the learning based method introduces many high frequency artifacts from training data. Our result does not have visible artifacts with strong edges close to the input low-resolution image.

Table 2 shows quantitative results by several algorithms, result by other algorithms are not given because their codes are not available. The measure is root mean error (RMS). Table 3 shows results with structural similarity (SSIM) [20] which is one of the most popular image quality measures. From these two tables, we can see that our algorithms performs the best overall.

4. CONCLUSION

In this paper, we have proposed a novel image super-resolution algorithm that can preserve edges well. First, we perform an up-sampling on the low-resolution image by combining both the soft-edge and hard-edge constraints. Then, a complex shock filter robust to noise is used to recover strong edges. Finally, we enforce a reconstruction constraint on the high-resolution result and obtain the final result by back projection. The main advantages of our algorithm are that it does not require image priors and that it preserves edges well. We have tested our algorithms qualitatively and quantitatively. Compared with several state-of-the-art super-resolution algorithms, ours performs the best overall.

5. ACKNOWLEDGMENTS

This work was supported by Introduced Innovative R&D Team of Guangdong Province (Robot and Intelligent Information Technology); Natural Science Foundation of China (60903117, 61070148); and Science, Industry, Trade, and Information Technology Commission of Shenzhen Municipality, China (JC201005270357A, ZYC201006130314A, JC201005270378A, ZYC201006130313A).

Table 3: SSIM values obtained by sveral methods. The best results are in bold.

Images	Bibubic	BP[8]	[13]	[21]	Ours
Man	0.8617	0.8905	0.5767	0.8716	**0.9205**
Zebra	0.8064	0.8885	0.4982	0.8477	**0.8912**
Fire	0.9299	0.9718	0.9667	0.9435	**0.9729**
KNhair	0.8451	**0.9226**	0.6657	0.8818	0.9225

6. REFERENCES

[1] J. Allebac and P. W. Wong. Edge-directed interpolation. In *Proc. ICIP*, 1996.

[2] S. Baker and T. Kanade. Limits on super-resolution and how to break them. In *Proc. CVPR*, 2000.

[3] D. Comaniciu and P. Meer. Mean shift: a robust approach toward feature space analysis. *IEEE Trans. on PAMI*, 24(5):603–619, May 2002.

[4] S. Dai, M. Han, W. Xu, Y. Wu, and Y. Gong. Soft edge smoothness prior for alpha channel super resolution. In *Proc. CVPR*, 2007.

[5] R. Fattal. Upsampling via imposed edges statistics. In *ACM SIGGRAPH*, 2007.

[6] W. Freeman and E. Pasztor. Learning low-level vision. *IJCV*, 40(1):25–47, 2000.

[7] G. Gilboa, N. A. Sochen, and Y. Y. Zeevi. Regularized shock filters and complex diffusion. *Lecture Notes in Computer Science*, pages 399–413, 2002.

[8] M. Irani and S. Peleg. Motion analysis for image enhancement: Resolution, occlusion, and transparency. *Journal of Visual Communication and Image Representation*, 40(4):324–335, 1993.

[9] X. Li and M. Orchard. New edge-directed interpolation.

[10] Z. Lin, J. He, X. Tang, and C.-K. Tang. Limits of learning-based superresolution algorithms. In *Proc. ICCV*, 2007.

[11] W. Liu, D. Lin, and X. Tang. Hallucinating faces: Tensorpatch super-resolution and coupled residue compensation. In *Proc. CVPR*, 2005.

[12] S. Osher and L. I. Rudin. Feature-oriented image enhancement using shock filters. *SIAM Journal on Numerical Analysis*, 27:919–940, 1990.

[13] Q. Shan, Z. Li, J. Jia, and C.-K. Tang. Fast image/video upsampling. In *ACM SIGGRAPH ASIA*, 2008.

[14] J. Sun, Z. Xu, and H.-Y. Shum. Image super-resolution using gradient profile prior. In *Proc. CVPR*, 2008.

[15] J. Sun, N.-N. Zheng, H. Tao, and H.-Y. Shum. Image hallucination with primal sketch priors. In *Proc. CVPR*, 2003.

[16] J. Sun, J. Zhu, and M. Tappen. Context-constrained hallucination for image super-resolution. In *Proc. CVPR*, 2010.

[17] C. Tomasi and R. Manduchi. Bilateral filtering for gray and color images. In *Proc. ICCV*, 1998.

[18] Q. Wang, X. Tang, and H. Shum. Patch based blind image super resolution. In *Proc. ICCV*, 2005.

[19] X. Wang and X. Tang. Hallucinating face by eigentransformation. *IEEE Trans. on SMC, Part C*, 35(3):425–434, 2005.

[20] Z. Wang, A. Bovik, H. Sheikh, and E. Simoncelli. Image quality assessment: from error visibility to structural similarity. *IEEE Trans. on IP*, 13(4):600–612, 2004.

[21] J. Yang, J. Wright, T. Huang, and Y. Ma. Image super-resolution as sparse representation of raw image patches. In *Proc. CVPR*, 2008.

Automatic Motion-Guided Video Stylization and Personalization*

Chen Cao[1], Shifeng Chen[1], Wei Zhang[1], Xiaoou Tang[1,2]
[1]Shenzhen Key Laboratory for Computer Vision and Pattern Recognition
Shenzhen Institutes of Advanced Technology,Chinese Academy of Sciences, China
[2]Department of Information Engineering, The Chinese University of Hong Kong, China
{chen.cao, shifeng.chen, zhangwei}@siat.ac.cn, xtang@ie.cuhk.edu.hk

ABSTRACT

Video stylization transfers a source video into an artistic version while maintaining temporal coherence between adjacent frames. In this paper, we formulate the unsupervised example-based video stylization with Markov random field model. In our algorithm, we implement an improved optical flow algorithm to maintain temporal coherence while improve the accuracy of estimation along motion boundaries. We also extend our algorithm to the application of video personalization, in which human faces keep clear and distinguishable. A series of techniques are fused in video personalization, including face detection and alignment, motion flow, skin detection, and illumination blending. Given a source video and a style template image, our algorithm produces the stylized and/or personalized video(s) automatically. Experimental results demonstrate that our algorithm performs excellently in both video stylization and personalization.

Categories and Subject Descriptors

I.4.9 [**Image Processing and Computer Vision**]: Applications

General Terms

Algorithms, Experimentation

Keywords

Non-Photorealistic Rendering, Video Stylization, Video Personalization

1. INTRODUCTION

Video stylization has many applications in multimedia entertainment. It is mainly based on image stylization while maintaining temporal coherence between adjacent frames. Compared with the original video, the stylized one would create a sense of beauty and inspire intense interests in human mind. As increasing attentions have been paid to personal artworks (e.g., home and campus DV), people would like to transfer their self-shot videos into a stylized one. Definitely the video would be blurred or distorted after stylization, people may hope to keep the face in the video clear and distinguishable. We develop an automatic algorithm to achieve these goals. Given a source video and a style template image, the system could produce stylized and/or personalized results. To the best of our knowledge, there is no work focusing on such a video personalization problem.

In stylization, we first consider single image rendering with an artificial style, and then extend image rendering to videos by processing the frames one by one while preserving temporal coherence. There are a number of existing methods in image style transfer. Some of them focus on using particular approaches to obtain specialized styles, such as [3] for line-drawing and [2] for watercolor. These approaches lay emphasis on analyzing the properties of the specified style, and design a particular non-photorealistic rendering model to simulate the artists' painting brush step by step. Another important classification of stylization is the example-based method [5], [7], [10]. Image analogies [5] is a representative algorithm among the example-based approaches. The main idea of example-based image stylization is that a source image B would be transferred into a stylized one B' by given a style template A'. The transfer algorithms could "learn" the style information from A' and then implement it on B to create a new image B' which has the same content as B and the similar style as A'.

Similar to [5], our algorithm is formulated in the model of Markov random fields (MRFs). In [5], both the template A' and its ground-truth image A should be given, while our approach needs only an arbitrary template image A' to create a simulated artwork, which reduces the algorithm limitations greatly. To improve the speed and performance, we use a coarse-to-fine belief propagation algorithm [8] to solve the global optimization of MRF, and use image quilting [4] to generate seamless patch boundaries.

For video stylization if we employ the image stylization algorithm to each frame of the video independently, the "flickering" effect (style textures randomly change in position and appearance frame by frame) would appear and make the result blinking and blurred. In order to preserve temporal coherence, we use the optical flow algorithm to find correspondences between frames.

Video stylization may blur or distort human faces in the video. Inspired by a cartoon personalization system called

*Area chair: Lei Chen

MM'11, November 28–December 1, 2011, Scottsdale, Arizona, USA.

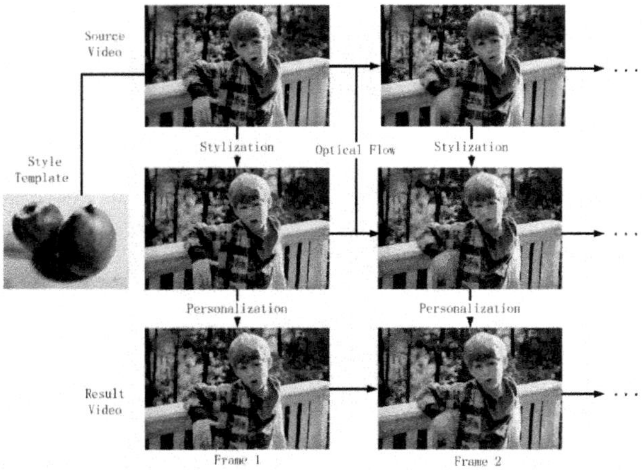

Figure 1: The framework of our algorithm. Top row: the first frame (left) and the second frame (right) of the source video. Middle row: the template image of watercolor style (left), the stylization result of the first frame as initialization (middle), and the stylization result of the second frame via optical flow (right). Faces are blurred in these frames. Bottom row: the final result of personalization.

EasyToon [11], we extract faces from the source video and process them separately from the non-facial parts. By using face detection and alignment, motion flow, skin detection, and illumination blending, we can get a result with recognizable faces in stylized video, i.e., the video personalization. The framework of our algorithm is shown in Fig. 1.

2. VIDEO STYLIZATION

The first step of video stylization is to initialize the first frame by using example-based image style transfer algorithm. Then the initialization is propagated to the following frames by optical flow. Our image stylization algorithm is inspired by image analogies [5]. In our algorithm, the well aligned ground-truth of the style template image A is not needed, which is necessary in [5]. We divided both A' and B into small patches and take patches from A' to replace the patches in B according to some rules. To solve this patch replacement problem, we build an MRF model and find its solution as follows. All steps of stylization is processed in luminance channel (Y channel) of YIQ color space. The final result is obtained by combining the changed Y channel and the unchanged I and Q channel.

2.1 Markov Random Field Model

The style template image A' could be divided into $w \times h$ patches and they are denoted as $L = \{l_1, l_2, \cdots, l_m\}$, here each l_i represents a $w \times h$ patch taken from A' and m is the patch number. The target image B (the first frame) is also divided into the same size patches, regarded as $\mathcal{V} = \{v_1, v_2, \cdots, v_n\}$. For every patch region v_i in $\mathcal{V}$, we paste a patch in L on v_i. The goal for style rendering is to find the best configuration $P = \{p_1, p_2, \cdots, p_n \mid p_i \in L\}$ (where p_i is the patch pasted on v_i) to minimize the energy function

$$E(P) = \sum_{v_i \in \mathcal{V}} D(p_i) + \mu \sum_{(v_i, v_j) \in \mathcal{E}} C(p_i, p_j), \qquad (1)$$

where $D(p_i)$ is the data cost of pasting patch p_i to region v_i, $C(p_i, p_j)$ is the consistency cost of a neighboring couple patches (v_i, v_j) to be pasted by (p_i, p_j), μ is a constant to balance D and C, and $\mathcal{E}$ is the set of edges linking each node in $\mathcal{V}$ to its four neighbors.

The data cost term $D(p_i)$ is defined as

$$D(p_i) = \sum_{(x,y) \in p_i} \left\| (p_i(x,y) - \overline{p_i}) - (v_i(x,y) - \overline{v_i}) \right\|^2, \qquad (2)$$

where (x, y) is the pixel coordinate in both patch p_i and the overlapping region v_i, $\overline{p_i}$ and $\overline{v_i}$ represent the mean value of all the pixel colors in p_i and v_i, respectively, and $\|\cdot\|$ is the L2 norm. The consistency cost term $C(p_i, p_j)$ is the sum of the squared differences (SSD) of pixel colors in the overlapping region between p_i and p_j.

We choose belief propagation (BP) to solve the energy minimization problem. The computational complexity of BP is the square of the number of label candidates in L. The large size of L makes BP intractable. Therefore, we propose two schemes to speed up the algorithm: selecting representative patches and utilizing two-step BP.

The number of elements in L could always be more than 10000 in our experiment. We select only 5000 representative patches. We define the quality of a patch l_i as

$$Q(l_i) = \sum_{(x,y) \in l_i} \left| Median(A'(x,y)) - A'(x,y) \right|, \qquad (3)$$

where $(x, y) \in l_i$ means that (x, y) is a pixel in patch l_i from the stylized sample A', and $Median()$ is the median filter. The larger $Q(l_i)$ is, the more style information the patch l_i contains. We take the top 5000 l_i with largest $Q(l_i)$ values as the patch candidates in the BP algorithm.

We utilize a two-step BP algorithm [8] to accelerate the BP process, i.e., to perform BP twice with N_1 and N_2 label candidates each time instead of operating BP once with N candidates, for that N_1 and N_2 are much smaller than N. Refer [8] for the details of two-step BP.

2.2 Image Quilting

After getting the result of P, we employ image quilting [4] to produce a seamless image from overlapping patches. The purpose of image quilting is to stitch together small patches by finding a ragged edge with the least inconsistencies between adjacent patches. The image quilting step is formulated as a min-cut problem. Suppose that a source node $\mathcal{S}$ and a sink node $\mathcal{T}$ represent the two adjacent patches. Then a graph is constructed whose nodes are the pixels in the overlapping region of the two adjacent patches. Each node (pixel) is connected to its four neighbors while the pixels in the boundaries are connected to $\mathcal{S}$ or $\mathcal{T}$. The weight of the edge connecting two neighbor pixels (s, t) is

$$W(s,t) = \|F_{sc}(s) - F_{sk}(s)\|^2 + \|F_{sc}(t) - F_{sk}(t)\|^2, \qquad (4)$$

where F_{sc} and F_{sk} represent the feature vectors of a pixel in source and sink patches, respectively.

2.3 Propagating to Succeeding Frames

After obtaining the initialization for the first frame, we propagate the stylized result to succeeding frames via motion flow. In this process, we use the optical flow algorithm in [1] to estimate the pixel-level correspondences between successive frames. Then we divided the currently processing frame into patches as in the image stylization step. For the patches that could be found corresponding patches in the

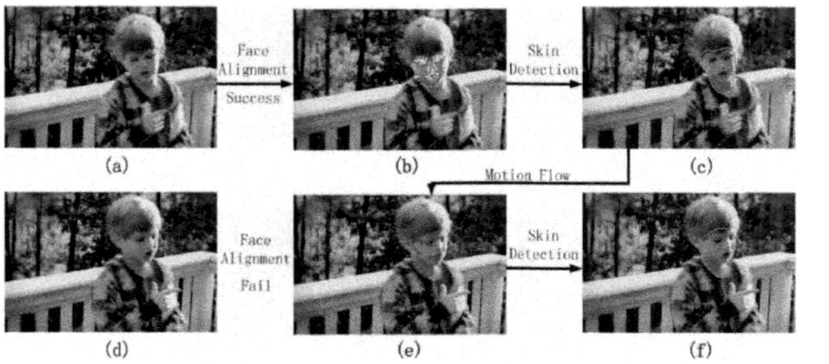

Figure 2: Example of the face extraction process. (a): The 10th frame in the source video. (b): The landmarks (white points) of the face alignment result. (c): The result of skin detection for (a). (d): The 11th frame. Face alignment fails due to the oblique orientation. (e): The face region obtained from the previous frame via motion flow. (f): The skin detection result based on the region in (e).

previous frame, we directly copy the patches in the previous frame into the current frame in the related positions. For the patches that has no relevant regions in its previous frame, we re-render them by using our image stylization approaches. To evaluate the reliability of correspondences between two patches, we calculate the SSD between them and set a threshold to judge the validation of correspondence.

In addition, a conspicuous artifact of optical flow is the over-smoothing or randomly dragging effect at occluded regions, which would visibly impair the quality of output video as mentioned in [12]. We adopt the algorithm of occlusion detection and bilateral diffusion in [12] to deal with this unsatisfactory phenomenon.

3. VIDEO PERSONALIZATION

3.1 Face Extraction

At first, a dynamic cascade method based face detection [13] is utilized to detect faces in frames. Then we employ an active shape model based face alignment [14] to locate the face feature points and a single Gaussian model based skin detection [9] to get the whole face region. The face extraction process is shown in Fig. 2.

Face alignment returns 87 landmarks of face features if succeed (see the white points in Fig. 2(b)). With these feature points, we could locate the face in the frame. However, these points do not surround the entire area of the face region. Thus we use a skin detection algorithm to obtain the whole face region after getting the face alignment results. We only detect skin in the area near the 87 landmarks of the face for high accuracy.

We use a Gaussian model for skin detection, which is:

$$p\left(c \mid skin\right) = \frac{1}{2\pi \left|\Sigma_S\right|^{1/2}} e^{-\frac{1}{2}(c-\mu_s)^T \Sigma_S^{-1}(c-\mu_s)}, \quad (5)$$

where c is a color vector of a pixel in the detected area. We perform the detection in YCrCb color space and c represents a two-dimensional vector indicates the values of Cr and Cb. The distribution parameters are

$$\mu_s = \frac{1}{n}\sum_{i=1}^{n} c_i, \quad \Sigma_S = \frac{1}{n-1}\sum_{i=1}^{n}\left(c_i - \mu_s\right)\left(c_i - \mu_s\right)^T, \quad (6)$$

where n is the number of skin color training data c_i. The pixels in the surrounded area of the landmarks of the face alignment result are set to be the training data. Of course we should firstly eliminate the dark points which might be the eyes or other shaded regions of the face in the training data set. $p\left(c \mid skin\right)$ represents the probability of a point with color vector c being a skin point. We set a threshold for $p\left(c \mid skin\right)$ to judge whether the point we detect belongs to skin or not. The red-line surrounded region in Fig. 2(c) is the result of skin detection.

An important and unavoidable issue is that face alignment might fail in some frames (see Fig. 2(d)) for the reason that a face is posed in an oblique orientation, or a part of the face is out of the camera screen, or the face is partially shaded by hands or other objects. This phenomenon is general in many cases. Address to this problem, we reuse the optical flow result obtained in the video stylization stage to trace the corresponding area of the face in the previous frame when face alignment fails in the current frame. The blue-line surrounded region in Fig. 2(e) is the corresponding area of face mask in Fig. 2(c) obtained via motion flow. After this step, we can get some regions of the face parts. We then set these parts as training data and conduct skin detection near these regions. Fig. 2(f) is the detection result.

(a) (b) (c) (d)

Figure 3: Template images: (a) Watercolor; (b) Oil on canvas; (c) Pastel; (d) Natural texture.

3.2 Face Blending

After the skin detection step, we obtain face masks in all frames. Then we simply combine the completely stylized face F' and not stylized face F with a coefficient α between 0 and 1 to control the amount of personal information on the final stylized face. The final stylized face F_{final} is:

$$F_{final} = \alpha F + \left(1 - \alpha\right) F'. \quad (7)$$

At last, We put the final stylized faces on the extracted face regions in the completely stylized result. Obviously, the seam boundary would occur between the face regions and the non-facial regions. To settle this problem, we use Poisson blending [6] to create merged and seamless boundaries between the faces and the other parts in the video.

4. EXPERIMENTAL RESULTS

To demonstrate the performance of our algorithm, we test it on some child-centered videos with four style templates (watercolor, oil-on-canvas, pastel, and natural texture in Fig. 3).

The first source video is about an active boy with exaggerated poses. Three frames from the video are shown in Fig. 4(a). The corresponding frames with watercolor style are given in Fig. 4(b). Notice that face regions are blurred after stylization. The final result of personalization is given in Fig. 4(c). Fig. 4(d) shows the personalized result on oil-on-canvas style. This style has a strong texture. Therefore we can see clearly that the temporal coherence is kept well: the texture on the same object (especially the background) maintained unchanged in different frames.

Fig. 5 is another result on the video about a girl who is chatting online. Fig. 5(b) includes the pastel-stylized frames

Figure 4: Example results by our algorithm. (a) The source video frames. (b) The stylized output in watercolor, faces are obscure. (c) The result artwork in watercolor after stylization and personalization. (d) The stylized and personalized artwork in oil-on-canvas style.

with obscure faces. The corresponding personalized result are given in Fig. 5(c). Fig. 5(d) is the result with natural texture style. From the result we can see that the faces are recognizable in a pleasing appearance and the non-facial parts show conspicuous texture similar to the style template.

5. CONCLUSION

In this paper, we propose an automatic algorithm to stylize and personalize videos into artistic works. It comprises two stages: video stylization and video personalization. Video stylization stylizes the first frame of the video for a given style template image and then propagates the result to all frames via motion flow. Video personalization extracts face regions in the video frames and processes them separately from the non-facial regions. Our stylization algorithm is example based and formulated with an MRF model. A two-step BP is used to solve the MRF energy minimization problem efficiently. We utilize an improved optical flow estimation method with occlusion detection and bilateral filtering to preserve temporal coherence and overcome the unsatisfactory artifacts in video stream. In video personalization stage, a method by combining face detection and alignment with skin detection is used to extract face region. Then the algorithm processes the face exclusively to make face clear and distinguishable. Our algorithm is robust even in the case that face alignment fails in some frames since we proposes a motion flow based face detection method to handle the problem. To the best of our knowledge, there is no existing work about such video personalization.

6. ACKNOWLEDGEMENTS

This work was supported by Introduced Innovative R&D Team of Guangdong Province (Robot and Intelligent Information Technology); Natural Science Foundation of China (60903117); and Science, Industry, Trade, and Information Technology Commission of Shenzhen Municipality, China (JC201005270357A, ZYC201006130314A).

Figure 5: More results of our algorithm. (a) The source video frames. (b) The stylized but blurred faces results in pastel style. (c) The stylized and personalized artwork in pastel style. (d) The stylized and personalized artwork in natural texture style.

7. REFERENCES

[1] T. Brox, A. Bruhn, N. Papenberg, and J. Weickert. High accuracy optical flow estimation based on a theory for warping. In *ECCV*, 2004.

[2] C. Curtis, S. Anderson, J. Seims, K. Fleischer, and D. Salesin. Computer-generated watercolor. In *SIGGRAPH*, 1997.

[3] D. DeCarlo and A. Santella. Stylization and abstraction of photographs. *ACM Trans. on Graphics*, 21(3):769–776, 2002.

[4] A. Efros, W. Freeman, et al. Image quilting for texture synthesis and transfer. In *SIGGRAPH*, 2001.

[5] A. Hertzmann, C. Jacobs, N. Oliver, B. Curless, and D. Salesin. Image analogies. In *SIGGRAPH*, 2001.

[6] P. Pérez, M. Gangnet, and A. Blake. Poisson image editing. *ACM Trans. on Graphics*, 22(3):313–318, 2003.

[7] R. Resales, K. Achan, and B. Frey. Unsupervised image translation. In *ICCV*, 2003.

[8] H. Ting, S. Chen, J. Liu, and X. Tang. Image inpainting by global structure and texture propagation. In *ACM MM*, 2007.

[9] V. Vezhnevets, V. Sazonov, and A. Andreeva. A survey on pixel-based skin color detection techniques. In *Graphicon*, 2003.

[10] B. Wang, W. Wang, H. Yang, and J. Sun. Efficient example-based painting and synthesis of 2d directional texture. *IEEE Trans. on Visualization and Computer Graphics*, 10(3):266–277, 2004.

[11] F. Wen, S. Chen, and X. Tang. Easytoon: cartoon personalization using face photos. In *ACM MM*, 2008.

[12] J. Xiao, H. Cheng, H. Sawhney, C. Rao, and M. Isnardi. Bilateral filtering-based optical flow estimation with occlusion detection. In *ECCV*, 2006.

[13] R. Xiao, H. Zhu, H. Sun, and X. Tang. Dynamic cascades for face detection. In *ICCV*, 2007.

[14] Y. Zhou, L. Gu, and H. Zhang. Bayesian tangent shape model: estimating shape and pose parameters via Bayesian inference. In *CVPR*, 2003.

On the Pooling of Positive Examples with Ontology for Visual Concept Learning *

Shiai Zhu†, Chong-Wah Ngo†, Yu-Gang Jiang‡
†Dept of Computer Science, City University of Hong Kong, Kowloon, Hong Kong
‡School of Computer Science, Fudan University, Shanghai, China
shiaizhu2@student.cityu.edu.hk, cwngo@cs.cityu.edu.hk, ygj@fudan.edu.cn

ABSTRACT

A common obstacle in effective learning of visual concept classifiers is the scarcity of positive training examples due to expensive labeling cost. This paper explores the sampling of weakly tagged web images for concept learning without human assistance. In particular, ontology knowledge is incorporated for semantic pooling of positive examples from ontologically neighboring concepts. This effectively widens the coverage of the positive samples with visually more diversified content, which is important for learning a good concept classifier. We experiment with two learning strategies: aggregate and incremental. The former strategy re-trains a new classifier by combining existing and newly collected examples, while the latter updates the existing model using the new samples incrementally. Extensive experiments on NUS-WIDE and VOC 2010 datasets show very encouraging results, even when comparing with classifiers learnt using expert labeled training examples.

Categories and Subject Descriptors

H.3.1 [**Information Storage and Retrieval**]: Content Analysis and Indexing

General Terms

Algorithms, Measurement, Experimentation

Keywords

Visual concepts, training set construction, semantic pooling

1. INTRODUCTION

Acquiring a sufficiently large amount of positive training examples is a key requirement for learning effective concept classifiers. Ideally we should have a training set that maximizes two criteria: coverage and diversity. Coverage specifies the inclusiveness of samples in describing different semantic facets of a concept. Diversity recounts the novelty of samples in presenting the diverse visual appearance of a semantic facet. Constructing a training set with good coverage and diversity is often difficult in practice due to the expensive cost in manual data sampling and labeling.

In recent few years, nevertheless, the proliferation of social media has made the low cost sampling and labeling of training examples a feasible idea [7, 8]. Flickr website, for example, has accumulated more than four billions of images and receives thousands of new uploads per minute. This repository alone already offers a tremendous pool of candidate images for the construction of training sets. However, due to the fact that most images are weakly (noisily) tagged, direct supplying these images for classifier learning without data cleaning will result in poor performance. One straightforward way for dealing with this problem is by bootstrap learning [7, 8]. In [8], an iterative framework that simultaneously learns classifiers and collects positive samples from the Web was proposed. Starting from a classifier learnt from a collection of expert labeled examples, iterative update of the classifier model is performed by including new web images which are predicted as positive by the model itself. Although the approach is expected to collect a clean and larger training set, the newly added images may be homogeneous and lack visual diversity. A similar idea of bootstrap learning was also proposed in [8], but interestingly, for collecting negative training samples from the Web. The sampled images are shown to be more suitable for concept learning than those collected by random sampling, leading to better classification performance. A variant of the bootstrapping strategy is active learning [9], where human intervention is required to iteratively provide manual labels to guide the learning process towards a good concept classifier. In general, bootstrap or active learning could suffer from high computational cost. For instance, as indicated in [8], the overall performance becomes stable after 50 rounds of learning, prediction and sample selection. As a result, the scalability of these learning strategies is in question especially for learning a large set of concept classifiers.

A more efficient way of sampling training examples is to rank the Web images according to their relevancy to a given target concept, and then select the top ranked ones [4, 12]. In [4], visual clustering is carried out to characterize the set of images as a cluster correlation network. Random walk is then performed on the network to rank the image clusters. Heuristics such as larger clusters are more relevant to the target concepts and noisy samples have weak visual correlation with other image clusters are adopted for relevancy reranking. In [12], instead of exploiting visual similarity, semantic field was proposed to predict the relevancy of tag lists

*Area chair: Lei Chen

to target concepts by exploiting external knowledge such as Wikipedia. The top-k ranked images are then used as positive examples for concept learning.

In this paper, different from [4, 7, 8, 12] which mainly focused on filtering noisy Web search results for training set construction, we address the issue of training sample enrichment, which is important for learning a good concept classifier with better generalization capability. Specifically, a semantic pooling technique is proposed to enlarge the coverage as well as to diversify the initial collection of sampled images by propagating positive examples among semantically related concepts using ontology. Two kinds of learning: aggregate and incremental learning, are then employed to train better concept classifiers using new samples. Ontology has been frequently adopted for boosting concept annotation performance [1, 5]. The existing works, however, are on the utilization of ontological relationship for concept label propagation or noise removal. Our work is different in the way that the ontology is employed to pool the freely obtained Web images for boosting the concept learning performance with a cleaner and more diverse training set.

2. SEMANTIC POOLING

Our proposed approach for collecting training examples consists two components: 1) collect and filter examples for each node in an ontological structure; and 2) hierarchical pooling of training examples based on the ontology. We elaborate each of the components below.

2.1 Positive Example Sampling

Given a concept node C_x, we first adopt a similar approach as [12] which considers tag-concept relevancy for training example acquisition. The probability of seeing a concept C_x in an image with a tag list $SF =< T_1, T_2, ..., T_n >$ is defined as $P(C_x|SF) = \frac{P(SF|C_x) \times P(C_x)}{P(SF)}$, where $P(C_x)$ is a constant for all the images under consideration when selecting examples for C_x, and thus can be ignored. The computation of $P(C_x|SF)$ is not very stable since the probability of the entire tag list $P(SF)$ is usually extremely small. Thus we approximate $P(SF|Cx)$ as $P(SF) \times (\sum_i P(T_i|C_x)/n)$, which combines the probabilities of observing SF as a whole and seeing each tag of SF in images tagged with concept C_x. With that, $P(SF)$ can be eliminated and $P(C_x|SF)$ can be approximated as:

$$P(C_x|SF) = \frac{\sum_{i=1}^{n} P(T_i|C_x)}{n} \quad (1)$$

where $P(T_i|C_x)$ denotes the likelihood of observing a tag T_i given a concept C_x, and n is the number of tags.

We employ two measures different from [12] for computing Equation (1). The first measure is Flickr Context Similarity (FCS), which was originally proposed in [6], for measuring the visual co-occurrence between two words. For instance, concept "car" is often tagged together with "road" in user labeling. Although both concepts are not closely related by ontological inference, their visual co-occurrence should be high. FCS is defined as $FCS(T_i, C_x) = e^{-NGD(T_i,C_x)/\rho}$, where $NGD(T_i, C_x) = \frac{max\{\log h(T_i), \log h(C_x)\} - \log h(T_i, C_x)}{\log N - \min\{\log h(T_i), \log h(C_x)\}}$, $h(T_i)$ is the number of Flickr images associated with tag T_i, and $h(T_i, C_x)$ is the number of images associated with both T_i and C_x.

The second measure is based on ontological similarity. For this, we adopt WUP [11], defined as $WUP(T_i, C_x) = \frac{2D(S_{T_i,C_x})}{L(T_i,C_x)+2D(S_{T_i,C_x})}$, where S_{T_i,C_x} is the lowest common ancestor of T_i and C_x in WordNet. The function D returns the depth of a concept, while the function L evaluates the path length by traversing from T_i to C_x in WordNet.

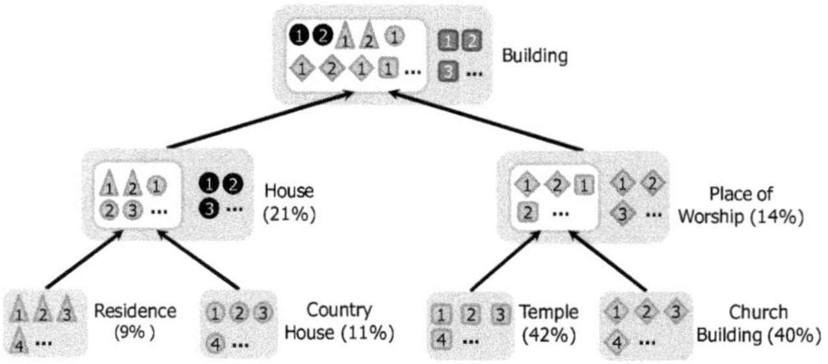

Figure 1: A toy example for illustrating the semantic pooling of training examples for concept "building". Positive samples of child nodes are hierarchically pooled in a bottom-up manner. The percentage in the parentheses indicates the proportion of examples to be propagated to the parent node, computed by Equation (2). The numbered small color boxes with various shapes represent images originally from different nodes, with rankings (indicated by the numbers) computed by Equation (1).

Based on the Bayesian theorem, the conditional probability in Equation (1) can be computed as $P(T_i|C_x) = P(T_i, C_x)/P(C_x)$, where $P(C_x)$ is ignored in our experiments since it is a constant when selecting images for concept C_x. Finally $P(T_i, C_x)$ can be estimated by $FCS(T_i, C_x) \times WUP(T_i, C_x)$. With Equation (1), each image has a $P(C_x|SF)$, based on which the top-k ones are selected as training samples for C_x.

2.2 Ontology-based Pooling

In ontologies like WordNet, child nodes are semantic subsets of parent nodes. Take concept "building" as an example, using the hyponymy relationship in WordNet, nodes under "building" are organized in a sub-tree structure of 6 layers and 268 child nodes. Intuitively, the coverage and diversity of training examples for "building" can be greatly enhanced, by also pooling the samples from the 268 child nodes. With this intuition, we employ WordNet ontology as the ground to propagate positive examples for concept learning.

According to WordNet hyponymy structure, as long as the target concepts are not leaf-nodes, each of them can form a multi-layer tree, with itself as the root node. Figure 1 shows the top three levels of a tree with root node "building". Sample pooling is performed on the tree structure in bottom-up manner. Specifically, taking a tree with only two-layers as an example, positive samples in the child nodes are propagated in proportion to the root node. The proportion is decided based on the popularity of the child node, which is measured based on the total number of images being returned from Flickr. Formally, the percentage of training samples to be propagated from a child node C_i to its parent node can be computed by:

$$P_{C_i} = \frac{f_{C_i}}{\sum_{C_j \in L_i} f_{C_j}} \quad (2)$$

where f_{C_i} is the number of Flickr images tagged with C_i,

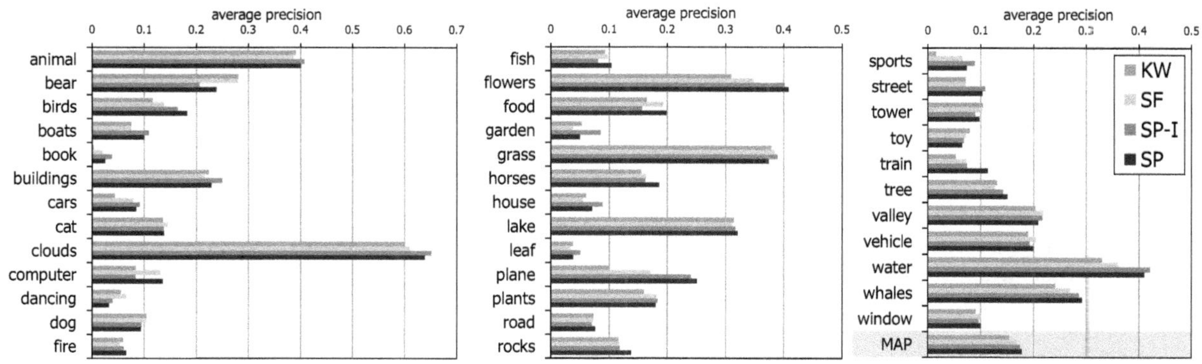

Figure 2: AP comparison on NUS-WIDE testing set

and L_i represents a set of concept nodes on the same layer with C_i in the tree.

The order of selecting samples for pooling is based on the rank list evaluated by Equation (1). In other words, the first image being picked up from a child node is always its top ranked image. Images propagated into a parent node are rescored by the following equation:

$$S(I_k) = (N - k)/N \tag{3}$$

where I_k is the image ranked at the k_{th} position among training examples of the child node C_i, and N is the number of images being propagated from C_i. After the bottom-up propagation process, samples arriving at the root node C^* are then aggregated with the original samples T_{C^*} in C^* as $\widetilde{T}_{C^*} \leftarrow T_{C^*} \cup T_{C_1} \cup T_{C_2} \cup \cdots$, where T_{C_i} denotes the set of positive examples propagated from the child node C_i, and $\widetilde{T}_{C^*}$ is the final set of examples for learning concept C^*. To facilitate successive propagations into nodes on the upper layers, the examples in $\widetilde{T}_{C^*}$ is then ranked by Equation (3), which guarantees that all the top ranked examples of child nodes will be distributed evenly in the ranked list of $\widetilde{T}_{C^*}$ and the orders are retained.

For a tree with more than two levels, similar procedure is carried out recursively from the leaf nodes to the root concept. Figure 1 gives a toy example to illustrate the procedure of semantic pooling for concept "building". The training set $\widetilde{T}_{C^*}$ is enriched with diverse examples from the child nodes.

3. CONCEPT LEARNING

Based on the pool of freely sampled images by ontology, we consider two scenarios for concept learning. Aggregate learning re-trains a classifier using the collection of training examples by semantic pooling. Incremental learning, on the other hand, uses the newly collected samples from the child nodes to update the existing models.

We adopt SVM for aggregate learning, and adaptive SVM (A-SVM) [10] for incremental learning. A-SVM learns a "delta function" $\Delta f(x)$ based on the new examples, and adapts the original SVM model $f^a(x)$ as $f(x) = f^a(x) + \Delta f(x) = f^a(x) + W^T\phi(x)$, where W^T are the parameters to be leant from new samples. A-SVM basically seeks for additional support vectors learnt from newly arrival data to adjust the original decision boundary of a classifier. It optimizes the trade-off that the new boundary should be close to the original one, and meanwhile, can correctly classify the new samples.

4. EXPERIMENT

We primarily use NUS-WIDE [2] which is a large-scale Web image dataset for performance evaluation. The dataset consists of 81 labeled concepts and we conduct experiments on the testing set which contains 107,859 images. Using WordNet, we construct 81 concept trees, with each of the concepts as root node. For each tree, we further remove the leaf nodes that have less than 1,000 images returned by Flickr. Eventually, we consider 37 concepts, each with a tree of depth more than two. Among the 37 concept trees, the average depth is 4 and the average number of child nodes is 55. For instance, concept "building" has 127 nodes of depth 6, and "sports" has 101 nodes of depth 7.

We compare our approach semantic pooling (SP) with two other approaches: 1) semantic field (SF) [12] based on the description in Section 2.1, and 2) simple keyword matching with query expansion (KW). In the experiments, SF and KW respectively sample 2,000 pseudo positive examples from Flickr. To ensure fair comparison such that each approach uses an equal number of training examples, SP also samples 2,000 positive examples. The first 1,000 examples are from the root node, while the remaining 1,000 examples are pooled from the child nodes. All the three approaches use the same set of negative examples, 5,000 per concept, randomly crawled from Flickr. Although there are better ways of collecting negative samples [8], we use random sampling for simplicity as our focus is on the collection of better positive training samples. For concept learning, we adopt the approach in [3] where three SVM models based on bag-of-visual-words, color moment and wavelet textures are trained respectively. Probability predictions from the three SVM models are linearly fused. For SP, in addition to training new SVM models using the newly pooled training sets, we also attempt an incremental learning method based on A-SVM [10]. Results from direct SVM training is indicated by SP, while those from A-SVM is marked by SP-I. Specifically, for SP-I, we use SVM classifiers learnt from SF filtering (without pooling) as original/source models. The models are updated by pooling 1,000 positive samples from child nodes using semantic pooling, and another 1,000 negative examples randomly acquired from Flickr.

We employ Average Precision (AP) to measure the performance of four different approaches. Figure 2 shows the results. SP, with mean AP (MAP) of 0.1774, exhibits better performance than SF (MAP=0.1655) and KW (MAP=0.1536). Among the tested concepts, there are 26 out of 37 concepts where SP shows higher AP than SF, and only 5 concepts suffer from performance degradation after pooling (around 5%). The performance degradation for these concepts is mostly due to different semantic interpretations between human labels and WordNet. For example, the ground-truth labels in NUS-WIDE regard "panda" as a kind of "bear", while in WordNet, "panda" is not a child node of "bear". Also, "beach ball" and "tree house" are two child nodes of "toy" in WordNet, but are rarely labeled as "toy" in NUS-WIDE. From our observation, the coverage and diversity of training examples for most concepts can be largely enhanced by semantic pooling. Figure 3 shows an example for concept "plane". In 3(a), the sampled examples for root node "plane" are mostly in close view and mixed with false positives. The samples from child nodes, as shown in 3(b), offer a more diverse view in terms of visual and semantic aspects. In addition, as the child node concepts are more specific, the chance of sampling false positives is usually lower than that for the parent concepts. As a result, the AP of concept "plane" is significantly boosted to 0.2402 (by SP) from 0.1715 (by SF). SP-I also improves both SF and KW significantly, with an MAP of 0.1744. Comparing SP-I to SP, there is no clear winner between the two. SP-I is computationally more efficient, but is more sensitive to parameter setting simply because it involves a few more parameters.

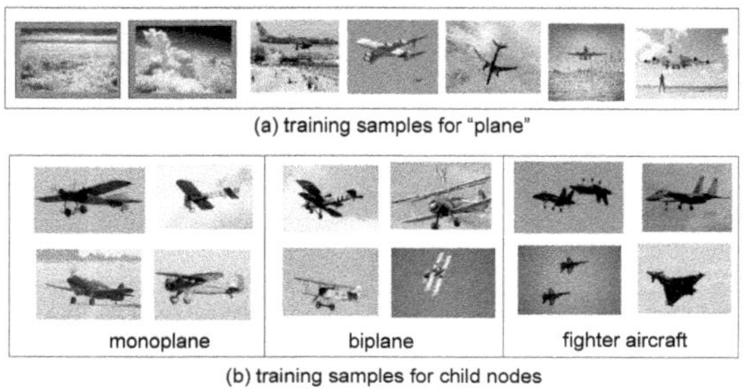

Figure 3: The automatically sampled training examples for "plane" and its child concepts. False positive examples are marked with red boxes.

Comparing our SP result (MAP=0.1774) with the publicly available VIREO-Web81* trained by expert labeled examples (MAP=0.2414) [12], there is still a performance gap. This is not surprising because the NUS-WIDE dataset was constructed two years ago by querying Flickr search engine — images downloaded at the same time may be visually more similar, resulting in the same data distribution (in feature space) between its official training and testing sets. Thus, we believe the performance gap between SP and VIREO-Web81 is partially due to the change of data characteristics of our newly downloaded training images. To verify this, we further conduct another experiment using VOC 2010 dataset. VOC 2010 provides labels for 20 semantic concepts. Among them, 8 concepts overlap with our constructed concept trees and VIREO-Web81. Thus, we evaluate the performance of the 8 concepts on the training set of VOC 2010 which has 10,103 images. Table 1 lists the experimental results. As shown in Table 1, the overall performance of SP (MAP=0.3284) is better than that of VIREO-Web81 (MAP=0.3230). This verifies our suspicion earlier that VIREO-Web81 is good on NUS-WIDE because

*http://vireo.cs.cityu.edu.hk/vireoweb81/

Table 1: Performance comparison of 8 concepts on VOC 2010 dataset.

Concept	SP	SP-I	SF	KW	VIREO-Web81
aeroplane	0.6628	**0.6760**	0.5671	0.4498	0.6519
bird	0.2266	0.2132	0.1924	0.1833	**0.2688**
boat	0.3041	0.3144	0.2461	0.2462	**0.3170**
car	0.3864	**0.4352**	0.3949	0.3274	0.3607
cat	**0.3712**	0.3700	0.3384	0.3253	0.3504
cow	0.1527	0.1344	**0.1630**	0.1556	0.1480
dog	0.3040	**0.3207**	0.3060	0.2706	0.2740
horse	**0.2194**	0.2067	0.1482	0.1513	0.2133
MAP	0.3284	**0.3338**	0.2945	0.2637	0.3230

of data domain over-fitting. In other words, our proposed approach SP is already able to produce training sets comparable to or even better than the expert labeled training sets. In addition, similar to the results on NUS-WIDE, in this experiment we also observe significant performance improvement from SP/SP-I over both SF and KW.

5. CONCLUSIONS

We have presented an ontology-based semantic pooling approach to enrich the coverage and diversity of freely sampled Web images for learning semantic concept detectors. By semantic pooling, consistent performance improvement is observed in our empirical studies on both NUS-WIDE and VOC 2010 datasets. In addition, when discounting the factor due to data distribution shift, the performance of classification models learnt using semantic pooling is comparable to that of detectors trained using expert labeled examples. Currently, we consider only semantic-level ontology for positive sample pooling. Future extension includes the pooling of positive and also negative examples by both semantic and visual co-occurrence relationships.

6. ACKNOWLEDGMENTS

The work described in this paper was fully supported by a grant from the Research Grants Council of the Hong Kong Special Administrative Region, China (CityU 119709).

7. REFERENCES

[1] L. Xie et al. Probabilistic visual concept trees. In *ACM Multimedia*, 2010.

[2] T.-S. Chua et al. NUS-WIDE: A real-world web image database from national university of singapore. In *CIVR*, 2009.

[3] Y.-G. Jiang et al. Representations of keypoint-based semantic concept detection: A comprehensive study. *IEEE Trans. on Multimedia*, 12(1):42–53, 2010.

[4] J. Fan, Y. Shen, N. Zhou, and Y. Gao. Harvesting large-scale weakly-tagged image databases from the web. In *CVPR*, 2010.

[5] R. Fergus, H. Bernal, Y. Weiss, and A. Torralba. Semantic label sharing for learning with many categories. In *ECCV*, 2010.

[6] Y.-G. Jiang, C.-W. Ngo, and S.-F. Chang. Semantic context transfer across heterogeneous sources for domain adaptive video search. In *ACM MM*, 2009.

[7] L.-J. Li and L. Fei-Fei. OPTIMOL: automatic object picture collection via incremental model learning. *Int. J. of Computer Vision*, 2009.

[8] X.-R. Li, C. G. M. Snoek, M. Worring, and A. W.M. Smeulders. Social negative bootstrapping for visual categorization. In *ICMR*, 2011.

[9] B. Settles. Active learning literature survey. Computer Sciences Technical Report 1648, University of Wisconsin–Madison, 2009.

[10] J. Yang, R. Yan, and A. G. Hauptmann. Cross-domain video concept detection using adaptive svms. In *ACM Multimedia*, 2007.

[11] W. Zhibiao and M. Palmer. Verb semantic and lexical selection. In *ACL*, 1994.

[12] S. Zhu, G. Wang, C.-W. Ngo, and Y.-G. Jiang. On the sampling of web images for learning visual concept classifiers. In *CIVR*, 2010.

Saliency-based Image Retargeting in the Compressed Domain*

Yuming Fang
School of Computer Engineering, Nanyang Technological University, Singapore
fa0001ng@e.ntu.edu.sg

Zhenzhong Chen
School of Electrical and Electronic Engineering, Nanyang Technological University, Singapore
zzchen@ntu.edu.sg

Weisi Lin⋆
School of Computer Engineering,Nanyang Technological University, Singapore
wslin@ntu.edu.sg

Chia-Wen Lin
Department of Electrical Engineering, National Tsing Hua University, Taiwan R.O.C
cwlin@ee.nthu.edu.tw

ABSTRACT

In this paper, we propose a novel image retargeting algorithm to resize images based on the extracted saliency information from the compressed domain. Firstly, we utilize DCT coefficients in JPEG bitstream to perform saliency detection with the consideration of the human visual sensitivity. The obtained saliency information is used to determine the relative visual importance of each 8×8 block for the image. Furthermore, we propose a new adaptive block-level seam removal operation for connected blocks to resize the image. Thanks to the directly derived saliency information from the compressed domain, the proposed image retargeting algorithm effectively preserves the objects of attention, efficiently removes the less crucial regions, and therefore significantly outperforms the relevant state-of-the-art algorithms, as demonstrated with the careful analysis and in the extensive experiments.

Categories and Subject Descriptors

I.4 [**Image Processing and Computer Vision**]: General—*image displays*

General Terms

Algorithms

Keywords

Image retargeting, saliency detection, human visual sensitivity, compressed domain

*Area chair: Lei Chen.
⋆Corresponding author.

1. INTRODUCTION

The content-aware image retargeting algorithms such as seam carving are popular and effective in resizing images. The performance for these algorithms greatly depends on the used visual significance maps which measure the visual importance for image pixels. The visual significance maps used in these algorithms include the gradient map, the saliency map and some high-level feature maps such as facial map, motion map and so on [1-6]. These existing image retargeting algorithms are implemented in the uncompressed domain. However, images are typically stored in a compressed domain such as JPEG. Thus, it is crucial to design an efficient image retargeting algorithm in the compressed domain.

In this paper, we propose a saliency-based image retargeting algorithm in the compressed domain. Firstly, we use DCT coefficients in the JPEG bitstream to obtain the saliency information with the consideration of the human visual sensitivity. In JPEG, an image is split into blocks of 8×8 pixels. Although the minimum coded unit (MCU) blocks can be as large as 16×16 (for 4:2:0 component subsampling format), we perform our saliency detection and retargeting at the 8×8 block level. After obtaining the saliency information, we determine the visual importance of each 8×8 block in the image. Based on the visual significance map, we design an adaptive seam removal approach for connected blocks to resize the image. Experimental results show the superior performance of the proposed saliency detection as well as image retargeting.

2. BACKGROUND AND MOTIVATIONS

The popular image retargeting algorithm of seam carving was proposed by Avidan *et al.* [1]. A seam is defined as 8-connected patch of low-energy pixels (from top to bottom or left to right) in images. These pixels include only one pixel in each row or column. The seam carving aims to reduce the width (or weight) by removing those unimportant seams. The visual importance map is used to determine the importance of each pixel in images. Based on seam carving, many other algorithms have been proposed to improve the performance for image retargeting [2,3].

Other advanced image retargeting algorithms have also been proposed. Wolf *et al.* [4] designed a video retargeting algorithm to resize videos by using the visual importance

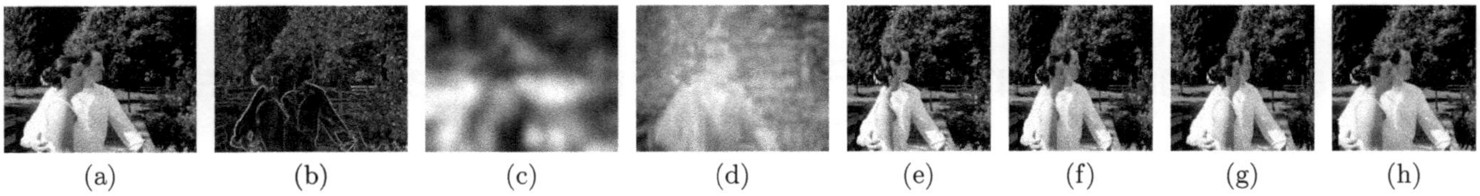

Figure 1: Comparisons of different image retargeting algorithms: (a) the original image; (b) the gradient map; (c) the saliency map from Itti's model [8]; (d) the saliency map from our proposed model; (e)-(h) the retargeted images from [2],[4],[5] and our proposed algorithm.

map composed of local saliency, face detection and motion detection. Ren *et al.* [5] proposed an image reatargeting algorithm based on global energy optimization, in which the saliency map and face detection were combined as the visual importance map. Jin *et al.* [6] presented a content-aware image resizing algorithm through warping a triangular mesh over images by regarding salient line features and curved features as important regions.

In this paper, we build a superior saliency detection model in the compressed domain to obtain the saliency map, which is used as the visual significance map for the proposed image retargeting. Thanks to the directly derived saliency map from the compressed domain, the proposed algorithm effectively preserves the objects of attention and remove the less crucial regions, as shown in Figure 1. From Figure 1, we can see our saliency map can detect the salient object more accurately than the gradient map and the saliency map from Itt's model [8]. More information and comparisons will be provided in the following sections.

3. THE FRAMEWORK

The proposed approach consists of two aspects. First, we propose a saliency detection model in the compressed domain, which is used to obtain the saliency map to measure the visual importance of each block in JPEG images. Second, based on the saliency detection in the compressed domain, we design a new block-level seam carving operation for connected blocks to resize JPEG images.

3.1 Saliency Detection in the Compressed Domain

Images are usually stored in a compressed domain such as JPEG. In this study, the saliency information is derived from the JPEG bitstream. The saliency detection model is built on the DCT coefficients with the consideration of the human visual sensitivity. The saliency value from feature k for each block S_i^k is determined by the differences between the block i and others in the image, and the weighting factors for these differences by the contrast sensitivities.

$$S_i^k = \sum_{j \neq i} \alpha_{ij} D_{ij}^k \tag{1}$$

where S_i^k is the saliency value from feature k for the block i; D_{ij}^k is the difference of feature k between the blocks i and j; α_{ij} is the weighting for the block difference D_{ij}^k. We use three features extracted from the JPEG bitstream to calculate the saliency values: intensity, color and orientation. The final saliency map is a combination of these feature maps.

3.1.1 Feature Extraction from JPEG Bitstream

In this study, we extract features from DCT coefficients. The DCT coefficients in one block are shown as Figure 2.

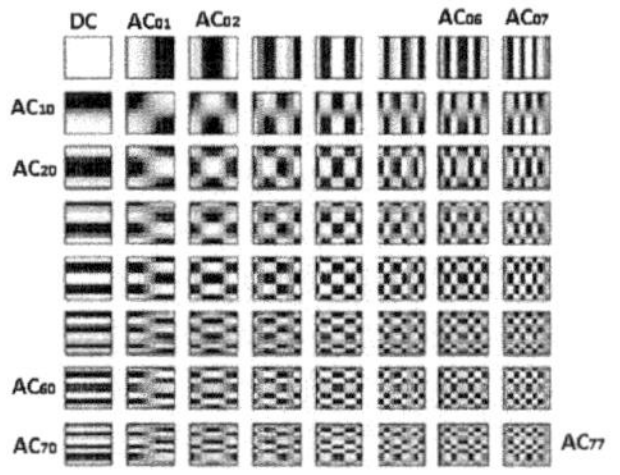

Figure 2: DCT coefficients in one 8×8 block.

DCT coefficients in one block are composed of the DC coefficient and AC coefficients. In this block, the DC coefficient is a measure of the average energy for the 8×8 pixels, while AC coefficients can represent the orientation information for this block. Thus, we use the DC coefficient to extract the intensity and color features for the block, and use the AC coefficients to extract the orientation feature of the block in the JPEG image.

Since the DC coefficients represent the Luminance and Chrominance information in YCrCb color space in the JPEG image, we firstly transfer the DC coefficients from YCrCb color space to the RGB color space to extract the intensity and color features for the JPEG image. We calculate the color and intensity features by following steps: let r, g and b denote the red, green and blue color components from DC coefficients, and four broadly-tuned color channels are generated as $R = r - (g + b)$ for new red component, $G = g - (r + b)/2$ for new green component, $B = b - (r + g)/2$ for new blue component and $Y = (r + g)/2 - |r - b|/2 - b$ for new yellow component. The intensity feature can be calculated as $I = (r + g + b)/3$. Each color channel is then decomposed into red/green and blue/yellow double opponency according to the related property of the human primary visual cortex [7, 8]: $C_{rg} = R - G$ and $C_{by} = B - Y$. I, C_{rg} and C_{by} are the extracted intensity and color features for an 8×8 block in the JPEG image. It is noted that a 16×16 MCU consists of four 8×8 Luminance blocks and two 8×8 Chrominance blocks (one for Cb and the other for Cr). Thus, four Luminance blocks share the same Chrominance blocks in a typical 4:2:0 component subsampling JPEG encoding system.

We use the AC coefficients in YCrCb color space to extract the orientation for each block. In YCrCb color space, Cr and Cb components represent the color information and their AC coefficients provide little information for orientation. Thus we use the AC coefficients of the Y component only to extract the orientation feature O. The AC coefficients used in this paper include the AC coefficients in the first row and first column in Figure 2: $O = AC_{0i} \bigcup AC_{i0} (i \in 1, 2 \ldots 6, 7)$.

3.1.2 Feature Maps in the Compressed Domain

In the next step, we use the intensity, color and orientation features to obtain the feature maps. Since we use the DC coefficients to calculate the intensity and color features for each block, the feature difference between blocks i and j can be calculated as:

$$D_{ij}^k = \mathfrak{C}_i^k - \mathfrak{C}_j^k \tag{2}$$

where $k = 1, 2, 3$ represent the intensity and color features respectively (one intensity feature and two color features); $\mathfrak{C}^k \in \{I, C_{rg}, C_{by}\}$.

As mentioned above, we use AC coefficients from the Luminance block to represent the orientation feature for each block in the JPEG image. The Hausdorff distance [9] is used here to calculate the difference between two AC coefficient vectors from two different blocks. The orientation difference D_{ij}^4 between two blocks i and j can be computed as follows:

$$D_{ij}^4 = \max(h(O_i, O_j), h(O_j, O_i)) \tag{3}$$

where O_i and O_j represent the AC coefficient vectors for blocks i and j, respectively. $h(O_i, O_j)$ is calculated as:

$$h(O_i, O_j) = \max_{o_i \epsilon O_i} \min_{o_j \epsilon O_j} \parallel o_i - o_j \parallel \tag{4}$$

where $\parallel . \parallel$ is the L2 norm.

We further propose to use the visual sensitivity to determine the weights for these feature differences. The model in [10] is adopted to measure the human contrast sensitivity as a function of eccentricity. The contrast sensitivity $C_S(f, e)$ is defined as:

$$C_s(f, e) = 1/(C_0 \exp(af(e + e_2)/e_2)) \tag{5}$$

where f is the spatial frequency (cycles/degree); e is the retinal eccentricity (degree) between blocks i and j; C_0 is the minimum contrast threshold; a is the spatial frequency decay constant; e_2 is the half-resolution eccentricity. Based on the study in [10], these parameters are set to $C_0 = 1/64$, $a = 0.106$, and $e_2 = 2.3$.

We let $a_{ij} = C_s(f, e)$ to represent the weights for the differences between blocks. According to (5), the weighting a_{ij} is dependent on the retinal eccentricity between blocks i and j. The weighting factor becomes smaller with increased retinal eccentricity from the block i that results in less contribution from D_{ij} in the final saliency value in (1).

3.1.3 *Saliency Map*

After obtaining the four feature maps S^k, the final saliency map for the JPEG image can be obtained by integrating these feature maps. According to (1), the four feature maps S^k can be calculated based on the D_{ij}^k ($k \in \{1, 2, 3, 4\}$) and a_{ij} in (2), (3) and (5). We use the coherent normalization based fusion method to combine these four feature maps into the final saliency map $\mathbb{S}$ as follows:

$$\mathbb{S} = \sum \gamma_\theta N_{(\theta)} + \prod \beta_\theta N_{(\theta)} \tag{6}$$

where N is the normalization operation; $\theta \in \{\mathrm{S}^k\}$; γ and β are parameters determining the weights for each components in (6). In this paper, we set $\gamma_\theta = \beta_\theta = 1/5$.

3.2 Block-based Seam Removal Operation

As we use the blocks with size of 8×8 to calculate the saliency map, the saliency map is only $1/64$ times of the original image and each value in the final saliency map represent the saliency value for one 8×8 block. When compared to traditional retargeting algorithms operating on the original

Figure 3: Comparisons of different image retargeting algorithms. The first column: the original images; The second to fifth columns: the retargeted images from [2], [4], [5], and our proposed algorithms.

size saliency map, the computational cost is much lower on the smaller saliency map. Moreover, we propose a block-based seam removal operation for resizing the JPEG image. Here we use the 'forward energy' method [2] in seam carving to determine the optimal seam. It is noted that since our saliency map is at block-level, each seam indicates connected blocks instead of connected pixels in the original image.

To reduce the block artifacts, we propose a new method to adaptively determine how many parallel strips in the block-level seams should be removed (8 strips in each 8-pixel wide block-level seam). As the optimal block-level seams are chosen according to their visual importance, the firstly chosen removal block-level seams are the least important areas in images. Therefore, we remove the the whole 8 strips for the block-level seams first. Then for other 8-pixel wide block-level seams, we remove part of them (less than 8 strips) according to their increased visual importance. So four different seam removal operations, i.e., remove 8, 6, 4, and 2 strips, are defined. The amount of removal block-level seams for each operation is determined as follows.

$$n = \arg\min_i(|R_i - T_m|) \tag{7}$$

where $m \in \{1, 2, 3, 4\}$ denotes the operation to remove 8, 6, 4, and 2 strips for the block-level seams; n is the amount of the removal block-level seams in the mth operation; N is the total amount of the removal block-level seams; R_i is the mean saliency value for the ith block-level seam; T_m is the threshold for the mth operation. With the superior saliency

Table 1: Comparisons of different saliency detection models.

Models	Precision	Recall	F-Measure
Hou's Model [12]	0.6152	0.2944	0.4916
Achanta's Model [13]	0.5450	0.3006	0.4288
Itti's Model [8]	0.5916	0.3784	0.4981
Our Model	0.6571	0.5961	0.6354

detection model, the artifacts are not obvious as they are typically located away from regions of attention, where the visual sensitivity is low.

4. EXPERIMENTS

In this section, we evaluate the overall performance of the proposed approach from two aspects: one is the performance of the proposed saliency detection algorithm, the other is the performance of the proposed image retargeting algorithm in resizing images.

4.1 Saliency Detection Evaluation

The performance of most existing image retargeting algorithms depends on the adopted visual significance maps which should be able to indicate the salient regions in images effectively, as demonstrated in Figure 1. In this experiment, we randomly select 500 images from the image database [11] to compare the performance of the saliency map from our proposed model with those from other existing saliency detection models [8, 12, 13]. The salient objects in the ground-truth maps are remarked by bounding boxes in this database. Similar with [11], we use precision, recall and F-measure to compare the performance of different saliency detection algorithms. Table 1 shows the comparison results in which we can see that the precision, recall and F-measure values from our saliency detection algorithm are higher than these from other algorithms. Our saliency detection algorithm in the compressed domain shows superior performance.

4.2 Image Retargeting Evaluation

In this experiment, we use the same 500 images to evaluate the performance of our proposed image retargeting algorithm. Three state-of-the-art image retargeting algorithms [2, 4, 5] are adopted for comparions. Some visual results are shown in Figure 3. We can observe that the retargeted images from our proposed algorithm are better than those from other existing algorithms.

The user study is performed to evaluate the performance of different algorithms. 10 participants (3 are female while others are male) involve in this experiment. The 500 original images are used as reference images. The experiments are conducted in the typical laboratory environment. All retargeted images from four different algorithms are displayed in the random order on the screen. Mean opinion scores (1-5) are recorded by participants where 1 means bad viewing experience and 5 means excellent viewing experience. Each participant votes for 50 images. The statistical results for the retargeted images are shown in Table 2. We can see that the mean score of the retargeted images from our proposed algorithm is higher than those from other algorithms. In Figure 4, we presents the number of the retargeted images under each score. Most of the retargeted images from our proposed algorithm provide better viewing experience for users.

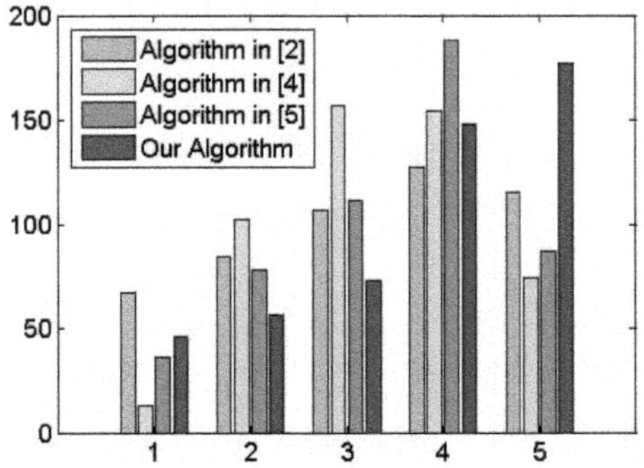

Figure 4: Score comparisons of retargeted images from different algorithms.

Table 2: Mean scores for the 500 retargeted images from different algorithms.

	[2]	[4]	[5]	Our Algorithm
Mean	3.278	3.348	3.424	3.708

5. CONCLUSIONS

In this paper, we have proposed a saliency-based image reatargeting algorithm in the compressed domain. We demonstrate the effectiveness of our novel saliency detection algorithm. Moreover, we propose a new block-based operation for resizing JPEG images. The user-study experiment shows that the proposed algorithm can obtain better results compared with existing ones in retargeting images.

6. REFERENCES

[1] S. Avidan, and A. Shamir. Seam carving for content-aware image resizing. *ACM TOG*, 26(3), 2007.

[2] M. Rubinstein, A. Shamir, and S. Avidan. Improved seam carving for video retargeting. *ACM TOG*, 2008.

[3] R. Achanta, and S. Susstrunk. Saliency detection for content-aware image resizing. *In ICIP*, 2009.

[4] L. Wolf, M. Guttmann, and D. Cohen-OR. Non-homogeneous content-driven video retargeting. *In ICCV*, 2007.

[5] T. Ren, Y. Liu, and G. Wu. Image retargeting based on global energy optimization. *In ICME*, 2009.

[6] Y. Jin, L. Liu, and Q. Wu. Nonhomogeneous scaling optimization for realtime image resizing. *In CGI*, 2010.

[7] S. Engel, X. Zhang, and B. Wandell. Colour tuning in human visual cortex measured with functional magnetic resonance imaging. *Nature*, 388(6), 1997.

[8] L. Itti, C. Koch, and E. Niebur. A model of saliency-based visual attention for rapid scene analysis. *IEEE TPAMI*, 20(11), 1998.

[9] R. T. Rockafellar, and R. J.-B. Wets. *Variational Analysis*. Springer-Verlag, 2005.

[10] W. S. Geisler, and J. S. Perry. A real-time foveated multi-solution system for low-bandwidth video communication. *SPIE*, 3299, 1998.

[11] T. Liu, J. Sun, N. Zheng, X. Tang, and H. Y. Shum. Learning to detect a salient object. *In CVPR*, 2007.

[12] X. Hou and L. Zhang. Saliency detection: a spectral residual approach. *In CVPR*, 2007.

[13] R. Achanta, S. Hemami, F. Estrada and S. Susstrunk. Frequency-tuned salient region detection. *In CVPR*, 2009.

Mining Concept Relationship in Temporal Context for Effective Video Annotation*

Jian Yi, Yuxin Peng† and Jianguo Xiao
Institute of Computer Science and Technology, Peking University
Beijing 100871, China
{yijian, pengyuxin, xjg}@icst.pku.edu.cn

ABSTRACT

We propose a new method to boost the performance of video annotation by exploiting concept relationship in temporal context. The motivation of our idea mainly comes from the fact that temporally continuous shots in video are generally with consistent content, so that concepts in these shots should be semantically relevant. We utilize a temporal model to describe the contributions of relevant concepts to the presence of a target concept. By connecting our model with conditional random field and adopting the learning and inference approaches of it, we could obtain the refined probability of a concept occurring in the shot, which is the leverage of temporal context and initial output of video annotation. Experimental results on the widely used TRECVID dataset exhibit the effectiveness of our method for improving video annotation accuracy.

Categories and Subject Descriptors

H.3.1 [**Information Storage and Retrieval**]: Content Analysis and Indexing—*indexing methods*

General Terms

Algorithms, Experimentation, Theory

Keywords

Video annotation, Context mining, Conditional random field

1. INTRODUCTION

In video annotation, concepts existing in video are not independent, but have relationship with each other, so that the performance of video annotation can be comparatively boosted by mining the concept relationship in video context. Generally, there are two kinds of contexts in video: Spacial context and temporal context. Spacial context describes relationship between concepts within a single shot, and temporal context describes relationship between concepts in different shots which are temporally continuous. In recent years, many works have been done for exploiting context information to improve the performance of video annotation. However, most of these works mainly concentrate on the spacial context [2, 3], and less works have been done for temporal context exploitation [10, 6, 5, 8]. Therefore, to fully use the context information in video and achieve better performance of video annotation, we mainly focus on the exploitation of temporal context in this paper.

In existing works for temporal context mining, Qi et al. [6] integrated a temporal kernel into Correlative Multi-Label (CML) framework to mine the rich temporal information in video. Computational cost could be a problem for this method when the number of concepts became large. In [10], Yang and Hauptmann used active learning with temporal sampling strategies to improve the accuracy of concept detectors. However, their smoothed score of a shot was simply a weighted combination of likelihood scores of three neighboring shots. Liu et al. [5] proposed an approach to generate probabilistic rules according to discovered temporal co-occurrence patterns. Weng et al. [8] utilized a recursive algorithm to learn temporal relationships from ground truth annotations. This method mainly focused on the consistent relationship between concepts in shots, but did not directly consider relationship between relevant concepts. To achieve better performance, our previous work [11] roughly classified video shots into four types according to their contained concepts, and encoded the temporal context information into the dependency of different shot types. This method treated all relevant concepts of target concept equally and model temporal context in shot level, which could not distinguish concepts having different contributions to the presence of target concept.

Based on the above considerations, we propose a novel temporal context model to improve the accuracy of video annotation, which could describe the contribution each relevant concept to a target concept. By connecting our model with conditional random field and adopting the learning and inference approaches of it, we could obtain the refined probability of a concept occurring in the shot, which is the leverage of temporal context information and initial output of video annotation, achieving impressive results.

2. OUR METHOD

The task of video annotation is to give each shot a prediction probability for each concept to be annotated. And we call this prediction probability as initial probability. However, it is difficult for many concepts to be annotated solely by these methods. As a result, the initial probability of video annotation is not always reliable. Therefore, to improve the video annotation accuracy, we turn to the temporal context mining in video, which is the main work of this paper. Our method for temporal context mining mainly contains two phases: training phase and inference

---

*Area chair: Lei Chen.
†Corresponding author.

MM'11, November 28–December 1, 2011, Scottsdale, Arizona, USA.

phase. In learning phase, we train a model of temporal context to capture relationship between concepts in different shots. In inference phase, we input the initial probability of test set into temporal context model to obtain the refined probability. Before describing our method, we firstly clarify the following notations: (1)$S = \{s_i\}, (1 \leq i \leq n)$ are the shots in video, n is the number of shots. The indices of the shots are assigned according to their temporal order in a video; (2)$Y = \{y_i^j\}, (1 \leq i \leq n, 1 \leq j \leq m)$ are the concept labels of S. y_i^j is the label of shot s_i for concept c_j. $y_i^j = 1$ denotes the presence of concept c_j in shot s_i, and otherwise $y_i^j = 0$. m is the number of concepts in the semantic lexicon; (3)$X = \{x_i^j\}, (1 \leq i \leq n, 1 \leq j \leq m)$ are the initial probabilities outputted the concept detectors in video annotation. $x_i^j =< p_i^j, \bar{p}_i^j >$ is the initial probability of shot s_i for concept c_j. p_i^j is the initial probability of labeling s_i with c_j, and $\bar{p}_i^j = 1 - p_i^j$.

2.1 Temporal Context Model

Let c_j be the target concept. Temporal context model for concept c_j is given as $M_j = \{\lambda^{j,k}\}, (c_k \in REL_j)$. REL_j is the set that contains the K concepts having the largest values of normalized mutual information ($NormMI$) [6] with c_j. In the experiments, we set K to be 5 by experience. Below gives the explanations:

- $\lambda^{j,k} =< \lambda^{j,k}_{l,l',h,1}, \lambda^{j,k}_{l,l',h,2} >, (l, l', h \in \{0,1\})$ could be explained as the relationship between initial probabilities of video annotation and concept label assignments in temporally continuous shots. $\lambda^{j,k}_{l,l',h,1}$ measures the contribution of initial probability $x_i^k =< p_i^k, \bar{p}_i^k >$ to the label assignments of $y_i^j = l$ and $y_{i+1}^j = l'$, and $\lambda^{j,k}_{l,l',h,2}$ measures the contribution of initial probability $x_{i+1}^j =< p_{i+1}^k, \bar{p}_{i+1}^k >$ to the label assignments of $y_i^j = l$ and $y_{i+1}^j = l'$ $(1 \leq i \leq n-1)$. x_i^k and x_{i+1}^k are the initial probabilities of shots s_i and s_{i+1} for concept c_k. y_i^j and y_{i+1}^j are labels of shots s_i and s_{i+1} for concept c_j. l, l' in $\lambda^{j,k}_{l,l',h,1}$ and $\lambda^{j,k}_{l,l',h,2}$ are the assigned values to y_i^j and y_{i+1}^j. h in $\lambda^{j,k}_{l,l',h,1}$ indicates the contribution is from initial probability p_i^k or $\bar{p}_i^k$, and h in $\lambda^{j,k}_{l,l',h,2}$ indicates the contribution is from the initial probability p_{i+1}^k or $\bar{p}_{i+1}^k$. Larger value of $\lambda^{j,k}_{l,l',h,1}$ ($\lambda^{j,k}_{l,l',h,2}$) means x_i^k (x_{i+1}^k) has a larger contribution to the assignments of $y_i^j = l$ and $y_{i+1}^j = l'$. For example, $\lambda^{j,k}_{l=1,l'=1,h=1,1}$ measures the contribution of initial probability p_i^k to the label assignments of $y_i^j = 1$ and $y_{i+1}^j = 1$ for shots s_i and s_{i+1}. Assuming concept c_j is "outdoor", and c_k is "road", $\lambda^{j,k}_{l=1,l'=1,h=1,1}$ measures how much the initial probability of s_i for concept "road" will contribute to the presence of "outdoor" in s_i and s_{i+1}.

Then we define a linear discriminative function based on M_j:

$$D(X,Y;M_j) = \sum_{i=1}^{n} \alpha(x_i^j, y_i^j) + \sum_{i=1}^{n-1} \sum_{c_k \in REL_j} < \theta(x_i^k, x_{i+1}^k, y_i^j, y_{i+1}^j), \lambda^{j,k} > \quad (1)$$

After the model $M_j = \{\lambda^{j,k}\}$ is learned from the training set, label vector Y^* can be obtained by maximizing over the argument Y as:

$$Y^* = \max_{Y} D(X,Y;M_j) \quad (2)$$

Inspecting the right part of Equ.1, the first item considers the relationship between initial probabilities of video annotation and concept label assignments within a single shot; The second item considers relationship between the initial probabilities of video annotation and concept label assignments in temporal context. The more appropriate the label assignments are, the larger value the two items have. $\alpha(x_i^j, y_i^j)$ and $\theta(x_i^j, x_{i+1}^k, y_i^j, y_{i+1}^k)$ in Equ.1 are two vectors. Follows give the definitions:

- Elements of $\alpha(x_i^j, y_i^j) =< \alpha_{l,h}(x_i^j, y_i^j) >$:

$$\begin{aligned} &\alpha_{l,h}(x_i^j, y_i^j) = \\ &p_i^j \cdot \delta(h=1) \cdot \delta(y_i^j = l) + \bar{p}_i^j \cdot \delta(h=0) \cdot \delta(y_i^j = l) \\ &l, h \in \{0,1\} \end{aligned} \quad (3)$$

  where $\delta(.)$ is an indicator function that takes on value 1 if the declared condition is true. These elements are used to model the connection between initial probability and the concept label. h in $\alpha_{l,h}$ is used to select p_i^j or $\bar{p}_i^j$ in Equ.3, and l is the value of label y_i^j.

- Elements of $\theta(x_i^k, x_{i+1}^k, y_i^j, y_{i+1}^j) = < \theta_{l,l',h,1}(x_i^k, y_i^j, y_{i+1}^j), \theta_{l,l',h,2}(x_{i+1}^k, y_i^j, y_{i+1}^j) >$:

$$\begin{aligned} &\theta_{l,l',h,1}(x_i^k, y_i^j, y_{i+1}^j) = \\ &p_i^k \cdot \delta(1=h)\delta(y_i^j = l)\delta(y_{i+1}^j = l') + \\ &\bar{p}_i^k \cdot \delta(0=h)\delta(y_i^j = l)\delta(y_{i+1}^j = l') \\ &l, l', h \in \{0,1\} \end{aligned} \quad (4)$$

$$\begin{aligned} &\theta_{l,l',h,2}(x_{i+1}^k, y_i^j, y_{i+1}^j) = \\ &p_{i+1}^k \cdot \delta(1=h)\delta(y_i^j = l)\delta(y_{i+1}^j = l') + \\ &\bar{p}_{i+1}^k \cdot \delta(0=h)\delta(y_i^j = l)\delta(y_{i+1}^j = l') \\ &l, l', h \in \{0,1\} \end{aligned} \quad (5)$$

  These elements sever to model relationship between the initial probability of video annotation and concept label in temporal context. $< \theta(x_i^k, x_{i+1}^k, y_i^j, y_{i+1}^j), \lambda^{j,k} >$ is the inner product of $\theta(x_i^k, x_{i+1}^k, y_i^j, y_{i+1}^j)$ and $\lambda^{j,k}$ as follows:

$$\begin{aligned} &< \theta(x_i^k, x_{i+1}^k, y_i^j, y_{i+1}^j), \lambda^{j,k} >= \\ &\sum \theta_{l,l',h,1}(x_i^k, y_i^j, y_{i+1}^j) \cdot \lambda^{j,k}_{l,l',h,1} + \\ &\sum \theta_{l,l',h,2}(x_{i+1}^k, y_i^j, y_{i+1}^j) \cdot \lambda^{j,k}_{l,l',h,2} \\ &l, l', h \in \{0,1\} \end{aligned} \quad (6)$$

After the above discriminative function is given, our task is to learn the parameters $M_j = \{\lambda^{j,k}\}, (c_k \in REL_j)$ from the training set, and predict the optimal probability of labeling shots with the target concept c_j. We will explain our model through a conditional random field, from which we could borrow some effective approaches for learning and inference to solve this problem.

2.2 Connecting Our Model with CRF

This section gives an intuitive explanation of our idea for temporal context modeling of the target concept c_j through a conditional random field (CRF) with chain structure as shown in Fig.1, which has been proposed in [4] to solve the problem of sequence labeling. Let $G = \{V, E\}$ denote this graph. G mainly consists of two parts: site set V and edge set E. In $V = \{v_i^j\}, (1 \leq i \leq n)$, v_i^j models concept c_j in shot s_i. n is the number of shots in video. In $E = \{e_{i,i+1}^j\}, (1 \leq i \leq n-1)$, $e_{i,i+1}^j$ models temporal context of c_j between s_i and s_{i+1}. Respecting to the graph in Fig.1, we

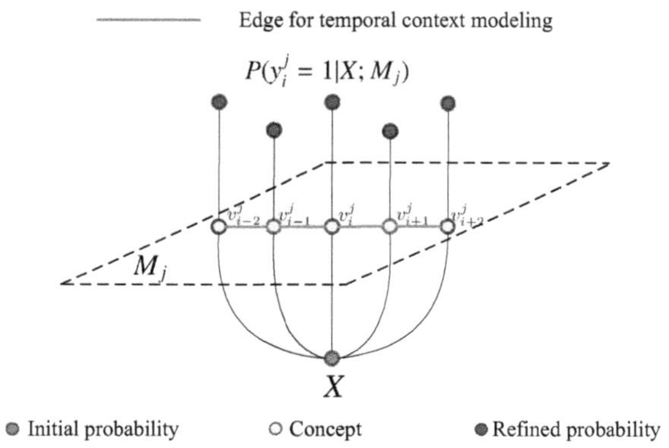

Figure 1: Chain structure graph of CRF to explain our temporal context model.

could give the conditional probability distribution over Y given X as follows:

$$P(Y|X; M_j) = \frac{1}{Z} exp(\sum_{i=1}^{n} A(x_i^j, y_i^j) + \sum_{i=1}^{n-1} I(\bar{x}_{i,i+1}^j, y_i^j, y_{i+1}^j; M_j)) \quad (7)$$

$\bar{x}_{i,i+1}^j = < x_i^k, x_{i+1}^k > (c_k \in REL_j)$ is the observed feature for edge $e_{i,i+1}^j$, integrating temporal context information. A models the dependency between initial probability and concept labels and I models temporal context.Then we give the definitions of A and I:

$$A(x_i^j, y_i^j) = \alpha(x_i^j, y_i^j)$$
$$I(\bar{x}_{i,i+1}^j, y_i^j, y_{i+1}^j, M_j) = \sum_{c_k \in REL_j} < \theta(x_i^k, x_{i+1}^k, y_i^j, y_{i+1}^j), \lambda^{j,k} > \quad (8)$$

where $\alpha(x_i^j, y_i^j)$ and $< \theta(x_i^k, x_{i+1}^k, y_i^j, y_{i+1}^j), \lambda^{j,k} >$ have been given in previous sections. Inspecting Equs 1, 7 and 8, we have:

$$P(Y|X; M_j) = \frac{1}{Z} exp(D(Y|X; M_j)) \quad (9)$$

It can be easily seen that inferring the best label vector Y, maximizing $P(Y|X; M_j)$ according to Maximum A Posteriori Probability (MAP) criterion is equal to maximizing $D(Y|X; M_j)$. Therefore, our model is essentially equivalent to the CRF based on the graph structure in Fig.1, and could be explained by it.

2.3 Learning and Inference

Learning: Given T videos with manual labels for training, denoted as $\{X_t, Y_t\}_{t=1}^T$, parameters of the above M_j, i.e. $\lambda^{j,k} =< \lambda_{l,l',h,1}^{j,k}, \lambda_{l,l',h,2}^{j,k} >$ could be learned by maximizing the log-likelihood of the given videos with respect to the conditional probability distribution:

$$\mathcal{L}(M_j) = \sum_{t=1}^{T} log(P(Y_t|X_t; M_j)) = \sum_{t=1}^{T}(\sum_{i=1}^{n_t} \alpha(x_i^j, y_i^j) + \sum_{i=1}^{n_t-1} \sum_{c_k \in REL_j} < \theta(x_i^k, x_{i+1}^k, y_i^j, y_{i+1}^j), \lambda^{j,k} > -logZ_t) \quad (10)$$

Below gives derivative of log-likelihood with respect to $\lambda_{l,l',h,1}^{j,k}$ and $\lambda_{l,l',h,2}^{j,k}$:

$$\partial\mathcal{L}/\partial\lambda_{l,l',h,1}^{j,k} = E_{\bar{P}(X,Y)}[\theta_{l,l',h,1}(x_i^k, y_i^j, y_{i+1}^j)] - \sum_{t=1}^{T} E_{P(Y|X_t)}[\theta_{l,l',h,1}(x_i^k, y_i^j, y_{i+1}^j)]$$
$$l, l', h \in \{0, 1\} \quad (11)$$

$$\partial\mathcal{L}/\partial\lambda_{l,l',h,2}^{j,k} = E_{\bar{P}(X,Y)}[\theta_{l,l',h,2}(x_{i+1}^k, y_i^j, y_{i+1}^j)] - \sum_{t=1}^{T} E_{P(Y|X_t)}[\theta_{l,l',h,2}(x_{i+1}^k, y_i^j, y_{i+1}^j)]$$
$$l, l', h \in \{0, 1\} \quad (12)$$

where $E_{\bar{P}(X,Y)}[\cdot]$ is the expectation with respect to the empirical distribution and $E_{P(Y|X)}[\cdot]$ is the expectation with respect to the conditional model distribution. Due to the combinatorial property of partition function Z, exact computation of marginal probability is problematic even for problems of moderate size. Various approximate inference algorithms, e.g., Markov Chain Monte Carlo (MCMC), loopy belief propagation (LBP) and mean field (MF), can be used to obtain the approximate marginal probabilities. We adopt mean field (MF) to calculate the approximate gradients and choose L-BFGS algorithm to maximize the log-likelihood because of their recent empirical success in training CRFs [13].

Inference: To refine the initial probability of video annotation, we input the initial probability X of the test set into the learned model, which could output marginal probability $P(y_i^j = 1|X; M_j)$ as the refined probability of labeling shot s_i with c_j by temporal context mining, using the inference method of CRF.

3. EXPERIMENTS AND RESULTS

3.1 Experimental Settings

To evaluate the performance of the proposed methods, we conduct our experiments on TRECVID 2006 data set [7]. The development set consists of 85 hours broadcast news video sources in Arabic, Chinese and English, including 137 videos with 43907 shots. We adopt the annotations of this development set from Columbia-374 [9], which has a lexicon of 374 semantic concepts. The test set contains 259 videos with 79484 shots. We adopt two popular sets of detection scores of 374 LSCOM concepts for refining: VIREO-374 [1] and Columbia-374 [9], both contain detectors for 374 concepts, and also supply the prediction results of the 374 concepts on TRECVID 2006 data set, including development and test set. By applying our method to these two baselines, we can evaluate the performance of our method for context mining. With the same setting as TRECVID 2006, we evaluate performance on the 20 officially selected concepts and use the mean inferred average precision (infAP) [12] as the metrics.

3.2 Experimental Results

Here we use the whole development set for training temporal context model, and evaluate results on the test set. The video annotation results of the baselines are refined using ours, Liu's [5], Weng's [8], and our previous [11] methods for temporal context mining respectively. As shown in Table 1, our method outperforms the existing methods with a 46.4% relative performance gain on the Columbia-374 baseline, and a 21.1% relative gain on the VIREO-374 baseline. The main reasons for this improvement are as follows. Comparing our method with Liu's approach, our method

Table 1: **Summary of overall performance gains on baseline using temporal context mining, compared with Liu's [5], Weng's [8], and our previous [11] methods.**

	Baseline	Columbia-374	VIREO-374
	Mean InfAP	0.0948	0.1542
Gains	Liu's method [5]	+16.9%	+10.6%
	Weng's method [8]	+17.3%	+14.6%
	Yi's method [11]	+32.1%	+18.9%
	Our method	+46.4%	+21.1%

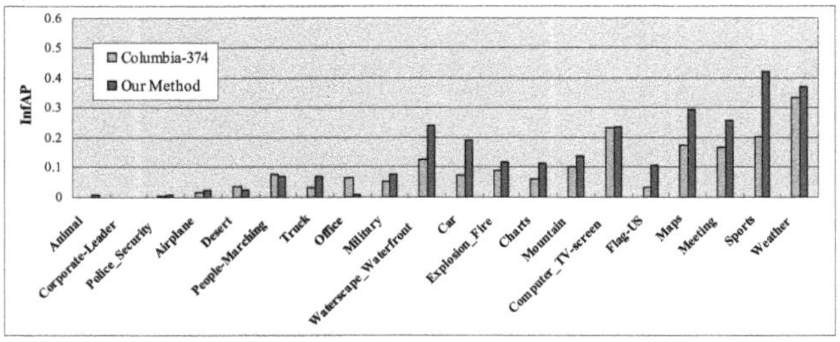

Figure 2: InfAP for 20 concepts in the official evaluation of TRECVID2006 benchmark, using our method for temporal context mining on Columbia-374 baseline.

could get optimal marginal probability by connecting our model with CRF. However, the approach in [5] had the problem that the prediction scores of detectors are directly used to infer the fused score, instead of using the optimal ones. Weng's method [8] mainly focused on the consistent relationship in temporal context, but did not consider directly relationship between relevant concepts. And our previous method [11] roughly classified shots into different types according to the contained concepts in shot. They treated all relevant concepts of target concept equally and model the temporal context in the shot level, which could not distinguish concepts having different contribution to the target concept. In this paper, we address this problem by integrating the temporal context into the observed feature for edges. Observed feature for the edge is a vector, where vector components are initial probabilities for relevant concepts. We learn a weight for each component to describe how much the corresponding concept could contribute to the presence of target concept. In this way, our model could capture relationship between target concept and other concepts more accurately than Weng's and our previous approaches.

Fig. 2 shows detailed results of our method on Columbia-374 baseline. 16 out of the 20 concepts in official evaluation are improved by using our method, and 14 concepts yield more than 20% relative improvements. Fig. 3 shows detailed results of our method on VIREO-374 baseline. 16 out of the 20 concepts in official evaluation are improved by using our method, and 12 concepts yield more than 20% relative improvements.

4. CONCLUSION

In this paper, we propose a new approach to boost the performance of video annotation by mining temporal context in video. The motivation of our idea mainly comes from the fact that temporally continuous shots in video are generally with consistent content. A temporal model is proposed to describe the contribution of each relevant concept to the presence of a target concept. By connecting our model with conditional random field and adopting the learning and inference approaches of it, we could obtain the refined probability of a concept occurring in the shot, which is the

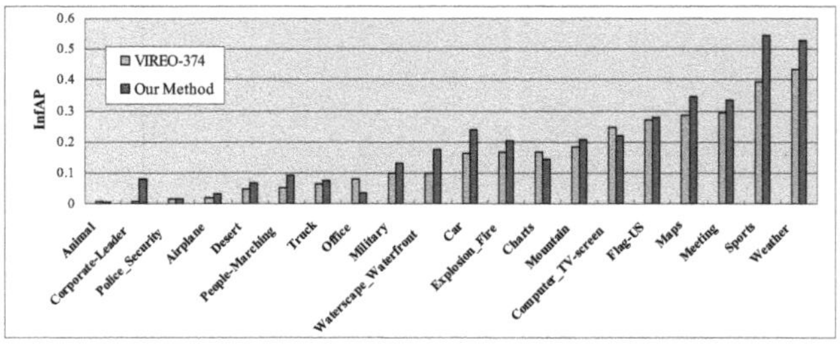

Figure 3: InfAP for 20 concepts in the official evaluation of TRECVID2006 benchmark, using our method for temporal context mining on VIREO-374 baseline.

leverage of temporal context information and initial output of video annotation, achieving impressive performance of video annotation. Experimental results on the widely used TRECVID dataset exhibit the effectiveness of our method.

5. ACKNOWLEDGE

The work described in this paper was fully supported by the National Natural Science Foundation of China under Grant Nos. 60873154 and 61073084, and the National Development and Reform Commission High-tech Program of China under Grant No. [2010]3044.

6. REFERENCES

[1] Y. G. Jiang, C. W. Ngo, and J. Yang. Towards optimal bag-of-features for object categorization and semantic video retrieval. *CIVR*, 2007.

[2] Y. G. Jiang, J. Wang, S. F. Chang, and C. W. Ngo. Domain adaptive semantic diffusion for large scale context-based video annotation. *ICCV*, 2009.

[3] L. Kennedy and S. F. Chang. A reranking approach for context-based concept fusion in video indexing and retrieval. *CIVR*, 2007.

[4] J. Lafferty, A. McCallum, and F. Pereira. Conditional random fields: Probabilistic models for segmenting and labeling sequence data. *ICML*, 2001.

[5] K. H. Liu, M. F. Weng, and et al. Association and temporal rule mining for post-processing of semantic concept detection in video. *IEEE Trans. on MM*, 10:240–251, 2008.

[6] G. J. Qi, X. S. Hua, and et al. Correlative multi-label video annotation with temporal kernels. *TOMCCAP*, 2009.

[7] A. F. Smeaton, P. Over, and W. Kraaij. Evaluation campaigns and trecvid. *MIR*, 2006.

[8] M. F. Weng and Y. Y. Chuang. Multi-cue fusion for semantic video indexing. *ACM Multimedia*, October 26-31 2008.

[9] A. Yanagawa, S. F. Chang, and et al. Columbia university's baseline detectors for 374 lscom semantic visual concepts. *Technical report, Columbia University*, 2007.

[10] J. Yang and A. G. Hauptmann. Exploring temporal consistency for video retrieval and analysis. *MIR*, 2006.

[11] J. Yi, Y. Peng, and J. Xiao. Refining video annotation by exploiting inter-shot context. *ACMMM*, 2010.

[12] E. Yilmaz and J. A. Aslam. Estimating average precision with incomplete and imperfect judgments. *CIKM*, 2006.

[13] J. Zhu, Z. Nie, J. Wen, B. Zhang, and W. Ma. 2d conditional random fields for web information extraction. *ICML*, 2005.

Structure Tensor Series-based Matching for Near-Duplicate Video Retrieval*

Xiangmin Zhou
CSIRO ICT Center, Canberra
ACT 2601 Australia
xiangmin.zhou@csiro.au

Lei Chen
Hong Kong University of Science and Technology,
Hong Kong, China
leichen@cs.ust.hk

Xiaofang Zhou
University of Queensland
Australia
zxf@itee.uq.edu.au

ABSTRACT

Near duplicate video retrieval has attracted much attention due to its wide spectrum of applications including copyright detection, commercial monitoring and news video tracking. In recent years, there has been significant research effort on efficiently identifying near duplicates from large video collections. However, existing approaches for large video databases suffer from low accuracy due to the serious information loss. In this paper, we propose a practical solution based on 3D structure tensor model for this problem. We first propose a novel video representation scheme, adaptive structure video tensor series (ASVT series), together with a robust similarity measure, to improve the retrieval effectiveness. Then, we prove the effectiveness of the proposed method by extensive experiments on hundreds hours real video data.

Categories and Subject Descriptors

H.3.1 [**Information Storage and Retrieval**]: Content Analysis and Indexing

General Terms

Design, Measurement, Experimentation, Performance

Keywords

ASVT Series, Similarity Measure, Near Duplicates

1. INTRODUCTION

With the expanding use of digital devices, more and more video data are being produced by individuals and organizations. In the meantime, with the rapid growth of broadband Internet service, videos have become a very popular Web medium. According to a recent report from YouTube, a video sharing website, there are around 65,000 new videos uploaded and more than 100 million video views per day [12]. The huge amount of videos together with its exponential growth raises critical challenges on many aspects including storage, search, navigation and categorization. Near-duplicate clip retrieval, as one of the challenges, has attracted attention due to its promising usage in many practical applications. For example, for video sharing websites, such as Youtube and Metacafe, to avoid copyright infringement, it is essential to quickly find whether or not near-duplicates exist in their large video databases whenever a new clip is uploaded. Practically, due to the high complexity and huge volume of video data, effective and efficient near duplicate video retrieval has been a challenging research problem.

Existing work on near duplicate clip detection focuses on designing effective video representations and similarity measure functions. Base on the visual features used for representing the videos, the previous approaches on near-duplicate video retrieval can be classified into two categories, global feature-based and local feature-based. Global feature-based approaches extracted visual features such as color histograms, motion features, gray intensities, and visual signatures to represent each video frame [3, 13, 8]. Since global feature-based approaches focus on capturing the global feature changes, many false alarms can be introduced due to lacking the mechanisms to differentiate local differences. Local feature-based approaches extracted visual features from a set of local interest points captured in each video frame and use these features to represent a video [6, 12]. Compared to global feature-based approaches, local feature-based ones have been proved to be more effective as reported in [12]. However, the existing local feature-based approaches all suffer from expensive computation cost of pair-wise comparison between video frames. Though [12] proposed indexing global features to speed up the retrieval efficacy, their methods ignore the temporal order between frames which leads to a low retrieval accuracy.

In this paper, we propose a tensor series-based approach to search near-duplicate videos. A number of frame samples are selected as the representatives of a clip. Each sample is described as multiple probability density functions (PDFs) over different dimensions of its extracted local descriptors. A series of consecutive samples in a video is then transformed into a volume of PDFs, which shows the distribution of their local descriptors and is further represented as a 3D structure tensor. The superiority of using 3D structure tensors is twofold. First, it captures the correlations of local interest points over the same dimension, across different dimensions and consecutive frame samples temporally. Thus, more discriminative information is preserved, leading to higher effectiveness of retrieval. Second, this tensor representation is highly compact, which guarantees the high efficiency of video matching. While tensor model has been successfully used for the video segmentation [10], to the best of our knowledge, this paper is the first effort on applying structure tensor model for video matching. Specifically, we propose a novel representation of video clips, adaptive structure video ten-

*Area chair: Hari Sundaram

MM'11, November 28–December 1, 2011, Scottsdale, Arizona, USA.

sor series (ASVT series), which captures both spatial and temporal visual features based on $variable$-length video segments. Meanwhile, an effective distance measure is proposed to improve the retrieval performance.

The rest of the paper is arranged as following. Section 2 presents a novel video representation scheme, adaptive tensor series, which captures both spatial and temporal characteristics, followed by the distance measure for tensor series. Extensive experimental results on hundreds hours of video data are reported in Section 3. Finally, we conclude the work in Section 4.

2. ADAPTIVE STRUCTURE VIDEO TENSOR REPRESENTATION

This section introduces a novel video representation scheme ASVT series. Specifically, the local descriptor distribution of each frame sample is first estimated in section 2.1. Then, the ASVT representation and a novel distance function to measure the similarity between ASVT series are respectively presented in section 2.2 and 2.3.

2.1 Local Descriptor Distribution

We exploit the distributions of high dimensional point sets to represent the extracted local interest descriptors of a frame sample into a properly defined feature space. Specifically, for each frame sample, we treat the set of extracted local interest descriptors as a set of random variables $X = \{X_1, X_2, ..., X_n\}$, where n is the number of local interest descriptors. Based on this set of random variables, we estimate the feature distribution of the frame sample. Since nonparametric density estimation offers a sophisticated solution for exploring large amounts of univariate or multivariate data without making specific distributional assumptions [4], in this work, we use a nonparametric estimation method, multivariate kernel density estimator, to extract the data distribution of local interest descriptors. Given that near-duplicate frame identification can be performed by comparing their similarity over each single dimension [2], we estimate the kernel density of local descriptors over each single dimension j to simplify the problem. Consider a set of variables $X^j = \{X_1^j, X_2^j, ..., X_n^j\}$, where X_i^j is the projected observation of d-dimensional local descriptor X_i over dimension j. The probability density function over X^j is:

$$\hat{f}_n(x) = \frac{1}{(nh)} \sum_{i=1}^{n} K(\frac{x - X_i^j}{h}) \quad (1)$$

where h denotes the bandwidth of the kernel-smoothing window, and K is the Gaussian kernel with unbounded support.

$$K(x) = \frac{1}{\sqrt{2\pi}} e^{-\frac{x^2}{2}}, \quad x \in R \quad (2)$$

After the probability density estimation, the whole descriptor set is described by a set of d PDFs, where d is the dimensionality of local descriptors. To represent a video frame, the constructed probability density over each dimension is sampled at d equally spaced points that cover the range of the data in the descriptor set. As a result, a frame is converted into a square feature matrix of size $d \times d$. We use $d \times d$ matrix to give same importance to two types of spatial information, the dimensions of local interest points and those of the PDFs, which is more diverse and robust to noise.

2.2 The ASVT representation

In this work, we plan to use *tensor model* to represent a short video segment and represent each video clip as a *tensor series*, which can be represented as

$$S = \{T_1, T_2, ..., T_m\} \quad (3)$$

where T_i is the 3D structure tensor of a video segment $\{p_1, p_2, ..., p_f\}$, p_i is a $d \times d$ matrix. A 3D structure tensor contains the gradient information of density distributions of a video segment in the spatial and temporal domain.

Clearly, representing a whole video sequence as a tensor is not acceptable because of the severe information loss. Borrowing the idea of q-grams used for approximate string matching [8], an alternative method to segment a video is to produce a series of $w - shingling$ by "sliding" a window of length w over this sequence. Thus each $w - shingling$ is a subclip of size w. However, directly using $w - shingling$ will suffer from two problems. First, due to the possible involvement of frame rate changes among near-duplicate videos, directly using $w - shingling$ will capture inconsistent patterns of tensor series among near-duplicate videos, thus leading to unacceptable results in tensor matching. Second, for videos with slow motions, this method will produce a number of redundant tensors, which raises up a challenge in fast tensor series matching. Therefore, extracting video subsequences of variable lengths is a good strategy for tensor series construction.

Given a clip, we construct its tensor series by the following steps. First, with the competitive shot boundary detection algorithm proposed by AT&T at TRECVID 2007 [7], a number of cuts are determined accurately. A segment between two adjacent cuts is called a video unit. Then, a series of local density distributions are extracted from the frame samples. We construct tensor representation over video units. Each video unit can cover variable number of frames because of the shrink of unit size. Thus, we call our video representation built on top of these units *a*daptive. The final ASVT series is obtained by transforming each video unit into a 3D structure tensor that captures the distribution change trends over this unit. Given that the neighboring frames are usually very similar, we build the 3D structure tensor of each video unit based on the frame samples instead of all the frames within it, so the cost of tensor series construction is reduced.

A video unit $V(v)$ can be considered as a volume data of $d*d*f$, where d is the dimensionality of the original local interest descriptors or the number of sampling points of the PDF over each dimension, and f the number of frame samples contained in a video unit. Suppose that x denotes the dimension id to a PDF, y is the id of a sample point over a PDF and t is the id of a frame sample. Each element of $V(v)$ is determined by a triple $v = \{x, y, t\}$, where x and y denote the spatial components and t is the temporal component. The spatio-temporal representation $I(v)$ of $V(v)$ is generated by convolving the volume data with a spatio-temporal filter $H(v)$ [10]. That is,

$$I(v) = V(v) * H(v) \quad (4)$$

where " $*$ " denotes convolution operation, and $H(v)$ is defined as

$$H(v) = \frac{1}{\sqrt{2\pi\sigma_x^2}\sqrt{2\pi\sigma_y^2}\sqrt{2\pi\sigma_t^2}} exp^{(-\frac{x^2}{2\sigma_x^2} - \frac{y^2}{2\sigma_y^2} - \frac{t^2}{2\sigma_t^2})} \quad (5)$$

Here, σ_x, σ_y and σ_t are standard deviations. Let $\nabla I(v)$ be the spatio-temporal derivatives of v in $V(v)$, a set of 3D structure tensors represented as matrixes are generated at different spatio-temporal locations of $V(v)$ according to the equation as follows.

$$\Sigma(v) = \nabla I(v).\nabla I(v)^T \quad (6)$$

The structure tensor for each spatio-temporal location (x, y, t) is the location value of $\Sigma(v)$ at this point. Given a location (x_i, y_i, t_i) of $V(v)$, its 3D structure tensor can be obtained by $\Sigma(x_i, y_i, t_i) = \nabla I(x_i, y_i, t_i).\nabla I(x_i, y_i, t_i)^T$. For a video unit $V(v)$, we define an ASVT that is a single 3D structure tensor representation.

Table 1: Comparison of series measures.

Distances	Hamming	ERP	DTW
Average precision	0.9471	0.9294	0.8606

The ASVT reflects the overall PDF change of a video unit along 3 dimensions (a 3×3 matrix), and can be computed by

$$T = \sum_{x=1}^{d}\sum_{y=1}^{d}\sum_{t=1}^{f} \frac{\nabla I(x,y,t).\nabla I(x,y,t)^T}{d*d*f} \quad (7)$$

Unlike the 3D structure tensors constructed over each image pixel for video segmentation [10], our tensor model is built on the top of variable-size video units, which makes the representation adaptive and highly compact.

2.3 Distance Measure for ASVT Series

We will define two functions that identify the similarity between S and Q jointly. The first, $D_T(T_s, T_q)$ is used to compute the similarity between two tensors. The second, $DTS(S, Q)$ is designed to measure the similarity of tensor series.

2.3.1 ASVT Distance Measure D_T

ASVT model is a probability distribution that captures the gradient information of local features. Applied to this near-duplicate video retrieval work, the local features refer to the PDFs of local descriptors of different frame samples over different dimensions. Given two ASVTs built on their video units, the similarity between them can be measured by their Jensen-Shannon(J) divergence. Let $p(x)$ and $q(x)$ be the density distributions of two ASVTs, the J-divergence between them is defined as

$$J(p||q) = \frac{1}{2} * (\int p(x) log \frac{p(x)}{q(x)} dx + \int q(x) log \frac{q(x)}{p(x)} dx) \quad (8)$$

The tensor distance can be measured by the J-divergence [11], which is simplified as:

$$D_T(T_q, T_s) = \frac{1}{4}(tr(T_q^{-1}T_s + T_s^{-1}T_q) - 2\gamma) \quad (9)$$

Where $tr(.)$ is the matrix trace operator, γ denotes the size of the square matrix T_q and T_s. The similarity measure $D_T(T_q, T_s)$ between two tensors T_q and T_s is the basic unit for measuring two tensor series.

2.3.2 ASVT Series Distance Measure DTS

Based on the tensor distance in formula 9, we can use various measures to compute the similarity between two tensor series, such as Hamming distance, DTW, and ERP. We use the leave-one-out classification test, which has been widely used for effective comparison of distance measures [1, 2]. We conduct the experiments on a 20-hour data set consisting of 1200 60s short video clips and the results on the average precision of three different measures are reported in Table 1. Based on the results, we can find out that Hamming distance performs as well as the other distance functions. Since Hamming distance is the "lightest" measure in terms of computation cost, we choose it for tensor series. Given two strings of equal length, the Hamming distance between them is determined by the number of positions for which the corresponding symbols are different. Applying Hamming distance to tensor series, we have:

Given two video tensor series Q and S of equal length, m ASVTs, respectively, DTS is a pairwise measure, defined as

$$DTS(Q, S) = \sum_{i=1}^{m} D_T(Q_i, S_i) \quad (10)$$

Where Q_i and S_i are the ith tensor of Q and that of S respectively. DTS is defined by extending Hamming distance from two aspects. Unlike a string where the difference between the corresponding symbols is a Boolean value, in the matching of tensor series, we find the matches by computing the distance between the corresponding tensor pairs.

For the similarity measure between two tensor series of different lengths, we add identity matrixes at the end of the shorter one. As such, the two tensor series have the same length. Given two tensor series Q and S of length m and m' respectively, assume $m < m'$, $DTS(Q, S)$ is defined as

$$DTS(Q, S) = \sum_{i=1}^{m'} D_T(Q'_i, S_i) \quad (11)$$

where Q' is the converted series of Q. Comparing with the quadratic time complexity of ERP and DTW, the time cost of DTS is linear.

3. EXPERIMENTAL EVALUATION

3.1 Experimental Setup

We conduct the experiments on a collection of 120-hour real videos from two sources: (1) A set of 20 hours 60s-clips consisting of the real videos from TV broadcasting and their transformed copies. Among them, 17.25 hours real videos are commercials, news and weather broadcasting reports captured from TV stations over months. Then, we produced 2.75 hours near-duplicates of these clips via 11 large variations, including 25% increase and decrease of contrast, 25% increase and decrease of brightness, 50% crop of frames, 50% alter of saturation, 2 times of scale decrease, left and right corner log insertion, vertical and horizontal flip. (2) 100 hours from the original TRECVID benchmark dataset (TRECVID_O).

We use the state-of-art algorithm proposed by AT&T to detect the video cuts and divide clips into segments [7]. Each frame is compressed using PLCVideo Mjpegs. Except the transformed data involving resize and cropping operations, all other videos are with the resolution of 352×288 pixels. We use the source code released by the authors of PCA-SIFT and follow all the parameter setting in [6] to extract 20-dimensional PCA-SIFT descriptors.

We select 15 clips from the first data source and the queries of ST1 for copy detection evaluation in TRECVID dataset as queries for the evaluation of our approach. The near-duplicate videos are those containing same content but with the following differences: (a) Formatting differences including encoding format, frame rate, bit rates; (b) Content differences including photometric variations listed as above and editing operations (logo insertion, adding borders around frames). The ground truth of queries over two datasets is obtained for effectiveness evaluation based on this near-duplicate definition. Three accessors participated in the user study with the direction of the definition. The ground truth is labeled based on inter-subject agreement on the relevance judgements.

The following matching approaches, including two state-of-art techniques STF-LBP and M-HIER for large video databases and three tensor based method we proposed, ASVT-DTS, ASVT-ERP and ASVT-DTW, are used in the experiments. Here, STF-LBP is spatial temporal signature matching [8]. M-HIER is hierarchical method combining global signatures and local features [12]. ASVT-DTS is our proposed matching that applies the ASVT model on DTS measure. ASVT-ERP is our alternative method that extends the conventional ERP to ASVT. ASVT-DTW is our alternative method that extends the conventional DTW to AVST.

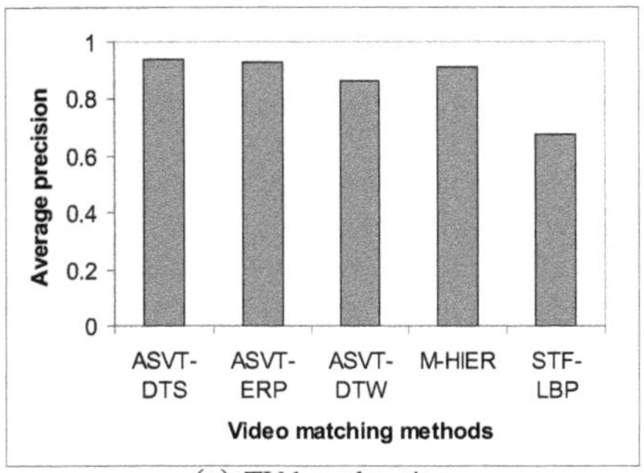

(a) TV broadcasting

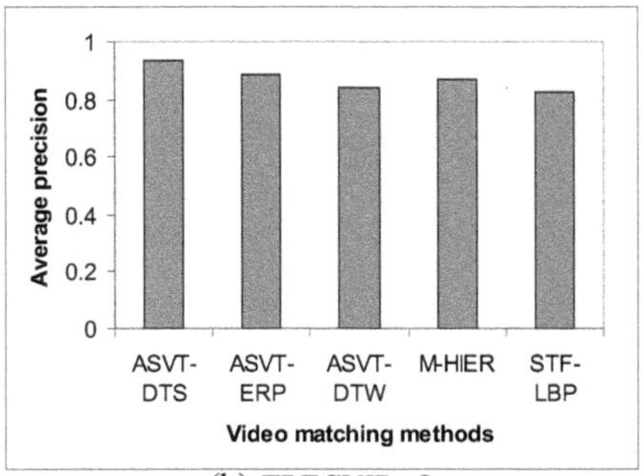

(b) TRECVID_O

Figure 1: Average precision comparison

To evaluate the effectiveness of our approach, we adopt the standard evaluation metric in TRECVID [9]. We evaluate the system based on the average precision, which is the average of the precision value obtained after each relevant clip is retrieved. The results of a query are ranked by their similarity values. The precision is calculated after each relevant clip is retrieved.

3.2 Evaluation on Effectiveness

We evaluate the effectiveness of our ASVT series matching by comparing the three proposed tensor series matching approaches with the state-of-art techniques. We compare the effectiveness of five video matching methods by testing the overall average precision of each approach over all the queries of two different datasets described in Section 3.1. Figure 1 (a)-(b) show the results.

Clearly, considering three tensor series matching approaches, on all the datasets, ASVT-DTS produces the best accuracy, nearly 98.7% overall average precision, with ASVT-ERP following it. The ASVT-DTW produces the worst results among three ASVT-based approaches. This is because ASVT can well handle the variations among near-duplicate videos. Thus, as a strict Humming based matching, the ASVT-DTS helps effectively reject the false positive clips during series matching. Moreover, ASVT-DTS takes the length difference between tensor series into consideration, the inherent information of tensor series as sequence data can be used to enhance the effectiveness of matching. For two other tensor series matching methods, ASVT-ERP measures the difference between tensor series in a flexible manner that possibly induces more false positive clips in the results, and ASVT-DTW neglects the effects of sequence length. Thus, the discriminative information of sequences is not effectively used in the matching.

Comparing with M-HIER and STF-LBP, the dominance of applying DTS on ASVT is more obvious. STF-LBP performs video matching by comparing the compact signature patterns. However, STF-LBP signatures are very sensitive to lightening change, which degrades the accuracy of near-duplicate video matching. More importantly, when processing the videos with local content shift such as local frame editing or frame rotation, these signatures can not work properly any more. As shown in Figure 1 (a)-(b), comparing with STF-LBP, our ASVT-DTS obtains much higher average precision on both the TV broadcasting dataset and the TRECVID_O dataset. Although M-HIER obtains similar average precision as our approach over all datasets, its high computation complexity becomes a barrier to real video retrieval applications.

4. CONCLUSION

In this paper, we first propose a novel video representation, called adaptive structure video tensor series (ASVT series), which captures the spatio-temporal gradient changes of the video data based on the distribution of local interest descriptors extracted from each frame sample. Then, an effective distance function is proposed to measure the similarity between two tensor series. We conduct the extensive experiments on hundreds hours of real video data to demonstrate the high effectiveness of the proposed distance measure. The experimental results have proved the superiority of our proposed approach over the state-of-art techniques.

5. ACKNOWLEDGMENTS

This work was supported by Hong Kong RGC GRF grant (No. 611608).

6. REFERENCES

[1] L. Chen and R. Ng. On the marriage of edit distance and L_p norms. In *VLDB*, pages 792–803, 2004.

[2] L. Chen, M. T. Özsu, and V. Oria. Robust and fast similarity search for moving object trajectories. In *SIGMOD*, pages 491–502, 2005.

[3] C. Chiu, C. Li, H. Wang, C. Chen, and L. Chien. A time warping based approach for video copy detection. In *ICPR*, pages 228–231, 2006.

[4] A. J. Izenman. Recent developments in nonparametric density estimation. *Journal of the American Statistical Association*, 86(413):205–224, 1991.

[5] A. Joly, J. Law-to, and N. Boujemaa. INRIA-IMEDIA TRECVID 2008: video copy detection. In *NIST TRECVID Workshop*, 2008.

[6] Y. Ke, R. Sukthankar, and L. Huston. An efficient parts-based near-duplicate and sub-image retrieval system. In *MM*, pages 869–876, 2004.

[7] Z. Liu, E. Zavesky, D. Gibbon, B. Shahraray, and P. Haffner. AT&T research at TRECVID 2007. In *TRECVID*, 2007.

[8] L. Shang, L. Yang, F. Wang, K.-P. Chan and X.-S. Hua. Real-time large scale near-duplicate web video retrieval. In *MM*, pages 531–540, 2010.

[9] A. F. Smeaton, P. Over, and W. Kraaij. Evaluation campaigns and trecvid. In *MIR*, 2006.

[10] H.-Y. Wang and K.-K. Ma. Spatio-temporal video object segmentation via scale-adaptive 3D structure tensor. *EURASIP J. Appl. Signal Process.*, 2004(1):798–813, 2004.

[11] Z. Wang and B. Vemuri. An affine invariant tensor dissimilarity measure and its applications to tensor-valued image segmentation. *CVPR*, 1:I-228–I-233 Vol.1, 2004.

[12] X. Wu, A. G. Hauptmann, and C. Ngo. Practical elimination of near-duplicates from web video search. In *MM*, pages 218–227, 2007.

[13] X. Zhou, X. Zhou, L. Chen, Y. Shu, A. Bouguettaya and J. A. Taylor. Adaptive Subspace Symbolization for Content-Based Video Detection. *TKDE*, 22(10):1372-1387, 2010.

[14] X. Zhou, and L. Chen. Monitoring near duplicates over video streams. In *MM*, pages 521–530, 2010.

A Smart Video Player with Content-Based Fast-Forward Playback

Junfeng Jiang
Department of Electrical and Computer Engineering, Ryerson University
350 Victoria Street, Toronto, Ontario, Canada, M5B 2K3
j7jiang@ee.ryerson.ca

Xiao-Ping Zhang
Department of Electrical and Computer Engineering, Ryerson University
350 Victoria Street, Toronto, Ontario, Canada, M5B 2K3
xzhang@ee.ryerson.ca

ABSTRACT
In this paper, we develop a video player to allow the users to do fast-forward playback based on the semantic video content. The whole system has two modules, processing and playing. In the processing part, we present a video time density function (VTDF) to describe the temporal dynamics of video data first. A VTDF-based temporal quantization method is then developed to find the best quanta and partition in the time domain. The optimal quanta are used to extract key frames. The optimal number of key frames is determined by a temporal mean square error (TMSE)-based criterion. In the playing module, we combine the key frame sequence and a set of parameters together and feed them into a triangle-based transition function to generate the sampled frames in a non-uniform way. A built video player will play all sampled frames in its intelligent fast-forward mode for a given fast-forward speed factor. The implementation of video player demonstrates the feasibility of proposed method in practice.

Categories and Subject Descriptors
H.5.1 [**Information Interfaces and Presentation**]: Multimedia Information Systems- *Video*; H.3.1 [**Information Storage and Retrieval**]: Content Analysis and Indexing.

General Terms
Algorithms, Design, Experimentation, Performance, Theory.

Keywords
Video content analysis, video time density function, temporal quantization.

1. INTRODUCTION
In recent years, we have witnessed a growing number of user-centric applications to allow ordinary people to record, edit, deliver, and publish their own home-made digital videos on social web or networks. The interaction with videos has become an important part of our life. However, the increasing availability of digital video has not been accompanied by an increase in its accessibility [1]. For example, one common requirement in rapid video playback is that before committing time to the full video, the users hope to do content-based fast-forward playback that preserves important semantic information. To meet that demand, effective and efficient technologies are required in practice.

A video summary is a condensed version of the video information [2]. The existing technologies can be roughly categorized into two main types, key frame extraction and video skimming [3]. Key frame extraction is to do video segmentation first (e.g., video shot boundary detection). For each segment, one or more key frames are extracted. The summarization result is to lay out those key frames sequentially or hierarchically, such as the methods used in [4][5][6]. Although the static summary can offer users a comprehensive view of video, it is susceptible to the smoothness problem, which means the users may feel uncomfortable while browsing the summary results [7]. Considering a video with long time duration, it is common to generate thousands of key frames. To layout those key frames sequentially is meaningless to understand the semantic video content [7].

Video skimming is an alternative solution to generate several video skims from the original video, such as the methods in [8][9]. However, the high computational complexity makes them infeasible in practice [3]. In current video players, the uniform fast-forward mode is still the main way for rapid video playback. Recently, some researchers try to implement content-based video players, such as the work in [10][11]. In [10], a non-uniform sampling solution is applied to sample frames and feed them into a video player for rapid video playback. However, when sampling few frames, experimental results show that it is hard to tell which one (uniform or non-uniform) is better. Therefore, new technique has to be developed for effective content-based rapid video playback by selecting the most salient set of frames.

In this paper, we build a smart video player to allow content-based rapid video playback before committing time to the original one. The new parameterized solution is to sample the frames non-uniformly. In particular, considering the rapid video playback problem is a generic sampling problem in nature, we employ the video time density function (VTDF) to explore the temporal dynamics of video first. A VTDF-based temporal quantization method is then developed to find the optimal key frame sequence. We then combine the key frame sequence and a set of parameters together and feed them into a triangle-based transition function to generate the sampled frames in a non-uniform way. The technique is integrated into a video player in practice. Before committing

*Area Chair: Xian-Sheng Hua

MM'11, November 28–December 1, 2011, Scottsdale, Arizona, USA.

time to the original video, users can do rapid video playback in two fast-forward modes freely.

The advantages of our method over existing methods can be summarized in three aspects. Firstly, unlike those existing model-based methods, our method does not need training data and parameter estimation. It is independent of domain features and knowledge. Secondly, we employ the VTDF and temporal quantization to generate a compact key frame sequence. Thirdly, the proposed solution is user-oriented. The users can set a set of parameters to specify how to do fast-forward playback in real time.

2. A SMART PLAYER WITH INTELLIGENT FAST-FORWARD PLAYBACK MODE

There are three steps in our method. First, the VTDF is employed to model video data in the time domain. Second, a VTDF-based temporal quantization is developed to generate the key frame sequence. The optimal number of key frames is determined by a temporal mean square error (TMSE)-based criterion. Third, a parameterized triangle transition function is applied to generate the sample frame sequence for rapid video playback.

2.1 Video Data Modeling Using the VTDF

A normalized chromaticity histogram, used in [12], is calculated to model each video frame in grey level. The illumination-invariant normalized chromaticity is defined as,

$$r = R/(R+G+B), \tag{1}$$

$$g = G/(R+G+B). \tag{2}$$

For one video with N frames, we build a 16(r) × 16(g), 256 bins histogram represent each video frame n ($0 \le n \le N$-1) in grey level, denoted by $H(n)$.

Considering frame n with N_p pixels, we explore the inter-frame dependency in pixel level using a class set C_{ij},

$$C_{ij} = \{k \mid g(n-1,k) = i, g(n,k) = j\}, \tag{3}$$

where $g(n, k)$ is the operator to get the grey value of frame n at pixel k ($1 \le k \le N_p$), and $0 \le i,j \le 255$.

The C_{ij} is used to calculate the joint probability $D(i,j)$,

$$D(i,j) = N(C_{ij})/N_p, \tag{4}$$

where $N(C_{ij})$ is the size of class set C_{ij}.

Note that $D(i,j)$ is to model that a pixel with grey value i at frame n-1 has a grey value j at frame n.

Therefore, we can build a matrix D (256×256) to model the grey value difference between two consecutive frames, n and n-1 in pixel level. And the VTDF of frame n can be calculated as,

$$f(n) = -\frac{1}{U}\sum_{i=0}^{255}\sum_{j=0}^{255} D(i,j)\log\frac{D(i,j)}{D(i,)D(,j)}, \tag{5}$$

$$f(0) = 0, \tag{6}$$

where $D(i,)$ and $D(,j)$ are the marginal probabilities. And U is the normalization factor.

For one video, its time density carries a lot of information and makes it different from other videos. It is uncommon that two different videos have the same time density rhythms. Therefore, the time density rhythms can be considered as an ID to index the video and measure the similarity between two videos. From this point of view, the time density can be used to explore the semantic information of video data. Considering the purpose of the VTDF is to explore the video density in the time domain by assigning a weight to each video frame based on the inter-frame dependency, the VTDF is effective to explore the semantic information of video in the time domain.

Inspired by the work in [13], we originally propose the VTDF to measure the association between two successive video frames [10]. Different from the work in [13] to calculate mutual information for video shot boundary detection, we calculate mutual information to measure the inter-frame dependency and give a weight to each video frame to solve the problems in rapid video playback. Note that other methods to calculate the inter-frame dependency rather than mutual information can be applied as well.

2.2 Video Key Frame Extraction Using the VTDF-Based Temporal Quantization

To extract M frames to represent the original N frames, a VTDF-based temporal quantization method is developed in this section.

The scheme of our temporal quantization can be represented by a set of quanta q, a set of boundary T and (2M-1) members,

$$q = \{q_1, \quad q_2, \quad \ldots, \quad q_M\}, \tag{7}$$

$$T = \{n_1, \quad n_2, \quad \ldots, \quad n_{M-1}\}, \tag{8}$$

$$q_1 < n_1 < q_2 < n_2 < \ldots < q_{M-1} < n_{M-1} < q_M, \tag{9}$$

where M is the quantization codebook size, and $M < N$.

The relationship between quanta and boundary is,

$$q_i = \sum_{n_{i-1}}^{n_i} nf(n) \Big/ \sum_{n_{i-1}}^{n_i} f(n), \tag{10}$$

$$n_i = \frac{q_i + q_{i+1}}{2}. \tag{11}$$

TMSE is calculated to measure the quantization error as,

$$TMSE = \frac{1}{M}\sum_{i=1}^{M} e(q_i), \tag{12}$$

$$e(q_i) = \sum_{n \in Q_i} (n - q_i)^2 f(n), \tag{13}$$

where the class set Q_i can be determined as,

$$Q_i = \{n \mid n_{i-1} \le n < n_i\}, \tag{14}$$

where $n_0 = 0$ and $n_M = N$.

Note that different from the conventional vector quantization method, all video frames within one class set have the temporal relationship in our method. In other words, they are consecutive in time.

Therefore, the whole quantization procedure is to find the optimal quanta and boundary iteratively. Termination is decided by the following criterion.

$$\frac{TMSE^{(j-1)} - TMSE^{(j)}}{TMSE^{(j-1)}} < \varepsilon_1, \tag{15}$$

where $TMSE^{(j)}$ is the value of TMSE using formula (12) in the j-th iteration ($j > 1$). ε_1 is a predefined small number.

The whole algorithm is summarized as follows,

1. Initialization: $q_1, q_2, \ldots, q_M$.
2. Iteration: calculate partition T using formula (11), update class set Q_i using formula (14), update q using formula (10), and calculate TMSE using formula (12).
3. Termination: formula (15).

A new TMSE-based criterion is applied to determine the optimal number of key frames, the value of M.

$$\frac{TMSE(M-1) - TMSE(M)}{TMSE(M-1)} < \varepsilon_2, \quad (16)$$

where $TMSE(M)$ is the TMSE value for a specific value of M ($M \geq 2$). Similarly, ε_2 is a predefined small number.

The value of M to terminate the formula (16) will be chosen as the optimal number of key frames.

After temporal quantization, we extract one frame K as the key frame to represent each partition.

$$K = round(q_i). \quad (17)$$

2.3 Video Frames Sampling Using a Triangle Transition

In this section, we combine the above key frame sequence and a set of parameters together and feed them into a triangle transition function to generate the sampled frames in a non-uniform way. The reason we apply the parameterized sampling function is that we hope to slow down when the video player is going to access key frames and speed up after the access. As a result, sampling more frames around each key frame will let the users see more details during fast-forward video playback.

Given total video frame number (before sampling) is N, the original video frame sequence can be indexed. The frame index at time n ($0 \leq n \leq N$-1) is denoted by $I(n)$,

$$I(n) = n. \quad (18)$$

A parameterized triangle transition is applied to find a transform from the original frame sequence domain to the time-based domain. Figure 1 demonstrates how the transition function works for non-uniform sampling.

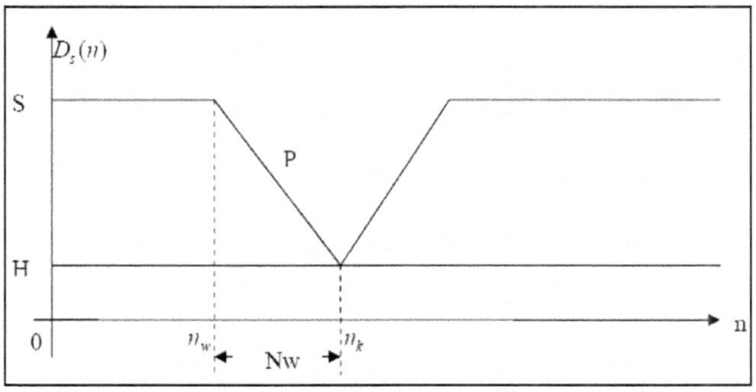

Fig. 1. Four parameters-based non-uniform sampling

The non-uniform sampled video frame sequence can be indexed by I_s (n; N_w, K, H, S) (for simple, we use $I_s(n)$) at time n, which depends on a parameter set θ,

$$\theta = (N_w, K, H, S), \quad (19)$$

where S is the fast-forward speed factor, $S \geq 1$ (e.g., given $S = 2$, the output for uniform sampling frame sequence is 2, 4, 6 ...). N_w (in the original frame sequence domain, we use W) is to model the non-uniform sampling interval for each key frame (how many terms between n_w and n_k). In other words, it is the size of sliding window. H is the non-uniform sampling factor to model the sub-sampling rate (how slow to do playback) at time n_k, $0 \leq H \leq S$.

Note that all parameters are in the time domain. In Fig. 1, $D_s(n)$ is the sampling period (distance) at time n defined by parameters S, N_w, and H, and K is the position of key frame in the original frame sequence (in time domain after sampling, we use the value of n_k as the time instance of K).

According to the above definitions of parameters in the time domain, we can calculate the slope P (left side, the right side can be calculated in a similar way) of our non-uniform sampling triangle by:

$$P = (H - S)/N_w. \quad (20)$$

Then we can calculate the $D_s(n)$ (left side, the right side can be calculated in a similar way) at time n:

$$D_s(n) = P \cdot (n - n_w) + S. \quad (21)$$

In here, we describe the sum of $D_s(n)$ by:

$$\sum_{n=n_w}^{n_w+n_k} D_s(n) = K - W. \quad (22)$$

Then we can derivate the equation (23) based on (21) and (22),

$$\sum_{n=n_w}^{n_w+n_k} [P \cdot (n - n_w) + S] = K - W. \quad (23)$$

Now, we can get the relationship between W and N_w by calculating the equation (23),

$$W = \frac{(S+H)(N_w+1)}{2}. \quad (24)$$

Now, we need to decide the value of n_w at time n, the boundary between uniform sampling and non-uniform sampling. We use the formula (25) to decide how to choose the value of n_w,

$$| I_s(n) - (K - W) | > S/2, \quad (25)$$

where if it is true, $n_w = I_s(n) + S$, otherwise, $n_w = I_s(n)$.

Then we know the value of n_k according to the value of n_w,

$$n_k = n_w + N_w. \quad (26)$$

Therefore, based on the above formulas, we can calculate $I_s(n)$ at time n in the non-uniform sampling as follows,

$$I_s^{real}(n) = I_s^{real}(n-1) + D_s(n), \quad (27)$$

where $I_s^{real}(n)$ is the frame index in continuous real domain. Then in practice we could take the round integers as the frame indices after sampling,

$$I_s(n) = round(I_s^{real}(n)). \quad (28)$$

The whole sampling algorithm can be described as follows:

1. For frame at time n (initialization: n = 0, $I_s(0)$ = 0) in the indexed video frame sequence and each key frame K, if $I_s(n) \notin [n_k - N_w, n_k + N_w]$, go to 2, else go to 3.

2. If $\mathrm{mod}(n/S) = 0$, n will be sampled (traditional uniform sampling), then $n = n + 1$, if $I_s(n) < N$-1, go back to 1.
3. Calculate $I_s(n+1)$ using formula (28), then $n = n + 1$, if $I_s(n) < N$-1, go back to 1.

The whole system for rapid video playback has two modules, processing and playing. In the processing module, a TXT file containing all extract key frame indices can be generated to feed into the playing module. In the playing module, the above triangle transition function is applied to generate the sampled frames non-uniformly. The built video player will only play the sampled frames and skip others in its intelligent fast-forward mode.

Note that given one video, only the key frame extraction part including VTDF calculation needs to be done offline at once. In other words, the parameterized non-uniform sampling using the triangle transition can generate the sample frames in real time.

3. EXPERIMENTAL RESULTS

To show the effectiveness of our method, we collect over 100 videos from YouTube and test them by arranging a group of users to watch the sampling results. After comparing with the traditional fast-forward, we conclude that our method can grasp the salient information ignored by the traditional method in addition to capturing the semantic information provided by it.

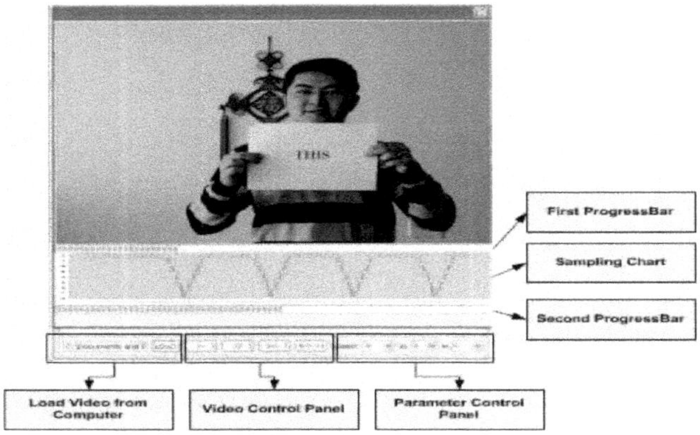

Fig. 2. Video Player GUI

Fig. 2 is the video player GUI built in Java. In Fig. 2, the X-axis of sampling chart is to model the sampled frame sequence and Y-axis is the sampling speed descriptor, denoted by s. For one video frame at time n (initialization, n = 0, $I_s(0)$ = 0) in the original video frame sequence, if $I_s(n) \notin [n_k - N_w, n_k + N_w]$, $s = S$, else $s = D_s(n)$. As a result, s is to model how slow to sample this frame. The first ProgressBar is to model the playback progress. After one frame is played, it will move $I_s(n)$. The second ProgressBar is to model the changes of $D_s(n)$. At time n, its selection value will be the value of $D_s(n)$.

To compare with existing solutions in literature, we refer to [11] for discussions. Its interactive video browsing model is designed for browsing video with predefined rules and preferences, thus lacking of generic.

4. CONCLUSION

In this paper, we present a new non-uniform sampling solution for content-based fast-forward video playback. It has two modules. In the processing module, we employ the VTDF and temporal quantization to generate the key frame sequence. The optimal number of key frames is determined by a TMSE-based criterion. In the playing module, the key frame indices will be fed into a parameterized triangle transition for non-uniform sampling to generate the sample frames for rapid video playback in the built video player. The new solution fully makes use of the visual-related information to explore the characteristics of video frames and provides a generic-oriented solution in rapid video playback. The proposed sampling method needs little offline processing effort and does not need model training and parameter learning before it is applied in practice.

5. REFERENCES

[1] C. Cotsaces, N. Nikolaidis and I. Pitas, "Video shot boundary detection and condensed representation: a review," *IEEE Signal Processing Magazine*, vol.23, No.2, 2006.

[2] Paul Over, Alan F. Smeaton, and Philip Kelly, "The trecvid rushes summarization evaluation pilot," in *Proc. of ACM Multimedia*, Sep. 2007.

[3] B.-T. Truong and S. Venkatesh, "Video abstraction: a systematic review and classification," *ACM Trans. on Multimedia Computing, Communications and Applications*, vol.3, No.1, Feb. 2007.

[4] B.-W. Chen, J.-C. Wang and J.-F. Wang, "A novel video summarization based on mining the story-structure and semantic relations among concept entities," *IEEE Trans. on Multimedia*, vol.11, No.2, pp.295-312, 2009.

[5] X. Zhu, J. Fan, A.-K. Elmagarmid, and X. Wu, "Hierarchical video summarization and content description joint semantic and visual similarity," *ACM Multimedia System*, 2003.

[6] J. Jiang, X.-P. Zhang, "Gaussian mixture vector quantization-based video summarization using independent component analysis," in *Proc. of IEEE Int. Work. on Multimedia Signal Processing (MMSP)*, Oct. 2010.

[7] Z. Xiong, R. Radhakrishnan, A. Divakaran, Y. Rui, and T.-S. Huang, "*A unified framework for video summarization, browsing and retrieval*," Elsevier Academic Press, 2006.

[8] S. Benini, P. Migliorati, and R. Leonardi, "Hidden Markov models for video skim generation," In *Proc. of the 8th Int. Work. on Image Analysis for Multimedia Interactive Services*, Jun. 2007.

[9] Y.-F. Ma, L. Lu, H.-J. Zhang, and M. Li, "A user attention model for video summarization," in *Proc. of ACM Multimedia*, Dec. 2002.

[10] J. Jiang, X.-P. Zhang, "A new player-enabled rapid video navigation method using temporal quantization and repeated weighted boosting search," in *Proc. of the 7th IEEE Computer Society Work. on Perceptual Organization in Computer Vision (POCV) in conjunction with CVPR 2010.*

[11] K-Y Cheng, S-J Luo, B-Y Chen, and H-H Chu, "SmartPlayer: user-centric video fast-forwarding," in *Proc. of the 27th Int. Conf. on Human Factors in Computing Systems,* 2009.

[12] J. Zhou and X.-P. Zhang. "An ICA mixture hidden Markov model for video content analysis," *IEEE Trans. on Circuits and Systems for Video Technology*, pp.1576-1586, 2008.

[13] Z. Cernekova, I. Pitas, and C. Nikou. "Information theory-based shot cut/fade detection and video summarization," *IEEE Trans. on Circuits and Systems for Video Technology*, 2006.

Video Anatomy: Cutting Video Volume for Profile

Hongyuan Cai
Department of Computer Science, IUPUI
723 W. Michigan St. SL280, Indianapolis, IN46202
hocai@cs.iupui.edu

Jiang Yu Zheng
Department of Computer Science, IUPUI
723 W. Michigan St. SL280Indianapolis, IN46202
jzheng@cs.iupui.edu

ABSTRACT

This work takes a new aspect view to profile a video volume to a video track as a digest for video preview. Our projected video profile contains both spatial and temporal information inclusively in a 2D image scroll that is continuous, compact, scalable, and indexing to each frame. To profile various types of video clips, we investigate the global flow field under all camera actions, and propose a uniformed scheme that uses a sampling line to cut the video volume across the major optical flow field. The resulting profile obtains an intrinsic scene space less influenced by the camera actions, and can be displayed in a video track to guide the access to video frames, and facilitate video browsing, editing, and retrieval.

Categories and Subject Descriptors

H.2.4 [**Database Management**] Database Applications – *Multimedia databases.* I.4.8 [**Image Processing and Computer Vision**]: Scene Analysis – *motion, time-varying imagery.*

General Terms

Algorithms, Measurement, Design, Experimentation.

Keywords

Video summary, video indexing, profile of video, camera motion, spatial-temporal slice, optical flow

1. INTRODUCTION

Current video indexing uses key frames for video clips/shots and their collection as story boards or scenes [1]. However, a key frame picks only a moment of the video clip. To index to each individual frame in a video summary, this work creates a 2D profile from the raw video data, which is an image belt containing one axis as the timeline and the other from a space dimension in the video. It is a novel aspect view of video that can index to each frame for video editing, and provides a view of entire scene space that a video captures for browsing. The created time belt can be presented in a video track in video editing and production, displayed in webpage for browsing, and used for video retrieval. Figure 1 displays a possible cutting for such a profile in the video.

To achieve above goals, this paper designs the cutting in the video volume to yield a planar or curved slice to reveal the video content in the video volume. It is implemented by sweeping a sampling line across the video volume. Our criteria to cut a profile from video are to include all the stable background space a video clip captures, to show meaningful shapes and identities of objects, and to reduce the distortion of target scenes in the profiles that obey different scene projections from the normal perspective projection. We analyze the typical camera works (motion styles), its underlying kinematics, and the generated optical flow in the video to ensure that our designed cutting and slicing strategy work for all types of video sequences. The significance to generate such a profile of video lies in its (i) compact size, (ii) reflecting temporal information, (iii) preserving shape to some extent, (iv) embracing static background and dynamic foreground, and (v) robustness in processing. Because dynamic video frames in a clip have overlaps on scenes, the reduction of redundant pixels in the 2D video profile becomes possible for video summarization. Our slicing of the video volume is designed to cut through every frame so that the continuous profile indexes to frames. The spatial information such as static environment and dynamic targets (objects, people, etc.) in the video is also visualized in the profile, although some deformation and changes in spatial ordering are brought in.

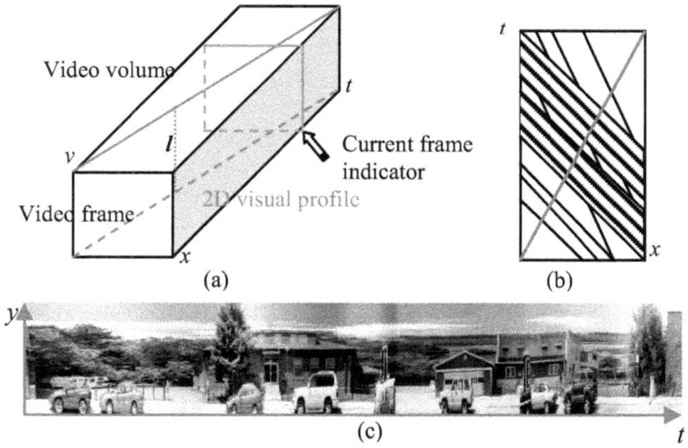

Figure 1. Video volume and a possible cutting of diagonal slice across the major flow in a video clip. (a) Video volume and a cutting slice, (b) an EPI showing flow traces of scenes, (c) profile of a video clip from a sideway translating camera.

The related works include *spatial* and *temporal video indexing.* The spatial indexing presents key frames [1] and its extension in a larger spatial domain generated by stitching camera panning views [2] and overlapping human actions in the same spatial domain [3-6]. These montage-based methods selectively stitch time-different regions into a video summary image. The drawbacks are as follows. (1) The camera motion is only limited to static and pan cases because no motion parallax is allowed (or single-depth background is required); (2) The extended key frame becomes cluttered if the video clip lasts for long or targets have a high complexity in the video; (3) The generated summary lacks of

*Area Chair: Lei Chen.

MM'11, November 28–December 1, 2011, Scottsdale, Arizona, USA.

temporal order; (4) The matching of background and segmentation of foreground are not robust for complex and dynamic scenes. In contrast, the *temporal indexing,* though under the controlled camera motion, has good results on camera rotation and translation by fixed [7,8] and dynamic slit scanning [9]. The shortcomings are (1) low temporal resolution for a short clip with fast motion; (2) views with a different projection from perspective projection; (3) deshaking of video or post smoothing [10,11,12].

Our proposed video summary in the profile is easy to be embedded into video software to enhance video editing, retrieval, analysis, and visualization in general. Compared with the related works, our video profile is a spatial-temporal slice to overcome the problems of related methods in the resolution, camera motion type, and robustness. It works for video clips from all kinds of camera works (operations). Our slice cutting strategy avoids image matching, flow segmentation, and other complex procedures in order to achieve the robustness. The computation involved is the global flow detection in a video clip. Moreover, the created video summary keeps the temporal order of video scalable in time, and has a higher resolution than spatial or temporal indexing method. Figure 1 gives an example of such profiles from a linear camera motion. As an initial result, our profiling method has been working on simple camera actions such as zoom, pan, and translation [13]. This paper focuses on building a uniformed framework for the video volume cutting on general camera alignments and motions that are the combination of simple motions. We analyze the intrinsic camera works (operations) and categorize video clips, and then examine the flow components of static background caused by the camera motion and the dynamic human/target/object motion against the background.

2. CAMERA MOTION AND IMAGE FLOW

A camera can be static or undergo motions such as zoom, rotation, translation, and their combinations. Practically, a video can be categorized by its camera works (operations) such as pan/tilt rotation, rail/vehicle based movement (camera facing forward/ backward/sideways), focusing and around-object motion (composed of simultaneous translation and rotation), forward moving or zooming, and so on. In addition, dynamic scenes in a static field of view (FOV) may further reveal a variety of motions as directional motion (e.g., marathon crowds) or diversified motion (e.g., random walking in a shopping mall). In general, we can describe the camera kinematics [13], which yields typical camera works generating distinct optical flows that can be classified as diversified flow or directional flow. This categorization helps us design a general cutting strategy to obtain the profile of video clips.

Now, let us examine some common properties of the categorized motions. For a video clip/shot with directional flow generated from a smooth camera ego-motion or a directional movement of target crowds, we can specify a *major flow* component in FOV (Figure 2). Moreover, we consider the flow component orthogonal to the major flow as the *minor flow*, and other flow components such as instantaneous rotation (camera roll) and shaking as the *unstable flow* component. Denoting a video clip by $\boldsymbol{C}$, and the optical flow vector by $\boldsymbol{u}(x,y,t)$ in the clip, the major flow $\boldsymbol{M} \in R^3$ in the video volume is computed as

$$M = \frac{1}{N} \sum_{x,y,t \in C} u(x,y,t) \qquad (1)$$

where N is the number of points in the clip. It shows direction if the scenes have a global motion or the camera motion is smooth.

The minor flow component $\boldsymbol{m}$ orthogonal to $\boldsymbol{M}$ is from particular styles of camera motion, hand shaking, unstable walking, and vehicle waving during the video capture. Its effect is visible in our profile as tilt changes during panning, translation, and zoom. Minor flow can be kept in the profile to reflect the dynamics of the camera, or can be removed by a video deshaking algorithm before and after profiling [10,11,12]. The *unstable motion*, $\boldsymbol{r}$, is from the instantaneous camera rolling, as well as the motion of dynamic targets against the background (BG) including non-rigid articulate motions and the deformation of human body and face, fire, smoke, water, etc. This type of motion is not dominant in the video clip for its smaller regions than background. Otherwise, it will be treated as major flow. The minor and unstable motion will not be used to determine the slice cutting. Although the unstable flow can be deshaked to some extent, we avoid cosmetic rectification since recording true motion in the profile is useful in clip editing.

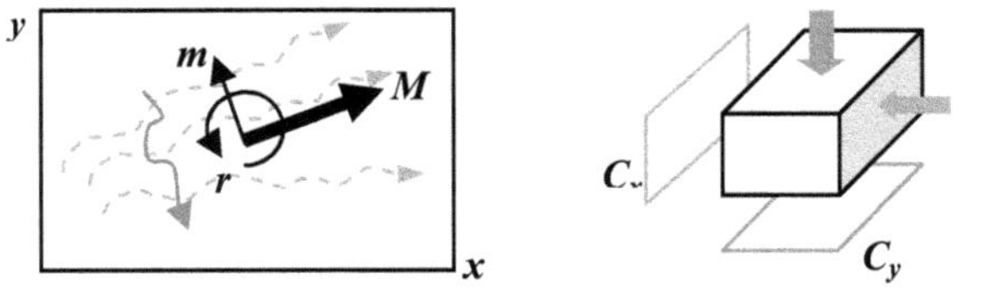

Figure 2. Major flow M, minor flow m and unstable flow including foreground motion (red) in video to be accumulated to condensed images.

We use *condensed image* used in vehicle video [10,11] to understand the distinct major flow in a video clip efficiently. In such slices, the motion is displayed as traces. Condensed images here are collected by averaging the intensities along the horizontal and vertical directions in the video. As an example in Figure 3, the major flow vector is close to horizontal direction. The long or high contrast features F_v perpendicular to $\boldsymbol{M}$ (i.e., in $\boldsymbol{m}$ direction) in the frames show their clear traces in one condensed image, while those features F_p parallel to $\boldsymbol{M}$ are blurred in it. Similarly, in the second condensed image, the condensing poses the stationary blur [14] on feature F_v but keeps F_p features sharp, and shows minor motion on them at the same time.

(a)

(b)

Figure 3. Two condensed images from a camera translating sideways. One is motion-oriented and the other is shape-orientated obtained by condensing intensities vertically and horizontally in the frames respectively. The time axes are horizontal.

If the major flow is non-parallel to either x or y axes ($\boldsymbol{M}$ in a slanted direction), both condensed images contain motion and shape information such as traces and shapes with stationary blur. Depending on the dominant information that the condensed images contain, we refer to one as *motion-orientated* and the other as *shape-orientated*, respectively. One displays more traces from the linear features in the video, and the other shows more blurred shape than traces. These properties are used in the profile cutting next.

3. CUT VIDEO VOLUME FOR PROFILE

This section explores a general slice cutting framework for the profiles of video clips from various simple or combined motions. Different from those methods of stitching regions from key frames, this work sets a sampling line $\boldsymbol{l}$ in the video frame to scan the major flow from one side to another across the frame. The ideal setting of $\boldsymbol{l}$ is to minimize $|\boldsymbol{l}\cdot\boldsymbol{M}|$ in the frame for cutting a sharp and complete shape (If $\boldsymbol{l}\perp\boldsymbol{M}$, then $|\boldsymbol{l}\cdot\boldsymbol{M}|=0$). At the same time, $\boldsymbol{l}$ should align with a set of structure lines in the frames, e.g., horizon, building rims, wall, etc., in order to preserve the scene structure in the generated profile. In real implementation, most clips are right side up aligning with structural lines in the 3D space, i.e., the video frame (axis or frame boundary) is aligned with structure lines in the scene. This is a reasonable condition for most video clips because of the gravity and the standing pose in taking and watching video. Now, we propose a qualitative cutting method for a general camera motion in taking a video clip.

1. Alignment of cutting slice: sampling line $\boldsymbol{l}$ for the slice will be parallel to one of the frame edges in either horizontal ($\boldsymbol{x}$ axis) or vertical direction ($\boldsymbol{y}$ axis), which results in a profile maximally compatible to the video orientation. We examine if the major flow vector is closer to vertical direction than horizontal direction to determine the line orientation in the frame. A vertical line $\boldsymbol{l}$ is selected if $|\boldsymbol{M}\cdot\boldsymbol{x}|\geq|\boldsymbol{M}\cdot\boldsymbol{y}|$, and a horizontal line is selected otherwise.
2. Diagonal Cutting: A slice will be cut with the evolving line $\boldsymbol{l}$ diagonally across the video volume for more scenes. Which direction to cut depends on the major flow, i.e., the slice should cut across the motion traces in the volume rather than aligning with them so as to include more scenes sharply in the slice. The moving direction of $\boldsymbol{l}$ is opposite to the major flow direction in the frame, and thus is most likely consistent to the camera moving direction.
3. Trajectory bending: The bending of the cutting slice (the speed change of scanning) is determined according to the zoom factor or the divergence of the flow. We will bend the diagonal slice towards the enlarged frame in the zoom clip.

We explain this algorithm using the traces in the condensed image in Figure 4, which displays the flow characteristics of general camera motions. For the simplicity, we assume here the major flow vector is horizontal, i.e., the camera motion is horizontal. From the simple camera motion such as zoom, rotation, and translation (abbreviated to Z, R, and T in bold) and their corresponding slice cutting [13], Figure 4 shows all the possible motion combinations. For example, a camera can zoom during translation (T+Z). A translating camera with its optical axis non-orthogonal to the path is also a case of T+Z. On a circular path around a center (T+R), the camera can face inside as $(T+R)_I$ to focus on a target [15], where the background generates the major flow. If the camera faces outward, i.e., $(T+R)_O$, which is usually obtained with a crane arm, the generated flow is more similar to translation with motion parallax [16]. Moreover, cases Z and S_D, as well as cases T and S_T in Figure 4 have inherently the same types of flow by looking at their flow traces.

For all composite camera motions above (in between simple motions Z, R, T), their traces and slice cutting trajectories in our algorithm are depicted. According to the additive property of optical flow from different camera motions, a composite motion generates flow traces deformed from that of the simple camera motions. It is noticeable in Figure 4 that the flow mostly has a consistent direction (leftward) inverse to the camera motion direction, even if the image velocities (trace orientations) vary. According to step 2 of our algorithm, the designed slices for composite motions are planes or curved surfaces across the flows

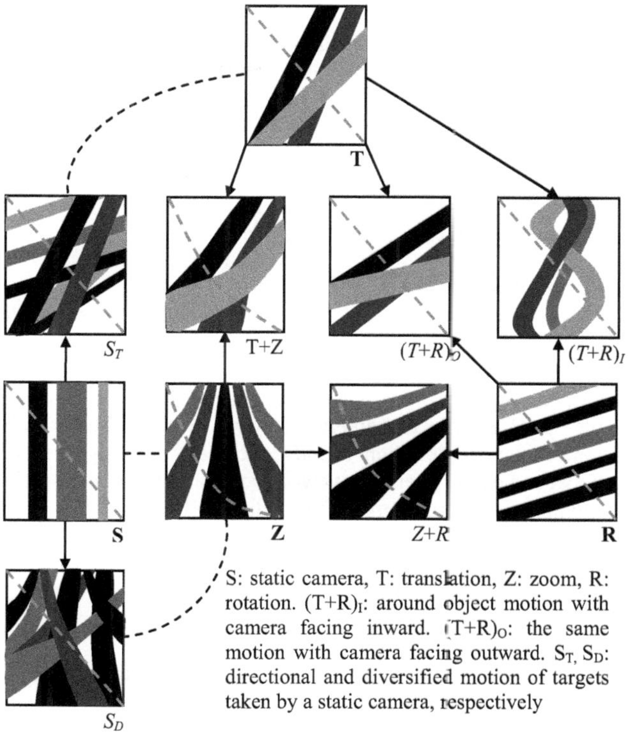

Figure 4. Possible cutting trajectories (red dotted lines) for major motion (traces in grey belts) in the condensed images. The downward vertical axis is the time axis. The camera motion is rightward if it is not static or zooming.

as indicated by dashed lines in red. The slice passes all the traces once to include the scenes stably appearing in the video clip.

4. EXPERIMENTS

When a video is read in, the color is condensed to two images, in which we segment video to clips according to the smooth camera motions. In the condensed image, edges orthogonal to the time axis leave clear footprint of clips. Based on the gradient values, horizontal and vertical components of the major flow vectors are computed and compared. This information is then used in selecting orientation of the sampling slice and its scanning direction. The slice is generated from the video volume accordingly. The test video clips are from YouTube and other video sharing websites. Figure 5 shows several profiles from the composite motions. Many TV programs are the concatenation of clips from static cameras. If the clip is short, the resulting profile is not very different from the key frame as in (a). The profile has a higher temporal resolution than key frame because the diagonal slice is longer than the frame in width. (b) is the diversified motion in a static view. Traces of people are displayed in the condensed image. The profile shows walking area crowded by people. The major flow vector is small for the static camera so that both horizontal and vertical cutting can be considered. We select a vertical slice for a profile. The same selection is performed on zooming in clip (c). The part zoomed up is enlarged and one side of scenes is also listed in the profile. If the cutting curve is bended in the opposite way, it will create reoccurrence at the other side of scenes in the profile. (d) is the zoom during pan. (e) and (f) are profiles from camera pan. (g) is an around-object video taken by a camera on a moving car. Such a camera orbiting around a target is also frequently adopted in shooting a static object such as sculpture or exhibit on a table, performer on a stage, etc. The camera motion contains translation and rotation simultaneously. (h) is a rotating object in a static background, which is similar as an around-object video. Object points rotate with respect to the camera and show the flow as segments of ellipse in the video frames. Their traces in the condensed image are sinusoidal curves [15]. The resulting profile is sharp and complete with a squeezed background. The foreground is extended to show its aspect views that are impossible to be covered by a perspective image or key frame.

5. CONCLUSION

This work proposed a general framework to cut video volume to obtain a profile of video. It is based on the analysis of camera kinematics and motion flow in the condensed images. A uniformed algorithm has been implemented on videos from simple and combined camera motions, which theoretically guarantees the profiles from various video clips. The significance of the work lies in generating new video profile with both spatial and temporal information. Further, the method is for general camera motions and is more robust than conventional mosaicing and onion-skinning. It can facilitate video browsing and editing when automatically applied to a video database.

6. REFERENCES

[1] Janvier, B., Bruno, E., et. al. Information-theoretic temporal segmentation of video and applications: multiscale keyframes selection and shot boundaries detection. *Multimedia Tools and Applications*, 30, 3 2006), 273-288.

[2] Taniguchi, Y., Akutsu, A., Tonomura, Y. PanoramaExcerpts: extracting and packing panoramas for video browsing. *ACM Multimedia* 1997, 427-436.

[3] Bartoli, A., Dalal, N. and Horaud, R. Motion panoramas. J. *CAVW*, 15, 5 2004, 501-517.

[4] Liu, F., Hu, Y. and Gleicher, M. L. Discovering panoramas in web videos. *16th ACM Multimedia* 08, 329-338.

[5] Pritch, Y., Rav-Acha, A. Peleg, S. Nonchronological video synopsis and indexing. *IEEE PAMI*, 30(11), 2008.

[6] Correa, C. D., Ma, K. L. Dynamic video narratives. *ACM SIGGRAPH 2010*, 29, 4.

[7] Zheng, J. Y. Digital route panoramas. *IEEE Multimedia*, 10(3) 57-67, 2003.

[8] Zheng, J. Y., Tsuji, S. Generating dynamic projection images for scene representation and understanding. *Computer Vision and Image Understanding*, 72, 3 1998, 237-256.

[9] Zomet, A., Feldman, D., Peleg, S. and Weinshall, D. Mosaicing new views: The crossed-slits projection. *IEEE PAMI (*2003), 741-754.

[10] Flora, G. R., Zheng, J. Y., Adjusting route panoramas with condensed image slices. *ACM Multimedia, 2007.*

[11] Zheng J. Y., Bhupalam, Y. and Tanaka, H., Understanding vehicle motion via spatial integration of intensities. *ICPR*08.

[12] Cai H., Zheng J. Y., Tanaka H. T., Acquiring shaking-free route panorama by stationary blurring. IEEE ICIP 2010: 921-924.

[13] Zheng J. Y., Cai H., Prabhakar K., Profiling video to visual track for preview, IEEE ICME 2011, 1-6.

[14] Zheng J.Y., Shi M., Scanning depth of route panorama based on stationary blur, IJCV, 78(2-3), 169-186, 2008

[15] Zheng, J. Y. Acquiring 3D models from sequences of contours. *IEEE PAMI,* 16(2),163-178, 1994.

[16] He, L., Shum, H. Y. Rendering with concentric mosaics. *SIGGRAPH*99, 299-306.

Figure 5. Profiles of video with end frames, profiles (time axes rightward), and condensed images (time axes downward).

Capture and Display for Live Immersive 3D Entertainment

Harlyn Baker, Nelson L. Chang, Arun Paruchuri
Hewlett-Packard Laboratories, Palo Alto CA
harlyn.baker;nelson.chang;arun.paruchuri@hp.com

ABSTRACT
We describe methods, accomplishments, and direction in a laboratory-corporate collaborative project over this past year and a half. With the goal of taking new immersive technologies to a growing customer base through in-situ demonstrations and experiments, we are combining novel capture and display capabilities in delivering life-sized immersive 3D entertainment experiences. We describe the adaptations and innovations needed in delivering immersive life-sized 3D to a large audience.

Categories and Subject Descriptors
C.3 [Computer Systems Organization] Special-purpose and application-based systems; Signal processing systems
J.5 [Arts and Humanities] Arts, fine and performing

General Terms
Algorithms, Design, Experimentation.

Keywords
Stereo display/capture, immersive experience, 3D entertainment.

1. INTRODUCTION
3D has become increasingly in demand for live reception of entertainment events such as sports and limited-run productions. The NBA playoffs, World Cup finals, and Masters Golf tournament are examples of recent such televised 3D events. The belief is that, if done well, premium viewing and interactive user experiences add value to the high-end fan base, extend the reach of the product, and create unique and memorable experiences for the talent and fan. The result could be life-like experiences that give fans the best view in the house: the prototypical Jack Nicholson seat at courtside. Delivering live 3D sporting events overseas could expand the fan base with life-like performances bypassing the huge overheads in moving two teams and the traveling production staff overseas. The opportunities are huge.

Nevertheless, capturing and delivering a compelling 3D experience for live events remains difficult and costly. Movies such as Avatar require a lot of advanced computer-generated (CG) modeling mixed with automated and interactive adjustments to achieve high quality 3D. Unlike CG, however, live events present only a single opportunity for acquiring the desired data, so acceptable capture can be challenging. Use of cameras with limited fields of view and the following of traditional 2D cinematography procedures such as rapid viewpoint, pan, zoom, and vergence adjustments tends to cause nausea and eye fatigue in 3D viewers [1,2]. Moreover, having multiple camera crews along with large life-sized displays can lead to extreme production costs.

We have been exploring ways to create compelling yet cost effective immersive 3D. Our solutions use scalable camera and projector arrays to deliver high quality, life-sized, immersive content. In contrast to standard entertainment formats such as 16:9 HD and 2.35:1 cinema, we consider alternate aspect ratios to bring an enhanced 3D experience. For example, a much wider panoramic 5:1 view with sufficient resolution to deliver the entire field of view (e.g. the full length of a basketball court or the breadth of a concert stage) gives a closer approximation to the in-arena experience.

The capture and display combination we present yields a rich, reduced-cost like-being-there 3D experience for live entertainment. The fan watches the action move across the screen rather than having the screen follow the action. As with the real venue, they are free to let their eyes explore–to the scoreboard, players on the sidelines, cheer-leaders, other local attendees, etc., all with sufficient resolution to be naturally drawn into the 3D scene.

2. THE CAPTURE CHALLENGE
Our intention in this effort has been to provide an immersive view of the event, one that cannot be acquired in its entirety in a single gaze; rather, we require the attendee to rotate the head to the left and right to encompass it all. In this model, the viewer will behave as though present at the event, seeing a nominal 50 degree field of view when looking ahead, and turning to the sides to take in the full-performance 100 degree context.

This act of self positioning to effect a change of view that a panorama enables has been seen to separate presence (and the sense of presence) from the more passive experience associated with choreographed viewing. In the latter situation, there is a "director" at the distribution point whose role is to select what the viewer will see. Equally, batteries of operators are positioned at the capture site to provide this director with a variety of streams and perspectives from which to select. Both are costly, and both detach the viewer from the experience of being there – presence.

2.1 Immersive Panoramic Imaging
For acquisition, we present the use of a synchronized camera array of numerous HD 1080p60 imagers driven from a single workstation [3]. Constraints on the placement of these imagers let us calibrate the camera system for both seamless high quality mosaicking and multi-viewpoint stereo [4] Moreover, we can configure the imagers in novel ways including interspersing portrait with landscape formats and providing variable baseline capture. Instead of using just two cameras, we use many; over

---

Area Chair: Xian-Sheng Hua

MM'11, November 28–December 1, 2011, Scottsdale, AZ, USA.

provisioning pixels in this way allows us to capture much wider fields of view while simultaneously capturing the two or more viewpoints needed for binocular 3D and beyond. Fig.1 shows a multiview camera capable of capturing triple-wide (each vertical column of lenses delivers a mosaicked panorama view) in five view zones. Deploying a few such fixed all-seeing camera systems can lead to much more flexible, competent, and inexpensive event capture, in contrast with the use of multiple crews and camera systems distributed over the space.

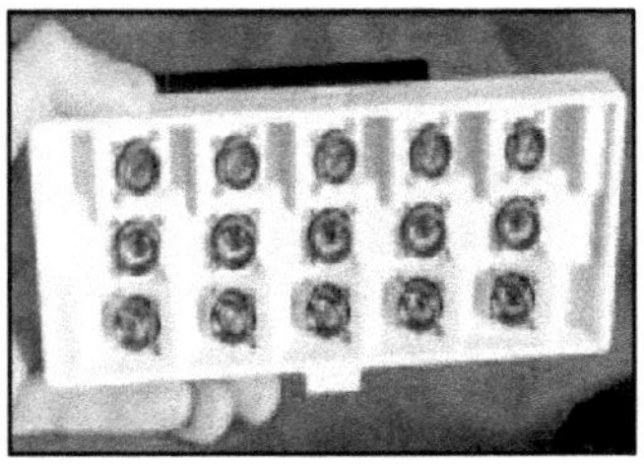

Figure 1. A triple-wide 5-view multi-imager camera.

To attain such a "super wide" view, we configure two or more HD imagers to share the capture at a given viewpoint, and combine their images. Such mosaicking is only exact when viewing a plane or when the imagers have coincident centers of projection, and this usually requires using mirrors [7]. Wishing to avoid the complication, expense, and fragility of a mirror solution for this mosaicking, we place our imagers as close to each other as possible in producing the panorama. Here, with our mounted HD imagers, this means about 23 mm. Wanting to minimize any effect of competing horizontal disparities which would come from laterally mounted imagers, we attain our panorama by placing one imager over the other (i.e., introducing a small amount of vertical disparity at the overlap).

2.2 Multi-view Imaging from a Distance

In most event capture situations, for logistics reasons, the provided camera placement differs from what may be preferred. Zoom lenses in traditional monoscopic capture permit camera crews to accommodate to this non-ideal placement, but the requirement of satisfying human 3D perception in a binocular setting puts constraints on the relationships between view distance, focal length, and perceived range, bringing another dimension to the task of reducing eye strain, fatigue, and visual discomfort in the viewing experience. With 3D cameras placed away from the ideal location, we are concerned about the visual veracity of what we can display, and specifically with the change in disparity associated with change in depth, a relationship that is often termed "roundness" in the 3D cinematography community. While there are many issues in delivering good 3D to viewers [1], we focus here on ensuring our camera system can provide what is essential so that subsequent software solutions can most easily meet the viewing needs.

Roundness describes the degree to which a viewed shape is perceived isotropically in 3D–that is, if a sphere is seen shaped spherically or has unintended spatial versus depth distortions. When the imagery is not acquired with this perceptual characteristic in mind, faces can become pancakes or noses can become de Bergerac-like. Additionally, mismatched focal lengths and baselines induce impressions of gigantism or miniaturism, where figures in the foreground or background are perceived with inappropriate size.

As Fig.2 sketches, we wish to reproduce the disparity (d) that would be observed at the desired locations (V□ and V□) using data acquired from the provided camera position. From a roundness perspective, we wish the change in disparity over some depth interval to be reproduced. Change in disparity with respect to distance is an inverse square relationship. In retaining the full stage in view for both viewer and acquiring camera (which determines the field of view and hence focal length of the lens to be employed), we can select an interocular (camera baseline) that will achieve this in an average (linearized) sense over the chosen depth interval. When we consider as controlling the round-ness, we can retain shape by scaling linearly with distance. This tells us how to build our cameras: while maintaining the framing (increasing the focal length, Hitchcock-like), we move back and broaden the baseline, while keeping fixed for each f and z, with a chosen Δz (other methods include [8]). The 3D multi-viewpoint cameras described in Section 4 were designed with this principle.

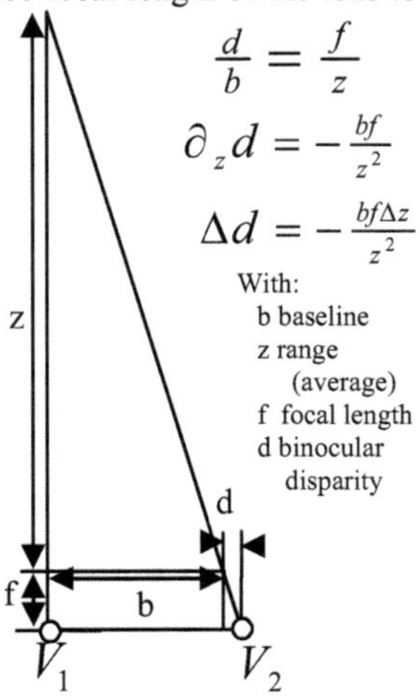

Figure 2. Correct roundness through maintaining Δdisparity with respect to range.

Viewer's eyes at V_1 and V_2

3. THE DISPLAY CHALLENGE

A truly immersive experience requires displays of sufficient resolution, size, and brightness, all of which don't easily scale. To address this, we use a similar approach for display, using a flexible 3D multi-projector platform that scales gracefully in size, aspect ratio, resolution, and cost. Multiple consumer-grade 1080P-WUXGA resolution projectors are configured in tiled and/or superimposed configurations to form a visually seamless high quality display [5]. With calibration patterns cast by the projectors and captured by a measurement camera, an automated modeling and optimization process derives one-pass per-pixel coefficients that can be applied in real-time to achieve synchronized 60 fps tiled rendering using GPU acceleration [6].

Key technical challenges we have met in our current work that extend our display capabilities include improved calibration algorithms for larger sized displays, synchronized live 4x1080p60 video ingestion, development of ambient-rejecting rear projection screens, and a scalable platform to support synchronized rendering across multiple workstations.

With dedicated polarization filters for each projector, the eyes get continuous images, overcoming the temporal-switching problems and low brightness typical in theater 3D systems. Additionally, the software solution for display frees us from fixed resolutions and aspect ratios, and helps reduce the fault intolerance and eye strain common in deployed commercial systems.

While personal glasses-free 3D devices are being introduced to consumers (e.g. Nintendo 3DS), glasses-based 3D is the preferred way to create life-sized displays supporting many viewers without highly restrictive view zones, ghosting, and other annoying artifacts. With our platform, we have created life-sized and selectable aspect ratio 3D event displays. With ambient light rejecting screens, these displays are sufficiently bright in room light to support comfortable simultaneous social interaction.

We have been demonstrating this display technology at numerous venues over the past year including an 11'x6' 3D rear-projection HD wall at both the Sundance Film Festival and an off-site briefing conference for corporate executives. Our in-lab demonstrations are moving from these smaller displays to much larger 3D displays for presenting the super-wide aspect ultra-high resolution scalable formats required for the immersive experience.

4. EXPERIMENTAL VALIDATION

Partner events at numerous locales over this year have provided the context for validating and advancing our 3D capture and 3D display technologies. The focus here has been on using these events to bring super-wide multi-view 3D capture and super-wide multi-view 3D display on line together.

4.1 Super-wide 3D Capture and Display

These partner events have presented a variety of capture scenarios calling for different aspect-ratio multi-view imaging, including basketball games from a 30' setback at center court, a fashion show viewing from 50' to the side at the end of the runway, and an R&B concert viewed from 160' back in a large hall. To satisfy these, we built several specialized super-wide multi-view HD cameras including a triple-wide stereo system (roughly 5760x1080 each) tailored for full-court basketball capture (Fig.3), a 12-imager varied-resolution system to cover the length of a fashion runway with consistent pixel resolution throughout, and a 19-imager system for varied-resolution concert capture (Fig.4). Various real-time 3D calibration tools are under development to help align the camera streams both in the field and in the lab. At the same time we developed matching display surfaces: extended the work to create a rear projection double-wide HD 22'x6' 3D display with 8 WUXGA projectors, supporting up to 4x1080P60 synchronized video via 3G HD-SDI over fiber, and most recently have built a 24-projector 36'x11' 3D screen.

As a first step in coupling 3D acquisition with 3D display, we demonstrated real-time live HD stereo 3D capture during an NBA Summer League game in Las Vegas, with local distribution over dark fiber to a double-wide HD 3D display. At the same event we captured double-wide triple-view and triple-wide double-view HD 3D content through designed multi-camera systems (Fig.1) which we displayed later, following image processing, on our 22' screen.

4.2 Multi-view capture example: the concert

Our last partner-event activity was an HD stereo simulcast of the R&B group Earth Wind and Fire at CES in Las Vegas, where we projected the group live in 3D on a 24'x11' display wall to a select audience. The video for this was from a selection of binocular stereo cameras. The invited guest and press response was uniformly positive, with a typical report [10] saying:

"... technology takes the experience of an intimate concert and scales it to a broader set of viewers, all while maintaining the authenticity and emotion of the experience."

Our current build is of a 36'x11' wall for presenting the double-wide video from the 19-imager ConcertCam, where we can mix immersive 3D display with overlays and inserts. The double-width 1080P25 stereo video (of which Fig.4 shows stills) has been cast across a 22'x6' display (Fig.5), enroute to presentation on the 36'x11' screen.

The viewing it delivers, with its encompassing and immersive feel requiring observers to turn to attend to different ongoing parts of the show, presents an experience that is, by today's standards, both novel and highly compelling – well beyond the usual. In permitting viewers to individually select where to direct their attention, it successfully demonstrates the *being-there* effect we have been discussing.

For the concert event capture, camera placement was to be centered, about 160 feet from the stage, while the desired view position was at about 30 feet. We chose a focal length to cover the stage (60-70 feet) and set our interoculars on those imagers so that its baseline (b) with the selected focal length (f) matched the roundness the viewer would experience when watching a performance at 30 + ~20 feet (mid stage Δz) with a human interocular of about 65mm. Fig.4 bottom left shows the initial design, with 6 banks of double-wide HD capture (about 11.5° FOV each), structured as two triple-views (for redundancy, and using 2 separate workstations) interspersed with 4° FOV telephoto lenses for close up detail capture. The bottom right shows the camera as deployed, where we replaced 3 of the long lenses with wider ones to obtain broader coverage at the overlap region, anticipating a sharpness requirement where the mosaic brings together the softer edges of the 2 adjoining lenses. The top row of Fig.4 shows the left mosaic view of the event; the second row shows a stereo view (crossed-eye viewing) of the mid length lenses, and the bottom shows 3 of the long high detail views (again, viewable in crossed-eye stereo). 36MP of video data were acquired per frame at 25fps (60fps capture became possible under Win7 with a bank of SATA3 RAID disks).

Until infinite resolution (or thereabouts) is available on our sensors, we expect to always be supplementing the static camera configuration with higher-resolution hot spots for isolating activities of interest inadequately captured with the homogeneous resolution of the multi-view mosaic. Capturing 3- or 4-view imagery (rather than simple 2-view binocular) by placing other imagers between the primary pair will enable us to synthesize other viewer positions [9] at the distance that baseline and focal length suggest, i.e., where the roundness and scaling best suit a human observer at the desired setback (recall that tradeoffs with such projective scale distortions as gigantism must also be considered).

Figure 3. Representative 5760x1080 image captured by prototype triple-wide HD 3D camera system in Figure 1 at the NBA Summer League engineered to capture the entire length of the basketball court.

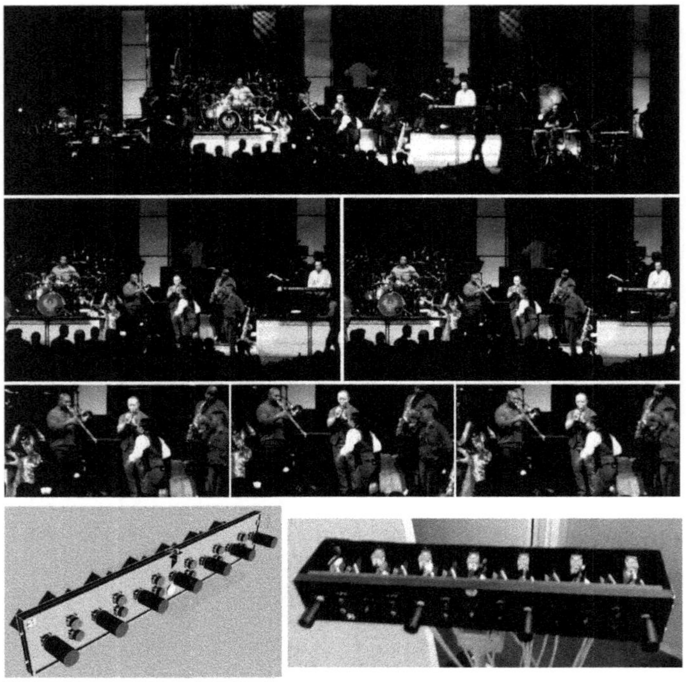

Figure 4: The Concert Cam. (top) Mosaicked double wide view (2x11□); (mid) Stereo pair (9□); (bottom) three long views (4□); (lower left) camera as designed; (lower right) cameras as deployed, replacing 3 long lenses with shorter mid range ones.

5. CONCLUDING REMARKS

Live 3D HD events such as the National Cinemedia Fathom [11], the Metropolitan Opera's Simulcasts to local cinemas, NBA playoffs, and the 2010 World Cup Finals all demonstrate fan interest and economic viability. Because individual cameras have limited field of view, multiple cameras and crews are needed to cover the extended experience, leading to high production costs. For 3D, camera crews require an extra operator to dynamically alter the viewpoint, focus, zoom, and vergence, which risk eye fatigue and strain for the audience. IMAX has developed immersive camera and display 2D technologies but they are primarily analog (film) and costly. Various camera companies such as 3alityDigital, PaceHD, Sony, and Panasonic have been developing dual-camera systems for capturing live 3D, but typically limit to 2K HD/ resolution and 1080i60 frame rates. Immersive multiview capture is an open area, with few competitors to the multi-HD camera systems we are deploying. Scalability is a major challenge in display, and competing multi-projector systems have not demonstrated the quality, flexibility, and adaptive scaling of the presented multi-projector technology.

Approaches such as those advocated and demonstrated here will lead to migration of these challenging burdens to the off-set production facility, increasing their flexibility while raising the bar on how viewers can enjoy events remotely – to the point where they may have individualized experiences as they attend to whatever aspects most draw their attention.

Figure 5. Prototype 22'x6' double-wide HD (3840x1080 @ 60 fps) 3D display using eight tiled+superimposed projectors.

6. ACKNOWLEDGEMENTS

We thank Henry Sang, Bob Cobene, and Ian Robinson for their contributions in management, organization and design in this effort.

7. REFERENCES

[1] F. Devernay, et al: Stereoscopic Cinema, Image & Geometry for 3-D Cinematography, Springer-Verlag, Berlin, 2010.

[2] B. Mendiburu, 3D Movie Making: Stereoscopic Digital Cinema from Script to Screen, Focal Press, 2009.

[3] H. Baker, D. Tanguay, A Multi-Imager Camera for Variable-Definition Video (XDTV*), Intl. Workshop on Multimedia Content, Rear, Class., and Security,* Istanbul, 2006.

[4] Z. Li, H. Baker et al., "Projective Epipolar Rectification for a Multi-imager Linear Array," *Proc. 3DPVT*, 2010.

[5] N. L. Chang and N. Damera-Venkata, "Scalable Large Format 3D Displays," *Proc. SPIE SDA XXI*, 2010.

[6] N. Damera-Venkata et al., "A Unified Paradigm for Scalable Multiple Projector Displays," *IEEE TVCG*, 13(6), 2007.

[7] C. Fehn, et al: Creation of High-Resolution Video Panoramas for Sport Events, Intl Jour Semantic Comp. (IJSC), 1:2, 2007.

[8] PePax http://nzphoto.tripod.com/stereo/3dtake/fbpepax.htm

[9] A. Katayama et al., A Viewpoint Dependent Stereoscopic Display Using Interpolation of Multi-Viewpoint Images, SPIE 2409, San Jose, 1995.

[10] http://www.progmic.com/2011/01/technology-from-big-platform-on-big-scale-for-big-events-is-hp-live-3d-technology-in-ces-2011-event-pictures/

[11] http://www.ncmfathom.com

A Real-time Bimanual 3D Interaction Method Based on Bare-hand Tracking

Junhao Shi
State Key Lab of CAD&CG
Zhejiang University
Hangzhou, China
99ellsworth@gmail.com

Mingmin Zhang
State Key Lab of CAD&CG
Zhejiang University
Hangzhou, China
zmm@cad.zju.edu.cn

Zhigeng Pan†
Digital Media and HCI Research Center, Hangzhou Normal University, Hangzhou, China
zgpan@cad.zju.edu.cn

ABSTRACT

We present a vision-based gesture interaction technique that is capable of tracking both hands in real-time. By only recovering features calculated from images, large amount of computation for 3D reconstructing and features tracking in 3D voxel grid is avoided. Thus, our system becomes an ideal tool for bimanual 3D gesture interaction, which needs neither markers nor gloves. Experimental results show that our method can complete the same pipeline with much less computational resource compared to existing ones. What's more, the application interface shows the effectiveness and intuitiveness of our bimanual tracking method.

Categories and Subject Descriptors

H.5.2 [**Information Interfaces and Presentation**]: User Interface – *theory and methods*; I.4.8 [**Image Processing and Computer Vision**]: Scene analysis – *Tracking.*

General Terms: Design, Experimentation, Human Factors.

Keywords

Computer vision, bare-hand interaction, 3D interaction.

1. INTRODUCTION

3D interaction, which enables users to carry out tasks by exchanging information with computer in 3D space, significantly improves immersive user experience. For a long time, researchers try to explore alternative input methods for 3D interaction besides using traditional cumbersome devices. Being frequently used in everyday life, gestures are familiar to people and natural to use. Yet approaches that utilize gestures with extra devices like special markers or data gloves [1,2] still burden users. Thus bare-hand tracking using computer vision technique is preferred in 3D interaction for its convenience, intuitiveness and flexibility. To design such a 3D interaction mode, the problem how to model a human hand, which is a highly articulated object with 26-27 DOF [3], is of particular importance. A variety of methods [4,5] have been proposed to model the structure and motion of hand.

In this paper, we propose a fast bare-hand tracking method which can fully support bimanual 3D interaction using only one personal computer. Our contributions are summarized as follows. Firstly, compared to some of the previous methods searching features in the whole 3D space [6], ours achieves lower cost by narrowing the searching space to 2D. Secondly, unlike in [7,8], all 6 DOF for hand pose can be determined. Finally, we present a robust way to distinguish among different gestures, allowing users to switch among them easily.

The paper is organized as follows: in Section 2 we review the existing methods for vision-based hand tracking. Section 3 is a brief introduction of our tracking algorithm. In Section 4 results of experiment are given, followed by conclusion.

2. RELATED WORK

Large amount of work try to solve the classic vision-based hand tracking problem. Besides methods using color gloves [9], bare-hand techniques also exist (see survey paper [4,5]), almost all of which can be classified as either model-based or appearance-based. Methods in the former category [10] take advantage of a priori knowledge built in the models so that image features can be looked as image observation of a 3D model. The most challenging task is recovering the joint angles, which is quite time consuming. Besides, the high temporal dependence indicates that lost tracking may happen if sudden changes of gesture occur.

Appearance-based model processes each new frame independently, thus avoiding the above initialization problem. Some only track and recognize 2D gestures which can be interpreted as pre-defined commands. System in [11] is able to recognize 26 letters by employing HMM, while [12] presents a template-based method that combines multiple cues for pose recognition. In [13] a 3-layer neural network is used to distinguish between different gestures and 3D pose. With two downward-pointing cameras, [7] describes a stereo vision system which acts as a multi-touch system. [8] introduces a vision-based interface for controlling a computer mouse via gestures determined by the number of detected fingertips. In [14] a similar fingertip tracking method is used with Kalman filter smoothing the tracking results. Problem the above systems suffer from is either unable to obtain all 6 DOF for hand pose or failing to provide bimanual interaction or both. In [6] researchers find a solution to the first problem by rebuilding the entire hand. However the computation load of this method is too high. Our work shows that with equal number of cameras as in [6], it is possible to achieve much acceleration by recovering extracted 2D robust feature points, while still maintaining tracking of all 6 DOF. Just as experiment shows, our method is able to track both hands on just one personal computer, instead of 3 in [15], which uses the same tracking method as in [6] for each of the two hands.

† Correspondence author.

*Area Chair: Lei Chen.

MM'11, November 28-December 1, 2011, Scottsdale, Arizona, USA.

3. 3D INTERACTION METHOD

3.1 Fingertip Detection

We choose the gestures depicted in Table 1 as target gestures, for the combination of them is capable of representing three classic 3D interaction modes: navigation, selection and manipulation.

Table 1. Target gestures of our system

Gesture	Posture		Tracked DOFs
point	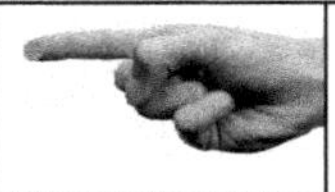	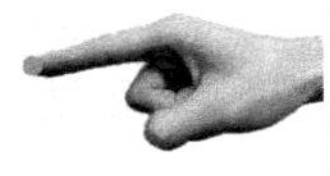	position (3 DOF) + direction (2 DOF)
pick	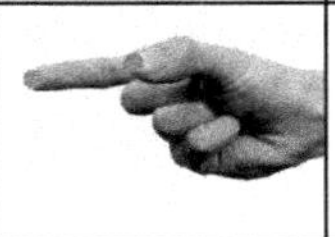	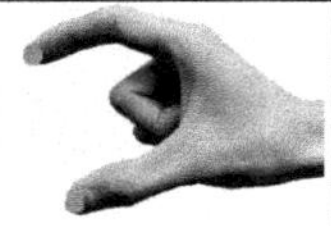	pose (6 DOF) + distance between two fingertips
release	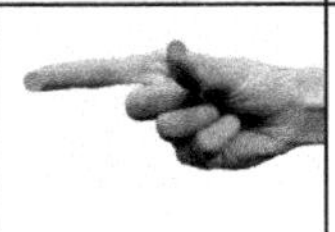	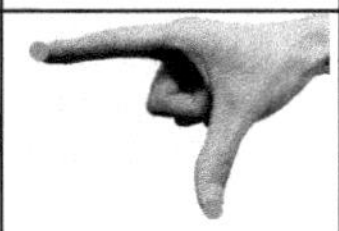	pose (6 DOF) + distance between two fingertips

New frames are segmented with Bayes Classifier [16], which works fine in laboratory environment. After mask images are smoothed, we find the largest blob [17] whose area is larger than *area_threshold*, and keep its contour information. Then Curvature based algorithm [18] is employed to find 2D fingertips. For the *i*th point P_i, we attach two attributes, namely the curvature value C_i and the direction flag F_i as follows:

$$C_i = \max_{l=threhold1}^{threshold2} (C_i(l))$$

$$C_i(l) = \frac{\overrightarrow{P_iP_{i-l}} \cdot \overrightarrow{P_iP_{i+l}}}{|\overrightarrow{P_iP_{i-l}}||\overrightarrow{P_iP_{i+l}}|}$$

$$F_i = sign(\overrightarrow{P_iP_{i-l_m}} \times \overrightarrow{P_iP_{i+l_m}}) \qquad (1)$$

$$l_m = \arg\max_{l=threhold1}^{threshold2} (C_i(l))$$

where l is the index displacement; P_{i-l} and P_{i+l} represent preceding and succeeding points of P_i. Only points with $C_i \geq$ *cur_threshold* and $F_i = 1$ are selected as candidates (see Figure 1). In our case, *threshould1* = 10, *thresuold2* = 30, cur_*threshould* = 0.7. Candidates close to each other are grouped and groups that satisfy the following requirements are reserved, otherwise rejected:

- Having largest or second largest number of elements.
- Element amount larger than *size_threshould* (10 in our case).

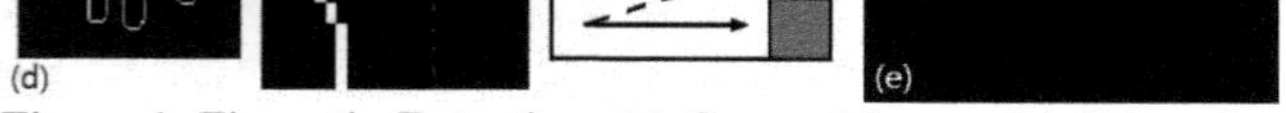

Figure 1: Fingertip Detection: (a) Current frame. (b) Skin color detection. (c) Contour of hand. (d) Packing of pixels on the contour. (e) Curvature test result, all colored dots have their *cur_threshold* larger than 0.7. The direction flag of red ones is 1, -1 for blue ones.

3.2 Gesture Recognition & Pose Estimation

With calibration data obtained as described in [19] and one pair of corresponding 2D fingertips, the position of the 3D fingertip can be recovered using triangulation technique. Only the index fingertip P_{index} will be detected if the current gesture is "point". Otherwise we have to tell whether the gesture is "pick" or "release". One solution [7] computes the direction of last phalanx of the fingers using local center of gravity, as shown in Figure 2 (a). Yet the method fails to provide accurate directions in our case, for the number of pixels involved in computing the 2D centroids is too small. Instead, we compare the distance between two 3D fingertips as in Figure 2 (b). Yet attention should be paid to various sizes of user's hand so that the distance threshold D_{th} is able to adapt to different people automatically. A user is asked to put the hand on table with all fingers fully outstretched in the initialization stage. We calculate the distance between fingertip of thumb P_{thumb} and that of little finger P_{thumb} as a measurement of hand size D_h.

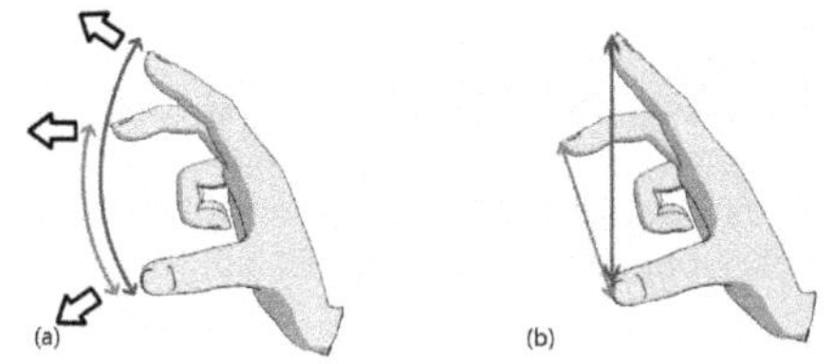

Figure 2: Distinguish between "pick" (red) and "release" (blue) (2D example): (a) using directions of the last phalanxes of the fingers; (b) using distance between two fingertips.

A survey is carried out to achieve a statistically persuasive mapping between off-line threshold $D_{th\text{-}off}$ and D_h with experimental results shown in Section 4.1. Based on the results, we generate a function $F_{th\text{-}off}$ that calculates $D_{th\text{-}off}$ given D_h:

$$D_{th\text{-}off} = F_{th\text{-}off}(D_h) = \frac{F_{pick}(D_h) + F_{release}(D_h)}{2}$$

$$D_h = \| P_{thumb} - P_{little} \| \qquad (2)$$

where F_{pick} and $F_{release}$ are curves constructed from above results using curve fitting process, and $\|\ \|$ represents Euclidean distance.

At time t given two detected fingertips P_1^t and P_2^t, the off-line result $D_{th\text{-}off}$ is combined with on-line result $D_{th\text{-}on}^{t-1}$ to get a more personal tailored threshold D_{th}^t, using the following functions:

$$D_{th}^t = wD_{th\text{-}on}^{t-1} + (1-w)D_{th\text{-}off}$$

$$D_{th\text{-}on}^t = \begin{cases} D_{th}^t - \beta \cdot G(D_f^t, D_{th}^t, \alpha) & \text{if current gesture is pick} \\ D_{th}^t + \beta \cdot G(D_f^t, D_{th}^t, \alpha) & \text{if current gesture is release} \end{cases} \qquad (3)$$

$$G(D_f^t, D_{th}^t, \alpha) = \begin{cases} 0 & \text{if } |D_f^t - D_{th}^t| \leq \alpha \\ |D_f^t - D_{th}^t| & \text{if } |D_f^t - D_{th}^t| > \alpha \end{cases} \quad D_f^t = \| P_1^t - P_2^t \|$$

where α, β and w are empirical parameters whose values are determined by experiments shown in Section 4.2.

Global center of gravity P_g is chosen as the third point to obtain rotation information. Now the position of hand T can be represented by P_g. For gesture "point", the pointing direction D can be computed:

$$D = \frac{P_{index} - P_g}{\| P_{index} - P_g \|} \qquad (5)$$

For the rest two gestures, we can derive the rotation matrix R as follows:

$$R = \left[(r_2 \times r_3)(r_2)(r_3)\right]$$

$$r_1 = \frac{P_{thumb} - P_g}{\| P_{thumb} - P_g \|},\quad r_2 = \frac{P_{index} - P_g}{\| P_{index} - P_g \|},\quad r_3 = \frac{r_1 \times r_2}{\| r_1 \times r_2 \|} \tag{6}$$

In summary, current gesture G_t can be defined as follows:

$$G_t = \begin{cases} \text{point} + T + D & P_1 \in \varnothing \vee P_2 \in \varnothing \\ \text{pick} + T + R & P_1 \notin \varnothing \wedge P_2 \notin \varnothing, D_f^t < D_{th}^t \\ \text{release} + T + R & P_1 \notin \varnothing \wedge P_2 \notin \varnothing, D_f^t \geq D_{th}^t \end{cases} \tag{7}$$

4. EXPERIMENTAL RESULT

4.1 Fingertip Distance Survey Result

50 subjects participated in our experiment. 26 are male and 24 are female, and their ages range from 7 to 55 years old (Figure 4 (a)). Since most people's hands stop growing after 20, a special favor is given to children and teenagers so that our data can cover a wide range of hand sizes. For each subject, the following data are measured (see Figure 3) and results are in Figure 4:

- The distance between fingertips of thumb and little finger when all fingers are fully outstretched
- The distance between the two fingertips under "pick".
- The distance between the two fingertips under "release".

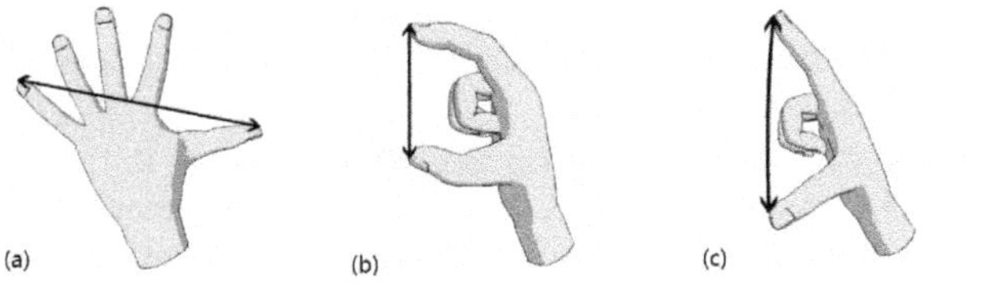

Figure 3: Distance measured in our experiment (2D example): (a) Distance when all fingers are outstretched. (b) Distance under "pick". (c) Distance under "release".

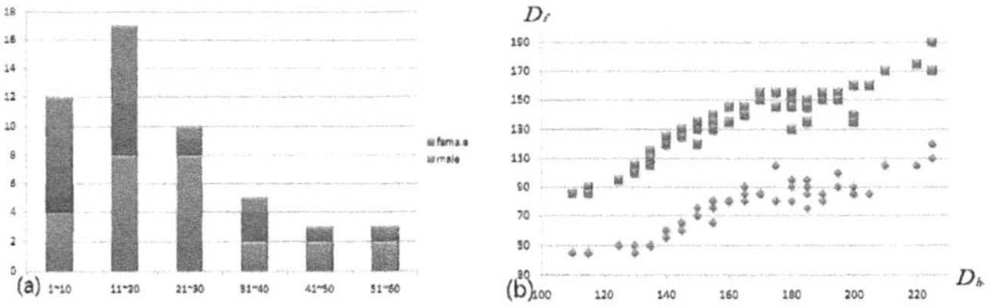

Figure 4: Distance measuring experimental result: (a) Age and gender of subjects. (b) X-axis denotes the distance when all fingers are outstretched. Red dots are distance under "pick" and blue ones for "release".

4.2 Threshold Parameter Experiment

In Section 4.3 3 parameters are used when computing distance threshold. α controls the discrepancy between threshold and fingertip distance to which the threshold can maintain its current value; β represents the update speed; w is a sensitivity parameter that controls the influence of on-line and off-line result. We first change α with β and w fixed, for we assume that update will complete anyway, with just several less or more frames.

Four α values were tested using the same 1600 frames. The subject's hand moved freely in the working space and only two gestures were allowed: either "pick" or "release". The subject was asked to switch between two gestures every 200 frames. For each α value, we recorded the distance between two fingertips and the threshold in each frame, both of which are depicted in Figure 5.

On the one hand, the results reveal that with smaller α value the threshold is more sensitive to the change of fingertip distance. However, too small a value leads to a tiny discrepancy between the fingertip distance and the threshold, producing more false recognition results. In Figure 5 segments between two black bars contain falsely determined gestures. On the other hand, system with α value too large lacks adaptability towards distance changes. Black circles in Figure 5 represent distance values that are significantly larger or smaller than current threshold, yet failing to cause adaption of the threshold. Further experiments show that values between 20mm and 30mm achieve equally good results. The rest two parameters are tested in a similar way. In conclusion, β from 0.05 to 0.15 and w from 0.2 to 0.4 work fine.

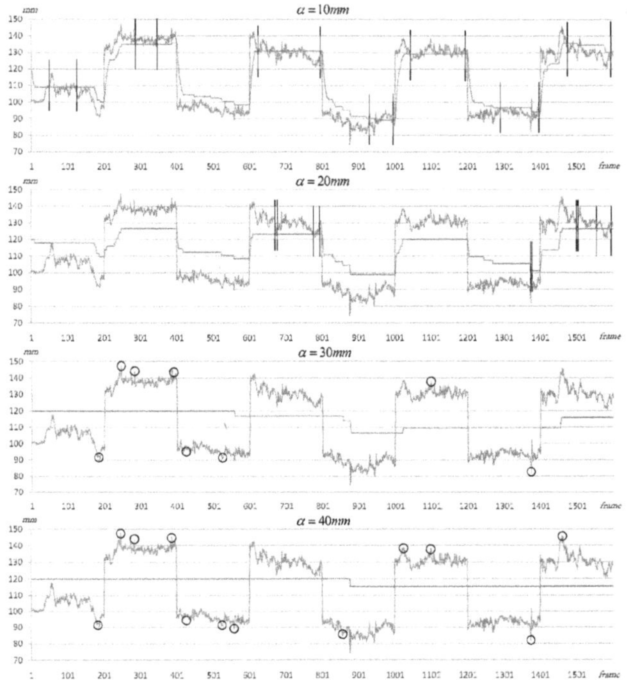

Figure 5: Fingertip distances and threshold values in each experiment. Blue lines represent the fingertip distance value, while red lines stand for threshold value.

4.3 Performance Test

In Figure 6, we show the fps of pipeline using our method (Method 1) and the one in [7] (Method 2, with 3D reconstruction and fingertips tracking on graphics card). Frames grabbed are 320×240. Both systems were tested on one same computer (Intel Core(TM) 2 Duo CPU E7500, Nvidia GeForce GTX 260). A total of three cameras (two Logitech QuickCam Communicate Deluxe, one Logitech QuickCam Pro 9000) are connected to the computer. It is clear that our method is much faster, while Method 2 spends too much time maintaining the voxel grid and tracking features.

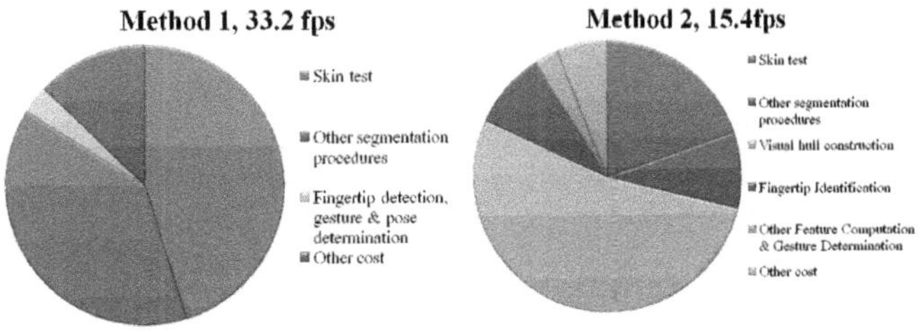

Figure 6: Frame rate and part each procedure occupied.

4.4 Interaction Interface

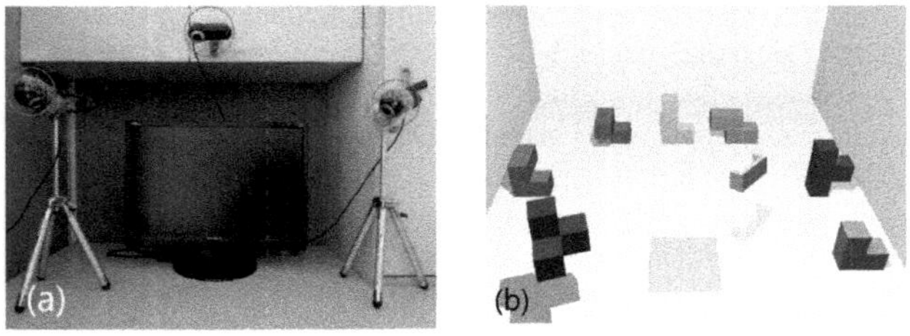

Figure 7: Interaction Interface: (a) System setup. (b) Shot of application scenario.

We developed an interface that requires a user to solve a Soma cube puzzle: to assemble all blocks to form an integral cube. The position and orientation of virtual robot hand is directly deduced from user's hand. Once a block changes its color, the user is able to grab it under gesture "pick". Once a block is picked up, it can be moved, rotated and placed. The second hand is used to enable or disable view modification mode by gesture "release". When it is enabled, viewpoint and the viewing direction can be changed with gesture "point". The attached video contains more details.

Several subjects who had never played Soma cube before tested this application and all were satisfied with its intuitiveness and accuracy. All the subjects were able to solve the puzzle with time spent ranging from several minutes to nearly half an hour. Yet from our observation we found that those who spent longer than fifteen minutes were stuck on the puzzle itself rather than on interaction. Furthermore, 4 subjects specially mentioned the effectiveness of bimanual interaction so that they could perform the task more smoothly through the coordination of two hands.

5. CONCLUSION

In this paper a real-time markerless bimanual hand tracking method is introduced, which is able to track the pose and 3 gestures of both hands. In the future, our plan is to enhance the collaboration of two hands. Also, it will be more satisfactory if other kind of gestures are recognized, which are required in more complex application scenarios. We hope we can get more promising results in this track.

6. ACKNOWLEDGMENTS

The project is supported by NSF of China on "3D interaction based on Gesture" (PI: Mingmin Zhang).

7. REFERENCES

[1] Benko, H., Ishak, E. W. and Feiner, S. 2005. Cross-dimensional gestural interaction techniques for hybrid immersive environments, *Proceedings of IEEE Virtual Reality*, 209-216.

[2] Sturman, D. J. and Zeltzer, D. 1994. A survey of glove-based input. *IEEE Computer Graphics and Applications*, 14, 1 (Jan. 1994.), 30-39.

[3] Kessler, G. D., Hodges, L. F. and Walker, N. 1995. Evaluation of the CyberGlove as a whole-hand input device. *ACM Transactions on Computer-Human Interaction*, 2, 4 (Dec. 1995.), 263-283.

[4] Pavlović, V. I., Sharma, R. and Huang, T. S. 1997. Visual interpretation of hand gestures for human-computer interaction: A review. *IEEE Transactions on Pattern Analysis and Machine Intelligence*, 19, 7 (Jul. 1997), 677-695.

[5] Wu, Y. and Huang, T. S. 2001. Hand modeling, analysis, and recognition. *IEEE Signal Processing Magazine*, 18, 3 (May 2001), 51-60.

[6] Schlattmann, M., Kahlesz, F., Sarlette, R. and Klein, R. 2007. Markerless 4 gestures 6 DOF real-time visual tracking of the human hand with automatic initialization. *Computer Graphics Forum*, 26, 3 (Sep. 2007), 467-476.

[7] Malik, S. and Laszlo, J. 2004. Visual touchpad: a two-handed gestural input device. *Proceedings of the 6th international conference on Multimodal interfaces*, 289-296.

[8] Argyros, A. A. and Lourakis, M. I. A. 2006. Vision-Based interpretation of hand gestures for remote control of a computer mouse. *Computer Vision in Human-Computer Interaction*, 40-51.

[9] Wang, R. Y. and Popović, J. 2009. Real-time hand-tracking with a color glove. *ACM Transaction on Graphics*, 28, 3 (Aug, 2009), 1-8.

[10] Stenger, B., Torr, P. H. S. and Cipolla, R. 2006. Model-based hand tracking using a hierarchical bayesian filter. *IEEE Transactions on Pattern Analysis and Machine Intelligence*, 28, 9 (Sep. 2006), 1372-1384.

[11] Liu, N., Lovell, B. C., Kootsookos, P. J. and Davis, R. I. A. 2004. Model structure selection and training algorithms for a HMM gesture recognition system. *International Workshop in Frontiers of Handwriting Recognition*, 100-105.

[12] Stenger., B. D. R. 2006. Template-based hand pose recognition using multiple cues. *Asian Conference on Computer Vision*, II, 551-560.

[13] Sato, Y., Saito, M. and Koik, H. 2001. Real-time input of 3D pose and gestures of a user's hand and its applications for HCI. *Proceedings of IEEE Virtual Reality*, 79-86.

[14] Conseil, S., Bourennane S. and Martin, L. 2005. Three dimensional fingertip tracking in stereovision. *International Conference on Advanced Concepts for Intelligent Vision Systems*, 9-16.

[15] Schlattman, M. and Klein R. 2007. Simultaneous 4 gestures 6 DOF real-time two-hand tracking without any markers. *Proceedings of the 2007 ACM symposium on Virtual reality software and technology*, 39-42.

[16] Pan, Z., Li, Y., Zhang, M., Sun, C., Guo, K., Tang, X. and Zhou, St. 2010. A real-time multi-cue hand tracking algorithm based on computer vision. *IEEE Virtual Reality 2010 Conference*, 219-222.

[17] Intel Corporation. Open Source Computer Vision Library Reference Manual v 2.2, December 2010.

[18] Lee, T. and Höllerer, T. 2007. Handy AR: markerless inspection of augmented reality objects using fingertip tracking. *IEEE International Symposium on Wearable Computers*, 83-90.

[19] J.-Y. Bouguet, Camera Calibration Toolbox for Matlab®, Standard Version, 2005, http://www.vision.caltech.edu/bouguetj/calib_doc/.

Learning"Verb-Object" Concepts for Semantic Image Annotation*

Xinming Zhang† ‡, Zheng-Jun Zha⋆, ChangSheng Xu † ‡
† National Laboratory of Pattern Recognition, Institute of Automation, CAS, Beijing, 100190, China
‡China-Singapore Institute of Digital Media, Singapore, 119613, Singapore
⋆School of Computing, National University of Singapore, 117417, Singapore
xmzhang@nlpr.ia.ac.cn, junzzustc@gmail.com,csxu@nlpr.ia.ac.cn

ABSTRACT

In real-world image understanding and retrieval applications, there exists a large number of images containing "verb-object" semantic. The most existing image annotation approaches which mainly focus on annotating images with "object" concepts may not well describe the image semantics. In this paper, we propose a novel image annotation approach by learning "verb-object" concepts. The "verb-object" concept learning method is developed based on the assumption that the classifiers of the "verb-object" concepts which contain the same object usually share a common structure. We formulate each "verb-object" concept classifier as a combination of a private part and a common part shared by all the "verb-object" concepts containing the same object. These classifiers are learned simultaneously through a joint optimization process. Experiments on a Web image data set containing 22,812 images with 28 concepts demonstrate that the proposed approach can achieve promising performance compared to the baseline method.

Categories and Subject Descriptors

H.3.3 [**Information Storage and Retrieval**]: Content Analysis and Indexing

General Terms

Algorithms, Experimentation

Keywords

Semantic Image Annotation, "Verb-Object" Concept

1. INTRODUCTION

Semantic image annotation, which aims to automatically assign semantic concepts to images, has become an active research topic owing to its great potentials in image understanding and retrieval. A number of image annotation approaches have been proposed in recent years. These methods can be roughly classified into three paradigms: the classification-based method which learns semantic concept classifiers to assign appropriate concepts to images [10, 3, 14, 18, 19]; the probabilistic modeling method that annotates images by inferring the joint probabilities between images and concepts [2, 6, 11, 8]; as well as the search-based approach which annotates an image by propagating the concepts of its visually similar images in a large-scale database [15, 16, 17].

Figure 1: Illustration of "verb-object" concepts

Despite the success of existing approaches, most of them mainly focus on annotating images with "object" concepts, such as "car", "lion" and "tree" etc. However, in real-world cases, a lot of images contain "verb-object" semantic, such as "repair car", "wash clothes" and "drink water", rather than only "object". Figure 1 shows some images that contain "verb-object" semantics. Modeling "verb-object" concepts is beneficial to understanding these images and is able to facilitate image search for the queries containing "verb-object" concepts.

Motivated by these observations, in this paper, we propose to learn "verb-object" concepts to better interpret image semantics. We assume that the classifiers of the "verb-object" concepts that contain the same object, such as "wash car", "drive car" and "repair car", usually share a common structure. We formulate each "verb-object" concept classifier as a combination of a private part and a common part shared by all the "verb-object" concepts that contain the same object. The classifiers of the concepts with the same object are simultaneously learned in an integrated optimization framework. We conduct experiments on a Web image corpus containing 22,812 images on 28 "verb-object" concepts. The experimental results demonstrate the effectiveness of our approach.

The rest of this paper is organized as follows. We review related works in Section 2 and elaborate the proposed "verb-object" concept learning approach in Section 3. Experimental results on a Web image corpus are reported in Section 4, followed by conclusions in Section 5.

*Area Chair: Xian-Sheng Hua

MM'11, November 28–December 1, 2011, Scottsdale, Arizona, USA.

2. RELATED WORK

In recent years, semantic image annotation has been found to be effective for image understanding and retrieval. A wealth of research efforts have been dedicated to this task. Existing image annotation methods can be typically categorized into three paradigms: classification-based [10, 3, 14, 18, 19], probabilistic modeling [2, 6, 11, 8] and search-based approaches[15, 16, 17].

Classification-based methods aim to build semantic concept classifiers and assign appropriate concepts to a given image based on the classification results. Many kinds of classifiers have been employed, such as Support Vector Machine [10], Mixture Hierarchical Model [3], two-dimensional multi-resolution hidden Markov models [14], and Graphical model [18] etc.

Probabilistic modeling approaches annotate images by inferring the joint probabilities between images and concepts. For example, Blei and Jordan [2] extended the Latent Dirichlet Allocation Model and proposed a Correlation Latent Dirichlet Allocation model which relates keywords and images. This model assumes that a Dirichlet distribution can be used to generate a mixture of latent factors. This mixture of latent factors is then used to generate keywords and image regions. Duygulu et al. [6] regarded image annotation as a machine translation problem. A statistical machine translation model is used to "translate" textual keywords to visual keywords, i.e., image blob tokens generated from image features using clustering. Some other works proposed relevance models for image annotation. Given a set of training images, relevance models are used to derive the probability of generating a textual keyword given the blobs in an image. The recent relevance models include Cross Media Relevance Model [11], Continuous Relevance Model [12], and Multiple Bernoulli Relevance Model [8].

Search-based image annotation methods attempt to annotate new images by exploiting the plentiful images on the Web [16, 5, 15]. Their assumption is that the visually similar images will possess certain semantic similarity, so their labels can be propagated in between and to annotate a new image. Wang et al. [16] collected 2.4 million high-quality Web images with abundant surrounding texts, and annotated a new image by mining common phrases from the surrounding texts of its visually similar images. Torralba et al. [15] collected around 80 million tiny images of 32×32 pixels and annotated new images using the nearest neighbor methods. They shown that the annotation performance improves when the image data set expands. Deng et al. [5] organized 3.2 million Web images and performed image annotation based on image ontology.

In addition, our work is also related to the multi-task learning technique [7]. Multi-task learning aims to improve learning performance by exploiting the relatedness between multiple tasks, i.e., the concepts in our work.

3. "VERB-OBJECT" CONCEPT LEARNING

In this section, we elaborate the proposed "verb-object" concept learning method. We first introduce the mathematical formulation and then provide the solution.

3.1 Formulation

Given a set of "verb-object" concepts $\{C_1, C_2, \ldots, C_K\}$ that contains the same object, such as "wash car","drive car", and "repair car" etc., we denote the training samples of the concept C_k as $\{\mathbf{x}_i^k, y_i^k\}_{i=1}^{N_k}$, where $\mathbf{x}_i^k$ is the d-dimensional feature vector of the i-th sample of concept C_k, y_i^k is its binary label which indicates $\{\mathbf{x}_i^k, y_i^k\}$ is a positive or negative sample, and N_k is the number of samples. Our goal is to learn a set of classifiers $\{f_k(\mathbf{x})\}_{k=1}^K$ for "verb-object" concepts $\{C_1, C_2, \ldots, C_K\}$. Since these concepts contain the same object, we assume that their classifiers share a common structure. We thus formulate each $f_k(\mathbf{x})$ as a combination of a private part and a common part shared by all the classifiers in $\{f_k(\mathbf{x})\}_{k=1}^K$. Here, we formulate $f_k(\mathbf{x})$ according to Support Vector Machine (SVM) [4] which has been proven effective in real applications.

$$f_k(\mathbf{x}) = \mathbf{w}_k^T \phi(\mathbf{x}) + \mathbf{w}^T \phi(\mathbf{x}) \tag{1}$$

where $\mathbf{w}_k$ and $\mathbf{w}$ are the model parameters of the private and common classifiers and ϕ is the feature mapping function that projects the original feature $\mathbf{x}$ into the transformed space.

The classifiers $\{f_k(\mathbf{x})\}_{k=1}^K$ can be jointly learned by solving the following optimization problem.

$$\min_{\mathbf{w}_k|_{k=1}^K, \mathbf{w}} \left(\frac{K}{2}||\mathbf{w}||^2 + \frac{K}{2}\sum_{k=1}^{K}||\mathbf{w}_k||^2 + C\sum_{k=1}^{K+1}\sum_{i=1}^{N_k}\xi_i^k \right)$$

$$\text{s.t.} \begin{cases} y_i^k(\mathbf{w}_k^T\phi(\mathbf{x}_i^k) + \mathbf{w}^T\phi(\mathbf{x}_i^k)) \geq 1 - \xi_i^k \\ \xi_i^k \geq 0, k = 1, 2, \ldots, K, i = 1, 2, \ldots, N_k \\ y_i^{K+1}\mathbf{w}^T\phi(\mathbf{x}_i^{K+1}) \geq 1 - \xi_i^{K+1} \\ \xi_i^{K+1} \geq 0, i = 1, 2, \ldots, N_{K+1} \end{cases} \tag{2}$$

where the first and second terms in the objective function are two regularization terms to prevent "overfitting" and the third term is the penalty on training errors. C is the tradeoff parameter and ξ_i^k is the slack variable. The first set of constrains are adopted for the training samples of "verb-object" concepts $\{C_1, C_2, \ldots, C_K\}$. The second set of constrains based on the training samples of the "object" concept are used to further facilitate the learning of $\{f_k(\mathbf{x})\}_{k=1}^K$. Here we assume that the positive samples of the "object" concept are the samples that are positive to any "verb-object" concepts in $\{C_1, C_2, \ldots, C_K\}$ and the negative samples are those which are negative to all the concepts in $\{C_1, C_2, \ldots, C_K\}$.

3.2 Solution

The objective function in Eq. (2) can be rewritten as the following primal Lagrange function:

$$\begin{aligned} L_p = & \frac{K}{2}||\mathbf{w}||^2 + \frac{1}{2}\sum_{k=1}^{K}||\mathbf{w}_k||^2 + \sum_{k=1}^{K+1}\sum_{i=1}^{N_k}\left(C - \mu_i^k\right)\xi_i^k \\ & - \sum_{k=1}^{K+1}\sum_{i=1}^{N_k}\alpha_i^k \left(y_i^k \left(\mathbf{w}_k^T\phi(\mathbf{x}_i^k) + \mathbf{w}^T\phi(\mathbf{x}_i^k) \right) - \left(1 - \xi_i^k\right) \right) \\ & - \sum_{i=1}^{N_{K+1}} \alpha_i^{K+1}\left(y_i^{K+1}\mathbf{w}_k^T\phi(\mathbf{x}_i^{K+1}) - \left(1 - \xi_i^{K+1}\right)\right) \end{aligned} \tag{3}$$

where $\alpha_i^k \geq 0$, $\alpha_i^k \geq 0$ are Lagrange multipliers. We minimize L_p by setting its derivatives with respect to $\mathbf{w}_k, \mathbf{w}$ and ξ_i^k to zero, which results in Eq. (4)

$$\begin{aligned} \mathbf{w}_k &= \sum_{i=1}^{N_k} \alpha_i^k y_i^k \phi(\mathbf{x}_i^k) \quad k = 1, 2, \ldots, K \\ \mathbf{w} &= \sum_{k=1}^{K} \mathbf{w}_k + \sum_{i=1}^{N_{K+1}} \alpha_i^{K+1} y_i^{K+1} \phi(\mathbf{x}_i^{K+1}) \end{aligned} \tag{4}$$

Substituting Eq. (4) into Eq. (3), we get the Lagrange dual objective function which is expressed in a matrix form as:

$$L(\mathbf{A}) = \max_{\mathbf{A}} \{-\mathbf{A}^T \mathbf{P} \mathbf{A} + \mathbf{1}\mathbf{A}\} \tag{5}$$

where

$$\mathbf{A} = [\alpha_1^1, \ldots, \alpha_{N_1}^1, \ldots, \alpha_1^{K+1}, \ldots, \alpha_{N_{K+1}}^{K+1}]^T$$

$$\mathbf{1} = [1, \ldots, 1]$$

$$\mathbf{P} = \frac{1}{2K} \begin{bmatrix} (K+1)\mathcal{K}_{1,1} & \ldots & \mathcal{K}_{1,K} & \mathcal{K}_{1,K+1} \\ \ldots & \ldots & \ldots & \ldots \\ \mathcal{K}_{K,1} & \ldots & (K+1)\mathcal{K}_{K,K} & \mathcal{K}_{K,K+1} \\ \mathcal{K}_{K+1,1} & \ldots & \mathcal{K}_{K+1,K} & \mathcal{K}_{K+1,K+1} \end{bmatrix}$$

$$\mathcal{K}_{m,n} = \begin{bmatrix} y_1^m \mathcal{K}(\mathbf{x}_1^m, \mathbf{x}_1^n) y_1^n & \ldots & y_1^m \mathcal{K}(\mathbf{x}_1^m, \mathbf{x}_{N_n}^n) y_{N_n}^n \\ \ldots & \ldots & \ldots \\ y_{N_m}^m \mathcal{K}(\mathbf{x}_{N_m}^m, \mathbf{x}_1^n) y_1^n & \ldots & y_{N_m}^m \mathcal{K}(\mathbf{x}_{N_m}^m, \mathbf{x}_{N_n}^n) y_{N_n}^n \end{bmatrix}$$

$$m, n = 1, 2, \ldots, K+1;$$

where $\mathcal{K}(\mathbf{x}_i, \mathbf{x}_j)$ is a kernel function and $\mathcal{K}_{m,n}$ is the kernel matrix of the training samples from concepts C_m and C_n. The optimization problem in Eq. (5) can be solved using SMO algorithm [9]. The resulted parameter matrix $\mathbf{A}$ is used to compute $\mathbf{w}_k$ and $\mathbf{w}$ in Eq. (4). Then we obtain the classifiers $\{f_k(\mathbf{x})\}_{k=1}^K$ according to Eq. (1).

4. EXPERIMENTS

In this section, we evaluate our approach on a Web image data set and compare it to a state-of-the-art method.

To evaluate the proposed "verb-object" concept learning approach, we conducted experiments on a Web image data set collected from Google image search engine [1]. We predefined 28 "verb-object" concepts for our evaluation. To construct the image data set, we generated a set of expanded concepts for each "verb-object" concept and submitted these concepts as queries to Google image search engine. For example, the expanded concepts for "drive car" include "driving car", "drive cars", and "man drive car" etc. The top 400 images in the search results were collected. To obtain the ground truth, we conducted a manual labeling process. We invited 20 subjects to manually label the images and filtered out the junk images that are irrelevant to the concepts. Finally, we obtained 22,812 images in total. There are 814 images for each concept on average. The ground truth was obtained through the majority voting of subjects' labeling. We separated the entire data set into three subsets: 60% as a training subset containing around 13 688 images, 20% as a validation subset with about 4562 images, and the remaining 20% for testing. The training subset was used to train the concept classifiers, the validation subset was used for tuning tradeoff parameters, and the testing subset was used to evaluate the annotation performance.

To describe the image content, we extracted a set of 128-dimensional SIFT features [13] from each image. We then employed K-Means clustering approach to cluster the SIFT features on training images into 500-dimensional visual words. The bag of visual words (BOW) features of validation and testing images were obtained by clustering their SIFT features into these 500-dimensional visual words.

For performance evaluation, we compared our approach to a baseline method, in which a SVM classifier was learned for each "verb-object" concept. We adopted RBF kernel $\mathcal{K}(\mathbf{x}_i, \mathbf{x}_j) = \exp\left\{-\frac{||\mathbf{x}_i - \mathbf{x}_j||^2}{\sigma}\right\}$ for the SVM baseline method and our approach. The kernel width σ and the tradeoff parameters C are obtained through a grid search on the validation subset. We adopted the widely-used non-interpolated Average Precision (AP) as the performance evaluation metric [1]. AP corresponds to the area under a non-interpolated recall/precision curve and it favors highly ranked relevant samples. We averaged the APs over all the 28 concepts to get Mean Average Precision (MAP) as the overall performance metric.

Figure 2 illustrates the annotation performance of our approach and the SVM baseline method. From these results, we can obtain the following observations:

- By jointly learning the "verb-object" concepts containing the same object, our approach outperforms the SVM baseline in terms of overall performance. It achieves a MAP of 0.31. Compared to the baseline with a MAP of 0.19, our approach achieves around 63.2% improvements.

- Our approach performs better on all the 28 concepts. Some of the improvements are significant. For example, our approach improves the AP by 154.8%, 120%, 107.1%, and 76.3% on concepts "buy car", "cook vegetable", "carry bike" and "carry bike", respectively.

In summary, our approach achieves better overall performance and consistently perform better on the diverse 28 concepts.

5. CONCLUSION

In this paper, we have proposed to learn "verb-object" concepts to better interpret image semantics. A novel "verb-object" concept learning algorithm has been developed based on the assumption that the classifiers of the "verb-object" concepts containing the same object usually share a common structure. These classifiers have been optimized through a joint learning process. Experiments on a Web image data set have demonstrated that our approach can improve the image annotation performance compared to the baseline method.

[1] http://images.google.com/

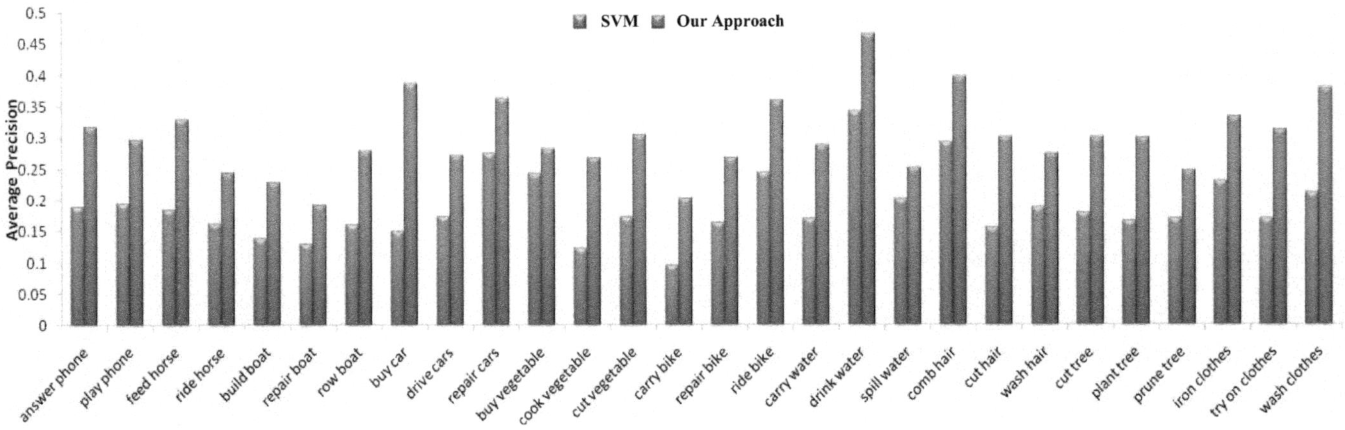

Figure 2: The annotation performance comparison between our approach and the SVM baseline method

Acknowledgement

This research was supported by National Natural Science Foundation of China (NSFC) Grant 60970092.

6. REFERENCES

[1] Trec video evaluation:. *http://trecvid.nist.gov/*.

[2] D. Blei and M. Jordan. Modeling annotated data. In *Proceedings of the ACM SIGIR conference*, pages 127–134, 2003.

[3] G. Carneiro, A. Chan, P. Moreno, and N. Vasconcelos. Supervised learning of semantic classes for image annotation and retrieval. *IEEE Transactions on Pattern Analysis and Machine Intelligence*, 29(3):394–410, 2007.

[4] C.-C. Chang and C.-J. Lin. Training nu-support vector classifiers: Theory and algorithms. *Neural Computation*, 13(9):2119–2147, 2001.

[5] J. Deng, W. Dong, R. Socher, L.-J. Li, K. Li, and L. Fei-Fei. Imagenet: a large-scale hierarchical image database. In *Computer Vision and Pattern Recognition, Proceedings of the IEEE Conference on*, 2009.

[6] P. Duygulu, K. Barnard, J. De Freitas, and D. Forsyth. Object recognition as machine translation: Learning a lexicon for a fixed image vocabulary. In *Proceedings of the European Conference on Computer Vision*, pages 97–112, 2002.

[7] T. Evgeniou, C. A. Micchelli, and M. Pontil. Learning multiple tasks with kernel methods. *Journal of Machine Learning Research*, 6:615–637, 2005.

[8] S. L. Feng, R. Manmatha, and V. Lavrenko. Multiple bernoulli relevance models for image and video annotation. In *Proceedings of the IEEE Conference on Computer Vision and Pattern Recognition*, pages 1002–1009, 2004.

[9] M. I. J. Francis R. Bach, Gert R. G. Lanckriet. Multiple kernel learning, conic duality, and the smo algorithm. In *Proceedings of the International Conference on Machine Learning*, 2004.

[10] Y. Gao, J. Fan, H. Luo, X. Xue, and R. Jain. Automatic image annotation by incorporating feature hierarchy and boosting to scale up svm classifiers. In *Proceedings of the ACM International Conference on Multimedia*, 2006.

[11] J. Jeon, V. Lavrenko, and R. Manmatha. Automatic image annotation and retrieval using cross-media relevance models. In *Proceedings of the ACM SIGIR Conference*, pages 119–126, 2003.

[12] J. Jeon and R. Manmatha. Automatic image annotation of news images with large vocabularies and low quality training data. In *Proceedings of the ACM International Conference on Multimedia*, pages 119–126, 2004.

[13] Y.-G. Jiang, J. Yang, C.-W. Ngo, and A. G. Hauptmann. Representations of keypoint-based semantic concept detection: A comprehensive study. *IEEE Transactions on Multimedia*, 12(1):42–53, 2010.

[14] J. Li and J. Z. Wang. Automatic linguistic indexing of pictures by a statistical modeling approach. *IEEE Transactions on Pattern Analysis and Machine Intelligence*, 25(9):1075–1088, 2003.

[15] A. Torralba, R. Fergus, and W. Freeman. 80 million tiny images: A large data set for nonparametric object and scene recognition. *IEEE Transactions on Pattern Analysis and Machine Intelligence*, 30(11):1958–1970, 2008.

[16] X. Wang, L. Zhang, X. Li, and W.-Y. Ma. Annotating images by mining image search results. *IEEE Transactions on Pattern Analysis and Machine Intelligence*, 30(11):1919–1932, 2008.

[17] X. Wang, L. Zhang, M. Liu, Y. Li, and W.-Y. Ma. Arista-image search to annotation on billions of web photos. In *Computer Vision and Pattern Recognition (CVPR), Proceedings of IEEE Conference on*, pages 2987–2994, 2010.

[18] Z.-J. Zha, X.-S. Hua, T. Mei, J. Wang, G.-J. Qi, and Z. Wang. Joint multi-label and multi-instance learning for imgae classification. In *Proceedings of the IEEE Conference on Computer Vision and Pattern Recognition*, 2008.

[19] Z.-J. Zha, T. Mei, J. Wang, Z. Wang, and X.-S. Hua. Graph-based semi-supervised learning with multiple labels. *Journal of Visual Communication and Image Representation*, 20:97–103, 2009.

A Novel Method for Semantic Video Concept learning using Web Images *

Yongqing Sun, Akira Kojima
NTT Cyber Solutions Laboratories, NTT Corporation, Japan
1-1 Hikarinooka Yokosuka Kanagawa,239-0847 Japan
yongqing.sun, kojima.akira@lab.ntt.co.jp

ABSTRACT

We propose a novel scheme to address video concept learning using web images, one that includes the selection of web training data and the transfer of subspace learning within a unified framework. Starting with a small set of video keyframes related to a video concept, we select web training data of good quality from the web by referring to the content of video keyframes. Then, by exploiting both the selected dataset and video keyframes, we train a robust concept classifier by means of a transfer subspace learning method. Experiment results demonstrate the robustness and effectiveness of our method.

Categories and Subject Descriptors

I.4.8 [**Scene Analysis**]: Object recognition

General Terms

Algorithms,Experimentation,Performance

Keywords

Visual concept modeling, Web image mining

1. INTRODUCTION

In recent years, exploring rich web image resources such as *Flickr* and *Youtube* has offered promising ways to perform low-manual-cost image concept learning and annotation. However, concept classifiers trained on web images perform poorly when they are directly applied to other domains such as *TRECVID* video concept detection. Such cross-domain learning based on web resources has been an active research method in recent years, but it still presents a number of unfulfilled research problems. The challenges of using web images for video annotation can be briefly broken down into two problems. First, it is difficult to select good quality training data from the web. Images gathered from the web are very "noisy" and contain images that are either duplicated or very similar to each other, which degrades training data quality. Data selection is an especially challenging problem when constructing training data of video concepts from the web using the framework of existing web image retrieval methods, which do not consider video frame properties at all. Second, the approach of switching knowledge between different domains is crucial since there are large differences in distribution between web images and video keyframes. Thus, a smarter algorithm is necessary to bridge the differences.

In this paper, we propose a new scheme to address these problems in a unified framework. It exploits the properties of both web images and TRECVID keyframes for video concept learning. First, the proposed method starts with a small set of images prepared from video keyframes of a concept called *reference images*. Then within the web images retrieved by concept words, noise filtering is conducted by exploiting the properties of reference images. Effective training data including representative images is then selected according to image salience and concept diversity. Finally, exploiting both the selected web data and TRECVID keyframes, transfer learning is adopted to build a robust classifier, which can also alleviate the over-fitting problem since it simultaneously conducts dimensionality reduction.

1.1 Related work

Our work is related to several research topics, including web image learning, canonical image selection from the web, and transfer learning. Due to limited space, we give only a brief overview here. There have been many studies on web image learning[6, 3]. For example, after web images are gathered using an object name, the visual concept is modeled as a constellation of parts using a probabilistic representation called *TSI-pLSA* developed by [6]. Regarding web canonical image selection, the work in [7] performs $K-means$ a clustering method on landmark related images leveraging both visual features and text metadata. Representative views are then selected as top-ranked images from top-ranked clusters. As mentioned above the main purpose of the existing web image learning and canonical image selection is to exploit web image properties to improve web image search results by current search engines. In contrast, new high-ranked web images are more content relevant and show a more representative overview of a concept. However, since the visual properties of video keyframes are different from those of web images, it is not appropriate to apply them directly to the application of video concept learning.

*Area chair: Xian-Sheng Hua

MM'11, November 28–December 1, 2011, Scottsdale, Arizona, USA.

Recently, cross-domain learning has been applied to solve the problem of training data scarcity in video concept detection in TRECVID. By leveraging the knowledge of a large amount of labeled training data from other domains called source domains, cross-domain learning methods make efforts to learn robust classifiers for the target domain. In [9], adaptive SVM is proposed to enhance the prediction performance of video concept detection, which adapts one or more existing classifiers trained from the source domain(program data in one TV channel data) to the target domain(other TV channel program data). Note that this method does not utilize the properties of the target domain, which is also useful in improving the classification performance. An instance-transfer approach is proposed in [10] to solve the cross-domain problem, in which the weights of the source domain data are estimated and a concept model is then trained based on the reweighted data. However, this approach is based on a strong assumption that both training and test data are drawn from the same feature distribution. Note that the above methods may perform desirably because they focus on cross learning between different TV channels or different TRECVID datasets, in which the distribution may be similar. However, in the context of web-based learning, since the difference between the properties of web images and TRECVID video keyframes is large, it is necessary to include information on both source and target domain data to build a robust classifier.

2. PROPOSED METHOD

According to [2], several visual properties of web images and TRECVID video frames have been observed. First, web image resolution is higher than that of TRECVID video keyframes. Second, web image objects are more salient and larger than those in TRECVID data. Third, backgrounds in TRECVID keyframes are more complicated than those in web images. As a result, in video concept learning it is not adequate to use the canonical images obtained by the existing web retrieval methods as training data directly. In this work we prepared a small set of images from video keyframes of the concept, which are denoted as $reference\ images$ and are used to introduce visual properties of the video concept to select training data from the web.

2.1 Training data selection from web

To alleviate the aforementioned visual differences between $reference\ images$ and web images, we propose a region-based method to capture the similarity of these two domains. We do so because we argue that their related images should share common regions although they may appear to be different in terms of size or location. Note that while local features like $SIFT$ may show effectiveness in concept learning conducted in the same domain, they may not present the relationship between two domains properly because of $SIFT$ descriptor difference due to the visual differences described above[2]. All images in this step are segmented into regions and characterized as region-based features reflecting image content from different viewpoints, which are presented in detail in [3]. All the regions are then normalized based on Gaussian normalization.

2.1.1 *Web image filtering*

First, by adopting the approach in [3], a classifier is trained from $reference\ images$, in which multiple visual patterns extracted from $reference\ images$ are used to describe the concept. Specifically, an efficient $K-means$ clustering algorithm is applied to cluster the regions of $reference\ images$ into several region clusters. These large-size clusters also include large-area regions that are then selected as salient region groups. Using the detected multiple salient region groups, an ensemble scheme based on discriminative analysis classifier is used to combine their corresponding visual patterns to describe the whole meaning of the concept. Then, if there are L salient groups, the same number of negative region groups is generated from TRECVID keyframes randomly. Using each salient region group and each negative group, a BDA classifier[3] V_i is built, $i = 1, \cdots, M$, $M = L \times L$. This classifier ensemble process is expected to describe semantic concepts in a more robust way.

Next, among web images gathered from the web using concept words, a noise filtering process is conducted exploiting the above classifiers. Given each web image I, the similarity between a region r_j in it and a visual model V_i is predicted by $D(r'_j, V_i)$. Here, $D()$ is Euclidean distance and r'_j is the projected r_j in discriminating space. The ensemble function given below is then used to determine whether or not a web image reflects the concept.

$$P(I) = \sum_{i=1}^{N} SS(i) \cdot \sum_{j=1}^{J} rw_j \cdot D(r'_j, V_i) \quad (1)$$

Here, $SS(i)$ are the weight values for the visual pattern classifier and rw_j are those for the regions in images that are set as their region ratios.

By introducing the visual properties of video keyframes and the region-based approach, regions sharing common visual patterns can be detected to bridge the relationship between two domains, which is used to enhance web image filtering. As a result, not only can irrelevant images be deleted, but also images that share a similar distribution with video keyframes can be selected.

2.1.2 *Training data selection*

Although irrelevant web images are suppressed, duplicate images are still prevalent, which impedes the generalization capacity of a classifier. In our work, we adopted the salience and diversity metrics proposed in Tang's work [4] to select regions from the filtered web images. We consider that the selected regions denoted as SR represent the concept from diverse viewpoints. Thus, we regard these web images including SR as web training data.

First, applying the $K - means$ clustering algorithm, all the regions of the filtered web images are clustered into N groups in an oversegmented way. Here, r_j indicates the region and the region's feature of the filtered images. It can be expected that these large-size region clusters contribute more discriminant power than smaller ones. That is, they can describe the concept in a more salient and representative way. The salience metric of SR including the selected region r_i is therefore defined as:

$$SAL = \frac{1}{N} \sum_{r_i \in SR} sal(r_i) \quad (2)$$

Here $sal(r_i)$ is the number of regions in the cluster corresponding to the i-th region in SR.

Regarding the diversity metric, the feature vector selection(FVS) algorithm proposed in [8] is used to find an orthogonal region set from the regions of the filtered web images, which compresses the redundancy information of the concept. According to the algorithm in [8], given a well selected SR, each region r_j in the filtered images can be approximated by a linear combination of regions in SR in kernel space. The diversity metric of SR can then be defined by minimizing the following normalized Euclidean distance in kernel space.

$$\frac{\| \phi(r_j) - \sum_{r_i \in SR} \alpha_{ji}\phi(r_i) \|^2}{\| \phi(r_j) \|^2} \tag{3}$$

Where α_{ji} are weights of the combination and can be optimized by the algorithm in [8].

Exploiting the above salience and diversity metrics, with a given size, an optimal region set SR is selected from the regions of the filtered web images by optimizing the following function, which is expected to maximize region diversity accompanied with salience.

$$\sum_{r_j \in WR} \frac{\| \phi(r_j) - \sum_{r_i \in SR} \alpha_{ji}\phi(r_i) \|^2}{\| \phi(r_j) \|^2 \cdot sal(r_j)} \tag{4}$$

Using the above selection process, the regions that belong to a large-size cluster and show dispersiveness in the span of feature space are selected from the filtered web images. Finally, the images including SR are regarded as the web training data. Images having multiple regions in SR are used only once in the web training data.

2.2 Cross-domain video concept learning

In many cases, the number of positive samples of TRECVID data(*target data*) is much lower than that of negative samples. Therefore, we want to find a cross-domain learning method which not only improves the classification performance by leveraging the knowledge of *source data*(web data), but also conducts dimensionality reduction that is expected to solve the overfitting problem due to the insufficiency of positive samples. The method proposed in [5],in which the age estimation problem is solved by a cross-domain subspace learning process, fits our goal well. In our work, by applying [5] with the web training images denoted as *source data* and video keyframes denoted as *target data*, a common subspace is learned based on a regularization subspace learning method by considering both distributions of both domains. For each image, a global visual feature or *BoW* is used; this will be described further in the Experiment section.

First, we adopted a mixture of Gaussian distributions to estimate the positive images in the combination of *source data* and *target data* referred to as CD and their common subspace. According to our empirical experience, the Gaussian component K is set from 15– 50. The objective function of the cross-domain subspace learning is modeled by finding an optimal projection or common subspace W, in which the projected features of both CD and its corresponding subspace share the same distribution. Using a regularization method the optimization can be carried out iteratively by the following function:

$$W_{k+1} = W_k + \kappa \left\langle \frac{\delta F(W)}{\delta W} + \lambda \frac{\delta H(W)}{\delta W} \right\rangle \tag{5}$$

Where $F(W)$ is the distribution of CD, $H(W)$ is a regularization term to adjust the likelihood function in subspace, and λ is the regularization weight. The above gradient of the distribution function of CD can then be obtained based the conventional discriminant subspace learning method, which is defined as:

$$\frac{\delta F(W)}{\delta W} = 2tr^{-1}(W^T S_w W) S_b W$$
$$-2tr^2(W_T S_w W) tr(W^T S_b W) S_w W$$

Here S_b and S_w denote the between-class and within-class scatter matrices, respectively. In [5], S_b and S_w are calculated according to the LDA algorithm. In our work, however, they are calculated according to the BDA proposed in [3], in which positive images are estimated by mixed Gaussian distribution and any distribution assumptions on negative images are relaxed. For actual applications this is more reasonable since negative images are very sparse within the span of feature space. With BDA, positive samples are clustered closely and the negative samples are pulled far away from the positive ones.

Let μ_k and Σ_k be the mean and covariance of the $k-th$ Gaussian component in CD and π_k be the mixing coefficient. Let $\mu_k^{'}$ and $\Sigma_k^{'}$ be the projected mean and covariance in the subspace. That is, $\mu^{'} = W^T \mu_k$ and $\Sigma_k^{'} = W^T \Sigma_k W$. Then the gradient of $H(W)$ follows the function, here $y_i = Wx_i$, G is the Gaussian probability density function:

$$\frac{\delta H(W)}{\delta W} = \sum_{i \in CD} \sum_{k=1}^{K} \gamma \Sigma^{'-1}(y_i - \mu_k^{'}) \mu_k^T \tag{6}$$

Where γ is:

$$\gamma = \frac{\pi_k G(y_i | \mu_k^{'}, \gamma'_k)}{\sum_{k=1}^{K} \pi_k G(y_i | \mu_k^{'}, \gamma'_k)} \tag{7}$$

Next using the above W, each image x_i of labeled *target data*(*target development data*) is then represented as a low-dimensional y_i. A SVR regression is then conducted on the *target data* to find the classification function $f(y)$. Here f can also be carried out by other linear or non-linear processes.

Finally, based on the above W and regression function f, for an unlabeled image from TRECVID keyframes(*target* test *data*),the classification of a video concept can be achieved.

2.3 Experiment

The performance of the proposed method is conducted by experiments on a subset of TRECVID 07 and 08 keyframes and web images. We use subset for experiments just because parameters can be tuned more efficiently. We also adopted the 20 video concepts used in the TRECVID 07 evaluation. Specifically, the development dataset includes two parts. One is keyframes collected from TRECVID 07 and 08 development data annotated by [1] that consists of about 10,000 keyframes. The other is web images gathered from the *Google* image search engine. In this work, given a concept, about 1000 – 2000 *JPEG* web images were gathered depending on the content relevance of the lower-ranked images. In total there are about 28,000 web images gathered for the 20 concepts. The test data is a subset of TRECVID 07 test data consisting of about 15,000 keyframes. Each concept model is learned independently using the proposed method. First, for each concept, about 30 – 100 *reference images* are selected from corresponding keyframes in the TRECVID development data. It can be conducted manually or automatically using a random rule. This number is determined considering computation efficiency and the number of positive samples. Our web filtering method is to some extent robust to the size of training data[3]. A concept classifier was then built based on *reference images* and used to conduct image filtering from the web images associated with the concept. Next, web training images were selected according to salience and diversity rules. As a result, 300 – 700 images were obtained as web training data. The negative samples used in this work were those obtained from TRECVID2007 and 2008. Finally, by exploiting positive samples in TRECVID data and the selected web training images,the concept learning was carried out by the aforementioned transfer subspace learning.

Due to limited space, Fig. 1 shows only one example to give an impression of how web training data likes. Using our method, the training data is obtained not only with less noise and redundancy, but also with an effort made to represent the content of video keyframes of a concept. To demonstrate the effectiveness of our method, we compared the proposed method with a baseline method that conducts concept learning using TRECVID data. Both our method and the baseline one make use of an average fusion of 2 SVM classification results for each concept using global image features and *BoW*. With respect to global features, for each image a total of 423- dimensional low level features are used, each of which consists of a color histogram (256), color moments (6), color coherence (128), texture MSRSAR (15), texture Tamura coarseness (10), and texture Tamura directionality(8). With respect to *BoW*, a *DoG* detector is used to extract the local keypoints from each image and a 128-dimensional *SIFT* descriptor is used. The $K - means$ clustering algorithm is then applied to generate 500 visual words. As a result, each image is represented as a 500-dimensional feature reflecting the histogram information of visual words. Spatial pyramid matching is also implemented in this work. Figure 2 summarizes the MAP scores. Me-

Figure 1: Part of reference images and web images related to "ComputerTVScreen"

dian is the median MAP scores obtained from the whole TRECVID 07 test data in all the submitted runs, which is shown here only to give a reference. As can be seen, our method performs generally better than or comparable to the baseline method for most concepts. It provides an average MAP score of 15.4% which is 5% higher than that of the baseline method. Our method provides better performance than the baseline method when concepts having not only sufficient positive samples in TRECVID data but also many related web images can be gathered, such as "office"and " waterscape". It is also advantageous in dealing with concepts when a large amount of related images can be gathered with good quality from the web though there are few keyframes in TRECVID data, e.g., "desert" and "US flag". There are only a few dozen positive images in TRECVID data, but the images obtained from the web are highly related. As a result, our method can successfully detect a concept in cases where the baseline method fails to do so. However for those concepts either having few keyframes in TRECVID or showing large diversity in web images, like "sports" and "police security", the performance is worse. It is very difficult to extract common visual patterns from "police security" keyframes because its content is represented diversely in video. Moreover, the "noise" level of this concept is also high in web images.

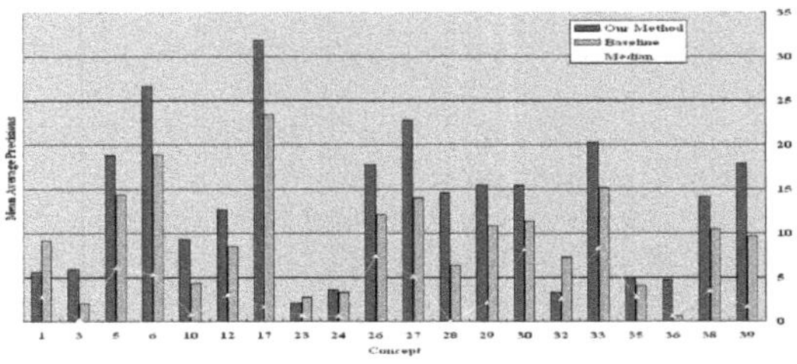

Figure 2: Performance of our method for 20 concepts of TRECVID 07 evaluation

The goal of this experiment on boosting classification results using web images provides an insight into the effectiveness of our method. The potential of using web images for video concept learning has been demonstrated in using our method. Although for some concepts there is still a performance gap compared with the best runs with high MAP scores, significant improvement was obtained in handling concepts with few TRECVID training data. In our future work, we will carry out a detailed investigation on training data selection and transfer learning methods to discover optimal solutions. We will also fine-tune parameters since they have a strong impact on classification results.

3. REFERENCES

[1] Wessel K.,et al. "TRECVID-2007 High-Level Feature task:Overview",*TRECVID Workshop*, Nov 2007.

[2] Jinqiao W., et al., "IVA-NLPR-IA-CAS TRECVID 2009: High LevelFeatures Extraction,"*TRECVID Workshop*, Nov 2009.

[3] Yongqing Sun,et al. "A Novel Region-based Approach to Visual Concept Modeling using Web Images", ACM Multimedia,08

[4] Jinhui T, et.al, "To construct optimal training set for video annotation," ACM Multimedia,06

[5] Ya Su, et.al. "Cross-database age estimation based on transfer learning," ICASSP 2010:1270-1273

[6] R. Fergus,et.al, "Learning Object Categories from Google's Image Search", ICCV, pp.1816 -1823, Vol.2,05

[7] Lyndon S. Kennedy, et.al " Generating diverse and representative image search results for landmarks", WWW 2008,pp.297-306

[8] Gaston Baudat, et. al, "Feature vector selection and projection using kernels", Neurocomputing, 55(1-2):21-38,2003

[9] Jun Yang, et al., "Cross-Domain Video Concept Detection using Adaptive SVMs", ACM Multimedia 07, pp.188-197

[10] S. Chang, et al. "Columbia University/VIREO-CityU/IRIT TRECVID2008 High-Level Feature Extraction and Interactive Video Search",*TRECVID Workshop*, Nov 2008.

[11] S. Tang, J.-T. Li, M. Li, C. Xie, Y. Liu, K. Tao, and S.-X. Xu, "TRECVID 2008 high-level feature extraction by MCG-ICT-CAS," *TRECVID Workshop*, Nov 2008.

Efficient Multi-modal Retrieval in Conceptual Space *

Jun Imura[1] Teppei Fujisawa[1] Tatsuya Harada[1,2] Yasuo Kuniyoshi[1]

[1] Grad. School of Information Science and Technology, The University of Tokyo

[2] JST PRESTO

{imura,fujisawa,harada,kuniyosh}@isi.imi.i.u-tokyo.ac.jp

ABSTRACT

In this paper, we propose a new, efficient retrieval system for large-scale multi-modal data including video tracks. With large-scale multi-modal data, the huge data size and various contents cause degradation of efficiency and precision of retrieval results. Recent research on image annotation and retrieval shows that image features based on the Bag-of-Visual Words approach with local descriptors such as SIFT perform surprisingly well with large-scale image datasets. Those powerful descriptors tend to be high-dimensional, imposing a high computational cost for approximate nearest neighbor searching in raw feature space. Our video retrieval method is focused on the correlation between image, sound, and location information recorded simultaneously, and to learn conceptual space describing the contents of the data to realize efficient searching. Experiments show good performance of our retrieval system with low memory usage and temporal complexity.

Categories and Subject Descriptors

H.3.3 [**Information Search and Retrieval**]: Retrieval Models

General Terms

Algorithms, Performance, Experimentation

Keywords

Generalized Canonical Correlation Analysis, Video Retrieval, Product Quantization

1. INTRODUCTION

In recent years, image and video sharing (e.g. Flickr and YouTube) have become popular. The popularization of smartphones is expected to accelerate the collection of personal life log data pervasively in daily life. The amount of multimedia data available on the web will continue its rapid growth into the future.

Several search algorithms have been proposed to process large amounts of image and video data. The most successful search method is the appearance-based approach, which is based on rapid similarity calculation by indexing low-level image features. However, a well-known semantic gap separates low-level image features and high-level image content. In general, the semantic similarity differs from similarity in the low-level image feature space. Because of the semantic gap, the appearance-based approach has limitations in terms of semantic search and the use of large amounts of visual data.

Extraction of rich features from images is crucial to search enormous amounts of data including diverse contents. Recently, large-scale generic object recognition is a rapidly evolving field. In this field, many Bag-of-Visual Words-based approaches have been proposed. They increase dramatically in recognition and retrieval performance [1]. Those features can represent diverse and complicated image contents. On the other hand, the dimensionality becomes huge. Therefore, the curse of dimensionality degrades the performance in similarity measures and increases the computational costs.

Proper evaluation of the similarity measure necessitates the selection of important elements representing contents from the high-dimensional space. In generic object recognition, kernel methods are typically used to learn the relation between images and labels from a tagged image dataset. The kernel methods can represent a nonlinear manifold in high-dimensional space. They are known to provide superior performance. However, the computational complexity and memory complexity of the kernel methods is no less than $O(N^2)$, where N is the training size. It is nontrivial to apply kernel methods to real-world data whose size is far beyond millions.

First, construction of a tagged image dataset is impractical for large amounts of real world data collected by individuals because the tagging of the huge amount of data is labor intensive. Other modality information collected through other sensors (e.g., audio and GPS) simultaneously with images is expected to represent contents that the image cannot capture by itself. Therefore, effective utilization of multimodal information is a key issue for practical large-scale semantic data search.

In summary, the following four points are important for practical large-scale semantic data search: 1) rich image features providing diverse contents, 2) extraction of crucial ele-

*Area chair: Xian-Sheng Hua

MM'11, November 28–December 1, 2011, Scottsdale, Arizona, USA.

ments from high dimensional data for proper semantic similarity calculation, 3) avoidance of labor-intensive dataset construction, and 4) scalability of large-scale real world data.

As described in this paper, we propose a new efficient retrieval system for large-scale multi-modal data including video tracks. Our method is designed to consider four key issues described above. Particularly, our retrieval method is focused on correlation between image, sound, and location information recorded simultaneously, and learns conceptual space, which describes contents of data to realize efficient searching. Moreover, the training complexity of learning the conceptual space from the large-scale multi-modal data is $O(N)$, without high-cost manual tagging, while achieving an even better search performance than that available with the traditional appearance-based approach.

2. RELATED WORKS

In recent research related to image retrieval, some efficient retrieval methods using compression and encoding of powerful image descriptors have been proposed.

[6] developed a rapid similar image retrieval method using a Fisher Vector compressed with Principal Component Analysis (PCA) and encoded by Locality Sensitive Hashing [2], Spectral Hashing [9], and $\alpha = 0$ Binalizing. The Fisher Vector is a descriptor that is computed by application of a Fisher Kernel [3] to Gaussian Mixture Models (GMM) in the feature space of a local descriptor. It can be regarded as an extension of BoVW. It uses the first-order and second-order statistics of local descriptors. Its dimension D equals to $(2N-1) \times d - 1$ or $N \times d$ for mean vectors, where N is the number of Gaussians and d is the dimension of the local descriptor. In this method, retrieval results are computed using the Hamming distance of the compact codes.

[5] proposed a powerful descriptor, Vector of Locally Aggregated Descriptor (VLAD), which approximates the GMM of Fisher Vector as hard quantization of local descriptors using the k-means method. It is a $D = N \times d$ dimensional vector corresponding to the components of mean vectors of the Fisher Vector. They achieved high accuracy of rapid similar image retrieval with severe limitation of memory usage by encoding the principal components of VLAD using Product Quantization (PQ) [4].

In these studies, PCA is used as a dimensionality reduction method to cut off noisy components to avoid the curse of dimensionality and to reduce the spatial and temporal complexity of approximate nearest neighbor (ANN) search for retrieval. However, PCA projection is based on the variance in raw feature space. It is difficult to lower the semantic gap. Consequently, PCA projection might lack components that are necessary to describe the contents of the data and which cause degradation of the retrieval accuracy.

[7] proposed learning of the semantic space of bi-modal data (images on the internet and texts linking to these images) using CCA and cross-modal retrieval in that space. Using data obtained from more than one modality enables us to use the structure between these modalities in addition to the information of the sample distribution in each feature space. This method is a scalable method to learn the space that represents its contents efficiently and which requires no labor for labeling data.

This approach, which efficiently estimates latent topics from bi-modal data and which learns a necessary representation of the contents, is expected to be applicable not only to images and text on the internet but also to large-scale multi-modal data in the real world.

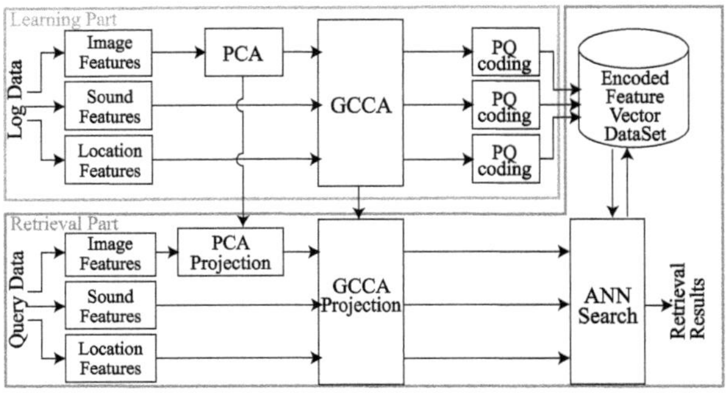

Figure 1: Illustration of the proposed multi-modal retrieval system.

3. APPROACH

In this section, we present a new method for efficient multi-modal retrieval. Using other modalities collected with images is reasonable to enrich features representing contents. Moreover, these multi-modal data are mutually related in accordance with their contents. Therefore, we first extract features expected to be related strongly to the contents and then learn crucial elements of high-dimensional features based on the structure between these modalities. For this research, we used three modalities: environmental sounds from audio tracks, locational categories from GPS, and visual features from video tracks.

3.1 Canonical Correlation Analysis

For scalability that can deal with large-scale data collection, learning methods must be simple and effective. We specifically examine the correlation of multi-modal data and used Canonical Correlation Analysis (CCA) for learning the conceptual space, representing the contents of multi-modal data. In fact, CCA is a linear dimensionality reduction method that maximizes the correlation of datasets. Because the original CCA is designed for two datasets, Generalized Canonical Correlation Analysis (GCCA) [8] is used to address three modalities.

As described in Figure 1, after extracting features from each modality, linear projection is calculated using GCCA. Let $\mathbf{X}_k \in \mathbb{R}^{N \times D_k}$ be feature matrices after centering for each modality and $\mathbf{R}_{kl} = \mathbf{X}_k^T \mathbf{X}_l$ be their correlation matrices where N is the number of samples, D_k represents the dimension of features, and k,l denotes the index of modality ($k = 1$ for image, $k = 2$ for sound, and $k = 3$ for location). Canonical vectors $\mathbf{h}_k$ are calculated to maximize the sum of correlation ρ between canonical components $\mathbf{z}_k = \mathbf{X}_k \mathbf{h}_k$ under normalization $\frac{1}{3}\sum_{k=1}^{3} \mathbf{h}_k^T \mathbf{R}_{kk} \mathbf{h}_k = 1$.

$$\arg\max_{\mathbf{h}_1,\mathbf{h}_2,\mathbf{h}_3} \rho = \frac{1}{6} \sum_{k,l=1,k\neq l}^{3} \mathbf{z}_k^T \mathbf{z}_l = \frac{1}{6} \sum_{k,l=1,k\neq l}^{3} \mathbf{h}_k^T \mathbf{R}_{kl} \mathbf{h}_l. \quad (1)$$

The canonical vectors $\mathbf{h} = [\mathbf{h}_1^T \mathbf{h}_2^T \mathbf{h}_3^T]$ are calculable by solving the following single Generalized EigenValue (GEV) problem.

$$\frac{1}{2}\begin{bmatrix} 0 & \mathbf{R}_{12} & \mathbf{R}_{13} \\ \mathbf{R}_{21} & 0 & \mathbf{R}_{23} \\ \mathbf{R}_{31} & \mathbf{R}_{32} & 0 \end{bmatrix} \mathbf{h} = \rho \begin{bmatrix} \mathbf{R}_{11} & 0 & 0 \\ 0 & \mathbf{R}_{22} & 0 \\ 0 & 0 & \mathbf{R}_{33} \end{bmatrix} \mathbf{h}. \quad (2)$$

For calculation stability, regularization terms $\beta\mathbf{I}$ can be added to correlation matrices $\mathbf{R}_{kk}$, where β is a small positive value. Canonical variables are calculated to be as many as the minimum of dimensions of three modalities. Thereby, we can obtain low-dimensional conceptual space by selecting canonical components from one corresponding to the largest correlation to an arbitrary dimension. Because the complexity of this GEV depends not on the number of learning samples but also on the total dimensions of features, this learning system of linear projection to the conceptual space is readily applicable to large-scale data.

For retrieval, vectors in the canonical space thus calculated are encoded by Product Quantization [4] and stored in RAM. PQ is a quantization method designed to efficiently search ANN data in high-dimensional space. It devides the feature vector into some lower-dimensional subvectors and k-means is applied to each subvectors. For each feature vector, it provides a small-size code representing combinations of the nearest centroids of each subvector. When a query feature vector is given, the system first calculates distances among all centroids in subspace, then estimates distances between the query and learning samples as sum of the distances between query subvectors and centroids using pre-calculated distances (Asymmetric Distance Calculation).

The system supports image query and multi-modal query for retrieval. We define the distance calculation for ANN searching as L2 distance for image query and sum of the L2 distance in all spaces for multi-modal query.

3.2 Features for each modality

Selecting appropriate features is an important part of designing the system. Because we use linear GCCA for the sake of scalability, some features must be evaluated properly with a linear metric for measuring similarity. Fast feature extraction is also important for an acceptable response of the retrieval procedure. For those purposes, we used VLAD for image features, Bag-of-Audio Words (BoAW) for sound features, and 1-of-k vector representation for location features.

As an image descriptor, VLAD estimates the distribution of local descriptors through hard clustering of k-means. Therefore, quantization of local descriptors and image description is conducted efficiently. From the perspective of complexity and performance, SURF128 features are densely sampled from points on a grid. For reduction of trivial elements for proper evaluation of correlation, VLAD is compressed into a high dimension (e.g., 1024 dim) using PCA before solving GCCA.

It is reasonably expected that environmental sounds are related strongly to contents. To represent continuous sounds in the environment, 100 samples of a 39-dimensional Mel-Frequency Cepstral Coefficients (MFCC) feature is extracted in each 1 s of the audio track. Then MFCC vectors are quantized to calculate a histogram of the 100 MFCC vectors in 1 s, just as in the BoVW method. This BoAW feature ignores short-term temporal changes in the frequency domain.

Feature for locational information is designed as a 1-of-k vector representation, where each dimension corresponds to one locational category (e.g., park, campus, street). Recent recording devices can easily attach location information to a video clip. Consequently, we can obtain information related to categories of the location data.

With GCCA projection of these features from multi-modal data, low-level features are mapped into conceptual space representing contents. Thereby, we obtain semantically important information from bottom-up features.

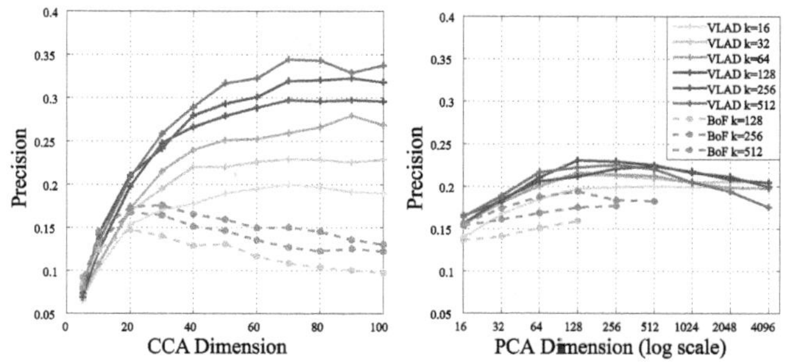

Figure 2: Effect of CCA and PCA for image features of Caltech256 dataset

4. EXPERIMENTS

In this section, we present the results of experiments on our method. First, we studied about the effect of CCA to image descriptors as a preliminary experiment. Then we evaluated proposed system with our original dataset for multi-modal data retrieval.

4.1 Effects of CCA

To make sure that CCA can find the essential elements representing contents, we did an experiment with CCA of image features and category labels of the images which are considered to have most strong relation to the contents. We used subset of Caltech256 - about 11,000 images in 100 categories , 80% of the data for learning and the rest for evaluation. BoVW and VLAD with grid sampled SIFT is extracted as image feature for the purpose of studying about the effect of CCA with different descriptors. Then canonical space considered as conceptual space is obtained by solving CCA of image feature and category labels given as 1-of-k vector representation. The evaluation is based on accuracy of recognition by nearest neighbor rule in this canonical space of image feature. We also did evaluation for PCA of BoVW and VLAD for comparison. Results are shown in Figure 2.

We can find a large advancement in performance of VLAD with CCA as compared with VLAD with PCA. This indicates that CCA can effectively work for selecting important elements and proposed system can achieve conceptual space representing semantic information by utilizing multi-modal information.

4.2 Multi-modal Dataset

We built a multi-modal dataset for evaluation of the retrieval performance. Some images in the dataset are portrayed in Figure 3. Our data are collected using a smartphone camera and microphone (640 × 480 resolution, 44.1 kHz monaural sound). This dataset includes about 2,100 frames sampled in 1.0 fps from about 35 min video clips. Features of each modality are extracted from each frame.

For image feature extraction, each frame is downsam-

Figure 3: example images of the multi-modal dataset

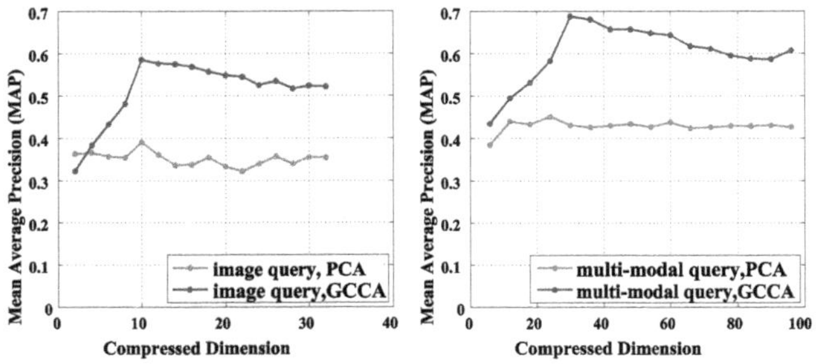

Figure 4: MAP vs. dimension with different query types

pled to 320 × 240 pixels preliminarily, then 128-dimensional SURF128 local descriptor is calculated at the 10 pixel grid point. About 1.5M in all SURF128 feature vectors are quantized using k-means++ into 64 clusters. The 8192-dimensional VLAD is calculated. For sound features, 2.1M MFCC feature vectors are quantized into 32 clusters. Therefore, we obtained 32-dimensional BoAW.

It is noteworthy that locational features are provided manually for each video clip in this experiment.

4.3 Multi-modal Retrieval Performance

We evaluated the accuracy of our multi-modal retrieval system. The compared method is based on the PCA of each feature. First, we evaluated both systems using a single-modal (only image) query. Queries are given as images. Only image features are extracted. Retrieval results are ranked by the approximated L2 distance of canonical components or principal components. Second, with multi-modal (image, sound and location) query, all features are extracted and the retrieval results are ranked by the sum of the approximated L2 distance in each space.

The compressed dimension is a critical parameter for accuracy and efficiency. Performance of the retrieval methods is measured using the Mean Average Precision (MAP). The results are shown in Figure 4.

Compared only with PCA, our method, which uses conceptual space composed using multi-modal correlation shows a better result in Figure 4. Our method performed highest MAP 0.69 at 30 dimension with multi-modal query where highest MAP of PCA-based method is 0.45. Even when the query is given as image, MAP of proposed system outperformed traditional approach.

4.4 Computational cost

Evaluation was calculated with dual Xeon quad-core processor @ 2.67GHz (Intel Corp.). In the feature extraction step, it took 10 min for local descriptor extraction, 44 sec for quantization and 100 sec for VLAD description. Additionally, 22 min were needed to load all SURF128 feature vectors from hard disk to RAM.

In the dimensionality reduction step, it took 110 sec for loading all VLAD features, 11 sec to solve the PCA of image features, less than 1 sec to estimate correlation matrices and 14 sec for solving GEV problem of CCA. It is noteworthy that we can obtain correlation matrices even faster by incremental calculation when adding new samples to the learned dataset. The retrieval cost for each query is estimated to be 120 ms including feature extraction.

5. CONCLUSION

As described in this paper, we have proposed an efficient retrieval system for large-scale multi-modal data based on the conceptual space calculated using Generalized Canonical Correlation Analysis of image, sound, and location features. Our method has scalability of $O(N)$ for learning and obviates costs of manual tagging. Experiment results for semantically similar data retrieval show that the proposed system performs better than the traditional appearance-based approach.

6. REFERENCES

[1] G. Csurka, C. R. Dance, L. Fan, J. Willamowski, and C. Bray. Visual categorization with bags of keypoints. In *ECCV SLCV Workshop*, 2004.

[2] P. Indyk and R. Motwani. Approximate nearest neighbors: towards removing the curse of dimensionality. In *ACM Symposium on Theory of Computing*, 1998.

[3] T. S. Jaakkola and D. Haussler. Exploiting generative models in discriminative classifiers. In *NIPS*, 1998.

[4] H. Jégou, M. Douze, and C. Schmid. Product quantization for nearest neighbor search. *IEEE PAMI*, 33(1):117–128, 2011.

[5] H. Jégou, M. Douze, C. Schmid, and P. Pérez. Aggregating local descriptors into a compact image representation. In *CVPR*, 2010.

[6] F. Perronnin, Y. Liu, J. Saándnchez, and H. Poirier. Large-scale image retrieval with compressed fisher vectors. In *CVPR*, 2010.

[7] N. Rasiwasia, J. Costa Pereira, E. Coviello, G. Doyle, G. R. Lanckriet, R. Levy, and N. Vasconcelos. A new approach to cross-modal multimedia retrieval. In *ACM Multimedia*, 2010.

[8] J. Vía, I. Santamaría, and J. Pérez. Canonical correlation analysis (CCA) algorithms for multiple data sets: Application to blind simo equalization. In *EUSIPCO*, 2005.

[9] Y. Weiss, A. Torralba, and R. Fergus. Spectral hashing. In *NIPS*, 2008.

Up-Fusion: An Evolving Multimedia Decision Fusion Method

Xiangyu Wang
National Univ. of Singapore
wang06@comp.nus.edu.sg

Yong Rui
Microsoft China R&D Group
yongrui@microsoft.com

Mohan S. Kankanhalli
National Univ. of Singapore
mohan@comp.nus.edu.sg

ABSTRACT

The amount of multimedia data available on the Internet has increased exponentially in the past few decades and is likely to keep on increasing. Given that a multimedia system has multiple information sources, fusion methods are critical for its analysis and understanding. However, most of the traditional fusion methods are static with respect to time. To address this, in recent years, several evolving fusion methods have been proposed. However, they can only be used in limited scenarios. For example, the context aware fusion methods need the context information to update the fusion model, but the context may not always be available in many applications. In this paper, a new evolving fusion method is proposed based on the online portfolio selection theory. The proposed method takes the correlation among different information sources into account, and evolves the fusion model when new multimedia data is added. It can deal with either crisp or soft decisions without requiring additional context information. Extensive experiments on concept detection task over TRECVID dataset have been conducted, and promising results have been obtained.

Categories and Subject Descriptors

H.3.1 [**INFORMATION STORAGE AND RETRIEVAL**]: Content Analysis and Indexing

General Terms

Algorithms

Keywords

multimedia fusion, online portfolio selection theory, evolving

1. INTRODUCTION

Multimedia techniques are developing at a very rapid pace. The amount of multimedia data available on the Internet has increased exponentially. Analysis of multimedia data is therefore needed in many applications such as information retrieval, education, and security. To perform multimedia analysis tasks, fusion methods are often employed.

There are still some open issues in multimedia fusion. One important issue is that the fusion model is not evolving. The evolution of the fusion model is of primary importance because of the nature of multimedia applications. First of all, most of multimedia data has limited or no labeled information. For example, on Flickr, the label for the multimedia document (image, tags and description) is not available or is quite noisy. The semantic label is important for multimedia analysis because many analysis tasks are based on classification and a large amount of labeled training data is necessary for good classification. Labeled examples are fairly expensive to obtain due to the high labor costs faced when annotating videos. Thus, little amount of training data is available at the beginning. The fusion performance may suffer as a result. Furthermore, the multimedia data keeps increasing with time. New instances of multimedia data are continuously added. For example, new videos are periodically uploaded on Youtube. The nature of the data collection can change. Thus, the fusion model may not always be valid or effective as the multimedia data increases. It will be quite useful to evolve the fusion model and improve the performance with new data. The previous methods generally cannot cope with the new data well. In this paper, an evolving fusion method, called Up-Fusion, is proposed.

2. RELATED WORKS

Most of the traditional decision fusion methods are static fusion methods [1]. That is, the fusion models in the methods stay unchanged no matter how the nature of data varies. For example, max / min / average fusion takes the max / min / average decision score of all information sources as the final decision score. The training-based super-kernel fusion method is proposed by Wu *et al.* in [9]. Not merely training on individual information sources to acquire individual classification models, the method determines the optimal combination of information sources by further training on the output decision scores of different information sources.

Generally speaking, the correlation and different performances of information sources are not considered. By considering correlation, a fusion method based on the portfolio selection theory is proposed in [8]. With the mean-variance analysis, the portfolio fusion finds the optimal weights for different sources by minimizing the correlation while maximizing the performance. But it is still a static method.

More importantly, once obtained, the fusion models in

*Area Chair: Marco Bertini

MM'11, November 28–December 1, 2011, Scotsdale, Arizona, USA.
Copyright 2011 ACM 978-1-4503-0616-4/11/11 ...$10.00.

these fusion methods are static over time. In reality, the correlation and reliability of information sources might vary with the changes of data or context. The static fusion methods cannot adapt to the changing data and environment, which may make the methods unreliable or even fail to work. Particularly, the portfolio fusion method [8] cannot be simply extended for evolution: simply applying portfolio fusion cannot guarantee the improvement in fusion performance and it is inefficient to update the fusion model whenever there is a new data instance.

Several evolving fusion methods have been proposed. An adaptive *crisp decision fusion method* is proposed in [4]. They modeled the decisions as conditional probabilities and used log-likelihood as weights for individual sources. The weights are updated according to their agreements with the fusion decision at each iteration. However, only crisp decisions (e.g., "yes / no") are considered, and it is not consistent with Principle of Least Commitment. The possible hypotheses are dropped in between and the performance may be degraded. A *confidence evolution method* is described in [2]. The method needs training for initial confidence for individual sources. Then, at each instance, the sources are divided into two subsets based on their decisions. The confidences are updated according to their agreement coefficients with the subsets. The methods need trusted sources and only confidence is updated. The fusion model is based on the underlying assumption that the media streams are independent, and the correlation among sources are not considered. The method needs to update the confidence for each new instance. It will be inefficient, and a significant restriction is that the labels may not be available online, as it may require manual intervention at every update step. A more realistic scenario is the update of the existing fusion model when a new batch of data becomes available. Recently, some context aware fusion methods have been proposed like [7, 5]. In *context weight fusion method* [7], adaptive weighting scheme was adopted for acoustic and visual speech recognition. The weights for audio and visual vary according to the noise level in speech. The method needs the context information which may not be available and dealing with all influential context factors is unrealistic. Again, correlation among information sources are not considered.

In this paper, we propose an evolving fusion method based on the online portfolio selection theory. Online portfolio selection [6] is a mechanism developed in economics. Consider a portfolio containing n stocks. Each trading day, the performance of the stocks can be described by a vector of price relatives, denoted by $\mathbf{x} = \{x_1, \ldots, x_n\}$, where x_i is the next day's opening price of the ith stock divided by its opening price on the current day. A portfolio is defined by a weight vector $\mathbf{w} = \{w_1, \ldots, w_n\}$ such that $w_i \geq 0$ and $\sum_{i=1}^{n} w_i = 1$. w_i is the proportion of the total portfolio value invested in the ith stock. The online portfolio selection strategy is as follows: At the start of each day t, the strategy gets the previous price relatives $\mathbf{x}^1, \ldots, \mathbf{x}^{t-1}$. From this information, the strategy immediately selects its portfolio $\mathbf{w}^t$ for the day. Over time, a sequence of daily price relatives $\mathbf{x}^1, \ldots, \mathbf{x}^T$ is observed and a sequence of portfolios $\mathbf{w}^1, \ldots, \mathbf{w}^T$ is selected. The mechanism aims to maximize the wealth on each day based on previous observations. Similarly, we want to improve the multimedia fusion performance as the data increasing in multimedia systems. Everyday we can observe the price and the return in the stock investment. In multimedia fusion, the scenario is similar if the "correct" labels of the new instances can be revealed for each update.

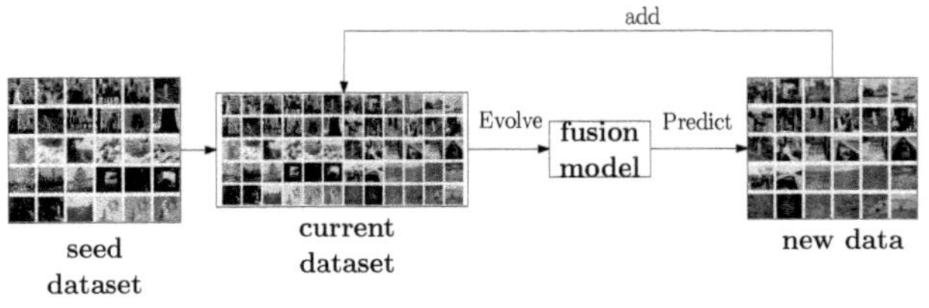

Figure 1: Framework of proposed Up-Fusion method

Compared to the static fusion methods, our proposed method is evolutionary. The fusion model evolves as new data being added. In this way, the fusion model can adapt to the changing data and environment. Suitable fusion models for different conditions should improve the performance as compared to a fixed model. Differing from the previous evolving fusion methods, our proposed method utilizes the correlation among different information sources, can deal with either crisp or soft decision (confidence score), and no context information is required.

3. UP-FUSION METHOD

$\mathcal{S}$ is a multimedia system designed for performing a task D. It consists of $n \geq 1$ correlated information sources $M_1, \ldots, M_n$. For $1 \leq i \leq n$, let $I_i(\mathbf{X}) \in [0, 1]$ be the decision of the task D based on M_i on instance $\mathbf{X}$. It is usually obtained by employing a detector on the features extracted from M_i. The final prediction I of $\mathcal{S}$ is modeled as the fusion of $I_i(\mathbf{X}), i = 1, \ldots, n$ based on the fusion model. Let $r_i(\mathbf{X})$ be the return of M_i at $\mathbf{X}$, and R_i be the expected return of M_i, which is defined as $R_i = E[r_i]$. More specifically, $r_{i;X_{\alpha:\beta}}$ denotes the returns for instances $\mathbf{X}_\alpha$ to $\mathbf{X}_\beta$ based on M_i. For $1 \leq i, j \leq n$, let $\Phi = [\Phi_{ij}]$ be the covariance matrix of information sources. The element Φ_{ij} is defined as $\Phi_{ij} = E[(r_i - E[r_i])(r_j - E[r_j])]$. It captures the correlations of different information sources. For $0 \leq t \leq T$, let f_i^t be the classification model of M_i at iteration t, and F^t be the multimedia fusion model obtained at iteration t. $y(\mathbf{X})$ is the true label of instance $\mathbf{X}$. The label is the class the data instance belongs to. The fusion flow is described in Algorithm 1, and the procedure can be illustrated in Figure 1.

The definition of return can be varied to different applications according to their aims. In the classification problem, since the aim of the classifier of information source is to accurately predict the labels and the performance is evaluated using accuracy, the return should be positive if the prediction is correct and negative otherwise. For M_i on instance $\mathbf{X}$, the return is defined as:

$$r_i(\mathbf{X}) = \begin{cases} 1 & \text{if } h_i(\mathbf{X}) == y(\mathbf{X}) \\ -1 & \text{otherwise} \end{cases} \tag{1}$$

where $h_i(\mathbf{X})$ is the predicted class of M_i on instance $\mathbf{X}$. For the retrieval problem, where we evaluate the performance using average precision, the definition of return can be:

$$r_i(\mathbf{X}) = \begin{cases} I_i(\mathbf{X}) - 0.5 & \text{if } y(\mathbf{X}) == 1 \\ -(I_i(\mathbf{X}) - 0.5) & \text{otherwise} \end{cases} \tag{2}$$

The expected return of ith information source R_i is ap-

Algorithm 1 Up-Fusion Method

Input: Seed dataset (the initial labeled dataset)

Initialization (Section 3.1)

- With the seed dataset, the classification model f_i for individual information source can be obtained
- The return $\mathbf{R}^0$, as well as the covariance matrix Φ^0 can be obtained according to Equation (3) and (4) based on the seed dataset
- The initial fusion model F^0 is constructed using Equation (5)

Evolution (Section 3.2)

- At iteration t, K new instances are added. The decisions can be obtained using the previous model F^{t-1}
- Consequently, the expectation $\mathbf{R}^t$ and correlation Φ^t for the information sources will be updated using Equation (6) and (7). The fusion model F^t will thus be updated according to Equation (8)

Output: Fusion model F^t

proximated as $R_i = E[r_i]$ over all the instances. The risk of information source is modeled as the standard deviation σ of return. For M_i, $\sigma_i^2 = E[(r_i - E[r_i])^2]$. The correlation ρ_{ij} between M_i and M_j over instances $\mathbf{X}_{1:\mathbf{N}}$ is defined as: $\rho_{ij} = \frac{E[(r_i - E[r_i])(r_j - E[r_j])]}{\sigma_i \sigma_j}$. Thus, the covariance matrix for n information sources is $\Phi = [\Phi_{ij}]_{n \times n}$, in which $\Phi_{ij} = \rho_{ij}\sigma_i\sigma_j = E[(r_i - E[r_i])(r_j - E[r_j])]$

With the portfolio fusion method, the optimal weights $\mathbf{w}$ are obtained by minimizing $\mathcal{F} = \mathbf{w}^{\mathrm{T}}\Phi\mathbf{w} - \lambda\mathbf{R}^{\mathrm{T}}\mathbf{w}$. Here, $\mathbf{w}^{\mathrm{T}}\Phi\mathbf{w}$ is the risk of the information sources. $\mathbf{R}^{\mathrm{T}}\mathbf{w}$ is the expected return. $\lambda \in [0, +\infty)$ is the "risk tolerance" factor.

3.1 Initialization

The method starts with a dataset of N_0 labeled instances. This dataset is called the *seed dataset*. The classification models for individual information sources can be obtained with the labeled data. Here, binary classification is considered because multi-class classification can be achieved by One-Versus-the-Rest strategy. The classification model for M_i is denoted as f_i^0. The decision according to f_i^0 on instance $\mathbf{X}$ is $I_i(\mathbf{X})$.

With the initial dataset, the expected return $\mathbf{R}^0$ and covariance Φ^0 are calculated. The initial expected return is

$$\mathbf{R}^0 = [R_i^0]_{n \times 1} \tag{3}$$

The initial covariance matrix for n information sources is $\Phi^0 = [\Phi_{ij}^0]_{n \times n}$, in which

$$\Phi_{ij}^0 = \rho_{ij}^0 \sigma_i^0 \sigma_j^0 \tag{4}$$

The optimal weights $\mathbf{w}^0$ for information sources are obtained by minimizing

$$\mathcal{F} = (\mathbf{w}^0)^{\mathrm{T}}\Phi^0(\mathbf{w}^0) - \lambda(\mathbf{R}^0)^{\mathrm{T}}(\mathbf{w}^0) \tag{5}$$

The initial fusion model $F^0 = \mathbf{w}^0 \cdot f_i^0$.

3.2 Evolution

The fusion model is updated every iteration when new data is added. It will be inefficient to update the fusion model whenever there is a new data instance. Moreover, a significant constraint is that the labels will not be discovered soon after the prediction is made. In our Up-Fusion method, we will update the fusion model when a batch of K new instances becomes available. In iteration $t (t = 1, 2, \ldots, T)$, K new instances are added into the dataset and the data instances are $\mathbf{X}_{1:N_t}$.

According to the definition, the return $\mathbf{R}^t = [R_i^t]_{n \times 1}$, in which R_i^t is defined as:

$$R_i^t = E[r_{i;X_{\alpha_t:\beta_t}}] \tag{6}$$

The covariance Φ_{ij}^t between M_i and M_j is updated as

$$\Phi_{ij}^t = \rho_{ij}^t \sigma_i^t \sigma_j^t = E[(r_{i;X_{\alpha_t:\beta_t}} - R_i^t)(r_{j;X_{\alpha_t:\beta_t}} - R_j^t)] \tag{7}$$

Here, the exact return and covariance method is used. That is, take all the current available data instances $\mathbf{X}_{1:N_t}$ into account, and calculate the return on the instance with Equation (1) or (2). Then, the new R_i^t and Φ^t is re-calculated on the whole available dataset based on the Equation (6) and (7). Here, $\alpha_t = 1$ and $\beta_t = N_t$.

The distribution of the newly added data instances may be largely different from the actual distribution, or the correlation of information sources on the newly added data instances varies from the actual correlation. The noisy new data instances may degrade the fusion performance. Thus, merely computing the exact return and covariance may not always improve the results. The performance may be unstable as the amount of data increases. To overcome this disadvantage, we refine the evolving fusion method by introducing a validation step. When the new data instances are added, the weights can be obtained with the Up-Fusion method. Then, the weights are validated on the initial seed dataset. If the performance on the initial seed dataset is improved compared to the previous weights, the new weights are updated. Otherwise, the weights remain unchanged. In this way, we can expect the fusion performance to be always improved.

Thus, the weights $\mathbf{w}^t$ at iteration t are obtained by minimizing

$$\mathcal{F} = (\mathbf{w}^t)^{\mathrm{T}}\Phi^t(\mathbf{w}^t) - \lambda(\mathbf{R}^t)^{\mathrm{T}}(\mathbf{w}^t) \tag{8}$$

Subject to:

- $\sum_{i=1}^{n} w_i^t = 1$, and $0 \leq w_i^t \leq 1$
- $\mathcal{P}(\mathbf{w}^t) \geq \mathcal{P}(\mathbf{w}^{t-1})$. Here, $\mathcal{P}(\mathbf{w})$ denotes the fusion performance on seed dataset with weights $\mathbf{w}$

To take prior knowledge into account, the initial point for minimization is set to be the previous weights. Starting from the initial weight vector, the formula is optimized as a quadratic programming problem. If the performance on validation dataset with new weights is better than that of the old weights, the fusion model is updated with new weights. Otherwise, the weights remain unchanged. In this way, the method evolves the fusion model to improve the fusion performance. The fusion model at iteration t is then expressed as: $F^t = \mathbf{w}^t \cdot f_i^t$. Here, $f_i^t = f_i^0$ because the classification model is not re-trained when adding new data instances.

The evolution is one of our contributions. Compared to static fusion method, the evolution updates the fusion model at every iteration when new data is added. Compared to the previous evolving fusion methods, the evolution utilizes the correlation among different sources, can deal with either crisp or soft decision, and no context information is required.

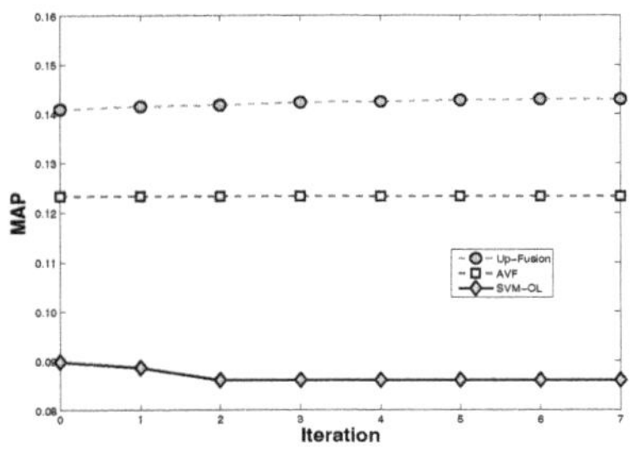

Figure 2: MAP based on whole exact return and covariance with true labels. Circle denotes the results of Up-Fusion method, square denotes average fusion method, while diamond denotes SKF-OL method

Methods	AVF	SKF	PTF	SKF-OL	Up-Fusion
MAP	0.123	0.09	0.141	0.086	0.143

Table 1: Performance of different fusion methods

4. EXPERIMENTS AND DISCUSSION

To show the effectiveness of the proposed Up-Fusion method, experiments have been conducted on concept detection on TRECVID 2007 dataset. Concept detection is an important task in information retrieval. The performance is compared with the popular state-of-the-art fusion methods: average fusion method (AVF), super-kernel fusion method (SKF) and portfolio fusion method (PTF). For complete comparison, we give an online version of super-kernel fusion method by re-training the fusion model with SVM at each iteration, which is denoted as SKF-OL. For SVM training, LIBSVM [3] is used with RBF kernel and default parameter values. $\lambda = 1$ is used.

For the concept detection, the models are trained using three features: edge direction histogram, Gabor, and grid color moment [10]. There are $21,532$ instances in the dataset. The data is evenly divided into three parts: initial part, new data part, and evaluation part. The initial part is taken as the initial seed dataset. The new data part is used to simulate adding new data instances. Then, we evaluate the performance for different concepts on the evaluation part of the dataset. In the evolution step, at each iteration, we sequentially include $K = 1,000$ instances from new data part into the available dataset and update the fusion models. A total of 32 concepts are evaluated. The mean average precision (MAP) for all concepts is used as the performance criteria. Here, the average precision for each concept is calculated over the $2,000$ retrieved relevant shots.

The MAP for each iteration is shown in Figure 2. The MAP results of different fusion methods are given in Table 1. Compared to the MAP of average fusion method, which is 0.123, the final MAP for Up-Fusion method on whole data is 0.143. Compared to the portfolio fusion method that utilizes the initial dataset only and stays unchanged as data increases, the Up-Fusion method improves the performance by evolving the fusion models as new data is added. The Up-Fusion method improves PTF by 1.4%(relative). Compared to other fusion methods, the improvement is more obvious.

Generally speaking, the proposed method obtains better performance than the average fusion method and super-kernel fusion method. The evolution phase generally improves the results. However, the improvement is not quite much. It could be because the distribution and nature of the data in this experiment does not change much, so does the correlation between different information sources. Thus, the update of correlation in each iteration only slightly improves the performance because of more data. Surprisingly, the performance of the online super-kernel fusion method generally decreases when it takes the new data into account. It may be because the generalization performance tends to suffer when there is too much noise and unbalanced data.

5. CONCLUSIONS

In this paper, an evolving fusion method has been proposed. Compared to the previous static fusion methods, especially the portfolio fusion method, as new data is continually added, the proposed Up-Fusion method evolves to adapt to the changing data and environment conditions. Evolved fusion models for different conditions can perform better than a fixed fusion model. Compared to the previous evolving fusion methods, our method utilizes the correlation among different information sources, can deal with either crisp or soft decision, and no context information is required. Experiments on representative concept detection tasks have shown the superiority of the proposed Up-Fusion method. Better updating methods will be studied in the future.

6. REFERENCES

[1] P. K. Atrey, M. A. Hossain, A. E. Saddik, and M. S. Kankanhalli. Multimodal fusion for multimedia analysis: A survey. *Multimedia Systems*, 16(6):345–379, 2010.

[2] P. K. Atrey and A. E. Saddik. Confidence evolution in multimedia systems. *IEEE Transanctions on Multimedia*, 10(7):1288–1298, November 2008.

[3] C.-C. Chang and C.-J. Lin. *LIBSVM: a library for support vector machines*, 2001. Software available at `http://www.csie.ntu.edu.tw/~cjlin/libsvm`.

[4] J.-G. Chen and N. Ansari. Adaptive fusion of correlated local decisions. *IEEE Transactions on Systems, Man, and Cybernetics*, 28(2):276–281, 1998.

[5] X. Geng, K. Smith-Miles, L. Wang, M. Li, and Q. Wu. Context-aware fusion: A case study on fusion of gait and face for human identification in video. *Pattern Recognition*, 43(10):3660–3673, 2010.

[6] D. P. Helmbold, R. E. Schapire, Y. Singer, and M. K. Warmuth. On-line portfolio selection using multiplicative updates. *Mathematical Finance*, 8(4):325–347, 1998.

[7] J.-S. Lee and C. H. Park. Adaptive decision fusion for audio-visual speech recognition. *Speech Recognition, Technologies and Applications*, pages 275–296, 2008.

[8] X. Wang and M. S. Kankanhalli. Portfolio theory of multimedia fusion. In *ACM International Conference on Multimedia*, pages 723–726, 2010.

[9] Y. Wu, E. Y. Chang, K. C.-C. Chang, and J. R. Smith. Optimal multimodal fusion for multimedia data analysis. In *ACM International Conference on Multimedia*, pages 572–579, 2004.

[10] A. Yanagawa, S.-F. Chang, L. Kennedy, and W. Hsu. Columbia university's baseline detectors for 374 lscom semantic visual concepts. TechReport 222-2006-8, Columbia University, 2007.

Robust Hand Gesture Recognition Based on Finger-Earth Mover's Distance with a Commodity Depth Camera *

Zhou Ren Junsong Yuan
Nanyang Technological University
50 Nanyang Avenue, Singapore 639798
{renzhou, jsyuan}@ntu.edu.sg

Zhengyou Zhang
Microsoft Research Redmond
Washington 98052-6399, USA
zhang@microsoft.com

ABSTRACT

The recently developed depth sensors, e.g., the Kinect sensor, have provided new opportunities for human-computer interaction (HCI). Although great progress has been made by leveraging the Kinect sensor, e.g. in human body tracking and body gesture recognition, robust hand gesture recognition remains an open problem. Compared to the entire human body, the hand is a smaller object with more complex articulations and more easily affected by segmentation errors. It is thus a very challenging problem to recognize hand gestures. This paper focuses on building a robust hand gesture recognition system using the Kinect sensor. To handle the noisy hand shape obtained from the Kinect sensor, we propose a novel distance metric for hand dissimilarity measure, called Finger-Earth Mover's Distance (FEMD). As it only matches fingers while not the whole hand shape, it can better distinguish hand gestures of slight differences. The extensive experiments demonstrate the accuracy, efficiency, and robustness of our hand gesture recognition system.

Categories and Subject Descriptors

H.1.2 [**User/Machine Systems**]: Human information processing; I.4.8 [**Scene Analysis**]: Depth cues, Shape

General Terms

Algorithm

Keywords

Hand Gesture Recognition, Human-Computer Interaction, Kinect Sensor, Finger-Earth Mover's Distance

1. INTRODUCTION

Hand gesture recognition is of great importance for human-computer interaction (HCI), because of its extensive applications in virtual reality, sign language recognition, and computer games [12]. Despite lots of previous work, traditional vision-based hand gesture recognition methods [4, 11] are still far from satisfactory for real-life applications. Because of the limitations of the optical sensors, the quality of the captured images is sensitive to lighting conditions and cluttered backgrounds, thus it is usually not able to detect and track the hands robustly, which largely affects the performance of hand gesture recognition.

Figure 1: Some challenging cases for hand gesture recognition, using depth cameras: the first and the second hands have the same gesture while the third hand confuses the recognition.

To enable a more robust hand gesture recognition, one effective way is to use other sensors to capture the hand gesture and motion, e.g. through the data glove [8]. Unlike optical sensors, such sensors are usually more reliable and are not affected by lighting conditions or cluttered backgrounds. However, as it requires the user to wear a data glove and sometimes requires calibration, it is inconvenient for the user and may hinder the naturalness of hand gesture. Also, such data gloves are expensive. As a result, it is not a very popular way for hand gesture recognition.

Thanks to the recent development of inexpensive depth cameras, e.g., the Kinect sensor, new opportunities for hand gesture recognition emerge. In spite of many recent successes in applying the Kinect sensor for face recognition [3] and human body tracking [10], it is still an open problem to use Kinect for hand gesture recognition. Due to the low-resolution of the Kinect depth map, typically, of only 640×480, although it works well to track a large object, e.g. the human body, it is difficult to detect and segment a small object from an image with this resolution, e.g., a human hand which occupies a very small portion of the image with more complex articulations. In such a case, the segmentation of the hand is usually inaccurate, thus may significantly affect the recognition step.

To illustrate the above problem, Fig.1 shows some examples. It can be seen that the contours have significant local distortions in addition to pose variations. Due to the low resolution and inaccuracy of the Kinect sensor, the two fingers in the second hand of Fig.1 are indistinguishable as they are close to each other. Unfortunately, classic shape recognition methods, such as shape contexts [2] and skeleton matching [1], cannot robustly recognize the shape contour with severe distortions. Clearly, recognizing noisy shapes is very challenging, especially if there are many gestures to recognize.

*Area chair: Alexander Hauptmann

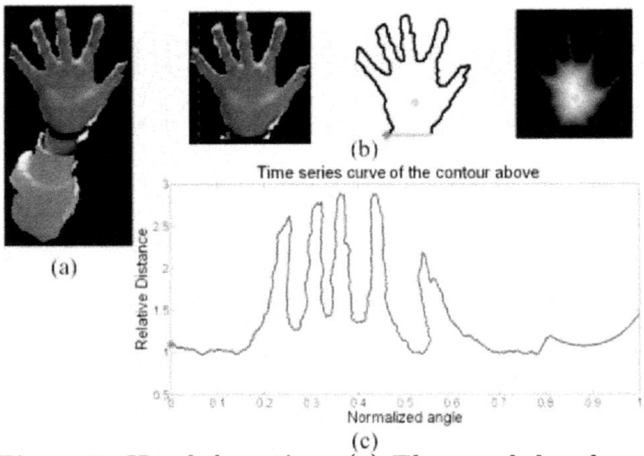

Figure 2: Hand detection. (a) The rough hand segmented by depth thresholding; (b) A more accurate hand detected with black belt (the green line), the initial point (the red point) and the center point (the cyan point); (c) Its time-series curve representation.

In order to address this problem, we propose a novel shape distance metric called Finger-Earth Mover's Distance (FEMD). FEMD is specifically designed for hand shapes. It considers each finger as a cluster and penalizes unmatched fingers. By testing on a 10-gesture dataset, our method is accurate, efficient, and performs robustly to articulations, local distortions, orientation and scale changes. To the best of our knowledge, this is the first attempt in real-life hand gesture recognition using Kinect sensor.

2. HAND DETECTION

We use Kinect sensor as the input device, which captures the color image and the depth map at 640×480 resolution.

2.1 Hand Segmentation

As for hand segmentation, we require the user to cooperate in two aspects (both are reasonable requirements in HCI): first, the user need to make sure that the hand is the frontmost object facing the sensor. Thus, by thresholding from the nearest depth position with a certain gap, a rough hand region can be obtained, as shown in Fig.2(a). Second, the user need to wear a black belt on the gesturing hand's wrist. We use RANSAC to locate the position of the black belt, and thus, a more precise hand shape can be detected, as shown in Fig.2(b). The hand shape is generally of 120×120 resolution, which may cause severe distortions.

2.2 Shape Representation

After detecting the hand shape, we represent it as a *time-series curve*, as shown in Fig.2(c). Such a shape representation has been successfully used for the classification and clustering of shapes [6]. The time-series curve records the relative distance between each contour vertex to a center point. We define the center point as the point with the maximal distance after Distance Transform on the shape (the cyan point), as shown in Fig.2(b); and the initial point (the red point) is defined according to the RANSAC line detected from the black belt (the green line).

In our time-series representation, the horizontal axis denotes the angle between each contour vertex and the initial point relative to the center point, normalized by 360°. The vertical axis denotes the Euclidean distance between the contour vertices and the center point, normalized by the radius of the maximal inscribed circle. As shown in Fig.2, the time-series curve captures nice topological properties of the hand, such as the fingers.

3. HAND GESTURE RECOGNITION

With the hand shape and its time-series representation, we apply template matching for robust recognition, i.e., the input hand is recognized as the class with which it has the minimum dissimilarity distance: $c = \arg\min_c \mathrm{FEMD}(H,\ T_c)$, where H is the input hand; T_c is the template of class c; $\mathrm{FEMD}(H,\ T_c)$ denotes the proposed Finger-Earth Mover's Distance between the input hand and each template.

3.1 Finger-Earth Mover's Distance

In [9], Rubner *et al.* presented a general and flexible metric, called Earth Mover's Distance (EMD), to measure the distance between signatures or histograms. EMD is widely used in many problems such as content-based image retrieval and pattern recognition.

EMD is a measure of the distance between two probability distributions. It is named after a physical analogy that is drawn from the process of moving piles of earth spread around one set of locations into another set of holes in the same space. The locations of earth piles and holes denotes the mean of each cluster in the signatures, the size of each earth pile or hole is the weight of cluster, and the ground distance between a pile and a hole is the amount of work needed to move a unit of earth. To use this transportation problem as a distance measure, i.e., a measure of dissimilarity, one seeks the least cost transportation — the movement of earth that requires the least amount of work.

Grauman and Darrell applied EMD to contour matching and contour retrieval [5], which represents the contour by a set of local descriptive features and computes the set of correspondences with minimum EMD costs between the local features. However, the existing EMD-based contour matching algorithms have two deficiencies:

1. Two hand shapes differ mainly in global features while not local features. As shown in Fig.3(a)(b), the fingers (global features) are their major difference. Besides, the large number of local features slows down the speed of contour matching. Therefore, it is better to consider global features in contour matching.
2. EMD allows for partial matching, i.e., a signature and its subset are considered to be the same in EMD measure: as in Fig.3(c)(d), the EMD distance of these two signatures is zero because the signature in Fig.3(d) is a subset of Fig.3(c). However, in many situations partial matching is illogical, such as in the case of Fig.3(a)(b), where the finger in Fig.3(b) is a partial set of the fingers in Fig.3(a). Clearly, they should be considered being very different.

Our Finger-Earth Mover's Distance (FEMD) can address these two deficiencies of EMD-based contour matching methods mentioned above. Different from the EMD-based algorithm [5], which considers each local feature as a cluster, we consider the input hand as a signature with each finger (the global feature) as a cluster. And we add penalty on empty holes to alleviate partial matches on global features.

Formally, let $R{=}\{(\mathbf{r}_1,\ w_{\mathbf{r}_1}),\ \ldots,\ (\mathbf{r}_m,\ w_{\mathbf{r}_m})\}$ be the first hand signature with m clusters, where $\mathbf{r}_i$ is the cluster representative and $w_{\mathbf{r}_i}$ is the weight of the cluster; $T{=}\{(\mathbf{t}_1,\ w_{\mathbf{t}_1}),\ \ldots,\ (\mathbf{t}_n,\ w_{\mathbf{t}_n})\}$ is the second hand signature with n clusters.

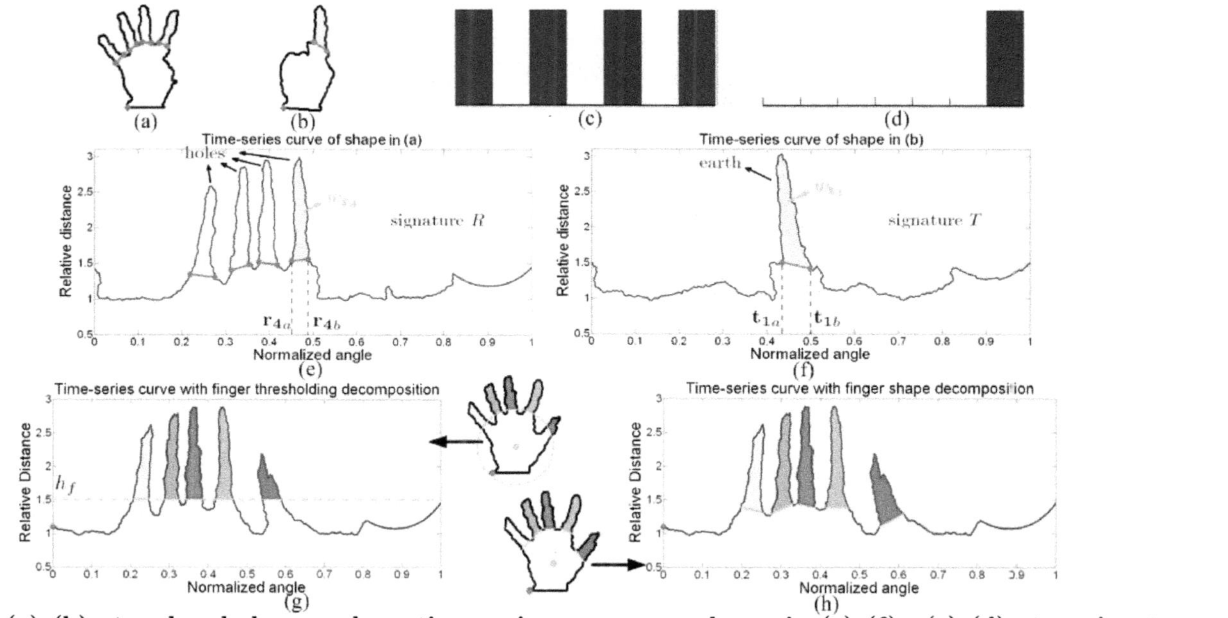

Figure 3: (a) (b): two hand shapes whose time-series curves are shown in (e) (f). (c) (d): two signatures that partially match, whose EMD cost is 0. (e) (f): the signature representations of the time-series curves. (g) (h): two finger detection methods, thresholding decomposition (g) and near-convex decomposition (h).

Now we show how to represent a time-series curve as a signature. Fig.3(e)(f) show the time-series curves of the hands in Fig.3(a)(b) respectively, where each finger corresponds to a segment of the curve. We define each cluster of a signature as the finger segment of the time-series curve: the representative of each cluster $\mathbf{r}_i$ is defined as the angle interval between the endpoints of each segment, $\mathbf{r}_i=[\mathbf{r}_{ia},\ \mathbf{r}_{ib}]$, where $0 \leq \mathbf{r}_{ia} < \mathbf{r}_{ib} \leq 1$; and the weight of a cluster, $w_{\mathbf{r}_i} \in (0,1)$, is defined as the normalized area within the finger segment.

$\mathbf{D}=[d_{ij}]$ is the ground distance matrix of signature R and T, where d_{ij} is the ground distance from cluster $\mathbf{r}_i$ to $\mathbf{t}_j$. d_{ij} is defined as the minimum moving distance for interval $[\mathbf{r}_{ia},\ \mathbf{r}_{ib}]$ to totally overlap with $[\mathbf{t}_{ja},\ \mathbf{t}_{jb}]$, i.e.:

$$d_{ij} = \begin{cases} 0, & \mathbf{r}_i \text{ totally overlap with } \mathbf{t}_j, \\ \min(|\mathbf{r}_{ia} - \mathbf{t}_{ja}|,\ |\mathbf{r}_{ib} - \mathbf{t}_{jb}|), & \text{otherwise.} \end{cases}$$

For two signatures, R and T, their FEMD distance is defined as the least work needed to move the earth piles plus the penalty on the empty hole that is not filled with earth:

$$\begin{aligned} \text{FEMD}(R,\ T) &= \beta E_{move} + (1-\beta)E_{empty}, \\ &= \frac{\beta \sum_{i=1}^{m}\sum_{j=1}^{n} d_{ij} f_{ij} + (1-\beta)|\sum_{i=1}^{m} w_{\mathbf{r}_i} - \sum_{j=1}^{n} w_{\mathbf{t}_j}|}{\sum_{i=1}^{m}\sum_{j=1}^{n} f_{ij}}, \end{aligned}$$

where $\sum_{i=1}^{m}\sum_{j=1}^{n} f_{ij}$ is the normalization factor, f_{ij} is the flow from cluster $\mathbf{r}_i$ to cluster $\mathbf{t}_j$, which constitutes the flow matrix $\mathbf{F}$. Parameter β modulates the importance between the first and the second terms. As we can see, E_{empty}, d_{ij} are constants given two signatures. To compute the FEMD, we need to compute the flow matrix $\mathbf{F}$. We follow the definition of the flow matrix $\mathbf{F}$ in EMD, which is defined by minimizing the work needed to move all the earth piles.

4. FINGER DETECTION

Before we can measure the FEMD distance between two hand shapes, we have to obtain the finger clusters in their time-series curves, namely to detect the fingers from the hand shapes. We propose two ways for finger detection:

4.1 Thresholding decomposition

As mentioned before, the time-series curve reveals a hand's topological information well. As shown in Fig.3(g), each finger corresponds to a peak in the curve. Therefore, we can apply the height information in time-series curve to decompose the fingers. Specifically, we define a finger as a segment in the time-series curve, whose height is greater than a threshold h_f. In this way, we can detect the fingers fast. However, choosing a good height threshold h_f is essential.

4.2 Near-convex hand decomposition

Thresholding decomposition is sensitive to the threshold h_f, and it may introduce segmentation errors, e.g., the thumb is incomplete in Fig.3(g). Now we introduce a more accurate finger detection method based on the near-convex shape decomposition scheme [8], as shown in Fig.3(h):

$$\min\ \alpha \parallel \mathbf{x} \parallel_{\mathbf{0}} + (1-\alpha)\mathbf{w}^{\top}\mathbf{x}, \quad s.t.\ \mathbf{A}\mathbf{x} \geq \mathbf{1},\ \mathbf{x}^{\top}\mathbf{B}\mathbf{x} = 0,\ \mathbf{x} \in \{0,1\}^{\overline{n}}.$$

It formulates shape decomposition as a integer optimization problem (details please refer to [8]). By relaxing $0<x_i<1$, the problem becomes a linear programming problem.

5. EXPERIMENTS

5.1 Dataset

We collect a new hand gesture dataset with a Kinect sensor (http://www.ntu.edu.sg/home/renzhou/HandGesture.htm). Our dataset is collected from 10 subjects, and it contains 10 gestures. Each subject performs 10 different poses for the same gesture. Thus in total our dataset has 10 subject × 10 gestures/subject × 10cases/gesture = 1000 cases, each of which consists of a color image and a depth map.

Our dataset is a very challenging real-life dataset, which is collected in uncontrolled environments. Besides, for each gesture, the subject poses with variations, namely the hand changes in orientation, scale, articulation, etc.

5.2 Performance Evaluation on Robustness

First, our hand gesture recognition system is robust to cluttered backgrounds, because the hand shape is detected

	Thresholding Decomposition+FEMD	Near-convex Decomposition+FEMD
Mean Accuracy	90.6%	93.9%
Mean Running Time	0.5004s	4.0012s

Table 1: The mean accuracy and the mean running time of the two proposed methods.

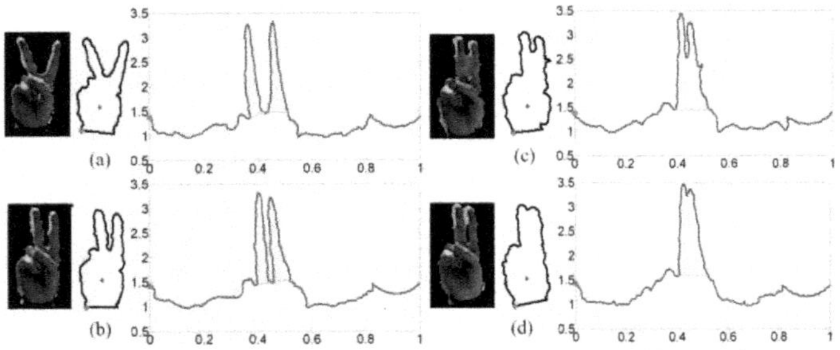

Figure 4: Our system is insensitive to the distortions and articulation.

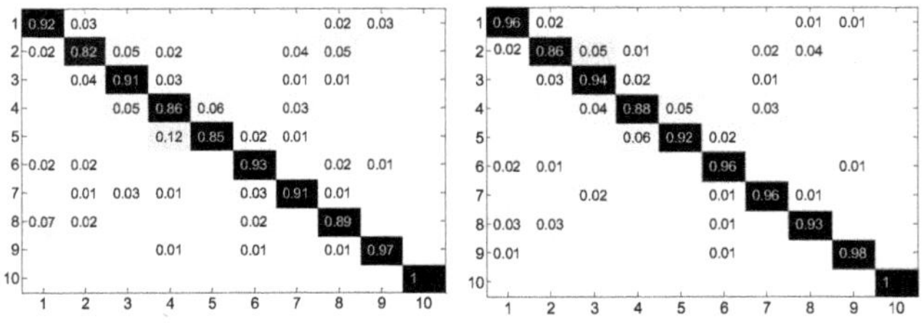

Figure 5: The confusion matrixes of thresholding decomposition based FEMD (left) and near-convex decomposition based FEMD (right).

using depth information and the backgrounds can be easily removed. Then, our hand gesture recognition system is robust to orientations changes. The reason is that the initial point and the center point are relatively fixed in each shape. Thus the time-series curves of the hands with different orientations are similar, and their distances are very small. Also, our hand gesture recognition system is robust to scale changes. Because the time-series curve and the FEMD distance are normalized, the hand shapes with scale changes can be correctly recognized as the same gesture.

Furthermore, our hand gesture recognition method is robust to the articulations and distortions due to imperfect hand segmentation. As the proposed FEMD distance metric uses global features (fingers) to measure the dissimilarity, local distortions are tolerable. As for the articulations, Fig.4 shows some examples: the color images show 4 hands of the same gesture; the next columns shows the corresponding hand shapes, and their time-series curves. As we can see, the hand shapes in Fig.4(c)(d) are heavily distorted. However, as illustrated in their time-series curves, by detecting the finger parts (the yellow regions), we represent each shape as a signature whose clusters are the finger parts. Particularly, the signatures of Fig.4(a)(b) have 2 clusters: $\{(\mathbf{r_1}, w_{\mathbf{r_1}}), (\mathbf{r_2}, w_{\mathbf{r_2}})\}$, and the signatures of Fig.4(c)(d) only have 1 cluster: $\{(\mathbf{t_1}, w_{\mathbf{t_1}})\}$. From Section 3.1, we can estimate that $(w_{\mathbf{r_1}}+w_{\mathbf{r_2}}) \approx w_{\mathbf{t_1}}$, and the ground distance d_{11}, $d_{21} \approx 0$. According to the definition, we know that the FEMD distances among the 4 shapes ≈ 0. Therefore, our FEMD metric is insensitive to distortions and articulations.

5.3 Accuracy and Efficiency

In Table 1, the mean accuracy and the mean running time of FEMD based on the two finger detection methods are given. The mean accuracy of near-convex decomposition based FEMD (93.9%) is higher than that of thresholding decomposition (90.6%), owing to more accurate finger decomposition. In terms of recognition error, the near-convex decomposition reduces the error rate from 9.4% of the thresholding decomposition to 6.1%, which is a 35% reduction. But on the other hand, the speed of the second method is slower than that of the first one, because of the more complex finger detection algorithm.

Fig.5 shows their confusion matrixes. Compared with the thresholding decomposition based FEMD, the near-convex decomposition based FEMD has less seriously confused categories. And the accuracies in all the classes are improved. Here we fix the near-convex decomposition parameter α=0.5, the FEMD parameter β=0.5, and the thresholding decomposition parameter h_f=0.6.

We have built a demo to demonstrate the superiority of our method in real-life applications [7].

6. CONCLUSIONS

Hand gesture recognition for real-life applications is very challenging because of the requirements on its robustness, accuracy and efficiency. In this paper, we presented a robust real-life hand gesture recognition system using the Kinect sensor. A novel distance metric, Finger-Earth Mover's Distance, is used for dissimilarity measure, which treats each finger as a cluster and penalize the empty finger-hole. In order to accurately detect the fingers, we presented two finger decomposition methods: thresholding decomposition and near-convex decomposition. Extensive experiments on a challenging 10-gesture dataset demonstrate that our hand gesture recognition system is accurate, efficient, and robust to articulations, distortions, and orientation, scale changes.

7. ACKNOWLEDGEMENT

This work was supported in part by the Nanyang Assistant Professorship (SUG M58040015) to Dr. Junsong Yuan.

8. REFERENCES

[1] X. Bai and L. J. Latecki. Path similarity skeleton graph matching. *IEEE Trans. on PAMI*, 30:1–11, 2008.

[2] S. Belongie, J. Malik, and J. Puzicha. Shape matching and object recognition using shape contexts. *IEEE Trans. on PAMI*, 24:509–522, 2002.

[3] Q. Cai, D. Gallup, C. Zhang, and Z. Zhang. 3d deformable face tracking with a commodity depth camera. In *Proc. of IEEE ECCV*, 2010.

[4] C. Chua, H. Guan, and Y. Ho. Model-based 3d hand posture estimation from a single 2d image. *Image and Vision Computing*, 20:191 – 202, 2002.

[5] K. Grauman and T. Darrell. Fast contour matching using approximate earth mover's distance. In *CVPR*, 2004.

[6] E. Keogh, L. Wei, X. Xi, S. Lee, and M. Vlachos. Lb_keogh supports exact indexing of shapes under rotation invariance with arbitrary representations and distance measures. In *Proc. of 32th International Conf. on VLDB*, 2006.

[7] Z. Ren, J. Meng, J. Yuan, and Z. Zhang. Robust hand gesture recognition with kinect sensor. In *Proc. of ACM MM*, 2011.

[8] Z. Ren, J. Yuan, C. Li, and W. Liu. Minimum near-convex decomposition for robust shape representation. In *Proc. of ICCV*, 2011.

[9] Y. Rubner, C. Tomasi, and L. J. Guibas. The earth mover's distance as a metric for image retrieval. *IJCV*, 40:99–121, 2000.

[10] J. Shotton, A. Fitzgibbon, and etc. Real-time human pose recognition in parts from single depth images. In *Proc. of IEEE CVPR*, 2011.

[11] B. Stenger, A. Thayananthan, P. Torr, and R. Cipolla. Filtering using a tree-based estimator. In *Proc. of IEEE ICCV*, 2003.

[12] J. P. Wachs, M. Kölsch, H. Stern, and Y. Edan. Vision-based hand-gesture applications. *Communications of the ACM*, 54:60–71, 2011.

Recognizing Clothes Patterns for Blind People by Confidence Margin based Feature Combination

Xiaodong Yang, Shuai Yuan, and YingLi Tian
Department of Electrical Engineering
The City College of New York, CUNY
New York, NY, 10031, USA
{xyang02, syuan00, ytian}@ccny.cuny.edu

ABSTRACT

Clothes pattern recognition is a challenging task for blind or visually impaired people. Automatic clothes pattern recognition is also a challenging problem in computer vision due to the large pattern variations. In this paper, we present a new method to classify clothes patterns into 4 categories: stripe, lattice, special, and patternless. While existing texture analysis methods mainly focused on textures varying with distinctive pattern changes, they cannot achieve the same level of accuracy for clothes pattern recognition because of the large intra-class variations in each clothes pattern category. To solve this problem, we extract both structural feature and statistical feature from image wavelet subbands. Furthermore, we develop a new feature combination scheme based on the confidence margin of a classifier to combine the two types of features to form a novel local image descriptor in a compact and discriminative format. The recognition experiment is conducted on a database with 627 clothes images of 4 categories of patterns. Experimental results demonstrate that the proposed method significantly outperforms the state-of-the-art texture analysis methods in the context of clothes pattern recognition.

Categories and Subject Descriptors

I.4.8 [**Scene Analysis**]: Object Recognition

General Terms

Algorithms, Design.

Keywords

Clothes pattern, recognition, computer vision, blind, visually impaired.

1. INTRODUCTION

Based on statistics from the World Health Organization (WHO), there are more than 161 million visually impaired people around the world, and 37 million of them are blind [9]. In everyday's life, choosing suitable clothes becomes a challenging task for blind or visually impaired people. They manage this task either through helping form their family members, or by using plastic Braille labels or different types of stitching patterns tags on the clothes, or just wearing clothes without any patterns. Recent advances in theories, sensors, and embedded computing hold the promise to enable computer vision technique to address their needs. Although some methods have been developed to determine whether clothes color and pattern are matched to help blind people [12], they cannot recognize the categories of clothes patterns.

Figure 1: Intra-class variations in traditional texture images and clothes patterns. Column 1-3: texture samples from three categories with less intra-class pattern variations. Column 4-6: clothes pattern samples of three categories with large intra-class variations. Samples of the same column belong to the same category.

Extensive research has been done for texture analysis to make representations of texture robust to viewpoint changes, non-rigid deformation, illumination variance, rotation, scaling, and occlusion [3, 11, 13]. A traditional representation of texture is the statistical features extracted from wavelet subbands of texture images. This method [11] utilizes the spectral information of texture images at different scales to characterize the global energy distribution property. However, such multiresolution approach ignores the local structural information. Most recent state-of-the-art texture recognition approaches [3, 13] represent texture as a histogram of textons by clustering local image features. Textons are the repetitive basic primitives to characterize a specific texture pattern. Because of the robustness to photometric and affine variations, SIFT [5] is commonly used to capture the structural information of texture. On the other hand, it was observed [13] that the combination of multiple complementary features usually achieves better results than the most discriminative individual feature.

As shown in Fig. 1, traditional texture analysis methods mainly focus on recognizing textures with large changes of viewpoint, orientation, and scaling, but with less intra-class pattern variations. However, for application of clothes pattern recognition, in addition to the above variations, there are large intra-class variations due to the huge number of clothes pattern

*Area Chair: Alexander Hauptmann

MM'11, November 28—December 1, 2011, Scottsdale, Arizona, USA.

designs of each specific clothes pattern. In this paper, we recognize clothes patterns into 4 categories: stripe, lattice, special, and patternless. The 4 categories are able to meet the basic requirements based on our initial survey with potential blind users. In order to handle the large intra-class variation and maintain the discrimination of inter-class variance, both statistical feature and structural feature are employed. While it is customary to simply concatenate multiple feature descriptors as feature combination strategy, we propose a confidence margin based scheme to combine individual features in a more compact and more discriminative way. Recognition experiments on the clothes pattern database validate the superiority of our proposed method over the-state-of-art texture analysis approaches.

2. MULTIPLE FEATURE CHANNELS

2.1 Primitive Feature

Statistical features are generally employed to analyze texture which lacks clutter and has uniform statistical properties. The most common approach is to extract energy values for all wavelet subbands of texture images. Wavelet subbands represent a generalization of multiresolution analysis tool. Several energy functions, such as magnitude, magnitude square, and rectified sigmoid [8], can be used to extract statistical features from each subband. Statistical features from wavelet subbands capture global spectral information of texture images at different scales. In this paper, we employ 5 statistical values including variance, smoothness, homogeneity, entropy, and laws energy [2] to constitute the statistical feature (STA).

Local image descriptors are able to capture the structural information that is ignored in the statistical features. The bag-of-words model [7] is then used to quantize local image descriptors to *visual words* in finite vocabularies. This technique treats texture images as loose collections of independent patches. The distribution of patches in the *visual words* vocabulary is then used to characterize the texture. Patches of texture images are represented by local image descriptors. In the performance evaluation of several local image descriptors [6], it was observed SIFT-based descriptor outperformed others because of its strong invariance to photometric change and affine transformation. SIFT descriptor is created by sampling gradient maps of a support region over a 4×4 grids, with 8 orientation bins for each grid. The magnitude of each point within the support region is weighted by a Gaussian window function to emphasize for the gradients closed to the center of the region and decrease the impact of small changes in the position of the region. The feature vector with 128 elements is then normalized and thresholded to remove elements with small values.

2.2 Multiple Features

In order to deal with the large intra-class variations presented in the clothes patterns, we employ both statistical feature (STA) and local structural feature (SIFT). Inspired by the spectral information and multiresolution provided by Wavelet subbands, we extract SIFT and STA from the original image and its associated wavelet subbands. Thus, for each local patch, STA and SIFT are constructed from original image, and its corresponding horizontal component, vertical component, and diagonal component of wavelet subbands. As shown in Fig. 2, the local patch surrounded by the red square is the support region to build SIFT descriptor; and the local patch surrounded by green square is the support region to compute STA descriptor. Note the support region of STA is larger than the support region of SIFT. This is because STA, the descriptor representing statistical property, needs larger region or more samples to be stable and meaningful. SIFT descriptor is built by sampling gradient map of its support region over 4×4 grids, with 8 orientation bins for each grid. Similarly, STA is calculated by sampling statistical properties of its support region over 4×4 grids. Each grid is further expended to 3 concentric grids with 5 statistical values (Sec. 2.1) representation for each grid. Therefore, SIFT descriptor and STA descriptor from each channel are of the dimensions of 128 and 240, respectively. We consider each descriptor/subband pair as a separate feature channel.

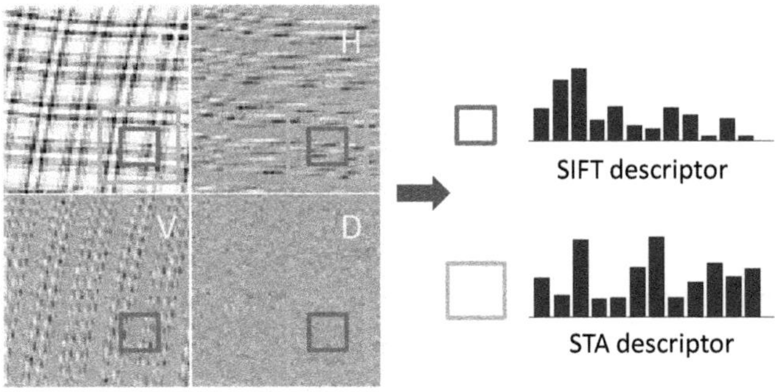

Figure 2: Multiple feature channels. SIFT and STA extracted from patches of wavelet subbands: original component (O), horizontal component (H), vertical component (V), and diagonal component (D).

3. FEATURE COMBINATION

Multiple complementary features capture properties of a phenomenon in different aspects. So, a combination of multiple complementary features is able to obtain better results than any individual feature channel. It is customary to directly concatenate feature vectors of multiple channels. While this method is simple and straightforward, it suffers the following drawbacks: 1) it cannot manifest the complementary relationships between different feature channels; 2) it always results in a very high feature dimension causing the curse of dimensionality [1]; 3) it might submerge some feature channels because of the imbalanced feature dimensions. In this paper, we employ a confidence margin based feature combination scheme to combine multiple feature channels. The final feature combined in this way has a low dimension but more discriminative power.

The confidence margin [4] is the measure of how close an instance is to the classification boundary of a classifier. It represents the reliability of prediction output based on a specific feature. In the context of classification, an instance close to the class boundary is less reliable than the one deep in the class territory. The Support Vector Machines (SVM) [10] is used as the classifier in our clothes pattern recognition system. SVM finds a maximum margin hyperplane in the feature space and can be solved by the Lagrange dual problem:

$$\min_{a} \frac{1}{2} \sum_{i=1}^{N} \sum_{j=1}^{N} a_i a_j y_i y_j K(x_i, x_j) - \sum_{i=1}^{N} a_i$$

$$s.t. \sum_{i=1}^{N} y_i a_i = 0, \qquad 0 \le a_i \le R$$

Here $K(x_i, x_j)$ is the kernel that generates an inner product of the transformed x_i and x_j in the feature space; y_i is the label of x_i; R

is the regularization parameter. SVM makes predictions of x by the sign of $g(x) = \sum_{i=1}^{N} a_i y_i K(x_i, x) + b$. $|g(x_i)|$ is defined as the magnitude of confidence margin of the instance x_i. SVM is fundamentally a two-class classifier. The one-versus-one [1] approach is used to recognize N $(N > 2)$ categories by training $N(N-1)/2$ different 2-class SVMs on all possible pairs of classes. An instance is recognized as the category with the highest number of votes. Accordingly, an instance x_i has $N(N-1)/2$ confidence margin values, which are used to constitute the confidence margin vector cm_i which is an alternate representation of x_i. There are four categories $(N = 4)$ in the clothes pattern dataset. So no matter what dimension of original features x_i, their confidence margin representations cm_i are all with the same dimension of 6. The proposed feature combination scheme, rather than using original feature vectors, employs their confidence margin representations to form the final combined feature. If F feature channels are used, $[x_i^1, x_i^2, \ldots, x_i^F]^T$ is the final feature vector generated by traditional feature combination method, and $[cm_i^1, cm_i^2, \ldots, cm_i^F]^T$ is the final feature vector obtained by our proposed method; where cm_i^f is the confidence margin vector of original feature x_i^f in the feature channel f.

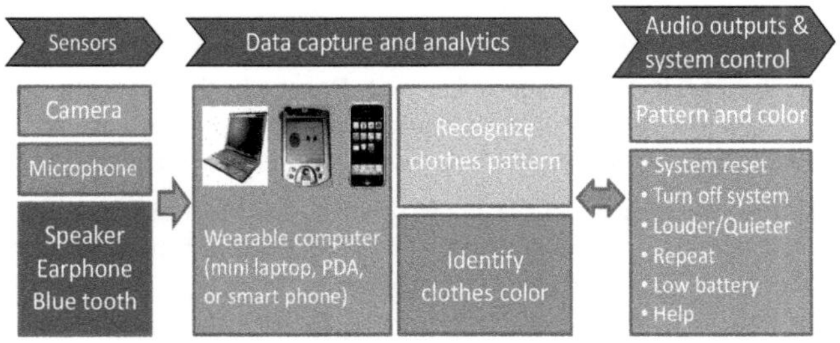

Figure 3: Prototype hardware and architecture design of clothes pattern recognition system for the blind and visually impaired persons.

4. SYSTEM AND INTERFACE

In addition to clothes patterns, color is also an important property of clothes. We apply the clothes color classification method in [12] to recognize clothes color to flowing categories: red, orange, yellow, green, cyan, blue, purple, pink, black, gray, and white. The system integrates both clothes pattern recognition and clothes color recognition.

The clothes pattern and color recognition system consists of three sections: 1) a camera connected to a computing machine to perform clothes pattern and color recognition; 2) speech commands for system control and configuration; 3) audio feedback to provide recognition results for both patterns and colors of clothes. The prototype of the proposed system integrates different sensors including a camera, a microphone, and audio output devices which can be an earphone, Bluetooth, or speakers. A camera is used to capture images of clothes. A wearable computer (can be a PDA or a smart phone) is used to capture and analyze data. The recognition results are described to the blind user by verbal display with minimal distraction of the user's hearing sense. The user can control the system by speech via microphones. The information is processed by the computing machine.

In our prototype, we develop a program based on Microsoft SDK tools for speech recognition and audio feedback to make it easy to use by blind users. As a user gives simple speech commands through a microphone, the system can directly recognize input commands, execute corresponding functions, and provide final audio outputs. In addition, the system can be set by a number of high priority speech commands such as *System reset*, *Turn off system*, *Repeat result*, *Help*, and speaker volume control commands (i.e. *Louder* and *Quieter*). To protect privacy and minimize masking environmental sounds, bone conduction earphones or small wireless blue tooth speakers can be used. The system will also check battery level and send out an audio warning when the battery level is low. Fig. 3 shows the system interface for development.

5. EXPERIMENTS AND DISCUSSIONS

A clothes pattern dataset with large intra-class variation is collected to evaluate our proposed clothes pattern recognition method and other state-of-the-art texture classification approaches. Experimental results demonstrate the complementary relationships of features from multiple channels, i.e. SIFT and STA features from original image and associated wavelet subbands. In addition, the recognition results also validate the superiority of the proposed confidence margin based feature combination scheme over the traditional feature combining method.

5.1 Datasets

To evaluate the recognition performances of our proposed method on clothes patterns, we collected a dataset including 627 images of 4 different typical clothes pattern designs: stripe, lattice, special, and patternless with 157, 156, 158, and 156 images in each category, respectively. This dataset will be released to public. The resolution of each image is 140×140. Fig. 4 illustrates sample images in each category. As shown in this figure, as well as lighting variances, scale changes, rotations, and surface deformations presented in traditional texture dataset, clothes patterns also demonstrate much larger intra-class variations, which augments the challenges for recognition.

Figure 4: Sample images in the clothes pattern dataset. Rows 1-4 correspond to the categories of lattice, special, stripe, and patternless.

5.2 Results and Discussions

We evaluate the recognition performance of our proposed method and state-of-the-art texture classification approaches on the clothes pattern dataset. In order to detect sufficient keypoints for each category, we evenly select keypoints in every 4 pixels. The sizes of support regions for STA and SIFT are empirically determined as 23x23 and 17x17. The final descriptors compared in recognition experiments include STA, SIFT, WSTA, WSIFT, WSIFT+WSTA, and WSIFT*WSTA. STA and SIFT are statistical descriptors and SIFT descriptors extracted from original images; WSTA and WSIFT correspond to statistical descriptors and SIFT descriptors extracted from original images and associated wavelet subbands; WSIFT+WSTA denotes the combined feature by simply concatenating the feature vectors of WSIFT and WSTA; WSIFT*WSTA refers the final feature combined by confidence margins of SIFT and STA from original images and wavelet subband images. The recognition experiments are evaluated by using 10%, 30%, 50%, and 70% of the dataset as training sets, and the rest as testing sets. The recognition results for different combinations of descriptors and training sets are demonstrated in Table 1. The reported recognition rates are the average over 100 random subsets. The number in bold correspond to the best recognition rate for different training volumes.

As shown in Table 1, the combination of multiple feature channels usually achieves better recognition results than individual feature channel. The recognition accuracy based on WSTA is better than STA, and WSIFT is better than SIFT as well, which verifies the complementary relationships of multiple feature channels. This is because that the horizontal, vertical, and diagonal images of wavelet subbands provide complementary frequency information to the spatial information of original images. On the other hand, the improvement of recognition rate based on WSIFT+WSTA over WSIFT or WSTA is not obvious. When only 10% of images are used as training set, WSIFT+WSTA even deteriorates the recognition performance. This is probably because the training set is too small compared to the large dimension of WSIFT+WSTA. However, if we use WSIFT*WSTA, or the descriptor combined by the confidence margin method, the recognition accuracy is significantly improved. This improvement benefits from confidence margin based combination method is able to manifest the complementary relationships between different feature channels, balance the feature dimensions of different feature channels, and generate feature vectors in a much lower dimension. Therefore, the final feature combined in this way has more discriminative power but far fewer feature dimensions. Furthermore, when the training set is larger than 10%, our proposed method is less sensitive to the volume of training data. For instance, our method can acquire comparable results by using 30% and 50% images as training set. In other words, we can train the proposed method to achieve comparable results by using less data.

Table 1. Recognition accuracy under different combinations of descriptors and volumes of training sets on clothes pattern dataset. The number in parenthesis of each descriptor denotes its dimensionality.

Method	10%	30%	50%	70%
STA (240)	62.50%	74.63%	76.81%	79.3%
SIFT (128)	69.66%	80.70%	84.30%	85.0%
WSTA (960)	70.40%	81.36%	85.78%	85.89%
WSIFT (512)	74.52%	83.17%	86.80%	87.70%
WSIFT+WSTA(1472)	72.30%	83.76%	86.00%	88.89%
WSIFT*WSTA (42)	**76.46%**	**87.50%**	**88.94%**	**91.86%**

6. CONCLUSION

In this paper, we have proposed a confidence margin based feature combination method to combine multiple feature channels to recognize clothes patterns which have large intra-class variations. Multiple feature channels are constructed by STA descriptors and SIFT descriptors from original images and associated wavelet subbands. The combination of multiple feature channels provides complementary information to improve recognition accuracy. Furthermore, the proposed confidence margin based feature combination method is able to represent the combined feature in a more compact and more discriminative format. The future research will focus on collection and recognition of more categories of clothes patterns.

7. ACKNOWLEDGEMENT

This work was supported by NIH 1R21EY020990, NSF grant IIS-0957016 and EFRI-1137172, and ARO grant W911NF-09-1-0565.

8. REFERENCES

[1] Bishop C. Pattern Recognition and Machine Learning. 2007. *Springer.*

[2] Harwood D., Ojala T., Pietikainen M., Kelman S., and Davis L. 1995. Texture Classification by Center-symmetric Auto-Correlation Texture Classification by Center-symmetric Auto-Correlation Using Kullback Discrimination of Distributions. *Patter Recognition.*

[3] Lazebnik S., Schmid C., and Ponce J. 2005. A Sparse Texture Representation Using Local Affine Regions. *IEEE Trans. on Pattern Analysis and Machine Intelligence.*

[4] Li L., Pratap A., Lin H., and Abu-Mostafa Y. 2005. Improving Generalization by Data Categorization. *Knowledge Discovery in Databases.*

[5] Lowe D. 2004. Distinctive Image Features from Scale-invariant Keypoints. *International Journal of Computer Vision.*

[6] Mikolajczyk K. and Schmid C. 2005. A Performance Evaluation of Local Descriptors. *IEEE Trans. on Pattern Analysis and Machine Intelligence.*

[7] Nowak E., Jurie F., and Triggs B. 2006. Sampling Strategies for Bag-of-Features Image Classification. *European Conference on Computer Vision.*

[8] Randen T., Husoy J. 1999. Filtering for Texture Classification: A Comparative Study. *IEEE Trans. on Pattern Analysis and Machine Intelligence.*

[9] Kocur I., Parajasegaram R., and Pokharel G. 2004. Global Data on Visual Impairment in the Year 2002. *Bulletin of the World Health Organization*, 82,844-851.

[10] Vapnik V.N. 1995. The Nature of Statistical Learning Theory. *Springer-Verlag.*

[11] Wang Z. and Yong J. 2008. Texture Analysis and Classification with Linear Regression Model based on Wavelet Transform. *IEEE Trans. on Image Processing.*

[12] Yuan S., Tian, Y., Arditi A. 2011. Clothes Matching for Visually Impaired Persons. *Journal of Technology and Disability.*

[13] Zhang J., Marszalek M., Lazebnik S., and Schmid C. 2007. Local Features and Kernels for Classification of Texture and Object Categories: A Comprehensive Study. *International Journal of Computer Vision.*

Dual-sensor fusion for indoor user localisation

Milan Redžić, Conor Brennan and Noel E O'Connor
CLARITY: Centre for Sensor Web Technologies
Dublin City University, Ireland
{milan.redzic,brennanc,oconnorn}@eeng.dcu.ie

ABSTRACT

In this paper we address the automatic identification of indoor locations using a combination of WLAN and image sensing. Our motivation is the increasing prevalence of wearable cameras, some of which can also capture WLAN data. We propose to use image-based and WLAN-based localisation individually and then fuse the results to obtain better performance overall. We demonstrate the effectiveness of our fusion algorithm for localisation to within a $8.9m^2$ room on very challenging data both for WLAN and image-based algorithms. We envisage the potential usefulness of our approach in a range of ambient assisted living applications.

Categories and Subject Descriptors

C.2.1 [**Network Architecture and Design**]: Wireless communication; H.4.3 [**Information Systems Applications**]: Communications Applications

General Terms

Algorithms, Measurement, Experimentation

Keywords

indoor localisation, WLAN, SURF vocabulary tree, fusion

1. INTRODUCTION

Wearable camera technology has evolved to the point whereby small unobtrusive cameras are now readily available, e.g. the Vicon Revue[1]. This has allowed research effort to focus on analysis and interpretation of the data that such devices provide [1]. Even in the absence of bespoke platforms such as the Vicon Revue, any smart phone can be turned into a wearable camera. The Campaignr[2] configurable micropublishing platform has shown the capability of mobile platforms to act as WLAN (and more general sensor) data gathering hubs. Our group is developing a device using an Android-based smart phone worn on a lanyard around the neck that in addition to image capture also senses a variety of other modalities e.g. motion, GPS, Bluetooth, WLAN. The idea is to use this platform in a variety of ambient assisted living applications as well as assistive technology for the memory and visually impaired. Whilst outdoor localisation is taken care of on this platform via GPS, indoor localisation is still an unsolved issue.

Although GPS has become synonymous with user localisation, indoors its signals are weak or non-existent. Using WLAN as a solution has given promising results, but its performance is subject to change due to multipath propagation and changes in the environment, such as number of persons present in a given location (see fig.1(a) which illustrates the effect of the presence of humans on WLAN received signal strength (RSS) data), variable orientation, temporary changes to building layout, etc. [2]. Performance also depends on the material the building is made from, size of spaces where measurements take place, antenna orientation, directionality, etc. [2]. Whilst image-based localisation techniques have provided some promising results, as in [3, 4], the limitations continue to be due to occlusion, changes in lighting, noise and blur [5]. In this paper, we propose an approach that combines image and WLAN data to leverage the best of both of these complementary modalities. We present the results for locating a user to within a specific office in a building or to a location within that office.

Most existing localisation methods are based on a single modality. In fact, to our best knowledge, even in other application domains there are only a few techniques based on fusion of RF and image sensing methods. In [6] the authors consider an active tracking system, consisting of a camera mounted on pan-tilt unit and a 360° RFID detection system to efficiently track humans in crowds. First they applied a particle filtering method to fuse heterogeneous data and then controlled the system motion to follow the person of interest. Other work describes an object tracking scheme using a different particle filtering model [7]. It consists of a camera observation method based on color features of the target and a WLAN-based localisation system.

In our previous work [8], we showed a proof of concept of how RSSs and image matching data could be fused to do coarse localisation for a small number of locations. Here we introduce a more precise WLAN-based algorithm, vocabulary tree concept for image-based localisation and a novel more complex and effective function in the fusion process.

*Area chair: Alexander Hauptmann
[1]http://www.viconrevue.com
[2]http://www.campaignr.com

MM'11, November 28–December 1, 2011, Scottsdale, Arizona, USA.

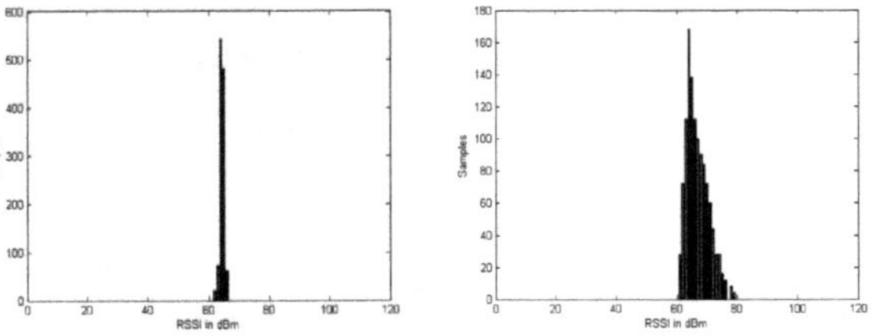

(a) Effect of users' presence on WLAN RSSI histogram in an office space: no users present (left), users present and moving (right)

(b) Sample images collected of office spaces

Figure 1: Examples of WLAN-based and visual sensing.

The approach is verified on a much larger and more challenging dataset. Our paper is structured as follows: Section 2 describes the experimental setup including data capture while section 3 discusses WLAN and image-based algorithms respectively. Section 4 introduces a novel fusion function while section 5 presents results for each modality individually and demonstrates that fusion outperforms any one modality leading to very accurate results overall.

2. EXPERIMENTAL SETUP

For our experimental test bed we use 20 offices on the second floor of a building (see fig. 2), where the average size of an office is $8.9m^2$. Within each office we use 5 calibrations points (CP), A, B, C, D & E. Each orientation of a CP (North, South, West and East) is represented with 8 (640×480 pixels) images taken with a camera (see fig. 1(b) for examples), and 300 RSSI (received signal strength indication) observations taken with a laptop. Every CP is represented using data from all four orientations together. In total we had $5,000$ images, of which $3,200$ were used for training and $1,800$ for testing, and $125,000$ signal strengths observations of which $120,000$ were used for training and $5,000$ for testing. One observation consists of received signal strengths from all active access points (in the best case the total number of access points: 14 in our case). Offices are chosen to be next to each other and moreover, look very similar inside, thus resulting in very challenging data for both WLAN and image-based localisation methods.

In a test we used one image and one signal strength observation per CP and tested how precisely we could localise to a given CP. Clearly, if we can localise to a CP, we can localise to within the office that contains that CP. We present results for localizing to a given office whereby the office selected is based on the 1st ranked results corresponding to one of the CPs for that office, even if the top ranked CP is incorrect. However, we wanted to understand how many

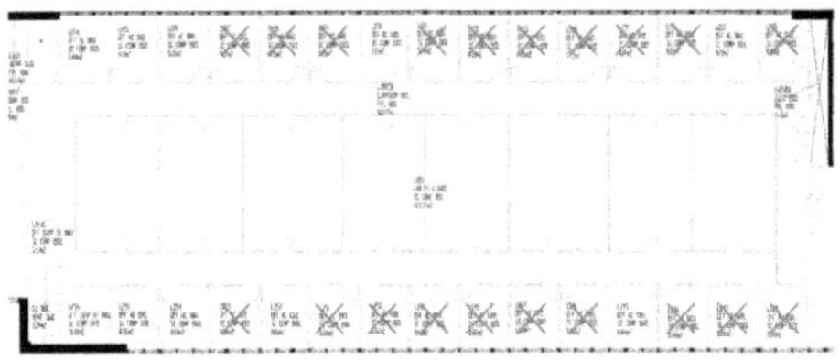

(a)

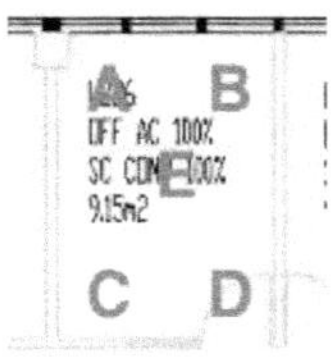

(b)

Figure 2: (a) Map of office locations – red crosses indicate offices used; (b) Calibration points $ABCDE$ within an office

(and which) CPs are necessary as this has an impact on the manual data collection effort required to perform accurate localisation. We examined localisation precision for 5 different combinations of 1, 2 and 3 CPs per office (giving 5 different sets of 20, 40 and 60 locations respectively in total). Precision (P) and average precision (AVP) were used as performance measures.

3. LOCALISATION METHODS

3.1 WLAN-based localisation

Probabilistic WLAN-based localisation techniques presume a priori knowledge of the probability distribution of the user's location [9, 2]. We decided to employ a Naive Bayes method [9] which takes into account the access points' (APs) signal strength values (RSSI) and also the frequency of the appearance of these APs. A signature for each CP is defined as a set of W distributions of signal strengths of W APs and a distribution representing the number of appearances of W APs received at this CP. We denote by $C \in \{1, 2, ..., K\}$ the CP random variable where K is the number of CPs, $X_m \in \{1, 2, ..., W\}$ represents the mth AP random variable, $Y_m \in \{1, ..., V\}$ is the signal strength that corresponds to m^{th} AP where W is number of APs, M is number of APs of an observation and V is number of discrete values of signal strength. From a set of N training observations $D = \{\mathbf{o}_1, \mathbf{o}_2, ..., \mathbf{o}_n\}$ where $\mathbf{o}_n = (c^{(n)}, x_1^{(n)}, y_1^{(n)}, ..., x_M^{(n)}, y_M^{(n)})$, $n = 1, .., N$ we can then estimate the signature parameters.

The joint distribution $P(C, X_1, Y_1, ..., X_M, Y_M)$ is given by

$$P(C) \prod_{m=1}^{M} P(X_m|C) P(Y_m|C, X_m) \quad (1)$$

where the distribution $P(C = c)$ could be assigned as uniform (without any loss of confidence).

If the identity function is $\mathbb{I}(a, b) = 1$ if $a = b$ else $= 0$, the sufficient statistics are:

$$n_c = \sum_{n=1}^{N} \sum_{m=1}^{M} \mathbb{I}(c^{(n)}, c) \quad (2)$$

$$n_c^{(x)} = \sum_{n=1}^{N} \sum_{m=1}^{M} \mathbb{I}(c^{(n)}, c) \mathbb{I}(x_m^{(n)}, x) \quad (3)$$

$$n_{c,x}^{(y)} = \sum_{n=1}^{N} \sum_{m=1}^{M} \mathbb{I}(c^{(n)}, c)\mathbb{I}(x_m^{(n)}, x)\mathbb{I}(y_m^{(n)}, y) \quad (4)$$

The parameters of $P(X_m|C)$ are estimated as

$$\hat{\pi}_c^{(x)} = \frac{n_c^{(x)} + 1}{n_c + W} \quad (5)$$

and the parameters of $P(Y_m|C, X_m)$ as

$$\hat{\gamma}_{c,x}^{(y)} = \frac{n_{c,x}^{(y)} + 1}{n_c^{(x)} + V} \quad (6)$$

Eventually at the prediction step we have:

$$l_i = P(c) \prod_{m=1}^{M} P(x_m|c)P(y_m|c, x_m) \quad (7)$$

The algorithm chooses the location which maximises l_i as being the user location. We rescaled these probabilities to sum to one and denoted their new values as the CP confidences, p_i.

3.2 Image-based localisation

Some efficient image retrieval and image-based localisation methods have been proposed so far [3]. Here we used a variation of the method shown in [10] to efficiently match query images that belong to a specific CP to the image training dataset of all CPs. Instead of SIFT, 64-dimensional SURF descriptors are used [4]. In our approach we make use of the sign of Laplacian (the trace of the Hessian matrix) which was already computed during the detection stage. Using the sign of the Laplacian we only compare those features that have the same type of contrast (dark on light background or light on dark background). All SURF features were extracted from all 3,200 images in the database, giving 794,146 feature descriptors. Each feature was associated with the image and the CP to which it belonged. To compare them we used the Euclidean distance. The features were split into two groups based on the sign of the Laplacian which halves our search time. For each group, we created a hierarchical tree clustering the descriptors using the K-means algorithm repeatedly. In the case of a query image, a match for each of its descriptor was found using the $+1$ or -1 hierarchical tree. Since each was labelled with the image and CP from which it was extracted, it therefore casts one vote for that CP. After each descriptor had voted for a CP, we then had a ranked list of CPs, from the most to the least likely. Similarly, we assigned a confidence for each CP (q_i) as the ratio of the number of votes associated with that CP and the total number of votes.

4. DATA FUSION

To perform fusion, we take confidences p_i and q_i from both sensing modalities P and Q into account, where in our case P and Q were WLAN and image sensing methods respectively. Here, i refers to a given CP. If we sort these confidences we can denote the first ranked, the second ranked, the third ranked, etc. (sorted) confidence by p_{max1}, p_{max2}, p_{max3}, etc. respectively (or by q_{max1},q_{max2}, etc. for the Q modality). We decided to use a large training dataset of confidences of different CPs. This would help in building a robust fusion function which would be reliably used on (unknown) testing data. First, let us define $P_{ij} = p_{maxi} - p_{maxj}$ and similarly $Q_{ij} = q_{maxi} - q_{maxj}$. Observing P_{12} and Q_{12} in many training confidence pairs we concluded that for values P_{12} and/or Q_{12} beyond some reliably large threshold, we were sure that the correct CP (location) was the 1st ranked one, based either on P or Q (or both). We established the thresholds T_1 and T_2 for P and Q and moreover we deduced that introducing multiplication and/or addition functions under some conditions can improve precision even more (or at least average precision). It is important to note that even if the 1st ranked confidence belongs to the correct location the algorithm would discard it if P_{12} (or Q_{12} or both) is below this(these) threshold(s). Also we found that the ranking of the correct location did not fall below some positions in both sets of rankings. In general, these are the mth position for P and the nth position for Q modality. The fusion function is thus as follows (eq. 8), where f_i represents fusion confidence and k_i confidence of the method to which $min(n, m)$ corresponds. The location output by the algorithm is the one with the maximum value of the fusion confidence:

$$f_i = \begin{cases} p_i, & P_{12} \geq Q_{12} \wedge P_{12} \geq T_1 \wedge Q_{12} \geq T_2 \\ q_i, & Q_{12} \geq P_{12} \wedge P_{12} \geq T_1 \wedge Q_{12} \geq T_2 \\ p_i, & P_{12} \geq T_1 \wedge Q_{12} < T_2 \\ q_i, & Q_{12} \geq T_2 \wedge P_{12} < T_1 \\ p_i q_i, & T_3 \leq P_{12} \leq T_4 \wedge T_5 \leq Q_{24} \leq T_6 \\ p_i + q_i, & T_7 \leq P_{12} \leq T_8 \wedge T_9 \leq Q_{24} \leq T_{10} \\ k_i, & \text{else} \end{cases} \quad (8)$$

5. RESULTS

An example of the benefits of fusion, when 2 CPs are observed as individual locations (BE), is shown in figure 3. It shows the behaviour of precision considering the top N ranked results, thus illustrating how often each modality returned the correct location as the top ranked result, 2nd ranked results, and so on (bars in the graph) and also how precision increases if the top N ranked results are considered (lines in the graph). In the top N, for $N = 1 \ldots 5$, the fusion approach outperforms both WLAN and image-based methods reaching precision of 91.82%. Also it can be seen that correct location rank doesn't drop below 8th for WLAN, and 12th for the image-based method. In this example we have $AVP_W = 75.18\%$, $AVP_I = 68.14\%$ and $AVP_F = 80.94\%$ for the WLAN, image-based and the fusion approach respectively.

The left hand side of table 1 shows results when using 1, 2 and 3 CPs per office (every CP represents a different location), using WLAN data only (P_W), image data only (P_I) and the fusion of both modalities (P_F). For 2 and 3 CPs we show a selection of results, corresponding to the best performing ones, rather than all possible combinations. The right hand side of the table shows results when we take into account the 1st ranked result that is not the correct one but that belongs to a CP within that particular office. This gives the precision to a particular office, denoted by P_{WO}, P_{IO} and P_{FO} obtained using WLAN-based, image-based and the fusion method respectively. From the table it is clear that fusion of WLAN and images significantly improves the performance of using either approach on its own. Moreover, on average, P_W, P_I and P_F decrease while P_{WO}, P_{IO} and P_{FO}

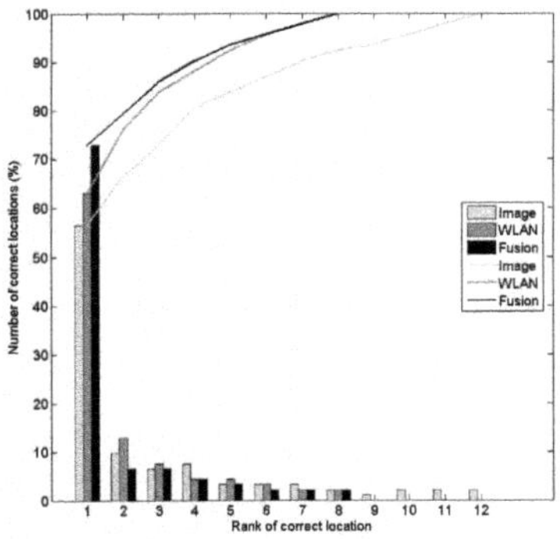

Figure 3: Number of correct locations (in %) found on the Nth rank (bars); Number of correct locations (in %) found in the top N ranks (lines)

CP	P_W	P_I	P_F	P_{WO}	P_{IO}	P_{FO}
A	65.22	50.00	69.57	65.22	50.00	69.57
E	69.57	60.87	73.91	69.57	60.87	73.91
C	69.57	56.52	78.26	69.57	56.52	78.26
B	73.91	58.70	82.61	73.91	58.70	82.61
D	71.74	63.04	76.09	71.74	63.04	76.09
AB	61.96	47.83	69.57	65.22	60.87	71.74
BE	63.04	56.52	72.83	71.74	70.65	76.09
ED	66.30	54.35	73.91	73.91	60.87	78.26
AC	64.13	46.74	71.74	75.00	53.26	78.26
BC	68.48	53.26	73.91	77.17	58.70	80.43
ABE	55.07	46.38	63.77	69.57	62.32	75.36
AEC	58.70	45.65	66.67	72.46	65.22	79.71
EBD	58.70	49.28	70.29	76.81	63.77	84.06
ABD	61.59	47.83	69.57	79.71	69.57	83.33
ACD	63.04	44.20	71.74	81.16	65.94	84.78

Table 1: Localisation results: P_W, P_I, P_F are precision results for considering each CP as a separate location; P_{WO}, P_{IO}, P_{FO} are precision results for localising to a specific office

increase when the number of CPs per office increases. This is expected since the data within an office are very similar, thus making the algorithms choose the nearby CP instead of the correct one. For images we have even more complex situation as locations that are not physically close by look similar as well. When we consider localisation to an office many incorrect 1st guesses become correct especially when the number of CPs in an office increases. Thus, in the case of 3 CPs, one can notice a large increase in precision, where on average it increased by 15.52%, 18.72% and 13.04% for WLAN-based, image-based and the fusion method respectively.

The performance variation for the localisation to within an office obtained by using a variable number of CPs also gives an interesting conclusion. Whilst the best results are naturally always obtained by using all 5 CPs for each office, we can see that using only one CP produces reasonably good performance: 82.61% precision for the best result (calibr. point B), 76.09% on average. This is important as it means that the manual data collection stage for model creation outlined in section 2 is viable as it only needs to be performed once (i.e. at one CP) per office in order to obtain reasonably accurate performance.

6. CONCLUSION

In this work, we presented results combining two complementary data sources for indoor localisation. By fusing WLAN signal strengths and image data, we achieve better performance than any individual modality. Future work will investigate the possibility of seamlessly tracking a user indoors, using dynamic and adaptive confidence-based weighting between these modalities, and more sophisticated classifiers such as neural networks.

7. ACKNOWLEDGMENTS

This work is supported by Science Foundation Ireland under grant 07/CE/I1147.

8. REFERENCES

[1] S. Karaman, J. Benois-Pineau, R. Meandgret, V. Dovgalecs, J.-F. Dartigues, and Y. Gaeandstel. Human daily activities indexing in videos from wearable cameras for monitoring of patients with dementia diseases. In *ICPR*, pages 4113–4116, 2010.

[2] A.S. Paul and E.A. Wan. RSSI-based Indoor Localization and Tracking Using Sigma-Point Kalman Smoothers. *IEEE Journal of Selected Topics in Signal Processing*, 3(5):860–873, 2009.

[3] J. Wolf, W. Burgard, and H. Burkhardt. Robust vision-based localization by combining an image-retrieval system with Monte Carlo localization. *IEEE Transactions on Robotics*, 21(2):208 – 216, 2005.

[4] H. Bay, T. Tuytelaars, and L. Van Gool. SURF: Speeded Up Robust Features. *Computer Vision and Image Understanding (CVIU)*, 110(3):346–359, August 2008.

[5] M. Redzic, C. O'Conaire, C. Brennan, and N. O'Connor. Multimodal Identification of Journeys. In *International Conference on Database and Expert Systems Applications (DEXA)*, pages 283–287, 2010.

[6] T. Germa, F. Lerasle, N. Ouadah, and V. Cadenat. Vision and RFID data fusion for tracking people in crowds by a mobile robot. *CVIU*, 114(6):641–651, June 2010.

[7] T. Miyaki, T. Yamasaki, and K. Aizawa. Tracking persons using particle filter fusing visual and Wi-Fi localizations for widely distributed camera. In *ICIP*, volume 3, pages 225–228, 2007.

[8] M. Redzic, C. O'Conaire, C. Brennan, and N. O'Connor. A hybrid method for indoor user localisation. In *4th European Conference on Smart Sensing and Context (EuroSSC)*, 2009.

[9] K. Tran, D. Phung, B. Adams, and S. Venkatesh. Indoor Location Prediction Using Multiple Wireless Received Signal Strengths. In *Proceedings of Australasian Data Mining Conference (AusDM)*, 2008.

[10] D. Nister and H. Stewenius. Scalable Recognition with a Vocabulary Tree. In *IEEE Conference on Computer Vision and Pattern Recognition (CVPR)*, 2006.

Document Dependent Fusion in Multimodal Music Retrieval

Zhonghua Li, Bingjun Zhang, Ye Wang
School of Computing, National University of Singapore, Singapore
{lizhongh, bingjun, wangye}@comp.nus.edu.sg

ABSTRACT

In this paper, we propose a novel multimodal fusion framework, document dependent fusion (DDF), which derives the optimal combination strategy for each individual document in the fusion process. For each document, we derive a document weight vector by estimating the descriptive abilities of its different modalities. The document weight vector also enables our framework to be easily integrated with existing multimodal fusion schemes, and achieve a better combination strategy for each document given a query. Experiments are conducted on a 17174-song music database to compare the retrieval accuracy of traditional query independent fusion and query dependent fusion approaches, and that obtained after integrating DDF with them. Experimental results indicate that DDF can significantly improve the retrieval performance of current fusion approaches.

Categories and Subject Descriptors

H.3.3 [**Information Search and Retrieval**]: Information filtering, Retrieval models; H.5.5 [**Sound and Music Computing**]: Systems

General Terms

Algorithms, Design, Experimentation

Keywords

Music, multimodal search, query dependent fusion, document dependent fusion, descriptive ability

1. INTRODUCTION

Since most documents (e.g., music, images, text documents) contain information or cues in different modalities, multimodal fusion, which aims to combine these modalities to better meet users' information needs, has been regarded as an effective approach to improve IR performance. Intensive research has been carried out aiming to estimate the optimal combination strategy of different modalities. Existing multimodal fusion approaches mainly include two categories: query independent fusion (QIF) and query dependent fusion (QDF). In the QIF scheme, the same fusion strategy is applied to combine different modalities for every query regardless of the query content and diversity. An example work of this category is CombSUM/CombMNZ method found in meta search [5]. However, this strategy is inadequate due to the fact that all queries are not equally created and they may have different information focuses. QDF emerges with the goal to improve the retrieval performance by adopting different fusion strategies for each query class (e.g., [1, 2, 7, 6]) or individual query (e.g., [9]). It is noted that these approaches focus on deriving the optimal fusion strategy by only considering queries. Once the fusion strategy is determined (either in QIF or QDF), all the documents adopt the same strategy to combine its modalities.

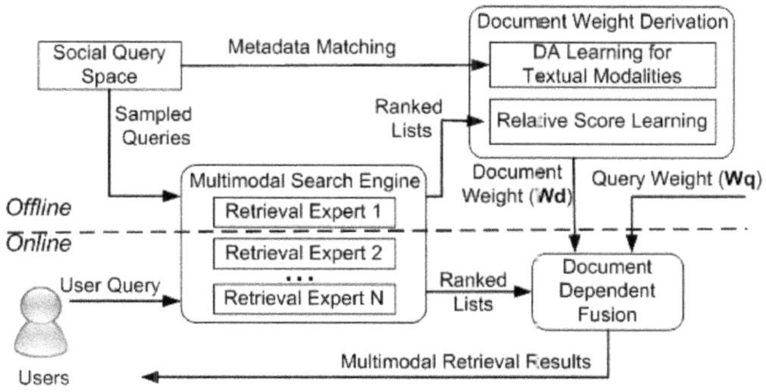

Figure 1: Document Dependent Fusion Framework for Multimodal Information Retrieval

In this paper, we propose a document dependent fusion (DDF) framework to derive the optimal fusion strategy for each document by considering influences of both queries and documents on the retrieval performance of IR applications. The structure of the framework is illustrated in Fig. 1. A document weight vector is derived for each document by learning the descriptive abilities of different modalities. This weight vector can be then integrated with QIF and QDF approaches. Confirmed by our experimental results, DDF significantly improves the performance of multimodal music retrieval.

The rest of the paper is organized as follows: Section 2 describes our approach from three main aspects: framework overview, document weight deviation, and document dependent fusion. Section 3 describes configurations of our experiments. Experimental results are presented and analyzed in Section 4, followed by the conclusion in Section 5.

*Area Chair: Alexander Hauptmann

MM'11, November 28–December 1, 2011, Scottsdale, Arizona, USA.

2. PROPOSED APPROACH

In this section, we first present an overview of the DDF framework based on the basic multimodal fusion structure. The fusion weight learning is then introduced in two phases: document weight deviation and document dependent fusion.

2.1 Document Dependent Fusion Overview

A multimodal retrieval system generally has N retrieval experts $\mathbf{RE} = [RE_1, ..., RE_N]$ to search relevant documents from different modalities. Given a query q , each retrieval expert RE_i returns a ranked list with the top n documents: $[d_{i1}, d_{i2}, ..., d_{in}]$. These ranked lists can be combined using a weight vector $\mathbf{W} = [W_1, ..., W_N]$, where $0 \leq W_i \leq 1$ and $\sum W_i = 1$. Each unique document d_k $(k \in [n, N * n])$ that appears in these ranked lists will be ranked by the final score

$$S_{d_k,q} = \sum_{i=1}^{N} s_{i_q,d_k} * W_i, \quad (1)$$

where s_{i_q,d_k} represents the score of document d_k in the ith ranked list given the query q, and it is generally normalized.

QIF approaches adopt the same fusion weight $\mathbf{W}$ for all the queries. The QDF scheme derives the optimal $\mathbf{W}$ for each query class or individual query. Both schemes provide a query-to-weight mapping in different resolutions. We format the fusion strategy in both cases as $\mathbf{W} = \mathbf{W_q}$. In this work, $\mathbf{W_q}$ and $\mathbf{W}$ are termed query weight and fusion weight.

We propose a document dependent fusion framework to derive the optimal fusion strategy for each document. A document weight vector ($\mathbf{W_d}$) is derived for each document according to the contributions of its different modalities. This weight vector can be integrated with the query weight to achieve a better fusion strategy (Eq. 2) for this document.

$$\mathbf{W} = f(\mathbf{W_q}, \mathbf{W_d}). \quad (2)$$

This fusion weight is used in the final score ranking in Eq. 1.

2.2 Document Weight Derivation

In this section, we derive a document weight vector which can reflect the importance of different modalities to a document. Since the formats of different modalities (e.g., textual, content) vary, we define a descriptive ability (DA) for each modality as a measure of its importance. Intuitively, a piece of information is considered useful only if it can meets users' information needs. The DA of a modality is defined as how well this modality meets users' information needs. We proceed to introduce the user information need space to lay the foundation of descriptive ability measures.

2.2.1 User Information Need Space

Since users' information needs are generally conveyed in queries, a large number of user queries need to be collected in order to construct a good user information need space. To save the effort of manually designing or collecting user queries, we construct a online folksonomy-based music social query space to simulate users' information needs in music retrieval.

The data information of this space is presented in Table 1 More detailed descriptions of this space can be found in [9].

2.2.2 Descriptive Ability of Textual Modalities by Metadata Matching

Textual metadata (e.g., title, descriptions) associated with music is an important modality of music documents. In multimodal music retrieval, there are generally several textual retrieval experts match music metadata with user queries on different music dimensions (e.g., genre, mood).

Table 1: Tag information in the music social query space. No. is the total number of tags in each music dimension

Dimensions	No.	Tag Clusters
Genre	244	Classical, Country, Electronic, HipHop, Jazz, Metal, Pop, Rock
Mood	286	Angry, Joy, Pleasure, Sad
Vocalness	13	Female, Male, Mixed, Nonvocal
Instrument	454	Brass, Percussion, Strings, Woodwinds

The metadata of each music document is compared with the music social query space. The binary occurrence count $n(d, w)$ of every word w from the music social query space (M) in document d is calculated. If word w appears in document d, $n(d, w)$ is set to 1, otherwise, we set it to 0. The descriptive ability of the kth textual modality of document d, can be derived as:

$$DA_T(d,k) = \frac{\sum_{w \in M_k} n(d,w)}{\sum_{w \in M} n(d,w)}, \quad (3)$$

where M_k is a subset of words in the music social query space M, and contains only words belong to the kth music dimension.

2.2.3 Descriptive Ability of Audio Modalities by Relative Score Learning

Audio modality refers to information derived from audio content, and is generally represented as feature vectors. Unlike metadata matching for textual modalities, these feature vectors are not directly comparable with the information needs represented using query keywords.

In this work, we utilize the relative score between audio and textual modalities to derive the descriptive ability of audio modalities. To estimate this relative score, we statistically analyze the retrieval results using a large number of user queries. For each query, N ranked lists are returned by all retrieval experts based on the similarity measure between the query and each modality of the documents. For each document d_k, we record the rank score s_{i_q,d_k} in the ith ranked list given a query q, and accumulate its total appearance over all the queries. The average score for the ith modality of this document can then be represented as:

$$S_{av}(i, d_k) = \sum_{q}^{N_Q} s_{i_q,d_k} / \sum_{q}^{N_Q} f_s(i_q, d_k), \quad (4)$$

where N_Q is the total number of queries; $f_s(i_q, d_k)$ is a selector function, which is set to 1(0) only when document d_k appears (does not appear) in the ith ranked list given a query q. We set $S_{av}(i, d_k)$ to 0 if document d_k never appears in the ith ranked list.

The average score provides an approximate importance of a modality over the tested queries. The relative score R_{j,d_k} between audio content and textual modalities on music dimension j $(j \in [1, N/2])$ is calculated as

$$R_{j,d_k} = \begin{cases} \frac{S_{av,C}(j,d_k)}{S_{av,T}(j,d_k)} & \text{if } S_{av,T}(j,d_k) \neq 0 \text{ and } S_{av,C}(j,d_k) \neq 0 \\ \kappa & \text{if } S_{av,T}(j,d_k) = 0 \text{ and } S_{av,C}(j,d_k) \neq 0 \\ 1/\kappa & \text{if } S_{av,T}(j,d_k) \neq 0 \text{ and } S_{av,C}(j,d_k) = 0 \\ 1 & \text{if } S_{av,T}(j,d_k) = 0 \text{ and } S_{av,C}(j,d_k) = 0, \end{cases} \quad (5)$$

where $S_{av,C}$ and $S_{av,T}$ are the average scores for content and textual modalities, respectively. Since the sampled queries may not cover all the cases in the music social query space, we introduce κ to balance the cases when any of the average scores is zero. In our experiments, κ is set to 1. The descriptive ability for the jth audio modality of document d_k can be calculated as

$$DA_C(d_k, j) = R_{j,d_k} * DA_T(d_k, j). \quad (6)$$

2.2.4 Document Weight Learning

Given the descriptive abilities of a document, document weight vector is derived by assigning higher weights to modalities with larger descriptive abilities. Assume W_{d,T_j} (W_{d,C_j}) is the weight for the jth textual (audio content) modality of document d, the document weight vector is represented as

$$\mathbf{W_d} = [W_{d,T_1}, ..., W_{d,T_{N/2}}, W_{d,C_1}, ..., W_{d,C_{N/2}}],$$

where $W_{d,T_j} = \lambda DA_T(j)$ and $W_{d,C_j} = \lambda DA_C(j)$; λ is the normalization constant, which can be calculated by solving the following equation:

$$\sum_{j=1}^{N/2} (W_{d,T_j} + W_{d,C_j}) = 1. \quad (7)$$

2.3 Document Dependent Fusion

The final fusion weight $\mathbf{W}$ integrates both query dependency and document dependency. Given a query q, with the query weight vector $\mathbf{W_q} = [W_{q,1}, ...W_{q,N}]$ estimated using existing approaches, all the unique documents returned by a retrieval expert share the same query weight. Assume the document weight for document d is $\mathbf{W_d} = [W_{d,1}, ..., W_{d,N}]$. Its final fusion weight $\mathbf{W} = [W_1, ..., W_N]$ is computed as:

$$W_i = \frac{W_{d,i} * W_{q,i}}{\sum_{j=1}^{N} W_{d,j} * W_{q,j}}, \quad (8)$$

where $i \in [1, N]$. From Eq. 8 we note that previous fusion schemes, QIF and QDF, are special cases of DDF when the document weight vector is set to $\mathbf{1}$ for every document.

3. EXPERIMENTAL CONFIGURATION

3.1 Data Collection

Our database contains 17174 music tracks together with their metadata. The metadata includes title, descriptions, keywords, comments from YouTube and tags from Last.fm. For each audio track, the ground truth music styles in four music dimensions (genre, mood, vocalness, instrument) were annotated and cross checked by amateur musicians.

Totally 236973 social queries were generated from the music social query space following the guidelines in [9]. We randomly sampled 200K queries for relative score learning (Section 2.2.3) and query weight training, and the remaining ones served as testing data.

3.2 Retrieval Methods

We consider both textual and audio retrieval experts for each music dimension being studied. Each incoming query is parsed by comparing it with the music social query space. The discovered keywords are then fed to corresponding textual and audio retrieval experts.

For textual retrieval expert, we adopt the standard text retrieval approach: first tokenize the metadata and eliminate the stop words, followed by stemming using Porter's algorithm [3] and ranking using OKAPI BM-25 [4].

In audio retrieval processes, each audio track is represented as an audio signature, which is Fuzzy Music Semantic Vector (FMSV) [8] representing the probabilities that a music item belongs to different music styles. Given a query keyword, a query FMSV is generated by filling 1 to the matched music style and 0 to other music styles. Euclidean distance is calculated between the query FMSV and the ones of all the audio tracks. A final ranked list is constructed by ranking tracks with smaller Euclidean distances higher in the list.

The score s_{i,d_k} ($k \in [1, N_d]$) of document d_k in the ith ranked list is normalized as: $s_{i,d_k} = 1 - Rank_i(d_k)/n$, where N_d is the number of unique music documents retrieved by all retrieval experts, and n is the number of music documents in each ranked list. We set n to 100 in our experiment.

As multiple music dimensions are considered, we adopt fractional relevance score to address the partial match between a music document and a query. This relevance score is determined as the number of matched dimensions to the total number of dimensions required by the query.

3.3 Comparison Methodology

To evaluate the proposed framework, we compared the performance of existing fusion schemes (QIF and QDF) with DDF using average precision (AP) and mean average precision (MAP). The MAP differences among various approaches were further assessed using t-test.

In the QDF scheme, we implemented *Regression-based QDF (RQDF-ORPegasos)*, which predicts a fusion strategy for each query using a regression model based on oracle combination weights [9]. After integrating document weights with this method, we named it *DRQDF-ORPegasos*.

We also implemented two QIF approaches. The first approach applies an optimal weight combination to all the queries based on oracle combination weights [2]. The second approach treats all retrieval experts with equal combination weights. We named these two approaches as QIF and equally weighted QIF (*EQIF*), and after integrating with DDF they were termed *DQIF* and *DEQIF*, respectively.

For each query, grid search was applied to derive the oracle combination weight which produced the highest AP. The query and its oracle combination weight formed a training sample and were used in *RQDF-ORPegasos* and *QIF* approaches. We examined the performance when different sizes of training datasets were used. Given a query in the testing dataset, each fusion method was tested three times, and the average AP of these three tests and MAP were computed over all the testing queries.

4. RESULTS AND ANALYSIS

Fig. 2 presents the retrieval accuracy (MAP) improvement of DQDF approaches compared to QDF approaches. Fig. 3 depicts the MAP comparisons between DQIF and QIF approaches. Table 2 illustrates the detailed retrieval accuracy improvement in different query types and the t-test results. *RQDF-ORPegasos* adopted 5 training samples to compute the sub-gradient in each iteration of ORPegasos [9].

4.1 QDF vs DQDF

When comparing with *RQDF-ORPegasos* (Fig. 2, Table 2), our approach performs much better when the training data size is below 6.4K, and fails to compete with *RQDF-ORPegasos* when the training query set becomes larger. This might be attributed to the relative score learning between textual and audio modalities. Since the relative score is learned from a subset of queries randomly selected from the original query

Table 2: Retrieval accuracy (MAP) improvement in different query types when integrating document weights with previous approaches. G, M, V, I represent genre, mood, vocalness, and instrument four music dimensions, while A indicates all four dimensions. t-test was conducted for the overall improvement, and p values are attached in column A. "<" means $p < 0.05$, and ">" means $p > 0.05$. No.(*) represents the size of training dataset, $* = \times 10^3$. The content in each column means the improvement in percentage (%). "-" means the performance decreases after integrating with document dependency.

Method	No.(*)	A(p)	G	M	V	I	GM	GV	GI	MV	MI	VI	GMV	GMI	GVI	MVI	GMVI
DRQDF-	0.1	3.1 (<)	-0.1	1.6	1.1	-0.3	6.9	6.5	0.8	3.6	2.1	6.5	4.0	1.8	4.0	4.0	2.3
ORPeg-	1.6	1.5 (<)	-0.1	1.6	0.7	-0.3	3.4	2.6	0.8	1.0	2.2	2.7	0.3	2.0	2.3	1.7	0.8
asos	25.6	-0.8 (<)	0	1.5	0.7	-0.3	1.9	1.0	-0.1	0.2	0.6	1.4	-2.9	-1	0.3	-0.6	-2.3
	200	-0.6 (<)	0	1.5	0.7	-0.3	2.3	1.6	0.1	0.1	0.6	1.5	-2.5	-1	0.7	-0.8	-2.2
DQIF	0.1	0.5 (>)	-0.1	1.6	0.8	-0.3	11.8	13.3	0.3	2.6	0.3	1.1	1.4	-0.9	-0.7	0.3	-1.9
	1.6	0.3 (>)	-0.1	1.6	0.8	-0.3	11.5	13.6	0.1	3.2	0.4	1.5	1.8	-1.1	-1.1	0.2	-2.7
	25.6	0.2 (>)	-0.1	1.6	0.8	-0.3	11.5	13.5	0.1	3.1	0.3	1.4	1.7	-1.1	-1.2	0.2	-2.8
	200	0.2 (>)	-0.1	1.6	0.8	-0.3	11.4	13.5	0	3.1	0.3	1.4	1.6	-1.2	-1.2	0.2	-2.8
DEQIF	N.A.	10.1 (<)	0.3	1.4	2.2	-0.2	9.7	13.7	12.9	5.6	15.4	19.3	6.2	17.0	17.3	10.9	5.6

dataset, it only provides an approximation of the relative importance between different modalities. The number of queries used in this process and the distributions among different music dimensions may affect relative scores in representing the real descriptive abilities of different modalities.

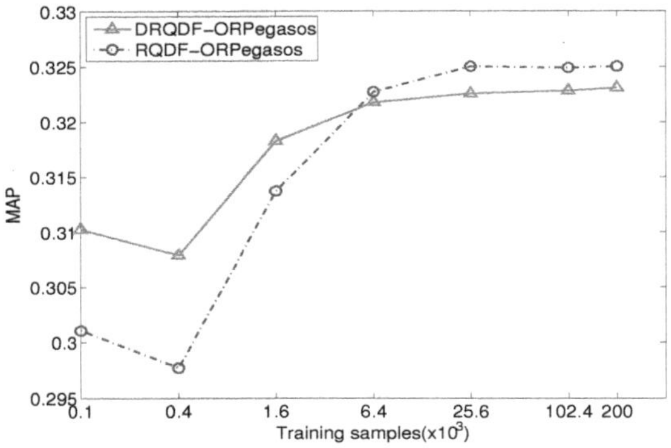

Figure 2: Retrieval accuracy (MAP) improvement when integrating DDF with RQDF-ORPegasos.

4.2 QIF vs DQIF

When comparing with QIF scheme, our approach outperforms QIF with an average improvement of 0.3% in MAP (Fig. 3). For *EQIF*, our approach increases the MAP by 10.1% (from 0.268 to 0.295). It indicates that the proposed framework unleashes the power of each document modality in multimodal fusion frameworks.

The MAP improvement in Table 2 illustrates the superior performance of our approach in estimating the optimal fusion weights in many query types. For instance, nearly all the 2-dimensional and 3-dimensional queries, and two single-dimensional (mood and vocalness) queries are improved using DDF approaches. The performance of query by genre and instrument is decreased with an almost constant ratio. This is mainly due to the insufficient number of queries in a particular query type while learning relative scores.

5. CONCLUSIONS

We have introduced a novel multimodal fusion framework, document dependent fusion (DDF), to derive the optimal fusion strategy for each individual document. We derive a document weight vector for each document, and integrate it into the fusion process. Confirmed by the experimental results, our proposed framework has significantly improved current multimodal fusion approaches. Moreover, in the process of DA derivation, relative scores of different modalities are learned from the retrieval results of a large number of

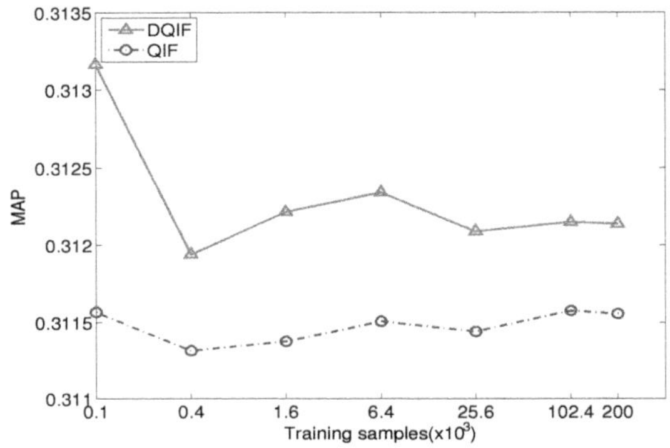

Figure 3: Retrieval accuracy (MAP) improvement when integrating DDF with QIF.

user queries. By combining with the DA of textual modalities, this method can derive DAs for modalities with various formats. Therefore, it can also be extended to other media documents in different multimodal retrieval applications, such as meta search, and video/image retrieval.

6. ACKNOWLEDGMENTS

The work was supported by Singaporean MOE grant R-252-000-381-112.

7. REFERENCES

[1] T. S. Chua, S. Y. Neo, K. Y. Li, G. Wang, R. Shi, M. Zhao, H. Xu, Q. Tian, S. Gao, and T. L. Nwe. Trecvid 2004 search and feature extraction task by nus pris. In *NIST TRECVID Workshop*, 2004.

[2] L. S. Kennedy, A. P. Natsev, and S. F. Chang. Automatic discovery of query-class-dependent models for multimodal search. In *Proc. of ACM Multimedia*, 2005.

[3] M. F. Porter. An algorithm for suffix stripping. *Program*, 14(3), 1980.

[4] S. E. Rrobertson, S. Walker, M. M. Beaulieu, M. Gatford, and A. Payne. Okapi at TREC-4. In *TREC*, 1995.

[5] J. A. Shaw and E. A. Fox. Combination of multiple searches. In *TREC-2*, 1994.

[6] L. Xie, A. Natsev, and J. Tesic. Dynamic multimodal fusion in video search. In *Proc. of IEEE ICME*, 2007.

[7] R. Yan and A. G. Hauptmann. Probabilistic latent query analysis for combining multiple retrieval sources. In *Proc. of ACM SIGIR*, 2006.

[8] B. Zhang, J. Shen, Q. Xiang, and Y. Wang. Compositemap: a novel framework for music similarity measure. In *Proc. of ACM SIGIR*, 2009.

[9] B. Zhang, Q. Xiang, H. Lu, J. Shen, and Y. Wang. Comprehensive query-dependent fusion using regression-on-folksonomies: a case study of multimodal music search. In *Proc. of ACM Multimedia*, 2009.

Finding Representative and Diverse Community Contributed Images to Create Visual Summaries of Geographic Areas

Stevan Rudinac, Alan Hanjalic, Martha Larson
Multimedia Information Retrieval Lab, Delft University of Technology, Delft, The Netherlands
{s.rudinac, a.hanjalic, m.a.larson}@tudelft.nl

ABSTRACT
This paper presents an automatic approach that uses community-contributed images to create representative and diverse visual summaries of specific geographic areas. Complex relations between images, extracted visual features, text associated with the images as well as users and their social network are modeled using a multimodal graph. To compute affinities between nodes in the graph we rely on the proven concept of random walk with restarts. The novelty of our approach lies in its use of the multimodal graph to create a diverse, yet representative, image set. Further, we introduce an edge-weighting mechanism for the fusion of heterogeneous modalities. We evaluate our summaries with a new protocol that tests for representativeness and diversity using image geo-coordinates and is independent of the need for human evaluators. The experiments, performed on a set of Flickr images, demonstrate the effectiveness of our approach.

Categories and Subject Descriptors
H.3.3 [**Information Storage and Retrieval**]: Information Search and Retrieval; H.3.5 [**Information Storage and Retrieval**]: On-line Information Services.

General Terms
Algorithms, Performance, Experimentation.

Keywords
Visual summaries of geographic areas, social media, image set representativeness, image set diversity, random walk with restarts.

1. INTRODUCTION
In this paper we present an approach to the automatic construction of visual summaries of geographic areas using social media from popular content sharing websites. Compact and informative visual summaries could significantly improve quality of experience for location recommendation systems, hotel booking websites and a variety of other services by helping users to gain an impression of the surroundings of a particular location. Our approach to visual summarization of geographic areas is illustrated by Figure 1.

*Area Chair: Marco Bertini.

MM'11, November 28–December 1, 2011, Scottsdale, Arizona, USA.

In the first step of our approach, we download Flickr images captured within a certain radius of a given location, together with the accompanying metadata, such as title, keywords, description, information on uploader and commentators. Similarly to [7,12,2,1], we link images and metadata together by constructing a graph, but propose a novel approach to edge weighting that takes into account the contribution of each individual modality to the overall summarization performance. A number of methods have been proposed for computation of affinities between nodes in the graph [13]. However, since these techniques are not our main focus, we adopt random walk with restarts (RWR), a state-of-the-art method [6,7,12,2]. In the next step, we compute image representativeness and select the final set of images for the visual summary in the iterative fashion, using a novel algorithm that jointly optimizes representativeness and diversity. By promoting diversity and representativeness of the images in the visual summary we aim at presenting all important aspects of a specific geographic area, e.g., landmarks, museums, restaurants, shops. Finally, we propose a novel evaluation protocol that assesses the necessary criteria for representativeness and diversity. Because it exploits only geo-coordinates associated with the images and does not require input of human evaluators, the method is particular useful to support the development of new approaches.

In the next section, we briefly address the related work. Our visual summarization algorithm is described in Section 3, while Section 4 addresses our proposed evaluation protocol. We report our experiments in Section 5 and conclude the paper with discussion of our findings.

2. RELATED WORK
Based on the assumption that users prefer diversified image search results [10], several approaches to diversifying the sets of representative images addressing a given search request have been proposed. In monomodal approaches, images were diversified either based on their visual features (e.g. selecting visual cluster centroids in [5]) or based on the associated text [11]. More recently, the ImageCLEF Photo Task 2009 focusing specifically on image search diversification concluded that multimodal approaches yield the highest performance [9]. We therefore adopt a multimodal approach in developing our method. Although several multimodal methods have already been proposed, e.g., selecting diverse and representative landmark images in [4] or using travelogues to create summaries of touristic destinations in [8], the geographic areas addressed there are of a different type and magnitude than in our work and therefore impose different diversification challenges and require a different methodological approach.

3. ALGORITHM DESCRIPTION

In this section, we describe the core of our visual summarization algorithm corresponding to the blocks (b) and (c) in the Figure 1.

3.1 Graph Construction

There are four types of nodes in our constructed graph G:

- *Image nodes V(I):* For each of N images of a given location an image node is added.
- *Visual feature nodes V(f):* For each image a visual feature node is added. Visual content of an image is described using local color moments extracted over a 5x5 regular rectangular grid and Gabor texture features.
- *Text nodes V(t):* For each image a text node is added. We index image title, keywords and description and represent them using a vector of TF-IDF weights.
- *User nodes V(u):* A user node is added for each of N_u image uploaders and commentators.

Attribute edges, marked with solid lines in Figure 1.b. link images with their attributes (visual feature, text and user nodes). Similarity edges (dashed lines) connect nodes of the same type. Edges linking visual feature nodes are weighted using Gaussian kernel similarity and the edges linking text nodes are weighted using cosine similarity between their TF-IDF vectors. The weights applied to the edges linking user nodes are proportional to the number of images "related" to both users:

$$W_u(i,j) = sim(u_i,u_j) = \frac{|S(u_i) \cap S(u_j)|}{|S(u_i) \cup S(u_j)|} \quad (1)$$

where $S(u_i)$ and $S(u_j)$ are the sets of images uploaded/commented by the users u_i and u_j and W_u is the resulting $N_u \times N_u$ matrix of user similarities. To obtain a better approximation of user links we consider images from all available locations and not only the ones for which we are constructing the graph.

Finally, we modify attribute and similarity edges using weights that reflect the contribution of each modality to the overall performance of the summarization algorithm. Weights are computed using subgraphs of the graph G (cf. Figure 1b.), consisting of image nodes and nodes of one other single modality, i.e., $V' = V(I) \cup V(f)$, $V' = V(I) \cup V(t)$ and $V' = V(I) \cup V(u)$. Modality dependant weights are then computed as:

$$\beta_f = \frac{\pi_f}{\pi_f + \pi_t + \pi_u}, \beta_t = \frac{\pi_t}{\pi_f + \pi_t + \pi_u}, \beta_u = \frac{\pi_u}{\pi_f + \pi_t + \pi_u}, \quad \text{where}$$

π_f, π_t and π_u indicate the performance of our visual summarization approach utilizing three unimodal subgraphs. The performance measure is discussed in Section 4. If the W_m is a matrix of edge weights linking nodes of the same modality m, we compute the final edge weights W'_m as $W'_m = \beta_m W_m, m \in \{f,t,u\}$.

3.2 Image Set Representativeness

If an image is similar to many other images in a given image set, we conjecture that it is representative of that set. Input to our module for selection of representative images are the affinities between image nodes $V(I)$ in the graph G described in the previous section. Similarly to [7,12,2], we compute multimodal affinities between image nodes using RWR algorithm. For each image, we compute a sum of similarities (affinities) with all other images of that location $p_{sum}(j) = \sum_{i=1:N, i \neq j} p_i(j)$, where $p_i(j)$ is a multimodal similarity between image nodes i and j, or more precisely a stationary probability of the image node i, when

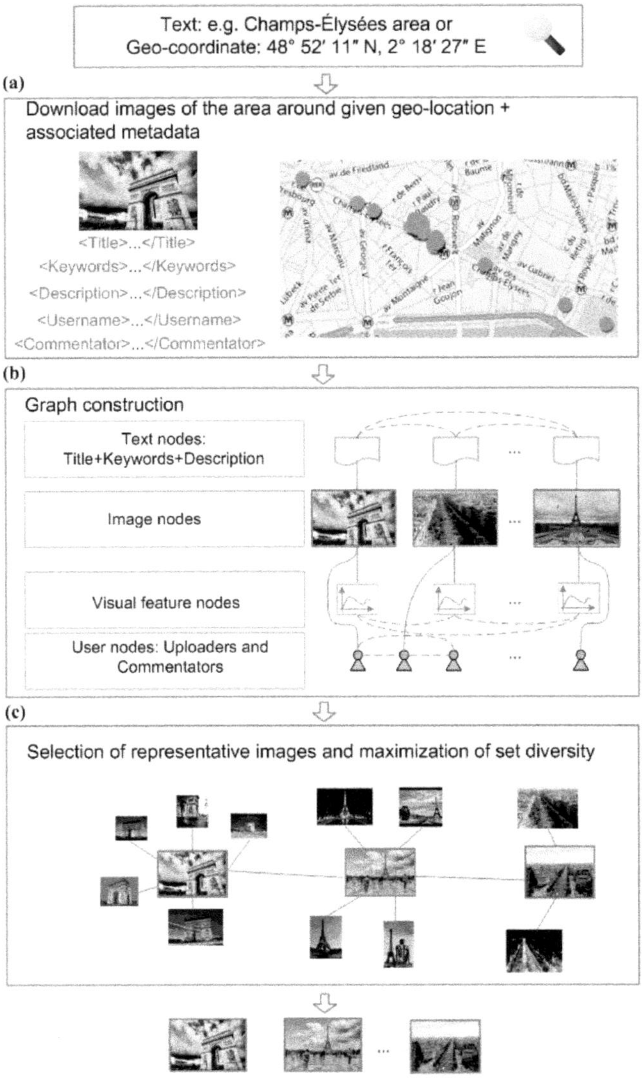

Figure 1. Creating visual summaries of geographic areas

the RWR is initialized from the image node j. Further, we sort images according to the increasing p_{sum} and for each image j define the representativeness score $RS(j)$ as the rank of the image in the sorted list. In this way, the image with the lowest p_{sum} will have RS=1 and the image with the highest p_{sum} will be assigned RS=N. As the first element of the target visual summary (optimal image set, OS), we select image with the highest RS.

3.3 Image Set Diversity

After the most representative image is selected for the visual summary, further images are selected in the iterative fashion. The next new image to be added to the summary should be as representative as possible, but at the same time as dissimilar as possible from already selected images. At each step, we initialize RWR from the image nodes of the images already selected for the OS and compute similarity of the set with all images of a given location $p_{OS}(j)$, $1 \leq j \leq N$. Images are then sorted according to the decreasing p_{OS} and for each image j diversity score $DS(j)$ is set to be equal to the rank of the image in the sorted list. In this way, the image that is most similar to the images in the OS receives DS=1 and the least similar image has DS=N. During each iteration, we select the image with the highest RS * DS score from amongst those that have not yet been selected for the OS. The process stops when the summary of a desired size is constructed.

4. EVALUATION PROTOCOL

We conjecture that a geographical spread of images collected from within a particular area reflects users' opinions with regard to popularity and attractiveness of the places in the area. Therefore, we expect a successful visual summarization algorithm to reproduce this geographical spread. We also believe that a larger geographical cluster reflects a higher popularity of a particular place and the possible existence of multiple "eye-catchers". On the other hand, our visual summary should cover all important aspects of a given area, and therefore it should include elements of the other clusters as well. In the first step of the evaluation protocol, we utilize affinity propagation clustering [3] to cluster images based on their geo-coordinates. This clustering has proven effective in the automatic estimation of the number of clusters. Further, we expect clusters to be represented in the final visual summary according to their relative frequency (size) in the entire collection of images of a given area. For example, if three clusters with 60, 30 and 10 elements each were detected, the final 10-image visual summary should ideally consist of 6, 3 and 1 images from those clusters. We propose to evaluate visual summaries using the well-known multinomial distribution PMF (MNPMF). We note here that the other evaluation metrics, e.g., Kullback Leibler divergence, could be utilized equally well, but we choose MNPMF because our evaluation problem is a good example of a multinomial distribution. We define MNPMF function $f(x \mid N_R, p_c)$ as:

$$f(x \mid N_R, p_c) = \binom{N_R}{x_1,\ldots,x_k} p_{c1}^{x_1} p_{c2}^{x_2} \ldots p_{ck}^{x_k} = \tag{2}$$

$$= \frac{N_R}{x_1! \cdots x_k!} p_{c1}^{x_1} p_{c2}^{x_2} \ldots p_{ck}^{x_k}$$

In the formula above, prior probabilities of k detected geo-clusters $p_c = (p_{c1}, p_{c2}, \ldots, p_{ck})$, $\sum_{i=1:k} p_{ci} = 1$ are defined as the relative sizes of those clusters and $x = (x_1, \ldots, x_k)$, $\sum_{i=1:k} x_i = N_R$ is the number of images in the final visual summary drawn from each cluster C_i, $i = 1 \ldots k$. The function f has a maximum when the number of images x in the visual summary corresponds to the clusters' prior probabilities p_c - $\forall i \in [1,k]: \frac{x_i}{N_R} = p_{ci}$. Another feature of MNPMF that makes it suitable for our purposes is a slight bias towards larger clusters. In other words, if the members of a particular cluster are not present in the visual summary, decrease in the value of function $f(x \mid N_R, p_c)$ will be proportional to the cluster size.

5. EXPERIMENTAL EVALUATION

We describe our experimental setup and report on experimental results investigating different aspects of our approach.

5.1 Experimenal Setup

We perform experiments on the collection of Flickr images captured within 1km of 500 locations in Paris, France, selected by a location recommender system [2]. We download images and the associated metadata, i.e., title, description, tags, geotags, information on uploaders and commentators. For the evaluation, we use 100 images from the 207 locations that have at least 100 images. We compare our approach to several alternatives, which we take to be conventional and sensible methods for selecting user-contributed images:

- *Random:* Images of a given location are randomly sampled for the visual summary. We use this approach as a naïve baseline, because we conjecture that random sampling of images would follow their geographical spread (e.g. geo-clustering). On the other hand, this approach is theoretically unaware of other factors influencing quality of a visual summary, such as e.g. visual representativeness/diversity, and appeal to the users.
- *View Count:* Visual summary is composed of the images with the highest view count. Sorting images according to their view count is a very common approach in commercial systems. For example, Flickr image search offers sorting according to the image "interestingness", which is derived from the view count, number of comments on that image and the number of people who selected that particular image as the "favorite" [4].
- *Number of Comments:* Images with the highest number of comments are selected for a visual summary. The reasoning behind selection of this alternative is similar to *View Count.*
- *Visual Clustering:* Similarly to [5], we utilize k-means clustering to cluster images based on their visual features and then select cluster centroids for the visual summary. Visual features used include local color moments extracted over 5x5 regular rectangular grid and Gabor texture features.

The remainder of this sections reports on our experimental results.

5.2 Evaluation of Visual Summaries

First, we evaluate the performance of our proposed approach (designated here RWR-RD) with regard to representativeness and diversity using the protocol from Section 4 and compare it to the four baselines described in Section 5.1: *Random*, *View Count*, *Nr. of Comments* and *Visual Clustering*. Here, we do not yet apply additional modality-dependant weights to the edges of our graph *G*, but rather we set $\beta_f = \beta_t = \beta_u = 1$.

Table 1. Performance (as MNPMF) of RWR-RD approach and the alternative approaches averaged over 207 locations

Selection Method	N_R=5	N_R=10	N_R=15	N_R=20
Random	0.0213	0.0116	0.0066	0.0045
View Count	0.0171	0.0084	0.0055	0.0039
Nr. of Comments	0.0030	0.0006	0.0001	0.0002
Visual Clustering	0.0154	0.0039	0.0014	0.0017
RWR-RD	**0.0320**	**0.0161**	**0.0092**	**0.0062**

Our proposed *RWR-RD* emerges as the best performer for the various sizes of the visual summary, i.e. N_R = 5, 10, 15 and 20 (cf. Table 1). *View Count* and *Nr. of Comments* dramatically fail to demonstrate representativeness and diversity, which may reflect users repeated viewing and commenting the same images or the same sorts of images of popular places. As "foretold" in the previous section, random baseline achieves a high performance with regard to geographic representativeness and diversity, but again, it is unaware of other factors comprising a good summary.

5.3 Improvement Distribution over Locations

Further, for the *RWR-RD* approach and the four alternatives we investigate distribution of performance over 207 locations. As shown in the Table 2, our proposed *RWR-RD* approach emerges as the best performer, with regard to representativeness and diversity, for the highest percentage of locations.

Table 2. Performance of RWR-RD approach and the alternatives as the percentage of locations for which a particular approach is the best performer as measured by MNPMF

Selection Method	N_R=5	N_R=10	N_R=15	N_R=20
Random	20.3	23.6	20.3	25.6
View Count	13.5	6.3	6.8	4.8
Nr. of Comments	11.6	6.3	1.4	1.4
Visual Clustering	19.3	17.9	21.3	22.8
RWR-RD	**35.3**	**45.9**	**50.2**	**45.4**

5.4 Usefulness of Additional Edge Weights

Finally, we investigate whether additional modality-dependent weighting described in the Section 3.1 brings a further improvement in the system. Performance of three unimodal graph-based approaches π_f, π_t and π_u is measured in terms of MNPMF averaged across 207 locations. Our exploratory experiments show that the performance of such unimodal *RWR-RD* variants, which exploit exclusively visual features, text or user modalities, cannot match the performance of the integrated multimodal *RWR-RD* approach.

Table 3. Performance of our summarization approach as a function of modality-dependant weights; as a performance measure MNPMF averaged over 207 locations is used

Selection Method	N_R=5	N_R=10	N_R=15	N_R=20
RWR-RD-W	**0.0339**	**0.0165**	**0.0101**	**0.0067**
RWR-RD	0.0320	0.0161	0.0092	0.0062

The results presented in Table 3 indicate that additional weighting of the edges in our graph (i.e. *RWR-RD-W* algorithm), based on modality analysis yields a moderate, but steady improvement across conditions.

6. DISCUSSION AND OUTLOOK

Our proposed approach to visual summarization of geographic areas succeeds in building summaries composed of diverse, yet representative images. Exploiting image content, automatically created metadata, user generated annotations as well as users' interactions with the content and their social networks, we demonstrate the full potential of data synergies in social media. Additional modality-dependent weights applied to attribute and similarity edges in the graph further improve performance of our summarization approach. The evaluation protocol we introduce holds potential for aiding development of image retrieval and visual summarization approaches, by testing whether criteria for representativeness and diversity are satisfied. It does not require involvement of human evaluators and relies solely on the analysis of geotags associated with the images. Finally, our experimental results demonstrate the viability of our approach. Other common or conventional approaches for choosing user-contributed images are shown to fail radically in demonstrating representativeness and diversity.

Our immediate next step will be to introduce a second method for evaluating the visual summaries that makes use of human input. This method, which we intend to implement using a crowdsourcing platform such as Mechanical Turk, will serve two purposes. First, it will allow us to confirm that our proposed automatic metric captures human perceptions of representativeness and diversity. Second, it will allow us to more accurately determine the extent to which our approach outperforms the conventional alternatives. As it stands now, we use the same evaluation metric to inform the estimation of additional, modality-dependent graph edge weights and to calculate the performance of our summarization approach. For this reason, we currently cannot guarantee complete independence of our summarization approach and our evaluation method.

Further future work will investigate factors influencing the performance of the approach. Although our visual summarization approach emerges as the overall best performer, on some locations alternate approaches perform better. Understanding of these differences will help us to refine the modality-dependent weighting of the edges in the graph and to improve the overall performance. Ultimately, we would like to investigate additional criteria relevant for visual summaries of location, such as the appeal of images to users.

7. ACKNOWLEDGMENTS

The research leading to these results has received funding from the European Commission's 7th Framework Programme (FP7) under grant agreement n° 216444 (NoE PetaMedia).

8. REFERENCES

[1] Bu, J., Tan, S., Chen, C., Wang, C., Wu, H., Zhang, L., and He, X. 2010. Music recommendation by unified hypergraph: combining social media information and music content. In *ACM MM '10*, 391-400.

[2] Clements, M. 2010. Personalised Access to Social Media. PhD Thesis, TU Delft, Delft, NL.

[3] Frey, B. J. and Dueck, D. 2007. Clustering by passing messages between data points. *Science*, 315 (5814), 972-976.

[4] Kennedy, L. S. and Naaman, M. 2008. Generating diverse and representative image search results for landmarks. In *WWW '08*, 297-306.

[5] Leuken, R. H. van, Garcia, L., Olivares, X., and Zwol, R. van. 2009. Visual diversification of image search results. In *WWW '09*, 341-350.

[6] Page, L., Brin, S., Motwani, R., and Winograd, T. 1999. The PageRank Citation Ranking: Bringing Order to the Web. Technical Report. Stanford InfoLab.

[7] Pan, J-Y., Yang, H-J., Faloutsos, C., and Duygulu, P. 2004. Automatic multimedia cross-modal correlation discovery. In *ACM KDD '04*, 653-658.

[8] Pang, Y., Hao, Q., Yuan, Y., Hu, T., Cai, R., and Zhang, L. 2011. Summarizing tourist destinations by mining user-generated travelogues and photos. *Comput. Vis. Image Underst.* 115, 3, 352-363.

[9] Paramita, M. L., Sanderson, M., and Clough, P. 2009. Diversity in photo retrieval: overview of the ImageCLEFPhoto task 2009. In *CLEF '09*, 45-59.

[10] Sanderson, M., Tang, J., Arni, T., and Clough, P. 2009. What Else Is There? Search Diversity Examined. In *ECIR '09*, 562-569.

[11] Song, K., Tian, Y., Gao, W., and Huang, T. 2006. Diversifying the image retrieval results. In *ACM MM '06*, 707-710.

[12] Urban, J. and Jose, J. M. 2006. Adaptive image retrieval using a Graph model for semantic feature integration. In *ACM MIR '06*, 117-126.

[13] Yen, L., Fouss, F., Decaestecker, C., Francq, P., and Saerens, M. 2009. Graph nodes clustering with the sigmoid commute-time kernel: A comparative study. *Data Knowl. Eng.* 68, 3, 338-361.

Fusing Object Detection and Region Appearance for Image-text Alignment *

Luca Del Pero Philip Lee James Magahern Emily Hartley Kobus Barnard
University of Arizona
{delpero, phlee, jamesmag, elh, kobus}@email.arizona.edu

ABSTRACT

We present a method for automatically aligning words to image regions that integrates specific object classifiers (e.g., "car" detectors) with weak models based on appearance features. Previous strategies have largely focused on the latter, and thus have not exploited progress on object category recognition. Hence, we augment region labeling with object detection, which simplifies the problem by reliably identifying a subset of the labels, and thereby reducing correspondence ambiguity overall. Comprehensive testing on the SAIAPR TC dataset shows that principled integration of object detection improves the region labeling task.

Categories and Subject Descriptors

I.4.8 [**Image processing and computer vision**]: Scene analysis—*Object recognition*

General Terms

Algorithms, Performance

1. INTRODUCTION

There has been much recent work on both training classifiers for object recognition, as well as learning models for automated image annotation, from weakly labeled data (e.g., [2, 5, 7, 13, 17, 16]). Such data consists of pictures with associated keywords, where it is not known which word corresponds to which part of the image (correspondence ambiguity). Learning from weakly labeled images is challenging, since it requires solving two problems at once: 1) locating the desired entity in the training data; 2) learning a model for appearance. Recent work suggests addressing the correspondence ambiguity in weakly labeled data as a separate problem from learning object appearance [3, 11]. Specifically, the goal is to align each label, initially associated with the whole picture, with the correct part of the image (Figure 1). We refer to this task as aligning the training data. Once this is done, this augmented data can be used for learning region or object models. Further, we agree with others that labels have to be localized in order to be useful for retrieval and recognition [1, 3].

In this work, we contribute a new strategy for aligning the training data. Specifically, we propose to combine object detectors, designed for robustly identifying a single specific entity, and existing methods for linking words to regions based on weak models. Previous work (e.g., [3, 11]) has relied on the latter, since it is not known in advance which models are good for which objects or regions. For example, some are better defined in terms of shape (e.g. "cup"), some in terms of color or texture ("zebra"), and some might require a part-based model ("bicycle"). However, developing a specific model for every word is impractical and does not scale. On the other hand, simple generic models can generalize over a large number of different entities, but cannot achieve the fine level of tuning required for robustly identifying a specific entity. It then seems natural to exploit existing detectors to reliably align some of the labels, relying on weak models for the remaining ones.

We also argue that detectors are useful for annotation when combined with exclusion reasoning [3], which posits that each word associated to an image should be assigned to at least one of its regions. Consider the example in Figure 1. If a car detector identifies the central region as "car", the labeling task becomes easier, as the choice for the two remaining regions is now restricted to "sky" and "snow". This also accommodates for the fact that detectors are usually available for common objects only. In fact, less common objects can be aligned via exclusion reasoning, thus producing data for training robust detectors for them.

The main contribution of this work is a principled strategy for integrating object detectors and exclusion reasoning into existing algorithms for region labeling. Specifically, we propose a probabilistic framework, as this is an effective way to combine different sources of information in this domain [6, 12, 15]. To test our ideas, we incorporate state-of-the art detectors [10] into a recent algorithm for region labeling [3].

Figure 1: Solving the correspondence ambiguity in weakly labeled data. See text for details

*Area chair: Alexander Hauptmann

MM'11, November 28–December 1, 2011, Scottsdale, Arizona, USA.

2. OVERVIEW OF OUR APPROACH

We start by defining a probabilistic framework for labeling the training data at the region level. Our input is a set of images, each with a set of associated keywords. We define the vocabulary V as the union of all such keywords $(w_1, ..., w_{|V|})$. Each image is subdivided into regions using a standard segmentation algorithm based on low level features, such as color and texture (for this work, we used NCuts [14]). We use the notation r_j to identify a generic image region produced by the segmenter.

Our goal is to compute a distribution $p(w|r_j)$ for each region over the whole vocabulary. The probabilistic constraints

$$\sum_{w \in V} p(w|r_j) = 1 \quad (1)$$

embody an additional manifestation of exclusion reasoning, which states that to the extent that we believe r_j is to be labeled with a word, it should not be labeled with other words. In fact, a word w_k with high $p(w_k|r_j)$ results in small $p(w_u|r_j)$ $\forall u \neq k$. For example, if a car detector outputs a low (high) probability $p(car|r_j)$ for region r_j, this will result in a high (low) probability $p(w_k|r_j) \forall w_k \neq$ "car". Note that this allows to smoothly integrate detectors, which are binary classifiers, into our region labeling scenario, which is a multiclass labeling problem. However, this requires mapping the output of detectors (typically scores) into probabilities using held out data, as discussed in Section 3.

Given $p(w|r_j, X)$ and $p(w|r_j, Y)$ computed using different sources of evidence X (e.g. detectors) and Y (e.g. appearance), we can combine them into $p(w|r_j, X, Y)$ by simple multiplication or by averaging [15]. When all information is incorporated into an output posterior distribution $p(w|r_j$, All constraints), we simply label r_j with the word w_k maximizing this distribution. In Section 4, we will discuss a strategy to integrate the calibrated output of a set D of detectors $p(w_k|r_j, D)$ with a posterior distribution $p(w_k|r_j)$, which can be computed using any other source of evidence. In order to test this approach, we will first use a state-of-the-art algorithm [3] that uses exclusion reasoning and image appearance to compute a first estimate of $p(w_k|r_j)$ $\forall j$, which we call $p(w_k|r_j, \mathit{baseline})$. This in fact the baseline we want to augment with $p(w_k|r_j, D)$, producing $p(w_k|r_j, \mathit{baseline}, D)$.

The baseline labeling algorithm. In this section, we summarize the labeling approach by Barnard and Fan [3], that we will extend with object detectors. Given the problem formulated above, this algorithm estimates the unknown posterior distributions $p(w|r_j)$ using four main constraints: 1) similar regions from different images are likely to be labeled with the same word, if they come from images sharing at least one keyword; 2) the label for a region should be chosen among the keywords associated with the image containing it; 3) each image label should have at least one region associated with it (exclusion reasoning); and 4) $\forall i$, $p(w|r_i)$ is a distribution over V, implying $\sum_{(w_v \in V)} p(w_v|r_i) = 1$; and $0 \leq p(w_v|r_i) \leq 1 \forall v, i$. See Barnard and Fan[3] for more detail. In what follows we will refer to the output of this algorithm as $p(w|r_j, \mathit{baseline})$. We now describe how we calibrate object detectors output so that it can be integrated with this distribution.

3. CALIBRATING DETECTOR OUTPUT

Existing object detectors typically attach detection scores to specific portions of images, such as bounding boxes or super-pixels (Figure 2, top row). Classification is then done by comparing the score for an image region against a threshold. We need to convert such scores into probabilities before they can be used in our probabilistic framework. Specifically, we need

$$p(w_k|r_j, d_k) \ , \quad (2)$$

which is the probability of assigning word w_k to image region r_j given the information provided by detector d_k (trained to recognize word w_k) for that particular region.

We develop a calibration procedure to map detection scores to probabilities based on training images where objects of interest have been manually identified. This is very different than simply scaling the score to the interval [0,1], and allows further reasoning when combined with probabilities coming from different sources, which the raw score alone would not.

We define s_{kj} to be the score assigned to r_j by a detector d_k. Our goal is to estimate $p(w_k|r_j, d_k) = p(w_k|s_{kj})$. Intuitively, we approximate these probabilities with the number of correct identifications at the given score (ie, the number of correct identifications at score s), divided by the number of times the detector output score s, at a suitable discretization. First, we define

$$K_m = \{r_1, ..., r_{|K_m|}\}, K_s = \{r_1, ..., r_{|K_s|}\} \ . \quad (3)$$

The former is the set of image regions in the training data that were manually labeled with word w_k, while the latter is the set of image regions in the training data for which the detector d_k output score s. We estimate $p(w_k|s)$ as the number of pixels for which d_k output score s AND that were also manually labeled with w_k, divided by the total number of pixels for which d_k output score s

$$p(w_k|s) = \frac{\sum_{r_i \in K_m, r_j \in K_s} size(r_i \cap r_j)}{\sum_{r_j \in K_s} size(r_j)} \ . \quad (4)$$

Here, the operator $size()$ measures the size of a region in terms of pixels, and $r_i \cap r_j$ is the overlap between r_i and r_j. The score is discretized using soft binning.

Given a score s_{kj} for a superpixel or bounding box r_j computed by detector d_k, we are now able to compute

$$p(w_k|r_j, d_k) = p(w_k|s_{kj}) \quad (5)$$

using the distribution calibrated with the procedure just described. However, we are usually interested in computing $p(w_k|r_i)$ for a region r_i produced by a segmentation algorithm (Figure 2, middle left), which does not directly correspond to detector output. Typically, given an image I, a detector d_k provides a set of possibly overlapping regions $K_I = (r_1, .., r_N)$ with corresponding scores $SK_I = (s_1, ..., s_N)$. We convert these scores into probabilities $PK_I = (p_1, ..., p_N)$. Last, the probability $p(w_k|r_i, d_k)$ for any region r_i in I can be computed either as the mean probability over the region

$$p(w_k|r_i, d_k) = \frac{\sum_{r_u \in K_I} (p_u * size(r_u \cap r_i))}{size(r_i)} \ , \quad (6)$$

or as the max

$$p(w_k|r_i, d_k) = \max_{(r_u \in K_I : size(r_u \cap r_i) > 0)} (p_u) \ . \quad (7)$$

Calibration at multiple scales. Several object detectors achieve scale invariance by providing scores at multiple scales. The procedure discussed in the previous section can be extended to calibrate $p_\sigma(w_k|s^\sigma)$ at a particular scale σ, provided that the size of the manual regions in K_I^σ used for calibration roughly match σ (s^σ is the score at scale σ). Given a detector d_k operating at multiple scales $\Sigma = (\sigma_1, ..., \sigma_{N_\sigma})$, we estimate $p_\sigma(w_k|s^\sigma) \forall \sigma \in \Sigma$. Then, we modify Equation 6 and 7 to

$$p(w_k|r_j, d_k) = \max_{\sigma \in \Sigma} \frac{\sum_{r_u^\sigma \in K_I^\sigma} (p_u^\sigma * size(r_u^\sigma \cap r_j))}{size(r_j)} \quad , \quad (8)$$

and

$$p(w_k|r_j, d_k) = \max_{\sigma \in \Sigma} \max_{(r_u^\sigma \in K_I^\sigma : size(r_u^\sigma \cap r_j) > 0)} (p_u^\sigma) \quad . \quad (9)$$

We use the max in both cases, since detectors perform classification by comparing the maximum over scale space against a threshold.

4. INTEGRATING OBJECT DETECTORS

In this section we propose a strategy for combining the posterior distribution $p(w|r_j, baseline)$ with the contributions of specific detectors, which we can now convert into probabilities. Combining $p(w|r_j, baseline)$ over the whole vocabulary, and probability $p(w_k|r_j, d_k)$ computed using detector d_k is not straightforward. While the former is a probability distribution over the vocabulary, and thus sums to one, $p(w_k|r_j, d_k)$ can be interpreted as the output of a binary classifier for word w_k, and does not allow to make any

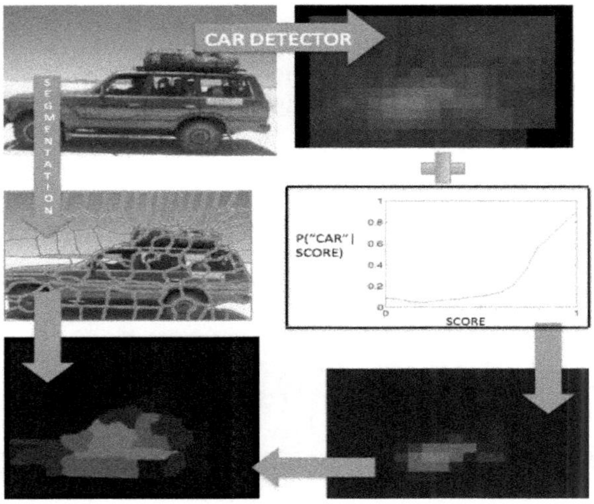

Figure 2: Mapping score into probabilities. Here, a car detector provided a score map (top right) for the original image, visualized by setting the red channel of each cell proportionally to the score (min score r = 0, max score r = 255). Using our calibration procedure, we found a mapping $p(\text{"}car\text{"}|score)$ (middle right), that we use to convert the score map into a probability map (bottom right), visualized by setting the red channel proportionally to the probability value (p("car"|s)=0 implies r = 0, p("car"|s)=1 implies r = 255). This is then used to compute probabilities for the image regions of interest (bottom left), for example the output of a segmentation algorithm (middle left).

Figure 3: Benefits of incorporating a car detector in the labeling process, see text for details

assumptions on the value $p(w_n|r_j, d_k)$ when $n \neq k$. However, we can assume that $(1 - p(w_k|r_{ij}, d_k))$ is the probability that the region is to be labeled with a word that is not w_k given the evidence provided by detector d_k. This suggests that we could weight $p(w_n|r_j, baseline)$ with $p(w_k|r_j, d_k)$ when $n = k$, and with $(1 - p(w_k|r_{ij}, d_k))$ otherwise

$$p(w_n|r_j, d_k, baseline) \propto p(w_n|r_j, baseline) * \\ p(w_k|r_j, d_k)^{\delta(n,k)} (1 - p(w_k|r_j, d_k))^{1-\delta(n,k)} \quad , \quad (10)$$

where $\delta(n, k) = 1$ if $n = k$, 0 if they are different. An example is shown in Figure 3. Here, we see the labels produces by the baseline algorithm (left), and the labels maximizing Equation 10 (right) after adding a car detector (middle).

Suppose now we have a set $D = d_1, ... \; d_{|D|}$ instead of a single one. We modify Equation 10 as

$$p(w_n|r_j, D, baseline) \propto p(w_n|r_j, baseline) * \\ \prod_{d_k \in D} (p(w_k|r_j, d_k)^{\delta(n,k)} (1 - p(w_k|r_j, d_k))^{1-\delta(n,k)}) \quad . \quad (11)$$

Importantly, this formulation is generic enough to augment any approach capable of computing a posterior distribution $p(w|r)$ over the vocabulary.

As described, we use a specific detector d_k on a region j only if w_k is in the label for the image containing r_j. However, we extend this by including words that are related to the detector that are likely to be visually similar. Specifically, we use a detector for a given word if any of its synonyms and hyponyms are in the image label set. For example, we use the detector for word w_k (eg, "car") on both its synonyms ("automobile") and its hyponyms ("Station Waggon", "Compact"). We use the WordNet semantic hierarchy [9] to get the hyponyms and synonyms.

5. RESULTS AND CONCLUSIONS

All our tests were performed on the SAIAPR TC-12 Benchmark [8], consisting of 20000 images, each annotated with 2 to 10 keywords. Ground truth manual segmentations and annotations are available for each image. We use a comprehensive evaluation strategy [4] for comparing the labels produced by our algorithm against ground truth annotations at the region level. In this scope, we used two different measures: 1) the frequency of correct labels predicted by an algorithm ("frequency"), and 2) the number of words an algorithm can reliably identify ("range") [4].

We tested our full approach on seven state-of-the-art detectors [10], listed in Table 2, for which we had enough images for both calibration and testing. First, each detector was calibrated on 80 positive and 40 negative images. We then tested on seven splits of 200 images where each image was labeled with at least one of the seven words we have a detector for. Each image was segmented using NCuts [14].

Table 1: Region word alignment performance

Algorithm	Range	Frequency
Empirical distribution	0.14	2.75
Baseline	1.08	4.60
Detectors (avg)	1.24	5.59
Detectors (max)	1.28	6.04
Theoretical maximum	4.41	19.96

Table 2: Results where each detector is relevant

Object	Range	Freq	Object	Range	Freq
Bicycle	+58.8%	+36.3%	**Car**	+22.4%	+46.3%
Bird	+3.0%	+0.1%	**Chair**	+17.8%	+39.5%
Boat	+8.4%	+33.7%	**Person**	+18.9%	+19.9%
Bottle	+10.2%	+44.9%			

The results in Table 1 show that adding detectors improves performance of the baseline, both in terms of range and frequency. We tested two different ways of computing $p(w_k|r_j, d_k)$ (Equation 8 and 9), and we found slightly better results when using the maximum over a region. A few qualitative results are shown in Figure 4.

Table 2 shows results restricted to images where a given detector was used, for each detector, using Equation 9 to combine results. Here we tabulate the improvement over the baseline, which is generally substantive. This validates that when we have an appropriate detector, using it generally improves alignment.

Conclusions. We developed a general approach to integrate object specific detectors with region labeling based on weak models for appearance. We advocate two contributions: 1) A generic formulation for converting the output of detectors into probabilities; 2) a way to integrate these probabilities, coming from binary classifiers for specific words, with posterior distributions over the whole vocabulary.

We plan to extend our strategy to incorporate additional sources of information. One example is where labels have associated adjectives such "red" or "white", which can provide prior probabilities on the label, and could be exploited similarly to the way we use detectors. A second source of information that we would like to exploit is prior knowledge from spatial context.

6. ADDITIONAL AUTHORS

Ping Wang, Atul Kanaujia, Niels Haering, ObjectVideo, {pwang, akanaujia, niels}@objectvideo.com

7. REFERENCES

[1] L. H. Armitage and P. G. B. Enser. Analysis of user need in image archives. *Journal of Information Science*, 23(4):287–299, 1997.

[2] K. Barnard, P. Duygulu, N. d. Freitas, D. Forsyth, D. Blei, and M. I. Jordan. Matching words and pictures. *Journal of Machine Learning Research*, 3:1107–1135, 2003.

[3] K. Barnard and Q. Fan. Reducing correspondence ambiguity in loosely labeled training data. In *IEEE CVPR*, 2007.

[4] K. Barnard, Q. Fan, R. Swaminathan, A. Hoogs, R. Collins, P. Rondot, and J. Kaufhold. Evaluation of localized semantics: data, methodology, and experiments. *IJCV*, 77:199–217, 2008.

[5] K. Barnard and D. Forsyth. Learning the semantics of words and pictures. In *International Conference on Computer Vision*, pages II:408–415, 2001.

[6] P. Carbonetto, N. d. Freitas, and K. Barnard. A statistical model for general contextual object recognition. In *ECCV*, volume I, pages 350–362, 2004.

[7] T. Deselaers, B. Alexe, , and V. Ferrari. Localizing objects while learning their appearance. In *ECCV*, volume 6314 of *LNCS*, pages 452–466. Springer, 2010.

[8] H. J. Escalante, C. A. Hernandez, J. A. Gonzalez, A. Lopez-Lopez, M. Montes, E. F. Morales, L. E. Sucar, L. Villasenor, and M. Grubinger. The segmented and annotated iapr tc-12 benchmark. *Computer Vision and Image Understanding*, 114(4, Special issue on Image and Video Retrieval Evaluation):419–428, 2010.

[9] C. Fellbaum, P. G. A. Miller, R. Tengi, and P. Wakefield. Wordnet - a lexical database for english.

[10] P. Felzenszwalb, R. Girshick, D. McAllester, and D. Ramanan. Object detection with discriminatively trained part-based models. *IEEE PAMI*, 2009.

[11] A. Gupta and L. S. Davis. Beyond nouns: Exploiting prepositions and comparative adjectives for learning visual classifiers. In *In ECCV*, 2008.

[12] Y. Jin, L. Khan, L. Wang, and M. Awad. Image annotations by combining multiple evidence & wordnet. In *ACM MM '05*, New York, NY, USA, 2005.

[13] V. Lavrenko, R. Manmatha, and J. Jeon. A model for learning the semantics of pictures. In *NIPS*, 2003.

[14] J. Shi and J. Malik. Normalized cuts and image segmentation. *IEEE Transactions on Pattern Analysis and Machine Intelligence*, 22(9):888–905, 2000.

[15] D. M. Tax, M. V. Breukelen, R. P. Duin, and J. Kittler. Combining multiple classifiers by averaging or by multiplying?, 2000.

[16] J. Verbeek, M. Guillaumin, T. Mensink, and C. Schmid. Image annotation with tagprop on the mirflickr set. In *MIR '10*, pages 537–546, New York, NY, USA, 2010. ACM.

[17] H. Zhang, A. C. Berg, M. Maire, and J. Malik. Svm-knn: Discriminative nearest neighbor classification for visual category recognition. In *In CVPR*, pages 2126–2136, 2006.

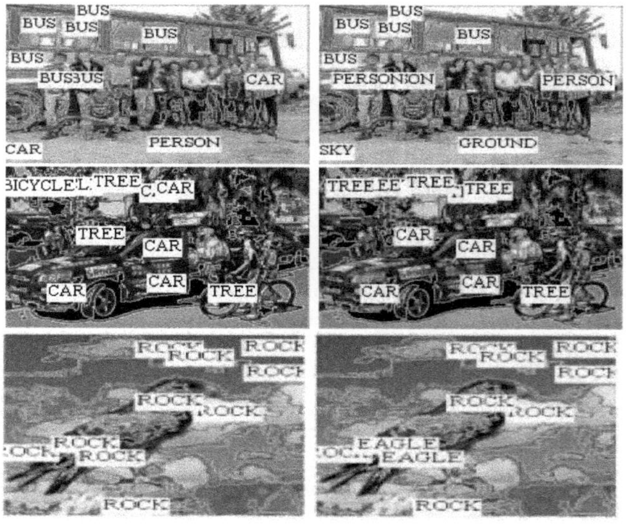

Figure 4: Adding detectors (right) improves the baseline algorithm (left). For better visibility, we only show the labels for the 10 largest regions

Bottom-up Saliency based on Weighted Sparse Coding Residual *

Biao Han
Digital Media Laboratory,
Shanghai University
Shanghai China
raintwoto@gmail.com

Hao Zhu
State Key Laboratory of
Cognitive Neuroscience and
Learning, Beijing Normal
University
Beijing China
zhuhao_hit@hotmail.com

Youdong Ding
Digital Media Laboratory,
Shanghai University
Shanghai China
ydding@shu.edu.cn

ABSTRACT

The guidance of attention helps the human vision system (HVS) to detect and recognize objects rapidly. In this paper, we propose a bottom-up saliency algorithm based on sparse coding theory. Sparse coding decomposes the inputs into two parts, codes and residual. From the viewpoint of biological vision and information theory, the coding length is closely related to the local complexity while the residual is closely related to the uncertainty. The proposed algorithm defines the weighted residual using sparse coding length as saliency. By multiplying the L0 norm of sparse codes and the residual, a saliency map is obtained. The performance of the proposed method is evaluated using ROC curves with two different scale datasets and is compared with state-of-the-art models. Our algorithm outperforms all other methods and the results indicate a robust and accurate saliency.

Categories and Subject Descriptors

I.2.10 [**ARTIFICIAL INTELLIGENCE**]: Vision and Scene Understanding Perceptual reasoning

General Terms

Algorithms, Experimentation

Keywords

Visual attention, Bottom-up saliency, Sparse coding

1. INTRODUCTION

What we see is determined by what we pay attention to. Humans are able to select the most relevant information from a large amount of visual data. Visual attention is used to reduce the redundancy and keep few but relevant information. Visual attention is widely studied by many researchers in the areas of psychology, neuroscience and computer vision. Koch and Ullman[8] proposed the original concept of visual saliency to represent visual attention. By calculating this visual saliency map, visual attention helps to solve computer vision problems such as thumbnail generation [11], video retargeting[16] and object recognition[13].

Bottom-up attention is a mechanism only driven by stimulus. Most of existing literature of bottom-up saliency are influenced by the idea of Feature Integration Theory (FIT)[15], such as [6], [5], [4]. These methods could lead to a good result, however, the relationship between FIT and the real neural mechanism is not clear. Other theories are also used to solve the problem of visual saliency, such as information theory[1], spectral theory[5], graph theory[4], and machine learning[7].

In this paper, we propose an algorithm based on sparse coding theory. As [12], sparse coding theory could explain what happened in the simple cells of primary visual cortex (V1). Sparse coding decomposes the inputs into two parts, codes and residual. From the viewpoint of information theory, sparse coding could reflect the flow of information. Sparse codes are the minimum entropy codes[12] which means that these codes contain the information of image parts with minimum entropy. So the residual are opposite, containing the information of the parts with maximum entropy . The higher the residual value is, the larger entropy is. The sparse coding length could be seen as the complexity when using specific sparse coding dictionary[9].

As shown in figure 1, we define the weighted sparse coding residual as saliency. The algorithm consists of following steps:

(1) Image inputs are divided into overlapping patches with the same size. For each patch, as [9], the sparse coding dictionary is calculated using the surrounding patches.

(2) Every patch is sparsely coded with its own dictionary. The patch is decomposed into two parts, the codes part and the residual part.

(3) By computing the l_0 norm of the sparse matrix, the weight is obtained. We get our saliency map by multiplying the weight and the residual. The higher the saliency value is, the more salient the area is.

The major contribution of this paper is proposing an efficient and effective algorithm based on weighted sparse coding residual. We define the multiply production of sparse coding length and residual as saliency, and get a good saliency map. This paper applies sparse coding theory to saliency

*Area chair: Alexander Hauptmann

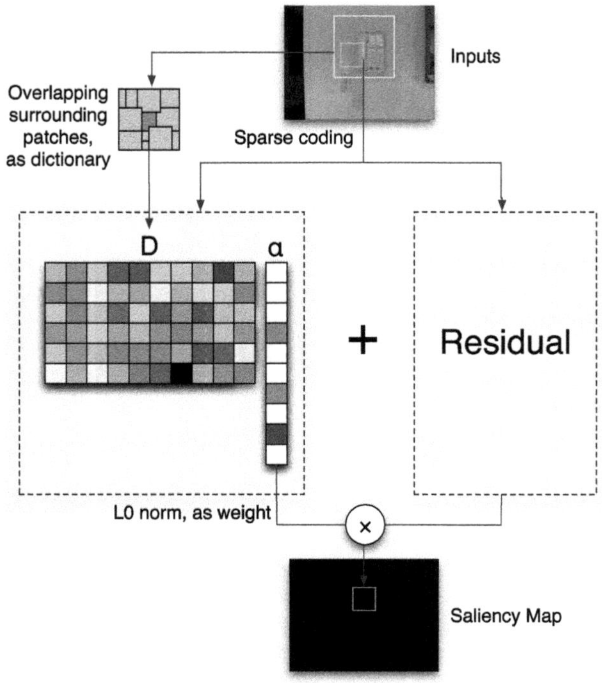

Figure 1: The framework of our method.

and tries to explain the internal relationship between sparse coding theory and visual saliency. Being compared with four state-of-the-art methods, our method outperforms all others and the results show the accuracy and robustness of our algorithm.

2. METHOD

Sparse coding theory helps to understand the response properties of simple cells in primate visual cortex and is an effective way to reduce the redundancy of input image. The basic assumption of this theory is that an image, X, can be represented by a linear superposition of bases in a dictionary, D. The sparse coding decomposes the image into two parts, the sparse codes and the residual. We calculated the saliency map by the weighted residual of sparse coding using the coding length of sparse codes. In following subsections, we will demonstrate our method.

2.1 Sparse Coding to Saliency Map

The first step of sparse coding is dividing image into patches, $X = \{x_1, x_2, \dots x_n\}$, n is the number of patches. Each patch of the input image could be represented as following:

$$x_i = D\alpha_i + r_i \tag{1}$$

$A = \{\alpha_1, \dots \alpha_i, \dots \alpha_n\}$ is the sparse codes for the image and $R = \{r_1, \dots r_i, \dots r_n\}$ is the residual of sparse coding. D is the dictionary. The goal of sparse coding is to find the optimal balance between information loss and sparseness. It could be seen as minimizing the following cost function:

$$E = -I(X; A) + \lambda \cdot [\text{sparseness of } A] \tag{2}$$

λ is the parameter of balancing between the sparsity and distortion. The problem of minimizing information loss could be solved by maximizing mutual information $I(X; A)$, where,

$$I(X; A) = H(X) - H(X|A) \tag{3}$$

Assuming that the residual R is independent of the image X, the information relationship among X, A and R could be described as following,

$$\begin{aligned} P(X|A) &= P(X|DA) \\ &= P(DA - X) \end{aligned} \tag{4}$$

while,

$$X = DA + R \tag{5}$$

hence,

$$\begin{aligned} H(X|A) &= H(DA - X) \\ &= H(R) = H(X) - I(X; A) \end{aligned} \tag{6}$$

Therefore, the $H(R)$ implies the uncertainty when knowing A to predict X. The higher the $H(R)$ is, the more uncertainty of the patch is.

By concluding the formulas above, we can see that there is a close connection between residual R and $I(X; A)$, the minimizing residual is closely related to maximizing $I(X; A)$[17]. In our algorithm, the residual is seen as an important component of saliency.

The other important component is the sparseness of the sparse codes. Sparseness could be measured by l_0 norm of the sparse codes. For each patch, the sparseness part of equation 2 could be reformulated as following,

$$[\text{sparseness of } A] = \|\alpha_i\|_0 \tag{7}$$

The l_0 norm in this equation means the number of the non-zero elements, in other words, the coding length. In our method, the dictionary is obtained by using overlapping surrounding patches. According to [9], the sparse coding length represents the similarity and novelty between patch and its surroundings. That is to say, the coding length represents local complexity. In our algorithm, the coding length is seen as the weight.

To sum up above arguments, the saliency of our method is the result of multiplying the l_0 norm of sparse codes and the residual of sparse coding, in other words, the product of local complexity and uncertainty. In our method, the l_1 norm of residual is used. The method could be represented by following function:

$$[\text{Saliency of } x_i] = \|\alpha_i\|_0 \cdot \|x_i - D\alpha_i\|^{L1} \tag{8}$$

2.2 Solution via l_1 Norm

To solve the sparse coding problem above, we use the method of l_1 norm minimization. The cost function of sparse coding (equation 2) could be reformulated as the problem of l_0 norm optimization:

$$\min \lambda\|\alpha_i\|_0 + \|x_i - D\alpha_i\|_2^2 \tag{9}$$

However, this optimization problem is also hard to solve. Related study[2] suggests that for most systems, the problem of sparest near-solution could be represented by the minimal l_1 norm near-solution. The l_0 norm optimization problem of equation 9 could be solved by minimizing the l_1 norm:

$$\min \lambda\|\alpha_i\|_1 + \|x_i - D\alpha_i\|_2^2 \tag{10}$$

This problem is a famous linear regression problem known as Lasso[14]. By using LARS algorithm[3], the l_1 norm minimizing problem could be solved. Therefore, the residual and the coding length could be obtained. By multiplying the residual and the coding length, the saliency value of each patch is obtained. After accumulation and normalization, we get the saliency map of our algorithm. The entire method is summarized as Algorithm 1.

Algorithm 1 Bottom-up Saliency based on Weighted Sparse Coding Residual

---

Input: Given image X
Output: The saliency map of X.

1: **for** each patch x_i of the image X **do**
2: Take patches from its surroundings to form dictionary D
3: Solve the Lasso problem

$$\min \lambda \|\alpha_i\|_1 + \|x_i - D\alpha_i\|_2^2$$

and get α_i
4: Calculate the local complexity $\|\alpha_i\|_0$ as weight and the l_1 norm of sparse coding residual $\|x_i - D\alpha_i\|^{L1}$
5: Calculate the patch saliency by

$$[\text{Saliency of } x_i] = \|\alpha_i\|_0 \cdot \|x_i - D\alpha_i\|^{L1}$$

6: **end for**
7: Get the saliency map by accumulating and normalizing the saliency by pixels.

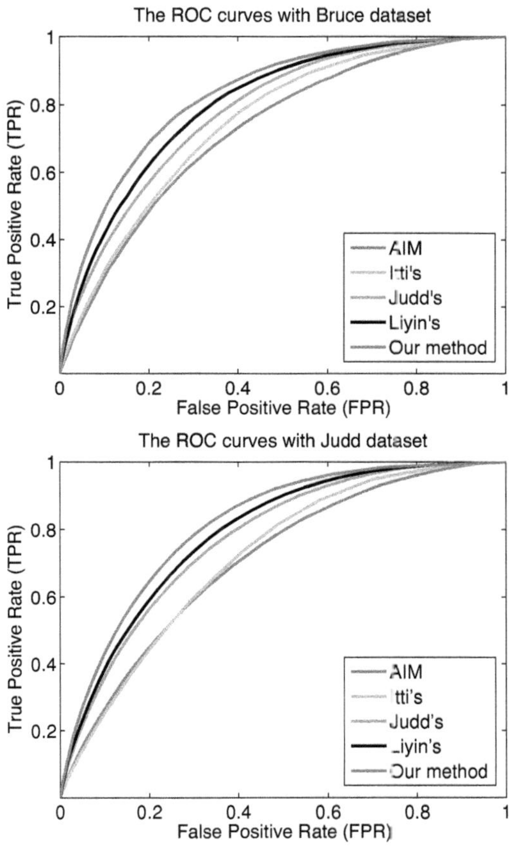

Figure 2: The ROC curves of four state-of-the-art methods and our method. The top one is with Bruce dataset and the bottom one is with Judd dataset.

3. EXPERIMENTS

In this section, we present the results of our method on extensive experiments with two public eye-tracking datasets. The datasets used in this paper is provided by Bruce[1] and Judd[7]. The Bruce dataset is a small-scale and popularly used dataset with 120 images, and the Judd dataset is a larger dataset with 1003 images. To evaluate the performance, we compared our algorithm with four state-of-the-art methods: AIM[1], Itti's[6], Judd's[7] and Liyin's[9]. Receiver Operating Characteristic (ROC) curve is used as evaluation criterion. By the quantitative analysis with ROC curves and Area Under the Curve (AUC) , proposed method shows good performance in different datasets.

3.1 Experimental Setup

The input images are down-sampled to 0.1 of original size for Bruce dataset and 0.08 for Judd dataset. Then, the input images are divided into patches of 8×8 pixels with an overlapping of 4 pixels in each direction. The dictionary of each patch is obtained by using the surrounding patches. Because we use surrounding patches for dictionary, there would be a boundary effect. Therefore, we also multiply the length of dictionary to reduce the impact. To realize the LARS algorithm, we use the fast implementation in SPAMS toolbox[10].

We realize Itti's method by using the reimplementation by Harel[4], which is a bit faster and more accurate in fixation prediction. For other methods, we use the default settings of their own implementation.

To evaluate the performance, we plot the ROC curves by computing the mean value of the output from toolbox provided by Harel[4]. The AUCs of each method is also computed.

3.2 Experimental Results

The results are evaluated by using quantitative and qualitative methods. On quantitative evaluation, we plot the ROC curves of different methods, by comparing the ROC curves and the AUCs, then the performance of each method is evaluated. On qualitative evaluation, we show some of the experiment results and compare them with saliency maps of other methods and the density maps of human fixation.

As shown in figure 2, we compare the ROC curves of our method with other methods. By observing the curves of the top one, we can see that our method shows competitive performance with Bruce dataset. To test the robustness of our method, we also evaluate the performance on Judd dataset, which is one of the largest public datasets. The results of our method with Judd dataset also outperform all others and the small decrease indicates the robustness of our algorithm. To know the results more directly, the AUCs for each method with two datasets are shown in table 1.

Our method is fast because we only use one scale of the input image (0.1 for Bruce dataset, 0.08 for Judd dataset) to calculate the saliency. For each image in the dataset, our method only spends about 1.5 seconds for each image in the two datasets on a Core 2 Duo 2.4GHz MAC.

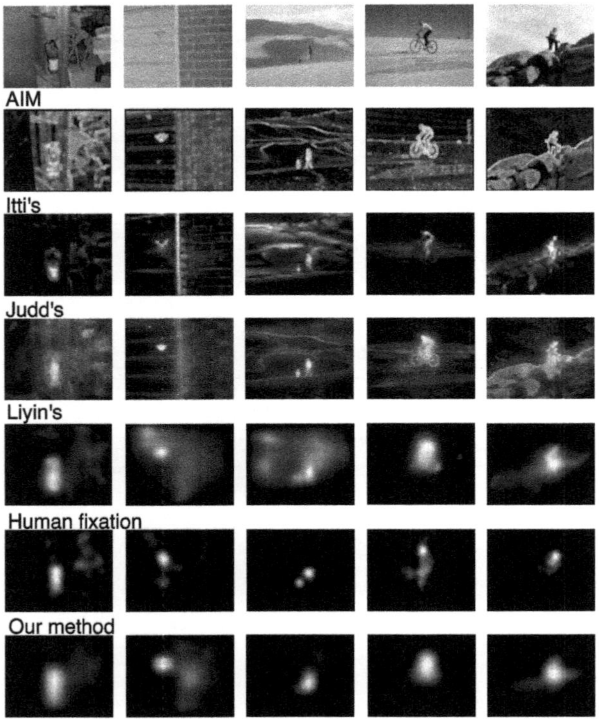

Figure 3: Some experiment results. The rows from top to down are: the original stimulus images, saliency maps generated by AIM[1], Itti's[6], Judd's[7] and Liyin's[9] methods, human fixation density maps and our saliency maps.

	Bruce Dataset	Judd Dataset
AIM[1]	0.7241	0.7076
Itti's[6]	0.7455	0.7169
Judd's[7]	0.7795	0.7732
Liyin's[9]	0.8006	0.7893
Our Method	**0.8264**	**0.8141**

Table 1: The AUCs comparison of all methods with different datasets.

We show some saliency map results in figure 3. By comparing with the results of AIM[1], Itti's[6], Judd's[7] and Liyin's[9] methods and human fixation, the saliency maps of our method could represent salient area accurately and show good ability in application.

4. CONCLUSION

In this paper, we propose a bottom-up saliency algorithm based on weighted sparse coding residual. The key of our method is sparse coding theory which is also regarded as a good way to understand vision. In the experiments, our method has the best performance and largest AUCs in comparison with four state-of-the-art methods. Our method is able to provide accurate and robust saliency maps for other applications. For future work, we will expand our method to temporal domain and apply our method to other computer vision problems.

5. REFERENCES

[1] N. Bruce and J. Tsotsos. Saliency based on information maximization. *Advances in Neural Information Processing Systems*, 2006.

[2] D. Donoho. For most large underdetermined systems of equations, the minimal l1-norm near-solution approximates the sparsest near-solution. *Communications on Pure and Applied Mathematics*, Jan 2006.

[3] B. Efron, T. Hastie, I. Johnstone, and R. Tibshirani. Least angle regression. *The Annals of Statistics*, Jan 2004.

[4] J. Harel, C. Koch, and P. Perona. Graph-based visual saliency. *Advances in Neural Information Processing Systems*, Jan 2007.

[5] X. Hou and L. Zhang. Saliency detection: A spectral residual approach. *IEEE Conference on Computer Vision and Pattern Recognition. CVPR*, 2007.

[6] L. Itti, C. Koch, and E. Niebur. A model of saliency-based visual attention for rapid scene analysis. *IEEE TPAMI*, Jan 1998.

[7] T. Judd, K. Ehinger, F. Durand, and A. Torralba. Learning to predict where humans look. *IEEE 12th International Conference on Computer Vision, ICCV*, 2009.

[8] C. Koch and S. Ullman. Shifts in selective visual attention: towards the underlying neural circuitry. *Hum Neurobiol*, 4(4):219–27, 1985.

[9] Y. Li, Y. Zhou, L. Xu, X. Yang, and J. Yang. Incremental sparse saliency detection. *The International Conference on Image Processing, ICIP*, Jan 2009.

[10] J. Mairal, F. Bach, J. Ponce, and G. Sapiro. Online learning for matrix factorization and sparse coding. *Journal of Machine Learning*, (11):19–60, Jan 2010.

[11] L. Marchesotti, C. Cifarelli, and G. Csurka. A framework for visual saliency detection with applications to image thumbnailing. *IEEE 12th International Conference on Computer Vision, ICCV*, 2009.

[12] B. Olshausen. Emergence of simple-cell receptive field properties by learning a sparse code for natural images. *Nature*, 381(6583):607–609, 1996.

[13] U. Rutishauser, D. Walther, C. Koch, and P. Perona. Is bottom-up attention useful for object recognition? *IEEE Computer Society Conference on Computer Vision and Pattern Recognition, CVPR*, 2004.

[14] R. Tibshirani. Regression shrinkage and selection via the lasso. *Journal of the Royal Statistical Society.*, Jan 1996.

[15] A. Treisman and G. Gelade. A feature-integration theory of attention. *Cognitive Psychology*, Jan 1980.

[16] L. Wolf, M. Guttmann, and D. Cohen-Or. Non-homogeneous content-driven video-retargeting. *IEEE 11th International Conference on Computer Vision. ICCV*, 2007.

[17] L. Zhaoping. Theoretical understanding of the early visual processes by data compression and data selection. *Network: Computation in neural systems*, 17(4):301–334, 2006.

Purposive Hidden-Object-Game: Embedding Human Computation in Popular Game

Yuzhao Ni, Jian Dong, Jiashi Feng, Shuicheng Yan
Dept. of Electrical and Computer Engineering, National University of Singapore, Singapore
{dcsniy, a0068947, a0066331, eleyans}@nus.edu.sg

ABSTRACT

Having su cient training images with known locations of objects is critical for modern image annotation, image retrieval, and object detection tasks. However, it is typically extremely labor-intensive to collect such data, as the process usually involves tedious manual-cropping and hand-labeling. In this work, following the principle of games with a purpose (GWAP), we design a so-called purposive hidden-object-game (P-HOG), which seamlessly embeds object localization into the enjoyable HOG gaming process. As indicated by its large number of online players and downloads, HOG is very popular and P-HOG thus possesses great potentials in aggregating massive informative annotations. For each gaming image, besides identifying the known hidden objects inserted automatically towards semantic and visual naturalness, players also imperceptibly locate the spatial positions of the unknown objects, which are indicated by the re ned user-provided tags from Flickr.com or other photo sharing websites. We conduct a pilot study of the game prototype and the comprehensive experiments show that the P-HOG appeals to general players, and is e ective for collecting massive object locations with satisfying accuracy.

Categories and Subject Descriptors

H.4 [**Information Systems Applications**]: Miscellaneous; D.2.8 [**Software Engineering**]: Metrics—*complexity measures, performance measures*

General Terms

Design

Keywords

Hidden Object Game, Human Computing, GWAP

Area chairs: Alexander Hauptmann, Marco Bertini and Cees Snoek

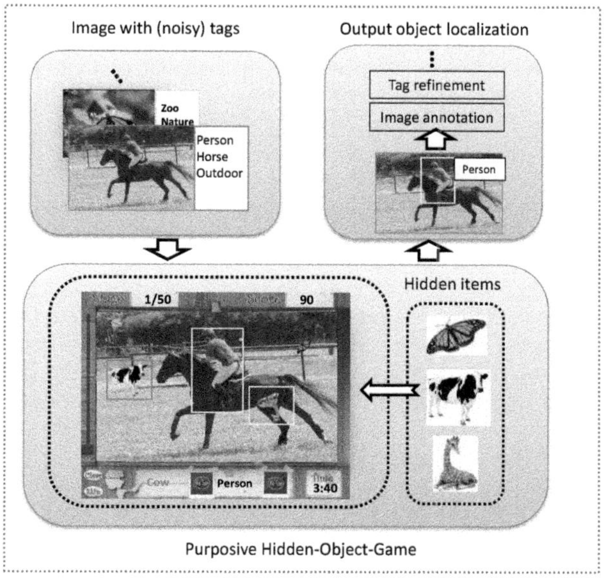

Figure 1: The system overview of the purposive hidden object game (P-HOG). The images from photo sharing websites with re ned user-provided tags are fed into the P-HOG, and the players imperceptibly annotate the positions of some tag objects.

1. INTRODUCTION

Many existing multimedia annotation, retrieval and recommendation algorithms will bene t from a large-scale dataset with accurate annotations. However, constructing such a dataset is generally tedious and labor-intensive, as it involves massive manual-cropping and hand-labeling. Recently the emerging trend of games with a purpose (GWAP) has paved another way for more e cient metadata collection [11] [2] [5]. GWAP is developed from the human computation technique which relies on the collaboration of game players to solve problems. Each player is required to perform a small part of a massive computation, similar to a processor in a distributed system. Unlike computer processors, however, humans require an incentive to participate such collective computation. GWAP aims at implicitly embedding the computational tasks in enjoyable and attractive games and meanwhile guaranteeing correct solutions to the problems. People play the games only for leisure purpose, and as a side e ect of their playing, informative metadata are produced and collected without sacri cing the game playability.

GWAP was pioneered by Luis Ahn *et al.* in their ESP

game [2]. In that work, they designed a game prototype to implicitly collect textual labels for images. In that game, two players are randomly paired and then view the same target image. The players are required to agree on an appropriate tag for the image as quickly as possible. And the tags agreed on simultaneously by them are collected as labels of the image. This e ort has collected over 10 million image labels since 2003, using the images randomly crawled from the web. While the amount of the data is impressive, they only collect textual labels without corresponding object position information.

In this work, we focus on developing the popular existing Hidden Object Game (HOG) towards the purpose of localizing the target objects which are indicated by the image tags, thus called purposive HOG (P-HOG). All the localizations are generated during the users' playing in the P-HOG game. HOG is a type of puzzle game and in this game, the players must nd speci ed hidden items by a tag list within an image. The P-HOG game developed in this work follows the same designing pattern as conventional HOG games. And an overview on it is provided in Figure 1. The gaming images associated with tags can be e ciently collected from photo sharing websites (*e.g.*, Flickr.com). As a single-player game, some evaluation mechanisms must be embedded into the P-HOG system to guarantee the quality of object localizations provided by the players. Inspired by the Captcha [1], some known items are added into P-HOG gaming images to control the quality of the collected metadata and prevent the players from providing misleading localizations. In this work, we present an algorithm to automatically add the known items in a natural manner.

2. AUTO-GENERATE GAMING IMAGES

Gaming images used in conventional HOG games are all generated manually, including the hidden items selection, nding appropriate places and changing their appearances. This process is time consuming and often requires speci c skills. Thus manual generation is not scalable to our speci c purpose which needs hiding known items to images from a large scale dataset. Therefore, in this work, we develop techniques for automatically generating gaming images to shield the arduous tasks.

2.1 Candidate Locations Selection

Shape is a useful cue for candidate location selection. Intuitively, it will be more natural for the object to be added into the region whose shape matches the item's. We rst segment the target image into several segments using the Mean Shift segmentation method [4]. Then an ellipse is used to t the shape of a segment and estimate the shape parameters. Here the geometry of the ellipse is determined based on the spatial distribution of the pixels falling in the speci ed region. By representing each pixel as a two dimensional vector $\mathbf{p}_i = [x_i, y_i]^T$, where x and y denote the horizontal and vertical coordinates respectively. Then a spatial distribution covariance matrix is constructed as follows, $C(i,j) = (\mathbf{p}_i \quad \boldsymbol{\mu})^T(\mathbf{p}_j \quad \boldsymbol{\mu})$, where $\boldsymbol{\mu}$ is the mean vector of all the vectors. According to the principle axis theorem, the axes can be calculated as the eigenvectors of the covariance matrix. Thus the shape can be well described by the two eigenvalues which represent the lengths of the two axes respectively. The shape for the item can also be estimated in the same way. After obtaining the shape descriptors, we calculate the shape di erence between a known item and a candidate patch in the target image. The results of incorporating the shape matching cues into hiding the known items are shown in Figure 2. It can be seen that for the items with relative large aspect ratio, they can be hidden naturally into the patches with similar shape.

2.2 Item Blending

To naturally add the known items to the selected locations of the target image, we employ the smoothed segmentation mask of the item as the alpha map [10] and blend the foreground item and background target image accordingly, namely,

$$I = \quad F + (1 \quad)B, \qquad (1)$$

where F, B, I denote the foreground item, background target image and the nal composite image respectively. The alpha map is the segmentation mask of the item which has been smoothed by a Gaussian lter. Before performing such image matting, several visual processings on the inserted item are applied to produce more natural composition results.

To ensure the color of the added known items is consistent with the local regions in the target image, namely the object and local target region possess the similar color distribution, we modify the color transfer method developed in [8] and impose the same color distribution on the known object as that of the target region. Following the method in [8], we rst convert the images from RGB to LMS color space. Then we enforce the two images to have the same color distribution in the sense of mean and variance statistics, by subtracting the mean value of the target region and scaling the color values based on the ratio of variances.

3. COLLECT IMAGE ANNOTATIONS

The purpose of this work is to seamlessly embed human computation into the enjoyable game playing process. The background program of the P-HOG records all the bounding boxes and automatically align them with the textual labels since the users are following the guidance in the tag list generated by the game. The object localization quality of each user will be accessed based on the accuracies on the known items automatically added by our algorithm. The localization results are less reliable if provided by the users with lower accuracies for the known items. The nal localization for each object comes from the weighted average of all the collected bounding boxes.

Though the game encourages the users to provide boundingbox as close to the object boundary as possible, there still exists a margin between the localization and the object true boundary. We adopt the segmentation method provided in [7] to re ne the bounding boxes considering its superiority in boundary detection. The target images are segmented into several superpixels and the bounding boxes will shrink or expand slightly to t the superpixel boundaries.

4. EVALUATIONS

In this section, we evaluate the e ectiveness of P-HOG in embedding human computing in popular games. The evaluations are two folds. Firstly, we qualitatively evaluate the naturalness of the images automatically generated from our

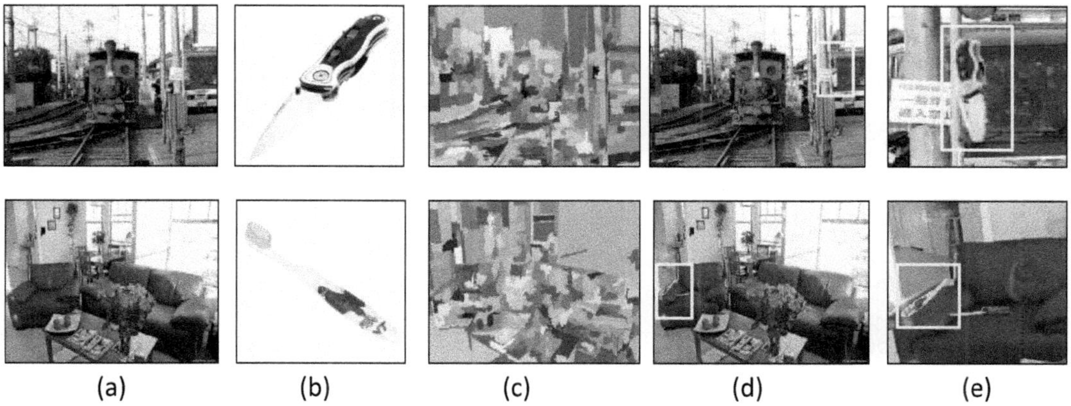

Figure 2: Examples of the composite images. (a) Target images. (b) Items selected from item image set. (c) Segmentation results from Mean Shift. (d) Composite results after item rotation and blending. (e) Closeup of the details. For better view, please refer to the color version.

algorithms by comparing with the images used in the online popular HOG games. Then we quantitatively evaluate the accuracies of the collected bounding boxes of the objects comparing with the groundtruth.

4.1 Datasets

Two widely used benchmark datasets, PASCAL-VOC-2007 and MIRFLICKR-25000 [6], are employed for the user study. The VOC2007 dataset includes 9,964 images and 20 annotated object categories in total. Precise bounding boxes for the objects from these 20 categories are also provided. We randomly sample a subset from the whole dataset which consists of 1,000 images. Each image includes 2 6 object labels. The MIRFLICKR dataset includes 25,000 images with user provided tags. Tags with low frequency are ltered out as in [12] and nally 198 tags are retained. The reason to select such a subset lies on that the contents of the images, which contain less than 3 tags, are usually simple and not suitable for the P-HOG game. Another consideration is too many "non exist" tags will decrease the playability and interestingness of the game.

The known item set we use in this work includes 263 manually collected item images. And the images are roughly partitioned into 3 subsets, sky, ground and others. Our algorithm adds 5 known items to each image from the VOC dataset and 2-4 items are added to the images from the MIRFLICKR dataset, proportional to the number of user-provided tags. 20 and 60 volunteers are invited for the annotation on VOC and MIRFLICKR images respectively. In average each image will be annotated 3 times.

4.2 User Gaming Experience

Playability and interestingness of the P-HOG are crucial for attracting enough players to contribute to the embedded human computing. However, ratings of the game playability and interestingness depend more on subjective factors and there lacks a quantitative criterion. Therefore, 30 volunteers are invited to attend user studies on the interestingness of the game, naturalness of the automatically generated gaming images and how challenging the game is. Each subject is required to play the P-HOG and another two online HOG games [1] at rst and then grades these three games on the

[1]`http://games-free-online.net/?a=game&id=558`
`http://games-free-online.net/?a=game&id=617`

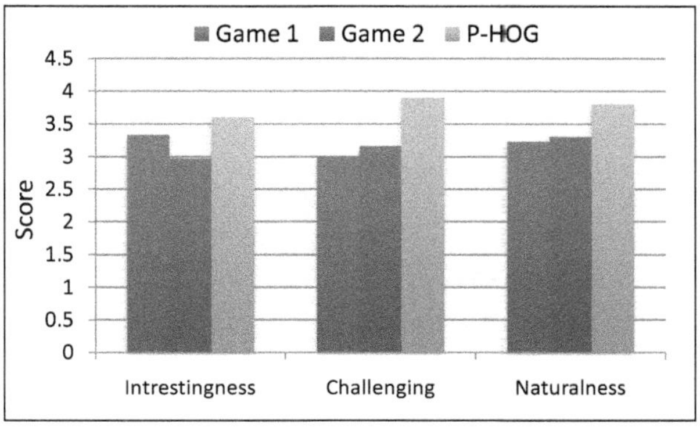

Figure 3: User study statistics on the ratings of the interestingness, challenging and naturalness of P-HOG compared with two other web HOG games.

above three factors. The grades range from 1 to 5, indicating the worst and best performance respectively. And the results are shown in Figure 3. From the gure, it can be seen that most of the subjects prefer to our P-HOG game on the interestingness and challengingness, and on the naturalness of the gaming images, the images automatically generated by our algorithm achieve superior slightly performance over the images from online games, which are manually generated. This veri es the e ectiveness of the developed automatically item inserting algorithm and the comparable attractiveness of P-HOG with common web HOG game and P-HOG is able to collect object localization metadata without sacri cing playability of the game. The P-HOG game is more challenging than the baseline web games due to the small size and appearance changing of some added components. And using computer generated item images to add in the two games decreases their interestingness and naturalness, since players prefer natural and realistic items hidden into the gaming images. We also investigate whether users are more glad to label images using P-HOG or conventional image labeling tools, such as LabelMe [9] and Peekaboom [3]. Results are shown in Figure 4, from which it can be seen P-HOG is more attractive than conventional labeling tools to users.

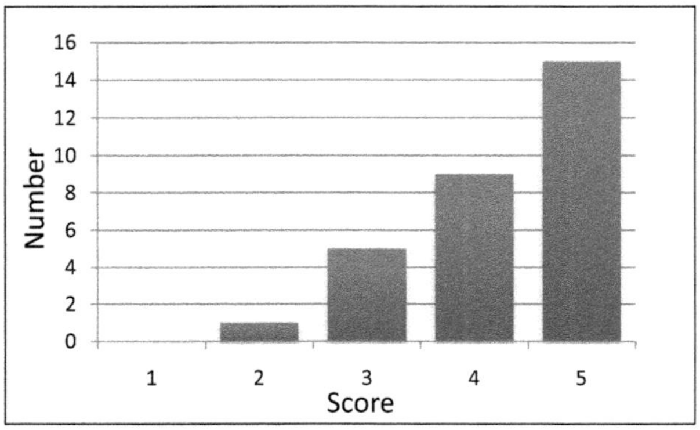

Figure 4: Voting statistics from users on that compared with image labeling tools, whether they are more glad to use P-HOG for image annotation.

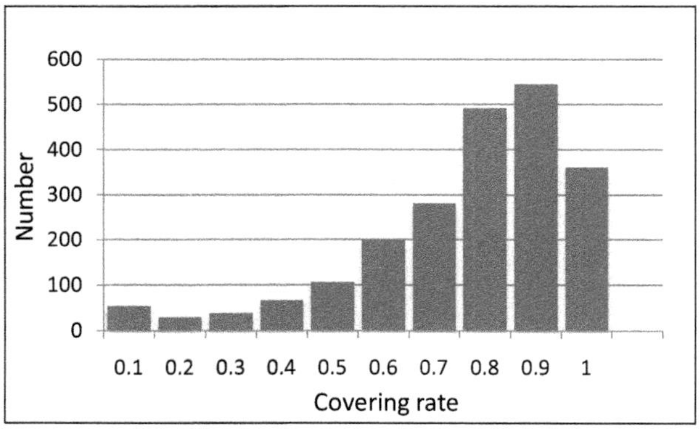

Figure 5: Histogram for the covering rates of the bounding boxes provided by the P-HOG player over the groundtruth bounding boxes.

4.3 Accuracy of Object Localizations

The object localization accuracy via P-HOG is evaluated on VOC2007 dataset. Images in the VOC2007 dataset have been annotated accurate bounding boxes for 20 classes of objects. The bounding boxes obtained from P-HOG players are compared with such groundtruth bounding boxes, measured by their covering rate. In the VOC2007 dataset, we randomly sample 1000 images and each image is labeled 3 times by the P-HOG players. The nal bounding boxes are averaged from all the provided bounding box. The evaluation results are shown in Figure 5. From the results, it can be seen that most of the bounding boxes provided by P-HOG players are comparable in accuracy with the bounding boxes accurately labeled in benchmark dataset, which demonstrates the e ectiveness of P-HOG in collecting accurate object location metadata.

5. CONCLUSIONS

In this work, we proposed a Purposive Hidden Object Game (P-HOG) to seamlessly embed localizing objects into the popular hidden object game. Through the P-HOG, massive object location information can be imperceptively collected during the game playing process, following the principles of human computing. Meanwhile, a built-in data quality controlling mechanism is also presented, which bene ts from an algorithm developed for automatically and naturally inserting known items into the target images. The algorithm takes semantic and visual consistency into considerations simultaneously and thus attractive gaming images can be produced e ciently. Comprehensive user study evaluations have demonstrated the high naturalness of the composition images and playability of the P-HOG.

6. ACKNOWLEDGMENTS

This work is supported by the CSIDM Project No.CSIDM-200803 partially funded by a grant from the National Research Foundation (NRF) administered by the Media Development Authority (MDA) of Singapore.

7. REFERENCES

[1] L. Ahn, M. Blum, and J. Langford. Telling humans and computers apart automatically. *Commun. ACM*, 47(2):56–60, 2004.

[2] L. Ahn and L. Dabbish. Labeling images with a computer game. In *Proceedings of the Conference on Human Factors in Computing Systems*, pages 319–326, 2004.

[3] L. Ahn, R. Liu, and M. Blum. Peekaboom: a game for locating objects in images. In *Proceedings of the Conference on Human Factors in Computing Systems*, pages 55–64, 2006.

[4] D. Comaniciu and P. Meer. Mean shift: A robust approach toward feature space analysis. *IEEE Trans. Pattern Anal. Mach. Intell.*, 24(5):603–619, 2002.

[5] C. Ho, T. Chang, J. Lee, J. Hsu, and K. Chen. Kisskissban: a competitive human computation game for image annotation. *SIGKDD Explorations*, 12(1):21–24, 2010.

[6] M. Huiskes and M. Lew. The mir ickr retrieval evaluation. In *ACM SIGMM International Conference on Multimedia Information Retrieval*, pages 39–43, 2008.

[7] G. Mori, X. Ren, A. Efros, and J. Malik. Recovering human body con gurations: Combining segmentation and recognition. In *IEEE Computer Society Conference on Computer Vision and Pattern Recognition*, pages 326–333, 2004.

[8] E. Reinhard, M. Ashikhmin, B. Gooch, and P. Shirley. Color transfer between images. *IEEE Computer Graphics and Applications*, 21(5):34–41, 2001.

[9] B. Russell, A. Torralba, K. Murphy, and W. Freeman. Labelme: A database and web-based tool for image annotation. *International Journal of Computer Vision*, 77(1-3):157–173, 2008.

[10] J. Wang and M. Cohen. Image and video matting: A survey. *Foundations and Trends in Computer Graphics and Vision*, 3(2):97–175, 2007.

[11] M. Yuen, L. Chen, and I. King. A survey of human computation systems. In *IEEE International Conference on Computational Science and Engineering*, pages 723–728, 2009.

[12] G. Zhu, S. Yan, and Y. Ma. Image tag re nement towards low-rank, content-tag prior and error sparsity. In *ACM Multimedia*, pages 461–470, 2010.

Geo-Localization of Street Views with Aerial Image Databases *

Mayank Bansal Harpreet S. Sawhney Hui Cheng
{mayank.bansal, harpreet.sawhney, hui.cheng}@sri.com
Vision Technologies Center
SRI International Sarnoff
Princeton, NJ 08540

Kostas Daniilidis
kostas@cis.upenn.edu
GRASP Laboratory
University of Pennsylvania
Philadelphia, PA 19104

ABSTRACT

We study the feasibility of solving the challenging problem of geo-localizing *ground level* images in urban areas with respect to a database of images captured from the air such as *satellite* and *oblique aerial images*. We observe that comprehensive aerial image databases are widely available while complete coverage of urban areas from the ground is at best spotty. As a result, localization of ground level imagery with respect to aerial collections is a technically important and practically significant problem. We exploit two key insights: (1) satellite image to oblique aerial image correspondences are used to extract building facades, and (2) building facades are matched between oblique aerial and ground images for geo-localization. Key contributions include: (1) A novel method for extracting building facades using building outlines; (2) Correspondence of building facades between oblique aerial and ground images without direct matching; and (3) Position and orientation estimation of ground images. We show results of ground image localization in a dense urban area.

Categories and Subject Descriptors

I.5.2 [**Pattern Recognition**]: Design Methodology—*Feature evaluation and selection*; I.4.9 [**Image Processing and Computer Vision**]: Applications; I.5.4 [**Pattern Recognition**]: Applications—*Computer vision, signal processing*

General Terms

Algorithms, Theory

1. INTRODUCTION

Given a ground level street view (SV) image in an urban area, we want to determine the geo-location of the camera in the absence of any metadata (GPS or camera parameters). We explore a novel approach: use commonly available satellite and oblique aerial image databases (e.g. Microsoft Bing [bing.com/maps], Google Maps [maps.google.com]) to match the SV image and in turn geo-locate the SV image. This problem is technically challenging and has not been addressed before, and practically satellite and aerial databases provide comprehensive coverage of large areas whereas SV databases are spotty at best.

Given an area-of-interest (AOI) such as a city, we create a feature database using both satellite (SAT) and oblique bird's eye-view (BEV) imagery covering the area. SAT provides orthographic top-down views of the scene while BEV provides oblique viewpoints. By combining the two, building outlines as well as building facades are extracted. SAT images provide the outlines while one or more of the BEV images are used to locate the corresponding buildings and extract facades. Appearance matching between images with widely different viewpoints (e.g. SV and SAT) is a challenging problem. Prior work using SIFT, MSER etc. has a low success rate, and is not robust to partial occlusions and appearance differences. Also matchable features must be discriminative enough for retrieval from a large database of indexable features along with the geo-coding (latitude-longitude) information in the BEV imagery. We approach the matching problem from a joint statistical and appearance viewpoint. We compute features that capture the statistical self-similarity (or dis-similarity) of local patches on a building facade with respect to other patches on the facade. Since these features essentially capture the local appearance statistics, they are robust to viewpoint and global appearance changes and can be computed in a similar manner for the SV image as well and then robustly matched with the features stored in the database.

Related Work: In [16] and [12], a street view image is matched to geo-tagged street view images. Chung et al. [2] extract MSER regions that are clustered to build adjacency matrices for matching with spectral graph approach. In [1], omnidirectional views are matched to building outline maps by detecting the tallest vertical corners of the buildings and matching them through 2D to 1D projection. Coorg & Teller [3] used vertical facades in combination with GPS and inertial sensors, to determine building orientations. Kosecka & Zhang [7] use facades to compute accurate camera orientation. The facades themselves are detected either by reasoning about their vertical projections [8] or by directly detecting lattice patterns after searching for repetitive features or image structure [10, 4, 6, 13, 9] followed by geometric or appearance-based validation. Schindler et al. [14] automatically geo-localize street images by matching repeated patterns on building facades. Recently, Park et al.[11] have focused on recovering the camera direction of a geo-tagged street image using either street views or satellite imagery. However, they rely on segmenting ground plane in the satellite imagery.

---

*Area Chair: Gang Hua

This material is based upon the work supported by the US Army RDECOM Acq Ctr under Contract No. 08-C-0117.

MM'11, November 28–December 1, 2011, Scottsdale, Arizona, USA.

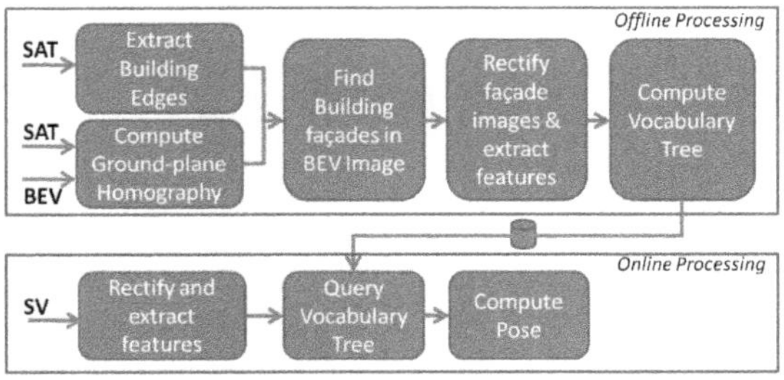

Figure 1: Overall system block diagram.

2. APPROACH

Fig. 1 depicts the flow of key processing modules in our approach. First, we align the ground plane between SAT and BEV imagery. Thus, BEV images can be rectified with respect to the ground plane with canonical axes (N-S, E-W) aligned. Then, we match building outlines extracted from SAT imagery with the corresponding outlines in the rectified BEV images. Subsequently, we use the identified building outlines to find the roofs of buildings thus identifying the facades. This allows extraction of ortho-rectified building facades from the BEV. Features that capture facade self-similarity are then extracted and stored in an adaptive vocabulary tree that hashes these features on the basis of mutual similarity. At run-time, for a query SV image, we first extract an ortho-rectified dominant facade region and then compute self-similarity features which are queried against the database to obtain a matching facade and its geo-location. Finally, point correspondences between the SV image and the BEV image for the identified location and direction are used to compute the 6 DOF pose of the SV camera using standard techniques.

2.1 Alignment

Input Imagery: We download both the overhead SAT and the oblique BEV imagery using Microsoft's Bing Web service. For computational management, each of these image types are downloaded as fixed size tiles, typically 100 meter square. Additionally, for both image types, we use the Web service to establish a map between pixel locations and their lat-long coordinates. For experiments in this work, we downloaded imagery for a 1 Km $\times$ 1 Km region in Ottawa, Canada. A few samples are shown in Fig. 2.

Imagery Alignment: Given the set of SAT and BEV image tiles and the mapping of their pixel coordinates to lat-long coordinates, we can warp the BEV images to the SAT coordinate system. To compute the warping transformation, we approximate it as a projective transformation between pixels in SAT and BEV – thus approximating the Earth's surface within each tile as a flat plane. Using the computed transformations, we warp each of the images to the SAT image coordinate system. As a result, the ground plane gets aligned well in all the images as shown in Fig. 3. To aid further processing, we also compute the dominant city block direction in the SAT imagery and rotate this image before warping the other images to its coordinate system. This renders most of the buildings parallel to the scan-lines in the image – a feature which will be exploited in further processing.

2.2 Facade Extraction

After initial imagery rectification, we extract regions from the BEV imagery corresponding to building facades. To ensure least distortion, we concentrate only on the facade planes which face the heading direction of the particular BEV image. Since the SAT imagery was previously rotated to align the city blocks with the image scan-lines, we can now restrict our attention to facade planes whose 2D projections are horizontal in the SAT images.

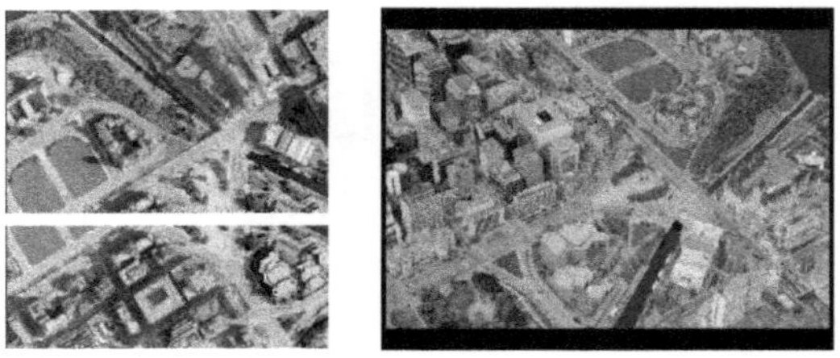

Figure 2: Sample SAT tiles (left) and BEV imagery (right) from Ottawa, Canada.

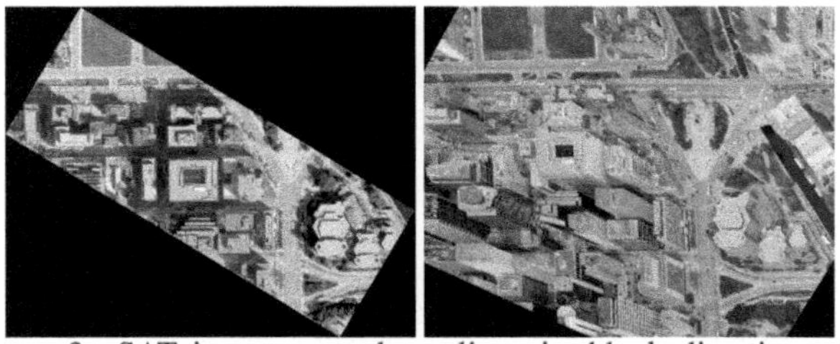

Figure 3: SAT image rotated to align city-block direction with the x-axis (left) and the corresponding BEV image automatically aligned to the SAT image w.r.t the ground-plane using the geo-coordinate information (right).

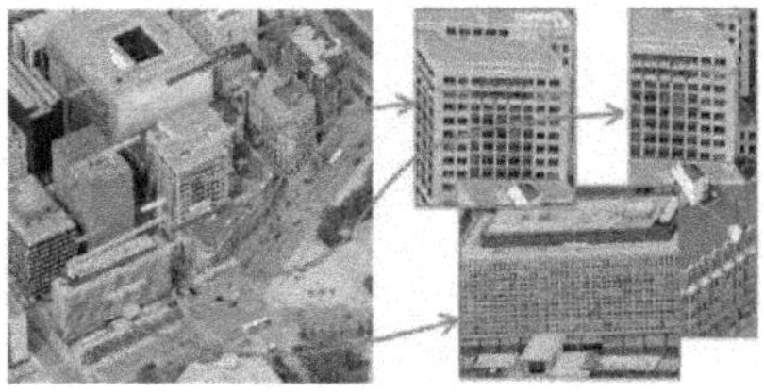

Figure 4: Example of the facade extraction process. a) detected building tops and bottoms, and b) extracted facade tiles.

Vertical Vanishing Point Estimation: In the ground-aligned BEV imagery, lines along the vertical (gravity) vanishing direction can be seen to be convergent. Before extracting affine corrected facades, we first rectify the BEV imagery so that these lines are rendered parallel. We detect canny edges in the BEV image and then group these edges into line segments. Lines along horizontal and vertical directions correspond to city block axes and can hence be rejected. From the remaining line segments, a RANSAC-based process then determines the inlier set of lines that intersect at the required vanishing point.

Image Rectification: Given the computed vanishing point, we now rectify the BEV image by mapping this vanishing point to a point at infinity (in particular to $v_x = [1,0,0]^t$), thus making the building edges parallel. This rectifying transformation is a projective warp which is computed by a method similar to the epipolar rectification method described in [5]. Due to the choice of v_x, the building facade edges in the rectified BEV become parallel to the image scan-lines.

SAT Edge Extraction: To extract building facades from BEV, we start by detecting building contours in the overhead SAT imagery. The contours need to be detected as chains of line-segments, each segment corresponding to one face of a building. We developed an iterative algorithm to extract these line segments from an initial canny edge-detector processed SAT image. Briefly, the algorithm links edges into edge-chains based on proximity and then fits line segments to these edge-chains, splitting wherever the deviation of the edges from the fitted line segment becomes greater than a threshold. Consistent line segments are merged into longer line segments and the overall process is iterated a few times.

Facade ROI Search: From the line segments extracted in the SAT imagery, we keep only the segments along the dominant facade direction in the BEV. Using the ground plane homography

Figure 5: Building top search. Line segments extracted from the SAT imagery are projected to the canny edge map of BEV where a sweep along the gravity direction is expected to give a maximal point at the top edge of the building.

between SAT and BEV, we warp these segments into the rectified BEV image coordinate system. These segments then map to approximately the bottom of the buildings in the BEV image because the transformation corresponds to the ground plane. In the rectified BEV imagery, the gravity vanishing direction is aligned with the scan lines and therefore the tops of these buildings can be found by sliding the mapped line segments horizontally (Fig. 5). Our algorithm to determine the building tops is described below. Once the building tops are determined, we obtain the coordinates of the four corners of each facade which can then be mapped back to the original (unrectified) BEV imagery for high-resolution texture retrieval. For each facade, we crop the texture from the original BEV imagery and then warp it into a rectilinear coordinate system. Fig. 4 shows an example of this process where a few of the facades are extracted and rectified to their orthographic representations.

Computation of Building Tops using GC: Given the nature of the rectified BEV imagery, the top of each building can be determined as a translation $\delta(s)$ for each segment s projected to the building bottom. We formulate this problem as a Graph Cut (GC) optimization of an objective function that consists of the usual data and smoothness costs. The data cost for a line segment is strictly a function of the hypothesized translation and is computed by measuring the average edge strength in the rectified BEV image when the line segment is translated by this value. Thus, when the segment lands on the top of a building, we incur a lower cost due to the high edge strength. To ensure smoothness in the translation values for connected line segments, we add a smoothness cost that penalizes difference in translation values for line segments that are spatially close to each other at their endpoints. For the typical polygonal chains of line segments that we detect for each building, the smoothness cost enforces a strong constraint that the entire building top be at a single translation and avoids the problem of local optima occurring at the numerous edges in the middle of the building facade. Fig. 6 shows an example of how this optimization approach helps the building extraction process.

2.3 Feature Detection & Matching

We represent each rectified facade with appearance features that are extracted over a uniformly sampled grid on the facade. Features from all the facades populate a feature database. We extract a similar set of features for a SV query image. Best matches between the query features and the database features are used to index facades in the database. The location corresponding to the best matching facade are used used to estimate the location and orientation of the coordinates of the query image.

Features: Features like MSER and SIFT do not work well for matching between the BEV and SV imagery due to their large viewpoint and appearance differences. We observe that even under large appearance and viewpoint changes, the layout of local patches within each facade can be used to create a statistical description of the facade pattern. Such statistical descriptions do not

Figure 6: Effect of Graph-Cuts Optimization. The green edges are the SAT edges directly projected to this view and they lie in the ground plane. The red edges are the estimated building top edges. The top row shows the estimates obtained by picking the maximum score for each edge pixel independently; the bottom row shows these estimates refined by the GC optimization.

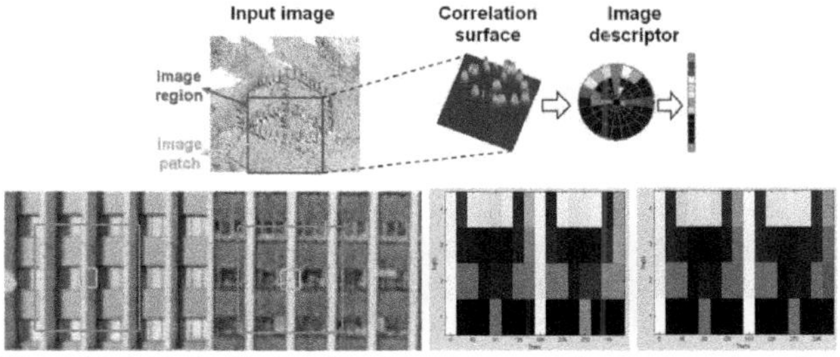

Figure 7: Self-similarity descriptor computation (top row), and example self-similarity descriptors for corresponding facades from the SV and BEV images respectively (bottom row).

get affected by the appearance and viewpoint changes as described by Shechtman et. al [15].

For a given pixel q, the local self-similarity descriptor d_q is computed by defining a patch centered at q and correlating it with a larger surrounding image region R_q to form a local 'correlation surface' (Fig. 7 top row) which is then transformed into a binned log-polar representation to account for local spatial affine deformations. For details, please refer to [15]. The bottom row of Fig. 7 shows rectified facades from corresponding SV and BEV images with the red ROI showing the region of support used for computing the self-similarity descriptor at the red pixel in the center. Also shown are the corresponding descriptors (computed at the center of the red ROIs, R_q) which are noticeably quite similar even with the large appearance difference between the images themselves.

Feature Detection: A single building facade may consist of multiple patterns at different scales. This variation is best captured by the self-similarity descriptor evaluated at the proper scale. We sample a uniform grid of points on the facade and extract the self-similarity descriptor at each of these points at a fixed set of scales. All the descriptors thus obtained are labeled with a unique number which we will refer to as the ID of the given facade. We repeat this process for each facade in our dataset and the descriptors are thus labeled with unique IDs equal in number to the number of facades.

Feature Matching: For scalable data retrieval using the self-similarity features, we use an Adaptive Vocabulary Tree (ADT). We push each of the feature vectors from each facade with the unique ID as the associated label into an ADT data structure. The ADT hashes the feature vectors according to the frequency of the IDs and the co-occurrence of the dimensions of the features resulting in a tree structure (Fig. 8). This tree structure is the database which we use at run-time for query search as described next.

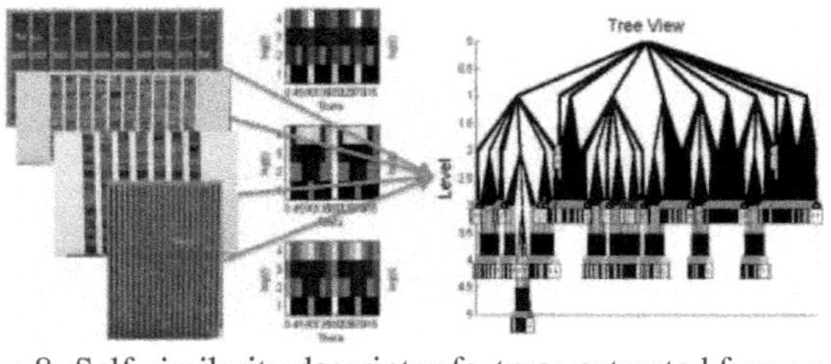

Figure 8: Self-similarity descriptor features extracted from various facades get pushed into an ADT data-structure.

Figure 9: Online processing of a SV image from Panoramio. Extracted and rectified facade returns these top three matching facades from the database. Using the top match, we estimate the camera pose (the point with the emanating rays) and compare it with the ground-truth location (red circle).

2.4 Query Processing & Pose Estimation

At run-time, we first rectify the query SV image by computing the vanishing points in the horizontal and vertical directions, and then extract any facade occupying a substantial portion of the image. For extracting the facades, we exploit the dominance of horizontal and vertical facade patterns; we compute HoG descriptors at a uniform sampling of pixels in the image and then cluster the resulting descriptors using K-Means. Self-similarity features are then extracted on a uniform grid like for the BEV image. These features are queried against the ADT database which returns matching candidates as the top few best matches. The score differential between the top two hits gives us an estimate of the confidence in the retrieval. If the retrieval is confident, we proceed to the geometric localization step with the best match; otherwise, we process both matches for pose estimation and use geometric consistency to prune out the bad match.

Pose Estimation: Facade matching is in itself good enough to localize the SV image within a constrained visibility zone defined by the facade. However, for precise localization of the SV camera we compute the 6 DOF pose of the camera to establish the efficacy of our method. We manually identify 7 point correspondences between the SV and BEV image in the structure surrounding the matched facade. These correspondences are used to estimate the fundamental matrix F [5] between the SV and BEV images. The epipole of the BEV image, as computed from F, then corresponds to the SV camera location in the BEV coordinate system.

The SV camera location in the BEV image is mapped to absolute lat-long coordinates using the ground plane correspondence with the SAT imagery. Finally, the metric (cms/pixel) information in the SAT image is used to estimate the camera focal length which can be used in conjunction with any knowledge about the CCD array dimensions to establish the camera field-of-view as well.

3. EXPERIMENTAL RESULTS

We tested our system on a region around Ridieu St. in Ottawa, Canada with a sample shown in Fig. 2. We used BEV imagery from the west and south heading directions to capture facades as seen from these two directions. For the test imagery, we used imagery from Panoramio and screen-shots from Google Street-view both of which contain lat-long information. Fig. 9 shows an example processing flow for a query SV image from Panoramio. The scores for the top three BEV facade matches shown were 5632.0, 1452.0 and 290.0 respectively. The magnitude difference between the first and second score suggests a good degree of confidence in the match. Pose estimation using the matched facade then gives us the final camera location of the SV image which is also shown in the figure along with the ground-truth location depicted as a red circle with a yellow center. Fig. 10 shows results on four more examples, the right column queries being screen-shots from Google Street-view.

Figure 10: Localization Results. Yellow boxes: input SV images, Red boxes: top 3 facade matches, and estimated and ground-truth pose on the BEV for each input.

In summary, this work establishes the feasibility of matching highly disparate street view images to aerial image databases to precisely geo-localize SV images without the need for GPS or camera metadata. In future work we plan to establish the quantitative efficacy of our method through large city-scale experiments.

4. REFERENCES

[1] T. Cham, A. Ciptadi, W. Tan, M. Pham, and L. Chia. Estimating camera pose from a single urban ground-view omnidirectional image and a 2D building outline map. In *CVPR*, 2010.

[2] Y. Chung, T. Han, and Z. He. Building recognition using sketch based representations and spectral graph matching. In *ICCV*, 2010.

[3] S. Coorg and S. Teller. Extracting textured vertical facades from controlled close-range imagery. In *CVPR*, 1999.

[4] P. Doubek, J. Matas, M. Perdoch, and O. Chum. Image Matching and Retrieval by Repetitive Patterns. *ICPR*, 2010.

[5] R. Hartley and A. Zisserman. *Multiple view geometry in computer vision*. Cambridge University Press New York, NY, USA, 2003.

[6] J. Hays, M. Leordeanu, A. Efros, and Y. Liu. Discovering texture regularity as a higher-order correspondence problem. *ECCV*, 2006.

[7] J. Kosecka and W. Zhang. Video compass. In *ECCV*, 2002.

[8] J. Kosecka and W. Zhang. Extraction, matching, and pose recovery based on dominant rectangular structures. *CVIU*, 2005.

[9] P. Mueller, G. Zeng, P. Wonka, and L. Van Gool. Image-based procedural modeling of facades. In *ACM SIGGRAPH*, 2007.

[10] M. Park, K. Brocklehurst, R. Collins, and Y. Liu. Deformed lattice detection in real-world images using mean-shift belief propagation. *TPAMI*, 31(10):1804–1816, 2009.

[11] M. Park, J. Luo, R. Collins, and Y. Liu. Beyond GPS: determining the camera viewing direction of a geotagged image. In *ACM-MM*, 2010.

[12] D. Robertson and R. Cipolla. An Image-Based System for Urban Navigation. *BMVC*, pages 819–828, 2004.

[13] F. Schaffalitzky and A. Zisserman. Geometric grouping of repeated elements within images. *Shape, Contour and Grouping in Computer Vision*, pages 81–81, 1999.

[14] G. Schindler, P. Krishnamurthy, R. Lublinerman, Y. Liu, and F. Dellaert. Detecting and Matching Repeated Patterns for Automatic Geo-tagging in Urban Environments. In *CVPR*, 2008.

[15] E. Shechtman and M. Irani. Matching local self-similarities across images and videos. In *CVPR*, 2007.

[16] W. Zhang and J. Kosecka. Image Based Localization in Urban Environments. In *Proc. Int. Symp. on 3D Data Processing, Visualization, and Transmission (3DPVT)*, 2006.

Exploiting User Information for Image Tag Refinement *

Jitao Sang[1,2], Jing Liu[1,2], Changsheng Xu[1,2]

[1]National Lab of Pattern Recognition, Institute of Automation, CAS, Beijing 100190, China

[2]China-Singapore Institute of Digital Media, Singapore, 119613, Singapore

{jtsang, jliu, csxu}@nlpr.ia.ac.cn

ABSTRACT

Photo sharing websites allow users to describe images with freely chosen tags. The user-generated tags not only facilitate the users in sharing and organizing images, but also provide large scale meaningful data for image retrieval and management. Extensive studies on improving the quality of user-generated tags for tag-based applications focused on exploiting the *image-tag*, *image-image* and *tag-tag* binary relationships. Considering that *user* is the originator of the tagging activity and *user* involves with *image* and *tag* in many aspects, in this paper we tackle the problem of tag refinement by leveraging *user* information. We propose a Tensor Decomposition framework to jointly model the ternary *user-image-tag* interrelation and respective intra-relations. The users, images and tags are represented in the corresponding latent subspaces. For a given image, the tags with the highest cross-space associations are reserved as the final annotation. The proposed method is validated on a large-scale real-world dataset.

Categories and Subject Descriptors

H.3.3 [**Information Storage and Retrieval**]: Information Search and Retrieval; I.2.8 [**Artificial Intelligence**]: Learning

General Terms

Algorithms, Theory, Experimentation

Keywords

Tag Refinement, Social Images, Factor Analysis

1. INTRODUCTION

With the popularity of Web 2.0 technologies, there are explosive photo sharing websites with large-scale image collections available online, such as Flickr, Picasa, Zooomr and Pinterest. These Web 2.0 websites allow users as owners, taggers, or commenters for their contributed images to interact and collaborate with each other in a social media dialogue. Typically, in a photo sharing website (Flickr as example), three types of interrelated entities are involved, i.e., *image*, *tag* and *user*. From this view, we can deem the user contributed tagging data as the products of the ternary interactions among images, tags and users.

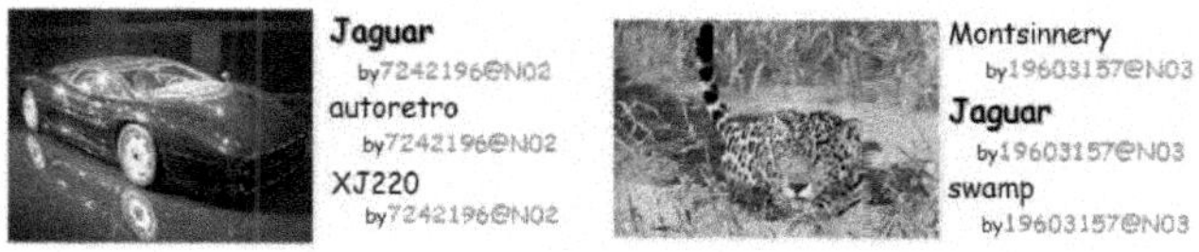

Figure 1: Example images from Flickr and their associated tags and taggers

Obviously, given such a large-scale web dataset, noisy and missing tags are inevitable, which limits the performance of social tag-based retrieval system. Therefore, the tag refinement to denoise and enrich tags for images is desired to tackle this problem. Existing efforts on tag refinement [1, 2, 3, 4, 5, 6, 7, 8] exploited the semantic correlation between tags and visual similarity of images to address the noisy and missing issues, while the user interaction as one of important entities in the social tagging data is neglected.

Users are the originator of the tagging activity and they involves with images and tags in many aspects. We believe that the incorporation of *user* information contributes to a better understanding and description of the tagging data. We take a simple example to explain this observation. As shown in Fig.1, the both images are tagged with "jaguar" by the two users (indicated by user ID), but they have different visual content, i.e., a luxury car and an animal respectively. Due to the well-known "semantic gap", traditional work on image content understanding cannot solve the problem well. In this case, users' interest and background information can be leveraged to specify the image semantics. That is, a car fan will possibly use "jaguar" to tag a 'car' image, while an animal specialist will use "jaguar" to tag a 'wild cat'. Note that it is not necessary to explicitly know the users' interests or profiles. What we are interested in is the variations in individual user's tagging patterns and preferences.

The goal of our work is to improve the underlying associations between the images and tags provided with the raw tagging data from photo sharing websites. To this end, in this paper, we solve it from a factor analysis perspective and aim at building the user-aware image and tag factor representations. With the user factor incorporated, the image and

*Area chair: Lexing Xie

MM'11, November 28–December 1, 2011, Scottsdale, Arizona, USA.

Copyright 2011 ACM 978-1-4503-0616-4/11/11 ...$10.00.

tag factors will be free to focus on their own semantics and we can obtain more semantics-specified image and tag representations. A novel method named *Multi-correlation Regularized Tensor Factorization* (MRTF) is proposed to tackle the tag refinement task. We utilize tensor factorization to jointly model the multiple factors. To alleviate the sparsity problem, the multiple intra-relations are employed as the smoothness constraints and then the factors inference is cast as a regularized tensor factorization problem. Finally, based on the learnt factor representations, which encode the compact users, images and tags representation over their latent subspaces, tag refinement is performed by computing the cross-space *image-tag* associations.

The main contributions of this paper are summarized as follows.

- We introduce *user* information into the social tag processing and jointly model the multiple factors of *user*, *image* and *tag* by tensor factorization.
- We propose the MRTF model to extract the latent factor representations. The sparsity problem is alleviated by imposing the smoothness constraints.
- The proposed framework is evaluated on a large-scale dataset and the advantage of incorporating user information is validated.

2. PROBLEM FORMULATION

The low-dimensional *user*, *image* and *tag* factor matrices can be viewed as compact representations in the corresponding latent subspaces. The latent subspaces capture the relevant attributes, e.g., the user dimensions are related to users' preferences or social interests, the image dimensions involve with visual themes and the tag dimensions are related to the semantic topics of tags. The basic intuition behind this work is: *The incorporation of user information will help extract more compact and informative image and tag representations in the semantic subspaces. The task of image tag refinement is then solved by computing the cross-space image-tag associations.* In this section we first introduce the idea of jointly modeling the *user*, *image* and *tag* factors into a regularized tensor factorization method, then explain how to employ the derived factors for tag refinement.

In the following, we denote tensors by calligraphic uppercase letters (e.g., $\mathcal{Y}$), matrices by uppercase letters (e.g., U, I, T), vectors by bold lowercase letters (e.g., $\boldsymbol{u}, \boldsymbol{i}$), scalars by lowercase letters (e.g., u, i) and sets by blackboard bold letters (e.g., $\mathbb{U}, \mathbb{I}, \mathbb{T}$).

2.1 Multi-correlation Regularized Tensor Factorization

There are three types of entities in the photo sharing websites. The tagging data can be viewed as a set of triplets. Let $\mathbb{U}, \mathbb{I}, \mathbb{T}$ denote the sets of users, images, tags and the set of observed tagging data is denoted by $\mathbb{O} \subset \mathbb{U} \times \mathbb{I} \times \mathbb{T}$, i.e., each triplet $(u, i, t) \in \mathbb{O}$ means that user u has annotated image i with tag t. The left image in Fig.1 corresponds to three triplets in $\mathbb{O}$ sharing the same image and user. The ternary interrelations can be viewed as a three-mode cube, where the modes are the user, image and tag. Therefore, we can induce a three dimensional tensor $\mathcal{Y} \in \mathbb{R}^{|\mathbb{U}| \times |\mathbb{I}| \times |\mathbb{T}|}$,

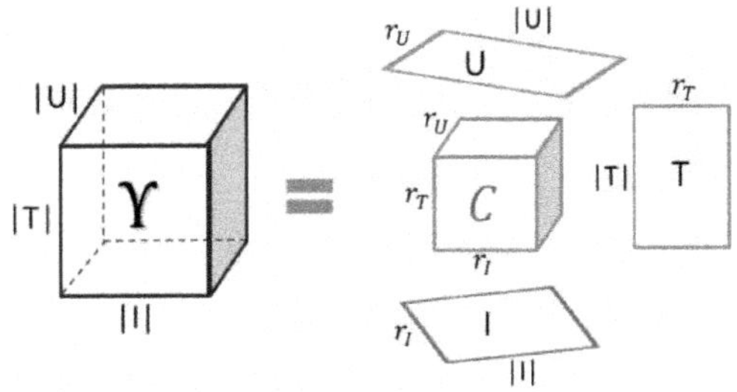

Figure 2: Tucker decomposition: the tensor $\mathcal{Y}$ is constructed by multiplying three factor matrices U, I, T to a small core tensor $\mathcal{C}$.

which is defined as:

$$y_{u,i,t} = \begin{cases} 1 & \text{if } (u,i,t) \in \mathbb{O} \\ 0 & \text{otherwise} \end{cases} \tag{1}$$

where $|\mathbb{U}|$, $|\mathbb{I}|$, $|\mathbb{T}|$ are the number of distinct users, images and tags respectively.

To jointly model the three factors of *user*, *image* and *tag*, we employ a tensor factorization model, Tucker Decomposition for the latent factors inference. In Tucker Decomposition, the tagging data $\mathcal{Y}$ are estimated by three low rank matrices and one core tensor (see Fig.2):

$$\hat{\mathcal{Y}} := \mathcal{C} \times_u U \times_i I \times_t T \tag{2}$$

where $\times_n$ is the tensor product of multiplying a matrix on mode n. Each low rank matrix ($U \in \mathbb{R}^{|\mathbb{U}| \times r_U}$, $I \in \mathbb{R}^{|\mathbb{I}| \times r_I}$, $T \in \mathbb{R}^{|\mathbb{T}| \times r_T}$) corresponds to one factor. The core tensor $\mathcal{C} \in \mathbb{R}^{r_U \times r_I \times r_T}$ contains the interactions between the different factors. The ranks of decomposed factors are denoted by r_U, r_I, r_T and this is called *rank-*(r_U, r_I, r_T) Tucker decomposition. An intuitive interpretation of Eq.2 is that the tagging data depends not only on how similar an image's visual features and tags' semantics are, but on how much these features/semantics match with the users' preferences.

Typically, the latent factors U, I, T can be inferred by directly approximating $\mathcal{Y}$ and the tensor decomposition problem is reduced to minimizing an point-wise loss on $\hat{\mathcal{Y}}$:

$$\min_{U,I,T,\mathcal{C}} \sum_{(\tilde{u},\tilde{i},\tilde{t}) \in |\mathbb{U}| \times |\mathbb{I}| \times |\mathbb{T}|} (\hat{y}_{\tilde{u},\tilde{i},\tilde{t}} - y_{\tilde{u},\tilde{i},\tilde{t}})^2 \tag{3}$$

where $\hat{y}_{\tilde{u},\tilde{i},\tilde{t}} = \mathcal{C} \times_u \boldsymbol{u}_{\tilde{u}} \times_i \boldsymbol{i}_{\tilde{i}} \times_t \boldsymbol{t}_{\tilde{t}}$.

In addition to the ternary interrelations, we also collect multiple intra-relations among users, images and tags. These intra-relations constitute the affinity graphs $W^U \in \mathbb{R}^{|\mathbb{U}| \times |\mathbb{U}|}$, $W^I \in \mathbb{R}^{|\mathbb{I}| \times |\mathbb{I}|}$ and $W^T \in \mathbb{R}^{|\mathbb{T}| \times |\mathbb{T}|}$, respectively. We assume that two items with high affinities should be mapped close to each other in the learnt subspaces. Therefore, the intra-relations are employed as the smoothness constraints to preserve the affinity structure in the low dimensional factor subspaces. In the following, we first introduce how to construct the affinity graphs, and then incorporate them into the tensor factorization framework.

User affinity graph W^U Generally speaking, the activity of joining in interesting groups indicate the users' interests and backgrounds. Therefore, we measure the affinity relationship between user u_m and u_n using the co-occurrence of their joined groups:

$$W^U_{m,n} = \frac{n(u_m, u_n)}{n(u_m) + n(u_n)} \tag{4}$$

where $n(u_m)$ is the number of groups user u_m joined and $n(u_m, u_n)$ is the number of groups u_m and u_n co-joined.

Image affinity graph W^I To measure the visual similarities between images, each image is extracted a 428-dimensional feature vector $\boldsymbol{d}$ as the visual representation [8, 7], including 225-d blockwise color moment features, 128-d wavelet texture features and 75-d edge distribution histogram features. The image affinity graph W^I is defined based on the following Gaussian RBF kernel:

$$W^I_{m,n} = e^{-||\boldsymbol{d}_m - \boldsymbol{d}_n||^2/\sigma_I^2} \tag{5}$$

where σ_I is set as the median value of the elements in W^I.

Tag affinity graph W^T. We build the tag affinity graph based on the tag co-occurrance relevance. The relevance of tag t_m and t_n is simply encoded by their weighted co-occurrence in the image collection:

$$W^T_{m,n} = \frac{n(t_m, t_n)}{n(t_m) + n(t_n)} \tag{6}$$

Note we have no rigid requirements for how to build the affinity graphs and other intra-relation measurements can also be explored.

The affinity graphs can be utilized as the regularization terms to impose smoothness constraints for the latent factors. All the affinity graphs are normalized. Take the image affinity graph W^I and the image factor matrix I as example, the regularization term is:

$$\sum_{m=1}^{|\mathbb{I}|}\sum_{n=1}^{|\mathbb{I}|} W^I_{m,n}||\boldsymbol{i_m} - \boldsymbol{i_n}||^2 \tag{7}$$

where $||\cdot||^2$ denotes the Frobenius norm. The basic idea is to make the latent representations of two images as close as possible if there exists strong affinity between them. We can achieve this by minimizing:

$$\begin{aligned} l &= \sum_{m=1}^{|\mathbb{I}|}\sum_{n=1}^{|\mathbb{I}|} W^I_{m,n}||\boldsymbol{i_m} - \boldsymbol{i_n}||^2 \\ &= \sum_{d=1}^{r_I}\sum_{m=1}^{|\mathbb{I}|}\sum_{n=1}^{|\mathbb{I}|} W^I_{m,n}(i_{m,d} - i_{n,d})^2 = tr(I^\top L_I I) \end{aligned} \tag{8}$$

where $tr(\cdot)$ denotes the trace of a matrix and L_I is the Laplacian matrix for the image affinity matrix W^I. We can build similar regularization terms for the user and tag factors. Combining with Eq.3, we obtain the following overall objective function:

$$\begin{aligned} \min_{U,I,T,\mathcal{C}} g = & \sum_{(\tilde{u},\tilde{i},\tilde{t})\in|\mathbb{U}|\times|\mathbb{I}|\times|\mathbb{T}|} (\hat{y}_{\tilde{u},\tilde{i},\tilde{t}} - y_{\tilde{u},\tilde{i},\tilde{t}})^2 \\ & + \alpha(tr(U^\top L_U U) + tr(I^\top L_I I) + tr(T^\top L_T T)) \\ & + \beta(||\mathbb{U}||^2 + ||\mathbb{I}||^2 + ||\mathbb{T}||^2) \end{aligned} \tag{9}$$

where $||\mathbb{U}||^2 + ||\mathbb{I}||^2 + ||\mathbb{T}||^2$ is l-1 regularization term to penalize large parameters, α and β are weights controlling the strength of corresponding constraints. Obviously, directly optimizing Eq.9 is infeasible and we use an iterative optimization algorithm. We propose an alternating learning algorithm (ALA) with gradient descent to learn the latent factors by iteratively optimizing each subproblems.

Table 1: The statistics of NUS-WIDE-USER15

	Users $\|\mathbb{U}\|$	Images $\|\mathbb{I}\|$	Tags $\|\mathbb{T}\|$	$\|\mathbb{O}\|$
USER15	3,372	124,099	5,018	1,223,254

2.2 Tag Refinement

From the perspective of subspace learning, the derived factor matrices U, I, T can be viewed as the feature representations on the latent *user*, *image*, *tag* subspaces, respectively. Each row of the factor matrices corresponds to one item (user, image or tag). The core tensor $\mathcal{C}$ defines a multi-linear operation and captures the interactions among different subspaces. Therefore, multiplying a factor matrix to the core tensor is related to a change of basis. We define $\mathcal{T}^{UI} := \mathcal{C} \times_t T$, then $\mathcal{T}^{UI} \in \mathbb{R}^{r_U \times r_I \times |\mathbb{T}|}$ can be explained as the tags' feature representations on the *user* $\times$ *image* subspace. Each $r_U \times r_I$ slice of matrix corresponds to one tag feature representation. By summing $\mathcal{T}^{UI}$ over the *user* dimensions, we can obtain the tags' representations on the *image* subspace. Therefore, the cross-space image-tag association matrix $X^{IT} \in \mathbb{R}^{|\mathbb{I}|\times|\mathbb{T}|}$ can be calculated as:

$$X^{IT} = I \cdot (\mathcal{C} \times_t T \times_u \mathbf{1}^\top_{r_U}) \tag{10}$$

The tags with K highest associations to image i are reserved as the final annotations:

$$Top(i, K) = \max_{t\in\mathbb{T}}{}^K X^{IT}_{i:} \tag{11}$$

In the experiment, we fix $K = 10$.

3. EXPERIMENTS

3.1 Data Set

We perform the experiments of social tag refinement on the large-scale web image dataset, NUS-WIDE [9]. It contains 269,648 images with 5,018 unique tags collected from Flickr. We crawled the owner information according to the image ID and obtained the owner user ID of 247,849 images[1]. The collected images belong to 50,120 unique users, with each user owning about 5 images. We select the users owning no less than 15 images and keep their images to obtain our experimental dataset, which is referred as NUS-WIDE-USER15. Table 1 summarizes the collected dataset. $|\mathbb{O}|$ is the number of observed triplets. The NUS-WIDE provides ground-truth for 81 tags of the images. In the experiments, we evaluate the performance of tag refinement by the F-score metric:

$$Fscore = \frac{2 \times Precision \times Recall}{Precision + Recall} \tag{12}$$

3.2 Performance Comparison

To compare the performances, five algorithms as well as the original tags are employed as the baselines:

- Original tagging (OT): the original user-generated tags.
- Random walk with restart (RWRW): the tag refinement algorithm based on random walk [10].
- Tag refinement based on visual and semantic consistency (TRVSC, [7]).

[1]Due to link failures, the owner ID of some images is unavailable

Table 2: Average performances of different algorithms for tag refinement

	OT	RWRW	TRVSC	M-E Graph	LR	MPMF	TF	MRTF
F-score	0.477	0.475	0.49	0.53	0.523	0.521	0.515	0.539

Figure 3: Example of tag refinement results. For each image, the top 5 annotations are shown.

- Multi-Edge graph (M-E Graph): a unified multi-edge graph framework for tag processing proposed in [11].
- Low-Rank approximation (LR): tag refinement based on low-rank approximation with content-tag prior and error sparsity [8].
- Multiple correlation Probabilistic Matrix Factorization (MPMF): the tag refinement algorithm by simultaneously modeling image-tag, tag-tag and tag-tag correlations into a factor analysis framework. [5].

In addition, we compared the performances of the proposed approach with different settings: 1) TF without smoothness constraints (TF) 2) TF with multi-correlation smoothness constraints (MRTF_0/1). Table 2 lists the average performances for different tag refinement algorithms.

It is shown that RWRW fails on the noisy web data. One possible reason is that the model does not fully explore the image-image intra-relations. The results of TRVSC and M-E Graph are taken from [11], which conducted tag refinement on a smaller subset of NUS-WIDE. Both TRVSC and M-E Graph suffer from the high computation problem and the performances are limited on large-scale applications. Using factor analysis methods, MPMF and LR perform well on sparse dataset, which coincides with the authors' demonstration. MRTF is superior than the other methods, showing the advantage of incorporating *user* information. Without smoothness priors, TF fails to preserve the affinity structures and achieves inferior results. Fig.3 further shows the tag refinement results for some exemplary images by the proposed MRTF framework. The experimental results validate our intuition that incorporation of *user* information with appropriate smoothness constraints contribute to a better modeling of the tagging data and derive compact *image* and *tag* factor representations.

4. CONCLUSIONS

We have presented a multi-correlation regularized factor analysis method that jointly models the *user*, *image* and *tag* factors. We argued that by exploiting the underlying structure of the photo sharing websites, our model is able to learn more semantics-specified image and tag descriptions from a corpus of social tagging data. The experimental results on collections from the photo sharing site Flickr show that our model performs well on the tag refinement task.

In the future, there exist different forms of metadata, such as descriptions, comments, and ratings. While we focus on tags in this paper, how to model other metadata for a overall understanding is one of our future works.

5. ACKOWNLEDGEMENT

This work was supported in part by the National Natural Science Foundation of China (Grant No. 60903146, 90920303), 973 Program (Project No. 2010CB327905) and Microsoft Research Asia UR Project.

6. REFERENCES

[1] Yohan Jin, Latifur Khan, Lei Wang, and Mamoun Awad. Image annotations by combining multiple evidence & wordnet. In *ACM Multimedia*, pages 706–715, 2005.

[2] Changhu Wang, Feng Jing, Lei Zhang, and Hong-Jiang Zhang. Content-based image annotation refinement. In *CVPR*, 2007.

[3] Dong Liu, Xian-Sheng Hua, Linjun Yang, Meng Wang, and Hong-Jiang Zhang. Tag ranking. In *WWW*, pages 351–360, 2009.

[4] Hao Xu, Jingdong Wang, Xian-Sheng Hua, and Shipeng Li. Tag refinement by regularized lda. In *ACM Multimedia*, pages 573–576, 2009.

[5] Zechao Li, Jing Liu, Xiaobin Zhu, Tinglin Liu, and Hanqing Lu. Image annotation using multi-correlation probabilistic matrix factorization. In *ACM Multimedia*, pages 1187–1190, 2010.

[6] Lin Chen, Dong Xu, Ivor Wai-Hung Tsang, and Jiebo Luo. Tag-based web photo retrieval improved by batch mode re-tagging. In *CVPR*, pages 3440–3446, 2010.

[7] Dong Liu, Xian-Sheng Hua, Meng Wang, and Hong-Jiang Zhang. Image retagging. In *ACM Multimedia*, pages 491–500, 2010.

[8] Guangyu Zhu, Shuicheng Yan, and Yi Ma. Image tag refinement towards low-rank, content-tag prior and error sparsity. In *ACM Multimedia*, pages 461–470, 2010.

[9] Tat-Seng Chua, Jinhui Tang, Richang Hong, Haojie Li, Zhiping Luo, and Yantao Zheng. Nus-wide: a real-world web image database from national university of singapore. In *CIVR*, 2009.

[10] Changhu Wang, Feng Jing, Lei Zhang, and HongJiang Zhang. Image annotation refinement using random walk with restarts. In *ACM Multimedia*, pages 647–650, 2006.

[11] Dong Liu, Shuicheng Yan, Yong Rui, and Hong-Jiang Zhang. Unified tag analysis with multi-edge graph. In *ACM Multimedia*, pages 25–34, 2010.

Known-Item Video Search via Query-to-Modality Mapping

Kong-Wah Wan
Institute for Infocomm Research
1 Fusionopolis Way
Singapore 138632
kongwah@i2r.a-star.edu.sg

Yan-Tao Zheng
Institute for Infocomm Research
1 Fusionopolis Way
Singapore 138632
yzheng@i2r.a-star.edu.sg

Lekha Chaisorn
Institute for Infocomm Research
1 Fusionopolis Way
Singapore 138632
clekha@i2r.a-star.edu.sg

ABSTRACT

We introduce a novel query-to-modality mapping approach to the TRECVid 2010 known-Item video search (KIS) task. To search for a specific target video, a KIS query is verbose with many multi-modal attributes. Issuing all search terms to a retrieval engine will confuse the search criteria in different modalities and result in "topic drift". We propose decomposing a KIS query into a set of short uni-modal subqueries and issue them to the search index of the corresponding modality features, such as text-based metadata, visual-based high-level features. To do so, we introduce novel syntactic query features and cast the query-to-modality mapping as a classification problem. Retrieval results on the TRECVid 2010 KIS dataset shows that our approach outperforms existing methods by a significant margin.

Categories and Subject Descriptors

H.3.3 [**Information Search and Retrieval**]: Query formulation

General Terms

Algorithms, Languages, Performance

Keywords

Multimedia Search, Query Segmentation

1. INTRODUCTION

The known-item video search (KIS) models the scenario in which the searcher has seen and known of a video before, but does not know where to look in the video corpus [1]. He begins his search session by issuing a lengthy text query describing the target video (Figure 1). The search engine returns a list of videos, where only one is the correct answer.

The average KIS query is verbose and comprises of many multi-modal search attributes. A running example is TRECV

* Area chair: Qi Tian

MM'11, November 28–December 1, 2011, Scottsdale, Arizona, USA.

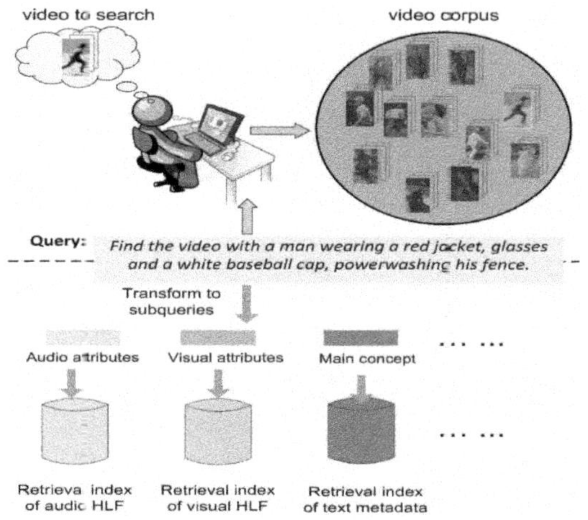

Figure 1: The Video Known-Item-Search scenario

KIS query 24: *"Find the video with a man wearing a red jacket, glasses and a white baseball cap, powerwashing his fence"*. Issuing all the search terms into a retrieval engine will confuse it with many search modalities and result in "topic drift". To address this problem, we propose decomposing a KIS query into short uni-modal subqueries, each embodying a different *attribute type* of the target object, and issued to a retrieval engine that is indexed on features of the corresponding modality type. Using our example, the query is segmented into a text-attribute set: {*"powerwashing fence"*}, and a visual-attribute-set: {*"red jacket", "glassess", "white baseball cap"*}. The former is issued to a metadata search engine, and the latter to a High-Level-Feature-(HLF)-based system. The two result lists can then be fused.

We assume there are grammatical and syntactic patterns governing the description of queried objects and their attributes, e.g. *"man in white shirt", "girl with brown hair"*, and use REGEX surface patterns [15] and syntactic features to capture these lexico-syntactic rules. On a text-attributed segment, we learn a classifier to identify the key concepts for text search. Query terms are represented by standard statistical and part-of-speech features, and dependency parsing. For visual-attributed segments, we apply visual detectors for the detected key concepts with query-to-detector mapping.

We validate our proposed method on the TRECVid 2010 dataset [1] comprising 8000 Internet Archive videos totaling 300 hours. Results show that our method outperforms standard baseline methods by a significant margin.

2. RELATED WORK

Known-item search (or known-item finding) has been a popular information seeking task in text retrieval. In this task, the user attempts to locate a web page, an email, or a report that he has known of [11]. Recently, the TRECVid forum extends this concept to formulate the known item search task for video. Because of the multi-modality nature of video, queries in video KIS are much more complex because they contain search terms on both the topical semantics and audio/visual attributes of video content.

There are recent attempts to apply existing video retrieval techniques on video KIS. Fusion of meta-data text and visual features are explored by Snoek *et. al* [14]. Ngo *et. al* applied query-to-concept mapping to leverage a set of 130 high level concepts for visual search [10]. In contrast, we focus on handling complex and verbose KIS queries and mapping query terms to their search modalities.

Analyzing complex queries has been a popular research topic in information retrieval. Risvik *et. al* first described web query term selection using mutual information and segment frequency [12]. Bendersky and Croft developed a probabilistic model to identify query keywords using features from TF, IDF, etc [2]. Bergsman and Wang applied supervised learning on similar features plus dependency features to segment a query into compound concepts [3]. In this paper, while we have used similar features and learning approach, we introduce additional novel syntactic dependency features to improve keyword extraction, and undertake the additional task of locating the A/V search terms.

3. QUERY-TO-MODALITY MAPPING

Without loss of generality, we constrain our discussion to two modality types: text (video metadata) and visual HLF.

3.1 Query Terms for Visual Modality

We introduce ways to identify the visual attributes (VA) of KIS queries as query terms of visual modality. First, there is a noticeable consistency in KIS queries: VA phrases are usually anchored by active verbs (VBG) such as *"wearing a..."*, *"standing by..."*, *"sitting on..."* or prepositions (PP) like *"with"*, *"in"*. Therefore, we first learn a set of surface patterns from an annotated data set of training queries manually marked with visual attributes.

Next, because surface patterns cannot handle long-range dependencies, we augment the REGEX rules with POS tags, and impose the rule that VA segments must not contain proper-noun (NNP) phrases. Then we analyze the term dependency relations from a dependency parser [9] to capture conjunctional constructs (Figure 2). For example, in *"a man wearing a red jacket, glasses, a white baseball cap"*, *"wearing"* is connected with *"red jacket"*, *"glassess"* and *"baseball cap"*, via the *dobj* relation. Semantically, it becomes: *"a man wearing a red jacket, wearing glassess, wearing a white baseball cap"*, making *"glasses"* and *"a white baseball cap"* part of the VA. In this expanded form, our surface patterns can properly identify all three *"wearing"* VA of the man.

3.2 Query Terms for Text Modality

The semantic content of a user's information need is usually expressed by the key terms in the query. In the following, we describe how the key terms can be selected. We also assume they can be captured by a ranking function.

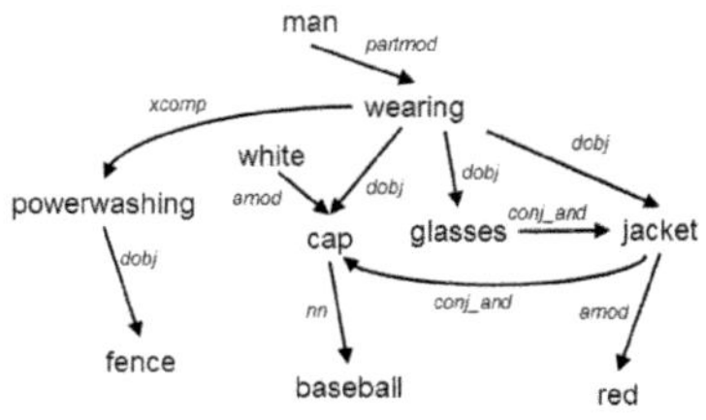

Figure 2: Typed dependency tree of KIS query 24

3.2.1 Selecting Key Query Terms

Noun Phrase (NP): The key concepts in a query are often embodied in the NP [2]. We extract NP using a parser [9]. If there are proper nouns (NNP), only they are selected as a compound keyword enclosed in quotes. Hence, given: *members of the Coast Guard sing the slow hit song*, the two resulting keywords are: {*"Coast Guard"*}, {*slow hit song*}

Dependency-Relations: Keywords are also extracted from the dependency parse (DP) tree. This can uncover related terms over multi-word and POS boundaries. For example, given: *tavern with round tables and dancing candlesticks*, the DP captures two keywords: {*tavern tables*}, {*tavern candlesticks*} connected by the *prep_with* relation.

3.2.2 Ranking Key Query Terms

We adopt a supervised learning approach and make use of the following term weighting features to derive the final key query term rank:

tf(K): frequency of term K in the corpus.

idf(K): inverse of the document frequency (*df*) of the query term in the corpus: $idf(K) = \log \frac{N}{df(K)}$

wig(K): weighted information gain of the query term K, based on the relative normalized entropy of the concept in corpus C and in the collection D of the top 50 retrieved documents when K is issued as query:

$$wig(K) = \frac{\frac{1}{50}\sum_{d \in D} p(K|d) - \log p(K|C)}{-\log p(K|C)} \quad (1)$$

ng_wiki(K): Given K, we form all valid segmentations S comprising n-gram (n=1..4) sub-segment s, and score S by an exponential sum of the frequency $count(s)$ of s in the English Wikipedia 2010-10-11 dump:

$$ng\_wiki(K) = \max_S \{ \sum_{s \in S} |s|^{|s|} \cdot count(s) \} \quad (2)$$

pos(K): the histogram of the POS tags of the three adjacent terms for each word of the key query term.

dp_in(K): total number of dependency links of K in the dependency tree. We expect that key terms are semantically related to many other terms, and characterized by their hub-like structures in the dependency tree.

3.3 Building HLF Detectors from Key Visual Query Terms

Similar to learning key concepts from textual attributes, key visual concepts in VA can be selected from noun phrases, e.g. *shirt, chair, sky, beach,* for which visual detectors can be built to augment retrieval. For this, we can turn to existing detectors [7]. However, there are problems with this

(a) beach, sky, country-side, **santa-cap**, hair (b) **brick-wall**, coat, screen, hair, apartment (c) screen, **apartment**, chair, computer, door

Figure 3: Top: Sample attribute images for training. Botton: The top five attribute predictons in images. Correct predictions are shown in bold.

approach. First, for many visual keywords such as *hair*, *santa-cap*, there is no detector available. Second, concepts in a VA segment are mostly local visual attributes of objects, and differ from the global descriptors in existing detectors.

For the purpose of showing the utility of visual-attributed analysis in this paper, we follow recent trends in describing objects with attributes [8], to learn new detectors for the key visual concepts. We choose 20 key visual concepts with the smallest semantic gap, estimated in terms of their inter- and intra-class visual variation [5]: *sky, beach, brick wall, santa-cap, country-side, shirt, chair, courtyard, pants, suit computer, screen, apartment, sofa, door, hair, coat, sunglass, beard, microphone*. For a keyword that is outside this list, we simply discard its visual detection.

For each keyword, we downloaded and manually prepared Google images for training. As negative examples, we randomly sampled from other keyword classes. All attribute images are resized to 128x128, and a broad variety of visual features is used: LAB-color, texton and SIFT visual words. Each feature type is respectively quantized into 64, 128, 300 K-means centroids, forming a 492-d bag-of-word image vector. A linear SVM is used as the classifier. To detect the presence of an attribute in an image, the attribute classifier is scanned over multiple locations and scales. The final output is a 20-d histogram score vector of keyword attributes. Figure 3 shows some examples of training attribute images, and the attribute predictions in images.

3.4 Fusion

We use linear fusion to combine retrieval results from all N attributes: Denote $f_k(x)$ to be the kth-modality retrieval score of input video x. The final retrieval score is: $R(x) = \sum_{k=1}^{N} \alpha_k f_k(x)$, where α_k is the weight of the kth-modality retrieval method and $\sum_k \alpha_k = 1$. The weights for α is determined by a grid-search maximizing the **AP** of R on the labeled training set, where each α_k is constrained to $\{0, 0.05, 0.1, \ldots, 1.0\}$.

4. EVALUATION

4.1 Query-to-Modality Mapping Results

We evaluate the proposed methods using the TRECVid 2010 dataset. This comprises of 8000 Internet Archive videos totaling 300 hours. Each video has a metadata text description averaging only 50 words. To facilitate the evaluation of intermediate results, we also develop two ground truth datasets: **D1**: annotation of query terms and its corresponding modality, and **D2**: optimal subqueries for text modality.

Table 1: Query-to-Modality Mapping results

Visual query term classification			
	Recall	Precision	Accuracy
CRF++ [13]	85.6	81.2	81.8
Our method	85.7	81.7	82.5

Textual query term classification			
	Proposed	*idf*	*wig*
Accuracy	72.3	52.4	65.7
Mean Reciprocal Rank	81.4	71.2	77.3

Query Terms for Visual Modality: The query dataset is splitted into a train-set (query 1 to 200), and the others used as test-set. To measure classification performance, we use standard precision, recall, and accuracy of correct assignment. We compare our method with an CRF++ stop-phrase removal method [13]. Comparable results are shown in Table 1, and indicate that a simple method based on surface patterns and syntactic features can produce competitive results with a state-of-art sequential tagger.

Query Terms for Text Modality: For the supervised learning tool, we use the TiMBL Memory-Based Learning software [4], We use 10-fold cross validation, and the average results over all ten runs are reported. Results are evaluated using *Accuracy* and *Mean Reciprocal Rank*. To see the advantage of our supervised learning approach, we also compare against a simple non-supervised weighting method based on two features: the inverse document frequency (*idf*) and the weighted information gain (*wig*) (see Section 3.2.2). Table 1 tabulates the results. They show that the supervised learning approach produces the best classifier.

4.2 Known-Item Video Search Results

In this sub-section and the next, we evaluate the performance of known-item search using the proposed method. The evaluation criteria for KIS is the mean inverted rank (MIR), at which the known item is found.

Retrieval on Text Modality: We first utilize the original query that undergoes standard query pre-processing such as stopword removal. We then issue the subqueries obtained from the proposed method, the human-annotated subqueries in **D1**, and the optimal subqueries in **D2** to the text-metadata-based retrieval indexes. For the subqueries generated from the proposed method, we adjust its length to make it include top 1, 2, 3 and 4 ranked key query terms.

Table 2 illustrates the accuracies of all the runs. We make three observations from the results. First, issuing using the original queries (with many modalities) yield the lowest retrieval, than issuing with sub-queries (with segmented modalities). This confirms the effectiveness of our proposed method. Second, retrieval using the proposed subqueries is only slightly lower than that from using human-annotated subqueries. This shows that our proposed method can effectively identify subqueries that is comparable to human annotation. Third, retrieval empirically peaks at a subquery of length two and deteriorates when more query terms are used. This is likely because most video metadata is very short and contain only one or two key concepts. For the

Table 2: Retrieval performance of text (video metadata) modality. Mean Inverted Rank @ 100 from the proposed method, human-annotation D1, and the optimal subqueries D2.

Original queries	Optimal queries **D2**	human-annotated **D1**	Proposed			
			top-1	top-2	top-3	top-4
27.7	38.5	36.7	33.8	35.7	35.4	35.2

rest of the paper, all reported text-attributed retrieval results are based on the top-2 ranked key terms.

4.3 Using More Modalities

In this section, we examine the retrieval benefit of using more attribute types. Here are the additional attribute types and their brief descriptions:

Auditory-based ASR modality: There are grammatical constructs common to spoken attributes, e.g. *"saying that..."*, that can detected using the surface pattern approach in Section 3.1. Spoken attributes are appropriately issued to a retrieval engine indexed on the spoken speech transcripts. As an Automatic Speech Recognition (ASR) engine, we use the HTK version 3.4 release from Cambridge University Engineering Department.

Visual-based OCR modality: These are characterized by the query snippets *"with the logo..."*, *"the text...appears on the screen"*, and are suitable for a retrieval engine indexed on the detected Optical Character Recognition (OCR) text in the video frames. We use a gray scale OCR engine, with multi-frame integration and a character segmenter using region-growing. The recognizer is a neural network trained using backpropagation.

Visual-based HLF concept detectors: Finally, we also use the 130-HLF-detectors from [7]. As discussed in Section 3.3, it is also important to note the difference between these global detectors and our VA detectors in Section 3.3. For query-to-HLF mapping, we match a query against an expanded gloss description with related Wikipedia text.

Table 3 shows the results of the various combination of modalities using linear fusion. It is clear that when more search modalities are utilized, we obtain better retrieval. The modality that contributes most to retrieval is the ASR modality. The modality with the least contribution is the 130-HLF-detectors. This concurs with the findings of other participants of the KIS tasks [10, 6, 14]. We also list the relevant results of these participants for comparison. The video-metadata-based retrieval results from [10, 14] are similar to the results that we obtain using the original query without any concept detection (See Table 2).

5. CONCLUSIONS

We have presented a query-to-modality mapping approach to the TRECVid 2010 known-Item video search (KIS) task. Our method deviates from the conventional query-to-HLF mapping by generalizing the query mapping to the various modality types in a multimedia domain, and formulating the mapping as a classification task based on surface pattern and syntactic features. This is in recognition that a sub-query of a particular modality type is better issued to a search engine that is indexed on features of the corresponding modality type. This query modality alignment can also be seen as a generalization of the query segmentation approach traditionally used by the text community for query analysis. We empirically show on the TRECVid 2010 KIS dataset that our approach can greatly enhance retrieval over existing methods.

Several issues are worthy of further investigation. The current retrieval is based on a linear fusion of search results by indexes of different modalities. The inter-relation among search attributes of different modalities can be further analyzed for a more intelligent fusion.

Table 3: Mean inverted rank (MIR) of different runs. Linear fusion is used to combine all modality. See text for the explanation of the acronyms.

Run modality	MIR@1	MIR@10	MIR@100
Original query	21.3	24.4	27.7
Text modality	27.3	33.4	35.7
Text + visual	28.0	34.5	37.3
Text+visual+ASR	32.5	37.5	39.2
Text+visual+ASR+OCR	33.4	39.2	41.0
Text+visual+ASR+OCR+HLF	33.4	39.8	41.3
BUPT text+ASR [6]	–	–	29.4
VIREO text+ASR [10]	–	–	25.8
Mediamill text+ASR [14]	–	–	25.0

6. REFERENCES

[1] *TRECVID 2010 Known-Item Search.* http://www-nlpir.nist.gov/projects/tv2010/tv2010.html#kis.

[2] M. Bendersky and W. B. Croft. Discovering key concepts in verbose queries. In *Proc of SIGIR*, pages 491–498, 2008.

[3] S. Bergsma and Q. I. Wang. Learning noun phrase query segmentation. In *Proc of EMNLP-CoNLL*, pages 819–826, 2007.

[4] W. Daelemans, J. Zavrel, K. van der Sloot, and A. van den Bosch. Timbl: Tilburg memory based learner version 6.3, reference guide. *ILK Technical Report ILK-1001*, 2010.

[5] J. Feng, Y. Zheng, and S. Yan. Towards a universal detector by mining concepts with small semantic gaps. In *Proc of ACM Multimedia*, pages 1707–1710, 2010.

[6] X. Guo, Y. Chen, W. Liu, Y. Mao, H. Zhang, K. Zhou, L. Wang, Y. Hua, Z. Zhao, Y. Zhao, and A. Cai. Bupt-mcprl at trecvid 2010. In *Proc of TRECVID Workshop*, 2010.

[7] Y.-G. Jiang, J. Yang, C.-W. Ngo, and A. G. Hauptmann. Representations of keypoint-based semantic concept detection: A comprehensive study. *IEEE Transactions on Multimedia*, 12:42–53, 2010.

[8] C. Lampert, H. Nickisch, and S. Harmeling. Learning to detect unseen object classes by between-class attribute transfer. *Proc CVPR*, 2009.

[9] M. Marneffe, B. MacCartney, and C. Manning. Generating typed dependency parses from phrase structure parses. In *Proc of LREC*, 2006.

[10] C.-W. Ngo, S.-A. Zhu, H.-K. Tan, W.-L. Zhao, and X.-Y. Wei. Vireo at trecvid 2010: Semantic indexing, known-item search, and content-based copy detection. In *Proc of TRECVID Workshop*, Nov 2010.

[11] P. Ogilvie and J. Callan. Combining document representations for known-item search. In *Proc of SIGIR*, SIGIR '03, pages 143–150, 2003.

[12] K. Risvik, T. Mikolajewski, and P. Boros. Query segmentation for web search. In *Proc of WWW*, 2003.

[13] H. Samuel and W. Bruce. Evaluating verbose query processing techniques. In *Proc of SIGIR*, pages 291–298, 2010.

[14] C. Snoek, K. Sande, O. Rooij, B. Huurnink, E. Gavves, D. odijk, M. Rijke, T. Gevers, M. Worring, D. Koelma, and A. Smeulders. The mediamill trecvid 2010 semantic video search engine. In *Proc of TRECVID Workshop*, 2010.

[15] M. Soubbotin and S. Soubbotin. Use of patterns for detection of likely answer strings: A systematic approach. In *Proc of TREC*, 2020.

Transfer Tagging from Image to Video*

Yang Yang
The University of Queensland
Brisbane, Australia
yang.yang@itee.uq.edu.au

Yi Yang
Carnegie Mellon University
Pittsburgh, United States
yiyang@cs.cmu.edu

Zi Huang
The University of Queensland
Brisbane, Australia
huang@itee.uq.edu.au

Heng Tao Shen
The University of Queensland
Brisbane, Australia
shenht@itee.uq.edu.au

ABSTRACT

Nowadays massive amount of web video datum has been emerging on the Internet. To achieve an effective and efficient video retrieval, it is critical to automatically assign semantic keywords to the videos via content analysis. However, most of the existing video tagging methods suffer from the problem of lacking sufficient tagged training videos due to high labor cost of manual tagging. Inspired by the observation that there are much more well-labeled data in other yet relevant types of media (e.g. images), in this paper we study how to build a "cross-media tunnel" to transfer external tag knowledge from image to video. Meanwhile, the intrinsic data structures of both image and video spaces are well explored for inferring tags. We propose a *Cross-Media Tag Transfer* (CMTT) paradigm which is able to: 1) transfer tag knowledge between image and video by minimizing their distribution difference; 2) infer tags by revealing the underlying manifold structures embedded within both image and video spaces. We also learn an explicit mapping function to handle unseen videos. Experimental results have been reported and analyzed to illustrate the superiority of our proposal.

Categories and Subject Descriptors

H.3.3 [**Information Storage and Retrieval**]: Information Search and Retrieval; I.2.6 [**Artificial Intelligence**]: Learning

General Terms

Algorithms, Experimentation, Performance

Keywords

Video Tagging, Cross-Media, Tag Transfer, Tag Inference

*Area chair: Marcel Worring

1. INTRODUCTION

In the most recent years, driven by the advances in the Internet and the digital camera techniques, a tremendous number of user-generated video clips have been emerging on the Web for publishing and sharing. To facilitate an effective and efficient video retrieval, it is significant for the modern video search engines to leverage the automatic video tagging techniques to index the video data with certain meaningful keywords, i.e. tags.

Figure 1: An illustration of the relevant Flickr[1] images and YouTube[2] videos on the topic of "*Football*".

Due to the expensive labor cost of manual tagging, it is not practical to provide sufficient labeled training data for most of the existing video tagging methods to build perfect tagging models, thereby leading to an unsatisfactory tagging performance. Currently, there are two advanced research directions aiming to address this problem: 1) The first one is the *transfer learning* (TL) model, which is motivated by the observation that tag information in relevant sources is helpful for generating better classifiers for the target data. However, most of the existing works only consider the same media type, i.e. video, for both the source and the target, where the tag insufficiency issue may still exist. It is natural to consider different media types as well, e.g. image. Noticing the recent success of cross media retrieval [9], we derive a strong motivation of developing a cross-media model for transferring tag knowledge from tagged image data to video data. Figure 1 illustrates Flickr images and YouTube videos both related to the topic "Football"; 2) The second way is to leverage both unlabeled data and labeled data in the same media. This is usually known as *semi-supervised learning*

[1]http://www.flickr.com/
[2]http://www.youtube.com/

(SSL) [10], which has shown great benefits to the applications in the multimedia research.

In this paper we aim to collaboratively take advantages of both transfer learning and semi-supervised learning to boost video tagging performance. The main contributions of our work are summarized as below:

- A cross-media video tagging scheme CMTT is proposed to transfer tag knowledge from image to video for improving video tagging performance.
- We explore the intrinsic manifold structures embedded in both image and video spaces by employing semi-supervised learning.
- Extensive experiments have been conducted to illustrate the effectiveness of our method.

The rest of this paper is organized as follows. In section 2, we describe the details of the CMTT model. Section 3 reports experimental results, followed by the conclusion in Section 4.

2. CROSS-MEDIA TAG TRANSFER

In this section we elaborate a novel cross-media video tagging scheme which is able to transfer tag knowledge from images to videos and infer video tags by exploring the intrinsic data structures of both images and videos as well.

2.1 Problem Formulation

Let $\mathbf{Z} = \{\mathbf{Z}^l \cup \mathbf{Z}^u\}$ denote a target video dataset. $\mathbf{Z}^l = \{(\mathbf{z}_i, y_i)\}|_{i=1}^{N_z^l}$ is the tagged video subset consisting of N_z^l tagged videos associated with their binary tag indicators $y_i \in \{-1,1\}^{c\times 1}$, where c is the number of the tags in the vocabulary. $\mathbf{Z}^u$ is the subset of N_z^u untagged videos. For each individual video $\mathbf{z}_i \in \mathbf{Z}$, it is represented as a sequence of keyframes $\{\mathbf{z}_{ij}\}|_{j=1}^{|\mathbf{z}_i|}$, where $\mathbf{z}_{ij}$ is the visual feature of the jth keyframe of $\mathbf{z}_i$, and $|\cdot|$ is the cardinality of a set. Suppose we are further given an auxiliary image dataset comprising of N_x well-tagged images $\mathbf{X} = \{(\mathbf{x}_i, y_i)\}|_{i=1}^{N_x}$, where $\mathbf{x}_i$ denotes the visual feature of the ith image, and $y_i \in \{-1,1\}^{c\times 1}$ is the corresponding tag indicator.

The primary goal of our work is to derive an effective tag transfer approach for assigning the untagged videos in $\mathbf{Z}^u$ with meaningful tags by simultaneously leveraging both the auxiliary image dataset $\mathbf{X}$ and the target video dataset $\mathbf{Z}$. An explicit mapping function is also required for handling the unseen videos.

2.2 Bridging Image and Video

To transfer tag knowledge, we need to bridge the gap between image and video. To this end, we employ a criterion based on *Maximum Mean Discrepancy* (MMD) [2]:

$$dist^2(\mathbf{X}, \mathbf{Z}) = tr(\mathbf{KT}) \tag{1}$$

where $\mathbf{T} = \mathbf{tt}^T$, $\mathbf{t} = [1/N_x, \ldots, 1/N_x, -1/N_z, \ldots, -1/N_z]^T$ and $\mathbf{K}$ is a compound kernel matrix over both $\mathbf{X}$ and $\mathbf{Z}$. $tr(\cdot)$ is the matrix trace.

Suppose we are given m basic kernels, to find an "optimal" kernel space, we use the multiple kernel MMD criterion:

$$dist^2(\mathbf{X}, \mathbf{Z}) = tr((\sum_i d_i \mathbf{K}_i)\mathbf{T}) = d^T\mathbf{p} \tag{2}$$

where $d = [d_1, \ldots, d_m]^T$ and $\mathbf{p} = [tr(\mathbf{K}_1\mathbf{T}), \ldots, tr(\mathbf{K}_m\mathbf{T})]^T$.

2.3 Cross Media Tagging

In this part we propose a cross-media tag inference model, which simultaneously transfers image tags as well as propagates video tags to the untagged videos by exploring the intrinsic image and video data structures.

To explore the manifold structure of image and video data, we can employ graph-based semi-supervised learning (SSL) over both image and video data:

$$\min_F \; tr((F-Y)^T U (F-Y)) + \alpha tr(F^T L F) \tag{3}$$

where the first component measures the distribution difference while the last two parts correspond to the SSL model. $Y = [y_1, \ldots, y_{N_x+N_z^l}, \mathbf{0}_c, \ldots, \mathbf{0}_c]^T \in \mathbb{R}^{(N_x+N_z)\times c}$ is the original tag matrix. $\mathbf{0}_c$ denotes an all-zero vector with c elements. $F = [f_1, f_2, \ldots, f_{N_x+N_z}]^T \in \mathbb{R}^{(N_x+N_z)\times c}$ is the corresponding predicted tag matrix. $U \in \mathbb{R}^{(N_x+N_z)\times(N_x+N_z)}$ is a diagonal matrix of which the ith diagonal element u_{ii} denotes the weight of the ith training sample. L is the composite Laplacian matrix defined over all the training data:

$$L = \begin{bmatrix} L_x & \mathbf{0} \\ \mathbf{0} & L_z \end{bmatrix} \tag{4}$$

where L_x and L_z are the sub-matrices over the image dataset and the video dataset, respectively.

However, this model can not handle unseen data. Inspired by [6], we add an additional component to simultaneously learn a mapping function, and integrate it into the above transfer model:

$$\begin{aligned} \min_{d,F,V,b} \; & d^T\mathbf{pp}^T d + tr((F-Y)^T U(F-Y)) + \alpha tr(F^T L F) + \\ & + \mu\left(\gamma \left\| (\sum_{i=1}^m d_i\mathbf{K}_i)V + \mathbf{1}b^T - F \right\|_F^2 + \right. \\ & \left. + \; tr(V^T(\sum_{i=1}^m d_i\mathbf{K}_i)V)\right) \\ & \textbf{s.t. } d \succeq \mathbf{0} \text{ and } d^T\mathbf{1} = 1 \end{aligned} \tag{5}$$

where the last two parts are multiple kernel ridge regression which helps to get a non-linear mapping function.

2.4 Laplacian Matrix and Multiple Kernels

The construction of Laplacian matrix and the choice of the base kernels are based on certain distance metric. However, since images and videos are heterogeneous data it is hard to directly utilize a unified metric to measure their distances. Therefore, we derive the following image-video and video-video distance metrics to handle this problem:

- ***Image-Video Distance.*** Given an image $\mathbf{x}$ and a video denoted as $\mathbf{z} = \{\mathbf{z}_i\}|_{i=1}^{|\mathbf{z}|}$, where $\mathbf{z}_i$ is the ith keyframe of $\mathbf{z}$. We define the distance between $\mathbf{x}$ and $\mathbf{z}$ as follows:

$$d_{IV}(\mathbf{x}, \mathbf{z}) = \min_{1\le i\le |\mathbf{z}|} d_{II}(\mathbf{x}, \mathbf{z}_i)$$

- ***Video-Video Distance.*** Given two videos $\mathbf{z}_p$ and $\mathbf{z}_q$, the pairwise distance between them is defined as below:

$$d_{VV}(\mathbf{z}_p, \mathbf{z}_q) = \frac{\sum_{i,j} d_{II}(\mathbf{z}_{pi}, \mathbf{z}_{qj})}{|\mathbf{z}_p||\mathbf{z}_q|}$$

2.4.1 *Construct Laplacian Matrix*

Based on these distance metrics, to obtain the Laplacian matrix, we first construct the k-nearest-neighbor graphs $\mathbf{W}_x = [w_x^{ij}] \in \mathbb{R}^{N_x \times N_x}$ and $\mathbf{W}_z = [w_z^{ij}] \in \mathbb{R}^{N_z \times N_z}$ for the image and video media, respectively.

$$\begin{cases} w_x^{ij} = \exp\left(-\frac{d_{II}^2(\mathbf{x}_i,\mathbf{x}_j)}{\gamma}\right), & \text{if } \mathbf{x}_i \in \mathcal{N}_k(\mathbf{x}_j) \text{ or } \mathbf{x}_j \in \mathcal{N}_k(\mathbf{x}_i) \\ w_z^{ij} = \exp\left(-\frac{d_{VV}^2(\mathbf{z}_i,\mathbf{z}_j)}{\gamma}\right), & \text{if } \mathbf{z}_i \in \mathcal{N}_k(\mathbf{z}_j) \text{ or } \mathbf{z}_j \in \mathcal{N}_k(\mathbf{z}_i) \\ 0, & \text{otherwise.} \end{cases}$$

where $\mathcal{N}_k(\cdot)$ is the function for searching the k nearest neighbors. Then the sub-Laplacian matrices L_x and L_z can be computed as:

$$\begin{cases} L_x = \mathbf{D}_x - \mathbf{W}_x \\ L_z = \mathbf{D}_z - \mathbf{W}_z \end{cases}$$

where $\mathbf{D}_x$ and $\mathbf{D}_z$ are diagonal matrices, and their i^{th} diagonal elements are calculated as $D_x^{ii} = \sum_j w_x^{ij}$ and $D_z^{ii} = \sum_j w_z^{ij}$, respectively. Recall the definition in Eq.(4), we get the composite Laplacian matrix $L = \begin{bmatrix} L_x & \mathbf{0} \\ \mathbf{0} & L_z \end{bmatrix}$.

2.4.2 *Construct Base Kernels*

Similarly, we derive the base kernels for our model by generalizing the existing kernels that are based on certain distance metrics. The generalized *Gaussian Kernel* should be computed as follows:

$$\begin{cases} k_{xx}^{ij} = \exp\left(-\frac{d_{II}^2(\mathbf{x}_i,\mathbf{x}_j)}{2\sigma^2}\right) \\ k_{xz}^{ij} = k_{zx}^{ij} = \exp\left(-\frac{d_{IV}^2(\mathbf{x}_i,\mathbf{z}_j)}{2\sigma^2}\right) \\ k_{zz}^{ij} = \exp\left(-\frac{d_{VV}^2(\mathbf{z}_i,\mathbf{z}_j)}{2\sigma^2}\right) \end{cases}$$

Similarly we can also construct other kernels, such as *Laplacian Kernel*, etc.

3. EXPERIMENTS

In this section we evaluate the effectiveness of our proposed model. Two web image datasets are used as the auxiliary sources while one video dataset is the target.

The proposed model is compared with two state-of-the-art transfer learning algorithms A-MKL[4] and A-SVM[8], and two baseline algorithms including SVM, and graph-based semi-supervised learning (SSL). The Mean Average Precision (MAP) is chosen as the evaluation metric.

3.1 Experiments Setup

3.1.1 *Datasets*

In our work, we employ two popular web image datasets, NUS-WIDE [3] and MIRFlickr [5] as the auxiliary sources, and two publicly available video datasets, Kodak Video Benchmark [1] and TRECVID 2007, as the targets. NUS-WIDE dataset has been widely used in the multimedia research. It consists of 269,648 images crawled from Flickr and tagging ground-truth for 81 semantic tags are provided for evaluation. The images in MIRFlickr are also collected from Flickr. Currently there are two versions: MIRFlickr-1M with 1 million web images and MIRFLICKR25000 with 25,000 images. Since there is no tagging ground-truth provided in the MIRFlickr-1M, we choose to use the MIRFLICKR25000, in

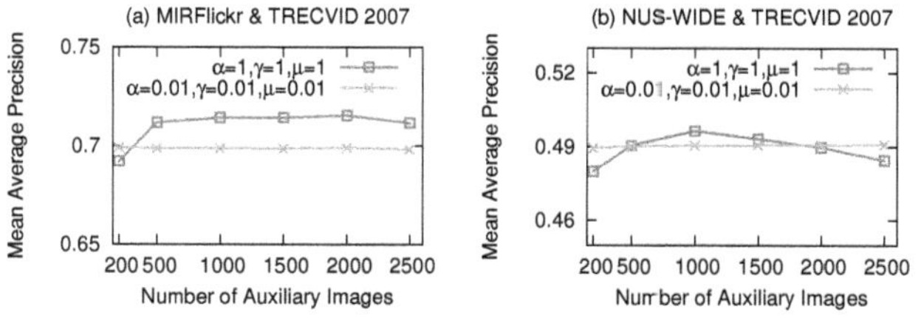

Figure 2: Effects of the Number of Auxiliary images on Video Tagging Performance.

which all the 25,000 images are manually tagged with 30 semantic tags. As to the targets, TRECVID 2007 includes 21,532 keyframes that are extracted from 110 videos. All the keyframes are manually annotated with 36 semantic tags.

Two image-video cross-media combinations are generated with the two auxiliary image datasets and TRECVID video dataset. In order to make consistency between the lexicon of the auxiliary image dataset and the target video dataset, we only consider the common tags between them. The images with at least one of these common tags are selected. This finally gives us 45,207 unique images.

3.1.2 *Visual Features*

Image visual features, such as 144-D color auto-correlogram (HSV), have been provided by NUS-WIDE and TRECVID 2007. For MIRFlickr and TRECVID 2007 combination, we represent visual content by Local Binary Patterns (LBP) feature [7]. LBP feature computes a value for each pixel by comparing its 8 neighbor pixels with the center pixel value and transforms the result to a binary value. The histogram of the values is summed up to form a local 256-D descriptor.

3.2 Parameters Setting

We choose the following four kinds of kernels to construct the basic kernel matrices: Gaussian Kernel, Laplacian Kernel, Inverse Square Distance Kernel and Inverse Distance Kernel. For each kernel, we set the bandwidth parameter $\sigma \in \{10^{-6}, 10^{-4}, \ldots, 10^4, 10^6\}$. Thus in total we obtain 28 basic kernels. These kernels are consistently used in all the MKL-based algorithms in the comparisons. The kernel used in the basic SVM and A-SVM [8] is chosen as the weighted average of all the basic kernels, and all the weights are set to $1/m$, where m is the number of the basic kernels.

There are three parameters in our proposed model: α, μ and γ. Here we set them all to $\{10^{-6}, 10^{-4}, \ldots, 10^4, 10^6\}$ to find the best setting. As to the construction of the Laplacian matrix, we empirically set the number of nearest neighbors to 5 and the similarity bandwidth to 1, respectively. For the comparing algorithm A-MKL, we tune both of its parameters θ and λ in the range of $[10^{-6}, 10^6]$ rather than the empirical fixed values. For all the SVM-based algorithms (i.e. the basic SVM, A-SVM, A-MKL), we set the cost parameter C to 1 by following the parameter settings in [4]. To achieve a fair comparison, we also tune the parameters of each comparing algorithm. The best experimental result for each algorithm is reported.

3.3 Effects of Auxiliary Web Images

We first study the effects of the auxiliary web images to video tagging. Intuitively, the larger the number of the auxiliary web images is, the more the improvement of the tagging performance is gained. Nevertheless, if the number of the auxiliary images is large, the distribution difference between image and video datasets may be hardly minimized, and the training cost also increases. We test the tagging performance trend along with the number (from 200 to 2500) of the images used in each cross-media combination.

To facilitate test on the effects of the auxiliary images, we simply fix γ, μ and α to 1 and 0.01 respectively. Figure 2 shows the results for all cross-media combinations, from which the following conclusions can be derived: 1) When $\gamma = 1, \mu = 1, \alpha = 1$, for each combination we can see an obvious increasing trend at the beginning of the corresponding curve. In (b), when the number becomes larger from 200 to 1000 the MAP keeps increasing. This strongly indicates that a relatively larger number of the auxiliary images would pose more positive effects on the tagging performance; 2) When $\gamma = 1, \mu = 1, \alpha = 1$, as the number continues increasing from 1000 to 2500, the performances either hold stable (case (a)) or begin to slightly decrease (cases (b)). This gives us a hint that too many auxiliary samples may even pose some negative effects on the tagging performance; 3) When $\gamma = 0.01, \mu = 0.01, \alpha = 0.01$, the MAP curves either keep stable or slightly decrease as the number grows, which further indicates that more auxiliary images do not necessarily help improve the tagging performance.

In summary, we conclude that the number of the auxiliary images should be determined carefully. Based on the analysis mentioned above, we consistently set the number 1000 in the following experiments to keep balance between tagging performance and the training cost. For a fair comparison we also choose to use 1000 images as the auxiliary source for both A-MKL and A-SVM.

Combination	SVM	SSL	A-MKL	A-SVM	CMTT
MIR&TREC	72.2 ± 1.4	71.7 ± 1.3	73.2 ± 1.7	72.4 ± 1.9	$\mathbf{77.6 \pm 0.9}$
NUS&TREC	53.0 ± 0.6	50.8 ± 1.6	48.6 ± 0.7	53.1 ± 1.0	$\mathbf{61.3 \pm 1.1}$

Table 1: Mean Average Precision (%) of all the comparing algorithms on two cross-media combinations of image and video datasets.

3.4 Comparisons with Existing Methods

In this part we compare the CMTT model with several existing learning methods. The results are shown in Table 1. We derive the following conclusions from these results: 1) In both cases, the proposed CMTT consistently gains the best performances among all the comparing algorithms. The CMTT gains around 6% and 10% performance improvement over these algorithms. This phenomenon clearly shows the general effectiveness of our proposal; 2) The CMTT always performs better than the SSL for both combinations. If we regard the SSL as the "non-transfer" version of our proposal, we have reasons to believe that our model really leads to positive knowledge transfer from images to videos. Figure 3 shows some examples of video tagging with and without tag transfer respectively; 3) As mentioned above, compared with two state-of-the-art transfer learning methods, the CMTT performs better all the time. We believe that it is because our model is able to explore the intrinsic data structure of both labeled and unlabeled data, and the information indeed helps build better tagging models; 4) When comparing the effects of different auxiliary image sources, we observe that for all the comparing algorithms, MIRFlickr always performs better than NUS-WIDE (around 10 – 16% improvement). The main reason lies in the different qualities of the tagging ground-truth. As far as we know, MIRFlicr is a full-manual tagged image dataset [5] while NUS-WIDE is a semi-manual tagged one [3].

4. CONCLUSION

In this paper, we derive a novel cross-media video tagging scheme, namely Cross-Media Tag Transfer (CMTT). which is able to transfer tag knowledge from image to video. It extends graph-based semi-supervised learning model for inferring tags by exploring the underlying image and video data structures. To handle the unseen videos, an explicit mapping function is learnt with multiple kernel ridge regression. Extensive experiments on two image and video cross-media combinations show the effectiveness of our proposal.

Figure 3: Examples of video tagging with tag transfer (CMTT) and without tag transfer (SSL).

5. REFERENCES

[1] J. L. Akira Yanagawa, Alexander C. Loui and S.-F. Chang. Kodak consumer video benchmark data set: concept definition and annotation, 2008.

[2] K. M. Borgwardt, A. Gretton, M. J. Rasch, H.-P. Kriegel, B. Schölkopf, and A. J. Smola. Integrating structured biological data by kernel maximum mean discrepancy. *Bioinformatics*, 22:e49–e57, 2006.

[3] T.-S. Chua, J. Tang, R. Hong, H. Li, Z. Luo, and Y.-T. Zheng. Nus-wide: A real-world web image database from national university of singapore. In *CIVU*, 2009.

[4] L. Duan, D. Xu, I. W.-H. Tsang, and J. Luo. Visual event recognition in videos by learning from web data. In *CVPR*, pages 1959–1966, 2010.

[5] M. J. Huiskes and M. S. Lew. The mir flickr retrieval evaluation. In *MIR*, 2008.

[6] F. Nie, D. Xu, I.-H. Tsang, and C. Zhang. Flexible manifold embedding: A framework for semi-supervised and unsupervised dimension reduction. *TIP*, 19(7):1921 –1932, 2010.

[7] T. Ojala, M. Pietikainen, and D. Harwood. A comparative study of texture measures with classification based on featured distributions. *PR*, 29:51–59, 1996.

[8] J. Yang, R. Yan, and A. G. Hauptmann. Cross-domain video concept detection using adaptive svms. In *ACM Multimedia*, pages 188–197, 2007.

[9] Y. Yang, Y. Zhuang, F. Wu, and Y. Pan. Harmonizing hierarchical manifolds for multimedia document semantics understanding and cross-media retrieval. *TMM*, 10(3):437–446, 2008.

[10] X. Zhu. Semi-supervised learning literature survey, 2008.

Detection of Pornographic Content in Internet Images*

Srinivasan H Sengamedu
Yahoo! Labs Bangalore
shs@yahoo-inc.com

Subhajit Sanyal
Yahoo! Labs Bangalore
subhajit@yahoo-inc.com

Sriram J. Sathish
Yahoo! Bangalore
thiru@yahoo-inc.com

ABSTRACT

Pornographic image detection is an important and challenging problem. Detection of pornography on the Internet is even more challenging because of the scale (billions of images) and diversity (small to very large images, graphic, grey scale images, etc.) of image content. The performance requirements (precision, recall, and speed) are also very stringent. Because of this, no single technique provides the required performance. In this paper, we describe a framework for detecting images with pornographic content. The framework combines various techniques based on object-level and pixel-level analysis of image content. To enable high-precision, we detect body parts (including faces) in images. For high-recall, low-level techniques like color and texture features are used. For adaptation to new datasets, we also support learning of appropriate color models from weakly-labeled datasets. In addition to image-based analysis, both text-based and site-level analysis are performed. Unlike many adult detection techniques, we explicitly leverage techniques like texture analysis and face detection for *non-adult* content identification. The multiple cues are combined in a systematic manner using ROC analysis and boosting. Evaluations on real world web data indicate that the system has the best performance among the systems compared.

Categories and Subject Descriptors

I.4.9 [**Computing Methodologies**]: Image Processing and Computer Vision—*Applications*

General Terms

Algorithms

Keywords

Adult Image Detection, Body part detection

*Area Chair: Marcel Worring

MM'11, November 28–December 1, 2011, Scottsdale, Arizona, USA.

1. INTRODUCTION

Image and video content and consumption on the Internet is increasing at a rapid rate. There is a proliferation of image and video sharing sites (Flickr, YouTube, etc.) and image and video search engines (Bing, Google, Yahoo, etc.). While pornographic content exists both in textual and media forms, it is hard to ignore visual forms of adult content. Hence all image and video sites have designated adult modes (like *SafeSearch Off*) and explicit adult content is permitted only in these modes. While these modes address the user intent problem, the content aspect – identification of adult content – is hard to address. Automatic detection of adult content is challenging because of the scale and diversity of image content on the Internet.

Scale: Internet today is estimated to contain about 100 billion images.

Diversity: There is a wide range in the size, resolution, and quality of images on the Internet (not to speak about the file formats). The nature of image content ranges from professionally created to user uploaded, very low to very high resolutions, very small to very large sizes, binary and gray scale images to full color images, cartoon and edited images to camera captured images, and so on.

Because of the large volume of media content on the web, it is impossible to editorially screen the content. Hence automated techniques for identifying adult visual (image/video) content are required. We have not come across a single system that grapples with this complexity.

The performance requirements are very stringent. False positives (non-adult images detected as adult) impact coverage while false negatives (adult images classified as non-adult) impact the user experience. Hence it is necessary to reduce both with higher emphasis on false negative reduction.

There has been a fair amount of research on this problem. See [1, 7, 5] for a representative sample. The following are the common disadvantages of these.

1) All of the approaches are based on low-level image processing techniques: use of color and edge features. While skin color models are fast and have shown some promise in face tracking in video applications, exclusive reliance on skin color models for the important problem of pornography detection is very limiting.

2) Most of the skin color models require pixel-level labels for learning. This makes it hard to adapt skin color models to new class of images like cell phone images or ethnicity/region-specific image collections.

3) Since all machine learning techniques "leak", most ap-

proaches use multiple techniques for pornography detection. Systematic combination of these techniques has also not been addressed.

While the challenges of Internet-scale adult detection have been emphasized so far, Internet also provides a unique opportunity: images do not occur in isolation. Images occur in web pages which often contain text. Images also occur in sites and adult images do not occur in isolation in adult sites.

The specific research contributions of this paper are listed in Section 2.

2. ADULT IMAGE DETECTION – FRAMEWORK

Before delving into the details of our solution, we list in this section the high-level principles that guide the solution.
Adult Images – Semantic view: An image is adult because it contains specific body parts and not because of skin exposure.
Non-adult Images – Semantic view: If a face (or any other object known to be non-adult) occupies a large part of an image, the image is less likely to be adult. A large fraction of web images contain faces and hence face detection is important.
Adult and Non-adult Images – Low-level view: While adult detection can be done in principle only with object detection, because of the limitations of object detection technologies, low-level features can be used to augment the semantic approach. Here again, we observe an interesting duality: Images which contain large amount of skin color are likely to be adult while images which contain large amount of texture are likely to be non-adult.
Learnable Models: To be applicable to a wide variety of datasets, it should be easy to learn the skin color and texture models with only weakly labeled training data.
Multiple Cues: In addition to image content, text provides an important signal in web applications.
Combining multiple cues: The cues should be combined in multiple ways for flexibility of application.
Site-level signals: We also use the information that images occur in sites for classification. For concreteness and simplicity of exposition, we describe a system that embodies the above principles. The next section provides an overview of the system.

3. SYSTEM OVERVIEW

Images on the Internet and in particular pornographic images have wide intra-class variability. In view of this, our system assembles a battery of techniques each of which addresses the problem from *complementary* aspects. In what follows we enumerate the various components of our system.

Stream identification: We broadly classify images as *photo* and *graphics*. Photos are images captured using cameras and graphics images are synthetic. Internet also contains images of mixed type – captioned images, photos with synthetic background, etc. Hence we further categorize the images into five different streams based on the applicability of techniques. The streams are listed below.
Stream 1: color photos which have some skin-colored regions.
Stream 2: color photos without any skin-colored regions.
Stream 3: gray-scale photos.
Stream 4: images with graphic/non-photorealistic content.
Stream 5: photos which are embedded in a synthetic background.
For *graphics/photo* classification, we use histogram-based techniques: graphic images have peaked histograms while for photos, the histogram is relatively flat. Entropy of histogram characterizes their shape: for flat histograms the entropy value is high while it is low if the histogram is sharply peaked. Apart from the entropy based disambiguation, we also use χ^2 test to ascertain how closely frequency distribution in the histogram is consistent with the uniform distribution. If the consistency with the uniform distribution is high, the image is likely to be natural while for low consistency, it is likely to be a graphics image. For *color/gray* scale classification, we explicitly check if for every pixel in the image the difference between the red and green values and red and blue values are both close to zero (and do not just rely on image headers). To detect *skin*-colored regions in an image, we use a combination of the skin-color models described in the works of Forsyth et al. [1] and Jones et al. [3].

Images with photographic content embedded large plain backgrounds are very common on the Internet. Because of the large flat background, the histogram is peaked and the images are classified as graphics. Since several adult images have this property, we postprocess Stream 4 images by removing the background. The rest of the image is subjected to Graphics/Photo classification. Any image classified as Photo in this stage is labeled Stream 5.

This categorization allows us to selectively apply various techniques to images of different types. As an obvious example, a technique based on skin color detection is not applicable for gray-scale images while body-part detection cannot be applied on graphics.

Body part detection: The presence of certain human body parts in an image can be indicative of whether the image is pornographic or otherwise. Our system utilizes techniques of object detection to detect and identify various body parts in images. Specifically, we have developed detectors for human face, female breasts and buttocks using the AdaBoost based object detection framework of Viola and Jones. We have developed detectors for three body parts in addition to faces: two breasts (2BR), single breasts (1BR), and buttocks (BU).

Texture analysis: A large class of benign (non-pornographic) images depict vegetation, natural and urban scenes. Such images are typically characterized by the presence of a lot of *clutter* in the images. On the other hand, a significant class of pornographic images on the Internet depict *smooth* skin-colored regions.

Since Gabor functions are non-orthogonal, one can define a carefully selected subset of Gabor functions for image description. [4] defines Gabor wavelets that are approximately complete and orthogonal. The coefficients of the Gabor representation then constitute the features to the classifier. In our work, we use a simple k-NN classifier for segregating adult and non-adult images.

Color analysis: We propose a new technique called *Bag of Colors* that represents an image as a bag of *scalar quantized* color values. Before computing Bag of Colors, each image is resized to a fixed size to address scale variations. The technique uses a normalized color representation for each pixel.

$$r = R/(R+G+B), \quad g = G/(R+G+B) \quad (1)$$

The color representation for each pixel (r, g) is scalar quantized to 12 bits (6 bits each for r and g). Each pixel is now represented by a color "word". An image is the collection of color words it contains.

We start from a training set of adult and non-adult images. Each image is converted into the bag of colors representation and an SVM (Support Vector Machine) is trained to discriminate between adult and non-adult images. This technique is very fast and has a throughput of 1000 image classifications per minute. The model based on bigrams of color words is more precise but is somewhat slower. In this model, bigram color words are computed by concatenating the color words of adjacent pixels p_i and p_{i+1}.

Blob analysis: Pornographic images often depict nude subjects in complex postures. Body part detectors typically fail to cover a wide range of poses. To handle such images, we adopt a skin color-based segmentation technique followed by characterizing the shapes of segmented regions.

The skin regions in adult images tend to be concentrated in contiguous regions. On the other hand, skin-colored pixels in non-adult images tend to be less contiguous. By quantifying the shape and distribution of the skin blobs, it is possible to distinguish between adult and non-adult images.

The shape of skin blobs in an image is characterized with statistical moments. To account for the changes in scale and orientation, we use affine invariant moments and Hu moments [6]. In addition to Hu moments, the distribution of the skin blobs in images is quantified with features like the relative size of the largest blob, the number of small, medium, and large blobs, etc. A decision tree is trained to discriminate between adult and non-adult images based on the skin blob features. The shape analysis stage flags both adult and benign images.

Text analysis: For images on the Internet, the textual context provides a wealth of information. This can be appropriately used to bridge the "semantic gap" in the algorithmic understanding of image content obtained by pixel level analysis. We use naive Bayes classifier for text classification.

Combined classification: The various components of our system as described above can independently classify whether an image is pornographic or not. An important aspect is to combine the verdicts of each of these component classifiers so as to optimize the performance of the composite system. In this context we have explored two different approaches, one optimized for speed and the other optimized for recall. Section 4 describes in detail these two approaches.

Site-based aggregation: Because of the inherent limitations of images processing techniques, it is not possible to detect *all* adult images in a site. Internet contains several adult sites in which most of the images are adult. Hence if we detect a large fraction of images in a site as adult, we blacklist the entire site. Section 5 contains a description of site-level blacklisting and site-level scoring of images.

4. COMBINED CLASSIFICATION

In the previous section, we discussed in detail the various components of our system. Each of the components is a classifier and there are several possible ways in which the classifier results can be combined to obtain a verdict about an image. The particular ordering of the various components can be determined through an *ROC analysis* or *boosting*.

Pipelined approach: Various orderings of the components and thresholds for each component classifiers provide a different operating points on an ROC. From the ROC, the optimal operating point is selected which in turn provides an ordering of the components and their respective thresholds. After the component ordering is selected, some of the stages (texture, blob-based, and bag of colors) are retrained to ensure that they performed well on the examples missed by the earlier stages.

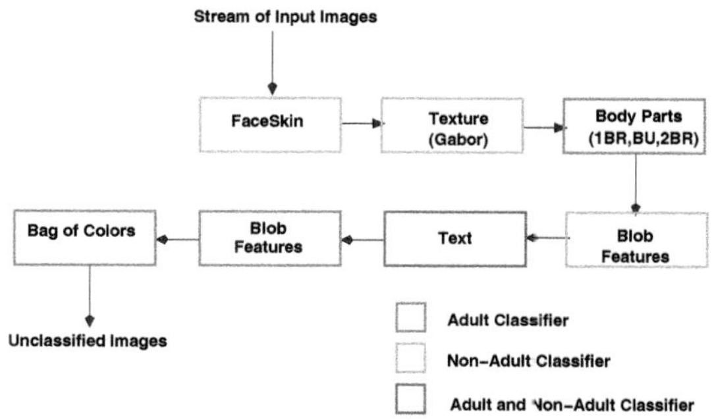

Figure 1: The adult image detection pipeline.

Boosting-based score combination: In this approach, the scores of individual techniques are combined to form a feature vector. A Gentle AdaBoost model [2] is trained as a binary classifier. This classifier is a decision tree compared to the decision stump of pipelined approach.

5. SITE-BASED AGGREGATION

Site blacklisting: Web sites rarely contain isolated adult images. If a Web site contains a large number of adult images, showing non-adult images from the site as search results often results in poor user experience: if the user wishes to examine the original image and visits the referring page, they are likely to see pornographic content. Hence blacklisting sites which contain a large number of adult images often leads to enhanced user experience. We calculate the *adult score* of a site as the fraction of images detected as adult. If the adult score of a site exceeds a threshold, we blacklist the site.

Site-based Image blocking: On the Internet, it is common for an image to be present in multiple contexts (webpages/web-sites). Hence with each image, we associate the adult scores of sites hosting the image. The final adult score of the image is the maximum or minimum scores of the associated site scores. Note that choosing the maximum increases the recall while choosing the minimum increases precision. If the adult score exceeds a threshold, the image is classified as adult.

6. EXPERIMENTAL RESULTS

In this section, we present the experimental results on the performance of the entire system as well those of individual components. The results show that the proposed system has the best performance among published systems.

Dataset: The dataset used for evaluation was obtained randomly sampling of 67850 images from a large image search index (of a few billion images in size). Hence this dataset

Dataset	Stream1	Stream2	Stream3	Stream4	Total
Full	45366	12369	3729	6386	67850
Adult	1155	14	18	19	1206
Non-adult	44211	12355	3711	6367	66644

Table 1: Database and Stream Statistics

Approach	TP	FP
Pipelined	86%	6%
Pipelined + Boosted + Site-based	95%	14%

Table 2: Performance of the system for two different approaches

Stage	Adult		Non-adult	
	TP	FN	FP	TN
Face & Skin	–	2.0	–	7.1
Texture	–	1.9	–	26.6
1BR	17.4	–	1.2	–
BU	26.8	–	1.3	–
2BR	4.4	–	0.4	–
BlobB	–	2.1	–	19.8
Text-A	27.5	–	4.3	–
Text-B	–	9.3	–	36.5
BlobA	0.43	–	0.11	–
BOC	6.8	–	1.1	–

Table 3: Performance of individual stages for Stream 1 images. The numbers are percentages.

is representative of the image composition on the Internet. The images in this dataset were editorially labeled as "Adult" or "Non-adult" images. The resulting dataset had 1206 adult-images and 66644 non-adult images. See Table 1 for the number of images in each stream for this dataset.

As can be seen, the ratio of pornographic to non-pornographic images is extremely skewed, with the pornographic images covering less than 2% of the database. Thus any system which classifies all the images as non-pornographic will have an accuracy of over 98%. Since the design goal is to have high adult-detection rate, we report TP rate and FP rate.

Training: To train the various body part detectors, we used approximately thousand cropped samples for each part and several thousand negative samples. For the negative samples special care was taken to ensure a good mix of natural scenes, objects and benign body parts (parts of faces, arms etc). To train and validate the other image based techniques, we used subsets of a database of approximately 7000 pornographic and 100000 non-pornographic images. Note that the training data requirements of low-level techniques are less demanding because of image-level labels and not region-level labels are required.

Performance: Table 2 gives the performance of the system for the pipeline based approach and the AdaBoost-based score combination strategy. It can be seen that the pipelined approach has higher precision (fewer false positives) while the boosting-based approach has high recall. The pipelined approach is twice as fast as the boosting-based approach. We are aware of only one *recent* system [5] which has been benchmarked on a similar test set. This system has 50% recall with 10% false positives or 90% recall with 35% false positives. Hence the system described in this paper has the best performance among the systems we are aware of.

To provide insights into the workings of the system, we provide stage-wise performance of Stream 1 images. Table 3 provides the percentage of adult and non-adult images detected by each stage of the pipeline – i.e., that each stage sees only the images left unclassified by the previous stage.

It can be seen from Table 3 that body parts are very effective in detecting adult images. In fact, almost 50% of adult images are detected by body part detectors. It can also be seen that texture plays a major role in detecting non-adult images. More than a quarter of non-adult images are detected by texture stage.

Another thing to note is the effectiveness of text – text classification is able to detect about a quarter of adult and about about a third non-adult images. Compared to image-based stages, text-stages are not very precise. The false detections are almost 5 times compared to image stages. And finally, blob-based detector are good in determining non-adult images.

The techniques described above have been implemented on the Hadoop platform. One run on a sample corpus of 1.2 billion images using a cluster with 4000 computational units takes about 100 hours.

7. DISCUSSION

In this paper, we have presented a framework and a system for detecting pornographic content in Internet images. To address the variability in the class of pornographic images, our system utilizes an assortment of both high-level and low-level image processing techniques. The high-level components address the problem from a "semantic" viewpoint by employing suitable detectors for various human body parts. The low-level techniques utilize color and texture information in a principled fashion to address pornographic images where the body part detectors are ineffective. The verdicts from the various components of our system are combined in various ways to get a consolidated judgment about an image. We have presented two different approaches for combining the verdicts/scores of the component classifiers: a pipelined approach which is designed for speed of processing, and a boosting-based scheme, which is suitable for high *recall*. Our system also uses textual content associated with the images. The experimental results show that our system has the best TP and FP rates among state of the art systems.

8. REFERENCES

[1] M. Fleck, D. Forsyth, and C. Bregler. Finding naked people. In *ECCV*, 1996.

[2] J. Friedman, T. Hastie, and R. Tibshirani. Additive logistic regression: a statistical view of boosting. Technical report, Dept. of Statistics, Stanford University, 2006.

[3] M. J. Jones and J. M. Rehg. Statistical color models with applications to skin detection. Technical report, Cambridge Research Laboratory, 1998.

[4] B. S. Manjunath and W. Y. Ma. Texture features for browsing and retrieval of image data. *PAMI*, 1996.

[5] H. A. Rowley, Y. Jing, and S. Baluja. Large scale image-based adult content filtering. In *Int. Conf. Computer Vision Theory & Applications*, 2006.

[6] M. Sonka, V. Hlavac, and R. Boyle. *Image Processing, Analysis and Machine Vision.* Prentice-Hall, 1999.

[7] J. Wang, J. Li, G. Wiederhold, and O. Firschein. System for screening objectionable images. *Computer Communications Journal*, 1998.

Effective Summarization of Large-Scale Web Images

Chunlei Yang
Dept of Computer Science
UNC-Charlotte
Charlotte, NC 28223, USA
cyang36@uncc.edu

Jialie Shen
School of Information Systems
Singapore Management University
Singapore, Singapore
jlshen@smu.edu.sg

Jianping Fan
Dept of Computer Science
UNC-Charlotte
Charlotte, NC 28223, USA
jfan@uncc.edu *

ABSTRACT

In this paper, we present a novel framework to achieve effective summarization of large-scale web images by treating the problem of automatic image summarization as the problem of dictionary learning for sparse coding, e.g., the summary of a given image set can be treated as a sparse representation of the given image set (i.e., sparse dictionary for the given image set). For a given semantic category (i.e., certain object class or image concept), we build a sparsity model to reconstruct all its relevant images by using a subset of most representative images (i.e., image summary); and a stepwise basis selection algorithm is developed to learn such sparse dictionary (i.e., image summary) by minimizing an explicit optimization function. By investigating their reconstruction ability, the reconstruction Mean Square Error (MSE) is adapted to objectively measure the performance of various algorithms for automatic image summarization. Our experimental results demonstrate that our dictionary learning for sparse representation algorithm can obtain more accurate summary as compared with other baseline algorithms for automatic image summarization.

Categories and Subject Descriptors

I.2.10 [**Artificial Intelligence**]: Vision and Scene Understanding - *Perceptual Reasoning.*

General Terms

Algorithms, Measurement, Experimentation

Keywords

Automatic image summarization, sparse coding, dictionary learning

*Area chair: Lexing Xie

1. INTRODUCTION

As a fundamental building block to enable interactive image navigation and exploration, automatic image summarization aims to select a small set of the most representative images for highlighting large amounts of images briefly.[3]. Most existing techniques focus on selecting a small set of the most representative images to highlight the most significant visual properties of a given image set in large size [3]. Thus the issue of automatic image summarization can be treated as an optimization problem, e.g., selecting a small set of the most representative images that can be used to reconstruct the original image set more effectively. If we define $\mathbf{X}$ as the original image set in large size and $\mathbf{D}$ as the summary of the given image set $\mathbf{X}$ in small size, automatic image summarization is to determine the summary $\mathbf{D}$ by minimizing the global reconstruction error:

$$\min_{\mathbf{D}} ||\mathbf{X} - f(\mathbf{D})||_F$$

The selection of the reconstruction function $f(\cdot)$ is to determine how each image in the original image set $\mathbf{X}$ can be reinterpreted by the most representative images in the summary $\mathbf{D}$. It is worth noting that all these images in the original image set $\mathbf{X}$ are represented as a set of visual features. In this paper, we define the reconstruction function $f(\cdot)$ as a small set of the most representative images in the summary $\mathbf{D}$ that can sparsely reinterpret all the images in the original image set $\mathbf{X}$. As a result, we can successfully reformulate the issue of automatic image summarization as the task of dictionary learning for sparse representation. Therefore, two research issues (automatic image summarization and dictionary learning for sparse representation) are linked together by their intrinsic coherence: both of them try to select an image subset in small size that can effectively and sufficiently reconstruct large amounts of images in the original image set.

Although automatic image summarization and dictionary learning for sparse representation have intrinsic coherence, we need to clarify that they have significant differences as well, e.g., the optimization function of the former has some unique constraints such as the fixed basis selection range, positive and L_0-norm sparsity of the coefficients. Based on this observation, we proposed a stepwise basis selection algorithm for dictionary selection and sparse coding to solve the reformulated optimization problem for automatic image summarization.

2. RELATED WORK

Existing algorithms can solve image summarization prob-

Figure 1: Demonstration for the additivity property of interest point feature.

lem simultaneously. Usually, the global distribution of an image set is investigated and image clustering is involved. In particular, Jaffe *et al.* [1] have developed a Hungarian clustering method by generating a hierarchical cluster structure and ranking the candidates according to their relevance scores. Denton *et al.*[2] have introduced the Bounded Canonical Set (BCS) by using a semidefinite programming relaxation to select the candidates, where a normalized-cut method is used for minimizing the similarity within BCS while maximizing the similarity from BCS to the rest of the image set. Other clustering techniques such as k-medoids [5] and affinity propagation [6] are also acknowledged. The global distribution of an image set can also be characterized by using a graphical model. Jing *et al.* [3] have expressed the relationship between the images with a graph structure, where the edges indicate their similarities and the nodes with the most connected edges are selected as the summary of the given image set.

On the other hand, there are iterative approaches. Some greedy-like algorithms are applied to select the best summary sequentially until sufficient number of the most representative images are picked out [4]. Simon *et al.* [4] have used a greedy method to select the best candidate by using some important summarization measurements such as likelihood, coverage and orthogonality. The greedy method focuses on selecting the most representative images while penalizing the appearances of the similar images.

Distinguished from the existing approaches, our proposed approach for automatic image summarization characterizes the representativeness of the image summary explicitly by optimizing a reformulated reconstruction function. We will demonstrate that automatic image summarization can be achieved more effectively by solving a problem of dictionary learning for sparse representation.

3. AUTOMATIC IMAGE SUMMARIZATION

The research aims to generate the visual summary for each semantic category (i.e., one certain object class or image concept). Given a semantic category, we extract a set of key-points from all the relevant images and the SIFT [7] descriptors are used for image content representation. All the key-points for the given semantic category are then partitioned into l clusters by using the affinity propagation algorithm and the cluster centroids for all these l clusters are used to construct a l-dimension codeword dictionary. For each relevant image, we further conduct a vector quantization of all its key-points according to the codeword dictionary. As a result, the feature vector for image representation is a normalized l-dimension histogram.

The normalized feature vector indicates the distribution of the codeword for the given image, or the probability of the appearance of the codewords in the given image. From this observation, we assume that the feature vector histogram of one given image can approximately be reconstructed by a weighted linear combination of the feature vector histograms of other images as demonstrated in Figure 1. To obtain the maximum reconstruction power, we try to minimize the overall reconstruction error:

$$\min \sum_{i=1}^{n} ||\mathbf{x}_i - \sum_{j=1}^{k} \mathbf{d}_j \alpha_{ji}||_2 \tag{1}$$

The codewords $\{\mathbf{d}_j\}$ are a set of most representative images that are selected from the original image set. The size of the most representative images $\{\mathbf{d}_j\}$ is determined by a trade-off between concise summarization and accurate reinterpretation: a small size of the most representative images $\{\mathbf{d}_j\}$ means more concise summary but the reinterpretation power may reduce; on the other hand, a large size of the most representative images $\{\mathbf{d}_j\}$ guarantees a better reinterpretation performance but the summary may be verbose. $\{\alpha_{ji}\}$ is a set of the sparse coefficients to guarantee that each image in the same semantic category can be represented by a limited number of the most representative images in the summary. Considering the reasonable complexity of the visual content of an image, bringing the sparsity is necessary (we will elaborate the choice of sparsity in the experiment section). To satisfy this condition, L_0-norm is taken into consideration. Given the image set X for the given semantic category, we formally rewritten Eq.(1) in the matrix form as follows:

$$\begin{aligned} \min_{\mathbf{D},\mathbf{A}} \quad & ||\mathbf{X} - \mathbf{DA}||_F \\ s.t. \quad & ||\alpha_i||_0 \leq t, i = 1, 2, ..., k. \end{aligned} \tag{2}$$

where $\mathbf{X} = \{\mathbf{x}_i | i = 1, 2, ..., n\} \in \mathbb{R}^{l \times n}$ is the original image set, l is the dimension of the feature vector, n is the total number of the images in the given semantic category, $\mathbf{D} = \{\mathbf{d}_i | i = 1, 2, ..., k\} \in \mathbb{R}^{l \times k}$ is the dictionary that we want to learn (i.e., summary for the given semantic category), k is the number of the codewords in this dictionary (i.e., the number of the most representative images), $\mathbf{A} \in \mathbb{R}^{k \times n}$ is the positive coefficient matrix that can be learned jointly, each column of $\mathbf{A} = \{\alpha_i | i = 1, 2, ..., n\}$ is the sparse representation for a given image and t is the corresponding sparsity. If t equals to k, the above formulation for automatic image summarization can be reduced to the k-medoids problem (the discrete form of k-means). The k-medoids algorithm is well known as one of the data summarization methods [5], thus our dictionary learning and sparse representation algorithm for automatic image summarization can be seen as an extension of the k-medoids.

In our reformulation, two aspects differ from the traditional sparse representation: 1) From the description of additivity of the local property we need to make sure the coefficients $\{\alpha_{ji}\}$ must be non-negative; 2) the dictionary $\mathbf{D}$ is selected from a group of the original images in $\mathbf{X}$ rather than a weighted combination of arbitrary images.

The optimization problem in Eq.(2) with L_0-norm penalty over the coefficients$\{\alpha_{ji}\}$ is "NP-hard"[9], thus the plan is to iteratively update the bases (codewords) and the coefficients while decreasing the reconstruction error until it stops at a stationary point. Our stepwise basis selection algorithm can be divided into two stages: (a) sparse coding stage; and (b) codeword updating stage.

Sparse coding stage: The dictionary $\mathbf{D}$ is fixed and the coefficients are updated as follows: The coefficients are learned individually for each image. For a given image x_i in the same semantic category, we initialize all its coefficients equal to zero and then find the basis of d_m which has the biggest inner product with x_i (the smallest angle between the two vectors). We gradually increase the coefficients of d_m at the positive sign direction until another basis d_o has a competitive inner product with the residual r as d_m, then we increase the coefficients at the joint direction of d_o and d_m. We repeat these operations until t coefficients are found or r decreases to zero.

Codeword updating (basis selection) stage: When the dictionary $\mathbf{D}$ and the coefficient matrix $\mathbf{A}$ are fixed, we sequentially release one of the k bases and update the released basis and the corresponding coefficient. The updating criteria is to choose the pair of $\mathbf{d}_o$ and α_o from all the $n-k+1$ candidates which can minimize the global reconstruction error e. e is calculated as :

$$\begin{aligned} e &= \sqrt{\sum_i (r_i - d_i\alpha)^2} \\ &= \sqrt{lr_i^2 + (\sum d_i^2)\alpha^2 - 2(\sum r_i d_i)\alpha} \end{aligned}$$

The minimum of $e = \sqrt{lr_i^2 - (\sum r_i d_i)^2}$ can be reached when $\alpha = \sum(r_i d_i) \backslash \sum d_i^2 = \sum(r_i d_i)$

After all the k codewords are updated, we fix the dictionary and go back to the sparse coding stage to update the coefficients. Such iteration process stops when the objective reaches a stationary point (no basis is being updated).

After the codeword updating (basis selection) stage, we have already got a set of coefficients that are good enough. The method used in sparse coding stage is greedy-like method and won't guarantee the decrease of the objective function. So we further perform another method which can guarantee the updated coefficients to decrease the objective function. This method starts matching pursuit from a given set of coefficients. It changes the values of the non-zero coefficients rather than the positions of these coefficients. The coefficient matrix A is updated by the result of two methods whichever reaches a smaller reconstruction error.

After the dictionary $\mathbf{D}$ is learned from the original image set $\mathbf{X}$ for the given semantic category, the codewords (basis) in the dictionary $\mathbf{D}$ are then treated as a good summary of the original image set $\mathbf{X}$ for the given semantic category.

4. ALGORITHM EVALUATION

To evaluate the proposed algorithm, we collected images from 1000 visual text terms and about 3000 relevant images are kept after image cleaning for each category. We then constructed a codeword dictionary of size 200. Then we apply the given codeword dictionary (200 dimensions) to quantize the key-points for each image and construct a 200-dimensional histogram of the feature vectors for each image, which can be the representation of $\mathbf{x}_i$ and $\mathbf{d}_i$ as appeared in Eq. (2). We denote the number of images in the given semantic category by N, the number of codewords by K and the sparsity by T. $\mathbf{D}$ represents the dictionary (summary) and $\mathbf{A}$ represents the coefficient matrix.

Three algorithms are introduced as the baseline algorithms in our experiments: k-medoids [5], affinity propagation [6] and Sparsifying Dictionary Selection (SDS) algorithm [8]. Our proposed algorithm are compared with the above three baseline algorithms objectively and subjectively.

The k-medoids is a typical clustering-based algorithm for automatic image summarization, k is the number of clusters (the size of the dictionary) and the medoids of each cluster is taken as the selected basis. The clustering process aims to partition the images in the original set into k clusters which can minimize the within-cluster sum of squares:

$$\min_{\mathbf{S}} \sum_{i=1}^{K} \sum_{\mathbf{x}_j \in \mathbf{S}_i} ||\mathbf{x}_j - \mathbf{d}_i||^2 \tag{3}$$

The affinity propagation algorithm partition the image set into multiple partitions. The number of partitions is affected by the preference value and thus can be binary searched. The element that has the minimum average distance to the rest of the cluster is selected as the basis.

$$\mathbf{d} = \arg\min_{\mathbf{d}_i \in \mathbf{C}} \sum_{\mathbf{x}_j \in \mathbf{C} \backslash \mathbf{d}_i} ||\mathbf{x}_j - \mathbf{d}_i||^2 \tag{4}$$

The SDS algorithm, on the other hand, represents a series of greedy algorithms which iteratively select the current best basis. Krause *et al.* suggested in [10] that if the data collection satisfy the submodular condition then the local optimal derived by greedy algorithm is a near-optimal solution. The greedy algorithm starts with an empty dictionary $\mathbf{D}$, and at every iteration i adds a new element by:

$$\mathbf{d}_i = \arg\min_{\mathbf{d} \in \mathbf{X} \backslash \mathbf{D}} F(\mathbf{D}_{i-1} \cup \mathbf{d}) \tag{5}$$

where F is the reconstruction function. The SDS algorithm is modified to satisfy our positive coefficients constraint.

Evaluation metric: We evaluate four algorithms for automatic image summarization based on their reconstruction abilities. Specifically, the performance is evaluated by the global reconstruction error in terms of Mean Square Error (MSE):

$$\begin{aligned} MSE := &\ \tfrac{1}{N} \sum_{i=1}^{N} ||\mathbf{x}_i - \mathbf{D}\alpha_i|_2 \\ s.t. &\ ||\alpha_i||_0 \leq T \end{aligned} \tag{6}$$

Smaller MSE value represents better reconstruction ability. Thus MSE is treated as the objective metric for evaluating the performance of various algorithms for automatic image summarization.

Objective evaluation : (1) The convergence of our proposed algorithm for automatic image summarization is evaluated in terms of the number of bases being updated and the change of MSE value. We set up the experiment with the size of the dictionary equals to 20 and the sparsity equals to 6. We have observed that there are large drops of the MSE curve in the steps of 11, 21 in the sparse coding stage. During each of the sparse coding stage, the decrease of the MSE value is caused by basis updating. After 3 or 4 iterations, no basis is being updated and the corresponding sparse coefficients gradually become stable. We repeated the experiment with random initials for over 20 times and observed similar results, thus our SBS algorithms can quickly converge after around 4 or 5 iterations.

(2) Our proposed SBS algorithm performs better than the other three baseline algorithms with a lower MSE value

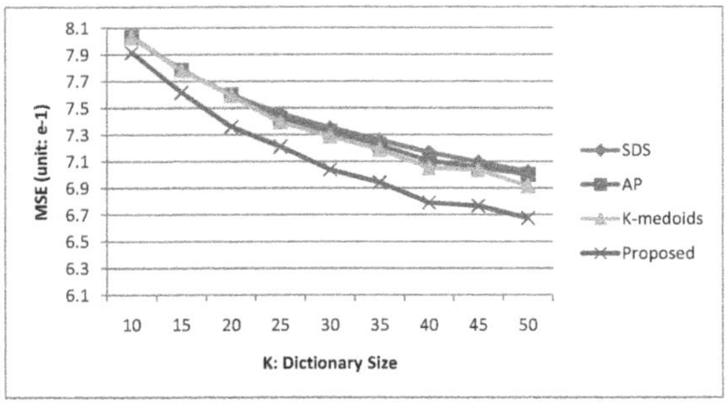

Figure 2: MSE performance evaluation in comparison with three baseline algorithms.

throughout the different choices of dictionary sizes. When the dictionary size is small (K=10), our proposed model performs similar to the baseline algorithms (with an improvement of 1.5%); as the K increases, the greedy-based algorithm performs the worst and our proposed SBS algorithm performs the best (with an improvement of 5.3%).

(3) We have also confirmed our assumption in section 3: as the dictionary size increases, the reconstruction error decreases and the summarization becomes less concise. The choice of K actually depends on the requirement of specific task.

(4) As explained in section 3, the sparsity in the image summarization problem indicates the use of a limited number of basic local visual attributes to reconstruct an image and we assumed that an image can only be composed by a limited number of salient local visual attributes. We increase the sparsity of T from 2 and observed that when T increases above 6, the reconstruction performance for the LPAR algorithm would not improve significantly, which means that most of the images in the same semantic category can sufficiently be reinterpreted by no more than 6 bases. This observation explains why we make T equals to 6 in the experiments.

Subjective evaluation: Because of the semantic gap, the MSE value may not be effective for evaluating the quality of image summary. Thus a user study is performed to evaluate the effectiveness of our proposed image summarization approach with the baseline approaches. The subjective evaluation metric is measured by the users' feedback on how well the summarization results represent the original images for the given semantic category. Our survey consists the following components : (1) 30 users (graduate students) are involved in this survey to investigate the summarization results for 15 semantic categories as listed in Table 1. In order to ease the burden from the user, the category size is reduced to 500. (2) The users are allowed to explore the image set and pick their own summary of 10 images. The summary from all the user are collected and counted, and the top 10 choices are selected as the ground truth. (3) The output from the 4 algorithms are compared with the ground truth and number of matches are reported. (4) The users will also give a relevance score scaled from 0 to 5 (5 being the best) to the four outputs based on their own judgement of relevancy. The algorithm name is hidden from the user during the process to avoid biased choice. The results reported in Table 1 indicates that our proposed dictionary learning approach has more matches and higher relevance score as compared with the baseline algorithms.

	K-med	AP	SDS	Proposed
coast	1/2.8	0/2.1	0/1.2	**5/4.8**
bridge	1/1.7	1/2.3	0/1.3	**3/3.8**
tower	1/2.2	1/2.3	0/1.0	**3/4.2**
pyramid	**2/2.8**	0/1.0	1/2.1	**2/3.6**
zoo	2/2.7	0/1.3	0/1.1	**3/4.3**
valley	0/1.5	**2/2.9**	1/1.7	1/2.2
trafficlight	0/1.4	0/1.2	1/2.1	**3/3.7**
sailboat	**2/2.7**	0/1.5	0/1.1	**2/3.2**
mountain	1/1.5	1/1.8	1/1.8	**2/3.5**
sunset	2/2.6	2/3.1	0/1.1	**4/4.7**
airport	1/1.7	**2/2.5**	0/1.1	1/2.1
streetview	0/1.5	0/1.4	1/2.3	**3/4.5**
skyscraper	0/1.2	0/1.3	1/1.9	**2/3.9**
stonehenge	**2/3.1**	1/1.6	1/2.1	1/2.7
waterfall	1/1.5	**2/2.8**	0/1.8	1/2.2
average	1.07/2.06	0.8/1.94	0.47/1.58	**2.4/3.56**

Table 1: Subjective evaluation results for 15 categories: (# of matches with the ground truth/relevance score from user)

5. CONCLUSION

Most existing algorithms for automatic image summarization have not formulated the problem explicitly and lack an objective evaluation metric. In this paper, we have discovered intrinsic coherence between the issue of automatic image summarization and the problem of dictionary learning for sparse representation, e.g., their ability to use an image subset in small size to sparsely reinterpret the original image set in large size. We utilize the knowledge from the research areas of dictionary learning and sparse coding, and explicitly reformulate the problem of automatic image summarization with a sparse representation model and solve an optimization problem by using our proposed stepwise basis selection algorithm. Our proposed algorithm outperforms the baseline algorithms in both objective and subjective evaluations.

6. REFERENCES

[1] E. Jaffe, M. Naaman, T. Tassa, M. Davis "Generating summaries for large collections of geo-referenced photographs", *Proc. Int. Conf. on World Wide Web*, 853-854, 2006.

[2] T. Denton, M. Demirci, J Abrahamson, A. Shokoufandeh, S. Dickinson, "Selecting Canonical Views for View-Based 3-D Object Recognition", *ICPR*, 2004.

[3] Y. Jing, S. Baluja, H. Rowley "Canonical Image Selection from the Web", *CIVR*, 2007.

[4] I. Simon, N. Snavelv, S. Seitz "Scene Summarization for Online Image Collections", *Intl. Conf on Computer Vision*, ICCV, pp. 1-8, 2007.

[5] Y. Hadi, F. Essannouni, R. Thami "Video Summarization by k-medoid Clustering", *ACM Symposium on Applied Computing*, SAC, 2006.

[6] B. Frey, D. Dueck "Clustering by Passing Messages Between Data Points", *Science*, 315, 972-977, 2007.

[7] D. Lowe, "Distinctive Image Features from Scale Invariant Keypoints", *Intl Journal of Computer Vision*, vol.60, pp.91-110, 2004.

[8] A. Krause, V. Cevher, "Submodular Dictionary Selection for Sparse Representation", *Proc. International Conference on Machine Learning*, ICML, 2010.

[9] B. Natarajan, "Sparse Approximate Solutions to Linear Systems", *SIAM J. COMPUT.* Vol. 24, No.2, pp.277-234, 1995.

Real-time Human Action Search using Random Forest based Hough Voting*

Gang Yu, Junsong Yuan
School of Electrical and Electronic Engineering
Nanyang Technological University, Singapore
gyu1@e.ntu.edu.sg, jsyuan@ntu.edu.sg

Zicheng Liu
Microsoft Research
Redmond, WA, USA
zliu@microsoft.com

ABSTRACT

Many existing techniques in content based video retrieval treat a video sequence as a whole to match it against a query video or to assign a text label. Such an approach has serious limitations when applied to human action retrieval because an action may occur only in a sub-region and last for a small portion of the video length. In situations like this, we essentially need to match the subvolumes of the video sequences against the query video. A naive exhaustive search is impractical due to large number of possible subvolumes for each video sequence. In this paper, we propose a novel framework for action retrieval which performs pattern matching at subvolume level and is very efficient in handling large corpus of videos. We construct an unsupervised random forest to index the video database, generate a score volume with Hough voting and then employ a max sub-path strategy to quickly search for the temporal and spatial positions of all the video sequences in the database. We present action search experiments on challenging datasets to validate the efficiency and effectiveness of our system.

Categories and Subject Descriptors

H.3.3 [[**Information Search and Retrieval**]: Retrieval models

General Terms

Algorithms, Experimentation, Theory

Keywords

Action Search, Hough Voting, Random Forest Indexing, Max Sub-path Search

1. INTRODUCTION

Human action search aims to search similar action segments from large database given a query action. It has a lot of practical uses in our daily lives, e.g., human computer interface, video surveillance, and medical diagnosis. However, this topic has been much less exploited than human action classification [3] and action detection [2] [9] [7].

[8] proposed a framework for action search which has promising experimental results on some existing benchmark datasets. With the help of random forest indexing, the problem that the limited query samples cannot model the large intra-class variations can be alleviated. Besides, by coarse-to-fine branch and bound search, the algorithm [8] can finish a one-hour database search in 26 seconds. Despite great speed advantage and superior performance, the algorithm [8] has two major drawbacks. First, it is still not acceptable to search one action in 26 seconds. For online applications, fast response is the inevitable property otherwise the user experiences would suffer. Second, there is one implicit assumption in [8]: the actions should be spatially fixed. For instance, it cannot handle the moving actions, e.g., walking. This is primarily due to the sliding window (branch and bound search) approach. If we relax the search space to include the moving volumes, it would be extremely computational prohibited.

To handle the two challenges in [8], we propose a novel action search system that can search and crop similar actions from a large corpus of video clips given an exemplar video clip. Videos are represented with spatio-temporal interest points [3]. To support fast search, we build a random forest to index all the STIP points in the database. Given a query video, we match each STIP in the query with the database based on the random forest. Given the matches, Hough voting is performed to generate a 3D score volume. The value of each element in the score volume refers to the likelihood of the region belonging to the same action type as query. By searching a sub-path within the volume, we can obtain an optimal sub-volume which is the most similar to the query action. There are three major contributions of our paper.

- We propose to use Hough voting to vote for candidate action centers, which integrates the spatial structure of interest points.
- The search problem is solved with the max sub-path search algorithm rather than the branch and bound search in [8] so that we can handle the moving actions.
- According to the experiments, we algorithm outperforms the state-of-the-art method [8] on both the accuracy and the speed.

Experiments on the benchmark MSR II [9] database and a drinking database validate the efficiency and effectiveness of our algorithm.

*Area chair: Qi Tian

MM'11, November 28–December 1, 2011, Scottsdale, Arizona, USA.

2. ALGORITHM

Our action search system mainly constitutes two components, Hough voting and max sub-path searching. Given a video database, $\mathcal{D} = \{\mathcal{V}_1 \cup \mathcal{V}_2 \cup \cdots \cup \mathcal{V}_N\}$, where $\mathcal{V}_i$ refers to a video clip and N is the number of videos. Each video can be represented by a set of spatio-temporal interest points (STIP) [3], $\mathcal{V} = \{d_i\}$. For each STIP point $d_i = [f_i, l_i]$, f_i refers to the feature description and l_i refers to its spatial-temporal location, $l_i = [\mathbf{x}_i, t_i]$. We use HOG (Histogram of Gradient) and HOF (Histogram of Flow) to describe f_i with feature dimension of 162. For action retrieval, our objective is to crop all the sub-volumes which are similar to the given query video $\mathcal{Q}$.

For simplicity, we denote $\mathcal{D} = \{d_i, i = 1, 2, \cdots, N_D\}$ as the database, where N_D is the total number of STIP points. Given a query $\mathcal{Q} = \{d_q, q = 1, 2, \cdots, N_Q\}$, we want to crop the sub-volumes with the maximum similarity score:

$$S(V^*, \mathcal{Q}) = max_{t\in[a,b],\mathbf{x},\rho} s(V_{t\in[a,b]}(\mathbf{x}, \rho), \mathcal{Q}), \quad (1)$$

where $V_{t\in[a,b]}(\mathbf{x}, \rho)$ refers to the sub-volume with temporal duration from frame a to frame b and spatial center at position $\mathbf{x}$ and spatial size at ρth level. For simplicity, we assume the spatial scale (ρ will be omitted in later discussion so that only $s(V_{t\in[a,b]}(\mathbf{x}), \mathcal{Q})$ is considered) and the spatial center does not change over time in the returned sub-volume. In the later discussion, we will show that our algorithm can be easily extended to handle different spatial scales and moving actions.

2.1 Random Forest Indexing

To index the database for fast STIP matches, we employ the unsupervised random forest structure [8]. In the off-line phase, we construct N_t trees independently and each tree is a partition over the feature space. Once a new query STIP arrives, we consider all the STIPs from the database which fall on the same leaf as the query STIP, and use those STIPs as the matches of the query STIP. There are several benefits of random forest based indexing. First of all, the trees are constructed in an unsupervised way so that they are class-independent. This is of great significance for action retrieval since we cannot determine ahead of time what kind of action a user is going to retrieve. Second, random forest based indexing is fast to evaluate. As shown in [8], it is over 300 times faster than the LSH (Local Sensitive Hashing)-accelerated nearest neighbor search scheme. Third, by adding more trees in the forest, we can make our matches more accurate. The outliers caused by the trees have little impact due to the robustness of Hough voting which will be discussed in the next section.

2.2 Hough Voting

To define the similarity function, we employ the frame based Hough voting score [4]:

$$\begin{aligned} s(V_{t\in[a,b]}(\mathbf{x}), \mathcal{Q}) &= \textstyle\sum_{t\in[a,b]} \sum_{d_q\in\mathcal{Q}} p([\mathbf{x}, t], f_q, l_q) \\ &= \textstyle\sum_{t\in[a,b]} \sum_{d_q\in\mathcal{Q}} p([\mathbf{x}, t]|f_q, l_q)p(f_q, l_q), \end{aligned} \quad (2)$$

where f_q and l_q refer to the feature description and location of the qth STIP point in the query video, respectively. $p([\mathbf{x}, t], f_q, l_q)$ is the probability that there exists a demanded action in position $[\mathbf{x}, t]$ and a matched STIP point d_q in the query. Since it is reasonable to assume a uniform prior over f_q and l_q, we have

$$s(V_{t\in[a,b]}(\mathbf{x}), \mathcal{Q}) \propto \sum_{t\in[a,b]} \sum_{d_q\in\mathcal{Q}} p([\mathbf{x}, t]|f_q, l_q). \quad (3)$$

In order to compute $p([\mathbf{x}, t]|f_q, l_q)$, the query STIP d_q should be first matched with the STIPs in $\mathcal{D}$. Although nearest neighbor search and its approximated algorithms, e.g. Local Sensitive Hashing (LSH), can give good match results, it is extremely time consuming. Thus, a random forest indexing is used here to improve the matching speed. Suppose we use N_t trees to partition the feature space, every query STIP d_q will fall into one of the leaves in tree T_i ($T_i \subset \mathcal{D}$) based on f_q. All the database STIPs that fall on the same leave as d_q are considered as the matches of d_q. Then we have

$$\begin{aligned} & s(V_{t\in[a,b]}(\mathbf{x}), \mathcal{Q}) \\ & \propto \sum_{t\in[a,b]} \sum_{d_q\in\mathcal{Q}} \textstyle\sum_i p([\mathbf{x}, t]|T_i, f_q, l_q)p(T_i|f_q, l_q) \\ & = \sum_{t\in[a,b]} \sum_{d_q\in\mathcal{Q}} \textstyle\sum_i \displaystyle\sum_{d_j\in\mathcal{D}, d_j\in T_i} p([\mathbf{x}, t], d_j|T_i, f_q, l_q)p(T_i|f_q, l_q), \end{aligned} \quad (4)$$

where $p(T_i|f_q, l_q) = \frac{1}{N_t}$. Denote N_{T_i} to be the number of points on the same leaf as d_q in tree T_i. For point j, denote its spatio-temporal location as $[\mathbf{x}^j_{(T_i)}, t^j_{(T_i)}], j = 1, 2, \cdots, N_{T_i}$. Then $p([\mathbf{x}, t]|T_i, f_q, l_q)$ can be computed with kernel density estimation:

$$p([\mathbf{x}, t]|T_i, f_q, l_q) = \frac{1}{Z} \sum_{j=1}^{N_{T_i}} exp(-\frac{||[\hat{\mathbf{x}}^j_q - \mathbf{x}, \hat{t}^j_q - t]||^2}{\sigma^2}), \quad (5)$$

where Z is a normalization constant and σ^2 is a bandwidth parameter. Suppose $l_q = [\mathbf{x}_q, t_q]$. Denote c_q to be the spatial center position of query action. Consider the video sequence from which the jth STIP point is extracted at position $[\mathbf{x}^j_{(T_i)}, t^j_{(T_i)}]$. This point casts a vote for the action position in this video sequence. The voted action position, $[\hat{\mathbf{x}}^j_q, \hat{t}^j_q]$, is computed as

$$\begin{aligned} \hat{\mathbf{x}}^j_q &= \mathbf{x}^j_{(T_i)} - \rho(\mathbf{x}_q - c_q) \\ \hat{t}^j_q &= t^j_{(T_i)}. \end{aligned} \quad (6)$$

By setting different ρ, we can handle action sub-volumes with different scales.

Although Hough voting is widely used in image analysis, it is much less exploited in the action retrieval literature. Our Hough voting strategy has the following advantages. First, its computational complexity is much lower than that of branch and bound search. Suppose the number of trees in a forest is N_t, the tree depth is t_d, the total number of STIPs in the database is N_D, and the number of STIPs in the query video is N_Q. Let us assume the STIPs in the database are unformly distributed over different leaves of each tree. Then the computational complexity of our Hough voting step is in average $O(N_t t_d N_Q + N_t \lceil \frac{N_D}{2^{t_d}} \rceil N_Q)$. In comparison, the complexity of branch and bound is at least proportional to the size of the spacetime volume, which is much larger than the number of interest points N_Q. As shown in Table. 2, the computational cost for Hough voting step is very small. Second, the Hough voting algorithm integrates the spatial context of different STIP into consideration. This enables us to have a more accurate search results compared with point based branch and bound search [7]. Third, the Hough voting step can be seamlessly integrated into our action search framework. In [7] Hough voting is utilized to refine the spatial locations of detections in the optional refine step. This is different from our work where Hough voting is to vote for the candidate action centers.

2.3 Sub-volume Search

After Hough voting, we have a 3D score volume (if we want to handle spatial scale changes of actions, it should be 4D score volume). What we need to do is to locate the temporal location a, b and spatial center $\mathbf{x}$ in Eq. 2. This problem is traditionally known as *Maximum Subarray Problem* [1]. Since the elements of our score volume are always non-negative, we constrain the size of the sub-volume by adding a regularization term. The score function Eq. 4 is further defined as:

$$\hat{s}(V_{t\in[a,b]}(\mathbf{x}), \mathcal{Q}) = s(V_{t\in[a,b]}(\mathbf{x}), \mathcal{Q}) + (b-a+1)\lambda S, \quad (7)$$

where λ is a small negative constant and S is spatial size of the action. Alg. 1 gives an illustration of our algorithm. We perform 1D sub-array search over different spatial position and locate a subarray with the maximum summation (Line 1 - 15). Based on the maximum summation, we can back-travel to locate the sub-path (Line 16 - 19). From the searched subarray, we can get the location of the retrieved sub-volume, i.e. a, b and $\mathbf{x}$.

In order to handle multiple scale action search, we can simply extend 3D score volume to 4D score volume with several scale levels and add another loop over different scales. Suppose our database is of spatial extent $M \times N$ and temporal duration T and further assume we consider the number of scale levels as S, the computational complexity of our sub-volume search is $O(MNTS)$. In our experiments below, S is fixed as 3. Hence, our sub-volume search is superior to branch and bound search in [7, 9] whose worst complexity is $O(M^2N^2T)$.

So far, we have assumed that the spatial position of an action does not change over time. We can relax this assumption by using the method of [6] to handle the moving actions, e.g., walking.

Algorithm 1 Maximum Sub-array Search

Input:
3D score volume $F \in \mathbb{R}^{M\times N\times T}$
Output:
Location of sub-volume $V_{t\in[a,b]}(\mathbf{z})$, i.e. $a, b, \mathbf{z} = (x, y)$
1: **for** $i = 1$ to M **do**
2: **for** $j = 1$ to N **do**
3: Set $c := 0$, $g := -\inf$
4: **for** $t = 1$ to T **do**
5: Set $c := c + F(i, j, t)$
6: **if** $c < 0$ **then**
7: Set $c := 0$
8: **end if**
9: **if** $c > g$ **then**
10: Set $g := c$
11: Set $b := t, x := i, y := j$
12: **end if**
13: **end for**
14: **end for**
15: **end for**
16: Set $a := b$
17: **while** $a > 1$ and $g > 0$ **do**
18: Set $g := g - F(i, j, t), a := a - 1$
19: **end while**

2.4 Implementation details

Since speed is an important aspect for action search system, we employ several methods to reduce the computational cost. Similar to [7], we down-sample the 3D score volume, both spatially and temporally. The difference between [7] and our Hough voting framework is that in [7], an interest point votes for any sub-volume that contains this point while in our framework, an interest point votes for a particular sub-volume whose center is specified. In other words, the relative spatial information is thrown away in [7] while we take advantage of the relative spatial information.

By spatial down-sampling of score volume, it is possible for us to handle high-resolution videos, e.g. 720p and 1080p, which are quite popular nowadays. Besides, with the help of temporal down-sampling, we can deal with extremely large datasets. In our experiments, we set the spatial-downsampling factor as 8 and temporal-downsampling factor as 2. As shown in Table. 1 and Table. 2, our action search system is superior to [8] not only on the precision but also on the speed.

3. EXPERIMENTS

Although action retrieval is extensively exploited before, action search with localization is little discussed in the literature. In order to evaluate our system, we compare with the recent work [8] and action detection [2]. Since they reported quantitative experiment results on MSR II dataset [9], it is easier for us to compare our results with theirs.

3.1 Experiments on MSRII

To give a quantitative results of our action retrieval system, MSR II is employed as a database for search. Three actions, handclapping, handwaving and boxing, are tested. The query videos are randomly drawn from KTH [5]. The evaluation measure is the same as [8]. To compute the precision we consider a true detection if: $\frac{\text{Volume}(V\cap G)}{\text{Volume}(G)} > \frac{1}{8}$, where G is the annotated ground truth subvolume, and V is the detected subvolume. On the other hand, to compute the recall we consider a hit if: $\frac{\text{Volume}(V\cap G)}{\text{Volume}(V)} > \frac{1}{8}$.

Three algorithms are evaluated. They are (i) branch & bound action retrieval [8], (ii) cross-dataset action detection [2] and (iii) our Hough voting based retrieval system. Since (ii) is a detection algorithm, it utilized all the available data (around 256 video clips) for training. Average precisions for handclapping, handwaving and boxing actions are listed in Table. 1. In order to handle boxing action with different directions, (i) flipped the query video and provide both clips as query. However, in our system (iii), we do not flip the query video, and only use the original clip as the query. According to the quantitative results, our algorithm outperforms the state-of-the-art action retrieval system. Due to the space limitation, we only give one illustrating example of handwaving action with top-7 retrieved results in Fig. 1. The regions marked with blue color indicate the retrieved spatial location of the action.

3.2 Experiments on wild videos

Another illustrating example is shown here with a wild video database. The database is downloaded from the Youtube

Figure 1: Top-7 retrieved results of handwaving action from MSR II database.

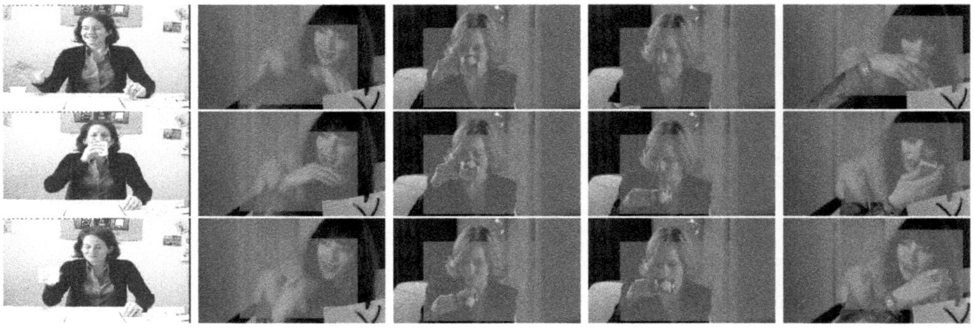

Figure 2: Action retrieval results on a Hollywood movie segment. A three second long query video with drinking action is shown in the first column where the images on the three rows in this column are its sample frames. The second to fifth column list the top-4 retrieved results, respectively.

Action Type	B&B Search [8]	Action Detection [2]	Our Method
handclapping	0.2397	0.1316	**0.3609**
handwaving	0.4301	0.3671	**0.5415**
boxing	0.3029	0.1748	**0.3166**

Table 1: Average precisions for action retrieval and action detection on MSR II database. The second and fourth columns are for action retrieval. The third column is for action detection.

and comes from one part of the movie called *"Coffee and Cigarettes"*. It contains 3415 frames and includes several drinking actions. We choose a query video with drinking action around 3 seconds long and 99 frames. Fig. 2 shows the top 4 retrieved results. The first column are the query video where the three rows in the column are the example frames from the video. The second to fifth columns are the top 4 retrieved videos. The second column and the fifth column are false detections. The reason for the false detections is that the motions in the two instances are similar to the drinking motion.

3.3 Computational Cost

Table. 2 shows the total computation cost (CPU time only) for branch and bound search system [8] and our system. We use a single PC with 2.6GHz CPU and 3G memory, which is almost the same environment as in [8]. We can see that our max sub-path search algorithm is 30 times faster than branch and bound action search. Overall, our system is over 10 times faster than [8].

4. CONCLUSION

We proposed an action search system which is superior to the state-of-the-art methods in terms of both the precision and the computational cost. By indexing the video database with a random forest, our frame-based Hough voting obtains a 3D score volume very efficiently. The computational cost can be further reduced by spatial and temporal down-sampling of the score volume. With the max sub-path search, our algorithm quickly detects the spatio-temporal positions of the action instances in the video database. The experiments validate the effectiveness and efficiency of our proposed system.

Method	B&B Search [8]	Our Method
Voting time (s)	0.6	1.5
Search time (s)	24.1	0.8
Total Time (s)	24.7	2.3

Table 2: Comparison of the total computation time of two action retrieval systems. The query video is 20 seconds long and the database consists of 54 high resolution videos with a total length of one hour. The task is to retrieve the 7 best matches from the database.

Acknowledgement

This work was supported in part by the Nanyang Assistant Professorship (SUG M58040015) to Dr. Junsong Yuan.

5. REFERENCES

[1] J. Bentley. Programming pearls: algorithm design techniques. *Communications of the ACM*, 27(9):865–873, 1984.
[2] L. Cao, Z. Liu, and T. S. Huang. Cross-dataset action detection. In *CVPR*, pages 1998–2005, 2010.
[3] I. Laptev. On space-time interest points. *International Journal of Computer Vision*, 64(2):107–123, 2005.
[4] B. Leibe, A. Leonardis, and B. Schiele. Robust object detection with interleaved categorization and segmentation. *International Journal of Computer Vision*, 77(1-3):259–289, 2008.
[5] C. Schüldt, I. Laptev, and B. Caputo. Recognizing human actions: A local svm approach. In *ICPR (3)*, pages 32–36, 2004.
[6] D. Tran and J. Yuan. Optimal Spatio-Temporal Path Discovery for Video Event Detection. *IEEE CVPR*, 2011.
[7] G. Yu, N. Goussies, J. Yuan, and Z. Liu. Fast action detection via discriminative random forest voting and top-k subvolume search. *Multimedia, IEEE Transactions on*, 13(3):507–517, 2011.
[8] G. Yu, J. Yuan, and Z. Liu. Unsupervised Random Forest Indexing for Fast Action Search. *IEEE CVPR*, 2011.
[9] J. Yuan, Z. Liu, and Y. Wu. Discriminative subvolume search for efficient action detection. *IEEE CVPR*, 2009.

Ensemble Multi-Instance Multi-Label Learning Approach for Video Annotation Task*

Xin-Shun Xu[1,2]
xuxs@lamda.nju.edu.cn

Xiangyang Xue[3]
xyxue@fudan.edu.cn

Zhi-Hua Zhou[1]
zhouzh@lamda.nju.edu.cn

[1]National Key Laboratory for Novel Software Technology, Nanjing University, Nanjing 210093, China
[2]School of Computer Science and Technology, Shandong University, Jinan 250101, China
[3]School of Computer Science, Fudan University, Shanghai 200433, China

ABSTRACT

Automatic video annotation is an important ingredient for video indexing, browsing, and retrieval. Traditional studies represent one video clip with a flat feature vector; however, video data usually has natural structure. Moreover, a video clip is generally relevant to multiple concepts. Indeed, the video annotation task is inherently a Multi-Instance Multi-Label (MIML) learning problem. In this paper, we propose the En-MIMLSVM approach for the video annotation task. It considers the class imbalance and long time training problems of most video annotation tasks. In addition, a temporally consistent weighted multi-instance kernel is developed to take into account both the temporal consistency in video data and the significance of instances of different levels in pyramid representation. The En-MIMLSVM is evaluated on TRECVID 2005 data set, and the results show that it outperforms several state-of-the-art methods.

Categories and Subject Descriptors

I.2.10 [**Artificial Intelligence**]: Vision and Scene Understanding—*video analysis*; I.2.6 [**Artificial Intelligence**]: Learning

General Terms

Algorithms, Design, Experimentation

Keywords

Video Annotation, Multi-Instance Multi-Label Learning, Ensemble Methods

1. INTRODUCTION

With the rapid development of storages devices, networks and compression techniques, large collections of digital videos are available publicly. How to effectively access large-scale video data, such as indexing, browsing and retrieval, has become a challenging task, and attracted more and more researchers. To tackle this issue, a common theme is to first annotate these videos with concepts which describe the information in the video content at semantic level, and then use these concepts to index or browse the video. Generally, it is labor-intensive and time-consuming to annotate large video data archives. Thus, annotating videos automatically (it is also called concept detection or high level feature extraction) has emerged as an active topic in the multimedia research community [12, 16].

A general approach is to first extract textual and/or visual features, and then train a model and use the trained model to predict concepts of new videos. Traditional methods represent each sample as a flat feature vector, and apply machine learning techniques such as support vector machine (SVM) [1, 21] and Hidden Markov Model [4] to construct classifiers which are then used for annotation. Recently, some researchers try to use structure-based representation, which represents each sample in a form beyond a flat feature vector, such as pyramid representation. In particular, multi-instance (MI) representation, which was originated from research on multi-instance learning [2], has attracted more and more attention. In MI, each sample is represented as a *bag* of instances, that is, feature vectors in the same feature space. In its standard form, it is assumed that a bag is positive if it contains at least one positive instance, and otherwise it is a negative bag. The relation between instances in each bag plays important roles [25]. MI has already been applied in many studies on video or image annotation tasks. For example, Naphade et al. [11] proposed a generalized multi-instance learning algorithm for video concept detection, Gu et al. [6] formulated the task as a multi-layer multi-instance learning problem, van de Sande et al. [18] represented each keyframe as a pyramid, and designed a kernel to measure the similarity between two keyframes.

It is important to notice that a keyframe usually contains more than one concept. For example, in TRECVID 2005 data set, according to LSCOM-Lite annotations [10], there are 39 concepts, and the largest number of concepts contained in one frame is 12. There are many studies trying to handle multi-labeled output. Generally, they try to annotate the video concepts separately. For example, one-vs-rest strategy can be used to train an SVM for each concept, and then the performance can be improved by techniques such as context-based concept fusion [12, 15]. The individual concepts and their correlations can also be treated simultaneously [14].

Recently, Zhou and Zhang [26] proposed the MIML (Multi-Instance Multi-Label learning) framework, where one object is represented by a bag of instances and the object is allowed to have multiple labels simultaneously. Such a framework is able to take the correlation among instances, correlation among labels, and correlation between instances and labels simultaneously, and provides a very rich representation and learning potential. It is evident that the video and image annotation tasks are naturally and inherently MIML tasks, and successful video and image annotation has al-

*Area Chair: Kiyoharu Aizawa. This research was supported by NSFC (61073097, 60970047, 61173068), 973 Program (2010CB327903), CPSF (20100470063), IIFSDU (2009TS033).

ready been developed in the MIML framework [8, 22]. A number of MIML algorithms have been developed during the past few years. For example, the MIMLBoost and MIMLSVM algorithms [26] solve MIML problems by degeneration. The D-MIMLSVM algorithm which solves MIML problems in regularization framework considers the inherent class-imbalance in multiple labels [27]. The M3MIML algorithm is a fast large-margin MIML approach [23]. There are also MIML distance metric learning approach [7], MIML approach based on Dirichlet-Bernoulli Alignment [20], and recently a powerful degeneration approach SISL-MIML [13].

By training and combining multiple classifiers, ensemble methods [24] are state-of-the-art techniques achieving strong generalization ability. In this paper, we propose the En-MIMLSVM approach, an ensemble multi-instance multi-label learning algorithm based on MIMLSVM. Inspired by [9], this method first samples several subsets from majority class independently, then trains multiple classifiers using the subsets and minority class, and finally combines all classifiers for final decision. It is able to exploit the majority class examples ignored by under-sampling, and make the training speed faster due to the small size training set. Thus, it can deal with the class imbalance problem and the long learning time of SVM simultaneously. Experiments on TRECVID2005 data set show that the proposed approach outperforms a number of state-of-the-art methods.

The rest of this paper is organized as follows: In section 2, we introduce the En-MIMLSVM method. In section 3, we report on experiments. Finally, we conclude this paper in section 4.

2. THE EN-MIMLSVM APPROACH

2.1 Basic Approach

There is serious class imbalance in most video annotation tasks. For instance, there are only 106 positive samples of concept "Prisoner" among 61901 samples in TRECVID 2005 development data set. In addition, training an SVM is usually posed as a quadratic programming problem, and becomes challenging when there are a large number of samples due to its high computational and memory requirement.

To deal with the problems above, under-sampling is an efficient method. It uses a subset of majority class samples to train a classifier. Although the training set becomes balanced and the training process becomes faster, standard under-sampling often suffers from the loss of helpful information concealed in the ignored majority class samples. In [9], Liu et al. proposed an ensemble method; rather than randomly removing majority class samples, this method tries to remove samples which have already been learned well, and thus reduces the risk of neglecting samples containing important information. Inspired by [9], our En-MIMLSVM method first samples several subsets from majority class independently; then AdaBoost is used to train a number of weighted SVMs from the union of each subset and the minority class, and finally all classifiers are combined for final decision.

The pseudo-code for En-MIMLSVM is shown in Algorithm 1. Here, for each class, SVM is used as base learner of an ensemble. In this paper, we use kernel which can capture both the structure and temporal information in the videos. The kernel is detailed in the next section.

Algorithm 1 En-MIMLSVM

1. For each class(concept)Input: In the training set, select all the positive samples $\mathcal{P}$, and all the negative samples $\mathcal{N}, |\mathcal{P}| < |\mathcal{N}|$, the number of subsets T to sample from $\mathcal{N}$, and s_i, the number of iterations to train an AdaBoost ensemble H_i
2. $i \Leftarrow 0$
3. repeat
4. $\quad i \Leftarrow i+1$
5. $\quad$ Randomly sample a subset $\mathcal{N}_i$ from $\mathcal{N}$, $|\mathcal{N}_i| = |\mathcal{P}|$.
6. $\quad$ Learn H_i using P and N_i. H_i is an AdaBoost ensemble with s_i weak classifier h_{ij} and corresponding weights α_{ij}.
   - a. $j \Leftarrow 0$
   - b. Input: a set of the weights of training samples:$w_{i1}^k \Leftarrow 1/(2 * |\mathcal{P}|), k \Leftarrow 1, ..., l = 2 * |\mathcal{P}|$
   - c. repeat
   - d. $\quad j \Leftarrow j+1$
   - e. $\quad$ Train an SVM component classifier, h_{ij} on the weighted training set.
   - f. $\quad$ Calculate the training error of $h_{ij} : \varepsilon_{ij} \Leftarrow \sum w_i^j, y_i \neq h_{ij}(x_i)$.
   - g. $\quad$ Set the weight of component classifier. $h_{ij} : \alpha_{ij} \Leftarrow \frac{1}{2} ln(\frac{1-\varepsilon_{ij}}{\varepsilon_{ij}})$
   - h. $\quad$ Update the weights of training samples if $j \neq s_i$: $w_i^{j+1} \Leftarrow \frac{w_i^j exp(-\alpha_{ij} y_i h_{ij}(x_j))}{C_i}$ where C_i is a normalization constant, and $\sum w_i^{j+1} = 1$
   - i. until $j = s_i$
7. $\quad$ Suppose the ensemble's threshold is θ_i, then the ensemble is: $H_i(x) = sgn(\sum_{j=1}^{s_i} \alpha_{ij} h_{ij}(x) - \theta_i)$
8. until $i = T$
9. Output: An ensemble: $H(x) = sgn(\sum_{i=1}^{T} \sum_{j=1}^{s_i} \alpha_{ij} h_{ij}(x) - \sum_{i=1}^{T} \theta_i)$

2.2 The Kernel Design

We represent each frame with pyramid style, and treat each patch as an instance. Several kernels have been designed for spatial pyramid representation [5, 18]; however, they usually compute the similarity between images/keyframes by using bin-by-bin method, and could not find the similarity between bins with different spatial positions. In addition, these kernels did not consider the property of temporal consistency in video data which has been shown very important in video annotation task [17, 19]. In order to leverage the spatial information in pyramid representation and the temporal consistency in video data, we design a new temporally consistent kernel.

Suppose that the bags of two keyframes are represented as:

$$P = \{p_1^1, p_2^1, ..., p_{m_1}^1, p_1^2, ..., p_{m_2}^2, ..., p_1^L, ..., p_{m_L}^L\}$$
$$Q = \{q_1^1, q_2^1, ..., q_{m_1}^1, q_1^2, ..., q_{m_2}^2, ..., q_1^L, ..., q_{m_L}^L\}$$

where m_i is the number of patches in level i in pyramid representation, L is the total number of levels, and p_j^i is the feature of the jth patch of level i, e.g., a histogram. Then the kernel for bags P and Q is defined as follows:

$$K_{WMI}(P, Q) = \sum_{i=1}^{L} w_i K_{MI}(P^i, Q^i) \tag{1}$$

where $P^i = \{p_1^i, p_2^i, ..., p_{m_i}^i\}$ and $Q^i = \{q_1^i, q_2^i, ..., q_{m_i}^i\}$, namely all the instances in level i, w_i the weight of the ith level instances which is defined according to the size of patches, and K_{MI} is a multi-instance kernel [3]. In this work, we use the following one:

$$K_{MI}(P^i, Q^i) = \frac{1}{(m_i)^2} \sum_{j=1}^{m_i} \sum_{k=1}^{m_i} k^{\rho}(p_j^i, q_k^i) \tag{2}$$

where ρ is a parameter, $k(.,.)$ is χ^2 kernel defined as:

$$k(p_j^i, q_k^i) = e^{-\frac{1}{A^i} D(p_j^i, q_k^i)} \tag{3}$$

where A^i is a scalar which normalizes the distances. In this paper, we set A^i to the average χ^2 distance between all elements of the ith level of all samples in the training set. $D(p_j^i, q_k^i)$ is the χ^2 distance, and can be defined as:

$$D(p_j^i, q_k^i) = \frac{1}{2} \sum_{t=1}^{d} \frac{(p_{jt}^i - q_{kt}^i)^2}{p_{jt}^i + q_{kt}^i} \tag{4}$$

where d is the dimension of feature vectors.

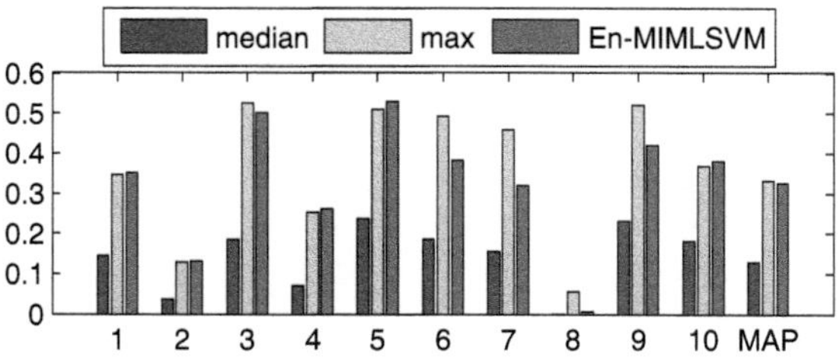

Figure 1: The results of En-MIMLSVM compared with median and max of TRECVID2005

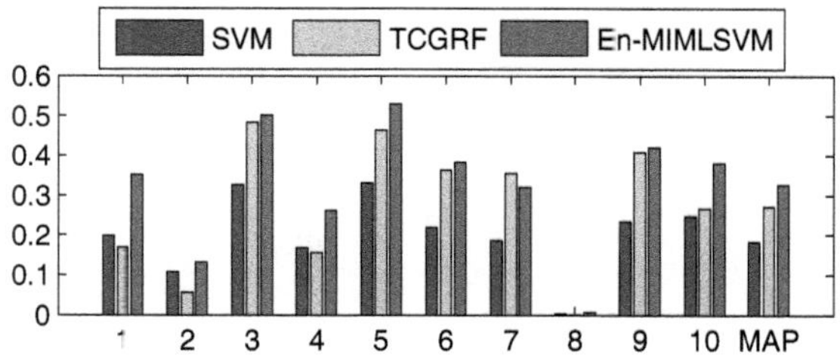

Figure 2: The results of En-MIMLSVM compared with SVM and TCGRF

It has been shown that adjacent video segments will be related to a same semantic concept [17, 19]. This intrinsic property of video data is usually called temporal consistency. To further incorporate the temporal consistency assumption into the kernel design, we propose the Temporally Consistent Weighted Multi-Instance Kernel (TCWMIK) for video annotation task. Here, an instance is represented as $p_j^i = (p_j^{iV}, p_j^{iT})$ in which p_j^{iV} is its visual feature vector and p_j^{iT} is its temporal information. Then the similarity between two instances can be calculated by

$$k_T(p_j^i, q_k^i) = e^{-\frac{\gamma_1}{A^i}D(p_j^{iV}, q_k^{iV}) - \gamma_2\|p_j^{iT} - q_k^{iT}\|} \quad (5)$$

where the first part of the exponent measures the similarity of visual features between two instances, and $\|p_j^{iT} - q_k^{iT}\|$ calculates the temporal distance between two instances. Parameters γ_1 and γ_2 balance the contribution of these two kinds of features. Note that, given a sample P, all its instances contain the same temporal information. This means that, given two samples P and Q, the second part in Eq. 5 is a constant for any instances between them. Thus, Eq. 5 can be rewritten as:

$$k_T(p_j^i, q_k^i) = e^{-\gamma_2 T_{PQ}} e^{-\frac{\gamma_1}{A^i}D(p_j^{iV}, q_k^{iV})} \quad (6)$$

where $T_{PQ} = \|T_P - T_Q\|$, and T_P is the temporal information of sample P, e.g., the temporal order of the subshot in this paper. Substituting Eq. 6 into Eq. 2, then we get

$$K_{TMI}(P^i, Q^i) = \frac{e^{-\gamma_2 \rho T_{PQ}}}{(m_i)^2} \sum_{j=1}^{m_i} \sum_{k=1}^{m_i} e^{-\frac{\gamma_1 \rho}{A^i}D(p_j^{iV}, q_k^{iV})} \quad (7)$$

Considering the significance of instances of different levels in pyramid representation, we finally get the following kernel:

$$K(P, Q)_{TCWMI} = \sum_{i=1}^{L} w_i K_{TMI}(P^i, Q^i) \quad (8)$$

From the above, we can find that this kernel can utilize both spatial and temporal information contained in samples. Moreover, it is not a bin-by-bin method, and can capture the information between all pairs of patches of the same level in pyramid representation.

3. EXPERIMENTS

To evaluate the proposed method, we conduct experiments on the benchmark data set of TRECVID2005. It consists of 170 hours of TV news videos from 13 different programs in Englich, Arabic and Chinese. After automatic shot boundary detection, the development (DEV) set contains 43970 shots, and the evaluation (EVAL) set contains 45755 shots. Some shots are further segmented into sub-shots. Finally, DEV and EVAL contain 61901 and 64256 sub-shots, respectively. The annotation task of TRECVID 2005 is to detect the presence or absence of 10 predetermined benchmark concepts in each shot of the EVAL set. These concepts are: *walking_running*, *explosion_fire*, *maps*, *flag-US*, *building*, *waterscape_waterfront*, *mountain*, *prisoner*, *sports* and *car* which are numbered from 1 to 10 in this paper. For each concept, systems are required to return a ranked-list of up to 2000 shots. The performance is evaluated by *Average Precision*(AP) and *Mean Average Precision*(MAP), which are the official performance metric in TRECVID evaluations. Each frame is represented by pyramid scheme: $1\times1, 2\times2, 1\times3$ and 3×1. From each patch, SIFT, OpponentSIFT and *rg*SIFT descriptors are extracted by Harris-Laplace and dense sampling methods. Then, codebook is generated from random selected descriptors. Finally, each patch is represented as a histogram.

A series of experiments are conducted to compare En-MIMLSVM with several state-of-the-art approaches including SVM, TCGRF [17] , MIMLSVM [26]. In the experiments, for En-MIMLSVM, we set the number of subsets $T = 10$, and the rounds of AdaBoost $s_i = 10$. During training, if the number of samples in minority class for one concept is more than 2000, 2000 samples are selected to represent the minority class. Other parameters, as well as parameters of the comparison algorithms are all selected by 5-fold cross-validations on training set.

Figure 1 shows the results of En-MIMLSVM compared with the *median* (the average results of all the participants in TRECVID05) and *max* (The best results for each concept of all the participants in TRECVID2005). From this figure, we can find that the performance of En-MIMLSVM always outperforms the *median*. It outperforms the *max* on 5 concepts.

Figure 2 compares En-MIMLSVM with TCGRF and SVM. Note that, for SVM, the features of all patches of a sample are firstly averaged so that each sample is represented as a vector; then, an SVM with RBF kernel is constructed. We can find that En-MIMLSVM beats SVM on all concepts, and beats TCGRF on 9 concepts.

Figure 3 compares the performance of En-MIMLSVM and MIMLSVM [26]. We can find that En-MIMLSVM performs much better than MIMLSVM on all concepts, as we have expected since En-MIML-SVM is an ensemble method using an improved version of MIMLSVM as base learner. It is important to note that, En-MIMLSVM is about 5~8 times faster than MIMLSVM because each classifier in En-MIMLSVM is built on a small data set.

For a further study, we also implement a variant, En-MIMSVM-v, in which only the visual features are used. In other words, Eq. 3 is used for training and testing. The results are shown in Figure 4. From this figure, we can observe that En-MIMLSVM outperforms En-MIMLSVM-v on all concepts. In particular, En-MIMLSVM performs much better on *walking_running*, *flag-US*, *building*, and *sports* than En-MIMLSVM-v due to the fact that the temporal consistency in these concepts is stronger than others. This confirms the effectiveness of incorporating temporal consistency.

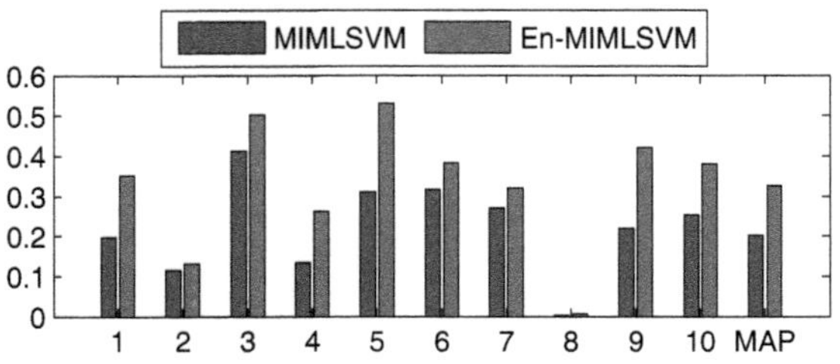

Figure 3: The results of En-MIMLSVM compared with MIMLSVM

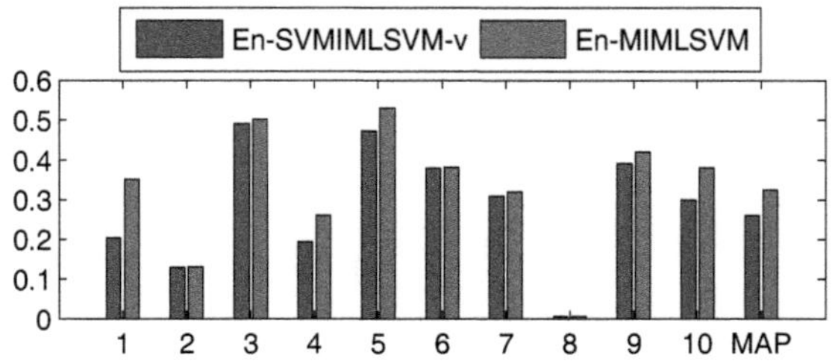

Figure 4: The results of En-MIMLSVM compared with En-MIMLSVM-v

4. CONCLUSION

In this paper, we propose the En-MIMLSVM approach for video annotation. This is an ensemble method developed in the MIML framework, and it is able to capture both the structure information and temporal information in the metadata. En-MIMLSVM is also endowed with the ability of dealing with class imbalance and improvement of learning efficiency. Experiments show that En-MIMLSVM outperforms a number of state-of-the-art methods. An interesting future work is to evaluate the proposed method on more concepts, such as the 39/374 LSCOM-lite concepts in TRECVID data.

5. REFERENCES

[1] A. Amir, M. Berg, and S.-F. Chang. IBM research TRECVID-2003 video retrieval system. In *TREVID*, 2003.

[2] T. G. Dietterich, R. H. Lathrop, and T. Lozano-Pérez. Solving the multiple-instance problem with axis-parallel rectangles. *Artificial Intelligence*, 89(1–2):31–71, 1997.

[3] T. Gartner, P. A. Flach, A. Kowalczyk, and A. J. Smola. Multi-instance kernels. In *ICML*, 179–186, 2002.

[4] A. Ghoshal, P. Ircing, and S. Khudanpur. Hidden markov models for automatic annotation and content-based retrieval of images and video. In *SIGIR*, 544–551, 2005.

[5] K. Grauman and T. Darrell. The pyramid match kernel: Efficient learning with sets of features. *Journal of Machine Learning Research*, 8:725–760, 2007.

[6] Z. Gu, T. Mei, X.-S. Hua, J. Tang, and X. Wu. Multi-layer multi-instance learning for video concept detection. *IEEE Transactions on Multimedia*, 10(8):1605–1616, 2008.

[7] R. Jin, S. Wang, and Z.-H. Zhou. Learning a distance metric from multi-instance multi-label data. In *CVPR*, 896–902, 2009.

[8] Y.-X. Li, S. Ji, J. Ye, and Z.-H. Zhou. Drosophila gene expression pattern annotation through multi-instance multi-label learning. In *IJCAI*, 1445–1450, 2009.

[9] X.-Y. Liu, J. Wu, and Z.-H. Zhou. Exploratory undersampling for class-imbalance learning. *IEEE Transactions on Systems, Man, and Cybernetics, Part B: Cybernetics*, 39(2):539–550, 2009.

[10] M. Naphade, L. Kennedy, J. R. Kender, S. F. Chang, P. Over, and A. Hauptmann. A light scale concept ontology for multimedia understanding for TRECVID 2005. In IBM Research Technical Report, 2005.

[11] M. Naphade and J. Smith. A generalized multiple instance learning algorithm for large scale modeling of multimedia semantics. In *ICASSP*, 341–344, 2005.

[12] M. R. Naphade, I. Kozintsev, and T. Huang. Factor graph framework for semantic video indexing. *IEEE Transactions on Circuits and Systems for Video Technology*, 12(1):40–52, 2002.

[13] N. Nguyen. A new SVM approach to multi-instance multi-label learning. In *ICDM*, 384–392, 2010.

[14] G.-J. Qi, X.-S. Hua, Y. Rui, J. Tang, T. Mei, M. Wang, and H.-J. Zhang. Correlative multilabel video annotation with temporal kernels. *ACM Transactions on Multimedia Computing, Communications and Applications*, 5(1):1–27, 2008.

[15] J. R. Smith, M. Naphade, and A. Natsev. Multimedia semantic indexing using model vectors. In *ICME*, 445–448, 2003.

[16] C. G. M. Snoek, M. Worring, J. C. van Gemert, J.-M. Geusebroek, and A. W. M. Smeulders. The challenge problem for automated detection of 101 semantic concepts in multimedia. In *MM*, 421–430, 2006.

[17] J. Tang, X.-S. Hua, T. Mei, G.-J. Qi, S. Li, and X. Wu. Temporally consistent gaussian random field for video semantic analysis. In *ICIP*, 525–528, 2007.

[18] K. E. van de Sande, T. Gevers, and C. G. Snoek. Evaluating color descriptors for object and scene recognition. *IEEE Transactions on Pattern Analysis and Machine Intelligence*, 32(9):1582–1596, 2010.

[19] J. Yang and A. G. Hauptmann. Exploring temporal consistency for video analysis and retrieval. In *MIR*, 33–42, 2006.

[20] S.-H. Yang, H. Zha, and B.-G. Hu. Dirichlet-bernoulli alignment: A generative model for multi-class multi-label multi-instance corpora. In *NIPS 23*, 2143–2150, 2009.

[21] J. Yuan, Z. Guo, and L. Lv et al. THU and ICRC at TRECVID. In *TRECVID*, 2007.

[22] Z.-J. Zha, X.-S. Hua, T. Mei, J. Wang, G.-J. Qi, and Z. Wang. Joint multi-label multi-instance learning for image classification. In *CVPR*, 1–8, 2008.

[23] M.-L. Zhang and Z.-H. Zhou. M3MIML: A maximum margin method for multi-instance multi-label learning. In *ICDM*, 688–697, 2008.

[24] Z.-H. Zhou. Ensemble learning. In S. Z. Li, editor, *Encyclopedia of Biometrics*, pages 270–273. Springer, 2009.

[25] Z.-H. Zhou, Y.-Y. Sun, and Y.-F. Li. Multi-instance learning by treating instances as non-i.i.d. samples. In *ICML*, 1249–1256, 2009.

[26] Z.-H. Zhou and M.-L. Zhang. Multi-instance multi-label learning with application to scene classification. In *NIPS 19*, 1609–1616, 2007.

[27] Z.-H. Zhou, M.-L. Zhang, S.-J. Huang, and Y.-F. Li. MIML: A framework for learning with ambiguous objects. *CoRR abs/0808.3231*, 2008.

Nonparametric Bottom-Up Saliency Detection Using Hypercomplex Spectral Contrast *

Ce Li, Jianru Xue, Nanning Zheng, Zhiqiang Tian
Institute of Artificial Intelligence and Robotics, Xi'an Jiaotong University
Xi'an, Shaanxi, P.R.China, 710049
{celi, jrxue, nnzheng, zqtian}@aiar.xjtu.edu.cn

ABSTRACT

Saliency detection is an useful technique for image semantic analysis such as auto image segmentation, image retargeting, advertising design and image compression. Inspired by two existing saliency detection algorithms, named spectral residual (SR) and phase spectrum of quaternion Fourier transform (PQFT), we propose a new bottom-up saliency detection method which is featured with the introduction of hypercomplex spectral contrast (HSC) in saliency detection. The proposed HSC algorithm introduces the HSV color image vector space in hypercomplex number, and is better comprehensive to consider amplitude spectral contrast into saliency model as well as phase spectral contrast. Meanwhile, we also incorporate the human vision nonuniform sampling into our model, which is a common phenomenon that directs visual attention to the logarithmic center of image in natural scenes. Experimental results on two public saliency detection datasets show that our approach performs better than four state-of-the art approaches remarkably.

Categories and Subject Descriptors

I.2.10 [**ARTIFICIAL INTELLIGENCE**]: Vision and Scene Understanding—*Perceptual reasoning*

General Terms

Algorithm, Experimentation, Performance

Keywords

Visual saliency, Hypercomplex Fourier Transform, Spectral Contrast, Nonuniform Sampling

1. INTRODUCTION

Selective visual attention is a important mechanism in human brain and visual system. Human always can quickly focus on some salient regions in an image or a video. These salient regions often include important semantic content, applied for image semantic analysis such as image segmentation [5], image editing [2] and image compression [14] etc.

Current methods of saliency detection are usually considered as a process of bottom-up or top-down. Most existing saliency detection models are based on the bottom-up computational framework. Among these models, Itti and Koch's model [9] is the most famous one. According to the Feature Integration theory [13], they detected saliency map by the center-surround operator and normalization a set of low-level features. Based on the model, N.Bruce et al. proposed an information maximization detection model [3]; Liu and Zheng decided visual attention by CRF learning algorithm[11]; Goferman introduced context information in salient object detection [6] etc. Recently, different from classic image statistical models, Hou [8] designed a quick Fourier spectral residual analysis algorithm for static image saliency. In this method, amplitude spectral residual is considered as an important key factor to stimulate visual attention. Furthermore, Guo [8] proposed saliency detection algorithm by phase spectrum of quaternion Fourier transform. Achanta [1] gave out a simple and effective solution of salient region detection by frequency tuned.

Compared with the above models, visual saliency detection in frequency domain has become one of research focus. But for saliency detection, it is a problem which is the amplitude spectrum important or phase spectrum important? From Piotrowski's viewpoint [12], We tend to think that the phase spectrum includes image structure information, and the amplitude spectrum carries the visual perception magnitude information. Hence, we propose a algorithm named HSC which is a comprehensive consideration with amplitude spectrum and phase spectrum to saliency detection in a multi-scale hypercomplex [4] HSV color space, supported by existing theories [13, 10]and existing saliency detection methods [9, 11, 8, 7, 1, 6]:

(1). In the frequency domain, amplitude spectrum and phase spectrum are both significant to saliency detection. Only salient amplitude or phase spectrum could not reconstruct whole saliency map.

(2). Saliency map is the product of various visual features of comprehensive stimulate. United Multi-feature vector expression would be a rapidly computation method.

(3). Pixel's position is important to saliency detection in an image. It is different that the visual attention with the different position in an image.

The contribution of this paper is twofold. On one hand,

*Area chair: Tat-Seng Chua

MM'11, November 28–December 1, 2011, Scottsdale, Arizona, USA.

we propose new saliency detection by hypercomplex spectral contrast (Section 2.1). On the other hand, we introduce a log-polar bias sampling mechanism to imitate a nonuniform sampling of human vision for visual attention (Section 2.2). Section 3 reports the experimental results carried out for comparing our proposed model with four state-of-the art methods on more than 1000 natural and psychological images. Finally, we conclude with a discussion in section 4.

2. OUR APPROACH

The framework of our approach is illustrated in Figure 1. Inspired by[7] and [8], we compute amplitude spectrum contrast and phase spectrum contrast in multi-scale HSV color space, by hypercomplex Fourier transform respectively . In this case, the saliency map could be produced using two hypercomplex spectral contrast map at same time by reconstruction and nonuniform sampling. Our HSC method mainly contains four steps:

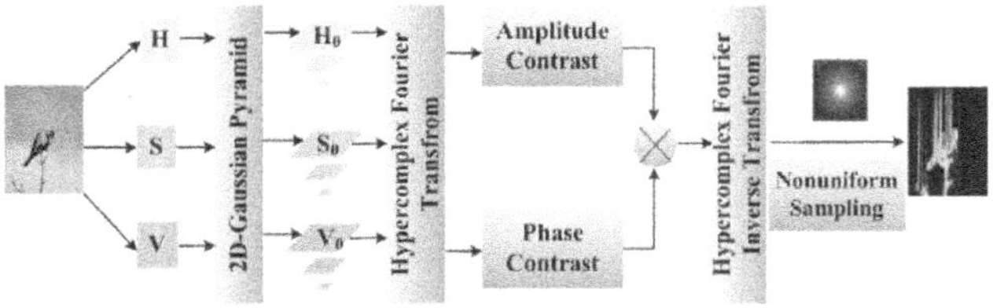

Figure 1: Overview of the HSC saliency detection framework.

Step 1: Converting a raw image **I** to the HSV color Space, then **I** was blurred by 2D Gaussian on three level pyramid to eliminate fine texture details as well as to average the energy of image **I**.

Step 2: Representing image pixels by pure quaternion (hypercomplex) on HSV color space, then we calculate the amplitude spectrum and phase spectrum of the image by hypercomplex Fourier transform[4] in different scales.

Step 3: Under various scales of raw image, we calculate the spectral contrast of amplitude and phase between raw image and blurred image then to reconstruct these contrast maps using amplitude spectral contrast and phase spectral contrast.

Step 4: Normalizing these reconstructed spectral contrast maps, and using log-polar nonuniform sampling, we could obtain the final saliency map.

2.1 Hypercomplex of HSV Color Image

Quaternion is a kind of hypercomplex numbers. Color image pixels have inherently 3-D components. And they can be represented in quaternion form using pure quaternion [4]. A commonly used color space that corresponds more naturally to human perception is the HSV color space, whose three components are hue, saturation and value. Therefore, in this paper, each pixel of the raw image is represented by hypercomplex numbers(quaternion)consisting of HSV three color components, which do not consider color opponent-component(RG or BY) and intensity, in diffierence to[7]. Thus a hypercomplex number HSV image $q(x,y)$ is defined as follows:

$$q{=}H\boldsymbol{i}+S\boldsymbol{j}+V\boldsymbol{k} \tag{1}$$

where$\boldsymbol{i}, \boldsymbol{j}, \boldsymbol{k}$ satisfies $\boldsymbol{i}^2 = \boldsymbol{j}^2 = \boldsymbol{k}^2 = -1, \boldsymbol{i} \perp \boldsymbol{j}, \boldsymbol{j} \perp \boldsymbol{k}, \boldsymbol{i} \perp \boldsymbol{k}, \boldsymbol{k} = \boldsymbol{ij}$.

In order to facilitate the next step, the hypercomplex number HSV image q*'s* pixel is given by pixel symplectic decomposition as Eq.(2):

$$q{=}f_1 + f_2\boldsymbol{j}; f_1 = H\boldsymbol{i}; f_2 = S + V\boldsymbol{i} \tag{2}$$

2.2 Saliency Detection Using HSC

Usually, salient visual stimulus is often generated by strong contrast signals in bottom-up model. These signals often have larger energy of spectrum. In other words, some strong spectral contrast of amplitude and phase are the main components in salient signals. In this paper, we calculate the amplitude spectrum and phase spectrum using hypercomplex Fourier Transform(HFT) [4] of HSV color image. Based on Eq.(2), HFT of the hypercomplex image q can be calculated by two complex Fourier transforms of the symplectic parts, such as Eq.(3):

$$Q[u,v]{=}F_1[u,v] + F_2[u,v]\boldsymbol{j} \tag{3}$$

We define each part of the forward and inverse hypercomplex Fourier Transform of Eq.(3)as follows Eq.(4):

$$\begin{aligned} F_i[u,v] &= \frac{1}{\sqrt{MN}} \textstyle\sum_{y=0}^{M-1} \sum_{x=0}^{N-1} e^{-j2\pi((xu/N)+(yv/M))} f_i(x,y) \\ f_i[x,y] &= \frac{1}{\sqrt{MN}} \textstyle\sum_{v=0}^{M-1} \sum_{u=0}^{N-1} e^{j2\pi((xu/N)+(yv/M))} F_i(u,v) \end{aligned} \tag{4}$$

where (x,y) is the spatial location of each pixel, (u,v) is the frequency domain. M and N are the image's height and width.

Furthermore, using above equations Eq.(1-4), we completed the transform from q to Q in hypercomplex frequency domain. Q is also defined in ploar form as follows:

$$Q{=}\left\|Q\right\| e^{j\phi} \tag{5}$$

where $\|Q\|$, ϕ and $\boldsymbol{j}$ are the amplitude spectrum, phase spectrum and unit pure hypercomplex number, respectively.

In the next subsection, we first define single-scale saliency of HSC. Furthermore, we would introduce multi-scale analysis into the HSC method in order to enhance our saliency detection result.

Single-scale saliency of HSC: First, we consider a single scale l, given input raw image **I**, we can obtain a blurred image $\mathbf{I}_b$ by 2D-gaussian filter($\sigma = 4$). Using Eq.(1-5), we calculate amplitude spectrum ($\|Q_I^l\|$,$\|Q_b^l\|$) and phase spectrum (ϕ_I^l, ϕ_b^l) of raw image and blurred image in HSV color space, respectively, as follows:

$$\begin{aligned} Q_I^l &= \|Q_I^l\| e^{j\phi_I^l} \\ Q_b^l &= \|Q_b^l\| e^{j\phi_b^l} \end{aligned} \tag{6}$$

Then, our amplitude spectral contrast CQ_{am}^l and phase spectral contrast CQ_{ph}^l are obtained by Eq.(7)

$$\begin{aligned} CQ_{ph}^l &= \|Q_I^l\| e^{j\phi_I^l} \;, \quad \|Q_I^l\| = 1 \\ CQ_{am}^l &= \frac{\|Q_I^l\|}{\|Q_b^l\|} e^{j\phi_I^l} \\ CQ^l &= CQ_{am}^l + CQ_{ph}^l \\ &= \{\|Q_I^l\| / \|Q_b^l\| + 1\} e^{j\phi_I^l} \end{aligned} \tag{7}$$

where CQ^l is the total of hypercomplex spectral contrast. Inspired by[8], the blurred image has average spectrum energy in hypercomplex frequency. Thus, the amplitude spectral contrast CQ^l_{am} could represent the salient energy in hypercomplex frequency domain. The phase spectral contrast CQ^l_{ph} could represent the salient structure information in hypercomplex frequency domain. According [8], the final hypercomplex spectral contrastCQ^l_{final} can be expressed as follows:

$$CQ^l_{final}= (log(\frac{\|Q^l_I\|}{\|Q^l_b\|}+1))e^{j\phi^l_I} \tag{8}$$

Hence, we use Eq.(4) to obtain the reconstruction of CQ^l_{final} as cq^l_I, represented as follows:

$$cq^l_I=a+bi+cj+dk \tag{9}$$

Finally, our HSC saliency map S^l at scale l is obtain by Eq.(10)

$$S^l=f_{gaussian} * \left\|cq^l_I\right\|^2, \quad \sigma=4. \tag{10}$$

Multi-scale saliency of HSC: Similarly as [6], in order to enhance our saliency detection result, using 2D-gaussian pyramid, we can obtain the set of multi-scale blurred images whose scales are $l=\{1,0.5,0.25\}$. Thus, the average of HSC saliency map at various scales can be obtained as follows:

$$S=\frac{1}{L}\sum_{l=1}^{L} S^l \tag{11}$$

2.3 Nonuniform Sampling and Saliency Map

Our understanding of nature is often through nonuniform observations in space or time. Usually, humans often browse one natural image from its center. This means that the pixel's position is important to saliency detection in a image. From these above views, we design a simple method of log center bias weight to simulate log-polar nonuniform sampling transform from starting the image center location. We can calculate the log-center-distance $D_log(x,y)$ between each pixel(x,y) and the image center. Hence, we obtain the final saliency map as follows:

$$SM_{final}(x,y) = S(x,y)/(1+D_{\log}(x,y)) \tag{12}$$

In the HSC algorithm, we use multi-scale hypercomplex spectral contrast and log-center-bias to implement the saliency detection. The method is simple and effective of image preprocessing to more digital media applications.

3. EXPERIMENTAL RESULTS

To evaluate the performance of our method, two comparison experiments on two publicly available datasets of more than 1000 images with correspondence ground-truth [1][8] and five psychological patterns [3].

We compare our approach with four state-of-art saliency detection approaches. They are classic model (IT[9]), recently excellent method(CA[6]) and two being related to our methods(SR[8], PQFT[7]). For the IT,CA,SR algorithm, we used the authors' provided code on the Web, while for PQFT, we implemente the method in Matlab using qtfm toolbox[4] since we could not have access to the author's

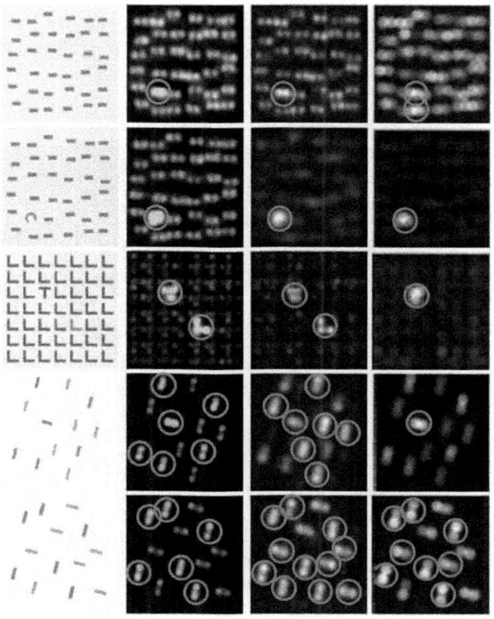

Figure 2: Comparison of our method with [7, 8]on psychological patterns,the frist column is the raw image, the second to fourth column are results produced by our method(HSC) and [7, 8], respectively.

code. All the tests are run at MATLAB 7.0 on Windows XP and are performed on the PC with P4 2.2G CPU and 2G Memroy.

3.1 Responses to Psychological Patterns

We test our model on various psychological stimulis which are commonly used to represent pre-attentive visual features and some mixted stimulis [3]. In this experiment, we use five stimulation patterns to test our approach, and our model does not include nonuniform Sampling technology for psychological testing of fairness. As shown in Figure 2, we compare our result with SR and PQFT. In Figure 2, the first and second rows are "color" and "curvature" basic stimulus test results, respectively. Ours and PQFT successfully find stimulus target, but SR finds one error "color". The third row is a pattern of combination stimulus with "intersection" and "color", our method is stronger salient stimulus than PQFT and SR. In particular, the last two rows are complex stimulis cases, which are stimulus patterns of combined with "line orientation" and "color", PQFT and SR almost fail to find them all because they consider amplitude spectral or phase spectral separately. Conversely, in the case, our method has a good performance for comprehensive considering contrast of amplitude and phase spectral in saliency detection model.

3.2 Natural Images

In this section, we test our method on salient object detection dataset provided by Achanta[1] and saliecny detection dataset based on frequecy domain provided by Hou[8].The total of two datasets have 1062 images with correspondence ground-truth. For fairly to test our method, we set the saliency map at the resolution of 320*240 in all experiments, then resize to raw size. For better visual effect, a 2D gaussian filter with $\sigma = 4$ is performed on all the results. We evaluate and compare our approach with four exiting methods using qualitative and quantitative performance evaluation, respectively.

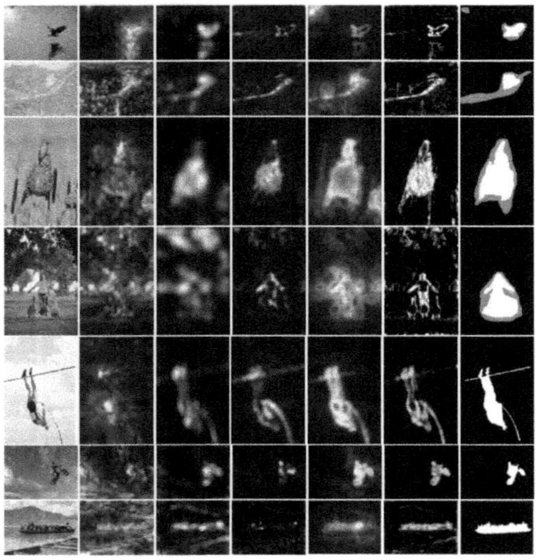

Figure 3: Comparison of our method with [9, 8, 7, 6], the frist column is the raw image, the last column is the hand-labeled image, the second to sixth column are results produced by [9, 8, 7, 6] and our method, respectively.

In qualitative comparison, we show our saliency map and compare to other four state-of-the-art algorithms (IT[9], SR [8], PQFT[7], CA[6]) in Figure 3. It can be seen that our approach is more robust and can detect saliency region which is closer to human hand-labeled images than other models.

Although similar as ours SR and PQFT use frequency domain to saliency detection, our method is better performance than the two methods since we consider not only amplitude spectral but also phase spectral for global contrast in an image. Although the saliency map from [6] is very similar to ours, our method average compute cost is 0.2 second to obtain a saliency map while CA needs 60 second average time, under the same computing conditions.

In quantitative performance evaluation, we compare our model with the above four methods using a measure introduced in [1]. The results are shown in Figure 4. Average values of precision, recall, and F-Measure are obtained over the same ground-truth datasets. F-Measure is defined as same as [1]:

$$F_\beta = \frac{(1+\beta^2) Precision \times Recall}{\beta^2 \times Precision + Recall} \tag{13}$$

In Eq.(13), $\beta^2 = 0.3$ according to [1]. From figure 4, we can see that our method performs better than other methods in human hand-labeled results.

4. CONCLUSIONS

This paper proposes a new saliency detection by using comprehensive amplitude and phase spectral contrast in hypercomplex Fourier domain and nonuniform sampling for natural images. The method is able to effective and quickly detect salient regions from an image and better responses to psychological patterns. Experimental results show that our method has better performance in comparison with other four state-of-the-art methods on two public static image datasets. For the future work, we are going to extend it to spatiotemporal salient object detection in video semantic analysis.

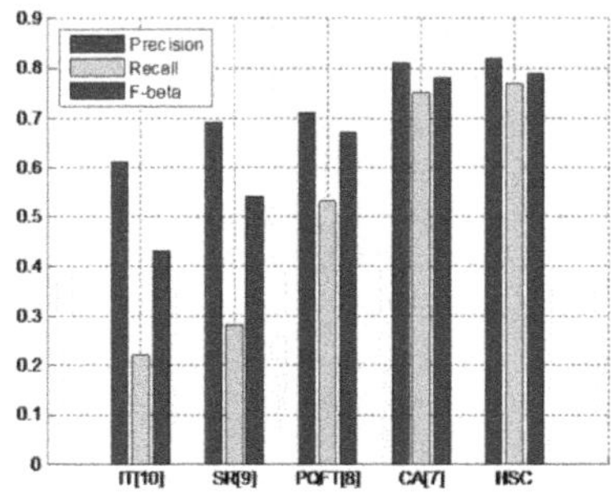

Figure 4: The precision-recall bar of HSC and the others methods on two datasets[1,8]

5. ACKNOWLEDGMENTS

This work was supported by the 973 Program under Grant No.2010CB327902, and the NSFC Nos.(60875008, 90920301 and 60805044).

6. REFERENCES

[1] R. Achanta, S. Hemami, F. Estrada, and S. Susstrunk. Frequency-tuned salient region detection. *CVPR*, 2009.

[2] R. Achanta and S. Susstrunk. Saliency detection for content-aware image resizing. *ICIP*, 2009.

[3] N. Bruce and J. Tsotsos. Saliency based on information maximization. *NIPS*, 2006.

[4] T. Ell and S. Sangwine. Hypercomplex Fourier transforms of color images. *IEEE TIP*, 16(1):22–35, 2007.

[5] Y. Fu, J. Cheng, Z.L. Li, and H.Q. Lu. Saliency cuts: An automatic approach to object segmentation. *ICPR*, 2008.

[6] S. Goferman, L. Zelnik-Manor, and A. Tal. Context-aware saliency detection. *CVPR*, 2010.

[7] C.L. Guo, Q. Ma, and L.M. Zhang. Spatio-temporal saliency detection using phase spectrum of quaternion fourier transform. *CVPR*, 2008.

[8] X.D. Hou and L.Q. Zhang. Saliency detection: A spectral residual approach. *CVPR*, 2007.

[9] L. Itti, C. Koch, and E. Niebur. A model of saliency-based visual attention for rapid scene analysis. *IEEE TPAMI*, 20(11):1254–1259, 1998.

[10] C. Koch and T. Poggio. Predicting the visual world: silence is golden. *Nature*, 2:9–10, 1999.

[11] T. Liu, J. Sun, N.N. Zheng, X.O. Xiao, and H.Y. Shum. Learning to detect a salient object. *CVPR*, 2007.

[12] L. Piotrowski and F. Campbell. A demonstration of the visual importance and flexibility of spatial-frequency amplitude and phase. *Perception*, 11:337-346, 1982.

[13] A. Treisman and G. Gelade. A feature-integration theory of attention. *Cognitive psychology*, 12(1):97–136, 1980.

[14] J.R. Xue, C. Li, and N.N. Zheng. Proto-object based rate control for JPEG2000: an approach to content-based scalability. *IEEE TIP*, 20(4):1177–1184, 2011.

Multiclass Object Detection by Combining Local Appearances and Context*

LiMin Wang[1,2], Yirui Wu[1], Tong Lu[1,*] and Kang Chen[1]
[1]State Key Lab for Novel Software Technology, Nanjing University, China
[2]Department of Information Engineering, The Chinese University of Hong Kong, Hong Kong
{07wanglimin,chenkangnobel}@gmail.com,wuyirui1989@163.com,lutong@nju.edu.cn

ABSTRACT

In this paper, we present a novel approach for multiclass object detection by combining local appearances and contextual constraints. We first construct a multiclass Hough forest of local patches, which can well deal with multiclass object deformations and local appearance variations, due to randomization and discrimination of the forest. Then, in the object hypothesis space, a new multiclass context model is proposed to capture relative location constraints, disambiguating appearance inputs in multiclass object detection. Finally, multiclass objects are detected with a greedy search algorithm efficiently. Experimental evaluations on two image data sets show that the combination of local appearances and context achieves state-of-the-art performance in multiclass object detection.

Categories and Subject Descriptors

I.4.8 [**IMAGE PROCESSING AND COMPUTER VISION**]: Scene Analysis

General Terms

Algorithms Experimentation

Keywords

Object Detection, Multiclass Hough Forest, Context Model

1. INTRODUCTION

Category-level object detection, i.e. predict the bounding boxes of object instances of a class in a test image, has been one of the most active areas in multimedia and computer vision. It has numerous applications such as driver assistance for automobiles by detecting pedestrians [5] and digital camera auto focus by using face detection [14]. There are two leading approaches to solve this problem: sliding windows [5, 14] and Hough voting [7, 10, 11]. Sliding windows scan over possible locations and scales, evaluate a classifier and use post processing to detect objects. Unfortunately, this procedure is a time-consuming work. Instead, Hough voting parametrizes object hypothesis and lets each local part vote for object centroid in the hypothesis space, greatly improving the detection efficiency. As a result, Hough voting has been successfully adapted to the problem of part-based object detection and obtained state-of-the-art results on some popular data sets in the past years. In [10], Leibe *et al.* introduce an *implicit shape model*(ISM), whose object part model is a set of visual words obtained generatively by clustering primitive image features. At running time, the interest point descriptors are matched against the visual words and each matching entry casts probabilistic votes about possible positions of the object in the scale space. In [7], Gall *et al.* present a discriminative Hough voting method called *Hough forest* for object detection. Rather than using a generative visual words, they learn a direct mapping between the appearance of an image patch and its Hough votes for object location.

Unlike single class object detection, there are less methods proposed for multiclass object detection [11, 6]. In [11], Opelt *et al.* present an incremental learning framework by combining shape features and local appearances for the problem of multiclass object detection. However, they ignore the contextual information, i.e. global scene statistics [13] or local interactions among objects [8] in the real world scene, which plays an important role in multiclass object detection. In [6], Desai *et al.* introduce an unified model for multiclass object detection that casts the problem as a structured prediction task. Their model learns statistics which capture the spatial arrangements of various object classes in real images. However, their method is still based on sliding windows and learns a window template for each object class, which cannot deal with object deformations and local appearance variations well .

In this paper, we present a novel approach for multiclass object detection by combining local appearances and context. We construct a multiclass Hough forest, which can efficiently model object deformations and local appearance variations. Meanwhile, contextual information, mainly the relative locations of different object classes, is incorporated into the multiclass Hough forest framework to disambiguate appearance inputs. Finally, we use a greedy search algorithm in the hypothesis space for multiclass object detection. Since our model considers both local appearances and object

*Area chair: Bernard Merialdo

MM'11, November 28–December 1, 2011, Scottsdale, Arizona, USA.

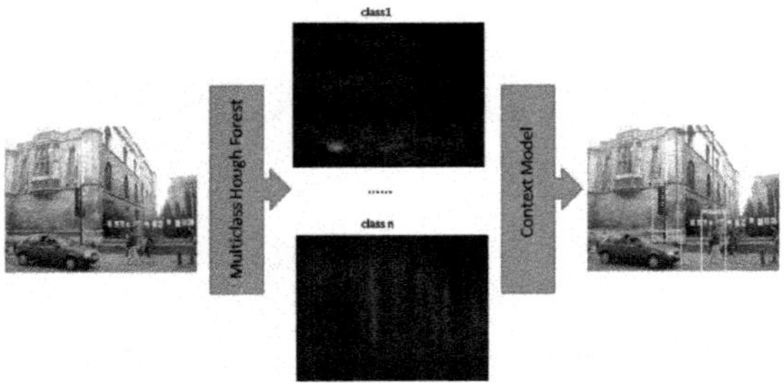

Figure 1: The detection processes of our approach.

interaction contexts, the greedy search algorithm efficiently improves the detection accuracy.

2. OUR APPROACH

We present a novel approach for multiclass object detection by combining local appearances and context. First, we establish a multiclass Hough forest and use local patches to vote for the possible locations of different objects. Then, we consider relative location constraints among objects in the Hough voting space and improve detection accuracy (See Fig. 1 for illustration).

2.1 Multiclass Hough Forest

Based on the single class Hough Forest proposed in [7], we introduce a multiclass Hough forest which can be used for multiclass object detection. Multiclass Hough forest is different from the single class Hough forest both in the training and detection processes. First, during the training phase, we train our forest by simultaneously modeling multiple object categories and thus different object classes can share common features. Second, in the detection phase, multiclass objects of interest can be directly detected by a single round of scanning over the image with our multiclass Hough forest.

Training data and leaf information. For our multiclass Hough forest, each tree $\mathcal{T}$ is constructed based on a set of patches from multiple object categories: $\{\mathcal{P}_i = (\mathcal{I}_i, c_i, \mathbf{d}_i)\}$, where $\mathcal{I}_i$ is the appearance of a local patch, c_i is the class label and $c_i \in \{0, 1, \ldots, |C|\}$, $\mathbf{d}_i$ is the offset of the patch. The training patches are randomly sampled from the training image collection and some of them contain examples of the class of interest with known bounding boxes. The patches from the background are assigned the class label $c_i = 0$ and the ones from interest objects are assigned class labels ranging from 1 to $|C|$, where $|C|$ is the total number of object classes. Every object patch is assigned a 2D offset vector $\mathbf{d}_i$, indicating the relative location of the patch from the object centroid.

For each leaf node L in the trees, the information about patches reaching this node is stored. We first introduce a portion list P_L to remember the portions of different class patches: $P_L = \{p_0, p_1, \ldots, p_{|C|}\}$, where p_i is the portion of the patches labeled with class i. Then we construct an offset matrix D_L to store the offsets of different class patches: $D_L = \{\mathbf{d}_{ij}\}$, where $\mathbf{d}_{ij}$ is the jth patch offset labeled with class i. During the detection, the information is used to cast probabilistic Hough votes about the existence of the object at different positions (see **Detection over scales**).

Multiclass tree construction. The construction of our multiclass Hough forest follows the common random forest framework [4]. Each of the tree is constructed recursively from the root until the stopping conditions are satisfied, e.g. the depth of a node is equal to maxima(d_{max}) or the number of the patches on a fixed node is relatively small(N_{min}). There are two key parts during the construction: binary test and evaluation of the binary test quality. We use the same features and binary test with the single Hough forest construction (see details in [7]). Meanwhile, we adapt the following two uncertainties for a set of patches $A = \{\mathcal{P}_i = (\mathcal{I}_i, c_i, \mathbf{d}_i)\}$ to our multiclass Hough forest to evaluate the binary test quality: class-label uncertainty and offset uncertainty. The class label uncertainty is defined as follows:

$$U_1(A) = |A| \times \sum_{i=0}^{|C|} p_i log \frac{1}{p_i} \tag{1}$$

where $|A|$ is the size of set A and p_i is the probability of class i. Then the offset uncertainty is defined as :

$$U_2(A) = \sum_{i=1}^{|C|} \sum_{j:c_j=i} (\mathbf{d}_j - \mathbf{d}_{Ai})^2 \tag{2}$$

where $\mathbf{d}_{Ai}$ is the mean offset vector over all the patches labeled with i. Finally, the split criteria is the same to the single Hough forest and we pick the binary test t^k with the minimal sum of the respective uncertainty:

$$\arg\min_k \Big(U_*(\{\mathcal{P}_i | t^k(\mathcal{I}_i) = 0\}) + U_*(\{\mathcal{P}_i | t^k(\mathcal{I}_i) = 1\}) \Big) \tag{3}$$

where $* = 1$ or 2 (depending on the random choice).

Detection over scales. During the detection phase, we use the leaf information of our multiclass Hough forest to vote for different class object centroids in the hypothesis space. Consider a patch $\mathcal{P}(\mathbf{y}) = (\mathcal{I}(\mathbf{y}), c(\mathbf{y}), \mathbf{d}(\mathbf{y}))$ centered at position $\mathbf{y}$. We are now interested in the probabilistic vote $p(E(\mathbf{x}), E(i) | \, \mathcal{I}(\mathbf{y}))$, which means the appearance $\mathcal{I}(\mathbf{y})$ of a patch casts for the possibility of detecting an object of class i in position $\mathbf{x}$. For a single tree $\mathcal{T}$, we define the probability as follows:

$$p(E(\mathbf{x}), E(i) | \, \mathcal{I}(\mathbf{y}); \mathcal{T}) =$$
$$\sum_{j:\mathbf{d}_{ij} \in D_L} \frac{1}{2\pi\sigma^2} \exp\left\{ - \frac{\| (\mathbf{y} - \mathbf{x}) - \mathbf{d}_{ij} \|^2}{2\sigma^2} \right\} \times \frac{p_i}{|D_L^i|} \tag{4}$$

where $|D_L^i|$ is the size of ith row of matrix D_L. For the whole forest $\{\mathcal{T}_t\}_{t=1}^{T}$, we just average the probabilistic vote coming from different trees.

To deal with object scale variations, we resize a test image to a scale space and detect by multiclass Hough forest in each scale. Finally, we use the mean shift to find the maxima in the scale space.

2.2 Context Model

Inspired by the work of Galleguillos *et al.* [8], we model relative location constraints among multi-class objects in the hypothesis space generated by the Hough voting and incorporates the spatial context to our multiclass Hough forest.

Modeling object relations. We use a subset of the LabelMe data set [12] for the training and test in our context model. The subset is mainly composed of street scenes. Like [6], we classify object pairwise relationships into five groups: *ontop*, *far*, *next to*, *above* and *below* (See Fig.2). For each object pairwise relationship $R^i (i = 1, 2, 3, 4, 5)$, we define a

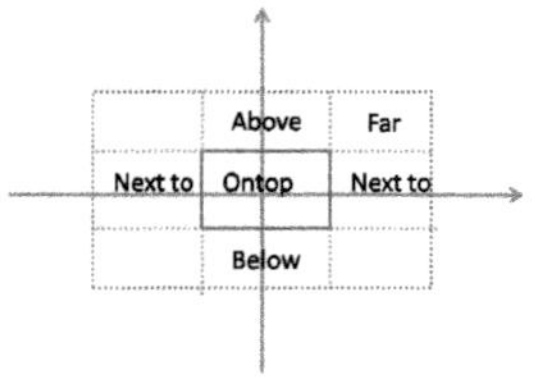

Figure 2: The location relationship between objects.

relationship matrix Φ^i, which captures the probability distribution of object class pairwises. The probability of an object class pairwise $< m, n >$ $(m, n = 1, \cdots, |C|)$ in the location relationship R^i is defined as follows:

$$p(< m, n >; \Phi^i) = \frac{1}{Z(\Phi^i)} \exp\{\phi^i_{mn}\} \quad (5)$$

where Φ^i is the relationship matrix and ϕ^i_{mn} is the entry (m, n) in the relationship matrix. $Z(\Phi^i)$ is the partition function. An object class pairwise $< m, n > \in R^i$ means two objects of class m and n satisfy the ith relative location constraint illustrated in Fig.2. Thus given a data set D, the probability of relationship R^i is :

$$p(D; \Phi^i) = \frac{1}{Z(\Phi^i)^{M^i}} \exp\{\sum_{m=1}^{|C|} \sum_{n=1}^{|C|} l^i_{mn} \phi^i_{mn}\} \quad (6)$$

where l^i_{mn} is the entry (m, n) of a frequency matrix for spatial relationship R^i in the data set D, which counts the times object pairwise $< m, n >$ appears in a training image, satisfying relationship R^i, and M^i is the total number of object pairwise of relationship R^i.

Learning model parameters. Given a data set D, we wish to find Φ^i maximizes the log likelihood of the observed object pairwise:

$$\mathcal{L}(\Phi^i) = \log p(D; \Phi^i) = \sum_{m=1}^{|C|} \sum_{n=1}^{|C|} l^i_{mn} \phi^i_{mn} - M^i \times \log Z(\Phi^i) \quad (7)$$

Since we must evaluate the partition function, maximizing the log likelihood is intractable. Like [8], we approximate the partition function using Monte Carlo integration. The importance sampling is used and the proposal distribution is equal to their observed frequency. Thus we can use the gradient descent to find Φ^i, which approximately optimizes the likelihood, and the gradient is as follows:

$$\nabla_{\Phi^i} \mathcal{L}(\Phi^i) = \begin{bmatrix} l^i_{11} & \cdots & l^i_{1|C|} \\ \vdots & \ddots & \vdots \\ l^i_{|C|1} & \cdots & l^i_{|C||C|} \end{bmatrix} \quad (8)$$

Due to the noise of estimating the partition function, it is difficult to check for the convergence and we adopt the same trick with [8]: training is terminated when 10 iterations of gradient decent go not yield averagely improved likelihood over the previous 10.

Greedy search method. Based on the candidates, i.e. some local maxima, in the object hypothesis space produced by the multiclass Hough forest, we propose a greedy search algorithm, which well combines local appearances and context for multiclass object detection. First, we define the probability $P(\mathbf{x}, c)$ as:

$$P(\mathbf{x}, c) = \alpha P_{app}(\mathbf{x}, c) + (1 - \alpha) P_{con}(\mathbf{x}, c) \quad (9)$$

Table 1: Greedy Search Algorithm.

Algorithm Greedy search for multiclass object detection by combining appearances and context.

Input. Some candidates: $(\mathbf{x}_1, c_1), \cdots, (\mathbf{x}_n, c_n)$ with the appearance probability: $P_{app}(\mathbf{x}_1, c_1), \cdots, P_{app}(\mathbf{x}_n, c_n)$.
Setp1. Set $R = \emptyset$ and initialize the context probability $P_{con}(\mathbf{x}_1, c_1), \cdots, P_{con}(\mathbf{x}_n, c_n)$ to be zero.
Step2. Search for $(\mathbf{x}_*, c_*) = \arg\max_{(\mathbf{x}, c_i) \notin R} P(\mathbf{x}_i, c_i)$. If $P(\mathbf{x}_*, c_*) > \theta$, $R = R \cup \{(\mathbf{x}_*, c_*)\}$, where θ is the detection threshold. Else stop.
Step3. For the remaining candidates, update the context probability:

$$P_{con}(\mathbf{x}_j, c_j) = \frac{1}{M} \left[(M-1) P_{con}(\mathbf{x}_j, c_j)) + \frac{\exp\{\phi^\star_{c_j c_*}\}}{Z(\Phi^\star)} \right]$$

where M is number of detecting objects and $\star \in \{1, \cdots, 5\}$. Go to **Step2**.
Output. The detection result $R = \{(\mathbf{x}_i, c_i)\}$.

where $P(\mathbf{x}, c)$ is the probability that an object of class c is present at position $\mathbf{x}$, $P_{app}(\mathbf{x}, c)$ indicates the evidence from local appearances and $P_{con}(\mathbf{x}, c)$ means the one from contextual information, α is a weight factor between appearances and context. For each candidate $(\mathbf{x}_i, c_i)$, the probability $P_{app}(\mathbf{x}_i, c_i)$ is calculated according to the Hough vote results and the probability $P_{con}(\mathbf{x}_i, c_i)$ is the average of the object pairwise probability $p(< c_i, j >)$ with other objects. Then, we propose a greedy search algorithm to find object class labels for the candidates (see Table 1. for details).

3. EXPERIMENTS

9 classes data set. We first collect a data set of 9 classes: Face, Plane, Motorbike, CarRear [9], CarSide [1], TUD pedestrian [2], CowSide [10], Weizmann Horse [3] and Bottles (from Google Image) to evaluate the detection accuracy of multiclass Hough forest. Each class has 200 training images and 100 test images. We extract 50 patches from each training image and train a multiclass Hough forest composed of 15 trees with $d_{max} = 20$ and $N_{min} = 20$. Then we use the multiclass Hough forest to detect the 9 classes objects in test images. See Fig. 3 for the detection results($precision = \frac{num\ of\ right\ detections}{num\ of\ total\ detections}$, $recall = \frac{num\ of\ right\ detections}{num\ of\ total\ instances}$). It is very encouraging that the detection precision is averagely higher than 0.8 for the 9 classes objects and even achieves a higher rate for some rigid object classes such as CarSide and Motobike. It indicates that the multiclass Hough forest is robust and efficient for multiclass object detection.

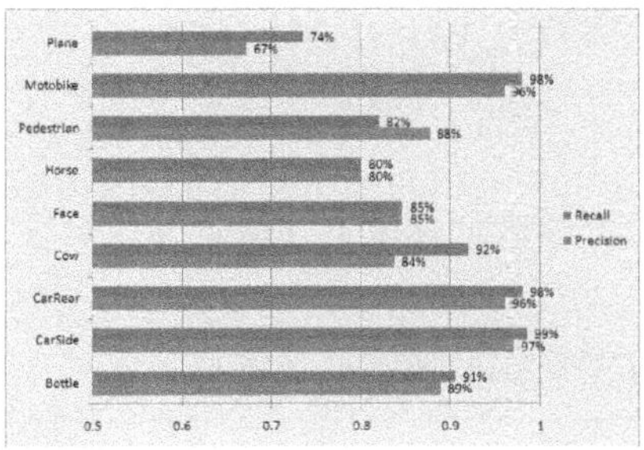

Figure 3: The detection result in 9 classes data set.

(a) Multiclass object detection results without the context model.

(b) Multiclass object detection results with the context model.

Figure 4: Examples of multiclass detection result in LabelMe data set.

Subset of LabelMe. Then, we use a subset of LabelMe data set [12] which is composed of 500 training images and 100 test images to evaluate whether our method is efficient for real world scenes. The subset is mainly composed of street scenes and we consider 6 class objects of interest in the scenes: Window, CarRear, CarSide, Pedestrian, Pole and Road. We use the object pairwise frequency matrix of the subset to train our context model. During the detection phase, we conduct two kinds of experiments: detection without context model and detection with context model. See Fig. 4 and Fig. 5 for the detection results. From the experiments, we find our multiclass Hough forest can accurately detect some rigid classes of objects from real scenes such as: Window, CarSide and Road. Meanwhile, from the left confusion matrix in Fig. 5, we find there exist wrongly detected instances or missed classes, such as Pedestrian and Pole. This is caused by the great variations or high deformations of the objects of these classes. After incorporating object relative location constraints with the appearances, we can successfully avoid such wrong detections and effectively decrease the false positive rate. The right confusion matrix in Fig. 5 illustrates our analysis.

One shortcoming of our method is the context model can now only help avoid wrong results after multiclass Hough forest detection, but can not improve the voting accuracy of our multiclass Hough forest (e.g. the missed instances due to occlusion in the last column in Fig. 4). The main reason is that our proposed greedy search algorithm is based on the local maxima in the hypothesis space and thus we can not find new instances if the votes are small. In the future work, we may consider combine our Hough forest and the context model into an unified model to solve the above problem.

4. ACKNOWLEDGEMENTS

The work was supported by Natural Science Foundation of China under Grant No. 60723003, 61021062 and 61003113, 973 Program of China under Grant No. 2010CB327903, and Natural Science Foundation of Jiangsu under Grant No BK 2009082.

5. REFERENCES

[1] S. Agarwal, A. Awan, and D. Roth. Learning to detect objects in images via a sparse, part-based representation. *TPAMI*, 26(11):1475 –1490, 2004.

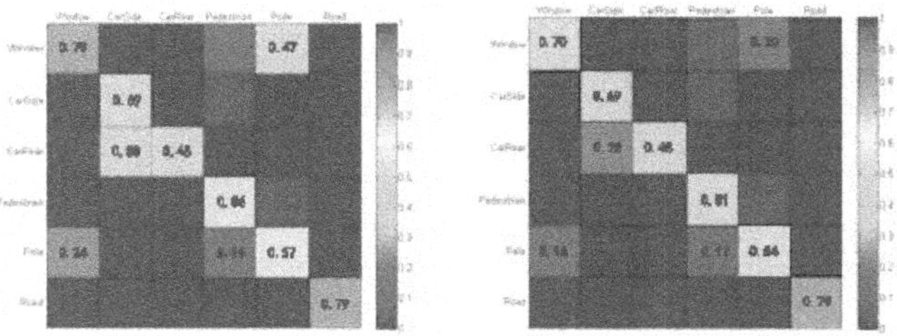

Figure 5: The confusion matrix for 6 classes. Left: results without context; Right: results with context.

[2] M. Andriluka, S. Roth, and B. Schiele. People tracking by detection and people detection by tracking. In *CVPR*, pages 1 – 8, 2008.

[3] E. Borenstein and S. Ullman. Learning to segment. In *ECCV*, pages 315–328, 2004.

[4] L. Breiman. Random forests. *Machine Learning*, 45(1):5–32, 2001.

[5] N. Dalal and B. Triggs. Histograms of oriented gradients for human detection. In *CVPR*, pages 886–893, 2005.

[6] C. Desai, D. Ramanan, and C. Fowlkes. Discriminative models for multi-class object layout. In *ICCV*, pages 229–236, 2009.

[7] J. Gall and V. S. Lempitsky. Class-specific hough forests for object detection. In *CVPR*, pages 1022–1029, 2009.

[8] C. Galleguillos, A. Rabinovich, and S. Belongie. Object categorization using co-occurrence, location and appearance. In *CVPR*, pages 1–8, 2008.

[9] G. Griffin, A. Holub, and P. Perona. Caltech-256 object category dataset. Technical Report 7694, 2007.

[10] B. Leibe, A. Leonardis, and B. Schiele. Robust object detection with interleaved categorization and segmentation. *IJCV*, 77(1-3):259–289, 2008.

[11] A. Opelt, A. Pinz, and A. Zisserman. Learning an alphabet of shape and appearance for multi-class object detection. *IJCV*, 80(1):16–44, 2008.

[12] B. C. Russell, A. Torralba, K. P. Murphy, and W. T. Freeman. Labelme: A database and web-based tool for image annotation. *IJCV*, 77(1-3):157–173, 2008.

[13] A. Torralba. Contextual priming for object detection. *IJCV*, 53(2):169–191, 2003.

[14] P. A. Viola and M. J. Jones. Robust real-time face detection. *IJCV*, 57(2):137–154, 2004.

Shared Feature Extraction for Semi-supervised Image Classification*

Yong Luo† , Dacheng Tao‡ , Bo Geng†, Chao Xu†, and Stephen Maybank§
†Key Laboratory of Machine Perception (Ministry of Education), Peking University, Beijing, China
‡Faculty of Engineering and Information Technology, University of Technology, Sydney, Sydney, Australia
§Department of Computer Science and Information Systems, Birkbeck College, Malet Street, London, UK
{luoyong, gengbo, xuchao}@cis.pku.edu.cn, Dacheng.Tao@uts.edu.au, sjmaybank@dcs.bbk.ac.uk

ABSTRACT

Multi-task learning (MTL) plays an important role in image analysis applications, e.g. image classification, face recognition and image annotation. That is because MTL can estimate the latent shared subspace to represent the common features given a set of images from different tasks. However, the geometry of the data probability distribution is always supported on an intrinsic image sub-manifold that is embedded in a high dimensional Euclidean space. Therefore, it is improper to directly apply MTL to multiclass image classification. In this paper, we propose a manifold regularized MTL (MRMTL) algorithm to discover the latent shared subspace by treating the high-dimensional image space as a submanifold embedded in an ambient space. We conduct experiments on the PASCAL VOC'07 dataset with 20 classes and the MIR dataset with 38 classes by comparing MRMTL with conventional MTL and several representative image classification algorithms. The results suggest that MRMTL can properly extract the common features for image representation and thus improve the generalization performance of the image classification models.

Categories and Subject Descriptors

I.4.7 [**Image Processing and Computer Vision**]: Feature Measurement—*feature representation*; I.5.2 [**Pattern Recognition**]: Design Methodology—*pattern analysis*

General Terms

Algorithm, Experimentation, Theory

Keywords

Image classification, manifold regularization, multi-task learning, semi-supervised

1. INTRODUCTION

In real image analysis applications, e.g. image classification and face recognition, labeling is time consuming while large amounts of unlabeled images are available. Semi-supervised learning (SSL) can improve the generalization ability of supervised learning by leverage of the unlabeled samples under some circumstances [4, 3]. Particularly, in semi-supervised image classification, we usually have to predict multiple labels and a typical method is to divide it into multiple binary classification tasks [16]. The traditional method is to learn each task separately. However, learning all of these tasks simultaneously can be advantageous by utilizing the multi-task learning (MTL) framework [1].

MTL is an approach to learn a task together with other related tasks at the same time, using a shared representation. This can often lead to a better model for the main task, because it allows the learner to use the commonality among the tasks. MTL has been widely used in various image analysis applications. In [5], it was applied to locating doors and recognizing door types from image pixel level features. Torralba et al. [13] applied MTL to object detection by utilizing the common features shared by different object classes. Since then, a lot of consequent results have been obtained for face recognition and image annotation.

MTL makes sense in these applications because we usually have a large number of classes but a limited number of the labeled training images from each class. By the use of MTL, images from related tasks can be combined together to jointly discover the shared features. These features are useful for each particular task. Besides, it has proven that the number of training samples required to train each task decreases linearly with the increasing number of tasks [2]. Therefore, given a large number of image classification tasks, it is feasible to obtain satisfied classification performance by using a very small number of labeled samples from each task.

However, it is not advisable to directly apply MTL to the high dimensional Euclidean space because images represented by a specific feature space, lie on a very low-dimensional image sub-manifold embedded in the ambient space. In this situation, a small amount of labeled samples cannot represent the true underlying data distribution. Thus the predictive function estimated with a risk minimization principle only using the labeled samples is not optimal. To solve this problem for MTL based image classification, we propose to minimize the joint empirical risks (JER) in MTL and approximate the sub-manifold together to obtain a robust model, which can smooth the predictive functions along the sub-manifold. This is motivated by the manifold regularization (MR) [3] framework. MR is a data-dependent regularization that exploits the geometry of the probability distribution. This geometry can be used to approximate the

*Area chair: Bernard Merialdo

MM'11, November 28–December 1, 2011, Scottsdale, Arizona, USA.

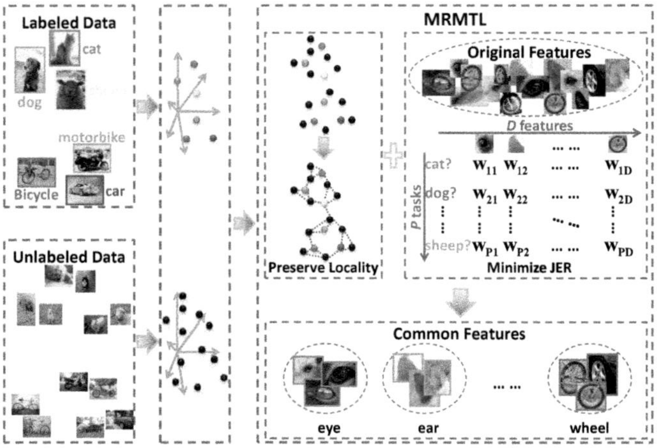

Figure 1: The framework of our proposed Manifold Regularized Multi-Task Learning algorithm.

true underlying image sub-manifold. MR has widely applied to many areas, e.g., image classification [7], image search ranking [8, 9], query suggestion [17], and video annotation [15, 14].

It is worthy emphasizing that the key in learning with MR is constructing a data adjacency graph to encode the low-dimensional sub-manifold. In single task learning, the amount of data may be insufficient for estimating the true underlying structure. The problem is lessened in MTL because the data used to construct the graph are from multiple tasks.

Therefore, we propose manifold regularized MTL (MRMTL) to discover the latent shared subspace of different tasks. Given several visual representations for image, we aim to learn a corresponding mapping by using MRMTL for each of them. We first calculate the graph Laplacian of the whole data set and conduct MRMTL to obtain the optimal transformation. Subsequently, original features are mapped to the low-dimensional shared subspace across labels by this transformation. Finally, we calculate kernels in the original features and cross-label features respectively and linearly combine the two kernels. We conduct extensive experiments on the PASCAL VOC'07 dataset with 20 classes [6] and the MIR dataset with 38 classes [11] by comparing MRMTL with conventional MTL [1] and several representative semi-supervised image classification algorithms [4, 10]. The experimental results demonstrate the effectiveness of the proposed MRMTL.

2. MANIFOLD REGULARIZED MULTI-TASK LEARNING

MRMTL is a particular implementation of SSL. Fig.1 shows the diagram of MRMTL for image classification: Given both labeled and unlabeled images, we first extract visual features for image representation. A data adjacency graph is then constructed by the use of all images from different tasks to generate a manifold regularization term. Multiple image classification tasks, e.g. "whether it is a dog or not?", are created and we can then find an optimal feature mapping by minimizing JER of these predictors with MR.

2.1 Notations

We use N, M, D and P to denote the number of training images, the number of different kinds of visual features for image representation, the data dimensionality, and the number of labels, respectively. The subscripts l, u and lu signify *labeled*, *unlabeled*, and *labeled + unlabeled*. The data matrix and the label indicator matrix for the mth visual feature are denoted as $X^m = [\mathbf{x}_1^m, \ldots, \mathbf{x}_N^m] \in \mathbb{R}^{D\times N}$ and $Y \in \mathbb{R}^{P\times N}$, where $\mathbf{x}_n^m \in \mathbb{R}^D$ is the nth instance, and $Y_{pn} = 1$ if the pth label is assigned to the nth instance, and -1 otherwise. The superscript m is omitted in our formulation because we handle each kind of feature in the same way.

2.2 Multi-Task Learning with MR

Given a set of N_l labeled samples $\{(\mathbf{x}_n, y_n)\}_{n=1}^{N_l}, y_n \in \{+1, -1\}$ drawn from a probability distribution $\mathcal{P}$ and a set of N_u unlabeled samples $\{\mathbf{x}_n\}_{n=N_l+1}^{N_l+N_u}$ generated according to the marginal distribution $\mathcal{P}_X$ of $\mathcal{P}$, the manifold regularization framework is to estimate an unknown function f by minimizing

$$\underset{f\in\mathcal{H}_K}{\operatorname{argmin}} \frac{1}{N_l}\sum_{n=1}^{N_l} L(\mathbf{x}_n, y_n, f) + \gamma_A\|f\|_K^2 + \gamma_I\|f\|_I^2, \quad (1)$$

where $\mathcal{H}_K$ is an associated Reproducing Kernel Hilbert Space (RKHS) and L is a prescribed loss function. $\|f\|_K^2$ penalizes the classifier complexities in the ambient space. $\|f\|_I^2$ is a smoothness penalty corresponding to the probability distribution. Both γ_A and γ_I are trade-off parameters. Following [3], $\|f\|_I^2$ can be approximated by $\frac{1}{(N_l+N_u)^2}\mathbf{f}^T\mathcal{L}\mathbf{f}$, where $\mathbf{f} = [f(\mathbf{x}_1), \ldots, f(\mathbf{x}_{N_l+N_u})]^T$, $\frac{1}{(N_l+N_u)^2}$ is the normalizing coefficient and $\mathcal{L}$ is the graph Laplacian given by $\mathcal{L} = \mathcal{D} - \mathcal{W}$. Here, $\mathcal{W}_{ij}$ is the edge weight, e.g., the heat kernel weight $\mathcal{W}_{ij} = e^{-\|\mathbf{x}_i - \mathbf{x}_j\|^2/4t}$ in the data adjacency graph constructed by using k nearest neighbors and the diagonal matrix $\mathcal{D}$ is given by $\mathcal{D}_{ii} = \sum_{j=1}^{N_l+N_u}\mathcal{W}_{ij}$.

The construction of the graph Laplacian needs large amounts of data. Now we learn multiple tasks at the same time and have enough data to construct a graph to approximate the true underlying data manifold. Thus, the proposed manifold regularized multi-task learning (MRMTL) can be written as:

$$\underset{\{f_p\}\in\mathcal{H}_K}{\operatorname{argmin}} \sum_{p=1}^{P}\left(\frac{1}{N_{lp}}\sum_{n=1}^{N_{lp}} L(\mathbf{x}_n^p, y_n^p, f_p) + \gamma_A\|f_p\|_K^2 + \gamma_I\|f_p\|_I^2\right), \quad (2)$$

where $y_n^p = Y_{pn}$.This formulation differs from the traditional MTL framework in the added MR term, which is helpful for learning with image features as illustrated in section 1.

In MTL, the predictive function for the pth task(label) is,

$$f_p(\mathbf{x}) = \mathbf{w}_p^T\mathbf{x} + \mathbf{v}_p^T\Theta\mathbf{x}, \quad (3)$$

where $\mathbf{w} \in \mathbb{R}^D$ and $\mathbf{v} \in \mathbb{R}^r$ are the weight vectors, $\Theta \in \mathbb{R}^{r\times D}$ is the linear transformation parameterizing the latent shared low-dimensional subspace, and r is the dimensionality of the latent shared subspace. The transformation Θ is common for all labels, and it has the orthogonality $\Theta\Theta^T = I$. We simplify the general formulation in (2) by assuming that the input data for each task are identical and we propose to learn an optimal feature map Θ from the data in the original feature space by minimizing the following regularized empirical risk:

$$\underset{\Theta}{\operatorname{argmin}} \sum_{p=1}^{P}\left(\frac{1}{N_l}\sum_{n=1}^{N_l} L(f_p(\mathbf{x}_n), y_n^p) + \alpha\|\mathbf{w}_p\|^2 + \beta\|\mathbf{w}_p + \Theta^T\mathbf{v}_p\|^2 + \frac{\gamma_I}{(N_l+N_u)^2}\mathbf{f}_p^T\mathcal{L}\mathbf{f}_p\right), \quad (4)$$

where $\mathbf{f}_p = [f_p(\mathbf{x}_1), \ldots, f_p(\mathbf{x}_{N_l+N_u})]^T$, $\|\mathbf{w}_p\|^2$ is the regularizer used in MTL and $\|\mathbf{w}_p + \Theta^T\mathbf{v}_p\|^2$ controls the complexity of the models. Both α and β are trade-off parameters. Let $\mathbf{u}_p = \mathbf{w}_p + \Theta^T \mathbf{v}_p$, This problem can be reformulated equivalently as

$$\min_{\Theta} \sum_{p=1}^{P} \left(\frac{1}{N_l} \sum_{n=1}^{N_l} L(\mathbf{u}_p^T \mathbf{x}_n, y_n^p) + \alpha \|\mathbf{u}_p - \Theta^T \mathbf{v}_p\|^2 + \beta \|\mathbf{u}_p\|^2 + \frac{\gamma_I}{(N_l + N_u)^2} \mathbf{f}_p^T \mathcal{L} \mathbf{f}_p \right), \quad s.t. \quad \Theta\Theta^T = I. \tag{5}$$

where $\mathbf{f}_p = [\mathbf{u}_p^T \mathbf{x}_1, \ldots, \mathbf{u}_p^T \mathbf{x}_{N_l+N_u}]^T$. We consider the least squares loss function,

$$L(\mathbf{u}_p^T \mathbf{x}_n, y_n^p) = (\mathbf{u}_p^T \mathbf{x}_n - y_n^p)^2.$$

Therefore, we can simplify (5) as:

$$\min_{\Theta} \frac{1}{N_l} \|X_l^T U - Y^T\|_F^2 + \alpha \|U - \Theta^T V\|_F^2 + \beta \|U\|_F^2 + \frac{\gamma_I}{(N_l + N_u)^2} tr((X_{lu}^T U)^T \mathcal{L} (X_{lu}^T U)) \quad s.t. \ \Theta\Theta^T = I. \tag{6}$$

where $\|\cdot\|_F$ denotes the Frobenius norm of a matrix, $U = [\mathbf{u}_1, \ldots, \mathbf{u}_P]$, and $V = [\mathbf{v}_1, \ldots, \mathbf{v}_P]$.

This is a convex optimization problem and we can get a closed form solution. Fixing (Θ, U), we obtain the optimal V by taking the derivative of the expression in (6) with respect to V and setting it to be zero.

$$V^* = \Theta U.$$

Similarly, substituting $V^* = \Theta U$ into (6) and fixing Θ, we obtain the optimal U,

$$U^* = \frac{1}{N_l}(M - \alpha\Theta^T\Theta)^{-1} X_l Y^T, \tag{7}$$

where M is defined as:

$$M = \frac{1}{N_l} X_l X_l^T + (\alpha + \beta) I + \frac{\gamma_I}{(N_l + N_u)^2} X_{lu} \mathcal{L} X_{lu}^T. \tag{8}$$

Finally, we can substitute the expression for (U^*, V^*) into (6) and obtain the optimal Θ. It is direct that this can be done by solving the following trace maximization problem:

$$\max_{\Theta} \ tr\Big((\Theta S_1 \Theta^T)^{-1} \Theta S_2 \Theta^T \Big) \quad s.t. \ \Theta\Theta^T = I, \tag{9}$$

where S_1 and S_2 are defined as:

$$S_1 = I - \alpha M^{-1} \tag{10}$$

$$S_2 = M^{-1} X_l Y^T Y X_l^T M^{-1}, \tag{11}$$

The obtained Θ^* can be used to induce a set of cross-label features, i.e., $\Theta^* \mathbf{x}$. We use these features to construct a visual kernel K_{v-comn} and combine it with the original kernel K_v, i.e.,

$$K_{v-new} = \lambda K_v + (1 - \lambda) K_{v-comn}, \tag{12}$$

where $\lambda \in [0, 1]$ is the combination parameter. The new visual kernel K_{v-new} contains both the shared information of different image classification tasks extracted by MRMTL and also the discriminative information in the original features. This kernel is further used for semi-supervised image classification.

3. EXPERIMENTS

We evaluate our method on two data sets, the PASCAL VOC'07 [6] and the MIR Flickr [11], which have been used in [10]. There are around 10,000 images of 20 different object categories in the PASCAL VOC'07 set and 25,000 images of 38 categories in the MIR Flickr set. The 15 different kinds of visual representations as described in [10] are extracted. We measure the performance using the average precision (AP) criterion for each class and the mean AP (mAP) over all classes. The number of labeled training examples is 100 (50 positive and 50 negative) in our experiments.

3.1 Extracting Shared Subspace

This set of experiments evaluates the effectiveness of MRMTL. We compare it with two popular methods for extracting shared subspace. The experiments are performed by the use of features in the shared subspace for semi-supervised image classification and the 15 different image representations are used for evaluation individually. The experimental setup is summarized as follows:

- **MRMTL:** The regularization parameters α, β and γ_I are tuned from the candidate set $\{10^i | i = -4, -3, \ldots, 3, 4\}$. The parameters k and t used in computing the Laplacian matrix are tuned from $\{1, 2, \ldots, 10, 20, \ldots, 100\}$ and $\{10^i | i = 2, 3, \ldots, 9\}$ respectively. The performance of the proposed method is not sensitive to the dimensionality of the shared subspace r as long as it is not too small. Hence, it is fixed to $5 \times \lfloor (m-1)/5 \rfloor$, where m is the number of labels.
- **ML-LS:** The multi-label formulation is presented in [12]. The regularization parameters α and β are tuned from the candidate set $\{10^i | i = -4, -3, \ldots, 3, 4\}$.
- **ASO-SVM:** The alternating structural optimization (ASO) algorithm proposed in [1] with hinge loss. The regularization parameter is tuned on the set $\{10^i | i = -4, -3, \ldots, 2, 3\}$.

The experimental results on the two data sets are presented in Figure 2. We observe that the proposed MRMTL approach perform the best for 9 features in the VOC set and 7 features in the MIR set.

3.2 Kernel Combination

In this subsection we use the shared features extracted with MRMTL to calculate a kernel and combine it with the kernel obtained from the original features. We choose the best combination parameter for combining the two kernels with this set of experiments. For the 15 kinds of original features, we average the distances between images based on these descriptors and use it to compute an RBF kernel. For the common features, we average the similarities which are computed based on a linear kernel. We simply combine the two kernels with varying λ to create the new kernel and apply it to classification, the results are shown in Figure 3.

The results indicate that common features ($\lambda = 0$) are not as good as the original features ($\lambda = 1$) for classification tasks on both PASCAL VOC'07 and MIR Flickr. However, by properly combining common features and original features, we can obtain significant performance improvement. In particular, by setting $\lambda = 0.8$, we can obtain 13.7% improvement on the PASCAL VOC'07 dataset and 7.8% improvement on the MIR Flickr dataset compared to the use of only original features.

3.3 Semi-supervised Image Classification with the New Kernel

With the best combination parameter, we calculate the new kernel described in (12) and use it for semi-supervised image classification to further verify the effectiveness of MRMTL. This set of experiments are based on the same setting as that used in [10]. In which, some additional textual information is used. We specifically compare the following methods:

- **SVM**: visual classifier learned on labeled examples.
- **Co-training**: learn a visual classifier and a textual classifier on the labeled data set, and bootstrap training ex-

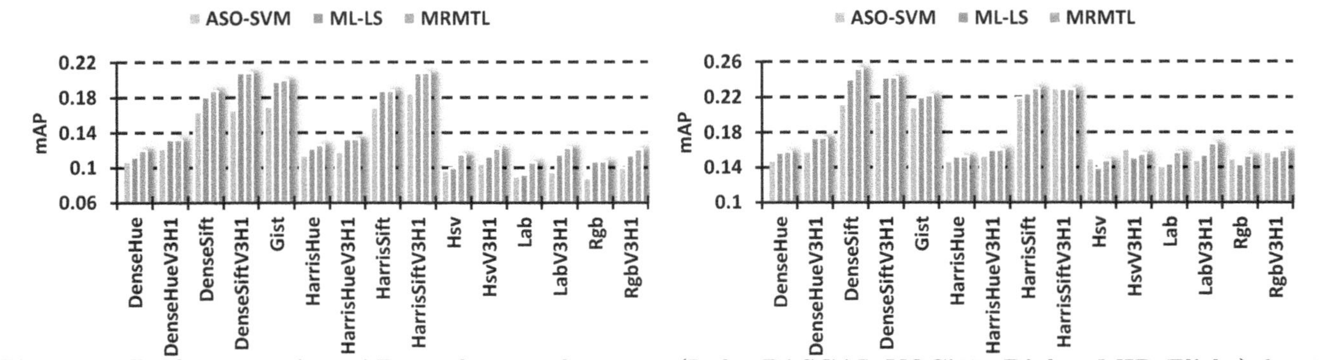

Figure 2: Performance in mAP on the two data sets (Left: PASCAL VOC'07; Right: MIR Flickr) for 15 kinds of features using 50 positive and 50 negative labeled examples for each class.

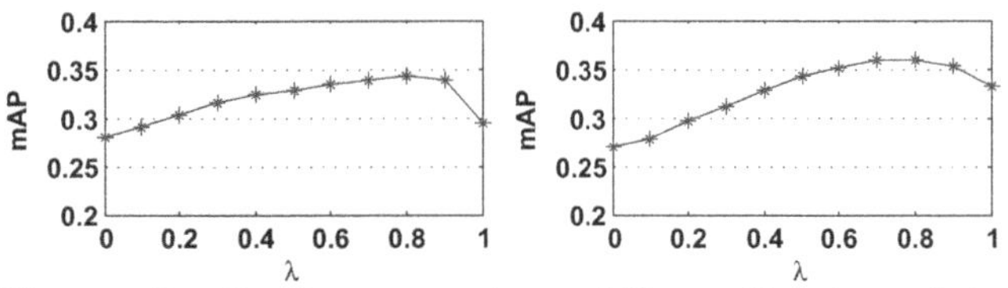

Figure 3: Performance in mAP on the two data sets (Left: PASCAL VOC'07; Right: MIR Flickr) of combining the original kernel and common kernel.

Table 1: Performance in mAP on the two data sets for different learning methods.

	PASCAL VOC'07	MIR Flickr
SVM	0.294	0.333
Co-training	0.323	0.351
MKL+LSR	0.366	0.367
MRMTL+CoTR	**0.385**	**0.386**

amples for each classifier based on the output of the other classifier.

• **MKL+LSR**: the approach proposed in [10]. A multiple kernel learning (MKL) classifier is learned on the labeled examples firstly. Then a classifier (only using the visual information) was obtained by the least squares regression (LSR) on the MKL scores for all examples.

• **MRMTL+CoTR**: simply replace K_v with K_{v-new} in the co-training setup.

The results of MKL+LSR, co-training and baseline SVM presented in [10] are directly used here because we use the same datasets and the same features. The experimental results shown in Table 1 show the superiority of the proposed MRMTL for image classification. The individual APs of the 58 classes are not reported due to the limited page length.

4. CONCLUSION AND DISCUSSION

We present a novel manifold regularized multi-task learning (MRMTL) based algorithm for semi-supervised image classification in this paper. In particular, the algorithm extracts the latent shared subspace among multiple tasks, in which a feature mapping is computed to discover this subspace for each kind of visual feature. Afterward, we transform the data into the shared subspace and a linear combination of the original features and the common features is used to get a new visual kernel. Our experiments demonstrate that 1) MRMTL outperforms popular algorithms for extracting shared subspace on image classification tasks, 2) it is effective to combine both the common features across different tasks with the original visual features.

5. ACKNOWLEDGMENTS

This paper is partially supported by NBRPC 2011CB302400, NSFC 60975014 and NSFB 4102024.

6. REFERENCES

[1] R. K. Ando and T. Zhang. A framework for learning predictive structures from multiple tasks and unlabeled data. *JMLR*, 2005.

[2] J. Baxter. A model of inductive bias learning. *JAIR*, 2000.

[3] M. Belkin, P. Niyogi, and V. Sindhwani. Manifold regularization: A geometric framework for learning from labeled and unlabeled examples. *JMLR*, 2006.

[4] A. Blum and T. Mitchell. Combining labeled and unlabeled data with co-training. In *COLT*, 1998.

[5] R. Caruana. Multitask learning. *Machine Learning*, 1997.

[6] M. Everingham, L. Van Gool, C. K. I. Williams, J. Winn, and A. Zisserman. The PASCAL Visual Object Classes Challenge 2007 (VOC2007) Results.

[7] B. Geng, C. Xu, D. Tao, L. Yang, and X. Hua. Ensemble manifold regularization. In *CVPR*, 2009.

[8] B. Geng, L. Yang, C. Xu, and X. Hua. Ranking model adaptation for domain specific search. In *CIKM*, 2009.

[9] B. Geng, L. Yang, C. Xu, and X. Hua. Content-aware ranking for visual search. In *CVPR*, 2010.

[10] M. Guillaumin, J. Verbeek, and C. Schmid. Multimodal semi-supervised learning for image classification. In *CVPR*, 2010.

[11] M. J. Huiskes and M. S. Lew. The mir flickr retrieval evaluation. In *MIR*, 2008.

[12] S. W. Ji, L. Tang, S. P. Yu, and J. P. Ye. Extracting shared subspace for multi-label classification. In *KDD*, 2008.

[13] A. Torralba, K. P. Murphy, and W. T. Freeman. Sharing features: efficient boosting procedures for multiclass object detection. In *CVPR*, 2004.

[14] M. Wang, X.-S. Hua, R. Hong, J. Tang, G.-J. Qi, and Y. Song. Unified video annotation via multi-graph learning. *TCSVT*, 2009.

[15] M. Wang, X.-S. Hua, J. Tang, and R. Hong. Beyond distance measurement: Constructing neighborhood similarity for video annotation. *TMM*, 2009.

[16] Z. Zha, X. Hua, T. Mei, J. Wang, G. Qi, and Z. Wang. Joint multi-label multi-instance learning for image classification. In *CVPR*, 2008.

[17] Z. Zheng-Jun, Y. Linjun, M. Tao, W. Meng, and W. Zengfu. Visual query suggestion. In *SIGMM*, 2009.

Difficulty Guided Image Retrieval using Linear Multiview Embedding *

Yangxi Li
Peking University, Beijing, China
liyangxi@gmail.com

Bo Geng
Peking University, Beijing, China
bogeng1985@gmail.com

Zheng-Jun Zha
National University of Singapore, Singapore
junzzustc@gmail.com

Dacheng Tao
University of Technology, Sydney, Australia
dacheng.tao@uts.edu.au

Linjun Yang
Microsoft Research Asia, Beijing, China
linjuny@microsoft.com

Chao Xu
Peking University, Beijing, China
xuchao@cis.pku.edu.cn

ABSTRACT

Existing image retrieval systems suffer from a radical performance variance for different queries. The bad initial search results for "difficult" queries may greatly degrade the performance of their subsequent refinements, especially the refinement that utilizes the information mined from the search results, e.g., pseudo relevance feedback based reranking. In this paper, we tackle this problem by proposing a query difficulty guided image retrieval system, which selectively performs reranking according to the estimated query difficulty. To improve the performance of both reranking and difficulty estimation, we apply multiview embedding (ME) to images represented by multiple different features for integrating a joint subspace by preserving the neighborhood information in each feature space. However, existing ME approaches suffer from both "out of sample" and huge computational cost problems, and cannot be applied to online reranking or offline large-scale data processing for practical image retrieval systems. Therefore, we propose a linear multiview embedding algorithm which learns a linear transformation from a small set of data and can effectively infer the subspace features of new data. Empirical evaluations on both Oxford and 500K ImageNet datasets suggest the effectiveness of the proposed difficulty guided retrieval system with LME.

Categories and Subject Descriptors

H.3.3 [**Information Search and Retrieval**]: Retrieval models

General Terms

Algorithms, Experimentation, Performance

Keywords

Spectral embedding, Reranking, Query difficulty estimation

---

*Area chair: Lexing Xie

1. INTRODUCTION

State-of-the-art image retrieval technologies suffer from a radical performance variance in response to different queries. Even for retrieval systems which perform well normally, their search results are unsatisfactory for some "difficult" queries. For these queries, the performance may be further degraded if they applied some query dependent strategies to refine the performance by mining the information from the query's search results. Taking pseudo relevance feedback based reranking [15] for instance, system suffers from performance deterioration greatly for "difficult" queries, because their search results may contain few relevant examples at top, which degrades the subsequent learning of robust classifiers to rerank the results.

One possible solution to this problem is to estimate the query's difficulty from the initial search results and utilize this information to guide the query dependent strategies. Query difficulty estimation(QDE) is proposed to quantitatively estimate the retrieval performance of a given query on a given dataset. Although various QDE methods have been proposed and perform well for text queries[18, 16], difficulty of image queries has rarely been studied for content based image retrieval(CBIR). That is because "a picture is worth more than a thousand words", whereas the well known semantic gap hinders the interpretation of rich high-level semantics from low-level visual features. Multiview representation, in which each image is expressed by various features as different views, could be used to narrow the semantic gap and boost the performance of retrieval and difficulty estimation. One natural issue related to multiview representation is: how to learn an optimal feature that can integrate the information from different views, to facilitate the similarity computation for retrieval and difficulty computation.

To resolve this issue, we apply spectral embedding algorithms for multiview features by encoding the neighborhood information in different feature spaces into a joint subspace. However, most multiview data mining algorithms[13, 14, 4] have some serious deficiencies which hinder their usage in multimedia search systems. The first difficulty lies in the online phase, because these algorithms cannot extract the feature representation for query images directly but require computing the embedding again, which is unacceptable for real time image retrieval systems. The second difficulty lies in the offline data processing phase caused by the spectral

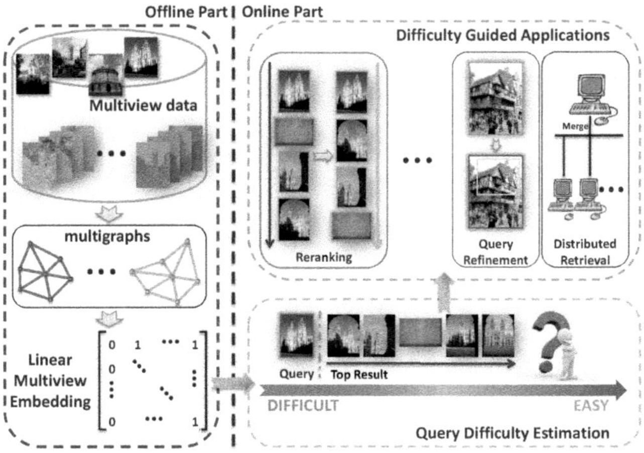

Figure 1: Proposed difficulty guided image retrieval system with LME.

decomposition over all the database images. This generally takes $O(n^3)$ time for database with n images [12]. It is infeasible for a practical CBIR system with millions or billions images in database.

To address the difficulties illustrated above, we propose a novel *linear* multiview embedding (LME) algorithm, which learns a linear transformation under the locality constraints on multiview data. With the low dimensional embedding derived from high dimensional data and the linear transformation, we design a query difficulty guided image retrieval system, which selectively performs reranking according to the estimated difficulty of the query image. This system is advantageous for several reasons:

- Performance perspective: since performing reranking on difficult queries tends to incur performance degradation due to the noisy initial results, difficulty guided image retrieval system brings performance improvement by preventing such degradations.
- Efficiency perspective: Both LME and difficulty estimation are easy to compute, while difficulty guided image retrieval system could avoid computational cost for unnecessary reranking.

2. SYSTEM OVERVIEW

Figure 1 illustrates the framework of LME based difficulty guided image retrieval system, which contains an offline module and an online module. In the offline part, a linear transformation is derived from LME. Firstly, different locality structures of multiview data are encoded in several graphs. Using the notion of graph Laplacian, we then get the multiview embedding and compute a linear transformation from it. This transformation optimally preserves local neighborhood information encoded in graphs.

In online part, the high dimensional features of query and its initial retrieval results are mapped into a certain subspace with above linear transformation effectively. These low dimensional embeddings are used together to estimate current query's difficulty. Then the estimated query difficulty is applied to the difficulty guided result refinement algorithm.

In this paper, Image QDE is defined as the degree of consistency between query image and its top results. The more inconsistent they are, the more difficult this query is. Formally, we could define one query's QDE score as

$$d(q, r_q) = \frac{1}{K}\sum\nolimits_{i=1}^{K} \|q - r_q(i)\|^2 \qquad (1)$$

where r_q is the query q's top K results. Some other methods in text QDE[18, 16] can also be borrowed here to boost the estimation. QDE provides valuable feedback to both retrieval system and users. A retrieval system could invoke alternative retrieval strategies according to queries' difficulties, e.g., selective query expansion, or guided image reranking. Users benefit from QDE by refining difficult query images to restate their search intention. Moreover, QDE is a useful clue for distributed image retrieval system to merge results from different datasets. Among all these applications, we focus on query difficulty guided reranking in this paper, and others will be left as our future work.

3. LINEAR MULTIVIEW EMBEDDING

In this section, we introduce the proposed linear multiview embedding (LME) in detail. We could describe LME formally: given a multiview dataset with n samples and m modalities, i.e., a set of data matrices $X = \{X^{(i)} \in \Re^{d_i \times n}\}_{i=1}^{m}$, where $X^{(i)}$ is the d_i-dimensional feature matrix for the ith representation. LME aims to find a linear transformation matrix U which could map the high dimensional data $X \in \Re^{d_t \times n}$ into a low dimensional embedding $Y \in \Re^{l \times n}(l < d_t)$, i.e., $Y = U^T X$, meanwhile keeps the neighborhood structures existed in the multiview dataset.

3.1 Multiview Spectral Embedding

In order to explore the complementary property among multiple views, each view's contribution is linearly combined with a set of nonnegative weights $\alpha = [\alpha_1, \ldots, \alpha_m], \sum_{i=1}^{m} \alpha_i = 1$. To avoid the trivial solution of α, we adopt the trick utilized in [13] which substitutes α_i with $\alpha_i^r, r > 1$. The optimization over all views is [14]:

$$\arg\min_{Y,\alpha} \sum\nolimits_{i=1}^{m} \alpha_i^r tr(Y L^{(i)} Y^T) \qquad (2)$$

The Laplacian matrix $L^{(i)} = D^{(i)} - W^{(i)}$, where $W^{(i)} \in \Re^{n \times n}$ is the similarity matrix of view ith and $W_{pq}^{(i)} = sim(x_p^{(i)}, x_q^{(i)})$ if $x_p^{(i)}$ is among the k-nearest neighbors of $x_q^{(i)}$ or vice versa; $W_{pq}^{(i)} = 0$ otherwise. $sim()$ is the similarity function between two data points. $W^{(i)}$ encodes the neighborhood information of the ith view. $D^{(i)}$ is a diagonal matrix and its entries are the column sum of $W^{(i)}$, $d_{jj}^{(i)} = \sum_p w_{pj}^{(i)}$.

3.2 Linear Approximation

As aforementioned, Optimization of equation (2) cannot apply to multimedia search directly. In this subsection, we get a linear transformation from equation (2) which can be easily applied to CBIR systems.

Given the data $X \in \Re^{d_t \times n}$ in the high dimensional space, suppose there is a linear transformation U can map X to a low dimensional embedding Y which satisfies the optimization of equation (2), i.e., $Y = U^T X$. Therefore, equation (2) can be rewritten as

$$\arg\min_{U,\alpha} \sum\nolimits_{i=1}^{m} \alpha_i^r tr(U^T X L^{(i)} X^T U) \qquad (3)$$

To uniquely determine U, the constraint $U^T X X^T U = I_d$ or $U^T U = I_d$ is imposed on equation (3). Formally, the objective function of LME is defined as follows:

$$\arg\min_{U,\alpha} \sum\nolimits_{i=1}^{m} \alpha_i^r tr(U^T X L^{(i)} X^T U)$$
$$\text{s.t. } U^T X X^T U = I_d; \sum\nolimits_{i=1}^{m} \alpha_i = 1, \alpha_i \geq 0 \qquad (4)$$

The transformation matrix U encodes the intrinsic locality structure existed in the multiview dataset. It is a linear approximation to the nonlinear spectral embedding algorithm.

3.3 Optimization

Equation (4) is a nonlinearly constrained nonconvex optimization problem. In this paper, we follow [14] using the alternating optimization to solve this problem.

For a fixed U, we can calculate α with Lagrange multiplier. The Lagrange function is

$$L(\alpha, \lambda) = \sum_{i=1}^{m} \alpha_i^r tr(U^T X L^{(i)} X^T U) - \lambda(\sum_{i=1}^{m} \alpha_i - 1) \quad (5)$$

By setting the derivative of $L(\alpha, \lambda)$ with respect to α_i and λ to zero, α_i can be obtained by

$$\alpha_i = \frac{(1/tr(U^T X L^{(i)} X^T U))^{1/(r-1)}}{\sum_{i=1}^{m}(1/tr(U^T X L^{(i)} X^T U))^{1/(r-1)}} \quad (6)$$

Afterwards, with a fixed α, equation (4) degenerates to

$$\arg\min_U tr(U^T X L X^T U), \quad \text{s.t. } U^T X X^T U = I_d \quad (7)$$

where $L = \sum_{i=1}^{m} \alpha_i^r L^{(i)}$. This optimization problem can be solved by conducting the generalized eigenvalue decomposition on XLX^T, i.e., $XLX^T\vec{\beta} = \lambda XX^T\vec{\beta}$. The optimal solution for equation (7) is the k eigenvectors associated with k smallest eigenvalues.

4. EXPERIMENTAL RESULT

In this section, we evaluate the effectiveness of proposed difficulty guided image retrieval system. We compare the proposed LME with the conventional linear feature dimensionality reduction algorithm PCA [9], and a nonlinear method LPP [8] in experiments.

4.1 Dataset

We conduct the experiments on two datasets. First is the *Oxford* dataset available from [1], which is a relative small set of 5K images with an extensive associated ground truth. For the local image features, the visual words are directly downloaded from their website, and the 1M codebook version is utilized for its best performance. We also build an *Oxford+500K* dataset which is composed of *Oxford* and 500K randomly selected unlabeled images from ImageNet dataset [2]. These 500K images are assumed not to contain images of the ground truth of *Oxford* and only used as "distractors" for the experiments.

We extract the multiview features from three different views. The first view feature is from the *global feature view*, a 428D concatenated feature which is used in [17] composed of the 225D block-wise color moment feature, the 75D edge distribution histogram feature, and the 128D wavelet texture feature. The second view feature is from the *biologically inspired feature view*[11]. The 544D biologically inspired feature is designed to mimic the human's process of visual cortex for computer vision applications. For these two views, Heat kernel is adopted to compute the similarity matrix $W^{(i)}$. The third view is the *bag-of-visual-words view*, which represents each image as a sparse bag-of-visual-words vector [10, 6, 5] where the length of vector equals to the number of unique visual words, and each dimension of vector records a specific weight of current visual word. Spatial consistency is adopted as similarity metric for this view. To calculate the spatial consistency between two images, we

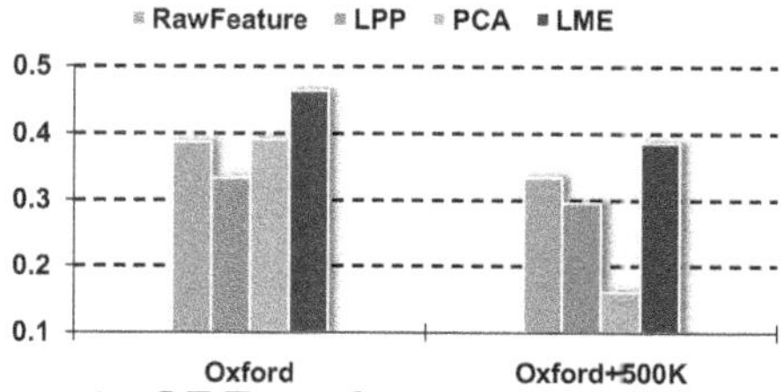

Figure 2: QDE performance comparison.

first conduct the RANSAC algorithm [3] to find out those "inlier" visual words which satisfy the affine transformation between two images. The spatial consistency similarity is defined as the sum of these visual words' IDF values. In addition, we concatenate each image's first two views as a 972D feature x which is high dimensional and needs dimensionality reduction.

Oxford dataset is evenly split into 5 folds, three are used for training the linear transformation U, one for validation and one for test. This U is directly used in large scale experiment on *Oxford+500K*.We conduct cross-validation five times and the average performance is reported.

4.2 Experimental Result and Analysis

4.2.1 Query Difficulty Estimation

Following the tradition in text query difficulty estimation realm, a query's difficulty is in correspondence with its retrieval performance, such as average precision(AP). So a general metric to evaluate the effectiveness of QDE algorithm is the correlation degree between estimated query difficulties and actual AP values of several queries. Spearman's ρ [7] is adopted in this paper. The Spearman's ρ varies within [-1, 1] as the correlation degree between the estimated difficulty and the actual performance changes from perfect reverse to perfect agreement. Note that we need to convert $d(q, r_q)$ in equation 1 to its reciprocal to calculate ρ.

Figure 2 shows the correlation coefficient ρ of QDE with raw high dimensional feature (denoted as "RawFeature"), PCA, LPP and LME, respectively. LME based QDE outperforms other methods on both datasets, which proves the reliability of LME to estimate the query's difficulty.

4.2.2 Difficulty Guided Reranking

In our difficulty guided reranking experiment, raw high dimensional feature x and its 100D low dimensional embedding are used in classic pseudo-relevance feedback based reranking [15], i.e., the top results of initial ranking list are taken as positive samples while the bottom results are taken as negative samples. A classifier is trained from these data and then the initial results are reranked with the scores of this classifier.

We compare mAP (mean average precision) of the reranking with PCA, LPP and proposed LME on both datasets. Figure 4 shows the reranking performance of these three methods as well as the reranking result with raw high dimensional feature, denoted as "RawFeature". The initial ranking result is denoted as "Baseline". From this result, we can see reranking with the proposed LME method consistently outperforms the Baseline and the other two algorithms on both datasets. Specifically, LME based reranking obtains about 6.8% and 11.8% relative improvements on mAP compared with the Baseline. In comparison, PCA and LPP based reranking only gain less than 3% on *Oxford* and 7% on *Oxford+500K*.

Subsequently, we test the effectiveness of proposed dif-

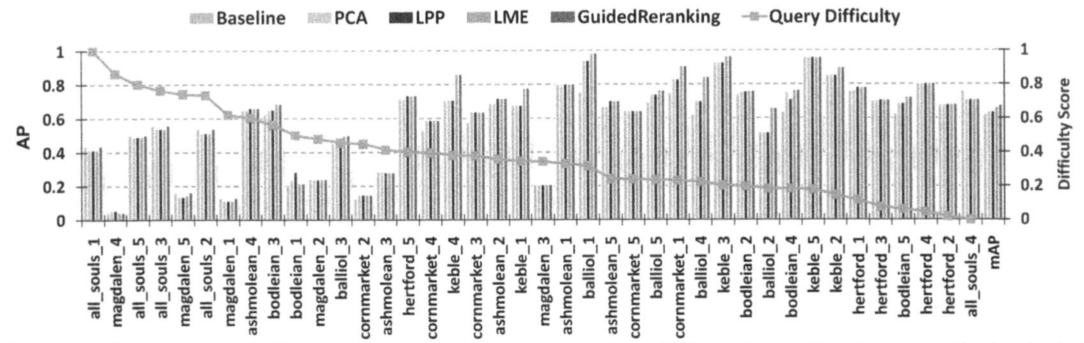

Figure 3: The performance of Baseline and Reranking with different methods over *Oxford* dataset. The queries are ranked from left to right according to the query difficulties from difficult to easy.

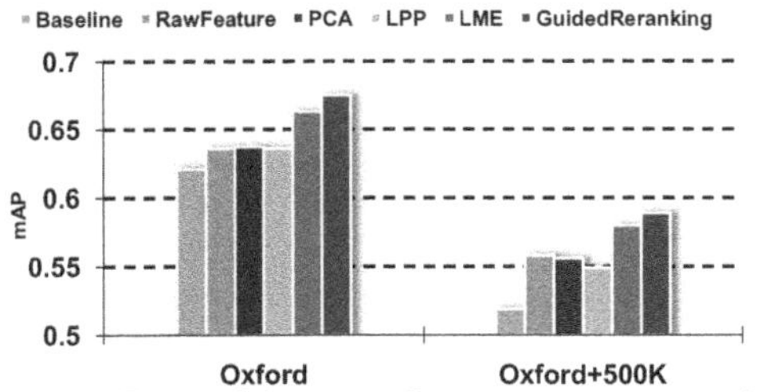

Figure 4: Reranking performance comparison.

ficulty guided reranking which utilizes the QDE scores to guide the performing of reranking. In pseudo relevance feedback based reranking, top results are supposed to be relevant and taken as positive examples in classifier learning. However, this is not always correct for difficult queries, since the irrelevant results may appear at very top of the list. Conducting reranking on these queries will further deteriorate the performance. In this experiment, we restrict the reranking is only applied to those "less difficult" queries, i.e., the ten most difficult queries are excluded from reranking in our settings.

The results of difficulty guided reranking are shown in figure 4 denoted as "GuidedReranking". Difficulty guided reranking brings further performance gain on both datasets, which are 8.7% and 13.5% over Baseline. Compared with LME, the average improvement of Guided Reranking is small, since only the performances of most difficult queries vary from LME to Guided Reranking. If only considering queries which performed reranking, the mAP of Guided Reranking improves 0.072 and 0.093 on both datasets, which are 11.6% and 17.9% better than Baseline. This improvement is quite significant.

Figure 3 demonstrates the average precision (AP) of Baseline and Reranking with different methods for each query respectively. We also show each query's QDE value calculated from equation 1, denoted as "Query Difficulty". Queries are ranked by their QDE scores with the difficult queries positioned at the left and the easy ones at the right. We can observe that reranking does not work well for those difficult queries, while most "less difficult" queries get improvement after reranking. This result demonstrates the correctness of QDE scores calculated with LME and the robustness of difficulty guided reranking.

5. CONCLUSION

In this paper, we proposed a query difficulty guided image retrieval system with linear multiview embedding(LME). The advantages of the proposed system are two-fold. Firstly, the proposed difficulty guided system solves the problem of performance and efficiency degradation of query dependent strategies caused by retrieval performance variance. Furthermore, the proposed linear transformation LME which encodes locality information from multiview data is suitable for online image retrieval applications. The experiments conducted on two datasets have demonstrated the superiority of the difficulty guided image retrieval system.

Acknowledgments

This paper is supported by NBRPC 2011CB302400, NSFC 60975014 and NSFB 4102024.

6. REFERENCES

[1] www.robots.ox.ac.uk/~vgg/data/oxbuildings/.

[2] J. Deng, W. Dong, R. Socher, L. Li, K. Li, and L. Fei-Fei. Imagenet: A large-scale hierarchical image database. In *CVPR*, 2009.

[3] M. A. Fischler and R. C. Bolles. Random sample consensus. *Comm. ACM*, 1981.

[4] B. Geng, C. Xu, D. Tao, L. Yang, and X. Hua. Ensemble manifold regularization. In *CVPR*, 2009.

[5] B. Geng, L. Yang, C. Xu, and X. Hua. Ranking model adaptation for domain specific search. In *CIKM*, 2009.

[6] B. Geng, L. Yang, C. Xu, and X. Hua. Content-aware ranking for visual search. In *CVPR*, 2010.

[7] J. D. Gibbons and S. Chakraborti. *Nonparametric Statistical Inference*. 1992.

[8] X. He and P. Niyogi. Locality preserving projections. In *NIPS*, 2003.

[9] H. Hotelling. Analysis of a complex of statistical variables into principal components. In *Journal of educational psychology*, 1933.

[10] J. Sivic and A. Zisserman. Video Google: A text retrieval approach to object matching in videos. In *ICCV*, 2003.

[11] D. Song and D. Tao. Biologically inspired feature manifold for scene classification. In *IEEE TIP*, 2010.

[12] A. Talwalkar, S. Kumar, and H. Rowley. Large-scale manifold learning. In *CVPR*, 2008.

[13] M. Wang, X. Hua, X. Yuan, Y. Song, and L. Dai. Optimizing multi-graph learning: towards a unified video annotation scheme. In *SIGMM*, 2007.

[14] T. Xia, D. Tao, T. Mei, and Y. Zhang. Multiview spectral embedding. In *IEEE TSMC-B*, 2010.

[15] R. Yan, A. Hauptmann, and R. Jin. Multimedia search with pseudo-relevance feedback. In *CIVR*, 2003.

[16] E. Yom-Tov, S. Fine, D. Carmel, and A. Darlow. Learning to estimate query difficulty: including applications to missing content detection and distributed information retrieval. In *SIGIR*, 2005.

[17] Z. Zha, X. Hua, T. Mei, J. Wang, G. Qi, and Z. Wang. Joint multi-label multi-instance learning for image classification. In *CVPR*, 2008.

[18] Y. Zhou and W. Croft. Query performance prediction in web search environments. In *SIGIR*, 2007.

Detection and Location of Near-Duplicate Video Sub-Clips by Finding Dense Subgraphs

Tianlong Chen [1], Shuqiang Jiang [1], Lingyang Chu [1], Qingming Huang [1,2]

[1] Key Lab of Intell. Info. Process., Inst. of Comput. Tech., CAS, Beijing, 100190, China

[2] Graduate University of Chinese Academy of Sciences, Beijing, 100049, China

{tlchen, lychu, qmhuang}@jdl.ac.cn , sqjiang@ict.ac.cn

ABSTRACT

Robust and fast near-duplicate video detection is an important task with many potential applications. Most existing systems focus on the comparison between full copy videos or partial near-duplicate videos. While it is more challenging to find similar content for videos containing multiple near-duplicate segments at random locations with various connections. In this paper, we propose a new graph based method to detect complex near-duplicate video sub-clips. First, we develop a new succinct video descriptor for keyframe match. Then a graph is established to exploit temporal consistency of matched keyframes. The nodes of the graph are the matched frame pairs; the edge weights are computed from the temporal alignment and frame pair similarities. In this way, the validly matched keyframes would form a dense subgraph whose nodes are strongly connected. This graph model also preserves the complex connections of sub-clips. Thus detecting complex near-duplicate sub-clips is transformed to the problem of finding all the dense subgraphs. We employ the optimization method of graph shift to solve this problem due to its robust performance. The experiments are conducted on the dataset with various transformations and complex temporal relations. The results demonstrate the effectiveness and efficiency of the proposed method.

Categories and Subject Descriptors

H.3.3 [**Information Search and Retrieval**]: Retrieval model

General Terms

Algorithms, Experimentation.

Keywords

Near-duplicate video detection, Sub-clip location, Graph shift

1. INTRODUCTION

With the rapid development of internet and multimedia technologies, the amounts of videos are growing explosively. Among these giant amounts of videos, there exist many duplicate video clips [16]. Detecting such near-duplicate video clips is desired by many potential applications such as web video retrieval [5, 9], automatic video tagging [5, 14] and large scale video database mining [13]. The common steps of this task can be summarized as follows. First, keyframes are extracted from videos by uniform sampling [7, 9] and shot-based method [5, 12]. Second, the keyframes are represented by a set of high dimensional feature vectors, including global features [7, 15] and local features [10, 11]. Finally, the similarity between two videos is determined by comparing the key frames in a pair wise manner.

Most existing systems focus on matching two full copy videos [9, 12, 13, 14] or partial near-duplicate videos [5, 6, 7, 15]. However, two similar videos may contain multiple near-duplicate segments in random locations due to temporal editing, such as inserting in or cutting out. Lifeng Shang *et al.* [9] constructed an efficient indexing structure and proposed a spatiotemporal feature to address the issues of real-time large scale near-duplicate web video retrieval. Their approach focuses on the running speed and accuracy, but fails to locate the similar sub-clips. The method of [15] focused on the robustness and uniqueness of the video signature, it propose a coarse-to-fine signature comparison scheme to locate a short query video clip in a long target video. Tan *et al.* [5] [6] presented an approach to detect and locate near-duplicate segments from two videos through the joint consideration of visual features and temporal coherency of frame sequence. All these methods perform not so well in the challenging situation when there are complex connections of similar segments from two videos. As shown in Figure 1, the near-duplicate segment connections could be one-to-one, one-to-many or many-to-many, and the order of those near duplicate sub-clips could be completely random.

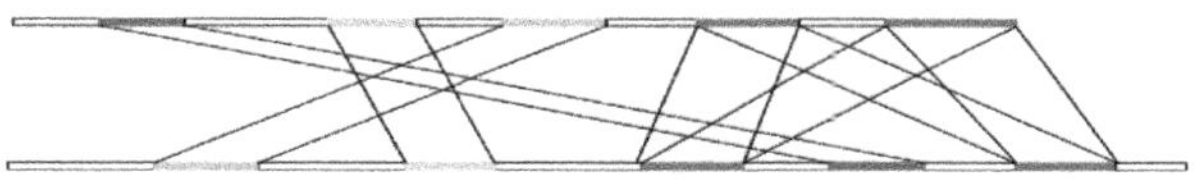

Figure 1. Near-duplicate videos containing complex connections.

In this paper, we propose a graph based method to robustly handle the challenging situation of videos with complex similar sub-clip connections. The main procedures are illustrated in Figure 2. After keyframe sampling and frame matching, a graph is established whose nodes represent matched keyframe pairs. By setting the temporal constraints into the edge weights, detecting complex near-duplicate sub-clips is transformed to the problem of finding all the dense subgraphs. We solve this optimization problem by using the method of graph shift [2]. Due to the intrinsic property of graph shift, our method is capable of detecting various conditions of near-duplicate sub-clip connections such as one-to-one, one-to-many or many-to-many. The proposed approach is fast and simple to implement. Compared with existing methods of partial-duplicate video detection, our approach has the following contributions:

1.The problem of near-duplicate sub-clip detection is converted to finding dense subgraphs.

*Area Chair: Lexing Xie

MM'11, November 28–December 1, 2011, Scottsdale, Arizona, USA.

2.We use a new succinct frame representation method called weighted histogram of gradient for similar key frame matching.

3.The boundaries of the complex similar sub-clips at random positions could be effectively located via subgraph analysis.

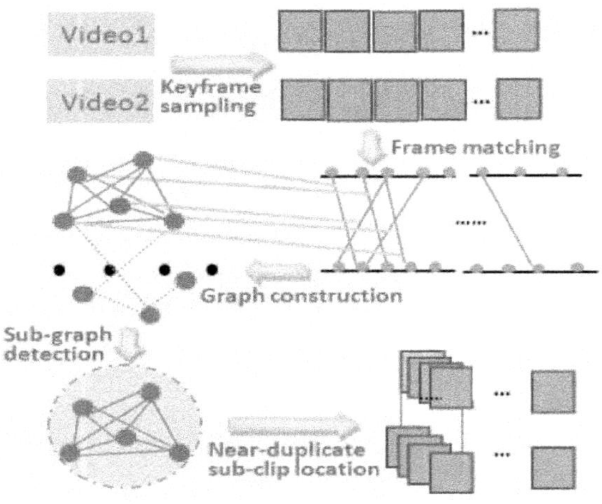

Figure 2. Illustration of the flowchart of our approach

2. WEIGHTED HISTOGRAM OF ORIENTED GRADIENT

In this paper we use a novel frame-level descriptor for video, combining the Histogram of Oriented Gradient (HOG) [8] and the Relative Mean Intensity (RMI) together by means of a weighting scheme. A frame is partitioned into rings which are invariant for the transformations such as rotation and flipping. Besides, instead of treating each frame as a whole, using a series of rings can save the local patterns and further make the descriptor more discriminative. RMI of each ring represents the bottom physical feature of a frame, and HOG, which is well-known for counting occurrences of orientation in localized portions of an image, has been improved in this paper with RMI as the weight. Compared with existing representations of video, the proposed descriptor offers several advantages. First, the combination of two naive features is succinct in concept. Second, it is compact in structure for encoding each frame at a certain sample rate. Third, it is invariant for common transformations such as: lighting, flipping, rotation, etc. Finally, it is also fast in extraction and matching procedure.

3. GRAPH CONSTRUCTION AND SUB-CLIP DETECTION

The idea of the graph model has been applied to various applications, such as image retrieval, image annotation and data clustering [2]. Liu at el. successfully used robust Graph model to detect common visual patterns in images [3]. In this paper, we extend the idea of finding dense subgraph in the temporal domain to detect and locate near-duplicate video sub-clips. A dense subgraph is a strongly connected subset of vertexes in a weighted undirected complete graph. The undirected graph is constructed by firstly using the detected similar keyframe pairs as the graph node, then associating the evaluation of temporal consistence and frame similarity with the edge weight. In this way, the validly matched frame pairs that are temporally consistent would form a dense subgraph and could be robustly detected by the method of graph-shift [3]. Thus the task of near-duplicate video sub-clip detection could be solved by detecting all the dense subgraphs in the previously mentioned complete graph.

3.1 Graph Construction

Given two sequences of keyframe points extracted from two videos, $V=\{v_1,v_2,...,v_n\}$ and $Q=\{q_1,q_2,...,q_m\}$, where m and n are the key frame numbers of V and Q respectively. Each keyframe is represented as a weighted histogram of oriented gradient as introduced in the last subsection. We conduct keyframe-pair comparison in the product space $P=V\times Q$, and obtain $n\times m$ keyframe pair, for a keyframe pair $p_i=(v_{i_1},q_{i_2})$ $v_{i_1}\in V$ $q_{i_2}\in Q$, we can calculate the feature similarity value by histogram intersection [9]. The function of the similarity value can be denoted as $S_{p_i}=f_1(i_1,i_2)$. The similarity value below a threshold ε means the two keyframes are not matched. The threshold parameter can be set relatively relax to include as much matched pairs as possible. In the experimental section, we will conduct an evaluation analysis on different threshold settings.

Given two keyframe pairs from two video, $p_i=(v_{i_1},q_{i_2})$ and $p_j=(v_{j_1},q_{j_2})$, we can compute the distance d_1 between keyframes v_{i_1} and v_{j_1} in the first video keyframe sequence. Likely, we can obtain d_2 between q_{i_2} and q_{j_2} in the second sequence. As there may exist various transformations in videos, and the frame per second may also change, we use the parameter s to represent the ratio between the two videos' frame rate. Now we can define a nonnegative monotonic decreasing function to encode this temporal information of keyframes.

$$T_{p_ip_j}(s)=f_2(|\,d_1-sd_2\,|) \tag{1}$$

Given two keyframe pairs, in other words, two nodes of the graph, the weight of the nodes is defined as

$$w_{ij}(s)=S_{p_i}S_{p_j}T_{p_ip_j}(s) \tag{2}$$

Suppose the set M contains k frame-pairs, and the graph G is $k\times k$ matrix. The adjacency matrix representation *A(s)* for the graph G is as follows:

$$A(i,j)(s)=\begin{cases}0, i=j\\ w_{ij}(s), i\neq j\end{cases} \tag{3}$$

Obviously the graph G is symmetric and nonnegative. Suppose a near-duplicate segment has r keyframe-pairs. It corresponds to a dense subgraph T of G with r vertices, which is a weighted countpart of maximal clique. If we represent a subgraph by a vector x, $x\in\Delta$, where $\Delta=\{x\in R^m : x\geq 0 and\,|\,x\,|_1=1\}$. x_i, the *i-th* component of x, denotes the probability of this subgraph contains the vertex i. the modes of a graph G are approximately local maximizers of graph density $g(x)=x^T A(s_0)x$. Given a vector x, the corresponding subgraph is *G(x)*. If x^* is a local maximizers of g(x), the $G(x^*)$ is a dense subgraph which is also a near-duplicate sub-clips. Therefore we need to calculate all local maximizers of this quadratic function:

$$\text{Maximize}\quad g(x)=x^T A(s_0)x \quad \text{Subject to}\quad x\in\Delta \tag{4}$$

The solution x^* is sparse. In the same solution, we can find that some components have relatively larger values, while other smaller values may correspond to noises or outliers. Therefore we can detect clusters according to the value of x^*, so the clusters may correspond to the near-duplicate segments.

3.2 Detection and Location of Near-duplicate Sub-clips

Given an initialization *x(0)*, the corresponding local solution x^* can be efficiently calculated. In [2], the authors proposed an algorithm to find all large local maximizers $\{x^*\}$. For a local maximizer x^*, they also presented an algorithm to find key pattern L from x^* in [3]. The algorithm is based on the fact that x^* is sparse and the number of its sufficiently large components usually indicates how large the key pattern is. For a key pattern L which consists of many matched frame-pair, we can detect the clusters according to the frame sequence number. Then we can discover the boundaries of the clusters to locate the boundaries of the similar segments.

The proposed method has the following advantages. First, temporal pattern detection is converted to dense subgraph seeking. The dense subgraph is a strongly connected subset of vertexes in a graph. According to the definition of the weight of graph edge in section 3.1, the correspondence between two frame pairs from the same similar connection is stronger than that from different connections or noises. Therefore this conversion is reasonable. Second, our approach could handle the complex situation shown in Figure 1. A dense subgraph only corresponds to a similar segment-pair. When two similar videos contain complex connections, there exists the same number of dense subgraphs corresponding to these similar sub-clips. The problem of finding dense subgraphs could easily be solved by the graph shift algorithm. Finally, the dense subgraph based method can accurately locate sub-clips. The localization of similar segments boundaries is through the analysis on the vertex set from the dense subgraph. This vertex set has less or no outlier, so we can obtain high overlap of the similar sub-clips from two videos.

The time complexity of keyframe matching is $O(n \times m)$ and $O(k \times k)$ for computing *A(s)*. A matching window is used to accelerate the matching of two video clips by aligning the two keyframe sequences [4]. However, it is less effective for the near-duplicate segments with random positions. The method of finding dense subgraphs is computationally efficient as discussed in [3]

4. EXPERIMENTS

To demonstrate the effectiveness and efficiency of our method, we conduct experiments in the dataset of 20 groups of videos. Every group consists of one query video and four reference videos which are all about ten minutes in length. The videos are edited manually consisting 4~6 sub-clips which is from TRECVID [1] with various transformations. These similar sub-clips may be sequential or cross at random temporal positions. The lengths of these sub-clips vary from tens of seconds to 3 minutes. We use two measures to evaluate the performance of our method: average precision and average recall. The precision and recall of each group is denoted as follows [6]:

$$Recall = \frac{\#Correctly\ detected\ near-duplicate\ frames}{\#Total\ near-duplicate\ frames}$$

$$Precision = \frac{\#Correctly\ detected\ near-duplicate\ frames}{\#Detected\ near-duplicate\ frames}$$

The nonnegative monotonic decreasing function f_2 in section 3.1 is denoted as:

$$f_2 = \exp(-\frac{|d_1 - sd_2|^2}{\phi})$$

In our experiments, $\phi = 100$.

4.1 Near-duplicate Video Sub-clips Detection

A total of 80847 keyframes are extracted from the whole database. We evaluate the sensitivity of the system with different parameter setting. The experiments are conducted by varying the respective parameters while fixing the others to $\varepsilon = 0.95$, $\eta = 0.01$, $\varphi = 0.83$. η and φ have been defined in [3], where η is the threshold to merge two similar local maximizers and φ is the threshold to drop some local maximizers with small $g(x^*)$. From Figure 3, we can see that, ε has a significant impact on the results. The average precision reaches the highest in $\varepsilon = 0.95$ while the average precision is highest in $\varepsilon = 0.94$. In general the precision and recall are not sensitive to η and φ. When the value of φ is higher than 0.83 or η is too small, the performance will be affected.

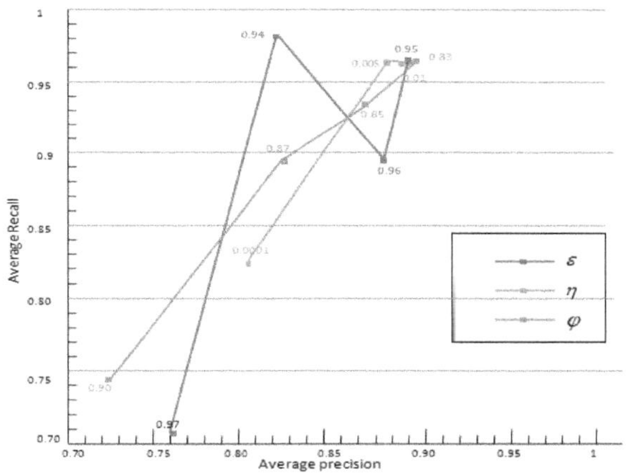

Figure 3. Sensitivity to parameters

From the above parameter analysis, we select these parameters to compare the performance of our method to a modification of Sub-Maximum Size Matching (SMSM) [7]. SMSM constructs a bipartite graph to identify the most suitable 1:1 mapping by optimizing the factors of visual content, temporal order and frame alignment together. We first extract dense segments of the first video and then apply SMSM. Table 1 shows the performance comparison. Our method outperforms SMSM in both average precision and average recall. This is because SMSM weakly handles videos containing complex connections.

Table 1. Result of method comparison

Approaches	Average Precision	Average Recall
Our method	89.00%	96.427%
SMSM	87.68%	85.40%

4.2 Complex Example

In this section, we use two long videos containing complex near duplicate sub-clip connections to demonstrate the performance of our approach. There are 2073 keyframes extracted from the first video, and 2394 key frames from the second video. The two videos containing complex sub-clips are shown in Figure 4(a). The numbers in the Figure represent the frame number. Then we use our approach and SMSM to detect the near-duplicate segments. The parameters in our approach are set as: ε =0.95, η =0.01, φ=0.83. The time of frame-pair comparison is 51s and the time of seeking temporal pattern is 57s. From Figure 4(b), lines with the same color denote the similar segments. We can see that our approach detects seven similar segments totally, six of which are correct, and the overlap is nearly 100% of the correct segments. The incorrect one is connected by two dotted lines. Figure 4(c) shows the result of SMSM. We can see our approach has higher overlap and precision. The experiments on many other video data also get similar results.

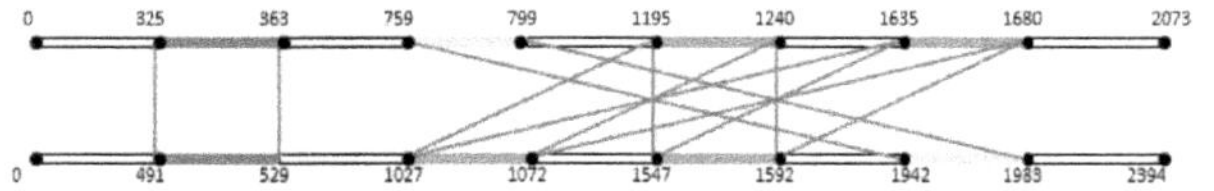

(a)

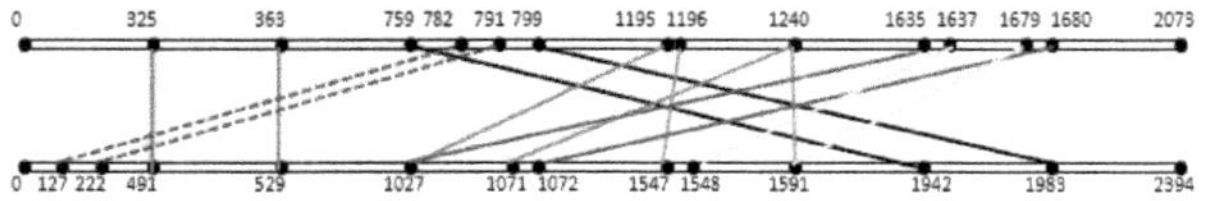

(b)

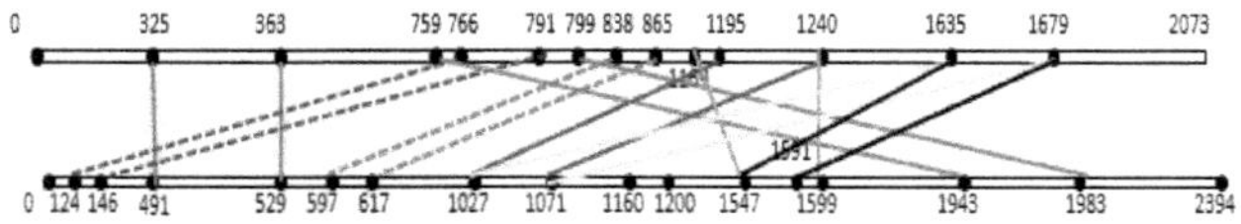

(c)

Figure 4. Illustration of complex example. (a) videos containing complex connections. (b) the result of our approach (c) the result of SMSM

5. CONCLUSION

In this paper, we present an effective solution to detecting and locating complex near-duplicate video sub-clips by finding dense subgraphs. The visual and temporal information are integrated and encoded to the established graph. The visual information is obtained by matching keyframes which are represented as the weighted histogram of oriented gradient, and the temporal information is taken into account in the weight of graph edge. In future work we shall try to speed up the computing time of the frame match.

6. ACKNOWLEDGMENTS

This work was supported in part by National Natural Science Foundation of China: 61025011, 60833006 and 61070108, in part by National Basic Research Program of China (973 Program): 2009CB320906, and in part by Beijing Natural Science Foundation: 4092042.

7. REFERENCES

[1] A.-F. Smeaton, P. Over, and W. Kraaij. Evaluation campaigns and trecvid. *In ACM MIR, 2006.*

[2] H.-R. Liu and S.-C. Yan. Robust Graph Mode Seeking by Graph Shift. *In ICML, 2010.*

[3] H.-R. Liu and S.-C. Yan. Common visual Pattern Discovery via Spatially Coherent Correspondences. *In CVPR, 2010.*

[4] H.-K. Tan, X. Wu, C.-W. Ngo and W.-L. Zhao. Accelerating near-duplicate video matching by combining visual similarity and alignment distortion. *In ACM Multimedia, 2008.*

[5] H.-K .Tan, C.-W. Ngo, Richang Hong and T.-S. Chua. Scalable Detection of Partial Near-duplicate Videos by Visual-Temporal Consistency. *In ACM Multimedia, 2009.*

[6] H.-K. Tan, C.-W. Ngo and T.-S Chua. Efficient mining of multiple partial near-duplicate alignments by temporal network. *IEEE Trans. On circuits and systems for video Technology, 2010.*

[7] H.-T. Shen, J. Shao, Z. Huang, X.-F. Zhou. Effective and Efficient Query Processing for Video Subsequence Identification. *IEEE Trans. Knowl. Data Eng. 21(3): 321-334 ,March 2009.*

[8] http://en.wikipedia.org/wiki/Histogram_of_oriented_gradients.

[9] L.-f. Shang, L.-j. Y.-F. Wang, K.-P. Chan and X.-S. Hua. Real-time large scale near-duplicate web video retrieval. *In ACM Multimedia, 2010.*

[10] J. Law-To, L. Chen, A. Joly, et al. Video copy detection: a comparative study. *In CIVR, 2007.*

[11] J. Sivic and A. Zisserman. Video google: A text retrieval approach to object matching in videos. *In Proc. ICCV, 2003.*

[12] P. Wu, T. Thaipanich, and C.-C. j. Kuo. A suffix array approach to video copy detection in video sharing social networks. *In Proc. ICASSP, 2009.*

[13] S. Poullot, M. Crucianu, and O. Buisson. Scalable mining of large video databases using copy detection. *In ACM Multimedia, 2008.*

[14] S. Siersdorfer, J. San Pedro, and M. Sanderson. Automatic video tagging using content redundancy. *In ACM SIGIR, July 2009.*

[15] X.S. Hua, X. Chen, H.J. Zhang. Robust video signature based on ordinal measure. *In Proc. ICIP, 2004.*

[16] X. Wu, A. G. Hauptmann, and C.-W. Ngo. Practical elimination of near-duplicates from web video search. *In ACM Multimedia, 2007.*

Query Expansion by Spatial Co-occurrence for Image Retrieval *

Yingfei Li [‡†], Bo Geng [‡], Zheng-jun Zha [#], Yangxi Li [‡], Dacheng Tao [§], Chao Xu [‡]
[‡] Key Laboratory of Machine Perception (Ministry of Education), Peking University, Beijing, P.R.China
[#] National University of Singapore, Singapore
[§] University of Technology, Sydney, Australia
{liyingfei, gengbo, liyangxi, xuchao}@cis.pku.edu.cn, junzzustc@gmail.com, dacheng.tao@uts.edu.au

ABSTRACT

The well-known bag-of-features (BoF) model is widely utilized for large scale image retrieval. However, BoF model lacks the spatial information of visual words, which is informative for local features to build up meaningful visual patches. To compensate for the spatial information loss, in this paper, we propose a novel query expansion method called Spatial Co-occurrence Query Expansion (SCQE), by utilizing the spatial co-occurrence information of visual words mined from the database images to boost the retrieval performance. In offline phase, for each visual word in the vocabulary, we treat the visual words that are frequently co-occurred with it in the database images as neighbors, base on which a spatial co-occurrence graph is built. In online phase, a query image can be expanded with some spatial co-occurred but unseen visual words according to the spatial co-occurrence graph, and the retrieval performance can be improved by expanding these visual words appropriately. Experimental results demonstrate that, SCQE achieves promising improvements over the typical BoF baseline on two datasets comprising 5K and 505K images respectively.

Categories and Subject Descriptors

H.3.3 [**Information Search and Retrieval**]: Retrieval Models

General Terms

Algorithms, Experimentation, Theory

Keywords

Image retrieval, query expansion

[†]This paper is supported by NBRPC 2011CB302400, NSFC 60975014 and NSFB 4102024.
*Area chair: Lexing Xie

MM'11, November 28–December 1, 2011, Scottsdale, Arizona, USA.

1. INTRODUCTION

Image retrieval has been a crucial research topic in multimedia and computer vision societies for years. Motivated by the text retrieval framework, Bag-of-features (BoF) technique [13, 9] is receiving growing popularity due to its well scalability. Within this framework, local features are firstly extracted from each image in the corpus. A codebook is subsequently constructed by clustering all the local features into "visual words". Based on this structure, each database image is represented as a BoF structure, and then indexed by an inverted file. In the online phase, a query is firstly transformed to BoF, and ad-hoc retrieval models are applied to return its similar images in the corpus in order.

However, with the scalability benefit brought by BoF, it suffers from performance degradation caused by the loss of spatial information. Such loss is especially severe for image data, which heavily relies on the spatial configuration of local patterns to form meaningful visual patches. In order to overcome this loss, many works [10, 1, 16] have been proposed to improve the BoF framework by incorporating spatial constraints.

Among these works, geometric verification [10] is a crucial step for post-processing, by using the features' spatial layout between two images. Query expansion by generative latent model is proposed [1], which employs the spatial configuration of visual words from query region, together with "background" distribution of words from initial top-ranked results. Multiple visual words with spatial information are bundled as grouped visual phrases [16] to gain geometric relationship between feature points. These methods focus on calculating geometric information between one or several images to boost feature matching performance. Such "local context" only utilizes the pattern extracted from single or a small number of images, hence it is not sufficiently robust. To solve this problem, we explore a new way to estimate the "global context" in the whole corpus.

We propose to find some spatial information mined from the entire corpus, i.e., by statistically analyzing the common patterns that frequently appear in multiple images. Considering the similar images which contain partially duplicate objects or/and scenes, context information that they frequently co-occurred with can be utilized, e.g., a query image contains a car without the road which usually showed up together with it in database images, thus the additional visual words of road expanded to the query could do a favor for the retrieval task. Based on this observation, we notice that by studying the spatial co-occurrence pattern of visual words in the training dataset, it is convenient to involve

Algorithm

1. Connect the closest visual words in the co-occurrence list iteratively to build a connected undigraph $G = (V, E)$.

2. Calculate the similarity matrix W defined by $W_{ij} = e^{\gamma||f(v_i,v_j)||^2}$, in the case that there is an edge $e(i,j) \in E$, otherwise, $W_{ij} = 0$, where $f(v_i, v_j)$ is the co-occurrence frequency of v_i and v_j, and γ is the propagation controlling parameter.

3. Calculate the normalized matrix N computed by $N = D^{-\frac{1}{2}}WD^{-\frac{1}{2}}$, where D is a diagonal matrix defined by $D = \sum_{j=1}^{m} W_{ij}$.

4. Denote S as the set of indices of zero items image histogram, and U the nonzero ones, as $H_U = [h_{s+1}, h_{s+2}, \ldots, h_m]^T$, iteratively calculate $H_U(t+1) = N_{US}H_S + \lambda N_{UU}H_U(t)$ until the series reach the converges.

5. Return the new weights assigned to H_U.

the "collocation" of the visual words in the query images for query expansion. The "collocation" of visual words reveals highly correlated connection between them, and is beneficial in boosting retrieval performance especially in the case of the queries with limited number of visual words.

The rich co-occurrence patterns mined from large image database can be informative data to expand the query representation and boost retrieval performance. Query expansion [12] is a technique commonly used in Information Retrieval to improve the retrieval performance by reformulating the original query. Typically, it identifies significant word associations (co-occurrences or collocations) from relevance feedback or pseudo-relevance versions by adding new terms or re-weighting the original terms. To model the spatial co-occurrence relationships between visual words, graph based manifold learning approach is considered here, which can expand the query representation through the manifold ranking on a constructed relationship graph [18]. Similar ideas have been successfully applied to image classification [5], image search ranking [3, 4], video annotation [15, 14], and image query suggestion [17].

In this paper, we propose Spatial Co-occurrence Query Expansion (SCQE) approach, which constructs the spatial co-occurrence relationship mined from database visual words off-line and expands the query image visual words by using the co-occurrence information online, to improve the image retrieval performance. Specifically, we construct a graph via the co-occurrence statistics obtained from the training image corpus. Then the visual words in the query propagate their weight to their close neighbors in the co-occurrence graph, re-evaluating the importance of the co-occurred neighboring visual words for retrieval. Experiment results show that our scheme achieves substantial improvement compared with the baseline in the Oxford5K dataset and imageNet505K dataset respectively.

2. SPATIAL CO-OCCURRENCE QUERY EXPANSION

In this section, we describe a novel Spatial Co-occurrence Query Expansion method in detail.

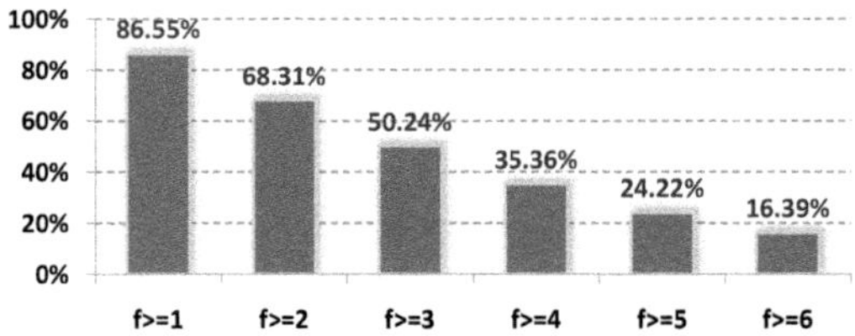

Figure 1: The histogram of visual word pair over their co-occurrence frequency on the Oxford5K dataset

2.1 Framework of Large Scale Image Retrieval

We concisely review the classic BoF large scale image retrieval system based on which we design the novel SCQE method. Both the query image and corpus images are represented as bags of visual words via the following procedure. First, Difference of Gaussian (DoG) [6] or Hessian Affine detectors [7] are used to detect key points in images of the corpus. Then 128-dimension SIFT (Scale Invariant Feature Transform) [6] descriptors are extracted to represent local region around each key point. Next, The SIFT descriptors are quantized into "visual words" through K-means method [10], and vocabulary composed of "visual words" is constructed. To lower loss of quantization, soft assignment (SA) [11] could be an improvement to K-means mapping, which assigns a weighted combination of visual words to each descriptor. As in [10], query and each image in the corpus is interpreted as a sparse vector of visual word occurrences expressing the BoF form. The tf-idf weighting scheme is adopted to evaluate the importance of a visual word to each image and its general importance in the corpus. For the efficiency consideration, an inverted file is used to store word occurrences mapped to the images in which it occurs.

2.2 Co-occurrence Statistic

In real visual world, each image contains thousands of local features, most of which are repetitive or similar patterns spatially co-occurred in local region. We define that two visual words which are frequently co-occurred in local regions of different images as co-occurred neighborhoods to each other. To analyze whether co-occurred neighborhoods universally exist in common images, we statistically compute their empirical distribution over Oxford5K dataset [10] which contains totally 16,344,070 local descriptors quantized by 100K visual words in 5062 images, and hence has 100K×100K visual word pairs.

We take the whole image as an integrated local region, and subsequently count how many times each pair of visual words co-occurred in one image. As is reported in Figure 1, it shows that more than 86.55% visual word pairs have at least 1 occurrence, 68.32% for 2 times and more than half of them co-occur for at least 3 times. These statistics verify that co-occurred neighborhoods generally exist in real world images, and can be utilized to enhance the BoF method for image retrieval.

To utilize this property, we design a novel query expansion method based on statistic of the co-occurred neighborhood. A co-occurred neighborhood table is constructed to record the co-occurrence of visual words pairs, storing both top-k neighbors with each visual word and their corresponding frequency of co-occurrence.

2.3 Query Expansion

Given the co-occurred neighborhood table, let X be a

Method	100k	1M
Hard assignment (HA)	0.517	0.614
HA+SCQE	**0.539**	**0.655**
Soft assignment (SA)	0.554	0.673
SA+SCQE	**0.596**	**0.708**

Table 1: Performance of SCQE method on Oxford5K dataset

group of SIFT descriptors in a D-dimension feature space, $X = [x_1, x_2, ..., x_N] \in R^{D \times N}$. Given a codebook with M entries, $B = [b_1, b_2, ..., b_M] \in R^{D \times M}$, different coding schemes convert each descriptor into an M-dimensional code $H = [h_1, h_2, ..., h_N] \in R^{M \times N}$ to represent image. The code H would be a sparse histogram due to the relative large vocabulary. Thus, taking the nonzero items of the image vector as $S = [s_1, s_2, ..., s_L] \in R^{M \times L} \subset H$, and the zero items as $U = [u_1, u_2, ..., u_K] \in R^{M \times K} \subset H$, and $S \bigcup U = H$, $S \bigcap U = \emptyset$.

According to the co-occurrence information, we build the graph structure of recorded co-occurred relationship among visual words. The weights of edges in the graph would be normalized through γ parameter. It controls the proportion of weights for the visual words to propagate to its neighbors. Notice that the iteration in step 4 is able to reach convergence, since H could be seen as the Markov stationary features (MSF) [8]. The nonzero visual words act as sources to disseminate their weights to their neighbors in the co-occurrence table until convergence. The regulation parameter $\lambda \in [0, 1]$ suggests the propagation strength of the weight to neighbors. The larger λ is, the more weight is spread from the original visual words to their neighbors, and the more important co-occurrence information is. We fix λ to 0.1 in our experiment practically. By setting these rules, new important visual words in terms of co-occurrence with the source visual words would gain weights to add spatial information to the BoF image vector representations. The ranking algorithm here is designed mainly by [18] which is described in details in the ***Algorithm*** table.

3. EXPERIMENT AND RESULT

To demonstrate the validity of our method, we compare it with the state-of-the-art results presented in [10] and [11] by using Average Precision (AP) score, and stress-test it on a 505K images dataset.

3.1 Dataset

Oxford5K Dataset. In this dataset [10], there are 5062 images covering 11 different Oxford "landmarks". 55 queries of 17 particular Oxford landmarks and an extensive associated ground truth is provided for testing. The bounding box to indicate region of interest is annotated on 55 query images.

ImageNet Dataset. We combine Oxford5K and 500K images sampled from imageNet [2] to construct the second dataset. 55 query images and the associated bounding boxes in Oxford5K as in the first corpus are used, where we assume that the 500K imageNet data barely contain relevant images to the queries.

The baseline procedure is composed of Hessian-Affine with SIFT description, HA quantization and tf-idf weighting scheme with inverted index. In Oxford5K, we test the SCQE based on both HA and SA, with 100K and 1M vocabulary. In the second dataset, we keep the entire retrieval system fixed with HA and 1M vocabulary, to stress-test retrieval performance of SCQE when scaling up.

mAP	HA	HA+SCQE	Effect
ImageNet105K	0.498	**0.565**	**+13.4%**
ImageNet505K	0.419	**0.494**	**+17.8%**

Table 2: Boost effect of SCQE method on the imageNet dataset with 1M vocabulary

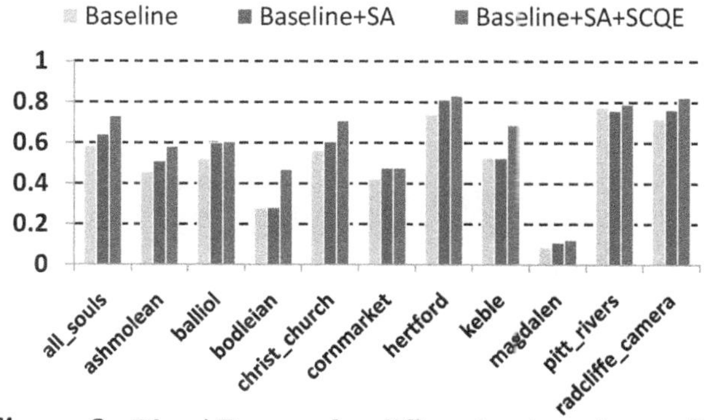

Figure 2: The AP score for different categories on Oxford5K dataset with 100K dictionary

3.2 Result

Retrieval mAP values of both baseline and SCQE are shown in Table 1. The results indicate that our approach gains an additional improvement on the small Oxford5K dataset by 3.7% and 6.7% with 100K vocabulary under HA and SA settings respectively, while 7.6% and 5.2% boost are achieved with 1M size vocabulary. It suggests that the co-occurrence information incorporated in the query leads to an almost consistent improvement in retrieval performance.

The performance of each 11 categories and all sample queries with 100K codebook on the Oxford5K dataset is illustrated in Figure 2 and Figure 3 respectively. 8 out of 11 landmarks on the dataset are beneficial from SCQE. Specifically, the class "bodleian" receives most performance rising by 65.6%, and "keble" improves by 31.0%, followed with "christ_chruch" by 16.7%. To gain more insight from the result, we inspect to the related query and find that those images with only partial or close-up of the query object or/and scene benefit most from SCQE. Understandably, queries with close-up content lacks more visual words to describe the integral object, and expanding such visual words through co-occurrence graph can help queries include additional relevant information.

When it comes to the three categories, i.e., "balliol", "cornmarket" and "magdalen", two factors can explain for the undesirable result. First, the queries in these two landmarks most include clear and integral buildings, thus, beneficial spatial co-occurrence information to be added is less. Second, in these queries, there are lots of messy elements which are commonly showing up in dataset, e.g. trees and pedestrians. Under these circumstances, SCQE is inclined to add visual words that co-occurred with the common elements in most images rather than the object-related ones, thus provides little improvement.

We also present two different results of queries that retrieved by the baseline with SA and our proposed SCQE

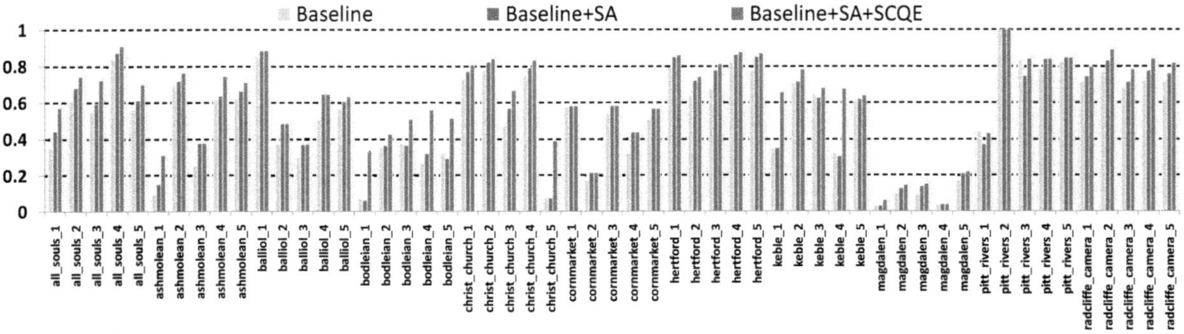

Figure 3: The AP for each query image on Oxford5K dataset with 100K vocabulary

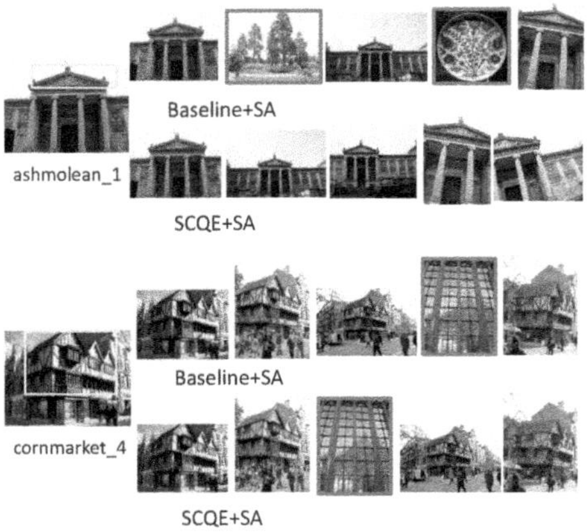

Figure 4: Two retrieval results using SCQE method and standard BoF with SA are presented, where yellow rectangles stand for bounding boxes and the red highlight image is "bad" in ground truth

method in Figure 4 to illustrate. For "ashmolean_1", the query region with tiny bounding box actually prevents a part of useful information with clear spatial structures of their surroundings. As a consequence, SCQE excludes the irrelevant pictures from the top returned list by the broader spatial information. But for the "cornmarket_4", SCQE has a small degradation due to the common visual factors like pedestrians of the image.

At last, Table 2 shows the performance of SCQE when the testing database is scaled-up to more than 100K images. It is evident that SCQE gains significant boost by 17.8% over the imageNet505K corpus.

3.3 Parameters Analysis

We take the number of co-occurrence neighbors k and the normalization factor γ as main parameters of our method. Since our model is set up upon large graph structure, the parameters are influential on the structure of graph in Riemannian Space. k measures the sparsity of the graph. Larger k leads the co-occurrence graph to be denser, and more computation time. γ determines the proportion of weights which the visual words disseminate to their co-occurred neighbors. Larger γ spreads more weights to its nearer neighbors and less to the further ones. The performance of the search engine changes in only small scope as the parameters varies, and propagating weights to more neighbors gains slightly increasing boost. Experiments are done with k=20 and γ=0.125.

4. CONCLUSION

In this paper, we propose a new query expansion method SCQE using the co-occurrence spatial information in image database to boost the performance of large scale image retrieval. The SCQE compensates for the loss of quantization brought by BoF model via the important co-occurrence information mined from the whole dataset. Furthermore, the proposed method brings performance boost consistently over different quantization settings and is scalable for large dataset. Experiments on both 5K and 505K dataset demonstrate that SCQE is effective in improving the CBIR system performance.

5. REFERENCES

[1] O. Chum, J. Philbin, J. Sivic, M. Isard, and A. Zisserman. Total recall: Automatic query expansion with a generative feature model for object retrieval. In *ICCV*, 2007.

[2] J. Deng, W. Dong, R. Socher, L.-J. Li, K. Li, and L. Fei-Fei. ImageNet: A Large-Scale Hierarchical Image Database. In *CVPR*, 2009.

[3] B. Geng, C. Xu, D. Tao, L. Yang, and X. Hua. Ensemble manifold regularization. In *CVPR*, 2009.

[4] B. Geng, L. Yang, C. Xu, and X. Hua. Content-aware ranking for visual search. In *CVPR*, 2010.

[5] B. Geng, L. Yang, C. Xu, and X. Hua. Ranking model adaptation for domain specific search. *IEEE TKDE*, 2010.

[6] D. Lowe. Distinctive image features from scale-invariant keypoints. *IJCV*, 2004.

[7] K. Mikolajczyk and C. Schmid. Scale and affine invariant interest point detectors. *IJCV*, 2004.

[8] B. Ni, S. Yan, and A. A. Kassim. Contextualizing histogram. In *CVPR*, 2009.

[9] D. Nistér and H. Stewénius. Scalable recognition with a vocabulary tree. In *CVPR*, 2006.

[10] J. Philbin, O. Chum, M. Isard, J. Sivic, and A. Zisserman. Object retrieval with large vocabularies and fast spatial matching. In *CVPR*, 2007.

[11] J. Philbin, O. Chum, M. Isard, J. Sivic, and A. Zisserman. Lost in quantization: Improving particular object retrieval in large scale image databases. In *CVPR*, 2008.

[12] G. Salton and C. Buckley. Improving retrieval performance by relevance feedback. *JASIS*, 1999.

[13] J. Sivic and A. Zisserman. Video Google: A text retrieval approach to object matching in videos. In *ICCV*, 2003.

[14] M. Wang, X. Hua, R. Hong, J. Tang, G. Qi, and Y. Song. Unified video annotation via multigraph learning. *IEEE TCSVT*, 2009.

[15] M. Wang, X. Hua, J. Tang, and R. Hong. Beyond distance measurement: constructing neighborhood similarity for video annotation. *IEEE TMM*, 2009.

[16] Z. Wu, Q. Ke, M. Isard, and J. Sun. Bundling features for large scale partial-duplicate web image search. In *CVPR*, 2009.

[17] Z. Zha, L. Yang, T. Mei, M. Wang, and Z. Wang. Visual query suggestion. In *SIGMM*, 2009.

[18] D. Zhou, J. Weston, A. Gretton, O. Bousquet, and B. Schölkopf. Ranking on data manifolds. In *NIPS*. 2004.

Social Image Tag Recommendation by Concept Matching*

Aixin Sun
axsun@ntu.edu.sg

Sourav S. Bhowmick
assourav@ntu.edu.sg

Jun-An Chong
chon0113@e.ntu.edu.sg

School of Computer Engineering, Nanyang Technological University, Singapore 639798

ABSTRACT

Tags associated with social images are valuable information source for superior image search and retrieval experiences. In this paper, we propose a novel tag recommendation technique that exploits the user-given tags associated with images. Each *candidate tag* to be recommended is described by a few *tag concepts* derived from the collective knowledge embedded in the *tag co-occurrence* pairs. Each concept, represented by a few tags with high co-occurrences among themselves, is indexed as a textual document. Then user-given tags of an image is represented as a text query and the matching concepts are retrieved from the index. The candidate tags associated with the matching concepts are then recommended. Leverages on the well studied Information Retrieval (IR) techniques, the proposed approach leads to superior tag recommendation accuracy and lower execution time compared to the state-of-the-art.

Categories and Subject Descriptors

H.3.3 [**Information Storage and Retrieval**]: Information Search and Retrieval—*Information filtering*

General Terms

Algorithms, Experimentation

Keywords

Flickr, social image, tag recommendation, tag concept

1. INTRODUCTION

The availability of user-given tags enables novel and superior tag-based techniques for social image retrieval. In this paper, we propose a novel approach that exploits the notion of *tag concepts* (or concepts for brevity) to recommend tags.

First, a set of *candidate tags* is selected from all tags in the social image collection. For each candidate tag t_c, a *tag relationship graph* (TRG) is constructed from the *tag co-occurrence* pairs. Each node in a TRG is a tag and an edge between two nodes indicates that the two tags have high co-occurrence measured by an *association measure* (e.g., Jaccard coefficient). Figure 1 depicts an example of

*Area chair: Kiyoharu Aizawa.
This work is supported by Singapore MOE AcRF Tier-1 Grant RG13/10.

MM'11, November 28–December 1, 2011, Scottsdale, Arizona, USA.

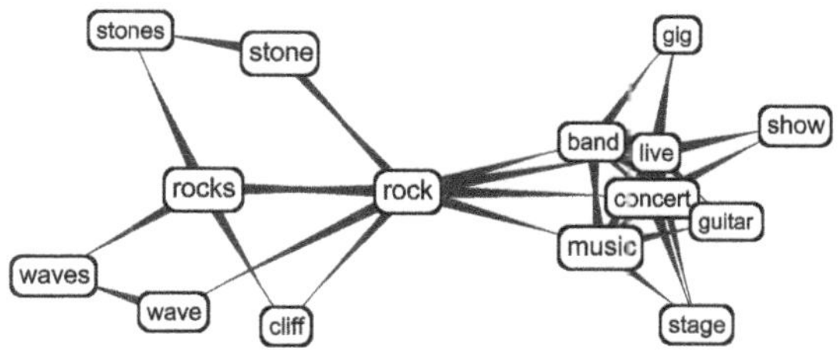

Figure 1: Tag relationship graph of rock.

TRG for the candidate tag rock. Next, a set of *concepts* associated with t_c through the collective knowledge embedded in the tag co-occurrence pairs is detected from the TRG using Modularity Clustering [7]. For example, two different concepts (*rock stone* and *rock music*) are evident in Figure 1 on the left and right hand sides of the `rock` node, respectively. Each concept is represented by a set of high co-occurrence tags. Lastly, we leverage on well-studied information retrieval techniques to recommend tags from the detected concepts. Specifically, the detected concepts are first indexed as textual documents, where a tag in the concept is treated as a word (or an index term). Then, the user-given tags of an image is represented as a text query and the matching concepts are retrieved from the index by exploiting cosine similarity. The candidate tags associated with the matching concepts are then recommended.

We have evaluated the impact of various issues on our proposed tag recommendation technique using NUS-WIDE dataset [1]. Specifically, we evaluated more than 190K test cases involving over 99K distinct images. To the best of our knowledge, this is the largest experiments conducted for social image tag recommendation with ground-truth labeling. Our experimental results suggest that the proposed concept-based strategy leads to superior tag recommendation accuracy as well as lower execution time compared to a state-of-the-art tag recommendation technique [8].

2. RELATED WORK

The efforts in social image tag recommendation can be broadly categorized into three types, namely, *model-based*, *example-based*, and *knowledge-based* approaches [2, 3, 4, 8, 9].

The *model-based* approach typically exploits the visual content component of images for tag recommendation. Methods based on this approach learn models from labeled examples of a predefined set of visual concepts. The learned models are then used to annotate new images according to their relevance to the concepts [2]. The *example-based* approach assumes that visually similar images are annotated by a similar set of tags. For a given image, tags are recommended among those associated with its nearest neighbors based on visual content similarity [3, 4, 9]. Nevertheless, computing nearest neighbors from a large image collection is often expensive. On the other hand, both approaches are particularly useful

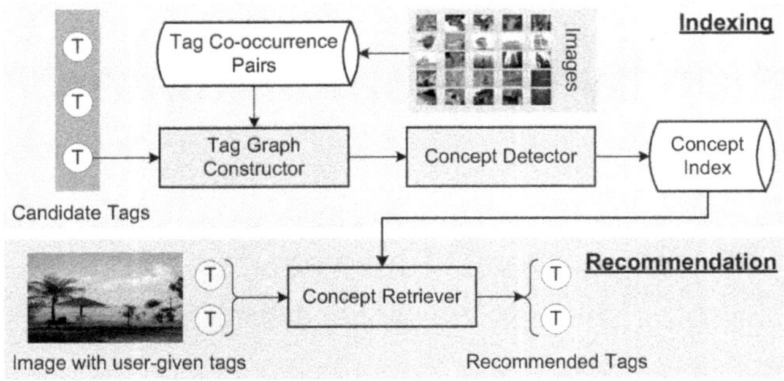

Figure 2: Architecture of the tag recommendation system.

when user-given tags are unavailable. The *knowledge-based* approach does not consider the visual content of images. Instead, it relies on the relationships (e.g., co-occurrence) among tags [8]. For instance, for each user-given tag, the method in [8] first selects its top-m co-occurring tags as candidate tags. Then, the candidate tags are re-ranked for recommendation based on strength of *co-occurrence*, *stability*, and *descriptiveness*.

In this paper, our proposed tag recommendation framework is also based on tag co-occurrence. In contrast to [8], we exploit the collective knowledge of *concepts* embedded in tag co-occurrence pairs to recommend tags. Also, given an association measure, our approach needs the user to define a single parameter (*hop threshold*) to facilitate tag recommendation. However, in [8] four parameters need to be tuned, which may not be practical for end users.

3. TAG RECOMMENDATION

The procedure of our *concepts-based* tag recommendation consists of three phases, namely the *tag relationship graph construction* phase, the *concept detection* phase, and the *tag recommendation* phase. Figure 2 depicts the architecture of our proposed tag recommendation system that realizes these phases.

3.1 Tag Relationship Graph (TRG)

First, we select a set of *candidate* tags from all tags in the social image collection. The selection criteria is application-dependent. For each selected candidate tag t_c, a *tag relationship graph* (TRG) is constructed from the *tag co-occurrence* pairs involving t_c and the pairs involving t_c's co-occurring tags. A *tag co-occurrence pair* of tags t_a and t_b is a 5-tuple $\langle t_a, t_b, f(t_a), f(t_b), f(t_a, t_b)\rangle$ where $f(t_a)$ (resp. $f(t_b)$) and $f(t_a, t_b)$ denote the numbers of images annotated by t_a (resp. t_b) and by both t_a and t_b, respectively. Given a collection of socially tagged images, the set of tag co-occurrence pairs forms the collective knowledge base. The TRG of t_c therefore captures the collective knowledge about t_c.

The construction of TRG requires two user-defined parameters, namely, *association measure* (denoted by α) and *hop threshold* (denoted by φ). The *association measure* specifies how to compute tag co-occurrence strength. Equation 1 gives three example association measures, namely, Jaccard coefficient, co-occurrence probability (*CoProb*), and Interest. The *hop threshold* φ specifies the number of co-occurring tags we need to consider for the TRG construction.

$$assoc(t_a, t_b) : \begin{cases} Jaccard(t_a, t_b) = \frac{f(t_a, t_b)}{f(t_a)+f(t_b)-f(t_a, t_b)} \\ CoProb(t_b|t_a) = \frac{f(t_a, t_b)}{f(t_a)} \\ Interest(t_b|t_a) = CoProb(t_b|t_a) - \frac{f(t_b)}{N} \end{cases} \quad (1)$$

In Equation 1, $assoc(t_a, t_b)$ denotes the association between two tags t_a and t_b, computed by one of the association measures on the right hand side, and N denotes the number of images in the collection. We now elaborate on the construction process.

Algorithm 1: Concept detection for candidate tag t_c

Input: TRG G_c of candidate tag t_c
Output: A set of concepts C_c for t_c

```
1 begin
2     obtain first hop tags H_c = firstHop(G_c, t_c);
3     remove t_c from G_c and get G'_c = removeTag(G_c, t_c);
4     detect concepts C_c = detectConcept(G'_c);
5     foreach concept c_p ∈ C_c do
6         foreach tag t ∈ c_p do
7             if t ∉ H_c then
8                 remove tag t from c_p
```

Given a candidate tag t_c, α, and φ, the TRG construction is initiated by creating t_c as the *central* node. Then the top-φ most co-occurring tags with t_c are included as the *first-hop* tags of t_c. Next, from the top-φ most co-occurring tags of each first-hop tag we select those tags that are associated with at least two first-hop tags and add them in the TRG as *second-hop* tags of t_c. Note that the association strength of the second-hop tags with the first-hop ones must be above the median of the association strength derived from all tag co-occurrence pairs. This constraint allows us to avoid adding too many tags that are not strongly associated. For example, Figure 1 depicts the TRG of candidate tag rock when $\alpha = Jaccard$ and $\varphi = 8$. Observe that rock is associated with 8 first-hop tags. Among the second-hop tags, stones is included in the graph as it is one of the top-8 most co-occurring tags of stone as well as of rocks (stones is associated with two first-hop tags rocks and stone).

3.2 Concept Detection

Concept detection is based on the intuition that tags often co-occur with other tags within the same concept but not with tags in a different concept. Hence, concept detection can be naturally formulated into a community detection or graph-cut problem. However, these techniques cannot be directly adopted as the central node (*i.e.*, candidate tag t_c) has strong associations with all the first-hop tags which often represent multiple concepts. The procedure to detect concepts is outlined in Algorithm 1. Observe that the removal of the central node from the TRG (line 3) is a key step for concept detection. This step ensures that associations between t_c and the first-hop tags do not affect the detection of concepts. For instance, the removal of tag rock leads to two disconnected components in Figure 1 and each component naturally forms a concept. The concept detection is then achieved by using a community detection or graph cut algorithm (line 4). In our implementation, we adopted Modularity Clustering, which has shown effectiveness in many community detection tasks and does not require to specify as input the number of clusters to be detected [7]. From the detected concepts (or subgraphs), the second-hop tags are removed as only the first-hop tags are strongly associated with t_c and hence can be used for recommendation (lines 5-8).

A concept is a 3-tuple $\langle t_c, assoc(t_c, c_p), c_p\rangle$ where $assoc(t_c, c_p)$ is the *association strength* between the candidate tag t_c and the concept c_p detected from its TRG (see Equation 2), and c_p is represented by a set of first-hop tags.

$$assoc(t_c, c_p) \quad = \quad \sum_{t \in c_p} assoc(t, t_c) \quad (2)$$

In the above equation $assoc(t, t_c)$ is computed based on one of the association measures defined in Equation 1. Table 1 illustrates representation of concepts. The first two records are the concepts for candidate tag rock whose TRG is depicted in Figure 1. The remain-

Table 1: **Example concepts for candidate tags** rock **and** sunset

⟨rock,	0.265,	{wave, cliff, rocks, stone}⟩
⟨rock,	0.247,	{concert, band, music, live}⟩
⟨sunset,	0.483,	{clouds, sun, sky, silhouette}⟩
⟨sunset,	0.341,	{beach, sea, ocean, water}⟩

ing two records represent the concepts for candidate tag sunset (the TRG is obtained using $\alpha = Jaccard$ and $\varphi = 8$). Due to space constraints, we do not display the TRG of sunset. The two concepts of sunset show two different aspects of the sunset scenes, *landscape* and *seascape*.

We index a concept as a textual document. Specifically, the set of tags in c_p is indexed as the content of the document in an inverted index where each tag is a word (or term) in the index [6]. Both the candidate tag t_c and the association strength $assoc(t_c, c_p)$ are indexed as attributes of the document (similar to *author*, *publication date* attributes of any textual document).

3.3 Tag Recommendation

The tag recommendation is modeled as a textual search problem and consists of two steps. First, it computes the *recommendation score* of each candidate tag with respect to the user-given tags of an image. Then, it sorts the candidate tags in descending order of their scores and recommends top-k tags to the user. As the second step is trivial, we elaborate on the first step further.

Let T_u be the set of user-given tags for a social image whose tags are to be recommended. All tags in T_u form a textual query, where each tag $t_u \in T_u$ is a term in the query and all terms are equally weighted. The *recommendation score* $score(t_c)$ of a candidate tag t_c is computed as follows.

$$score(t_c) = \sum_{c_p \in C} match(T_u, c_p) \cdot assoc(t_c, c_p) \qquad (3)$$

In this equation, $match(T_u, c_p)$ is the *match score* between a concept of t_c and T_u, computed using widely adopted cosine similarity between the textual query and the document content. We use Lucene as the indexer and its default similarity setting.

4. EXPERIMENTS

Evaluation of social image tag recommendation is a challenging task partially due to the lack of a benchmark dataset. Existing studies have largely engaged in user study for evaluation. However, this impose practical limits to number of test cases. Recommending tags that are syntactically removed from existing user-tagged images may not truly reflect the accuracy of a tag recommendation method. This is because these syntactically removed tags may not be strongly related to the image due to the noisy nature of user-assigned tags. In our evaluation, we use the NUS-WIDE dataset, which is the largest publicly available human-annotated dataset [1].

4.1 Dataset

In the NUS-WIDE dataset, ground-truth images of 81 categories were manually labeled. These categories were carefully selected such that they (i) correspond to some frequent tags in Flickr, (ii) cover both general concepts like "animal" and specific ones like "dog" and "flowers", and (iii) belong to different genres including scene, object, event, program, people and graphics [1]. All the three aforementioned criteria and the ground-truth labeling make NUS-WIDE a fairly good dataset for tag recommendation evaluation. Importantly, although many images in the dataset have been manually labeled to one or more categories, they may not be tagged by the corresponding category labels. For instance, an image is manually labeled under tiger category because it contains a tiger object. However, it may not contain tiger as a tag due to incompleteness of user tagging. Fortunately, this creates a good *test case* for our tag recommendation method as we just need to evaluate whether the method can effectively recommend tag tiger to the image.

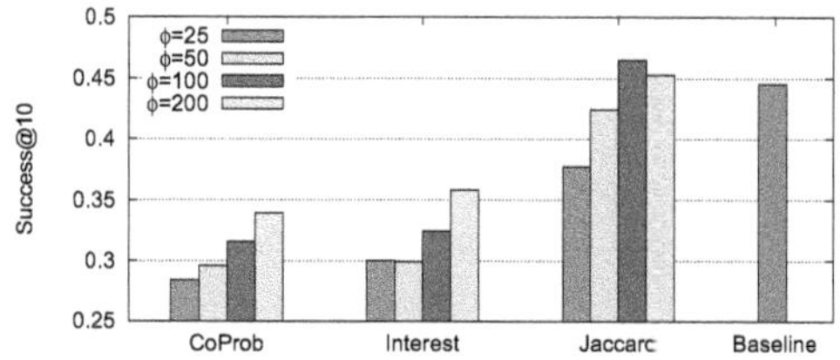

(a) Accuracy using Success@10 for all methods.

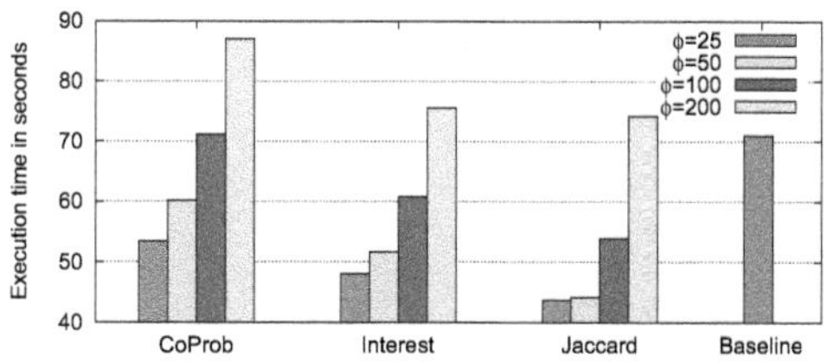

(b) Execution time of all methods

Figure 3: Time and accuracy (Success@10).

In our experiments, we used the 81 category labels as candidate tags and their corresponding ground-truth for evaluation. To generate the tag co-occurrence pairs, we select 5981 frequent tags, each of which has been used to tag at least 100 images, among the 420K distinct tags appeared in the dataset. A tag co-occurrence pair is recorded if two tags co-occurred for at least 10 times, resulting in more than 527K pairs[1]. The infrequent tags are not considered in the knowledge base (*i.e.*, tag co-occurrence pairs).

For each of the 81 categories, all images that belong to the category but are not tagged by the category label are selected as test cases. Among them, we further select images containing *at most* 10 frequent tags[2] for recommendation leading to 190,288 test cases. These test cases involve 99,106 distinct images as an image may belong to more than one category.

4.2 Methods

We evaluate three association measures, namely, Jaccard, CoProb, and Interest (defined in Equation 1) for TRG construction. For each association measure, we use $\varphi = \{25, 50, 100, 200\}$. Hence, 12 methods are evaluated based on the proposed tag recommendation framework. In the sequel, for a given φ we denote a method using association measure α as $\alpha\varphi$ (*e.g.*, *Jaccard100*).

We compare our proposed technique with the state-of-the-art tag recommendation algorithm for Flickr reported in [8]. In the sequel, we refer to this algorithm as the *baseline* approach. For fair comparison, the tags recommended by the baseline method that are not among the 81 category labels (*i.e.*, candidate tags in our methods) are excluded as there is no ground-truth labeling for these tags.

4.3 Results

S@10. We evaluate the recommendation accuracy of our approach using *Success@K* (or simply *S@K*), which is the probability of finding a labeled category among the top *K* recommended tags.

[1]Tag pairs $\langle t_a, t_b\rangle$ and $\langle t_b, t_a\rangle$ are considered the same as co-occurrence is unidirectional.

[2]The infrequent tags have no impact on tag recommendation as they are not included in the knowledge base.

Table 2: **Number of concepts indexed.**

Assoc measure α	$\varphi = 25$	$\varphi = 50$	$\varphi = 100$	$\varphi = 200$
CoProb	309	356	418	506
Interest	353	438	520	600
Jaccard	387	503	596	709

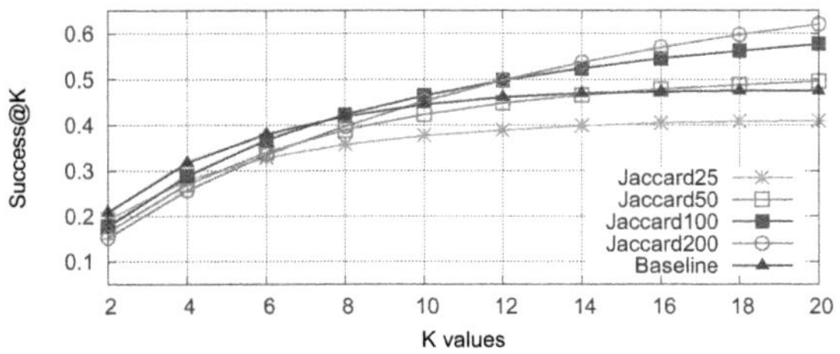

(a) Effect of K on Success@K.

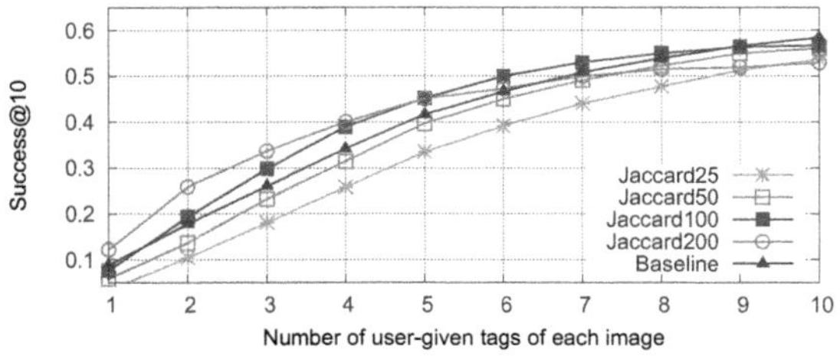

(b) S@10 vs number of user-given tags.

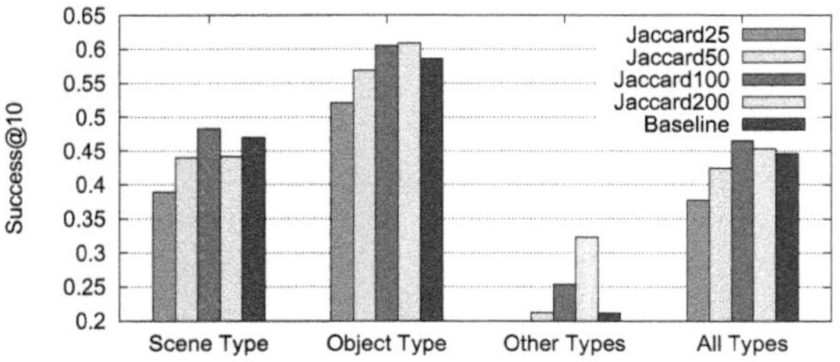

(c) Effect of candidate tags types on S@10.

Figure 4: Tag recommendation performance comparison.

Note that it is also used in [8]. Figure 3(a) plots the $S@10$ values of the baseline and our proposed method based on the three association measures. We can make the following observations. Firstly, Jaccard-based method outperforms its counterparts based on CoProb or Interest by a large margin. In other words, symmetric association measure performs better than asymmetric association measure in tag recommendation, consistent with that reported in [8]. Secondly, *Jaccard100* and *Jaccard200* both outperform the baseline method. Particularly, *Jaccard100* is the winner among all methods.

Execution time. Figure 3(b) reports the execution times for processing 190,288 test cases for all methods executed on the same computer. Observe that CoProb-based methods are the slowest and methods based on Jaccard are the most efficient ones among the 12 proposed methods. Larger φ leads to larger TRG and consequently more concepts need to be indexed (Table 2). Obviously, potentially more concepts are then matched for a given image, leading to a longer execution time. Observe that *Jaccard100* not only achieves better tag recommendation accuracy ($S@10$) compared to the baseline method, its execution time is also 24% lower than the latter. In the following experiments we shall compare the 4 methods with Jaccard association measure (*Jaccard25*, *Jaccard50*, *Jaccard100*, and *Jaccard200*) and the baseline.

Effect of K in $S@K$. Figure 4(a) reports the $S@K$ values for K ranging from 2 to 20. The baseline method achieves the best $S@K$ for $K \leq 8$ and then reaches a plateau for $K \geq 10$. Both *Jaccard100* and *Jaccard200* achieve slightly better $S@10$ and then significant better $S@K$ values for $K > 10$ compared to the baseline. Note that for a tag recommendation system, a larger K indicates that its users might be overloaded with too many recommended tags. Therefore, in the sequel we discuss our results for $K = 10$, which is a reasonable number for tag recommendation and has been used in several recent works such as [5].

Number of user-given tags. Figure 4(b) reports the effect of number of user-given tags an image already has on $S@10$. Clearly, more user-given tags means that a tag recommendation method can leverage on more information about the image for better recommendation, leading to higher $S@10$ values. Observe that *Jaccard100* outperforms the baseline when the number user-given tags is between 2 and 8. *Jaccard200* is the best performing method when the number of tags is fewer than 5. However, it did not benefit as much as other methods when more user-given tags are available.

Tag types. The 81 candidate tags include 33 tags apiece in *scene* and *object* categories. These two major categories cover 63% and 19% of the test cases, respectively. Figure 4(c) reports the values of $S@10$ for these categories of objects. Observe that tags in *object* category have highest $S@10$ values for all methods.

5. CONCLUSIONS

In this paper, we propose a novel knowledge-based approach for image tag recommendation that exploits tag concepts, which are derived based on the collective knowledge embedded in tag co-occurrence pairs. Our proposed tag recommendation framework is generic in nature. In particular, the candidate tags maybe selected based on various criteria most important to the target application; the TRG may be constructed based on different association measures and hop threshold values; the tag concepts can be detected by alternative graph-cut algorithms; and the matching score between the user-given tags and the concepts are based on well-studied techniques in Information Retrieval. This enables not only customized matching score computation (*e.g.,* query term weighting and similarity definitions between the user-given tags and the matching concepts), but also boost efficiency and scalability of the tag recommendation process. It is therefore part of our future work to investigate techniques along these dimensions to further improve tag recommendation accuracy.

6. REFERENCES

[1] T.-S. Chua, J. Tang, R. Hong, H. Li, Z. Luo, and Y.-T. Zheng. NUS-WIDE: A real-world web image database from National University of Singapore. In *Proc. CIVR*, 2009.

[2] J. Li and J. Z. Wang. Real-time computerized annotation of pictures. *IEEE TPAMI*, 30(6):985–1002, 2008.

[3] X. Li, C. G. M. Snoek, and M. Worring. Learning social tag relevance by neighbor voting. *IEEE TMM*, 11(7):1310–1322, 2009.

[4] D. Liu, X.-S. Hua, L. Yang, M. Wang, and H.-J. Zhang. Tag ranking. In *Proc. WWW*, 2009.

[5] Y.-T. Lu, S.-I. Yu, T.-C. Chang, and J. Y.-J. Hsu. A content-based method to enhance tag recommendation. In *Proc. IJCAI*, 2009.

[6] C. D. Manning, P. Raghavan, and H. Schütze. *Introduction to Information Retrieval*. Cambridge University Press, 2008.

[7] M. E. J. Newman. Modularity and community structure in networks. *Proc. of Nat. Aca. of Sci. of USA*, 103:8577–8582, 2006.

[8] B. Sigurbjörnsson and R. van Zwol. Flickr tag recommendation based on collective knowledge. In *Proc. WWW*, 2008.

[9] G. Zhu, S. Yan, and Y. Ma. Image tag refinement towards low-rank, content-tag prior and error sparsity. In *Proc. MM*, 2010.

Automatic Image Annotation with Weakly Labeled Dataset*

Wei Zhang[1], Yao Lu[1], Xiangyang Xue[1], Jianping Fan[2]
[1]School of Computer Science, Fudan University, Shanghai, China
[2]Department of Computer Science, UNC-Charlotte, NC28223, USA
{weizh, yaolu, xyxue}@fudan.edu.cn jfan@uncc.edu

ABSTRACT

It is very attractive to exploit weakly-labeled image dataset for multi-label annotation applications. In our paper the meaning of the terminology *weakly labeled* is threefold: i) only a small subset of the available images are labeled; ii) even for the labeled image, the given labels may be uncorrect or incomplete; iii) the given labels do not provide the exact object locations in the images. A novel method is developed to predict the multiple labels for images and to provide region-level labels for the objects. We cluster the image regions to learn several region-exemplars and predict the label vector for each image region as a locally weighted average of the label vectors on exemplars. By investigating the label confidence matrix for the region-exemplars from different perspectives (*column picture* and *row picture*), we sufficiently leverage the visual contexts, the semantic contexts, and the consistency between similarities in the visual feature space and semantic label space. Experimental results on real web images demonstrate the effectiveness of the proposed method.

Categories and Subject Descriptors

H.3.1 [**Information Storage and Retrieval**]: Content Analysis and Indexing

General Terms

Algorithms, Experimentation, Performance

Keywords

Multi-Label Image Annotation, Weakly-Labeled Dataset, Region-Level Labels

1. INTRODUCTION

With the massive explosion of web images, how to access these images efficiently is an important research task, and automatic image annotation has become more and more attractive. In real image annotation applications, multiple semantic concepts may occur simultaneously in an image; each individual label of one image is actually related to local regions rather than the whole image. It is attractive to learning the image classifiers from *weakly labeled* images available on the web. Herein the terminology *weakly labeled* can be investigated from three perspectives: i) Since manually annotating is time-consuming and labor-intensive, only a subset of images are labeled, and the number of available labeled images is much smaller than that of unlabeled ones; ii) In a collaborative image tagging system, people can tag the images according to their personal expertise and perception, and the label set for each labeled image may be uncorrect or incomplete; iii) The multiple labels are given loosely at the image level rather than at the object level (i.e., without providing the exact object locations in the images). Our goal is to precisely predict the multiple labels for images and to provide region-level labels for the objects, simultaneously.

In [2] a framework was proposed to improve the retrieval performance by refining noisy labels of a group of Flickr photos. [17] proposed a label refinement formulation considering the label characteristics from the points of view of low-rank, error sparsity, content consistency and label correlation. [15] and [14] both proposed graph-based semi-supervised learning frameworks, which can simultaneously explore the correlations among multiple labels and the label consistency over the graph. Those methods above inferred the correspondence between the images and their associated labels only at the image level rather than at the region level. [8] proposed a unified formulation to implement various tag analysis tasks including label-to-region assignment in a coherent way; however the correlations between labels are not exploited in [8].

In this paper a novel method is developed to simultaneously perform label prediction and label-to-region assignment based on weakly-labeled web image dataset. Each image is firstly segmented into several regions. We cluster the image regions to learn a small number of region-exemplars and predict the label vector for each image region as a locally weighted average of the label vectors on exemplars. By investigating the label confidence matrix for the region-exemplars from different perspectives (*column picture* and *row picture*), our method sufficiently leverages the visual contexts, the semantic contexts, and the associations between image-level and region-level labels. Different from [8], the correlations between the semantic concepts are effec-

*Area chair: Bernard Merialdo

MM'11, November 28–December 1, 2011, Scottsdale, Arizona, USA.

tively captured in our method, which is of significance to the performance of multi-label image annotation. Experimental results on the real web images demonstrate the effectiveness of the proposed method.

2. ALGORITHM

Suppose that $\{(\mathbf{x}^1, \mathbf{y}^1), ..., (\mathbf{x}^l, \mathbf{y}^l)\}$ are l labeled images for training. Each image includes r_i regions: $\mathbf{x}^i = \{\mathbf{x}^i_1, ..., \mathbf{x}^i_{r_i}\}$, where the number of regions r_i may vary across images. Let $\mathcal{C} = \{c_1, ..., c_m\}$ be a semantic lexicon of m concepts, and let $\mathbf{y}^i = [\mathbf{y}^i_1, \dots, \mathbf{y}^i_m]^\top \in \{0,1\}^m$ be the initial m−dimensional label vector corresponding to the image $\mathbf{x}^i$, where $\mathbf{y}^i_s = 1 (s = 1, \dots, m)$ if the concept c_s is associated with the image $\mathbf{x}^i$, and 0 otherwise. Our goal is to predict the label vector for any new image and to predict the region-level label simultaneously.

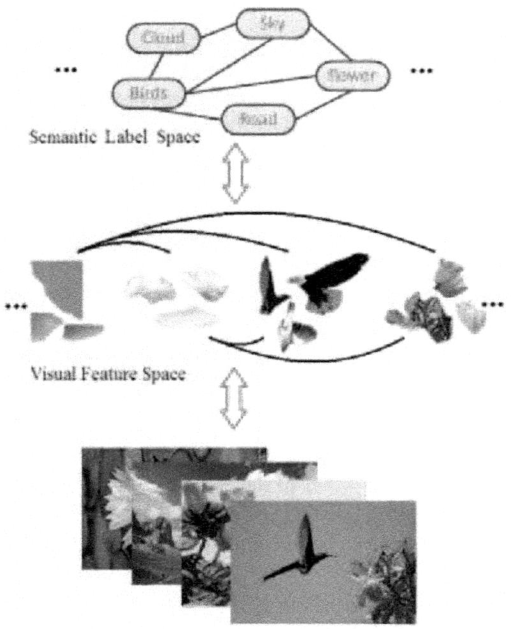

Figure 1: An overview of our method. Each image is firstly segmented into regions. All regions are clustered into several groups. In the visual feature space, region-exemplars are used to construct the visual context graph. In the semantic label space, concepts form the semantic context graph which captures the correlations between concepts.

Each image is firstly segmented into several regions. Let $\mathbf{h}^i_j \in [0,1]^m (j = 1, ..., r_i)$ denote the label confidence vector of $\mathbf{x}^i_j$ (the j−th region in the i−th image), and the s−th component of $\mathbf{h}^i_j$ just measures the probability that the concept c_s is associated with the region $\mathbf{x}^i_j$. To address the scalability issue, all the image regions are clustered into several groups by clustering algorithms such as *Affinity Propagation* [6] based on the visual similarity. Suppose that n clusters are obtained, and one region-exemplar is learned for each cluster, then we get n region-exemplars $\{\dot{\mathbf{x}}_1, ..., \dot{\mathbf{x}}_n\}$. Inspired by [12], we approximately reconstruct each image region as a convex combination of its nearest exemplars:

$$\mathbf{x}^i_j \approx \sum_{q \in \langle \mathbf{x}^i_j \rangle} \pi_{ijq} \dot{\mathbf{x}}_q, \tag{1}$$

where $\langle \mathbf{x}^i_j \rangle$ denotes the index set of k closest exemplars for $\mathbf{x}^i_j$, and the combination coefficients π_{ijq} can be learned by quadratic programming (QP) as follows:

$$\min \frac{1}{2} \|\mathbf{x}^i_j - \sum_{q \in \langle \mathbf{x}^i_j \rangle} \pi_{ijq} \dot{\mathbf{x}}_q\|^2, s.t. \quad \pi_{ijq} \geq 0, \sum_{q \in \langle \mathbf{x}^i_j \rangle} \pi_{ijq} = 1 \tag{2}$$

Let $\dot{\mathbf{h}}_q \in [0,1]^m$ denote the label confidence vector for the exemplar region $\dot{\mathbf{x}}_q, (q = 1, ..., n)$, which can be viewed as a point in the semantic label space. It it reasonable to preserve the neighborhood contexts when mapping image regions from the visual feature space to the semantic label space. Then, the label confidence vector for the image region $\mathbf{x}^i_j$ can be estimated as a locally weighted average of the labels on exemplars:

$$\mathbf{h}^i_j = \sum_{q \in \langle \mathbf{x}^i_j \rangle} \pi_{ijq} \dot{\mathbf{h}}_q, \tag{3}$$

Let $\pi_{ijq} = 0$ if $q \notin \langle \mathbf{x}^i_j \rangle$ and denote $\vec{\alpha}^i_j = [\pi_{ij1}, ..., \pi_{ijn}]^\top$, $\dot{H} = [\dot{\mathbf{h}}_1, ..., \dot{\mathbf{h}}_n] \in [0,1]^{m \times n}$, then Eq. (3) can be expressed as:

$$\mathbf{h}^i_j = \dot{H} \vec{\alpha}^i_j, \tag{4}$$

Once the region-level label confidence vectors are learned, the image-level label confidence vectors can be estimated by $\sum_{j=1}^{r_i} \omega^i_j \mathbf{h}^i_j$ (herein ω^i_j is the voting weight and can be selected as the percentage of covered area of each region). To achieve the coherence between region-level labels and image-level labels, and thus realize the cross-level label propagation, we minimize the following loss function:

$$\min \sum_{i=1}^{l} \|\mathbf{y}^i - \sum_{j=1}^{r_i} \omega^i_j \mathbf{h}^i_j\|^2 = Tr((Y - \dot{H}A)^\top (Y - \dot{H}A)) \tag{5}$$

where $Y = [\mathbf{y}^1, ..., \mathbf{y}^l] \in \{0,1\}^{m \times l}$, $\dot{H} = [\dot{\mathbf{h}}_1, ..., \dot{\mathbf{h}}_n] \in [0,1]^{m \times n}$, and $A = [\sum_{j=1}^{r_1} \omega^1_j \vec{\alpha}^1_j, ..., \sum_{j=1}^{r_l} \omega^l_j \vec{\alpha}^l_j] \in R^{n \times l}$.

The label confidence matrix for the region-exemplars $\dot{H} = [\dot{\mathbf{h}}_1, ..., \dot{\mathbf{h}}_n] \in [0,1]^{m \times n}$ can be investigated from different perspectives: i)*column picture*: Each column of $\dot{H}$ corresponds to the label distribution for one region-exemplar , and $\dot{\mathbf{h}}_q (q = 1, ..., n)$ can be viewed as the high-level feature vector of the q−th region-exemplar in the semantic label space, which differs from the low-level feature vector $\dot{\mathbf{x}}_q$ in the visual feature space; ii)*row picture*: Each row of $\dot{H}$ can be viewed as the voting scores from all the region-exemplars for each concept, and can also be viewed as the feature vector of the concept. By constructing different graphs from above two perspectives, we can sufficiently leverage visual context, semantic context, and the consistency between visual features and semantic concepts, to improve the performance of image annotation.

Let $G = (\{\dot{\mathbf{x}}_q\}_{q=1}^n, S)$ be the visual context graph with the vertex set corresponding to the region-exemplars $\{\dot{\mathbf{x}}_q\}_{q=1}^n$ and the adjacent matrix S measuring the visual similarities between region pairs. S is an $n \times n$ sparse symmetric matrix and can be defined using visual features as follows:

$$S_{pq} = \begin{cases} exp\{-\rho \mathbf{d}(\dot{\mathbf{x}}_p, \dot{\mathbf{x}}_q)\} & \dot{\mathbf{x}}_p \in \langle \dot{\mathbf{x}}_q \rangle \vee \dot{\mathbf{x}}_q \in \langle \dot{\mathbf{x}}_p \rangle \\ 0 & otherwise \end{cases} \tag{6}$$

where $\langle \dot{\mathbf{x}}_q \rangle$ denotes the set of k closest exemplars for $\dot{\mathbf{x}}_q$, $\mathbf{d}(\dot{\mathbf{x}}_p, \dot{\mathbf{x}}_q)$ is the distance between exemplars $\dot{\mathbf{x}}_p$ and $\dot{\mathbf{x}}_q$, and ρ is the scaling parameter. The visual and semantic consistency for the exemplar regions can be achieved by solving the following problem:

$$\min \frac{1}{2} \sum_{pq} S_{pq} \left\| col(\dot{H}, p) - col(\dot{H}, q) \right\|^2 = Tr\left(\dot{H}(\widetilde{S} - S)\dot{H}^\top\right) \tag{7}$$

where $col(\dot{H}, p)$ denotes the $p-$th column of $\dot{H}$, i.e., $\dot{\mathbf{h}}_p$, and $\widetilde{S}$ is an $n \times n$ diagonal matrix with $\widetilde{S}_{qq} = \sum_{p=1}^{n} S_{pq}$.

On the other hand, let $G' = (\{c_s\}_{s=1}^{m}, W)$ be the semantic context graph with the vertex set corresponding to the concepts $\{c_s\}_{s=1}^{m}$ and the adjacent matrix W measuring the correlations between concepts. W is an $m \times m$ sparse symmetric matrix and can be defined as follows:

$$W_{st} = \begin{cases} exp\{-\sigma \mathbf{d}(c_s, c_t)\} & \mathbf{d}(c_s, c_t) < \epsilon \\ 0 & otherwise \end{cases} \tag{8}$$

where σ and ϵ are the parameters, and $\mathbf{d}(c_s, c_t)$ is the Normalized Google Distance (NGD) [4] between concepts c_s and c_t:

$$\mathbf{d}(c_s, c_t) = \frac{max\{logf(c_s), logf(c_t)\} - logf(c_s, c_t)}{logN - min\{logf(c_s), logf(c_t)\}} \tag{9}$$

where $f(c_s)$ is the numbers of the webpages returned by Google search engine when typing c_s as the search term, $f(c_s, c_t)$ is the number of webpages returned when typing c_s and c_t together as the search term, and N is the total number of the images in Google. The smaller the NGD is, the stronger the semantic relation is; so, the weight W_{st} measures the affinity between concepts c_s and c_t. At the same time, each row of $\dot{H}$ corresponds to the voting scores from all the region-exemplars for each concept and can be viewed as the feature vector of the concept. Strongly correlated concepts concepts should have similar voting scores, which can be achieved by solving the following problem:

$$\min \frac{1}{2} \sum_{st} W_{st} \left\| row(\dot{H}, s) - row(\dot{H}, t) \right\|^2 = Tr\left(\dot{H}^\top (\widetilde{W} - W)\dot{H}\right) \tag{10}$$

where $row(\dot{H}, s)$ denotes the $s-$th row of $\dot{H}$, and $\widetilde{W}$ is an $n \times n$ diagonal matrix with $\widetilde{W}_{tt} = \sum_{s=1}^{m} W_{st}$.

Therefore, by incorporating various contextual relations in a single framework as shown in Figure. 1, the proposed model for automatic image annotation takes the formulation as:

$$\begin{aligned} \min_{\dot{H}} \quad & Tr\left((Y - \dot{H}A)^\top (Y - \dot{H}A)\right) + \\ & \theta_1 Tr\left(\dot{H}(\widetilde{S} - S)\dot{H}^\top\right) + \theta_2 Tr\left(\dot{H}^\top (\widetilde{W} - W)\dot{H}\right) \end{aligned} \tag{11}$$

where θ_1 and θ_2 are the controlling parameters. Let the derivative of the above cost function with respect to $\dot{H}$ be zero, we have

$$\dot{H}(\theta_1(\widetilde{S} - S) + AA^\top) + \theta_2(\widetilde{W} - W)\dot{H} = YA^\top \tag{12}$$

which is essentially a Sylvester equation [15] widely used in control theory. Vectorizing the unknown matrix $\dot{H}$, Eq. (12) can be transformed to a linear system:

$$\begin{aligned} & [(\theta_1(\widetilde{S} - S) + AA^\top) \otimes I_m + I_n \otimes (\theta_2(\widetilde{W} - W))]vec(\dot{H}) \\ & = vec(YA^\top) \end{aligned} \tag{13}$$

where $vec(.)$ is the vectorization of the matrix, $\otimes$ is the Kronecker product, and I_m and I_n are $m \times m$ and $n \times n$ identity matrices, respectively. We can efficiently solve $vec(\dot{H})$ in Eq. (13) by a generalized minimal residual algorithm [13], and then obtain $\dot{H}$ from $vec(\dot{H})$. For any new image, we predict its region-level labels using $\dot{H}$ via Eq. (1) and Eq. (3), and then the image-level label vector is derived as well.

3. EXPERIMENTS

In this section, we evaluate the proposed method on the NUS-WIDE-SUB dataset [3, 8] which is a challenging collection of real-world web images from Flickr containing 18,325 images with 81 labels. We focus on evaluating our method when the number of labeled images is much smaller than that of unlabeled ones, and randomly split the dataset into the 10% subset for training and the 90% subset for testing. Since the user-provided tags is noisy, the training images are precisely re-annotated at first. We use Felzenswalb's graph cut algorithm [5] to segment each image into several regions. Four kinds of visual features are extracted for each region: 1) 14-dim color feature including mean RGB, HSV conversion, HUE histogram and SAT histogram; 2) 30-dim texture feature including LM-filter mean response [7] and LM-filter response histogram; 3) 8-dim geometric feature encoding the position and size information of the segment; 4) 500-dim BoW histogram. Based on the above visual features, the composite distance between image regions is computed using JEC[10]. Employing Affinity Propagation algorithm [6], we cluster the regions from the training images and obtain the region-exemplars.

Method	Training%	Precision	Recall
ML-LGC	50%	0.28	0.29
CNMF	50%	0.29	0.31
SMSE	50%	0.32	0.32
MISSL	50%	0.27	0.33
MEG	50%	**0.35**	0.37
Ours	**10%**	0.31	**0.41**

Table 1: Performance comparisons of different automatic annotation methods on NUS-WIDE-SUB.

We compare the proposed method with the state-of-the-art algorithms: 1) ML-LGC[16], 2) CNMF[9], 3)SMSE[1], 4)MISSL[11], 5)MEG[8]. In the label prediction task, we aim at predicting the labels of the testing images and use the provided 81 semantic concepts as the ground truth annotations for evaluation. We calculate the average precision and average recall to measure the performance. Table 1 gives the performance comparisons of the image annotation algorithms. The results of the state-of-the-art were reported in [8]. From the results we can clearly see that our algorithm is better than or comparable with the state-of-the-art algorithms even though much fewer training examples are required than the state-of-the-art, which demonstrates the

Image	Before	After
	Road, sunset, sun, plane, airport	Plane, sky, sun, sunset, clouds, road, vehicle, airport
	Sky, lake, tree, water, grass, leaf, glacier	Tree, lake, boat, mountain, grass, sky, water
	House, tower, window, buildings, sky	House, buildings, sky, tree, grass, garden, leaf

Figure 2: The refined label rank lists are obtained according to the learned label confidence vector.

Figure 3: Region-level labeling results of our method for some images from NUS-WIDE-SUB dataset.

effectiveness of strategy to sufficiently leverage various contextual relations. Figure 2 gives the refined label rank lists obtained by the learned label confidence vector in comparison with the initial labels provided by the users. Moreover, the proposed algorithm is also suitable for the task of label-to-region assignment. Since the NUS-WIDE-SUB dataset has no ground truth for this task, we merely give some results in Figure 3. The results demonstrate that by learning the label confidences for the region-exemplars, our method can effectively estimate the label confidences for each image region, then the tasks of predicting both image-level and region-level labels are accomplished simultaneously.

4. CONCLUSIONS

In this paper a novel method is proposed to perform automatic image annotation with weakly-labeled image dataset. Clustering technique is employed to learn a small number of region-exemplars, and the labels for each image region are predicted as a locally weighted average of the labels on exemplars. By investigating the label confidence matrix for the region exemplars from *column* and *row* pictures, we sufficiently leverage the consistency of similarities between samples in the visual feature space and semantic label space, the correlations among the semantic concepts, and the associations between image-level and region-level labels, which are of significance to the performance of image annotation.

5. ACKNOWLEDGMENTS

We would like to thank the anonymous reviewers for their helpful comments. This work was supported in part by the 973 Program (No.2010CB327906), the NSF of China (No.60903077 and No.60873178), and the STCSM's innovation program(No. 10511500703).

6. REFERENCES

[1] G. Chen, Y. Song, F. Wang, and C. Zhang. Semi-supervised multi-label learning by solving a sylvester equation. In *SDM*, 2008.

[2] L. Chen, D. Xu, I. W. Tsang, and J. Luo. Tag-based web photo retrieval improved by batch mode re-tagging. In *CVPR*, 2010.

[3] T.-S. Chua, J. Tang, R. Hong, H. Li, Z. Luo, and Y.-T. Zheng. Nus-wide: A real-world web image database from national university of singapore. In *CIVR*, 2009.

[4] R. Cilibrasi and P. Vitany. The google similarity distance. In *TKDE*, 2007.

[5] P. Felzenszwalb and D. Huttenlocher. Efficient graph-based image segmentation. *IJCV*, 59(2):167–181, 2004.

[6] B. Frey and D. Dueck. Clustering by passing messages between data points. *Science, vol. 315, 2007.*

[7] T. Leung and J. Malik. Representing and recognizing the visual appearance of materials using three-dimensional textons. *IJCV*, 43(1):29–44, 2001.

[8] D. Liu, S. Yan, Y. Rui, and H.-J. Zhang. Unified tag analysis with multi-edge graph. In *ACM MM*, 2010.

[9] Y. Liu, R. Jin, and L. Yang. Semi-supervised multi-label learning by constrained non-negative matrix factorization. In *AAAI*, 2006.

[10] A. Makadia, V. Pavlovic, and S. Kumar. A new baseline for image annotation. In *ECCV*, 2008.

[11] R. Rahmani and S. Goldman. Missl: Multiple-instance semi-supervised learning. In *ICML*, 2006.

[12] S. T. Roweis and L. K. Saul. Nonlinear dimensionality reduction by locally linear embedding. *Science, vol. 290, 2000.*

[13] Y. Saad and M. H. Schultz. Gmrs: A generalized minimal residual algorithm for solving nonsymmetrci linear systems. In *SIAM JSSC.*, 1986(7).

[14] J. Tang, S. Yan, R. Hong, G.-J. Qi, and T.-S. Chua. Inferring semantic concepts from community contributed images and noisy tags. In *ACM MM*, 2009.

[15] Z.-J. Zha, T. Mei, J. Wang, Z. Wang, and X.-S. Hua. Graph-based semi-supervised learning with multiple labels. *J. Vis. Commun. Image R., 2009.*

[16] D. Zhou, O. Bousquet, T. Lal, J. Weston, and B. Scholkopf. Learning with local and global consistency. In *NIPS*, 2003.

[17] G. Zhu, S. Yan, and Y. Ma. Image tag refinement towards low-rank, content-tag prior and error sparsity. In *ACM MM*, 2010.

Efficient Approximate Nearest Neighbor Search with Integrated Binary Codes

Wei Zhang[1,2], Ke Gao[1], Yongdong Zhang[1], and Jintao Li[1]
[1]Advanced Computing Research Laboratory, Institute of Computing Technology
Chinese Academy of Sciences, Beijing, China
[2]Graduate University of the Chinese Academy of Sciences, Beijing, China
{zhangwei, kegao, zhyd, jtli}@ict.ac.cn

ABSTRACT
Nearest neighbor search in Euclidean space is a fundamental problem in multimedia retrieval. The difficulty of exact nearest neighbor search has led to approximate solutions that sacrifice precision for efficiency. Among such solutions, approaches that embed data into binary codes in Hamming space have gained significant success for their efficiency and practical memory requirements. However, binary code searching only finds a big and coarse set of similar neighbors in Hamming space, and hence expensive Euclidean distance based ranking of the coarse set is needed to find nearest neighbors. Therefore, to improve nearest neighbor search efficiency, we proposed a novel binary code method called Integrated Binary Code (IBC) to get a compact set of similar neighbors. Experiments on public datasets show that our method is more efficient and effective than state-of-the-art in approximate nearest neighbor search.

Categories and Subject Descriptors
H.3.3 [**Information Storage and Retrieval**]: Information Search and Retrieval

General Terms
Algorithms, Performance.

Keywords
Similarity Search, Approximate Nearest Neighbor Search.

1. INTRODUCTION
Nearest neighbor search for large-scale data in high-dimensional space is a fundamental requirement in many multimedia retrieval applications. Currently most nearest neighbor search approaches are on the basis of Euclidean metric. Focusing on the Euclidean space, given a dataset $X \subset R^D$, the nearest neighbor of a vector x from X is defined as $NN(x) = \{x' : \min(d(x,x')) \wedge (x' \in X)\}$ where d is a Euclidean distance metric. The difficulty of exact NN (nearest neighbor) search has led to various indexing methods. The early tree-structure based NN methods such as kd-tree, R-tree, etc. are suffered from "curse of dimensionality" [1]. As noises and approximate factors always exist in high-dimensional data extraction processes in multimedia, Approximate Nearest Neighbor (ANN) algorithms that sacrifice precision for efficiency achieve remarkable success in multimedia retrieval field.

*Area Chair: Marcel Worring

MM'11, November 28–December 1, 2011, Scottsdale, Arizona, USA.

One of the most famous ANN methods is Locality Sensitive Hashing (LSH) [2]. LSH uses hash-table structures to filter most false positives, and then re-ranks the leftover data by Euclidean distances. LSH can achieve ANN search efficiently with a controllable high probability. However, the heavy memory consumption is a barrier to apply LSH to large-scale database.

Consequently, in recent years many approaches [3-8] use binary codes to limit memory consumption. These approaches embed high-dimensional data into Hamming space, satisfying the conditions that neighborhood relationships are retained in the embedded space as much as possible. Then distance computations of binary codes can be executed by hardware, which enable fast retrieval.

For these binary code methods, searching nearest neighbors in Euclidean space is approximated by searching similar neighbors in terms of Hamming distances between codes. However, binary codes are generated with information loss. Thus re-ranking by exact Euclidean distances is needed to find nearest neighbors, which consumes time heavily and has become the efficiency bottleneck.

Therefore, we put forward a novel binary code method called Integrated Binary Code (IBC) to get a compact set of similar neighbors and hence improve query efficiency ultimately. The IBC is based on two novel and complementary binary code methods called as Uni-bicode and Quanti-bicode respectively. Figure 1 demonstrates our method. The set of similar neighbors obtained using the IBC is the intersection of the two sets returned by Uni-bicode and Quanti-bicode. In this way, Euclidean distance computations of the similar neighbors can be reduced significantly. As a result ANN search efficiency can be improved.

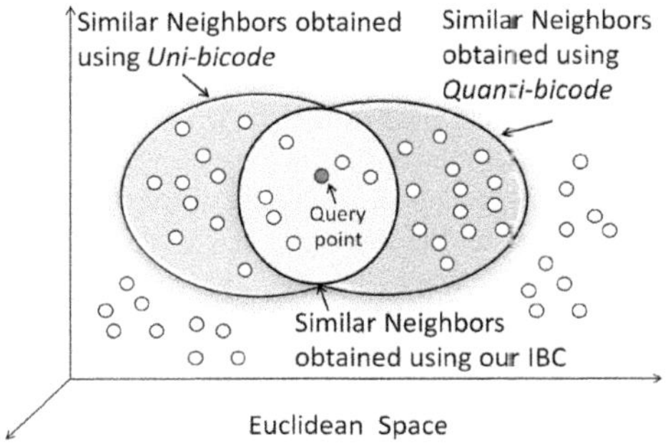

Figure 1. Illustration of our Integrated Binary Code (IBC) method. The set of similar neighbors obtained by IBC is the intersection of Uni-bicode and Quanti-bicode.

2. RELATED WORK

A simple method of binary codes generation is to randomly choose projection directions and threshold projection values as in [3]. Hamming Embedding (HE) [4] produces binary codes using random orthogonal projections. Machine learning approaches [5, 8] always report more compact and higher quality codes than random approaches. One is Spectral Hashing [5] (SH), which achieves significant improvement on LSH in Euclidean space and reports comparable results to [8] with much greater simplicity.

All these approaches retrieve similar neighbors by restricting Hamming distances between codes. Ideally, the nearest neighbors in Euclidean space should be returned. However, binary code searching strategy returns a coarse set number of similar neighbors in Hamming distance, which will obviously decrease the search quality. An example is cited to explain this specifically. With 10k SIFT [9] vectors from INRIA BIGANN [7] database (refer to section 4.1 for detail), 32-bit codes are generated using source codes provided by the authors of SH [5]. The searching results by restricting Hamming distances between codes are showed in Table 1.

Table 1. Nearest Neighbors in Euclidean Space returned by restricting Hamming distance

Hamming distance	Similar Neighbors returned (%)	Nearest Neighbor returned (%)
2	0.0089	16
4	0.1641	42
8	5.6769	80
10	16.4539	96

Searching binary codes does not guarantee the nearest neighbors can be found, except within a large Hamming distance which also increases false positives. As is shown in Table 1, when the nearest neighbor is returned with probability 96%, there will be 16.4% similar points returned. The situation exists for other binary code methods. As reported by [4], Hamming distance restriction keeps 94% of the 5-NN and filters 77% points, there are still 23% points returned as search result.

Consequently, for ANN search re-ranking process by Euclidean distance computations should be provided to find nearest neighbors. Nevertheless, such computations consume time heavily and hence reduce efficiency. This motives us to increase the proportions of nearest neighbors to search results that are returned by Hamming distance restriction of binary codes. In the experimental section, Hamming Embedding (HE) [4] and SH [5] will be used as baseline for IBC evaluation.

3. INTEGRATED BINARY CODE

In this section, we will introduce two novel binary code methods: Uni-bicode and Quanti-bicode. Uni-bicode utilizes percentiles to partition data in principal component space while Quanti-bicode uses clustering techniques. Based on the complementary properties of the two approaches, Integrated Binary Code (IBC) method is proposed and demonstrated in section 3.3.

3.1 Percentiles Based Uni-bicode

In order to generate compact codes of high quality, Uni-bicode transforms data into principal component space as other high-dimensional indexing algorithms [4, 6, 11] using Principle Component Analysis (PCA). Assigning the number of bits is known as bit allocation. In transform space, an adaptive bit allocation algorithm is adopted. Assume a bit allocation array $B=\{ b_1, b_2, \ldots\}$ stores the assignment on each component. Instead of allocating equal bits to different components as in [12], components with larger variances should be assigned more bits to produce a better partition. In practice, variances can be estimated as Eigen values of covariance matrix of training data. As discussed in [6], an optimal allocation is achieved when $b_i \sim \log_2 \lambda_i$, where λ_i is the corresponding Eigen value. We adopt this allocation algorithm for its simplicity and effectiveness, and the details can be referred in [6].

After bit allocation, binary codes are generated by partitioning thresholds on each principal component. The thresholds are produced in Algorithm 1.

Algorithm 1. Thresholds Generation for Uniform Partition

Input: Bits Allocation Array B, training dataset D after PCA
Output: T as a two dimensional array of thresholds
  For each $B(i)$ >0 on component i
    For j=1 to $B(i)$
      Estimate *percentile* of $\lfloor 100 * (j/(B(i)+1)) \rfloor$ from D;
      save T(i)(j) = *percentile*,
    End
  End

Percentile provides a way of estimating proportions of the data that should fall below a certain percent. Percentiles split a set of ordered data into hundredths. Usage of percentiles can ensure the partition works well.

After thresholds generation, binary codes of query points or dataset points can be computed as follows: (1) on each component i, set the value of bit on position B(i-1)+j to 1 if data point is larger than T(i)(j) and otherwise 0; (2) congregate all bits together.

3.2 Clustering Based Quanti-bicode

The Quanti-bicode method is similar to Uni-bicode, except that the thresholds are generated in a different way. Firstly, Quanti-bicode transforms data into principle component space. Then the adaptive bit allocation algorithm (refer to 3.1 for detail) is executed. After generating thresholds by clustering based quantization, Quanti-bicode produces binary codes as Uni-bicode. An unsupervised clustering method is adopted for data quantization, i.e. k-means is executed on each principal component direction. The thresholds are produced as follows:

Alogorithm2. Thresholds Generation for Clustering Partition

Input: Bits Allocation Array B, training dataset D after PCA
Output: T as a two dimensional array of thresholds
  For each B(i)>0 on component i
    Set the number of clustering centers k to $B(i)$;
    Execute k-means on component i of training data.
    Save the array of k-means centers in T(i)
  End

Binary codes of [6] are generated by assigning data to the index number of clustering centers. The problem of such a method is that Hamming distances between binary codes are not reflecting similarity of original data any more. To exploit similarity in Hamming space, our algorithm takes each cluster center as a threshold and generates binary codes as Uni-bicode method.

3.3 IBC based on Uni-bicode and Quanti-bicode

Integrated Binary Code (IBC) is a novel binary code search method to improve query efficiency. As is shown in Figure 1, the set of similar neighbors obtained using IBC is the intersection of the two sets from Uni-bicode and Quanti-bicode.

Uni-bicode uses percentiles to generate thresholds for partitioning data. Percentiles make the partitioning quantity of data to be equal. On the other hand, Quanti-bicode uses clustering technique, and hence the spatial information of data distribution is utilized, which is complementary to percentiles. Using data projected on a principle component from [11], four sample thresholds are generated using percentile and k-means clustering respectively. The distinction is exhibited in Figure 2.

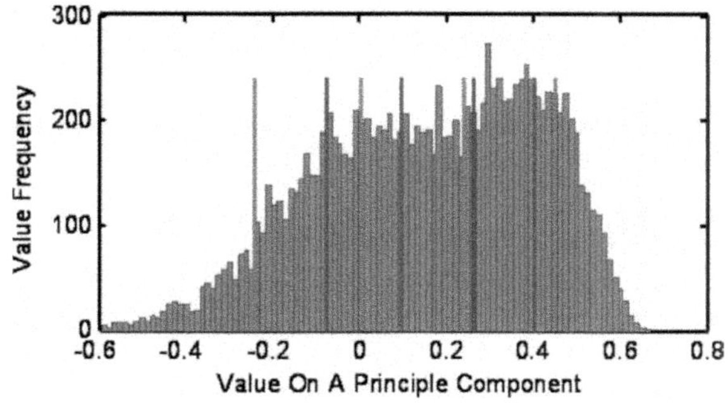

Figure 2. Different partitions by Uni-bicode and Quanti-bicode on a sample principle component from [11]. The blue line indicates Uni-bicode and the red Quanti-bicode.

As can be observed, the two methods partition data differently. Taking advantage of the complementary properties, IBC search can return a refined set of similar neighbors. Thus, IBC is efficient and effective for ANN search.

3.4 ANN Search Using IBC

The ANN search algorithm using IBC is listed in Algorithm 3. The order of Uni-bicodes and Quanti-bicodes in IBC searching is almost uninfluential on the search result.

Alogorithm3. ANN Search Algorithm

1. Compute *Uni-bicode* and *Quanti-bicode* of query point y.

2.IBC searching :

Compute Hamming distances between y and points in dataset S_1 using *Uni-bicodes*. After filtering points whose Hamming distances are larger than *dist*, a sub-set S'_1 is obtained. Then Compute Hamming distances between y and points in S'_1 using *Quanti-bicodes*. If Hamming distance between $p \in S'_1$ and y is less than *dist*, add p to candidate list S_2.

3. For ANN search, re-rank S_2 by exact Euclidean distances, and return the nearest one.

The ANN algorithm requires only a few parameters. As for IBC searching, the number of total bits and Hamming distance threshold are trade-offs between query efficiency and accuracy. Take Hamming distance *dist* for example. If *dist* is large, there will be more candidates returned and the query will achieve higher accuracy. Besides, if *dist* is small, there will be fewer neighbors to be processed and the query will be efficiency.

4. EXPERIMENTAL RESULTS

Our algorithms are evaluated on two datasets. One is from INRIA BIGANN dataset [7], which is a public benchmark for approximate nearest neighbor search. We use one sub-dataset of 1M 128-d SIFT descriptors for performance comparison. The other is [10] used for image retrieval. This dataset contains about 2680 images, and are categorized into 8 outdoor scene categories. *Filtered-Ratio* and *NN-Recall* are defined to illustrate the search quality. The higher of *Filtered-Ratio* means more noises are filtered after searching and query efficiency is improved. And higher *NN-Recall* means more correct nearest neighbors are found and effectiveness is improved.

$$Filtered-Ratio=\frac{Number\ of\ Points\ Filtered\ After\ Search}{Size\ of\ Dataset}$$

$$NN\text{-}Recall=\frac{Number\ of\ Nearest\ Neighbors\ Returned\ by\ Search}{Size\ of\ Query\ Set}$$

The experiments are performed on a workstation with 24G memory, 2.13GHz Intel CPU and 64-bit Operating system.

4.1 Approximate Nearest Neighbor Search

To show the efficiency of our algorithm, we perform nearest neighbor search on 1M SIFT vector dataset from BIGANN, using SH [5] and HE [4] as baseline.

Firstly, since SH achieves significant improvement on LSH and reports comparable results to [8] with much greater simplicity, we compare Quanti-bicode, Uni-bicode and IBC with SH in Figure 3. When hamming distance is 10, Quanti-bicode filters 94.7% points and finds 97% nearest neighbors, Uni-bicode filters 92.8% and finds 99%, while SH filters 83.5% and finds 100%. With all binary codes set to 32-bit, our two novel binary code methods are more efficient than SH with comparable precision. Moreover, IBC achieves the best *Filtered-Ratio* with additional memory consumption. The efficiency is improved by integration of the two complementary methods.

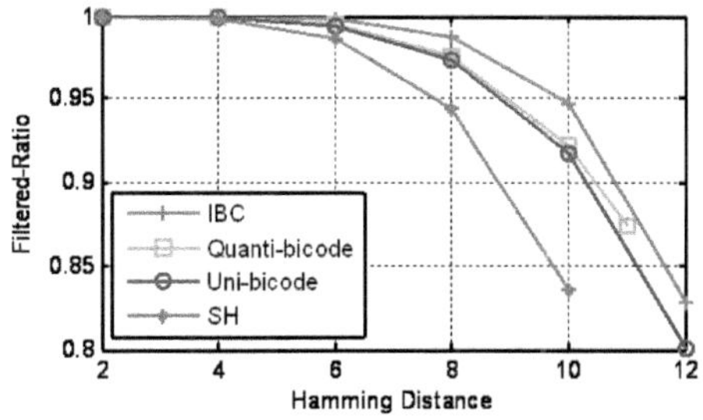

Figure 3. Comparison of IBC, Quanti-bicode, Uni-bicode and Spectral Hashing (SH) [5].

Secondly, to compare the binary code methods more objectively, vector quantization with multiple assignments is applied to both HE and IBC using the same parameters. In the following experiments the length of binary codes is evaluated and set to 32 bit and 64 bit respectively. The quantization process filters 92.088% of dataset points and achieves 100% NN-Recall. By varying hamming distances, Figure 4 demonstrates ANN search results of different approaches.

As can be seen from Figure 4, IBC achieves both higher NN-Recall and Filtered-Ratio than HE, i.e. IBC remains more correct nearest neighbors with less false positives. The red ellipse in the figure corresponds to a region that is well balanced between efficiency and precision. When the NN-Recall is near to 1.0, points are mainly filtered by quantization and binary code methods filter few points for large hamming distances.

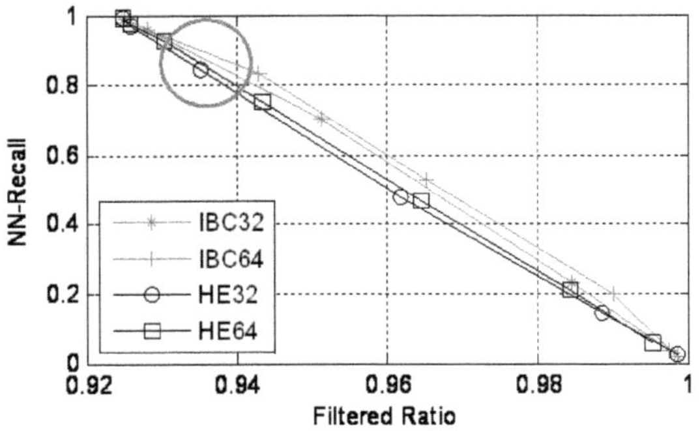

Figure 4. Comparison of IBC and Hamming Embedding (HE) [4] with multi-assignment vector quantization using 32-bit and 64-bit binary codes respectively.

Moreover, IBC with both binary code methods using 32-bit performs better than HE using 64-bit. This indicates that with the same memory consumption, our IBC method achieves both higher Filtered-Ratio and NN-Recall than HE. And thus IBC is more effective and efficient on the dataset.

4.2 Image Retrieval

To further verify our algorithm, we perform image retrieval on an open dataset [10] using the original 960-d GIST [10] descriptor. GIST is a global descriptor and different from SIFT in the pre experiments. To compare these methods in accuracy, we also re-rank the results returned by HE [4] and SH [5] using exact Euclidean distances. The linear scan method computes nearest neighbors using exact Euclidean distances and is used as baseline.

In this experiment, we set *dist* =16 for all methods. The length of all binary codes is set to 64-bit. Under these parameters, the search results of our IBC method are almost the same as liner scan. Table 2 shows the average search time and precision of queries. The sample retrieval results are illustrated in Figure 5. Some query results of SH are different from linear scan in Figure 5, but still relevant to the queries. However, the time usage of IBC is only 55.1% of SH.

Table 2. Absolute search time and precision (5NN-Recall) comparisons of Linear Scan, IBC, SH [5] and HE [4] with searching results re-ranked by Euclidean distances. The time is measured in seconds.

	Linear Scan (Base line)	IBC+ Re-Rank	SH+ Re-Rank	HE+ Re-rank
Time	0.0453	**0.0076**	0.0138	0.00267
5NN-Recall	1.0	**0.982**	0.889	0.451

Since HE only quantizes query point to the closest cluster, many nearest neighbors are lost for the quantization borders. With significant improved precision over HE, IBC is only 1.85 times slower. To conclude, our method achieves better performance than SH both in efficiency and effectiveness, and much better search quality than HE on the dataset.

5. CONCLUSION

To find nearest neighbors more efficiently in multimedia retrieval, we have proposed a novel IBC binary code method. The experiments on open datasets showed that the IBC can achieve better performance in terms of the trade-off between search quality and efficiency than existing methods.

Figure 5. Sample retrieval results on an open dataset using the original GIST descriptor.

6. ACKNOWLEDGMENTS

This work was supported by the National Basic Research Program of China (973Program, 2007CB311100), National Nature Science Foundation of China (61003163), Co-building Program of Beijing Municipal Education Commission.

7. REFERENCES

[1] Arya, S., Mount, D. M., et al. 1998. An optimal algorithm for approximate nearest neighbor searching fixed dimensions. *J. ACM*, 45 (6): 891-923.

[2] Datar, M., Immorlica, N., Indyk, P.,et al.2004.Locality-sensitive hashing scheme based on p-stable distributions. *SCG* '2004, 253-262.

[3] Min, K., Yang, L., et al. 2010. Compact Projection: Simple and Efficient Near Neighbor Search with Practical Memory Requirements. *CVPR*'2010.

[4] Jegou, H., Douze, M. and Schmid, C. 2008.Hamming embedding and weak geometric consistency for large scale image search. *ECCV*'2008, 304-317.

[5] Weiss, Y., Torralba, A. , et al. 2008. Spectral Hashing. *Advances in Neural Information Processing Systems.*

[6] Brandt, J. 2010.Transform Coding for Fast Approximate Nearest Neighbor Search in High Dimensions. *CVPR*'2010.

[7] Jegou H., Douze M., et al. 2011.Product Quantization for Nearest Neighbor Search. *PAMI*, 33(1), 117-128.

[8] Torralba, A., Fergus, R. and Weiss, Y. 2008.Small codes and large image databases for recognition. *CVPR*'2008.

[9] Lowe, D. 2004.Distinctive image features from scale-invariant keypoints. *IJCV*, 60 (2): 91–110.

[10] Oliva, A., Torralba, A. 2001.Modeling the shape of the scene: a holistic representation of the spatial envelope. *IJCV*, 42(3): 145-175.

[11] Zhang, W., Gao, K., Zhang, Y.D. and Li J.T. 2010.Data-Oriented Locality Sensitive Hashing. *ACM MM*'2010.

[12] Wang, X.J., Zhang, L., Jing, F., Ma W.Y.2006. AnnoSearch: Image Auto-Annotation by Search. *CVPR*'2006, 1483-1490.

Content Quality Based Image Retrieval With Multiple Instance Boost Ranking *

Peng Yang, Hui Li, Qingshan Liu, Lin Zhong, Dimitris Metaxas
Piscataway, NJ, United States
peyang@cs.rutgers.edu, lih9@umdnj,qsliu@cs.rutgers.edu, linzhongzl@gmail.com, dnm@cs.rutgers.edu

ABSTRACT

Most previous works treated image retrieval as a classification problem or a similarity measurement problem. In this paper, we propose a new idea for image retrieval, in which we regard image retrieval as a ranking issue by evaluating image content quality. Based on the content preference between the images, the image pairs are organized to build the data set for rank learning. Because image content generally is disclosed by image patches with meaningful objects, each image is looked as one bag, and the regions inside are the corresponding instances. In order to save the computation cost, the instances in the image are the rectangle regions and the integral histogram is applied to speed up histogram feature extraction. Due to the feature dimension is high, we propose a boost-based multiple instance learning for image retrieval. Based on different assumptions in multiple instance setting, Mean, Max and TopK ranking models are developed with Boost learning. Experiments on the real-world images from Flickr, Pisca, and Google shows that the power of the proposed method.

Categories and Subject Descriptors: B.X.X [Pattern Recognition]: Statistical

General Terms: Algorithms.

Keywords: Image Retrieval, Ranking, Multiple Instance.

1. INTRODUCTION

An image retrieval system is for browsing, searching and retrieving images from a large database of digital images or on line. Most traditional methods of image retrieval utilize the methods of adding meta data such as captioning, keywords, or descriptions to the images, so that retrieval can be performed over the annotation words. To search for the specific images, users may provide query terms such as keyword, and then the search engine will return images "satisfied" to the query. However, textual descriptions can not always capture the very essence of content in the images. In recent years, the increase in social web applications and the semantic web have inspired the development of image search technologies. More researchers focus on visual interpretation of picture content, and try to do image retrieval through understanding the visual content inside the images. Content-based image retrieval (CBIR), also known as query by image content (QBIC) and content-based visual information retrieval (CBVIR), aims to use computer vision techniques to handle the image retrieval problem [11][4][16].

In order to understand the visual content in the image, in the past years, much research effort has been done on image classification [17] and automatic image annotation [12][18]. Although lots of methods have been proposed on CBIR [4][11], most of these methods look image retrieval as a classification problem or a similarity measurement issue between the query image and the images in the database or online. These kind of methods still do not touch the visual content quality evaluation among the images.For example, in Figure 1, three images are returned by Flickr through the key word "Tiger". The perfect ranking order of these three images should be (a) > (b)> (c), because image (a) contains the full body of a tiger, but image (b) has part of the occluded head of a tiger, and image (c) is not a tiger at all. However, this kind of perfect list is not always available for the current image search engine due to the searching procedure heavily depends on the keyword on the tag, not the true visual content in the image. In order to alleviate negative impaction of the annotations, clustering and classification methods are used on visual features extracted from images as a pre-processing step [4], but they can not provide the good visual content order relation too. Taking the advantage of the user's relevance feedback

(a) (b) (c)

Figure 1: Three tigers images with the tag "tiger" returned by Flickr. The ranking of image (a) should be higher than image (b), and image (b) is higher than image (c).

[15] is another solution, but its idea is to re-organize the data set by the user's labeling such as relevance or irrelevance and to train the classifier again, so the above mentioned problem still exists. As shown in Figure 1, (a) and (b) are relevant to key word "Tiger", but (a) is obviously much better than (b). Therefore, more detail feedback is necessary. In this paper, both the relative and the quality of the images are taken into account. We not only indicate whether the images are relevant or not, but also predicts how relevant the images are. In other words, besides retrieving the relevant images based on the query, we list them in an order with the best relevant on the top one at the same time. In practices, it is hard to label how the interested image is relevant to the query with an exact score on

*Area chair: Qi Tian

MM'11, November 28–December 1, 2011, Scottsdale, Arizona, USA.

the training set. However, it is easy to label the preference between the images, based on the preference relationship, and the image pairs are readily available for learning[10]. In order to realize this function, the pairwise based ranking model is proposed based on the training set which contains the preference on each image pair. Recently ranking model learning has been widely explored in text information retrieval [2][10][6], but the related work on image retrieval are a few[13][8].

Inspired by [3][8], we extend ranking model learning into into multiple instance setting. One image is looked as one bag, and the potential regions in the image are looked as the instances. Normally, image segmentation should be applied to separate images into sub-regions. Although reliable segmentation is especially helpful for feature representations, some issues plaguing current techniques are computational complexity, reliability of good segmentation and acceptable segmentation quality assessment methods. In this paper, we do not depend on image segmentation, and we simply take the rectangle region with difference scale and at different positions as the instances. Besides avoiding the uncertainties of image segmentation, using the rectangle regions as the instances have two-fold advantages: 1) save the computation cost with no segmentation;2) fast feature extraction algorithm could be applied on the statistical feature extraction, such as, integral histogram technique used in this paper. Three different schemes are proposed to multiple instance ranking learning. We test the proposed method by extensive experiments on the images from Flickr, Pisca, and Google, and the experimental results demonstrate it effectiveness and power.

2. MULTIPLE INSTANCE BOOST RANKING

Multiple instance learning is first introduced in the context of drug activity prediction in [5]. Different from traditional pattern-based learning, training class labels are only associated with sets of samples (or bags), instead of individual samples (or instances). The labels of instances are only indirectly associated with the labels of bags. If a bag is labeled as positive, it means that at least one instance inside the bag is positive. On the other hand, a bag is labeled as negative if and only if all the instances in the bag are negative. The most of previous work on image retrieval, it tired to learn a classifier to label the images into being relevant or irrelevant to the query. However, even two images are relevant in content, they also exist the difference from content quality. It is well known that the semantic content of image is generally disclosed by one or some interesting objects in the image, and it is not easy to localize the interest objects automatically. To handle these issues, we propose to integrate multiple instance learning into Boost ranking in this section.

Assuming there have lots of images from the same category, each image in the training set has one rank score to evaluate its content quality, i.e., whether this image contains high-quality interested objects, but the locations of the interested objects in the images are unknown. In other words, the dominant regions in the image are unknown, which play an important role in making rank score. From the view of the multiple instance setting, the ranking order is on the bag level (image), and the ranking order on the instances(regions) in the bag is not known, but it is implicity represented by the ranking order on its bag. Define the bag set B_i and the corresponding orders O_i, where $i \in [1, n]$. Without losing generality, the orders decrease monotonously and are satisfied with $O_1 \geq O_2 \geq ... \geq O_n$. Organize the pairwise data with the bag pairs (B_i, B_j) with the associated order information (O_i, O_j). For convenience, we rearrange and index the bag pairs as $(B_{k,1}, B_{k,0})$ with $(O_{k,1} \geq O_{k,0})$, where k indexes the bag pair, and $O_{k,1}$ and $O_{k,0}$ are the order scores of the bag $B_{k,1}$ and $B_{k,0}$ respectively.

2.1 Mean-based Model

In this model, we define the function F as the mean of the instance scores by equation: $O(B_k) = \frac{R(x_{k,1})+R(x_{k,2})+...+R(x_{k,m})}{m}$ The ranking score $R(x)$ on each instance can be defined as $R(x) = \sum_{t=1}^{T} \alpha_t r_t(x)$. We can rewrite equation as

$$O(B_k) = \frac{\sum_{i=1}^{m} \sum_{t=1}^{T} \alpha_t r_t(x_i)}{m} = \sum_{t=1}^{T} \alpha_t \frac{\sum_{i=1}^{m} r_t(x_i)}{m} \quad (1)$$

Therefore, in the boosting framework, in each round, we just need to learn the optimal weak ranker $r_t(x)$ and the corresponding weight α_t. We take simple threshold as the weak ranker, and the output of $r_t(x)$ is $\{1, 0\}$. The optimal weak ranker is the one which minimizes the rank error on the bag pairs, and the corresponding coefficient $\alpha_t = \frac{1}{2}log(\frac{1+\Re}{1-\Re})$, where $\Re = \sum_k D(B_{k,0}, B_{k,1})(O(B_{k,1}) - O(B_{k,0})$. The weight on each bag pair is $D(B_{k,0}, B_{k,1})$, and the rank score on the bag $B_{k,1}$ is $O(B_{k,1}) = \frac{1}{m}\sum_j r(x_{k,j,1})$.

Algorithm 1 *Multiple Instance Ranking Based on Max Score*

1: Give example image(bag) pairs $(B_{1,0}, B_{1,1})$,...,$(B_{n,0}, B_{n,1})$. Each bag contains instances $\{x_{i,j}\}$, where $j = 1, ..., m$.
2: Initialize weight $D_t(B_{k,0}, B_{k,1}) = 1/N$.
3: **for** $t = 0 .... T$ **do**
4: Get weak ranker $r_t : r_t(x) \rightarrow H$, s.t equation **??**.
5: Choose $\alpha_t \in R$.
6: Base on current weak ranker, choose the instances with max rank score as the available instances $\{x^*_{i,j}\}$
"E"-Step:
1) Get optimal weak ranker $r^*_t(x)$ based on the available instances $\{x^*_{i,j}\}$, and α^*_t.
2) Update the rank score on all instances
$R_t(x_{i,j}) = R_{t-1}(x_{i,j}) + \alpha^*_t r^*_t(x_{i,j})$.
"M"-Step:
1) Keep up the instances with max rank score in each bag and save these instances as the available instances $\{x^*_{i,j}\}$, and check the stop conditions.
7: Update:
$\alpha_t = \alpha^*_t, r_t = r^*_t, O_t(B_i) = max(r_t(x_{i,j}))$.
$D_{t+1}(B_{i,0}, B_{i,1}) = \frac{D_t(B_{i,0}, B_{i,1}) \exp(\alpha_t(O_t(B_{i,0}) - O_t(B_{i,1})))}{Z_t}$
where Z_t is a normalization factor.
8: **end for**
9: Output the final ranking $H(x) = \sum_t^T \alpha_t r_t(x)$.

2.2 MAX-based Model

The MAX-based model defines the function F based on the max of the instance score as: $O(B_k) = max(R(x_{k,1}), R(x_{k,2}), ..., R(x_{k,m}))$. Therefore, in each round the max rank score is picked up from the rank score of the potential best instances in each bag. As we know, most of the instances in the bag have little contributions to ranking bag, so it is reasonable to remove these instances during the training procedure. The greedy strategy is to keep the instances with maximum ranking score and withdraw the other instances in each bag. However, this greedy strategy is too aggressive to lose the potential good instances. Therefore, we adopt an "EM"-based instance selection scheme in each round. In each iteration, the weak ranker $r_t(x)$ is learned based on the available instances in each bag, and then the learned strong ranker $\sum_{t-1} \alpha_i r_i + \alpha_t r_t(x)$ by this iteration is used to cut off the instances which are not best ones in each bag. In "E" step, the ideal weak ranker $r^*_t(x)$ is learned based on the remained instances, and α_t^* is the corresponding weight. In "M" step, based on the updated strong ranker $\sum_{t-1} \alpha_i r_i + \alpha_t^* r_t^*(x)$, all the instances is checked to see whether they are with max rank score, and the remained instances go to "E" step again. The stop condition of the "EM" is the change rate of the available instance is less than δ or the maximum iteration is reached. The whole process is summarized in algorithm 1.

2.3 Top K-based Model

The top K-based model is a compromise between the Mean-based model and Max-based model, which defines the function as the mean of the top K of the instance scores, described in equation ??

$$O(B_k) = max_{TopK}(R(x_{k,1}), R(x_{k,2}), ..., R(x_{k,m})) \tag{2}$$

Similar to the Max-based model, an EM strategy is used to select the top K instances in each bag during the training procedure. The details of the algorithm is similar to algorithm 1. The same stop condition of "EM" step is used to choose the top K instances. We set $K = 5$ in the experiments.

3. IMAGE REPRESENTATION

As described above, each image is taken as one bag, and some potential regions that may contain interesting objects in the image are regarded as its instances. In [8], they used image segmentation as preprocessing, and took each segmented region as one instance. However, image segmentation has some uncertainties. For example, same object is often segmented into several regions, so the region-based instant can only describe limited local information of the object. Additionally, extra computation cost is needed for image segmentation. In our experiments, we take rectangle regions as the instance, and we use rectangles with difference scales to slide over one image to build instances. For the real images, the size of interested object inside the image is always not too small for the high quality images. Based on this prior, the rectangle size is in the proper range. For one image whose size is mxn, the range of the height of the rectangle is $[\frac{1}{3}m, m]$, and the range of the width is $[\frac{1}{3}n, n]$.

The statistical features are used to represent the instances as in most previous work. We use popular statistical features including RGB, HSV, LAB, rg, opponent, Gabor, and Haar-like features. For each feature, we map it into a normalized histogram, and finally we obtain totally 1200-dimensional histogram features to describe each instance. Because we use rectangles to present instances, we can easily adopt the integral histogram technique to speed up the histogram computation for each kind of feature [14]. After building the integral histogram, for any rectangle in this image, the histogram could be obtained by calculating three times plus-minus operations. Thus, our feature extraction is very fast, and moreover, we can produce a large number of instances for an image bag and some of instances can exactly capture the interesting objects in the image.

4. EXPERIMENT

Same as [8], we send 10 category animal queries to Flickr, which are Alligator, Dalmatian, Dolphin, Elephant, Giraffe, Goat, Horse, Kangaroo, Leopard, and Penguin. For each category, we download around 200 images. We also test the proposed method on the images collected from Google image searching engine and Picasa, which are another two popular photo sharing services. We download the same 10 category animal images from both Google and Picasa. Animals are demonstrably among the most difficult classes to recognize. There has been much fascination with searching animals on the web recently[1][7].

We manually assign one of the three following labels to the images: (1) Good image: a good example of the animal category. The animal(animals) is the most salient object in the image and is well delineated. (2) Intermediate image: the image contains the desired animal. However, the animal is not the dominant object or the image has extensive occlusion or the view is not good. (3) Junk image: the image does not contain real animal. Figure 1 shows an example, where three tiger images are labeled as three different levels respectively.

Table 1: Average Precisions for different queries on Flickr

Query	Flickr	Our Methods		
		Mean	Max	Top K
Alligator	0.4092	0.6244	0.7368	0.7232
Dalmatian	0.4088	0.6368	0.697	0.5198
Dolphin	0.6571	0.7078	0.7938	0.852
Elephant	0.5264	0.4425	0.6021	0.5085
Giraffe	0.5943	0.8874	0.7293	0.8366
Goat	0.5487	0.5991	0.5699	0.5083
Horse	0.683	0.8341	0.7287	0.7847
Kangaroo	0.3516	0.475	0.6282	0.5431
Leopard	0.5735	0.6172	0.6628	0.727
Penguin	0.2074	0.6949	0.5439	0.7107
mean	0.4960	0.6519	0.6692	0.6914

4.1 Performance Measures

To evaluate the performance of the learned ranking model for the testing images, we adopt two performance measures. The first measure is the Normalized Discounted Cumulative Gain (NDCG)[9]. For a list of images sorted in descending order of the scores output by a ranking model, the NDCG score at the m_{th} image is computed as

$$N_m = C_m \sum_{j=1}^{m} \frac{2^{r(j)-1}}{log_2(1+j)}, \tag{3}$$

where $r(j)$ is the rating of the j_{th} image, C_m is the normalization constant which equals to $1/INDCG$, INDCG is the NDCG scores on the ideal list ranked by its ground truth ratings. The second measurement is Average Precision (AP). AP is calculated as:

$$AP = \frac{1}{N_{pos}} \sum_{j=1}^{N} P(j) \times rel(j), \tag{4}$$

where N_{pos} is the number of the positive images, N is the number of total retrieved images, $rel(j)$ is a binary function indicating whether the j_{th} image is relevant, and $P(j)$ is the precision at j. We regard the good images as the positive, the intermediate and the junk images as the negative images.

4.2 Experiment Setting

Each image is regarded as a bag, and we extract many rectangle regions from it with different size and scale and take these rectangle regions as the instances in the bag. The width of the rectangle is set as $\{\frac{1}{3}m, \frac{1}{2}m, \frac{2}{3}m, m\}$, and the corresponding height is also $\{\frac{1}{3}m, \frac{1}{2}m, \frac{2}{3}m, m\}$. The sample step is half of the width and height, so totally there are 121 instances in one bag. Half of the images are randomly selected from the collected data sets as the training set and the others as the testing data.

On the Flickr data set, we first compare the rankings obtained by our method with the original Flickr ranking result. Flickr ranks the images in descending order of "relative", which should be determined according to the click-through, comments and some other factors. We also compare our method with Hu's work by using their experimental results directly [8]. To evaluate the generality of the proposed ranking model, we use the ranking model learned on the Flickr data set to test the images from Google and Picasa. On the

Table 2: Average Precision for different query at Nth Image

Query	Google Image			Ours (Mean)			Ours (Max)			Ours (TopK)		
	@5th	@10th	@20th	@5th	@10th	@20th	@5th	@10th	@20th	@5th	@10th	@20th
Alligator	0.8056	0.7608	0.7243	1.0000	0.8556	0.7310	1.0000	1.0000	1.0000	1.0000	0.7440	0.7766
Dalmatian	1.0000	1.0000	1.0000	1.0000	1.0000	0.9886	0.9167	0.8228	0.8146	1.0000	0.9526	0.9186
Dolphin	1.0000	0.9526	0.8871	1.0000	0.9889	0.9151	1.0000	1.0000	0.7528	1.0000	1.0000	0.8772
Elephant	1.0000	0.9294	0.8515	1.0000	1.0000	0.9445	1.0000	1.0000	0.9719	0.9167	0.8339	0.8376
Giraffe	0.9167	0.8073	0.8401	1.0000	1.0000	1.0000	1.0000	0.9617	0.9232	1.0000	1.0000	0.9568
Goat	1.0000	0.9283	0.8890	1.0000	1.0000	0.9914	1.0000	1.0000	1.0000	1.0000	1.0000	0.9917
Horse	0.8875	0.8044	0.7810	1.0000	0.9617	0.8657	1.0000	1.0000	0.8980	1.0000	0.9889	0.9468
Kangaroo	1.0000	0.9415	0.8501	1.0000	1.0000	0.9510	1.0000	1.0000	1.0000	1.0000	0.9379	0.8752
Leopard	1.0000	0.9160	0.8726	1.0000	1.0000	0.9764	1.0000	1.0000	0.9917	1.0000	1.0000	0.9308
penguin	0.9500	0.9068	0.8370	1.0000	0.9765	0.9438	1.0000	0.9750	0.8986	1.0000	0.9283	0.9287
mean	0.9560	0.8947	0.8533	1.0000	0.9783	0.9308	0.9917	0.9760	0.9251	0.9917	0.9386	0.9040

Table 3: Average Precisions for different query

Query	Google Image	Ours	Picasa	Ours
Alligator	0.6465	0.6580	0.1213	1.0000
Dalmatian	0.9528	0.9031	0.3492	0.8056
Dolphin	0.7793	0.6529	0.6456	0.8863
Elephant	0.7055	0.8154	0.2188	0.5246
Giraffe	0.8101	0.8832	0.4728	0.7198
Goat	0.7677	0.8944	0.4985	0.4889
Horse	0.7319	0.8119	0.5349	0.8606
Kangaroo	0.7455	0.8220	0.2634	0.4455
Leopard	0.8247	0.8887	0.4136	0.6120
penguin	0.7204	0.8442	0.1421	0.8373
mean	0.768	0.820	0.418	0.724

Google and Picasa testing data sets, we compare the results from our method with the ranking results provided by them respectively. We download the top 60 images for each category from Google search and the images in the first page returned by Picasa, and we assign one of the three level to each image as the ground truth.

4.3 Experiment Result

First, we test the proposed method on the Flickr data set and compare it with [8]. Table 1 reports the experiment results. Compared with the outputs of Flickr, both our method and Hu's work are much better. This means multiple instance ranking method can improve the ranking performance significantly. Due to different setting such as Mean, Max and Top K are used in both methods, we list the comparison result according to these three setting respectively in Table 1. It can be found that our method obtains a competitive performance compared to [8]. On average, 40 features are used for each category in our method. Comparing with [8], much less features are used to get similar performance.

In order to investigate the generality of our method, we apply the ranking model trained on the Flickr data set to the data set from Google and Picasa respectively. Table 1 reports the results on Google images and Picasa images respectively. For Google image, we label the top 60 images returned by Google, and we compare our method with the TopK model. From the result of table 3, it is clear to see that our method could further improve the performance of Google search engine. We also apply the TopK model to Picasa images. Here, the images returned in the first page are used for testing, normally 24 images are returned in the first page for our setting. We can see that our ranking model can significantly improve the performance of Picasa search engine too. For information retrieval, the users are more interested in the top N returned samples. We focus on the top 5, 10, and 20 images, and the corresponding average precision and NDCG are shown in table 2 . The results in these two tables further demonstrate the effectiveness and power of our method.

5. CONCLUSION

In this paper, we proposed a new multiple instance ranking algorithm to attack the content based image retrieval problem. According the preference between the images, the pairwise image sets are organized to build the data set for rank learning. Each image is looked as one bag, and the possible rectangle regions inside are taken as the corresponding instances. Based on the assumption: if one bag is better than the other one, the bag contains at least one instance which is better than all the other instances in the other bag. We take the max strategy into ranking consideration. Relaxing the assumption to take the average score or the scores of the best K instances in the bag, we built the models called the Mean, Max, and TopK models to do ranking. Because the statistical features are used as the raw feature, we applied integral histogram to speedily extract the histogram features in rectangle regions. Experiments on the data from Flickr, googe image search engine and Pisca demonstrated the effectiveness and robustness of our methods.

6. REFERENCES

[1] T. L. Berg and D. A. Forsyth. Animals on the web. *Proceedings of the 2006 IEEE Computer Society Conference on Computer Vision and Pattern Recognition*, 2006.

[2] C. Burges, T. Shaked, E. Renshaw, A. Lazier, M. Deeds, N. Hamilton, and G. Hullender. Learning to rank using gradient descent. pages 89–96, 2005.

[3] Y. Chen, J. Z. Wang, and D. Geman. Image categorization by learning and reasoning with regions. *Journal of Machine Learning Research*, 5:913–939, 2004.

[4] R. Datta, D. Joshi, J. Li, and J. Z. Wang. Image retrieval: Ideas, influences, and trends of the new age. *ACM Comput. Surv.*, 40, 2008.

[5] T. G. Dietterich, R. H. Lathrop, T. Lozano-Perez, and A. Pharmaceutical. Solving the multiple-instance problem with axis-parallel rectangles. *Artificial Intelligence*, 1997.

[6] Y. Freund, R. Iyer, R. E. Schapire, and Y. Singer. An efficient boosting algorithm for combining preferences. *J. Mach. Learn. Res.*, vol.4:933–969, 2003.

[7] E. Hörster, M. Slaney, M. Ranzato, and K. Weinberger. Unsupervised image ranking. *Proceedings of the ACM workshop on Large-scale multimedia retrieval and mining*, 2009.

[8] Y. Hu, M. Li, and N. Yu. Multiple-instance ranking: Learning to rank images for image retrieval. *Computer Vision and Pattern Recognition*, 2008.

[9] K. Järvelin and J. Kekäläinen. Cumulated gain-based evaluation of ir techniques. *ACM Transactions on Information Systems*, 20, 2002.

[10] T. Joachims. Optimizing search engines using clickthrough data. *ACM Knowledge Discovery and Data Mining.*

[11] M. S. Lew. Content-based multimedia information retrieval: State of the art and challenges. *ACM Trans. Multimedia Comput. Commun. Appl*, 2:1–19, 2006.

[12] J. Li and J. Z. Wang. Real-time computerized annotation of pictures. *IEEE Transactions on Pattern Analysis and Machine Intelligence*, 30(1), June 2008.

[13] J. S. M. Merler, Rong Yan. Imbalanced rankboost for efficiently ranking large-scale image/video collections. *Computer Vision and Pattern Recognition*, 2009.

[14] F. Porikli. Integral histogram: A fast way to extract histograms in cartesian spaces. *in Proc. IEEE Conf. on Computer Vision and Pattern Recognition*, 2005.

[15] Y. Rui, T. S. Huang, M. Ortega, and S. Mehrotra. Relevance feedback: A power tool for interactive content-based image retrieval. *IEEE Transactions on Circuits and Systems for Video Technology*, pages 644–655, 1998.

[16] N. Sebe, M. S. Lew, X. Zhou, T. S. Huang, and E. M. Bakker. The state of the art in image and video retrieval. CIVR'03, 2003.

[17] A. W. M. Smeulders, S. Member, M. Worring, S. Santini, A. Gupta, and R. Jain. Content-based image retrieval at the end of the early years. *IEEE Transactions on Pattern Analysis and Machine Intelligence*, 22:1349–1380, 2000.

[18] L. von Ahn and L. Dabbish. Labeling images with a computer game. 2004.

Detecting Motion Synchrony by Video Tubes *

Ying Zheng
Duke University
Durham, NC, 27708
yuanqi@cs.duke.edu

Steve Gu[†]
Duke University
Durham, NC, 27708
steve@cs.duke.edu

Carlo Tomasi
Duke University
Durham, NC, 27708
tomasi@cs.duke.edu

ABSTRACT

Motion synchrony, *i.e.*, the coordinated motion of a group of individuals, is an interesting phenomenon in nature or daily life. Fish swim in schools, birds fly in flocks, soldiers march in platoons, etc. Our goal is to detect motion synchrony that may be present in the video data, and to track the group of moving objects as a whole. This opens the door to novel algorithms and applications. To this end, we model individual motions as *video tubes* in space-time, define motion synchrony by the geometric relation among video tubes, and track a whole set of tubes by dynamic programming. The resulting algorithm is highly efficient in practice. Given a video clip of T frames of resolution $X \times Y$, we show that finding the K spatially correlated video tubes and determining the presence of synchrony can be solved optimally in $O(XYTK)$ time. Preliminary experiments show that our method is both effective and efficient. Typical running times are $30-100$ VGA-resolution frames per second after feature extraction, and the accuracy for the detection of synchrony is more than 90% as evaluated in our annotated data set.

Categories and Subject Descriptors

I.2.10 [**Artificial Intelligence**]: Vision and Scene Understanding; I.4.9 [**Image Processing and Computer Vision**]: Applications; I.5 [**Pattern Recognition**]: Design Methodology, Applications

General Terms

Algorithms, Design, Experimentation, Measurement

1. INTRODUCTION

We study the new problem of finding motion synchrony in a video stream. Motion synchrony is an interesting phenomenon in both nature and daily life. For example, fish synchronize their swimming behavior in order to increase their chance for survival. People can synchronize their motions as well. Group dancing or marching often exhibit ordered motion with rhythms and harmonies. In soccer or basketball, people coordinate with each other to either launch an attack or defend against the other team.

*Area chair: Qi Tian

[†]Ying Zheng and Steve Gu contribute equally to this paper.

MM'11, November 28–December 1, 2011, Scottsdale, Arizona, USA.

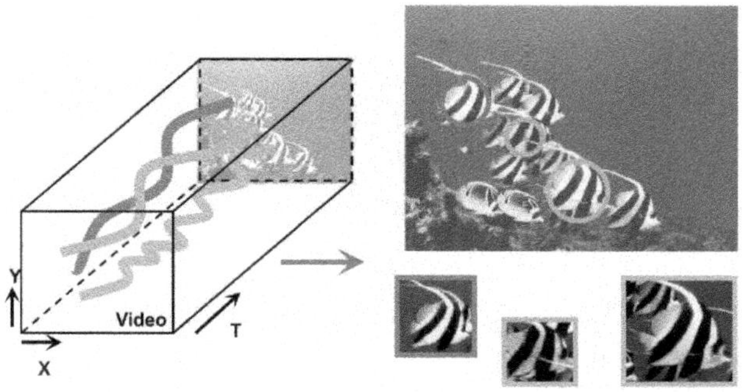

Figure 1: Video tube decomposition for selected fish in a school. These fish move in synchrony.

Finding motion synchrony is challenging, because telling individuals apart is often difficult. For example, each fish in a school looks like the others. How can each be tracked and distinguished reliably? Moreover, given that we know the position of each fish, how to determine if their motions are in synchrony or not? We introduce a few innovations to answer these questions. The general idea is to track the coordinated motions in a collective way and use the geometric relations between individuals to measure the degree of synchrony.

To represent coordinated motion, we decompose an image sequence into a set of disjoint *video tubes* of interest. A video tube is a space-time volume that groups the regions for a single object in consecutive frames into a long, twisting tube. Video tubes are richer than point trajectories. We model each video tube as a generalized cylinder that is equipped with a learnt object model. Different video tubes can share the same object model and hence are not independent of each other. The main novelty of our work is that we allow different video tubes to be spatially correlated and we model their spatial relation explicitly with a minimal spanning tree.

Explicit modeling of synchronous motion thus helps in two ways: First, it keeps tubes of similar objects explicitly distinct from each other, thereby making tracking reliable in the face of severe and widespread ambiguity, whether one is interested in *detecting* synchrony or not. Second, this new type of motion model allows measuring synchrony when its detection is of interest.

1.1 Literature Review

Synchronization has been studied in both audio and video signals [6, 1, 19, 17, 5, 7]. For instance, synchrony measures have been derived [17, 7] for associating the movement of mouths to the oscillation of sound waves. To the best of our knowledge, detecting motion synchrony, *i.e.*, a coordinated motion of separate individuals within a single video, has not been well explored in the literature. Since synchrony is measured in the visual domain, the challenge is equivalent to that of tracking individual objects well. Multiple-object tracking has been studied in the literature [15, 12, 13, 11, 18, 14, 8] but most of this work focuses on people or vehicle detection. In one exception [8], spatial relations are used to track similar objects. We move a step further by defining the video tubes and using the geometric relations among them to measure and detect motion synchrony.

1.2 Our Contributions

Our contributions are as follows: First, we propose to detect the motion synchrony within a single video stream. This opens door to novel algorithms and applications. Second, we introduce the notion of coordinated video tubes to capture and measure motion synchrony. Third, we give an efficient algorithm to compute the K geometrically correlated video tubes in a video block of T frames of resolution $X \times Y$ in $O(XYTK)$ running time with a small constant. The efficiency of the algorithm makes our method highly practical for fast video processing. Fourth, we collect and annotate a data set for evaluating synchrony detection. This data set can serve as a benchmark for further study.

Preliminary experiments show that our method for detecting motion synchrony is both effective and efficient. A set of video tubes in an image sequence can be found at $30 - 100$ (VGA) frames per second, and the accuracy of synchrony detection is better than 90% in our annotated data set.

2. FINDING VIDEO TUBES

Let V be a $X \times Y \times T$ space-time block where T is the number of frames and each image frame has $X \times Y$ pixels. A tube $U \subset V$ is modeled as a generalized cylinder that passes through each frame exactly once. Specifically, a tube U is represented as a tuple $U = (\mathcal{X}, \mathcal{M}, r)$ where $\mathcal{M}$ is the object model, and the sequence $\mathcal{X} = (x_1, x_2, \cdots, x_T)$ specifies the location of disk centers with radius r in each frame. The model $\mathcal{M}$ is a set of suitably defined appearance features that describes the objects of interest.

2.1 Geometric Relation among Tubes

To specify the geometric relations among multiple video tubes, we compute the Euclidean minimal spanning tree (EMST) among tube centers in the first frame and the tree deforms when tracked through the video sequence. The amount of deformation measures the deviation from synchrony. The reason for working with EMST is to group all tubes into a single component by edges of minimal lengths.

Denote the tree $\mathcal{T}_f = \langle \mathcal{V}_f, \mathcal{E} \rangle$ as the result of tracking the EMST $\mathcal{T}_1$ in the first frame all the way to frame f. Here $\mathcal{V}_f = \left\{x_1^f, x_2^f, \cdots, x_k^f\right\}$ is the set of centers of tubes $U_1, U_2, \cdots, U_k$ in frame f, and $\mathcal{E}$ specifies the $k-1$ spatial constraints among the k tubes, as captured by the constant topology of the spanning tree computed in the first frame.

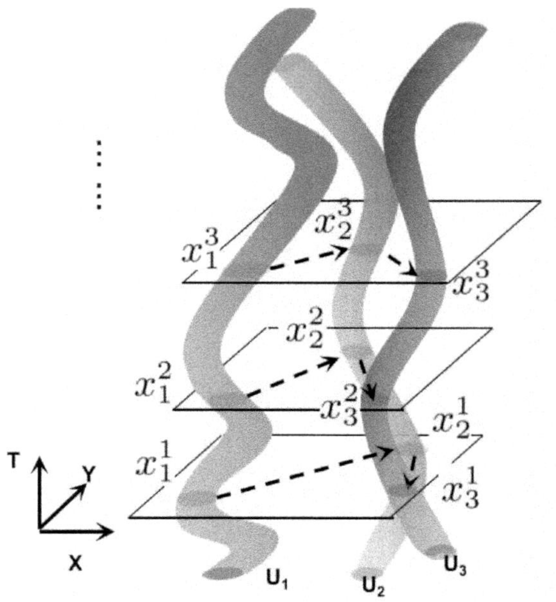

Figure 2: Video tubes and their geometric relations in the spatial and temporal domain.

2.2 The Coordinated Motion Model

We build video tubes frame by frame. Let $\mathcal{M}_1, \cdots, \mathcal{M}_k$ be the object models for tubes $U_1, \cdots, U_k$. Given the set $\mathcal{V}_f$ of positions of the k tube centers in frame $f-1$, the cost of extending these tubes to frame f is:

$$\text{Cost}(\mathcal{V}_f) = \sum_{i=1}^{k} E(x_i^f; \mathcal{M}_i) + \lambda \sum_{(i,j)\in\mathcal{E}} \|\delta(i,j,f)\|^2 \quad (1)$$

where the *visual inconsistency* term $E(x_i^f; \mathcal{M}_i)$ measures the visual dissimilarity between the disk centered at x_i^f and the object model $\mathcal{M}_i$ associated to the ith tube, as measured in previous work [9, 8], and the norm of the vector

$$\delta(i,j,f) = (x_i^f - x_j^f) - (x_i^{f-1} - x_j^{f-1}) \quad (2)$$

measures the *pattern deformation* of an edge in the minimal spanning tree between frames $f-1$ and f. The constant λ is a regularization parameter that balances the penalties between visual inconsistency and pattern deformation.

The objective is therefore to find the optimal arrangement $\hat{\mathcal{V}}_f$ for which the cost $\text{Cost}(\hat{\mathcal{V}}_f)$ is minimal among all possible choices of configuration $\mathcal{V}_f$:

$$\hat{\mathcal{V}}_f = \arg\min_{\mathcal{V}_f} \text{Cost}(\mathcal{V}_f) \,. \quad (3)$$

This optimization problem is solved in Section 4 below.

3. MEASURES FOR SYNCHRONY

We use the spatial relation determined by the spanning tree to measure the synchrony and account for the *structural difference* between two consecutive trees. Two measures, μ_1 and μ_2, are used to capture first-order and second-order

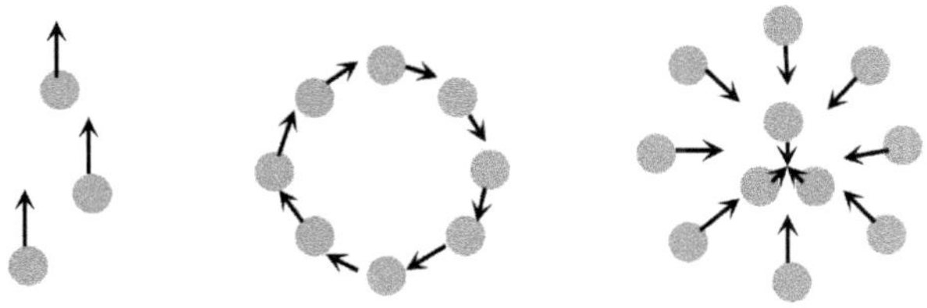

Figure 3: Left: First-order synchrony pattern. Middle and right: Examples of second-order synchrony. Each red dot represents a frame of the video tube and the vector indicates the motion direction.

deformation (lack of synchrony), respectively.

$$\mu_1 = \frac{1}{(K-1)(T-1)} \sum_{f=2}^{T} \sum_{(i,j)\in\mathcal{E}} \|\delta(i,j,f)\| \quad (4)$$

The measure μ_1 for the degree of first-order deformation of a video clip of T frames accumulates pairwise vector differences of the form (2) in consecutive frames. The actual position of each tube is irrelevant. What matters is the changes of their relative positions. For instance, μ_1 is zero for pure translation. However, μ_1 cannot capture nonlinear motions (see Figure 3 for illustration). We hence introduce the other measure μ_2 for the degree of second-order deformation:

$$\mu_2 = \frac{1}{(K-1)(T-2)} \sum_{f=2}^{T-1} \sum_{(i,j)\in\mathcal{E}} \|\delta(i,j,f+1) - \delta(i,j,f)\| \,. \quad (5)$$

In practice, both deformation measures are used to determine the synchrony state by comparing μ_1, μ_2 to a fixed threshold. Those video clips with sufficiently low μ_1 or μ_2 are declared to have motion synchrony.

4. THE ALGORITHM

We give an efficient algorithm to solve the optimization in Equation (3). The speedup is significant thanks to the use of the generalized distance transform [2], similarly to what is done for the matching of pictorial structures in human body parsing [3] and object recognition [4] and tracking [10].

The visual inconsistency $E(x_i^f; \mathcal{M}_i)$ can be evaluated in $O(1)$ or constant time [9, 8] with the help of the integral-image structure. In order to optimize the cost model, we start from the leaves in the spanning tree. We compute the optimal position for each leaf $x_l^f \in \mathcal{V}_f$, given each possible position x_p^f of the leaf's parent:

$$\text{opt}_l(x_p^f) = \arg\min_{x_l^f} [E(x_l^f; \mathcal{M}_l) + \|\delta(l,p,f)\|^2] \,. \quad (6)$$

Then, recursively, we compute the minimum-cost position for each intermediate node x_i^f – tracing back from leaf nodes – for all the possible positions x_p^f of that node's parent:

$$\text{opt}_i(x_p^f) = \arg\min_{x_i^f} [E(x_i^f; \mathcal{M}_i) + \|\delta(i,p,f)\|^2 + \sum_{j\in C_i} \text{opt}_j(x_i^f)] \quad (7)$$

where C_i is the set of the children of x_i^f in the spanning tree. Finally, we compute the cost of the root x_r^f:

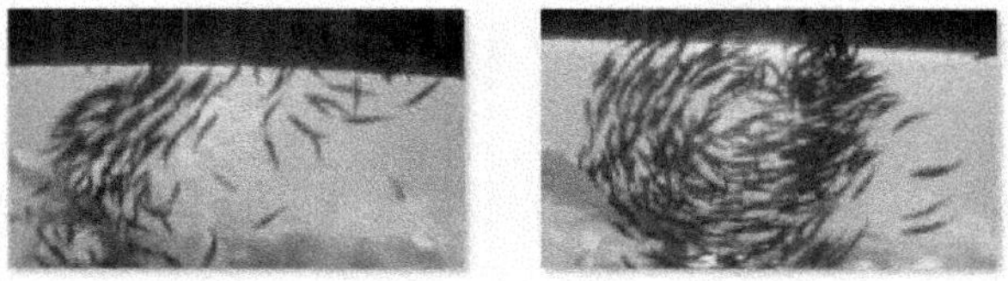

Figure 5: The *Fish* data set contains random fish motion (left) and fish circling in synchrony (right).

$$\text{opt}_r(x_r^f) = \arg\min_{x_r^f} \left\{ E(x_r^f; \mathcal{M}_r) + \sum_{j\in C_r} \text{opt}_j(x_r^f) \right\} \,. \quad (8)$$

If implemented naively, this dynamic programming scheme would take time $O(X^2Y^2K)$. The complexity is further lowered to $O(XYK)$ by using the generalized distance transform. We refer to the paper [2] for details.

The overall algorithm is simple: First, compute tube models $\mathcal{M}_i$ and their minimum spanning tree $\mathcal{T}_1$ in the first frame. For subsequent frames, do the following:

Step 1: Use the algorithm above to find the optimal $\mathcal{V}_f$ defined in Equation (3)

Step 2: Extend the video tubes to frame f and update deformation measures (4) and (5)

Step 3: Set $f \leftarrow f+1$ and repeat until $f = T$.

Computing EMST takes $O(K \log K)$ time. In applications, $\log K \ll XY$, so the overall running time is $O(XYKT)$.

5. EXPERIMENTS

Typical video sequences are very long and objects often come in and out of the field of view. We therefore chop long sequences into clips of small duration and apply our method for finding correlated video tubes and motion synchrony to these short video clips. We collect 4 video sequences and chop them into 200 short video clips. We annotate each video clip by visual inspection as to whether it contains motion synchrony (See Figure 5 for examples).

We use SIFT features [16] for the tube models $\mathcal{M}_i$ and nearest neighbor matching [9] to evaluate visual inconsistency in Equation (1). Object models are constructed from a few windows specified by a user around some of the object in the first frame. Except for SIFT feature detection, running times range from 30 to 100 frames per second depending on how many video tubes are found. The program is mostly written in C++/MEX with the visual interface implemented in MATLAB.

Sample results are shown in Figure 4 and synchrony detection accuracy is shown in Table 1. The average accuracy for detecting synchrony is more than 90%. The code and data are available at `http://www.cs.duke.edu/~yuanqi/`.

6. CONCLUSIONS

We give an efficient algorithm to track synchronous motions in video, and use variations in the spatial pattern of the objects to measure the degree of motion synchrony. Preliminary results show that our method achieves more than 90% detection accuracy.

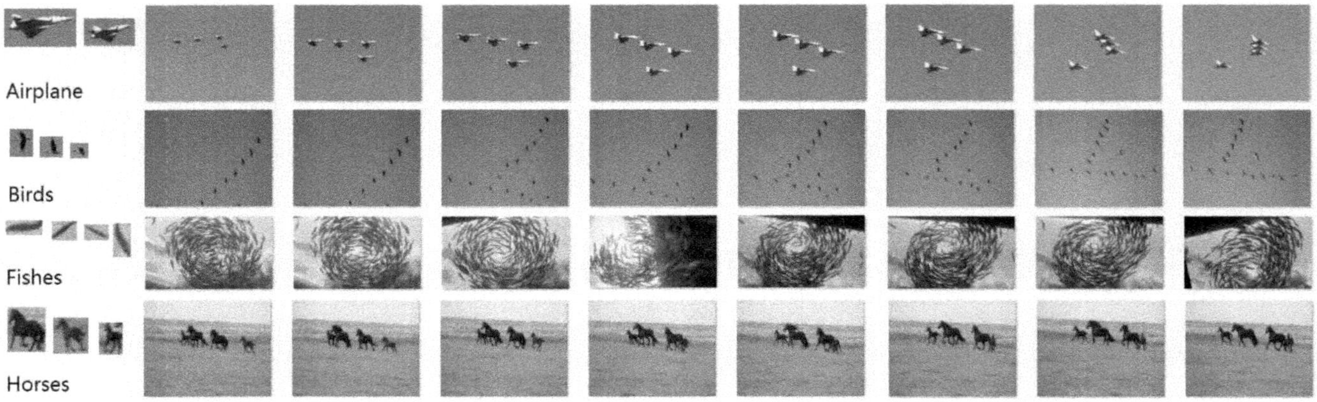

Figure 4: The left column show the query images. The rest show detected examples of motion synchrony.

Table 1: Motion synchrony for 4 categories.

Sequences	Airplane	Birds	Fish	Horses
# frames in the video	1025	2000	2200	1875
# chopped clips	50	50	50	50
# synchronous clips	35	21	23	30
# true positive	31	19	15	28
# true negative	14	28	26	20
# correctly classified	45	47	41	48
Detection accuracy	0.90	0.94	0.82	0.96

Video tubes can also be used in other applications such as automatic object highlighting, interactive object retrieval, and efficient memory storage of video segments. Our algorithm is efficient for these tasks. We leave the investigation of these applications for future work.

7. ACKNOWLEDGMENTS

This work is supported by the National Science Foundation under Grant No. IIS-1017017 and by the Army Research Office under Grant No. W911NF-10-1-0387.

8. REFERENCES

[1] M. Beal, N. Jojic, and H. Attias. A graphical model for audiovisual object tracking. *PAMI*, 25(7):828–836, 2003.

[2] P. Felzenszwalb and D. Huttenlocher. Distance transforms of sampled functions. Technical Report TR2004-1963, Cornell Computing and Information Science, 2004.

[3] P. Felzenszwalb and D. Huttenlocher. Pictorial structures for object recognition. *IJCV*, 61(1):55–79, 2005.

[4] P. Felzenszwalb, D. McAllester, and D. Ramanan. A discriminatively trained, multiscale, deformable part model. In *CVPR*, 2008.

[5] J. Fisher and T. Darrell. Speaker association with signal-level audiovisual fusion. In *IEEE Transaction on Multimedia*, 2004.

[6] J. Fisher, T. Darrell, W. Freeman, and P. Viola. Learning joint statistical models for audio-visual fusion and segregation. In *NIPS*, 2001.

[7] S. Gu and C. Tomasi. Phase diffusion for the synchronization of heterogenous sensor streams. In *ICASSP*, pages 1841–1844, 2009.

[8] S. Gu and C. Tomasi. Branch and track. In *CVPR*, 2011.

[9] S. Gu, Y. Zheng, and C. Tomasi. Efficient visual object tracking with online nearest neighbor classifier. In *ACCV*, pages 267–277, 2010.

[10] S. Gu, Y. Zheng, and C. Tomasi. Linear time offline tracking and lower envelope algorithms. In *ICCV*, 2011.

[11] R. Hess and A. Fern. Discriminatively trained particle filters for complex multi-object tracking. In *CVPR*, pages 240–247, 2009.

[12] Z. Khan, T. Balch, and F. Dellaert. Mcmc-based particle filtering for tracking a variable number of interacting targets. *PAMI*, pages 1805–1918, 2005.

[13] B. Leibe, K. Schindler, and L. V. Gool. Coupled detection and trajectory estimation for multi-object tracking. In *ICCV*, pages 1–8, 2007.

[14] K. Li, E. Miller, M. Chen, T. Kanade, L. Weiss, and P. Campbell. Computer vision tracking of stemness. In *ISBI*, pages 847–850, 2008.

[15] Y. Li, C. Huang, and R. Nevatia. Learning to associate: Hybridboosted multi-target tracker for crowded scene. In *CVPR*, pages 2953–2960, 2009.

[16] D. Lowe. Object recognition from local scale-invariant features. In *ICCV*, pages 1150–1157, 1999.

[17] H. Nock, G. Iyengar, and C. Neti. Assessing face and speech consistency for monologue detection in video. In *Proc. ACM Multimedia*, pages 303–306, 2002.

[18] A. Perera, C. Srinivas, A. Hoogs, G. Brooksby, and W. Hu. Multi-object tracking through simultaneous long occlusions and split-merge conditions. In *CVPR*, pages 666–673, 2006.

[19] M. Sargin, Y. Yemez, E. Erzin, and A. Tekalp. Audiovisual synchronization and fusion using canonical correlation analysis. *IEEE Transactions on Multimedia*, 9(7):1396–1403, 2007.

Automatic Image Tagging through Information Propagation in a Query Log Based Graph Structure*

Teresa Bracamonte
tbracamo@dcc.uchile.cl

Barbara Poblete
bpoblete@dcc.uchile.cl

KDW-PRISMA Research Group, Department of Computer Science, University of Chile
Yahoo! Research Latin America
Santiago, Chile

ABSTRACT

Annotating or tagging multimedia objects is an important task for enhancing multimedia information retrieval processes. In the context of the Web, automatic tagging deals with many issues, such as loosely tagged images and huge collections of images with no textual data at all. Recently, graph representations have been shown useful for modeling relationships between images and their associated semantics. Using these types of graphs, it is possible to represent images and their textual labels as nodes, and the relationship between them as edges, under the assumption that visual similarity implies semantic similarity. In this work, we present an algorithm for automatic tag propagation in such a graph structure, called the *visual-semantic graph.* This graph has been used in prior work only for the task of image retrieval re-ranking. The goal of our work, is to show how the visual-semantic graph can be used for efficient tag propagation to unlabeled images. More specifically, our contributions are: (1) An algorithm to propagate tags automatically based on the breadth-first traversal and (2) A set of heuristics for pruning this approach for large size collections.

Categories and Subject Descriptors

H.3.3 [**Information Storage and Retrieval**]: Information Search and Retrieval; H.2.8 [**Database Management**]: Applications—*Image databases*

General Terms

Algorithms, Design, Experimentation, Human Factors

Keywords

Automatic tagging, tag propagation, query log analysis, Web mining

*Area chair: Marcel Worring

1. INTRODUCTION

Tagging multimedia objects, such as images, music and video, is a relevant task for multimedia information retrieval (MIR) processes. The amount of multimedia objects on the Web, in particular images, is continuously increasing, which represents several challenges for MIR. One of the issues is that the application of content-based information retrieval (CBIR) methods in such growing environments is not scalable. Instead of performing CBIR algorithms, commercial search engines use the context information of multimedia objects (e.g. URL, surrounding text, annotations and tags) to determine their relevance with respect to a query. Besides the diverse computational representation of multimedia objects, Web users can express the same idea with different words and in different levels of specificity, and interpret different concepts from a single image. This difference between the computational representation of multimedia, what we understand from its content and what we express in written or spoken language is known as the *semantic gap* [9].

In addition to the problems mentioned before, there is an enormous number of images which do not have any textual information. Therefore, Web search engines are unable to index all those elements in order to make them available for Web users. Also, the relatively small amount of tagged images found on the Web have mostly been manually annotated. In most cases, these tags depict the publishers' point of view instead of relevant information about the image contents. Besides, tags are commonly noisy and sparse.

Thus, *a mechanism for automatically tagging Web multimedia objects with highly descriptive expressions is necessary.* Several studies (e.g. [2], [3], [5], [6], [8]) have focused on the automatic image tagging problem, but their effectiveness rely on the soundness of their initial set of tags and their criteria to establish similarity between images.

In this work we address the challenge of automatic tagging, focusing on finding a proper relationship between image content and the concepts it represents. To achieve this, we extend the work of Poblete et al. [7], which uses the relationship of user search engine query clicks and images. Therefore, using queries as tags contributes with valuable information, due to the aggregation of large click volumes.

Following this motivation, we propose an algorithm to automatically propagate tags in a graph structure. In this case, we use the visual-semantic graph proposed by Poblete et al. in [7] to establish the relationship between image similarity and user preferences. Our goal is to explore the capabilities of the visual-semantic graph for the propagation of queries as labels.

Our main contributions are: (1) An algorithm to tag images automatically, based on the breadth-first traversal and (2) A set of heuristics for pruning the breadth-first traversal when confronted to very large image collections. Our approach can be generalized to graphs in which the textual labels, content-based similarity criteria, and multimedia objects vary. For instance, we can use news videos instead and images and apply an ad-hoc similarity criteria. Then we could link them to the keywords of their transcriptions.

Road map: We describe our algorithm for propagating tags using the visual-semantic graph in Section 2. In Section 3, we describe the dataset and the evaluation methodology. Then, in Section 3.4 we present experimental results. We discuss conclusions and future work in Section 4.

2. AUTOMATIC TAGGING BASED ON INFORMATION PROPAGATION

In this section, we describe the graph structure we use to propagate information and our tag propagation method. First, we describe the visual-semantic graph structure which is the graph structure we use in this case. Then, we present our algorithm; providing a description of the algorithm and explaining the main variables.

2.1 Visual-Semantic Graph

The visual-semantic graph [7] aims at representing the relationship between semantics and visual similarity based on user search preferences. The visual-semantic graph, denoted $G_{\nu,S}$, is the result of the union of two graphs. The first graph (S) represents the relationship between the queries submitted to a Web search engine and the images from the result list that were selected as relevant. Edges are weighted according to their normalized number of clicks. The graph S can be any graph that represents a well-established semantic relationship between text and multimedia objects. The second graph (ν) represents the visual similarity between images in the selected result set. The graph ν ca be built using one or more content descriptors. In this work we employ OMD (Ordinal Measure Distance) [1] as the visual descriptor and the distance of Hamming as similarity measure. In order to optimize the size of ν, it contains only the edges which value is higher than a threshold.

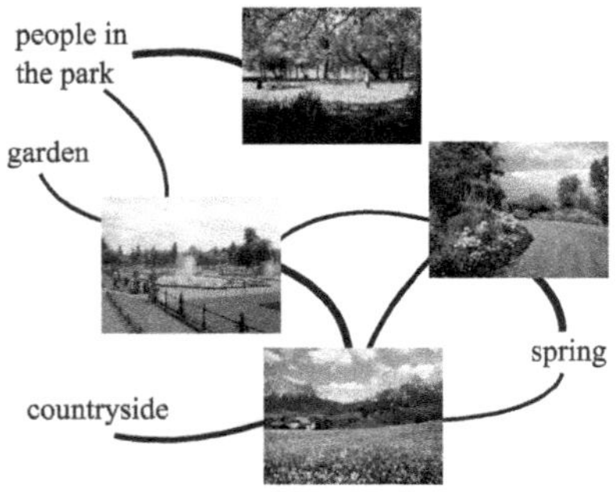

Figure 1: Visual-semantic graph representation (edge weight are depicted by their thickness).

After merging the visual graph and the semantic graph, the edge weight of the resulting visual-semantic graph are normalized with respect to each node so that edges represent the probabilities of jumping from one node to another node. Fig. 1 illustrate the structure of the visual-semantic graph.

2.2 Automatic Tag Propagation Algorithm

We automatically assign tags to images by propagating tags through the visual-semantic graph. We found that the visual descriptor and the measure we employ to build the graph conveys to a Zipf's-law-like edge frequency distribution (Fig. 4). In an analogy to "stop-words", we define *"stop-images"* which are images with many similar images (nodes with many edges). We empirically determined that "stop-images" are not good candidates to propagate information, so we dismiss their output edges.

Since the original weight of a nodes' output edges is stochastic-normalized, there is a inversely proportional relationship between the maximum weight of all output edges of node and the amount of a node's output edges. We reweigh the edges of the graph in order to reduce the effect of edge weight minimization in nodes with many connections.

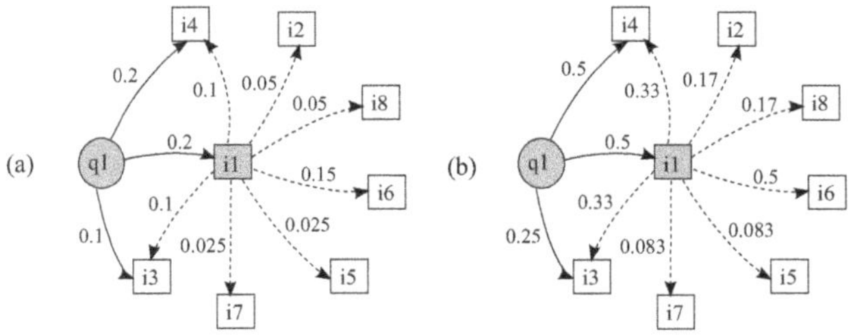

Figure 2: Graph Preprocessing. (a) original edges, (b) re-weighted edges

Let $w_{i,j}$ and $w'_{i,j}$ be the original and new weight, respectively, of the edge that connects nodes i and j. $w'_{i,j}$ is inversely proportional to the max value of all output edges of node i ($w_{i,k}$); and proportional to the sum of all the output edges of node i. Formally, each node's output edge is normalized using:

$$w'_{i,j} = \frac{w_{i,j} * \sum w_{i,k}}{\max\ w_{i,k}} \tag{1}$$

This equation maintains the idea that the edges' weights are probabilities and it adds weight independence to edges. Weight independence is required to propagate tags uniformly. Fig. 2 shows the application of our re-weighting scheme.

Once we have reweighed the visual-semantic graph, we perform our method. The proposed method consists on traversing the graph. This traversal process starts at each query and it is independent of other queries' traversal processes. Our method is highly parallelizable. For each query q, we propagate it to its connected images i passing as much energy as the edge's weight. Let, $t_{q,i}$ the energy of tag q with respect to an image i, the first propagation step consists of:

$$t_{q,i} = w'_{q,i} \tag{2}$$

Then, we propagate the tag q associated to a image j to all its neighbors i. We choose only the neighbors that fulfill the *edge probability threshold* (α). If there are nodes that have been already tagged with q, we keep the one with the maximum value. Formally, each image i is tagged with q using the following expression:

$$t_{q,i} = \max(t_{q,j} * w'_{j,i}, t_{q,i}) \tag{3}$$

We repeat this propagation scheme following a breadth-first traversal until the energy of the tag associated to a image

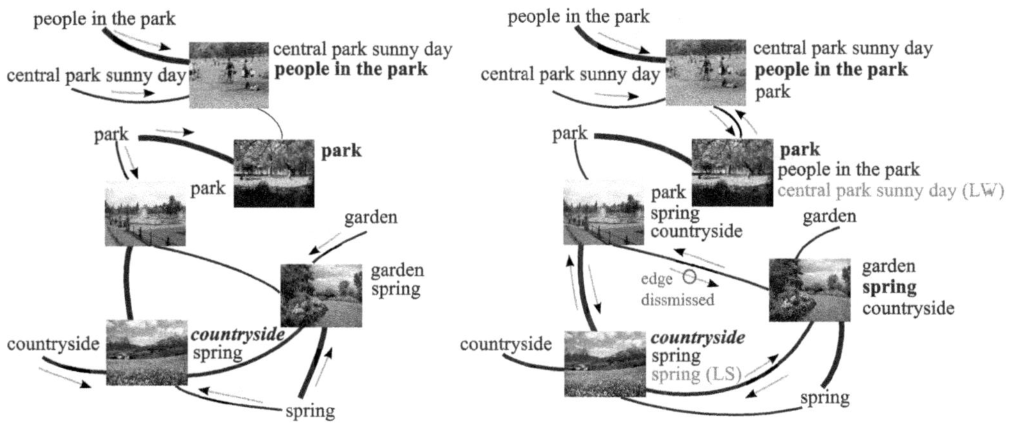

Figure 3: Example of tag propagation. (LS): tag has less energy than current, (LW): energy value of propagation lower than ϵ.

does not reach the *tagging energy threshold* (ϵ). The variables α and ϵ are employed to prune the graph's traversal path. Fig. 3 shows the propagation process performed by our algorithm. In Fig. 3, tags propagated and marked with LS are discarded because they do not have an energy value higher than the current value. Additionally, tags marked with LW are not propagated a further step because their energy value is lower than the threshold ϵ.

Variables. Since our approach focuses on providing an approximation to the automatic tagging problem, in our algorithm we use variables which allow us to prune edges which do not contribute to good tag assignment.

Edge connectivity threshold(α). This variable is used to determine whether we propagate tags between two nodes connected by an edge which value must be higher than α.

Propagation energy threshold(ϵ). This variable represents the minimum energy value required to propagate a tag from the current node to its descendants. The value of ϵ is inversely proportional to the propagation path length.

3. EVALUATION

In this section, we perform an initial evaluation to explore the effectiveness of our algorithm to propagate tags on the visual-semantic graph. We describe our working dataset, the baseline approach and the experimental framework that we will use in future work for more in-depth analysis.

3.1 Dataset

In order to test our algorithm with real world data, we use the visual-semantic graph corresponding to the Yahoo! query log from March, 01st 2010 to March, 06th 2010. The chosen week contains approximately 7 million unique clicked images (images clicked in at least one session). Overall, that week registered about 11.2 million unique-session clicks on images, and 2.7 million queries.

Next, we define the set of "stop-images", which are images that have a *huge* amount of similar images adjacent to them. Fig. 4 shows the distribution of the amount of edges connected to an image sorted in descending order. We filter the output edges of the nodes that appear in the first third part of the ranking list. As a result, we keep the images that have at most 32 output edges. Then, we preprocess the edges of the original dataset using the Eq. 1.

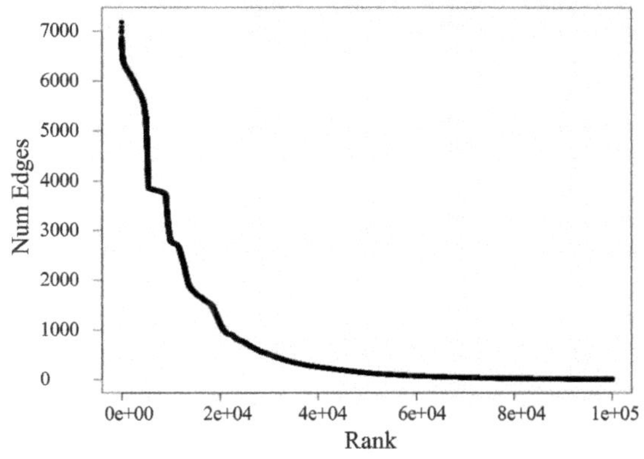

Figure 4: Distribution of the amount of edges connected to an image sorted in descending order.

3.2 Baseline

The selected baseline approach consists of what we call a naïve propagation technique. The naïve propagation scheme propagates queries to all images connected to them through a path of length not longer than three. In future work, we plan to use a more competitive algorithm as a baseline, such as the proposed by Wang et al.[10]. The Linear Neigborhood Propagation (LNP) algorithm has shown to be more robust than other algorithms based on random walks.

3.3 Evaluation

In our experimental design we consider executing our algorithm with many different configurations of the pruning variables. We present a preliminary evaluation of the tags obtained for a random sample of images. We assess each configuration in terms of Precision against the baseline approach. We also evaluate the influence of the variables used for pruning. To perform a preliminary evaluation, we took a sample of 150 images and their corresponding tags after performing the baseline approach and the proposed algorithm. The distribution of the tag amounts of the images from the sample is the same distribution as that of the complete dataset. The evaluation configuration we establish are combinations of $\alpha = 0.5, 0.375, 0.25$ and $\epsilon = 0.25, 0.1875, 0.125$. For the edges of the visual-semantic graph we have a maximum α value of 0.5. This value of α means that we have equal confidence for propagating tags in the semantic and the visual portions of the graph. We calculate the Precision of the assigned tags of each image using:

$$Precision = \frac{Number\ of\ correct\ tags}{Total\ amount\ of\ tags}$$

We calculate the average of all the Precision values we obtained for the different configurations.

3.4 Preliminary Results

Table 1 summarizes the Precision values obtained when evaluating the accuracy of the tags associated to a sample of images, after executing our algorithm and the naïve approach. First, we notice that the pruning variables have an immediate effect improving the Precision of the tags assigned. Also, we notice that as the values assigned to the pruning variables increase, the effect of these variables in the Precision measure decreases. The maximum Precision value our approach achieves is about 0.8. Even increasing the pruning of the propagation of tags set we do not improve the Precision.

We notice that increasing α improves Precision quicker than increasing ϵ. However, ϵ provides good improvements when the value of α is small. As a matter of fact, these pruning variables represent a good complement for effectively propagating tags in a graph structure. In our propagation algorithm, α controls the width of the spanning tree resulting from the breadth-first traversal, and ϵ controls the depth of the propagation paths.

Table 1: Precision of our algorithm and baseline approach.

Variables	$\epsilon = 0.125$	$\epsilon = 0.1875$	$\epsilon = 0.25$
$\alpha = 0.25$	0.398	0.415	0.488
$\alpha = 0.375$	0.526	0.717	**0.810**
$\alpha = 0.5$	0.730	0.798	**0.799**
Baseline		0.357	

4. CONCLUSIONS AND FUTURE WORK

We have presented an automatic tagging algorithm based on tag propagation. Our method considers frequent queries clicked from images in a search engine as initial tags, and we define a propagation scheme based on the existing visual-semantic graph structure. We conclude that the use of a good pruning criteria improves the quality of the results. Therefore, the value of α and ϵ are important for the efficiency of our algorithm. We propose a re-weighting scheme which helps to easily generalize the variable values, depending on the visual similarity measure used to build the graph.

We believe that the Precision values obtained can be improved by using a combination of visual descriptors to determine edges between images, as opposed to only one descriptor. Additionally, the combination of descriptors could contribute to smoothing the long tail distribution we found in the number of image edges.

As we mentioned in the previous section, in future work we plan to perform a large scale user evaluation of the tags assigned to images. For the large scale evaluation we will use a Web-based crowdsourcing service such as Mechanical Turk[1]. We will consider only those tags that do not correspond to direct clicks represented in the semantic section of the graph. The assessor's agreement to the tags assigned by the propagation methods will be measured using a Likert-type scale [4]. This scale will allow us to determine whether users have a positive or negative response to the tags related to each image. We will also evaluate results using a combination of visual descriptors, focusing on descriptors that work at region level instead of at image level (such as OMD). Previous work ([6], [8]) have shown good results in this direction.

5. ACKNOWLEDGMENTS

This work has been partially supported by FONDEF-CONICYT project D09I1185. The authors thank Benjamin Bustos, Ivan Sipiran and Juan Barrios from the KDW-Prisma Research Group at the University of Chile for their valuable comments.

6. REFERENCES

[1] D. Bhat and S. Nayar. Ordinal measures for images correspondence. *IEEE transactions on pattern analysis and machine intelligence*, 20(4):415–423, 1998.

[2] X. Chen, Y. Mu, S. Yan, and T.-S. Chua. Efficient large-scale image annotation by probabilistic collaborative multi-label propagation. In *Proceedings of the international conference on Multimedia*, MM '10, pages 35–44, New York, NY, USA, 2010. ACM.

[3] S. Gao, Z. Wang, L.-T. Chia, and I. W.-H. Tsang. Automatic image tagging via category label and web data. In *Proceedings of the international conference on Multimedia*, MM '10, pages 1115–1118, New York, NY, USA, 2010. ACM.

[4] R. Likert. A technique for the measurement of attitudes. *Archives of psychology*, 1932.

[5] D. Liu, X.-S. Hua, M. Wang, and H.-J. Zhang. Image retagging. In *Proceedings of the international conference on Multimedia*, MM '10, pages 491–500, New York, NY, USA, 2010. ACM.

[6] D. Liu, S. Yan, Y. Rui, and H.-J. Zhang. Unified tag analysis with multi-edge graph. In *Proceedings of the international conference on Multimedia*, MM '10, pages 25–34, New York, NY, USA, 2010. ACM.

[7] B. Poblete, B. Bustos, M. Mendoza, and J. Barrios. Visual-semantic graph: Towards reducing the semantic gap in web image retrieval. 2010.

[8] Y. Shen and J. Fan. Leveraging loosely-tagged images and inter-object correlations for tag recommendation. In *Proceedings of the international conference on Multimedia*, MM '10, pages 5–14, New York, NY, USA, 2010. ACM.

[9] A. W. M. Smeulders, M. Worring, S. Santini, A. Gupta, and R. Jain. Content-based image retrieval at the end of the early years. *IEEE Transactions on Pattern Analysis and Machine Intelligence*, 22(12):1349–1380, 2000.

[10] J. Wang, F. Wang, C. Zhang, H. C. Shen, and L. Quan. Linear neighborhood propagation and its applications. *IEEE Transactions on Pattern Analysis and Machine Intelligence*, 31:1600–1615, 2009.

[1] https://www.mturk.com/mturk/welcome

Identifying Authoritative Sources of Multimedia Content *

Lyndon Kennedy
Yahoo! Labs
4301 Great America Parkway
Santa Clara, CA 95054
lyndonk@yahoo-inc.com

Malcolm Slaney
Yahoo! Research
4301 Great America Parkway
Santa Clara, CA 95054
malcolm@ieee.org

ABSTRACT

We present a framework for identifying authoritative sources (such as web sites or individual users) that are likely to produce high-quality or interesting images. We construct a directed graph across sources based on the propensity of one source to "cite" the content from another. A graph-centrality measure scores the authority for each source, which could then be applied for retrieval purposes. We apply this method to web image retrieval, where web sites are the sources, and citations are found via copy detection; and on a photo sharing site, where individuals are the sources and citations are users' favorites. We are able to identify primary or influential sources of media while avoiding the computational cost of other approaches.

Categories and Subject Descriptors

H.3.1 [**Information Search and Retrieval**]: Content Analysis and Indexing

General Terms

Algorithms, Human Factors

1. INTRODUCTION

Multimedia retrieval is a challenging problem. Millions of images are added to the web every day and users increasingly require mechanisms for navigating these massive collections. The challenge is that the actual information contained in images and videos (matrices of pixels and streams of audio) does little to reveal the semantic meaning of the media.

There are four popular signals for ranking objects: image features, the text around the object, the (web) links, and popularity. In this paper we propose another signal based on citations.

1) Pioneering approaches to visual search relied upon content cues extracted from the image itself: typically distributions of low-level features, such as colors, textures, and edges in the images. These signals are difficult to exploit due to the "semantic gap" between content and high-level meaning.

2) Currently web-scale multimedia search uses text around the object. This works because a web page containing an image often contains words describing the content. But this information doesn't necessarily tell us which image of the Golden Gate Bridge, for example, is the best one.

3) People often credit PageRank [7] for making it possible for users to navigate the modern web. The key insight is that a hyperlink is essentially an editorial judgement by a real person that the linked-to document is somehow important and PageRank provides a mechanism for aggregating these recommendations from millions of web authors.

4) Objects can also be ranked based on popularity. This is important since most multimedia objects do not come with links. Flickr, for example, uses a (secret) combination of view counts and lists of personal favorites to create a measure of interestingness. Then one can sort images that match a keyword by interestingness or popularity.

In this work, we propose a new cue based on how multimedia documents are *produced*. We focus on the *source* of the document, meaning the specific web site, user, or IP address that is providing the piece of media. We aim to characterize how *authoritative* this source is and how likely it is to provide media that are frequently relevant, interesting, or otherwise *reliably* relevant.

The primary contribution of this work is a new cue for measuring image citation and a framework for leveraging this cue to determine the importance of the *source* of an image. We propose that authoritative sources can be found via an adaptation of traditional analyses of citation networks. If we can construct a graph of sources and their relative propensities to "cite" each other, then we can apply ranking techniques, such as PageRank [7], to determine the authority of each source. We evaluate the proposed framework by examining the propensity of web sites to copy images from each other. We define this copying behavior as a form of citation and find that we are able to identify sites that are often primary sources for iconic images. We also show that users marking photos as favorites on social media sites is a signal which can be used to identify authoritative users.

2. RELATED WORK

An important piece of related work is the well-known PageRank algorithm [7]. In its initial application, PageRank computes the authority of web pages by interpreting hyperlinks as a sort of citation. The web pages are taken as nodes and the hyperlinks between them as directed edges and the

*Area chair: Bernard Merialdo

MM'11, November 28–December 1, 2011, Scottsdale, Arizona, USA.

resulting ranking of pages is roughly the stationary probability of a random walk over that graph. This approach is not limited to only web pages and hyperlinks. Several previous works have shown applications of this technique for multimedia retrieval. In these works, the nodes are multimedia documents in a search result, such as video clips [1], web images [3], or video stills [5] and the edges between the nodes are weighted by the visual similarity between them. Applying a random walk technique, like PageRank, over these types of graphs shows improvements in the overall relative ranking of documents.

Some prior work has looked at creating the graph structure not at the level of the document, itself, but at the level of the *sources* of the documents. These "SiteRank" solutions are applied to web documents, where web pages are treated as documents and the *sites* (typically the domain names from which the pages come) as the sources. The relative strength of links between any two sources is typically weighted by the number of hypertext documents in one source with hyperlinks to documents from the target source. The resulting ranking of sources can be applied to making crawling mechanisms more efficient [2], enabling persistent search systems [8], or browsing peer-to-peer networks [10].

Our proposed approach is different from previous work in that we propose to characterize multimedia documents not by their individual content, but by the quality of the sources from which they are drawn. We believe this is the first work to apply random-walk techniques to multimedia sources rather than the documents themselves.

3. PROPOSED FRAMEWORK

In our proposed system, we construct a citation network between a set of sources. "Sources" are persons, publications, or any other entities that produce, disseminate, or consume multimedia content and a "citation" occurs when one source references a piece of media from another source. We reason that some sources are more likely to be producers of high-quality, relevant, or interesting multimedia documents than others and we hypothesize that this quality will be reflected by the centrality of the source in this resulting source citation network. Intuitively, sources that are frequently cited are likely to continually produce high-quality media.

We construct the citation network such that each node represents a source and edges are placed between nodes and weighted based on the propensity of one source to cite another source. Edges are directed towards the source being cited and the weights of all outgoing edges for each node are normalized to sum to one. We then apply the PageRank algorithm across this network, which is essentially a random walk over the citation graph with random restarts. The stationary probability distribution of this random walk over nodes is then interpreted as a ranking of each of the sources according to their relative authority.

If we conduct the process as described above over a heterogeneous collection of sources, then we will ultimately arrive at a query-independent ranking of sources. However, some sources may be more specialized than others, meaning that this general ranking of authority might not be applicable for all types of queries. We then propose to further improve the approach by enabling ourselves to find more-specific subgraphs, where the sources are likely to be constrained to certain classes of topics. If we apply PageRank to these subgraphs, then we will expect the resulting rankings of nodes to be different from the general case and unique to the specific topics of the sources that we have sub-selected. We call these analyses over topic-sensitive subgraphs query-class-dependent rankings, as they can be utilized separately based on the type of query being addressed.

4. APPLICATION TO IMAGE SEARCH

A key insight of the original PageRank work is that hyperlinks between websites are functionally equivalent to citations. That is, a link from one website to another is essentially a vote of confidence conferred upon the target page. When website authors wish to mention or utilize an image, however, they do not typically just create a hyperlink to the original. Instead, they will make a copy of the image and re-post it. We observe that these copied images are effectively citations of the original image and that the most frequently copied images on the web are often more likely to be relevant to the query and subjectively of higher quality or more iconic. In this application, we go a level higher to the *sources* that are actually providing the images. In this case, the sources are individual web sites and we aggregate individual cases of image copying across various websites into an overall propensity for citation between these sources.

4.1 Overall Approach

Our approach to tracing citation patterns across sources relies heavily on the detection of near-duplicate images across the entire web. With these image near-duplicate detection results, we would like to aggregate inter-source citations and construct a source citation graph across which to conduct PageRank. This is, unfortunately, infeasible across all of the billions of images available on the web. Instead, we propose to populate the lists of possible sources by issuing queries against a commercial web image search engine and to detect near-duplicates within the resulting images returned. Specifically, we limit near-duplicate detections to be conducted solely within the images returned for each query, which greatly reduces the computational complexity with a very small expense of decreased recall in the discovery of near-duplicate images: multiple copies of the same image are far more likely to be returned within the same query rather than across disparate queries.

4.2 Citation Detection

A citation occurs when an image is copied and reposted elsewhere. To detect this, we have to detect whether two images are copies of each other and if they are, then resolve which one is citing which.

Copy detection has seen a great deal of interest and a number of workable proposed solutions. In this work, we opt for a simple approach, which matches scale-invariant feature transform (SIFT) [6] descriptors across candidate image pairs. A version of this method is included in a freely-available SIFT toolkit [9].

Given two instances of an image, both of which are detected as copies of each other, we are still left with the question of which image was copied from which, or more pointedly, which source is the originator of the image and which source is merely citing that original image. We have solved this with a very simple approach: we extract the 'Last-Modified' date from the HTTP headers for the images and project that the older file is being cited by the newer file. This, of course, may not actually reflect the reality of

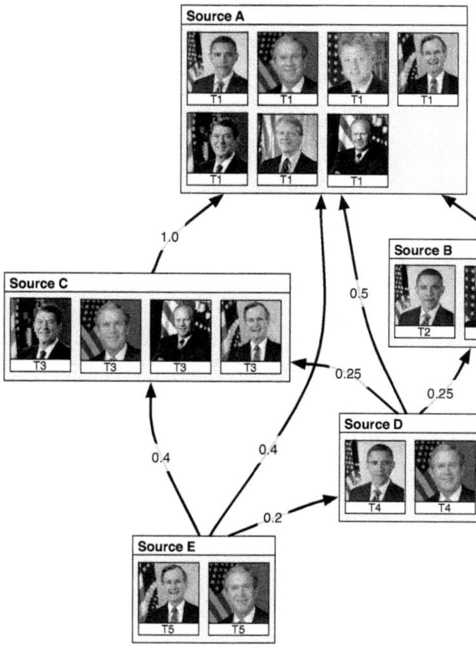

Figure 1: A source citation network is extracted from repeated images across multiple sources. The edges from a source are weighted according to how many images are being reused between the two sources. The out-links from one source are normalized to sum to one.

how the images were discovered and repurposed, but it is a reasonable approximation.

4.3 Graph Construction

Once we have pairwise citations detected between individual images, we need to move on to constructing a graph between sources. The graph consists of sources (nodes) and citation propensities (weighted, directed edges). For each pair of near-duplicate images that we have detected, we draw an edge between the sources (domains) of the images, directed from the citing source to the original source. If multiple such pairs are discovered between two sources, the weight of the edge between the two sources is weighted proportionally. Finally, the weights of the edges are normalized such that the outlink weights from each node sum to unity.

To illustrate this citation network construction process, Figure 1 shows a hypothetical source graph across sources of images for recent United States presidents. There are seven images in total dispersed across five different sources. In each source, the image is also tagged with a timestamp. (For simplicity, the times are simply T1-T5 and all images within a source have identical timestamps.) The weight of the edges between any two sources is proportional to the amount of images that they have in common between them.

The queries used to seed the graph construction dictate the types of authorities that we will find. We propose to leverage this to arrive at different authority scores for different classes of queries. For example, if we choose to seed the model with only queries for professional athletes, then the resulting citation graph structure will be highly specific to sources likely to provide sports images. We seed the process with several popular query classes.

5. EVALUATION

To evaluate our approach for detecting source authority for web images, we amass a collection of over 10 million images. This data set is collected by issuing over 12,000 queries against a commercial web image search engine (in this case, Yahoo! image search) and collecting the top-1,000 returned images, which is the maximum number of results returned by such engines. In addition to the images, themselves, we also retain information about the sources of the images, such as the URL of the image and the URL of the web page that refers to the image itself. We further obtain the HTTP headers for each image in order to identify the 'Last-Modified' date for the image files.

5.1 Primary Sources

We hypothesize that the high-authority sources that we are identifying are actually often the originators of images, or the "primary sources." To investigate this, we offer some qualitative analysis of these sources. Figure 2 shows the top-ranked sources for a few classes of queries as predicted by our system. Within these results, we see a tendency for intuitively-identified primary sources to come up towards the top. In the "Athletes" category, we see "assets.espn.go.com" and "sportsillustrated.cnn.com," respectively the locations of images for the official ESPN and Sports Illustrated websites. For the "Actors" category, we see "us.movies1.yimg.com" and "mtv.com," which are the sources for images for Yahoo! Movies and MTV, respectively. Interestingly, for the "Pets" category, users on Flickr are providing the most authoritative content.

5.2 Relevance

Previous work [4] has established that the detection of near-duplicate images in image search results is a key cue for determining the relevance of images. In particular, images can be clustered into groups in which are all the images are near-duplicates of each other. The relative size of each cluster will reflect the number of times that the image has been copied, so more-frequently copied images can be ranked above less-frequently copied ones. A problem with this approach, like many other reranking techniques [1, 3, 5] is that it is required to be run over the results for every query. However, the process takes far too long to be suitable for use in an actual retrieval system.

We take 80% of our queries and construct citation networks and to yield rankings of websites. We then use these rankings against the search results for the remaining 20% of queries. We also apply an expensive duplicate-based reranking approach to the results of these test queries. We compare the relative rankings that would result from the duplicate reranking (the size of the duplicate clusters that each image would appear in) against the authority scores for the sources of each image. We find that these two values are highly correlated ($p << .001$), so we are able to approximate the results of a computationally expensive operation at very little run-time cost.

5.3 Fresh Images

There is a time lag between the creation of an image and the point at which it has become largely copied and redistributed across the web, so for a relatively new image, there would only be one or two instances of the image: not enough to warrant a high rank in reranking based approaches. Can

Athletes	Movies	Games	Actors	Automotive	Pets
assets.espn.go.com	images.rottentomatoes.com	img.jeuxvideo.fr	us.movies1.yimg.com	img2.netcarshow.com	farm1.static.flickr.com
sportsillustrated.cnn.com	soundtrackcollector.com	tothegame.com	mtv.com	farm1.static.flickr.com	z.about.com
i.a.cnn.net	cinema.com	xboxmedia.ign.com	l.yimg.com	zercustoms.com	farm4.static.flickr.com
images.sportsline.com	moviegoods.com	gamershell.com	cinema.com	s2.desktopmachine.com	farm3.static.flickr.com
onlinesports.com	us.movies1.yimg.com	dignews.com	img2.timeinc.net	seriouswheels.com	lionking.org
canmag.com	z.about.com	gameslave.co.uk	images.zap2it.com	canadiandriver.com	eugenewei.com
firstshowing.net	kino.ural.ru	ps3media.ign.com	filmweb.no	mondeo.fordclubs.org	farm2.static.flickr.com
sportsmed.starwave.com	impawards.com	totalmortalkombat.com	img.timeinc.net	allcarwallpapers.com	icicom.up.pt
espn.go.com	dvdactive.com	pcmedia.ign.com	a69.g.akamai.net	farm4.static.flickr.com	arcatapet.com
espn-att.starwave.com	collider.com	xbox360media.ign.com	artistdirect.com	autogaleria.pl	snakesonablog.com

Figure 2: Top-ranked web sources for several classes of queries.

we trust certain sources enough to believe that new images from the sources will still be likely to relevant? To investigate this question, we re-use the 80/20 training/testing split described in the previous evaluation. Here, we rank all of the images in the test set according to their "Last-Modified" date. We then take the 1% most-recent images and subsample two sets of 100 images: the first set are images from sites ranked to be the single most authoritative for their class and the second set is randomly sampled, regardless of site. We find that these fresh images are, on average, 71% relevant to the query, while the images from authoritative sites are relevant 95% of the time.

5.4 Citation in Social Media

We also conduct one further experiment (orthogonal to the above-described ones) to evaluate an application where the quotation action is more explicit. On Flickr, users can mark other users' photographs as "favorites," which is also effectively a citation. To experiment with this signal, we take a snapshot of Flickr as of April 2008: 25.5 million users, 2.5 billion photos, and 112 million instances of users marking photos as favorites. We construct a graph between users by building an edge from user A to user B if user A has marked one of user B's photos as a favorite. The edges are weighted by the total number of user B's photos that user A has favorited. 2.2 million users have marked a favorite or had one of their photographs marked as a favorite.

With a random walk over this graph of users, we can arrive at a listing of the most authoritative users: those most likely to be cited or favorited. We test this by ranking users according to their authority scores and gauging their propensity to produce highly interesting photographs (as determined by Flickr's "interestingness" algorithm). We gather the top 500 most-interesting photographs for the month following the end of our data set and find that more than 80% of the most-interesting photographs for that time period are produced by the top 2% most-quoted users. The top 10% produce nearly 100% of those photographs. Therefore, we can predict photographs of future interest based on the past frequency with which a particular photographer was cited.

6. CONCLUSIONS AND FUTURE WORK

We have proposed a new citation cue and a framework for judging the relevance of images based on the authority of the sources that provide the images. We have found our proposed approach is able to approximate relevance improvements that can be derived from other content-based post-query processing techniques without requiring significant computational resources at query time. The approach is also able to find brand new content that is relevant. We further apply the approach to photographs on a social photo sharing site and find that we are able to find users that often produce interesting content.

Thus far we have simply demonstrated the potential impact of source authority as derived through the proposed methods for ranking. Future work might deploy the source authority cue as a feature in a machine-learned-ranking application to fully utilize it in combination with any number of other factors.

7. REFERENCES

[1] W. H. Hsu, L. Kennedy, and S.-F. Chang. Video Search Reranking through Random Walk over Document-Level Context Graph. In *ACM Multimedia*, Augsburg, Germany, September 2007.

[2] Q. Jiang and Y. Zhang. SiteRank-Based Crawling Ordering Strategy for Search Engines. In *Proceedings of the 7th IEEE International Conference on Computer and Information Technology*, pages 259–263. IEEE Computer Society, 2007.

[3] Y. Jing and S. Baluja. PageRank for product image search. In *Conference on the World Wide Web*. ACM New York, NY, USA, 2008.

[4] L. Kennedy. *Advanced techniques for multimedia search: Leveraging cues from content and structure.* PhD thesis, Columbia University Graduate School of Arts and Sciences, 2009.

[5] J. Liu, W. Lai, X.-S. Hua, Y. Huang, and S. Li. Video search re-ranking via multi-graph propagation. In *MULTIMEDIA '07: Proceedings of the 15th international conference on Multimedia*, pages 208–217, New York, NY, USA, 2007. ACM.

[6] D. Lowe. Distinctive Image Features from Scale-Invariant Keypoints. *International Journal of Computer Vision*, 60(2):91–110, 2004.

[7] L. Page, S. Brin, R. Motwani, and T. Winograd. The pagerank citation ranking: Bringing order to the web. Technical report, Computer Science Department, Stanford University, 1998.

[8] E. Schmidt and J. Singh. SiteRank: Link-Based Relevance Computation for Persistent Search. Technical report, 745-06, Department of Computer Science, Princeton University, 2006.

[9] SIFT demo program, David Lowe. http://www.cs.ubc.ca/~lowe/keypoints/.

[10] J. Wu and K. Aberer. Using SiteRank in p2p information retrieval. Technical report, IC/2004/31, Swiss Federal Institute of Technology, Lausanne, Switzerland, 2004.

Semantic Point Detector

Kuiyuan Yang*
Dept. of Automation
Univ. of Sci. & Tech. of China
Hefei, Anhui, 230027 China
ustc_yky@hotmail.com

Lei Zhang
Microsoft Research Asia
No. 5 Danling Street
Beijing, 100080 China
leizhang@microsoft.com

Meng Wang
School of Computing
National Univ. of Singapore
Singapore 117417, Singapore
eric.mengwang@gmail.com

Hong-Jiang Zhang
Microsoft Adv. Tech. Center
No. 5 Danling Street
Beijing, 100080 China
hjzhang@microsoft.com

ABSTRACT

Local features are the building blocks of many visual systems, and local point detector is usually the first component for local feature extraction. Existing local point detector are designed with target for matching and it may not perform well when applied in image content representation. Actually many existing studies demonstrate that the simple dense sampling strategy can achieve better performance than many local point detection methods in image classification tasks. In this paper, we propose a novel point detector named semantic point detector, which detects a set of semantically meaningful patches from each image and yields more compact and complete image representation. It is learned from an set of images with concepts from a large ontology. We conduct extensive experiments based on the proposed detector, and the experimental results demonstrate the effectiveness of our approach.

Categories and Subject Descriptors

H.3.1 [**Information Storage and Retrieval**]: Content Analysis and Index

General Terms

Algorithms, Experimentation

Keywords

Semantic point detector

1. INTRODUCTION

Local features not only help to find correspondences in spite of large changes in viewing conditions, occlusions, and background clutter, but also yield an interesting description of the image content for image retrieval and object or scene recognition [13]. Generally, there are two main steps for extracting local features, the first is point detection, and the next is point descriptor extraction. Point detection can be viewed as a task of selecting a set of points from all possible candidates on the image grid. The widely used point detectors can be divided into two categories, namely interest point detector and dense sampling. Interest point detector is originally designed for recognizing specific objects or finding correspondence between two or more wide baseline views. It selects a set of points based on the local image structures, such as corners [4] and blobs [7], these points tend to be sparse and stable in images of the same object or scene. Recently, these detectors have been successfully used in near-duplicate detection and landmark retrieval [12, 15].

However, these detectors are designed with the purpose of finding points that are invariant under a certain family of transformations. This principle makes robust the correspondence establishment between images with the same object or scene , but it is not necessarily optimal for describing the image content and revealing semantic meanings. Actually, many recent studies have shown that the simplest dense sampling method, which provides a more complete image representation, is able to perform much better than interest point detector in many image classification tasks [10]. However, the good performance is actually achieved based on the good discriminative ability of the subsequent classifiers, as they will need to mine the useful information. Intuitively, it is not necessary to use all the patches and reasonable point selection approach is required.

In this work, we propose a learning-based point detector called semantic point detector which aims to select a set of points that can better represent the image. The point detector is built based on a patch-level binary classifier that distinguishes the informative patches from the non-informative ones. The definition of informativeness depends on the specific application. Existing local point detectors define informativeness for matching purpose. The points that are the invariant to a group of transformations are defined as informativeness, and thus different hand-designed classifiers are proposed to detect such points. Semantic point detector is designed for image interpretation tasks, and the informativeness is thus defined as the semantic representativeness.

*This work was performed when Kuiyuan Yang was visiting Microsoft Research Asia as a research intern.
∗Area Chair: Lexing Xie

MM'11, November 28-December 1, 2011, Scottsdale, Arizona, USA.

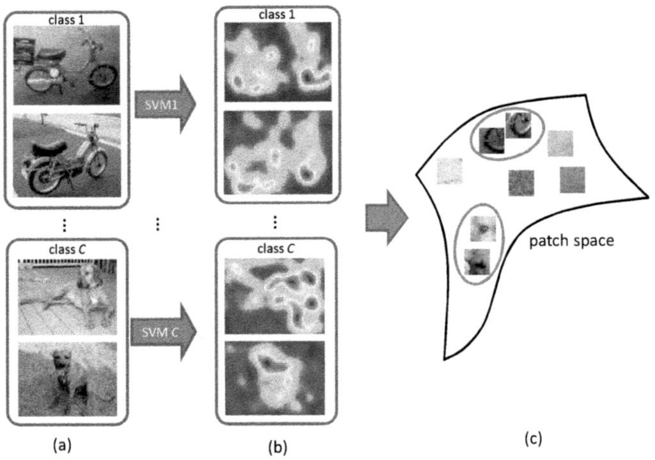

Figure 1: Schematic illustration of the proposed method. We use a set of images from C categories (a) to train a set of linear SVMs, and the patch-level classifiers are directly derived from them. (b) shows the patch-level classification scores, the hot colors are corresponding to high scores. Finally, in (c) the patch-level classifiers jointly determine semantically representative regions in the patch space, which are illustrated with red ellipses.

The semantic representative patches are with clear semantic meanings independent of the context. To find such patches, we learn the semantic point detector from an image dataset with the concepts from a large ontology. First, each image is represented as a linear combination of all its patches' representations. Second, the image-level linear classifier is learned for each concept. Since these two steps only perform linear operations on the patch representation, the patch-level classifier can be directly derived from the image-level classifier. It classifies each patch according to its relevance to the concept. With a large set of such patch-level classifiers, we can distinguish a lot semantically meaningful regions in the patch space. Considering the validated hypothesis "useful patches are likely to be shared across categories" [1, 14], a large set of such patch level classifiers can form a reasonably complete semantic point detector. It selects a patch based on its semantic representativeness, which can generate a more compact and complete image representation.

As a summary, the main contributions of the paper include:

(1) we propose a semantic point detector;

(2) we suggest a semantically meaningful patch gathering process; and

(3) we evaluate and compare a number of different local point detectors on image classification and demonstrate that the semantic point detector can generate more compact and complete image representation.

The rest of the paper is organized as follows. In Section 2, we detail the proposed semantic point detector. The experimental validations are presented in Section 3. Finally, we conclude the paper in Section 4.

2. SEMANTIC POINT DETECTOR

As introduced above, semantic point detector is a semantic classifier for image patches. It is intuitive to train such classifier using a set of semantically meaningful and meaningless patches. However, such labeling process is of high cost and hard to label enough patches to well cover the semantically meaningful regions in the whole patch space. Here, we directly derive such patch-level classifiers from a set of image-level classifiers which can be easily obtained from a set of images with labels. In this section, we detail the construction process of the semantic point detector. First, we introduce the patch and image representation. Then we introduce the method to derive the patch-level classifiers.

2.1 Patch and Image Representation

Bag-of-visual-words representation has been successfully used in image interpretation tasks. However, it is with limited representation power of the patch space as all the patches belong to the same visual words are treated the same after quantization step, and many methods have been proposed to overcome the quantization problem [5, 11, 16]. Here we use the Super-Vector coding introduced by Zhou et al. [16] for patch and image representation, which achieved state-of-the-art performance on the standard datasets. This representation was shown to extend bag-of-visual-words: it is not limited to the number of occurrence of each visual word but it also provides discrimination to the descriptors belong the same visual word, which yields a better representation of the patch space.

Let $I = \{I_p\}_{p=1}^{P}$ be the set of P local patch descriptors extract from an image, and visual vocabulary $V = \{v_k\}_{k=1}^{K}$ is a set of visual words generated by a unsupervised learning algorithm. The Super-Vector coding of descriptor I_p is defined by

$$\phi(I_p) = [\phi_1(I_p), \ldots, \phi_K(I_p)] \tag{1}$$

$$\phi_k(I_p) = [\gamma_k(I_p), s\gamma_k(I_p)(I_p - v_k)] \tag{2}$$

where

$$\gamma_k = \begin{cases} 1, & if\ k = \arg\min_j \parallel I_p - v_j \parallel \\ 0, & otherwise \end{cases}, \tag{3}$$

and s is a nonnegative constant and $I_p - v_k$ is the quantization error. The Super-Vector coding degenerates into bag-of-visual-words representation when $s = 0$.

Finally, image I is represented by linearly combining the patch descriptors,

$$\Phi(I) = \frac{1}{P}\sum_{p=1}^{P}\phi(I_p) \tag{4}$$

2.2 Image and Patch Level Classifiers

For a category with a set of positive and negative images, linear SVM that employs a hinge loss is used to learn the image-level classification function $f(I) = w^T\Phi(I)$. As only linear operation are performed on the patch descriptors, by a simple mathematics transformation, the image-level classification function can be directly transferred to the patch level,

$$f(I) = w^T\Phi(I) = \frac{1}{P}\sum_{p=1}^{P} w^T\phi(I_p) = \frac{1}{P}\sum_{p=1}^{P} f(I_p) \tag{5}$$

Then we obtain the patch-level classifier, i.e.,

$$f(I_p) = w^T\phi(I_p) \tag{6}$$

AP(%)	DoG	KB	HarLap	Random	SPD
aeroplane	0.488	0.216	0.533	0.545	0.599
bicycle	0.277	0.248	0.421	0.373	0.475
bird	0.230	0.146	0.245	0.220	0.291
boat	0.290	0.306	0.446	0.474	0.516
bottle	0.114	0.122	0.095	0.121	0.124
bus	0.177	0.283	0.302	0.325	0.381
car	0.420	0.391	0.603	0.559	0.642
cat	0.273	0.274	0.248	0.348	0.371
chair	0.283	0.309	0.355	0.337	0.351
cow	0.139	0.086	0.223	0.200	0.266
diningtable	0.154	0.195	0.235	0.198	0.143
dog	0.212	0.237	0.210	0.304	0.322
horse	0.440	0.428	0.593	0.541	0.516
motorbike	0.219	0.191	0.457	0.313	0.450
person	0.637	0.636	0.699	0.682	0.717
pottedplant	0.126	0.084	0.114	0.173	0.113
sheep	0.144	0.148	0.265	0.235	0.221
sofa	0.182	0.140	0.202	0.200	0.281
train	0.375	0.442	0.492	0.501	0.480
tvmonitor	0.242	0.225	0.292	0.287	0.321
average	0.271	0.255	0.351	0.347	0.379

Table 1: Comparison of different detectors on PASCAL VOC 2007 test set.

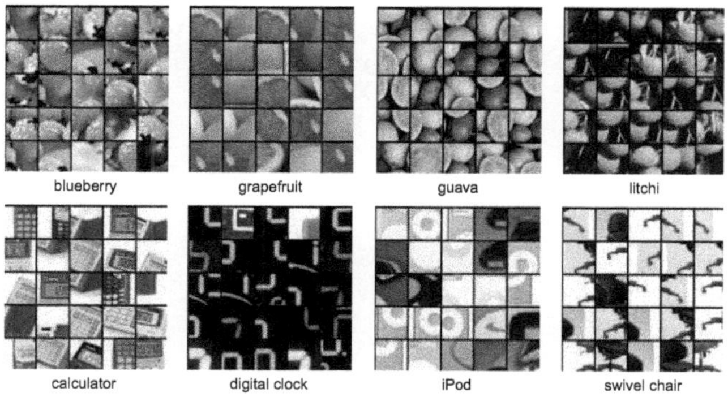

Figure 3: Some exemplar semantically representative patches learned from ImageNet50K. From top to bottom, the two rows show semantically representative patches of some categories from fruit and artifacts, respectively.

The patch-level classifier equips us with the ability of telling the semantic representativeness of a patch for the category.

2.3 Semantic Point Detector

It is intuitive that learning more patch classifiers will find more semantic regions in the patch space. Suppose we have C categories and a set of training images for each category $c \in \{1, \ldots, C\}$, which is a typical multi-class problem and we train a set of one-versus-rest image-level linear classifiers denoted by $\{w_c\}_{c=1}^{C}$, and a set of patch-level classifiers is derived via Eq. 6. The classifier w_c is learned to identify the useful patches for representing category c and these patches are denoted by,

$$\mathcal{P}_c = \{I_p : w_c^T \phi(I_p) > t\} \quad (7)$$

then all the useful patches jointly identified by all these patch classifiers is denoted by,

$$\mathcal{P} = \bigcup_{c=1}^{C} \mathcal{P}_c = \bigcup_{c=1}^{C} \{I_p : w_c^T \phi(I_p) > t\} \quad (8)$$

which can cover a larger and larger semantically meaningful area in the image space as more categories are used. We define $\max_c w_c^T \phi(I_p)$ as the semantic representativeness score of a patch, the score indicate the confidence of a patch belongs to the useful patch set $\mathcal{P}$.

The semantic point detector selects points according to the semantic representativeness score.

3. EXPERIMENTAL RESULTS

We first introduce the experiment for learning semantic point detector. Then we apply it to image classification. In all the following experiments, 128-dimensional SIFT vectors are extracted to represent the image patches.

3.1 Semantic Point Detector Learning

We relied on the ImageNet50K as the training database for semantic point detector, which consists of 50,000 images from a large ontology of 1000 visual concepts, including about 500 kinds of living things and the other about 500 kinds of artifacts [2]. For each image, a set of 32x32 patches over a grid with spacing of 4 pixels are extracted, and a visual vocabulary V of size 1024 is trained on one million randomly sampled descriptors. Then each image is represented with Eq. 1, and a one-versus-rest linear SVM is trained for each category. In Fig. 3 we visualize the learned semantic representative patches of some exemplar categories from fruit and artifact.

3.2 Image Classification

To evaluate the performance of the proposed semantic point detector in applications, an image classification experiment was carried out on the PASCAL VOC2007 dataset [3]. The images in the dataset contain objects from 20 object categories. It contains 9963 images which are split into three subsets: training data (2501 images), validation data (2510 images), and test data (4952 images). All the following experiment results are obtained on the test data. We use the PASCAL toolkit to evaluate the classification accuracy, measured by Average Precision based on the precision/recall curve. Our goal is to compare different point detectors with respect to their recognition performance. To minimize other affects, we use a basic scheme to perform the classification task (not using any spatial information, not using multiple kernels, etc). The method consists of the following steps: a) a set of local points with descriptors are detected for each image; b) a visual vocabulary is constructed by clustering local descriptors; c) image representation is computed via Eq. 1; and d) an one-versus-rest linear SVM is trained for each category.

We conduct a set image classification experiments with the following local point detectors: DoG [8], Kadir Brady (KB) [6] , Harris-Laplace (HarLap) [9], Random: 32x32 patches are selected randomly over the image grid, Semantic Point Detector (SPD): this is our proposed detector. Figure 2 illustrates an example of points detected by different detectors.

The visual vocabulary of size 1024 was constructed in each experiment respectively, as the detected local points changed when using different detectors. To ensure fair comparison, the number of points of Random and SPD are kept the same with DoG which detects the fewest points on average ($\approx$ 600

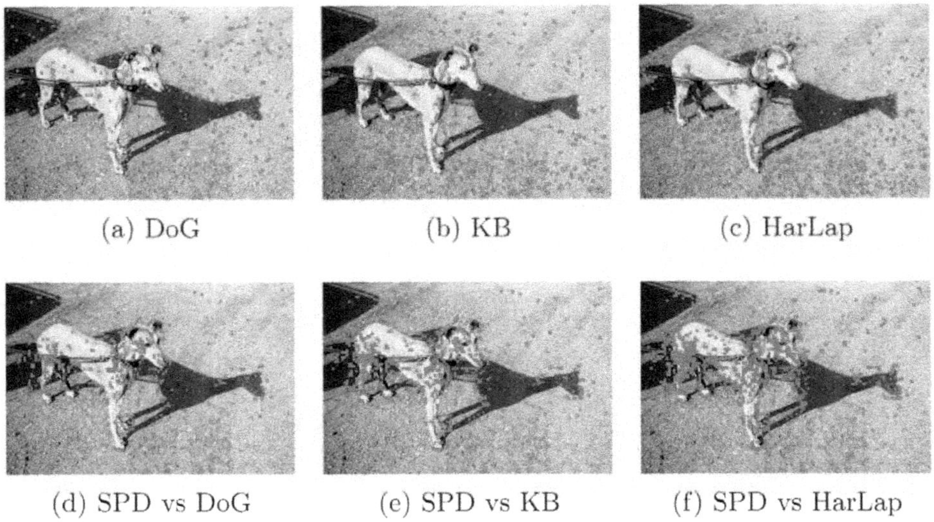

Figure 2: Examples of comparison between different detectors, the results of existing detectors (DoG, KB, and HarLap) are shown in the top row, the bottom row shows results of SPD compared with the above detectors by keeping the same number of points.

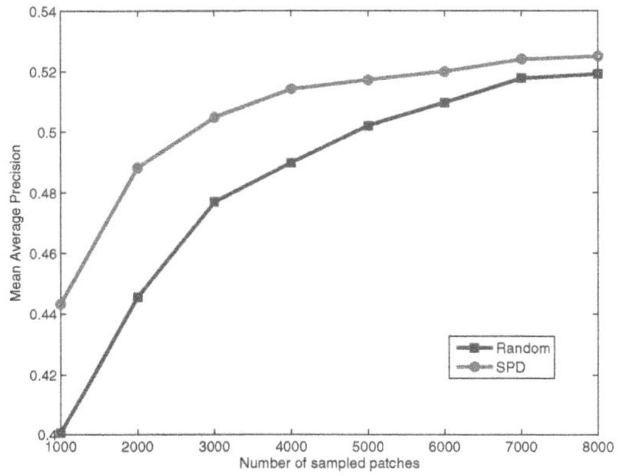

Figure 4: Mean Average Precision as a function of the number of sampled patches used for classification.

points). The comparison results are shown in Table 1, from which it is clear that SPD significantly outperform the other detectors on classification accuracy.

As dense sampling has been proved to be the most effective sampling strategy for image classification. The Random and SPD will converge to dense sampling as more points sampled. We conduct another group of experiments to investigate the converge rate of the two sampling strategy. Figure 4 shows the effects on mean average precision of varying the number of patches sampled per image. It can be seen that the SPD converges much faster than random sampling, this is also demonstrate that the SPD can select a set patches that are more compact and complete.

4. CONCLUSIONS

In this paper, we have proposed a novel semantic point detector to find semantically representative patches. It is learned from an image dataset for a large ontology of visual concepts. And the extensive experiments validate the effectiveness of the new detector. Compared with existing detectors that designed for matching purpose, the semantic point detector provides a more compact and complete image representation and works much better in image interpretation tasks.

5. REFERENCES

[1] E. Bart and S. Ullman, "Cross-generalization: learning novel classes from a single example by feature replacement," in *CVPR*, 2005.

[2] J. Deng, W. Dong, R. Socher, L.-J. Li, K. Li, and L. Fei-Fei, "ImageNet: A Large-Scale Hierarchical Image Database," in *CVPR*, 2009.

[3] M. Everingham, L. Van Gool, C. K. I. Williams, J. Winn, and A. Zisserman, "The PASCAL Visual Object Classes Challenge 2007 (VOC2007) Results," http://www.pascal-network.org/challenges/VOC/voc2007/workshop/index.html.

[4] C. Harris and M. Stephens, "A combined corner and edge detector," in *Alvey vision conference*, 1988.

[5] H. Jegou, M. Douze, and C. Schmid, "Hamming embedding and weak geometric consistency for large scale image search," in *ECCV*, 2008.

[6] T. Kadir and M. Brady, "Saliency, scale and image description," *IJCV*, 2001.

[7] T. Lindeberg, "Detecting salient blob-like image structures and their scales with a scale-space primal sketch: a method for focus-of-attention," *IJCV*, 1993.

[8] D. G. Lowe, "Distinctive image features from scale-invariant keypoints," *IJCV*, 2004.

[9] K. Mikolajczyk and C. Schmid, "Scale & affine invariant interest point detectors," *IJCV*, 2004.

[10] E. Nowak, F. Jurie, and B. Triggs, "Sampling strategies for bag-of-features image classification," in *ECCV*, 2006.

[11] F. Perronnin, J. Sánchez, and T. Mensink, "Improving the fisher kernel for large-scale image classification," in *ECCV*, 2010.

[12] J. Philbin, O. Chum, M. Isard, J. Sivic, and A. Zisserman, "Object retrieval with large vocabularies and fast spatial matching," in *CVPR*, 2007.

[13] T. Tuytelaars and K. Mikolajczyk, "Local invariant feature detectors: A survey," *Foundations and Trends® in Computer Graphics and Vision*, 2008.

[14] K. Yang, M. Wang, X.-S. Hua, S. Yan, and H.-J. Zhang, "Assemble new object detector with few examples," *IEEE Transactions on Image Processing*, 2011.

[15] S. Zhang, Q. Huang, G. Hua, S. Jiang, W. Gao, and Q. Tian, "Building contextual visual vocabulary for large-scale image applications," in *Proceedings of the international conference on Multimedia*, 2010.

[16] X. Zhou, K. Yu, T. Zhang, and T. Huang, "Image classification using super-vector coding of local image descriptors," in *ECCV*, 2010.

Scenic Photo Quality Assessment with Bag of Aesthetics-Preserving Features *

Hsiao-Hang Su[1], Tse-Wei Chen[1], Chieh-Chi Kao[1], Winston H. Hsu[2], Shao-Yi Chien[1]
[1]Graduate Institute of Electronics Engineering and Department of Electrical Engineering
[2]Department of Computer Science and Information Engineering
National Taiwan University, Taipei, Taiwan
{waterhangg, variant, chiehchi.kao, sychien}@media.ee.ntu.edu.tw[1]
winston@csie.ntu.edu.tw[2]

ABSTRACT

In this paper, an aesthetic modeling method for scenic photographs is proposed. A bottom-up approach is developed to construct an *aesthetic library* with *bag-of-aesthetics-preserving features* instead of top-down methods that implement the heuristic guidelines (*rule-specific features*) listed in the photography literature, which is employed in previous works. The proposed method can cover both implicit and explicit aesthetic features with a learning process. The experimental results show that the proposed features in the library (92.06% in accuracy) outperform the state-of-the-art rule-specific features (83.63% in accuracy) significantly in the aesthetic quality assessment for scenic photos, and the rule-specific features are also proved to be encompassed by the proposed features. Meanwhile, it is observed from experiments that the features extracted for contrast information are more effective than those for absolute information, which is consistent with the properties of human visual systems.

Categories and Subject Descriptors

H.4 [**Information Systems Applications**]: Miscellaneous

General Terms

Experimentation, Human Factors

Keywords

Aesthetic Modeling, Photo Aesthetic Quality Assessment

1. INTRODUCTION

There are more and more works focusing on the problems of modeling photographic aesthetics. Most existing works [6, 2, 3, 8, 4, 11] adopt a rule-based feature extraction approach for aesthetic modeling, which is a top-down process, to implement heuristic photographic guidelines individually, such as "Rule of Thirds" and "Visual Weight Balance" (cf. Figure 2). These individual features are called *rule-specific features* in this paper. However, these ad hoc rule-specific features with low-dimensionality may lose some aesthetic characteristics. For example, the visual attention information modeled in the rule-specific features are extracted with a saliency map [11]. However, because scenic photographs considered in our work lack distinct foreground objects, the information from saliency map is not enough. Thus, these features may not provide good description for high quality scenic photos.

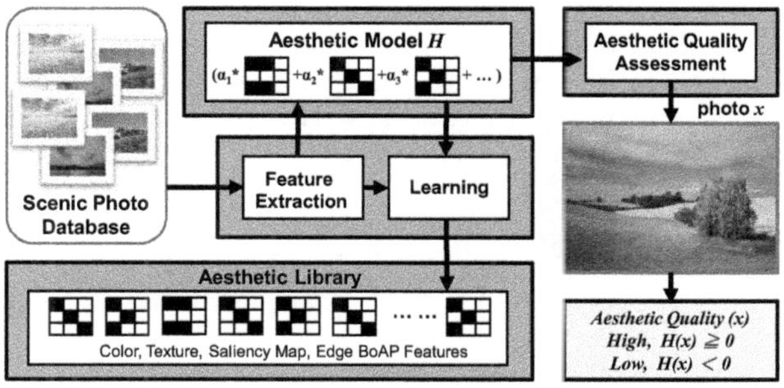

Figure 1: Overview of the proposed method. Given the aesthetic library with the proposed BoAP features, a preference-aware aesthetic quality classifier is learned through the learning process. The experimental results demonstrate that the proposed features outperform the state-of-the-art rule-specific features utilized in previous works.

In contrast to previous works, a bottom-up aesthetic modeling methodology is proposed to comprehensively analyze and mimic the essence of aesthetics. The idea of the proposed approach is that although the aesthetics is sophisticated, there still exists an *aesthetic library*, which covers all possible implicit rules (some are too complicated to be listed in photographic manuals), adhered to by high quality scenic photos. Based on the idea of constructing a library, a new image representation, denoted as *bag-of-aesthetics-preserving* (BoAP) feature image representation, is proposed, as shown in Figure 1. The proposed BoAP features in the aesthetic library are extracted from different feature spaces to model color, texture, saliency, and edge information jointly.

This paper is organized as follows. The details of the aesthetic modeling procedure are given in Section 2. In Section

*Area chair: Kiyoharu Aizawa

(a) Rule of Thirds. (b) Visual Weight Balance.

Figure 2: Two famous aesthetic rules in the photography literature. (a) The primary subject's center of mass (indicated by red cross-hair) is placed at the position near one of the four stress points (yellow cross-hairs). (b) The visual weights of different regions (indicated by red and green dashed lines) satisfy the Golden Ratio (approximately equal to 1.61803). We will show that such ad-hoc rules can be systematically included in the proposed bag-of-aesthetics-preserving features.

3, the experimental results and analyses are discussed. Finally, the conclusion is presented in Section 4.

2. PROPOSED METHOD

The proposed feature set is constructed by a bottom-up approach, which includes two steps: 1) partitioning an image into multi-size image patches and 2) extracting the bag-of-aesthetics-preserving (BoAP) features by systematically manipulating the patches in different feature spaces. The extracted BoAP features constitute the feature set.

2.1 Multi-Resolution Image Decomposition

A multi-resolution grid-based decomposition method, which partitions an image into predefined basic patches of different grid sizes, is proposed to model images in a coarse-to-fine manner. In contrast to the linear-time decomposition methods utilized in [10] (k-means) and [3] (graph-based), the proposed approach divides images into grids of different sizes in a constant time with very low timing overhead. There are four simple types of geometric compositions defined in this paper, as illustrated in Figure 3. These black and white patches are further utilized to extract BoAP features in Section 2.2. For Figure 3(a), the images are not divided or are divided into several horizontal/vertical lines at the global scope. For Figure 3(b)–(d), denoted as n×n composition, the images are partitioned into n×n spatial grids, i.e., n×n basic image patches. The concept of this image decomposing step is to utilize these coarse-to-fine geometric compositions to model and further mine the correlation among all the decomposed patches. With this approach, structural arrangement in the images can be captured at multiple resolutions.

2.2 Bag-of-Aesthetics-Preserving Feature Extraction

The BoAP features are extracted after an image is transformed into numerous multi-size patches. The extracting process consists two steps: 1) describe multi-size image patches using feature vectors and 2) generate different sets of BoAP features by applying a few simple patch-wise operations on the feature vectors of patches for different feature spaces.

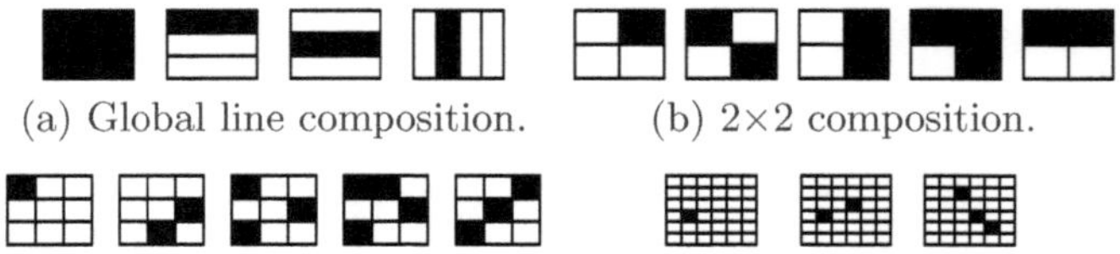

(a) Global line composition. (b) 2×2 composition.

(c) 3×3 composition. (d) 6×6 composition.

Figure 3: Some examples in four types of geometric compositions: The black patches can be viewed as the pre-defined foreground regions while the white patches can be seen as the background regions.

Figure 4: Illustration of patterns generated by permutation $\binom{4}{2}$ in 2×2 composition. The image is decomposed into four patches P, where $P = A, B, C, D$. Each patch is represented by feature vectors $f_k(P)$, where k denotes the kinds of feature images.

2.2.1 *Feature vectors of image patches*

Inspired by the relation between the feature space and its corresponding modeled rules built by prior works (e.g., a saliency map corresponds to rules about composition, contrast, and clarity; HSV or other color spaces correspond to colorfulness and color harmony), we propose to elaborate and analyze photographic aesthetics from different aspects by applying BoAP feature extraction to different feature spaces separately [7]. There are four types of information modeled in the proposed approach: color, texture, saliency, and edge information. To begin with, an image I is transformed into a number of *feature images* I_k, where k denotes the kinds of feature images extracted from the aforementioned information. Based on the feature images I_k, each decomposed patch P in an image I is represented by feature vectors $f_k(P)$. The feature images and the corresponding patch feature vectors for each information type are introduced as follows.

For color information, HSV color space is utilized. H, S, and V feature images are extracted and analyzed separately [7]. A local binary pattern (LBP) feature image is extracted to model the texture information. Each location is assigned a decimal value by encoding the neighboring eight pixels with respect to the pixel value at that location. In order to model the importance of each pixel and the locations of salient regions in an image, a saliency map [5] is also employed as a feature image.

For feature images I_k, where k = H, S, V, LBP, and saliency map, the first two moments, mean (μ) and variance (σ^2) descriptors, are utilized to describe the statistic properties of the decomposed patches within an image. The mean and variance within the patch P can be calculated from the following equations:

$$\mu_k(P) = \frac{1}{N}\sum_{i=1}^{N} I_k(i), \tag{1}$$

$$\sigma_k^2(P) = \frac{1}{N-1}\sum_{i=1}^{N}(I_k(i) - \mu_k(P))^2, \tag{2}$$

$$f_k(P) = (\mu_k(P), \sigma_k^2(P)), \tag{3}$$

where N is the pixel number in the patch P and $\forall i \in P$; k is the feature image type. Therefore, for each basic patch P in a specific feature image I_k, it is represented by a two-dimensional vector $f_k(P)$.

For edge information, each basic patch P in an image is represented by a histogram of oriented gradient (HOG). HOG features are obtained by accumulating gradient values over pixels in one patch into a histogram of D gradient directions. There are three kinds of bin number D (i.e., defined by orientations) extracted in the experiment; the value of D is set to 2 (horizontal/vertical), 4, and 8. That is, for k = HOG, each patch P is represented and described by a D−dimensional vector $f_k(P)$, where D =2, 4, and 8.

2.2.2 *Generation of BoAP Features by patch-wise operations*

Up to now, lots of feature vectors representing multi-size patches have been extracted in each analyzed feature space. For each geometric composition type illustrated in Figure 3, some simple and fast *patch-wise operations* are defined to generate thousands of BoAP features including **absolute** and **contrast** information. By applying the defined patch-wise operations on $f_k(P)$, a set of BoAP features is extracted for one type of feature image I_k (denoted as BoAP_k features). First, a **permutation** operation is utilized to generate lots of patterns by rearranging a number of patches in an organized order. That is, there are a number of $\binom{n\times n}{m}$ patterns to be generated for one type of n×n composition ($n \times n$ stands for the total patch number, m for the black patch number, and $n \times n - m$ for the white patch number in Figure 3). The m black patches can be viewed as the predefined foreground regions, and the $n \times n - m$ white patches can be seen as the background regions. Taking the 2×2 composition type for example, the permutation operator first generates $\binom{4}{1}+\binom{4}{2}+\binom{4}{3}$ patterns. Figure 4 illustrates the feature extraction procedure of patterns from $\binom{4}{2}$. In this example, an image is partitioned into four patches. Each patch is represented by feature vectors $f_k(P)$, where $P = A, B, C, D$ in this case. Based on applying patch-wise operations on feature vectors of patches, the **absolute** and **contrast** features are extracted per pattern, as shown in Table 1, where the top-left pattern in Figure 4 is taken as an example. The **absolute** features model the absolute value distribution of m black patches while the **contrast$_1$** features model the within-contrast among multiple black patches and **contrast$_2$** features model the relative contrast between multiple black patches and white patches. The contrast is shown

Table 1: Absolute and contrast features of top-left pattern in Figure 4. Features are generated by patch-wise operations on feature vectors of patches $f_k(P)$, where $P = A, B, C, D$.

Features Type	Operation
absolute	$\frac{1}{2}(f_k(A) + f_k(D))$
contrast$_1$	$f_k(A) - f_k(D)$
contrast$_2$	$f_k(A+D) - f_k(B+C)$

more consistent with human visual perceptions [1, 9]. Therefore, the proposed approach models multiple patches at different image resolutions simultaneously. The final BoAP features are obtained by including all features from color, texture, saliency, and edge together (i.e., k = H, S, V, LBP, saliency map, and HOG).

The advantages of the proposed BoAP image representation are: 1) images can be viewed in multiple resolutions by the proposed decomposition method; 2) images can be described from different aesthetic aspects, including color, texture, saliency, and edge, by applying the proposed patch-wise operations on all feature spaces; 3) contrast information, which humans are more sensitive to, is taken into consideration; 4) the computation process is highly efficient via patch-wise operations.

2.3 Aesthetic Model Learning

Considering the performance in photo quality classification tasks, Adaboost is the most suitable choice [8] and is utilized for discriminating feature selection in this paper to explore and analyze the relation between the extracted BoAP features and landscape photos.

In the algorithm, each of the BoAP features in the library serves as a hypothesis (denoted as h) and corresponds to a weak classifier. The selection process chooses the most discriminative feature $h_n(\cdot)$ with the minimum classification error in differentiating high aesthetic quality and low aesthetic quality photos at each iteration, and assigns a weight α_n to it at the same time based on its discriminating power. Finally, all N selected features $h_n(\cdot)$ are integrated and boosted together to form a strong aesthetic model H using the following equation:

$$H(x) = \text{sign}(\sum_{n=1}^{N} \alpha_n \cdot h_n(x)), \tag{4}$$

where x denotes the a photo in the training database; H is the learned model, a weighted combination of all of the selected discriminative BoAP features $h_n(\cdot)$ from the aesthetic library. The final learned model H in Equation (4) is the formulized judging criterion for scenic photographs. That is, photograph x can be assessed by a set of selected aesthetic features the high quality photos adhere to.

$H(x) = 1$ indicates that the testing photo represented by the proposed BoAP features possesses the high aesthetic quality while $H(x) = -1$ means the testing photo is of low aesthetic quality.

3. EXPERIMENTAL RESULTS

3.1 Database Collection

Most of the previous works evaluate their photo aesthetic quality assessment systems using their own private photo

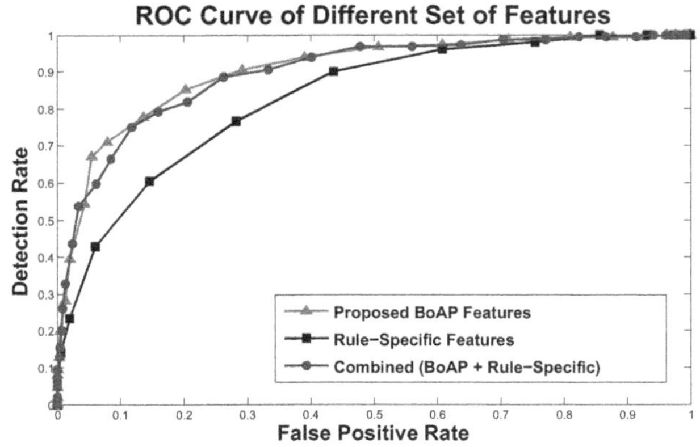

Figure 5: Comparison in the classification performance of the rule-specific features, the proposed BoAP features, and the combined (i.e. rule-specific + BoAP) features. The result shows that the proposed BoAP features outperform the state-of-the-art rule-specific features significantly. The performance of the combined features, including rule-specific features into the proposed BoAP feature library, does not improve. It shows that the proposed BoAP features encompass the professional photographic guidelines (i.e. encoded in the rule-specific features).

collections. In this paper, we utilize the same public available dataset used in both [12] and [8]. Because we focus on mining and characterizing the underlying aesthetic rules for landscape photos, only photos from the landscape category of this database are used in the experiments. In addition to this dataset, high and low aesthetic quality photos are collected from the online photo sharing website *Flickr* and the photograph contest website *DPChallenge*.

Because high quality photos in different topics still have some underlying aesthetic properties in common, in contrast to the previous work by Cheng et al. [3], a prior knowledge of the topic represented by a photo is not needed in this work. The database utilized in this paper contains all kinds of landscape classes without performing scene topic classification a priori.

3.2 Photo Aesthetic Quality Classification

To evaluate the effectiveness of the proposed BoAP features, the learned model H in Equation (4) serves as an aesthetic quality classifier to perform photo quality assessment. Photos in the database are split into training set and testing set. The training set has 340 high quality photos and 680 low quality photos, while the others (up to 3000 photos) constitute the testing set. Based on the BoAP features, the corresponding built model can achieve the highest accuracy 92.06%, which beats the performance achieved by the rule-specific features (83.63% accuracy), which combines the works in [6, 12, 8]. Moreover, among the selected features in the model, **contrast** features (75.31% in percentage) are more effective than **absolute** features (24.69% in percentage). This result is consistent with the fact that humans are more sensitive to contrast [1, 9].

3.2.1 Evaluation with ROC Curve

To further compare the classification performance with the rule-specific features and the proposed BoAP features, the receiver operating characteristic (ROC) curves are plotted by adjusting the threshold of the learned aesthetic model with Adaboost from $-\infty$ to ∞. As Figure 5 demonstrates, the proposed BoAP features achieve better performance than the rule-specific features. Moreover, if these two types of features are combined by adding the rule-specific features into the proposed BoAP feature library, the performance is almost the same as that with the proposed features. Therefore, a conclusion can be drawn from experiments that the proposed features encompass the guidelines listed in photographic manuals (i.e. encoded in the rule-specific features). That is, the rule-specific features extracted by rule-based method are well covered by ours.

4. CONCLUSION

An aesthetic modeling method for scenic photos is proposed in this paper. A new image representation with bag-of-aesthetics-preserving (BoAP) features is developed, and the aesthetic model is built by a learning process with scenic photo database. The experimental results show that the proposed features (92.06% in accuracy) outperform the state-of-the-art rule-specific features (83.63% in accuracy). In addition, these experiments further demonstrate that the rule-specific features are covered by the proposed features. Meanwhile, it is observed from experiments that the features extracted for contrast information are more effective than those for absolute information, which is consistent with the fact that humans are more sensitive to contrast in the visual perception systems.

5. REFERENCES

[1] B. T. Barrett et al. Nonveridical visual perception in human amblyopia. *Investigative Ophthalmology Vis. Sci.*, 2003.

[2] S. Bhattacahrya et al. A framework for photo-quality assessment and enhancement based on visual aesthetics. In *ACM MM*, 2010.

[3] B. Cheng et al. Learning to photograph. In *ACM MM*, 2010.

[4] R. Datta et al. Studying aesthetics in photographic images using a computational approach. In *ECCV*, 2006.

[5] J. Harel et al. Graph-based visual saliency. In *NIPS*. 2007.

[6] Y. Ke et al. The design of high-level features for photo quality assessment. In *IEEE CVPR*, 2006.

[7] C. Li et al. Aesthetic visual quality assessment of paintings. *IEEE J. of Selected Topics in Signal Processing*, 2009.

[8] Y. Luo et al. Photo and video quality evaluation: Focusing on the subject. In *ECCV*, 2008.

[9] A. McNamara. Visual perception in realistic image synthesis. *Comput. Graph. Forum*, 2001.

[10] M. Nishiyama et al. Sensation-based photo cropping. In *ACM MM*, 2009.

[11] X. Sun et al. Photo assessment based on computational visual attention model. In *ACM MM*, 2009.

[12] C.-H. Yeh et al. Personalized photograph ranking and selection system. In *ACM MM*, 2010.

Hybrid Image Summarization* †

Hao Xu† Jingdong Wang‡ Xian-Sheng Hua‡ Shipeng Li‡
†University of Science and Technology of China xuhao657@ustc.edu
‡Microsoft Research Asia {jingdw, xshua, spli}@microsoft.com

ABSTRACT

In this paper, we address a problem of managing tagged images with hybrid summarization. We formulate this problem as finding a few image exemplars to represent the image set semantically and visually, and solve it in a hybrid way by exploiting both visual and textual information associated with images. We propose a novel approach, called Homogeneous and Heterogeneous Message Propagation (H^2MP), which extends affinity propagation that only works over homogeneous relations to heterogeneous relations. The summary obtained by our approach is both visually and semantically satisfactory. The experimental results demonstrate the effectiveness and efficiency of the proposed approach.

Categories and Subject Descriptors

H.3.1 [**Information Storage and Retrieval**]: Content Analysis and Indexing; I.2.10 [**Artificial Intelligence**]: Vision and Scene Understanding

General Terms

Algorithms, Experimentation

Keywords

Image summarization, image presentation, affinity propagation, homogeneous and heterogeneous message propagation

1. INTRODUCTION

The increasing development of image search engines, photo-sharing web sites, and desktop photo management tools, has made people easily access a large amount of images. However, image collections are usually unorganized, which makes finding desired photos and quick overview of an image collection very difficult. This unstructured nature of image collections has attracted great effort on computing visual summaries. On the other hand, most image collections are provided with rich text information, and such image collections are called tagged image collections in this paper. For example, images on Flickr are titled, tagged, and commented by users. Images from the Web are often associated with surrounding texts. The text information usually reflects the semantic content of images and is helpful for summarization.

In this paper, we address the image management task through a hybrid summarization scheme. The key is to find the summary in a hybrid way to exploit both visual and textual information. An example is shown in Fig. 1. Given rich tag information associated with images, there are three useful relations from images and tags: two homogeneous relations within images and tags, i.e., image similarity and tag similarity, and one heterogeneous relation between images and tags, i.e., their association relations. We propose a hybrid summarization approach to find image exemplars through investigating all three relations together, especially the information from the associated tags, i.e., association relations between images and tags and relations within tags, so that the generated summary is both visually and semantically satisfactory.

1.1 Related work

Most existing image sharing web sites present an overview of an image collection by showing the latest images (e.g., Flickr group [4]), which obviously does not present a good summary, or allowing consumers to manually select images (e.g., Picassa web album [1]), which is inconvenient for consumers particularly in a large number of images.

Rother et al. [16] summarize a set of images with a "digital tapestry". They synthesize a large output image from a set of input images, stitching together salient and spatially compatible blocks from the input images. Wang et al. [20, 12] create a "picture collage", a 2D spatial arrangement of the images in the input set chosen to maximize visible salient regions. These works do not address the problem of selecting the set of images to appear in the summary. Wang et al. [19] present a hierarchical clustering scheme that can benefit the browsing of large image collections.

Recently, there are a few works to deal with the selection problem. Jia et al. [11] present a hierarchical affinity propagation approach to image collection summarization. Xu et al. [22] propose to describe images using cross-media information and perform an affinity propagation based image clustering approach. Simon et al. [18] selects a set of images using the greedy k-means algorithm, by examining the distribution of images to select a set of canonical views only based on visual features without exploiting the associated tags. Raguram and Lazebnik [14] select iconic images to summarize general visual categories using a simple joint clustering technique from both appearance and semantic aspects. It first obtained two independent clusters from the visual feature and the textual feature, respectively, and then takes their intersection to get

†Area Chair: Marcel Worring.
*This work was performed at Microsoft Research Asia.

MM'11, November 28–December 1, 2011, Scottsdale, Arizona, USA.

(a) (b)

Figure 1: An example of a visual summary for an image collection. (a) shows randomly selected images and their associated texts from the input, a set of tagged images, and (b) shows its summary identified by our hybrid summarization scheme.

the final clustering, but the joint process is obtained sequentially instead of simultaneously. Surrounding texts are limitedly exploited for image grouping [9, 15] by considering the association relations between words and images using the co-clustering technique, but without investigating interior relations over tags.

Image summarization is also studied in the information retrieval community. Clough et al. [5] construct a hierarchy of images using only textual caption data, and the concept of subsumption. Schmitz [17] uses a similar approach but relies on Flickr tags. Jaffe et al. [10] summarize a set of images using only tags and geotags. By detecting correlations between tags and geotags, they are able to produce tag maps, where tags and related images are overlaid on a geographic map at a scale corresponding to the range over which the tag commonly appears. All these approaches could be used to further organize the images. However, none of them exploits the visual information.

1.2 Our approach

In this paper, we present a hybrid summarization approach to find a few image exemplars to represent the image collection, which is both visually and semantically satisfactory. Toward this end, we propose an effective scalar hybrid message propagation scheme over images and tags, Homogeneous and Heterogeneous Message Propagation (H^2MP), to exploit simultaneously homogeneous relations within images and tags and heterogeneous relations between images and tags. It is beyond the affinity propagation algorithm [8] that only can handle homogeneous data, and H^2MP can effectively exploit the heterogeneous relations between images and tags as well as the interior relations within tags. Besides, our approach is superior over existing co-clustering algorithms [6, 7] that only utilize the heterogeneous relations because 1) it directly obtains the exemplars instead of performing the necessary postprocess to find the centers followed by a clustering procedure and 2) it takes advantage of homogeneous relations with images and tags as well as heterogeneous relations between them.

2. IMAGE SUMMARIZATION

Given a set of n images, $\mathcal{I} = \{I_1, I_2, \cdots, I_n\}$, a set of corresponding texts, $\mathcal{T} = \{\mathcal{T}_1, \mathcal{T}_2, \cdots, \mathcal{T}_n\}$, $\mathcal{T}_k = \{W_1^k, W_2^k, \cdots, W_{m_k}^k\}$, and the union set of tags $\mathcal{W} = \{W_1, \cdots, W_m\} = \mathcal{T}_1 \cup \mathcal{T}_2 \cup \cdots \cup \mathcal{T}_n$, we aim to find a summary, a set of image exemplars, $\bar{\mathcal{I}} \in \mathcal{I}$. There are three types of relations over images and tags as depicted in Fig. 2. The heterogeneous relations between all pairs of associated images and tags are represented by the edges, $\mathcal{E}^R$. The homogeneous relations within images are represented by the edges, $\mathcal{E}^I$, and the similarity between a pair of images i and k is denoted by $s'_I(i,k)$. The homogeneous relations within tags are represented by the edges, $\mathcal{E}^W$, and the similarity between a pair of tags j and k is represented by $s'_W(j,k)$.

Suppose a set of image exemplars to be identified be denoted as $\bar{\mathcal{I}} = \{I_{c_1}, I_{c_2}, \cdots, I_{c_n}\}$, where $c_k \in \{1, 2, \cdots, n\}$ is the index of image I_k's exemplar, and $\mathbf{c} = [c_1\ c_2\ \cdots\ c_n]^T$ is a label vector over images. If such a label vector satisfies a valid constraint that an image should also serve as the exemplar of itself if it is the exemplar of any other image, it would uniquely correspond to a set of image exemplars. In other words, identifying the exemplars can be viewed as searching over valid labels.

2.1 H^2 message propagation

H^2MP is different from the original affinity propagation algorithm [8] in that H^2MP transmits not only the homogeneous messages within images and tags, i.e., responsibility and availability depicted in Figs. 3(a) and 3(b), but also the heterogeneous messages between images and tags, i.e., discardability and contributability depicted in Figs. 3(c) and 3(d). In the following, we will present these four kinds of messages. For convenience, we would only present the homogeneous messages over images as the messages over tags are similar, and present the heterogeneous messages by standing at the image side as the messages on the tag side can also be similarly obtained. For presentation simplicity, we drop the subscripts I.

Homogeneous message propagation

The "responsibility" and "availability" messages in H^2MP are updated as follows,

$$r(i,k) = \bar{s}(i,k) - \max_{i':i' \neq k}[\bar{s}(i,i') + a(i,i')]. \quad (1)$$

$$\bar{s}(i,k) = \begin{cases} \sum_{j \in \mathcal{E}^R_{i\cdot}} v(i,j) + s(i,i) & k = i, \\ s(i,k) & k \neq i. \end{cases} \quad (2)$$

$$a(i,k) = \begin{cases} \sum_{i':i' \neq k} \max(0, r(i',k)) & k = i, \\ \min[0, r(k,k) + \sum_{i':i' \neq i,k} \max(0, r(i',k))] & k \neq i. \end{cases} \quad (3)$$

The key difference in the two messages from the original affinity propagation lies in the responsibility $r(i,j)$, which involves the heterogeneous message, i.e., the "contributability" message $v(i,j)$ from tag j to image i. This serves as a bridge in which the affect from tags will be transmitted to images. In the iteration process, $v(i,j)$ would become relatively larger when the probability of tag j being an exemplar becomes larger, and become smaller otherwise. Looking at Eqn. (2), we can observe that the contributability message takes effect when $k = i$, which means that it affects the preference of image i being an exemplar. Hence, the probability of image i, selecting itself as its exemplar, would be affected posi-

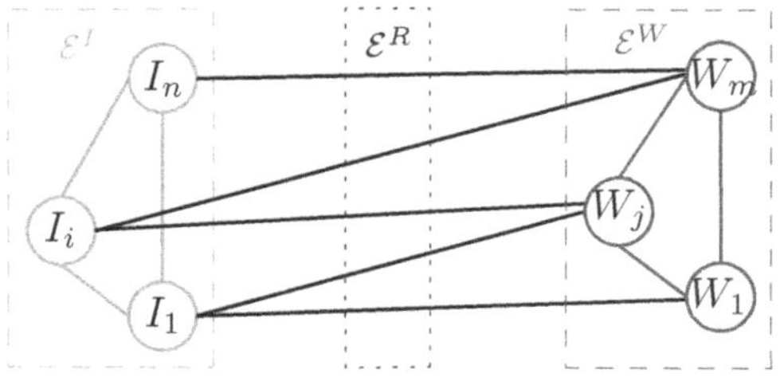

Figure 2: Heterogeneous graph over images and tags.

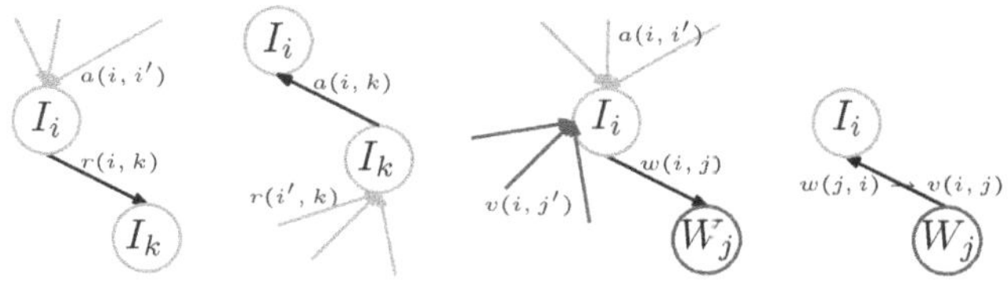

(a) $r(i, k)$ (b) $a(i, k)$ (c) $w(i, j)$ (d) $v(i, j)$

Figure 3: Illustration of message propagation.

tively monotonically by the probability that tags linking to image i serve as exemplars.

Heterogeneous message propagation

There are two kinds of message exchanged between images and tags. The "discardability" $w(i, j)$, sent from image i to tag j, which reflects how much it is affected that image i selects itself as its exemplar when the contribution of word j is discarded and helps tag j make better decision whether to select itself as its exemplar. The "contributability" $v(i, j)$, sent from tag j to image i, which reflects how well image i serves as an exemplar considering whether tag j is an exemplar. The two messages are updated as

$$\begin{aligned} w(i, j) &= r(i, i) + a(i, i) - v(i, j) \\ &= t(i, i) - v(i, j). \end{aligned} \tag{4}$$

$$\begin{aligned} v(i, j) =& \max\{p(i, j), q(i, j) + w(j, i)\} \\ & - \max\{\bar{q}(i, j), p(j, i) + w(j, i)\}. \end{aligned} \tag{5}$$

Here, in Eqn. (4), $r(i, i) + a(i, i) = t(i, i)$ is the belief that image i selects itself as its exemplar, and $w(i, j)$ aims to evaluate the affect degree if the contribution from tag j to image i is discarded and help tag j make better decision whether to select itself as its exemplar. In evaluating the contributability message $v(i, j)$ from tag j to image i in Eqn. (5), $w(j, i)$ means that the belief that tag j selects itself as its exemplar without considering the contribution from image i, and $q(i, j) + w(j, i)$ evaluates the contribution from tag j to the probability that image i serves as an exemplar. $\max\{p(i, j), q(i, j)+w(j, i)\}$ essentially means that the degree that image i serves as an exemplar whether tag j serves as an exemplar. Similarly, $\max\{\bar{q}(i, j), p(j, i) + w(j, i)\}$ means that the degree that image i does not serve as an exemplar whether tag j serves as an exemplar. Their difference, called contributability, hence can evaluate how well image i serves as an exemplar considering the contribution from tag j. $v(i, j) > 0$ means positive contribution from tag j, and negative contribution otherwise.

Exemplar assignment

The belief that image i selects image j as its exemplar is derived as the sum of the incoming messages,

$$t(i, j) = r(i, j) + a(i, j). \tag{6}$$

Then the exemplar of image i is taken as

$$\hat{c}_i = \arg\max_{j \in \mathcal{E}_i^I \cup \{i\}} t(i, j). \tag{7}$$

It should be noted that the heterogeneous relations are latently involved in assigning the exemplars because the responsibility $r(i, j)$ already counts the contribution from tags that is indicated in Eqn. (1) and Eqn. (2).

To summarize, H^2MP is an iterative algorithm, and at the beginning all the eight kinds of messages are initialized as 0, and the eight messages are repeatedly updated until the iteration number reaches T or the identified exemplars do not change. The algorithm is described in the following,

Algorithm 1 Hybrid summarization

1. Initialize all the 8 messages as 0.
2. Compute 4 homogeneous messages for images and tags according to Eqn. (1) and Eqn. (3).
3. Compute 4 heterogeneous messages between images and tags according to Eqn. (4) and Eqn. (5).
4. Repeat steps 2 and 3 till the iteration number reaches T or the identified exemplars do not change.
5. Make image exemplar assignments according to Eqn. (7).

2.2 Implementation

Similar to AP [8], the self-similarity $s_I'(i, i)$ of an image i, i.e., the preference of an image being an exemplar, is set as $\lambda\,\mathrm{Med}[s_I'(i, k)]$ with $\mathrm{Med}[s_I'(i, k)]$ being the median image similarity. λ is useful to control the exemplar number. For tags, we adopt the WordNet similarity [2], a variety of semantic similarity and relatedness measures based on a large lexical database of English, WordNet [3]. The self-similarities of words are similarly set.

Let's consider $p(i, j)$ in the heterogeneous message. $p(i, j)$ is the weight describing the case $c_i = i, b_j \neq j$, and $p(j, i)$ is the weight describing the case $c_i \neq i, b_j = j$. We set $p(i, j) = \theta/|\mathcal{E}_{i\cdot}^R|$, and $p(j, i) = \theta/|\mathcal{E}_{\cdot j}^R|$, where θ is a constant negative value, fixed as 15 in this paper, to control the mutual affect degree for image and tag exemplar identification, and the division by the tag number connecting image i, $|\mathcal{E}_{i\cdot}^R|$, aims to averagely separate its affect to connected tags. $q(i, j)$ and $\bar{q}(i, j)$ are the weights corresponding to the case $c_i \neq i, b_j \neq j$ and $c_i = i, b_j = j$.

3. EXPERIMENTS

In our experiment, we present the performance comparison of our approach with several relate approaches. This collection consists of about 11k images and associated tags and is crawled from the popular photo sharing Web site Flickr, using the queries, including flower, city, building, dog, cat, plants, mountain, river, sunset, and so on. We filter out some noisy tags that few images are associated with and finally get 816 tags. On average, each image has 6.1 tags and each tag is assigned to 15.9 images. We extract a GIST scene descriptor [13], which has been shown to work well for scene categorization, as the image feature with 3 by 3 spatial resolution where each bin contains that image region's average response to steerable filters at 6 orientations and 3 scales, and use the negative Euclidean distance as the image similarity.

We investigate the performances from both the visual and semantic perspectives. In the literature of image summarization and clustering, most evaluation criteria use the class labels of the images to test the performance. However, they are not adoptable for our hybrid summarization because hybrid summarization has multiple objectives, visual and sematic objectives and no simple la-

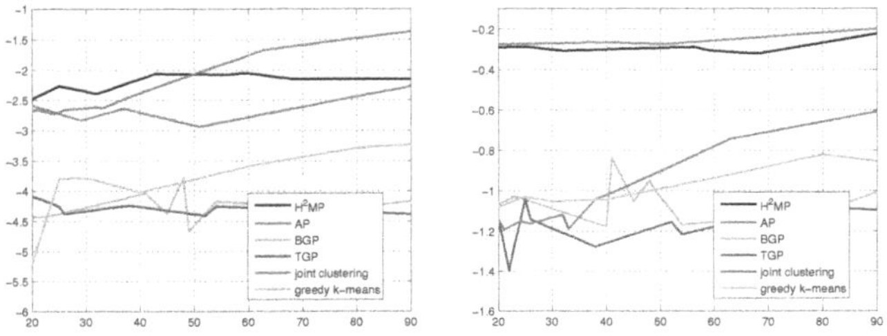

(a) (b)

Figure 4: Performance comparison. The x-axis represents the exemplar number, the y-axis in (a) and (b) represent the semantic exemplarness and visual exemplarness.

bels can be applied here. Instead, we present two straightforward measures, visual exemplarness and sematic exemplarness. Visual exemplarness is defined as the average value of visual similarities between each image and its corresponding exemplar, and semantic exemplarness is defined as the average value of textual similarities between the associated tags of each image and its corresponding exemplar.

We present a quantitative comparison of our approach (H^2MP) with several representative approaches, AP (affinity propagation [8]), BGP (Bipartite graph partitioning [6]), TGB (Tripartite graph partitioning [15]), and recently developed two methods: greedy k-means [18] and joint clustering [14]. Fig. 4(a) and Fig. 4(b) illustrate the performances of different approaches in terms of semantic and visual exemplarness with different number of exemplars.

For semantic exemplarness, H^2MP constantly outperforms the other approaches except the joint clustering approach [14] and its performance is a little worse than the joint clustering approach when the number of exemplars exceeds 50. This is understandable because our approach balances the visual and semantic performances while joint clustering generates results by taking intersection between the results using visual feature and text feature to cluster images, and hence may get superiority for semantic performance when the cluster number is very large. However, the performance for modest number of exemplars is more meaningful, because too many exemplars are not preferred in summarization. From this sense, our approach is more satisfactory in semantic performance.

For visual exemplarness, both AP and H^2MP show significant advantages over the other approaches. The visual performance of H^2MP is only a little worse than that of AP that purely uses visual feature, which is reasonable since our approach also takes into consideration the semantic information. In summary, H^2MP achieves satisfactory semantic and visual performance compared with other approaches.

4. CONCLUSION

In this paper, we present a hybrid image summarization scheme to manage image collections. Toward this end, we propose a novel approach, homogeneous and heterogeneous message propagation, which extends the affinity propagation algorithm from homogeneous data to heterogeneous data. The reduction from vector-valued messages to scalar-valued messages is more complicated than in affinity propagation because it involves additional heterogeneous relations and details can be found from [21]. The application of our approach to hybrid image summarization can effectively exploit image similarities, the association relations between images and tags and the relations within tags. The experimental results demonstrate its effectiveness and efficiency.

5. REFERENCES

[1] `http://picasaweb.google.com/.`

[2] `http://search.cpan.org/dist/WordNet-Similarity.`

[3] `http://wordnet.princeton.edu/.`

[4] `http://www.flickr.com/groups/.`

[5] R. Clough, H. Joho, and M. Sanderson. Automatically organising images using concept hierarchies. In *SIGIR Workshop on Multimedia Information Retrieval*, 2005.

[6] I. S. Dhillon. Co-Clustering Documents and Words using Bipartite Spectral Graph Partitioning. In *KDD*, pages 269–274, 2001.

[7] I. S. Dhillon, S. Mallela, and D. S. Modha. Information-Theoretic Co-Clustering. In *KDD*, pages 89–98, 2003.

[8] B. J. Frey and D. Dueck. Clustering by Passing Messages Between Data Points. *Science*, 315:972–976, February 2007.

[9] B. Gao, T.-Y. Liu, T. Qin, X. Zheng, Q. Cheng, and W.-Y. Ma. Web Image Clustering by Consistent Utilization of Visual Features and Surrounding texts. In *ACM Multimedia*, pages 112–121, 2005.

[10] A. Jaffe, M. Naaman, T. Tassa, and M. Davis. Generating Summaries for Large Collections of Geo-Referenced Photographs. In *WWW*, pages 853–854, 2006.

[11] Y. Jia, J. Wang, C. Zhang, and X.-S. Hua. Finding image exemplars using fast sparse affinity propagation. In *ACM Multimedia*, pages 639–642, 2008.

[12] T. Liu, J. Wang, J. Sun, N. Zheng, X. Tang, and H.-Y. Shum. Picture collage. *IEEE Transactions on Multimedia*, 11(7):1225–1239, 2009.

[13] A. Oliva and A. B. Torralba. Modeling the Shape of the Scene: A Holistic Representation of the Spatial Envelope. *International Journal of Computer Vision*, 42(3):145–175, 2001.

[14] R. Raguram and S. Lazebnik. Computing Iconic Summaries for General Visual Concepts. In *First IEEE Workshop on Internet Vision*, 2008.

[15] M. Rege, M. Dong, and J. Hua. Graph Theoretical Framework for Simultaneously Integrating Visual and Textual Features for Efficient Web Image Clustering. In *WWW*, pages 317–326, 2008.

[16] C. Rother, S. Kumar, V. Kolmogorov, and A. Blake. Digital Tapestry. In *CVPR (1)*, pages 589–596, 2005.

[17] P. Schmitz. Inducing Ontology from Flickr Tags. In *Proceedings of the Workshop on Collaborative Tagging at WWW*, 2006.

[18] I. Simon, N. Snavely, and S. M. Seitz. Scene Summarization for Online Image Collections. In *ICCV*, 2007.

[19] J. Wang, L. Jia, and X.-S. Hua. Interactive browsing via diversified visual summarization for image search results. *Multimedia Systems*, pages 1–13, 2010.

[20] J. Wang, J. Sun, L. Quan, X. Tang, and H.-Y. Shum. Picture Collage. In *CVPR (1)*, pages 347–354, 2006.

[21] J. Wang, H. Xu, X.-S. Hua, and S. Li. Hybrid image summarization. Technical report, MSR-TR-2010-176, 2010.

[22] H. Xu, J. Wang, X.-S. Hua, and S. Li. Summarizing tagged image collections by cross-media representativeness voting. In *ICME*, pages 922–925, 2009.

Multimodal Fusion for Video Copy Detection*

Xavier Anguera
Telefonica Research
Torre Telefonica Diagonal 00
08019 Barcelona, Spain
xanguera@tid.es

Juan Manuel Barrios
PRISMA Research Group
Department of Computer Science, University of Chile
jbarrios@dcc.uchile.cl

Tomasz Adamek
Telefonica Research
Torre Telefonica Diagonal 00
08019 Barcelona, Spain
tomasz@tid.es

Nuria Oliver
Telefonica Research
Torre Telefonica Diagonal 00
08019 Barcelona, Spain
nuriao@tid.es

ABSTRACT

Content-based video copy detection algorithms (CBCD) focus on detecting video segments that are identical or transformed versions of segments in a known video. In recent years some systems have proposed the combination of orthogonal modalities (e.g. derived from audio and video) to improve detection performance, although not always achieving consistent results. In this paper we propose a fusion algorithm that is able to combine as many modalities as available at the decision level. The algorithm is based on the weighted sum of the normalized scores, which are modified depending on how well they rank in each modality. This leads to a virtually parameter-free fusion algorithm. We performed several tests using 2010 TRECVID VCD datasets and obtain up to 46% relative improvement in min-NDCR while also improving the F1 metric on the fused results in comparison to just using the best single modality.

Categories and Subject Descriptors

H.3 [**Information Storage and Retrieval**]: Content Analysis and Indexing

General Terms

Algorithms

Keywords

Content-Based Video Copy Detection, Multimodal, Fusion

1. INTRODUCTION

Content-based video copy detection systems aim at finding video segments that are identical or transformed versions of segments in an known video. Joly et al. [4] propose a definition of video copy based on a subjective notion of tolerated transformations. A tolerated transformation is a function that creates a new version of a document where the original document "remains recognizable". CBCD systems perform the detection by processing visual and/or audio content of videos, ignoring any metadata and avoiding to embed watermarks into the original videos.

Traditionally, CBVCD systems have relied only on the visual information in the videos, driving research towards new features that allowed for scalable systems and fast retrieval. In recent years systems started incorporating features derived from the audio modality. Through the fusion of multimodal information, CBVCD systems can obtain improved performance levels and be more robust to errors (e.g. one of the modalities is severely damaged or missing in the video copy). An important step in the combination of multiple input streams (which can be more than two, including several system results from audio and from video) is how their fusion is performed. Typically, there are significant differences in how the different modalities internally produce their results. Hence, most systems perform the fusion at the decision level by combining the individual outputs.

In this paper we propose a novel weighted-sum decision-level multimodal fusion system that is able to effectively combine an unlimited number of monomodal outputs, consisting of lists of the best matches sorted by scores. The main strengths of the proposed approach are three-fold: (1) The use of a *flooring bias* on the individual output scores, combined with an area-preserving normalization, ensures that all individual modalities have an equivalent impact in the final scores, which is dependent on the ratio between the different matching segments; (2) the *rank* of each individual result is used as extra information in the fusion; (3) as a side result, the weights in the final sum of scores can be set to trivial values with no significant decrease in performance, therefore turning our system into virtually *parameter-free*.

2. MULTIMODAL FUSION APPROACHES

To the present day, most of the proposed combinations consist on the fusion at decision level. They can be classified into two, rather fuzzy, classes: rule-based fusion and weighted sum of the output scores.

On the one hand, rule-based fusion approaches apply some

*Area chair: Kiyoharu Aizawa

MM'11, November 28–December 1, 2011, Scottsdale, Arizona, USA.

heuristic rules to choose which of the results from each modality should be considered in the final results. Saracoglu et al. [11] return the single match with highest score between both modalities. Liang et al. [6] combine the multiple outputs from each modality either through the union (less restrictive) or the intersection (more restrictive and less prone to false alarms) of all results. Mukai et al. [9] obtain very good performance by considering the overlap between video matches in both modalities and giving priority to the audio results when selecting the output results.

On the other hand, many systems do a weighted sum of the scores obtained from each modality. Like in [6], Le et al. [5] apply the union/intersection of the two modalities, and then in the overlapping segments they apply a weighted sum of the scores with manually set weights (emphasizing the audio scores). One important step that is many times overlooked by the systems is the dynamic range of scores obtained by each modality, which makes direct comparison of system outputs difficult. Among the few systems that describe the scores normalization being applied are Narsev et al. [10] who normalize each modality by the median scores obtained on a development set, and Uchida et al. [13] who normalize scores by the second-best score in the resulting list of matches and then apply some rules for score boosting depending on how many modalities contain the same match.

Probably the closest work to our proposal is from Jegou et al. [3] who perform an initial normalization of the features and then combine them using a weighted sum with equal weight for each modality. In addition, they include a score weighting dependent on the ratio of each match with the best match in that modality. Our approach is different in that our normalization already takes into account the best-matching score and in addition we consider the position of the match within the ranked list in each modality.

3. MULTIMODAL VIDEO COPY DETECTION SYSTEM

In this section we briefly describe the parallel audio and video processing modules that run at the core of our system to obtain the outputs that are later fused with the proposed multimodal fusion algorithm. Each of the modules finds, for each given query, a list of up to N potential copies within a reference database, and returns the start-end times for both query and reference videos in the matching segment, and a score. Note that at this point the output range of the scores is not enforced to match in all cases, which will be dealt with by the fusion preprocessing step. The fusion system presented in this paper has been tested using the output of three individual modules: a global video module, a local video module and a local audio module. These modules were developed independently by two TRECVID 2010 participating teams and obtained good results individually.

3.1 Visual Global Features Module

The visual global features module was developed by PRISMA Research Group at the University of Chile [1]. It defines a distance between video segments as a weighted combination of global descriptors and uses a pivot-based indexing structure to perform approximate searches. It is divided in five tasks: Preprocessing (which tries to minimize the effect of visual transformations by normalizing video frames), Video Segmentation (which partitions every video into small segments of nearly $\frac{1}{3}$ seconds length), Feature Extraction (which represents each segment with the average Edge Histogram [7] and the average Gray Histogram), Approximate Search (which for every query segment performs an approximate k-NN search retrieving the most similar reference segments), and Copy Localization (which looks for chains of similar reference segments, and returns a list copy candidates each one with a location and a score).

3.2 Visual Local Features Module

The local visual features processing module was developed at Telefonica Research [14]. It compares all query keyframes with all reference keyframes using a state-of-the-art image retrieval engine relying on local features [8] and then combines the obtained ranked lists of matched keyframes into copied video segments by performing a temporal consistency post-processing. The module is divided in three tasks: Feature Extraction (which samples every video with one frame per second and extracts novel local features called DART [8]), Keyframe Matching (by using hierarchical dictionaries of visual words and inverted files to locate matching frames, which are then refined through a spatial verification stage), and Temporal Consistency (which computes the time differences between matches, and returns a list copy candidates each one with a location and a score).

3.3 Audio Local Features Module

The audio local features module was also developed at Telefonica Research [14]. Our implementation is similar to Philips [2]. First, the feature extraction computes the short-time FFT of the acoustic data every 10ms, converts the frequency bins into Mel scale, and codifies the first bands with a 15-bit fingerprint. Then we insert the data into a hash table and search for exact matches between query and reference information. Finally, a temporal consistency step (similar to the video one) is used to obtain the matching segments between videos.

4. MULTIMODAL FUSION ALGORITHM

Once all individual modules have computed their N_k-best matching results for any given query, the fusion module merges all these results into a single output ranking in order to a) reduce the false alarm rate from matches present in any of the outputs, and b) reduce the miss rate of any individual modality. The final result of the fusion algorithm is a ranked list of the N-best overall matches, together with their final score. Such scores are normalized to the range [0,1] to make it easier to later apply a copy decision threshold, regardless of how many (and which) modalities have been merged. The output of N_k-best results is convenient to compute optimal score curves, while in a real-case scenario we would only output those matches (if any) exceeding a given application-specific decision threshold.

The fusion algorithm performs two main tasks. First, it finds and merges the matching results coming from different modalities when they are in overlap. Then, it computes a final matching score for all segments, both the merged ones and also those coming from only one modality. When doing do, we take into account both the similarity score and the ranking obtained by the videos in each modality. Next we describe in detail each of the steps involved in the fusion.

4.1 Scores Preprocessing and Normalization

The inputs to the algorithm are the lists of N_k-best reference video matches from the available K input modalities for a given query, ordered by their matching score $S_k(r)$ $|r\epsilon\{1\dots N_k\}$, $k\epsilon\{1\dots K\}$. Note that the dynamic range of the scores for every modality does not need to be the same, but all need to represent a similarity, where value 0 represents an exact match. In the case that any of the input modalities is not able to return the same number of matches as the other modalities (*i.e.* $N_k < N$) it causes a potential problem as the following normalization steps would artificially emphasize these modalities more than the others. To void this problem we apply a preprocessing step, that we call N-best match flooring, which consists of adding a small value α to all scores, and extending the number of results to have $N_k = N$ output scores, as shown in Eq. 1. The value of α can be fixed for all modalities or set dynamically depending on their statistics. In our case we set $\alpha = 0.1$ for all cases.

$$S'_k(r) = \begin{cases} S_k(r) + \alpha & 1 \leq r \leq N_k \\ \alpha & N_k < r \leq N \end{cases} \quad (1)$$

Next, the matching scores of each modality k, $S'_k(r)$, are independently L1-normalized in order to make them comparable with each other. For each score in modality k we normalize it as $\hat{S}_k(r) = \frac{S'_k(r)}{\sum_{j=1}^{N} S'_k(r)}$. Note that the underlying distribution of scores within each modality remains intact with such normalization.

4.2 Fusion of Normalized Scores

After preprocessing all scores we fuse them by considering their ranking r within each modality, their normalized scores and the temporal limits.The parameters associated with each matching segment $c_k(r)$ in each of the computed modalities are: $c_k(r) = \{B_k^Q(r), E_k^Q(r), B_k^R(r), E_k^R(r), \hat{S}_k(r), I_k(r)\}$, where $B_k^Q(r) \dots E_k^R(r)$ are the start-end times of the matching segments both for query and reference videos, $\hat{S}_k(r)$ is the matching score and $I_k(r)$ is the ID of the reference video the segment matches with.

Given all matching segments found in the different modalities, in this step we want to create a set of L fused segments $C = \{c_1 \dots c_L\}$ containing both new segments created from the overlap of original segments in individual modalities and the rest of original matching segments that did not overlap with others. For any two matching segments $c_{k_1}(r_1)$ and $c_{k_2}(r_2)$ (or alternatively between a matching segment and a partially fused segment) we determine they are in overlap if $I_{k_1}(r_1) = I_{k_2}(r_2)$ and

$$\frac{\min\{E_k^Q(r), E_k^R(r)\} - \max\{B_k^Q(r), B_k^R(r)\}}{\max\{E_k^Q(r), E_k^R(r)\} - \min\{B_k^Q(r), B_k^R(r)\}} > 0.5$$

Note that the way that matches are retrieved in every individual modality makes it impossible to obtain multiple matches from the same modality in the same final segment. When two segments are in overlap we fuse their segment boundaries (both for query and reference) selecting as start time the minimum between all segments' start times, and as end time the maximum between all end times. Finally, given all matching segments $c_k(r)$ that have been fused into a c_l, we obtain the final score of c_l as

$$S(c_l) = \frac{\sum_{c_k(r)\epsilon c_l} W_k \cdot \frac{N_k - r + 1}{N_k} \cdot \hat{S}_k(r)}{\sum_{k=1}^{K}(W_k \cdot \hat{S}_k(1))} \quad (2)$$

where the ranking r of the segment within a given modality k affects the final score through the term $\frac{N_k - r + 1}{N_k}$, which is 1 for the best match and $\frac{1}{N_k}$ for the worst. Additionally, the term W_k is an optional weight parameter to manually emphasize some modalities versus others in the final score. As will be seen in the evaluation, we only use this parameter to balance the impact of the audio versus the video modalities. Note that the scores are normalized by the sum of all best matching scores for each modality $\hat{S}_k[1]$, such that fused segments lacking matching segments for some of the modalities will incur in some penalty, and also all scores will be in the $[0, 1]$ range.

Once all $S(c_l)$ have been computed, they are ranked and the matching clusters with the N-best scores are returned, discarding the rest. Alternatively, an application-dependent threshold could be used to output the matches (if any) that exceed its value.

5. EXPERIMENTS

We tested the suitability of the proposed algorithm using the content-based copy detection dataset used in the 2010 NIST TRECVID benchmarking campaign [12]. For a set of 11,256 query videos the task consists on finding whether (and which) portions appear in any in any of the 11,524 videos in the reference dataset. In the creation of the queries 8 possible video transformations and 7 possible audio transformations from the reference videos have been used.

To evaluate the performance we use the The Normalized Detection Cost Rate (NDCR) and the F1 score like in the TRECVID evaluations. Perfect results would obtain NDCR=0 and F1=1. In addition, we also report the percentage of videos with correct matches appearing within the N-best results, independently of their score. Even if some of these matches might have a low score and never be chosen without incurring in a very high false alarm rate, this metric gives an upper bound of the number of true positives that each system can achieve.

5.1 Experimental Results

We performed experiments both in the individual modalities and in all possible combinations of two and three modalities. Given that we fuse two video-based modalities with one audio modality, when combining all three modalities we decided to balance the contribution of audio and video by setting $W_k = 0.5$ for the video modalities. Otherwise we set $W_k = 1$. In all the experiments we set $N = 20$.

Table 1: *NDCR and F1 results for the combination of multiple modalities*

Output conmbination	Min NDCR	Opt F1	%hits
Local Audio (LA)	0.928	0.952	75.5%
Local Video (LV)	0.928	0.930	84.7%
Global Video (GV)	0.715	0.893	65.5%
LA + GV	0.664	0.954	93.3%
LV + GV	0.824	0.949	90.8%
LA + LV	**0.590**	0.950	91.9%
LA + LV + GV	0.598	**0.964**	96.9%

Table 1 presents the minimum NDCR, optimum F1 scores and the percentage of hits for all possible combinations of input modalities being considered. The first block of results show the scores for each modality output independently, namely for the local audio system (LA), the local video system (LV) and the global video system (GV). In the second and third blocks we do the proposed fusion in groups of two and three modalities, respectively.

In terms of the NDCR and F1 metrics (second and third columns on the Table), the global video system obtains significantly better NDCR results than any of the local features systems, but its F1 score is the lowest. This indicates that the matching start-end times for this modality are not as accurately found as in the other modalities. In the second block we observe that any combination of *audio and video* features yields a significant improvement in NDCR score over any individual modality. However, the NDCR score of the local and global video combination is worse than the best individual video result (GV). This result shows the correlation of the two approaches, even if they focus on different characteristics of the video modality. Still, the improvement in F1 score obtained when combining LV+GV makes it worthwhile to use the fusion. Similarly, the F1 score is already very good when using LA alone and remains similar when combining these with any of the video features.

Finally, the combination of all individual systems obtains a slightly worse NDCR score than the best combination of two modalities (LA + LV), while the F1 score obtains an important improvement.

In terms of (*%hits*), they progressively increases as more modalities are taken into account. This indicates that the fusion algorithm can incorporate and give higher scores to the useful information in each individual modality.

Table 2: *Overlap between matches in single modalities and LA+LV+GV*

	LA	LV	GV
total matches	5664	6349	4914
Shared with LA+LV+GV	99.9%	100%	99.8%
Only in LA+LV+GV	28.5%	14.4%	48.1%

Next we analyze how well the real matches get transferred from the N_k-best results on the individual modalities to the final N-best results, given that the final number of results is $\frac{1}{K}$ the size of the sum of results of all individual modalities. Table 2 shows the matches overlap between correct matches found by each individual modality (found within the N-best returned results) and by the combination of all three modalities. The first line in the table shows the number of total correct matches that each individual modality returns (local video is the one that returns the biggest number). The second line shows how many of these individual matches are present in the results from the fusion algorithm. We see how in all cases most matches found in the individual modalities are contained in the fused results. This ensures that our fusion system does incorporate correctly the information present in the individual modalities. Finally, for completeness purposes, we show the percentage of matches in the fusion results that do not appear in the individual modalities.

6. CONCLUSIONS AND FUTURE WORK

In this paper we propose a fusion algorithm for the combination of multiple modalities at the decision level. The final list of possible matches is obtained through the weighted sum of the normalized scores for each modality, modified depending on how well they rank in each modality. We perform extensive tests with the TRECVID 2010 dataset and show that the fused results improve by more than 46% relative the min-NDCR results. We also observe that the results are more stable in the multimodal system than in any of the multimodal modules. Finally, we show that the F1 scores improve when considering multiple overlapping segments. Future work will include testing the proposed approach with more monomodal processing outputs to see whether our conclusions hold for more than 3 modalities, and to further investigate the role that different modalities and features play on the CBCD task.

7. REFERENCES

[1] J. M. Barrios and B. Bustos. Content-based video copy detection: PRISMA at trecvid 2010. In *Proc. NIST-TRECVID Workshop*, 2010.

[2] J. Haitsma and T. Kalker. A highly robust audio fingerprinting system. In *Proc. ISMIR*, 2002.

[3] H. Jegou, M. Douze, G. Gravier, C. Schmid, and P. Gros. INRIA LEAR-TEXMEX: Video copy detection task. In *Proc. NIST-TRECVID Workshop*, 2010.

[4] A. Joly, O. Buisson, and C. Frélicot. Content-based copy retrieval using distortion-based probabilistic similarity search. *IEEE Trans. on Multimedia*, 9(2):293–306, 2007.

[5] D.-D. Le, S. Poullot, M. Crucianu, X. Wu, M. Nett, M. E. Houle, and S. Satoh. National institute of informatics, japan at TRECVID 2009. In *Proc. NIST-TRECVID Workshop*, 2009.

[6] Y. Liang, B. Cao, J. Li, C. Zhu, Y. Zhang, C. Tan, G. Chen, C. Sun, J. Yuan, M. Xu, and B. Zhang. THU-ING at TRECVID 2009. In *Proc. NIST-TRECVID Workshop*, 2009.

[7] B. S. Manjunath, J.-R. Ohm, V. V. Vasudevan, and A. Yamada. Color and texture descriptors. *IEEE Trans. on Circuits and Systems for Video Tech.*, 11(6):703–715, 2001.

[8] D. Marimon, A. Bonnin, T. Adamek, and R. Gimeno. DARTs: Efficient scale-space extraction of daisy keypoints. In *Proc. CVPR*, 2010.

[9] R. Mukai, T. Kurozumi, K. Hiramatsu, T. Kawanishi, H. Nagano, and K. Kashiro. NTT communications science laboratories at TRECVID 2010 content-based copy detection. In *Proc. NIST-TRECVID Workshop*, 2010.

[10] A. Narsev, S. Bao, J. Chang, M. Hill, M. Merler, J. R. Smith, D. Wang, L. Xie, R. Yan, and Y. Zhang. IBM research TRECVID-2009 video retrieval system. In *Proc. NIST-TRECVID Workshop*, 2009.

[11] A. Saracoglu, E. Esen, T. Ates, B. O. Acar, U. Zubari, E. C. Ozan, E. Ozalp, A. A. Alatan, and T. Ciloglu. Content based copy detection with coarse audio-visual fingerprints. In *Proc. CBMI*, pages 213–218, June 2009.

[12] A. F. Smeaton, P. Over, and W. Kraaij. Evaluation campaigns and trecvid. In *MIR*, pages 321–330, New York, NY, USA, 2006. ACM Press.

[13] Y. Uchida, S. Sakazawa, M. Agrawal, and M. Akbacak. KDDI labs and SRI international at trecvid 2010: Content-based copy detection. In *Proc. NIST-TRECVID Workshop*, 2010.

[14] E. Younessian, X. Anguera, T. Adamek, N. Oliver, and D. Marimon. Telefonica research at trecvid 2010 content-based copy detection. In *Proc. NIST-TRECVID Workshop*, 2010.

Pedestrian Detection with Geometric Context from a Single Image *

Junqiang Wang, Huadong Ma
Beijing Key Laboratory of Intelligent Telecommunications Software and Multimedia,
Beijing University of Posts and Telecommunications, Beijing 100876, China
boyjunqiang@gmail.com, mhd@bupt.edu.cn

ABSTRACT

We address the problem of pedestrian detection in still images. Many current pedestrian detection systems limit their performance by ignoring the underlying 3D geometric context in the image. We can estimate the geometric context by learning appearance-based method. We propose a novel context feature and local integrable features. These features are used for building many candidate weak classifiers by using linear SVM. Finally, MPL-Boost method selects the best weak classifiers suited for detection and construct the rejector-based cascade detector. We provide a thorough quantitative evaluation of our method on TUD-Brussels dataset and demonstrate that it outperforms the state-of-the-art pedestrian detector in recall rate, meanwhile, shows faster speed than other context incorporation method.

Categories and Subject Descriptors

I.4.8 [**Image Processing and Computer Vision**]: Scene Analysis—*object recognition*; I.4.9 [**Image Processing and Computer Vision**]: Applications; I.5.4 [**Pattern Recognition**]: Applications—*computer vision, signal processing*

General Terms

Algorithms, Design, Experimentation

Keywords

Pedestrian detection, Multi-pose learning boost, Intersection kernel SVM, Geometric context

1. INTRODUCTION

The ability to automatically detect pedestrians in images is key to a number of application domains such as surveillance and intelligent vehicles. However, because of variations of clothing, pose, lighting conditions, and cluttered backgrounds, the task of pedestrian detection is challenging.

*Area chair: Bernard Merialdo

MM'11, November 28–December 1, 2011, Scottsdale, Arizona, USA.

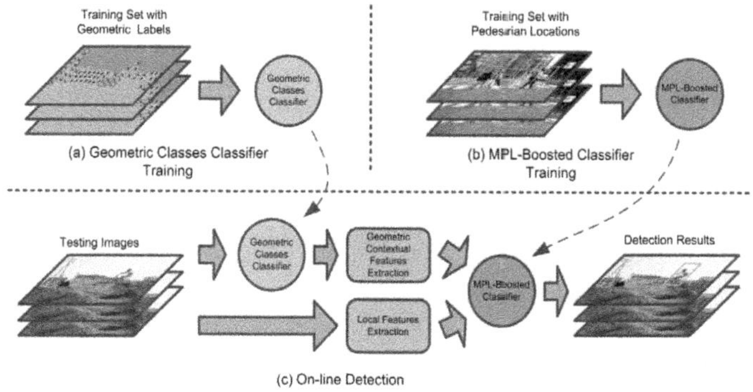

Figure 1: An illustration of the proposed system.

Currently popular object detection methods [2, 10, 8] try to recognize objects using local information alone, which assume that all useful information about an object is contained within the detection window in the image. The detection window is scanning over all locations and scales to find the target. However, that may lead to error - car will not fly in the sky. Learning from human vision, there is strong evidence that context plays an important role in object detection [7], so we must consider the context of entire image for the detection task.

In contrast, our method combines local features with geometric context features to improve the detection performance. As we can see in the Figure 1, we take the first steps toward building the geometric classes map by adopting a technique to estimate the orientations of surfaces from a single image, then a novel feature extraction method is applied on the map to extract many context features. These context features will combine with local features to build many candidate weak classifiers by using linear SVM. Finally, we use MPL-Boost [1] method to select the best weak classifiers suited for detection and build the rejector-based cascade detector.

2. RELATED WORK

Dalal & Triggs [2] presented a well-known overlapped and dense local descriptor, Histograms of Oriented Gradients (HOG), to represent a detection window. Zhu *et al* [10] combined the AdBoost with weak linear SVM classifier of variable-size blocks. The cascade strategy speeds up processing time more than 70 times. Wang *et al* [8] proposed an HOG-LBP detector. Although above methods have succeeded in some detection tasks, geometric context, which

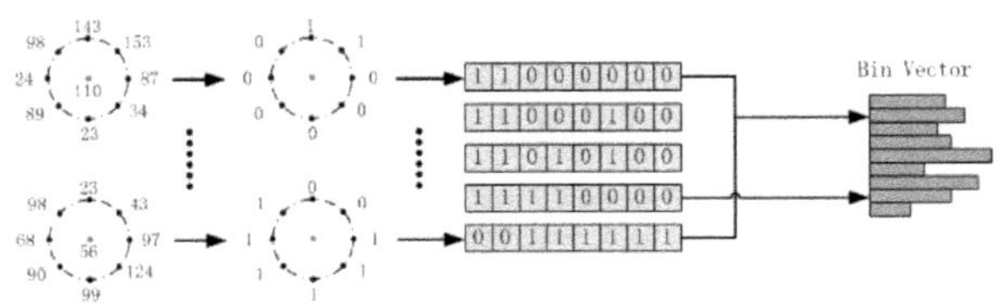

Figure 2: S-LBP feature extraction process.

can further improve the representation effectiveness and efficiency, is not fully investigated in these works.

Several researchers have recently begun to consider the use of contextual information for object detection. The work of Torralba et al. [6] got a sense of the viewpoint and mean scene depth, which provides a useful prior for object detection. Hoiem et al. [5] proposed a mechanism for estimating rough 3D scene geometry from a single image and use this information as extra features to improve object detection. Although above methods have succeeded in improving detection performance by incorporating context, the processing speed and contextual features optimizing, is not fully investigated in these works.

3. LOCAL FEATURES

To form local features, we take the notion of integral channel features [3], and use different types of Channel Generation Function (CGF) [3], including a novel simplified local binary pattern (S-LBP), LUV color, gradient histograms, and gradient magnitude.

We define two types of feature for different CGFs. (1) *First feature type is for S-LBP*, which is defined as a weighted histogram where bin index is determined by LBP pattern and weight by the amount of the specific pattern in a rectangular region. (2) *Second feature type is for other CGFs*, which is defined as a sum of pixels in a fixed rectangular region in the result image of CGF [3]. We can produce many features by adjusting the location, size and aspect ratios of rectangular regions. In order to improve calculation speed of these features, we adopt the notion of integral image.

1) Simplified Local Binary Pattern (S-LBP) Histogram: We build LBP feature similar to [8], but we simplify the classical LBP feature by treating every uniform bit pattern equally to its bit inverse representation (see Figure 2). Exceptions are the two bit patterns 00000000 and 11111111 which are highly discriminative and very common in real world images. The use of inversion operation on 56 of 58 patterns leaves us with $(58 - 2)/2 + 2 = 30$ values to sort into bins (see Figure 2). For each bin we use an integral image for quick calculation.

2) Gradient Magnitude: We compute gradients by convolving simple centered mask $M_x = [-1, 0, 1]$ with image I in x direction $G_x(x, y) = M_x * I$ and mask $M_y = [-1, 0, 1]^T$ in y direction $G_y(x, y) = M_y * I$. The gradient magnitude at the point (x, y) is $G(x, y) = \sqrt{G_x(x, y)^2 + G_y(x, y)^2}$.

3) Gradient Histograms: A gradient histogram is a weighted histogram where bin index is determined by gradient angle and weighted by gradient magnitude. The gradient angle can be computed via the following formula:

$$O(x, y) = \arctan\left(G_x(x, y)/G_y(x, y)\right) \tag{1}$$

Let $\Theta(x, y)$ denote quantized gradient angle of $O(x, y)$, θ denotes possible gradient angles of $\Theta(x, y)$. R_θ for every θ is $R_\theta(x, y) = G(x, y) \cdot \mathbf{1}[\Theta(x, y) = \theta]$, where $G(x, y)$ is the gradient magnitude at $I(x, y)$. By default, 8 gradient angles are used. We use binary search to approximate the angle of a 2D vector by finding the maximum value of its dot product with vectors spaced uniformly along a unit circle.

4) LUV Color: A appropriate color space can provide useful cue for pedestrian detection. We use LUV color in our method. Because the bottleneck of LUV color transform is cube root computation, so we use a fast estimate [3].

4. CONTEXTUAL FEATURES

We propose a context encoding method, which is inspired by the work of Hoiem *et al.* [5].

As shown in Figure 3, the first step is to apply the over-segmentation method of Felzenszwalb *et al.* [4] to obtain a set of "superpixels". Each superpixel is assumed to correspond to a single label. Multiple segmentation hypotheses based on different kinds of features are evaluated to form multiple potential groupings of superpixels. Finally, the final geometric labels are estimated by using the logistic regression version of Adaboost. The superpixel label confidences are determined by averaging the label likelihoods of the regions that contain it, weighted by the homogeneity likelihoods:

$$C\left(y_i = v|\mathbf{x}\right) = \sum_{j}^{n_h} P\left(y_i = v|\mathbf{x}, \mathbf{h}_{ji}\right) P\left(\mathbf{h}_{ji}|\mathbf{x}\right) \tag{2}$$

where C is the label confidence, y_i is the superpixel label, v is a possible label value, $\mathbf{x}$ is the image data, n_h is the number of hypotheses, $\mathbf{h}_{ji}$ defines the region that contains the ith superpixel for the jth hypothesis, and y_j is the region label. The sum of the label likelihoods for a region and the sum of the homogeneity likelihoods for all regions containing a particular superpixel are normalized to sum to one.

However, there exist two problems in [5]: **1)** the processing speed is slow, which take 30 seconds for a 640×480 image by using a 2.13GHz CPU. **2)** the contextual features, which used by object detection, are computed on some prefixing window regions. So these features are not well encoding the contextual information. So we improve their method in two major aspects:

1) Combining the contextual features extraction and local features extraction: For texture feature calculation of [5], we use S-LBP feature, rather than DOOG filters, because computing speed of DOOG filter is slow. For color feature calculation of [5], the HSV color is replaced by LUV color. Because the S-LBP feature and the LUV color feature are also used in local features extraction, so these features do not need double-counting, which is help to improve the computing speed of the entire detection.

2) Using multiple candidate Haar-like features: During object detection phase, the contextual features used by Hoiem *et al.* [5] are the average confidence for the object window region (center), average confidences for the windows above and below the object, and the above-center and below-center differences for each geometric classes. Since the locations and types of feature are prefixed by hand, it can't be the optimized selection. To optimize the feature selection, we built multiple candidate Haar-like features computed on top of the confidence map of geometric regions.

(a) Input (b) Superpixels (c) Geometric Labels

Figure 3: To obtain geometric classes, we build structural knowledge of the image: from pixels(a), to superpixels (b), to the final geometric labels(c).

We use two kinds of candidate features for each geometric class: first-order features and higher-order features. The first-order features are the average confidence for rectangular regions in the object window region or near the object window region. Higher-order features are defined as any feature that can be computed by using multiple first-order features (e.g., the difference of two first-order features). The features are extremely fast to compute by using integral image. We produce many features by adjusting the location, size and aspect ratios of rectangular regions. Then we use Adaboost classifier to select most discriminative subset of these features. During detection, only those features in the discriminative subset are computed.

5. DETECTION WITH MPL-BOOST

Local features and contextual features form the Candidate Features Pool (CFP) which are used for building a large number of candidate weak classifiers by using linear SVM [10]. Finally, MPL-Boost [1] method selects the best weak classifiers suited for detection and construct the rejector-based cascade detector. We will give a short description of our learning method.

We simultaneously learn K strong classifiers, while the response to an input pattern is given as the maximum response of all K strong classifiers. We are given n samples $x_i \in \Re^n_+$ and n corresponding labels $y_i \in \{-1, +1\}$. We assume that there are K latent variables $y_i^k \in \{-1, +1\}$ associated with each sample. Each latent variable defines membership to one of the K groups. A sample is considered positive if it belongs to at least one of these groups, which can be expressed as $y_i = \max_k \left(y_i^k\right)$.

Our goal is to simultaneously split the positive data into K groups and train K classifiers $h^1, ..., h^K$, one per group, so that $\max_k \left(h^k(x_i)\right) = y_i$. In our experiment, the number of groups K is 4. We define the probability $p_i^k \equiv p^k(y_i = 1|x_i)$ according to a single classifier h^k as $p_i^k = \sigma\left(2h_i^k\right)$, where $h_i^k = h^k(x_i)$. Given all the classifiers, we define the probability $p_i \equiv p(y_i = 1|x_i)$ as the maximum over the probabilities p_i^k. Consider $\mathbf{h}$ as an n-vector whose i^{th} component h_i has the value $h(x_i)$. The loss Γ is a function over $\mathbf{h}$.

$$\Gamma(\mathbf{h}) = -\sum_{i=1}^{n} \left(\mathbf{1}(y_i = 1)\log\, p_i + \mathbf{1}(y_i = -1)\log(1 - p_i)\right)$$

The training algorithm is summarized in Algorithm 1. We optimize $\Gamma(\mathbf{h})$ by coordinate descent, cycling through k, where in each phase we train weak linear SVM classifier by using randomly selected features in CFP. h_t^k use weights $\left|w_i^k\right|$ and add the weak classifier to h^k while keeping all other weak classifiers fixed.

Algorithm 1 Training the cascade

for $t = 1$ to T **do**
  for $k = 1$ to K **do**
    Compute weights $w_i^k = -\frac{\partial \Gamma}{\partial h_i^k}$
    Train weak linear SVM classifier h_t^k by using randomly selected features in CFP using weights $\left|w_i^k\right|$
    Find a_t via line search to minimize $\Gamma\left(\cdot, h^k, \cdot\right)$
      $a_t = \arg\min_a \Gamma\left(\cdot, h^k + a h_t^k, \cdot\right)$
    Update strong classifier $h^k \leftarrow h^k + a_t^k h_t^k$.
  end for
end for

6. EXPERIMENTS

For following experiments, we randomly generate 6000 candidate local features and 1000 candidate contextual features. We train our cascade classifier by using MPL-Boost on the resulting representation with 2000 weak SVM classifiers. Negative windows are generated by training the default classifier with 6000 random negative windows, bootstrapping 6000 hard negative windows, and repeating the entire process twice.

6.1 Dataset

Our test set is the publicly available TUD-Brussels [9] dataset. The set contains 508 image pairs at a resolution of 640×480 with overall 1326 annotated pedestrians. The wide variety of object pose, size and the frequency of occlusions make detection extremely challenging.

6.2 Results

We use a sliding window over multiple scales. The scale step is $2^{\frac{1}{10}}$. Non-maximal suppression (NMS) is used to suppress multiple nearby detections. As baseline classifiers, we evaluate the HOG with linear SVM approach of [2], the Adboost cascade of HOG with L1 norm approach of [10], the Integral HOG-LBP approach of [8] and the method of [5], which combined HOG with context. We call them HOG, Adboost HOG, HOG-LBP, and Context HOG respectively in our experiment.

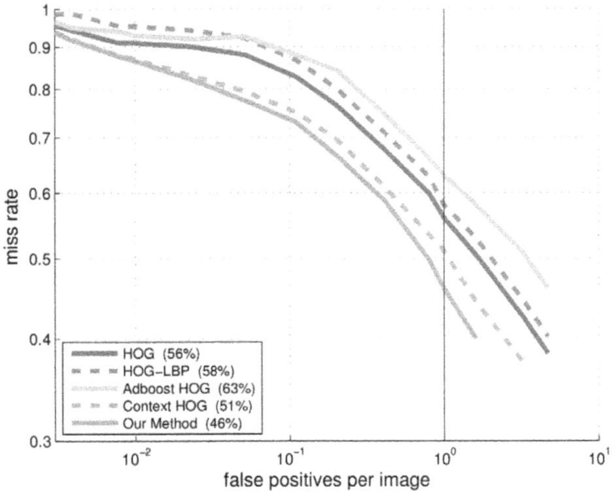

Figure 4: Performance on TUD-Brussels dataset.

Table 1: Time Required for a 640×480 Image

Methods	800 windows per image	12800 windows per image
Context HOG [5]	18sec	61sec
Our method	5sec	17sec

The results in terms of miss rate-FPPI performance are given in Figure 4. The best performance is reached by our method, which is 54% detection rate at 1 FPPI. The HOG classifier achieves 44% detection rate. It seems we could not gain anything with LBP feature on this dataset. Compared to HOG classifier, the HOG-LBP gives slightly worse performance, which is 42% detection rate. The AdBoost HOG achieves worst performance which only gives 37% detection rate. The method of [5] adds geometric context to HOG classifier, and improves the performance of HOG classifier by 5%.

We only compare the processing time to [5] (because other method [2, 10, 8] not incorporate contextual information, which will lead to unfair comparison). The average time (on a PC with a 2GHz Dual-core CPU) required to evaluate a 640×480 image is summarized in Table 1. Our method only needs 5-second for a sparse scan. It's almost 4 times faster than Context HOG. Some sample detections are shown in Figure 5

Figure 5: Sample detections on the TUD-Brussels dataset and other dataset. True positives are green, false positives are red.

7. CONCLUSIONS AND FUTURE WORKS

In this paper, we proposed an pedestrian detection method, which incorporated geometric context from a single image. Experimental results have validated the effectiveness of the method, which shows that our method can reach more than 54% detection rate at 1 FPPI on TUD-Brussels dataset, which is much higher than the performance of HOG and HOG-LBP methods. Our method improves the performance by 5% relative to other detector that with context, meanwhile, improves the processing speed almost 4 times.

Since the geometric contextual feature computation is still the computation bottleneck of our detector, we will further investigate speeding methods.

ACKNOWLEDGMENT: The research reported in this paper was supported in part by the National 973 Project of China under Grant No.2011CB302700; the National Natural Science Foundation of China under Grant No.60833009, No.60903072, and No.61003280; the National Science Fund for Distinguished Young Scholars under Grant No.60925010.

8. REFERENCES

[1] B. Babenko, P. Dollár, Z. Tu, and S. Belongie. Simultaneous learning and alignment: Multi-instance and multi-pose learning. In *ECCV workshop on Faces in Real-Life Images*, 2008.

[2] N. Dalal and B. Triggs. Histograms of oriented gradients for human detection. In *IEEE International Conference on Computer Vision and Pattern Recognition*, volume 1, pages 886–893, 2005.

[3] P. Dollár, Z. Tu, and P. Perona. Integral channel features. In *Proceedings of the British Machine Vision Conference*, 2009.

[4] P. F. Felzenszwalb and D. P. Huttenlocher. Efficient Graph-Based Image Segmentation. *International Journal of Computer Vision*, 59(2):167–181, Sept. 2004.

[5] D. Hoiem and A. Efros. Geometric context from a single image. *IEEE International Conference on Computer Vision*, 2005.

[6] A. Torralba. Contextual Priming for Object Detection. *International Journal of Computer Vision*, 53(2):169–191, 2003.

[7] A. Torralba. Contextual Influences on Saliency. *Neurobiology of Attention*, pages 586–593, 2005.

[8] X. Wang, T. Han, and S. Yan. An HOG-LBP human detector with partial occlusion handling. In *IEEE International Conference on Computer Vision*, pages 32–39, 2010.

[9] C. Wojek, S. Walk, and B. Schiele. Multi-cue onboard pedestrian detection. In *IEEE International Conference on Computer Vision and Pattern Recognition*, pages 794–801, 2009.

[10] Q. Zhu, M. Yeh, K. Cheng, and S. Avidan. Fast human detection using a cascade of histograms of oriented gradients. In *IEEE International Conference on Computer Vision and Pattern Recognition*, volume 2, pages 1491–1498, 2006.

Risk Management for Video-on-Demand Servers leveraging Demand Forecast *

Di Niu, Hong Xu, Baochun Li
Department of Electrical and Computer Engineering
University of Toronto
{dniu, henryxu, bli}@eecg.toronto.edu

Shuqiao Zhao
Multimedia Development Group
UUSee, Inc.
shuqiao.zhao@gmail.com

ABSTRACT

Video-on-demand (VoD) servers are usually over-provisioned for peak demands, incurring a low average resource efficiency. However, bandwidth shortage may still occur for individual videos as they share and contend for server resources. In this position paper, we propose a predictive workload management system for VoD servers targeting bandwidth. The system draws belief about future demand as well as demand volatility based on demand history using time series forecasting techniques. The prediction enables dynamic and efficient server bandwidth reservation with QoS guarantees. More importantly, we use a hedging technique similar to investment portfolio management and distribute workloads to multiple servers exploiting demand anti-correlation. The proposed system consolidates the workloads, enhances resource utilization, while in the meantime effectively controlling risk of server overload. The proposed methods are evaluated based on real-world VoD traces.

Categories and Subject Descriptors

C.2.3 [**Network Operations**]: Network Management; Network Monitoring; C.4 [**Performance of Systems**]: Modeling Techniques

General Terms

Algorithms, Measurement, Performance, Reliability

Keywords

Video-on-Demand, Risk Management, Hedging, Demand Prediction, Bandwidth Reservation

1. INTRODUCTION

A large-scale Video on Demand (VoD) system involves millions of users watching movies, TV episodes and other videos streamed from a huge library of video channels. As a user must download at a rate no smaller than the video playback rate to watch a video smoothly, bandwidth constitutes the performance bottleneck in these systems. VoD servers therefore require abundant egress bandwidth as well as disk I/O speed to read and deliver video continuously.

VoD server capacity is usually overly provisioned for the anticipated peak demand, incurring low utilization during non-peak hours. Despite over-provision, bandwidth shortage can still occur for an individual video, if the instantaneous demand for it exceeds the aggregate capacity of the servers hosting the video. Undoubtedly, in the presence of demand fluctuation and uncertainty, one challenge facing all VoD services is to economically plan the capacity, minimizing unnecessary over-provision costs while in the meantime controlling risk of under-provision or server overload.

Dynamic *bandwidth reservation*, if realized, can enhance resource efficiency and control quality at the same time, because now we can limit the server bandwidth dedicated for each video channel, allowing efficient and safe use of the remaining idle bandwidth by other channels or applications. Specifically, if the bandwidth reserved for a channel exceeds the demand for it, other channels/applications can use the unreserved bandwidth or the idle part in the reserved bandwidth. On the other hand, if the demand for the channel exceeds the reserved bandwidth, the aggregate downloading rate of the video will be capped by the reserved bandwidth. The above bandwidth reservation function can be readily implemented with software rate limiting at network interfaces of servers.

Apparently, there is a tradeoff between QoS and resource efficiency: when more bandwidth is reserved, the risk of shortage is lowered, yet the unreserved bandwidth that can be promised for other purposes is reduced undesirably. Therefore, an important research problem is to judiciously decide the right amount of server bandwidth to be reserved for each channel as demand evolves, with two major challenges. First, bandwidth reservation must be predictive instead of reactive, since when bandwidth shortage occurs in a channel, a delay is needed to replicate the video to other servers in order to increase the capacity available for this video. With the presence of configuration and replication delays, a reactive scheme is too slow to match demand changes closely. Second, since video servers are usually distributed, decisions have to made regarding how to split the workload among multiple servers as well as where to place the content.

In this paper, from a novel perspective, we view the bandwidth demand for each video in short-term future as a random variable with predictable mean and variance, just as

*Area chair: Reza Rejaie

MM'11, November 28–December 1, 2011, Scottsdale, Arizona, USA.

investments in financial markets are assumed to have an expected return subject to random risks. We propose to book bandwidth for video channels that accommodates not only their projected mean demands but also the demand variation. We formulate a mean-variance optimization problem through which each server consolidates workloads based on demand anti-correlation, by maximizing the expected demand it can serve while confining the probability of server overload to a small threshold. Such a formulation is inspired by investment diversification theory [5], according to which, a stock investor chooses a diversified portfolio of stocks to minimize her return uncertainty given a certain expected return level. However, we modify such a portfolio theory to adapt to our scenario of video server management. Before introducing our workload portfolio management framework, we also briefly mention how to make prediction about demand statistics using seasonal ARIMA models [7] and GARCH models [2], widely used in econometrics.

The resulted workload management system makes decisions with respect to bandwidth reservation, content placement, and load direction, which are updated at 10-minute frequency and readily implementable in real-world systems. Trace-driven simulations show that, our algorithm can enhance utilization of the reserved bandwidth resource while providing probabilistic service guarantees to users.

2. SYSTEM OVERVIEW

We propose a predictive and adaptive workload management system that works periodically at 10-minute frequency, alternating between phases of *demand estimation* and *workload management.* Suppose there are N video channels and S (possibly distributed) servers.

In the demand estimation phase, we monitor the total number of bytes streamed from servers in each video channel i in each 10-minute period, from which the average bandwidth demand of channel i is calculated. Based on demand history, the expected bandwidth requirement of each channel in the next 10 minutes is predicted. Demand prediction is fundamentally backed up by the fact that the population in a video channel follows diurnal evolution [7]. The system not only forecasts the expected demand, but also outputs a *volatility* estimate which represents the degree that the demand may fluctuate around its expectation, as well as the demand *correlation* between different channels.

We illustrate demand forecast using real-world traces. Our demand traces come from UUSee [4], an operational large-scale VoD service based in China. The dataset contains bandwidth demands in UUSee video channels sampled every 10 minutes during 2008 Summer Olympics. We make 10-minutes-ahead (one-step-ahead) prediction of bandwidth demand $\{S_t\}$ in a typical video channel released at time period $t_0 = 264$ (2008-08-10 10:47:39) in UUSee [1, 4]. The channel has a maximum online population of 2664. The bandwidth consumption series of the first 1.25 days is used as the training data starting from time period 81. The initial 80 time periods are excluded which may not conform to later evolution patterns. We use the seasonal ARIMA model [7] to predict the expected bandwidth demand in each time period. The test period is the 3 days following the training period. Fig. 1(a) shows the prediction results, with zero-mean prediction errors plotted in Fig. 1(b). We further use the GARCH model elaborated in [6] to predict demand variation around its mean. Fig. 1(c) shows the estimated

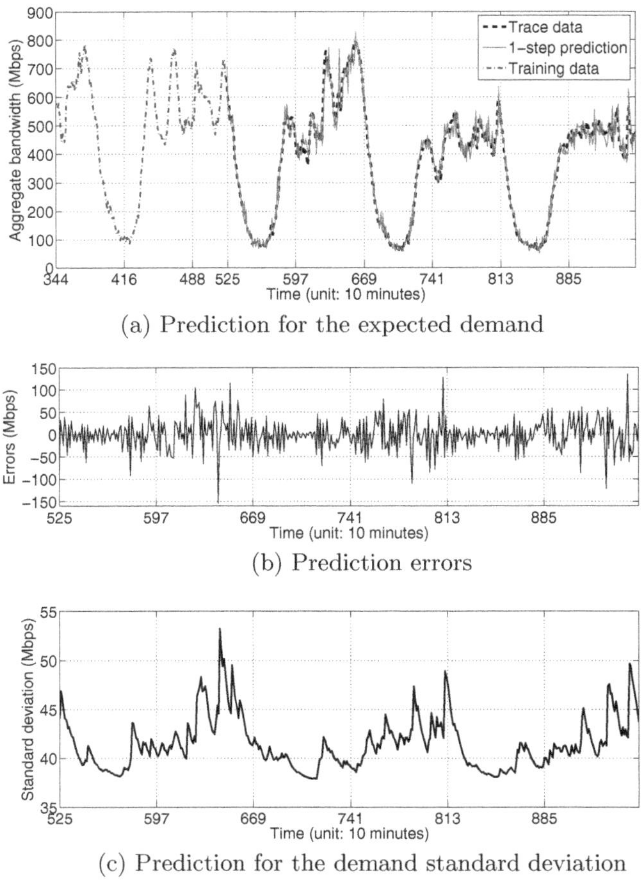

(a) Prediction for the expected demand

(b) Prediction errors

(c) Prediction for the demand standard deviation

Figure 1: 10-minutes-ahead prediction for bandwidth demand S_t in a popular UUSee video channel.

time-varying demand standard deviation relative to its expectation. It will be clear that the reserved bandwidth for a workload will be its expected demand plus a risk premium depending on the demand variation.

In the workload management phase, the system takes the predicted statistics about future demands as the input and generates a *load direction matrix* $\mathbf{W} = [w_{si}]$, where w_{si} represents the proportion of channel i's workload directed to server s. The output matrix $\mathbf{W}$ essentially corresponds to a joint decision of bandwidth reservation, content placement and load direction, updated every 10 minutes. If a server s has $w_{si} = 0$ for all i, the server is not employed. Thus, the total number of servers used can be determined from $\mathbf{W}$. Moreover, video i is replicated to server s only if $w_{si} > 0$, constituting a content placement decision. Apparently, we have $\sum_s w_{si} = 1$ if the aggregate server capacity is sufficient. In practice, load direction matrix $\mathbf{W}$ can be readily implemented by routing the requests for video channel i to server s with probability w_{si}.

Afterwards, the system proceeds to demand estimation again for the next 10 minutes. It strives to ensure probabilistic service guarantees so that the load imposed on each server does not exceed its bandwidth capacity with a high probability, *e.g.*, 0.98. Under quantitatively confined risks, the system aims to reserve as little bandwidth as possible to enhance resource efficiency. This is achieved by consolidating workloads onto multiple servers based on anti-correlation through mean-variance optimization.

3. WORKLOAD MANAGEMENT

In this section, we focus on using demand statistics and predictions to guide workload management to enhance utilization while hedging server overload risk. Suppose before time t, we have obtained the estimates about demands in the coming $\Delta t = 10$ minutes. Our objective is to decide load direction matrix $\mathbf{W}$ so as to minimize total bandwidth reservation while confining risk of overload at each server.

We first introduce a few useful notations. Recall that N denotes the number of videos in the system. Let random variable D_i denote the bandwidth demand for video i, with estimated expectation $\mu_i = \mathbf{E}[D_i]$ and variance $\sigma_i^2 = \mathbf{Var}[D_i]$, $i = 1, \ldots, N$. Note that the random demands $D_1, \ldots, D_N$ may be highly correlated due to the correlation between video genres, viewer preferences and video release times. Denote ρ_{ij} the correlation coefficient of D_i and D_j, with $\rho_{ii} \equiv 1$. For convenience, let $\boldsymbol{\mu} = [\mu_1, \ldots, \mu_N]^\mathsf{T}$, and $\mathbf{\Sigma} = [\sigma_{ij}]$ be the $N \times N$ symmetric covariance matrix with $\sigma_{ii} = \sigma_i^2$ and $\sigma_{ij} = \rho_{ij}\sigma_i\sigma_j$ for $i \neq j$.

Consider S available servers in the system. Denote C_s the upper bound on bandwidth capacity available on server s, $s = 1, \ldots, S$. C_s may be limited by the egress bandwidth capacity of server s. It can also be manually configured to spread the workload across multiple servers and avoid booking bandwidth from a single server.

Recall that the load direction matrix is denoted $\mathbf{W} = [w_{si}]$, $s = 1, \ldots, S$, $i = 1, \ldots, N$, where w_{si}represents the proportion of video i's demand directed to and served by server s, with $\sum_s w_{si} = 1$. We define $\mathbf{w}_s := [w_{s1}, \ldots, w_{sN}]^\mathsf{T}$ as the *workload portfolio* of server s. Given $\mathbf{w}_s$, the aggregate load imposed on server s is a random variable $L_s = \sum_{i=1}^N w_{si}D_i$, with expectation and variance given by

$$\mathbf{E}[L_s] = \mathbf{E}[\textstyle\sum_{i=1}^N w_{si}D_i] = \mu_1 w_{s1} + \ldots + \mu_N w_{sN} = \mu^\mathsf{T}\mathbf{w}_s,$$
$$\mathbf{Var}[L_s] = \mathbf{Var}[\textstyle\sum_{i=1}^N w_{si}D_i] = \sum_{i,j}\rho_{ij}\sigma_i\sigma_j w_{si}w_{sj} = \mathbf{w}_s^\mathsf{T}\mathbf{\Sigma}\mathbf{w}_s.$$

3.1 A Single Server's Decision

When a single server s forms its workload portfolio, it aims to serve as many demands as possible, while making sure that enough egress server bandwidth is allocated. For random demands, this goal corresponds to maximizing the expected load $E[L_s]$, while confining $\Pr(L_s > C_s)$ to a small value δ. We thus obtain the following optimization problem:

$$\max \boldsymbol{\mu}^\mathsf{T}\mathbf{w}_s, \tag{1}$$
$$\text{s.t.} \quad \Pr(L_s > C_s) \leq \delta, \tag{2}$$
$$\mathbf{0} \preceq \mathbf{w}_s \preceq \mathbf{1}, \tag{3}$$

where $\mathbf{0} = [0, \ldots, 0]^\mathsf{T}$, $\mathbf{1} = [1, \ldots, 1]^\mathsf{T}$ are N-dimensional vectors.

When L_s is normally distributed (which can be observed from the UUSee traces), constraint (2) is equivalent to

$$\mathbf{E}[L_s] + \theta\sqrt{\mathbf{Var}[L_s]} = \boldsymbol{\mu}^\mathsf{T}\mathbf{w}_s + \theta\sqrt{\mathbf{w}_s^\mathsf{T}\mathbf{\Sigma}\mathbf{w}_s} \leq C_s, \tag{4}$$

where $F(\cdot)$ is the CDF of normal distribution $\mathcal{N}(0,1)$, and $\theta = F^{-1}(1-\delta)$ is a constant.

To serve the load L_s, $\mathbf{E}[L_s] + \theta\sqrt{\mathbf{Var}[L_s]}$ bandwidth is reserved on server s, where we call $\theta\sqrt{\mathbf{Var}[L_s]}$ the "cushion bandwidth" needed to accommodate load fluctuation. Constraint (4) essentially requires that the total booked resource be bounded by C_s. Note that problem (1) is a second-order conic program and can be solved efficiently using interior point method [3].

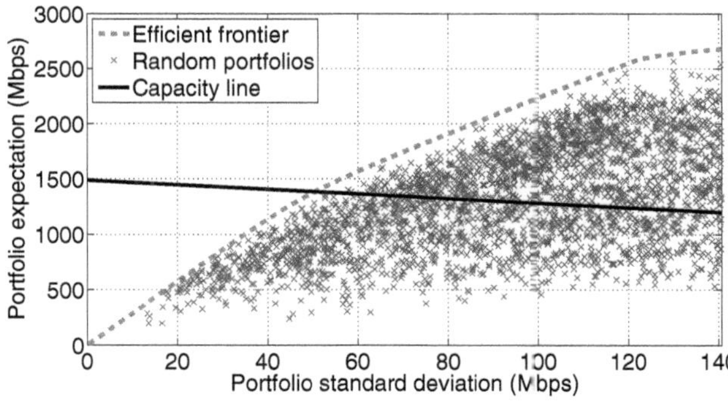

Figure 2: The efficient frontier for portfolios of 5 videos and a single server s on the $\sqrt{\mathbf{Var}[L_s]}$-$\mathbf{E}(L_s)$ plane. Random portfolios are formed by uniformly choosing w_{si} in $(0,1)$ for $i = 1, \ldots, 5$. The capacity line represents (4) with $C_s = 1500$ Mbps and $\delta = 2\%$.

Alternatively, we can explain problem (1) in terms of the efficient portfolio frequently used in investment theory [5]. Among all $\mathbf{w}_s$ that achieves a certain $\mathbf{E}[L_s]$, there is a $\mathbf{w}_s^*$ that leads to the minimum load standard deviation $\sqrt{\mathbf{Var}[L_s]}$. Portfolio $\mathbf{w}_s^*$ is preferred because it achieves the least load variation and thus requires the least cushion bandwidth to be reserved. Therefore, the curve of the minimum $\sqrt{\mathbf{Var}[L_s]}$ as a function of $\mathbf{E}[L_s]$ is called the *efficient frontier*. In a $\sqrt{\mathbf{Var}[L_s]}$-$\mathbf{E}(L_s)$ plane, every possible portfolio is represented by a point lying on or below the efficient frontier.

For example, we consider 5 video channels, with known demand expectation and covariance matrix. The efficient frontier is plotted in Fig. 2, where we also plot random portfolios formed by uniformly choosing w_{si} from $(0,1)$. In addition, there is a capacity line corresponding to the QoS constraint (4), which passes $(0, C_s)$. The intersection of the capacity line with efficient frontier leads to the optimal solution to problem (1), i.e., the maximum expected load serviceable under a very small overload risk. For example, in Fig. 2, we have $\delta = 2\%$ and $\theta = 2.05$, which means that with probability $F(\theta) = 0.98$, the load on server s is satisfied.

3.2 Multiple Servers

When S servers share the load, we can let the servers optimize their workload portfolios one after another as follows. Initially, let $s = 1$ and solve (1) to obtain $\mathbf{w}_1^*$. We then update D_i to $(1 - \sum_{r=1}^s w_{ri}^*)D_i$ for all i and calculate the new $\boldsymbol{\mu}$ and $\mathbf{\Sigma}$ based on the new D_i's. Afterwards, we can update s to $s+1$, and re-solve (1) to obtain $\mathbf{w}_{s+1}^*$ for the next server. Such a process is repeated until $s = S$.

As a result, the bandwidth to be reserved from server s is

$$\boldsymbol{\mu}^\mathsf{T}\mathbf{w}_s^* + \theta\sqrt{\mathbf{w}_s^{*\mathsf{T}}\mathbf{\Sigma}\mathbf{w}_s^*}, \tag{5}$$

and the aggregate bandwidth reserved from all servers is

$$S_{\text{booked}} = \textstyle\sum_{s=1}^S(\boldsymbol{\mu}^\mathsf{T}\mathbf{w}_s^* + \theta\sqrt{\mathbf{w}_s^{*\mathsf{T}}\mathbf{\Sigma}\mathbf{w}_s^*}), \tag{6}$$

The algorithm enhances the utilization of each server, one after another, by pushing the cushion bandwidth $\theta\sqrt{\mathbf{w}_s^\mathsf{T}\mathbf{\Sigma}\mathbf{w}_s}$ on each server to the minimum. As each server s accommodates more expected demand $\boldsymbol{\mu}^\mathsf{T}\mathbf{w}_s$, the necessary aggregate bandwidth reservation is reduced.

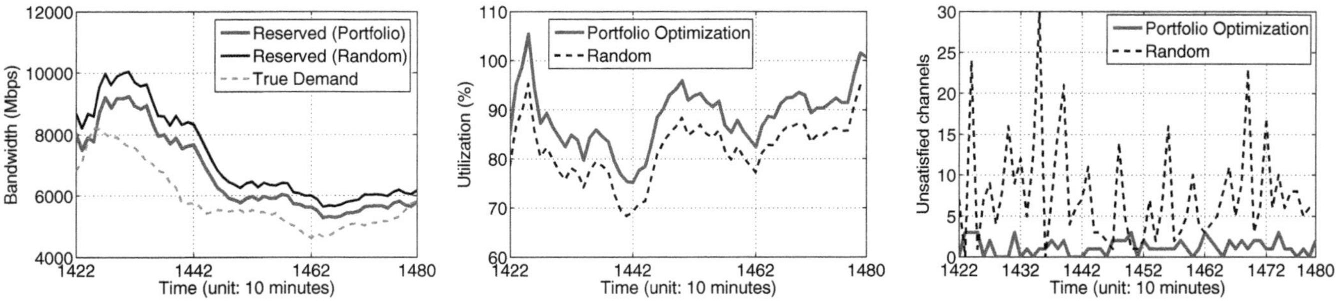

(a) Reserved Bandwidth vs. True Demand (b) Utilization of Reserved Bandwidth (c) Channels with Unsatisfied Requests

Figure 3: Workload portfolio optimization vs. random load direction for a typical peak period.

4. PERFORMANCE EVALUATION

We conduct trace-driven simulations to evaluate the performance of workload portfolio optimization, in comparison with *random load direction* described below. Initially, let $s = 1$. We randomly generate $\mathbf{w}_s$ in $(\mathbf{0}, \mathbf{1})$, and rescale it to $\mathbf{w}'_s$ such that QoS constraint (4) is achieved with equality. Update $\boldsymbol{\mu}$ and $\boldsymbol{\Sigma}$ in the same way as in workload portfolio optimization. We then update s to $s+1$, and repeat the above process to obtain $\mathbf{w}'_{s+1}$ for the next server until $s = S$.

In our evaluation, bandwidth reservation is carried out online every $\Delta t = 10$ minutes. Before time t, the system has obtained estimates $\boldsymbol{\mu}_t = [\mu_{1t}, \ldots, \mu_{Nt}]$ and $\boldsymbol{\Sigma}_t = [\sigma_{ijt}]$ for the coming period $[t, t+\Delta t)$ using forecasting methods mentioned in Sec. 2. We then take $\boldsymbol{\mu}_t$ and $\boldsymbol{\Sigma}_t$ as inputs and calculate $\mathbf{W}_t$ under both workload portfolio optimization and random load direction. Based on $\mathbf{W}_t$, the bandwidth to be reserved from each server is calculated. Once completed, the above demand prediction and workload management process is repeated for the next period $[t + \Delta t, t + 2\Delta t)$. To intentionally distribute workloads across multiple servers, we set the available capacity of each server to be 300 Mbps. We set $\theta = 2.05$ to confine the under-provision probability below $\delta = 2\%$ on each server.

We consider time periods 1422—1480, a typical peak usage period, containing 161 concurrent channels (after certain aggregation). Fig. 3 shows a detailed comparison between workload portfolio optimization and random load direction. Fig. 3(a) plots the aggregate reserved bandwidth under both methods as well as the true demand. We see that the aggregate reserved bandwidth under random load direction is larger than that under portfolio optimization. The former also represents significant over-provisioning as compared to the true demand. Fig. 3(b) further plots the utilization of the aggregate reserved bandwidth by true demand under both methods, substantiating the fact that portfolio optimization enhances resource efficiency.

Based on Fig. 3(a) and Fig. 3(b), under-provision does occur if the utilization exceeds 100% or if the aggregate reserved bandwidth is less than the true demand, but not vice versa: even if the aggregate reserved bandwidth suffices, provision shortage can still occur in individual channels. This motivates us to check the number of unsatisfied channels (with provision shortage) at each point of time. We observed that portfolio optimization guarantees better QoS than random load direction, although δ is set to 2% for both methods. The former confines unsatisfied channels to less than 5 throughout the period.

5. CONCLUDING REMARKS

In this position paper, we propose a predictive and dynamic bandwidth management framework for VoD servers, focusing on controlling quality risks and enhancing resource efficiency. The system predicts the expected future demand as well as demand volatility in each video channel, and estimates demand correlations between channels, by monitoring and learning from demand history. Based on demand prediction, the system jointly makes decisions regarding the capacity to be reserved from each server, content placement, as well as load direction across distributed servers.

Borrowing insights from correlation-based hedging techniques in investment theory, our system strives to leverage demand anti-correlation between video channels to consolidate the workload, thus saving the total bandwidth reservation required while diversifying out risks of under-provision or server overload. Specifically, we formulate the workload portfolio management problem as a mean-variance optimization with probabilistic service level guarantees. We evaluate the performance of the proposed algorithm against random workload mixing through simulations driven by a real-world video access dataset from UUSee VoD services.

6. REFERENCES

[1] UUSee. http://www.uusee.com.

[2] T. Bollerslev. Generalized Autoregressive Conditional Heteroskedasticity. *Journal of Econometrics*, 31:307–327, 1986.

[3] S. Boyd and L. Vandenberghe. *Convex Optimization.* Cambridge University Press, 2004.

[4] Z. Liu, C. Wu, B. Li, and S. Zhao. UUSee: Large-Scale Operational On-Demand Streaming with Random Network Coding. In *Proc. IEEE INFOCOM*, 2010.

[5] H. Markowitz. Portfolio Selection. *The Journal of Finance*, 7(1):77–91, March 1952.

[6] D. Niu, B. Li, and S. Zhao. Understanding Demand Volatility in Large VoD Systems. In *Proc. the 21st International workshop on Network and Operating Systems Support for Digital Audio and Video (NOSSDAV)*, 2011.

[7] D. Niu, Z. Liu, B. Li, and S. Zhao. Demand Forecast and Performance Prediction in Peer-Assisted On-Demand Streaming Systems. In *Proc. IEEE INFOCOM Mini-Conference*, 2011.

Prefetching Strategy in Peer-Assisted Social Video Streaming * †

Zhi Wang[1], Lifeng Sun[1], Shiqiang Yang[1], and Wenwu Zhu[2]
[1]Tsinghua National Laboratory for Information Science and Technology
Department of Computer Science and Technology, Tsinghua University, Beijing, China
[2]Microsoft Research Asia, Beijing, China
{wangzhi04@mails., sunlf@, yangshq@}tsinghua.edu.cn, wenwuzhu@microsoft.com

ABSTRACT

Online social network has emerged as the most popular approach for people to directly access multimedia contents. Among these contents, video sharing is a challenging task due to the demand on a large amount of uplink bandwidth at the dedicated server. We leverage a P2P paradigm to alleviate the server to distribute shared videos. By investigating traces obtained from a popular online social network in China, we observe that users' preferences can be predicted. We design a user preference guided prefetching strategy to reduce video startup delays, enabling smooth playback. Simulation experiments show that our design achieves high prefetch accuracy and short startup delay with conservative storage and bandwidth capacities at peers.

Categories and Subject Descriptors

J.4 [**Computer Applications**]: Social and behavioral sciences; C.2.4 [**Distributed Systems**]: Distributed applications

General Terms

Design, Measurement

Keywords

P2P, Social Network, Prefetching, Streaming

1. INTRODUCTION

As one of the most popular applications on the Internet, online social network allows users to establish and maintain their social connections, and to present themselves by posting and sharing various contents [6]. In this paper, we focus on the video sharing in online social network. We have obtained traces from the administrator of Renren [1], one of the largest online social network sites in China. We observe that videos that are originally hosted on video sharing sites, such as Youku [2] and Youtube [3], are aggregating into Renren. It is clear that online social network has emerged as a new platform where users can access video contents conveniently.

Information hosted by online social network can be used to identify users' interests. Cheng *et al.* [4] have proposed a reputation model based on trust between friends to guide users to browse desirable contents, and Yang *et al.* [9] have proposed a movie recommendation system based on rating information shared among friends. In this paper, we make use of such information hosted in the online social network, to guide peers to prefetch videos to enable high-quality social video streaming.

First, we leverage a P2P (Peer-to-Peer) paradigm to enable video streaming to large-scale users in the online social network with conservative server bandwidth. In P2P streaming, each peer (user or client) is capable to cache media chunks of videos it has watched, and distribute these chunks to other peers, saving the server uplink bandwidth. P2P has been proven successful in distributing both live [8] and VoD (Video-on-Demand) contents [7]. Cheng *et al.* [5] also proposed peer-assisted distribution of short videos on video sharing sites like Youtube.

Second, we design a prefetching strategy to enable high-quality streaming. By prefetching the prefix chunks of a video that is likely to be viewed by a user, a short startup delay and smooth playback can be achieved. Our prefetching strategy is based on users' *preferences* gradually learnt from their historical video access patterns. In the online social network, users' preferences of videos are predicted by (1) users' historical selections of *source* users who share the videos, (2) social closenesses between the *viewing users* and the source users, and (3) popularities of the videos. For a user, the un-watched videos are ranked according to the user's preferences of them, such that videos with higher ranks are more likely to be viewed by the user. After that, the user (peer) downloads prefix chunks of the ranked videos in order. The startup delays thus can be reduced when the user plays videos that have been prefetched.

The remainder of this paper is organized as follows. We investigate traces of Renren in Sec. 2. We present our prefetching design in Sec. 3. In Sec. 4, we give the evaluation results. And we conclude the paper in Sec. 5.

---

*Area chair: Surender Chandra

†Supported in part by National High-Tech Research and Development Plan of China (863) under Grant No. 2009AA01Z328, the National Natural Science Foundation of China under Grant No. 60833009 and No. 60773158, and the National Basic Research Program of China (973) under Grant No. 2006CB303103.

MM'11, November 28–December 1, 2011, Scottsdale, Arizona, USA.

Table 1: Trace Item of Content Viewing

Field	Definition
T	The time stamp of this trace item
Viewer	The user who views the content item
Source	The user who posts or shares the content item
Content	The ID and URL of the content item

2. MEASURING VIDEO SHARING/VIEWING ON RENREN

As one of the largest online social network sites in China, Renren has attracted more than 160 million users as of Feb. 2011. The traces we obtained from Renren contain about 100,000 users, their social connections, and their interactions. From the traces, we try to understand users' preferences of videos shared by others.

2.1 Traces from Renren

On Renren, users are allowed to share video links from other video sharing sites, *e.g.*, Youku, so that users can directly view these videos on their Renren pages. In the traces, about 21,000 videos are imported from Youku between July 1st and July 31st, 2010. After videos are imported to Renren, how users view them are recorded by the content viewing trace items, each of which contains four fields as illustrated in Table 1.

2.2 Measurement Results

We are interested to know the impact of *social relationship* on users' preferences of videos, *i.e.*, how users select videos shared on Renren. In Renren's traces, we have made the following observations:

Videos Aggregate in the Online Social Network. Many video sharing sites have provided an easy "share-in-a-click" function for users to share videos with their friends in the online social network. We retrieve the original video sharing sites from the trace items. As shown in Fig. 1, videos on Renren are imported from many external popular video sharing sites. It is clear that videos of traditional video sites are *aggregating* in the online social network. On the other hand, the social relationship and users' preferences hosted by the online social network can improve the video recommendation, making users more likely to access videos directly via the social network.

Users' Preferences of Videos shared by Friends. On Renren, a user is allowed to watch not only videos shared by his friends, but also a much larger number of other popular videos shared by strangers, and automatically recommended by the system. However, we observe that more than 12% of videos views are between friends, *i.e.*, the source and viewing users are socially connected. Considering the huge number of strangers to a user on Renren, this observation indicates clear preferences of users to watch videos shared by their friends.

Weak Correlation between Video and Blog Viewings. Since blog and video are two important types of contents on Renren, we wonder if the access patterns of blogs can be used to predict the access patterns of videos. We investigate the correlation between blog viewing and video viewing. In Fig. 2, each sample shows the number of video views versus the number of blog views between a pair of users during a week. We observe that the correlation is quite weak. Thus, in our design, how users view blogs is not used to predict how they view videos.

Predicting Users' Preferences from Historical Selections. Since users' interests can be relatively stable, a pair of users who have similar interests should be likely to view videos shared by each other for a long period. We select trace items spanning two consecutive weeks to verify it. We calculate the number of views between a pair of users for each week. In Fig. 3, each sample illustrates the number of views between a pair of users in a week versus that in the previous week. The relatively strong correlation indicates that users' historical selections can predict users' future preferences.

Next, we make use of the historical video selection and social closeness information to guide the video prefetching, so that startup delays can be reduced in the video streaming.

3. PREFETCH FOR SOCIAL VIDEO STREAMING

As observed in Renren's traces, users' selections of videos depend on not only what the videos are, but also who share the videos with. As a promising approach to reduce video startup delay, prefetching the prefix chunks of videos has to solve a key problem: among the huge number of un-watched videos, which ones are more likely to be viewed by a user?

According to the observations in Sec. 2, we design a prefetching strategy based on users' preferences guided by information from the online social network. We first discuss how a user's preference is predicted, then give the detailed prefetching design.

3.1 Choosing Videos to Prefetch

In the social video streaming, a viewing user has to choose among many videos to prefetch. In our design, the viewing user's video preference is predicted by (1) who share the videos and (2) what the videos are.

3.1.1 Preference of Source Users

We use the following metrics to predict a viewing user's preference of a source user: (1) His historical selection of the source user, which has been observed to have strong correlation with his future selection; (2) Social closeness between the viewing user and the source user, since friends are observed to be more likely to view each other's shared videos.

Historical Selection of the Source User. In the online social network, viewing user i chooses videos shared by multiple source users in set Y_i, which is the set of source users whose shared videos are likely to be viewed by user i. In our design, Y_i contains all i's friends, and strangers whose shared videos have been watched by i before. We define a pair-wise index h_{ij} to evaluate i's historical selection level of source user j as $h_{ij} = \frac{c_{ij}}{\sum_{k\in Y_i} c_{ik}}$, where $j \in Y_i$ and c_{ij} is the number of historical views that peer i watches videos shared by peer j. Large h_{ij} indicates that user i prefers videos shared by user j, such that user i can still choose videos shared by user j in the future.

Social Closeness between the Viewing User and the Source User. We observe that users are more likely to watch videos shared by their friends on Renren. In our design, such social preference between friends is evaluated by a straightforward metric, which is the fraction of their common friends over their total friends. The social closeness f_{ij} between user i and user j is defined as $f_{ij} = \frac{|F_i \cap F_j|}{|F_i \cup F_j|}$, where $j \in Y_i$ and F_i

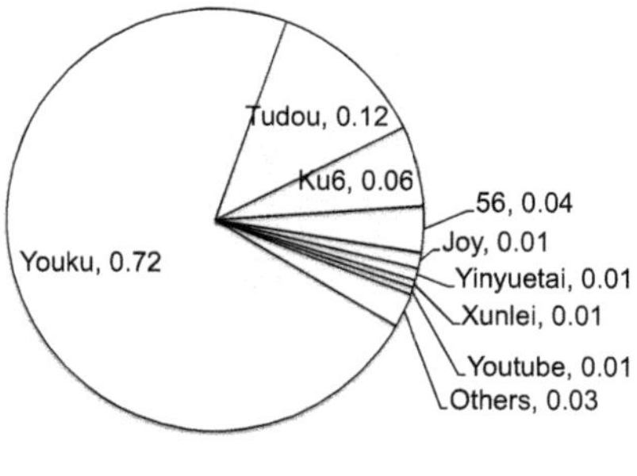

Figure 1: Videos are aggregating in online social network

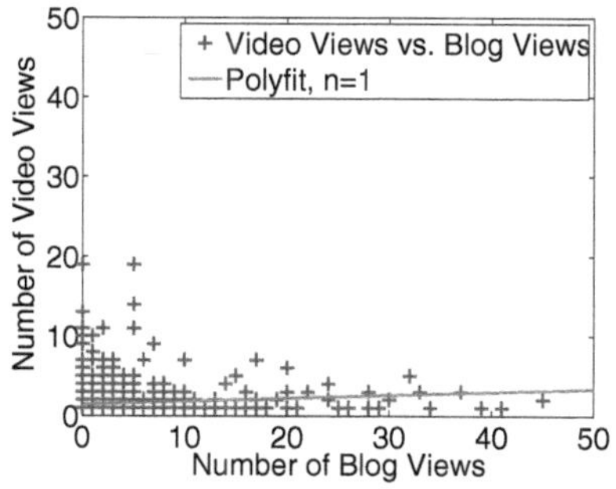

Figure 2: Video views vs. blog views

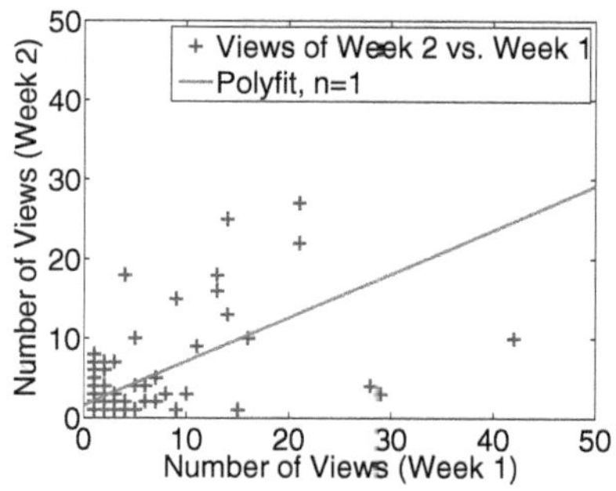

Figure 3: Video preference vs. historical selection

is the set of friends of user i. Intuitively, larger f_{ij} indicates stronger social closeness between i and j.

Preference of a Source User. According to our observations from Renren's traces, both historical selection and social closeness predict a viewing user's future preference of source users. We define a source preference index e_{ij} to evaluate how much viewing user i likes to watch videos shared by source user j as $e_{ij} = w_i f_{ij} + (1 - w_i)h_{ij}$, where w_i is a parameter for a peer to adjust the weights of historical selection and social closeness. Larger w_i indicates that i selects videos more according to friend links. In our design, w_i is dynamically tuned by peer i in each round. At the end of each round, if j' is discovered to be the "best" source user, *i.e.*, the view number of videos shared by j' is the largest, then w_i will be increased by a small amount δ if $f_{ij'} > h_{ij'}$ and $w_i < 1$, or decreased by a δ if $f_{ij'} < h_{ij'}$ and $w_i > 0$. In our experiments, w_i is initially set to 0.5, δ is set to 0.01, and each round is 30 minutes long.

3.1.2 Preference of Videos

Video Popularity. Source preference index e_{ij} evaluates viewer i's preference to choose source user j. However, a source can share multiple videos; while for a viewing user, only being able to select the "best" source users is not enough to do the prefetching. We next give the video rank scheme based on video popularities and source preference indices. The popularity of a video reflects how much viewing users like the video. In our design, the popularity of video k is defined as p_k, which is the number of views that users watch the video.

When a user logs in his account, he is provided a list of un-watched videos shared by his friends and other users. The number of these videos can be very large for a viewing user. We define V_{ji} as the set of source j's shared videos that have not been watched or prefetched by peer i. We give each video $k \in \cup_{j \in Y_i} V_{ji}$ a video preference index $s_i(k)$ as follows:

$$s_i(k) = p_k \sum_{j|k \in V_{ji}} e_{ij}, \quad k \in \cup_{j \in Y_i} V_{ji}.$$

Larger $s_i(k)$ indicates that viewing user i is more likely to watch video k in the future.

3.2 Prefetching The Selected Videos

3.2.1 Downloading The Prefix Chunks

When prefetching a video, a peer actively downloads the prefix chunks of that video, *i.e.*, the first several chunks. The prefetching strategy is carried out by a peer locally when the buffered chunks for the current video can be played for at least 5 seconds (*i.e.*, enough to resist network jitters), or it idles (*i.e.*, no video is being played). The peer keeps a sliding window for the current video, expecting to receive urgent chunks, which are for the next 5 seconds. Only when the sliding window is fully filled, the peer carries out the prefetching. The un-prefetched videos in set $\cup_{j \in Y_i} V_{ji}$ are ranked in $s_i(k)$'s descending order. Videos with larger $s_i(k)$ will be prioritized to be prefetched. When underflow of the sliding window occurs, the peer will suspend the prefetching and focus on downloading chunks of the current video.

Table 2: Bandwidths of Peers [10]

Fraction of Peers	20%	50%	30%
Downlink (kbps)	784	1500	3000
Uplink (kbps)	128	384	1000

3.2.2 Cache Strategy

As a peer's local storage capacity is limited, stale video chunks have to be eliminated to make room for new ones. We divide the whole storage at a peer into 3 regions and give them different priorities as follows: (1) The region for current video (*high priority*): chunks in this region are never eliminated whether they have been played or not, to enable fast seek forward/backward, which are found to be quite normal [11]. (2) The region for prefetching (*normal priority*): we fix the number of maximum chunks for prefetching to K, *i.e.*, a user will stop prefetching when this region is fully filled. In this region, a *FIFO* scheme is used to eliminate stale chunks. (3) The region for other chunks (*low priority*): this region occupies the remained room of the storage, where an *LFU* replacement scheme is used to eliminate the stale chunks. In our design, the dedicated server and peers also prioritize to serve chunks for current video playback over prefetching chunks.

4. PERFORMANCE EVALUATION

We evaluate the performance of our design by simulation experiments driven by Renren's traces.

4.1 Experiment Setup

We choose 500 active users who have viewed the largest numbers of videos. The bitrate and duration of a video are set to 600 Kbps and 10 minutes, respectively. Peers' uplink and downlink capacities are configured in Table 2. The uplink capacity of the dedicated server, who stores all videos,

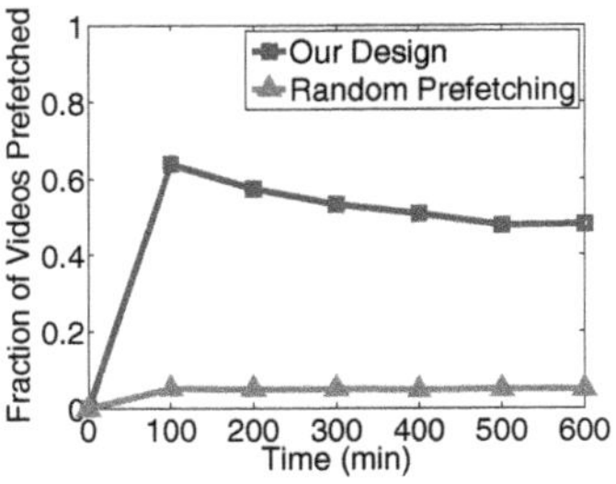

Figure 4: Prefetching accuracy vs. time

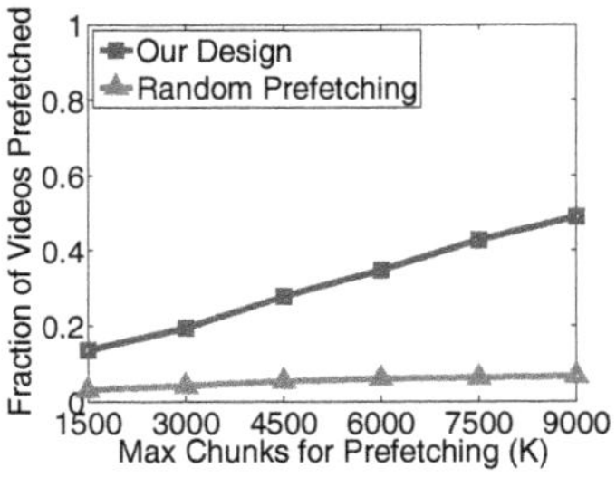

Figure 5: Prefetching accuracy vs. max chunks for prefetching

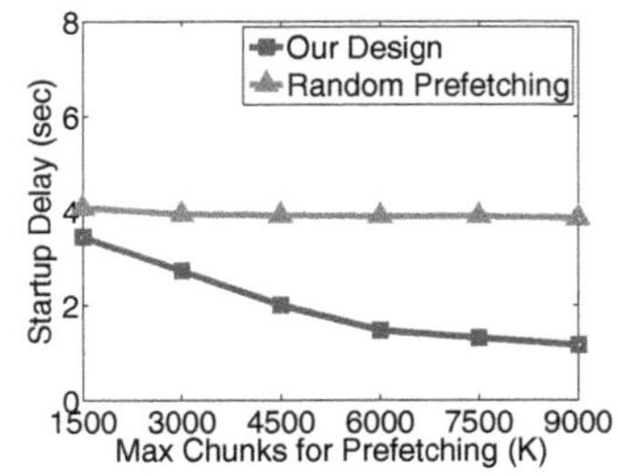

Figure 6: Startup delay vs. max chunks for prefetching

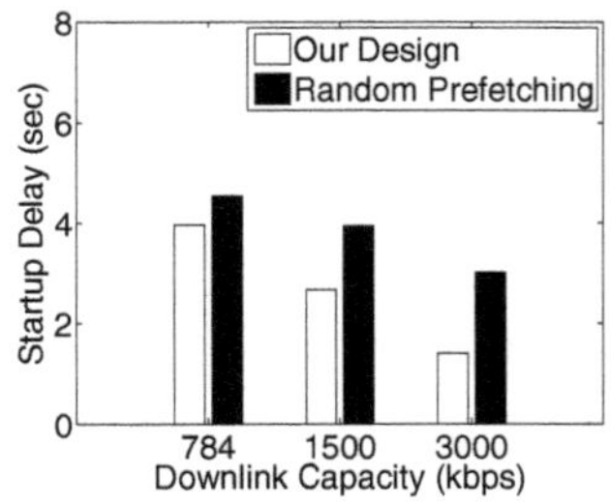

Figure 7: Startup delay vs. downlink capacities at peers

is set to 100 Mbps. The size of each chunk is 1200 bytes. A user chooses the videos to watch as indicated in the traces. A user caches the chunks it has downloaded according to the cache strategy discussed in Sec. 3. Neighboring peers who can help each other are discovered by a tracker server. When downloading chunks, users make use of their neighboring peers, and only download the urgent chunks from the dedicated server to reduce the startup delays.

4.2 Experiment Results

4.2.1 Prefetching Accuracy

We first evaluate the prefetching accuracy, which is defined as the fraction of the prefetched videos (at least one of whose prefix chunks has been downloaded *before watching*), over all videos watched by peers. We compare our design with a random prefetching scheme, in which peers download prefix chunks of videos randomly chosen among all videos shared by its friends. Fig. 4 illustrates the prefetching accuracy versus the simulation time. We observe that our design achieves much higher prefetching accuracy than the random scheme. And the prefetching accuracy can reach a stable value after a short period when peers have learnt their interested sources and video popularities.

We also evaluate the impact of the maximum number of chunks for prefetching on the prefetching accuracy. Fig. 5 depicts the average prefetching accuracy versus the maximum number of chunks for prefetching (K). We observe that larger storage capacity leads to higher prefetching accuracy in our design; while storage capacity has little impact on the random prefetching scheme. The reason is that peers have downloaded too many chunks that are never played in the random prefetching.

4.2.2 Startup Delay

We also evaluate the startup delays, which are caused by initial buffering when users start videos. Fig. 6 illustrates the average startup delay versus K. From this figure we can see that our design achieves smaller startup delays than the random prefetching scheme. We also observe that larger K leads to shorter startup delays in our design, and has little impact on the random prefetching scheme, mainly due to the much lower prefetching accuracy of the random scheme.

Startup delays are also determined by the downlink capacities at peers. Peers with larger downlink capacities are able to download more chunks, so that more candidate videos can be covered. As illustrated in Fig. 7, we observe that larger downlink capacities in both our design and the random scheme lead to shorter startup delays, and similar downlink capacity achieves much shorter startup delays in our design than in the random prefetching scheme. The reason is that prefetching only works when peers have extra capacities to download prefix chunks of other videos, and our design chooses the most effective chunks for prefetching.

5. CONCLUDING REMARKS

Videos from video sharing sites like Youku are aggregating into online social networks like Renren. In Renren's traces, we observe that users' video viewing preferences can be predicted by their historical selection of source users, social closenesses and the videos' popularities. We design prefetching strategy based on the users' video preferences. Our simulation results verify the effectiveness of our prefetching design, which achieves short startup delays, enabling fast video switching and smooth playback.

6. REFERENCES

[1] http://www.renren.com.

[2] http://www.youku.com.

[3] http://www.youtube.com.

[4] R. Cheng and L. E.K. Bring Order to Online Social Networks. In *Proc. of IEEE INFOCOM*, 2011.

[5] X. Cheng and J. Liu. Nettube: Exploring social networks for peer-to-peer short video sharing. In *Proc. of IEEE INFOCOM*, 2009.

[6] L. Guo, E. Tan, S. Chen, X. Zhang, and Y. Zhao. Analyzing Patterns of User Content Generation in Online Social Networks. In *Proc. of ACM SIGKDD*, 2009.

[7] Y. Huang, T. Fu, D. Chiu, J. Lui, and C. Huang. Challenges, Design and Analysis of A Large-scale P2P-VoD System. In *Proc. of ACM SIGCOMM*, 2008.

[8] S. Xie, B. Li, G. Keung, and X. Zhang. Coolstreaming: Design, Theory, and Practice. *IEEE Transactions on Multimedia*, 9(8):1661–1671, 2007.

[9] X. Yang, G. Y., and L. Y. Bayesian-inference Based Recommendation in Online Social Networks. In *Proc. of IEEE INFOCOM*, 2011.

[10] M. Zhang, Y. Xiong, Q. Zhang, L. Sun, and S. Yang. Optimizing the Throughput of Data-driven Peer-to-Peer Streaming. *IEEE Transactions on Parallel and Distributed Systems*, 20:97–110, 2008.

[11] C. Zheng, G. Shen, and S. Li. Distributed Prefetching Scheme for Random Seek Support in Peer-to-Peer Streaming Applications. In *Proc. of ACM MM*, 2005.

Resource Allocation for Cloud-based Free Viewpoint Video Rendering for Mobile Phones*

Dan Miao
Dept. of EEIS, University of Science and Technology of China, Hefei, China
miaodan@mail.ustc.edu.cn

Wenwu Zhu, Chong Luo
Microsoft Research Asia
Beijing, China
wenwuzhu,cluo @microsoft.com

Chang Wen Chen
Dept. of CSE, State University of New York at Buffalo
Buffalo,USA
chencw@buffalo.edu

ABSTRACT

Free viewpoint video (FVV) / Free viewpoint TV (FTV) on mobile devices over cellular networks is very challenging due to the requirement for large bandwidth and limitations in computation and battery life on mobile phones. To address such challenges, in this paper we propose a cloud-based FVV / FTV rendering framework for mobile devices over cellular networks. In this framework, cloud performs rendering for mobile devices. In order to achieve maximum QoE (Quality of Experience) for mobile users, we propose a novel resource allocation scheme, which jointly considers rendering allocation between cloud and client based on user's QoE and rate allocation among texture, depth, and channel rate based on rate-distortion analysis. We formulate this resource allocation scheme as an optimization problem which can then be transformed into a convex optimization for the given rate ratio. Experimental results demonstrate that the proposed cloud-based FVV rendering solution can substantially improve video quality on mobile devices comparing with traditional approaches.

Categories and Subject Descriptors

H.5.1 [**Multimedia Information Systems**]: Video

General Terms

Design, Measurement

Keywords

FVV, Mobile devices, Cloud computing, Resource allocation

1. INTRODUCTION

With recent advances in computer vision, computer graphics, and display technologies, free viewpoint video (FVV) / free viewpoint TV (FTV) services are drawing great attention. In general, people desire to watch free viewpoint contents using different types of devices that are convenient for users. These devices can be PC, laptops and mobile phones depending on where the users currently locate. Rendering and displaying FVV on fat device such as PC have gained great progress in the past decades. However, rendering and viewing it on mobile phone in real-time remain very challenging due to the bandwidth bottleneck in cellular networks and limited resources in computation of mobile phones.

On FVV/FTV, several research groups have developed various warping-based view rendering schemes with multi-view video texture and depth [1] [2]. These schemes addressed the rendering quality of generated views for PC users in the wired networks. Shi et al. recently proposed a remote rendering scheme for mobile phone [3]. Their novel viewpoint stream is rendered in proxy and transmitted to mobile devices over a Wi-Fi network.

As emerging cloud computing, multimedia cloud computing can provide a variety of computing and storage services for mobile devices [4]. In this research we study cloud-based free viewpoint video over cellular networks. Remote rendering using cloud computing can provide an effective way to resolve the bandwidth and computation limitation problems by rendering novel view in cloud in real-time and sending it back to mobile devices. To accomplish this goal, a key challenge encountered in cloud-based rendering is how to allocate the resources between cloud and mobile clients to achieve an optimal tradeoff between computation and communication while maximize quality of experience (QoE).

In this paper, we propose a novel cloud-based FVV/FTV rendering framework for mobile devices over cellular networks. In this framework, we develop a novel resource allocation scheme that jointly considers rendering allocation and rate allocation to optimize the quality of user experience. More specifically, we jointly perform rendering allocation between cloud and mobile device based on QoE to reduce interaction delay and rate allocation among texture and depth of two reference views based on the Rate-Distortion analysis to improve the quality of the novel view. We formulate the proposed scheme as an optimization problem which can be transformed into a convex optimization for the given rate ratio.

2. CLOUD BASED RENDERING ARCHITECTURE

In this section, we illustrate the architecture of cloud-based rendering for mobile device over cellular networks. Figure 1 depicts the concept diagram of cloud-based rendering for

*Area Chair: Surender Chandra

MM'11, November 28–December 1, 2011, Scottsdale, Arizona, USA.

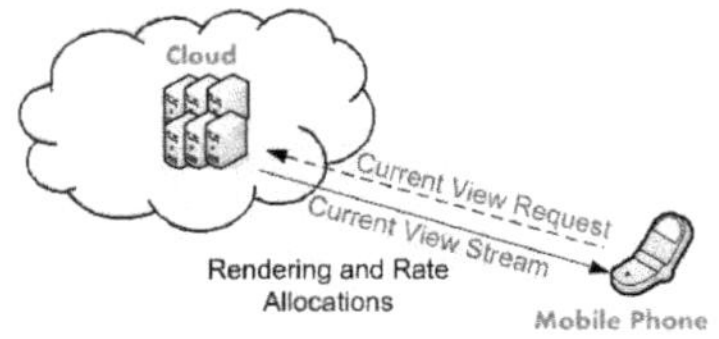

Figure 1: Cloud-based FVV rendering for mobile phone

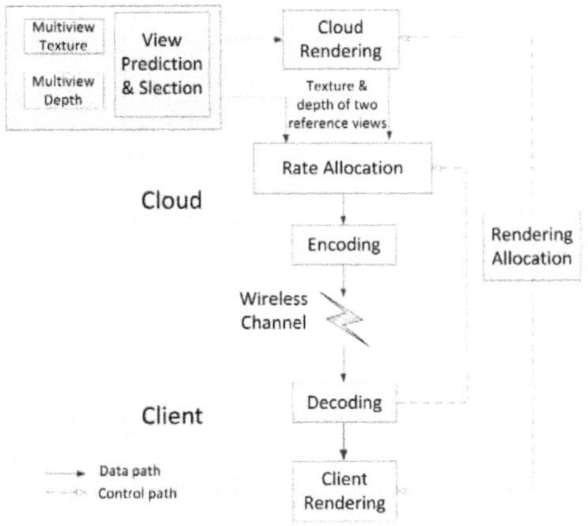

Figure 2: Architecture of resource allocation for cloud-based FVV rendering for mobile phones

mobile phone. In this concept architecture, each time when user requests a new viewpoint, the novel view will be rendered in the cloud and then sent to the client.

Figure 2 depicts the architecture of our proposed resource allocation between the cloud and the client. The rendering module is employed in both cloud and client. Based on the rendering allocation scheme, the novel view is generated in the cloud, and the client will do local rendering if the user wants minimized interaction delay. The rate allocation module encodes the selected view(s) from the View Prediction & Selection module according to the viewpoint request. The rate allocation is performed under the rendering allocation scheme using the wireless channel information such as packet-loss ratio fed back from the decoder.

3. RESOURCE ALLOCATIONS FOR CLOUD-BASED RENDERING

In this section, we present resource allocation for cloud-based rendering. The proposed resource allocation scheme jointly considers rendering allocation between the cloud and the client as well as rate allocation among texture and depth of two reference views.

3.1 Rendering Allocation

Traditionally, rendering is conducted on client side. However, rendering on mobile devices imposes significant challenges due to limitation on computing capability and battery life of mobile devices. To address the challenges, we propose cloud-based video rendering for mobile devices. A key problem in cloud-based rendering is how to allocate resources between the cloud and the client to optimize QoE. For FVV, from QoE perspective the mobile users mainly care view quality and interaction delay.

To achieve optimal view quality, we propose quality-optimal cloud rendering in which all rendering is performed in the cloud. It works as follows. The user sends viewpoint request

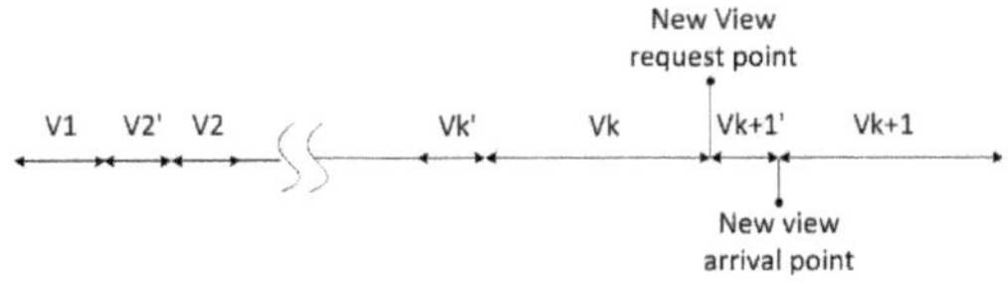

Figure 3: Viewing time representation

to the cloud, and the novel view is rendered and encoded in the cloud and then transmitted to the user. Then the corresponding stream is decoded and displayed directly on the mobile phone. High quality rendering algorithm can be produced, since the cloud can offer abundant computation resource. Comparing with client rendering in which at least two views of texture and depth need to be transmitted to the user and the rendering is performed on client side using compressed reference views under the computation constraint, our cloud-based rendering can offer best view quality.

To minimize viewer's interaction delay, we propose delay-optimal cloud rendering. The idea is to perform local rendering for the novel view on mobile device while waiting for the requested view coming, thereby concealing the interaction delay. We partition the entire viewing time into two categories: stationary-viewing-time and switching-viewing-time, as shown in Figure 3 in which V_k represents stationary-viewing-time and $V_k^{'}$ represents switching-viewing-time of the kth viewpoint. Switching-viewing-time starts when user requests a novel viewpoint. It lasts until the response stream can be received from the cloud on local devices. We perform cloud rendering during the stationary-viewing-time while local rendering during switching-viewing-time on the mobile device. On local rendering, we employ 3D warping on the mobile device. Usually two reference views with texture and depth are necessary to be sent to client for rendering to avoid severe occlusion artifacts and to guarantee good rendering quality. In our approach, one is the requesting view while the other one is the camera view selected from the View Selection and Prediction module in Figure 2. Specifically, we first perform the prediction for the next viewpoint. The prediction is made based on the user profile. The viewpoint position is recorded each time when the user request is received in the cloud. We maintain and update the user profile of the viewpoint's location distribution. We assume that the next viewpoint is located at the viewpoint which has the largest probability in the profile. Based on the prediction result, we select the camera view which is near this predicted one and ensure that the predicted view can fall in between the current view and the selected camera view.

3.2 Rate Allocation

As aforementioned, to optimize the view quality we propose a novel rate allocation scheme. To cope with the high error rate in wireless channel, Forward Error Correction (FEC) is employed to combat the errors. For delay-optimal cloud rendering, the video quality during stationary-viewing-time is determined by texture quality of current view and during switching-viewing-time by texture and depth quality of the two reference views. Therefore, the problem becomes distortion-minimized rate allocation between source and channel, between two reference views, and between texture and depth. As rate allocation for quality-optimal cloud rendering can be viewed as part of delay-optimal rendering between source and channel, we focus on rate allocation of delay-optimal cloud rendering in the following.

3.2.1 Formulation

To minimize total distortion for entire viewing time, we formulate the rate allocation problem as

$$\min_{R_V, R_V^{'}, R_i, R_i^{'}, R_c} D(R_s, R_c) = \alpha D_1(R_V, R_c) + \beta D_2(R_V, R_V^{'}, R_i, R_i^{'}, R_c)$$
$$st. R_V + R_V^{'} + R_i + R_i^{'} + R_c \leq R_0, \quad (1)$$

where D_1 and D_2 represent average distortion of stationary-viewing-time and switching-viewing-time, respectively, R_s, R_c represent total source and channel rate, respectively, $R_V, R_V^{'}$, $R_i, R_i^{'}$ represent texture and depth rates of current view and the selected camera view, respectively, and R_0 represents total transmission rate. The parameters α,β represent view-time length of the two types of viewing proportional to the entire viewing time. Their values are updated by the user profile of each viewpoint's viewing time recorded each time when the viewpoint is changed.

3.2.2 Rate-Distortion Analysis

For cloud-based FVV, end-to-end distortion includes texture source distortion, depth source distortion, and channel distortion. We choose the view synthesized in the cloud without compression and transmission as the reference in order to solve the problem of no-reference evaluation. To calculate D_1, we assume the streams are rendered, compressed and transmitted in order. According to the quality evaluation criteria, the overall distortion of D_1 consists of source distortion D_s and channel distortion D_c. That is

$$D_1 = D_s + D_c. \quad (2)$$

The rendered video distortion of D_2 is introduced by texture and depth of the two decoded reference views, since the stream is interpolated by two views. We employ the distortion model adopted in [5]. Therefore, the distortion of predicted view can be represented by the distortions of the two reference view as follows:

$$D_2 = \omega_V^2(D_V + \tau\psi_V D_{depth_V}) + \omega_i^2(D_i + \tau\psi_i D_{depth_i}), \quad (3)$$

where D_V and D_i represent texture distortions of the current view and the camera view, respectively; while D_{depth_V} and D_{depth_i} represent depth distortions of these two views, respectively. ω_V and ω_i represent the distance-dependent blending weights with $\omega_V + \omega_V = 1$, τ is a constant determined by the sequence, and ψ_V,ψ_i represent the motion sensitivity factor of the two reference views, which can be computed as

$$\psi_{(.)} = 1/(2(2\pi)^2) \cdot \iint S_{(.)}(\omega_1, \omega_2) \cdot (\omega_1^2 + \omega_2^2) d\omega_1 d\omega_2. \quad (4)$$

In Eq.(4), $S_{(.)}(\omega_1, \omega_2)$ denotes the energy density of the reference views and (ω_1, ω_2) is the two-dimensional frequency vector. According to the above R-D analysis, we represent rendering distortion, determined by compression and transmission, as source distortion and channel distortion of texture and depth. We represent the source rate and distortion as the function of quantization step-size. Next we will investigate D-Q and R-Q model. The relation between source distortion and quantization step-size can be represented as [6]

$$MSE = \rho \cdot (Q_{step}), \quad (5)$$

Table 1: Rate Allocation Algorithm

1.Initialize model parameter $\tau, \rho, \mu, \nu, \psi$
2.Update parameter α, β
3.Compute rate ratio r based on packet-loss ratio
4.Compute source rate R_s
5.Compute Q according to (8) using the Lagrange method

where ρ in Eq.(5) is a model parameter. The relation between source rate and quantization step-size can be represented as [7]

$$R = \frac{\mu}{Q_{step}} + \nu. \quad (6)$$

In Eq.(6), μ and ν are model parameters.
In this work, we consider a random binary channel (BSC) model, as in many cases burst errors can be converted into random errors with pre-interleaving. We use Reed-Solomon Codes as the FEC code to protect the data from the packet loss. The (N,K) RS block code with 8 bits per symbol is employed. Note that in the RS code, any error pattern with no more than $T = \lfloor (N-K)/2 \rfloor$ symbol errors can be corrected. When the channel packet-loss ratio is known, the channel distortion behaves like an on-off threshold, i.e., the lost packet is either enable to be recovered completely if loss ratio is within the error pattern or is unable to be corrected completely if loss ratio is beyond the correction ability. We can determine the rate ratio r based on the packet-loss ratio fed back from the decoder to guarantee that RS code can just correct the error under this packet-loss ratio.

3.2.3 Rate Allocation Algorithm

Given the rate ratio r, the optimization problem of Eq.(1) then can be represented as

$$\min_{R_V, R_V^{'}, R_i, R_i^{'}} D = \alpha D_1(R_V) + \beta D_2(R_V, R_V^{'}, R_i, R_i^{'})$$
$$st. (R_V + R_V^{'} + R_i + R_i^{'})(1 + r) \leq R_0. \quad (7)$$

Substituting Eqs.(2)(3)(5)(6) into Eq.(7), we obtain

$$\min_{Q_V, Q_V^{'}, Q_i, Q_i^{'}} D = (A \cdot Q_V + B \cdot Q_V^{'} + C \cdot Q_i + D \cdot Q_i^{'})$$
$$st. \eta/Q_V + \theta/Q_V^{'} + \gamma/Q_i + \delta/Q_i^{'} \leq R_s, \quad (8)$$

where $Q_V, Q_V^{'}, Q_i, Q_i^{'}$ represent quantization step-sizes of texture and depth of current view and camera view, respectively, R_s represents available source rate, and A, B, C, D, $\eta, \theta, \gamma, \delta$ are parameters that can be obtained by derivation. Due to the page limitation, we omit their expressions here. The problem now becomes a convex optimization problem, which can be solved using the Lagrange method. We develop a close-form solution of quantization step-size determination at GOP level. The RD-based rate allocation algorithm is summarized in Table 1.

4. SIMULATION RESULTS

We have carried out simulations to evaluate the effectiveness of the proposed resource allocation scheme. We use *Network Emulator for Windows toolkit* [8] to simulate the cellular networks. We use HTC HD (QUALCOMM(R) 7201A 528MHz

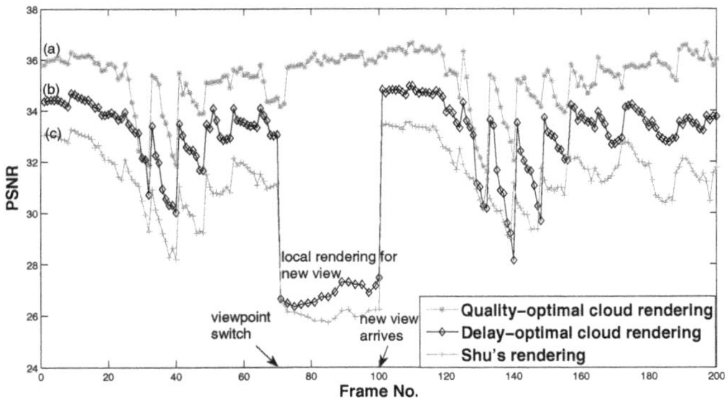

Figure 4: PSNR comparison of the rendered frame under the condition of 250kbps bandwidth and 3% packet-loss ratio

CPU and 288MB memory) mobile phone. The texture and depth views are coded with simulcast coding using MVC software JMVM6.0. The 3D video sequence *BookArrival* is used in the experiments with resolution 320*240. The view range includes 4 camera viewpoints 8, 10, 12, 14. The wireless channel bandwidth is set to 250kbps and packet-loss ratio is 3%.

We select one period from the entire viewing process in the simulation. In this period, viewpoint is changed from view11 to view13. Figure 4(a) shows the PSNR value of each frame for quality-optimal cloud rendering with 20fps. Figure 4(b) shows the PSNR value of each frame for delay-optimal cloud rendering. During the stationary-viewing-time, the frame rate can also achieve 20fps, but it drops to 10fps during local rendering. Comparing with Figure 4(a) and 4(b), we can see that the quality of quality-optimal cloud rendering is best, followed by delay-optimal cloud rendering. Note that when viewpoint is changed, quality-optimal cloud rendering will introduce little interaction delay. For delay-optimal cloud rendering, due to the view selection algorithm and local rendering, the new viewpoint will fall between the two reference views and the interaction delay can be concealed. We compare the rendering video quality of our proposed delay-optimal cloud rendering scheme with that of Shu's approach [3]. In Shu's approach, two reference views are transmitted to user based on prediction for next viewpoint. In the simulation, we use the best condition of Shu's approach in which one reference view equals to the current viewpoint. For the sake of comparison, two reference views are assigned equal rate in Shu's approach while the rate ratio between texture and depth is set to 4:1, 5:1, 6:1, respectively. Figure 4(c) shows the PSNR value of each frame for Shu's approach. As the performance of different rate ratios between texture and depth is similar, we select the best case 5:1 in Shu's approach. From Figure 4(b) and 4(c) we can see that our approach greatly outperforms Shu's one with equal rate for the two reference views. Figure 5 displays the 70th frame of the rendered sequence using three schemes. The image on top left, top right, and bottom is generated by the quality-optimal cloud rendering, delay-optimal cloud rendering, and Shu's rendering (rate ratio is 5:1), respectively. Form Figure 5, we can see that our proposed cloud rendering schemes can achieve much better quality than Shu's approach subjectively.

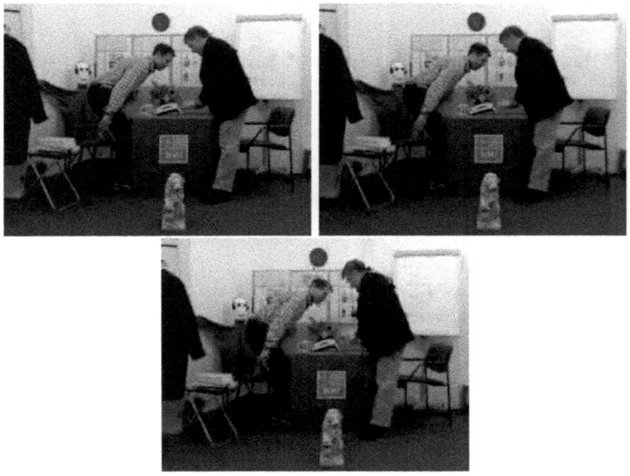

Figure 5: Comparisons of the 70th rendered frame

5. CONCLUSIONS

In this paper, we have presented a novel cloud-based free viewpoint video rendering framework for mobile phones over cellular networks. More specifically, we proposed a novel resource allocation scheme that jointly considers rendering and rate allocations between cloud and client to optimize the quality of experience. Simulation results have demonstrated the effectiveness of the proposed quality-optimal cloud rendering and delay-optimal cloud rendering approaches.

6. REFERENCES

[1] Y. Mori, N. Fukushima, T. Yendo, T. Fuji, and M. Tanimoto. View generation with 3d warping using depth information for ftv. *Signal Processing: Image Communication*, 24(1-2):65–72, Jan. 2009.

[2] A. Smolic, K. Muller, K. Dix, P. Merkle, P. Kauff, and T. Wieg. Intermediate view interpolation based on multiview video plus depth for advanced 3d video system. *in Proc. IEEE ICIP 2008*, pages 2448–2451.

[3] S. Shi, W. J. Jeon, K. Nahrstedt, and R. H. Campbell. Real-time remote rendering of 3d video for mobile devices. *in Proc. ACM Multimedia 2009*, pages 391–400.

[4] W. Zhu, C. Luo, J. Wang, and S. Li. Multimedia cloud computing: Directions and applications. *Special Issue on Distributed Image Processing and Communications, IEEE Signal Processing Magazine*, 28(3):56–69, Apr. 2011.

[5] Y. Liu, Q. Huang, S. Ma, D. Zhao, and W. Gao. Joint video/depth rate allocation for 3d video coding based on view synthesis distortion model. *Signal Processing: Image Communication*, 24(8):666–681, Sept. 2009.

[6] H. Wang and S. Kwong. Rate-distortion optimization of rate control for h.264 with adaptive initial quantization parameter determination. *IEEE Trans. CSVT*, 18(1):140–144, Jan. 2008.

[7] S. Ma, W. Gao, and Y. Lu. Rate-distortion analysis for h.264/avc video coding and its application to rate control. *IEEE Trans. CSVT*, 15(12):1533–1544, Dec. 2005.

[8] http://research.microsoft.com/en us/about/techtransfer/techtransfer2008.aspx.

APRICOD: A Distributed Caching Middleware for Fast Content Discovery of Non-continuous Media Access *

Zhen Wei Zhao
NUS Graduate School for Integrative Sciences and Engineering
National University of Singapore, Singapore
zhaozhenwei@nus.edu.sg

Wei Tsang Ooi
School of Computing
National University of Singapore, Singapore
ooiwt@comp.nus.edu.sg

ABSTRACT

We propose an access pattern-driven distributed caching middleware named APRICOD, which can be built on top of any existing content discovery system. APRICOD caters for fast and scalable content discovery in peer-to-peer media streaming systems, especially when user interactions that leads to non-continuous media access (such as random seek in video and teleportation in virtual environment) are present. APRICOD caches query results based correlations among media objects accessed by users, reducing the content discovery time. Our evaluation using a VoD access trace shows that close to 70% of non-continuous access queries can be resolved with a single hop using APRICOD.

Categories and Subject Descriptors: H.2.4 [**Systems**]: Query processing; H.3.4 [**Systems and Software**]: Distributed systems

General Terms: Design, Performance

Keywords: Content discovery system, user interaction, caching, non-continuous media access, peer-to-peer

1. INTRODUCTION

Content discovery is a process by which a peer identifies where to retrieve a required object from. The requirement for content discovery time varies across different applications. File sharing applications can tolerate long content discovery time, while interactive media streaming applications such as VoD and networked virtual environment, require shorter lookup time to ensure a smooth user experience. For instance, De Silva *et al.* [4] show that over 95% of users can tolerate a delay up to only 1 second in progressive mesh streaming.

Approaches to content discovery can be classified into either *centralized*, *DHT-based*, *gossip-based*, or *cell-based* approaches. The centralized approach relies on a central server to index the content and to respond to content discovery queries. Media streaming systems such as Kangaroo [8] adopt this approach. With the centralized approach, queries take only one hop to resolve, but it is not scalable and has a single-point of failure.

DHT is a scalable and distributed content discovery approach. It employs a structured overlay to route queries to their destination through intermediate nodes. Queries can be resolved within maximal $log(N)$ hops, where N is the number of nodes in the DHT overlay. DHT is highly scalable, but is not suitable for content discovery in interactive media streaming applications due to its potentially long lookup time.

The gossip-based approach is widely used in media streaming systems. With this approach, peers periodically exchange data availability information with their neighbors. To support non-continuous access, gossip-based approach often groups peers into clusters according to their playback point. A peer maintains neighborhood relationship with not only peers in its own cluster, but also some peers in other clusters. If the peer jumps to another cluster due to non-continuous access, it reestablishes its new neighborhood through either its current neighbors or through a neighborhood discovery mechanism (such as through a centralized server or DHT). Different variations of this approach are adopted by systems such as InstantLeap [7] and RINDY [1]. Gossip-based approach works effectively when the number of clusters is small. When the number of clusters increases, however, the content discovery time and neighborhood maintenance overhead increase.

In the cell-based approach, resources are managed distributedly by selected nodes, usually called super peers or cell managers. Each cell manager behaves like a central server for the resource it manages. Hence, the content discovery problem is converted to the problem of finding the cell manager that manages the required resources. Unlike DHT, which routes queries based on the hashed key value, the cell-based approach directs peers to the right cell manager based on temporal or spatial adjacency relations among the cells. For instance, Cheng *et al.* [2] group vertices in a progressive mesh into cells and use this approach to enable content discovery in peer-to-peer progressive mesh streaming. Fast discovery of the right cell manager during non-continuous access, however, remains a problem.

Given the drawbacks of existing content discovery approaches, a fast and scalable content discovery system that supports non-continuous media access is needed. In this paper, we propose such a system called APRICOD. APRICOD is a distributed caching middleware that exploits the access correlations among media objects so as to shorten the content discovery time, especially for non-continuous media access.

We say object Obj_2 is correlated with Obj_1 if peers are likely to access Obj_2 after accessing Obj_1. In media systems, the two basic sources of data correlation are spatial and temporal relations. For instance, in a virtual environment, two nearby objects are correlated spatially. Two consecutive video segments are correlated

*Area chair: Wu-chi Feng

MM'11, November 28–December 1, 2011, Scottsdale, Arizona, USA.

temporally. Such obvious correlations are results of continuous access to media.

Other forms of correlations exist due to non-continuous access. Such correlations can be caused by reasons such as features in user interfaces (bookmarked playback point in a video or teleporters and landmarks in a virtual environment). These correlations can be exploited for provision of fast content discovery during non-continuous access. Existing systems, however, do not exploit such correlations. In particular, DHT-based approaches are unable to exploit these correlations since $\langle key, value \rangle$ pairs are looked up independently of each other. Existing gossip-based and cell-based systems only exploit those obvious correlations, which support continuous media accesses effectively, but incur longer latency for non-continuous access.

APRICOD is the first system that exploit the non-obvious correlations for content discovery. In APRICOD, the convolving correlations (including those non-obvious correlations) are mined in a black-box way, making our system application-independent. More specifically, we use the user interaction history to infer the correlations. The mined correlations are further used to facilitate content discovery. In contrast to the existing data-driven content discovery systems such as DHT and many others, APRICOD is user access pattern driven. To the best of our knowledge, we are the first to explore this new paradigm for content discovery.

We now describe the design philosophies of APRICOD, which lead to the improvements of APRICOD over the existing content discovery systems. Firstly, APRICOD is a caching middleware on top of an underlying content discovery system. It tries to resolve as many queries as possible with merely a single hop. Secondly, APRICOD resolves popular queries faster than unpopular ones. Thirdly, instead of viewing queries issued from different peers as independent from each other, we allow peers (even those offline ones) to collaborate by sharing their query information. Fourthly, APRICOD does not use a fixed overlay structure, rather it adapts to user access pattern by automatically changing its overlay structure over time. Finally, the APRICOD overlay is conceptually separate from either the data dissemination or the content discovery overlay, which makes it general and can be used for various applications and attached to different existing content discovery systems.

2. RELATED WORK

We now briefly discuss related work that considers non-continuous access in peer-to-peer media streaming.

Qiu *et al.* [7] design a content discovery scheme called InstantLeap for P2P VoD streaming. It divides peers into groups according to their playback point and each peer maintains connections to a portion of those groups. Content discovery is achieved through neighbor list exchange. Even though theoretically a constant number of hop is needed at high probability, it is at the cost of scalability because the number of connections a peer has to keep grows linearly with respect to the number of groups. Yang *et al.* [8] adopt a centralized approach to perform content discovery. As a result, it requires peers to continuously update the server about their data availability, which places significant amount of workload on the server when the peer population is large.

MOPAR [9] supports non-continuous access such as teleportation by using DHT to provide global connectivity. When peers teleport to another location, MOPAR discovers peers around the destination by querying the DHT. As a result, it is hard to ensure fast response to user interactions due to the potentially long lookup time of DHT. Cheng *et al.* [2] propose a content discovery scheme specifically for progressive mesh streaming by exploiting the parent-child relation among vertices. However, similar techniques cannot be applied to other systems where such elegant hierarchical relation does not exist.

Several recent research work investigated into exploiting social relationship among users for content discovery. These systems assume that two users who are in the same social group are likely to be interested in the same set of files. Based on this assumption, Pouwelse *et al.* [6] develop Tribler, a social-based peer-to-peer file sharing system. Cheng *et al.* [3] develop NetTube, which exploits social relations to assist in streaming of YouTube videos. It is not clear, however, how social relationship relates to non-continuous access patterns in media.

3. SYSTEM MODEL

As a caching middleware, APRICOD should be used together with an underlying content discovery system that provides query resolution guarantees so as to ensure global connectivity. Fig. 1 shows two possible configurations, where APRICOD provides support for a centralized content discovery system and a DHT-based system respectively.

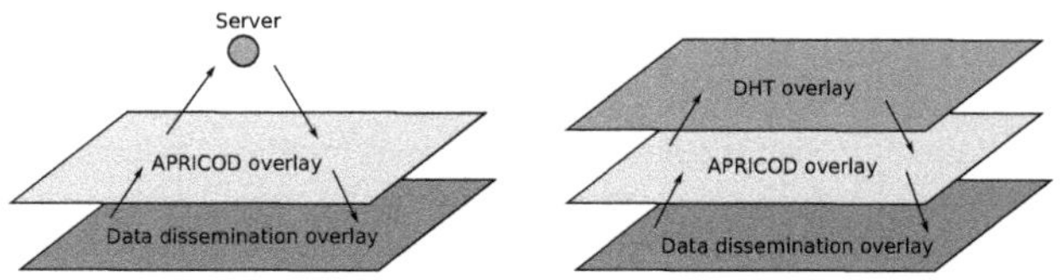

(a) Attached with server (b) Attached with DHT

Figure 1: APRICOD used together with underlying content discovery systems. (Arrows indicate query resolution path. Queries are passed to the upper layer if they cannot be resolved by APRICOD.)

Fig. 1 shows that the APRICOD overlay is designed separately from the data dissemination and the content discovery overlay. All layers in Fig. 1 are conceptually independent of each other, even though in real implementation they may be combined together. The data dissemination layer issues query to the APRICOD layer. If APRICOD cannot resolve the query, it relays the query to the content discovery layer. Both configurations in Fig. 1 have their respective advantages and drawbacks: the system architecture shown in Fig. 1(a) trades scalability for shorter lookup time. It is the other way round for Fig. 1(b). Our work focuses on the APRICOD overlay and we treat the content discovery layer as a black box.

The key construct behind APRICOD is a resource map. All media objects accessible by users constitute a n-dimensional resource space, which is partitioned into small cells. For instance, in a VoD system, a video is partitioned in the temporal dimension. A cell is thus a video segment. In a virtual environment, the virtual space can be partitioned in the spatial dimension, where a cell is an area. Each cell is managed by a logical node called *cell manager*. Content discovery in APRICOD is achieved by exploiting correlations among media objects managed by these cell managers. Recall that object Obj_2 is correlated with Obj_1 if peers are likely to access Obj_2 after accessing Obj_1. Accordingly, two cell managers are correlated if the objects they manage are correlated. Each cell manager maintains a small number of links pointing to their most correlated cell managers. Links can be either fixed links, which corresponds to the obvious correlations, or dynamic links, which corresponds to non-obvious correlations and are updated on the fly. These cell managers and the links they maintain constitute the resource map.

Suppose a peer is currently accessing resources managed by a cell manager H. The peer attaches to the cell manager H, and uses it as the query resolver to perform content discovery. Every cell manager maintains a content provider list for objects it manages. Therefore, if the peer queries for a list of content providers for objects managed by H, H would be able to answer the query directly. If the peer starts accessing objects in a cell that is out of the responsibility of H, the peer should find the corresponding cell manager K who is in charge of that cell first and then request a list of content providers from K. To discover K, the peer queries cell manager H as well, because it is very likely that H has a link pointing to K given the way we construct the resource map. If so, the query is a hit and resolves in just a single hop.

When H does not have a link to K, it resorts to the content discovery layer to find K and return K's IP address to the peer. In addition, H should establish a dynamic link pointing to K, since the query indicates that K is correlated to H. Even though establishing the dynamic link does not help the querying peer, it will help future peers issuing the same query. In other words, H caches the query result. As the peer moves to access resources managed by another cell manager, it changes the cell manager it is attaching to and repeats the same querying process as described above.

We can observe that the resource map is constructed incrementally: a new dynamic link is established if a query misses. This construction process is indeed a learning process, which learns the correlations among cell managers, reflecting user access patterns. Due to the capacity limitation at each cell manager, we may want to limit the number of links a cell manager can maintain. If the capacity limit is reached, an existing dynamic link should be replaced. State-of-the-art cache replacement policies (such as LRU/k and LFU) can be used to determine which dynamic link to replace.

If the peer has cached enough content managed by a cell manager, it registers itself as a content provider to that cell manager for those media objects it has cached. Accordingly, deregistration should be carried out when deleting the content from its cache.

Note that cell managers are logical nodes, which can be mapped to different peers in real implementation. Cell managers employ appropriate replication scheme (and thus logically never fail) to preserve the learnt correlations in the system.

4. EVALUATION

We evaluate APRICOD by collecting traces from a VoD flash player, which log the seeking behavior of 54 users while watching a lecture video over one semester. The $857s$ video is quantized into segments with equal length of $10s$. Each segment is managed by a cell manager. Whenever the playhead moves from segment S_A to segment S_B, a query is issued to M_A (the cell manager in charge of segment S_A) to discover M_B. Each cell manager maintains two fixed links pointing to its neighbors, i.e., the cell managers that manage the previous segment and next segment in temporal order in the video. Apart from that, each cell manager also maintains n dynamic links pointing to non-neighboring cell managers ($n = 10$ by default), using LFU as the cache replacement policy.

First, we examine the correlations among non-neighboring segments since that is the fundamental assumption APRICOD is built on. Correlations among neighboring segments are obvious, so we do not examine them. Fig. 2 shows the correlations among non-neighboring segments mined from the trace. The X-axis denotes the top x portion of most popular non-continuous access links, and the Y-axis denotes the portion of queries attracted by the top x portion of most popular non-continuous access links. Meanwhile, the green *dotted line* denotes random user access pattern. The red *solid line* denotes user access pattern observed in the trace. Within the huge non-continuous access link space, only a small portion of them get accessed. From the figure, we can conclude that there is significant amount of correlations even among non-neighboring segments. By knowing a small number of non-continuous access links, we would be able to answer a significant portion of non-continuous access queries.

Next we use the trace data to demonstrate how APRICOD evolves over time and to show how APRICOD works. For clarity, we limit the number of dynamic links to 5 and focus on the cell managers in charge of segments $60, 61, 62, 63$ and 64 only (shown as blue nodes). Fig. 5 shows a serial of snapshots of the system states. Outgoing links of black nodes are not shown in Fig. 5. Neighbor links are not shown as well since they are always present. Each link is labeled with its access count. The thicker the link is, the more often it is accessed, indicating a stronger correlation.

When the simulation starts (Fig. 5(a)), there are no dynamic links in the system. After receiving 700 queries, dynamic link starts appearing. From Fig. 5(b) to 5(c) we start observing link replacement. For instance, the links $62 \rightarrow 55$ and $62 \rightarrow 57$ in Fig. 5(b) are replaced by $62 \rightarrow 59$ and $62 \rightarrow 69$ in Fig. 5(c). As more queries are received, the dynamic links adapt automatically to the user access pattern. One phenomenon that can be easily observed from Fig. 5(a) to 5(f) is that those links that indicate strong correlations tend to be kept over time. Note that access count of each link may not increase monotonically from Fig. 5(a) to 5(f). For instance, the link $62 \rightarrow 65$ has an access count of 3 in Fig. 5(e), but only 1 in Fig. 5(f). This is because the link is replaced and later added back between the $2800th$ and $3500th$ query. When adding back a previously replaced link, its access count restarts from 1.

Finally, the trace is fed into an APRICOD simulator to examine the caching efficiency. We group every 50 queries into a round according the order they are issued, and then compute the hit rate of each round. Fig. 3 plots the CDF of query hit rate, including both continuous access queries and non-continuous access queries. The green line denotes the query hit rate when only neighboring links (fixed links) exist, handling only continuous access queries. The red line shows the hit rate when we have 10 dynamic links in addition to the fixed links to handle non-continuous access queries. Fig. 3 shows that the median hit rate increases from about 0.6 to 0.85 with the dynamic links introduced by APRICOD. The improvement is achieved by exploiting the correlations among non-neighboring segments as shown in Fig. 2.

Since neighboring links will always be present, continuous access queries will always hit with peer failure as an exception. Thereby, we focus our evaluation below on non-continuous access queries. Fig. 4 shows the hit rate of non-continuous access queries over time. We can observe the learning process from the curve. At the beginning of the simulation, the hit rate of non-continuous access queries is almost 0. After receiving 15 rounds of queries (each round consists of 50 queries), the hit rate increases to 0.7. We observe 1464 non-continuous access queries with 781 hits and 683 misses. Majority of the missed queries (668 out of 683) are due to the fact that they are seen for the first time. This observation suggests that we can get a higher query hit rate by training the system with more data.

We also evaluated APRICOD in a peer-to-peer virtual environment using traces from Second Life [5]. Similar improvement is observed. We omit the details here due to space constraint.

5. CONCLUSION

In this work, we proposed a general distributed content discovery caching middleware named APRICOD, aiming at shortening the content discovery time for non-continuous media access. APRICOD exploits the correlations among media objects, and is general

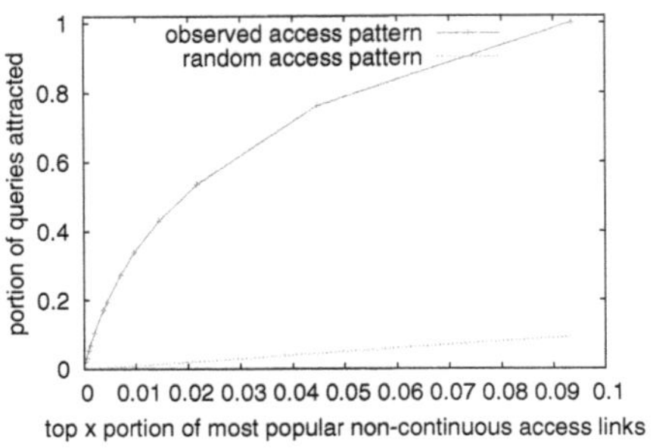

Figure 2: Correlations among non-neighboring segments observed in the trace

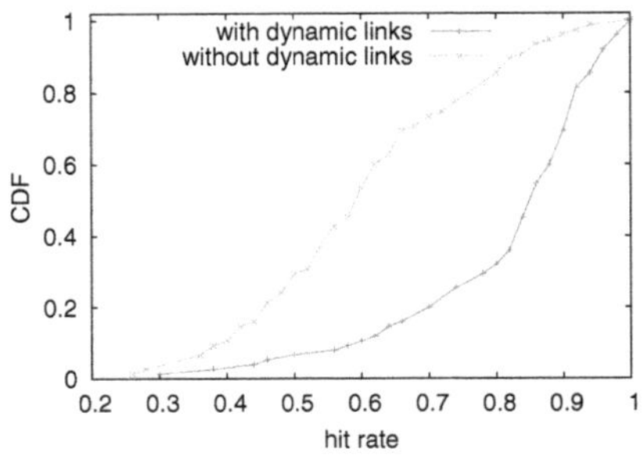

Figure 3: CDF of query hit rate

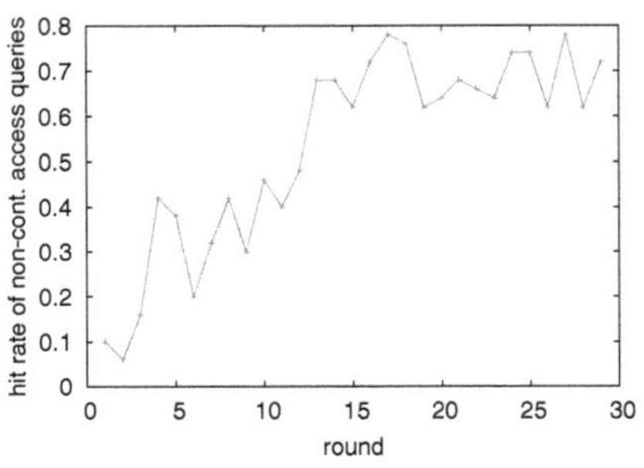

Figure 4: Non-continuous access query hit rate over time

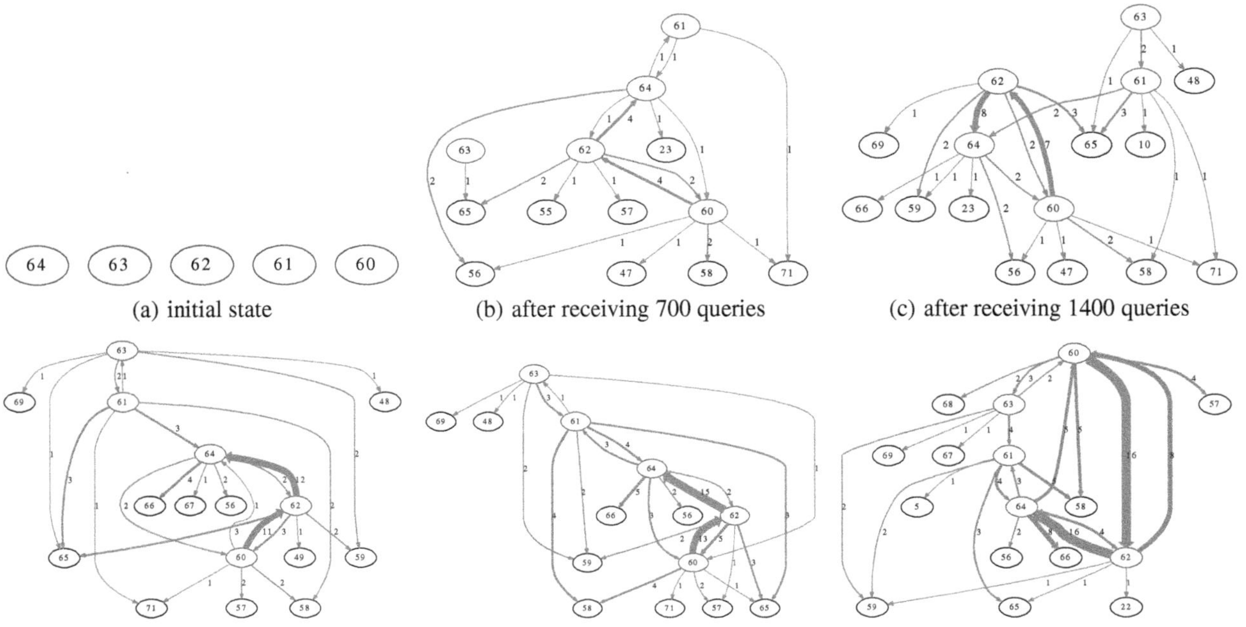

(a) initial state

(b) after receiving 700 queries

(c) after receiving 1400 queries

(d) after receiving 2100 queries

(e) after receiving 2800 queries

(f) after receiving 3500 queries

Figure 5: Evolution of dynamic links over time

enough to be used for various P2P media streaming applications such as VoD, virtual environment, zoomable video, and many others. The evaluation of APRICOD by user traces collected from a VoD player shows that it is able to shorten the content discovery time for a significant portion of non-continuous access queries to just one hop.

Acknowledgments: This research is supported by NExT Search Center, funded by the Singapore National Research Foundation & Interactive Digital Media R&D Program Office, MDA under the research grant WBS:R-252-300-001-490.

6. REFERENCES

[1] B. Cheng, H. Jin, and X. Liao. Supporting VCR Functions in P2P VoD Services Using Ring-Assisted Overlays. In *ICC '07*, pages 1698–1703, Glasgow, Scotland, UK, June 2007.

[2] W. Cheng, D. Liu, and W. T. Ooi. Peer-assisted view-dependent progressive mesh streaming. In *MM '09*, pages 441–450, Beijing, China, 2009.

[3] X. Cheng and J. Liu. NetTube: Exploring Social Networks for Peer-to-Peer Short Video Sharing. In *INFOCOM '09*, pages 1152–1160, Rio de Janeiro, Brazil, Apr. 2009.

[4] R. N. De Silva, W. Cheng, W. T. Ooi, and S. Zhao. Towards understanding user tolerance to network latency and data rate in remote viewing of progressive meshes. In *NOSSDAV '10*, pages 123–128, Amsterdam, Netherlands, 2010.

[5] H. Liang, R. De Silva, W. Ooi, and M. Motani. Avatar mobility in user-created networked virtual worlds: measurements, analysis, and implications. *Multimedia Tools and Applications*, 45:163–190, 2009.

[6] J. A. Pouwelse, P. Garbacki, J. Wang, A. Bakker, J. Yang, A. Iosup, D. H. J. Epema, M. Reinders, M. R. van Steen, and H. J. Sips. TRIBLER: a social-based peer-to-peer system: Research Articles. *Concurr. Comput. : Pract. Exper.*, 20:127–138, February 2008.

[7] X. Qiu, C. Wu, X. Lin, and F. C. Lau. InstantLeap: fast neighbor discovery in P2P VoD streaming. In *NOSSDAV '09*, pages 19–24, Williamsburg, VA, 2009.

[8] X. Yang, M. Gjoka, P. Chhabra, A. Markopoulou, and P. Rodriguez. Kangaroo: video seeking in P2P systems. In *IPTPS'09*, Boston, MA, 2009.

[9] A. P. Yu and S. T. Vuong. MOPAR: a mobile peer-to-peer overlay architecture for interest management of massively multiplayer online games. In *NOSSDAV '05*, pages 99–104, Stevenson, Washington, 2005.

Robust Image Registration and Tampering Localization Exploiting Bag of Features Based Forensic Signature *

Sebastiano Battiato, Giovanni Maria Farinella, Enrico Messina, Giovanni Puglisi
Dipartimento di Matematica e Informatica, Università degli Studi di Catania, Italy
{battiato, gfarinella, emessina, puglisi}@dmi.unict.it

ABSTRACT

The distribution of digital images with the classic and newest technologies available on Internet (e.g., emails, social networks, digital repositories) has induced a growing interest on systems able to protect the visual content against malicious manipulations that could be performed during their transmission. One of the main problems addressed in this context is the authentication of the image received in a communication. This task is usually performed by localizing the regions of the image which have been tampered. To this aim the received image should be first registered with the one at the sender by exploiting the information provided by a specific component of the forensic hash associated with the image. In this paper we propose a robust alignment method which makes use of an image signature based on the Bag of Features paradigm. The alignment is based on a voting procedure in the parameter space of the model used to recover the geometric transformation occurred into the manipulated image. Experiments show that the proposed approach obtains good margin in terms of performances with respect to state-of-the art methods.

Categories and Subject Descriptors

I.4.10 [**Image Processing and Computer Vision**]: Image Representation; I.4.9 [**Image Processing and Computer Vision**]: Applications

General Terms

Algorithms, Security, Verification

Keywords

Image Forensics, Forensic Hash, Bag of Features, Image Registration, Tampering Localization, Image Authentication.

*Area chair: Tian-Tsong Ng

MM'11, November 28–December 1, 2011, Scotsdale, Arizona, USA.

1. INTRODUCTION AND MOTIVATIONS

The importance of digital visual data is reflected by their increasing and systematically use in the communication platforms offered by Internet to the today's society. The growing demand of techniques useful to protect digital visual data against malicious manipulations is induced by different episodes that make questionable the use of visual content as evidence material [3]. Specifically, methods useful to establish the validity and authenticity of a received image are needed in the context of Internet communications. To this aim different solutions have been recently proposed in literature [1, 2, 5, 6, 7]. Most of them share the same basic scheme: i) a hash code based on the visual content is attached to the image to be sent; ii) the hash is analyzed at destination to verify the reliability of the received image.

In order to perform tampering localization, the receiver should be able to filter out all the geometric transformations (e.g., rotation, scaling, translation) added to the tampered image by aligning the received image the one at the sender [2, 6]. The alignment should be done in a semi-blind way: at destination one can use only the received image and the image hash to deal with the alignment problem since the reference image is not available. The challenging task of recovering the geometric transformations occurred on a received image from its signature motivates this paper.

Building on the technique described in [2] and [6], we propose a new method to detect the geometric manipulations occurred on an image starting from the hash computed on the original one. Differently than [2] and [6], we exploit replicated matchings and a voting procedure in the parameter space of the transformation model employed to establish the geometric manipulation (i.e., rotation, scale, translation). As pointed out by the experimental results, the proposed approach obtains the best results with a significant margin in terms of estimation accuracy with respect to [2] and [6]. The effectiveness of the proposed method is also reflected through tampering detection tests in which a block-wise approach based on histograms of oriented gradients representation has been employed [7].

The remainder of the paper is organized as follows: Section 2 presents the proposed alignment signature and the registration framework. Section 3 reports experiments and discuss the registration and tampering localization results. Finally, conclusion are given in Section 4.

2. REGISTRATION COMPONENT

As in [2, 6], we adopt a Bag of Features based representations to reduce the dimensionality of the descriptors to be used as hash component for the alignment. A codebook is generated by clustering the set of SIFT extracted on training images. The pre-computed codebook is shared between sender and receiver. It should be noted that the codebook is built only once, and then used for all the communications between sender and receiver (i.e., no extra overhead for each communication). The sender extracts SIFT features and sorts them in descending order with respect to their contrast values. Afterward, the top n SIFT are selected and associated to the *id* label corresponding to the closest prototype belonging to the shared codebook. The final signature for the alignment component is created by considering the *id* label, the dominant direction θ, and the keypoint coordinates x and y for each selected SIFT. The source image and the corresponding hash component for the alignment (h_s) are sent to the destination. The system assumes that the image is sent over a network consisting of possibly untrusted nodes, whereas the signature is sent upon request through a trusted authentication server which encrypts the hash in order to guarantee its integrity [5]. The image could be manipulated for malicious purposes during the untrusted communication.

Once the image reaches the destination, the receiver generates the related hash signature for registration (h_r) by using the same procedure employed by the sender. Then, the entries of the hashes h_s and h_r are matched by considering their *id* values.The alignment is hence performed by employing a similarity transformation of keypoint pairs corresponding to matched hashes entries:

$$x_r = x_s\lambda\cos\alpha - y_s\lambda\sin\alpha + T_x \tag{1}$$

$$y_r = x_s\lambda\sin\alpha + y_s\lambda\cos\alpha + T_y \tag{2}$$

The above transformation is used to model the geometrical manipulations which have been done on the source image during the untrusted communication. The model assumes that a point (x_s, y_s) in the source image I_s is transformed in a point (x_r, y_r) in the image I_r at destination with a combination of rotation (α), scaling (λ) and translation (T_x, T_y). The aim of the alignment phase is the estimation of the quadruple $(\widehat{\lambda}, \widehat{\alpha}, \widehat{T_x}, \widehat{T_y})$ by exploiting the correspondences $((x_s, y_s), (x_r, y_r))$ related to matchings between h_s and h_r. We propose to use a cascade approach; first an initial estimation of the parameters $(\widetilde{\alpha}, \widetilde{T_x}, \widetilde{T_y})$ is accomplished through a voting procedure in the quantized parameter space $\overline{\alpha} \times \overline{T_x} \times \overline{T_y}$. Such procedure is performed after filtering outlier matchings by taking into account the differences between dominant orientations of matched entries. The initial estimation is then refined considering only reliable matchings in order to obtain the final parameters $(\widehat{\alpha}, \widehat{T_x}, \widehat{T_y})$. Afterward, the scaling parameter $\widehat{\lambda}$ is estimated by means of the parameters $(\widehat{\alpha}, \widehat{T_x}, \widehat{T_y})$ which have been previously estimated on the reliable information obtained through the filtering described above. The overall estimation procedure is detailed in the following.

Moving T_x and T_y on the left side and making the ratio of (1) and (2) the following equation is obtained:

$$\frac{x_r - T_x}{y_r - T_y} = \frac{x_s\cos\alpha - y_s\sin\alpha}{x_s\sin\alpha + y_s\cos\alpha} \tag{3}$$

Solving (3) with respect to T_x and T_y we get the formulas to be used in the voting procedure:

$$T_x = \left(\frac{x_s\cos\alpha - y_s\sin\alpha}{x_s\sin\alpha + y_s\cos\alpha}\right)(T_y - y_r) + x_r \tag{4}$$

$$T_y = \left(\frac{x_s\sin\alpha + y_s\cos\alpha}{x_s\cos\alpha - y_s\sin\alpha}\right)(T_x - x_r) + y_r \tag{5}$$

Each pair of coordinates (x_s, y_s) and (x_r, y_r) can be used together with (4) and (5) to represent two lines in the parameter space $\alpha \times T_x \times T_y$. The initial estimation of the parameters $(\widetilde{\alpha}, \widetilde{T_x}, \widetilde{T_y})$ is hence obtained by considering the densest bin of a 3D histogram in the quantized parameter space $\overline{\alpha} \times \overline{T_x} \times \overline{T_y}$. This means that the initial estimation of $(\widetilde{\alpha}, \widetilde{T_x}, \widetilde{T_y})$ is accomplished in correspondence of the maximum number of intersections between lines generated by matched keypoints.

As said before, to discard outliers (i.e., wrong matchings) the information coming from the dominant directions (θ) of the SIFT is used during the voting procedure. In particular $\Delta\theta = \theta_r - \theta_s$ is a rough estimation of the rotational angle α. Hence, for each fixed triplet $(\overline{\alpha}, \overline{T_x}, \overline{T_y})$ of the quantized parameter space, the voting procedure considers only the matchings between h_s and h_r such that $|\Delta\theta - \overline{\alpha}| < t_\alpha$. The threshold value t_α is chosen to consider only matchings with a rough estimation $\Delta\theta$ which is closer to the considered $\overline{\alpha}$ (e.g., consider just matchings with a small initial error of ± 3.5 degree). In this way we obtain an initial estimation of rotation angle $\widetilde{\alpha}$, and translation vector $(\widetilde{T_x}, \widetilde{T_y})$ by taking into account the quantized values used to build the 3D histogram into the parameter space.

To refine the initial estimation we exploit the m matchings which have generated the lines intersecting in the selected bin. Specifically, for each pair $((x_{s,i}, y_{s,i}), (x_{r,i}, y_{r,i}))$ corresponding to the selected bin of the 3D histogram, we consider the following translation vectors

$$(\widehat{T_{x,i}}, \widetilde{T_{y,i}}) = \left(\left(\frac{x_{s,i}\cos\widetilde{\alpha} - y_{s,i}\sin\widetilde{\alpha}}{x_{s,i}\sin\widetilde{\alpha} + y_{s,i}\cos\widetilde{\alpha}}\right)(\widetilde{T_y} - y_{r,i}) + x_{r,i}, \widetilde{T_y}\right) \tag{6}$$

$$(\widetilde{T_{x,i}}, \widehat{T_{y,i}}) = \left(\widetilde{T_x}, \left(\frac{x_{s,i}\sin\widetilde{\alpha} + y_{s,i}\cos\widetilde{\alpha}}{x_{s,i}\cos\widetilde{\alpha} - y_{s,i}\sin\widetilde{\alpha}}\right)(\widetilde{T_x} - x_{r,i}) + y_{r,i}\right) \tag{7}$$

together with the subsequent equations

$$x_{r,i} = x_{s,i}\lambda_i\cos\alpha_i - y_{s,i}\lambda_i\sin\alpha_i + T_{x,i} \tag{8}$$

$$y_{r,i} = x_{s,i}\lambda_i\sin\alpha_i + y_{s,i}\lambda_i\cos\alpha_i + T_{y,i} \tag{9}$$

The parameters values $(\widetilde{\alpha}, \widetilde{T_x}, \widetilde{T_y})$ in (6) and (7) are the ones obtained through the voting procedure.
Solving (8) and (9) with respect to $a_i = \lambda_i\cos\alpha_i$ and $b_i = \lambda_i\sin\alpha_i$ we obtain:

$$a_i = \frac{y_{r,i}y_{s,i} + x_{r,i}x_{s,i} - x_{s,i}T_{x,i} - y_{s,i}T_{y,i}}{x_{s,i}^2 + y_{s,i}^2} \tag{10}$$

$$b_i = \frac{x_{s,i}y_{r,i} - x_{r,i}y_{s,i} + y_{s,i}T_{x,i} - x_{s,i}T_{y,i}}{x_{s,i}^2 + y_{s,i}^2} \tag{11}$$

Since the ratio $\frac{b_i}{a_i}$ is by definition equals to $\tan\alpha_i$, for each pair of matched keypoints we can estimate $\widehat{\alpha_i}$ by exploiting the following formula:

$$\begin{aligned}\widehat{\alpha_i} = &\frac{1}{2}\arctan\left(\frac{x_{s,i}y_{r,i} - x_{r,i}y_{s,i} + y_{s,i}\widehat{T_{x,i}} - x_{s,i}\widetilde{T_{y,i}}}{y_{r,i}y_{s,i} + x_{r,i}x_{s,i} - x_{s,i}\widehat{T_{x,i}} - y_{s,i}\widetilde{T_{y,i}}}\right)\\ &+\frac{1}{2}\arctan\left(\frac{x_{s,i}y_{r,i} - x_{r,i}y_{s,i} + y_{s,i}\widetilde{T_{x,i}} - x_{s,i}\widehat{T_{y,i}}}{y_{r,i}y_{s,i} + x_{r,i}x_{s,i} - x_{s,i}\widetilde{T_{x,i}} - y_{s,i}\widehat{T_{y,i}}}\right)\end{aligned} \tag{12}$$

Once $\widehat{\alpha_i}$ is obtained, the equation (13) (derived from (8) and (9) by considering (6) and (7)) is used to estimate $\widehat{\lambda_i}$.

$$\begin{aligned}\widehat{\lambda_i} = &\frac{1}{4}\frac{x_{r,i} - \widetilde{T_{x,i}}}{x_{s,i}\cos\widehat{\alpha_i} - y_{s,i}\sin\widehat{\alpha_i}} + \frac{1}{4}\frac{y_{r,i} - \widetilde{T_{y,i}}}{x_{s,i}\sin\widehat{\alpha_i} + y_{s,i}\cos\widehat{\alpha_i}} \\ &+ \frac{1}{4}\frac{x_{r,i} - \widetilde{T_{x,i}}}{x_{s,i}\cos\widehat{\alpha_i} - y_{s,i}\sin\widehat{\alpha_i}} + \frac{1}{4}\frac{y_{r,i} - \widetilde{T_{y,i}}}{x_{s,i}\sin\widehat{\alpha_i} + y_{s,i}\cos\widehat{\alpha_i}}\end{aligned} \tag{13}$$

The above method produces m quadruples $(\widehat{\lambda_i}, \widehat{\alpha_i}, \widehat{T_{x,i}}, \widehat{T_{y,i}})$, one for each matching pair $((x_{s,i}, y_{s,i}), (x_{r,i}, y_{r,i}))$ corresponding to the bin selected with the voting procedure. The final transformation parameters $(\widehat{\lambda}, \widehat{\alpha}, \widehat{T_x}, \widehat{T_y})$ to be used for the registration are computed by averaging over all the m produced quadruples.

It should be noted that some *id* values may appear more than once in h_s and/or in h_r. Even if a small number of SIFT are selected during the image hash generation process, the conflict due to replicated *id* can arise. For example, it is possible that a selected SIFT has no unique dominant direction; in this case the different directions are coupled with the same descriptor, and hence will be considered more than once by the selection process which generates many instance of the same *id* with different dominant directions.

Differently than [6], the described approach considers all the possible matchings in order to preserve the useful information. The correct matchings are hence retained but other wrong pairs could be generated. Since the noise introduced by considering correct and incorrect pairs can badly influence the final estimation results, the presence of possible wrong matchings should be considered during the estimation process. The approach described in this paper deals with the problem of wrong matchings combining in cascade a filtering strategy based on the SIFT dominant direction (θ) with a robust estimator based on a voting strategy on the parameter space (see further details in [1]). In this way the information of spatial position of keypoints and their dominant orientations are jointly considered, and the scale factor is estimated only at the end of the cascade on reliable information.

3. EXPERIMENTAL RESULTS

This section reports a number of experiments on which the proposed approach has been tested and compared with respect to [2] and [6]. In order to cope with scene variability the tests have been performed considering a subset of the fifteen scene category benchmark dataset used in [4]. The training set used in the experiments is built through a random selection of 150 images from the aforementioned dataset. Specifically, ten images have been randomly sampled from each scene category. The test set consists of 15750 images generated through the application of different manipulations on the training images (Tab. 1). The registration results obtained employing the proposed approach considering an alignment hash component of different size (i.e., different number of SIFT) are reported in Tab. 2.

To demonstrate the effectiveness of the proposed approach, and to highlight the contribution of both, the replicated matchings and cascade filtering during the estimation, we have performed comparative tests by considering our method, the approach proposed in [6], and the method proposed in [2] which exploits both replicated matchings and a cascade filtering approach.

Table 1: Image manipulations.

Operations	Parameters
Rotation (α)	3, 5, 10, 30, 45 degrees
Scaling (σ)	factor = 0.5, 0.7, 0.9, 1.2, 1.5
Orizontal Traslation (T_x)	5, 10, 20 pixels
Vertical Traslation (T_y)	5, 10, 20 pixels
Cropping	19%, 28%, 36%, of entire image
Tampering	block size 50x50
Malicious Tampering	block size 50x50
Linear Photometric Transformation (a*I+b)	a = 0.90, 0.95, 1, 1.05, 1.10 b = -10, -5, 0, 5, 10
Compression	JPEG Q=10
Various combinations of above operations	

Table 2: Registration results of the proposed approach.

	Mean Error σ			
Number of SIFT	**15**	**30**	**45**	**60**
Unmatched Images	3.17%	1.50%	0,96%	0.84%
Mean Error α	1.3826	0.7970	0.5153	0.4255
Mean Error σ	0.0421	0.0237	0.0161	0.0134
Mean Error T_x	1.9704	0.9131	0.6012	0.4866
Mean Error T_y	1.6857	0.8880	0.6271	0.5540

The approach proposed in [6] has been reimplemented. The Ransac thresholds used in [6] to perform the geometric parameter estimation have been set to 3.5 degrees for the rotational model and to 0.025 for the scaling one. These thresholds values have been obtained through data analysis (inliers and outliers distributions). Although Lu et al. [6] claim that further refinements are performed using the matchings that occur more than once, actually they do not provide any implementation detail. Hence, to further refine the results obtained by Lu et al. [6] without replicated matchings, we have re-considered all the previous discarded matchings belonging to $[\widehat{\theta} - 3.5, \widehat{\theta} + 3.5]$ and $[\widehat{\sigma} - 0.025, \widehat{\sigma} + 0.025]$, with $\widehat{\theta}$ and $\widehat{\sigma}$ coming from the estimation without replicates. In order to perform a fair comparison, the threshold t_α used in our approach to filter the correspondences (see Section 2) has been set with the same value of the threshold employed by Ransac to estimate the rotational parameter in [6]. The quantized values $\overline{T_x}$ and $\overline{T_y}$ needed to evaluate the right side of (4) and (5) have been quantized considering a step of 2.5 pixels. Similar considerations have been done to properly set the parameters of the approach proposed in [2] in order to guarantee a fair comparison. Specifically, the bin size used in [2] has been obtained doubling the corresponding Ransac thresholds: a histogram with bin size of 7 degrees ranging from -180 to 180 degrees has been used for the rotation estimation step, whereas a histogram with bin size equal to 0.05 ranging from 0 to $\max_\sigma = 10$ was employed to estimate the scale. Finally, a codebook with 1000 visual words has been employed to compare the different approaches. The codebook has been learned through k-means clustering on the overall SIFT descriptors extracted on training images.

First, let us examine the typically cases on which registration approaches could fail. Two cases can be distinguished: i) no matchings are found between the hash built at the sender (h_s) and the one computed by the receiver (h_r); ii) all the matchings are replicated. The first problem can be mitigated considering a higher number of features. The second one is solved by allowing replicated matchings (see Section 2).

As reported in Tab. 3, by increasing the number of SIFT

Table 3: Comparison with respect to unmatched images.

	Unmatched Images			
Number of SIFT	15	30	45	60
Lu et al. [6]	7.54%	2.79%	1.63%	1.17%
Battiato et al. [2]	1.00%	0.57%	0,30%	0.10%
Proposed approach	3.17%	1.50%	0,96%	0.84%

points there is a decreasing of the number of unmatched images (i.e., image pairs that the algorithm is not able to process because there are no matchings between h_s and h_r) for all the approaches. In all cases the percentage of images on which our algorithm is able to work is higher than the one obtained by the approach proposed in [6]. Despite the percentages of unmatched images obtained employing [2] is less than the one obtained by the proposed approach, the tests reported in the following reveal that our method strongly outperforms the other two in terms of parameter estimation error and robustness with respect to the different transformations.

Table 4: Average rotational error.

	Mean Error α			
Number of SIFT	15	30	45	60
Unmatched Images	**10.81%**	**4.10%**	**2.17%**	**1.66%**
Lu et al. [6]	5.9700	6.5225	6.7614	6.6574
Battiato et al. [2]	3.0408	2.1747	2.0613	1.6890
Proposed approach	0.9213	0.6525	0.3548	0.2756

Table 5: Average scaling error.

	Mean Error σ			
Number of SIFT	15	30	45	60
Unmatched Images	**10.81%**	**4.10%**	**2.17%**	**1.66%**
Lu et al. [6]	0.0543	0.0512	0.0533	0.0551
Battiato et al. [2]	0.0241	0.0211	0.0182	0.0165
Proposed approach	0.0295	0.0191	0.0125	0.0102

Tab. 4 and Tab. 5 show the results obtained in terms of rotational and scale estimation through mean error. In order to properly compare the methods, the results have been computed taking into account the images on which all approaches were able to work (the number of unmatched images is reported into the tables). The proposed approach outperforms [2] and [6] obtaining a considerable gain in terms of rotational accuracy. Moreover, the performance of our approach significantly improves with the increasing of the extracted feature points (SIFT). On the contrary, the technique in [6] is not able to take advantage from the information coming from an increasing number of extracted SIFT points. The rotational estimation gain obtained by employing our approach instead the one in [6] is about 5 degree exploiting the minimum number of SIFT, and reaches 6 degree with 60 SIFT. A good gain in terms of performance is also obtained with respect to the scale factor (Tab. 5).

Finally, experiments have been done to validate the tampering localization performances after image registration. To this aim, the 1500 images of the test set containing a tampering patch have been considered. As in [7], a uniform quantization of orientation histograms has been used to represent non-overlapping blocks of images. Euclidean distance is used to discriminate between tampered and not tampered blocks. The different registration approaches have been compared through ROC curves. The area under the curves indicates a biased estimation of the expected tampering detection accuracy of the different methods. As shown

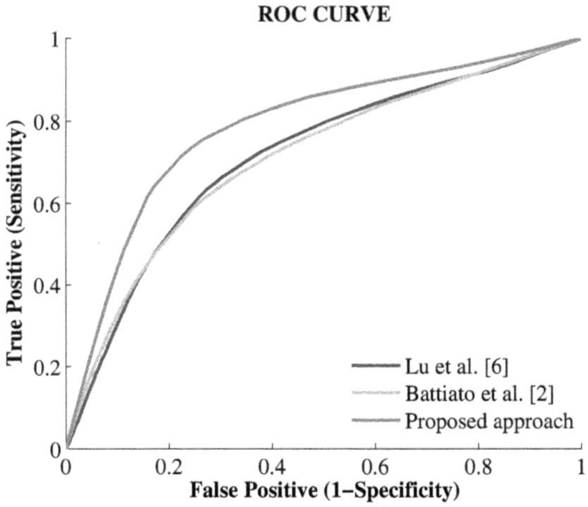

Figure 1: Tampering detection comparison.

in Fig. 1, our approach strongly outperforms the other techniques.

4. CONCLUSIONS AND FUTURE WORKS

The assessment of the reliability of an image received through the Internet is an important issue in nowadays society. This paper addressed the image alignment and tampering detection tasks in the context of distributed forensic systems. A robust image registration component which exploits an image signature based on the Bag of Features paradigm has been introduced. Comparative tests show that the proposed approach outperforms recently appeared techniques by obtaining a significant margin in terms of performances.

5. REFERENCES

[1] S. Battiato, G. M. Farinella, E. Messina, and G. Puglisi. A robust forensic hash component for image alignment. In *International Conference on Image Analysis and Processing*, 2011.

[2] S. Battiato, G. M. Farinella, E. Messina, and G. Puglisi. Understanding geometric manipulations of images through BOVW-based hashing. In *IEEE International Workshop on Content Protection &Forensics*, 2011.

[3] H. Farid. Digital doctoring: how to tell the real from the fake. *Significance*, 3(4):162–166, 2006.

[4] S. Lazebnik, C. Schmid, and J. Ponce. Beyond bags of features: Spatial pyramid matching for recognizing natural scene categories. In *IEEE Computer Society Conference on Computer Vision and Pattern Recognition*, pages 2169–2178, 2006.

[5] Y.-C. Lin, D. Varodayan, and B. Girod. Image authentication based on distributed source coding. In *IEEE Computer Society International Conference on Image Processing*, pages 3–8, 2007.

[6] W. Lu and M. Wu. Multimedia forensic hash based on visual words. In *IEEE Computer Society International Conference on Image Processing*, pages 989–992, 2010.

[7] S. Roy and Q. Sun. Robust hash for detecting and localizing image tampering. In *IEEE Computer Society International Conference on Image Processing*, pages 117–120, 2007.

Towards Content-based Audio Fragment Authentication

Xiangyang Xue, Wei Li, Yue Yin
School of Computer Science and Technology, Fudan University, Shanghai 201203, P. R. China
xyxue@fudan.edu.cn, weili-fudan@fudan.edu.cn, hello.yueyin@gmail.com

ABSTRACT

Audio authentication is a technique to protect the integrity and originality of audio signals. Due to the long duration, it is often desirable to authenticate only a segment of audio signal. To the authors' knowledge, this important issue has not been seriously researched so far. In this paper, a novel authentication algorithm is proposed for the purpose of audio fragment authentication. SIFT descriptor originated from computer vision field is introduced and calculated on audio spectrogram to accomplish the tasks of fragment alignment, time-domain blocking, cropping and inserting identification etc. Experiments show reliable discrimination between admissible and malicious manipulations, precise tamper localization and classification.

Categories and Subject Descriptors

K.6.5 [**Management of Computing and Information Systems**]: Security and Protection – *authentication*

General Terms

Algorithms, Experimentation

Keywords

Audio, fragment authentication, SIFT, spectrogram

1. INTRODUCTION

The semantic meaning of audio can be easily altered by audio editing and processing tools. Therefore, audio authentication has become an emerging technique in recent years, aiming at effectively protect the originality and integrity of audio signals.

In the literature, only few audio authentication algorithms have been published [1-6]. One desirable feature of audio authentication is to determine authenticity of a received segment [7]. However, to the authors' knowledge, this important issue has not been addressed by the research community so far. In this paper, we propose a novel audio authentication algorithm which is specially designed for the purpose of audio fragment authentication. The audio segment to be authenticated is first aligned to its corresponding position of the original signal by matching the SIFT (scale invariant feature transform) descriptors of audio spectrograms. Then by investigating the time-stretching factors obtained from SIFT key points, the dubious audio segment and the reference audio are divided into one or more homogeneous blocks in terms of stretching factors. Time-domain blocking can be directly used for recognizing malicious cropping or inserting. Combined with pitch-shifting factor estimation, it can also be used in mapping the corresponding time-frequency units between the dubious and the original audio, thus facilitate the subsequent robust hash calculation. Experimental results show that given a 10s long received audio segment, its integrity and originality can be reliably authenticated. Moreover, maliciously modified regions can be precisely located, and the type of illegal operations can also be classified.

Area Chair: Tian-Tsong Ng.
Corresponding author: weili-fudan@fudan.edu.cn

MM'11, November 28-December 1, 2011, Scottsdale, Arizona, USA.

2. FRAGMENT ALIGNMENT

To authenticate a dubious audio segment, the first thing to be done is to find its original time position in the reference audio. In order to accomplish the task of fragment alignment, we introduce the SIFT local descriptor that has been widely used in computer vision technique. The output of the SIFT feature extractor is a set of key points invariant to image stretching and translation, with their location, scale, orientation and 128-dimensional descriptor.

To exploit SIFT descriptors on audio, a prerequisite is to transform the 1-dimensional audio signal into the form of 2-dimensional spectrogram image using short-time Fourier transform (STFT). In spectrogram, the y axis is log-scaled frequencies ranging from 100 to 3000Hz considering that low-middle frequency coefficients are more robust against occasional disturbance and this frequency range can cover the band width of speech and the main components of most musical instruments; the x axis is time, represented with frame number (frame length and hop size are 4096 and 2048 points respectively in experiment). Then SIFT features are calculated on the spectrogram of the dubious and the reference audio respectively, and the 128-dimensional descriptors are compared with each other to obtain the matched key point pairs, as shown in Figure 1.

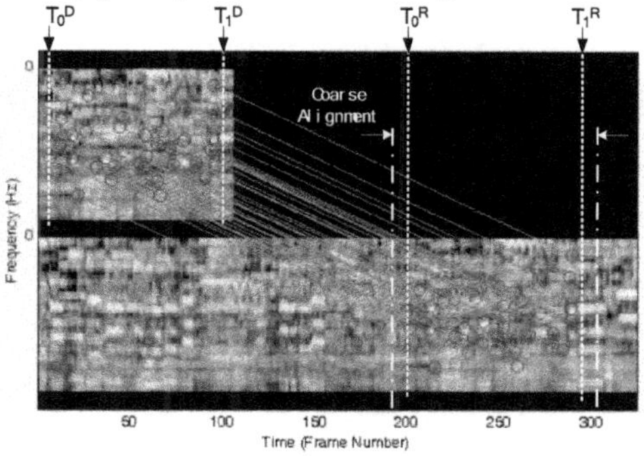

Figure 1. Matching of SIFT key points between spectrograms of the dubious and the reference audio signal

To be specific, let $\{(\boldsymbol{P}_1^D, \boldsymbol{P}_1^R), (\boldsymbol{P}_2^D, \boldsymbol{P}_2^R), \ldots, (\boldsymbol{P}_N^D, \boldsymbol{P}_N^R)\}$ denotes the N pairs of matched SIFT key points, then the leftmost and rightmost point positions of the two signals are written as,

$$T_0^D = \min\{\boldsymbol{P}_1^D.x,, \ldots, \boldsymbol{P}_N^D.x\} \quad T_1^D = \max\{\boldsymbol{P}_1^D.x,, \ldots, \boldsymbol{P}_N^D.x\}$$
$$T_0^R = \min\{\boldsymbol{P}_1^R.x,, \ldots, \boldsymbol{P}_N^R.x\} \quad T_1^R = \max\{\boldsymbol{P}_1^R.x,, \ldots, \boldsymbol{P}_N^R.x\}$$

Suppose the length of the dubious audio is L_D, then the space between the left (right) boundary and the leftmost (rightmost) SIFT point is T_0^D and $L_D - T_1^D$ respectively. Therefore, the corresponding mapped spaces on the reference audio are calculated according to Eq. (1) and marked as Δ_0^R and Δ_1^R.

After the SIFT key points are ascendingly sorted by their time coordinate, the dubious audio's estimated location on the reference audio is given by Eq. (2).

$$\begin{cases} \overline{\Delta_D} = \dfrac{1}{N-1} \displaystyle\sum_{i=1}^{i=N-1} (\boldsymbol{P}_{i+1}^D.x - \boldsymbol{P}_i^D.x) \\ \overline{\Delta_R} = \dfrac{1}{N-1} \displaystyle\sum_{i=1}^{i=N-1} (\boldsymbol{P}_{i+1}^R.x - \boldsymbol{P}_i^R.x) \\ \Delta_0^R = (T_0^D)\, \overline{\Delta_R}/\overline{\Delta_D}, \\ \Delta_1^R = (L_D - T_1^D)\, \overline{\Delta_R}/\overline{\Delta_D} \end{cases} \quad (1)$$

where L_R, SR_R and P_R are the frame number, sampling rate, and the time length (s) of the reference audio, respectively.

$$\begin{cases} T_{start}^R = \dfrac{(T_0^R - \Delta_0^R) \times (P_R \times SR_R)}{L_R} \\ T_{end}^R = \dfrac{(T_1^R + \Delta_1^R) \times (P_R \times SR_R)}{L_R} \end{cases} \quad (2)$$

3. ROBUST HASHING

Because the received audio segment might have experienced various distortions such as time stretching, pitch shifting, time-domain cropping and inserting etc., two preprocessing i.e. time-domain blocking and frequency alignment are first performed to overcome the above problems before robust hash generation.

3.1 Time-domain Blocking

The aim of time-domain blocking is to partition the dubious and the reference audio into one or more blocks within each the time-stretching factors are approximately the same, thus facilitate the discovery of maliciously cropped/inserted regions and the following robust hashing.

(1). For SIFT key point pairs $\{(\boldsymbol{P}_1^D, \boldsymbol{P}_1^R), (\boldsymbol{P}_2^D, \boldsymbol{P}_2^R), \dots, (\boldsymbol{P}_N^D, \boldsymbol{P}_N^R)\}$, the time distance between two neighboring key points of the dubious and the reference audio and the time-stretching factor are defined as

$$\begin{cases} L^{\{D,R\}} = \left\{ L_i^{\{D,R\}} \middle| L_i^{\{D,R\}} = \boldsymbol{P}_{i+1}^{\{D,R\}}.x - \boldsymbol{P}_i^{\{D,R\}}.x, i = 1, \dots, N-1 \right\} \\ R_i = \dfrac{L_i^D}{L_i^R}, i = 1, 2, \dots, N-1 \end{cases} \quad (3)$$

Next these factors are grouped into several subsets $\{C_i\}$ like $\underbrace{\{\mathrm{R}_1, \dots, \mathrm{R}_i\}}_{C_1} \dots \underbrace{\{\mathrm{R}_j, \dots, \mathrm{R}_k\}}_{C_i} \dots \underbrace{\{\mathrm{R}_m, \dots, \mathrm{R}_{N-1}\}}_{C_M}$. In each subset, the ratios inside are almost the same, while with two successive subsets e.g. $\mathrm{C}_i = \{\mathrm{R}_j, \dots, \mathrm{R}_k\}$ and $\mathrm{C}_{i+1} = \{\mathrm{R}_{k+1}, \dots, \mathrm{R}_l\}$ the mean time-stretching factor will have a big change as Eq. (4).

$$\left| \left(\frac{1}{k-j+1} \sum_{n=j}^{k} R_n \middle/ \frac{1}{l-k} \sum_{n=k+1}^{l} R_n \right) - 1 \right| > T_h, \\ j < k < l-1 < N-1 \quad (4)$$

where N is the number of key point pairs, T_h represents the threshold used in partitioning subsets. Small T_h is more sensitive to tiny changes of time-stretching factors and hence facilitates the discovery of cropped/inserted local regions, while larger value will accommodate occasional variation of stretching factors. In experiment, we choose T_h=0.3 to comprise the two aspects.

(2). According to the SIFT key points grouped into each subset $\underbrace{\{\boldsymbol{P}_1^{\{D,R\}}, \dots, \boldsymbol{P}_i^{\{D,R\}}\}}_{C_1} \dots \underbrace{\{\boldsymbol{P}_j^{\{D,R\}}, \dots, \boldsymbol{P}_k^{\{D,R\}}\}}_{C_i} \dots \underbrace{\{\boldsymbol{P}_m^{\{D,R\}}, \dots, \boldsymbol{P}_{N-1}^{\{D,R\}}\}}_{C_M}$ and the fragment alignment method introduced in section 2, the dubious and the reference audio are partitioned into corresponding blocks $\{B_1, B_2, \dots, B_M\}$. To explain the blocking procedure more clearly, we show several special cases as examples. If the dubious audio only experienced common signal processing such as lossy compression which does not affect the time structure, all R_i will be approximately the same (≈1), and both the dubious audio snippet and its aligned reference counterpart have only one block; if the dubious audio is time-stretched, all R_i are still approximately the same (>1 or <1), thus only one block exists on both sides; if the middle third of the dubious audio is cropped, R_i around the cutting point will be very small, accordingly form a concavity since R_i on both sides are approximately 1. In this case, the reference and the dubious audio are divided into three blocks, the left and the right third blocks can still be linked together without the influence of cutting, as shown in Figure 2.

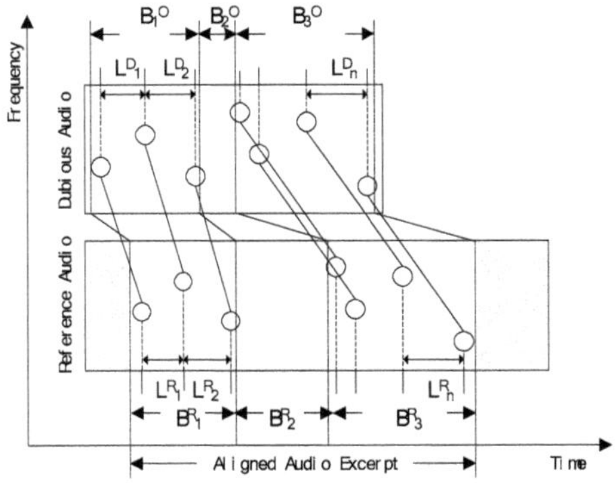

Figure 2. Illustration of time-domain blocking based on time-stretching factor when cropping exists on the dubious audio

3.2 Frequency Alignment

If the dubious audio is pitch shifted, its frequency values will pro rata derivate from their counterpoint of the reference audio. To map the frequency components, first we need to estimate the pitch shifting factor. Given two matched SIFT key points $\{\boldsymbol{P}_i^R, \boldsymbol{P}_i^D\}$, their frequency component is $\{\hat{F}_i^R = \boldsymbol{P}_i^R.y,\ \hat{F}_i^D = \boldsymbol{P}_i^D.y\}$. Then, the pitch shifting factor is calculated according to Eq. (5) and frequency alignment is performed in terms of Eq. (6)-(7).

$$\hat{R}_i = 2^{\hat{F}_i^D - \hat{F}_i^R/12}, i = 1, 2, \dots, N \quad (5)$$

$$\hat{R} = median(\{\hat{R}_i \mid i = 1, 2, \dots, N\}) \quad (6)$$

$$F_{start}^R = \frac{F_{start}^D}{\hat{R}} \quad (7)$$

where $\hat{R}$ is the pitch shifting factor, $F_{start}^{\{R,D\}}$ represents the base frequency of the reference/dubious audio, as shown in Figure 3.

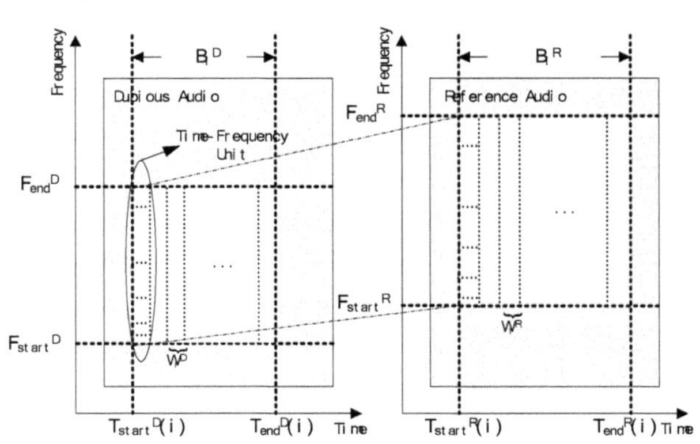

Figure 3. Frequency alignment between the spectrograms of the dubious and the reference audio block

3.3 Robust Hashing

In this section, we adapt the famous Philips audio fingerprinting algorithm [8] to generate robust hashes under the above framework. For each aligned block pair $B_i^{\{D,R\}}$, the frame length W_i^R and frequency range $F_{\{start,end\}}^R$ are adjusted in light of Eq. (8)

$$\begin{cases} W_i^R = \dfrac{W_i^D}{\bar{R}_i}, i = 1,2,\dots,M \\ F_{start}^R = \dfrac{F_{start}^D}{\hat{R}} \\ F_{end}^R = \dfrac{F_{end}^D}{\hat{R}} \end{cases} \quad (8)$$

where $\bar{R}_i$ and $\hat{R}$ are the average time-stretching and pitch-shifting factor of block B_i, respectively.

Let $E^{\{D,R\}}(k,n)$ be the energy of the k-th frequency bin, the n-th frame. After dividing the frequency range $F_{start}^{\{D,R\}} \sim F_{end}^{\{D,R\}}$ into 33 non-overlapping bark-scale subbands, 32-bit robust hash of each frame is calculated in terms of Eq. (9).

$$H^{\{D,O\}}(k,n) = \begin{cases} 1, if\ E^{\{D,R\}}(k,n) > E^{\{D,R\}}(k+1,n), \\ 0, if\ E^{\{D,R\}}(k,n) \leq E^{\{D,R\}}(k+1,n) \end{cases} \quad (9)$$

$$\text{for } k = 1,2,\dots 32 \text{ and } n = 1,2,\dots,N_f,\ N_f = \left\lfloor \sum_{i=1}^{M} \frac{T_{start}^D(i) - T_{end}^D(i)}{W_i^D} \right\rfloor$$

where k is the number of frequency subband, n means the frame number among all blocks.

4. AUTHENTICATION DECISION AND TAMPER CLASSIFICATION

Given a short dubious audio segment $x^D(\cdot)$ and a long reference audio signal $x^R(\cdot)$, the task of fragment authentication is to judge whether $x^D(\cdot)$ is a part of $x^R(\cdot)$ with the semantics not having been maliciously modified. Malicious modifications typically include time-domain cropping/inserting and frequency-domain band-stop filtering, which can be first identified by virtue of the above introduced time-stretching factor and the histogram of SIFT matching points vs. frequency described below. If at least one malicious operation is detected, authentication fails. If no malicious operations is recognized, we go on comparing robust hashes of $x^D(\cdot)$ and its aligned part in $x^R(\cdot)$. If the bit error rate (BER) is not more than a threshold T, authentication succeeds. In this case, distortions probably occurred on the dubious audio may be content-preserving operations such as lossy compression, time-scale modification (TSM) and pitch shifting etc. Of course, very serious such distortions may change to be malicious operations. Compared with conventional authentication algorithms that mainly differentiate admissible and malicious operations from a single BER point of view, this method open a new road for authentication judgment and distortion classification in virtue of the power of SIFT spectrogram descriptor, as detailed below.

4.1 Malicious Cropping/Inserting

As stated in section 3.1, time-stretching factor can be used to describe whether the dubious audio's time structure has been altered compared with its original part of the reference audio. In the case of common signal processing or time stretching, the factors are closely around 1 or a constant number. However, if malicious cutting or inserting occurs, the dubious audio's time structure will be changed and show a concavo or convex in the factor curve, as shown in Figure.4. Therefore, based on the stretching factors, cropping/inserting can be reliably identified.

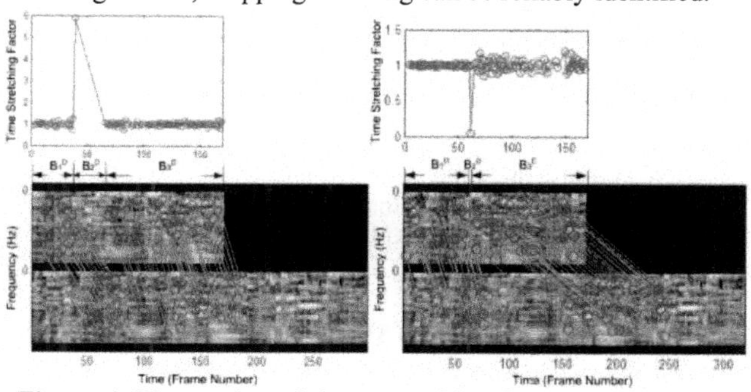

Figure 4. Illustration of time-stretching factor curve under cropping (right)/inserting (left)

4.2 Malicious Frequency Modification

Band-stop filtering is a typical malicious frequency modification. In the affected spectrogram regions, the number of SIFT key points that can be matched with those of the reference audio will drop dramatically. Based on this fact, we construct a histogram to intuitively judge whether band-stop filtering has occurred, and estimate the central frequency of the modified band. The x axis of the histogram is partitioned into 30 bins ranging from 100 to 3000 Hz, each SIFT key point's frequency component is quantized into an appropriate bin. The y axis of the histogram is the number of matched SIFT key points in each frequency bin. Figure 5 is an example of band-stop filtering, it can be seen that around 800-900 Hz no matched points exist, and around this region matched number is also affected more or less. Local histogram similarity can also be used to quantitatively describe this phenomenon, that is, if in certain places the histogram similarity is very low, then it is very possible that the dubious audio has been maliciously band-stop filtered.

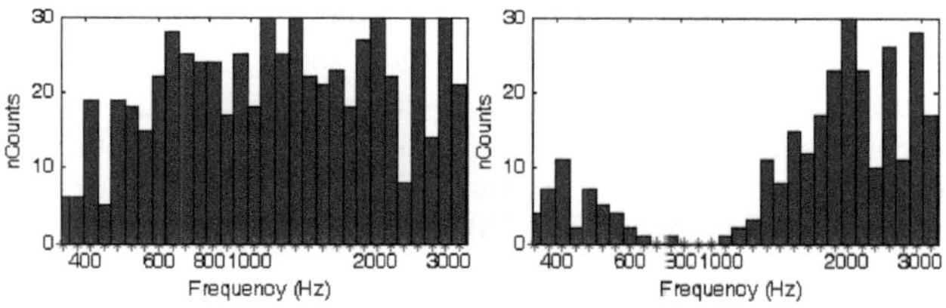

Figure 5. Histogram (number of matched SIFT key points vs. frequency bin) illustration before and after band-stop filtering

4.3 Content Preserving/Changing Operations

This kind of operations typically indicate common audio processing, e.g. MP3 compression, filtering, time stretching, pitch shifting etc., to name a few. Generally speaking, such operations are admissible under middle to low extent, and might change to be malicious if they become stronger. Such modifications cannot be detected in the blocking stage, for their time-stretching factors keep nearly unchanged without obvious singular points as in cropping or inserting. As such, the whole dubious audio fragment is still treated as one block. In this case, BER between the dubious audio snippet and its aligned reference part are used for authentication decision in terms of Eq. (10).

$$\mathrm{BER} = \frac{1}{N_f}\sum_{n=1}^{N_f} \mathbf{H}^D(n) \oplus \mathbf{H}^R(n)$$
$$\begin{cases} \mathrm{BER} > T, \text{authentication fails} \\ \mathrm{BER} \leq T, \text{authentication succeeds} \end{cases} \quad (10)$$

where T is a BER threshold to distinguish admissible with malicious operations, and set as 0.35 in experiment. Follow the probabilistic method of calculating false positive rate in reference [8], theoretic FPR is 5.129477×10^{-6}, acceptable in practice.

5. EXPERIMENTAL RESULTS

5.1 Dataset

A dataset of 1030 audio pieces is collected to evaluate the proposed system, including diverse speech and music signals. Each audio piece is 2 minutes long, wave format, sampled at 44.1 kHz, and monophonic. Audio snippets to be authenticated are 10s long and randomly cut from the original signals.

5.2. Authentication Results and Statistics

The task of experiment is to check the algorithm's ability of differentiating admissible operations from malicious modifications. In Table 1, the true positive rates under acceptable manipulations and true negative rates under illegal modifications are summarized. It can be seen that by virtue of SIFT descriptor of audio spectrogram, in most cases the dubious audio fragment can be correctly authenticated, that is, authentication passes under admissible operations and fails under malicious modifications.

To be specific, under acceptable operations like MP3 at 32kbps, TSM at ±10%, pitch shifting up to ±20%, and low-pass filtering at 4kHz and 8kHz, at least 81% of the dubious audio signals are correctly authenticated. When TSM goes up to ±20%, the true positive rate drops a little bit, but still close to 80%. Note that in the situation of fragment authentication, for audio segment to be authenticated there is a prerequisite distortion i.e. cropping. Utilizing SIFT descriptor of spectrogram cannot guarantee a hundred percent precise alignment between the audio fragment and its true position in the original audio, and in some cases the misplacement is non-negligible. Subsequently, of the 1030 original non-modified audio segments, only 968 (93.98%) pieces are successfully authenticated.

With regards to the three time-domain malicious tampering, i.e. replacing, cropping, and inserting, the true negative rates are surprisingly as high as 99.4%, 99.6% and 100% respectively. This proves the effectiveness of time-stretching factor on recognizing cropping/adding and robust hashing on replacing. As for the two frequency-domain malicious band-stop filtering (one is centered at 800-900 Hz and the other 1500-1600 Hz), the true negative rate are 82.9% and 76.7% respectively, which are relatively low compared with the above time-domain cases.

Table 1. True positive/negative rates of authentication

Modification	TPR/TNR	Modification	TPR/TNR
No attack	94.0%	Pitch Shift -20%	81.2%
MP3 32kbps	85.6%	Pitch Shift -10%	87.7%
TSM -20%	77.5%	Pitch Shift +10%	81.6%
TSM -10%	82.6%	Pitch Shift +20%	83.7%
TSM +10%	83.1%	Low Pass 4 kHz	89.3%
TSM +20%	78.0%	Low Pass 8 kHz	89.1%
Replace	99.4%	Band-Stop 800-900 Hz	82.9%
Crop	99.6%	Band-Stop 1500-1600 Hz	76.7%
Insert	100%		

In a practical authentication system, two important false statistics must be taken into consideration. One is false positive rate (FPR), which is the rate of considering an audio signal as authentic when it has been maliciously modified; the other is false negative rate (FNR), which is the rate of judging a piece of audio as inauthentic when it has actually undergone content-preserving operations. Below we adopt confusion matrix to demonstrate the overall system performance. Of the 14420 admissible operations, 2340 of them are falsely judged as malicious so that authentication fails, thus the false negative rate is 0.1623. In contrast, of the 3090 malicious modifications, only 10 of them are falsely determined as admissible so that authentication succeeds, therefore the false positive rate is 0.00324. From the matrix it can be seen that the authentication system is able to make distinction between admissible and malicious operations pretty well. Also in experiment we find that most cases of false negative are caused by large-scale pitch shifting and time stretching which may seriously change the audio content so that authentication fails.

Table 2. Confusion matrix of authentication errors

Confusion Matrix		Predicted	
		Malicious	Admissible
Actual	Malicious	a=3080	b=10
	Admissible	c=2340	d=12080

5.3 Statistics on Localization Precision

If authentication fails, it is often required to locate the maliciously tampered time-frequency regions. As a first quantitative evaluation, we take ±0.2s and ±10% of the central frequency as the error range, and obtain precision of 87.9%, 76.9%, 77.4%, 81.0% and 73.8% for replacing, cropping, inserting, and band-stop filtering at 800-900 Hz, 1500-1600 Hz respectively.

6. CONCLUSION

This paper initiates the research on audio fragment authentication. Its main feature is to accomplish multiple tasks by introducing SIFT feature into spectrogram. Experiments are encouraging, with good discriminability between acceptable and malicious operations. One inadequacy is that SIFT-based method cannot assure absolutely accurate fragment alignment so that a minority of original audio segments triggers the authenticator. This is also what to be solved in future work.

7. ACKNOWLEDGEMENTS

This work is supported by NSFC (60873255, 61171128), Shanghai Municipal R&D Foundation (No. 08dz1500109, 10dz1201605), and 973 Program (2010CB327900).

8. REFERENCES

[1] C. P. Wu and C. C. Kuo, "Fragile speech watermarking based on exponential scale quantization for tamper detection," *ICASSP* 2002, pp. 3305-3308.

[2] R. Radhakrishnan and N. Memon, "Audio content authentication based on psycho-acoustic model," *SPIE Security and Watermarking of Multimedia Contents*, 4675: 110-117, 2002.

[3] M. Steinebach and J. Dittmann, "Watermarking-based digital audio data authentication, " *EURASIP Journal on Applied Signal Processing*, 10: 1001-1015, 2003.

[4] S. Zmudzinski and M. Steinebach, "Perception-based audio authentication watermarking in the time-frequency domain," *IH* 2009, pp. 146-160.

[5] D. Varodayan, Y. C. Lin and B. Girod, "Audio authentication based on distributed source coding, " *ICASSP* 2008, pp. 225-228.

[6] G. Valenzise, G. Prandi, M. Tagliasacchi and A. Sarti, "Identification of sparse audio tampering using distributed source coding and compressive sensing techniques, " *EURASIP Journal on Image and Video Processing*, 2009: 1-12.

[7] B. B. Zhu, M. D. Swanson and A. H. Tewfik, "When seeing isn't believing," *IEEE Signal Processing Magazine*, 21(2): 40-49, 2004.

[8] J. Haitsma and T. Kalker, "A highly robust audio fingerprinting system, " *ISMIR* 2002, pp. 107-115.

Cap Detection for Moving People in Entrance Surveillance

Rui Min
Multimedia Communications Dept.
EURECOM
Sophia Antipolis, France
(+33) 04 93 00 82 69
min@eurecom.fr

Jean-Luc Dugelay
Multimedia Communications Dept.
EURECOM
Sophia Antipolis, France
(+33) 04 93 00 81 41
jld@eurecom.fr

ABSTRACT
While there has been an enormous amount of research on face recognition under pose/illumination changes and image degradations, problems caused by occlusions are mostly overlooked. Moreover, most of the existing approaches of face recognition under occlusion conditions focus on overcoming facial occlusion problems due to sunglasses and scarf. To the best of our knowledge, occlusion due to cap has never been studied in the literature, but the importance of this problem should be emphasized since it is known that bank robbers and football hooligans take advantage of it for hiding their faces. This paper presents a solution to this newly identified face occlusion problem – the time-variant occlusion due to cap in entrance surveillance, in the context of face biometrics in video surveillance. The proposed approach consists of two parts: detection and tracking of occluded faces in complex surveillance videos; detecting the presence of cap by exploiting temporal information. The detection and tracking part is based upon body silhouette and elliptical head tracker. The classification of cap/non-cap faces utilizes dynamic time warping (DTW) and agglomerative hierarchical clustering. The proposed algorithm is evaluated on several surveillance videos and yields good detection rates.

Categories and Subject Descriptors
I.4.8 [**Scene Analysis**]: Object recognition, Time varying imagery, Tracking; I.2.10 [**Vision and Scene Understanding**]: Video Analysis.

General Terms: Algorithms, Experimentation, Security

Keywords: Entrance surveillance, face recognition, occlusion detection, security management.

1. INTRODUCTION
Face recognition, the least intrusive biometric technique from the sampling point of view, has been applied to a wide range of commercial and law enforcement applications. With the emphasis on real world scenarios (e.g. face recognition in video surveillance), in the last decade, an enormous amount of research on face recognition under pose/illumination changes and image degradations has been conducted. However, problems caused by occlusions are mostly overlooked, although facial occlusions are quite common in non-cooperative systems such as video surveillance applications.

*Area Chair: Tian-Tsong Ng

MM'11, November 28–December 1, 2011, Scottsdale, Arizona, USA.

Facial occlusions, which might also occur for benign behaviors, are often related to several severe security issues. For example, ATM criminals and football hooligans tend to wear scarf, sunglasses and/or cap to prevent their faces been recognized. Therefore, face recognition robust to partial occlusions is an essential technique for security management and forensics. Among most of the existing solutions, local features and local components based methods (e.g. [1][2]) become prominent, since locality emphasized algorithms are less sensitive to partial occlusions in comparison with conventional holistic algorithms. Nevertheless, information from occluded parts can still hinder the recognition performance in those approaches. More recently, researchers have revealed that prior knowledge of occlusions can significantly improve the accuracy of local feature based face recognition [3][4], since the harmful information from occluded parts can thus be excluded explicitly. Hence, accurate occlusion detection is crucial to achieve occlusion robust face recognition.

It should be noted that the state-of-the-art of occluded face recognition addresses the time-invariant occlusions only (e.g. scarf, sunglasses or artificially generated occlusions) from a single image. Time-invariant indicates that the occlusion is not changing without external forces within a certain period of time. In this paper, we identify a new type of occlusion: the time-variant occlusion, specifically speaking the occlusion due to cap in entrance surveillance (though headdresses like hard hat in [5] is not considered as an occlusion problem). Nowadays, Closed-Circuit Television (CCTV) cameras are deployed everywhere for security purpose. The most common deployment of such cameras is at the room ceiling in order to monitor the entrances of various

Figure 1. Illustration of Entrance surveillance scenarios

places (e.g. banks, ticket machine of subway station, supermarkets, libraries, and stadium) (see Figure. 1). With videos captured by such cameras, the identities of people inside the restricted place can be recorded and later recognized by automatic face recognition (AFR) systems or human observers. However, according to many recent police reports, bank robbers, shop thieves and football hooligans usually wear a cap when entering the places where they commit crimes. Due to the viewing angle problem, a close-distance face captured by a CCTV camera is often occluded by the visor, whereas a far-distance face is not occluded but it has a low resolution. The occlusion caused by cap with a visor is therefore varying along with people moving. Because of the trade-off between occlusion and image quality, obtained face images are usually unrecognizable from the recorded videos. Thus, it is imperative to equip automatic cap detection systems in entrance surveillance, which cannot only detect suspicious persons, but also provide prior knowledge of occlusion to improve the face recognition of criminals.

In this paper, we address then the occlusion detection due to cap for entrance surveillance. The proposed approach consists of first detect and track the face region and then detect the presence of cap within the tracked face. The detection and tracking part is based upon silhouette analysis and elliptical head tracker [6]. The classification of cap/non-cap faces adopts dynamic time warping (DTW) and agglomerative hierarchical clustering.

2. CHALLENGES AND INNOVATIONS

There are many challenges for the proposed cap detection system. First of all, in entrance surveillance, even a close-distance face is relatively far away from the camera (in comparison with the traditional biometric scenario). In addition, various variations due to occlusion, rotation, low resolution and complex backgrounds make the correct detection of face region a difficult problem. In the targeted entrance surveillance scenario, the most common approach – Viola-Jones algorithm [7] implemented in OpenCV cannot even find a non-occluded face correctly (mainly due to the resolution problem). For this reason, we implemented a customized method to detect and track the face region, which exploits more robust features such as body silhouette and head geometry.

Secondly, occlusion due to cap is time-variant. Unlike the time-invariant occlusions (such as scarf and sunglasses), the occlusion caused by cap is varying along time. When a face is approaching, the occluded area on the face increases accordingly. The changing of occluded area mainly depends on the speed and pause of people walking. Since the walking habit is non-homogeneous and largely different among individuals, the occlusion situation is also diverse for different people or even the same people in different videos. In addition, the occluded area is also changing because of the rigid head movements (e.g. head nodding and looking way). For above reasons, occlusion detection using a single image is very unlikely to get accurate results. In our approach, we exploit all the frames in the video to reduce the effects of different variations and tracking errors; furthermore, the temporal information is preserved by using DTW to distinguish the characteristics of occlusion varying from the occluded and non-occluded faces.

Last but not least, the proposed system is supposed to work in real time, since the computational capability is limited in distributed sensor networks. The flowchart of the proposed system is given in Figure 2. The simplicity of each of the steps ensures the overall performance of our system.

3. HEAD DETECTION AND TRACKING

The customized head detection and tracking is based on silhouette image and elliptical head tracker. The accuracy of detection and tracking thus largely depends on the quality of extracted body silhouette. Following the well established silhouette analysis in gait recognition [8]; our system is able to achieve good detection and tracking of non-optimal faces in textured background.

3.1 Background Modeling

The first step is to construct a reliable background model for silhouette extraction. Here, the LMedS (Least Median of Squares) method [9] is applied to build the background from a small portion of video sequences, thanks to its power of filter moving objects.

3.2 Silhouette Extraction

Once the background image is correctly constructed, the foreground detection can be achieved by differencing and thresholding between the background image and the current frame. Because the background subtraction step may introduce noise and distortions in the segmented foreground, post-processing including morphological operations and connected component selection are applied in order to obtain a clear body silhouette.

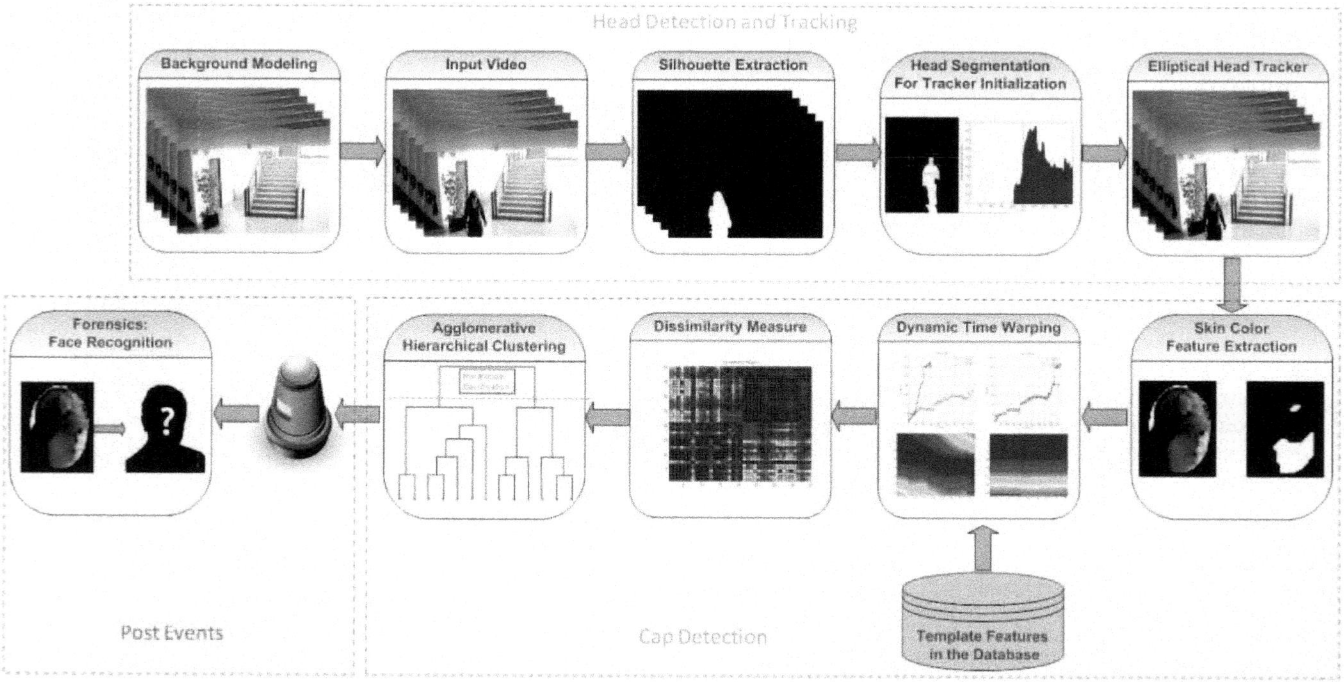

Figure 2. Flowchart of the proposed cap detection system

3.3 Head Segmentation
Correct segmentation of head from the body silhouette is critical to initialize a head tracker. The bounding box of walking body is naturally obtained from the silhouette. To segment the head from the other part of the body, we apply a horizontal projection to the silhouette image. Then the head-shoulder detection is achieved via selecting the histogram steep rise.

3.4 Scalable Elliptical Head Tracker
The tracking part is directly adopted from [6]. The choice of the elliptical head tracker is based on the fact that it is robust to occlusion, rotation, tilting and textured background to some extent. In addition, the merits of scalability, reacquisition and low complexity encourage us to integrate it into our system. However, instead of applying the elliptical head tracker to a gradient map, we fit the ellipse to the body contour which is extracted by a Canny edge detector from the silhouette image. The reason is due to the gradient map of a low resolution head is indistinguishable from the textured background. In the prediction part, the monotonic increment assumption is made. This assumption can accelerate the system speed as well as automatically exclude the person who is leaving the entrance (in which case the face is invisible and also redundant, it was recorded during entering).

In our experiments, the elliptical head tracker correctly tracked the head in 84% of all the frames (of 40 video clips) for 10 different people with and without cap under 2 illumination conditions (morning and evening). Errors are due to incorrect ellipse fitting (23%) or lost tracking (77%).

4. Cap Detection
Because facial components, such as eyes, nose and mouth, are almost undetectable in the entrance surveillance scenario, the only reliable feature for occlusion classification is the skin color. In this paper, a novel Spatial-Temporal (ST) feature representation based on skin color is proposed. Inspired by the work from [10], DTW and agglomerative hierarchical clustering are employed to classify the unsynchronized ST features.

4.1 Skin Color based Feature Extraction
A traditional way [11] to extract skin pixels which is fast and stable is applied. Skin pixels are differentiated from the non-skin pixels in the *YCbCr* color space by pre-defined thresholds. In this paper, we tested two types of features: 1. the number of skin pixels in the region of interest (ROI); 2. the ratio of number of skin pixels to number of all pixels in the ROI. Then the extracted features from all frames of one video clip are concatenated to construct a ST representation. The perceptual classifications between features extracted from the occluded and non-occluded video clips are shown in Figure 3.

4.2 Dynamic Time Warping
Dynamic time warping, also called curve registration, is widely used in various applications (e.g. speech recognition, musical information retrieval and bioinformatics), thanks to its capability of measuring the similarity between two sequences varying in time or speed. The optimal match between two feature vectors is found by stretching and compression under the constraint of monotonicity. First, a difference matrix $D[i,j] = |Q[i] - T[j]|$ of the query feature vector $Q[i]$ and the template feature vector $T[j]$ is calculated. Then a cost matrix M is recorded by keeping a running tab on the dissimilarities of elements while summing up to a minimum accumulated cost measure via dynamic programming [10]. The formation of M can be written as:

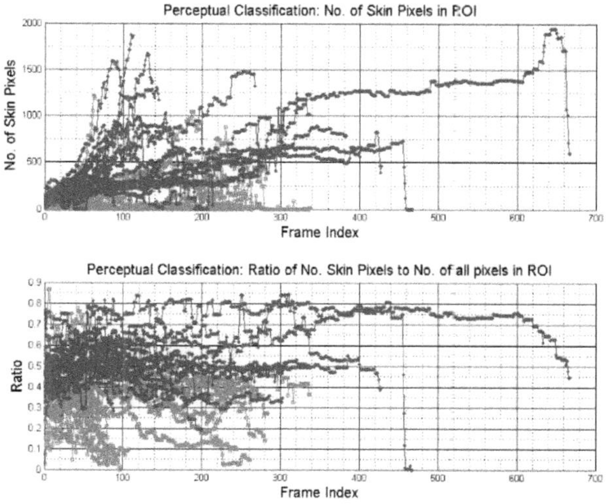

Figure 3. Perceptual classification of the proposed features (Blue: faces without cap, Red: faces with cap)

$$M[i,j] = min\begin{pmatrix} M[i-1,j-1] \\ M[i-1,j] \\ M[i,j-1] \end{pmatrix} + D[i,j] \quad (1)$$

With matrix M, a minimum cost path can be retraced along diagonal. The final dissimilarity between the query and template is thus the summation of all costs on the path, normalized by the length of the longer feature vector between Q and T.

4.3 Dissimilarity Matrices
In our cap detection system, a number of features extracted from video clips of occluded and non-occluded faces serve as the templates. When a query video comes in, the dissimilarities between the query and all templates are computed via DTW. To reduce computation, the dissimilarities between all pairs of templates are pre-calculated and stored as dissimilarity matrices in the database. The system also support online updating by integrating the dissimilarities computed from the query into the matrices. A visual presentation of the dissimilarity matrices is shown in Figure 4.

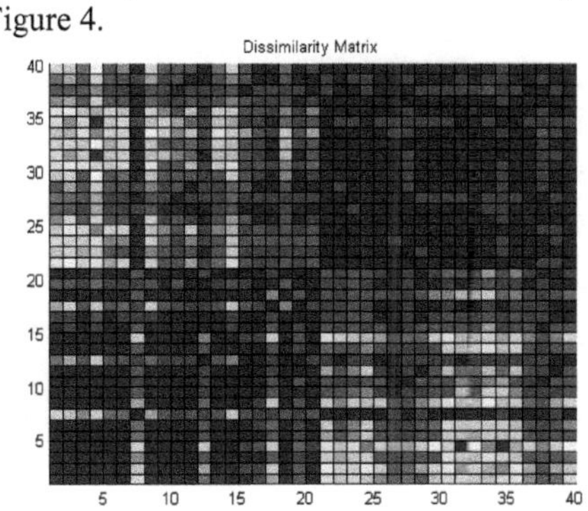

Figure 4. Dissimilarity Matrices of 40 video clips (1-20 without cap, 21-40 with cap, cold color indicates low dissimilarity)

4.4 Agglomerative Hierarchical Clustering
Knowing the dissimilarity matrices, the agglomerative hierarchical clustering algorithm is applied for classification. A dendrogram is returned by the clustering algorithm. In the dendrogram we choose the level with two clusters for decision making. The class label of each cluster is decided by the number

of template features within the same cluster; as an example, a cluster belongs to the cap class when there are more template features from cap videos in the cluster and vice versa. A query feature is thus classified according to the cluster's class label. Ward's method is chosen empirically for the clustering task.

4.5 Post Events

Here we briefly discuss the post events after cap detection. In the entrance surveillance scenario, the presence of cap is undesirable for security management. In the cooperative case (e.g. in airport security check), the system can provide information so that guards can kindly ask the passenger to remove his/her cap. In the non-cooperative case (e.g. in bank), it can identify the suspicious person so that increase the security level or draw the attention from a human observer. For forensics purpose from recorded videos, it can be easily combined with local feature based face recognition system as described in [4].

5. EXPERIMENTS

In this paper, we built a rather challenging dataset to simulate the environment of entrance surveillance in real-world. 40 videos (length varying from 60 to 666 frames) have been recorded using an Axis P1343 IP camera fixed at the room ceiling in an indoor terrace (with sunlight during the daytime and artificial lights in the evening). 10 people were asked to walk toward to the camera and enter the door of office below the camera. Each person had twice recording, one time wearing a cap and another time without wearing a cap. The caps have different colors and textures in order to maximize the variations. The experiments are organized in 2 sessions, one session in the morning and another one in the evening. In sum, 40 videos are comprised of 20 with cap and 20 without cap, under 2 different illumination conditions. The dataset is publically available at URL: http://image.eurecom.fr/pub/mm11.

In our experiment, we tested 2 different features within 3 different ROI. The features are: 1. number of skin pixels (Skin) in ROI, 2. ratio of number of skin pixels to number of all pixels (Ratio) in ROI. Three ROI are selected automatically according to the minor diameter of ellipse returned by the head tracker. Illustrations of ROI are given in Figure 5.

Table 1. Results of the proposed system

Feature	FAR	FRR	*Classification Accuracy*
Skin_ROI1	15%	40%	72.5%
Skin_ROI2	15%	40%	72.5%
Skin_ROI3	35%	5%	80%
Ratio_ROI1	5%	30%	82.5%
Ratio_ROI2	5%	20%	**87.5%**
Ratio_ROI3	0%	25%	**87.5%**

Table 1 shows the results of our experiment. Here we define that a people without wearing cap is "accepted" and the one wearing cap is "rejected". It is clear that Ratio has better classification accuracy than Skin. Ratio_ROI2 and Ratio_ROI3 lead to the best result (up to 87.5%). For Ratio_ROI2, 1 person is wrongly "accepted" and 4 people are wrongly "rejected", whereas nobody is wrongly "accepted" using Ratio_ROI3.

6. CONCLUSIONS

This paper presents a solution to a newly identified occlusion problem: time-variant occlusion due to cap in entrance surveillance. The proposed system can be applied to a wide range of applications for security management in nowadays video surveillance. In particular, it can provide prior information of occlusion to face recognition system of identifying suspicious persons. It overcomes several challenges due to sensor and human behaviors in the imperfect world. In addition, it exploits the temporal information to analyze the characteristics of occlusion varying. Future works include the cap detection in crowed scenes, as well as face selection in the trade of occlusion and resolution.

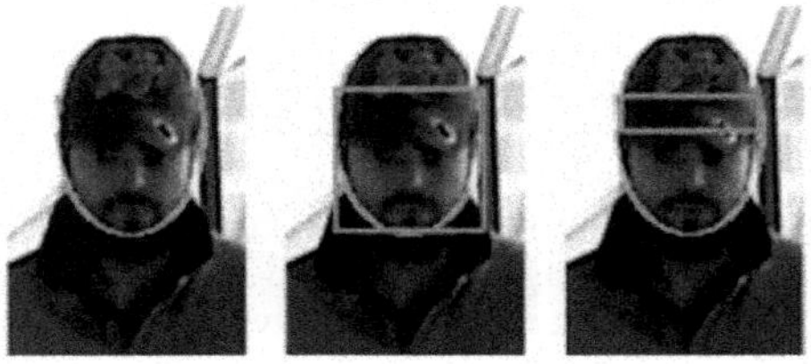

Figure 5. Pre-defined ROI 1-3 (from left to right: the whole ellipse, the face region, the upper-eyebrow region)

7. ACKNOWLEDGMENTS

This work is partially funded by the French national project FR OSEO BIORAFALE. The authors also would like to thank Mr. Monir Azraoui for his help in simulations.

8. REFERENCES

[1] Martinez, A. M. 2002. Recognizing Imprecisely Localized, Partially Occluded, and Expression Variant Faces from a Single Sample per Class. *IEEE Trans. Pattern Anal. Mach. Intell.* 24, 6 (June 2002), 748-763. DOI=10.1109/TPAMI.2002.1008382

[2] Kim, J., Choi, J., Yi, J., and Turk., M. 2005. Effective Representation Using ICA for Face Recognition Robust to Local Distortion and Partial Occlusion. *IEEE Trans. Pattern Anal. Mach. Intell.* 27, 12 (December 2005), 1977-1981. DOI=10.1109/TPAMI.2005.242

[3] Rama, A., Tarres, F., Goldmann, L., and Sikora, T. 2008 More robust face recognition by considering occlusion information, In *Proceedings of the 8th IEEE International Conference on Automatic Face & Gesture Recognition* (Sept. 2008), vol., no., pp.1-6, 17-19.

[4] Min, R., Hadid, A., and Dugelay, J.-L. 2011. Improving the recognition of faces occluded by facial accessories, In *Proceedings of the 9th IEEE International Conference on Automatic Face & Gesture Recognition* (Santa Barbara, CA, USA, March 21-25, 2011)

[5] Du, S., Shehata, M., and Badawy, W. 2011 , "Hard hat detection in video sequences based on face features, motion and color information," In *Proceedings of the 3rd International Conference on Computer Research and Development* (March 2011) vol.4, no., pp.25-29, 11-13

[6] Birchfield, S. 1998. Elliptical Head Tracking Using Intensity Gradients and Color Histograms. In *Proceedings of the IEEE Computer Society Conference on Computer Vision and Pattern Recognition* (CVPR '98). Washington, DC, USA, 232-.

[7] Viola, P. and Jones, M. J. 2004. Robust Real-Time Face Detection. *Int. J. Comput. Vision* 57, 2 (May 2004), 137-154. DOI=10.1023/B:VISI.0000013087.49260.fb

[8] Wang, L., Tan, T., Ning, H. and Hu, W. 2003. Silhouette Analysis-Based Gait Recognition for Human Identification. *IEEE Trans. Pattern Anal. Mach. Intell.* 25, 12 (December 2003), 1505-1518. DOI=10.1109/TPAMI.2003.1251144

[9] Yang, Y.-H. and Levine, M. D. 1992. The background primal sketch: an approach for tracking moving objects. *Mach. Vision Appl.* 5, 1 (January 1992), 17-34. DOI=10.1007/BF01213527

[10] Brown, J. C., and Miller, P. J. O. 2007 Automatic classification of killer whale vocalizations using dynamic time warping. *J. Acoust. Soc. Amer.* v122. 1201-1207.

[11] Chai, D. and Ngan, K N. 1999 Face Segmentation Using Skin Color Map in Videophone Applications, *IEEE Trans. Circuits and Systems for Video Technology*, vol. 9, no. 4, pp. 551-564, 1999.

High Efficient Distributed Video Coding with Parallelized Design for Cloud Computing

Han-Ping Cheng[1], Yun-Chung Shen[1], Ja-Ling Wu[1], and Kiyoharu Aizawa[2]

[1] Graduate Institute of Networking and Multimedia, National Taiwan University
National Taiwan University, Taipei 10617, Taiwan, R.O.C

[2]Department of Information and Communication Engineering, The University of Tokyo

+886-2-3366-4888

{plokm, cazindo, wjl}@cmlab.csie.ntu.edu.tw, aizawa@hal.t.u-tokyo.ac.jp

ABSTRACT

In this work, by combining coding tools developed in recent literatures on transform domain WZ video coding with some newly developed modules on both encoding and decoding sides, an efficient and practical WZ video coding architecture, dubbed as DIStributed video coding with PArallelized design for Cloud computing (DISPAC), is proposed to better the corresponding rate-distortion (RD) performance. Another unique feature of DISPAC, lies in the parallelizability of the modules used by its WZ decoder which increased the decoding speed largely. Experimental results conducted on an emulated Could computing environment reveal that DISPAC codec can gain up to 3.6 dB in the RD measures and 60.97 times faster in the decoding speed as compared with the-state-of-art WZ video codec, respectively

Categories and Subject Descriptors

I.4.2 [**Image Processing and Computer Vision**]: Compression (Coding) *–Approximate methods, Exact coding.*

General Terms

Algorithms, Design

Keywords

Distributed video coding, Wyner-Ziv video coding, parallel, Cloud computing, CUDA, multi-core, block mode selection, side information refinement

1. INTRODUCTION

Distributed video coding (DVC) has recently attracted a vast amount of attention from the video coding community all around the world. The new coding paradigm is also known as Wyner-Ziv (WZ) video coding, which is based on Slepian-Wolf and Wyner-Ziv theorems. These theorems mainly state that separate encoding and joint decoding of two correlated sources, X and Y, can be encoded to the same minimum rate as joint encoding and decoding in the conventional video coding. DVC codec subverts the traditional prediction-based standard video coding scheme by exploiting the source statistics at the decoder with the development of simpler encoders. These features are effectively utilized in several application domains, e.g. video conferencing with mobile devices, wireless video cameras and wireless low-power surveillance.

The DISCOVER codec [1], which improved the architecture developed in [2] with more advanced coding tools, has been known as the state-of-the-art WZ video codec for years. It uses advanced frame interpolation techniques to create the so-called side information (SI). The performance of the SI creation process based on adjacent previously decoded frames is limited by the quality of the past and the future reference frames as well as the distance and motion behavior between them. These limitations explain the typical poor RD performance of WZ coding for high motion or large group of pictures (GOP) size sequences.

Most recently, Martins et al. [3] applied new information about the WZ frame during the decoding process to overcome some of the limitations mentioned above and achieve better WZ coding RD measures, especially for high and complex motion content. Nevertheless, the RD performance gap between the existing WZ video codecs and conventional video codec (e.g. H.264/AVC) still exists.

On the other hand, since DVC can successfully shift the computational complexity from the encoder to the decoder, it has been expected to provide a video codec solution for Cloud computing mobile devices (such as mobile phones), where Cloud computing is a technology that uses the internet and large amounts of central remote servers to maintain data and applications. With appropriate transcoding techniques, it is possible to let the Cloud take charge of the most complex part of video coding so that the low-complexity encoder (e.g. DVC encoder) and decoder (e.g. conventional decoder) are sufficient to support a large variety of video services for the client sides of the Cloud. However, most reported WZ codecs have a high time delay in decoder, which hinders its practical application in real-time systems.

In this work, by combining some most recently proposed efficient coding tools with some newly proposed coding modules and taking into account the parallelizability of the modules used by the WZ decoder, DISPAC effectively reduces the RD performance gap between the existing WZ codecs and the most-known predictive video codec. Moreover, it achieves much faster decoding speed on an emulated Could computing environment (consisting of multi-core CPU and GPU processors).

2. DISPAC Video Codec

The architecture of DISPAC codec is illustrated in Fig. 1, which is based on the architecture of MLWZ codec [3] with some additional modules. Instead of using Turbo codes to realize the Slepian-Wolf codec as in [3], we used LDPCA codes [4] based on the motivation that the decoding algorithm of LDPCA code is much suitable for parallel computing. The additional two function

*Area Chair: Wei-Tsang 0oi

MM'11, November 28-December 1, 2011, Scottsdale, Arizona, USA.

modules, 1) block mode selection module and 2) SI re-creation module, are highlighted in grey in Fig. 1, which are used to further improve the RD performance. Since the architecture of DISPAC codec is very similar to the architecture of MLWZ codec, only the functions of the newly added modules will be addressed.

2.1 Block Mode Selection Module in the DISPAC Encoding

Blocks within a frame can have very different characteristics and these characteristics have a great impact on the coding performance. In this module, we classify the block of WZ frame to three modes: 1) Skip mode, 2) Intra mode and 3) WZ mode. Blocks with a very low motion and a very high motion are classified to the Skip mode and Intra mode respectively, while others are classified to the WZ mode, which are coded the same as described in [3].

2.1.1 Skip Mode Selection

The WZ frame is first divided into N by N ($N \geq 4$) non-overlapped blocks. Then, the mean squared error (MSE) between a given block in the WZ frame to be encoded and the co-located block in the reference frame (which is the past frame of the hierarchical coding structure [5]) is computed. If $MSE < T_1$, the block to be encoded is classified as Skip mode. The value of T_1 is empirically chosen as 10. In current implementation, we use N=8 and for each block, 1 bit is used to indicate whether the block is Skip mode or not, which is called the binary decision map (BDM) in this work. Therefore, for a QCIF sequence, the BDM bits required to be sent to the decoder for block classification is 396 bits per WZ frame (because the number of 8×8 blocks in a QCIF frame is 396). The BDM bits could be compressed efficiently by applying any kind of low complexity bi-level lossless coding techniques. Here, we use JBIG, which is a lossless image compression standard proposed by the Joint Bi-level Image experts Group, to compress the bits spent for BDM as suggested in [6].

For the frame having few Skip blocks or even no Skip blocks, the additional bits used to stand for the block classifications may be wasted. Hence the encoder uses 1 bit for each WZ frame to tell the decoder whether the Skip mode is enabled or not. If the number of Skip blocks in the frame is less than a threshold T_2, the Skip mode is disabled, which means the whole blocks in the frame are WZ or Intra coded, and the bits for BDM would not be sent to the decoder. T_2 is defined by

$$T_2 = \tau M/\mathrm{BitplaneNum}\,, \qquad (1)$$

where M is the bit spend of BDM after JBIG compression, BitplaneNum is the number of bitplanes in the WZ frame according to the quantization table in [3] (i.e. BitplaneNum = 63 when table is Q_8) and τ is a scale factor (empirically set $\tau = 3$ in our implementation).

2.1.2 Intra Mode Selection

The Intra blocks are selected as in [6], which applied the fast motion compensated interpolation to create the estimated SI at the encoder side with little encoding complexity increase. After the estimated SI is created, it is used to estimate the rate of WZ coding block by considering the correlation noise between the SI frame and the WZ frame to be coded. In [6], a parameter for adjusting the existing gap between estimated rate and real rate of WZ coding is used. It is set to 2.0 empirically in DISPAC codec. On the other hand, the rate of the Intra coding block is estimated by considering the fraction of zeros among the DCT quantized coefficients in a block, DC quantized coefficient of the block and

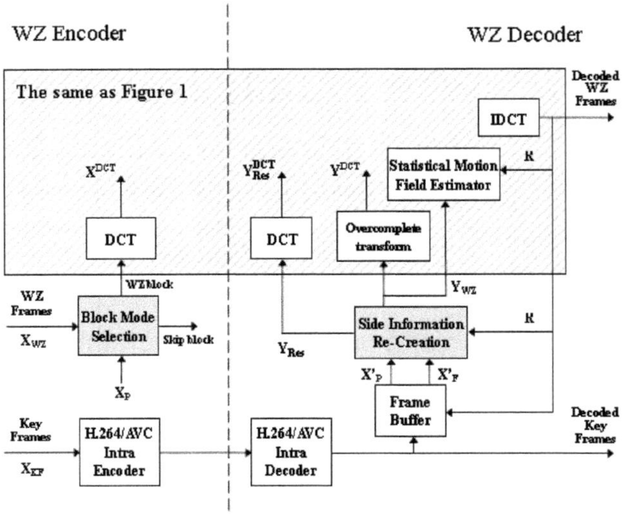

Figure 1. DISPAC codec architecture.

previous Intra encoded data. Then, the Intra/WZ mode is chosen if the estimated rate of the Intra/WZ coding block is lower than another one. The Intra blocks are coded with the efficient H.264/AVC Intra coding techniques. To simplify the encoder and lower the encoding complexity, the prediction mode of H.264/AVC Intra coding is restricted only to the 4×4 DC mode.

As the Skip mode mentioned in Section 2.1.1, the BDM for Intra mode is compressed by JBIG and Eq. (1) is applied to determine whether the Intra mode is enabled in this WZ frame or not.

When LDPCA encoding, the bit values corresponding to the blocks which are classified to the Skip or Intra mode are set to zero and their log-likelihood ratios at the LDPCA decoder are set to a relatively high value indicating that those bits are zero with a very high confidence. Hence, the LDPCA decoder only cares about correcting the bits of WZ blocks.

In DISPAC codec, the decoded Intra blocks are also used to replace the co-located blocks in the SI frame created at the decoder to further improve the motion learning performance described in [3]. On the contrary, the Skip block is not copied to SI since the co-located blocks in the SI frame are accurate enough due to having low motion activities under most conditions.

2.2 Side Information Re-creation Module in the DISPAC Decoding

The MLWZ applies the motion learning process to the same SI during the whole decoding process. But for high motion sequences, the initial SI may be poor due to lack of information about the current decoding frame and it would influence the motion learning performance much. However, new information is available at the decoder side during decoding process, band by band. Hence we use SI re-creation module to further improve the learning process.

After decoding the previous $b-1$ bands, the reconstructed block R_n^{b-1} can be obtained. Now, perform bidirectional motion estimation (BME) using block matching algorithm which computes the matching error of the reconstructed block R_n^{b-1} and the blocks within $\pm S$ ($S = 32$ is used in our codec) search range in the nearest future and past decoded frames, X'_F and X'_P respectively. The forward motion vector and the backward motion vector at integer pixel precision are calculated as

$$(m_x, m_y) = \underset{d_x, d_y}{\operatorname{argmin}} CF(d_x, d_y), d_x, d_y \in [-S, S] \ , \quad (2)$$

where

$$CF(d_x, d_y) = MAD(d_x, d_y) \times \left(1 + K \times \sqrt{{d_x}^2 + {d_y}^2}\right), \quad (3)$$

$$MAD(d_x, d_y) = \frac{1}{16} \sum_{x=0}^{3} \sum_{y=0}^{3} \left| X'_{n+(d_x, d_y)}(x, y) - R_n^{b-1}(x, y) \right| . \quad (4)$$

(d_x, d_y) denotes candidate motion vectors within the search range, and (m_x, m_y) is the best motion vector. Notice that $X'_{n+(d_x,d_y)}$ is the block in the future or the past reference frame displaced by (d_x, d_y). CF in Eq. (3) includes a penalty term, K, as in [5], which favors motion vectors closer to the origin. K controls how much penalty is introduced when the motion vectors go to extreme positions of the search range (we use K = 0.05 as suggested in [5]). After finding both motion vectors at integer precisions, the half-pixel precision motion estimation is further applied, which searches 8 half-pixel points around the integer-pixel motion vector without the penalty term (K = 0). Finally, bidirectional motion compensation is performed to obtain new SI. This new SI is then utilized by the subsequent motion learning process to contribute RD performance gain for high motion sequences.

3. Parallelizing the DISPAC Decoder

After simple profile analysis, the bottleneck components of our current codec in terms of decoding time are 1) SI creation [1], 2) correlation noise modeling [3], 3) LDPCA decoding, 4) SI re-creation and 5) statistic motion learning modules [3]. Therefore, we focus on parallelizing these modules on GPGPU though Compute Unified Device Architecture (CUDA) and on multi-core CPU though Open Multi-Processing (OpenMP). Due to the page limitation, we omit the implementation detail and only describe which part in the decoding module is parallelized on GPGPU and which part is parallelized on multi-core CPU.

3.1 Parallel Side Information Creation

The SI creation process consists of forward motion estimation, bidirectional motion estimation, spatial motion smoothing and bidirectional motion compensation. Among them, the most time-consuming parts are the forward motion estimation (FME) stage and bidirectional motion estimation (BME) stage. In FME, the time complexity comes from large motion search range (± 32). On the other hand, the BME uses adaptive search range which is small at most of the times, so the motion search operation is fast at this stage. However, since both the BME and SI re-creation described in Section 2.2 are performed at half-pixel precision, we applied the FIR filter [7], which is also adopted in H.264/AVC, to perform the up-sampling on the whole past and future reference frames at the BME stage. Therefore, the result of up-sampling can be reused at the SI re-creation stage and the decoding of subsequent WZ frames. In this way, the operation of FIR filtering makes the time spend on the BME stage become non-negligible. Here, the FME is parallelized on GPGPU and the operation of FIR filter is parallelized on multi-core CPU.

3.2 Parallel Correlation Noise Modeling

The correlation noise modeling (CNM) module comprises three components: 1) correlation noise parameter estimation, 2) correlation noise distribution modeling and 3) conditional bit probabilities computation. The main bottleneck is on the correlation noise distribution modeling because the probability density function (pdf) of CNM for each of the coefficients in the WZ blocks should be pre-computed by using the sum of Laplacian which was defined in [3]. We parallelized the correlation noise distribution modeling and the conditional bit probabilities computation on GPGPU. In this way, the pdf of correlation noise obtained by the correlation noise distribution modeling stage can be utilized directly by the conditional bit probabilities computation stage and needs not to be transferred back to the host.

3.3 Parallel LDPCA Decoding

The LDPCA decoding is the most time-consuming part in the WZ video decoder as will be shown in Section 4. Here, the method of [8] is adopted, which parallelized the message-passing algorithm in each LDPC decoding iteration on GPGPU through CUDA. It uses two kernels: 1) horizontal processing kernel and 2) vertical processing kernel to accelerate the horizontal process and vertical process in the message-passing algorithm. Moreover, the convergence (syndrome check error) is tested at host after 100 iterations instead of each iteration to save the time spend on data transition between host and device.

3.4 Parallel Side Information Re-Creation

The SI re-creation is used to improve the accuracy of the SI used by the motion learning process. However, it also increases the decoding complexity because the bidirectional 4×4 block size full search motion estimation algorithm at half pixel precision is involved in the process. Fortunately, the structure of the algorithm is suitable for parallel computing so that the time complexity can be much reduced. In this work, we only parallelized integer pixel full search on GPGPU

3.5 Parallel Statistic Motion Learning

The statistic motion learning process includes 1) updating statistic motion field (SMF) probabilities and 2) SI re-estimation, which are described in [3]. Here, we parallelized updating statistic motion field probabilities on GPGPU and SI re-estimation on multi-core CPU.

4. Experimental Results

The test condition of rate-distortion (RD) performance of DISPAC codec is the same as in [1,3,9], which adopts four sequences, Foreman, Soccer, Coastguard and Hall Monitor, with GOP size 2, 4 and 8. Each sequence corresponds to a potential application scenario of WZ coding: Soccer and Foreman sequences can simulate the situations of video recording and video conversation using cell phones, respectively. Coastguard and Hall Monitor sequences are “easier” sequences corresponding to well-behaved and lower motion contents, which are in some way the representative situations of video surveillance applications. Due to page limitation, only the Foreman sequence with 150 frames, QCIF resolution, 15Hz frame rate and GOP size 8 is shown in Fig. 2. The RD gains of the DISPAC codec against the MLWZ codec can go up to 3.1 dB for Soccer, 2.6 dB for Hall Monitor, 1.6 dB for Foreman and 0.2 dB for Coastguard. The RD gains of DISPAC codec against DISCOVER codec are even larger. It can go up to 3.6 dB for Soccer, 3.1 dB for Foreman, 2.6 dB for Hall Monitor and 0.9 dB for Coastguard. Comparing with selected benchmarking standard video codecs, H.264/AVC Intra and H.264/AVC No Motion [9], the RD performance of DISPAC codec outperforms H.264/AVC Intra and is comparable to H.264/AVC No Motion for most sequences under all test conditions, except for Soccer sequence which has the most complex motion activities of all sequences.

We evaluated decoding speed of DISPAC codec against other WZ codecs on a workstation equipped with an Intel Xeon E5530 CPU at 2.4GHz and an NVIDIA Tesla C1060 graphics card which is used to emulate the basic unit of a Could computing environment. One of the results is shown in Table 1. The decoding time spent by each module of every codec is shown in seconds. In Table 1, "SIC" denotes the time spent by SI creation, "SML" denotes the time spent by statistic motion learning, "CNM" denotes the time spent by correlation noise modeling, "LDPCA" denotes the time spent by LDPCA decoding, "SIR" denotes the time spent by SI re-creation, "Others" denotes the time spent by remaining modules and "Total." denotes the total decoding time. In, all sequences, the LDPCA decoding dominates the total decoding time for all WZ codecs. For MLWZ codec, the decoding time for CNM becomes non-negligible due to more complex noise modeling, which even exceeds the LDPCA decoding time for Hall Monitor sequence (which takes the least time for LDPCA decoding, thanks to the accuracy of SI). For DISPAC codec, the module of CNM is the same as that of MLWZ codec, so it also becomes one of the bottlenecks for decoding. Another bottleneck of DISPAC codec is the SIR module, which involves the operations of bidirectional motion estimation at half pixel precision.

The total decoding time of DISPAC decoder are smaller than that of the DISCOVER and MLWZ for most sequences in sequential decoding. One reason is that some numbers of blocks are classified as Skip or Intra mode and, in turn, reduces the time spend for LDPCA decoding, CNM, SIR and SML, which process the WZ blocks only. Another reason results from that the motion learning SI is improved much by adding the SIR module and by involving the decoded Intra block in the initial SI. When considering the WZ decoding under the condition that multi-core CPU and GPGPU are provided, DISPAC decoder is always the fastest one.

Table 2 shows the speed up ratio of the DISPAC decoder against the DISCOVER decoder according to the total decoding time. We can see the maximum speed up appeared in the Soccer sequence, which is 60.97 times faster by making use of both 8 core and GPGPU, because of the effect of block mode selection module and relative large improvement on the accuracy of SI.

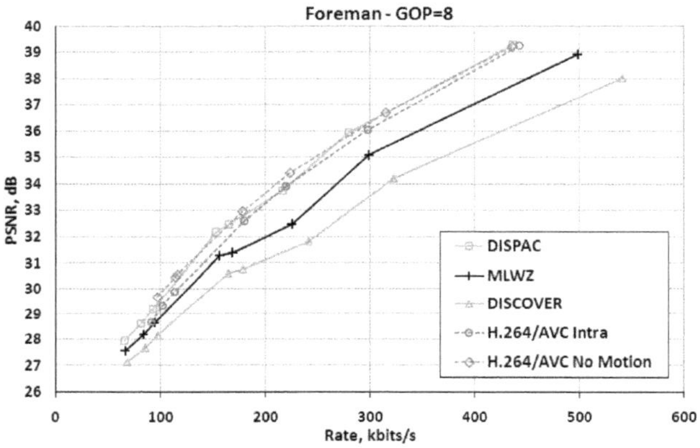

Fig. 2. Rate-distortion for the Foreman sequence.

Platform	Sequential (single core)			8core + GPGPU
Codec	DISCOVER	MLWZ	DISPAC	DISPAC
SIC	24.47	24.72	22.32	0.69
SML	-	35.66	8.06	0.94
CNM	39.8	1836	1079.07	4.65
SIR	-	-	1041.53	8.66
LDPCA	10957.19	7895	4106.09	179.98
Others	1.96	3.94	11.98	3.92
Total.	11021.46	9789.39	6284.9	199.94

Table 1. Decoding time for Foreman sequence.

Parallel Mode	Sequential (single core)			8core + GPGPU
Codec	DISCOVER	MLWZ	DISPAC	DISPAC
Foreman	1	1.13	1.75	55.12
Soccer	1	0.96	2.73	60.97
Coastguard	1	0.83	0.8	32.79
Hall Monitor	1	0.42	0.87	11.57

Table 2. The speed up ratio comparing to DISCOVER

5. CONCLUSIONS

By shifting the computational complexity from the encoder to the decoder and integrating with appropriate trascoding techniques, DVC has been expected to provide a video codec solution for Cloud computing mobile devices (such as mobile phones). This expectation comes from the fact that if the high complexity decoding and transcoding tasks could be handled by the Cloud, then both the video encoder and decoder of the mobile device would be very simple, and therefore, consuming low power. The proposed DISPAC codec moves on step toward this goal. Experimental results show that the DISPAC codec not only makes new steps to narrow down the RD performance gap between WZ coding and conventional prediction-based video coding, but also can be executed much faster than all the-state-of-art WZ decoders on an emulated Cloud computing platform. As far as the authors could track, it is the best performing transform domain WZ video codec with respect to the RD performance and decoding speed.

6. REFERENCES

[1] A. Aaron, R. Zhang, B. Girod, "Wyner–Ziv coding of motion video", Asilomar Conf. on Signals, Systems and Computers, November 2002.

[2] X. Artigas, J. Ascenso, M. Dalai, S. Klomp, D. Kubasov, M. Ouaret: "The DISCOVER codec: architecture, techniques and evaluation", Picture Coding Symp. November 2007.

[3] R. Martins, C. Brites, J. Ascenso, F. Pereira, "Statistical Motion Learning for Improved Transform Domain Wyner-Ziv Video Coding", IET-IPR(4), No. 1, 28-41, February 2010.

[4] D. Varodayan, A. Aaron and B. Girod, "Rate-Adaptive Codes for Distributed Source Coding", EURASIP Signal Processing Journal, Special Section on Distributed Source Coding, vol. 86, no. 11, November 2006.

[5] J. Ascenso, C. Brites, F. Pereira, "Content Adaptive Wyner-Ziv Video Coding Driven by Motion Activity", IEEE International Conf. on Image Processing, October 2007.

[6] B.-R. Chiou, Y.-C. Shen, H.-P. Cheng, J.-L. Wu, "Performance improvement of distributed video coding by using block mode selection", *ACM International Conf. on Multimedia*, 2010.

[7] ISO/IEC 14496-10 2003, "Coding of audio-visual objects– part 10: advanced video coding" (July 2003).

[8] Y.-S. Pai, H.-P. Cheng, Y.-C. Shen, J.-L. Wu, "Fast decoding for LDPC based distributed video coding", *ACM International Conf. on Multimedia*, 2010.

[9] Test condition of DISCOVER codec - http://www.img.lx.it.pt/~discover/test_conditions.html

Real-time Decoding for LDPC Based Distributed Video Coding

Tse-Chung Su[1], Yun-Chung Shen[2] and Ja-Ling Wu[1,2], Fellow, IEEE
[1] Department of Computer Science and Information Engineering, National Taiwan University
[2] Graduate Institute of Networking and Multimedia, National Taiwan University
National Taiwan University, Taipei 10617, Taiwan, R.O.C.
{jsrf, cazindo, wjl}@cmlab.csie.ntu.edu.tw

ABSTRACT
Wyner-Ziv (WZ) video coding – a particular case of distributed video coding (DVC), is well known for its low-complexity encoding and high-complexity decoding characteristics. Although some works have been made in recent years, especially for improving the coding efficiency, most reported WZ codecs have high time delay in the decoder, which hinders its practical values for applications with critical timing constraint. In this paper, a fully parallelized sum-product algorithm (SPA) for low density parity check accumulate (LDPCA) codes is proposed and realized through Compute Unified Device Architecture (CUDA) based on General-Purpose Graphics Processing Unit (GPGPU). Simulation results show that, through our work, QCIF (surveillance) videos can be decoded in real-time with extremely high quality and without rate-distortion (RD) performance loss.

Categories and Subject Descriptors
I.4.2 [**Image Processing and Computer Vision**]: Compression (Coding) – *Exact coding and Approximate methods*; D.1.3 [**Software**]: Programming Techniques – *Parallel programming*

General Terms
Algorithms, Design, Experimentation, Performance.

Keywords
DVC, LDPC, SPA, parallel computing, GPGPU, CUDA.

1. INTRODUCTION
Distributed video coding (DVC) has recently attracted a vast amount of attention from the video coding communities all around the world. DVC codec subverts the traditional prediction-based standard video coding scheme by exploiting the source statistics at the decoder with the development of simpler encoders. These features are effectively utilized in several application domains, e.g. video conferencing with mobile devices and wireless low-power surveillance systems. The new coding paradigm is also known as WZ video coding, which is based on Slepian-Wolf [1] and Wyner-Ziv [2] theorems. These theorems mainly state that separate encoding and joint decoding of two correlated sources, X and Y, can achieve the same compression rate as joint encoding and decoding conducted in the conventional source coding schemes. The first WZ video codec [3] was developed in 2002. This popular WZ codec architecture divides the video frames into WZ frames and key frames. The key frames are coded using a conventional Intra codec such as JPEG or H.264/AVC intra. These coded key frames are treated as references, for the WZ decoder, which are used to create an estimation of the original WZ frame, the so-called side information (SI), to help conducting the decoding process. The Slepian-Wolf decoder, which is the core module of WZ codec, treats the difference between WZ and SI as correlation noise and tries to do an error correction on SI to recover the decoded WZ frame. Typically, Slepian-Wolf codec is realized by channel codes [4], especially codes with capacity near the Shannon limit, such as turbo and low-density parity-check (LDPC) codes. The evaluation on WZ codec [5] shows that LDPC codes outperform turbo codes in terms of RD performance and complexity, especially at the decoder side.

While the errors between the SI and the WZ frame are different frame by frame, the structure of LDPC code needs to be adapted to the varying statistics of the pre-described correlation noise. The LDPC accumulate (LDPCA) codes with rate- compatible scheme [6] is a well-designed solution for this issue by requesting more syndrome bits once the attempt to decode each coding unit fails for the given SI. In such case, the encoder replies to each request by sending additional syndrome bits, which combined with the previously sent ones, until they are sufficient for successful decoding. However, such a decode-check-request process usually loops tens of times through the feedback channel, especially in high motion or large group of pictures (GOP) size videos, which leads to high time-delay of WZ decoding and hinders the practical values of DVC for real-time applications. Actually, in DVC, more than 90% of decoding complexity is contributed by Slepian-Wolf decoder [4]. In this paper, we proposed an optimized DVC decoder by parallelizing the LDPCA decoding using CUDA interface. Simulation results show that the maximal speed-up ratio can reach to 400, for CIF size sequences, as compared with the sequential counterpart.

This paper is organized as follows. The SPA algorithm used in LDPCA decoder is introduced in Section 2. Then, the fully parallelized SPA algorithm is described in Section 3. In Section 4, the RD performance and the decoding complexity are investigated. Finally, some concluding remarks are presented in Section 5.

*Area Chair: Wei Tsang Ooi

MM'11, November 28–December 1, 2011, Scottsdale, Arizona, USA.

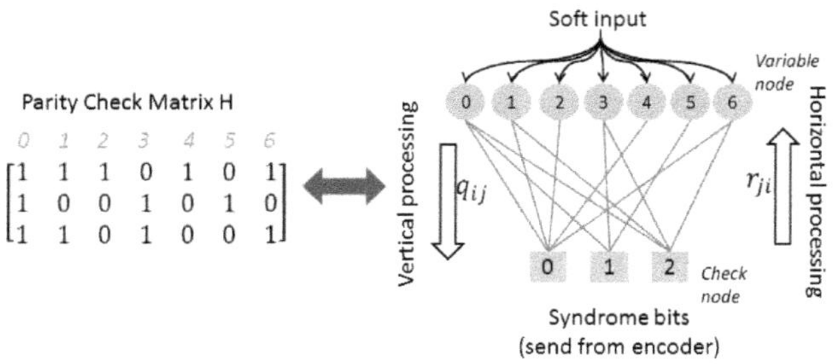

Figure 1. Parity Check Matrix and its tanner graph.

2. SUM-PRODUCT ALGORITHM

Sum-Product algorithm (SPA) [7] is an iterative algorithm for computing joint probabilities (messages) on graphs. Messages are passed between the variable nodes and the check nodes, which represent the codeword bits and the syndrome bits, respectively. The message passing behavior are often visualized by a bipartite graph (tanner graph), as illustrate in Figure 1. Each SPA iteration consists of two phases: horizontal processing and vertical processing. The vertical processing computes messages q_{ij} sent from variable node i to check node j by

$$q_{ij} = p_i + \sum_{j' \in C_i \backslash j} r_{j'i}\ , \quad \text{for } (i,j) \in E, \tag{1}$$

where E is the set containing edges between variable node i and check node j in a parity check matrix H, p_i is the initial probability (soft input) of variable node i, and $C_i \backslash j$ stands for all check nodes connected to variable node i except check node j. The horizontal processing, on the other hand, updates the message r_{ji} from each check node j to each variable node i by the following equations:

$$r_{ji} = sign_{ij} \times mag_{ij}, \quad \text{for } (i,j) \in E \tag{2}$$

$$sign_{ij} = (1 - 2S_j) \times \prod_{i' \in V_j \backslash i} signof(q_{i'j}) \tag{3}$$

$$mag_{ij} = \varphi\left(\sum_{i' \in V_j \backslash i} \varphi(|q_{i'j}|)\right) \tag{4}$$

$$signof(x) = \begin{cases} 1, \text{if } x \geq 0 \\ -1, \text{if } x < 0 \end{cases} \tag{5}$$

$$\varphi(x) = -\log\left(\tanh\left(\frac{x}{2}\right)\right), \tag{6}$$

where $V_j \backslash i$ stands for variable nodes connected to check node j except variable node i and S_j is the syndrome bit for check node j, which is sent from the DVC encoder.

3. PARALLEL LDPCA DECODING IN CUDA

The SPA algorithm fits for SIMD (single instruction, multiple data) operation well. All edges are updated according to the same equations (1)-(6) but only with different index information (C_i, V_j) and messages q_{ij} and r_{ji}. In [8], two fast LDPCA decoding kernels, vertical processing kernel (VPK) and horizontal processing kernel (HPK) have been designed, which correspond to the vertical processing and horizontal processing, respectively. Each message can be updated per CUDA thread according to its SIMD structure. The simulation results of [8] showed about 20~30 times speed-up gain can be obtained as compared with the naïve sequential decoder for the same test sequence. It is our believe that further performance improvement in CUDA is essential because LDPCA decoding is still the bottleneck of the overall codec system.

3.1 Parallel Partial Reduction (PPR) in HPK

There are in total 65 tanner graphs (codes) with different number of check nodes to cope with different correlations between WZ and SI [9]. LDPCA decoder picks one of the codes for Slepian-Wolf decoding for each request. Table 1 shows the average decoding time for part of codes derived from [8]. From Table 1, it is more time-consuming obviously when codes with high row degrees (check node degrees) in parity check matrix (tanner graph) are adopted. The reason is that the usage of φ function, and the instructions in (3) and (4), increase linearly as the set V_j (i.e. check node degree) increase. More precisely, in (4) for example, the number of additions and φ functions computed by each CUDA thread is ($|V_j \backslash i|$-2) and $|V_j \backslash i|$, respectively. It is remarkable that these facts are critical for sequences with high-compression ratio (e.g., Hall Monitor). Because high compression ratio means that codes with less check nodes are more frequently adopted, and the row degrees of these codes are always very high.

Table 1. LDPCA decoding time on CUDA derived from [8]

Code ID	LDPC(n, m)	Check node (row) degree (ρ(x) distribution)	HPK+VPK Decoding time for100 iterations (ms)
0	(1584, 48)	x^{98}	8.29+1.49
6	(1584, 192)	$0.75x^{23}+0.25x^{26}$	3.40+1.52
12	(1584, 336)	$0.71x^{11}+0.14x^{14}+0.14x^{13}$	3.04+1.53
18	(1584, 480)	$0.3x^{5}+0.1x^{8}+0.6x^{11}$	2.31+1.55
30	(1584, 768)	$0.94x^{5}+0.06x^{8}$	2.00+1.52
42	(1584, 1056)	$0.5x^{2}+0.5x^{5}$	1.81+1.52
60	(1584, 1488)	$0.94x^{2}+0.06x^{5}$	1.78+1.56

To reduce the complexity of HPK, the edge messages (q_{ij} and r_{ji}) were stored in row-major order, so all threads within a row could utilize the same shared memory. Second, because all threads within a row execute almost the same input messages except their own messages (set $V_j \backslash i$), we can re-write (3) and (4) as

$$\begin{cases} sign_{ij} = (1 - 2S_j) \times \text{SignQ}_j \times \text{signof}(q_{ij}) & (7) \\ mag_{ij} = \varphi(\text{MagQ}_j - \varphi(|q_{ij}|)) & (8) \end{cases},$$

where SignQ_j and MagQ_j stand for

$$\begin{cases} \text{SignQ}_j = \prod_{i \in V_j} \text{signof}(q_{ij}) & (9) \\ \text{MagQ}_j = \sum_{i \in V_j} \varphi(|q_{ij}|) & (10) \end{cases},$$

respectively. Equation (9) and (10) show that all edge messages connected to check node j share the same data MagQ_j and SignQ_j. Therefore, superfluous arithmetic computations in HPK can be significantly reduced because the computation of MagQ_j and SignQ_j can be further parallelized as addressed in the rest of this section.

We present a Parallel Partial Reduction (PPR) scheme to compute $MagQ_j$ and $SignQ_j$. The technique is very similar to parallel reduction, which is a common and important data parallel primitive in CUDA [10], except for doing multiple reductions (i.e., summarizing into multiple MagQj and SignQj) within a CUDA block. The procedure of acquiring $MagQ_j$ is illustrated in the shared memory portion of Figure 2. The number of threads we used for each iteration is equal to half of the number of the elements in a given array of the shared memory. Every thread adds the values of two elements up and brings the result to the next iteration until all values of elements are summed together as illustrated. The number of additions in (4) computed by each CUDA thread is reduced to $\lceil \log(\|V_{j'}\|) \rceil + 1$, where j' is the variable node with the highest degree (row degree) in a CUDA block. Furthermore, since the computation of φ functions have been shared in the shared memory, the number of φ function computed by each CUDA thread is largely reduced to 2 for all code IDs in LDPCA.

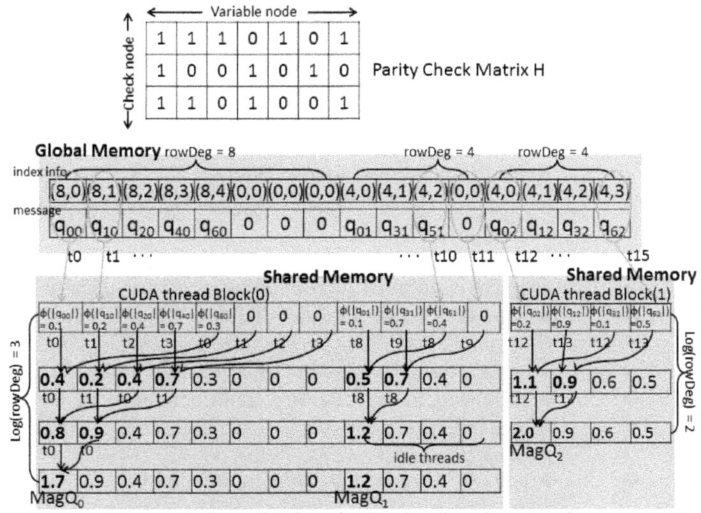

Figure 2. Parallel Partial Reduction for $MagQ_j$.

3.2 Combination of VPK and HPK

CUDA kernel combination is a very useful performance optimization strategy when kernels are invocated consecutively without interleaving with CPU instructions. Kernel invocations have additional overhead [11] due to the parallelism of application being broken by CUDA inter-block synchronization and the inevitable global memory access at the beginning and the end of the kernels. These overheads would slow down the LDPCA decoding process. In order to reduce the number of kernel invocations during the decoding process, the HPK and VPK are replaced by a kernel named update message kernel (UMK), which is constructed by appending VPK after HPK. The UMK eliminates the synchronization between HPK and VPK and will not cause any race condition. The reason is that instructions in HPK (first half of UMK) only share data within the same CUDA block. However, the UMKs can't be further combined together. We still have to separate each vertical processing in different iterations into different kernel invocation (UMK) to keep CUDA blocks synchronized, because instructions in VPK (latter half of UMK) have to read r_{ji} across other CUDA blocks due to row-major data structure. To further minimize global memory read latency of variable r_{ji}, we alternatively read global memory through texture fetch, which is cached and is used to avoid uncoalesced data loads from the global memory [11].

4. SIMULATION RESULTS

The following simulations are performed with our transform domain Wyner-Ziv (TDWZ) video codec, called DISPAC [12], which has combined most recently proposed efficient TDWZ coding tools. Most of the critical modules have been parallelized on GPU or multi-core CPU. The UMK kernel is executed using 128 threads per block to obtain the best LDPCA decoding speed.

4.1 Average Decoding Time of the Parallelized LDPCA Decoder

To verify the speedup of our implementation of parallelized LDPCA decoder, the average LDPCA decoding time per feedback is calculated during the WZ decoding process, which is shown in Table 3. We use Forman sequence with both QCIF and CIF resolutions, which are applied with block length N=1584 and N=6336, respectively. For providing fair comparison, the simulations are performed in 3 different GPU devices: GeForce 9800 GTX+, Tesla C1060, and Tesla C2050 disabling ECC (the detail specification of the device can be seen in Tables 2). Table 4 also shows the decoding time of the sequential (CPU) version and two recently proposed paralleled LDPCA decoder on GPGPU [13][8]. Although the devices used by [13] and [8] are better than some devices of ours like 9800 GTX+ (cf. Table 2), our parallelized LDPCA decoder outperforms [13] and [8] significantly in term of decoding time in all conditions.

Table 2. Hardware specifications of various GPU Devices

	GeForce 9800 GTX+	Tesla C1060	GeForce GTX260	Tesla C2050
Compute Capability	1.1	1.3	1.3	2.0
MP x Cores/MP	16x8	30x8	27x8	14x32

Table 3. Average decoding time of proposed parallelized LDPCA decoder per feedback

	9800GTX	Tesla C1060	Tesla C2050
100 iteration(QCIF)	1.93~1.83ms	1.23~1.26ms	0.55~0.60ms
50 iteration(QCIF)	1.09~1.27ms	0.67~0.70ms	0.29~0.31ms
100 iteration(CIF)	3.26~3.34ms	2.39~2.52ms	1.25~1.34ms
50 iteration(CIF)	1.87~2.12ms	1.27~1.34ms	0.65~0.69ms

Table 4. Average decoding time of other implementations of LDPCA decoder per feedback

	Intel Xeon X5650 @ 2.66 GHz	[13] using GTX260	[8] using Tesla C1060
100 iteration(QCIF)	129.40 ms	35ms	6.34 ms
50 iteration(QCIF)	67.51 ms	18ms	3.23 ms
100 iteration(CIF)	519.87 ms	46ms	18.79 ms
50 iteration(CIF)	272.65 ms	24ms	9.50 ms

4.2 RD Performance and Overall Decoding Speed

We also measure the RD performance and the decoding complexity of the whole system with 4 sequences, Foreman, Soccer, Coastguard, and Hall Monitor, with GOP size 8 as adopted in [14, 15], which is the most critical case in terms of decoding complexity. The resolution of the sequences are QCIF and 15 Hz frame rate, as adopted in [14, 15]. On the other hand, only the luminance component of each frame is used to compute the bitrate, PSNR, and decoding speed; moreover, both key frames and WZ frames are included in the evaluation. The system is executed on a workstation with an Intel Xeon E5530 CPU at 2.4GHz (8MB cache) and a Tesla C2050 (cf. Table 2). The number of LDPCA iterations per feedback is fixed to 50. As shown in Table 5, the decoding speed raises as the quality (Qindex) decreases. It is because the number of coding unit drops when the quality decreases, easing the burden of LDPCA decoding. Another influence on the decoding speed is the number of requests through feedback channel. Table 5 also shows that the Hall sequence can be decoded in real time with very good video quality, which implies that it has become practical to apply Wyner-Ziv video codec to some real applications such as in video surveillance systems. More importantly, the RD performance remains unchanged because we did not alter any algorithm of the SPA algorithm.

Table 5. RD performances and decoding speed

Qindex	1	2	3	4	5	6	7	8
Hall Monitor (142 WZ frames, 22 key frames)								
rate(kbits/s)	33.58	37.45	42.64	63.51	68.74	86.61	101.2	147.5
PSNR(dB)	30.54	31.01	31.18	33.6	33.66	35.04	36.51	39.46
WZ fps	63.02	59.25	41.37	24.86	22.05	17.84	16.75	13.2
Overall fps	**72.05**	**67.34**	**47.55**	**28.6**	**25.34**	**21.01**	**20.57**	**15.19**
Foreman (130 WZ frames, 20 key frames)								
rate(kbits/s)	66.67	81.93	93.11	153.7	165.7	217.0	280.2	437.3
PSNR	27.95	28.62	29.21	32.18	32.48	33.74	35.94	39.3
WZ fps	18.49	18.26	14.26	10.24	9.84	8.63	7.62	6.52
Overall fps	**21.25**	**21.01**	**16.38**	11.77	11.3	9.93	8.75	7.5
Soccer (130 WZ frames, 20 key frames)								
rate(kbits/s)	77.85	92.09	98.41	157.7	162.6	199.4	263.2	475.0
PSNR	28.47	28.85	29.60	32.38	32.50	33.57	35.34	39.08
WZ fps	18.62	19.66	19.23	15.01	15.71	15.80	14.00	8.95
Overall fps	**21.49**	**22.69**	**22.20**	**17.34**	**18.15**	**18.27**	**16.19**	10.36
Coastguard (130 WZ frames, 20 key frames)								
rate(kbits/s)	52.97	68.47	76.09	127.9	139.4	197.8	260.0	462.1
PSNR	26.66	27.13	27.44	29.53	29.85	30.89	32.60	36.15
WZ fps	21.49	20.67	13.65	8.44	7.35	6.07	5.64	4.57
Overall fps	**24.81**	**23.86**	**15.77**	9.76	8.51	7.03	6.54	5.32

5. CONCLUSION

This paper represents a parallelized LDPCA decoder on GPGPU with various features. The fully parallelized PPR scheme reduces the intensive operations of LDPCA decoder, while the technique of CUDA kernel combination reduces the global memory bandwidth and removes the superfluous synchronization barrier. Simulation shows that by integrating the proposed LDPCA decoder to the DISPAC decoder, videos in surveillance sequence (e.g. hall monitor) can be decoded in real-time. As for other video sequences (e.g. coastguard, soccer, and foreman), at least 5.32 frames per second decoding speed can be obtained. All videos are decoded with very high quality and without RD performance loss.

6. REFERENCES

[1] Slepian, D. and Wolf, J, 1973. Noiseless coding of correlated information sources. *IEEE Trans. on Information Theory*. 19, 4, 471- 480.

[2] Wyner, A. and Ziv, J. 1976. The rate-distortion function for source coding with side information at the decoder. *IEEE Trans. on Information Theory*. 22, 1, 1-10.

[3] Aaron, A., Rui, Z. and Girod, B. 2002. Wyner-ziv coding of motion video. In *Proc.* of *Conference Record of the Thirty-Sixth Asilomar Conference on Signals, Systems and Computers, 2002.*, 240-244.

[4] Girod, B., Aaron, A. M., Rane, S. and Rebollo-Monedero, D. 2005. Distributed video coding. *Proceedings of the IEEE*. 93, 1, 71-83.

[5] Varodayan, D. and Aaron, A. 2006. Rate-adaptive codes for distributed source coding. *EURASIP Signal Processing Journal, Special Issue on Distributed Source Coding*. 86, 11, 3123-3130.

[6] Varodayan, D., Aaron, A. and Girod, B. 2005. Rate-adaptive distributed source coding using low-density parity-check codes. In *Proc.* of *Signals, Systems and Computers, 2005. Conference Record of the Thirty-Ninth Asilomar Conference on*, 1203-1207.

[7] Kschischang, F. R., Frey, B. J. and Loeliger, H. A. 2001. Factor graphs and the sum-product algorithm. *Information Theory, IEEE Trans. on*. 47, 2, 498-519.

[8] Pai, Y.-S., Cheng, H.-P., Shen, Y.-C. and Wu, J.-L. 2010. Fast decoding for ldpc based distributed video coding. In *Proc.* of *ACM international conference on Multimedia*,

[9] Ldpca c source: http://www.stanford.edu/~divad/software/ldpca.zip.

[10] Optimizing parallel reduction in cuda: http://developer.download.nvidia.com/compute/cuda/1_1/Website/projects/reduction/doc/reduction.pdf.

[11] Cuda programming guide 3.2: http://developer.download.nvidia.com/compute/cuda/3_2/toolkit/docs/CUDA_C_Programming_Guide.pdf.

[12] H.-P. Cheng,Y.-C. Shen, J.-L. Wu. 2011. High Efficient Distributed Video Coding with Parallelized Design for Cloud Computing, *ACM International Conf. on Multimedia.*

[13] Ryanggeun, O., Jongbin, P. and Byeungwoo, J. 2010. Fast implementation of wyner-ziv video codec using gpgpu. In *Proc.* of *IEEE International Symposium on Broadband Multimedia Systems and Broadcasting*, 1-5.

[14] Artigas, X., Ascenso, J., Dalai, M., Klomp, S., Kubasov, D. and Ouaret, M. 2007. The discover codec: Architecture, techniques and evaluation. In *Proc.* of *Picture Coding Symposium*.

[15] Discover - test material: http://www.img.lx.it.pt/~discover/test_conditions.html

Mixing Remote Locations using Shared Screen as Virtual Stage *

Shingo Uchihashi
Communication Technology Laboratory
Fuji Xerox Co., Ltd.
Yokohama, Japan
shingo.uchihashi@fujixerox.co.jp

Tsutomu Tanzawa
Computer Science and Media Engineering
University of Yamanashi
Kofu, Japan
ttanzawa@yamanashi.ac.jp

ABSTRACT

This paper introduces a visual communication system that integrates images displayed on a shared screen and people in front of the screen using depth information obtained from a stereo camera. Conventional video conferencing systems convey PC screen contents and video of local and remote participants in different channels, making interactions among them difficult. The proposed system maps persons in the foreground onto the screen preserving relative position and size. A series of preliminary experiments is conducted to compare the performance of the proposed system against conventional systems.

Categories and Subject Descriptors

H.4.3 [**Communications Applications**]: Computer conferencing, teleconferencing, and videoconferencing

General Terms

Experimentation, Performance

Keywords

Remote collaboration, mixed reality

1. INTRODUCTION

Recent advancements in network bandwidth have allowed visual communication systems to flourish. People at remote locations can see each other using high-definition video streams and discuss presentation materials that are shared among all participating sites.

Nevertheless, there still exist difficulties in communicating over a distance. Typical visual communication systems convey PC screen contents and video of people on separate channels. This scheme adds extra workload in understanding events at remote sites. Imagine a situation where a presenter is giving a talk using slides that are shared remotely, and a person at a different location comes up to ask a question pointing at a certain area in the slide. A person in a third location has to carefully choose which display to watch or lose track of the discussion.

This indicates a limitation of a conventional approach where remote people appear on screens which work as *windows* to their sites [3]. The HyperMirror system pushes every site to the other side of the window [5]. This approach has its own limitation. Since participants see themselves and remote participants in a large screen as if all of them are co-located and looking at a large mirror, so participants have to adjust their movements from visual feedback.

To enable smooth discussions among distributed participants, we propose integrating images displayed on a shared screen and people in front of the screen. A common solution for this approach is to cast shadows of varying size onto a screen to provide their awareness [1][4]. Other solutions deal only with hands [7], restrict environments to be identically configured [8], or ignore real world completely [2]. Instead, we use depth information to extract people in front of the screen and normalize them in size, allowing participants from every location and the contents of the shared screen to be displayed in a single frame, and eliminating the burden of choosing the right one to watch from multiple screens.

2. PROPOSED SYSTEM

2.1 Generating Reconstructed View

We propose a visual communication system that extracts images of people in front of a screen at each location, transforms the images to align with the screen, and exchanges them among the remote sites so that a person in front of any screen shows up in other screens along with the shared screen contents (See Figure 1). Transparency of extracted regions may be adjusted to avoid hiding screen contents and people at different locations.

To implement the concept, depth information is used in two ways. First, it is used as a cue to segment foreground image regions from the screen in the background where appearance changes dynamically. Second, the extracted image regions of people are adjusted in size and shape based on their distance from the camera so that their relative sizes to the screen area are preserved and images from different locations can be easily aligned.

A regular RGB image associated with a depth map is obtained using a stereo camera. Each depth measurement is turned into a point in the screen-centered coordinate space, where the y-axis and the z-axis are taken perpendicular to

*Area chair: Pal Halvorsen

MM'11, November 28–December 1, 2011, Scottsdale, Arizona, USA.

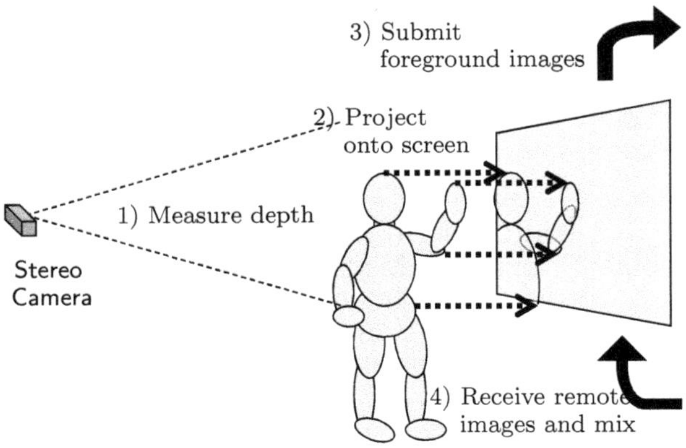

Figure 1: Overview of the proposed system.

Figure 2: Our stereo camera.

the floor and the screen respectively. To construct an image of people aligned with the screen, corresponding regions of the RGB image are orthogonally projected onto the screen by ignoring z information and putting everything onto x-y plane. We refer to the generated image as a "reconstructed view".

2.2 Stereo Camera

We have built our own stereo camera to obtain RGB images associated with the depth information (See Figure 2). Two USB 2.0 cameras are mounted 200 mm apart. Each camera is equipped with a 1/3 CCD and captures an image of a resolution of 1024×768. Stereo correspondences are computed using area-based matching scheme with the area size of 4×4 pixels. The equiangular line fitting with sum of the absolute differences (SAD) is used for fast sub-pixel registration [6]. The outputs of the processes are a RGB image of the resolution of 800×600 associated with a depth map at 14.6 frames per second. The images cover 49.0 degrees of the viewing angle horizontally.

3. EXPERIMENT 1 : INSTRUCTIONS

We conducted a series of user experiments to evaluate the performance of the proposed system. The first set of experiments tested capabilities of the system for conveying basic instructions and perception of size from one site to the others by comparison with regular camera images typically used for video conferencing systems. We consider basic instructions, including pointing and gesturing, must be conveyed correctly, and perception of size is hard to achieve for remote participants since apparent size of objects varies depending on distance from a camera.

3.1 General Procedures

We recruited 18 volunteer subjects and asked them to watch video clips and write out what was perceived from the video clips. A video clip contains outputs produced by one of the three methods: a camera looking at a screen from a front position (front view), a camera looking at a screen from an angled position (angled view), and the proposed system (reconstructed view). For each task, a subject was asked to watch three video clips that contained a different combination of a method and an instruction problem on 27-inch LCD monitor. The presenting order of methods and problems were counterbalanced among participants.

Video clips were taken in a conference room with an 80-inch rear-projection display. A high-definition camera was placed in front of the screen. Another high-definition camera was placed in the right-front of the screen for capturing the angled view. Our stereo camera was placed by the camera for the angled view. All cameras were adjusted to have the same height position to align with the center of the screen. When capturing, the scenes were simultaneously shot by the three cameras. The captured video was compressed with H.264 codec to have 1024×768 at 15 fps.

3.2 Pointing instruction

In a video clip, a person pointed at eight randomly selected positions from an array of circled alphabet letters with colors displayed on the large screen. Each letter was on 5-cm grids. Three sets of letter positions were prepared for the task. Sample images are shown in Figure 3.

Subject were asked to write out letters that were perceived to be pointed in the video. The obtained letters were then matched against the letters actually pointed when shooting the video clips. The averages of mean errors from the 18 subjects for front, angled, and reconstructed views are 0cm, 0.1cm, and 3.71cm respectively. ANOVA on the results indicated that there is a significant difference among the three methods ($F(2,34)=137.82$, $p<0.01$). Further LSD test revealed that the mean error for the reconstructed view, 3.71cm, was significantly larger than the errors of the other methods that were effectively 0 ($p<0.01$).

3.3 Gesturing Instruction

In a video clip for gesturing instructions, a person pointed at one of the edges of a cube displayed on the screen, and then made a gesture of either opening or pushing in a side of the cube with the selected edge as an axis. Three different combinations of an edge and a side were used for each of opening and pushing gestures. See Figure 4(a) for sample images from the clips.

Each time a subject finished watching a clip, the subject was asked to write out which edge was selected and which side was moved to which direction. The answers were then matched against the ground truth to compute an accuracy measure that indicates how many answers out of the three were correct. Subject watched both opening gesture video clip and pushing in gesture video clip for each method, and we averaged the accuracy for the two gestures to obtain an accuracy for a method.

The average of accuracy scores from the 18 subjects for front, angled and reconstructed views are 0, 0.963, and 0.963

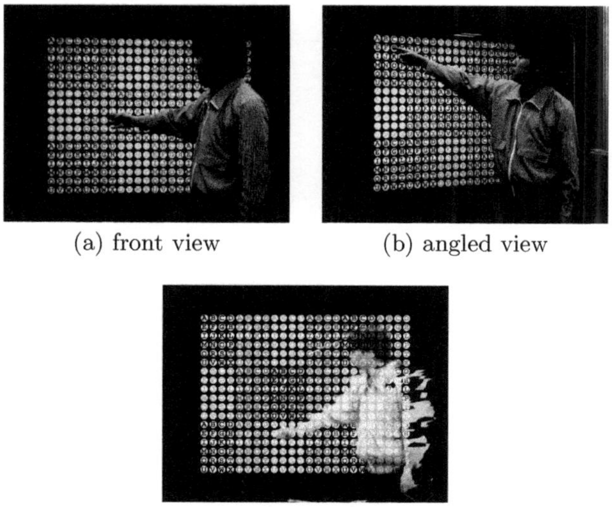

(a) front view (b) angled view

(c) reconstructed view

Figure 3: Pointing instructions

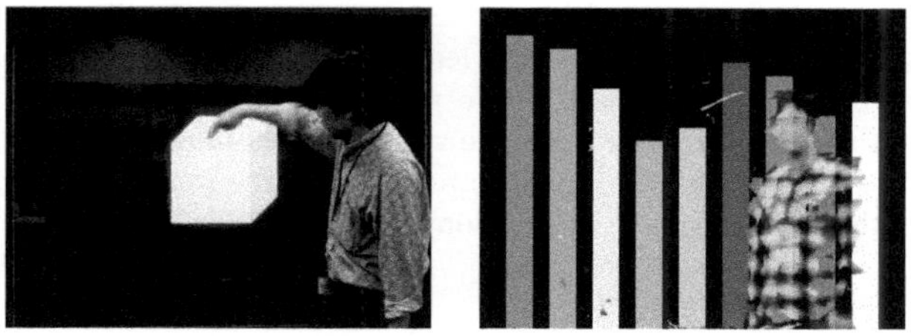

(a) Gesturing instructions (b) Height comparisons

Figure 4: Sample images from video clips.

respectively. ANOVA on the results indicated that there is no significant difference among the three methods suggesting that all the methods conveyed the instructions perfectly ($F(2,34)=2.12$, $p>0.1$).

3.4 Size Perception

In the video clips, nine colored bars were displayed on the large screen. Each bar had one of heights between 150cm and 190cm stepped by 5cm. One of the three persons walked around in front of the screen area. The order of bar heights was randomly selected for each person.

After watching a video clip, each subject was asked to write out which color bar was perceived to be equal in height with the person in front of the screen. A difference between the height of the obtained bar and the actual height of the person was recorded.

The averaged errors of the 18 subjects for the three methods are shown with 95% confidence intervals in Figure 5. ANOVA on the results indicated that there is a significant difference among the methods ($F(2,34)=6.84$, $p<0.01$). Further LSD test revealed that the mean error for the reconstructed view is significantly smaller than the errors of the other methods ($p<0.01$). No significant difference is detected between the front view and the angled view.

3.5 User Preference

Upon completing the above series of experiments, we asked the subject to provide pair-wise comparisons of the three methods in a five-point scale as well as reasons for the judgements in free form. Figure 6 summarizes the results.

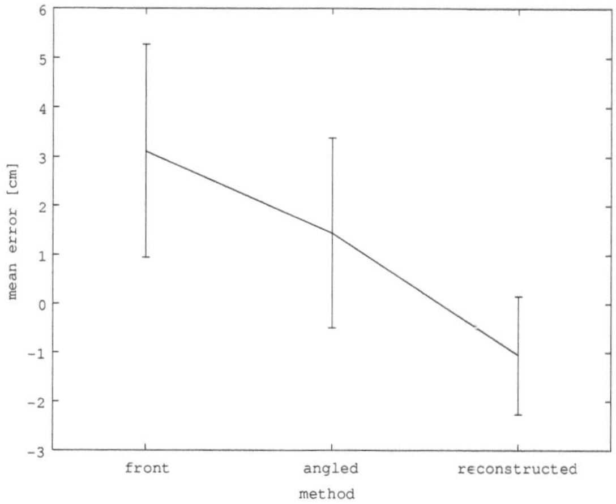

Figure 5: Averaged errors for direct height matching from video images.

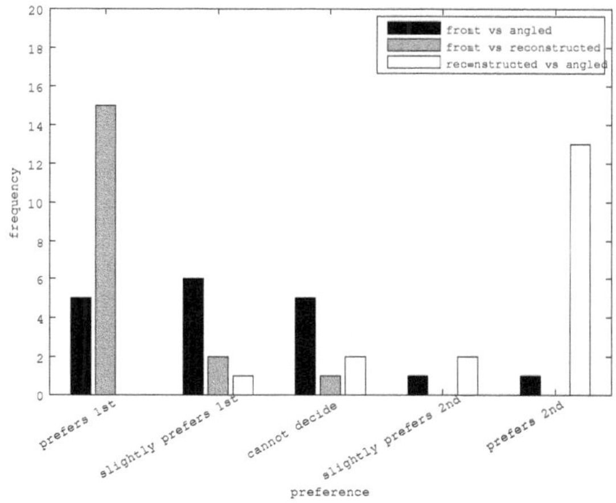

Figure 6: User preferences.

Most of the feedback for the reconstructed view had negative tones such as "Could not see clearly where the person is pointing at" and "Distorted images with flickers were distracting." Split opinions were collected for the comparison between the front view and the angled view. Some participants preferred the angled view because the view looked familiar to them and/or they felt that they could perceive depth better. Others preferred the front view simply because it was nice and square. Few expressed they did not mention the difference at all.

4. EXPERIMENT 2 : COLLABORATION

The second experiment was conducted to verify the benefit of reconstructing separate views into a single view in terms of communication efficiency. A comparison with a typical video conferencing setting was demonstrated. Subjects actually interacted with the systems instead of just watching the video clips as in the first set of experiments.

Figure 7: A scene from the remote collaboration experiment.

4.1 Procedures

We set up a simple task to be conducted collaboratively between two sites. At each of the two locations, the same image with randomly placed numbers from 1 to 25, roughly on 20cm-grid, was displayed on a 80-inch screen. Two subjects, one at each site, were asked to point at the numbers in incremental order starting from 1. At one site, the subject was also asked to act as a presenter showing where the numbers were to a local audience, the experimenter in the same room.

For each pair of subjects, four sessions were carried in total to let the two subjects to use both systems and experience both roles for each system. The task completion time was recorded for every session. We had 12 subjects or 6 pairs of subjects participating the experiment. The order of the systems used was counterbalanced among subject pairs to cancel the order effects. Figure 7 shows a typical scene from the experiment sessions. Note that the remote person in Figure 7 is presented semi-transparently to avoid hiding the screen contents.

4.2 Results

The average of the task completion time over 12 subjects for each system are shown with 95% confidence intervals in Figure 8. The averaged time for the video conferencing setting and our reconstructed view setting were 51.5 seconds and 48.17 seconds respectively. Although the result of the t-test did not show a significant difference between them, it indicated a certain tendency for our proposed method to require less amount of time (p=0.09).

5. CONCLUSIONS AND FUTURE WORK

This article proposed a visual communication system that integrates images displayed on a shared screen and people in front of the screen at multiple sites into a single frame using depth information. The results of our user experiments reveal that the proposed system can carry gesturing instructions equally well with conventional teleconferencing systems, and it allows perceiving size from remote sites better. Although pointing accuracy has rooms for improvement, remote collaboration using our system is demonstrated to be more efficient.

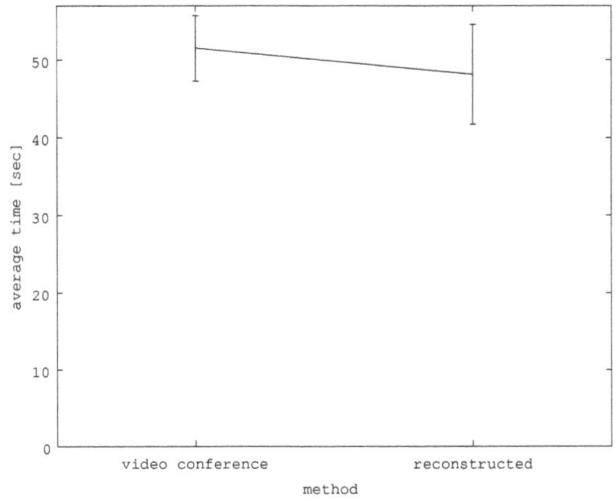

Figure 8: Comparison of averaged task completion time.

Despite the reasonable performance, our proposed system turned out to be favoured the least in our preference test due to its poor image quality. We plan to improve accuracy of depth measurements from the stereo camera and introduce noise reduction techniques to achieve better image quality. Further performance evaluation is also planned.

6. REFERENCES

[1] M. Apperley, L. McLeod, M. Masoodian, L. Paine, M. Phillips, B. Rogers, and K. Thomson. Use of video shadow for small group interaction awareness on a large interactive display surface. In *Proc. of the Fourth Australasian User Interface Conference on User Interfaces*, volume 18, pages 81–90, 2003.

[2] M. Hirose, T. Ogi, T. Yamada, and K. Tamagawa. Development of stereo video avatar in networked immersive projection environment. In *Proc. of IEEE ICIP*, volume 3, pages 21–25, 1999.

[3] H. Ishii and M. Kobayashi. Clearboard: A seamless medium for shared drawing and conversation with eye contact. In *Proc. of ACM CHI*, pages 525–532, 1992.

[4] Y. Miwa and C. Ishibiki. Shadow communication: System for embodied interaction with remote partners. In *Proc. of ACM CSCW*, pages 467–476, 2004.

[5] O. Morikawa and T. Maesako. Hypermirror: Toward pleasant-to-use video mediated communication system. In *Proc. of ACM CSCW*, pages 149–158, 1998.

[6] M. Shimizu and M. Okutomi. Sub-pixel estimation error cancellation on area-based matching. *International Journal of Computer Vision*, 63(3):207–224, 2005.

[7] A. Tang, C. Neustaedter, and S. Greenberg. Videoarms: Embodiments for mixed presencs groupware. In *Proc. of HCI 2006*, pages 85–102, 2006.

[8] N. Yamashita, K. Hirata, T. Takada, Y. Harada, Y. Shirai, and S. Aoyagi. Effects of room-sized sharing on remote collaboration on physical task. *IPSJ Digital Courier*, 3:788–799, 2007.

Measuring the Latency of Cloud Gaming Systems*

Kuan-Ta Chen[1], Yu-Chun Chang[12], Po-Han Tseng[1],
Chun-Ying Huang[3], and Chin-Laung Lei[2]
[1]Institute of Information Science, Academia Sinica
[2]Department of Electrical Engineering, National Taiwan University
[3]Department of Computer Science, National Taiwan Ocean University

ABSTRACT

Cloud gaming, i.e., *real-time game playing via thin clients*, relieves players from the need to constantly upgrade their computers and deal with compatibility issues when playing games. As a result, cloud gaming is generating a great deal of interest among entrepreneurs and the public. However, given the large design space, it is not yet known which platforms deliver the best quality of service and which design elements constitute a good cloud gaming system.

This study is motivated by the question: *How good is the real-timeliness of current cloud gaming systems?* To address the question, we analyze the response latency of two cloud gaming platforms, namely, OnLive and StreamMyGame. Our results show that the streaming latency of OnLive is reasonable for real-time cloud gaming, while that of StreamMyGame is almost twice the former when the StreamMyGame server is provisioned using an Intel Core i7-920 PC. We believe that our measurement approach can be generally applied to PC-based cloud gaming platforms, and that it will further the understanding of such systems and lead to improvements.

Categories and Subject Descriptors

C.4 [**Performance of Systems**]: Measurement techniques; J.7 [**Computers in Other Systems**]: Command and control, Consumer products, Real time; K.8.0 [**Personal Computing**]: General—*Games*

General Terms

Measurement, Performance

1. INTRODUCTION

Thin clients have become increasingly popular in recent years, primarily because of the high penetration rate of broadband Internet access and the use of cloud computing technology to build large-scale data centers. The massive computation and storage resources of data centers enable users to shift their workload to remote servers. As a result, thin clients are more convenient and also more powerful (with the supply from remote servers) than traditional fat clients. Thus, today, it is not uncommon for people work and play by accessing remote computers via thin clients.

Although the advantages of thin clients have been demonstrated in many applications, *computer games* in particular have benefited from the advances in the thin client technology. One of the reasons is that the *overhead* of setting up a game can be significant because game software is becoming increasingly complex. As a result, players are often restricted to one computer and cannot play games anywhere, anytime. In addition, trying a new game can be difficult because there may have software and hardware *compatibility issues* between the game and players' computers. Hence, players may be faced with a dilemma of whether to upgrade their computers or forgo the opportunity to try a new game.

Cloud gaming, i.e., *real-time game playing via thin clients*, offers solutions for all the above-mentioned issues. Cloud gaming frees players from the need to constantly upgrade their computers as they can now play games that host on remote servers with a broadband Internet connection and a thin client. Here a thin client can be a lightweight PC, a TV with a set-top box, or even a mobile device. Consequently, there are no set up overheads or compatibility issues if players wish to try a game because all the hardware and software is provided in the data centers by the game operators. Given these potential advantages for both game developers and consumers, cloud gaming has been seen a possible paradigm that would change the way computer games are delivered and played.

Cloud gaming has already generated a great deal of interest among entrepreneurs, venture capitalists, and the general public. Several startup companies offer or claim to offer cloud gaming services, such as OnLive[1], StreamMyGame[2], Gaikai[3], G-Cluster[4], OTOY[5], and T5-Labs[6], though their realizations may be very different. Some of the services are only accessible via thin clients on a PC (either native or browser-based applications), while others can be accessed via a TV with a set-top box. Quite a few design alternatives

*Area chair: Wei Tsang Ooi

†This work was supported in part by the National Science Council under the grant NSC100-2628-E-001-002-MY3.

MM'11, November 28–December 1, 2011, Scottsdale, Arizona, USA.

[1]`http://www.onlive.com/`
[2]`http://www.streammygame.com/`
[3]`http://www.gaikai.com/`
[4]`http://www.gcluster.com/`
[5]`http://www.otoy.com/`
[6]`http://www.t5labs.com/`

can be adopted when implementing a cloud gaming service, such as 1) the way the existing game software is modified and run on the server; 2) the way the game screen is encoded (on the server) and decoded (on the client); 3) the way game streaming data is delivered to the client; and 4) the way short-term network instability is handled to maintain the game's responsiveness and graphical quality. Because of the large design space of such systems, *it is not yet known which platforms deliver the best quality of service and which design elements constitute a good cloud gaming system.*

In this paper, we perform an anatomic analysis of the latency of two cloud gaming platforms, namely, OnLive and StreamMyGame. We chose them because they were the only PC-based cloud gaming platforms on the market at the time of writing (April 2011). Measuring the latency of cloud gaming systems is challenging because most of the systems are *proprietary and closed*, i.e., none of the source codes and internals of the cloud servers, game software, and thin clients are available. In addition, cloud servers and the game software running on them cannot be modified because they are managed centrally by the service operators. Despite of these restrictions, we propose a measurement methodology that can assess the delay components of a cloud gaming system even if the system is proprietary and closed. To the best of our knowledge, this work is the first to anatomically analyze the delay components of cloud gaming systems.

Our contribution of this work is two-fold: 1) We propose a methodology for measuring the latency of cloud gaming systems. It can be applied even if the system is closed and not modifiable. 2) We profile two commercial cloud gaming platforms, OnLive and StreamMyGame, and show that the streaming latency of OnLive is reasonable for real-time cloud gaming, while that of StreamMyGame is almost twice the former when the StreamMyGame server is provisioned using an Intel Core i7-920 (2.66 GHz) PC.

The remainder of this paper is organized as follows. The next section provides a review of related works. We present our measurement methodology and the measured results in Section 3. Section 4 contains our concluding remarks.

2. RELATED WORK

Nieh and Laih [4] proposed using slow-motion benchmarking to evaluate the performance of several thin client platforms on various tasks. Unfortunately, the technique cannot be applied to cloud gaming systems because games would have to be modified so that they could run in slow motion. Besides, the performance metrics used, i.e., the amount of data transferred, are not sufficient to accurately assess the temporal and spatial quality of cloud gaming services.

3. LATENCY MEASUREMENT

3.1 Evaluated Platforms and Games

When OnLive[1] was introduced at the Game Developer's Conference in 2009, it attracted a significant amount of attention from the mass media and the public. The service is well-known partly because of its high-profile investors and partners, including Warner Bros, AT&T, Ubisoft, Atari, and HTC. It was released in June 2010 and now offers more than 120 games as of September 2011. OnLive's client is available on Microsoft Windows, Mac OS X, and as a TV set-top box. The minimum bandwidth requirement is 3 Mbps, but an Internet connection of 5 Mbps or faster is recommended. All the games are delivered in HDTV 720p format.

Unlike OnLive, which hosts game servers in its own data centers, StreamMyGame[2] (SMG) offers software solutions for remote game playing. The service was launched in October 2007 and currently supports more than 120 games from Windows to Windows- and Linux-based clients as of September 2011. It supports game streaming in a variety of resolutions, from 320x240 to 1920x1080 (1080p), which require an Internet connection between 256 Kbps (320x240) and 30 Mbps (1080p). Although StreamMyGame offers a software-based platform rather than a centralized service, we consider it a perfect fit for this present study because we focus on the performance of game streaming mechanisms rather than the capacity of service providers.

Because of the architectural differences of OnLive and SMG, their system configurations in our experiments are not identical. The main difference is that the OnLive server is operated by OnLive Inc., while the SMG server is operated by ourselves and installed with the SMG server software developed by Tenomichi/SSP Ltd. For a fair comparison, the OnLive client and SMG server/client are running on desktop computers equipped with two Intel Core i7-920 processors running at 2.66 GHz; in addition, both platforms are configured to provide remote gaming in 1280x720 resolution with same 3D effect settings.

We used three games, namely, Lego Batman: The Videogame (Batman), Warhammer 40,000: Dawn of War (DOW), and F.E.A.R. 2: Project Origin (FEAR) in this work. We chosen the games because they are supported by both platforms and they represent three game genres. Lego Batman is an action-adventure game, FEAR is a typical first-person shooter (FPS) game, and Warhammer is a real-time strategy (RTS) game. FPS games normally require a high rate of game screen updates, whereas the pace of adventure and RTS games is relatively slower with an omnipresent viewpoint [3].

3.2 Anatomy of Delay Components

We segment a cloud gaming system's response delays (RD) to players' commands into three components:

- **Network delay** (ND): the time required to deliver a players' command to the server and return a game screen to the client. It is usually referred to as the network round-trip time (RTT).
- **Processing delay** (PD): the difference between the time the server receives a player's command (from the client) and the time it responds with a corresponding frame after processing the command.
- **Playout delay** (OD): the difference between the time the client receives the encoded form of a frame and the time the frame is decoded and presented on the screen.

Unlike the network delay, which can be measured using tools like `ICMP` ping, the processing delay (at the server) and playout delay (at the client) occur *internally* in the cloud gaming system and are not accessible from outside. Our goal is to measure both delays accurately by using only external probes.

3.3 Response Delay Measurement

To measure the response delay (RD), which equals to ND+PD+OD, of a cloud gaming system, we exploit the fact

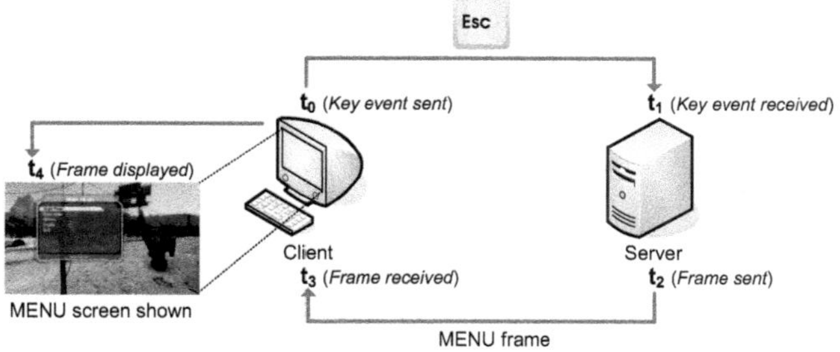

Figure 1: The key events in the measurement of the response delay of a cloud gaming platform by invoking the menu screen.

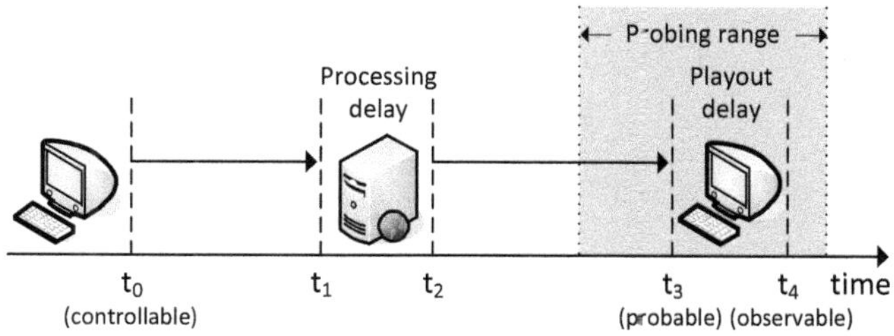

Figure 2: The decomposition of the response delay. The gray area represents the range in which the `recv()` call may be started to be blocked in order to probe the exact location of t_3.

that most games support a hot key, which is used to access a menu screen anytime during game play. The key is usually the **ESC** key for computer games and the **START** button for console games. Without loss of generality, we assume the ESC key is the hot key for invoking the menu screen. As illustrated in Figure 1, assuming the ESC key is pressed at time t_0 and the menu screen is shown to the user at time t_4, the time difference $(t_4 - t_0)$ corresponds to the response delay of the ESC key. However, the processing delay $(t_2 - t_1)$ and the playout delay $(t_4 - t_3)$ are not visible and cannot be measured directly.

To determine the response delay, we utilize the hooking mechanism[7] in Windows to inject our instrumentation code into the OnLive and SMG clients. We use the **detours** library to intercept the **IDirect3dDevice9::EndScene()** function, which is called when a Direct3D application finishes drawing graphics on a hidden surface and is about to present the surface on the screen. We then use the following procedure to measure the response delay:

1. Simulate an **ESC** key press event by calling the **SendInput()** function at time t_0.
2. Each time the game screen is updated, we examine the colors of a specific set of pixels to determine if the menu screen is displayed.
3. Wait until the menu screen appears (and note the time as t_4).

We can therefore calculate the response delay by subtracting t_0 from t_4[8]. Each run of the procedure yields a sample of the response delay; thus, we can repeatedly execute the procedure to obtain a set of response delay samples.

3.4 Response Delay Decomposition

During the experiments, we periodically measure the network round-trip time using **ICMP** ping as ND samples. Since we have ND and the sum of ND, PD, and OD constitutes the response delay, we only need to determine either PD (processing delay) or OD (playout delay) in order to decompose all the components. More specifically, we need to further determine the occurrence of t_3 (shown in Figure 2) in order to obtain PD and OD.

The rationale behind probing t_3 is that it is the time the menu screen delivered to the client from the server. Thus, if incoming data is (intentionally) blocked (by us) on the client earlier than t_3, the menu screen will not be shown until the blocking is cancelled. On the other hand, if incoming data is blocked later than t_3, the menu screen will be displayed despite that no further screen updates are received and shown as long as the incoming data blocking is sustained.

To facilitate the data blocking mechanism, we hook the **recvfrom()** function, which is called when the thin clients attempt to retrieve a UDP datagram from the UDP/IP stack. The measurement procedure is as follows:

1. Simulate an **ESC** key press event by calling the **SendInput()** function at time t_0. Also, compute t_{block} as a random time between $RD - 100$ ms and $RD + 50$ ms[9], assuming the playout delay shorter than 100 ms.
2. If the menu screen appears before t_{block}, record the time as t_{menu} and terminate the procedure. Otherwise, at t_{block}, temporarily block all the subsequent **recvfrom()** calls for one second[10].
3. Wait until the menu screen appears (and note the time as t_{menu}).

If t_{menu} is later than t_{block} + 1 sec, we consider that the blocking is successful and t_3 should be some time later than t_{block}. In this case, t_{block} is added to the set $t_{block\_succeeded}$. On the other hand, if t_{menu} is earlier than t_{block}, we consider that the blocking is failed and t_3 must be some time earlier than t_{menu}. In this case, t_{menu} is added to the set t_{block_failed}. By repeating the procedure a number of times, we can obtain a set $t_{block\_succeeded}$ that are earlier than t_3, and another set t_{block_failed} that are later than t_3, where t_3 must lie approximately at the boundary of the two sets.

We then estimate t_3 as the point that yields the minimum sum of the two density functions formed by $t_{block\_succeeded}$ and t_{block_failed} respectively, where each density function is computed as the mixture of the Gaussian density functions centered at each element with a standard deviation of any reasonable magnitude[11]. After estimating t_3, we can com-

[7]The Windows hooking mechanism is invoked by calling the **SetWindowsHookEx** function. It is frequently used to inject code into other processes.

[8]Certain games, such as FEAR, intentionally postpone the appearance of the menu screen for a short period of time. Thus, we have calibrated the response delays by subtracting the intentional menu appearance delay from the measured delays obtained using the procedure.

[9]The 50-ms interval is chosen arbitrarily in order to leave a "safe zone" that ensures the menu screen will be blocked with a non-zero probability.

[10]The one-second interval is chosen arbitrarily in order to determine whether or not the menu screen is blocked. Other values can also apply without affecting the measurement results.

[11]In our experiment, we use a standard deviation of 20 ms; however, other values of the same order of magnitude would yield nearly identical t_3 estimates.

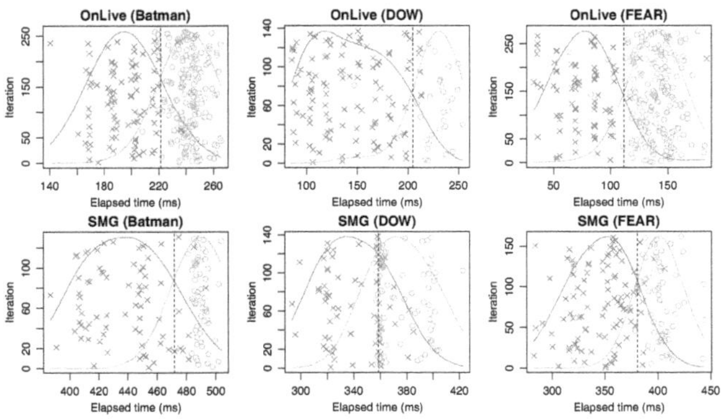

Figure 3: The scatter plots of $t_{block\_succeeded}$ and t_{block_failed} samples, denoted by red crosses and blue circles respectively. The vertical dashed lines denote the estimates of t_3 minus the network delay.

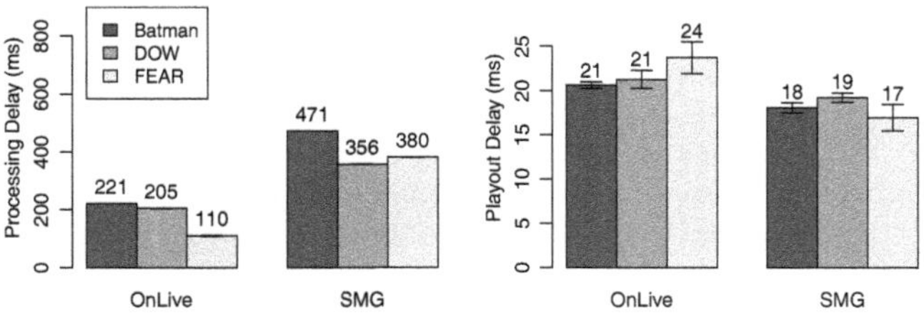

Figure 4: The estimated processing delays and playout delays of both cloud gaming platforms.

pute PD (server processing delay) as $t_3 - t_0 -$ ND and OD (playout delay) as $t_4 - t_3$.

3.5 Measurement Results

Figure 3 shows the scatter plots of $t_{block\_succeeded}$ and t_{block_failed} samples, denoted by red crosses and blue circles respectively. Note that we have subtracted all the samples by ND in order to remove the effect of network delay between our PC and the OnLive data center. We can observe that the ranges of $t_{block\_succeeded}$ and t_{block_failed} sets are not disjoint. This is reasonable because there may be fluctuations in the server's and client's workloads, and the network delay may vary due to network congestion. Because t_3 (and consequently PD and OD) are inferred based on a set of iterations, we validate the robustness of t_3 by cross-validation. That is, instead of using the data from all iterations, we select 50 iterations at random and use them to estimate t_3. The procedure is repeated at least 30 rounds. If the estimated values for t_3 in different rounds are close, we can confirm that the estimated PD and OD are reliable and not susceptible to measurement noises.

Figure 4 shows the average processing delays and playout delays as well as their 95% confidence bands of OnLive and SMG when Batman, DOW, and FEAR are played. As can be seen, the confidence bands of both processing and playout delays are fairly small, which indicates that our proposed measurement technique produces robust estimates of the delay components. From the graph, OnLive's processing delays are approximately half of those of SMG. This should be because OnLive utilizes a more efficient, possibly hardware-based, H.264 encoder to encode game screens in real time. It could also simply because the processing power of our SMG server is much lower than that of the OnLive server. Taking a closer look at OnLive, its processing delay is approximately 200 ms for Batman and DOW and 100 ms for FEAR. We consider FEAR's shorter processing delay is an intentional arrangement by OnLive because FPS games are known especially susceptible to lags [1,3], and the shorter delay may be the consequence of using higher-performance servers[12] for the game. Considering action and RTS games are slower-paced, OnLive's differential resource provisioning looks a reasonable strategy to provide an overall satisfactory gaming experience to players [2].

As to the average playout delays of both platforms, OnLive spends 20–30 ms and SMG spends ≈15–20 ms in frame decoding and display. Both systems perform similarly well in this aspect, as such short playout delays would not have a serious impact on the gaming experience.

To summarize, OnLive's overall streaming delay (i.e., the processing delay at the server plus the playout delay at the client) for the three games is between 135 and 240 ms, which is acceptable if the network delay is not significant. On the other hand, real-time encoding of 720p game frames seem to be a burden to SMG on an Intel i7-920 server because the streaming delay can be as long as 400–500 ms. Investigating whether the extended delay is due to design/implementation issues of SMG or it is an intrinsic limit of software-based cloud gaming platforms will be part of our future work.

4. CONCLUSION AND FUTURE WORK

In this paper, we have proposed a general methodology to measure the latency components of cloud gaming systems, even those that are proprietary and closed. We applied the methodology on two platforms, OnLive and StreamMyGame, and identified that OnLive implements a game-genre-based differential resource provisioning strategy to provide sufficiently short latency for real-time gaming. On the other hand, StreamMyGame takes almost twice latency to provide 720p real-time game graphics with an Intel Core i7-920 PC, which leaves us an issue to investigate whether the extended delay is due to an intrinsic limit of software-based cloud gaming systems.

In our future work, we will continue to improve the applicability and accuracy of the proposed methodology. In addition, we plan to apply the methodology to more platforms for understanding their strengths and weaknesses, and derive general guidelines for designing quality cloud gaming systems.

5. REFERENCES

[1] Y.-C. Chang, K.-T. Chen, C.-C. Wu, C.-J. Ho, and C.-L. Lei. Online game QoE evaluation using paired comparisons. In *Proceedings of IEEE CQR 2010*, June 2010.

[2] K.-T. Chen, P. Huang, and C.-L. Lei. How sensitive are online gamers to network quality? *Communications of the ACM*, 49(11):34–38, Nov 2006.

[3] M. Claypool and K. Claypool. Latency and player actions in online games. *Commun. ACM*, 49:40–45, November 2006.

[4] A. M. Lai and J. Nieh. On the performance of wide-area thin-client computing. *ACM Trans. Comput. Syst.*, 24:175–209, May 2006.

[12] http://blog.onlive.com/2009/05/12/hopping-through-cloud-onlive/

Distributed Video Coding with Compressive Measurements

Hsiao-Yun Tseng[1], Yun-Chung Shen[2] and Ja-Ling Wu[1,2], Fellow, IEEE

[1]Department of Computer Science and Information Engineering, National Taiwan University
[2]Graduate Institute of Networking and Multimedia, National Taiwan University

National Taiwan University
Taipei 10617, Taiwan, R.O.C.

{kumokay, cazindo, wjl}@cmlab.csie.ntu.edu.tw

ABSTRACT

This paper presents a novel distributed video coding (DVC) scheme using compressive sensing (CS) that achieves low-complexity for encoding and efficient signal sensing. Most CS recovery algorithms rely only on signal sparsity. Yet, under DVC architecture, additional statistical characterization of the signal is available, which offers the potential for more precise CS recovery. First, a set of random measurements are acquired and transmitted to the decoder. The decoder then exploits the statistical characterization of the signal and generates the side information (SI). Finally, utilizing the SI, a Bayesian inference using belief propagation (BP) decoding is performed for signal recovery. The proposed CS-DVC system offers a more direct way of signal acquisition and the potential for more precise estimation of the signal from random measurements. Experimental results indicate that SI can improve the signal reconstruction quality in comparison with a CS recovery algorithm that relies only on the sparsity.

Categories and Subject Descriptors

I.4.2 [**Image Processing and Computer Vision**]: Compression (Coding) – *Approximate methods, Exact coding.*

General Terms

Algorithms, Design

Keywords

Compressive sampling, Wyner-Ziv video coding, distributed video coding, side information, sparse representations.

1. INTRODUCTION

With the increasing development of wireless networks and the widespread popularity of handheld devices, a vision of video acquisition, processing, and sharing across applications such as battery-powered mobile devices, disposable video cameras, and visual sensor networks has emerged. To realize this vision, a variety of technical challenges must be overcome, including reducing the signal sampling cost, lowering the encoding complexity, and improving compression efficiency.

Fortunately, a video coding paradigm known as Distributed Video Coding (DVC) opens a door for new coding solutions [1]. Based on Slepian-Wolf and Wyner-Ziv information-theoretic results – the minimum rate to encode two correlated sources separately is the same as the minimum rate for joint encoding of the source -- practical implementations of DVC have been proposed since 2002 [2], [3]. While all standardized video coding schemes follow the approach that the encoder exploits the statistics of the source signal, DVC algorithms exploit source statistics at the decoder, and therefore promise a substantial savings in encoder complexity.

Meanwhile, compressive sensing (CS) has emerged as a novel signal processing framework, which provides an alternative to Shannon/Nyquist sampling. CS builds on the ubiquitous compressibility of signals [4]; that is, most of the information contained in a signal often resides in just a few large coefficients according to some specific basis. In CS, a signal that can be compressed using classical methods, such as transform coding, can also be efficiently acquired via a small set of random linear projections, and hence significantly reduce the signal acquisition cost.

Benefit from DVC and CS, we propose a video coding solution to fulfill the requirements of low-complexity, efficient signal sensing and encoding; other CS-based DVC schemes have been proposed in [5-7]. Starting from acquiring a set of CS measurements, we design a codec architecture built on the DVC paradigm. In this work, we concentrate on exploiting the statistical characterization of the signal for decoding. Not only the spatio-temporal correlations along the video sequence are exploited, but also the statistical characterizations of the signal are investigated together with the received compressive measurements, which provide side information (SI) for further improvement of decoding process. Based on SI, a Bayesian inference using belief propagation (BP) decoding [8] is performed for signal recovery.

The proposed CS-DVC system offers a more direct way of signal acquisition and the potential for more precise estimation of the signal from random measurements. We demonstrate the benefits of using SI by comparing the performance of a CS decoding algorithm relies only on the sparsity of the signal to our system. Experimental results show that SI can improve the signal reconstruction quality, and the proposed approach achieves better performance in comparison with that of [5] and [6].

2. BAYESIAN COMPRESSIVE SENSING

In CS, considering a discrete-time signal $x \in \mathbb{R}^N$ that is of the form $x = \Psi s$, where $\Psi \in \mathbb{R}^{N\times N}$ is an orthonormal basis and $s \in \mathbb{R}^N$ is the sparse representation of x that has $K \ll N$ non-zero coefficients. To measure x, we compute the measurement vector $y \in \mathbb{R}^M$ as M linear projections of x via a sensing matrix Φ by

$$y = \Phi x = \Phi\Psi s. \qquad (1)$$

*Area Chair: Pal Halvorsen.

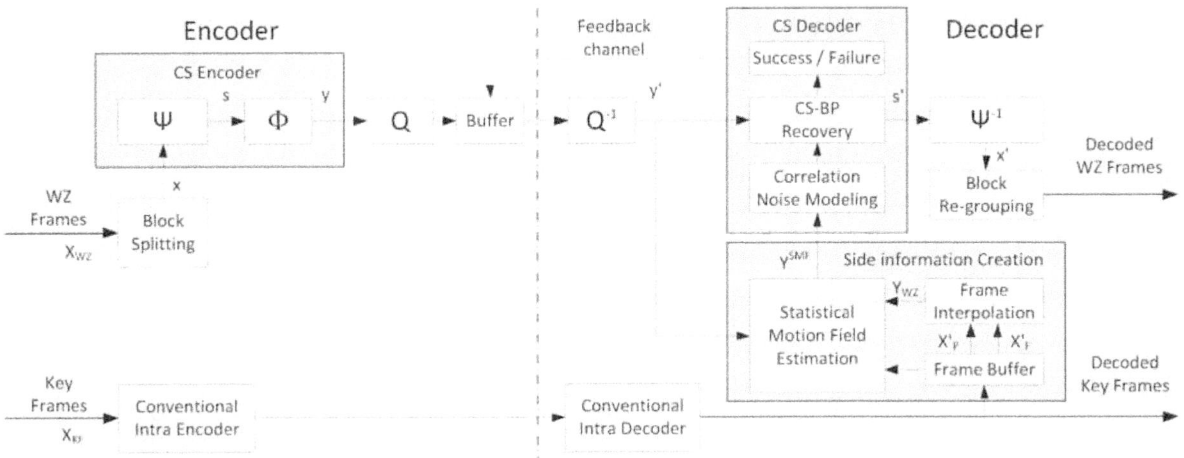

Figure 1: The CS-DVC codec architecture

Although the reconstruction of x given y and Φ using $M \ll N$ measurements appears to be an ill-posed problem, with the prior knowledge of sparsity, we can obtain the solution to s via l_0 minimization

$$\hat{s} = \arg\min\|s\|_0 \text{ s.t. } y = \Phi\Psi s \quad (2)$$

, which is unfortunately an NP-complete problem. Yet a much easier linear programing problem, the l_1-optimization problem,

$$\hat{s} = \arg\min\|s\|_1 \text{ s.t. } y = \Phi\Psi s \quad (3)$$

yields an equivalent solution, and hence x can be efficiently reconstructed by $x = \Psi\hat{s}$.

Besides sparsity, in some applications we have other signal characterizations available, which provide a potential for a more precise and efficient signal reconstruction.

By applying a Bayesian inference, the signal is modeled by some probability distribution, and we seek a solution that best matches our prior signal model. The maximum *a posteriori* (MAP) estimate is formulated as follows:

$$\hat{s}_{MAP} = \arg\max_s f(s' = s) \; s.t. \; y = \Phi\Psi s \quad (4)$$

where $f(s)$ is the probability distribution function (pdf) of s. By choosing Φ as a sparse matrix, a low-complexity message-passing methods can be employed to solve the MAP problem.

Clearly, to obtain a more precise estimate of s via the MAP method, we need a prior knowledge of the signal, which is known as SI in DVC. Also, the quality of SI dominates the performance of the reconstruction.

3. CS-DVC CODEC ARCHITECTURE

3.1 The Basic Idea

In a nutshell, the overall codec architecture illustrated in Figure 1 works as follows. The input sequence is divided into key frames (X_{KF}) and WZ frames (X_{WZ}). The key frames are H.264/AVC Intra coded [9]. Following the coding architecture a rather different way to compress the WZ frames is obtained: each WZ frame is divided into non-overlapping 16×16 blocks; each block (the signal x) is independently sampled in the DCT domain via a CS encoding matrix Φ. The resulting measurement vector y is quantized and stored in the buffer. The encoder sends fixed amounts of measurements upon the decoder requests.

The decoding process starts by creating the SI for each WZ frame. With the past (X'_P) and the future (X'_F) decoded key frames closest to X_{WZ}, the SI frame (Y_{WZ}), an estimate of the original WZ frame X_{WZ}, is obtained by performing a motion compensated frame interpolation process. The statistical motion field estimation is performed using the de-quantized measurements and, hence the SI frame is re-estimated and contributes to a quality increase. Each block is decoded using a belief propagation (BP) decoder with the a posteriori probabilities of signals approximated by a Laplacian distribution. The decoder requests more measurements via feedback channel until the decoding task is considered successful. Finally, the key frames and WZ frames together generate the decoded video sequence.

Further details of the highlighted modules: the CS encoder, the side information creation module, and the CS decoder, are provided in the following sections.

3.2 The CS Encoder

In the encoding of a WZ frame, each block is transformed into a $n \times 1$ vector x and sampled by a measurement matrix Φ in a domain Ψ, in which x can be sparsely represented by a vector s, yielding a vector $y = \Phi s = \Phi\Psi^{-1}x$. Here, at the CS encoder, we choose Ψ to be the DCT domain; thus, x represents the pixels and s is the set of DCT coefficients of a block. For each block, two sets of measurements y_0 and y_1 are acquired using two matrices Φ_0 and Φ_1 respectively.

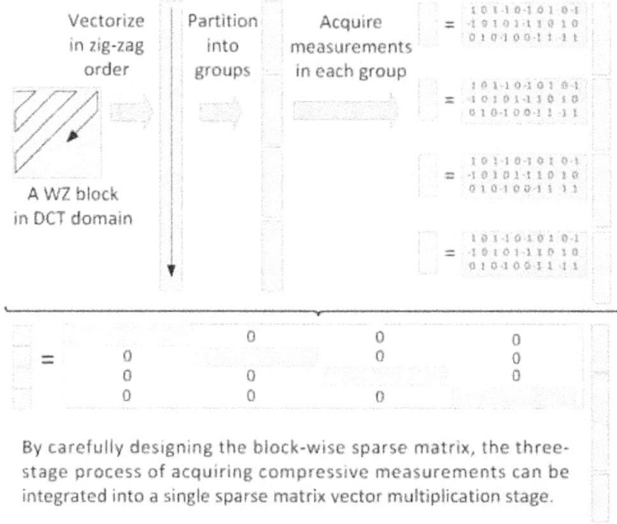

Figure 2: The block-wise sparse matrix

At the first step, a set of compressive measurements y_0 sampled in DCT domain by a dense CS encoding matrix Φ_0 with +1/-1 entries drawn from uniform Bernoulli distribution, are sent to the SI creation module to improve the SI quality, and to the CS decoder to check if the decoding is successful.

To correct the errors in the SI, another set of measurements y_1 is acquired and sent to the CS-BP decoder. Here, the CS encoding matrix Φ_1 is a block-wise sparse matrix, where the off-diagonal blocks are zero matrices. Each diagonal block is dominated by zero entries with nonzero entries $\{-1,+1\}$ randomly placed in each row and each column. By carefully designing the encoding matrix Φ_1, the DCT coefficients s are split into groups and, hence are measured, quantized, and transmitted group by group in response to the requests from the decoder. Observing the varying dynamic range distribution of each DCT coefficient band, each group of coefficients can be more efficiently encoded varying the quantization step size. Also, each group of coefficients can be reconstructed independently, which allows the decoder to parallelize the decoding process. Fig 2 shows the construction of the block-wise sparse matrix Φ_1 and the partition process of the coefficients.

3.3 Side Information Creation

The side information creation module generates an estimate (Y_{WZ}) of the WZ frame (X_{WZ}). The quality of SI influences significantly the rate-distortion performance. First, SI is generated by frame interpolation using decoded key frames. After the decoder received y_0, the statistical motion field estimation method is applied to improve the quality of SI.

Frame Interpolation: Two major approaches -- hash-based motion estimation and motion compensated interpolation – are employed to create side information; see [10] for further details.

Statistical Motion Field Estimation: Motivated by the motion estimation (ME) and motion compensation (MC) techniques in conventional video compression, that is, a block is composed of a best match block from the previous frame and the residual signal, we use the received measurements to find the possible motion vector (MV) of a WZ block.

On receiving the measurement vector y_0 of a WZ block, we search the previous decoded key frame in a neighborhood defined around the WZ block position to find the best match block by comparing the measurements of each block; that is, we employ ME in the measurement domain, and thus obtain a possible MV (m_x, m_y) pointing to the referenced block. Then a set of probabilities associated with the MV regarding the WZ block compose the statistical motion field (SMF). Each SMF probability expresses the likelihood of a MV describing the displacement for the WZ block in the SI. The set of relevant MVs is confined to all possible positions around the referenced block within a search window size of $\pm S$, as represented in Fig. 3, and the SMF probability of a block in the window is computed as

$$SMF(m_x + d_x, m_y + d_y) = e^{-\mu \cdot SSE(m_x+d_x, m_y+d_y)} \quad (5)$$

, where $|d_x| \leq S, |d_y| \leq S$, μ is a smoothing factor, and $SSE(m_x, m_y)$ is the sum of the square errors between the measurement vector of the referenced block and y_0. The SMF probabilities are then normalized as

$$\overline{SMF}(m_x + d_x, m_y + d_y) = \frac{SMF(m_x+d_x, m_y+d_y)}{\sum_{u=-S}^{S}\sum_{v=-S}^{S} SMF(m_x+u, m_y+v)} \quad (6)$$

Finally, the WZ block in SI is updated by

$$Y^{SMF}(x,y) = \sum_{u=-S}^{S}\sum_{v=-S}^{S} X'_{KF}(x+m_x+u, y+m_y+v)\overline{SMF}(m_x+u, m_y+v) \quad (7)$$

The SMF method for DVC has been proposed in [10]. Notice that we explore the SMF method in two different viewpoints: (i) from ME/MC viewpoint, SMF expresses the likelihood of the motion vector for a block; (ii) from CS viewpoint, blocks in the neighborhood form a dictionary in which a WZ block can be sparsely represented. Under the CS scenario, SMF provides an approximate solution for sparse signal recovery.

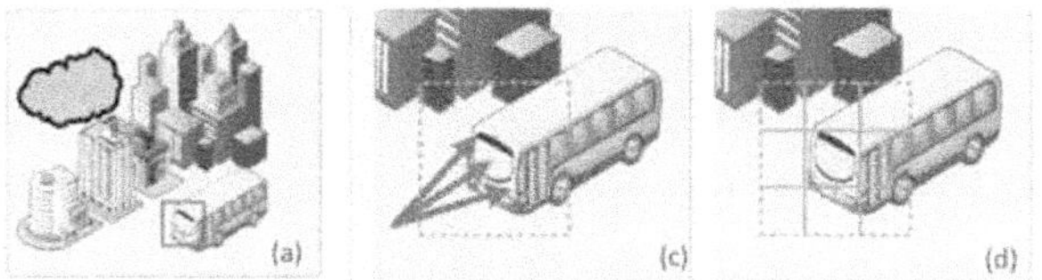

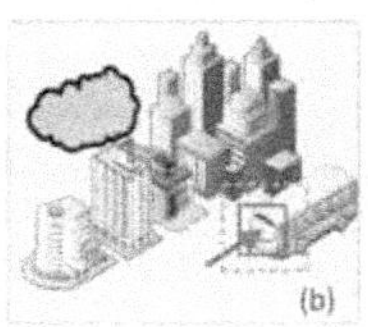

(a) The WZ frame and the WZ block. (b) The motion vector and the SMF window in previous key frame. (c) From ME/MC viewpoint: SMF expresses the likelihood of the motion vector for a block. (d) From CS viewpoint: Blocks in the neighborhood form a dictionary in which a WZ block can be sparsely represented.

Figure 3: The SMF estimation

3.4 The CS Decoder

The CS decoding process begins with the modeling of the probability distribution for the signal values at each block. The obtained *a priori* probability then sent to the CS-BP recovery module for signal reconstruction.

Correlation Noise Modeling: Given SI, as in [11], a Laplacian distribution is used to model the correlation noise between X_{WZ} and Y_{WZ}, which expresses the amount of confidence for a given value in SI. First, the residual frame R is computed as the difference between the motion compensated versions of the future (X_F) and the past (X_P) frames:

$$R(x,y) = \frac{X'_F(x+d_{xf}, y+d_{yf}) - X'_P(x+d_{xp}, y+d_{yp})}{2} \quad (8)$$

Secondly, to obtain the transformed frame T, a DCT transform is applied to each block in R frame: $T_n(u,v) = \mathrm{DCT}[R_n(x,y)]$, where R_n and T_n represents the coefficients inside the n_{th} block of R frame and T frame. Finally, the Laplacian probability density function at position (u,v) of the n_{th} block is given by

$$p_n(X_n(u,v)) = \frac{1}{2b} e^{-\frac{|X_n(u,v) - Y_n(u,v)|}{b}}, b = \begin{cases} \sqrt{\frac{\sigma^2}{2}} & D_n^2(u,v) < \sigma_n^2 \\ \sqrt{\frac{D_n^2(u,v)}{2}} & D_n^2(u,v) > \sigma_n^2 \end{cases} \quad (9)$$

where $\sigma_n = E[T_n] - E[T_n]^2$ and $D_n = |T_n| - E[T_n]$. $E[.]$ is the expectation operator.

CS-BP recovery: The CS decoder employs belief propagation (BP) method to reconstruct signals by iteratively passing messages over a graphical model [8].

In the beginning, a factor graph is constructed based on the sparse CS encoding matrix Φ_1 with two types of nodes: the variable nodes and the check nodes. The variable nodes v are initialized with the signal prior, and the check nodes are associated with the constraint nodes c. Two types of messages – messages from v to c and messages from c to v -- are computed and are placed on the bipartite graph:

$$\mu_{v\to c}(v) = \prod_{u\in n(v)\{c\}} \mu_{u\to v}(v) \quad (10)$$

$$\mu_{c\to v}(v) = \sum_{\sim\{v\}}\left(con(n(c))\prod_{w\in n(c)\{v\}} \mu_{w\to c}(w)\right) \quad (11)$$

where $n(v)$ and $n(c)$ are sets of neighbors of v and c respectively, $con(n(c))$ is the constraint on the set of variable nodes $n(c)$, and $\sim\{v\}$ is the set of neighbors of c excluding v. After some iteration, the marginal distribution $f(v)$ for a variable node is computed as

$$f(v) = \prod_{u \in n(v)\{c\}} \mu_{u \to v}(v), \quad (12)$$

and hence an estimate of the signal is obtained.

At each iteration, the CS-BP recovery module obtains an estimate of the signal x, and computes $y'_0 = \Phi_0 s' = \Phi_0 \Psi^{-1} x'$ and check the minimum mean square error (MMSE) of y'_0 and y_0. If the MMSE is below a threshold, no more requests are sent to the encoder. Otherwise, the decoder requests another group of measurements.

4. EXPERIMENTAL RESULTS

The rate-distortion (RD) results presented here were obtained with following test conditions: all frames of Foreman and Hall Monitor with QCIF resolution, a GOP of length 2, and a frame rate of 15 frames/second. Key frames are encoded by H.264/AVC intra, and the quantization parameters (QP) for each RD point are chosen such that the average quality (PSNR) of the WZ frames is similar to the quality of the key frames. WZ frames are divided into blocks of 16×16 pixels, and measured with a Bernoulli matrix Φ_0 of $\{-1, +1\}$ and a block-wise sparse matrix Φ_1 with nonzero values $\{-1, +1\}$. The acquired measurements y_0 and y_1 are quantized using a uniform quantizer of 7 bits. For motion interpolation, ± 32 pixels are adopted as the search range; for SMF estimation, the search range is ± 10 pixels and a SMF window of size ± 2 pixels is used.

For coding efficiency, we employ skip-mode selection in encoding. A block is referred to a skipped block if it is changed very little with respect to its co-located block in the previous key frame. Also, in decoding, the SMF is performed only for SI blocks with large displacement to the referenced block. At each RD point, different measurement rate and thresholds are chosen.

Figs. 4 and 5 show the average PSNRs as a function of the average rates of the two test sequences respectively. Compared with the existing CS coders simply using l_1 minimization [6], with SI, our signal reconstruction quality is much improved. Fig. 6 shows the average PSNR as a function of average measurement rates of the Foreman test sequence. In this case, both key frames and WZ frames are captured via CS, and more measurements are allocated for key frames as in [5]. As shown in the figure, our method outperformed the method in [5].

5. CONCLUSIONS

In this paper, we proposed a video coding solution via CS based on the DVC paradigm. Specially, the proposed CS-DVC framework exploits the statistical characterizations of both spatio-temporal correlation of a video sequence, and the correlations between measurements and the prior knowledge of the signal. We develop a SI generation algorithm to exploit the statistical characterization of signal in both pixel domain and measurement domain. The obtained SI is then used to compute the decoding input probabilities for further CS-BP decoding. A Bayesian inference framework with SI of good quality can be more efficient and precise to reconstruct a signal from compressive measurements than performing a CS recovery algorithm merely relies on signal sparsity. Experimental results indicate that with the aid of the proposed SI generation, the signal reconstruction quality can be much improved as compared with the existing CS-based DVC codecs.

6. REFERENCES

[1] B. Girod, A. M. Aron, S. Rane, and D. Rebollo-Monedero, Distributed video coding, *Proc. IEEE*, vol. 93, no. 1, pp. 71-83, Jan. 2005.

[2] R. Puri and K. Ramchandran, PRISM: A New Robust Video Coding Architecture Based on Distributed Compression Principles, *Proc. Allerton Conf.*, October 2002.

[3] X. Artigas, J. Ascenso, M. Dalai, S. Klomp, D. Kubasov, M. Ouaret, The DISCOVER codec: Architecture, Techniques and Evaluation, *Picture Coding Symposium* 2007

[4] E. J. Candes and M. B. Wakin, An introduction to compressive sampling, *IEEE Signal Processing Magazine*, vol. 25, no. 2, pp. 21-30, March 2008.

[5] H. W. Chen, L. W. Kang, and C. S. Lu, Dynamic Measurement Rate Allocation for Distributed Compressive Video Sensing, in *Proc. IEEE/SPIE Visual Communications and Image Processing*, July 2010.

[6] J. Prades-Nebot, Y. Ma, and T. Huang, Distributed video coding using compressive sampling, in *Proc. of Picture Coding Symposium*, USA, May 2009.

[7] T. T. Do, Y. Chen, D. T. Nguyen, N. Nguyen, L. Gan, and T. D. Tran, Distributed compressed video sensing, in *Proc. of IEEE Int. Conf. on Image Processing*, Nov. 2009.

[8] D. Baron, S. Sarvotham, R. G. Baraniuk, Bayesian Compressive Sensing Via Belief Propagation, *IEEE Trans. on Signal Processing*, vol.58, no.1, pp.269-280, Jan. 2010.

[9] ISO/IEC 14496 – 10 2003: Coding of audio-visual objects – part 10: advanced video coding

[10] R. Martins, C. Brites, J. Ascenso, F. Pereira, Statistical motion learning for improved transform domain Wyner-Ziv video coding, *IET-IPR*, No. 1, pp. 28-41, Feb. 2010.

[11] C. Brites, F. Pereira, Correlation noise modeling for efficient pixel and transform domain Wyner–Ziv video coding, *IEEE Trans. Circuits Syst. Video Technol.*, vol. 18, no. 9., pp. 1177–1190, September, 2008

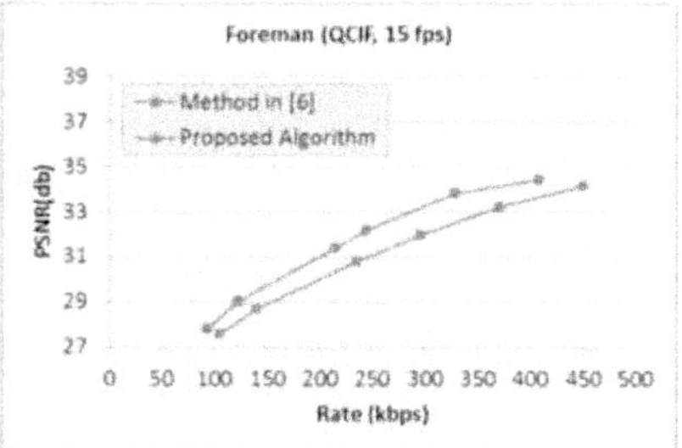

Figure 4: RD performance with Foreman

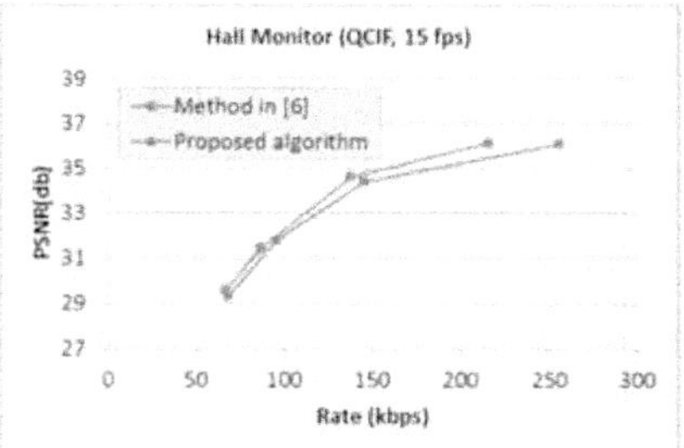

Figure 5: RD performance with Hall Monitor

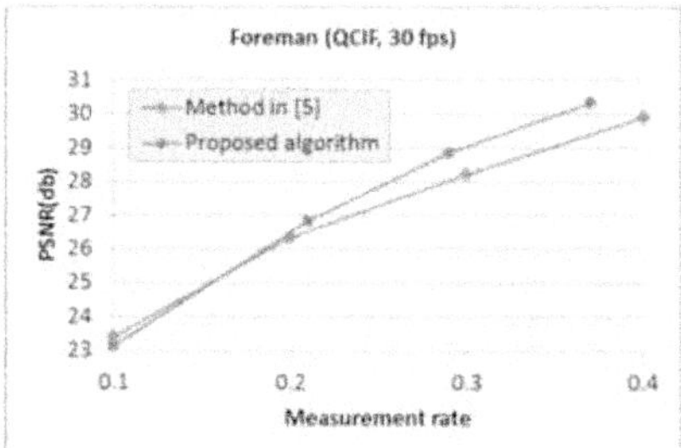

Figure 6: RD performance with Foreman

Personalized Portraits Ranking

Lei Huang[1,2], Tian Xia[1], Ji Wan[1,2], Yongdong Zhang[1], Shouxun Lin[1]
[1]Institute of Computing Technology, Chinese Academy of Sciences, Beijing 100190, China
[2]Graduate University of Chinese Academy of Sciences, Beijing 100049, China
{huanglei, txia, wanji, zhyd, sxlin}@ict.ac.cn

ABSTRACT

Portraits, also known as images of people, constitute an important part of consumer photos. Existing methods manage portraits based on either explicit objectives, e.g., a specified person or event, or aesthetics, i.e., the aesthetic quality of portraits. This paper presents a novel system for personalized portraits ranking. First, four kinds of personalized features, i.e., composition, clothing style, affection and social relationship are proposed to quantify users' intent. Then, example-based and sketch-based user interfaces (UI) are developed, which are capable of capturing users' personal intent hardly described by queries or aesthetics. Finally, portraits ranking is implemented by combing these features together with the developed user interfaces. Experimental results show that the system performs well in providing personalized preferences and the proposed features are effective for portraits ranking. From the user study, our system gets promising results.

Categories and Subject Descriptors

I.4.9 [**Image Processing and Computer Vision**]: Applications; H.5.2 [**Information Interfaces and Presentation**]: User Interfaces – *Graphical user interfaces (GUI)*

General Terms

Algorithms, Performance

Keywords

Portraits ranking, Personalized ranking, Example-based ranking, Sketch-based ranking, Social relationship features, Affection features, Clothing style features

1. INTRODUCTION

With the proliferation of digital cameras, the volume of portraits is growing rapidly. Therefore, selecting and managing portraits in a personalized manner, e.g., finding portraits which have similar appearance with an example portrait is becoming a common demand. Personalized portraits ranking aims to display portraits in a way better fits users' intent, which leads to more convenient organization and access of portraits repositories.

Portraits management and ranking has received lots of research focuses in recent years. Generally, existing approaches mainly fall into three categories: face-based, event-based and aesthetic-based. Face-based methods have received the most research focus and they can be further divided into two genera. For the first genus, researchers try to manage portraits based on face clustering. For

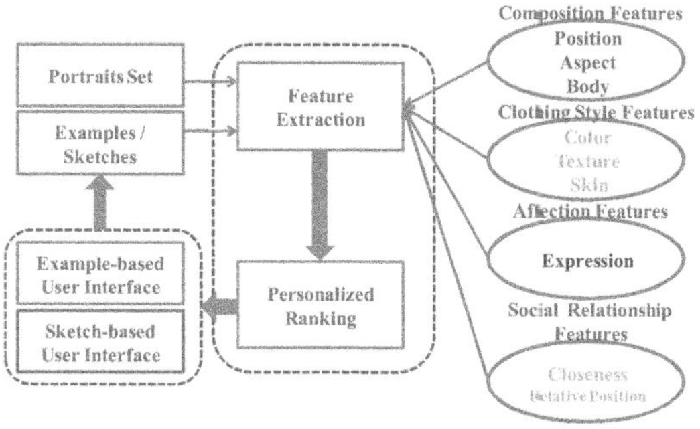

Figure 1. Overview of the proposed system.

example, Chen et al. [1] explored face similarities to semi-automatically annotate faces in family photo albums. For better performance, many researchers explored context information to aid face clustering. For example, Song et al. [2], Gallagher et al. [3] and Zhang et al. [4] explored clothing feature for face clustering; Zhao et al. [5] and Wang et al. [6] combined the social context and clothing context for face clustering. In addition, some commercial software, e.g. "Google Picasa", use people clustering methods. For the second genus, researchers try to manage portraits by attributes of the face. For example, Kumar et al. [7] and Siddiquie et al. [8] proposed approaches for ranking portraits based on attribute queries like "Middle-aged, Eyeglasses", etc. The event-based methods manage portraits through event clustering. In Ref. [9], Lin et al. jointly considered the people, events and locations for inferring event labels. Liu et al. [10] clustered people by community analysis in news video. The aesthetic-based methods rank portraits based on aesthetic features. In Ref. [11], Li et al. proposed features for predicting the aesthetic quality of portraits.

The methods mentioned above are very useful in portraits management and have largely facilitated the selection of portraits. It is observed that these methods ranking portraits mainly towards a specified person, event or general aesthetic quality. However, people are usually with diverse intents and there are cases that the intents cannot be precisely described by either specified objectives or aesthetic merely. Typical scenarios are: finding portraits with similar appearance to an example portrait, or finding images containing two people in scheduled positions. Yeh et al. [12] proposed a photograph ranking system that incorporate certain image patterns e.g., percentage of a certain color, black-and-white ratio, as personalized features. With these features, users can find photographs in accordance with their personal taste. However, these patterns are toward general sets of photos and they are only able to configure personalization in limited ways. Portraits have unique properties, it is not surprised that the patterns are hardly effective for portraits. Therefore, method that ranks portraits in a personalized way is of great demand and significance.

In this paper, we propose a novel system for personalized portraits ranking. To address the issue of the measurement for personalized requirements, four kinds of features, i.e., composition, clothing style, affection of people and social relationship (when there are

*Area Chair: Wei Tsang Ooi

MM'11, November 28- December 1, 2011, Scottsdale, Arizona, USA.
Copyright 2011 ACM 978-1-4503-0616-4/11/11...$10.00.

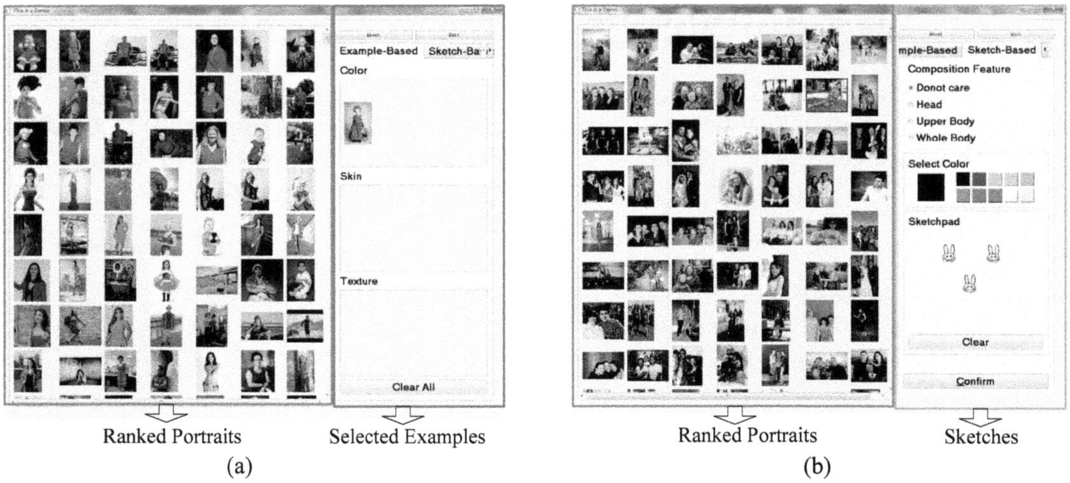

Figure 2. Two novel UIs of our system support personalized portraits ranking. (a) Example-based UI: ranking portraits by dragging the example image to the three sub-windows on the right, i.e., color, skin and texture. (b) Sketch-based UI: ranking portraits by selecting options and sketching. The details are presented in section3.1.

more than one people are detected in an image) are proposed. In order to solve the representation issue of personalized demands, we design two user interfaces: the example-based one and the sketch-based one. For the example-based user interface the user can rank portraits by example portraits. And for sketch-based user interface the user can rank portraits by sketching. The overview of our system is shown in Fig.1. The user interfaces are shown in Fig.2.

2. PERSONALIZED FEATURES EXTRACTION

2.1 Face Region Location and Clothing Region Location

Before features extraction, the face regions and the clothing regions should be located. A modified version of [13] which can handle rotated faces is performed first to get the face regions. And the clothing regions are acquired in rectangular regions below the faces [2]. All images are normalized by the face size.

2.2 Features Extraction

2.2.1 Composition Features

The most famous photograph composition guideline is the "Rule of Thirds" which means to place main subjects at roughly one third of the horizontal or vertical dimension of the photography. In portraits, the main subjects are always the people and we propose three measurements to denote the composition: position ratio, aspect ratio and body ratio.

Position Ratio. The position ratio which presents the position of people in images is defined as follows:

$$PR_x = \frac{x}{I_{width}}, PR_y = \frac{y}{I_{height}} \tag{1}$$

where, (x, y) is the coordinate of the face center in the images, I_{width} and I_{height} is the width and height of images.

Aspect Ratio. The aspect ratio we used is the same with [12] which is defined as $AR = I_{width} / I_{height}$.

Body Ratio. Body ratio means the ratio of the body part appearing in the photograph which is defined in Eq. (2).

$$BR = \frac{Length_{body}}{Length_{face}} \tag{2}$$

where, $Length_{body}$ is the length of body appearing in images, $Length_{face}$ is the length of face in images. The most common forms of this feature are face portraits, upper body portraits and whole body portraits.

2.2.2 Clothing Style Features

Clothing style is an important feature for portraits ranking. Actually, recognizing the style of clothing is a very hard task. Therefore, we do not attempt to recognize the style of clothing, but use three effective features to denote it. Color features, texture features and skin features are proposed. All these three features are computed within the body region (i.e., clothing region).

Color features. To solve the influence caused by the illumination, the color of clothing region is transferred from RGB to HSV firstly. Then the HSV color space is quantified to 256 bins. A three-level color histogram pyramid [4] is computed to represent the spatial relations as shown in Fig.3. Skin regions [14] are ignored when computing color features.

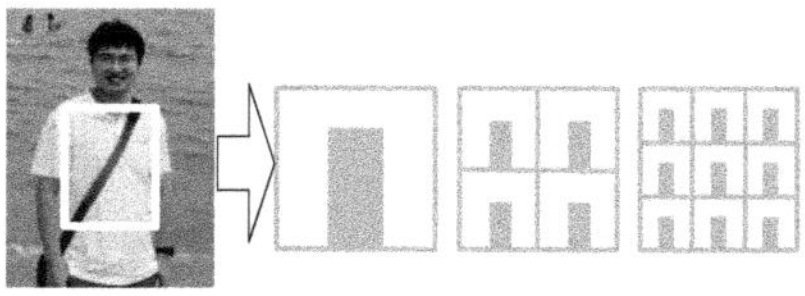

Figure 3. Color histogram pyramid.

Texture features. Since clothes usually have complex texture patterns that represent certain degrees of personalization, we extract texture features from the clothing region as follows. Firstly, Gaussian smooth filtering is carried out to reduce the influence of self-fold of clothes. Secondly, canny edge detector is employed to detect the edges. Thirdly, the direction of each edge pixel is computed by Eq. (3) [15]. The direction values are qualified into 4 bins and the body area is divided into 3*3 blocks as illustrated in Fig.3. Finally, 4-dimensional descriptors are extracted in the whole body region and nine blocks of body region respectively which represent the ratio of edge pixels for each bin. All descriptors formed the final texture feature which is 10*4-dimensional.

$$\theta(x, y) = \arctan((I_{(x,y+1)} - I_{(x,y-1)}) / (I_{(x+1,y)} - I_{(x-1,y)})) \tag{3}$$

Skin features. Skin feature is another salient feature to denote the clothing style for clothed people. In our system, the Bayes skin detection method [14] is used to detect the skin regions. And the skin features is defined as a 10-dimensional descriptor which represent the ratio of skin in the whole body and nine blocks of body region.

2.2.3 Affection Features
Face expression is used to illustrate the affection features which are similar to Ref. [11]. The face expression feature is computed by the measurement of mouth openness and eye openness computed as distances between corresponding ASM facial points [16] as is shown in Fig.4 (a).

Figure 4. Affection features and social relationship features. (a) Face expression features. (b) Closeness features and relative position features.

2.2.4 Social Relationship Features
Closeness feature and relative position feature are proposed to represent the social relationship of people in images which inspired by the work in Ref. [6] and [11]. The closeness and the relative position of people in the photos show the social relationships of the people. For example, a couple may stand closeness and the face that located at higher position in the image is more likely to be the husband. To get the closeness feature and relative position feature, we first connect all faces with an undirected complete graph, then the MST (Minimal Spanning Tree) is computed by the Prim algorithm. The average distances of all of the edges in the MST is used to represent the closeness of people. An array of differences of height of people in the portraits is used to represent the relative position feature. Fig.4 (b) shows the example of social relationship features.

3. PERSONALIZED RANKING

3.1 User Interfaces
Two user interfaces are designed for personalized ranking: Example-based and Sketch-based (Fig.2).

Example-based: In the Example-based user interface, three panels are available: color, skin and texture which means three clothing style features. Example dragged into the color panel means the color feature is more prior than others. The other two panels are as the same.

Sketch-based: In the sketch-based user interface, the user can rank portraits by options, colors and sketches. The options denote the body ratio and the colors denote the clothing colors. For the sketches, one can draw the position of each person by click mouse on the sketch-pad. The sketch-based user interface is very useful when there are no approving examples.

3.2 Distance Metric
The distance metric for the color features is the histogram interaction. We assign a larger weight for the center areas than surrounding areas of body to reduce the influence by the background areas at the body boundary. And the Euclidean distance is used as distance metric for other features. All the distances are normalized to [0, 1], 0 means the most similar and 1 means the least similar.

The distance score for each ranked image is computed as follows:

$$D_j = \frac{1}{N}\sum_{i=1}^{N} w_i \cdot d(f_i) \tag{4}$$

where, D_j indicates the distance between example-selected/sketch and the jth image in the portraits set. w_i is the weight of each feature i, the default value of w_i for each feature is 1. $d(f_i)$ denotes the distance between example-selected/sketch and the ranked image of each feature f_i. N is the feature number. In this paper, N is 9.

When more than one example is selected, the distance score for each ranked image is computed as follows:

$$MD_j = \frac{1}{M}\sum_{k=1}^{M} (D_j)_k \tag{5}$$

where, MD_j is the distance between examples-selected and the jth image in the portraits set, M is the number of selected-examples, D_j is defined in Eq.(4).

4. EXPERIMENTS AND USER STUDY
A consumer photo collection of 1816 portraits is used in our experiments. All the images are downloaded from "Flickr" by using "portraits", "portraits+couple", "portraits+family" as queries. Some samples of our data set can be seen in Fig 2.

4.1 Ranking Results
To show the effect of the proposed system, some ranking results of example-based and sketch-based UIs are showed in Fig.5 and Fig. 6, respectively. In both figures, the first column is example or sketch queries, while the rest columns correspond to the top ranked images. It is seen that quite good ranking results are obtained. In example-based results, the people in the example image wearing naked shoulder clothes can find results with similar clothes in skin priority setting (Fig.5 (b)). Analogously, all returned images having a smiling face as the example one in "face portrait" setting (Fig.5(e)). While in sketch-based results, arbitrary combination of input items always generates results that satisfy sketch items. The proposed system explicitly exhibits its personalization in both cases.

To further evaluate the features' performance, we have annotated the color features, skin features and social relationship features on our data set. Specifically, the color feature is annotated for "Red", "Black" and "White". The social relationship feature is annotated for images with four people, three people and two people. The skin feature is annotated for clothes with bare shoulder. We use the sketch-based UI for the color and social relationship features evaluation and the example-based UI for the skin features evaluation. The results are shown in Fig.7. From the results we can see that the performances of our features are promising.

There also have a few unsatisfactory results, as shown in Fig.5 and Fig.2. Most of them are caused by various poses, false face detection and self-fold of clothing. Furthermore, the performance of the affection feature depends on the accuracy of ASM.

4.2 User Study
We conducted user-based studies to evaluate the effectiveness of the proposed system. Specifically, a total of 10 users were recruited in this study. They were asked to randomly submit example or sketch queries to the user interfaces and then commented the quality of the returned portrait rankings. The

Figure 5. Ranking results by examples. (1) Selected example images. (2)-(6) First five ranking results. (a)-(c) Experiments for color priority, skin priority, texture priority each. (d) Experiments for both color and skin priority. (e) Experiments for "face portrait" examples. (f) Experiments for examples with two people. Images in red dashed box are error ranked results.

Figure 6. Ranking results by sketches. The top row is the ranking results by sketch. The bottom is the ranking results by "color+composition+sketch".

rating score ranged from 0 to 10 and a higher score indicated more satisfactory. The average scores of the 10 users for the example-based and sketch-based interfaces were 8.9 and 9.0, respectively. In addition, most users gave affirmative answers to questions like *Whether the user interfaces are easy to use*? or *Do you want to use such a interface to search portraits*, showing the usefulness of the proposed system.

5. CONCLUSION AND FUTURE WORK

In this paper a novel system for personalized portraits ranking is proposed. The system presents two novel user interfaces, which record a user's personalization via the selected example images or the input sketch items. Four kinds of personalized portraits features, i.e., composition, clothing style, affection and social relationship, are firstly proposed to describe the recorded images or items for ranking. Both objective and subjective experimental results show that the proposed system effectively and robustly ranks portraits in a personalized way. However, personalization is a subjective and challenging issue, more research will be done on discovering personalized features and we anticipate more exciting work in the future.

6. ACKNOWLEDGMENTS

This work is supported by the National Basic Research Program of China (973 Program, 2007CB311100); National High Technology and Research Development Program of China (863 Program, 2009AA01A403); National Nature Science Foundation of China (61100087); Beijing Natural Science Foundation (4112055); Co-building Program of Beijing Municipal Education Commission.

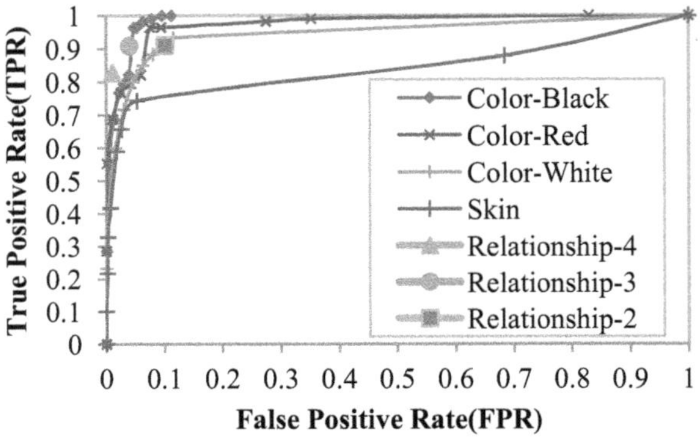

Figure 7. Performance of our features.

7. REFERENCES

[1] Chen, L., Hu, B., Zhang, L., Li, M. and Zhang, H. Face annotation for family photo album management, IJIG, 2003.

[2] Song, Y. and Leung, T. Context-aided human recognition-clustering, ECCV, 2006.

[3] Gallagher, A.C. and Chen, T. Clothing cosegmentation for recognizing people, CVPR, 2008.

[4] Zhang, W., Zhang, T. and Tretter, D. Clothing-based person clustering in family photos, ICIP, 2010.

[5] Zhao, M., Teo, Y.W., Liu, S., Chua, T. and Jain, R. Automatic person annotation of family photo album, ICIVR, 2006.

[6] Wang, G., Gallagher, A. C., Luo, J.B. and David, F. Seeing people in social context: recognizing people and social relationships, ECCV, 2010.

[7] Kumar, N., Belhumeur, P. and Nayar, S. Facetracer: a search engine for large collections of images with faces, ECCV, 2008.

[8] Siddiquie, B., Feris, R.S. and Davis, L.S. Image ranking and retrieval based on Multi-Attribute queries, CVPR, 2011.

[9] Lin, D., Kapoor, A., Hua, G. and Baker, S. Joint people, event, and location recognition in personal photo collections using cross-domain context, ECCV, 2010.

[10] Liu, C.X., Huang, Q.M., Jiang, S.Q. and Xu, C.S. Event based news video people classification and ranking using multimodality features, ICME, 2010.

[11] Li, C.C., Gallagher, A., Loui, A.C. and Chen, T. Aesthetic quality assessment of consumer photos with faces, ICIP, 2010.

[12] Yeh, C.H., Ho, Y.C., Barsky, B.A. and Ouhyoung, M. Personalized photograph ranking and selection system, ACM MM, 2010.

[13] Viola, P. and Jones, M. Rapid object detection using a boosted cascade of simple features, CVPR, 2001.

[14] Jones, M.J. and Rehg, J.M. Statistical color models with application to skin detection, IJCV, 2002.

[15] Lowe, D.G. Distinctive image features from scale-invariant keypoints, IJCV, 2004.

[16] Cootes, T. F., Taylor, C. J., Cooper, D. H. and Graham, J. Active shape models—their training and application, CVIU, 1995.

A New Analysis Method for Paired Comparison and Its Application to 3D Quality Assessment*

Jong-Seok Lee
School of Integrated Technology
Yonsei University
406-840 Incheon, Korea
jong-seok.lee@yonsei.ac.kr

Lutz Goldmann, Touradj Ebrahimi
Multimedia Signal Processing Group (MMSPG)
Ecole Polytechnique Fédérale de Lausanne (EPFL)
1015 Lausanne, Switzerland
{lutz.goldmann, touradj.ebrahimi}@epfl.ch

ABSTRACT

Among various subjective quality evaluation methodologies, paired comparison has the advantage of improved simplicity of the subjects' evaluation task due to simplified rating scales and direct comparison of two stimuli. Thus, it may lead to more reliable results when individual quality levels are difficult to define, quality differences between stimuli are small or multiple quality factors are involved. This paper proposes a new method to analyze results of paired comparison-based subjective tests. By assuming that ties convey information about significant differences between two stimuli being compared, the confidence intervals for the quality scores are estimated using a maximum likelihood criterion, which enables us to intuitively examine the significance of quality score differences. We describe the complete test methodology including the test procedure, outlier detection and score analysis applied to quality assessment of 3D images acquired using varying camera distances. Experimental results demonstrate the usefulness of the proposed analysis method, as well as the enhanced quality discriminability of the paired comparison methodology in comparison to the conventional single stimulus methodology.

Categories and Subject Descriptors

H.1.2 [**Models and Principles**]: User/Machine Systems—*Human Factors*; I.4.1 [**Image Processing and Computer Vision**]: Digitization and Image Capture—*Camera Calibration*

General Terms

Algorithms

Keywords

paired comparison, quality of experience, statistical significance, maximum likelihood estimation, stereoscopic image

*Area chair: Wei Tsang Ooi

MM'11, November 28–December 1, 2011, Scottsdale, Arizona, USA.

1. INTRODUCTION

Subjective multimedia quality assessment is to measure quality of experience (QoE) of multimedia content through subjective experiments. Its results provide knowledge about the way that human subjects perceive quality for the type of media considered. Such understanding can be exploited in various applications of multimedia, e.g. determination of content distribution strategies, development and benchmarking of multimedia processing algorithms, and development of objective quality metrics.

In general, it is important to utilize an appropriate test methodology for an experiment in order to exclude undesirable external factors, assess the targeted quality aspect accurately, and ensure reproducibility of the results. For this, there have been efforts to standardize test methodologies, e.g. [8]. Examples of frequently used methodologies are single stimulus and double stimulus methodologies. However, these methodologies have been developed mainly in the context of quality assessment for traditional 2D image/video content. Thus, applying them directly to assessment of new types of media such as 3D images/videos and high dynamic range images may not be as effective as for 2D image/video due to inherent differences in perception mechanisms. Often, quality differences between stimuli are too small, multiple quality factors are involved simultaneously, or individual quality levels are difficult to define, which may cause unreliable quality ratings by the subjects.

Paired comparison is one of the standardized test methodologies [8], which has potential to improve reliability of subjective tests due to the simplicity of the subjects' rating task. Instead of choosing a value on a discrete or continuous scale as in single stimulus or double stimulus methodologies, a subject only needs to indicate which one between a pair of stimuli has better quality. Results of paired comparison tests appear as winning frequencies between each pair and, thus, an additional analysis step is required to estimate a quality score and the corresponding confidence information for each stimulus.

In this paper, we propose a new method for analysing the ratings of the paired comparison in order to obtain quality scores equivalent to traditional mean opinion scores (MOS) and, more importantly, to the corresponding confidence intervals. The method is based on the assumption that ties carry information about significant differences of paired stimuli. Thereby, obtaining the confidence intervals is formulated as a maximum likelihood estimation problem in such a way that the intervals increase in proportion to the number of ties. The most important features of the proposed method is that it enables intuitive examination of significant quality score differences.

To evaluate the proposed method, it is applied to the quality assessment of stereoscopic images acquired with varying inter-camera distances. Although 3D content is gaining popularity as a new type of media, many people still do not have much experience. Therefore, it is usually quite difficult for them to understand various quality factors involved in 3D perception and distinguish between quality variations in specific aspect under consideration. Through experiments, it is shown that the paired comparison methodology combined with the proposed analysis method can be successfully applied to 3D image quality evaluation and offers several advantages in comparison to the popular single stimulus methodology.

The rest of this paper is organized as follows. Section 2 provides a general overview of the paired comparison-based test methodology. Section 3 focuses on the novel analysis method to derive mean opinion scores and confidence intervals from the results of a paired comparison experiment. In Section 4, the effectiveness of the proposed method is demonstrated through a quality evaluation study for 3D images. Finally, concluding remarks are given in Section 5.

2. SIMULTANEOUS PAIRED COMPARISON

2.1 Test procedure

The basic idea of paired comparison is to present two stimuli simultaneously or sequentially and to ask subjects about their relative preferences of the stimuli. In general, a preference of stimulus A against stimulus B can be expressed on a continuous scale, e.g. [-10, 10], or a discrete scale, e.g. {'much better', 'better', 'same', 'worse', and 'much worse'} [8]. In our case, however, we use a ternary scale, i.e. {'better', 'same', 'worse'}, in order to keep the subjects' rating task as simple as possible. Note that a weighting scheme can convert ratings done on a more subdivided scale to equivalent ratings on the ternary scale.

Inclusion of a tie (i.e. 'same') in the scale is useful for several reasons. First, it simplifies the subjects' ranting task, especially when the quality difference between the given two stimuli is not easily noticeable. Moreover, if ties are not allowed, subjects are forced to choose between 'better' and 'worse' even when the quality difference of two stimuli appears unclear. This may result in biased results due to (possibly non-uniform) randomness. More importantly, ties provide useful information regarding the ambiguity in quality difference between two stimuli, which will be exploited for significance analysis in our method.

During the test session, each subject is asked to observe a pair of stimuli (A and B) and choose his/her preference between 'A is better', 'B is better', and 'same'. Especially, we employ simultaneous viewing by using two identical 3D displays, so that direct comparison between stimuli is possible and the reliability of ratings is enhanced.

2.2 Outlier detection

In single or double stimulus methodologies, the reliability of a subject is examined by comparing his/her ratings to those of other subjects. If the individual ratings deviate too much from the overall ratings, the subject is regarded as an outlier and his/her ratings are not considered further.

On the other hand, a subject's reliability in paired comparison can be evaluated by examining only his/her individual ratings across different pairs. Let $i > j$ indicate that stimulus i is rated better than j by a subject If $i > j$, $j > k$ and $k > i$, a circular triad is formed, which violates the transitivity rule. If the number of circular triads is too large, the subject is regarded as an outlier. Since a tie (noted as $i = j$) is allowed in our rating scale, the following four cases are considered as circular triads: (1) $i > j$, $j > k$ and $k > i$, (2) $i > j$, $j > k$ and $k = i$, (3) $i > j$, $j = k$ and $k > i$, and (4) $i = j$, $j > k$, and $k > i$. If the ratio of the number of circular triads among all possible triads is larger than a threshold, the subject's ratings are discarded.

2.3 Quality score estimation

When ties are not allowed and the rating scale is binary, ratings by M subjects for a set of stimuli appear as winning frequencies, w_{ij}, $\forall i, j \in \{1, ..., N\}$, representing the number of subjects who chose stimulus i against j. These frequencies need to be converted to quality scores equivalent to MOS for further quality examination and comparison.

A popular method for this is to use the Bradley-Terry (BT) model [1] that relates the empirical winning probability of stimulus i against j, $P_{ij} = w_{ij}/M$, with their quality scores, π_i and π_j, as:

$$P_{ij} = \frac{\pi_i}{\pi_i + \pi_j} \tag{1}$$

The scores π_i $(i = 1, ..., N)$ satisfying $\pi_i \geq 0$ and $\sum_i \pi_i = 1$ can be obtained via maximum likelihood estimation.

When ties are included in the rating scale (as in our study), winning frequencies w_{ij} and tie frequencies $t_{ij} = t_{ji}$ summarize ratings of M subjects, where $w_{ij} + w_{ji} + t_{ij} = M$.

A few approaches have been proposed to accommodate ties in the framework of the BT model. A simple solution is to consider a tie as a half way between the other two preference options, i.e. $w_{ij} \leftarrow w_{ij} + t_{ij}/2$, and then to use the original BT model [3, 5]. The approaches proposed in [2, 6] introduced additional parameters that need to be estimated together with π_i.

3. PROPOSED ANALYSIS METHOD

Unlike the aforementioned approaches accommodating ties, the proposed method uses ties to infer the confidence of converted quality scores. Such confidence is important in analyzing and interpreting the quality scores. A higher quality score does not necessarily mean that the corresponding stimulus has a better quality than another stimulus if the score difference is not statistically significant. Therefore, confidence information enables us to prevent misleading judgment in such a case.

In our method, it is assumed that the ambiguity of quality differences between two stimuli is found in ties. The two extreme cases where the ties supposedly belong to one of the other two preference options are used to obtain the upper and lower bounds of the confidence intervals for the quality scores. Therefore, significance of quality differences between stimuli can be easily examined by checking whether their confidence intervals overlap. In other words, the fact that the confidence intervals of two stimuli overlap implies that the dominance of a score against the other may have been inverted and thus the quality difference is not significant.

First, the winning frequencies are used to obtain quality scores by using the BT model without considering ties. Then, the confidence interval for the score of each stimulus, $[\pi_i - \Delta\pi_i^-, \pi_i + \Delta\pi_i^+]$, is obtained as follows. The lower and upper bounds of the empirical winning probability of stimulus i, P_{ij}^- and P_{ij}^+ are obtained as

$$P_{ij}^- = w_{ij}/M \tag{2}$$

$$P_{ij}^+ = (w_{ij} + t_{ij})/M \tag{3}$$

assuming that the ties have been the preferences of stimulus j or i, respectively. These probabilities are related to the new parameters $\Delta\pi_i^-$ and $\Delta\pi_i^+$ as

$$P_{ij}^- = \frac{\pi_i - \Delta\pi_i^-}{\pi_i - \Delta\pi_i^- + \pi_j + \Delta\pi_j^+} \tag{4}$$

$$P_{ij}^+ = \frac{\pi_i + \Delta\pi_i^+}{\pi_i + \Delta\pi_i^+ + \pi_j - \Delta\pi_j^-} \tag{5}$$

A maximum likelihood criterion is used to estimate the values of $\Delta\pi_i^-$ and $\Delta\pi_i^+$ where the log-likelihood function to be maximized can be written as

$$L = \sum_{i=1}^{N}\sum_{j=1}^{N}\left\{P_{ij}^- \log\left(\frac{\pi_i - \Delta\pi_i^-}{\pi_i - \Delta\pi_i^- + \pi_j + \Delta\pi_j^+}\right)\right.$$
$$\left. + P_{ij}^+ \log\left(\frac{\pi_i + \Delta\pi_i^+}{\pi_i + \Delta\pi_i^+ + \pi_j - \Delta\pi_j^-}\right)\right\} \tag{6}$$

The aforementioned existing methods also reflect uncertainty in the resultant quality scores and the additional parameters in a way that their values change according to the number of ties. However, such relationship is less intuitive to examine significant quality score differences between stimuli in comparison to our method.

4. EXPERIMENT

4.1 Task and dataset

The EPFL 3D Image Database [4] was used in our study. It contains stereoscopic images with a resolution of 1920×1080 pixels covering diverse indoor and outdoor scenes with a large variety of colors, textures and depth structures. Each scene was captured using a stereo camera setup with six different inter-camera distances from 10 cm to 60 cm with a step size of 10 cm.

The camera distance is an important parameter in acquisition of stereoscopic images, which has significantly impact on the perceived 3D quality. A larger camera distance usually produces more 3D depth, but if it gets too large, it may cause unnaturalness and discomfort. The optimal camera distance depends on various factors including scene characteristics as well as the display size and viewing conditions.

In our experiments, six scenes were chosen from the database, i.e. sofa, tables, sculpture, moped, bikes, and construction. The other scenes were used for training. All possible pairs of each scene were considered to perform paired comparison tests. Thus, each subject watched $\binom{6}{2} \times 6 = 90$ pairs.

4.2 Environment

The tests were conducted at our laboratory designed for professional subjective quality tests according to the recommendations in [8]. The room walls were painted in gray 128 and the ambient lighting is achieved through a set of neon lamps with a color temperature of 6500 K. Two 46" LCD polarized stereoscopic displays with a native resolution of 1920×1080 pixels were used to present two stimuli simultaneously. Each subject sat in front of the two screens at a distance of approximately 2 m that is equivalent to 3 times the height of the screen. The subject was allowed to turn his/her head freely to watch the individual stimulus on each screen alternatively.

4.3 Procedure

Sixteen subjects (12 males and 4 females) participated in the tests. They were screened for visual acuity, color vision and binocular vision according to [7]. All of them were non-expert viewers with a marginal experience of 3D image and video viewing. Their ages ranged from 25 to 36 with an average of 29.9.

Prior to a test session, a training session was held to introduce the test procedure and rating task to the subject by using a set of training stimuli. In the middle of the test, a short break was given to prevent the fatigue of the subject.

The method described in Section 2.2 was used to detect outliers. Since the transitivity violation rates were less than 0.05 for all subjects, no subject was rejected as an outlier.

Quality scores and confidence intervals were obtained from the subjective ratings by using the method presented in Section 3. The scores were logarithmically scaled for better visualization, and then normalized so that the minimum and maximum scores for each content are 0 and 100, respectively.

4.4 Results and analysis

Figure 1 compares the results of paired comparison with those of single stimulus reported in [4][1]. In the latter case, the MOS and 95% confidence interval values are shown. For better comparison, the results of single stimulus tests were re-scaled to the same range as the paired comparison for each scene.

Overall, the results of the two test methodologies show a similar trend, i.e. the best quality for each scene is obtained for small camera distances that lead to a good 3D effect with comfortable disparity levels. As the camera distance increases, the quality decreases considerably due to the uncomfortable amount of disparity. Content-dependence of this trend is also observed, e.g. the construction scene shows relatively moderate quality decrease for camera distances of 20 cm to 40 cm due to the more distant background when compared to other scenes, which appears in both single stimulus and paired comparison results. For the case of paired comparison, the confidence intervals appear asymmetric around the quality scores because two separate variables were defined for the lower and upper bounds. This enables us to easily examine the significance of quality difference between two stimuli by checking the overlap between the confidence intervals of two stimuli.

An important advantage of paired comparison over the single stimulus methodology is that ambiguity between stimuli is decreased. In [4], it was mentioned that the subjects of the single stimulus tests had difficulty in discriminating quality differences especially for mid-range camera distances. However, such difficulty could be alleviated by simplifying the subjects' task through paired comparison,

[1]Due to the page limit, the results for only three scenes are shown here.

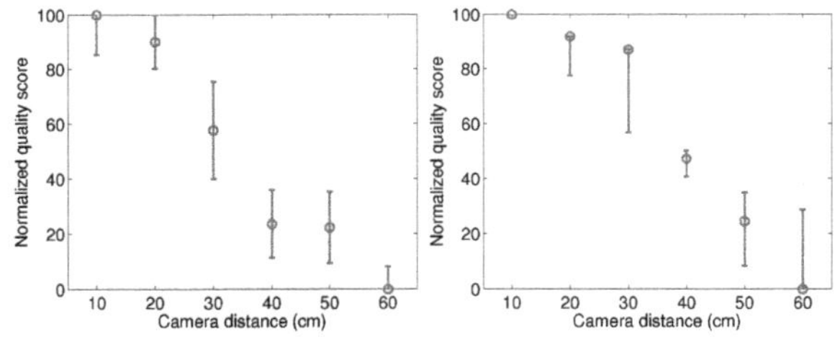

(a) sofa

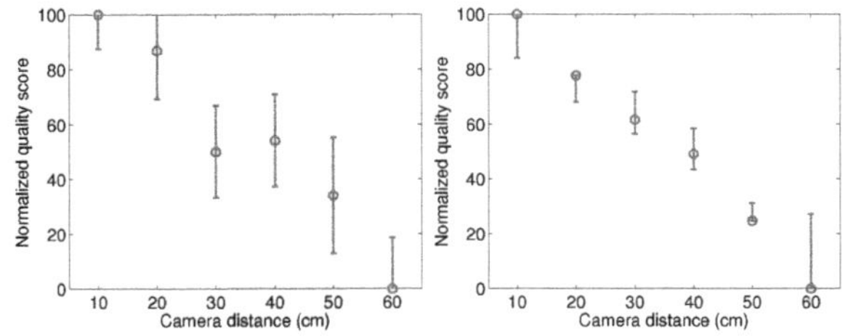

(b) sculpture

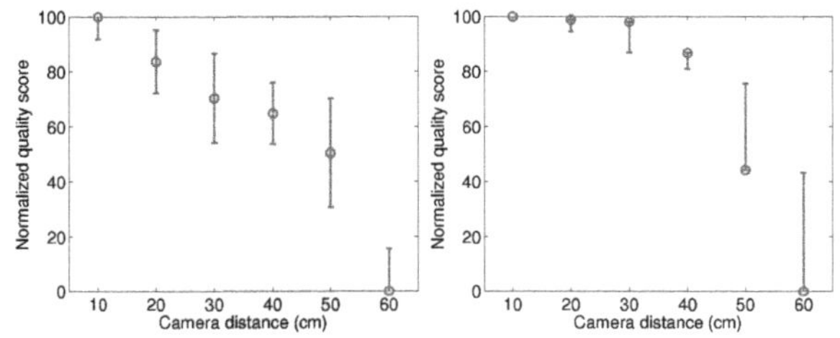

(c) construction

Figure 1: Comparison of the results of the single stimulus (left column) and paired comparison (right column) tests.

which resulted in enhanced discriminability between stimuli as it can be seen from the figure.

In order to compare the two methodologies in terms of discriminability, pair-wise comparison results were simulated from the quality scores of the single stimulus tests. In other words, the scores of a subject for each pair of stimuli were compared and, if the score difference is larger than a threshold, the one having a higher score was considered as the winner of the comparison, otherwise, a tie was recorded. By adjusting the threshold, we generated simulated comparison results having the same probabilities of ties to those of the paired comparison experiment. This procedure was repeated for all subjects involved in the single stimulus experiment. Then, we computed a discriminability measure defined as the absolute difference between the probabilities for the preference of each of two stimuli, i.e. $D_{ij} = |P_{ij} - P_{ji}|$. Table 1 compares the average values of the discriminability measure of the single stimulus and paired comparison methodologies. Overall, the paired comparison tests achieve higher discrimination between stimuli than the single stimulus tests.

5. CONCLUSIONS

We have proposed a new analysis method for paired comparison-based subjective quality assessment, which was applied to 3D image quality evaluation. The complete methodology including the test procedure, outlier detection, score calculation and significant analysis was described. Exploiting the ambiguity residing in ties, the proposed method facilitates intuitive examination of significant quality difference without any additional statistical hypothesis test. A case study on 3D image quality evaluation demonstrated that the paired comparison test methodology improves quality discriminability between stimuli in comparison to the single stimulus methodology.

It is worth mentioning that the improved discriminability was obtained at the expense of an increased test duration (i.e. 36 stimuli to be evaluated in a single stimulus test versus 90 stimulus pairs to be compared in a paired comparison test). In our future work, we will work on improving efficiency of paired comparison. We also plan to apply the proposed method to other evaluation tasks where conventional single or double stimulus methodologies have difficulty in obtaining reliable results.

Table 1: Average discriminability measures of single stimulus (SS) and paired comparison (PC) for each scene.

Method	sof.	tab.	scu.	mop.	bik.	con.	Avg.
SS	**0.75**	0.69	0.63	0.69	0.73	0.71	0.70
PC	0.73	**0.72**	**0.75**	**0.84**	**0.79**	**0.83**	**0.78**

6. ACKNOWLEDGMENTS

This work was support in part by the Ministry of Knowledge Economy, Korea, under the IT Consilience Creative Program (NIPA-2010-C1515-1001-0001), in part by Yonsei University Research Fund of 2011, in part by the European Network of Excellence PetaMedia (no. 216444), and in part by the COST Action IC1003 Qualinet.

7. REFERENCES

[1] R. A. Bradley and M. E. Terry. Rank analysis of incomplete block designs: I. the method of paired comparisons. *Biometrika*, 39:324–345, 1952.

[2] R. R. Davidson. On extending the Bradley-Terry model to accommodate ties in paired comparison experiments. *J. Am. Stat. Assoc.*, 65(329):317–328, Mar. 1970.

[3] M. E. Glickman. Parameter estimation in large dynamic paired comparison experiments. *J. R. Stat. Soc., Ser. C (Appl. Stat.)*, 48(3):377–394, 1999.

[4] L. Goldmann, F. D. Simone, and T. Ebrahimi. Impact of acquisition distortions on the quality of stereoscopic images. In *Proc. Int. Workshop on Video Processing and Quality Metrics for Consumer Electronics*, Scottsdale, Arizona, USA, Jan. 2010.

[5] J.-S. Lee, F. D. Simone, N. Ramzan, Z. Zhao, E. Kurutepe, T. Sikora, J. Ostermann, E. Izquierdo, and T. Ebrahimi. Subjective evaluation of scalable video coding for content distribution. In *Proc. ACM Multimedia*, Firenze, Italy, Oct. 2010.

[6] P. V. Rao and L. L. Kupper. Ties in paired-comparison experiments: A generalization of the Bradley-Terry model. *J. Am. Stat. Assoc.*, 62(317):194–204, 1967.

[7] Subjective assessment of stereoscopic television pictures. Recommendation ITU-R BT.1438, 2000.

[8] Methodology for the subjective assessment of the quality of television pictures. Recommendation ITU-R BT.500-11, 2002.

ImagiLight: a Vision approach to Lighting Scene Setting *

Tommaso Gritti
Video & Image Processing group
Philips Research Eindhoven, The Netherlands
tommaso.gritti@philips.com

Gianluca Monaci
Video & Image Processing group
Philips Research Eindhoven, The Netherlands
gianluca.monaci@philips.com

ABSTRACT

The advent of integrated lighting installations, consisting of individually controllable lamps with advanced rendering capabilities, is fundamentally transforming lighting. This brings a need for an intuitive control capable of fully exploiting the rendering capabilities of the complete lighting infrastructure. In this paper we present a new method to automatically create lighting atmospheres in any type of environment, that allows for an natural interaction with the lighting system and generates unique, suggestive effects. To prove the effectiveness and versatility of the proposed solution, we deploy the system in several application scenarios, and discuss the results.

Categories and Subject Descriptors

J.5 [**Computer Applications**]: Arts and humanities—*Architecture*; I.4.8 [**Computing Methodologies**]: Image processing and computer vision—*Scene Analysis*

General Terms

Algorithms, Design

Keywords

Light atmosphere creation, solid state lighting, sparse image approximation, lighting design

1. INTRODUCTION

Lighting plays a pivotal role for the perception of the environment. Light affects the appearance of buildings, the mood of rooms, as well as people's behavior and well-being [3, 10]. Until recently, advanced lighting systems were mainly constrained to niche applications, where a light designer typically predefines a set of light atmospheres, selects and deploys the required lighting modules and establishes the controls to create the desired effects. Even though these steps are usually supported by computer-aided light simulation software [2, 7], they are complex and time consuming.

More intuitive and powerful light control can be achieved by the transition of traditional light controls to new "effect-driven" controls. In this new approach, the desired effect is specified, and the controls are automatically determined for the existing lighting infrastructure. In this paper we propose a new system, *ImagiLight*, to identify the available resources of the lighting infrastructure and accordingly calculate the settings of its lighting modules to match the intended light scene. The target light scene is specified by an input image or video. The proposed system comprises a set of controllable luminaires and a camera that is used to capture the effect of each light module on the scene. These pictures are used by the control algorithm as *basis functions* to map the input image into the environment. This approach allows to control an arbitrarily complex light infrastructure intuitively through visual content, while automatically accounting for complex interactions of multiple lights among them and with the environment. The proposed control algorithm is fast and scalable, allowing scalability in the number of controllable lights and flexibility of adapting to new setups.

Few camera-based solutions for lighting control have been developed recently [6, 8, 9]. These works focus on white light management systems, e.g. for energy saving in office environments. They describe the use of a calibrated digital camera to control electric lighting and blinds in response to daylight availability and occupancy of the room. The major contribution of this paper, and the main difference from [6, 8, 9], is that the proposed system collects not only few working points, but pictures of the effect of each light on the environment. In this way the system calibration step can be simplified, because the global effect of each light on the scene is captured. Furthermore, the atmosphere rendering, although not extremely accurate from a colorimetric point of view (which could be alleviated at the calibration phase, as in [8, 9]), can capture the complex interplay between several light sources and the environment, as will be demonstrated in the experimental section of the paper.

2. IMAGILIGHT

The proposed solution, ImagiLight, consists of four basic steps: 1. Installation; 2. Basis functions acquisition; 3. Computation of the solution; 4. Rendering of solution.

Installation: A room is fitted with a lighting system composed by luminaires individually controllable via wireless or wired communication (e.g. DALI, DMX). We require each luminaire to be dimmable at any desired value between

*Area chair: Pal Halvorsen

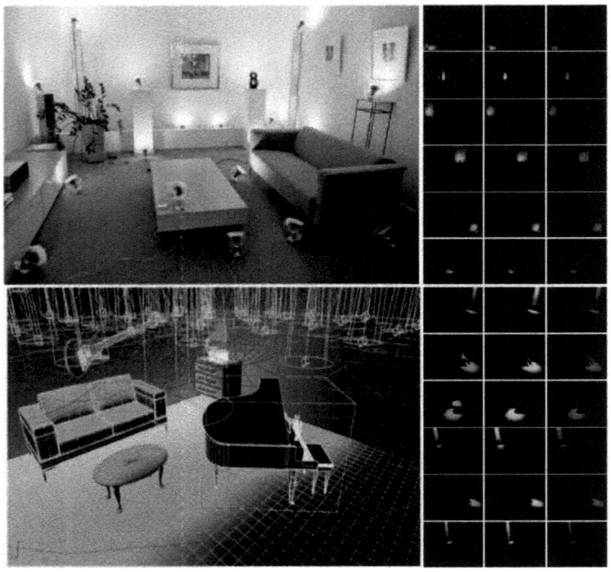

Figure 1: Real (top) and synthetic (bottom) rooms used for testing the proposed approach. The right side shows some of the calibration images for the two setups.

0 and 1, 0 being completely off, 1 being the maximum intensity possible. In the case of colored RGB light sources, each channel should be individually addressable, i.e. RGB luminaires are treated as three independent red, green and blue luminaires. In this work we tested the proposed approach in two different setups: a real and a virtual room. Both test rooms are shown in Fig. 1. More details about the experimental setup are given in Section 3.

Basis functions acquisition: A camera, placed at the position from which the light atmospheres should be enjoyed, acquires the contributions of each individual lamp on the scene. To allow for an affordable solution, we adopt a standard RGB camera as capturing device. During the acquisition process, each light primary is flashed individually at maximum intensity. We assume that the lighting elements are linear and acquire one image per channel, activated to its maximum driving value. The light effect at any value between 0 and the maximum is approximated as a linearly scaled version of the image captured at the maximum value. At the end of the process, a basis function set composed of N images showing the effect of each primary of each light source on the environment is available. The right side of Fig. 1 shows some of the calibration images acquired in a real (top) and a virtual room (bottom).

Computation of the solution: The user selects any desired image or video, which should be rendered by the lighting system, from the point of view from which the basis functions set was acquired. Using these images, an optimal solution is automatically computed. We devote Section 2.1 to the description of the algorithm.

Rendering of solution: The computed solution is rendered by the system, sending to each lamp the optimal activation value for each channel.

2.1 Optimal sparse solution

We adopt a notation in which matrices are expressed as bold capital letters and vectors as bold letters. We resize the input RGB digital image, $\mathbf{Y}$, and the basis functions to identical dimensions $u \times v \times 3$. We reshape $\mathbf{Y}$ into a column vector $\mathbf{y} \in \mathbb{R}^w$, while the basis functions are arranged into a matrix $\mathbf{D} = \mathbb{R}^{w \times N}$, of which the columns contain all the reshaped basis functions $\mathbf{d}_i \in \mathbb{R}^w$, with $w = 3uv$.

Assuming the lights to behave linearly with respect to dimming levels, and relying on the Grassmann's law of additive color matching, we can rewrite the problem of approximating the target image $\mathbf{Y}$ using the lights in the room as $\mathbf{y} = \mathbf{Dx}$. $\mathbf{x} \in \mathbb{R}^N$ is a vector of coefficients expressing the activations of each channel of each lamp, thus $\mathbf{x} \in [0, 1]$. Since we typically have fewer basis vectors than measurements (number of color pixels w), $N < w$. To find the optimal $\hat{\mathbf{x}}$ we have thus to solve the over-determined system of equation with constraints:

$$\hat{\mathbf{x}} = \arg\min \|\mathbf{y} - \mathbf{Dx}\|_2, \text{ subject to } \mathbf{x} \in [0, 1]. \quad (1)$$

One option to solve the problem (1) is to use Non-negative Least Squares (NNLS), scaling the coefficients to the interval $[0, 1]$, as in [8, 9]. In Sec. 3 we will briefly discuss results obtained using the NNLS method in our framework.

One alternative to Non-negative Least Squares is Matching Pursuit (MP) [4]. MP is a greedy algorithm that solves Eq. (1) iteratively. MP is an iterative method that selects the weighting coefficients in order of importance. Thus the first coefficient computed is the one corresponding to the light with the highest contribution to the scene, and so on. This makes the representation scalable, meaning that the process can be stopped at any moment, being sure that at the time (one of) the best possible solution is available. Furthermore, the algorithm is simple enough to allow for real-time implementation on common hardware.

Let us initialize a residual image $\mathbf{r}^0 = \mathbf{y}$ at iteration $i = 1$. Standard MP solves Eq. (1) according to the following 2 steps procedure:

1. **Basis selection:** at iteration i the index of the optimal light to be activated, $\hat{\jmath}$, is found. The inner products between all the basis functions $\mathbf{D}$ and the current residual $\mathbf{r}^{i-1}$ are computed as:
$$\mathbf{c}^i = |\mathbf{D}^T \mathbf{r}^{i-1}|, \quad (2)$$
where $\cdot^T$ indicates the transposition operator. The index of the optimal light, $\hat{\jmath}$, is selected as the one that gives the largest inner product between basis functions and residual, $\hat{\jmath} = \arg\max |\mathbf{c}^i|$. The contribution for lamp $\hat{\jmath}$ at iteration i is thus $\hat{c}^i_{\hat{\jmath}} = \mathbf{d}^{i^T}_{\hat{\jmath}} \mathbf{r}^{i-1}$.
2. **Residue and coefficient update:** remove from the residue the contribution of the basis function just selected, weighted by the corresponding coefficient:
$$\mathbf{r}^i = \mathbf{r}^{i-1} - \hat{c}^i_{\hat{\jmath}} \cdot \mathbf{d}^{i^T}_{\hat{\jmath}}, \quad (3)$$
and update the activation coefficient $\hat{x}^i_{\hat{\jmath}} = \hat{x}^i_{\hat{\jmath}} + \hat{c}^i_{\hat{\jmath}}$.

The procedure stops when the number of iterations i is larger than a predefined value K or when the value of the activation coefficient $\hat{c}^i_{\hat{\jmath}}$ falls below a certain threshold.

As already remarked, standard MP cannot be used here because the activation of each light component should be positive and not exceed 1. The modified algorithm, that we call Bounded-Non-negative Matching Pursuit (BNNMP), is described in detail in Algorithm 1. The main difference between the original MP algorithm and Algorithm 1 resides in step 4: this modification enforces that, after each iteration, no light is activated outside the physical limits $[0, 1]$.

Algorithm 1: Pseudo-code of the Bounded-Non-negative Matching Pursuit (BNNMP) algorithm.

Input: Basis vectors $\mathbf{D}$ and target image $\mathbf{y}$
Output: Lights activation coefficients $\hat{\mathbf{x}}$

– Normalize basis functions and target image
– Initialize cumulative light activation coefficients $\hat{x}_j = 0, j = 1, \ldots, N$

foreach *iteration* (i) **do**
  1. ValidCoefficientFound = FALSE
  2. Compute $c^i_j, j = 1, \ldots, N$, as in (2)
  3. Sort all $c^i_j, j = 1, \ldots, N$: $c^i_{j_s}$, $s = 1, \ldots, N$, $|c^i_{j_1}| \geq |c^i_{j_2}| \geq \ldots \geq |c^i_{j_N}|$
  for $s = 1$ **to** N **do**
    if $(\hat{x}_j = 1 \wedge c^i_{j_s} > 0) \vee (\hat{x}_j = 0 \wedge c^i_{j_s} < 0)$ **then**
      4. Continue
    else
      if $(\hat{x}_j + c^i_{j_s} \geq 0$ *AND* $\hat{x}_j + c^i_{j_s} \leq 1)$ **then**
        4. $\hat{c}^i_j = c^i_{j_s}$
      else
        if $\hat{x}_j + c^i_{j_s} > 1$ **then**
          4. $\hat{c}^i_j = 1 - \hat{x}_j$
        else
          4. $\hat{c}^i_j = -\hat{x}_j$
      5. ValidCoefficientFound = TRUE
  if *ValidCoefficientFound = FALSE* **then**
    6. Stop
  else
    6. Update cumulative activation coefficient: $\hat{x}_j = \hat{x}_j + \hat{c}^i_j$
    7. Update residue, as described in (3)

3. EXPERIMENTAL RESULTS

3.1 Experiments in virtual and real rooms

The target atmospheres are specified through input images. We use a database of 1000 input images automatically retrieved from the web using the query "colorful", "saturated", "panorama". The real room is fitted with 19 RGB Philips LivingColors lamps, for a total of 57 addressable channels. All light channels can be set using a DMX controller. We use a Philips SPC900 webcam as capturing device. The DMX controller, webcam and rendering algorithms run on a standard PC. A picture of the test room is shown in Fig. 1 (top). To easily test more complex lighting installations we designed a virtual room using Autodesk 3D Studio Max 9. Once the geometry and the materials in the room were defined, 46 RGB light spots were added, for a total of 138 addressable channels. Fig. 1 (bottom) shows an image of the design of the virtual room. To simulate the presence of a camera capturing the effect of the lights on the room, a separate rendering of each light channel was calculated. Please note that these renderings were directly adopted as images captured by a real camera, and the same algorithm used for the real setup was used to generate light activation values. The final light atmosphere can be obtained by combining the rendered basis functions with the activation coefficients computed with *ImagiLight.*

Figure 2 shows rendering results obtained with the proposed method applied to few target images selected from our database, for the two setups. In all cases the input images were down-sampled to 30×20 pixels and the results were computed with the BNNMP algorithm run for 200 iterations. As expected, the availability of more lights makes the rendering in the virtual room more faithful. To this regard, it is important to keep in mind that the images of the rendering in the real room were acquired with a standard webcam with limited dynamic range.

Figure 2: Results obtained with the proposed method. First column: target image. Second column: rendering in the virtual room setup. Third column: rendering in the real room setup.

Algorithm	PSNR	Time
BNNMP (0.5)	11.96 ± 1.30	$0.12s$
BNNMP (0.7)	12.35 ± 1.30	$0.16s$
BNNMP (1.0)	12.64 ± 1.31	$0.22s$
BNNMP (2.0)	12.90 ± 1.33	$0.38s$
NNLS	12.94 ± 1.31	$2.30s$

Table 1: Performance of the BNNMP algorithm with $0.5N$, $0.7N$, N and $2N$ iterations ($N = 138$), and NNLS, for the virtual room setup.

In order to quantify the quality of the rendered atmospheres, the target image and the picture of the rendered atmosphere are converted into the CIELab color space. CIELab is a more perceptually uniform color space than RGB, meaning that a change of the same amount in a color value produces a change of about the same visual importance. As a measure of rendering quality, we use the peak signal-to-noise ratio (PSNR) between the target and rendered images. We do not expect this metric to be utterly precise, the PSNR should rather reflect the relative differences between the different algorithmic settings.

Table 1 lists the PSNR values (average $\pm$ standard deviation (STD)) computed for the complete image database using BNNMP and NNLS on the virtual room. Four different settings for the maximum number K of iteration of BNNMP are used: $0.5N$, $0.7N$, N and $2N$, where N is the number of controllable light channels (138 for the virtual room). In addition to PSNR, the table shows the average time required to compute the solution. Computational time

Figure 3: Example of light painting interface realized using ImagiLight. A computer screen on the bottom right corner of each image shows the target image. Sequence is from left to right, top to bottom.

is estimated with unoptimized Matlab code, on a Intel Core 2.0 Ghz. All values are averaged over the 1000 test images.

As expected, PSNR values are extremely low in all cases, given the low number of controllable lights and the high dimensionality of the target images. PSNR values are close for all algorithmic settings, with NNLS and BNNMP with $K = 2N$ iterations exhibiting essentially similar rendering accuracy. In terms of speed of computation, the BNNMP method greatly outperforms NNLS. An attractive feature of the proposed BNNMP control algorithm is its scalability which allows to set the desired trade-off between rendering quality, energy consumption and speed. Table 1 also shows that the proposed method consistently and substantially outperforms NNLS in terms of computation speed.

For further results, illustrating extensions to video content rendering, please visit [1].

3.2 Application 1: Light painting

We developed a painting interface to allow a user to iteratively set the desired lighting atmosphere by simply painting the desired image content. While the example in Fig. 3 shows such interface running on a standard PC, future implementations would fit perfectly on touch-based tablet devices. We believe this scenario to be particularly attractive for light designers, allowing an extremely intuitive interface to test very advance lighting effects, focusing on the desired effect instead of the control parameters for each luminaire.

3.3 Application 2: Interactive installations

ImagiLight has been chosen as the core technology for the Flower Power interactive installation [5] at the 2010 STRP Festival in Eindhoven, one of the largest art and technology festivals in Europe. The installation involved 110 LED luminaires placed along the walls and on the ceiling of a large space surrounding a flower bed. Presence detectors located around the flower bed control the position of a camera suspended over the flowers, allowing visitors to move the camera location in a fun and cooperative interaction. Live images captured by the camera are fed into *ImagiLight* to control the overall lighting atmosphere as shown in Figure 4. The overall light scene is faithful to the input image, while being a suggestive abstraction of it with its saturated colors and its smooth, abstract shades.

4. CONCLUSIONS

ImagiLight extends traditional light control systems, providing an intuitive and powerful way of setting atmospheres

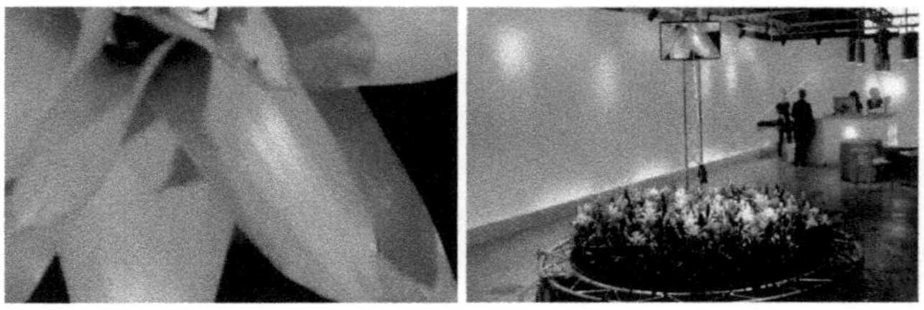

Figure 4: Image captured by the installation's camera [left] and rendered light atmosphere [right].

in arbitrarily complex lighting systems by automatically approximating user-defined input images representing the desired light atmospheres. The proposed method is fast and can be implemented in real time with common hardware. The method allows for scalability, so that the new capabilities of an updated lighting system can be quickly exploited. Despite its simplicity, *ImagiLight* can reproduce rich, evocative atmospheres. The effectiveness of the system was shown in the example applications of light painting, and interactive installations. We foresee that the versatility of the proposed method allows its deployment in several contexts: personalized atmosphere creation for home, retail, hospitality, museums and art installations.

The quality of obtained renderings could be further improved by adopting a combination of HDR image acquisition [8,9] to increase the available dynamic range and color-calibrating the camera to linearize its response [6,8,9].

5. REFERENCES

[1] Imagilight videos, 2011. [Online] Available: `https://sites.google.com/site/tommasogritti/publications/imagilight_videos`.

[2] ERCO. Erco guide. Technical report, 2007. [Online] Available: `http://www.erco.com`.

[3] S. Leppämäki. *The effect of exercise and light on mood.* PhD thesis, University of Helsinki, 2006.

[4] S. Mallat. *A Wavelet Tour of Signal Processing.* Academic Press, 1998.

[5] G. Monaci, T. Gritti, F. Vignoli, W. Walmink, and M. Hendriks. Flower Power. In *Proc. of ACM Multimedia*, 2011.

[6] G. Newsham and C. Arsenault. A camera as a sensor for lighting and shading control. *Lighting Research and Technology*, 41(2):143–163, 2009.

[7] G. Nichols, J. Shopf, and C. Wyman. Hierarchical image-space radiosity for interactive global illumination. *Comput. Graph. Forum*, 28(4):1141–1149, 2009.

[8] A. Sarkar, M. Fairchild, and C. Salvaggio. Integrated daylight harvesting and occupancy detection using digital imaging. In *Proc. of SPIE Sensors, Cameras and Systems for Industrial/Scientific Applications IX*, volume 6816, 2008.

[9] A. Sarkar and R. Mistrick. A novel lighting control system integrating high dynamic range imaging and dali. *LEUKOS*, 2(4):307–322, 2006.

[10] W. van Bommel and G. van den Beld. Lighting for work: A review of visual and biological effects. *Lighting Research and Technology*, 36(4):255–266, 2004.

Consensus-based Cross-correlation*

Florian Schweiger[1], Georg Schroth[1], Michael Eichhorn[1], Eckehard Steinbach[1], Michael Fahrmair[2]
[1]Technische Universität München, Munich, Germany
[2]DOCOMO Euro-Labs, Munich, Germany
florian.schweiger@tum.de

ABSTRACT

Cross-correlation is a classical similarity measure with broad applications in multimedia signal processing. While it is robust against uncorrelated noise in the input signals, it is severely affected by systematic disturbances which lead to biased results. To overcome this limitation, we propose in this paper consensus-based cross-correlation (ConCor) to deal with heavily corrupted signal parts that derail regular cross-correlation. ConCor builds upon the widely adopted RANSAC algorithm to reliably identify and eliminate corrupt signal parts at limited additional complexity. Our approach is universal in that it can be combined with existing cross-correlation variants. We apply ConCor in two example applications, namely video synchronization and template matching. Our experimental results demonstrate the improved robustness and accuracy when compared to classical cross-correlation.

Categories and Subject Descriptors: I.5.4 [Pattern Recognition]: Applications — signal processing, computer vision

General Terms: Algorithms

Keywords: Robust correlation, synchronization, template matching

1. INTRODUCTION

Cross-correlation is an important standard tool in signal processing, with applications ranging from image, video and audio processing to econometrics and physics. The cross-correlation function of two N-dimensional, discrete sequences is defined as

$$c(\Delta t) = \sum_{t \in \mathcal{T}} a(t+\Delta t)\, b^{*}(t), \quad t, \Delta t \in \mathbb{Z}^N \tag{1}$$

where the asterisk denotes complex conjugation and $\mathcal{T}$ is the set of sample indices where both $a(t+\Delta t)$ and $b(t)$ are defined.

*Area chair: Wei Tsang Ooi

MM'11, November 28–December 1, 2011, Scottsdale, Arizona, USA.

For every offset Δt, the cross-correlation function measures the similarity between the first signal and the second, accordingly shifted signal. If there is a statistical correlation between the two signals, the cross-correlation function will attain high values for the respective offsets. More precisely, if the random processes generating the samples of a and b are jointly ergodic and zero-mean, then $c(\Delta t)$ is an estimate for the covariance of the two processes shifted with respect to each other by Δt.

A variant commonly used in image processing is *zero-mean normalized cross-correlation (ZNCC)* where the input signals are normalized with their mean and standard deviation over the region defined by $\mathcal{T}$. It is equivalent to the Pearson correlation coefficient between the accordingly shifted signals, and has the advantage of fair comparison even if the signals are on different overall levels.

Cross-correlation is prone to failure if the signals are excessively corrupted. While it is relatively insusceptible to additive white noise, the effects of non-stationary disturbances are more severe. If the signals include burst-wise errors, *e.g.*, due to dominant crosstalk components or occlusions, the cross-correlation function can contain side maxima in the same order of magnitude as the peak at the true offset.

A robust alternative are *rank correlation* approaches which do not consider the actual values of the input signals but rather their ranked order. They increase robustness against isolated errors, comparable to the advantage of the median filter over regular averaging, but reach their limit in the case of burst errors. Two widely used rank correlation measures are *Spearman's Rho* and *Kendall's Tau* [6].

Our *consensus-based cross-correlation (ConCor)* approach presented in Section 2 specifically addresses the problem of burst disturbances. Most notably, it is compatible with the above mentioned cross-correlation variants. Initially developed for 1-D time series encountered in the video synchronization application discussed in Section 3.1, ConCor has proved to be a versatile tool applicable to other classes of signals as well.

1.1 Applications

The basic purpose of cross-correlation is to retrieve the fundamental similarities between two signals which are otherwise obscured by adverse effects such as noise. Generally speaking, it is employed whenever a certain pattern needs to be detected in a signal or when the shift between two matching signals is to be determined.

In image processing, for instance, two-dimensional cross-correlation is used in template matching, *i.e.*, in order to identify known shapes in an image, or to determine the disparity of pixels between images [2].

Another application is beat detection in audio processing. In [8], music tracks are analyzed in this respect by cross-correlating them with reference signals of known tempo.

One of the example applications discussed in Section 3 deals with the problem of video synchronization. Based on one-dimensional time-series extracted frame-wise from two videos [12, 10], cross-correlation is used to find their temporal offset.

Outside the multimedia domain, cross-correlation is used, for instance, in telecommunications to detect template signals of known shape in a noisy receive signal. In econometrics, cross-correlation serves as an important tool to examine the relationships between time series [9]. In physics, cross-correlation is used among others to determine astronomical Doppler shifts from observed spectra, *e.g.*, [11].

1.2 Related Work

There are several works which aim at robust cross-correlation in the presence of errors in either of the input signals. The mentioned rank correlation measures are examples of correlation approaches robust against single spurious samples.

The case where contiguous samples are corrupted is often encountered in image processing, in the form of occlusions. In fact, many cross-correlation variants robust against burst disturbances originate from that field. An extensive overview of correlation measures for the purpose of template matching can be found in [3] and [1]. The general approach is to determine a mask identifying corrupted samples, either prior to or while performing the actual cross-correlation. In [5], for every examined shift Δt, corresponding pixels are judged with regard to their incremental behavior. Only if the gray values of both behave qualitatively the same compared to their left neighbors, they are considered in the correlation measure, otherwise masked out. In another approach, presented in [7], the first signal is transformed into the second, following an affine model which is robustly fitted using LMedS, again repeatedly for every shift Δt. Only at the true offset, this fit is meaningful. For all other shifts, the affine model does not hold and can only be established by force. This is inefficient and time-consuming, and results in completely unfounded cross-correlation values. This fundamental problem is also inherent to [5].

A main difference of ConCor is that robust model fitting is not performed based on the original data samples but on precomputed partial cross-correlation functions. Instead of trying to establish a model between the sample values of both signals for every hypothesized shift, we fit a simple offset model seeking support from the majority of signal parts.

2. CONCOR

Our assumption is that major parts of the signals are free of errors, and only some, locally limited portions are corrupted. The input data can hence be divided into good and bad segments, and we will use the established RANSAC algorithm [4] to determine this separation.

2.1 Principle

The basic idea behind consensus-based cross-correlation is to split one of the signals into shorter segments b_i of length M, and to cross-correlate each of them individually with the second signal. Explicitly, for the 1-D case:

$$b_i(t) = \begin{cases} b(t) & : (i-1)M \le t < iM \\ 0 & : \text{else} \end{cases}$$

$$c_i(\Delta t) = \sum_t a(t + \Delta t)\, b_i^*(t)$$

The so obtained partial cross-correlation functions (PCCF) c_i are then combined in a RANSAC motivated manner in order to separate the corrupted segments from the valid ones. In terms of RANSAC, the model to be fitted is the offset, hence an N-D vector. The data points are the PCCFs which are combined, *i.e.*, summed up in order to determine potential offset candidates. Obviously, the sum of all PCCFs yields the cross-correlation function of the original signals:

$$\sum_i c_i(\Delta t) = \sum_i \sum_t a(t+\Delta t)\, b_i^*(t) = \sum_t a(t+\Delta t) \sum_i b_i^*(t)$$
$$= \sum_t a(t+\Delta t)\, b^*(t) = c(\Delta t)$$

By omitting outlier PCCFs in the above summation, we are able to exclude their influence on the resulting cross-correlation function.

The algorithm below summarizes our proposed *consensus-based cross-correlation* approach given two input sequences $a(t)$ and $b(t)$.

The ConCor Algorithm:

1	Chop shorter signal in segments $b_i(t)$ of length M.
2	Compute the PCCFs $c_i(\Delta t) = \sum a(t+\Delta t)\, b_i^*(t)$.
Repeat	
3 a	Make a random selection of s PCCFs and compute their sum.
3 b	Extract candidate offsets from that sum.
3 c	For every offset candidate, evaluate the number of consenting PCCFs (inliers).
.... *until confidence is reached that at least one outlier-free PCCF set has been selected.*	
4	Select the offset with most inlier PCCFs.
5	Recompute the offset from the sum of inlier PCCFs.

As is usual for RANSAC, the stop criterion for the loop over steps 3abc is determined online, based on the worst case estimate of the outlier ratio.

A side benefit of ConCor is that it still yields meaningful results for large offsets where the overlap between a and b decreases. In regular cross-correlation, when the set $\mathcal{T}$ in Eq. (1) becomes significantly smaller, less and less samples contribute, and any kind of normalization becomes unstable. With ConCor, this issue is taken care of automatically. Segments b_i that fall outside the overlap region defined by $\mathcal{T}$ are simply deemed outliers, while the remaining segments still have the chance to vote for or against a given offset.

2.2 Model Fitting and Outlier Identification

In principle, a single PCCF is sufficient to determine the offset between the input signals. The minimum number of data points required to fit the model is hence $s=1$. However, PCCFs and their combinations are more trustworthy when more samples have been involved in their computation. Consequently, the total number of samples sM should be raised to a maximum. In general, increasing s, hence combining several small segments rather than using a single large segment, leads to a better chance of avoiding corrupted signal parts. Of course, including more samples always increases the risk of introducing corrupt samples. This trade-off in the choice of s and M is application-specific and depends on the burst error distribution expected for the considered class of signals.

A combination of PCCFs does not necessarily exhibit a single, conclusive peak. Instead, it will contain several local maxima of comparable strength, leading to more than one candidate offset. In our implementation, all candidates are kept, and each one undergoes a consensus check with respect to the remaining PCCFs. Several consensus measures are conceivable, including the absolute or relative PCCF value at the examined offset, or even its curvature. In the examples presented in Section 3, a PCCF votes for an offset candidate if it has a local maximum in close proximity to it.

Depending on the application, it might be necessary to mitigate noise effects in order to reduce the number of spurious offset candidates. This can be accomplished by morphological closure which preserves the exact position of the surviving, most meaningful peaks.

3. EXAMPLE APPLICATIONS

In the following, we present results obtained with ConCor in two very different scenarios. The first one introduces the video synchronization application ConCor was initially developed for. Here, 1-D signals are cross-correlated to determine their temporal offset. To emphasize its generality, we also apply ConCor to 2-D signals, namely in the context of template matching in the presence of occlusions.

3.1 Video Synchronization

In order to find the temporal offset between two video sequences, a common approach is to reduce the video data to one-dimensional time series that reflect characteristic scene changes over time. In the following, we use the method proposed in [10] to generate such time series, where, in a nutshell, high signal values correspond to scene motion in the video. The signals are zero-mean and normalized by their standard deviation.

The videos used in this example were captured with stationary cameras and show the same scene of a person acting in front of a static background, eventually hiding inside a paper bank. In the course of the action, a group of passers-by traverse the scene. Figure 1 shows the two input signals together with example frames from the respective videos. In this experiment, we segment the second signal into snippets containing $M = 100$ frames (step 1 of the above described algorithm). The computed PCCFs (step 2) are plotted in Figure 2. During the random selection process (step 3a), $s = 3$ of the segments are combined to determine potential offsets. Prior to local maximum extraction (step 3b), and the consensus check (step 3c), we apply morphological closure to the respective signals using a structuring element which is 51 frames wide. This is necessary to eliminate the effects of parasitic oscillations specific to this kind of signals. A PCCF votes for a given offset candidate if its closest local maximum is no further than 10 frames away. Eventually, the offset is determined from the unsmoothed combination

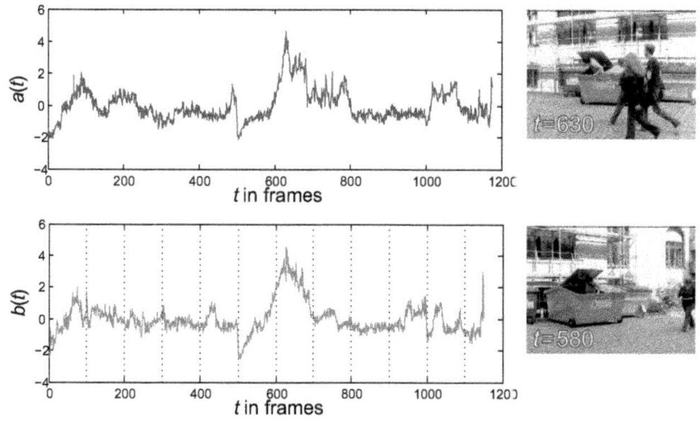

Figure 1: The two input signals a and b and synchronous frames from the video sequences they have been derived from. The segmentation of b is indicated by the dotted vertical lines.

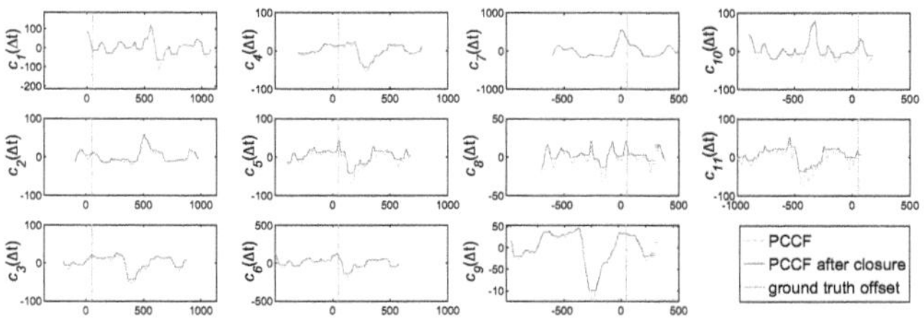

Figure 2: The partial cross-correlation functions (PCCF) corresponding to the signals in Fig. 1

of the largest set of inlier PCCFs (step 5), achieving frame accurate synchronization, which is illustrated in Figure 4.

For comparison, Figure 3 shows the results obtained by zero-mean normalized cross-correlation (ZNCC) of the sequences $a(t)$ and $b(t)$. The deviation of the found offset from ground truth is caused by effects at the image borders. Due to the different viewpoints of the involved cameras, people entering and leaving the scene trigger fluctuations which occur slightly delayed in the 1-D signals. The rather strong peak around frame 700 is a result of this effect, caused by the group of passers-by. Regular cross-correlation approaches tend to align such dominant signal parts at any rate, ignoring the smaller yet more consistent parts in the signals.

ConCor deals with this problem by expelling singular segments. Figure 4 shows the cross-correlation function computed from inlier segments only, *i.e.*, $c_2 + c_3 + c_5 + c_8 + c_{11}$, together with the resulting alignment.

3.2 Template Matching

We now turn to the template matching application illustrated in Figure 6, where a book cover with 357×500 pixels is to be recovered in a 1280×960 pixel image. Working with four-fold down-sampled versions of the images, normalized by their global mean and standard deviation, we segment the template into a grid of 6×8 blocks and run ConCor as described previously. In every iteration, $s = 3$ blocks are combined and the inlier threshold is set to 5 pixels. In this case, morphological filtering is not required.

In Figure 5, the conventional cross-correlation function is compared to the one obtained from the inliers determined by ConCor. While the correct peak would otherwise be obscured, ConCor succeeds in retrieving it.

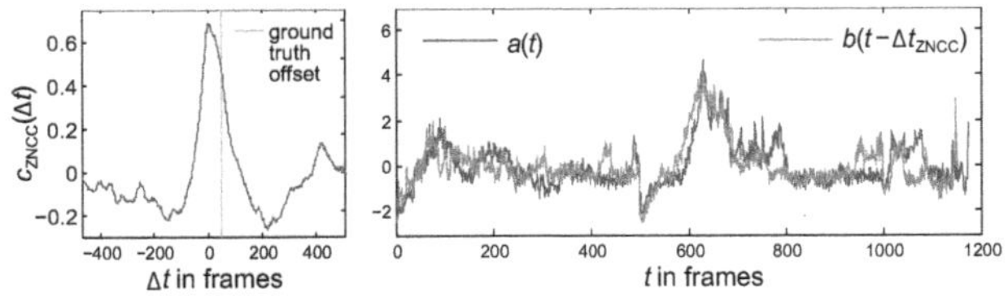

Figure 3: Conventional ZNCC of signals a and b yields an incorrect offset of $\Delta t_{\mathrm{ZNCC}} = 1$ frame. This is due to the dominant, erroneous peak between frames 500 and 700 whose alignment is enforced.

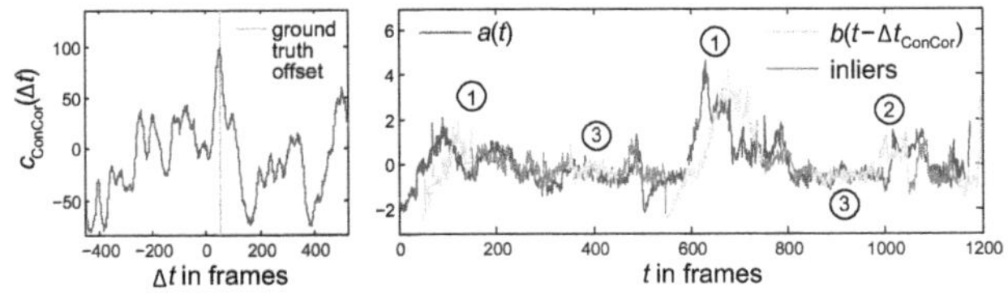

Figure 4: ConCor yields the correct offset $\Delta t_{\mathrm{ConCor}} = 50$ frames. In particular, it discards segments b_i where ① people enter the scene from the right, ② people walk in from the left, and ③ where there is not enough scene motion to reasonably establish temporal relationships between both videos.

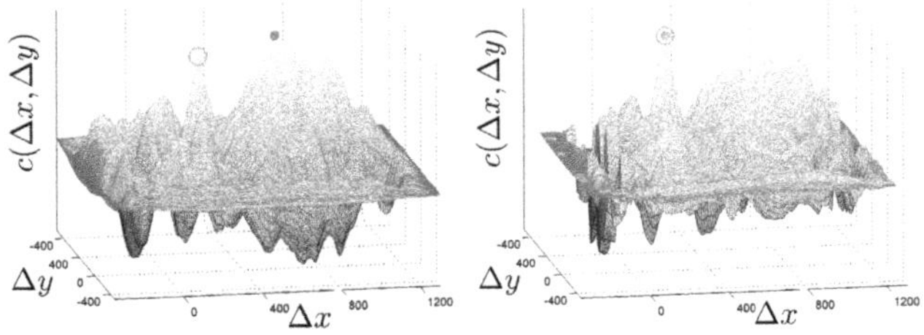

Figure 5: Regular cross-correlation (left) versus ConCor (right). The highest peaks are marked with bullets, the correct one with a circle (see Fig. 6).

Figure 6: The template (left) and its position in the right image as found by regular cross-correlation (dashed red) and by ConCor (solid green). The highlighted template blocks are deemed outliers, either due to occlusion or the lack of distinctiveness.

Compared to approaches in the style of [7], the complexity of ConCor is significantly lower. The initial computation of PCCFs requires the same number of operations as conventional cross-correlation for the entire signals. On top of that, RANSAC needs to be applied on a relatively small data set, here consisting of 48 blocks. The method of [7] works on all the template pixels, repeatedly fitting an affine model between the shifted template and the image. Except at the true offset, this is highly inefficient as the outlier ratio increases tremendously with the displacement, which requires a maximum number of random draws in the model fitting process.

Both [5] and [7] yield pixel-wise occlusion masks. In this respect, masking by ConCor is more conservative. Not only does it dismiss occluded parts that would impair cross-correlation, it also excludes regions which are not distinctive enough to make a relevant contribution. If required, a precise occlusion mask can be obtained from the ConCor result by pixel-wise comparison.

4. CONCLUSION

The consensus-based cross-correlation strategy we have proposed is a versatile extension to achieve robustness to burst errors in the input signals. It can replace conventional cross-correlation approaches irrespective of the application at hand. Initially conceived for 1-D time-series encountered in video synchronization, we have shown that ConCor can also be applied to higher dimensional data. The outlier classification strategy and the involved parameters might need to be adapted to the specific signal class. However, these parameters have not proved overly critical in our experiments.

5. REFERENCES

[1] P. Aschwanden and W. Guggenbühl. Experimental results from a comparative study on correlation-type registration algorithms. In *ISPRS Workshop*, pages 268–282, Washington, D.C., Aug. 1992.

[2] R. Brunelli. *Template matching techniques in computer vision*. John Wiley & Sons Ltd, Mar. 2009.

[3] S. Chambon and A. Crouzil. Similarity measures for image matching despite occlusions in stereo vision. *Pattern Recognition*, 2011.

[4] M. Fischler and R. Bolles. Random sample consensus: A paradigm for model fitting with applications to image analysis and automated cartography. *Communications of the ACM*, 24(6):381–395, June 1981.

[5] S. Kaneko, Y. Satoh, and S. Igarashi. Using selective correlation coefficient for robust image registration. *Pattern Recognition*, 36(5):1165–1173, May 2003.

[6] M. Kendall and J. D. Gibbons. *Rank correlation methods*. A Charles Griffin Title, 5th edition, Sept. 1990.

[7] Z. Lan, R. Mohr, and P. Remagnino. Robust matching by partial correlation. In *British Machine Vision Conference*, pages 651–660, Birmingham, U.K, Sept. 1995.

[8] J. Laroche. Efficient tempo and beat tracking in audio recordings. *Journal of the Audio Engineering Society*, 51(4):226–233, Apr. 2003.

[9] D. Pierce. Relationships – and the lack thereof – between economic time series, with special reference to money and interest rates. *Journal of the American Statistical Association*, 72(357):11–26, Mar. 1977.

[10] G. Schroth, F. Schweiger, M. Eichhorn, E. Steinbach, M. Fahrmair, and W. Kellerer. Video synchronization using bit rate profiles. In *International Conference on Image Processing*, Hong Kong, Sept. 2010.

[11] S. Simkin. Measurements of velocity dispersions and doppler shifts from digitized optical spectra. *Astronomy and Astrophysics*, 31(2):129–136, Mar. 1974.

[12] J. Yan and M. Pollefeys. Video synchronization via space-time interest point distribution. In *Advanced Concepts for Intelligent Vision Systems*, Brussels, Belgium, Aug. 2004.

Modeling Motion Visual Perception for Video Quality Assessment

Junyong You
Norwegian University of Science and Technology
Trondheim, Norway
junyong.you@acm.org

Touradj Ebrahimi
École Polytechnique Fédérale de Lausanne
Lausanne, Switzerland
touradj.ebrahimi@epfl.ch

Andrew Perkis
Norwegian University of Science and Technology
Trondheim, Norway
andrew@iet.ntnu.no

ABSTRACT

Contrast sensitivity of Human Visual System (HVS) plays an important role in perceiving visual stimuli, and consequently, it has a significant impact on the perceived video quality. This paper proposes a visual perception model based on foveated vision and motion perception. The reference and the distorted video sequences are processed by the visual perception model to generate the perceived stimuli in HVS. The perceived difference of the processed sequences is measured in spatial and temporal domains considering the visual sensitivity. An advanced pooling scheme is proposed based on the visual attention mechanism, eye movement type, and influence of temporal quality variation, in order to estimate the perceived video quality. Experimental results demonstrate that the proposed metric significantly outperforms state-of-the-art quality models with respect to a combined eye-tracking and subjective video quality assessment data set.

Categories and Subject Descriptors

I.4.10 [**IMAGE PROCESSING AND COMPUTER VISION**]: Image Representation

General Terms: Algorithms, measurement

Keywords: Contrast sensitivity, foveated vision, motion perception, Quality of Experience, visual attention

1. INTRODUCTION

With the advent of multimedia evolution, a critical task for multimedia services is to provide consumers with the best Quality of Experience (QoE). Consequently, perceived video quality assessment plays a kernel role in visual signal processing chain starting from acquisition, to compression, transmission, and finally to display, as different artefacts might be introduced at each stage in the whole chain. Some traditionally and widely used metrics, such as MSE and PSNR, have been demonstrated to be poorly correlated with subjective quality judgment, as the characteristics of Human Visual System (HVS) are not taken into account in their design. In order to accurately evaluate and then monitor the perceived quality of visual signals in the processing chain, more accurate quality metrics are expected considering high-level characteristics of human visual and perception systems.

*Area Chair: Pål Halvorsen.

MM'11, November 28–December 1, 2011, Scottsdale, Arizona, USA.

In normal situations when viewing a scene, the visual perception is always guided by an integral mechanism in the HVS, called visual attention, as the human brain is not able to process all the potentially available stimuli at once when subjected to different sources of sensory information. Therefore, viewers track and gaze at interesting regions by different eye movements, such as smooth pursuit and fixation. Subsequently, visual signals are processed by the visual perception mechanisms in the HVS to generate the perception in the brain, among which the contrast sensitivity function plays an important role in filtering the original signals. Due to the non-uniform distribution of the photo-receptors and in particular cone cells on the retina, the HVS has the highest resolution around the fixation point of eyes and dramatically decreases away from this point, as a function of eccentricity [1]. This is usually called foveated vision, which indicates that the HVS has different sensitivities to different spatial frequencies and locations when perceiving static visual stimuli. On the other hand, motion also has a significant impact on the contrast sensitivity when viewing video. Generally speaking, the contrast sensitivity reduces with increasing motion velocity, which is usually modeled by the spatiotemporal contrast sensitivity function. In [2], Kelly has proposed an engineering model to formulize the contrast sensitivity as a function of spatial frequency and retinal velocity. However, to the best of our knowledge, there are no integrated models proposed to combine the static foveated vision and motion guided sensitivity, in the literature. Even though the spatio-temporal contrast sensitivity function is non-separable, some visual experiments have observed that the decrease slope of the sensitivity with increasing eccentricity is independent of temporal frequency [3]. This observation motivates us to develop an accurate motion tuned foveation model in this work to generate accurate perception of video stimuli in the HVS.

Since the contrast sensitivity plays an important role in generation of visual perception, it naturally influences the assessment of quality degradations. Video quality models based on the static foveated vision mechanism have been proposed, and demonstrate better performance when compared to other metrics that do not consider such a mechanism [4]. However, the motion perception is not taken into account when developing these models, which might degrade their performance for evaluation of the perceived video quality. In [5], the authors use retinal velocity to adjust the maximum visible frequency at a given eccentricity. This approach might be unnatural because human vision has prior sensitivity to moving stimuli than static ones when viewing video sequences. Additionally, both the visual attention mechanism and temporal quality distortions are ignored in [5]. The importance of applying visual attention mechanism in quality assessment is twofold. First, determining fixation points is mainly driven by the attention mechanism. Viewer's fixation always gazes at the regions that can attract their attention. Actually, visual attention mechanism is usually ignored in existing foveated-based solutions for visual signal compression and quality assessment [4, 5], in which the center of images is often selected as the fixation point. Second, visual attention itself also has a significant impact on quality assessment, as one can assume that less attentive regions have more tolerance to quality degradations when compared to attended regions. In this work, a combined eye-tracking and quality assessment experiment [6] is employed to develop a video quality metric based on fixation points recorded in the eye-tracking experiment and to derive attentive information.

The remainder of the paper is organized as follows. Section 2 presents an improved visual perception model. The proposed quality metric based on spatial-temporal distortions and pooling scheme is presented in Section 3. Section 4 reports the experimental results. Concluding remarks are given in Section 5.

2. VISUAL PERCEPTION MODEL

When viewing a visual stimulus in a quasi-static scene, the visual perception generated in the human brain is always guided by the foveated vision mechanism. The contrast threshold can be modeled by the spatial frequency (f) and retinal eccentricity (e) at different locations, as defined in Eq. (1):

$$CT(f,e) = CT_0 \cdot \exp(\alpha \cdot f \cdot \frac{e+e_2}{e_2}) \quad (1)$$

where the retinal eccentricity e in degrees is computed from the viewing distance and the distance between individual location and the fixation point. CT_0 is the minimum contrast threshold, α is the spatial frequency decay constant, and e_2 is the half-resolution eccentricity. In this work, we have chosen the best fitting values for the three parameters from the literature as: CT_0=1/75, α=0.106, e_2=2.3. The contrast sensitivity function is defined as the reciprocal of CT. For a given location and accordingly the eccentricity e, the highest visible frequency in static scenes can be estimated by setting CT to 1.0 (maximum possible contrast):

$$f_{\text{static}}(e) = \frac{e_2 \cdot \ln(1/CT_0)}{\alpha \cdot (e+e_2)} \text{ (cycles/degree)} \quad (2)$$

In order to generate the perception of a video frame in static scenes, we have built a 2D Gaussian pyramid on the frame image. At each decomposition level, the decomposed image is blurred and up-sampled to its original resolution. The blurred image is finally interpolated with the maximum visible frequency to generate the foveated presentation of the frame. This approach is similar to a foveated multi-resolution system developed in [1].

Furthermore, motion can significantly influence the contrast sensitivity when viewers watch a moving scene. Daly [2] fit a contrast sensitivity model to his experimental data based on the spatial frequency (f) and retinal velocity (v_R), defined as follows:

$$CSF(f,v_R) = k \cdot c_0 \cdot c_2 \cdot v_R \cdot (2\pi f c_1)^2 \cdot e^{-(4\pi f c_1)/\rho_{\max}}$$
$$k = 6.1 + 7.3 \cdot |\log(c_2 \cdot v_R/3)|^3,\ \rho_{\max} = 45.9/(c_2 \cdot v_R + 2) \quad (3)$$

The retinal velocity can be measured by compensating the eye movement from the object movement, i.e. $v_R = v_O - v_E$, in which v_O and v_E are the physical velocity of the object and the velocity of eye movement, respectively. In this work, the constants $\{c_0, c_1, c_2\}$ were set to 1.14, 0.67, and 1.7, respectively, following the experiments conducted by Daly [2]. The model achieves the maximum contrast sensitivity when the retinal velocity is near the drift eye movement (0.15 deg/sec). When the retinal velocity is above the drift eye movement, the contrast sensitivity will be reduced as the velocity increases.

Therefore, given a retinal velocity of an object, the maximum visible frequency of the object can be estimated by setting CSF to 1.0. The solution can be found by the Lambert's W function, noted as $f_{\text{motion}}(v_R)$. However, Eq. (3) is to measure the contrast sensitivity of the HVS to the object that the eyes are tracking. For other objects away from the fixation point, the maximum visible frequencies can also be influenced by the eccentricities, in addition to the motion velocities. As explained in Section 1, we first estimate the maximum visible frequency f_{motion} of each pixel determined by the retinal velocity, and then tune the maximum frequency by the eccentricity of an individual location.

$$f_{\max}(v_R,e) = f_{\text{motion}}(v_R) \cdot f_{\text{static}}(e) / f_{\text{static}}(0) \quad (4)$$

where $f_{\max}$ indicates the maximum visible frequency of a pixel at the retinal velocity v_R and the eccentricity of e. This model is reduced to the regular velocity-based contrast sensitivity when the eyes are gazing at a moving object; on the other hand, if the retinal velocity of a visual scene is close to the drift or fixation movement, Eq. (4) is then reduced to regular foveation-based contrast sensitivity as defined in Eq. (2). Subsequently, the maximum visible frequency determined by retinal velocity and eccentricity is interpolated with the decomposed frame image in the 2D Gaussian pyramid decomposition to generate the foveated presentation of the frame image in a moving scene.

In this work, we have employed the optical flow estimated by the Lucas-Kanade algorithm to simulate the physical velocity of an object. Eye movement velocity is measured between two fixation points in two frames. If the physical velocities of all the pixels in the frame are below the maximum drift velocity (0.8 deg/sec), this frame is assumed to be part of a static scene. The foveation-based operation is then performed to generate the foveated presentation. Otherwise, if the physical velocity is above drift movement, the frame is processed by the motion tuned foveation operation. Figure 1 illustrates a moving frame superimposed with the optical flow (down-sampled from the original flow for visualization) and the fixation point (red cross), the perceived presentation in HVS without considering the influence of motion on the sensitivity, and the perceived presentation when considering both the motion perception and foveated vision mechanism (from left to right).

Figure 1. Perceived presentations of a video frame image.

3. VIDEO QUALITY ASSESSMENT

3.1 Spatial-temporal Distortion Model

Existing foveation-based visual quality metrics are mainly based on comparing the difference between a reference signal and its distorted version filtered by the foveation operation [4, 5]. That means the quality degradation is evaluated using the form: $F(D)$, in which D denotes the difference and F is the foveation operation. However, visual quality evaluation is performed by comparing the difference of the perceived stimuli, generated through stimulation on retina and visual cortex, between the distorted and reference signals. Therefore, a visual quality metric can also be modeled as: $D(F)$, which indicates that the difference between two processed stimuli is used in the perception of quality. The results from the two different methodologies might also be different, as the foveation operation is non-linear.

The perception of each frame in the reference and the distorted sequences can be generated by the proposed visual perception model, in which the optical flow estimated from the reference video is used for both sequences. In this work, only the luminance plane is used in quality evaluation. On the other hand, the fixation point in a frame in the distorted video might be different from that in the reference video, because visual attention can be affected by localized distortions. In this case, we use two different fixation points for the reference and the distorted frames, and then generate their respective perceived presentations. Let the perceived presentations of reference and distorted frames be *F_R* and *F_D*, respectively. The squared-error is used to measure the perceived difference (*PD*) of the two presentations, defined as:

$$PD = (F\_D - F\_R)^2 \tag{5}$$

PD models the perceived difference of two sequences in spatial domain. For video quality assessment, it is also important to consider the distortion in temporal domain. Viewers can perceive smooth motion if there are no unexpected distortions along the motion directions of objects. Therefore, distortions interrupting smooth motion perception can significantly degrade the perceived video quality. As explained earlier, the contrast sensitivity at a given retinal velocity v_R and eccentricity e is defined as follows:

$$CS(f, v_R, e) = \begin{cases} CSF(f, v_R) \cdot f_{\max\_static}(e) / f_{\max\_static}(0), & f \le f_{\max} \\ 0, & f > f_{\max} \end{cases} \tag{6}$$

Subsequently, a temporal window spanning over several frames (8 in this work) is defined, within which an individual vector (*V*) for each pixel is generated composed of 8 elements along the motion direction. The 1D Gabor transform is performed on the vector to calculate the frequency response $R(k)=V*G(k)$, in which * denotes convolution, and $G(k)$, k=1,2,…,8 are the central frequencies of all the Gabor filters. Thus, the temporal perception of a moving pixel is calculated as follows in Eq. (7):

$$TP = \sum_{k=1}^{8} R(k) \cdot CS(k, v_R, e) \tag{7}$$

The temporal distortion is then evaluated by measuring the relative difference of the temporal perception between the reference and the distorted presentations, defined as follows:

$$TD = \frac{TP\_D - TP\_R + C}{TP\_R + C} \tag{8}$$

where *TP_D* and *TP_R* denote the temporal perception of the reference and distorted presentations, respectively, and *C* is a small constant (set as 0.01 in this work) to avoid instability when *TP_R* is close to zero. Finally, the temporal distortion measure *TD* is multiplied with the spatial difference *PD* to model the overall distortion between a reference frame and its distorted version.

3.2 Video Quality Metric based on Spatial-temporal Pooling Scheme

A perceived distortion map between each reference frame and the distorted frame is generated by the spatial-temporal distortion model. In order to calculate a single quality measure of a distorted video, the quality map should be pooled both in space and in time.

Before starting the pooling scheme, video frames under the saccadic movement (160-300 deg/sec) are first eliminated from quality computation, because the HVS has virtually no sensitivity during saccades. While during other two eye movement types: drift and smooth pursuit, the HVS usually has high sensitivity to visual stimuli. The eye movement types can be determined by the velocity between two consecutive fixation points: if it is larger than 160 deg/sec, we assume that the saccadic movement occurs.

Additionally, the visual attention mechanism is also taken into account in the spatial-temporal pooling, because less attended regions can be more tolerant to distortions. Attention intensity over different spatial locations in a frame can be expressed in the form of a fixation density map derived from all the fixation points recorded in the combined eye-tracking and quality assessment experiment [6]. For each fixation point, a 2D Gaussian filter with the same resolution as in the video frame is generated. The filter is centered at the fixation point and its variance is derived from the viewing angle (2° approximating the size of the fovea) and the viewing distance. Finally, all the Gaussian filters corresponding to all the effective fixation points are summed and normalized into the range [0, 1], that is taken as the fixation density map (FDM). Figure 2 illustrates an example of a frame image with all the fixation points (yellow circles), a single 2D Gaussian filter, and the fixation density map (from left to right).

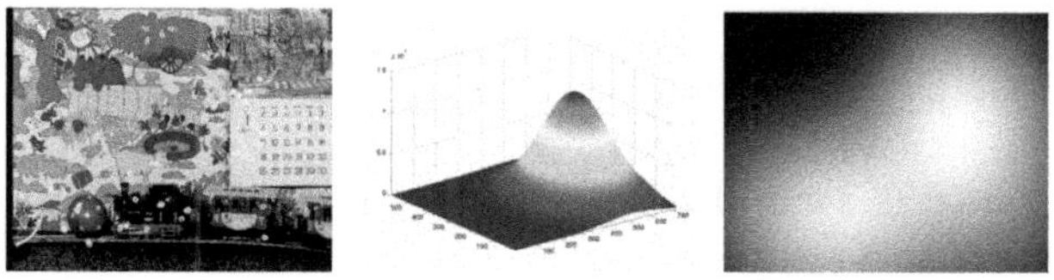

Figure 2. Image, 2D Gaussian filter, and fixation density map.

The frames, in which only fixation, drift, smooth pursuit movement, or both, exist, are divided into different segments. The segment duration is set to 250 ms, the average fixation duration. Moreover, if the correlation between two consecutive FDMs in a segment is below an empirical threshold (0.95 in our experiments), that segment is then sub-divided into two shorter segments. Thus, we can assume that the attention intensities of different frames in a segment are similar to each other. The first pooling step is a short-term temporal pooling performed in each segment. The large temporal variations of distortions are usually more annoying for viewers than limited temporal variations of distortions. We adopt a pooling scheme proposed in [7] to model the influence of temporal quality variations on the quality evaluation in each segment. The distortion gradient *D'* is first computed at each pixel, and then the short-term pooling is performed as follows:

$$Q_1 = mean(D) \cdot \{1 + 3 \cdot \max(D') \cdot fs[sign(D')]\} \tag{9}$$

where *mean*(*D*) denotes the average of the distortion map values over all the frames in the segment, *sign*(*D'*) is the number of sign changes of *D'*, and *fs* is the response of the following filter dependent on the number of sign changes (*n*):

$$fs(n) = \frac{e^{-(n-1)^2/(2\cdot\sigma^2)}}{\sigma \cdot \sqrt{2\pi}} \tag{10}$$

The short-term temporal pooling generates a single pooled distortion map in a segment, which is then pooled in space with the fixation density map: $Q_2=\sum(Q_1 \cdot \text{AFDM})$ to calculate a single quality value for each segment, in which AFDM denotes the averaged fixation density map over all the frames in the segment.

Finally, the quality measure of the distorted video is calculated by a long-term temporal pooling over all the segments as follows:

$$Q = (1 + \frac{1}{TV}) \cdot \sum(Q_2 \cdot TPF) \tag{11}$$

where *TV* denotes the total variation of Q_2 over all the segments, and *TPF* is the filtered result of a function defined in Eq. (12) by the Gaussian filter for several times (typically 8) [8].

$$F(k)=\begin{cases}1/L, & k \le L/3 \quad (k\text{: segment index}) \\ 1/(2L), & L/3 < k < 2L/3 \quad (L\text{: number of segments}) \\ 3/(2L), & k \ge 2L/3\end{cases} \qquad (12)$$

4. EXPERIMENT

A combined eye-tracking and video quality assessment data set [6] was employed in our experiments. In this data set, twenty video sequences were compressed with H.264/AVC and then four different packet loss patterns were introduced to each stream. The eye-tracking and video quality assessment was performed by 30 non-expert participants seated at a distance of about 150 cm. Because only one single fixation point is used in the proposed visual perception model, the point achieving the peak value in the fixation density map of each video frame is selected as the fixation point of that frame. The velocity of eye movement is computed between two consecutive fixation points.

To evaluate the performance of the proposed quality metric, we implemented other two foveation-based video quality models, FWSNR [4] and FMSE [5]. Additionally, two popular video quality metrics were included in our experiments, namely VQM [9] and MOVIE [10]. PSNR was also used as a benchmark. VQM and MOVIE are not based on the foveation operation, but visual sensitivity is also taken into account. As different metrics often produce their results in different scales, a non-linear regression operation between the metric results and the subjective scores was performed using a logistic function, as suggested by VQEG. Subsequently, the fitted metric results were compared against the actual subjective quality scores leading to four evaluation criteria: Pearson linear correlation, Spearman rank-order correlation, root-mean-squared error (RMSE), and outlier ratio.

Table 1. Evaluation results of video quality models

Models	Pearson	Spearman	RMSE	Outlier
Proposed	*0.725*	*0.694*	*0.568*	*0.048*
FWSNR	0.494	0.441	0.716	0.09
FMSE	0.505	0.44	0.711	0.105
VQM	0.485	0.482	0.721	0.063
MOVIE	0.485	0.593	0.724	0.088
PSNR	0.416	0.451	0.75	0.073

Table 1 gives the evaluation results of different video quality models, which demonstrates that the proposed metric significantly outperforms other quality models with respect to the employed quality assessment data set. A possible drawback of FMSE and FWSNR is that the fixation point is always set to the image center, and therefore, the foveated video presentation is different from the real perceived presentation in the HVS if the eyes were not gazing at the image center. Furthermore, neither the attention mechanism nor temporal distortions are taken into account in these two quality metrics. Opposite to them, the proposed model is based on a more accurate visual perception model and also considers other important mechanisms, such as visual attention and perception to smooth motion. PSNR has the worst performance because it does not consider the characteristics of HVS. VQM and MOVIE perform rather poorly with respect to the employed data set, though their performance is usually promising for other video databases as reported in literature. A potential improvement of their performance might be achieved by including the attention information in external weighting operations. Generally speaking, none of the quality metrics showed excellent performance for the employed data set. In our opinion, the possible reason is that the subjective quality assessment was performed using an eye tracker, and therefore, the quality judgment might not be as accurate as those quality assessment experiments without using eye trackers.

In this work, we have used the recorded fixation points in modeling visual perception and deriving attentive intensity. However, the information about fixation points is not always available in a normal subjective video quality database. In another work, we have developed attention models to derive the attention map and predict fixation points without the need for an eye-tracker. Therefore, in future work, the predicted fixation and derived attention map designed in that work can be integrated into the proposed perception and quality models for evaluating the perceived video quality, in which eye-tracking is needless.

5. CONCLUSION

A visual perception model based on motion tuned foveated vision has been proposed in this paper. Based on the perceived presentations of a reference video and its distorted version, we presented a quality metric considering the contrast sensitivity of HVS in spatial and temporal domains. A carefully designed pooling scheme was then applied to the quality maps to model the important influence of quality variations and visual attention mechanism on the perceived video quality. The experimental results with respect to a combined eye-tracking and quality assessment data set have demonstrated a significant increase in the performance of the proposed metrics when compared to other foveation-based video quality models and some popular metrics.

6. REFERENCES

[1] Geisler, W. S., and Perry, J. S. 2002. Real-time simulation of arbitrary visual fields. *ACM Symposium on Eye Tracking Research & Applications*. ETRA'02. ACM, Louisiana, USA.

[2] Daly, S. 1998. Engineering observations from spatiovelocity and spatiotemporal visual models. *SPIE Int. Conf. Human Vision and Electronic Imaging III*. San Jose, USA.

[3] Wright, M. J., and Johnston, A. 1983. Spatiotemporal contrast sensitivity and visual field locus. *Vision Res.* 23, 10 (1983), 983-989.

[4] Lee, S. Pattichis, M. S., and Bovik, A. C. 2002. Foveated video quality assessment. *IEEE Trans. Multimed.* 4, 1 (Mar. 2002), 129-132.

[5] Rimax-Drlje, S., Vranješ, M., and Žagar, D. 2010. Foveated mean squared error - a novel video quality metric. *Multimed. Tools Appl.*, 49, 3 (Sep. 2010), 425-445.

[6] Engelke, U., Barkowsky, M., Le Callet, P., et al. 2009. *IRCCyN/IVC Eyetracker SD 2009_12 Database*. Available online: http://www.irccyn.ec-nantes.fr/spip.php?article550.

[7] Ninassi, A., Le Meur, O., Le Callet, P., and Barba, D. 2009. Considering temporal variations of spatial visual distortions in video quality assessment. *IEEE J. Sel. Top. Signal Process.* 3, 2 (Apr. 2009), 253-265.

[8] You, J., Korhonen, J., and Perkis, A. 2010. Attention modeling for video quality assessment: balancing global quality and local quality. *IEEE Int. Conf. Multimed. & Expo.* ICME'10. Singapore.

[9] Pinson, M., and Wolf, S. 2004. A new standardized method for objectively measuring video quality. *IEEE Trans. Broadcast.* 50, 3 (Sep. 2004), 312-322.

[10] Seshadrinathan, K., and Bovik, A. C. 2010. Motion tuned spatio-temporal quality assessment of natural videos. *IEEE Trans. Image Process.* 19, 2 (Feb. 2010), 335-350.

Automatic Object Segmentation from Large Scale 3D Urban Point Clouds through Manifold Embedded Mode Seeking*

Zhiding Yu[1,2], Chunjing Xu[1], Jianzhuang Liu[1], Oscar C. Au[2] and Xiaoou Tang[1,3]
[1]Shenzhen Key Laboratory for Computer Vision and Pattern Recognition, Shenzhen Institutes of Advanced Technology, Chinese Academy of Sciences
[2]Department of Electronic and Computer Engineering, The Hong Kong University of Science and Technology
[3]Department of Information Engineering, The Chinese University of Hong Kong
{zd.yu, cj.xu, jz.liu}@siat.ac.cn, eeau@ust.hk, xtang@ie.cuhk.edu.hk

ABSTRACT

This paper presents a system that can automatically segment objects in large scale 3D point clouds obtained from urban ranging images. The system consists of three steps: The first one involves a ground detection process that can detect relatively complex terrain and separate it from other objects. The second step superpixelizes the remaining objects to speed up the segmentation process. In the final step, a manifold embedded mode seeking method is adopted to segment the point clouds. Even though the segmentation of urban objects is a challenging problem in terms of accuracy and problem scale, our system can efficiently generate very good segmentation results. The proposed manifold learning effectively improves the segmentation performance due to the fact that continuous artificial objects often have manifold-like structures.

Categories and Subject Descriptors

I.4.6 [**Image Processing and Computer Vision**]: Segmentation—*Pixel classification*

General Terms

Algorithms, Experimentation

Keywords

3D point cloud, clustering, mode seeking, manifold

1. INTRODUCTION

3D models with geographical locations and semantical labels are the key for urban modeling that is widely used in a variety of applications, such as urban planning, simulation and visualization. Compared to modeling with traditional tedious and time-consuming CAD tools to create and visualize 3D digital urban models, many methods have been developed in recent years to obtain 3D information automatically. With these methods, it becomes possible that large scale 3D data can be obtained and processed.

*Area chair: Pal Halvorsen

MM'11, November 28–December 1, 2011, Scottsdale, Arizona, USA.

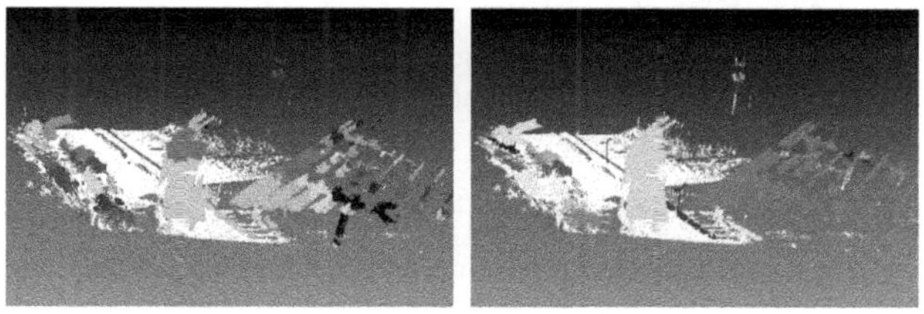

(a) (b)

Figure 1: An example of urban object segmentation. (a) Mean shift segmentation. (b) Segmentation obtained by our system with manifold embedded mode seeking, which improves the result in (a) significantly.

As a common method to obtain 3D information, systems equipped with LIDAR (light detection and ranging) sensors are widely used. The obtained data, also called ranging images, can be represented by 3D point clouds. However, a cloud as a whole reveals only limited structure of the urban scene and is far from being an informative visualization. To further utilize it, a necessary step is to label and categorize the points in the cloud object by object.

Object segmentation plays a crucial role in the point cloud processing routine. By segmentation, the points composing an object is extracted from the scene for recognition and a semantical tag is then attached to it. Despite the abundant previous works, only a few are related to large scale urban scene object localization [5]. Most methods are designed for a much confined scenario, such as focusing on a specific class of objects like roads [6], vehicles [4, 10], trees [15, 14, 9], and buildings [7, 3, 11]. In these cases, either the scenario is relatively simple that contains only a few objects [8], or the input objects have been segmented from the scene. The theme of these papers is mainly related to recognition and reconstruction of a specific class of objects where object recognition (or classification) techniques play a central role.

The urban object recognition system proposed in [5] uses normalized cuts [13] and min cut [1] to localize and partition point cloud objects. Other graph partitioning methods such as graph cut [2] are also useful tools for partitioning a set of points into subgroups. Our data, however, consist of much more complicated urban scenes, which render these methods fail in our experiments. The major challenge is basically twofold: First, point clouds typically consist of complicated, densely aligned objects with large size variation. Second, the inherent computation consuming nature of segmentation further leads to difficulties in dealing with large scale problems, reducing the practicality of a method. In this paper, we develop a system that can automatically segment objects in a 3D cloud of a large scale urban scene that contains billions of points. An example of the segmentation using our system is illustrated in Fig. 1(b). It is worth mentioning that Golovinskiy et al. [5] and Lim et al. [8] also developed a system for similar purpose. The differences between our work and theirs include that 1) our system can extract complicated terrain maps, while [5] and [8] assume relatively simple, flat terrains. Without accurate terrain extraction, segmentation of some objects is easy to fail, 2) buildings that later can be used for further mesh reconstruction are included and segmented, 3) our data are highly noisy and heterogeneous due to the data acquisition and preprocessing method[1], and 4) the objects in our data are highly occluded since the data are generated by going through the streets once.

2. THE PROPOSED METHOD

Fig. 2 shows how our method works. The three main steps, ground (terrain) detection, superpixelization, and object segmentation, are described as follows.

2.1 Terrain Detection

The first step of our system is to detect terrain from a point cloud. The terrain of a scene is related to the resolution we consider:

DEFINITION 2.1. *Let $C = \{p_i = (x_i, y_i, z_i) | i = 1...N\}$ be a perfectly captured scene without occlusion and noise where N is the number of points in C, and Δ be the resolution with which each pixel on a terrain map represents a $\Delta \times \Delta$ square in the real scene. The terrain map T^Δ with resolution Δ is defined as:*

$$T^\Delta(k,l) = \min_{\{p \in C | (x_\Delta(p), y_\Delta(p)) = (k,l)\}} z(p), \tag{1}$$

where $z(p)$ is the function to have the z-coordinate, along with $x_\Delta(p)$ and $y_\Delta(p)$ being the functions that retrieve the grid indices along the x-axis and the y-axis respectively when the xy-plane is masked with a $\Delta \times \Delta$ grid.

It is not difficult to develop a simple algorithm to generate the terrain map based on the definition if a perfectly captured scene is given. In real cases, however, occlusion and noise are ubiquitous. For example, parts of the ground hidden under cars cannot be detected. We use the following techniques to overcome this problem: 1) a maximum threshold is set to detect an abrupt change of the local minimum of heights for points, 2) paved road detection, and 3) expansion from paved road to obtain a better terrain.

The ground extraction algorithm is a two-pass process consisting of rough ground extraction and further refinement. In the first step, we divide the xy-plane into regular grids of size $\Delta \times \Delta$. For each grid, we eliminate points higher than the lowest point with a height difference larger than $Thre_1$. Mathematically, we define the roughly extracted ground as a set of extracted points satisfying the following condition:

$$\begin{aligned} T_1^\Delta(k,l) = \{z(q) | q \in C, (x_\Delta(q), y_\Delta(q)) = (k,l), \\ z(q) - \min_{\{p \in C | (x_\Delta(p), y_\Delta(p)) = (k,l)\}} z(p) \le Thre_1\}, \end{aligned} \tag{2}$$

[1]The ranging images are obtained by driving a vehicle loaded with LIDAR censors on the street. Due to the local traffic, the objects in the scene, such as vehicles and working people, are not stationary, causing some objects distorted. Another reason for low quality of the data is that our scene covers a much larger urban area, with the spanning about 10 kilometers. So the density of the data at many locations is low where it is hard to define objects.

The first step can effectively remove the majority of the objects while preserving uneven portions of the ground. Since we set Δ to 1.5 and $Thre_1$ to 1.7 in this paper, our system can tolerate inclination up to approximately 40 degrees. The method can also eliminate vertical structures with abrupt rise. Most of these structures correspond to building facades, walls, overpass pillars and trunks and should be considered as objects.

The second step aims at eliminating undesired object residues. Since the detected point clouds show an elongated shape along the road, we perform principal component analysis (PCA) with the cloud points on the xy-plane and select the eigenvector corresponding to the largest eigenvalue to indicate the road direction. We then divide the points into stripes of width Δ_s along the road direction, using multiple hyperplanes perpendicular to the road. Within each stripe, the points are further divided into grids of size $\Delta_g \times \Delta_s$.

Suppose we use l_k to indicate the l_kth grid in the k stripe, T_1^k to indicate the point set in the kth stripe, and T_1^{k,l_k} to indicate the point set corresponding to the l_kth grid. To locate the expansion starting point, the grid containing the paved road in the kth stripe is detected as:

$$l_{Road} = \arg\min_{l_k} \frac{1}{|T_1^{k,l_k}|} \sum_{p \in T_1^{k,l_k}} (z(p) - z_{Road})^2, \tag{3}$$

where the road height z_{Road} is defined as:

$$z_{Road} = \text{mean}(\{z(q) | q \in T_1^k, z(q) \in Bin_{max}(q)\}) \tag{4}$$

and the maximum bin Bin_{max} is defined as the largest bin of the histogram of point heights ranging from $\min_{p \in T_1^k}(z(p))$ to $\min_{p \in T_1^k}(z(p)) + Thre_2$. Experiments show that most road points are well detected, with similar heights densely concentrated in the height histogram to form the largest bin. Thus it is reasonable to estimate the road height by calculating the mean of the largest bin.

The detected grid is taken as the starting point. We eliminate points within this grid that are higher than the lowest point with height difference more than $Thre_3$ and mark this grid as "refined". We then propagate the refinement from the starting grid in a spatially continuous manner along the stripe. For each unrefined grid, we refer to the highest point that is identified as the ground in the previously refined grid and denote it as the reference point. Each unidentified point in the unrefined grid is compared with the reference point. Those higher with height differences larger than $Thre_3$ are eliminated and the rest are identified as ground. The highest among these points is selected as the new reference point. If there are no newly identified ground points, the reference point is not changed. The above process is repeated until all grids are refined in the map. We select Δ_s, Δ_g, $Thre_2$ and $Thre_3$ respectively as 10, 1, 10 and 1 and set the bin size as 1.

2.2 Point Cloud Superpixelization

The residual $C - T$ by removing the detected terrain T from a given cloud C is to be segmented. In order to solve large scale segmentation problem, a necessary step prior to the segmentation of objects is superpixelization. We first use mean shift oversegmentation with a bandwidth 5. The obtained clusters are further refined by recursively performing cluster split using 2-cluster k-means clustering, until each cluster contains less than 300 points.

2.3 Segmentation of Objects

Since the number of objects in a given urban scene is unknown, a clustering algorithm that needs this number known is not suitable for such a task. Mode seeking methods such as mean shift can serve as an appropriate tool. Besides the ability to automatically

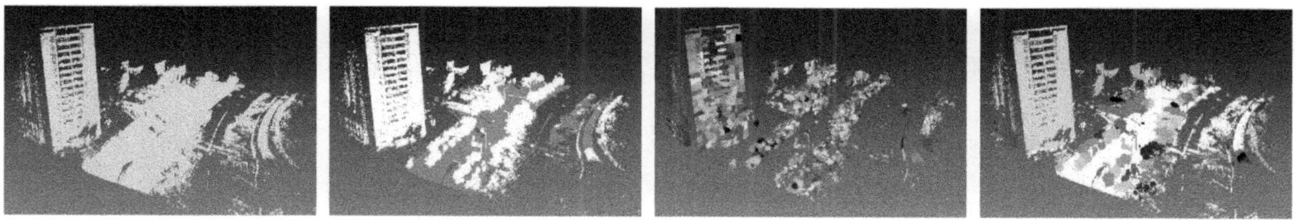

(a) (b) (c) (d)

Figure 2: An example illustrating the segmentation process. From left to right are figures of the original point cloud, ground (in red) detection, superpixelization and object segmentation.

determine the cluster number and the potential for parallelization, mode seeking can accurately detect many objects (such as trees) even though they are densely aligned. We observe that these objects tend to have high point density at their centers while showing low density at their boundaries, which particularly favors such method.

Our method is closely related to mean shift but has many additional features that prove to be essential for obtaining good segmentations: 1) a directional biased kernel bandwidth with z axis suppression, 2) minimum panning tree (MST) embedded mode seeking [16] that can detect compact structures and favor point connectivity with manifold-like point clouds, and 3) a large size prior for buildings with adaptive kernel size.

The observation for introducing the first feature is that points tend to have larger correlation along the vertical direction than horizontal directions. It inspires us to increase the kernel bandwidth along the vertical direction to strengthen point connectivity. This is equivalent to suppressing the z-axis coordinates for all the points and performing subsequent operations including MST construction and mode seeking in the z axis suppressed coordinate space. In this paper, we suppress the z coordinates with a ratio of 0.5.

Suppose the superpixels of a point cloud are represented by a set $\mathbf{V} = \{\mathbf{v}_i | i = 1, \ldots, N, \mathbf{v}_i \in \mathbf{R}^d\}$, where N is the total number of superpixels. The dimensionality d equals 3 in our case and $\mathbf{v}_i$ is the mean z-suppressed space coordinate of the points belonging to the ith superpixel. For a given set of superpixels, we construct its full connection graph $\mathbf{G} = (\mathbf{V}, \mathbf{E})$ where $\mathbf{E} = \{e_{i,j} | i, j = 1, ..., N, i \neq j\}$ and $|e_{i,j}| = \|\mathbf{v}_i - \mathbf{v}_j\|$. Using Kruskal algorithm we are able to extract the minimum spanning tree (MST) $\mathbf{S} = (\mathbf{V}, \mathbf{E_S})$, which is a connected graph of $\mathbf{G}$ with $\mathbf{E_S} \subseteq \mathbf{E}, |\mathbf{E_S}| = N - 1$. For any node pair (i, j), $i \neq j$, there exists a unique path $\mathbf{E}_{ij}$ such that $\mathbf{E}_{ij} \subseteq \mathbf{E_S}$, i and j are connected sequentially by elements of $\mathbf{E}_{ij}$ and deleting any one of the elements results in the disconnection of i and j. In addition, we define $\mathbf{E}_{ij}$ to be $\emptyset$, if $i = j$.

We propose to use a joint representation of the MST distance space ("MST space" for short) and the feature space (the coordinate space) to define the density estimator. Consider the simplest case where the MST space kernel center is located exactly at a tree node $\mathbf{v}_j$. Then the density estimator can be written as follows:

$$f(\mathbf{v}) = c_0 \sum_i k\left(\frac{d(\mathbf{v}_j, \mathbf{v}_i)^2}{h_1^2}\right) k\left(\left\|\frac{\mathbf{v} - \mathbf{v}_i}{h_2}\right\|^2\right), \quad (5)$$

where $d(\mathbf{v}_j, \mathbf{v}_i)$ is the cumulative length of the path connecting node $\mathbf{v}_i$ and $\mathbf{v}_j$, defined as:

$$d(\mathbf{v}_j, \mathbf{v}_i) = \sum_{e_{m,n} \in \mathbf{E_{ij}}} \min_{p_k \in \mathbf{V}_m, p_l \in \mathbf{V}_n} ||p_k - p_l||. \quad (6)$$

In (6), p_k is the single point coordinate of the kth point and $\mathbf{V}_m$ represents the set of points belonging to the mth superpixel. We use the above form instead of $d(\mathbf{v}_j, \mathbf{v}_i) = \sum_{e_{m,n} \in \mathbf{E_{ij}}} ||v_m - v_n||$ defined in [16] to further reward attraction along manifolds. In (5), $\mathbf{v}$ is the feature space kernel center, h_1 and h_2 are the bandwidth parameters controlling the window size, c_0 is a constant determined by the sample size and bandwidth, and $k(x) = \exp(-\frac{1}{2}x)$ is the profile of a normal kernel.

The inference of mode seeking for the tree-embedded density estimator is well described in [16]. We employ the fast approximation of the mode seeking process by iteratively shifting the MST space kernel and the feature space kernel, which is described in [16]. We also employ an adaptive bandwidth, utilizing a large size prior for buildings. We re-cluster superpixels from clusters containing at least one superpixel higher than the road height for 7.5 in the z axis suppressed space, with the same superpixel set and MST structure as those in the previous step, but the bandwidths for re-clustered superpixels are enlarged to 7.2 and 12, which are six times the original bandwidths. Combining the cluster label for low altitude superpixels together with the re-clustered result, we can obtain the final cluster label for each point in the point clouds.

Finally, we emphasize again that our method can automatically label different objects without object recognition after the terrain detection. One example is given in Fig. 2(d), and more can be seen in the next session.

3. EXPERIMENTS

We conduct comprehensive experiments to test the proposed system on a data set containing 176 images obtained by scanning some streets of our city. To better illustrate its performance, the results are compared with results obtained by mean shift, a standard segmentation method widely adopted in the literature for point cloud segmentation [5, 12]. The mean shift algorithm is operated on the same object superpixels obtained through the first and second steps of our method. It also uses adaptive bandwidth in the our experiments, with the same parameter adaptivity settings to our method.

3.1 Qualitative Evaluation

We randomly illustrate some ranging images with representative urban scenes and perform ground detection and segmentation. The results indicate our system can generate very good segmentation under a variety of complicated scenes. The scenes illustrated in Figs. 1 and Fig. 2 contain complex terrain which is hard to extract. Our system can accurately extract the majority of the ground. It is also worth mentioning that the embedding manifold structure helps to improve segmentation on spanning objects, particularly overpasses and buildings, as illustrated in Fig. 1, Fig. 4(a) and Fig. 4(d). Notice that for the data illustrated in Fig. 1, there is no way for mean shift to segment the whole bridge without erroneously including nearby objects (the pylon on the right). Fig. 4(e) illustrates our segmentation result on a challenging task where large buildings are densely aligned while the scanned points are sparse on these buildings. The buildings are difficult to separate but our system can generate very accurate segmentation. Fig. 3(f) and Fig. 3(g) contains densely aligned trees difficult to separate. Our method works

(a) (b) (c) (d) (e) (f) (g)

Figure 3: A portion of the segmentation results obtained by our system. The test data contains typical urban scenes.

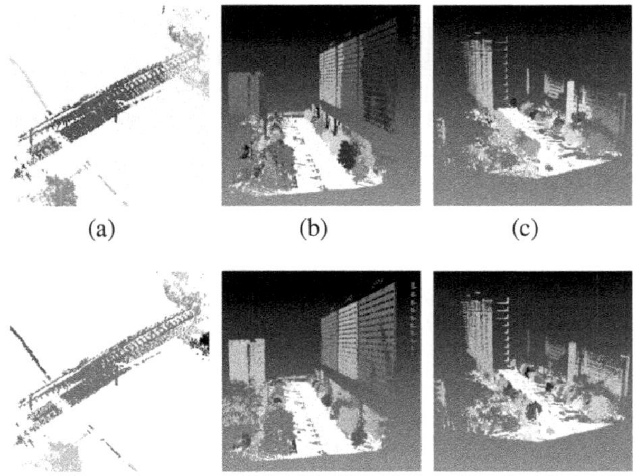

(a) (b) (c)

(d) (e) (f)

Figure 4: A comparison of segmentations obtained by our system and mean shift. The second row contains better results obtained by our system, while results obtained by mean shift contain both serious oversegmentation and oversmoothing.

well on such kind of data. Tested on the whole data set containing hundreds of scenes similar to the above illustrated ones, the visual examination suggests that our system has similar performance to the illustrated ones. In all our experiments, the bandwidth for mean shift is set to 4 and the two bandwidths h_1 and h_2 for our method are respectively set to 1.2 and 2. These parameters are empirically selected to optimize the performance of the two methods.

3.2 Quantitative Evaluation

We compare each automatic segmentation against the ground truth [2] segmentation by finding (a) how much of the automatic segmentation contains the whole object (precision), and (b) how much of the object is not oversmoothed with other objects (recall). The result is illustrated in Fig. 5. Results show that our method significantly outperforms mean shift.

4. DISCUSSION AND CONCLUSION

In this paper, we have developed a system that can automatically segment objects in complicated urban scenes. The system can separate single, relatively small objects while preserving the connectivity of large, spanning ones. It provides good initial interpretations of the urban scenes, based on which 3D object reconstruction, visualization and recognition can be carried out.

5. ACKNOWLEDGEMENTS

This work was supported by grants from Introduced Innovative R&D Team of Guangdong Province (Robot and Intelligent Information Technology), Natural Science Foundation of China (61005011, 60975029, 61070148), and Science, Industry, Trade and Information Technology Commission of Shenzhen Municipality, China (JC201005270358A, JC201005270350A, JC200903180635A, JC201005270378A, ZYC201006130313A).

[2]Since the work load is huge, we only label a portion of the data set and select objects that are easy to label.

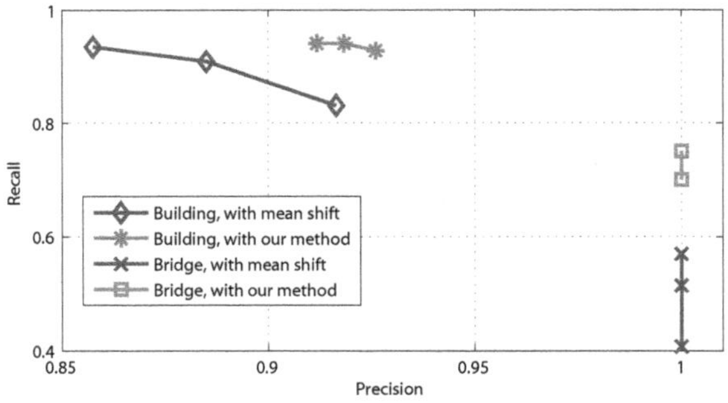

Figure 5: A quantitative comparison of segmentations obtained by our system and mean shift.

6. REFERENCES

[1] Y. Boykov and G. Funka-Lea. Graph cuts and efficient n-d image segmentation. *IJCV*, 70(2):109–131, 2006.

[2] Y. Boykov, O. Veksler, and R. Zabih. Fast approximate energy minimization via graph cuts. *IEEE T-PAMI*, 23(11):1222–1239, 2002.

[3] J. Chen and B. Chen. Architectural modeling from sparsely scanned range data. *IJCV*, 78(2):223–236, 2008.

[4] A. Frome, D. Huber, R. Kolluri, T. Bulow, and J. Malik. Recognizing objects in range data using regional point descriptors. *ECCV*, 2004.

[5] A. Golovinskiy, V. Kim, and T. Funkhouser. Shape-based recognition of 3d point clouds in urban environments. *ICCV*, 2009.

[6] A. Jaakkola, J. Hyyppa, H. Hyyppa, and A. Kukko. Retrieval algorithms for road surface modelling using laser-based mobile mapping. *Sensors*, 8(9):5238–5249, 2008.

[7] F. Lafarge, X. Descombes, J. Zerubia, and M. Pierrot-Deseilligny. Building reconstruction from a single DEM. *CVPR*, 2008.

[8] E. Lim and D. Suter. Conditional random field for 3D point clouds with adaptive data reduction. *Int'l. Conf. on Cyberworlds*, 2007.

[9] Y. Livny, F. Yan, M. Olson, B. Chen, H. Zhang, and J. El-Sana. Automatic reconstruction of tree skeletal structures from point clouds. *ACM Transactions on Graphics*, 29(5), 2010.

[10] E. Meier and F. Ade. Object detection and tracking in range image sequences by separation of image features. *IEEE International Conference on Intelligent Vehicles*, 1998.

[11] L. Nan, A. Sharf, H. Zhang, D. Cohen-Or, and B. Chen. SmartBoxes for interactive urban reconstruction. *ACM SIGGRAPH*, 2010.

[12] X. Shao, K. Katabira, R. Shibasaki, and Z. H.J. Multiple people extraction using 3D range sensor. *SMC*, 2010.

[13] J. Shi and J. Malik. Normalized cuts and image segmentation. *IEEE T-PAMI*, 22(8):888–905, 2002.

[14] Y. Wang, H. Weinacker, and B. Koch. A lidar point cloud based procedure for vertical canopy structure analysis and 3D single tree modelling in forest. *Sensors*, 8:3938–3951, 2008.

[15] H. Xu, N. Gossett, and B. Chen. Knowledge and heuristic-based modeling of laser-scanned trees. *ACM Transactions on Graphics*, 26(4):19, 2007.

[16] Z. Yu, O. Au, K. Tang, and C. Xu. Nonparametric Density Estimation on A Graph: Learning Framework, Fast Approximation and Application in Image Segmentation. *CVPR*, 2011.

Key Object-based Static Video Summarization *

Zhiqiang Tian, Jianru Xue, Xuguang Lan, Ce Li, Nanning Zheng
Institute of Artificial Intelligence and Robotics, Xi'an Jiaotong University
Xi'an, Shaanxi, P.R. China, 710049
{zqtian,jrxue,xglan,celi,nnzheng}@aiar.xjtu.edu.cn

ABSTRACT

In this paper, we present a system for object-based video summarization facilitated by an efficient video object segmentation system. We eliminate the redundancy not only from spatial and temporal domain, but also from content domain. First, we detect shot boundaries and extract video objects by a 3D graph-based algorithm. Once the objects are obtained, the shape of the objects need to be represented. The key objects are extracted in a global manner by K-means clustering of shapes. Experimental results on the proposed object-based scheme combined with efficient video object segmentation show desirable summarization.

Categories and Subject Descriptors

I.2.10 [**Artificial Intelligence**]: Vision and Scene Understanding—*Video analysis*

General Terms

Algorithms, Experimentation

Keywords

Video object summarization, graph cuts, video object segmentation, key actions

1. INTRODUCTION

To date, a great demand for video data in applications due to the significant improvement in the processing technology and availability of large storage systems. It is necessary and important to allow the computer to automatically manage the parts of interest form videos. In recent years, video summary for efficient browsing, retrieval, and storage is becoming more and more popular. It is a video content service to make videos easier or faster to understand.

*Area chair: Pal Halvorsen

Generally speaking, a video summary is defined as sequence of still or short dynamic video presenting the content of the video in compact and brief manner. The target summary is rapidly provided with concise information about original content. From the viewpoint of presentation style, the existing methods can be classified into two categories, i.e., static video summarization and dynamic video skimming. Static video summaries are consist of several keyframes, while dynamic video summaries are composed of a set of thumbnail movies (with or without audio) extracted from the original video, our method belongs to the first category. Li [6], Truong [10] and Money [7] have present comprehensive surveys of video abstract.

Since the proposed approach in this paper falls into the static video summarization, we mainly focus the review on this category hereinafter. There has been a rich literature on static video summarization [1, 3], These existing methods provide effective solutions to summary video into a concise representation. However, they focus on low frame-level processing. Object-based or content-based video summarization has been rarely addressed, though content-based videos are widely used in surveillance systems, retrieval systems and second generation video coding systems.

Erol and Kossentini [2] present an automatic key video object plane selection in the MPEG-4 compressed domain using the Hamming and the Hausdorff distance measures. The shape of the objects are approximated using the shape coding modes that can be determined from MPEG-4 bitstream. Nevertheless, most object-based video systems perform processing in the uncompressed domain. Our paper addresses the object-based video summarization in the uncompressed domain which is independent on the video coding standards.

Similarly, Kim [5] presents an integrated scheme for object-based video abstraction. Their object-based keyframes are extracted in a sequential manner through the sequence and first frame in a shot is always chosen as a keyframe. Unlike our system, their work focuses more on static background videos. Our work in contrast focuses on summarizing long films with an global manner, and we allow for both static and moving background. For all frames in one shot are clustered into several segments based on shape similarity without considering the order of frames position. The frames that are closest to the center of each segment are considered as keyframes. This make our scheme more compact than Kim's, and will not yield analogous keyframes, especially for long shots.

In this paper, we proposed key object-based video summarization (KOBVS) scheme, combined with an efficient video

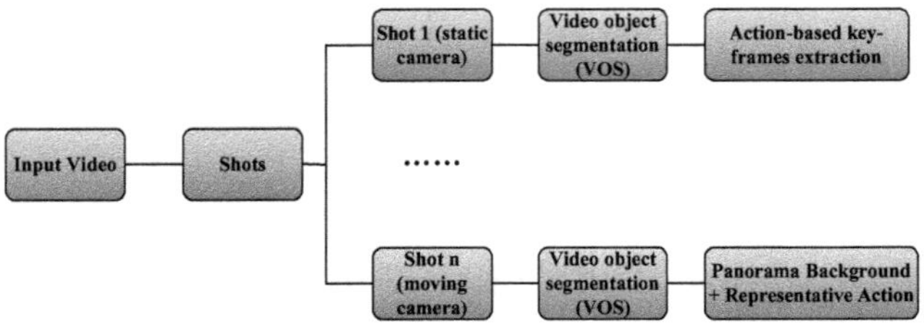

Figure 1: System overview

objects segmentation system, generates desirable summarization of the videos containing semantic representative actions for static background and moving background. For the shot with static background, keyframes are presented based on key objects extraction using 3D graph-based segmentation and shapes comparison. And the shot with moving background is decomposed by 3D graph-based segmentation, and depicted as a combination of background panorama and representative foreground objects. Our proposed framework of video summarization is shown in Figure 1.

This paper is organized as follows. In Section 2, we present an efficient video objects segmentation algorithm that is the preprocess of the content-based video summarization system. The key object-based video summarization for static and moving camera is introduced in Section 3. Experimental results are shown in Section 4. Finally, Section 5 concludes this paper.

2. VIDEO OBJECT SEGMENTATION

2.1 Shot detection

Shot detection is an essential step involved in video summarization. A shot is a continuous strip of motion picture that runs for an uninterrupted period of time. We use Zhang's method [13] to detect shot boundaries. Once shots are extracted it is possible to analyze video content based on color, motion, texture and others features.

2.2 Video object segmentation

Motivation of video segmentation can be classified as the application in retrieval, coding, recognition, scenes understanding, summarization, editing and so on. As widely used, many video object segmentation algorithms have been recently proposed [12, 8]. Due to their high complexity, these methods are not efficient for multimedia application, e.g. video summarization.

We have proposed an efficient video object segmentation method in [9] for static camera. In this work we extend this method to moving camera video sequences. Firstly, we oversegment each frame and take the oversegmented regions as the vertices in the 3D spatio-temporal graph. Then multiple cues are fused together to extract objects accurately. Finally, accurate foreground and background segmentation are efficiently achieved by graph cut.

We segment frames use the mean shift method for its good performance and fast speed compared to other methods. Once obtain the over-segmented frames, we construct spatio-temporal graph in the video volume. Then we define the object segmentation as assigning a label to each region. Our 3D graph cuts algorithm solves the labeling problem by minimizing the following energy function:

$$E(l) = \sum_{r \in R} D_r^c(l_r) + \gamma \sum_{r \in R} D_r^m(l_r) + \alpha_1 \sum_{\{i,j\} \in N_s} V_{i,j}^s(l_i, l_j) + \alpha_2 \sum_{\{i,j\} \in N_t} V_{i,j}^t(l_i, l_j) \quad (1)$$

where l stands for the label of each region, $l = 1$ if region r belongs to the foreground, and $l = 0$ otherwise. R is the set of regions in 3D spatio-temporal video volume. $D_r^c(l_r)$ and $D_r^m(l_r)$ represent the conformity of color and motion of a region to the foreground/background respectively. $V_{i,j}^s$ measures color differences between two neighbor regions in the spatial domain (intra frame), $V_{i,j}^t$ measures color differences between two neighbor regions in the temporal domain (inter frame), both encourage two similarity adjacent regions to be assigned same label. N_s is the spatial neighborhood, N_t is the temporal neighborhood, $\{i, j\}$ represent two neighbor regions. γ is responsible for balancing the importance of color cue and motion cue. We normalized D_r^c and D_r^m to the scale of $[0, 1]$, and set the $\gamma = 0.5$ in all of our experiments. The parameters α_1 and α_2 specify the importance of the spatial smoothness term $V_{i,j}^s$ and temporal smoothness term $V_{i,j}^t$. The default values are fixed to $\alpha_1 = 0.05, \alpha_2 = 0.05$ in all of our experiments.

We model the foreground/background color likelihoods in a non-parameter manner, as histogram in the HSV color space. The color likelihood term $D_r^c(l_r)$ is defined as:

$$D_r^c(l_r) = -\log p(C_k | l_r) \quad (2)$$

where C_k represents the mean color of the kth region. Probabilistic normalization requires that $\sum_C p(C|l_r = 1)$, and similarly for the background likelihood.

The construction of motion likelihood based on the assumption that camera are static. So we need to preprocess the moving background sequence. In this work, we register consecutive frames assuming a geometric transformation to estimate global motion. We choose the affine motion model A defined at point $p(x, y)$ by $A(p) = (a_1 + a_2x + a_3y, a_4 + a_5x + a_6y)$ sine it is a good tradeoff between representative and complexity. We employ a feature-based method to estimate the parameter vector $\Theta = (a_1, a_2, a_3, a_4, a_5, a_6)$ between frame I_t and I_{t+1}. We first detect the feature points of each frame by SIFT, which is reported to perform best among popular feature descriptors. SIFT provides a 128-dimensional local descriptor for each keypoint. Next, for each pair of consecutive frames, we match keypoint descriptors using the approximate nearest neighbors *kd*-tree initially. We build a *kd*-tree from the feature descriptors in frame I_{t+1}, and for each feature in frame I_t we find two nearest neighbors in I_{t+1} that are $dist1$ and $dist2$. If the ratio of closest distance to 2nd closest distance less than Th_r then accept this match, e.g. $dist1/dist2 < Th_r$. We used $Th_r = 0.6$ and it works well in most of our experiments. After initial matching for consecutive frames I_t and I_{t+1}, we use RANSAC to robustly extract the feature correspondence between the frames and estimate the restricted model (i.e., eliminating outlier that feature correspondence lies on moving objects, and estimating the scaling and translation parameters). Once we obtain the transformations between each pair of consecutive frames. We can warp I_{t+1} to I_t

using transformations to align background (global motion compensation).

The optical flow method of Werlberger et al. [11] is adopted as it runs close to real-time and has very good results on the Middlebury Optical Flow Data set. Then we can use the magnitude of optical flow to describe the motion likelihood of a oversegmented region. The larger magnitude of optical flow of a region, the more likely the region is foreground objects. The motion term $D_p^m(l)$ is defined as:

$$D_r^m(l_r) = -\log p(O_k|l_r) \quad (3)$$

where O_k represents the mean magnitude of optical flow of the kth region. Probabilistic normalization requires that $\sum_O p(O|l_r = 1)$, and similarly for the background likelihood.

The prior term $V_{i,j}^s$ and $V_{i,j}^t$ are well-known Ising prior and can be defined as follow.

$$V_{i,j}^s(l_i, l_j) = \sum_{\{i,j\}\in N_s} (1 - \delta(l_i - l_j))e^{-\beta_1\|C_i - C_j\|^2} \quad (4)$$

$$V_{i,j}^t(l_i, l_j) = \sum_{\{i,j\}\in N_t} (1 - \delta(l_i - l_j))e^{-\beta_2\|O_i - O_j\|^2} \quad (5)$$

where δ is Kronecker delta function $\delta((l_i - l_j) \neq 0) = 0$. C_i and O_i are the color and motion expectation of all pixels in the region i repectively, and $\|\cdot\|$ is the L_2 norm. The contrast parameters are set to $\beta_1 = (2 <\| C_i - C_j \|>)^{-1}$, $\beta_2 = (2 <\| O_i - O_j \|>)^{-1}$, where $< \cdot >$ denotes expectation over all pairs of neighbors in video volume.

3. KEY OBJECTS EXTRACTION

The object is detected in a sequence of frames, and each action is represented by a sequence of object masks in those frames. The number of video objects obtained by 3D graph cuts is too big to represent the video content efficient. For example, a people walk on the square, there are many object masks obtained from VOS phase. All of these shapes (actions) are very similar, we can use few representative shapes to depict the video content.

We reduce the number of representative actions to a small fixed number N_r by K-means clustering, N_r is set to 3 in our experiments. This idea is motivated by the fact that any significant actions of video objects are very likely to result in changes in the object's shape and variance of this change can potentially describe the type of object action.

For grouping the actions, we need a shape descriptor or feature vector to represent each object mask. Seven Hu moments [4] is selected which are known to be invariant to translation, rotation and scale change. Mahalanobis distance as distance metric is calculated between the moment description of two shapes. Figure 6 and Figure 9 shows the representative actions of two video Longjump and Stefan.

4. EXPERIMENTAL RESULTS

In this section, we present experimental results on the test sequence 'Hall' (352x288x200) for static background, while 'Longjump' (360x288x100) and 'Stefan' (352x240x250) for moving background. They are shown in Figure 2, Figure 4 and Figure 7, respectively. The most time-consuming part of our method is extract shapes of video objects. Given a video of resolution 352x288 and length 200 frames, it took about 120 seconds to process using a AMD 2.1GHz PC.

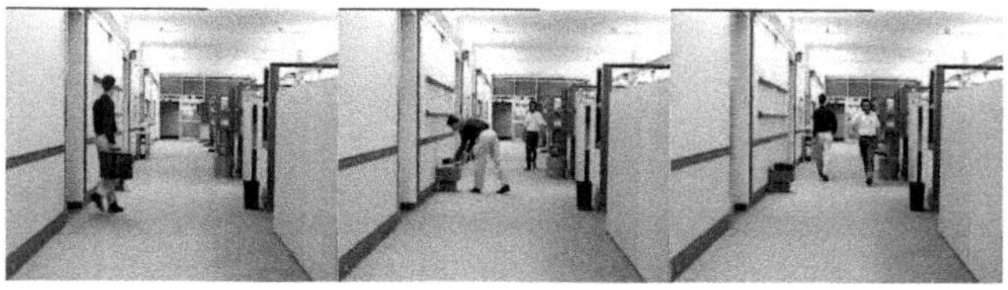

Figure 2: Hall sequence

Figure 3: Further summarization of Hall into 3 representative actions by K-means clustering

The experimental results are shown in Figure 3, 5, 6, 8, 9. From the results, we can see that important events are shown. For Hall sequence, the people walk with briefcase, bending to put and walk without briefcase are shown (only use one object for distinct show).

Figure 5 and Figure 8 show the panorama background of long jump scene and tennis court scene. From the panorama view, we can catch the comprehensive surroundings fleetly without browsing every frame of videos. In our experiment, we use the public panorama software to generate background panorama. From these results, we can see that the video content are highly compact in the spatial domain and temporal domain.

Figure 6 reports representative actions of Longjump, such as running up, prancing and dropping. Figure 9 also shows the representative actions which are waiting, hitting and running. These results show that the video information are condensed in content domain effectively.

5. CONCLUSIONS

We have proposed an action-aware scheme for key object-based video summarization. The contribution and characteristics of our scheme are as followings. First, our video object segmentation method is efficient and the KOBVS is easy to implement. Second, it is effective to capture key actions. Third, videos are highly condensed not only in spatial and temporal domain, but also in content domain. In the future, our scheme should be able to discriminate the

Figure 4: Longjump sequence

Figure 5: Panorama background of Longjump

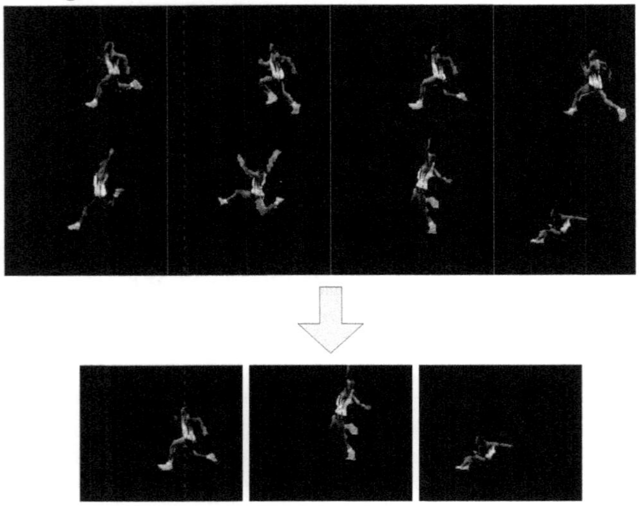

Figure 6: Further summarization of Longjump into 3 representative actions by K-means clustering

Figure 7: Stefan sequence

Figure 8: Panorama background of Stefan

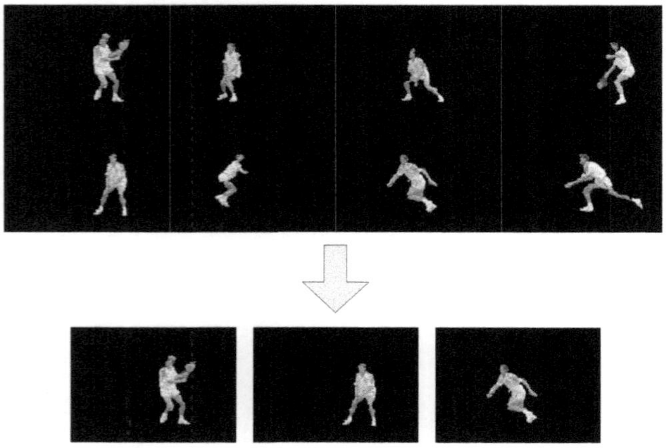

Figure 9: Further summarization of Stenfan into 3 representative actions by K-means clustering

higher level semantic aspects of different activity and events for better summarization of image sequences.

6. ACKNOWLEDGMENTS

This work was supported in part by the National Basic Research Program of China (973 Program) under Grant No. 2010CB327902, the "863" of P.R.China under Grant No. 2009AA011709, and NSFC Nos. 60875008, 90920301 and 60805044.

7. REFERENCES

[1] S. de Avila, A. Lopes, et al. VSUMM: A mechanism designed to produce static video summaries and a novel evaluation method. *Pattern Recognition Letters*, 32(1):56–68, 2011.

[2] B. Erol and F. Kossentini. Automatic key video object plane selection using the shape information in the MPEG-4 compressed domain. *Multimedia, IEEE Transactions on*, 2(2):129–138, 2000.

[3] M. Furini, F. Geraci, M. Montangero, and M. Pellegrini. STIMO: STIll and MOving video storyboard for the web scenario. *Multimedia Tools and Applications*, 46(1):47–69, 2010.

[4] M. Hu. Visual pattern recognition by moment invariants. *Information Theory, IRE Transactions on*, 8(2):179–187, 1962.

[5] C. Kim and J. Hwang. An integrated scheme for object-based video abstraction. In *Proceedings of the eighth ACM international conference on Multimedia*, pages 303–311. ACM, 2000.

[6] Y. Li, S. Lee, C. Yeh, and C. Kuo. Techniques for movie content analysis and skimming: tutorial and overview on video abstraction techniques. *Signal Processing Magazine, IEEE*, 23(2):79–89, 2006.

[7] A. Money and H. Agius. Video summarisation: A conceptual framework and survey of the state of the art. *Journal of Visual Communication and Image Representation*, 19(2):121–143, 2008.

[8] B. L. Price, B. S. Morse, and S. Cohen. Livecut: Learning-based interactive video segmentation by evaluation of multiple propagated cues. In *ICCV*, 2009.

[9] Z. Tian, J. Xue, N. Zheng, X. Lan, and C. Li. 3d spatio-temporal graph cuts for video objects segmentation. In *International Conference on Image Processing*, 2011.

[10] B. Truong and S. Venkatesh. Video abstraction: A systematic review and classification. *ACM Transactions on Multimedia Computing, Communications, and Applications (TOMCCAP)*, 3(1):3, 2007.

[11] M. Werlberger, W. Trobin, T. Pock, A. Wedel, D. Cremers, and H. Bischof. Anisotropic huber-l optical flow. In *The British Machine Vision Conference*, 2009.

[12] B. Xue, W. Jue, S. David, and S. Guillermo. Video snapcut: Robust video object cutout using localized classifiers. In *ACM SIGGRAPH*, 2009.

[13] H. Zhang, A. Kankanhalli, and S. Smoliar. Automatic partitioning of full-motion video. *Readings in multimedia computing and networking*, page 321, 2002.

Example-based Human Motion Extrapolation Based on Manifold Learning

Nick C. Tang
Inst. of Information Science, Academia Sinica
128, Sec. 2, Academia Rd., Taipei, Taiwan
nickctang@gmail.com

Chiou-Ting Hsu
Dep. of Computer Science, National Tsing Hua Univ.
101, Sec. 2, Kuang-Fu Rd., Hsinchu, Taiwan
cthsu@cs.nthu.edu.tw

Tsung-Yi Lin
Inst. of Information Science, Academia Sinica
128, Sec. 2, Academia Rd., Nankang, Taipei, Taiwan
tsungyi@iis.sinica.edu.tw

Hong-Yuan Mark Liao
Inst. of Information Science, Academia Sinica
128, Sec. 2, Academia Rd., Nankang, Taipei, Taiwan
liao@iis.sinica.edu.tw

ABSTRACT
In this paper, we propose a new framework to synthesize human motions based on only one single posture given in the input image. To generate visually pleasing motion sequences, the proposed framework consists of two key techniques. One is *motion retrieval*, which retrieves reference motions from a human motion database on a low-dimensional motion manifold. Another one is *human motion extrapolation,* which first generates new postures by deforming the shape of the input posture according to the retrieved motions and then synthesizes the corresponding motion sequence. To demonstrate the efficacy of the proposed method, we generate several human motion sequences using input images with different postures and show that the results are indeed visually pleasing.

Categories and Subject Descriptors
I.3.5 Computational Geometry and Object Modeling, I.3.6 Methodology and Techniques.

General Terms: Algorithms, Design, Experimentation.

Keywords: manifold learning, shape matching, mesh deformation, human motion synthesis.

1. INTRODUCTION
In recent years, human motion synthesis [3,4] has become a popular research topic. Many methods have been proposed to edit or recover missing human motions with minimum user intervention. For example, Kover *et al.* [4] proposed an example-based approach to synthesize new motions according to existing motion data. In [3], Kobayashi *et al.* proposed an interactive framework to help user manipulate a human motion from a video sequence by dragging its multiple feature points. However, when only a small number of example images are available, the synthesized motions usually have poor quality because of the lack of postures and their corresponding texture information.

In this paper, we propose a new framework to automatically and efficiently synthesize motion sequences from a human motion database based on only one single input image. To have a visually pleasing result, we need to tackle a number of challenging issues. Firstly, when given one input image O, we need to retrieve its reference motions from the motion database. Since motion representation usually involves high-dimensional data, we propose to learn a low-dimensional manifold to characterize the high-dimensional motions. Each motion sequence in the database is then represented as a trajectory in the manifold. After projecting the input posture O into the low-dimensional space, we first determine a reference posture as its most similar one and then retrieve the reference motions along the trajectory of the reference posture in the manifold space. Once having a reference motion, the next issue is to generate the human motion via extrapolation. We propose to apply a shape transformation process to estimate the displacement of each contour point on the shape of O and then use a mesh deformation process to generate the new postures of O. Finally, we conduct a simple texture transferring process to generate the deformation result.

The remainder of this paper is organized as follows. Section II describes the procedure of motion retrieval. In Section III, we present the proposed human motion extrapolation algorithm. Section IV details the experiment results. Concluding remarks are drawn in section V.

2. MOTION RETRIEVAL
Human motion is difficult to synthesize and manipulate because of its high dimensional representation. Nevertheless, since its intrinsic dimension is usually much lower, we propose to learn a low dimensional motion manifold by preserving the temporal continuity in the high dimensional human motion. The motion manifold provides a means to manipulate human motion in the low dimensional space with better computational efficiency and motion consistency.

2.1 Description of Human Motion
We adopt the shape context descriptor [1] to represent each human posture in a high-dimensional space First, as shown in Fig. 1(a), a set of contour points P is uniformly sampled around the contour of a human posture. For each contour point p_i, a spatial diagram h_i is computed in a log-polar space (as shown in Fig. 1(b)) to describe the shape context of p_i.

*Area Chair: Wei Tsang Ooi

This research was supported in part by Taiwan E-learning and Digital Archives Programs (TELDAP) sponsored by the National Science Council of Taiwan under NSC Grants: NSC100-2631-H-001-020, NSC100-2631-H-001-013.

MM'11, November 28–December 1, 2011, Scottsdale, Arizona, USA.

(a) (b)

Fig. 1. Shape context computation. (a) Contour points on human posture. (b) Diagram of log-polar space.

In [1], the matching cost between two contour points p_i^α and p_i^β, which belong to different postures α and β respectively, is defined as follows:

$$C(p_i^\alpha, p_j^\beta) = \frac{1}{2}\sum_{k=1}^{K}\frac{[h_i(k)-h_j(k)]^2}{h_i(k)+h_j(k)}, \tag{1}$$

where $h_i(k)$ and $h_j(k)$ denote the kth bin of the normalized histograms of p_i^α and p_i^β respectively. Next, matching of two postures α and β is accomplished by minimizing the total matching cost,

$$E(\pi) = \sum_i C(p_i^\alpha, p_{\pi(i)}^\beta), \tag{2}$$

where π is a permutation. In Eq. (2), because the matching is constrained to the one-to-one matching, the posture matching is considered as an assignment problem and is solved by the bipartite graph matching. Finally, after determining the matching between the two postures α and β, we define their distance as follows:

$$D_S(\alpha,\beta) = \frac{1}{n}\sum_{i\in\alpha} C(p_i^\alpha, p_{\pi(i)}^\beta) + \frac{1}{m}\sum_{j\in\beta} C(p_j^\beta, p_{\pi(j)}^\alpha). \tag{3}$$

2.2 Manifold Learning with Isomap Algorithm

The goal of isometric feature mapping (Isomap) algorithm is to seek a Euclidean space that preserves the geodesic distance between any two data points in the original high-dimensional space. Given a human motion database, we first use the distance measurement defined in Eq. (3) to calculate the distance between any two postures and obtain the pairwise distance matrix D_S.

The Isomap algorithm includes three major steps: construction of neighboring graph, computation of geodesic distance and construction of low-dimensional embedding. Given the distance matrix D_S, the first step is to construct an adjacency graph G according to the neighboring relations defined in $D_S(\alpha, \beta)$ between any two postures α and β. In the second step, Isomap estimates the geodesic distances between all pairs of postures on the manifold M by computing the shortest path distances $D_G(\alpha, \beta)$ in the graph G. Finally, the Isomap algorithm applies multidimensional scaling (MDS) on D_G to construct an embedding of the data in a d-dimensional Euclidean space Y. The lower-dimensional embedding points in Y are chosen to minimize the cost function:

$$E = \|\tau(D_G) - \tau(D_Y)\|_{L^2} \tag{4}$$

where D_Y denotes the matrix of Euclidean distances, L^2 represents the L^2 matrix norm, and the τ operator converts the distances to inner products. Let $y_\alpha = [y_{\alpha1}, y_{\alpha2}, \ldots, y_{\alpha d}]^T$ be the coordinate of the ith point in the space Y. The distance between the αth and β^{h} points is computed as follows:

$$d_{\alpha\beta}^2 = (y_\alpha - y_\beta)^T(y_\alpha - y_\beta) = y_\alpha^T y_\alpha + y_\beta^T y_\beta - 2y_\alpha^T y_\beta. \tag{5}$$

To overcome the indeterminacy of the solution due to arbitrary translation, the following zero-mean constraint is assumed.

$$\sum_{\alpha=1}^{n} y_\alpha = 0. \tag{6}$$

From Eq. (5) and (6), the inner product of y_α and y_β is derived as follows:

$$y_\alpha^T y_\beta = -\frac{1}{2}(d_{i\alpha\beta}^2 - \frac{1}{n}\sum_{\alpha=1}^{n} d_{\alpha\beta}^2 - \frac{1}{n}\sum_{\beta=1}^{n} d_{\alpha\beta j}^2 + \frac{1}{n^2}\sum_{\alpha=1}^{n}\sum_{\beta=1}^{n} d_{\alpha\beta}^2). \tag{7}$$

Let $D = [d_{\alpha\beta}]$ denote the distance matrix. The inner product of D, $\tau(D)$, is obtained by

$$\tau(D) = -\frac{1}{2}HDH, \tag{8}$$

where $H = I - \frac{1}{n}11^T$ is the centering matrix with $\mathbf{1}=[1,1,1,\ldots,1]^T$. The global minimum of Eq. (4) is achieved by setting the coordinates y_i to the top d eigenvectors of the matrix $\tau(D_G)$.

In MDS, the dimensionality of Y can be estimated from the decrease in error with increased dimensionality. The residual variance R_d, which is usually used to evaluate the error of dimensionality reduction, is defined as

$$R_d = 1 - r^2(D_G, D_Y), \tag{9}$$

where $r(D_G, D_Y)$ is the correlation coefficient of D_G and D_Y. As shown in Fig. 2, the value of d is determined when the curve ceases to decrease and is selected as three in this paper.

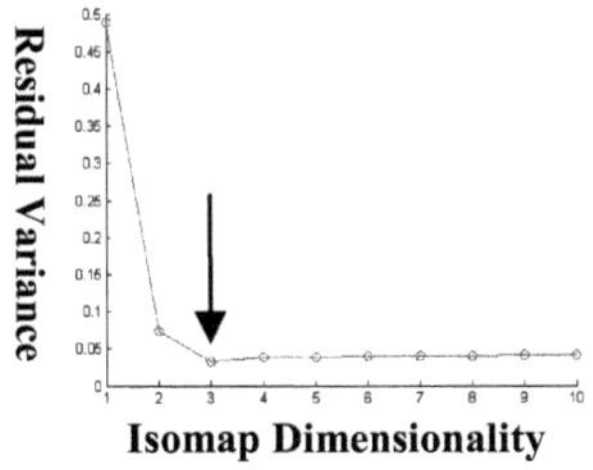

Fig. 2. The residual value R_d of Isomap on the training data.

2.3 Motion Retrieval

Using the method described in Sec. 2.2, we construct a low-dimensional Isomap space Y to represent all the postures in the human motion database. Therefore, each posture is transformed into a low-dimensional point in Y and each human motion sequence is represented as a trajectory in Y, as shown in Fig. 3.

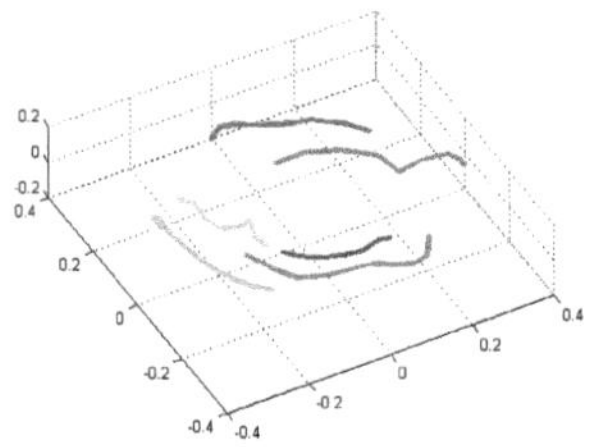

Fig. 3. The constructed Isomap space for human motion database.

Whenever the user input a human posture O, we first calculate the shape distance between O and all the postures in the database and then map it into the constructed Isomap space Y. Next, in the manifold space, we could efficiently determine the most similar posture by the nearest neighbor rule and then retrieve the reference motions $M_{t,t+1..,n}^{m}$ along the trajectory on the motion manifold m. Fig. 4 shows an example of the retrieval result when given only one human posture from the user.

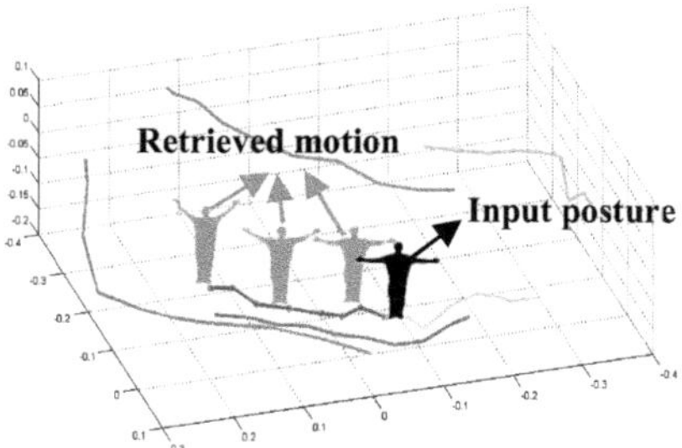

Fig. 4. An example of motion retrieval.

3. HUMAN MOTION EXTRAPOLATION

With the reference motions $M^m_{t,t+1..,n}$ retrieved from the human motion database, we then start to extrapolate new motions of the user input image O according to $M^m_{t,t+1..,n}$. We conduct three major steps to automatically accomplish the motion extrapolation task. The first step, *shape transformation based on contour point matching*, determines the correspondences of contour points between M^m_t and M^m_{t+1} so as to compute the displacement Δp^t_i of each contour point p^t_i on the shape of M^m_t. The second step, *triangular mesh deformation*, first decomposes O into a set of triangular mesh T^O and then deforms each mesh according to the handle constraints on O and the point displacement Δp^t_i to extrapolate new posture O'. The third step, *texture transferring*, transfers the texture from O to the new posture O'.

3.1 Shape Transformation Based on Contour Point Matching

Automatic estimation of correspondences between two different human postures is a challenging task, because human motion usually contains free-form deformation. To overcome this difficulty, we propose a new matching algorithm to estimate the correspondence of contour points between different postures in terms of shape context descriptor.

First, we obtain an initial guess of the correspondence between p^t and p^{t+1} by minimizing the total cost of their shape context:

$$E(\pi)=\sum_i C(p^t_i, p^{t+1}_{\pi(i)}). \qquad (10)$$

However, as shown in Fig. 5(a), the estimate of correspondences contains several error-matches, because the cost function merely considers the matching cost between isolated points while ignores the global consistency. Hence, we adopt an error-match correction mechanism to solve this problem. First, we assume that correct correspondences should preserve the ordering of contour points induced from shape to maintain the global consistency. Hence, we propose to detect error-matches as those pairs which disobey the following rule::

$$if\ i_1 < i_2 < ... < i_n, then\ \pi(i_1) < \pi(i_2) < ... < \pi(i_n). \qquad (11)$$

After we determine all the error-matches in π, we then re-estimate the correspondence between those contour points by minimizing the coordinate transformation error:

$$\arg\min_{\pi'(i)\in p^{t+1}} \left\{ \frac{1}{n}\sum_i^n \sqrt{(p^{t+1}_{(\pi'(i),x)} - T(p^t_{(i,x)}))^2 + (p^{t+1}_{(\pi'(i),y)} - T(p^t_{(i,y)}))^2} \right\}, \qquad (12)$$

where *T(.)* denotes the estimated TPS transform by using [6]. Fig. 5(b) shows an example of corrected correspondence π' between p^t and p^{t+1}. Once π' is computed, we then calculate the displacement $\Delta p^t_i = T(p^t_i) - p^t_i$ of each contour point and use the displacement as a guidance to deform the input image O.

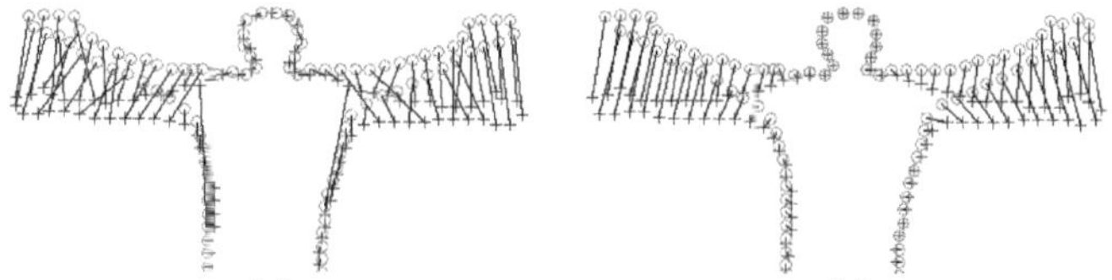

(a) (b)

Fig. 5. An example of (a) inconsistent contour point matching and (b) error-match correction.

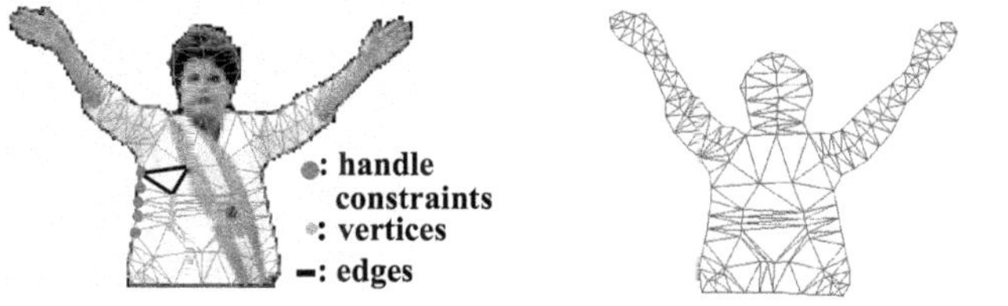

(a) (b)

Fig. 6. An example of triangular mesh deformation. (a) the result of mesh triangulation and the illustration of handle constraint, vertex and edge. (b) the result of mesh deformation.

3.2 Triangular Mesh Deformation

Next, to generate a new posture O' from O, we propose to first decompose O into a set of triangular mesh T^O and then deform each triangular mesh on O according to the handle constraints and the corresponding displacement Δp^t_i. Our approach includes three major steps: mesh triangulation, handle constraints computation and mesh deformation. In the first step, a set of contour point p^O is uniformly sampled on the shape contour of O. Then we apply the constrained conforming Delaunay triangulation based on p^O to decompose O into a set of triangular mesh T^O (as shown in Fig. 6(a)). In the second step, we obtain the displacement between p^O and p^t using technique described in Section II.A and then use p^O and its corresponding target position $p^{O}_i{'} = p^O_i + \Delta p^t_{\pi(i)}$ as inputs to deform each triangular mesh on O. In the third step, we adopt an edge-based mesh deformation technique [2] to deform the computed triangular meshes to generate new posture O' of O. The deformation task is accomplished by minimizing the distortion of the edge vectors under the handle constraints p^O:

$$\arg\min_{v'\in V}\left\{ \sum_{\{i,j\}\in E}\left\|(v_j'-v_i') - T_{ij}(v_j - v_i)\right\|^2 + \omega\sum_{i\in P^O}\left\|(v_i'-P^O_i)\right\|^2 \right\}. \qquad (13)$$

where v_i is the vertex coordinate of the original shape of O, v_i' is the vertex coordinate of deformed shape, E is the set of edges of all triangular meshes, ω is a weight factor, and T_{ij} is the rotation matrix used to map the vertices around the edge to new positions as closely as possible.

Fig. 6(a) shows an example of the handle constraints p^O, vertexes V and edges E of O. Since the target position $P^{O}_i{'}$ of p^O_i is computed in the previous step, the new coordinate of each vertex can be easily obtained according to Eq. (13). Fig. 6(b) shows an example of mesh deformation.

3.3 Texture Transferring

After the new vertex coordinate v_i' of v_i is obtained, we next start to transfer the texture from O to O'. In other words, we need to map the original triangular mesh T_i^O to the deformed triangular mesh $T_i^{O}{'}$ so as to complete the texture transferring task. We first convert every point $r(x,y)$ in the mesh $T_i^O(v_{i1}(x_1,y_1), v_{i2}(x_2,y_2), v_{i3}(x_3,y_3))$ into the barycentric coordinate system by computing the vector of barycentric coordinate $(\lambda_1, \lambda_1, \lambda_1)$:

$$\begin{aligned} \lambda_1 &= \frac{(y_2-y_3)(x-x_3)+(x_3-x_2)(y-y_3)}{(y_2-y_3)(x_1-x_3)+(x_3-x_2)(y_1-y_3)}, \\ \lambda_2 &= \frac{(y_3-y_1)(x-x_3)+(x_1-x_3)(y-y_3)}{(y_3-y_1)(x_2-x_3)+(x_1-x_3)(y_2-y_3)}, \\ \lambda_3 &= 1-\lambda_1-\lambda_2. \end{aligned} \tag{14}$$

Then, we use the computed coordinate $(\lambda_1, \lambda_1, \lambda_1)$ to map $r(x,y)$ into $r'(x',y')$, which are in T_i^O and $T_i^{O}{'}$ respectively, by

$$\begin{bmatrix} x' \\ y' \end{bmatrix} = [\lambda_1, \lambda_2, \lambda_3] \times \begin{bmatrix} v_1'(x_1', y_1') \\ v_2'(x_2', y_2') \\ v_3'(x_3', y_3') \end{bmatrix} \tag{15}$$

where $v_i'(x_i', y_i')$ is the vertex coordinate of $T_i^{O}{'}$. Fig. 7 shows an example of the texture transferring result.

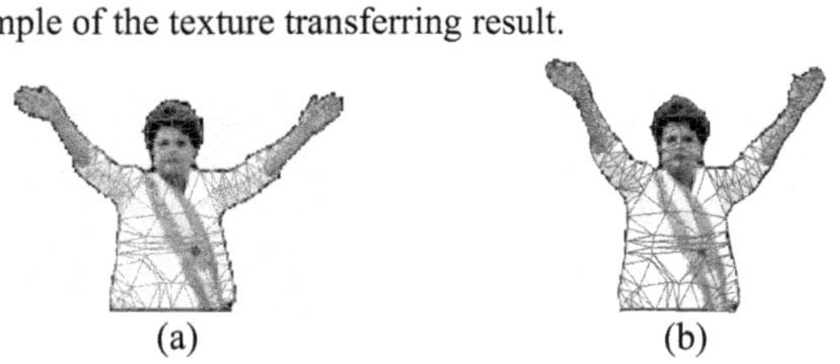

Fig. 7. An example of texture transferring. (a) input object image *O*. (b) result of texture transferring.

4. EXPERIMENT RESULTS

To test the effectiveness of the proposed human motion extrapolation method, we conducted two sets of experiment. In each experiment, we only use an object image as input to generate a new motion sequence according to the retrieved motions. In Fig. 8, the first column is the input image. The results of motion retrieval are shown in the odd rows and the corresponding motion extrapolation results are shown in the even rows.

5. CONCLUSIONS

We proposed a new framework to automatically and efficiently generate new motion sequence based on an input image. Two major steps are involved in this work: motion retrieval and human motion extrapolation. The first step, *motion retrieval*, efficiently retrieves reference motions from a human motion database and also guarantees the motion consistency. The second step, *human motion extrapolation*, synthesizes new postures according to the retrieved motions by deforming the triangular mesh and transferring the texture of input image consecutively. The limitation of our proposed algorithm is that the result of motion extrapolation heavily relies on the retrieved motions. If there exists no similar posture in the human motion database, users are suggested to collect more reference postures to improve the performance.

6. REFERENCES

[1] S. Belongie, J. Malik and J. Puzicha, "Shape matching and object recognition using shape contexts," *IEEE Transactions on Pattern Analysis and Machine Intelligence*, vol. 24, issue 4, pp. 509 – 522, 2002.

[2] T. Igarashi and Y. Igarashi "Implementing as-rigid-as-possible shape manipulation and surface flattening," *Journal of Graphics Tools*, vol. 14, number 1, pp. 17-30, 2009.

[3] L. Kovar , M. Gleicher and F. Pighin, "Motion graphs," *in Proc. of the 29th annual conference on Computer graphics and interactive techniques*, vol. 21, issue 3, July 2002.

[4] J. Kobayashi, C. K. Bi and S. Takahashi, "Sophisticated Construction and Search of 2D Motion Graphs for Synthesizing Videos," *Fourth Pacific-Rim Symposium on Image and Video Technology*, pp. 487-494, 2010.

[5] J. B. Tenenbaum, V. de Silva, and J. C. Langford, "A global geometric framework for nonlinear dimensionality reduction," *Science*, Vol. 290, pp. 2319- 2323, 2000.

[6] F. L. Bookstein, *Morphometric Tools for Landmark Data: Geometry and Biology.* Cambridge Univ. Press, 1991.

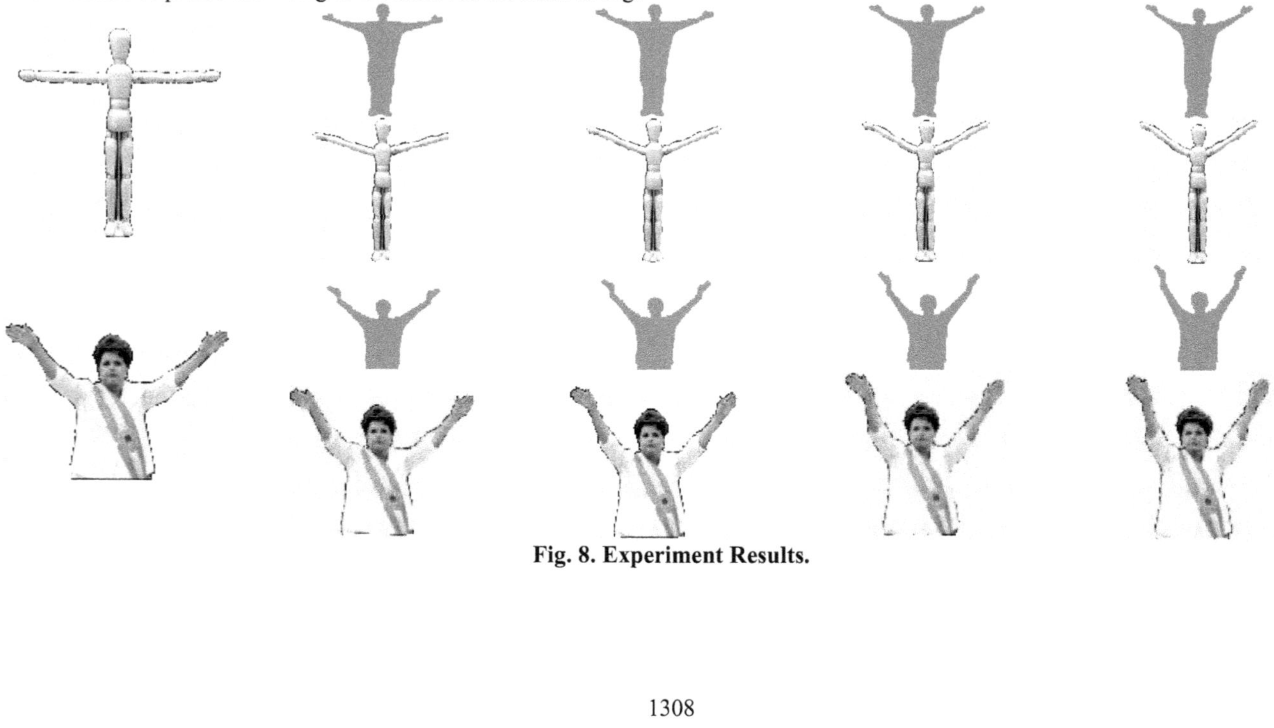

Fig. 8. Experiment Results.

CuteChat: A Lightweight Tele-immersive Video Chat System* †

Jiangbo Lu[1], Viet Anh Nguyen[1], Zeping Niu[2], Bhavdeep Singh[2], Zhiping Luo[1], Minh N. Do[3]
[1]Advanced Digital Sciences Center, Singapore
[2]Nanyang Technological University, Singapore
[3]University of Illinois at Urbana-Champaign, IL, USA
{jiangbo.lu,vanguyen}@adsc.com.sg, {niuz0003,bhav0004}@e.ntu.edu.sg
luozhipi@gmail.com, minhdo@illinois.edu

ABSTRACT

This paper presents a lightweight tele-immersive video chat system named *CuteChat*. Based on our recently developed video object cutout technology, the CuteChat system is designed and optimized to provide a radically new video chat experience by merging each participant in the same shared space, allowing them to interact more naturally in an integrated manner. With the goal to make the system easily accessible by massive consumers, we address the challenges in the whole pipeline of video processing, coding, communication, composition, and playback. Extensive experiments have shown that the proposed CuteChat system runs reliably and comfortably in real time on one's laptop or desktop PC, and it needs only a commodity webcam for video acquisition and just public Internet for tele-immersive video conferencing. With such a really minimal deployment requirement, we present a variety of interesting applications and user experiences created by the CuteChat system.

Categories and Subject Descriptors

H.5.1 [**Multimedia Information Systems**]: Video; I.4.9 [**Image Processing and Computer Vision**]: Applications

General Terms

Design, Experimentation, Performance

Keywords

Video chat, tele-immersive system, video object cutout

1. INTRODUCTION

Internet-based video chat and conferencing have become increasingly popular these years, thanks to easy access to the Internet, free PC to PC video call services, and easily available commodity webcams. However, the functionality and user experience that existing commercial video chat systems can provide are still rather limited and sometimes unsatisfying. For instance, a user may dislike showing his private space during a video conferencing session. Another case is that a business user may like to make his live presentation more engaging if two separate pieces of content to share (slides and his own video) can be seamlessly integrated into one. For these reasons and also more, tele-immersive (TI) systems have attracted many research interests in the last decade. The ultimate goal of TI systems is to capture full-body human motion in 3D and transmitting this information over the networks, and finally render the 3D photorealistic representations of remote users into a virtual space at interactive rates. Although recently some 3D TI systems that demonstrate interesting remote collaboration applications have been developed, such as the National Tele-Immersion Initiative [4] and TEEVE [9], there are still several barriers that hinder their wide deployment in real life. Typically, these 3D TI systems require bulky and expensive 3D video capturing setup, high transmission bandwidth, and a number of extra hardware and high-performance computers.

(a) (b)

Figure 1: (a) CuteChat system setup. (b) An example composited video frame merging two remote users into a common background environment. (All the figures in this paper are best viewed in color.)

Motivated by the lack of a practical TI solution to meet users' real desires in experiencing immersive video chat and remote collaboration, we present in this paper a lightweight TI video chat system based on a minimal setup requirement, i.e., a webcam, a PC plus the public Internet. We call this system *CuteChat*. As shown in Figure 1, the CuteChat system allows merging two or multiple video conferencing participants into the same shared background environment, and they can interact with each other or with the selected background content (e.g., presentation slides, online photo albums) in a more natural and integrated manner.

Taking a holistic system design and optimization approach, this

*Area chair: Pal Halvorsen.

†This work was done when Zeping Niu and Bhavdeep Singh were interning at Advanced Digital Sciences Center.

MM'11, November 28–December 1, 2011, Scottsdale, Arizona, USA.

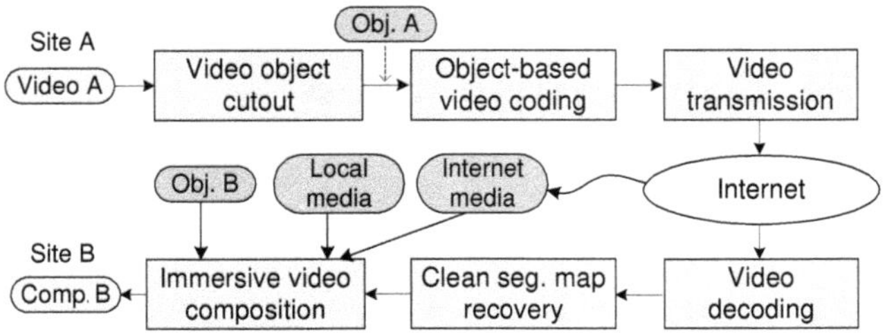

Figure 2: System overview.

paper addresses the challenges in the key components of the CuteChat system including real-time video object cutout with a single webcam, object-based video coding, low-latency video communication and multiparity video conferencing, immersive video composition and mixed-reality. As an end result, the proposed CuteChat system is able to perform a two-way, Internet-based immersive video conferencing between two remote users, and it deals with VGA-sized (640 × 480) video object cutout, encoding and decoding in real time on a commodity laptop or desktop PC.

1.1 Related Work

As discussed in the introduction, the existing 3D TI systems [4, 9] are usually very bulky, bandwidth-demanding, and computationally intensive, which seriously limit their wide applications in daily practice. Wu *et al.* [8] recently attempted to enhance the portability of the existing TI systems, but their system still demands nontrivial setups. Prior research has also been conducted to develop 2D TI systems (e.g., [3]) based on commodity cameras and computers. However, the key foreground segmentation techniques adopted are often very rudimentary and cannot generate high-quality TI compositions as provided by our system.

Segmenting a foreground layer from a live video, or video object cutout, in real time is a challenging research problem. Though recent years have witnessed some important advances in this research field [1, 2, 6, 7], the technology existing today is still distant from what a practical solution really desires, especially when it is put under a context of live video teleconferencing. Some known issues are small video resolutions e.g., 320 × 240, inaccurate foreground segmentation under challenging test conditions, and requiring stereo cameras [2] or additional depth sensors [7].

2. CUTECHAT SYSTEM

2.1 Overview

Figure 2 gives an overview of the CuteChat system, where only a pair of a sender and a receiver is shown for simplicity. In reality, our system actually supports multiparty, two-way video conferencing. At the sender site (site A in Figure 2), a commodity webcam is used to capture a live video stream, which is processed with our video object cutout technique to segment out object A in real time. Next, object-based video coding is performed to encode the foreground object stream using blue color as the background chroma key. Then, the compressed object video with a default resolution of 640 × 480 is transmitted over the public Internet, reaching the receiver site under the management of an enhanced video delivery scheme. After decoding the object video, a clean segmentation map recovery method is applied to reconstruct a clean foreground segmentation map, which would otherwise contain boundary artifacts caused by compressing object video with background chroma keying. Lastly, the user has a range of options regarding how to composite the final video to be displayed on screen. She can choose to

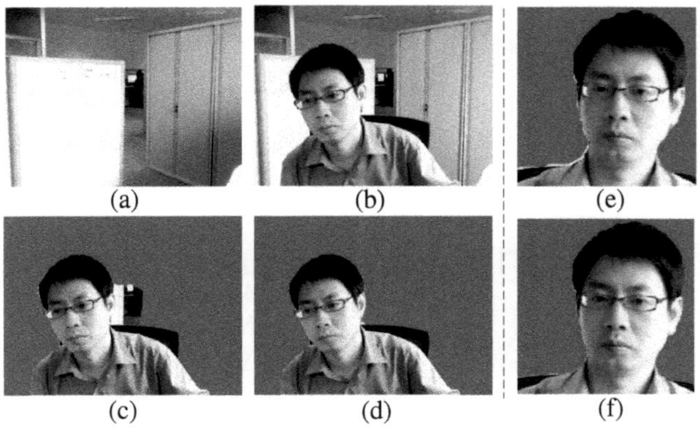

Figure 3: Video object cutout. (a) Known background. (b) A live video frame where a background person with similar colors was moving. (c) Cutout result yielded by our implementation of [6]. (d) Our cutout result. Close-up of the result without (e) and with (f) using our labeling refinement technique.

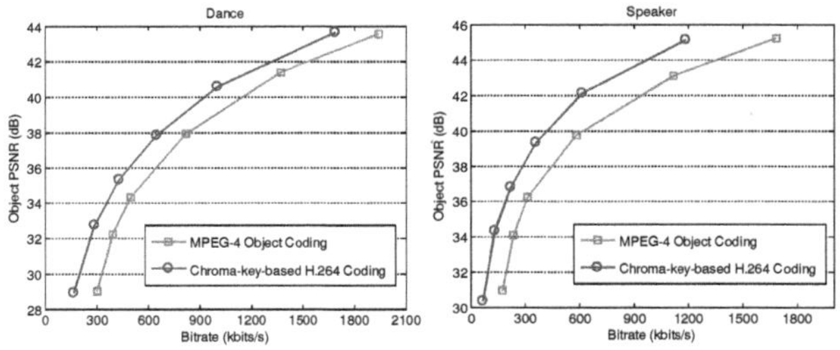

Figure 4: Performance comparison of implicit shape and object coding using H.264 and MPEG-4.

merge her own object video into the final frames, while the background content (e.g., slides, photos) can be selected either from the local store, or streamed dynamically from somewhere in the Internet as shared by the site A.

2.2 Video object cutout

As illustrated in Figure 2, video object cutout is the very first processing step that is critical to the proposed CuteChat system. Assuming that the background is known and the webcam is static, we have developed a practical solution for real-time segmenting a foreground layer from a live video captured by a single webcam. Though this assumption appears somewhat constrained, a good solution can be widely deployed and it enables aforementioned exciting applications with no additional cost. In fact, segmenting the foreground layer accurately from a complex scene where various changes can happen in the background is still rather challenging. A presentation of our video cutout technology is out of the scope of this paper (also due to the IP protection process). Basically, our technology consists of two major steps, i.e., *layer estimation* and *labeling refinement.* Figure 3 shows some video object cutout results (with background in blue).

2.3 Object-based video coding

Implicit H.264 object coding. For standard compliance and higher coding efficiency, a chroma-key-based scheme using H.264 is adopted over MPEG-4 object coding to encode the cutout object. Background is replaced by a special color prior to encoding by H.264 and chroma keying is used to recover the object region at

Figure 5: Chroma keying-based clean shape recovery without and with using the proposed method.

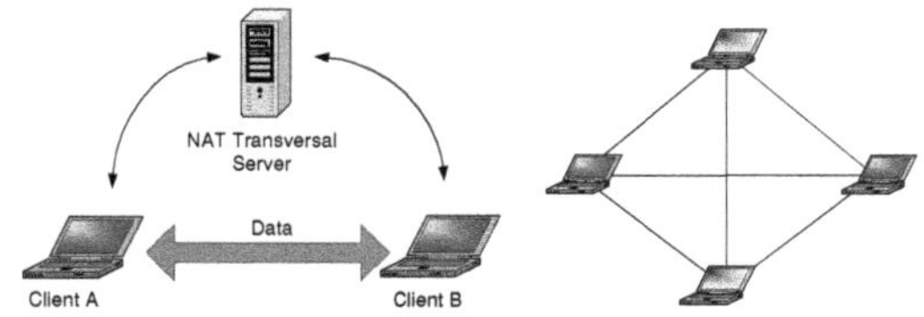

Figure 6: NAT traversal mechanism and multiparty conferencing architecture in CuteChat.

the receiver site. Figure 4 shows the superior coding performance of chroma-key-based H.264 over MPEG-4 object coding.

Effective chroma keying. Due to quantization artifact, background color can cross the boundary and bleed into the object region. Simple thresholding in the shape recovery will result in many outliers and undesirable boundary (see Figure 5). To handle these misclassified pixels, a robust nonlinear filter is applied to the binary mask obtained by the chroma keying. Essentially, the current pixel is reassigned as a background pixel if the number of neighboring background pixels exceeds a certain threshold.

Fast encoding scheme. To speed up the encoding process, computational power is mostly reserved for the object region. Extensive mode decision process for the background region is eliminated with the early skip mode detection.

2.4 Networking and multiparty conferencing

A P2P connection is established between two clients in CuteChat for exchanging media data. To traverse NAT, a server in public domain with the basic implementation of a UDP hole punching technique is deployed to establish the P2P connection. Actual media data is exchanged in the P2P session without going through the NAT traversal server (see Figure 6). For low-cost and flexible setup, a full mesh architecture is utilized for multiparty conferencing instead of a complex and expensive centralized solution. That is each client connects to every other client for sending and receiving media data from remote sites, which is similar to [5].

2.5 Immersive video composition

As shown in Figure 2, immersive video composition is the module where a variety of contents from different sources are merged together. Specifically, we have implemented two different content composition and sharing options. First, users can select to immerse only the incoming video object or both remote and local video objects into a background scene. Second, the user can opt for sharing her local media (e.g., presentation slides) or any online public media (e.g., photos in Flickr). For the latter, a keyword-based image search and sharing panel will pop up next to the main output window (Figure 1(a)). With one click the user can easily share with her conversing party personal photos or other digital medias in the Internet. Instead of transmitting the photo itself, only the corresponding URL associated with the user's click will be sent to the

Table 1: Execution speed of our algorithm in FPS

Resolution	w/o multi-threading		w/ multi-threading	
	Laptop	Desktop	Laptop	Desktop
640×480	12.3	12.1	17.1	18.4
1280×960	9.6	9.3	13.9	17.5

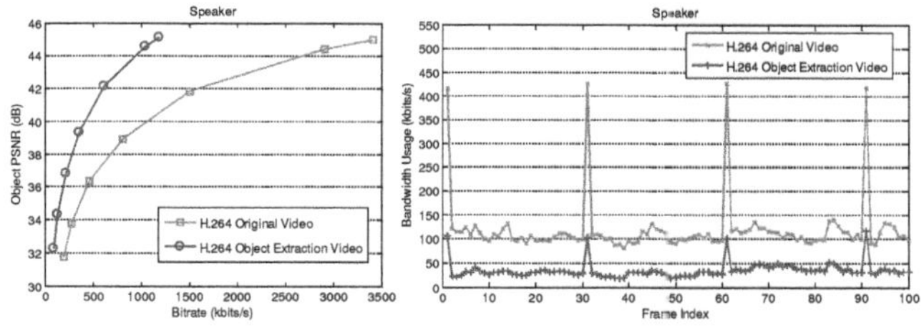

Figure 8: Bandwidth savings given by object cutout coding compared with the original video content.

remote site. After receiving this URL command from the socket, a worker thread is invoked to download the specified photo from the Internet automatically, and it will update the remote site's background image when it is ready. Our experiments show that users like this new feature of instantly sharing photos as the background while conducting video chats at the same time.

2.6 Software Implementation

Microsoft DirectShow framework is utilized to implement CuteChat due to the flexible and scalable media content manipulation through the filter concept. Video object cutout and fast chroma-key-based H.264 object coding are wrapped into the customized filters. Received video data from the other site is put into a buffer that is queried by a merge filter to integrate them into a virtual space. This architecture makes it straightforward and easy to extend to multiparty conferencing.

3. EXPERIMENTS

This section first evaluates the performance of the key components and then presents overall user experience study.

Video object cutout quality and speed. Figure 7 shows foreground segmentation results achieved by our video cutout technique under a variety of challenging test conditions. It deals with these cases very well. Table 1 reports the execution speeds of the proposed algorithm tested on a laptop and a desktop PC. Both CPUs contain four cores, each running at 2.7GHz. We have measured the speed of using a single CPU core and also that after exploiting the multi-threading (MT) technique to parallelize two selected modules. However, the code has not been fully optimized yet. For the VGA resolution, even our single-core version is able to segment the foreground object accurately at a real-time speed. After MT acceleration, our method can even process 1280×960 videos at 14 FPS on the mainstream CPU in one's laptop, while the CPU load is just around 37%.

Object-based video coding. By throwing out the undesired background and non-interesting objects, it allows both to reduce the required bitrate and to speed up the encoding process. Figure 8 shows the rate-distortion curves obtained by encoding the original video content and object cutout, respectively. For the same visual quality, about *three* times bandwidth savings can be achieved at the medium bitrate range; moreover, smaller sizes of I frames (spikes in the right figure) will ease the network congestion and delay in transmitting video contents. Table 2 reports the coding

(a) (b) (c) (d) (e) (f)

Figure 7: Foreground segmentation results for various test cases. (a) A large number of similar black pixels in the background. (b) Picture changes on the TV set and time-varying cast shadow of a ceiling fan. (c) A rotating fan in front of the clutter background. (d) A intruder of bigger size walked toward the camera. (e) A lamp in the up-left corner switched on. (f) A moving person in the background (a video clip from [1]).

Table 2: Video coding performance comparison

Resolution	Bitrate (Kbits/s)	Encoding frame rate (fps)	
		Object cutout	Original frames
640 × 480	1,200	34.3	12.4
	600	41.2	16.5
1280 × 960	2,400	16.2	6.7
	1,200	18.4	8.3

Figure 9: Multiparty immersive video conferencing.

speeds for different video quality with and without object cutout. The encoding process is significantly accelerated, hence leaving more CPU resources for other tasks running concurrently.

Multiparty immersive video conferencing. With the compressed video bitrate of 350 kbits/s, CuteChat can easily support up to five participants over the public Internet with acceptable and smooth video quality thanks to the bandwidth savings mentioned earlier. Figure 9 shows the immersive and interactive communication features in CuteChat, where remote conferees are integrated in the same virtual sharing space. While remote conferees are merged at the bottom of the shared space, a user-selectable conferee can be picked and displayed with a higher quality in the main window. The virtual space can be easily changed to local or remote resources (e.g., document, image, or video) to provide enjoyable and effective communication experiences.

User experience. We have conducted user experience study to find out how users perceive the CuteChat system. We observed that users are very interested in this system. They are impressed by the real-time segmentation of foreground at high quality from live videos, feeling that his/her webcam has been transformed into an intelligent one magically. Users also really enjoy the immersive video chat features. They feel more tightly connected with remote conferees and selected background content, after replacing the distractive original backgrounds with a shared 2D space.

4. CONCLUSION

In this paper, we have presented the design and implementation of a lightweight tele-immersive video chat system based on truly commodity capturing, computing, and networking setups. We addressed the challenges in the key components of the proposed CuteChat system, but also exploited the synergy between different modules to maximize the overall system performance. Our future plan is to further improve the current system and related key technology, and conduct a more extensive user experience evaluation.

5. REFERENCES

[1] A. Criminisi, G. Cross, A. Blake, and V. Kolmogorov. Bilayer segmentation of live video. In *Proc. of CVPR*, 2006.

[2] V. Kolmogorov, A. Criminisi, A. Blake, G. Cross, and C. Rother. Bi-layer segmentation of binocular stereo video. In *Proc. of CVPR*, 2005.

[3] C. W. Lin, Y. J. Chang, C. M. Wang, Y. C. Chen, and M. T. Sun. A standard-compliant virtual meeting system with active video object tracking. *EURASIP Journal on ASP*, 2002.

[4] D. E. Ott and K. Mayer-Patel. Coordinated multi-streaming for 3D tele-immersion. In *Proc. of ACM Multimedia*, 2004.

[5] R. Sheppard *et al.* New digital options in geographically distributed dance collaborations with teeve: Tele-immersive environments for everybody. In *ACM Multimedia*, 2007.

[6] J. Sun, W. Zhang, X. Tang, and H.-Y. Shum. Background cut. In *Proc. of ECCV*, 2006.

[7] L. Wang, C. Zhang, R. Yang, and C. Zhang. Tofcut: towards robust real-time foreground extraction using a time-of-flight camera. In *Proc. of 3DPVT*, 2010.

[8] W. Wu, R. Rivas, A. Arefin, S. Shi, R. Sheppard, B. Bui, and K. Nahrstedt. MobileTI: A portable tele-immersive system. In *Proc. of ACM Multimedia*, 2009.

[9] Z. Yang, Y. Cui, B. Yu, J. Liang, K. Nshrstedt, S. H. Jung, and R. Bajscy. TEEVE: The next generation architecture for tele-immersive environments. In *Proc. of 7th ISM*, 2005.

Energy-aware Complexity Adaptation for Mobile Video Calls

Haiyang Ma†, Deepak Gangadharan‡, Nalini Venkatasubramanian§, Roger Zimmermann‡
† Graduate School for Integrative Sciences and Engineering,‡ School of Computing
†‡National University of Singapore, Singapore
§ Dept. of Computer Science, University of California, Irvine
§nalini@ics.uci.edu
†‡{haiyang,gdeepak,rogerz}@comp.nus.edu.sg

ABSTRACT

High energy consumption has become a challenge for multimedia applications on mobile platforms. We propose a cross layer framework that integrates complexity adaptation and energy conservation for mobile video calls. First we select the most utility-aware encoding and decoding parameters for videos of different motion levels through extensive offline profiling and analysis. Then we design a feedback algorithm to adaptively apply different coding parameters while monitoring the system performance online during a video call. To minimize energy consumption, we utilize Dynamic Voltage and Frequency Scaling (DVFS) for the CPU and buffered transmissions for the network. Our experimental results show an effective saving on energy consumption, with on average 52% savings on the CPU and 30% on the wireless network, while still maintaining high quality service.

Categories and Subject Descriptors

C.3 [**Special-purpose and application-based systems**]: Real-time and embedded systems; C.4 [**Performance of Systems**]: modeling techniques

General Terms

Algorithms, Design, Experimentation

Keywords

Energy-use optimization, adaptation, mobile video calls

1. INTRODUCTION

In recent years we have witnessed the explosive increase and widespread adoption of mobile devices such as smartphones and tablet PCs as entertainment hubs where multimedia applications have been emerging as a dominant usage pattern. For such applications sufficient processing power needs to be provided and a specific level of QoS (Quality of Service) should be sustained. As a result, they pose huge burdens for mobile devices with only constrained resources such as battery capacity, memory and processing capability.

Recently video calling has been introduced into mobile platforms, which we refer to as *Mobile Video Calls*, such as Apple's FaceTime. Compared with traditional multimedia applications, mobile video calls entail both an encoder and a decoder in simultaneous execution on energy-consuming hardwares such as CPU, graphical display, wireless network interface card (NIC) and integrated camera. Therefore mobile devices are more susceptible to fast draining of the battery and severe degradation in QoS. While past research has concentrated on workload reduction for either an encoder or a decoder, complexity adaptation of dual coding algorithms on mobile platforms has not been explored yet.

We propose an integrated framework based upon complexity adaptation and energy conservation for mobile video calls. We explore the complexity-quality design space for MPEG-4 [1] through detailed profiling and choose the most utility-aware coding parameters with regard to the video's context changes in a mobile scenario. We design a feedback-based adaptation mechanism where execution conditions of coding work, such as video quality, buffer size, coding delay, etc., are continuously fed back. In this way we manage to sustain QoS while considerably reducing the workload and energy consumption of mobile video calls.

2. RELATED WORK

Various methods to reduce the workloads of different functional components of video coding have been proposed. For the decoder, Peng [6] suggests properly pruning the DCT data within macroblocks to scale the computational complexity. Ji *et al.*[5] propose substitution of pixel interpolation modes in motion compensation. The complexity of the decoder could also be adapted in cooperation with the encoder, as put forth by Wang *et al.*[9] who adopt decoding-complexity aware encoding. For encoding, most research efforts have been devoted to motion estimation scaling. Ji *et al.*[4] propose to decrease the search range and motion vector resolution for complexity reduction. Shafique *et al.*[7] adopt a pixel decimation pattern and adaptive stopping criteria. Zhou *et al.*[11] propose a fast inter mode decision to curtail the set of possible coding modes.

Power management for resource-demanding multimedia applications on mobile platforms has long been an impor-

*Area Chair: Pal Halvorsen

MM'11, November 28–December 1, 2011, Scottsdale, Arizona, USA.

tant research focus. Some researchers try to minimize energy consumption on hardware components, such as Cao *et al.*[2] who designed a DVFS algorithm for the CPU and, Tamai *et al.*[8] who proposed to shorten the working time of the network card using periodic bulk transfer. Some researchers seek the best tradeoff between QoS and energy consumption so that battery life can be extended without sacrificing much service quality. Typical methods include the one by Yuan *et al.*[10] who trade off multimedia quality against energy by leveraging a hierarchy of global and internal adaptations and, Hsu *et al.*[3] who utilize scalable video coding in video streaming service. However, these approaches either focus on one particular hardware component or coding functionality, and concurrent encoder and decoder optimization has not been considered. In contrast, our work provides a solution for a dual coding scenario with energy savings contributed by multiple components.

3. SYSTEM OVERVIEW

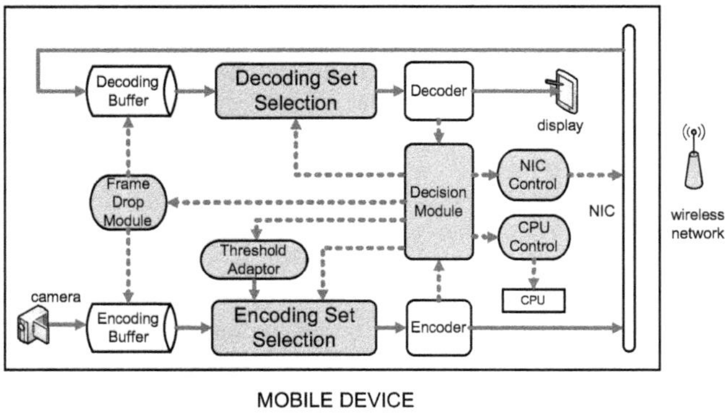

Figure 1: System framework. The white blocks illustrate the coding module and the solid arrows show its workflow. The blue (dark) blocks illustrate the proposed feedback module with its workflow indicated in dashed arrows.

The structure of our video call system on a mobile device is shown in Figure 1. The white blocks illustrate the coding module with its workflow indicated in solid arrows. Like other video conferencing systems, the coding module has an encoder and a decoder. The encoder continuously reads frames from the front-facing camera and encodes them into a compressed bitstream that is to be transmitted to the receiver through a wireless network. The decoder, on the other hand, reads the received bitstream from the network and decodes it into complete frames for display on the screen.

The blue (dark) blocks show the feedback module proposed in this paper and the dashed arrows indicate its workflow. The feedback module consists of a Frame Drop Module that decides when and how to drop frames, a Threshold Adaptor as well as an Encoding and a Decoding Set Selection module that decide which coding parameters should be selected for the current frames. The CPU and the NIC Control Module implement DVFS and buffered transmissions. The Decision Module controls all other modules' behaviors. Next we take a deeper look at the coding module for the workload reduction while the control mechanism and algorithm for the feedback module will be explained in Section 5.

4. VIDEO CODING COMPLEXITY SCALING

Most video codecs adopt a macroblock-oriented motion compensation approach and can be decomposed into several modules. The complexity of each module can be fine-tuned with different control parameters, generating videos of various qualities at different workloads. In order to explore the quality-complexity (energy) design space, we conducted extensive experiments and profiled the output and workloads of the main functional modules with various coding options. We utilize Xvid, an open source implementation of MPEG-4, as the video codec for analysis and experiments. We selected ten 150-frame video sequences in QCIF (176x144) format from a set of standard MPEG test videos[1]. We ran all profiling work on the SimpleScalar platform configured with the MIPS instruction set. The results are discussed in the following parts separately for the encoder and the decoder.

4.1 Encoder Adaptation

Motion Estimation (ME) is the most computationally intensive component of the encoding process, therefore we focus on the workload scalability in ME. During motion estimation, the encoder searches through the reference frames, trying to find a best matching motion vector (MV) for the current macroblock in terms of minimal pixel SAD (Sum of Absolute Difference). We define Motion Level $MotionL$ to be the average SAD between two consecutive raw frames, and show that video sequences with similar $MotionL$ show comparatively similar workloads under the same encoding parameters. For a frame, the workload of the ME module is controlled by three parameters: the search precision, the search range and the compensation mode. In Table 1 we list all the workload reduction options for encoding in MPEG-4 and there are 12 combinations in total, each of which is referred to as an *encoding set*. To select the most appropriate encoding set for different videos, we encode the ten test videos with all encoding options and record the resulting complexity and quality. To quantitatively evaluate the tradeoff between quality and complexity we define a utility function $Util$:

$$Util = \frac{\overline{\Delta COUNT}}{\overline{\Delta SAD}}.$$

$\overline{\Delta SAD}$, the average percentage by which the final matching SAD value increases compared to the original approach in Xvid, serves as the indicator of quality loss due to simplification in the ME process. Similarly, $\overline{\Delta COUNT}$ is the average reduction in the number of performed searches and SAD computations per macroblock. After processing all videos we observe that videos with similar motion levels tend to have similar performances for the same encoding options and the selected encoding sets fall into three clusters. As a result, we create three sets L1, L2 and L3 as listed in Table 2, which provide the best optimizations for video frames with high, medium and low $MotionL$ values.

4.2 Decoder Adaptation

Like the encoder, the decoder can also be decomposed into several components and the receiver may choose to simplify or ignore some components to decrease the workload. The primary mechanisms are Huffman Coefficient Discard and

[1]media.xiph.org/video/derf/

Item	Parameter
Search Range	original, half range, quarter range
Precision	fullpel, half and quarter pel
Coding Mode	all, DIRECT and INTER only

Table 1: Available encoding options.

Level	Range	Precision	Mode	MotionL
L1	full	subpel	all	high
L2	half	fullpel	Direct,Inter only	medium
L3	quarter	fullpel	Direct,Inter only	low

Table 2: Selected encoding sets for adaptation.

Fullpel Compensation Replacement. To test the efficacy of these two approaches, we first decode the ten test videos with the standard decoding process (SDP) where no workload reduction measure is taken. We refer to this decoding set as D0. Then four decoding optimizations are tested, namely 30%, 50% and 70% Huffman codes drop and Fullpel MC replacement, respectively. The workloads are measured as average processor cycles per frame, and $\overline{\Delta WorkRed}$ denotes the percentage of the workload reduction compared to D0. For the decoder, we define the relative quality difference $\overline{\Delta RelQ}$ to be the average PSNR between the output frames produced by SDP and the complexity reduction measures mentioned above. An upper bound of 50 dB is set for output frames of identical content. We select four videos from our test set with different *MotionL* (*grandma*: 2.57; *labvideo*: 9.91; *cityvideo*: 19.76; *husky*: 26.03). The decoding results of $\overline{\Delta WorkRed}$ and $\overline{\Delta RelQ}$ are depicted in Figure 2.

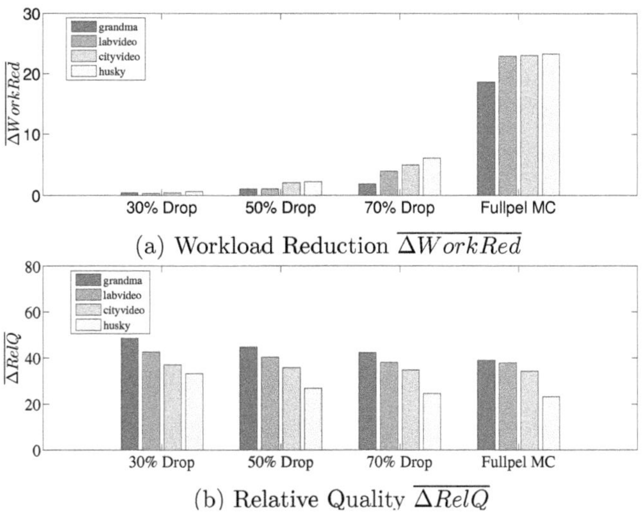

(a) Workload Reduction $\overline{\Delta WorkRed}$

(b) Relative Quality $\overline{\Delta RelQ}$

Figure 2: Workload Reduction $\overline{\Delta WorkRed}$ (a) and Relative Quality $\overline{\Delta RelQ}$ (b) for different decoding sets.

We can see from Figure 2 that when dropping Huffman codes the workload reduction rarely exceeds 5%, while Fullpel MC can reduce the workload by about 20% on average. Therefore, we will adopt Fullpel MC as the only workload reduction approach at the decoder side and refer to this decoding set as D1.

5. DECISION MODULE

Algorithm 1 illustrates the workflow of the decision module. Once a frame's coding work has been completed, its corresponding statistics (execution time, frame size, buffer queue size, etc.) are sent to the decision module, which keeps collecting statistics until the GOP size threshold is reached. *Line* 6 predicts the motion level for the next GOP based on the amount and change rate of recent GOPs. *Line* 7 calculates the difference between the averaged encoding time of current GOP frames and the standard encoding time (the inverse of the frame rate), which is used for motion level threshold adaptation in lines 9 and 10. *Line* 8 computes a similar value for the decoder. Based on the current threshold and predicted motion level, a proper coding set is assigned to the encoder and the decoder for the next GOP, as lines 11 to 22 show. We use adaptive instead of fixed thresholds to maintain a fair use of computational resources in the system.

Algorithm 1 Workflow of Decision Module

```
1:  for each frame do
2:     CollectStats(Encoder,Decoder);
3:     if !GOP_Size_Reached then
4:        continue;
5:     end if
6:     MotionL = α × prevMotionL + β × (MotionL − prevMotionL);
7:     ΔEncTime = EncTime − StdEncTime;
8:     ΔDecTime = DecTime − StdDecTime;
9:     Thresh_L = Thresh_L + λ × ΔEncTime;
10:    Thresh_H = Thresh_H + λ × ΔEncTime;
11:    if MotionL < Thresh_L then
12:       SetEncoderSet(L3);
13:    else if MotionL > Thresh_H then
14:       SetEncoderSet(L1);
15:    else
16:       SetEncoderSet(L2);
17:    end if
18:    if ΔDecTime/StdDecTime > θ then
19:       SetDecoderSet(D1);
20:    else
21:       SetDecoderSet(D0);
22:    end if
23:    FrameDropHardwareControl();
24:    ResetStats(Encoder,Decoder);
25: end for
```

To optimize network usage, the NIC is set to sleep mode when the buffer is emptied. When frames of a GOP have been encoded, the NIC is transitioned into working mode to send and receive data. The frame drop rate is proportional to buffer occupancy rate *BOR* and DVFS. The CPU frequency will be adjusted to the next lower or higher level if *BOR* is below or higher than some thresholds. If the highest frequency level has been reached in the previous round and *BOR* still remains high, more frames will be dropped and the coding set will be further lowered.

6. EXPERIMENTAL EVALUATION

We established a video call connection between a server and a ThinkPad laptop through a WiFi network, which was measured to have sufficient bandwidth and a negligible loss rate. The laptop was equipped with a 2.8GHz Intel® Core 2

Vid.	Res.	App	EDrop [%]	NPSNR [dB]	EQT [ms]
lab	640x360	S	0	33.992	1.24
		A	0	34.024	2.12
	640x480	S	0	32.768	18.96
		A	0.331	32.713	18.92
city	640x360	S	0	28.571	25.04
		A	0	29.325	27.36
	640x480	S	1.466	28.281	44.04
		A	3.864	28.294	51.72

Table 3: Performance comparison at 400kbps with standard (S) and adaptive (A) approaches.

Duo processor and an Intel® Wireless WiFi Link 5300AGN NIC. The processor supports DVFS through the ACPI interface[2] at four frequency levels: 0.8GHz, 1.6GHz, 2.13GHz and 2.8GHz. The energy model for the CPU and the NIC are derived from prior work. We recorded two 2-minute-long videos in raw YUV format at resolution 640x480, then rescaled them to 640x360. The bitrate was fixed at 400kbps. For the standard approach (S), we set the frequency to the highest available value (2.8GHz) and sent every frame once it was encoded. For the adaptive approach (A), DVFS and buffered transmission are both employed. We performed our tests five times and the results were averaged. The performances are shown in Table 3. Figure 3 shows the energy consumption of the CPU and the NIC. In Table 3 *EDrop*, *NPSNR* and *EQT* stand for encoder drop rate, encoder nominal PSNR and encoder drop rate, respectively.

From Table 3 we observe that the adaptive, energy saving mode shows comparable performance to the standard mode (at the highest CPU frequency) while its energy consumption is impressively decreased. With DVFS, the CPU energy consumption is reduced by 52.04% on average, and NIC energy is reduced by 30.88% through buffered transmission.

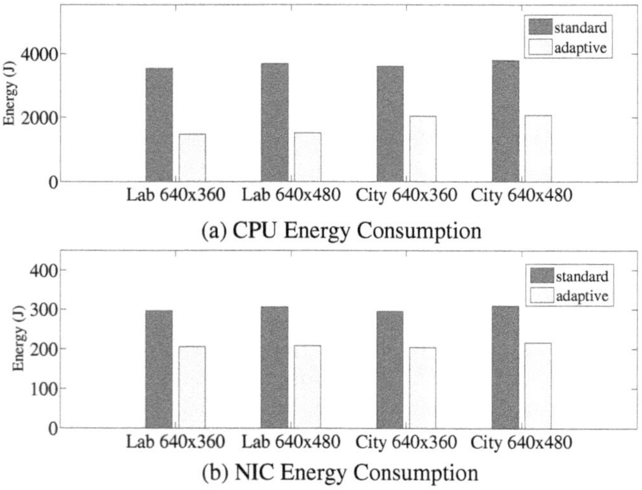

Figure 3: Energy consumption of CPU and NIC.

7. CONCLUSIONS AND FUTURE WORK

We have proposed an integrated framework for complexity adaptation and energy conservation for mobile video calls, combining selected encoding and decoding sets for videos of different motion levels into a feedback algorithm. We also utilize hardware energy saving techniques such as DVFS for the CPU and buffered transmissions for the wireless network to reduce the energy consumption while still achieving satisfactory system performance, which is validated by our experimental results under two scenarios.

Going forward, we plan to extend and implement the feedback mechanism with a holistic decision on the execution conditions of both participants. Moreover, wireless networks can be unstable, which may result in frequent data loss and varied bandwidth. Therefore, error correction and concealment must be employed.

[2]www.acpi.info

8. ACKNOWLEDGEMENT

We would like to acknowledge that this research was carried out at the Centre of Social Media Innovations for Communities (COSMIC), sponsored and supported by the Singapore National Research Foundation and Interactive & Digital Media Program Office, MDA.

9. REFERENCES

[1] ISO/IEC 14496-2:2004 - Information technology – Coding of Audio-Visual Objects – Part 2: Visual, 2004.

[2] Z. Cao, B. Foo, L. He, and M. van der Schaar. Optimality and Improvement of Dynamic Voltage Scaling Algorithms for Multimedia Applications. In *45th Design Automation Conference*, pages 179–184, 2008.

[3] C. Hsu and M. Hefeeda. Achieving Viewing Time Scalability in Mobile Video Streaming Using Scalable Video Coding. In *1st ACM SIGMM Conference on Multimedia Systems*, pages 111–122, 2010.

[4] W. Ji, M. Chen, X. Ge, P. Li, and Y. Chen. A Perceptual Macroblock Layer Power Control for Energy Scalable Video Encoder Based on Just Noticeable Distortion Principle. *Journal of Network and Computer Applications*, 34(5), 2010.

[5] W. Ji, M. Chen, X. Ge, P. Li, and Y. Chen. ESVD: An Integrated Energy Scalable Framework for Low-power Video Decoding Systems. *EURASIP Journal on Wireless Communications and Networking, Special Issue on Multimedia Communications over Next Generation Wireless Networks*, 2010.

[6] S. Peng. Complexity Scalable Video Decoding via IDCT Data Pruning. In *IEEE International Conference on Consumer Electronics (ICCE)*, pages 74–75, 2001.

[7] M. Shafique, L. Bauer, and J. Henkel. 3-Tier Dynamically Adaptive Power-Aware Motion Estimator for H.264/AVC Video Encoding. In *13th International Symposium on Low Power Electronics and Design (ISLPED)*, pages 147–152, 2008.

[8] M. Tamai, T. Sun, K. Yasumoto, N. Shibata, and M. Ito. Energy-Aware Video Streaming with QoS Control for Portable Computing Devices. In *14th International Workshop on Network and Operating Systems Support for Digital Audio and Video*, pages 68–73, 2004.

[9] Y. Wang and S. Chang. Complexity Adaptive H.264 Encoding for Light Weight Streams. In *IEEE International Conference on Acoustics, Speech and Signal Processing*, pages II25–28, 2006.

[10] W. Yuan, K. Nahrstedt, S. Adve, D. Jones, and R. Kravets. GRACE-1: Cross-layer Adaptation For Multimedia Quality and Battery Energy. *IEEE Transactions on Mobile Computing*, pages 799–815, 2006.

[11] Z. Zhou and M. Sun. Fast Macroblock Inter Mode Decision and Motion Estimation for H.264/MPEG-4 AVC. In *International Conference on Image Processing (ICIP)*, pages 789–792. IEEE, 2004.

Fast Frame-rate Up-conversion of Depth Video via Video Coding *

Yanjie Li, Lifeng Sun
Information Science and Technology Department
Tsinghua University, Beijing, 100084
carol.lyj@gmail.com,sunlf@tsinghua.edu.cn

Tianfan Xue
Department of Information Engineering
The Chinese University of HongKong
xtf009@ie.cuhk.edu.hk

ABSTRACT

Recent development of depth sensors has facilitated the progress of 2D-plus-depth methods for 3D video representation, for which frame-rate up-conversion (FRUC) of depth video is a critical step. However, due to the computational cost of state-of-the-art FRUC methods, real time applications of 2D-plus-depth is still limited. In this paper, we present a method of speeding up the FRUC of the depth video by treating it as part of a video coding process, combined with a novel color-mapping algorithm is adopted to improve the quality of temporal upsampling. Experiments show that the proposed systems saves up to 99.5% of the frame interpolation time, while achieving virtually identical reconstructed depth video as state-of-the-art methods.

Categories and Subject Descriptors

I.4.9 [**Image Processing and Computer Vision**]: Applications

General Terms

Design, Performance

Keywords

Depth video, Frame-Rate Up-Conversion (FRUC), Video coding, Motion-Compensated Frame Interpolation (MCFI)

1. INTRODUCTION

Depth video representing the relative distance of objects to the video camera are useful in many multimedia applications, especially in 3DTV. The recent development of depth sensors for capturing depth maps has drawn great interests to 2D-plus-depth methods [4]. However, due to the computational and physical complexities, most methods for capturing depth video, such as stereoscopic and range sensors based systems, can only provide information at a low frame-rate, which severely limits the applications of 2D-plus-depth. Therefore, temporal upsampling of depth videos, also known as frame-rate up-conversion (FRUC), has become an emerging research area [1, 2, 3, 5].

State-of-the-art researches utilize motion-compensation assisted block-based frame interpolation (MCFI) [2, 5, 6] for FRUC of depth video. Conventional algorithms conduct motion estimation using the depth video itself, and are therefore unreliable because depth video lacks texture for conducting accurate motion estimation. Recently, Choi et al. exploited the idea of sharing motion information from 2D video data in [2], and significantly improves the interpolation results.

Although improvement of visual quality has been achieved by applying MCFI to FRUC, a major problem of all current MCFI based methods is the time cost, especially for high-resolution fast moving 2D videos, as exhaustive search of motion directions by calculating pairwise similarities between blocks is usually necessary.

In this paper, we propose a highly efficient FRUC system, by re-using motion information extracted from the 2D video that is available in many applications. At the encoding side, motion information of 2D blocks is estimated and stored in the bitstream, and can be used directly by the decoder, thereby by-passing the majority of the time consuming motion estimation during FRUC. As motion estimation is an integral part of most video coding algorithms, our proposed algorithm introduces virtually no additional cost. Experimental results demonstrate that our method reaches state-of-the-art performance and cuts 99.5% processing time of Choi et. al.'s method.

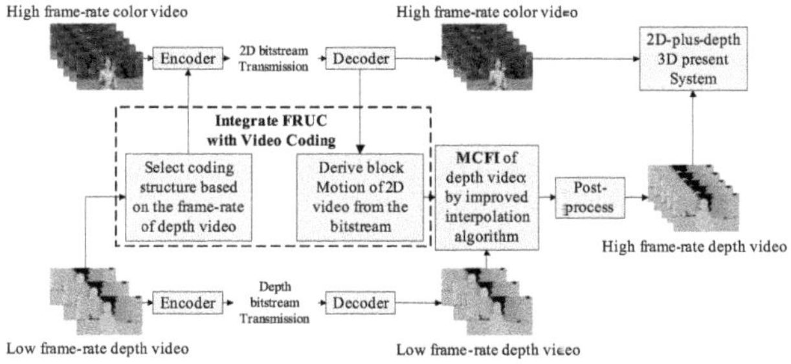

Figure 1: Proposed FRUC framework

Figure 1 illustrates the proposed algorithm on a high level. Although the H.264 AVC video coding standard was used in the experiments reported in this paper, other codecs are also applicable. On the encoder side, the coding structure selected for 2D video depends on the frame-rate of the depth

*Area chair: Pal Halvorsen

video, so that the interpolated depth frames correspond to B-frames in 2D video. On the decoder side, motion information of 2D video derived from decoder is directly used for MCFI, which greatly reduces the time cost for motion estimation. In addition, we also propose an improved interpolation algorithm, namely the color-mapping algorithm, for MCFI, leading to both subjective and objective quality improvements.

The paper is organized as follows. Section 2 gives detailed description of the proposed algorithm, with experimental results and analysis given in Section 3. Finally, Section 4 contains the conclusion.

2. PROPOSED FRAMEWORK

2.1 Integration FRUC with video coding

2.1.1 2D video coding structure selection

In performing 2D video coding, our algorithm selects a coding structure so that interpolated depth frames correspond to non-reference B-frames, whereas captured depth frames correspond to I-frames or P-frames in the 2D video. As an example, if we capture one depth frame for every three depth frames, we would choose the coding structure shown in Figure 2, so that captured (and therefore deemed more reliable) information from two temporally neighboring frames are used to represented an interpolated frame, leading to improved quality. Furthermore, the interpolated depth frames corresponding to non-reference B frames are not used for the construction of other frames, so as to reduce interpolation error propagation.

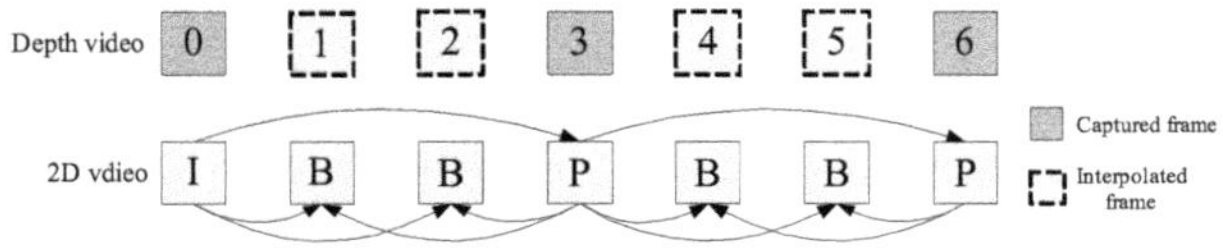

Figure 2: Example of coding structure selection

2.1.2 Motion information derivation from decoder

H.264/AVC standard divides a frame into blocks of different size and each block can be intra-predicted or inter-predicted. Block of size 4×4 is the smallest block used in H.264/AVC standard, and larger blocks can be viewed as multiple 4×4 blocks with the same prediction mode. In this paper, we choose block of size 4×4 as *basic-block* for interpolation, and use coordinate of its top-left pixel to tab a basic-block. For example, basic-block $B(x, y)$ denotes the 4×4 block with top-left pixel (x, y), and pixel $(i, j), i, j \in [0, 3]$ in $B(x, y)$ denotes the pixel $(x + i, y + j)$ in the frame.

The proposed framework divides the interpolated depth frame into basic-blocks and applies MCFI to them using the motion information of corresponding blocks in 2D map derived by H.264/AVC decoder.

Basic-blocks in the 2D B-frame can be inter-predicted or intra-predicted. The inter-predicted block is either an uni-direction predicted block which has a single pair of reference frame and motion vector, or a bi-direction predicted block which has two pairs of reference frame and motion vector, forward and backward. Block $B(x,y)$ with motion vector mv is matched to $B(x+mv_x, y+mv_y)$ in its reference frame. The intra-predicted block has no motion information between frames.

We interpolate the depth block corresponding to an inter-predicted block in 2D map by MCFI, while we fill the depth block corresponding to an intra-predicted block in the post processing described in Section 2.3.

2.2 MCFI for depth blocks corresponding to inter-predicted 2D blocks

For a depth block corresponding to an uni-direction predicted block in a 2D B-frame, we apply the improved interpolation algorithm described in Section 2.2.1, to fill it using a single pair of reference frame and motion vector.

For the depth block corresponding to a bi-direction predicted block in the 2D B-frame, we fill it by weighted average of the interpolation results of two pairs of reference frame and motion vetor. Let $B(x, y)$ denote the interpolated basic-block; $d(i, j)$ denotes pixel (i, j) in $B(x, y)$, $i, j \in [0, 3]$; and $d_f(i, j)$ and $d_b(i, j)$ denote pixel (i, j) in $B(x, y)$ filled using forward motion information and backward motion information respectively. Then $d(i, j)$ is filled as:

1) If $d_f(i, j)$ and $d_b(i, j)$ are not filled, $d(i, j)$ is not filled;
2) If $d_f(i, j)$ is filled and $d_b(i, j)$ not, $d(i, j)$ will be $d_f(i, j)$;
3) If $d_b(i, j)$ is filled and $d_f(i, j)$ not, $d(i, j)$ will be $d_b(i, j)$;
4) If both $d_f(i, j)$ and $d_b(i, j)$ are filled, the value of $d(i, j)$ will be

$$d(i, j) = \frac{T_b}{T_f + T_b} d_f(i, j) + \frac{T_f}{T_f + T_b} d_b(i, j) \tag{1}$$

where T_f and T_b denotes temporal distances from the interpolated depth frame to forward reference depth frame and backward reference depth frame, respectively.

2.2.1 Improved interpolation algorithm

As shown in Figure 3, D and F denote the interpolated depth frame and its corresponding 2D frame. Each basic block B in D has a co-located basic block B' in F. B' is matched to a block B'_R in its reference 2D frame F_R using its motion vector mv. Then we can get block B_R, co-located with B'_R, in the depth frame D_R corresponding to F_R.

Traditional interpolation algorithm just copies B_R to B. However, because shape of boundaries may change and since block motion vectors, generated in the encoder for compression purpose, may not absolutely correlate with real object motion, copying the block directly will cause distortions especially around the boundaries of objects. The distortions affect the quality of rendered 3D video seriously.

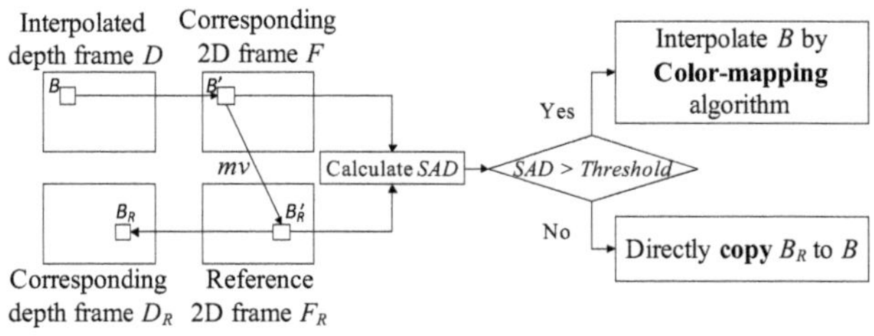

Figure 3: Improved interpolation algorithm

To solve such problem, this paper proposes an improved interpolation algorithm shown in Figure 3.

SAD in Figure 3 is calculated as:

$$SAD = \sum_{i=0}^{3} \sum_{j=0}^{3} \left| \left| c_{B'}(i, j) - c_{B'_R}(i, j) \right| \right| \tag{2}$$

where $c_{B'}(i, j)$ denotes the color value of pixel (i, j) in B' and $c_{B'_R}(i, j)$ denotes the color value of pixel (i, j) in B'_R.

Color-mapping algorithm is a novel interpolation algorithm proposed by us, which is more correct but consumes more time than block copying. Whether block copying or color-mapping algorithm is finally used depends on the similarity between B' and B'_R. When the blocks match well, we simply copy B_R to B. Otherwise, which means the motion information is not reliable or the shape of objects changes, color-mapping algorithm is selected. The threshold is chosen by considering the requirement of interpolation. Large threshold is chosen if high efficiency is required, while small value is selected if high quality is desired. In later experiments, we choose 15 because it promises satisfactory quality under ideal speed.

Basic idea of color-mapping is to map each color with a depth value locally, and interpolate each pixel according to its color in the corresponding 2D map. The process is described in Algorithm 1 and shown in Figure 4.

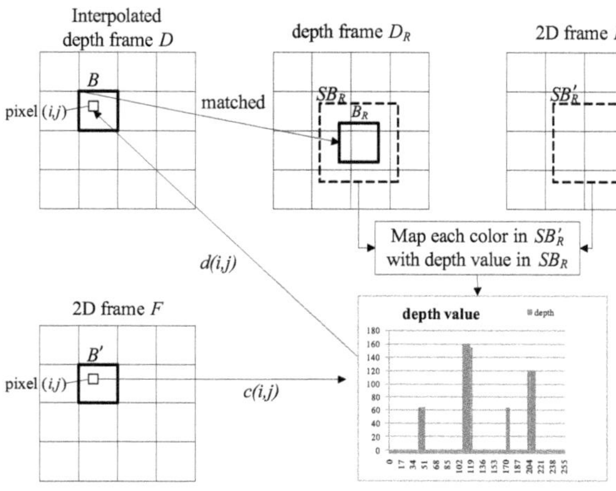

Figure 4: Process of color-mapping

The algorithm expands basic-block to super-block because 4×4 is too small to provide reliable color-depth mapping.

It is easy to understand that false motion vector will lead to larger color error and the pixel will not be filled because $weightSum = 0$. And the algorithm can also make clearer edges because pixels are filled based on color values in F.

2.3 Post processing

After MCFI, there are still pixels not filled because their color have no depth value mapped or belong to intra-predicted blocks. We fill such pixel as weighted average value of its neighboring pixels filled at the previous step. The weight depends on the distance and the color difference in 2D map between the interpolated pixel and the already filled pixel.

3. EXPERIMENTS AND RESULTS

To demonstrate the effectiveness of the proposed framework, we up-converse different sequences under different low frame-rates by using several FRUC approaches.

The testing sequences are provided by MSRA (1024×768) and Philips 3DTV website (960×540). The original frame rate of each sequence is 30 fps, and is temporally down-sample to 15, 10 and 7.5 fps. The characters of the sequences are shown in Table 1.

Because depth video is not directly used for display, we measure the quality of depth video by calculating the PSNR between the rendered free-viewpoint video at the position of nearby viewpoint and the standard free-viewpoint video rendered by the original high frame-rate depth video.

Algorithm 1 Color-mapping

Input: Interpolated basic-block B in depth frame D; matched basic-block B_R in depth frame D_R; 2D frame F and F_R corresponding to D and D_R respectively; a Gaussian filter kernel g.
Initialization: Set $m[c]$ records whether color c has a mapped depth value and set $dv[c]$ saves the depth value mapped to it

```
Expand B_R to super-block SB_R of size 8 × 8
Find super-block SB'_R co-located to SB_R in F_R
for color value c ∈ [0, 255]
    if at least one pixel in SB'_R have value c
        m[c] ← 1
        dv[c] ← average depth value of all the pixels in SB_R
                correspond to the pixels having value c in SB'_R
    else
        m[c] ← 0 and dv[c] ← 0
endfor
Find B', which is the co-located basic-block of B in F
for each pixel (i, j) in B
    Find color value c(i, j) for pixel (i, j) in B'
    Define Ω as the searching color range centered over c(i, j)
    depthSum = Σ_{c∈Ω} dv(c)m(c)g(||c − c(i, j)||)
    weightSum = Σ_{c∈Ω} m(c)g(||c − c(i, j)||)
    if weightSum ≠ 0
        d(i, j) = depthSum / weightSum
    else
        Do not fill d(i, j)
endfor
```

Table 1: Test Sequences

Sequence	*Video description*
Girl	Both 2D and depth video move slowly
Ballet	A few objects in 2D and depth video move fast
Football	2D video moves fast, depth video moves slowly
Frisbee	Both 2D and depth video move fast

3.1 Comparison with other approaches

This paper compares performance of the proposed framework with other two FRUC approaches: 1) MCFI using 2D motion information derived by full-search block matching algorithm (FBMA) as in [2], abbreviated as MCFI-F; 2) conventional MCFI using motion information of depth video in [6], which is abbreviated as MCFI-D.

PSNR of the rendered video and average time cost to dispose per frame are used to evaluate the three FRUC approaches. The experiment is done on depth video of 15 fps by CPU of 2.56GHz without any speedup by hardware or parallelism. The results are listed in Table 2.

It is obvious that our framework has the highest efficiency among the three approaches. Compared with MCFI-F, it saves up to 99.5% running time per frame. For sequences with high motion in 2D video, the advantage is notable. Our framework achieves satisfactory rendering quality, which is comparable with MCFI-F. Especially, for sequence *Football* and *Frisbee*, our framework outperforms MCFI-F obviously. This is because high motion in the 2D video of these sequences makes the motion estimation in MCFI-F unreliable and time-consuming.

Although speed of MCFI-D on some sequences is acceptable, distortion of its rendered free-viewpoint video is serious. This is mainly because the motion estimated from

Table 2: Performance Comparison

Sequence	*PSNR Time*	*Approaches*		
		ours	MCFI-F	MCFI-D
Girl	*PSNR*	26.82	26.84	26.44
	ms/f	68	1989	104
Ballet	*PSNR*	28.01	28.16	26.74
	ms/f	53	4151	241
Football	*PSNR*	26.94	26.69	26.40
	ms/f	117	13313	76
Frisbee	*PSNR*	22.86	22.88	20.96
	ms/f	88	18950	302

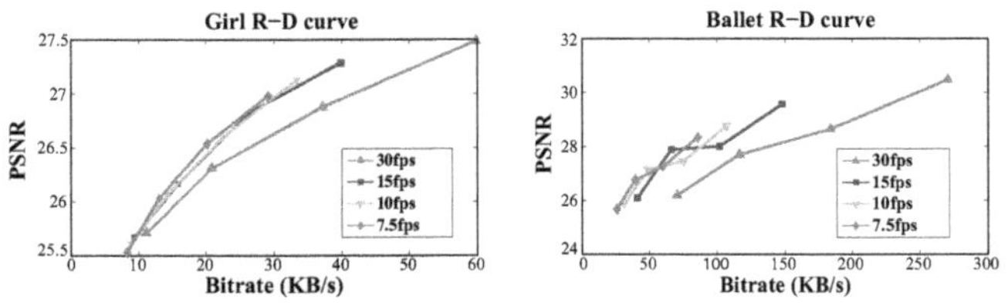

Figure 5: R-D curve under different up-conversion rate for *Girl* and *Ballet*

depth video is unreliable. For the depth video with a large motion, MCFI-D is also time consuming.

3.2 Compression by temporal down-sampling

We further compress depth video at the frame rate of 15, 10 and 7.5fps respectively and up-converse them by our framework. We also compress it at the original frame rate. For each condition, we set QP parameters from 24 to 36 in step 4. Figure 5 shows the Rate-Rendering Distortion (R-D) result of *Girl* and *Ballet*. Curves of low frame-rate are above the curves of original frame-rate, which demonstrates that we can compress depth video by temporal down-sampling it and up-conversing it using the proposed framework. The lines show that it can save up to approximately 37% bitrates of depth video while achieving the same rendering quality. We can also find that our framework is robust to large up-conversion scale. Moreover, compression under 7.5fps performs the best under small bitrates.

3.3 Subjective improvement

The visual quality of rendered images also improves when the proposed framework is exploited. Figure 6 shows the comparison between the rendered free-viewpoint samples of different compression conditions for depth video under approximate the same bitrates 68.33KB/s. It can be found that the proposed framework provides more accurate motion estimation than MCFI-D (see the arm of the lady). Moreover, compared with compression at the original 30fps, compressing low frame-rate depth video and using the proposed framework can provide clearer edges of objects (see the head of the man).

Figure 7 shows the effect of the novel color-mapping algorithm. From magnified local parts, we can see that blocks with false motion information are also interpolated correctly and boundaries are much smoother than block copying.

4. CONCLUSION

This paper speeds up the MCFI based FRUC of depth video by viewing it as part of the video coding process. This

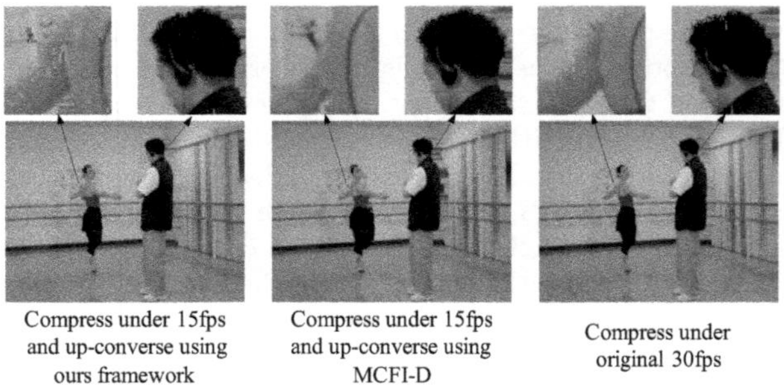

Figure 6: Visual quality of rendered frame of *Ballet*

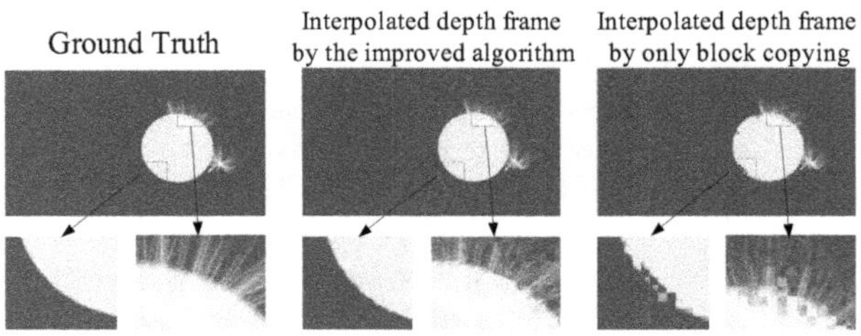

Figure 7: Effect of color-mapping algorithm

assumption is natural as video coding is commonly used in most video applications. The framework selects the coding structure for 2D video, which maps the interpolated depth frames to B frames in 2D video. And at the decoder side, motion information of corresponding 2D video are directly derived as motion estimation of depth video for MCFI, so that time cost for the motion estimation is significantly reduced. The framework also proposes a novel color-mapping interpolation algorithm, which enhances quality of interpolated depth frames.

5. ACKNOWLEDGEMENT

This work is supported by the Development Plan of China (973) under Grant No.2011CB302206, the National Natural Science Foundation of China under Grant No.60833009, and the National High-Tech Research and Development Plan of China (863) under Grant No.2009AA01Z328.

6. REFERENCES

[1] R. Cheng and K. Nahrstedt. Empirical study of 3D video source coding for autostereoscopic displays. In *Proceedings of the 15th international conference on Multimedia*, pages 573–576. ACM, 2007.

[2] J. Choi, D. Min, B. Ham, and K. Sohn. Spatial and temporal up-conversion technique for depth video. In *Image Processing (ICIP), 2009 16th IEEE International Conference on*, pages 3525–3528. IEEE, 2009.

[3] E. Ekmekcioglu, S. Worrall, and A. Kondoz. A temporal subsampling approach for multiview depth map compression. *Circuits and Systems for Video Technology, IEEE Transactions on*, 19(8):1209–1213, 2009.

[4] C. Fehn et al. Depth-image-based rendering (DIBR), compression and transmission for a new approach on 3D-TV. In *Proceedings of SPIE Stereoscopic Displays and Virtual Reality Systems XI*, volume 5291, pages 93–104. San Jose, CA, USA, 2004.

[5] H. Wang, C. Huang, and J. Yang. Depth maps interpolation from existing pairs of keyframes and depth maps for 3D video generation. In *Circuits and Systems (ISCAS), Proceedings of 2010 IEEE International Symposium on*, pages 3248–3251. IEEE, 2010.

[6] Y. Yang, Y. Tung, and J. Wu. Quality enhancement of frame rate up-converted video by adaptive frame skip and reliable motion extraction. *Circuits and Systems for Video Technology, IEEE Transactions on*, 17(12):1700–1713, 2007.

Multimodal QoE Evaluation in P2P-based IPTV Systems

Mu Mu* Johnathan Ishmael Keith Mitchell Nicholas Race Andreas Mauthe
School of Computing and Communications, InfoLab21
Lancaster University, Lancaster, LA1 4WA, United Kingdom
{m.mu, j.ishmael, k.mitchell, n.race, a.mauthe}@lancaster.ac.uk

ABSTRACT

Peer-to-Peer (P2P) technologies provide efficient and low-cost delivery for commercial and user-generated content. Although a number of audio-visual content distribution services have been developed using P2P-based mechanisms, it is still a challenge to guarantee satisfactory user experience on high quality video streaming services due to the dynamic nature of P2P distribution. An objective assessment service is the key enabler of service quality monitoring and management. However, this complex task can not be achieved by any individual objective model that only captures a certain aspect of service quality. This paper introduces a multimodal quality evaluation framework that is specifically designed and implemented for the assessment of video streaming services in P2P-based IPTV systems. Results of initial experiments show the effectiveness of this framework.

Categories and Subject Descriptors

H.5.1 [**Multimedia Information Systems**]: [Evaluation /methodology]; I.4 [**Image Processing and Computer Vision**]: Miscellaneous

General Terms

Measurement, Human Factors

Keywords

P2P-based IPTV, Quality of Experience

1. INTRODUCTION

Peer-to-peer (P2P)-based distribution mechanisms have recently become popular for video distribution, due to its high efficiency of data exchange and low cost of supporting infrastructure. Video contents are fragmented into small pieces of *chunks* before they are distributed over a meshed overlay topology. Unlike file-sharing services where the integrity of files is not affected by the receiving order or arrival time of individual chunks, chunks for a video streaming service must be delivered on time and intact for video decoding. Therefore maintaining a satisfactory level of user experience on P2P-based video services is still challenging. End users' experience of video content can be influenced by distortions caused by impairments from several entities within a P2P-based service including link quality, packet networks, P2P overlay, end system and video coding. Although a number of advanced mechanisms (e.g., [5, 6]) have been designed to better manage the user experience of video service in P2P networks, there is still a lack of a working quality evaluation service to effectively assess service quality. This paper introduces a multimodal quality evaluation framework that is specifically designed and implemented for the assessment of video streaming services in P2P-based IPTV systems. Multiple types of subjective and objective evaluation models are integrated to measure key metrics that are relevant to user experience in a collaborative way. Using the timestamps associated with different measurements, profound analysis of evaluation results can be conducted to establish service diagnosis tools, which are valuable to identify root-causes of detrimental distortions. Results of initial experiments show the effectiveness of our design.

*Area chair: Wei Tsang Ooi
*Corresponding Author

MM'11, November 28–December 1, 2011, Scottsdale, Arizona, USA.

2. BACKGROUND AND RELATED WORK

A P2P system is a self-organising system of equal, autonomous peers that aims for the shared usage of distributed resources in a networked environment, while avoiding central services [14]. In P2P systems, content data is partitioned into tagged chunks. The information about chunks are then exchanged between peers so that each peer can download data chunks from other peers concurrently [13].

Recently P2P networking is becoming popular in consumer networks where self-generated data is shared. However, it is still challenging to exploit a P2P system for commercial video streaming services due to the nature of the P2P distribution paradigm. Distributed content is usually resembled from fragments received from a number of intermediate receivers. Therefore, an excessive end-to-end delay may be experienced. The behaviour of receivers is also unpredictable. Peers are free to join and leave the service at any time, thus abandoning descendant peers [15]. Furthermore, extra overheads are introduced at the receiver to maintain storage and exchange state information.

Commercial video services such as IPTV have strict QoE requirements to guarantee a high quality level as specified by service level agreement (SLA) recognised between service providers and content consumers. In [4] the quality requirements for IPTV services are specified. It is concluded that video streams are highly sensitive to information loss and that the QoE impact is in turn correlated to a number of variables including: type of data loss, codec, loss profile and decoder concealment algorithms. QoE requirements must therefore be defined with regard to discrete quality violation events [8]. In the ITU Focus Group on IPTV, quality target metrics have been extended to consider the actual quality as perceived by end users. User level quality metrics such as "*Maximum one visible artifact per x hours*" were defined to evaluate the delivery of IPTV services [1]. The Broadband Forum has also defined a set of user level QoE metrics in [11]. For example, a criterion of "*one impairment event per 12 hours or better*" is defined for HDTV services.

3. PROBLEM SPACE AND MOTIVATION

End users' experience of video content can be deteriorated by distortions caused by impairments of several entities of a P2P-based service including link quality, packet networks, P2P overlay, end system and video coding. In order to fulfill users' expectation of service quality and to provide a benchmarking platform that compares different designs of P2P systems, a quality evaluation service is required. This evaluation service must provide accurate assessment of video service with respect of user perception while supporting service diagnosis to effectively identify root-causes of any detected quality degradation.

The quality of user experience is ultimately determined by users' subjective opinions. To collect users' opinions subjective experiments are usually carried out using well-specified test plans in dedicated test environments (e.g. [3]). However, conventional subjective experiments are time-consuming, costly and therefore not suitable for an in-service evaluation, especially in commercial IPTV services.

A number of objective quality evaluation models have been designed to conduct quality assessment. Objective models analyse video content displayed at the receiver and evaluate visual distortions using image and video signal processing tools [17, 2]. However, the analysis at end systems is not able to support comprehensive service diagnosis to identify the causes and network location of quality degradation.

Network QoS model are widely used to evaluate the impact of network impairments to services. Some advanced QoS models have been recently developed by integrating application-level metrics [18, 7]. Discrete analysis of perceptual impact of individual packet loss has also been designed to better capture user-level QoE [8, 9]. However these models are not specifically designed to evaluate impairments within the P2P overlay layer and within end systems. Furthermore, the compression distortions caused by lossy video coding can not be evaluated directly using network-layer models.

Overall, current QoE models are not able to fully support quality assessment and service diagnosis for P2P-based IPTV services. The objective is only achievable by the collaboration of multiple subjective and objective quality models, with each providing a required type of evaluation function. Service diagnosis is enabled by comparing and matching the evaluation results of relevant quality models. For instance, when an objective distortion measurement model detects a visual artefact in video frames, measurement from both network and end system can be used to efficiently identify the cause of this distortion. If the cause has been the decoder error, specific actions can be taken to examine decoding procedures.

4. MULTIMODAL QOE EVALUATION IN P2P-BASED IPTV SYSTEMS

This section gives an overview of our design of a multimodal evaluation process as well as current implementation activities. The implementation work is based on our P2P-based IPTV distribution service, which has been widely deployed on the campus of Lancaster University for both live and VoD programs. The service is received using a purpose-built P2P IPTV set-top box.

4.1 Overview

Figure 1 gives the framework for the evaluation system, which works with five key elements of a video distribution system including original source content, encoder (transcoder), distribution network, end system and end user. Two assessment scenarios are defined to provide pre-service (trial) analysis and in-service QoE evaluation.

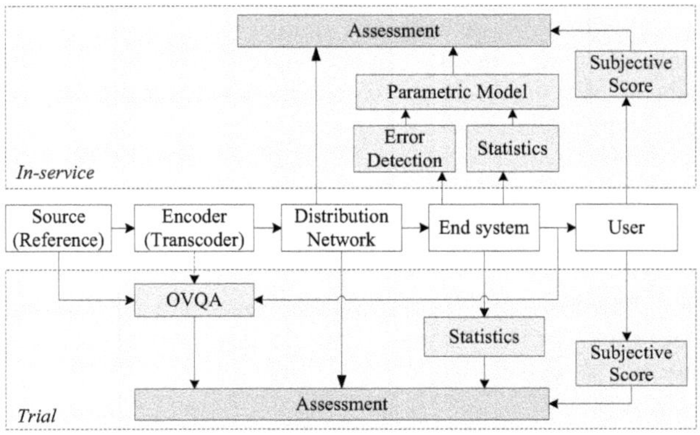

Figure 1: Framework for multimodal QoE evaluation

For the trial assessment services, objective video quality assessment models provide evaluation of picture quality at the source, the video encoder as well as the end system. By comparing the results from the three monitoring processes, the influence of video compression and transmission impairments to video frames can be investigated. In users' end systems, delivered content packets are assembled and decapsulated before video decoding is carried out. Report engines are implemented in end systems (set-top boxes) to provide decoding statistics such as buffer level and decoding syntax error that are relevant to quality of video services. A special user interface is also established in end systems to collect users' ratings of service quality. For instance, a user can instantaneously report a perceived distortion by pressing a designated button on the remote controller.

Figure 2 illustrates a use case of a multimodal evaluation to analyse the influence of network impairments to our P2P-based IPTV services. Using the time-stamp information that is associated with all evaluation processes, we are able to investigate how some packet losses are repaired by retransmission mechanisms of the P2P overlay, while others reach the video decoder and are eventually perceived by human users as visual distortions. This test plan can be used to benchmark the robustness of different overlay designs.

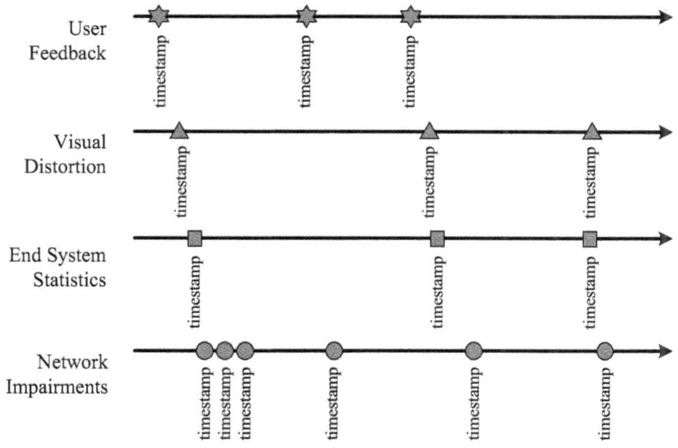

Figure 2: Multimodal evaluation associated by timestamp information

For the in-service scenario, resource-intensive image analysis on consumer devices is not practical. Due to the nature of P2P distribution, measurement and management in network layer is only effective on access aggregation points, where all corresponding packets of a given media stream pass through. Light-weighted statistics along with error detection functionality is provided by end systems. An objective parametric model can be employed to evaluate the impairments monitored in end system. Compared with the intensive subjective feedback module employed for the trial scenario, the collection of user opinion for the in-service scenario requires less interaction and causes less interference to video service.

Figure 3 shows a ongoing in-service quality evaluation. End users give instantaneous feedback when a visual distortion is perceived. Meanwhile the IPTV set-top box periodically reports light-weight decoding statistics to a statistics server.

Figure 3: An ongoing in-service quality evaluation

The following sections introduce our recent development and evaluations under the multimodal evaluation framework.

4.2 User Feedback and Questionnaire

User feedback function is integrated in the IPTV set-top box to provide a mean for end users to efficiently send feedback regarding the service quality. A user can conveniently report a perceived audio or video distortion by pressing the dedicated *blue button* on the remote controller. A small icon appears on screen for a short period of time as an acknowledgement of user feedback (Figure 4). This instantaneous feedback is logged locally and also reported immediately to a QoE management service.

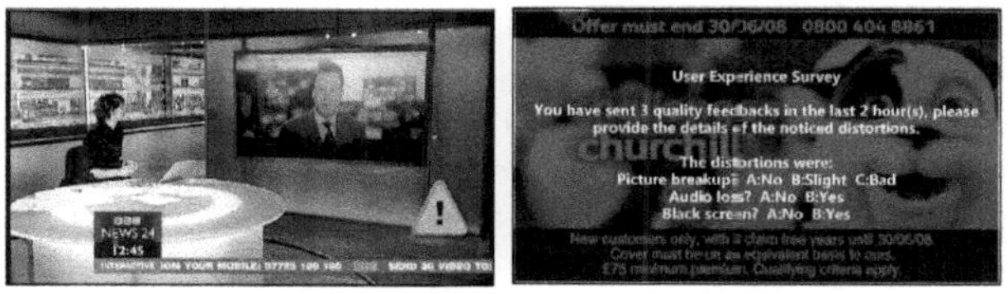

Figure 4: Instantaneous feedback and questionnaire

The overall impact of multiple distortions is also monitored considering relevant psychological effects. For instance, a forgiveness effect (a.k.a. memory effect [10]) exists due to the fact that the objection felt by an observer immediately following an impaired video segment is compensated after a long period of unimpaired video [12]. Our system recognises the forgiveness effect using a sliding "attention window", which defines a certain period of time backwards from the current time. If the number of feedbacks triggered within this "attention window" reaches a predefined threshold, an QoE notification is activated and a questionnaire can be initiated to collect details of corresponding service disruption (Figure 4).

4.3 Visual Distortions

Visual distortions on video frames are measured using objective assessment models. A HDMI-splitter is employed to relay video signal from set-top box to a display unit (LCD TV set) and a video capture card of an evaluation terminal simultaneously. Multiple quality assessment models are implemented at the evaluation terminal for different measurement strategies. For instance, a no-reference perceptual quality assessment model introduced in [16] is exploited to evaluate picture quality based on the measurement of both blurring and blocking effects. Figure 5 presents real-time monitoring results using this no-reference model. It is also noticed that the quality level remains nearly constant between frame number 110 and 190. This usually indicates a frame freezing distortion on screen. Further joint analysis of user feedback, network measurement and statistics verifies that this is in fact a frame freezing event caused by syntax errors of decoding process due to a sequence of severe network impairments.

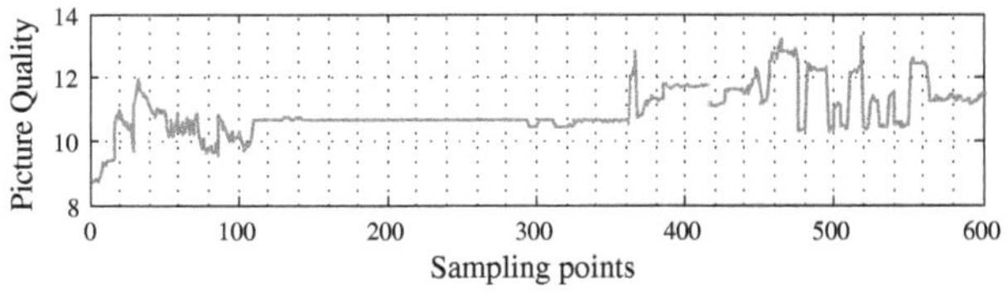

Figure 5: No-reference picture quality assessment

4.4 Network Impairments

In order to test system performance under different network conditions, various types of controlled transmission impairments are emulated using either *Netem* or radio signal management between wireless mesh boxes within our wireless P2P-based distribution services. Content packets associated with a given video stream are monitored at access aggregation points. For complex distribution topologies, deep packet inspection (DPI) may be utilised for packet analysis.

4.5 End System Statistics

Using a report engine in our IPTV set-top box, a large number of system status statistics regarding packet handling and video decoding are gathered for service evaluation. Examples of status information are *total number of decoded I,P,B frames*, *min, max and average bit-rate*, *buffer overflow and underflow events*, and *decoder syntax error*. The syntax error reported by decoder is commonly an indication of detrimental distortions appeared in video frames. Figure 6 shows an error detection analysis giving the cumulative syntax errors reported. Using time-stamp information to correlate multimodal evaluations, we can efficiently identify which error event(s) caused the frame freezing distortions shown in Figure 5.

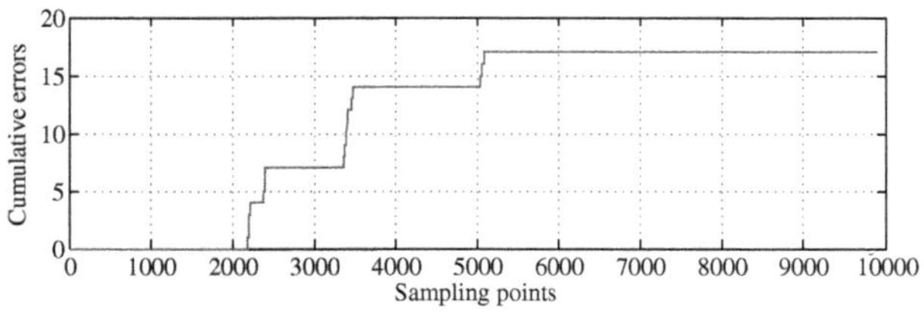

Figure 6: Decoder syntax error reported in statistics

5. CONCLUSION

This paper introduces a multimodal QoE evaluation framework that is specifically designed for trial and in-service quality assessment in P2P-based IPTV service. A number of subjective and objective evaluation methods are defined and implemented within this framework. Through initial experiments, a joint service quality evaluation and diagnosis process using multiple evaluation models is demonstrated. For future work, the evaluation framework will be further integrated into our Livinglab environment. An analysis service is also under construction aiming to conduct automated service evaluation without human intervention and participation.

6. ACKNOWLEDGEMENTS

The work presented in this paper is supported by European Commission within the FP7 Project: P2P-Next and FIRM project (Framework for Innovation and Research in MediaCityUK).

7. REFERENCES

[1] Application layer reliability solutions for IPTV services. *ITU-T FG Working document IPTV-ID-0097*, 2006.

[2] Perceptual evaluation of video quality. Technical report, OPTICOM

[3] Final report of VQEG's Multimedia phase I validation test. *Video Quality Experts Group*, 2008. http://www.its.bldrdoc.gov/vqeg/.

[4] Quality of experience requirements for IPTV services. *ITU-T FG IPTV Recommendation G.1080*, 2008.

[5] R. Fortuna, E. Leonardi, M. Mellia, M. Meo, and S. Traverso. QoE in Pull Based P2P-TV Systems: Overlay Topology Design Tradeoffs. In *IEEE Tenth International Conference on Peer-to-Peer Computing*, pages 1–10. 2010.

[6] C. Kiraly, L. Abeni, L. Cigno, et al. Effects of P2P streaming on video quality. In *IEEE International Conference on Communications*, pages 1–5. 2010.

[7] T. Lin, S. Kanumuri, Y. Zhi, D. Poole, P. Cosman, and A. Reibman. A versatile model for packet loss visibility and its application to packet prioritization. *IEEE Transactions on Image Processing*, 19(3):722–735, 2010.

[8] M. Mu, A. Mauthe, R. Haley, and F. Garcia. Discrete quality assessment in IPTV content distribution networks. *Elsevier Journal of Signal Processing: Image Communication*, 2011.

[9] M. Mu, R. Gostner, A. Mauthe, F. Garcia, and G. Tyson. Visibility of individual packet loss on H.264 encoded video stream. In *Proceedings of Sixteenth Annual Multimedia Computing and Networking (MMCN'09)*, San Jose, California, USA, 2009.

[10] M. Pinson and S. Wolf. Comparing subjective video quality testing methodologies. In *Proceedings of SPIE Video Communications and Image Processing Conference, Lugano, Switzerland*. SPIE, 2003.

[11] T. Rahrer, R. Fiandra, and S. Wright. Triple-play services quality of experience (QoE) requirements and mechanisms - For architecture and transport. Technical Report TR-126, Broadband Forum, 2006.

[12] V. Seferidis, M. Ghanbari, and D. E. Pearson. Forgiveness effect in subjective assessment of packet video. *IET Journal of Electronics Letters*, 28(21):2013–2014, 1992.

[13] T. Silverston and O. Fourmaux. Measuring P2P IPTV systems. In *Proceedings of ACM International Workshop on Network and Operating Systems Support for Digital Audio and Video (NOSSDAV), Urbana-Champaign, Illinois, USA*. ACM, 2007.

[14] R. Steinmetz and K. Wehrle. Peer-to-peer networking & computing. *Informatik-Spektrum*, 27(1):51–54, 2004. Springer.

[15] D. Tran, K. Hua, and T. Do. A peer-to-peer architecture for media streaming. *IEEE Journal on Selected Areas in Communications*, 22(1):121–133, 2004.

[16] Z. Wang, H. R. Sheikh, and A. C. Bovik. No-reference perceptual quality assessment of JPEG compressed images. In *Proceedings of IEEE International Conference on Image Processing*. 2002.

[17] S. Wolf and M. H. Pinson. Spatial-temporal distortion metrics for in-service quality monitoring of any digital video system. *Proc. SPIE International Symposium on Voice, Video, and Data Communications*, 3845:266–277, 1999.

[18] F. You, W. Zhang, and J. Xiao. Packet loss pattern and parametric video quality model for IPTV. In *Proceedings of the 2009 Eigth IEEE/ACIS International Conference on Computer and Information Science*, pages 824–828, 2009.

Blind Navigation with a Wearable Range Camera and Vibrotactile Helmet

Steve Mann, Jason Huang, Ryan Janzen, Raymond Lo, Valmiki Rampersad, Alexander Chen, Taqveer Doha
University of Toronto, Department of Electrical and Computer Engineering
http://wearcam.org/blindvision.htm

ABSTRACT

We present a way finding system that uses a range camera and an array of vibrotactile elements we built into a helmet.

The range camera is a Kinect 3D sensor from Microsoft that is meant to be kept stationary, and used to watch the user (i.e., to detect the person's gestures). Rather than using the camera to look at the user, we reverse the situation, by putting the Kinect range camera on a helmet for being worn by the user. In our case, the Kinect is in motion rather than stationary.

Whereas stationary cameras have previously been used for gesture recognition, which the Kinect does very well, in our new modality, we take advantage of the Kinect's resilience against rapidly changing background scenery, where the background in our case is now in motion (i.e., a conventional wearable camera would be presented with a constantly changing background that is difficult to manage by mere background subtraction).

The goal of our project is collision avoidance for blind or visually impaired individuals, and for workers in harsh environments such as industrial environments with significant 3-dimensional obstacles, as well as for use in low-light environments.

Categories and Subject Descriptors

I.4.8 [**Image Processing and Computer Vision**]: Scene Analysis—*Depth cues, Range data, Motion*; I.4.9 [**Image Processing and Computer Vision**]: Applications; H.1.2 [**Models and Principles**]: User/Machine Systems—*Human factors*

General Terms

Design, Experimentation, Human Factors

Keywords

personal safety devices, blind navigation, depth sensor, Microsoft Kinect, vibrotactile helmet, collision avoidance

*Area Chair: Pal Halvorsen

MM'11 November 28–December 1, 2011, Scottsdale, Arizona, USA.

1. INTRODUCTION

1.1 Microsoft Kinect

The Microsoft Kinect was designed for use with Microsoft's Xbox 360 gaming console. It allows the gamer to interact with games without the need for physical controls. It accomplishes this by tracking the gamer's movements and position in three-dimensional space, with respect to itself, in real-time. In normal use, the Kinect sits stationary and observes the gamer as he/she moves.

We propose the use of the Kinect in a different manner, where the Kinect moves with the user, so that it observes the world in a similar fashion as the user observes (or would have observed, in the case of a blind individual). Rather than having the Kinect watch the user, the user uses it to watch their environments.

Microsoft's Kinect employs PrimeSense's 3-D sensing technology. PrimeSense's 3-D sensor uses light coding to code the scene volume, using active IR (infrared) illumination [2, 3, 4]. The sensor then uses a CMOS image sensor to read the coded light back from the scene. The coded light is processed by PrimeSense's SoC chip [5], contained in the 3-D sensor, to give the depth information.

In our implementation, the Kinect is used to extract the 3D depth information of the environment being observed by the user. This depth information is passed to the user in the form of tactile feedback, using an array of vibrotactile actuators as shown in Figure 2.

1.2 Other head-mounted navigational aids

Most previous head-mounted navigational aids have used standard camera systems, to present tactile information to the user. One such example is called "seeing with the tongue" [8].

Standard camera systems work well for gesture recognition because the stationary background can be subtracted from the image, so that people can be clearly seen with simple computer image processing. However, when the camera is wearable, the background is constantly changing, making it difficult to separate distant background clutter from nearby objects.

Some specialized blind collision avoidance aids such as the VibraVest [1] provided 3D range information but required expensive special-purpose hardware such as a miniature radar system.

The Kinect is a new widely deployed commercial off-the-shelf technology that provides a low-cost solution to the problems associated with sensitivity to distant background

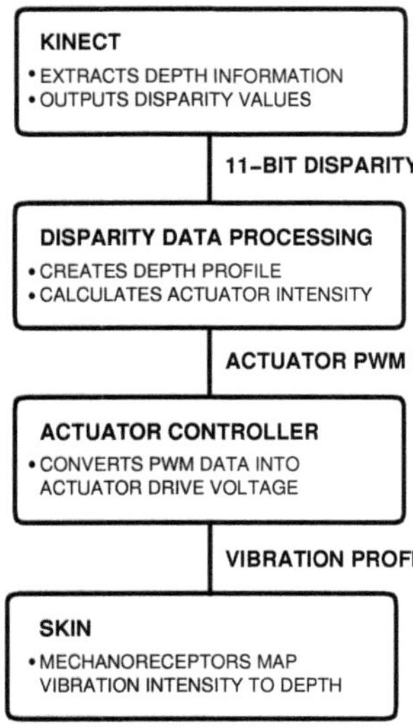

Figure 1: System signal flow path overview

clutter. Since background clutter is especially prevalent in a wearable camera situation, the technology used in the Kinect shows great promise in wearable vision systems.

2. PHYSICAL SETUP

Figure 1 shows the signal flow path in our system architecture. Our goal is to convert depth information obtained using Kinect into haptic feedback so that users can perceive depth within a range that matters most for collision avoidance, while not being overwhelmed by distant background clutter.

An array of six vibrating actuators mounted inside a helmet are controlled using the depth values using an algorithm that calculates the vibration intensity profile for each of these actuators. The intensity profile is transmitted to an Arduino microcontroller which drives each of the actuators using Pulse-Width Modulation (PWM). PWM allows voltage on the actuators to be regulated for varying degrees of vibration.

This sense of depth moves with the head in a natural manner. Thus, the user can scan the head back and forth to get a natural understanding of subject matter in their environment. The general layout of our helmet is depicted in Fig 2.

We mounted the Kinect securely on top of a welding helmet. An array of 6 vibration actuators were positioned along the head strap of the helmet. The helmet is placed on the head as shown in Fig 2.

For testing by sighted users, a dark welding shade was used, which could either entirely stop light from passing through, or under computer program control, vary the amount of light passing through. In this way, the device could function as a switchable blindfold for testing purposes.

2.1 Vibrotactile actuators, and motor controllers

To provide haptic feedback, we used a set of vibrating actuator motors. The vision processing algorithm controls the motors through a serial connection to an Arduino. These values correspond directly to PWM output from pins 2 to 7 on the microcontroller. Each output pin is used as control signal in motor driver circuit which determines the actuator

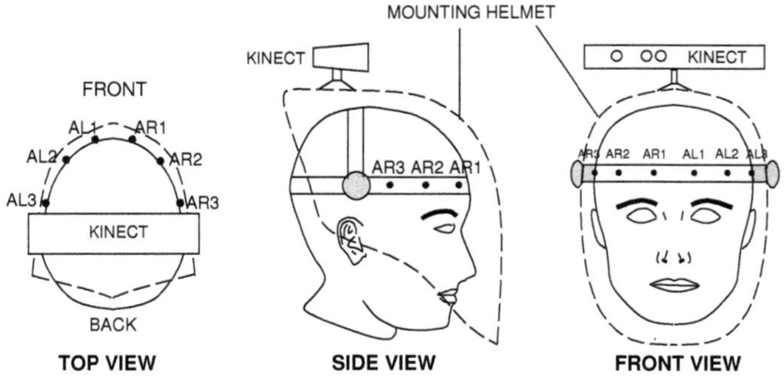

Figure 2: Wearable sensor and actuator configuration on a helmet, showing placement of the motor actuators around the forehead.

vibration response for AL3 to AR3 as shown in Fig 2.

For our setup, we used 10x3.4mm shaftless vibration motor for each of the actuators. The motor is rated to be driven at a maximum voltage of 3.6V. Depending on the PWM value from each of the Arduino pins, the corresponding actuator can be driven at voltages calculated as:

$$V_{\text{actuator}} = \text{PWM}/255 * 3.6, \quad \text{PWM} \in [0, 255] \quad (1)$$

The actuator Voltage and Current response was tested to be linear. Based on this, we determined that the vibrating actuator also had a linear response, when driven between voltages from 0 to 3.6V.

3. REAL-TIME IMAGE PROCESSING TO CONTROL VIBRATION ACTUATORS

3.1 Distance map recovered from Kinect

We accessed the Kinect data in real-time with a wearable laptop computer on a backpack. The Kinect provides data in a proprietary data format called "disparity" values.

To recover the actual distance from the raw depth data in the proprietary format, we used the following conversion equation

$$\text{distance} = R = \frac{1}{\alpha \cdot \text{disparity} + \beta} \quad (2)$$

The parameters have been empirically found in [7] to be: $\alpha = -0.0030711016$ and $\beta = 3.3309495161$. As a result, the range extremities become:

	disparity	distance
MIN distance detectable	0	0.30 m
MAX distance detectable	1030	5.96 m

At distances closer than 30cm, the Kinect is not able to measure disparity. The disparity values are calibrated such that the device is able to read values up to 6m without significant loss of resolution within acceptable error margin while operating indoors. We found this range of 0.3 to 6 metres to be useful for collision avoidance at typical walking speeds.

This range is also greater than the range of a typical cane used by visually impared users, and permits a warning sooner in advance of collision, at a given walking speed. It is the relatively near range (just beyond an arm's length) where the greatest sensitivity is needed.

3.2 Partitioning the distance map

The Kinect operates with horizontal field of view of 57° horizontally and 43° vertically. A distance map across this field (akin to a 2D video feed) was computed in real-time based on the disparity values.

In our setup, the depth sensing region was divided into six smaller zones, three on the left (SL1, SL2, and SL3) and three on the right (SR1, SR2, SR3). Each of the zones corresponds to the vibration in one actuator.

3.3 Controlling a 1-dimensional array of actuators

Fig 2 and 3 show the layout of the actuators and viewable area of sensing regions respectively. Our setup allows the user to scan their head back and forth and feel various objects as if they were pressing against their forehead. While not providing high resolution imaging, we found that it was possible to navigate a hallway and find various doors, doorways, etc., and also avoid collision with other people in a crowded hallway.

3.4 Transfer function with 1-to-1 mapping from each sensing region to each actuator

We desired objects in the visual field to cause the vibrations to become stronger as the objects get closer. In this way the system creates the sensation of objects pressing against the forehead at-a-distance, i.e. before collision occurs. The sensation increases in strength as collision becomes more imminent.

This can be accomplished by making the vibration (as sensed) be inversely proportional to distance, i.e. $V \propto 1/R$.

Alternately we can make the sensed vibration vary as $V \propto 1/R^2$, as with a force field such as a magnetic field. For example, when holding two magnets close to each other, the magnetic repulsion (or attraction) is inversely proportional to the separation distance squared. Thus we can mimic nature, in this regard, in order to make the effect comprehensible and intuitive.

We now partition the depth map for each of the different vibration actuators. For an inverse-square law, we make the total vibration a weighted integral across the sensing region:

$$v_n = \frac{1}{S_{FOV}} \int_{S_{FOV}} \frac{1}{R^2(\theta,\phi)} a_{\theta,n}(\theta) a_{\phi,n}(\phi) dS \qquad (3)$$

for actuator n. $a_{\theta,n}$ and $a_{\phi,n}$ are aperture functions, weightings which vary depending on the horizontal and vertical locations, respectively. They are different for each sensing region n. S is sensing surface in steradians (sr).

We found empirically that the background noise from Eqn. 3, coming from objects in the background behind the subject matter, was distracting. Our second implementation simply used the closest object in zone, still weighted by the aperture functions:

$$v_n = \min_{S_{FOV}} \frac{1}{R^2(\theta,\phi)} a_{\theta,n}(\theta) a_{\phi,n}(\phi) \qquad n \in 1...N \qquad (4)$$

We also experimented with the following 1/R law, which gave an improved advance warning of faraway objects approaching (> 3m).

$$v_n = \min_{S_{FOV}} \frac{1}{R(\theta,\phi)} a_{\theta,n}(\theta) a_{\phi,n}(\phi) \qquad n \in 1...N \qquad (5)$$

The result is a center-weighted mapping, as illustrated in Fig 3.

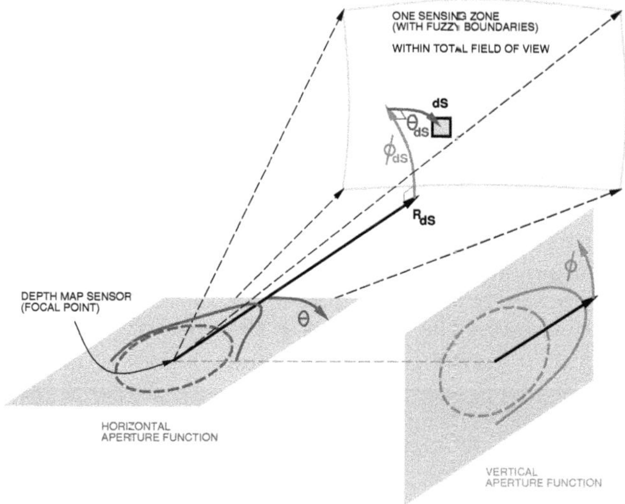

Figure 3: The viewable area of the depth sensor was divided into zones, each of which corresponded to one of the actuator motors. The sensitivity profile was center-weighted as illustrated.

3.5 Fuzzy zone boundaries

It is also possible to go beyond a simple 1-to-1 mapping from each spatial sensing region to each actuator. For example, we experimented with making fuzzy boundaries on each sensing region, using a horizontal aperture function that extended beyond the boundaries of each sensing region (see horizontal aperture function in Fig 3). As a result, each actuator was slightly responsive to neighbouring sensing regions. The overlap and center-weighting, combined with natural exploratory motions of the user's head, gave some sub-pixel accuracy that allowed the user to sense some degree of fine detail.

3.6 Compensating for non-linear behavior of motors and human perception

One challenge of our design is to convert the depth map values to another sensory mode such as tactile feedback using an actuator.

It is clear to see that using a linear model for mapping raw depth value to the actuator is inadequate for several reasons. For many of the sensory modalities, our sensory perceptions are non-linear and have a highly compressive nature. For example, humans perceive loudness of sound in a logarithmic scale. This logarithmic scale recurs often in the human senses and comes from Weber's analysis of "just-noticeable differences" [6]. A perceived sensation P results from fractional changes in a physical quantity I as in:

$$\Delta P \propto \frac{\Delta I}{I} \qquad (6)$$

After setting $P = 0$ at the minimum perceptible physical quantity I_0, the solution becomes:

$$P = k \log\left(\frac{I}{I_0}\right) \qquad (7)$$

Weber found this logarithmic law to exist for the sense of touch [6]. Therefore, we needed to modify the vibrations outlined earlier, into an exaggerated actuator stimulus that

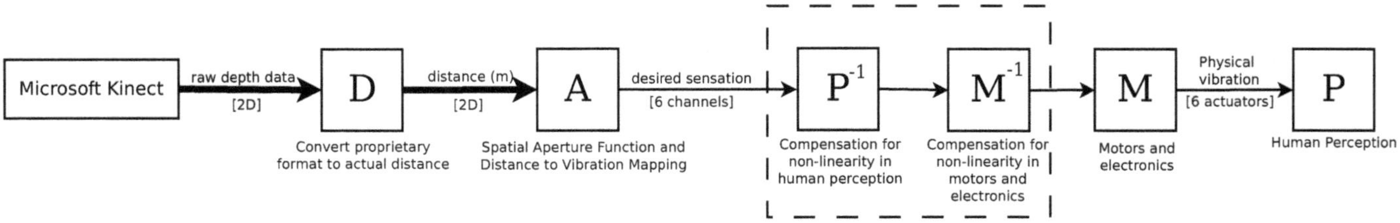

Figure 4: This figure shows the conversion of the depth map data to the actual physical vibration of the 6 actuators in the helmet. The underlying non-linear relationships among the raw depth sensor, motor and electronics, and human perceptions are estimated empirically. By aggregating the M^{-1} and P^{-1} functions, we can determine the mapping of the vibrating intensity to the sensitivity range of human senses experimentally.

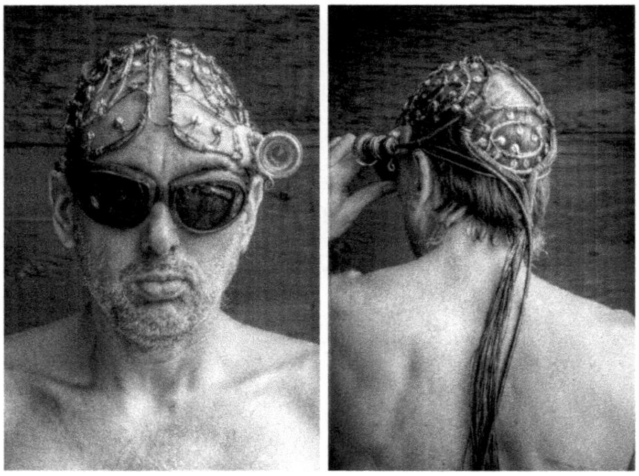

Figure 5: The MindMesh^{TM} BCI (Brain Computer Interface) FPGA mesh-computing architecture has 64 electrodes, so that various items such as the Kinect or more conventional cameras can be "plugged into the brain".

would properly be *perceived* by the user as the given $1/R$ law or $1/R^2$ law, as desired.

An additional compensation was necessary because the raw depth data collected from the Kinect is not a direct measurement of the actual distance in the real world.

Since the non-linearities and the underlying interactions between the actuator and human perception are difficult to recover, we estimated these relationships experimentally by performing trials on different users. We have found that using an exponential decade function as follows provides adequate results, and also conforms with the non-linear response of the human senses that we desired to overcome:

$$w = (0.978)^{255d} \tag{8}$$

where d is the measured distance normalized with 1 indicating the maximum range, and w the PWM value which controls the electrical actuator.

Figure 4 shows the conversions and compensation we have introduced in the signal flow path. Notice that our system has aggregated the inverse of the non-linear responses of the motor and electronics as well as human perception for simplicity. With the proper calibration and compensation for non-linearity and sensory thresholds, users were able to learn the relationship between the distance and the vibration intensity after several minutes of training with the system.

4. FUTURE WORK

In further variations of the system, we implemented various 2-dimensional arrays, such as a 3 by 4 array of 12 actuators, and a 2 by 6 array of 12 actuators (the Arduino has 12 PWM outputs). In further explorations, we also experimented with larger arrays using multiple microcontrollers. However, we found that a small number of actuators was often sufficient.

We are currently completing a BCI (Brain Computer Interface) in place of the vibrotactile devices. Our system, which we call the MindMesh^{TM}, is depicted in Figure 5.

5. CONCLUSION

We have proposed a novel way of using the Microsoft Kinect 3-D camera, for navigation which we hope will someday assist the visually impaired. Rather than having the Kinect observe a user, we put the Kinect on the user to observe the user's environment. We found that the typical operating range of the Kinect (30cm to 6m) was well suited to indoor navigation in typical crowded corridors, and the like. This preliminary work suggests that eyeglasses could be made using PrimeSense's 3-D sensing technology, for potential use by the visually impaired. Videos of the helmet in action can be viewed at: **http://wearcam.org/blindvision/**

6. REFERENCES

[1] S. Mann. *Intelligent Image Processing*. John Wiley and Sons, November 2 2001. ISBN: 0-471-40637-6.

[2] A. Shpunt. DEPTH MAPPING USING MULTI-BEAM ILLUMINATION, Jan. 21 2008. US Patent App. 12/522,172.

[3] A. Shpunt and B. Pesach. OPTICAL PATTERN PROJECTION, July 21 2010. US Patent App. 12/840,312.

[4] A. Shpunt and Z. Zalevsky. Depth-varying light fields for three dimensional sensing, Mar. 13 2007. US Patent App. 11/724,068.

[5] E. Spektor, Z. Mor, and D. Rais. INTEGRATED PROCESSOR FOR 3D MAPPING, Mar. 4 2009. US Patent App. 12/397,362.

[6] E. Weber, H. Ross, and D. Murray. *EH Weber on the tactile senses*. Psychology Press, 1996.

[7] Wikipedia. Ros (robot operating system) — wikipedia, the free encyclopedia, 2011. [Online; accessed 12-April-2011].

[8] P. B. y Rita, M. E. Tyler, and K. A. Kaczmarek. *Seeing with the Brain*, volume 15(2), pages 285–295. Hillsdale, NJ: Lawrence Erlbaum Associates Inc, 2003.

Recognizing Interaction Between Human Performers Using 'Key Pose Doublet'*

Snehasis Mukherjee †
Electronics and
Communication Sciences Unit,
Indian Statistical Institute
203 B.T. Road, Kolkata
snehasismukho@gmail.com

Sujoy Kumar Biswas
Electronics and
Communication Sciences Unit,
Indian Statistical Institute
203 B.T. Road, Kolkata
skbhere@gmail.com

Dipti Prasad Mukherjee
Electronics and
Communication Sciences Unit,
Indian Statistical Institute
203 B.T. Road, Kolkata
dipti@isical.ac.in

ABSTRACT

In this paper, we propose a graph theoretic approach for recognizing interactions between two human performers present in a video clip. We watch primarily the human poses of each performer and derive descriptors that capture the motion patterns of the poses. From an initial dictionary of poses (visual words), we extract key poses (or key words) by ranking the poses on the centrality measure of graph connectivity. We argue that the key poses are graph nodes which share a close semantic relationship (in terms of some suitable edge weight function) with all other pose nodes and hence are said to be the central part of the graph. We apply the same centrality measure on all possible combinations of the key poses of the two performers to select the set of 'key pose doublets' that best represent the corresponding action. The results on standard interaction recognition dataset show the robustness of our approach when compared to the present state of the art method.

Categories and Subject Descriptors

I.4 [**Image Processing and Computer Vision**]: Applications

General Terms

Experimentation

Keywords

graph centrality, bag of words, human poses, human interaction, key pose doublet

1. INTRODUCTION

Detecting human activities in video is an active research area [5, 12, 15]. Semantic analysis of human activities in videos leads to various vision-based intelligent systems, including smart surveillance systems, intelligent robots, action-based human computer interfaces, etc. For instance, a good method to automatically distinguish suspicious or unusual activities such as punching, pushing or kicking from normal activities can be useful in places like rail station, airport or shopping mal. Multiple activities must be recognized, even when the background is non-uniform (for pedestrians and/or other moving objects). Figure 1 shows examples of some interactions.

(a) (b) (c) (d)

Figure 1: Examples of some interactions (a)hugging, (b)punching, (c)pushing, (d)kicking taken from [14]

Several approaches exist in recognizing human action focusing on either low and mid-level feature collection ([5, 12]) or modeling the high level interaction among the features [8, 7]. Following bag-of-words model [5, 12], Niebles *et. al.*, automatically learns the probability distributions of the visual words using graphical models like probabilistic Latent Semantic Analysis (pLSA) and Latent Dirichlet Allocation (LDA) to form the dictionary of visual words. Also there are good efforts of combining global and local video features for action recognition [15].

There are approaches studying pose specific video features [2, 4] but modeling visual senses associated with poses in videos is largely an unexplored research area. In [9], a new pose descriptor is proposed using a gradient weighted optical flow feature combining both global and local features. They mine the pose descriptors using Max-diff *kd*-tree [10] to form the initial dictionary of poses. The initial pose dictionary contains both ambiguous and unambiguous (or key poses) poses. The poses in the initial dictionary are ranked using the centrality measure (a measure of ambiguity) of graph connectivity [11] to select the key poses. The approach made by [9] is limited to solo performer, and since they bank on the repetitive nature of the human actions by introducing *action cycles*, their methodology does not perform well (see Section 3 for results) in case of interactions like punching (once) or pushing away. However, if we consider each individual separately, one can observe a recurring pattern in the motion patterns of limbs. But it complicates the inferencing as action cues from two different actions need to be combined for semantic analysis. Our methodology tries to utilize this cue, i.e., motion and pose pattern of individual

*Area chair: Wei Tsang Ooi

†Corresponding author

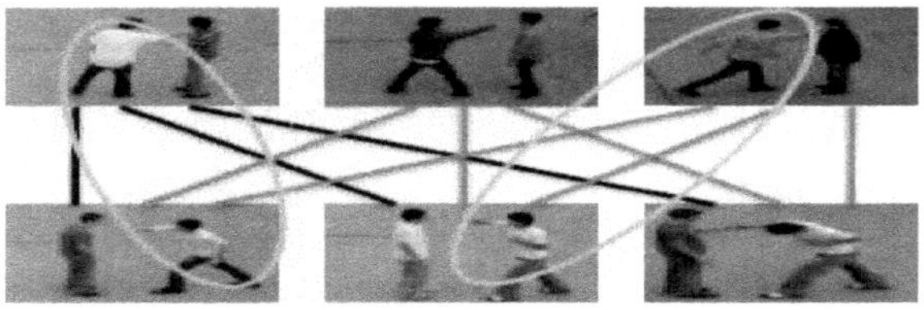

Figure 2: Bipartite graph representing key poses for two performers for 'punching' interaction. Green ellipses show examples of 'key pose doublets' concatenating key poses of left and right performers.

performer, in order to build a pose based recognition model for interaction types.

We make a two-fold contribution to enhance the approach of [9] for recognizing interaction between multiple human performers. First, we apply the procedure of [9] on each of the performers present in the video to select the key poses for both the performers. Second, for each action we primarily take all possible combination of key poses of the two performers to form 'pose doublets'. We again apply the centrality measure of graph connectivity [11] to rank the 'pose doublets' and select the 'key pose doublets' best representing the corresponding interaction. Figure 2 shows examples of some key poses for the two performers in the interaction 'punching'. The key poses are represented as nodes in the bipartite graph shown in Figure 2. After ranking the 'pose doublets' we select the 'key pose doublets' shown by the green ellipses.

We show the accuracy of our approach compared to the state-of-the-art in Section 3 followed by conclusions in Section 4. Before that we discuss the proposed approach in the next Section.

2. PROPOSED METHODOLOGY

The proposed methodology consists of three steps. First we discuss the method for constructing the initial dictionary. Next we discuss the process of extracting key poses for each person in the video. Lastly we describe the method for constructing 'key pose doublet'.

2.1 Forming Initial Pose Dictionary

We use multidimensional pose descriptor corresponding to each performer of each frame of an action video as suggested in [9]. We have used the method of Gilbert *et. al.* [3] to draw the best fit rectangular window around each performer.

The initial pose dictionary is constructed [9] from the multidimensional pose descriptors in two steps. First, the descriptors are derived by combining motion cue from the optical flow field (using Lucas-Kanade algorithm [6]) and pose cue from the gradient field of a particular video frame. Second, the pose descriptors, upon data condensation, result into a moderately compact representation and we call it the initial dictionary of visual poses. The initial pose dictionary contains pose clusters that may be equated with words in a *document*, where the *document* stands for a video in our version of the bag-of-words model. In the following, we briefly describe the descriptor extraction process as well as the formation of initial pose dictionary.

The pose descriptor combines the benefit of motion information from optical flow field and pose information from the gradient field. The optical flow field is weighted with the strength of the gradient field to produce a resultant flow field. Next the resultant flow vectors are quantized into 8 bins of an angular histogram. Now this same process is carried out for three different layers, where first layer is the whole image matrix, second layer splits the image into four equal blocks and the third layer splits it into 16 blocks each producing 8 bin vector resulting to a 168-dimensional pose descriptor after concatenation.

Once we evaluate the pose descriptor, a *kd*-tree based data condensation technique eliminates much of the redundancies in the repetitive motion pattern of human actions and provides a moderately compact pose dictionary. The idea of data condensation is preferred to clustering because in data condensation one may afford to select multiple representatives from the same cluster, whereas in clustering the objective lies in identifying true number of clusters. The leaf nodes of the *kd*-tree denote one pose cluster or the visual pose word; one can choose multiple samples from each leaf node to construct the initial pose vocabulary $S_j = \{p_i \in \Re^d | i = 1, 2, ..., k\}$ where $j = 1, 2$, and d denotes the dimensionality of the pose descriptors with k representing the cardinality of S_j, $j = 1, 2$. The algorithm to construct the *kd*-tree is explained in details in [10]. In our experiment we choose the mean of each leaf of the kd-tree as our pose word and learn the dictionaries S_1, S_2 of poses of the two persons. Next we outline the scheme for ranking the poses of S_1, S_2 using centrality theory of graph connectivity.

2.2 Formation of Compact Dictionary

The poses in S_1 and S_2 are often ambiguous and our goal is to identify the unambiguous poses (or key poses) from both S_1 and S_2 and produce compact dictionaries $\Xi_j, j = 1, 2$. The poses from $S_j, j = 1, 2$ are placed in a graph as nodes and the edge between each two poses stands for the dissimilarity in terms of a semantic relationship between them, measured using some form of weight function [9]. Let $\rho(u, v)$ denote how many times the pose words $u, v \in S_j$ both occur together in all video sequences of a particular action type. Then the edge weight $\omega(u, v)$ is given by

$$\omega(u, v) = \begin{cases} \frac{1}{\rho(u,v)} & when\ \rho(u, v) \neq 0 \\ \infty & \text{otherwise} \end{cases} \quad (1)$$

According to (1), the lower the edge weight, the stronger is the semantic relationship between the pose words. Next we calculate the eccentricity measure [16] of graph connectivity to measure the semantic difference between the poses in a pose graph. Floyd-Warshall algorithm [1] computes all-pair-shortest path between pose nodes. If the distance $d(u, v)$ between two pose words $u, v \in S_j$ is the sum of the edge weights $\omega(u, v)$ on a shortest path from u to v in the pose graph, then the eccentricity $e(u)$ of a pose u is given by

$$e(u) = max\{d(u, v) \mid v \in S_j\}, \quad (2)$$

for $j = 1, 2$.

Hence we have ranked the poses in S_j by their eccentricity measure, used as a measure of ambiguity. For each performer in video sequences of each action type, we choose the N-best poses by selecting poses with N-lowest eccentricity in a pose graph. We call the selected poses as key poses and include the key poses in the compact dictionaries Ξ_j. Once we identify the key poses for a particular kind of action we repeat the same process for all kinds of actions. The key poses $p_1, p_2, \ldots, p_k$ extracted from all the action types are grouped together to form Ξ_j.

$$\Xi_j = \{p_1, p_2, \ldots, p_k\} \;\forall\; p_i \in S_j, \;\; i = 1, 2, \ldots, k \;\; j = 1, 2. \tag{3}$$

Next we discuss the process of selecting 'key pose doublet'.

2.3 Selecting 'Key Pose Doublets'

We have two compact dictionaries $\Xi_j, j = 1, 2$ for each performers. These two dictionaries contain key poses of the corresponding action type. Each of the key poses can best represent the pose of a single performer during the corresponding interaction with the other performer. Our next task is to model these poses to represent the interaction between the two performers. An easy way for this is to make joint poses concatenating two 168-dimensional pose vectors $\xi_1 \in \Xi_1$ and $\xi_2 \in \Xi_2$. Now the question is, which combination of poses (ξ_1, ξ_2) we should take? To answer this question, we first take the all possible combinations $(\xi_{1,i}, \xi_{2,j})$ where $\xi_{1,i} \in \Xi_1, i = 1, 2, \ldots, m$ and $\xi_{2,j} \in \Xi_2, j = 1, 2, \ldots, n$, m and n being the cardinalities of Ξ_1 and Ξ_2 respectively. We call these concatenated combinations as 'pose doublets', where a set Y of mn 'pose doublets' represents a particular interaction type. For better recognition of the interaction, we have to choose a smaller set $\Psi \subseteq Y$ of 'pose doublets'. We call the elements of Ψ as 'key pose doublets'.

We represent the poses in Ξ_1 and Ξ_2 by a weighted undirected graph (Figure 2). The key poses are represented by nodes in the graph. There is no edge between the pose nodes of the same compact dictionary. Hence the weighted undirected graph constructed by poses in Ξ_1 and Ξ_2 is basically a bipartite graph. The two sets of poses may be thought of as a coloring of the graph with two colors: if we color all poses in Ξ_1 red, and all poses in Ξ_2 green, each edge has endpoints of differing colors, as is required in the graph coloring problem. But each pose node has an edge to all pose nodes of the other compact dictionary. In Figure 2, the two rows of nodes represent the pose nodes of the two different dictionaries Ξ_1 and Ξ_2.

If $x_{i,j}$ is the number of times the key poses $\xi_{1,i} \in \Xi_1$ and $\xi_{2,i} \in \Xi_2$, $i = 1, 2, \ldots, m$, $j = 1, 2, \ldots, n$ occur simultaneously in the video sequences of the same action, then the edge weight $w_{i,j}$ between $\xi_{1,i}$ and $\xi_{2,i}$ is defined as follows

$$w_{i,j} = \frac{1}{x_{i,j}}. \tag{4}$$

It is clear from (4) that the edge weight between any two poses indicate the likeliness of the two poses to occur simultaneously for the particular type of interaction. Better the likeliness of two poses of two different dictionaries, lower the edge weight between them. We rank the 'pose doublets' according to the edge weight between the corresponding pair of key poses. We choose the N-best 'pose doublets' to represent the corresponding interaction. We call them 'key pose doublets' for that interaction type and include them in Ψ. Hence learning phase of our approach is complete. Next we describe our experiments on the proposed approach and the results obtained from the experiments.

3. EXPERIMENTS AND RESULTS

We get a complete set of 'key pose doublets' for all action types by taking the union of the Ψs of all types of interactions. For a training video, we just extract the 'pose doublets' and find the nearest 'key pose doublet' (in terms of Euclidean distance) from the union set of all 'key pose doublets'. We construct a histogram of the occurrences of the 'key pose doublets' in the video sequence. This histogram can be used as a signature of a particular interaction (as in bag of words model). The histogram is called the interaction descriptor. For a test video, we construct the interaction descriptor and find the closest match of the test descriptor among the descriptors of all the interactions.

We test our method on a standard dataset known as UT-Interaction dataset [14]. We find two sets of video data of 60 video sequences (two performers in each sequence) in each of them. Each set contains 10 video sequences of 6 different interactions 'Handshaking (Hs)', 'Hugging(Hg)', 'Kicking(Kc)', 'Pointing(Pt)', 'Punching(Pn)' and 'Pushing(Ps)'. The only exception is, 'Pt', which is a single performer action. We consider the same performer as both left and right performers in case of 'Pt'. Set 1 of the UT-Interaction dataset contains video with almost uniform background whereas set 2 contains more challenging video sequences with non-uniform background and poor lighting condition.

We follow the leave-one-out experiment. We construct the interaction descriptors (as action descriptors in [9]) from the dictionary of 'key pose doublets' Ψ for recognition. The average time consumed for learning key poses and learning the pose doublet by each interaction amounts to little less than one minute. After the detection of 'key pose doublets', our approach takes only a few seconds for both learning and testing in our MATLAB^{TM} version 7.0.4 implementation in a machine with processor speed 2.37 GHz, 512MB RAM.

We tested our method separately on both set 1 and set 2 of the UT-Interaction dataset. The confusion matrices for set 1 and set 2 are given in Tables 1 and 2 respectively. Table 3 shows the efficacy of the proposed approach over the method of Ryoo *et. al.* [13]. Accuracy is measured by the percentage of correct detections.

The first and second rows of Figure 3 represent key poses

Table 1: Confusion matrix of set 1 of UT-Interaction dataset (entries given in %)

	Hs	Hg	Kc	Pt	Pn	Ps
Hs	80	0	0	20	0	0
Hg	0	90	0	0	0	10
Kc	0	0	90	0	10	0
Pt	10	0	0	90	0	0
Pn	10	0	0	20	70	0
Ps	0	10	0	0	0	90

Table 2: Confusion matrix of set 2 of UT-Interaction dataset (entries given in %)

	Hs	Hg	Kc	Pt	Pn	Ps
Hs	70	0	0	10	20	0
Hg	0	80	0	0	0	20
Kc	0	0	80	0	20	0
Pt	10	0	0	70	20	0
Pn	10	0	10	20	60	0
Ps	0	20	0	0	0	80

Table 3: Recognition accuracy on UT-Interaction dataset compared to [13] (accuracy given in %)

Interactions	Hs	Hg	Kc	Pt	Pn	Ps	Overall
[9]	50	60	30	60	20	40	43.33
[13]	75	87.5	75	62.5	50	75	70.8
Proposed	75	85	85	80	65	85	79.17

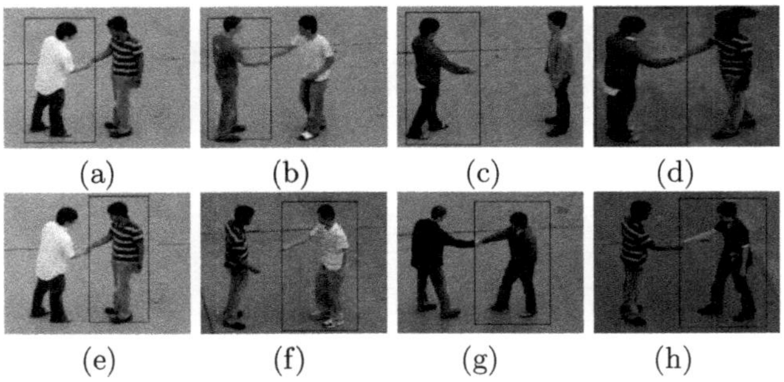

Figure 3: Top and bottom rows show the key poses for left and right performer respectively for interaction 'Hs'. (a)sequence 2, frame 53, (b)sequence 4, frame 48, (c)sequence 5, frame 41, (d)sequence 10, frame 48, (e)sequence 2, frame 54, (f) sequence 6, frame 36, (g)sequence 8, frame 60 and (h)sequence 9, frame 33 from UT-Interaction dataset

Table 4: 'Key pose doublets' (K) for interaction 'Hs' with their centrality values (C) obtained by (4)

Figures of (K)	(C)	Figures of (K)	(C)
3(a), 3(e)	0.009	3(b), 3(h)	0.018
3(d), 3(h)	0.014	3(a), 3(f)	0.019
3(d), 3(g)	0.015		

of the left and right performers respectively for the interaction 'Hs' of the UT-Interaction dataset.

Table 4 shows the 'key pose doublets' selected for the interaction 'Hs' with their centrality values. For interaction 'Hs' we get 4 key poses for both the performers yielding 16 possible combinations of 'pose doublets'. We rank them according to the centrality measure given by (4) and select the top 5 as 'key pose doublets'. Figure 4 shows how the percentage of accuracy changes over the number of 'key pose doublets' per interaction. We get highest accuracy when number of 'key pose doublets' is 5 per interaction (i.e., $N = 5$).

4. CONCLUSIONS

We develop an efficient method to recognize the interaction between human performers in video. From an initial vocabulary of poses, the proposed approach builds a small but highly discriminatory dictionaries of key poses for two different performers. By the notion of centrality theory of graph connectivity we extract the key poses for each performers. Among the all possible combinations of key poses for two different performers, we select most relevant pairs of poses called 'key pose doublets' to form a dictionary. In future, we want to fix a suitable threshold to select the 'key pose doublets'. Presently our algorithm works for two performers; extending it to recognize multiple performers in the same scene may be another future research direction.

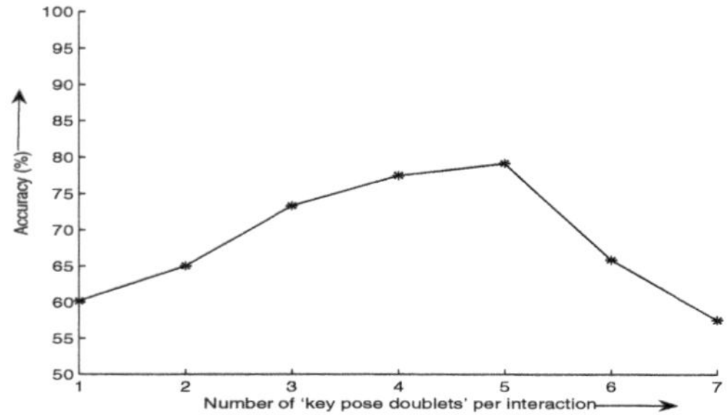

Figure 4: Accuracy plot with number of 'key pose doublets' per interaction for UT-Interaction dataset.

5. REFERENCES

[1] T. H. Cormen, C. E. Leiserson, R. L. Rivest, and C. Stein. *Introduction to Algorithms.* MIT Press, 2003.

[2] L. Fengjun and R. Nevatia. Single view human action recognition using key pose matching and viterbi path seraching. In *CVPR*. IEEE Computer Society, 2007.

[3] A. Gilbert and R. Bowden. Multi person tracking within crowded scenes. In *conference on Human motion: understanding, modeling, capture and animation*, pages 166–179. Springer, 2007.

[4] N. Ikizler and P. Duygulu. Histogram of oriented rectangles: A new pose descriptor for human action recognition. *Image and Vision Computing*, 27(10):1515–1526, September 2009.

[5] J. Liu, S. Ali, and M. Shah. Recognizing human actions using multiple features. In *CVPR*. IEEE Computer Society, July 2008.

[6] B. D. Lucas and T. Kanade. An iterative image registration technique with an application to stereo vision. In *International Joint Conference on Artificial Intelligence*, pages 674–679. Morgan Kaufmann Publishers Inc., 1981.

[7] G. Mori and J. Malik. Estimating human body configurations using shape context matching. In *ECCV (volume 3) LNCS 2352*, pages 666–680. Springer, January 2002.

[8] G. Mori, X. Ren, A. Efros, and J. Malik. Recovering human body configurations: Combining segmentation and recognition. In *CVPR (volume 2)*, pages 326–333. IEEE Computer Society, June 27-July 2 2004.

[9] S. Mukherjee, S. K. Biswas, and D. P. Mukherjee. Modeling sense disambiguation of human pose: Recognizing action at a distance by key poses. In *Asian Conference on Computer Vision, Volume 1, LNCS 6492*, pages 244–255, November 2010.

[10] B. L. Narayan, C. A. Murthy, and S. K. Pal. Maxdiff kd-trees for data condensation. *Pattern Recognition Letters*, 27(3):187–200, February 2006.

[11] R. Navigli and M. Lapata. An experimental study of graph connectivity for unsupervised word sense disambiguation. *IEEE T-PAMI*, 32(4):678–692, April 2010.

[12] J. C. Niebles, H. Wang, and L. Fei-Fei. Unsupervised learning of human action categories using spatial-temporal words. *International Journal of Computer Vision*, 79(3):299–318, June 2008.

[13] M. S. Ryoo and J. K. Aggarwal. Spatio-temporal relationship match: Video structure comparison for recognition of complex human activities. In *IEEE ICCV*, 2009.

[14] M. S. Ryoo and J. K. Aggarwal. UT-Interaction Dataset, ICPR contest on Semantic Description of Human Activities (SDHA). http://cvrc.ece.utexas.edu/ SDHA2010/ Human_Interaction.html, 2010.

[15] Y. Wang and G. Mori. Hidden part models for human action recognition: Probabilistic vs. max-margin. *IEEE T-PAMI*, 33(7):1310–1323, July 2011.

[16] D. B. West. *Introduction to Graph Theory.* Prentice Hall, 2000.

High-Efficient Software Parallel CAVLC Encoder Based on Programmable Stream Processor

Huayou Su, Chunyuan Zhang, Jun Chai, Mei Wen, Nan Wu, Ju Ren
School of Computer, National University of Defense Technology
Changsha, China
Huayousu@163.com, {cyzhang, chaijun200306, meiwen, nanwu, renju}@nudt.edu.cn

ABSTRACT

This article presents an efficient software parallel CAVLC encoder based on programmable stream processors (Storm- SP16 and GPU). For static processor Storm SP16, a block-based 16 ways parallel CAVLC is presented with streaming processing. A component-oriented CAVLC encoder is proposed aiming at dynamic stream processor GPU. Experiments results show that, compared to the CPU version, more than 70 times of speedup can be obtained for the CAVLC based on Storm and over 50 times for GPU-based component-oriented CAVLC encoder. The throughput of the presented CAVLC encoder is more than 10 times higher over that of published software CAVLC encoders on DSP and multi-core platforms.

Categories and Subject Descriptors

D.1.3 [Programming Techniques]: Concurrent Programming – Parallel programming

General Terms

Algorithms, Design, Experimentation, Performance

Keywords

CAVLC; software parallel; stream processor; real-time; HD

1. INTRODUCTION

In the H.264/AVC [3] Baseline Profile, CAVLC [1] provides considerable improvement of coding efficiency over the conventional coding of UVLC. However, the high coding gain increase comes mainly from its high computational complexity. In the past few years, many works are concerned with accelerating the CAVLC encoder by dedicated hardware. An optimization of CAVLC based on FPGA is proposed in [8]. Dedicated ASIC CAVLC encoders are developed for real-time video encoding in [2,10]. Though high efficiency can be gained, dedicated ASIC designs are inflexible, time-consuming, and expensive.

Stream architecture, an emerging architecture, can achieve high efficient performance by decoupling the data transfers and the computation. There are many stream processors, including Imagines Imagine, STORM-SP16 (STORM), Cell, Merrimac, GPU, and so on. All of these processors character with powerful computational capacities. Considerable high performance has been achieved in signal processing and scientific computation when using stream processors [4,6,7].

In this paper, an efficient parallel CAVLC encoder of H.264 baseline version is proposed based on programmable stream processor. A block-based CAVLC encoder is implemented on static stream processor Storm. For massively parallel architecture GPU, a component-oriented CAVLC is proposed. The whole process is divided into three stages: two scans, coding, and lag packing. The experiments show that the proposed parallel CAVLC encoder gains 70 times of speedup compared with the CPU only version when using Storm and 50 times of speedup for using GeForce 260+ GTX. Both of them can support real-time HDTV encoding.

The rest of the paper is organized as follows. Section 2 briefly describes the CAVLC of H.264/AVC. A block-based parallel CAVLC encoder is proposed based on Storm using SIMD method in section 3. In section 4 a component-oriented CAVLC encoder is implemented based on GPU. Section 5 shows the performance analysis and results. Finally, a conclusion is drawn in Section6.

2. OVERVIEW OF CAVLC

CAVLC is employed to encode the quantized residual data of the 4x4 or 2x2 blocks. Figure 1 shows the encoding process of the CAVLC. First, the encoder scans the quantized coefficients in zigzag order block by block and obtains the statistic symbols. Then, five different steps are employed sequentially to encode the symbols. For each MB, there are altogether 27 blocks needed to be encoded, including 1 Luma DC block, 16 Luma AC blocks, 2 Chroma DC blocks (size of 2x2) and 8 Chroma AC blocks. The statistic symbols are shown as following:

- **Coeff_token**: the number of nonzero coefficient and number of signed trailing
- **Trailing_Sign_trail**: the sign of trailing ones
- **Levels**: the remaining nonzero coefficients
- **Total_zeros**: the total number of zeros before the last coefficient
- **Run_before**: the number of run zeros preceding each nonzero level in reverse zigzag order.

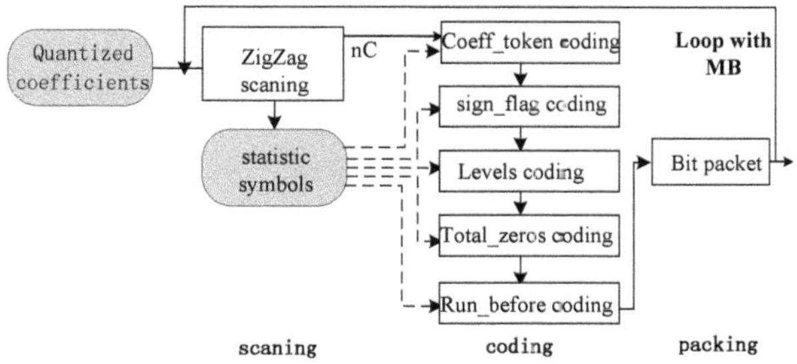

Figure 1. CAVLC encoder process flow

*Area Chair: Wei Tsang Ooi

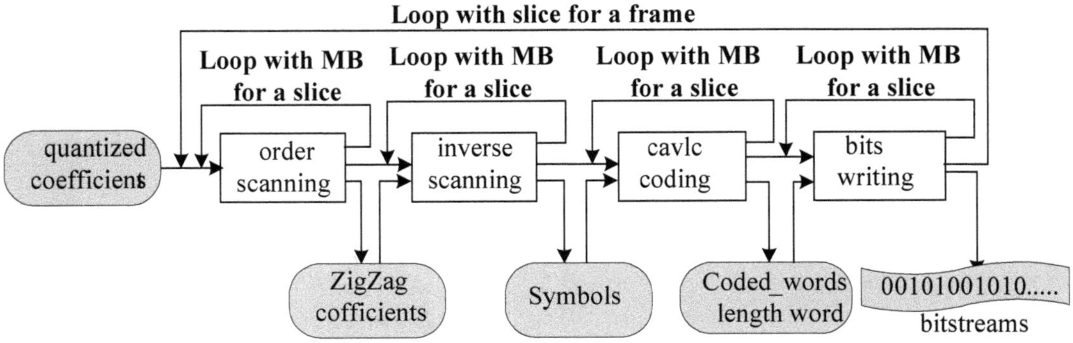

Figure 2. The proposed CAVLC based on STORM

3. PARALLEL CAVLC ENCODER ON STASTIC PROGRAMMABLE PROCESSOR

3.1 Optimization of CAVLC Architecture

In order to execute the parallel CAVLC encoder, the first step is optimizing the structure of the conventional CAVLC. In this article, The CAVLC encoder is divided into three stages: two scans, parallel coding and lag packing. We segment the loops in term of slice according to the three stages. The proposed CAVLC encoder based on Storm-SP16 is shown in Figure 2. ***Two scans***: two scans are employed to gain the statistic symbols: a positive scan and a reverse scan. First, a positive scan is executed to the quantized coefficients which are stored in zigzag order then. Second, a reverse scan is employed to the zigzagged coefficients and the values of nC are calculated based on the total_coeffs gained in the first scan. Two advantages are won. The first one is avoiding the redundancy of accessing the quantized coefficients of the adjacent blocks when computing the value of nC. The second is reducing the zigzag operations by using clever storage strategy. ***Parallel coding:*** lookup the tables and coding the symbols of an MB in raster order. The results contain two parts: the coded-words and their valid length. ***Lagging packing:*** though the length of bit-stream of each MB is not constant, it is fixed after the symbols are encoded completely. According to the valid length of bit-stream of each MB, the output position can be obtained and a parallel packing can be performed. It can not only eliminate the constraint of accessing dependence, but also improve the performance of bit-stream.

3.2 Implementation Based on Storm-SP16

STORM-SP16 is a high efficient DSP aiming at signal processing and video coding based on Imagine processor. The program is executed in SIMD on 16 Data Parallel Units, which is also called Lane. For CAVLC, maximum 27 blocks (4x4 block or 2x2 block) need to be coded for an MB. In this paper, the 27 blocks are allocated into 16 Lanes of the STORM processor shown in Figure 3. For simplifying the programming, two blocks are allocated to a Lane. Owing to only 27 blocks within an MB while the target processor contains 16 Lanes, some Lanes process useless data. As is shown, one block is valid in Lane0, which is the Luma DC block. From Lane1 to Lane8, two luma AC blocks are processed. The Lane9 deals with the two Chroma DC blocks. The Chroma AC blocks are assigned to Lanes from 10 to 13. Lane14 and Lane15 are invalid. For STORM, the parallel degree is constant and is always 16, therefore the whole process adopt the same allocation method showing in Figure 3. Five kernels are designed to perform the CAVLC coding process. The kernels are organized as Figure 4. It is one kind of producer-consumer relation. Limited by the capacity of the LRF, the kernels process one row of MBs in each time.

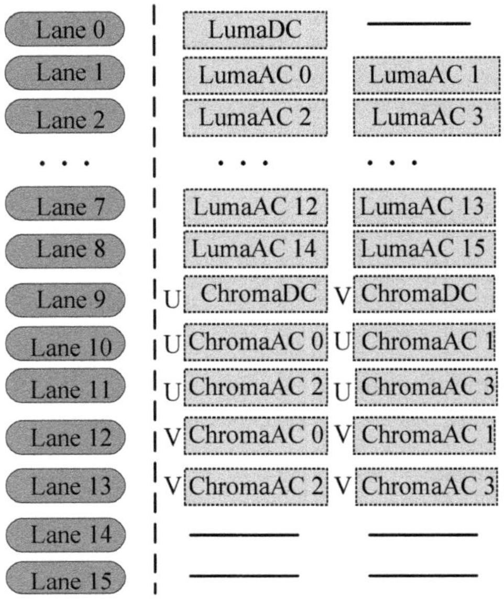

Figure 3. The allocation of data of CAVLC encoder

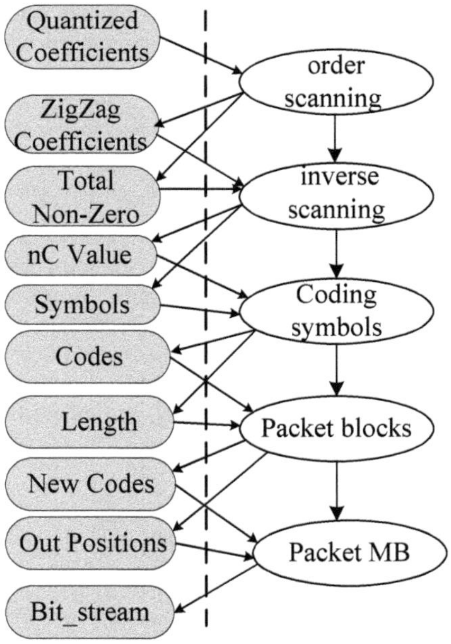

Figure 4. The organization of the kernels and streams

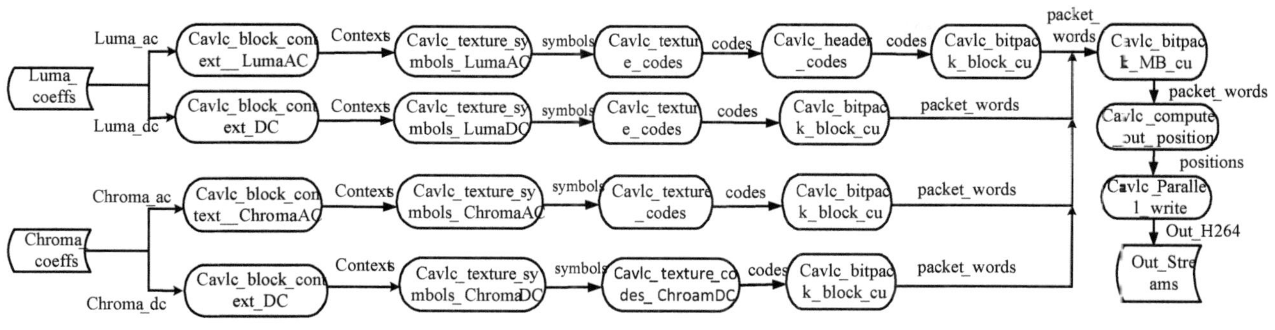

Figure 5. The component-oriented CAVLC

4. THE PROPOSED CAVLC ENCODER BASED ON GPU

GPU can offer more powerful computational capacity and much larger memory spaces. Large amounts of parallelism and efficient hiding delay strategy are critical for high efficient performance on such architecture. However, there are two major factors affecting the parallelizing of the CAVLC efficiently. One is the intensive control operations resulted from the processing for different components (luma and chroma) and symbols (total_coefficients, run, levels, and so on). The more important is the variable length coding. To solve the problems, beside the strategy of lagging packing mentioned above, an innovative CAVLC is proposed based on GPU, which is called component-oriented CAVLC, shown as figure 5. It processes the coefficients frame by frame in order of Luma DC, Luma AC, Chroma DC, Chroma AC, instead of processing the four components MB by MB. For example, until all the coefficients of Luma DC of a frame are executed, the component of Luam AC can be encoded, and so on. The unnecessary branches can be effectively reduced by this way. In this article, the CAVLC encoder is divided into two stages: parallel coding and parallel packing.

4.1 Parallel coding

It can be seen from the Figure 5, the processing is divided into 4 independent paths according to components (luminance, chrominance) and the coefficient type (DC, AC), before packing the bit-streams. Especially, we divided each path into two parts: scanning the coefficients and coding the symbols. Because the processings for all the four paths are very similar, in this paper, the processing for Luma AC is chosen as example to illustrate our parallel implementation of CAVLC encoder. In CAVLC, the process is organized for a 4x4 sub_block. There is strong data dependency between coefficients of the same sub_block. Naturally, the processing granularity of the parallel algorithm is a 4x4 sub_block. In our implementation, each thread was assigned to deal with a 4x4 block. We configure the thread block with 128 threads. 16 sequential threads take charge of an MB together and 8 MBs are encoded by a thread block.

4.2 Parallel packing

In this section, two steps are employed to accomplish the parallel packing. The first step is packing the bit-stream of different blocks of an MB to form an integrated one and computes the output position for bit-streams of each MB. In order to implement parallel output, some parameters are needed as follows. According to the length (n*8+m), the start position of output for each MB can be obtained.

- The number of integral byte of bit-stream for each MB (n)
- The number of the remaining bits less than one byte of each MB (m, m < 8)
- The shift mode and shift bits for each MB

In the second stage, each thread writes the bit-stream of MBs back to the final results. If the remaining bits of the current MB are less than a byte, then the rest bits is fetched from the next MB. Figure 6 shows the parallel writing course. In our implementation, a composed byte is generated by shifting the previous bit-stream towards left and the next bit-stream towards right. The bit-shifted is 8-m for left-shift and m for right-shift. Though the lengths of different bit-stream of MB are varied, it will result in branch within a warp. The high parallelism and less data transformed can improve the speed of packing.

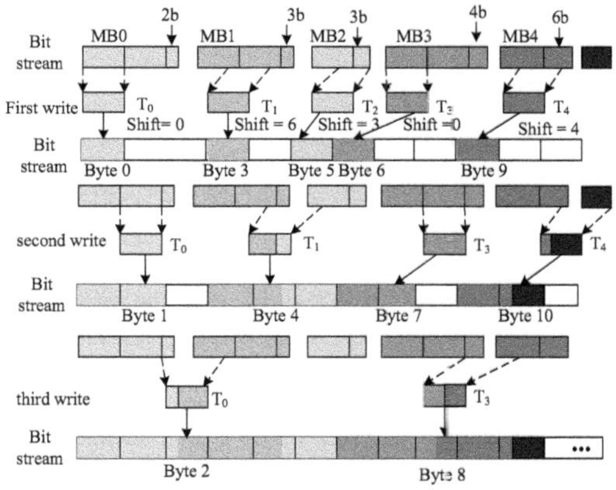

Figure 6. Parallel writing packing

5. EXPERIMENTAL RESULTS

To evaluate the performance of the proposed parallel CAVLC encoder, the following development environment is used: AMD Athlon 5200+ X2 Dual Core 2.7 GHz with 2GB memory, stream processor STORM G220 (700 MHz), NVIDIA GeForce 260+ GTX (1.29GHz) with 889MB DRAM. Since our target is real-time HDTV, 1080P (blue_sky) and 720P (into_tree) are selected as test sequences.

We evaluate the performance of the proposed CAVLC encoder and compare the results with those of using CPU only. The detailed information is shown in Table 1. The time of the column others includes transforming time and startup costs for kernels. As can be seen from the Table, compared with execution time when using CPU only, the parallel CAVLC can achieve 72.27X speedup when using STORM and 48.4X speedup with the assistance of GPU for 1080p format picture.

Currently, optimization implementation of CAVLC encoder by software methods mainly concentrated in using the DSP, multi-processor, stream processor platform. The compare between the proposed CAVLC encoders and other published software ones can be seen in Table 2. It can be seen from the table, compared with the CAVLC encoder on DSP, 17.18 and 11.17 times of speedup can be gained for the CAVLC based on STORM and the one based on GPU. Compared to AsAP[9], the speedup are 9.68 and 6.29 times.

Table 1. Percentage and speedup of various parts of the proposed CAVLC encoder

Test sequences	Encoder	Execution time per frame (ms)					Speed up
		scan	coding	packet	others	total	
720P	CPU only	NA	NA	NA	NA	201	1
	storm-1	1.03	0.66	1.48	0.29	3.44	58.43
	GTX 260+	1.47	1.10	1.35	1.37	5.29	38
1080P	CPU only	NA	NA	NA	NA	438	1
	storm-1	1.81	1.15	2.72	0.38	6.06	72.27
	GTX 260+	2.82	1.86	2.61	1.85	9.14	48.4

Table 2. Performance of CAVLC encoder on different platforms

Platforms	Processor type	Frequency	Test sequence	Execution time per frame
DSP TI C642 [5]	8-way VLIW	600MHz	720P QP = 24	59.1ms
Multicore AsAP [9]	15 cores MIMD	1.07GHz	720P QP = 20	33.3ms
Stream processor our work	16 lane SIMD	700MHz	720P QP = 30	3.44
GPU our work	216 SP MIMT	1.29GHz	720P QP = 30	5.29ms

6. CONCLUSION

In this article, a high-performance software CAVLC encoder based on static stream processor STORM and an efficient parallel one based on GPU are presented. For STORM processor, a segmentation of functional model is introduced in term of slice. Aiming at the GPU architecture, a component-oriented CAVLC is proposed. Experiments results show that the proposed parallel CAVLC encoders can achieve significant performance. Compared to the CPU version, more than 70 times of speedup can be obtained for STORM and over 50 times for GPU. In addition, the proposed architecture is both flexible and scalable in that its parallel degrees can change with the architecture of the target processor.

7. ACKNOWLEDGMENTS

The authors gratefully acknowledge support from National Nature Science Foundation of China under NSFC No. 61033008 and 60703073, Research Fund for the Doctoral Program of Higher Education of China under SRFDP No. 20104307110002.

8. REFERENCES

[1] Bjoietegaard, G., Lillcvold, K. Context-adaptive VLC (CAVLC) coding of coefficients. *Doc.JVT-C028, JVT of ISO MPEG&ITU VCEG, 3rd Meeting*, Rairfax, Virginia, USA, May, 2002.

[2] Han, C. S., Lee, J. H. Area efficient and high throughput CAVLC encoder for 1920×1080@30p H.264/AVC. *In Proceedings of International Conference on Consumer Electronics*, pp.1-2. January, 2009.

[3] Joint Video Team (JVT) of ISO/IEC MPEG and ITU-T VCEG. Draft ITU-T recommendation and final draft international standard of joint video specification (ITU-T Rec. H.264/ISO/IEC 14 496-10 AVC). JVT-G050, 2003.

[4] Khailany, B., Dally, W. J., Rixner, S. Imagine: signal and imagine processing with streams. *Hotchips2000*. Stanford, CA. August, 2000.

[5] Taheni D., Imen W., Amine A. DSP CAVLC implementation and optimization for H.264-AVC baseline encoder. *In Proceedings of IEEE International Conference on Electronics, Circuits and Systems*, pp.45-48. August, 2008.

[6] Thies, W., Karczmarek, M, Amarasinghe, S. Streamlt: A language for streaming applications. *In Proceedings of International Conference on Compiler Construction*, pp.1-17. April, 2002.

[7] Wu, N., Wen, M., Wu, W., Ren, J., Zhang, C. Y. Streaming HD H.264 encoder on programmable processors. *In Proceedings of ACM International Conference on Multimedia 2009*, pp.362-371. October, 2009.

[8] Xu, M. H., Li, K., Xuan, X.G., Fan, Y.L. Optimization of CAVLC algorithm and its FPGA implementation. *In Proceedings of International Conference on Electronic Packaging Technology & High Density Packaging*, pp.1-4. July, 2008.

[9] Xiao, Z., Baas, B. A high-performance parallel CAVLC encoder on a fine-grained many-core system. *In Proceedings of ICCD '08*, pp.248-254. October, 2008.

[10] Yi, Y., Song, B. C. High-speed CAVLC encoder for 1080p 60-Hz H.264 codec. *Signal Processing Letters*, vol. 15, pp.891-894. November, 2008.

A Real-time Database Architecture for Motion Capture Data

Pengjie Wang[1,2] Rynson W.H. Lau[3] Mingmin Zhang[1] Jiang Wang[3] Haiyu Song[2] Zhigeng Pan[1,4]
[1]State Key Laboratory of CAD & CG, Zhejiang University, Hangzhou, 310027, China
[2]College of Computer Science & Engineering, Dalian Nationalities University, Dalian, 116600, China
[3]Department of Computer Science, City University of Hong Kong, Hong Kong
[4]Digital Media and HCI Research Center, Hangzhou Normal University, Hangzhou, 310023, China
wpj@dlnu.edu.cn, rynson@cs.cityu.edu.hk, zmm@cad.zju.edu.cn, {wj11hk, songhaiyu, zhigengpan}@gmail.com

ABSTRACT
Due to the popularity of motion capture data in many applications, such as games, movies and virtual environments, huge collections of motion capture data are now available. It is becoming important to store these data in compressed form while being able to retrieve them without much overhead. However, there is little work that addresses both issues together. In this paper, we address these two issues by proposing a novel database architecture. First, we propose a lossless compression algorithm to compress the motion clips, which is based on a novel Alpha Parallelogram Predictor (APP) to estimate the degree of freedom (DOF) of each child joint from its immediate neighbors and parents that have already been processed. Second, we propose to store selected eigenvalues and eigenvectors of each motion clip, which only require a very small amount of memory overheads, for faster filtering of irrelevant motions. Based on this architecture, real-time queries become a three-step process. In the first two steps, we perform a quick filtering to identify relevant motion clips in the database through a two-level indexing structure. In the third step, only a small number of candidate clips are uncompressed and accurately matched with a Dynamic Time Warping algorithm. Our results show that users can efficiently search clips from this losslessly compressed motion database.

Categories and Subject Descriptors
H.3.3 [**Information Storage and Retrieval**]: Information Search and Retrieval – *retrieval models*

General Terms
Algorithms, management, performance, design, experimentation.

Keywords
Motion capture data, motion compression, motion indexing.

1. INTRODUCTION
Motion capture (mocap) data are now widely used in many applications, including movies, games, animation and virtual environments. As huge collections of mocap data are being produced, there is a need to design effective motion compression and retrieval methods for the storage and retrieval of these data. However, there is little work that considers both the indexing and compression of mocap data.

*Area Chair: Wei Tsang Ooi

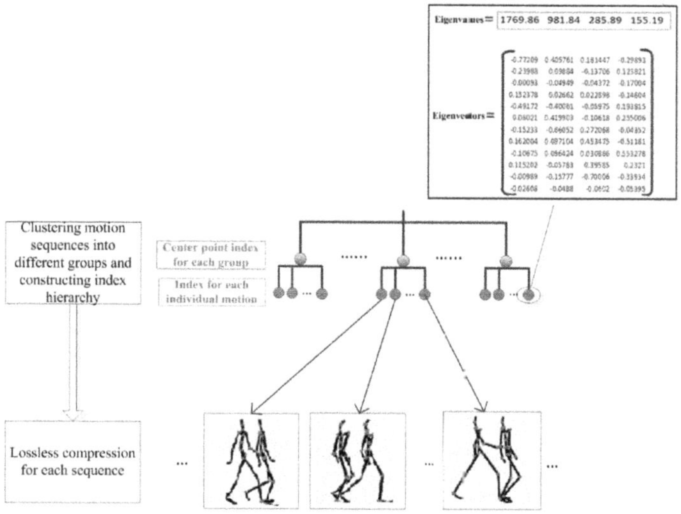

Figure 1. System Overview.

In this paper, we try to address these two problems by proposing a novel database architecture for motion capture data. Our architecture is composed of two levels, the index level and motion clips level, as shown in Figure 1. First, motion clips are clustered into many groups using the proposed novel distance measure, EigenDis, which is defined in the eigenspace of motion clips. Second, the two-level indexing structure is defined. The high-level of the indexing structure is represented by the center point index of each cluster, while each node in low level of the indexing structure stores the leading eigenvectors and the eigenvalues of a motion clip and a pointer to the corresponding motion clip. Each motion clip in the database is compressed losslessly by using our novel Alpha Parallelogram Predictor (APP), which estimates the degree of freedom (DOF) of each child joint from its immediate neighbors and parents that have been processed. The prediction parameter, alpha (α), is adaptively chosen from a carefully designed lookup table. Our results show that the user can efficient search the motion data from the losslessly compressed motion database, as our two-level indexing structure can filter irrelevant motion clips effectively and reduce the candidate set, and only the final set of clips need to be decompressed.

2. RELATED WORKS
The need for compact motion representation has resulted in a number of compression techniques for mocap data. Arikan [1] uses Bezier curves to represent motion clips, and then applies clustered PCA to reduce dimensionality. Beaudoin et al. [3] adapt standard wavelet compression on joint angles to compress mocap data. Tournier et al. [12] use principal geodesics analysis to build

a descriptive model of the pose data of a motion, keeping only the leading principal geodesics. This model is then used in an inverse kinematics system to synthesize poses that not only match the end-joint constraints but also with the interior joint positions. Given this pose model, only the compressed end-joint trajectories and the root joint's position and orientation need to be stored in order to recover the motion. All these methods are lossy method. Therefore, they throw away some information from the data in order to achieve high compression ratios.

On the other hand, automatically searching for similar motions is of great importance in motion synthesis and reusing. Since motion data are multi-attribute time-series, it is straightforward to apply dynamic time warping (DTW) [4, 6] or uniform scaling [8] for motion retrieval. However, these methods are based on numerical comparison and are typically very slow. Kovar and Gleicher [9] propose pre-computing "match webs" to describe potential matches among motion subsequences, in order to improve run-time retrieval efficiency. However, this method has a very high pre-processing time. In addition, if a query is not already in the database, this method will need to compute the match webs between the query and all the motions in the database. Deng et al. [5] propose to decompose motions into body parts and extract common motion patterns for each part. A motion clip can be represented as a string of pattern indices, and so motion retrieval becomes simple string matching. However, the data structures used amount to nearly 5% of the size of the motion database, which can be expensive for large databases. Muller et al. [11] propose an efficient semantics-based motion retrieval method, where the user inputs a query motion as a set of time-varying geometric feature relationships. It essentially transforms the motion retrieval problem into a binary matching problem in a geometric relationship space. However, specifying well-defined geometric (semantic) relationships for highly dynamic motions, such as boxing, is non-trivial, especially for novice users.

In summary, current state-of-art motion retrieval algorithms do not work with current compression algorithms, since compression algorithms introduce an overhead to real-time applications – the motion files need to be decompressed before use. In addition, all existing compression methods for motion capture data are lossy. However, if we want to edit a motion file compressed with a lossy compression method, we will need to uncompress it before editing and then compress it again afterwards. Each time we compress the motion file, the lossy compression method will introduce additional error to the file. Hence, a motion file needed to go through a number of such editing operations at different times will result in a compound error. Thus, a lossless compression method is needed. In this paper, we address these two problems by proposing a database architecture that integrates our proposed lossless compression method with our two-level indexing structure and a tree-step motion retrieval method.

3. DATABASE CONSTRUCTION

The raw motion data are high-dimensional time-series, which need dimension reduction. In this paper, we accomplish dimension reduction by adopting the feature set defined by [10], which uses positions of four end effectors and head as the features of the motion. After this process, the curve simplification algorithm is applied to reduce the number of frames to 20% of the original one. Finally, an adaptive *k*-means clustering algorithm is used to group similar motion clips together. To cluster motions, we need an effective and efficient distance measure. We propose to compute a matching score of two clips in eigenspace as our distance measure, called *EigenDis*.

4. Motion Index and EigenDis

In [2], it is observed that different actions within a single motion have different eigenspaces, and motion segmentation can be achieved by taking advantage of this. Inspired by this observation that each type of motion has its unique eigenvector "pattern", we propose to extract these "patterns" as motion index, and define EigenDis as the pattern matching score of two clips. In run-time, the matching scores between the input query clip and the clips in the database are used to pre-filter irrelevant clips.

First, we represent the original motion clips as a low-dimensional matrix composed of d vectors:

$$\mathbf{F} = (f_1, f_2, f_3, ..., f_d) \quad (1)$$

where $f_1, f_2, \ldots, f_d$ are the position vectors, d indicates the total number of angles, each defined as $f_i = (f_{1,i}, f_{2,i}, ..., f_{n,i})^{\mathrm{T}}$, and n is the number of frames in the motion. We define a mean vector:

$$\overline{\mathbf{F}} = (\overline{f}_1, \overline{f}_2, \overline{f}_3, ..., \overline{f}_d)$$

where $\overline{f}_i = \frac{1}{n}\sum_{j=1}^{n} f_{j,i}$, and a difference vector:

$$\hat{\mathbf{F}} = \mathbf{F} - \overline{\mathbf{F}} = (\hat{f}_1, \hat{f}_2, \hat{f}_3, ..., \hat{f}_d)$$

We compute the covariance matrix of $\hat{\mathbf{F}}$ as:

$$\mathbf{R} = (r_{j,k})_{d \times d} \quad (2)$$

where $r_{j,k} = \frac{1}{n}\sum_{i=1}^{n} \hat{f}_{i,j} \cdot \hat{f}_{i,k}$. We then obtain the s eigenvalues of $\mathbf{R}$, $\lambda_1 \geq \lambda_2 \geq \ldots \geq \lambda_s \geq 0$, and the corresponding eigenvectors $v_1, v_2, \ldots, v_s$, where s is the rank of $\mathbf{R}$. The weight of an eigenvalue is defined as: $\alpha_i = \frac{\lambda_i}{\sum_{k=1}^{s} \lambda_k}$.

We keep the leading m ($m \leq s$) largest eigenvalues until the accumulated weight is higher than a threshold *AccThr*. (In our implementation, we set it to 0.9.) We refer to m as the *length of the motion index*. Then, the final eigenvector matrix becomes:

$$\mathbf{V} = (v_1, v_2, \ldots, v_m) \quad (3)$$

We store $\mathbf{V}$ and the corresponding eigenvalues as the motion index of this motion, as shown in Figure 1. Assuming that the query motion is **VQ** and a motion in the database is **VD**, we compute the matching score of these two indexes as,

$$\rho = \sum_{i=1}^{m} w_i \rho_{i,\,i} \quad (4)$$

where w_i is defined as the ith eigenvalue over the total eigenvalues of the query index, and $\rho_{i,\,i}$ is the correlation coefficient between the ith eigenvector of **VD** and the ith eigenvector of **VQ**.

4.1 Two-level Index Construction

After the clustering process, a two-level indexing structure is constructed. The low level is the index for a specific motion clip. The content of an index node includes eigenvectors (Eq. (3)) and the corresponding eigenvalues. At the high level, each cluster stores a center point index. This center point is computed from the *k*-means clustering process. Each motion clip, as pointed to by a low level index node, is compressed losslessly using our Alpha Parallelogram Predictor (APP) method.

4.2 Lossless Compression of Motion Data

We adapt and extend the traditional parallelogram predictor [7] of mesh compression to compress the motion capture data in a lossless way, by introducing a prediction parameter, alpha (α), and its lookup table.

The motion data is first split into some equal-sized clusters before prediction, with each cluster having t poses. Figure 2 shows a human skeleton model and an example of APP. The right hand side of Figure 2 only shows two columns and some rows of cluster i. Assuming that c is a DOF index of child joint C, p is the DOF index of the parent of joint C. The numbers of DOFs of joint 18 and joint 16 are indexed by c and p, respectively. For cluster i, we can predict $DOF_{b+j,c}$ using the following formula:

$$P_{b+j,c} = DOF_{b+j-1,c} + \alpha\,(DOF_{b+j,p} - DOF_{b+j-1,p}) \qquad (5)$$
$$b = t(i-1)$$

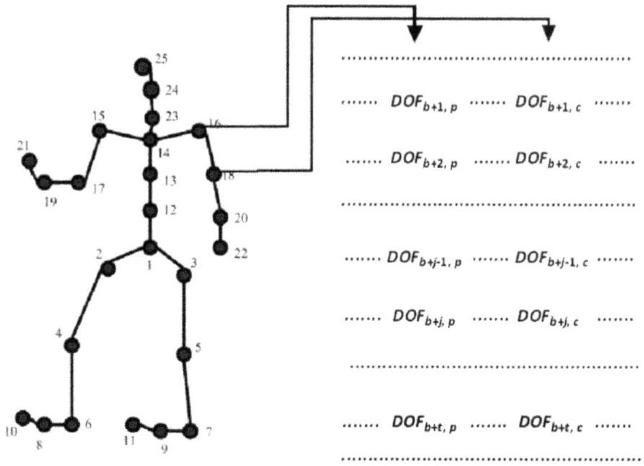

Figure 2. The virtual human skeleton and an example of APP.

When using Eq. (5) for prediction, the prediction error of DOF index c of cluster i is:

$$\varepsilon_{i,c} = \sum_{j=1}^{t}\left(DOF_{b+j,c} - P_{b+j,c}\right)^2$$
$$= \sum_{j=1}^{t}\left((DOF_{b+j,c} - DOF_{b+j-1,c}) + \alpha(DOF_{b+j-1,p} - DOF_{b+j,p})\right)^2 \qquad (6)$$

where $DOF_{b+j,c}$ is the actual value corresponding to the prediction value $P_{b+j,c}$. We obtain the minimum of $\varepsilon_{i,c}$, when:

$$\alpha = \frac{\sum_{j=1}^{t}(DOF_{b+j,p} - DOF_{b+j-1,p})(DOF_{b+j-1,c} - DOF_{b+j,c})}{\sum_{j=1}^{t}\left(DOF_{b+j,p} - DOF_{b+j-1,p}\right)^2} \qquad (7)$$

The α value computed from Eq. (7) is referred to as the ideal α value, since we can obtain a minimum error if we use it for prediction. Unfortunately, each ideal α value will occupy 32 bits to store. With a lot of α values to store, it will offset the compression ratio significantly. To address this problem, we first construct a α lookup table. Given an ideal α value, we simply look up the nearest α value from this lookup table and use it for prediction as described in Eq. (5). In this way, we only need to store the indices to the lookup table.

5. A TREE-STEP RETRIEVAL METHOD FOR COMPRESSED MOTIONS

Based on our database architecture, we can elaborate our run-time three-step motion retrieval algorithm as follows:

1. ***Group-filtering*** – This step is to branch the query motion to candidate groups by calculating matching score (EigenDis) between the query index and the center point index of each group. We set a threshold *FilterThrLel1* to remove all groups which scores are below this threshold. Others are returned as the resulting candidate groups.
2. ***Clip-filtering*** – This step is to identify the candidate clips from the candidate groups obtained from the first step. For each clip in the candidate groups, we compute one final matching score, which is the EigenDis between the query index and the index of the candidate clip. The matching is between the eigenvalues and eigenvectors of the two indices as in Eq. (4). We set a threshold *FilterThrLel2* to filter all clips which scores are below this threshold. Others are returned as the resulting candidate set.
3. ***Motion decompression and comparison*** – This step performs a detailed matching. We first uncompress each candidate motion clip and then use a time-series matching algorithm to compare between the query motion and this candidate motion. In our implementation, we use the DTW algorithm to perform the time-series matching.

With the above three-step retrieval algorithm, we can quickly remove a large number of irrelevant motion clips without involving decompression. We only need to decompress and execute the expensive DTW algorithm for a small number of motion clips to identify the matched motion clips.

6. RESULTS AND DISCUSSIONS

To evaluate the performance of the proposed method, we have implemented it in C++ and performed our experiments on a PC with an Intel Core Duo 2.26GHz CPU and 2GB RAM. Figure 3 shows our system interface. The red motion is the query. The blue motions are the best three motions and the remaining matched motions are in green. In this section, we first study the performance on the database construction process. We then study the run-time query performance of our method.

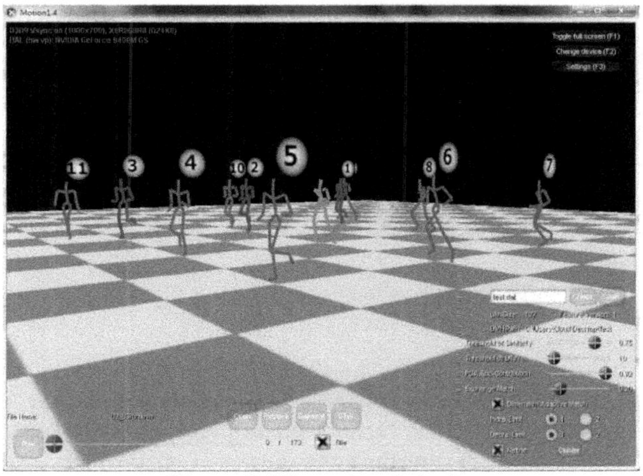

Figure 3. The system interface.

6.1 Performance of Database Construction

To examine the storage requirement and computation times of the proposed method, we have tested it on three databases of different sizes. In Table 1, column 1 shows the size of the input databases and the number of motion files. Columns 2, 3 and 4 show the index size, α look up table size and the compressed motion data size, respectively. Column 5 shows the total database size. Columns 6, 7 and 8 show the index extraction time, clustering time and compression time for constructing the database, respectively. Column 9 shows the total database construction time, which is the sum of columns 6, 7 and 8. During the clustering process, the EigenDis threshold (***ClsThr***) that we use to determine if a clip should belong to a group is 0.75. There are also two compression parameters that we need to determine: the number of groups, t, and the α lookup table. Here, we set t=10 and the α lookup table is {-1, -0.5, -0.25, 0, 0.25, 0.5, 1, 2}. From Table 1, we can see that by using our lossless compression method, we can effectively reduce the sizes of the databases to roughly a quarter of their original sizes.

Table 1. Database size and construction time, with *ClstThr* = 0.75, *t*=10 and α lookup table={-1, -0.5, -0.25, 0, 0.25, 0.5, 1, 2}.

Orig. DB Size (MB) / No. of Files	Size (MB)				Time (s)			
	Index size	Alpha size	Comp. size	Total size	Indexing time	Clustering time	Comp. time	Total time
39 / 134	0.23	0.25	9.76	10.24	2.23	0.23	14.79	17.25
172 / 121	0.21	0.23	45.25	45.69	9.98	0.17	63.67	73.82
290 / 233	0.40	0.52	72.78	73.70	15.90	0.45	107.49	123.84

6.2 Run-time Retrieval Performance

In this experiment, we apply some random queries from four types of motion on the first database mentioned in Table 1. This database includes 39 walking, 33 running, 14 jumping, 10 basketball-dribbling, 5 kicking ball, 3 drinking, 4 climbing, 8 cartwheeling, 5 picking up, 10 hoping and 3 dancing motions. Figure 4 compares the *precision* and *recall* of the proposed method with the non-filtering method (full search with the DTW matching process), and the non-DTW method (simply filtering the motion clips with the proposed indexing structure). We can see that with the proposed indexing structure, the recall values of our method (as well as the non-DTW method) are similar to those of the non-filtering method. When applying the non-DTW method, the precision values are not very good as some irrelevant motions still exist. By using our proposed method, the precision values are almost the same as the non-filtering method.

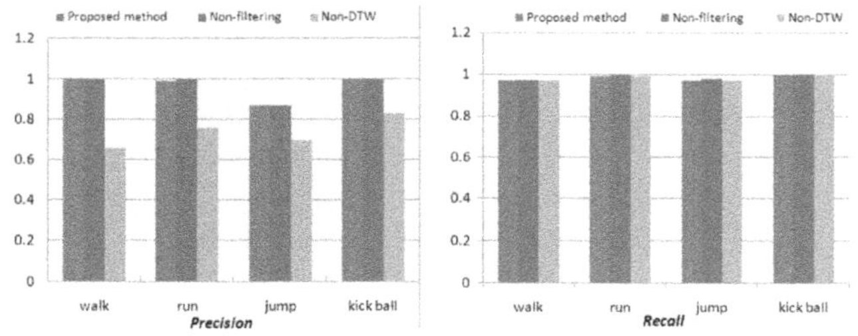

Figure 4. The *precision* and *recall* comparison between the proposed method (*FilterThrLel1*=0.2 and *FilterThrLel2*=0.45), the non-filtering method and the non-DTW method.

Table 2 shows the *response time per query* comparison of the proposed method, the non-filtering method (full search with the DTW matching process on the compressed motions) and non-compression method (our method but without compressing the motions). We use the same three databases as shown in Table 1 for this experiment. We can see that the proposed method can significantly reduce the *response time per query* through the filtering process with the indexing structure, as compared with the non-filtering method. The reduction is even more significant when the size of the database is large.

Table 2. The *response time per query* comparison between the proposed method, the non-filtering method and the non-compression method with number of candidate clips = 5.

DB Size(MB)	Proposed method (s)	Non-filtering (s)	Non-compression (s)
39	0.28	3.06	0.1
172	0.76	69.81	0.24
290	0.81	142.54	0.28

7. CONCLUSIONS

In this paper, we have looked at both compression and retrieval of motion capture data and proposed a database architecture to address both issues at the same time. We have proposed a lossless compression method for motions with a compression ratio of 25% of the original database size. We have also introduced a three-step motion retrieval method to effectively accelerate the retrieval process by filtering irrelevant motions with the proposed indexing structure. We have demonstrated the performance of the architecture by a number of experiments.

8. ACKNOWLEDGMENTS

The correspondence author of this paper is Zhang Mingmin. This paper was partially supported by NSFC (61170318, 61173124), two Fundamental Research Funds for the Central Universities (DC10040113, DC10040111), and two SRG grants from City University of Hong Kong (7002576 and 7002664).

REFERENCES

[1] O. Arikan. Compression of motion capture databases. *ACM Trans. on Graphics*, 25(3): 890–897, 2006.

[2] J. Barbic, A. Safonova, J. Pan, C. Faloutsos, J. Hodgins, N. Pollard. Segmenting motion capture data into distinct behaviors. *Proc. Graphics Interface*, pp.184-193, 2004.

[3] P. Beaudoin, P. Poulin, M. van de, Panne. Adapting wavelet compression to human motion capture clips. *Proc. Graphics Interface*, pp. 313–318, 2007.

[4] C. Chiu, S. Chao, M. Wu, S. Yang, H. Lin. Content-based retrieval for human motion data. *Visual Communication and Image Representation*, 15(3):446-466, 2004.

[5] Z. Deng, Q. Gu, Q. Li. Perceptually consistent example-based human motion retrieval. *Proc. ACM I3D,* pp.191-198, 2009.

[6] K. Forbes, E. Fiume. An efficient search algorithm for motion data using weighted PCA. *Proc. ACM SCA*, pp.67-76, 2005.

[7] M. Isenburg, P. Alliez. Compressing polygon mesh geometry with parallelogram prediction. *Proc. IEEE Visualization*, pp. 141-146, 2002.

[8] E. Keogh, T. Palpanas, V. Zordan, D. Gunopulos, M. Cardle, Indexing Large Human-Motion Databases, *Proc. VLDB*, 2004.

[9] L. Kovar, M. Gleicher. Automated extraction and parameterization of motions in large data sets. *ACM Trans. on Graphics*, 23(3):559–568, 2004.

[10] B. Krüger, J. Tautges, A. Weber, A. Zinke. Fast local and global similarity searches in large motion capture databases, *Proc. ACM SCA*, pp. 1-10, 2010.

[11] M. Muller, T. Roder, and M. Clausen. Efficient content-based retrieval of motion capture data. *ACM Trans. on Graphics*, 24(3):677–685, 2005.

[12] M. Tournier, X. Wu, C. Nicolas, A. Élise, R. Lionel. Motion Compression using Principal Geodesic Analysis. *Proc. Eurographics*, pp. 355-364, 2009.

Once Upon a Time, I Bought a Movie and it Played Everywhere in My Home

Jay Geagan, and Dulce Ponceleon
IBM Almaden Research Center
650 Harry Road, San Jose CA 95120
jgeagan@us.ibm.com, dulce@almaden.ibm.com

ABSTRACT

As digital media replaces analog, consumers are beginning to discover that their devices no longer interoperate in the way they were accustomed to. For example, they may find it impossible to transfer a DVR-recorded show onto a portable media player from a different manufacturer. Content creators are weary from supporting myriad ecosystems, each with different rules, restrictions, DRM systems, and file formats. To address these issues, IBM has developed the Advanced Secure Content Cluster Technology (ASCCT), which provides the highest levels of DRM protections for content owners, while at the same time being completely invisible to the user, allowing them to freely move, play, and backup content from any and all ASCCT devices within their home network. We describe the plug-and-play automatic construction of an interoperable secure cluster of heterogeneous devices using a minimal message protocol.

Categories and Subject Descriptors

K.5.1 [**Hardware/Software Protection**]

General Terms

Algorithms, Management, Security, Verification.

Keywords

ASCCT, NNL, Interoperability, broadcast encryption, content protection, home networking, audio/video, digital media, consumer electronics.

1. INTRODUCTION

Not long ago, content could be played everywhere. Broadcasts were recorded and later played back to any device in the home. Any purchased or rented content played on any player. Analog audio and video formats remained mostly unchanged for decades, and consumers amassed vast libraries of purchased audio and video tapes. Tthere was no such thing as non-interoperability.

*Area Chair: Tian Tsong Ng.

MM'11, November 28-Decemeber 1, 2011, Scottsdale, Arizona, USA.

Fast-forward to 2011. The first "analog sunsets" have happened (and more are coming) and although digital media has improved media quality and form factors, interoperability and simplicity and convenience have been sacrificed for the legal paying consumer. A purchased Blu-ray disk cannot (legally) be converted to the format that today's most popular portable media player requires. Consumers who desire to play a movie in full HD on their TV, and on a hand-held player, and on a netbook, and in the minivan DVD player discover that to (legally) do so it requires four purchases. When it is legally possible to transcode, it is often a complex process involving confusing terminology or cabling that varies with the source and destination devices.

Most of this non-interoperability is a consequence of Digital Rights Management (DRM) systems, which content producers require to prevent rampant copying of purchased content. Though some believe that the content producers lock people into non-interoperable DRM islands in order to force consumers to purchase copies of the same content for each of their home systems, the reality is that this is an unintended consequence. As evidence, note that many Blu-ray disks also contain a transcoded copy for the most popular portable player(s), and hybrid DVD/Blu-ray disks have been announced. However, even in cases like this, the island has merely become a small temporary archipelago, but cannot include the not-yet-invented popular player formats of tomorrow.

IBM developed the Advanced Secure Content Cluster Technology (ASCCT) to eliminate this ever-growing digital quagmire. Though it provides the strongest DRM to make content producers comfortable, it also includes an automatic clustering protocol that brings back the interoperability and ease of use that pre-digital-age consumers enjoyed, while allowing for forward-compatibility with future formats.

2. ASCCT EXTENDS INDUSTRY-ACCEPTED DRM TO A NETWORK

The DRM used in ASCCT is an enhanced version of the AACS[1] broadcast encryption security techniques[2] used for Blu-ray media. Broadcast encryption allows one-way transmission of protected content to authorized but anonymous recipients. Just as any Blu-ray player plays any Blu-ray disk without the owner having to register the disk or player with an authorization server, any ASCCT-compliant device can transparently join any cluster and automatically unlock the DRM secrets to access the content. Consumers are unaware that DRM is being enforced unless they try to circumvent it.

The fundamental encryption data structure used in ASCCT is the Media Key Block (MKB), similar to that used in AACS. This NNL-tree data structure [3] allows compactly encrypting a secret (a shared encryption key) for any exact combination of enabled (authorized) and disabled (revoked) members of a set of billions of leaf nodes in the NNL tree. Each leaf node corresponds to a single ASCCT device, which is assigned a particular set of NNL decryption keys, that are securely embedded into the device

An important feature of ASCCT is that it does not specify any particular media encoding formats (codecs, file formats, etc.) which allows any ASCCT-certified device to freely transcode to any media format, as long as it maintains the encryption and DRM protections and rules specified by the source content. This guarantees forward-compatibility and eliminates format-specific islands and archipelagos without content producers needing to "bless" every specific new format that is developed. Figure 1 shows a sample ASCCT Home Cluster with several devices and four possible ways to import content.

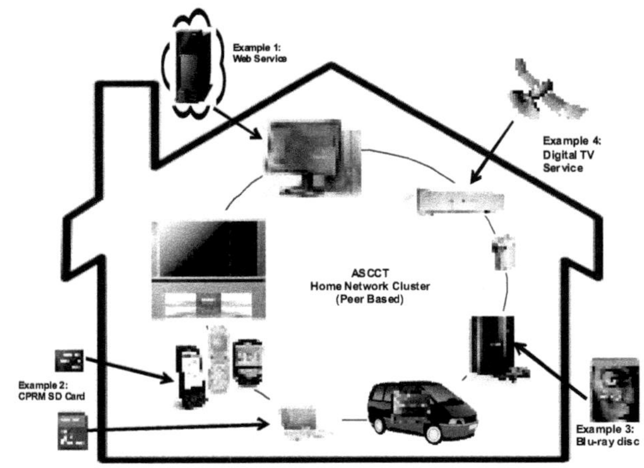

Figure 1: ASCCT Home-based cluster

Another feature of ASCCT is that the basic messages can be sent in the clear. Because the critical secret (derived from the current MKB) is shared only by valid devices, it is never necessary to transmit other secrets directly – these are encrypted or calculated from that shared secret. Integrity and validity of messages is also ensured by values calculated from this MKB secret

The main feature of ASCCT is that is a peer-to-peer system. Any compliant device can join any cluster and access its content. Devices may un-join a cluster, and they are no longer able to decrypt content from their former cluster(s). All of this happens without checking in with a central big-brother DRM authority – the devices perform the authentication by themselves. This has tremendous implications for user privacy, network topological flexibility, and allowing cluster changes when disconnected from the internet, or if the central authority would have been down, or even permanently out of business.

Other DRM systems "bind" a piece of content to a particular physical device or media [1,], but ASCCT binds content to a cluster of devices – for example, several devices found in one home. More precisely, instead of cryptographically binding to a unique device or media ID, the cluster devices automatically negotiate a single unique shared cluster key, and content is bound to that. Because this cluster binding key is shared among all of the devices that are members of that cluster (and not known by non-member devices) then any member of the cluster knows how to decrypt any and all content that is bound to that cluster. To a non-member of the cluster, files that contain cluster-encrypted content are useless random blobs, so this encrypted content can be backed up just like any other file to any storage media (hard disk, network cloud, etc.) without any concerns about unauthorized use. The owner does not have to worry about their "one copy" being lost. All devices of the cluster can decrypt the content files for playback.

3. SIMPLIFIED AUTOMATIC SECURE CLUSTERING

3.1 Simple Messages Enable Portability

Messages are semantically minimal, allowing them to be implemented with any syntax wrapper and transmitted via TCP, or even connectionless protocols such as UDP, SMS, or carrier pigeon. Messages are loss-tolerant: state information in a dropped request or response is recovered by subsequent requests. Not all devices need to be on the same network or speak all of the protocols – e.g. an ethernet-only cluster member syncs with an ethernet-or-SMS member which syncs with a SMS-only member.

3.2 Device Initialization

An ASCCT device starts life being in a singleton cluster containing only itself, initialized with a randomly-generated secret "binding key" used to encrypt its content files. As with AACS (Blu-ray) Broadcast Encryption, each ASCCT device has a unique set of secret keys that allow it to process a Media Key Block (MKB) to compute a shared secret, unless the device has been revoked in the MKB. ASCCT message authenticity is verified by using that MKB secret to compute the Message Authentication Code (MAC) value for messages:

```
mac = AES_hash(MKB-secret + header-values)
```

3.3 Cluster Discovery and MKB Viral Update

Devices automatically discover information about other devices, clusters, and updates to the MKB via IMHERE information, which is registered in a directory, or broadcasted over a network using a common autodiscovery or directory protocol such as UPnP , Zeroconf, Bonjour, or LDAP.

All the examples presented in this paper use 128-bit identifiers and 128-bit cryptographic functions. As follows is an example of device A broadcasting its basic information via an IMHERE message, so that other devices can discover it:

```
A-)) IMHERE:
device=aaaaaaaaaaaaaaaaaaaaaaaaaaaaaaaa
cluster=a1a1a1a1a1a1a1a1a1a1a1a1a1a1a1a1
MKBhash=9adaa6d1bb259cb7772d16e03326971f
AThash=1b9b586ce0fa1e5ff075b26af3d82a13
address=192.168.3.111:45337
```

Newer versions of MKBs (which revoke compromised devices) are periodically introduced on newly-released content and devices, and are automatically detected when a device sees an IMHERE containing an MKBhash different from that computed from its current MKB. When this occurs, the devices exchange GetMKB messages with each other, and retain the most recent MKB version. This propagates rapidly through any network, with all non-revoked ASCCT devices quickly updating to the newest MKB containing a new secret value.

3.4 Cluster Discovery and Joining

Fundamentally, the cluster-build protocol contains only two messages: AUTHORIZEME and GetAT.

When Device B wants to join Device A's cluster (which it learned about from an IMHERE message) it simply sends a message to Device A, asking to join:

```
B->A  AUTHORIZEME:
device=bbbbbbbbbbbbbbbbbbbbbbbbbbbbbbbb
cluster=a1a1a1a1a1a1a1a1a1a1a1a1a1a1a1a1
address=192.168.3.222:45337
mac=b39f7723b2361c2185412d8351e21c82
```

Device A verifies that MAC was computed correctly, adds Device B to cluster `a1a1a1a1a1a1a1a1a1a1a1a1a1a1a1a1`, and tells Device B the encryption of the cluster's secret:

```
A->B  AUTHORIZED:
cluster=a1a1a1a1a1a1a1a1a1a1a1a1a1a1a1a1
device=bbbbbbbbbbbbbbbbbbbbbbbbbbbbbbbb
binding= 40c230fc5bdcf29f65ec13f1dc6ff60c
mac= 418f7943e939730f1f77eab302abbaac
```

Once Authorized, Device B needs to know the cluster members (which now includes itself) so it sends a GetAT message:

```
B->A  GetAT:
cluster=a1a1a1a1a1a1a1a1a1a1a1a1a1a1a1a1
mac=b39f7723b2361c2185412d8351e21c82
```

Device A verifies that MAC was computed correctly, and tells B the Authorization Table for the cluster:

```
A->B  AT:
cluster=a1a1a1a1a1a1a1a1a1a1a1a1a1a1a1a1
AT=<base64-encrypted-authorization-table>
mac= 418f7943e939730f1f77eab302abbaac
```

The Authorization Table is decrypted using the shared secret and now contains both devices, i.e. Device B joined the cluster::

```
cluster=a1a1a1a1a1a1a1a1a1a1a1a1a1a1a1a1
device=aaaaaaaaaaaaaaaaaaaaaaaaaaaaaaaa
device=bbbbbbbbbbbbbbbbbbbbbbbbbbbbbbbb
```

In the Authorized response, the binding value is AES-encrypted using the result of a function, f(MKBsecret,AT, that includes the MKB secret and the Authorization Table. The receiving Device B can calculate the same f(MKBsecret,AT, but uses the inverse AES function to decrypt the actual secret cluster binding key. The two devices now share a secret private binding key and can now freely exchange and play any content encrypted with it. Since the content is strongly encrypted, it needs no further protection and can be freely transmitted, copied, and stored anywhere.

All of the above was made possible because both devices shared a common (latest version) MKB, and therefore they can both use the same secret value stored in that MKB to exchange messages.

3.5 Content Binding and Migrations

So far, the explanation has focused on the secure exchange of a binding key. The other component is the "content directory" which maintains a list of items (media files) that are bound to the cluster, using indirect encryption keys which are referenced only via the current binding key. When the binding key is recalculated (when devices join or leave, or when a new MKB is discovered) the content itself remains unchanged – only the encryption indirection (from the old binding key to the new binding key) needs to be updated in the directory for each content item. This is a fast operation (per content title) which each device performs as it re-negotiates (or discovers the new value of) its binding key. Compliant ASCCT devices must honor this general requirement, in order to solve certain challenging "socio-topological" cluster issues described below.

Because of the peer-to-peer nature of ASCCT, any cluster device can authorize any other device to join the cluster. This is true even if some or all of the other cluster devices are not currently on or online, or not present – they will learn about the new member (and update the binding key) once they are exposed to any device that knows about the added member(s). Because of this, you can have a perfectly viable cluster where some devices have never directly communicated with each other – e.g. the "vacation home" or "kid goes to college" scenarios. A mobile device that is part of a cluster can be exposed to devices in other remote locations, and consequently they can be added to its cluster. Adding such devices changes the binding key, and re-binds the content, and the changes eventually propagate back to the rest of the cluster when the device returns. Figure 2 shows an example of a disconnected topology, connected by the occasional appearance of a mobile cluster member that communicates changes across three islands.

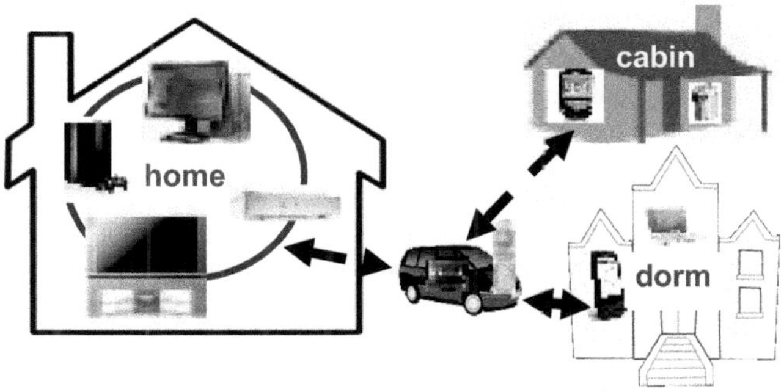

Figure 2: Disjoint Cluster in Operation

However, having an unbounded cluster size would inevitably lead to the pathological "dorm room scenario" with a cluster of thousands of devices, all in the same cluster, sharing a single purchased copy of some content. Hence, an arbitrary upper bound *N* (e.g. 10) on the cluster size is imposed. This *N* is part of the Authorization Table, and generally read-only (for rejecting an AUTHORIZEME that would exceed *N*) for normal compliant devices, but can be adjusted (by ASCCT service "virtual devices") in special circumstances – e.g. by paying a license fee for a larger cluster, proving you actually have 20 family members, etc. These services are another category of ASCCT cluster member, which provide and bind content or services (for example a subscription to HBO) to a cluster without counting as one of the *N* devices.

In order to remove a device from a cluster, the device must "abandon" the cluster it is a member of. In practical terms, it means informing one or more cluster members that it is leaving, and internally creates a new "singleton cluster" containing only itself cluster. The deleted member notification automatically propagates to the other cluster members (who may not even be online at the moment) by its disappearance from the Authorization Table, which changes the AThash in the IMHERE message, as described earlier. As part of the compliance requirements, a device must forget the binding key of its former cluster, and therefore cannot decrypt any content from its former cluster. It is now ready to join another cluster, or have other devices join its new cluster.

Another scenario is the "divorce scenario" where one or more cluster devices wish to leave the cluster but still retain access to one or more content items from the previous cluster. Instead of re-binding (and discarding the old binding) the content, the content remains bound to the old cluster, but also an additional binding to the new cluster is generated. The mechanism to perform this is provided in ASCCT, but the cost of this transaction is up to the content owner – they may choose to charge full price for the copy for the new cluster, or offer a discounted rate since the content itself does not need to be re-downloaded – it is essentially similar to purchasing a new download, or acquiring rights to a copy from another cluster.

3.6 Broadcast Encryption and Security Levels

Earlier implementations of ASCCT assigned equal access rights to all compliant devices, i.e. devices could (fully) play all encrypted content available in the cluster. The latest AACS system incorporates *security classes,* a relatively recent broadcast encryption feature where devices are no longer all equal. Instead each device is assigned to a specific class, a security class, based upon the level of "trust". There is no limit to the number of security classes that can be defined. There is a hierarchy of devices and consequently a hierarchy of keys. Devices that are more secure or trustworthy are given a higher-security set of Device Keys, while devices that are considered less secure are given a lower-security set of Device Keys. ASCCT protects content such that only the devices associated to the appropriated security classes can decrypt and access such content. For example, one could define two security classes to protect two different types of movies, high-definition and standard-definition movies.

ASCCT supports security classes while still using a *single* MKB by defining a different "cluster binding key" for each security class. Only the binding key associated to the top security class is generated randomly. Devices in higher security classes can derive the binding key associated to lower security classes using a chain of one-way functions *F(x).* Devices in the lowest security class process the MKB and generate the cluster binding key, *Km,* like when there was only one class of devices. The rest of the devices process the MKB and generate a *precursor of Km.* All compliant devices can process the same MKB and interact using the cluster binding key *Km.* For example, consider a cluster with three device security classes *(C0, C1,C2),* each class protecting different movie types (A,B,C) respectively. Less secure devices in *C0* generate *Km* and can only playback movies of type A. Devices in class C2 can play all content, while devices in C1 can play all but type-C movies. Devices in C2 process the MKB and generate precursor K_m^{-2} that enables them to playback type-C movies. C2 devices derive K_m^{-1} and K_m^{0} as follows to access type-B and type-A movies respectively:

$$K_m^{-1} = F(K_m^{-2})\text{; and } K_m = K_m^{0} = F(K_m^{-1})$$

Although it might not be obvious at first, there are plenty of cases where devices do not need to know the decryption key(s) associated to the content they hold. For example, in the case of a flash memory card, there is no need for the card microcontroller to decrypt the content, instead the player or host device will be the one doing so. The external drive where a user chooses to store his movie library does not need to decrypt the movies. By definition, storage devices do not need to decrypt content they hold. There are other scenarios where it would be useful to authenticate participating devices, but not required for such devices to decrypt content. By using security classes in broadcast encryption it is possible to define a specific class that captures the requirements for such devices.

3.7 Additional ASCCT Features

The ASCCT system includes commands not described here, such as those for cluster device removal and binding key updating, as well as features for content import-export, and suggested rules for handling other real-world disjoint topological home and business scenarios not described above. ASCCT can protect static content as well as streamed content. The MKB security foundations and mechanics can be found in [2, 3, 4].

CONCLUSION

In this paper, we have given an overview of ASCCT, including some of its unique characteristics and capabilities. We have also described some of the technical details of the ASCCT messaging protocol and cryptographic foundations. Finally, we have shown how these techniques combine to invisibly protect content, while simultaneously providing effortless-to-use automatic clustering for sharing content among every device in a home.

4. REFERENCES

[1] Advanced Access Content System, (AACS) http://www.aacsla.com/specifications

[2] A. Fiat, M. Naor, "Broadcast Encryption", Advances in Cryptography (Crypto 93), Lecture Notes in Computer Science 773, Springer-Verlag, New York, pp.480-491

[3] D. Naor, M. Naor, and J. Lotspiech, "Revocation and Tracing Routines for Stateless Receivers," Advances in Cryptology (Crypto 2000), Lecture Notes in Computer Science 2139, Springer-Verlag, New York, 2001, pp. 41-62.

[4] G. Deen, D. Ponceleon, D. Leake Jr, "Broadcast Encryption: Paving the Road to Practical Content Protection Systems", SPIE, January, 2009 San Jose CA.

Learning Frame Relevance for Video Classification*

Hua Wang
Department of Computer Science and Engineering
University of Texas at Arlington, TX 76019, USA
huawangcs@gmail.com

Feiping Nie
Department of Computer Science and Engineering
University of Texas at Arlington, TX 76019, USA
feipingnie@gmail.com

Heng Huang
Department of Computer Science and Engineering
University of Texas at Arlington, TX 76019, USA
heng@uta.edu

Yi Yang
School of Computer Science
Carnegie Mellon University, Pittsburgh, PA 15213, USA
yiyang@cs.cmu.edu

ABSTRACT

Traditional video classification methods typically require a large number of labeled training video frames to achieve satisfactory performance. However, in the real world, we usually only have sufficient labeled video clips (such as tagged online videos) but lack labeled video frames. In this paper, we formalize the video classification problem as a Multi-Instance Learning (MIL) problem, an emerging topic in machine learning in recent years, which only needs bag (video clip) labels. To solve the problem, we propose a novel Parameterized Class-to-Bag (P-C2B) Distance method to learn the relative importance of a training instance with respect to its labeled classes, such that the instance level labeling ambiguity in MIL is tackled and the frame relevances of training video data with respect to the semantic concepts of interest are given. Promising experimental results have demonstrated the effectiveness of the proposed method.

Categories and Subject Descriptors

I.2.6 [**Artificial Intelligence**]: Learning; H.3.1 [**Information Storage and Retrieval**]: Content Analysis and Indexing; I.2.10 [**Artificial Intelligence**]: Vision and Scene Understanding—*Video Analysis*

General Terms

Algorithms, Performance, Experimentation

Keywords

Video Classification, Multi-Instance Learning

*Area chair: Lexing Xie

MM'11, November 28–December 1, 2011, Scottsdale, Arizona, USA.

1. INTRODUCTION

Many existing video annotation approaches label every frame of a video clip and traditional video classification methods are usually designed to use the frame labels. However, frame level labeling requires expensive human labors, which often makes training an accurate video classification model very cost prohibitive. On the other hand, due to the rocketing growth of online videos with user tags at video clip level, we have abundant inexpensive coarsely labeled video training data. Therefore, devising video classification methods relying on only video clip labels is of great practical interest. In this paper, we explore this challenging, yet important, multimedia content analysis problem.

Given a video clip, the associated semantic labels usually arise from only a few of its frames but not all. For example, for the video clip in Figure 1, the "Studio" concept only comes from the two left frames, while the "Outdoor" concept is only attached to the three right frames. Apparently, labeling all the frames of this video clip is neither cost effective nor necessary. Therefore, identifying the relevances of the frames of coarsely labeled video clips to the semantic concepts of interest could potentially reduce the labeling cost while maintaining satisfactory video classification performance. To this end, we propose a novel Parameterized Class-to-Bag (P-C2B) Distance method by placing video classification under the framework of Multi-Instance Learning (MIL) that only leverages video clip labels, such that we are able to predict labels for unseen video clips as well as to learn frame relevances for the training video clips.

MIL [2] is an emerging topic in machine learning to address the classifications of data bags, in which each *bag* is a collection of *instances* with features associated to the instance. The aim of MIL is to infer bag labels based on the assumption that a positive bag contains at least one positive instance, while a negative bag contains negative instances only. MIL has attracted a lot of attention in recent years, and has been applied to many real-world applications [4, 9, 10, 11]. In the scenario of video classification, as illustrated in Figure 1, a video clip is considered as a bag and its frames are considered as instances. Our goal is to predict labels for a new coming bag (video clip) using the classification model learned from training bags and their associated labels.

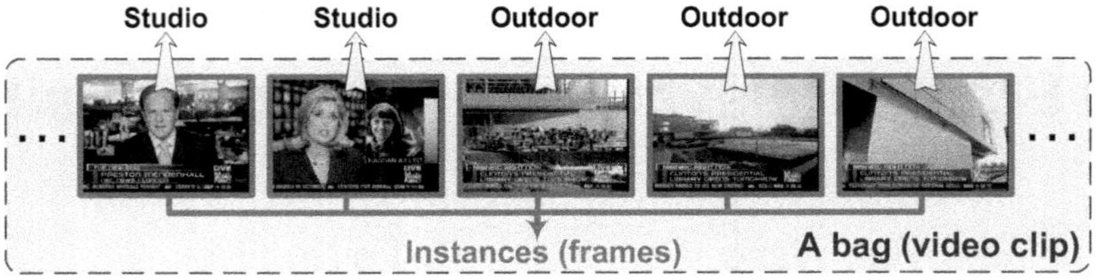

Figure 1: In multi-instance learning a video clip is represented as a bag and its frames are represented as instances. The semantic concepts associated with a video clip, *e.g.*, "Studio" and "Outdoor", usually arise only from a few of its frames but not all.

In the proposed method, we aim to address the two main challenges of MIL [9]: measuring set-to-set distance and weak label association. For the former, instead of computing the traditional Bag-to-Bag (B2B) distance that often does not truly reflect the semantic relationships between data objects [1], we consider to directly assess the relevance between classes and data objects, and propose to use *Class-to-Bag (C2B) distance*. For the latter, we take into account the relative importance of a training instance with respect to its labeled classes by assigning it with a weight for each of its labeled classes, called as *Significance Coefficient (SC)*. Ideally, the learned SCs of an instance, *i.e.*, frame relevance, with respect to its true associated classes should be large, whereas its SCs with respect other classes should be small. Parameterizing the C2B distance by the learned SCs, our P-C2B distance method for multi-instance data is proposed.

2. PARAMETERIZED CLASS-TO-BAG DISTANCE FOR MULTI-INSTANCE DATA

In this section, we first introduce a novel Parameterized Class-to-Bag (P-C2B) Distance to address the challenges of multi-instance data, followed by the objective and optimization procedures to learn it.

Problem formalization. Given a video classification task, we have N training video clips $\mathcal{X} = \{X_1, \ldots, X_N\}$ and K conceptual classes. Each video clip contains a number of frames represented by a bag of instances $X_i = \left[\mathbf{x}_i^1, \ldots, \mathbf{x}_i^{n_i}\right] \in \mathbb{R}^{d \times n_i}$, where n_i is the number of the frames (instances) in video clip X_i. Each instance is abstracted as a vector $\mathbf{x}_i^j \in \mathbb{R}^d$ of d dimensions. We are also given the class memberships of the input data, denoted as $Y = [\mathbf{y}_1, \ldots, \mathbf{y}_N]^T \in \{0,1\}^{N \times K}$ where $\mathbf{y}_i$ is the label indicator of X_i. In the setting of MIL, if there exists $j \in \{1, \ldots, n_i\}$ such that $\mathbf{x}_i^j$ belongs to the k-th class, X_i is assigned to the k-th class and $Y_{ik} = 1$, otherwise $Y_{ik} = 0$. Yet the concrete value of the index j is unknown. More specifically, the following assumptions are held in the settings of MIL: (1) bag X is assigned to the k-th class $\Longleftrightarrow$ at least one instance of X belongs to the k-th class; (2) bag X is not assigned to the k-th class $\Longleftrightarrow$ no instance in X belongs to the k-th class. Our goal is to learn from the training data $\mathcal{D} = \{X_i, \mathbf{y}_i\}_{i=1}^N$ a classifier that is able to predict labels for a new query video clip X.

2.1 Parameterized Class-to-Bag Distance

To tackle the two major difficulties of MIL, the estimation of set-to-set distances and instance level labeling ambiguity [9], we first propose a novel P-C2B distance for multi-instance data.

Class-to-Bag (C2B) Distance. We first represent every class as a *super-bag* that comprises the instances of all its training bags: $C_k = \left\{\mathbf{x}_i^j \mid i \in \pi_k\right\}$ where $\pi_k = \{i \mid Y_{ik} = 1\}$ is the index set of all the training bags belonging to the k-th class. We denote the number of instances in C_k as m_k, *i.e.*, $|C_k| = m_k$. Note that, in single-label video data sets where each video clip belongs to exactly one class, *i.e.*, $\sum_{k=1}^K Y_{ik} = 1$, therefore $C_k \cap C_l = \varnothing$ $(\forall\, k \neq l)$ and $\sum_{k=1}^K m_k = \sum_{i=1}^N n_i$. In multi-label video data sets where each video clip (thereby each instance) may belong to more than one class, *i.e.*, $\sum_{k=1}^K Y_{ik} \geq 1$, thus $C_k \cap C_l \neq \varnothing$ $(\forall\, k \neq l)$ and $\sum_{k=1}^K m_k \geq \sum_{i=1}^N n_i$, *i.e.*, different super-bags may overlap and one instance $\mathbf{x}_i^j$ may appear in multiple super-bags.

Then we define the elementary distance from an instance $\mathbf{x}_i^j$ of a super-bag C_k to a data bag $X_{i'}$ by the distance between $\mathbf{x}_i^j$ and its nearest neighbor instance in $X_{i'}$:

$$dist_k\left(\mathbf{x}_i^j, X_{i'}\right) = \left\|\mathbf{x}_i^j - \mathcal{N}_{i'}\left(\mathbf{x}_i^j\right)\right\| \quad , \quad \forall i \in \pi_k \; , \qquad (1)$$

where $\mathcal{N}_{i'}\left(\mathbf{x}_i^j\right)$ denotes the nearest neighbor of $\mathbf{x}_i^j$ in $X_{i'}$.

Finally, the C2B distance from C_k to $X_{i'}$ is computed as:

$$Dist\left(C_k, X_{i'}\right) = \sum_{i \in \pi_k} \sum_{j=1}^{n_i} dist_k\left(\mathbf{x}_i^j, X_{i'}\right) = \sum_{i \in \pi_k} \mathbf{e}^T \mathbf{d}_{ii'k} \; , \qquad (2)$$

where $\mathbf{e} = [1, \ldots, 1]^T$ is a constant vector, and $\mathbf{d}_{ii'k} \in \mathbb{R}^{n_i}$ in which the j-th element is $\left\|\mathbf{x}_i^j - \mathcal{N}_{i'}\left(\mathbf{x}_i^j\right)\right\|$.

Parameterized Class-to-Bag (P-C2B) Distance. Because the C2B distance defined in Eq. (2) does not take into account the the instance level labeling ambiguity in MIL, we further develop it by weighting the instances in a super-bag upon their relevance to a concerned class.

Due to the ambiguous associations between instances and labels, not all the instances in a super-bag really characterize the corresponding class. For example, in Figure 1 the rightmost instance (frame) is in the super-bag of "Studio" class, because the entire video clip is labeled with both "Studio" and "Outdoor". Intuitively, we should give it a smaller, or even no, weight when determining whether to assign "Studio" label to a query video clip; and give it a higher weight when deciding "Outdoor" label. To be more precise, let w_{ik}^j be the weight for $\mathbf{x}_i^j$ with respect to the k-th class, we compute the parameterized C2B distance from C_k to $X_{i'}$ as:

$$Dist\left(C_k, X_{i'}\right) = \sum_{i \in \pi_k} \mathbf{w}_{ik}^T \mathbf{d}_{ii'k} \; , \qquad (3)$$

where $\mathbf{w}_{ik} = \left[w_{ik}^1, \ldots, w_{ik}^{n_i}\right]^T$. As can be seen, different from Eq. (2) in which all the elementary distances are equally weighted by $\mathbf{e}$, the C2B distance defined in Eq. (3) gives different weights to the instances in a super-bag upon their relevances by $\mathbf{w}_{ik}$. Because w_{ik}^j reflects the relative importance of instance $\mathbf{x}_i^j$ when determining the label for the k-th class, we call it as the Significance Coefficient (SC) of $\mathbf{x}_i^j$ with respect to the k-th class, and the resulted C2B distance computed by Eq. (3) as the proposed Parameterized Class-to-Bag (P-C2B) Distance.

2.2 Objective and Optimization Algorithm

Armed with the P-C2B distance defined in Eq. (3), we learn w_{ik}^j by maximizing the data separability, *i.e.*, we minimize the overall P-C2B distance from a class to all its belonging bags, whilst maximizing the overall P-C2B distance from the same class to all the bags not belonging to it. Formally, for a given class C_k, we solve the following optimization problem:

$$\min_{\mathbf{w}_{ik}\geq 0,\ \mathbf{w}_{ik}^T\mathbf{e}=1} \frac{\sum_{i'\in\pi_k}\sum_{i\in\pi_k}\mathbf{w}_{ik}^T\mathbf{d}_{ii'k}}{\sum_{i'\notin\pi_k}\sum_{i\in\pi_k}\mathbf{w}_{ik}^T\mathbf{d}_{ii'k}} . \quad (4)$$

Let $\mathbf{d}_{ik}^w = \sum_{i'\in\pi_k}\mathbf{d}_{ii'k} \in \mathbb{R}^{n_i}$ and $\mathbf{d}_{ik}^b = \sum_{i'\notin\pi_k}\mathbf{d}_{ii'k} \in \mathbb{R}^{n_i}$, we rewrite the problem in Eq. (4) as:

$$\min_{\mathbf{w}_{ik}\geq 0,\ \mathbf{w}_{ik}^T\mathbf{e}=1} \frac{\sum_{i\in\pi_k}\left(\mathbf{w}_{ik}^T\mathbf{d}_{ik}^w + \alpha\mathbf{w}_{ik}^T\mathbf{w}_{ik}\right)}{\sum_{i\in\pi_k}\mathbf{w}_{ik}^T\mathbf{d}_{ik}^b} , \quad (5)$$

where the second term in the numerator is added to avoid the degenerate solution.

To solve the optimization objective in Eq. (5), we derive an iterative algorithm as following.

Algorithm 1: The algorithm to solve the problem (5).

$t=0$. Randomly initialize $\mathbf{w}_{ik}^{(0)}$ satisfying $\mathbf{w}_{ik}^{(0)} \geq 0$, $\left(\mathbf{w}_{ik}^{(0)}\right)^T\mathbf{e} = 1$.

while *not converge* **do**

1. Calculate $\lambda^{(t)} = \frac{\sum_{i\in\pi_k}\left[\left(\mathbf{w}_{ik}^{(t)}\right)^T\mathbf{d}_{ik}^w + \alpha\left(\mathbf{w}_{ik}^{(t)}\right)^T\mathbf{w}_{ik}^{(t)}\right]}{\sum_{i\in\pi_k}\left(\mathbf{w}_{ik}^{(t)}\right)^T\mathbf{d}_{ik}^b}$.
2. Calculate

$$\mathbf{w}_{ik}^{(t+1)} = \arg\min_{\substack{\mathbf{w}_{ik}\geq 0,\\ \mathbf{w}_{ik}^T\mathbf{e}=1}} \sum_{i\in\pi_k}\left(\mathbf{w}_{ik}^T\mathbf{d}_{ik}^w + \alpha\mathbf{w}_{ik}^T\mathbf{w}_{ik}\right) - \lambda^{(t)}\sum_{i\in\pi_k}\mathbf{w}_{ik}^T\mathbf{d}_{ik}^b . \quad (6)$$

3. $t = t+1$.

end

Let $\mathbf{d}_{ik} = \mathbf{d}_{ik}^w - \lambda^{(t)}\mathbf{d}_{ik}^b$, we may rewrite the optimization problem in Eq. (6) as following:

$$\min_{\mathbf{w}_{ik}\geq 0,\ \mathbf{w}_{ik}^T\mathbf{e}=1} \sum_{i\in\pi_k}\left(\mathbf{w}_{ik}^T\mathbf{d}_{ik} + \alpha\mathbf{w}_{ik}^T\mathbf{w}_{ik}\right) . \quad (7)$$

We can see that the problem in Eq. (7) can be decoupled to solve the following subproblems separately for each $i \in \pi_k$:

$$\min_{\mathbf{w}_{ik}\geq 0,\ \mathbf{w}_{ik}^T\mathbf{e}=1} \mathbf{w}_{ik}^T\mathbf{d}_{ik} + \alpha\mathbf{w}_{ik}^T\mathbf{w}_{ik} , \quad (8)$$

which are convex quadratic programming (QP) problems, and can be efficiently solved because $\mathbf{w}_{ik} \in \mathbb{R}^{n_i}$ and the value of n_i, *i.e.*, the bag size of X_i, is usually not large.

Given the learned w_{ik}^j $(1 \leq k \leq K, 1 \leq i \leq N, 1 \leq j \leq n_i)$, we can compute $D(C_k, X)$ $(1 \leq k \leq K)$ for a query video clip X using Eq. (3), based on which the classification can be conducted following the same rules as in [9].

3. EXPERIMENTAL RESULTS

In this section, we experimentally evaluate the proposed P-C2B method in automatic video classification tasks, where we emphasize its effectiveness in low-cost conditions.

3.1 Data Preparation

We conduct our experiments using **TRECVID 2005** video data set[1], which contains 277 video clips with 61,901 shots labeled by 39 LSCOM-Lite concepts. Each shot (key frame) is considered as an instance in our study. For each instance, following [8] we extract a 384-dimensional low-level visual feature vector by dividing the corresponding key frame into 64 blocks by a 8×8 grid and computing the first and second moments (mean and variance) of each color band. We split each video clip into 5 consecutive parts and end up with 1385 bags. Different bags have different numbers of instances. In average, each bag comprises 44.7 instances. Because in TRECVID 2005 data set, each video clip is annotated with more than one semantic label, it is a multi-label data set.

3.2 Experimental Settings

Because the main purpose of the proposed P-C2B distance method is to deal with low-cost video classification, we evaluate it in the conditions where we only have video clips labels but not frame labels. We employ standard 5-fold cross-validation for evaluation and report the average performance over the 5 trials. For each video clip, we randomly select a fraction of its frames and assign their labels to the video clip, while the labels of both selected and not-selected frames are assumed to be unknown. We emulate two different conditions when the amount of selected frames are 80% and 50%, and the corresponding results are reported in the top and bottom halves of Table 1 respectively.

The proposed P-C2B method has only one parameter, *i.e.*, the regularization parameter α in Eq. (5). Empirically, we set $\alpha = 0.01$ throughout our experiments.

We first compare our method to two baseline classification methods including support vector machine (SVM) method and transductive support vector machine (TSVM) [3] method. The former is one of the most widely used supervised classification method in statistical learning, while the latter is an extension of the former and is a semi-supervised classification method. Because both of these two methods are designed for single-instance data, they are not able to handle data objects with varied sizes. To this end, we assign the bag labels to all its component frames. This brings instance level labeling ambiguity, which, on the other hand, significantly reduces required labeling cost for training, because we only need human experts to label either the whole video clips or a fraction of their frames instead of all. For each class we train a one-vs-others classier using the frames in the training video clips, and classify the frames in the test video clips. Gaussian kernel is used for the both methods, *i.e.*, $\mathcal{K}(\mathbf{x}_i, \mathbf{x}_j) = \exp\left(-\beta\left\|\mathbf{x}_i - \mathbf{x}_j\right\|^2\right)$, where β and the regularization parameter C are fine tuned by searching the grid of $\left\{10^{-5}, \ldots, 10^{-1}, 1, 10, \ldots, 10^5\right\}$ via an internal 5-fold cross-validation using the training data of each of the 5 trails. The both methods are implemented using SVM-light[2].

We also compare our method to two most related methods, *i.e.*, two recent MIL methods including miGraph [11]

[1]http://www-nlpir.nist.gov/projects/trecvid/
[2]http://svmlight.joachims.org/

Table 1: Video classification performances (mean ± standard deviation) comparison when only 80% (top half) and 50% (bottom half) of the frames are labeled.

Method	Hamming loss ↓	One-error ↓	Coverage ↓	Rank loss ↓	Average precision ↑
SVM	0.239 ± 0.014	0.448 ± 0.010	1.323 ± 0.010	0.240 ± 0.012	0.335 ± 0.020
TSVM	0.235 ± 0.012	0.444 ± 0.012	1.312 ± 0.016	0.233 ± 0.014	0.338 ± 0.022
SML	0.228 ± 0.013	0.441 ± 0.015	1.308 ± 0.011	0.229 ± 0.016	0.342 ± 0.025
miGraph	0.215 ± 0.012	0.366 ± 0.016	1.202 ± 0.015	0.213 ± 0.010	0.386 ± 0.021
MIMLSVM+	0.208 ± 0.010	0.357 ± 0.015	1.116 ± 0.018	0.205 ± 0.012	0.398 ± 0.021
P-C2B	**0.191 ± 0.011**	**0.341 ± 0.010**	**1.093 ± 0.007**	**0.188 ± 0.010**	**0.420 ± 0.012**
SVM	0.282 ± 0.012	0.515 ± 0.013	1.585 ± 0.019	0.289 ± 0.017	0.240 ± 0.019
TSVM	0.280 ± 0.013	0.511 ± 0.015	1.580 ± 0.020	0.283 ± 0.015	0.245 ± 0.020
SML	0.276 ± 0.010	0.505 ± 0.013	1.574 ± 0.015	0.277 ± 0.013	0.249 ± 0.018
miGraph	0.233 ± 0.012	0.418 ± 0.015	1.310 ± 0.019	0.244 ± 0.012	0.306 ± 0.020
MIMLSVM+	0.227 ± 0.014	0.404 ± 0.015	1.293 ± 0.016	0.237 ± 0.013	0.318 ± 0.018
P-C2B	**0.209 ± 0.011**	**0.373 ± 0.012**	**1.183 ± 0.014**	**0.214 ± 0.011**	**0.354 ± 0.013**

method and MIMLSVM+ [4] method. Because miGraph method is a single-label classification method, one-vs-others strategy is used to conduct classification, one class at a time. Note that, because both of these two method and the proposed P-C2B method are multi-instance classification methods, thus we perform classification at bag, *i.e.*, video clip, level. Namely, although we know the ground truth instance labels, these three methods do not use them. They only use bag labels following standard MIL settings.

Finally, we report the performance of a most recent video classification method, *i.e.*, supervised manifold learning (SML) [5] method which has demonstrated state-of-the-art classification performance. Since this method is designed to work at frame level, we employ the same strategy as that for SVM to conduct classification. We implement the method following its original work and set the parameters as optimal.

3.3 Experimental Results

Because TRECVID 2005 data set is a multi-label data set, we evaluate the classification performances of the compared methods using five widely used multi-label evaluation metrics, as shown in Table 1, where "↓" indicates "the smaller the better" while "↑" indicates "the bigger the better". We refer readers to [6] for details of these evaluation metrics.

The average classification performances (mean ± standard deviation) of the compared methods over the 5 trials of the experiments are reported in Table 1, from which we can see that the proposed method is consistently better than the other compared methods, sometimes very significantly. Moreover, when labeling cost is reduced, *i.e.*, the amount of labeled frames are reduced, the classification performance degradations of the multi-instance methods, including the proposed P-C2B distance method, are not very significant, whereas those of the single-instance methods are considerably large. These results concretely demonstrate the usefulness of multi-instance learning in cost effective video classification, as well as the effectiveness of the proposed method.

4. CONCLUSION

In this paper, we proposed a novel Parameterized Class-to-Bag (P-C2B) Distance method to solve the video classification problem under the framework of Multi-Instance Learning (MIL). The Significance Coefficients (SCs) are learned to assess the relative importance of a training instance with respect to its labeled classes, which thus solves the notorious instance label assignment ambiguity in MIL. Moreover, through the learned SCs, the frame relevances to the concerned semantic concepts of the coarsely labeled video clips are explicitly given to reveal the insight of the input data set. The promising experimental results were reported in empirical evaluations, which validated the proposed method.

Acknowledgment.

This research was supported by NSF-IIS 1117965, NSFCCF-0830780, NSF-DMS-0915228, NSF-CCF-0917274.

5. REFERENCES

[1] O. Boiman, E. Shechtman, and M. Irani. In defense of nearest-neighbor based image classification. In *IEEE CVPR*, 2008.

[2] T. Dietterich, R. Lathrop, and T. Lozano-Pérez. Solving the multiple instance problem with axis-parallel rectangles. *Artificial Intelligence*, 89(1-2):31–71, 1997.

[3] T. Joachims. Transductive inference for text classification using support vector machines. In *ICML*, pages 200–209.

[4] Y. Li, S. Ji, S. Kumar, J. Ye, and Z. Zhou. Drosophila Gene Expression Pattern Annotation through Multi-Instance Multi-Label Learning. *ACM/IEEE TCBB*, 2011.

[5] Y. Liu, Y. Liu, and K. Chan. Supervised manifold learning for image and video classification. In *ACM Multimedia*, 2010.

[6] R. Schapire and Y. Singer. BoosTexter: A boosting-based system for text categorization. *Machine learning*, 39(2):135–168, 2000.

[7] R. Tibshirani. Regression shrinkage and selection via the LASSO. *Jouranl of Royal Statistics Society B.*, 58:267–288, 1996.

[8] H. Wang, H. Huang, and C. Ding. Image annotation using multi-label correlated green's function. In *IEEE ICCV*, 2009.

[9] H. Wang, F. Nie, and H. Huang. Learning instance specific distance for multi-instance classification. In *AAAI*, 2011.

[10] C. Zhang and P. Viola. Multiple-instance pruning for learning efficient cascade detectors. In *NIPS*, 2008.

[11] Z. Zhou, Y. Sun, and Y. Li. Multi-instance learning by treating instances as non-I.I.D. samples. In *ICML*, 2009.

Large Scale Image Search with Geometric Coding

Wengang Zhou[1], Houqiang Li[1], Yijuan Lu[2], Qi Tian[3]
Dept. of EEIS, University of Science and Technology of China[1], Hefei, P.R. China
Dept. of Computer Science, Texas State University[2], Texas, TX 78666
Dept. of Computer Science, University of Texas at San Antonio[3], Texas, TX 78249
zhwg@mail.ustc.edu.cn[1], lihq@ustc.edu.cn[1], yl12@txstate.edu[2], qitian@cs.utsa.edu[3]

ABSTRACT
Bag-of-Visual-Words model is popular in large-scale image search. However, traditional Bag-of-Visual-Words model does not capture the geometric context among local features in images. To fully explore geometric context of all visual words in images, efficient global geometric verification methods are demanded. In this paper, we propose a novel geometric coding algorithm to encode the spatial context among local features of an image for large scale partial duplicate image retrieval. Our approach is not only computationally efficient, but also can effectively detect duplicate images with rotation, scale changes, occlusion, and background clutter with low computational cost. Experiments show the promising results of our approach.

Categories and Subject Descriptors
I.2.10 [Vision and Scene Understanding]: VISION

General Terms
Algorithms, Experimentation, Verification.

Keywords
Image retrieval, partial-duplicate, large scale, rotation-invariant, geometric square coding, geometric fan coding.

1. INTRODUCTION
With the emergence of Tineye [1] and Google Image Search [2], partial-duplicate image search has been attracting more and more attention in recent years. Partial-duplicate images are referred as those images, part of which are usually cropped from the same original image, but edited with modification in color, scale, rotation, partial occlusion, *etc.* Fig. 1 shows some instances of partial-duplicate Web images. Partial-duplicate image search can be widely used in many applications, such as image/video copyright violation detection, tracking the appearance of an image online and duplicate image annotation.

Large scale image retrieval [5~17] with local features has been significantly improved based on Bag-of-Visual-Words (BOW) model. BOW model achieves scalability for large scale image retrieval by quantizing local features to visual words. Popular local features include SIFT [4], MSER [23], *etc.* Local feature quantization makes image representation very compact. However, it also reduces the discriminative power of local descriptors. And the unavoidable quantization error will cause false matches of local features between images and decrease retrieval accuracy.

Figure 1. Examples of partial-duplicate Web images.

To reduce the quantization error, some approaches improve the discrimination power of local features, such as soft-quantization [12, 15], Hamming Embedding [6]. Some other approaches focus on utilizing geometric information in images to improve retrieval precision in a pre-processing or post-processing way.

The motivation of pre-processing approaches is to encode spatial context of local features into image representation. In [17], a spatial-bag-of-features scheme is used to encode geometric information of objects within an image and generate ordered bag-of-features for image search. Due to the large amount of local features in images, it is hard for the pre-processing approaches to fully encode various spatial relationships.

To avoid these problems, post-processing approaches use geometric consistency to filter those false matches. In [3], the locally spatial consistency of some spatially nearest neighbors is used to filter false matches. However, such loose geometric constraint is sensitive to the image noise from background clutter. Bundled-feature [16] is to assemble features in local MSER [20] regions to increase the discriminative power of local features. Geometric min-hashing [14] constructs repeatable hash keys with loosely local geometric information for more discriminative description. All of the above post-processing approaches only verify spatial consistency of features in local areas instead of the entire image. Although they are computationally efficient, they cannot capture the spatial relationship between all features, which makes it hard to detect all false matches.

To capture geometric relationships of all features in a whole image, global geometric verification method such as RANSAC

*Area Chair: Nicu Sebe.

MM'11, November 28–December 1, 2011, Scottsdale, Arizona, USA..

[11, 18, 19] is often used for this task. RANSAC can greatly improve retrieval precision. However, it is computationally expensive. It is usually applied on the subset of the top-ranked candidate images, which may not be sufficient in large scale image retrieval systems. The spatial coding approach [8] is another global geometric-verification method to remove false matches based on spatial maps. The drawback of spatial coding is that it requires that the duplicated patches in the query and the matched image share the same or very similar spatial configuration and it cannot handle rotation very efficiently.

In this paper, our motivation is to design an efficient global geometric verification approach, which can achieve rotation-invariant and is insensitive to background clutter. We propose two coding schemes, *i.e.*, geometric square coding and geometric fan coding, to encode the geometric relationships of local features for global spatial verification. Our approach can efficiently and effectively address images with free rotation changes.

2. OUR APPROACH

2.1 Geometric Coding

The spatial context among local features of an image is critical in identifying duplicate image patches. After SIFT quantization, SIFT matches between two images can be obtained. However, the matching results are usually polluted by some false matches. To refine the matching results effectively and efficiently, we propose the geometric coding scheme.

The key idea of geometric coding is to encode the geometric context of local SIFT features for geometric consistency verification. Our geometric coding is composed of two types of coding strategies, *i.e.*, geometric square coding and geometric fan coding. The difference between the two strategies lies in how the image plane is divided. Before encoding, the image has to be divided with a certain criterion that can address both rotation-invariance and scale-invariance. We design the criterion via the intrinsic invariance merit of SIFT feature.

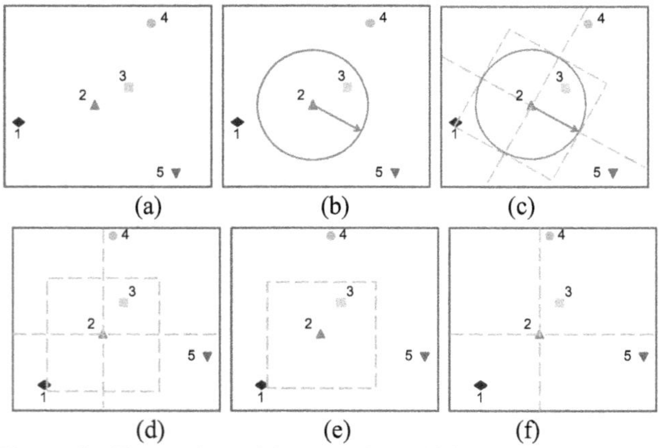

Figure 2. Illustration of image plane division. (a) Five SIFT features in image; (b) Key point of feature 2 displayed as vector indicating scale, orientation, and location (red arrow); (c) Image plane division with lines and square (green dashed lines) with feature 2 as reference point; (d) Image plane rotation from (c); (e) and (f): Image subdivisions from (d).

Fig. 2 gives a toy example of image plane division with feature 2 as reference point. Fig. 2(b) illustrates an arrow originated from feature 2, which corresponds to a vector indicating the scale and orientation of the SIFT feature. With feature 2 as origin and direction of the arrow as major direction, two lines horizontal and vertical to the arrow are constructed. Besides, centered at feature 2, a square is also drawn along these two lines, as shown in Fig. 2(c). For comparison convenience, we rotate the locations of all features to align the arrow to be horizontal, as shown in Fig. 2(d). After that, the image plane division with the two lines and the square can be decomposed into two kinds of sub-divisions, as shown in Fig. 2(e) and (f), which are used for geometric square coding and geometric fan coding, respectively.

2.1.1 *Geometric Square Coding*

Geometric square coding (GSC) encodes the geometric context in axial direction of reference features. In GSC, with each SIFT feature as reference center, the image plane is divided by regular squares. A square coding map, called *S*-map, is constructed by checking whether other features are inside or outside of the square.

To achieve rotation-invariant representation, before checking relative position, we have to adjust the location of each SIFT feature according to the SIFT orientation of each reference feature. For instance, given an image I with M features $\{f_i(x_i, y_i)\}$, $(i = 1,2,\ldots,M)$, with feature $f_i(x_i, y_i)$ as reference point, the adjusted position $f_j^{(i)}(x_j^{(i)}, y_j^{(i)})$ of $f_j(x_j, y_j)$ is formulated as follows:

$$\begin{pmatrix} x_j^{(i)} \\ y_j^{(i)} \end{pmatrix} = \begin{pmatrix} \cos(\phi_i) & -\sin(\phi_i) \\ \sin(\phi_i) & \cos(\phi_i) \end{pmatrix} \cdot \begin{pmatrix} x_j \\ y_j \end{pmatrix}, \quad 0 \le i, j < M \qquad (1)$$

where ϕ_i is a rotation angle equal to the SIFT orientation of the reference feature f_i.

S-map describes whether other features are inside or outside of a square defined by the reference feature. For image I, its *S*-map is defined as:

$$Smap(i,j) = \begin{cases} 1 & \text{if } \max\left(\left|x_j^{(i)} - x_i^{(i)}\right|, \left|y_j^{(i)} - y_i^{(i)}\right|\right) < s_i \\ 0 & otherwise \end{cases} \qquad (2)$$

where s_i is a half-square-length proportional to SIFT scale of feature $f_i : s_i = \alpha \cdot scl_i$, α is a constant.

To more strictly describe the relative positions, we advance to general squared maps. For each feature, n squares are drawn, with an equally incremental step of the half side length on the image plane. Then, the image plane is divided into $(n+1)$ non-overlapping parts. Correspondingly, according to the image plane division, a generalized geo-map should encode the relative spatial positions of feature pairs. The general *S-map* is defined as follows,

$$GS(i,j) = \frac{\max\left(\left|x_j^{(i)} - x_i^{(i)}\right|, \left|y_j^{(i)} - y_i^{(i)}\right|\right)}{s_i} \qquad (3)$$

where s_i is the same as that in Eq. (2), $k = 1,2,\ldots,r$.

2.1.2 *Geometric Fan Coding*

Geometric square coding (GSC) encodes the geometric context perpendicular to axial direction of reference features. In geometric fan coding, we take each SIFT feature as reference point and divide the image plane into some regular fan regions. Then two fan coding maps, *i.e.*, *H*-map and *V*-map, are constructed by checking which fan region other features fall into.

Based on the adjusted new positions of SIFT feature in Eq. (1), two binary geometric maps, called *H*-map and *V*-map, are generated. *H*-map and *V*-map describe the relative spatial positions between each feature pair along the horizontal and vertical directions, respectively. They are formulated as follows,

$$H(i,j)=\begin{cases}0 & \text{if } x_j^{(i)} \le x_i^{(i)} \\ 1 & \text{if } x_j^{(i)} > x_i^{(i)}\end{cases} \tag{4}$$

$$V(i,j)=\begin{cases}0 & \text{if } y_j^{i} \le y_i^{i} \\ 1 & \text{if } y_j^{i} > y_i^{i}\end{cases} \tag{5}$$

We can put forward the geometric fan coding to more general formulations to impose stricter geometric constraints. The image plane is divided into $4 \cdot r$ parts, with each quadrant evenly divided into r fan regions. We decompose the division into r independent sub-divisions, each dividing the image plane into four quadrants. Each sub-division is encoded independently and their combination leads to the final fan coding maps.

The general fan coding maps *GH* and *GV* are both 3-D and defined as follows. With feature f_i as reference, the location of feature f_j is rotated counterclockwise by $\theta_i^{(k)} = \frac{k \cdot \pi}{2 \cdot r} + \phi_i$ degree $(k = 0,1,...,r-1)$ according to the image origin point, yielding the new location $f_j^{(i,k)}(x_j^{(i,k)}, y_j^{(i,k)})$. ϕ_i is the SIFT orientation angle of f_i, as used in Eq. (1). Then *GH* and *GV* are formulated as,

$$GH(i,j,k)=\begin{cases}0 & \text{if } x_j^{(i,k)} \le x_i^{(i,k)} \\ 1 & \text{if } x_j^{(i,k)} > x_i^{(i,k)}\end{cases} \tag{6}$$

$$GV(i,j,k)=\begin{cases}0 & \text{if } y_j^{(i,k)} \le y_i^{(i,k)} \\ 1 & \text{if } y_j^{(i,k)} > y_i^{(i,k)}\end{cases} \tag{7}$$

2.2 Spatial Verification

Denote that a query image I_q and a matched image I_m are found to share N pairs of matched features through SIFT quantization. Then the corresponding sub-geo-maps of these matched features for both I_q and I_m can be generated and denoted as (GS_q, GH_q, GV_q) and (GS_m, GH_m, GV_m) by Eq. (3), Eq. (6) and Eq. (7), respectively. After that, the comparison of geometric maps is performed as follows. We do logical Exclusive-OR (XOR) operation on GH_q and GH_m, GV_q and GV_m, respectively:

$$V_H = GH_q \oplus GH_m ; \qquad V_V = GV_q \oplus GV_m \tag{8}$$

If some false matches exist, the entries of these false matches on GH_q and GH_m may be inconsistent, and so are that on GV_q and GV_m . These inconsistencies will cause the corresponding exclusive-OR result of V_H and V_V to be 1. We define the inconsistency from geometric fan coding as follows,

$$F_H(i,j) = \bigcup_{k=1}^{r} V_H(i,j,k) \; ; \quad F_V(i,j) = \bigcup_{k=1}^{r} V_V(i,j,k) \tag{9}$$

The inconsistency from geometric square coding is defined as:

$$F_S(i,j) = \left| GS_q(i,j) - GS_m(i,j) \right| \tag{10}$$

Consequently, by checking F_H , F_V and F_S , the false matches can be identified and removed. Denote:

$$T(i,j)=\begin{cases}1 & \text{if } F_S(i,j) > \tau \text{ and } F_H(i,j)+F_V(i,j) > \beta \\ 0 & \text{otherwise}\end{cases} \tag{11}$$

where β and τ are constant integers.

Ideally, if all N matched pairs are true positives, T will be zero for all entries. If false matches exist, the entries of these matches on those geometric coding maps may be inconsistent. We can iteratively remove such match that causes the largest inconsistency, until all remained matches are consistent to each other.

3. EXPERIMENTS

We construct our basic dataset by crawling one million images from the Web. To build the ground truth dataset, we collected and manually labeled 1104 partial-duplicate Web images of 33 groups from the Web. These ground-truth images are shared to the public and can be downloaded from: [21]. In our experiments, 100 representative query images are selected from the ground truth dataset for evaluation comparison. We use mean average precision (mAP) to evaluate the accuracy performance of all experiments.

We use an inverted-file index structure to index images. Each visual word is followed by an entry in the index that contains the list of images in which the visual word appears. For each indexed feature, we store its image ID, SIFT orientation, scale and the *x*- and *y*- coordinate, which will be used for generating geometric coding maps for retrieval. Similar to [8], the image similarity is formulated by the number of true matches.

Two approaches are considered for comparison. The first one is the Bag-of-Visual-Words approach with visual vocabulary tree [3], denoted as the "baseline" approach. The second one is re-ranking via geometric verification, which is based on the estimation of an affine transformation by a variant of RANSAC [19] as used in [11]. We call this method "RANSAC". In the experiment, all candidate images are involved in the RANSAC-based re-ranking.

We perform the experiments on a server with 2.4 GHz CPU and 8 GB memory. Fig. 3 illustrates the mAP performance of the comparison algorithms and our geometric coding (GC) approach. Table 1 shows the average time cost per query of all approaches. The time cost of SIFT feature extraction is not included.

Compared with the baseline, our approach is more time-consuming, since it is involved with geometric coding and verification. It takes the baseline 0.095 second to perform one image query on average, while for our approach the average query time cost is 0.155 second, 0.06 second more than the baseline. However, our approach increases the MAP from 0.37 to 0.54, a 46% improvement over the baseline. RANSAC is the most time-consuming approach, due to the affine estimation from many random samplings. It costs 1.052 second on average per query, which is 6.7 times more than our approach. Also, it is notable that our approach achieves even better mAP performance than the "RANSAC" method.

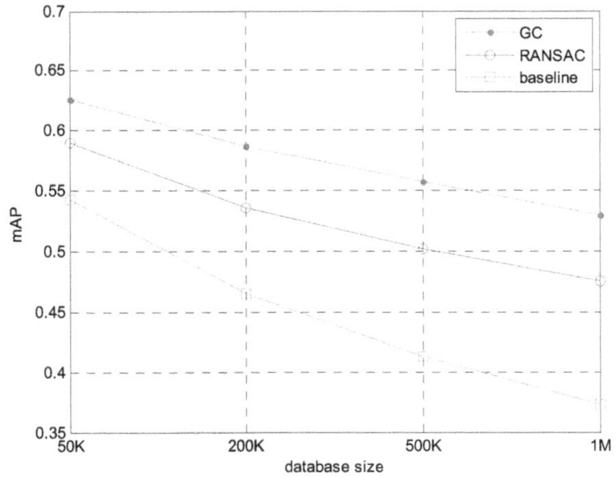

Figure 3. Comparison of mAP for different methods on the 1M database. (Best viewed in color PDF)

Table 1. The average time cost of the comparison methods and our geometric coding (GC) approach.

approach	baseline	RANSAC	GC
time cost (s)	0.095	1.052	0.155

4. CONCLUSION

In this paper, we propose a novel geometric coding scheme for SIFT match verification in large scale partial-duplicate image search. The geometric coding consists of geometric square coding and geometric fan coding. It efficiently encodes the relative spatial locations among features in an image and effectively discovers false feature matches between images. Our approach can effectively detect duplicate images with rotation, scale changes, occlusion, and background clutter.

In our future work, we will study better quantization strategy for visual codebook generation. Also, we will move on from duplicate image search to video copy detection, and explore its potential on image and video annotation [22].

5. ACKNOWLEDGMENTS

This work was supported in part to Dr. Li by NSFC under contract No. 60672161 and 863 Program under contract No. 2006AA01Z317, in part to Dr. Lu by Research Enhancement Program (REP) and start-up funding from the Texas State University, and in part to Dr. Tian by NSF IIS 1052851, Faculty Research Awards by Google, FXPAL and NEC Laboratories of America, respectively.

6. REFERENCES

[1] http://www. Tineye.com

[2] http://similar-images.googlelabs.com/

[3] J. Sivic and A. Zisserman. Video Google: A text retrieval approach to object matching in videos. In *Proc. ICCV*, 2003.

[4] D. Lowe. Distinctive image features from scale-invariant key points. In *IJCV*, 60(2):91-110, 2004.

[5] D. Nister and H. Stewenius. Scalable recognition with a vocabulary tree. In Proc. CVPR, pages 2161-2168, 2006.

[6] H. Jegou, M. Douze, and C. Schmid. Hamming embedding and weak geometric consistency for large scale image search. In *Proc. ECCV*, 2008.

[7] S. Zhang, Q. Tian, G. Hua, Q. Huang, and S. Li. Descriptive Visual Words and Visual Phrases for Image Applications. In *Proc. ACM Multimedia*, 2009.

[8] W. Zhou, Y. Lu, H. Li, Y. Song, and Q. Tian. Spatial coding for large scale partial-duplicate web image search. In *Proc. ACM Multimedia*, 2010.

[9] S. Zhang, Q. Huang, G. Hua, S. Jiang, W. Gao, and Q. Tian. Building Contextual Visual Vocabulary for Large-scale Image Applications. In *Proc. ACM Multimedia*, 2010.

[10] O. Chum, J. Philbin, J. Sivic, M. Isard, and A. Zisserman. Total recall: Automatic query expansion with a generative feature model for object retrieval. In *Proc. ICCV*, 2007.

[11] J. Philbin, O. Chum, M. Isard, J. Sivic and A. Zisserman. Object retrieval with large vocabularies and fast spatial matching. In *Proc. CVPR*, 2007.

[12] J. Philbin, O. Chum, M. Isard, J. Sivic and A. Zisserman. Lost in quantization: Improving particular object retrieval in large scale image databases. In *Proc. CVPR*, 2008.

[13] O. Chum, J. Philbin, M. Isard, and A. Zisserman. Scalable near identical image and shot detection. In *Proc. CIVR*, 2007.

[14] O. Chum, M. Perdoch, and J. Matas. Geometric minhashing: Finding a (thick) needle in a haystack. In *Proc. CVPR*, 2009.

[15] H. Jegou, H. Harzallah, and C. Schmid. A contextual dissimilarity measure for accurate and efficient image search. In *Proc. CVPR*, 2007.

[16] Z. Wu, Q. Ke, M. Isard, and J. Sun. Bundling Features for Large Scale Partial-Duplicate Web Image Search. In Proc. CVPR, 2009.

[17] Y. Cao, C. Wang, Z. Li, L. Zhang, L. Zhang. Spatial-bag-of-features. In Proc. CVPR, 2010.

[18] M. A. Fischler and R. C. Bolles. Random Sample Consensus: A paradigm for model fitting with applications to image analysis and automated cartography. Comm. of the ACM, 24: 381–395, 1981.

[19] O. Chum, J. Matas, and S. Obdrzalek. Enhancing RANSAC by generalized model optimization. In Proc. ACCV, 2004.

[20] J. Matas, O. Chum, M. Urban, and T. Pajdla. Robust wide baseline stereo from maximally stable extremal regions. In Proc. BMVC, 2002.

[21] http://home.ustc.edu.cn/~zhwg/download/DupGroundTruth Dataset.rar .

[22] M. Wang, X.-S. Hua, R. Hong, J. Tang, G.-J. Qi, Y. Song. Unified Video Annotation via Multi-Graph Learning. *IEEE Transactions on Circuits and Systems for Video Technology*, vol. 19, no. 5, 2009.

Clothes Search in Consumer Photos via Color Matching and Attribute Learning *

Xianwang Wang and Tong Zhang
Hewlett-Packard Laboratories
1501 Page Mill Rd.
Palo Alto, CA, USA, 94304
{xianwang.wang, tong.zhang}@hp.com

ABSTRACT

Automatic clothes search in consumer photos is not a trivial problem as photos are usually taken under completely uncontrolled realistic imaging conditions. In this paper, a novel framework is presented to tackle this issue by leveraging low-level features (e.g., color) and high-level features (attributes) of clothes. First, a content-based image retrieval (CBIR) approach based on the bag-of-visual-words (BOW) model is developed as our baseline system, in which a codebook is constructed from extracted dominant color patches. A reranking approach is then proposed to improve search quality by exploiting clothes attributes, including the type of clothes, sleeves, patterns, etc. The experiments on photo collections show that our approach is robust to large variations of images taken in unconstrained environment, and the reranking algorithm based on attribute learning significantly improves retrieval performance in combination with the proposed baseline.

Categories and Subject Descriptors

H.3.3 [**Information Search and Retrieval**]: Retrieval models

General Terms

Algorithms, Design, Experimentation

Keywords

Clothes search, reranking, attribute learning, color matching

1. INTRODUCTION

Clothes recognition, due to its wide applications from automatic tagging to e-commerce of clothes, is a very active topic in computer vision and multimedia research. For example, clothes have been investigated as an important cue for boosting face recognition performance [4, 7]. Given a clothes image as a query, our goal is to retrieve images containing the same clothes appeared in the query image. However, visual search of dressed clothes in photo collections is a challenging task, even for humans. There is high variability in clothes appearance, which stems from the variation of the realistic imaging condition: (1) two instances of the same clothes may be of different scales and orientation due to viewpoint changes; (2) there may be large geometric deformation across images; (3) there may be significant occlusion from objects and other subjects; (4) there may exist many changes of cluttered background; and (5) the photos may be captured with different lighting conditions. These variations are the major factors complicating the matters for visual clothes search algorithms.

The text-based image retrieval has demonstrated its effectiveness and efficiency in large-scale image search. However, the performance of such a system degrades significantly when applied on consumer photos, i.e., many of the query results from text-based image search engines contain irrelevant and noisy images. The reranking framework [9] is recently proposed to address the weakness of text-based image search by leveraging visual cues of the photos to refine the initial text-based search result such that the images are re-ordered in relevance. In essence, visual search reranking resorts to low-level image features to measure the visual similarity. However, dressed clothes are often folded and may easily create non-rigid deformation, false edges and self-shadows, which bring false low-level features. Therefore, none of the visual reranking methods can be applied directly to visual clothes search.

In this paper, we propose a novel framework to address the issues of clothes search in the approaches of text-based and reranking-based visual search. First, we present an efficient visual codebook generation scheme that uses a dominant color extraction algorithm to capture the major patterns of dressed clothes. The basic idea is to select the most representative patches instead of all the patches in the dataset to build the codebook, because some patches such as those from the background clutter may bring noise and non-descriptive visual codewords. Moreover, dominant color patch representations characterize the appearance of each clothes image with the major colors, which provides robustness to the internal and external clothes variations to some extent.

Motivated by [3], we further use attribute information of clothes to rerank and improve our color-based CBIR results. A query image always reflects the specific intention of a user. For example, if the user submits a T-shirt image with other clothes features such as collar, button, and horizontal stripe, most likely he/she wants to search for T-shirt images with similar features. We call these high-level visual features as attributes. Attributes as high-level visual features are less sensitive to pose, illumination, deformation, background clutter, and other variations than the low-level features. Furthermore, attributes carry semantic meaning, providing large gains in clothes recognition. One detector is independently trained to detect the probability of the presence for each clothes attribute (T-shirt, collars, button, horizontal stripe, etc.). In this work, we build twenty-five de-

*Area chair: Tat-Seng Chua

MM'11, November 28–December 1, 2011, Scottsdale, Arizona, USA.

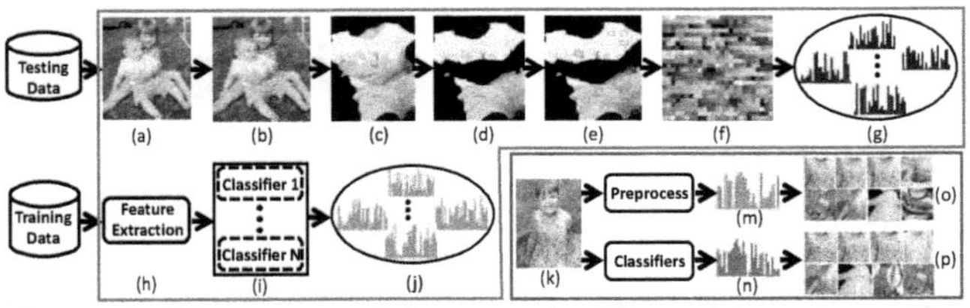

Figure 1: The proposed framework. The red box shows the flowchart of the offline process, while the blue box describes the flowchart of the online process. (a) Face detection; (b) Clothes extraction; (c) Clothes segmentation; (d) Skin elimination; (e) Dominant color patch extraction; (f) Code-book construction; (g) Quantization; (h) Feature extraction; (i) Attribute classifiers; (j) Trait vectors of the testing dataset; (k) A query image; (m) The histogram of visual words corresponding to the query image; (n) The trait vector corresponding to the query image; (o) The initial search result from color matching; (p) The final reranking result using attribute learning.

tectors for clothes attributes based on large sets of training data.

While human recognition using clothes as contextual information [7] has been studied reasonably well in recent years, there is, to our best knowledge, no method that explicitly and efficiently solves the problem of clothes search in the presence of the variations. The main contribution of this paper is to introduce a novel framework by combining color matching and attribute learning to address this issue. The attribute classifiers are used to infer the intention behind the query image, through which the relevance and ranking of search results from color matching can be further improved.

2. SYSTEM OVERVIEW

The scheme of our approach is to learn a color-based BOW model from the testing dataset and general reranking models of clothes attributes from the labeled training dataset at the offline stage, and then apply the learned modules online to handle all queries. The detailed algorithm procedure using color matching and attribute learning for clothes search is shown in Fig. 1. In the offline stage, the outline of processing pipeline is as follows,

1. Estimate the rough clothes location in each photo from the test database by running face detection [5] (Fig. 1a) and taking certain parts below the head (Fig. 1b).
2. Apply clothes segmentation with the Grabcut method [6] (Fig. 1c) and skin detection [11] (Fig. 1d) to eliminate the noisy non-clothes pixels, e.g., human skin, cluttered background, and occlusion from other subjects or objects.
3. Extract the dominant color patches and describe each of them with a high-dimensional descriptor (Fig. 1e).
4. Build a visual codebook from the high-dimensional descriptions by quantizing and clustering them into a vocabulary of visual words using an unsupervised clustering algorithm such as K-means (Fig. 1f). Each clothes image is then represented as a histogram of visual words (Fig. 1g).
5. Extract three types of visual features from each clothes image in the labeled dataset and concatenate the features into the unified feature (Fig. 1h).
6. Build the attribute classifier for each attribute based on the united features (Fig. 1i).
7. Extract visual features from each extracted photo after step 1, and concatenate the features into the unified feature.
8. Run all the learned attribute classifiers on the united features from the step above. Each clothes image can then be described as a trait vector by concatenating the output of each classifiers (Fig. 1j).

For a query image (Fig. 1k), we first apply step 1 and step 2 of the offline stage to remove the noisy pixels, and build its corresponding histogram of visual words using the generated codebook (Fig. 1m). The initial search result (Fig. 1o) can then be obtained by comparing the histogram to the ones of the testing dataset (Fig. 1g) using the technique of similarity measurement as described in Section 3. Similarly, we can build its corresponding trait vector (Fig. 1n) using step 7 and step 8 of the offline stage. Finally, the reranking results (Fig. 1p) can be generated by simply comparing the trait vector to the ones of the top ω clothes images (Fig. 1j) in the initial search result (in our case, $\omega = 60$).

3. COLOR MATCHING

3.1 Dominant Color Patch Extraction

We propose one more powerful clothes descriptor based on dominant color (DC) patches. DC is one of the most distinguishing features, and It is also robust against internal and external variations of clothes to some extent. There are five successive steps to extract DC patches from each clothes (Fig. 1e):

- Generate the 3D histogram in the RGB color space with 16 bins on each axis for each clothes. The colors in the same bin are assumed to be similar, and the centroid of each bin is selected as its quantized color, denoted as $c_i = (\mathbf{x}_i^R, \mathbf{x}_i^G, \mathbf{x}_i^B)$.
- Select the quantized colors of bins with $M_i/M > \tau$ as DCs, where M_i is the number of pixels in the ith bin, M is the number of all pixels in the image, and τ is the predefined threshold (e.g., $\tau = 0.008$). We denote the DCs as $\{(\mathbf{x}_{(dc,j)}^R, \mathbf{x}_{(dc,j)}^G, \mathbf{x}_{(dc,j)}^B)\}_{j=1}^K$, where K is the number of DCs.
- Divide the clothes image into 7×7 non-overlapping patches; Go through all patches, and select the patch p as one candidate of dominant color patches for DC j, if $|\overline{\mathbf{x}}_p^R - \mathbf{x}_{(dc,j)}^R| < T_R$ and $|\overline{\mathbf{x}}_p^G - \mathbf{x}_{(dc,j)}^G| < T_G$ and $|\overline{\mathbf{x}}_p^B - \mathbf{x}_{(dc,j)}^B| < T_B$, where $(\overline{\mathbf{x}}_p^R, \overline{\mathbf{x}}_p^G, \overline{\mathbf{x}}_p^B)$ is the mean color of patch p, T_R, T_G, and T_B are thresholds in R, G, B components respectively (e.g., $T_R = T_G = T_B = 2$), and $1 \le j \le K$.
- Sort the candidate patches for each DC j in order by the number of pixels (in the patch) which colors are close to $(\mathbf{x}_{(dc,j)}^R, \mathbf{x}_{(dc,j)}^G, \mathbf{x}_{(dc,j)}^B)$; select γ patches (i.e., γ is up to 20) as DC patches for each DC j of this clothes.
- Perform illumination normalization on each DC patch using $(R/(R+G+B), G/(R+G+B), B/(R+G+B)$.

3.2 Clothes Representation

Even after the preprocessing with the previous steps, there is no guaranty that all the regions in the image left belong to the clothes. Moreover, the extracted clothes regions may include various decoration, wrinkle, folding, and shading, which will still cause interferences on visual search. Therefore, we use BoW representation to increase tolerance of these variations. To do that, DC patches from all the clothes in the dataset are collected to form the data matrix $Y = (y_1, \cdots, y_{\mathcal{M}}) \in \Re^{D\times\mathcal{M}}$, where $y_i \in \Re^D (i = 1, \cdots \mathcal{M})$ is the D-dimensional DC patches. In our case, D is equal to 147 ($7 \times 7 \times 3$). K-means clustering is then run on Y to obtain the clothes codebook (Fig. 1f), which contains $k = 500$ code words (i.e., the number of clusters for K-means).

The 2-level vector quantization, pixel-based and patch-based, is then performed on each clothes in the testing dataset after the preprocessing. We first quantize the clothes in pixel level using the color map from the codebook. Next, we perform patch-based quantization with the generated codebook. Particularly, we divide the quantized clothes with pixel level into 7×7 patches, and each patch is mapped into its nearest code word after illumination normalization. Therefore, by mapping the clothes patches to the codewords, each clothes in the testing dataset can be represented by the k-dimensional frequency histogram over the codebook (Fig. 1g). It is expressed $H = [h_1, \cdots, h_k]$, where $h_i = n_i / \sum_{j=1}^{k} n_j$, and n_i is the number of occurrence of codeword i in this clothes.

For a new query image q (Fig. 1k), we perform the preprocessing steps (a-d) in Fig. 1 and generate the histogram of visual words H^q (Fig. 1m) using the built codebook. The objective of this step is to define a measure of similarity between H^q and the codeword histogram of the jth clothes $H^{(p,j)}$ from the testing dataset. In this work, we adopt Jeffrey Divergence as follows,

$$\begin{aligned} D(H^{(p,j)}, H^q) &= KL(H^{(p,j)} \| (H^{(p,j)} + H^q)/2) \\ &\quad + KL(H^q \| (H^{(p,j)} + H^q)/2) \quad (1) \end{aligned}$$

$$KL(H^{(p,j)} \| H^q) = \sum_{i=1}^{k} (h_i^{(p,j)} \log \frac{h_i^{(p,j)}}{m_i} + h_i^q \log \frac{h_i^q}{m_i}) \quad (2)$$

where KL is Kullback-Leibler divergence, and $m_i = (h_i^{(p,j)} + h_i^q)/2$. After the comparison of H^q to each clothes $H^{(p,j)}$ in the testing dataset, we sort the clothes with the similarity degree in ascending order and obtain the initial search result (Fig. 1o) corresponding to the query image q .

4. ATTRIBUTE LEARNING

We use three types of semantic attributes to describe clothes images. **Categories** attributes refer to the type of clothes such as "jacket", "coat", "shirt", etc. **Adjective** attributes describe what kind of patterns are on the surface of clothes like "vertical or horizontal stripe", "small flowers", and "characters". **Part** attributes identify parts of clothes such as "tie", "gallus", "collar", and so on. We have $N = 25$ auxiliary training sets, $\Im_i = \{(x_1^i, y_1^i), \ldots, (x_{N_i}^i, y_{N_i}^i)\}$ for $i = 1 \ldots N$, where x_j^i is the jth image in the ith auxiliary training set, $y_j^i \in \{-1, +1\}$ is the label of that image, and N_i is the number of examples in the ith training set. The goal of attribute learning is to improve the initial search result from color matching using a set of high-level features (semantic attributes) computed from low-level features, which are extracted from $\{x_j^i\}$.

Three types of low-level features are used to locally or globally model the shape and appearance information of clothes in our experiments. The local shape of each cloth is represented by Pyramid Histogram of Oriented Gradients (PHOG [2]). Pyramid Histogram of Visual Words(PHOW [1]) are also used to model the local appearance of clothes. Furthermore, we employ the GIST descriptor to describe clothing textures. Therefore, for each clothes image x_j^i, we have the unified feature $f_j^i = [f_{(j,1)}^i, f_{(j,2)}^i, f_{(j,3)}^i]$ which is a concatenation of PHOG feature $f_{(j,1)}^i$, PHOW feature $f_{(j,2)}^i$, and GIST feature $f_{(j,3)}^i$ (Fig. 1h).

4.1 Attribute Classifier

Training Dataset. We built a clothes database with 12,823 images, which are extracted from 26,324 consumer photos using the technique of clothes extraction (Fig. 1a-b) as described in Section 2. We have manually labeled each clothes image for N attributes.

We treat attribute classification as a supervised learning problem, i.e., build attribute classifier C_i to detect the describable attribute i of clothes images from the training set $\{(f_j^i, y_j^i)\}_{j=1}^{N_i}$ (Fig. 1i). The least-squares posterior classifiers (LSPC [8]) is adopted here. LSPC is an efficient non-linear probabilistic classification method, which employs a linear combination of Gaussian kernels centered at the training points for modeling the class-posterior probability. Different from SVM which learns the decision boundaries between different classes, the LSPC can provide the confidence of class prediction. Please refer to [8] for a detailed discussion.

For the jth clothes image in the testing dataset, we extract the PHOG, PHOW, GIST features to construct the unified feature $\{f_j^t\}$. We then compute the output of each attribute classifier $C_i (i = 1, \ldots, N)$, and concatenate the outputs to form a trait vector $\mathbf{C}(f_j^t)$, i.e., $\mathbf{C}(f_j^t) = [C_1(f_j^t), \ldots, C_N(f_j^t)]$ $= [\widehat{p}(y = 1 | f_j^t, \beta_{1,y}), \ldots, \widehat{p}(y = 1 | f_j^t, \beta_{N,y})]$. Therefore, we have the collections of trait vectors with one-to-one correspondence with the images in the testing dataset (Fig. 1j).

Besides of the prediction of a few individual attributes for a query image, the final goal of attribute learning is to improve the initial search results from color matching. That is, for the query image q (Fig. 1k), we can also extract the low-level appearance and shape features to build the unified feature $\{f^q\}$. The trait vector of the query image $\mathbf{C}(f^q)$ will be obtained by applying the learned attribute classifiers on $\{f^q\}$ (Fig. 1n). Finally, we match $\mathbf{C}(f^q)$ against the top ω trait vectors of the clothes images in the search result of color matching using similarity measurement discussed above, and move the 'closer' ones to the top to get the final search result corresponding to the query image q (Fig. 1p).

5. SYSTEM EVALUATION

Testing Dataset. A publicly available dataset [4] was employed to evaluate the proposed approach. This dataset contains 589 images, in which 1008 faces with 32 identities are labeled. Therefore we have 1008 clothes images for testing. We also labeled the identities of clothes corresponding to these faces to evaluate clothes retrieval. The clothes images include a variety of variations such as pose, illumination, cluttered background, occlusion, and etc. The retrieval performance is evaluated in terms of the average precision rate $PR = R_r/R$ and the average recall rate $RC = R_r/R_t$, where R_r is the number of returned images considered as relevant, R_t is the number of total relevant images in the dataset and R is the number of all returned images (e.g., $R = 12$).

Result. To demonstrate its effectiveness, we compare the proposed reranking method (color matching + attribute learn-

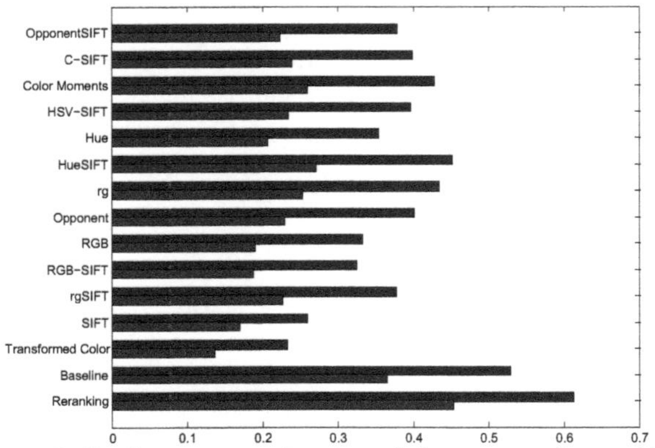

Figure 2: Performance evaluation of the proposed reranking method (color matching + attribute learning) against the baseline alone (color matching) and CBIR using the different descriptors in [10] on the dataset [4]. Blue bars indicate the average recalls, while red bars indicate the average precisions.

ing) against our search baseline alone (color matching) and the traditional Content-Based Image Retrieval (CBIR) using the state-of-the-art descriptors [10] such as C-SIFT, Opponent-SIFT, RGB-SIFT, etc. We randomly select 200 images from the testing dataset for this experiment. The overall performance is shown in Fig. 2. From this result, we can see that the proposed method outperforms CBIR as well as the color matching based search baseline. Specifically, compared with CBIR with HueSIFT and color matching, our method obtains about 16.15% and 8.4% relative improvements in the average recall respectively. Moreover, the proposed reranking method improves the performance over CBIR with HueSIFT by 18.16% and over the baseline by 8.82% in terms of the average precision. The results indicate that the proposed supervised attribute learning method can learn a good reranking function and that the learned reranking model can generalize well across a broad range of clothes with large appearance variations. Furthermore, The results show that our color matching method alone also has better tolerance to variability of clothes appearance.

Fig. 3 gives an example result for the convincing illustration of the advantages of our supervised reranking method over the CBIR with HueSIFT and the color matching baseline. It can be observed that the proposed method promotes highly relevant images (the images marked by the red rectangle), which are ranked in the bottom in the initial list, to the top. Moreover, the proposed method increases the average precision by moving the missing relevant images (the images marked by the green rectangle) in the initial list to the top. Therefore the approach can help us infer the implicit user intention behind the query image and pick up a smaller subset of visual features that are significant to such intention. In other words, it puts the semantic restriction in the visual search space and improves the retrieval performance. For example, this query puts emphasis on the local shape features ("horizontal stripe") and color features (red clothes). From the result, we can see that the first 11 items retrieved by the proposed method (the bottom row) share both local color and shape features, while items in the baseline result set (the middle row) deviate their emphasis onto the local color only, and items in the CBIR result set (the top row) onto shape features only.

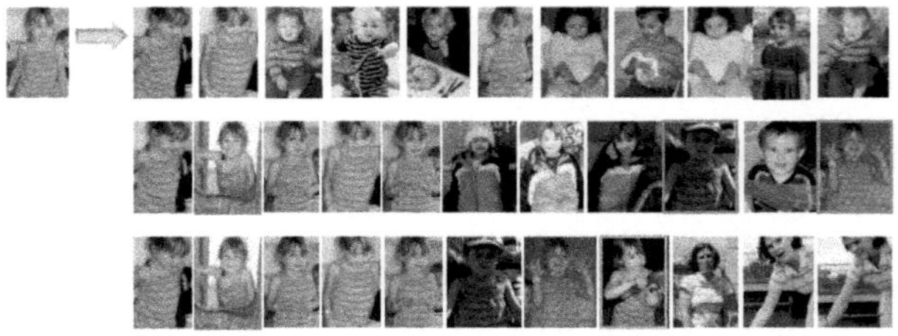

Figure 3: The left column shows the query image. The right column shows the final search results with 11 nearest neighbors using CBIR with HueSIFT (the top row), color matching (the middle row), and the proposed reranking method (the bottom row).

6. CONCLUSION

In this paper, we present a novel framework for automatic visual clothes search. We first build two types of models at the offline stage, including a color-based BOW model from the testing dataset and general reranking models of clothes attributes from the labeled training dataset. The BOW model is used for color matching to obtain the initial search result, while the general reranking models are employed to infer user intention behind query images, and re-sort the images in the initial list in relevance. It has been demonstrated that our method improves the retrieval performance with clothes taken under a variety of realistic imaging conditions.

7. REFERENCES

[1] A. Bosch, A. Zisserman, and X. Muoz. Image classification using random forests and ferns. In *ICCV*, pages 1–8, 2007.

[2] N. Dalal and B. Triggs. Histograms of oriented gradients for human detection. In *CVPR*, pages 886–893, 2005.

[3] A. Farhadi, I. Endres, D. Hoiem, and D. Forsyth. Describing objects by their attributes. In *CVPR*, pages 1778–1785, 2009.

[4] A. Gallagher and T. Chen. Clothing cosegmentation for recognizing people. In *CVPR*, pages 1–8, June 2008.

[5] M. J. Jones and P. Viola. Fast multi-view face detection. In *CVPR*, 2003.

[6] C. Rother, V. Kolmogorov, and A. Blake. Grabcut - interactive foreground extraction using iterated graph cuts. *ACM Siggraph*, 23:309–314, August 2004.

[7] Y. Song and T. Leung. Context-aided human recognition: Clustering. In *ECCV*, pages 382–395, 2006.

[8] M. Sugiyama. Superfast-trainable multi-class probabilistic classifier by least-squares posterior fitting. *IEICE Tran. on Information and Systems*, 93-D(10):2690–2701, 2010.

[9] X. Tian, L. Yang, J. Wang, Y. Yang, X. Wu, and X.-S. Hua. Bayesian video search reranking. In *ACM Multimedia*, pages 131–140, 2008.

[10] K. van de Sande, T. Gevers, and C. Snoek. Evaluating color descriptors for object and scene recognition. *PAMI*, 32(9):1582–1596, September 2010.

[11] P. Yogarajah, J. Condell, K. Curran, A. Cheddad, and P. McKevitt. A dynamic threshold approach for skin segmentation in color images. In *ICIP*, pages 2225–2228, September 2010.

A Fast MAP Adaptation Technique for GMM-supervector-based Video Semantic Indexing Systems

Nakamasa Inoue, Koichi Shinoda
Dept. of Computer Science,
Tokyo Institute of Technology, Japan
{inoue, shinoda}@ks.cs.titech.ac.jp

ABSTRACT

We propose a fast maximum a posteriori (MAP) adaptation technique for a GMM-supervectors-based video semantic indexing system. The use of GMM supervectors is one of the state-of-the-art methods in which MAP adaptation is needed for estimating the distribution of local features extracted from video data. The proposed method cuts the calculation time of the MAP adaptation step. With the proposed method, a tree-structured GMM is constructed to quickly calculate posterior probabilities for each mixture component of a GMM. The basic idea of the tree-structured GMM is to cluster Gaussian components and approximate them with a single Gaussian. Leaf nodes of the tree correspond to the mixture components, and each non-leaf node has a single Gaussian that approximates its descendant Gaussian distributions. Experimental evaluation on the TRECVID 2010 dataset demonstrates the effectiveness of the proposed method. The calculation time of the MAP adaptation step is reduced by 76.2% compared to that of a conventional method and resulting accuracy (in terms of Mean average precision) was 10.2%.

Categories and Subject Descriptors

I.4.9 [**Computing Methodologies**]: Image processing and computer vision—*Applications*

General Terms

Algorithm, Experimentations

Keywords

Video Semantic Indexing, GMM Supervectors, MAP Adaptation

1. INTRODUCTION

Video semantic indexing is one of the fundamental challenges in the field of computer vision. Its goal is to develop a generic method for automatically assigning semantic tags to video data. Detecting semantic concepts including objects, events and scenes is a challenging task due to within-class variations in shapes, colors, illuminations and backgrounds.

Many studies have started to focus on large-scale video recognition—a problem that requires a large amount of computational resources in recent years. For example, in the TREC Video Retrieval Evaluation (TRECVID) [1] workshop, which provides researchers with common tasks of video analysis, the size of target video resources has been doubling every year. While developing an accurate classification method is a top priority, a fast method for processing such a large amount of data is also needed. In response to these requirements, the motivation of the present study is to develop a fast and accurate semantic indexing system.

In recent researches, supervector coding of local features [2] has been proposed as an image-annotation method and applied to video recognition. For example, using a combination of Gaussian mixture model (GMM) supervectors and support vector machines (SVMs) has achieved better performance than that achieved by the bag-of-visual-words approach [3, 4]. With this method, a probability density function (pdf) of extracted local features is estimated by a GMM using maximum a posteriori (MAP) estimation. This MAP estimation step is called MAP adaptation. Aiming to reduce computational costs, most previous studies focused on reducing the cost of feature extraction (e.g., GPU implementations in [5]). The calculation time of the MAP adaptation step, however, has become the bottleneck of a system.

In the present study, we propose a fast maximum a posteriori (MAP) adaptation technique for a GMM-supervectors-based video semantic indexing system. We evaluated the technique by testing it on the TRECVID 2010 dataset.

2. PROPOSED METHOD

2.1 Gaussian Mixture Model

A probability distribution function (pdf) of local visual (or audio) features is estimated for each video shot. Here, Gaussian mixture models (GMMs), whose pdf is given by

$$p(x|\theta) = \sum_{k=1}^{K} w_k g_k(x), \quad g_k(x) = \mathcal{N}(x|\mu_k, \Sigma_k), \qquad (1)$$

are employed where x is a local feature, $\theta = \{w_k, \mu_k, \Sigma_k\}_{k=1}^{K}$ is a set of parameters, K is the number of mixture components, w_k is a mixture coefficient, and $g_k(x)$ is a pdf with a mean vector μ_k and a covariance matrix Σ_k.

*Area chair: Qi Tian

MM'11, November 28–December 1, 2011, Scottsdale, Arizona, USA.

The GMM parameters are estimated by using an expectation maximization (EM) algorithm with a maximum a posteriori (MAP) criterion. For MAP adaptation, a GMM for prior distribution, namely a universal background model (UBM), is first needed. The UBM presents how the features are distributed in the general case: therefore, the parameters used for the UBM, $\hat{\theta}^{(\mathrm{U})}$, is estimated by applying the EM algorithm to all features in training videos.

With the proposed method, only mean vectors are adapted for each shot. The MAP solution gives the following equations:

$$\hat{\mu}_k^{(s)} = \frac{\tau \hat{\mu}_k^{(\mathrm{U})} + \sum_{i=1}^{n} c_{ik} x_i}{\tau + \sum_{i=1}^{n} c_{ik}}, \quad c_{ik} = \frac{w_k g_k(x_i)}{\sum_{k=1}^{K} w_k g_k(x_i)}, \tag{2}$$

where $X_s = \{x_i\}_{i=1}^{n}$ is a set of (one type of) feature vectors extracted from the s-th shot, $\hat{\theta}^{(\mathrm{U})}$ is the UBM parameter, and τ is a predefined hyper-parameter.

2.2 Tree-structured GMMs

Given the UBM, a tree structure of Gaussian components that makes calculation of Eq. (2) efficient is constructed. The basic idea is to cluster Gaussian components by a single Gaussian. For given Gaussian components $g_m = \mathcal{N}(\cdot|\mu_m, \Sigma_m)$ and combination coefficients α_m ($\alpha_m \geq 0, \sum \alpha_m = 1$) ($m = 1, 2, \cdots, M$), we define a combined single Gaussian by

$$\alpha_1 g_1 \oplus \alpha_2 g_2 \oplus \cdots \oplus \alpha_M g_M = \mathcal{N}(\cdot|\bar{\mu}, \bar{\Sigma}), \tag{3}$$

$$\bar{\mu} = \sum_{m=1}^{M} \alpha_m \mu_m, \quad \bar{\Sigma} = \sum_{m=1}^{M} \alpha_m (\Sigma_m + \mu_m \mu_m^{\mathsf{T}}) - \bar{\mu}\bar{\mu}^{\mathsf{T}}. \tag{4}$$

If only a set of Gaussians components $G = \{g_1, g_2, \cdots, g_M\}$ is given,

$$g(G) = \frac{1}{M} g_1 \oplus \frac{1}{M} g_2 \oplus \cdots \oplus \frac{1}{M} g_M. \tag{5}$$

is simply used. Figure 1 shows an example of a tree-structured GMM. Each leaf node corresponds to a Gaussian component of the GMM, and each other node has a single Gaussian obtained by combining corresponding Gaussian pdfs of descendant nodes. As for the following tree-construction algorithm, it is assumed that the maximum number of child nodes for each layer (with the exception of the leaf layer) is given. For example, if the maximum number of child nodes for the first layer is two and that for the second layer is three, the resulting tree will be designed as shown in Figure 1. In this case, a tree with a depth of three (including the leaf layer) is obtained. This tree-structured GMM is denoted as $\mathcal{T}_{(2,3)} = (V, E, G_{\mathrm{TREE}})$ where V is a set of nodes, E is a set of edges, and $G_{\mathrm{TREE}} = \{g^{(v)} | v \in V\}$ is a set of Gaussian pdfs. In general, a node at the t-th layer of a tree $\mathcal{T}_{(P_1, P_2, \cdots, P_T)}$ has, at most, P_t child nodes.

The node pdfs $g^{(v)}$ of a tree $\mathcal{T}_{(P_1, P_2, \cdots, P_T)}$ are created by the following algorithm. Note that $G_{\mathrm{GMM}} = \{g_1, g_2, \cdots, g_K\}$ is a set of mixture components of the UBM, $G^{(v)}$ is a subset of G_{GMM} corresponding to node v, $g^{(v)}$ is a Gaussian pdf for node v, and $d(g_m, g_n)$ is the sum of Kullback-Leibler divergence from g_m to g_n and that of from g_n to g_m.

1. Prepare a queue and enqueue $(r, G^{(r)})$, where r is the root node, and $g^{(r)} \leftarrow g(G^{(r)})$ $(G^{(r)} = G_{\mathrm{GMM}})$.

2. (Min-max Initialization) Dequeue $(v, G^{(v)})$. Let $\{c_p\}_{p=1}^{P}$ be the child nodes of node v. For $p = 1, 2, \cdots, P$, initialize child Gaussian pdfs as follows:

$$g^{(c_p)} \leftarrow \alpha \tilde{g}^{(c_p)} \oplus (1 - \alpha) g^{(v)} \tag{6}$$

where $0 \leq \alpha \leq 1$, and $\tilde{g}^{(c_p)}$ is chosen from $G^{(v)}$ by

$$\tilde{g}^{(c_p)} = \begin{cases} \underset{g \in G^{(v)}}{\operatorname{argmax}}\ d(g, g^{(v)}) & (p = 1) \\ \underset{\substack{g \in G^{(v)} \\ g \neq \tilde{g}^{(c_1)}, \cdots, \tilde{g}^{(c_{p-1})}}}{\operatorname{argmax}}\ \min_{1 \leq p' < p} d(g, \tilde{g}^{(c_{p'})}) & (\text{otherwise}) \end{cases} .$$

3. (Clustering by k-means) Assign each Gaussian component in $G^{(v)}$ to the nearest child node, i.e.

$$G^{(c_p)} \leftarrow \{g \in G^{(v)} \mid p = \underset{p'}{\operatorname{argmin}}\, d(g, g^{(c_{p'})})\}. \tag{7}$$

Update $g^{(c_p)}$ by using Eq. (5) as $g^{(c_p)} \leftarrow g(G^{(c_p)})$. Repeat this step until the following sum converges:

$$D = \sum_{p=1}^{P} \sum_{g \in G^{(c_p)}} d(g, g^{(c_p)}). \tag{8}$$

4. For $p = 1, 2, \cdots, P$, enqueue $(c_p, G^{(c_p)})$ if c_p is not in the $(T+1)$-th layer and $|G^{(c_p)}| > 1$. Go to step 5 if the queue is empty; otherwise, return to step 2.

5. For each node v in the $(T+1)$-th layer, create leaf nodes ℓ for each $g_k \in G^{(v)} \subset G_{\mathrm{GMM}}$ and set $g^{(\ell)} = g_k$.

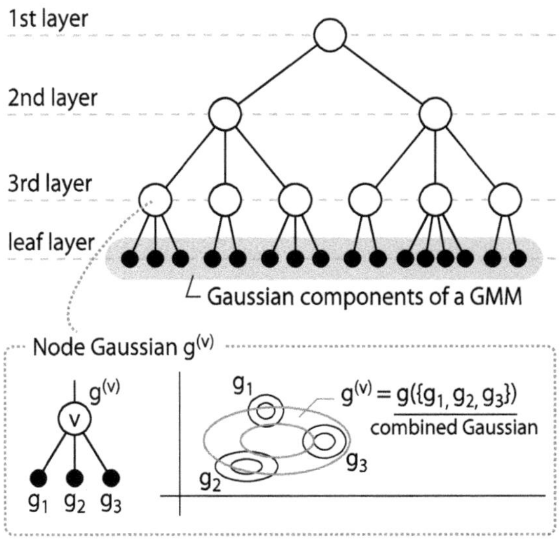

Figure 1: An example of a tree-structured GMM.

2.3 Fast MAP Adaptation

A fast MAP adaptation technique which estimates c_{ik} in Eq. (2) efficiently by using a tree-structured GMM is explained in the following. For a constructed tree-structured GMM $\mathcal{T}_{(P_1, P_2, \cdots, P_T)}$, node weights are first defined as follows:

1. For each leaf node, set $w^{(\ell)} = w_k$ if $g^{(\ell)} = g_k \in G_{\mathrm{GMM}}$.

2. Calculate weights for $t = T+1, T, \cdots, 1$ as follows. For each node v in the t-th layer,

$$w^{(v)} = \sum_{c \in C(v)} w^{(c)}, \tag{9}$$

Table 1: The 30 target semantic concepts in the TRECVID 2010 dataset

Airplane Flying	Animal	Asian People	Bicycling	Boat ship	Bus
Car Racing	Cheering	Cityscape	Classroom	Dancing	Dark-skinned People
Demonstration Or Protest	Doorway	Explosion Fire	Female Human Face Closeup	Flowers	Ground Vehicles
Hand	Mountain	Nighttime	Old People	Running	Singing
Sitting down	Swimming	Telephones	Throwing	Vehicle	Walking

where $C(v)$ is a set of child nodes of the node v.

The algorithm for estimating c_{ik} for feature vector x_i is described as follows. The key idea is to construct a GMM of active nodes V_A, which means vector x_i will be assigned to descendants of nodes in V_A. $|V_A|$ is kept small by obtaining active nodes from the root node.

1. Set $V_A \leftarrow \{r\}$, where r is the root node.
2. Expand active nodes by making child nodes of the active nodes active:
$$V_A \leftarrow \bigcup_{v \in V_A} C(v), \tag{10}$$
where $C(v)$ is a set of child nodes of the node v. Here, $C(\ell) = \{\ell\}$ is used for leaf nodes ℓ to keep the leaf nodes active.
3. Consider an active GMM given by
$$p(x|V_A) = \sum_{v \in V_A} \tilde{w}^{(v)} g^{(v)}(x), \quad \tilde{w}^{(v)} = \frac{w^{(v)}}{\sum_{v \in V_A} w^{(v)}}.$$
Calculate
$$c_i^{(v)} = \frac{\tilde{w}^{(v)} g^{(v)}(x_i)}{\sum_{v \in V_A} \tilde{w}^{(v)} g^{(v)}(x_i)} = \frac{w^{(v)} g^{(v)}(x_i)}{\sum_{v \in V_A} w^{(v)} g^{(v)}(x_i)}.$$
4. Keep a node v active if $c_i^{(v)}$ is larger than the predetermined threshold c_{TH}, i.e.
$$V_A \leftarrow \{v \in V_A \mid c_i^{(v)} > c_{\mathrm{TH}}\} \tag{11}$$
5. If all nodes in V_A are leaf nodes, output
$$\hat{c}_{ik} = \begin{cases} c_i^{(\ell)} & (\ell \in V_A,\ g^{(\ell)} = g_k) \\ 0 & (\text{otherwise}) \end{cases}. \tag{12}$$
Otherwise, return to step 2.

Since the observed $\hat{c}_{ik}$ for non-active nodes is 0, the sum in Eq. (2) can be calculated for non-zero $\hat{c}_{ik}$ only. Moreover, calculation speed and levels of approximation can be controlled by selecting the threshold in $0 < c_{\mathrm{TH}} \leq 1$. Note that the same c_{ik} as given by Eq. (2) is obtained if c_{TH} is set to 0 (because all leaf nodes will be active at the final step).

2.4 GMM Supervector

The combination of GMM supervectors and support vector machines (SVMs) was first proposed as a speaker recognition method [6] and has been applied to image and video recognition [3, 4]. GMM supervectors are created for each shot given by

$$\phi(X_s) = \begin{pmatrix} \tilde{\mu}_1^{(s)} \\ \tilde{\mu}_2^{(s)} \\ \vdots \\ \tilde{\mu}_K^{(s)} \end{pmatrix}, \quad \tilde{\mu}_k^{(s)} = \sqrt{w_k^{(\mathrm{U})}} \left(\Sigma_k^{(\mathrm{U})}\right)^{-\frac{1}{2}} \hat{\mu}_k^{(s)}, \tag{13}$$

where $\hat{\mu}_k^{(s)}$ is an adapted mean vector obtained from Eq. (2), and $\theta^{(\mathrm{U})}$ is the GMM parameter for the UBM. Finally, SVMs are trained for each semantic concepts and for each type of features by using RBK kernels.

Note that while the scope of this paper is fast creation of the GMM supervectors, the proposed technique can be used for creating the Fisher vectors [7].

3. EXPERIMENTS

3.1 Database and Task

Our experiments were conducted on the TRECVID 2010 dataset [1]. The dataset consists of 400 hours of Internet archive videos with creative commons licenses. The shot boundaries are automatically detected and provided with the video data. Half of the videos were used for training, and the others were used for testing. The number of shots was 119,685 for training and 146,788 for testing. The task of semantic indexing in the experiment is to detect the 30 semantic concepts listed in Table 1. The target 30 concepts (including objects, events and scenes) were selected at the TRECVID 2010 workshop. They are considered to be useful for video searching.

The evaluation measures are Mean average precision (Mean AP) and calculation time (CT) of the testing phase. Mean AP is defined as the mean of APs over all 30 target concepts, and APs are estimated by using a method called inferred average precision (Inf AP), proposed in [8].

3.2 Experimental Conditions

The following four types of visual and audio features are extracted from video data: 1) SIFT features with Harris-Affine detector (SIFT-Har), 2) SIFT features with Hessian-Affine detector (SIFT-Hes), 3) SIFT and hue histogram with dense sampling (SIFTH-Dense), and 4) MFCC audio features (MFCC).

The number of mixtures (vocabulary size) K for GMMs was 512 for visual features and 256 for audio features. For computational efficiency, it was assumed that covariance matrices are diagonal. Hyper parameter τ in the MAP adaptation was set to 20.0. SVMs were trained for each semantic concepts by using the libSVM implementation [9]. For tree-structured GMMs, the optimal tree structure $\mathcal{T}_{\mathrm{opt}}$ was selected as

$$\mathcal{T}_{\mathrm{opt}} = \operatorname*{argmin}_{\mathcal{T} \in \mathcal{S}} \mathrm{CT}(\mathcal{T}), \tag{14}$$
$$\mathcal{S} = \{\mathcal{T}_{(P_1, P_2, \cdots, P_T)} \mid 1 \leq T \leq 5, 1 \leq P_t \leq 5\}, \tag{15}$$

where $\mathrm{CT}(\mathcal{T})$ is calculation time when the tree $\mathcal{T}$ is used. The trees $\mathcal{T}_{(4,4,5)}$, $\mathcal{T}_{(4,5,5)}$, $\mathcal{T}_{(3,4,4,5)}$ and $\mathcal{T}_{(3,3)}$ were selected for SIFT-Har, SIFT-Hes, SIFTH-Dense and MFCC, respectively. Parameter α in Eq. (6) was fixed to 0.1. Threshold c_{TH} for the fast MAP adaptation was set to 0.001. Here, a low threshold was set so as to keep detection performance

Table 2: Comparison of Mean Inf AP (%) in terms of different features.

Feature	No tree	$\mathcal{T}_{\text{opt}}$
SIFT-Har	6.30	6.32
SIFT-Hes	5.96	6.08
SIFTH-Dense	7.10	6.95
MFCC	1.99	2.00
Fusion	10.15	10.16

Table 3: Calculation time (sec) for MAP adaptation.

Feature	No tree	$\mathcal{T}_{\text{opt}}$	$\mathcal{T}_{\text{binary}}$
SIFT-Har	1.62	0.49	0.98
SIFT-Hes	1.67	0.48	1.00
SIFTH-Dense	2.89	0.81	1.89
MFCC	0.22	0.03	0.08

high. Experiments using different thresholds were also conducted (see Subection 3.3.3).

In the experiments, calculation time was measured by using one Intel Xeon 2.93 GHz CPU.

3.3 Results

3.3.1 Mean Inf APs

Table 2 summarizes obtained Mean Inf APs for each features and a fusion method. The Fusion combines four features by calculating the weighted sum of detection scores (fusion weights were optimized by using two-fold cross validation on training data). As a result, we can see that the Mean Inf APs using tree-structured GMMs are comparable to those using no trees.

Estimation errors of c_{ik} were also evaluated from the mean absolute error (MAE), given as follows:

$$\text{MAE} = \frac{1}{n}\sum_{i=1}^{n}\sum_{k=1}^{K}|\hat{c}_{ik} - c_{ik}|, \qquad (16)$$

where $\hat{c}_{ik}$ and c_{ik} are given by Eq. (12) and Eq. (2), respectively. The MAE for SIFTH-Dense was 0.32 on average (note that $0 \leq \text{MAE} \leq 2$). Although we have estimation errors of c_{ik} in the fast MAP adaptation algorithm, they can be cancelled when the distance between two GMM supervectors is calculated since the same errors occur in training and testing phases.

3.3.2 Calculation Time

Table 3 lists calculation times for MAP adaptation using different features and different trees. The results for binary trees ($\mathcal{T}_{\text{binary}}$) are also listed in the table. The calculation speed when the optimal tree is used on average 4.2 times faster than when trees were not used; that is, calculation time was reduced by 76.2%. The MAP adaptation step took, on average, 0.055 msec per feature.

3.3.3 Effect of using different thresholds

Table 4 lists the results obtained using different thresholds c_{TH} for the fast MAP adaptation. The number of leaf nodes that are active (at least once in Eq. (10)) and MAE are also listed in the table.

Table 4: Comparison of Mean Inf AP (%), calculation time (sec) for MAP adaptation (CT), number of leaf nodes $|V_A|$ and Mean absolute error (MAE) by using different thresholds c_{TH} (for SIFTH-Dense).

c_{TH}	Mean Inf AP	CT	$\|V_A\|$	MAE
0.001	6.95	0.81	17.0	0.32
0.01	6.99	0.68	11.2	0.53
0.1	6.60	0.59	7.3	0.80
0.5	6.41	0.53	5.4	0.98

As c_{TH} gets higher, the calculation time shortens, but Mean Inf AP was decreased when $c_{\text{TH}} = 0.1$ and 0.5. Moreover, the number of active leaf nodes decreases, and MAE increases. It can thus be concluded that calculation time should be reduced not by setting a high threshold c_{TH} but by selecting a better-structured tree to keep detection performance high. In particular, c_{TH} should be equal to or smaller than 0.01 in this case.

4. CONCLUSION

A fast MAP adaptation technique using tree-structured GMMs for a video semantic indexing system was proposed. The detection time was reduced by 56.6%, compared to that of convention method, while high detection performance was maintained. The best result, in terms of Mean Inf AP, attained by our fusion method tested on the TRECVID 2010 dataset was 10.16% when tree-structured GMMs were used and 10.15% when no trees were used. Our future work will focus on a GPU implementation of the fast MAP adaptation. As a result, feature extraction and MAP adaptation will be independently conducted for each local feature by GPUs.

5. REFERENCES

[1] A. F. Smeaton, and et al. Evaluation campaigns and trecvid. In Proc. of *ACM Multimedia MIR* workshop, pages 321–330, 2006.

[2] X. Zhou, and et al. Image classification using super-vector coding of local image descriptors. In Proc. of *ECCV*, 2010.

[3] X. Zhou, and et al. Sift-bag kernel for video event analysis. In Proc. of *ACM Multimedia*, 2008.

[4] N. Inoue, and et al. High-Level Feature Extraction using SIFT GMMs and Audio Models. In Proc. of *ICPR*, 2010.

[5] C. Wu. SiftGPU: A GPU implementation of sift. http://cs.unc.edu/~ccwu/siftgpu, 2007.

[6] W. M. Campbell, and et al. Support vector machines using gmm supervectors for speaker verification. In *IEEE Signal Processing Letters*, 13:308–311, 2006.

[7] T. Jaakkola and D. Haussler. Exploiting generative models in discriminative classifiers. In *In Advances in Neural Information Processing Systems 11*, pages 487–493. MIT Press, 1998.

[8] E. Yilmaz, and et al. A simple and efficient sampling method for estimating ap and ndcg. In Proc. of *ACM SIGIR*, pages 603–610, 2008.

[9] C.-C. Chang and C.-J. Lin. Libsvm: a library for support vector machines. Software available at http://www.csie.ntu.edu.tw/cjlin/libsvm, 2001.

Compositional Object Pattern: A New Model For Album Event Recognition*

Shen-Fu Tsai
Coordinated Science Laboratory
University of Illinois at Urbana-Champaign
stsai8@illinois.edu

Liangliang Cao
Multimedia Group
IBM Watson Research Center
liangliang.cao@us.ibm.com

Feng Tang
Hewlett-Packard Labs
1501 Page Mill Road, Palo Alto, CA 94304 USA
feng.tang@hp.com

Thomas S. Huang
Coordinated Science Laboratory
University of Illinois at Urbana-Champaign
t-huang1@illinois.edu

ABSTRACT

In this paper, we study the problem of recognizing events in personal photo albums. In consumer photo collections or on-line photo communities, photos are usually organized in albums according to their events. However, interpreting photo albums is more complicated than the traditional problem of understanding single photos, because albums generally exhibit much more varieties than single image. To solve this challenge, we propose a novel representation, called Compositional Object Pattern, which characterizes object level pattern conveying much richer semantic than low level visual feature. To interpret the rich semantics in albums, we mine frequent object patterns in the training set, and then rank them by their discriminating power. The album feature is then set as the frequencies of these frequent and discriminative patterns, called Compositional Object Pattern Frequency(COPF). We show with experimental result that our algorithm is capable of recognizing holidays with accuracy higher than the baseline method.

Categories and Subject Descriptors

I.4 [**Image Processing and Computer Vision**]: Feature Measurement, Image Representation

General Terms

Algorithms, Experimentation

*Area chair: Kiyoharu Aizawa

Keywords

Photo Albums, Event Recognition, Compositional Object Pattern

1. INTRODUCTION

In vision and multimedia community, many studies have been dedicated to single image understanding, especially object recognition and scene classification. In contrast, there are less attention paid to album-level event classification, although most consumer photos are kept in the form of albums. Because people usually organize their photo albums corresponding to different events, it is crucial for consumer photo management systems to recognize the underlying event within each album. However, the task of album event recognition is harder than conventional single image understanding, as a collection of photos exhibits more variety than single image. From another viewpoint, event is a higher level concept than other subject like object and scene, and therefore to interpret the event in an album is a more challenging task. In particular, albums often consist of "typical" and "non-typical" photos. "Typical" photos are those when viewed individually the event can be recognized by human. Conventional image-based classification techniques will probably fail to recognize the non-typical photos and hence decrease the accuracy of album event recognition.

Since an event involves many high level concepts, it is difficult for low level feature to capture its rich semantic. However, most previous image understanding methods mostly use low level features for high level semantic analysis. The semantic gap between low-level features and high level concepts impose a serious problem for current event recognition methods. As suggested in [1], low-level feature based image classification is not able to achieve very high accuracy in event classification. The work [1] relies on meta information such as time or GPS to improve the recognition accuracy, however, those meta data might be changed due to image format change or photo redistribution. In this paper, we explore another way to bridge the semantic gaps, which employs high level object detection for high level semantic inference.

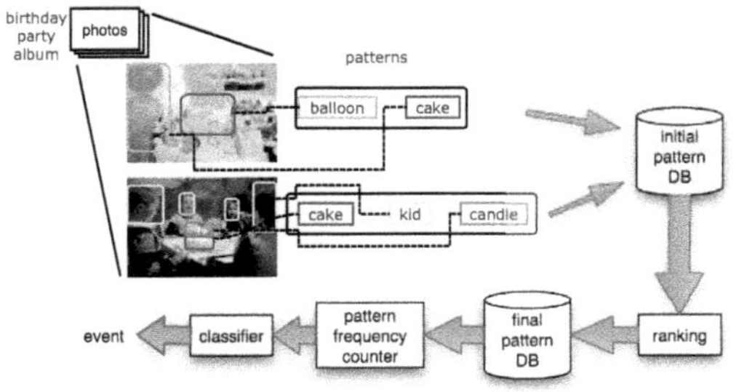

Figure 1: Overview of our proposed algorithm

Our work is partly motivated by [10], which employed an object detector bank to extract object semantic as the image feature for classification. The resulting image feature works well on "typical" images, however, could not be used for "non-typical" ones. In contrast, this paper explores middle level concepts in the album level, and proposed a new model called Compositional Object Patterns to mine the context information within a photo albums, which could reliably recognize the event robustly subject to the affects of "non-typical" images.

We propose to solve the problem of album event classification by mining relevant and discriminative object patterns in the albums. The large number of the mined frequent patterns are further ranked by their discriminating power, and the top ranked ones are the final patterns that are used to represent each album. We show that our algorithm discovers semantically meaningful object pattern, and yields satisfying performance on a photo album dataset from real life.

The rest of the paper is organized as follows. Section 2 reviews previous relevant works. Section 3 describes how itemset mining is used to explore object patterns. Section 4 presents the proposed pattern ranking followed by album representation. Section 5 and Section 6 present experimental results and conclusion, respectively.

2. RELATED WORKS

Collection-level analysis of cosumer photos has not drawn too much attention in the past. In [2, 3] the authors explored relationship between collection-level annotation and image-level annotation with help of GPS and time information associated with the photos, whereas in our work we are more interested in understanding image based on only visual content. Authors of [8] proposed to describe images and video frames by a set of scores of visual concepts. Then, unlike our pattern mining approach, they cluster the resulting image features directly to build event feature vocabulary, which may be affected by irrelevant visual feature and noisy output of visual concept detector, while the patterns we discover should be more robust to these two factors.

In recent years, there has been a couple of works on mining compositional feature. The authors of [5] pointed out that compositional feature, viewed as a combination of primitive features, is a non-linear transformation from the primitives and thus can have higher discriminative power. They propose Fisher score and information gain to measure relevance of the mined compositional feature. In [14], the authors mine frequent compositional patterns in the whole training set followed by multiclass Adaboost to select feature for image-based classification. Combined with decision tree classifier, [7] proposes to discover frequent yet discriminative pattern while growing the decision tree during training process. While these mentioned works assume general feature vector, [15] explicitly explores frequent quantized visual patterns with self-discovered distance metric used by clustering algorithm. Note that none of these works explicitly uses object detection. The feature closest to middle level concept detection is the PCA-SIFT[9] visual primitive used in [15].

3. ITEMSET MINING

3.1 Itemset Terminology

A *transaction database* $\mathcal{T}$ is a set of *transactions*, where each transaction T, associated with a unique transaction id, is a set of distinct *items*. Let $I = \{i_1, \ldots, i_{|I|}\}$ be the complete set of distinct items appearing in $\mathcal{T}$. An *itemset* D is a non-empty subset of I. A transaction T is said to *contain* itemset D if $D \subseteq T$. The number of transactions in $\mathcal{T}$ containing itemset D is the *support* of itemset D, denoted as $sup(D)$. Given a minimum support threshold min_sup, an itemset D is *frequent* if $sup(D) \geq min\_sup$. An itemset D is a *frequent closed itemset* if it is frequent and there does not exist any proper superset $D' \supset D$ such that $sup(D') = sup(D)$.

3.2 Proposed Object Itemset

3.2.1 Object Detection

For each image I, N object detectors are run against it, each producing a set of detections with some score. For each detector we keep only the maximum response (score) it generates, resulting in a N-dimensional feature vector $m(I) = (m_1(I), \ldots, m_N(I))$ where $m_n(I)$ is the maximum response of detector n within image I.

3.2.2 Itemizing Object Detection

To convert each continuous-valued $m_i(I)$ in $m(I)$, for each dimension(object) we apply Lloyd's algorithm[11] to compute least square quantization based on training set, assuming k quantization levels. Hence the quantized features is $q(I) = (q_1(I), \ldots, q_N(I))$, where $q_n(I) \in \{1, \ldots, k\}, \forall n$. With quantized detector responses $q(I)$, we then convert it to a transaction $T(I) = \{t(q_1(I)), \ldots, t(q_N(I))\}$, where function $t()$ transforms a quantized response from a specific detector to a unique item based on $t(q_n(I)) = k * (n-1) + q_n(I) \in \{1, \ldots, Nk\}$. Therefore, there are totally Nk distinct items, numbered from 1 to Nk. Each transaction has exactly N items.

3.2.3 Closed Itemset Mining

We apply mining algorithm $|\mathcal{E}|$ times, once for each event E_i from images in the training albums labeld as E_i, where $\mathcal{E} = \{E_1, \ldots, E_{|\mathcal{E}|}\}$ denotes the set of distinct events.

4. COMPOSITIONAL OBJECT PATTERN FREQUENCY (COPF) ALGORITHM

4.1 Pattern Ranking

For each event E_i, the set of patterns $\mathcal{D}_{E_i}$ thus mined are candidates for the final patterns used for recognizing E_i. To pick up the most discriminative patterns, we rank them

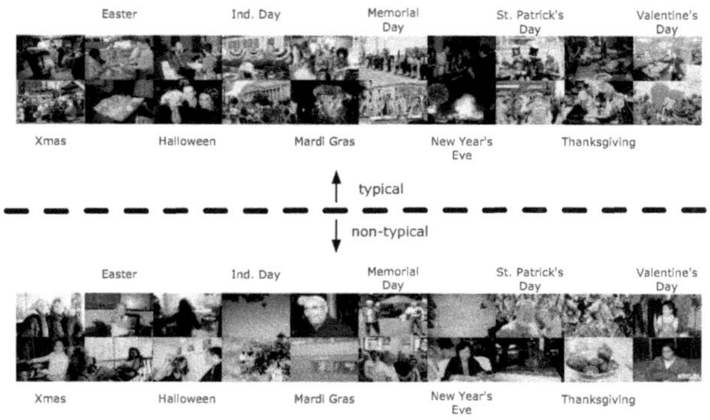

Figure 2: Sample typical and non-typical photos in the 10-Holiday dataset

according to their relevance to E_i. For each $D_j^{E_i} \in \mathcal{D}_{E_i}$ and for each album a_m in training set, we obtain the relative frequency f_j^m which is the percentage of photos containing itemset $D_j^{E_i}$ in album a_m, so $0 \leq f_j^m \leq 1$. Every album a_m is also associated with a binary variable $y_m^{E_i} \in \{0, 1\}$ depending on whether it is labeled E_i. Thus we can compute the average precision(AP) of detecting E_i based solely on f_j^m. We thus select the top patterns for each event E_i and form the final set of primitive patterns $\mathcal{P} = \{P_j\}_{j=1}^{|\mathcal{P}|}$ as the union of the top relevant patterns of all events.

4.2 Pattern Frequency And Classification

The final feature for album a_m is then computed as $f_m = (f_1^m, \ldots, f_{|\mathcal{P}|}^m)^T$ where each f_j^m is the relative frequency of photos containing P_j in album a_m. We call it Compositional Object Pattern Frequency (COPF). We train multiclass Support Vector Machine(SVM) classifier for event classification.

5. EXPERIMENTS

We collected a 10-Holiday dataset, came up with a list of 38 relevant objects semi-automatically, and trained the corresponding object detectors. For more details see [12]. Some typical and non-typical holiday photos are shown in Figure 2.

5.1 Implementation

5.1.1 Compostional Object Pattern Frequency(COPF)

The proposed Compositional Object Pattern Frequency (COPF) algorithm described in Section 4 is applied, where the number of quantization level is set to $k = 7$. When mining frequent closed itemsets, we use the program of CLOSET+ [13] provided by its authors, with threshold of support set to 30. For multiclass SVM classifier we adopt LIBSVM package provided at [4], using 5-fold cross validation on training set for parameter tuning.

5.1.2 Image-based Multiclass Adaboost (SAMME)

As a baseline model for comparison, we implement the algorithm in [14] as it is the most similar work to ours. The authors of this work proposed to mine frequent and discriminative compositional patterns from the whole training set in contrast of our mining frequent patterns with respect to each class seperately followed by pattern ranking. In their work, the mined patterns are then used by multiclass Adaboost[16] to find the most discriminative features for classification. When implementing their algorithm, we set k, the number of quantization level, to 7, same as COPF. However, the algorithm is only for image-based classification. So we attach the album label to all of its images for training, and when testing the album label is the majority vote of all its estimated image labels.

5.2 Results

5.2.1 Mined patterns

Before checking the classification accuracy, we first examine some top ranking object patterns. In Figure 3, we show some of the top patterns for each event. Here the number of quantization is set to $k = 7$, and each parenthesis encloses a corresponding level from 1 to k. By definition, objects that are absent in the pattern are "unimportant" or "irrelevant", i.e. whether they appear or not do not help distinguishing the event from others, just like the concept "person" does not help very much in recognizing "outdoor", as previously explained. We observe in the figure that most of the mined patterns are meaningful, in that they match our common knowledge and understanding of the holidays and objects. Moreover, these patterns are indeed sparse in objects, enabling our algorithm to get rid of detection noise, especially from the detectors of the irrelevant objects. Nonetheless, there is some noise in the patterns as well, mostly due to imperfect object detectors.

Holiday	top ranking patterns
Christmas	christmas tree(7) christmas tree(7) feather boa(3)
Easter	attire(3) firework(3) rabbit(6) flag(1) turkey(5)
Halloween	jack-o-lantern(7) pumpkin(7) uniform(3) food(3) jack-o-lantern(7) pumpkin(7)
Independence Day	child(1) easter egg(1) firework(7) child(1) firework(7) uniform(2)
Mardi Gras	attire(6) drum(4) light source(3) uniform(5) bassoon(2) champagne(3) easter egg(2) food(3) table(2)
Memorial Day	euphonium(3) jack-o-lantern(1) uniform(5) stage(6) uniform(6)
New Year's Eve	food(2) room light(4) room light(4) uniform(3)
St. Patrick's Day	child(3) cross(4) easter egg(3) french horn(3) military uniform(4) bouquet(4) food(5) rabbit(4) uniform(4)
Thanksgiving	christmas tree(1) easter egg(4) room light(2) attire(2) christmas tree(1) jack-o-lantern(2)
Valentine's Day	american flag(2) basket(3) heart(6) american flag(2) basket(3) christmas tree(1) heart(6)

Figure 3: Top ranking patterns for each holiday. Full response is 7.

5.2.2 Accuracy comparison

Figure 4 compares the accuracy performances of the baseline and proposed algorithms. Overall, COPF works significantly better with its average accuracy being 46.2%, which is 24.2% higher than SAMME. In fact, SAMME virtually breaks down with accuracy mostly under 30%. This is because it attempts to distinguish individual image before voting, while many images are common to more than one events, i.e. the overlapping between events is quite significant and it is impossible to classify these photos into one single event. SAMME works the best with New Year's Eve photo album because it is the only event composed of many night scene pictures taken at night. It is also observed that, COPF does not work well on St. Patrick's Day, probably because its main feature, various green objects, is not well captured as the general object detectors we use are based on HOG feature[6].

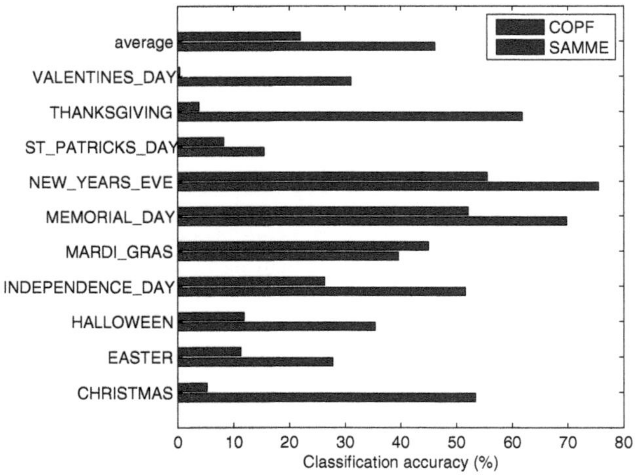

Figure 4: Classification accuracy comparison between the proposed algorithm COPF and the baseline algorithm SAMME

6. CONCLUSION AND FUTURE WORK

In this paper, we propose a novel model named Compositional Object Pattern to attack the problem of album event recognition. To accommodate the scenario of photo albums, we propose a novel object pattern mining algorithm which mines and ranks the discriminative object patterns for event classification. Based on mined patterns, albums are characterized by the relative frequencies of discriminative patterns. Experimental results show that our algorithm can distinguish events more accurately than baseline of the single image based classification. The object patterns discovered by our algorithm verify that object level semantic are meaningful and reliable.

In the future, we are interested in incorporating pattern itemset with the relative location of object detection, and we believe such context information will be useful in many visual applications.

7. ACKNOWLEDGEMENT

This research was supported in part by HP Innovation Research Program and the National Science Council, Taiwan, R.O.C. under contract NSC-095-SAF-I-564-035-TMS (to Shen-Fu Tsai).

8. REFERENCES

[1] L. Cao, J. Luo, and T. Huang. Annotating photo collections by label propagation according to multiple similarity cues. In *Proceeding of the 16th ACM international conference on Multimedia*, pages 121–130. ACM, 2008.

[2] L. Cao, J. Luo, H. S. Kautz, and T. S. Huang. Annotating collections of photos using hierarchical event and scene models. In *CVPR*. IEEE Computer Society, 2008.

[3] L. Cao, J. Yu, J. Luo, and T. S. Huang. Enhancing semantic and geographic annotation of web images via logistic canonical correlation regression. In W. Gao, Y. Rui, A. Hanjalic, C. Xu, E. G. Steinbach, A. El-Saddik, and M. X. Zhou, editors, *ACM Multimedia*, pages 125–134. ACM, 2009.

[4] C.-C. Chang and C.-J. Lin. *LIBSVM: a library for support vector machines*, 2001. Software available at `http://www.csie.ntu.edu.tw/~cjlin/libsvm`.

[5] H. Cheng, X. Yan, J. Han, and C.-W. Hsu. Discriminative frequent pattern analysis for effective classification. In *ICDE*, pages 716–725, 2007.

[6] N. Dalal and B. Triggs. Histograms of oriented gradients for human detection. In *CVPR*, pages 886–893, 2005.

[7] W. Fan, K. Zhang, H. Cheng, J. Gao, X. Yan, J. Han, P. Yu, and O. Verscheure. Direct mining of discriminative and essential frequent patterns via model-based search tree. In *Proceeding of the 14th ACM SIGKDD international conference on Knowledge discovery and data mining*, KDD '08, pages 230–238, New York, NY, USA, 2008. ACM.

[8] W. Jiang and A. C. Loui. Semantic event detection for consumer photo and video collections. In *ICME*, pages 313–316. IEEE, 2008.

[9] Y. Ke and R. Sukthankar. Pca-sift: a more distinctive representation for local image descriptors. *Proceedings of the 2004 IEEE Computer Society Conference on Computer Vision and Pattern Recognition 2004 CVPR 2004*, 2:506–513, 2004.

[10] E. P. X. Li-Jia Li, Hao Su and L. Fei-Fei. Object bank: A high-level image representation for scene classification & semantic feature sparsification. In *Neural Information Processing Systems (NIPS)*, Vancouver, Canada, December 2010.

[11] S. Lloyd. Least squares quantization in pcm. *Information Theory, IEEE Transactions on*, 28(2):129–137, Mar. 1982.

[12] S.-F. Tsai, F. Tang, and T. S. Huang. Album-based object-centric event recognition. *Workshop on Visual Content Identification and Search in 2011 IEEE International Conference on Multimedia and Expo (ICME 2011)*.

[13] J. Wang, J. Han, and J. Pei. Closet+: searching for the best strategies for mining frequent closed itemsets. In *Proceedings of the ninth ACM SIGKDD international conference on Knowledge discovery and data mining*, KDD '03, pages 236–245, New York, NY, USA, 2003. ACM.

[14] J. Yuan, J. Luo, and Y. Wu. Mining compositional features for boosting. In *IEEE Conf. Computer Vision and Pattern Recognition*, 2008.

[15] J. Yuan, Y. Wu, and M. Yang. From frequent itemsets to semantically meaningful visual patterns. In *Proceedings of the 13th ACM SIGKDD international conference on Knowledge discovery and data mining*, KDD '07, pages 864–873, New York, NY, USA, 2007. ACM.

[16] J. Zhu, H. Zou, S. Rosset, and T. Hastie. Multi-class adaboost. Technical report, 2005.

Learning from Search Engine and Human Supervision for Web Image Search*

Linjun Yang
Microsoft Research Asia
Beijing, China
linjuny@microsoft.com

Alan Hanjalic
Delft University of Technology
Delft, The Netherlands
a.hanjalic@tudelft.nl

ABSTRACT

Visual reranking aims at improving the precision of text-based Web image search. In this paper we propose to combine two learning strategies for deriving the reranking model: *learning from search engine* and *learning from human supervision.* The first strategy learns the reranking model in a pseudo-supervised fashion by interpreting parts of the initial text-based search result as pseudo-relevant. The second strategy involves manual relevance labeling of the text-based search results obtained for a limited number of representative queries. While learning from search engine is query dependent and can therefore adapt better to individual queries, it is essentially unsupervised and noisy. While human supervision can better relate the search results to true relevance criteria, it needs to be deployed in a way to keep the reranking scalable. A combination of the two is expected to benefit from their respective advantages and reduce the impact of their individual deficiencies. We propose a two-stage learning approach to visual reranking, where in the online stage multiple query-relative meta rerankers are learned in a pseudo-supervised fashion from the search results and in the offline stage human supervision is used to derive the final reranking function based on these meta rerankers. The experimental results demonstrate that the proposed method significantly outperforms the existing reranking approaches.

Categories and Subject Descriptors

H.3.3 [**Information Search and Retrieval**]: Retrieval models

General Terms

Algorithm, Experimentation, Performance

*Area chair: Tat-Seng Chua

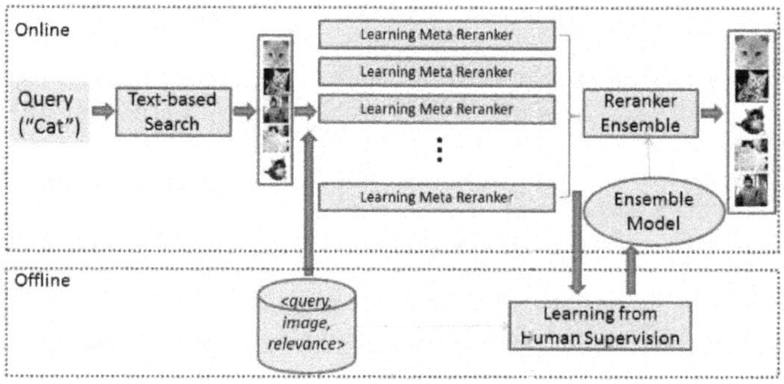

Figure 1: The framework of the proposed two-stage learning approach to visual reranking.

Keywords

image search reranking, learning to rerank, visual reranking

1. INTRODUCTION

The existing web image search engines [1][2][3] retrieve and rank images mostly based on the text in the corresponding web pages. This, however, often leads to unsatisfactory results due to the mismatch between the text and image content [25]. To improve the precision of the text-based image search ranking, visual reranking has been proposed to refine the search result from the text-based image search engine by incorporating the additional information conveyed by the visual modality.

A large number of existing visual reranking approaches are based on the so-called PRF (Pseudo Relevance Feedback) assumption [24][5][16][6][20][13], where the top-N images of the initial result list are regarded as pseudo-relevant and used to learn a reranking model (visual classifier). We refer to this scheme as *learning from search engine* (or *pseudo-supervised*). Even though such methods can improve the precision over the initial text-based result in some cases, the assumption that the top-N images are all equally relevant can be seen as too rigorous to be satisfied well by any arbitrary text-based image search engine. Since the text-based image search is far from perfect (which is the reason to perform the reranking in the first place), the top result will inevitably contain irrelevant images, which may introduce noise into the learning of reranking models and lead to sub-optimal search result being returned after reranking. Although this assumption can be relaxed in graph-based reranking methods [21], it remains difficult to accurately specify the importance for each of the individual images in the initial text-based result.

To better discover the relationship between the visual features and the targeted (objective) ranking, Yang and Hanjalic [25] and Krapac and et al. [13] recently proposed to introduce human supervision into the learning of reranking models. We refer to these methods as *learning from human supervision* (or *supervised*), since they rely on manual relevance labeling of a training data set built from the search results obtained for a number of representative queries. These human-labeled results are used to train a query-independent reranking model that can be employed later on to rerank the initial search result obtained for an arbitrary query. The main challenge there lies in designing a suitable number of query-relative reranking features. In [25], eleven features were hand-designed based on the insights obtained from the visual context and PRF, while in [13] these features were extracted by averaging the visual features of the top images in the text-based search result. Although experiments demonstrated the effectiveness of these features to capture the relevance between the textual query and the images, the fact that the features are heuristic and rule-based indicates that further improvement toward more robust and generic reranking performance could be obtained.

In this paper, we propose a two-stage learning approach to visual reranking that combines the advantages of learning from search engine and learning from human supervision. In the first (online) stage, pseudo-supervised learning is deployed to automatically discover relevant information contained in the text-based search result for each individual query, based on which multiple meta rerankers can be constructed. In the second (offline) stage, we learn in a supervised fashion an ensemble model that combines the meta rerankers into the targeted reranking model. Due to the human supervision, the obtained model will be compatible with true search relevance criteria and avoid the noise characterizing purely pseudo-supervised methods. At the same time, the scalability of the method will not be affected by human supervision because a query-independent model is learned.

The paper is organized as follows. In Section 2 we describe the proposed two-stage learning approach, which is followed by the experimental analysis in Section 3. We conclude the paper with Section 4, in which we provide a brief overview of the main results of the paper and the prospects for our future work.

2. VISUAL RERANKING BASED ON TWO-STAGE LEARNING

The general framework of the proposed two-stage learning approach is illustrated in Fig. 1. In the online stage, when a textual query is submitted to the image search engine by a user, initial search can be performed using any contemporary text-based search technique [18]. Then, L meta rerankers are learned from the initial text-based search result. Finally, for each of the top-N images in the initial result, an L-dimensional score vector is obtained comprising the scores from all L meta rerankers when applied to that image. The score vector is then used as input to a reranker ensemble model, which has already been trained offline, to estimate the ranking scores in the reranked image search list.

The offline stage is devoted to learning the reranker ensemble model from human supervision, i.e., based on manually labeled training data. Since the learned ensemble model will be used for reranking the text-based search result, the training set is constructed from these results through the following steps. First, several representative queries sampled from the query log are selected. Then, using these queries the top N images are retrieved from the text-based image search engine and downloaded for processing. Finally, for each query-image pair, the annotator is invited to label the relevance between them to form the ground truth. After the training data is collected, the score vector can be computed from the meta rerankers, for each image and the corresponding query. Then the reranker ensemble model is learned and stored in the memory to be used in the online stage for responding to users' submitted queries.

In summary, we can say that while in the online stage of the proposed approach we learn the query-dependent meta rerankers for each individual query in a pseudo-supervised fashion from the search engine, the offline stage serves to learn the query-independent reranker ensemble model in a supervised fashion that optimally combines the multiple meta rerankers.

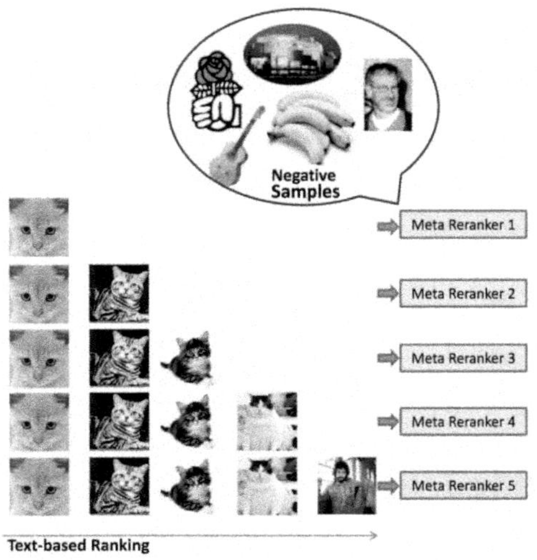

Figure 2: Illustration of learning multiple meta rerankers in a pseudo-supervised fashion from the search engine.

2.1 Learning from search engine

Our proposed strategy for learning from the search engine aims at refining the PRF assumption stating that the top images in the text-based search result can be regarded as pseudo-relevant. While most of the existing approaches treat these images equally, the images at different ranked positions in the text-based result should have different probabilities to be relevant. We therefore propose an effective method to learn multiple meta rerankers from the text-based search result, to take the different relevance probabilities of images at different initial ranks into consideration. As shown in Fig. 2, we construct the meta rerankers by iteratively adding images along the ranked list in the descending order into the set of positive training samples. In other words, the first meta reranker is learned using only the topmost image as positive sample, and the ith meta reranker using the top i images. In such a way we can achieve multiple meta rerankers trained using data with the varying trade-off between the robustness and accuracy. The less of the top images are used for learning the meta reranker, the more accurate the training data is. However, when more images are involved, the robustness of the trained meta reranker will be improved, though the data quality (accuracy) may be reduced.

Since a discriminative learning method is usually more effective for learning a visual model, we adopt SVM (Support Vector Machine) [10] in this paper. Since also negative samples are needed for training, we further select the images which are ranked at the bottom of the ranked list for each query as negative samples.

2.2 Learning from human supervision

After the meta rerankers are learned, we need to learn an ensemble model to combine them. This problem can be addressed using a learning-to-rank method [15], by regarding the score vector from the meta rerankers as ranking features.

Ranking SVM [11] is among the most popular learning-to-rank algorithms and we also adopt it in this paper. This algorithm adapts the widely-used SVM classifier to handle the ranking problem. The basic idea is to decompose ranking into a set of pair-wise preferences and then to reduce the learning-to-rank problem into a pair-wise classification problem. Ranking SVM learns the ranking model by solving an optimization problem that can be defined as follows:

$$\begin{aligned} &\min \ \frac{1}{2}W^T W + C\sum \xi^i_{jk} \\ &s.t.\ \forall q_i, I_j \succ I_k : W^T(M(I_j) - M(I_k)) \geq 1 - \xi^i_{jk} \\ &\quad \forall i,j,k : \xi^i_{jk} \geq 0, \end{aligned} \tag{1}$$

where W is the model weight vector, $M(I_j)$ is the score vector from the L meta rerankers for the image I_j, and where $I_j \succ I_k$ means that image I_j is more relevant than I_k for the query q_i.

Standard efficient approaches to learning an SVM classifier, such as SMO (Sequential Minimal Optimization) [19], can be directly employed for learning a Ranking SVM. Moreover, a fast algorithm, e.g., the cutting-plane algorithm [12], can be adopted to speed up the training of a linear Ranking SVM.

3. EXPERIMENTS

In this section, we demonstrate the effectiveness of the proposed reranking approach by means of an experimental study performed on the publicly available Web Queries dataset.

3.1 Experimental setup

To make the experimental results reported in this paper reproducible, we used the publicly available Web Queries dataset[1] comprising a large amount of representative and diverse image search queries. The dataset contains in total 353 queries. For each query, tens or hundreds of images are retrieved and downloaded using a web search engine, which resulted in a total of 71478 images. For each query and an image in its text-based search result, a binary relevance is labeled as the ground-truth.

To illustrate the effectiveness of the proposed method, we compare it with the text-based search baseline from the search engine as well as with the state-of-the-art supervised and unsupervised (including pseudo-supervised) reranking methods. The supervised approaches include the recently proposed supervised-reranking [25] and query-relative classifier [13]. The unsupervised reranking methods include the PRF reranking [24], random walk reranking [7][9], and Bayesian reranking [21][22]. In the PRF reranking, top-ranked images in the initial search result for a given query are used as positive samples and the negative samples are selected using the strategy described in Section 2.1. For Bayesian reranking, the best performing local learning consistency and pair-wise ranking distance are used. As suggested in [13], 400 ordered visual words are used to construct the binary features for query-relative classifier.

The reranking models in the supervised reranking methods [25][13] and the proposed approach in this paper are trained using Ranking SVM [11]. To validate the parameter C in Ranking SVM, the entire dataset is randomly split into 10 folds to generate the training, validation, and test data. The reranking methods are tested in a round robin way for 10 times. At each time, one among the 10 folds is used for testing, 8 folds for training, and the rest one for validating the parameter C.

For the purpose of computing visual similarity between images, the SIFT features [17] with dense sampling are extracted from the images and then quantized together with the spatial layout to represent the images as bags of visual words [23]. For the methods including random walk reranking, Bayesian reranking, and supervised-reranking, histogram intersection is used as the similarity measure between two images. For PRF reranking and the proposed two-stage learning approach to visual reranking, the linear kernel is adopted for SVM due to efficiency reasons.

Average Precision (AP) [4] and Normalized Discounted Cumulative Gain (NDCG) [8] are adopted to measure the ranking performance. AP is defined as the average of precisions at various recall levels. The APs for all queries in the dataset are averaged to obtain the Mean Average Precision (MAP). NDCG emphasizes more on the relevance of top results through discounting the gain by the ranked position, which is defined as

$$\text{NDCG@}k = \frac{\text{DCG@}k}{\text{IDCG@}k}, \tag{2}$$

where

$$\text{DCG@}k = \sum_{i=1}^{k} \frac{2^{r_i} - 1}{\log_2(i+1)}, \tag{3}$$

r_i is the relevance of the corresponding image and IDCG@k is a normalization term used to make the NDCG normalized to be between 0 and 1.

3.2 Performance comparison

Table 1 shows the performance comparison of the proposed approach and the selected representatives of the existing reranking methods in terms of MAP, NDCG@10, and NDCG@40. It can be clearly observed that all the visual reranking methods outperform the *Text-baseline* with performance improvements larger than 12% in terms of MAP. This demonstrates the effectiveness of the visual reranking concept. Furthermore, all the reranking methods incorporating human supervision, including *Supervised-reranking* and *Query-relative*, as well as our proposed approach outperform the unsupervised ones, which once again justifies

[1] http://lear.inrialpes.fr/~krapac/webqueries/webqueries.html

Table 1: Performance comparison of various reranking methods.

Methods	MAP	NDCG@10	NDCG@40
Text-baseline	0.569	0.682	0.633
PRF [24]	0.658 (+15.64%)	0.772 (+13.20%)	0.718 (+13.43%)
Random walk [7][9]	0.641 (+12.65%)	0.766 (+12.32%)	0.704 (+11.22%)
Bayesian [21]	0.643 (+13.01%)	0.766 (+12.32%)	0.709 (+12.01%)
Supervised-reranking [25]	0.665 (+16.87%)	0.769 (+12.76%)	0.733 (+15.80%)
Query-relative [13]	0.666 (+17.05%)	0.768 (+12.61%)	0.729 (+15.17%)
Proposed approach	0.705 (+23.90%)	0.828 (+21.41%)	0.778 (+22.91%)

the integration of a human supervision step in the reranking process.

Compared to the supervised reranking methods, our proposed approach outperforms both *Supervised-reranking* and *Query-relative* methods significantly. Since the employed learning algorithm and the visual feature representation are nearly the same for these reranking methods, this result shows that our approach is the most successful one in effectively utilizing the information extracted from the text-based search result. Since the *Query-relative* classifier uses the average of the visual features from top images as the visual representation of the query, the performance may be influenced by the outliers in the top result. Also a differentiation of images at different ranked positions is not taken into consideration there. Compared to this, our approach is hardly affected by outliers, since the weights for different meta-rerankers are learned from human-labeled data. Compared to the *Supervised-reranking* approach, which extracts eleven carefully designed reranking features based on the domain knowledge from the image search context, our approach can be said to generalize better since the knowledge about the image search is discovered automatically.

4. CONCLUSIONS

In this paper, we proposed a two-stage learning approach to visual reranking, to integrate the respective advantages of two learning strategies, namely *learning from search engine* and *learning from human supervision*, when deriving an effective image search reranking model. We learned multiple meta rerankers from the initial text-based search result by using different numbers of top images as positive samples, which are then combined using an ensemble model learned from human supervision by labeling search results obtained for representative queries. We found that a pseudo-supervised learning process can discover more comprehensive information contained in the noisy text-based search result, while the human supervision can help the process to learn to optimally turn this information into an effective reranking model. The experimental results on the Web Queries dataset demonstrate that the proposed method outperforms all the existing supervised and unsupervised reranking approaches. It improves the performance by 23.9% over the text-based search result.

The approach described in this paper could be naturally applied to learning concept models from image search engines in a semi-automatic fashion. Compared to the fully automatic methods [14], the semi-automatic approach could learn the concept models for any arbitrary concept better with only little human supervision.

5. REFERENCES

[1] http://images.bing.com/.

[2] http://images.google.com/.

[3] http://images.yahoo.com/.

[4] Trec-10 proceedings appendix on common evaluation measures. *http://trec.nist.gov/pubs/trec10/appendices/measures.pdf.*

[5] R. Fergus, L. Fei-Fei, P. Perona, and A. Zisserman. Learning object categories from google's image search. In *ICCV*, 2005.

[6] M. Fritz and B. Schiele. Decomposition, discovery and detection of visual categories using topic models. In *CVPR*, 2008.

[7] W. H. Hsu, L. S. Kennedy, and S.-F. Chang. Video search reranking through random walk over document-level context graph. In *ACM Multimedia*, 2007.

[8] K. Järvelin and J. Kekäläinen. IR evaluation methods for retrieving highly relevant documents. In *SIGIR*, 2000.

[9] Y. Jing and S. Baluja. Visualrank: Applying pagerank to large-scale image search. *IEEE Trans. on PAMI*, 30(11):1877–1890, 2008.

[10] T. Joachims. *Making large-scale support vector machine learning practical*, pages 169–184. MIT Press, Cambridge, MA, USA, 1999.

[11] T. Joachims. Optimizing search engines using clickthrough data. In *KDD*, 2002.

[12] T. Joachims. Training linear svms in linear time. In *KDD*, 2006.

[13] J. Krapac, M. Allan, J. Verbeek, and F. Jurie. Improving web-image search results using query-relative classifiers. In *CVPR*, 2010.

[14] L.-J. Li and L. Fei-Fei. OPTIMOL: automatic Online Picture collecTion via Incremental MOdel Learning. *Int. J. Comput. Vision*, 2009.

[15] T.-Y. Liu. Learning to rank for information retrieval. *Found. Trends Inf. Retr.*, 3:225–331, March 2009.

[16] Y. Liu, T. Mei, X.-S. Hua, J. Tang, X. Wu, and S. Li. Learning to video search rerank via pseudo preference feedback. In *ICME*, 2008.

[17] D. G. Lowe. Distinctive image features from scale-invariant keypoints. *Int. J. Comput. Vision*, 60(2), 2004.

[18] C. D. Manning, P. Raghavan, and H. Schütze. *Introduction to Information Retrieval.* Cambridge University Press, July 2008.

[19] J. C. Platt. Fast training of support vector machines using sequential minimal optimization. In *Advances in kernel methods: support vector learning.* MIT Press, 1999.

[20] F. Schroff, A. Criminisi, and A. Zisserman. Harvesting image databases from the web. In *ICCV*, 2007.

[21] X. Tian, L. Yang, J. Wang, Y. Yang, X. Wu, and X.-S. Hua. Bayesian video search reranking. In *ACM Multimedia*, 2008.

[22] X. Tian, L. Yang, X. Wu, and X.-S. Hua. Visual reranking with local learning consistency. In *MMM*, 2010.

[23] A. Vedaldi and B. Fulkerson. VLFeat: An open and portable library of computer vision algorithms. http://www.vlfeat.org, 2008.

[24] R. Yan, A. G. Hauptmann, and R. Jin. Multimedia search with pseudo-relevance feedback. In *CIVR*, 2003.

[25] L. Yang and A. Hanjalic. Supervised reranking for web image search. In *ACM Multimedia*, 2010.

Semi-Supervised Face Image Retrieval using Sparse Coding with Identity Constraint

Bor-Chun Chen, Yin-Hsi Kuo, Yan-Ying Chen, Kuan-Yu Chu, and Winston Hsu
National Taiwan University, Taipei, Taiwan
{siriushpa, kuonini, yanying}@gmail.com, b96902119@ntu.edu.tw, winston@csie.ntu.edu.tw

ABSTRACT

We aim to develop a scalable face image retrieval system which can integrate with partial identity information to improve the retrieval result. To achieve this goal, we first apply sparse coding on local features extracted from face images combining with inverted indexing to construct an efficient and scalable face retrieval system. We then propose a novel coding scheme that refines the representation of the original sparse coding by using identity information. Using the proposed coding scheme, face images with large intra-class variances will still be quantized into similar visual words if they share the same identity. Experimental results show that our system can achieve salient retrieval results on LFW dataset (13K faces) and outperform linear search methods using well known face recognition feature descriptors.

Categories and Subject Descriptors

H.3.3 [**Information Search and Retrieval**]: Retrieval models

General Terms: Algorithms, Performance

Keywords: Face, retrieval, Sparse coding, Semi-supervised, Identity

1. INTRODUCTION

The goal of face image retrieval is to find the ranking result from most to least similar face images in a face image database given a query face image. Such work has many applications in different areas. For instance, when it applies on personal multimedia, it can enable automatic face tagging and face image clustering; while in forensics, it can help with crime investigation.

Face retrieval task is closely related to face recognition task, a problem has been investigated for decades. Pentland and Turk introduced the concept of eigenfaces [13] which has been widely used; Ahonen et al. proposed using local texture descriptors: local binary pattern (LBP) [10] for face recognition [2]. The descriptor proposed is efficient and has good performance. The difference between face recognition and face retrieval is that face recognition task requires completely labeled data in the training set, and it uses learning based approach to find classification result while neither training set nor learning process is needed in face retrieval task, and it provides a ranking result. Although descriptors used in face recognition can be directly applied on retrieval task, it is not trivial to apply it on an indexing system due to its high dimensionality. One might consider using traditional image retrieval system such as bag-of-words (BoW) model [12] constructed by local descriptors like SIFT features [7] for this

*Area Chair: Kiyoharu Aizawa.

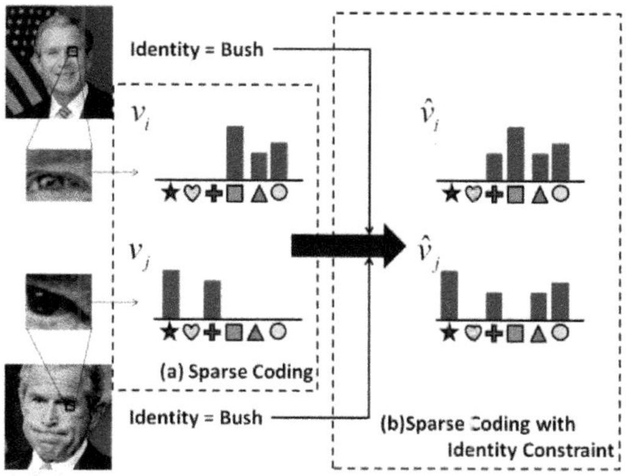

Figure 1. (a) Because face images have high intra-class variance, patches from two bush images are quantized into different sparse representations (v_i, v_j). (b) Augment face sparse coding with identity constraint. Even though the original sparse representations are different, the proposed coding scheme will propagate identity-related visual words between images of the same identity and construct more semantic sparse representations ($\hat{v}_i, \hat{v}_j$). In this example, number of overlapped visual words increase from zero to three.

problem. But when applying these methods on face images the performance is unsatisfactory. It is because face images have higher intra-class variance and these methods neglect the important spatial information in face images.

Wu et al. proposed a face image retrieval framework using identity based quantization and multi-reference re-ranking [16] to solve this problem. Motivated by their work, we propose a framework using more general coding scheme with the help of partial identity information to form a semi-supervised face image retrieval system. Similar idea was discussed in [15] for semantic hashing. It is easy to see the work has its necessity because in most of application for face retrieval, we might have some side information about our database images, including identity information, gender information, social network, etc. It is important if we can properly use such (noisy and partially available) information in the retrieval system to improve the results. To the best of our knowledge, little work aims to deal with this problem.

Recently, sparse coding has shown promising results on many different applications such as image denoising and classification. Raina et al. proposed a machine learning framework using unlabeled data to learn basis of sparse coding for classification task [11]. Yang et al. [17] further improved it by applying on SIFT descriptors along with spatial pyramid matching [6]. Gao et al. proposed a variant of sparse coding called laplacian sparse coding [4] by adding a locality constraint in the objective function. All of them show that sparse representations are well adapted to natural signals. Taking advantage of sparse coding, we introduce a face retrieval system using inverted index built from sparse representation of face images.

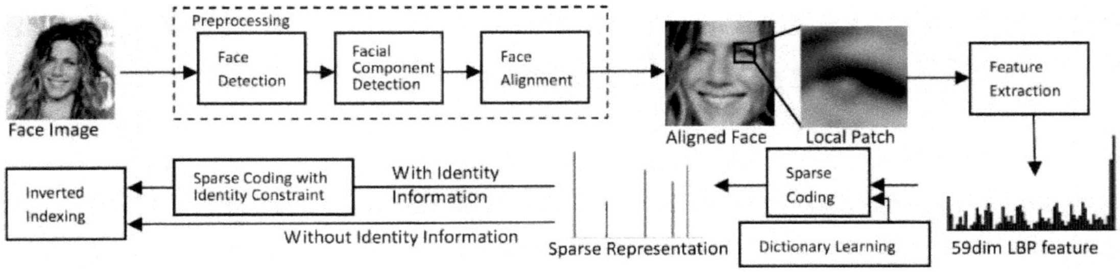

Figure 2. The proposed system framework. 59 dimension uniform local binary pattern feature descriptors are extracted from 175 grids in an aligned face image. These features then are quantized into visual words using sparse coding. Images with identity information are further refined via the proposed method. Finally, inverted index is built using the final sparse representation.

Although using sparse coding combined with inverted indexing results in an efficient retrieval framework, it does not take advantage of using identity information. To address this point, we propose a novel coding scheme to refine the result of sparse coding based on identity information. One might think our method is similar to [4], but they are essentially different. Firstly, no template features and large laplacian matrix is needed in our method. Secondly, since we quantize each person separately, we can scale up to as many people as we want. Last but not least, we integrate (partially available) identity information to automatically derive semantic-related visual words.

Figure 1 illustrates the proposed method. Using sparse coding with identity constraint, a query will be able to retrieve most images with the same identity as long as it is similar to one of them. To sum up, our contributions include identifying the problem of semi-supervised face image retrieval, introducing a general coding scheme for face retrieval problem, and further improving the performance by using identity information in the coding scheme. Extensive experiments show that the proposed method significantly outperforms linear search methods (cf. Table 1).

2. SYSTEM FRAMEWORK

For every face image in database, we first employ a frontal face cascade detector [14] to find the location of the face, and then active shape model [9] is applied to locating five facial components, including two eyes, two mouth corners and nose tip. The face image is then aligned using the locations of the eyes. After alignment, we define 5x7 grids around each facial component to get a total of 175 grids using the same procedure in [16]. From each grid, we extract a 59 dimension uniform LBP feature descriptor. All 175 descriptors then are first quantized into visual words separately by using sparse coding (Nonzero entries in the sparse representation are considered as visual words). Images with identity information are further refined using coding scheme described in section 3 to embed the information. Inverted index is built using the final sparse representation. Note that each descriptor from different grid locations will be quantized separately, hence two visual words will match only if it is extracted from the same grid location. Through this way, we can encode important geometric information of face into visual words.

Given a query image, we apply the same detection, alignment, and feature extraction methods described above. The extracted features are then quantized into visual words by sparse coding and used for retrieving inverted index. In the retrieval stage, we simply use histogram intersection to compute similarity score. The system overview is shown in Figure 2.

3. SPARSE CODING WITH IDENTITY CONSTRIANT

3.1 Sparse Coding (SC)

Traditional BoW model use k-means clustering algorithm to learn dictionary for quantization. The algorithm solves the following optimization problem:

$$\min_{D,V} \sum_{i=1}^{n} \|x_i - Dv_i\|^2 \quad (1)$$

$$\text{subject to } Card(v_i) = 1, \|v_i\|_1 = 1, v_i \succcurlyeq 0, \forall i$$

where $D = [d_1, \ldots, d_k]$ is a dictionary matrix with the size of $59\times K$, each column represents a centroid (totally K); $V = [v_1, \ldots, v_n]$ is the centroid indicator matrix, each v_i indicates that the original feature x_i belongs to a centroid in D. The constraint $Card(v_i) = 1$ means each feature can only be assigned to one centroid. This constraint is considered to be too strict because some features might be at boundary of two or more centroids, therefore many people suggest relaxing the constraint and putting L1 regularization term on v_i instead. This then turn into another optimization problem known as sparse coding:

$$\min_{D,V} \sum_{i=1}^{n} \|x_i - Dv_i\|^2 + \lambda \|v_i\|_1 \quad (2)$$

$$\text{subject to } \|v_i\| \leq 1, \forall i$$

This optimization problem can be efficiently solved by an online optimization algorithm [8]. We adopt this method to learn dictionary D for later use. Because we quantize feature descriptors from each grid separately, we have to learn different dictionary from them. Consequently, there are total 175 dictionaries learned.

Once the dictionary is learned, we can fix D in the above formulation and minimize the objective function along with v_i separately to find the sparse representation of each feature. When D is fixed, the optimization problem turns into a least square problem with L1 regularization. Since the L1 regularization term makes the objective function non-differentiable when v_i contains zero elements, we cannot solve it by standard unconstraint optimization method. This challenge has led to many literatures using different approaches to solve this problem. Here we use LARS algorithm [3] to solve this problem. Because of the L1 regularization term, each sparse representation v_i will only contain several nonzero elements out of K dimension. These nonzero entries are then considered as the visual words from the descriptor x_i. Since there are 175 grid locations, total dictionary size is $175\times K$.

3.2 Sparse Representation Refinement using Identity Constraint (SC+I)

Sparse representations computed from section 3.1 are ready for inverted indexing, but it does not embed the identity information. Hence, the retrieval results suffer from low recall rate due to high intra-class variance. Therefore, we introduce a method to reduce the intra-class variance by using identity information. Intuitively, the sparse representation extracted from the images of the same identity should be alike. To achieve this, we propose to add an identity constraint into the original sparse coding problem to refine each sparse representation v_i separately:

$$\min_{\hat{v}_i} \beta\|x_i - D\hat{v}_i\|^2 + (1-\beta)\|V^P - \hat{v}_i 1^T\|_F^2 + \gamma\|\hat{v}_i\|_1 \quad (3)$$

where $V^p = [v_{p1},\ldots,v_{pm}]$ are m sparse representations computed from section 3.1 which share the same identity with v_i, β is a parameter for adjusting weight between identity information and visual feature, and γ is another parameter for adjusting the sparsity of the result. Since there are two different parameters and each term in the objective function is in different scales, it is hard to set the parameters. Hence we propose a simply way to normalize the objective, the results are as follow:

$$\min_{\hat{v}_i} \beta\frac{\|x_i - D\hat{v}_i\|^2}{\|x_i\|^2} + (1-\beta)\frac{\|V^P - \hat{v}_i 1^T\|_F^2}{m\|v_i\|^2} + \gamma\frac{\|\hat{v}_i\|_1}{\|v_i\|_1} \quad (4)$$

Although the objective function is non-differentiable, the objective function without L1 regularization term is twice differentiable and convex. Therefore we can still solve this problem by using generalized algorithms for L1 constraint optimization problem. Specifically, we use a projected scaled sub-gradient algorithm [1] proposed by Schmidt.

After refinement, sparse representations from the same identity will propagate visual words to each other, and query will be able to retrieve most images from the same identity as long as it is similar to at least one of them (cf. Figure 1 (b)).

4. EXPERIMENTS

4.1 Experimental Setting

4.1.1 Data Set

We use all the images from LFW dataset [5] for our experiments. There are total 13,233 face images among 5,749 people in this dataset, while 1,680 people with two or more images and 12 people with 50 or more images. We take ten images each from these 12 people, total 120 images, as our query set. Figure 3 shows some example images from the dataset. Throughout the experiments we use mean average precision (MAP) and precision at one (p@1) as our performance measurement.

4.1.2 Face Retrieval Baselines

We use two kinds of face descriptors with linear search as baselines to compare with our system[1]. The first one is based on the face recognition descriptor proposed in [2]. We divided the face into 7 by 7 fixed grids, extract 59 dimension uniform LBP

[1] We also implemented the method in [16] and found that the performance relative to linear search system is the same but MAP of our linear search system is lower than the number they reported. The possible reason might be that we use different descriptors and query set.

Figure 3. Example images from LFW dataset. Images in the same column are of the same person.

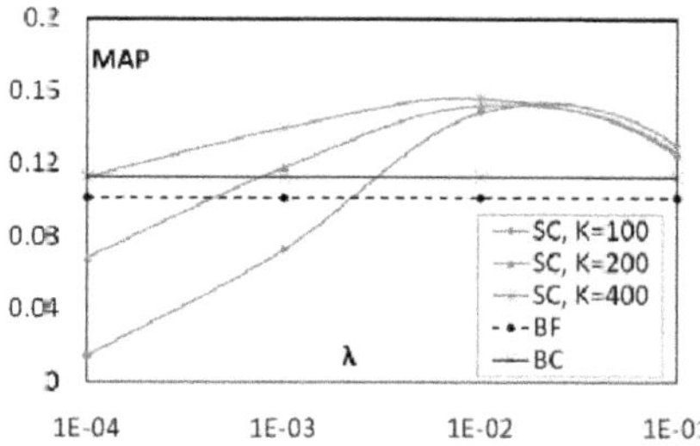

Figure 4. Comparison between sparse coding with linear search baselines. Sparse coding outperforms baselines in different dictionary size *K*, this is because the baselines suffer from curse of dimensionality.

from each grid, and then concatenate the features from each grid to form a global descriptor with 2,891 dimension, we call it baseline – fixed grids (BF) in the following experiments. The second one is the simple concatenation of local descriptors extracted in our proposed method, it has 175 grids with 59 dimension feature, total 10,325 dimension, and we call it baseline – component based (BC) in the following experiments.

For fair comparison, in the experiments with one hundred percent identity information, after retrieving images using linear search in baselines, we perform re-ranking by using the identity information to retrieve images from top 10 ranked identities and only use these images as ranking results. (BF+R, BC+R)

4.2 Sparse Coding Retrieval Performance

In sparse coding, we need to decide the size of dictionary K and sparsity parameter λ. In our experiments, we have tried different dictionary size from 100 to 400 with λ range from 10^{-4} to 10^{-1}. Results are shown in Figure 4. We find out that if λ is properly set (around 10^{-1} to 10^{-2}) the performance affects little by the size K. When λ is big (around 10^{0}), it penalizes the nonzero entry so much that all the entries in sparse representation become zero, therefore, the MAP drops to zero. When λ is small (around 10^{-4}), the performance drops faster with smaller dictionary size, this is because the sparse representation are so dense that each visual word lost its discriminative power.

When λ is chosen properly, the performance of sparse coding exceeds baselines because the baselines with high dimensional features suffer from the curse of dimensionality. Note that in Figure 4 the component based baseline (BC) outperforms the fixed grids baseline (BF) , this is because that grids from component based baseline have many overlaps in the central face area where contains more information, this overlapping acts like the weight in the fixed grid method, and proper weight increasing the performance agrees with the finding in [2]. In the following experiments, we use K=100, λ=0.1 as our default parameters.

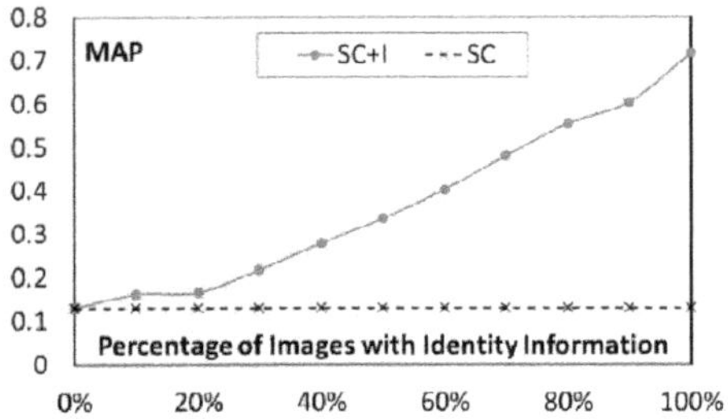

Figure 5. Performance of sparse coding with identity information under different percentages of images with identity information. It shows that our method can effectively leverage (partial) identity information.

4.3 Sparse Coding with Identity Constraint Retrieval Performance

In sparse coding with identity constraint, we need to decide β, the weight between visual features and identity information, and sparsity parameter γ. In our experiments, we have tried different β range from 0.1~0.9 with γ range from 0.1~0.5 and find out it performs best when β is 0.1 and γ is 0.15 in the case of one hundred percent images with identity information. The best β is small indicating that we weight toward the identity information. This is probably because the identity information used in our experiments is reliable. The results are shown in Table 1. We can see that sparse coding with identity constraint achieve 70% relative improvement in MAP over the baselines using the same feature descriptors (BC+R). It suggests that our method effectively utilizes the identity information for the retrieval task while maintaining an efficient and scalable index structure.

In the case of partial information, the performance decreases when the information is less, but as long as there is some identity information, using sparse coding with identity constraint always outperforms using sparse coding only. Figure 5 shows the performance of sparse coding with identity constraint under different percentage of identity information compares with sparse coding without identity constraint. Note that the query images do not carry any identity information.

Intuitively, adding the identity constraint will increase the number of visual words in sparse representation and increase the retrieval time. Figure 6 shows the relationship between average number of visual words and performance by fixing β=0.1 and adjusting γ. We find out that under the same sparsity with sparse coding, sparse coding with identity constraint can achieve much higher performance.

Table 1 summarizes the performance of the proposed method and baselines under the best setting. Note that the performance of proposed method outperforms the linear search method in both cases while using an efficient index structure.

5. CONCLUSIONS

We propose a face retrieval method based on inverted index structure with sparse coding and achieve better performance than linear search based on well-known face recognition descriptors. We then show how to extend the proposed method into semi-supervised case. In the experiments, we show that using the identity information, we can achieve higher performance while maintain the same sparsity. In the future, we will test the scalability of our system and combine more context information into the proposed framework to further boost up the performance.

Table 1. Performance of the proposed method. Sparse coding outperforms linear search no matter with or without identity information. The left three columns are without any identity information while the right are with 100% identity information. Note that we did not compare the result that using partial information because the baselines cannot deal with partial identity labels.

Method	BF	BC	SC	BF+R	BC+R	SC+I
MAP	0.10	0.12	**0.16**	0.33	0.42	**0.72**
P@1	0.61	0.71	**0.80**	0.61	0.71	**0.86**

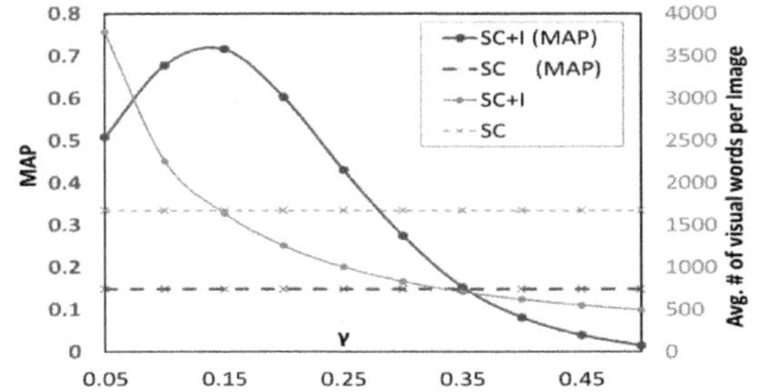

Figure 6. Relationship between sparsity and performance in sparse coding and sparse coding with identity information. Using identity constraint can achieve much higher performance while maintaining roughly the same sparsity.

6. REFERENCES

[1] http://www.cs.ubc.ca/~schmidtm/Software/L1General.html
[2] T. Ahonen, A. Hadid, and M. Pietikainen, Face recognition with local binary patterns. In ECCV, 2004.
[3] B. Efron, T. Hastie, I. Johnstone, and R. Tibshirani. Least angle regression. In ANN STAT, 2004.
[4] S. Gao, I. W.-H. Tsang, L.-T. Chia, P. Zhao. Local features are not lonely – laplacian sparse coding for image classification. In CVPR, 2010
[5] G. B. Huang, M. Mattar, T. Berg, and E. Learned-Miller. Labeled faces in the wild: A database for studying face recognition in unconstrained environments. In ECCV, 2008.
[6] S. Lazebnik, C. Schmid, and J. Ponce. Beyond bags of features: Spatial pyramid matching for recognizing natural scene categories. In CVPR, 2006.
[7] D. Lowe. Distinctive image features from scale-invariant keypoints. In IJCV, 2003.
[8] J. Mairal, F. Bach, J. Ponce, and G. Sapiro. Online dictionary learning for sparse coding. In ICML, 2009.
[9] S. Milborrow and F. Nicolls. Locating Facial Features with an Extended Active Shape Model. In ECCV, 2008.
[10] T. Ojala, M. Pietikainen, and T. Maenpaa. Multiresolution gray-scale and rotation invariant texture classification with local binary patterns. In IEEE T PATTERN ANAL, 2002.
[11] R. Raina, A. Battle, H. Lee, B. Packer, and A. Y. Ng. Self-taught learning: Transfer learning from unlabeled data. In ICML, 2007.
[12] J. Sivic and A. Zisserman. Video Google: A text retrieval approach to object matching in videos. In ICCV, 2003.
[13] M. Turk and A. Pentland. Eigenfaces for recognition. In J COGNITIVE NEUROSCI, 1991.
[14] P. Viola and M. Jones. Rapid object detection using a boosted cascade of simple features. In CVPR, 2001.
[15] J. Wang, S. Kumar, and S.-F. Chang. Semi-supervised hashing for scalable image retrieval. In CVPR, 2010.
[16] Z. Wu, Q. Ke, J. Sun and H.-Y. Shum. Scalable Face Image Retrieval with Identity-Based Quantization and Multi-Reference Re-ranking. In CVPR, 2010.
[17] J. Yang, K. Yu, Y. Gong, and T. Huang. Linear spatial pyra-mid matching using sparse coding for image classification. In CVPR, 2009.

Level Influence of Spatial Pyramid Matching in Object Classification*

Hong Lu†, Renzhong Wei, Yanran Shen, Xiangyang Xue
Shanghai Key Lab of Intel. Info. Processing
School of Computer Science
Fudan University, Shanghai, China
{honglu, 09210240083, yanran, xyxue}@fudan.edu.cn

ABSTRACT

In this paper we propose to effectively consider the shape and size variations for object classification. Specifically, a novel image matching method is proposed to incorporate the image segmentation with Spatial Pyramid Matching (SPM), and test our method on flower classification. A Level Influence Factor (LIF) is introduced to represent weights of different pyramid levels based on the statistical information of each segmented image. Then the images are classified based on the LIF weighted spatial pyramid bag-of-visual-words feature, and some levels with weight values zeros are not needed to be compared further. Also, in SPM matching stage, the block in one image is compared with not only its corresponding block in another image, but also the spatially neighboring blocks of the corresponding blocks to find the best match. This fuzzy matching method can incorporate some translation of objects. Experiments are performed on a flower dataset containing 1360 images from 17 different categories. And experimental results demonstrate that our proposed method has better time efficiency than traditional SPM and outperforms the state-of-art flower classification methods.

Categories and Subject Descriptors

I.4.7 [**Image Processing and Computer Vision**]: Feature Measurement—*feature representation*; H.3.1 [**Information Storage and Retrieval**]: Content Analysis and Indexing—*indexing method*

General Terms

Algorithms, Experimentation, Performance

Keywords

Level influence, spatial pyramid, adaptive matching, flower classification

†Corresponding author: honglu@fudan.edu.cn
*Area chair: Tat-Seng Chua

MM'11, November 28–December 1, 2011, Scottsdale, Arizona, USA.

1. INTRODUCTION

How to effectively incorporate shape and scale diversities with visual feature extraction and matching is important for object classification. Take flowers as example, different sizes of calyx, petal and pistil make different appearances. Even for the same kind of flower, different viewpoints and view distances also greatly influence the appearance. For flower classification, usually color, shape, texture [1] are computed on global image, then various machine learning methods are used for classification based on these features. Previous study shows that local features like Scale Invariant Feature Transform (SIFT) [8] has good performance on flower classification [9]. Specifically, SIFT features are quantized under a bag-of-visual-words (BoW) [7] framework. And an image is represented by histogram of these features over the whole image. However, these words completely disregard the spatial layout information, and cannot take advantage of the regularities in image composition and the spatial arrangement.

Considering the layout or spatial information, Lazebnik *et al.* extended bag-of-features with a spatial pyramid matching (SPM) method for image matching [6]. Specifically, an image is partitioned into increasingly fine sub-regions, *e.g.* 1×1, 2×2, 4×4, etc., and concatenating histograms of local features which are computed inside each sub-region as the feature of the image. Images are matched by matching features of the corresponding blocks at the same level. Then the level matching results are weighted and fused together. Chum *et al.* [11] also consider the scales of local features in SPM, and compute small and large scale feature histograms separately. However, the weights in SPM for different levels are chosen empirically, ignoring the characteristic of each image. Due to size and scale differences of objects, the importance of each level to each image should be different in SPM. In this paper, we propose a method to measure the pyramid level influence to the understanding of the whole image.

For flower classification, several methods were proposed in previous works [9, 10]. One of the state-of-art methods was proposed by Nilsback *et al.* in [10]. Specifically, pistils and petals of flowers are first detected to cooperate with flower segmentation. Then foreground flowers are segmented out from backgrounds and the background parts are dropped in feature generating and learning step. Nilsback *et al.* [10] followed this work, and tried more local features in the BoW framework. Both of their works show that, segmentation is an effective pre-step before flower classification. Uijlings *et al.* [12] proved that background information is also helpful in object classification. And for most flowers, backgrounds usually appear to be leafs and solid ground. Flowers differ from each other not only in petals and pistil, but also in leaf shape, leaf size, solid ground, etc. So segmenting background is also helpful for recognizing different flowers.

In this paper, we propose to combine image segmentation with BoW model, and improve SPM by incorporating our proposed level influence factor (LIF) for image matching and classification. The paper is organized as follows. Section 2 gives the idea of LIF from biological view and uses it for image representation. Section 3 introduces an adaptive matching method in SPM. Section 4 gives both LIF statistical data and classification performance of our proposed method. And we conclude our work in Section 5.

2. LEVEL INFLUENCE FACTOR

Before the computation of level influence of different levels, we first segment an image into regions with different sizes. Specifically, mean shift is proposed for density estimation and clustering in [5, 15]. And it is used for image segmentation in [4]. Experiments demonstrate that mean shift is both effective and efficient. Thus we adopt mean shift for image segmentation.

Our proposed Level Influence Factor (LIF) is a statistical index describing the influences of different spatial levels for an image. We compute the LIF based on a segmentation prestep that segment an object and its background into several parts with various sizes. If an image contains many small flowers, small segmented regions should be more helpful than big regions for flower classification. On the other hand, if a flower appears to be a large part, large segmented regions should be more helpful. Thus LIF is proposed to describe the importance of different scale levels for different kinds of flowers.

To define LIF, we adopt a Clark Evans (CE) index [3], which is commonly used in biological research. CE was first proposed to describe population distribution of a species in a given area, and it is an effective method in ecology statistics [3, 14]. CE is defined in Equ. (1) as below.

$$\begin{aligned} CE &= r_A/r_E \\ &= \frac{\frac{1}{N}\sum_{i=1}^{N} r_i}{0.5\sqrt{\frac{A}{N}}+0.204\frac{P}{N}+0.041\frac{P}{N^{\frac{3}{2}}}} \end{aligned} \quad (1)$$

In r_A, N is the number of individuals for this species in the area, r_i the distance from the i_{th} individual to its nearest neighbor. And the denominator r_E is the average nearest neighbor distance theoretically following Poisson distribution, where A the size of the area, P the perimeter of the area. For Equ. (1), a ratio value $CE > 1$ suggests ordering, while $CE < 1$ suggests clustering, and $CE = 1$ suggests random distribution.

For flower segmentation, different kinds of flowers are segmented into different sizes of segments due to the diversity of shape and scale. We propose a method to weight the segments from an ecological view on region size. As the species concept in ecology, we group the segments with similar size together to be a species. All segments in an image can be assigned to several groups. At the same time we partition the images into regular grids, and intersection points between grid lines are considered to be individuals. We define a level influence factor(LIF) similarly to CE to represent the

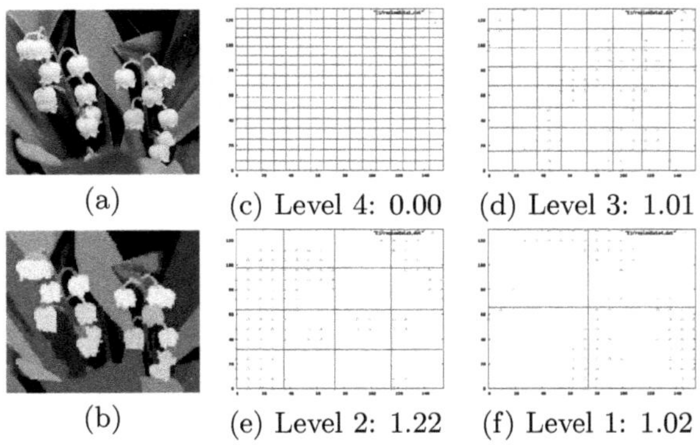

Figure 1: An example of Clark Evans index for a typical segmented image; Left column: (a) is the original image, (b) is segmented image; Middle and right column: points belonging to different levels and CEs of these levels

influence of different kinds of groups for the understanding of the whole image.

We give a group label i to each segment according to the size of the segment, as introduced below.

$$\frac{S}{2^{2N-2i+2}} < s < \frac{S}{2^{2N-2(i+1)+2}} \quad (2)$$

where S is the size of the whole image, s the size of current segment, N the number of the levels.

As shown in Figure 1, image in (a) is segmented into different sizes of segments as shown in (b). The individuals, i.e. the intersections points of the partitioned regular grids are assigned into one of the segments according to their location. And the segments are grouped into 4 levels. (c), (d), (e), (f) show the points that belonging to different scale levels. LIF index on each level i is then computed based on segments and grid points as below.

$$LIF(i) = \frac{\frac{1}{N_i}\sum_{j=1}^{N_i} r_j}{0.5\sqrt{\frac{A_i}{N_i}} + 0.204\frac{P_i}{N_i} + 0.041\frac{P_i}{N_i^{\frac{3}{2}}}} \quad (3)$$

Similar to the CE index, N_i is the number of points for level i, A_i the area of all segments which belong to level i, P_i the sum of lengths of edges surrounding the segments which belong to level i, r_j the distance from the j_{th} individual to its nearest neighbor.

We compute LIF for each level of the image to represent the importance of this level to the whole image. We will later use LIF to replace the weight in traditional SPM for image matching and classification.

3. IMAGE MATCHING METHOD

3.1 Spatial Pyramid Matching with LIF

In image retrieval or classification, SPM is proposed to incorporate spatial information for image representation and matching [6]. An image is partitioned into several levels with increasingly finer grids, e.g. 1×1, 2×2, 4×4, etc. blocks. Image matching is performed by matching visual feature of blocks at different levels and fuse the results together.

SPM works by penalizing matches found in larger cells. Specifically, it assigns the weight $w(i) = \frac{1}{2^{L-i}}$ for level i

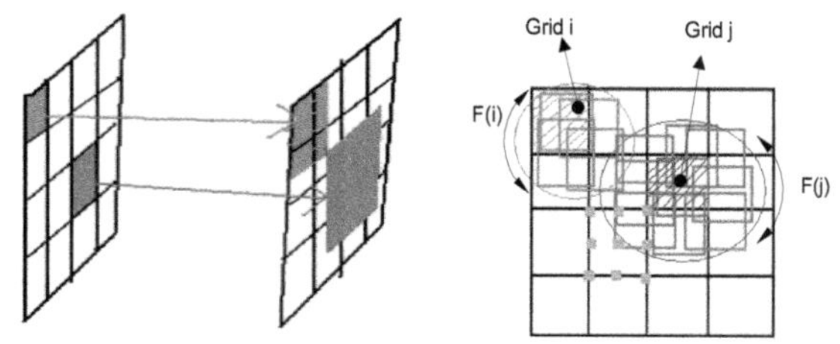

(a) (b)

Figure 2: Adaptive spatial pyramid matching method.

$(i = 0, 1, 2, \cdots, L-1)$, and L represents the total number of levels. The distance measure D_L below is used for matching two images X and Y.

$$D_L(X,Y) = \sum_{i=1}^{L} w(i) \sum_{j=1}^{N_i} d\left(V_j^i(X), V_j^i(Y)\right) \quad (4)$$

where N_i is the block number on the i_{th} level, V_j^i the visual feature of block j on level i.

And our proposed LIF indicates the importance of different levels to the whole image. We use $LIF(i)$ to replace the weights $w(i)$ of different levels in image matching.

3.2 Adaptive Block Matching in SPM

The second innovation of our paper is to propose a new searching method between block pairs. Traditional SPM method directly matches a block with its corresponding one in the target image. The sum of the block distances at all levels is regarded as the distance of two images. Considering the object translation, blocks from the source image do not match blocks with the same location of the target image. Usually, the most possible matching pair is the blocks around the corresponding block.

We propose an adaptive matching method under the framework of SPM. As illustrated in Figure 2, for red block on (a), we search over the red area for all the possible locations on the target area. The possible blocks are chosen by moving a sliding window around the corresponding block, as shown in Figure 2 (b) and the location with the minimum distance is selected as the most matched block. Figure 2 (b) shows the searching areas for image grids i and j as shown in Figure 2 (a). The adaptive search method improves the classification performance with some tolerance to translation.

The new distance for a block a with the block in target image is described as below.

$$d(V(a), V(b)) = \min_{j \in F(b)} d(V(a), V(j)) \quad (5)$$

where $F(b)$ is all the possible searching blocks in the target image around b, and b is the corresponding block of source block a in the target image. Suppose a block with size $m \times n$ in the source image, where m is the width and n the height, the location of the block is defined by the top left and bottom right points (x_0, y_0, x_1, y_1). In our proposed method, 8 extra blocks need to be compared with the source block in the target images. Specifically, blocks with the center point in $(\frac{x_0+x_1}{2} \pm a, \frac{y_0+y_1}{2} \pm b)$, where $a \in [\frac{m}{2}, -\frac{m}{2}, 0]$, $b \in [\frac{n}{2}, -\frac{n}{2}, 0]$. The minima of these distances is considered to be the final distance of the block a with that in the target image.

Figure 3: Example of LIF difference for different flowers, including both big and small species. Left column gives the flower samples and the corresponding graph is the LIF distribution over the 80 samples.

4. EXPERIMENT

We apply our proposed method on flower classification. We use the dataset introduced in [9], which composes 1360 images of 17 classes of flowers, each class includes 80 samples with various viewpoints and gestures. This dataset is challenging for two reasons. First, large number of flower species are included in this dataset. Second, for each species, the variation is challenging enough for the variations of scale, color, shape, texture, etc. The flower database is suitable for testing our proposed image matching method.

4.1 Segmentation and LIF

In our experiment, we separate the segments into 5 levels, and compute LIF by Equ. (3) for each level. We compute the LIF distribution for each level from 80 images for each class. The distribution for 4 classes are shown in Figure 3. In the figure, the left columns are the sample images. And the right columns are the corresponding LIF distributions of the classes. Specifically, the 4 classes are two with small flowers and two big ones. The results in Figure 3 validate our assumptions that different kinds of flowers have different LIF properties. Specifically, For big flowers, low levels such as level 1, level 2 give high LIF values in average. While high levels such as level 3, level 4 give low LIF values in average. In SPM, low levels represent large segments in the image. Then for images with large flowers, large segments are more useful for image matching. On the contrary, for small flowers, high levels give high LIF values in average. Then for images with small flowers, small segments are more useful for image matching.

Furthermore, we can get from first row of Fig. 3 that, LIFs of level 0 and level 4 are zeros for most flowers. Then we can omit the matching of these levels for image matching, which greatly reduces computational cost. Specifically, if we compute 5-level SPM, usually we should compare each block in each level, that means 341 times, i.e. $1+4+16+64+256$. When we use the proposed LIFs as weights, we should only compare 84 times, i.e. $4+16+64$, since LIF values for level 0 and level 4 are all zeros. Statistics show that, 72% images have LIFs near *zero*. And for level 5, about LIFs of 51% images are near *zero*. Figure 4 shows LIF value distribution for all 1360 images. For a five level SPM framework, in average, only 187 block comparisons are needed instead of 341.

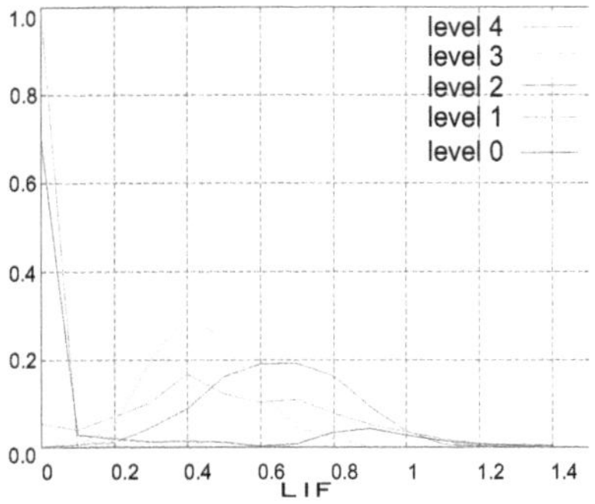

Figure 4: LIF value distribution for 1360 images. For level 0 and level 4, most LIFs are nearly *zero*.

Figure 5: Some good results for the top similar images on the rank list.

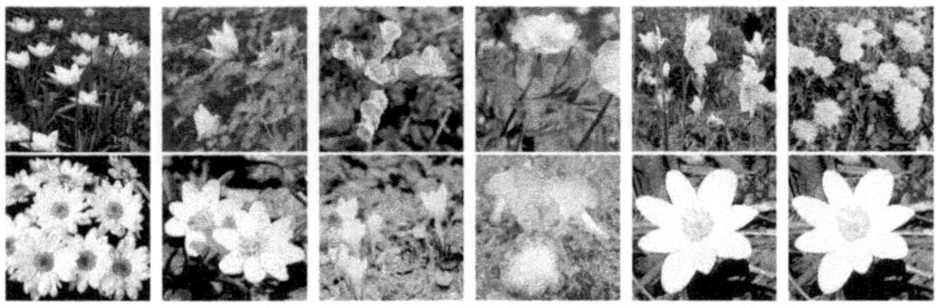

Figure 6: Some bad results for the top similar images on the rank list.

4.2 LIF-based Classification

We use 384 dimensional HSV-SIFT [2, 13] to describe visual feature of key points on dense sampled grids. A codebook with 1,000 visual words is generated from those visual features by k-means clustering. For each image, we compute LIF by Equ. (3) from a 5-level spatial pyramid representation. In classification, we compute the distance of image pair by summing $L2$ feature distances of each level, which are weighted by LIF we computed before. In our experiment, 75% of the flowers are used for training visual vocabulary, i.e. 60 images for each class. Nearest neighbor classifier is chosen for its efficacy [9].

The performance of classification algorithm is measured from the remaining 25% testing images, i.e. 20 images for each class. We use the measurement introduced in [9]: given a testing image I_i^{test}, the classifier returns a ranked list of training images I_j^{train}, $j = 1..M$, with $j = 1$ being the highest ranked, M is size of training set. If the highest ranked correct classification is at $j = p$ in the list, then the performance score W_i for I_i^{test} is:

$$\begin{cases} 100 - 20 \times \frac{p-1}{S-1}, & if \;\; p \leq S \\ 0, & otherwise \end{cases}$$

Since we only care about a short list of correct matches, we define S to be the length of the short list, i.e. $S = 5$. Over all performance on the testing set is $\frac{1}{N}\sum_{i=1}^{N} W_i$, which represents the average score for all the N testing images.

We get a 83.2% average precision over 340 testing images. Compared with performance reported in [9] 81.3% by combining color and shape feature, our method can obtain 1.9% improved performance while greatly reduce the time cost.

Figure 5 and Figure 6 give some good and bad results for some testing samples. In the figure, the first column is the testing sample. And the rest are ranked by the $L2$ distance with the testing sample. Our proposed method gives a good performance on most of the testing samples, especially for big flowers, as showed in Figure 5. For these flowers, LIFs of low levels usually appear to be a large value, that of high levels appear to be near *zero*, which means low levels on SPM representation are more important.

5. CONCLUSION

In this paper, we have introduced LIF to represent the importance of different levels to the whole image, which is different from other SPM framework with a fixed weight for each level. Experiments demonstrate that, flowers with different scales and shapes have different LIFs. Furthermore, we also introduced an adaptive matching method for block matching. Our proposed method is shown to possess better time efficiency than traditional SPM and outperform the state-of-art flower classification methods.

Acknowledgment

This work was supported in part by 973 Program (Project No. 2010CB327900), Natural Science Foundation of China (No. 60875003 and 60873178), Shanghai Committee of Science and Technology (No. 11ZR1403400), and 211-Project Sponsorship for Young Professors.

6. REFERENCES

[1] Text of ISO/IEC 15938-3/FCD Information Technology - Multimedia Content Description Interface - Part 3 Visual. *Internation Organization for Standardization*, ISO/IEC JTC1/SC29/WG11/N4062, March 2001.

[2] A. Bosch, A. Zisserman, and X. Munoz. Scene classification using a hybrid generative/discriminative approach. *IEEE Trans. PAMI*, 30(4):712–727, 2008.

[3] P. J. Clark and F. C. Evans. Distance to Nearest Neighbor as a Measure of Spatial Relationships in Populations. *Ecology*, 35(4):445–453, Oct. 1954.

[4] D. Comaniciu and P. Meer. Mean shift: A robust approach toward feature space analysis. *IEEE Trans. PAMI*, 24(5):603–619, 2002.

[5] K. Fukunaga and L. Hostetler. The estimation of the gradient of a density function, with applications in pattern recognition. *IEEE Transactions on Information Theory*, 21(1):32–40, 1975.

[6] S. Lazebnik, C. Schmid, and J. Ponce. Beyond bags of features: Spatial pyramid matching for recognizing natural scene categories. In *CVPR*, volume 2, pages 2169–2178, 2006.

[7] F.-F. Li and P. Perona. A bayesian hierarchical model for learning natural scene categories. In *CVPR*, pages 524–531, 2005.

[8] D. G. Lowe. Distinctive image features from scale-invariant keypoints. *IJCV*, 60(2):91–110, 2004.

[9] M.-E. Nilsback and A. Zisserman. A visual vocabulary for flower classification. In *CVPR*, 2006.

[10] M.-E. Nilsback and A. Zisserman. Delving into the whorl of flower segmentation. In *BMVC*, volume 1, pages 570–579, 2007.

[11] O.Chum and A. Zisserman. An examplar model for learning object classes. In *CVPR*, 2007.

[12] J. Uijlings, A. Smeulders, and R. Scha. Real-time bag of words, approximately. In *Proc. ACM Int'l Conf. on Image and Video Retrieval*, 2009.

[13] K. van de Sande, T. Gevers, and C. Snoek. Evaluation of color descriptors for object and scene recognition. In *CVPR*, pages 1–8, 2008.

[14] B. Wang and S. Yu. Multi-scale analysis of population distribution patterns. *Journal of Plant Ecology*, 29(2), 2005.

[15] C. Yizhong. Mean shift, mode seeking, and clustering. *IEEE Trans. PAMI*, 17(8):790–799, 1995.

Ensemble Approach Based on Conditional Random Field for Multi-Label Image and Video Annotation*

Xin-Shun Xu[1,2]
xuxinshun@sdu.edu.cn

Yuan Jiang[2]
jiangy@lamda.nju.edu.cn

Liang Peng[1]
pengliang.sdu@gmail.com

Xiangyang Xue[3]
xyxue@fudan.edu.cn

Zhi-Hua Zhou[2]
zhouzh@lamda.nju.edu.cn

[1]School of Computer Science and Technology, Shandong University, Jinan 250101, China
[2]National Key Laboratory for Novel Software Technology, Nanjing University, Nanjing 210093, China
[3]School of Computer Science, Fudan University, Shanghai 200433, China

ABSTRACT

Multi-label image/video annotation is a challenging task that allows to correlate more than one high-level semantic keyword with an image/video-clip. Previously, a single model is usually used for the annotation task, with relatively large variance in performance. The correlation among the annotation keywords should also be considered. In this paper, to reduce the performance variance and exploit the correlation between keywords, we propose the En-CRF (Ensemble based on Conditional Random Field) method. In this method, multiple models are first trained for each keyword, then the predictions of these models and the correlations between keywords are incorporated into a conditional random field. Experimental results on benchmark data set, including Corel5k and TRECVID 2005, show that the En-CRF method is superior or highly competitive to several state-of-the-art methods.

Categories and Subject Descriptors

I.2.10 [**Artificial Intelligence**]: Vision and Scene Understanding—*video analysis*; I.2.6 [**Artificial Intelligence**]: Learning

General Terms

Algorithms, Design, Experimentation

Keywords

Image Annotation, Video Annotation, Conditional Random Field, Multi-Label Learning, Ensemble Methods

1. INTRODUCTION

With the fast accumulation of image and video data, how to effectively access large-scale multimedia database, such as indexing, browsing and retrieval, has become a challenging task. As most users prefer textual queries, a common theme is to first annotate these images/videos with keywords which describe the content in the images, and then use these keywords for indexing or browsing. Manual annotation is labor-intensive and time-consuming. Thus, automatic image/video annotation has emerged as an important topic, and become an active research topic in recent years. This paper focuses on multi-label image/video annotation task in which an image/video-clip is associated with more than one keyword simultaneously. The learning framework to tackle such scenario is called multi-label learning in machine learning community which has attracted more and more attentions during the past few years [21, 30, 31, 23].

Many techniques have been developed for the image/video annotation task. For image annotation, Jeon et al. [8] proposed the cross-media relevance model (CMRM) which tries to estimate the joint probability of the visual keywords and the annotation keywords on the training data set. This relevance model was further improved through continuous-space relevance model (CRM) [11], multiple Bernoulli relevance model (MBRM) [4], and dual cross-media relevance model [13]. Carneiro et al. [3] proposed a probabilistic approach for this task. Guillaumin et al. [7] proposed a discriminatively trained nearest neighbor model in which tags of test images are predicted using a weighted nearest-neighbor model to exploit labeled training images. In [32], Zhang et al. introduced a regularization based feature selection algorithm to leverage both the sparsity and clustering properties of features, and incorporated it into the image annotation task.

To consider multiple labels, a common approach is to learn a separate classifier for each keyword on training data, and use them to predict whether a new image belongs to some classes. In this paradigm, SVM based methods have been shown effective [1, 26]. Gao et al. proposed a hierarchical boosting algorithm by incorporating feature hierarchy and boosting to scale up SVM image classifier. Yanagawa et al. [25] built a set of baseline detectors for 374 LSCOM concepts by using SVM. Those methods also treat the concepts independently. In most image/video annotation tasks, there are significant correlations in keywords. To exploit the correlation, and improve the performance of the binary concept classifiers, some methods try to construct models with a context-based concept fusion strategy [9, 14, 18, 22, 28]. Qi et al. [20] simultaneously modeled both the individuals as well as their correlations with a unified formulation. Recently, a new machine learning framework named MIML (Multi-Instance Multi-Label learning) was proposed [34], which represented each object as multiple

*Area Chair: Kiyoharu Aizawa. This research was supported by NSFC (60975043,61173068), CPSF (20100470063), Jiangsu PPPRF (1001001B), IIFSDU (2009TS033), and NSF of Shandong Province (Q2008G06).

instances and allowed the object to have multiple labels simultaneously. This framework was soon applied to and found well useful in image annotation [27].

Ensemble methods are a kind of powerful learning paradigm which is able to achieve strong generalization ability by using multiple learners [33]. Usually, ensemble methods combine the individual learners by voting, averaging, or their variants. In this paper, we propose the En-CRF method, which combines multiple models, as potential functions, with a conditional random field [10]. In addition to the profit from combining multiple models, the En-CRF method also takes benefit from using CRF to exploit the correlations between the keywords.

The rest of this paper is organized as follows: In section 2, we introduce the En-CRF method, including the training and testing processes. In section 3, we report on the experimental results on benchmark data set Corel5k and TRECVID 2005. Finally, we conclude this paper in section 4.

2. THE EN-CRF METHOD

2.1 The Framework

Given a feature vector X, let $Y \in \mathcal{Y}$ denote the label vector with length m, and y_i is the ith element of Y, taking the value in {-1, +1} with +1 denotes that the corresponding label is a proper one for X, while -1 denotes that the corresponding label is irrelevant to X. For each keyword, we construct r classifiers. These classifiers can be different models, e.g., SVM with different kernels, neural networks with different number of hidden units, etc. The posterior probability for label Y is of the following form:

$$p(Y|X) = \frac{1}{Z(X)} \exp\left(-E(Y|X)\right) \quad (1)$$

where $E(Y|X)$ is the energy function defined as:

$$E(Y|X) = \sum_{i}^{r}\sum_{j}^{m} w_{ij} f_{ij}(X, y_j) + \sum_{i}^{m}\sum_{j}^{m}\sum_{k=0}^{3} w_{ijk}\delta(y_i, y_j, k) f'_{ij}(y_i, y_j) \quad (2)$$

where $f_{ij}(X, y_j)$ is defined to measure how likely the result of the ith classifier for the jth label is positive. For instance, as used in this paper, its value can be the signed distance to the hyperplane when SVM is used as the classifier. $f'_{ij}(y_i, y_j)$ measures the correlation between the ith and jth keywords, $k \in \{0, 1, 2, 3\}$ corresponds to four combinatorial states of two labels, e.g., 0 corresponding to the state that both labels are negative, and $\delta(y_i, y_j, k)$ is defined as:

$$\delta(y_i, y_j, k) = \begin{cases} 1 & y_i = -1 \text{ and } y_j = -1 \text{ and } k = 0 \\ 1 & y_i = -1 \text{ and } y_j = +1 \text{ and } k = 1 \\ 1 & y_i = +1 \text{ and } y_j = -1 \text{ and } k = 2 \\ 1 & y_i = +1 \text{ and } y_j = +1 \text{ and } k = 3 \\ 0 & \text{otherwise} \end{cases} \quad (3)$$

Similarly, $Z(X)$, the partition function, is defined by:

$$Z(x) = \sum_{Y \in \mathcal{Y}} \exp\left(-E(X|Y)\right) \quad (4)$$

2.2 Training Process

The training process of En-CRF consists of two steps: (1) setting up $f_{ij}(X, y_j)$ and $f'_{ij}(y_i, y_j)$; (2) learning the parameters w.

As mentioned above, $f_{ij}(X, y_i)$ is defined to measure how likely the result of the ith classifier for the jth label is positive. For this, we first train r SVM's with different kernels for each class, and therefore get r hyperplanes for each class. Then, $f_{ij}(X, y_j)$ takes the value of the signed distance of X to the ith hyperplane. $f'_{ij}(y_i, y_j)$ measures the correlation of the ith and jth keywords, and it can be realized by the co-occurrence of the ith and jth keywords. Notice that some keyword pairs may have rather weak interactions. That is, the presence/absence of one keyword would not affect the presence/absence of another keyword. Thus, it is not necessary to involve all classes during training process. Here, we adopt the normalized mutual information [20] to determine which label pairs should be selected. For keywords p and q, the normalized mutual information is defined as

$$NormMI(p, q) = \frac{MI(p, q)}{min\{H(p), H(q)\}} \quad (5)$$

where $MI(p, q)$ is the mutual information of words p and q, and $H(p)$ is the marginal entropy of word p as defined respectively,

$$MI(p, q) = \sum\nolimits_{y_p, y_q} P(y_p, y_q) log \frac{P(y_p, y_q)}{P(y_p)P(y_q)} \quad (6)$$

$$H(p) = -\sum\nolimits_{y_p \in \{0,1\}} P(y_p)P(y_q) \quad (7)$$

Based on the normalized mutual information, the pairs whose correlations are larger than a threshold are considered.

Once we get $f_{ij}(X, y_j)$ and $f'_{ij}(y_i, y_j)$, given the training set $D = \{(X^1, Y^1), (X^2, Y^2), ..., (X^n, Y^n)\}$, the penalized log likelihood of parameters w is

$$L(w|D) = \log\left(\prod_{i=1}^{n} p(Y^i|X^i)\right) - \sum_{i,j} \frac{w_{ij}^2}{2\sigma^2} - \sum_{i,j,k} \frac{w_{ijk}^2}{2\sigma^2} \quad (8)$$

where the last two terms are introduced to reduce overfitting. Given the gradient of the log likelihood at w_{ij} or w_{ijk}, optimization methods such as BFGS [2] can be used to find the optimal w.

2.3 Testing and Ranking Process

A trained En-CRF model can be easily used to annotate a new example X. There are also two steps to annotate a new example. First, we should calculate $f_{ij}(X, y_j)$, and δ used in Eq. 2 (note that f'_{ij} can be computed in advance). $f_{ij}(X, y_j)$ can be easily computed based on the hyperplane of ith classifier for the jth label. The second step is to infer a label vector Y for this X according to

$$Y = \underset{Y \in \mathcal{Y}}{argmax}\; p(Y|X). \quad (9)$$

This inference problem can be executed efficiently by some dynamic programming algorithms, e.g., the Viterbi-like algorithm used in this paper.

It would be nice if the annotated keywords can be ranked according to their relevancy to the example. This requires us to give a score to every annotated keyword. Here we can get this by computing the conditional expectation [20] of a keyword. Suppose that the predicted label vector for an image is Y, and $\wp$ is the keyword set, the conditional expectation of y_p for keyword p can be computed by

$$\mathcal{E}(y_p|X, Y_{\wp\backslash p}) = P(y_p = +1|X, Y_{\wp\backslash p}) - P(y_p = -1|X, Y_{\wp\backslash p}) \quad (10)$$

According to Eq. 1, $P(y_p|X, Y_{\wp\backslash p})$ is defined as

$$P(y_p|X, Y_{\wp\backslash p}) = \frac{1}{Z_p} \exp\left(-E(y_p \circ Y_{\wp\backslash p}|X, w)\right) \quad (11)$$

where

$$Z_p = \sum\nolimits_{y_p \in \{+1,-1\}} \exp\left(-E(y_p \circ Y_{\wp\backslash p}|X, w)\right) \quad (12)$$

and the circle operator means to concatenate two parts of labels into one.

The En-CRF method is summarized in Algorithm 1.

Algorithm 1 En-CRF

Training

1. Input: The training data set D
2. Train r SVM's for each class label, and get the hyperplanes H.
3. Compute f_{ij}, f'_{jl} and δ for all data in D
4. Get w by optimizing Eq. 8.

Testing

1. Input: a test example X
2. Compute f_{ij} according to the hyperplanes H, and δ.
3. Infer the label vector $Y = argmax_{Y \in \mathcal{Y}}\ p(Y|X)$.
4. Output: Y

3. EXPERIMENTS

3.1 Experiments on Image Data

In this section, En-CRF is tested on the Corel data set which contains 5,000 images collected from larger Corel CD set. Each image has been annotated by an average of 3–5 keywords from a dictionary of 371 keywords. The data set is further divided into two parts: training set and testing set which contains 4500 and 500 images, respectively. Finally, the dictionary contains 260 words that appear in both the training and testing set.

Similar to the routine in [24], images are first represented with pyramid structure in which the division scheme is 1×1, 2×2, 1×3. From each region, SIFT, C-SIFT, rgSIFT, and OpponentSIFT descriptors are first extracted with both Harris-Laplace point sampling and dense sampling methods. Then, k-means is used to generate a dictionary with size 2000. Finally, for each type of feature, a region is represented as a 'bag-of-words' histogram.

For each keyword, 6 SVM's with different kernels are trained on the training set. These kernels include (1)Spatial pyramid kernel with weighted χ^2 distances of multiple features [24]; (2)Spatial pyramid kernel with weighted earth mover distance (EMD) [29] of multiple features, in which EMD is used instead of χ^2 distance; (3)Pyramid match kernel [6]; (4)Multiple instance kernel [5], in which each feature is treated as an instance; (5) RBF kernel, in which all features are sequentially combined into a flat vector. (6)Polynomial kernel, in which all features are also combined into one vector as in (5). Note that the features used in (2)&(3) is a little different from those used in other kernels. For saving space, here we do not give the detail.

The results are shown in Table 1. The left part is the annotation results in which 'P' is mean precision, 'R' is mean recall and 'N+' denotes the number of keywords with non-zero recall value. The right part is the retrieval results in which the Mean Average Precision (MAP) is used to measure the performance. From Table 1, we can find that En-CRF is superior or highly competitive to state-of-the-art methods.

3.2 Experiments on Video Data

In this section, we evaluate En-CRF on the video benchmark data set TRECVID2005. In the experiments, only the development set is used which contains 80 hours international broadcast news in Arabic, English and Chinese. These news videos are first automatically segmented into 61901 subshots [19]. For each subshot, a keyframe is extracted to represent the subshot, and associated with one or more concepts of 39 concepts according to LSCOM-Lite annotations [17]. Most videos are multi-labeled, e.g., 75.7% shots/subshots have more than one concept. The feature extraction scheme and kernels are as same as those used in subsection 3.1. The performance is evaluated by Average Precision (AP) and MAP which are the official performance metrics in TRECVID evaluations. The AP corresponds to the area under a non-interpolated recall/precision curve and it favors highly ranked relevant subshots.

Table 1: Comparison of En-CRF and state-of-the-art methods on Corel5K. 'P' denotes mean precision, 'R' denotes mean recall, 'N' denotes the number of keynotes with non-zero recall, and 'MAP' means mean average precision

Annotation				Retrieval (MAP)	
Method	P	R	N+	260 words	recall≥ 0
infNet[16]	0.17	0.24	112		
JEC[15]	0.27	0.32	139		
LASSO[15]	0.24	0.29	127		
TagProp[7]	0.33	0.42	160		
GS[32]	0.30	0.33	146		
CRM[11]	0.16	0.19	107	0.26	0.30
SML[3]	0.23	0.29	137	0.31	0.49
TGLM[12]	0.25	0.29	131	0.29	0.52
MBRM[4]	0.24	0.25	122	0.30	0.35
En-CRF	0.32	0.33	148	0.32	0.42

In this paper, the AP is calculated on the top-ranked 2000 shots returned from these methods. The MAP are calculated by averaging the AP's of all concepts. We compare En-CRF with CML (II) and CMLT [20], both are popular methods which considering correlations among concepts, where CMLT incorporates temporal information into a kernel. All parameters are selected by 3-fold cross-validation on training set. The AP and MAP are shown in Figure 1. From Figure 1, we can find that

- En-CRF achieves the best performance on 28 concepts, and performs better on 32 concepts than CML(II), and 28 than CMLT. En-CRF obtains the best MAP.
- En-CRF performs much better than CML(II) and CMLT on some concepts, e.g., "Office"(82.34% better than CML(II), 65.37% better than CMLT), and "Urban"(68.57% better than CML(II), and 52.88% better than CMLT).
- En-CRF deteriorates on some concepts, e.g., "Sports" due to the fact the there are strong temporal consistency in video data for such concepts, and such information is not considered in En-CRF.

4. CONCLUSIONS

In this paper, we propose the En-CRF method for image and video annotation. In En-CRF, multiple classifiers are trained for each keyword, and all classifiers are combined with a conditional random field. Experimental results on benchmark data sets, including Corel5k and TRECVID 2005, show that En-CRF is superior or highly competitive to several state-of-the-art methods. An interesting future work is to improve En-CRF by incorporating helpful temporal and structured information in video/image annotation tasks.

5. REFERENCES

[1] A. Amir, M. Berg, and S.-F. Chang et al. IBM research TRECVID-2003 video retrieval system. In *TRECVID*, 2003.

[2] R. H. Byrd, J. Nocedal, and R. B. Schnabel. Representations of quasi-newton matrices and their use in limited memory methods. *Mathematical Programming*, 63(2):129–156, 1994.

[3] G. Carneiro, A. B. Chan, P. J. Moreno, and N. Vasconcelos. Supervised learning of semantic classes for image annotation and retrieval. *IEEE Transactions on Pattern Analysis and Machine Intelligence*, 29(3):394–410, 2007.

[4] S. Feng, R. Manmatha, and V. Lavrenko. Multiple bernoulli relevance models for image and video annotation. In *CVPR*, 1002–1009, 2004.

[5] T. Gartner, P. A. Flach, A. Kowalczyk, and A. J. Smola. Multi-instance kernels. In *ICML*, 179–186, 2002.

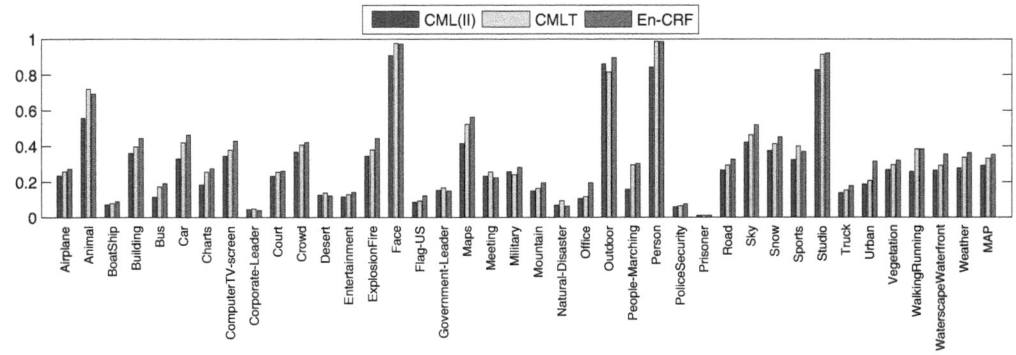

Figure 1: The performance of CML(II), CMLT and En-CRF

[6] K. Grauman and T. Darrell. The pyramid match kernel: Discriminative classification with sets of image features. In *ICCV*, 1458–1465, 2005.

[7] M. Guillaumin, T. Mensink, J. Verbeek, and C. Schmid. Tagprop: Discriminative metric learning in nearest neighbor models for image auto-annotation. In *ICCV*, 309–316, 2009.

[8] J. Jeon, V. Lavrenko, and R. Manmatha. Automatic image annotation and retrieval using cross-media relevance models. In *SIGIR*, 119–126, 2003.

[9] W. Jiang, S.-F. Chang, and A. C. Loui. Context-based concept fusion with boosted conditional random fields. In *ICASSP*, 949–952, 2007.

[10] J. D. Lafferty, A. McCallum, and F. C. N. Pereira. Conditional random fields: Probabilistic models for segmenting and labeling sequence data. In *ICML*, 282–289, 2001.

[11] V. Lavrenko, R. Manmatha, and J. Jeon. A model for learning the semantics of pictures. In *NIPS 16*, 553–560, 2003.

[12] J. Liu, M. Li, Q. Liu, H. Lu, and S. Ma. Image annotation via graph learning. *Pattern Recognition*, 42(2):218–228, 2009.

[13] J. Liu, B. Wang, M. Li, Z. Li, W.-Y. Ma, H. Lu, and S. Ma. Dual cross-media relevance model for image annotation. In *MM*, 605–614, 2007.

[14] Z. Lu, H. H. Ip, and Q. He. Context-based multi-label image annotation. In *CIVR*, 279–287, 2009.

[15] A. Makadia, V. Pavlovic, and S. Kumar. A new baseline for image annotation. In *ECCV*, 316–329, 2008.

[16] D. Metzler and R. Manmatha. An inference network approach to image retrieval. In *CIVR*, 42–50, 2004.

[17] M. Naphade, L. Kennedy, J. R. Kender, S. F. Chang, P. Over, and A. Hauptmann. A light scale concept ontology for multimedia understanding for TRECVID 2005. In IBM Research Technical Report, 2005.

[18] M. R. Naphade, I. Kozintsev, and T. Huang. Factor graph framework for semantic video indexing. *IEEE Transactions on Circuits and Systems for Video Technology*, 12(1):40–52, 2002.

[19] C. Petersohn. Fraunhofer HHI at TRECVID 2004: Shot boundary detection system. In *TRECVID*, 2004.

[20] G.-J. Qi, X.-S. Hua, Y. Rui, J. Tang, T. Mei, M. Wang, and H.-J. Zhang. Correlative multilabel video annotation with temporal kernels. *ACM Transactions on Multimedia Computing, Communications and Applications*, 5(1):1–27, 2008.

[21] R. E. Schapire and Y. Singer. Boostexter: A boosting-based system for text categorization. *Machine Learning*, 39(2-3):135–168, 2000.

[22] J. R. Smith, M. Naphade, and A. Natsev. Multimedia semantic indexing using model vectors. In *ICME*, 445–448, 2003.

[23] G. Tsoumakas and I. Katakis. Multi-label classification: An overview. *International Journal of Data Warehousing and Mining*, 3(3):1–13, 2007.

[24] K. E. van de Sande, T. Gevers, and C. G. Snoek. Evaluating color descriptors for object and scene recognition. *IEEE Transactions on Pattern Analysis and Machine Intelligence*, 32(9):1582–1596, 2010.

[25] A. Yanagawa, S.-F. Chang, L. Kennedy, and W. Hsu. Columbia universityąŕs baseline detectors for 374 lscom semantic visual concepts. Technical report, Columbia University ADVENT, 2007.

[26] J. Yuan, Z. Guo, and L. L. et al. THU and ICRC at TRECVID. In *TRECVID*, 2007.

[27] Z.-J. Zha, X.-S. Hua, T. Mei, J. Wang, G.-J. Qi, and Z. Wang. Joint multi-label multi-instance learning for image classification. In *CVPR*, 1–8, 2008.

[28] Z.-J. Zha, T. Mei, X.-S. Hua, G.-J. Qi, and Z. Wang. Refining video annotation by exploiting pairwise concurrent relation. In *MM*, 345–348, 2007.

[29] J. Zhang, S. Lazebnik, and C. Schmid. Local features and kernels for classification of texture and object categories: a comprehensive study. *International Journal of Computer Vision*, 73(2):213–238, 2007.

[30] M.-L. Zhang and Z.-H. Zhou. Multilabel neural networks with applications to functional genomics and text categorization. *IEEE Transactions on Knowledge and Data Engineering*, 18(10):1338–1351, 2006.

[31] M.-L. Zhang and Z.-H. Zhou. ML-KNN: A lazy learning approach to multi-label learning. *Pattern Recognition*, 40(7):2038–2048, 2007.

[32] S. Zhang, J. Huang, Y. Huang, Y. Yu, H. Li, and D. Metaxas. Automatic image annotation using group sparsity. In *CVPR*, 3312–3319, 2010.

[33] Z.-H. Zhou. Ensemble learning. In S. Z. Li, editor, *Encyclopedia of Biometrics*, 270–273, Springer, 2009.

[34] Z.-H. Zhou and M.-L. Zhang. Multi-instance multi-label learning with application to scene classification. In *NIPS 19*, 1609–1616, 2007.

Refining Local Descriptors by Embedding Semantic Information for Visual Categorization*

Yingbin Zheng, Renzhong Wei, Hong Lu†, Xiangyang Xue
Shanghai Key Lab of Intel. Info. Processing
School of Computer Science
Fudan University, Shanghai, China
{ybzh, 09210240083, honglu, xyxue}@fudan.edu.cn

ABSTRACT

Local descriptor extraction and vector quantization are the important components of widely-used Bag-of-Features (BoF) model for visual categorization. This paper proposes a simple and efficient approach to refine the local descriptors for vector quantization by embedding semantic information. The original local descriptors are integrated by a sequence of category-independent and category-dependent basis. Particularly, the category-dependent basis is learned by minimizing the joint loss minimization over local descriptors from different categories with a shared regularization penalty, which can be formulated as a linear programming problem. The transferred descriptors are further quantized and aggregated to the visual vocabulary. Experiments are performed on PASCAL VOC 2007 benchmark and the quantitative comparisons with several state-of-the-art approaches demonstrate the effectiveness of our proposed approach.

Categories and Subject Descriptors

I.4.7 [**Image Processing and Computer Vision**]: Feature Measurement—*feature representation*; H.3.1 [**Information Storage and Retrieval**]: Content Analysis and Indexing—*indexing method*

General Terms

Algorithms, Experimentation, Performance

Keywords

Local descriptor, semantic information, visual categorization

1. INTRODUCTION

Recently, Bag-of-Features (BoF) model becomes a popular representing scheme for visual categorization [16, 5]. Standard BoF pipeline contains three steps: (1) local descriptors (e.g. SIFT [9] and HoG [6]) are extracted from the images; (2) parameters of the vector quantization algorithm are learned from the training descriptors and each image is mapped from continuous high-dimensional local descriptor space into the discrete histogram of vocabulary with visual words; (3) the histograms are matched based on some metrics, e.g., $L1$-norm or $L2$-norm. In this paper, we focus on the second step of the pipeline.

Standard BoF frameworks use k-means clustering as vector quantization method [16, 5]. k-means and some of its extension methods are trained without class information. Recent works [13, 10] with category labels show the use of semantic information can improve the categorization performance. Specifically, Perronnin et al. [13] construct category-specific histograms in a similar manner to k-means, while Moosmann et al. [10] build a different tree structure for quantization. Here we also aim to develop a category-specific structure for the BoF framework to enhance the visual categorization results.

In this paper, we propose a novel framework for vector quantization by refining the local descriptors. Specifically, we employ a two-step projection on original local descriptors: the category-independent projection for dimensionality reduction, and the category-dependent projection for embedding the semantic information. After projections, we further quantize and aggregate the transferred descriptors to form the visual vocabulary. The highlights of this representation are: (i) the lightweight randomized method for category-independent projection is simple and extremely fast; (ii) the basis for category-independent projection is learned by minimizing the joint loss minimization over local descriptors from different categories with a shared regularization penalty, which can be formulated as a linear programming problem and solved efficiently; (iii) the visual words are generated without running clustering or taking extra training process.

The remainder of this paper is organized as follows. Section 2 reviews the related work on task of vector quantization for visual categorization. Section 3 describes our proposed approach. In Section 4 we demonstrate the quantitative study on PASCAL VOC 2007 dataset. And finally, we conclude our work in Section 5.

2. RELATED WORKS

A number of attempts to improve k-means exist in the literature [12, 14, 13, 10, 17, 11]. As discussed above, we can roughly summarize them into two groups unsupervised and

†Corresponding author: honglu@fudan.edu.cn
*Area chair: Tat-Seng Chua

MM'11, November 28–December 1, 2011, Scottsdale, Arizona, USA.

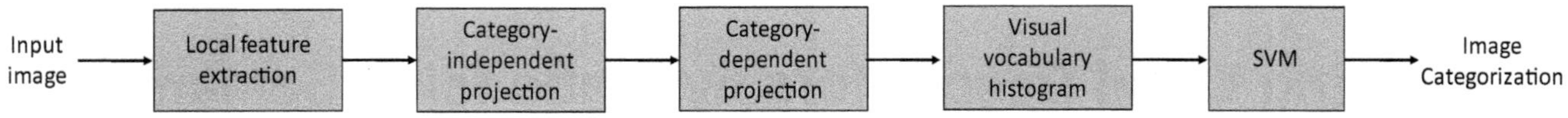

Figure 1: The flowchart of our image representation.

supervised methods. The unsupervised ones try to accelerate the vector quantization speed without semantic labels. For example, Nister et al. [12] replaced k-means by the hierarchical k-means clustering to obtain the tree structure vocabulary. Philbin et al. [14] employed approximated k-means by using the randomized k-d trees for the local feature assignment in the nearest-neighbor search.

Another group of methods incorporate category information into the learning of vector quantization procedure [13, 10, 17, 11]. Perronnin et al. [13] represent images using general histogram and a set of category-specific histograms. Moosmann et al. [10] and Uijlings [17] build discriminative visual word vocabularies using Random Forest methods. Probably most similar to our approach is the work of Ma et al. [11] on combining the idea of Locality Sensitive Hashing (LSH, [1]) and Random Forest, which makes a balance between accuracy and efficacy. Our proposed approach is also simple and effective and can achieve better categorization results.

3. METHODOLOGY

In this section we describe our framework to refine the local descriptors by embedding the semantic information. An overview of our image representation chain is summarized in Figure 1.

3.1 Embedding Semantic Information

Let $\mathbf{X}^c = \{\mathbf{x}_1^c, \mathbf{x}_2^c, ..., \mathbf{x}_{n_c}^c\}$ denote the set of training local descriptors for category c where n_c is the total number of descriptors. The local descriptor $\mathbf{x}_i^c \in \mathbb{R}^d$ is a d dimensional vector extracted from one local region of training images of category c. Our initial motivation is the local descriptor refinement by mapping the descriptors into a more discriminant feature space. Many previous dimensionality reduction or projection-based methods enable the mapping by linear functions. For example, Principal Component Analysis (PCA), one of the standard methods for dimensionality reduction, has been applied to local descriptors [8]. Another potential solution is the randomized projection, which has been applied to image data [3]. Formally, linear projection on the local descriptors can be computed as

$$\mathbf{f}(\mathbf{x}_i) = \mathbf{W}^T \mathbf{x}_i$$

where the $d \times p$ matrix $\mathbf{W}$ denotes the projection parameters (e.g. basis of PCA or randomized basis) and $\mathbf{f}(\mathbf{x}_i) \in \mathbb{R}^p$ is the transformed descriptor. Different with this approach above, our strategy is to get $\mathbf{W}^c$ for each category c separately, i.e.,

$$\mathbf{f}^c(\mathbf{x}_i) = (\mathbf{W}^c)^T \mathbf{x}_i$$

Let $\mathbf{f}^c(\mathbf{x}_i) = (f_1^c(\mathbf{x}_i), f_2^c(\mathbf{x}_i), ..., f_p^c(\mathbf{x}_i))^T$ and we consider the single linear project function $f^c(\mathbf{x}) = \mathbf{w}^T\mathbf{x}$ for late descriptions and $\mathbf{f}^c(\mathbf{x}_i)$ are generated by repeating the procedure p times. In order to construct a more discriminant representation, we aim to learn $f^c(\mathbf{x})$ by a linear classifier determines the relevance of the descriptor $\mathbf{x}$ to category c.

Instead of learning $\mathbf{w}$ directly, a two-step projection is employed here: the category-independent projection for dimensionality reduction, and then the category-dependent projection to embed the semantic information. There are two reasons for incorporating the category-independent projection: (i) category-independent projection reduces the parameter number and makes the framework more efficient; (ii) learning procedure under such methods can embed information about categories. In fact, the two-step projection can be degenerated to single-step one if we set the projection matrix of category-independent projection as an identity matrix.

3.1.1 *Category-Independent Projection*

We choose random projection for its simplicity and efficiency. Let random functions be $r_j(\mathbf{x}) = \Phi_j^T\mathbf{x} - b_j$ ($j = 1, ..., k$), where $\Phi_j \in \mathbb{R}^d$ are randomly sampled from normal distribution $\mathcal{N}(0, 1)$, and b_j is the threshold determined based on the information gain. Note that $r_j(\cdot)(j = 1, ..., k)$ is produced in an unsupervised setting and all the categories share the random functions. To find the proper threshold b_j, we group the training descriptors $\mathcal{D}$ with different categories into two subset $\mathcal{D}^+$ and $\mathcal{D}^-$ according to whether $r_j(\mathbf{x}) = \Phi_j^T\mathbf{x} - b_j \geq 0$ or not. We calculate the entropy $E(\mathcal{D}^+)$ and $E(\mathcal{D}^-)$ of the categories in each descriptor subset. The final score is defined as in [15], i.e.

$$Score(b_j) = -\frac{|\mathcal{D}^+|}{|\mathcal{D}|}E(\mathcal{D}^+) - \frac{|\mathcal{D}^-|}{|\mathcal{D}|}E(\mathcal{D}^-) \quad (1)$$

We randomly generate several candidates for threshold b_j and the one that maximizes Equ. (1) is chosen.

3.1.2 *Category-Dependent Projection*

Linear project functions $f^c(\mathbf{x})$ are further defined as $f^c(\mathbf{x}) = \sum_{j=1}^k \alpha_j^c r_j(\mathbf{x})$, where α_j^c are the category-dependent parameters, and k is the number of random functions described above.

Intuitively, learning the optimal parameters $\alpha_j^c (j = 1, ..., k)$ can be formatted as follows:

$$\min_{\alpha^c} \sum_{\mathbf{x}_i \in \mathbf{X}^c \cup \mathbf{X}_n^c} L(f^c(\mathbf{x}_i), y_i) + \lambda \sum_{j=1}^k |\alpha_j^c| \quad (2)$$

where $\mathbf{X}_n^c$ means a descriptor subset randomly selected from training set except for $\mathbf{X}^c$ (note that $|\mathbf{X}^c| = |\mathbf{X}_n^c|$ to balance the weight of positive and negative samples). We set $y_i = 1$ if $\mathbf{x}_i \in \mathbf{X}^c$ and $y_i = -1$ if $\mathbf{x}_i \in \mathbf{X}_n^c$. The first term measures the training errors of each training descriptors (here we use the hinge loss, i.e. $L(f^c(\mathbf{x}_i), y_i) = \max(0, 1 - y_i f^c(\mathbf{x}_i))$). The second term promotes sparsity of parameter α^c.

Inspired by the multi-task feature learning framework [2], we propose to solve Equ. (2) for different categories simultaneously. we consider the following optimization problem

$$\min_{\alpha} \sum_c \sum_{\mathbf{x}_i^c \in \mathbf{X}^c \cup \mathbf{X}_n^c} L(f^c(\mathbf{x}_i^c), y_i^c) + \lambda \sum_{j=1}^k \max_c |\alpha_j^c| \quad (3)$$

Figure 2: Sample images of the PASCAL VOC 2007 dataset [7].

The left hand term in Equ. (3) is the empirical error across different categories while the right hand term is a shared regularization penalty which suppresses the importance of some random function $r_j(\cdot)$ for all the categories.

The optimization problem in Equ. (3) can be formulated as a linear programming problem:

$$\min_{\alpha,\beta,\xi} \sum_{c} \sum_{\mathbf{x}_i^c \in \mathbf{X}^c \cup \mathbf{X}_n^c} \xi_i^c + \lambda \sum_{j=1}^{k} \beta_j \tag{4}$$

$$\text{s.t.} \quad y_i^c \sum_{j=1}^{k} \alpha_j^c r_j(\mathbf{x}_i^c) \geq 1 - \xi_i^c, \ \forall c \forall i$$

$$\xi_i^c \geq 0, \ \forall c \forall i$$

$$\beta_j \geq \alpha_j^c \geq -\beta_j, \ \forall c \forall j$$

$$\beta_j \geq 0, \ \forall j$$

3.2 Computing Visual Vocabulary Histogram

Given an image $\mathcal{I} = \{\mathbf{x}_1, ..., \mathbf{x}_m\}$, the visual vocabulary histogram for category c is generated based on category-specified projected descriptors $\{\mathbf{f}^c(\mathbf{x}_1), ..., \mathbf{f}^c(\mathbf{x}_m)\}$ in Section 3.1. Due to design of category-dependent projection, we can employ a function $I : \mathbb{R} \in \{0, 1\}$, i.e.

$$I(f^c(\mathbf{x})) = \begin{cases} 1, & f^c(\mathbf{x}) \geq 0 \\ 0, & f^c(\mathbf{x}) < 0 \end{cases} \tag{5}$$

Since $\mathbf{f}^c(\mathbf{x})$ is p-dimensional, the vocabulary with at most 2^p unique visual words is generated. We then compute the representation for the image $\mathcal{I}$ by counting the number of descriptors assigned to each visual words.

4. EVALUATION

We evaluate the proposed approach on PASCAL Visual Object Classes Challenge (VOC) 2007 dataset [7]. There are 9,963 images in total, including 2,501 images for training, 2,510 for validation, and 4,952 images for testing. The dataset contains annotation of 20 different object categories (as illustrated in Figure 2).

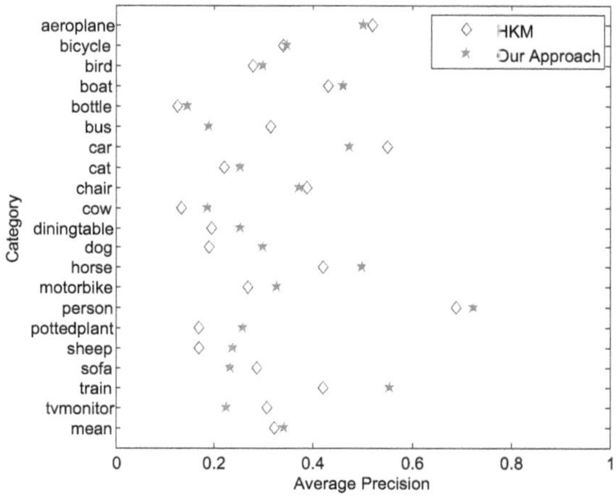

Figure 3: Performance comparison between proposed method and unsupervised method.

4.1 Implementation

For each image in the dataset, we use dense sampling strategy to find the local regions. Then SIFT descriptor is applied to generate the 128-dimensional local feature. About 2,500 local descriptors are extracted for each image. We empirically set the number of random functions for each $f^c(\mathbf{x})$ as $k = 32$ and the dimension of $\mathbf{f}^c(\mathbf{x})$ is $p = 12$. The visual word filtering strategy [11] is applied and finally we have a vocabulary with $1,000$ selected visual words.

To get the object categorization accuracy, support vector machine (SVM) with χ^2 kernel is used in our experiment: $d_{\chi^2}(f_1, f_2) = \frac{1}{2}\sum_{i=1}^{d} \frac{(f_{1i}-f_{2i})^2}{f_{1i}+f_{2i}}$, where f_1 and f_2 are two d-dimensional image features. Specifically, libSVM [4] is used to train and test the categorization models.

The categorization performance is evaluated using average precision (AP), defined as $AP(c) = \frac{1}{m_c}\sum_{k=1}^{n} p(k) I_c(k)$, where n is the dataset size, m_c is the image number of category c, $p(k)$ indicates the precision at position k, $I_c(k) = 1$ indicates the the image with rank k-th belonging to category c and $I_c(k) = 0$ otherwise.

4.2 Results and Discussions

Our approach is compared with several state-of-art methods, containing both unsupervised and supervised strategies.

Unsupervised method We employ the hierarchical k-means (HKM, [12]) on SIFT descriptors. 200,000 local descriptors are randomly chosen from the training images. In our experiments, the hierarchical k-means builds a vocabulary tree with the branch factor (number of children of each node) $k = 10$ and maximum number of levels $L = 3$; then 1,000 clusters are obtained for the comparison. Comparison between our proposed method and hierarchical k-means is shown in Figure 3. We can clearly see the superiority of proposed method over hierarchical k-means with the same number of vocabulary. The improvement of mean average precision is 2%. Our method performs better for 14 out of the 20 categories, which suggests the effectiveness by embedding semantic information.

Supervised methods We also follow the setup of Random Forest (RF, [17]) and Randomized Locality Sensitive

Vocabularies (RLSV, [11]) to construct the visual word vocabulary. The same 200,000 local descriptors as that for hierarchical k-means are used for training the trees. Here each vector also has a category information from the annotation of its original image. For RF approach, learning the supervised tree is done recursively and finally each tree is with maximum number of levels $L = 3$ and about 1,000 visual words. Figure 4 illustrates the categorization results between RLSV, RF, and our approach for all the categories. Our method performs better than RLSV for 14 categories, and RF for 13 categories out of 20 categories. Overall, the results demonstrate that our method outperforms previous supervised methods.

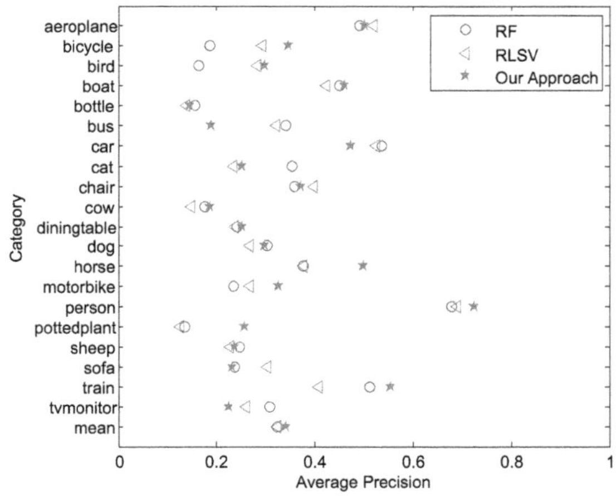

Figure 4: Performance comparison between proposed method and supervised methods.

5. CONCLUSION

In this paper, we have introduced a method to embed semantic information into local descriptors for visual categorization. The local descriptors are integrated by a sequence of category-independent and category-dependent basis. The category-independent basis are selected from random projection, and the category-dependent basis is learned by an optimization problem which minimizes the joint loss minimization over the descriptors from different categories. The transferred descriptors are further quantized and aggregated to the visual vocabulary for categorization. Preliminary evaluation on PASCAL VOC 2007 dataset have confirmed the effectiveness of our method.

Currently, we only implemented a basic system with only 20 categories and the linear programming problem Equ. (4) can be solved efficiently. However, since the number of variables and constraint conditions of the problem are proportional to the category numbers, solving it may be computationally expensive with the increasing of categories. Our future work will incorporate the hierarchy taxonomy structure on large number of categories. Another potential direction may be the using of the non-linear function (instead of the random linear functions in Section 3.1.1), which may be beneficial to some object categories (as suggested in [18]).

Acknowledgment

This work was supported in part by 973 Program (Project No. 2010CB327900), Natural Science Foundation of China (No. 60875003 and 60873178), Shanghai Committee of Science and Technology (No. 11ZR1403400), and 211-Project Sponsorship for Young Professors. Y. Zheng is also supported by the outstanding doctoral research funding of Fudan University.

6. REFERENCES

[1] A. Andoni and P. Indyk. Near-optimal hashing algorithms for approximate nearest neighbor in high dimensions. *Commun. ACM*, 51:117–122, 2008.

[2] A. Argyriou, T. Evgeniou, and M. Pontil. Multi-task feature learning. In *Advances in Neural Information Processing Systems*, 2006.

[3] E. Bingham and H. Mannila. Random projection in dimensionality reduction: Applications to image and text data. In *Annual ACM SIGKDD Conference on Knowledge Discovery and Data Mining*, 2001.

[4] C.-C. Chang and C.-J. Lin. *LIBSVM: a library for support vector machines*, 2001. Software available at `http://www.csie.ntu.edu.tw/~cjlin/libsvm`.

[5] G. Csurka, C. R. Dance, L. Fan, J. Willamowski, and C. Bray. Visual categorization with bags of keypoints. In *Workshop on Statistical Learning in Computer Vision, ECCV*, pages 1–22, 2004.

[6] N. Dalal and B. Triggs. Histograms of oriented gradients for human detection. In *Conference on Computer Vision and Pattern Recognition*, 2005.

[7] M. Everingham, L. Van Gool, C. K. I. Williams, J. Winn, and A. Zisserman. The PASCAL Visual Object Classes Challenge 2007 (VOC2007) Results. http://www.pascal-network.org/challenges/VOC/voc2007/workshop/index.html.

[8] Y. Ke and R. Sukthankar. PCA-SIFT: a more distinctive representation for local image descriptors. In *Conference on Computer Vision and Pattern Recognition*, volume 2, pages 506–513, 2004.

[9] D. G. Lowe. Distinctive image features from scale-invariant keypoints. *International Journal of Computer Vision*, 60(2):91–110, 2004.

[10] F. Moosmann, B. Triggs, and F. Jurie. Fast discriminative visual codebooks using randomized clustering forests. In *Advances in Neural Information Processing Systems*, pages 985–992, 2006.

[11] Y. Mu, J. Sun, T. X. Han, L.-F. Cheong, and S. Yan. Randomized locality sensitive vocabularies for bag-of-features model. In *ECCV*, 2010.

[12] D. Nister and H. Stewenius. Scalable recognition with a vocabulary tree. In *Conference on Computer Vision and Pattern Recognition*, pages 2161–2168, 2006.

[13] F. Perronnin, C. Dance, G. Csurka, and M. Bressan. Adapted vocabularies for generic visual categorization. In *ECCV*, 2006.

[14] J. Philbin, O. Chum, M. Isard, J. Sivic, and A. Zisserman. Object retrieval with large vocabularies and fast spatial matching. In *Conference on Computer Vision and Pattern Recognition*, 2007.

[15] J. Shotton, M. Johnson, and R. Cipolla. Semantic texton forests for image categorization and segmentation. In *Conference on Computer Vision and Pattern Recognition*, 2008.

[16] J. Sivic and A. Zisserman. Video google: a text retrieval approach to object matching in videos. In *ICCV*, pages 1470–1477, 2003.

[17] J. Uijlings, A. Smeulders, and R. Scha. Real-time bag of words, approximately. In *ACM International Conference on Image and Video Retrieval*, 2009.

[18] L. Yang, R. Jin, R. Sukthankar, and F. Jurie. Unifying discriminative visual codebook generation with classifier training for object category recognition. In *Conference on Computer Vision and Pattern Recognition*, 2008.

Common Visual Pattern Discovery via Graph Matching

Hongtao Xie[1,2], Ke Gao[1],Yongdong Zhang[1], Jintao Li[1], Huamin Ren[3]
[1]Institute of Computing Technology, Chinese Academy of Sciences, Beijing, 100190, China
[2]Graduate University of Chinese Academy of Sciences, Beijing, 100049, China
[3] Information Center, Beijing University of Chinese Medicine, Beijing, 100029,China
{xiehongtao, kegao, zhyd, jtl, renhuamin}@ict.ac.cn

ABSTRACT
Discovering common visual patterns (CVPs) between two images is a challenging problem, due to the significant photometric and geometric transformations, and the high computational cost. In this paper, we formulate CVPs discovery as a graph matching problem, depending on pairwise geometric compatibility between feature correspondences. To efficiently find all CVPs, we propose two algorithms--Preliminary Initialization Optimization (PIO) and Post Agglomerative Combining (PAC). PIO reduces the search space of CVPs discovery based on the internal homogeneity of CVPs, while PAC refines the discovery result in an agglomerative way. Experiments on object recognition and near-duplicate image retrieval validate the effectiveness and efficiency of our method.

Categories and Subject Descriptors
I.4.9 [Image Processing and Computer Vision]: *Applications.*

General Terms
Algorithms, Performance, Experimentation

Keywords
Common Visual Pattern, Graph Matching.

1. INTRODUCTION
A common visual pattern (CVP) is the common parts of two images, and these parts have coherent spatial layout and similar visual content. Discovering CVPs from the images are becoming increasingly important for various applications, such as object retrieval [1], point set matching [2], near-duplicate image detection [3] and image database browsing [4].

Discovering CVPs is a difficult task, and there are several challenges. Firstly, significant photometric and geometric transformations usually take place between two images, such as occlusions, cropping, adding noise, changes of illumination, scale, viewpoint, and contrast. Sometimes, even nonrigid deformations occur. Under the combinations of transformations and deformations, two instances of a CVP differ not only in visual appearance, but also in 2D layout. Secondly, it lacks a priori knowledge of the CVPs, thus not known in advance the total number of CVPs and the number of their instances. Finally, it is complex to detect a single CVP between two images, and thus evaluating all candidate CVPs will inevitably be computationally expensive. Figure 1 shows such a challenging example with two CVPs between two images.

Figure1: Two CVPs between two images. Our method can reliably locate all the CVPs and establish spatially coherent correspondences between local features (illustrated as ellipses) as demonstrated in the second row.

Recently, several CVPs discovery methods have been proposed [2][3][4][5][6][8]. However, existing approaches can only deal with weakly supervised cases with relatively slight occlusions and deformations, hence limiting the target image categories [2], rely on the initialization and do not guarantee the global optimal solution [3][4], or have complicated constraints and high computational cost [5][6][8].

In this paper, we formulate CVPs discovery as a graph matching problem by defining an objective function based on pairwise geometric compatibility between feature correspondences. Firstly, we extract local features [7] in each image and get potential feature correspondences between two images. Then, a similarity graph is built. The nodes of the graph represent potential correspondences, and the edges represent the pairwise geometric consistency between corresponding correspondences. So, the spatially coherent feature correspondences (a CVP) constitute a dense subgraph [8], which is a weighted counterpart of maximal cliques of un-weighted graph [9]. Finally, to efficiently find the dense subgraphs (CVPs discovery), two algorithms--Preliminary Initialization Optimization (PIO) and Post Agglomerative Combining (PAC) are proposed. PIO reduces the search space of CVPs discovery and improves time performance, while PAC refines the final result and enhances discovery accuracy.

*Area Chair: Qi Tian

MM'11, November 28- December 1, 2011, Scottsdale, Arizona, USA.

There are several advantages of our method. First, it works well under the circumstance of significant transformations. As shown in the second row of Figure 1, our method can precisely locate the two CVPs, even when severe clutters and deformations take place. Second, it can discovery all CVPs, no matter the manner of mappings between them. Third, it is effective and efficient. It is faster than the previous methods [8][9], and has higher accuracy.

2. COMMON VISUAL PATTERN DISCOVERY

In this section, we first elaborate how to formulate CVPs discovery as a graph matching problem. Then two algorithms-- PIO and PAC are proposed to solve the graph matching problem in an effective and efficient way.

2.1 Problem Formulation

Given two sets of local features P and Q, obtained from two images respectively. Each feature point p is represented by $p = \{p_d, p_l\}$. p_d is the local descriptor and $p_l = (x, y)$, which is the coordinate of point p. Then, we can get the potential feature correspondences $C = \{c_i \mid c_i = (i, i'), i \in P \text{ and } i' \in Q\}$, between these two images. C can be obtained by comparing the similarity of local descriptors [7] or returned by bag-of-feature scheme [10]. For correspondence c_i, the transformation matrix H_i from i to i' can be easily calculated [11]. Then for two correspondences $c_i = ((i,i'), H_i)$ and $c_j = ((j,j'), H_j)$, the pairwise geometric similarity $d_{pgc}(c_i, c_j)$ between c_i and c_j is defined by:

$$T = \max_{c_i, c_j \in C} \left(\frac{1}{2}\left(\left|j_l' - H_i j_l\right| + \left|i_l' - H_j i_l\right|\right)\right)$$

$$d_{pgc}(c_i, c_j) = T - \frac{1}{2}\left(\left|j_l' - H_i j_l\right| + \left|i_l' - H_j i_l\right|\right), \quad (1)$$

where $|\cdot|$ denotes the Euclidean distance function. Obviously, $d_{pgc}(c_i, c_j)$ will be large if H_i and H_j are similar to each other.

Suppose set C contains m correspondences, $C = \{c_1, c_2, ..., c_m\}$ and we build a graph G with m vertices. Each vertex of G represents a correspondence in C and the weight of its edge between node i and node j is set to be $d_{pgc}(c_i, c_j)$. The weighted adjacency matrix of graph G is a $m \times m$ matrix, denoted by M, and defined as:

$$M(i,j) = \begin{cases} 0, & i = j \\ d_{pgc}(c_i, c_j), & i \neq j \end{cases}. \quad (2)$$

Obviously, M is symmetric and nonnegative.

For a CVP with n feature points, it corresponds to a dense subgraph T of G with n vertices [8], which is a weighted counterpart of maximal clique [9]. In [9], Pavan establishes a connection between the weighted maximal cliques and the local maximizers of following quadratic function:

$$\text{maximize } f(x) = x^T M x, \quad (3)$$
$$\text{subject to } x \in \Delta$$

where $\Delta = \{x \in R^m : x \geq 0 \text{ and } |x|_1 = 1\}$. It indicates that a subset V of vertices of G is the maximal clique if and only if its corresponding vector x^V is a local maximizer of $f(x)$, where $x_i^V > 0$ if $i \in V$ and $x_i^V = 0$ if $i \notin V$. x_i represents the probability of a dense subgraph containing node i. That is the probability of CVP V including correspondence c_i.

As a CVP corresponds to a local maximizer of $f(x)$, to discover all CVPs, it has to find all local maximizers of $f(x)$, or local maximizers with relatively large values $f(x)$, which correspond to the true CVPs. To solve (3), [8] and [9] use replicator equation:

$$x_i(t+1) = x_i(t)\frac{(Mx(t))_i}{x(t)^T Mx(t)}, \quad i = 1,...m. \quad (4)$$

That is, given an initialization vector $x(1)$, the corresponding local solution x^* of (3) can be obtained by iteratively executing (4). In [8], for each vertex v of G a set T is built, and T is composed of v and its neighboring vertices. Then $x(1)$ is initialized in T, where $x_i(1) = 1/|T|$ if $i \in T$ and $x_i(1) = 0$ if $i \notin T$. So in [8], the number of initialization vectors is equal to the number of vertices in G. With x^*, the corresponding CVP can be recovered easily, according to the values of x^*_i [8].

2.2 Algorithms

With sufficient initialization vectors and equation (4), the solutions of quadratic function (3) can be obtained [8][9]. However, they have two major shortcomings:

- They have to initialize $x(1)$ at each vertex v of G, which is computational expensive. For example, if there are m vertices in graph G, they have to initialize $x(1)$ m times. Thus at each vertex of a CVP, [8] initializes $x(1)$ once. As these initializations usually converge to the same local maximum, it is a great waste of time.
- Usually, quadratic function (3) has many local maximizers. Some of the maximizers represent CVPs and the others are sets of false correspondences. To reduce the influence caused by false correspondences, [8] just drops all the local maximizers with small function values $f(x)$. In fact, many small maxima correspond to parts of the true CVPs. So dropping all small maxima directly will reduce the accuracy of CVPs discovery.

To solve the above two problems, we propose two algorithms: PIO and PAC. PIO can reduce the search space of CVPs discovery and improve time performance, while PAC can refine the discovery result and enhance accuracy effectively.

2.2.1 Preliminary Initialization Optimization

Intuitively, for the correspondences in each CVP, as they have coherent spatial distribution, the pairwise geometric similarity values among them are high. For a false correspondence, as it is distributed randomly, the pairwise similarity values between it and the other correspondences are low. Based on this property, we can find the confident vertices of graph G. For each vertex i, we calculate its total similarity value with all the other vertices:

$$v(i) = \sum_{j \in G} M(i,j), \quad (5)$$

and get the average similarity value:

$$v_{ave} = \frac{1}{|G|}\sum_{i \in G} v(i). \quad (6)$$

Then, if $v(i)$ is larger than v_{ave}, i is the confident vertex. In this way, most of the false correspondences can be separated out. However, as the amount of confident vertices is still huge, we cannot simply initialize $x(1)$ just on the basis of the confident vertices.

For a CVP, the correspondences in it have high pairwise geometric similarity, and the similarity values between the correspondences in it and those outside are low. As a cluster should have high internal homogeneity and there should be high inhomogeneity between the entities in a cluster and those outside [9]. So a CVP has the same property of a cluster [12]. Thus, to approximately find the CVPs, we can use a clustering method. As we already have the similarity matrix M, we use affinity propagation [13] to cluster the vertices of G and take the confident vertices as "preferences" [13]. For efficiency, the maximum number of iterations of affinity propagation is set to be 30-50. For each cluster, a set T is made up of the vertices in this cluster and their neighboring vertices. Then, $x(1)$ is set in T and the local maximizer of (3) is got by (4). Compared to [8], for a graph G of 3000 vertices the number of $x(1)$ returned by PIO is about 300 times less, which significantly improves the efficiency of CVPs discovery. What's more, as PIO initializes $x(1)$ in a meaningful way (clustering), it has higher CVPs discovery accuracy, as illustrated in the experiment section.

2.2.2 *Post Agglomerative Combining*

As the amount of initialization vectors obtained by PIO is still large, quadratic function (3) has many local maximizers. Thus, we propose post agglomerative combining algorithm to refine the final result. For the candidate patterns C_i and C_j returned by (4), we define their similarity $S(C_i,\ C_j)$ as:

$$S(C_i,\ C_j)=\begin{cases}\dfrac{1}{|C_i||C_j|}\sum_{a\in C_i}\sum_{b\in C_j}M(a,b)+|C_i\cap C_j|, & i\neq j\\ 0, & i=j\end{cases},\quad (7)$$

The PAC algorithm is summarized in Algorithm 1. At each agglomerating step, for two candidate patterns corresponding to a same CVP, as the similarity value between them is large, they are likely to merge into a larger pattern. For patterns with false correspondences, as the similarity values between them and other patterns are small, they are likely to remain as smaller patterns. The agglomerating step is iterated until the maximum similarity is lower than a threshold σ_D. Typically, a CVP is likely to get enough numbers of correspondences. Thus, we can select reliable CVPs by choosing well-formed large patterns with a threshold σ_N. Besides, other information, such as location and geometric consistency of correspondences [11] can be applied to further refine the final result.

3. EXPERIMENTS

In this section, we evaluate our method on two tasks: object recognition and near-duplicate image retrieval. In our experiments local features are obtained by the Hessian-Affine detector [14] and the SIFT descriptor [7]. The parameters are set as: $\sigma_D=15$ and $\sigma_N=20$.

3.1 Object Recognition

In this experiment, we test our method on object recognition problem with the Toys dataset [15]. The performance is quantified by processing all pairs of model and test images, and compared with Liu's method [8] and Ferrari's method [15]. The initial feature

Algorithm1. Post Agglomerative Combining

```
Set S_0 = {C_i}, i = 1,...,n returned by (4) as the initial candidate patterns;
t=0;
(Hierarchical Pattern agglomerating)
Repeat
    t= t+1;
    Among all possible pairs(C_i, C_j) in S_{t-1}, find (C_a, C_b)
    such that S(C_a, C_b) = max_{i,j} S(C_i, C_j);
    If S(C_a, C_b) ≥ σ_D
        Merge C_a and C_b into a single pattern C_q;
        S_t = (S_{t-1} − {C_a, C_b}) ∪ {C_q};
    End
Until |S_t| == 1 or max_{i,j} S(C_i, C_j) < σ_D;
CVPs = {C_i | C_i ∈ S_t and |C_i| > σ_N}
```

correspondences between two images are obtained in the same manner as described in [7], and our method and [8] have the same adjacency matrix M .The ROC curves in Figure 2 depicts the detection rate versus false positive rate of different methods. As shown in Figure 2, our method outperforms the methods of [8] and [15]. On average, our method only need 0.68 second to find the CVPs between a pair of image, while [8] needs 1.7 second. Examples of discovered CVPs are shown in Figure 3, we can see that despite large deformations, our method can correctly detect all the CVPs and has higher detection accuracy than the method of [8]. Besides, for the effect of PAC, the CVPs detected by our method cover more areas than the CVPs detected by [8].

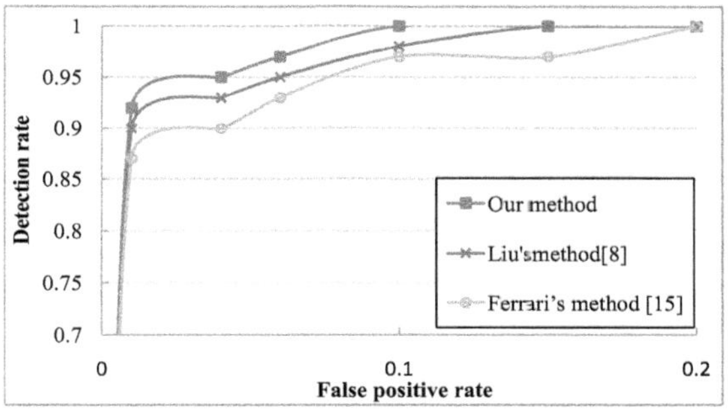

Figure2: ROC curves for three methods on Toys dataset [15].

3.2 Near-duplicate Image Retrieval

In this experiment we show an application of CVPs discovery in near-duplicate image retrieval, which plays an important role in many applications. For near-duplicate images, they have obvious CVPs. The experiment is conducted on Ukbench dataset [16] and Toys dataset [15]. The near-duplicate image retrieval system is built upon the scheme proposed by [11]. For a query image, we first get the candidate similar images with the method in [11], then we re-rank the top 50 candidate images based on the size of detected CVPs. The performance metric applied in our experiment is mean average precision (mAP) [1[illegible]]. We compare our method with the following approaches: 1) Baseline, the method in [11]; 2) Baseline+Ransac, the search result of Baseline is refined by Ransac [17] and 3) Baseline + [8], the search result of Baseline is re-ranked based on the size of CVPs detected by [8]. For 2) and 3), we both re-rank the top 50 candidate images.

Table 1: Search accuracy for four methods on Ukbench [16] and Toys [15] datasets.

	Ukbench	Toys
Baseline	0.842	0.445
Baseline+Ransac	0.864	0.472
Baseline+ [8]	0.885	0.785
Our method	**0.923**	**0.917**

Table 1 compares the above four approaches, leading to two major observations:

(1) Our method significantly improves the search precision. Compared to Baseline + [8], our method achieves 4.3% and 16.8% improvements in mAP on the two sets respectively.

(2) Compared to Baseline + Ransac, our method has much better performance. This is because that Ransac is based on the global geometric changes between the query image and the candidate images. But nonrigid deformations and viewpoints changes take place in these sets. So our method is more suitable for dealing with significant viewpoints changes and nonrigid deformations.

These two experiments illustrate the effectiveness and efficiency of our method in CVPs discovery.

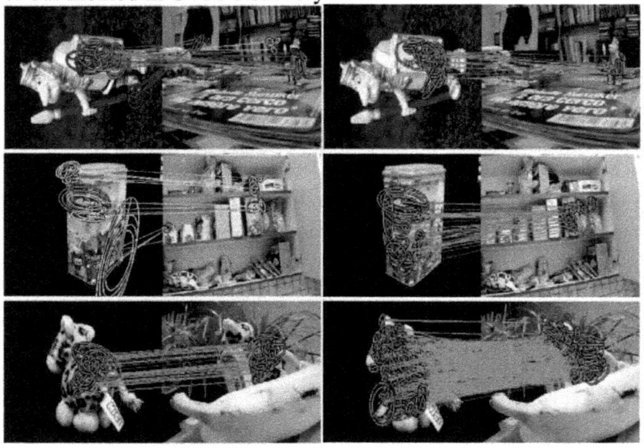

Figure3: CVPs discovery results on the image pairs of Toys dataset [15]. Left: the CVPs discovered by [8]. Right: the CVPs discovered by our method. All the detected CVPs are indicated by different colors.

4. CONCLUSION

We have introduced two algorithms: PIO and PAC, to discovery CVPs in two images. Our method takes advantage of internal homogeneity of CVPs and refines discovery result in an agglomerative way. Compared to the state-of-the-art methods, we can not only reduce the search space of CVPs discovery, but also improve the discovery accuracy. Experiments on both object recognition and near-duplicate image retrieval show that our method can effectively and efficiently detect all CVPs automatically, despite variations caused by transformations and deformations. In future work, we will develop methods of using CVPs to provide query expansion and database browsing.

5. ACKNOWLEDGEMENT

We would like to thank Dr. Hairong Liu (National University of Singapore) for providing us the code of [8] and for giving us precious suggestions. This work is supported by the National Basic Research Program of China (973 Program, 2007CB311100); National Nature Science Foundation of China (61003163, 60873165); Beijing New Star Project on Science & Technology (2007B071); National High Technology and Research Development Program of China (863 Program, 2009AA01A403); Co-building Program of Beijing Municipal Education Commission.

6. REFERENCES

[1]. Berg, T. Berg, and J. Malik. Shape matching and object recognition using low distortion correspondences. CVPR, 2005.

[2]. J. Yuan and Y. Wu. Spatial random partition for common visual pattern discovery. ICCV, 2007.

[3]. Gangqiang Zhao, Junsong Yuan. Mining and Cropping Common Objects from Images. ACM MM 2010.

[4]. H.-K. Tan and C.-W. Ngo. Localized matching using earth mover's distance towards discovery of common patterns from small image samples. IVC, 2009

[5]. T. Tuytelaars, C. H. Lampert, M. B. Blaschko, and W. Buntine. Unsupervised object discovery: A comparison. IJCV, 88:284–302, 2010.

[6]. P. Hong and T. S. Huang. Spatial pattern discovery by learning a probabilistic parametric model from multiple attributed relational graphs. JDAM, 139:113–135, 2004.

[7]. D. Lowe. Distinctive image features from scale-invariant keypoints. IJCV, 2004.

[8]. H. Liu, S. Yan. Common Visual Pattern Discovery via Spatially Coherent Correspondences. CVPR, 2010.

[9]. M. Pavan and M. Pelillo. Dominant sets and pairwise clustering. PAMI, 2007.

[10]. J. Sivic and A. Zisserman. Efficient visual search of videos cast as text retrieval. PAMI, 2009.

[11]. H. Jegou, M. Douze and C. Schmid. Improving bag-of-features for large scale image search. IJCV, 2010.

[12]. Minsu Cho, Jungmin Lee and Kyoung Mu Lee. Feature Correspondence and Deformable Object Matching via Agglomerative Correspondence Clustering. ICCV, 2009.

[13]. Frey, J. and Dueck, D. Clustering by passing messages between data points. Science, 315:972-974, 2007.

[14]. K. Mikolajczyk, Binaries for affine covariant region descriptors, http://www.robots.ox.ac.uk/vgg/research/affine/, 2007.

[15]. V. Ferrari, T. Tuytelaars, and L. Gool. Simultaneous object recognition and segmentation from single or multiple model views. IJCV, 67(2):159–188, 2006.

[16]. D. Nister, H. Stewenius, Scalable recognition with a vocabulary tree. CVPR, 2006.

[17]. O. Chum, J. Matas and S. Obdrzalek. Enhancing RANSAC by generalized model optimization. ACCV, 2004

Environmental Sound Classification for Scene Recognition Using Local Discriminant Bases and HMM *

Feng Su
suf@nju.edu.cn

Li Yang
mf1033035@stu.nju.edu.cn

Tong Lu
lutong@nju.edu.cn

Gongyou Wang
mf1033024@stu.nju.edu.cn

State Key Laboratory for Novel Software Technology
Nanjing University
Nanjing, 210093, China

ABSTRACT

Analysis and classification of auditory scenes or contexts play important roles in content-based indexing and retrieval of multimedia databases and context-aware applications. In this paper, we propose an environmental sound and auditory scene recognition scheme that focuses on efficient feature representation and classfication of the unstructured composition of a scene (for example, restaurant, street, beach, etc.). We propose to use the local discriminant bases (LDB) technique to identify the discriminatory time-frequency subspace for environmental sounds and then use it for corresponding feature extraction. Based on LDB, we present two recognition models, with or without explicit sound event modeling, for auditory scenes, in which the hidden Markov model (HMM) is used to depict the characteristics and correlations among various events that constitute the scene. The experimental results demonstrate the effectiveness of the proposed approach for auditory scene classification.

Categories and Subject Descriptors

H.3.1 [**Information Storage and Retrieval**]: Content Analysis and Indexing

General Terms

Algorithms, Experimentation

Keywords

Auditory scene recognition, environmental sound, HMM, local discriminant bases

*Area chair: Bernard Merialdo

MM'11, November 28–December 1, 2011, Scottsdale, Arizona, USA.

1. INTRODUCTION

The rapid increase in speed and capacity of smart mobiles and various embedded devices equipped with acoustic sensors and powerful CPUs has allowed the inclusion of sound as a common type of data in many exciting applications such as content-based indexing and retrieval of multimedia databases, robotics systems and context-aware applications. Compared with vision-based approaches in these applications, audio signals are robust in situations like visual obstruction or weak lighting and are relatively inexpensive in storing and computing, thereby are widely exploited either independently or as an important component in multi-modal processing.

For context aware processing that this work is mainly targeted, we want to simulate our own abilities to reconstruct from sounds an accurate perception of objects and events present in our natural environment by computation modeling. More specifically, we want to automatically recognize an auditory scene, which involves efficiently retrieving and classifying semantic information about the environment or conetxt that a sound segment is acquired. The term auditory scene here refers to the acoustic modeling of a specific location or site such as restaurant, bus station, conference hall, or forest, which is similar to what an image of the same location provides visually. An auditory scene usually contains and is characterized by various sound events occurring in it, which are short audio segments with distinct acoustic patterns corresponding to specific object or event in the scene, such as laughing, whistling or gunfire, as illustrated in Fig. 1. The semantic information extracted from an auditory scene and the knowledge about the category of surrounding environment can inspire new forms of multimedia services or augmentations to existing ones. For example, a mobile phone can automatically switch the operational mode or provide customized information with the change of circumstances.

Research in general audio signal analysis and recognition has received long time interests in the past years [5, 6, 8] and a variety of audio features and processing models have been proposed in temporal or spectral domain such as the popular Mel-frequency cepstral coefficients (MFCCs). Most of previous efforts deal with speech or music, which can be categorized to structured sounds due to their formantic or harmonic structure characteristic. Environmental sounds,

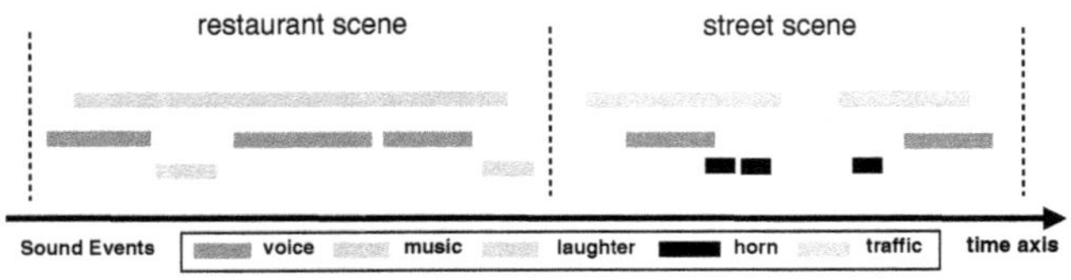

Figure 1: Illustration of auditory scenes and sound events.

on the other side, are typically unstructured, which may have a broad noise-like flat spectrum and diverse variety of signal composition and are difficult to build models.

Compared to the works on speech or music, research in environmental sound and auditory context recognition are relatively less. In [1], a set of key audio effects are modeled with HMMs and a Bayesian network-based approach is proposed to discover the high-level semantics of an auditory context embedded in key effect sequences. In [2], general acoustic environment types are characterized as a whole rather than collections of discrete sound events pre-extracted. The author proposed to use the matching pursuit (MP) algorithm to select effective time-frequency features as the supplementation to MFCC for audio environment characterization. Eronen et al. [4] developed a system to evaluate the recognition accuracy of various audio features (ZCR, MFCC, Band-energy, Spectral flux, etc.), feature transforms (PCA, ICA, LDA), classifiers (k-NN and HMM) on 24 audio contexts and compared the results with human listeners. In [9], a hybrid SVM/KNN classifier is used for environmental sound classification based on MPEG-7 low-level audio descriptors.

In this paper, we propose an automatic recognition scheme for unstructured auditory scenes using local discriminant bases (LDB) features and HMM-based scene models. The remainder of this paper is organized as follows. Section 2 describes the LDB-based audio feature extraction. Section 3 describes the HMM-based recognition model for auditory scenes. Performance evaluation and some discussions are given in Section 4.

2. AUDIO FEATURE EXTRACTION BY LOCAL DISCRIMINANT BASES

The LDB algorithm proposed by Saito and Coifman [7] is one kind of "best-basis" method to select an orthonormal optimum basis or subspace from a large collection of bases, which minimizes entropy or maximizes a certain discriminant measure among classes. Once such a basis is selected, a small number of most significant coordinates (features) can be used to enhance the performance of the classifier without losing important information of the problem.

LDB has been successfully applied to various classification problems in signal and image processing. In [8], LDB algorithm with wavelet packet bases is exploited to identify the subspaces that exhibit high discrimination between audio signal classes. The block diagram of the LDB-based algorithm used in audio classification is depicted in Fig. 2.

2.1 Local Discriminant Bases Computation

In LDB, an audio signal x_i is decomposed into a binary wavelet packets tree $\{\Omega_{j,k}\}$, where j indicates the level of the tree, k indicates the node index in level j, $\Omega_{j,k}$ denotes the

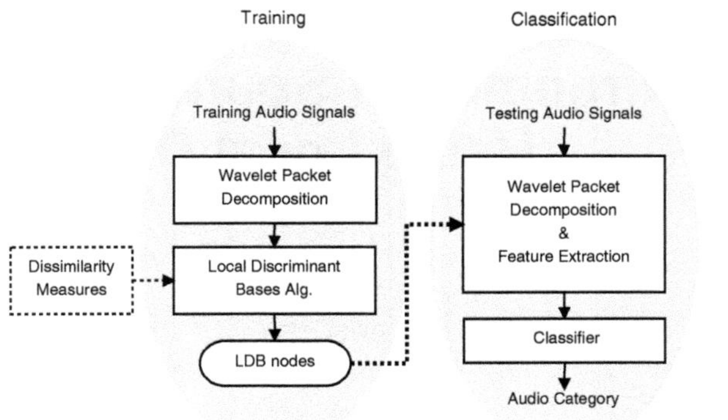

Figure 2: Block diagram of the LDB-based sound classification algorithm.

subspace spanned by a set of wavelet packet basis vectors $\{\mathbf{w}_{j,k,l}\}_{l=0}^{l=2^{u-j}-1}$ and 2^u corresponds to the length of the signal x_i. The signal x_i can then be expressed as

$$x_i = \sum_{j,k,l} [a_{j,k,l}]_i \cdot \mathbf{w}_{j,k,l} \tag{1}$$

where, $a_{j,k,l}$ are the basis vector coefficients at node (j,k).

The goal of LDB is to identify the set of best subspaces (nodes) that provides maximum dissimilarity information between different signal classes, from all 2^J mutually orthogonal subspaces (J is the number of decomposition levels). This is a pruning process on the wavelet packet tree based on the discriminative capability of a wavelet packet node (subspace) (j,k) on P signal classes. As in [8], we adopt following steps in this process:

1. Compute the dissimilarity values $M_\beta^{(j,k)}$ of node (j,k) on the $\beta^{th} \in \binom{P}{2}$ combination of two signal classes, which is formulated as the mean of the dissimilarity values $\{D^{(j,k)}\}_{t\in[1..T]}$ between a set of T pairs of sample signals extracted randomly from the training sets of the two classes respectively.

   On the node (j,k) of wavelet packets decompositions of two samples being compared, $D^{(j,k)}$ takes one of two forms: 1) the difference of the normalized energy, $E_1^{(j,k)} - E_2^{(j,k)}$, which reveals the variance of energy concentration locations on the TF plane; 2) the difference of temporal variance of local statistics of basis vector coefficients, $var[\mathbf{v}_1^{(j,k)}]/var[\mathbf{v}_2^{(j,k)}]$, which reveals two samples' dissimilarity on nonstationarity. $\mathbf{v}_{1,2}$ are vectors of the piecewise variances of the coefficients.

2. Choose Q LDB nodes with consistently high values of $M_\beta^{(j,k)}$ over the random trials of training samples of the βth class combination.

3. From the pool of $Q \times \binom{P}{2}$ LDB nodes collected from all class combinations, choose the H most frequently occurring LDB nodes.

Repeating this process for each form of the dissimilarity measurement $D^{(j,k)}$ and combining the resulting nodes, we finally obtain a set of best discriminative LDB nodes, from which we extract the wavelet packet basis coefficients or the

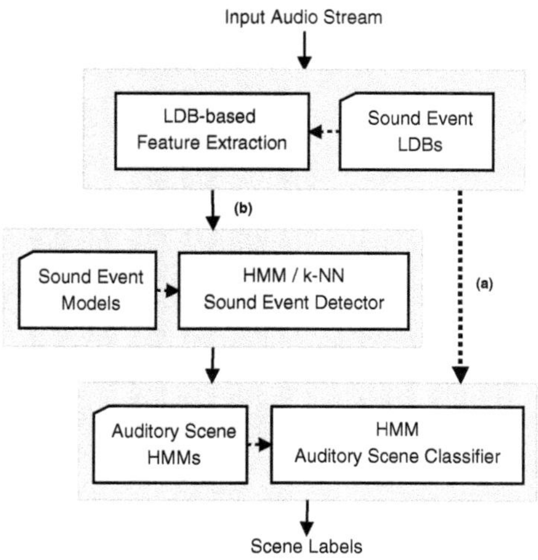

Figure 3: Block diagram of the proposed auditory scene recognition algorithm. (a) and (b) denote two alternative models in handling sound events.

energy/variance value forementioned to form the final feature vector of an input audio signal.

Optionally, to reduce the influence of fixed-size analysis window that may cause interruption of sound events due to their varied durations and unstructed occurrences, an unsupervised analysis of the temporal similarity of audio signals or features at any two time slices can be applied to the audio stream, which adaptively align the analysis window of appropriate length at the boundaries between two sequences of self-similar signals.

3. HMM-BASED AUDITORY SCENE MODELING AND RECOGNITION

Based on the LDB audio feature, we propose an HMM-based auditory scene recognition scheme, which has two alternative models as shown in Fig. 3. The main difference lies in whether or not having a separate explicit model for discrete sound events.

In the first scene recognition model (Fig. 3(a)), we integrates the implicit detection of individual sound events in the scene recognition, on the basis of the LDB's inherent discriminability resulting from the adaptive learning (node selection) process on the sound event training samples, and LDB's capability of depicting multiscale temporal signatures and audio spectral shape. The LDB feature vectors extracted from the input audio steam are directly used as the observations of the HMM-based scene model for training and classification.

3.1 Sound Event Modeling

In the second scene recognition model (Fig. 3(b)), an explicit sound event modeling is proposed as an intermediate layer, for which we adopt a generative HMM-based method as well as a K-nearest neighbor (kNN) method.

For the former, we train one HMM model $\mathrm{HMM}_e^{(i)}$ for each sound event class $i \in [1..K]$ (K is the number of event classes), capturing the timbre (by HMM states) and rhythm (by state transitions) of the sound event and modeling the observation density of the LDB features by the mixture of Gaussian. The model size and initial probability of HMM are decided by clustering algorithm on the training samples. For an input audio segment, the extracted LDB feature vectors are given to each $\mathrm{HMM}_e^{(i)}$, and the corresponding log-likelihood values $[l_1, l_2 \dots, l_K]$ are computed using the Forward algorithm. For the kNN method, similar pseudo-likelihood values are calculated based on the distances between sample points.

The likelihood $[l_1, l_2 \dots, l_K]$ of an audio segment belonging to each specific sound event model is used as the feature vector fed into the scene recognition model. For more robustness, we can further build a *pseudo-semantic feature* as in [3] based on *likelihood ratio test*, which derives an inner-class distribution $f_i(x|\theta_1)$ and outer-class distribution $f_i(x|\theta_0)$ of the likelihood value x for the ith event class, based on training samples from the ith event class and all other classes, respectively. Then, $[f_i(x|\theta_1)/f_i(x|\theta_0)]_{i=1..K}$ is considered the pseudo-semantic feature vector and used in place of the likelihood in scene recognition.

3.2 Auditory Scene Recognition

Auditory scenes are characterized by the occurrences and correlations of specific events. For each auditory scene class $j \in [1..C]$ (C is the number of scene classes considered), we construct and train an HMM model $\mathrm{HMM}_s^{(j)}$ to capture its composition (i.e. sound events) and temporal variation characteristics through HMM states and their transitions. In the training stage, the specification of the HMM including the model size (state number), the number of observation Gaussian mixtures and the initial probability in each state are determined experimentally based on the training samples collected, reflecting the complexity and variations of different scenes, and the transition and emission probabilities of HMM are estimated with the Baum-Welch algorithm.

In recognition, the input audio is divided into overlapping event detection windows, from which the features of either the LDB for recognition model (a), or the likelihood or pseudo-semantic feature for recognition model (b), are extracted. The feature sequence is then fed into each $\mathrm{HMM}_s^{(j)}$ and the model with the maximum output likelihood is considered the recognized scene class.

4. EXPERIMENTAL RESULTS

We evaluated the proposed auditory scene recognition model on natural (unsynthesized) test data collected from Internet and some movie/TV clips. Ten scene types that are distinct enough to be perceived, including 6 outdoor scenes and 4 indoor scenes, are considered in this work: inside moving vehicles, beach, train station, street with traffic, restaurant, auditorium, forest, raining with thundering, playground, and war field. Total 21 sound event types are considered, including engine, car-braking, siren, horn, gun-shot/explosion, dishware/cutlery, music, running water, bird twittering, thundering, people talking, applause, laughter, cheer, traffic and crowd background, etc.

The training set for proposed models contains around 100 audio clip samples for every sound event and auditory scene class, while the test set contains around 150 samples for each class. The clip length ranges 1-3s for sound events and 15s-2min for scenes. To extract audio features, we first learn a 40-dimensional LDB subspace (20 for node energy and 20 for coefficient variance) based on the sound event training

Table 1: Confusion Matrix for 10-Class Scene Classification using LDB Features with HMM

Actual Classes	Classified Scenes % (in same order as rows)									
	1.	2.	3.	4.	5.	6.	7.	8.	9.	10.
1. vehicle	47		33		5			4	11	
2. beach		54			6	11		20	9	
3. station	3		81		4				12	
4. street		1	28	51	14			2	4	
5. restau.		7	1		82				10	
6. audito.		6	3	1		68		7	15	
7. forest		1					97	2		
8. raining		2	7					90	1	
9. playgnd		24	4	2	7			1	62	
10. war		1	17	4				4		74

set. Then, for an input audio stream, we apply a sliding event detection window of around 1s length on it, which are further divided into overlapping 100ms frames, and extract the 40-dim LDB feature vector from each frame.

For the explicit sound event modeling, the average recognition accuracy of 21 sound events on the test set is about 81%. The worst case is for crowd background (28.6%), followed by running water (52%) and traffic (66.7%), since they are usually covered by other events and noise.

Table 1 gives the confusion matrix of auditory scene classification, constructed by applying the recognition model (a) to the test set in a single arbitrary trial. The model size of the HMM for each auditory scene type listed in Table 1 are experimentally chosen as 4, 3, 4, 5, 4, 5, 3, 3, 4, 3, respectively, while the number of observation mixtures is set as four in this work, which can also be learned from samples.

In Fig. 4, we compared the overall recognition accuracy for considered scene classes, using LDB with two HMM-based scene models, MFCC and LDB+MFCC with scene model (a), respectively. The latter is the hybrid feature vector formed by concatenating 20-dim LDB (energy) and 20-dim MFCC features.

As shown by the figure, the two proposed scene models have comparable performances, while model (a) is simpler and more efficient in computation (without explicit training of the sound event models), thereby potentially more suitable for limited computing resources. The figure also shows some complementary aspects of LDB and MFCC features in characterizing auditory scenes. As stated in [2], MFCC is relatively weak to characterize sounds with narrow spectral band structure, which could be the simple, relatively monochromatic but characteristic environmental sound composition in certain scenes, such as some samples of the beach or inside-vehicle scenes in our experiments, for which LDB features can be more effective after efficient learning on the sound event samples. By combining LDB and MFCC features, we achieved an averagely enhanced accuracy rate.

5. ACKNOWLEDGMENTS

Research supported by the National Science Foundation of China under Grant Nos. 61003113, 61021062 and the Natural Science Foundation of Jiangsu Province of China under Grant Nos. BK2009082 and the 973 Program of China under Grant No. 2010CB327903.

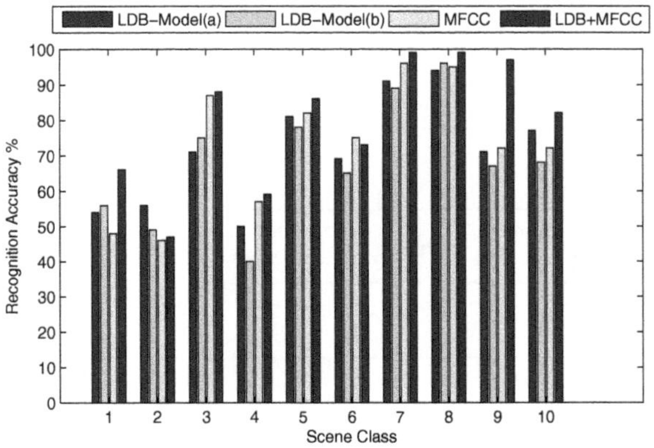

Figure 4: Overall recognition rate comparing 10 classes using LDB with model (a), LDB with model (b), MFCC, and LDB+MFCC features. Scene classes are arranged in the same order as in Table 1.

6. REFERENCES

[1] R. Cai, L. Lu, A. Hanjalic, H.-J. Zhang, and L.-H. Cai. A flexible framework for key audio effects detection and auditory context inference. *IEEE Trans. on Audio, Speech, and Language Processing*, 14(3):1026–1039, May 2006.

[2] S. Chu, S. Narayanan, and C.-C. J. Kuo. Environmental sound recognition with time-frequency audio features. *IEEE Trans. on Audio, Speech, and Language Processing*, 17(6):1142–1158, August 2009.

[3] W.-T. Chu, W.-H. Cheng, and J.-L. Wu. Generative and discriminative modeling toward semantic context detection in audio tracks. In *MMM 2005*, pages 38–45, 2005.

[4] A. J. Eronen, V. T. Peltonen, J. T. Tuomi, A. P. Klapuri, S. Fagerlund, T. Sorsa, G. Lorho, and J. Huopaniemi. Audio-based context recognition. *IEEE Trans. on Audio, Speech, and Language Processing*, 14(1):321–329, January 2006.

[5] S. Kiranyaz, A. F. Qureshi, and M. Gabbouj. A generic audio classification and segmentation approach for multimedia indexing and retrieval. *IEEE Trans. on Audio, Speech, and Language Processing*, 14(3):1062–1081, May 2006.

[6] C.-C. Lin, S.-H. Chen, T.-K. Truong, and Y. Chang. Audio classification and categorization based on wavelets and support vector machine. *IEEE Trans. on Speech and Audio Processing*, 13(5):644–651, September 2005.

[7] N. Saito and R. R. Coifman. Local discriminant bases and their applications. *Journal of Mathematical Imaging and Vision*, 5(4):337–358, 1995.

[8] K. Umapathy, S. Krishnan, and R. K. Rao. Audio signal feature extraction and classification using local discriminant bases. *IEEE Trans. on Audio, Speech, and Language Processing*, 15(4):1236–1246, May 2007.

[9] J.-C. Wang, J.-F. Wang, K. W. He, and C.-S. Hsu. Environmental sound classification using hybrid SVM/KNN classifier and mpeg-7 audio low-level descriptor. In *IJCNN 2006*, pages 1731–1735, 2006.

Semi-Supervised Manifold Ordinal Regression for Image Ranking*

Yang Liu, Yan Liu, Shenghua Zhong, Keith C.C. Chan
Department of Computing, The Hong Kong Polytechnic University
Hung Hom, Kowloon, Hong Kong, P. R. China
{csygliu,csyliu,csshzhong,cskcchan}@comp.polyu.edu.hk

ABSTRACT

In this paper, we present a novel algorithm called manifold ordinal regression (MOR) for image ranking. By modeling the manifold information in the objective function, MOR is capable of uncovering the intrinsically nonlinear structure held by the image data sets. By optimizing the ranking information of the training data sets, the proposed algorithm provides faithful rating to the new coming images. To offer more general solution for the real-word tasks, we further provide the semi-supervised manifold ordinal regression (SS-MOR). Experiments on various data sets validate the effectiveness of the proposed algorithms.

Categories and Subject Descriptors

I.5.2 [**Pattern Recognition**]: Design Methodology—*pattern analysis*

General Terms

Algorithms

Keywords

Manifold learning, ordinal regression, manifold ordinal regression, semi-supervised learning, semi-supervised manifold ordinal regression, image ranking

1. INTRODUCTION

Image ranking has attracted much attention in the last decade [11, 6, 12]. Many learning algorithms have been developed to tackle this problem, such as the regression based methods [2], the manifold learning based approaches [5, 8], and the probability based models [6].

In this paper, we present a novel algorithm called manifold ordinal regression (MOR) for image ranking, which is motivated by two observations. First, image ranking can be naturally formulated as an ordinal regression problem. Suppose that a human being is asked to rank the images according to a given query. There might be several rating scales in one's mind, such as "very relevant", "relevant", "partially relevant", or "irrelevant". Unlike the multi-class classification, ordinal regression not only recognizes whether the data points belong to the same group or not, but also provides the rank information of different data groups. Moreover, compared with the regular regression, the range of ordinal regression function is discrete and finite, which matches the rating scales in the human mind.

Second, manifold learning is an appropriate tool for image analysis. As an important category of nonlinear feature extraction technologies, manifold learning uncovers the intrinsic structure of data sets by assuming that the high-dimensional observations lie on or close to a low-dimensional manifold [14, 10, 1]. Many image data sets hold the nonlinear structures in their original high-dimensional feature spaces [14, 10, 18], which makes manifold learning being an appropriate tool for the image analysis task [5, 8, 9].

Although some effective manifold learning methods have been developed for clustering and classification [15, 9], they are not directly applicable to ordinal regression. Figure 1 provides an illustration. Given the query "man wearing glasses", we can rank the images accordingly: 1) the images of the man wearing glasses are ranked as very relevant; 2) the images of the man not wearing glasses are ranked as partially relevant; and 3) the images of the woman not wearing glasses are ranked as irrelevant. For clustering or classification, we prefer the projection that maximizes the

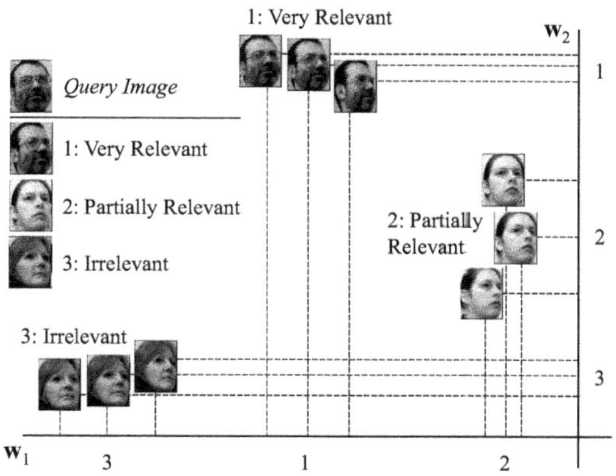

Figure 1: Schematic illustration of manifold ordinal regression on the data set with nonlinear geometry.

*Area chair: Bernard Merialdo

MM'11, November 28–December 1, 2011, Scottsdale, Arizona, USA.

separability, so $\mathbf{w}_1$ is the optimal axis for data mapping. However, the projection on $\mathbf{w}_1$ cannot preserve the ranking information of different data blocks, which is of great importance in our task. To keep both ranking information and manifold structure, the projection on $\mathbf{w}_2$ is preferred.

According to above considerations, we proposes a novel algorithm MOR to seek the explicit function that projects the original data to the one-dimensional ranking axis. To offer more general solution for real-word tasks, we further develop the semi-supervised manifold ordinary regression (SS-MOR), which learns the ordinal regression function using both labeled and unlabeled data under the proposed model.

2. MANIFOLD ORDINAL REGRESSION

Let $\{(\mathbf{x}_i, y_i)\}$ $(i = 1, ..., n)$ be the training set, where $\mathbf{x}_i \in \mathbb{R}^d$ denotes the input data point and $y_i \in \{1, ..., k\}$ denotes the corresponding rank label. In order to perform ordinal regression under the manifold learning framework, we formulate the objective function of MOR as follows:

$$\begin{aligned} &\min\ J(\mathbf{w},\gamma) = \sum_{i,j=1}^{n} (\mathbf{w}^T\mathbf{x}_i - \mathbf{w}^T\mathbf{x}_j)^2\mathbf{A}_{ij} - C\gamma \\ &s.t.\ \ \mathbf{w}^T(\mathbf{m}_{r+1} - \mathbf{m}_r) \geq \gamma,\ r = 1, ..., k-1, \end{aligned} \tag{1}$$

where $\mathbf{w} \in \mathbb{R}^d$ is the projection vector, $\mathbf{A}$ is the $n \times n$ adjacency matrix constructed to model the neighborhood relationship between data points, $\mathbf{m}_r$ denotes the mean vector of samples from rank r, n_r is the number of data samples in rank r, γ is the margin between the projected means of two consecutive ranks, and $C \geq 0$ is a penalty coefficient used to balance the manifold structure and order information.

2.1 Neighborhood Graph Construction

In MOR, we use the Heat kernel [1] to assign the weight on the neighborhood graph, i.e., $\mathbf{A}_{ij} = \exp(-d(\mathbf{x}_i, \mathbf{x}_j)^2/2\sigma)$ if $j \in \mathcal{N}_i$ and $i \in \mathcal{N}_j$; and $\mathbf{A}_{ij} = 0$ otherwise. Here $d(\mathbf{x}_i, \mathbf{x}_j)$ denotes the distance between $\mathbf{x}_i$ and $\mathbf{x}_j$, $\mathcal{N}_i$ is the index set of the K nearest neighbors of $\mathbf{x}_i$, and $\sigma = \sum_{i=1}^{n} d(\mathbf{x}_i, \mathbf{x}_{i_K})^2/n$, where $\mathbf{x}_{i_K}$ is the Kth nearest neighbor of $\mathbf{x}_i$.

To integrate the order information into the neighborhood graph, we define $d(\mathbf{x}_i, \mathbf{x}_j) = (|y_i - y_j| + 1)||\mathbf{x}_i - \mathbf{x}_j||_2$, where $|\cdot|$ denotes the absolute value operator and $||\cdot||_2$ denotes the L_2-norm operator. Compared with the L_2 distance, the distance between data points within each rank is kept unchanged while the distance between data points from different ranks is enlarged. Furthermore, the rank difference is properly reflected by the extent of enlargement.

In the neighborhood graph construction procedure, we utilize the order information from the local perspective. In the objective function (1), we aim to maximize the distance between two consecutive ranks, which considers the order information using a global manner. By incorporating the order information from both local and global perspectives, a unified manifold learning model is formulated for ranking.

2.2 Optimization Procedure

We first rewrite (1) as follows:

$$\begin{aligned} &\min\ J(\mathbf{w},\gamma) = \mathbf{w}^T\mathbf{X}\mathbf{L}\mathbf{X}^T\mathbf{w} - C\gamma \\ &s.t.\ \ \mathbf{w}^T(\mathbf{m}_{r+1} - \mathbf{m}_r) \geq \gamma,\ r = 1, ..., k-1, \end{aligned} \tag{2}$$

where $\mathbf{X} = [\mathbf{x}_1, ..., \mathbf{x}_n]$ is the data matrix, $\mathbf{L} = \mathbf{D} - \mathbf{A}$ is the $n \times n$ Laplacian matrix [1], and $\mathbf{D}$ is a diagonal matrix defined as $\mathbf{D}_{ii} = \sum_{j=1}^{n} \mathbf{A}_{ij}$ $(i = 1, ..., n)$. Then we obtain the Lagrangian equation of (2):

$$\begin{aligned} L(\mathbf{w},\gamma,\alpha) = \ &\mathbf{w}^T\mathbf{X}\mathbf{L}\mathbf{X}^T\mathbf{w} - C\gamma \\ &- \sum_{r=1}^{k-1} \alpha_r\big(\mathbf{w}^T(\mathbf{m}_{r+1} - \mathbf{m}_r) - \gamma\big), \end{aligned} \tag{3}$$

where α_r are the Lagrange multipliers which satisfy $\alpha_r \geq 0$. The necessary conditions for the optimality are:

$$\begin{cases} \dfrac{\partial L}{\partial \mathbf{w}} = 0 \ \Rightarrow\ \mathbf{w} = \dfrac{1}{2}(\mathbf{X}\mathbf{L}\mathbf{X}^T)^{\dagger}\displaystyle\sum_{r=1}^{k-1} \alpha_r(\mathbf{m}_{r+1} - \mathbf{m}_r), \\ \dfrac{\partial L}{\partial \gamma} = 0 \ \Rightarrow\ C = \displaystyle\sum_{r=1}^{k-1} \alpha_r, \end{cases} \tag{4}$$

where $(\mathbf{X}\mathbf{L}\mathbf{X}^T)^{\dagger}$ is the Moore-Penrose pseudoinverse of $\mathbf{X}\mathbf{L}\mathbf{X}^T$.

Based on Eq. (4), (2) could be converted to:

$$\begin{aligned} &\min \sum_{r=1}^{k-1} \alpha_r(\mathbf{m}_{r+1} - \mathbf{m}_r)^T(\mathbf{X}\mathbf{L}\mathbf{X}^T)^{\dagger}\sum_{s=1}^{k-1} \alpha_s(\mathbf{m}_{s+1} - \mathbf{m}_s) \\ &s.t.\ \ \sum_{r=1}^{k-1} \alpha_r = \sum_{s=1}^{k-1} \alpha_s = C,\ \alpha_r, \alpha_s \geq 0,\ r, s = 1, ..., k-1. \end{aligned} \tag{5}$$

Above is a convex quadratic programming (QP) problem with linear constraints, which can be solved by some standard optimization algorithms. Then we can obtain $\mathbf{w}$ by substituting α_r into the first equation in (4). For any data point $\mathbf{x}$, we can determine its rank by the k nearest neighbor classifier or by the decision function $f(\mathbf{x}) = \min_{r \in \{1,...,k\}} \{r : \mathbf{w}^T\mathbf{x} - b_r < 0\}$, where b_r is defined as:

$$b_r = \begin{cases} \dfrac{\mathbf{w}^T(n_{r+1}\mathbf{m}_{r+1} + n_r\mathbf{m}_r)}{n_{r+1} + n_r} & r = 1, ..., k-1, \\ \max\limits_{i \in \{1,...,n\}} \{\mathbf{w}^T\mathbf{x}_i\} & r = k. \end{cases} \tag{6}$$

2.3 Semi-Supervised Manifold Ordinal Regression

In many multimedia applications, labeled samples are often very expensive to obtain. Meanwhile, unlabeled samples are relatively easy to get and can be very helpful in discovering the global distribution of the data set [3, 19]. As shown in Figure 2, the optimal axis for data mapping is $\mathbf{w}_3$ if we consider both labeled and unlabeled images in the learning procedure, which is different from the axis $\mathbf{w}_2$ learned using only labeled images.

To offer more general solution for the real-world tasks, we develop the semi-supervised manifold ordinal regression (SS-MOR), which learns the ordinal regression function using both labeled and unlabeled data under the proposed model.

Given the training set $\{\mathbf{x}_1, ..., \mathbf{x}_l, \mathbf{x}_{l+1}, ..., \mathbf{x}_n\} \subset \mathbb{R}^d$, the first l data points $\mathbf{x}_i$ $(i = 1, ..., l)$ are labeled as $y_i \in \{1, ..., k\}$ and the remaining $n - l$ data points $\mathbf{x}_u$ $(u = l+1, ..., n)$ are unlabeled. We minimize the following cost function [17]:

$$J(\mathbf{F}) = \frac{1}{2}\sum_{i,j=1}^{n} \|\frac{\mathbf{F}_i}{\sqrt{\mathbf{D}_{ii}}} - \frac{\mathbf{F}_j}{\sqrt{\mathbf{D}_{jj}}}\|^2\mathbf{A}_{ij} + \mu\sum_{i=1}^{n} \|\mathbf{F}_i - \mathbf{Y}_i\|^2, \tag{7}$$

where $\mathbf{Y}$ denotes the $n \times k$ label matrix with $\mathbf{Y}_{ij} = 1$ if $y_i = j$, and $\mathbf{Y}_{ij} = 0$ otherwise; $\mathbf{F}$ denotes the final label matrix;

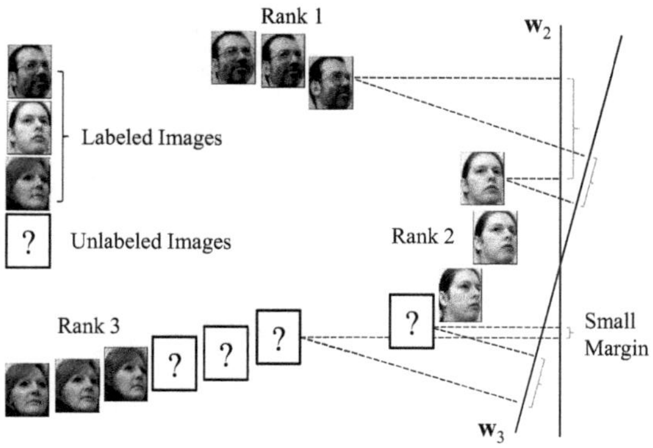

Figure 2: Schematic illustration of semi-supervised manifold ordinal regression on the data set with both labeled and unlabeled data.

$\mathbf{F}_i$ and $\mathbf{Y}_i$ denote the ith row of $\mathbf{F}$ and $\mathbf{Y}$, respectively; and $\mu > 0$ is the regularization parameter. The first term of $J(\mathbf{F})$ ensures that nearby data points have similar labels, while the second term of $J(\mathbf{F})$ requires the consistency between final labels and initial labels.

Differentiating $J(\mathbf{F})$ with respect to $\mathbf{F}$, we have

$$\frac{\partial J}{\partial \mathbf{F}} = \mathbf{F} - \mathbf{D}^{-\frac{1}{2}}\mathbf{A}\mathbf{D}^{-\frac{1}{2}}\mathbf{F} + \mu(\mathbf{F} - \mathbf{Y}) = 0. \quad (8)$$

Then we can obtain $\mathbf{F} = \mu((1+\mu)\mathbf{I} - \mathbf{D}^{-\frac{1}{2}}\mathbf{A}\mathbf{D}^{-\frac{1}{2}})^{-1}\mathbf{Y}$. If the matrix is singular, we can use its Moore-Penrose pseudoinverse to replace the regular inverse. Finally, the label $\tilde{y}_i$ of each data point $\mathbf{x}_i$ $(i = 1, ..., n)$ can be assigned by $\tilde{y}_i = \text{argmax}_{j=1,...,k}\, \mathbf{F}_{ij}$.

According to the new labels of originally unlabeled data, we can calculate the new mean vector of each class: $\tilde{\mathbf{m}}_r = \frac{1}{\tilde{n}_r}\sum_{\tilde{y}_i=r}\mathbf{x}_i$, where $\tilde{n}_r$ is the number of data samples in class r (including the newly classified unlabeled data points). Replacing $\mathbf{m}_r$ with $\tilde{\mathbf{m}}_r$ in (1) - (5), we can obtain the optimal $\tilde{\mathbf{w}}$ and the new decision function: $\tilde{f}(\mathbf{x}) = \min_{r\in\{1,...,k\}}\{r : \tilde{\mathbf{w}}^T\mathbf{x} - \tilde{b}_r < 0\}$, where $\tilde{b}_r$ is defined as follows:

$$\tilde{b}_r = \begin{cases} \dfrac{\tilde{\mathbf{w}}^T(\tilde{n}_{r+1}\tilde{\mathbf{m}}_{r+1} + \tilde{n}_r\tilde{\mathbf{m}}_r)}{\tilde{n}_{r+1} + \tilde{n}_r} & r = 1, ..., k-1 \\ \max\limits_{i\in\{1,...,n\}}\{\tilde{\mathbf{w}}^T\mathbf{x}_i\} & r = k \end{cases} \quad (9)$$

3. EXPERIMENTS

In this section, we evaluate the performance of MOR and SS-MOR on three data sets: the UMIST face data set [4], the USPS digit data set [7], and the MSRA-MM image data set [16]. The mean absolute error (MAE, i.e., $\frac{1}{n}\sum_{i=1}^{n}|\hat{y}_i - y_i|$) [13] is used as the evaluation criterion. Here $\{\hat{y}_1, ..., \hat{y}_n\}$ denote the predicted ranks and $\{y_1, ..., y_n\}$ are the true targets. For all the statistical experiments, we repeat them for 20 times and report the average results. For simplicity, we set the nearest neighbor number $K = 10$ and the regularization parameter $\mu = 0.5$ in our experiments.

3.1 UMIST Face Data Set

To intuitively illustrate that MOR is capable of preserving both rank information and manifold structure, we conduct an experiment using the data samples from the UMIST face data set [4]. Consider the query "man wearing glasses".

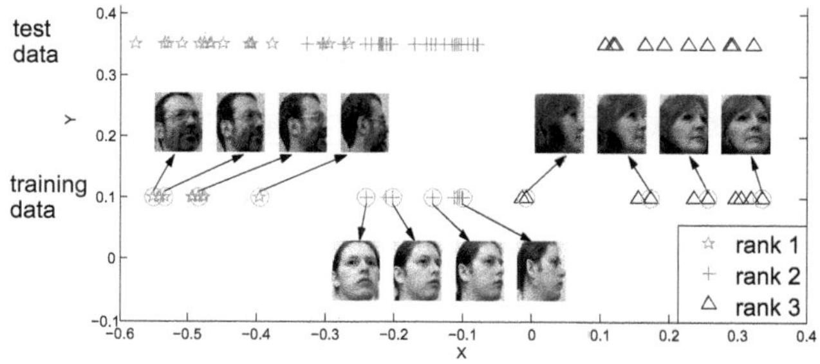

Figure 3: Projection results of training and test data on UMIST face data set using MOR.

Table 1: MAE of four algorithms on USPS data set with different training/test partition sizes.

Train/Test	MOR	KDLOR	SR	LPP
100/10900	2.73 ± 0.22	$\mathbf{2.50 \pm 0.11}$	2.85 ± 0.20	3.05 ± 0.28
200/10800	$\mathbf{2.47 \pm 0.08}$	2.48 ± 0.16	2.71 ± 0.16	2.90 ± 0.20
500/10500	$\mathbf{2.00 \pm 0.09}$	2.17 ± 0.09	2.44 ± 0.13	2.68 ± 0.12
1000/10000	$\mathbf{1.75 \pm 0.04}$	1.82 ± 0.03	2.29 ± 0.10	2.60 ± 0.11

Clearly, the images from three given classes can be ranked accordingly: 26 images of the man wearing glasses are ranked as totally match; 38 images of the man not wearing glasses are ranked as partially match; and 20 images of the woman not wearing glasses are ranked as unmatch.

Figure 3 shows the projection results of MOR. Each image is gray scale and the resolution is 56×46, so the original dimension is 2576. For each rank, 10 images are used for training and the rest are used for test. Obviously, the projected training data are arranged orderly with clear margins between consecutive ranks. Furthermore, the manifold structure within each rank, i.e., the pose variation of each person, is preserved in the projected space smoothly. For test data, although there are overlaps between rank 1 and rank 2, most of the samples are sorted correctly according to their ranks, which means that the proposed algorithm provides a faithful prediction on test data.

3.2 USPS Digit Data Set

We conduct two experiments on the United State Postal Service (USPS) data set [7]. This data set of hand written digital characters comprises 11000 normalized grayscale images of size 16×16, with 1100 images per class.

In the first experiment, our target is ranking the data according to the true digit shown in the images. We compare MOR to three representative algorithms: kernel discriminant learning for ordinal regression (KDLOR) [13], spectral regression (SR) [2], and locality preserving projections (LPP) [5]. For MOR and KDLOR, ten-fold cross validation is employed to determine the parameter C. For each class, p $(= 10, 20, 50, 100)$ images are selected for training and the rest are used for test. As shown in Table 1, MOR achieves the best results in most of the cases.

In order to demo how the performance of proposed model could be improved further when the labeled data are insufficient, in the second experiment, we test the SS-MOR by fixing the number of labeled training data and introducing the unlabeled training data. For each class, 10 images are selected as labeled training data and u $(= 10, 40, 90)$ images are selected as unlabeled training data. As shown in Table 2, the MAE of SS-MOR keeps decreasing when the number of

Table 2: MAE of SS-MOR on USPS data set with different numbers of unlabeled training data.

Labeled/Unlabeled Train	100/100	100/400	100/900
MAE of SS-MOR	2.68 ± 0.19	2.39 ± 0.16	2.21 ± 0.19

Table 3: MAE of three algorithms on MSRA-MM data set with different original feature spaces.

Features	SS-MOR	MOR	KDLOR
BWCM	$\mathbf{0.393 \pm 0.072}$	0.423 ± 0.078	0.456 ± 0.061
HSV-CH	$\mathbf{0.396 \pm 0.037}$	0.429 ± 0.019	0.440 ± 0.046
CC	$\mathbf{0.402 \pm 0.027}$	0.425 ± 0.035	0.463 ± 0.038
EDH	$\mathbf{0.379 \pm 0.026}$	0.398 ± 0.028	0.431 ± 0.063
WT	$\mathbf{0.403 \pm 0.024}$	0.421 ± 0.036	0.430 ± 0.018

unlabeled training data increases, which indicates that utilizing the unlabeled data in the training phase can improve the performance of the proposed model.

3.3 MSRA-MM Image Data Set

We conduct two experiments on a heterogeneous data set, which consists of 10 categories from the MSRA-MM image data set [16]. These categories are: baby, car, dragons, football, fruit, panda, party, school, tiger, and tree, each of which contains about 1000 images. For each image, its relevance to the corresponding query is labeled with three levels: very relevant, relevant and irrelevant.

The first experiment demonstrates the performance of the proposed MOR and SS-MOR on five different types of original feature spaces: 225-D block-wise color moment (BWCM); 64-D HSV color histogram (HSV-CH); 144-D color correlogram (CC); 75-D edge distribution histogram (EDH); and 128-D wavelet texture (WT) [16]. We compare the proposed algorithms to KDLOR, which has already shown its effectiveness in Table 1. For MOR and KDLOR, we randomly select 10 labeled images from each category for training and uses the rest for test. For SS-MOR, besides the 10 labeled images, we further use 90 randomly selected images without corresponding labels for training and uses the rest for test. Table 3 shows the MAE of SS-MOR, MOR, and KDLOR. By jointly optimizing the manifold structure and the order information, MOR outperforms the KDLOR. By incorporating the unlabeled data into the learning procedure, SS-MOR further enhances the performance.

In the second experiment, we construct the original feature space by combining aforementioned five types of features, and thus obtain a 636-dimensional vector for each image. The other settings are the same as those in the first experiment. Figure 4 shows the top ranking results generated by the SS-MOR for three categories: car, party, and tiger, respectively. The proposed algorithm obtains good results.

4. CONCLUSION

In this paper, we present a manifold ordinal regression (MOR) approach for image ranking. The first term of MOR objective function intends to preserve the manifold structure of the data set, while the second term aims to maximize the margin between the projected means of two consecutive ranks. By jointly optimizing these two terms, the projected data are orderly sorted while the intrinsic manifold structure of the data set is well preserved. To adapt the real-world applications, we present the semi-supervised manifold ordinal regression (SS-MOR). Experiments on several standard image data sets demonstrate that the proposed methods achieve good performance on the image ranking task.

Figure 4: Top ranking results of the proposed SS-MOR for car, party, and tiger, respectively.

5. ACKNOWLEDGMENTS

This work was supported by grant PolyU 5204/09E.

6. REFERENCES

[1] M. Belkin and P. Niyogi. Laplacian eigenmaps and spectral techniques for embedding and clustering. In *NIPS 14*, 2002.

[2] D. Cai, X. He, and J. Han. Spectral regression: a unified subspace learning framework for content-based image retrieval. In *Proc. 15th ACM Multimedia*, pages 403–412, 2007.

[3] O. Chapelle, B. Schölkopf, and A. Zien, editors. *Semi-Supervised Learning*. MIT Press, 2006.

[4] D. B. Graham and N. M. Allinson. Characterizing virtual eigensignatures for general purpose face recognition. In *Face Recognition: From Theory to Applications, NATO ASI Series F, Computer and Systems Sciences 163*, pages 446–456, 1998.

[5] X. He. Incremental semi-supervised subspace learning for image retrieval. In *Proc. 12th ACM Multimedia*, pages 2–8, 2004.

[6] E. Hörster, M. Slaney, M. Ranzato, and K. Weinberger. Unsupervised image ranking. In *Proc. 1st ACM LS-MMRM Workshop*, pages 81–88, 2009.

[7] J. J. Hull. A database for handwritten text recognition research. *IEEE TPAMI*, 16(5):550–554, 1994.

[8] Y.-Y. Lin, T.-L. Liu, and H.-T. Chen. Semantic manifold learning for image retrieval. In *Proc. 13th ACM Multimedia*, pages 249–258, 2005.

[9] Y. Liu, Y. Liu, and K. C. C. Chan. Supervised manifold learning for image and video classification. In *Proc. 18th ACM Multimedia*, pages 859–862, 2010.

[10] S. Roweis and L. K. Saul. Nonlinear dimensionality reduction by locally linear embedding. *Science*, 290(5500):2323–2326, December 2000.

[11] Y. Rui, T. S. Huang, and S.-F. Chang. Image retrieval: Current techniques, promising directions, and open issues. *J. Visual Commun. Image Represent.*, 10:39–62, 1999.

[12] B. Siddiquie, R. Feris, and L. Davis. Image ranking and retrieval based on multi-attribute queries. In *CVPR*, 2011.

[13] B.-Y. Sun, J. Li, D. D. Wu, X.-M. Zhang, and W.-B. Li. Kernel discriminant learning for ordinal regression. *IEEE Trans. Knowl. and Data Eng.*, 22:906–910, 2010.

[14] J. B. Tenenbaum, V. de Silva, and J. C. Langford. A global geometric framework for nonlinear dimensionality reduction. *Science*, 290(5500):2319–2323, December 2000.

[15] H. Wang, S. Yan, T. Huang, and X. Tang. Maximum unfolded embedding: formulation, solution, and application for image clustering. In *Proc. 14th ACM Multimedia*, pages 45–48, 2006.

[16] M. Wang, L. Yang, and X.-S. Hua. Msra-mm: Bridging research and industrial societies for multimedia information retrieval. *Microsoft Technical Report*, 2009.

[17] D. Zhou, O. Bousquet, T. N. Lal, J. Weston, and B. Schölkopf. Learning with local and global consistency. In *NIPS 16*. 2004.

[18] D. Zhou, J. Weston, A. Gretton, O. Bousquet, and B. Schölkopf. Ranking on data manifolds. In *NIPS 16*. 2004.

[19] X. Zhu, Z. Ghahramani, and J. D. Lafferty. Semi-supervised learning using gaussian fields and harmonic functions. In *ICML*, pages 912–919, 2003.

Blurred Image Region Detection and Classification *

Bolan Su*+ subolan@comp.nus.edu.sg

Shijian Lu+ slu@i2r.a-star.edu.sg

Chew Lim Tan* tancl@comp.nus.edu.sg

*School of Computing, National University of Singapore
Computing 1(COM1), 13 Computing Drive, Singapore 117417
+Institute for Infocomm Research, Singapore
1 Fusionopolis Way #21-01 Connexis, Singapore 138632

ABSTRACT

Many digital images contain blurred regions which are caused by motion or defocus. Automatic detection and classification of blurred image regions are very important for different multimedia analyzing tasks. This paper presents a simple and effective automatic image blurred region detection and classification technique. In the proposed technique, blurred image regions are first detected by examining singular value information for each image pixels. The blur types (i.e. motion blur or defocus blur) are then determined based on certain alpha channel constraint that requires neither image deblurring nor blur kernel estimation. Extensive experiments have been conducted over a dataset that consists of 200 blurred image regions and 200 image regions with no blur that are extracted from 100 digital images. Experimental results show that the proposed technique detects and classifies the two types of image blurs accurately. The proposed technique can be used in many different multimedia analysis applications such as image segmentation, depth estimation and information retrieval.

Categories and Subject Descriptors

I.4.6 [**IMAGE PROCESSING AND COMPUTER VISION**]: Segmentation—*Pixel classification*; I.5.4 [**PATTERN RECOGNITION**]: Application—*Computer Vision*

General Terms

Algorithms

Keywords

Image Blur, Blurred Region Detection and Classification, Singular Value Decomposition, α Channel Map

1. INTRODUCTION

There exists blur in many digital images due to defocus or motion, which is illustrated in Figure 1(a) and (c). Sometimes blur may be produced by the photographer to strengthen photo's expressiveness, but unintentional blur will decrease the image quality, which is caused by incorrect focus, object motion, hand shaking and so on. In any cases, automatic image blurred region detection and classification are useful for learning the image information, which can be used in different multimedia analysis applications such as image segmentation, depth recovery and image retrieval.

(a) defocus blur image (b) image blur map

(c) motion blur image (d) image blur map

Figure 1: Illustration of the blur map constructed by a singular value feature: (a,c) show a pair of example images that suffer from defocus blur and motion blur; (b,d) show the corresponding blur maps that are constructed based on the proposed singular value feature.

Many blur detection techniques are based on edge sharpness information [7, 9]. However, these edge sharpness based methods cannot distinguish either the blurred/non-blurred image regions or the type of image blurs. And Kovacs and Sziranyi's method [3] extract the unblur region using blind deconvolution. Based on the observation that blurred images usually lack high frequency information, some techniques [8, 6] detect image blurs using low pass filtering, without applying the decovolution.

In this paper, we propose an automatic image blurred detection and classification technique that first detects blurred regions within a single image and then identifies the blur type of the blurred image regions. The contributions of our work can be summarized in several aspects.

- First, we observe the connection between image blurs and

*Area chair: Bernard Merialdo

MM'11, November 28–December 1, 2011, Scottsdale, Arizona, USA.

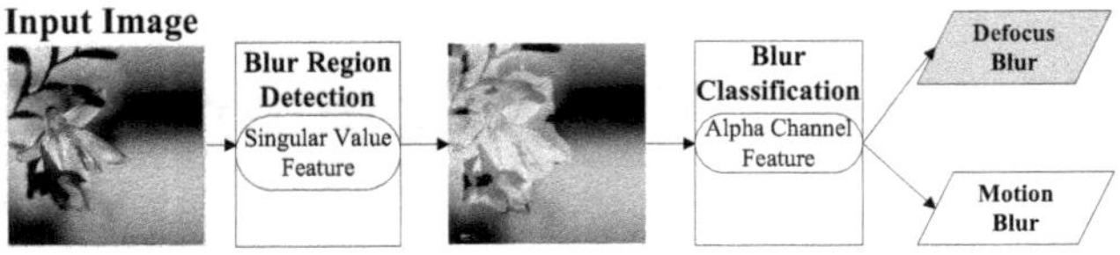

(a)

Figure 2: Framework of the proposed image blurred region detection and classification technique.

singular value distributions and accordingly design a blur metric that detects blurred regions from a single image accurately.

- Second, we capture the distribution pattern of the gradient of the alpha channel to differentiate motion and defocus blur effectively.
- Third, we build an automatic blur detection and classification system that requires neither image deblurring nor blur kernel estimation. The built system can also be used in many other applications such as image segmentation, image enhancement and image retrieval.

2. THE PROPOSED SYSTEM

The proposed technique first constructs a blur map that encodes the blur degree of an image. The blur degree is estimated by the ratio between the first few most significant singular values and all singular values that are computed over a local image patch surrounding each image pixel. Such estimation is based on the observation that the first few most significant eigen-images of a blurred image patch usually have higher weights (i.e. singular values) than an image patch with no blur (because image blurs often suppress the high-frequency image details that is reflected within those less significant eigen-images). Once the blurred image regions are extracted, the blur types of those blurred regions are further identified based on the gradient distribution patterns of the alpha channels.

The overall framework is illustrated in Figure 2. The non blurred region is first extracted from the input image, which is marked by green color, and then the blurred region is classified into defocus blur as highlighted in the blue box.

3. IMAGE BLUR FEATURES

This section describes the two image features that are used in our proposed blur detection and classification technique. One feature is a singular value feature that can be used as a blur metric to detect image blur effectively and accurately. The other feature is an alpha channel feature that can be used for blur type classification.

3.1 Singular Value Feature

Singular value decomposition (SVD) is one of the most useful techniques in linear algebra, and has been applied to different areas of computer science. Given an image I, its SVD can be represented by $I = U\Lambda V^T$ where U, V are orthogonal matrices and Λ is a diagonal matrix that is composed of multiple singular values arranged in decreasing order. The image can therefore be decomposed into multiple rank 1 matrices (which are also called eigen-images) [1] as follows:

$$I = \sum_{i=1}^{n} \lambda_i \mathbf{u}_i \mathbf{v}_i^T \qquad (1)$$

(a) motion blur image (b) defocus blur image

Figure 3: a pair of example images suffering from motion blur image and defocus blur and their corresponding $\nabla\alpha$ distributions in Hough space (a clear white circle region appears in $\nabla\alpha$ distribution of the defocus blur image as highlighted by a red color circle in (b)).

where the $\mathbf{u}_i, \mathbf{v}_i$, and λ_i are the column vectors of U, V and diagonal terms of Λ. Under the framework of digital image compression, the image I can be approximated by I_k that sums up the first k components.

As Equation 1 shows, the singular value decomposition actually decomposes an image into a weighted summation of a number of eigen-images where the weights are exactly the singular values themselves. Therefore, the compressed image which omits the small singular value in tail actually replaces the original image by a coarse approximation. Those eigen-images with a small singular value which often capture detailed information are instead discarded.

Such situation is similar to the image blurring that keeps shape structures at large scales but discards image details at small scales. From another viewpoint, those eigen-images in Equation 1 provide different scale-space analysis of the image [1], i.e., the first few most significant eigen-images work on large scales that provide rough shapes of the image while those latter less significant eigen-images encode the image details. Suppose that an image I is convoluted with a Point Spread Function(PSF) H as follows:

$$I * H = \sum_{i=1}^{n} \lambda_i (\mathbf{u}_i \mathbf{v}_i^T) * H \qquad (2)$$

where the convolution operator $(\mathbf{u}_i \mathbf{v}_i^T) * H$ tends to increase the scale-space of eigen-images and accordingly causes a loss of high-frequency details. In other word, those small singular values that match to small scale space eigen-images correspond to larger scale-space eigen-images after convolution. As a result, the image details are weakened and those large scale-space eigen-images get higher weights. For a blurred image, the first few most significant eigen-images therefore usually have much higher weights (i.e. singular values) compared with that of a clear image. We thus propose a singular value feature that measures the blurry degree of an image as follows:

$$\beta 1 = \frac{\sum_{i=1}^{k} \lambda_i}{\sum_{i=1}^{n} \lambda_i} \qquad (3)$$

where λ_i denotes the singular value that is evaluated within a local image patch for each image pixel. As Equation 3 shows, the singular feature is actually the ratio between the first k most significant singular value and all singular values.

Generally, blurred image regions have a higher blur degree compared with clear image regions with no blurs, which is shown in

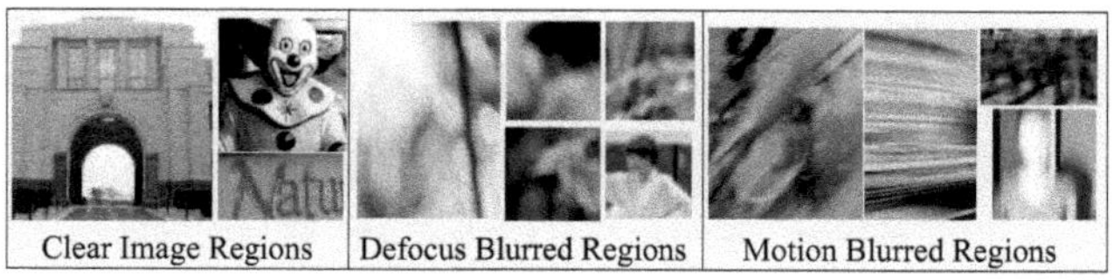

Figure 4: Selected samples of blurred/non-blurred image regions from our dataset.

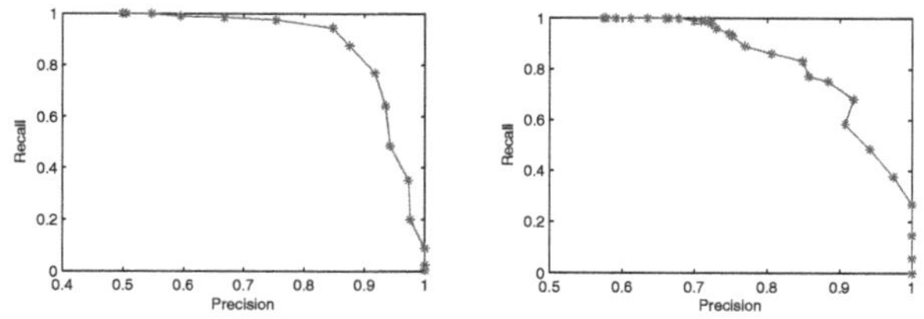

(a) (b)

Figure 5: Illustration of the Recall-Precision curve of our classification method. (a) the recall-precision curve of 'blur' in blur/nonblur classification using singular value feature. (b) the recall-precision curve of 'defocus blur' in motion/defocus blur classification using alpha channel feature.

Figure 1(b) and (d). So an image pixel will be classified into blurred region if its $\beta 1$ is larger than a threshold, otherwise, it will be categorized as non blurred region.

3.2 Alpha Channel Feature

Once the image blur is detected, the image blur type needs to be identified as either motion blur or defocus blur. We use the two-layer image composition model [5], in which an image I is viewed as a combination of an image foreground F and an image background B as follows:

$$I = \alpha F + (1 - \alpha)B \quad (4)$$

where α lies between 0 and 1. In a clear image, most of the values of α are either 1 or 0. But in a blurred image, the foreground and background tend to mix together, most of the value of α lie at the boundary between foreground and background become pure decimal.

An alpha channel model constraint [2] has been reported for motion blur images, which is defined as $\nabla\alpha \cdot \mathbf{b} = \pm 1$. $\mathbf{b}$ is a 2×1 vector, denotes the blur extension in horizontal and vertical direction. The blur kernels $\mathbf{b}$ of motion blurred images are usually directional, so the distribution of $\nabla\alpha$ will be lines, which is shown in Figure 3(a). But the image pixel intensities will spread out with constant steps at every directions after blurred for defocus blurred images, so the elements of $\nabla\alpha$ will have similar magnitude values but different angles. And then the $\nabla\alpha$ distribution will look like a circle, as shown in Figure 3(b).

So we evaluate the circularity of shape pattern of $\nabla\alpha$ distribution. We calculate the distances from the center to nearest salient points(dark spot) at different directions on the $\nabla\alpha$ distribution to obtain an array $d_1, d_2, \cdots, d_n$, where d_i denotes the estimated distance at one direction, which is shown in Figure 3. We define the alpha channel feature $\beta 2$ as the variation of the distance array, which is shown in Equation 5.

(a) (b)

Figure 6: Illustration of blurred and non-blurred image region extractions by several example images: the red curves separate the blurred and non-blurred images regions where the image in (a) has a blurred background and the image in (b) has a blurred foreground.

$$\beta 2 = Var\{d_1, d_2, \cdots, d_n\} \quad (5)$$

The motion blurred image regions will have much larger $\beta 2$ values compared with defocus blurred image regions. So a threshold is used on $\beta 2$ to classify the type of blurred regions into either motion or defocus.

4. EXPERIMENTS AND DISCUSSIONS

4.1 Blur Region and Type Classification

Our blur detection and classification features are tested on different images. Those images are first cropped into smaller regions so that they contain only blur or clear region. We generate 200 clear image regions, 100 defocus blur image regions, and 100 motion blur image regions in total from 100 digital images. Some examples of our dataset are shown in Figure 4.

Figure 5 shows the recall-precision curve of our method. The threshold for singular value feature varies from 0 to 1, with a step 0.05, while the threshold of alpha channel feature changes in a range [0,0.4], the interval is 0.01. And the method produce best accuracy for blur/nonblur classification when singular value threshold is 0.75, the accuracy is 88.78%. The best accuracy for motion/defocus classification is 80% when the alpha channel threshold is 0.12. Compared with Liu et.al.'s method [6], which reports maximum 76.98% accuracy for blur/nonblur classification and 78.84% for motion/defocus blur classification, our method is simpler yet performs great.

4.2 Blur Region Segmentation

We then use our technique to extract blurred regions of images. A blurred region is extracted based on the constructed singular value blur map. And a blur mask is built based on the threshold obtained in the previous subsection to divide blurred/non blurred regions. To evaluate the accuracy, we first manually extracted the blurred regions of 10 partially blurred images as ground truth. The blurred image regions extracted by our proposed method is then evaluated based on their comparison with the ground truth image regions. The accuracy measurement of our region extraction is defined as the ratio of the correctly segmented pixels and the total image pixels. Our experiments show that the blurred region extraction accuracy (by our proposed method) is 83% on averaged over the 10 images. Our method can successfully extracts the blurred image regions, as shown in Figure 6.

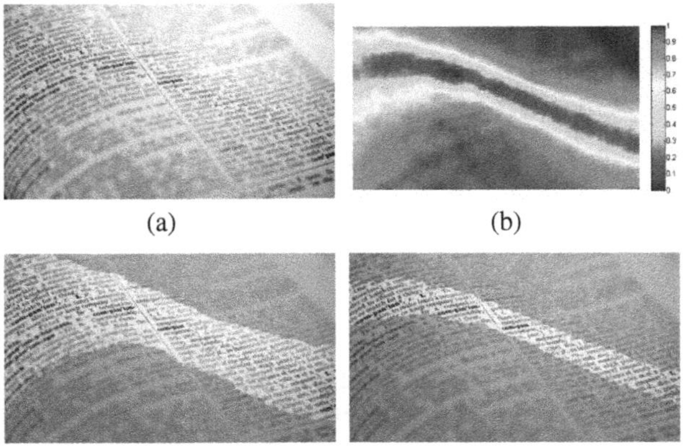

(a) (b)

(c) (d)

Figure 7: The document image in (a) contains defocus blur of different extents. Its corresponding singular value map is shown in (b), those regions with different blur degrees are highlighted in different color. (c) and (d) show the two extracted blurred image regions of (a) when the threshold is set at 0.91 and 0.76, respectively.

(a) (b) (c)

Figure 8: Comparison of blurred image region extraction: (a-c) show the blurred image regions that are extracted by using Levin's method [5], Liu et al.'s method [6], and our proposed method, respectively.

On the other hand, the size of extracted blurred image regions depends on the singular value threshold because there is no clear boundary between blurred and non-blurred image regions. Figure 7(a) shows a blurred document image example and Figure 7(b) shows the singular value blur map of the example image that illustrates blur degree variation. Different blurred image extraction results can be obtained when different thresholds are set. As shown in Figure 7, two different blurred image regions in (c) and (d) can be extracted from (a) based on the thresholds of 0.91 and 0.76, respectively. We also compare our proposed technique with Liu et al. [6] and Levin's [4] based on a public image shown in Figure 8, which also produces good segmentation result.

4.3 Blur Degree Estimation

Lastly, we can use our blur detection features to rank the blur level of images. The blur degree of an image is affected by two aspects: one is the blur extent of the whole image, which can be evaluated by the singular value feature $\beta 1$; the other is the ratio of the size of blur area to the whole image size. The blur degree of an image is then given as follows:

Figure 9: Images ranked based on the estimated blurry degree D: the proposed D in Equation 6 captures the image blurry degree properly, i.e., images are blurred more severely with the increase of D.

$$D = k\beta 1 + (1-k)(\frac{\Omega_b}{\Omega}) \tag{6}$$

where k is a weight that is set at 0.5 to give equal weights to the two aspects, Ω_b denotes the size of blurred image regions, Ω denotes the whole image size. Those severely blurred images should have large values on $\beta 1$ and $\frac{\Omega_b}{\Omega}$, and then the degree D. Figure 9 shows an array of example images that are ranked by the blur degree estimated by our proposed technique, which are sorted properly.

5. CONCLUSION

In this paper, we propose an image blurred region detection and classification method that can automatically detect blurred image regions and classifies the blur types without either image deblurring or kernel estimation. We construct a new blur metric: singular value feature, and use it to detect the blurred regions of an image. We also analyze the alpha channel information and classify the blur type of the blurred image regions into defocus blur or motion blur, respectively. Our proposed method is simple and effective. Experiments show that our method works for different kinds of images and can also be used for different multimedia analysis applications such as depth recovery, information retrieval and segmentation.

6. REFERENCES

[1] H. Andrews and C. Patterson. Singular value decompositions and digital image processing. *IEEE Transaction on Acoustics, Speech and Signal Processing*, 24:26–53, 1976.

[2] S. Dai and Y. Wu. Motion from blur. *CVPR*, 2008.

[3] L. Kovács and T. Szirányi. Focus area extraction by blind deconvolution for defining regions of interest. *IEEE Transaction on Pattern Analysis and Machine Intelligence*, 29:1080–1085, 2007.

[4] A. Levin. Blind motion deblurring using image statistics. *Advances in Neural Information Processing Systems*, 2007.

[5] A. Levin, A. Rav-Acha, and D. Lischinski. Spectral matting. *IEEE Transactions on Pattern Analysis and Machine Intelligence*, 30:1699–1712, 2008.

[6] R. Liu, Z. Li, and J. Jia. Image partial blur detection and classification. *CVPR*, 2008.

[7] P. Marziliano, F. Dufaux, S. Winkler, and T. Ebrahimi. A non-reference perceptual blur metric. *ICIP*, 3:57–60, 2002.

[8] J. D. Rugna and H. Konik. Automatic blur detection for metadata extraction in content-based retrieval context. *SPIE*, 5304:285–294, 2003.

[9] H. Tong, M. Li, H. Zhang, and C. Zhang. Blur detection for digital images using wavelet transform. *In Proceedings of IEEE International Conference on Multimedia&Expo*, pages 17–20, 2004.

Human Group Activity Analysis with Fusion of Motion and Appearance Information

Zhongwei Cheng[1], Lei Qin[2], Qingming Huang[1,2], Shuqiang Jiang[2], Shuicheng Yan[3], Qi Tian[4]

[1]Graduate University of Chinese Academy of Sciences
Beijing 100190, China

[2]Key Lab of Intelli. Info. Process., Inst. of Comput. Tech., CAS
Beijing 100190, China

[3]Electrical and Computer Engineering, National University of Singapore
Singapore, 117576

[4]Department of Computer Science, University of Texas at San Antonio
TX 78249, U.S.A.

{zwcheng, lqin, qmhuang, sqjiang}@jdl.ac.cn, eleyans@nus.edu.sg, qitian@cs.utsa.edu

ABSTRACT
Human activity analysis is an important and challenging task in video content analysis and understanding. In this paper, we focus on the activity of small human group, which involves countable persons and complex interactions. To cope with the variant number of participants and inherent interactions within the activity, we propose a hierarchical model with three layers to depict the characteristics at different granularities. In traditional methods, group activity is represented mainly based on motion information, such as human trajectories, but ignoring discriminative appearance information, e.g. the rough sketch of a pose style. In our approach, we take advantage of both the motion and the appearance information in the spatiotemporal activity context under the hierarchical model. These features are inhomogeneous. Therefore, we employ multiple kernel learning methods to fuse the features for group activity recognition. Experiments on a surveillance-like human group activity database demonstrate the validity of our approach and the recognition performance is promising.

Categories and Subject Descriptors
H.3.1 [**INFORMATION STORAGE AND RETRIEVAL**]: Content Analysis and Indexing – *Abstracting methods*;

I.2.10 [**ARTIFICIAL INTELLIGENCE**]: Vision and Scene Understanding – *Video analysis*

General Terms
Algorithms, Design, Experimentation

Keywords
Human Group Activity, Activity Analysis, Feature Fusion

1. INTRODUCTION
As the amount of digital media grows rapidly, the demand of analyzing, understanding and utilizing these data is rising. Human activity analysis, as an important and challenging task in video content analysis, has drawn growing attention of worldwide researchers for its great potential and promising applications in industry, entertainment, security and medical domains. In recent years, human activity analysis has made notable progress and the representative state-of-the-art approaches are reviewed in [1].

*Area Chair: Kiyoharu Aizawa

MM'11, November 28–December 1, 2011, Scottsdale, Arizona, USA.

(a) human action (b) group activity (c) crowd behavior

Figure 1. Human activity categorization

Human activity is a complex concept with diverse semanteme, various expressions and different scales. To present our work clearly, we categorize human activities into three levels: human action, group activity and crowd behavior according to the number of participants and the complexity of the activity. Fig.1 illustrates instances of the three categories. The methods to analyze these activities should be different and be adjusted to their inherent characteristics. As the smallest scale of activity, human action covers single person action and the interaction between a pair of persons. For the movements of human body are significant properties of action, the related methods aim at modeling the action pattern with localized features of motion or appearance information [2, 3]. Group activity is the intermediate level activity with countable people and complex interactions. The "group" here is also mentioned as "small group", which consists of three or more persons with possible occlusions. To recognize group activity, the analysis of actions of individuals as well as their overall relations becomes essential [1]. For crowd behavior which consists of visually uncountable people, it is impossible to track individuals and recognize their actions to understand the whole crowd. Thus a reasonable choice is to model the entire crowd with motion information [4], such as optical flows or motion trajectories.

In this paper, we focus on the group activity. It is difficult to handle the structured property of human group activity through single models. Therefore, researchers have attempted to take advantage of layered models. Three level localized causalities are introduced to characterize relations within, between and among motion trajectories [5]. Cheng *et al.* proposed a three layered model to describe the activity patterns [8]. However, the top level of their models, which is to depict the holistic activity pattern, is not represented properly. Interactions of person-person and person-group are considered in [7], but the complete layered structure is not explicitly defined.

To represent the activity patterns of human group, motion information is widely utilized. Ni *et al.* describes motion information by digital filter responses on participants' motion trajectories [5], while Gaussian Process regression is applied to represent motion patterns in [8]. Although the motion information is proper to depict the activity pattern, appearance information can

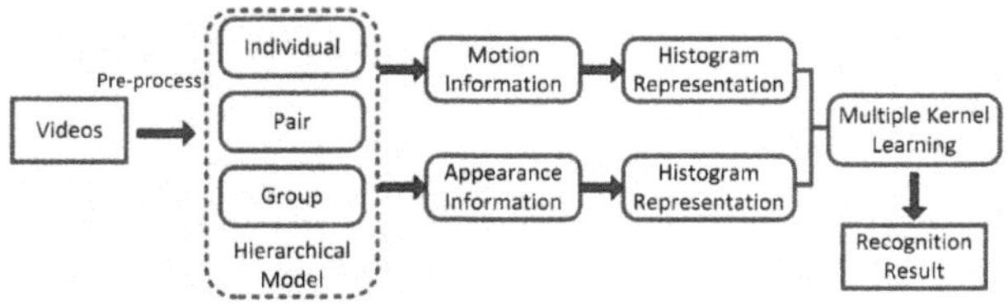

Figure 2. Framework of our approach

be a complementary to draw the discriminative characters for promoting the understanding of group activity. Zhu *et al* utilized localized appearance, SIFT, as a descriptor of activity [6]. But localized features can be unreliable due to appearance variance and noise. Thus the holistic appearance features are more appropriate to represent activity patterns.

In this paper, we propose a new approach to analyze human group activity, with the framework demonstrated in Fig.2. Different to previous works, by considering spatiotemporal context information of the activity, we construct a hierarchical model for human group activity and represent activity pattern with both the motion and the appearance information. The inhomogeneous features are expressed in histogram form respectively and fused with Multiple Kernel Learning methods.

The remainder of this paper is organized as follows. In section 2, we introduce the hierarchical model of group activity. The representations of motion and appearance information are described in section 3. Experimental validation and conclusions come with the last two sections.

2. HIERARCHICAL MODEL FOR HUMAN GROUP ACTIVITY

As introduced in the previous section, group activity has more participants and interactions than human action and more visible individual movements than crowd behavior. To analyze the group activity, we need to recognize the individual actions, the pairwise interactions, and the overall motion pattern of the group. Semantically, they are mutual promotional components for understanding the group activity. However, due to the diversity of participants and their variant numbers, it is hard to cope with the patterns of human group activity. Jointly considering different granularities of activity pattern is a reasonable solution for modeling the activity. In this paper, we introduce a three layered hierarchical model for group activity recognition. Fig.3. illustrates an activity instance represented under our hierarchical model. The bottom row shows all components of activity patterns in three granularities. The corresponding realistic examples of video frames are demonstrated in the top row. The three levels represent the group activity pattern from different aspects, and they are complementary for analyzing the group activity. Details of the model levels are introduced in the rest of this section.

Individual Level: This level focuses on the action pattern of a single participant. By depicting the individual movements of people within a group activity, we can obtain a general knowledge of that activity. It should be noted that appearance information is useful to represent discriminative individual patterns, which is consistent with human cognition. Especially, the general holistic appearances of people's movements can properly describe the style of key poses in actions. Different with usual human action representation, action patterns of a single participant do not work separately for group activity. As our target is to represent the group activity, knowing a participant doing a specific type of action is not of much significance. While to present the frequency of an action appearing in a category of activities makes more sense.

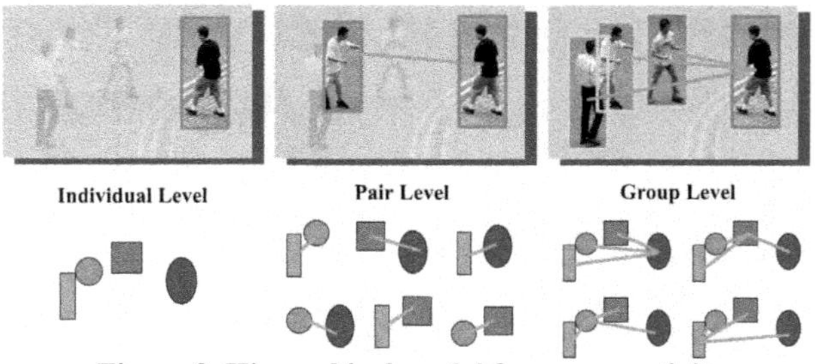

Figure 3. Hierarchical model for group activity

Pair Level: Pairwise representations are designed to handle the internal interactions of group activity. Each pair of participants reveals some kind of interaction within the activity, no matter if it is semantically significant. These pairwise patterns can be regarded as medial level components of group activity pattern. Although some pairs may connect unrelated persons in the activity, it is reasonable that the discriminative pairwise patterns for a specific activity class have statistical significance.

Group Level: The top level of group activity model is to express the pattern of the entire group, with handling the great diversification of group activity instances. We introduce a representation of the holistic pattern, noted as grouptron. The grouptron can be taken as high level component of the activity pattern. To treat a specific person as a reference, the grouptron represents the relativities in action with all other participants. One grouptron indicates a specific view of the group activity. Thus we think that collection of the grouptrons of a group activity can depict the activity pattern properly in group level.

As presented above, our hierarchical model of group activity employs statistical property of component patterns in each level to handle variations and generate discriminative representations. The decomposition of group level pattern into different personal views of the group is different from directly modeling of the entire group, which makes our model more expressive. This model also provides a framework for considering different types of information at multiple granularities.

3. FEATURE REPRESENTATION

We adopt different features for different levels of the hierarchical model. Both motion and appearance information are taken into account. Motion features are based on trajectories of participants, and as object tracking is not the topic of this paper, it is considered as a pre-processing step. To ease the complexity of tracking, we split videos into smaller video segments according to the timelines. Thus motion features are extracted from video segments. Nevertheless, appearance features are extracted on the basis of video frames.

3.1 Motion Representation

Motion information, especially the motion trajectories of people [5, 6, 8], is effective for activity representation. In this paper, we step forward by not just describing the trajectory pattern itself but also representing the context information of the activity as well. For the individual level, motion pattern lies in the time-variant locations of the humans, or specifically their motion trajectories. For the pair level, as pairwise motion patterns reflect the interactions, we represent it through the time-variant distances between the pair of humans. As to the group level, the

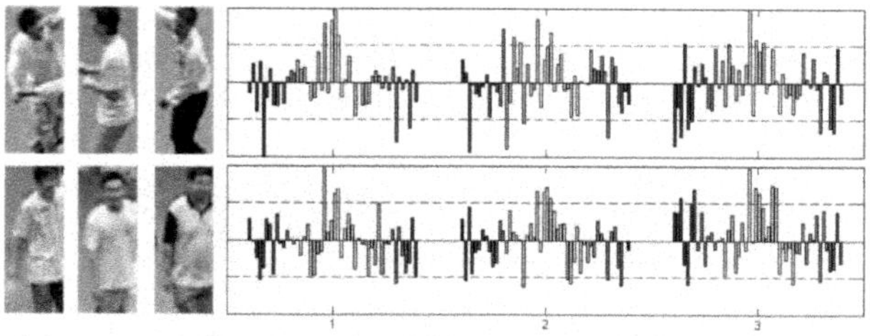

(a) Appearance samples (b) 50D PCA of corresponding HoG features

Figure 4. Appearance information in activity

representation of a grouptron needs to cover the characters of all pairwise relationships between the reference person and all the other ones. Thus we present it through the statistics of all the pairwise information (the time-variant distances). As all motion representations are extracted from unified form (time-variant data, which can be treated as some kind of trajectory), we apply the same feature extracting paradigm for all the three levels of the activity model. To simplify the explanation, we take the physical meanings of motion trajectory in the individual level to introduce the motion features extracted.

Given a set of motion trajectories within a video segment, we have $\{T_i(t_j) \mid i=1,..,n \text{ and } j=1,..,m\}$, where n is the number of trajectories and m is the length of trajectories. The motion representation consists of two parts:

Movement Property: This part depicts the characteristic of a trajectory itself. Actually, a trajectory consists of temporal conjunctive positions, which can be regarded as a kind of temporal context of the activity. Inspired by [8], we employ Gaussian Process (GP) to represent the probabilistic variation of the trajectory. With modeling a trajectory as a GP over time and applying the squared exponential covariance function, which is denoted in Eq.1, the hyper-parameters $\theta = [\sigma_f, l, \sigma_n]$ are utilized to represent the character of the trajectory. Please refer to [9] for the details of GP regression to obtain the hyper-parameters θ.

$$T(t) \sim \mathcal{GP}(0,\Sigma),\ \Sigma=\sigma_f^2 \exp\left(-\frac{(t-t')^2}{2l^2}\right) + \sigma_n^2\delta_{jj'} \quad (1)$$

Moreover, location change of the person within a trajectory is used to express the movement scale.

$$c_i = |T_i(t_1) - T_i(t_m)| \quad (2)$$

Velocity is also an important property of movement. We adopt the average velocity ϑ and velocity ratio r to represent the intensity and the complexity of the movement respectively.

$$\vartheta_i = \frac{1}{m-1}\sum_{j=2}^{m} v_j \quad (3)$$

$$r_i = |\vartheta_i| \Big/ \frac{1}{m-1}\sum_{j=2}^{m}|v_j| = \left|\sum_{j=2}^{m} v_j\right| \Big/ \sum_{j=2}^{m}|v_j| \quad (4)$$

where $v_j = T(t_j) - T(t_{j-1})$.

Movement Context: For group activity, individual's movement is influenced by other participants. By considering it in the feature view, we bring the activity context information into the motion representation. This activity context is a kind of spatial context of one's movement in a group activity, which indicates the movements of other persons in the same activity and the influence to him/her. The relative location change rc and relative average velocity rv are used to depict the context.

$$rc_i = c_i - \frac{1}{n}\sum_{p=1}^{n} c_p \quad (5)$$

$$rv_i = \vartheta_i - \frac{1}{n}\sum_{p=1}^{n} \vartheta_p \quad (6)$$

Therefore, the motion information of a trajectory T_i can be represented as the feature vector of $[\theta_i, c_i, \vartheta_i, r_i, rc_i, rv_i]$.

3.2 Appearance Representation

Besides motion, general appearance, like shape, is also an important clue for activity recognition. It provides additional discriminative information which is complementary to motion information. For example, we can estimate the activity in Fig.1(b) without motion information. We employ the Histograms of Oriented Gradients (HoG) [10] to represent the shape information in this paper. The appearance of activity may be diverse majorly due to the reason that an activity usually consists of several individual actions. To grab the holistic, or as to say the 'style', of the appearance information of activity, we apply Principal Components Analysis (PCA) to the HoG features. And we believe these principal components can reflect the general appearance characters. As illustrated in Fig.4(a), in the top row are three samples of *fight* activity, and in the bottom are of *walk-in-group*. These samples are visually discriminative. And Fig.4(b) demonstrates 50 dimensions (50D) PCA to the HoG features corresponding with samples in Fig.4(a). It can be observed that the appearance representations can supply some discriminative information.

In this paper, we apply appearance representation just to the individual level of our activity model. It may be a possible way to compose pair of samples to a new pairwise sample and then apply the representation on it for the pair level. And other appearance descriptors, like GIST, can be employed to represent the activity appearance "style".

With motion and appearance feature representations on the hierarchical activity model, multiple inhomogeneous features are extracted for the group activity recognition. The way to fuse these features affects the recognition performance. Directly concatenating them into a larger feature is a practicable method, but would not be suitable for the inconsistent dimensions of different features. In this paper, we deal with the fusion of features by Multiple Kernel Learning with different features generating kernel matrix respectively.

4. EXPERIMENTS

Experiments are performed on Human Group Activity (HGA) dataset in [5] to validate our approach. The HGA dataset consists of 476 videos in total with 6 categories of group activities. Each activity instance contains 4-8 participants. The trajectories of people in videos are generated by blob tracking with manual initializations [5]. According to different collecting conditions, the dataset is organized in 5 sessions. In the experiments, we test the performance with the average classification accuracy of the 6 activity categories through leave-one-session-out strategy. We first test the performance of motion feature, then the appearance feature, and finally we compare our approach with the state-of-the-art methods.

To generate motion features of activities, we extract motion representations from three model levels respectively. Then we apply Bag of Words (BoW) method to obtain statistical histogram features from every activity video [2]. About 50% of data are selected randomly for codebook generation. K-means clustering is applied separately for different model levels. Multi-

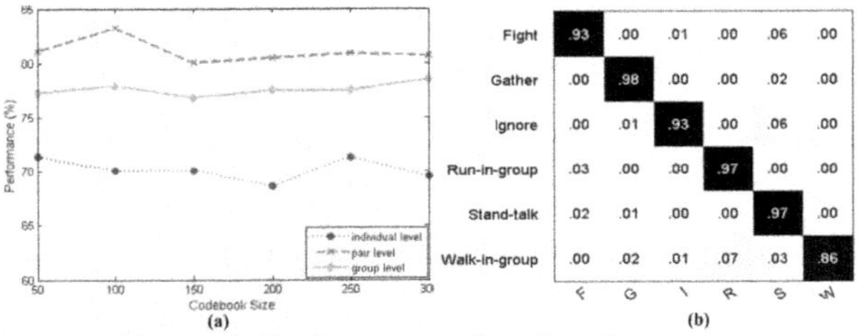

Figure 5. Performance of motion feature

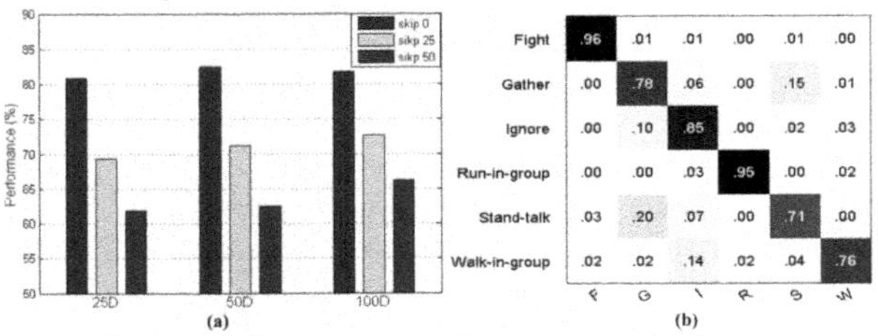

Figure 6. Performance of appearance feature

class Support Vector Machines with a χ^2 distance based kernel are employed to recognize the group activities. Fig.5(a) shows the performance under different codebook sizes with motion features from our three model levels. The performance of pair and group level features is obviously better than individual level, which implies the interaction and holistic patterns are more discriminative for group activity. We can notice that the performances of three levels reach optimum at different codebook sizes, probably due to diverse sparseness of the histograms caused by the varied feature amount in different model levels. The confusion matrix of recognition results with all motion information is shown in Fig.5(b).

Appearance features are extracted just in individual level for this dataset. We assign a bounding box to a person according to his/her center point from the trajectory to get an appearance sample. With an estimated vertical compensation for the affine transformation, size of bounding box varies to get proper sample size. These samples are resized to the same scale, and then 972D HoG features are extracted. Then the HoG features are projected to lower dimensionality by PCA and clustered to generate codebook. As appearance feature is based on frames, samples from a small number of video data are sufficient. Thus we randomly choose only 10% of data to generate PCA coefficients and the codebook of BoW. The size of codebook is set to 512 for the plentiful appearance samples. Different dimensions and component selection strategies of PCA are tested and results are presented in Fig.6(a). The "skip M" stands for dropping the top significant M principle components and selecting the following N as features, demonstrated with M=0, 25, 50 and N=25, 50, 100. Performance of "skip 0" outperforms the others, illustrating the top principle components, which present the general and holistic appearance, are more expressive than those in the rear, which present the specific and detailed appearance. Another observation is that the performance of the appearance features is superior to motion feature in individual level, expressing the value of appearance in activity recognition. From the confusion matrix in Fig.6(b), we can discover that appearance information is more effective for intense activities such as *fight* and *run-in-group*.

Feature fusion is achieved by multiplication of kernel matrices of motion and appearance features in different model levels respectively (totally four kernels, one for appearance and three for motion). The performance of ours and other methods are listed in Table.1. It shows that our approach outperforms previous methods. And it can be observed that combining both motion and appearance features is better than just using motion information with over 3% performance gain, which reveals the impact of appearance.

Table 1. Performance comparison with other methods

Methods	*Performance*
Ni. *et al* [5]	73.5%
Cheng. *et al* [8]	91.8%
Zhu. *et al* [6]	87%
motion	93.7%
motion + appearance	**96.8%**

5. CONCLUSION

We propose an approach for the analysis of human group activity in this paper. With a hierarchical model, we represent the group activity pattern from three complementary levels. Other than previous work, we consider both the motion and appearance information with activity context. Experiments on HGA dataset validate the effectiveness of our approach and the recognition performance is notable.

To design informative descriptors for grouptrons is nontrivial and worth of interests in the future work. We will also investigate appearance representations for pair and group levels and explore effective expressions of discriminative components of group activity pattern.

6. ACKNOWLEDGMENTS

This work was supported in part by National Natural Science Foundation of China: 61025011, 61035001 and 61003165, in part by National Basic Research Program of China (973 Program): 2009CB320906, and in part by Beijing Natural Science Foundation: 4111003. This work was supported in part to Dr. Qi Tian by NSF IIS 1052851, Faculty Research Awards by Google, FXPAL and NEC Laboratories of America, respectively.

7. REFERENCES

[1] Aggarwal, J.K. and Ryoo, M.S. 2011. Human activity analysis: A Review. ACM Computing Surveys (CSUR), v.43 n.3, p.1-43.

[2] Niebles, J.C., Wang, H. and Fei-Fei, L. 2008. Unsupervised learning of human action categories using spatial-temporal words. International Journal of Computer Vision (IJCV) 79, 3(Sep).

[3] Ryoo, M.S. and Aggarwal, J.K. 2009. Spatio-temporal relationship match: Video structure comparison for recognition of complex human activities. In ICCV.

[4] Mahadevan, V., Li,W., Bhalodia, V. and Vasconcelos, N. 2010. Anomaly Detection in Crowded Scenes. In IEEE Conference on Computer Vision and Pattern Recognition.

[5] Ni, B., Yan, S. and Kassim, A. 2009. Recognizing Human Group Activities with Localized Causalities. In IEEE Conference on Computer Vision and Pattern Recognition.

[6] Zhu, G., Yan, S., Han, T.X. and Xu, C. 2011. Generative group activity analysis with quaternion descriptor. In International Conference on Advances in Multimedia Modeling.

[7] Lan, T., Wang, Y., Yang, W. and Mori, G. 2010. Beyond Actions: Discriminative Models for Contextual Group Activities. In Annual Conference on Neural Information Processing Systems.

[8] Cheng, Z., Qin, L., Huang, Q., Jiang, S. and Tian, Q. 2010. Group Activity Recognition by Gaussian Process Estimation. In International Conference on Pattern Recognition.

[9] Rasmussen, C. E. and Williams, C. K. I.2006. Gaussian Processes for Machine Learning. The MIT Press.

[10] Dalal, N. and Triggs, B. 2005. Histograms of oriented gradients for human detection. In IEEE Conference on Computer Vision and Pattern Recognition.

Exploring Latent Class Information for Image Retrieval using the Bag-of-Feature Model *

Lingqiao Liu
School of Engineering, Australian National University, ACT 0200, Canberra, Australia
lingqiao.liu@anu.edu.au

Lei Wang
School of Computer Science & Software Engineering,University of Wollongong
NSW 2522, Australia
leiw@uow.edu.au

ABSTRACT

Recently, the Bag-of-Feature (BoF) model has shown promising performance in object and generic image retrieval. The similarity between two images is typically measured by the distance between the two histograms. Due to the imperfection of local descriptor and quantization error, visually similar image patches can be wrongly quantized into different visual words, making this distance-based measure less accurate. To address this issue, this paper explores the information of *latent class*, which is formed by all the database images that share the same visual concept with the one being compared to a given query. We then cast image similarity as the probability of the query and a database image belonging to a same latent class. Considering that a class of images together can better depict a visual concept, the shift from image-to-image to image-to-class comparison is expected to bring a more robust similarity measure. Because the ground truth of the latent class is not accessible in image retrieval, we define a latent class prior in our probabilistic model and derive its marginal distribution. This gives rise to a novel and efficient image similarity measure. It can significantly improve retrieval performance without prolonging retrieval process. Experimental study on multiple benchmark data sets demonstrates its advantages.

Categories and Subject Descriptors

H.3.1 [**Information Storage and Retrieval**]: Context Analysis and Indexing

General Terms

Algorithms, Experimentation

Keywords

Similarity, Image Retrieval, Neighborhood

*Area chair: Bernard Merialdo

1. INTRODUCTION

Recently, the Bag-of-Feature (BoF) model has demonstrated its superior performance in object image retrieval [12, 16, 11] and established itself as the state-of-the-art. Usually, the BoF model extracts local patches from images, represents them with a patch descriptor, and quantizes all the descriptors into a set of "visual words". Each image is then characterized by a histogram indicating the frequency of occurrence of different "visual words". In retrieval, the similarity between a query and a database image is measured via a properly chosen distance between the two histograms.

However, the distance between histograms may not accurately reflect visual similarity as expected due to i) the current patch descriptor e.g. SIFT [9] or HOG [17] is not perfect and visually similar patches are not necessarily close to each other in the descriptor space; ii) when quantizing the descriptors to visual words, quantization error makes two close descriptors be assigned to different visual words. Efforts have been made to improve this situation. To handle the imperfection of the local descriptor and reduce the quantization error, methods of using soft-assignment [13] and learning the possible appearance changes of an image patch [10, 14] have been proposed. To improve the efficiency of histogram-based similarity measure, sophisticated measures have been developed, for example, the Earth Mover distance [15], contextual dissimilarity [5] and the one that counteracting the negative effect of visual word's "burstiness" phenomenon [4].

The above methods evaluate image similarity by focusing on the information of two individual images. It ignores the potential help of the images in the database. This paper argues that in an image database, there are many latent classes each of which consists of a set of images sharing a same visual concept. To attain a better similarity measure, we propose to explore the information of the latent class for each database image because a class of images together can better depict a visual concept. With this information, we define the image similarity between a query and a database image as the probability that they belong to a same latent class and shift from the image-to-image comparison to an image-to-class comparison. A key difficulty is that in practice the ground truth of a latent class is not accessible. To handle this situation, we utilize a latent class prior in our probabilistic analysis and derive its marginal distribution. This gives an efficient image similarity measure which can be as simple as a weighted average of the exponential similarity score between a query and the neighbors of a compared image. The new measure can significantly improve retrieval performance without prolonging retrieval process because the major computation is done offline. Also, it supports the mechanism of inverted file, which is essential to the efficiency of image retrieval with the BoF model. Experimental study on multiple benchmark data sets verifies the superior performance of the proposed image similarity measure for both object and generic image retrieval.

2. RELATED WORK

This section reviews some work related to this paper. The idea of using class information to boost retrieval has long been explored by a large body of research on image retrieval with relevance feedback [18, 3]. Our method is different at that it does not require a user to provide labeled examples but implicitly infers the latent class information in a totally unsupervised way. Such a difference also distinguishes our method from the image-to-class distance recently proposed for image classification [1]. Moreover, the work in [1] compares two images at image patch level, incurring heavy computational load. Differently, our method works at the histogram level which can better meet the fast response requirement of image retrieval. Considering relevant objects to help object similarity evaluation has also been explored in [19, 6, 7]. However, the method in [6] is mainly developed for web application, in which the relevant objects can be conveniently and clearly identified via hyperlinks or shared properties, while the relevant database images in our work have to be modeled in a probabilistic sense. Also, the similarity score in [6] is computed in an iterative way while ours can be obtained in one shot, making it potentially more attractive in terms of computational load. In [19], the similarity between two points is defined as the similarity of the distributions of their neighboring points. Our method employs a likelihood-based similarity measure, which can directly evaluate the similarity of a query, as a single point, to a set of database images. The class or cluster concept has also been considered in [7]. It requires a pre-clustering of database images, which critically depends on the number of clusters to be formed and does not scale well with large-sized data sets and high-dimensional image representations. Finally, our method can be linked to the query expansion method [2] when it synthesizes a new query $\mathbf{q}_{\text{new}}$ online based on a set of top-ranked retrieved images and conducts a second round of retrieval with $\mathbf{q}_{\text{new}}$. Comparing $\mathbf{q}_{\text{new}}$ with each database image can be viewed as a class (the set of top-ranked retrieved images)-to-image (a database image) similarity measure. Our method is different at that i) it only needs a single round of retrieval and ii) it identifies the latent-class information offline. These make our method more computationally efficiency than the above query expansion.

3. OUR METHOD

Let I_q and I_i denote a query image and the ith database image, respectively, and $\mathbf{q}$ and $\mathbf{x}_i$ represent their histograms obtained from the BoF model. I_0 is the image being compared with I_q. Let $\mathcal{C}_0 = \{I_i \mid y(I_i) = y(I_0), i = 1, \cdots, N\}$ be the set of the database images sharing the same latent class label with I_0, where $y(I_i)$ is the label of I_i and N is the database size. Assuming that $\mathcal{C}_0$ is known, we define *our similarity score as the likelihood of $y(I_q) = y(I_0)$, which is equivalent to class-conditional probability $P(\mathbf{q}|y(I_0))$*. By using the kernel density estimation to model this probability, our similarity score can be expressed as

$$\begin{aligned} P(\mathbf{q}|y(I_0)) &= \frac{1}{nh}\sum_{I_i \in \mathcal{C}_0} K\left(\frac{\mathbf{q}-\mathbf{x}_i}{h}\right) \\ &= \frac{1}{nh}\sum_{i=1}^{N} \delta_i K\left(\frac{\mathbf{q}-\mathbf{x}_i}{h}\right), \end{aligned} \quad (1)$$

where n is the cardinality of $\mathcal{C}_0$ and δ_i is an indicator for I_i. $\delta_i = 1$ if $y(I_i) = y(I_0)$ and zero otherwise. K is the kernel function and it is defined as $\exp\left(\frac{\mathcal{S}(\mathbf{q},\mathbf{x}_i)}{h}\right)$ in this work, where h is the bandwidth and $\mathcal{S}(\mathbf{q}, \mathbf{x}_i)$ is a pre-chosen similarity measure between $\mathbf{q}$ and $\mathbf{x}_i$.

A key difficulty is that $y(I_i)$ is not accessible in practice, making $\mathcal{C}_0$ and δ_i unknown. To handle this, we treat all δ_i $(i = 1, \cdots, N)$ as latent variables and derive the marginal distribution $P(\mathbf{q}|y(I_0))$. Defining $\mathbf{\Delta} = \{\delta_1, \cdots, \delta_N\}$, the marginal distribution can be expressed as the expectation of the similarity score for a given $\mathbf{\Delta}$, denoted as $P(\mathbf{q}|y(I_0), \mathbf{\Delta})$, under all possible configurations:

$$P(\mathbf{q}|y(I_0)) = \sum_{\delta_1=0}^{1}\sum_{\delta_2=0}^{1}\cdots\sum_{\delta_N=0}^{1} P(\mathbf{q}|y(I_0), \mathbf{\Delta})P(\mathbf{\Delta}), \quad (2)$$

where $P(\mathbf{\Delta})$ denotes the prior distribution of the configuration $\{\delta_1, \cdots, \delta_N\}$. We can reasonably assume $\mathbf{x}_1, \cdots, \mathbf{x}_N$ to be i.i.d, and this allows $P(\mathbf{\Delta})$ to be factorized as $\prod_{i=1}^{N} P(\delta_i)$. Also, we model the probability of $\{\delta_i = 1\}$ as

$$P(\{\delta_i = 1\}) = \frac{1}{Z}\exp\left(-\beta\mathcal{D}(I_0, I_i)\right), \quad (3)$$

where Z is the normalization factor and β is the scaling factor. Any distance function $\mathcal{D}(\cdot, \cdot)$ measuring the closeness between I_0 and I_i can be applied. Possible choices include a simple bin-to-bin histogram distance, the Earth Mover distance, the spatial matching score of two images, or even the distance from their caption information. Here we use the bin-to-bin histogram distance and express it as $\mathcal{D}(\mathbf{x}_0, \mathbf{x}_i)$. Also, we use its "local" version to define $\mathcal{D}(I_0, I_i)$

$$\mathcal{D}(I_0, I_i) = \begin{cases} \mathcal{D}(\mathbf{x}_0, \mathbf{x}_i) & \text{if } \mathbf{x}_i \in \mathcal{N}_k(\mathbf{x}_0) \\ \infty & \text{otherwise,} \end{cases} \quad (4)$$

where $\mathcal{N}_k$ is defined as the set of k nearest neighbors of $\mathbf{x}_0$. The "local" version is preferred due to i) when represented in a high-dimensional histogram space, the database images likely reside on a sub-dimensional manifold, which makes a large distance less reliable in reflecting image similarity [8]; ii) it significantly saves computation by avoiding considering a large number of database images that unlikely share the same latent class label with I_0.

Let P_i^+ denote $P(\{\delta_i = 1\})$ and then $P(\{\delta_i = 0\}) = 1 - P_i^+$. We obtain

$$P(\mathbf{\Delta}) = \prod_{i=1}^{N} P(\delta_i) = \prod_{i=1}^{N} P_i^{+\delta_i}(1 - P_i^+)^{(1-\delta_i)}. \quad (5)$$

Now $P(\mathbf{q}|y(I_0))$ can be obtained by substituting Eq.(5) and Eq.(1) into Eq.(2). The last issue is that the n in Eq.(1) changes with the configuration Δ (note that $n = \sum_{i=1}^{N} \delta_i$). This issue can be tackled by considering the case of $n \approx k$ only because: i) for $n > k$: the local version of P_i^+ implies that $P(\mathbf{\Delta}) = 0$ in this case; ii) for $n < k$: in a high-dimensional space the distance $\mathcal{D}(\mathbf{x}_O, \mathbf{x}_i)$ becomes similar for different $\mathbf{x}_i$. This makes P_i^+ uniformly large for all $\mathbf{x}_i \in \mathcal{N}_k(\mathbf{x}_O)$ because a proper β ensures large P_i^+ for all $\mathbf{x}_i$ in $\mathcal{N}_k(\mathbf{x}_O)$. As a result, the probability of the configuration $\Delta' = \{\Delta | \sum_{i=1}^N \delta_i \approx k\}$ will dominate over other configurations because more "$\delta_i = 0$" terms introduce more smaller probability $(1 - P_i^+)$ to the product in Eq. (5), significantly decreasing $P(\mathbf{\Delta})$. Hence, we can safely consider the case $n \approx k$ only without losing much precision. With this approximation, we can rewrite $P(\mathbf{q}|y(I_O))$ in Eq.(2) as:

$$
\begin{aligned}
&P(\mathbf{q}|y(I_O)) \propto \\
&= \sum_{\mathbf{\Delta}} \left(\sum_i \delta_i K \left(\frac{\mathbf{q} - \mathbf{x}_i}{h} \right) \right) \left(\prod_{i=1}^N P_i^{+\delta_i} (1 - P_i^+)^{(1-\delta_i)} \right) \\
&= \sum_i \sum_{\mathbf{\Delta}} \delta_i K \left(\frac{\mathbf{q} - \mathbf{x}_i}{h} \right) \prod_{i=1}^N P_i^{+\delta_i} (1 - P_i^+)^{(1-\delta_i)} \\
&= \sum_i \left(\prod_{j \neq i} \sum_{\delta_j} g_j \right) \left(\sum_{\delta_i = 0}^1 \delta_i K \left(\frac{\mathbf{q} - \mathbf{x}_i}{h} \right) g_i \right) \\
&= \sum_i P_i^+ \exp \left(\frac{\mathcal{S}(\mathbf{q}, \mathbf{x}_i)}{h} \right), \qquad (6)
\end{aligned}
$$

where we define $g_i = P_i^{+\delta_i} (1 - P_i^+)^{(1-\delta_i)}$ and utilize the fact that $\sum_{\delta_i=0}^1 g_i = 1$. Eq.(6) indicates that to calculate the proposed similarity score $P(\mathbf{q}|y(I_O))$, we find all $\mathbf{x}_i$ in $\mathcal{N}_k(\mathbf{x}_O)$ and compute $\mathcal{S}(\mathbf{q}, \mathbf{x}_i)$ for each of them. Then the k individual similarity scores are aggregated by summing weighted exponentials. According to Eq.(4), images more likely to share the latent class with I_O have higher P_i^+.

Our similarity measure can be efficiently implemented in a BoF-model-based image retrieval system by:

- (Offline) Determine $\mathcal{N}_k(\mathbf{x}_O)$ for each database image I_O and their P_i^+ values with the distance $\mathcal{D}(I_O, I_i)$.
- Given a query $\mathbf{q}$, compute $\mathcal{S}(\mathbf{q}, \mathbf{x})$ for all database images $\mathbf{x}$.
- Obtain $P(\mathbf{q}|y(I_O))$ for all database images to rank.

Compared with retrieval using image-to-image similarity measure, only the last step is extra. Its computational cost is low, only at the order of $\mathcal{O}(kN)$.

4. EXPERIMENTAL RESULT

Three benchmark data sets, Oxford5K, Caltech101 and Scene15, are used to verify the advantages of our similarity measure over the image-to-image measure. Oxford5K [12] contains 5062 images which comprise 11 landmarks and irrelevant scenes. The task of Oxford5K is to retrieve the images of the same landmark in a query. We directly download the one million visual words from the author's webpage and follow the same experiment protocol in [12]. The mean Average Precision (mAP) and average Recall are used to evaluate retrieval performance. For Caltech101 and Scene15 which have well-defined image classes, we use them to retrieve the images having the same semantic concept as the query. For each of their images, a single scale of 16×16 patches with the step size of 8 are densely sampled and represented by the HOG features [17]. The extracted features are clustered into 1000 visual words since it performs best in the literature. Precision of top 10 retrieved image (Precision@10) is used to evaluate retrieval performance [1]. We choose the best image-to-image similarity measure for each data set that is computationally feasible for large-scale retrieval. To make comparison fair, the same image-to-image similarity is used to calculate $\mathcal{S}(\mathbf{q}, \mathbf{x})$ in Eq.(6). In detail, the cosine angle between the tf-idf weighted histograms of a query and a database image is chosen for Oxford 5K, while the minus χ^2 distance is chosen for Caltech 101 and Scene 15. For Oxford 5K, the bandwidth $h = 1.0$ and the scaling factor $\beta = 0.01$. They are set as 4.0 and 0.025 for Caltech 101 and Scene 15, respectively. Using different h and β is due to the different feature dimensions and normalization schemes.

Table 1 compares the proposed measure to the image-to-image measure with different neighborhood size. As seen, on all the three databases the proposed measure consistently outperforms the image-to-image measure. The improvement is especially significant in Oxford 5K, as large as 10%. Cross-referencing the result reported in [12], such improvement is even larger than that obtained by employing an extra local-descriptor-based spatial verification. Figure 1 plots the average Recall under different neighborhood size k, which further verifies the superior performance of the proposed measure. Also, it is worth mentioning that the exponential model currently used in Eq.(3) for estimating P_i^+ is a very simple one. Higher retrieval performance can be expected when more sophisticated models, e.g. the one based on spatial matching score of two images, are applied. To give a more detailed evaluation, we further compare the proposed measure with the image-to-image measure in terms of "Precision at top 10" for every class of query. For Oxford5K, there are 11 query classes, each of which has 5 query images. For Scene15, there are 15 query classes consisting of 4485 query images. As seen, the proposed measure achieves high Precision value on most of classes for both data sets (Caltech101's result is not presented due to its large class number, 102).

Table 1: Retrieval performance vs. neighborhood size k (The "baseline" is the image-to-image similarity measure)

Dataset	baseline	k=5	10	15	20	25
Oxford5K	61.8	70.2	70.7	71.3	**72.1**	71.8
Scene15	52.5	53.0	54.9	56.6	57.2	**57.6**
Caltech101	33.5	34.6	36.3	37.1	37.6	**37.9**

Finally, we give a true example in Figure 3 to better illustrate the advantage of the proposed similarity. The first row shows that when using an image-to-image histogram similarity measure, $\mathcal{S}_{\text{direct}}$, to directly compare the query to two database images 1 (true match) and 2 (false match), image 2 appears to be more similar, leading to a wrong retrieval. To look into this mistake, the shared visual words between the query and each database image are displayed. The presence of more shared visual words approximately implies a higher histogram similarity. When image 1 undertakes a large viewpoint change from the query image, their shared

[1]We use "Precision of top 10" because retrieving relevant images is more difficult in Caltech101 and Scene15 than in Oxford5K, making all mAP values too low to compare.

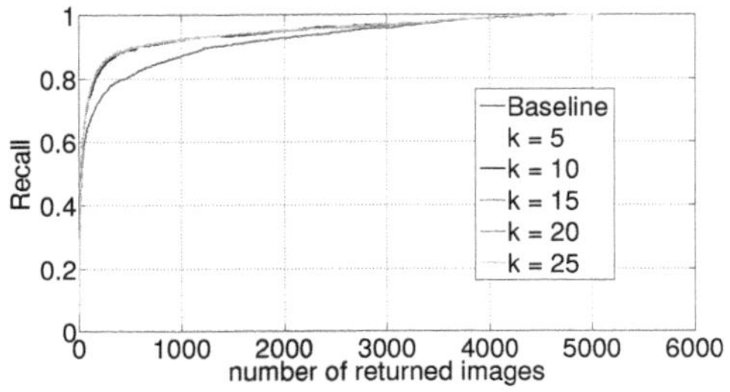

Figure 1: Recall on Oxford5K with different neighborhood size k (The "baseline" is the image-to-image similarity measure)

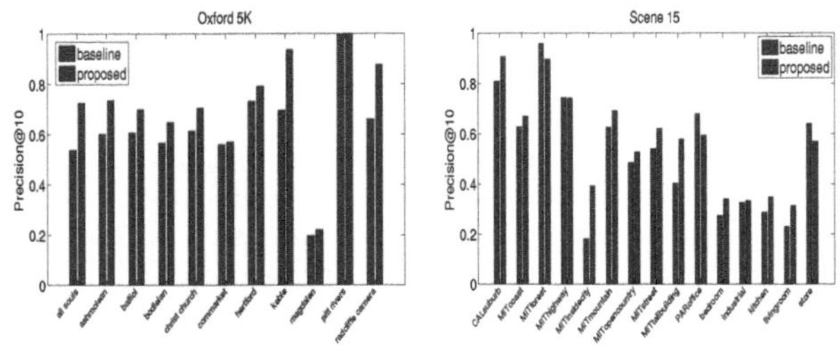

Figure 2: Precision of top 10 for each query class

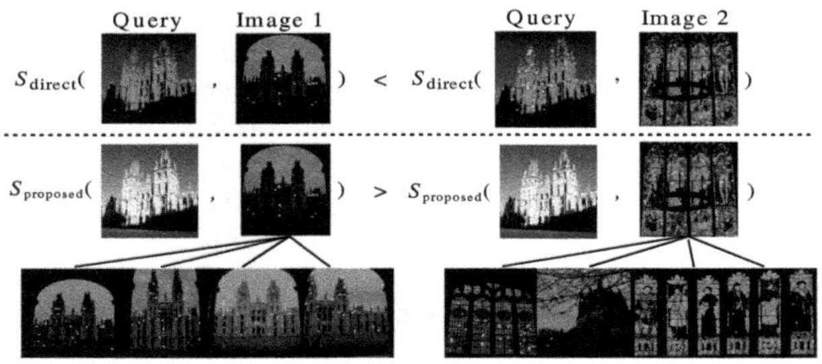

Figure 3: A true example demonstrating the advantage of the proposed similarity measure. Please see the text of the last paragraph of Section 4.

visual words tend to be less. Meanwhile, image 2, an irrelevant image, may incidentally match the query by a higher histogram similarity. However, if taking the neighborhood (4 neighbors here) of each database image into account, we can find that the query actually has a reasonably large number of visual words shared with all the neighbors of image 1, while this number drops significantly for some of the neighbors of image 2. By adopting the proposed similarity measure to incorporate this information, a higher similarity score can be obtained between the query and image 1, giving a correct retrieval.

5. CONCLUSION

We propose to cast image similarity as the likelihood of the query sharing a same latent class with a database image. By adopting a probabilistic formulation and taking a set of assumptions, our analysis ends up with an efficient image-to-class similarity measure which demonstrates superior retrieval performance to traditional image-to-image similarity measure. In our future work, we plan to enrich the proposed similarity measure by incorporating more sophisticated models to better infer the neighborhood structure.

6. REFERENCES

[1] O. Boiman, E. Shechtman, and M. Irani. In Defense of Nearest-Neighbor Based Image Classification. In *CVPR*, 2008.

[2] O. Chum, J. Philbin, J. Sivic, M. Isard, and A. Zisserman. Total recall: Automatic query expansion with a generative feature model for object retrieval. In *ICCV*, 2007.

[3] G.-D. Guo, A. K. Jain, W.-Y. Ma, and H.-J. Zhang. Learning similarity measure for natural image retrieval with relevance feedback. *IEEE TRANSACTIONS ON NEURAL NETWORKS*, 13(4):811–820, 2002.

[4] H. Jégou, M. Douze, and C. Schmid. On the burstiness of visual elements. In *CVPR*, 2009.

[5] H. Jégou, H. Harzallah, and C. Schmid. A contextual dissimilarity measure for accurate and efficient image search. In *CVPR*, 2007.

[6] G. Jeh and J. Widom. SimRank: a measure of structural-context similarity. In *SIGKDD*, New York, NY, USA, 2002.

[7] F. Kang, R. Jin, and S. C. H. Hoi. Similarity beyond distance measurement. In *Recherche dInformation Assistlęe par Ordinateur*, 2007.

[8] L. Liu, L. Wang, and X. Liu. In defense of soft-assigment coding. In *ICCV*, 2011.

[9] D. G. Lowe. Object recognition from local scale-invariant features. In *ICCV*, 1999.

[10] A. Mikulĺĭk, M. Perdoch, O. Chum, and J. Matas. Learning a fine vocabulary. In *ECCV*, 2010.

[11] D. Nister and H. Stewenius. Scalable recognition with a vocabulary tree. In *CVPR*, 2006.

[12] J. Philbin, O. Chum, M. Isard, J. Sivic, and A. Zisserman. Object retrieval with large vocabularies and fast spatial matching. In *CVPR*, 2007.

[13] J. Philbin, O. Chum, M. Isard, J. Sivic, and A. Zisserman. Lost in quantization: Improving particular object retrieval in large scale image databases. In *CVPR*, 2008.

[14] J. Philbin, M. Isard, J. Sivic, and A. Zisserman. Descriptor learning for efficient retrieval. In *ECCV*, 2010.

[15] Y. Rubner, C. Tomasi, and L. J. Guibas. The Earth Mover's Distance as a Metric for Image Retrieval. *IJCV*, 40(2):99–121, Nov 2000.

[16] J. Sivic and A. Zisserman. Video Google: A text retrieval approach to object matching in videos. In *CVPR*, 2003.

[17] C. S. Svetlana Lazebnik and J. Ponce. Beyond bags of features: Spatial pyramid matching for recognizing natural scene categories. In *CVPR*, 2006.

[18] L. Wang, X. Li, P. Xue, and K. L. Chan. A novel framework for svm-based image retrieval on large databases. In *ACM MM*, 2005.

[19] M. Wang, X.-S. Hua, J. Tang, and R. Hong. Beyond distance measurement: constructing neighborhood similarity for video annotation. *IEEE Transcation on MultiMedia*, 11:465–476, April 2009.

Combining Latent Semantic Learning and Reduced Hypergraph Learning for Semi-Supervised Image Categorization*

Zhiwu Lu and Yuxin Peng†
Institute of Computer Science and Technology, Peking University, Beijing 100871, China
{luzhiwu,pengyuxin}@icst.pku.edu.cn

ABSTRACT

This paper presents a novel framework that can combine latent semantic learning and reduced hypergraph learning for semi-supervised image categorization. To improve the traditional bag-of-features representation, we first propose a semantics-aware representation which can learn latent semantics automatically from a large vocabulary of abundant visual keywords through contextual spectral embedding. The learnt latent semantics can be readily used to define a histogram intersection kernel. Based on this semantics-aware kernel, we further develop a reduced hypergraph-based semi-supervised learning method to exploit both labeled and unlabeled images for image categorization. Experimental results have shown that the proposed framework can achieve significant improvements with respect to the state of the arts.

Categories and Subject Descriptors

H.3.3 [**Information Storage and Retrieval**]: Information Search and Retrieval—*retrieval models*

General Terms

Algorithms, Experimentation, Performance

1. INTRODUCTION

Semi-supervised image categorization has many applications such as image annotation and retrieval where a large number of unlabeled images are available. However, this task still remains challenging due to the well-known semantic gap. Hence, several influential attempts based upon bag-of-features (BOF) [9, 5] have been made to give rise to encouraging results, which may be due to the intermediate representation formed with visual keywords. In this paper, we refer to the visual keywords as mid-level features in order to distinguish them from the low-level visual features and high-level semantics of images.

*Area chair: Marcel Worring

†Corresponding author.

MM'11, November 28–December 1, 2011, Scottsdale, Arizona, USA.

A distinct disadvantage of BOF is that it may suffer from the redundancy of mid-level features, since typically thousands of visual keywords are generated to obtain better performance on a relatively large image dataset [9]. Moreover, these mid-level features are exploited independently and the first-order statistics is mainly considered. Intuitively, the semantic correlation of mid-level features is very useful for bridging the semantic gap in image categorization.

Although the semantic information can be incorporated into the visual vocabulary using either local region annotation or image annotation, such manual labeling is too expensive and tedious for a large image dataset. In this paper, we focus on automatically extracting, from the abundant mid-level features, high-level features that are fewer in number but more representative in terms of descriptive power. Previously, several unsupervised approaches to latent semantic learning [2, 3] have been developed based on topic models such as probabilistic latent semantic analysis (PLSA). However, very few attempts have been made to explicitly preserve the manifold geometry of the mid-level feature space which is very important for latent semantic learning. To our best knowledge, [6] is the first attempt to extract high-level latent semantics from videos for action recognition by manifold learning based on diffusion maps [4]. Although some promising results have been reported on human action datasets, its advantage on scene images is not obvious.

To deal with the above issues associated with image representation, we propose a novel contextual spectral embedding (CSE) method which can exploit both intra-image and inter-image context for discovering the local intrinsic geometric structure of the mid-level features. Here, we represent the intra-image context by the spatial layout of mid-level features. For inter-image context, we consider a representation based on the Pearson product moment (PPM) correlation, which serves to quantify the similarity between mid-level features. These two types of context are further used to construct a contextual graph for spectral embedding (SE) [8]. A distinct advantage of our method is that it does not require any tuning of the parameters for graph construction because the PPM correlation is a nonparametric measure. On the contrary, in previous work [6], the mid-level features are represented as vectors of point-wise mutual information and their similarity is typically characterized via a Gaussian function. As reported in [6], the choice of the variance in this function affects the performance significantly.

In this paper, we evaluate the effectiveness of the learnt high-level features by applying them to semi-supervised image categorization through defining a histogram intersection kernel. Although graph-based semi-supervised learning (SSL) [11] has been shown to be effective in dealing with small sample problems by exploiting both labeled and unlabeled data, we develop a reduced hypergraph-based SSL method for image categorization instead so that the higher order correlation between images [1, 12] can be incorporated into semi-supervised learning. Finally, we successfully combine latent semantic learning and reduced hypergraph learning for semi-supervised image categorization

2. LATENT SEMANTIC LEANING BY CONTEXTUAL SPECTRAL EMBEDDING

In this section, we first present our approach to contextual graph construction by exploiting both intra-image and inter-image context. This contextual graph is subsequently used for spectral embedding so that we can learn latent semantics by spectral clustering in the new embedding space.

2.1 Contextual Graph Construction

To apply spectral embedding to learning high-level latent semantics from mid-level features, we need first to construct a graph. Given a vocabulary of mid-level features $\mathcal{V}_m = \{m_i\}_{i=1}^M$, we can define a graph $G = \{V, W\}$ with its vertex set $V = \mathcal{V}_m$ and $W = [w_{ij}]_{M\times M}$, where w_{ij} denotes the similarity between two mid-level features m_i and m_j. In [6], W is defined by a Gaussian function when each mid-level feature is represented as a vector of point-wise mutual information. However, the choice of the variance in the Gaussian function affects the performance significantly.

In this paper, we adopt a nonparametric function called Pearson product moment (PPM) correlation to define the similarity measure between mid-level features. Let the bag-of-features representation for image n be $\{c_n(m_i) : i = 1, ..., M\}$, where $c_n(m_i)$ is the count of times that m_i occurs in image n $(n = 1, ..., N)$. We can define the PPM correlation between m_i and m_j by:

$$w_{ij} = \frac{\sum_{n=1}^N (c_n(m_i) - \mu(m_i))(c_n(m_j) - \mu(m_j))}{(N-1)\sigma(m_i)\sigma(m_j)}, \quad (1)$$

where $\mu(m_i)$ and $\sigma(m_i)$ are the mean and standard deviation of $\{c_n(m_i) : n = 1, ..., N\}$, respectively. The distinct advantage of using this measure is that we have eliminated the need to tune any parameter for graph construction.

Since the PPM correlation matrix is collected across different images, we have actually exploited the inter-image context between mid-level features to construct a graph for spectral embedding. Here, we also consider the intra-image context, which can be captured by placing a series of increasingly finer grids over an image. That is, each sub-image at level l is divided into 2×2 parts at level $l + 1$, where $l = 0, ..., L - 1$ and L is the finest scale. Let $W_s^{(l)}$ be the PPM correlation matrix obtained according to the s-th sub-image on the $2^l \times 2^l$ grid. The PPM correlation matrix at level l can be defined as $W^{(l)} = \sum_s W_s^{(l)}$. We combine the PPM correlation matrices at multiple scales by:

$$W = \frac{1}{2^L} W^{(0)} + \sum_{l=1}^{L} \frac{1}{2^{L-l+1}} W^{(l)}, \quad (2)$$

where a coarser scale is assumed to be less important. Finally, we incorporate both inter-image and intra-image context between mid-level features into graph construction.

2.2 Spectral Learning of Latent Semantics

After a contextual graph has been constructed by exploiting the context between mid-level features, we perform spectral embedding on this graph. In the new low-dimensional embedding space, we learn high-level latent semantics by spectral clustering. The algorithm is summarized as follows:

(1) Find K largest nontrivial eigenvectors $\mathbf{v}_1, ..., \mathbf{v}_K$ and associated eigenvalues $\lambda_1, ..., \lambda_K$ of $\bar{\mathcal{L}} = D^{-1/2} W D^{-1/2}$.

(2) Form $E = [\lambda_1 \mathbf{v}_1, ..., \lambda_K \mathbf{v}_K]$, and normalize each row of E to have unit length. Here, the i-th row $E_{i.}$ denotes the new feature vector of m_i.

(3) Perform k-means clustering on the new feature vectors $E_{i.} (i = 1, ..., M)$ to partition the vocabulary $\mathcal{V}_m$ into K clusters. Here, each cluster of mid-level features denotes a new high-level feature.

The above contextual spectral embedding method will be denoted as CSE in the following. Since the time complexity of the above algorithm is $O(M^3 + KM)$, our CSE for latent semantic learning can be run very efficiently even on a large dataset with the data size $N \gg M$.

Let $\mathcal{V}_h = \{h_j\}_{j=1}^K$ be the vocabulary of high-level features learnt from the vocabulary of mid-level features $\mathcal{V}_m = \{m_i\}_{i=1}^M$. The bag-of-features representation with $\mathcal{V}_h$ for each image can be derived from the original bag-of-features representation with $\mathcal{V}_m$ as follows. Given the count of times $c_n(m_i)$ that mid-level feature m_i occurs in image n $(n = 1, ..., N)$, the count of times $c_n(h_j)$ that high-level feature h_j occurs in this image can be computed by:

$$c_n(h_j) = \sum_{i=1}^M c_n(m_i) c(m_i, h_j), \quad (3)$$

where $c(m_i, h_j) = 1$ if mid-level feature m_i occurs in cluster j (i.e. high-level feature h_j) according to spectral clustering and $c(m_i, h_j) = 0$ otherwise. That is, each image is now represented as a histogram of high-level features. This semantics-aware image representation can be used to define a histogram intersection kernel A:

$$A(x_n, x_{\tilde{n}}) = \sum_{j=1}^K \min(c_n(h_j), c_{\tilde{n}}(h_j)), \quad (4)$$

where n (or $\tilde{n}$) $= 1, ..., N$. We can further exploit the spatial information of high-level features using spatial pyramid matching [5]. The resulting multi-scale kernel adopts the same scale L as contextual spectral embedding.

3. IMAGE CATEGORIZATION BY REDUCED HYPERGRAPH LEARNING

In this section, we apply our semantics-aware kernel to hypergraph-based semi-supervised image categorization. Particularly, we propose a reduced hypergraph learning algorithm to accelerate semi-supervised learning.

3.1 Semi-Supervised Image Categorization

We further formulate the semi-supervised image categorization problem as follows. Given an image dataset $\mathcal{X} = \{x_1, ..., x_{N_l}, x_{N_l+1}, ..., x_N\}$ and a label set $\{1, ..., C\}$, the first N_l images x_i $(i \leq N_l)$ are labeled as $z_i \in \{1, ..., C\}$ and the remaining images x_u $(N_l + 1 \leq u \leq N)$ are unlabeled. The goal is to predict the labels of the unlabeled images. Although graph-based semi-supervised learning [11] has been shown to be effective in dealing with small sample problems, this paper focuses on developing a hypergraph-based method so that the higher order correlation between images can be incorporated into semi-supervised learning.

Given the affinity matrix A^* defined by normalizing our kernel $A^*_{ij} = A(x_i, x_j)/(\sqrt{A(x_i, x_i)}\sqrt{A(x_j, x_j)})$, the hypergraph $\mathcal{G} = \{\mathcal{V}, \mathcal{E}, \mathbf{w}\}$ for semi-supervised learning can be constructed as follows. We first set $\mathcal{V} = \{v_i : i = 1, ..., N\} = \mathcal{X}$ and $\mathcal{E} = \{e_j : e_j = \mathcal{N}(x_j), j = 1, ..., N\}$, where $\mathcal{N}(x_j)$ is the k-nearest neighborhood of x_j. This means that each hyperedge has $k+1$ vertices. The incidence matrix H of the hypergraph $\mathcal{G}$ is defined as: $H_{ij} = A^*_{ij}$ if $v_i \in e_j$ and 0 otherwise. Moreover, we define the hyperedge weights $\mathbf{w} = \{w(e_j) : j = 1, ...N\}$ by

$$w(e_j) = \frac{1}{k+1} \sum_{v_i \in e_j, v_{i'} \in e_j} A^*_{ii'}, \tag{5}$$

which accumulates the similarity between each vertex in hyperedge e_j and its center in the kernel space (determined by A^*). Given these hyperedge weights $\mathbf{w}$, we can define the vertex degree as $d(v_i) = \sum_{e_j \in \mathcal{E}} w(e_j) H_{ij}$. Moreover, the hyperedge degree is defined as $\delta(e_j) = \sum_{v_i \in \mathcal{V}} H_{ij}$.

The semi-supervised image categorization problem can now be solved through semi-supervised learning based on the hypergraph discussed above. Let F be a $N \times C$ matrix corresponding to a classification on the dataset $\mathcal{X}$ by labeling each image x_i as a label $z_i = \arg\max_{j \le C} F_{ij}$. Define a $N \times C$ matrix Z with $Z_{ij} = 1$ if x_i is initially labeled as $z_i = j$ and $Z_{ij} = 0$ otherwise. The hypergraph-based semi-supervised learning algorithm is summarized as follows:

(1) Compute the matrix $\Theta = D_v^{-1/2} H W D_e^{-1} H^T D_v^{-1/2}$, where Dv, De, and W denote the diagonal matrices of the vertex degrees, the hyperedge degrees, and the hyperedge weights, respectively.

(2) Iterate $F(t+1) = \alpha \Theta F(t) + (1-\alpha) Z$ for label propagation until convergence, where α is a parameter in the range $(0, 1)$.

(3) Let F^* denote the limit of the sequence $\{F(t)\}$. Label each image x_i with a label $z_i = \arg\max_{j \le C} F^*_{ij}$.

3.2 Reduced Hypergraph Learning

Since Θ may have much more nonzero entries than the incidence matrix H, the above hypergraph-based SSL may become too time-consuming for a large dataset. To accelerate it, we then propose a reduced hypergraph learning algorithm based on the clique expansion method [1].

More concretely, we first construct a traditional graph $\mathcal{G}_c = \{\mathcal{V}_c, \mathcal{E}_c\}$ from the original hypergraph $\mathcal{G} = \{\mathcal{V}, \mathcal{E}, \mathbf{w}\}$. Suppose $\mathcal{V}_c = \mathcal{V}$ and $\mathcal{E}_c = \{(u, v) | u, v \in e, e \in \mathcal{E}\}$. The edge affinity $A_c(u, v)$ of the traditional graph $\mathcal{G}_c$ is defined by

$$A_c(u, v) = \sum_{u, v \in e, e \in \mathcal{E}} w(e) H(u, e) H(v, e). \tag{6}$$

The above definition means that the affinity matrix A_c can be expressed by $A_c = HWH^T$. Here, the similarity measure between data can be updated with this affinity matrix A_c. The distinct advantage of using this new similarity measure for semi-supervised learning is that the high order correlation between data can be exploited. Based on the new affinity matrix A_c, we can construct a traditional $\tilde{k}$-nearest neighbors graph by defining the edge weight matrix $\tilde{W}$ as:

$$\tilde{W}(u, v) = \begin{cases} A_c(u, v), & v \in \mathcal{N}(u); \\ 0, & \text{otherwise}, \end{cases} \tag{7}$$

where $\mathcal{N}(u)$ is the $\tilde{k}$-nearest neighborhood of vertex u. Finally, we compute $\tilde{\Theta} = \tilde{D}^{-1/2} \tilde{W} \tilde{D}^{-1/2}$ for label propagation, where $\tilde{D}$ is a diagonal matrix with its (u, u)-element equal to the sum of the u-th row of $\tilde{W}$.

In fact, we can obtain our reduced hypergraph learning by replacing Θ in Step (2) of the original hypergraph-based SSL algorithm with this new sparse matrix $\tilde{\Theta}$. In the following, our reduced hypergraph learning is denoted as Reduced HSSL, while the original algorithm is denoted as Original HSSL. Different from Original HSSL with a quadratic time complexity $O(N^2)$ in worst cases, our Reduced HSSL only has a linear worst-case time complexity $O(\tilde{k}N)$.

4. EXPERIMENTAL RESULTS

4.1 Experimental Setup

We select two image datasets, i.e. scenes 8 [10] and Caltech 101, for performance evaluation. The SIFT descriptors are then extracted the same as [5]. Finally, we perform k-means clustering on the extracted SIFT descriptors to form a visual vocabulary of M mid-level features.

Our CSE method is first compared with spatial pyramid matching (SPM) [5] and diffusion map (DM) [6]. We set $L = 2$ for both CSE and SPM, while set $M = 2,000$ for both CSE and DM. Here, we do not directly compare with PLSA, since PLSA requires large memory for $M = 2,000$. In fact, many previous results (e.g. [7]) have shown that SPM outperforms PLSA. Hence, our CSE can be indirectly demonstrated to outperform PLSA, given the gain of our CSE over SPM reported in the later experiments.

Moreover, we also compare our reduced hypergraph-based semi-supervised learning (HSSL) with the traditional graph-based semi-supervised learning (SSL) [11]. In the experiments, we set $\alpha = 0.8$, $k = 30$ and $\tilde{k} = 300$ for our reduced HSSL. In fact, our Reduced HSSL is not sensitive to these parameters, and we select relatively smaller values for k and $\tilde{k}$ to ensure its efficient running even on a large dataset.

For semi-supervised image categorization, only a small number of labeled images are provided initially, i.e., 10 labeled images are randomly selected from each category for the two image datasets. Each experiment is randomly run 100 times, and the mean average precision (MAP) measure is used for the performance evaluation.

4.2 Results on the Image Datasets

We first compare our Reduced HSSL with the Original HSSL and the traditional graph-based SSL on the scene dataset. The affinity matrix for these graph-based methods is defined by the SPM kernel with varying vocabulary size M. In the experiments, we set $k = 30$ and $\tilde{k} = 300$ for our Reduced HSSL. For fair comparison, we set $k = 30$ for Original HSSL, and the traditional SSL is configured with $k = 300$. From Figure 1, we can find that our Reduced HSSL is significantly more efficient than the Original HSSL

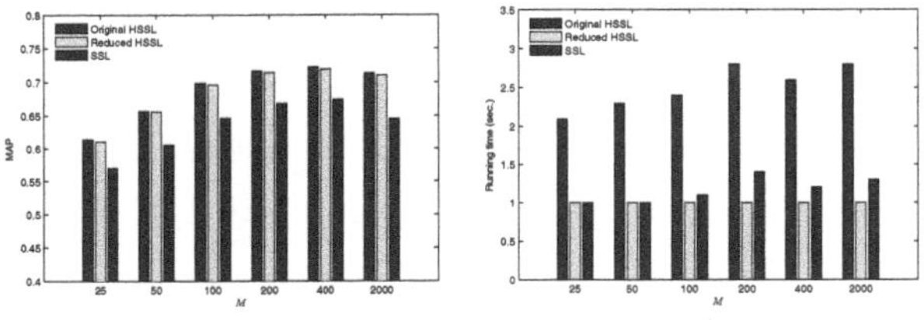

(a) (b)

Figure 1: Comparison of different graph-based methods on the scene dataset: (a) categorization results measured by MAP; (b) running time.

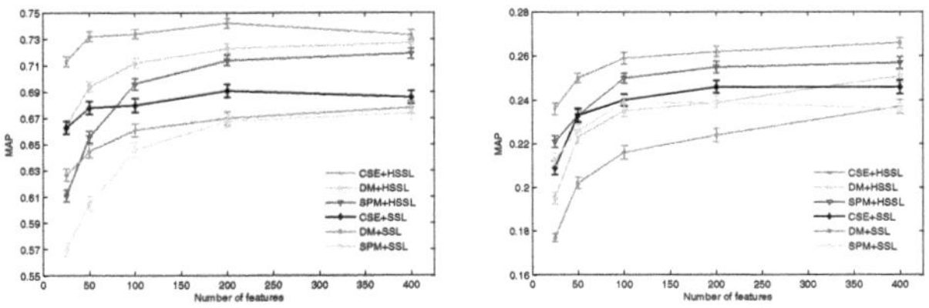

(a) (b)

Figure 2: The categorization results on the two image datasets: (a) scene; (b) Caltech. The error bars indicate 95% confidence intervals.

but with little performance degradation. More importantly, our Reduced HSSL can achieve much better results than the traditional SSL but without incurring extra time cost. In the following, we will only consider our Reduced HSSL, i.e., HSSL only denotes our Reduced HSSL.

Moreover, to show the effectiveness of the high-level features learnt by our CSE method, we compare the three methods CSE, DM [6], and SPM on the two image datasets. Figure 2 gives the comparison. Overall, our CSE method is shown to perform the best among the three methods, whenever HSSL or SSL is used for semi-supervised image categorization. More concretely, the significant gain over SPM achieved by our CSE method verifies that the learnt high-level features can provide a semantically more succinct representation but a richer descriptor than the mid-level features, while the significant gain over DM achieved by our CSE method may be due to the fact that our CSE method has eliminated the need to tune any parameter for graph construction which has been shown to affect the performance of graph-based methods significantly. To the best of our knowledge, our CSE method has been demonstrated to achieve the most outstanding performance in the challenging task of semi-supervised image categorization among all the latent semantic learning approaches.

Finally, we can further observe from Figure 2 that the use of hypergraphs for semi-supervised image categorization leads to significantly improved performance (see CSE+HSSL vs. CSE+SSL, DM+HSSL vs. DM+SSL, or SPM+HSSL vs. SPM+SSL) over the traditional SSL. The reason may be that hypergraph-based methods can exploit higher order correlation between images for semi-supervised learning as compared to graph-based methods. That is, the higher order correlation between images can help to reconcile the contradictory propagated label information for certain images and thus achieve more accurate label predictions.

5. CONCLUSIONS

We have proposed a novel framework that can combine latent semantic learning and hypergraph learning for semi-supervised image categorization. The proposed framework has the following advantages: 1) our contextual spectral embedding method can learn latent semantics by discovering the manifolds hidden among visual keywords using both inter-image and intra-image context, quite different from other related methods; 2) our reduced hypergraph-based SSL for image categorization significantly outperforms the traditional graph-based methods for the use of the higher order correlation between images; 3) both our latent semantic learning and reduced hypergraph learning are scalable with respect to the data size and can be applied to large image datasets. For future work, the proposed framework will be applied to other image understanding tasks.

6. ACKNOWLEDGEMENTS

The work described in this paper was fully supported by the National Natural Science Foundation of China under Grant Nos. 60873154 and 61073084, and the National Development and Reform Commission High-tech Program of China under Grant No. [2010]3044.

7. REFERENCES

[1] S. Agarwal, K. Branson, and S. Belongie. Higher order learning with graphs. In *ICML*, pages 17–24, 2006.

[2] A. Bosch, A. Zisserman, and X. Muñoz. Scene classification via pLSA. In *ECCV*, pages 517–530, 2006.

[3] L. Fei-Fei and P. Perona. A Bayesian hierarchical model for learning natural scene categories. In *CVPR*, pages 524–531, 2005.

[4] S. Lafon and A. Lee. Diffusion maps and coarse-graining: A unified framework for dimensionality reduction, graph partitioning, and data set parameterization. *PAMI*, 28(9):1393–1403, 2006.

[5] S. Lazebnik, C. Schmid, and J. Ponce. Beyond bags of features: Spatial pyramid matching for recognizing natural scene categories. In *CVPR*, pages 2169–2178, 2006.

[6] J. Liu, Y. Yang, and M. Shah. Learning semantic visual vocabularies using diffusion distance. In *CVPR*, pages 461–468, 2009.

[7] Z. Lu, H. Ip, and Q. He. Context-based multi-label image annotation. In *CIVR*, pages 1–7, 2009.

[8] A. Ng, M. Jordan, and Y. Weiss. On spectral clustering: Analysis and an algorithm. In *NIPS 14*, pages 849–856, 2002.

[9] E. Nowak, F. Jurie, and B. Triggs. Sampling strategies for bag-of-features image classification. In *ECCV*, pages 490–503, 2006.

[10] A. Oliva and A. Torralba. Modeling the shape of the scene: A holistic representation of the spatial envelope. *IJCV*, 42(3):145–175, 2001.

[11] D. Zhou, O. Bousquet, T. Lal, J. Weston, and B. Schölkopf. Learning with local and global consistency. In *NIPS 16*, pages 321–328, 2004.

[12] D. Zhou, J. Huang, and B. Schölkopf. Learning with hypergraphs: Clustering, classification, and embedding. In *NIPS 19*, pages 1601–1608, 2007.

Optimal Batch Selection for Active Learning in Multi-label Classification *

Shayok Chakraborty, Vineeth Balasubramanian and Sethuraman Panchanathan
Center for Cognitive Ubiquitous Computing (CUbiC), Arizona State University
Tempe, Arizona, USA
schakr10@asu.edu, vineeth.nb@asu.edu, panch@asu.edu

ABSTRACT

Multi-label classification is a generalization of conventional classification, where it is possible for a single data point to have multiple labels. Manual annotation of a multi-label data point requires a human oracle to consider the presence/absence of every possible class separately, which involves significant labor. Active learning techniques are effective in reducing human labeling effort to induce a classification model. When exposed to large quantities of unlabeled data, such algorithms automatically select the salient and representative instances for manual annotation. Further, to address the high redundancy in data such as image or video sequences as well as the availability of multiple labeling agents, there have been recent attempts towards a batch mode form of active learning, where a batch of data points is selected simultaneously from an unlabeled set. In this work, we propose a novel optimization based batch mode active learning strategy to minimize human labeling effort in multi-label classification problems. To the best of our knowledge, this is the first attempt to develop such a scheme primarily intended for the multi-label context. The proposed framework is computationally simple, easy to implement and can be suitably modified to perform batch mode active learning in other formulations, such as single-label classification or problems involving hierarchical label spaces. Our results corroborate the efficacy of the proposed algorithm and certify the potential of the framework in being used for real world applications.

Categories and Subject Descriptors

I.2.6 [**Artificial Intelligence**]: Learning; I.5.4 [**Pattern Recognition**]: Applications—*Computer Vision*

General Terms

Algortihms,Theory

*Area chair: Bernard Merialdo

Keywords

Batch Mode Active Learning, Multi-label classification, Optimization

1. INTRODUCTION

Conventional classification problems assume each data instance to be associated with a single class label. However, many applications require a more generalized setting where it is possible for a single data point to be associated with multiple classes simultaneously. This is referred as the *multi-label classification* setting. For instance, classifying the contents of a natural scenery image is a multi-label problem, as a single image can have multiple contents (like sunset, ocean, mountains etc.) associated with it. To develop a reliable classification model for multi-label data, a large amount of labeled data is necessary in the form of a training set. However, annotating a data point in a multi-label scenario requires a human oracle to check the presence/absence of every possible class in the data point. Thus, while gathering a large amount of unlabeled data is cheap and easy, labeling a data point in a multi-label problem entails significant manual effort. Hence, developing a strategy to minimize human annotation effort in a multi-label problem is of paramount practical importance.

Active learning algorithms have gained popularity to reduce human annotation effort to induce a classifier. When exposed to large quantities of unlabeled data, such algorithms automatically select the promising and exemplar instances to be labeled manually. This tremendously reduces the annotation effort and also endows the model with greater generalization capability as it gets trained on the salient examples from the underlying data population [15]. In addition to the large quantities of data that are generated each day (for example, YouTube videos), the presence of multiple labeling agents (for example, the vast consumer population) necessitates a scheme to simultaneously select and learn from multiple data points. To address this need, *batch mode active learning* (BMAL) techniques, which attempt to select a batch of data points simultaneously from an unlabeled set, have been proposed in recent years.

In this paper, we propose a novel framework for optimal batch selection for active learning in multi-label classification. To the best of our knowledge, this is the first effort to develop a BMAL framework for multi-label problems. Sample applications of such a framework include image retrieval, video search and expression recognition. Although validated only on image data in this work, the proposed approach can be used in any multimedia application involving multi-label data. Also, the framework is generic and can be adapted to other formulations such as single-label classification or problems involving hierarchical label spaces.

2. RELATED WORK

Several active learning frameworks have been proposed in the pattern recognition literature. They can be broadly categorized into 2 groups: (*i*) *pool-based* active learning methods, which query a single data instant at a time from an unlabeled pool [15], [5],[1],and (*ii*) *batch mode* active learning methods, which query a batch of unlabeled points simultaneously. Since BMAL is the focus of this work, we briefly review the few methods that have been published in this context. Brinker [3] proposed a BMAL strategy which queried a diverse batch of points where diversity was measured as the angle between the hyperplane of the selected point to all the other hyperplanes of the already selected points. Hoi *et al.*[10], [9],[11] used the Fischer information matrix as a measure of model uncertainty and proposed to select a batch of points which reduced the Fischer information. Guo and Schuurmans [8] formalized the problem by defining an objective function and selecting a set of unlabeled points which optimized the value of that function.

Previous work on active learning for multi-label classification is mainly based on greedy heuristics, where a score is computed for every point in an unlabeled set and the point having the maximum score is queried for its class label. Brinker [4] proposed an active learning scheme for multi-label problems, where an SVM was trained for every possible class and the unlabeled point having minimum distance to all the separating hyperplanes was queried for its class labels. Singh *et al.* [14] used the posterior probabilities to derive an uncertainty score for every unlabeled point and proposed to query the most uncertain point. Zhang *et al.* [16] presented a multi-view active learning algorithm where intra-view uncertainty represented the sample and label uncertainties and inter-view uncertainty reflected the uncertainty across multiple views. Based on the aggregated uncertainty, the most informative sample-label pair was queried for manual annotation. Li *et al.* [12] computed a loss value for every instance in an unlabeled set and proposed to query the point furnishing the maximum expected loss.

All the aforementioned techniques for active learning in the multi-label scenario are based on heuristic score functions and query only a single instance at a time from an unlabeled set. They can be extended to batch selection by querying the top k points based on the score rankings, k being the batch size. However, this will not consider the information overlap among the selected points, i.e., if a set of data points produce a high aggregate uncertainty score but also have a high redundancy among them, then the information gained by querying the set is not substantial. In this paper, we propose a novel optimization based BMAL scheme for multi-label classification problems, which also addresses this issue. We now describe the mathematical formulation of our approach.

3. PROPOSED FRAMEWORK

Consider a batch mode active learning problem, where we are given a multi-label training set L_t and an unlabeled set U_t at time t. Let w^t be the classifier trained on L_t. The objective is to select a batch B (containing k points) from U_t in such a way that the future learner w^{t+1}, trained on $L_t \bigcup B$, has maximum generalization capability. Let Y denote the set of possible classes in the problem.

The fundamental idea behind the proposed algorithm is to select a batch of points in such a way that each individual point furnishes high information and the selected batch of points have minimal redundancy among them. The rationale behind this is that we need to query highly informative points from the unlabeled set; however, if two points separately furnish useful information but they provide the same information, then querying one point makes the other redundant. Hence, besides choosing informative points, we need to ensure that the selected points have minimal redundancy among them, i.e., each of them provides useful, but different pieces of information.

To achieve this, we compute an uncertainty vector $C \in \Re^{|U_t| \times 1}$, where $C(i)$ denotes the uncertainty value of point x_i in the unlabeled pool. A redundancy matrix $R \in \Re^{|U_t| \times |U_t|}$ is also defined whose $(i,j)^{th}$ entry is a measure of redundancy between unlabeled points x_i and x_j (details on the computation of these parameters are given later). We now need to decide which specific points need to be queried from the unlabeled set. Exhaustive search is not feasible due to the exponential nature of the search space. Hence, we solve this problem using numerical optimization-based techniques. We define a binary vector M with $|U_t|$ entries ($M \in [0,1]^{|U_t| \times 1}$) where each entry M_i denotes whether the corresponding unlabeled point x_i will be included in the batch ($M_i = 1$) or not ($M_i = 0$). We would like to select points which furnish high uncertainty scores (as given by the entries in vector C) and have high divergence (less redundancy) among them (as given by the entries in R). We formulate an optimization problem to satisfy these two conditions:

$$\max_M C^T M + \frac{1}{2} M^T R M \tag{1}$$

subject to the constraints:

$$M_j \in \{0,1\}, \forall j \tag{2}$$

$$\sum_{j=1}^{|U_t|} M_j = k \tag{3}$$

where k is the specified batch size. This is an integer programming problem due to constraint 2 and so, we relax the constraint and derive a continuous optimization problem:

$$\max_M C^T M + \frac{1}{2} M^T R M \tag{4}$$

subject to the constraints:

$$0 \leq M_j \leq 1, \forall j \tag{5}$$

$$\sum_{j=1}^{|U_t|} M_j = k \tag{6}$$

This is a quadratic programming (QP) problem and can be efficiently solved using a standard QP solver. Once we solve M, we set the top k entries in M as 1 and the remaining as 0 to greedily recover the integer solution. Our formulation ensures that such an ordering also considers the redundancy among the selected points besides their uncertainties (unlike earlier work in multi-label active learning, as discussed in Section 2).

Computing the Uncertainty Vector C: The uncertainty of the model w^t on a point x_i is used as a measure

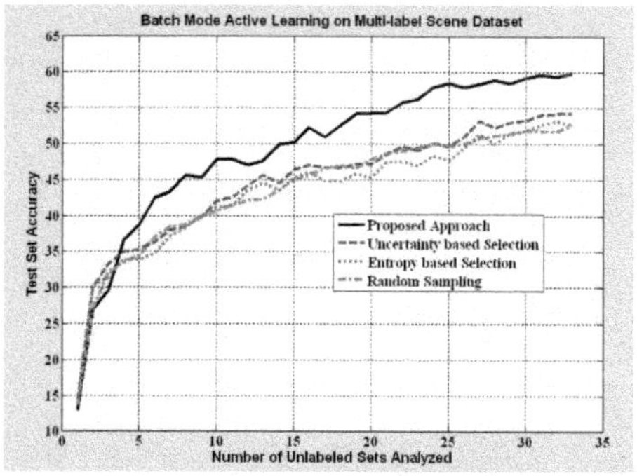

(a) Accuracy on the Scene dataset

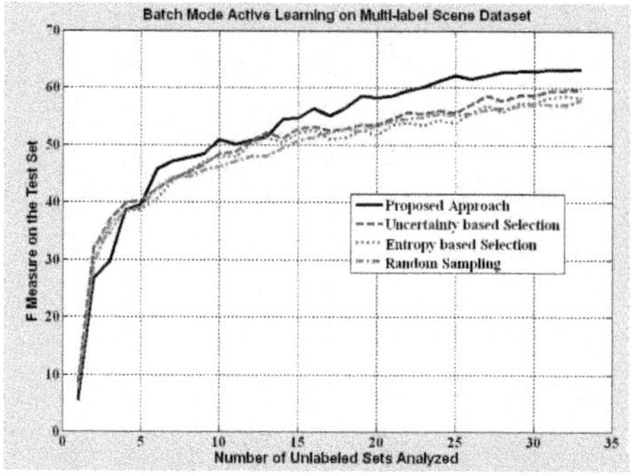

(b) F-Measure on the Scene dataset

Figure 1: Multi-label Batch Mode Active Learning on the Scene Dataset

of the informativeness of that point; higher values of uncertainty denote a high degree of information. Entropy is taken as a measure of uncertainty in this work. To compute $C(i)$, the model w^t is applied on point x_i in the unlabeled pool to yield posterior probabilities p^i with respect to all the $|Y|$ classes. Since this is a multi-label problem, the entropy $S(Y|x_i, w^t)$ of point x_i is computed as the average entropy over the individual classes:

$$S(Y|x_i, w^t) = \frac{1}{|Y|}\sum_{j=1}^{|Y|}[p_j^i \log p_j^i + (1-p_j^i)\log(1-p_j^i)] \quad (7)$$

Hence, $C(i)$ is set to be equal to $S(Y|x_i, w^t)$.

Computing the Redundancy Matrix R: The redundancy measure between two points is an estimate of the amount of information overlap between the points. The symmetric Kullback Leibler divergence is used to compute the redundancy between two points. Let p^i and p^j denote the sets of posterior probabilities of two points x_i and x_j in the unlabeled pool. Then, the $(i,j)^{th}$ entry in matrix R is set to be equal to the symmetric KL divergence between the two sets of probability values:

$$R(i,j) = \sum_{c=1}^{|Y|}(p_c^i - p_c^j)\log\frac{p_c^i}{p_c^j} \quad (8)$$

Note that, to compute both the uncertainty vector C and the redundancy matrix R, we merely need to apply the current model w^t on every unlabeled point to derive the posterior probabilities. This does not involve classifier retraining (unlike [8])and hence is computationally very efficient.

The proposed framework is generalizable and by suitably modifying the uncertainty vector and the redundancy matrix, it can be used in applications other than multi-label learning. For instance, consider a learning problem with hierarchical label space, i.e., each class has subclasses and the labels are organized in the form of a tree. The uncertainty of a point can then be computed as the weighted sum of the uncertainties at each level in the label hierarchy. The redundancy between two points can also be defined analogously. Thus, by a simple modification, the framework can be used to perform batch mode active learning in problems involving hierarchical label spaces.

4. EXPERIMENTS

Heuristic approaches of BMAL: The performance of the proposed approach was compared against three other multi-label active learning techniques, which were extended to the BMAL context: (*i*) *Random Sampling*, where a batch of unlabeled data points is selected at random from an unlabeled set, (*ii*) *Uncertainty based Selection*, in which an SVM is trained for each possible class and the top k uncertain points (k being the batch size) are selected from an unlabeled set, where uncertainty of a point is computed as the minimum distance of the point to all the hyperplanes in the feature space (extending Brinker's [4] method for batch selection) and (*iii*) *Entropy based Selection*, where the entropy is computed for every unlabeled instance and the top k points are queried based on the entropy ranking (extending Singh *et al*'s. [14] method for batch selection).

Evaluation Metrics: We used two metrics to evaluate the performance of the active learning algorithms - (*i*) *Accuracy* and (*ii*) *F-Measure*. For the detailed definition of these metrics in a multi-label context, please refer [7].

Classification Model: SVM was used as the base classifier because of its established performance in multi-label learning [12] [4]. A polynomial kernel of degree 2 was used in all our studies, based on preliminary experiments.

4.1 Datasets Used and Results

1. The Scene Dataset: This dataset consists of 2407 natural scene images, where each image contains one or more of 6 possible classes - beach, sunset, foliage, field, mountain and urban. A 294 dimensional feature vector was extracted from each image (similar to [2]). The images were randomly permuted and a model was trained on an initial set containing 10 images. Unlabeled sets containing 30 images each were then presented to the learner and the model was asked to query a batch of 10 images. The selected points were appended to the training set. The model was then updated and tested on a test set containing about 1400 images. The goal was to study the growth in performance on the test set as batches of unlabeled samples were added to the training set from the unlabeled pools. The results are shown in Figure 1 where the x-axis denotes the number of unlabeled data streams that have been analyzed and the y axis denotes the accuracy / F-measure on the test set. We note that both the accuracy and F-measure grow at the fastest rate for the proposed approach. This corroborates the fact that the proposed algorithm succeeds in selecting the salient images and attains a given level of accuracy with the least number of labeled examples.

2. The FacePix Dataset: This dataset (*www.facepix.org*) contains images of subjects under natural conditions, with head poses ranging from $-90°$ (extreme left) to $90°$ (extreme right). Automatically determining the pose of a sub-

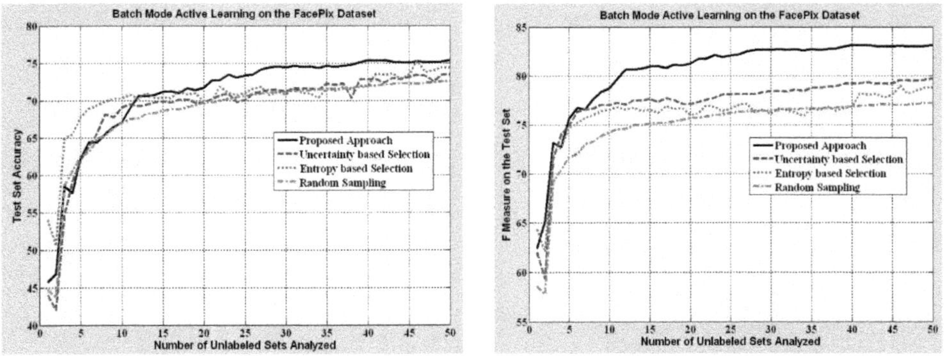

(a) Accuracy on the FacePix dataset (b) F-Measure on the FacePix dataset

Figure 2: Multi-label Batch Mode Active Learning on the FacePix Dataset

ject is important in applications ranging from robotics to assistive technology. Since head pose is a continuous variable, it is possible that a pose angle of say, $-60°$ can be considered as far left or left (as shown in Figure 3). Due to

Figure 3: Pose images from the FacePix dataset

the fuzziness in the label boundaries, the following rubric was used to discretize the classes in this work: ($-90°$ to $-66°$: Far Left), ($-65°$ to $-46°$: Far Left and Left), ($-45°$ to $-21°$: Left), ($-20°$ to $-6°$: Left and Frontal), ($-5°$ to $5°$: Frontal), ($6°$ to $20°$: Frontal and Right), ($21°$ to $45°$: Right), ($46°$ to $65°$: Right and Far Right), ($66°$ to $90°$: Far Right). The Gabor feature was extracted from each image (similar to [6]). Unlabeled video streams, containing varied poses of subjects, were presented to the learner and a batch of 10 images was queried from each. The performance was evaluated on a test set containing 2000 images with all kinds of poses. The results are depicted in Figure 2 and further emphasize the superiority of the framework in practical applications.

5. CONCLUSION

In this work, we proposed a simple and efficient strategy for batch mode active learning for multi-label problems. The results obtained are superior when compared to the batch-mode extensions of previously published techniques in the literature. The proposed framework is flexible and by defining the uncertainty vector C and the redundancy matrix R suitably, it can be adapted to different applications.

Our future work will focus on further improving the running time of the proposed algorithm. Solving the QP problem may be time consuming when dealing with large datasets. However, there have been recent efforts to efficiently solve QP problems [13] by using a pivoting algorithm and the KKT conditions; these can be incorporated in our approach to make it feasible and efficient even for large scale data.

6. REFERENCES

[1] Y. Baram, R. El-Yaniv, and K. Luz. Online choice of active learning algorithms. *JMLR*, 5, 2004.
[2] M. Boutell, J. Luo, X. Shen, and C. Brown. Learning multi-label scene classification. *Pattern Recognition*, 2004.
[3] K. Brinker. Incorporating diversity in active learning with support vector machines. *ICML*, 2003.
[4] K. Brinker. On active learning in multi-label classification. In *SpringerLink*, 2006.
[5] D. Cohn, Z. Ghahramani, and M. Jordan. Active learning with statistical models. *JAIR*, 1996.
[6] B. Gokberk, L. Akarun, and E. Alpaydin. Feature selection for pose invariant face recognition. In *IEEE ICPR*, 2002.
[7] G.Tsoumakas and I. Katakis. Multi-label classification: An overview. In *International Journal of Data Warehousing and Mining*, 2007.
[8] Y. Guo and D. Schuurmans. Discriminative batch mode active learning. In *NIPS*, 2008.
[9] S. Hoi, R. Jin, and M. R. Lyu. Large-scale text categorization by batch mode active learning. In *International Conference on World Wide Web*, 2006.
[10] S. Hoi, R. Jin, J. Zhu, and M. Lyu. Semi-supervised SVM batch mode active learning for image retrieval. In *IEEE CVPR*, 2008.
[11] S. Hoi, R. Jin, J. Zhu, and M. R. Lyu. Batch mode active learning and its application to medical image classification. In *ICML*, 2006.
[12] X. Li, L. Wang, and E. Sung. Multi-label svm active learning for image classification. *IEEE ICIP*, 2004.
[13] Y. Liu and Z. Zhang. A fast algorithm for linearly constrained quadratic programming problems with lower and upper bounds. In *International Conference on Multimedia and Information Technology*, 2008.
[14] M. Singh, E. Curran, and P. Cunningham. Active learning for multi-label image annotation. In *Technical Report, University College Dublin*, 2009.
[15] S. Tong and D. Koller. Support vector machine active learning with applications to text classification. *JMLR*, 2000.
[16] X. Zhang, J. Cheng, C. Xu, H. Lu, and S. Ma. Multi-view multi-label active learning for image classification. In *IEEE ICME*, 2009.

Extracting Intentionally Captured Regions Using Point Trajectories*

Yuta Nakashima Noboru Babaguchi
Graduate School of Engineering Osaka University
2-1 Yamadaoka, Suita, Osaka 565-0871, Japan
{nakashima, babaguchi}@nanase.comm.eng.osaka-u.ac.jp

ABSTRACT

When camera persons take videos with mobile video cameras, they usually have capture intentions, i.e., what they want to express in their videos, and there are intentionally captured regions (ICRs) in the video frames that are essential for the capture intentions. Extracting ICRs is thus beneficial for wide range of applications such as video summarization and video adaptation for small displays. In this paper, we present a novel method for automatically extracting ICRs. A camera person usually moves his/her camera so that ICRs can be arranged in appropriate positions in video frames; therefore, ICRs can yield specific motion. This observation indicates that such specific motion is a vital cue for extracting ICRs. The proposed method represents motion by point trajectories, which are long-term trajectories of spatially dense points in video frames, and extracts ICRs using an ICR model based on the point trajectories. We experimentally evaluate the proposed method to demonstrate its potential applicability.

Categories and Subject Descriptors

I.4.9 [**Computing Methodologies**]: Image processing and computer vision—*applications*

General Terms

Algorithms, Design, Experimentation

Keywords

Intentionally captured region, capture intention, point trajectory

1. INTRODUCTION

Automatic extraction of regions of interest (ROIs) is an important task of video content analysis and has been extensively applied to many applications such as video summarization [12] and video adaptation for small displays [5]. Many methods for automatic ROI extraction have been proposed based on visual attention models [6, 2, 3], which simulate the visual system of animals when they watch images/videos; therefore, ROIs based on visual attention models can be deemed as those from viewers' perspective.

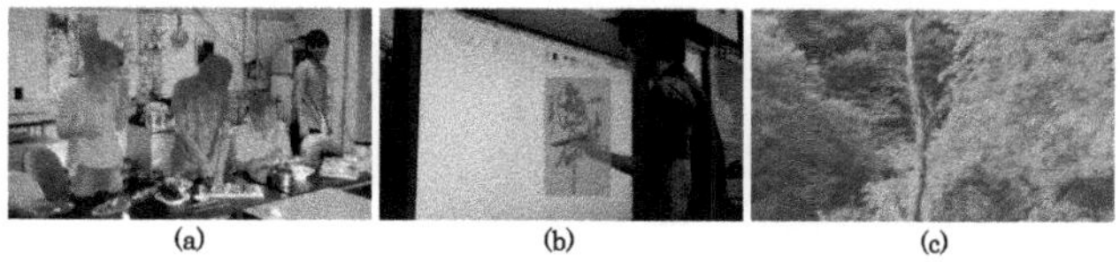

Figure 1: Examples of ICRs.

When camera persons take videos with mobile video cameras, they determine what they want to express in their video, which is referred to as camera persons' capture intentions [7]. For example, to record people cooking or beautiful scenery can be a capture intention. For such a capture intention, the regions of the people as in Fig. 1(a) or the scenery as in Fig. 1(c) are essential, and the video can become meaningless without these regions. We refer to such a region as an intentionally captured region (ICR).

ICRs are a new type of ROIs that are based on camera persons' perspective in contrast to visual attention models, and are also beneficial for above mentioned applications; nevertheless, only a few number of works have been done for this type of ROIs. For example, Nakashima et al. have proposed to detect intentionally captured human objects [9] and applied it to automatic privacy protection in videos [8]. However, their method is incapable of extracting ICRs, which is not limited to human objects.

This paper proposes a novel method for extracting ICRs in videos. The proposed method is based on the observation that a camera person's capture intention induces specific camera motion against motion of objects in the scene; therefore, motion in video frames is a vital cue for automatically extracting ICRs. Inspired by point trajectory-based object segmentation techniques [1, 11], we represent such motion by long-term and spatially dense point trajectories obtained from the method [10]. This representation enables us to model ICRs without explicitly detecting particular objects such as human objects and thus frees the proposed method from the limitation of [9].

The contributions of this paper are summarized as follows: (i) We introduce a novel concept of ICRs, which are regions essential for camera persons' capture intention. ICRs can be arbitrary regions in video frames so that, for example,

*Area chair: Bernard Merialdo

MM'11, November 28–December 1, 2011, Scottsdale, Arizona, USA.

(a) (b)

Figure 2: (a) Example frame. (b) Point trajectories.

scenery that usually occupies all pixels in a video frame as shown in Fig. 1(c) can be an ICR. (ii) To model ICRs, we propose new features that are extracted from point trajectories. We evaluate the discrimination ability of each feature. (iii) The proposed method is experimentally evaluated to show its potential applicability.

2. OVERVIEW

As mentioned in the previous section, a camera person's capture intention induces specific camera motion. For example, when the camera person captures a moving person, she moves her camera so that the person can be in the frame, or when she captures scenery, she slowly pans her camera to record the panoramic view. Such camera motion as well as object motion in the scene results in the motion in video frames. We represent the motion using point trajectories. An example video frame with an ICR indicated by the pale red region and its point trajectories are shown in Fig. 2(a) and (b). As can be seen, the point trajectories in the ICR indicated by the red lines are obviously different from those in the background indicated by the blue lines.

Based on this observation, we extract the ICRs using point trajectories. The flowchart of the proposed method is shown in Fig. 3. We first extract point trajectories using [10]. Features are then extracted from each point trajectories and the decision value for the features is calculated by a support vector machine (SVM) trained as an ICR model. Finally ICRs are extracted by graph cuts algorithm [4]. In the following sections, we describe each component.

3. FEATURES AND ICR MODEL

Let $\tilde{\mathbf{w}}_i = (\mathbf{p}_{B_i,i}^\top \cdots \mathbf{p}_{E_i,i}^\top)^\top$ denote the i-th point trajectory where B_i and E_i are the indexes of the beginning video frame and the last video frame, respectively. The point in $\tilde{\mathbf{w}}_i$ on the t-th video frame is denoted by $\mathbf{p}_{t,i} = (x_{t,i}\ y_{t,i})^\top$. Since the lengths of point trajectories $N_i = E_i - B_i + 1$ are different from each other, to extract features, we excerpt a point trajectory $\mathbf{w}_{t,i}$ with a fixed length T centered at the t-th frame from $\tilde{\mathbf{w}}_i$. The following features are extracted from these point trajectories.

Position of Point (POX and POY) is the coordinates of the point, i.e., $x_{t,i}$ and $y_{t,i}$. These features are considered to be the most informative because camera persons usually try to arrange ICRs around the center of the video frame.

Difference from Dominant Rigid Motion (DRM) represents whether or not $\mathbf{w}_{t,i}$ is in the dominant rigid motion. DRM is beneficial for modeling an ICR that corresponds to a foreground object. Based on [11], we measure how likely the point trajectory $\mathbf{w}_{t,i}$ is in the dominant rigid motion as follows: Let $W_t = (\mathbf{w}_{t,1} \cdots \mathbf{w}_{t,I})$ denote a subset of excerpted point trajectories. If all point trajectories in W_t are on rigid objects, the rank of W_t is three. Therefore, three trajectories, which are denoted by $W_t' = (\mathbf{w}_t^1\ \mathbf{w}_t^2\ \mathbf{w}_t^3)$,

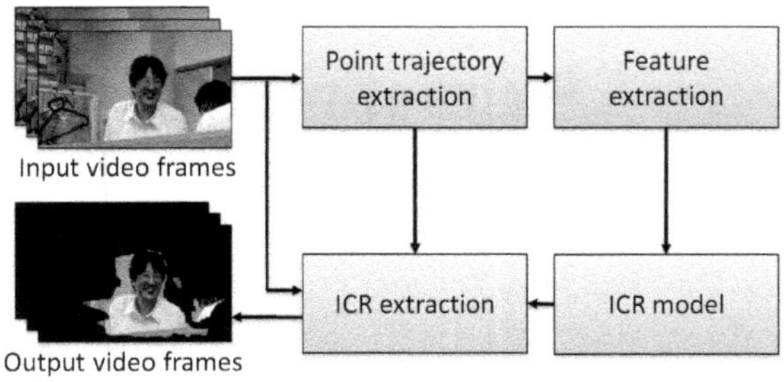

Figure 3: Flowchart of the proposed method.

are randomly chosen from the excerpted point trajectories, and the following criterion is calculated as in [11]:

$$F_t = \sum_{i=1} \|P_t' \mathbf{w}_{t,i} - \mathbf{w}_{t,i}\|_2 \tag{1}$$

where $P_t' = W_t'(W_t'^\top W_t')^{-1} W_t'^\top$ and $\|\cdot\|_2$ is the Euclidean distance. This process is repeated K times to find W_t^* that minimizes F_t. The excerpted point trajectories in W_t^* are expected to be in the dominant rigid motion. We use $f_{t,i} = \|P_t^* \mathbf{w}_{t,i} - \mathbf{w}_{t,i}\|_2$ as a feature.

Stability of Motion (SOM) represents whether the point largely moves or not. SOM can tell when the point become intentionally captured because camera persons first move their cameras to arrange ICRs at appropriate positions with relatively rapid camera motion, and then try to stabilize the ICR. Let $d_{t,i}$ denote the Euclidean distance between $\mathbf{p}_{t,i}$ and $\mathbf{p}_{t-1,i}$, i.e., We calculate the weighted mean $\boldsymbol{\nu}_i$ and covariance matrix Θ_i for $\tilde{\mathbf{w}}_i$ as

$$\boldsymbol{\nu}_i = \sum_{\mathbf{p}_{\tau,i} \in \tilde{\mathbf{w}}_i} \omega_{\tau,i} \mathbf{p}_{\tau,i}, \quad \Theta_i = \sum_{\mathbf{p}_{\tau,i} \in \tilde{\mathbf{w}}_i} \omega_{\tau,i} (\mathbf{p}_{\tau,i} - \boldsymbol{\nu}_i)(\mathbf{p}_{\tau,i} - \boldsymbol{\nu}_i)^\top \tag{2}$$

where $d_{t,i} = \|\mathbf{p}_{t,i} - \mathbf{p}_{t-1,i}\|_2$ and

$$\omega_{\tau,i} = \begin{cases} \frac{1}{N_i} & \text{if } d_{\tau,i} < \mathit{MED}_i \\ \frac{1}{N_i} e^{\mathit{MED}_i - d_{\tau,i}} & \text{otherwise} \end{cases}. \tag{3}$$

MED_i is the median of $d_{t,i}$ over t. SOM is calculated as the Mahalanobis distance given by

$$m_{t,i} = \sqrt{(\mathbf{p}_{t,i} - \boldsymbol{\nu}_i)^\top \Theta_i^{-1} (\mathbf{p}_{t,i} - \boldsymbol{\nu}_i)}. \tag{4}$$

We use the weighted mean and covariance matrix based on median of $d_{t,i}$ given by (2) so that SOM can be small even when a camera person follows a moving object, which yields relatively rapid motion in video frames.

Motion along Major Axis (MMA) represents the width of the distribution of the points in the point trajectory along the major axis. MMA together with the following two features, i.e., MMI and AMD, are useful for roughly describing overall motion of $\mathbf{w}_{t,i}$. MMA is given as the largest eigenvalue $\lambda_{t,i}$ of the covariance matrix of $\mathbf{w}_{t,i}$, that is,

$$\Sigma_{t,i} = \frac{1}{T} \sum_{\mathbf{p}_{\tau,i} \in \mathbf{w}_{t,i}} (\mathbf{p}_{\tau,i} - \ _{t,i})(\mathbf{p}_{\tau,i} - \ _{t,i})^\top. \tag{5}$$

The mean $\ _{t,i}$ is calculated by $\ _{t,i} = \sum \mathbf{p}_{\tau,i}/T$, where the summation is calculated for $\mathbf{p}_{\tau,i}$ in $\mathbf{w}_{t,i}$.

Motion along Minor Axis (MMI) is given as the smallest eigenvalue of $\Sigma_{t,i}$, denoted by $\kappa_{t,i}$.

Angle of Major Axis (AMD) is calculated from the eigenvector $\mathbf{v}_{t,i} = (v_{t,i}^x, v_{t,i}^y)^\top$ corresponding to the largest eigenvalue $\lambda_{t,i}$ by $a_{t,i} = \tan^{-1}(v_{t,i}^y / v_{t,i}^x)$.

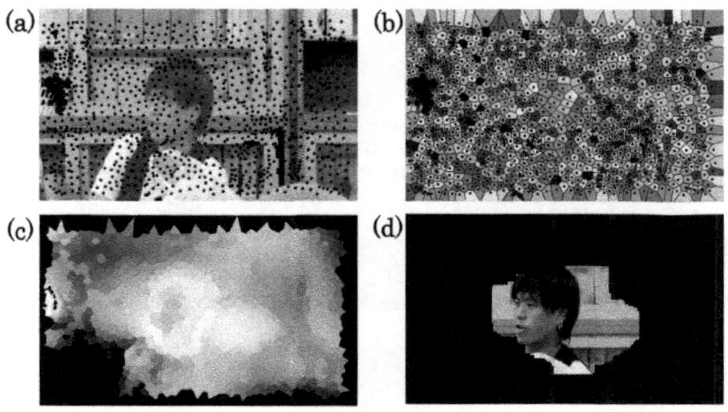

Figure 4: Examples of (a) original frame with corresponding points, (b) Voronoi diagram based on the points, (c) data term, and (d) extracted ICR.

Curvature of Trajectory (COT) represents how frequently the excerpted point trajectory changes its direction. COT can be beneficial for discriminating pan from the other camera motion, and is calculated by

$$c_{t,i} = \sum_{\mathbf{p}_{\tau,i} \in \mathbf{w}_{t,i}} \frac{(\mathbf{p}_{\tau,i} - \mathbf{p}_{\tau+k,i})(\mathbf{p}_{\tau,i} - \mathbf{p}_{\tau-k,i})^\top}{\|\mathbf{p}_{\tau,i} - \mathbf{p}_{\tau+k,i}\|_2 \, \|\mathbf{p}_{\tau,i} - \mathbf{p}_{\tau-k,i}\|_2}, \quad (6)$$

which is a sum of curvatures in $\mathbf{w}_{t,i}$. The parameter k is empirically set to 5.

We define an eight-dimensional feature vector for $\mathbf{p}_{t,i}$ as

$$\mathbf{v}_{t,i} = (x_{t,i} \; y_{t,i} \; f_{t,i} \; m_{t,i} \; \lambda_{t,i}, \; \kappa_{t,i} \; a_{t,i} \; c_{t,i}). \quad (7)$$

As an ICR model, we train an SVM with a set of labeled feature vectors. We denote the decision value given the feature vector $\mathbf{v}_{t,i}$ by $g(\mathbf{v}_{t,i})$. A greater decision value indicates that the point trajectory is likely to be in an ICR.

4. ICR EXTRACTION

To extract ICRs, we assign a label $l_n \in \{-1, +1\}$ to each pixel, which represents whether the n-th pixel is in ICRs ($l_n = +1$) or not ($l_n = -1$), using the ICR model and graph cuts algorithm [4] considering spatial continuity of the original video frame.

Let A denote the set of adjacent pixels. For each video frame, the graph cuts algorithm minimizes the energy given by

$$E = \sum_n D_n(l_n) + \sum_{(n,n') \in A} V_{n,n'}(l_n, l_{n'}) \quad (8)$$

where $D_n(l_n)$ is the data term that represents how likely the n-th pixel is in an ICR and $V_{n,n'}(l_n, l_{n'})$ is the smooth term to confirm continuity among adjacent pixels.

Since the decision values are obtained for a subset of all pixels in a video frame, i.e., $\mathbf{p}_{t,i}$, we divide a video frame into small regions as shown in Fig. 4(b) to spread the decision values on the video frame. For this, a Voronoi diagram are generated based on Delaunay triangulation, in which all $\mathbf{p}_{t,i}$ in the video frame are deemed a vertices of the triangles. We denote the region corresponding to $\mathbf{p}_{t,i}$ by $\Omega_{t,i}$, and define the data term for the n-th pixel in $\Omega_{t,i}$ as

$$D_n(l_n) = \begin{cases} \sigma(g(\mathbf{v}_{t,i}) - \alpha) & \text{for } l_n = +1 \\ 1 - \sigma(g(\mathbf{v}_{t,i}) - \alpha) & \text{otherwise} \end{cases} \quad (9)$$

where $\sigma(z) = 1/[1 + \exp(-z)]$ is a sigmoid function and α is a parameter to control how much the algorithm favors $l_n = -1$. An example of the data term is shown in Fig. 4(c).

Table 1: Kullback-Leibler divergences.

POX	POY	DRM	SOM	MMA	MMI	AMD	COT
0.037	0.0077	0.010	0.0016	0.0075	0.0040	0.0027	0.0077

Table 2: FPR and TPR for various values of α and β (FPR, TPR).

	$\beta = 1$	$\beta = 30$	$\beta = 100$
$\alpha = -3$	(0.47, 0.64)	(0.46, 0.64)	(0.45, 0.63)
$\alpha = -2$	(0.38, 0.57)	(0.37, 0.57)	(0.34, 0.55)
$\alpha = -1$	(0.20, 0.39)	(0.17, 0.37)	(0.12, 0.30)
$\alpha = 0$	(0.08, 0.19)	(0.06, 0.16)	(0.03, 0.08)

The smooth term $V_{n,n'}$ is given by

$$V_{n,n'}(l_n, l'_n) = \begin{cases} 0 & \text{for } l_n = l_{n'} \\ \beta(M - \|\boldsymbol{\gamma}_n - \boldsymbol{\gamma}_{n'}\|_1) & \text{otherwise} \end{cases} \quad (10)$$

where $\boldsymbol{\gamma}_n$ represents the color of the n-th pixel in the RGB color space, $\|\cdot\|_1$ is the Manhattan distance, and M is the upper bound of $\|\boldsymbol{\gamma}_n - \boldsymbol{\gamma}_{n'}\|_1$. The contribution of the smooth term is determined by β. This term penalizes the different labels assigned to adjacent pixels in similar colors. The pixels with $l_n = +1$ are extracted as ICRs as in Fig. 4(d).

5. EXPERIMENTAL RESULTS

We evaluated the performance of the proposed method as well as the contribution of each feature. We used 16 videos at 30 frames per second taken by several camera persons. The average duration of the videos is 48.1 seconds. The camera persons who took the videos assigned a label indicating ICRs to each pixel in video frames as shown in Fig. 1. Since this is a time consuming task, the camera persons assigned labels every ten frames. Labels of excerpted point trajectories are determined based on these labels. According to [11], the values of T and K were set to 30 and 1000, respectively. To evaluate the performance, we employed 16-fold cross-validation, where 15 videos were used for training the SVM and 1 video was used for evaluation. To reduce the computational cost, we chose 20000 feature vectors out of those extracted from 15 videos to train the SVM.

To evaluate the contribution of each features, we generated the histograms p_j and q_j of each feature for excerpted point trajectories labeled as intentionally captured and not, respectively, where j is the index of histogram bins. The Kullback-Leibler (KL) divergence defined as follows are calculated as a measure of discrimination ability:

$$D_{\mathrm{KL}}[p, q] = \sum_j p_j \log \frac{p_j}{q_j}. \quad (11)$$

Table 1 shows the results. As can be expected, POX gives the highest discrimination ability, followed by DRM, while SOM is the worst. We consider that this is because SOM is adopted to tell when the region becomes intentionally captured, and the value of SOM hardly differs between ICRs and other regions. Therefore, we need to evaluate the discrimination abilities of combinations of the features to show usefulness of SOM. The distributions of AMD also do not yield much difference compared to the other features.

The performance of the proposed method was evaluated by the false positive rate (FPR) and true positive rate (TPR) that are defined as follows:

$$\mathrm{FPR} = \frac{|\bar{\Omega}_{\mathrm{GT}} \cap \Omega_{\mathrm{EXT}}|}{|\bar{\Omega}_{\mathrm{GT}}|}, \quad \mathrm{TRP} = \frac{|\Omega_{\mathrm{GT}} \cap \Omega_{\mathrm{EXT}}|}{|\Omega_{\mathrm{GT}}|} \quad (12)$$

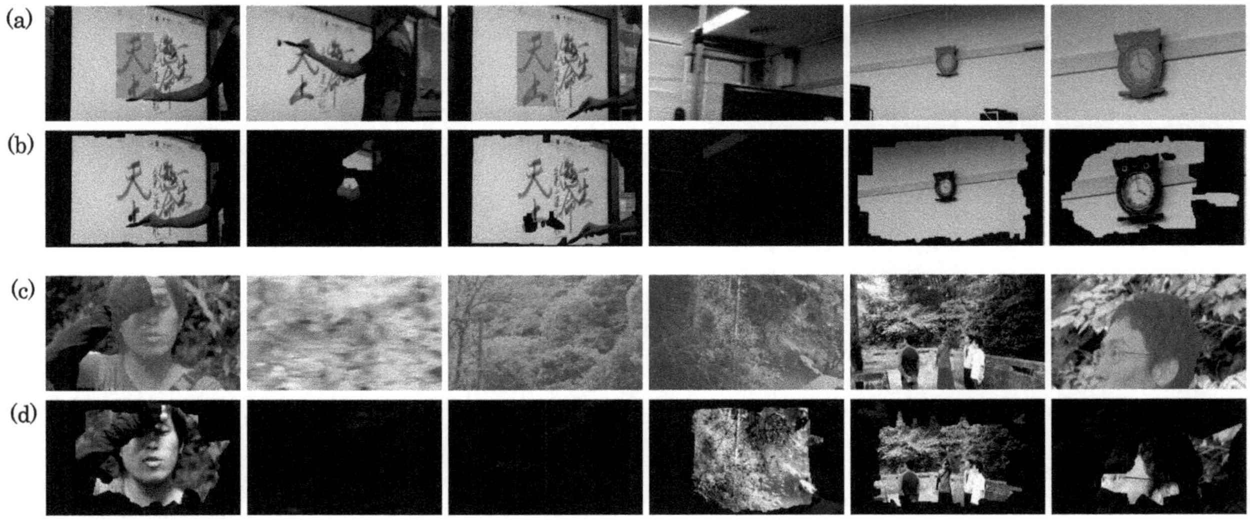

Figure 5: Results of ICR extraction for two videos. (a) and (c) are the original frames with ground truth regions highlighted in pale red. (b) and (d) show extracted ICRs, and the other regions are shaded.

where Ω_{GT} and Ω_{EXT} denote ICRs labeled by the camera persons and extracted ICRs, respectively. The number of the pixels in Ω is denoted by $|\Omega|$ and $\bar{\Omega}$ is the complementary set of Ω. We used several values of the parameters α and β to show the effects of these parameters.

The results are shown in Table 2. The proposed method does not extract any regions in most cases when the value of α is large because $g(\mathbf{v}_{t,i})$ is biased toward negative values. The performance is the best when $\alpha = -2$ and $\beta = 100$ in terms of the distance from the point (0, 1) in the FPR versus TPR space. Figure 5 shows example frames and extracted ICRs. The proposed method successfully discriminates presence and absence of ICRs as in Fig. 5(a) and (b). However, the exact shapes of ICRs cannot be extracted. This problem can be partly solved by revising the smooth term in (10). In the third frame of Fig. 5(d), the proposed method is incapable even of presence/absence discrimination. This is because the camera person rapidly panned his camera when capturing scenery, which is tough to discriminate from motion when the camera person changes ICRs as in the fourth frame of Fig. 5(a) and the second frame of Fig. 5(c).

6. CONCLUSION

In this paper, we presented a novel concept of intentionally captured regions (ICRs), which are a new type of regions of interest from camera persons' perspective, and proposed a method for automatically extracting ICRs in videos taken with mobile video cameras. The proposed method uses features extracted from point trajectories to model ICRs, and extract ICRs based on the model. Our experimental results indicated that the horizontal position is the most informative cue for ICR extraction. We also demonstrated that the proposed method can extract ICRs with 0.34 of false positive rate and 0.55 of true positive rate. We consider that these results are encouraging although the performance should be improved. Our future work is as follows: We should leverage temporal continuity of ICRs to improve the performance. A feature that represents coherency of motion, which can be useful when a camera person captures scenery, should be developed. This work is partly supported by a Grant-in-Aid for scientific research from the Japan Society for the Promotion of Science.

7. REFERENCES

[1] T. Brox and J. Malik. Object segmentation by long term analysis of point trajectories. In *Proc. European Conf. Computer Vision*, pages 282–295, 2010.

[2] L. Itti and P. Baldi. A principled approach to detecting surprising events in videos. In *Proc. IEEE Computer Society Conf. Computer and Vision Pattern Recognition*, pages 631–637, June 2005.

[3] L. Itti, C. Koch, and E. Niebur. A model of saliency based visual attention for rapid scene analysis. *IEEE Trans. Pattern Anal. Mach. Intell.*, 20(11):1254–1259, Nov. 1998.

[4] V. Kolmogorov and R. Zabih. What energy functions can be minimized via graph cuts? *IEEE Trans. Pattern Anal. Mach. Intell.*, 26(2):147–159, Feb. 2004.

[5] F. Liu and M. Gleicher. Video retargeting: automating pan and scan. In *Proc. ACM Int'l Conf. Multimedia*, pages 241–250, Oct. 2006.

[6] T. Liu, Z. Yuan, J. Sun, J. Wang, N. Zheng, X. Tang, and H.-Y. Shum. Learning to detect a salient object. *IEEE Trans. Pattern Anal. Mach. Intell.*, 33(2):357–367, Feb. 2011.

[7] T. Mei, X.-S. Hua, H.-Q. Zhou, and S. Li. Modeling and mining of users' capture intention for home video. *IEEE Trans. Multimedia*, 9(1):66–77, Jan. 2007.

[8] Y. Nakashima, N. Babaguchi, and J. Fan. Automatically protecting privacy in consumer generated videos using intended human object detector. In *Proc. ACM Int'l Conf. Multimedia*, pages 1135–1138, Oct. 2010.

[9] Y. Nakashima, N. Babaguchi, and J. Fan. Detecting intended human objects in human-captured videos. In *Proc. Conf. Computer Vision and Pattern Recognition Workshop*, pages 1–8, Aug. 2010.

[10] P. Sand and S. Teller. Particle video: long-range motion estimation using point trajectories. In *Proc. IEEE Computer Society Conf. Computer Vision and Pattern Recognition*, pages 2195–2202, June 2006.

[11] Y. Sheikh, O. Javed, and T. Kanade. Background subtraction for freely moving cameras. In *Proc. IEEE Int'l Conf. Computer Vision*, pages 1219–1225, Sept. 2009.

[12] T. Wang, T. Mei, X.-S. Hua, X.-L. Liu, and H.-Q. Zhou. Video collage: a novel presentation of video sequence. In *Proc. Int'l Conf. Multimedia and Expo*, pages 1479–1482, July 2007.

Exploring Self-Similarities of Bag-of-Features for Image Classification*

Chih-Fan Chen
Research Center for IT Innovation
Academia Sinica, Taipei, Taiwan
ryanchen@citi.sinica.edu.tw

Yu-Chiang Frank Wang
Research Center for IT Innovation
Academia Sinica, Taipei, Taiwan
ycwang@citi.sinica.edu.tw

ABSTRACT

The use of bag-of-features (BOF) models has been a popular technique for image classification and retrieval. In order to better represent and discriminate images from different classes, we advance BOF and explore the self-similarities of visual words for improved performance. The proposed *self-similarity hypercubes* (SSH) model, which observes the concurrent occurrences of visual words in an image, is able to describe the structural information of the BOF in an image. Our experiments confirm that our SSH provides additional and complementary information to BOF and thus results in improved classification performance. Unlike most prior methods requiring extraction or integration of multiple types of features for similar improvements, our SSH works in the same domain as the BOF does. Moreover, we do not limit the use of our SSH to any particular type of image descriptors, and its generalization is also verified.

Categories and Subject Descriptors

H.3.1 [**Information Storage & Retrieval**]: Content Analysis and Indexing; I.4.7 [**Image Processing & Computer Vision**]: Feature Measurement—*feature representation*

General Terms

Algorithms, Experimentation, Performance

Keywords

Image classification, bag-of-features, self-similarity

1. INTRODUCTION

Due to the growth of Web-based image applications such as Flickr and Google Images, lots of attention has been directed to image classification and retrieval for researchers in multimedia communities. Among existing methods, the *bag-of-features* (BOF) model [1, 16, 10] has been a popular technique due to its simplicity and effectiveness. BOF quantizes local image descriptors into distinct visual words, and it uses a histogram representation to show the number of occurrences of each word for each image. Several works have been proposed to improve the BOF model [9, 10]. Some proposed to preserve the spatial information of descriptors, while others combined different features to boost the performance [6, 12]. Although promising results were reported, the increase of computation complexity in extracting and fusing different features, plus high feature dimensionality, would prohibit the use of these methods in large-scale problems.

*Area chair: Lexing Xie

MM'11, November 28–December 1, 2011, Scottsdale, Arizona, USA.

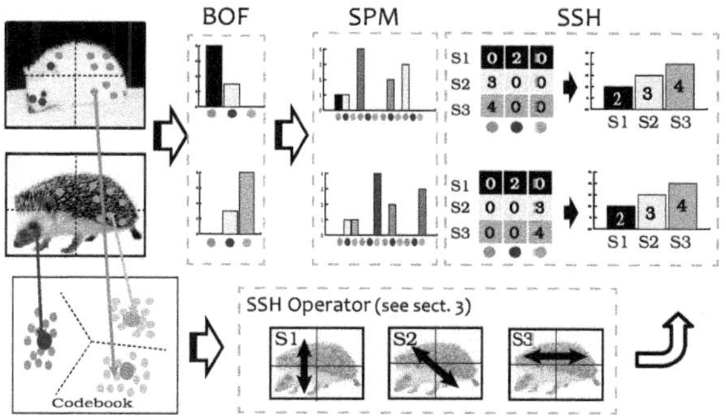

Figure 1: Advantages of our self-similarity hypercube (SSH) model over standard BOF and SPM (see Sect. 2).

In this paper, we utilize the *self-similarities* of visual words and propose the *self-similarity hypercubes* (SSH) feature model (see Section 3). We aim at utilizing the *related* spatial information of visual words present in images (see Figure 1 for example), and such structural information will provide additional representation ability to the standard BOF. As a results, improved classification performance can be expected. While the self-similarities of image *patches* or *descriptors* have been investigated in literature (e.g., [15, 3], these prior approaches typically required extraction and processing of self-similarity features in the associated feature domains. In our work, we explore the self-similarity of existing visual words; in other words, we do not require additional feature extraction or selection processes. Our experiments will verify that our method is not limited to the use of appearance features (e.g., SIFT [11]), and we can extend our SSH to HoG [2] or other image descriptors.

2. RELATED WORK

2.1 BOF and SPM for Image Classification

Among approaches for image classification, the *bag-of-features* (BOF) model [1, 16, 10] has demonstrated its success in recent years. BOF considers each image as a collection of *unordered* local image descriptors. To represent an image, BOF quantizes these descriptors into distinct *visual words*, and it uses a histogram to indicate the number of occurrences of each visual word. To determine the visual words (i.e., *dictionary* or *codebook*) from images, one typically performs k-means, etc. clustering algorithms and divide the image descriptors into distinct groups, and the representative of each group (e.g., cluster mean) is thus considered as a visual word. Once the BOF is obtained, one can design classifiers such as SVM for classification.

As mentioned in [9], BOF discards the spatial order of image descriptors and thus limits the classification performance. To address this problem, spatial pyramid matching (SPM) is proposed to partition an image into several grids in different scales. The BOF models pooled from different grids are concatenated as the final SPM model to preserve the spatial order of local descriptors (and the associated visual words) [9]. However, take a SPM with three image scales for example, the dimension of a SPM feature vector will be $(1+2^2+4^2) = 21$ times larger than that of the BOF, which inevitably increases the computation time.

2.2 Self-Similarity

Figure 1 shows an example in which standard BOF/SPM models are not sufficient to represent different images from the same object category. Comparing the two BOF (or SPM) models, it is obvious that they are not similar to each other due to texture, etc. appearance variations. Shechtman and Irani [15] first proposed to utilize the *local self-similarity* (LSS) of patches present in an image. By exploring the neighborhood of each pixel, LSS uses such information to detect object images containing similar local structures as the query input does. Later, Deselaers *et al.* [3] advocated to construct BOF models on LSS. They learned a codebook based on LSS descriptors, and they utilized the *global* self-similarity to describe the structural information of the entire image. In order to achieve improved performance, their method needs to determine and extract self-similarity features prior to the integration of their resulting features and the standard BOF (e.g., from SIFT, HoG [2], or GIST [14] descriptors). In this paper, we advance the self-similarity of the existing BOF models. Unlike [15, 3], our method need not extract different types of features or learn extra codebooks. We aim at exploring the self-similarity of existing visual words, and we do not limit our method to the use of any particular image descriptors. Therefore, our proposed feature model is computationally more preferable than prior works requiring combination of different types of features (e.g., [6]) for improved performance.

3. OUR PROPOSED METHOD

3.1 Learning of BOF via Sparse Coding

Since our approach extracts the self-similarities of visual words from the existing BOF model, we briefly discuss the construction of BOF in this subsection. Take the codebook constructed from SIFT features for example (see Figure 2(a)), we first extract dense SIFT descriptors from images, and we quantize these descriptors into distinct visual words. Figure 2(b) shows example quantization results, in which each colored number indicates the visual word assigned to the associated descriptor. Instead of using vector

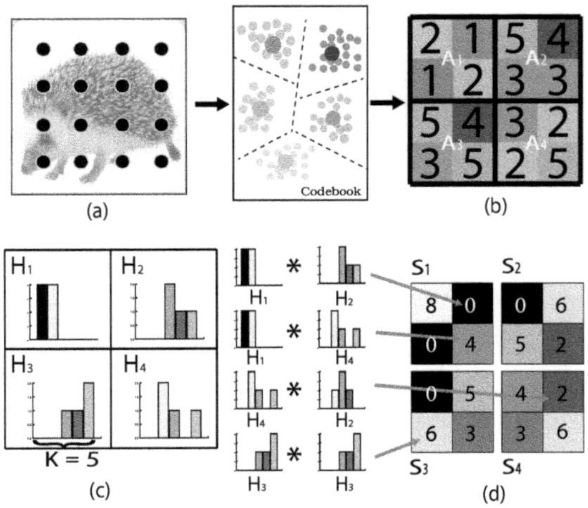

Figure 2: Our proposed SSH model. (a) Extracting dense image descriptor for codebook learning. (b) Encoding the descriptors with the associated visual words. (c) Construction of BOF for each grid. (d) Performing inner products S_1, S_2, etc. between BOF from different grids to obtain visual word self-similarities. The final SSH model is determined by Eq. (2).

quantization (VQ), we apply sparse coding (SC) [13] to construct an over-complete codebook and encode the descriptors accordingly. The final BOF model is produced by the *max-pooling* operation on the encoded descriptors. It has been verified in [17] that such SC-based BOF models outperform those constructed by VQ.

Since the detailed discussion of SC is beyond the scope of this paper, we only highlight this BOF learning process. Suppose that we have N SIFT descriptors extracted from images, SC learns an over-complete codebook with size K, which solves the following optimization problem:

$$\min_{D,\alpha} \sum_{i=1}^{N} \frac{1}{2} \|x_i - A\alpha_i\|_2^2 + \lambda \|\alpha_i\|_1, \tag{1}$$

where x_i is the image descriptor, A is the codebook with K visual words, α_i is the associated sparse coefficient vector, and λ controls the sparsity. To produce the final K-dimensional BOF model for an image, all encoded α_i vectors will be summed up by a dimension-wise max-pooling operation. Once the codebook A is learned during training, we only need to encode the descriptors of the test image and calculate its BOF accordingly. If a SPM model is of interest, a K-dimensional BOF will be pooled from each grid in each image scale. For example, a SPM model with three image scales will result in a $21K$ dimensional feature vector.

3.2 Learning of Self-Similarity Hypercubes

In this paper, we advocate to explore the *self-similarity* of visual words within the BOF model. We propose to construct the *self-similarity hypercubes* (SSH) features for each image. The purpose of our SSH is to preserve the structural information of visual words present in images, and our experiments will confirm that such information results in improved classification performance. While the term SSH has been used by Deselaers and Ferrari [3], they focus on extracting the global structure of local self-similarity features in *pixel* domain. Our work is very unique, since our SSH extends the existing BOF and does not require to determine/extract additional self-similarity features in other domains as [15, 3] did.

To construct our SSH model, we first divide an image into several sub-regions. For example, we segment the input image in Figure 2(a) into $D \times D = 2 \times 2 = 4$ grids, which are denoted as A_1 to A_4 in Figure 2(b). Recall that the numbers in each grid indicate the visual words assigned to the corresponding image descriptors. As suggest by [17], we construct the BOF models for each grid by max-pooling and produce the four histogram representations $\{H_1, H_2, H_3, H_4\}$ accordingly (as shown in Figure 2(c)).

Instead of directly concatenating these representations (like SPM), we exploit the self-similarity of visual words present in different grids. More precisely, we start from H_1 and calculate *inner products* between H_1 and different H_i. The resulting vector is denoted as $S_1 = [s_{11}, s_{12}, s_{13}, s_{14}]^T$, which contains structural information of visual words present in this image. Recall that each attribute in the BOF model H_i indicates the number of occurrences of each visual word, and the inner product between different H_i implies the similarity between those BOF models (and the associated visual words) present in an image.

Take s_{14} for example, $s_{14} = H_1^T H_4 = 4$, which calculates the visual word similarity between H_1 and H_4 in Figure 2(c). More precisely, s_{14} sums up the numbers of occurrences of each visual word *concurrently* present in grids A_1 and A_4. Therefore, we have $s_{14} = 2 \times 2 + 0 = 4$ (i.e., visual word 2 occurs twice, while none of the remaining words are present in both grids). Similarly, we have $s_{11} = H_1^T H_1 = 2 \times 2 + 2 \times 2 = 8$ representing the visual word self-similarity of grid H_1. After the calculation for the inner product vector S_1 is complete, we repeat this process for S_2, S_3, etc. We note that, since $s_{ij} = H_i^T H_j = s_{ji}$, the final SSH feature can be calcualted as follows:

$$SSH = [s_{11}, s_{12}, \ldots, s_{1D^2}, \ldots, s_{(D^2-1)D^2}]^T, \qquad (2)$$

where $s_{ij} = H_i^T H_j$, and D is the number of grids in each direction. As a result, if we divide an image into $D \times D = 4 \times 4 = 16$ grids, the dimension of SSH is $d_{SSH} = C_2^{D^2} + D^2 = D^2(D^2+1)/2 = 16 \times 17/2 = 136$. It is worth noting that, although our SSH is based on the existing BOF model, the dimensionality of SSH is a function of the number of grids D^2 and is *independent* of the dictionary size K. Once the SSH model is obtained, we simply concatenate the BOF/SPM and SSH models and produce the final feature representation for training and testing.

4. EXPERIMENTS AND RESULTS

4.1 Datasets

We consider two datasets for object recognition tasks: Caltech-101 [5] and Caltech-256 [7]. We randomly select 15 or 30 images per class for training (i.e., N_T =15 or 30). For the remaining images, no more than 50 per class are used for testing. All tests are repeated 10 times, and we present the averaged results with standard deviations. The longer side of each image is resized to 300 pixels ([17] also did this). For dense SIFT extraction, we extract SIFT descriptors from 16 $\times$ 16 pixel patches of each image, and the spacing between adjacent patches is 6 pixels. We set λ in (1) as 0.2 for codebook learning. Since we only consider linear SVMs (trained by *liblinear* [4]) for our SSH, our method provides excellent scalability for larger-scale classification problems.

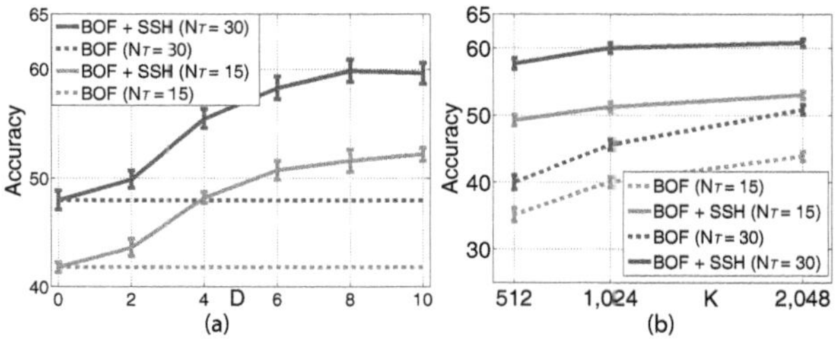

Figure 3: Performance comparisons on Caltech-101 with different SSH and codebook sizes. Note that $D = 0$ corresponds to the use of standard BOF.

4.2 Parameters of SSH

As discussed in Sect. 3.2, our SSH exploits visual word self-similarity, and the dimensionality of SSH is a function of the number of grids in an image, i.e., $d_{SSH} = D^2(D^2+1)/2$. Since the construction of our SSH is based on BOF, we also need to select its codebook size K. Once these parameters are determined (which can be done via cross-validation in practice), we concatenate both BOF and SSH models to form the final feature for classification.

Figure 3(a) shows the recognition performance on Caltech-101 using different D values. We note that $D = 0$ represents the standard BOF (we choose $K = 2048$), and the corresponding accuracy is considered as the baseline (shown in dotted lines). For $D > 0$, our method produces a feature vector BOF + SSH, which is of size $K + d_{SSH}$. From this figure, we observe the increase of accuracy when D goes up. However, for the use of finer grids ($D > 8$ or $D^2 > 64$) in SSH, we did not observe remarkable improvement in accuracy (while a much longer feature vector will be produced). Therefore, we choose $D = 8$ for our SSH, and the dimension of the final feature vector BOF + SSH is $K + d_{SSH} = 2048 + 64(64+1)/2 = 2048 + 2080 = 4128$.

Figure 3(b) shows the recognition performance using different codebook sizes K. It can be seen that, compared with the standard BOF, our approach consistently achieved improved recognition, and such improvements become more significant when smaller K values are of use. From the above results, we validate that additional structural information of visual words provided by our SSH indeed exhibits complementary classification ability, and thus improved performance can be obtained. Some example object categories which benefit from our SSH and thus achieve significant performance improvements are shown in Figure 4.

4.3 SSH of Different BOF models

While one of the advantages of our SSH is the extension of the current BOF model without further extraction or processing of features from other domains, we need to evaluate our SSH on BOF models constructed by different image descriptors. This is to show the generalization of our SSH. Besides the performance on Caltech-101 using BOF of SIFT descriptors, we also consider the use of dense HoG features [2]. To extract HoG for an image, we first divide each image patch into $4 \times 4 = 16$ grids, and each grid is of size 8×8, 6×6, or 4×4 pixels. In other words, the size of each patch is 32×32, 24×24, 16×16 pixels. For the 16 grids of each patch, we calculate 8 directional responses and concatenate the outputs into a 128-dimensional HoG descriptor. Table 1 shows the performances using standard BOF/SPM models using SIFT or HOG descriptors, and those with our method

Table 1: Classification performance using BOF, SPM and SSH with different image descriptors ($N_T = 30$).

Type	BOF	BOF+SSH	SPM	SPM+SSH
Dimension	K (2048)	$K + d_{SSH}$ (4128)	$21K$ (43008)	$21K + d_{SSH}$ (45088)
SIFT	51.5 ± 1.8	64.4 ± 0.8	73.3 ± 0.6	74.7 ± 0.9
HOG (8×8)	48.9 ± 0.6	59.4 ± 1.6	68.4 ± 1.0	69.4 ± 0.9
HOG (6×6)	39.5 ± 1.6	54.2 ± 1.3	64.3 ± 0.9	66.3 ± 0.6
HOG (4×4)	29.0 ± 0.8	47.8 ± 1.1	56.9 ± 0.7	58.7 ± 0.8

Table 2: Performance comparisons.

Database	Caltech 101		Caltech 256	
N_T	15	30	15	30
Griffin [7]	~ 59.0	67.6 ± 1.4	~ 28.10	34.1 ± 0.2
German [8]	$--$	66.2 ± 0.5	$--$	27.2 ± 0.5
Yang [17]	67.0 ± 0.5	73.2 ± 0.5	27.7 ± 0.5	34.0 ± 0.4
Ours	$\mathbf{68.2 \pm 0.7}$	$\mathbf{74.7 \pm 0.9}$	$\mathbf{33.0 \pm 0.3}$	$\mathbf{39.7 \pm 0.3}$

(denoted as BOF+SSH and SPM+SSH). From this table, we see that the use of our BOF+SSH or SPM+SSH consistently outperformed that of standard BOF or SPM, and this observation holds for both SIFT and HoG. Therefore, the robustness of our method is confirmed.

It is also worth noting that, although SPM is expected to outperform BOF (see [17]), the dimensionality of SPM is 21 times larger than that of BOF. For large-scale problems, K is typically very large (beyond thousands even millions) and thus the use of SPM is not preferable. From Table 1, one can see that our approach with BOF+SSH results in the feature model whose dimensionality is in *the same order* as that of BOF, while a remarkable improvement (64.4% vs. 51.5%) in accuracy was still achieved.

4.4 Comparisons

Table 2 compares our SSH with state-of-the-art methods on the two datasets. We only consider those using a single type of features (such as BOF and its extensions) for comparisons. Griffin *et al.* [7] first applied the SPM on both datasets, and we use their results as baselines. Although Germent *et al.* [8] proposed a kernel codebook to encoding the SIFT descriptors with more flexibility, negligible differences were observed from the results between [8] and [7]. Yang *et al.* [17] applied the sparse coding technique for BOF and SPM. While their approach achieved improved recognition on Caltech-101, marginal improvements were observed on Caltech-256. Using our SSH (SPM+SSH to be more precise), we obtained recognition rates at 74.7% and 39.7% on the two datasets, and the improvements over the aforementioned works are significant. We note that, although recent methods combining multiple types of features for improved performance exist (e.g., 77.7% and 45.8% on the same datasets were reported in [6]), these methods need to extract features from different domains and typically require more complicated or nonlinear classifiers to combine those features. Our method aims at utilizing the visual word self-similarity, which is not limited to any particular descriptor and does not require additional feature extraction or selection processes. From the above experiments, we successfully confirm the effectiveness of our SSH.

5. CONCLUSIONS

In this paper, we advocated the visual word self-similarity for image classification. Based on the BOF model of interest, our proposed SSH model explores the structural information of visual words present in an images by observing concurrent occurrences of the associated visual words. Unlike most prior methods which typically integrate multiple types of features for improved classification performance, our SSH is constructed in the same feature domain as the BOF model does, and thus we do not need extra feature extraction, selection, or fusion processes. From the experimental results, we confirmed that our SSH provides additional and complementary representation and classification ability, and thus both the effectiveness and generalization of our SSH model were successfully verified.

Figure 4: Selected object categories with improved performance by SSH.

Acknowledgements This work is supported in part by the National Science Council of Taiwan via NSC 100-2221-E-001-018-MY2 and NSC 100-2631-H-001-013.

6. REFERENCES

[1] G. Csurka et al. Visual categorization with bags of keypoints. In *ECCV Workshop*, 2004.

[2] N. Dalal and B. Triggs. Histograms of oriented gradients for human detection. In *IEEE CVPR*, 2005.

[3] T. Deselaers and V. Ferrari. Global and efficient self-similarity for object classification and detection. In *IEEE CVPR*, 2010.

[4] R.-F. Fan et al. Liblinear: A library for large linear classification. In *JMLR*, 9:1871-1874, 2008.

[5] L. Fei-Fei, R. Fergus, and P. Perona. Learning generative visual models from few training examples: An incremental bayesian approach tested on 101 object categories. In *IEEE CVPR WorkShop*, 2004.

[6] P. Gehler and S. Nowozin. On feature combination for multiclass object classification. In *IEEE ICCV*, 2009.

[7] G. Griffin, A. Holub, and P. Perona. Caltech-256 object category dataset. Technical report, 2007.

[8] C. V. J. Gemert et al. Kernel codebooks for scene categorization. In *ECCV*, 2008.

[9] S. Lazebnik, C. Schmid, and J. Ponce. Beyond bags of features: Spatial pyramid matching for recognizing natural scene categories. In *IEEE CVPR*, 2006.

[10] D. Li et al. Large-scale robust visual codebook construction. In *ACM MM*, 2010.

[11] D. Lowe. Object recognition from local scale-invariant features. In *IEEE ICCV*, 1999.

[12] H. Ma et al. Bridging the Semantic Gap Between Image Contents and Tags. In *IEEE Trans. Multimedia*, 2010.

[13] J. Mairal, F. Bach, J. Ponce, and G. Sapiro. Online dictionary learning for sparse coding. In *ICML*, 2009.

[14] A. Oliva and A. Torralba. Modeling the shape of the scene: A holistic representation of the spatial envelope. In *IJCV*, 42:145-175, 2001.

[15] E. Shechtman and M. Irani. Matching local self-similarities across images and videos. In *IEEE CVPR*, 2007.

[16] J. Yang et al. Evaluating bag-of-visual-words representations in scene classification. in *ACM MIR*, 2007.

[17] J. Yang et al. Linear spatial pyramid matching using sparse coding for image classification. In *IEEE CVPR*, 2009.

Non-rigid 3D Model Retrieval Using Multi-Scale Local Features *

Pengjie Li
Beijing Key Laboratory of Intelligent Telecommunications Software and Multimedia
Beijing University of Posts and Telecommunications
Beijing 100876, China
lipj16@gmail.com

Huadong Ma
Beijing Key Laboratory of Intelligent Telecommunications Software and Multimedia
Beijing University of Posts and Telecommunications
Beijing 100876, China
mhd@bupt.edu.cn

Anlong Ming
Beijing Key Laboratory of Intelligent Telecommunications Software and Multimedia
Beijing University of Posts and Telecommunications
Beijing 100876, China
minganlong@bupt.edu.cn

ABSTRACT

The number of available non-rigid 3D models in various areas increases steadily. The local features are more effective than global features for the search of these non-rigid 3D models. Global descriptors fail to consistently compensate for the intra-class variability of non-rigid 3D models. To solve this problem, we propose a non-rigid 3D model retrieval method based on multi-scale local features. Firstly, we extract keypoints at multiple scales automaticlly. Then, the Heat Kernel Signature (HKS) local descriptors are computed for each keypoint. However, the HKS descriptors are sensitive to scale. In order to solve this problem, the HKS descriptors are put into the Bag-of-Features (BOF) framework. In the BOF framework, we use a kind of histogram equalization technique to make our feature descriptor robust to model scaling. Experimental results on two public benchmarks show that our algorithm can achieve satisfactory retrieval performance for the non-rigid 3D models.

Categories and Subject Descriptors

H.3.3 [**Information Search and Retrieval**]: Retrieval model; I.3.5 [**Computational Geometry and Object Modeling**]: Curve, surface, solid, and object representations.; I.4.8 [**Scene Analysis**]: Object recognition.

General Terms

Algorithms, Experimentation

Keywords

Non-rigid 3D model retrieval, local features, multi-scale, heat kernel signature (HKS), scale invariant.

*Area chair: Tat-Seng Chua

MM'11, November 28–December 1, 2011, Scottsdale, Arizona, USA.

1. INTRODUCTION

With the rapid development of visualization technologies, a large number of digital 3D models are distributed widely on the Internet. Moreover, 3D models have been widely used in CAD, virtual reality, medicine and entertainment. This makes it an urgent need to organize and retrieve the 3D models effectively and efficiently. Especially the non-rigid 3D models are increasing steadily and used in many areas. However, previous efforts have been mainly devoted to the retrieval of rigid 3D models, and how to efficiently and effectively compare non-rigid 3D models is still a challenging problem in the field of content-based 3D model retrieval.

A number of methods for 3D model retrieval have been proposed already. So far, the dominant researches have been to use global features, i.e. features that need the complete, isolated shape for their extraction. Examples are Fourier or spherical harmonics [1], shape moments [2], shape histograms [3]. These global features are successful at handling rigid 3D models. However, most of these approaches fail to consistently compensate for the intra-class variability of non-rigid 3D models. This occurs because a global descriptor is sensitive to non-rigid transformations like bending or stretching, thus, resulting in an erroneous matching. The non-rigid 3D models, some parts of which may be more deformable than other rigid parts. One of the biggest challenges in non-rigid 3D model retrieval and comparison is the design of a shape descriptor that would maintain invariance under a wide class of transformations the 3D model can undergo. For non-rigid 3D model retrieval, the use of local rather than global features is advantageous. A few methods based on local features have been proposed [4, 5]. In [4], each local feature descriptor uses a representation of image information in the neighborhood of the salient feature points. For each feature point, a 128-dimensional vector descriptor was constructed by using the Scale Invariant Feature Transform (SIFT) method. The SIFT feature extraction and vector quantization are computational expensive. Further, the SIFT feature descriptor is not intrinsic. For non-rigid model retrieval, an ideal feature descriptor first of all should be intrinsic and deformation-invariant. Second, it should be insensitive to topological noise and sampling. Finally, the descriptor should be scale-invariant. Recently, the HKS descriptor was introduced as an intrinsic local shape descriptor [5]. The HKS descriptor satisfies the first two properties of an ideal feature descriptor. But HKS descriptor is sensitive to scale variance. Ovsjanikov et al. [5] used the HKS to construct shape descriptors. The HKS descriptor is computed at every point of the 3D model, which is computational expensive. In [5], the original HKS descriptor is used, which is sensitive to scale.

In this paper, we develop a new non-rigid 3D model retrieval method based on multi-scale local features. Firstly, we extract keypoints at multiple scales automatically. If keypoints are detected at a fixed scale, it is possible that keypoints may never appear on the less curved or featured parts of certain 3D models. In order to solve this problem, we detect keypoints at multiple scales. Then, the HKS local descriptors are computed for each keypoint. The HKS descriptor is intrinsic and deformation-invariant. Moreover, it is insensitive to topological noise and sampling. However, a notable disadvantage of the HKS descriptor is the sensitivity to scale. To solve this problem, the HKS descriptors are integrated into the BOF framework. In the BOF framework, a kind of histogram equalization technique is adopted to make our feature descriptor robust to model scaling. The experiments show that our method can achieve satisfactory retrieval results for the non-rigid 3D models.

2. KEYPOINT DETECTION AT MULTI-SCALE

Let $P = \{v, p\}$ be the data structure of a 3D model containing vertices v and polygons p. Vertices are the coordinates of each point and polygons are index numbers of the points which compose individual polygons. Firstly, each 3D model is sampled at uniform intervals. At each sample point $v' = [x\ y\ z]$, a local surface is cropped from the 3D model using a sphere of radius r centered at v'. The value of r is a trade off between the feature's descriptiveness and sensitivity to occlusions. Small values of r will be less sensitive to occlusions but will contain less information about the underlying surface and hence the feature will be less descriptive. The value of r is also related to the scale of the 3D models. For small size models, r should be small and for large models it should be large.

For each sample point, local surface is cropped to extract a local coordinate frame that is robust to occlusions and other global perturbations. However, we extract the reference frame directly from the data points for computational efficiency and later for feature extraction only if the point qualifies as a keypoint. Then, the cropped surface is rotated so that the normal of the point is aligned with the positive z-axis. Since we are dealing with complete 3D models, the cropped surface may also contain polygons that are occluded. These polygons are removed using hidden surface removal [6]. Points only shared by occluded polygons are removed. Let $L_j = [x_j\ y_j\ z_j]\ (j = 1, 2, \ldots, n)$ be the remaining points. The mean of the remaining points is given by

$$M = \frac{1}{n}\sum_{j=1}^{n} L_j \tag{1}$$

and the covariance matrix of is given by

$$C = \frac{1}{n}\sum_{j=1}^{n} L_j {L_j}^T - MM^T \tag{2}$$

where L_j is the j-th column of matrix L. Performing Principal Component Analysis (PCA) on the covariance matrix C gives us

$$CV = DV \tag{3}$$

where V is the matrix of eigenvectors, D is the diagonal matrix of the eigenvalues of C. The matrix L can be aligned with its principal axes using the Hotelling transform [7]:

$$L'_j = V(L_j - M)\ (j = 1, 2, \ldots n) \tag{4}$$

Let X and Y represent the x and y components of the point cloud L', respectively i.e.

$$X = \{x_1, x_2, \ldots, x_n\}\ and\ Y = \{y_1, y_2, \ldots y_n\} \tag{5}$$

$$\sigma = \frac{\max(X) - \min(X)}{\max(Y) - \min(Y)} \tag{6}$$

where σ is the ratio between the first two principal axes of the local surface. We proceed with the keypoint detection if $\sigma > \sigma_0$. However, to eliminate noise we choose a threshold $\sigma_0 > 1$. We choose $\sigma_0 = 1.05$ in our experiments.

3. MULTI-SCALE LOCAL FEATURES

In this paper, we take the HKS descriptor to extract the local features from the multi-scale keypoints. The HKS local descriptor is intrinsic and thus deformation-invariant. Further, it is insensitive to topological noise and sampling. However, HKS descriptor is sensitive to scale variance. To make the feature vector invariant to scale, we put the HKS local descriptors into the bag-of-features (BOF) framework. In the BOF framework, a kind of histogram equalization technique is adopted to make our feature descriptor robust to model scaling.

3.1 HKS Local Features Extraction

After the keypoints are extracted at multiple scales, the HKS local descriptor is computed at every keypoint. The HKS descriptors are based on the heat kernel on a Riemannian manifold, which has the following expansion in terms of the eigenvalues and eigen-functions of the Laplace-Beltrami operator [8]:

$$K_t(x, y) = \sum_{i=0}^{\infty} e^{-t\lambda_i}\phi_i(x)\phi_i(y) \tag{7}$$

where λ_i is the eigenvalues, ϕ_i is the eigenfunctions, $t \in R^+$ is the time parameter and x, y, are two points on the manifold. The heat kernel can be interpreted as the amount of heat transferred from x to y in time t given a heat source at x (see Figure 1). The HKS of a point x is a function of one parameter t, and defined as the restriction of the heat kernel to the diagonal: $K_t(x, x)$. For each keypoint X of the 3D model, we define its discrete HKS as an n-dimension vector descriptor:

$$F(x) = (f_1(x), f_2(x), \ldots, f_n(x))^T \tag{8}$$

whose elements are $f_i(x) = c(x)K_{\alpha^{i-1}t_0}(x, x)$. We select the value of $c(x)$ in such a way that $\|f_i(x)\|_2 = 1$. In our experiments, we set $t_0 = 512$ and $\alpha = 1.2$.

3.2 Scale-invariant HKS descriptor in BOF

The HKS descriptors are sensitive to scale. In the BOF framework, a kind of histogram equalization technique is

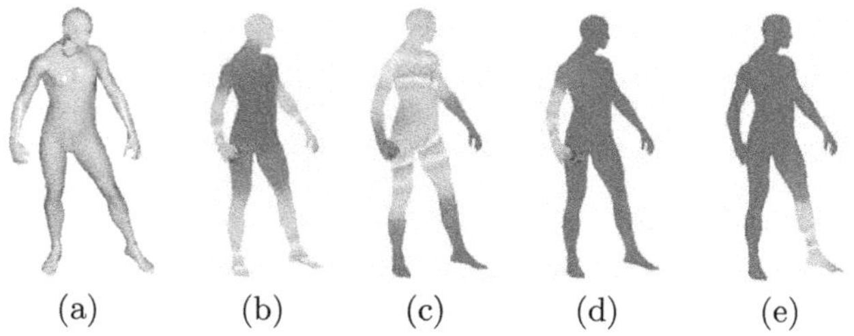

Figure 1: Illustrations of HKS descriptor. (a) is a 3D human model. (b) are the values of $K_t(x,x)$ mapped on the 3D human model in (a). (c) (d) and (e) are the values of $K_t(x,y)$ for three different choices of y on the side, hand, and leg of the 3D human model in (a).

adopted to make our feature descriptor robust to model scaling. Meanwhile, the HKS descriptors are vectorized and normalized to unity which means that the feature vector is effectively scale invariant.

In the BOF framework, a vocabulary $W = \{F_1, F_2, \ldots, F_N\}$ of size N is a set of representative vectors in the descriptor space, obtained by means of unsupervised learning (vector quantization) using the k-means algorithm. Larger vocabulary size provides higher discriminative power at the expense of increase in storage and processing time. Given a vocabulary W, for each keypoint with the descriptor $F(x)$, we define the feature distribution by:

$$\mu(x) = (\mu_1(x), \mu_2(x), \ldots, \mu_N(x))^T \tag{9}$$

whose elements are

$$\mu_i(x) = c(x)e^{-\frac{\|F(x)-F_i\|_2^2}{2\delta^2}} \tag{10}$$

and the value of $c(x)$ is selected in such a way that $\|\mu(x)\|_1 = 1$. $\mu_i(x)$ can be interpreted as the probability of the keypoint x to be associated with the descriptor F_i from the vocabulary W. Equation (10) can be interpreted as a process of vector quantization. Each HKS descriptor is quantized into a word of the vocabulary W. Integrating the feature distribution over the entire 3D model Q yields a $W \times 1$ vector:

$$\eta(Q) = \int_S \mu(x)da(x) \tag{11}$$

which is refered to as a BoF descriptor. $\mu_i(x)$ is the set of all keypoints of a 3D model, and $x \in S$. Then, the quantized HKS local descriptors are accumulated into a histogram.

A notable disadvantage of the HKS descriptors is their sensitivity to scale. In order to make our feature vector robust to model scaling, a kind of histogram equalization technique is adopted. The word frequency h^{b_o} which originally belongs to bin b_o is relocated to bin b_n by:

$$b_n = \left\lceil \frac{\sum_{i=1}^{b_o} h^i}{\sum_{i=1}^{K} h^i} \right\rceil \tag{12}$$

where K is the number of bins. By equation (12), adjacent bins could be merged together in some feature channels [9]. In this way, we can obtain a new histogram, in which the distribution of each feature channel extends to the whole space and the new BOF vectors are less sensitive to scaling.

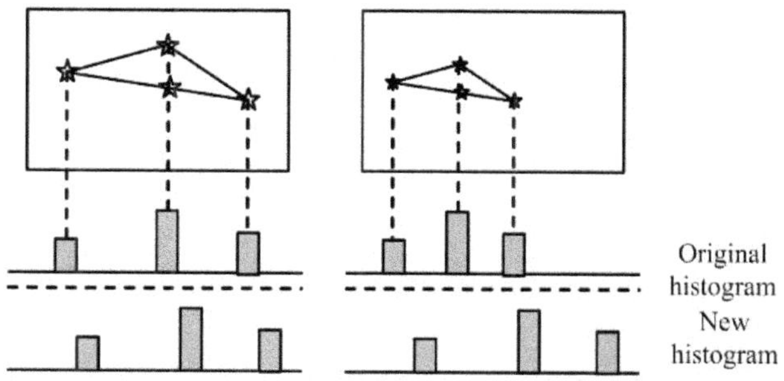

Figure 2: Illustration of the histogram equalization technique. A triangle is composed of 4 local features represented by stars. Due to different scales, the original histograms are not matched. By equalization, the histograms expand to have the same distribution and all the correspnding parts are matched.

As shown in Figure 2, after equalization, all the parts of the identical model in different scales are matched.

3.3 Similarity Computation

Using the vector representation in Section 3.2, a quantified histogram H is generated for each 3D model. We can define the similarity between two models M_q and M_p as the similarity between the corresponding histograms H_q and H_p. We take the histogram intersection as the similarity measure.

$$SIM(M_q, M_p) = HI(H_q, H_p) \tag{13}$$

Where $HI(\cdot,\cdot)$ is the histogram intersection function.

4. EXPERIMENTS

4.1 The Testing Data Set

In this paper, the 3D model databases used are the McGill Benchmark (MGB) database [10] and the ShapeGoogle Benchmark (SGB) database [5]. The MGB database contains a rich variety of non-rigid 3D models. These models are articulated shapes with articulating parts. The database contains 255 models which are divided into ten categories, namely, 'Ants', 'Crabs', 'Spectacles', 'Hands', 'Pliers', 'Octopuses', 'Humans', 'Snakes', 'Spiders' and 'Teddy-bears'. The SGB database consists of 1061 models with simulated transformations. As far as we know, this is the largest non-rigid 3D model retrieval benchmark. The database contains 469 different classes.

4.2 Experimental Results

To evaluate the retrieval performance of the proposed method for the non-rigid 3D models, the retrieval results are compared to the following two methods:

- The BF-SIFT method [4].
- The Shape Google method [5].

The retrieval performance was evaluated in terms of "precision" and "recall" (as shown in Figure 3), where precision is the proportion of the retrieved models relevant to the query and recall is the proportion of relevant models in the entire database retrieved in the query.

From Figure 3, we can see that our method get better retrieval performance than the other two methods on both

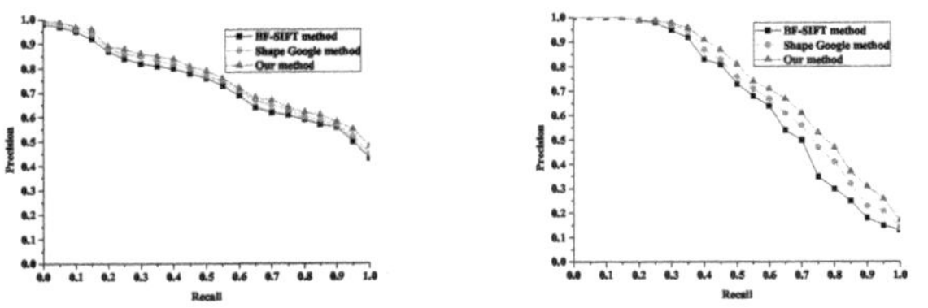

(a) (b)

Figure 3: Comparison of our method against other methods: BF-SIFT [4], and the Shape Google method [5] on the two benchmarks in terms of precision-recall diagram. (a) Performance comparison for models on the MGB database. (b) Comparison for non-rigid models on the SGB database.

Figure 4: Partial results using our method on MGB

the two shape benchmarks. Figure 4 illustrate the partial retrieval results (two classes "humans" and "teddy-bears") produced by using our method on the MGB database.

Figure 5 illustrate the partial retrieval results produced by using our method on the SGB database. Experiments are implemented for this benchmark on four classes "horses", "centaurs", "dogs" and "humans". Experiments are tested on multi-scale 3D models.

In Figures 4 and 5, the query models are depicted in the first column. The first five retrieval models are depicted in the subsequent columns in accordance with the similarity. The best match model is the query model itself, since the query is also in the database. This also is a criteria for testing the effectiveness of retrieval algorithm. From the retrieval performance above, we can see that our method is effective on both of the two benchmarks.

5. CONCLUSIONS

In this paper, we presented a novel retrieval method for non-rigid 3D models. Our method is based on multi-scale local features. By using multi-scale local features, our descriptor can compensate for the intra-class variability of non-rigid 3D models. Moreover, our descriptor keeps the advantage of HKS, and we adopt a kind of histogram equalization technique to make the descriptor robust to scale variance. Through a large set of experiments we have shown that our method can achieve satisfactory retrieval performance for the non-rigid 3D models.

Figure 5: Partial results using our method on SGB

6. ACKNOWLEDGMENTS

This work is supported by the National Natural Science Foundation of China under Grant No. 60833009 and No. 60903072; the National Natural Science Foundation for Distinguished Young Scholars under Grant No. 60925010; the Fundamental Research Funds for the Central Universities under Grant No. 2009RC0213 and the 111 Project under Grant No. B08004.

7. REFERENCES

[1] L. Kobbelt, P. Schrder, M. Kazhdan, T. Funkhouser, and S. Rusinkiewicz. Rotation invariant spherical harmonic representation of 3d shape descriptors. In Proceeding of the Symposium on Geomery Processing, pp. 156-164, 2003.

[2] M. Elad, A. Tal, and S. Ar. Content based retrieval of VRML objects - an iterative and interactive approach. In Proceeding of Eurographics Workshop on Multimedia, pp. 97-108, 2001.

[3] R. Osada, T. Funkhouser, B. Chazelle, and D. Dobki. Shape distributions. ACM Transactions on Graphics. pp. 807-832, 2002.

[4] R. Ohbuchi, K. Osada, T. Furuya, and T. Banno. Salient local visual features for shape-based 3D model retrieval. In Proceeding of IEEE International Conference on Shape Modeling and Applications (SMI), pp. 93-102, 2008.

[5] Maks Ovsjanikov, Alexander M. Bronstein, Michael M. Bronstein and Leonidas J. Guibas. Shape Google: a computer vision approach to invariant shape retrieval. In Proceeding of IEEE International Conference on Computer Vision Workshops (ICCV Workshops), 2009.

[6] A. Mian, M. Bennamoun, and R. Owens. On the repeatability and quality of keypoints for local feature-based 3D object retrieval from cluttered scenes. International Journal of Computer Vision, 2009.

[7] Ajmal Mian, Mohammed Bennamoun, and Robyn Owens. Keypoint identification and feature-bassed 3D face recognition. In Proceedings of International Conference on Biometrics (ICB). pp.163-171, 2007.

[8] J. Sun, M. Ovsjanikov, and L. Guibas. A concise and provably informative multi-scale signature based on heat diffusion. In Proceedings of Eurographics Symposium on Geometry Processing (SGP). pp.1383-1392, 2009.

[9] Yang Cao, Changhu Wang, Zhiwei Li, Liqing Zhang, and Lei Zhang. Spatial-bag-of-features. In Proceedings of IEEE Conference on Computer Vision and Pattern Recognition (CVPR), 2010.

[10] J. Zhang, R. Kaplow, R. Chen, K. Siddiqi, The McGill Shape Benchmark, 2005.

Marginal-based Visual Alphabets for Local Image Descriptors Aggregation*

Miriam Redi
EURECOM, Sophia Antipolis
2229 route des crêtes
Sophia-Antipolis
redi@eurecom.fr

Bernard Merialdo
EURECOM, Sophia Antipolis
2229 route des crêtes
Sophia-Antipolis
merialdo@eurecom.fr

ABSTRACT

Bag of Words (BOW) models are nowadays one of the most effective methods for visual categorization. They use visual dictionaries to aggregate the set of local descriptors extracted from a given image. Despite their high discriminative ability, one of the major drawbacks of BOW still remains the computational cost of the visual dictionary, built by clustering in the high dimensional feature space.

In this paper we introduce a fast, effective method for local image descriptors aggregation that is based on marginal approximations, i.e. the approximation of each descriptor component distribution. We quantize each dimension of the feature space, obtaining a visual *alphabet* that we use to map the image descriptors in a fixed-length visual signature. Experimental results show that our new method outperforms the traditional BOW model in both accuracy and efficiency for the scene recognition task. Moreover, we discover that the marginal-based aggregation provides complementary information with respect to BOW, by combining the two models in a video retrieval system based on TRECVID 2010 [8].

Categories and Subject Descriptors

I.4.7 [**Artificial Intelligence**]: Scene Analysis

General Terms

Algorithms

Keywords

Scene Recognition, Feature Extraction, CBIR

1. INTRODUCTION

Effective techniques for automatic image categorization are essential to manage large collections of digital images and video. The general approach is to model the redundant image information with a low-dimensional description, namely an image signature, and then classify such signatures with supervised learning techniques. Visual descriptions based on quantized local invariant features (e.g. [4]) have been extensively used for image categorization and retrieval. Among these approaches, the Bag-Of-Visual-Words [1] model has been proven to be a very successful method to aggregate discriminative local image properties. The image is first represented with a set of independent local patches encoded by robust local descriptors. The resulting representation is a high-dimensional, variable length description of the image. Visual dictionaries are then used to map each image to a fixed length feature vector that can be used as input for traditional classifiers (e.g. Support Vector Machines).

Many methods have been proposed to generate such dictionaries. Generally, they use clustering techniques on the local descriptors of a set of training images to define visual words. K-means [1] clustering is nowadays the most common technique for creating BOW, but recently more efficient methods based on mean-shift [2], hierarchical clustering [5], or fixed quantization based on lattices [?] have been proposed to improve the model performances.

Despite their good performances in image recognition and retrieval, one of the major drawbacks of all these approaches is their computational cost, for both clustering in the high dimensional feature space (determined by the descriptors distribution) and visual words assignment.

In this paper we present a simple, fast and effective algorithm for local feature quantization that we name MEDA (Marginal Estimation for Descriptors Aggregation). This approach provides a different way of aggregating local descriptors that does not involve any clustering or operation in the high-dimensional space, leading to an image signature that requires much less computation and provides better accuracy compared to traditional BOW models.

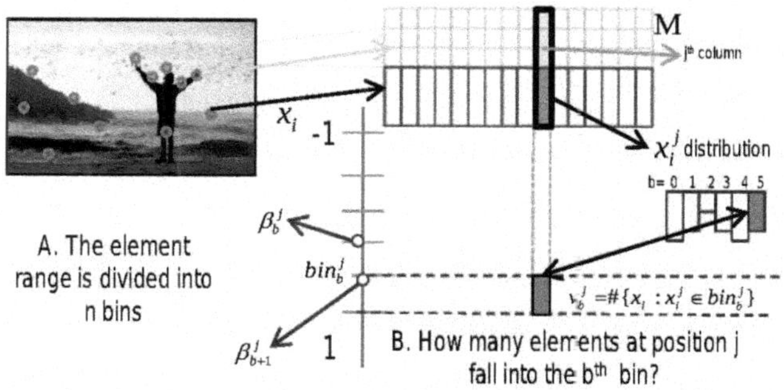

Figure 1: MEDA: a histogram representing the component distribution over unidimensional bins.

*Area chair: Nicu Sebe

MM'11, November 28–December 1, 2011, Scottsdale, Arizona, USA.

Similar to the BOW model, a k-dimensional local invariant descriptor (LID) is used to describe a set of interest points in the image. While generally the quantization is performed in a k-dimensional space determined by the LID length, the basic idea of our approach is to model the k-dimensional space by the k marginal distributions approximations. This is obtained with an aggregation process that involves (see Fig. 1 for a visual explanation) two steps: (a) we quantize the range of each dimension of the LID into n bins, defining a reduced set of possible values that each of the k components of a described point can take; (b) given an image and its set of descriptors, we count the frequencies of the computed bin values, and we collect them in a $k \times n$ histogram, i.e. the MEDA image signature. Therefore, the marginal, i.e. the probability distribution of each component of the LID is approximated by a histogram representing its frequency over unidimensional bins.

Following the textual metaphor of the BOW, our method defines, for each component of the LID, a set of possible 1-d visual *letters*, namely the bin values; the collection of such *letters* is a *visual alphabet* that allows the mapping of an image to a fixed-length attribute vector. In this paper, we present and compare three different methods that define the values in the visual *alphabet*, based on different types of range quantization, namely uniform quantization, quantile-based quantization and an entropy-based quantization we perform using a decision tree.

In order to test the effectiveness of MEDA for image representation we first choose the indoor (67 classes) [7] and outdoor (8 classes) [6] scene recognition task. Results show that, in both databases, our technique outperforms in accuracy and efficiency the classical BOW model for the same feature size. We also evaluate the performances of our technique for the Trecvid 2010 [8] Semantic Indexing Task. We show that BOW and MEDA model achieve the same results for concept detection. Moreover, when combining MEDA with the BOW, we also discover that our new technique brings a new, complementary source of discriminative information in the local image analysis, improving the final retrieval precision by 25 %.

The remainder of this paper is organized as follows: Sec. 2 presents a detailed implementation of the MEDA model for local features quantization; we then explain, in Sec. 3, a variety of methods to approximate the range of the components; finally, in Sec. 4 we evaluate the performances of our model comparing it with traditional BOW.

2. MARGINALS ESTIMATION FOR DESCRIPTORS AGGREGATION

We propose an image representation that collects in a histogram the frequency of each component of the locally extracted vectors. While the BOW model quantizes the local features in a multi-dimensional space (*words*) determined by the descriptor length, here the quantization is performed in a 1-d space, for each component (*letter*) of the LID.

Given an image I, a set of w salient points is automatically detected in the image. Then, local descriptors $x_1, x_2, \ldots, x_w$ of length k are computed over the surrounding regions; we therefore obtain a set of normalized vectors $x_i = (x_i^1, \ldots, x_i^k)$, where each element x_i^j represents the value of the descriptor x_i at position j, $j = 1, \ldots, k$.

After normalization, each element x_i^j can take a value in the finite interval $R = [-1, 1]$, which covers a very large set of possible discrete values $a_1, a_2, \ldots, a_m$. The idea here is to quantize R by mapping it into a smaller set of discrete values $\beta^j \in R$, corresponding to a set of bins $bin_1^j, \ldots, bin_n^j$, i.e. our *alphabet*, defined for each dimension of the LID:

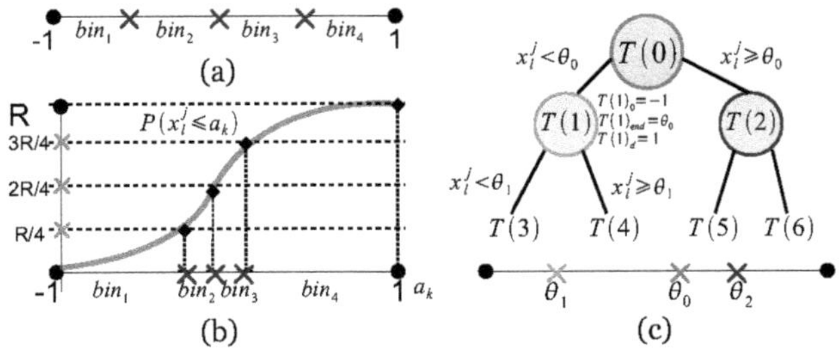

Figure 2: Three versions of the MEDA alphabet

$$bin_b^j = [\beta_b^j, \beta_{b+1}^j[, b=0, \ldots, n-1, n<m \quad (1)$$

(+1 is added to the last bin). By doing so, each element in the image can be represented by the index of corresponding bin $bin_b^j : \beta_b^j \leq x_i^j < \beta_{b+1}^j$. The choice of the bin boundaries values will be discussed in the next Section.

We have therefore defined a set of shared visual *letters* that can be used to approximate the marginal distribution of the jth element of the descriptors in the image. We can now represent the image as the collection of the number of elements x_i^j, $\forall i, j$ that fall into each of the identified bins.

The resulting signature for the image I is a vector

$$v = (v_1^1, v_2^1, \ldots, v_n^1, v_1^2, \ldots, v_n^k)$$

with $v_b^j = \#\{x_i : x_i^j \in bin_b^j\}$, $\forall i, j,$[1] The dimension of the MEDA signature is therefore $n \times k$.[2]

3. ALPHABET CONSTRUCTION

How to define the boundaries of such bins, our *letters*, so that the marginal of the jth component, $\forall j$ is properly estimated? In this section we tackle this issue using three different approaches, namely: (1) **uniform quantization**: the range is divided into n equally spaced bins (2) **quantile-based quantization**: the range is divided so that the probability of a sample to fall into a bin is equal for all the n bins in the quantized space (3) **tree-based quantization**: for each bin, the boundaries are learnt by minimizing the overall entropy given a progressively smaller interval of R. Each of these methods leads to a different version of the MEDA histogram, that will be evaluated in Sec 4.

3.1 Uniform Bins

The most simple approach to define the bin boundaries over the data range is the uniform quantization. The advantage of such a simple approach is that it does not require prior knowledge of the marginal distribution of the components. As every component of the LID can take values in the same interval [-1,1], the resulting *alphabet* is an identical set of *letters* for every j. The range R is divided into n equal intervals of length $2/n$, and the set of bins valid for every component (see Fig. 2(a)) is defined as:

[1] $\#\{\cdot\}$ is a function that counts the number of the elements that satisfy the condition in brackets.

[2] Intuitively, if we define a matrix M whose rows are the descriptors x_i, v represents the concatenation of the n-dimensional histograms of the set of points stored in each column of a M

$$bin_b = [-1 + \frac{2b}{n}, -1 + \frac{2(b+1)}{n}[$$

3.2 Quantile-Based Bins

Here we try to adapt the width of each bin to the probability distribution of the component over the data range. This process requires a learning phase in which we identify the probability of the jth component of the descriptors to take the value a_r, $r = 1, \ldots, m$ in the range R, i.e. the marginal distribution of x_i^j (see Fig. 2(b)). We need a dataset of N images over which we collect W described points x_l, $l = 1, \ldots, W$; we can then define the marginal:

$$p(a_r^j) = \#\{x_l : x_l^j = a_r\}$$

and the cumulative probability $P(x_l^j \le a_r) = \sum_{s=1}^{r} p(a_s^j)$. We want each component x_l^j to be equally probable for all the bins in the range: we need therefore to find those values in the interval for which $p(x_l^j \in bin_b^j) = W/n$ for all b, being $\sum p(a_r^j) = W$. The final set of bins is defined as:

$$bin_b^j = [a_r^j : P(x_l^j \le a_r) = \frac{bW}{n}, a_r^j : P(x_l^j \le a_r) = \frac{(b+1)W}{n}[$$

3.3 Entropy-Based Bins

We propose a partition of the data range into a set of unbalanced bins, selected based on the minimization of the overall entropy. Here again we need a learning phase on a training set of N images and a total of W keypoints x_l. We build, for each position j of the LID, a decision tree T^j, with n splits built in n iterations, that progressively learns the boundaries of each bin_b^j.

Each node $T^j(t)$, at depth $T_d^j(t)$ of the tree considers the set of x_l^j that take values between $T_0^j(t)$ and $T_{end}^j(t)$. The tree growing starts from the root node $T^j(0)$, corresponding to the whole set of $x_l^j \in R$ and, at each step, finds the value θ_t^j in R for which the resulting partition of the data has the minimum entropy, i.e. the optimum bin boundary.

If we assume the dataset is categorized in c classes $y_1, .., y_c$, the general entropy of the data for a split $a_r \in R$ is:

$$H(y|a_k) = -p(x_l^j{<}a_r) \sum_{p=1}^{c} p(y_p|x_l^j{<}a_r) log(p(y_p|x_l^j{<}a_r))$$
$$-p(x_l^j{\ge}a_r) \sum_{p=1}^{c} p(y_p|x_l^j{\ge}a_r) log(p(y_p|x_l^j{\ge}a_r))$$

with $p(y_p|x_l^j{<}a_r)$ and $p(y_p|x_l^j{\ge}a_r)$ being the probability of a component belonging to an image labeled with category y_p to fall into the low/high bin generated by the split.[3] The following is the pseudo-code that summarizes how to grow a decision tree to learn the *alphabet* for the jth component:

```
Grow_Tree
  T^j(0) = {root}
  repeat
    choose unmarked leaf T^j(t)
    find θ_t^j = arg min_{a_r} H_t(y|a_r), T_0^j(t) ≤ x_l^j < T_e^j nd(t)
    if T(t)_d^j < max_depth then
      T_0^j(t+1) ← T_0^j(t), T_end^j(t+1) ← θ_t^j {left child}
      T_0^j(t+2) ← θ_t^j, T_end^j(t+2) ← T_end^j(t) {right child}
    else
      mark T^j(t)
    end if
  until all leaves are marked
  β_b^j ← in order tree walk on θ_t^j
```

3 $p(y_p|x_l^j < a_r) = \frac{\#\{x_l^j : x_l^j < a \in y_p\}}{\#\{x_l^j : x_l^j < a_r\}}$; $p(y_p|x_l^j \ge a_r) = \frac{\#\{x_l^j : x_l^j \ge a \in y_p\}}{\#\{x_l^j : x_l^j \ge a_r\}}$

Two child nodes $T^j(1)$ and $T^j(2)$ are created as the result of the split at the first iteration (see Fig. 2 (c)); at the second iteration, $T^j(1)$ will find the best split for the set of elements for which holds $-1 \le x_l^j < \theta_0$, while $T^j(2)$ will consider those x_l^j that lie between θ_0^j and 1. The process is iterated until the maximum depth (*max_depth*) required to identify n bins is reached. Finally, the set of boundaries θ_t^j found is sorted and the bin values are assigned according to Eq. (1).

4. EXPERIMENTAL VALIDATION

This section presents an evaluation of the different versions of MEDA on a variety of challenging datasets. We compare accuracy and computational efficiency of MEDA and BOW on two datasets built for the scene recognition task. We then test the effectiveness of the two approaches for a video retrieval system built for the TRECVID 2010 [8] database.

4.1 Scene Recognition Task

We evaluate the performances of our model for image recognition in two challenging datasets, for indoor and outdoor scene categorization. First, we extract the image local descriptors using the PCA-SIFT method described in [3], which reduces the dimensionality ($d = 36$) of the original SIFT (as proposed in [4], with $d = 128$) by applying PCA on the gradient image around the salient point. Once the local descriptors are extracted, we aggregate them using both BOW, by clustering a subset of training images using a standard k-means algorithm, and MEDA models (we implement the three different versions of the MEDA model according to the methods in Sec. 3). A one vs all SVM is indeed built to separate each class from the others, using a chi-square kernel of degree 2. As evaluation measure, we use the average multiclass prediction accuracy.

Experimental Setup

The **Outdoor Scenes Dataset**, first introduced in [6], is composed of 2600 color images organized in 8 categories of natural scenes. We split such dataset using 100 images per class for training and the rest for testing. For evaluation, we compute: MEDA uniform quantization, 20 bins (*uniform* 20 × 36), quantile-based, 20 bins (*quantile* 20 × 36). entropy-based, 16 bins (*tree* 16 × 36). In order to compare the performances with MEDA, we create a set of visual dictionaries with 500/720 visual words (BOW 500/BOW 720). The **Indoor Scenes Dataset**,with 67 categories and 15620 images, was proposed in [7] as a new, unique database for indoor scene recognition, . For this second group of experiments, we follow the experimental setup in [7]: 20 images for testing and the rest for training. We define for this experiment: *uniform* 10 × 36, MEDA with uniform quantization, 10 bins ; *quantile* 10 × 36, quantile-based, 10 bins and *tree* 8 × 36, tree-based, 8 bins. Moreover, we build dictionaries of 360/500 visual words (BOW 360, BOW 500).

Results

As we can see from Table 1, the most complex version (*tree* · × 36) of the MEDA model is more than 150 times less computationally expensive compared to the BOW model corresponding to the same feature size. Moreover, we show in Fig 3(a-b) that MEDA is not only efficient, but it outperforms in accuracy the BOW model by 10% for the Indoor Scenes Dataset and 3% for the Outdoor Scenes.

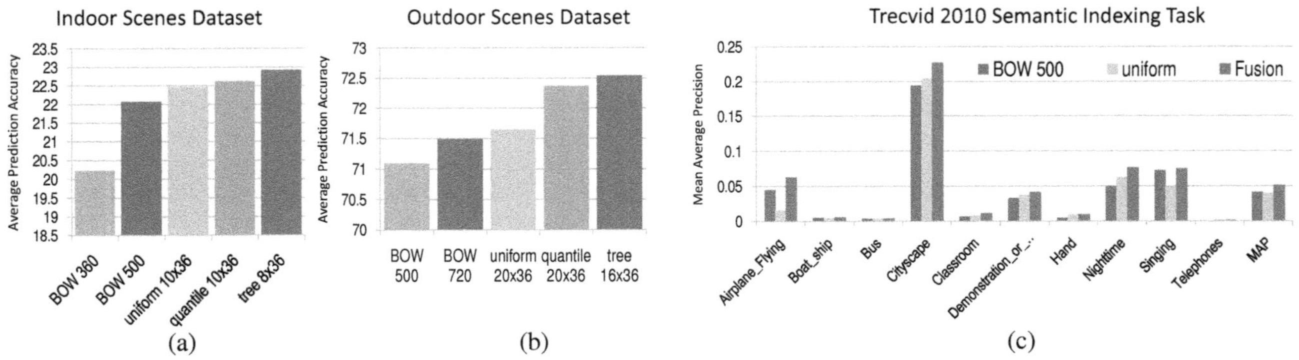

Figure 3: Comparing BOW with MEDA: (a-b) scene recognition (c) video retrieval

Table 1: Training Set Processing Times (s) for BOW vs MEDA models

Indoor 67 Dataset			Outdoor 8 Dataset		
BOW	360 500	62503 86685	BOW	500 720	10027 14429
MEDA	uniform (10 × 36) quantile (10 × 36) tree (8 × 36)	135 163 401	MEDA	uniform (20 × 36) quantile (20 × 36) tree (16 × 36)	55 23 87

4.2 Video Retrieval Task

For the Light Semantic Indexing Task of TRECVID (SIN), participants are required to build a retrieval system that produces a ranked list of relevant shots ten semantic concepts.

Experimental setup

The training set of TRECVID 2010 contains 3200 videos that we split in 1617 for training and 1616 for test. For our experiments, we extract SIFT [4] descriptors from the video keyframes and quantize them using BOW with 500 words (*BOW 500*), as in [?], and MEDA with uniform quantization (*uniform*)[4]. A set of SVM-based classifiers is trained to detect the concept presence, for each concept. The concepts score of MEDA and BOW are then linearly fused (*fusion*) to evaluate the effectiveness of the combination of the two approaches. As evaluation measure, we use the mean average precision.

Results

Despite its simplicity and efficiency, MEDA achieves retrieval results comparable with the BOW model, as shown in Fig.3(c). The most interesting result here is the improvement we obtain on the BOW-based retrieval (+25% on the final MAP) by combining it with the MEDA-based retrieval. Our technique for descriptor aggregation brings new, complementary information to a traditional BOW model. As a matter of fact, MEDA calculates the frequency of each component (visual *letter*), while BOW calculate the frequency for the whole vector (visual *word*). Similar explanation can justify the poor results we obtain with MEDA for some concepts e.g. Airplane_Flying.

5. CONCLUSIONS

Bag of Words is an effective method for image description. Despite its accuracy, one of the major drawbacks of such model is its high computational cost. In this paper we introduced a new model for local descriptor aggregation based on descriptor marginal distribution approximation, namely the MEDA model, and demonstrated that it represents a fast and reliable approach for image categorization. Moreover, we showed that its combination with BOW improve the performances of a video retrieval system by 25 %, making MEDA a promising cue for content based multimedia retrieval. Possible tracks for future work include the usage of base LIDs other than SIFT, and the addition spatial information in the MEDA model. Moreover, a possible solution against the high dimensionality of the final image signature could be the use of techniques such as PCA. Finally, given the good performances of our 1-d quantization technique when combined with k-d quantization, we could explore the possibility of 2 or 3-d quantization and build multi-dimensional visual dictionaries.

[4]The number of bins is optimeized per concept in the training phase

6. REFERENCES

[1] G. Csurka, C. Dance, L. Fan, J. Willamowski, and C. Bray. Visual categorization with bags of keypoints. In *Workshop on statistical learning in computer vision, ECCV*, volume 1, page 22. Citeseer, 2004.

[2] F. Jurie and B. Triggs. Creating efficient codebooks for visual recognition. In *In Proceedings of the IEEE International Conference on Computer Vision.*

[3] Y. Ke and R. Sukthankar. PCA-SIFT: A more distinctive representation for local image descriptors. In *Proceedings of the 2004 IEEE conference on Computer vision and pattern recognition.*

[4] D. Lowe. Distinctive image features from scale-invariant keypoints. *International journal of computer vision*, 60(2):91–110, 2004.

[5] D. Nister and H. Stewenius. Scalable recognition with a vocabulary tree. In *Computer Vision and Pattern Recognition, 2006 IEEE Computer Society Conference on*, volume 2. IEEE, 2006.

[6] A. Oliva and A. Torralba. Modeling the shape of the scene: A holistic representation of the spatial envelope. *International Journal of Computer Vision*, 42(3):145–175, 2001.

[7] A. Quattoni and A. Torralba. Recognizing indoor scenes. In *Computer Vision and Pattern Recognition, IEEE Conference on.* IEEE, 2009.

[8] A. F. Smeaton, P. Over, and W. Kraaij. Evaluation campaigns and trecvid. In *MIR '06*, New York, NY, USA, 2006. ACM Press.

Modeling Multimedia Contents through Probabilistic Feature Signatures*

Christian Beecks, Anca Maria Ivanescu, Steffen Kirchhoff and Thomas Seidl
Data Management and Data Exploration Group
RWTH Aachen University, Germany
{beecks, ivanescu, kirchhoff, seidl}@cs.rwth-aachen.de

ABSTRACT

We introduce a new family of flexible feature representations for content-based multimedia retrieval: *probabilistic feature signatures.* While conventional *feature histograms* and *feature signatures* aggregate the multimedia objects' feature distributions exhibited in some feature space according to a partitioning, probabilistic feature signatures model these feature distributions by means of discrete or continuous probability distributions. In this way, they combine the advantages of high expressiveness and compactness, for instance through *Gaussian mixture models.* In this paper, we introduce the concept of probabilistic feature signatures and provide the empirical evidence of high retrieval performance when using this feature representation type. We show that probabilistic feature signatures are able to outperform conventional feature signatures.

Categories and Subject Descriptors

H.3.3 [**Information Search and Retrieval**]: Retrieval models, Search process

General Terms

Experimentation, Performance, Theory

Keywords

probabilistic feature signature, content-based multimedia retrieval, signature quadratic form distance

1. INTRODUCTION AND RELATED WORK

Reflecting multimedia object properties by a compact and expressive feature representation is a challenging task for today's content-based retrieval systems [5, 10, 20, 21]. While numerous approaches aim at aggregating extracted features into an equi-length feature vector [12], namely *feature histogram* [22], which can be compared by using vector-based distance functions [8, 17], recent approaches tend to approximate the objects' contents through flexible feature representations, so-called *feature signatures* [18]. This type of feature representation reasonably adjusts to the contents of individual multimedia objects and can be compared by making use of adaptive distance functions [3], such as the Earth Mover's distance [18] or the Signature Quadratic Form distance [2, 4]. Although feature signatures exhibit high applicability to various contents of multimedia objects, they typically aggregate the object's features individually according to an adaptive partitioning of the feature space. For this purpose, the features are frequently partitioned through a clustering algorithm, such as *k-means*, and each partition is stored by a representative with the corresponding weight reflecting the number of features belonging to the current partition.

*Area chair: Lexing Xie

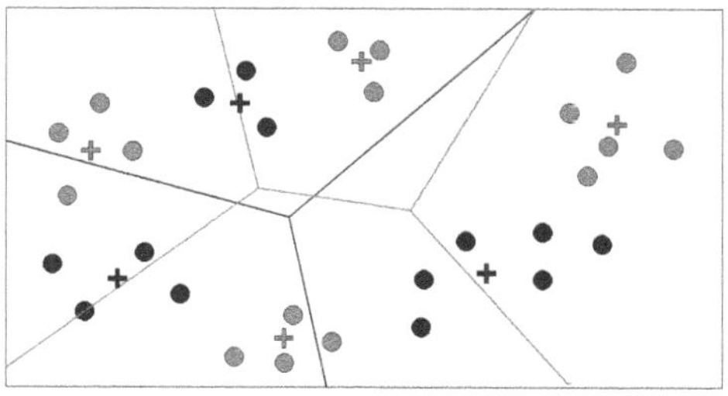

Figure 1: A feature space with two feature distributions and the resulting partitionings

Formally, a feature signature S is defined over a feature space $\mathbb{F} = \mathbb{R}^d$ as a finite set of tuples from $\mathbb{F} \times \mathbb{R}$ comprising representatives and weights:

$$S \subset \{\langle r, w\rangle \mid r \in \mathbb{F} \wedge w \in \mathbb{R}\}.$$

We elucidate the idea of feature signatures in Figure 1 where we depict two feature distributions by means of blue and green points as well as the resulting partitions yielding the feature signatures. As can be seen in the figure, the size of both feature signatures differ from each other and it is dependent on the partitioning/clustering algorithm. Given this example, we make the following observations: first the expressiveness of a feature signature depends on the number of representatives which are shown as plus symbols. More representatives will result in higher approximation quality of the original feature distribution. Second, the partitions' inherent feature distributions are completely neglected, i.e. each partition is represented by exactly one representative. Finally, the partitions are non-overlapping, i.e. each feature is assigned to exactly one partition which is due to the hard-assignment clustering approach [9].

In order to counteract the issues mentioned above, we introduce a generic family of flexible feature representations, the *probabilistic feature signatures*, which approximate feature distributions by means of discrete or continuous probability distributions. By making use of arbitrary probability distributions, they have the ability to model the partitions' internal structure more accurately, for example through multiple components of a *Gaussian mixture model* [14, 15, 25]. Besides these properties, probabilistic feature signatures are also more convenient for content-based analysis and retrieval techniques, since describing multimedia objects by discrete or continuous functions provides the advantage of having solid algebraic properties already defined.

We structure the remainder of this paper as follows: we introduce probabilistic feature signatures in Section 2 where we also define one distance-based similarity measure in order to determine distance values between these probabilistic feature signatures. In Section 3, we provide the empirical evidence of high retrieval performance when using probabilistic feature signatures and show that this feature representation type is able to outperform conventional feature signatures, before we conclude the paper in Section 4.

2. PROBABILISTIC FEATURE SIGNATURES

Representing multimedia objects by features in some feature space is a basic task for nearly all content-based analysis and retrieval techniques. Whereas specific computer vision tasks, such as object recognition, require the features to be accessible in an unaggregated way, content-based retrieval approaches frequently require some degree of generalization in order to cope with different similarity notions. As a consequence, feature distributions are aggregated and approximated by so-called feature representations. As mentioned in the previous section, we introduce *probabilistic feature signatures*, which are generally defined as *probability distributions* over some feature space $\mathbb{F}$, as follows:

$$\tilde{S} : \mathbb{F} \to \mathbb{R}^{\geq 0}$$

In this abstract way, a probabilistic feature signature $\tilde{S} \in \mathbb{R}^{\mathbb{F}}$ is a function assigning each point in the feature space $\mathbb{F}$ a value greater than or equal to zero. In particular, the probability distribution can either be *discrete* or *continuous*. Whereas a *discrete probability distribution* is characterized by a *probability mass function* specifying the likelihood of each feature in the feature space to occur in the corresponding multimedia object, a *continuous probability distribution* is characterized by a *probability density function* specifying a density for each feature in the feature space.

We illustrate an example of a continuous probabilistic feature signature in Figure 2. We depict an image of a picturesque sunset and its corresponding probabilistic feature signature. The probabilistic feature signature can be obtained by clustering the extracted color features with the *expectation maximization* algorithm [6] which generates a Gaussian mixture model $\tilde{S}(x) = \sum_{i=1}^{n} w_i \cdot \mathcal{N}_{\mu_i,\Sigma_i}(x)$. This model is defined for each $x \in \mathbb{F} = \mathbb{R}^d$ and comprises the components $\mathcal{N}_{\mu_i,\Sigma_i}(x) = \frac{1}{\sqrt{(2\pi)^d|\Sigma_i|}} e^{-\frac{1}{2}(x-\mu_i)\Sigma_i^{-1}(x-\mu_i)^T}$ with mean $\mu_i \in \mathbb{F} = \mathbb{R}^d$ and covariance matrix $\Sigma_i \in \mathbb{R}^{d \times d}$. As can be seen in the figure, the smooth color gradient, which is slightly disturbed by the small dark landing stages, is well

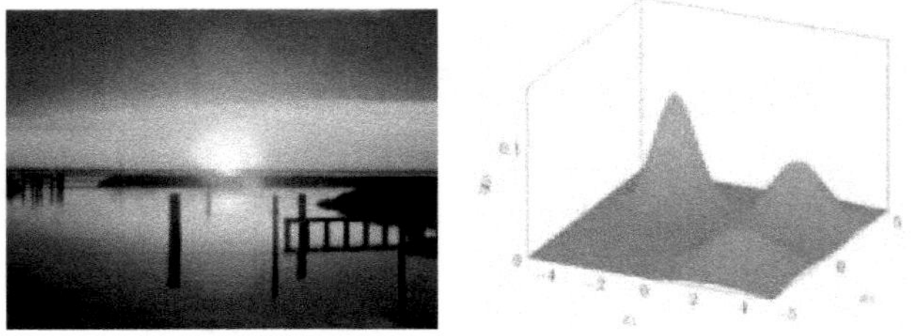

(a) Picturesque sunset (b) Continuous distribution

Figure 2: An image with its continuous probabilistic feature signature

reflected through the components of the Gaussian mixture model. Following the principle of the soft-assignment clustering [9], which has also been investigated and shown to improve the retrieval/classification performance in [16] and [24], the components of the Gaussian mixture model overlap and define a probability for regions in the feature space depending on all components. Hence, probabilistic feature signatures offer both high expressiveness and a compact description at the same time.

In order to exemplify how to determine a distance value between two probabilistic feature signatures using the Signature Quadratic Form distance [2, 4], we replace this distance's inherent similarity function $f_s : \mathbb{F} \times \mathbb{F} \to \mathbb{R}$, which compares representatives of conventional feature signatures, with a *component similarity function* $f_{\mathcal{N}} : \mathbb{R}^{\mathbb{F}} \times \mathbb{R}^{\mathbb{F}} \to \mathbb{R}$, which compares components of the Gaussian mixture models. This component similarity function is defined as follows:

$$f_{\mathcal{N}}(\tilde{S}^q, \tilde{S}^p) = \prod_{i=1}^{d} \frac{e^{-\frac{\alpha(\mu_i^q - \mu_i^p)^2}{1+2\alpha((\sigma_{ii}^q)^2 + (\sigma_{ii}^p)^2)}}}{\sqrt{1 + 2\alpha((\sigma_{ii}^q)^2 + (\sigma_{ii}^p)^2)}},$$

where $\sigma_{ii} \in \mathbb{R}$ and $\mu_i \in \mathbb{F} = \mathbb{R}^d$ denote the standard deviation and mean of dimension i, respectively. Furthermore, the parameter $\alpha \in \mathbb{R}^+$ is used to adapt the component similarity function to the underlying feature space. While [1] thoroughly investigates the Signature Quadratic Form distance for Gaussian mixture models based on high-dimensional local feature descriptors [23], such as SIFT [11], this paper additionally introduces the generic family of probabilistic feature signatures and further shows their benefits over conventional feature signatures when using low-dimensional color descriptors. Therefore, the next section is devoted to the experimental evaluation including perceptual examples.

3. PRELIMINARY EXPERIMENTS

In this section, we compare the retrieval performance based on conventional feature signatures with that based on the proposed probabilistic feature signatures. To this end, we make use of the following image databases: *Corel Wang* [26], *UCID* [19], and *COIL-100* [13]. We extracted probabilistic feature signatures by using the WEKA [7] implementation of the expectation maximization clustering algorithm [6] to obtain Gaussian mixture models with 10 components over a five-dimensional position and color feature space. In order to guarantee a fair and comparable setting, we use the same clusterings to generate conventional feature signatures by defining the representatives as the corresponding means of the Gaussian mixture models.

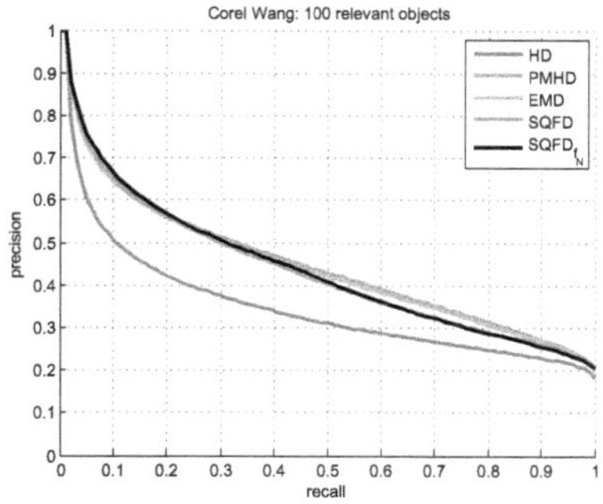

(a) *Corel Wang* database

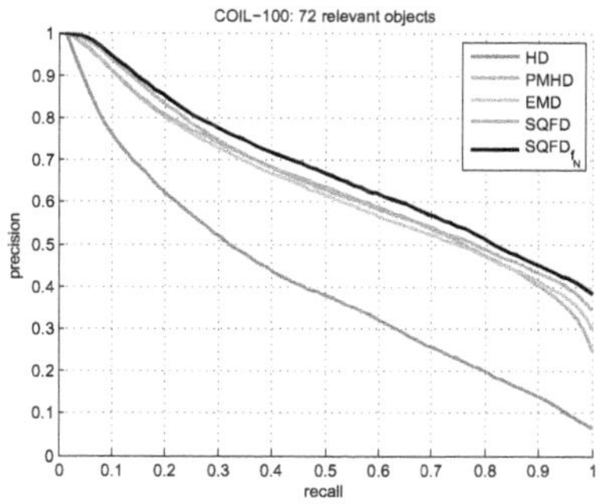

(b) *COIL-100* database

Figure 3: Precision and recall curves for 1,000 randomly chosen similarity queries

We evaluated the retrieval performance by measuring *mean average precision* values [12] for 1,000 distinct random queries.[1] For this purpose, we used the ground truth provided with the aforementioned databases. The results are reported in Table 1 for the Hausdorff distance (HD), perceptually modified Hausdorff distance (PMHD), Earth Mover's distance (EMD), and Signature Quadratic Form distance (SQFD) on conventional feature signatures and the presented Signature Quadratic Form distance (SQFD$_{f_\mathcal{N}}$) with the component similarity function $f_\mathcal{N}$ on probabilistic feature signatures.

Table 1: Mean average precision values

	HD	PMHD	EMD	SQFD	SQFD$_{f_\mathcal{N}}$
Corel Wang	0.339	**0.442**	0.435	0.425	0.429
UCID	0.458	0.560	0.552	0.540	**0.577**
COIL-100	0.407	0.642	0.630	0.644	**0.675**
⌀MAP:	0.401	0.548	0.539	0.536	**0.560**

As can be seen in the table, the average retrieval quality improves when using probabilistic feature signatures, in particular within the *UCID* and *COIL-100* databases. In the *Corel Wang* database, the average retrieval quality of the SQFD$_{f_\mathcal{N}}$ is below that of the PMHD and EMD, but as can be seen in Figure 3 (a) the first part of the precision and recall curve of the SQFD$_{f_\mathcal{N}}$ is slightly higher than those of the other distances on conventional feature signatures in the *Corel Wang* database. Furthermore, on the *COIL-100* database, probabilistic feature signatures outperform conventional feature signatures as can also be seen at the higher precision and recall curve of the SQFD$_{f_\mathcal{N}}$ in Figure 3 (b).

Let us now investigate the perceptual retrieval quality by means of several perceptual retrieval results. In Figures 4 - 6 we depict three different content-based similarity queries and their resulting 10 nearest neighbors from left to right. In general, the perceptual retrieval results correspond to the measured mean average precision values reported in Table 1 and the precision and recall curves depicted in Figure 3. Regarding the query image depicting the colorful bus in Figure 4, it can be seen that the combination of probabilistic feature signatures with the SQFD$_{f_\mathcal{N}}$ reveals 8 bus images. Similarly, in Figure 5 where the query image depicts pink roses in full bloom, the retrieval results based on probabilistic feature signatures show a high visual similarity with respect to the query image. Even in Figure 6 where the query image depicts a panoramic mountain view, the resulting 10 nearest neighboring images appear visual similar with respect to the query image.

[1]In fact, the *UCID* database only contains 262 queries.

Figure 4: A query image depicting a colorful bus and the resulting 10 nearest neighboring images

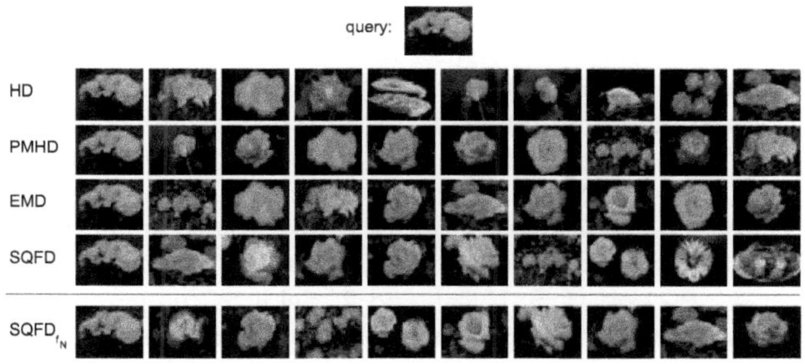

Figure 5: A query image depicting pink roses in full bloom and the resulting 10 nearest neighboring images

To sum up, we have shown that probabilistic feature signatures are an appropriate feature representation type for multimedia and, particularly, image data. Based on compact descriptions of continuous feature distributions, for instance Gaussian mixture models, probabilistic feature signatures are able to outperform conventional feature signatures which represent the contents of multimedia objects in a discrete way in terms of retrieval quality for the purpose of content-based retrieval.

4. CONCLUSIONS

Probabilistic feature signatures are generalized feature representations independent of any feature space partitioning.

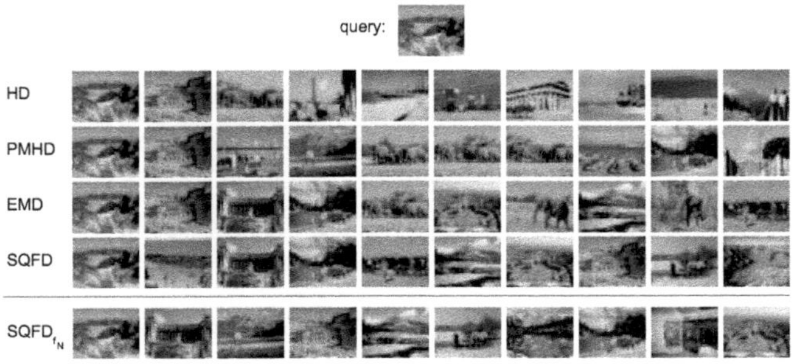

Figure 6: A query image depicting a panoramic mountain view and the resulting 10 nearest neighboring images

Approximating feature distributions through discrete and continuous probability distributions results in a higher retrieval quality compared to that when making use of conventional feature signatures. Therefore, we conclude that probabilistic feature signatures are a compact feature representation type with promising applicability to content-based multimedia retrieval.

5. ACKNOWLEDGMENTS

The authors gratefully acknowledge the financial support of the Deutsche Forschungsgemeinschaft (DFG) within the Collaborative Research Center SFB-686.

6. REFERENCES

[1] C. Beecks, A. M. Ivanescu, S. Kirchhoff, and T. Seidl. Modeling image similarity by gaussian mixture models and the signature quadratic form distance. In *Proc. IEEE ICCV*, 2011.

[2] C. Beecks, M. S. Uysal, and T. Seidl. Signature quadratic form distances for content-based similarity. In *Proc. ACM Multimedia*, pages 697–700, 2009.

[3] C. Beecks, M. S. Uysal, and T. Seidl. A comparative study of similarity measures for content-based multimedia retrieval. In *Proc. IEEE ICME*, pages 1552–1557, 2010.

[4] C. Beecks, M. S. Uysal, and T. Seidl. Signature quadratic form distance. In *Proc. ACM CIVR*, pages 438–445, 2010.

[5] R. Datta, D. Joshi, J. Li, and J. Z. Wang. Image retrieval: Ideas, influences, and trends of the new age. *ACM Computing Surveys*, 40(2):1–60, 2008.

[6] A. Dempster, N. Laird, D. Rubin, et al. Maximum likelihood from incomplete data via the EM algorithm. *Journal of the Royal Statistical Society. Series B (Methodological)*, 39(1):1–38, 1977.

[7] M. Hall, E. Frank, G. Holmes, B. Pfahringer, P. Reutemann, and I. H. Witten. The weka data mining software: an update. *SIGKDD Explor. Newsl.*, 11:10–18, 2009.

[8] R. Hu, S. Rüger, D. Song, H. Liu, and Z. Huang. Dissimilarity measures for content-based image retrieval. In *Proc. IEEE ICME*, pages 1365 -1368, 2008.

[9] M. J. Kearns, Y. Mansour, and A. Y. Ng. *An information-theoretic analysis of hard and soft assignment methods for clustering*, pages 495–520. MIT Press, Cambridge, MA, USA, 1999.

[10] M. S. Lew, N. Sebe, C. Djeraba, and R. Jain. Content-based multimedia information retrieval: State of the art and challenges. *ACM Transactions on Multimedia Computing, Communications, and Applications*, 2(1):1–19, 2006.

[11] D. G. Lowe. Distinctive image features from scale-invariant keypoints. *Int. J. Comput. Vision*, 60:91–110, 2004.

[12] C. D. Manning, P. Raghavan, and H. Schtze. *Introduction to Information Retrieval.* Cambridge University Press, New York, NY, USA, 2008.

[13] S. Nene, S. K. Nayar, and H. Murase. Columbia Object Image Library (COIL-100). Technical report, Department of Computer Science, Columbia University, 1996.

[14] H. Permuter, J. Francos, and I. Jermyn. Gaussian mixture models of texture and colour for image database retrieval. In *Proc. IEEE ICASSP*, volume 3, pages 569 – 572, 2003.

[15] H. Permuter, J. Francos, and I. Jermyn. A study of gaussian mixture models of color and texture features for image classification and segmentation. *Pattern Recogn.*, 39:695–706, 2006.

[16] J. Philbin, O. Chum, M. Isard, J. Sivic, and A. Zisserman. Lost in quantization: Improving particular object retrieval in large scale image databases. *Proc. IEEE CVPR*, pages 1–8, 2008.

[17] Y. Rubner, J. Puzicha, C. Tomasi, and J. M. Buhmann. Empirical evaluation of dissimilarity measures for color and texture. *Comput. Vis. Image Underst.*, 84:25–43, 2001.

[18] Y. Rubner, C. Tomasi, and L. J. Guibas. The Earth Mover's Distance as a Metric for Image Retrieval. *Int. J. Comput. Vision*, 40(2):99–121, 2000.

[19] G. Schaefer and M. Stich. Ucid: an uncompressed color image database. In *Proc. of SPIE, Storage and Retrieval Methods and Applications for Multimedia*, pages 472–480, 2004.

[20] N. Sebe, M. S. Lew, X. Zhou, T. S. Huang, and E. M. Bakker. The state of the art in image and video retrieval. In *Proc. ACM CIVR*, pages 1–8, 2003.

[21] A. W. M. Smeulders, M. Worring, S. Santini, A. Gupta, and R. Jain. Content-based image retrieval at the end of the early years. *IEEE TPAMI*, 22:1349–1380, 2000.

[22] M. J. Swain and D. H. Ballard. Color indexing. *Int. J. Comput. Vision*, 7:11–32, 1991.

[23] K. van de Sande, T. Gevers, and C. Snoek. Evaluating color descriptors for object and scene recognition. *IEEE TPAMI*, 32(9):1582–1596, 2010.

[24] J. C. van Gemert, C. J. Veenman, A. W. Smeulders, and J.-M. Geusebroek. Visual word ambiguity. *IEEE TPAMI*, 32:1271–1283, 2010.

[25] N. Vasconcelos and A. Lippmann. Feature representations for image retrieval: Beyond the color histogram. In *Proc. IEEE ICME*, pages 899–902, 2000.

[26] J. Z. Wang, J. Li, and G. Wiederhold. Simplicity: Semantics-sensitive integrated matching for picture libraries. *IEEE TPAMI*, 23(9):947–963, 2001.

Bag-of-colors for Improved Image Search *

Christian Wengert
kooaba AG
Förrlibuckstrasse 178
8005 Zürich, Switzerland
wengert@kooaba.com

Matthijs Douze
INRIA Grenoble
655 avenue de l'Europe
38334 Saint Ismier, France
matthijs.douze@inria.fr

Hervé Jégou
INRIA Rennes
Campus de Beaulieu
35042 Rennes, France
herve.jegou@inria.fr

ABSTRACT

This paper investigates the use of color information when used within a state-of-the-art large scale image search system. We introduce a simple yet effective and efficient color signature generation procedure. It is used either to produce global or local descriptors. As a global descriptor, it outperforms several state-of-the-art color description methods, in particular the bag-of-words method based on color SIFT. As a local descriptor, our signature is used jointly with SIFT descriptors (no color) to provide complementary information. This significantly improves the recognition rate, outperforming the state of the art on two image search benchmarks. We provide an open source package of our signature[1].

Categories and Subject Descriptors: I.4.10 [Image processing and computer vision]: Image representation; H.3.3 [Information storage and retrieval]: Information search and retrieval

General Terms: Algorithms

Keywords: Image retrieval, color descriptor

1. INTRODUCTION

We consider the problem of content-based image retrieval, for applications such as object recognition or similar image retrieval. This problem requires to produce a description of the image, typically a fixed-size vector. This description must be discriminative, but sufficiently invariant to handle the transformations the image may have undergone (cropping, different viewpoints, rotation, etc).

Most of the recent state-of-the-art large scale image search systems [7, 3] rely on local descriptors, in particular the SIFT descriptors [4] and its variants. They are extracted from regions of interest using a scale-invariant detector [4, 6, 5]. These descriptors are often used jointly with the bag-of-words (BOW) framework [11], which produces a single vector from a set of local descriptors.

Surprisingly and despite its assessed relevance for image classification [13], most of the recent papers on large scale image search ignore color information. The best results reported for this task on popular benchmarks, such as the UKB [7] or Holidays datasets [1], which both contain colorful images, are reported for techniques based on grey-level SIFT descriptors only.

Related work on color descriptors: The body of literature dealing with color descriptors is vast. Some of these descriptors have been normalized in the MPEG7 standard. The color version of the GIST descriptor [8] is widely used for scene recognition. For the sake of conciseness, two color signatures will be used as reference, namely color GIST [8] and color SIFT [13]. The color SIFT descriptor is the counterpart of SIFT [4] with color integrated. Its best variant [13] is the OpponentSIFT [14]. Similar to SIFT, it describes regions of interest extracted by a detector. It has mainly be considered for image and video classification tasks. For this reason, it is used in conjunction with the BOW aggregation framework [11]. However, this paper shows that much better results can be achieved using these descriptors by combining them with the state-of-the-art local descriptor matching method of [3].

The main contribution of our paper is a simple color description method, which is used to produce either global or local descriptors. In the first case (global), computing the image signature is much faster than producing a BOW vector with [13]: the main bottleneck is the computation of a color histogram, which is fast. Most importantly, improved search results are obtained on the evaluation datasets compared to other global descriptors.

The paper is organized as follows. Section 2 introduces our color signature generation procedure and analyzes the impact of several parameters and variants. As a global descriptor, our signature outperforms other global descriptors, including BOW generated from SIFT or color SIFT descriptors. Section 3 explains how the signature is used to describe local patches. Our color signature used jointly with SIFT descriptors outperforms the state of the art for the same memory usage and complexity. It is also better than color SIFT used within a comparable search system.

2. BAG-OF-COLORS SIGNATURES

In this section, we propose a method to extract a color signature, called bag-of-colors (BOC). This signature is extracted either for the whole image, producing a global descriptor, or from a patch (extracted by a region detector [6, 5]), in which case we obtain local color descriptors.

Since the method relies on computing a color histogram, the proposed signature is conceptually close to the work of [12]. However it departs from this method in several ways that drastically improve the recognition results. First, instead of using a regular color partition as in [12], the color codebook is learned on a set of real-world images. Most importantly, the histogram is constructed and normalized in a way inspired by the successful ingredients of the BOW framework [11] and recent improvements proposed for the

*Area chair: Bernard Merialdo

[1] `http://www.kooaba.com/en/learnmore/labs/`

MM'11, November 28–December 1, 2011, Scottsdale, Arizona, USA.

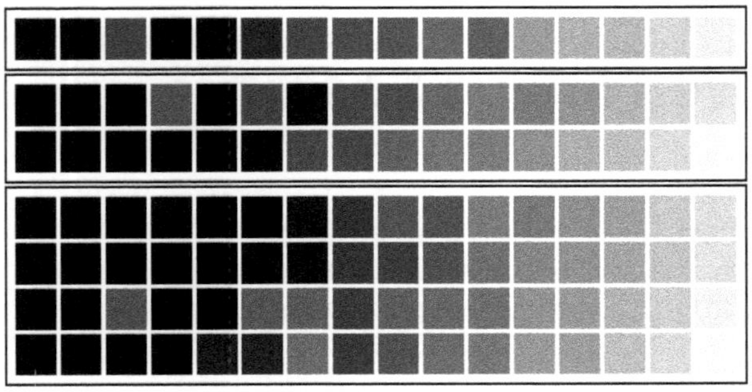

Figure 1: Color dictionaries learned by our procedure for $k_c = 16, 32, 64$. *Best viewed in color.*

Fisher kernel [10], but here applied to color components. As a result, the signature is more robust and avoids the typical problem of [12], where the most frequent colors dominate the other colors in the final representation and deteriorate the performance.

Hereafter, we introduce the signature generation procedure, analyze its results, and finally give a comparison with a BOW approach which shows that our signature provides consistently better results.

2.1 Color descriptor pipeline

Our color signature generation pipeline includes several steps. Different choices of parameters are investigated and evaluated.

Color space: Similar to most color descriptors, we use the CIE-Lab[2] color space in all our methods. This space is preferred to, e.g., the opponent space because it is more consistent with the Euclidean space structure, in particular the color dictionary generation procedure, which is based on k-means.

Color codebook: Our method needs a color dictionary $\mathcal{C} = \{c_1, \ldots, c_{k_c}\}$, defined as a set of k_c colors (often referred to as a *palette*). We first consider building a codebook by quantizing each L, a and b components separately and regularly in 4 or 8 bins, leading to $k_c = 64$ or 512 colors in total.

Then, we also learn a color dictionary that is more adapted to natural images. It is obtained by selecting and clustering typical colors from real-world images. In order to reduce the impact of some images containing large uniformly colored areas, we propose the following procedure in order to collect typical and unique colors for producing the color dictionary.

1) Collect 10000 random images from Flickr.
2) Resize each image to 256×256 pixels, convert it to CIE-Lab and split it in blocks of 16×16 pixels (i.e., 256 blocks in total).
3) For each block, find the most occurring color. Ties are randomly resolved. If this color corresponds to less than 5 occurrences (out of 256), select an arbitrary color from the block.
4) At this point, we have extracted 256 Lab colors per image. The set of 256×10000 colors from all images is clustered using a k-means algorithm, producing a k_c Lab colors palette.

The palettes learned by our procedure are shown in Figure 1 for different values of k_c. Some colors (e.g., dark grey/brown) are more represented than others in the palette, due to the unbalanced color statistic of natural images.

Color signature: The first step of our color signature method consists in computing the histogram of colors in the image for the fixed color codebook $\mathcal{C}$. This is done by first resizing (isotropic scaling) the image to a fixed number (≈16384) of pixels. For each pixel p we select the closest color (w.r.t. the Euclidean distance) in the codebook $\mathcal{C}$, and increment the corresponding bin of the output k_c-dimensional histogram.

Inverse document frequency is a successful technique in BOW. It downweights the contribution of the most common visual words and increases the importance of rare visual words by multiplying the frequency component with its corresponding *idf* weighting term. Similar to this technique, we update the histogram components by applying color *idf* weighting terms.

Normalization: power-law and normalization. Two techniques are considered. First, the "power-law" transformation proposed in [10] for Fisher vectors is applied component-wise. For a vector $x = (x_1, ..., x_d)$, it consists in updating each component as $x_i := \sqrt{x_i}$.

Similar to *idf*, the objective of the power-law update is to downweight colors in images that have very high frequencies, but in contrast to *idf* it does not take into account the statistics of other images in the dataset. The empirical distribution of colors gives very limited importance to less occurring colors, for instance those associated with small objects. The power-law method regularizes the contribution of each color in the final descriptor.

Finally, a L1 vector normalization is performed to make the vectors more comparable. The vector is updated as $x := x / \sum_{i=1..d} x_i$. Although an Euclidean normalization is often adopted in the BOW framework (e.g., in [11, 1]), the L1 normalization provides consistently better results for our color signatures.

Comparison metric: Signatures are compared to find the nearest neighbors of the query image in a database of signatures. The choice of the comparison metric is therefore critical. We compare the simple Manhattan (L1) and Euclidean (L2) distances, as well as distances specifically used for histograms: the fast Earth-Mover-Distance of [9], the χ^2 distance, the Shannon-Jenson divergence (SJD). The histogram intersection (HI) which were used in [12] for color histograms are equivalent to the L1 distance if the vectors are L1-normalized.

2.2 Evaluation

To motivate our final method, we analyze the impact of the choices involved in the bag-of-colors generation process. The search quality is evaluated as the mAP on the INRIA Holidays dataset [1], computed using the evaluation package available online. In this section, for the sake of exposition, our analysis is conducted on global descriptors only. The results for local descriptors obtained with the same signature generation method are analyzed in Section 3.

Dictionary, normalization and comparison metric have an impact that is summarized in Table 1. First observe that a learned vocabulary gives much better results that the original scheme by Swain which regularly splits the L, a and b axes (leaving many bins empty, as the Lab colorspace is not a cube). Second, the power-law transform has an important impact: an improvement of at least +8% of mAP is achieved by this simple component-wise preprocessing, showing that it is important not to consider dominant colors only. Third, the *idf* weighting provides a slight improvement of 1 point of mAP, comparable to what is typically observed for the standard SIFT-based BOW framework.

Overall, the best comparison metric is the L1 distance, which is slightly better than the χ^2 distance and JSD. The HI and FastEMD distances provide poor results on our features.

The RGB space has also been investigated. Results are consistently worse than for the CIE-Lab space in all our experiments: for reference, using this color space provides mAP=59.9% at best, compared to 63.8% in the CIE-Lab space.

[2] More precisely, we used the ITU-R recommendation BT.709 using the D65 white point reference.

exp no.	palette	k_c	metric	power-law	idf	mAP
#1	structured	64	L1			38.0
#2	structured	512	L1			45.3
#3	structured	512	FastEMD			43.1
#4	structured	512	L1	x		54.4
#5	learned	256	L1			54.5
#6	learned	256	L1	x		62.8
#7	learned	256	L1	x	x	**63.8**
#8	learned	256	χ^2	x	x	63.5
#9	learned	256	SJD	x	x	63.3
#10	learned	256	FastEMD	x	x	59.6

Table 1: Color signature construction in CIE-Lab space. Impact of the dictionary: *structured* refers to a typical palette (Lab is split in either 4x4x4 or 8x8x8 components, leading to $k_c = 64$ or 512), *learned* refers to our color learning procedure for natural images. Our BOC method is #8.

k_c	16	32	64	128	256	512	1024
mAP	41.2	51.8	57.1	61.0	63.8	64.0	64.6
ms/signature	22	25	27	47	65	128	220
ms/search	31	59	112	223	432	851	1692

Table 2: Impact of the palette size on accuracy (mAP on Holidays), signature extraction time and search time for querying a dataset of 1 million vectors (one processor core).

The number k_c of colors in the learned palette is the key parameter of the method. Its impact on both quality and timings is given by Table 2. We measured the signature extraction time with our Matlab implementation (the image is assumed to be resized already to 16k pixels). The search timings correspond to the cost of finding the 100 nearest L1-neighbors in a dataset of 1 million vectors. They have been measured by querying 500 k_c-dimensional vectors using exhaustive search.

Our bag-of-colors method is denoted by BOC in the following. It corresponds to the best choices for the global color signature: a palette learned with our procedure, the power-law, *idf* weighting and L1 normalization. The best comparison metric is L1, which is fortunate as the triangle inequality can therefore be exploited for indexing purpose.

A comparison with the standard BOW method [11] directly applied on raw color pixels (i.e., using CIE-Lab, Euclidean normalization, cosine similarity and idf, but without power-law) leads to mAP=38.4%. This score is comparable with that of Swain's method (Experiments #1 to #4), which gives a mAP between 38.0% and 45.3%, for $k_c = 64$ and 512, respectively.

The comparison with the state of the art is provided in Table 3. It is carried out on two benchmarks: the INRIA Holidays dataset and the UKB benchmark [7]. On UKB the accuracy is measured as the average number of images correctly ranked in top four positions (best score=4).

BOC significantly outperforms BOW: [1] reports mAP=54.9% for this BOW baseline on Holidays and [3] a score=2.99 on UKB. Besides, it does not achieve the best results of [3], which reports mAP=81.3% and score=3.42, respectively, with an improved matching scheme based on geometry and Hamming Embedding. However, our approach is significantly simpler, the descriptor extraction orders of magnitude faster, and our descriptors requires only 256

Method ↓	base descriptor	D	Holidays	UKB
Results reported in the literature				
BOW [3]	SIFT	20,000	46.9	2.88
BOW [3]	SIFT	200,000	57.2	2.95
HE [3]	SIFT	N/A	74.5	3.30
Results with other methods (reimplemented)				
color GIST [8]	RGB pixels	960	37.6	2.06
BOW	color SIFT	20,000	57.9	2.28
HE	color SIFT	N/A	76.5	2.58
Proposed approach				
BOC	Lab pixels	256	63.8	3.34
LBOC	SIFT+BOC	N/A	78.9	3.50

Table 3: Comparison with the state of the art. quality: mAP on Holidays and score/4 on UKB (higher is better). All schemes are compared without the spatial verification re-ranking scheme. N/A means that the image is not represented by a single vector of fixed length D but by a set of descriptors' signatures (typically requires 30kB/image in memory).

floats, while [3] requires about 30KB per images. In the next section, we will comment the other results of Table 3, which shows that BOC is also a powerful descriptor for local patches.

3. LOCAL COLOR SIGNATURE

The color descriptor proposed in the previous section has been shown to provide excellent performance on standard benchmarks. However, because at this point we used it only as a global descriptor, it is not able to cope with the most difficult cases such as strong cropping. Moreover, it does not capture texture information which had made the success of gradient based descriptors such as SIFT.

In this section, our color signature is applied directly on patches and used in conjunction with SIFT descriptors [4] to provide a rich combination of both color and texture, which was shown successful in the recent color extension of SIFT descriptors [13]. It is integrated within the image matching method of [3], called Hamming Embedding (HE), which is a state-of-the-art extension of BOW.

3.1 Binary signatures

In [3], the SIFT descriptors are assigned to visual words, but are additionally described by a binary signature of 64 bits. Each binary signature is computed from the SIFT descriptor, complementing the information given by the visual word. The Hamming distance between binary signatures is used to remove non-matching feature pairs and assign a voting score to the selected matches.

Since this distance removes mismatches, it offers an alternative to the dramatic increase in visual vocabulary sizes required by other approaches (up to 1M visual words in [7]). It is also an elegant way of taking into account the density variations in descriptor space. Indeed, the Hamming distance is implicitly normalized with respect to the local density in the BOW quantization cell. This property facilitates the early fusion of heterogeneous binary signatures, including the color signature described below.

3.2 Color binary signatures

Our approach follows the guidelines of [3], but instead of using the 64 bits to describe the SIFT, some of the bits are dedicated to represent color information. A local BOC descriptor is extracted from the elliptical region on the image that is used to compute the SIFT descriptor. We use a palette of k_c=256 colors. The vector is then binarized into a short binary signature of fixed size. The Hamming distance between two binary color signature should, at best, reflect the similarity between the original BOC descriptors.

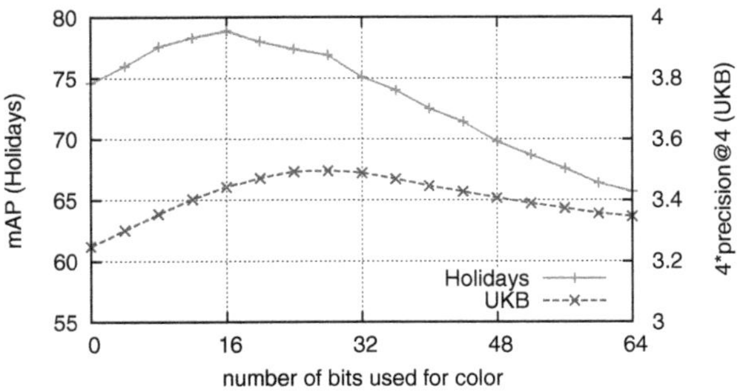

Figure 2: Trade-off between SIFT and color on Holidays and UKB. Each detected region is represented by 64 bits in total, shared by the representation of the SIFT and the LBOC descriptor. The performance scale on the left is for the Holidays dataset, on the right it is for UKB.

The 256-dimensional BOC vector needs to be reduced to a small number of bits b_c ($b_c = 0..64$, depending on the balance between SIFT and color). This descriptor tends to be sparse because it is computed on small regions: on average 80 % of its components are 0. We therefore adopt a dimensionality reduction inspired by [2], which was shown effective to reduce sparse BOW vectors. We first generate a sparse binary matrix B of size $k_c \times k_c$ such that each row and each column of B sum up to 8, and keep only the first b_c rows, producing a sparse binary matrix B' of size $b_c \times k_c$.

The color binary signature is obtained from a given local BOC vector x by first computing the projected vector $x' = B' \times x$. Second, each component of x' is compared to the median value for this component (learned on a training set), which produces a bit. *Note:* From our experiments, this strategy is better than using a projection obtained by principal component analysis. This might be due to the fact that our sparse projection is more consistent with the L1 distance, which is clearly better than L2 for BOC vectors. It is also better than binarizing a BOC vector generated by a palette comprising $k_c = b_c$ colors.

3.3 Experiments

As in Section 2.2, our evaluation is performed on Holidays and UKB. To obtain a fair comparison, we have adjusted the threshold of the color SIFT detector so that, on average, it approximately produces the same number of descriptors per image, as shown below:

Benchmark	Holidays	UKB
Hessian-Affine + SIFT	2988	1048
color SIFT	3244	1066

The trade-off between color and texture is shown by Figure 2 for a fixed signature of 64 bits, where b_c bits are used for color and the remaining $64 - b_c$ bits are the ones defined for SIFT by HE. The importance of color clearly depends on the dataset: SIFT alone performs better than the LBOC descriptor on Holidays, but this observation is reversed for UKB[3]. Overall, the optimum is clearly obtained when sharing the bits between these descriptors, with approximately 70 to 75% of the signature dedicated to SIFT and the rest used to represent color.

The comparison with the state of the art is shown by Table 3. Abusing the notation, the method that uses jointly SIFT and our binarized color signature is denoted by LBOC (local bag-of-colors). The color SIFT descriptor provides better results than SIFT on Holidays. However on UKB this descriptor suffers from not being invariant to rotation. The results of HE are significantly better than those obtained with BOW, as reported in the literature. The best results are clearly obtained with our LBOC approach, outperforming the reference method (SIFT+HE) and color SIFT by 4.4 and 2.4 points of mAP, respectively.

Large scale experiments have been performed on Holidays merged with 100K images from Flickr. With SIFT+LBOC, we obtain mAP=65.3 % against 61.2 % for HE with SIFT only. Querying the inverted file takes 0.56 s using a single processor core (2.5Ghz). This timing and the memory usage, about 30 kB/image, do not depend on the input descriptor (SIFT, LBOC or a combination).

[3]Note, however, that even for UKB with all 64 bits allocated to color in the signature, the visual word already provides a partial information about the SIFT descriptor. Therefore one should not conclude that color is more important than SIFT on this benchmark.

4. CONCLUSION

We have proposed a color signature inspired by the bag-of-words framework, and used it either as a global or a local descriptor. Our experiments show that color information significantly improves the retrieval quality in large scale image search, although it is often ignored in this context. Our global descriptor exhibits very competitive performance compared to more sophisticated methods. Used as a local descriptor, the results are better than those obtained by a state-of-the-art system based on SIFT or color SIFT descriptors.

Acknowledgments: This work was realized as part of the Quaero Project, funded by OSEO, a French State agency for innovation.

5. REFERENCES

[1] H. Jégou, M. Douze, and C. Schmid. Hamming embedding and weak geometric consistency for large scale image search. In *ECCV*, October 2008.

[2] H. Jégou, M. Douze, and C. Schmid. Packing bag-of-features. In *ICCV*, September 2009.

[3] H. Jégou, M. Douze, and C. Schmid. Improving bag-of-features for large scale image search. *IJCV*, 87(3):316–336, February 2010.

[4] D. Lowe. Distinctive image features from scale-invariant keypoints. *IJCV*, 60(2):91–110, 2004.

[5] J. Matas, O. Chum, U. Martin, and T. Pajdla. Robust wide baseline stereo from maximally stable extremal regions. In *BMVC*, pages 384–393, September 2002.

[6] K. Mikolajczyk, T. Tuytelaars, C. Schmid, A. Zisserman, J. Matas, F. Schaffalitzky, T. Kadir, and L. V. Gool. A comparison of affine region detectors. *IJCV*, 65(1/2):43–72, 2005.

[7] D. Nistér and H. Stewénius. Scalable recognition with a vocabulary tree. In *CVPR*, June 2006.

[8] A. Oliva and A. Torralba. Modeling the shape of the scene: a holistic representation of the spatial envelope. *IJCV*, 42(3):145–175, 2001.

[9] O. Pele and M. Werman. Fast and robust earth mover's distances. In *ICCV*, 2009.

[10] F. Perronnin, J.Sánchez, and T. Mensink. Improving the fisher kernel for large-scale image classification. In *ECCV*, 2010.

[11] J. Sivic and A. Zisserman. Video Google: A text retrieval approach to object matching in videos. In *ICCV*, October 2003.

[12] M. J. Swain and D. H. Ballard. Color indexing. *IJCV*, 7:11–32, 1991.

[13] K. E. A. van de Sande, T. Gevers, and C. G. M. Snoek. Evaluating color descriptors for object and scene recognition. *PAMI*, 32(9):1582–1596, 2010.

[14] J. van de Weijer, T. Gevers, and A. Bagdanov. Boosting color saliency in image feature detection. *PAMI*, 28(1):150–156, January 2006.

Asymmetric Hamming Embedding*

Taking the best of our bits for large scale image search

Mihir Jain
INRIA Rennes
mihir.jain@inria.fr

Hervé Jégou
INRIA Rennes
herve.jegou@inria.fr

Patrick Gros
INRIA Rennes
patrick.gros@inria.fr

ABSTRACT

This paper proposes an asymmetric Hamming Embedding scheme for large scale image search based on local descriptors. The comparison of two descriptors relies on an vector-to-binary code comparison, which limits the quantization error associated with the query compared with the original Hamming Embedding method. The approach is used in combination with an inverted file structure that offers high efficiency, comparable to that of a regular bag-of-features retrieval system. The comparison is performed on two popular datasets. Our method consistently improves the search quality over the symmetric version. The trade-off between memory usage and precision is evaluated, showing that the method is especially useful for short binary signatures.

Categories and Subject Descriptors: I.4.10 Image processing and computer visionImage representation; H.3.3 Information storage and retrievalInformation search and retrieval

General Terms: Algorithms

Keywords: Image search, Hamming Embedding

1. INTRODUCTION

Large scale image search is still a very active domain. The task consists in finding in a large set of images the ones that best resemble the query image. Typical applications include searching images on the web [15], location [13] or particular object [11] recognition, or copy detection [8]. Earlier approaches were based on global descriptors such as color histograms or GIST [12]. These are sufficient in some contexts [3], such as copy detection, where most of the illegal copies are very similar to the original image. However, global description suffer from well-known limitations, in particular they are not invariant to significant geometrical transformations such as cropping. Here we focus on the bag-of-words (BOW) framework [14] and its extension [6], where local descriptors are extracted from each image [9] and used to compare images.

The BOW representation of images was proved to be very discriminant and efficient for image search on millions of images [5, 11]. Different strategies have been proposed to improve it. For instance, [11] improves the efficiency in two ways. Firstly, the assignment of local descriptors to the so-called visual words is much faster thanks to the use of a hierarchical vocabulary. Secondly, by considering large vocabularies (up to 1 million visual words), the size of the inverted lists used for indexing is significantly reduced. Accuracy is improved by a re-ranking stage performing spatial verification [9], and by query expansion [1], which exploits the interaction between the relevant database images.

Another way to improve accuracy consists in incorporating additional information on descriptors directly in the inverted file. This idea was first explored in [5], where a richer descriptor representation is obtained by Hamming Embedding (HE) and weak geometrical consistency [5]. HE, in particular, was shown successful in different contexts [15], and improved in [6, 7]. However, this technique has a drawback: each local descriptor is represented by relatively large signatures, typically ranging from 32 [15] to 64 bits [6].

In this paper, we propose to improve HE in order to better exploit the information conveyed by the binary signature. This is done by exploiting the observation, first made in [2], that the query should not be approximated. We therefore adapt the voting method to better exploit the precise query location instead of the binarized query vector. This requires, in particular, two regularization steps used to adjust the dynamic of the local query distribution. This leads to an improvement over the reference symmetric HE scheme. As a complementary contribution, we evaluate how our approach trades accuracy against memory with smaller number of bits. To our knowledge, such a comparison has never been published.

The paper is organized as follows. The datasets representing the application cases and the evaluation protocol are introduced in Section 2. Section 3 briefly describes the most related works: BOW and HE. Our asymmetric method is introduced in Section 4. Finally, experiments in Section 5 compare the performance of our asymmetrical method with the original HE, and provides a comparison with the state of the art on image search. It shows a significant improvement: we obtain a mean average precision of 70.4% on the Oxford5K Building dataset before spatial verification, i.e., +4% compared with the best concurrent method.

2. EVALUATION DATASETS

This section introduces the datasets used in our experiments, as well as the measures of accuracy used to evaluate the different methods. These datasets reflect two application use-cases for which our method is relevant, namely place and object recognition. They are widely used to evaluate image search systems.

Oxford5K and Paris. These two datasets of famous building in Oxford and Paris contain 5,062 and 6,412 images, respectively. We use Paris as an independent learning set to estimate the parame-

*Area chair: Bernard Merialdo

MM'11, November 28–December 1, 2011, Scottsdale, Arizona, USA.

ters used by our method. The quality is measured on Oxford5K by mean average precision (mAP), as defined in [13]: for each query image we obtain a precision/recall curve, and compute its average precision (the area under the curve). The mAP is then the mean for a set of queries.

INRIA Holidays. This dataset contains 1491 images of personal holiday photos, partitioned into 500 groups, each of which represents a distinct scene, location or object. The first image of each group is the query image and the correct retrieval results are the other images of the group. Again, the search quality is measured by the mAP, see [13, 5] for details. A set of images from Flickr is used for learning the vocabulary, as done in [5].

Flickr1M. In order to evaluate the behavior of our method on a large scale, we have used a set of up to one million images. More precisely, we have used the descriptors shared online[1] by Jegou et al., which were downloaded from Flickr and described by the same local descriptor generation procedure as the one used for Holidays. This dataset is therefore merged with Holidays and the mAP is measured using the Holidays ground-truth, as in [7].

The recall@R measure is used for this large scale experiment. It measures, at a particular rank R, the ratio of relevant images ranked in top R positions. [3] states that it is a good measure to evaluate the filtering capability of an image search system, in particular if the large scale image search is followed by a precise spatial geometrical stage, as classically done in the literature.

3. RELATED WORK

3.1 Bag-of-features representation

The BOW framework [14] is based on local invariant descriptors [10, 9] extracted from covariant regions of interest [10]. It matches small parts of images and can cope with many transformations, such as scaling, local changes in illumination and cropping.

The feature extraction is performed in two steps: detecting regions of interest with the Hessian-Affine detector [10], and computing SIFT descriptors for these regions [9]. We have used the features provided by the authors for all the datasets.

The fingerprint of an image is obtained by quantizing the local descriptors using a nearest-neighbor quantizer, produced the so-called *visual words* (VW). The image is represented by the histogram of VW occurrences normalized with the L2 norm. A *tf-idf* weighting scheme is applied [14] to the k components of the resulting vector. The similarity measure between two BOW vectors is, most often, cosine similarity. The visual vocabulary of the quantizer is produced using k-means. It contains a large number k of visual words. In this paper, $k = 20,000$ for the sake of consistency with [5] and [6]. Therefore, the fingerprint histograms are sparse, making queries in the inverted file efficient.

3.2 Hamming embedding

The Hamming Embedding method of [5] is a state of the art method derived from BOW. A better representation of the images is obtained by adding a short signature that refines the representation of each local descriptor. In this approach, a descriptor x is represented by a tuple $(q(x), b(x))$, where $q(x)$ is the visual word and $b(.)$ is a binary signature of length m computed from the descriptors to refine the information provided by $q(x)$. Two descriptors are assumed to match if

$$\begin{cases} q(x) = q(y) \\ h\left(b(x), b(y)\right) = \sum_{i=1..m} |b_i(x) - b_i(y)| \leq h_t \end{cases}, \quad (1)$$

[1]http://lear.inrialpes.fr/people/jegou/data.php

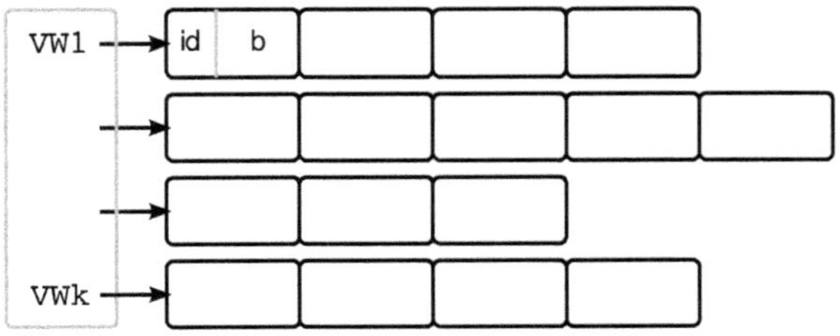

Figure 1: Overview of the HE indexing structure: it is a modified inverted file. Each inverted list is associated with a visual word. Each local descriptor is stored in a cell containing both the image identifier and a binary signature (from 4 to 64 bits in our paper). This indexing structure is also used in our AHE method: only the score similarity is modified.

where $h(b, b')$ is the Hamming distance between binary vectors $b = [b_1, .., b_m]$ and $b' = [b'_1, .., b'_m]$, and h_t is a fixed threshold. The image score is obtained as the sum [5] or weighted sum [7] of the distances of the matches satisfying (1), then normalized as with BOW.

As BOW, the method uses an inverted file structure, which is modified to incorporate the binary signature, as illustrated by Figure 1. The matches associated with the query local descriptors are retrieved from the structure and used as follows.

- Find the nearest centroid of the query descriptor x, producing quantized indexes $q(x)$, i.e., the visual word (VW). The entries of the inverted list associated with $q(x)$ are visited.
- Compute the vector $\mathbf{Q} \times x = b^* = [b_1^*(x), \dots, b_m^*(x)]$ associated with descriptor x, where $\mathbf{Q}$ is a rotation matrix for which only the first m rows are kept so that $\mathbf{Q} \times x \in \mathbb{R}^m$.
- The binary signature is obtained by comparing each component $b_i^*, i = 1..m$ with a threshold $\tau_{q(x),i}$. This amounts to selecting $b_i = 1$ if $b_i^* - \tau_{q(x),i} > 0$, else $b_i = 0$. The thresholds $\tau_{c,i}$ are the median values of b_i^* measured on an independent learning set for all VWs c and all bit components i.
- Only the database descriptors satisfying Equation 1 make a vote for the corresponding image, i.e., they vote only if their Hamming distance is below a pre-defined threshold h_t. The vote's score is 1 in [5]. Scoring with a function of the distance improves the results [6]. We therefore adopt this choice.
- All images scores are finally normalized (divided by the L2 norm of the BOW vector).

Additionally, we consider in this paper two techniques [6] that improve the results. First, multiple assignment (MA) reduces the number of matches that are missed due to incorrect quantization indexes. Second, the so-called *burstiness* (denoted by "burst") handling method regularizes the score associated with each match, to compensate the bursty statistics of regular patterns in images.

4. ASYMMETRIC HAMMING EMBEDDING

This section introduces our approach. It is inspired by the works of Dong [2] and Gordo [4], where the use of asymmetric distances was investigated in the context of Locality Sensitive Hashing. This method has to be significantly adapted in our context. Using the distance to hyperplanes may suffice for pure nearest neighbor search, where the objective is the find the Euclidean k-nearest neighbor of a given query [2]. However, in our case, this is not sufficient, because computed distances are used as match quality measurements. Our goal is therefore to provide a soft weighting strategy that bet-

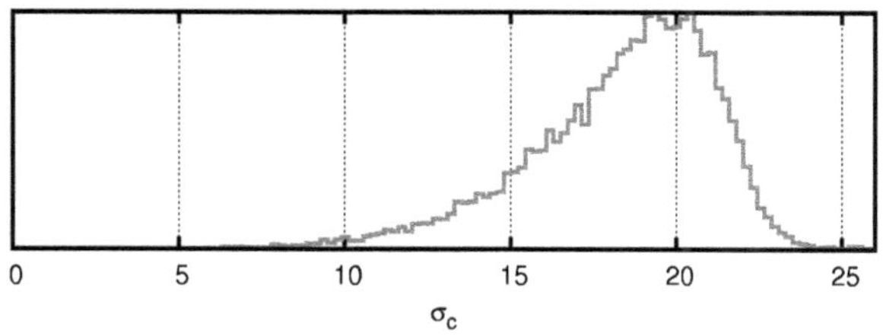

Figure 2: Empirical probability distribution function of σ_c measured for all visual words. The large variation of density across cells shows the need for a per-cell variance regularization.

ter exploits the confidence measures of all matches to produce the aggregated image scores.

Intra-cell distance regularization. We first adapt the local distances so that they become more comparable for different visual words. This is done, in our AHE scheme, by computing the standard deviation σ_c of the distance $b_i^* - \tau_{c,i}$ to the separating hyperplanes for each of the k visual words c. This estimation is carried out using a large set of vectors from an independent learning set. We used 50M Flickr descriptors for Holidays and all the descriptors from Paris for Oxford5K. The standard deviation is either computed component-wise (one per bit dimension) or for the whole cell. In our case we chose the simple choice of estimating a single parameter per cell used for all bits (isotropic assumption).

As observed in Figure 2, the standard deviations significantly vary from one cell to another. It is then worth obtaining more comparable values when using distances as quality measurements.

Distance to hyperplanes. In the symmetric version, the query projected by $\mathbf{Q}$ is binarized and compared with the database descriptors. We instead compute the distance between the projected query ($b^*(x) = \mathbf{Q} \times x$) and the database binary vectors that lie in the same cell (associated with $q(x)$). The "distance" between the ith component of $b^*(x)$ and the binary vector $b(y)$ is given by

$$d_{\mathrm{a}}^{\mathrm{i}}\left(b_i^*(x), b_i(y)\right) = |b_i^*(x) - \tau_{q(x),i}| \times |b_i(x) - b_i(y)| \,. \quad (2)$$

This quantity is zero when x is on the same side of the hyperplane associated with the ith component. The distances are added for all the m components to get an asymmetric "distance" between a query descriptor x and a database descriptor y, defined as

$$h_{\mathrm{a}}\left(b^*(x), b(y)\right) = \frac{1}{\sigma_{q(x)}} \times \sum_{i=1..m} d_{\mathrm{a}}^{\mathrm{i}}\left(b_i^*(x), b_i(y)\right). \quad (3)$$

The descriptors are assumed to match if $h_{\mathrm{a}}\left(b^*(x), b(y)\right) \leq h_t$, as for the symmetric version. For a given query x, the values $|b_i^*(x) - \tau_{q(x),i}|$ are precomputed before being compared to the database vectors. The similarity is penalized according to the distance from the hyperplane in the embedded Hamming space, providing improved measurements, as illustrated by Figure 3. In the symmetric case, it does not matter how far b_i^* lies from $\tau_{q(x),i}$. In contrast, the distance is a continuous function in our method.

Score weighting. Similar to what is done in [6] for the symmetric case, the distance obtained by Equation 3 is used to weight the voting score. In [6] weights are obtained as a gaussian function of Hamming distance. Here the weights are simply the difference $h_t - h_{\mathrm{a}}\left(b^*(x), b(y)\right)$ between the threshold and the normalized "distance". We also apply the burstiness regularization method of [6]. As we will show in Section 5, its impact is very important in our case because the aforementioned variance regularization does not sufficiently balance the amount of score received by the different *query* vectors, leading individual descriptors from the query

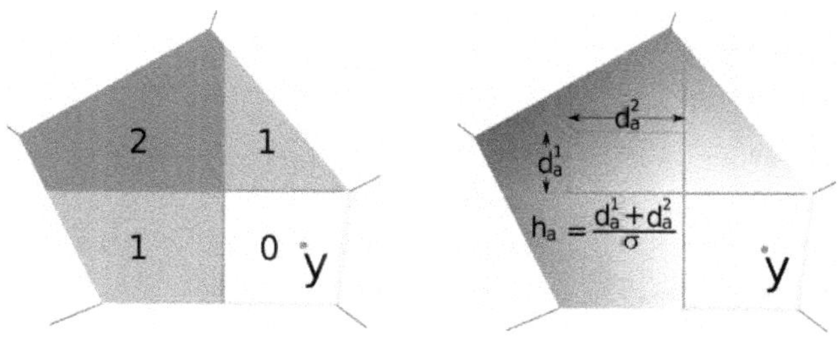

Figure 3: Illustration of HE and AHE for binary signatures of length 2. In the symmetric case, only three distances are possible (0, 1 or 2) between query and database descriptor y. AHE gives a continuous distance (reflected by the intensity of blue).

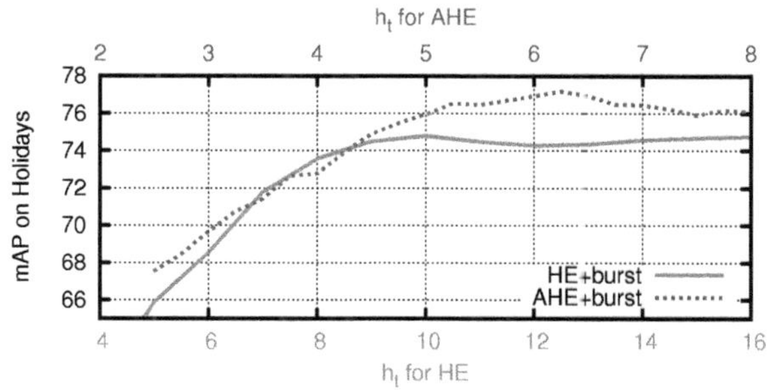

Figure 5: Impact of the threshold on accuracy (m = 32 bits). Note that the ranges for h_t differ for HE (Hamming distance) and AHE (derived from normalized distance to hyperplanes).

image to have a very different impact in the final score. The burstiness regularization effectively addresses this issue.

5. EXPERIMENTS

Search quality: HE *vs* AHE. Figure 4 evaluates our AHE method introduced in Section 4 against the original HE one, for varying numbers of bits. For both HE and AHE, we report the results obtained with the best threshold. As shown by Figure 5, the performance is stable around this best value.

Using the asymmetric version significantly improves the results. As stated in Section 4, the burstiness regularization of [6] is important in our case: without it AHE only achieves a slight improvement for short signatures.

Observe the important trade-off between the search accuracy and the signature length: using more bits clearly helps. However it is important to keep this signature short so that database images remain indexed in memory. Multiple Assignment helps in all cases, at the cost of increased query time. Unless specified, we used MA to the 5 nearest visual words, denoted by MA5.

Comparison with the state of the art. Table 1 compares our results with, to our knowledge, the best ones reported in the literature. Our approach clearly outperforms the state of the art on both Holidays and Oxford5K. Interestingly, for symmetric HE, our results (*in italics*) on Oxford5K are better than those reported in [6] with a geometry check. This is because on these datasets, the features used in [6] are not as good as those we used here. We only include in our comparison the results reported with learning done on an independent dataset itself. Some papers shows that learning on the test set itself improves the results, as to be expected. But as stated in [7] such results do not properly reflect the expected accuracy when using the system on a large scale.

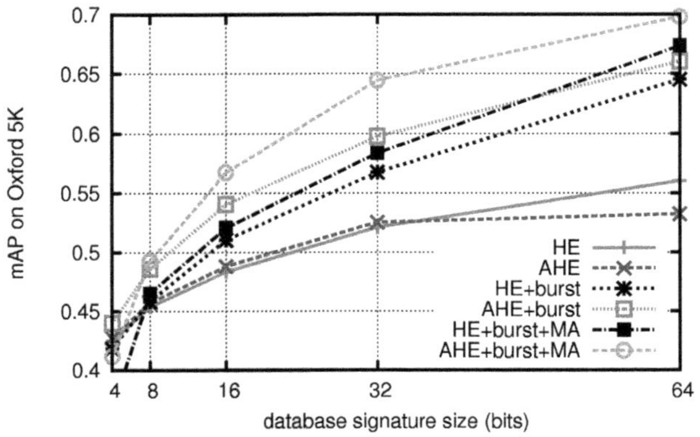

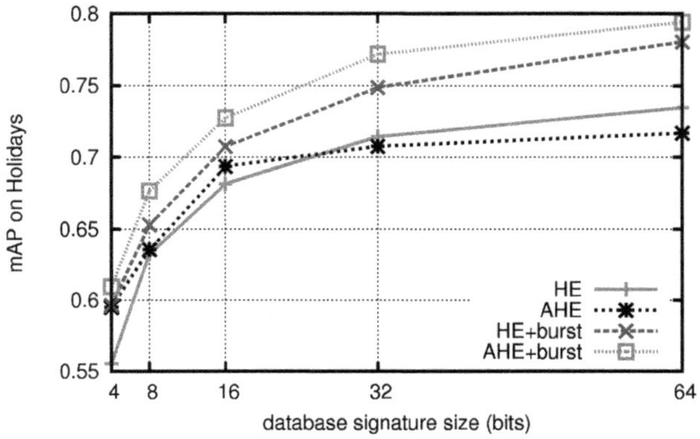

Figure 4: HE vs AHE: Trade-off between memory usage (per descriptor) and search quality.

	Oxford5K	Holidays
BOW [14]	40.3	-
BOW+soft MA [14]	49.3	-
HE+MA5 [6]	61.5	77.5
HE+burst [5]	*64.5*	*78.0*
HE+burst+MA5 [5]	*67.4*	*79.6*
AHE+burst	66.0	79.4
AHE+burst+MA5	69.8	**81.9**
AHE+burst+MA10	**70.4**	81.7

Table 1: State of the art. For [5], we report *in italics* the results obtained with the best descriptors ([5] reports inferior results with different descriptors and with geometrical information only).

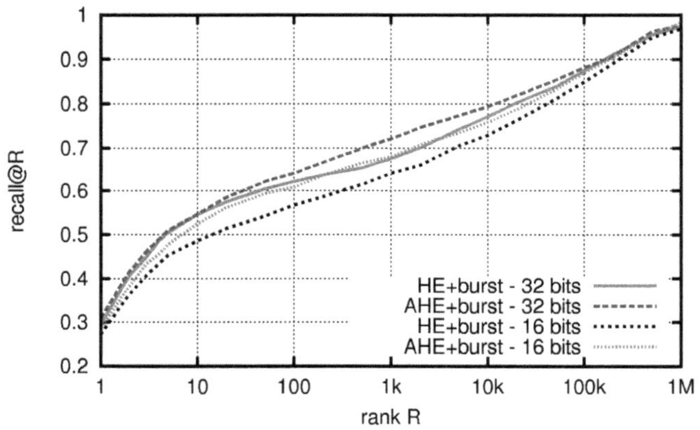

Figure 6: Search quality on a large scale (1 million images): Holidays merged with Flickr1M.

Large scale experiments. As shown in Figure 6, the filtering capability of AHE is better than HE: the recall@R measure is almost as good for AHE with 16 bits as HE with 32 bits. Equivalently, the performance is much better for a given memory usage.

The complexity of the method is increased compared to the original symmetric method. In both HE and AHE, the vector has to be projected. The main difference appears in the similarity computation, which is a simple `XOR` operation following by a bit count in HE, while we need to add pre-computed floating point values to get h_a in Equation 3. As a result, on 1 million images the search time is roughly 1.7 times slower in the asymmetric case, on average, compared to [6]: on average searching in one million images (using 64 bits) with AHE it takes 2.9s on one processor core, against 1.7s for HE.

Acknowledgments: This work was realized as part of the Quaero Project, funded by OSEO, French State agency for innovation.

6. CONCLUSION

This paper shows that a vector-to-binary code comparison significantly improves the state-of-the-art Hamming Embedding technique by reducing the approximation made on the query. This is done by exploiting the vector-to-hyperplane distances. The improvement is obtained at no additional cost in terms of memory. As a result, we improve the best results ever reported on two popular image search benchmarks before geometrical verification.

7. REFERENCES

[1] O. Chum, J. Philbin, J. Sivic, M. Isard, and A. Zisserman. Total recall: Automatic query expansion with a generative feature model for object retrieval. In *ICCV*, October 2007.
[2] W. Dong, M. Charikar, and K. Li. Asymmetric distance estimation with sketches for similarity search in high-dimensional spaces. In *SIGIR*, July 2008.
[3] M. Douze, H. Jégou, H. Singh, L. Amsaleg, and C. Schmid. Evaluation of GIST descriptors for web-scale image search. In *CIVR*, July 2009.
[4] A. Gordo and F. Perronnin. Asymmetric distances for binary embeddings. In *CVPR*, June 2011.
[5] H. Jégou, M. Douze, and C. Schmid. Hamming embedding and weak geometric consistency for large scale image search. In *ECCV*, October 2008.
[6] H. Jégou, M. Douze, and C. Schmid. On the burstiness of visual elements. In *CVPR*, June 2009.
[7] H. Jégou, M. Douze, and C. Schmid. Improving bag-of-features for large scale image search. *IJCV*, 2010.
[8] J. Law-To, L. Chen, A. Joly, I. Laptev, O. Buisson, V. Gouet-Brunet, N. Boujemaa, and F. Stentiford. Video copy detection: a comparative study. In *CIVR*, 2007.
[9] D. Lowe. Distinctive image features from scale-invariant keypoints. *IJCV*, 60(2):91–110, 2004.
[10] K. Mikolajczyk and C. Schmid. Scale and affine invariant interest point detectors. *IJCV*, 60(1):63–86, 2004.
[11] D. Nistér and H. Stewénius. Scalable recognition with a vocabulary tree. In *CVPR*, pages 2161–2168, June 2006.
[12] A. Oliva and A. Torralba. Modeling the shape of the scene: a holistic representation of the spatial envelope. *IJCV*, 42(3):145–175, 2001.
[13] J. Philbin, O. Chum, M. Isard, J. Sivic, and A. Zisserman. Object retrieval with large vocabularies and fast spatial matching. In *CVPR*, June 2007.
[14] J. Sivic and A. Zisserman. Video Google: A text retrieval approach to object matching in videos. In *ICCV*, 2003.
[15] Z. Wu, Q. Ke, M. Isard, and J. Sun. Bundling features for large scale partial-duplicate web image search. In *CVPR*, pages 25–32, 2009.

Spatially-coherent Pyramid Matching Based on Max-pooling*

Xiangang Cheng
School of Computer Engineering, Nanyang Technological University
Singapore 639798
xiangang@pmail.ntu.edu.sg

Liang-Tien Chia
School of Computer Engineering, Nanyang Technological University
Singapore 639798
asltchia@ntu.edu.sg

ABSTRACT

This paper presents a method of max-pooling spatially-coherent pyramid matching (MpScPM). Higher-layer representations are generated from lower-layer subregions, by a biologically-inspired max pooling strategy. Second, instead of reshaping the pyramid representation into a vector (used in generic SPM), the layer and location information of each subregion are kept and weak geometrical correspondences between matched subregions are explored to enhance our pyramid matching method. To enhance the possibility of finding the best matches at different scales and locations, cross-layer region similarities are computed, while the correspondences (either spatial neighbors or adjacent layers) are also incorporated. We evaluate our proposed MpScPM method on several existing benchmark datasets and it achieves excellent performances.

Categories and Subject Descriptors

H.4 [**Information Systems Applications**]: Miscellaneous; D.2.8 [**Software Engineering**]: Metrics—*complexity measures, performance measures*

General Terms

Algorithms

Keywords

max pooling, spatial coherent, pyramid matching

1. INTRODUCTION

High level image representation is crucial for image retrieval and classification. Among different methods, "Bag-of-Words" model [9] is a widely-used approach for generic image categorization and retrieval, which represents an image with a histogram by assigning all the descriptors of local regions to "visual word" frequency. The weakness of this model is that it takes all the features into account, including the "noises". In addition, it also brings in variations when the proportion of object size or the number of objects are different between images. Different from BOW models, parts-based models [1] focus on the discriminative parts within an image. If significant parts of an object are detected in the image, one can conclude that the object exists in the image. Thus the part-based models give us an important indication that the image can be efficiently represented with partial content instead of the global summations of all parts.

Both objects and scenes have their own structures, that is why human brain can easily identify objects which have been seen before. Researchers have proved that spatial information plays an important role in image representation. Lazebnik et al. [4] extended the Pyramid Matching Kernel (PMK) [2] by incorporating the spatial information of local regions. One image is partitioned into increasingly fine sub-areas and formed as a hierarchical tree representation. This Spatial Pyramid Matching (SPM) method implicitly assumes a fixed tree structure. That is, corresponding subregions of images from the same class share the same visual properties, that is the reason why SPM works exceptionally well for scene classification. However, for object classification the assumption may not hold because objects may have different scales and locations. It is therefore not appropriate to compare the image by reshaping the hierarchical tree in a plain vector.

What we've observed is that the pyramid representation shows not only the rigid hierarchical structure of the image, but also the correspondences between subregions within a pyramid layer and even cross layers. Their dependency information is relax but robust for most images. In this paper, our objective is to formulate the image similarity as a hierarchical tree similarity problem. The motivation behind this work is to build the hierarchical image representation by a bottom-up maximum pooling strategy, which uses the saliency characteristics in lower-layer regions to describe higher-layer regions. The main advantage is that it is robust to clutter and the image is not dominated by large area of similar pattern. What's more, we incorporate the invariant properties among the hierarchical tree structure. That is, within-layer and cross layers dependencies between close regions are exploited.

The rest of the paper is organized as follows: Section 2 gives the details of building an image representation by max-pooling based bottom-up strategy. In Section 3, we extend the pyramid matching of images by incorporating cor-

*Area chair: Marcel Worring.

MM'11, November 28–December 1, 2011, Scotsdale, Arizona, USA.

respondences between regions, thereby achieving spatially-coherent. The experiment results are reported and compared in Section 4. Finally, we conclude the contributions of this paper in Section 5.

2. BIO-INSPIRED PYRAMID

Traditional bag-of-words model [9] uses the mean of the visual words in the whole region. Such methods take all features including "noise" points into consideration. As the spatial pyramid matching is based on the BoW model, it is also not clutter-tolerant. Researchers [7, 8, 14] working with biological techniques adopted the max pooling procedure to minimize the clutter problem. It is formalized mathematically as an operation which returns the largest value of its inputs. Thus a neuron that performs a maximum operation on its pooled inputs will respond to the strongest of its inputs only and will not be affected by other weaker inputs. The max pooling procedure is well established by biophysical evidence in visual cortex (V1) [8] and is empirically justified by many algorithms applied to image categorization.

In this section, we will describe the construction of a hierarchical tree by a biological-inspired max pooling strategy. Usually, an object is formed by various parts. However, to differentiate one object from another, only the distinctive parts are required to generate the object model, while the other parts of the image can be neglected. For example, we can judge whether an image is in the face category when we successfully detect the patches of eyes, nose and mouth. In most general cases, we might not know what the characteristics of each category is in prior knowledge. Therefore, it is better to build the structure by bottom-up procedure in the cognitive process of understanding an image.

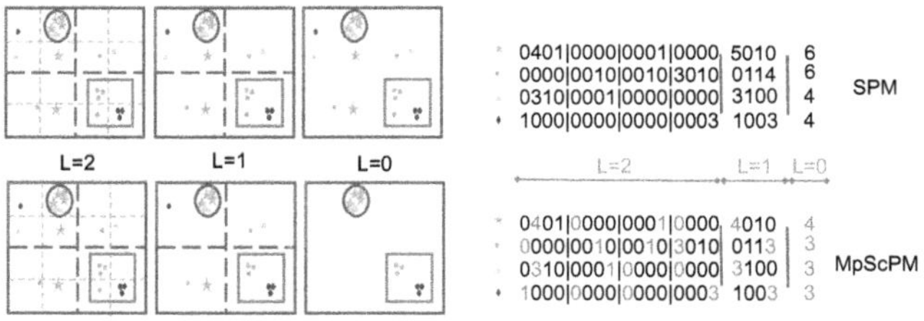

Figure 1: Comparison of bio-inspired spatial pyramid and the general spatial pyramid. The blue circle and red square stand for two different patterns in the image.

2.1 Subregions to describe the image structure

Currently, most of the methods take the single feature as the basic element. However, single feature is limited due to its descriptive power. It is sensitive to noises and object deformations. Instead of feature points, we use subregions with a number of features as the element of an image, which contain sufficient statistics of the local region. To be exact, the image is divided into small subregions. Each subregion contains one or limited parts of the object/scene. We mine the image information based on these subregions. In order to get sufficient statistics, the dense sampling patches are adopted. Each patch is then describe by the SIFT feature [6]. The SIFT features are quantized to a fixed-sized visual words and the subregion is represented by the bag-of-words histogram. To be exact, we represent it as $H = (h_1, h_2, \ldots, h_K)$, where K is the number of visual words by clustering algorithms.

2.2 Maximum spatial pooling

For each upper layer region, it contains several lower subregions. In SPM model, it is the mean of the lower regions. However, as we analyzed above, the mean operation is not robust to clutter. All the noise features will be taken into consideration. Meanwhile, maximum operation has been proven to be clutter-tolerant. This max pooling procedure is well established by biophysical evidence in visual cortex. Given the subregion representation $H_{i1}, H_{i2}, \ldots, H_{iM}$, The upper layer representation will be $H_i = max\{H_{i1}, H_{i2}, \ldots, H_{iM}\}$ That is, for each bin in the histograms of lower layer regions, the maximum value is adopted as the bin value in the higher layer. The maximum operation is in fact using the salient characteristics of object/scene to represent the whole image. See Fig. 1 for illustration. The red numbers in MpScPM indicate the maximum-pool value for the region in the respective layer and location.

To handle the problem that one structure might be partitioned into different subregions, we adopt the overlapping strategy. See Fig. 2 for illustration. That is, the subregions are specified with a fixed step which is smaller compared to their sizes. For each visual word, the value of the higher layer is equal to the max of the values in the lower subregions. The overlapping strategy ensures that most of the important patterns are not segmented in different regions. What's more, the features will not be counted repeatedly because of the maximum spatial pooling procedure. For SPM, it cannot handle objects that are cut across by the fixed subregions in the lower layer.

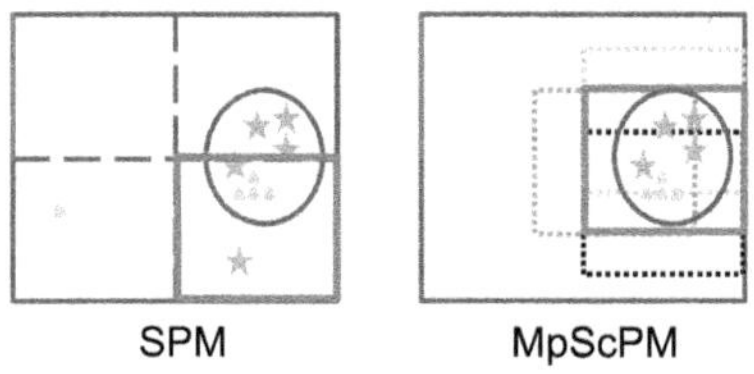

Figure 2: An illustration of how object pattern that is not aligned to subregions is handled by SPM & our MpScPM. The red box is the selected subregion.

3. SPATIALLY-COHERENT MATCHING

The pyramid representation shows the hierarchical properties of the image. Our objective here is to formulate the image similarity as a modified hierarchical tree similarity. Due to the transition, rotation and scale variances, images do not follow a rigid hierarchical tree structure. Therefore, we do not treat image matching as the traditional hierarchical tree matching. Instead, we incorporate the invariant properties within the structure of hierarchical tree.

3.1 One-to-one subregion matching

In order to better explain the problem, we use $G = (V, E)$ to represent the hierarchical tree, which can be seen as a directed graph. V is the vertex corresponding to the regions and E is the edge indicating if two regions are co-occurrent. In details, we link not only the nodes between children and parent, but also sibling nodes which are spatial neighbors.

Without loss of generality, we represent an image with the hierarchical regions, noted as $V = \{v_1, v_2, \ldots, v_N)\}$, in which N is the total number of subregions from all the layer L and $N = L(L-1)/2$. Each v_n is a histogram representation by maximum pooling. Given two images V_p and V_q, we measure the feature similarities of all the subregions:$s_{ij} = f(v_{pi}, v_{qj})$. The equation shows the visual similarity of different regions from different layers and spatial locations.

Any two images have the same cardinality, that is they have the same number of subregions. On the other hand, the correspondence can be shown to exist between any two sets that have the same cardinality. Our objective is to maximize the following equation,

$$\begin{aligned} &\textit{maximize} \ \sum\nolimits_{i,i'} w_{ii'} s_{ii'} \\ &\textit{subject to} \ w_{ii'} \in \{0,1\}, \ \ 1 \le i \le N, \ 1 \le i' \le N \\ &\qquad \sum\nolimits_{i'=1}^{N} w_{ii'} \le 1, \ \ 1 \le i \le N \\ &\qquad \sum\nolimits_{i=1}^{N} w_{ii'} \le 1, \ \ 1 \le i' \le N \end{aligned} \tag{1}$$

From Eq. 1, we see that there are one-to-one correspondences between images. That is, each subregion in the first image is paired with one and only one subregion in the second, while each subregion in the second image is paired with one and only one subregion in the first. None of the subregions from either set are left unpaired. To solve the one-to-one matching problem, we follow the Hungarian Algorithm [3]. That is, given a weighted bipartite graph $G_b = (V_b, E_b)$, the max-weight matching M is to be found, in which every vertex is adjacent to one edge in M.

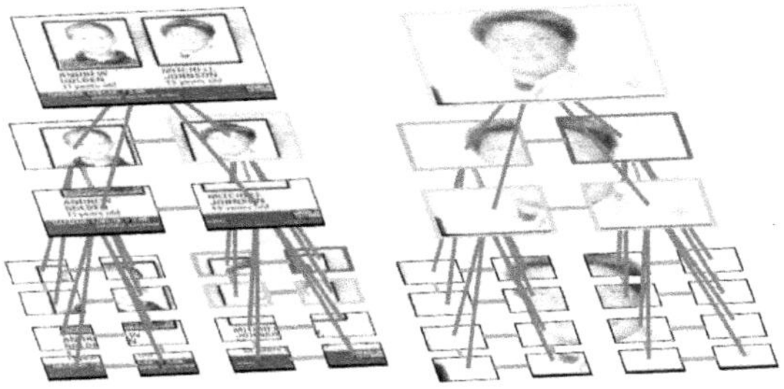

Figure 3: Spatially-coherent Pyramid Matching. The subregions with colored outline are matched pairs.

3.2 Spatially-coherent region correspondence

The correspondence between patches is an important factor in the hierarchical tree. Compared to the "global" tree structure, the correspondence between regions can be seen as "local". The nodes are not isolated from each other. For two pairs $M_i = (i, i')$ and $M_j = (j, j')$, if i and j have a link and i' and j' also have a link, they give extra support for matching the tree. To explore this dependence, we define two types of correspondences:

1. Correspondence between parent and children. As the child node is a subregion of the parent, it shows a dependence in the scale space (cross layers). See the red lines in Fig. 3.
2. Correspondence between siblings. The sibling correspondences show the spatial dependence within a layer. See the blue lines in Fig. 3.

To indicate the correspondence, we have,

$$\delta_{ij} = \begin{cases} 1 & \text{if there is a link between } i \text{ and } j \\ 0 & \text{otherwise} \end{cases} \tag{2}$$

To show the coherence of two pairs, we use

$$c_{ii'jj'} = \delta_{ij}\delta_{i'j'} s_{ii'} s_{jj'}. \tag{3}$$

That means in the matched pairs (i, i') and (j, j'), $c_{i,j}$ is nonzero if and only if there are correspondence links between i and i' as well as j and j'.

Finally, the similarity of two images can be measured as:

$$\hat{S} = \sum\nolimits_{i,i'} w_{ii'} s_{ii'} + \sigma \sum\nolimits_{i,i',j,j'} c_{ii'jj'} w_{ii'} w_{jj'} \tag{4}$$

In the above objective function, the first part measures the similarities of the subregion pairs. And the second part is to evaluate the correspondence of different matched pairs, either spatial or scale dependencies. The parameter σ is the trade-off between the two parts.

4. EXPERIMENTS

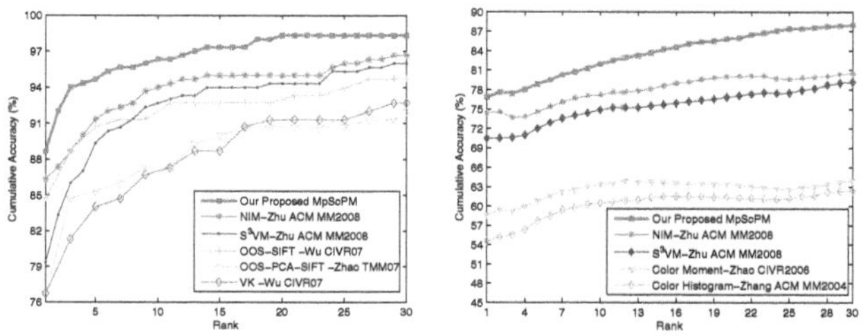

(a)Columbia Dataset (b)CityU Dataset

Figure 4: Top-k IND retrieval performance of our proposed method and relevant methods on the Columbia dataset and CityU dataset.

In our experiment, we adopt the dense sampling strategy with 16×16 patch size. For each patch, we use the SIFT [6] representation. The general k-means clustering method is used and a vocabulary of 500 visual words is generated. To measure the similarity between subregions, we take the RBF kernel. For the retrieval problem, we use Eq. 4 to measure similarity of query images and the candidates. For classification problem, we use it as the kernel and the LIBSVM is used to train the model.

4.1 Image Near-Duplicate Retrieval

In this section, we evaluate our proposed method on two Image Near-Duplicate(IND) datasets which were extracted from the keyframes of TRECVID corpus. The Columbia dataset is provided by [15], which are the keyframes extracted from TRECVID 2003 corpus. Each dataset includes 150 IND pairs (300 images) and 300 non-duplicate images. The second dataset CityU dataset is a much larger dataset from TRECVID 2004 corpus, with 7006 keyframes including 3388 near-duplicate image pairs. To compare with other state-of-art method, we adopt the same experiment setup for IND retrieval. All IND pairs are used as queries to evaluate performance. To evaluate the retrieval performance of our proposed MpScPM and comparison with other state-of-art methods, we estimate the probability of the successful top-k retrieval $P(k)$ as follows:$P(k) = \frac{Q_c}{Q}$, where Q_c is the number of queries that rank their INDs within the top-k position, and Q is the total number of queries.

We compare our MpScPM with other state-of-the-art methods: (i) the NIM [18] (ii) the S^3VM [18], (iii) the LIP-IS+OOS [17], (iv) the OOS-SIFT approach [12] (v) the Visual Keywords(VK) methods [12] and (vi) color moment [16] or color histogram [15] based retrieval. Figure 4 shows the results of these methods for top-k IND retrieval on the

Table 1: Top-1 retrieval performance comparison of our proposed method, SAPM, SPM and TPM on both Columbia Dataset.

Methods	Accuracy(%)
SPM	78.0
TPM	75.7
SAPM	80.7
Our MpScPM	88.7

Columbia dataset and cityU dataset where k changes from 1 to 30. From the figure, we can see that our MpScPM significantly outperforms the other methods in terms of accuracy.

We also compare our proposed approach with Spatial Pyramid Matching (SPM)[4], Temporal Pyramid Matching (TPM) and Spatially Aligned Pyramid Matching (SAPM)[13], which are related methods to ours as they also incorporate some kind of spatial information. Table 1 shows the top-1 retrieval performance on the Columbia Dataset. Our results significantly outperform the other three approaches, which shows that our strategy of using bottom-up spatial maximum pooling and spatially-coherent correspondence exploring in the hierarchical tree did provide more discriminative information for determining IND.

4.2 Event Classification

Our algorithm is tested on the sports event dataset [5]. This dataset was collected from the Internet, and was later annotated thoroughly by Lotus Hill Research Institute. There are 8 sports categories in the dataset. The number of images in each category varies from 137 to 250. In each image, there are always one or more athletes, and the poses and sizes of these athletes differ significantly. In this work, we take the same classification protocol setup as in [5]: For each event class, 70 randomly selected images are used for training and 60 of the remaining images are used for testing. We compare our method with other corresponding methods.

Table 2: Comparison of classification results on Princeton 8-sports event dataset.

Methods	Accuracy(%)
PMK[2]	78.84±0.55
scene/object[5]	73.4
Spatial PACT[11]	78.50
HIK[10]	77.54
HIK2[10]	84.21
Our MpScPM	84.79±0.53

The experiment results are reported in Table 2. A single scale for dense sampling points extraction is adopted. In the sports event dataset, our proposed method achieves an accuracy of 84.79 ± 0.53. The Pyramid Matching Kernel(PMK) [2] has an accuracy of 78.84 ± 0.55. Comparing with other state-of-arts methods reported on this dataset, our proposed method also show better performance. The result in [5] is 73.4, which is based on scene environment classification and object categorization. The spatial PACT, which adopts a spatial pyramid of PACT feature, achieved 78.50 accuracy. We also compared with Histogram Intersection Kernel(HIK) [10] (Note HIK and HIK2 adopted one scale and multi-scales of dense sampling points, respectively). If both methods use only one scale of dense sampling points, our proposed method greatly outperforms HIK (77.54). And our result is as good as HIK2 (84.21), when it adopted 5 scales of dense sampling points, as well as the Sobel images.

5. CONCLUSION

This paper presents a biologically-inspired max-pooling pyramid strategy for image representation, as well as the spatially-coherent pyramid matching for image similarity measuring. By applying max pooling of salient characteristics from the lower-layer subregions, the representation of higher-layer region has been shown to be more clutter-tolerant. By matching the regions at different layers and incorporating geometry correspondences between matched regions, the results enforced our claims of scale and position invariant. The experiments have shown that our proposed MpScPM achieves excellent performance.

6. REFERENCES

[1] R. Fergus, P. Perona, and A. Zisserman. Object class recognition by unsupervised scale-invariant learning. *CVPR*, 2003.

[2] K. Grauman and T. Darrell. The Pyramid Matching Kernel: Discriminative Classification with Sets of Image Features. In *ICCV*, 2005.

[3] H. Kuhn. The Hungarian method for the assignment problem. *Naval research logistics quarterly*, pages 83–97, 1955.

[4] S. Lazebnik, C. Schmid, and J. Ponce. Beyond bags of features: Spatial pyramid matching for recognizing natural scene categories. In *CVPR*, 2006.

[5] L. Li and L. Fei-Fei. What, where and who? classifying event by scene and object recognition. In *ICCV*, 2007.

[6] D. G. Lowe. Distinctive image features from scale-invariant keypoints. *International Journal of Computer Vision*, 60:91–110, 2004.

[7] T. Serre, M. Riesenhuber, J. Louie, and T. Poggio. On the role of object-specific features for real world object recognition in biological vision. In *Biologically Motivated Computer Vision*, pages 387–397, 2002.

[8] T. Serre, L. Wolf, and T. Poggio. Object recognition with features inspired by visual cortex. In *CVPR*, 2005.

[9] J. Sivic and A. Zisserman. Video Google: A Text Retrieval Approach to Object Matching in Videos. In *ICCV*, 2003.

[10] J. Wu and J. Rehg. Beyond the Euclidean distance: Creating effective visual codebooks using the histogram intersection kernel. *ICCV*, 2009.

[11] J. Wu and J. M. Rehg. Where am i: Place instance and category recognition using spatial pact. In *CVPR*, 2008.

[12] X. Wu, W. Zhao, and C. Ngo. Near-duplicate keyframe retrieval with visual keywords and semantic context. In *CIVR*, 2007.

[13] D. Xu, T. Cham, S. Yan, and S. Chang. Near Duplicate Image Identification with Spatially Aligned Pyramid Matching. In *CVPR*, 2008.

[14] J. Yang, K. Yu, Y. Gong, and T. Huang. Linear spatial pyramid matching using sparse coding for image classification. *CVPR*, 2009.

[15] D. Zhang and S. Chang. Detecting Image Near-Duplicate by Stochastic Attribute Relational Graph Matching with Learning. In *ACM Multimedia*, 2004.

[16] W. Zhao, Y. Jiang, and C. Ngo. Keyframe retrieval by keypoints: Can point-to-point matching help? *International Conference on Image and Video Retrieval*, 2006.

[17] W.-L. Zhao, C.-W. Ngo, H.-K. Tan, and X. Wu. Near-Duplicate Keyframe Identification with Interest Point Matching and Pattern Learning. *Trans. on Multimedia*, 2007.

[18] J. Zhu, S. C. Hoi, M. R. Lyu, and S. Yan. Near-Duplicate Keyframe Retrieval by Nonrigid Image Matching. *ACM Multimedia*, 2008.

Text and Image Subject Classifiers: Dense Works Better

Daan T.J. Vreeswijk Bouke Huurnink Arnold W.M. Smeulders

Intelligent Systems Lab Amsterdam, Informatics Institute, University of Amsterdam
Science Park 904, 1098XH Amsterdam, The Netherlands
{d.t.j.vreeswijk,b.huurnink,a.w.m.smeulders}@uva.nl

ABSTRACT

We investigate the feasibility of training visual concept detectors for such abstract subject categories as *biology* and *history* with the aim of employing these for full-text to image linking. We show that using dense sampling methods can lead to image classifiers that perform well enough for interactive search. Echoing this dense sampling in the image domain, we also show that using term frequencies as text features outperforms using a topic abstraction method. Finally, we use these monomodal classifiers for the task of linking texts to images, improving more than 50% over the state-of-the-art, thereby showing that dense is better.

Categories and Subject Descriptors

I.5.2 [**Design Methodology**]: [Feature evaluation and selection]; H.3.3 [**Information Search and Retrieval**]: [Retrieval Models]

General Terms

Experimentation, Measurement, Performance

Keywords

Multimedia subject classification, multimedia linking, retrieval, feature representation

1. INTRODUCTION

The state-of-the-art in image search engines is such that physical objects like car, bicycle, and boat have reached very good recognition rates. For concepts like these, the state-of-the-art has reached an average precision in the range of 30–80%, well over the threshold of what is generally considered to be useful for interaction [10]. In fact, performance figures typically increase with 7% average precision points per year [10] due to better features, better machine learning and more and better examples. We aim to bring these state-of-the-art image classifiers into subject-based multimedia linking between images and text narratives.

The way physical object classifiers work is through recognizing that all boats have a mast against the sky (or at least vertical gradients against the horizontal gradients water brings), or that bicycles' wheels and spokes against street texture are the obvious details uniquely identifying that class [12]. In contrast, for *abstract subjects* like history, music, and geography less progress has been made. Few have dared to venture into building image subject classifiers, as it is hard to see which elements of visual appearance would be shared by these abstract concepts. In addition, to cover all internal class variation, the number of training examples would be very big. Yet, subject classification is what professionals do first if they index a picture or a text. Bookstores, libraries, and archives are organized by subjects like history and music, while these are the hardest categories for current day image search engines.

Meanwhile, the state-of-the-art in text analysis is such that subject classification may be considered a solved problem [7]. Once the words in a full text are known, the subject(s) of the text may follow from on the basis of, for example, underlying topical models obtained using Latent Dirichlet Analysis (LDA) [1], or on the basis of vectors of normalized document terms [7].

We aim to generate subject classifiers using multimedia sources, i.e. images embedded in full texts. The natural approach to abstract subject classification is multi-modal, which was performed in [6]. There, the authors show that using canonical correlation analysis (CCA) on their representations of images and texts is beneficial for the performance of the multimedia linking system. However attractive this model may be from a conceptual point of view, the state-of-the-art in both image concept classification and text subject classification is to use as many raw features as possible [5, 7].

Thus the question arises: What is more beneficial for the full-text to image linking task: training state-of-the-art, but monomodal, image- and text classifiers for the same set of subjects and then performing linking in subject space, or to use less informative feature sets but jointly model the information from both modalities?

The novelty over [6] is as follows. The authors demonstrated that it is possible to classify texts and images by cross correlation analysis. It won them the best student paper award at ACM Multimedia 2010 and rightfully so. They reduced the text and the images to a small feature set. In

---

Area chair: Tat-Seng Chua

MM'11, November 28–December 1, 2011, Scottsdale, Arizona, USA.

contrast, in this paper we will demonstrate for the same dataset that using a dense description of the text using many words works better. In addition, we demonstrate that using image features which sample the image densely at each pixel rather than at salient points alone further improves the result. This, together with the use of better classifiers, makes the average precision of multimedia linking improve from 51% to 56%. Dense works better.

2. RELATED WORK

To provide context for our work, we review related work in the multimedia linking task, and zoom in briefly on the state-of-the-art in classifying physical objects in images.

Early efforts on linking between text and images did so on the basis of text; i.e., keywords were manually assigned to images, and this text (rather than the image content itself), was used to identify images that should be linked to a textual article [2]. In [6], a method for cross-modal retrieval of images and large bodies of text has been proposed. The authors compare several ways of mapping textual and linguistic information to correlated subspaces, and test the strength of these correlations by using image queries to find bodies of text as well as vice versa. Here, images were represented by SIFT features and narrative texts were represented by a model derived using Latent Dirichlet Allocation (LDA) [1]. The authors experimented with *correlation matching*, using canonical correlation analysis to find texts similar to an image, and *semantic matching*, using an intermediate representation of both images and documents as a set of classes. They found that a combination of correlation matching and semantic matching yielded the best results. In this paper we adopt the task and dataset of this paper, but the feature extraction and model training is performed differently.

The state-of-the-art in image classification is the Bag-of-Words approach [3, 8], which is still dominant [11] in major image- and video retrieval benchmarks [4, 9]. The goal of this paper is to apply this state-of-the-art to the text to image linking domain, so we adopt this approach. This approach samples feature patches from the image, and considers each patch separately, disregarding any spatial information. These patches form the input for a kernel-based SVM classifier, for a detailed explanation see [13].

3. APPROACH AND SETUP

The main research question of this paper is: *What is more beneficial for the full-text to image linking task: training state-of-the-art, but monomodal, image- and text classifiers for the same set of subjects and then performing linking in subject space, or to use less informative feature sets but jointly model the information from both modalities?* To investigate this, we first train monomodal subject classifiers using the SIFT and LDA features from [6]. To extend beyond this baseline, we will show the benefit of using dense sampling methods in both modalities.

Wikipedia Dataset We use the dataset provided by [6], which consist of images and texts from 2700 of Wikipedia's featured articles and was kindly provided by the authors. Each article has been classified into one of 10 categories. The articles are split into sections, with each section consisting of a piece of text and an accompanying image. The final dataset consists of a set of 2,866 texts and a set of 2,866 images. Each set is split into 2173 training examples and 693 test examples. In addition, the dataset contains LDA features for the texts and SIFT features for the images.

Feature Extraction The standard practice in the state-of-the-art image- and text classification is to sample very dense features from both modalities. For the images, this is implemented by creating a SIFT-descriptor for every pixel in the image. Following [13], the feature extraction process uses a codebook of 4096 visual words, and a 2-layered spatial pyramid consisting of a 1x1 and a 1x3 layer. We call this feature set *D-SIFT*. For the text features, the most dense sampling one can perform is counting the words in the document. Since this would lead to a very sparse feature vector for a document, we removed all words that occurred less than three times in the dataset. This feature set will be referred to as *TF*.

Classifier Training To train the image classifiers, we employ support-vector machines using a histogram-intersection kernel. For a detailed explanation of the mechanisms used, we refer to [13]. The LDA-based text classifier was trained using a parzen-classifier, while for the TF-based classifier, an SVM using a polynomial kernel was trained.

Linking After creating the image- and text classifiers, we have obtained a mapping for items in both of these input modalities to the subject space. This gives a representation of the input items as N-dimensional vectors in this subject-space. Given a distance measure, it is now possible to calculate the distances between all texts and images. The goal of the method is to produce a ranked list of images for each text, and to produce a ranked list of texts for each image. This means that we take a retrieval approach, viewing each text as an image query, and each image as a text query. For each query, we then sort all elements of the other modality ascending by distance, which gives us the desired ranked list.

Performance Metric The linking performance of ranked lists for individual texts and images, as well as the intermediate performance of image and text subject classifiers, is calculated using the well-known Mean Average Precision (MAP) metric. This measure rewards the placement of correct results at the top of the list. Note that for each combination of features two MAP-scores are obtained: one when using the images as query, and one when using the texts.

4. RESULTS

In this section, we will first show the performance of the image- and text classifiers separately, before turning our attention to the linking task.

Classification Results Table 1 shows the performance of subject classification for images using SIFT and Dense-SIFT features, and for texts using LDA and (dense) term features. As can be seen, the results for both modalities confirm that denser sampling leads to better subject classification performance, increasing AP by 50% for images and 31% for texts.

Taking a closer look at the performance of subject classification for images, the subject that improves the most using dense sampling of pixels is *Sport & recreation* (+140%). The *History* performance increase, on the other hand, is negligible (+1%). This reflects the intuition that sports images have a more consistent visual appearance than historical images; almost any image can be "historical". Overall, the best classified subject is *Biology*, while *Art & architecture* is the

Table 1: Performance in AP of image classification and text classification for the 10 subject classes, compared to the approach of Rasiwasia et al [6]. Classes are sorted in ascending order of the number of training examples (top to bottom).

	Image class.		**Text class.**	
Subject	*SIFT*	*D-SIFT*	*LDA*	*TF*
Art & architecture	0.072	0.108	0.229	0.795
Royalty & nobility	0.164	0.180	0.682	0.804
Media	0.234	0.353	0.393	0.858
Music	0.148	0.287	0.659	0.958
Literature & theatre	0.239	0.318	0.673	0.816
Sport & recreation	0.201	0.496	0.982	0.986
Geography & places	0.382	0.468	0.768	0.921
History	0.200	0.201	0.427	0.662
Biology	0.417	0.607	0.943	0.970
Warfare	0.287	0.480	0.901	0.961
MAP	0.234	0.350	0.666	0.873

Figure 1: The five highest ranked images per subject, according to the worst, median and best performing image classifier. Images that have been incorrectly classified according to the subject label are indicated by the red border. Note that although the images for *Art & architecture* are of the wrong category, their appearances do not seem unreasonable, indicating the high visual ambiguity of the class.

most difficult to classify. Figure 1 gives an indication of the classifier performance. Turning to texts, classification performance here is always higher than for images in the same category. This confirms that, with the long history of research in text analysis, text subject classification is an easier task than image subject classification. Dense sampling brings the classification performance of all but one classifier to above 0.75 in AP. The exception is *History*, which is the most difficult kind of text to classify. The best classified subjects are *Music*, *Biology*, *Sport & Recreation*, and *Warfare*, all with an AP score of over 0.95. The categories that benefit the most from dense sampling of terms are *Art & architecture* (+245%) and *Media* (+118%). These two subjects were particularly badly classified using LDA, suggesting that the underlying topic model of the LDA features did not capture the characteristics of these subject classes well.

Table 2: Cross-modal mean linking performance in MAP for image-to-texts linking (*I2T*), and for text-to-images linking (*T2I*). The best score per linking type is highlighted in bold.

	I2T		**T2I**	
	LDA	*TF*	*LDA*	*TF*
SIFT-SCM	0.277	—	0.226	—
SIFT	0.305	0.339	0.229	0.242
D-SIFT	0.387	**0.418**	0.325	**0.353**

Cross-modal Linking Results Recall that for image-to-texts linking, the vector of subject probabilities for a given image is used to retrieve texts with similar distributions of subject probabilities, resulting in a ranked list of linked texts. The inverse is the case for text-to-images linking. Table 2 show the final results when applying the subject classifiers in the image-to-texts and the text-to-images linking tasks. Our baseline is the combination of the *SIFT* image features with *LDA* text features from [6], which uses logistic-regression based subject classification and CCA (indicated by *SIFT-SCM*). The best overall linking performance is obtained using the best image and text subject classifiers from Table 1: D-SIFT for images and TF for texts. This improves image-to-texts linking by 51% and text-to-images linking by 56% over the baseline. Furthermore, it is interesting to see that our SVM-based method of learning separate image and text detectors already slightly outperforms the baseline.

A detailed view per category of linking performance is given in Figure 2. Our results here show that image-to-texts linking and text-to-images linking performs similarly over the different subjects, with image-to-text consistently outperforming text-to-image. *Biology* images and texts obtain the highest absolute linking scores, while *Art & architecture* texts obtain the lowest linking scores. Furthermore, the performance of the linking is closely related to the performance of the intermediate image subject classifiers, which obtained the highest and lowest scores for these very subjects. This suggests that as we improve subject classification performance, our linking performance will also improve.

5. DISCUSSION AND CONCLUSIONS

In this paper we have focused on achieving the linking task through monomodal subject classification. Here we used state-of-the-art dense feature sampling in combination with state-of-the-art classification techniques to classify images and texts into the same subject categories, and then linked between images and texts by calculating similarity in subject space. This monomodal approach has proven successful in terms of improving linking performance, and it would be interesting to investigate whether incorporating a joint modelling framework by means of combination with CCA, as suggested by [6] further increase performance. Furthermore, to extend the linking task, we plan to expand this work to a larger dataset, with multiple subject labels per image-text pair.

In improving the multimedia linking task, we have shown that dense feature sampling is very effective when training classifiers for abstract subjects. For some categories (e.g. *Biology* and *Sport & recreation*), average precision scores reach

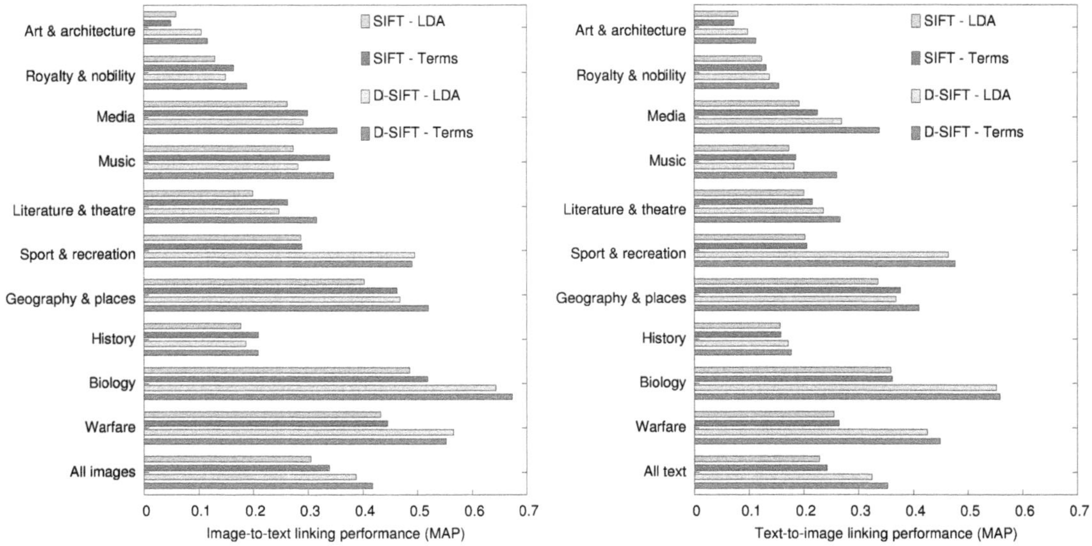

(a) Linking an image to full-text narratives.

(b) Linking a full-text narrative to images.

Figure 2: Category-level average performance of cross-modal linking between full-text narratives and images. Note that overall, linking from an image to full-text narratives gains gains higher performance than linking from a full-text narrative to images.

the level of those of detectors for physical objects, while the mean average precision increases by 50% when compared to the sparse-featured approach. In the text classification, we also have reconfirmed the "denser is better" adage, using a full term feature representation to improve the mean average precision score over LDA-based classification. Turning to the full multimedia linking task, we have shown that detectors based on dense feature descriptions from different modalities can be successfully applied to link these modalities together. We have achieved an improvement over the state of the art of 51% relative (14% absolute) for the task of linking texts to an image query, and 56% relative (13% absolute) for the task of linking images to a text query. These results show that combining densely modelled, monomodal classifiers vastly outperforms the joint modelling of sparse features for the multimedia linking of texts and images.

Acknowledgements

This research was partially supported by the Center for Creation, Content and Technology (CCCT), and by the Dutch Ministry of Economic Affairs and Amsterdam Topstad under the Krant van Morgen project.

6. REFERENCES

[1] D. Blei, A. Ng, and M. Jordan. Latent Dirichlet allocation. *The Journal of Machine Learning Research*, 3:993–1022, 2003.

[2] C. Carrick and C. Watters. Automatic association of news items. *Information Processing & Management*, 33(5):615–632, 1997.

[3] G. Csurka, C. Dance, L. Fan, J. Willamowski, and C. Bray. Visual categorization with bags of keypoints. In *Workshop on Statistical Learning in Computer Vision, ECCV*, pages 1–22, 2004.

[4] M. Everingham, L. Van Gool, C. K. I. Williams, J. Winn, and A. Zisserman. The PASCAL Visual Object Classes Challenge 2010 (VOC2010) Results. `http://www.pascal-network.org/challenges/VOC/voc2010/workshop/index.html`.

[5] E. Nowak, F. Jurie, and B. Triggs. Sampling strategies for bag-of-features image classification. *ECCV*, pages 490–503, 2006.

[6] N. Rasiwasia, J. Costa Pereira, E. Coviello, G. Doyle, G. R. Lanckriet, R. Levy, and N. Vasconcelos. A new approach to cross-modal multimedia retrieval. In *ACM MM*, pages 251–260, 2010.

[7] F. Sebastiani. Machine learning in automated text categorization. *ACM Computing Surveys)*, 34(1):1–47, 2002.

[8] J. Sivic and A. Zisserman. Video Google: A text retrieval approach to object matching in videos. In *ICCV*, pages 1470–1477, 2003.

[9] A. F. Smeaton, P. Over, and W. Kraaij. Evaluation campaigns and TRECVid. In *MIR*, pages 321–330, 2006.

[10] C. G. M. Snoek and A. W. M. Smeulders. Visual-concept search solved? *IEEE Computer*, 43(6):76–78, June 2010.

[11] C. G. M. Snoek and M. Worring. Concept-based video retrieval. *Foundations and Trends in Information Retrieval*, 4(2):215–322, 2009.

[12] J. R. R. Uijlings, A. W. M. Smeulders, and R. J. H. Scha. What is the spatial extent of an object? In *CVPR*, pages 770 –777, 2009.

[13] J. R. R. Uijlings, A. W. M. Smeulders, and R. J. H. Scha. Real-time visual concept classification. *IEEE Transactions on Multimedia*, 12(7):665 –681, 2010.

Automatic Concept-to-Query Mapping for Web-based Concept Detector Training *

Damian Borth
University of Kaiserslautern
D-67663 Kaiserslautern, Germany
d_borth@cs.uni-kl.de

Adrian Ulges
German Research Center for Artificial Intelligence (DFKI)
D-67663 Kaiserslautern, Germany
adrian.ulges@dfki.de

Thomas M. Breuel
University of Kaiserslautern
D-67663 Kaiserslautern, Germany
tmb@cs.uni-kl.de

ABSTRACT

Nowadays, online platforms like YouTube provide massive content for training of visual concept detectors. However, it remains a difficult challenge to retrieve the right training content from such platforms since the underlying query construction can be arbitrarily complex. In this paper we present an approach, which offers an automatic *concept-to-query mapping* for training data acquisition from such platforms. Queries are automatically constructed by a keyword selection and a category assignment using ImageNet and Google Sets as external sources. Our results demonstrate that the proposed method is able to reach retrieval results comparable to queries constructed by humans providing 76% more relevant content for detector training than a one-to-one mapping of concept names to retrieval queries would do.

Categories and Subject Descriptors

H.3.3 [**Information Storage and Retrieval**]: Information Retrieval and Indexing

General Terms

Algorithms, Measurement, Experimentation

Keywords

Web Video, Concept Detection, Query Refinement, Query Expansion, Query Mapping

1. INTRODUCTION

As current video collections are growing in size [?] the demand for robust search and retrieval tools increases. One successful approach to provide such tools is concept detection [16], which employs supervised machine learning to build an index of semantic concepts for retrieval. Due to the very time consuming acquisition of positive samples for detector training, socially tagged images and video have been considered as a valid alternative to expert labeled training data [8, 20]. Such data is publicly available at large scale from online platforms like Flickr or YouTube and is associated with a noisy but rich corpus of tags, comments and ratings that are provided by their online communities.

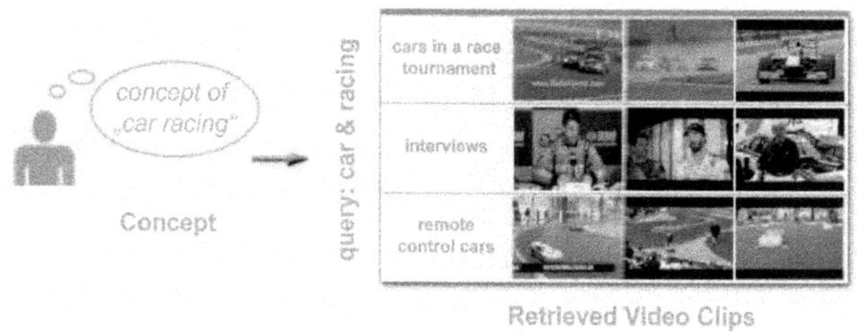

Figure 1: To learn the concept "car racing" a query is formulated to retrieve training material from online portals like YouTube. Unfortunately, a simple query mapping of the concept name will deliver a wide range of related video clips which are not all suitable for visual learning of the concept.

Consequently, prior detector training, such systems must send a query to the desired online platform for training data retrieval. Often, these queries are predefined by a human operator [19] facing the following conditions: First, a proper mapping between a concept definition and a set of keywords is essential as it determines strongly the quality of the retrieved training data and therefore the performance of the resulting system [21]. Second, since good queries can be arbitrarily complex – including tags, category restrictions or time/date constraints – a large set of possible configurations for a query exists, demanding a significant amount of time for query analysis and manual refinement.

This is illustrated in Figure 1, a straightforward mapping of the *concept* "car racing" to the *query* "car racing" may lead to a training set containing non-relevant videos about race driver interviews or clips about remote controlled cars. Knowing this, a query refinement to "car racing tournament -rc -interview" and a restriction to the category "Autos & Vehicle" or "Sports" would reduces ambiguity and increase the amount of relevant content for detector training and finally improve system performance.

*Area chair: Lexing Xie

MM'11, November 28–December 1, 2011, Scottsdale, Arizona, USA.

The key contribution of this paper is a novel approach offering such a *concept-to-query mapping*. This is accomplished by two key features:

1. **Automatic Keyword Selection**: The initial query is expanded by additional keywords based on a combination of tag statistics, ImageNet [5] and GoogleSets.
2. **Automatic Category Assignment**: The second feature is the assignment of a category to a query. This is achieved by utilizing the hierarchical structure of ImageNet in combination with tag statistics from YouTube.

Using the proposed approach, we demonstrate that the fraction of relevant content from retrieved training data using automatically constructed queries is comparable to human constructed queries. Also, query construction can be performed on the fly as it stays within the time span of two seconds, which is a tolerable waiting time for web retrieval [11]. Additionally, this functionality was also build into *lookapp*, a public available demo system for construction of web-based concept detectors [4][1].

This paper is organized as follows: first we discuss related work in the context of visual learning and query formulation (Section 2). After this, the proposed approach is presented (Section 3) and evaluated in quantitative experiments on real-world web video data (Section 4). A discussion concludes the paper (Section 5).

2. RELATED WORK

Web data can be considered as an attractive source for visual learning [13, 14, 15, 17, 18, 20] as it allows to train more flexible and scalable visual recognition systems. However, its exploitation is particular challenging due to its subjective and ambiguous nature containing significant amounts of non-relevant material as reported for Google Image Search [14], Flickr images [9] and web video from YouTube [19].

Different approaches have been presented to cope with this challenge. One group of approaches apply relevance learning, where label relevance is modeled either by kernel density estimation [3, 19], or nearest neighbor voting [8]. Another group of methods tackles the problem by tag re-ranking using graph based random walks [6, 10]. An alternative direction of getting more relevant training material can be the improvement of the initial retrieval by directly manipulating the query, an area related to concept-based query expansion or mapping [12, 22, 24]. Here, methods like relevance feedback, lexical approaches including synonyms, hypernyms or statistical approaches including local or global term frequencies and co-occurrences are employed to identify the most relevant concept for a given query. However, in this paper our main goal is not to satisfy users information need during retrieval but to retrieve video material which is suitable for visual learning of concept detectors. Therefore - from our point of view - we aim not to find the most relevant combination of concept detectors for a given query but to find a *proper* query formulation for a given concept definition.

One part of query construction for e.g. YouTube is the assignment of a category. Research in the area of web video categorization was performed based on visual and tag information [2], text and social information [23] and large-scale web crawling and search engine log data [18]. The proposed

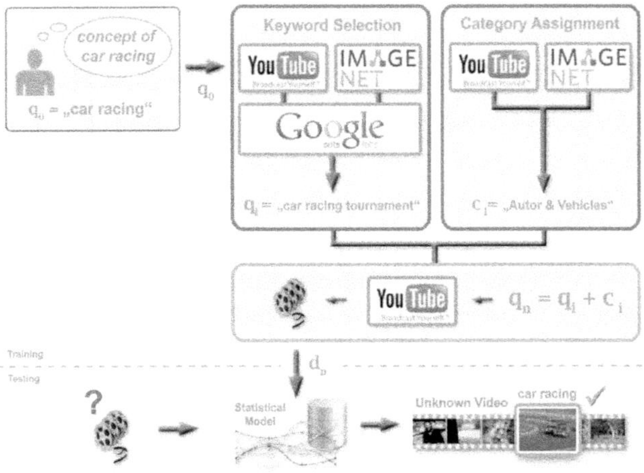

Figure 2: Illustration of the approach. Concepts are trained on downloaded material from online portals like YouTube. To retrieve a list of videos the query q_n must be constructed and send to YouTube (green box). Triggered by an initial concept name q_0 the system performs an automatic keyword selection leading to $q_i = \{car\ racing\ tournament\}$. This keywords are then used to infer a proper category $c_i = \{Autos\ \&\ Vehicles\}$ (red boxes). Both, q_i and c_i, are now used to construct q_n

category assignment is similar to [18], where first tags are recommended and according to this information categories are assigned. However, the setting is different compared to our approach: we select tags and assign categories purely based on concept information and not the visual content of an uploaded video.

3. APPROACH

In the following, a framework for query construction in the context of visual learning from the web is described. The system is outlined in Figure 2: to learn a concept like "car racing" video clips are retrieved from YouTube. This is realized by the construction of a query, which is send to the YouTube API. The core of the proposed approach is an automatic keyword selection and category assignment to a given concept. This process is referred to as *concept-to-query mapping* and is highlighted by the red boxes in Figure 2. Taking the original LSCOM [7] concept name as initial query q_0, an automatic selection of keyword terms leads to an expanded query $q_i = \{car\ racing\ tournament\}$. This query is then used to infer a proper category $c_i = \{Autos\ \&\ Vehicles\}$ for the concept. Finally, the query q_n is constructed from q_i and c_i (green box) used to retrieve training data for concept learning.

3.1 Basic Concepts

In the following, a query q represents the set of parameters which is used to retrieve videos from the YouTube API. This set of parameters may including text, tags, category restrictions and limitations to a particular time span or specific country. In this paper we focus on the most distinctive parameter: keywords and categories leading to the query representation $q = \{t_0, ..., t_n\} * \{c_0, ..., c_m\}$ with n keywords t_i and m category assignments c_j. It should be kept in mind

[1]Lookapp: http://lookapp.appspot.com

that the presented approach is general as it could be applied to all web video portals that allow access to their database through a similar API like YouTube.

3.2 Automatic Keyword Selection

The first step for the *concept-to-query mapping* is to transfer a concept to a set of keywords. The entry point is given by the concept name forming the initial query q_0. It is important to note that this initial query is expected to retrieve a significant amount of non-relevant videos. Based on q_0 a set of synonyms s_{q_0} is retrieved from ImageNet. Here, ImageNet is preferred over WordNet because it covers concepts suitable for visual learning. Additionally, tag statistics are calculated from the set of videos retrieved by q_0. We calculate tag frequencies for each tag appearing in this initial dataset leading to a ranked list t_{q_0} of top tags for q_0. Although we employ stop word removal and neglect digits and dates, this tag list can be considered noisy and less reliable than s_{q_0} for the purpose of disambiguation of concepts. However, with t_{q_0} we expect to capture specific wording of the YouTube community. Fusing s_{q_0} and t_{q_0} we receive a new query $q_1 = \{s_0, ..., s_{n_s}\} \cup \{t_0, ..., t_{n_t}\} \subseteq s_{q_0} \cup t_{q_0}$ with $n_s + n_t = n$ keywords. This query is now send to Google Sets providing additional semantic relations in the context of q_1. Google Sets is a experimental prototype to generate lists of similar items. Its underlying probability model ranks these items according to their appearance in specific HTML structures as found in the world wide web. As a result we receive a ranked list l_{q_1} of keywords, which we limit to n keywords resulting in the final query $q_i = \{t_0, ..., t_n\} \subseteq l_{q_1}$.

3.3 Automatic Category Assignment

As a second step we automatically assign categories to the previously constructed query q_i. Given q_i, a second set of videos is retrieved from YouTube and its category distribution $p(c|videos)$ is calculated. Additionally, for each keyword $t \in q_i$ its corresponding ImageNet synset is found. If no synset is found for $t \in q_i$, this term will not contribute to the category assignment. For each found synset the path from the synset node to the ImageNet root is build and mapped to a YouTube category according to a manual constructed mapping function $map(p)$. This mapping function maps ImageNet's first (and partially second) level synsets to YouTube categories allowing to transfer all $17k$ synsets to all 15 YouTube categories by only providing roughly 60 manual mappings. A mapping – in this context – may just be as straightforward as $Animal \rightarrow Animals$ or as complex as $University \rightarrow Education$. The final step in the category assignment is a ranking of the mapped YouTube categories according to their query dependent distribution $p(c|videos)$ providing the set $c_i = \{c_0, ..., c_m\}$.

The final query q_n can now be constructed by $q_n = \{t_0, ..., t_n\} * \{c_0, ..., c_m\}$ providing an unambiguous query for training data retrieval.

4. EXPERIMENTS

Experiments are performed on a dataset of real-world web video content retrieved from YouTube. For this, we evaluate the 30 concepts from the TRECVID 2011 benchmark, which have been selected by NIST for evaluation. For each concept three experiments have been performed:

- **[exp-1]** query construction by a simple one-to-one mapping of concept name to a YouTube query. Here, concept names from LSCOM are taken.
- **[exp-2]** query construction by manual refinement from a human according to a visual inspection on YouTube.
- **[exp-3]** query construction performed by the proposed automatic concept-to-query mapping from Section 3. Queries were limited to $n = 3$ keywords and $m = 1$ category assignments.

For each query and experiment 100 videos have been retrieved from YouTube and manually reviewed for relevance according to the LSCOM concept definition. This manual inspection – which was based on three keyframes per video clip – evaluates how many of the retrieved video clips truly contain the concept. Since it has been shown that this fraction $x \leq 1.0$ directly influences detector performance [19], it serves as a metric for the quality of the constructed query.

Table 1 illustrates the results of the evaluation. For each concept the fraction $x \leq 1.0$ of relevant content is shown and additionally for **[exp-3]** the automatically constructed queries are printed (for a full overview of used queries including the manually constructed ones, please refer to the website: `http://lookapp.appspot.com/evaluation_mm11`). When comparing these three experiments, we can see that **[exp-1]** queries perform weak i.e. they contain the most non-relevant content when retrieving videos from YouTube. Further, manual refined queries **[exp-2]** and automatically constructed queries **[exp-3]** perform comparable to each other improving the fraction of relevant content by 76%.

For some concepts like "airplane flying" or "boat ship" the approach particularly benefits from ImageNet synonyms whereas for concepts, where no synonyms could be found the focus on frequent YouTube tags may lead query construction into the wrong direction like observed for the concept "throwing" or "singing". Also, for concept with a uncommon concept name like "female human face closeup" the method was not able to retrieve any content from YouTube. However, for the majority of concepts the selected keyword terms were semantically meaningful and related to the concept. Also, for most category assignments the method selected the same category a human operator would do.

5. DISCUSSION

In this paper, we have addressed the challenge of automatically mapping concepts to queries for training data retrieval from sources like YouTube. To achieve this we utilize differed external sources like YouTube, ImageNet and Google Sets. In quantitative experiments with web video retrieved from YouTube, it was shown that the proposed approach is able to achieve comparable results to human constructed queries improving the fraction of relevant material by 76% as compared to a simple one-to-one mapping of a concept name to a YouTube query. Future work will extend the approach by relevance feedback to further improve training data retrieval.

6. ACKNOWLEDGMENTS

This work was supported by the German Research Foundation (DFG), project MOONVID (BR 2517/1-1).

Table 1: Results of the evaluation. Fractions of relevant material i.e fraction of videos containing the concept are displayed for each concept and each of the three experiments. The last line displays the relevance as average over all 30 concepts.

Concept Name	[exp-1]	[exp-2]	[exp-3]	**[exp-3] Queries (keywords; category)**
airplane flying	0.30	0.47	**0.56**	airplane flying aircraft; Autos/Vehicles
animal	0.40	0.89	**0.93**	animal nature; Pets/Animals
Asian people	0.36	**0.52**	0.40	asian people asians; People/Blog
bicycling	0.29	**0.63**	0.62	bicycling city; Sport
boat ship	0.30	0.57	**0.68**	boat ship water; Autos/Vehicles
bus	0.15	0.57	**0.72**	bus buses; Autos/Vehicle
car racing	0.48	0.50	**0.64**	car racing cars; Autos/Vehicles
cheering	0.48	0.27	**0.54**	cheering cheer; Sports
cityscape	0.13	0.12	**0.14**	cityscape architecture; Travel/Events
classroom	0.13	**0.39**	0.36	classroom students; Education
dancing	0.53	0.56	**0.61**	dancing live; None
dark-skinned people	0.62	0.65	**0.79**	dark skinned people; People/Blogs
demonstration or protest	**0.76**	0.72	0.41	demonstration protest funny; News/Politics
doorway	0.07	**0.20**	0.15	doorway vent; Howto/Style
explosion fire	0.33	0.35	**0.61**	explosion fire gasoline; How/Style
female human face closeup	0.04	**0.64**	0.36	female human face closeup; None
flowers	0.11	**0.53**	0.42	flowers green; Howto/Style
ground vehicle	0.31	0.47	**0.70**	ground vehicle military; Autos/Vehicles
hand	0.19	0.51	**0.59**	hand; Science/Technology
mountain	0.11	0.61	**0.70**	mountain peak; Travel/Events
nighttime	0.05	0.28	**0.53**	nighttime building; Travel/Events
old people	0.23	0.23	**0.36**	old people; Comedy
running	0.28	0.35	**0.63**	running basketball; Sports
singing	0.78	**0.88**	0.63	singing fun; None
sitting down	0.02	**0.10**	0.06	sitting down the; Travel/Events
swimming	0.48	**0.78**	0.70	swimming water; Sport
telephones	0.04	**0.67**	0.46	telephone call; Science/Technology
throwing	0.13	**0.65**	0.16	throwing to;None
vehicle	0.31	**0.64**	**0.64**	vehicle car; Autos/Vehicles
walking	0.20	**0.44**	0.09	walking alternative; None
average	0.29	**0.51**	**0.51**	

7. REFERENCES

[1] Thanks, YouTube community, for two BIG gifts on our sixth birthday!. The YouTube Blog; available from http://youtube-global.blogspot.com/2011/05/thanks-youtube-community-for-two-big.html (retrieved: June'11), 2011.

[2] D. Borth, J. Hees, M. Koch, A. Ulges, C. Schulze, T. Breuel, and R. Paredes. TubeFiler – an Automatic Web Video Categorizer. In *Proc. Int. Conf. on Multimedia*, 2009.

[3] D. Borth, A. Ulges, and T.M. Breuel. Relevance Filtering meets Active Learning: Improving web-based Concept Detectors. In *Int. Conf. on Multimedia Information Retrieval (MIR)*, 2010.

[4] D. Borth, A. Ulges, and T.M. Breuel. Lookapp - Interactive Construction of web-based Concept Detectors. In *Int. Conf. on Multimedia Retrieval (ICMR)*, 2011.

[5] J. Deng, W. Dong, R. Socher, L.J. Li, K. Li, and L. Fei-Fei. ImageNet: A Large-Scale Hierarchical Image Database. In *Int. Conf. Computer Vision and Pattern Recognition (CVPR)*, 2009.

[6] W.H. Hsu, L.S. Kennedy, and S.F. Chang. Reranking Methods for Visual Search. *IEEE Transactions on Multimedia*, 14(3):14–22, 2007.

[7] L. Kennedy, A. Hauptmann, M. Naphade, J. Smith, and S.-F. Chang. LSCOM Lexicon Definitions and Annotations Version 1.0. Technical report, Columbia University, 2006.

[8] X. Li, C.G.M. Snoek, and M. Worring. Unsupervised Multi-Feature Tag Relevance Learning for Social Image Retrieval. In *Int. Conf. on Image and Video Retrieval (CIVR)*, 2010.

[9] Xirong Li, Cees G. M. Snoek, and Marcel Worring. Learning social tag relevance by neighbor voting. *IEEE Transactions on Multimedia*, 11(7):1310–1322, 2009.

[10] D. Liu, X.S. Hua, L. Yang, M. Wang, and H.J. Zhang. Tag Ranking. In *Int. Conf. on World Wide Web*, 2009.

[11] F.F.H. Nah. A study on tolerable waiting time: how long are Web users willing to wait? *Behaviour & Information Technology*, 23(3):153–163, 2004.

[12] A.P. Natsev, A. Haubold, J. Tešić, L. Xie, and R. Yan. Semantic Concept-based Query Expansion and Re-ranking for Multimedia Retrieval. In *Int. Conf. on Multimedia*, 2007.

[13] C. Ramachandran, R. Malik, X. Jin, J. Gao, K. Nahrstedt, and J. Han. VideoMule: a Consensus Learning Approach to Multi-label Classification from Noisy User-Generated Videos. In *Int. Conf. on Multimedia*, 2009.

[14] F. Schroff, A. Criminisi, and A. Zisserman. Harvesting Image Databases from the Web. In *Int. Conf. Computer Vision (ICCV)*, 2007.

[15] A. Setz and C. Snoek. Can Social Tagged Images Aid Concept-Based Video Search? In *Int. Conf. on Multimedia and Expo (ICME)*, 2009.

[16] C. Snoek and M. Worring. Concept-based Video Retrieval. *Foundations and Trends in Information Retrieval*, 4(2):215–322, 2009.

[17] Y. Sun, S. Shimada, Y. Taniguchi, and A. Kojima. A Novel Region-based Approach to Visual Concept Modeling using Web Images. In *Int. Conf. on Multimedia*, 2008.

[18] G. Toderici, H. Aradhye, M. Pasca, L. Sbaiz, and J. Yagnik. Finding meaning on YouTube: Tag Recommendation and Category Discovery. In *Int. Conf. on Computer Vision and Pattern Recognition (CVPR)*, 2010.

[19] A. Ulges, D. Borth, and T. Breuel. Visual Concept Learning from Weakly Labeled Web Videos. In *Video Search and Mining*. Springer-Verlag, 2009.

[20] A. Ulges, C. Schulze, M. Koch, and T. Breuel. The Challenge of Tagging Online Video. *Comp. Vis. Img. Underst.*, 2009.

[21] A. Ulges. *Visual Concept Learning from User-tagged Web Video*. Phd-thesis, University of Kaiserslautern, 10 2009.

[22] D. Wang, X. Li, J. Li, and B. Zhang. The Importance of Query-Concept-Mapping for Automatic Video Retrieval. In *Int. Conf. on Multimedia*, 2007.

[23] C.W. Ngo X. Wu, W.L. Zhao. Towards Google Challenge: Combining Contextual and Social Information for Web Video Categorization. In *Int. Conf. on Multimedia*, 2009.

[24] R. Yan and A.G. Hauptmann. A Review of Text and Image Retrieval Approaches for Broadcast News Video. *Information Retrieval*, 10(4):445–484, 2007.

Hypergraph Spectral Hashing for Similarity Search of Social Image * †

Yueting Zhuang, Yang Liu, Fei Wu, Yin Zhang, Jian Shao
College of Computer Science, Zhejiang University
Hangzhou, China
{yzhuang, liuy, wufei, jshao, zhangyin98}@cs.zju.edu.cn

ABSTRACT

The development of social media brings great challenges to image retrieval on both efficiency and accuracy. In addition to achieving fast similarity search over large scale data, it is very crucial to represent the complex and high-order relationships among the social contents to improve the semantic understanding of social images. In this paper, unified hypergraph is implemented to model the various relationships among images and other contexts in social media. Moreover, we extend traditional spectral hashing to hypergraph to accelerate similarity search of social images by mapping semantically related vertices into similar binary codes within a short Hamming distance. Furthermore, the proposed HSH approach is extended to out-of-sample data in a supervised manner. We evaluated our approach on the dataset crawled from *Flickr* and the experiment results indicate that our proposed HSH approach is both efficient and effective.

Categories and Subject Descriptors

H.3.3 [**Information Storage and Retrieval**]: Information Search and Retrieval

General Terms

Algorithms, Experimentation, Performance

1. INTRODUCTION

During last few years, many photo sharing websites, such as *Flickr*, *Picasa Web Album*, have become popular with numerous photos uploaded everyday. These photo sharing websites not only provide a platform for photo sharing but also enable users to create photo galleries, add comments or tags as well as join into user communities, *etc.* The social resources contributed by users can greatly facilitate the browsing and searching of social images. For example, images uploaded by the same user or annotated by the same tag are more likely to be related in semantic.

Over the past decades, many advances have been made on text and content based image retrieval [7, 4]. However, the explosion of social media brings new challenges because more cues can be utilized to understand the semantic of images. The various types of features(such as the low-level features and social contents contributed by users) among social images complement each other to exactly express the semantics of images. It is therefore critical to find a appropriate representation mechanism that integrates homogenous and heterogenous features to improve the understanding of high-level semantics of social images.

Moreover, fast finding the similar images to a given query from large scale social images is another important issue. Accordingly, a better similarity index structure to encode the complicated correlations is very desirable for building scalable content-based search systems in social media.

Recently, hashing technologies [8, 1, 9, 10] were widely adopted on scalable image retrieval applications. In these approaches, each item in the database is transformed into compact binary codes that preserve the original structure of data and the similarity of two items is measured by the Hamming distance between their corresponding binary codes which is extremely fast to calculate. Nevertheless, these approaches have two drawbacks when they are directly introduced to social image indexing:

1. The current hashing approaches only utilize the pairwise distances to represent the relations among images while the relationships in real social media settings tend to be complex and high-order.

2. The social contents of different images are widely divergent. Some images contain tags and uploader information while some do not. Hence it is infeasible to measure the similarity of these images from a same metric space.

In this paper, we aim to take the social contents of images into consideration and design a better semantic hashing algorithm to achieve fast similarity search of large scale social images. We first represent complex and higher-order relationships in social media by hypergraph [3] in which an edge can connect more than two vertices. Then *Hypergraph Spectral Hashing* (HSH) is proposed so that semantically related images are mapped to similar codes within a short Hamming

*This work is supported by National Natural Science Foundation of China (No. 90920303, No. 60833006), 973 program (2010CB327904).

†Area chair: Tat-Seng Chua

MM'11, November 28–December 1, 2011, Scottsdale, Arizona, USA.

distance. In order to gain the binary codes of out-of-sample data, a supervised learning method is conducted to learn the hashing functions for novel inputs. The effectiveness and superiority of our proposed approach are demonstrated by experiments conducted on our crawled *Flickr* dataset.

2. HYPERGRAPH SPECTRAL HASHING

In this section we introduce our proposed hypergraph representation and its corresponding hashing mechanism.

2.1 Hypergraph Construction

In this work, we use unified hypergraph [6] to model the objects and relationships in social media where different type of objects can be uniformly viewed as vertices in the hypergraph. More specifically, we use five types of vertices corresponding to the images, users, tags, locations and user groups, which constitute the vertex set V.

Furthermore, we introduce edge set E which contains homogeneous and heterogeneous hyperedges to represent the various similarities and relationships among these vertices.

- **Homogeneous hyperedges:** The *homogenous hyperedges* are utilized here to connect similar homogenous vertices, *i.e.*, similar images measured by low-level visual feature, such as color, edge and shape.
- **Heterogeneous hyperedges:** The *heterogeneous hyperedges* are conducted to connect image vertices with other vertices to represent the complex and high-order relationships induced by social media. For example, a user vertex and image vertices can be connected by a *heterogenous hyperedges* to represent the relationship that the user is an owner of these images.

In particular, a weight parameter $w(e_i)$ is assigned to each hyperedge $e_i \in E$ according to its importance in the hypergraph. By adding all hyperedges to the hyperedge set E with weight function w, we can construct the complete unified hypergraph denoted as $G(V, E, w)$.

2.2 Spectral Hashing on Hypergraph

Given the constructed unified hypergraph $G(V, E, w)$, for each vertex $v_i \in V$, semantic hashing seeks to find a mapping function $\mathbf{f}$ that can map vertex v_i into an l dimension binary code $\mathbf{y}_i$ defined as follows[1]:

$$\mathbf{f} : v_i \to \mathbf{y}_i \in \{-1, 1\}^l \tag{1}$$

According to [9], the mapping function should have the following good merits: (1) The similarity is preserved by mapping similar vertices in the hypergraph into similar binary codes that have a small hamming distance; (2) The mapping function tends to generate compact binary codes and only a small number of bits are required to code the whole dataset; (3) The mapping function could handle the out-of-sample inputs.

To keep the similarity of vertices in binary hashing code, the mapping function is expected to map vertices in the same hyperedge with more similar binary codes. Motivated by this idea, we seek to find the hashing function that can minimize the average Hamming distance between binary codes of vertices in the same hyperedge. Moreover, we require each bit of the binary code to have a 50% probability of being 1 or -1 for the sake of coding efficiency.

[1]In this stage, hashing code for all kinds of vertices in the hypergraph are generated while only the hashing code of image vertices are actually used in later stage

Let $\{\mathbf{y}_i\}_{i=1}^n$ be the list of binary codes of all n vertices, for vertex $v_i, v_j \in V$ in hyperedge $e_k \in E$, as in [11], the normalized hamming distance between v_i and v_j on e_k is $\frac{w(e_k)}{\delta(e_k)}(\mathbf{y}_i/\sqrt{d(v_i)} - \mathbf{y}_j/\sqrt{d(v_j)})^2$. To minimize the average distance of all the vertices and hyperedges, we obtain the following optimal objective function of *Hypergraph Spectral Hashing*:

$$minimize : \frac{1}{2} \sum_{e_k \in E} \sum_{\{v_i, v_j\} \subseteq e} \frac{w(e_k)}{\delta(e_k)} (\frac{\mathbf{y}_i}{\sqrt{d(v_i)}} - \frac{\mathbf{y}_j}{\sqrt{d(v_j)}})^2 \tag{2}$$

$$s.t. : \{\mathbf{y}_i\}_{i=1}^n \in \{-1, 1\}$$

$$\sum_{i=1}^{n} \mathbf{y}_i = 0$$

$$\frac{1}{n} \sum_{i=1}^{n} \mathbf{y}_i \mathbf{y}_i^T = I$$

By introducing the *hypergraph laplacian* from [11], the average distance over all vertices can be rewritten as:

$$\sum_{e_k \in E} \sum_{\{v_i, v_j\} \subseteq e_k} \frac{w(e_k)}{\delta(e_k)} (\frac{\mathbf{y}_i}{\sqrt{d(v_i)}} - \frac{\mathbf{y}_j}{\sqrt{d(v_j)}})^2 = 2Y^T \Delta Y \tag{3}$$

where Y is a $n \times k$ matrix whose jth row is $\mathbf{y}_j^T$ and

$$\Delta = I - \frac{1}{2} D_v^{-1/2} H W D_e^{-1} H^T D_v^{-1/2} \tag{4}$$

Accordingly, we can rewrite the above optimal function as:

$$minimize : trace(Y^T \Delta Y) \tag{5}$$

$$s.t. : Y(i, j) \in \{-1, 1\}$$

$$Y^T 1 = 0$$

$$Y^T Y = I$$

According to [9], the solution of Equation (5) is an NP hard problem. However, we can remove the constraint $Y(i, j) \in \{-1, 1\}$ and convert this solution of Equation (5) into a hypergraph partition problem. Equation (3) shows that Δ is positive semi-definite and the smallest eigenvalue of Δ is 0. So the solutions of the simplified problem is the k eigenvectors of Δ with minimal eigenvalue(after excluding the eigenvectors which has eigenvalue 0). To obtain the binary codes, we just need threshold these eigenvectors to binary values.

2.3 Extension for Novel Input

The stage mentioned above only obtains the binary codes of images already contained in the hypergraph. However, given novel query images which are not represented in the hypergraph, it would be time-consuming and unrealistic to update the constructed hypergraph to produce the binary hashing codes of novel images.

Obtaining hashing code for novel query input is closely related to the *out-of-sample-extension* problem in manifold learning. Traditionally Nystörm methods [2] and Spectral Hashing [9] are involved to resolve this challenge. However, these methods are either computing expensive or depend on a very restrictive assumption of the distribution of data.

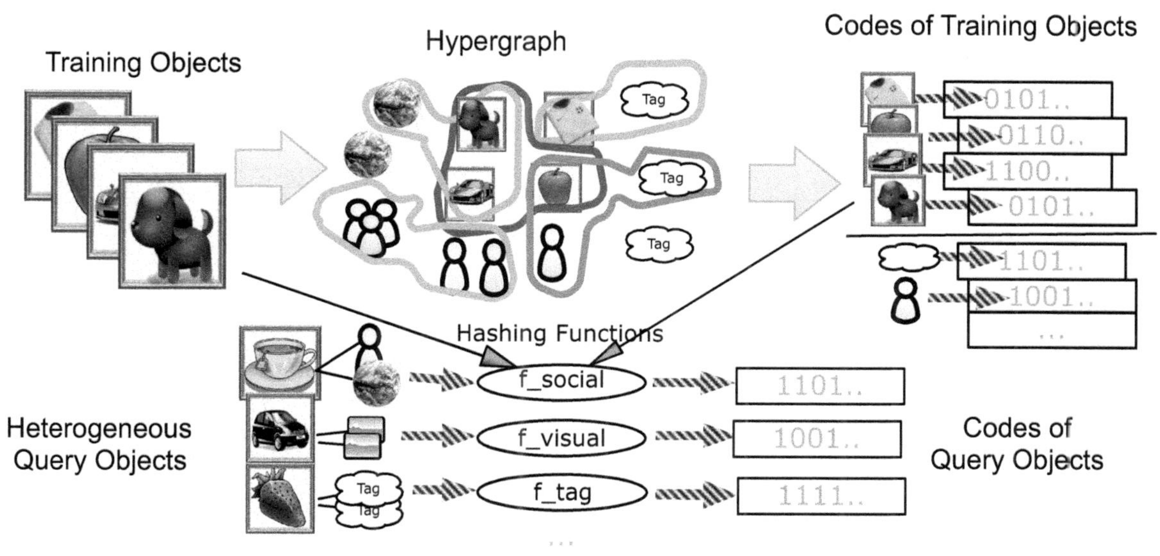

Figure 1: The training images and their corresponding features are first constructed as a hypergraph and Hypergraph Spectral Hashing is conducted to obtain the compact binary codes of the image vertices. Then we learn different hashing functions by different types of features to handle various querying modalities

As the features in social media objects are widely divergent and the retrieval of social media need to be very efficient, above methods are not suitable for our application. In [10], Zhang *et al.* considered this problem as a supervised process and proposed *Self-Taught Hashing* approach. In this paper, we extend this supervised learning approach to *Hypergraph Spectral Hashing* for novel query inputs. Given the obtained l dimension binary codes $\mathbf{y}_i$ of each training image, we think of each bit $\{\mathbf{y}_i^p\}_{p=1}^l \in \{+1, -1\}$ in $\mathbf{y}_i$ as a binary class label of image v_i and train a binary classifier $f^p(x)$ by the features of training images. Then the l learned binary classifiers $f^1(x), f^2(x), \ldots, f^l(x)$ are concatenated as a hashing function $\mathbf{f}(x)$ to predict the l-bit binary code of each query image. Moreover, we train different hashing functions using different feature vectors including visual feature, text feature(tags), and other social context(users and locations).

In this work, we used Support Vector Machine(SVM) with non-linear kernels as the classifier to achieve non-linear mappings from different feature vectors to their binary codes. Figure 1 shows the whole procedure of the proposed *Hypergraph Spectral Hashing.*

3. EXPERIMENTS

In this section, we evaluated the performance of our proposed algorithm on social image datasets and demonstrate the advantage of our method by comparing to some *state-of-the-art* approaches.

3.1 Data Preparation

To make our evaluation more practical and reasonable, we collected our own dataset from *Flickr* using *Flickr* public API. Firstly, we selected 100 popular photo sharing groups on different topics from *Flickr*. Furthermore, we crawled images from these groups as well as their social contexts (uploaders, tags, user communities and locations). As the images in the same photo group are similar in content, the group labels of the images were used as the ground-truth to evaluate relevance between query image and retrieved images.

The whole image collection for experiments consists of more than 50,000 images. We selected those images with rich social information as the training images to learn the hashing functions. To achieve a better performance of image retrieval, users, tags and locations were also preprocessed to filter irrelevant information. Moreover, we extracted the following five kinds of low-level visual features from our image collection: Color histogram and color moments, Edge histogram, Gabor wavelets coefficients, Local Binary Pattern, and GIST.

To construct the hypergraph, for each image vertex, we added *homogenous hyperedges* to connect it with its k nearest neighbors vertices based on the similarity of different low-level visual features. In our experiment, k is set to 300 and we set the weight of each *homogeneous hyperedge* by using the average distance of its neighbors, which assumes that the closer its neighbors are, the higher weight the hyperedge will have. Besides, we also connected semantically similar tag vertices measured by word-net similarities[2] with *homogenous hyperedges* .

In addition, five *heterogenous hyperedges* were adopted to represent the relationships among images and different social objects:

- Hyperedges that connect tag vertices with image vertices annotated by this tag.
- Hyperedges that connect user, image and tags vertices together to represent the high-order tagging activity.
- Hyperedges that connect location vertices with image vertices taken by this location.

[2]http://wn-similarity.sourceforge.net/

	visual			tag			social		
Method	8bit	16bit	32bit	8bit	16bit	32bit	8bit	16bit	32bit
LSH	0.1640	0.1652	0.1634	0.1680	0.1675	0.1683	0.1644	0.1644	0.1644
SSC	0.2154	0.2264	0.2323	0.1690	0.1828	0.1879	0.1651	0.1654	0.1653
SpH	0.2513	0.2558	0.2563	0.1952	0.2555	0.3134	0.1981	0.1981	0.2176
STH	0.2194	0.2264	0.2283	0.2850	0.3011	0.3009	0.2749	0.2854	**0.3074**
HSH	**0.2716**	**0.2899**	**0.2915**	**0.3229**	**0.3665**	**0.3927**	**0.2859**	**0.2883**	0.2868

Table 1: The performance comparison of algorithms in terms of F1-score at different code length by different features

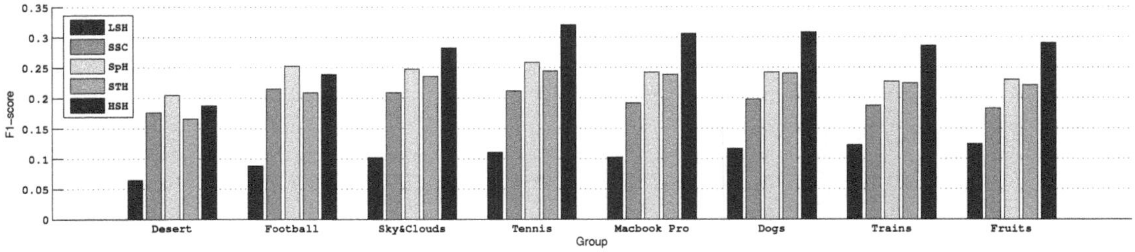

Figure 2: The performance comparison of algorithms in terms of F1-score on different photo groups

- Hyperedges that connect user vertices with image vertices uploaded by this user.
- Hyperedges that connect user community vertices with user vertices belong to this user community.

The weights of all the heterogenous hyperedges are set to 1 equally.

3.2 Experimental Results and Analysis

In our experiment, all of the training images were encoded into compact binary codes by our proposed *Hypergraph Spectral Hashing* (HSH) and other competitive methods, including LSH [5], Boosting-SCC [8], Spectral Hashing (SpH) [9] and Self-Taught Hashing (STH) [10]. For each query image, we used its hashing codes to find the similar images in the training set by comparing their Hamming distances F1-scores were calculated to evaluate the retrieval results. The experiments were performed on the binary codes generated by three different individual features. We used 500 queries from 20 groups in our dataset as query images and the result on different features at different code length are reported in Table 1. Moreover, Figure 2 gives out the retrieval results on 8 photos groups selected from the whole dataset.

The experiment results indicate that *Hypergraph Spectral Hashing* outperforms other hashing methods on different features at different code length. The main reason is probably that the hashing functions of HSH are learned from hypergraph which captures the high-order relations between different features. Although the hashing codes are generated by different features individually, the hashing functions already captures the latent information of other features and therefore the performance of HSH is boosted.

4. CONCLUSIONS

In this paper, we introduce a novel hashing framework for image search on social media. We first model the relationships in social media by hypergraph and obtain the binary codes of vertices using spectral hashing on hypergraph. Furthermore, we extend our model to novel inputs by different hashing functions learned in a supervised manner. The experiment results on our *Flickr* dataset demonstrate the effectiveness and efficiency of our proposed method. This work also inspired us that the accuracy of the social image search can be greatly improved by utilizing the social content of images. As a general framework, it is easy to extend our approach to other media and social media environments.

References

[1] A. Andoni and P. Indyk. Near-optimal hashing algorithms for approximate nearest neighbor in high dimensions. In *Annual Symposium on Foundations of Computer Science*, pages 459–468, 2006.

[2] Y. Bengio, O. Delalleau, N. L. Roux, J.-F. Paiement, P. Vincent, and M. Ouimet. Learning eigenfunctions links spectral embedding and kernel pca. *Neural Computation*, 16(10):2197–2219, 2004.

[3] C. Berge. *Graphs and hypergraphs.* North-Holland Public Company, 1973.

[4] R. Datta, D. Joshi, J. Li, and J. Z. Wang. Image retrieval: Ideas, influences, and trends of the new age. *ACM Comput. Surv.*, 40:5:1–5:60, May 2008.

[5] A. Gionis, P. Indyk, and R. Motwani. Similarity search in high dimensions via hashing. In *VLDB*, pages 518–529, 1999.

[6] C. C. C. W. H. W. L. Z. Jiajun Bu, Shulong Tan and X. He. Music recommendation by unified hypergraph: combining social media information and music content. In *ACM Multimedia*, 2010.

[7] Y. Rui, T. S. Huang, and S. fu Chang. Image retrieval: Current techniques, promising directions and open issues. *Journal of Visual Communication and Image Representation*, 10:39–62, 1999.

[8] G. Shakhnarovich, P. A. Viola, and T. Darrell. Fast pose estimation with parameter-sensitive hashing. In *ICCV*, pages 750–759, 2003.

[9] Y. Weiss, A. Torralba, and R. Fergus. Spectral hashing. In *NIPS*, pages 1753–1760, 2008.

[10] D. Zhang, J. Wang, D. Cai, and J. Lu. Self-taught hashing for fast similarity search. In *SIGIR*, pages 18–25, 2010.

[11] D. Zhou, J. Huang, and B. Schölkopf. Learning with hypergraphs: Clustering, classification, and embedding. In *NIPS*, pages 1601–1608, 2006.

Selecting the Best Faces to Index Presentation Videos *

Michele Merler
Department of Computer Science
Columbia University
New York, NY 10027
mmerler@cs.columbia.edu

John R. Kender
Department of Computer Science
Columbia University
New York, NY 10027
jrk@cs.columbia.edu

ABSTRACT

We propose a system to select the most representative faces in unstructured presentation videos with respect to two criteria: to optimize matching accuracy between pairs of face tracks, and to select humanly preferred face icons for indexing purposes. We first extract face tracks using state-of-the-art face detection and tracking. A small subset of images are then selected per track in order to maximize matching accuracy between tracks. Finally, representative images are extracted for each speaker in order to build a face index of the video. We tested our approach on 3 unstructured presentation videos of approximately 45 minutes each, for a total of a quarter million frames. Compared to the standard min-min approach, our method achieves higher track matching accuracy (94.22%), while using 6% of the running time. Using an optimal combination of 3 user preference measures, we were able to build face indexes containing 54 speakers (out of the 58 present in the videos) indexing into 795 detected tracks.

Categories and Subject Descriptors H.3 [Information Storage and Retrieval]: H.3.1 Content Analysis and Indexing; D.2.8 [Content representation]:
General Terms Algorithms, Human Factors
Keywords Video Indexing, Face Tracking and Matching

1. INTRODUCTION

Various systems have been proposed to automatically index professional videos such as movies, TV shows, and news based on characters appearing in them [4]. Likewise, in the surveillance and biometrics fields, there is great interest in building high quality compact yet complete face logs from large unstructured static camera footage, to be presented to analysts for further processing[10]. Our work lies at the convergence of these two trends, as it aims at indexing unstructured presentation videos based on speaker appearances, and uses quality measures to select representative face images.

Not much attention has been given instead to unstructured videos shot in uncontrolled environments. The determination of the "best" faces for recognition purposes (especially in terms of pose) has been studied both from a psychological [3] and computational point of view [8].The results suggest that humans are able to infer the full 3D information about the head of a person when seeing a 3/4 view of their face. Liu et al. [8] analyzed the same problem from the computer vision point of view and verified that a 32° pose provides the best generalization performance for face matching algorithms. In the surveillance domain, Fourney et al. [5] present a series of quality measures (based on pose,illumination,sharpness, resolution and skin) to reduce face tracks into face logs.

To the best of our knowledge, the only work trying to assess the quality of speakers video indexes for unstructured presentation videos is the one by Haubold et al. [7], who have conducted user studies comparing head vs. head and shoulders person representation indexes. However, such indexes were created manually and not automatically.

2. FACE TRACKS GENERATION

Face tracks are sequences of consecutive frames in which a face is tracked. Since the videos we investigate are unedited and unstructured, we cannot rely on standard shot detection algorithms to segment the video into shots. We therefore implemented a simple loose shot boundaries detector, which splits each frame into 9x5 regions, and then thresholds mean gray scale differences between corresponding regions in frames separated by a step 3 frames. While simple, this loose shot boundaries detection algorithm is 98% accurate and prevents inconvenient behaviors of the tracker.

In order to find "seed" faces (where to initialize the tracker), we use the Viola Jones face detector. To alleviate the significant amount of false detections originating from the noisy videos, we applied the skin color filter introduced by Gomez et al. [6] to each pixel in the candidate face regions. The resulting skin model in the RGB colorspace is the following:

$$Pixel = skin \iff \begin{cases} R/G > 1.185 & and \\ \frac{R*B}{(R+G+B)^2} > 0.107 & and \\ \frac{R*G}{(R+G+B)^2} > 0.112 \end{cases} \quad (1)$$

We then empirically evaluated that restricting a face track seed to require that more than 20% of the pixels in a candidate region had skin tone, resulted in doubling face track detection precision performances with respect to the default

*Area chair: Bernard Merialdo

This research was supported in part by NSF grant IIS-0713064.

MM'11, November 28–December 1, 2011, Scottsdale, Arizona, USA.

Video	#Frames	#Speak.	#GTracks	#DTracks	GATL	DATL	TPrec.	TRecall	TF1	Radius
1	85K	19	77	213	1718	830	0.896	0.637	0.745	7.11
2	103K	19	77	378	2249	640	0.916	0.584	0.713	6.01
3	65K	20	72	204	1367	551	0.921	0.581	0.713	5.92
Total	253K	58	226	795	1787	673	0.911	0.6	0.723	5.34

Table 1: Experiments videos ground truth information and tracking performances: number of frames, number of speakers, number of ground truth (G) and detected (D) tracks and Average Track Length (ATL, in frames). Tracking performances in terms of Precision, Recall, F1 and average Euclidean distance(Radius) between ground truth region and system region.

Viola Jones face detector, while maintaining the same level of recall. Once the seed has been established for a face track, we track the face in both temporal directions, until the track exits the frame borders or one of the detected shots boundaries is encountered.

We use the appearance based online multiple instance learning tracker (MILTrack) recently introduced by Babenko et al. [2], integrating it with face detections to alleviate the drifting effect in the following way. We start at a track seed, and initialize MILTrack with it. At each frame t, if we are within the loose shot boundaries determined as described above and the predicted position of the tracked region is not outside the frame, we proceed with the tracking step.

In case the Viola Jones detector finds a region $\mathbf{f}_t^O$ overlapping the output of MILTrack $\mathbf{f}_t^P = (x, y, w)$, we then consider $\mathbf{f}_t^P$ to be the noisy prediction part of a simplified, steady-state Kalman filter, while the Viola Jones detection provides a noisy observation $\mathbf{f}_t^O$. A parameter α determines how to optimally weight the prediction over the observation, and it is fixed a priori between 0 and 1. Therefore at each frame t the position of the tracked face will be fixed according to the following Equation:

$$\mathbf{f}_t \leftarrow \alpha \mathbf{f}_t^P + (1 - \alpha)\mathbf{f}_t^O \qquad (2)$$

The tracking process is re-initialized in case another face track seed $\mathbf{S}_t$ is encountered while tracking, since the confidence of being correctly on target in a track seed is extremely high. In Table 1 we report the tracking precision, recall and F1, as well as the average L2 distance between ground truth and tracked region face centers, obtained with the best $\alpha = 0.6, 0.5, 0.8$ for videos 1, 2 and 3 respectively.

3. OPTIMAL FACE SELECTION

We propose to process face tracks to select the most useful faces for both track matching and indexing purposes. We perform such selection based on the following three quality measures [5, 8].

Pose. We select faces presenting a 3/4 view, following the literature [3, 8] and the results of an informal user study in which we asked people which pose representation of a face they preferred to be shown to them as part of a visual face index. In order to do so, we trained a left 3/4 and right 3/4 pose detector using 1200 images from the FaceTracer[1] dataset. Each classifier is an SVM with RBF kernel based on edge histogram extracted in 5x5 uniformly split regions in an image.

SkinRatio. We select faces with a high fraction of the image occupied by skin pixels, using the filter introduced in Equation 1. This measure is useful to exclude samples where the tracker drifted away from the face of a speaker.

Resolution. We select faces that are large. The low resolution of the videos in our dataset (in particular video 3, 432x240) demands that the index must contain face images with as much close-up as possible.

We want to stress that our approach for face selection within a track is independent from the matching descriptor choice across tracks. In order to perform across tracks matches, we chose to represent each face with the Local Binary Pattern (LBP) descriptor [1]. We split each face into a 7x7 grid and concatenate LBP histograms computed from all the regions into a 2891 dimensional feature vector $\mathbf{v}$. Finally, we use the square root of the Euclidean distance between feature vectors as a metric to evaluate the similarity between two feature vectors $\mathbf{v1}$ and $\mathbf{v2}$.

In order to select faces for the final speakers visual index, we took into account another result of our informal user study: people preferred to be shown a head-and-shoulder representation of a speaker, rather than simply the face by itself. Therefore, while the quality analysis was conducted on the face region, when producing the visual indexes reported in Figure 3 we enlarged the face bounding box by 20% horizontally and vertically, and further duplicated its height to include a head and shoulder view.

4. EXPERIMENTS

We ran experiments on 3 different MPEG videos containing student presentations, for a total of more than 2 hours of footage and one quarter of a million frames. The videos were recorded by non-professionals and are unedited. They also present challenges in that the camera is rarely steady, there are not clean cuts to identify shots, resolution is low, and they lack structure. Table 1 presents the information about number of speakers and tracks of the inspected videos.

4.1 Face Tracks Extraction and Matching

In order to perform matching between tracks, a standard approach used among others by Everingham et al. [4] consists in computing the min-min distance between tracks T1 and T2, that is, compute the distance between each possible pair of elements $t1 \in T1$ and $t2 \in T2$.

We tested two methods to selection subsets of elements to match in each track: the first one involves a simple temporal sampling of the faces in the track, while the second consists in an unsupervised method based on image quality measures. For temporal sampling, we simply selected one face every n examples, and we tried values of $n = 1, 3, 10, 100$.

We evaluated track matching accuracy for each video, using the extracted tracks with best tracking precision in each video. Matching is performed in a Nearest Neighbor classification framework: given a reference track T_r, we compute the distance between the reference and all the tracks T_i in

[1]http://www.cs.columbia.edu/CAVE/projects/face_search

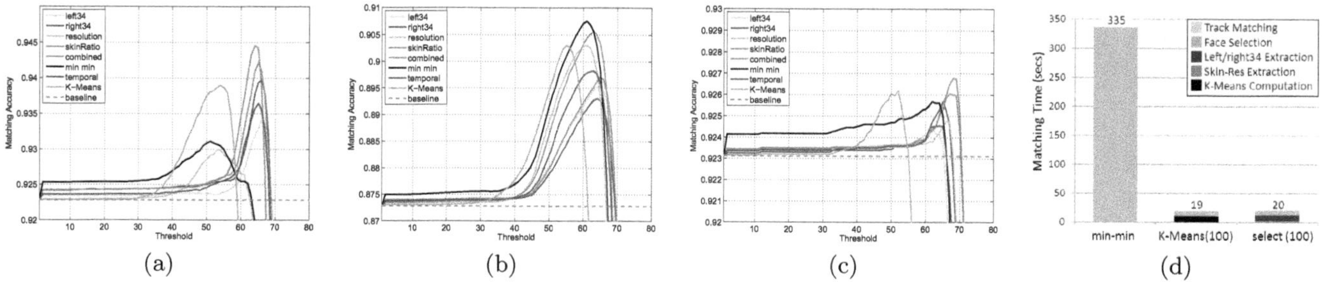

Figure 1: (a)-(c) Matching accuracy performance for the three investigated videos. (d) Average processing time (in seconds) for track matching. Comparison between the min-min standard approach, K-means clustering (in dark blue) and the proposed selection method, which is based of 4 steps: skinRatio and image resolution extraction (2.46 seconds, in red), pose classifier evaluation (9.08 seconds, in violet), face selection (0.02 seconds, in green) and track matching (8.18 seconds when the top 100 faces for each track are retained, in light blue). Note that, unlike our proposed method, K-means does not provide face indexes.

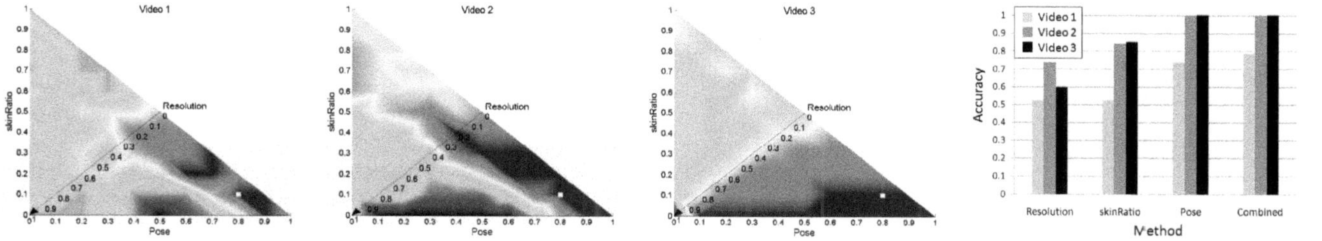

Figure 2: Selection accuracy for index building on the three investigated videos. Heat map of the accuracy given combinations of quality measures in Equation 3. The white squares represent the optimal combination, which is $\mathbf{w} = (0.8, 0.1, 0.1)^T$, interestingly shared across all three videos.

the video which do not temporally overlap with it (we consider that if two tracks overlap temporally, they must belong to different individuals). We retain the track T_i which has the smallest distance $d(r, i)$ to T_r to be a candidate match, and if $d(r, i)$ is smaller than a matching threshold, we consider that T_r and T_i are a match. We compared four different modalities to compute the distance between two tracks.

The first modality (min-min) is to compute the distance between all pairs of images $d(\mathbf{v}_r^m, \mathbf{v}_i^n)$, where $\mathbf{v}_r^m \in T_r$ and $\mathbf{v}_i^n \in T_i$, and keep the minimum distance to represent the distance between the tracks. This method presents two limitations in our unconstrained domain. The first one is efficiency, given the large amount of redundancy present in each track due to the temporal domain of a video. The second is accuracy, since the face tracks generation module returns a set of tracks which can be considered noisy, containing false positives from the seeds detection stage, and drifts in tracking caused cutting of face regions.

The second modality involves using a temporal sampling of n faces in each track, computing the distances between these reduced sets and retain the minimum one.

The third modality employs K-means clustering in the LBP feature space, as suggested by Mau et al.[9]. The $K = n$ cluster centers are used to compute the distances between tracks, and the minimum distance is kept.

The last modality consists in computing the distances only between the n top track faces which are selected based on the response to our quality measure filters (see Section 3).

For temporal, K-means, and selection matching we retained $n = 100$ samples from each track (or the whole track in case the length of the track is smaller than 100). Experiments with $n = 1, 3, 10$ were also conducted and provided worse matching accuracy results, which we omit for brevity.

Figure 1 reports track matching accuracy as the threshold varies in percentage of the range of values of the track distances. In the Figure we report a baseline which predicts all pairs to be non-matches. For all videos, all selection-based matching methods present a global maximum in the accuracy with respect to the chosen threshold. The optimal threshold seems to be consistently located between 60% and 70% of the range of distances between tracks. From the results shown in Figure 1, not only the computational cost of computing the distances between tracks is reduced when using filtering techniques to reduce the number of image pairs to match, but matching accuracy increases in two out of three videos. This is due to the reduction or removal of noisy, drifted, or partially cut images from the tracks which is accomplished through sampling. The the skin color-based filter provides the best results in such videos. In fact, proper face matching requires a full face occupying most of the image, which is best guaranteed by the skin color filter.

Figure 1(d) shows the computational gain of using the proposed face selection method within tracks before matching. Notwithstanding the overhead introduced by feature extraction and face selection before matching, the proposed approach achieves a higher level of track matching accuracy while needing approximately 6% the running time of min-min matching. This is due to the greatly reduced computational complexity of matching each pair of tracks: $O(k^2)$ (with $k = 100$ in our experiments) versus $O(n^2)$ for min-min, where n is the number of frames in a track. According to Table 1 the relationship between k and n is on average of 1 to 6.7, which is quite significant when squared.

We tested a series of possible combinations of the three

Figure 3: Generated visual speaker index. Most of the images show the desired 3/4 head and shoulder view of the speaker. Some fail, either by portraying the wrong person (in red) with respect to the ground truth or by presenting a full profile (in magenta), from which is hard to identify the person.

quality measures according to the following formula (each quality measure is normalized between 0 and 1):

$$Q = w1 \cdot pose + w2 \cdot resolution + w3 \cdot skinRatio \quad (3)$$

with *pose* being either $left34$ or $right34$. We empirically found that the best combinations of $\mathbf{w} = (w1, w2, w3)^T$ were $(0.0, 0.3, 0.7)^T$, $(0.3, 0.1, 0.6)^T$ and $(0.0, 0.7, 0.3)^T$ for video 1, 2 and 3 respectively, and $pose = right34$ for all videos. It is interesting to notice how $resolution$ is much more important for the low resolution video 3, while *pose* does not seem to be fundamental, probably because faces with different poses were matched against each other.

We also note that the performance of our selection method is comparable with K-means clustering both in terms of accuracy and efficiency. However, our selection method provides us also with the candidate faces for the speakers visual index, whereas the average faces returned by K-means do not hold any meaning to a human.

4.2 Representative Index Extraction

In order to obtain the faces to build the speakers visual index, we took the results of the 3 filters presented in Section 3 to all the images in each track and retained the ones returning the best combined scores, following Equation 3 (with the modification that $pose = max\,|left34, right34|$, since differently from matching we do not care which direction the face is facing, as long as it is a 3/4 view). The best face among all those in the tracks representing the same speaker (resulting from track matching) is expanded to include a head and shoulder view of the person.

In Figure 2 is reported the accuracy of the indexes obtained with different combinations of the three quality measures, as well as their individual performances. Accuracy is measured as the fraction (out of the possible 58 speakers) of selected images representing a 3/4, head and shoulder view of a speaker. In this framework, differently from matching, the *pose* measure is the predominant factor in performance. This is because from the perspective of the visual index, a full frontal or full profile view of a person is considered an error. It is also interesting to notice that while in video 1 and 2 $resolution$ seems to hurt in combination with the other two measures, on the lowest resolution video 3 this effect is not registered (lower triangle of the heat map).

Figure 3 shows the head and shoulders views of speakers selected for the visual index. The system is able to automatically generate a qualitatively pleasing index consisting of 54 out of the 58 speakers present in the videos. One speaker was never detected, and in some cases the wrong person or view were selected since tracks were not matched properly or *resolution* and *skinRatio* prevailed over *pose*.

5. CONCLUSIONS

We have presented a system to select the most representative faces in unstructured presentation videos with respect to two criteria: to optimize matching accuracy between pairs of face tracks, and for indexing purposes.

We were able, by using quality metrics, to build face indexes of the speakers in 3 unstructured presentation videos, with a head and shoulders, 3/4 view, which is the pose preferred by humans. In the future we plan to evaluate the performance of the generated indexes through user studies.

6. REFERENCES

[1] T. Ahonen, A. Hadid, and M. Pietikainen. Face recognition with local binary patterns. In *ECCV*, pages 469–481, 2004.

[2] B. Babenko, M.-H. Yang, and S. Belongie. Visual Tracking with Online Multiple Instance Learning. In *CVPR*, 2009.

[3] D. Burke, J. Taubert, and T. Higman. Are face representations viewpoint dependent? a stereo advantage for generalizing across different views of faces. *Vision Research*, 47(16):2164 – 2169, 2007.

[4] M. Everingham, J. Sivic, and A. Zisserman. Taking the bite out of automated naming of characters in tv video. *Image and Vision Computing*, 27(5):545 – 559, 2009.

[5] A. Fourney and R. Laganiere. Constructing face image logs that are both complete and concise. In *CRV*, pages 488–494, 2007.

[6] G. Gomez and E. F. Morales. Automatic feature construction and a simple rule induction algorithm for skin detection. In *ICML Workshop on Machine Learning in Computer Vision*, pages 31–38, 2002.

[7] A. Haubold and J. R. Kender. VAST MM: multimedia browser for presentation video. In *CIVR*, pages 41–48, 2007.

[8] X. Liu, J. Rittscher, and T. Chen. Optimal pose for face recognition. In *CVPR*, pages 1439–1446, 2006.

[9] S. Mau, S. Chen, C. Sanderson, and B. Lovell. Video face matching using subset selection and clustering of probabilistic multi-region histograms. In *ICIVC*, pages 1 – 8, November 2010.

[10] K. Nasrollahi and T. Moeslund. Complete face logs for video sequences using face quality measures. *Signal Processing, IET*, 3:289 – 300, 2009.

A Biologically Inspired Computational Model for Image Saliency Detection

Sheng He[1], Junwei Han[1], Xintao Hu[1], Ming Xu[1], Lei Guo[1], Tianming Liu[2]
[1]School of Automation, Northwestern Polytechnical University, Xi'an, Shaanxi 710072 China.
[2]Department of Computer Science, Bioimaging Research Center, the University of Georgia, Athens, GA 30602, USA.
{heshengxgd, junweihan2010, xintao.hu,xuming406}@gmail.com; lguo@nwpu.edu.cn; tliu@uga.edu

ABSTRACT

Image saliency detection provides a powerful tool for predicting where human tends to look at in an image, which has been a long attempt for the computer vision community. In this paper, we propose a biologically-inspired model for computing image saliency. At first, a set of basis functions that accords with visual responses to natural stimuli is learned by using eye-fixation patches from an eye-tracking dataset. Three features are then derived based on the learned basis functions including continuity, clutter contrast, and local contrast. Finally, these three features are combined into the saliency map. The proposed approach is easy to implement and can be used in many image and video content analysis applications. Experiments on a large-scale benchmark dataset and comparisons with a number of the state-of-the-art approaches demonstrate its superiority.

Categories and Subject Descriptors

I.4.8 [**Image Processing and Computer Vision**]: Scene Analysis

General Terms

Algorithms, Performance, Experimentation

Keywords

Image saliency detection, Biologically-inspired, Sparse coding.

1. INTRODUCTION

Due to the ability of automatically estimating where human tends to focus on in the viewing field, computational modeling of visual saliency is gradually becoming the cornerstone of many multimedia applications such as video summarization [1], image resizing [2], and object segmentation [3]. It has been thus extensively studied in recent years. Existing algorithms can be broadly classified into two categories: biologically inspired and computationally inspired approaches. Inspired by the neuronal architecture of the early primate visual system, Itti [4] proposed the first biologically plausible framework, which implemented the saliency map by "center-surround" operating on three contrast-based features across multi-scales. Motivated by the evidence that the receptive fields of simple-cells in the primary visual cortex (V1) are similar to sparse codes learned from natural image patches, another school of methods [5-7] built the saliency map based on sparse codes mining. The mining schemes include Information Maximization [5], Incremental Coding Length [6], and Site Entropy Rate [7].

More algorithms are purely computationally inspired. The work in [8-10] detected the saliency in the frequency domain. Yu et al. [11] proposed a complementary saliency map by combining sketch-like and envelop-like features. Ren et al. [12] considered super-pixels as the basic unit and adopted the clustering technique to improve the performance of saliency detection. More recently, Cheng et al. [15] developed an elegant histogram descriptor indicating global contrast under the assumption that large objects are more attentive than tiny ones. Other approaches pose saliency modeling as a classification problem. Supervised learning algorithms, such as Support Vector Machines [13] and Conditional Random Fields [14], were used to optimize features guided by a ground truth dataset labeled by human or obtained from human eye-tracking data.

In some sense, the purely computationally inspired approaches are ad hoc. Their performance largely relies on the image database they work on since many attention factors, features, and the learning procedure are oriented towards the prior assumptions built on the image database. The human visual attention mechanism is much more complicated than what we can understand so far. This limits the performance of biologically inspired approaches to some extent. However, this category of methods is to mimic the capability of human and attempts to discover the intrinsic cues of visual attention. As long as the related areas like biology, psychology, and neurology make the breakthrough in visual attention mechanisms, it is certainly to benefit the biologically inspired methods significantly. Therefore, biologically inspired methods are potentially more promising.

The saliency map computed by many methods still suffers from such drawbacks as low resolution, ill-defined salient object boundary, non-uniform entire salient object, which also has been pointed out in [10, 11]. These problems may arise from the fact that many existing approaches only take either local contrast or global contrast into consideration. They do not balance these two aspects of cues well. The emphasis on local contrast tends to produce higher saliency values near salient object boundaries. The use of global contrast leads to ill-defined boundaries.

This paper proposes a biologically inspired bottom-up computational model to detect image saliency based on sparse representations that have been acknowledged to be similar to the receptive fields of simple cells in V1. The proposed model is motivated by the following three commonly agreed biological evidences: 1) According to Gestalt principles, continuous objects

*Area Chair: K. Selcuk Candan.

MM'11, November 28-December 1, 2011, Scottsdale, Arizona, USA.

are more likely to attract attentions. The continuity is one of key factors for saliency detection. 2) The clutter contrast of a scene can influence visual search and perception of the stimuli [16]. 3) A neuron's activities are mostly driven by its neighbors [4].

Three features are derived based on the sparse coding theory to reflect the above evidences and then combined to yield the saliency map. The first two features emphasize the global consideration and the last one is to detect the local contrast. The major contributions of the proposed work can be summarized as follows: 1) The sparse codes are learned from eye-fixation patches obtained from eye tracking data rather than arbitrary patches, which is demonstrated to be able to achieve better results. 2) All features are extracted based on sparse coding coefficients, which is simple, efficient, and analogous to neuron's activities. 3) Clutter contrast features are modeled using sparse coding and formally applied to detect image saliency. 4) Empirical comparisons of the proposed work with a number of state-of-the-art approaches are performed on a publicly available database.

The remainder of this paper is organized as follows. Section 2 describes sparse coding representations. Section 3 presents the development of the saliency map. Experimental results are given in Section 4. Finally, conclusions are drawn in Section 5.

2. SPACE CODING RESPRESENTATIONS

It has been mostly agreed that the sparse coding principle is an appropriate simulation to the intrinsic activation property of visual neurons in V1 [17]. An image patch $\mathbf{I}$ can be represented as a linear superposition of a set of patch bases:

$$\mathbf{I} = \sum_{k=1}^{n} \alpha_k \mathbf{B}_k \quad (1)$$

where $\mathbf{B}_k$ and α_k denote the kth basis function and the corresponding coefficient, respectively. Let $\mathbf{F}_k = \mathbf{B}_k^{-1}$ be the kth filter function and α_k can be calculated by:

$$\alpha_k = \sum_{(x,y)} \mathbf{F}_k(x,y)\mathbf{I}(x,y) \quad (2)$$

The sparse coding principle believes the receptive fields of simple cells in V1 can be characterized by basis functions each accounting for a neuron's response. As studied in [17], finding a complete set of basis functions which spans the image space is a critical issue. Traditionally, basis functions are learned using Independent Component Analysis (ICA) from a set of general-purpose image patches randomly selected from a large-scale database [5-7]. In principle, this strategy can obtain a complete set of bases approximately if we have boundless training data. However, in practice, with a view to limited computation resource, a task-oriented scheme may achieve better performance for the specific task. In this paper, we propose to learn basis functions using eye-fixation patches obtained from a publicly available eye tracking database [13], instead of using patches randomly selected from a general-purpose database. The learned bases account for image structures gaining attentions more likely.

88918 eye-fixation patches which are more attractive from all 1000 images in the eye tracking database proposed in [13] are collected. ICA algorithm is utilized to learn the basis functions with the size of 7×7×3 =147. Fig. 1 illustrates basis functions learned from fixation patches and learned from image patches randomly selected from the same database, respectively.

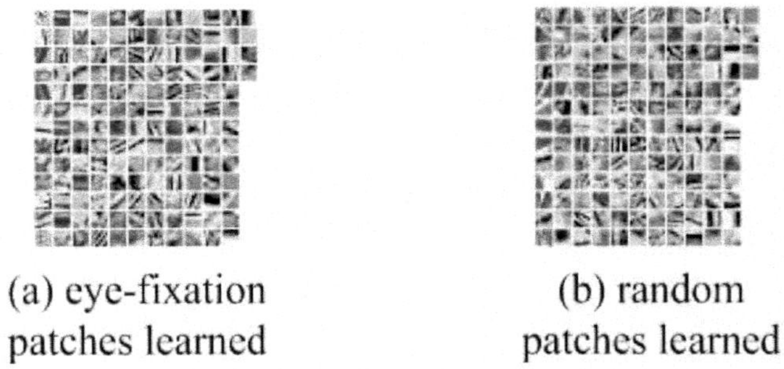

Figure 1: The basis functions learned from (a) eye-fixation patches and (b) random-selection patches.

3. THE SALIENCY MODEL

3.1 Continuity-based Features

According to Gestalt principles, continuity is an important property for attentive objects. This paper proposes to model it based on sparse codes. The framework is shown in Fig. 2.

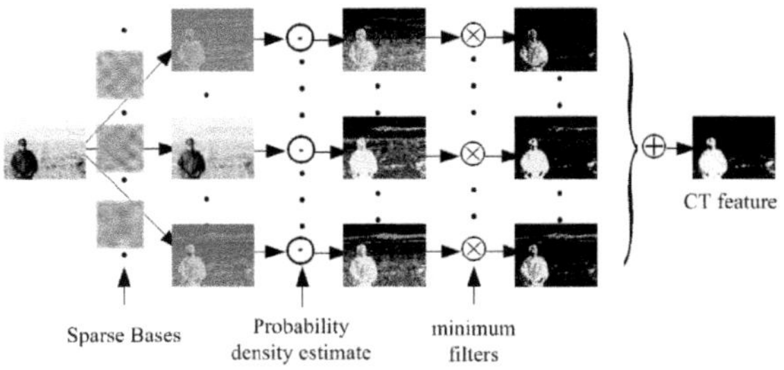

Figure 2: The proposed framework of generating continuity-based features.

At first, the input image is filtered by the set of learned basis functions (according to Eq. (2)) to obtain the corresponding coefficient maps. Afterwards, in the kth coefficient map, we construct the coefficient histogram. The counts in the histogram bins are converted to a discrete probability distribution $H_k(x,y)$, where (x,y) is a location in the map. $H_k(x,y)$ is modified by a Gaussian kernel as:

$$P_k(x,y) = \exp(-\frac{H_k(x,y)}{2\sigma^2}) \quad (3)$$

Since the coefficient histogram technique only models the coefficient coherence without taking spatial connectivity into account, a post-process is utilized to remove the isolated patch noise. Due to its simplicity, the minimum filter is applied within the neighborhood of 5×5. Finally, the continuity-based feature map is generated as the summation of all coefficient maps:

$$CT(x,y) = \sum_{k} P_k(x,y) \quad (4)$$

3.2 Clutter Contrast Features

As mentioned in [16], visual clutter contrast is one of inherent factors to decide the image saliency. In [16], a feature congestion measure is proposed to estimate the clutter of any scene. To the best of our knowledge, very little work of saliency detection has formally adopted clutter contrast as a feature. In this paper, we define clutter as the complexity of the structure of the patches in images, which is measured based on the sparse representations.

The framework of generating clutter-based features is displayed in Fig. 3. Given an input image and a set of basis functions, each location (x, y) can be represented by a set of coefficients $\boldsymbol{\alpha}(x, y)$ according to the Eq. (2). Then, the clutter contrast features are calculated as follows:

$$CC(x,y) = \exp(-\frac{(\lambda A(x,y)+(1-\lambda)E(x,y))}{2\sigma^2}) \quad (5)$$

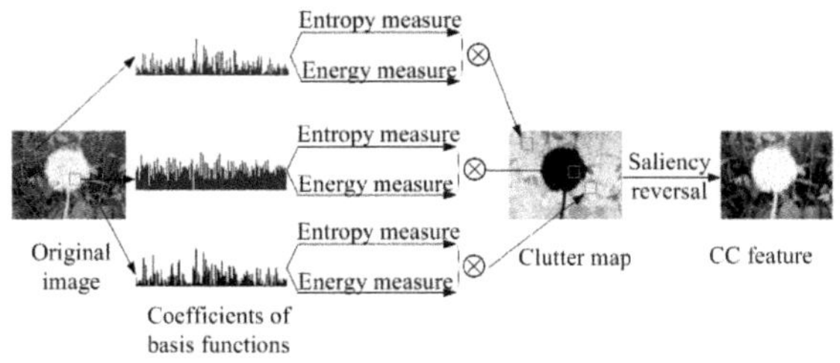

Figure 3: The framework of generating clutter contrast features.

Here, $A(x, y)$ and $E(x, y)$ are entropy and energy over $\boldsymbol{\alpha}_{(x,y)}$, respectively, which are formulated as:

$$A(x,y) = \sum_i p_i \log p_i, \quad p_i = \frac{|\alpha_i|}{\sum_j |\alpha_j|}, \quad \alpha_i, \alpha_j \in \boldsymbol{\alpha}(x,y) \quad (6)$$

$$E(x,y) = \sum_i \alpha_i^2 \quad (7)$$

In our implementation $\lambda = 0.4$.

As pointed out in [20], there are two kinds of contrast patterns generally: smooth background with cluttered salient objects and smooth salient objects with cluttered background. The clutter contrast calculation by Eq. (5) can handle the former contrast pattern only but is inappropriate for the latter pattern for the purpose of highlighting salient objects. A saliency reversal procedure [14, 20] is utilized to refine the results, which is based on variance comparison between background and salient object.

3.3 Local Contrast Features

Local contrast is a major cue to detect saliency. It is normally obtained by center-surround differencing (CSD). This paper models local contrast by means of CSD over sparse coding coefficients, which is defined as follows:

$$LC(x,y) = \sum_{l=1}^{n} \Theta_l(x,y) \quad (8)$$

$$\Theta_l(x,y) = \sum_{(x',y')\in\Omega} \left\{ \exp(\frac{\|\boldsymbol{\alpha}(x,y) - \boldsymbol{\alpha}(x',y')\|_2}{2\sigma^2}) - 1 \right\} \quad (9)$$

Here Θ is the CSD operator and Ω is the neighborhood of (x, y), and l is the scale. In our implementation, the size of Ω was set to 5×5 and the scale number was set to 5. The framework of obtaining local contrast is shown in Figure 4.

3.4 Feature Combination

In visual attention modeling, the feature combination is a tricky problem as biological theories behind it are still unclear. Although many algorithms [13, 14] adopted learning-driven scheme, they are ad hoc and require an extensive training stage. In the proposed work, inspired by the conclusion in [21] that V1 cells tuned to different features interact through lateral connections and activity in cells responding to stimuli is suppressed through mutual inhibition, we develop a novel combination strategy to reveal the mutual interaction across features.

$$S(x,y) = \frac{1}{N}(CT^2(x,y) + CC^2(x,y) + LC^2(x,y) + CT(x,y)\cdot CC(x,y) + CT(x,y)\cdot LC(x,y) + CC(x,y)\cdot LC(x,y)) \quad (10)$$

Here N is a normalizator.

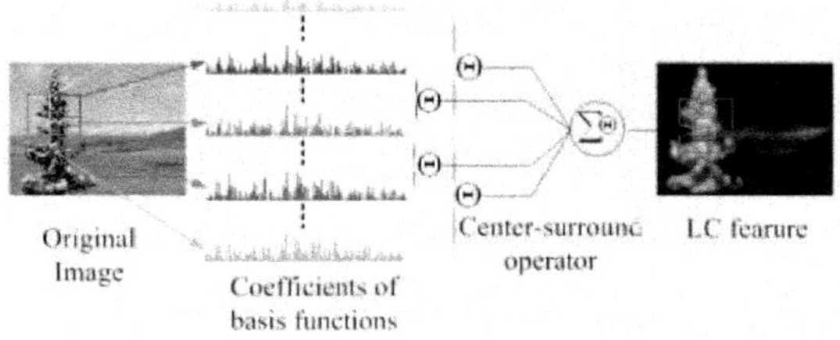

Figure 4: Framework of obtaining local contrast features.

4. EXPERIMENTAL RESULTS

Two evaluation studies were conducted to test the proposed work. The first evaluation is to compare the performance of two basis functions learning strategy: eye-fixation patches based and random patches based methods. The second test is to quantitatively evaluate the proposed saliency detection algorithm by comparing with a number of state-of-the-art algorithms. In our experiments, 1000 images in the benchmark dataset presented in [10] with their ground truth which is manually labeled by subjects, were utilized as testing data.

4.1 Evaluations of Eye-fixation Patches based Learning

Fig. 5 shows the ROC curves of saliency detection computing on all testing data by using basis functions learned from eye-fixation patches and learned from random patches, respectively. As can be seen from the comparison, eye-fixation patches learning strategy can improve the performance of sparse coding representations for the task of visual saliency detection.

4.2 Evaluations of the Proposed Algorithm

To objectively evaluate the proposed work, we compare it with a number of state-of-the-art algorithms including the Information Maximization (IM) [5], Coding Length Increments (CLI) [6], Special Residual (SR) [8], Frequency-Tuned (FT) [10], Feature Congestion Measure (FCM) [16], Self-ReSemble (SRS) [18], SUN [19]. Fig. 6 shows the comparison results and Fig. 7 shows the ROC curves of saliency detection calculating on all testing data. The results can demonstrate the superiority of our work.

5. CONCLUSIONS

In this paper, a computational model of visual saliency motivated by biological evidences was reported. Three attention-oriented features were derived based on sparse coding representations and then combined to generate the saliency map. Comprehensive experimental results on a benchmark dataset and comparisons with state-of-the-art approaches have demonstrated the effectiveness of the proposed work.

Acknowledgements
This research was supported by the National Science Foundation of China under Grant 61005018 and by NPU Foundation for Fundamental Research under Grant NPU-FFR-JC201041.

6. REFERENCES

[1] Ma, Y., Lu, L., Zhang, H. and Li, M. A user attention model for video summarization. *ACM Multimedia* 2002.

[2] Avidan,S. and Shamir, A.. Seam carving for content-aware image resizing. *ACM Transactions on Graphics.* 26(3), 2007.

[3] Han, J., Ngan, K., Li, M. and Zhang, H. Unsupervised extraction of visual attention objects in color images. *IEEE Trans. Circuits Syst. Video Techn.* 16(1): 141-145, 2006.

[4] Itti, L., and Koch, C. and Niebur, E. A model of saliency-based visual attention for rapid scene analysis. *IEEE Transactions on Pattern Analysis and Machine Intelligence.* 20(11): 1254-1259, 1998.

[5] Bruce, N. and Tsotsos, J. Saliency based on information maximization. In *Advances in neural information processing systems.* 18: 155, 2006.

[6] Hou, X. and Zhang, L. Dynamic visual attention: Searching for coding length increments. In *Advances in neural information processing systems.* 21: 681–688, 2008.

[7] Wang, W., Wang, Y., Huang, Q. and Gao, W. Measuring Visual Saliency by Site Entropy Rate. In *Proceeding of the IEEE Conference on Computer Vision and Pattern Recognition,* 2010.

[8] Hou, X. and Zhang, L. Saliency detection: A spectral residual approach. In *Proceeding of the IEEE Conference on Computer Vision and Pattern Recognition,* 2007.

[9] Guo, C., Ma, Q., and Zhang, L. Spatio-temporal saliency detection using phase spectrum of quaternion fourier transform. In *Proceeding of the IEEE Conference on Computer Vision and Pattern Recognition,* 2008.

[10] Achanta, R., Hemami, S., Estrada, F. and Susstrunk, S. Frequency-tuned salient region detection. In *Proceeding of the IEEE Conference on Computer Vision and Pattern Recognition,* 2009.

[11] Yu, H., Li, J., Tian, Y. and Huang, T. Automatic Interesting Object Extraction From Images Using Complementary Saliency Maps. *ACM Multimedia* 2010.

[12] Ren, Z., Hu, Y., Chia, L. and Rajan, D. Improved saliency detection based on superpixel clustering and saliency propagation. *ACM Multimedia* 2010.

[13] Judd, T., Ehinger, K., Durand, F. And Torralba, A. Learning to predict where humans look. In *Proceeding of International Conference on Computer Vision.* 2009.

[14] Liu, T., Yuan, Z., Sun, J., Wang, J., Zheng, N., Tang, X. and Shum, H. Y. Learning to detect a salient object. In *Proceeding of the IEEE Conference on Computer Vision and Pattern Recognition,* 2007.

[15] Cheng, M., Zhang, G., Niloy, J., Huang, X. and Hu, S. Global Contrast based Salient Region Detection. In *Proceeding of the IEEE Conference on Computer Vision and Pattern Recognition,* 2011.

[16] Ruth, R., Li, Y. and Lisa, N. Measuring visual clutter. *Journal of Vision.* 7(2):17, 2007.

[17] Olshausen, B. Emergence of simple-cell receptive field properties by learning a sparse code for natural images. *Nature.* 381(6583): 607-609, 1996.

[18] Seo, H. and Milanfar, P. Nonparametric bottom-up saliency detection by self-resemblance. In *Proceeding of the IEEE Conference on Computer Vision and Pattern Recognition,* 2009.

[19] Zhang, L., Tong, M., Marks, T., Shan, H. and Cottrell, G. SUN: A Bayesian framework for saliency using natural statistics. *Journal of Vision* 8(7):32, 2008.

[20] Wang, Z. and Li, B. A two-stage approach to saliency detection in images. In *Proceeding of IEEE International Conference on Acoustics, Speech, and Signal Processing,* 2008.

[21] Koene, A. and Zhaoping, L. Feature-specific interactions in salience from combined feature contrasts: Evidence for a bottom–up saliency map in V1. *Journal of Vision.* 7(7):17, 2007.

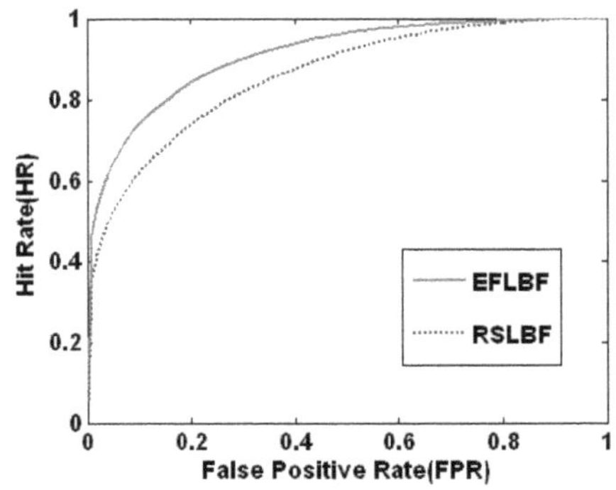

Figure 5: The ROC curve of saliency detection by using Eye-Fixation Learned Basis Functions (EFLBF) and Random-Selection Learned Basis Functions (RSLBF).

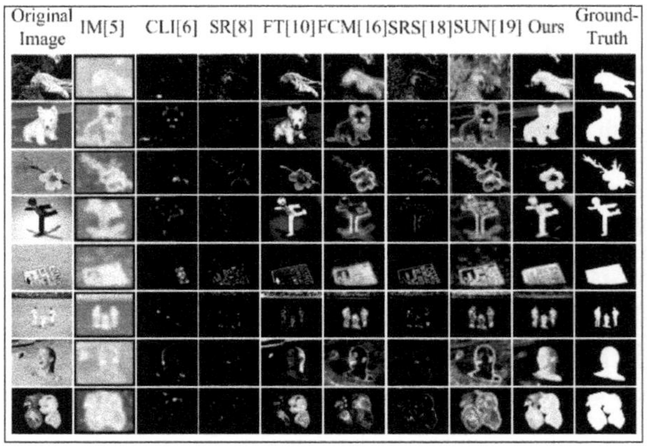

Figure 6: Saliency maps by different algorithms.

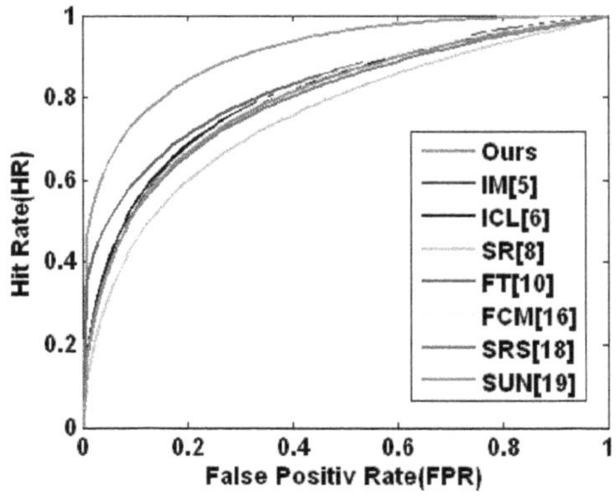

Figure 7: ROC curves of saliency detection by different algorithm.

Unsupervised Fast Anomaly Detection in Crowds

Xiaoshuai Sun, Hongxun Yao, Rongrong Ji, Xianming Liu, Pengfei Xu
Department of Computer Science, Harbin Institute of Technology
No.92, West Dazhi Street, Harbin, P. R. China, 150001
{xiaoshuaisun, h.yao, rrji, xmliu, pfxu}@hit.edu.cn Tel: +86-451-86416485

ABSTRACT
In this paper, we proposed a fast and robust unsupervised framework for anomaly detection and localization in crowed scenes. Our method avoids modeling the normal state of the crowds which is a very complex task due to the large within class variance of the normal target appearance and motion patterns. For each video frame, we extract the spatial temporal features of 3D blocks and generate the saliency map using a block-based center-surround difference operator. Then, motion vector matrix is obtained by adaptive rood pattern search block-matching algorithm and distance normalization. Attractive motion disorder descriptor is proposed to measure the global intensity of anomalies in the scene. Finally, we classify the frames into normal and anomalous ones by a binary classifier. In the experiments, we compared our method against several state-of-the-art approaches on UCSD dataset which is a widely used anomaly detection and localization benchmark. As the only unsupervised approach, our method outputs competitive results with near real-time processing speed.

Categories and Subject Descriptors
H.3.1 [**Information Systems**]: Content Analysis and Indexing; H.5.1 [**Multimedia information Systems**]: Video

General Terms
Algorithms, Experimentation, Human Factors

Keywords
Unsupervised anomaly detection, motion estimation, attractive motion disorder descriptor

1. INTRODUCTION
As reviewed in [1, 2], monitoring surveillance videos, especially for videos of crowded scene, is a very expensive and tiring task. Thus, automatic detection of anomalous events in crowds has become an attractive topic in computer vision and pattern recognition research. Due to the unreliability of trajectory analysis in crowded scene [3], recent works focus on designing robust dynamic scene representations that avoid multiple targets tracking [4, 5, 6, 7, 8]. Adam *et al.* [4] maintain probabilities of optical flow in local regions, using histograms. Kim and Grauman

*Area Chair: Kiyoharu Aizawa

MM'11, November 28-December 1, 2011, Scottsdale, Arizona, USA.

(a) Normal moving targets (b) The crowed scene

Figure 1. Large within-class variance of the normal target appearance and motion patterns in crowded scene.

[5] utilized a mixture of probabilistic **PCA** models to model local optical flow patterns, and enforce global consistency using a Markov Random Field (**MRF**). Inspired by classical studies of crowd behavior, Mehran *et al.* [6] characterized crowd behavior using concepts such as social force. These concepts lead to optic flow measurement of target interaction within the crowds, which are combined with a latent Dirichlet Allocation (**LDA**) model for anomaly detection. Mahadevan *et al.* [8] proposed a unified framework for joint modeling of appearance and dynamics of the scene, under which the outliers are labeled as anomalies.

However, scene representation is not the only problem for anomaly detection task. Modeling the normal state of the crowded scene is another challenging problem due to the large within-class variance of the normal target appearance and motion patterns. Figure 1 shows the moving targets appeared in a 20 seconds video clip, which contains different target appearances and movements. In real-world applications, the length of the video with normal crowd behaviors will be much longer than 20 seconds, thus it's nearly impossible to model the normal state containing thousands of patterns with different spatial temporal appearance. Compared with supervised or semi-supervised learning of the normal states [2, 3, 4, 5, 6, 7, 8, 9], it may be more practical to directly model the global intensity of anomalous events in a purely unsupervised manner.

From experimental observations, we found that abnormal contents or unusual human behaviors will consistently attract the attention of human observers, which means most of the anomalies are more attractive or more salient compared with the other contents in the environment. Besides, the presence of anomalies will probably turn the ordered crowd movements into a disordered state. Based on these observations, we proposed an unsupervised framework for anomaly detection and localization task, which uses *Attractive Motion Disorder descriptor* to directly measure the overall intensity of anomalies and avoids modeling of the crowd's normal behavior. Our descriptor is constructed by fusing the statistical features of visual saliency and motion vectors, which is inspired by both the perceptual and computational observations on normal and anomalous videos.

2. METHOD

The proposed unsupervised anomaly detection framework is shown in Figure 2. Temporal derivatives of spatial temporal video blocks are extracted as visual features. Saliency is then computed by block-based center-surround difference operator. Motion disorder is measured by the standard deviation of the motion vectors estimated by adaptive block-match algorithm. By analyzing the statistical distribution of visual saliency and the motion vector matrix, we construct attractive motion disorder descriptor to measure the global anomalous intensity, with which video frames are classified into normal or anomalous frames by a binary classifier. Localization of the detected anomalies is achieved using the spatial temporal saliency map.

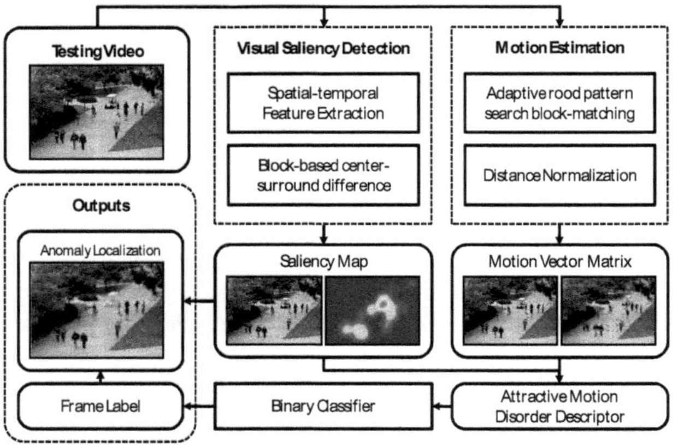

Figure 2. The framework of the proposed method.

2.1 Center-Surround Saliency Detection

Saliency is an important concept for computational visual attention modeling, which could be quantitatively measured by center-surround difference [10, 11], information maximization [12], incremental coding length [13] and site entropy rate [14], *etc.* In our case, we first extract spatial-temporal local features from the video, then generate the saliency map using a block-based center-surround operation, which is more computational efficient and shares the plausibility of previous works. The visual field is segmented into 24×32 3D sub-blocks represented by a gradient-based spatial-temporal descriptor. The descriptor of a sub-block is constructed by the absolute values of the temporal derivatives in all pixels in the block. These values are stacked into a 1-D feature vector. A center-surround difference operator, akin to the visual receptive fields of human vision system, is adopted as a quantitative measurement for visual saliency. In traditional models [10, 11], the center-surround difference was computed across different spatial scales using Difference of Gaussian filters. In our case, we only compute the difference between center block and its surrounding eight-neighborhoods for the concern of computation efficiency. The saliency of a given block is defined as the average center-surround difference measured by the Manhattan Distance between the features of the center and its surrounding blocks:

$$S_{i,j} = \sum_{m=-1}^{1} \sum_{n=-1}^{1} \left| F_{i,j} - F_{i+m,j+n} \right|_1 \tag{1}$$

Figure 3 shows some examples of the spatial temporal saliency maps computed using the temporal gradient features and block-based center-surround difference operator. It's easy to notice that the anomalies tend to appear at the locations with the largest saliency value in the scene.

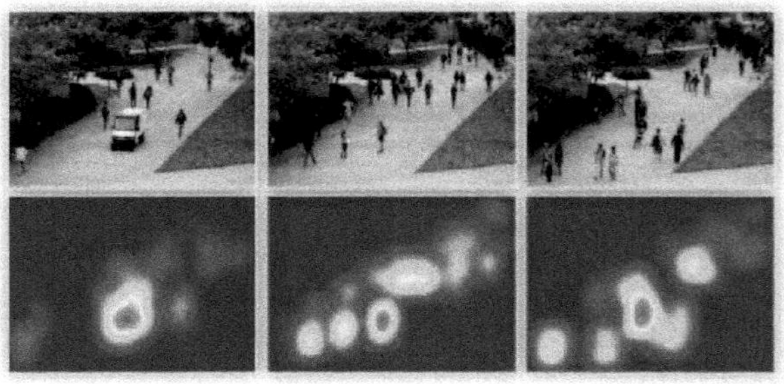

Figure 3. Examples of the spatial temporal saliency maps.

2.2 Attractive Motion Disorder Descriptor

The motion vectors obtained by adaptive rood pattern search block-matching algorithm [15] are used as motion descriptors for each sub-block. The visual field is segmented into 12×16 sub-blocks with equal size. Note that, motion vectors can also be directly obtained from the compression domain data if the video is compressed using motion compensation technique. Let $M_{i,j}$ denote the motion vector of the sub-block in *i*th row and *j*th column, we apply distance normalization to eliminate the scale variance of the motion vector caused by the geometrical setting of the camera:

$$M'_{i,j} = \left(\frac{\beta \cdot (H-i)}{H} + \beta \right) \cdot M_{i,j}, \tag{2}$$

where M is the motion vector matrix, H is the height of M, $\beta = 0.5$ is a distance compensation parameter which has been fixed in our experiment. After normalization, object moments appeared in all sub-blocks can be near equally measured by M'. Figure 4 illustrates motion estimation and normalization results.

Figure 4. Motion estimation. From left to right: input video frame, motion estimation result by adaptive rood pattern search block-matching [15] and normalized motion vectors.

There are various measurements for system disorder such as *Entropy* and *Standard Deviation*. *Entropy* is an important concept in physics and information theory, which is also widely used as a quantitative measurement for uncertainty or unpredictability. *Standard Deviation* is an easy to compute statistical feature describing the variance or diversity of a group of data. Practically, we use standard deviation to measure the motion disorder, because it leads to a better overall performance while costing much less computations compared with other measurements. Given the spatial temporal saliency map *S*, the motion vector matrix *M'*, we define the **A**ttractive **M**otion **D**isorder **(AMD)** descriptor *A* by:

$$A = \alpha \cdot \max(S) + (1-\alpha) \cdot \mathrm{std}(M'), \tag{3}$$

where $\alpha \in [0,1]$ is a fusing parameter, std(.) denotes the standard deviation of the input matrix. The descriptor can be regarded as a quantitative measurement for global intensity of all the anomalous events appeared in the visual field. Higher value for the **AMD** descriptor indicates larger probability for the appearance of anomalies. Figure 5 illustrate the distribution of **AMD** descriptor ($\alpha \in 0.5$) in normal and anomalous videos.

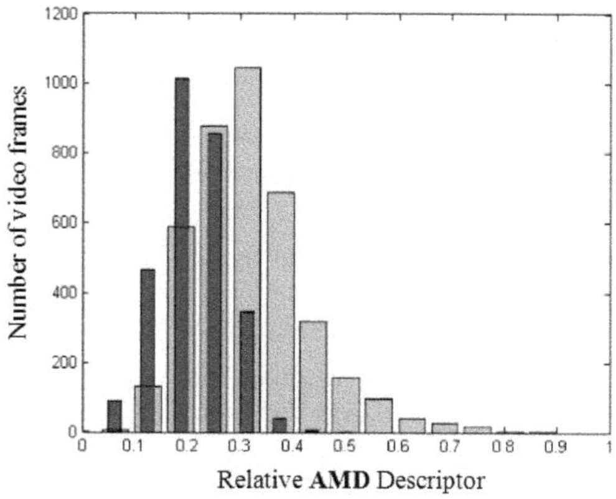

Figure 5. Distribution of AMD descriptor in normal (blue) and anomalous (green) video frames of UCSD Ped_1 dataset.

2.3 Anomaly Detection and Localization

Video frames can be classified into normal or abnormal frames by a binary classifier using the **AMD** descriptor. As described in Section 1, anomalous regions tend to attract more visual attention compared with the other events happened in the scene. Thus, saliency map can be used as a reference for localization and segmentation of the anomalous regions. In practice, we adopt Equation 4 to segment the anomalies, which is first proposed in [16] for non-parametric proto-object segmentation.

$$O(x,y)\begin{cases}1 & \text{if } S'(x,y) > \text{threshold,}\\ 0 & \text{otherwise.}\end{cases} \quad (4)$$

where O is the localization binary map, $S' = S * G$ is a refined saliency map smoothed by a Gaussian filter G ($3\times3, \sigma = 1$). We set the threshold to be $7\times\mathbf{E}(S)$ empirically, where $\mathbf{E}(S)$ is the mean intensity of the saliency map. Examples of anomaly detection and localization results are shown in Figure 6.

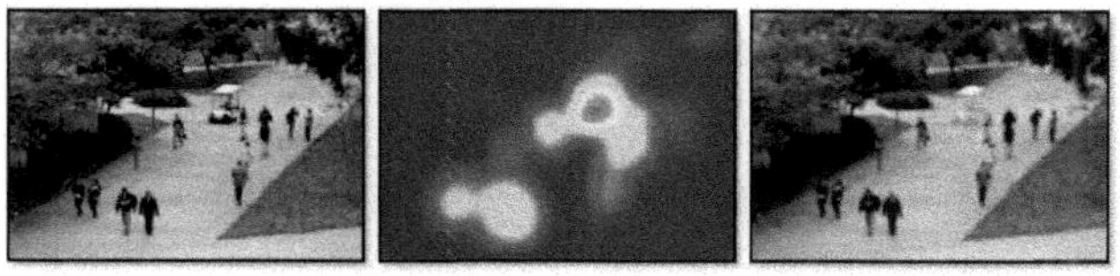

Figure 6. Anomaly detection in crowded videos. From left to right: Detected abnormal frame, corresponding saliency map and localization result of the anomalous region.

3. EXPERIMENTS

We evaluate the proposed approach on UCSD dataset [8][1], which is a well annotated publicly available dataset for the evaluation of abnormal detection and localization in crowded scenes. The dataset was acquired with a stationary camera mounted at an elevation at a resolution of 238 × 158 with 10 fps, overlooking pedestrian walkways. The circulation of non pedestrian entities in the walkways, and anomalous pedestrian motion patterns are regarded as abnormal events. Commonly appeared anomalies include bikers, skaters, small carts, and people walking across a walkway or in the grass. Videos were split into 2 subsets: **Ped_1** and **Ped_2**, each corresponding to a different scene. Videos recorded from each scene were split into various clips each of which has around 200 frames. **Ped_1** contains 34 training clips and 36 testing clips, while **Ped2** contains 16 training clips and 14 testing clips. For each clip, the ground truth annotation includes a binary flag per frame, indicating whether an anomaly is present in that frame.

Practically, all video frames are resized to 120×160 in order to reduce the computation cost. For each frame, we extract the spatial temporal features of 5×5×3 3D video blocks, and generate a 24×32 saliency map using the proposed block-based center-surround difference operator. A 12×16 motion vector matrix is then obtained based on adaptive rood pattern search block-matching algorithm and distance normalization. Based on the saliency map and the motion vector matrix, we compute the **AMD** descriptor using Equation 3 ($\alpha = 0.5$), which is proposed to describe the overall intensity of anomalies appeared in the frame. Finally, the video frame is classified into normal or anomalous frame by a binary classifier.

The evaluation on **UCSD** dataset contains two components: anomaly detection and localization. By varying the parameters of the tested approach, an **ROC** curve can be drawn to intuitively evaluate the anomaly detection performance. Figure 7 illustrates the **ROC** curves for **UCSD** dataset of various state-of-the-art approaches and our approach, while Figure 8 shows some visual examples of anomaly localization and segmentation results of the tested approaches. In addition to Figure 7, Table 1 shows the area under **ROC** curve (**AUC**) of the tested methods, in which a larger **AUC** score means better classification performance. According to the experimental results, our method, as the only completely unsupervised training-free approach, outputs competitive results against the state-of-the-art methods with near real-time processing speed. Visual results indicate that our method is able to accurately localize the anomalous events in the crowded scene and outputs better segmentation results with well defined boundaries.

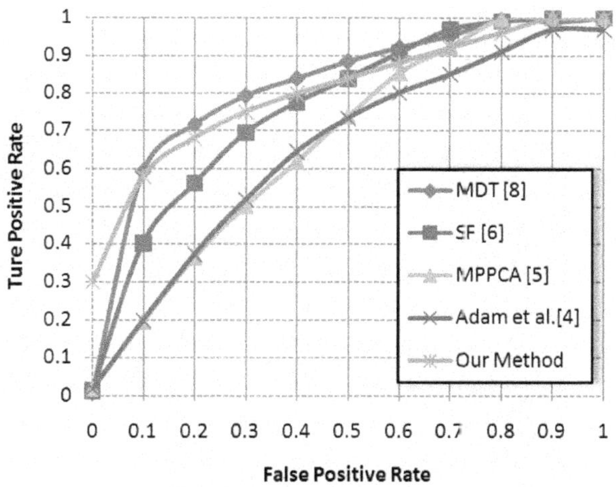

Figure 7. ROC curves of tested approaches on UCSD Ped_1 dataset. Tested approaches include our method, MDT-based approach [8], the Social Force Model [6], the mixture of optical flow (denoted as MPPCA [5]) and optical flow monitoring method (Adam *et al.* [4]).

Table 1. Area Under ROC Curves

Method	MDT	SF	MPPCA	Adam	Ours
AUC	0.7895	0.7413	0.6554	0.6350	**0.7919**

[1] http://www.svcl.ucsd.edu/projects/anomaly/dataset.htm

4. CONCLUSION

In this paper, we proposed an unsupervised framework for fast anomaly detection and localization in crowded scene. Instead of modeling the normal states, we directly model the intensity of anomalies using attractive motion disorder descriptor, which is constructed by fusing the statistical features of saliency map and motion vector matrix. Saliency detection and motion estimation are conducted by block-based center-surround difference operator and adaptive rood pattern search block-matching algorithm, both of which are highly efficient and lead to a near real-time overall processing speed. Experimental results on a widely used bench-mark dataset demonstrate the effectiveness of the proposed framework. Our future work lies in integrating other reliable features, such as location distribution prior, into the framework to further improve the overall performance.

5. ACKNOWLEDGEMENT

This work was supported by the National Natural Science Foundation of China (Grant No. 61071180 and Key Program Grant No. 61133003).

6. REFERENCES

[1] N. Haering, P. Venetianer, and A. Lipton. "The evolution of video surveillance: an overview". *Machine Vision and Applications*, 19(5-6):279–290, 2008.

[2] L. Seidenari, M. Bertini. "Non-parametric anomaly detection exploiting space-time features". *ACM Multimedia*, pp.1139–1142, 2010.

[3] F. Jiang, Y. Wu, and A. Katsaggelos. "A dynamic hierarchical clustering method for trajectory-based unusual video event detection". *IEEE TIP*, 18(4):907–913, 2009.

[4] A. Adam, E. Rivlin, I. Shimshoni, and D. Reinitz. "Robust real-time unusual event detection using multiple fixed location monitors". *IEEE TPAMI*, 30(3):555–560, 2008.

[5] J. Kim and K. Grauman. "Observe locally, infer globally: A space-time MRF for detecting abnormal activities with incremental updates". *CVPR*, pp. 2921–2928, 2009.

[6] R. Mehran, A. Oyama, and M. Shah. "Abnormal crowd behavior detection using social force model". *CVPR*, pp.935–942, 2009.

[7] L. Kratz and K. Nishino. "Anomaly detection in extremely crowded scenes using spatio-temporal motion pattern models". *CVPR*, pp.1446–1453, 2009.

[8] V. Mahadevan, W. Li, V. Bhalodia and N. Vasconcelos. "Anomaly Detection in Crowded Scenes". *CVPR*, 2010.

[9] O. Boiman and M. Irani. "Detecting irregularities in images and in video". *IJCV*, 74(1):17–31, Aug. 2007.

[10] L. Itti, C. Koch and E. Niebur. "A model of saliency-based visual attention for rapid scene analysis". *IEEE TPAMI*, 20(11), 1998.

[11] D. Gao, V. Mahadevan, and N. Vasconcelos. "The discriminate center-surround hypothesis for bottom-up saliency". *Advances in Neural Information Processing Systems*, pp.497-504, 2007.

[12] N. Bruce and J. Tsotsos. "Saliency based on information maximization". *Advances in Neural Information Processing Systems*, pp.155–162, 2006.

[13] X. Hou and L. Zhang, "Dynamic visual attention: searching for coding length increments. *NIPS,* pp. 681–688, 2008.

[14] W. Wang, Y. Wang, Q. Huang, and W. Gao, "Measuring Visual Saliency by Site Entropy Rate". *CVPR*, pp. 2368–2375, 2010.

[15] Y. Nie, and K. Ma. "Adaptive rood pattern search algorithm for fast block matching motion estimation". *IEEE TIP.* 11(12), pp.1442--1448, 2002.

[16] X. Hou and L. Zhang, Saliency detection: a spectral residual approach. *CVPR*, 2007.

Figure 8. Comparisons of abnormal localization results from (i) our approach; (ii) MDT approach and (iii) SF-MPPCA approach. The results of MDT and SF-MPPCA are provided by Mahadevan *et al.* [8]

Video Indexing and Recommendation Based on Affective Analysis of Viewers

Sicheng Zhao, Hongxun Yao, Xiaoshuai Sun, Pengfei Xu, Xianming Liu, Rongrong Ji
Department of Computer Science, Harbin Institute of Technology
No.92, West Dazhi Street, Harbin, P. R. China, 150001
{zsc, h.yao, xiaoshuaisun, pfxu, xmliu, rrji}@hit.edu.cn Tel: +86-451-86416485

ABSTRACT
Most previous works on video indexing and recommendation were only based on the content of video itself, without considering the affective analysis of viewers, which is an efficient and important way to reflect viewers' attitudes, feelings and evaluations of videos. In this paper, we propose a novel method to index and recommend videos based on affective analysis, mainly on facial expression recognition of viewers. We first build a facial expression recognition classifier by embedding the process of building compositional Haar-like features into hidden conditional random fields (HCRFs). Then we extract viewers' facial expressions frame by frame through the videos, collected from the camera when viewers are watching videos, to obtain the affections of viewers. Finally, we draw the affective curve which tells the process of affection changes. Through the curve, we segment each video into affective sections, give the indexing result of the videos, and list recommendation points from views' aspect. Experiments on our collected database from the web show that the proposed method has a promising performance.

Categories and Subject Descriptors
H.3.1 [**Information Systems**]: Content Analysis and Indexing

General Terms
Algorithms, Experimentation, Human Factors

Keywords
Video indexing, segmentation, recommendation, affective analysis, facial expression recognition, viewers

1. INTRODUCTION
With the widespread use of cameras, videos have become more and more popular, being an indispensable part of our daily life. Meanwhile, on-line services for sharing personal or professional videos such as YouTube, YouKu [1] are developing rapidly, as shown in Figure1.

How to organize videos into categories, how to segment each video into affective sections and how to recommend videos of high quality, whether of one's interest or of high clearness, have become a difficult and nerve-wracking question, but of paramount importance for managing website and improving user experience. Song *et al.* [2] presented a large scale video taxonomic classification system, utilizing the category taxonomic structure in training and interpreting the classification results, and integrating video content based features with text features. Wang *et al.* [3] provided an effective way of integrating data from diverse sources, and proposed three-DRF model for fusing models trained from individual data sources when combined with small amount of manually labeled data in a pairwise fashion. Irie [4] proposed a latent topic driving model to movie affective scene classification. Rho [5] reasoned about the user's mood and situation using both collaborative filtering and ontology technology and implemented a prototype music recommendation system.

Figure 1. Examples of on-line videos from [1]. Videos in the two lines are comedies and exciting moves respectively, both sorted in order of recommendation points, in proportion to image area. The right column are typical affections when viewers are watching these videos: happiness and surprise.

On the other hand, affective computing has been paid much attention and widely spread, since R. W. Picard introduced the idea [6]. And facial expression is the key method to express one's affections. Facial expression analysis and recognition has attracted much research attention in the community of psychology and computer science for more than 40 years. And a lot of perfect results have been obtained, including high recognition accuracy, fast recognition speed, mature feature extraction method, such as Haar-like features [7], Gabor features [8], local binary patterns (LBPs) [9], and effective classifier building method, such as SVM [9], AdaBoost [7]. Yang et al. [10] applied compositional features into facial expression recognition to avoid the AU detection due to its ambiguity. Chang et al. [11] adopted hidden conditional random fields (HCRFs) to classify facial expression and expanded it into partially-observed hidden conditional random fields (POHCRFs), in which POHCRF9 got the highest accuracy.

*Area Chair: Kiyoharu Aizawa

MM'11, November 28-December 1, 2011, Scottsdale, Arizona, USA.

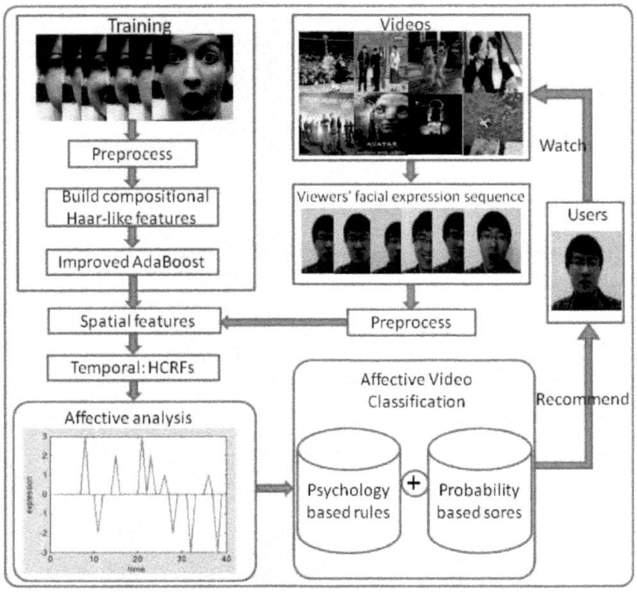

Figure 2. The architecture of the proposed method

However, most previous works only focus on increasing the recognition accuracy, based on normal facial expression database, in which expressions are too exaggerated, unavailable in daily life. Though widely reported that facial expression recognition has many potential applications, few concrete and practical systems based on facial expression recognition have been developed.

In this paper, we propose a novel method to index, segment and recommend videos based on affective analysis, mainly on facial expression recognition of viewers, considering spatio-temporal context. The architecture of our proposed method is shown in Figure 2.

Our contribution lies in three aspects: 1.We index, segment and recommend videos especially web videos based on affective analysis, mainly on facial expression recognition of viewers. To the best of our knowledge, this is the first time to employ viewers' affections for indexing and recommending videos. 2. We propose affective curve model in the form of function and combine it with videos' affection flow. We also explain the meanings of inflection points of the curve. 3. We analyze and recognize expressions from spatio-temporal aspect simultaneously by embedding the process of building compositional Haar-like features into HCRFs, and develop a practical system of expression recognition to reflect viewers' affections, which are crucial to evaluate videos' quality.

2. SPATIO-TEMPORAL FACIAL EXPRESSION RECOGNITION

Here we adopt Yang's [10] compositional feature strategy, which achieves high recognition accuracy even when recognizing expressions with low intensity. The most two important steps are calculating the training error of each feature with the following popular weak classifier

$$s(x)=\begin{cases}1 & if \quad p\cdot f_{p,i}(x)>p\cdot\theta_{p,i}\\ 0 & otherwise\end{cases} \tag{1}$$

where $\theta_{p,i}$ minimizes the weighted error, and the combination updating rule shown in Equation (2). The feature f_i is to be added to the combined feature if the training error is reduced after combination.

$$f_i\rightarrow[f_1,\cdots,f_m] \quad if\ \varepsilon[f_1,\cdots,f_m,f_i]<\varepsilon[f_1,\cdots,f_m] \tag{2}$$

Different from Yang [10], our combined features won't stop until Equation (2) is not satisfied instead of growing up to the maximum length.

Then the process of building compositional features is embedded into HCRFs. In nature, the main idea behind HCRFs is to enrich CRFs by adding hidden states to capture complex dependencies or implicit structures in the training samples. The effect can be enhanced by using more hidden variables, or by increasing the number of possible hidden states [11]. Equation (3) and (4) list the probability and feature function, and Equation (5) gives the objective function in training parameters θ [11, 12].

$$P(y\mid x,\theta)=\frac{\sum_h \exp(\varphi(y,h,x;\theta))}{\sum_{y'}\sum_h \exp(\varphi(y',h,x;\theta))} \tag{3}$$

$$\varphi(y,h,x;\theta)=\sum_j f(x,j)\cdot\theta(h_j)+\sum_j\theta(y,h_j) + \sum_{(j,k)\in E}\theta(y,h_j,h_k), f(x,j)=[f_{j-1}^T,f_j^T-f_{j-1}^T]^T \tag{4}$$

$$L(\theta)=\sum_i \log P(y_i\mid x_i,\theta)-\frac{1}{2\sigma^2}\|\theta\|^2 \quad \theta^*=\arg\max_\theta L(\theta) \tag{5}$$

The detailed training algorithm is listed in Algorithm1.

Algorithm 1 *Facial expression recognition training procedure*

Input: Image samples, labels *(x_1,y_1), (x_2,y_2), ... , (x_n,y_n)*, x_i *is a expression sequence,* $y_i\in\{-3,-2,-1,0,1,2,3\}$

Output: Classifier $P(y\mid x,\theta)$

1 for *i=1* to *n*

2 Build candidate set *{F}* and encode it as a binary vector, similar with the method in [10];

3 **for each** $f_i\in F$ do

4 **if** $\varepsilon[f_1,\cdots,f_m,f_i]<\varepsilon[f_1,\cdots,f_m]$ do

$f_i\rightarrow[f_1,\cdots,f_m]$;

Update the training error;

end if

end for

5 According to (3) and (4), calculate $P(y_i\mid x_i,\theta)$;

end for

6 According to (5), train parameters θ;

7 Return θ.

3. VIDEO INDEXING AND RECOMMENDATION

3.1 Viewers' Facial Expression Recognition

What is the most different from previous works and the most difficult is that the videos of views' facial expression usually consist of several different categories of expression. How to segment the videos into image sequences, each of which consist of only one prototype expression, becomes the most important question. Here we adopt the optimization strategy: we calculate the probability of the sequence from the first frame to present frame, until the probability comes to the maximum and then update the first frame. The detailed is shown in Algorithm 2.

Algorithm 2 *Facial expression recognition testing procedure*

Input: Image sequence $(x_1, x_2, \ldots, x_n)$

Output: Expression recognition result $(y_{11}, y_{12}, \ldots, y_{1m}), y_i$□$\{-3,-2,-1,0,1,2,3\}$

1 **Initialization** $i=1$, $count=1$;

2 while i<=n do

3 Calculate compositional Haar-like features f_i;

4 According to the results of **Algorithm 1**, calculate the probability $P(y_k|x_i)$, y_k□$\{-3,-2,-1,0,1,2,3\}$;

5 Calculate the maximum sequence probability $j^*=\arg\max_j P(y_k|x_i,\ldots,x_j)$,□$\{-3,-2,-1,0,1,2,3\}$;

6 $l(count)=j$;

Record expression category: $y(j)=y_k$;

7 Update the first image of sequence: $i=j+1$;

8 $count=count+1$;

end while

9 Return y.

3.2 Affective Curve

An affective curve can be created by manipulating goals, obstacles, and solutions to produce feelings like fear, disgust, anger, surprise, happiness, and sadness. These components can be coordinated with many different attractions, such as the attraction of a particular star, an act of spectacular violence, a sad song, and a dangerous stunt.

Definition An affective curve is a trinary function $A=f(t,p,e)$, in which t, p, e and A are short for *time, person, event and affective valence(affections)* respectively. As we consider facial expression for affective valence only, A belongs to the seven basic categories of facial expressions. That is,

$$A\in\{\text{'fear'}, \text{'sadness'}, \text{'surprise'}, \text{'happiness'}, \text{'disgust'}, \text{'anger'}, \text{'neutral'}\}.$$

For a particular person in a special event, the affective curve turns into $A=f(t)$, as shown in Figure 5. From the figure, we can see that there are many inflection points, which are the transitions of viewers' affections, meaning the transitions of video, the key part of the story, determining the results of the story.

Table 1. Indexing and recommendation criteria of videos.

	main facial expressions	terminal expression	recommendation standard
comedy	neu, hap	hap	P(hap)> θ_1
tragedy	neu,hap, sad	sad	P(sad)> θ_{21} &P(hap)< θ_{22}
horror	neu, fea, sur	fea, sur	P(fea)+P(sur)> θ_3
moving	neu, sad	sad	P(sad)> θ_4
boring	neu, dis	neu,dis	don't recommend at all
exciting	neu, hap, sur	hap	P(hap)+P(sur)> θ_6

3.3 Video Indexing and Recommendation

Video indexing is done according to viewers' affective curve and affective segmentation. Here we classify videos into six affective categories: comedy, tragedy, horror films, moving movies, boring films, and exciting movies. Take comedy for example, if there are only two facial expressions- happiness and neutral, and the percentage of happiness reaches the trained threshold, we classify it to comedy.

Video recommendation is done through the percentage of viewers' main facial expression and the terminal facial expression. Take comedy for example, if the percentage of happiness reaches 10% and the terminal facial expression is happiness, we can say the video is good enough to recommend to others, for it achieves its aim to make viewers happy. The detailed indexing and recommendation criteria are shown in Table 1. Hap, sad, dis, sui, ang, fea stand for happiness, sadness, disgust, surprise, anger, fear respectively (the same below).

4. EXPERIMENTS

We conduct our training experiments of expression recognition on the Cohn-Kanada expression database [13], a popular database widely used to evaluate facial expression analysis and recognition algorithms. The detailed description is shown in [13].

We conduct our video indexing and recommendation experiments on our own selected database. It consists of 100 short videos of different categories from YouKu [1], such as comedy 30%, tragedy 15%, horror film 15%, moving movies 18%, boring films 10%, exciting movies12% and so on. Fig.1 shows the examples. We also collected related videos of 10 viewers most students of 20 to 30, 40% female and 60% male, watching the selected web videos as the reflection of viewers' affection. They also gave their evaluation including recommendation points after watching videos. Corresponding examples of viewers' facial expressions (original) are shown in Figure 4.

4.1 Facial Expression Recognition

We compare our method with [11]'s POHCRFs + Gabor method, which adopted POHCRFs with Gabor features and [10]'s Boosting + compositional method, which integrated the procedure of building compositional features into boosting. The experimental results on the testing set are illustrated in Table 2. It is clear to see that our proposed method outperforms the other two. Our method obtains the average recognition accuracy of 96.6%, while that of POHCRF + Gaobr is 90.0% and that of Boosting + Compositional is 92.3%. This is reasonable because we combine temporal and spatial context together in a unified framework.

Table 2. Comparison of performance on the testing set (%)

	hap	sad	dis	sur	ang	fea
POHCRF+Gabor[11]	98.0	97.5	98.6	69.4	87.7	88.9
Boosting+Comp[10]	95.6	90.4	91.7	98.3	84.4	93.2
HCRF+Comp(ours)	100.0	98.2	98.7	99.4	92.4	95.5

Based on the training on Cohn-Kanada database, we test our viewers' facial expression sequence and also get a satisfying performance, with accuracy reaching 90% Some recognition result examples can be found in Figure 4.

4.2 Video Indexing and Recommendation

Take comedy< Got the Money Anyway>, tragedy <Titanic>, horror < Ferocious bell at the midnight>, moving < old soldier: Wu Dehou> , boring < There is a graduate home>, exciting <MBA: Kebi> for example, part of the affective curves are drawn in Figure 3. To explain it, we take the famous comedy and tragedy for example. It is clear to see that the curve of the opusculum is filled with happiness, completely fitting the effect of comedy. The affections of viewers watching the tragedy are happy and finally sad, and this is the criteria of tragedy.

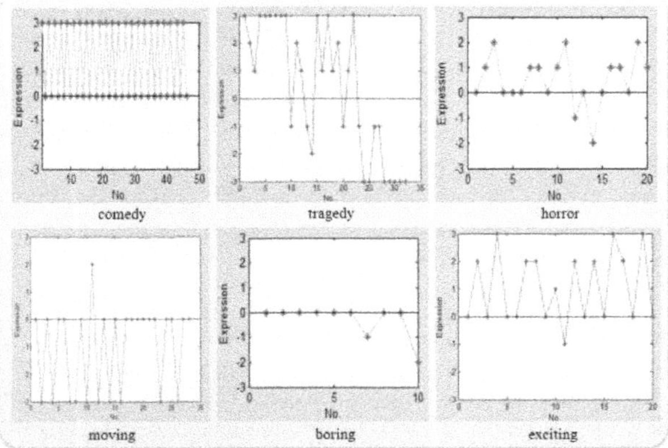

Figure 3. Affective Curves. -3,-2, -1, 0, 1, 2, 3 stand for sadness, anger, disgust, neutral, fear, surprise, happiness respectively.

Then we segment each video into affection sections, according to viewers' expressions. Some of the examples are listed in Figure 4. The detailed indexing confusion matrix is listed in Table 3. We can see that the average accuracy reaches 85.4%. Some of the videos are incorrectly classified, not because of the algorithm but because of videos' quality. Take comedy <There is a graduate home > for example, it is classified as boring, because it doesn't make viewers laugh at all. So we won't recommend it at all too.

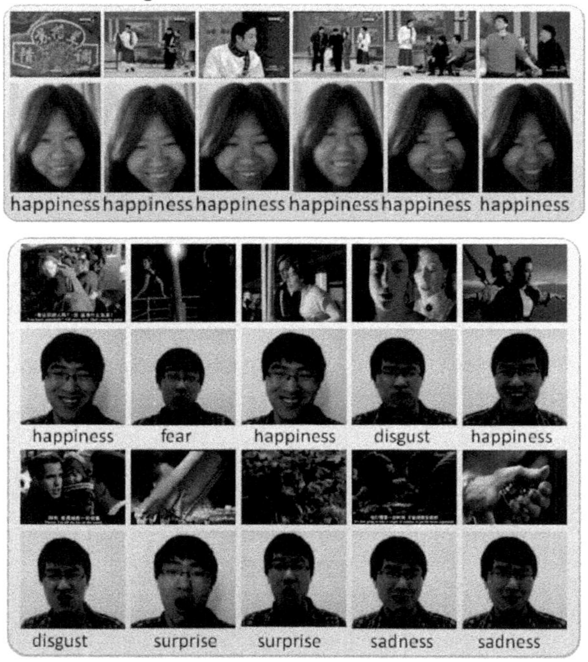

Figure 4. Examples of the affective scene of comedy <Got the Money Anyway> and tragedy <Titanic>

According to the recommendation criteria listed in Table 1, we give recommendation points according to the proportion. Some results are shown in figure 1.

5. CONCLUSION AND FUTURE WORK

In this paper, we propose a novel method to index and recommend video based on affective analysis, mainly on facial expression recognition of viewers. By building a spatio-temporal facial expression recognition classifier, drawing affective curve and segmenting each video into affective sections, we obtain perfect results of video indexing and recommendation.

Table 3. Indexing confusion matrix (%)

	comedy	tragedy	horror	moving	boring	exciting
comedy	93.33	0	0	0	3.33	3.33
tragedy	0	80	0	6.66	13.33	0
horror	0	0	86.66	0	3.33	3.33
moving	0	5.56	0	88.88	5.56	0
boring	10	10	0	0	80	0
exciting	8.33	0	8.33	0	0	83.33

We only consider facial expression as the method of expressing affections without considering verbal, vocal and other parts. Affections are generated through series of methods, including facial expressions, verbality, vocality, sounds, and actions. Combining them together effectively may further improve the performance of analyzing viewers' actual affections, which can increase the accuracy of video indexing and recommendation. In addition, it is also possible to build a general dataset of various methods of expressing affections. Integrating an iterative co-training framework of incrementally adding additional unlabeled data is also a possible way of further expanding the training data set and improving the classification performance. We can also classify videos into more detailed categories in the form of affections to index and recommend videos better.

6. ACKNOWLEDGEMENT

This work was supported by the National Natural Science Foundation of China (Grant No. 61071180 and Key Program Grant No. 61133003).

7. REFERENCES

[1] YouTube. www.youtube.com
YouKu. www.youku.com

[2] Y. Song, M. Zhao, Jay Yagnik, and X. Wu. 2010. "Taxonomic Classification for Web-based Videos," *CVPR*.

[3] Z. Wang, M. Zhao, *et al.* 2010. "YouTubeCat: Learning to Categorize Wild Web Videos," *CVPR*.

[4] Go Irie, Kota Hidaka, Takashi Satou. 2009. "Latent Topic Driving Model for Movie Affective Scene Classification," *MM*, pp. 565-568.

[5] Seungmin Rho, Byeong-jun Han, Eenjun Hwang. 2009. "SVR-based Music Mood Classification and Context-based Music Recommendation," *MM*, pp. 713-716.

[6] Picard R.W. 1997.Affective Computing [M].London , England: MIT Press.

[7] P. Yang, Q. Liu, and D. N. Metaxas. 2009. "Boosting encoded dynamic features for facial expression recognition," *Pattern Recognition Letters*, 30(2).

[8] G. Littlewort, M. S. Bartlett, I. Fasel, J. Susskind, and J. Movellan. 2006. "Dynamics of facial expression extracted automatically from video," *Image and Vision Computing*.

[9] C. Shan, S. Gong, and P. W.McOwan. 2005. "Robust facial expression recognition using local binary patterns," *ICIP*.

[10] P. Yang, Q. Liu, and D. N. Metaxas. 2010. "Exploring Facial Expressions with Compositional Features," *CVPR*.

[11] K.Chang, T. Liu,S. Lai. 2009. "Learning Partially-Observed Hidden Conditional Random Fields for Facial Expression Recognition," *CVPR* , pp. 533-540.

[12] A. Quattoni, M. Collins, and T. Darrell. 2004. "Conditional random fields for object recognition," *NIPS*.

[13] T. Kanade, J. Cohn, and Y.-L. Tian.2000. "Comprehensive database for facial expression analysis," *FG*, pp. 484-490.

Eventscapes: Visualizing Events over time with Emotive Facets

Brett Adams, Dinh Phung, Svetha Venkatesh
Curtin University, Perth, 6845, W. Australia
{b.adams,d.phung,s.venkatesh,}@curtin.edu.au

ABSTRACT

The scale and dynamicity of social media, and interaction between traditional news sources and online communities, has created challenges to information retrieval approaches. Users may have no clear information need or be unable to express it in the appropriate idiom, requiring instead to be oriented in an unfamiliar domain, to explore and learn. We present a novel data-driven visualization, termed *Eventscape*, that combines time, visual media, mood, and controversy. Formative evaluation highlights the value of emotive facets for rapid evaluation of mixed news and social media topics, and a role for such visualizations as pre-cursors to deeper search.

Categories and Subject Descriptors: H.3.1 [Information Storage and Retrieval]: Content Analysis and Indexing; H.5.1 [Information Interfaces and Presentation]: Multimedia Information Systems

General Terms: Algorithms, Human Factors, Experimentation

Keywords: Event, social media, sentiment, visualization

1. INTRODUCTION

One interesting characteristic of Web 2.0 is the symbiosis that has emerged between traditional news and social media discussion of that news. Breaking news can be broadcast further by interested people, diffusing in social media feeds; conversely, "citizen journalists" can be the first to scoop news on social media platforms, such as blogs or Twitter, and subsequently have it picked up by traditional news publishers. In addition to this dynamic, once news has diffused, social media often hosts discussion of it, which is enriched and provoked by evolving events, and in the interplay of opinions. The amount, diversity, and detail of news available on the web today far exceeds what was available a generation ago.

But this cataract of information comes at a cost: the average user often lacks the knowledge and/or awareness of the context of news to interpret its significance. There is a need for tools that help users rapidly orient themselves in an unfamiliar domain (e.g., US politics, climate change, mobile technology, or multiple sclerosis), and generate insights in familiar domains. Such tools can be conceived of as sitting between web search (e.g., Google keyword search) and manually authored digests (Wikipedia pages).

For example, social media has been avidly adopted by communities of people with health impairments. These communities often digest and discuss news with implications for their malady. But for those unfamiliar with a specific community, the history of salient events will not be readily apparent, which involve significant personalities, and might use alien language, idioms or jargon.

Research into systems that engender not simply information discovery, but learning, has been urged from an information retrieval perspective, where they are termed *exploratory search interfaces* [8]. Systems fitting this description have emerged from Multimedia and HCI research, including event-driven summarization of web video [5]; spatial representation of social media events [6]; and emotion polarity in real-time annotated debate [3]. The Blews system, which uses blogs to provide context for political news articles [4], is closest in spirit to this work. But it differs from Eventscapes in key aspects stemming from their assumed domain of politics: Blews only presents aggregates, manually identified political affiliation of blogs, and a politics-specific formulation of sentiment.

We present a novel visualization called *Eventscapes*. Eventscapes aim to represent the history of an information domain comprising news and related social media discussion, as a potential precursor to further exploration. An eventscape ingests multimedia in the form of feeds, performs topic modelling and clustering to discover topics and events, and arranges the discovered events in time. The primary visualization uses visual media–images and video stills–for rapid and casual browsing. In addition, eventscapes include two mood-related facets: document mood and event controversy, which is a composite function of mood-related features and social media features. Mood is a useful characteristic of "ego-centric" social media, where unlike mediated news, which often strives for objective neutrality, the author is prominent; and controversy is useful for crystallizing the issues causing friction in a debate. Eventscape generation is entirely data-driven and makes minimal assumptions.

2. EVENTSCAPE CREATION

Eventscapes visualize the history of events in a domain as evidenced by traditional news sources and corresponding discussion in social media. The aim, like all information visualization, is to transform a large amount of complex information into a form more readily digested; in particular, events, timing, persons involved, the diversity of sentiment expressed, and degree of controversy. Visualization should help orient a user new to a domain, or enable new insights to one familiar to the domain.

We use 'domain' in its loosest sense, to be whatever collection of documents a user submits to Eventscapes. These documents might be of a common class, such as politics news, opinion pieces, and blogs, or be the combined output social media–blogs, forum posts, tweets, and flickr uploads–of a user's friends. Text processing in Eventscapes is agnostic to the document source. Below we detail Eventscapes' document ingestion, visualization and interaction.

*Area Chair: Bernard Merialdo

MM'11, November 28–December 1, 2011, Scottsdale, Arizona, USA.

2.1 Information extraction

The visualization takes as input a collection of documents, D, that are about a topic of interest. Document collections are created in a web application that is a related project , by a subscription model. Eventscapes ingests documents in the form of RSS feeds, a simple, lightweight web publishing format. As noted above, nothing is assumed about the make-up of this document set, but we are interested in exploring the interactions between news and social media, and so have chosen feeds from each. For the examples in this paper we have used feeds created by Google Alerts, Twitter search, Youtube search, and manually subscribed feeds from news sites, opinion blogs and personal blogs.[1]

The set of documents, D, can be viewed as evidence for an ongoing topic of discussion and/or temporally restricted events. To extract these topics and events, we use a time-sensitive topic model, Topic Over Time (TOT), which is of the Latent Dirichlet family. The output of the model is a number of topics, which are probability distributions over a lexicon, together with topic assignments to words in all documents. These topic mixtures form the basis of a document similarity measure which is subsequently used to cluster documents. We use negative Jensen-Shannon divergence of topic mixtures, and Affinity Propagation to cluster, but there exist many alternative similarity measures and clustering algorithms. The resulting clusters, $C = \{d_1, d_2, \ldots, d_c\}$, where $D = d_1 \cup d_2 \ldots \cup d_c$, capture topics that are ongoing, and/or time-bound events, and are extracted both for their utility in filtering the visualization, and calculation of a measure of per-topic/event controversy.

In addition, for every document in D we extract the following information: timestamp, links to embedded visual media (images and video, the primary element in visualization), emotion valence and arousal of document text (calculated with the Affective Norms for English Words, ANEW, lexicon [1]), author or publisher of the document, and, if possible, the number, depth, and content of comments attached to the document. Post and comment parsing is performed using the web application mentioned above.

Finally, we calculate a measure of controversy for every document cluster. Merriam-Webster Dictionary offers the following definition of controversy: a *discussion* marked especially by the expression of *opposing views* : dispute (emphasis added). We propose a generic formulation of controversy, $c()$, for a cluster of documents, d_i, relative to clusters C:

$$c(d_i|C) = w_e.e(d_i|C) + w_x.x(d_i|C) + w_i.i(d_i|C) \quad (1)$$

where $e()$ measures the nature of *emotions* expressed in the documents; $x()$ measures the amount of *exchange* between those participating in discussion about the documents; $i()$ measures the degree of *interest* shown in the topic; and $w_e + w_x + w_i = 1$ weight the contribution of each measure.

We have used the following specific formulations of the above measures. Each is a weighted sum of one or more logistic functions, $l(x|\alpha, \beta) = \frac{1}{1+e^{-\alpha x+\beta}}$, where x is the normalized distance of a cluster feature, and α and β are parameters that effect the shape of the logistic curve.

$$e(d_i|C) = w_{e_1}.l(x_i^{ASL}) + w_{e_2}.l(x_i^{VAL}) + w_{e_3}.l(x_i^{ANGER}) \quad (2)$$

where x_i^{ASL} is normalized distance from the cluster mean of mean document arousal for cluster i; likewise, x_i^{VAL} refers to *standard deviation* of document valence; and x_i^{ANGER} refers to the ratio of documents in the angry quadrant of the valence–arousal plane (i.e., valence < 5, arousal > 5; top left of the mood map in Figure 2). Intuitively, $e()$, tends toward its maximum of 1 when cluster documents have relatively high arousal, diverse valence, and large proportion of angry sentiment. Conversely, $e()$, tends toward its minimum of 0 when cluster documents have low arousal, uniform valence, and low proportion of angry sentiment.[2]

$$x(d_i|C) = l(x_i^{COM}) \quad (3)$$

where x_i^{COM} is normalized distance from cluster mean of comments per document for cluster i. Intuitively, $x()$ tends toward its maximum when the documents in the cluster provoke much discussion in the form of comments, and vice versa.

$$i(d_i|C) = l(x_i^{DOC}) \quad (4)$$

where x_i^{DOC} is normalized distance from cluster mean of documents per cluster for cluster i. Intuitively, $i()$ tends toward its maximum when there are more documents discussing the topic correlated with cluster i, and vice versa.

The above formulations of controversy are not definitive, and might be elaborated in many ways. E.g., a richer formulation of $e()$ might include rhetorical features, such as modal verbs like 'should', which indicate level of commitment, [2]; a more precise formulation of $x()$ would reflect comment exchanges and comment thread depth, rather than simply count, where comment authors have repeated exchanges; and a richer formulation of $i()$ might use web services to gauge interest in a topic, such as Google Trends (e.g., for web video summarization, [7]).

2.2 Visualization

Eventscapes visualization and interface has been implemented in JavaScript for ease of prototyping and deployment. An example eventscape, for the domain *Australian Politics*, can be seen in Figure 1. It is composed of three distinct areas: timeline, event/topic clusters, and selected cluster documents, which correspond to the boxed annotations in Figure 1.

The primary artifacts rendered in the timeline are images (or video stills). Imagery is primary, rather than text (e.g., tag clouds or n-grams) because they can quickly convey a lot of information– "a picture is worth a thousand words". Moreover, specific images in news and social media are typically chosen to encapsulate the most salient elements of the textual content; if the story is about an election result, it may be the winning or losing personality; if it is about the discovery of potential viral cause of a disease, the image may be a representation of a virus. Documents without an image are represented as small squares, and can be navigated to and read like any other document.

Mood is represented in the timeline and documents list. Images are positioned horizontally according to valence: low valence images (e.g., from documents expressing anger or depression) tend to the left, and vice versa. Mood is also mapped to colour according to the mood map in Figure 2. Documents are colour-coded, images are bordered by the same colour, and mood "blooms" of documents in the selected cluster mingle in the timeline to provide a sense of the diversity of mood in the current cluster at the current time. Divergent sentiment can indicate important elements of a debate, such as bias and confusion.

The controversy measure, Equation 1, is mapped to a colour, from white for low controversy to red for high controversy, and displayed behind each cluster in the list.

[1]Feed collation need not be manual; recommenders group feeds.

[2][3] suggest that Pearson correlation between negative and positive tweets (in their case) can suggest controversy.

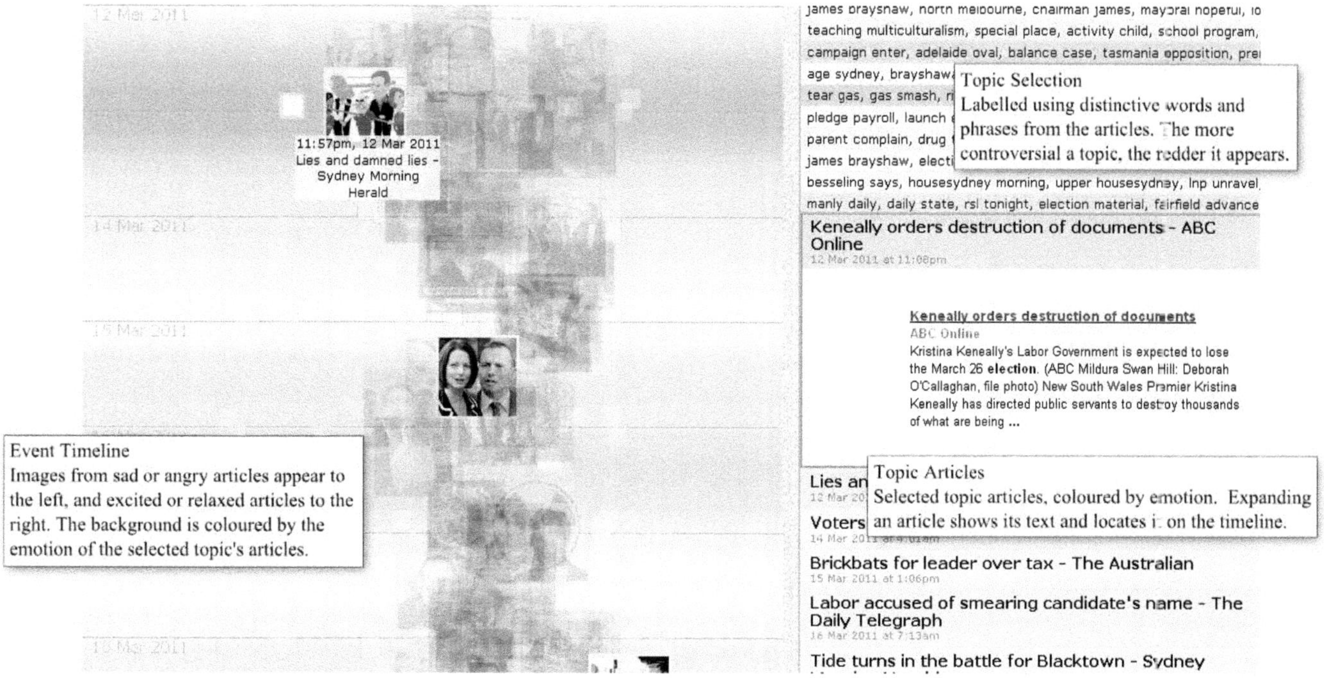

Figure 1: Example eventscape from AUSPOL corpus. The selected cluster corresponds to a recent state election.

All three panes can be interacted with, and actions are propagated to the others. Clicking on an image selects that image's enclosing cluster; clicking a cluster scrolls the timeline to the cluster's mean time and fades all images not in that cluster, and clicking a document in the document list opens that document, and scrolls the timeline to its published time. Eventscapes aim to be accessible to the casual user, and information analyst under time constraints, as a launch pad into further search. Below we discuss two examples to indicate the kinds of insights Eventscapes can engender.

First, for the domain of *Australian Politics*, with reference to Figure 1, a cluster of high controversy has been selected. The cluster's documents show a high degree of sentiment diversity; the images not faded indicate the involved personalities; and a quick sift through the document titles and truncated content indicate, at the very least, the cluster has something to do with a state election. In fact, the election was a landslide against the incumbents, and involved a subsequent period of acrimony.

Second, for the domain of *Chronic Fatigue Syndrome/Sufferers*, with reference to Figure 2, a period is indicated that saw publication of medical research shedding doubt on previous findings that pointed to a retro-viral cause (the virus is called XMRV). That the topic in question has to do with *viruses* can be rapidly ascertained from the images chosen to embellish the articles, one highlighted with mouse-over, and another below un-faded because part of the selected cluster. For reference, news citing the article can be seen at annotation ***E*** in Google Trends. Social media response to this publication is constrained to the calm/depressed quadrants of the mood plane, as indicated by the dominant blue/purple colour-coding.

3. FORMATIVE EVALUATION

We performed a small formative evaluation of Eventscapes to assess its strengths and weaknesses, and elicit new features.[3] Past experience with developing web applications has shown us the value of a participatory design process, so the evaluation emphasizes the elicitation of suggestions for improvement. Four participants were obtained from the Department by invitation. Each was given two eventscapes to view in the browser of their choice.

The eventscapes for the study were built from these corpora:

1. *Australian Politics* (AUSPOL), covers news, tweets, and blog feeds: this set covers a close federal election, a state election, and a number of controversial policy issues. The corpus contains 21017 posts/articles, and 89663 comments.
2. *Chronic Fatigue Syndrome* (CFS), news and blogs: this set covers a number of contentious medical findings, and related commentary in professional and personal blogs. The corpus contains 3672 posts/articles and 21807 comments.

All documents (posts and comments) were used to generate topic models, but only posts and articles were clustered. TOT parameters were 30 topics for AUSPOL, 25 for CFS, using 5000 Gibbs samples for both. Controversy weights were set once for all: $w_e = 0.6$, $w_{e1} + w_{e_2} + w_{e_3} = 0.25 + 0.5 + 0.25$; $w_x = 0.2$; $w_i = 0.2$; $\alpha = 1.5$, $\beta = 1$. Clusters below 5 documents were culled.

Participant feedback was via online survey. Questions focused on evaluating four aspects of the visualization: event/topic discovery; the usefulness of timeline presentation of discovered events/topics; mood facet; and controversy facet. Questions were posed to explicitly isolate the performance/utility of each aspect from others as much as possible. In addition, participants were asked for an overall judgment of the visualizations.

Overall response to Eventscapes was positive: the statement "I like Eventscapes" received an average rating of 4.33 on a Likert-scale from 1 (strongly disagree) to 5 (strongly agree); "I understand Eventscapes" received an average rating of 3.33.

In more detail, the response to the timeline and emotive facets was uniformly positive: timeline usefulness had an average rating of 4; image layout by valence an average rating of 3.5; and precision of controversy estimation an average rating of 3.5; and usefulness of controversy for navigation, an average rating of 4.5.

[3]Indeed, formal evaluation of such systems is acknowledged as a challenge in its own right, [8, 5].

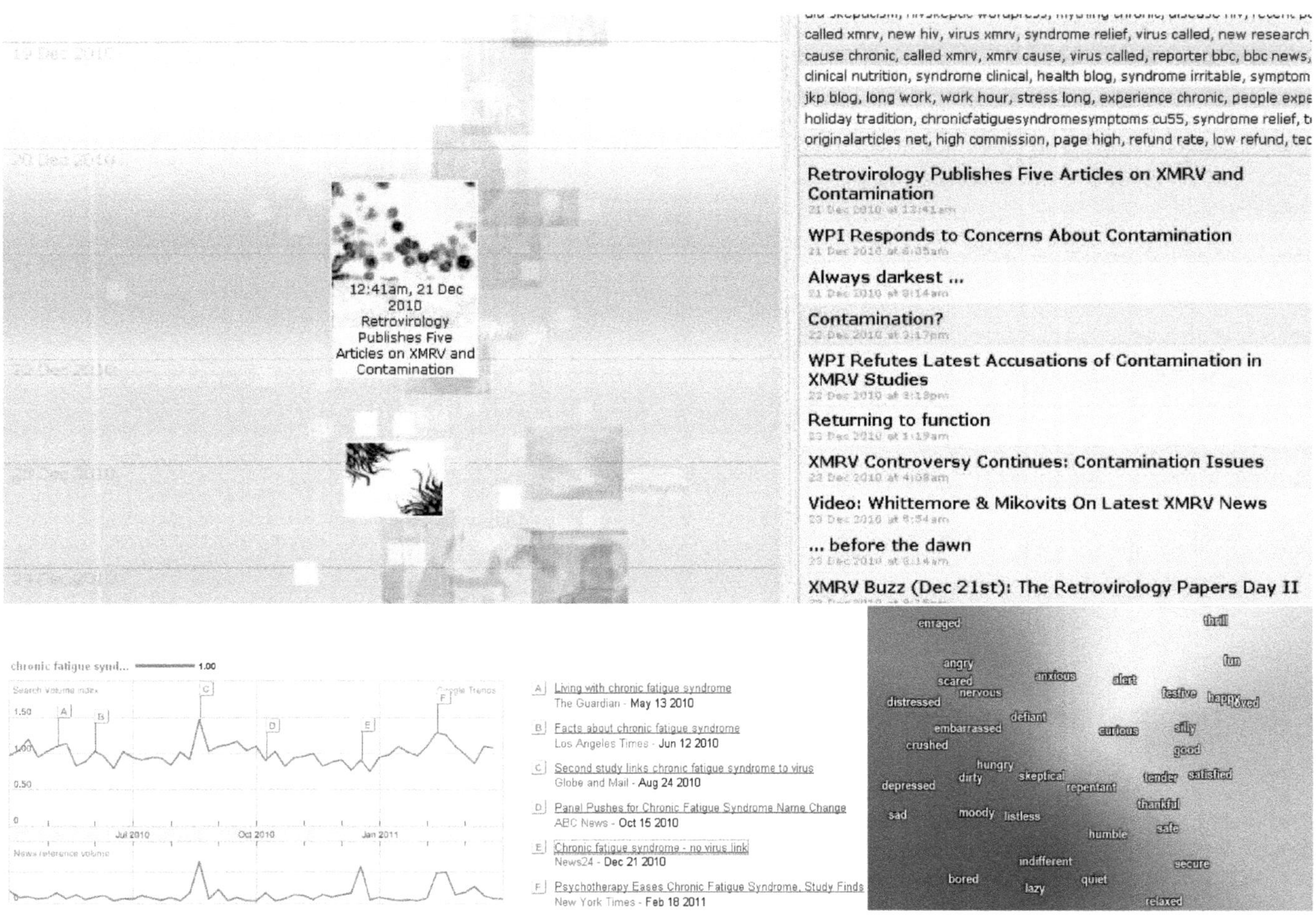

Figure 2: Top: Example eventscape from CFS corpus. Doubt about a retro-viral cause for CFS (the virus is called XMRV), article *E* in Google Trends (bottom left), provoke a subdued response. Bottom right: Map of valence (x-axis) and arousal (y-axis) to colour.

Document clustering was the weakest link, receiving an ambivalent average rating of 3. Clustering performance affects controversy calculation and document filtering and will be targeted in future. Better topic models will come from using the whole text of news articles when only snippets are published via feeds. One participant commented that there were many clusters. Use of non-parametric topic models, and similarity measures that result in fewer clusters will be explored. The same participant also desired a means of ranking clusters. Clusters are ranked by mean time, but an option to rank by controversy would be useful. Automatic recognition of clusters as either topics (spread in time) or events (constrained in time), and explicit classification as such, is another option.

When asked which applications they would add Eventscapes to, 4 people voted for their feed reader of choice (e.g., Google Reader), and one for online forums (the other option being Wikipedia).

4. CONCLUSION AND FUTURE WORK

Motivated by the emerging interaction between traditional news publication and social media, we have presented Eventscapes, which uses visual media and emotive facets, including sentiment and topic controversy, to visualize a document collection. It aims to enable users lacking contextual awareness of a news/topic domain a grasp of salient events and personalities, and further exploration within the domain via the same interface. A small formative evaluation for the domains *Australian Politics* and *Chronic Fatigue Syndrome*, reflected positively on novel use of visual depiction of event history, mood and controversy. Future work will involve a larger, longitudinal study, ideally with a portion of journalism students; implement an on-demand version of eventscapes; and a community facet that enables the user to see if divergent opinions correlate with online communities (e.g., arising from homophily in online networks), or fall along different boundaries (e.g., pre-existing political bias).

5. REFERENCES

[1] M. Bradley and P. Lang. Affective Norms for English Words (ANEW) Instruction Manual and Affective Ratings. *Technical Report C-1, The Center for Research in Psychophysiology*, 1999.

[2] N. Diakopoulos, S. Goldenberg, and I. Essa. Videolyzer: quality analysis of online informational video for bloggers and journalists. In *Proc. Int Conf. on Human factors in Comp. Sys.*, CHI '09, pp. 799–808, NY, NY, USA, 2009.

[3] N. Diakopoulos and D. Shamma. Characterizing debate performance via aggregated twitter sentiment. In *Proc. Int. Conf. on Human factors in Comp. Sys.*, CHI '10, pp. 1195–1198, NY, NY, USA, 2010.

[4] M. Gamon, S. Basu, D. Belenko, D. Fisher, M. Hurst, and A. König. Blews: Using blogs to provide context for news articles. In *Proc. of the Int. Conf. on Weblogs and Social Media, ICWSM 2008*, March 2008.

[5] R. Hong, J. Tang, H. Tan, C. Ngo, S. Yan, and T. Chua. Beyond search: Event driven summarization for web videos. *Accepted for pub. in ACM Trans. on Multimedia Computing, Communications, and Applications.*

[6] V. Singh, M. Gao, and R. Jain. Social pixels: genesis and evaluation. In *Proceedings of the international conference on Multimedia*, MM '10, pp. 481–490, New York, NY, USA, 2010. ACM.

[7] S. Tan, H.-K. Tan, and C.-W. Ngo. Topical summarization of web videos by visual-text time-dependent alignment. In *Proc. Int. Conf. on Multimedia*, MM '10, pp. 1095–1098, NY, NY, USA, 2010. ACM.

[8] R. White, B. Kules, S. Drucker, and M. Schraefel. Supporting exploratory search: Intro. *Commun. ACM*, 49:36–39, April 2006.

Signature-Image-Based Event Analysis for Personal Photo Albums * †

Minh-Son Dao Duc-Tien Dang-Nguyen‡ Francesco De Natale

mmLAB - Department of Information Engineering and Computer Science
University of Trento
Via Sommarive, 14I-38123 POVO(TN), Italy
(dao, dangnguyen, denatale)@disi.unitn.it

ABSTRACT

Quick reorganizing and draft annotating personal photo albums under event scheme is an emerging trend. In this research, a method has been developed to meet such requirements using the idea of *gist* and mosaic art so that viewers could understand the meaning of a whole scene without paying much attention in individual details. First, given a photo album, all chronologically ordered images are normalized to a smaller size, and then mosaicked side-by-side to create a signature image representing for that album. Next, by integrating the optimized linear programming with the color descriptor of the signature image, not only the event-type of the album but also all sub-event-types of the sub-sequence photos are decided. More than 19,000 images of five varied event-types have been used to evaluate the proposed method. Experimental results show that the proposed method could detect events towards annotation and re-organization of personal photo albums with high accuracy at a rapid speed.

Categories and Subject Descriptors

I.4 [**Image Processing and Computer Vision**]: Scene Analysis; H.3 [**Information Storage and Retrieval**]: Content Analysis and Indexing

General Terms

Algorithms

Keywords

Gist, Mosaic art, Optimization Linear Programming, Event Analysis, Personal Photo Album

*Area chair: Tat-Seng Chua

†This work is supported by GLOCAL project (www.glocal-project.eu)

‡co-author

MM'11, November 28–December 1, 2011, Scottsdale, Arizona, USA.

1. INTRODUCTION

It has been said that a picture is worth a thousand words. Thus, there is no surprise when people prefer to use photos to index events they have been involved in. Studies in cognitive psychology have shown that when looking at photos, the first thing people recall is the event itself, then who was involved in, and where and when that event happened [9]. Therefore we could say that personal photo albums are indexes of the events in life.

We have witnessed a vast increase in uploading, sharing and tagging personal photo albums on social networks within a decade. Billion of photos can be found over the Internet, on social network websites like Facebook[1], or public photo-sharing websites such as FlickR[2] and Photobucket[3], to name a few. Nevertheless, the more images people share on social networks, the more difficult to retrieve what they need. This is because of the big difference between human vision system and computer vision w.r.t understanding well the semantic meaning conveyed by images. Although content-based media retrieval has been developed significantly these days, there is still lack of successfully automatic tools to support systems as well as users to control their data [5][7]. Therefore, we would like to propose a new method to meet such an emerging requirement. The proposed method is based on two observations:

- **Common Patterns**: One of the most interesting users' habits is taking a series of images around the places where events happened. That leads to the assumption that inside one event's episode, there might be some common patterns (e.g. colors, landmarks, perspective, or objects) that could help us understand events holistically.

- **Common Structures**: In social life, there are a lot of spoken and unspoken rules human beings must follow without questioning or thinking about it. Thus, it should be reasonable to assume that real-life events should have structures. Consequently, their photo albums should also have the same structures.

Based on those two observations, we propose a method to detect event-type, organize, and annotate personal photo albums into a set of subfolders associated with the structure of

[1]www.facebook.com
[2]www.flickr.com
[3]www.photobucket.com

event-types. To distinguish from previous approaches focusing on individuals of events, we process these individuals as a whole - a holistic event. That helps us bypass the complexity of existing problems in computer vision, such as object detection, image segmentation, concept detection.

The rest of the paper is organized as follows. In section 2 we overview the related work on this problem. Section 3 describes our methodology for personal photo album analysis. We also introduce *Signature Image*, a low-level feature representing the gist of an event. Experimental results are shown in section 4. In section 5 includes conclusions and ideas for future work.

2. RELATED WORK

In this section, we briefly review some existing literature related to Personal Photo Collections analysis.

In [3], a method for event detection of a single photo from specific sport events is presented. Compared to previous work, authorsmade a significant improvement by using a graphical model for labeling and adding SIFT features for matching. By using only a single photo, their approach can only apply to certain events with certain photo types.

In [10], Yu et al. presented an approach for photos grouping based on the similarity of photos among users on the network based on SimRank and spectral clustering. The results of real users' collections showed accuracy significantly improved (up to 63%). Another interesting method with the same approach was introduced in [1]. This research used the conditional random field models to calculate correlation among photos in a collection in terms of time, location, and scene of the collection.

In [4] an event detection method was proposed for home photos using a conceptual graph where concepts must be detected from photos. This method used weighted histogram-intersection-based measurements to match the concepts with the event models to estimate the event type. Experimental results on 2400 photos with an event taxonomy of 5 layers and 20 categories showed that the average precision is approximately 60%.

Nevertheless, none of all information used in these methods could be easily found in photo-sharing social networks due to lack of popular input devices (e.g. GPS) as well as high accuracy of user-generated-content data being generated and shared. Besides, the complexity of these methods is very high due to a high computational cost of each member's problem (e.g. object detection, image segmentation, concept detection). Moreover, most of these methods treat images as individuals instead of considering as a part of the whole event, though we know that "The whole is different from the sum of its parts" (Aristotle in the Metaphysics).

3. METHODOLOGY

In this section, a series of algorithms to create signature images (SIB), and to analyze photo albums by using SIB are introduced and discussed thoroughly. For clarification, before discussing our methodology in details, we clarify some terminologies and assumptions as follows: (1) a personal photo album or photo album is used to describe a set of images taken by a single digital image device during the time a certain real-life event happened. All images must have UTC time, and (2) Let E_k, P_i^k, and $I_j^{k,i}$ denote k^{th} event type, i^{th} photo album of event type E_k, and j^{th} image of photo album P_i^k, respectively. Let γ, λ, and T denote *similar* threshold, *updating* threshold, and size of normalized image, respectively.

Figure 1: SIB of *Cricket* Event Type

3.1 SIB:Signature Image

Given an unknown event photo album P contained N images $\{I_j\}_{j=1..N}$, the SIB of this event is created by using Alg. 1.

Algorithm 1: *Creating Signature Image for a Given Event*

1. Init SIB as 0x0 color pixels
2. FOR ALL I_j DO
   (a) Scale all images I_j to TxT color pixels
   (b) Sort time ascending these images. Let $\widehat{I_j}$ denotes images after sorting so that $\forall j$, $time(\widehat{I}_{j-1}) < time(\widehat{I_j})$
   (c) Resize SIB to $(T \times |P|) \times T$
   (d) Mosaic time ascending all images $\widehat{I_j}$ to SIB at region (left, top, right, bottom)=$(0, 0, T \times |P|, T)$
3. END ALGORITHM

Torralba et al [8] proposed a research method which allows us to scale an image to a smaller one without losing significat information. They prove that the ability of gathering information is remarkably tolerant to degrations in image solution. Moreover, psychophysics has shown that with a single glance of an image, human can perceive the meaning of event conveyed in such an image [6]. Thus, mosaicking all images of an event into one big picture could help to understand that event better - in a gist manner, or even to create a new perspective of an event similar to the way the mosaic arts work.

Given N photo albums $\{P_i^k\}_{i=1..N}$ of event type E_k, a new set of *Signature Image* of this event type, $SIB^k = \{SIB_i\}_{i=1..N}$, is created. For visualization and storage, we mosaic all SIBs row by row to create an unique image SIB^k. Fig. 1 illustrates the image SIB^k of kth event type, in this case E_k=*Cricket*, and N=12. It should be noted that each row in Fig. 1 denotes one *Cricket* photo album.

3.2 Event Type Classification

Now we focus on the issue of event type classification using SIB. Assume that there are K signature images $\{SIB^k\}_{k=1..K}$, each SIB^k represents an event type E_k. Given an unknown-event-type photo album P, the Alg. 2 is used to decide to which event type the photo album P belongs.

Algorithm 2: *Classifying event type using SIBs*

1. Calculate SIB of photo album P using Alg. 1
2. $D = 0$

3. FOR ALL SIB^k DO
    (a) Calculate dissimilarity distance between SIB and SIB^k: $d_k = d(SIB, SIB^k)$
    (b) $D = D \cup \{d_k\}$
4. Calculate $d_{min} = min(d_k)$, and $idx = argmin_k(d_k)$, where $d_k \in D$
5. IF $d_{min} \leq \gamma$ THEN
    (a) $SIB^{temp} = SIB^{idx}$
    (b) Update $SIB^{temp} = SIB^{idx} \cup SIB$
    (c) IF $d(SIB^{temp}, SIB^{idx} > \lambda)$ THEN $SIB^{idx} = SIB^{temp}$
    (d) Return idx (the given photo album belongs to event type E_{idx})
6. ELSE the given photo album is assigned as *unknown event type*
7. END ALGORITHM

In fact, the main idea of using SIB to detect event type of an unknown event is to measure the similarity between two SIBs: one identifies event type (SIB^k), and the other represents the unknown event SIB_i. The larger the distance similarity is, the better accuracy for event type classification. Therefore, using SIB can simplify the complexity of event type classification by turning the problem to color image retrieval with a small number of images (SIBs).

SIB event type classification is an unsupervised method. It also has an ability to enhance its knowledge throughout its life. The more photo albums the users update to a certain event type, the more characteristic information of such event type accrues by simply increasing its SIB's size. However, to prevent the oversize of SIB^k, when an incoming unknown event is classified successfully into a certain event type, whether or not its SIB image could be mosaicked to SIB^k is decided by updating threshold (see 5.c in Alg. 2).

Color feature is also popular in content-based image retrieval community due to its straightforward information and low computational cost [5]. There are several state-of-the-art methods using color feature as the main feature for comparing two images. Thus, we decided to use colors as the main descriptor to calculate $d(SIB, SIB^k)$.

3.3 Event Analysis

This section introduces a method by which a photo album could be divided into a set of subfolders sharing the same semantic meaning. As we mentioned earlier, most of real-life events have their own structure influenced by their culture, education, or social life level. For example, one western marriage often has a rehearsal party, a ceremony with a bride, a groom, and a priest, and a party at the end; a soccer match usually starts with the first half and is followed by the second half. Therefore, if we can define the structure of those events, we can reorganize and annotate photo albums by using SIB.

Assuming that there is a set of photo albums $P^k = \{P_i^k\}$, $i = 1..N$ belongs to event E_k where N is the number of photo albums. We can also assume that there is an event model of event E_k: $ME_k = \{SE_{k,j}\}$, $j = 1..M$ where M is the number of sub-event-types, and $SE_{k,j}$ is the jth sub-event-type of E_k. Infact, event type and sub-event-type are equal with regards to semantic meaning. They are used to express the meaning of social activities or complex actions. Hence, we can use Alg. 2 to create SIBs for sub-event-types.

For each photo album P_i^k, based on event model, we manually group temporally successive images into different sub-photo-albums whose contents share the same semantics; each sub-photo-album represents for each sub-event-type SE. Then, we using Alg. 2 to create SIBs for these sub-photo-albums. Let $SIB^{k,j}$ denote the SIB of $SE_{k,j}$.

At this point, if we consider:(1) the event model ME_k as a *corpus*; (2) each $SIB^{k,j}$ as a *chunk of speech units* in the corpus ME_k; and (3) SIB of the photo album P as a *sentence* whose characters are I_j (see Alg. 1), our problem could be seen as *text to speech synthesis* problem. There are several techniques to solve this problem, such as HMM, Maximum Expectation, or Maximum Matching Algorithm [2]. We, however, choose the last one to create sub-photo-albums due to its simplicity and popularity.

4. EXPERIMENTAL RESULTS

The dataset used in our experiment is downloaded from Picasa[4]:207 photo albums (19101 images) of five various event-types covering sport, social, and natural landscape categories are downloaded from Picasa Web Albums to form the testbed: *Basketball* (30 albums, 2498 images), *Cricket* (35 albums, 3525 images), *SkiHoliday* (33 albums, 3165 images), *Graduation* (34 albums, 3634 images), and *Marriage* (75 albums, 3634 images). We have also obtained a thorough ground truth annotation for every photo album as well as UTC time information for each image.

We have also obtained a thorough ground truth annotation for every photo album as well as UTC time information for each image.

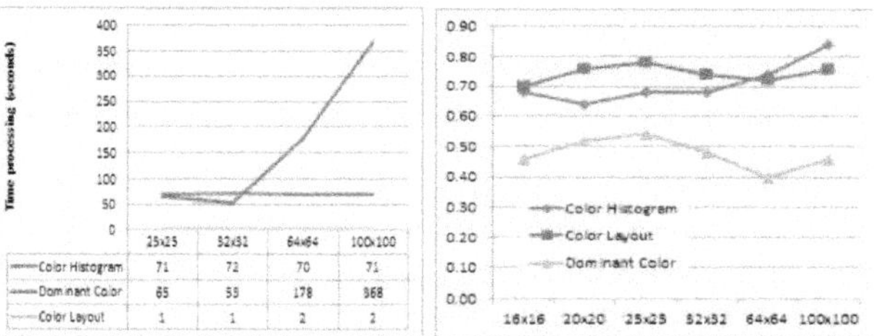

Figure 2: (left)Comparing Time Processing with Different Color Descriptors; (right)Average Recall of Event-type Classification with Different Color Descriptors and Image Size

First, we would like to discuss the accuracy and time processing of the proposed method. The results are illustrated in Fig. 2. In general, the accuracy of classification is very high, and the time processing is fast.

Second, we checked the misclassification rate among event types (see Fig. 3). Noted that each cell of diagram denotes the dissimilarity degree between two event types, and is normalized to [0,1]. It means that the higher the cell's value is, the smaller misclassification rate.

Third, we discuss the convergence of SIB's size and the method for choosing *updating* threshold. In Fig. 4, after 10-15 updating times, the distance similarity between the SIB before updating and the SIB after updating, $d(SIB_{i-1}^k, SIB_{i-1}^k \cup SIB)$, starts converging to a small value (see the

[4]www.picasa.com

	Basket Ball	Cricket	Graduation	Marriage	Ski Holiday
Basket Ball	0.00	0.64	0.40	0.43	0.82
Cricket	0.64	0.00	0.68	0.50	0.46
Graduation	0.40	0.68	0.00	0.25	0.87
Marriage	0.43	0.50	0.25	0.00	0.69
Ski Holiday	0.82	0.46	0.87	0.69	0.00

(a) Color Layout

	Basket Ball	Cricket	Graduation	Marriage	Ski Holiday
Basket Ball	0.00	0.40	0.57	0.63	0.77
Cricket	0.40	0.00	0.34	0.36	0.59
Graduation	0.57	0.34	0.00	0.35	0.76
Marriage	0.63	0.36	0.35	0.00	0.89
Ski Holiday	0.77	0.59	0.76	0.89	0.00

(b) Color Dominant

	Basket Ball	Cricket	Graduation	Marriage	Ski Holiday
Basket Ball	0.00	0.87	0.86	0.81	0.87
Cricket	0.87	0.00	0.87	0.82	0.83
Graduation	0.86	0.87	0.00	0.79	0.86
Marriage	0.81	0.82	0.79	0.00	0.80
Ski Holiday	0.87	0.83	0.86	0.80	0.00

(c) Color Histogram

Figure 3: Distance matrices of Event-type Classification with Different Color Descriptors, T=25

average line in diagrams). Therefore, after a certain number of updating times, we easily detect the *updating* thresholds by calculating the average of the total range of $d(SIB_{i-1}^k, SIB_{i-1}^k \cup SIB)$ during the stabilizing period.

Finally, we compare our method with two existing methods focusing on photo album analysis: (a) Lim et al [4], and (b) Cao et al [1] (please refer to previous sections to have more information how these methods work). From the comparison (Fig. 5), we could conclude that our method works better than the others.

5. CONCLUSION

We have presented SIB method, and a novel event type analysis for personal photo collections. Our method shows the advantages of fast computing and is easy to implementation. Moreover, it is an unsupervised method and has the ability to enhance its knowledge throughout its life. This is the first time the mosaic art and the advantages of human visual system are integrated to classify event type towards organizing personal photo albums. With our method, there is no need to detect objects, landmarks or the meaning of tags to understand the global information of events. The experiments show that our method has very high accuracy and is extremely fast. Since event type classification plays an important role in many problems of event mining in multimedia, such asevent detection or event recognition, our method could be used not only in event type classification but also for other relevant problems. In future work, we will create better SIBs by integrating spatial information in terms of number of photos with geo-tag increasing, and also by finding the suitable distances as well as features for the improved SIBs qualifications.

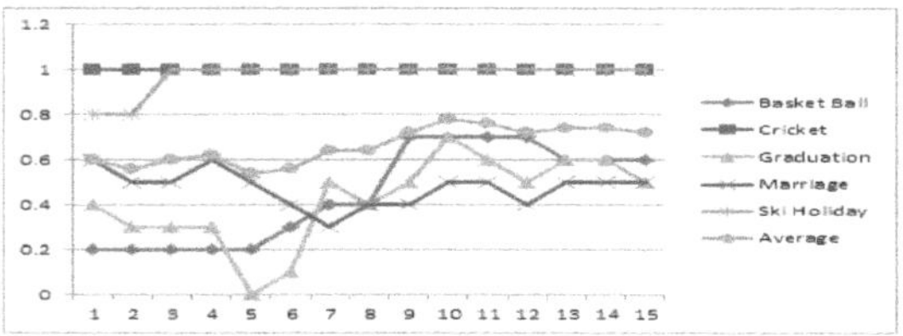

(a) Recall

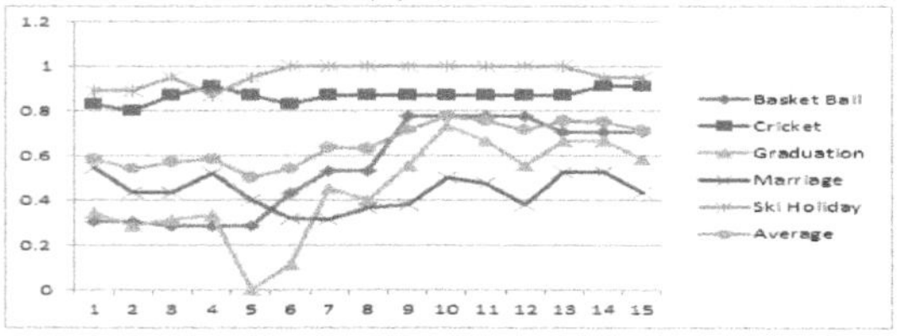

(b) F-scores

Figure 4: Convergence of SIB's size

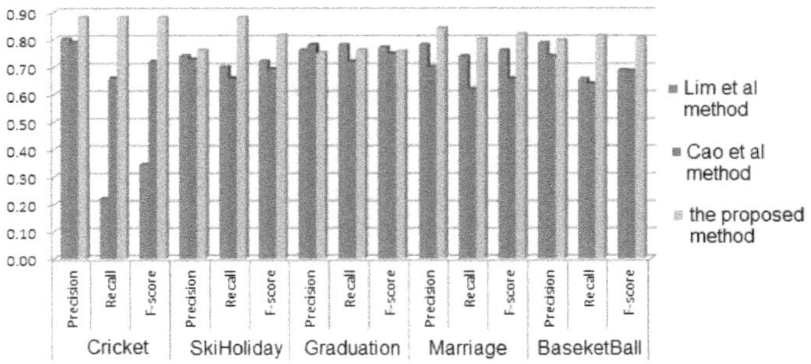

Figure 5: Photo album analysis; Comparing to other methods

6. REFERENCES

[1] L. Cao, J. Luo, H. Kautz, and T. Huang. Image annotation within the context of personal photo collections using hierarchical event and scene models. *IEEE Trans. on Multimedia*, 11(2):208–219, Feburary 2009.

[2] T. Dutoit. *An Introduction to Text-to-Speech Synthesis*. Kluwer Academic Publishers, Norwell, MA, USA, 2001.

[3] L. Li and L. Fei-Fei. What, where and who? classifying events by scene and object recogntion. In *ICCV*, pages 1–8, 2007.

[4] J. H. Lim, Q. Tian, and P. Mulhem. Home photo content modeling for personalized event-based retrieval. *IEEE Multimedia*, 10:28–37, 2003.

[5] Y. Liu, D. Zhang, G. Lu, and W.-Y. Ma. A survey of content-based image retrieval with high-level semantics. *Journal of Pattern Recognition*, 40:262–282, 2007.

[6] A. Oliva and A. Torralba. Building the gist of a scene: the role of global image features in recognition. In *Progress in Brain Research*, pages 23–36, 2006.

[7] P. Sandhaus and S. Boll. Semantic analysis and retrieval in personal and social photo collections. *Journal of Multimedia Tools and Application*, 51:5–33, 2011.

[8] A. Torralba, R. Fergus, and W. Freeman. Tiny images. *MIT Technical Report - MIT-CSAIL-TR-2007-24*, 2007.

[9] W. Wagenaar. My memory: A study of autobiographical memory over six years. *Cognitive Psychology*, 18(2):225–252, 2004.

[10] J. Yu, X. Jin, J. Han, and J. Luo. Mining personal image collection for social group suggestion. In *IEEE ICDMW*, pages 202–207. IEEE, 2009.

Leveraging Collective Wisdom for Web Video Retrieval through Heterogeneous Community Discovery

Lin Pang[1, 2], Juan Cao[1], Yongdong Zhang[1], Shouxun Lin[1]
[1]Institute of Computing Technology, Chinese Academy of Sciences, Beijing 100190, China
[2]Graduate University of Chinese Academy of Sciences, Beijing 100049, China
{panglin,caojuan, zhyd, sxlin} @ict.ac.cn

ABSTRACT
With the exponential growth of social media, web video retrieval based on contextual information associated with videos has attracted wide attention recently. However, state-of-the-art methods mainly focus on limited kinds of context cues and lack of unified exploration towards multiple heterogeneous contexts. In this paper, we propose a novel web video ranking framework called ***CommunityRank*** by leveraging the collective wisdom from a community perspective. Firstly, it formulizes various social relations among users, videos and tags in a heterogeneous context network and further detects its latent community structure. Then the algorithm maps videos into the community space and performs a community-oriented re-ranking through a bipartite graph model. By aggregating the multiple relations, ***CommunityRank*** can make the most of textual, visual and social contexts and leads to better search results. The encouraging performances of the proposed method on YouTube video collection demonstrate that the discovered communities reveal topics of interest emerging in collective behaviors and can facilitate web video retrieval.

Categories and Subject Descriptors
H.3.3 [**Information Storage and Retrieval**]: Information Search and Retrieval – *Retrieval models*

General Terms
Algorithms, Experimentation

Keywords
Social Media; Video Retrieval; Heterogeneous Community Discovery

1. INTRODUCTION
With the rapid advancements in Web 2.0 technology, a huge and ever increasing amount of digital videos are stored, shared, and accessed across Internet. Aside from visual signals, videos in social networking sites such as YouTube are accompanied by varied types of contextual information such as tags, titles, related videos and even user information and social network data. These contextual recourses provide complementary information to the video content itself, which presents new challenge and exciting opportunity to web video retrieval.

*Area Chair: Tat-Seng Chua

MM'11, November28–December1, 2011, Scottsdale, Arizona, USA

Recently, contextual information from different viewpoints such as textual, visual and social context has been actively discussed. Some work [1, 2] has focused on investigating and improving the use of tags. Given the ambiguity, subjectivity and noise in tags, several methods such as visual neighbor voting [1], tag co-occurrence analysis [2] are proposed to help refine the tag list. In [3, 4], both visual and textual cues are jointly explored for social image re-ranking. In [5], visual context and some simple social contextual information such as time duration, number of views are combined for near-duplicate video retrieval. Besides that, the user and social network context are also used for image annotation [6] and video re-ranking [7]. Although previous studies have shown promising performances by leveraging different aspects of context respectively, exploring multiple heterogeneous contexts in a unified framework to facilitate video retrieval still has not been reported in the literature.

As a matter of fact, due to the various social activities in YouTube, there are complex relations among different entities such as users, videos and tags which can provide meaningful contextual cues to understand video content. However, single type of relation is usually sparse and noisy, and thus not reliable in determining the accurate context. For example, in our statistics of a dataset with around 80000 videos and 40000 users, only 43.9% videos are commented by users while only 38.8% users ever label a video as favorite. The social network among users is particular sparse with only 28.1% users having friends. On the other hand, integrating multiple types of relations that evolved in YouTube can complement each other as well as reduce the noise and thus can obtain more reliable context information. However, given that different relations are heterogeneous, how to make the most of multiple types of social context to optimize web video search is still a big challenge.

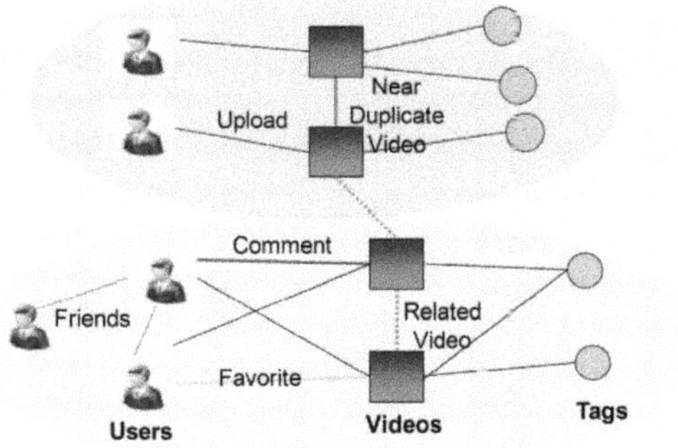

Figure 1. Communities in Heterogeneous Context Network. Edge represents social relationship between nodes, and different relations have been assigned with different colors.

Motivated by the research work of community structure [8] in network analysis, we try to explore the collective wisdom that emerges in multiple aspects of contexts in YouTube from a community perspective. A community consists of a group of nodes that are densely connected to each other but sparsely connected to other dense groups. Community structure in networks usually reveals the common topic or interest that emerges as a result of the collective activities among masses of nodes. For example, a community in the WWW indicates a group of pages with closely related topics. To leverage multiple social contexts in YouTube for web video retrieval, in this paper we propose a novel web video ranking framework called ***CommunityRank***. Firstly, it models the various social relations among users, videos and tags in a heterogeneous context network and detects the latent community structures. As shown in Figure 1, the various contexts among different entities in YouTube are modeled in a heterogeneous context network, where the vertices represent different entities including users, videos and tags, and different kinds of edges represent the relation between vertices. Furthermore, the two communities in this network which represent groups of related user, video and tags are marked by ellipses with different colors. Based on the discovered communities, ***CommunityRank*** further maps the videos into the community space and performs a community-oriented re-ranking through a bipartite graph model. By aggregating the rich yet noisy data from multiple relations, ***communityRank*** reveals the most informative context embedded in social networks and thus can provide reliable social cues for web video retrieval.

The rest of this paper is organized as follows: Section 2 describes the proposed ***CommunityRank*** framework; Section 3 presents the experimental results; At last, Section 4 concludes the paper.

2. *COMMUNITYRANK* FRAMEWORK

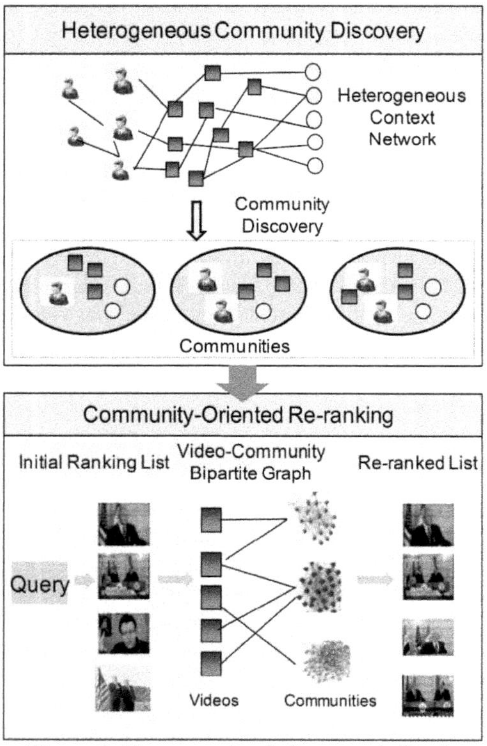

Figure 2. Framework of *CommunityRank*.

As shown in Figure 2, our ***CommunityRank*** framework consists of two stages: Heterogeneous Community Discovery and Community-Oriented Re-ranking. The first stage aims to mine the heterogeneous community structure embedded in multiple contexts which reveals the latent groups of interest formed by densely interacted users, videos and the corresponding tags. Based on the discovery communities, the second stage utilizes the community-level context which is more informative and reliable to re-rank the initial ranking list.

2.1 Heterogeneous Community Discovery

2.1.1 Heterogeneous Context Network (HCN)

As shown in Figure 1, there are multiple types of relations among different entities in YouTube. In general, we utilize six contextual relations to construct the heterogeneous context network.

Firstly, we exploit three kinds of relations between users and videos, which are generated by users' actions on videos including uploading, commenting and marking as favorite video.

R1: upload relation between user and video.

R2: comment relation between user and video.

R3: favorite relation between user and video.

Secondly, we extract two kinds of relations among videos.

R4: related video relation. The related videos are usually similar or relevant videos, which provide useful hints for video retrieval.

R5: near-duplicate video relation. We adopt SIFT-BOW based near-duplicate detection method to estimate the visual relations.

At last, we extract the user social network.

R6: user friendship relation among users.

2.1.2 Community Discovery in HCN

The multiple relations among users, videos and tags in heterogeneous context network are from different view points, that is, semantic meaning, video relevance, and user interest, which provide complementary clues for understanding video contents. Therefore their combination could give a more accurate and confident estimation of the community of interest.

We adopt the MetaFac algorithm in [9] to detect the community structure in the heterogeneous context network. Based on relational hypergraph factorization, MetaFac is efficient to extract meaningful communities from the multi-relation multi-dimension network. This algorithm is motivated by the intuition that multiple relations tend to be consistent with each other inside latent communities.

First of all, formulate the heterogeneous context network in a metagraph $G=(V, E)$, where $V=\{v^{(q)}\}$ and $E=\{e^{(r)}\}$ stands for the set of vertices and edges in G respectively. Here define a set of entities with the same type as a facet. The three facets in our network are denoted as $v^{(q)}$ (q=1, 2, 3 for the user facet, video facet, and the tag facet respectively). The different six relations are denoted as $e^{(r)}$ (r=1, 2, 3, 4, 5, 6). Besides, if relation $e^{(r)}$ is associated with entities from facet $v^{(q)}$, we denote it as $v^{(q)} \rightarrow e^{(r)}$. In addition, the observations of an *M*-way relation $e^{(r)}$ among different facets are represented as an *M*-way data tensor $\chi^{(r)}$.

Assume a process as follows: the probability of a relation x_{ij} between any two entities i and j involved in a community k can be viewed as a function of the relationships between community k with entity i, and k with j. Let $p(i|k)$ *indicate* how likely an interaction in the *k-th* community involves the *i-th* entity and $p(k)$ is the probability of an interaction exist in the *k-th* community, we can express x_{ij} by $x_{ij}=\sum_k p(k)p(i|k)p(j|k)$. Likewise a three way relation such as an upload relation among entity *i*1, *i*2 and *i*3 can be represented by $x_{i_1 i_2 i_3}=\sum_k p(k)p(i_1|k)p(i_2|k)p(i_3|k)$. Thus, the relation set χ among the facets $v^{(1)}$ $v^{(2)}$ $v^{(3)}$ can be represent by

$$\chi \approx \sum_{k=1}^{K} p(k) u_k^{(1)} \circ u_k^{(2)} \circ u_k^{(3)} = [z] \prod_{m=1}^{3} \times_m U^{(m)} \quad (1)$$

where χ is the data tensor representing the observed three-way interactions among facet $v^{(1)}$ $v^{(2)}$ and $v^{(3)}$. $p(i_m|k)$ is written as an (i_m,k)-element of $U^{(m)}$ for m=1,2,3. $U^{(m)}$ is an $I_m \times K$ matrix, where I_m is the size of $v^{(m)}$ *and* K is the number of communities in the network. The probabilities of communities are elements of **z**, i.e. $p(k)=\mathbf{z}_k$. This is a process of tensor decomposition where core tensor [**z**] and the factor matrices $\{U^{(m)}\}$ are constrained to contain nonnegative probability values. Based on the above analysis, the community discovery problem in the multi-relation network can be transferred to factorize all data tensors $\chi^{(r)}$ such that all tensors can be approximated by a common nonnegative core tensor [**z**] and a shared set of nonnegative factors $\{U^{(m)}\}$.With respect to the above goal, a cost function is defined as follows to simultaneously reduce all the approximation costs in tensor decomposition.

$$J = \min_{z,\{U^{(q)}\}} \sum_{e^{(r)}} D(\chi^{(r)} \| [z] \prod_{m: v^{(m)} \to e^{(r)}} \times_m U^{(m)}) \quad (2)$$
$$s.t \;\; z \in R_+^{1*k}, U^{(q)} \in R_+^{Iq*K} q = 1,2,3$$

where K is the number of communities, and $D(\cdot\|\cdot)$ is the KL-divergence. By using the proposed interactive update algorithm in [9] to solve the above optimization problem, we can finally get the core tensor [**z**]and facet matrices $U^{(m)}$ as a community model. Here, each (i, k)-element of a facet matrix **U** is p ($i|k$) (i.e. how likely an interaction in the community k involves entity i), and each element $\mathbf{z}_k = p(k)$ is the probability of an interaction involved in community k). Based on this, we can easily compute $p(k|i)$ in Eq. 3 to indicate the soft membership of entity i with respect to community k

$$p(k|i) = \frac{p(i|k)*p(k)}{\sum_{k'} p(k')p(i|k')} \quad (3)$$

2.2 Community-Oriented Re-ranking

Since the discovered communities capture the most informative and consistent context emerging in multiple relations, we can project the videos to community space to get more reliable social context of videos. We implement a Bipartite Graph Model [10] to re-rank the videos with respect to their community-oriented context. It is intuitive to model the relationship between video and communities as a bipartite graph, where one side is video node; the other side is the community node. Different from the model in [10], the video-community bipartite graph here is a directed graph, where the weight of edge from video i to community k is $p(k|i)$,and the weight from community k to video j is p (j|k). Firstly, the video nodes get the initial ranking scores from their textual relevance with the query. Then, perform two-step propagation. After one-step propagation, the community nodes get their relevance with query from the related videos. The more video nodes with higher relevance distributed in the community, the higher score it will get. Then, in the second propagation step the videos are re-ranked with the community-oriented context, where videos belong to the most relevant communities will be promoted. The two-step propagation process can be formulized in Eq. (4). After the propagation in the bipartite graph, we can get the score $r_{context}$ of videos oriented to the community context.

$$w_{ij} = \frac{1}{\sum_k p(k|j)} \sum_{k'=1}^{m} \frac{p(i|k')p(k'|j)}{\sum_t p(t|k')}$$
$$r_{context}(i) = \sum_{j=1}^{n} w_{ij} r_{initial}(j); \quad (4)$$

Then, we combine the contextual score with the initial score to re-rank the videos as follows, where α is a weight parameter that belongs to (0, 1).

$$r_{all} = \alpha r_{initial} + (1-\alpha) r_{context} \quad (5)$$

In addition, it is worth noting that the heterogeneous community discovery is computed offline and do not contribute to the time cost of the retrieval process. As w_{ij} can be pre-computed, the re-ranking step just takes linear time.

3. EXPERIMENTS

3.1 Data Set and Evaluation Measure

We conduct the experiments on a web video benchmark MCG-WEBV (Version 2.0) [11]. We choose part of the collection as our dataset, including 82352 videos uploaded from Dec. 2008 to Feb. 2009 on YouTube which retain the social contexts such as related video and same author relationships. We consider the 39555 users that uploaded these videos as the user set, and further collect multiple relations among users and videos including the commenting, marking a video as favorite and even the user friendship network using YouTube API. There are 59902 unique tags in the dataset which have frequency between 5 and 4,000.We choose 10 hot topics from the proposed 73 topics in MCG-WEBV, and use the topic description as queries to perform video retrieval. The details of the queries are shown in Table 1. The top 100 videos in the ranking list are evaluated by manually labeled ground truth. At last, we adopt the Mean Average Precision (MAP) as evaluation metric.

Table 1. The selected 10 queries

Bush attacked by shoes	HotForWords
New York Hudson river airplane crash	Israel attacks Gaza Palestine
Miley Cyrus's show	Highway hero dog
Barack Obama's inaugural speech	Eye makeup
Madonna's concert in Brazil	Iphone advertisement

3.2 Performance of Discovered Communities

First of all, we intuitively demonstrate the characteristic of community structure. As shown in Figure 3, part of the context network including 10 communities marked with different colors is illustrated. It is obvious that in the context network, nodes are densely connected with each other within the community and thus reveal the collective behaviors among different entities. Especially, we choose two communities and investigate the entities involved in them. We show the key frames of the top representative videos and the most likely tags with respect to the community based on p ($i|k$) as computed in Section 2.1. From Figure 3, we can see the two communities are respectively related to two particular topics, namely "Football" and "Eye makeup". By mining the multiple interactions embedded in the context network, the discovered communities represent the most consistent topics of interest among different entities, which provide meaningful cues for understanding web videos.

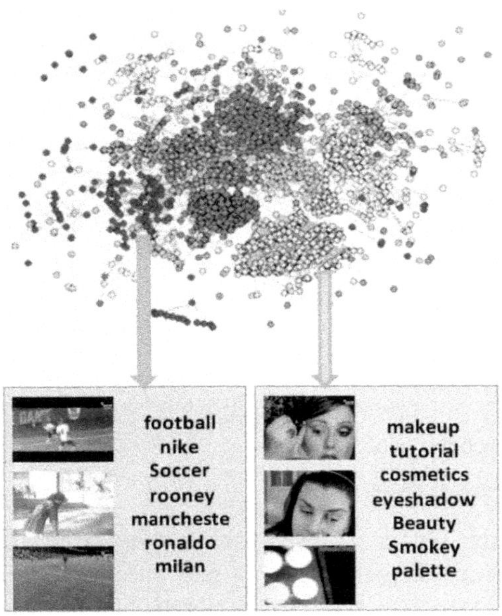

Figure3. Discovered Community Structure and the representative videos and tags in two communities

3.3 Effects of *CommunityRank*

In the heterogeneous community discovery step, the community size K plays an important role in the video retrieval framework. Here, we compare the performances of ***CommunityRank*** with respect to different choices of K. As shown in Figure 4, it gets the optimal results when K is set to 600. On one hand, if K is too small, there will be very large communities which may represent ambiguous topics and mislead the community-oriented re-ranking. On the other hand, if K is too large, there will be many isolated local units of nodes which are meaningless to understand the social context of videos.

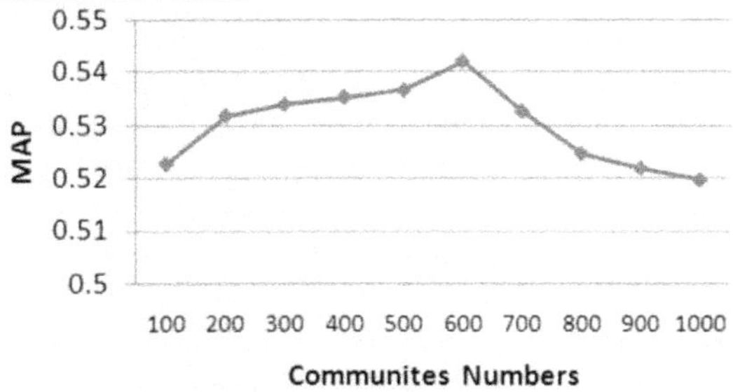

Figure4. Performance with different community numbers

In the re-ranking step, the parameter α is empirically set to be 0.5 to fully combine contextual and initial scores. To further investigate the effects of different cues, we compare the results of *CommunityRank* methods by using different relation sets such as *CommuntiyRank* using visual relations (R5) and *CommunityRank* using the other five social relations. In addition, the initial textual based method is considered as baseline. As shown in Table 2 , it is obvious that the three community based runs show the superior performances compared with the textual baseline. Especially, the full *CommunityRank* has achieved 6.3% improvement over the textual baseline. Besides, the *CommunityRank* using social relations outperforms the visual relation based method. That is because web videos related to the same topic usually vary in visual appearances, which makes the visual context unreliable. At last, the full *CommunityRank* method as a fusion of both visual and social relations can reveal the most informative context and achieves the best performance.

Table 2. Comparison of performance with different context

	Baseline	Visual Relation	Social Relations	Full *CommunityRank*
MAP	0.510	0.520	0.534	0.542

4. CONCLUSION

In this paper, we propose a framework to mine the collective wisdom embedded in social networking websites to facilitate web video retrieval from a community perspective. Multiple context relations such as uploading, commenting, labeling as favorite, make friends as well as the visual context between near duplicate videos are integrated in a heterogeneous context network. Then we perform a community discovery method on the network to extract the latent community structures which reveal topics of interest. Furthermore, by leveraging the community level context, we re-rank the videos through a bipartite graph model. Experiments on a YouTube dataset show that the discovered heterogeneous communities are able to capture the collective behaviors emerging in social networks, and provide meaningful summary of the collection. Based on this, the ***CommunityRank*** framework can take advantage of both the textual, visual and social context, and thus leads to better ranking results.

5. ACKNOWLEDGMENTS

This work was supported by the National Basic Research Program of China (973Program, 2007CB311100), National Nature Science Foundation of China (60902090), Beijing New Star Project on Science & Technology (2007B071), and Co-building Program of Beijing Municipal Education Commission.

6. REFERENCES

[1] Li, X., Snoek, C. and Worring, M. Learning social tag relevance by neighbor voting. *IEEE Trans. Multimedia*, 2009

[2] Wang, C., Jing, F. , Zhang, L.and Zhang, H. Content-based image annotation refinement. In *CVPR*, 2007

[3] Wang, M., Yang, K., Hua, X.and Zhang, H. Towards Relevant and Diverse Search of Social Images. *IEEE Trans. Multimedia*, 2010.

[4] Yao, T., Mei, T. and Ngo, C. Co-reranking by mutual reinforcement for image search. In *CIVR*, 2010.

[5] Wu, X., Ngo, C., Hauptman, A. and Tan, H. Real-Time Near-Duplicate Elimination for Web Video Search with Content and Context. *IEEE Trans. Multimedia*, 2009

[6] Shevade, B., Sundaram, H.and Xie, L. Modeling personal and social network context for event annotation in images. In *JCDL*, 2007

[7] Gou, L., Chen, H., Kim, J.and Zhang, X. SNDocRank: a Social Network-Based Video Search Ranking Framework. In *ACM MIR* ,2010

[8] Porter, M., Onnela,J. and Mucha,P. Communities in Networks. *Notices of the AMS*, 2009.

[9] Lin, Y.R., Sun, J., Castro, P. et al. MetaFac: Community Discovery via Relational Hypergraph Factorization. In *SIGKDD*,2009

[10] Zhou, T., Ren,J., Medo, M.and Zhang,Y. Bipartite network projection and personal recommendation. *Phys Rev E*, 2007

[11] Cao, J., et al. MCG-WEBV: A Benchmark Dataset for Web Video Analysis. Technical Report. Institute of Computing Technology, Chinese Academy of Sciences, 2009

Automatic Preview Generation of Comic Episodes for Digitized Comic Search *

Keiichiro Hoashi, Chihiro Ono
KDDI R&D Laboratories Inc.
2-1-15 Ohara Kamifukuoka
Saitama 356-8502 Japan
{hoashi,ono}@kddilabs.jp

Daisuke Ishii, Hiroshi Watanabe
GITI, Waseda University
1011 Nishitomida Honjo
Saitama 367-0035 Japan
dai.ishii@fuji.waseda.jp
hiroshi.watanabe@waseda.jp

ABSTRACT

This research proposes a novel method to present "thumbnails" of episodes of digitized comics, in order to improve the efficiency of comic search. Comic episode thumbnails are generated based on image analysis technologies developed especially for comic images. Namely, the following procedures are developed for our system: automatic comic frame segmentation, text balloon extraction, and a linear regression based model to calculate the importance score of each extracted frame. The system then selects frames from each episode with high importance score, and aligns the selected frames to create the episode thumbnail, which is presented to the system user as a compact preview of the episode. User experiments conducted with actual Japanese comic images prove that the proposed method significantly decreases the time necessary to search for specific episodes from a large scaled comic data collection.

Categories and Subject Descriptors

H.3.3 [**Information Systems**]: Information Search and Retrieval—*retrieval models, search process*; H.2.4 [**Database Management**]: Systems—*multimedia databases*

General Terms

Algorithms, Experimentation.

1. INTRODUCTION

Recently, digital distribution of comics (especially for mobile phones) has developed into a huge business in Japan. Furthermore, the spread of content over the Web has increased the worldwide popularity of Japanese comics, which indicates the potential growth of the global comic distribution market. As the amount of digitized comics increases, technology to support comic search is expected to become more and more important. However, the search function of existing online comic distribution sites is basically restricted to metadata search, *e.g.*, keyword search of comic title/artist.

The objective of this research is to improve the usability of digitized comic search systems. In order to achieve this goal, we propose a novel method to generate "thumbnails" of comic episodes, by selecting and aligning significant comic frames from a given comic episode, *i.e.*, a series of comic page images. Component technologies based on image analysis are developed to extract features from comic images, such as automatic segmentation of frames and text balloon extraction. Features extracted from the frames and text balloons are input to a linear regression based model, which calculates the importance score of each frame. Finally, frames with high importance score are presented to the user as the preview of the comic episode. User experiments are conducted to evaluate this method on a virtual comic distribution site. Results of this experiment indicate that our proposal significantly improves the efficiency of comic episode search.

2. BACKGROUND

By far, the most popular format of Japanese comics is the "story comic," which is typically serialized on weekly/monthly issued comic magazines. The basic unit of a story comic, *i.e.*, an *episode*, typically consists of 20-30 pages, depending on the publication which the comic is serialized on. In most digital comic distribution services, comic titles are sold in units of episodes. However, especially in comic distribution services for mobile devices, users can only search for comics based on their metadata, *e.g.*, comic title, author name, genre, etc. This means that, while users can easily search for specific titles of comics, it is extremely difficult for them to search for specific episodes from the title, which is a major user need. In fact, most existing services merely present a list of numbered episodes for each title, making it virtually impossible for users to find episodes without (mistakenly) downloading undesired ones.

Presenting a preview of comic episodes is assumed to be a helpful method for users who want to find specific episodes from a large scaled comic data collection. A typical way to generate such previews is to provide access to the first few pages of a comic episode, similar to the approach implemented for digital book distribution sites, such as Amazon.com. However, the pages presented in the preview may not be sufficient for users to grasp the story of the episode.

*Area chair: Bernard Merialdo

MM'11, November 28–December 1, 2011, Scottsdale, Arizona, USA.

This is especially true for comics, since the amount of (textual) information on a page is sparse compared to usual books. Furthermore, browsing through numerous comic pages is expected to be a time-consuming process, especially when the users' demand is to find an episode from a large data collection, and/or when users are using digital comic distribution services on mobile devices with limited screen size.

3. RELATED WORK

Existing research efforts in the area of content-based analysis of comic images have focused on automatic frame segmentation. The mainstream approach is to iteratively segment frames from the input comic image based on density gradient, as proposed in [1, 2]. These methods enable the extraction of individual frames from a given comic page image. Furthermore, methods which utilize comic frame segmentation results to transform comics for viewing on mobile devices have also been developed [3, 4, 5].

Extraction of text information from comic page images is also an essential technology. Most existing text extraction research [6, 7] utilize edges as features to localize regions which include text. This approach is effective for general photographs, but is difficult to be applied for comics, since all elements (including the non-textual areas) of a typical comic image consist of strong edges. Thus, text extraction methods which are specialized for comics images becomes necessary. Guo *et al.* have developed a method to extract text balloons from comic strips, by extracting areas which are not connected with the frame boundary lines [8]. The efficacy of this method has only been evaluated on comic strips in relatively fixed formats, thus may not be able to handle the wide variety of expressions in story comics.

4. COMIC EPISODE SUMMARIZATION

4.1 General framework

The main proposal of this research is the automatic generation of comic episode "thumbnails," and its presentation to comic search system users for previewing comic episodes. The general framework of our proposal is illustrated in Figure 1[1]. The proposed system consists of four major steps. First, for each page (image) of the input comic episode, frame segmentation (*ref.* (1) of Figure 1) is conducted. A set of features is extracted from each segmented frame (*ref.* (2)), which is then used to calculate the frame importance score (*ref.* (3)). Frames with high importance scores are selected (*ref.* (4)) and presented to the user as the thumbnail of the input episode.

A conceptual image which illustrates the implementation of comic episode summarization results for an online comic distribution service, is shown in Figure 2. In existing comic distribution sites, users access to their favorite comic titles by text-based search (as illustrated in the "Top page" and "Title search result" screens of Figure 2), and select the episode which they want to purchase from the list of episodes in the search result. By utilizing our proposal, a summary of each episode can be generated beforehand, so that users can confirm the content of an episode by clicking on the preview link, as illustrated in the "Preview" screen in Figure 2. This user interface is expected to reduce erroneous

[1]Comic images in this paper are provided from the website "Manga no Shimbun" (http://manganews.com/)

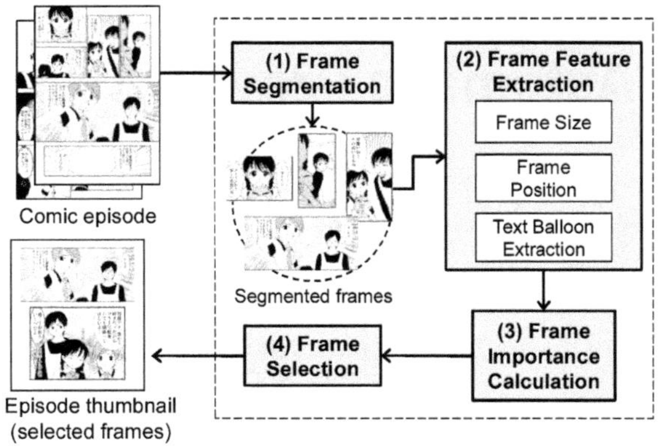

Figure 1: Outline of proposed system, which selects frames from comic images to generate a thumbnail summarization for each episode.

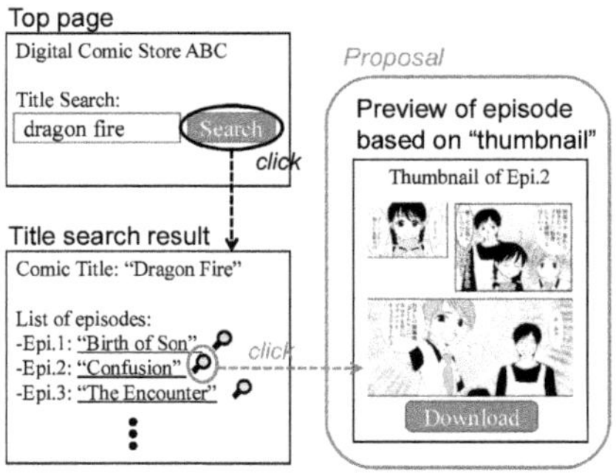

Figure 2: Conceptual illustration of comic search interface using summarization results

downloading/purchasing of unwanted comic episodes, and improve the overall usability of comic distribution services. Details of each step are provided in the following sections.

4.2 Frame segmentation

The frame segmentation method developed for our system utilizes the results of two existing approaches: iterative frame separation (IFS), and frame corner detection (FCD). The combination of these two methods has been proved to improve frame segmentation accuracy in [2].

First, IFS is conducted to obtain a rough estimation of segmented frames, following the method proposed in [1]. The basic approach of this method is to recursively split the input comic image to two sub-regions until no separation line can be detected. Next, FCD is implemented by extracting corners from the comic image based on two methods: selecting intersection points of lines extracted by Hough transformation, and Harris's corner detection method. Based on the IFS results, a multiple number of frame boundary candidates are generated by drawing lines which intersect with the corners detected by FCD. The average density of gradient values for all frame candidates are calculated, based on the result of applying the Sobel filter to the page image. Finally, the candidate with the highest score is selected as the optimal segmentation result for each of the initially segmented frames.

4.3 Text balloon extraction

Japanese text consist of a wide variety of characters, especially compared to English. Furthermore, as mentioned in

Figure 3: Example images of text balloon extraction steps: (a) text character extraction, (b) paint bucket filling, (c) gradual expansion.

Table 1: Extracted frame features

Type	Feature
Frame	width (pixels)
	height (pixels)
	area (pixels)
	coordinates of upper left corner (x, y)
Text balloon	area (pixels)
	number of characters
	mean character size (pixels)

Section 3, text character extraction from comic images is not a trivial problem. Therefore, development of a technology to extract text balloons from Japanese story comics for feature extraction of comic images is necessary. The method we have developed to achive this goal is based on the following two steps. First, initial text character regions are extracted from the input comic image, based on text character detection. Next, the area of the text balloon is determined by expanding the extracted candidate regioins.

The first step is to extract text character candidates from the comic page image. This procedure is implemented by utilizing the face detection method of Viola *et al* [9]. A text detector is built based on training data, which consists of images of Japanese text characters as the positive data set, and randomly extracted non-textual sub-regions from the comic images, as the negative data set. Haar-like features are extracted from all images in the training data, and the text detector is constructed by Adaboost learning.

Next, the area of the text balloon is determined by expanding the region of the extracted text characters. Area expansion is conducted by a hybrid of two methods. One is the paint bucket filling approach, which simply fills the white space surrounding each extracted character. However, there are many cases which result in over-filling errors, due to small gaps in the balloon boundaries. In order to compensate with such errors, we also implement the gradual expansion method, where the candidate area is gradually expanded until all edges of the surrounding area become white. This approach is applied when the result of the paint bucket method verges to multiple edges of the comic page image. All overlapping results are merged to obtain the final text balloon area. Example images of each step in the text balloon extraction procedure are shown in Figure 3.

4.4 Frame feature extraction

Based on the results of the frame segmentation and text balloon extraction steps, a feature vector is generated for each segmented frame. The frame features extracted in this process are listed in Table 1.

As written in Table 1, frame features are roughly categorized to two types: features of the frame itself, and features of the text balloon associated with each frame. The number of characters per text balloon is derived by applying a commercial Japanese optical character recognition (OCR) module. The mean character size is estimated by dividing the text balloon area by the number of characters in the OCR results. As a result, the features of frame F are expressed by an 8-dimensional feature vector $\vec{F} = (f_1, \cdots, f_8)$, where each element of $\vec{F}$ expresses the value of the features.

4.5 Frame importance score calculation and episode summarization

Features extracted from each frame are then used to calculate the importance score of the frame in question. A linear regression model is constructed to calculate the importance score of each frame F, denoted as follows: $Score(F) = \sum_{i=1}^{8} \beta_i \cdot f_i + \epsilon$, where β_i denotes the regression coefficient of the i-th feature.

In order to construct the importance score calculation model, we prepared a training data set by collecting subjective evaluation data of significant comic frames. In this process, 5 subjects were asked to read 8 episodes of Japanese comics, and select up to a maximum of 5 frames which they judged to be important for the episode. The ratio of subjects who selected each frame as important, and the feature vector of each frame are used as the regressand and regressors to estimate the coefficients β_i, and ϵ.

The thumbnail of a comic episode is generated by calculating the importance score of all frames of the episode, and selecting the frames with high importance. Namely, the top N frames, according to their importance scores, are selected to represent the episode. Since the chronological order of the frames is essential to express the episode content, the selected N frames are sorted according to their order of appearance, when the thumbnail is presented to the user.

5. EXPERIMENTS

A subjective user experiment is conducted to evaluate the efficacy of our proposal for comic search systems. For this experiment, we simulate a situation where users of a virtual comic distribution site are searching for a specific comic episode, from comic titles which consist of a large number of episodes. The subjects are assigned to use one of the following two methods to preview the content of comic episodes during the search task: our proposed thumbnail generation method, and the conventional (Amazon-like) previewing method, in which the subjects browse the first few pages of an episode. The overall efficiency required to successfully search the target episode is measured for evaluation. Details of the experiment are as follows.

5.1 Framework of experiment

In this experiment, the subjects are asked to search for specific episodes of popular Japanese comic titles. Namely, a short text abstract of the target episode is presented to the subjects as the query. The list of all episodes from the specified comic title is also presented to the subjects on a Web-based interface. By clicking on an episode link, subjects are able to see the "preview" of the episode. The episode preview is generated on one of the two previously mentioned methods. Based on the content of the episode preview, the subject judges whether or not the selected episode matches with the query. If the subject decides that the current episode

Table 2: Summary of comic titles used for evaluation experiments

ID	# of episodes	Avg page #	Avg # frames/page
T_1	64	26.3	4.65
T_2	276	19.5	4.47
T_3	108	21.4	4.61
T_4	233	18.8	5.61

matches the query, he/she clicks the button to "download" the episode. The search task concludes if the downloaded episode is a correct match. If not, the subject can browse the entire content of the downloaded episode, in order to grasp the story of the comic title.

For comparison of the proposed and conventional methods, the following measures are recorded for each experiment: time required to search target episode, and the number of episodes browsed per task. These measures are used to evaluate the efficiency of the episode search task for both methods. In addition to these objective measures, all subjects were asked to answer a questionnaire after the experiment. The main objective of the questionnaire is to collect information about each subjects' familiarity to the comic titles used for this experiment. Namely, the subjects are asked if they have read each comic title prior to the experiment, and also their general acquaintance with (both digital and paper) comics.

5.2 Experimental data

Four popular Japanese comic titles $T_1, \cdots, T_4$ are used for our experiments. The number of episodes per title, average number of pages per episode, and average number of frames per page are presented in Table 2.

84 subjects have cooperated for the experiment (41 male, 43 female, age range from late teens to 50s). All subjects have general experience in reading Japanese story comics. Two queries are given to the subject for each title $T_1, \cdots, T_4$, thus, each subject is asked to conduct the search task eight times. The preview method for each title in the experiment is decided so that each subject previews two of the four titles by the proposed method, and the other two by the conventional method. The combination of the title and preview method is determined randomly for each subject.

5.3 Results

Table 3 lists the average time (secs), and the number of previewed episodes that were necessary for each user to search for a single query. As clear from this result, the proposed method has enabled users to search for comic episodes in significantly less time, compared to the conventional method. It is also notable that the number of episode previews for the proposed method is higher than that of the conventional method. These results indicate that the conventional method to present the first few pages of a comic episode is more time-consuming than the proposal, which is assumed to be the main cause of the search time difference between the two methods.

Furthermore, we focus on the time required for users to search for episodes of comic titles which they are familiar with. Table 4 lists the average search time per title, for the subjects who have read more than half of all episodes of each comic title. The number of such familiar subjects per title is also written in this Table.

Table 3: Average time and number of browsed episodes in search experiment

Method	Avg time (secs)	# of browsed episodes
Preview	324.7	34.1
Conventional	373.5	22.7

Table 4: Average search time (secs) for subjects familiar to each comic title

	Title ID				
Avg time	T_1	T_2	T_3	T_4	Avg
Prev	306.4	200.2	221.9	328.2	264.2
Conv	365.9	405.8	295.4	341.4	352.1
# of subjects	36	51	44	33	41.0

As clear from Table 4, the average time difference between the proposed and conventional methods is 87.9 secs, which is significantly higher than that of all experiments (48.8 secs, see Table 3). This result indicates that the proposed method is especially effective for users who understand the general outline of the comic title.

6. CONCLUSIONS

This paper proposes a novel method to generate and present thumbnail-like summaries of episodes for digitized comics. This method is expected to improve the efficiency to search comic episodes on online comic distribution services. Subjective experimental results conducted with actual Japanese comic data have proved that our proposal can reduce the time necessary to search for specific comic episodes from a large-scaled data collection. We believe our research will contribute to improve the usability of digitized comic distribution services, and support the future prosperity of the comic distribution industry.

7. REFERENCES

[1] T. Tanaka, K. Shoji, F. Toyama, J. Miyamichi: "Layout analysis of tree-structured scene frames in comic images," Proceedings of IJCAI 2007, pp. 2885-2890, 2007.

[2] D. Ishii, H. Watanabe: "A study on frame position detection of digitized comics images," 2010 Workshop on Picture Coding and Image Processing (WPCIP), pp. 124-125, 2010.

[3] M. Yamada, R. Budiarto, M. Endo, S. Miyazaki: "Comic image decomposition for reading comics on cellular phones," IEICE Trans. Info. Sys., Vol. E87-D, No. 6, pp. 1370-1376, 2004.

[4] K. Arai, H. Tolle: "Method for automatic e-comic scene frame extraction for reading comic on mobile devices," Proceedings of ITNG 2010, pp. 370-375, 2010.

[5] K. Arai, H. Tolle: "Automatic e-comic content adaptation," Int'l Journal of Ubiquitous Computing, Vol. 1, Issue 1, pp. 1-11, 2010.

[6] K. Junga, K.I. Kimb, A.K. Jainc: "Text information extraction in images and video: a survey," Pattern Recognition, Vol. 37, Issue 5, pp. 977-997, 2004.

[7] V. Wu, R. Manmata, E.M. Riseman: "TextFinder: an automatic system to detect and recognize text in images," IEEE Trans PAMI, Vol. 21, No. 11, pp. 1224-1229, 1999.

[8] Q. Guo, K. Kato, N. Sato, Y. Hoshino: "An algorithm for extracting text strings from comic strips," Proc. of ACM SIGGRAPH 2006, 2006.

[9] P. Viola, M. J. Jones: "Robust real-time face detection," Int. J. Comput. Vis. Vol. 57, No. 2, pp. 137-154, 2004.

2D Geon Based Generic Object Recognition *

Xiangqian Yu,
Vincent Oria
NJ Institute of Technology
University Heights
Newark, NJ 07102
{xy35,oria}@njit.edu

Pierre Gouton
Universite de Bourgogne
Aile Science de l'Ingénieur
21078 Dijon Cedex, France
pgouton@u-bourgogne.fr

Geneviève Jomier
Universite de Paris-Dauphine
LAMSADE, UMR CNRS 7024
place du Marechal de Lattre
de Tassigny75 775
Paris Cedex 16, France
genevieve.jomier@dauphine.fr

ABSTRACT

The Recognition by Components(RBC) is a theory in Psychology introduced by Biederman in the late 80s, by which humans perceive scenes through simple 3D objects with regular shapes such as spheres, cubes, cylinders, cones, or wedges, called Geons (geometric ions). Extracting geons from 2D images is a very challenging task as it requires a good segmentation and the recognition of the 3D geons in a 2D space. In this paper, we propose a novel approach for extracting 2D geons from 2D images. The process is composed of three major parts: image preprocessing which includes image background removal and segmentation, arc-geon detection, and polygon-geon detection. We also propose a general procedure for matching the extracted 2D geons to given models for object recognition. Experiment results show that our approach is competitive compared to existing object recognition methodologies in general.

Categories and Subject Descriptors

H.2 [**Media Analysis and Search**]: Miscellaneous—*Extract meaningful Geons from images and compare them with given models*

General Terms

Algorithm

Keywords

geon extraction, segmentation, levenshtein distance, object recognition

1. INTRODUCTION

The recognition of objects from images remains one of the most challenging problem in computer vision although it plays a significant role in intelligent systems(e.g. multimedia retrieval, robotics, etc). The previous works on object recognition can be grouped into two different categories: feature-based[5], and component-based as discussed in [1],[3]. Component-based have drawn much less attentions compared to feature-based approaches.

Shortly after the RBC theory[1] was proposed, several research projects were launched to find efficient and accurate approaches to geon extractions from images. The literature on geon extraction can also be divided into two categories: line drawing-based and image-based, depending on the type of input data.

The line drawing-based approach assumes that the contour information of the objects are given and focuses on identifying the geons. For example, Munk Fairwood [3] proposed an approach which uses logical program to extract geons from manually drawn objects.

The image-based approach aims at providing a full procedure of recognition with the entire image as input. For example, Du and Munck Fariwood[2] presented a feature grouping approach, which takes a set of straight lines collected from a segmented image to form geons. In [9], Wu and Levine used parametric geons as coarse descriptors of objects and defined seven 3D geon types.

Nevertheless, all those approaches have focused on very simple objects created from hand drawing or simple models, with monotonous backgrounds which makes them not applicable to general objects recognition in complex scenes. This paper defines a finite 2D geon set based on the parametric representation of 3D geons presented in [9], and proposes a systematic approach for 2D geon extraction. For object recognition purpose, we are proposing an object matching method in addition. The rest of the paper is organized as follows: Section 2 introduces 2D geons and the geon extraction procedure; Section 3 discusses how the geons are compared to given object models; Section 4 presents the results and Section 5 concludes the paper.

2. 2D GEON DEFINITION AND EXTRACTION

We first discuss the mapping of 3D geons into a 2D space, and then present the geon extraction procedure we are proposing.

2.1 Mapping 3D Geons into 2D Spaces

Parametric 3D geons are a finite set of distinct volumetric shapes, which are used to describe the shapes of object parts. Wu and Levines defined seven types of parametric geons according to equation.1. Fig.1(a) shows the parametric 3D geons defined in [9]. The parameter ϵ_1 defines the *squareness* in the north-south direction and ϵ_2 controls the *squareness* in the east-west direction. The parameters a_1, a_2, a_3 control

*Area Chair: Lexing Xie.

MM'11, November 28–December 1, 2011, Scottsdale, Arizona, USA.

the scale of the 3D shape along x, y, z axes.

$$\left(\left| \frac{x}{a_1} \right|^{2/\epsilon_2} + \left| \frac{y}{a_2} \right|^{2/\epsilon_2} \right)^{\epsilon_1/\epsilon_2} + \left| \frac{z}{a_3} \right|^{2/\epsilon_1} = 1 \qquad (1)$$

A 3D geon needs too much information to identify while what an image contains is quite limited. We define six types of 2D geons from 3D parameter geons discussed above. Compared to a 3D geon, a 2D geon needs less information to identify. By projecting the 3D geons onto a 2D space, we get three basic 2D geon types: Ellipse, parallelogram, and trapezoid as shown in Fig.1(b). The other three extended types (circle, rectangle, and triangle) are special cases of the three basic ones. An ellipsoid can be mapped into an ellipse(circle is a special case of ellipse); a cylinder can be mapped into a parallelogram from the side-view (along Y-axes) or an ellipse from sky-view(along Z-axis); a tapered cylinder (a corn is a special case of tapered cylinder) can be mapped into a trapezoid (a triangle is a special case of trapezoid) from the side-view or an ellipse from the sky-view; a distorted cylinder can be mapped into part of an ellipse; a cuboid can be mapped into multiple parallelograms; a tapered cuboid can be mapped to a combination of trapezoid and parallelogram; and a distorted cuboid can be mapped to a combination of a partial-ellipse and a parallelogram.

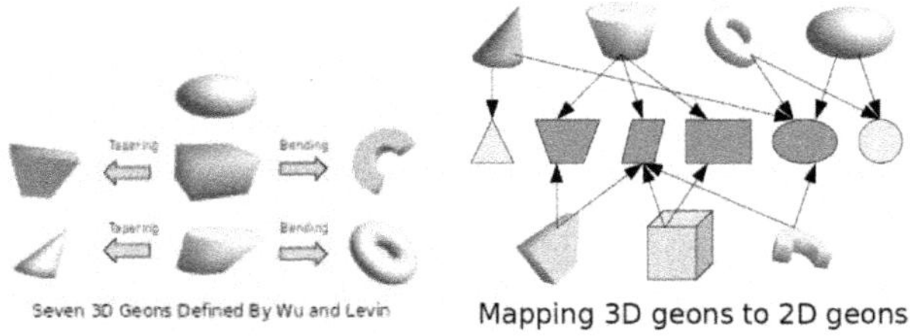

(a) 3D Geons (b) 2D Geons

Figure 1: 3D Geons and Corresponding 2D Geons

2.2 2D Geon Extraction

We group the six types of 2D geon types into two categories: arc-geon, which includes ellipse and circle geons, and polygon-geon, which includes triangle, trapezoid, rectangle, and parallelogram. In order to extract 2D geons from an image, we first pre-process the image to remove the background pixels and segment the image into regions; then the arc-geons are extracted first during the arc-geon detection phase and detect all other geons in polygon-geon detection phase; and finally we validate all extracted geons.

2.2.1 Image Preprocessing

The image pre-processing comprises two parts: background removal and image segmentation. Since we are more concerned about objects which in most cases are in the foreground of an image, we first remove as many background pixels as possible. We use the background removal algorithm proposed by Lu and Gou[7]. The background in an image is defined[7] based on two hypotheses: 1) Background regions are normally connected to borders and are of relatively smaller sizes; 2) the regions occupying the corners are most likely to be part of the background.

We believe that a geon raw contour can be extracted through grouping the pixels in an image by their color or grey intensity which can be achieved through image segmentation. It is true that a perfect image segmentation algorithm remains to be found. Nevertheless, choosing a good segmentation algorithm is critical to the success of the geon detection. In this paper, we used Felzenszwalb's efficient graph-basic image segmentation[4]. It segments an image based on color-distances between pixels and produces a list of regions.

The extraction of geons operates as a multi-level special filter on the list of regions with each filter aiming at discovering a type of geon.

2.2.2 Arc-Geon Detection

Ellipse and circle are the two types in the arc-geon group. The arc-geon detection extracts all arc-geons from the list of regions produced by the segmentation (Let us denote by Γ that region list). Some of the regions obtained from the segmentation may already have their shapes close to an arc-geon. We first retrieve them following some heuristics before applying an ellipse detection algorithm to the remaining regions.

Detecting Arc-Geons Using Simple Heuristic Rules: Some regions in Γ may have shapes close to an arc-geon. To reduce the complexity of future steps, we try to detect as many of those regions as possible. The rules are based on the observation that given a region obtained from the segmentation phase, if the region is an ellipse or a circle region, its center abscissa and ordinate should respectively be equal to the average abscissa and the average ordinate of all points that lie in the region; similarly its major and minor axes should respectively be the longest and shortest diameters of it respectively. From the observation we can get a clear idea of the location the arc-geon to be found if any. So we construct an arc-geon from the observation parameter and try to see if the shape of the arc-geon constructed is close to a contour in the region.

Detecting Arc-Geons Using Ellipse Detection Algorithm: The previous step although fast cannot handle irregular shapes caused by the overlapping or the physical connections between two or more geons. To extract all other arc-geons, we apply an ellipse detection algorithm on the remaining regions. A number of methods for ellipse detection exist, and we have chosen the ellipse detection approach introduced by Xie and Ji in[10] for efficiency.

2.2.3 Polygon-Geon Detection

Under the assumption that all arc-geons have been extracted in the arc-geon detection procedure, we can conclude that the remaining detectable 2D geons (if any) are polygon-geons with at most four edges. Similar to the arc-geon detection, we first try to remove as many regions by detecting rectangle geons using simple heuristic rules; then we apply our Extract Geon From Line Pieces(EGFL) to detect all remaining polygon-geons.

Detecting Rectangle Geons Using Simple Heuristic Rules: Some regions in Γ may have shapes that looks like a polygon-geon. Note that, polygon-geons other than rectangle have too many flexibilities in their shapes that makes them more difficult to identify. Rectangle geons corresponding to parts of real life objects normally have one of their edges parallel to the ground (X-axis). A car body, a cabinet, a building are a few examples. For a rectangle region with one edge parallel to the ground, its lower left corner vertex should have the smallest abscissa and ordinate among all points that lie in it, and its upper right corner vertex should have the largest abscissa and ordinate among all points that lie in it. From the observation, we create a rectangle and try to see if there is a contour that is close to the rectangle we create.

Detecting Polygon-Geons Using EGFL: We first extract straight line pieces from each remaining region in Γ, and then create all possible geons from different spatial combinations of the detected line pieces.

We analyse the possible spatial relationships between two line pieces and listed all possible eight cases as shown in Fig.2. EGFL acts differently according to the spatial relationship between two given line pieces.

Fig.2(a), 2(b), and 2(c) describe situations where two line pieces are parallel to each other. We project both two line pieces onto the X-axis and the Y-axis. If the projection of one line locates completely inside of the other as shown in the left of Fig.2(a), we construct a trapezoid by connecting the end points of two lines as shown in the right of Fig.2(b). Otherwise if the projection of one line locates partially inside or completely outside of the other as shown in the left of Fig.2(b) and Fig.2(c) respectively, we construct a parallelogram and a triangle if two line pieces differentiate in length as shown in the right of Fig.2(b) and Fig.2(c).

Fig.2(d) to Fig.2(h) describe all other situations. In Fig.2(d), the two line pieces cross each other. In this case, we create four triangles since all of them are possible geons. In Fig.2(e), the two line pieces have one identical end point. They can be two edges of a triangle or a parallelogram; so we create a triangle and a parallelogram. Fig.2(f) shows the situation that two line pieces will intersect on the extensions of both of them. They can come from a triangle or a trapezoid, but since the cost of substituting a triangle with a trapezoid is negligible as explained in Section3.2.1, we construct a trapezoid. In Fig.2(g), an end point of one of the line pieces (Let us denote by l_1 the line piece) also belongs to the other line piece, and in Fig.2(h), the two line pieces will intersect if we extend one of them (Let us denote by l_2 the line piece that need to be extended). None of the defined six 2D geons contains edges with spatial relationships in these two cases, however, it is possible that there exist two geons that share the line piece l_1 in the case of Fig.2(g) or the line piece l_2 in the case of Fig.2(h). In this case, we create two more line pieces which are parallel to l_1 or l_2 as shown in the right of Fig.2(g) or Fig.2(h) respectively and add them into the line piece list.

For any polygon-geons, EGFL needs only two of its edges to extract it. Consequently, even for a geon of irregular shape, EGFL is capable of detecting it if any two of its composing edges have been extracted.

A geon extracted from a region should have most of its pixels within the region. For each geon, let us denote by n_g the number of pixels that lie in both the geon and the region that the geon extracted from, and let us denote by a_g the area of the geon. To validate a geon, we compute the ratio between its n_g and a_g and check whether the result is larger than some predefined threshold.

3. MATCHING GEON SEQUENCE AND OBJECT MODELS

This section discusses the method we used to map a geon list to given models. We represent the geon list with a 2D string [6] with each character representing a geon. The order of characters is determined based on the geometrical positions of the geons. The object models are also converted

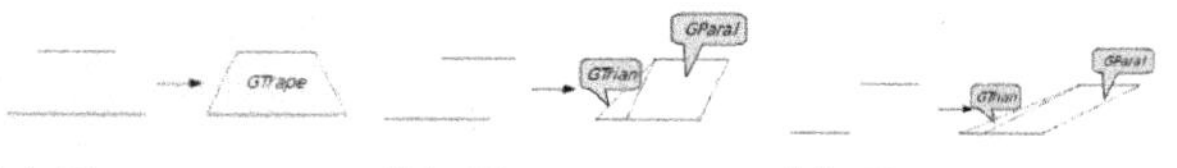

(a) Form a trapezoid (b) Form a parallelogram and a triangle (c) Form a parallelogram and a triangle

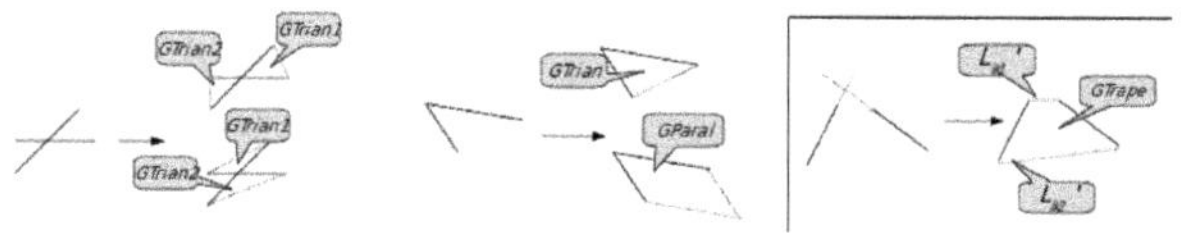

(d) Form four triangles (e) Form a triangle and a parallelogram (f) Form two lines and construct a trapezoid if possible

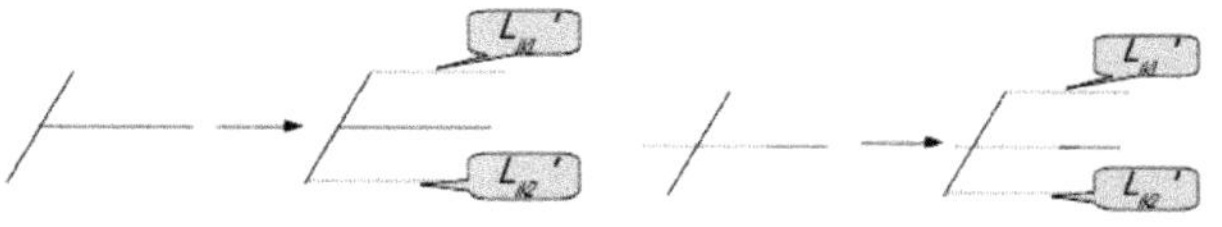

(g) Form two lines and add them into line list (h) Form two lines and add them into line list

Figure 2: Geon Construction From Two Line Pieces

to a 2D string. Then, we compute the weighted levenshtein distance between the two 2D strings.

3.1 Generating Geon 2D String

We define a geon 2D string as two lists of geons sorted in ascending order of their center ordinates firstly and then their center's abscissas as in [6]. The raw geon list extracted is unsorted, and it does not contain any position relationship information. Representing geons in a 2D string ensures that the spatial relationships among the geons is taken into account.

3.2 Distance Function

We need to calculate the distances between the geon 2D string and a model 2D string first. We then categorize the image based on the distances. We calculate the distance using an adapted levenshtein distance algorithm(ALDA).

3.2.1 Adapted Levenshtein Distance Algorithm

For a given geon 2D string a model 2D string, we compute the distance between them using an adapted levenshtein distance algorithm. The levenshtein distance, also called edit distance, measures the level of difference between two sequences. The original levenshtein distance for two strings represents the minimum number of insertion, deletion, or substitution operations to transfer one string to another, and operation weights for all those three operations are the same.

Assigning the same weight to all operations for our case won't be appropriate. 2D geons are extracted in an approximate way, which means, a rectangle geon could be extracted as an ellipse or a trapezoid. One main reason for this phenomena is that a target object might get blocked by other objects in an image; another reason is the segmentation algorithm cannot always be trusted; and also, different view points of an object can produce different types of geons. So we need to assign different weights to different operations. For example, the cost of substituting a rectangle to a parallelogram should be less than the cost of substituting a rectangle to a triangle since rectangle is more similar to

Table 1: Experiment results on CalTech dataset

Type	Size	2DPCA(%)		OurApproach(%)	
		precision	recall	precision	recall
Car-Rear	30	**75.7778**	91.1111	59.5385	**100.000**
	45	**70.9036**	90.0000	61.5385	**100.000**
Leaf	30	**86.6667**	**78.6667**	44.4350	57.1429
	45	**85.9206**	**76.6667**	40.4353	70.0000
Air Plane	30	**54.3095**	52.0000	44.6675	**80.0000**
	45	**80.0317**	62.8571	53.8461	**86.6667**

parallelogram than to triangle. We defined different weights for different operations in our ALDA.

3.2.2 *Generating Sub Geon Strings*

An extracted geon list might contain noisy geons as shown in Fig.3. Fig.3(a) is the input image, Fig.3(b) is the extracted geon list, and in Fig.3(c) is a model of bottle. As discussed in 3.2.1, when computing the distance, if we need to delete some geon from the geon string, the deletion operation cost will be added into the distan

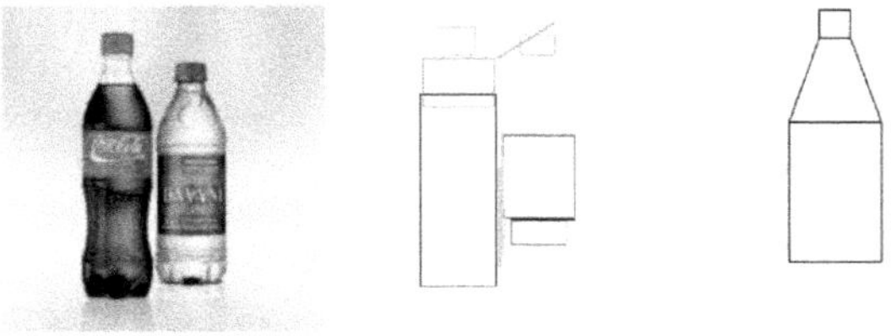

(a) Input Image (b) Raw Geons (c) Bottle Model

Figure 3: Matching Failure Caused by Noises

The presence of noisy geons increases the distances inappropriately. To address this problem, we compute the distances between all combinations(a n choose i problem) of an extracted geon string and a model, and select the minimum distance as the final result. When generating sub geon strings, we also make sure not to remove a geon which is part of an object by restricting that geons being removed can only be outliers.

After we have calculated the distances between a geon string and all given models, we can recognize the object as the type of the model which gives the smallest distance.

4. EXPERIMENT RESULTS

We compared our matching method with the 2DPCA(2 Dimensional Principle Component Analysis)[11]. Compared to other feature-based object recognition competitors, our approach does not need any training data, but it does require pre-defined object models. We have constructed an image dataset *CSID*(Complex Small Image Dataset). Images in *CSID* have relative more complex scenes, smaller number of images when compared to modern image datasets, such as calTech, COIL-100[8]. There are currently 3 types of objects in *CSID*: car, lamp, and bottle, each type contains 20 images. Experiments have been carried on the *CSID* and COIL-100.

Table.1 shows the experimental results based on COIL-100 and Table.2 shows the experimental results based on *CSID*. In general, we can find that 2DPCA-SVM has better performance on **precision** than our approach on COIL-100 dataset, and our approach has better performance on **recall** for **car-rear** and **airplane**. We also discovered that the 2DPCA's performance drops when the size of dataset drops.

Table 2: Experiment Result on CSIDataSet

Object Type	Our Approach(%)		2DPCA(%)	
	Recall	Precision	Recall	Precision
Bottle	**100.00**	**58.323**	33.000	25.000
Car	**100.00**	58.822	50.000	**66.667**
Lamp	**100.00**	44.383	50.000	**75.000**

Our approach is less performant on the **leaves** dataset compared to the 2DPCA. On one hand, all images in the **leaves** dataset have been taken from the same or very similar leaf object in different backgrounds. On the other hand, it is very hard for our approach to decompose leaves into geons, and also hard to design proper models for leaves.

Table.2 shows that 2DPCA has poor performance on our **CSID** and our approach almost obtained the same performance as for the calTech dataset shown in table.1. Our approach gives perfect **recall** values for all classes, which means our approach can retrieve all images of a certain class from the dataset.

5. CONCLUSION AND FUTURE WORK

In this paper, we first defined a novel parametric 2D geon set based on existed 3D geon set. Then we presented a scheme to extract 2D geons from 2D images. Experiment results showed that the scheme worked for not only synthetic images, but also for complex real world images in most cases. However, our approach is restricted by the segmentation result of images. In the future, we will focus on finding a way to replace the segmentation part and obtaining more stable results.

6. REFERENCES

[1] I. Biederman. Recognition by components: A theory of human image understanding. *Psychological Review*, 94(5):115–147, November 1987.

[2] L. Du and R. Munck-Fairwood. Geon recognition through robust feature grouping. *Image Processing, 9th Scandinavian Conference on Image Analysis, Uppsala, Sweden*, June 1995.

[3] R. Fairwood. Recognition of generic components using logic-program relations of image contours. *Image and Vision Computing*, 9(2):113–122, April 1999.

[4] P. F. Fekzebszwakv. Efficient graph-based image segmentation. *IJCV*, 59(2), 2004.

[5] P. J. Lazebnik S., Schmid C. Beyond bags of features: Spatial pyramid matching for natural scene catergories. *CVPR*, pages 2169–2178, 2006.

[6] A. J. Lee and H. Chiu. 2d z-string: A new spatial knowledge representation of image databases. *IEEE Transactions on Pattern Analysis and Machine Intelligence*, 26(1):131–137, Jan 2004.

[7] Y. Lu and H. Guo. Background removal in image indexing and retrieval. *Proceedings 10th Int.Conf, Image and Processing, IEEE Computer Society*, pages 933–938, 1994.

[8] M. H. Nene S.A., Nayar S.K. Coil 100 database. 1996.

[9] K. Wu and M. D. Levin. 3-d shape approximation using parametric geons. *Image and Vision Computing archive*, 15(12), Jan 1996.

[10] Y. Xie and Q. Ji. A new efficient ellipse detection method. *International Conference on Pattern Recognition 2002*, (2):859–862, 2004.

[11] J. Yang, D. Zhang, A. F.Frangi, and J. Yang. Two dimensional pca: A new approach to appearance based face reprensentation and recognition. *IEEE Transactions on Pattern Analysis and Machine Intelligence*, 26(1):131–137, Jan 2004.

Image Annotation by Composite Kernel Learning with Group Structure *

Ying Yuan
College of Computer Science
Zhejiang University, China
tracy1108@zju.edu.cn

Fei Wu
College of Computer Science
Zhejiang University, China
wufei@cs.zju.edu.cn

Yueting Zhuang
College of Computer Science
Zhejiang University, China
yzhuang@cs.zju.edu.cn

Jian Shao
College of Computer Science
Zhejiang University, China
jshao@zju.edu.cn

ABSTRACT

We can obtain more and more kinds of heterogeneous features (such as color, shape and texture) in images which can be extracted to describe various aspects of visual characteristics. Those high-dimensional heterogeneous visual features are intrinsically embedded in a non-linear space. In order to effectively utilize these heterogeneous features, this paper proposes an approach, called Composite Kernel Learning with Group Structure (CKLGS), to select groups of discriminative features for image annotation. For each image label, the CKLGS method embeds the nonlinear image data with discriminative features into different Reproducing Kernel Hilbert Spaces (RKHS), and then composes these kernels to select groups of discriminative features. The utilization of CKLGS for image annotation shows the proposed approach achieves a better performance.

Categories and Subject Descriptors

H.3.3 [**Information Search and Retrieval**]: Retrieval models

General Terms

Algorithms, Experimentation

Keywords

Composite Kernel Learning, Feature Selection, Group Structure, Image Annotation

1. INTRODUCTION

One image is often associated with multiple visual features, such as global features (e.g., color, shape, and texture) or local features (e.g., SIFT and Local Binary Pattern (LBP)). Different kinds of heterogenous features have their intrinsic discriminative power to characterize a certain semantics. That is to say, only limited distinct groups of heterogenous features distinguish each semantics from others. Therefore, how to select out most discriminant subgroups of heterogeneous visual features for image annotation is an important problem.

Meanwhile, high-dimensional heterogeneous features extracted from the image are often embedded in a nonlinear and inseparable subspace and it is essential to discern the embedded subspace of original high-dimensional heterogenous features. Therefore, some kernel-based methods are utilized to discover the embedded subspace. However, the classical kernel-based methods like SVM are based on a single kernel and the group structure insides multiple heterogenous features is ignored by only one kernel function.

Inspired by the *lasso* (least absolution shrinkage and selection operator) [9] which was proposed for feature selection in high-dimensional settings, some *sparsity*-based kernel approaches were proposed for kernel learning. Lanckriet et al. [5] considered conic combinations of kernel matrices. But this method can only solve problems with small number of kernels and data. Bach et al. [1] proposed Multiple Kernel Learning (MKL) to overcome such deficiency. The MKL method embedded the nonlinear image data with discriminative features into RKHS, and then utilized the kernel function in RKHS to select groups of discriminative features. However, MKL does not take the group structure of features into account. Recently, Szafranski et al. [8] put forth an approach of composite kernel learning to overcome the deficiency of MKL.

As we know, the heterogenous features in images are naturally grouped. For example, color and shape respectively discern the aspects of visual characteristics. Hence, this paper integrates the MKL and the grouping effect in images to propose an approach for nonlinear feature selection during image annotation by the composite kernel learning, called Composite Kernel Learning with Group Structure (CKLGS). The basic idea of CKLGS is to map original features into different RKHS and utilize the group structure inside heterogenous features to adaptively select out most important nonlinear features.

*Area Chair: Lexing Xie

MM'11, November 28–December 1, 2011, Scottsdale, Arizona, USA.

2. THE PROPOSED APPROACH

Assume that we have a set of n annotated images with C labels $\{(\mathbf{x}_i, \mathbf{y}_i) \in \mathbb{R}^p \times \{-1,1\}^C : i = 1, 2, \ldots, n\}$, where $\mathbf{x}_i = (x_{i1}, \ldots, x_{ip})^T \in \mathbb{R}^p$ represents the feature vector for the ith image, p represents the dimensionality of features, and $\mathbf{y}_i = (y_{i1}, \ldots, y_{iC})^T \in \{-1,1\}^C$ is the corresponding label vector, $y_{ij} = 1$ if the ith image has the jth label and $y_{ij} = -1$ otherwise. Since different kinds of features can be obtained from images, we further assume that p-dimensions features are divided into G disjoint groups. Therefore, the feature vector of the ith image x_i can be rewritten as $x_i = (x_{i,1}^T, x_{i,2}^T, \ldots, x_{i,G}^T)^T$.

We also assume that we are given m_i kernel matrices $K_{g,1}, K_{g,2}, \ldots, Kg, m_i$ obtained from evaluating m_i kernel functions on the data $\{x_{i,g}\}$ respectively. Then we can get $\sum m_i$ distinct kernel matrices $(K_{1,1}, \ldots, K_{1,m_i}, \ldots, K_{G,1}, \ldots, K_{G,m_G})$.

2.1 Composite Kernel Learning with Group Structure

In the multiple kernel learning method [1], the problem of learning the best linear combination of kernels is given as follows:

$$K(x_i, x_j) = \sum_{m=1}^{M} \eta_m K_m(x_i, x_j)$$

with coefficients subjected to

$$\sum_{m=1}^{M} \eta_m = 1, \eta_m \geq 0, 1 \leq m \leq M.$$

As we can see, the MKL framework fails to capture the group structure within features. In order to handle the selection of kernels within predefined groups, it is desirable to define a group structure among kernels, and guide the selection process through group structure of kernels. Therefore, this paper introduces the group structure of heterogeneous features into composite kernel learning for image annotation.

For each label $c \in \{1, \ldots, C\}$, we tend to train a regression model to select out salient features mapped by kernel functions at group level as follows:

$$\begin{aligned}
\min_{f_u, b, \xi, \eta_1, \eta_2} \quad & \frac{1}{2} \sum_{g=1}^{G} \eta_{1,g}^{-p} \sum_{u=1}^{m_g} \eta_{2,u}^{-q} ||f_u||_{\mathcal{H}_u}^2 + C \sum_i \xi_i \\
\text{s.t.} \quad & y_{ic}(\sum_u f_u(x_i) + b) \geq 1 - \xi_i, 1 \leq i \leq n \\
& \xi_i \geq 0, 1 \leq i \leq n \\
& \sum_g d_g \eta_{1,g} = 1, \eta_{1,g} \geq 0, 1 \leq g \leq G \\
& \sum_u \eta_{2,u} = 1, \eta_{2,u} \geq 0, 1 \leq u \leq M
\end{aligned} \tag{1}$$

Here, $||f||_{\mathcal{H}}^2 = \sum_{i=1}^{\infty} \sum_{j=1}^{\infty} \alpha_i \alpha_i K(x_i, x_j)$ is the smoothness function, p and q are parameters of CKLGS to be set, C is the regularization parameter, and d_g is the size of group g. The $\boldsymbol{\eta_1} = (\eta_{1,1}, \ldots, \eta_{1,G})$ in (1) which makes the weight of each group either non-zero or zero will give rise to the sparsity between groups, and $\boldsymbol{\eta_2} = (\eta_{2,1}, \ldots, \eta_{2,M})$ which makes the coefficients in each group either non-zero or zero will give rise to the sparsity in groups. Therefore, the parameter vectors $\boldsymbol{\eta_1}$ and $\boldsymbol{\eta_2}$ together can be able to identify which groups of homogeneous features are selected as salient features for label c. Simultaneously, some kinds of homogeneous features may be dropped out for the representation of cth label due to their irrelevance.

Algorithm 1: CKLGS

```
For each label c(c = 1, 2, ..., C) do
Initialize η
solve the classical SVM problem → J(η)
For t = 1, 2, ... do
  compute d = −∇J(η)
  compute descent direction D_t and optimal step γ_t
  η^{t+1} ← η^t + γ_t D_t
  if stopping criterion then
  break
  end
end
```

2.2 Algorithm of CKLGS

In order to solve the optimization problem (1), we replace the two shrinking coefficients $\boldsymbol{\eta_1} = (\eta_{1,1}, \ldots, \eta_{1,G})$ and $\boldsymbol{\eta_2} = (\eta_{2,1}, \ldots, \eta_{2,M})$ by $\boldsymbol{\eta} = (\eta_1, \ldots, \eta_M)$ where $\eta_u = \eta_{1,g}^p \eta_{2,u}^q (u = 1, \ldots, M)$. Thus, the problem of (1) can be represented as:

$$\begin{aligned}
\min_{f_u, b, \xi, \boldsymbol{\eta}} \quad & \frac{1}{2} \sum_u \frac{1}{\eta_u} ||f_u||_{\mathcal{H}_u}^2 + C \sum_i \xi_i \\
\text{s.t.} \quad & y_{ic}(\sum_u f_u(x_i) + b) \geq 1 - \xi_i, 1 \leq i \leq n \\
& \xi_i \geq 0, 1 \leq i \leq n \\
& \sum_g (d_g^p (\sum_{u \in m_g} \eta_u^{1/q})^q)^{1/(p+q)} \leq 1 \\
& \eta_u \geq 0, 1 \leq u \leq M
\end{aligned} \tag{2}$$

We use one two-step alternate optimization algorithm to solve the problem of (2).

We define $J(\boldsymbol{\eta})$ as the objective value of

$$\begin{aligned}
\min_{f_u, b, \xi, \boldsymbol{\eta}} \quad & \frac{1}{2} \sum_u \frac{1}{\eta_u} ||f_u||_{\mathcal{H}_u}^2 + C \sum_i \xi_i \\
\text{s.t.} \quad & y_{ic}(\sum_u f_u(x_i) + b) \geq 1 - \xi_i, 1 \leq i \leq n \\
& \xi_i \geq 0, 1 \leq i \leq n
\end{aligned} \tag{3}$$

Then, the problem of (2) is equal to the following optimization problem:

$$\begin{aligned}
\min_{\boldsymbol{\eta}} \quad & J(\boldsymbol{\eta}) \\
\text{s.t.} \quad & \sum_g (d_g^p (\sum_{u \in m_g} \eta_u^{1/q})^q)^{1/(p+q)} \leq 1 \\
& \eta_u \geq 0, 1 \leq u \leq M
\end{aligned} \tag{4}$$

In the inner loop, we fix the coefficients $\boldsymbol{\eta}$ and solve the optimization problem (3) with respect to $f_1, , f_M$, b and ξ. In the outer loop, we fix f_m,b and ξ and update $\boldsymbol{\eta}$ of the optimization problem (4) by an efficient projected gradient descent method. The CKLGS algorithm is presented in Algorithm 1. Here, the step size γ_t is determined by a one-dimensional line search with Armijo's rule, which ensures global convergence.

3. EXPERIMENTS

In this section, we evaluate the proposed framework CKLGS with other *state-of-the-art* algorithms on multi-label image annotation, and analyze the sparsity of different setting of parameters.

3.1 Experimental Datasets and Evaluation Criterion

To evaluate the performance of the proposed CKLGS algorithm, we conduct experiments on two open benchmark image datasets, i.e., MSRA-MM 2.0 [6] and NUS-WIDE [2], as well as a personal image collection, i.e., Kodak [7]. Images in these datasets may be associated with more than one labels and the labels can be used as ground truth for image annotation.

For each image in the datasets, we extract its heterogeneous features and concatenate those heterogeneous features as a vector. Each kind of homogeneous features is taken as a group. We describe the three evaluated datasets with the number of feature groups as follows:

- Kodak [7] with 3590 images and 22 labels: 657-D features are divided into 7 groups. Namely, 144-D Color Correlogram, 16-D Co-occurrence Texture, 73-D Edge Direction Histogram, 7-D Face Feature, 64-D Color Histogram, 225-D Block-Wise Color Moments, and 128-D Wavelet Texture.

- MSRA-MM 2.0 [6] with 42266 images and 100 labels: 899-D features are divided into 7 groups. Namely, 144-D Color Correlogram, 75-D Edge Direction Histogram, 7-D Face Feature, 64-D Color Histogram, 225-D Block-Wise Color Moments, 256-D RGB and 128-D Wavelet Texture.

- NUS-WIDE [2] with 50000 images and 81 labels: 1134-D features are divided into 6 groups. Namely, 144-D Color Correlogram, 73-D Edge Direction Histogram, 500-D Bag of Words, 64-D Color Histogram, 225-D Block-Wise Color Moments and 128-D Wavelet Texture.

ROC curve which used to characterize compromise relations between TP and FP is derived from the ROC space which regards False Positive Rate (FPR) as the horizontal axis and True Positive Rate (TPR) as the vertical axis. As the ROC curves can not be compared with each other directly for their overlap, we use the area under the ROC curve, called AUC, to compare performance. We use the MacroAUC and the MicroAUC scores to measure the performance across multiple labels.

3.2 Experiment Setup

First, we embed the data into reproducing kernel Hilbert space via mappings $\phi(x) = (\phi_1(x), ..., \phi_G(x))$. That is for each group, there is a different mapping function. Without loss of generality, we use the Gaussian Kernel Function $K(x_i, x_j) = e^{-\frac{(x_i - x_j)^2}{2\sigma}}$ as the mapping function. For each group, we set four different values of $\sigma(10^{\{-1,0,1,2\}})$ to build four different kernel matrices. Thus the data in RKHS can be represented as a linear combination of $4 \times G$ kernel matrices where G is the number of groups. For each label c, we utilize the CKLGS algorithm to obtain the weight $\eta_{1,g}$ of feature groups and the weight $\eta_{2,u}$ of kernel matrices within each group. Then we can predict the class label $y = \sum_u f_u(x_i) + b$ for each testing image x_i.

For each dataset, we randomly select $5 \times C$ images for training where C is the number of labels, and the remaining for testing. During the sampling process, each label is guaranteed to appear in at least one image. This process is repeated ten times to generate ten random training/test partitions, and we report the average results.

3.3 Performance Comparison for Image Annotation

The CKLGS algorithm utilizes the kernel matrices in RKHS and introduces the group structure in images into kernel mapping. We compare our algorithm with the following six methods for multi-label annotation, and the parameters of all the methods are tuned using 5-fold cross-validation based on MacroAUC:

- **SVM**: Linear SVM is applied on each label using the one vs. all scheme.
- **CCA + SVM**: Canonical Correlation Analysis (CCA) is applied first to reduce the data dimensionality before linear SVM is applied.
- **CCA + RR**: Canonical Correlation Analysis (CCA) is applied first to reduce the data dimensionality before ridge regression is applied.
- **JDRMC**: Joint Dimensionality Reduction for Multi-label Classification [4] performs dimensionality reduction and multi-label classification simultaneously.
- **SSMC**: Shared Subspace for Multi-label Classification [3] presented a framework for extracting shared subspace in multi-label classification.
- **GLLR**: Group lasso with logistic regression [10] encoded a sparse grouping prior to seek after a more interpretable model for feature selection and could identify most of discriminative groups of homogeneous features.

Table 1 shows the performance in terms of MacroAUC and MicroAUC. We can observe that the feature selection with CKLGS for image annotation outperforms all other six compared algorithms in terms of two evaluation metrics.

3.4 Sparsity Analysis

We conduct experiments to evaluate the performance under the settings of CKLGS with different sparsity by the parameters p and q. Three pairs of p and q are designed for the experiments.

- $p = 0$, $q = 1$, which equals to a group lasso kernel method called Multiple Kernel Learning (MKL) [1].
- $p = 1/2, q = 1/2$, which is a convex version of our algorithm, named as $\text{CKLGS}_{1/2}$.
- $p = 1$, $q = 1$, which is a non-convex version of our algorithm, named as CKLGS_1.

The experiment is repeated ten times to obtain the average MacroAUC, MicroAUC, the number of selected groups and that of kernels. The results are depicted in Table 2. We can observe that $\text{CKLGS}_{1/2}$ achieves the highest performance, and CKLGS_1 is more sparse than the others.

We also adjust the regularization parameter C which control the penalization in this procedure to obtain the best

Table 1: Performance comparison(mean MacroAUC ± Standard Deviation and mean MicroAUC ± Standard Deviation) when $5 \times C$ labeled data for training. The results shown in boldface are better than others.

A. Performance of the 7 compared methods in terms of MacroAUC

	Kodak	MSRA-MM 2.0	NUSE-WIDE
$\text{CKLGS}_{1/2}$	**0.8124 ± 0.0133**	**0.6348 ± 0.0024**	**0.7265 ± 0.0063**
SVM	0.7892 ± 0.0157	0.6228 ± 0.0055	0.6746 ± 0.0065
CCA+SVM	0.7217 ± 0.0165	0.5365 ± 0.0013	0.5933 ± 0.0054
CCA+RR	0.7288 ± 0.0176	0.5377 ± 0.0009	0.5960 ± 0.0052
JDRMC	0.6790 ± 0.0162	0.5339 ± 0.0117	0.5312 ± 0.0045
SSMC	0.7294 ± 0.0146	0.5496 ± 0.0010	0.5610 ± 0.0053
GLLR	0.7426 ± 0.0113	0.5551 ± 0.0026	0.6256 ± 0.0024

B. Performance of the 7 compared methods in terms of MicroAUC

	Kodak	MSRA-MM 2.0	NUSE-WIDE
CKLGS1/2	**0.8644 ± 0.0070**	**0.8859 ± 0.0023**	**0.8966 ± 0.0017**
SVM	0.8061 ± 0.0239	0.7996 ± 0.0074	0.7693 ± 0.0055
CCA+SVM	0.7039 ± 0.0100	0.5981 ± 0.0154	0.7065 ± 0.0134
CCA+RR	0.7330 ± 0.0064	0.6056 ± 0.0148	0.7016 ± 0.0204
JDRMC	0.7216 ± 0.0187	0.6753 ± 0.0157	0.5819 ± 0.0052
SSMC	0.7411 ± 0.0079	0.6591 ± 0.0104	0.6626 ± 0.0072
GLLR	0.7809 ± 0.0015	0.7745 ± 0.0136	0.7750 ± 0.0023

Table 2: The performance under the settings of CKLGS with different sparsity by the parameters p and q.

A. Performance and sparsity on data KODAK.

	MacroAUC	MicroAUC	Group selected	Kernel selected
MKL	0.7571 ± 0.0249	0.8410 ± 0.0134	5.37 ± 0.2579	10.3545 ± 0.6904
$\text{CKLGS}_{1/2}$	**0.8048 ± 0.0133**	**0.8639 ± 0.0111**	3.4909 ± 0.5372	12.9545 ± 1.8016
CKLGS_1	0.7163 ± 0.0178	0.8334 ± 0.0055	**1.1000 ± 0.0813**	**2.0909 ± 0.2273**

B. Performance and sparsity on data MSRA-MM 2.0.

	MacroAUC	MicroAUC	Group selected	Kernel selected
MKL	0.5764 ± 0.0038	0.8897 ± 0.0012	4.9960 ± 0.1585	9.0600 ± 0.4682
$\text{CKLGS}_{1/2}$	**0.6349 ± 0.0062**	**0.8862 ± 0.0009**	3.7660 ± 0.1537	14.0100 ± 0.5817
CKLGS_1	0.5520 ± 0.0040	0.8756 ± 0.0030	**1.3960 ± 0.1828**	**2.3080 ± 0.5139**

C. Performance and sparsity on data NUS-WIDE.

	MacroAUC	MicroAUC	Group selected	Kernel selected
MKL	0.6498 ± 0.0083	0.8846 ± 0.0017	5.0963 ± 0.1809	10.7407 ± 0.4088
$\text{CKLGS}_{1/2}$	**0.7265 ± 0.0063**	**0.8966 ± 0.0017**	3.3975 ± 0.0797	11.9679 ± 0.3077
CKLGS_1	0.5816 ± 0.0078	0.8709 ± 0.0026	**1.2938 ± 0.0512**	**2.4296 ± 0.1615**

performance of our algorithm. The results are reported in Table 3 which state that this algorithm is nonsensitive to the values of the regularization parameter C.

4. CONCLUSIONS

This paper proposes a feature selection approach, called CKLGS. CKLGS embeds groups of heterogeneous visual features into RKHS and utilizes the kernel functions in RKHS with group structure of visual features to select out most salient groups of features for image annotation. Our proposed method introduces group structure of heterogeneous high-dimensional features within images into multiple kernel learning for image annotation. Experiments with six other state-of-the-art methods for image annotation on three image datasets show the effectiveness of our algorithm.

5. ACKNOWLEDGMENTS

This work is supported by National Natural Science Foundation of China (No. 61070068, No. 90920303), 973 program (2009CB320801).

Table 3: The performance and the sparsity of the proposed algorithm in terms of MacroAUC and MicroAUC to the regularization parameter C.

A. Performance and sparsity on data KODAK.

	C=10	C=100	C=1000	C=10000
MacroAUC	0.8089 ± 0.0110	0.8038 ± 0.0127	0.8048 ± 0.0133	0.8048 ± 0.0133
MicroAUC	0.8593 ± 0.0090	0.8583 ± 0.0105	0.8639 ± 0.0111	0.8639 ± 0.0111

B. Performance and sparsity on data MSRA-MM 2.0.

	C=10	C=100	C=1000	C=10000
MacroAUC	0.6440 ± 0.0054	0.6369 ± 0.0055	0.6344 ± 0.0061	0.6349 ± 0.0062
MicroAUC	0.8105 ± 0.0283	0.8486 ± 0.0123	0.8836 ± 0.0014	0.8862 ± 0.0009

C. Performance and sparsity on data NUS-WIDE.

	C=10	C=100	C=1000	C=10000
MacroAUC	0.7253 ± 0.0071	0.7247 ± 0.0073	0.7249 ± 0.0072	0.7265 ± 0.0063
MicroAUC	0.8918 ± 0.0023	0.8918 ± 0.0023	0.8962 ± 0.0015	0.8966 ± 0.0017

6. REFERENCES

[1] F. Bach, G. Lanckriet, and M. Jordan. Multiple kernel learning, conic duality, and the SMO algorithm. In *Proceedings of the twenty-first international conference on Machine learning*, page 6. ACM, 2004.

[2] T. Chua, J. Tang, R. Hong, H. Li, Z. Luo, and Y. Zheng. Nus-wide: A real-world web image database from national university of singapore. In *Proceeding of the ACM International Conference on Image and Video Retrieval*, pages 1–9. ACM, 2009.

[3] S. Ji, L. Tang, S. Yu, and J. Ye. Extracting shared subspace for multi-label classification. In *Proceeding of the International Conference on Knowledge Discovery and Data Mining*, pages 381–389. ACM, 2008.

[4] S. Ji and J. Ye. Linear dimensionality reduction for multi-label classification. In *Proceedings of the International Joint Conference on Artifical Intelligence*, pages 1077–1082. Morgan Kaufmann Publishers Inc., 2009.

[5] G. Lanckriet, N. Cristianini, P. Bartlett, L. Ghaoui, and M. Jordan. Learning the kernel matrix with semidefinite programming. *The Journal of Machine Learning Research*, 5:27–72, 2004.

[6] H. Li, M. Wang, and X. Hua. MSRA-MM 2.0: A Large-Scale Web Multimedia Dataset. In *2009 IEEE International Conference on Data Mining Workshops*, pages 164–169. IEEE, 2009.

[7] A. Loui, J. Luo, S. Chang, D. Ellis, W. Jiang, L. Kennedy, K. Lee, and A. Yanagawa. Kodak's consumer video benchmark data set: concept definition and annotation. In *Proceedings of the International Workshop on Multimedia Information Retrieval*, page 254. ACM, 2007.

[8] M. Szafranski, Y. Grandvalet, and A. Rakotomamonjy. Composite kernel learning. In *Proceedings of the 25th international conference on Machine learning*, pages 1040–1047. ACM, 2008.

[9] R. Tibshirani. Regression shrinkage and selection via the lasso. *Journal of the Royal Statistical Society. Series B (Methodological)*, 58(1):267–288, 1996.

[10] F. Wu, Y. Yuan, and Y. Zhuang. Heterogeneous feature selection by group lasso with logistic regression. In *Proceedings of the international conference on Multimedia*, pages 983–986. ACM, 2010.

Video-to-Shot Tag Allocation by Weighted Sparse Group Lasso *

Xiaofeng Zhu Zi Huang Heng Tao Shen
School of Information Technology and Electrical Engineering
The University of Queensland
QLD 4072, Australia
{zhux,huang,shenht}@uq.edu.au

ABSTRACT

Traditional shot tagging techniques are focused on learning and propagating the tags at the same level, that is from labeled training shots to the unknown test shots. Due to the lack of sufficient labeled video shots, effective shot tagging remains challenging. By observing that video-level tags are more widely provided, we design a novel approach to propagate video-level tags to the test shots. A weighted sparse group lasso method (WSGL) is proposed for shot reconstruction, which well preserves the structural sparsity to reduce the noise in tag propagation. Meanwhile, it simultaneously considers the spatial-temporal information within the video corpus to enhance the tagging performance. Extensive experiments are conducted on two public video datasets to demonstrate the effectiveness of the proposed method.

Categories and Subject Descriptors

H.3.1 [**Information Storage and Retrieval**]: Content Analysis and Indexing methods

General Terms

Algorithms, Performance, Experimentation

Keywords

Video tagging, Structure sparsity

1. INTRODUCTION

With the major developments on network and multimedia technologies, and the open nature of online content publishing and sharing, the amount of videos on the Internet is incredible today. To facilitate efficient keyword-based video search, automatic video tagging is in high demand. In recent decades, lots of research efforts have been made towards an effective video tagging [3, 5]. However, most of the existing methods are only focused on propagating tags on video level, while a more fine-grained tagging at shot-level is also important for many real applications.

Fig.1 gives an example video about Queensland flood, with video-level tags such as "Queensland flood", "city", "car", "clean-up", etc. By performing video-to-shot tag allocation, "clean-up" is assigned to the last shot, which will be retrieved directly when searching the event of "clean-up". The scan against the entire video would be avoided.

Figure 1: A video clip of Queensland flood consisting of four shots.

To achieve the video-to-shot tag allocation, this paper proposes a novel weighted sparse group lasso (WSGL) method to linearly reconstruct a given shot by regarding the video corpus as the bases and each video as a group of shots. A reasonable hypothesis that the videos selected for the reconstruction process shall preserve both intra-group sparsity and inter-group sparsity. The WSGL model involves certain prior knowledge within the video corpus into the shot reconstruction process, such as spatial-temporal information of videos, etc. Based on the learnt reconstruction correlation between the given test shot and the video corpus bases, a statistical model is further designed to assign the video-level tags to the test shot with the corresponding probabilities.

We apply the proposed WSGL in two scenarios. On the one hand, given an video with video-level tags, we aim to localize these tags to each individual shot. On the other hand, considering a set of the annotated videos as a video corpus, we assign a test shot with semantic tags automatically by analyzing the correlation between the test shot and the video corpus.

To the best of our knowledge, the WSGL is the first method proposed to achieve the video-to-shot tag allocation with an efficient solution. There is no generative model or training process in our tagging procedure, thus it is scalable. Moreover, the WSGL is the first method that simultaneously considers spatial-temporal prior information within the video corpus and two sparsity features (i.e., intra-group sparsity and inter-group sparsity) in one single reconstruction model.

*Area Chair: Marcel Worring

MM'11, November 28–December 1, 2011, Scottsdale, Arizona, USA.

2. THE APPROACH

Given a test shot and a video corpus $\boldsymbol{V} = \{(V_g, T_g)|g = 1..G\}$ consisting of G videos, each of which V_g is associated with its video-level tags T_g, the shot tagging relies on analyzing the correlation between the test shot and the videos in the corpus based on their content features.

Each video in the corpus is essentially a list of shots, denoted as $V_g = (\mathbf{v}_{g,1}, ..., \mathbf{v}_{g,n_g})$, where $\mathbf{v}_{g,j}$ is the key frame standing for the jth shot of the gth video, which can be represented as a vector in the predefined d-dimensional feature space. The duration of each shot is denoted as $t_{g,j}$.

By considering the test shot as an observation and the shots from the video corpus as variables, the original V2S problem can be firstly transformed into a shot reconstruction problem based on which the tag allocation is then performed. The key point for such a reconstruction model is to effectively find the correlations between the test shot and the videos based on their intrinsic characteristics. To achieve that, a novel weighted sparse group lasso is proposed (Sec 2.2). A statistical model is further designed for tag allocation according to the shot correlations discovered in the first step (Sec 2.3).

2.1 Preliminary

The existing sparse coding methods are widely used in the applications of variable selection, model reconstruction,etc, which includes the lasso, the group lasso and the sparse group lasso. The lasso is a popular variable selection method in linear regression models. Each shot of the video in the corpus can be considered as a variable in the shot reconstruction. The group lasso is an extension of lasso to handel the case that the variables are categorized into several groups. In our case, the variables (i.e., shots) can be naturally grouped by their parent video.

While the group lasso takes into account the inter-group sparsity, the sparse group lasso further considers the sparsity within a group. When applying sparse group lasso (SGL) to shot reconstruction, the objective function can be defined as follows.

$$\arg\min_{\mathbf{s}} \frac{1}{2}\|\mathbf{v}_q - \sum_{g=1}^{G} \mathbf{V}_g \mathbf{s}_g\|_2^2 + \lambda_1 \sum_{g}^{G} \|\mathbf{s}_g\|_1 + \lambda_2 \sum_{g=1}^{G} \|\mathbf{s}_g\|_2 \quad (1)$$

where the first term penalizes the whole reconstruction error of all encoding shots, i.e., to control the overall sparsity of the reconstruction model (or intra-group sparsity), and the second term receives the inter-group sparsity. It combines ℓ_1 penalty and $\ell_{2,1}$ penalty together to select a part of videos from the corpus as well as limits the influence of the selected videos to only some (but not necessarily all) shots.

However, further improvement on sparse group lasso is desired. Firstly, sparse group lasso penalizes each factor with same weight as lasso and group lasso. That is, same weight for each component on λ_1 (or λ_2) is used to assess their relative importance. In real applications, such a scenario will also produce bias towards the large coefficients. Secondly, we expect to take advantages of prior knowledge (i.e., the spatial-temporal information in the training videos) to strengthen the performance of the reconstruction model.

2.2 Weighted Sparse Group Lasso

In this paper, we propose a novel method named weighted sparse group lasso (WSGL) by considering both video temporal and spatial information for shot reconstruction.

We assign a temporal weight on each shot for alleviating the bias issue and a spatial weight for penalizing non-dense videos. Both the information within individual shots (i.e., the temporal weight) and the relationship among the shots within each video (i.e., the spatial weight) are utilized for achieving an effective WSGL to solve the V2S problem.

The objective function of the weighted sparse group lasso (WSGL) is defined as:

$$\arg\min_{\mathbf{s}} \frac{1}{2}\|\mathbf{v}_q - \sum_{g=1}^{G} \mathbf{V}_g \mathbf{s}_g\|_2^2 + \lambda_1 \sum_{g=1}^{G} \|\mathbf{w}_g^t \mathbf{s}_g\|_1 + \lambda_2 \sum_{g=1}^{G} \mathbf{w}_g^s \|\mathbf{w}_g^t \mathbf{s}_g\|_2 \quad (2)$$

where $\mathbf{w}_g^t$ and $\mathbf{w}_g^s$ are the temporal weight and the spatial weight respectively, which will be further discussed in the following sections.

In shot reconstruction, WSGL regards the entire video corpus as the bases space, where each video V_g, $g = 1..G$ is naturally a group consisting of a set of variables - shots. Given a test shot $\mathbf{v}_q$, WSGL aims to reconstruct $\mathbf{v}_q$ by the shots from $V_g|g = 1..G$ taking into account the predefined weights on each shot. The weighting issue is the key point to distinguish our method from the conventional SGL methods. Moreover, the parameter includes prior knowledge within the bases space. Such a flexibility in turn can produce different amounts of shrinkage for different factors. Hence, WSGL is more practical than SGL in real applications.

In the next subsections, we will explain the details on temporal weight $\mathbf{w}_g^t$ and the spatial weight $\mathbf{w}_g^s$.

2.2.1 *Temporal Weighting*

It is natural that long shots within a video contribute more to video tagging than short shots. In other words, given a video with a set of tags, generally, most of the tags could be used for describing the content of the long shots.

Thus, in shot reconstruction, long shots are preferred which have stronger association with the video-level tags, to provide a more accurate shot tagging. By taking into account this issue, we define the temporal weight for each shot (i.e., variable) while the existing methods consider variables equally.

The temporal weight of the i-th shot in the g-th video is defined as $w_{g,i}^t = (t_{g,i}/\sum_{j=1}^{n_g} t_{g,j})^{-1}$, while the weight vector over the the gth video is denoted as $\mathbf{w}_g^t = (w_{g,1}^t, ..., w_{g,n_g}^t)$.

2.2.2 *Spatial Weighting*

Besides the temporal information extracted from individual shots, we also consider the spatial information within each videos. A new concept named Spatial Standard Deviation (SSD) is proposed to reveal the intrinsic relationships among the shots in a video. For the gth video consisting of n_g shots, its SSD is formally defined as $SSD_g = \frac{1}{d}\sum_{j=1}^{d}\sqrt{\frac{1}{n_g}\sum_{i=1}^{n_g}(v_{g,i}^j - \mu_g^j)}$, where $v_{g,i}$ is the ith key frame and μ_g is the mean frame feature vector of the gth video, and the superscript j stands for the jth dimension of the corresponding vectors.

According to the mathematical meaning of the standard

deviation, smaller the SSD_g is, closer the shots in the gth video are. The video with a small SSD is called dense video (or dense group). We assume that dense videos should be selected with higher priority resulting in a higher group sparsity in shot reconstruction. Less the videos being selected can reduce the noise introducing to the reconstruction model to some extend. Thus, SSD can be used as a penalty to the non-dense videos in the WSGL model. It is formally called spatial weight, which is denoted as $\mathbf{w}_g^s = (\underbrace{SSD_g, ..., SSD_g}_{n_g})$.

2.2.3 *Objective Function and Implementation*

By setting $\mathbf{b}_g = \mathbf{w}_g^t \times \mathbf{s}_g$, $g = 1..G$, the objective function in Eq.2 is converted into

$$\arg\min_{\mathbf{s}} \frac{1}{2}\|\mathbf{v}_q - \sum_{g=1}^{G} \mathbf{V}_g^{'}\mathbf{b}_g\|_2^2 + \lambda_1 \sum_{g=1}^{G} \|\mathbf{b}_g\|_1 + \lambda_2 \sum_{g=1}^{G} \mathbf{w}_g^s \|\mathbf{b}_g\|_2 \quad (3)$$

where $\mathbf{V}_g^{'} = \mathbf{V}_g \mathbf{w}_g^{t^{-1}}$. In WSGL, each weight coefficient implies the contribution of the corresponding component to the reconstruction model. First, the weighted ℓ_1 norm is used to penalize each shot such that the coefficients of irrelevant shots (i.e., with higher weight) are shrunken to zero. At the same time, the weighted ℓ_1 norm reduces the shrinkage bias towards the larger coefficients of significant variable. Second, the weighted $\ell_{2,1}$ norm penalizes the coefficients of significant videos such that the dense videos are firstly selected.

The implementation of WSGL follows the idea in [1] that separates the general optimization procedure in Eq.3 into two sequential steps, i.e., inter-group sparsity selection followed by intra-group sparsity selection, which are repeated until a convergence condition is met. Note that, for convenient parameter setting, we scale the domain of λ_1 and λ_2 into [0,1] in our implementation.

2.3 Tag Allocation

By solving the objective function Eq.3, we obtain an optimal $s = \{s_g | g = 1..G\}$, which represents the correlations between the test shot and the corpus videos. The importance of the gth video in the shot reconstruction is measured by $sc_g = \frac{\sum_{j=1}^{n_g} s_{g,j} t_{g,j}}{\sum_{j=1}^{n_g} t_{g,j}}$, which is an integration of the importance of each shot (i.e., s_g) within the video. The length of each shot is also taken into account. The higher the score is, the more important the gth video is to reconstruct the test shot.

As each video in the corpus is associated with a set of tags, the probability of the ith tag in the vocabulary assigned to the test shot is calculated by $P_i = \sum_{g=1}^{G} sc_g \times c$, $c = 1$ when the ith tag belongs to the gth video while $c = 0$, otherwise. After ranking the probability of each tag in descending order, the tags at the top k (k=5 in our experiments) are allocated to the test shot as the most possible tags.

3. EXPERIMENTS

In this section, we evaluate the performance of the proposed method with other state-of-the-art algorithms on solving the V2S issue by testing average accuracy and Hamming loss on two real video datasets, Kodak's Consumer Video Benchmark dataset [4] and TREC Video Retrieval Evaluation 2007.

Datasets	kNN	GLasso	LRA	SGL	WSGL
Kodak-s	0.3195	0.3140	0.3079	0.3751	**0.3969**
Kodak-l	0.3980	0.3672	0.3729	0.4012	**0.4232**
Trecvid07	0.5716	0.5618	0.5933	0.5936	**0.6226**

Table 1: Average accuracy comparison of different parameters setting on three datasets. Note that, we illustrate out the best result in all algorithms.

Datasets	kNN	GLasso	LRA	SGL	WSGL
Kodak-s	0.2042	0.2031	0.2048	0.1893	**0.1848**
Kodak-l	0.1812	0.1938	0.1896	0.1848	**0.1784**
Trecvid07	0.1952	0.1624	0.1580	0.1576	**0.1518**

Table 2: Hamming loss comparison of different parameters setting on three datasets. Note that, we illustrate out the best result in all algorithms.

3.1 Experimental Setting

Kodak dataset has 25 concepts over 1358 videos including 5166 shots. The entire videos are considered as the first video corpus named Kodak-l, while a number of 395 videos containing more than five shots each are selected as the second video corpus named Kodak-s. We select 285 shots whose number of tags is larger than two as the test data[1].

Dataset Trecvid07 has 36 concepts over 110 videos with 21532 shots. We select all 110 videos as the training data and 551 shots whose number of tags is larger than two as the test data. Thus, two groups of experiments with two different video corpus on Kodak dataset and one group of experiment on Trecvid 07 dataset are conducted. We characterize the visual content of each key frame by extracting their Local Binary Patterns (LBP).

Four baseline methods including kNN[2], group lasso (GLasso), Bi-layer sparse coding (LRA) [2], sparse group lasso (SGL) are compared with the proposed method WSGL. Both Hamming loss and average accuracy are used in the experiments as the indicators of the effectiveness.

3.2 Parameter Setting

We test different parameter settings in our model for achieving the best experimental results. There are two parameters in the WSGL: 1) λ_1 is used to control intra-group sparsity; 2) λ_2 is used to control inter-group sparsity. By default, here we set $\lambda_1, \lambda_2 \in \{10^{-1}, ..., 10^{-6}\}$.

We choose tagging average accuracy and Hamming loss as the evaluation metrics. The results on the effects of λ_1 and λ_2 are illustrated in Figure 2. As can be seen, in most cases, as λ_1 and λ_2 increase the average accuracy goes up. We believe larger λ_1 and λ_2 lead to a higher degree of both intra-group sparsity and inter-group sparsity, thereby introducing in less tag propagation noise.

We can also observe that the Hamming loss shows similar trends with the change of λ_1 and λ_2. This gives a further verification of the above analysis.

[1]The test shots have no overlapping with Kodak-s

[2]The better performance with the setting between $k = 50$ and $k = 100$ is reported in the performance study.

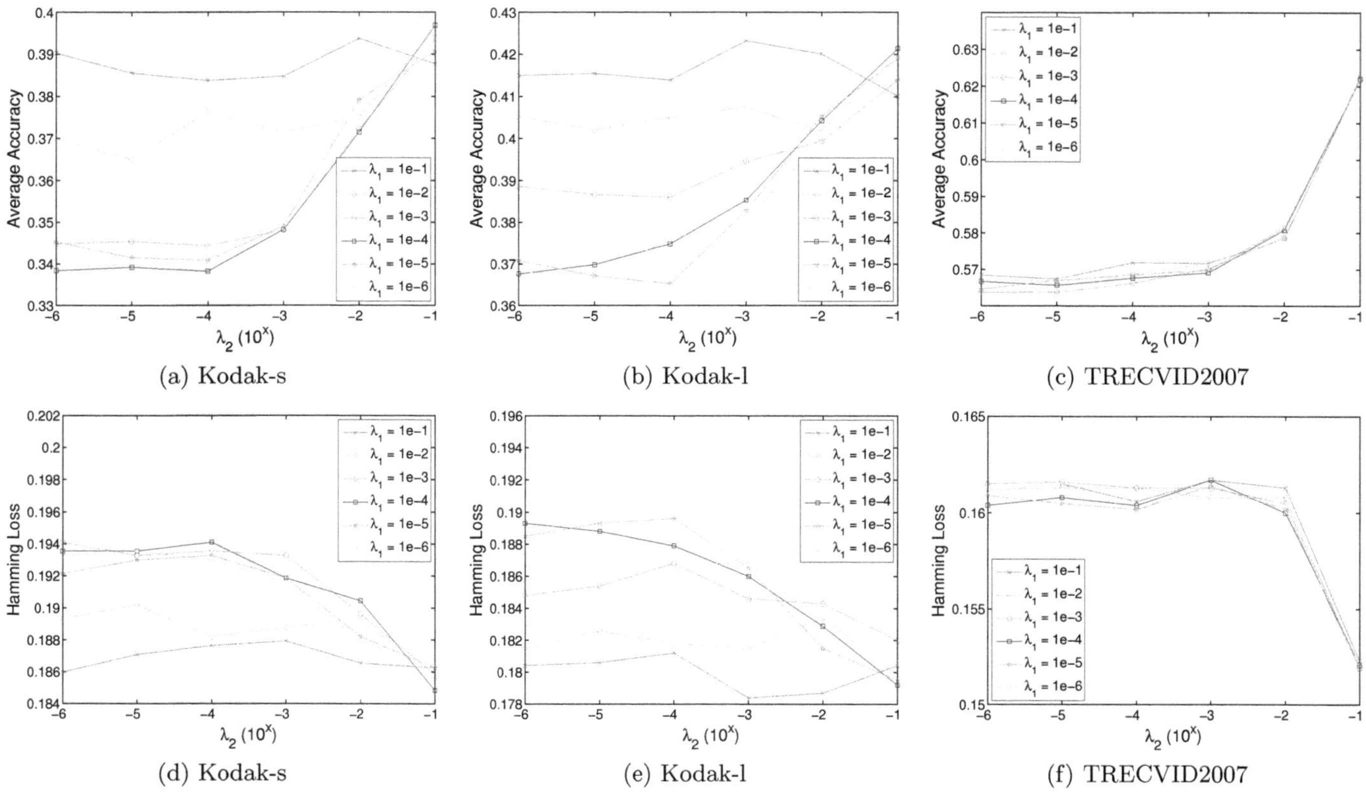

(a) Kodak-s (b) Kodak-l (c) TRECVID2007

(d) Kodak-s (e) Kodak-l (f) TRECVID2007

Figure 2: Average accuracy (upper row) and Hamming loss (lower row) of WSGL on the different datasets with different parameters setting.

3.3 Comparison and Analysis

Observed from Table 1 and Table 2, the proposed method WSGL outperforms the other existing methods at different evaluations on the different datasets. This clearly illustrates the effectiveness of out proposed method.

We can observe that the group lasso mostly performs worst in all the comparing sparse coding algorithms, and sometimes even worse than the kNN method in our experiments. We believe that the group lasso just considers inter-group sparsity but neglects intra-group sparsity. Since the LRA algorithm contains implicit group effects and uses Bi-layer sparsity to filter the redundancy, it is better than the group lasso. Sparse group lasso takes both inter-group sparsity and intra-group sparsity into account. Thus, sparse group lasso is better than group lasso and LRA. However, sparse group Lasso does not utilize spatial-temporal prior information within the video corpus, while the WSGL includes certain prior knowledge as well as handles the magnitude bias issue to achieve the best performance.

Intuitively, it is feasible to involve the spatial-temporal information into the shot reconstruction model. Two groups of experiments are conducted to test the effects of the temporal weight and the spatial weight separately. Due to the space limit, the detailed report is omitted.

4. CONCLUSION

In this paper we firstly introduce a practical yet challengeable problem, i.e., the video-to-shot tag allocation which aims to assign the known video-level tags to the unknown shots. A novel weighted sparse group lasso is proposed to perform effective video-to-shot tag allocation. The proposed method achieves two sparsity features, inter-group sparsity and intra-group sparsity, and takes prior knowledge in the video corpus into account, resulting in a relatively better performance compared with the existing methods. In future we will extend the proposed framework to deal with the video-to-shot tag allocation problem by employing information from cross-media domains.

5. REFERENCES

[1] J. Friedman, T. Hastie, and R. Tibshirani. A note on the group lasso and a sparse group lasso. *ArXiv e-prints*, 2010.

[2] X. Liu, B. Cheng, S. Yan, J. Tang, T.-S. Chua, and H. Jin. Label to region by bi-layer sparsity priors. In *ACM Multimedia*, pages 115–124, 2009.

[3] S. Siersdorfer, J. S. Pedro, and M. Sanderson. Automatic video tagging using content redundancy. In *ACM SIGIR*, pages 395–402, 2009.

[4] A. Yanagawa, A. C. Loui, J. Luo, S.-F. Chang, D. Ellis, W. Jiang, L. Kennedy, and K. Lee. Kodak consumer video benckmark data set: concept definition and annotation. *Columbia University ADVENT Technical Report 246-2008-4*, 2008.

[5] W.-L. Zhao, X. Wu, and C.-W. Ngo. On the annotation of web videos by efficient near-duplicate search. *IEEE Transactions on Multimedia*, 12(5):448 –461, 2010.

Extracting Key Frames from Consumer Videos Using Bi-layer Group Sparsity

Zheshen Wang[1], Mrityunjay Kumar[2], Jiebo Luo[2], Baoxin Li[1]

[1]Computer Science, Arizona State University
699 S. Mill Ave., Tempe, AZ, 85281
{zheshen.wang, baoxin.li}@asu.edu

[2]Eastman Kodak Company
1999 Lake Ave., Rochester, NY, 14650
{mrityunjay.kumar, jiebo.luo}@kodak.com

ABSTRACT
Compared to well-edited videos with predefined structures (e.g., news or sports videos), extracting key frames from unconstrained consumer videos remains a much more challenging problem due to their extremely diverse contents (no pre-imposed structure) and uncontrolled video quality (e.g., due to poor lighting or camera shake). In order to exploit spatio-temporal correlation present in the video for key frame extraction, we propose a bi-layer group sparse representation in which the input video frames are first segmented into homogeneous patches and group sparsity is imposed at two levels simultaneously: (i) patch-to-frame, and (ii) frame-to-sequence. The grouped sparse coefficients are further combined with frame quality scores to generate key frames. Extensive experiments are performed on videos from actual end users. Results obtained by the proposed approach compare favorably with existing methods to confirm its effectiveness.

Categories and Subject Descriptors
I.2.10 [**Vision and Scene Understanding**]: Video Analysis.

General Terms
Algorithms, Design, Experimentation.

Keywords
Key frame extraction, group sparsity, consumer video.

1. INTRODUCTION
Rapid growth in the use of digital cameras and camcorders has made automatic key frame extraction a necessity for managing, and browsing huge amounts of video data. The key frame extraction problem has been investigated for years [1, 2], primarily targeting structured and clean videos (e.g., sports and news videos [3]). However, such algorithms are sub-optimal for consumer videos as the latter record extremely diverse contents, often lack pre-imposed structure, and usually exhibit low quality due to factors such as poor lighting and camera shake. In addition, sound track or metadata are typically not available for unedited consumer videos.

*Area Chair: Bernard Merialdo.

MM'11, November 28–December 1, 2011, Scottsdale, Arizona, USA.

This paper presents a bi-layer group sparse representation to exploit spatio-temporal correlation present in the video data for key-frame extraction from consumer videos. Specifically, the input video frames are first segmented into visually homogeneous patches and the proposed bi-layer group sparsity, which is derived by combining the traditional group sparse Lasso and Moreau-Yosida regularization, is used to enforce group sparsity at two levels simultaneously: (i) patch-to-frame, and (ii) frame-to-sequence. The patch-to-frame level group sparsity captures the spatial correlation among the frames whereas the inter-frame temporal correlation is taken into account at the frame-to-sequence group sparsity step. The grouped sparse coefficients are further combined with high-level semantic-based frame quality scores to select key frames.

In the rest of this paper, we first describe the proposed approach in Section 2. Experiments, results, and analysis are presented in Section 3. We conclude the work in Section 4.

2. BI-LAYER GROUP SPARSE REPRESENTATION
In this paper, we propose a bi-layer group sparse representation for key frame extraction from general consumer videos. Different from traditional clustering-based methods, this approach relies on signal-reconstruction perspective for key frame selection. In particular, the proposed approach exploits the fact that frames selected as key frames should reconstruct the input video with minimum reconstruction error.

Due to the fact that the expected number of key frames is always very small compared to the length of the input video (i.e., sparse selection of video frames), a sparse representation framework for making such selection is appropriate.

2.1 Sparse Group Lasso
Recently, sparse learning via L_1 regularization [4] and its various extensions has received increasing attention in computer vision, pattern recognition, and multimedia computing [5]. Specifically, based on an over-complete dictionary $A \in R^{m \times n}$ $(m<n)$ with n bases

$$y = Ax \tag{1}$$

where $y \in R^{m \times 1}$ is the target signal to be approximated, $x \in R^{n \times 1}$ is the unknown (sparse) coefficient vector. The sparsest solution can be obtained by solving a L_1 optimization problem in polynomial time by the standard linear programming method [6]:

$$\min_x \| Ax - y \|_2^2 + \lambda \| x \|_1 \tag{2}$$

where λ is a regularization parameter.

However, for cases when group attributes are present (e.g., categorical information of images, image sources of sub-image patches), the Lasso solution is not satisfactory as it only selects variables without considering the grouping factors. To overcome this problem, sparse group Lasso [7, 8] was proposed, which imposes an additional group sparse constraint upon the original Lasso penalty. Using Moreau-Yosida regularization, we consider the sparse group Lasso criterion [9]

$$\min_x \frac{1}{2} \| Ax - y \|_2^2 + \lambda_1 \| x \|_1 + \lambda_2 \sum_{k=1}^{g} w_{G_k} \| x_{G_k} \|_2 \tag{3}$$

where $A \in R^{m \times n}$, $y \in R^{m \times 1}$, $x \in R^{n \times 1}$ is divided into g non-overlapping groups x_{G_1}, x_{G_2}, ..., x_{G_g} and w_{G_k} is the weight for the kth group. In Eq. (3), $\lambda_1 \| x \|_1$ indicates traditional element-level sparse penalty and $\lambda_2 \sum_{i=1}^{g} w_{G_i} \| x_{G_i} \|_2$ further imposes group-level sparsity in computing the cost to reconstruct y. λ_1 and λ_2 control the relative contributions of the two terms, respectively. Intuitively, Eq. (3) computes a sparse coefficient vector to approximate y, where nonzero coefficients exhibit a grouping effect.

2.2 Sparse Group Lasso for Frame Reconstruction

Due to the temporal redundancy present in videos, it is possible to reconstruct each frame of the input video as a sparse linear combination of the remaining frames. Formally, given an input video containing n frames $y^{(1)}$, $y^{(2)}$, ..., $y^{(n)}$, where $y^{(j)} \in R^{m \times 1}$ and m is the dimension of features representing frame $y^{(j)}$, we can find a sparse set of coefficients

$$x^{(j)} = [x_1^{(j)}, x_2^{(j)}, ..., x_n^{(j)}]^T, \; j = 1, ..., n \tag{4}$$

to reconstruct frame $y^{(j)}$ based on dictionary $A^{(j)} \in R^{m \times n}$, which consists of all frames from y except $y^{(j)}$

$$A^{(j)} = [a_1^{(j)}, a_2^{(j)}, ..., a_n^{(j)}]^T, \; j = 1, ..., n \tag{5}$$

where

$$a_i^{(j)} = \begin{cases} y^{(i)}, & i \neq j \\ 0^{m \times 1}, & i = j \end{cases}, \; i, j = 1, ..., n \tag{6}$$

To exploit the local spatial information present in the input video frames, we first segment each frame into homogeneous subimage patches:

$$y^{(j)} = \{p_1^{(j)}, p_2^{(j)}, ..., p_{l_j}^{(j)}\} \tag{7}$$

where $p^{(j)}$ are the patches from frame $y^{(j)}$ and the total number of patches in $y^{(j)}$ is l_j. Then, frame reconstructions are performed on the patch level with both patch-level and frame-level sparsities imposed by using the sparse group Lasso formulation in Eq. (3):

$$\min_{x'^{(j)}} \frac{1}{2} \| A'^{(j)} x'^{(j)} - y^{(j)} \|_2^2 + \lambda_1 \| x'^{(j)} \|_1 + \lambda_2 \sum_{k=1}^{n} w_{G_k} \| x'_{G_k} \|_2 \tag{8}$$

in which $A'^{(j)} \in R^{m \times n'}$ consisting of patches from all frames except $y^{(j)}$ and $n' = \sum_{r=1}^{n} l_r$ denotes the number of total patches (for a consistent representation for all frames, we set the dimensions of patches from frame j in $A'^{(j)}$ as zeros instead of removing them from the dictionary) and $x'^{(j)} \in n' \times 1$ are the patch-level sparse coefficients. All patches belong to n non-overlapping groups, which corresponds to n input frames. Intuitively, Eq. (8) seeks a set of sparse coefficients $x^{(j)}$ to reconstruct frame $y^{(j)}$ by using a small amount of patches from a limited number of frames except $y^{(j)}$ itself. (Note that we use a quantized histogram of grid-based SIFT features, so the dimensions of features that represent patches and frames are the same. More details about features will be described in Section 3.1).

2.3 Bi-layer Sparse Group Lasso for Video Reconstruction

As described in Section 2.2, traditional group sparse representation can be applied to reconstruct each frame of the input video separately, so that sparse coefficients are optimized for each frame independently (i.e., a set of coefficient $x^{(j)}$ obtained for the entire sequence). Due to the visually continuous nature of video, the sparse solver turns to select patches from temporally nearby frames to reconstruct the target frame. Hence, overall, it is difficult to differentiate the relative contributions of each frame to reconstruct the entire sequence.

In this work, we propose to introduce another layer of *grouping* by accumulating the reconstruction errors of each frame with its corresponding dictionary, which yields a bi-layer group sparsity formulation:

$$\min_x \frac{1}{2} \sum_{j=1}^{n} \| A'^{(j)} x' - y^{(j)} \|_2^2 + \lambda_1 \| x' \|_1 + \lambda_2 \sum_{k=1}^{n} w_{G_k} \| x'_{G_k} \|_2 \tag{9}$$

Compared to Eq. (8), Eq. (9) sums reconstruction errors for each frame $y^{(j)}$ based on the corresponding dictionary $A'^{(j)}$ which contains patches from all frames except $y^{(j)}$. Note that, in Eq. (9), the expected coefficients x' are shared by all of the n frames, which requires a global optimization over the entire group (i.e., all frames of the input sequence) to solve the sparse representation problem. By stacking the target frames and their corresponding dictionaries

$$A' = [A'^{(1)}, A'^{(2)}, ..., A'^{(j)}]^T, \; A' \in R^{m \cdot n \times n'} \tag{10}$$

$$Y = [y^{(1)}, y^{(2)}, ..., y^{(n)}], \; Y \in R^{m \cdot n \times 1} \tag{11}$$

Eq. (9) can be further written as

$$\min_x \frac{1}{2} \| A' x' - Y \|_2^2 + \lambda_1 \| x' \|_1 + \lambda_2 \sum_{k=1}^{n} w_{G_k} \| x'_{G_k} \|_2 \tag{12}$$

which can be solved by using the regular group sparse solver (e.g., [9]). In other words, the multi-task group sparse representation problem can be viewed as a single-task group sparse representation problem with dimension-concatenated target signals and dictionaries.

With the obtained sparse coefficients x' on the patch level, frame-level coefficients x can be further computed as a weighted summation of patch-level coefficients (weighted by the sizes of patches) involved in the current frame.

$$x'_j = \sum_{r=a}^{b} x_r, \; j = 1, \dots, n \tag{13}$$

in which $a = \sum_{q=1}^{j-1} l_q + 1$ and $b = \sum_{q=1}^{j} l_q$, which are the number of patches of the first j-1 frames and j frames, respectively.

2.4 Proposed Approach for Key Frame Extraction

Using the obtained frame-level sparse coefficients x from Eq. (13), key frames can be selected according to the relative importance of each frame to reconstruct the input video. However, sparse representation is typically appropriate for only low-level features. To compensate for high-level semantics (e.g., high-quality frames preferred to blurry frames with the same visual contents for key frames), we incorporate three frame quality scores to regulate the obtained sparse coefficients to finally select key frames. The three scores are introduced below:

Image quality score computes *BIQI* image quality score [10]

$$s_i^{(IQ)} = \exp(-BIQI(f_i)) \tag{14}$$

Frames with high image quality score (the larger the better image quality) are preferred as key frames.

Scene complexity score of a single frame is defined as its Kolmogorov complexity measured by the normalized (to the frame size) length of its Bzip2 sequence [11].

$$s_i^{(SC)} = BZIP2(f_i) / size(f_i) \tag{15}$$

Frames with high scene complexity scores (i.e., informative frames) are more likely to be key frames.

Color histogram change score is defined as the maximum Euclidean distance between the color histograms (we use concatenated hue histograms in HSV space over a two-level image pyramid, 1X1 and 2X2) of the current frame and the $(i-\tau)^{th}$ and the $(i+\tau)^{th}$ frames, respectively.

$$s_i^{(CC)} = \exp\left(-\max\left\{\sqrt{(H_i - H_{i-\tau})^2}, \sqrt{(H_i - H_{i+\tau})^2}\right\}\right) \tag{16}$$

This score captures salient visual scene changes of the input video. According to an assumption that transition frames are of less interest, frames with high color histogram change scores (i.e., frames that appear in the relatively more continuous portions of the videos) are better candidates for key frames.

The above scores are normalized to [0, 1] for the given video before further computation. Finally, the frame important score is defined as a weighted summation of the above three scores

$$s_i = \eta \cdot [s_i^{(IQ)}, s_i^{(SC)}, s_i^{(CC)}]^T \tag{17}$$

where η is a vector of constant weights for balancing the three components. Overall, we expect frames with high frame quality scores to be selected as key frames. We set $\eta = [1/3, \; 1/3, \; 1/3]$ in our experiments.

To select final key frames, we combined the obtained frame-level sparse coefficients x and frame quality score s by following the strategy below:

Initial an empty set Ω. Loop for the following steps until Ω contains K indices (we used the number of ground-truth key frames to specify K in our experiments):

(1) Choose the index with the largest coefficient

$$i_1 = \arg\max_i \{x_i \mid i = 1, \dots, n\} \tag{18}$$

(2) Check the surrounding region of i_1 in s and choose the index i_2 with the largest frame quality score

$$i_2 = \arg\max_i \{s_i \mid i \in [i_1 - \tau, i_1 + \tau]\} \tag{19}$$

(3) Set the surrounding region of i_2 in both x and s as zero

$$x_i = 0, \; s_i = 0, \; i \in [i_2 - \tau, i_2 + \tau] \tag{20}$$

(4) Add i_2 to set Ω.

Frames from the original video with indexes in Ω are selected as final key frames.

3. EXPERIMENTS

To verify the effectiveness of the proposed approach, we conducted experiments on video from actual users and compared the results to human-labeled ground-truth and results from other methods. A total of 17 videos provided by the authors of [2] were originally selected from 3000+ home videos [12] with resolution 640X480 or 320X240, frame rates from 24 to 30, and average length of 29 seconds. Contents of the videos range from natural sceneries, trips, sports, and outdoor activities to concerts, weddings, birthday parties, and card games, and therefore span reasonably the space of general consumer videos, with each video clip containing a single shot. Note that this assumption is generally true for videos captured using digital or phone cameras, thus removing the need for shot boundary detection.

3.1 Experimental Settings

For a given video, we first segment the sequences into frames according to their original frame rates. For spatio-temporal data reduction, extracted frames are further down-sampled to 320X240 (if the original resolution is 640X480) spatially and temporally with a step of 5 frames (i.e., each group of 5 consecutive frames is defined as a snippet and the first frames are used as representatives for each snippet). Dense SIFT descriptions [13] are then extracted on an image grid (*GridSpacing*=5, *PatchSizes*=8 and 16 in our experiments) for H, S, V color channels of each frame and further quantized to 100 dimensions by k-means clustering on randomly selected samples over the entire video. Histograms of quantized features are then computed over a three-level spatial pyramid to yield a 2100-dimension feature vector for each frame.

Results from the proposed approaches and other competitive methods are evaluated by comparing them with the ground-truth key frames that were selected by three third-party human judges [2]. We follow the same evaluation rules as proposed in [2]. Specifically, by comparing two sets of ordered key frames, two fames that occurr within a short period of time and similar in scene content and composition are considered as equivalent, score=1; otherwise, score=0 (0.5 is used when there is ambiguity). Accuracies are reported as the number of matched key frames (i.e., total score for the entire video) over the number of total ground-truth key frames.

3.2 Results and Analysis

Results from the proposed approach on the 17 videos (which were used in [2]) are presented in Table 1. Compared to the accuracies reported in [2] (we removed video#14-"wedding" which is missing and recomputed the accuracies for fair comparisons): Evenly spaced (ESKF) 48%, Motion-based (MKFE) 55% and Histogram-based (UCF) 48%, our approach outperforms ESKF and UCF by 7.7% and slightly better than the performance of MKFE. Visual results from different approaches on Video-"SoloSurfer" are presented in Figure 1.

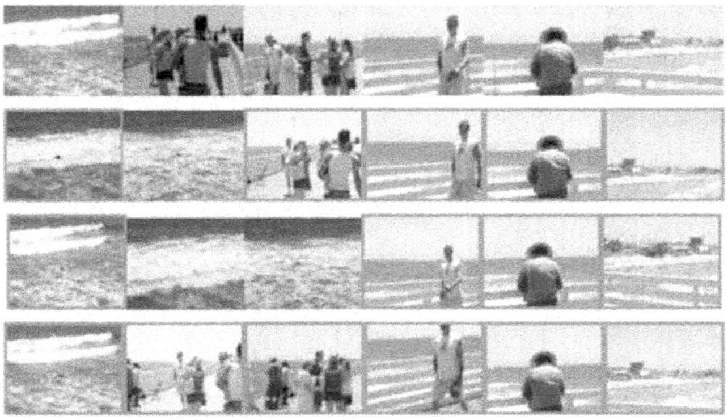

Figure 1. "SoloSurfer" (Red solid borders indicate match score=1, dashed borders indicate score=0.5): Comparison is between ground truth (1st row), MKFE (2nd row), ESKF (3rd row) and the proposed approach (4th row). As reported in [2], the UCF method resulted in a total match score=2. Visual results from the UCF method are not available.

Table 1. Results from the proposed approach.

Video Name	Score of matches over number of total key frames
SchoolBand	3/6
Asian Exhibit	3/6
CardsAroundTable	5.5/7
ReporterTour	2/9
SoloSurfer	5/6
SkylineFromOverlook	4/6
FireworkAndBoat	1/4
EatingSardines	4/6
BusTour	1.5/5
LiquidChocolate	5/6
OrnateChurch	4/4
LawnchairDance	1.5/6
KnockKnockPrincess	2.5/7
HappyDog	4/4
MuseumExhibit	3/4
PoolAcrobat	2 /7
BoatUpsideDown	7.5/12
Total	**58.5/105 = 55.7%**

4. CONCLUSION

In this work, we propose a bi-layer group sparse representation approach to extract key frames from consumer videos by relying solely on visual content. The bi-layer group sparse representation is based on the traditional group sparse Lasso with Moreau-Yosida regularization and models the spatio-temporal correlation present in the input video for key frame extraction by jointly imposing the group sparsity at two levels: (i) patch-to-frame, and (ii) frame-to-sequence. The grouped sparse coefficients are further combined with high-level semantic-based frame quality scores to select key frames. The proposed approach does not rely on any non-visual data or domain knowledge and is more robust than existing approaches for general consumer videos. Results on videos from actual end users and comparisons to existing approaches demonstrate the effectiveness of the proposed approach.

5. REFERENCES

[1] Truong, B. T., and Venkatesh, S. 2007. Video abstraction: A systematic review and classification. *ACM Transactions on Multimedia Computing, Communications and Applications*, 3(1).

[2] Luo, J., Papin, C., and Costello, K. 2009. Towards extracting semantically meaningful key frames from persona video clips: From humans to computers. *IEEE Trans. on Circuits and Systems for Video Technology*, 19(2): 289-301.

[3] Rasheed, Z., and Shah, M. 2005. Detection and representation of scenes in videos. *IEEE Transactions on Multimedia*, 7(6): 1097-1105.

[4] Tibshirani, R. 1996. Regression shrinkage and selection via the Lasso. *Journal of the Royal Statistical Society: Series B* 58(1): 267–288.

[5] Mairal, J., Bach, F., Ponce, J., Sapiro, G., and Zisserman, A. 2009. Non-local sparse models for image restoration. *IEEE International Conference on Computer Vision*.

[6] Chen, S., Donoho, D., and Saunders, M. 2001. Atomic decomposition by basis pursuit. *Society for Industrial and Applied Mathematics*, 43(1): 129-159.

[7] Yuan, M., and Lin, Y. 2006. Model selection and estimation in regression with grouped variables. *Journal of the Royal Statistical Society: Series B*, 68(1): 49-67.

[8] Meier, L., Geer, S., and Buhlmann, P. 2008. The group Lasso for logistic regression. *Journal of the Royal Statistical Society: Series B*, 70: 53-71.

[9] Liu, J., and Ye, J. 2010. Moreau-Yosida Regularization for Grouped Tree Structure Learning. *Annual Conference on Neural Information Processing Systems*.

[10] Moorthy, A. K., and Bovik, A. C. 2010. A two-step framework for constructing blind image quality indices. *IEEE Signal Processing Letters*, 17(5): 513-516.

[11] Sundaram, H., Xie, L., Chang, S. 2002. A utility framework for the automatic generation of audio-visual skims. *ACM International Conference on Multimedia*.

[12] Loui, A., Luo, J., Chang, S., Ellis, D., Jiang, W., Kennedy, L., Lee, K., and Yanagawa, A. 2007. Consumer video benchmark data set: concept definition and annotation. *International Workshop on Multimedia Information Retrieval*.

[13] Lazebnik, S., Schmid, and C. Ponce, J. 2006. Beyond bags of features: Spatial pyramid matching for recognizing natural scene categories. *IEEE Conference on Computer Vision and Pattern Recognition*.

Spatial Pooling for Transformation Invariant Image Representation

Xia Li
Dept. of Computer Science
University of Texas
at San Antonio
TX, 78249, U.S.A
xial@cs.utsa.edu

Yan Song
Department of EEIS
University of Science and Technology of China, Hefei, 230027, China
songy@ustc.edu.cn

Yijuan Lu
Dept. of Computer Science
Texas State University
San Marcos, TX, 78666, U.S.A
yl12@txstate.edu

Qi Tian
Dept. of Computer Science
University of Texas
at San Antonio
TX, 78249, U.S.A
qtian@cs.utsa.edu

ABSTRACT
Spatial Pyramid Matching (SPM) [2] has been proposed to extend the Bag-of-Word (BoW) model for object classification. By reserving the finer level information, it makes image matching more accurate. However, for not well-aligned images, where the object is rotated, flipped or translated, SPM may lose its discrimination power. To tackle this problem, we propose novel spatial pooling layouts to address various transformations, and generate a more general image representation. To evaluate the effectiveness of the proposed approach, we conduct extensive experiments on three transformation emphasized datasets for object classification task. Experimental results demonstrate its superiority over the state-of-the-arts. Besides, the proposed image representation is compact and consistent with the BoW model, which makes it applicable to image retrieval task as well.

Categories and Subject Descriptors
I.4.8 [Scene Analysis]: Object recognition.

General Terms
Algorithms, Experimentation, and Verification.

Keywords
Image Representation, Spatial Transformation, and Object Classification.

1. INTRODUCTION
Bag-of-Word model (BoW) has shown its superiority over many conventional global features in image classification and retrieval systems [5, 7, 11-13, 19, 20]. However, it has been shown that quantization error may degrade the performance of image classification and retrieval. To address this issue, many methods have been proposed recently. They can be categorized into three groups: 1) improving the codebook quality and reducing quantization error [5, 7], 2) constructing a robust visual representation, *e.g.* visual phrase [11], and 3) utilizing the geometric information to remove false matched feature pairs, *e.g.* bundled feature [12], spatial coding [13], and spatial matching [14].

In this paper, we mainly focus on image matching method for object recognition. As BoW discards the spatial order of local features, the descriptive power of its image representation is limited. The previously proposed spatial pyramid matching (SPM) [2] provides a good solution for this problem. Typically, SPM partitions the image into regions on multiple resolution levels. As shown in Fig. 1, each column displays the 3-level SPM partition. The final image representation is the concatenation of the BoW representations of all the regions. This "subdivide and reorder" strategy achieves more accurate matching by reserving the spatial information. Although SPM can greatly improve the performance of image classification on some benchmark datasets, including Caltech101 [3] and Scenes15 [15], it cannot handle object transformations. Three object transformations are illustrated in Fig. 1. The guitars in image (a) and (b) are rotated different angles. The ducks in image (c) and (d) are flipped horizontally. The bottles in image (e) and (f) appears at different locations. We can see that the corresponding SPM regions of similar images fail to match in the three cases. Our experiments demonstrate that SPM performs even worse than BoW with translation variance. Spatial Bag-of-Visual Word (SBoW) [8] is proposed to extend SPM. The image retrieval experiments show the effectiveness of SBoW. However, its image representation consists of thousands of long histograms, which are too complex for real-time application. So labeled data and boosting algorithm are used to select the most useful histograms for a given dataset.

Different from SBoW, this paper aims to find out a compact image representation robust to rotation, flipping and translation variances. We propose three kinds of spatial layouts: spatial pyramid ring, reordered SPM, and relative SPM, which are evaluated by extensive experiments on different transformation datasets. Experimental results show that compared with SPM and SBoW, our approaches can handle these spatial variances more efficiently and effectively. Furthermore, the simplicity of the proposed layouts makes it a promising potential for real time applications.

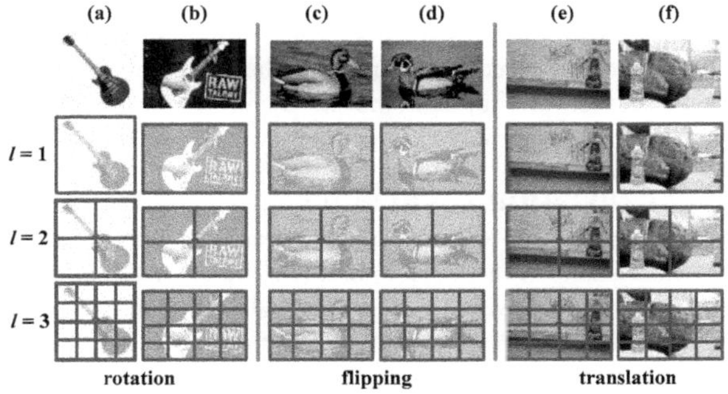

Figure 1. SPM division on rotated, flipped and translated objects.

*Area Chair: Nicu Sebe.

MM'11, November 28–December 1, 2011, Scottsdale, Arizona, USA.

We will introduce our approaches in Section 2. In Section 3, the experiments and results are given. Finally, discussion and future work are concluded in Section 4.

2. THE PROPOSED APPROACH

Our objective is to construct a spatial transformation invariant image representation. We will first introduce our rotation- and flip- invariant method, and then the translation-invariant method will be introduced next.

2.1 Rotation and Flipping Invariance

An object may rotate any angle on the image plane, like the exemplars of electronic guitar in Fig. 1(a) and (b), or flip horizontally or vertically, like the duck images in Fig. 1(c) and (d). We can see that different spatial transformations may cause the same visual features fall into different SPM bins, which degrades the discrimination power of SPM. Note that in this section, we assume images are well-aligned after rotation or flipping.

2.1.1 Spatial Pyramid Ring (SPR)

To handle object rotation like image (a) and (b) in Fig. 1, SBoW calibrates sectors according to a certain structure pattern. However, to deal with any rotation angle in the meanwhile avoiding being too strict, the appropriate sector number needs to be predetermined, which is a challenging task. Furthermore, SBoW is not flipping free. As we can see from the flipping example in Fig. 1, when object structure is flipped, partial shifting method cannot find matching pairs, as the order of sectors is reversed.

In order to solve this problem, we propose a pooling method based on spatial pyramid ring, which can better handle both rotation and flipping transformations. This is inspired from the observation that visual words falling into a spatial ring area remain stable on rotated or flipped objects.

We first partition the image into concentric rings on the polar coordinate. Then we compute BoW histogram within each ring. Motivated from the "subdivide and reorder" strategy of SPM, we also build a spatial pyramid to represent the image. Assume we have L-level pyramid, on the l-th level; the image is divided into 2^{l-1} concentric rings from the image center. The step size between rings is set to D/2^{l-1}, where D denotes the half diagonal length of the image. Fig. 2 displays our spatial pyramid ring partitions on the horizontally flipped duck images. This method will yield $\sum_{l=1}^{L} 2^{l-1}$ histograms for one image based on the rings. All the histograms can be concatenated to form a long histogram for representing the entire image.

Fig. 2 illustrates that this simple ring layout is flipping invariant as the corresponding rings of the two images are still matched. It also works for rotations. This mainly benefits from the fact that the same parts of an object will remain within a certain ring area in spite of rotation or flipping. And the pyramid representation can be matched on different resolution levels of the rings structure.

2.2 Translation Invariance

In this section, we will address the translation transformation problem. As shown in Fig. 1(e) and (f), objects may appear anywhere in an image, which cannot be handled by the layout based on SPM. Hence, we further propose two schemes: Reordered SPM and relative SPM.

2.2.1 Reordered SPM

The reason that SPM fails under translation transformation is that SPM requires matching each region pairs correspondingly between any two images. This problem can be fixed to some extent by resetting the matching order of SPM cells.

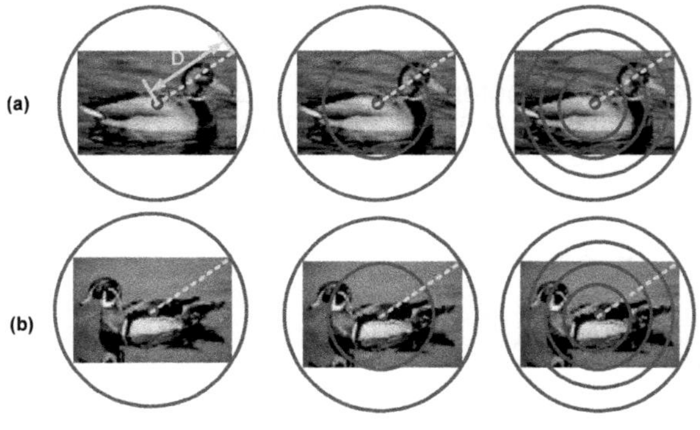

Figure 2. Illustration of SPR on image (a) and (b). From left to right are 1st, 2nd, and 3rd pyramid level.

First, we build SPM with L levels, which are $\sum_{l=1}^{L} 2^{2\times(l-1)}$ cells in total. Then on the l-th level, we sort the $2^{2\times(l-1)}$ bins for each visual word channel according to either ascending or descending order and form the re-ordered histogram for each visual word channel. For example, Fig. 3 contains three visual words (represented by yellow triangle, green star, and blue square) in the image (a) and (b), and it displays the SPM partition on the 2nd level. The right of the image shows the term frequency of each visual word in every region in descending order. Then the histograms of all visual word channels are connected to form the l-th level histogram representation, and finally representations of all the levels are concatenated together to form the entire image representation. With reordered SPM, objects appearing within different regionss will be matched because their histograms on each word channel have been aligned well.

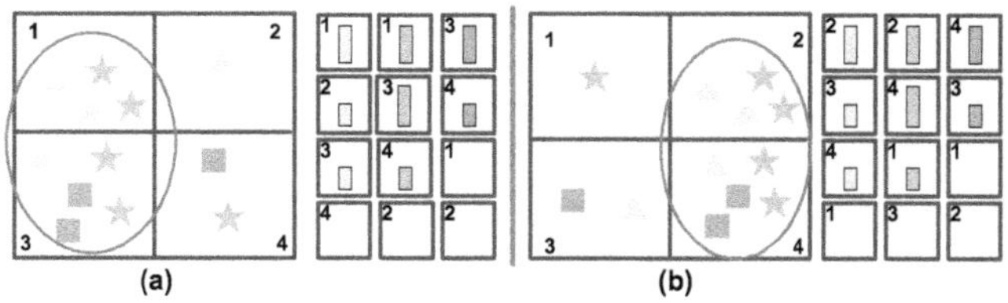

Figure 3. Illustration of Reordered SPM for translation invariance. Image (a) and (b) have the same object circled by a red ellipse. Images are divided into 2×2 grids. Their right parts show the reordered histograms from top to bottom for each visual word colored in yellow, green and blue separately.

2.2.2 Relative SPM

In the quantization and pooling step of image classification, some recent work has shown that Locality-constrained Linear Coding (LLC) [7] with max pooling [6] can yield good performance. LLC softly quantizes local features to their k nearest words. Max pooling then selects the nearest one feature for a certain visual word. Hence the selected feature can be regarded as salient points and we are able to derive the specific location where a visual word appears in an image.

We propose to utilize the geo information of salient points generated from the coarser level of SPM to generate the current level grids. For example, after max pooling on the l-th level, we can compute the center of the selected salient points within each region on this level, then each center is used as the origin point to divide its belonging region into another 2×2 grids for the (l+1)-th level. See the toy example in Fig. 4 for reference.

We call this method relative SPM as its grid division is relative to the distribution of salient points. This method benefits from the approximate tracking of the object position.

3. EXPERIMENTS

In this section, we will verify the proposed spatial pooling methods for object classification on three different spatial transformation datasets including flipping, rotation and translation variance datasets.

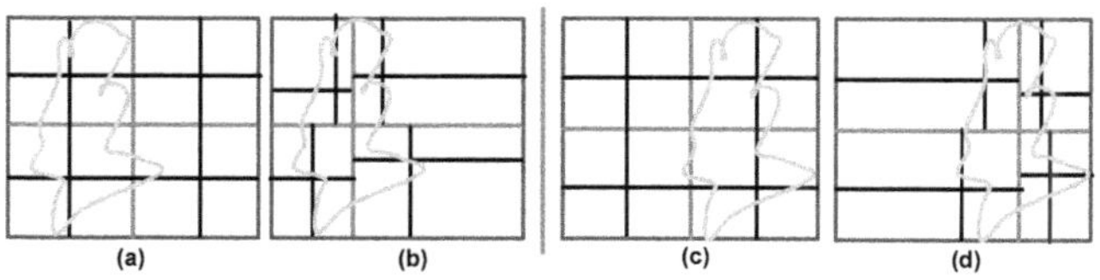

Figure 4. Illustration of Relative SPM. The same object is sketched in green curve. (a) and (c) are the original SPM partition. (b) and (d) show the partition of our approach. Red line is the 2nd level partition and black line is the 3rd level partition.

3.1 Experimental Settings

Image representation: The Bag-of-Word histogram is adopted. We use *K*-Means clustering to generate visual codebooks of size from 512 to 2048. After quantizing local feature descriptors into visual words, each image is represented by a visual word histogram. Here, Locality-constrained Linear Coding [7] is used for feature quantization, and max pooling [6] is used for histogram generation due to their sound performance on standard image classification benchmarks. To extract local feature descriptors, we adopt two popular methods: SIFT [1] detected from sparse regions and densely sampled SIFT. It has been shown that dense SIFT sampling gives better performance than sparse region of interest detectors, especially for object classification. This is because the so called "brute force" metric of dense sampling which covers all the information with overlap. However, the SIFT descriptors generated by dense sampling are not scale and orientation invariant. So we choose the appropriate one to avoid the feature level influence in different experiments. For dense sampling, we extract SIFT descriptors from 16×16 patches with step size 4. For sparse region of interest detection, we use the open source software VLFeat [9] with default parameters.

Model training: Three datasets are generated to test flipping, rotation, and translation variances respectively. We use LIBSVM [10] with linear kernel for object classification. For every object, we randomly select 30 images for training. The left data are used for testing. We run the experiments five times and calculate the average classification accuracy of all categories for each run.

Baseline system: We use BoW to denote the baseline image level classification. SPM denotes adding SPM on the baseline method, where max pooling is performed within each cell. Three-level SPM is adopted with 1+4+16=21 cells.

3.2 Flipping Invariance Experiment

Flipping Dataset: To test flipping invariant methods, we assume no other spatial variance exists, *e.g.* objects are center-aligned, and occupy the most part of an image with similar scale. We use Caltech101 [3] with 9144 images of 101 categories in this experiment and we randomly flip images horizontally or vertically. Flipping samples are shown in Fig. 5.

We use dense SIFT descriptors to cover the whole image. Although dense SIFT is not flipping invariant, It has been proposed in [18] to combine the metrics of both dense sampling and sparse detectors to make the extracted feature more stable and repeatable. Therefore, in our experiments, we make an assumption that there is a good way to address the feature level variance to avoid its influence on feature matching. With this assumption, we can focus on analyzing the spatial transformation. Hence, the descriptors from the non-flipped images are used for the flipped images instead, but the location information of descriptors are flipped.

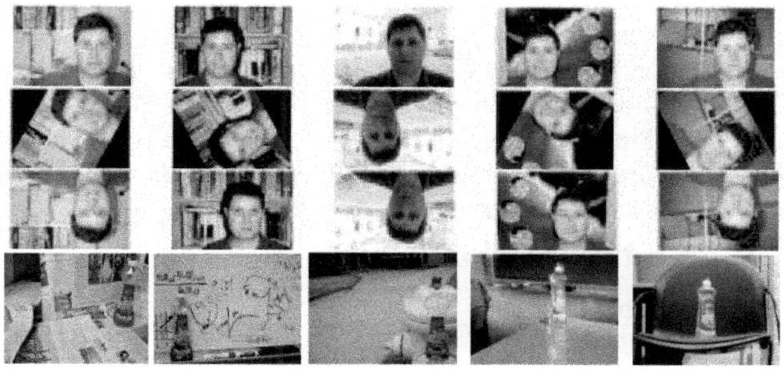

Figure 5. Image samples. The first three rows are from Caltech101: 1st row shows the original images; 2nd row shows images after random rotation; 3rd row shows images after randomly horizontal or vertical flipping. The last row shows sample images from the "AjaxOrange" category of SIVAL.

In the experiment, we combine BoW model with three different spatial coding algorithms: SPM [2], calibrated circular projection (CCP) in SBoW [8], and spatial pyramid ring (SPR) pooling. The codebook size is 2048 as it is widely used in previous work [6]. For CCP, the images are divided into 1, 4, and 16 sectors. In our spatial pyramid ring pooling, 1, 2, 4, and 8 rings are constructed from the 1st to 4th level, which yields 1+2+4+8=15 rings. We test the three algorithms on the flipping dataset and obtain the average classification accuracy shown in Table 1.

Table 1. Caltech101 classification accuracy comparison on flipping and rotation data

Method	Before transformation	After flipping	After rotation
BoW	52.17%	-	26.81%
SPM[2]	74.34%	57.94%	29.84%
CCP[8]		57.04%	29.23%
SPR		**66.61%**	**34.95%**
SPR + SPM		**70.19%**	**35.20%**

The accuracy of SPM drops to 57.94% from 74.34% after flipping. The performance of CCP is close to SPM. Our proposed SPR gives the best improvement of 14% over the image level classification, *i.e.*, BoW, and about 8.6% improvement over SPM and CCP. These results clearly demonstrate that spatial pyramid ring pooling is very effective against flipping variances.

3.3 Rotation Invariance Experiment

Rotation Dataset: We randomly rotate the images in Caltech101 with an angle between 0 and 360 counterclockwise. See Fig. 5 for sample images.

In this section, we want to show that spatial pyramid ring pooling also works well with rotation variance. As we mentioned above, dense SIFT is not rotation invariant. So in this experiment, we use the sparse region of interest detector to extract SIFT features.

Experimental results of the three spatial pooling methods are shown in the last column of Table 1. Both SPM and CCP improve the performance. However, spatial pyramid ring pooling method achieves the best performance. We further test combining SPM with SPR pooling by connecting their histograms together to form the final image representation. It outperforms all other methods on both flipping and rotation.

3.4 Translation Invariance Experiment

Translation Dataset: To test translation invariant methods, we use SIVAL benchmark [17]. This dataset contains 1, 500 images in 25 categories. An image contains a primary object located randomly and independently on the image with diverse backgrounds. Objects do not occupy the entire image, but have similar scale at most time. Since the biggest variance of this dataset is translation, we use it to evaluate the methods for handling translation variance only. Fig. 5 shows some sample images from this dataset.

Table 2. SIVAL classification accuracy

Codebook Size	512	1024	2048
BoW	51.03%	64.86%	76.22%
SPM[2]	26.39%	32.63%	39.57%
Relative SPM	34.31%	40.27%	46.15%
Reordered SPM	59.50%	69.94%	77.83%
Reordered Relative SPM	61.29%	71.53%	78.94%

We test BoW, SPM, Relative SPM, Reordered SPM, and Reordered Relative SPM on this dataset. Their classification accuracy with different codebook sizes are listed in Table 2. We can see SPM fails on this dataset. It is even worse than image level classification. The Relative SPM method is designed for adjusting the division of SPM to make it focus on the object. This method does improve the SPM performance by about 7%. The most effective method is Reordered SPM, which gains improvement over the image level classification. Combining the two methods together achieves the best performance on this dataset. This improvement is relatively less than what can be gained by using SPM on well-aligned image datasets as can be seen from Table 1. This means without object localization, it is hard to do fine level matching globally due to the large translation variance of objects and irrelatively diverse background noise. We don't compare our methods with SBoW on translation problem, as it requires a complex learning process to determine which line projections should be used.

4. CONCLUSIONS

In this paper, we propose several effective spatial pooling methods to handle various spatial transformations. The generated spatial transformation invariant image representation can improve the entire image matching very well. Experimental results show that Spatial Pyramid Ring (SPR) pooling works best for rotation and flipping variances. A refined version of SPM (Relative Reordered SPM) can improve the matching accuracy with large translation variance.

Furthermore, the proposed approaches are not limited to classification task. They also can be applied on object detection and image retrieval applications as well. That is because we invariantly embed the spatial layout information into classical BoW image representation, which ensures that all current techniques following the image representation step can be seamlessly applied.

In the future, we will continue to address other spatial transformations of objects, *e.g.* scale and view angle change. We also would like to fuse these methods together to design a unified representation, which can be tolerant with all kinds of layout variances.

5. ACKNOWLEDGEMENT

This work is supported in part to Dr. Qi Tian by NSF IIS 1052851, Faculty Research Awards by Google, FXPAL and NEC Laboratories of America, in part to Dr. Yan Song by Anhui Provincial Natural Science Foundation under grant 090412056, and in part to Dr. Yijuan Lu by Research Enhancement Program (REP) and start-up funding from the Texas State University respectively.

6. REFERENCES

[1] D. Lowe, "Distinctive image features from scale-invariant keypoints," *IJCV*, 2004.

[2] S. Lazebnik, C. Schmid, and J. Ponce, "Beyond bags of features: Spatial pyramid matching for recognizing natural scene categories," *In proc. CVPR*, 2006.

[3] L. Fei-Fei, R. Fergus, and P. Perona, "Learning generative visual models from few training examples: an incremental Bayesian approach tested on 101 object categories," *CVPR Workshop on Generative-Model Based Vision*, 2004.

[4] L. Fei-Fei and P. Perona, "A Bayesian hierarchical model for learning natural scene categories," *In proc. CVPR*, 2005.

[5] D. Nister and H. Stewenius, "Scalable recognition with a vocabulary tree," *In proc. CVPR*, 2006.

[6] Y. Boureau, F. Bach, Y. LeCun, J. Ponce, "Learning mid-level features for recognition," *In proc. CVPR*, 2010.

[7] J. Wang, J. Yang, K. Yu, F. Lv, T. Huang, and Y. Gong, "Locality-constrained linear coding for image classification," *In proc. CVPR*, 2010.

[8] Y. Cao, C. Wang, Z. Li, L. Zhang, "Spatial-bag-of-features," *In proc. CVPR*, 2010.

[9] A. Vedaldi and B. Fulkerson, "VLFeat: An Open and Portable Library of Computer Vision Algorithms," 2008, http://www.vlfeat.org/

[10] C.-C. Chang and C.-J. Lin. LIBSVM: a library for support vector machines, 2001. Software available at http://www.csie.ntu.edu.tw/-cjlin/libsvm.

[11] S. Zhang, Q. Tian, G. Hua, Q. Huang, and S. Li, "Descriptive Visual Words and Visual Phrases for Image Applications," *In ACM MM*, 2009.

[12] Z. Wu, Q. Ke, M. Isard, and J. Sun, "Bundling features for large scale partial-duplicate web image search," *In proc. CVPR*, 2009.

[13] W. Zhou, Y. Lu, H. Li, Y. Song, Q. Tian, "Spatial coding for large scale partial-duplicate web image search," *In ACM MM*, 2009.

[14] J. Philbin, O. Chum, M. Isard, J. Sivic and A. Zisserman, "Object retrieval with large vocabularies and fast spatial matching," *In proc. CVPR*, 2007.

[15] A. Oliva and A. Torralba, "Modeling the shape of the scene: a holistic representation of the spatial envelope," *IJCV*, 2001.

[16] M. Everingham, L.V. Gool, C.K.I. Williams, J. Winn, A. Zisserman, "The PASCAL Visual Object Classes (VOC) Challenge," *IJCV*, 2009

[17] SIVAL: http://accio.cse.wustl.edu/sg-accio/SIVAL.html

[18] T. Tuytelaars, "Dense interest points," *In proc. CVPR*, 2010.

[19] M. Wang, X. Hua, R. Hong, J. Tang, G. Qi, Y. Song, "Unified Video Annotation Via Multi-Graph Learning," *IEEE CSVT*, 2009.

[20] M. Wang, X. Hua, T. Mei, R. Hong, G. Qi, Y.Song and L. Dai, "Semi-Supervised Kernel Density Estimation for Video Annotation," *CVIU*, 2009.

Multi-Feature pLSA for Combining Visual Features in Image Annotation *

Rui Zhang, Ling Guan
Ryerson Multimedia Research Laboratory
Toronto, Canada
rzhang,lguan@ee.ryerson.ca

Lei Zhang, Xin-Jing Wang
Microsoft Research Asia
Beijing, China
leizhang,xjwang@microsoft.com

ABSTRACT

We study in this paper the problem of combining low-level visual features for image region annotation. The problem is tackled with a novel method that combines texture and color features via a mixture model of their joint distribution. The structure of the presented model can be considered as an extension of the probabilistic latent semantic analysis (pLSA) in that it handles data from two different visual feature domains by attaching one more leaf node to the graphical structure of the original pLSA. Therefore, the proposed approach is referred to as multi-feature pLSA (MF-pLSA). The supervised paradigm is adopted to classify a new image region into one of a few pre-defined object categories using the MF-pLSA. To evaluate the performance, the VOC2009 and LabelMe databases were employed in our experiments, along with various experimental settings in terms of the number of visual words and mixture components. Evaluated based on the average recall and precision, the MF-pLSA is demonstrated superior to seven other approaches, including other schemes for visual feature combination.

Categories and Subject Descriptors

I.5.1 [**Computing Methodologies**]: Pattern Recognition—*Models;Statistical*

General Terms

Algorithms, Experimentation, Performance

Keywords

Image Annotation, Descriptor Combination

1. INTRODUCTION

Within the past few years, we have appreciated the accessibility of the plentiful multimedia information thanks to those powerful search engines, such as Google^{TM}, Bing^{TM}, and Baidu^{TM}, to name only a few. A further inspection on the retrieval paradigm employed by these search engines shows that the keyword-based search of multimedia data still serves as the mainstream enabling technology due to the straightforwardness of natural language in terms of the initial query formulation during a typical search process. To improve users' experience with the multimedia search technology, effective indexing is critical considering the ever-increasing amount of multimedia data on the Internet.

In correspondence to the keyword-based search, indexing is desired to be achieved by labeling available images with textual description, a.k.a. image annotation. Because of the inefficiency of manual annotation, there has been much effort devoted to automatic image annotation [11, 2]. Converting the image representation from visual to textual domain also facilitates exposing the semantic structure of a database to users for browsing [1]. Throughout years of intensive study on visual recognition, it has been well-recognized that utilizing the information from multiple modalities and multiple types of features in each modality results in performance improvement [5].

Therefore, it is nontrivial to effectively utilize multiple low-level visual features. To address this problem in image region annotation, we propose a generative model which combines texture and color features via a mixture model of their joint distribution. The selection of these two types of features is based on the consideration that they have proven discriminative and complementary for representing images capturing the semantics in the general scope of real life. The SIFT [7] and local transformed color histogram (LTCH) [10] calculated around key points detected using the Harris-Laplace key point detector [8] are chosen as the descriptors for the texture and color features, respectively. These descriptors are selected in that they encode texture and color information and are invariant to rotation and light color change and shift, respectively. In terms of the specific structure of the model, it can be considered as an extension to pLSA, where the two types of visual descriptors extracted from the same key point location are jointly modeled yet with their conditional distributions constrained via a single latent variable. Therefore, the proposed model is referred to as multi-feature pLSA (MF-pLSA). Although we only targeted the image region annotation, the model is also applicable to other visual recognition tasks such as scene classification. In the experiment, we employed the VOC2009 and LabelMe databases and compared the MF-pLSA with seven other approaches, including the vector concatenation of different low-level descriptors as well as their bag-of-visual-

*Area chair: Tian Qi-add appropriate name

MM'11, November 28–December 1, 2011, Scottsdale, Arizona, USA.

word (BOVW) representations. The results based on the average recall and precision demonstrate the superior overall performance of the MF-pLSA.

2. RELATED WORKS

Essentially, existing approaches to combining information from multiple sources for image annotation can be grouped into two categories. Featuring lower complexity, vector concatenation has been applied to combing the low-level descriptor vectors from multiple visual feature domains, such as color, texture and position. Examples falling into this category can be found in the visual components of the variants of latent Dirichlet allocation (LDA) proposed by Blei [2] and the multi-modal hierarchical models in Barnard [1]. Moreover, in both [10] and [3], the SIFT descriptor is extracted within different color channels separately and the resulting descriptors at the same key point are stored in a longer vector. Despite the higher discriminative power of cascading different visual descriptors than that of each individual descriptor, the computational complexity is shifted to the subsequent steps, e.g. constructing a visual codebook if BOVW is used or estimating the class-specific probability density function. The other category of methods also model the joint distribution of multiple features; however, a hidden variable is introduced to make the less correlated features conditionally independent, such as text and visual features. Following this principle, prominent document analysis approaches, such as pLSA and LDA, have been successfully adapted to handle the joint modeling of visual and textual information, as in [2, 1]. In addition, Lienhart [6] proposed a multi-layer multi-modal pLSA, where the topics of the textual pLSA and visual pLSA are selected conditionally on the topic chosen for the top level pLSA. The layered structure is considered to be consistent with the generative process of local visual patterns, i.e. image contains objects which in turn are composed of parts.

Different from the afore-mentioned approaches, we explore the potential of the second feature combination strategy in the low-level visual domain. While taking advantage of the reduced complexity of this kind of methods associated with the modeling step, the MF-pLSA outperforms the other way of feature integration, i.e. vector concatenation of both low-level descriptors and their BOVW representations. Meanwhile, it should be noted that there is another subtle difference between feature fusion within visual domain and across visual and textual domains. For the latter, a strict correspondence between a keyword and a visual word might not be available. On the other hand, two different visual descriptors can be calculated at one key point location, resulting in the fact that such two descriptors can be considered as sampled from two distributions conditional on the same state of the hidden variable.

3. MF-PLSA FOR IMAGE ANNOTATION

Prior to the discussion on the training and testing of the MF-pLSA, it should be noted that this model is built upon the BOVW image representation. Based on the discrete nature of the domain of the MF-pLSA and the graphical representation of the model in Fig. 1, we define the following notation for explaining the algorithms. The variable z is a hidden variable, which, if observed, leads to the conditional independence of the SIFT visual word v and the LTCH visual word w, respectively. The root node d denotes an image region in the present context. Thus, the joint distribution of all the observed regions and visual words, denoted $\boldsymbol{d}$, $\boldsymbol{v}$ and $\boldsymbol{w}$, can be formulated as

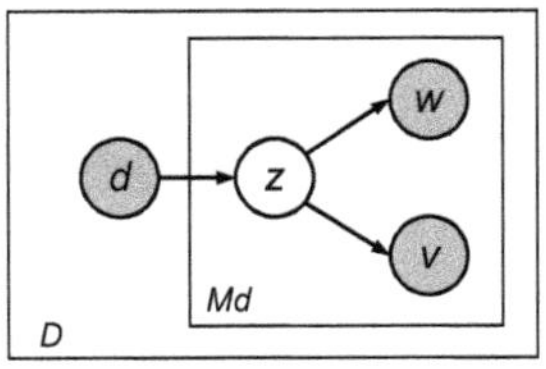

Figure 1: The structure of the MF-pLSA depicted using a directed graphical model. D denotes the number of documents and M_d denotes the number of visual word pairs in document d. A shaded node indicates the corresponding variable has its value observed during the data acquisition process.

$$P(\boldsymbol{w},\boldsymbol{v},\boldsymbol{d}) = \prod_{d} P(d) \prod_{(w,v)} P(w,v|d)^{\mathcal{N}(w,v,d)}, \quad (1)$$

where $\mathcal{N}(w,v,d)$ is the frequency of occurrence of the 3-tuple (w,v,d) in the observed data.

Given that there are C color visual words, S SIFT visual words, Z mixture components and D image regions, in view of clarity, we denote the set of parameters of the model as Θ and define

$$\begin{aligned}\Theta \triangleq\ & \{P(w|z)|(w,z)\in\{1,2,\dots,C\}\times\{1,2,\dots,Z\}\} \quad (2)\\ \cup\ & \{P(v|z)|(v,z)\in\{1,2,\dots,S\}\times\{1,2,\dots,Z\}\}\\ \cup\ & \{P(z|d)|(z,d)\in\{1,2,\dots,Z\}\times\{1,2,\dots,D\}\}.\end{aligned}$$

To use the maximum likelihood (ML) principle and assuming $P(d)$ is uniform, the log likelihood of $(\boldsymbol{w},\boldsymbol{v},\boldsymbol{d})$ with respect to Θ can be written as

$$\begin{aligned}L(\Theta) &= \sum_{d=1}^{D}\sum_{w=1}^{W}\sum_{v=1}^{V}\mathcal{N}(w,v,d)\log P(w,v|d) \quad (3)\\ &= \sum_{d=1}^{D}\sum_{w=1}^{W}\sum_{v=1}^{V}\mathcal{N}(w,v,d)\log\sum_{z=1}^{Z}P(w|z)P(v|z)P(z|d).\end{aligned}$$

In terms of the estimation of Θ, as the hidden variable z is not observed, the expectation-maximization (EM) procedure is an effective tool. Interleaving the E-step and M-step, the resulting estimates of the parameters can be written as

$$\begin{aligned}P(w|z) &= \frac{\sum_{d=1}^{D}\sum_{v=1}^{V}\mathcal{N}(w,v,d)P(z|w,v,d,\Theta^{i-1}_{w,v|d})}{\sum_{d=1}^{D}\sum_{w=1}^{W}\sum_{v=1}^{V}\mathcal{N}(w,v,d)P(z|w,v,d,\Theta^{i-1}_{w,v|d})} \quad (4)\\ P(v|z) &= \frac{\sum_{d=1}^{D}\sum_{w=1}^{W}\mathcal{N}(w,v,d)P(z|w,v,d,\Theta^{i-1}_{w,v|d})}{\sum_{d=1}^{D}\sum_{w=1}^{W}\sum_{v=1}^{V}\mathcal{N}(w,v,d)P(z|w,v,d,\Theta^{i-1}_{w,v|d})},\\ P(z|d) &= \frac{\sum_{w=1}^{W}\sum_{v=1}^{V}\mathcal{N}(w,v,d)P(z|w,v,d,\Theta^{i-1}_{w,v|d})}{\mathcal{N}(d)},\end{aligned}$$

where $\mathcal{N}(d) = \sum_{w=1}^{W}\sum_{v=1}^{V}\mathcal{N}(w,v,d)$ and i is the iteration index.

3.1 Supervised Classification with the Model

To annotate regions of images, we exploit the MF-pLSA with the supervised classification paradigm. First, we define the set of class labels as $\Omega = \{\omega|1,2,\dots,|\Omega|\}$, where $|\Omega|$ is the number of classes. Then, representing the parameter set and the joint distribution of SIFT and LTCH visual words of class ω by Θ_ω and $P_\omega(w, v)$ respectively, the ML principle is employed to classify a new image region d' through

$$\hat{\omega} = \arg\max_{\omega \in \Omega} f(d'; \Theta_\omega), \tag{5}$$

where

$$\begin{aligned} f(d'; \Theta_\omega) &= \sum_{w=1}^{W} \sum_{v=1}^{V} \mathcal{N}(w, v, d') \log P_\omega(w, v) \qquad (6) \\ &= \sum_{w=1}^{W} \sum_{v=1}^{V} \mathcal{N}(w, v, d') \log \sum_{d=1}^{D_\omega} P_\omega(w, v|d) P_\omega(d) \\ &= \sum_{w=1}^{W} \sum_{v=1}^{V} \mathcal{N}(w, v, d') \\ &\quad \cdot \log \frac{1}{D_\omega} \sum_{d=1}^{D_\omega} \sum_{z=1}^{Z} P_\omega(w|z) P_\omega(v|z) P_\omega(z|d), \end{aligned}$$

$P_\omega(w|z)$, $P_\omega(v|z)$ and $P_\omega(z|d)$ are the specific elements in Θ_ω, D_ω is the number of regions in class ω and $\hat{\omega}$ is the predicted label of d'.

4. EXPERIMENTS

4.1 Databases

The first database is VOC2009 [4]. It includes 7818 images in total, which are annotated using 20 concepts. All of them were used for the experiments. The resulting training and testing sets include 9298 and 9390 image regions, respectively. The second database is LabelMe [9], which has 51285 images and 306005 regions in total, which are annotated using 210 concepts. Only 16 classes were selected for the experiments because they have significantly more annotated object regions than those unselected. The images of each of the 16 classes were randomly split into two disjoint sets to prepare the training and testing data. As a result, the training set and the testing set include 36547 and 58176 regions, respectively. For both databases, each semantic class is represented using a keyword.

4.2 Experimental Setup

4.2.1 Approaches Compared with the MF-pLSA

The MF-pLSA was compared with seven other approaches. The first four are based on nearest-neighbor using histogram of the SIFT visual word (S-Hist), histogram of the LTCH visual word (C-Hist), histogram of the visual word of concatenated SIFT and LTCH descriptors (SC-Hist), and the concatenated S-Hist and C-Hist (Concat-Hist). The other three are pLSA with the SIFT visual word (S-pLSA), pLSA with the LTCH visual word (C-pLSA) and pLSA with the visual word of concatenated SIFT and LTCH descriptors (SC-pLSA). Among them, the SC-Hist, Concat-Hist and SC-pLSA are methods capable of integrating the SIFT and LTCH descriptors. For the approaches based on mixture modeling, such as pLSA and MF-pLSA, we set the number of hidden topics Z to 5, 20 and 50 in order to study the performance variation as the model order changes. To test how the level of fineness of the descriptor quantization affects the overall performance, we conducted experiments with 100, 200 and 500 visual words.

4.2.2 Performance Evaluation Criteria

Regarding the performance evaluation criterion, we adopted average recall and precision, defined by $\mathcal{R}_\omega^{avg} = \frac{1}{|\Omega|} \sum_\omega \mathcal{R}_\omega$ and $\mathcal{P}_\omega^{avg} = \frac{1}{|\Omega|} \sum_\omega \mathcal{P}_\omega$, where $\mathcal{R}_\omega = \frac{R_\omega^{corr}}{R_\omega}$ and $\mathcal{P}_\omega = \frac{R_\omega^{corr}}{R_\omega^{targ}}$, and R_ω^{corr}, R_ω, and R_ω^{targ} are the number of correctly classified regions of the ω-th class, the number of regions of the ω-th class, and the number of regions categorized into the ω-th class.

4.3 Results

The comparison in terms of the average recall and precision are shown in Fig. 2. For the VOC2009 database, according to Fig. 2(a) through Fig. 2(f), about 3% improvement in terms of $\mathcal{R}_\omega^{avg}$ is obtained compared with the best of the other approaches. In terms of $\mathcal{P}_\omega^{avg}$, the improve-ment falls between 1.5% and 2.0%, increasing as the number of visual words is raised. As shown in Fig. 2(g) through Fig. 2(l), improvement in terms of $\mathcal{R}_\omega^{avg}$ and $\mathcal{P}_\omega^{avg}$ for the LabelMe database range from 4.4% to 6.5% and 3.5% to 5.2%, respectively. It can be observed that the performance based on the LabelMe database is better than that based on the VOC2009 database under different experimental settings, which is primarily due to the fact that the object boundary of the LabelMe database is much more accurate than that of the VOC2009. To visually inspect the annotation results, some examples of the classification using SC-pLSA and MF-pLSA are provided in Fig. 3.

5. CONCLUSION AND FUTURE WORK

In this paper, we have presented a novel model, MF-pLSA, for combining descriptors in the low-level visual domain, which is applied to the problem of annotating regions of images. Having the image data represented as SIFT and LTCH descriptors extracted from key points, the MF-pLSA jointly learns the distributions of these descriptors with a mixture model for each of the semantic classes. The mixture models are used along with the supervised classification paradigm to classify previously unseen image regions into one of several pre-defined categories. Through extensive experimental evaluation using the VOC2009 database and the LabelMe database as well as different experimental settings regarding the numbers of visual words and mixture components, the superiority of the MF-pLSA to seven other approaches has been demonstrated. We believe introducing contextual information, which encodes the co-occurrence of different object categories, or a hierarchical organization of them into the presented framework should be worth exploring and potentially able to further improve the performance.

6. REFERENCES

[1] K. Barnard et al. Matching words and pictures. *JMLR*, 3:1107–1135, 2003.

[2] D. M. Blei and M. I. Jordan. Modeling annotated data. In *Proc. ACM SIGIR*, pages 127–134, 2003.

[3] A. Bosch, A. Zisserman, and X. Muoz. Scene classification using a hybrid generative/discriminative approach. *IEEE TPAMI*, 30(4):712–727, Apr. 2008.

[4] M. Everingham and et al. The PASCAL Visual Object Classes Challenge 2009 (VOC2009) Results.

[5] L. Guan and et al. Multimodal information fusion for

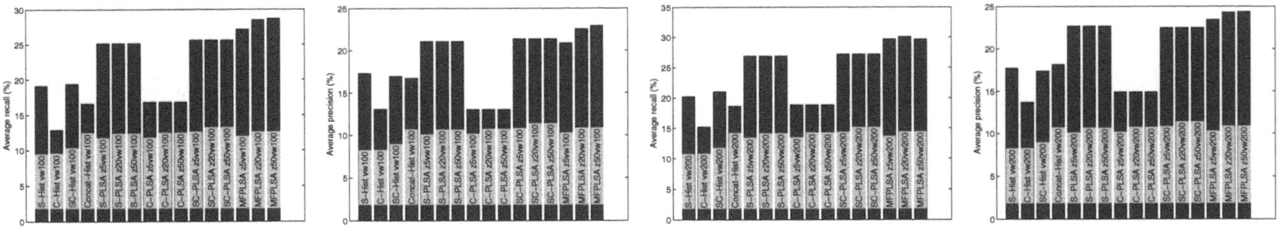

(a) 100 visual words (b) 100 visual words (c) 200 visual words (d) 200 visual words

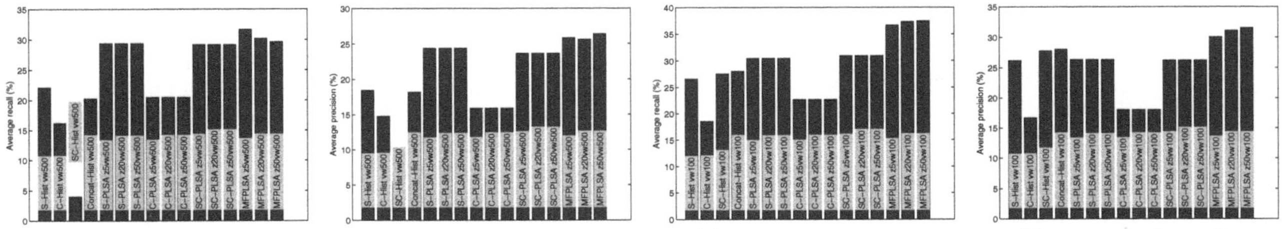

(e) 500 visual words (f) 500 visual words (g) 100 visual words (h) 100 visual words

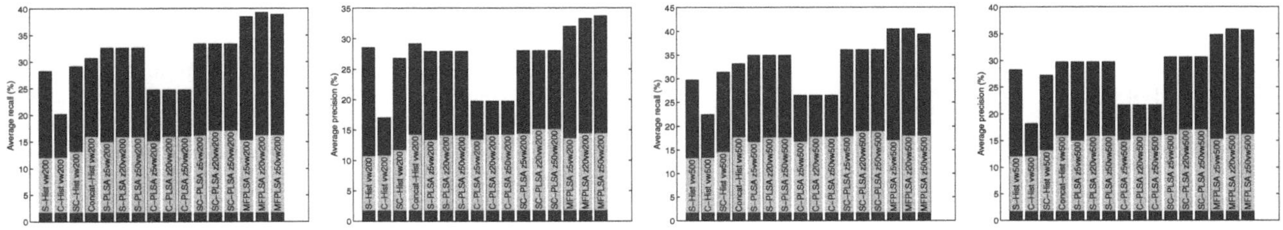

(i) 200 visual words (j) 200 visual words (k) 500 visual words (l) 500 visual words

Figure 2: The comparison in terms of average recall and precision. (a)-(f): VOC2009. (g)-(l): LabelMe.

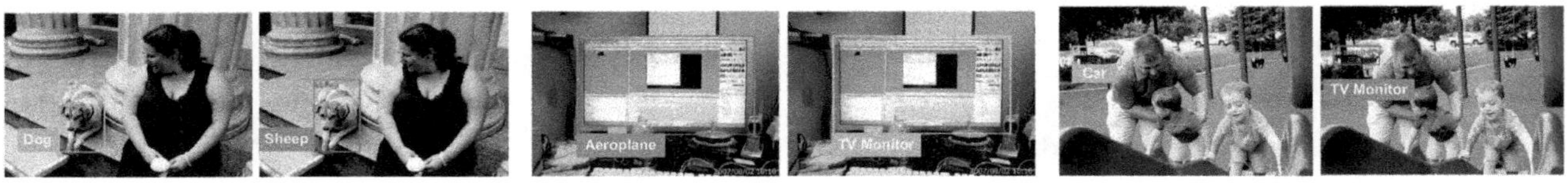

(a) Dog (b) TV Monitor (c) Car

(d) Table (e) Tree (f) Chair

Figure 3: Examples of annotation results. The figure on the left-hand side of each class is the result of MF-pLSA and the one on the right-hand side is the result of SC-pLSA. In addition, the boundary of a successfully classified object is shown in green. (a)-(c):VOC2009. (d)-(f):LabelMe.

selected multimedia applications. *IJMIS*, 1(1):5–32, 2010.

[6] R. Lienhart, S. Romberg, and E. Hörster. Multilayer pLSA for multimodal image retrieval. In *Proc. ACM CIVR*, pages 9:1–9:8, 2009.

[7] D. G. Lowe. Distinctive image features from scale-invariant keypoints. *IJCV*, 60:91–110, Nov. 2004.

[8] K. Mikolajczyk and C. Schmid. Scale affine invariant interest point detectors. *IJCV*, 60:63–86, Oct. 2004.

[9] B. C. Russell and et al. Labelme: a database and web-based tool for image annotation. *IJCV*, 77:157–173, May. 2008.

[10] K. E. A. van de Sande et al. Evaluating color descriptors for object and scene recognition. *IEEE TPAMI*, 32(9), Sept. 2010.

[11] X.-J. Wang and et al. Annotating images by mining image search results. *IEEE TPAMI*, 30(11):1919–1932, 2008.

Tag-Based Social Image Search with Visual-Text Joint Hypergraph Learning

Yue Gao [†], Meng Wang [♯], Huanbo Luan [‡], Jialie Shen [◇], Shuicheng Yan [‡], Dacheng Tao [§]
[†] TNLIST, Dept. of Automation, Tsinghua University, Beijing, China
[♯] Hefei University of Technology, Hefei, China
[‡] National University of Singapore, Singapore
[◇] School of Information Systems, Singapore Management University, Singapore
[§] Centre for Quantum Computation and Intelligent Systems, University of Technology, Sydney, Australia
kevin.gaoy@gmail.com, {mengwang,luanhb}@comp.nus.edu.sg
jlshen@smu.edu.sg, eleyans@nus.edu.sg, dacheng.tao@gmail.com

ABSTRACT

Tag-based social image search has attracted great interest and how to order the search results based on relevance level is a research problem. Visual content of images and tags have both been investigated. However, existing methods usually employ tags and visual content separately or sequentially to learn the image relevance. This paper proposes a tag-based image search with visual-text joint hypergraph learning. We simultaneously investigate the bag-of-words and bag-of-visual-words representations of images and accomplish the relevance estimation with a hypergraph learning approach. Each textual or visual word generates a hyperedge in the constructed hypergraph. We conduct experiments with a real-world data set and experimental results demonstrate the effectiveness of our approach.

Categories and Subject Descriptors

H.3.3 [**Information Search and Retrieval**]: Content Analysis and Index; H.4 [**Information Systems Applications**]: Miscellaneous

Keywords

Tag-based image search, hypergraph learning, visual-text

1. INTRODUCTION

In recent years, the amount of social media grows in an explosive way due to the fast development of multimedia and network technology, such as Flickr and Youtube. The development of efficient search for these media corpus becomes highly desired. On these websites, users are allowed to not only upload multimedia data but also annotate their content with tags. Therefore, many social media entities are associated with user-provided tags. By indexing media data with these tags, tag-based search becomes a solution for users in interesting data on social media websites.

However, the performance of existing tag-based search methods is usually not satisfactory. This can mainly be attributed to the following two facts. First, user-provided tags are usually noisy. Second and more important, there lacks a good ranking strategy to order the multimedia entities that contain a query tag. For example, currently Flickr provides two ranking options for tag-based image search, one is time-based ranking and the other is interestingness-based ranking. However, they both rank images according to measures that are not related to relevance and thus in many cases the search results are not good enough in terms of relevance.

Several research efforts have been dedicated to developing relevance-based ranking for social media search. Given a query tag, the task is to estimate the relevance levels of the images that contain the tag. The visual content of images and tags have both been explored. However, existing methods usually use the two information sources separately or sequentially. For example, the method in [10, 19] mainly works as follows. First, an initial relevance score of each image is learned according to the similarity between the query tag and the image's tag set. A graph-based learning is then performed to refine the relevance scores based on the pairwise visual similarities of images. Therefore, tag and visual information is actually used in the first and second steps, respectively. This is due to the fact that visual features and tags are different characteristics and are not easy to be integrated.

In this work, we propose a visual-text joint hypergraph learning approach to simultaneously explore the two information sources. Each image can be represented by bag-of-words and bag-of-visual-words, which are generated from the image's tags and visual content, respectively. A hypergraph is constructed to model the relationship of all images, in which each vertex denotes an image and a hyperedge is a visual or textual word (i.e., tag), and a hyperedge connects to multiple vertices. We define the weight of each edge based on the visual similarities of images belonging to the edge. The relevance scores of images are learned based on the hypergraph and then we can order the images with their relevance scores in descending order. Experiments on a Flickr data set demonstrates the superiority of our approach over the state-of-the-art methods.

*Area chair: Lexing Xie

MM'11, November 28–December 1, 2011, Scottsdale, Arizona, USA.

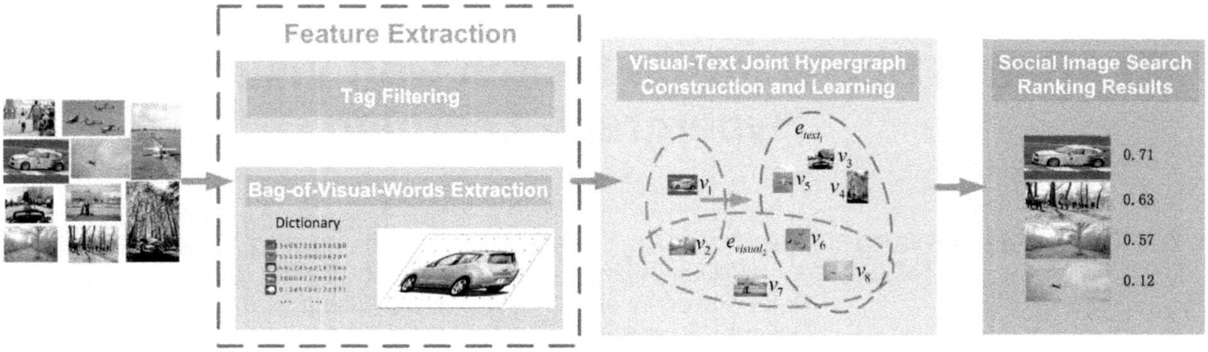

Figure 1: The flowchart of the proposed method.

The rest of the paper is organized as follows. Section 2 briefly reviews related work. In Section 3, we introduce the tag-based image search with visual-text joint hypergraph learning approach. Experiments on a Flickr data set are provided in Section 4. Finally, we conclude the paper in Section 5.

2. RELATED WORK

Multimedia analysis and retrieval [5,6,14,15,17,18,20,21] has attracted a lot of attention recently, and extensive research efforts have been dedicated to topics related to web image search in the past years [3, 4, 16]. Different from these web images, social images can be indexed with user-contributed tags and tag-based image search is an effective approach for social image search. However, user-provided tags are usually noisy. Therefore, several research has been conducted towards improving search performance by tag refine or tag relevance learning [2, 9, 11–13, 19, 24]. Liu et al. [?] proposed a relevance-based ranking method for social image search. It first learns relevance scores based on images' tags and then refines the scores by exploring images' visual content. In [19], a diverse relevance ranking scheme was proposed to re-rank images by exploring the content of images and their associated tags. The first component of their approach estimates the relevance scores of images and it is actually the same with [10]. However, these methods usually use visual and tag information separately or sequentially, whereas our approach integrates them in a hypergraph learning scheme such that they can be simultaneously investigated. Experiments will demonstrate the superiority of our approach.

Hypergraph has been widely investigated in information retrieval and pattern recognition tasks [1, 3, 7, 23] for its capability of capturing high-order relationship of samples. A probabilistic hypergraph matching method was proposed in [22] to match two feature sets. In the transductive learning framework for image retrieval [8], each image was represented by a vertex in a probabilistic hypergraph, and the image retrieval was formulated as a hypergraph ranking task.

Considering the capability of hypergraph in high-order relationship mining and unified modeling (the hyperedge can be generated based on different information sources), our work employs the hypergraph learning method for a tag-based image search with joint visual-text information.

3. VISUAL-TEXT JOINT HYPERGRAPH LEARNING

We introduce the proposed tag-based image search with visual-text joint hypergraph learning in this section. Figure 1 demonstrates the schematic illustration.

3.1 Feature extraction

By feature extraction, we aim to generate the bag-of-words and the bag-of-visual-words representations for each social image.

For bag-of-words representation, we simply generate it by selecting several informative tags. From our dataset, which will be introduced in the next section, we have 12,921 unique tags. We first perform a filtering with the help of Wikipedia, and those tags that do not have coordinate in Wikipedia are removed (they are usually misspelling or meaningless words). Then we select 2,000 tags that are with the highest TF-IDF values. With the 2,000 tags, we generate the bag-of-words representation for each image.

For bag-of-visual-words representation, we perform Difference-of-Gaussian (DoG) method to detect keypoints in each image and then employ 128D SIFT descriptor. A 1,000-D codebook is built by grouping the keypoint features with hierarchical K-means and in this way a 1000-D bag-of-visual-words representation is generated for each image.

3.2 Hypergraph construction

A hypergraph $\mathcal{G} = (\mathcal{V}, \mathcal{E}, w)$ is composed by the vertex set $\mathcal{V}$, the hyperedge set $\mathcal{E}$, and the hyperedge weight w . Each hyperedge e_i is given a weight $w(e_i)$. The hypergrpah G can be denoted by a $|\mathcal{V}| \times |\mathcal{E}|$ incidence matrix $\mathbf{H}$ with entries:

$$h(v,e) = \begin{cases} 1 & if\ v \in e \\ 0 & if\ v \notin e \end{cases} \quad (1)$$

For a vertex $v_i \in \mathcal{V}$, the vertex degree is estimated by:

$$d(v_i) = \sum_{e \in \mathcal{E}} \omega(e)\, h(v_i, e). \quad (2)$$

For a hyperedge $e_i \in \mathcal{E}$, the edge degree is estimated by

$$\delta(e_i) = \sum_{v \in \mathcal{V}} h(v, e_i). \quad (3)$$

We let $\mathbf{D}_v$ and $\mathbf{D}_e$ denote the diagonal matrices of the vertex degrees and the hyperedge degrees, respectively, and we let $\mathbf{W}$ denote the diagonal matrix of the hyperedge weights.

In our approach, we regard each image in the database as

a vertex in the visual-text hypergraph $G = (\mathcal{V}, \mathcal{E}, w)$. For example, assuming there are totally n images in the database, the generated hypergraph $G = (\mathcal{V}, \mathcal{E}, w)$ thus contains n vertices. Taken both the visual content and the text information into consideration, there are two types of hyperedges generated from the visual content and the tags respectively.

For visual content-based hyperedge, each visual word is selected as a hyperedge, and the images that contain the same visual word are connected by the hyperedge. These visual-content based hyperedge is denoted by $\mathcal{E}_{visual}$. Analogously, for tag-based hyperedge, each tag is selected as a hyperedge, and the images containing the same tag are connected by the hyperedge. These tag-based hyperedges is denoted by $\mathcal{E}_{text}$. Let n_{visual} and n_{text} denote the number of the two types of hyperedges, there are totally $n_E = n_{visual} + n_{text}$ hyperedges.

We let $\mathbf{D}_v$ and $\mathbf{D}_e$ denote the diagonal matrices of the vertex degrees and the hyperedge degrees respectively, and the incidence matrix $\mathbf{H}$ is constructed using Equation (1). The weight of a hyperedge w is estimated based on the similarity of images connected by the hyperedge, i.e.,

$$w(e_i) = \sum_{I_a, I_b \in e_i} \exp\left(-\frac{\|I_a - I_b\|^2}{\sigma^2}\right), \tag{4}$$

3.3 Hypergraph Learning

For hypergraph learning, the Normalized Laplacian method proposed in [23] is employed, and it is formulated as a regularization framework:

$$\arg\min_f \{\lambda R_{emp}(f) + \Omega(f)\}, \tag{5}$$

where f is the classification function to be learned, $\Omega(f)$ is a regularizer on the hypergraph, $R_{emp}(f)$ is empirical loss, and $\lambda > 0$ is a weighting parameter. The regularizer on the hypergraph is defined as

$$\begin{aligned}\Omega(f) &= \frac{1}{2}\sum_{e\in\mathcal{E}}\sum_{u,v\in\mathcal{V}} \frac{w(e)h(u,e)h(v,e)}{\delta(e)}\left(\frac{f(u)}{\sqrt{d(u)}} - \frac{f(v)}{\sqrt{d(v)}}\right)^2 \\ &= \frac{1}{2}\sum_{e\in\mathcal{E}_{visual}}\sum_{u,v\in\mathcal{V}} \frac{w(e)h(u,e)h(v,e)}{\delta(e)}\left(\frac{f(u)}{\sqrt{d(u)}} - \frac{f(v)}{\sqrt{d(v)}}\right)^2 \\ &+ \frac{1}{2}\sum_{e\in\mathcal{E}_{text}}\sum_{u,v\in\mathcal{V}} \frac{w(e)h(u,e)h(v,e)}{\delta(e)}\left(\frac{f(u)}{\sqrt{d(u)}} - \frac{f(v)}{\sqrt{d(v)}}\right)^2\end{aligned} \tag{6}$$

Let $\mathbf{\Theta} = \mathbf{D}_v^{-\frac{1}{2}}\mathbf{H}\mathbf{W}\mathbf{D}_e^{-1}\mathbf{H}^T\mathbf{D}_v^{-\frac{1}{2}}$, and $\mathbf{\Delta} = \mathbf{I} - \mathbf{\Theta}$, the normalized cost function can be written as

$$\Omega(f) = f^T\mathbf{\Delta}f. \tag{7}$$

Here $\mathbf{\Delta}$ is a positive semi-definite matrix, and it is usually called hypergraph Laplacian.

The transductive inference is formulated with a regularization on hypergraphs $\arg\min_f \{\lambda R_{emp}(f) + \Omega(f)\}$, and the loss term is defined as follows:

$$\|f - y\|^2 = \sum_{u\in\mathcal{V}} (f(u) - y(u))^2, \tag{8}$$

where y is the label vector. Assuming the number of all images in the database is n, and the i-th image is selected as the query image. Denote by y an $n \times 1$ vector, where all elements of y are 0 except its i-th value is 1. Then the learning task for social image search is to minimize the sum of the two terms:

$$\Phi(f) = f^T\mathbf{\Delta}f + \lambda\|f - y\|^2, \tag{9}$$

where $\lambda > 0$ is the regularization parameter. Differentiating $\Phi(f)$ with respect to f, we can obtain:

$$f = \left(\mathbf{I} + \frac{1}{\lambda}\mathbf{\Delta}\right)^{-1} y. \tag{10}$$

After obtaining the relevance score vector f, we can rank the images that contain the query tag with the scores in descending order.

3.4 Analysis of computational cost

According to the process introduced above, it can be analyzed that the computational cost of hypergraph learning scales as $O(n^3)$, where n is the number of images in the hypergrpah learning procedure. But in fact we can solve Eq. (10) can be solved with an iterative process, which can reduce the computational cost to $O(n^2)$.

4. EXPERIMENTS

4.1 Experimental Settings

To evaluate the proposed tag-based image search method with visual-text joint hypergraph learning, we conduct experiments on the dataset in [19]. The data are collected from Flickr with the search results of 52 tags: *airshow, apple, beach, bird, car, cow, dolphin, eagle, flower, fruit, jaguar, jellyfish, lion, owl, panda, starfish, triumphal, turtle, watch, waterfall, wolf, chopper, fighter, flame, hairstyle, horse, motorcycle, rabbit, shark, snowman, sport, wildlife, aquarium, basin, bmw, chicken, decoration, forest, furniture, glacier, hockey, matrix, Olympics, palace, rainbow, rice, sailboat, seagull, spider, swimmer, telephone,* and *weapon.* Time-based ranking is used in the data collection process and thus we can estimate the search relevance of time-based ranking. Mean Average Precision (MAP) is adopted as our performance evaluation metric.

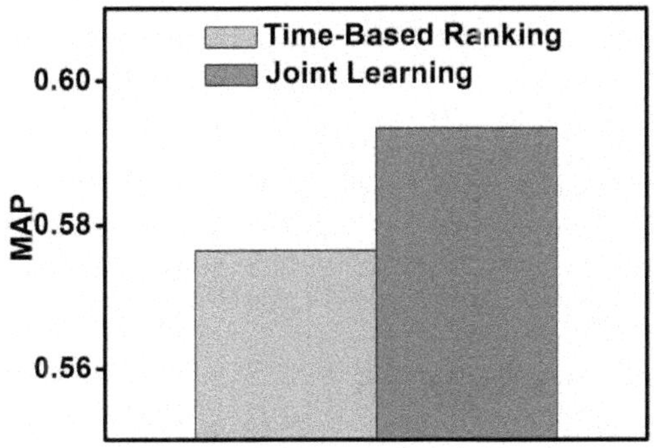

Figure 2: The MAP comparison of the two compared methods.

4.2 Experimental Results

We compare the following methods in the experiment:

- Time-Based Ranking. Time-based ranking orders the images according to their uploading time.
- Tag-Based Image Search with Visual-Text Joint Hypergraph Learningčň i.e., the proposed method. We denote it as "Joint Learning".

In our "Joint Learning" method, the parameter λ is simply set to 0.9, and the parameter σ in Eq. (4) is simply set to the median value of the pairwise distances of all images. For each query tag, we only randomly select 2000 images that do not contain the tag as negative samples.

Figure 2 demonstrates the results. From the results we can see that, time-based ranking performs worse than the "Joint" method. Among the 52 tags, there are 21 queries where the improvement of search performance is more than 10%. The MAP measures of the two compared methods are 0.576 and 0.593, respectively. Figure 3 demonstrate the top 10 search results of the two compared ranking methods of an example query "Forest".

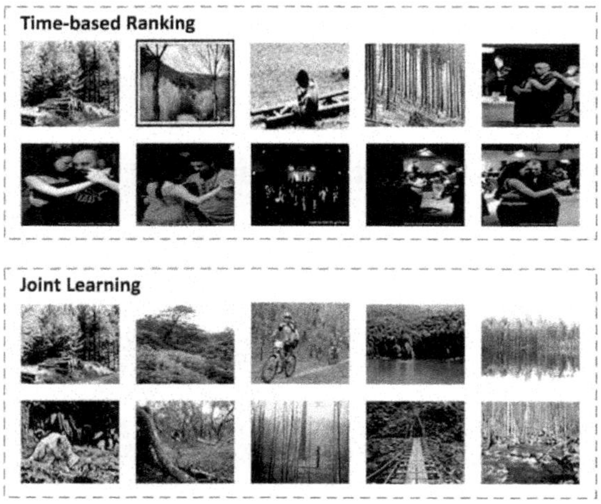

Figure 3: The top 10 results of the two ranking methods of an example query "Forest".

5. CONCLUSION

In this work, we propose a tag-based image search with visual-text joint hypergraph learning. In this method, we simultaneously investigate the visual and text information of images with a hypergraph learning approach. Hyperedges are generated based on visual and textual words. We conduct experiments on a Flickr data set and compare the proposed approach with existing methods. Experimental results show that our method can achieve better performance.

6. REFERENCES

[1] J. Bu, S. Tan, C. Chen, C. Wang, H. Wu, L. Zhang, and X. He. Music recommendation by unified hypergraph: combining social media information and music content. In *Proceedings of the ACM International Conference on Multimedia*, 2010.

[2] L. Chen, D. Xu, W. Tsang, and J. Luo. Tag-based web photo retrieval improved by batch mode re-tagging. In *Proceedings of the IEEE International Conference on Computer Vision and Pattern Recognition*, 2010.

[3] T. Chen, M.-M. Cheng, P. Tan, A. Shamir, and S.-M. Hu. Sketch2photo: Internet image montage. *ACM Trans. Graph*, 28, 2009.

[4] M.-M. Cheng, G.-X. Zhang, N. J. Mitra, X. Huang, and S.-M. Hu. Global contrast based salient region detection. In *Proceedings of the IEEE International Conference on Computer Vision and Pattern Recognition*, pages 409–416, 2011.

[5] Y. Gao, M. Wang, Z. Zha, Q. Tian, Q. Dai, and N. Zhang. Less is more: Efficient 3d object retrieval with query view selection. *IEEE Transactions on Multimedia*, 11, 2011.

[6] B. Geng, L. Yang, C. Xu, and X.-S. Hua. Ranking model adaptation for domain-specific search. *IEEE Transactions on Knowledge and Data Engineering*, 2010.

[7] Y. Huang, Q. Liu, S. Zhang, and D. Metaxas. Video object segmentation by hypergraph cut. In *Proceedings of the IEEE Computer Society Conference on Computer Vision and Pattern Recognition*, pages 1–6, Miami, USA, 2009.

[8] Y. Huang, Q. Liu, S. Zhang, and D. Metaxas. Image retrieval via probabilistic hypergraph ranking. In *Proceedings of the IEEE Computer Society Conference on Computer Vision and Pattern Recognition*, pages 1–6, 2010.

[9] X. Li, C. G. Snoek, and M. Worring. Unsupervised multi-feature tag relevance learning for social image retrieval. In *Proceedings of the ACM International Conference on Image and Video Retrieval*, 2010.

[10] D. Liu, X.-S. Hua, L. Yang, M. Wang, and H.-J. Zhang. Tag ranking. In *Proceedings of the International Conference on World Wide Web*, 2009.

[11] D. Liu, M. Wang, X.-S. Hua, and H.-J. Zhang. Semi-automatic tagging of photo albums via exemplar selection and tag inference. *IEEE Transaction on Multimedia*, 13:82–91, 2011.

[12] D. Liu, M. Wang, L. Yang, X.-S. Hua, and H. Zhang. Tag quality improvement for social images. In *Proceeding of IEEE International Conference on Multimedia*, pages 350–353, 2009.

[13] D. Liu, S. Yan, X.-S. Hua, and H.-J. Zhang. Image tagging via collaborative tag propagation. *IEEE Transaction on Multimedia*, 13:702–712, 2011.

[14] J. Shen, J. Shepherd, B. Cui, and K.-L. Tan. A novel framework for efficient automated singer identification in large music databases. *ACM Transactions on Information Systems*, 27, 2009.

[15] J. Shen, D. Tao, and X. Li. Modality mixture projections for semantic video event detection. *IEEE Transactions on Circuits and Systems for Video Technology*, 18:1587–1596, 2008.

[16] A. Smeulders, M. Worring, S. Santini, A. Gupta, and R. Jain. Content-based image retrieval at the end of early years. *IEEE Transactions on Pattern Analysis and Machine Intelligence*, 22:1349–1380, 2000.

[17] M. Wang and X.-S. Hua. Active learning in multimedia annotation and retrieval: A survey. *ACM Transactions on Intelligent Systems and Technology*, 2:10–31, 2011.

[18] M. Wang, X.-S. Hua, J. Tang, and R. Hong. Beyond distance measurement: Constructing neighborhood similarity for video annotation. *IEEE Transactions on Multimedia*, 11:465–476, 2009.

[19] M. Wang, K. Yang, X.-S. Hua, and H.-J. Zhang. Towards relevant and diverse search of social images. *IEEE Transactions on Multimedia*, 12:829–842, 2010.

[20] Y. Yang, D. Xu, F. Nie, S. Yan, and Y. Zhuang. Image clustering using local discriminant models and global integration. *IEEE Transactions on Image Processing*, 10:2761–2773, 2010.

[21] Y. Yang, Y. Zhuang, F. Wu, and Y. Pan. Harmonizing hierarchical manifolds for multimedia document semantics understanding and cross-media retrieval. *IEEE Transactions on Multimedia*, 10:437–446, 2008.

[22] R. Zass and A. Shashua. Probabilistic graph and hypergraph matching. In *Proceedings of the IEEE Computer Society Conference on Computer Vision and Pattern Recognition*, Alaska, USA, 2008.

[23] D. Zhou, J. Huang, and B. Schokopf. Learning with hypergraphs: Clustering, classification, and embedding. In *Proceedings of Advances in Neural Information Processing Systems 19*, pages 1601–1608, 2007.

[24] G. Zhu, S. Yan, and Y. Ma. Image tag refinement towards low-rank, content-tag prior and error sparsity. In *Proceedings of the ACM International Conference on Multimedia*, 2010.

Integrating Rich Information for Video Recommendation with Multi-Task Rank Aggregation*

Xiaojian Zhao†, Guangda Li‡, Meng Wang‡
Jin Yuan‡, Zheng-Jun Zha‡, Zhoujun Li†, Tat-Seng Chua‡
State Key Laboratory of Software Development Environment, Beihang University†
School of Computing, National University of Singapore‡
{zhaoxj01, guanda10, eric.mengwang, jinjinyuan1981, junzzustc}@gmail.com,
lizj@buaa.edu.cn, chuats@comp.nus.edu.sg

ABSTRACT

Video recommendation is an important approach for helping people to access interesting videos. In this paper, we propose a scheme to integrate rich information for video recommendation. We regard video recommendation as a ranking problem and generate multiple ranking lists by exploring different information sources. A multi-task rank aggregation approach is proposed to integrate the ranking lists for different users in a joint manner. Our scheme is flexible and can easily incorporate other methods by adding their generated ranking lists into our multi-task learning algorithm. We conduct experiments with 76 users and more than 10, 000 videos. The results demonstrate the feasibility and effectiveness of our approach.

Categories and Subject Descriptors

H.3.3 [**Information Storage and Retrieval**]: Information Search and Retrieval

General Terms

Algorithm, Experimentation, Performance

Keywords

Video Recommendation, Multi-Task Rank Aggregation

1. INTRODUCTION

With the rapid advances in storage devices, networks and compression techniques, video data from different domains are growing at an explosive rate. For example, the most popular video sharing site, YouTube[1], hosts over 150,000,000 videos [1]. As a result, users are often bewildered by the vast quantity of videos when they want to find some interesting video contents. Therefore, automatic video recommendation becomes highly desirable to tackle this information-overload problem by presenting lists of potentially interesting videos to the users.

*Area chair: Hari Sundaram
[1]http://www.youtube.com

MM'11, November 28–December 1, 2011, Scottsdale, Arizona, USA.

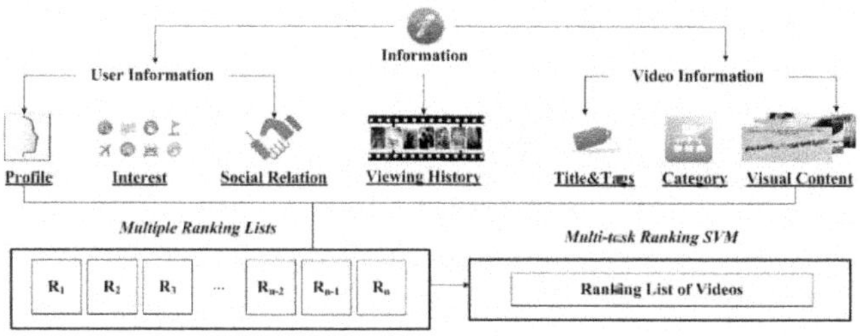

Figure 1: The schematic illustration of the proposed video recommendation scheme that explores multi-source information

Several efforts have been dedicated to video recommendation that explore different information sources. The recommendation services on commercial video websites, such as YouTube, Yahoo! Video[2] and Bing Videos[3], are usually built based on the textual information of videos or users' profiles (only for registered users) [12]. Some methods analyze the interest relationship of users by mining the viewing history [3] [15], while several others recommend videos based on the users' profile [11] or utilize users' viewing histories [19]. However, they all lack an unified scheme that is able to integrate multiple information sources for video recommendation.

In this paper, we propose a personalized video recommendation scheme by integrating rich information. Figure 1 demonstrates the schematic illustration of the approach. We regard video recommendation as a ranking task, i.e., to rank videos in a database with the expectation that interesting videos for a specific user can be prioritized in the list. We explore rich information of both the users and videos, including the education background, occupation, location, interests, past viewing history, social network of users; as well as the title, description, tags and visual content of videos. Multiple ranking lists are generated based on different information sources and we employ a multi-task rank aggregation approach to fuse the ranking lists to generate the final recommendation.

The main contributions of this paper are as follows:

- To the best of our knowledge, this is the first work that integrates rich information for video recommendation. We do not only provide a solution but also analyze the effectiveness of different information sources for video recommendation.
- We propose a multi-task rank aggregation algorithm that is able to accomplish user-adaptive rank aggregation. We show that it is superior to approaches that learn a global rank aggregation model as well as those that learn rank aggregation for each user individually.

[2]http://video.yahoo.com
[3]http://www.bing.com/videos/browse

2. RELATED WORK

Research on video recommendation mainly focuses on three typical approaches, namely, *collaborative filtering* (CF), *content-based filtering* (CBF), and *hybrid filtering* (HF) that combines the above approaches [2]. The CF approaches compare a user's ratings of videos with those of hundreds of others, find people who share similar preferences, and then recommend videos that are interesting for those people with similar preferences. For example, Setten et al. [14] proposed to use different social filtering methods to predict user interest based on other users' information, and designed a combination of prediction techniques. Baluja et al. [3] built a user-video graph which represents the co-view information among different users and its recommendation was performed by a graph propagation in which the label of each note was obtained from its neighbors. For CBF approaches, videos can be recommended based on previous user viewing information for the videos. For example, Mei et al. [13] presented an online video recommendation system, VideoReach, using multimodal relevance between videos and users' click-through data. They considered three modalities, textual, visual and aural, and combined the relevance scores from them by using attention fusion function. HF approaches combine the above two approaches in a single framework [2]. For example, Burke [4] employed mixture models which build the recommendation based on a linear combination, voting, or selection of the content-based prediction and collaborative prediction. Our proposed approach is a flexible approach and is able to integrate different methods. In fact, we can generate ranking lists with different methods or information sources and then employ the multi-task ranking approach to integrate all the ranking lists.

3. RANKING LIST GENERATION WITH RICH INFORMATION

In this section, we introduce the ranking lists generated with rich information. Here we organize them according to the involved information sources about the users including profile, viewing history and social network, as well as the videos. In addition, we also generate ranking lists based on collaborative filtering, the most typical recommendation approach.

3.1 Profile Based Ranking

We collect a set of profile for each user, including major, degree, occupation, interests and location. The user's profile information is represented with texts. Table 1 gives an example. Since we have the text information of each video, including title, description and tags, we can rank videos based on their textual similarity with user's profile information. Here we generate 3 ranking lists, which are based on user's interests, location and other information respectively.

Table 1: The profile information of an exemplary user

Profile Item	Information
Major	Computer Science
Degree	Ph.D.
Occupation	Researcher
Interests	Reading;Swimming;Movie;Travel
Hometown	San Francisco, California
Working Place	Mountain View, California

3.2 History Based Ranking

The viewing history contains the list of videos that have been accessed by the user previously. It is able to reflect the interests of the user. We thus rank videos by estimating their similarities with the history. Here we consider three types of viewing history: recent (i.e., the most recent video viewed by the user), short-term history (the videos viewed on that day), and long-term history (all the past history). For each type of viewing history, we generate 2 ranking lists, one by measuring the visual similarity of videos and the other by textual similarity. Therefore, we generate 6 ranking lists based on the user's history information.

3.3 Social Network Based Ranking

Many recommendation algorithms, such as collaborative filtering, are built by mining the interest relationship of a large number of users [2] [10] [18]. But in fact, a user usually has close interests with his/her friends. For example, when a user wants to enjoy some videos, it is natural for him/her to turn to friends for suggestions. With the rapid advances of social network, we can easily collect information on a user's friends and explore their video viewing histories. Our approach is as follows. We denote $\mathcal{V}_i$ as the video set that has been viewed by the i-th friend. We integrate all the videos viewed by the users' friends into a video set $\mathcal{V}$, i.e., $\mathcal{V} = \mathcal{V}_1 \bigcup \mathcal{V}_2 \bigcup \ldots\ldots \bigcup \mathcal{V}_r$, where r is the number of friends. We then generate ranking lists with two methods. For the first method, we set the ranking score of 1 to videos in $\mathcal{V}$ and the score of 0 to all the other videos. Since we can set $\mathcal{V}_i$ to either the recent one, short-term history, or long-term history of the i-th friend, we can obtain 3 ranking lists with this method. Note that these ranking lists are actually not stable as there are only two scores, 0 and 1, for the videos. But it is not a problem for generating the final recommendation list since our rank aggregation, which will be introduced in the next section, is a score-based fusion approach. In the second method, we still put the videos in $\mathcal{V}$ on top of the ranking list, but for the other videos, we rank them according to their similarities with $\mathcal{V}$. Since we can adopt visual and textual similarity respectively, so we can generate 3 ranking lists for each. Therefore, we generate 9 ranking lists based on users' social network information.

3.4 Collaborative Filtering Based Ranking

Collaborative filtering is the most widely-adopted approach for recommendation. It is usually accomplished by mining a user-item matrix. There are two typical approaches, one is estimating the similarity of users [2] and the other is estimating the similarity of items. Here we employ these two methods to generate two ranking lists and integrate them into our approach.

4. MULTI-TASK RANK AGGREGATION

After generating multiple video ranking lists using different information sources, our next task is to aggregate these video lists into an optimized video list such that the top items can be recommended to the users. It can be formulated as a rank aggregation problem [9]. Rank aggregation methods usually can be categorized into two approaches, namely, the rank-based approach and score-based approach [16]. Here we adopt the score-based approach, i.e., we fuse ranking lists according to the ranking scores of each video instead of their ranking positions. There are two straightforward approaches, one is to learn a global rank aggregation model and the other is to learn a rank aggregation model for each user. However, for the first approach, the behavioral differences of different users are overlooked; while the second approach does not consider the dependency among users and this may make the learned model unreasonable if training data are limited to a user. Therefore, we propose a multi-task learning approach that is able to simultaneously learn models for multiple users such that the correlation of the users can be explored [7]. We build our approach based on ranking SVM [5], and the method is named multi-task ranking SVM.

We first introduce several notations. We denote $\mathbf{v}_i \succ \mathbf{v}_j$ and $(\mathbf{v}_i, \mathbf{v}_j) \in \mathcal{R}$, if a video $\mathbf{v}_i$ is ranked higher than a video $\mathbf{v}_j$ in an order $\mathcal{R}$. Otherwise, we denote $(\mathbf{v}_i, \mathbf{v}_j) \notin \mathcal{R}$. We assume for simplicity that $\mathcal{R}$ has strict ordering, which means that, for all pair $\mathbf{v}_i$ and $\mathbf{v}_j$ in $\mathcal{R}$, we have either $\mathbf{v}_i \succ \mathbf{v}_j$ or $\mathbf{v}_i \prec \mathbf{v}_j$. Let $\mathcal{R}^*$ be the optimal ranking of video in which the video is ordered perfectly according to the user's preference. A training set for multi-task ranking SVM is a set of partial orders $\mathcal{R}^* \subset \mathcal{R}$, which are the total number of pair wise orderings. The target of the multi-task ranking SVM is to learn a function f_k that satisfies $f_k(\mathbf{v}_i) > f_k(\mathbf{v}_j)$ for all pairs of $(\mathbf{v}_i, \mathbf{v}_j) \in \mathcal{R}$ given the k-th user. For simplicity, we assume $f_k(\mathbf{v}) = \mathbf{w}_k \cdot \mathbf{v}$. For every user, all $\mathbf{w}_k$ can be defined:

$$\mathbf{w}_k = \mathbf{w}_0 + \Delta\mathbf{w}_k \tag{1}$$

where $\mathbf{w}_0$ can be viewed as a common part of all users and $\Delta\mathbf{w}_k$ indicates the distinct difference of the k-th user. The vectors $\Delta\mathbf{w}_k$ are usually enforced to be *small*, i.e. we assume that the tasks are related in a way that the true models are all close to some model $\mathbf{w}_0$. We then estimate all $\Delta\mathbf{w}_k$ as well as $\Delta\mathbf{w}_0$ simultaneously. To this end, we solve the following optimization problem, which is analogous to SVM [7]:

$$\begin{aligned} \min \sum_{k=1}^{K}\sum_{i=1}^{n_k} \xi_{ki} + \lambda_1 \sum_{k=1}^{K} ||\Delta\mathbf{w}_k||^2 + \lambda_2||\mathbf{w}_0||^2 \\ s.t.\ (\mathbf{w}_0 + \Delta\mathbf{w}_k)(\mathbf{v}_{ki}^{(1)} - \mathbf{v}_{ki}^{(2)}) \geqslant 1 - \xi_{ki}\ \ \xi_{ki} \geqslant 0 \end{aligned} \tag{2}$$

where n_k denotes the number of training sample pairs for the k-th user, $(\mathbf{v}_{ki}^{(1)}, \mathbf{v}_{ki}^{(2)})$ refers to the k-th training pair for the i-th user, λ_1 and λ_2 are the positive regularization parameters, and the ξ_{ki} are slack variables that measure the error of the final models $\mathbf{w}_k$.

The optimal solution to the optimization problem is:

$$\begin{aligned} \Delta\mathbf{w}_k^* = \tfrac{T}{2\lambda_1}\sum_{i=1}^{m} \alpha_{ik}(\mathbf{v}_{ik}^{(1)} - \mathbf{v}_{ik}^{(2)}) \\ \mathbf{w}_0^* = \tfrac{\lambda_1}{K\lambda_2}\sum_{k=1}^{K} \Delta\mathbf{w}_k^* \end{aligned} \tag{3}$$

where α_{ik} is the nonnegative Lagrange multipliers. The dual formulation for the above problem is:

$$\begin{aligned} \max_{\alpha_{ik}}\{-\tfrac{1}{2}\sum_{i=1}^{m}\sum_{s=1}^{K}\sum_{j=1}^{m}\sum_{k=1}^{K} \alpha_{is}\alpha_{jk}K_{sk}(\mathbf{v}_{is}^{(1)} - \mathbf{v}_{is}^{(2)}, \mathbf{v}_{jk}^{(1)} - \mathbf{v}_{jk}^{(2)}) \\ + \textstyle\sum_{i=1}^{m}\sum_{k=1}^{K} \alpha_{it}\} s.t.\ 0 \leq \alpha_{ik} \leq T/2\lambda_1 \end{aligned} \tag{4}$$

where

$$K_{sk}(\mathbf{y}, \mathbf{z}) := (\tfrac{\lambda_1}{K\lambda_2} + \delta_{sk})\mathbf{y}\cdot\mathbf{z},\ \ s, k = 1, \ldots, T$$

Accordingly, we can obtain the optimal $\mathbf{w}_0$ and $\Delta\mathbf{w}_k$. By performing rank aggregation with the weight vector $\mathbf{w}_0 + \Delta\mathbf{w}_k$, we can obtain the final ranking list for recommendation.

5. EXPERIMENTS

5.1 Experimental Settings

We conduct experiments with 76 participants from two countries. They are all active YouTube and Facebook users from different backgrounds. The video viewing behavior on YouTube of these users were tracked in a one-month period (from Dec. 2010 to Jan. 2011). It is shown that there are about 150 videos viewed per user on average. The profile and social relationship information among the 76 users are collected. It is shown that the number of friends of the users can vary from 3 to 18. The videos and their associated information, including title, description and tags are all collected. In this way, we have collected 11400 videos. For each user, we split the viewed videos into two parts: the videos viewed in the first two weeks, and the videos viewed in the next two weeks. The second part is used for testing. That means, we regard videos in the second part as relevant samples for recommendation[4]. We assign the relevance scores of 1 and 0 to the videos in the second part and the other videos for a user, respectively.

Table 2: The comparison of exploring different information sources for video recommendation (For the history type, R, S and L indicate the recent video, short-term history, and long-term history respectively).

Ranking method		Textual Information			Visual Information		
User Information	interest	0.34			-		
	location	0.23			-		
	profile	0.22			-		
		R	S	L	R	S	L
History-Based		0.36	0.33	0.30	0.29	0.28	0.26
SN-Based		0.31	0.34	0.32	0.25	0.27	0.27
CF Based	item	0.22					
	user	0.23					
All Information		**0.41**					

In our ranking list generation method, we estimate the similarity of two sets of textual terms and the visual similarity of two videos. For calculating the similarity of two sets of textual terms (it needs to be used in our ranking list generation approach), we first compute the similarity of each pair of textual terms across the two sets based on Google distance [6] and then use the average result. To estimate the visual similarity of two videos, we first segment each video into shots and extract a representative key-frame from each shot. For each key-frame we extract 428-dimensional global visual features for each image [20], including 225-D block-wise color moments generated from a 5-by-5 fixed partition of the image [17], 128-D wavelet texture, and 75-D edge direction histogram [8] [21]. Then the visual similarity of two videos is calculated by averaging the similarities of all key-frame pairs across the two videos.

For the training of multi-task rank aggregation model, we further split the videos of the first two weeks for each user into two parts, one is the videos viewed in the first week and the rest videos form the second part. We generate ranking lists and learn the rank aggregation model based on the videos of the second part. The parameters λ_1 and λ_2 in Eq. 2 are jointly tuned with 5-fold cross-validation (note that here cross-validation is accomplished by dividing users into different folds). For performance evaluation metric, we adopt normalized discounted cumulative gain (NDCG) [18].

5.2 Experimental Results

We first compare our approach that integrates all information sources with methods that only use part of the information. We compare our approach with 17 methods that use only part of the information by combining different information sources. For the methods that involve multiple ranking lists, we employ the multi-

[4]It is worth noting that this setting actually makes the performance underestimated, as the users may also be interested in the videos out of the second part. So a most rigorous approach for ground truth establishment is to let users label all videos with interestingness. But our approach is still reasonable for comparing different algorithms and it is a widely-adopted approach for avoiding the intensive labeling cost.

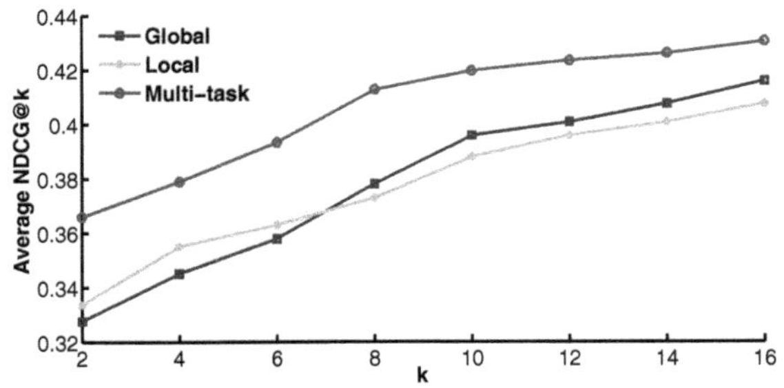

Figure 2: The performance variation of different ranking strategies in different depth

task rank aggregation approach to fuse them. Table 2 illustrates the comparison of average NDCG@10. From the results, we have the following observations. First, text-based recommendation consistently achieves better performance than visual content based recommendation. Second, among the three types of history information, recent based recommendation performs better than short-term history and long-term history. This is because many users' interests are temporally continuous and thus the continuously viewed videos are usually close. However, it is not the case for SN-based method because the longer viewing histories from friends' can better reveal the user's interest. Finally, we can see that integrating all information sources can achieve the best result.

We also compare our multi-task rank aggregation approach with the following two methods for rank aggregation:

(1) Learning a global rank aggregation model for all users, i.e., the weighting vectors of all users are identical.

(2) Learning a specific rank aggregation model for each user, i.e., $\mathbf{w}_0$ is removed in Eq. 2.

We denote our approach and these two methods as "Multi-Task", "Global" and "Local", respectively. Both of the "Global" and "Local" methods are based on Ranking SVM; the only difference is that, one learns a model for all users and the other learns a model for each individual user. In these two methods, the parameter of Ranking SVM is tuned to its optimal value. These three methods are used to fuse the 20 ranking lists introduced in Section 3. Figure 2 illustrates the comparison of average NDCG at different depths. We can see that our approach consistently outperforms the other two methods. Figure 3 illustrates the detailed NDCG@10 results for the 76 users. We can see that for most users our approach achieves the best results. But it is worth noting that, by adopting the multi-task rank aggregation approach, we also introduce a problem for new users. That is, how to learn rank aggregation model for the new user. We can adopt the following strategy. If a new user is associated with enough training data, we can learn a rank aggregation model for the user individually. Otherwise, we can employ several recently proposed model adaptation methods that are able to adapt the models of existing users to this new user.

6. CONCLUSION AND FURTHER WORK

In this paper, we proposed a video recommendation scheme that is able to integrate multiple information sources with a multi-task rank aggregation approach. Ranking lists are generated by exploring different information sources and we then fuse the ranking lists with a multi-task learning approach. We conducted experiments on more than 11,000 videos and the results demonstrated the feasibility and effectiveness of our approach. Our scheme is flexible and different ranking methods can be easily integrated as we only need to fuse several ranking lists in the aggregation step. In future, we will conduct experiments with more users and videos, and investigate the problem of new users with empirical justification.

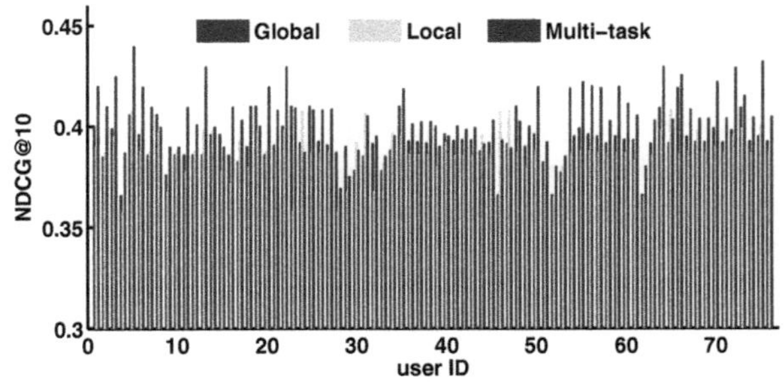

Figure 3: The performance comparison of the three rank aggregation methods for each user. NDCG@10 is used as the performance evaluation metric here.

7. ACKNOWLEDGEMENTS

This work was supported by the National Natural Science Foundation of China (61170189, 60973105), the Fund of the State Key Laboratory of Software Development Environment under Grant No. SKLSDE-2011ZX-03 and the Singapore National Research Foundation & Interactive Digital Media R&D Program Office, MDA under research grant (WBS:R-252-300-001-490).

8. REFERENCES

[1] Encyclopedia. *http://en.wikipedia.org/wiki/YouTube/*.

[2] G. Adomavicius and A. Tuzhilin. Toward the next generation of recommender systems: a survey of the state-of-the-art and possible extensions. *IEEE Transactions on Knowledge and Data Engineering*, 17(6):734–749, 2005.

[3] S. Baluja, R. Seth, D. Sivakumar, Y. Jing, J. Yagnik, S. Kumar, D. Ravichandran, and M. Aly. Video suggestion and discovery for youtube: taking random walks through the view graph. In *WWW*, pages 895–904, 2008.

[4] R. Burke. Hybrid web recommender systems. *Lecture Notes in Computer Science*, pages 377–408, 2007.

[5] Y. Cao, J. Xu, T.-Y. Liu, H. Li, Y. Huang, and H.-W. Hon. Adapting ranking SVM to document retrieval. In *ACM SIGIR*, pages 186–193, 2006.

[6] R. L. Cilibrasi and P. M. Vitányi. The google similarity distance. *IEEE Transactions on Knowledge and Data Engineering*, 19(3):370–385, 2007.

[7] T. Evgeniou and M. Pontil. Regularized multi–task learning. In *ACM KDD*, pages 109–117, 2004.

[8] B. Geng, L. Yang, C. Xu, and X. Hua. Content-aware ranking for visual search. In *CVPR*, pages 3400–3407, 2010.

[9] B. Geng, L. Yang, C. Xu, and X.-S. Hua. Ranking model adaptation for domain specific search. *IEEE Transactions on Knowledge and Data Engineering*, 2010.

[10] X. Hu, L. Tang, and H. Liu. Enhancing accessibility of microblogging messages using semantic knowledge. In *ACM CIKM*, 2011.

[11] H. Luo, J. Fan, and D. A. Keim. Personalized news video recommendation. In *ACM MM*, pages 1001–1002, 2008.

[12] T. Mei and K. Aizawa. Video recommendation. In *Chapter of Internet Multimedia Search and Mining*. Bentham Science Publisher, 2011.

[13] T. Mei, B. Yang, X.-S. Hua, L. Yang, S.-Q. Yang, and S. Li. Videoreach: an online video recommendation system. In *ACM SIGIR*, pages 767–768, 2007.

[14] M. van Setten, M. Veenstra, and et.al. Prediction strategies in a TV recommender system-method and experiments. In *WWW*, pages 203–210, 2003.

[15] M. Wang and X.-S. Hua. Active learning in multimedia annotation and retrieval: A survey. *ACM Transactions on Intelligent Systems and Technology*, 2(2):10, 2011.

[16] M. Wang, X.-S. Hua, R. Hong, J. Tang, G. Qi, and Y. Song. Unified video annotation via multigraph learning. *IEEE Transactions on Circuits and Systems for Video Technology*, 19(5):733–746, 2009.

[17] M. Wang, X.-S. Hua, J. Tang, and R. Hong. Beyond distance measurement: constructing neighborhood similarity for video annotation. *IEEE Transactions on Multimedia*, 11(3):465–476, 2009.

[18] M. Wang, K. Yang, X.-S. Hua, and H. Zhang. Towards a relevant and diverse search of social images. *IEEE Transactions on Multimedia*, 12(8):829–842, 2010.

[19] B. Yang, T. Mei, X.-S. Hua, L. Yang, S.-Q. Yang, and M. Li. Online video recommendation based on multimodal fusion and relevance feedback. In *ACM CIVR*, pages 73–80, 2007.

[20] Z.-J. Zha, X.-S. Hua, T. Mei, J. Wang, and Z. Wang. Joint multi-label multi-instance learning for image classification. In *CVPR*, pages 1–8, 2008.

[21] Z.-J. Zha, L. Yang, T. Mei, M. Wang, and Z. Wang. Visual query suggestion. In *ACM MM*, pages 15–24, 2009.

Quantifying Human Reconstruction Accuracy for Voxel Carving in a Sporting Environment *

David Monaghan, Philip Kelly, and Noel E. O'Connor
CLARITY: Centre for Sensor Web Technologies
Dublin City University, Ireland
david.monaghan@dcu.ie

ABSTRACT

Whilst voxel carving approaches exist that allow non-invasive 3D human reconstruction, their performance is heavily dependent on the number of cameras used and the placement of these cameras around the subject. We present a technique to quantify the fall-off in accuracy of spatially carved volumetric representations of humans based on real world constraints. We describe an example of such a quantitative evaluation using a synthetic dataset of typical sports motion in a tennis court scenario, created using computer graphics techniques and motion capture data. Experiments are performed using a baseline voxel carving technique that includes player tracking, background subtraction and player voxel carving. This type of quantitative evaluation could be used by amateur sporting clubs without a sophisticated capture infrastructure to understand how best to instrument a camera network in order to obtain a good trade-off between reconstruction accuracy and installation cost.

Categories and Subject Descriptors

I.4.5 [**Computing Methodologies**]: Image Processing and Computer Vision—*Reconstruction*

General Terms

Algorithms, Measurement, Experimentation

Keywords

Image processing, 3D Reconstruction, Space Carving

1. INTRODUCTION

In order for coaches to both technically and tactically improve a player's performance they must be able to ascertain the deficiencies in an athlete's abilities and effectively communicate to the player how to correct these. In our on-going work, we aim to maximise the impact of coaching feedback by developing tools for both performance analysis and visualisation of player performance. In tennis, for example, 3D visualisation could be used to provide detailed feedback on an athlete's biomechanical movement during specific actions crucial to overall performance. Such a visualisation would be useful for coaches for identifying faults in a player's stroke mechanics during serves, drop shots, etc as well a useful means of conveying this information back to the athlete.

Clearly, 3D human reconstruction is a key component in achieving this, as it forms a core element of both performance analysis and visualisation. For example, Zhao et.al. [10] fit a human skeletal poses to a temporal series of 3D volumetric representations, resulting in the acquisition of the movement of a human's limbs and body over time. This technique could be employed as the basis for the evaluation of sporting performance, for example determining how parameters, such as fatigue, affect an athlete technique over time. However, the accuracy of such skeletal fitting techniques are intrinsically linked to the precision of the 3D human representations. Similarly, an accurate reconstruction of the player at any point in time would allow the coach flexibility when clarifying a tactical or technical issue by allowing the game to be viewed from any angle; or enabling highly beneficial tactical information to be obtained by an athlete from reliving a match from their own viewpoint, a spectator's viewpoint, and from their opponent's viewpoint. The usefulness of this depends on the accuracy of the visualisation.

In an ideal scenario, the 3D human volumetric models would be acquired from voxel carving techniques using a camera network consisting of numerous high quality cameras, with the cameras in the network positioned on the surface of a virtual sphere around the athlete. Real world constraints, however, do not normally allow for this. In a low cost amateur set-up, the quality and number of cameras available is limited. Furthermore, the physical constraints of retro-fitting a camera network to an existing environment will often mean the non-linear placement of cameras that do not provide full 360 degree encirclement. For such a scenario, deciding the optimum camera placement positions can lead to significant gains in the accuracy of generated volumetric models. To the best of our knowledge, however, no tools exist to help inform how best to instrument the camera network in order to ensure maximum quality given a limited budget (number of cameras) and real world practical mounting constraints.

In this work, we describe a technique that, starting from

*Area chair: Qi Tian

MM'11, November 28–December 1, 2011, Scottsdale, Arizona, USA.

an idealized capture scenario, can quantify the fall off in accuracy of a 3D reconstruction as the number of cameras is reduced. Using this as a tool, the number, placement and cost of the camera network could be optimised, allowing the highest quality 3D volumetric models to be acquired given a defined budget and the physical constraints of the capture environment (note that we do not claim to address this complex optimization problem here, it is targeted for future work). The paper is organised as follows: Section 2 provides a brief overview on previous work conducted in the area 3D reconstruction techniques. Section 3 gives an overview of the proposed approach. Section 5 provides quantitative and subjective evaluation of the approach and conclusions and future work are outlined in section 6.

2. RELATED WORK

The 3D reconstruction techniques described in the literature range from emerging techniques based on wearable cheap sensors [8] to well-known and broadly used light scanning and infra-red optical motion capture systems. Although systems such as Vicon [2] are generally regarded as being the *gold standard* in accurate motion reconstruction, they can be impractical and cumbersome in some scenarios. Athletic motion, in particular, is challenging because subjects often move very quickly through large spatial volumes that may be difficult to densely and safely populate with enough cameras to ensure adequate coverage and resolution. The practicalities of installing a large number of expensive cameras in such spaces may also be impractical due to the inherent cost of the hardware. Within the context of real world sporting environments, where athletes tend not to be permitted to be instrumented or wear restrictive motion capture suits, a non-invasive technique that does not disturb or distract the athlete is the most desirable solution.

Space carving [3, 5, 6, 7], or voxel (a 3D pixel) carving, techniques can provide such a non-invasive solution and can be implemented on a low-cost camera network allowing the approach to be feasibly employed by both amateur and elite level sports clubs. Space carving techniques create a 3D representation of a subject from a temporally calibrated sequence of 2D images captured from a number of cameras at multiple viewing angles. In each image, a silhouette of the region of interest (i.e. the athlete) is identified and segmented. A virtual cube is drawn around the volume a subject occupies in 3D space and this volume is subsequently populated with voxels. Each voxel is analogous to a virtual lump of clay that is carved by iterating through each of the cameras and eliminating inconsistent voxels from this predefined initial volume using the extracted silhouettes from each image [6]. The resultant voxels occupy the space that corresponds to the most probable 3D spatial location of the subject. However, the accuracy of the resultant 3D representation is heavily dependent on the number of cameras used and their placement.

3. GENERATING A GROUND TRUTH

In this paper, we present a technique to quantify the fall-off in accuracy of a spatially carved volumetric representation based on real world constraints. In this case study, these constraints are derived from (i) a modest budget that will support a limited number of our preferred cameras, and (ii) based on the capture environment that imposes a physical restriction on the placement of these cameras (for example, cameras cannot be placed in areas where they will be damaged, or located where no physical structures exist on which they can be mounted). However, in order to quantitatively calculate the expected error of a space carving from a given camera set-up, a *groundtruth* 3D representation is needed. The groundtruth represents the best possible space carving that could be achieved in the environment, given a near unlimited budget (i.e. a large number of cameras). This groundtruth data can be used to quantify the fall-off in accuracy resulting from the reduction in the number of cameras from an ideal scenario to a scenario governed by real world constraints. However, the generation of this dataset in a real-world scenario is highly complicated as the groundtruth volume of the region of interest is generally unknown to a high degree of accuracy, and acquiring and positioning a very high number of cameras is unrealistic due to budgetary and engineering constraints (it is what we are trying to avoid in the first place!).

We therefore propose the use of synthetic datasets. We first accurately model the capture area in an OpenGl graphical environment. Using this graphical model, a high number of plausible camera positions (and camera intrinsic parameters) can be identified. This number is set to be sufficiently high to ensure saturation in coverage within the required area of capture. By using a hypothetical camera's intrinsic and extrinsic parameters, a camera viewpoint in a real world scenario can be mimicked to a high degree of accuracy in the virtual graphical environment.

In order to generate a groundtruth human, we captured a typical sample set of the types of motions that the subject is expected to perform at capture time. For example, in this work, the area of interest is a tennis court, so we used typical human tennis movements captured in a Vicon motion capture studio. However, a variety of publicly available motions [1] could have been used for different scenarios. The data allows synthetic human motion to be rendered within the virtual reconstruction. Using this virtual environment, synthetic video streams of expected human animation from each of the virtual cameras can be generated. The voxel carving of the synthetic player is then be performed (as described in section 4) from all of the virtual camera viewpoints for any individual time instant or complete video sequence. The resulting volumetric representations are taken as a groundtruth dataset, as they can be seen as the highest quality 3D reconstruction that could be achieved given an unlimited number of cameras.

Using this setup, the carvings from any subset of the camera positions can also be acquired. We quantify the resulting error by calculating the Normalised Mean Square Error (NMSE) of the groundtruth volumetric reconstruction against any reconstruction from an inferior camera setup. The 3D NMSE between the two volumes is possible as the space carvings are written in real world Euclidean coordinates. In this work, the MSE is normalised with respect to the number of voxels used in a carving, typically of the order of 10^5 voxels, to allow for a direct comparison. The NMSE cost function will be 0 if the two volumes are identical, rising to 1 if there is no spatial volume in common between the two volumes.

4. VOXEL CARVING APPROACH

We use our own approach to the acquisition of the 3D

Figure 1: Real-world reconstruction; (Row 1) 5 camera views; (Row 2) Model from 5 camera views.

human volumetric representations that is tailored towards a tennis scenario [4]. The approach is completely autonomous and requires no human interaction. There are several components of this system including player tracking, background subtraction, silhouette extraction and voxel carving. An overhead camera is used for player tracking. Player tracking is required as it automatically approximates player position on the tennis court groundplane, allowing for a choice of the initial virtual cube for voxel carving – note that a good choice can have a considerable impact on the results of the reconstruction process [6]. Using the tracked players bounding box, a cube is then drawn around the player and this represents the most probable spatial volume that is occupied by the player. The cube height is set to a standard player height, in this study 2.4 metres. The *number* of voxels dynamically changes with each frame so as to maintain a constant voxel spatial resolution.

Using intrinsic and extrinsic camera calibration parameters the cameras in which the player-cube appears can be easily identified. The real-world coordinates of this spatial volume can then be transformed into camera coordinates for any of the cameras and specific region where the player appears in each image can be isolated from the rest of the image. By restricting the silhouette extraction algorithm to only search within the bounds of the player-cube in each image the computational effort of the silhouette extraction is significantly reduced. The silhouette extraction algorithm is based on an approximate median background subtraction model [4] and the entire process is autonomous.

After the player silhouettes are constructed, the space carving technique, which follows from the technique of Yang *at el* [9], is performed. To reduce the strain on available computer memory that traditional voxel carving techniques can have, an initial carving is carried out at a low voxel spatial resolution. The spatial volume surrounding the player can therefore be optimised and a second, more accurate, player-cube is calculated. A second space carving is then carried out at a higher voxel spatial resolution. An example carving for a single time instant in a real-world setup with 5 cameras using this approach can be seen in figure 1.

5. QUANTITATIVE EVALUATION

For this study, we evaluate the trade-off between cost (i.e. number of cameras) and reconstruction accuracy using the NMSE measure in a specific application scenario, namely our real-world a tennis court facility. For this analysis, we focused 50 virtual cameras on a single side of a tennis court – cameras were positioned according to the physical constraints of the environment (for example, cameras were not placed on the court, or located in areas where there are no physical structures – as such, cameras could only be placed on a 220 degree arch around the court due to the presence of other tennis courts). Taking several still frames from a video sequence (see figures 3(a), (b) and (c) for example), we implemented the voxel carving algorithm using all 50 cameras to perform the carving operation. The resultant volumetric representation of the tennis player represents the best possible, or groundtruth, space carving that could be obtained. Three such acquired models can be seen in figure 3, rows (i), (iii) and (v), in each of these figures the reconstruction is a volumetric shape and is shown at 8 different angles, each separated by 45 degrees.

We then randomly remove a virtual camera and perform the voxel carving again. This new volumetric representation is slightly different to the previous one as it has been cut with fewer cameras and the decrease in accuracy from the groundtruth carving is quantitatively evaluated using the NMSE measure, as outlined in section 3. Figure 2 shows how the NMSE error indicates the fall off in accuracy of the space carving as the number of cameras is reduced. It can be seen that by using only 5 cameras a space carving with an NMSE of 0.4729 with respect to the groundtruth can be obtained. Some example carvings for synthetic data from our 5 real-world cameras positions, as shown in figure 1, are illustrated in figure 3, rows (ii), (iv) and (vi). It should be noted that the results in figure 3(vi) are noisier than those in rows (ii) and (iv) due the increased complexity of the pose, as the player is leaning forwards and his arms are folded inward generating occlusions. From figure 2 we could thus infer that better quality representations may be achievable by adding another camera (to bring the NMSE < 0.4) but that no further significant improvements beyond this would be obtained until we reached 9 cameras.

6. CONCLUSIONS

In this study we presented a technique to quantify the accuracy achievable via spatially carved volumetric representations based on real world constraints. We used a 3D reconstruction technique developed for an amateur sporting environment and illustrated how we could quantitatively evaluate its performance by simulating realistic human motion and virtual placement of a large number of cameras.

Figure 3: Synthetic data volumetric reconstruction; (a)/(b)/(c) Example viewpoint of model pose; (i)/(iii)/(v) Reconstruction produced from 50 cameras; (ii)/(iv)/(vi) Reconstruction produced from 5 cameras.

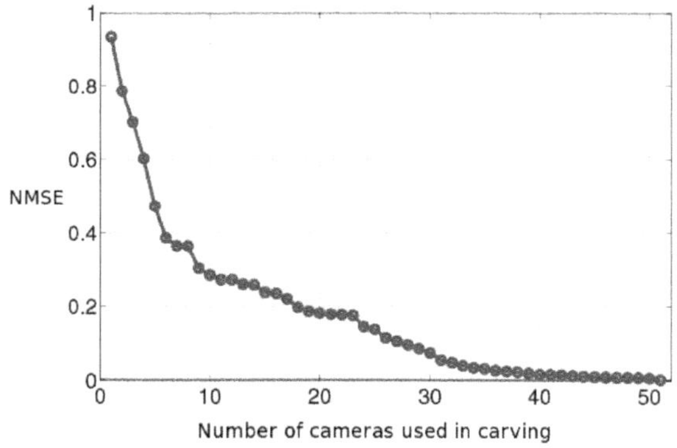

Figure 2: Quantitative evaluation of space carvings with regard to the number of cameras used.

7. ACKNOWLEDGMENTS

This research was partially supported by the European Commission under FP7-247688 3DLife. This work is supported by Science Foundation Ireland under grant 07/CE/I1147

8. REFERENCES

[1] Cmu graphics lab motion capture database. http://mocap.cs.cmu.edu/, 2011.

[2] Vicon. http://www.vicon.com, 2011.

[3] A. Broadhurst, T. Drummond, and R. Cipolla. A probabilistic framework for space carving. In *Conf on Computer Vision*, volume 1, page 388, 2001.

[4] C. O. Conaire, P. Kelly, C. Kim, and N. E. O'Connor. Automatic camera selection for activity monitoring in a multi-camera system for tennis. In *ACM/IEEE Conference on Distributed Smart Cameras*, 2009.

[5] W. B. Culbertson, T. Malzbender, and G. Slabaugh. Generalized voxel coloring. In *Intern. Workshop on Vision Algorithms: Theory and Practice*, pages 100–115, 1999.

[6] K. N. Kutulakos and S. M. Seitz. A theory of shape by space carving. *Intern. Journal of Computer Vision*, 38:199–218, July 2000.

[7] S. M. Seitz, B. Curless, J. Diebel, D. Scharstein, and R. Szeliski. A comparison and evaluation of multi-view stereo reconstruction algorithms. In *IEEE Conference on Computer Vision and Pattern Recognition*, volume 1, pages 519–528, 2006.

[8] J. Tautges, A. Zinke, B. Krüger, J. Baumann, A. Weber, T. Helten, M. Müller, H.-P. Seidel, and B. Eberhardt. Motion reconstruction using sparse accelerometer data. *ACM Trans on Graphics*, 2011.

[9] Y.-K. Yang, J. Lee, S.-K. Kim, and C.-H. Kim. Adaptive space carving with texture mapping. In *ICCSA (3)*, pages 1129–1138, 2005.

[10] X. Zhao and Y. Liu. Generative tracking of 3d human motion by hierarchical annealed genetic algorithm. *Pattern Recognition*, 41:2470–2483, August 2008.

Time-aware Co-Training for Indoors Localization in Visual Lifelogs *

Vladislavs Dovgalecs Rémi Mégret Yannick Berthoumieu
University of Bordeaux
IMS, UMR 5218 CNRS
F33400 Talence, France
{vladislavs.dovgalecs, remi.megret, yannick.berthoumieu}@ims-bordeaux.fr

ABSTRACT

In this paper we address the problem of location recognition from visual lifelogs by leveraging visual features and temporal information in an unified framework. The proposed method features a co-training approach that takes advantage of both labeled and unlabeled data using a confidence measure we propose for this task. It exploits jointly two SVM classifiers on two types of visual features as well as the temporal continuity of the video through temporal accumulation scheme. We demonstrate experimentally on the publicly available IDOL2 dataset that the algorithm yields performance improvement due to its ability to exploit jointly multiple cues, time and unlabeled data.

Categories and Subject Descriptors

H.3.1 [**Information Storage and Retrieval**]: Content Analysis and Indexing – Indexing methods; I.5.2 [**Pattern Recognition**]: Design Methodology – Classifier design and evaluation, Feature evaluation and selection.

General Terms

Algorithms, Design, Experimentation.

Keywords

Lifelog indexing, semi-supervised learning, co-training, temporal information.

1. INTRODUCTION

Lifelogging and ego-centric video monitoring is now a practical way for activity and behavior monitoring [7] as well as a mean for memory aid. Although there exist technical solutions for activity log acquisition, the need for efficient content structuring is still of great importance and remains an open question. To search multiple hour recordings efficiently, an indexing method is required. In our study we focus on the estimation of the location of the monitored person using visual information captured by a wearable wide angle camera attached to the person's shoulder.

Indoors localization using image-based approaches is a widely researched topic in computer vision and robotics. Discrete features [12] can be used for indoors and outdoors localization but require explicit matching of local features which can be costly. Signature based approaches such as Bag of Features (BOF) [8] or CRFH [5], which are based on the distribution of quantized local features, produce global image description that is more easily amenable to efficient use for video analysis.

An important issue concerns the discrimination power. A single type of features may not be efficient in all conditions. Fusion of multiple cues is a way to improve the discriminability by exploiting several feature types that exhibit complementary properties with respect to selectivity and invariance. A multiple cue integration method exploiting confidence measure for place classification was proposed in [9], which uses the late fusion of SVM scores obtained on diverse visual cues. They also propose temporal accumulation of the scores over time, which allows to smooth out isolated misclassifications.

Another specificity of lifelog indexing is the low amount of training data. Semi-supervised learning is a way to profit from abundant unlabeled data together with small labeled data set. It was used for instance in [3] to improve BOF and feature matching recognition in the case of sparse labeling.

In this paper we investigate how to combine both semi-supervised, temporal and multiple visual cues for location recognition. We show that appearance-based model can be refined iteratively in a semi-supervised manner using predictions and a confidence measure. Secondly, we show how two cues can be fused to train a classifier in a co-training setup for image-based localization while taking into account both unlabeled data and temporal information.

The paper is organized as follows. In section 2, we introduce a supervised approach featuring multiple cue fusion and temporal accumulation that is representative of the state of the art and will serve as a baseline. In section 3, we propose semi-supervised time-aware co-training method. Results are presented in section 4.

*Area Chair: Kiyoharu Aizawa
Acknowledgment: This work is partially supported by a grant from Agence Nationale de la Recherche with reference ANR-09-BLAN-0165-02, within the IMMED project http://immed.labri.fr/

MM'11, November 28–December 1, 2011, Scottsdale, Arizona, USA.

2. SUPERVISED FUSION OF MULTIPLE CUES AND TIME INFORMATION

In this section we review a multiple cue fusion method proposed in [9]. We complement it with a non-linear dimensionality reduction step, which allows the rest of the framework to work on low dimensional features with linear SVM kernel, and temporal accumulation. This method is used as a final stage module in the proposed framework.

2.1 Feature extraction and preparation

For each image of the video we extract two visual features: BOF [8] (hierarchical vocabulary with 1111 words) and very high dimensional but sparse CRFH [5] gist-like features. The intersection kernel [1] is used to evaluate affinities between such distribution based features. Other image kernels such as local feature matching [12] are not considered here because of their higher computational cost, but could also be used.

The extracted visual features are of high dimensionality which poses a problem of over-fitting when the number of training samples is low. We reduce the dimensionality using KPCA [11] to 100 dimensions which decreases the risk of over-fitting. The selected intersection kernel also takes into account the non-linearity of the original feature spaces, yielding a linear embedding space that approximates the original affinities.

Additionally, we noticed that affinity matrix pruning help improving the results. A simple k-Nearest Neighbor pruning decreased harmful influence of distant and non-similar images. Computation of linear kernel from KPCA embeddings ensures positive definite kernel for linear kernel classifier.

In the rest of this paper, classification will be done using linear SVMs applied on the KPCA embeddings.

2.2 SVM-based Discriminative Accumulation

Let $\mathbf{x}$ be a pattern (an embedding vector obtained from the preprocessing step) and $y \in \{-1, 1\}$ the corresponding label in a two-class context. Given a test pattern $\mathbf{x}$, the SVM learns a decision function

$$f(\mathbf{x}) = \sum_{i=1}^{n} y_i \alpha_i k(\mathbf{x}_n, \mathbf{x}) + b$$

where we selected a linear kernel $k(\mathbf{x}_n, \mathbf{x}) = \mathbf{x}_n^T \mathbf{x}$.The patterns$\{\mathbf{x}\}_{i=1}^{n}$ and associated $\{\alpha\}_{i=1}^{n}$ are the training patterns and learned coefficients.

For $C > 2$ classes, we train C functions $\{f_j\}_{j=1}^{C}$ in a one-versus-all setup. For a test pattern $\mathbf{x}_i$ we therefore obtain C decision values or scores $s_j^i = f_j(\mathbf{x}_i), j = 1, \ldots, C$. The class estimation is obtained as

$$\hat{y}_i = \arg \max_{j=1..C} s_j^i$$

The Discriminative Accumulation Scheme (DAS) proposed in [9] improves the performance by fusing the information from two different classifiers in a late fusion approach: the new scores are built by combining linearly the two independent SVM classifier outputs

$$s_{j,DAS}^i = \beta\, s_{j,BOF}^i + (1 - \beta)\, s_{j,CRFH}^i$$

As pointed out by the authors and reference in [9], the accumulation scheme makes the decision more robust compared to the majority vote approach.

2.3 Temporal Accumulation Scheme

Additionally, images from the video that are close in time are likely to belong to the same class. This can be taken into account by using Temporal Accumulation (TA)

$$s_{j,TA}^i = \sum_{\Delta i = -\tau}^{\tau} w(\Delta i) s_j^{i+\Delta i}$$

where $w(\Delta i)$ represents the weight of a temporal window of size $2\tau + 1$. Effectively, large score variation for neighbor images is lessened by this operation of smoothing.

3. SEMI-SUPERVISED TIME-AWARE CO-TRAINING APPROACH

We now extend the previously introduced supervised framework to a semi-supervised approach using the co-training paradigm.

3.1 Co-training Architecture

The idea of self-training [10] consists in supplying the most confident estimations to the labeled set where the procedure can be repeated on the remaining unlabeled patterns. This type of learning can be extended to two visual cues, giving rise to co-training [2] where each single classifier trains another one with the most confident estimates. For a single view, [4] proposed a method which trains two learners by using two different learning algorithms. Tri-training [14] teaches a third classifier the consensus obtained of two other classifiers. The co-training approach is interesting for our application as it brings together the advantages of multi-cue fusion with semi-supervised learning [13].

We now review the co-training algorithm which iteratively learns two SVM classifiers. The method is part of architecture shown in Fig. 1.

At round $t = 0$ two SVM classifiers are learned independently on the training set in a one-against-all setup. Initial estimations are produced on the unlabeled data set. Applying the DAS method on theses two outputs represent a baseline supervised method.

At round $t = n$ the p most confident estimates from each view are selected and appended to the opposite training set. The concerned patterns are then removed from both testing sets and a new pair of classifiers is learned after this feedback loop. The procedure may be repeated until exhaustion of unlabeled patterns. Applying the DAS method on the SVM scores produced by these new classifiers corresponds to what we call the co-training-DAS approach (CO-DAS).

In the experimental section we will consider only one iteration of CO-DAS in order to investigate the gain of the proposed feedback loop compared to other approaches.

The performance of the approach is highly dependant on the selection of the most confident estimates to be used in the feedback loop. Ideally, only correct estimates should be used. Finally, complementary visual cues will allow to learn an enriched model in order to avoid over-fitting. For this task, in the following discussion, we contribute a confidence measure, and introduce the framework incorporating time information which provides more diverse training patterns into the learning loop.

3.2 Selection of confident predictions

The proposed selection scheme exploits the SVM scores to construct a scalar confidence measure $z_i = z(\mathbf{x}_i)$. It is

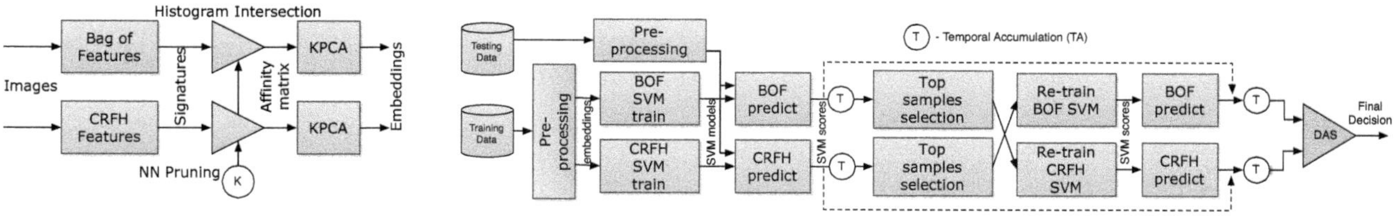

Figure 1: (Left) Pre-processing for embedding computation. (Right) Time-aware co-training workflow

designed to be positive and larger for confident and close to zero for less confident estimates. Our confidence measure z_i is computed in two steps. First the contrast between the best score and the rest is computed

$$z_i^0 = s_{j^*}^i - \sum_{j \neq j^*} s_j^i$$

It is then penalized in case of class overlap

$$z_i = z_i^0 \max\left(0, 1 - \frac{p_i - 1}{C}\right)$$

where $p_i = Card(\{j = 1..C | s_j^i > 0\})$ represents the number of classes for which $\mathbf{x}_i$ has positive scores. In the degenerate case of all positive or negative scores values, we set zero confidence ($z_i \leftarrow 0$).

3.3 Time-aware feedback

Time information can be injected using the Temporal Accumulation Scheme (TA) proposed in section 2.3 prior the final decision. The main contribution of this paper shows that temporal information should be used in the co-training loop. It is done by applying TA on the scores in the inner feedback loop, thus defining a new time-aware co-training approach. One of the main advantages is that TA is not a mere post-processing, but can help bringing new patterns that are visually different from the training samples, provided they are temporally close to confident samples. More diversity is introduced, thus yielding models that generalize better. The temporal window should not be selected too large, in order to avoid accumulating over the temporal boundaries between classes. The experiments presented in the next section confirm the interest of this approach.

4. EXPERIMENTAL PERFORMANCES

In this section we report the performances obtained on public real-world data to evaluate the gain brought by the proposed approach.

4.1 Considered approaches

All approaches compared in this section can defined from a set of building blocks that have been defined previously.

We define three main categories. In each of them the TA variant appends Temporal Accumulation as a post-processing before taking final decision on the class. For the sake of readability, only the DAS decision approach is considered here, as it provides consistently better results than classifying the BOF or CRFH features separately.

- DAS, TA-DAS: supervised approaches;
- CO-DAS, CO-TA-DAS: semi-supervised approaches; the confidence values used in co-training are based on the raw scores from the individual classifiers;
- TA-CO-DAS, TA-CO-TA-DAS: semi-supervised time-aware approaches; the confidence values used in co-training are based on temporally accumulated scores.

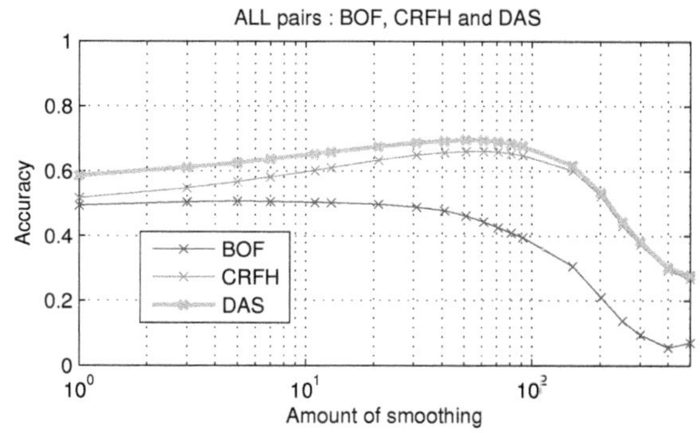

Figure 2: Effect of both multi-cue fusion and temporal accumulation on supervised classifier

4.2 Data corpus

In our experiments we used the IDOL2 video database [6] which is representative of the appearance of a camera moved across an indoor environment. It includes visual variabilities due to different lighting conditions (sunny, cloudy, night) and natural change of scene due to human activities over time. We used the part called "minnie", which contains 12 individual sequences captured at 5 fps, for a total duration of 38 minutes, representing repeated visits through 5 different rooms at various times and light conditions. More details on this corpus can be found in [6].

All possible pairs of sequences have been tested, using one sequence for training and one for testing. 12 pairs represent same light conditions with close in time recording, 48 pairs represent different light conditions with several weeks between the recording. Average performances are considered.

4.3 Effect of temporal smoothing

In Fig. 2 the effect of both multi-cue fusion using DAS and Temporal Accumulation is shown.

The results show that the TA scheme yields an improvement over the DAS baseline by around 10% where no smoothing corresponds to the leftmost value (temporal window of 1 sample). This is true in cases of different levels of annotations,for different light conditions and sequence capture times. The optimal values is around 50 frames which is not surprising if we take into account the fact that the robot was constantly moving and did not spend more than 10 seconds in the same room. Larger temporal window may result in severe misclassifications around class boundaries. For subsequent tests we selected a temporal window of 50 frames.

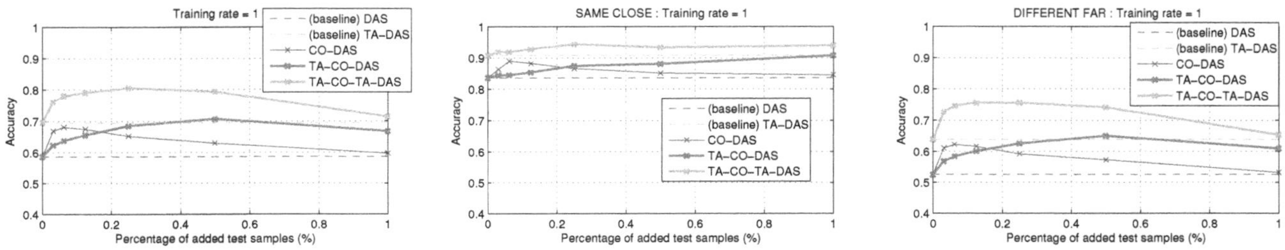

Figure 3: Performance of co-training and its interaction with temporal accumulation schemes.

4.4 Effect of co-training

In Fig. 3 the performance of the proposed approach is shown, as well as a detailed comparison to other approaches including temporal information. The figure shows a summary of average performance for all possible sequence pairs (a), as well as the average performance for the most extreme cases: same light, close in time sequence pairs (b) and different light, far in time sequence pairs (c). In each summary the baseline DAS scheme is compared to the TA-DAS baseline and three extended methods involving co-training, temporal accumulation and DAS scheme in different setups. We plot the average performance for each method as a function of the amount of training samples used for the co-training feedback loop.

First, we can note strikingly different performances due to different light conditions and complexity of the scenes caused by a difference in time for certain sequence pairs. Nevertheless, the relative ranking of the studied approaches remains the same in both extreme cases, which is why we will discuss only the global average.

Indeed, the TA-CO-DAS and TA-CO-TA-DAS methods show a consistent improvement compared to their respective baselines (DAS and TA-DAS) not using co-training.

It is of interest to note that co-training without any temporal information (CO-DAS) improves on its baseline, reaching almost the level of TA-DAS. Nevertheless, temporal information is best used both in the co-training loop and at post-processing step yielding TA-CO-TA-DAS method. This yields the best performances, showing the ability of the proposed method to include all considered sources of information.

5. CONCLUSION

In this paper, we have presented a semi-supervised approach within the co-training framework for video lifelog indexing which profits both from discriminative kernel learning methods and from the complementarity of two visual features integrated in a time-aware semi-supervised framework.

The proposed approach, by selecting the most reliable samples for the iterative co-training steps, allows us to adapt the model initially trained to the characteristics of the unlabelled data, thus improving the performances. Based on our experiments on the IDOL2 database, the improvement in performance is larger when time information is taken into account, both during co-training feedback and as a post-processing. This confirms that the semi-supervised closed-loop brings relevant information, that could not be extracted in the supervised approach, and that the use of time information is a central part of this improvement.

6. REFERENCES

[1] A. Barla, F. Odone, and A. Verri. Histogram Intersection Kernel for Image Classification. *Int. Conf. on Image Processing (ICIP)*, 2003.

[2] A. Blum and T. Mitchell. Combining Labeled and Unlabeled Data with Co-Training. *Int. Conf. on Learning Theory (COLT)*, 1998.

[3] V. Dovgalecs, R Mégret, H. Wannous, and Y. Berthoumieu. Semi-Supervised Learning for Location Recognition from Wearable Video. *Content-Based Multimedia Indexing (CBMI)*, 2010.

[4] S. Goldman and Y. Zhou. Enhancing Supervised Learning with Unlabeled Data. *Int. Conf. on Machine Learning (ICML)*, 2000.

[5] O. Linde and T. Lindeberg. Object Recognition using Composed Receptive Field Histograms of Higher Dimensionality. *Int. Conf. on Pattern Recognition (ICPR)*, 2004.

[6] J. Luo, A. Pronobis, B. Caputo, and P. Jensfelt. The KTH-IDOL2 Database. Technical report, Kungliga Tekniska Hoegskolan, CVAP/CAS, 2006.

[7] R. Mégret, V. Dovgalecs, H. Wannous, S. Karaman, J. Benois-Pineau, E. El Khory, J. Pinquier, P. Joly, R. André-Obrecht, Y. Gaëstel, and J.-F. Dartigues. The IMMED Project: Wearable Video Monitoring of People with Age Dementia. *ACM Multimedia*, 2010.

[8] D. Nister and H. Stewenius. Scalable Recognition with a Vocabulary Tree. *Conf. on Computer Vision and Pattern Recognition (CVPR)*, 2006.

[9] A. Pronobis and B. Caputo. Confidence-Based Cue Integration for Visual Place Recognition. *Int. Conf. on Intelligent Robots and Systems (IROS)*, 2007.

[10] C. Rosenberg, M. Hebert, and H. Schneiderman. Semi-Supervised Self-Training of Object Detection Models. *7th IEEE Workshop on Applications of Computer Vision (WACV)*, 2005.

[11] A. J. Smola, B. Scholkopf, and K.-R. Muller. Nonlinear Component Analysis as a Kernel Eigenvalue Problem. *Neural computation*, 10(6):1299–1319, 1998.

[12] C. Valgren and A. J. Lilienthal. SIFT, SURF & Seasons: Appearance-Based Long-Term Localization in Outdoor Environments. *Robotics and Autonomous Systems*, 58(2):149–156, 2010.

[13] Z. H. Zhou. When Semi-Supervised Learning meets Ensemble Learning. *Workshop on Multiple Classifier Systems (MCS)*, 2009.

[14] Z. H. Zhou and M. Li. Tri-training : Exploiting Unlabelled Data using Three Classifiers. *IEEE Trans. on KDE*, 17(11):1529–1541, 2005.

Automatic Sentence Generation from Images *

Yoshitaka Ushiku
Grad. School of Information Science and Technology
The University of Tokyo
ushiku@isi.imi.i.u-tokyo.ac.jp

Tatsuya Harada
Grad. School of Information Science and Technology
The University of Tokyo / JST PRESTO
harada@isi.imi.i.u-tokyo.ac.jp

Yasuo Kuniyoshi
Grad. School of Information Science and Technology
The University of Tokyo
kuniyosh@isi.imi.i.u-tokyo.ac.jp

ABSTRACT

For the overwhelming amounts of multimedia used on the Web, methods of *search* and *understanding* with sentences are necessary. Representing the contents not only using labels but also using sentences including labels' relations enables users to *search* with a story and to *understand* multimedia deeply. However, few existing works describe such sentences because obtaining objects' relations and grammar is difficult. We specifically examine captions of images that are similar to an input image. They are expected to explain the input image to some degree. Therefore, we propose a novel approach to generate a sentential caption for the input image by summarizing those captions. Our experiment using a dataset consisting of images and text demonstrates that the proposed method can generate sentential captions.

Categories and Subject Descriptors

I.2.10 [**Artificial Intelligence**]: Vision and Scene Understanding

General Terms

Algorithms, Theory, Experimentation

Keywords

Similarity measure, Probabilistic canonical correlation analysis, Multi-stack decoding

1. INTRODUCTION

Multimedia, such as images and videos, are increasing explosively. For efficient usage, technologies with which users can *search* and *understand* each datum are required. Although many methods can be used for *search* and *understanding* the form of multimedia (e.g., similar image retrieval and video summarization), technologies that use natural language for *search* and *understanding* are also studied widely.

*Area chair: Qi Tian

MM'11, November 28–December 1, 2011, Scottsdale, Arizona, USA.

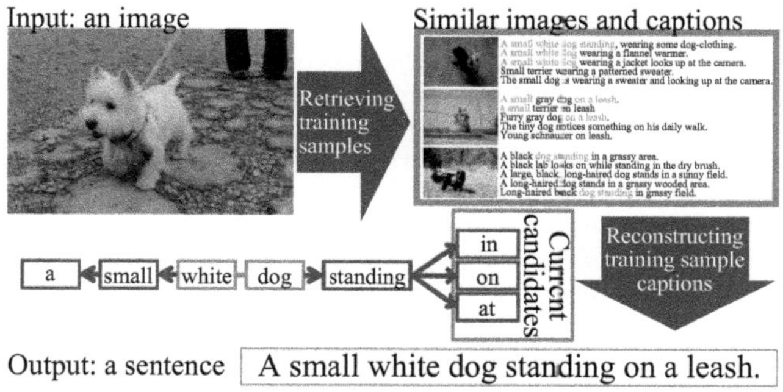

Figure 1: Methodology overview.

To represent multimedia with natural language, output as a sentential caption that includes each relation is more useful than output with independent labels. Moreover, when enabling search by representing multimedia with natural language, sentential representation can realize flexible query, by which each relation includes isolated words: to *understand* and *search* multimedia, output in a sentence is useful.

Captioning images is very difficult because estimating not only objects of images but also objects' relations and correct grammar is required. For example, one-to-one relations of a thousand objects run into the millions. In existing research of sentence outputs from a video, character recognition of subtitles, and speech recognition of conversation have been used instead of descriptions of the visual contents.

Images are explained sententially in [2], which describes collection of labeled pairs of an image and a caption. A suitable caption is sought through label estimation of an input image. Because labels are necessary, however, the cost for data collection is large. To caption general images, more training samples must be used. In image recognition, usage of a vast quantity of data from the Web can yield good results [14]. Although images and captions are collectable from the Web, labels cannot be extracted automatically.

In this paper, we developed an algorithm to generate sentential captions for general images using data which consist of images and texts only. To generate captions, we devote attention to images, the contents of which resemble the contents of an inputted image. In captions accompanying these similar images, some representations also explain the inputted image. Not only the objects in an image but the relations among them and grammatical knowledge are already embedded there. If such representations are extracted and if a sentence is reconstructed, then the contents of the image can be explainable both grammatically and correctly. Therefore we propose an approach that reconstructs the training sample captions of images that resemble an inputted image.

2. SENTENTIAL CAPTION GENERATION

In this section, we present the details of the proposed approach. Sec. 2.1 describes similarity learning used to search for similar training samples, and Sec. 2.2 describes caption generation for an input image from the retrieved captions.

2.1 Retrieving training samples

Generally, a gap separates the similarity of image appearance and the similarity of contents. To search for training samples with contents resembling the input image from large data, scalable similarity learning must be done. Ushiku et al. [11] proposed the improvement of the gap by combining the similarity of an image and the similarity of a text. This method is an extension of the image annotation method Canonical Contextual Distance (CCD) [4] to images and texts. The algorithm can calculate the similarity between images as a distance of that context. Then we can search more precisely than when using the similarity of visual appearance. Moreover, the method is scalable because this similarity learning is independent of a data number.

We denote an image/text feature as $\boldsymbol{x}$ or $\boldsymbol{y}$, and the latent variable as $\boldsymbol{z}$. It is realized that $\boldsymbol{x}$ or $\boldsymbol{y}$ has appeared as a stochastic representation of an image or a text from $\boldsymbol{z}$ based on a certain contents. Then, a similar image retrieval turns into a nearest neighbor approach using the distance between probability distributions $p(\boldsymbol{z}|\boldsymbol{x})$ from an input image and $p(\boldsymbol{z}|\boldsymbol{x},\boldsymbol{y})$ from the training sample pair of an image and a text. These distributions are expressed as a normal distribution as $\boldsymbol{z}|\boldsymbol{x},\boldsymbol{y} \sim \mathcal{N}(\boldsymbol{\mu}_{xy}, \Phi_{xy})$ and $\boldsymbol{z}|\boldsymbol{x} \sim \mathcal{N}(\boldsymbol{\mu}_x, \Phi_x)$. For an exponential family such as a normal distribution, Kullback–Leibler Divergence (KLD) is used as a pseudo-distance. We denote i.i.d. $p(\boldsymbol{z}|\boldsymbol{x})$ with mean $\boldsymbol{\mu}_x$ and with variance Φ_x, and $p(\boldsymbol{z}|\boldsymbol{x},\boldsymbol{y})$ with mean $\boldsymbol{\mu}_{xy}$ and variance Φ_{xy}. Then CCD is defined by excepting constant terms from KLD from an input image $\boldsymbol{x}_q$ to a training sample $\{\boldsymbol{x}_t, \boldsymbol{y}_t\}$ as

$$\mathrm{CCD}(\boldsymbol{x}_t, \boldsymbol{y}_t|\boldsymbol{x}_q) = \left\|\Phi_{xy}^{-\frac{1}{2}}(\boldsymbol{\mu}_x - \boldsymbol{\mu}_{xy})\right\|^2. \quad (1)$$

When we define latent variables $\boldsymbol{r}_t$ for a training sample and $\boldsymbol{r}_q$ for the input image, this is equivalent to a neighbor search using Euclidean distance with $\boldsymbol{r}$ defined as

$$\boldsymbol{r}_t = \Phi_{xw}^{-\frac{1}{2}}\boldsymbol{\mu}_{xy}, \boldsymbol{r}_q = \Phi_x^{-\frac{1}{2}}\boldsymbol{\mu}_x. \quad (2)$$

As described above, it is reduced to the estimation of $\boldsymbol{\mu}_{xy}$, $\boldsymbol{\mu}_x$ and Φ_{xy}. If maximum likelihood estimation is performed with training samples, then it is derived as

$$\boldsymbol{\mu}_x = M_x^T A^T(\boldsymbol{x} - \bar{\boldsymbol{x}}), \Phi_x = I - M_x M_x^T, \quad (3)$$

$$\boldsymbol{\mu}_{xy} = \begin{pmatrix} M_x \\ M_y \end{pmatrix}^T \begin{pmatrix} (I-\Lambda^2)^{-1} & -(I-\Lambda^2)^{-1}\Lambda \\ -(I-\Lambda^2)^{-1}\Lambda & (I-\Lambda^2)^{-1} \end{pmatrix} \begin{pmatrix} A^T(\boldsymbol{x}-\bar{\boldsymbol{x}}) \\ B^T(\boldsymbol{y}-\bar{\boldsymbol{y}}) \end{pmatrix}, \quad (4)$$

$$\Phi_{xy} = I - \begin{pmatrix} M_x \\ M_y \end{pmatrix}^T \begin{pmatrix} (I-\Lambda^2)^{-1} & -(I-\Lambda^2)^{-1}\Lambda \\ -(I-\Lambda^2)^{-1}\Lambda & (I-\Lambda^2)^{-1} \end{pmatrix} \begin{pmatrix} M_x \\ M_y \end{pmatrix}, \quad (5)$$

where $\bar{\boldsymbol{x}}$ and $\bar{\boldsymbol{y}}$ are feature averages, and where M_x and M_y are arbitrary matrices satisfying $M_x M_y^T = \Lambda$ and for which the spectrum norm of each matrix is less than 1. Here we denote them with $0 < \beta < 1$ as $M_x = \Lambda^\beta$ and $M_y = \Lambda^{1-\beta}$, which is exactly like probabilistic canonical correlation analysis (pCCA): a probabilistic interpretation of canonical correlation analysis (CCA). In fact, CCA maximizes the correlation between canonical variables $\boldsymbol{s} = A^T(\boldsymbol{x} - \bar{\boldsymbol{x}})$ and $\boldsymbol{t} = B^T(\boldsymbol{y} - \bar{\boldsymbol{y}})$. These are derived from the following generalized eigenvalue problem: $R_{XY}R_Y^{-1}R_{YX}A = R_X A\Lambda^2$, $R_{YX}R_X^{-1}R_{XY}B = R_Y B\Lambda^2$, where Λ^2 is a diagonal matrix of eigenvalues, $R_X = \sum_{i=1}^n(\boldsymbol{x}_i - \bar{\boldsymbol{x}})(\boldsymbol{x}_i - \bar{\boldsymbol{x}})^T$, $R_Y = \sum_{i=1}^n(\boldsymbol{y}_i - \bar{\boldsymbol{y}})(\boldsymbol{y}_i - \bar{\boldsymbol{y}})^T$, and $R_{XY} = \sum_{i=1}^n(\boldsymbol{x}_i - \bar{\boldsymbol{x}})(\boldsymbol{y}_i - \bar{\boldsymbol{y}})^T = R_{YX}^T$.

2.2 Reconstructing training sample captions

We define the training sample pair $\boldsymbol{s}_i$ of an image $\boldsymbol{x}_i$ and a caption $\boldsymbol{y}_i$, caption set of $\boldsymbol{s}_i$ as $\mathcal{W}_i$, and each caption as $\boldsymbol{w} = w_1^l = (w_1 w_2 \dots w_l)$, where l is the length and w_i represents the i-th word. Here, $\boldsymbol{s}_i$ is obtained using a neighborhood search with CCD described in the preceding section. Some phrases (word sequences) that explain the input image's own objects and those relations correctly and grammatically are expected in $\mathcal{W}_i$.

We generate captions of desired length l_{tar} to the input image. The scores of candidate captions are computed from the input image; then the caption having the highest score is output. Our objectives are 1) searching for explanatory phrases and 2) captioning for the desired length. Consequently, two feature functions are defined for each purpose. The first is a score $\phi(p_{hr}|\boldsymbol{x}_q)$ when phrase p_{hr} is selected for the input image $\boldsymbol{x}_q$. The second is a score for the current sentence length. Although other scores such as those of a grammar model with n-gram are usable, here we investigate the captioning ability accomplished solely by reconstruction of training sample captions.

We define the probability of retrieving $\boldsymbol{s}_i$ from an input image $\boldsymbol{x}_q$ as $p(\boldsymbol{s}_i|\boldsymbol{x}_q)$, and define the probability of selecting a phrase p_{hr} from the pair $\boldsymbol{x}_q$ as $p(p_{hr}|\boldsymbol{s}_i)$. The phrase score is defined as a logarithm with those probabilities as

$$\phi(p_{hr}|\boldsymbol{x}_q) = \left(1 - \frac{o(p_{hr})}{o_{max}(p_{hr})}\right)\log\left(\sum_i p(p_{hr}|\boldsymbol{s}_i)p(\boldsymbol{s}_i|\boldsymbol{x}_q)\right), \quad (6)$$

where $o_{max}(p_{hr})$ is the maximum occurrence of p_{hr} in one sentence, and $o(p_{hr})$ is the occurrence of p_{hr} in the currently generating sentence. The coefficient of the logarithm has a control for a specific dominant phrase so as not to produce meaningless repetition. The probability $p(\boldsymbol{s}_i|\boldsymbol{x}_q)$ of selecting a pair $\boldsymbol{s}_i$ is retrieved from the input image $\boldsymbol{x}_q$ is defined as,

$$p(\boldsymbol{s}_i|\boldsymbol{x}_q) = \frac{\exp(-\mathrm{CCD}(\boldsymbol{s}_i|\boldsymbol{x}_q))}{\sum_i \exp(-\mathrm{CCD}(\boldsymbol{s}_i|\boldsymbol{x}_q))}. \quad (7)$$

The probability $p(p_{hr}|\boldsymbol{s}_i)$ of selecting p_{hr} from each pair $\boldsymbol{s}_i$ is defined using tf-idf [10], the product of the frequency of each term in a document and the inverse of the appearance frequency of that term in all documents, as follows.

$$p(p_{hr}|\boldsymbol{s}_i) = \frac{\text{tf-idf}(p_{hr})}{\sum_{p_{hr}\in\mathcal{W}_i}\text{tf-idf}(p_{hr})}. \quad (8)$$

Therein, Tf-idf represents how well each word distinguishes the text.

We denote the length score as a logarithm of the probability of current length $l \sim \mathcal{N}(l_{tar}, \sigma)$. Qualitatively, σ represents the tolerance level of caption length. In this paper, we define that $l_{tar} = 12$ and $\sigma = 1$.

Because generable captions increase exponentially with vocabularies, comparison of all captions is difficult. Consequently, output is determined with graph search. In a typical approach [6] to statistical machine translation, scores are first calculated using various feature functions from both languages. Then the translations are generated to maximize the sum of the scores using a graph search such as a multi-stack beam search.

Beam searching saves some high rank candidate sentences in one stack. The stack size can adjust the accuracy of graph search and the computational complexity. In a multi-stack beam search, a stack is divided according to the translated word amounts in the input sentence. The highest-ranked sentence in the last stack is output. In this paper, however, the input not as a sentence but as an image causes problems.

First, because there is nothing equivalent to word position correspondence of an input sentence and a translation, left-to-right expansion is impossible. Therefore, we take an approach to expand a sentence to both sides. We consider the l_s words' phrase which has the highest probability of explaining the input image as a seed. Then we expand a caption to both sides.

As another problem, because the judgment of *untranslated* portion of an image is difficult, neither the end of the translation and division of the stack based on the translated words' length is possible. Therefore, we divide a stack based on the sentence being generated. An index on which can be ended is given to the candidate captions in each stack. In the caption set $\mathcal{W}$, EDGE of Sentence (EOS) is added beforehand to the head and end of each caption. When the phrase that is connectable to EOS exists in $\mathcal{W}$, it is unrelated with the score when connected with EOS at the time, but the index and the score when connected to the EOS are memorized. When the expansion is finished, the word sequence that is inserted by EOS will be output as

$$\boldsymbol{w} = \underset{\boldsymbol{w}=(w_{i_s} w_{i_s+1} \cdots w_{i_e-1} w_{i_e})}{\arg\max} \sum_k \phi_k(w_{i_s}^{i_e} | \boldsymbol{x}_q), \quad (9)$$

where i is an index connectable to EOS. i_e and i_s are found in left-to-right and right-to-left expansion respectively.

3. EXPERIMENTAL EVALUATION

For the experiment, PASCAL Sentence [2] dataset are used. This dataset has 20 categories; each category has 50 images. Each image has about five captions of around 10 words each. 45 pairs of an image and a text per category are chosen as training samples. Training samples are prepared at random five times, and all evaluations are averaged.

As image features, the use of shape information and texture information of an image are required. Consequently, HLAC [5], Gist [8], and LBP [7] are adopted for texture information, and SIFT [3] is adopted for shape information. Using SIFT, global features are obtained using Locality-constrained Linear Coding (LLC) [13], which expresses a local descriptor by two or more neighbor code books. In addition, texture information differs by the color space. Therefore, each global feature is extracted from the image expressed by each color space (gray scale, RGB, Transformed color, Opponent color, C-invariant color) used in [12].

As a text feature, use of word/phrase usage information in each caption is required. In detail, the word/phrase which appeared in the whole captions is expressed with one dimension of vector space model, and a characteristic word/phrase of each caption is weighted by tf-idf. In this research, features of seven kinds with tf-idf to words/phrases, which is a 2–7 word sequence, are used.

Furthermore kernel principal component analysis (KPCA) with a partial sample is performed for each feature referencing to [4] to embed nonlinear metric into Euclidean space keeping scalability. We employ a string kernel as a structure kernel for text, L1/L2, χ^2, Bhattacharya, Jeffrey, Hellinger, and histogram intersection kernel as distance kernels.

In [2], image captions themselves are manually evaluated, which makes fair comparison difficult. Therefore, we investigate automatic evaluation with which matching to the reference given to the input image in the dataset is quantified. Captions are evaluated with match of n-gram using BiLingual Evaluation Understudy (BLEU) [9] and NIST [1].

The CCD parameter used to search for a training sample is optimized by maximizing BLEU/NIST of the caption which originally accompanied the input image and the retrieved caption. Concurrently, Mean Average Precision (MAP) is also used as a typical retrieval evaluation This calculates the match rate of the category of an input image and the retrieved sample. However, this evaluation can not be calculated without the category label to images and captions. For caption generation from images and captions only, optimization without MAP, which needs labels, is desirable.

Table 1: Evaluation of training sample retrieval.

Image feature	Image feature only			CCD		
	MAP	NIST	BLEU	MAP	NIST	BLEU
SIFT	0.11	0.45	0.0066	0.14	0.49	0.014
HLAC	0.080	0.45	0.0064	0.13	0.47	0.012
Gist	0.081	0.45	0.0065	0.14	0.47	0.013
LBP	0.084	0.45	0.0068	0.13	0.49	0.012

3.1 Evaluation of training sample retrieval

The accuracy with CCD depends on the kernel and reduced dimensions with KPCA, β and reduced dimensions with pCCA, as well as the kind of feature. We optimized them by maximizing evaluation scores with image features only, and with CCD, respectively. Maximized evaluation scores for each image feature are shown in Table 1.

The training samples are retrieved with better accuracy than when using each feature independently. *Hereinafter, we concatenate image features using each best parameter.*

3.2 Evaluation and discussion of captions

Examples of images are presented on the left side of Fig.2. Bad examples are shown on the right of Fig.2. Automatic evaluation was compared with evaluation by hands in advance of evaluating the proposed method. Six captions output to each image are shown to 10 subjects. The order of captions is random. For that reason, subjects cannot understand which system output which caption. Each caption is evaluated using a five-level rating according to how well it explains the image. The evaluations are standardized. The correlations between each of BLEU and NIST and hand evaluation are 0.63 and 0.82, respectively, showing that NIST especially is appropriate for evaluation of captions.

As described in this paper, three scores are used in the parameter optimization for CCD. The evaluation of generated captions with parameters for each score and using each length phrase is shown in Fig.3. Results show the best score when CCD parameters is determined using NIST, showing that our method is useful with images and texts only.

Moreover, when using a phrase of a certain length independently, a resultant short phrase is better. Therefore, scores obtained when using phrases of two kinds, of which lengths differ, and two or more lengths sequentially from short length are investigated. The results are shown respec-

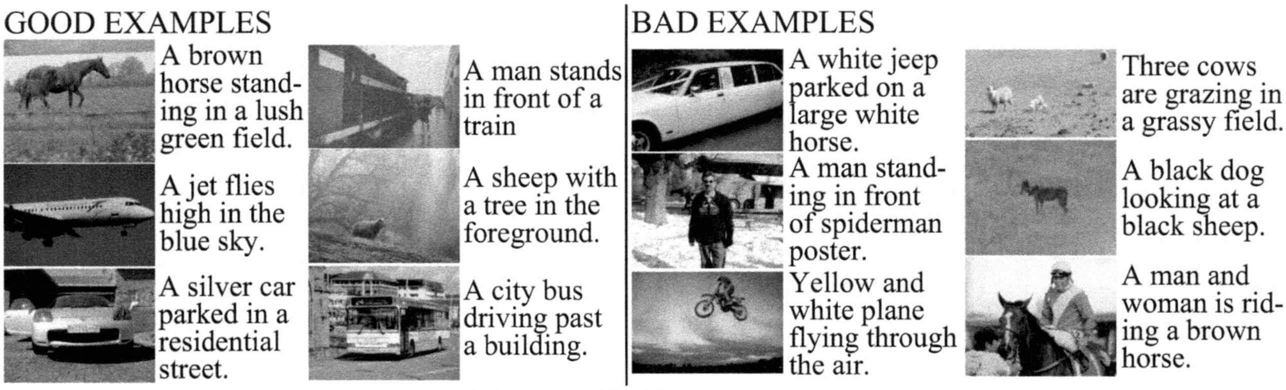

Figure 2: Caption examples.

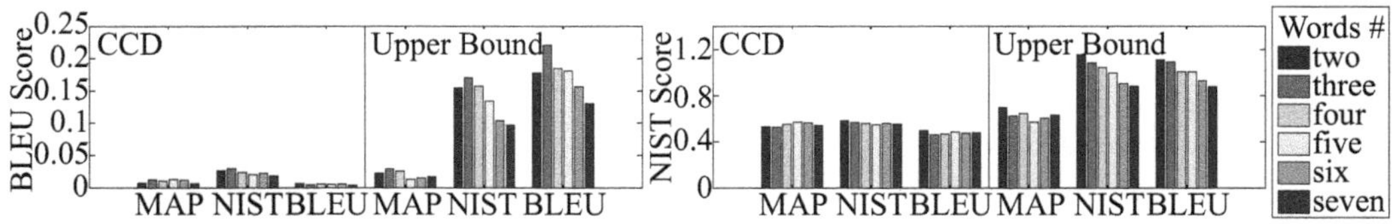

Figure 3: Score comparison. "Upper Bound" means that captions are generated from retrieved samples with ideal similarity.

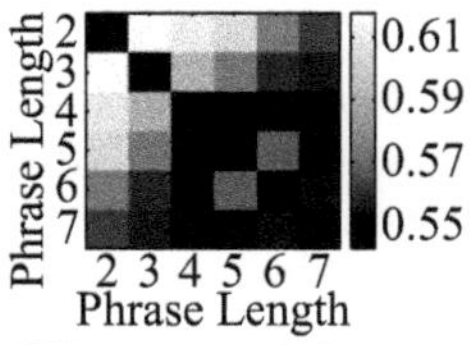

Figure 4: Phrase combinations.

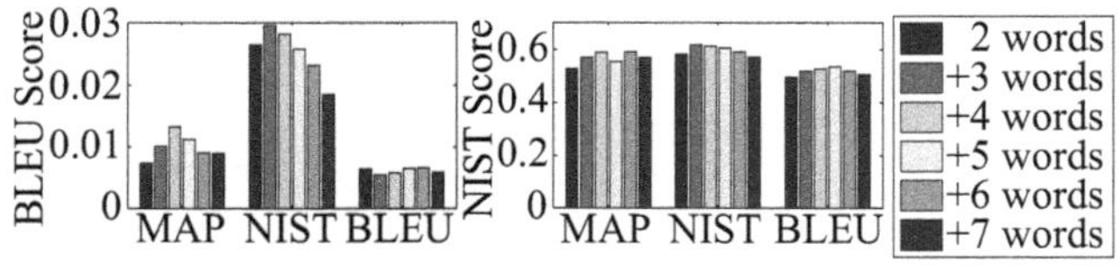

Figure 5: NIST scores related to phrase combinations.

tively in Fig.4 and Fig.5. Generally, when using the two-word and three-word phrases, generated captions have the best score. When using longer phrases, an almost identical caption to the training sample captions is generated, and it comes to describe different contents from those of the input image. As datasets become larger, longer phrases will increase rapidly. The better result obtained with the short phrase shows the best applicability to large-scale data.

4. CONCLUSION

In this paper, we proposed an approach that is useful to generate sentential captions of images for efficient understanding and searching for increasing images. Using the proposed method, captions are generated only from images and texts, whereas the existing caption generation method requires manual labeling. We devote attention to the captions of the training samples. The objects are assumed to be handled by the image, its relations, and grammatical knowledge that is embedded in the phrases of such captions. Then the image captions are generated by putting phrases together. Results of the experiment verified that the proposed method can explain images sententially. Evaluation showed a correlation between its results and those of manual evaluation.

Experimental results demonstrate that the caption accuracy is sensitive to the retrieval precision of training samples. Future work will be undertaken to make this retrieval precision higher in a scalable range, incorporating the use of other models such as n-grams for sentence generation. Regarding future prospects, this work creates a foothold for captioning of videos containing other information modalities.

5. REFERENCES

[1] G. Doddington. Automatic evaluation of machine translation quality using n-gram co-occurrence statistics. In *HLT*, pages 138–145, 2002.

[2] A. Farhadi, M. Hejrati, M. A. Sadeghi, P. Young, C. Rashtchian, J. Hockenmaier, and D. Forsyth. Every picture tells a story: Generating sentences from images. In *ECCV*, pages 15–28, 2010.

[3] D. G. Lowe. Distinctive image features from scale-invariant keypoints. *IJCV*, 60(2):91–110, 2004.

[4] H. Nakayama, T. Harada, and Y. Kuniyoshi. Evaluation of dimensionality reduction methods for image auto-annotation. In *BMVC*, pages 94.1–94.12, 2010.

[5] O. Nobuyuki and T. Kurita. A new scheme for practical flexible and intelligent vision systems. In *IAPR Workshop on Computer Vision*, pages 431–435, 1988.

[6] F. J. Och and H. Ney. Discriminative training and maximum entropy models for statistical machine translation. In *ACL*, pages 295–302, 2002.

[7] T. Ojala, M. Pietikäinen, and D. Harwood. A comparative study of texture measures with classification based on feature distributions. *Pattern Recognition*, 29(1):51–59, 1996.

[8] A. Oliva and A. Torralba. Modeling the shape of the scene : A holistic representation of the spatial envelope. *IJCV*, 42(3):145–175, 2001.

[9] K. Papineni, S. Roukos, T. Ward, and W.-J. Zhu. Bleu: a method for automatic evaluation of machine translation. In *ACL*, number July, pages 311–318, 2002.

[10] G. Salton and C. S. Yang. On the specification of term values in automatic indexing. *Journal of documentation*, 29(4):351–372, 1973.

[11] Y. Ushiku, T. Harada, and Y. Kuniyoshi. Improving image similarity measures for image browsing and retrieval through latent space learning between images and long texts. In *ICIP*, pages 2365–2368, 2010.

[12] K. E. A. van De Sande, T. Gevers, and C. G. M. Snoek. Evaluating color descriptors for object and scene recognition. *PAMI*, 32(9):1582–96, 2010.

[13] J. Wang, J. Yang, K. Yu, F. Lv, T. Huang, and Y. Gong. Locality-constrained linear coding for image classification. In *CVPR*, pages 3360–3367, 2010.

[14] X.-J. Wang, L. Zhang, M. Liu, Y. Li, and W.-Y. Ma. Arista - image search to annotation on billions of web photos. In *CVPR*, pages 2987–2994, 2010.

Audio-Visual Fusion Using Bayesian Model Combination for Web Video Retrieval *

Vasant Manohar, Stavros Tsakalidis, Pradeep Natarajan, Rohit Prasad, and Prem Natarajan
Speech, Language, and Multimedia Business Unit
Raytheon BBN Technologies
10 Moulton Street, Cambridge, MA 02138
{vmanohar, stavros, pradeepn, rprasad, pnataraj}@bbn.com

ABSTRACT

Combining features from multiple, heterogeneous, audio visual sources can significantly improve retrieval performance in consumer domain videos. However, such videos often contain unrelated overlaid audio content, or have significant camera motion to reliably extract visual features. We present an approach, which overcomes errors in individual feature streams by combining classifiers trained on multiple, heterogeneous feature streams using Bayesian model combination (BAYCOM). We demonstrate our method, by combining low-level audio and visual features, for classification of a large 200 hour web video corpus. The combined models outperform any of the individual features by 10%. Further, BAYCOM consistently outperforms traditional early and late fusion methods.

Categories and Subject Descriptors

I.4.9 [**Computing Methodologies**]: IMAGE PROCESSING AND COMPUTER VISION—*Applications*

General Terms

Algorithms, Experimentation

Keywords

Bayesian Model Combination, Audio-Visual Fusion, Web Video Retrieval

1. INTRODUCTION

Ability to efficiently represent and effectively exploit content from multiple audio-visual feature streams is crucial for search and retrieval from large video databases. The large volume of user-generated videos uploaded daily on websites, like YouTube, has generated considerable interest in developing such capabilities. However, progress has been limited due to the difficult challenges created by the unstructured nature of such videos. The large variations in lighting, viewpoints, and camera motion in such videos complicate the processing of the visual stream. On the other hand, the accompanying audio track's feature stream has lower dimensionality and can provide complementary information to the visual stream. However, in web videos the audio track is frequently quite noisy and often has unrelated content overlaid on the video.

Thus, classifiers and concept detectors trained on feature streams from different modalities are susceptible to large errors. Techniques that are robust to such errors in the individual streams and that can effectively combine their output have attracted significant interest. Early fusion of audio-visual feature vectors by concatenation as well as late fusion by combining the output of classifiers trained on individual feature streams were compared in [15]. Techniques for determining the optimal combination of multimodal information were proposed in [17] including gradient-descent linear fusion and super-kernel nonlinear fusion. Several statistical multi-modal fusion techniques were evaluated in [3], while The MediaMill semantic video search engine was presented in [14]. These approaches work by extracting low-level audio and visual features, and then combining them at the feature or the hypothesis levels. In contrast, a novel short term audio-visual atom (S-AVA) representation was proposed in [8] that associates a short-term region track with regional visual features and background audio features.

In addition to the challenges involved in combining multiple, error prone classifiers, there are also several system level difficulties while processing large multimedia corpora. Bag-of-words techniques using low-level visual features have found significant success in image and video classification [4, 9, 2, 5]. Such approaches represent each image in a video using hundreds of multi-dimensional vectors creating overwhelming storage and processing requirements. Some attempts have been made to address this in recent literature [7, 9, 2] by learning compact mid-level features. However, even fundamental tasks like learning a representative codebook remains a challenge.

In this paper, we evaluate several techniques for combining the audio-visual features for type classification on a large web video corpus with ≈200 hours of data. We present our video processing module in Section 2, audio processing in Section 3, codebook learning in Section 4, model combination in Section 5, experimental results in Section 6, and conclude in Section 7.

*Area chair: Bernard Merialdo

2. VIDEO PROCESSING

Our module for processing the visual stream consists of two stages: low-level feature extraction and compact mid-level feature extraction.

2.1 Low-level Feature Extraction

Bag-of-words approaches (e.g. [4, 6, 9, 5]) based on interest point features like SIFT, SURF, etc., have had significant success in computer vision. Here, these methods first identify salient points in an image and then extract local gradient information to transform an image into a set of feature vectors. In our work we tested the performance of SIFT [10], SURF [1], and D-SIFT [2] features.

SIFT: These features are among the most widely used in vision and work by first detecting interest points at different scales using a difference of Gaussians (DoG) approach and then extracting a 128 dimensional feature descriptor at each point to capture local image gradients. These descriptors are scale invariant and robust to affine distortion.

SURF: The speeded-up robust features (SURF) are similar in principle to SIFT, but are several times faster to extract. They are extracted using sums of 2D Haar Wavelet response and are potentially more robust to image transformations compared to SIFT.

D-SIFT: This is a dense version of SIFT where, instead of detecting interest points, the 128-dimensional feature vectors are extracted by uniformly sampling over the image. D-SIFT typically generates 3× the number of points generated by SIFT and has been shown to outperform SIFT for image classification [2].

2.2 Mid-Level Spatio Temporal Features

The interest point approaches discussed so far typically extract hundreds of points in each frame of the video, creating overwhelming storage requirements. For example, storing an average of 200 SIFT interest points/frame would require 880MB of storage space for a 5 minute video clip at 30fps on a machine using 4 bytes per floating point number. It is not scalable to use such large amounts of data for downstream processing, including codebook learning, classifier training, and classification. To address this, we compress the video features by successively clustering raw features into a hierarchy of spatio-temporal volumes (STVs). We first split the video into shots based on the color histogram difference between successive frames [18]. Next, we partition the shot volume into STVs and cluster all the raw interest point features that lie within a given STV using weighted *k-means*. The resulting centroids are again clustered based on a coarser STV partitioning at the next level and so on. This successive clustering generates a single STV hierarchy for each shot. Based on empirical testing, we found the STV hierarchy illustrated in Figure 1 to have the best performance.

3. AUDIO PROCESSING

To represent the audio content, we first transform the raw audio into a 45 dimensional feature stream using the following steps. Features were extracted from overlapping frames of audio data, each 29 ms long, at a rate of 100 frames per second. Each frame was windowed with a Hamming window and a 36-pole LPC smoothed power spectrum was computed for the frequency band 80-6000 Hz. From this, 14

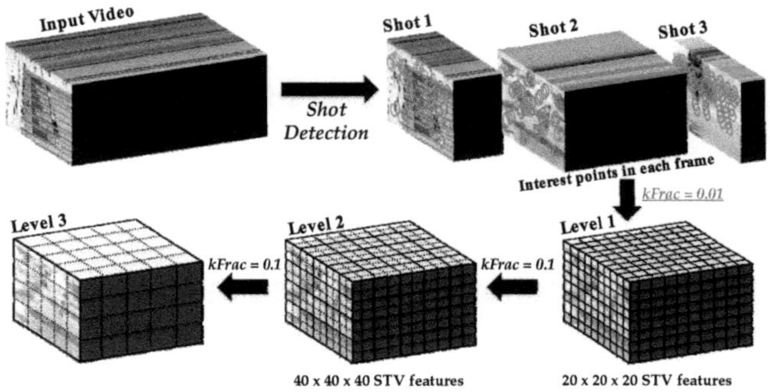

Figure 1: STV Pyramid: The raw features are successively clustered in 20×20×20 STVs, then 40×40×40 STVs, and at the highest level over the entire shot. At level 1, *kFrac*=0.01 and at levels 2 and 3, *kFrac*=0.1.

Mel-warped cepstral coefficients were computed. The mean cepstrum and peak energy of each segment of speech was removed non-causally from the appropriate sub-vector, removing any long term bias due to the channel. In addition, the feature vectors were scaled and translated such that for each video, the data has zero mean and unit variance. These base cepstral features with their first and second derivatives, together with the energy and its first and second derivatives, compose the 45-dimensional feature vector.

4. CODEBOOK LEARNING

We learn codewords to represent the audio and video content by clustering a set of feature vectors extracted from different videos of the dataset, using k-means or similar unsupervised clustering algorithm. Given a new video, we assign each feature vector x_i to the nearest codeword:

$$\alpha_i \in \{0,1\}^K, \alpha_{i,j} = 1 \Leftrightarrow j = arg \min_{k \leq K} ||x_i - c_k||^2 \tag{1}$$

where, c_k is the kth codeword. Then, we take the average of the α_i assigned to different codewords for different feature vectors and represent each video by the vector $\mathbf{h}$:

$$\mathbf{h} = \frac{1}{N}\sum_{i=1}^{N} \alpha_i \tag{2}$$

where, N is the total number of feature vectors. This approach is similar to the commonly used *vector quantization* [11]. Given a set of training videos and their class labels, we first obtain their codebook histogram representation as in equation (2), and then train suitable classifiers. In our experiments we train SVM with radial basis function (RBF) kernels. These classifiers were then used to classify test videos.

5. BAYESIAN MODEL COMBINATION

Once we train classifiers using the visual and audio features, we combine their output using Bayesian decision theoretic approach (BAYCOM) as suggested in [12]. Let M be the number of models to combine, and r_i denote the output generated by model i. Here, r_i consists of the classification c_i generated by system i, along with the associated confidence score s_i, i.e. r_i=(c_i,s_i). Let the event c mean "hypothesis c

is correct" and C be the set of unique classes proposed by all systems. Then, the model selects the optimal hypothesis according to

$$c^{\star} = \underset{c \in C}{\operatorname{argmax}}\, P(c \mid r_1, \ldots, r_M) \tag{3}$$

According to Bayes theorem the probability term in equation 3 can be written as

$$P(c \mid r_1, \ldots, r_M) = P(c) \frac{P(r_1, \ldots, r_M \mid c)}{P(r_1, \ldots, r_M)} \tag{4}$$

Assuming that the system hypotheses are independent of each other and ignoring the denominator since it is independent of c, equation 4 becomes

$$P(c) \prod_{i=1}^{M} P(r_i \mid c) = P(c) \prod_{i=1}^{M} P(s_i \mid c_i, c) P(c_i \mid c) \tag{5}$$

The first term $P(c)$ is the prior probability of c being the correct class. The second term $P(s_i \mid c_i, c)$ is the conditional score distribution and can be decomposed in two disjoint events. If $c_i = c$, then this term denotes the probability the system i is correct with a score s_i. If $c_i \neq c$, then this term denotes the probability the system i is incorrect with a hypothesis c_i and a score s_i. Similarly, the third term $P(c_i \mid c)$ can be decomposed in two disjoint events.

The approach followed in the original BAYCOM formulation assumes that the conditional probabilities are independent of the particular hypothesis c_i and determined only by whether the hypothesis is correct or incorrect. In this work, we use class specific conditional probabilities. To overcome data sparseness, we smooth the conditional probabilities with the class independent probabilities using the Witten-Bell smoothing [16]. For example, the $P(c_i \mid c)$ was smoothed as

$$P(c_i \mid c) = (1 - \lambda) * P_{ML}(c_i \mid c) + \lambda * P(c_i) \tag{6}$$

where, $P_{ML}(c_i|c)$ is the Maximum Likelihood (ML) estimate of the conditional probability and

$$\lambda = \frac{N_{c_i,c}}{N_{c_i,c} + \sum_{c_i} c(c_i, c)} \tag{7}$$

where, $N_{c_i,c} = |\{c_i : \#(c_i, c) > 0\}|$. The term $P(c_i)$ in equation 6 denotes the class independent probability.

6. EXPERIMENTS

For our experiments, we used 2794 videos of varying duration (ranging from 2 min to more than an hour) downloaded from YouTube using different queries. We aggregated these videos based on the queries into 9 classes: *Baking*, *Baseball*, *Military Parade*, *Protest*, *Robbery*, *Building Shelter*, *Sports*, *Traffic*, *War Footage*. The videos returned by YouTube for different queries had significant error in each of the classes including wrong retrievals, cartoon videos simulating robbery/fighting, news reports, etc. We had human annotators manually analyze the videos we downloaded and remove the erroneous retrievals. The total duration of the audio-visual corpus was 200 hours.

We learned our codebooks from a held out set of 61 videos, which was randomly selected with a uniform distribution across the different classes. The remaining video set (of 2733 videos) was used to train and test SVM classifiers based on the codeword histogram projections. We split the data into 10 different partitions at 6:2:2 train:dev:test separation. We ensured that videos from each class were also split with the same ratio. Throughout all experiments we train SVM with RBF kernels and set the parameters γ to 0.5, c to 10^5, and ϵ to 0.001. We conducted three sets of experiments to validate our audio, visual, and audio-visual feature combinations.

Performance of Audio Features: We compared our audio features with two baseline approaches. The first approach automatically segments the input speech to 8 broad classes: *voiced continuents*, *fricatives and sibilants*, *obstruents*, *laughter*, *breath*, *lipsmack*, *music*, and *silence*. This is done using a dual-gender phoneme-class recognizer trained over 150 hours of broadcast news data, and then adapted to web audio on the held out 61-video set. For the second approach, we used a segmental Gaussian mixture model tokenizer following the approach described in [13], which first segments the audio stream based on spectral discontinuities and then clusters the audio features within the segments. Table 1 compares the performance of different approaches. Clearly, the unsupervised audio codebook approach outperforms other standard techniques.

Approach	Accuracy (%)
Phoneme Recognition	40.5±1.1
SGMM	56.7±2.3
Unsupervised Codebook (k=1024)	**66.1±2.6**

Table 1: Comparison of the various approaches for audio label generation for classification.

Performance of Visual Features: Next, we compared the performance of our visual features. Table 2 compares their performance. D-SIFT, which extracts the maximum number of feature points per frame shows the best performance.

Feature	SURF	SIFT	D-SIFT
Accuracy(%)	60.8±2.0	64.6±2.1	**68.6±1.8**

Table 2: Comparison of different visual features for classification.

Performance of Feature Combinations: We considered several possible methods to combine different audio and visual features. For each combination, we tested early and late fusion strategies. In early fusion (Early), we simply concatenated the codeword histograms of different features for each video and then trained an SVM classifier on the combined feature vector. For late fusion, we first output the class probabilities generated by each individual feature's SVM and then considered 5 approaches - 1) Training an SVM by concatenating the class probability vectors (late SVM) 2) Choosing the output of the model with maximum confidence in a prediction (late Max) 3) Choosing the class based on the sum of confidences (late Sum) 4) Voting based on the model predictions (late Voting) 5) Bayesian combination (BAYCOM) as described in Section 5 by training on the confidence scores of the individual feature SVMs on the dev partition. First, we compared the impact of audio features on the overall performance by comparing combination of only the visual features (SIFT+SURF+D-SIFT) against both audio and visual features in the combination. Table 3 compares the performance of visual only and audio-visual combinations, for both early and late fusion. As expected, audio-visual combination outperforms visual-only combination in all cases.

	All Visual	Audio-Visual
Early Fusion	75.3±1.6	**79.8±1.2**
Late Fusion (SVM)	77.5±2.0	**79.2±1.7**

Table 3: Comparison of visual only feature combination with audio-visual combination.

Next, we compared the performance of different feature combination strategies. Table 4 summarizes the performance of different approaches. Here, the BAYCOM approach we outlined in Section 5 outperforms other strategies.

Approach	Accuracy (%)
Early Fusion	79.8±1.2
late SVM	79.2±1.7
late Max	78.3±1.1
late Sum	79.7±1.6
late Voting	77.3±1.4
BAYCOM	**81.4±1.2**

Table 4: Comparison of different audio-visual feature combinations.

Figure 2 shows the classwise performance of the various methods described in this paper. We observe that audio-visual combinations improve upon individual features even for less frequent classes such as *baking*, *baseball*, and *shelter* events. We also present the performance of an Oracle system which picks the best feature among the visual and the audio features for a particular video. The overall performance of the Oracle is 88.72 ± 1.44 reiterating the fact that the individual features capture complimentary information that can be harnessed in combinatorial framework.

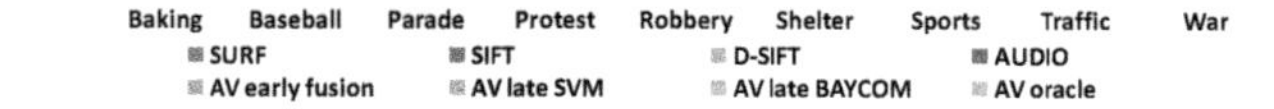

Figure 2: Comparison of different approaches for different classes, with oracle.

7. CONCLUSIONS

We presented an approach to efficiently process and combine the audio and the visual content from large video corpora. Our experiments show that unsupervised audio codebooks significantly outperform traditional phoneme segmentation based approaches. Further, combination of multiple diverse feature streams outperform any of the individual features, with audio-visual combinations producing the largest gains. Finally, Bayesian model combination consistently outperforms traditional early and late fusion approaches. We plan to build on this by analyzing co-occurrence statistics of codewords from different feature streams and also localize occurrences of events in the video.

8. REFERENCES

[1] H. Bay, A. Ess, T. Tuytelaars, and L. V. Gool. Surf: Speeded up robust features. *CVIU*, 110(3):346–359, 2008.

[2] Y. Boureau, F. Bach, Y. Le Cun, and J. Ponce. Learning mid-level features for recognition. In *CVPR*, pages 2559–2566, 2010.

[3] S.-F. Chang et al. Large-scale multimodal semantic concept detection for consumer video. In *MIR*, pages 255–264, 2007.

[4] G. Csurka, C. R. Dance, L. Fan, J. Willamowski, and C. Bray. Visual categorization with bags of keypoints. In *In Workshop on Statistical Learning in Computer Vision, ECCV*, pages 1–22, 2004.

[5] L. Duan, D. Xu, I. Tsang, and J. Luo. Visual event recognition in videos by learning from web data. In *CVPR*, pages 1959–1966, 2010.

[6] L. Fei-Fei and P. Perona. A bayesian hierarchical model for learning natural scene categories. *CVPR*, pages 524–531, 2005.

[7] H. Jegou, M. Douze, and C. Schmid. Packing bag-of-features. In *ICCV*, pages 2357–2364, 2009.

[8] W. Jiang, C. V. Cotton, S.-F. Chang, D. Ellis, and A. C. Loui. Short-term audio-visual atoms for generic video concept classification. In *ACM Multimedia*, pages 5–14, 2009.

[9] J. Liu, Y. Yang, and M. Shah. Learning semantic visual vocabularies using diffusion distance. In *CVPR*, pages 461–468, 2009.

[10] D. G. Lowe. Distinctive image features from scale-invariant keypoints. *IJCV*, 60:91–110, 2004.

[11] J. Makhoul, S. Roucos, and H. Gish. Vector quantization in speech coding. *Proceedings of the IEEE*, 73(11):1551 – 1588, Nov. 1985.

[12] A. Shankar. Bayesian model combination (baycom) for improved recognition. *ICASSP*, pages 845–848, 2005.

[13] M.-H. Siu, H. Gish, A. Chan, and W. Belfield. Improved topic classification and keyword discovery using an HMM-based speech recognizer trained without supervision. In *Interspeech*, 2010.

[14] C. G. M. Snoek et al. The MediaMill TRECVID 2009 semantic video search engine. In *Proceedings of the 7th TRECVID Workshop*, 2009.

[15] C. G. M. Snoek, M. Worring, and A. W. M. Smeulders. Early versus late fusion in semantic video analysis. In *ACM Multimedia*, pages 399–402, 2005.

[16] I. Witten and T. Bell. The zero-frequency problem: Estimating the probabilities of novel events in adaptive text compression. 37(4):1085–1094, 1991.

[17] Y. Wu, C. Lin, E. Chang, and J. Smith. Multimodal information fusion for video concept detection. In *ICIP*, pages IV: 2391–2394, 2004.

[18] H. Zhang, A. Kankanhalli, and S. Smoliar. Automatic partitioning of full-motion video. *Multimedia Systems*, 1(1):10–28, 1993.

Enriching and Localizing Semantic Tags in Internet Videos*

Lamberto Ballan, Marco Bertini, Alberto Del Bimbo, and Giuseppe Serra
Media Integration and Communication Center, Università degli Studi di Firenze
Viale Morgagni 65 - 50134 Firenze, Italy
{ballan, bertini, delbimbo, serra}@dsi.unifi.it

ABSTRACT

Tagging of multimedia content is becoming more and more widespread as web 2.0 sites, like Flickr and Facebook for images, YouTube and Vimeo for videos, have popularized tagging functionalities among their users. These user-generated tags are used to retrieve multimedia content, and to ease browsing and exploration of media collections, e.g. using tag clouds. However, not all media are equally tagged by users: using the current browsers is easy to tag a single photo, and even tagging a part of a photo, like a face, has become common in sites like Flickr and Facebook; on the other hand tagging a video sequence is more complicated and time consuming, so that users just tag the overall content of a video. In this paper we present a system for automatic video annotation that increases the number of tags originally provided by users, and localizes them temporally, associating tags to shots. This approach exploits collective knowledge embedded in tags and Wikipedia, and visual similarity of keyframes and images uploaded to social sites like YouTube and Flickr.

Categories and Subject Descriptors

H.3.1 [**Information Systems**]: Content Analysis and Indexing; H.3.5 [**Information Storage and Retrieval**]: Online Information Services

General Terms

Algorithms, Design, Experimentation

Keywords

Tag refinement, tag relevance learning, internet videos, social video retrieval

1. INTRODUCTION

In the last years, social media repositories such as Flickr and Youtube have become more and more popular, allowing users to upload and share media content[1], annotating it with personal keywords called *tags*. Tags provide contextual and semantic information which can be used to organize and facilitate media content search and access. The performance of social image and video retrieval systems depends mainly on the availability and quality of tags. However, these are often imprecise, ambiguous and overly personalized [2], and also very few (typically one-three tags per image) [13].

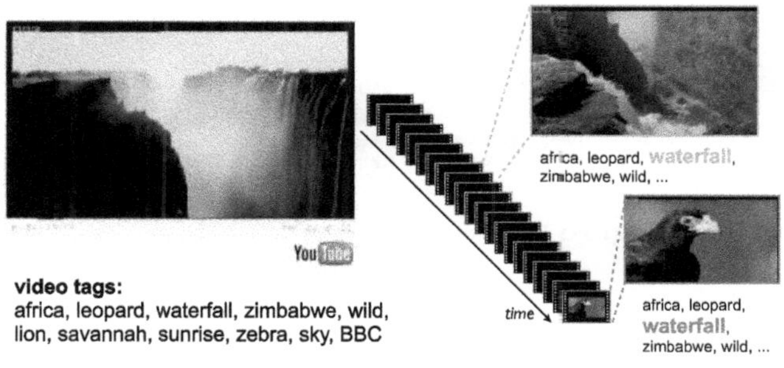

Figure 1: *left)* Example of a YouTube video with its related tags; *right)* localization of tags in shots.

Several efforts have been recently done in the area of content-based tag processing for social image retrieval [7]. The main focus of these works has been put on three aspects: *i)* tag ranking/relevance, *ii)* tag refinement and *iii)* tag-to-region assignment. Li *et al.* [4] addressed the problem of tag relevance estimation by accumulating votes from visually similar images. The basic idea is that if different users label similar images with the same tags, these tags truly represent the actual visual content. This method has been recently extended to a multi-feature relevance learning approach, obtained by combining global and local features to better represent visual image content [5]. In the tag ranking approach proposed by Liu *et al.* [6], tags are ranked according to their relevance to the content of images. First is adopted a Kernel Density Estimation approach to estimate the initial relevance score for each tag, then score values are refined by using a random walk process that explores the relationship of tags (represented using a graph model).

Most of the recent works on internet videos have addressed problems like near duplicate detection [11], training concept detectors [15] or topic detection [12]. Currently, only a few works have considered the problem of tag suggestion and

*Area chair: Nicu Sebe.

[1]For instance, YouTube reported in March 2011 that about 24 hours of video are uploaded every minute and more than 2 billion views per day have been registered.

MM'11, November 28–December 1, 2011, Scottsdale, Arizona, USA.

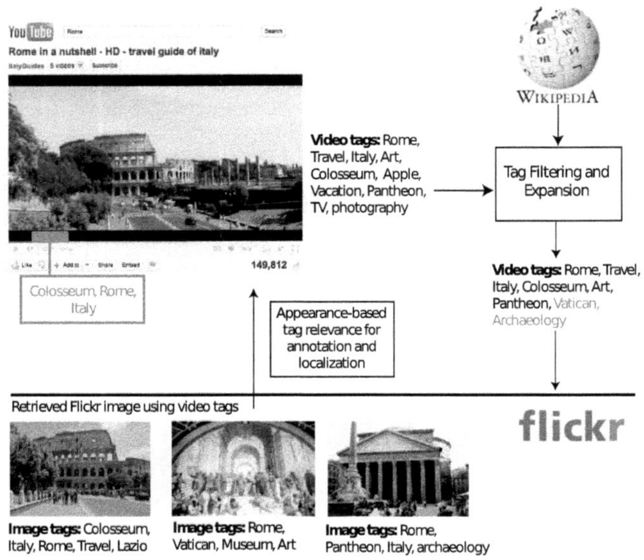

Figure 2: Overview of the system.

localization (see Fig. 1) in internet videos [1,3,10]. In [1] shots of YouTube videos are automatically annotated using Flickr images, with a tag relevance algorithm that, exploiting visual similarity of keyframes and images, can also add new tags that were not originally available in videos. Localization of video tags is addressed in [3]; a multiple instance learning approach that considers semantic relatedness of co-occurring tags is used to model shots and videos. In [10] video shots are annotated with 34 concept detectors, using their results to build a semantic representation for each shot. The same detectors are applied to Flickr images and semantic similarity with video keyframes is used to suggest tags selected from those of the images.

In this paper we propose a method for video tag suggestion and temporal localization based on social knowledge. The system exploits the tags associated to user-generated videos and images uploaded to social sites (such as YouTube and Flickr), their visual similarity and the Wikipedia folksonomy, to suggest new tags that can be associated at the shot level to a particular keyframe. Fig. 2 shows an overview of the system. The rest of the paper is organized as follows: tag filtering and suggestion is described in Sect. 2; visual analysis and tag relevance are presented in Sect. 3; experimental results are presented in Sect. 4. Conclusions are finally drawn in Sect. 5.

2. SOCIAL AND SEMANTIC TAG FILTERING AND EXPANSION

The first step of our approach is the expansion of the tags associated with the video to be annotated. This is required because, as noted in [16], YouTube videos are annotated with an average of five tags, a number that would not allow to produce a thorough annotation of all the shots. Tag expansion is also needed to ease the alignment of different folksonomies in YouTube and Flickr, to select the images that will be used to associate the tags to keyframes.

Filtering. We filter the video tags that are candidate for expansion, to reduce the risk of semantic drift. Given a video V let $U = \{u_1, \cdots u_n\}$ be the user-defined tags, after discarding stopwords, dates and numbers. We determine a relevance score based on the following method. The tags u_t that appear in the video title get the maximum score ($score(u_t) = 1$), a behavior similar to that of web search engines, while the scores of other tags are determined using the related videos, provided by YouTube.

The basic intuition is that the score of a tag in the video can be inferred from tags of the related videos: the more frequently a tag occurs in the related videos, the more relevant it might be. In particular, consider the m related videos of V and their tags. Let n_u be the number of occurrences of tag u in the related videos, we compute its relevance as $r_u = n_u/m$. Tags with low values are discarded ($r < 0.15$), while tags with high relevance ($r > 0.85$) take scores equal to 1 and are called "strong" tags. For all the other "weak" tags we consider their co-occurrence and semantic relation with the "strong" tags. Co-occurrence between two tags is the number of videos where both tags are used. This value is not very meaningful, as it does not consider the frequency of the individual tags. Therefore we normalize the co-occurrence using the asymmetric normalization method, i.e. with the frequency of one of the tags as in: $o(u_1, u_2) = n_{(u_1,u_2)}/n_{u_1}$, where $n_{(u_1,u_2)}$ is the number of times that the tag u_1 co-occurs with tag u_2. This normalization has been found to improve the diversity of the tags [13]. In particular we compute the co-occurrence between each "weak" tag and the "strongest" tag (i.e. the tag with maximum r). Then we evaluate the *semantic relatedness* with "strong" tags, considering the hyperlinks between the corresponding Wikipedia articles using the method in [9]; the maximum value, s_u, is considered. Finally, the scores of the "weak" tags is computed as the weighted sum of their relevance in related videos, their co-occurrence with the "strongest" tag $\bar{u}$ and their semantic relationship with the "strong" tags as:

$$score(u) = w_1 \cdot r_u + w_2 \cdot o(u, \bar{u}) + w_3 \cdot s_u$$

Tags with a score less than a threshold ($\tau_{filtering}$) are discarded, while the others are used in the next step.

Expansion. Tag expansion is done considering two aspects: *i)* social information, using tags of the related videos, and *ii)* semantic information and folksonomies, using Wikipedia. For the first aspect we consider the occurrences of the tags in the related videos: those with a high number of occurrences, that are not in the list of filtered tags of the analyzed video, are inserted. For the second step we use Wikipedia articles to expand semantically the tags. First we choose the search terms to select Wikipedia resources. Search terms are defined by a single tag or by a combination of two tags (initial experiments have shown that larger combinations are ineffective). The combination of tags is useful for the disambiguation of concepts (e.g. consider the combination of "golden" and "gate"). Two tags are combined if their co-occurrence in related videos, $o(u_1, u_2)$, is high; experimentally we found that an effective threshold is 0.9. Search terms are used to select relevant Wikipedia articles, using Wikipedia Miner toolkit [8]. For each Wikipedia resource we consider the list of *anchors*, i.e. text used within links to Wikipedia articles, as candidate tags. The anchors that are more frequently used are added to the tag list.

3. APPEARANCE-BASED TAG RELEVANCE

Videos are segmented in shots using a fast algorithm that

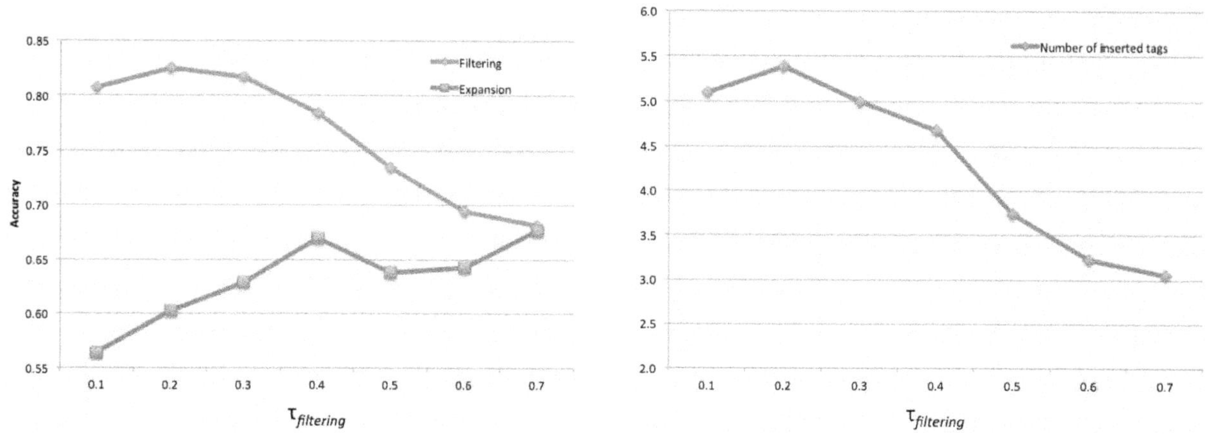

Figure 3: *left)* Mean accuracy of the filtering and expansion steps at different score thresholds; *right)* Mean number of tags added correctly to a video.

analyses the frame luminance. For each shot we extract the middle frame, creating a set of keyframes $K = \{K_1, \ldots, K_l\}$. The list of filtered and expanded tags obtained in the previous step is used to start the annotation process, selecting from Flickr a set of images $I = \{I_1, \ldots, I_m\}$ that have been annotated at least with one of them; each I_d has the tags $\{u_1^i, \ldots u_p^i\}$, and the union of these tags is the vocabulary used for video annotation. Due to the fact that user-generated tags are noisy, it is necessary to determine the tag relevance in order to obtain a correct annotation. For this reason we have followed, in principle, the approach for evaluating tag relevance in similar images of [4], adapting it to deal with the problem of locating tags in videos. In our approach keyframes do not have any tag associated to them, since the tags associated to the whole video may not refer to the specific content of a shot; applying the approach of [4] to the shots and tags of a video would simply result in their reordering [1]. The relevance of a tag u_j^i is computed by counting the presence of u_j^i in the visual neighbors of the keyframe K_l, minus its prior frequency. This is based on the consideration that tags that occur frequently in the visual neighborhood of K_l are important for the keyframe being analyzed. In our approach we compute relevance as the weighted sum of the presence of a tag in the neighbors, where weights are inversely proportional to the visual distance between keyframe K_l and the I images. Since we are treating keyframes as unlabeled images, we estimate tag relevance for each candidate tag w.r.t. the keyframe and select those whose relevance score is above a threshold $\tau_{relevance}$. We found that this approach is more consistent with the distance-based weighting of tag relevance, rather than selecting a fixed number of the highest ranking tags independently from their distance from the keyframe, as in [4]. Moreover, it has to be considered that we are working with images from very diverse sources and tagging practices, so that we want to be able to avoid adding tags that are not relevant enough, or add all the relevant tags in the neighborhood. All the tags added to the shots in this step are used to annotate the video also at the global level.

To compute visual similarity between keyframes K and Flickr images I we use a 370-dimensional feature vectors that includes local and global features. This feature vector is composed by a 50 dimensional color correlogram computed in the HSV color space, a 80 dimensional vector for the MPEG-7 Edge Histogram Descriptor and a 240 dimension vector for the TOP-SIFT descriptor. This latter descriptor is a variation of TOP-SURF [14], a compact image descriptor that combines interest points with visual words, designed for fast content-based image retrieval.

The Flickr images are clustered using k-means, to use the cluster centers as indexes for a fast approximate nearest neighbor search. For each keyframe of the video the nearest cluster center based on the visual similarity is retrieved. Images belonging to this cluster are considered as neighbors.

4. EXPERIMENTS

We evaluate our approach on a dataset created to represent the diversity of content on YouTube. As in [1] the dataset is composed by four YouTube videos for each of the 15 categories (*Auto & Vehicles, Comedy, Education, Entertainment, Film and Animation, Gaming, Howto & Style, Music, News and Politics, Nonprofits & Activism, Pets & Animals, Science & Technology, Sports, Travel & Events*). The total duration of videos is three hours and eight minutes and the number of detected shots is 4196. The number of tags per video varies from 8 to 22.

Experiment 1: Tag Filtering/Expansion. In the first experiment we analyzed the performance of our system to filter and expand the initial tags related to a video. Evaluation results is reported in terms of accuracy, computed as the ratio between the number of correct operations (addition/deletion of tags) and the number of tags. Fig. 3-*left* presents the mean accuracy of filtering and expansion steps at different threshold scores ($\tau_{filtering}$); Fig. 3-*right* shows the mean number of the tags correctly added to the video. Note that accuracy of expansion increases for high values of the threshold. This is due to the fact that with a high threshold the filtering step maintains only very relevant tags, thus reducing the semantic drift that may happen during the expansion process. However, in this case only few new tags are added. To select a good threshold it also necessary to consider the mean number of tags added correctly. Based on these data a good value for $\tau_{filtering}$ is 0.40, that allows to have a mean accuracy of 78.4% (filtering) and of 67% (expansion) adding an average of 4.6 tags to the original set.

YouTube category	$\tau_{relevance}$=1		$\tau_{relevance}$=3		$\tau_{relevance}$=5		$\tau_{relevance}$=7		$\tau_{relevance}$=11	
	Acc.	Tags	Acc.	Tags	Acc.	Tags	Acc.	Tags	Acc.	Tags
Auto & Vehicles	0.41	10.99	0.65	4.09	0.78	2.13	0.86	1.36	0.93	0.66
Comedy	0.58	5.49	0.85	2.68	0.95	1.68	0.92	0.89	0.77	0.16
Education	0.49	3.97	0.62	1.83	0.76	0.84	0.72	0.39	0.69	0.11
Entertainment	0.60	4.46	0.84	2.98	0.99	1.94	1	0.89	1	0.03
Film & Animation	0.54	2.16	0.93	1.28	0.99	0.59	1	0.19	1	0.01
Gaming	0.47	3.85	0.85	2.13	0.93	0.97	0.99	0.60	1	0.2
Howto & Style	0.39	3.91	0.61	2.02	0.69	1.04	0.71	0.45	0,71	0.31
Music	0.39	2.48	0.69	0.48	1	0.10	1	0.012	1	0.06
News & Politics	0.62	5.32	0.87	2.40	0.97	1.04	1	0.46	1	0.04
No-profit & Activism	0.61	2.62	0.93	1	0.98	0.42	1	0.17	1	0.04
People & Blogs	0.40	5.70	0.67	2.74	0.79	1.22	0.82	0.58	0.50	0.15
Pets & Animals	0.56	4.83	0.75	2.28	0.86	1.04	0.85	0.55	0.94	0.23
Science & Technology	0.44	4.80	0.64	1.67	0.81	0.84	0.89	0.44	0.87	0.16
Sport	0.41	4.49	0.74	2.63	0.82	1.39	0.92	0.62	0.94	0.14
Travel & Events	0.61	12.57	0.79	7.34	0.87	4.21	0.91	2.45	0.98	1.18
Average	0.50	5.18	0.76	2.50	0.88	1.30	0.91	0.67	0.90	0.23

Table 1: Results for tag localization and suggestion for each YouTube category, in terms of accuracy and average number of correctly added tags, as $\tau_{relevance}$ varies.

Experiment 2: Localizing Tag. In the second experiment we analyze the performance of the system in adding and locating of relevant tags to shots. The performance is measured in terms of accuracy: i.e. ratio between the number of tags correctly suggested and the total number of suggested tags. For each tag, resulting from the filtering and expansion process, the system downloads the first 15 Flickr images ranked according the "relevance" criterion provided by the Flickr API. Table 1 reports, for different relevance threshold scores, the accuracy and the mean number of correctly suggested tags for shot. The overall performance of the system is promising. We can observe that the mean accuracy on the entire dataset increases until score equals to seven and slightly decreases for higher scores, remaining close to 0.9; while the mean number of suggested tags correctly decreases significantly for high scores (e.g. when requiring a threshold above 5). From the experimental results we can also note that some categories are more tractable than the others. In the "Auto & Vehicle" and "Travel & Events" categories, the extracted Flickr images are very relevant and similar to the shots analysed. This can be seen from the number of suggested tags which is quite large. In "Film & Animation" we saw that it is difficult to retrieve Flickr images similar to trailer scenes of feature films. "Howto & Style" collects very diverse content that is hard to be correctly annotated.

5. CONCLUSIONS

In this work we have presented a method for semantic video annotation based on social knowledge embedded in YouTube, Flickr and Wikipedia. The tags provided by the users that share videos on internet are localized within the shots and new tags are added. The preliminary results are encouraging for almost all the categories of videos uploaded to YouTube. Our future work will deal with the improvement of the features used to evaluate the visual similarity of keyframes and with evaluation of visual similarity among videos. We plan also to further improve the use of semantic relations between tags, adding other structured sources of social knowledge, like DBPedia, to improve tag expansion.

Acknowledgments. This work is partially supported by the EU euTV Project (Contract FP7-226248).

6. REFERENCES

[1] L. Ballan, M. Bertini, A. Del Bimbo, M. Meoni, and G. Serra. Tag suggestion and localization in user-generated videos based on social knowledge. In *Proc. of ACM WSM*, 2010.

[2] L. S. Kennedy, S.-F. Chang, and I. V. Kozintsev. To search or to label? Predicting the performance of search-based automatic image classifiers. In *Proc. of ACM MIR*, 2006.

[3] G. Li, M. Wang, Y.-T. Zheng, and T.-S. Chua. ShotTagger: Tag location for internet videos. In *Proc. of ACM ICMR*, 2011.

[4] X. Li, C. G. M. Snoek, and M. Worring. Learning social tag relevance by neighbor voting. *IEEE Transactions on Multimedia*, 11(7):1310–1322, 2009.

[5] X. Li, C. G. M. Snoek, and M. Worring. Unsupervised multi-feature tag relevance learning for social image retrieval. In *Proc. of ACM CIVR*, 2010.

[6] D. Liu, X.-S. Hua, L. Yang, M. Wang, and H.-J. Zhang. Tag ranking. In *Proc. of WWW*, 2009.

[7] D. Liu, X.-S. Hua, and H.-J. Zhang. Content-based tag processing for internet social images. *Multimedia Tools and Applications*, 51(1):723–738, 2011.

[8] D. Milne and I. H. Witten. An open-source toolkit for mining Wikipedia. In *Proc. of NZCSRSC*, 2009.

[9] D. Milne and I. H. Witten. An effective, low-cost measure of semantic relatedness obtained from Wikipedia links. In *Proc. of AAAI*, 2008.

[10] H.-S. Min, J. Choi, W. De Neve, Y. M. Ro, and K. N. Plataniotis. Semantic annotation of personal video content using an image folksonomy. In *Proc. of IEEE ICIP*, 2009.

[11] S. Paisitkriangkrai, T. Mei, J. Zhang, and X.-S. Hua. Scalable clip-based near-duplicate video detection with ordinal measure. In *Proc. of ACM CIVR*, 2010.

[12] J. Shao, W. Yin, S. Ma, and Y. Zhuang. Topic discovery of web video using star-structured k-partite graph. In *Proc. of ACM Multimedia*, 2010.

[13] B. Sigurbjörnsson and R. van Zwol. Flickr tag recommendation based on collective knowledge. In *Proc. of WWW*, 2008.

[14] B. Thomee, E. M. Bakker, and M. S. Lew. TOP-SURF: a visual words toolkit. In *Proc. of ACM Multimedia*, 2010.

[15] A. Ulges, C. Schulze, M. Koch, and T. M. Breuel. Learning automatic concept detectors from online video. *Computer Vision and Image Understanding*, 114(4):429–438, 2010.

[16] W. Zhao, X. Wu, and C.-W. Ngo. On the annotation of web videos by efficient near-duplicate search. *IEEE Transactions on Multimedia*, 12(5):448 – 461, 2010.

Scene Segmentation of Wedding Party Videos by Scenario-based Matching with Example Videos

Kazuki Sawai*
Graduate School of I.S., Nagoya University
ksawai@murase.m.is.nagoya-u.ac.jp

Tomokazu Takahashi
Faculty of Econ. & Info., Gifu Shotoku Gakuen Univ.
ttakahashi@gifu.shotoku.ac.jp

Daisuke Deguchi
Graduate School of I.S., Nagoya University
ddeguchi@is.nagoya-u.ac.jp

Ichiro Ide
Graduate School of I.S., Nagoya University
ide@is.nagoya-u.ac.jp

Hiroshi Murase
Graduate School of I.S., Nagoya University
murase@is.nagoya-u.ac.jp

ABSTRACT

We propose a method for scene segmentation of a wedding party video. Recently, it has become popular to take videos of a wedding ceremony and its party. Especially, because of its length, each scene of a wedding party video needs to be indexed with each event for efficient browsing. The proposed method segments a wedding party video into scenes of events by scenario-based matching with example videos that are synthesized by combining scenes from other wedding party videos according to a scenario.

Categories and Subject Descriptors

H.5.1 [**Multimedia Information Systems**]: Video; H.3.1 [**Content Analysis and Indexing**]: Indexing methods; I.5.4 [**Applications**]: Computer vision

General Terms

Algorithms

Keywords

Wedding party, scene segmentation, dynamic time warping

1. INTRODUCTION

Wedding is one of the most important events in a person's life. With the rapid popularization of video cameras, it has become popular to take videos of a wedding ceremony and its party. Especially, wedding parties takes a long time compared to wedding ceremonies. Therefore, to quickly browse video segments of particular events, each video segment needs to be indexed with each event in the wedding party. Currently, this process is performed as a part of services by bridal agencies. However, there is a demand to perform this automatically because it takes much cost in terms of effort and time.

*Currently at NTT COMWARE CORPORATION.
*Area chair: Qi Tian

MM'11 November 28–December 1, 2011, Scottsdale, Arizona, USA.

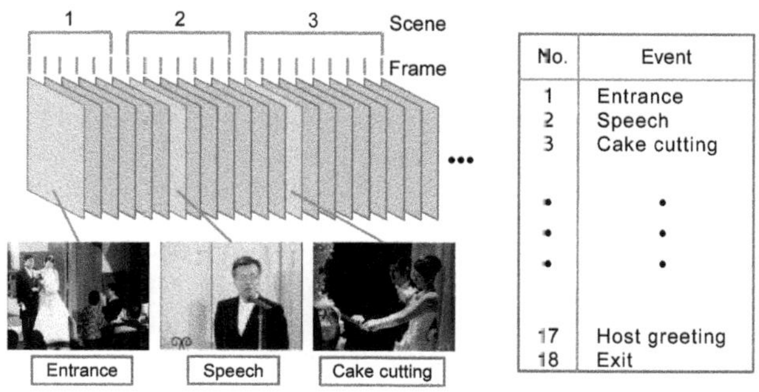

(a) Video (b) Scenario

Figure 1: Video of a wedding party and its scenario.

As shown in Fig. 1 (a), a wedding party video consists of various scenes. Here, we use the term "scene" to represent a video segment associated with an event. Generally, a wedding party is organized along a scenario which describes the order of events as shown in Fig. 1 (b). The proposed method segments a wedding party video into scenes and indexes them by associating the scenes with the events based on the scenario.

Wedding parties share the following characteristics:

- The same kinds of events are performed in various ways and length.
- Different kinds of events with similar characteristics could be performed.

Figures 2 (a) and (b) show sample images of the same kind of events in different wedding parties. Although these images are captured in the same kind of events, they differ in composition, lighting, background, and subject. Therefore, the proposed method selectively uses appropriate audio

(a) Speech A (b) Speech B

(c) Candle touching (d) Groom greeting

Figure 2: Sample images of wedding party events.

and visual features for each kind of events. The proposed method also employs a segmentation strategy that could accept the difference of the length in the same kind of events. On the other hand, Figs. 2 (c) and (d) show sample images of different events in the same wedding party. Their characteristics are similar although these images are captured in different kinds of events. To improve segmentation accuracy in such cases, the proposed method uses the information of the order of events written in the scenario.

2. RELATED WORK

Cheng et al. [1] proposed a method for scene segmentation of wedding ceremony videos. This method segments a wedding ceremony video into scenes associated with events using audio and visual features. To obtain the features, various techniques are used, such as speech/music classification [3] and camera flash detection. The proposed method also uses these techniques because their features would also be effective for scene segmentation of wedding party videos. The method in [1] constructs a single common model of temporal variation of the features for each kind of events to achieve scene segmentation with a model-based matching method. However, it is difficult in case of wedding parties to construct a single model for each kind of events because the events are performed in various ways and length. Therefore, the proposed method takes not the model-based approach but an example-based approach.

The proposed method calculates the dissimilarity between two video segments based on a DTW (Dynamic Time Warping) method. The DTW method is a sequence matching method that could be applied to two sequences with different lengths, and has also been used for video segment matching [2, 4, 6]. When two video segments $\mathbf{X}$ and $\mathbf{Y}$ are represented as sequences of feature vectors $(\mathbf{x}_1, \ldots, \mathbf{x}_P)$ and $(\mathbf{y}_1, \ldots, \mathbf{y}_Q)$, the dissimilarity is calculated by using the DTW method as below. First, the dissimilarity between two vectors $\mathbf{x}_p$, $\mathbf{y}_q$ is defined as

$$d(p,q) = \sqrt{\sum_{n=1}^{N} (x_{p,n} - y_{q,n})^2}, \quad (1)$$

where $x_{p,n}$ and $y_{q,n}$ represent the n-th element of $\mathbf{x}_p$ and $\mathbf{y}_q$, respectively. The dissimilarity $D(\mathbf{X}, \mathbf{Y})$ is calculated as $D(P, Q)$ by the following recurrence formula:

$$D(1,1) = d(1,1), \quad (2)$$

$$D(p,q) = \min \begin{cases} D(p-1,q) + \omega_1 d(p,q) \\ D(p-1,q-1) + \omega_2 d(p,q) \\ D(p,q-1) + \omega_3 d(p,q) \end{cases}. \quad (3)$$

Here, ω_1, ω_2, and ω_3 are weight factors for the matching.

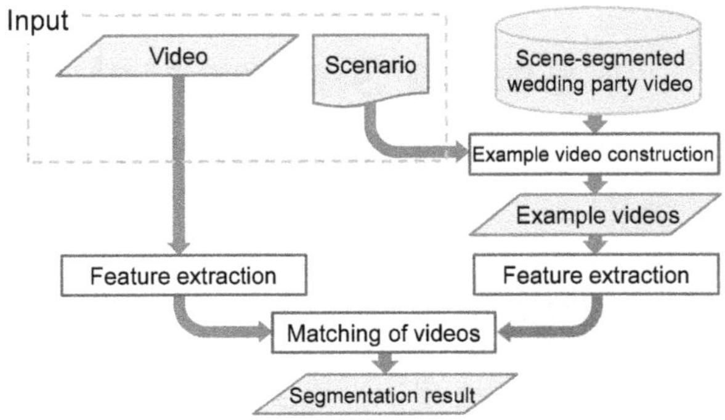

Figure 3: Flow diagram of the proposed method.

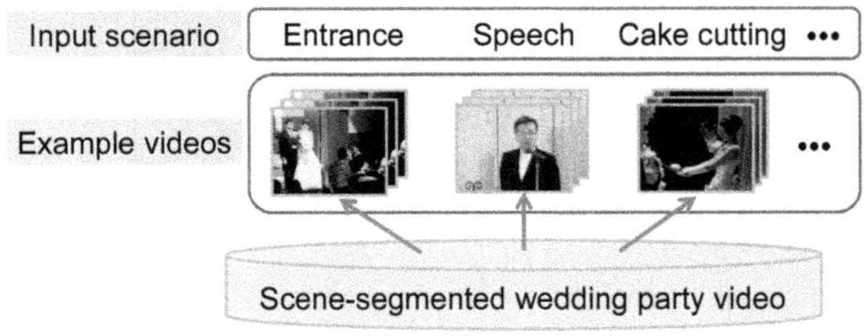

Figure 4: Construction of example videos.

3. PROPOSED METHOD

Figure 3 shows the flow diagram of the proposed method. The proposed method consists of the following three parts.

3.1 Construction of example videos

Figure 4 illustrates the construction of the example videos. As a preparetory process, multiple wedding party videos other than the input video are segmented into scenes of events manually. Thus we obtain a large number of labeled scenes $\{\mathbf{S}_{e,i_e} | e = 1, \ldots, E, i_e = 1, \ldots, I_e\}$. Here, E represents the number of events, I_e, the number of labeled scenes of an event e. The proposed method constructs example videos by arranging the labeled scenes along the event sequence $\mathbf{e} = (e_1, \ldots, e_M)$ described in the input scenario.

3.2 Feature extraction

Multiple audio and visual features are used. A feature vector is constructed from the features extracted from each unit segment consisting of T frames; a video is represented as (number of frames)$/T$ feature vectors. The proposed method extracts the features as follows:

Face detection

Faces are useful information to recognize events. The proposed method uses the average and variance of the number, size, and position of faces as visual features. A famous face detector [7] is used to detect the faces.

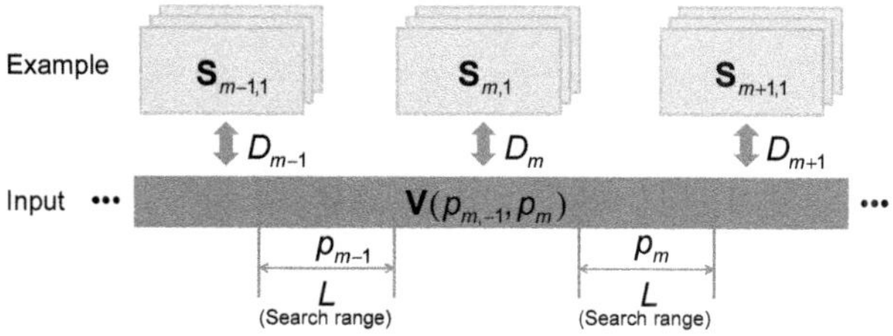

Figure 5: Matching between input and example videos.

Camera flash detection

Many camera flashes are observed in important events. Therefore, the number of flashes and the maximum difference of pixel intensities before and after the flashes are extracted by using a flash detection method [5].

Pixel intensities

Various lighting effects are used depending on events. Also, most male guests wear black suits and cover a large area of a frame in particular events. Therefore, the proposed method uses the average and the variance of pixel intensities.

Speech/music classification

Music plays loudly in some events. On the other hand, a person speaks in other events. The proposed method classifies sound sequences into speech, music, and silence by using the method proposed in [3], then uses the classification result as an audio feature. The root mean square and zero crossing frequency of speech power are used in the classification, which are also used as audio features.

3.3 Matching between videos

3.3.1 *Dissimilarity between video segments*

The proposed method calculates the dissimilarity between two video segments based on the DTW method described in Section 2. The effective features for matching between example and input videos depend on events. Therefore, to improve the accuracy of the matching, the proposed method uses a weighted Euclidian distance instead of Equation (1):

$$d(p, q) = \sqrt{\sum_{n=1}^{N} w_{e,n}(x_{e,p,n} - y_{q,n})^2}, \quad (4)$$

where $x_{e,p,n}$ is the n-th element of the p-th vector of a scene of an event e in example videos, $y_{q,n}$, the n-th element of the q-th vector of a video segment of an input video, $w_{e,n}$, the n-th element of the weight vector for the event e.

The weight vectors $\mathbf{w}_e(e = 1, \ldots, E)$ are learned beforehand for each event from a large number of labeled scenes in example videos.

3.3.2 *Scene segmentation*

Scene segmentation is performed by the following steps:

Step 1. Initial segmentation

We represent the beginning and the ending times of the m-th event in the input scenario as p_{m-1} and p_m ($p_{m-1} < p_m, m = 1, \ldots, M$), respectively. Here, p_0 and p_M are given as the beginning and the ending times of the input video. The initial segment positions $\mathbf{p}_0 = (p_0, \ldots, p_M)$ are calculated by the following equation:

$$\mathbf{p}_0 = \arg\min_{\mathbf{p}} \sum_{m=1}^{M} \frac{(p_m - p_{m-1} - \mu_m)^2}{\sigma_m^2}, \quad (5)$$

Table 1: Event names and number of scenes (Total: 216).

Event name (Number of scenes)
Bouquet casting (17), Bride and groom entrance (5), Bride and groom exit (15), Cake cutting (5), Candle touching (15), Congratulatory telegram (8), Exit for changing costumes (7), Groom greeting (14), Guest speech (22), Host greeting (14), Intermission (19), Message from bride to parents (15), Other show (19), Photo session (3), Singing show (22), Slide show (16)

where μ_m and σ_m^2 represent the mean length and the variance of an event e_m, respectively, which are calculated beforehand from labeled scenes of example video for each event.

Step 2. Updating by video segment matching

Figure 5 shows an overview of the video segment matching. $\mathbf{S}_{m,i}$ denotes the i-th labeled scene of an event e_m in the example videos. On the other hand, $\mathbf{V}(p_{m-1}, p_m)$ denotes a video segment from p_{m-1} to p_m in the input video. This step finds the position of each event that minimizes the dissimilarity between input and example videos by searching for p_m from a range in a width of L. The positions $\mathbf{p}_{t+1} = (p_0, \ldots, p_M)$ are obtained by the following equation:

$$\mathbf{p}_{t+1} = \arg\min_{\mathbf{p}_t} \min_{i} \sum_{m=1}^{M} \left\{ \frac{(p_m - p_{m-1} - \mu_m)^2}{\sigma_m^2} + \alpha_m D(\mathbf{S}_{m,i}, \mathbf{V}(p_{m-1}, p_m)) \right\}. \quad (6)$$

Here, α_m represents the weight of the event e_m, which is learned beforehand from example videos for each event so that Equation 6 can be minimized.

Step 3. Iteration

The segmentation process increments t by one and returns to Step 2 if the difference between $\mathbf{p}_{t+1}$ and $\mathbf{p}_t$ is greater than a threshold, otherwise outputs $\mathbf{p}_{t+1}$ as the results.

4. EXPERIMENT

Two experiments were conducted on actual wedding party videos. The first experiment evaluated the accuracy of scene segmentation. On the other hand, the second experiment investigated the effectiveness of each of the visual and the audio features used in the proposed method.

4.1 Setup

15 videos from different wedding parties were used for the experiments. Each video was 1.2 to 1.8 hours long and included 11 to 19 events. Table 1 shows event names and the number of scenes included in the videos. For example, 17 scenes of different bouquet casting events were included in the 15 videos. The unit video length for the segmentation was set to $T = 10$ sec. and the range width for the video segment matching was set to $L = 150$ sec. For each video, we used the video for input and the other 14 videos for the construction of example videos.

To evaluate the segmentation accuracy, we calculated the success rate by the following equation:

$$\text{success rate [\%]} = \frac{\text{number of correct units}}{\text{number of all units}} \times 100. \quad (7)$$

As a comparative method, we used a method that performs only the initial segmentation step described in 3.3.2.

Table 2: Segmentation accuracy.

Method	Proposed	Comparative
Success rate [%]	82.6	69.8

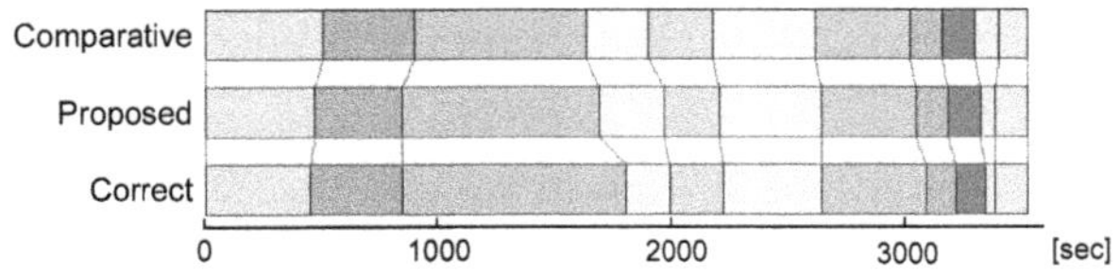

Figure 6: Example of successful segmentation results.

4.2 Segmentation accuracy

Table 2 shows the segmentation accuracy of the proposed method. This result indicates that the scenario-based matching with example videos improved the segmentation accuracy. From this result, we confirmed the effectiveness of the proposed method. Figure 6 shows an example of successful segmentation results. Each colored segment represents each segmented scene. In this case, the success rates of the comparative method and the proposed method were 84.5% and 95.7%, respectively. Similarly, Fig. 7 shows an example of segmentation results with low success rates. In the case where the same kinds of events occurred successively, it is difficult to achieve accurate segmentation by video segment matching based on the dissimilarity of visual and audio features because similar features are extracted from them. Other approaches would be required to solve this problem, such as scene boundary detection using speech detection of the MC and handclap detection. In the case where the initial segmentation result differed largely from the correct one, the result may fall into a local solution before reaching the correct answer. If estimated times of events are described in the wedding party scenario, use of this information could be effective to improve the accuracy.

4.3 Effectiveness of visual and audio features

Figure 8 shows the segmentation accuracy when only one kind of feature was used. For each kind of features, the accuracy was higher than that of the comparative method. The proposed method which is a combination of features, was even better than any of the features used indivisually. From this result, we confirmed the effectiveness of the features used in the proposed method.

5. SUMMARY

We proposed a method for scene segmentation and indexing of a wedding party video. The proposed method segments the video into scenes associated with events by scenario-based video segment matching between input and example videos. Experiments were conducted on actual wedding video party videos. As a result, the proposed method achieved an accuracy of 82.6% for scene segmentation.

Future work will include further improvement of the segmentation accuracy by use of a scene boundary detection technique and the information of estimated times of events planed in the wedding party scenario.

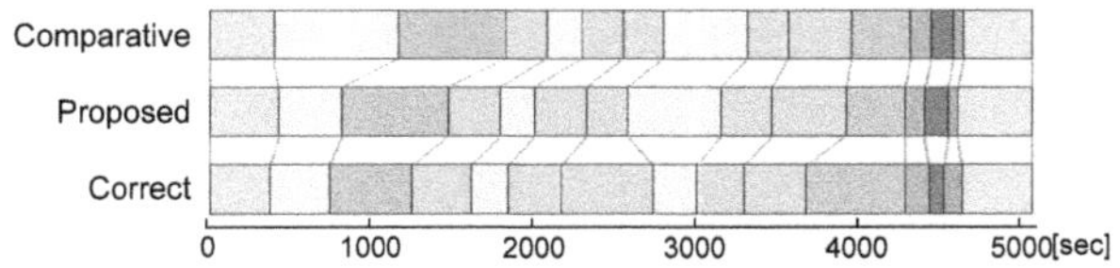

Figure 7: Example of failed segmentation results.

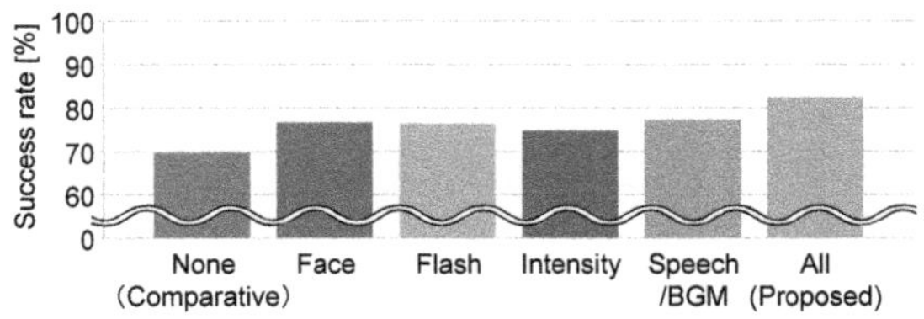

Figure 8: Success rates for each kind of features.

6. ACKNOWLEDGMENTS

Parts of this work were supported by the Grants-in-Aid for Scientific Research. The videos used in the experiments were provided by ClimBcube Co., Ltd.

7. REFERENCES

[1] W.-H. Cheng, Y.-Y. Chuang, and M.-C. Tien. Semantic-event based analysis and segmentation of wedding ceremony videos. In *Proc. Int. Workshop on Multimedia Information Retrieval 2007*, pages 95–104, March 2007.

[2] C.-Y. Chiu, C.-H. Li, H.-A. Wang, C.-S. Chen, and L.-F. Chien. A time warping based approach for video copy detection. In *Proc. IAPR 18th Int. Conf. on Pattern Recognition*, pages 228–231, September 2006.

[3] C. Panagiotakis and G. Tziritas. A speech/music discriminator based on RMS and zero-crossings. *IEEE Trans. Multimedia*, 7(1):155–166, February 2004.

[4] J. Sato, T. Takahashi, I. Ide, and H. Murase. Change detection in streetscapes from GPS coordinated omni-directional image sequences. In *Proc. IAPR 18th Int. Conf. on Pattern Recognition*, pages 935–938, August 2006.

[5] M. Takimoto, S. Satoh, and M. Sakauchi. Identification and detection of the same scene based on flashlight patterns. In *Proc. 2006 IEEE Int. Conf. on Multimedia and Expo*, pages 9–12, January 2006.

[6] H. Uchiyama, D. Deguchi, T. Takahashi, I. Ide, and H. Murase. Ego-localization using streetscape image sequences from in-vehicle cameras. In *Proc. 2009 IEEE Intelligent Vehicles Symposium*, pages 185–190, June 2009.

[7] P. Viola and M. Jones. Robust real-time face detection. *Int. J. Computer Vision*, 57(2):137–154, May 2004.

Content-aware Photo-on-photo Composition for Consumer Photos*

Aibo Tian
Department of Computer Science
The University of Texas at Austin
atian@cs.utexas.edu

Xuemei Zhang
Hewlett-Packard Labs
1501 Page Mill Road
Palo Alto, CA 94304 USA
xuemei.daxin@gmail.com

Daniel R. Tretter
Hewlett-Packard Labs
1501 Page Mill Road
Palo Alto, CA 94304 USA
dan.tretter@hp.com

ABSTRACT

We propose an approach to automatically generate photo-on-photo compositions using only a consumer's own image collection, without imposing a strong theme constraint dictated by typical background art designs. Our goal is to ensure adequate foreground and background photo sizing, avoid occlusion of important background photo content, and respect simple aesthetic rules in photo arrangement. We propose a novel image content redundancy measure to extract the informative zone, which is a rectangular region of the background photo that should not be occluded by foreground content. Background photo layout and foreground layout regions are then calculated based on a placement algorithm that deals with possible aspect ratio mismatch of the canvas and background photo, as well as cases of insufficient foreground photo layout area.

Categories and Subject Descriptors

H.5.1 [**Information Interfaces and Presentation**]: Multimedia Information System

General Terms

Algorithms, Design

Keywords

Photo composition, Informative zone, Salience map, Content redundancy

1. INTRODUCTION

With the rapid growth of consumer digital photo collections, users are shifting from simple printing to personal creation and publication of photo composition products such as photobooks. Current commercial photo composition services are still mostly based on templated pages, with the final appearance of the composition constrained by background artwork and template style (MagicPhotobook[6][2], snapfish[1], shutterfly[2]). AutoCollage[5] does not rely on templates, but the composition loses substantial user photo content by cropping. To achieve the twin goals of high aesthetic quality and showcasing of personal photos, we aim to create a tool that does not rely on strongly-themed background artwork that dominates a page, but rather uses only photos from the user's collection for page composition. Our system will allow rapid automatic composition of photo-on-photo pages that respect simple aesthetic rules to give the composition a designed yet highly personal look.

Our goal is to automatically generate photo compositions in a photo-on-photo style (Figure 3). Given a set of candidate photos for a composition and a user-specified canvas, we extract a rectangular informative zone for each photo based on a novel content redundancy measure. We define an "informative zone" as the smallest rectangular zone that contains the most unique content in the image. Areas outside of the informative zone are layout regions where foreground photos can be placed. When given multiple photos to place on a page, we can automatically select a background photo by choosing the one with the largest area outside the informative zone. Based on the informative zone results, we also propose a placement algorithm to arrange the background photo onto a target canvas of arbitrary dimensions to optimize background and foreground photo sizing as well as visual balance of the composition. Foreground photos can then be arranged on the page using any layout algorithm that accepts "exclusion zones" such as ExBRIC [1]. The user can choose any photo as the background photo, and put any number of foreground photos on it. Our content redundancy measure and layout style are inspired by composition samples generated by a professional design artist.

2. INFORMATIVE ZONE EXTRACTION USING CONTENT REDUNDANCY

The key part of a photo-on-photo composition style is partial occlusion of the background photo by the foreground content. However, important portions of the background photo must not be covered by foreground content. Our informative zone extraction algorithm is designed to divide any user photo into informative zones (parts that should not be occluded by foreground content) and safe layout zones (parts where foreground photos can safely cover).

*Area chair: Dick Bulterman

[1]www.snapfish.com
[2]www.shutterfly.com

MM'11, November 28–December 1, 2011, Scottsdale, Arizona, USA.

Figure 1: Examples of redundancy images. The left image is the original image, the middle one is horizontal redundancy image, and the right one is vertical redundancy image.

What is "informative" or "important" content is a highly subjective concept, and requires high-level understanding of an image. Computer vision algorithms today are far from being able to understand an image like a human viewer. Instead, many heuristic methods are proposed in the literature [4][3] that find important parts of an image based on low-level features. These methods generally define busy regions (e.g. high gradient regions) in an image as the informative zone, and assume the blank parts are unimportant. However, we find that layouts that cover blank regions of a background image produce very poor compositions. Professional designers we talk to all argue that for photo composition, it is important to leave ample blank space visible. Without spaces, the compositions appear cluttered and unprofessional. They suggest that covering "useless" busy regions would produce much better results than covering blank spaces.

We propose that informative zones are better defined by content redundancy instead of salience. Specifically, our informative zone extraction algorithm is motivated by the following two observations. First, regions in the photo with repetitive or predictable image features can be mentally recovered by an observer through visual inference, and therefore can often be safely covered. For example, Figure 3(b) shows a background scene dominated by horizontal repetitive pattern, and artists typically choose to cover a vertical slice of the background with foreground photos, instead of covering blank regions. Second, casual photographers generally do not put the most interesting objects at the periphery when composing a shot. Thus, periphery regions of images are more likely to be safe for occlusion. Combining the two observations together, we propose an algorithm that calculates horizontal and vertical content redundancy of an image, and trims away the redundant regions at the periphery to get an "informative zone" for each image. Examples can be seen in Figure 2. For now, we constrain the informative zone to be a single rectangular region for simplicity, but the redundancy principle can be easily extended to produce multiple informative zones of different shapes for an image.

2.1 Generating Redundancy Map

We call a pixel as redundant if it is perfectly predicted by the progression of its neighboring pixels. For a pixel value v_n at horizontal location x_n, we define it's left-redundancy as the deviation from a linear prediction from the values v_0 to v_{n-1}. between the coordinates and pixel values (1).

$$\mathbf{D_n} = \Delta E\{t_n'(T_{n-1}'T_{n-1})^{-1}(T_{n-1}'V_{n-1}), v_n\}, \quad (1)$$

where t_n is a vector of 2 elements $(1, x_n)'$, $T_n = (t_1, ..., t_n)'$, and x_n is the pixel coordinate at location n. It is easy to see that T_n is just the standard predictor term used in linear regression. The term v_n is a vector of CIEL*a*b* values after the S-CIELAB transformation [7], at location n, and $V_n = (v_1, ..., v_n)'$. The operation ΔE is the CIEL*a*b* color difference [7]. S-CIELAB is a perceptual pre-filtering step in color opponent channels to model the different spatial sensitivity to luminance and chromatic features in an image. This step improves redundancy estimates in color textured areas and generally helps with stability of the informative zone calculation.

The redundancy calculation in (1) can be easily generalized to get right-, top- and bottom-redundancy. For each pixel, we can calculate its horizontal redundancy as the minimum ΔE of its left and right redundancy, and its vertical redundancy as the minimum ΔE of its top and bottom redundancy values. Figure 1 shows an image and its horizontal and vertical redunancy maps R^x and R^y constructed this way.

2.2 Informative Zone Extraction

Once we have the redundancy maps for an image, an informative zone can be determined by trimming away high-redundancy areas on the four sides of the image.

We collapse the R^X and R^Y images into one dimensional profiles P^X and P^Y, which indicate the general informative level at each location along the horizontal and vertical dimensions. Using $mean_X$ and $mean_Y$ to denote the averaging operation along the X and Y dimensions, we have:

$$P^X = \{mean_Y([R^X]^{c_X})\}^{\frac{1}{c_X}} \quad (2)$$

$$P^Y = \{mean_X([R^Y]^{c_Y})\}^{\frac{1}{c_Y}} \quad (3)$$

where c_X and c_Y are constants greater than one, which are used to emphasize larger values in the final average so that highly informative regions are not left out of the informative zone even if they occupy a relatively small region in the image.

Once we have both profiles of informative level on each location, we "push in" the boundaries of informative zones on each direction (left/right/top/bottom), and stop on the first location where the P^X and P^Y values exceed their respective thresholds t_X and t_Y, which are also determined adaptively for each image. Methods for determining these thresholds are straightforward and usually application-specific, therefore we will not go into details in this paper.

After obtaining the initial zone boundaries, we expand the informative zone by one fourth of the redundant area in each direction, to make sure that users have enough visible content to infer the parts that will be covered by foreground photos. Some examples of the extracted informative zones are shown in Figure 2.

2.3 Background Photo Selection

Once we have the informative zone for each photo, we can use them to automatically select one photo that is most suitable to be used as background. In our implementation we choose the photo with the largest proportion of area outside the informative zone as the best background photo, since it is likely to give more area (and thus more flexibility) for foreground photo layout.

3. BACKGROUND PHOTO LAYOUT AND COMPOSITION

In a practical system, the selected background photo seldom has exactly the same aspect ratio as the composition

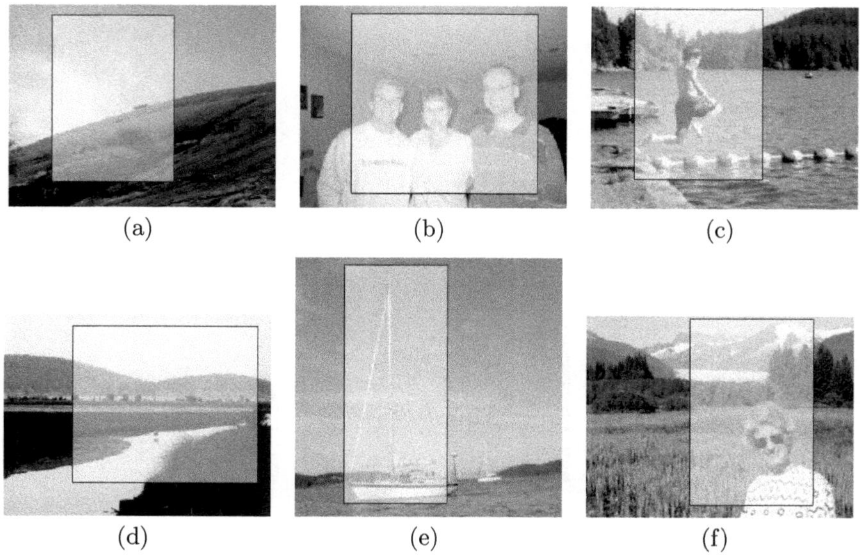

Figure 2: Results of informative zone extraction.

Algorithm 1 Background photo sizing and placement.

Input: Canvas size l_c^X and l_c^Y, background photo size l_b^X and l_b^Y, and foreground photo number n

Output: Background photo scale s, and coordinates x, y

$S_{back}^{max} = l_b^X \cdot l_b^Y \cdot [\min(\frac{l_c^X}{l_b^X}, \frac{l_c^Y}{l_b^Y})]^2$
$s = 1.0$
while true do
  Compute x, y using (5)
  Compute $ratio$ using (7)
  if (6) is **true then**
    return s, x, y
  else
    $s \leftarrow s - \delta$
    $S_{back} = S_{back}^{max} \cdot s^2$
  end if
end while

canvas. Proper sizing and placement of a background photo onto a canvas with mismatched dimensions is critical in achieving a pleasing composition, as it affects how well the foreground photos can be laid out, and the overall balance of the final composition.

3.1 Background Photo Sizing and Placement

A high quality photo-on-photo composition should have background and foreground photos of adequate sizes, and a balanced layout. Algorithm 1 illustrates the proposed approach for determining background sizing and placements.

We search optimal background configuration in the scale space first. Given a background photo scale, we propose a balance measure to compute the background placement. Balance measure is a one-dimensional measure (either horizontal or vertical) that reflects how good the weights are distributed. The weight is proportional to the area, and weighted differently for foreground, background and informative zone. We use the uniform distribution as the ideal distribution for the whole composition. The balance score is calculated as the average deviation of the cumulative weight distribution and cumulative uniform distribution. In practice, we only sample several special points, such as center of informative zone and centers of foreground photo layout areas, to compute the deviation (4).

$$B = 1 - \frac{\sum_{i=1}^{k} |C_{w_i} - C_{u_i}|^{c_B}}{k} \tag{4}$$

where C_{w_i} and C_{u_i} are the cumulative weight at the ith sample points of canvas and ideal uniform distribution, k is the total number of sample points, c_B is a coefficient.

Background photo layout is solved by optimizing a placement score that is the product of foreground photo area and balance scores (5). The foreground photo area can be estimated in many ways given the background placement and informative zone. One way is to run the foreground layout algorithm to obtain the real area. We can also approximate the area by making simplifying assumptions such as assuming tight packing rectilinear layout, without going through an actual layout algorithm.

In practice we seldom optimize over all possible placements, but only choose a few configurations and pick the one with the highest placement score. The choice of candidate placements could be guided by aesthetics constraints, or by computational cost considerations.

$$(x, y) = argmax_{x,y} S_{fore}(s, x, y)(B^X(x, y)B^Y(x, y))^{c_p} \tag{5}$$

where s is the scale of background photo, x and y are coordinates of background photo, S_{fore} is the estimated foreground area for this arrangement, B^X and B^Y are the horizontal and vertical balance scores, and c_p is an exponent that roughly indicates the "importance" of balance relative to foreground photo area.

After obtaining a plausible background configuration, we determine the quality of it by giving constraints of foreground photo area. We want to ensure that the ratio of foreground photo area and background photo area is big enough (6), and the total foreground photo area should be increased as the number of foreground photos (7), though individual foreground photo area may be decreased. If the current configuration is satisfied by the constraints (6)(7), we return the scale and placement as the final results.

$$S_{back} \leq \frac{S_{fore}(s, x, y)}{ratio} \tag{6}$$

(a) (b) (c) (d) (e) (f)

Figure 3: Results of automatic photo composition using consumer photos.

$$ratio = \min(\frac{c_{r1}}{n^{c_{r2}}}, \frac{1}{n}) \quad (7)$$

where s is the background photo scale, x and y are background coordinates, S_{back} and S_{fore} are background and estimated average individual foreground photo area, n is the number of foreground photos, c_{r1} and c_{r2} are coefficients between [0,1].

3.2 Foreground Photo Layout

After selecting, sizing and placing the background photo on the canvas, many existing photo layout algorithms could be used to arrange foreground photos in the safe region (outside the informative zone). For a first implementation of our system, we select the ExBric algorithm [1] for foreground photo layout.

4. EXPERIMENTS

In this section, we illustrate the performance of informative zone extraction algorithm and demonstrate final photo-on-photo compositions using real user photo sets.

4.1 Experimental Setup

The proposed system is tested on 25 photo sets from 8 users. The photo sets contain a total of 1627 photos, with the sets ranging in size from 10 to 138 photos. The topics of the photos include travel, party, daily life and natural scenes. Over 78% of the photos contain people.

Each photo set first goes through an automatic selection and clustering step [6], which assigns up to 6 photos to each page of a photobook. A background photo is automatically chosen and placed on each page, and the foreground photos are laid out with background photo to form a photo-on-photo composition for each page.

4.2 Experimental Results

Figure 2 shows some examples of the proposed informative zone extraction. For those photos only with natural scene (Figure 2(a), 2(d), 2(e)), the proposed algorithm captures the redundant area effectively. It is worth noting that for photos containing people (Figure 2(b), 2(c), 2(f)), our algorithm preserves faces and people within informative zones accurately and consistently without the aid of any face-detection algorithm.

Figure 3 demonstrates the photo compositions generated by our system. These examples show different variations of the composition, depending on the number of foreground photos and the informative zone of background photo. Figure 3(c) and 3(e) illustrate our stylistic treatments for the regions that cannot be covered by background photo. In these two examples, we use reflection and fading. We demonstrate the automatic composition of these whole photo sets to a professional artist. She considers most of them as good compositions, and all of them as acceptable.

5. CONCLUSIONS

We propose an approach to automatically generate photo composition in photo-on-photo style. The background photo is selected based on the informative zone extraction using a novel content redundancy measure. The scale and position of background photo are adapted to arbitrary canvas. For future work, we may extend the algorithms to support multiple informative zones and non-rectangular shapes.

6. REFERENCES

[1] H. Chao, C. Atkins, X. Zhang, and D. Tretter. Blocked recursive image composition with exclusion zones. In *ACM symposium on Document engineering*, 2010.

[2] Y. Gao, C. B. Atkins, P. Cheatle, J. Xiao, X. Zhang, H. Chao, P. Wu, D. Tretter, D. Slatter, A. Carter, R. Penny, and C. Willis. Magicphotobook: Designer inspired, user perfected photo albums. In *ACM Multimedia*, 2009.

[3] T. Liu, J. Sun, N. Zheng, X. Tang, and H. Shum. Learning to detect a salient object. In *CVPR*, 2007.

[4] L. Itti, N. Koch, and E. Niebur. A model of saliency-based visual attention for rapid scene analysis. *IEEE Transactions on PAMI*, 1998.

[5] C. Rother, L. Bordeaux, Y. Hamadi, and A. Blake. Autocollage. In *SIGGRAPH*, 2006.

[6] J. Xiao, X. Zhang, P. Cheatle, Y. Gao, and C. B. Atkins. Mixed-initiative photo collage authoring. In *ACM Multimedia*, 2008.

[7] X. Zhang and B. A. Wandell. A spatial extension of cielab for digital color-image reproduction. *Journal of the Society for Information Display*, 1997.

PhotoFeel: Feeling Your Photo Collection with Graph-based Audiovisual Flocking

Cheng-Te Li, Hsun-Ping Hsieh, Shou-De Lin
Graduate Institute of Networking and Multimedia
National Taiwan University, Taipei, Taiwan
{d98944005, d98944006, sdlin}@csie.ntu.edu.tw

ABSTRACT
This paper proposes an audiovisual presentation system, called *PhotoFeel*, to not only give users pleasant browsing atmosphere but also deliver a quick sense conveyed by given photo collection. While conventional photo display systems aim at improving the styles of presentation, we explore the visual and semantic feelings to create a space exhibiting the feelings from photographers. This is achieved by simulating the interactions among photos to emerge some flocking behaviors, where each photo is regarded as a simulated agent. To present the feelings of photos on the flocking, we construct two graphs by investigating the visual contents and tag semantics respectively. In addition, to enhance the diverse feelings of a photo collection, three audiovisual effects are composed to have rich presentation of feelings. Experimental results show that our *PhotoFeel* truly exhibits potential feelings for given photos and people comparatively favor our system.

Categories and Subject Descriptors
H.5.1 [**Information Interface and Presentation**]: Multimedia Information Systems – *Animation*; I.6 [**Simulation and Modeling**]: Types of Simulation – *Visual.*

General Terms
Design, Human Factors.

Keywords
Photo feelings, audiovisual presentation, flocking simulation, visualization, photo-based artwork.

1. INTRODUCTION
Nowadays, taking photos has become a popular activity for people to record what they experience in daily life. At the instant of pressing the shutter of camera, the photograph captures things ranging from physical impressions to personal feelings and moods, called "a picture is worth a thousand words." And thus we browse photo albums as if tasting our stories. This motivates us to devise an application which not only provides rich presentation for users to browse the visual contents but also allows users to experience the diverse feelings conveyed by the given collection of photos (e.g. album) from photographers.

--
Area Chair: Susanne Boll

MM'11, November 28--December 1, 2011, Scottsdale, Arizona, USA.

There are lots of tools and studies on photo browsing or exploring. A common used technique is the photo browser, like ACDSee[1] and Picasa[2] which provides a thumbnail manner to facilitate management of photo collections. Recently, some intelligent systems are devised to express rich browsing experience. Photo Tourism [12] presented an interactive navigation manner to explore photos in 3D scene. Photo Navigator [4] exploited the spatial relations among photos to create a feeling of space for users. In [13], a 2D virtual canvas was developed to easily browse desired photos based on visual similarities. On the other hand, the photo slideshow with music accompaniment is another prevalent form to experience photos. Photo2Video [5] applied "Ken Burns" effect to produce motion clips with incidental music to highlight some attentive regions. Tiling Slideshow [2] generated a music-driven slideshow where each frame is tiled by multiple photos. These techniques, however, mainly focus on improving the style of presentation for those who see the photos. The diverse feelings conveyed from the photos are not considered. Although the works [7][8] exploited music generation and accompaniment to present the feelings expressed in visual contents, they primarily riveted on illustrations and paintings, respectively.

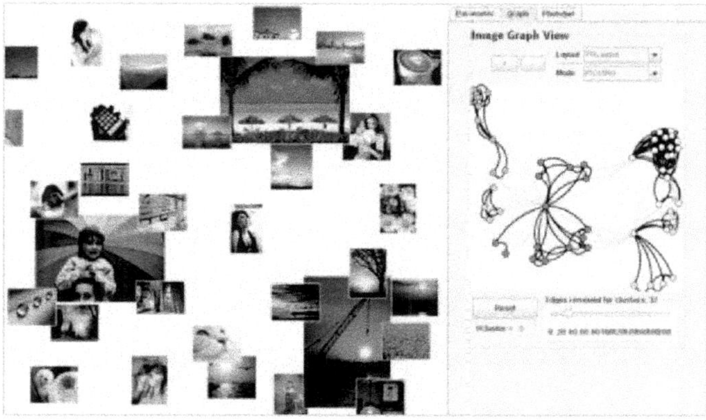

Figure 1. A snapshot (partial) for the proposed *PhotoFeel* audiovisual flocking simulation.

In this paper, we propose a novel audiovisual system, *PhotoFeel*, for users to not only browse the visual contents easily but also taste the feelings conveyed by the given collection of photos. The central idea of *PhotoFeel* is that by regarding each photo as a simulated character, termed photo agent, we create the physical interactions among photos to emerge some flocking behaviors, which exhibits a kind of movement process of "birds of a feather flock together" for characters. An atmosphere of feeling or mental picture will be created by viewing the emerging behaviors among photo agents. Since the feelings are physically characterized by

[1] ACDSee: http://www.acdsystems.com
[2] Picasa: http://picasa.google.com/

visual contents and tag semantics of photos, we model the feelings by constructing two *graphs* using visual and semantic similarities among photos. Such graphs are used to guide the flocking simulations and provide the feelings of photos from two diverse perspectives. We further compute three audiovisual effects to enhance the browsing and feeling experience as the simulation proceeds: (1) detecting photo clusters to direct the interactions among photo agents, (2) highlighting the representative photo for each flock of photo agents, and (3) calculating the affinity values between photos to generate real-time sound effects based on a series of psychological color-music mappings. Figure 1 shows a snapshot of *PhotoFeel* audiovisual flocking system.

2. SYSTEM OVERIEW

There are three components in the proposed *PhotoFeel* system, including content processing, graph-based computation, and audiovisual flocking simulation, as shown in Figure 2. First, given a collection of photos (e.g. album), where each photo is associated with some tags, we extract both some global and local visual features from them. And then we construct two graphs to capture the hidden feelings from two aspects: visual contents and tag semantics. Second, to present the feeling of photos during the simulation, based on the visual and semantic graphs, we develop three audiovisual effects, (a) photo clustering, (b) representative photo determination, and (c) feeling affinity calculation, which are integrated into the following flocking simulation. Finally, by considering each photo as a simulated agent, we combine item (a) and (b) to simulate and guide the interactions among photo agents to emerge flocking behaviors of photos for visualization, and we also use item (c) to generate real-time sound effects conforming to the captured feelings based on the two graphs. People can view and listen into the flocking behaviors to taste the feelings or atmosphere created by the given collection of photos.

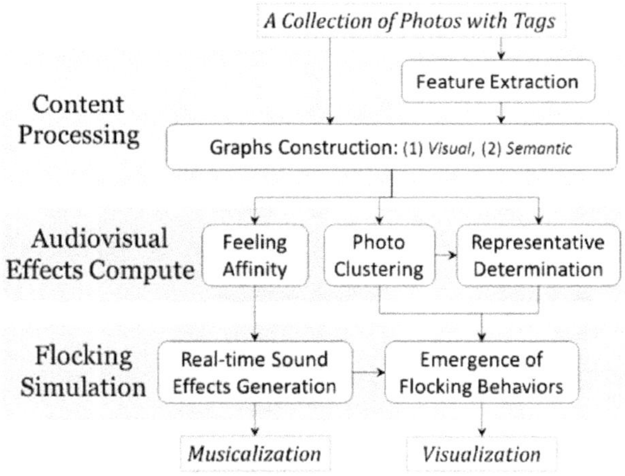

Figure 2. System flowchart of the proposed *PhotoFeel*.

3. CONTENT PROCESSING

In this section, we build the foundation of our system using the graph representation to capture the feelings among photos from the visual and semantic points of view. We first elaborate the visual features we employ for the constructions of graphs.

3.1 Visual Feature Extraction

We combine the global features of colors and texture and local geometric features to model the visual contents. The global features capture the photographic visual composition while the local ones identify the actual structural elements of objects. Such mixed global and local features have been shown to provide significant complementary information in recognition tasks [1].

- **Global Features.** We extract color histograms and color moments as global features of photos to capture theirs visual and spatial color distributions. We also utilize the Gabor textures to model the textural information. A feature vector will be produced for each photo by concatenating these features. The similarity between two photos is calculated according to normalized Euclidean distance.
- **Local Features.** We also represent the photos by local interest point descriptors, given by the scale-invariant feature transform (SIFT) with a Difference of Gaussian (DoG) process. Given two photos p_i and p_j with the descriptor vectors, $D_i=(d^1{}_i, d^2{}_i, ..., d^n{}_i)$ and $D_j=(d^1{}_j, d^2{}_j, ..., d^n{}_j)$, we define the similarity between two photos as the number interest points shared between two photos divided by their average number of interest points.

3.2 Graph Constructions

Based on the extracted visual features and the associated semantic tags on photos, we intend to model the feelings conveyed from photos by means of constructing a visual graph and a semantic graph. Both visual and semantic graphs contain photos as nodes, and the links between two photos are connected if their defined similarity exceeds a given threshold. The first one is the *visual graph*, which is designed to capture the visual feelings and impressions conveyed by the given photo collection. If two photos exhibit similar visual contents and resemble each other in appearance, they tend to express similar visual feelings, and thus we gather and connect them together in the graph. The second one is the *semantic graph*, which considers the photo feelings from the viewpoint of semantic tags. If two photos possess more common conceptual tags (e.g. object names, emotional terms, events, persons, and locations), they have high potential to convey similar meanings or reflect the same feelings, and thus we link them together in the sematic graph. In next section, we will elaborate how to exploit the visual and semantic graphs to compute diverse audiovisual effects for audiovisual flocking simulation. What follows describes how to construct these graphs in our system.

- **Visual Graph.** Given a collection of photos, the visual graph is constructed by estimating the similarity between photos using the extracted visual features. Since there are global and local features, we define the *visual similarity* between two photos p_i and p_j by using a convex function as

$$VisualSim(p_i, p_j)=\alpha \times GlobalSim(p_i, p_j) + (1-\alpha) \times LocalSim(p_i, p_j). \quad (1)$$

  This similarity definition provides a flexible preference when the given photo collection is characterized by either global or local part. Two photos are linked if their similarity exceeds a given *visual threshold* δ_v which controls the strength of visual feelings.

- **Semantic Graph.** We regard the tags associated on each photo as a kind of semantic features to construct the semantic graph. We modify the *Normalized Google Distance* (*NGD*) [3], which is a measure of semantic interrelatedness derived by calculating the correlation from Google search results, to define the *semantic similarity* between photos. Given two photos p_i and p_j with tag sets $T(p_i)$ and $T(p_j)$, we define the semantic similarity

$$SemanticSim(p_i, p_j) = \sum_{t_a \in T(p_i), t_b \in T(p_j)} \frac{1}{1+NGD(t_a, t_b)} \quad (2)$$

where $NGD(t_a, t_b) = \frac{\max\{\log f(t_a), \log f(t_b)\} - \log f(t_a, t_b)}{\log N - \min(\log f(t_a), \log f(t_b))}$, in which $f(t_a)$, $f(t_b)$, and $f(t_a, t_b)$ denotes the number of photos containing t_a, t_b, both t_a and t_b, separately in a photo corpus. N is the total number of photos in our corpus. Likewise, a *semantic threshold* δ_s is given to allow the extent of semantic feelings.

4. AUDIOVISUAL EFFECTS

To present the feelings conveyed by the given photos collection, in this section, based on the visual and semantic graphs, we attempt to create three audiovisual effects, including photo clustering, representative photo determination, and feeling affinity calculation. The first two parts are used to guide the interactions among photo agents to emerge some flocking behaviors from the visual aspect while the last one is used to generate real-time sound effects to create a kind of atmosphere consistent with the feelings behind given photos.

4.1 Photo Clustering

The first part is to group the photos according to visual and semantic graphs. Since a photo collection could deliver some different impressions, we gather photos with similar visual feelings to a cluster for further simulation so that the mental image of each flock can appear clearly during simulation. We perform the photo cluster by employing the *Fast Newman algorithm* [9], which a graph-based clustering method finding some tightly intra-connected and loosely inter-connected subgraphs as final clusters.

4.2 Representative Photos Determination

To enhance the feelings of each detected photo cluster, we find a representative photo for each cluster to be the central impression. The representative photos will be highlighted and enlarged during flocking simulation so that users can not only browse the diverse visual topics but also easily understand the feeling of each cluster. Based on the induced subgraph of each photo cluster, we provide three diverse importance measures to determine the representative photos from different aspects, including *degree*, *closeness* [15], and *PageRank* centrality. Degree is a local measure and thus served as a first glance or feeling for the feeling of a cluster. Both closeness and PageRank are global measures to find essential ones relatively in such subgraph of photos.

4.3 Feeling Affinity Estimation

While the above two parts are used to guide the flocking effects visually, we exploit this feeling affinity to generate sound effects in auditory perception. Specifically, if two photo agents are too close or collide during simulation, our system will produce some harmonious or discord sound effects according to their affinity of feelings. Two photos in the visual or semantic graph could deliver different feelings and the corresponding photo agents could meet during flocking simulation. We propose the feeling affinity to estimate their resemblance of mental impressions for sound effects generation. The basic idea of feeling affinity is that if two photos have higher structural proximity to one another in the graph, they tend to obtain higher affinity score. We employ the *Random Walk with Restart* (*RWR*) [14] to compute the feeling affinity. Given two photos p_i and p_j in the graph, the feeling affinity is defined as

$$FeelingAffinity(p_i, p_j) = RWR(p_i, p_j) + RWR(p_j, p_i). \quad (3)$$

where $RWR(p_i, p_j)$ is the steady-state probability that a random surfer walks from p_i and finally stay at p_j in the graph.

5. AUDIOVISUAL FLOCKING

Equipped with the three audiovisual effects capturing different mental impressions carried by the given photo collection, now we intend to present the audiovisual presentation system for feeling photos. We realize the idea of "birds of a feature flock together" to create a space of feelings for these photos. By taking each photo as an agent, we exploit the technique of flocking simulation to exhibit the sentimental interactions among photos for sensing. We employ a typical flocking model, *Reynolds' model* [11], in our system. This flocking model consists of three basic rules to lead agents to produce flocking behaviors. The first is *separation* rule steering agents to avoid crowding local flockmates, the second is *alignment* steering agents towards the average heading of local flockmates, and the third is *cohesion* steering agents to move forward the average position of local flockmates. On the other hand, by using the audiovisual effect of photo clusters, we devise a probability P_c to guide the interactions among photos agents to produce sentimental flocks during simulation process. That is, if P_c is set to higher, photos with similar feelings will have higher potential flock together. Moreover, we enhance the central feeling of each photo cluster by highlighting the corresponding representative photo to display. Some sound effects will be generated based on the audiovisual effect of feeling affinities among photo agents. What follows elaborates the emergent flocking behaviors exhibited in visual aspect, and describes how to generate sound effects to enhance the feeling in auditory aspect.

5.1 Emergence of Flocking Behaviors

We utilize two produced emergent flocking behaviors (i.e., visual and semantic) to illustrate and demonstrate the photo feelings delivered by our system. Figure 3 shows an example of flocking behaviors using the visual graph. That is, agents of photos with similar visual impressions tend to flock and move together. We can see there are four diverse appearances, including red, green, blue, and black-white. Besides, photo agents with no visual attributions wander among these four crews. Note that though the wandering agents could move toward some visual flock, they tend to leave the flock since they are affected by such cluster. Figure 4 shows the emergent flocking behaviors by the semantic graph. Likewise, photo agents with similar semantic feelings or concepts, including sunset, flower, cup, girl, and colorful, flock together controlled by P_c. Some agents belonging to no major clusters wander in the simulating space.

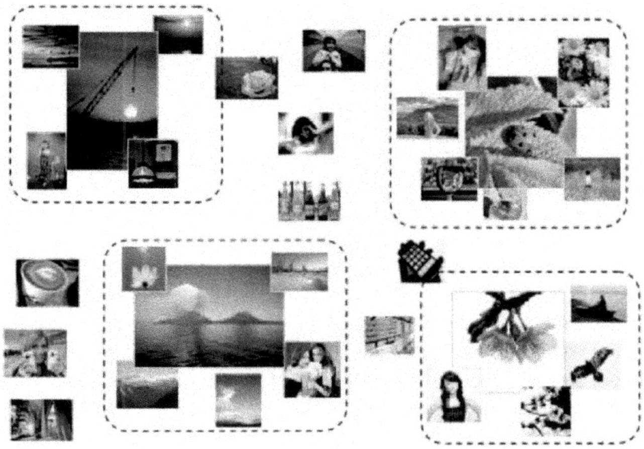

Figure 3. Flocking behavior using the *visual graph*.

Figure 4. Flocking behavior using the *semantic graph*.

6. EVALUATIONS

We evaluate our *PhotoFeel* system by subjective experiments, as the evaluation methods in [2][4][5][7][8]. We compare the flocking simulation produced by our *PhotoFeel* to the slideshows generated by ACDSee[1] and Photo Story[3] in terms of satisfaction. And the slideshows are accompanied with sentimental music. The dataset we use is the MIR Flickr 25000 collection [6]. We manually select two photo sets with number of photos = 100 for the evaluation.

Table 1. List of five criteria for evaluation.

Feeling (Sen)	Does the presentation convey feelings for photos?
Fun (Fun)	Is it a funny presentation?
Experience (Exp)	Does the presentation reach appreciation aesthetics?
Atmosphere (Atm)	How do you feel the audiovisual effects?
Acceptance (Acc)	Do you want to use it to taste your photos?

We invited 25 persons to participate this subjective experiment. Each person is asked to view the slideshows and our audiovisual flocking simulation. Then they are asked to give scores from 1 to 10 to express their satisfaction for the questions listed in Table 1. Higher score indicates better satisfaction for that criterion. Note that since our *PhotoFeel* provides two feelings (i.e., visual and semantic) to display, we compute average score of the two aspects for each criterion.

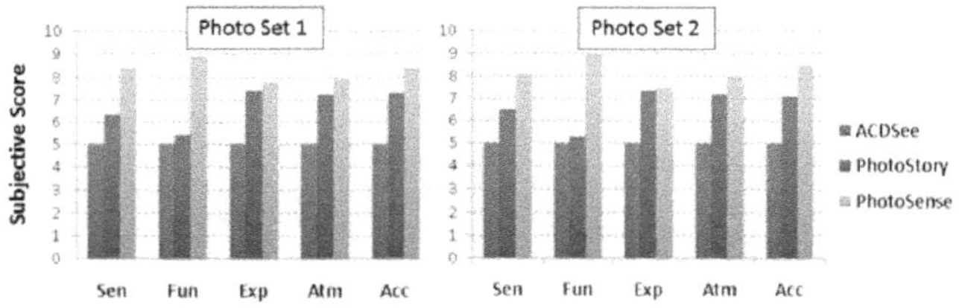

Figure 5. Results of subjective evaluation for two photo sets.

We set the score of ACDSee to 5 as the baseline. Figure 5 shows the results of subjective evaluation. We can observe our system outperform other two on average, especially for the criterion of feelings and fun. This comes from the exhibition of the space of central feelings by the emergent flocking behaviors among photo agents with audiovisual and animated effects. However, we nearly have no difference on the criterion of experience. We think it is because sometimes the movement of photo agents becomes a little complicated and not intuitive for users to explore.

[3] Photo Story: http://www.microsoft.com/athome/morefun/photostory.mspx

7. CONCLUSIONS

We present an audiovisual presentation system, *PhotoFeel*, to capture and exhibit the feelings conveyed by the given photos. The central idea is presenting flocking behaviors emerged from the interactions among photos to create a space of photo feelings. The feelings are modeled by visual and semantic graphs from visual contents and tag semantics. And then we embed the impressions of photos on our system by computing three audiovisual effects and applying them to guide the simulation in both visual and auditory aspects. Experimental results demonstrate the satisfaction of this new kind of photo presentation.

8. REFERENCES

[1] S. Chang, W. Hsu, L. Kennedy, L. Xie, A. Yanagawa, E. Zavesky, and D. Zhang. Columbia University TRECVID-2005 Video Search and High-Level Feature Extraction. *NIST TRECVID Workshop*, 2005.

[2] J. C. Chen, W. T. Chu, J. H. Kuo, C. Y. Weng, and J. L. Wu, Tiling Slideshow. In *Proc. of ACM Intl. Conference on Multimedia (MM'06)*, 25–34, 2006.

[3] R. L. Cilibrasi, and P. B. M. Vitanyi. The Google Similarity Distance. *IEEE Transactions on Knowledge and Data Engineering (TKDE)*, 19(3), 370–383, 2007.

[4] C. C. Hsieh, W. H. Cheng, C. H. Chang, Y. Y. Chuang, and J. L. Wu. Photo Navigator. In *Proc. of ACM International Conference on Multimedia (MM'08)*, 419–428, 2008.

[5] X. S. Hua , L. Lu, and H. J. Zhang. Photo2Video - A System for Automatically Converting Photographic Series into Video. In *Proc. of ACM Intl. Conference on Multimedia (MM'04)*, 708–715, 2004.

[6] M. J. Huiskes and M. S. Lew. The MIR Flickr Retrieval Evaluation. In *Proc. of ACM Intl. Conf. on Multimedia Information Retrieval (MIR'08)*, 39–43, 2008.

[7] K. Ishizuka and T. Onisawa. Generation of Variations on Theme Music Based on Impressions of Story Scenes. In *Proc. of ACM International Conference on Game Research and Development*, 129–136, 2006.

[8] C. T. Li and M. K. Shan. Emotion-based Impressionism Slideshow with automatic music accompaniment. In *Proc. of ACM International Conference on Multimedia (MM'07)*, 839–842, 2007.

[9] M. E. J. Newman. Fast Algorithm for Detecting Community Structure in Networks. *Physical Review*, E 69, 066133, 2004.

[10] R. W. Pridmore. Music and Color: Relations in the Psychophysical Perspective. *Colour Research and Application*, 17(1), 57–61, 1992

[11] C. W. Reynolds. Flocks, Herds and Schools: A Distributed Behavior Model. *ACM SIGGRAPH*, 25–34, 1987.

[12] N. Snavely, S. M. Seitz, and R. Szeliski. Photo Tourism: Exploring Photo Collections in 3D. *ACM Transactions on Graphics*, 25(3), 835–846, 2006.

[13] G. Strong and M. Gong. Organizing and Browsing Photos using Different Feature Vectors and Their Evaluations. In *Proc. of ACM Intl. Conference on Image and Video Retrieval (CIVR'08)*, No.3, 2008.

[14] H. Tong, C. Faloutsos, and J. Y. Pan. Fast Random Walk with Restart and Its Application. In *Proc. of IEEE Intl. Conference on Data Mining (ICDM'06)*, 613–622, 2006.

[15] S. Wasserman and K. Faust. Social Network Analysis: Methods and Applications. *Cambridge University Press*, 1994.

Learning to Produce 3D Media from a Captured 2D Video *

Minwoo Park, Jiebo Luo, Andrew Gallagher, Majid Rabbani
Corporate Research and Engineering
Eastman Kodak Company
{minwoo.park, jiebo.luo, andrew.gallagher, majid.rabbani}@kodak.com

ABSTRACT

Due to the advances in display technologies and the commercial success of 3D motion pictures in recent years, there is renewed interest in enabling consumers to create 3D content. While new 3D content can be created using more advanced capture devices (i.e., stereo cameras), most people still use 2D capture devices. Furthermore, enormously large collections of captured media exist only in 2D. We present a system for producing stereo images from captured 2D videos. Our system detects "good" stereo frames from a 2D video, which was captured *a priori* without any constraints on camera motion or content. We use a trained classifier to detect pairs of video frames that are suitable for constructing stereo images. In particular, for a given frame I_t at time t, we determine if $\hat{t}$ exists such that $I_{t+\hat{t}}$ and I_t can form an acceptable stereo image. We verify the performance of our method for producing stereo media from captured 2D videos in a psychovisual evaluation using both professional movie clips and amateur home videos. To the best of our knowledge, detecting good stereo pairs from a captured 2D video has been adequately addressed in the literature.

Categories and Subject Descriptors

I.4.0 [IMAGE PROCESSING AND COMPUTER VISION]: General

General Terms

Algorithms

Keywords

2D to 3D, Stereo Image

1. INTRODUCTION

Shortly after the dawn of photography (from roughly the 1850s), stereoscopes and anaglyph images were invented to convey to the user a scene with depth and realism [1]. The fundamental insight was that by presenting to each eye of a human viewer its own image of the scene from a unique viewpoint, the viewer will experience depth perception. Imaging systems have incorporated innumerable technological innovations in the century and a half since, and now, such innovations as 3D television (requiring 3D glasses or no glasses) and handheld devices are available to consumers. However, despite these achievements, the vast majority of captured images and video are monocular. Although a few stereo cameras exist, they have yet to gain wide-spread market penetration. It is possible to use multiple captures from a monocular camera to obtain the effect of stereo views, but great care must be taken to position the camera to replicate the arrangement of the human eyes, and also to ensure that the objects in the captured scene remain fixed in their positions during the time lapse between captures. However, this situation hinders the freedom of image and video capture. More importantly, there is already a huge volume of monocular video and stereo that have already been captured and that available source can be leveraged to produce new 3D media.

In this work, we propose to produce a set of good-quality stereo images from any input video. Our method relies on a classifier that determines whether a proposed stereo pair meets geometric constraints to ensure that a human viewer will have a pleasant 3D viewing experience. The classifier uses features related to keypoint matching across the two images in the proposed pair, and it considers both epipolar geometric and global motion descriptions. For each frame in a video we find potential stereo matches. The classifier

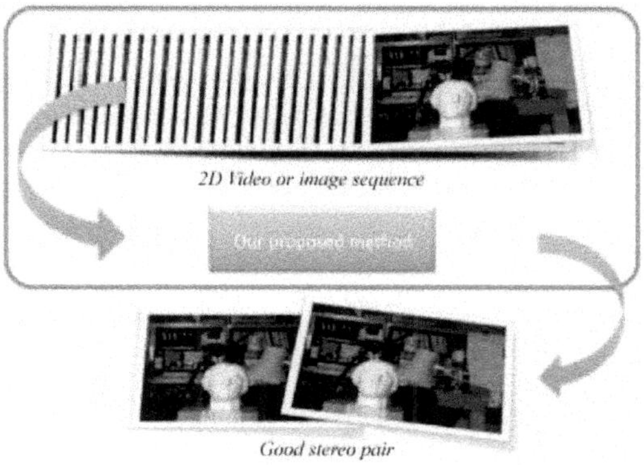

Figure 1: Our goal is to identify from a 2D video the content that would present appreciable 3D effect to a human observer as opposed to recovering 3D depth.

*Area chair: Susanne Boll

is used for two purposes, which are two of the main contributions of this paper:

- find, for each frame of the video, another frame to serve as its stereo match
- find, across all frames of the video, frame pairs with a stereo match that leads to very good stereo quality

Our algorithm takes a monocular video (or a time sequence of image frames such as photos shot in a burst) and produces from the video a small set of stereo images of high stereo quality. Note that the produced stereo images can induce an impression of 3D but it may not have true-to-life 3D depth. Our goal is to identify from a 2D video the content that would present an appreciable 3D effect on a human observer as opposed to recovering 3D depth from a stereo pair.

This work is justified by the renewed and growing interest in 3D media. Clearly, 3D content is in critical need. While new 3D content can be created using more advanced capture devices such as stereo cameras (e.g., Fuji Real3D), most people still own 2D capture devices and also possess enormous amounts of legacy content in 2D forms. The methods that we present in this paper are useful for allowing people to produce and see 3D media that originates from any video captured in 2D.

2. RELATED WORK

There is a great deal of research devoted to the analysis of stereo (or multi-view) captures of a scene through stereo matching or structure-from-motion algorithms. We refer the reader to [9] for a description of algorithms in this area. In general, this line of work is devoted to processing multiple images of a scene to compute either dense or sparse depth. However, recovering accurate and dense 3D range information has yet to be realized for pairs of images captured from a similar vantage point. Conversely, our proposed work aims to detect a good candidate stereo image pair, or to produce a good stereo image pair rather than reconstruct a dense 3D map of the scene. Namely, the proposed work aims to mine good stereo image pairs from a 2D video. Please see Figure 1. We also point out that structure from motion and stereo matching both assume that input pair images are captured with no nonrigid motion in the scene, and problems arise when this is not the case. Our algorithm explicitly seeks out objects that move in a non-consistent manner with respect to the background, and performs recomposition to produce a perceptually consistent stereo image pair.

Our work is related to several other areas. First, we produce a set of "key frames" from a video in common with key frame extraction methods such as [15]. However, our key frames are actually stereo images. Further, we consider the quality and geometric consistency of the stereo pair, which has not been previously addressed.

Second, our work is related to approaches that aim to convert 2D media to 3D [2, 12, 13, 14]. Guttmann et al., [2] present a semi-automatic method to convert a 2D video to a stereoscopic video pairs. The system requires user-scribbles to identify relative depths of background and foreground objects, and a depth map is generated by these scribbles and propagated over several frames. If there are many objects that are at different depths, this method requires more complex user scribbles. Ward et al. [14] combine temporally coherent segmentation, structure from motion (SFM), and user input to convert existing 2D captured videos to 3D videos. These methods [2, 12, 13, 14] all require user input. In contrast, we seek to find and produce only high-quality stereo images, instead of converting every frame of a video from 2D to 3D using user interactions.

Third, the work by Saxena et al. [8] and the work by Hoiem et al., [5] are somewhat related in that they consider the problem of estimating 3D scene structure from a single still image of an unconstrained environment.

3. METHOD

Symbol	Description
$v_x^{(a)}$ & $v_y^{(a)}$	All of horizontal & vertical optical flows
$v_x^{(i)}$	Epipolar inliers' horizontal optical flow
$v_y^{(i)}$	Epipolar inliers' vertical optical flow
$v_x^{(o)}$	Epipolar outliers' horizontal optical flow
$v_y^{(o)}$	Epipolar outliers' vertical optical flow
Feature	**Description**
$a(v_x^{(i)}), a(v_y^{(i)})$	Average of $v_x^{(i)}$ and $v_y^{(i)}$
$v(v_x^{(i)}), v(v_y^{(i)})$	Variance of $v_x^{(i)}$ and $v_y^{(i)}$
$a(v_x^{(o)}), a(v_y^{(o)})$	Average of $v_x^{(o)}$ and $v_y^{(o)}$
$v(v_x^{(o)}), v(v_y^{(o)})$	Variance of $v_x^{(o)}$ and $v_y^{(o)}$
$a(v_x^{(a)}), a(v_y^{(a)})$	Average of $v_x^{(a)}$ and $v_y^{(a)}$
$\lambda_{max}^{(i)}, \lambda_{min}^{(i)}$	Eigen values of 2D scatter matrix of $v_x^{(i)}$ and $v_y^{(i)}$
$\mathbf{u}_{max}^{(i)}, \mathbf{u}_{min}^{(i)}$	Eigenvectors of 2D scatter matrix with respect to epiploar inliers' flows.
$\lambda'^{(i)}_{max}, \lambda'^{(i)}_{min}$	Eigen values of 2D scatter matrix of epipolar inliers.
$\mathbf{u}'^{(i)}_{max}, \mathbf{u}'^{(i)}_{min}$	Eigenvectors of 2D scatter matrix of epipolar inliers.
$a(\angle E)$	Average angle of epipolar lines
$v(\angle E)$	Variance of angle of epipolar lines
$\mathbf{e_1}, \mathbf{e_2}$	Locations of epipole 1 and 2
$\angle\overline{\mathbf{c_1 e_1}}, \angle\overline{\mathbf{c_2 e_2}}$	Angle of line between centers of image and epipoles.
$\#N_{3D}$	The number of reconstructed 3D points
${}^{\#in}/_{\#all}$	Ratio of the number of $v^{(i)}$ over the number of $v^{(a)}$
T_x^{3D} T_y^{3D} T_z^{3D}	The x, y, and z components of the relative camera location in 3D, respectively
$v(X_{3D})$ $v(Y_{3D})$ $v(Z_{3D})$	Variance of x, y, and z components in 3D points, respectively
b_E	Is epipole inside image?
R_1, R_2, R_3, R_4	$\frac{a(v_x^{(i)})}{a(v_y^{(i)})}, \frac{v(v_x^{(i)})}{v(v_y^{(i)})}, \frac{a(v_x^{(a)})}{a(v_y^{(a)})}, \frac{\lambda_{max}^{(i)}}{\lambda_{min}^{(i)}}$

Table 1: A subset of entire 42 features and their descriptions. Please refer to the supplemental material for a complete set of the proposed features.

We first collect positive stereo pair samples and negative samples. Positive samples are: 1) stereo image pairs from Middlebury stereo websites [9], 2) stereo image pairs captured by a Fuji Real3D stereo camera, 3) image pairs from a single lens video camera where there are mostly translational horizontal movements with small rotations but no independent moving objects, and 4) image pairs from a single lens video camera where there are mostly translational horizontal movements and small rotations with independent moving objects. Negative samples are: 1) image pairs from a single lens video camera where the camera only rotates about the camera origin, and 2) image pairs from a single lens video camera where there are only vertical movements. The negative image pair samples have overlapping image content; however, they do not contain views of the scene from horizontally translated viewpoints. The resulting number of positive samples and negative samples are 332 and 403, respectively.

Feature Extraction: We first detect Kanade-Lucas-Tomasi (KLT) features in I_t, track KLT features over $I_{t+\hat{t}}$ using the KLT tracking algorithm [10], and we extract several features from the computed optical flows. To extract the features, we first perform the RANSAC algorithm to compute epipolar geometry [4], and recover the camera positions using tracked KLT features and classify each tracked KLT feature using RANSAC. Inliers are tracked points that are consistent with the estimated epipolar geometry, and outliers are the remaining tracked points. Figure 2 shows the optical flow field found by tracking feature points [6] where green arrows show epipolar inliers' flow and the white arrows show epipolar outliers' flow.

Next, a suite of features is computed from the tracked points to characterize the relative camera motion with respect to the scene. For example, the number of 3D points ($\#N_{3D}$), the x, y, and z components of the relative camera location in 3D (T_x^{3D},T_y^{3D},T_z^{3D}), and variance of x, y, and z components in 3D points ($v(X_{3D}), v(Y_{3D}), v(Z_{3D})$) can be computed using a structure from a epipolar geometry algorithm [4]. The complete list of all computed features and their descriptions can be seen in Table 1 and the computation of other quantities are straightforward.

To discuss the significance of some of the features, measuring $a(\angle E)$ and $v(\angle E)$ in Table 1 can indicate whether there is camera rotation only, translation only, or both. The $a(\angle E)$ and $v(\angle E)$ close to 0 means that there exists only a horizontal translation of the camera. However, if the scene does not contain objects at different depths, it does not make an interesting stereo frame pair (as all objects appear to be on a single plane). This condition is detected by $std(v_x^{(i)}), std(v_y^{(i)}), std(v_x^{(o)}), std(v_y^{(o)})$, and so on.

Figure 2: Green: estimated epipolar inliers' flow. White: estimated epipolar outliers' flow. Other features are further computed using these inliers and outliers.

Training and Testing a Classifier: We found that a classification using a decision tree based machine learning algorithm performs best among several machine learning algorithms available in [3]. Therefore, we use random trees originally introduced by Leo Breiman and Adele Cutler [11] for our Phase I algorithm. The random trees classifier takes the input feature vector $\mathbf{X}$, classifies it with each tree $y_i = Tr_i(\mathbf{X})$ in the forest, and outputs the level label C that receives the majority of votes. Positive and negative samples are represented by $C = 1$ and $C = -1$, respectively. For this purpose, we use the OpenCV library. Formally, the trained prediction function using a random tree is given as:

$$C_{learned} = R_{forest}(\mathbf{X}) \tag{1}$$

We evaluate the trained prediction model using 10-fold cross validation and measure the classification accuracy. The precision/recall rate for correct positive and negative samples are 94.2%/95.87% and 98.01%/96.70%, respectively. The overall accuracy of the trained prediction model is 96.33%.

Quality of the Detection: Once the pairs are identified by the classifier as positive samples, we evaluate the quality of the samples by:

$$Q = v(v_x^{(i)}) \tag{2}$$

where $v_x^{(i)}$ is the horizontal flow of epipolar inlier points (Table 1). Although this quality measure is simple, it is powerful when used on the identified stereo frame pairs. A higher value indicates more scene objects at different depths, resulting in a richer 3D effect. Therefore, we select a stereo frame pair $(I_t, I_{t+\hat{t}})$ with the highest Q from pairs $\{(I_t, I_{t+\hat{t}}) \,|\hat{t} = 1 \sim 4\}$.

Left and Right View Determination: We determine the left and the right views by the one of the features T_x^{3D} that is already computed. If $T_x^{3D} > 0$, then $I_{t+\hat{k}}$ is a right-hand view, or otherwise a left-hand view. Next, we generate stereo image for the proper target display.

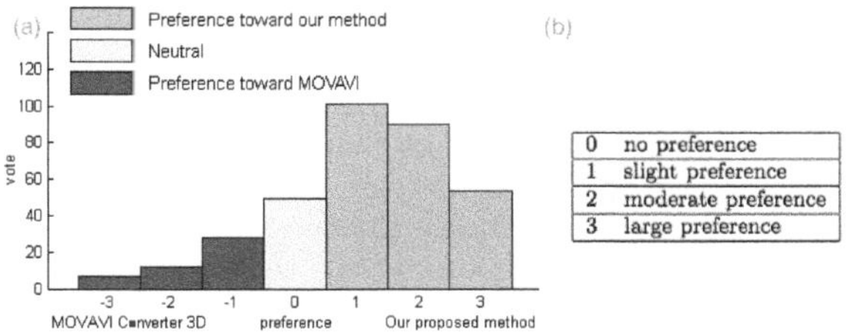

Figure 3: Histogram of preference where each of 10 judges is asked to express his or her degree of preference for 34 stereo images generated by both algorithms.

4. USER STUDY

We compare our proposed system to a fully automatic off-the-shelf package called MOVAVI Video Converter 3D [7]. Our test is designed to compare the perceived quality of our system with MOVAVI for 34 images. We randomly select results of both algorithms applied to six different videos including TV shows, movies, and home videos when the results of both algorithms are available (our proposed method produces frame pairs only when it considers there is a good enough 3D effect in the frame pair).

In the psychovisual study, a subject was presented with two different stereo versions of the same scene from the same video, one from our proposed method and the other from MOVAVI, in succession on screen (we choose not to display both stereo images side by side to eliminate inference; the subject can toggle back and forth between the two stereo versions). See Figure 3. All images were presented in a blind random order such that the subject cannot discern

(a) MOVAVI [7]　　(b) Ours

Figure 4: Left column shows the results by MOVAVI video converter 3D [7] for generating anaglyphs. Right column shows the results by our proposed method. Note that how the depth difference among objects in the right column are nicely presented (e.g the fence and the cars, the light post and the house).

which version is produced by which method. The subject is asked to select the stereo image that provides better stereo perception. Further, the subject is required to first make a forced choice and then indicate the magnitude of preference for the preferred image on a scale of 0 to 3, shown in Figure 3b.

For the purpose of the psychovisual test, stereo quality was defined as referring to the three-dimensional aspects of depicted objects in a scene. In particular, the following factors contribute to the perceived stereo quality: *the range of the depth of a scene, the vividness of the depth of the scene, the sense of volume in the scene, the sense of distance between objects and within objects (such as the folds in clothing, facial features), the consistency in the sense of depth across the scene, and the ease of perceiving all of the above.*

A total of 10 judges participated in the study, including imaging scientists who have experience judging 2D or 3D image quality, as well as typical consumers we recruited. It is interesting that there is only a slight difference in the preference and the magnitude of preference between the technical judges and nontechnical consumers.

In analyzing the judge responses, the ratings were coded such that preferences in favor of our proposed method were given positive scores (+1, +2, +3) while ratings favoring the MOVAVI Video Converter 3D [7] were given negative scores (-1, -2, -3). As can be seen in Figure 3a, there is a strong preference toward our proposed method. The 90% confidence interval for a preference toward our proposed method is (77.94%, 83.65%).

Some of the results used in the user study can be seen in Figure 4. The first to last rows in Figure 4 show a clear depth difference between the fence and the cars, the light post and the house, the person facing back and the person facing front, the child in the back and the person in the front, respectively. In addition, the speed of our method is real-time, although as the search range $\hat{t}$ increases the computation time increases linearly.

Finally, we emphasize that the anaglyph image composition procedure described in this paper is only one way to display the produced 3D media content by our method. Alternatively, the composite left and right views can be displayed on many other current 3D devices (e.g., polarized stereo displays or shutter-glasses).

5. CONCLUSIONS

In this work, we first introduce a learning-based method to detect video frames that can make good stereo pairs from a captured 2D video. Experiments using both professional and amateur videos show that our proposed approach produces higher quality stereo images when compared with existing methods. In the future, we plan to further extend this work to include temporal information to produce a realistic 3D video from a 2D video.

6. REFERENCES

[1] H. Gernsheim. *A Concise History of Photography*. Dover Publications, Inc., 1986.

[2] M. Guttmann, L. Wolf, and D. Cohen-Or. Semi-automatic stereo extraction from video footage. In *IEEE International Conference on Computer Vision*, pages 136–142, 2009.

[3] M. Hall, E. Frank, G. Holmes, B. Pfahringer, P. Reutemann, and I. H. Witten. The weka data mining software: An update. In *SIGKDD Explorations*, 2009.

[4] R. I. Hartley and A. Zisserman. *Multiple View Geometry in Computer Vision*. Cambridge University Press, second edition, 2004.

[5] D. Hoiem, A. A. Efros, and M. Hebert. Automatic Photo Pop-up. In *ACM SIGGRAPH*, pages 577–584, 2005.

[6] B. D. Lucas and T. Kanade. An Iterative Image Registration Technique with an Application to Stereo Vision. In *Joint Conference on Artificial Intelligence*, pages 674–679, 1981.

[7] MOVAVI. MOVAVI Video Converter 3D, http://www.movavi.com/videoconverter3d/.

[8] A. Saxena, M. Sun, and A. Y. Ng. Learning 3-D Scene Structure from a Single Still Image. *IEEE International Conference on Computer Vision*, pages 1–8, 2007.

[9] D. Scharstein and R. Szeliski. A taxonomy and evaluation of dense two-frame stereo correspondence algorithms. *Int. J. Comput. Vision*, 47(1-3):7–42, 2002.

[10] J. Shi and C. Tomasi. Good features to track. In *IEEE Conference on Computer Vision and Pattern Recognition*, pages 593–600, 1994.

[11] L. B. Statistics and L. Breiman. Random forests. In *Machine Learning*, pages 5–32, 2001.

[12] W. J. Tam and L. Zhang. 3d-tv content generation: 2d-to-3d conversion. In *IEEE International Conference on Multimedia and Expo*, 2006.

[13] C. Varekamp and B. Barenbrug. Improved depth propagation for 2D to 3D video conversion using key-frames. *IET Conference Publications*, (534):29–29, 2007.

[14] B. Ward, S. B. Kang, and E. Bennett. Depth director: A system for adding depth to movies. *IEEE Transactions on Computer Graphics and Applications*, 31(1):36–48, 2011.

[15] Y. Zhuang, Y. Rui, T. Huang, and S. Mehrotra. Adaptive key frame extraction using unsupervised clustering. In *IEEE International Conference on Image Processing*, volume 1, pages 866–870, Oct. 1998.

A Tool for Authoring Unambiguous Links from Printed Content to Digital Media

Andreas Girgensohn[1], Frank Shipman[2], Lynn Wilcox[1],
Qiong Liu[1], Chunyuan Liao[1], Yuichi Oneda[3]

[1]FX Palo Alto Laboratory, Inc.
3174 Porter Drive
Palo Alto, CA 94304, USA

[2]Department of Computer Science
Texas A&M University
College Station, TX 77843, USA

[3]Fuji Xerox
6-1, Minatomirai, Nishi-ku
Yokohama, 220-8668, Japan

{andreasg, wilcox, liu, liao}@fxpal.com, shipman@cs.tamu.edu, oneda.yuichi@fujixerox.co.jp

ABSTRACT

Embedded Media Markers (EMMs) are nearly transparent icons printed on paper documents that link to associated digital media. By using the document content for retrieval, EMMs are less visually intrusive than barcodes and other glyphs while still providing an indication for the presence of links. An initial implementation demonstrated good overall performance but exposed difficulties in guaranteeing the creation of unambiguous EMMs. We developed an EMM authoring tool that supports the interactive authoring of EMMs via visualizations that show the user which areas on a page may cause recognition errors and automatic feedback that moves the authored EMM away from those areas. The authoring tool and the techniques it relies on have been applied to corpora with different visual characteristics to explore the generality of our approach.

Categories and Subject Descriptors

H.5.1 [**Information Interfaces and Presentation**]: Multimedia Information Systems.

General Terms

Algorithms, Design, Human Factors.

Keywords

Vision-based paper interface, authoring tool, document retrieval.

1. INTRODUCTION

Embedding links to on-line content in printed documents is one approach to bridging the gap between people's consumption of digital and paper content. Such links need to be easy to use, highly accurate, and minimize the disturbance of the aesthetics of the printed medium. Our work on Embedded Media Markers (EMMs) is an approach to achieving these goals [5]. To indicate to users the presence of links and to avoid accuracy issues inherent in pure content-based retrieval approaches, EMMs are deliberately authored and are visualized on the page. To address issues of aesthetics, EMMs are semi-transparent overlays included in printed documents that make use of the existing content of the printed material as a "fingerprint" that is used to identify the EMM during retrieval (see Figure 1). Readers photograph the printed matter including the EMM to retrieve the associated digital content.

Our initial implementation of EMMs showed much potential but showed that authors of documents embedding EMMs need support to be sure that the EMMs authored are distinct enough that they can be accurately identified. This paper describes a new EMM authoring interface that leverages the analysis of the printed content and already authored EMMs in order to provide feedback and support for authors placing EMMs in a document or set of documents.

The next section describes related and prior work. This leads into a presentation of the design of a new EMM authoring interface. We conclude with a discussion of our findings and future work.

2. RELATED WORK

There are two common approaches for creating links between paper documents and digital content. One approach is to print markers on the document. Examples are 2D bar codes [8] or printed grids of dots [3]. The second approach uses content analysis to recognize the particular portion of a paper document and determine the link based on that content. The second common approach to linking between paper and digital content is to compute features of the document content itself that identify the document patch in order to create a media link. HotPaper [1] and Mobile Retriever [6] use features based on document text such as the spatial layout of words. Other systems such Bookmarkr [4] and MapSnapper [2] use pixel level image features, such as SIFT [7], to recognize generic document content. With these systems, visually obtrusive marks are not required for identification. As a result, in most content-based retrieval systems, there is no on-paper indication to the user that there is media linked to the document.

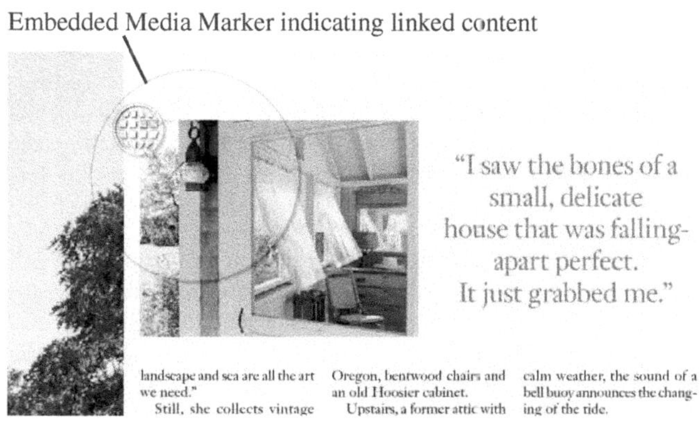

Figure 1. Part of a page with EMM as seen by the reader.

*Area Chair: Dick Bulterman

MM'11, November 28–December 1, 2011, Scottsdale, Arizona, USA.

EMMs combine the characteristics of barcode-based and visual content-based approaches to improve their usability and accuracy while reducing their impact on the aesthetics of the paper document. EMMs rely on deliberately placed markers, like barcode and glyph approaches, but do not rely on encoding information in the marker (see Figure 1). Instead, the marker indicates to the reader the location and size of the link anchor. The destination of the link is determined via the content of the paper document in the region of the link. By only indexing subregions of the document page, this approach reduces the size of the index for the document. In contrast with barcodes and glyphs, the EMM icon indicates the type of media associated with the marker.

3. EMM AUTHORING SUPPORT

Authoring an EMM is a process of identifying a location in a collection of pages that is a source anchor for a link and the media content to which it links. Support for the authoring process is needed to help users create useful and unambiguous EMMs. We designed a web-based authoring tool to aid EMM placement and assuring that the EMM can be accurately recognized.

The authoring tool supports the user in placing EMMs on document pages to ensure recognition and to avoid conflicts. It first lets users select the page to author and then matches the keypoints on the page to those on other pages. The authoring tool uses that information to identify page regions that have a sufficient density of keypoints that would not be confused with previously authored EMMs or pages in the collection. Because of the way the recognition process works, regions that contain a group of keypoints matching the same EMM are especially undesirable. The authoring tool uses this information to guide the user with visualization and assistive techniques.

There are several components of the authoring tool. The top level manages a collection of document pages by displaying page thumbnails that a user can select for authoring. Selected pages are displayed in a center region, and can be zoomed for easier authoring. A sidebar supports creation of media links by displaying thumbnails representing links that the user can drag onto the page being authored. The authoring component allows users to place an EMM at a desired location in the page while indicating whether or not that location can be recognized accurately (see Figure 2).

The interactive authoring tool uses shading to indicate page areas that are unsuitable for EMMs. In addition to the shading, users may also turn on the display of individual keypoints that are colored in shades between blue (good) and red (bad) to indicate how well they match keypoints on other pages (see Figure 3). In the tool, a user clicks on a desired location of the page and an EMM is automatically placed near that location optimizing the recognizability. The size of the EMM is determined by a score computed from the keypoints in the region. At this point, the user can drag the EMM to other more desirable areas of the document.

An authored collection of EMMs comes from a corresponding collection of document pages. Such a collection may consist of the pages of a single book or an issue of a magazine. A collection may also encompass the pages of all the issues of a magazine published during a time period. In the latter case, the collection may change over time when new issues of the magazine are added. Readers of such books, magazines, or other documents start by identifying the

Figure 2. EMM authoring interface indicating unsuitable areas in shades of brown and a newly authored EMM in green.

collection. They then take a picture of an EMM using a portable device such as a smartphone that uploads the picture to the EMM server which redirects the device to the linked content.

The next sections describe how the authoring tool supports the authoring of unambiguous EMMs by determining suitable page regions, visualizing them, and guiding the user towards them.

3.1 Adjusting EMMs for Better Recognition

Once EMM authors select a page for placement of a new EMM or editing of an existing EMM, they are presented with a zoomable view of the page that shows the existing EMMs and an overlay indicating areas to avoid (shown in brown) when placing EMMs, as shown in Figure 2. EMMs are placed by clicking on the page image. They are visualized as by translucent green circles.

When an EMM is first placed, the smallest area with a sufficient keypoint score that contains the click position is identified. This ensures that authored EMMs includes enough distinguishable keypoints to satisfy the retrieval algorithm. Unlike the approach of simply counting the number of keypoints [5], a score is computed that measures potential confusion with other EMMs in the database. This score represents both the presence of keypoints and the confusability with other EMMs and other pages in the database.

The authoring interface is interactive, providing visual feedback of the location, size, and uniqueness of the EMM as the user moves the mouse to the desired link anchor. As the EMM is dragged, its size increases or decreases based on the score, and is shown in red when the score is below the recognition threshold and green otherwise. The computation of the score is optimized such that it can be recomputed quickly enough in JavaScript to give immediate feedback to the user in the middle of a drag operation. A lower bound of 2 by 2 inches is enforced for the region to accommodate the minimal focal distance of mobile phone cameras. If the resulting regions would be very large, the authoring tool attempts to move the EMM to avoid unsuitable regions, such as blank portions of pages. If no suitable region can be found, the EMM is colored red to indicate its unsuitability. Both assistive techniques, i.e., resizing and moving EMMs, can be turned off by the author. If the score

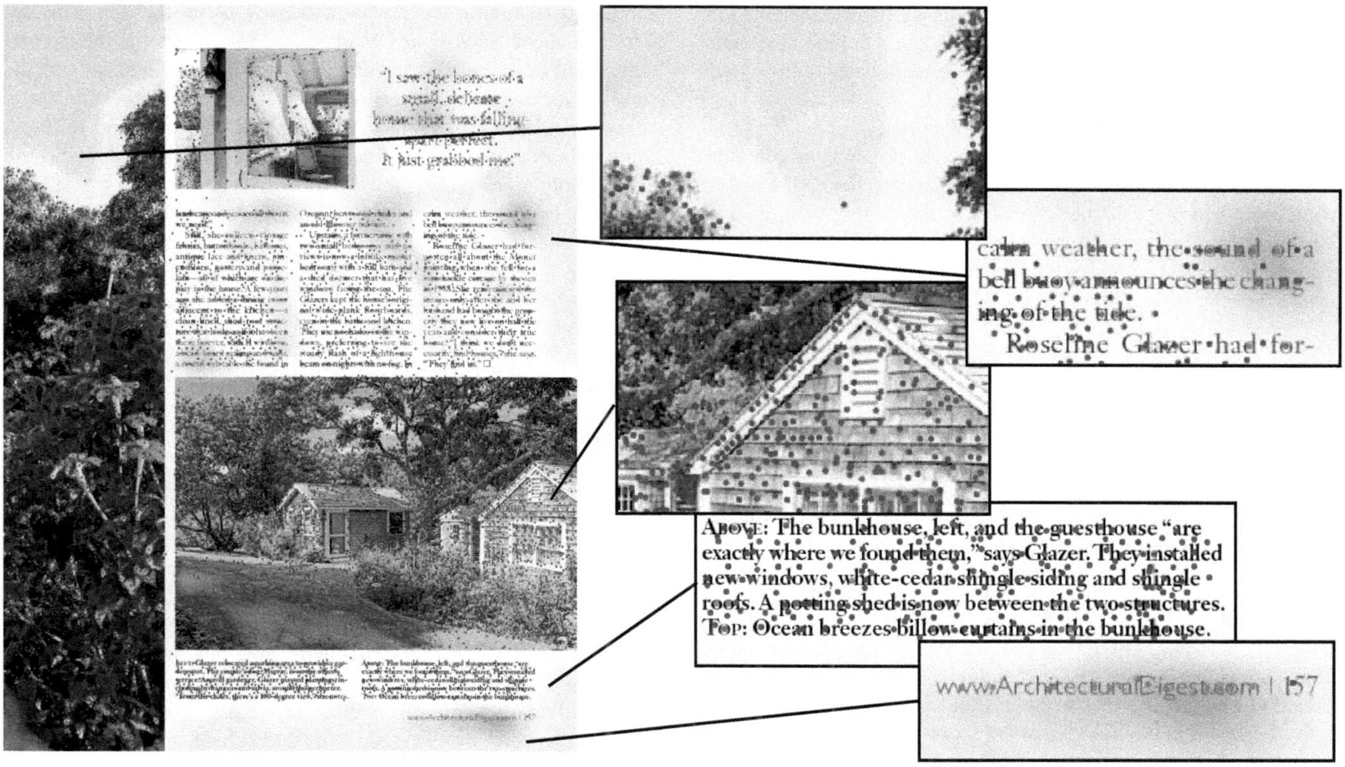

Figure 3. Visualization of keypoint conflicts and unsuitable page regions.

represents just the presence of keypoints, this support prevents the user from placing an EMM in a region with too few keypoints. However, it does not guarantee recognition accuracy. Other EMMs in the database may be associated with very similar keypoints. The following section discusses how to detect such conflicts.

3.2 Detecting Potential Conflicts

Rather than just counting keypoints in a region to determine the total score, the authoring tool determines how distinguishable those keypoints are from keypoints already in the database. The tool checks both against previously authored EMMs for actual conflicts and against other pages in the document page collection for potential conflicts. Each keypoint is given a score based on how well it matches keypoints of other EMMs and document pages. The scores of keypoints are taken into consideration when determining a suitable location for an EMM and when automatically adjusting an EMM after a user interaction. For each keypoint, the distance to the closest keypoint among keypoints in other EMMs and pages is determined. If this distance is zero, the keypoint is given a score of negative one, indicating that it does not provide good discrimination. As the distance to the neighboring keypoint increases, the score increases to a maximum of positive one. Other keypoints are assigned a score based on the distance and the maximum match distance. The normalized distance between 0 and 1 is linearly mapped to a score between -1 and 1.

When evaluating a region of a page during authoring, the scores of keypoints in that region are added. A large positive sum indicates that the region is suitable for placing an EMM. A neutral or negative sum indicates that the region is unsuitable. We use a threshold to determine if a page region for a potential EMM contains enough good keypoints. For example, we may require that the page region contains keypoints with a total score of at least 100. By using the sum of keypoint scores instead of the keypoint count, we incorporate the notion of conflicts with other pages and EMMs. For example, either 100 keypoints with a score of 1 or 200 keypoints with an average score of 0.5 would be sufficient for a page region.

Placing two EMMs too close to each other is detrimental for retrieval because keypoints from the undesired EMM may be included in the photo of the desired EMM. While keypoint scores could be used to discourage authors from placing EMMs too close to each other on the same page by using the score density, it is simpler to check for sufficient spacing and to alert the author.

Comparing the EMM authoring page against the other pages in the collection has both advantages and disadvantages. An advantage is that regions that are ambiguous, such as text passages in the default font, can be avoided. The same words appear on many different pages so that another EMM may provide a better match to a low-quality picture of an EMM containing those words. Such regions can be found without requiring the authoring of previous EMMs. On the other hand, such an approach, if used to block the authoring of EMMs, may prevent attaching an EMM to a distinctive region that is repeated across pages.

Instead of blocking the user from authoring potentially ambiguous EMMs, the system provides support for authoring multiple source anchors for the same destination. When a user authors an EMM for a region that is repeated some number of times, the system can ask if the EMM should be added for all instances of this region. This makes it possible to map all instances of a corporate logo to the same destination and make it clear to the author that visually similar EMMs must link to the same location. The retrieval of regions similar to a selected region is a two-step process. First, all pages with a large number of matching keypoints are located. Second, on each of those pages, regions containing many matching keypoints are located. Those regions are presented as candidates to the user.

3.3 Spreading Penalty Scores

When multiple keypoints matching the same previous or potential EMM are located in the region being considered for EMM placement, there is a much higher chance that the current location and that other location will be confused during retrieval. To reduce such conflicts, the nearby keypoints that map to the same EMM are further reduced in their score.

We call the difference between the perfect score of 1 and the actual score of a keypoint the penalty score. As the keypoint score lies between -1 and 1, that penalty score ranges from 0 to 2. The system spreads this penalty to nearby keypoints that match the same EMM. The penalty score is weighted by a distance function and the weighted sum of matching penalty scores is accumulated at each keypoint. This weighted sum of penalty scores is subtracted from the original score of the keypoint.

The spread penalty score is weighted by a normalized distance within a given radius. We use 25% of the radius of a typical EMM as the spread radius. The spread penalty score is accumulated separately and added to each keypoint score in a separate step to avoid spreading beyond the distance threshold or spreading back and forth. As shown in Figure 3, keypoint scores of -1 are visualized as red dots, scores of 1 as blue dots, and scores in between as shades of purple. Depending on the source material, other colors can be used to be noticeable on the displayed page. While keypoint dots are not shown by default, the user can turn them on to get a more detailed view of potential conflicts.

3.4 Visualizing Suitable Page Regions

In the authoring tool, the document page is displayed with an overlay that gradually shades out regions of the page with low keypoint density scores. Regions suitable for EMMs contain many keypoints not similar to those used by other EMMs and few keypoints similar to those already used. The average keypoint score density in a region indicates its suitability. A threshold for this density is used for visualization. We experimentally determined that a score threshold of 100 for a 2-inch by 2-inch region produced good results and converted that to a density threshold.

To determine the average keypoint density while taking keypoint scores into consideration, we compute a density score over a circular region with a weight that linearly decreased with distance. We use 50% of the radius of a typical EMM for the circular region. The integral under the two-dimensional curve should be normalized to one with this function.

This approach can be used with the negative keypoint scores described earlier. When combining positive and negative scores, both an empty region and a region with an equal amount of positive and negative scores would have a neutral suitability. When all keypoints have a score of 1, any region where the keypoint density exceeds the threshold has the maximum suitability. A higher density of keypoints with lower positive scores would also lead to the maximum suitability. Conversely, a high density of keypoints with negative scores produces a region with a negative suitability.

When spreading the penalty score to keypoints in the same vicinity matching the same EMM, keypoint scores can drop below -1. When determining the keypoint density using the approach described above, such scores would cause a larger part of the circular region to be visualized as completely unsuitable, indicating to the user that this region should really be avoided. Figure 3 illustrates this visualization technique using shades of brown and different amounts of transparency. The close-ups of Figure 3 demonstrate that empty areas such as the sky are covered by a semi-translucent overlay. In contrast, the picture of the house contains a high density of blue dots representing keypoints that match nothing else so that no overlay is added. The body text at the top of the page has regions with predominately red dots that are covered with a solid overlay. This is even more the case for the page footer that only contains red dots. The figure caption with bold text does not match much else so that it would be suitable for placing an EMM.

4. CONCLUSIONS

In this paper, we motivated why unambiguous marks linking paper to digital documents are important. We described cases where Embedded Media Markers (EMMs) could be confused with one another if they were authored on top of similar content or near each other. We presented an authoring tool that uses a combination of visualization and assistive techniques to guide the user. It steers users away from potentially confusing page regions. It does this by analyzing previously authored EMMs and other pages in the document collection to identify regions in the page being authored that can be confused with keypoints in the database.

EMMs already provide a means for placing links on paper that offer excellent retrieval performance while indicating the presence of links with minimal impact on the document aesthetics. We expect that the support for simple authoring of unambiguous EMMs will make EMMs even better suited for linking from paper documents to associated digital content.

5. REFERENCES

[1] B. Erol, E. Antunez, J. Hull. HOTPAPER: multimedia interaction with paper using mobile phones. *Proc. of Multimedia '08*, 399-408, 2008.

[2] J. Hare, P. Lewis, L. Gordon, G. Hart. MapSnapper: Engineering an efficient algorithm for matching images of maps from mobile phones. *Proc. of Multimedia Content Access: Algorithms and Systems II*, 2008.

[3] B. Hecht, M. Rohs, J. Schöning, A. Krüger. Wikeye – Using Magic Lenses to Explore Georeferenced Wikipedia Content. *Proc. of Pervasive Mobile Interaction Devices Wrkshp*, 2007.

[4] N. Henze, S. Boll. Snap and share your photobooks. *Proc. of Multimedia '08*, 409-418, 2008.

[5] Q. Liu, C. Liao, L. Wilcox, A. Dunnigan, B. Liew. Embedded media markers: marks on paper that signify associated media. *Proc. of Intelligent User Interfaces,* 149-158, 2010.

[6] X. Liu, D. Doermann, Mobile Retriever: access to digital documents from their physical source. *Int. Jour. on Document Analysis and Recognition*, 11(1): 19-27, 2008.

[7] D.G. Lowe. Distinctive image features from scale-invariant keypoints, *Int. Jour. of Computer Vision*, 60(2), 91-110, 2004.

[8] J. Rekimoto, Y. Ayatsuka. CyberCode: designing augmented reality environments with visual tags. *Proc. of DARE 2000*, 1-10, 2000.

Interactive Digital Scrapbook Generation for Travel Photos Based on Design Principles of Typography

Jung-Yu Yeh[2], Min-Chun Hu[1,3], Wen-Huang Cheng[3], and Ja-Ling Wu[1,2]

[1]Graduate Institute of Networking and Multimedia, National Taiwan University
[2]Department of Computer Science and Information Engineering, National Taiwan University
[3]Research Center for Information Technology Innovation, Academia Sinica
Taipei, Taiwan (R.O.C.)

{gina, trimy, wisley, wjl}@cmlab.csie.ntu.edu.tw

ABSTRACT

To facilitate the photo management and sharing tasks, many application tools have been developed to generate pleasant photo slideshows, collages, or scrapbooks by applying simple templates/layouts and visual effects. In this work, we propose a convenient digital scrapbook generating system for travel photos, named as IS-Scrapbook, which keeps the virtues while dismisses the drawbacks of conventional digital photo presentation styles. The IS-Scrapbook system has three friendly attributes compared to other photo presentation tools. First, aiming to attract the audience, we highlight objects more meaningful or familiar to the viewer, e.g. the landmark and the protagonist in the photos. Second, five basic design principles of typography, i.e. proximity, contrast, balance, color harmony and repetition, are applied to produce more vivacious layouts. Third, the system automatically generates a digital scrapbook with a default layout, and the user can further adjust photo positions and enrich each page by sketching or inserting dialog bubbles with the aid of the developed user interface. User study shows that the proposed work enhances the experiences of photo browsing and gives a brand-new way of photo sharing.

Categories and Subject Descriptors

H.5.2 [**Information Interfaces and Presentation**]: User Interfaces – *Evaluation/methodology, Graphical user interfaces (GUI)*

General Terms

Algorithms, Design, Human Factors, Management.

Keywords

Design principle, image content analysis, photo browsing, photo sharing, scrapbook, slideshow

1. INTRODUCTION

1.1 Motivation

With the popularity of digital camera and the advanced technology in storage, people can take photos at will for recording and sharing their wonderful journey. The captured photos can serve as memory cues for recalling the traveling experiences in the future since they record not only the object/scene/event but also the corresponding time information. On the other hand, sharing, referred to a real-time interaction around photos [1], has been shown to be one of the main goals of taking photos. Kirk *et al.* [2] studied on the activities people usually performed with their digital photos after capturing, and this study proposed a photowork lifecycle including the following three stages: pre-download stage, at-download stage, and pre-share stage. There is a substantial amount of work at the pre-share stage, such as selecting, editing, annotating, and organizing photos for sharing. The time-consuming tasks at this stage usually make people leave their photos unused for a long time, and finally degrade the merit of taking photos in their journey. Therefore, we aim at developing a handy tool for sharing travel photos in a fascinating style.

1.2 Related Work

Lots of applications have been proposed either to help the user manage his/her huge photo collections, or to relieve the tedious editing work. Studies on these applications can be classified into the following categories.

- ***Conventional slideshow.*** A conventional slideshow can be automatically generated by showing photos one by one. Plenty of software tools, such as *ACDSee*, *Picasa*, and even the web application like *Flickr* provides the slideshow functionality as a basic service. In order to catch the audiences' attention, some commercial software tools, e.g. *MediaShow*, offer abundant special transition effects between photos and add accompanying music to build up a pleasant atmosphere. For the sake of enriching the presentation style, *Photo Story* further includes a camera motion-like transition effect (e.g., panning or zooming) within each photo. All the above-mentioned applications, to some extent, have the same attribute that only one picture is displayed at one time still.

- ***Collage.*** Collage is widely used for constructing a short summary of a photo collection since it can show abundant photos in one frame. The target of a collage is to keep Regions of Interest (ROIs) of each picture not being occluded, so as to result in a fertile and visually pleasing image. In the early stage, collage tools, such as *PhotoScape*, usually provided a number of fixed templates for the user, and manually assigning photos were required. However, picking out satisfactory photos and choosing appropriate templates are fairly time-consuming and difficult for non-designers and/or amateur users. Therefore, *AutoCollage* and *Picture Collage* take visual contents of input photos into consideration to automatically design a suitable layout. Besides, *miCollage* provides a middle ground to generate a collage between the fully automatic and the fully manual ones.

*Area Chair: Susanne Boll

MM'11, November 28–December 1, 2011, Scottsdale, Arizona, USA.

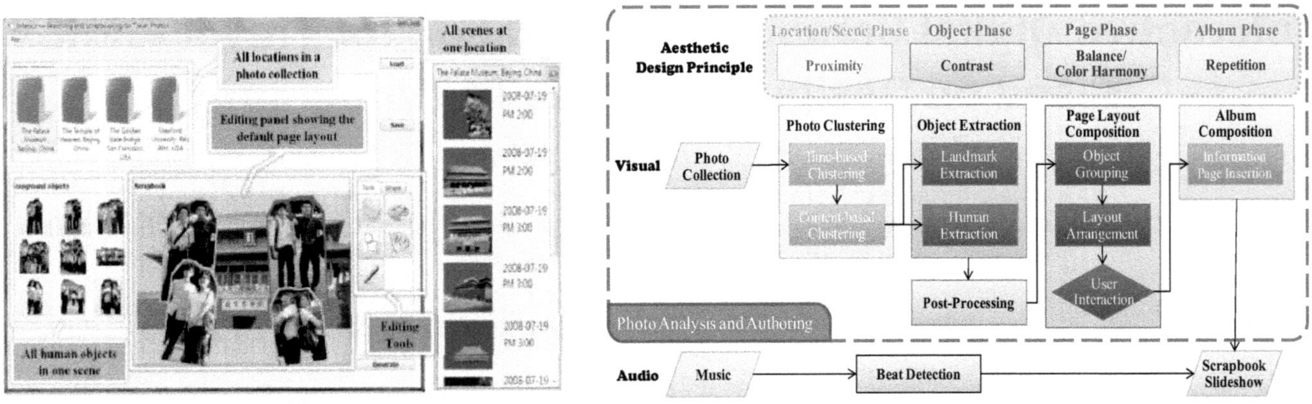

(a) (b)

Figure 1. (a)The user interface of the IS-Scrapbook system. (b) The proposed framework of the IS-Scrapbook system.

● ***Hybrid Slideshow.*** In conventional slideshows, only one picture is shown at a time, whereas, the number of images in a collage has a wide range from tens to hundreds. Since neither displaying pictures individually nor squeezing excessive images on screen is an appealing photo presentation style, the hybrid slideshow strikes to balance the pros and cons of them. *Tiling Slideshow* is a classic example of hybrid slideshow. Time-based clustering and content-based clustering are combined to organize the photos automatically, and then collages are generated by the time- and color-related photos. Finally, all collages are encoded into a music-driven slideshow. In addition, the transition effects among images in the same collage are enhanced in *iSlideshow* to form a story-telling presentation.

● ***Digital Scrapbook.*** Scrapbook is a notebook where a series of photos are glued, and some information of the recorded events, such as the dates, the travel partners, and the locations/ landmarks is written on the pages. Sometimes, even a short paragraph would be appended to describe details about the journey, or some illustrations and adornments would be put to add the diversity of interests. This is a fabulous method for recording a journey since a set of complete memory cues are included in a scrapbook, and that's why the travel scrapbook has been popular for a long time. With the aid of digital photography, a huge amount of digital scrapbook software with new scrapbook techniques, ideas, and products are born to meet the great demands in recent years. These digital scrapbook software tools provide lots of design features, such as, themed pages/packages, photo editor, and photo embellishments. Note that although finely designed features are provided, the whole editing work is time-consuming since it is still made manually.

1.3 Contribution

The forementioned motivation and related work urge us to develop a travel photo presentation tool, IS-Scrapbook, which has the following properties: 1) the tool lightens the user's burden at the photo pre-share stage, 2) an adequate number of photos are put together with proper layout in each page as the hybrid slideshow does, and 3) the produced output records important information about the journey and adds personal aesthetics elements like the scrapbook does. Meanwhile, three contributions are made in this work: 1) we highlight objects more meaningful or familiar to the viewer, e.g. the landmark and the protagonist in the photos, so that the audience will be more interested in the photo presentation, 2) five basic design principles of typography, i.e. proximity, contrast, balance, color harmony and repetition, are first time in the literature applied to produce a piece of visually pleasing digital scrapbook, and 3) an interactive user-friendly interface, as shown in Figure 1 (a), is developed to facilitate adjusting of the automatically generated results, so as to adding personal aesthetics elements into the final scrapbook. For more demonstration of the proposed system, please refer to https://sites.google.com/site/isscrapbook/.

The rest of this paper is organized as follows. The system framework of IS-Scrapbook is introduced in Section 2. Section 3 briefly presents five basic design principles of typography and expounds how to construct a digital scrapbook based on these principles. Section 4 shows the evaluation results and Section 5 concludes this work.

2. THE PROPOSED FRAMEWORK

We make an investigation into the travel photo collections and design the framework of IS-Scrapbook as illustrated in Figure 1 (b). A photo collection and a music file are taken as the input of our system. The photos are processed through four phases, including the location/scene phase, the object phase, the page phase, and the album phase. In each phase, we adopt different aesthetic design principles and corresponding procedures to generate a good-looking scrapbook slideshow (details will be introduced in Section3).

Music plays an important role in sharing presentation. It not only helps to build up pleasant atmosphere during the sharing, but also enhances the browsing experience. To harmonize the audio-visual effect, we slightly adjust the showing up speed of IS-Scrapbook to be aligned with the beat of input music by using the techniques developed in [3].

3. PHOTO ANALYSIS AND AUTHORING

How to automatically crop and arrange photos is the main issue of generating a pleasing photo presentation. Presentation styles like collage and hybrid slideshow purpose to keep ROIs of each photo not being occluded or cropped; however, the domain knowledge about "design" is barely applied to the existing photo presentation applications. The IS-Scrapbook system analyzes and authors the input photo collection through four phases and adopts the following five aesthetic design principles which have been widely used in typography [4, 5].

● ***Proximity*** means that relative items should be grouped close together to be one visual unit. Following the proximity helps to give the reader a clear structure of the content.

● ***Contrast*** adds interest to the visual content and emphasizes what is important or directing the reader's eyes by making it look very different (in typeface, color, size, etc.) from others.

● ***Balance*** is a sense that the focal point of the viewer should not be pulled too much by any specific part. It is usually achieved by adjusting positions, sizes and colors of objects.

● ***Color harmony*** is a set of color relationships that has been found to be visually pleasing. Following the color harmony principle, the character of a design work can be enhanced.

● ***Repetition*** of design elements (such as color, shapes, spatial relationships, fonts, sizes) strengthens the unity and adds visual interest of a design work.

3.1 Location/Scene Phase

At the location/scene phase, we make photos of the same location (e.g. a popular tourism attraction) or of the same scene (e.g. a distinct view of a landmark) closely appear in the presentation slideshow to achieve the design principle of *proximity*. Given a photo collection $\boldsymbol{C}$ taken in a journey, we assume photos of the same location are taken closely in terms of time. Therefore, we first partition a photo collection $\boldsymbol{C}$ into several photo sets $\{\boldsymbol{L_i}\}$ by applying a simple time-based clustering method [6] according to the timestamp extracted from EXIF (Exchangeable image file format) of each photo. Moreover, a photo set L_i can be further partitioned into photo sets $\{\boldsymbol{S_j}\}$, where each photo set $\boldsymbol{S_j}$ comprises photos of the same scene. Photos taken in the same scene usually have similar background in terms of visual content, resulting in a certain degree of near-duplication. Hence, content-based clustering based on the near-duplicate detection (NDD) technique [7] is employed to partition each photo set L_i. A representative photo for each photo set $\boldsymbol{S_j}$ is simultaneously obtained after clustering, and we observe that the representative photo is the one containing most part of the scene/landmark since the applied NDD technique is based on matching SIFT feature points.

3.2 Object Phase

A conventional slideshow consisting of plenty near-duplicate photos will easily bore the audience. Therefore, it is unnecessary to show the entire part of each photo especially when many photos are taken in the same scene. To minimize the redundant visual content and preserve important portion of the photos, the object phase extracts meaningful objects, i.e. the landmark and the human, for each photo set $\boldsymbol{S_j}$ to be displayed. We take the representative photo of $\boldsymbol{S_j}$ as the landmark object (cf. Section 3.1) and the face detection technique is used for estimating regions of human objects. Some human objects may be relative small compared to the landmark object, resulting in being easily ignored by the audience. At the object phase, we follow the design principle of *contrast* by applying post-processing such as adjusting object sizes and adding borders to human objects with colors very different from the dominant color of the landmark object, so that the protagonist of photos can be noticed.

3.3 Page Phase

For each photo set $\boldsymbol{S_j}$, we now have a bunch of informative objects (including one landmark object and more than one human objects) to be displayed. However, showing too much content in the same page will make the page in a state of chaos. At the page phase, we define the visual weight of a page $\boldsymbol{P}$ as

$$\boldsymbol{VW_P} = \textstyle\sum_{o \in G} \boldsymbol{VW_o}, \quad (1)$$

where $\boldsymbol{G}$ is a group of human objects that will be presented in the page $\boldsymbol{P}$, and $\boldsymbol{VW_o}$ denotes the visual weight of an human object $\boldsymbol{o}$ in the group $\boldsymbol{G}$. In this work, $\boldsymbol{VW_o}$ is defined by the area of the human object. Given all human objects of a photo set $\boldsymbol{S_j}$ and an expected page visual weight $\boldsymbol{VW_e}$, we first sort all human objects in descending order according to their visual weight, and a greedy algorithm is employed to divide human objects into groups. One page is created for each group of human objects such that $\boldsymbol{VW_P} \leq \boldsymbol{VW_e}$ for all pages. Moreover, the landmark object will be displayed as the background of each created page.

After determining what to be shown in each page, we arrange the page layout based on the design principle of *balance*. Give a group of human objects, $\boldsymbol{G}$, we adopt the method proposed by Liu et al. [8] with a little modification to automatically compose a page layout. A page is first divided into grids with $\boldsymbol{N_R}$ rows and $\boldsymbol{N_C}$ columns, where $\boldsymbol{N_R}$ and $\boldsymbol{N_c}$ are defined by

$$\boldsymbol{N_R} = (\textstyle\sum_{o \in G} \boldsymbol{width_o})/\boldsymbol{W}, \quad (2)$$

$$\boldsymbol{N_C} = (\textstyle\sum_{o \in G} \boldsymbol{height_o})/\boldsymbol{H}, \quad (3)$$

$$\text{subject to} \quad \boldsymbol{N_O} \leq \boldsymbol{N_R} \times \boldsymbol{N_C}. \quad (4)$$

$\boldsymbol{W}$ and $\boldsymbol{H}$ are the width and height of the page, respectively, and $\boldsymbol{N_O}$ is the number of human objects in the group $\boldsymbol{G}$. Each human object is assigned to a unique grid to make the page *balance*. Hence, we find the best permutation of objects to fit the $\boldsymbol{N_R} \times \boldsymbol{N_C}$ grids according to the following two physical concepts: (1) the total width/height of objects in each row/column should be similar, and (2) the geometric center of a page should be kept close to the center bottom part of the page for preserving a steady appearance.

At the object phase, colored borders are used for enhancing the *contrast* between human objects and the landmark object. However, border colors of human objects appearing in the same page should follow the design principle of *color harmony*. Harmonic colors can be described by the degrees of area around the HSV color wheel and their angle(s) of separation, and we adopt eight types of harmonic colors proposed in [9].

Moreover, IS-Scrapbook randomly rotates each human object with a small angle to enhance the diversity of a page layout and suggests this default layout for the user. It is still able to accommodate manual changes such as deleting, translating, and/or rotating an object through an interactive user interface. With the friendly user interface, the editor can also insert personal style adornments, such as dialogue bubbles, polygons, illustrations, and specific colors, to enrich the page layout.

3.4 Album Phase

At the album phase, we transcode all pages produced above into a digital scrapbooking slideshow. Moreover, an additional page is inserted between pages of different locations/landmarks, so that the editor can write a brief introduction of the upcoming location/landmark on it. Note that, dates and timestamps extracted at the location phase will be automatically appended to this page. Last but not least, we employ the design principle of *repetition* to unify the digital scrapbooking slideshow. For example, the typeface, the font size, and the position of added texts are fixed throughout the slideshow.

4. EVALUATION

Since objective evaluation of the proposed system is difficult, a series of subjective tests were undertaken to evaluate the performance of our system. The detailed information of the photo collections used in our experiments can be found at https://sites.google.com/site/isscrapbook/experimental-results. Generally speaking, the photo-sharing presentations can be categorized into three kinds: *slideshow*, *collage*, and *hybrid slideshow*. In this experiment, we generate five photo sharing results using different tools: 1) A conventional slideshow automatically generated by the commercial software *ACDSee*. The display order is alphabetically determined. 2) A collage automatically produced by the commercial software *Shape Collage*. Photos have to be manually categorized first, and photos in the same category are used for generating a collage. Few parameters could be adjusted for providing visually pleasing results. 3) A collage manually made with the commercial software *PhotoScape*, which provides about one hundred layout templates for users. The size and the position of each photo have to be assigned one by one by the editor. 4) A hybrid slideshow automatically created by *Tiling Slideshow*. The photos are clustered by timestamp and content information and are cropped based on ROI. The display order and timing are synchronized with the beats of the input music. 5) A scrapbooking slideshow automatically constructed by our system, *IS-Scrapbook*. To more strictly evaluate the default result created by our system, no extra decoration or adjustment is manually made by the editor, and no special transition effects are applied between pages.

Fourteen evaluators were invited to join the user study, and the production results were presented to them by projecting onto a 60-inch screen. Evaluators were requested to grade from 1 to 10 to show their satisfaction regarding to the following five perspectives, and the results are shown in Figure 2.

- **Clearness.** Do you think the region of interest is prominent?
- **Attractiveness.** Do you think it attracts the audiences' attention?
- **Summarization.** Is it a good visual summary of the travel photos?
- **Richness.** How do you think the variety of page layouts?
- **Creativeness.** Do you think it is a creative presentation?

In general, *IS-Scrapbook* outperformed the other four tools with high average scores (*i.e.*, 3.17, 5.12, 7.12, 7.32, and 7.76 in terms of the five perspectives respectively), and the conventional slideshow, like *ACDSee*, got the lowest scores among all the photo presentations. In addition, browsing a slideshow consisting of multiple collages is not an enjoyable experience because too much information is shown at a time, with seriously occlusion among photos. The rank of *PhotoScape*, *Tiling Slideshow*, and *IS-Scrapbook* are slightly different in each perspective. *IS-Scrapbook* performs well with respect to the clearness because we cut out the ROIs first to remove the irrelative noises from the photos. Moreover, the result of *IS-Scrapbook* is evaluated as the most creative slideshow among all. With regard to the richness of page layout, the difference between *Tiling Slideshow* and ours is tiny, whereas the performance of *PhotoScape* is relatively low even though it provides hundred of templates for the user. Both *PhotoScape* and *IS-Scrapbook* are evaluated as suitable for editing a summary of travel photos since humans and the landmarks are scaled and shown appropriately. Furthermore, in *IS-Scrapbook*, the basic travel information, such as dates, is automatically added to the presentation to help the audiences comprehend the context of the journey. Referring to the attractiveness, *Tiling Slideshow* outperforms the others because of fade-in/fade-out effects and music-driven playing speed.

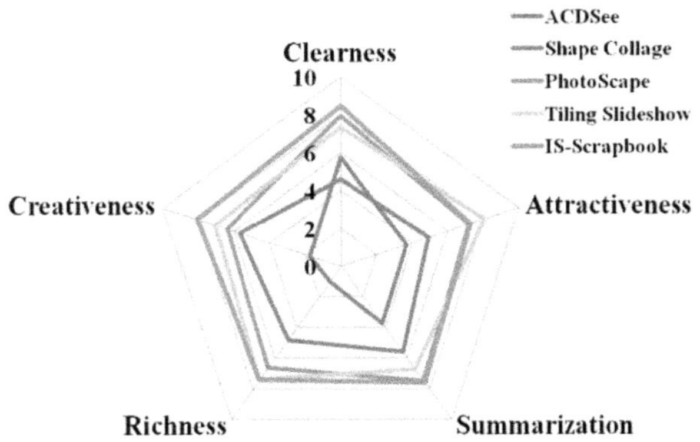

Figure 2. Comparisons of ACDSee, Shape Collage, PhotoScape, Tiling slideshow, and IS-Scrapbook in five perspectives.

5. CONCLUSIONS

Digital scrapbook is not a new presentation style, but previously developed tools require a lot of human effort to complete the organizing and editing tasks for a large photo set, especially the travelling photos. In this paper, an automatic framework of digital scrapbook, named IS-Scrapbook, is proposed to analyze and author photos through four phases. The domain knowledge about design is adopted to generate a pleasing presentation, and a user-friendly interface is also provided to extend its flexibility. For professional designers, our system saves a lot of time on organizing and choosing photos; for non-professional designers, the system not only provides recommendations for making a delicate work with design elements, but also offers a user-friendly interface for editing and adding personal style. The subjective evaluation results exhibit the satisfaction of this scrapbook-based presentation of photo sharing from the viewpoint of the audience. Lots of related issues are worthy of further investigation, for example, the boundary of foreground objects could be smoother and fancy transition effects could be applied to gradually change scenes for enhancing the viewing experience. We will devote ourselves to them continuously.

6. References

[1] Frohlich, D., Kuchinsky, A., Pering, C., Don, A. and Ariss, S. 2002. Requirements for photoware. In *Proc.* of *ACM CSCW'02*, 166-175.

[2] Kirk, D., Sellen, A., Rother, C. and Wood, K. 2006. Understanding photowork. In *Proc.* of *Human Factors in computing systems*, 761-770.

[3] Scheirer, E. D. 1998. Tempo and beat analysis of acoustic musical signals. *J. Acoust. Soc. Am.* 103, 1, 588-601.

[4] Williams, R. 2008. The non-designer's design book.

[5] Wikipedia: Design elements and principles.

[6] Platt, J. C., Czerwinski, M. and Field, B. 2003. Phototoc: Automating clustering for browsing personal photographs. In *Proc.* of *IEEE PCM'08*, 6-10.

[7] Chu, W.-T. and Lin, C.-H. 2009. Automatic summarization of travel photos using near-duplication detection and feature filtering. In *Proc.* of *ACM MM'09*, 1129-1130.

[8] Liu, T., Wang, J., Sun, J., Zheng, N., Tang, X. and Shum, H.-Y. 2009. Picture collage. *IEEE Trans. Multimedia*. 11, 7, 1225-1239.

[9] Cohen-Or, D., Sorkine, O., Gal, R., Leyvand, T. and Xu, Y.-Q. 2006. Color harmonization. *ACM Trans. Graph.* 25, 3, 624-630.

Augmented Makeover based on 3D Morphable Model*

Patricia Wang
Intel Labs China
patricia.p.wang@intel.com

Xiaofeng Tong
Intel Labs China
xiaofeng.tong@intel.com

Yangzhou Du
Intel Labs China
yangzhou.du@intel.com

Jianguo Li
Intel Labs China
jianguo.li@intel.com

Wei Hu
Intel Labs China
wei.hu@intel.com

Yimin Zhang
Intel Labs China
yimin.zhang@intel.com

ABSTRACT

Avatar is the virtual representation of user's facial, body, and motion characteristics in computer game, social network, and augmented reality. Facial modeling needs enormous efforts to achieve immersive experience in applications like avatar chatting or online makeover. Great challenge exists in robust detection of 2D facial prominent points and mapping them to 3D models in a parameterized manner. Another challenge is how to characterize semantic components of eyes, mouth, nose, and cheek rather than low level mesh geometries. In this paper, we proposed an augmented makeover framework to deal with aforementioned challenges. Aiming to provide amateurs with flexible customizations, morphable model is constructed from a set of scanned 3D face data set. Appearance personalization is carried out in the offline phase where single image and multiple views are discussed respectively to generate deformative shape in a progressive manner. Augmentation is implemented in the online phase where a fast and robust 3D tracking is used to balance the tradeoff between accuracy and real-time requirements. By this means, immersive Human Computer Interaction such as virtual makeover and photo-realistic avatar chatting could be achieved.

Categories and Subject Descriptors

I.4.9 [**Image Processing and Computer Vision**]: Applications; I.5.4 [**Pattern Recognition**]: Applications—*Computer vision*

General Terms

Algorithm, Design, Experimentation, Performance

Keywords

Morphable model, structure analysis, surface reconstruction, face landmark, augmented reality, virtual makeover

*Area Chair: Susanne Boll

MM'11, November 28–December 1, 2011, Scottsdale, Arizona, USA.

1. INTRODUCTION

Avatar technology has increasingly appealing usages in virtual world (Second Life, Google Earth), online makeover (TAAZ), virtual dressing on digital signage, etc. Controlling and driving avatar's action and gesture in real time could be fairly tackled with depth sensing technology and underlying range camera (PrimeSense) as demonstrated by Kinect. In comparison to body mimic, the expression and facial feature of avatar is quite challenging to handle. From the network service perspective, bandwidth issue has to be well considered to avoid transmitting enormous 3D geometry data. In various usage scenarios or considering privacy issues, consumers may require different styles of avatar, photo-realistic, cartoon, anthropomorphic face, etc. Aiming to provide immersive experience, this paper focuses on the photo-realistic face augmentation for amateurs.

Face modeling techniques could be roughly categorized into four categories: 3D scanner, generic model, surface reconstruction, and statistical morphable model [2]. Besides the static neutral model, online avatar animation requires to track deformations (novel identities, expressions, and poses) not included in prior database. Normally in human faces, there are non-ambiguous landmarks (nose tip) and ambiguous landmarks (points along the jaw contour). Therefore the local structure of these prominent components is more distinctive in avatar personalization.

This paper addresses the face makeover problem in adapting to both offline prior database and online personal deformation. Using the morphable model approach, a neutral avatar is presented to consumers as initialization in which basis shape and texture components have been statistically learnt from prior data set. Considering to provide a flexible solution, an integrated scheme is deployed to meet various demands on capturing image or video, stationary or animation enhancement, limited or sufficient computation resource. Our main contribution lies in three aspects: i) the *parameterized generation* highly reduces the bandwidth consumption; ii) the *multi-view stereo* characterizes geometry-realistic as well as photo-realistic appearances; iii) the *model-based 3D tracking* well handles with non-rigid expression beyond rigid pose.

The remainder of this paper is organized as follows. Section 2 briefly introduces related work on morphable model, face alignment, and tracking-based augmentation. Section 3 presents our adaptive framework of face model personalization and augmentation, and articulates our main contributions. Section 4 depicts the technical details. Section 5 evaluates our virtual makeover performances.

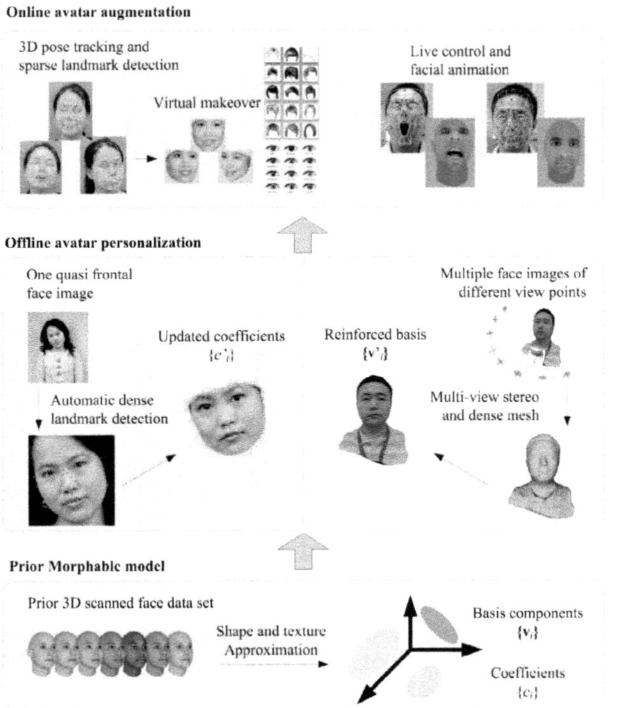

Figure 1: Workflow of offline face personalization and online augmentation. Two options for personalization quality: single image or multi-view images.

2. RELATED WORK

Morphable model has been used for synthesis and recognition of face, teeth and mouth data. It is usually derived from an example set of 2D images or 3D scanned mesh. Geometric surface is represented with vertices of shape and texture. Parameters of morphable model could be learnt with a non-iterative statistical approach such as Singular Value Decomposition, or stochastic gradient descent and Support Vector Regression [2].

Alignment means to position an object into a canonical pose, so the position of features (e.g., facial key points) relative to a fixed coordinates system can be examined. Classic methods are based on Active Shape Model and Active Appearance Model. Further methods treat localization of facial landmarks as a pattern recognition task (adopting boosted-based classifiers) [7].

Surface reconstruction could use time-of-flight lasers [1] or image based methods. In stereo vision, structure from motion techniques have been studied to find correspondence points between image pair, and feature trajectories overtime are then used to reconstruct their 3D positions and the camera external parameters. Previous face augumentation work normally requires manual labeling of feature points on a few photos [2].

3. FRAMEWORK OVERVIEW

Figure 1 illustrates the workflow of our avatar personalization and augmentation framework. It consists of three stages: i) morphable model construction based on prior 3D scanned face data set, learning the shape and texture basis components and coefficients for neutral faces; ii) offline personalization based on one quasi frontal face image or multiple face images covering different view points; iii) online augmentation based on real-time 3D pose tracking.

The aim of constructing a morphable model is to represent 3D faces in a vector space and estimate the space spanned by the exemplar faces. As prior data set hardly cover variations of age, gender, race, expression, we need to infer deformative information for personalization. When taking one single face image as input, the inference is to estimate new coefficients of shape and texture basis components. When taking multi-view face images as input, the inference is to reinforce the shape and texture basis components. As offline generated avatar is hard to capture dynamic and expressional motion, we need to track real-time pose and compensate non-rigid transformation to enhance avatar appearance.

4. MAJOR COMPONENTS

This section depicts the three major components of our augmented makeover framework.

4.1 Morphable Face Model

Morphable model is constructed based on a data set of 3D faces. Morphing between faces requires full correspondence between all exemplar faces. Having defined a reference scan of mesh with v vertices, dense point-to-point correspondence with all other scans could be established with an automated technique. Mathematically, we define the shape vector $\mathbf{S}$ of an exemplar 3D face as the coordinates of the v vertices that make up the mesh:

$$\mathbf{S} = (x_1, y_1, z_1, x_2, y_2, \cdots, y_v, z_v)^T. \quad (1)$$

For simplicity, we assume that the number of valid texture values in texture map is equal to the number of vertices. We therefore represent the texture of a face by a texture vector $\mathbf{T}$ that contains the color values of the v corresponding vertices:

$$\mathbf{T} = (r_1, g_1, b_1, r_2, g_2, \cdots, g_v, b_v)^T. \quad (2)$$

Arbitrary new faces can be generated by varying the parameters $\mathbf{a} = (a_1, a_2 \cdots a_n)^T$ and $\mathbf{b} = (b_1, b_2 \cdots b_n)^T$ that control shape and texture. Different from the definition in [2], we also consider to reinforce the basis vectors $[\mathbf{s}_1, \mathbf{s}_2, \cdots]^T$ and $[\mathbf{t}_1, \mathbf{t}_2, \cdots]^T$ in the generation of new faces. This is significant to deal with the problem that prior face data set is lack of identity or expression variability. In this paper, we define the morphable face model as a multidimensional linear combination function:

$$\phi = (\sum_i a_i \mathbf{s}_i, \sum_i b_i \mathbf{t}_i), \quad (3)$$

with the constraints $0 \leq a_i, b_i \leq 1$, that is we stay in the convex hull of the exemplar faces.

4.2 Offline Face Personalization

The morphable face model describes the shape and texture variations. This section presents how to generate a model instance by optimizing the model parameters. In the next two subsections, we discuss the case for single image and multiple views, respectively.

4.2.1 Matching to Single Image

Suppose we are given a new image as input, personalization means that the reparameterized model instance should look as similar to the face image as possible in appearance. Previous works on matching a morphable model to image are based on manually-labeled 2D feature points [2, 7].

In this paper, the positions of 88 prominent points are automatically detected. The hierarchical classifier network [6] is employed to detect face landmarks in a coarse-to-fine continuum strategy. Instead of searching all possible feature points in the face region simultaneously, we construct the feature point set of coarser layer by merging the feature points in the finer layer. Having detected the positions of 88 feature points, the task of matching a morphable model to single image is to find the 3D coordinates of all other vertices. Similar to Equation (1), we define landmark vector $\mathbf{L}$ as the 2D coordinates of 88 feature points:

$$\mathbf{L} = (x_1, y_1, x_2, \cdots, x_{88}, y_{88})^T. \quad (4)$$

The mapping from 3D shape model to 2D landmark vector $\Gamma : \mathbf{S} \mapsto \mathbf{L}$ is assumed as a linear transformation:

$$\mathbf{L} = \Gamma\mathbf{S} = \Gamma(\bar{\mathbf{s}} + \sum_{i=1}^{n} a_i \mathbf{s}_i). \quad (5)$$

Let $\mathbf{r} = \mathbf{L} - \Gamma\bar{\mathbf{s}}$, in order to solve the mapping function Γ, we minimize a cost function:

$$E(\mathbf{S}) = \|\Gamma \sum_{i=1}^{n} a_i \mathbf{s}_i - \mathbf{r}\|^2. \quad (6)$$

The optimum can be found by Singular Value Decomposition [2].

4.2.2 *Reinforcement with Multiple Views*

Let us consider now that we have multiple face images representing several instances of identical deformable 3D shape. Using a RTS (rotation-translation-scale) camera model, we can express the projection of the 3D shape $\mathbf{S}$ onto 2D image plane $\mathbf{p}$ as:

$$\mathbf{p} = [x, y]^T = k\mathbf{R}\mathbf{S} + \mathbf{t}, \quad (7)$$

where k is a scale parameter, $\mathbf{R}$ is a matrix containing the first two rows of 3D rotation matrix, $\mathbf{t} = (t_x, t_y)^T$ is the translation.

To reinforce shape basis given multiple views, we minimize the following objective function:

$$\min_{\mathbf{s}_i, a_i, k_j, \mathbf{R}_j, \mathbf{t}_j} \sum_{j=1}^{m} \|\mathbf{p}_j - k_j \mathbf{R}_j (\bar{\mathbf{s}} + \sum_{i=1}^{n} a_i \mathbf{s}_i) - \mathbf{t}_j\|^2. \quad (8)$$

This could be solved by joint estimation of the camera parameters and deformative shape parameters [2].

In this paper, the bundled depth-map merging algorithm [4] is employed to generate high quality point cloud and geometric structure. To get a new shape basis update, we compute a set of 3D shape corrections $\Delta\mathbf{S}$ to refine the shape estimate ($\mathbf{S} \leftarrow \mathbf{S} + \Delta\mathbf{S}$). To minimize the reprojection error in Equation (15), we define

$$\mathbf{p}_j - k_j \mathbf{R}_j (\bar{\mathbf{s}} + \sum_{i=1}^{n} a_i \mathbf{s}_i) - \mathbf{t}_j = k_j \mathbf{R}_j \Delta\mathbf{S}. \quad (9)$$

Let us denote the 3D shape estimate of image plane $\mathbf{p}_j$ by $\mathbf{S}^{(j)}$ (obtained by approach in Section 4.2.1). We incorporate prior information in the form of a set $\mathbf{\Pi}_0 = [\mathbf{S}^{(1)}, \cdots, \mathbf{S}^{(m)}]$ of m 3D shapes. And then compute a prior shape basis $\mathbf{S}_0$ (with associated eigenvalues λ_0) by applying Principal Component Analysis on these concatenated shapes.

After having 3D shape description, we employ Thin Plate Spline algorithm for coordinate transformation. And procrustes analysis is used to align two geometric models by optimally translating, rotating and scaling the shapes. We construct a view independent cylindrical texture and blend the pixels in border areas to avoid texture artifacts [3].

4.3 Online Avatar Augmentation

This section describes how to deal with motion pictures enabling live applications when a deformative face model has been generated. In live applications such as online makerover and avatar animation, real-time tracking and pose estimation are the crucial modules to superimpose computer generated content on live video.

3D tracking is to continuously recover all six degrees of freedom that define the 3D displacement of an object relative to the camera. Different from general tracking tasks, in this paper we in particular are dealing with face. That means we may take advantage of prominent facial points as robust feature to track. And we may make use of a generic head model to handle non-planar movements. As run time performance badly influences user satisfaction in Augmented Reality applications, we have to balance the tradeoff between tracking accuracy and computational workload. Therefore we reduce the number of facial points to track, and simply the geometry of head model.

In this paper, we employ Haar cascade classifiers to detect seven landmark points and estimate six parameters of face pose. The seven landmarks are 4 eye corners, 2 mouth corners, and 1 nose tip. The face pose is parameterized by 3D rotation (roll α, pitch β, yaw γ), 2D translation (t_x, t_y), and scaling (s). The approach we used is considering the detection and tracking task as a pattern recognition task. The face rectangle region is cropped and scaled to a normalized size after a fast face detection module. For each facial point, an individual cascade classifier is trained and the classifier is able to output a probabilistic score for a test image.

We use standard Gauss-Newton algorithm to minimize the cost function and find the optimal shape parameters. Given an initial estimation of parameters, it generally converges within 10 steps in our experiments. To prevent a sensitive initialization from falling into local minimum, POSIT algorithm is employed to generate multiple initializations. With the recovered pose, we are able to render a personalized avatar by adjusting a virtual camera. And with the detected position of facial landmarks, we are able to augment computer-generated content to live video of moving face. Beyond the seven landmarks online detected, we could leverage the dense shape model offline generated.

5. EXPERIMENTS AND DISCUSSIONS

In this section, we describe the experiment details and discuss key findings. In our experiments, we have utilized two major 3D face data sets: Binghamton University 3D Facial Expression (3DFE) and the BJUT-3D Large-Scale Chinese Face Database (BJUT) [5]. Basic information about these two data set is summarized in Table 1. The summary includes the number of female (#Female) and male (#Male) in the subjects, their ranging age (Age), variety of ethnic (#Ethnic), and prototypic expressions (#Expr.). In 3DFE data set, ethnic/racial ancestries include White, Black, East-Asian, Middle-east Asian, Indian, and Hispanic Latino. Six prototypic expressions are happiness, disgust, fear, angry, surprise and sadness. In BJUT data set, only Chinese faces are available and four expressions are neutral, happy, angry,

Table 1: **Information of the two 3D face data sets we used in constructing morphable model**

	#Female	#Male	Age	#Ethnic	#Expr.
3DFE	56	44	[18,70]	6	6
BJUT	250	250	[16,49]	1	4

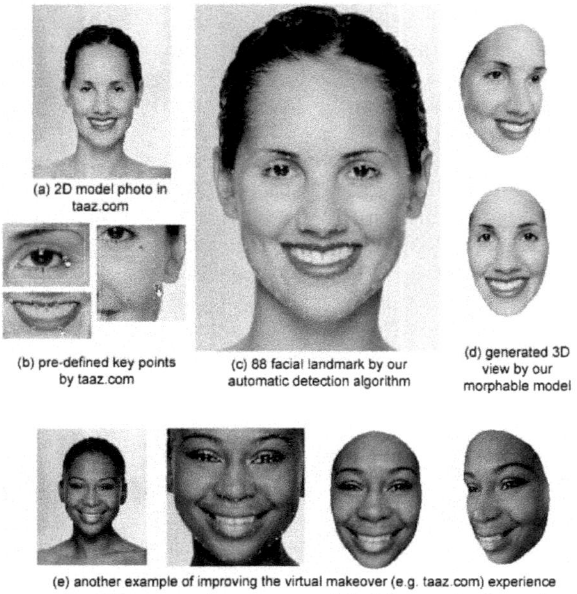
(a) 2D model photo in taaz.com
(b) pre-defined key points by taaz.com
(c) 88 facial landmark by our automatic detection algorithm
(d) generated 3D view by our morphable model
(e) another example of improving the virtual makeover (e.g. taaz.com) experience

Figure 2: 2D experience provided by existing virtual makeover website vs. 3D experience provided by our automatic single image based avatar personalization.

and surprise. They both use CyberWare Laser Scanner [1] to acquire high-resolution 3D faces.

After all scanned face data were transformed into a unified coordinate system, average face shape is calculated. Through Delaunay triangulation [3], we get the mesh of 88 facial points on average face. This mesh shares same topology across all scanned faces, and therefore each scanned face has same number of triangles. Apparently the sparse mesh of 88 facial points is not fine enough to generate smooth face shape. We then perform re-mesh to generate dense mesh of more facial vertices. This is done in a cylinder surface, where each triangle's three edges in a sparse mesh go through a midpoint interpolation. By finding the nearest neighbors in the corresponding X-Y-Z coordinate system, we get the vertices of next level of dense mesh, which consist of 88 points, 326 points, and 1255 points respectively.

As illustrated in Figure 2 (a), we employed one 2D model photo in taaz.com as the single image to generate avatar. Be noted that this model photo is used to preview a user-specified lipstick effect. Shown in Figure 2 (b), taaz.com has provided a tool for users to adjust the positions of a set of pre-defined key points in eye, mouth/lip, and cheek areas. In comparison to their tool, we could automatically detect 88 facial points as marked in Figure 2 (c). The number of key points are more than their predefined ones, and the accuracy is satisfied for frontal face. Wit h the algorithm stated in Section 4.2.1, we estimated the shape and texture coefficients and generated the new face. Figure 2 (d) shows the 3D view rendered from different angles.

Figure 2 (e) listed another example, in which we show the original 2D model photo, the automated detected 88 facial points by our algorithm, and the 3D views rendered

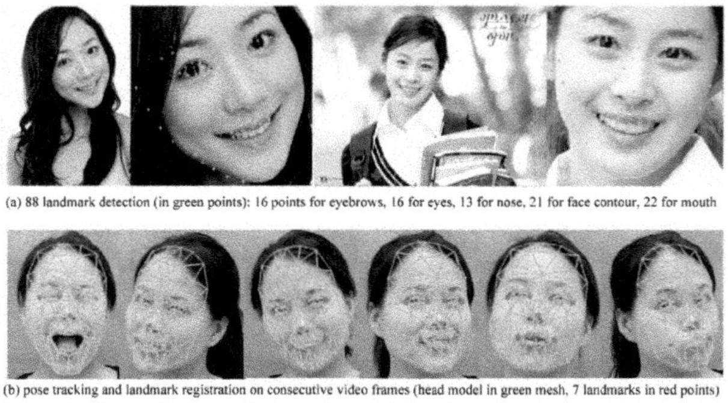
(a) 88 landmark detection (in green points): 16 points for eyebrows, 16 for eyes, 13 for nose, 21 for face contour, 22 for mouth
(b) pose tracking and landmark registration on consecutive video frames (head model in green mesh, 7 landmarks in red points)

Figure 3: Examples of 88 landmark detection and pose tracking using a simplified head model.

after morphable model mapping. Apparently, existing still planar experience could be greatly enhanced by our photo-realistic avatar personalization. One major limitation of our approach so far is that we haven't handle hair quite well.

We tested our algorithm on faces with various expressions, poses, moustache, sunglasses, and also occluded by hand or hair. Figure 3 shows representative results out of 1891 frames. The green mesh indicates the Candide-3 head model, and the red points indicates the detected seven landmarks. It shows that our approach is able to accurately locate the landmarks as well as tracking the 3D poses given expression variations.

6. CONCLUSIONS AND FUTURE WORK

This paper aims to solve content generation problems in augmented reality applications. Specifically we focus on human face which is quite challenging as we have to deal with variations in identity, expression, pose, race, age, gender, etc. The proposed framework is scalable by extending prior face data set and partitioning the computation workload on personalization and augmentation stages. In next step we would put more efforts on texture analysis. Effective texture generation could directly improve surface characteristics because rectify texture artifacts and aliasing are more pleasing to the viewer. Another future work is to incorporate with mirror world creation and enhance social interaction experiences.

7. REFERENCES

[1] Cyberware rapid 3d scanners. In *www.cyberware.com.*

[2] V. Blanz and T. Vetter. A morphable model for the synthesis of 3d faces. In *26th International Conference on Computer Graphics and Interactive Techniques (Siggraph)*, pages 187–194. ACM Press, August 1999.

[3] M. de Berg, O. Cheong, and et al. *Computational Geometry: Algorithms and Applications.* Otfried Cheong, Reading, Massachusetts, 2008.

[4] J. Li, E. Li, Y. Chen, L. Xu, and Y. Zhang. Bundled depth-map merging for multi-view stereo. In *IEEE CVPR*, pages 2769–2776. IEEE, June 2010.

[5] B. U. of Technology. The bjut-3d large-scale chinese face database. pages 211–216, 2005.

[6] L. Zhang, H. AI, and S. LAO. Robust face alignment based on hierarchical classifier network. In *HCI/ECCV 2006, LNCS 3979*, pages 1–11, June 2006.

[7] Z. Zhang, Z. Liu, and et al. Robust and rapid generation of animated faces from video images: A model-based modeling approach. *International Journal of Computer Vision*, 58(1):93–119, June 2004.

Static and Dynamic Video Summaries

Yingbo Li, Bernard Merialdo
EURECOM
Sophia-Antipolis, 06560, France
{yingbo.li, bernard.merialdo}@eurecom.fr

Mickael Rouvier, Georges Linares
University of Avignon
Avignon, 84911, France
{mickael.rouvier, georges.linares}@univ-avignon.fr

ABSTRACT
Currently there are a lot of algorithms for video summarization; however most of them only represent visual information. In this paper, we propose two approaches for the construction of the summary using both video and text. One approach focuses on static summaries, where the summary is a set of selected keyframes and keywords, to be displayed in a fixed area. The second approach addresses dynamic summaries where video segments are selected based on both their visual and textual content to compose a new video sequence of predefined duration. Our approaches rely on an existing summarization algorithm, Video Maximal Marginal Relevance (Video-MMR), and its extension Text Video Maximal Marginal Relevance (TV-MMR) proposed by us. We describe the details of those approaches and present experimental results.

Categories and Subject Descriptors
I.2.10 [**Artificial Intelligence**]: Vision and Scene Understanding – *video analysis.*

General Terms
Algorithms, Design.

1. INTRODUCTION
Video summarization has attracted a lot of attention from researchers these years, because of the unimaginable explosion of multimedia information. For example, the benchmark activity, the TREC Video Retrieval Evaluation (TRECVid), is important in the area of multimedia now. Many algorithms have been proposed to summarize single and multiple videos [2]. Some algorithms only depend on visual information [2], while others use visual and audio information [3], visual and text information, or all three kinds of information [4] [6]. The information used in the summarization algorithms may be diverse, but the summary itself is often built simply from the video frames [7].

A video summary can take two forms [5]: a static storyboard summary, which is a set of selected keyframes, or a dynamic video skim, composed by concatenating short video segments. According to their intrinsic properties, static summaries can contain video frames, possibly some keywords, but cannot include the audio track; while in dynamic summaries, all three kinds of information can be present.

*Area Chair: Hari Sundaram

*MM'*11, November 28–December 1, 2011, Scottsdale, Arizona, USA.

In this paper we consider the construction of the static summary composed of keyframes and keywords. We assume that the display space has a fixed size, which has to be optimized between keyframes and keywords. A keyframe occupies more space than a keyword, but also generally contains more information. We search for an algorithm to optimally decide the percentage of keyframes and keywords that provide the maximum information inside the available display space. This allows building a static summary which contains the maximum information presented to the user.

For dynamic summary, we consider the synchronized summary, where the audio-visual segments are extracted from the original sequence and concatenated. We explore the issue of the optimal segment duration, since a short duration is generally sufficient to represent the visual content of a video segment, while a longer audio segment provides more information.

2. Linguistic information measure
In our approach, the information content of the audio track is evaluated based on the text transcription of the audio channel by an Automatic Speech Recognition (ASR) system from LIA (Laboratoire d'Informatique d'Avignon, France). The LIA ASR system is using context-dependent Hidden Markov Models for acoustic modeling and *n*-gram Language Models (LM). Training corpora comes from broadcast news records and large textual materials: acoustic models are estimated on 180 hours of French broadcast news. Language Models are trained on a collection of about 109M words, from French newspapers and large newswire collections. The ASR system is run on the audio track of the video sequences. The result is a sequence of words, with the beginning and ending times of their utterance. These timecodes allow synchronizing the audio and the video information in the summarization algorithm. They also allow providing candidate boundaries for audio-visual segments to be selected.

By analogy with text information retrieval techniques, the audio information content is measured according to the words that appear in the selected segment. We construct a word document vector d for the whole transcription of a video (or the transcriptions of a set of videos), as in the Vector Space model. We construct a similar vector for the text transcription t of a segment extracted from an audio-visual sequence. The audio information content of the segment is defined as the cosine between these two vectors:

$$sim(t,d) = cos(t,d) = \frac{t \cdot d}{\|t\|\|d\|} \qquad (1)$$

The results are provided as lists of sliding windows of n words, (with n ranging from 1 to 10), together with windows covering complete sentences. For each window, the beginning and end times are provided, together with the similarity score. An example of such list for 3-grams is shown in Table 1.

Table 1. Some examples of 3-gram

Score	Begin	End	3-gram
0.06	51.53	52.18	on craint on
0.07	51.58	52.28	craint on s'
0.07	51.94	52.86	on s' exprimer
0.15	52.25	53.44	s' exprimer comédien
0.15	52.46	53.54	exprimer comédien ce
0.15	52.86	53.94	comédien ce matin
0.07	53.47	54.21	ce matin les

3. TV-MMR

3.1 Video-MMR

By analogy with text summarization, we have proposed to adapt the Maximal Marginal Relevance (MMR) [1] principle to design a new algorithm, Video-MMR [2], for multi-video summarization. When iteratively selecting keyframes to construct a summary, Video-MMR selects a keyframe whose visual content is similar to the content of the videos, but at the same time different from the frames already selected in the summary. By analogy with the MMR algorithm, we define the Video Marginal Relevance (Video-MR) of a keyframe at any given point of the construction of a summary S by:

$$\textit{Video-MR}(f) = \lambda\, Sim_1(f, V \backslash S_k) - (1-\lambda) \max_{g \in S_k} Sim_2(f, g) \quad (2)$$

where V is the set of all frames in all videos, S is the current set of selected frames, g is a frame in S and f is a candidate frame for selection. λ allows adjusting the relative importance of relevance and novelty. Sim_2 is just the similarity $sim(f, g)$ between frames f and g. And

$$Sim_1(f, V \backslash S) = \frac{1}{|V \backslash (S \cup f)|} \sum_{g \in V \backslash (S \cup f)} sim(f, g) \quad (3)$$

A summary S_{k+1} can be constructed by iteratively adding the frames with Video-MMR into the summary:

$$S_{k+1} = S_k \cup \underset{f \in V \backslash S_k}{argmax}(\lambda\, Sim_1(f, V \backslash S_k) - (1-\lambda) \max_{g \in S_k} Sim_2(f, g)) \quad (4)$$

3.2 TV-MMR

The Video-MMR algorithm only uses visual information. In order to exploit the textual information obtained by the Speech Recognition, we propose an extension which we call Text Video Maximal Marginal Relevance (TV-MMR). TV-MMR selects video segments corresponding to n-grams by using both the textual and the visual content. By mimicking the formula of Video-MMR, the formula of TV-MMR is proposed as:

$$S_{k+1} = S_k \cup \underset{f \in V \backslash S_k}{argmax}\{ \beta[\lambda\, Sim_{I1}(f, V \backslash S_k) - (1-\lambda) \max_{g \in S_k} Sim_{I2}(f, g)] + (1-\beta)[\mu\, Sim_{T1}(f, V \backslash S_k) - (1-\mu) \max_{g \in S_k} Sim_{T2}(f, g)]\} \quad (5)$$

where f and g are audio-visual segments corresponding to n-grams. The definitions of Sim_{I1} and Sim_{I2} are the same as in Eq. 2. Sim_{T1} and Sim_{T2} are the textual similarities from ASR results, and they play a similar role for the text as Sim_{I1} and Sim_{I2} for the video. The parameter β allows adjusting the relative importance between visual information and textual information.

While in Video-MMR, the basic information unit was a single keyframe, in TV-MMR it is an n-gram segment. The visual content of an n-gram segment is composed of all the keyframes which appear between the beginning and ending times of the utterance. For faster computation, we subsample the video at the rate of 1 frame per second, so that a 5 second utterance will be represented by a set of 5 keyframes. The similarity between keyframes that is used in Video-MMR is extended to a similarity between sets of keyframes by computing the average of keyframes similarities.

The procedure of TV-MMR summarization is explained as the following sequence of steps:

1) The initial video summary S_1 is initialized with one segment, defined as:

$$S_1 = arg \max_{f_i, f_i \neq f_j} [\prod_{j=1}^{n} Sim_I(f_i, f_j) \cdot \prod_{j=1}^{n} Sim_T(f_i, f_j)]^{\frac{1}{n}} \quad (6)$$

where f_i and f_j are n-gram segments from the video set V and n is the total number of segments except f_i. Sim_I computes the similarity of visual information between f_i and f_j; while Sim_T is the similarity of text information between f_i and f_j.

2) Select the segment f_k by TV-MMR formula, Eq. 5.
3) Set $S_k = S_{k-1} \cup \{f_k\}$.
4) Iterate to step 2) until S has reached the predefined size.

4. STATIC AND DYNAMIC SUMMARIES

4.1 Static Summaries

A static video summary is basically composed of selected keyframes. However, it can be useful to use also some of the display space to show some keywords which are related to the content of the video sequence. In our work, we use the speech transcription of the audio track, as described in Section 2. The summary is often presented inside a display space with predefined size, for example a web page. Therefore, the summarization algorithm has to select a predefined number of keyframes to fit inside this space, while maximizing the amount of information which is presented to the user. When keywords are also possible, the summarization algorithm should decide, not only on which keywords to display, but also about the relative number of keywords and keyframes to fit in the predefined space. The diversity of the visual and the textual content is different from video to video, so that a fixed choice for the number of keywords and keyframes cannot be optimal.

In our work, we have considered that keyframes are of fixed size (another option would be to allow some keyframes to shrink, but we leave it for future exploration), and that the space occupied by a keyframe is equal to the space occupied by 60 characters. Selecting more keyframes reduced the number of words which can be displayed, and vice-versa. For a fixed display space, only combinations of keyframes and keywords which fit inside this space are considered. The task of the summarization algorithm is to find the combination that provides the most information.

Our video summarization algorithm, Video-MMR, is incremental, and produces a sequence of video summaries where one keyframe is added at each step. This provides a sequence of keyframes with decreasing visual importance, out of which we can easily consider the first k, for any value of k. During the Video-MMR, the marginal relevance $k_V(i)$ of a keyframe f_i as defined in Eq. 2, decreases as the iterations proceed. We fix a threshold and stop the Video-MMR iterations when the marginal relevance falls below the threshold. For a given video, this provides a number M of keyframes. We normalize the visual relevance of the keyframe:

$$k'_V(i) = k_V(i) / \sum_{j \in M} k_V(j) \quad (7)$$

From the speech transcription, we can associate each video keyframe with an n-gram, based on the timecodes. This allows defining the text similarity $k_T(i)$ of the text segment associated to the keyframe f_i as the cosine measure introduced in Section 2. Again, we normalize these values over the selected set:

$$k'_T(i) = k_T(i) / \sum_{j \in M} k_T(j) \quad (8)$$

We take the size of a keyframe as the basic unit, and assume that the available display size is P times the size of a single keyframe. As mentioned previously, size of a character is taken as 1/60 of the keyframe size. With these figures, the optimal summary will be composed of the set of keyframes ρ_V and the set of keywords ρ_T which maximize:

- The optimal summary to be presented in a display space best combination of frames and text is the one that maximizes the total visual and textual information that is presented, as is described in the following formula:

  $$max_{\rho_V, \rho_T}[K_V(\rho_V) + K_T(\rho_T)] \quad (9)$$

  With the constraint $size(\rho_V) + size(\rho_T) \leq P$, and the definitions:
- $K_V = \sum_{j \in \rho_V} k'_V(j)$,
- $K_T = \sum_{j \in \rho_T} k'_T(j)$,
- $size(\rho_V) = |\rho_V|$,
- $size(\rho_T) =$ (number of characters of words in ρ_T)/60.

4.2 Dynamic Summaries

Our dynamic summaries are the concatenation of audio-visual segments extracted from the original videos. The candidate segments out of which we select are the segments corresponding to the utterances of *n*-grams. In this paper, we only discuss the dynamic summaries from the viewpoint of maximizing the information in summaries, though the story flow and rhythm are also important for the dynamic summary.

A specific difficulty comes from the fact that the rate of information flow is different between the audio and the visual media. For the visual part, videos are a succession of shots. Those shots are often rather long (on the order of 10 seconds or more), with slow motion (with the exception of music clips). In this case, a visual presentation of 1 or 2 seconds of the shot is sufficient to convey most of the visual content of the shot. Any longer presentation is a wasteful usage of the visual information channel for the summary. On the contrary, for the textual part, redundancy is extremely rare, so that longer extracts provide greater information content. Therefore, the choice of the optimal duration of *n*-grams is lead by two opposite constraints:

- Smaller values of *n* favor more visual content to be presented (for a given summary duration),
- Higher values of *n* allow more coherent text information to be included.

Based on this analysis, we explore the use of TV-MMR to find the best compromise between those constraints. For each value of *n*, we can build a summary from the *n*-gram segments. We can then compare the quality of these different summaries and select the best one according to a combination of its visual and textual content. We propose the following equation for this optimization:

$$argmax_n\, K(S_n) = argmax_n\left[K'_V(S_n) + K'_T(S_n)\right] \quad (10)$$

where S_n is the summary built by TV-MMR from the *n*-gram segments, $K(S_n)$ is the quality of its audio-visual content, defined as the sum of K'_V, the similarity of video segments in the summary with the original video and K'_T, the similarity between text words in the summary and all the text. Before applying TV-MMR, we define the expected duration of the summary.

We then perform experiments to compare the values of text similarities and visual similarities from different values of *n*, in order to find the best compromise.

5. EXPERIMENTAL RESULTS

In the experiments the video sets are collected from Internet news aggregator website "wikio.fr". Totally we have 21 video sets, each of which contains between 3 and 15 videos, whose durations vary from a few seconds to more than 10 minutes. The genres of the videos are various including news, advertisement and movie, to ensure the diversity of the experimental videos.

In the experiment, the similarity of two video frames, $sim(f_i, f_j)$, is defined as cosine similarity of visual word histograms:

$$sim(f_i, f_j) = cos\left(H_{f_i}, H_{f_j}\right) = \frac{H_{f_i} \cdot H_{f_j}}{\|H_{f_i}\|\|H_{f_j}\|} \quad (11)$$

where H_{f_i} and H_{f_j} are histogram vectors of frame f_i and f_j. And for the similarity of text of two segments in TV-MMR, it uses the same definition with Eq. 11 but the text histogram of an utterance is defined as:

$$H = (w_1, w_2, \ldots, w_T) \quad (12)$$

where w_T is the number of $T st$ word in the utterance, and the number of the words is T.

5.1 TV-MMR

To remain consistent with Video-MMR, we still use Summary Reference Comparison (SRC) in [2] to select the best parameters μ and β. First we vary μ from 0.1 to 0.9, each step being 0.1. Then we get a figure for 2-gram as the basic unit in Figure 1:

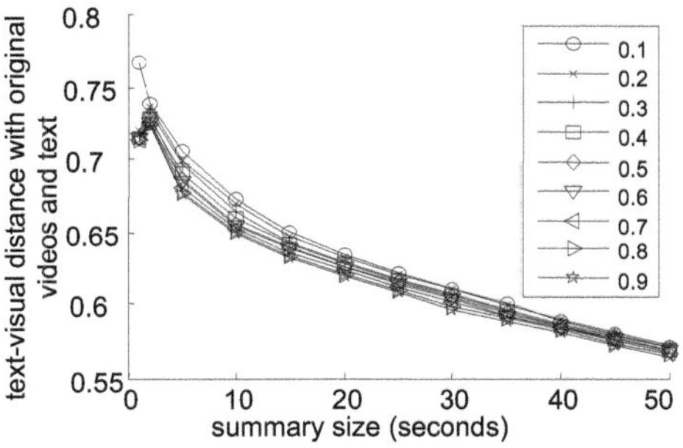

Figure 1. SRC of parameter μ

It is obvious that $\mu = 0.9$ is the best in Figure 1. For the other *n*-grams, the figures are similar with $\mu = 0.9$ owning the best curves, but they are not shown because of the limited pages. Therefore in Eq. 5 we prefer $\mu = 0.9$. And we vary β like μ and consider βs for different *n*-grams, finally we choose $\beta = 0.1$.

Because we have known $\lambda = 0.7$ in Video-MMR [2], in Eq. 5 $\lambda = 0.7$, $\mu = 0.9$ and $\beta = 0.1$. After the best parameters are decided, we can compare the text-visual distances with original videos of TV-MMR and Video-MMR in Figure 2. In Figure 2, we only show the examples of 2-gram and 8-gram, but the other *n*-grams have similar curves. It is obvious that our TV-MMR outperforms the existing algorithm Video-MMR.

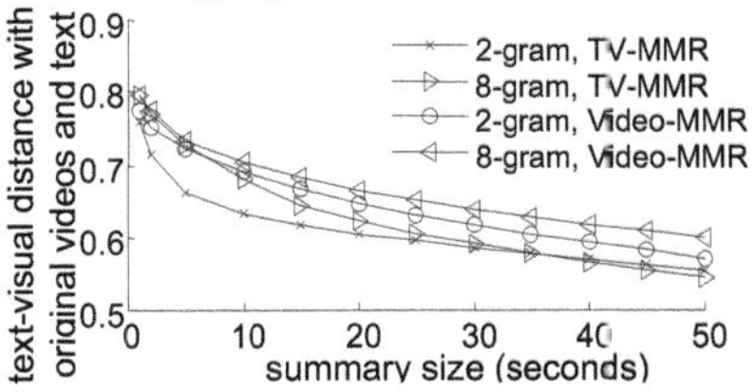

Figure 2. TV-MMR and Video-MMR

5.2 Static Summaries

For our experiments, we consider several display size:

- *P*=12, as a reasonable value when the display space is a full screen on a computer,

- P=6, a common value when using the display of a smart phone,
- P=3 and P=4, as often found when a single line of keyframes is considered, inside a larger page.

We perform experiments over 21 different video sets, representing more than 200 videos. For each set, we consider different values of $|\rho_V|$, select the corresponding keyframes and keywords, and plot the value of the total visual and textual information in the summary, as defined in Eq. 9. Figure 3 is the curve for the case where the display size is P=12, the text segments are 2-grams, and $|\rho_V|$ varies from 0 to 12. The maximum value is obtained for $|\rho_V| = 5$. Table 2 shows the overall results of the optimal value of $|\rho_V|$ for various values of P and various lengths of n-grams. We can see that the optimal number of keyframes has little variations when different lengths of n-grams are considered. However, when full sentences are considered for the text segments, selecting a complete sentences force to select both important and unimportant keywords, which is suboptimal, and only keyframes are selected in the final summary.

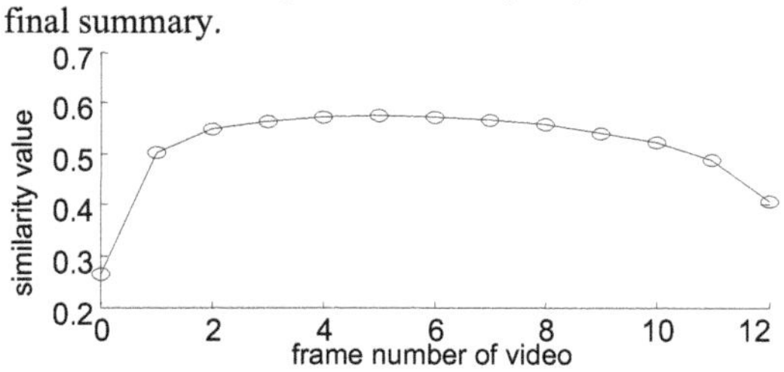

Figure 3. Information value of different $|\rho_V|$ when P=12 and $gram_n = 2$

Table 2. Statistical data of the best frame number in P

frame	1-gram	2	3	4	5	6	7	8	9	10	sentence
P=12	4	5	5	5	4	4	5	4	5	5	8
P=6	2	2	2	2	2	2	3	2	3	3	4
P=4	1	2	2	2	1	2	1	2	1	2	4
P=1	1	1	1	1	1	1	1	1	2	2	3

In Figure 4 we show an example of the static summary for $P = 6$ and 1-gram (For better visualization, the total space is not exactly 6 times the space of an image).

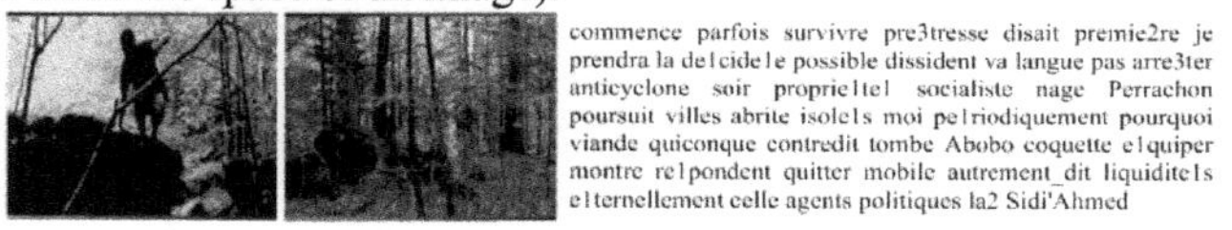

Figure 4. An example of the static summary

5.3 Dynamic Summaries

To obtain dynamic summaries with the duration D=10, 30, 50, 60, 70, or 80 seconds, we carry out TV-MMR with different grams, 1~10-gram or sentence, as the basic unit. Then we compute text similarities with utterance collection and visual similarities with the original videos for dynamic summary as Eq. 11 and Eq. 12. The mean text similarities and visual similarities of 21 video sets from different n-grams are shown in Figure 5. When the summary time is short like 10 seconds and 30 seconds, text scores don't increase with the increase of $gram_n$. However, when the summary time is around 60 seconds, $gram_n$ begins to influence on text similarity. The points of 7-gram are inflection and moderate points which maximize both text and video similarities for D=50, 60, 70, or 80 seconds.

Therefore, 7-gram is the best length of the basic unit/segment for dynamic summary, maximizing both text and visual information in a dynamic summary with a duration more than and around 60 seconds. A short basic unit, like 1-gram, seems to be better when the summary size is shorter than 50 seconds. According to our experimental data, the average durations are 2.1 seconds for 7-gram and 0.3 seconds for 1-gram. Therefore in dynamic summary of 60 seconds, every basic segment should last for 2.1 seconds.

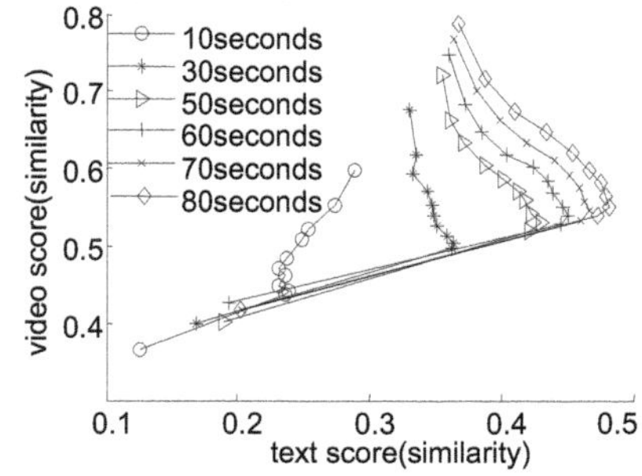

Figure 5. Dynamic summaries: the points from top to down are the values of 1~10-gram and sentences in each curve

6. CONCLUSION

We have proposed two strategies for maximizing the amount of audio, text and video information provided by a summary.

For static summaries we have presented a summarization algorithm which selects keyframes and keywords to maximize the visual and textual information presented in a predefined display space. Our algorithm automatically chooses the optimal number of keyframes. The visual and textual information of the candidates are evaluated, normalized, and the best selection is selected based on Video-MMR.

For dynamic summaries based on the concatenation of selected short video segments, we have proposed a novel summarization algorithm for text and video, TV-MMR, by which we decide the best segment duration by maximizing the summary information. With our models we can optimally construct dynamic summary of audio and video.

7. Acknowledgements

This research was partially funded by the national project RPM2 ANR-07-AM-008.

8. REFERENCES

[1] J. Carbonell and J. Goldstein. The Use of MMR, Diversity-Based Reranking for Reordering Documents and Producing Summaries. *ACM SIGIR conference*, Australia, 1998.

[2] Yingbo Li and Bernard Merialdo. Multi-Video Summarization based on Video-MMR. *WIAMIS*, 2010.

[3] M. Furini and V. Ghini. An Audio-Video Summarization Scheme Based on Audio and Video Analysis. *IEEE Cosumer Communications and Networking Conference*, USA, 2006.

[4] Y. Ma, L. Lu, H. Zhang and M. Li. A User Attention Model for Video Summarization. *ACM Multimedia*, USA, 2002.

[5] B. Truong and S. Venkatesh. Video abstraction: A Systematic Review and Classification. *ACM Transactions on Multimedia Computing, Communications and Applications*, Vol. 3, No. 1, Article 3, February 2007.

[6] Changsheng Xu et al. Automatic Music Video Summarization Based on Audio-Visual-Text Analysis and Alignment. *ACM SIGIR*, Brazil, 2005.

[7] M. Furini, F. Geraci, M. Montangero. VISTO: VIsual STOryboard for Web Video Browsing. *CIVR*, 2007.

Author Index

www.ingramcontent.com/pod-product-compliance
Ingram Content Group UK Ltd.
Pitfield, Milton Keynes, MK11 3LW, UK
UKHW051455290926
15471UKWH00008B/1215

9 781450 313612